BENCHMARK SERIES

Microsoft® Office 2016

Nita Rutkosky • Audrey Roggenkamp • Ian Rutkosky

PARADIGM
EDUCATION SOLUTIONS
St. Paul

Senior Vice President	Linda Hein
Editor in Chief	Christine Hurney
Director of Production	Timothy W. Larson
Production Editor	Jen Weaverling
Cover and Text Designer	Valerie King
Copy Editors	Communicáto, Ltd.; Page to Portal, LLC
Senior Design and Production Specialist	Jack Ross; PerfecType
Assistant Developmental Editors	Mamie Clark, Katie Werdick
Testers	Janet Blum, Fanshawe College; Traci Post
Instructional Support Writers	Janet Blum, Fanshawe College; Brienna McWade
Indexer	Terry Casey
Vice President Information Technology	Chuck Bratton
Digital Projects Manager	Tom Modl
Vice President Sales and Marketing	Scott Burns
Director of Marketing	Lara Weber McLellan

Cover Photo Credits: © Photomall/Dreamstime.com. **Getting Started Photo Credits:** Page 3: Leungchopan/Shutterstock.com.

ISBN 978-0-76386-913-7 (print)
ISBN 978-0-76386-914-4 (digital)

875 Montreal Way
St. Paul, MN 55102
Email: educate@emcp.com
Website: ParadigmCollege.com

Printed in the United States of America

23 22 21 20 19 18 17 2 3 4 5 6 7 8 9 10 11 12

Contents

Preface

Benchmark Series: Microsoft® Office 2016 is designed for students who want to learn how to use the new version of Microsoft's popular suite to enhance their productivity at school, work, and home. Throughout this text, students are expected to develop and execute strategies for solving information processing and management problems using Word 2016; for solving numeric and mathematical problems using Excel 2016; for organizing, querying, and retrieving data using Access 2016; and for writing, creating, and producing presentations using PowerPoint 2016. After successfully completing a course using this textbook and digital courseware, students will be able to:

- Analyze, synthesize, and evaluate school, work, or home information-processing needs and use application software to meet those needs efficiently and effectively
- Create, design, and produce professional documents using word processing software
- Process, manipulate, and represent numeric data using spreadsheet software
- Plan, structure, and create databases for efficient data access and retrieval using database software
- Design and create informational and motivational slide shows that contain hyperlinks, tables, images, and animation using presentation software
- Learn strategies for merging and integrating source data from different applications

Upon completing the text, students can expect to be proficient in using the major applications of the Office 2016 suite to organize, analyze, and present information.

Well-designed textbook pedagogy is important, but students learn technology skills through practice and problem solving. Technology provides opportunities for interactive learning as well as excellent ways to quickly and accurately assess student performance. To this end, this textbook is supported with SNAP 2016, Paradigm's web-based training and assessment learning management system. Details about SNAP as well as additional student courseware and instructor resources can be found on page xv.

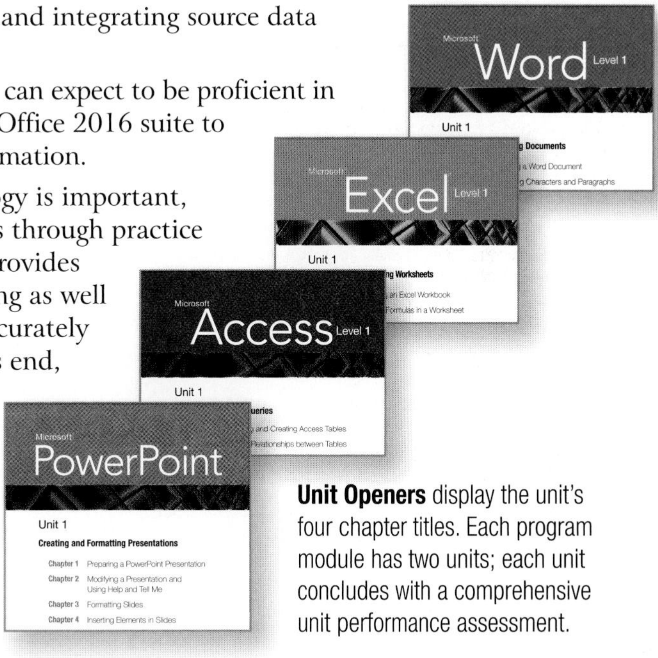

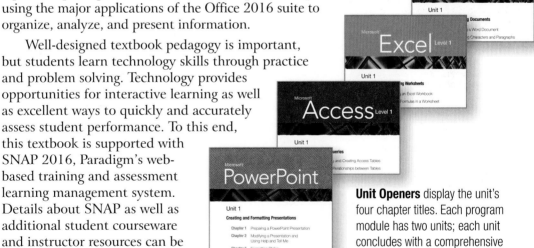

Unit Openers display the unit's four chapter titles. Each program module has two units; each unit concludes with a comprehensive unit performance assessment.

Achieving Proficiency in Office 2016

Since its inception several Office versions ago, the *Benchmark Series* has served as a standard of excellence in software instruction. Elements of the *Benchmark Series* function individually and collectively to create an inviting, comprehensive learning environment that produces successful computer users. The following visual tour highlights the structure and features that comprise the highly popular *Benchmark* model.

Student Textbook and eBook

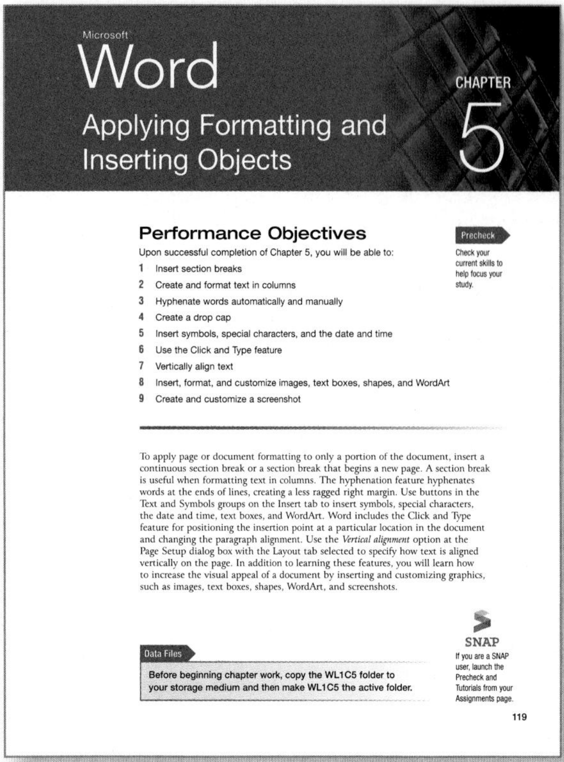

Microsoft

Word

CHAPTER 5

Applying Formatting and Inserting Objects

Performance Objectives

Upon successful completion of Chapter 5, you will be able to:

1 Insert section breaks
2 Create and format text in columns
3 Hyphenate words automatically and manually
4 Create a drop cap
5 Insert symbols, special characters, and the date and time
6 Use the Click and Type feature
7 Vertically align text
8 Insert, format, and customize images, text boxes, shapes, and WordArt
9 Create and customize a screenshot

Precheck

Check your current skills to help focus your study.

To apply page or document formatting to only a portion of the document, insert a continuous section break or a section break that begins a new page. A section break is useful when formatting text in columns. The hyphenation feature hyphenates words at the ends of lines, creating a less ragged right margin. Use buttons in the Text and Symbols groups on the Insert tab to insert symbols, special characters, the date and time, text boxes, and WordArt. Word includes the Click and Type feature for positioning the insertion point at a particular location in the document and changing the paragraph alignment. Use the *Vertical alignment* option at the Page Setup dialog box with the Layout tab selected to specify how text is aligned vertically on the page. In addition to learning these features, you will learn how to increase the visual appeal of a document by inserting and customizing graphics, such as images, text boxes, shapes, WordArt, and screenshots.

Data Files

Before beginning chapter work, copy the WL1C5 folder to your storage medium and then make WL1C5 the active folder.

SNAP

If you are a SNAP user, launch the Precheck and Tutorials from your Assignments page.

119

Chapter Openers present the performance objectives and an overview of the skills taught.

Precheck quizzes allow students to check their current skills before starting chapter work.

Data Files are provided for each chapter from the ebook. A prominent note reminds students to copy the appropriate chapter data folder and make it active.

Students with SNAP access are reminded to launch the Precheck quiz and chapter tutorials from their SNAP Assignments page.

Projects Build Skill Mastery within Realistic Context

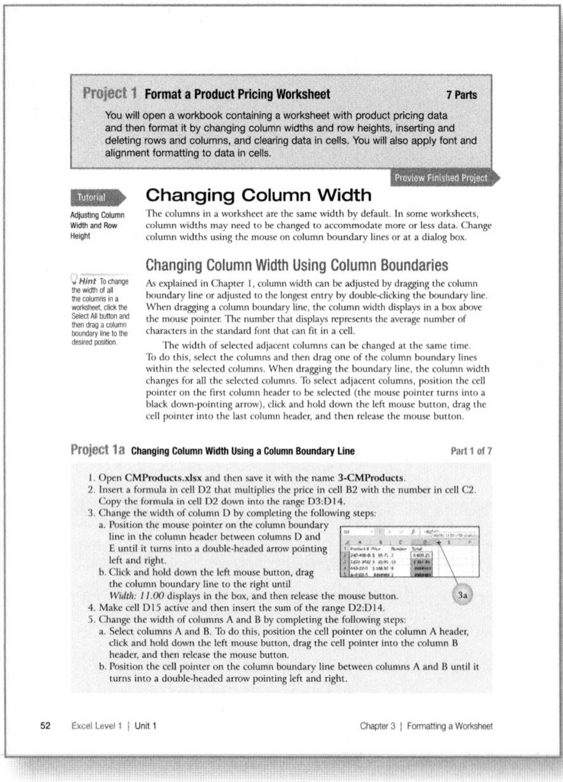

Project 1 Format a Product Pricing Worksheet 7 Parts

You will open a workbook containing a worksheet with product pricing data and then format it by changing column widths and row heights, inserting and deleting rows and columns, and clearing data in cells. You will also apply font and alignment formatting to data in cells.

Preview Finished Project

Tutorial

Adjusting Column Width and Row Height

Changing Column Width

The columns in a worksheet are the same width by default. In some worksheets, column widths may need to be changed to accommodate more or less data. Change column widths using the mouse on column boundary lines or at a dialog box.

Changing Column Width Using Column Boundaries

Hint To change the width of all the columns in a worksheet, click the Select All button and then drag a column boundary line to the desired position.

As explained in Chapter 1, column width can be adjusted by dragging the column boundary line or adjusted to the longest entry by double-clicking the boundary line. When dragging a column boundary line, the column width displays in a box above the mouse pointer. The number that displays represents the average number of characters in the standard font that can fit in a cell.

The width of selected adjacent columns can be changed at the same time. To do this, select the columns and then drag one of the column boundary lines within the selected columns. When dragging the boundary line, the column width changes for all the selected columns. To select adjacent columns, position the cell pointer on the first column header to be selected (the mouse pointer turns into a black down-pointing arrow), click and hold down the left mouse button, drag the cell pointer into the last column header, and then release the mouse button.

Project 1a Changing Column Width Using a Column Boundary Line Part 1 of 7

1. Open **CMProducts.xlsx** and then save it with the name **3-CMProducts**.
2. Insert a formula in cell D2 that multiplies the price in cell B2 with the number in cell C2. Copy the formula in cell D2 down into the range D3:D14.
3. Change the width of column D by completing the following steps:
   a. Position the mouse pointer on the column boundary line in the column header between columns D and E until it turns into a double-headed arrow pointing left and right.
   b. Click and hold down the left mouse button, drag the column boundary line to the right until *Width: 11.00* displays in the box, and then release the mouse button.
4. Make cell D15 active and then insert the sum of the range D2:D14.
5. Change the width of columns A and B by completing the following steps:
   a. Select columns A and B. To do this, position the cell pointer on the column A header, click and hold down the left mouse button, drag the cell pointer into the column B header, and then release the mouse button.
   b. Position the cell pointer on the column boundary line between columns A and B until it turns into a double-headed arrow pointing left and right.

3a

52 Excel Level 1 | Unit 1 Chapter 3 | Formatting a Worksheet

Multipart Projects provide a framework for instruction and practice on software features. A project overview identifies tasks to accomplish and key features to use in completing the work.

Preview Finished Project shows how the file will look after students complete the project.

Tutorials provide interactive, guided training and measured practice.

Hint margin notes offer useful tips on how to use features efficiently and effectively.

Typically, a file remains open throughout all parts of the project. Students save their work incrementally. At the end of the project, students save, print, and then close the file.

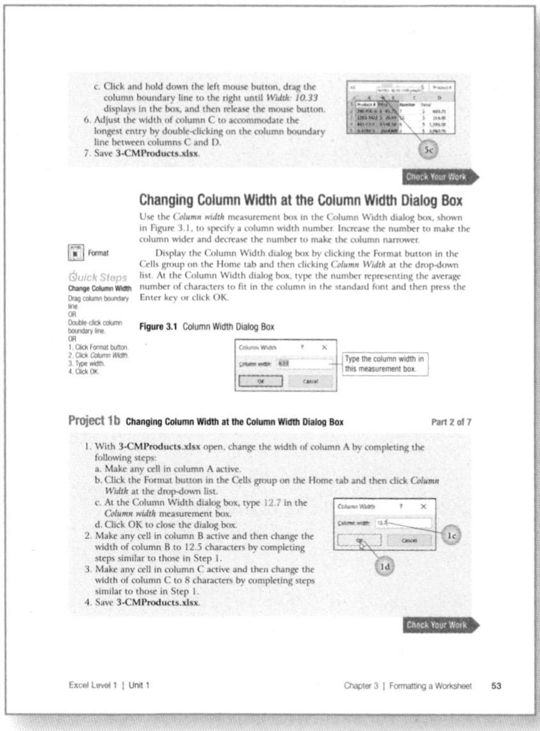

c. Click and hold down the left mouse button, drag the column boundary line to the right until *Width: 10.33* displays in the box, and then release the mouse button.
6. Adjust the width of column C to accommodate the longest entry by double-clicking on the column boundary line between columns C and D.
7. Save **3-CMProducts.xlsx**.

Check Your Work

Changing Column Width at the Column Width Dialog Box

Use the *Column width* measurement box in the Column Width dialog box, shown in Figure 3.1, to specify a column width number. Increase the number to make the column wider and decrease the number to make the column narrower.

Format

Display the Column Width dialog box by clicking the Format button in the Cells group on the Home tab and then clicking *Column Width* at the drop-down list. At the Column Width dialog box, type the number representing the average number of characters to fit in the column in the standard font and then press the Enter key or click OK.

Quick Steps
Change Column Width
Drag column boundary line.
OR
Double-click column boundary line.
OR
1. Click Format button.
2. Click *Column Width*.
3. Type width.
4. Click OK.

Figure 3.1 Column Width Dialog Box

Type the column width in this measurement box.

Project 1b Changing Column Width at the Column Width Dialog Box Part 2 of 7

1. With **3-CMProducts.xlsx** open, change the width of column A by completing the following steps:
   a. Make any cell in column A active.
   b. Click the Format button in the Cells group on the Home tab and then click *Column Width* at the drop-down list.
   c. At the Column Width dialog box, type 12.7 in the *Column width* measurement box.
   d. Click OK to close the dialog box.
2. Make any cell in column B active and then change the width of column B to 12.5 characters by completing steps similar to those in Step 1.
3. Make any cell in column C active and then change the width of column C to 8 characters by completing steps similar to those in Step 1.
4. Save **3-CMProducts.xlsx**.

Check Your Work

Excel Level 1 | Unit 1 Chapter 3 | Formatting a Worksheet 53

Check Your Work allows students to confirm they have completed the project activity correctly.

Quick Steps provide feature summaries for reference and review.

Between project parts, the text presents instruction on the features and skills necessary to accomplish the next section of the project.

Step-by-Step Instructions guide students to the desired outcome for each project part. Screen captures illustrate what the screen should look like at key points.

Magenta Text identifies material to type.

Chapter Review Tools Reinforce Learning

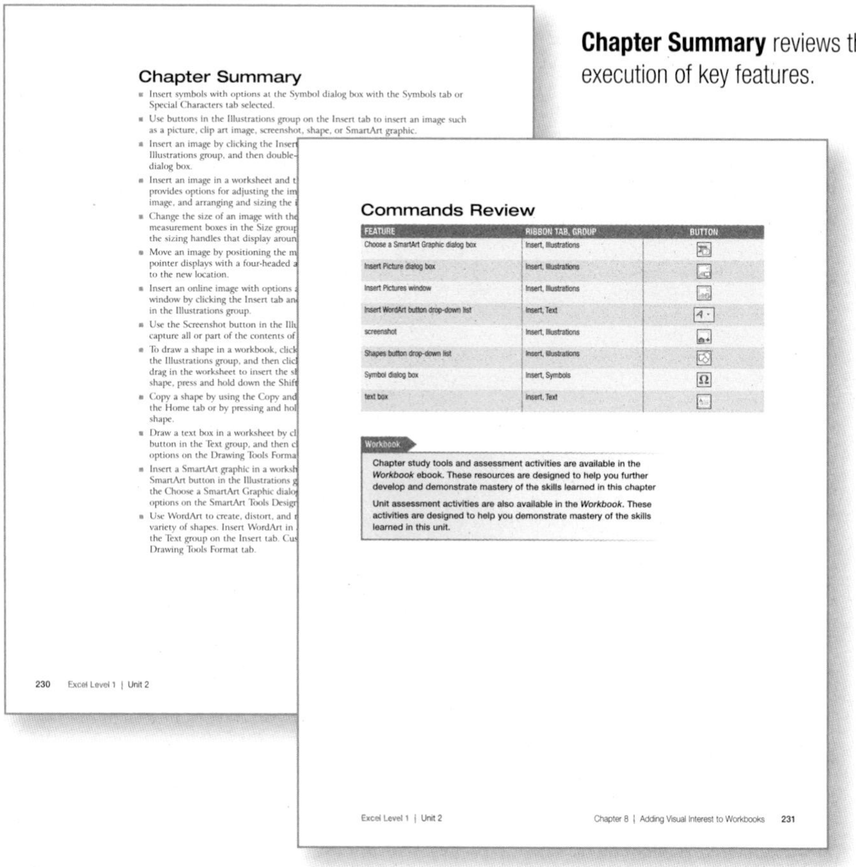

Chapter Summary

- Insert symbols with options at the Symbol dialog box with the Symbols tab or Special Characters tab selected.
- Use buttons in the Illustrations group on the Insert tab to insert an image such as a picture, clip art image, screenshot, shape, or SmartArt graphic.
- Insert an image by clicking the Insert
Illustrations group, and then double-
dialog box.
- Insert an image in a worksheet and t
provides options for adjusting the im
image, and arranging and sizing the
- Change the size of an image with the
measurement boxes in the Size group
the sizing handles that display aroun
- Move an image by positioning the m
pointer displays with a four-headed a
to the new location.
- Insert an online image with options a
window by clicking the Insert tab an
in the Illustrations group.
- Use the Screenshot button in the Illu
capture all or part of the contents of
- To draw a shape in a workbook, click
the Illustrations group, and then clic
drag in the worksheet to insert the sh
shape, press and hold down the Shift
- Copy a shape by using the Copy and
the Home tab or by pressing and hol
shape.
- Draw a text box in a worksheet by cl
button in the Text group, and then cl
options on the Drawing Tools Forma
- Insert a SmartArt graphic in a worksh
SmartArt button in the Illustrations g
the Choose a SmartArt Graphic dialo
options on the SmartArt Tools Design
- Use WordArt to create, distort, and m
variety of shapes. Insert WordArt in
the Text group on the Insert tab. Cus
Drawing Tools Format tab.

230 Excel Level 1 | Unit 2

Commands Review

FEATURE	RIBBON TAB, GROUP	BUTTON
Choose a SmartArt Graphic dialog box	Insert, Illustrations	
Insert Picture dialog box	Insert, Illustrations	
Insert Pictures window	Insert, Illustrations	
Insert WordArt button drop-down list	Insert, Text	
screenshot	Insert, Illustrations	
Shapes button drop-down list	Insert, Illustrations	
Symbol dialog box	Insert, Symbols	Ω
text box	Insert, Text	

Workbook

Chapter study tools and assessment activities are available in the *Workbook* ebook. These resources are designed to help you further develop and demonstrate mastery of the skills learned in this chapter

Unit assessment activities are also available in the *Workbook*. These activities are designed to help you demonstrate mastery of the skills learned in this unit.

Excel Level 1 | Unit 2 Chapter 8 | Adding Visual Interest to Workbooks 231

Chapter Summary reviews the purpose and execution of key features.

Commands Review summarizes visually the major features and alternative methods of access.

At the end of each chapter, students are encouraged to go to the Workbook *ebook to access study tools and assessment activities.*

Workbook eBook Activities Provide a Hierarchy of Learning Assessments

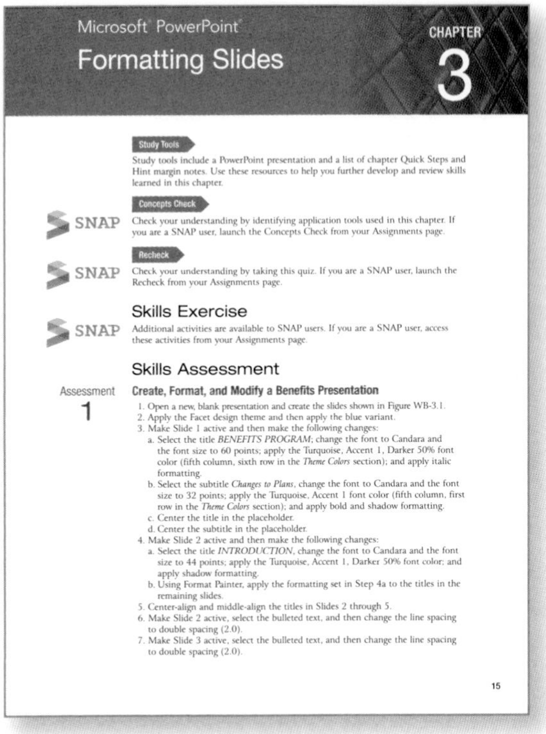

Microsoft PowerPoint

CHAPTER 3

Formatting Slides

Study Tools

Study tools include a PowerPoint presentation and a list of chapter Quick Steps and Hint margin notes. Use these resources to help you further develop and review skills learned in this chapter.

Concepts Check

SNAP Check your understanding by identifying application tools used in this chapter. If you are a SNAP user, launch the Concepts Check from your Assignments page.

Recheck

SNAP Check your understanding by taking this quiz. If you are a SNAP user, launch the Recheck from your Assignments page.

Skills Exercise

SNAP Additional activities are available to SNAP users. If you are a SNAP user, access these activities from your Assignments page.

Skills Assessment

Assessment 1

Create, Format, and Modify a Benefits Presentation

1. Open a new, blank presentation and create the slides shown in Figure WB-3.1.
2. Apply the Facet design theme and then apply the blue variant.
3. Make Slide 1 active and then make the following changes:
   a. Select the title *BENEFITS PROGRAM*; change the font to Candara and the font size to 60 points; apply the Turquoise, Accent 1, Darker 50% font color (fifth column, sixth row in the *Theme Colors* section); and apply italic formatting.
   b. Select the subtitle *Changes to Plans*, change the font to Candara and the font size to 32 points; apply the Turquoise, Accent 1 font color (fifth column, first row in the *Theme Colors* section); and apply bold and shadow formatting.
   c. Center the title in the placeholder.
   d. Center the subtitle in the placeholder.
4. Make Slide 2 active and then make the following changes:
   a. Select the title *INTRODUCTION*, change the font to Candara and the font size to 44 points; apply the Turquoise, Accent 1, Darker 50% font color; and apply shadow formatting.
   b. Using Format Painter, apply the formatting set in Step 4a to the titles in the remaining slides.
5. Center-align and middle-align the titles in Slides 2 through 5.
6. Make Slide 2 active, select the bulleted text, and then change the line spacing to double spacing (2.0).
7. Make Slide 3 active, select the bulleted text, and then change the line spacing to double spacing (2.0).

15

Study Tools are presentations with audio support and a list of chapter Quick Steps and Hint margin notes designed to help students further develop and review skills learned in the chapter.

Concepts Check is an objective completion exercise that allows students to assess their comprehension and recall of application features, terminology, and functions.

Recheck concept quizzes for each chapter enable students to check how their skills have improved after completing chapter work.

Skills Exercises are available to SNAP 2016 users. SNAP will automatically score student work, which is performed live in the application, and provide detailed feedback.

Skills Assessment exercises ask students to develop both standard and customized types of word processing, spreadsheet, database, or presentation documents without how-to directions.

Visual Benchmark assessments test problem-solving skills and mastery of application features.

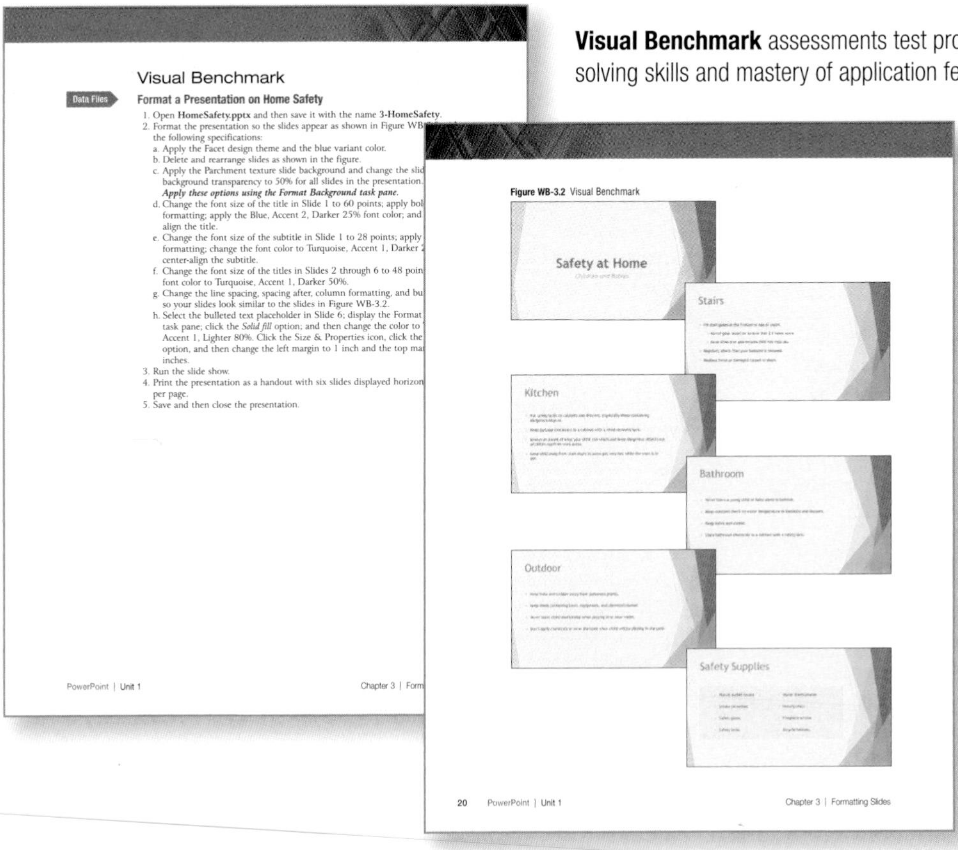

Visual Benchmark

Data Files

Format a Presentation on Home Safety

1. Open **HomeSafety.pptx** and then save it with the name **3-HomeSafety**.
2. Format the presentation so the slides appear as shown in Figure WB
   the following specifications:
   a. Apply the Facet design theme and the blue variant color.
   b. Delete and rearrange slides as shown in the figure.
   c. Apply the Parchment texture slide background and change the slid
   background transparency to 50% for all slides in the presentation.
   Apply these options using the Format Background task pane.
   d. Change the font size of the title in Slide 1 to 60 points; apply bol
   formatting; apply the Blue, Accent 2, Darker 25% font color; and
   align the title.
   e. Change the font size of the subtitle in Slide 1 to 28 points; apply
   formatting; change the font color to Turquoise, Accent 1, Darker
   center-align the subtitle.
   f. Change the font size of the titles in Slides 2 through 6 to 48 poin
   font color to Turquoise, Accent 1, Darker 50%.
   g. Change the line spacing, spacing after, column formatting, and bu
   so your slides look similar to the slides in Figure WB-3.2.
   h. Select the bulleted text placeholder in Slide 6; display the Format
   task pane; click the *Solid fill* option; and then change the color to
   Accent 1, Lighter 80%. Click the Size & Properties icon, click the
   option, and then change the left margin to 1 inch and the top ma
   inches.
3. Run the slide show.
4. Print the presentation as a handout with six slides displayed horizon
   per page.
5. Save and then close the presentation.

PowerPoint | Unit 1 Chapter 3 | Form

Figure WB-3.2 Visual Benchmark

20 PowerPoint | Unit 1 Chapter 3 | Formatting Slides

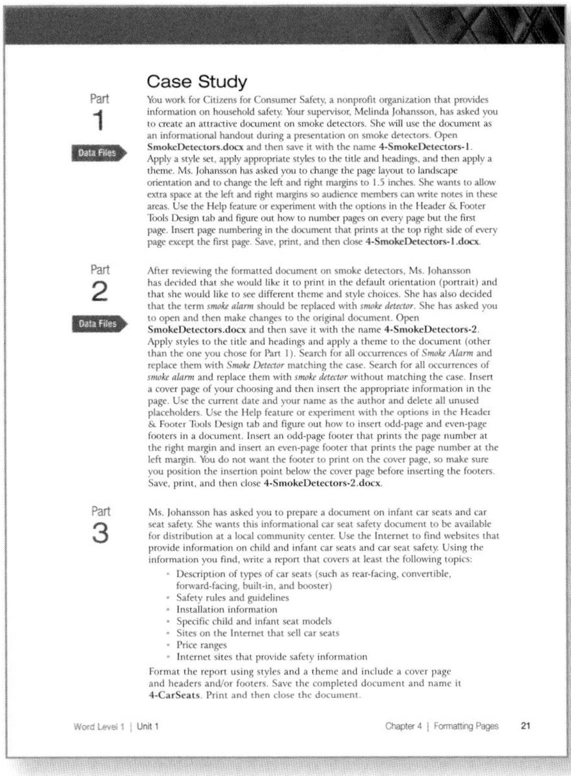

Case Study

Part 1

Data Files

You work for Citizens for Consumer Safety, a nonprofit organization that provides information on household safety. Your supervisor, Melinda Johansson, has asked you to create an attractive document on smoke detectors. She will use the document as an informational handout during a presentation on smoke detectors. Open **SmokeDetectors.docx** and then save it with the name **4-SmokeDetectors-1**. Apply a style set, apply appropriate styles to the title and headings, and then apply a theme. Ms. Johansson has asked you to change the page layout to landscape orientation and to change the left and right margins to 1.5 inches. She wants to allow extra space at the left and right margins so audience members can write notes in these areas. Use the Help feature or experiment with the options in the Header & Footer Tools Design tab and figure out how to number pages on every page but the first page. Insert page numbering in the document that prints at the top right side of every page except the first page. Save, print, and then close **4-SmokeDetectors-1.docx**.

Part 2

Data Files

After reviewing the formatted document on smoke detectors, Ms. Johansson has decided that she would like it to print in the default orientation (portrait) and that she would like to see different theme and style choices. She has also decided that the term *smoke alarm* should be replaced with *smoke detector*. She has asked you to open and then make changes to the original document. Open **SmokeDetectors.docx** and then save it with the name **4-SmokeDetectors-2**. Apply styles to the title and headings and apply a theme to the document (other than the one you chose for Part 1). Search for all occurrences of *Smoke Alarm* and replace them with *Smoke Detector* matching the case. Search for all occurrences of *smoke alarm* and replace them with *smoke detector* without matching the case. Insert a cover page of your choosing and then insert the appropriate information in the page. Use the current date and your name as the author and delete all unused placeholders. Use the Help feature or experiment with the options in the Header & Footer Tools Design tab and figure out how to insert odd-page and even-page footers in a document. Insert an odd-page footer that prints the page number at the right margin and insert an even-page footer that prints the page number at the left margin. You do not want the footer to print on the cover page, so make sure you position the insertion point below the cover page before inserting the footers. Save, print, and then close **4-SmokeDetectors-2.docx**.

Part 3

Ms. Johansson has asked you to prepare a document on infant car seats and car seat safety. She wants this informational car seat safety document to be available for distribution at a local community center. Use the Internet to find websites that provide information on child and infant car seats and car seat safety. Using the information you find, write a report that covers at least the following topics:

- Description of types of car seats (such as rear-facing, convertible, forward-facing, built-in, and booster)
- Safety rules and guidelines
- Installation information
- Specific child and infant seat models
- Sites on the Internet that sell car seats
- Price ranges
- Internet sites that provide safety information

Format the report using styles and a theme and include a cover page and headers and/or footers. Save the completed document and name it **4-CarSeats**. Print and then close the document.

Word Level 1 | Unit 1 Chapter 4 | Formatting Pages 21

Case Study requires analyzing a workplace scenario and then planning and executing a multipart project.

Students search the web and/or use the program's Help feature to locate additional information required to complete the Case Study.

Unit Performance Assessments Deliver Cross-Disciplinary, Comprehensive Evaluation

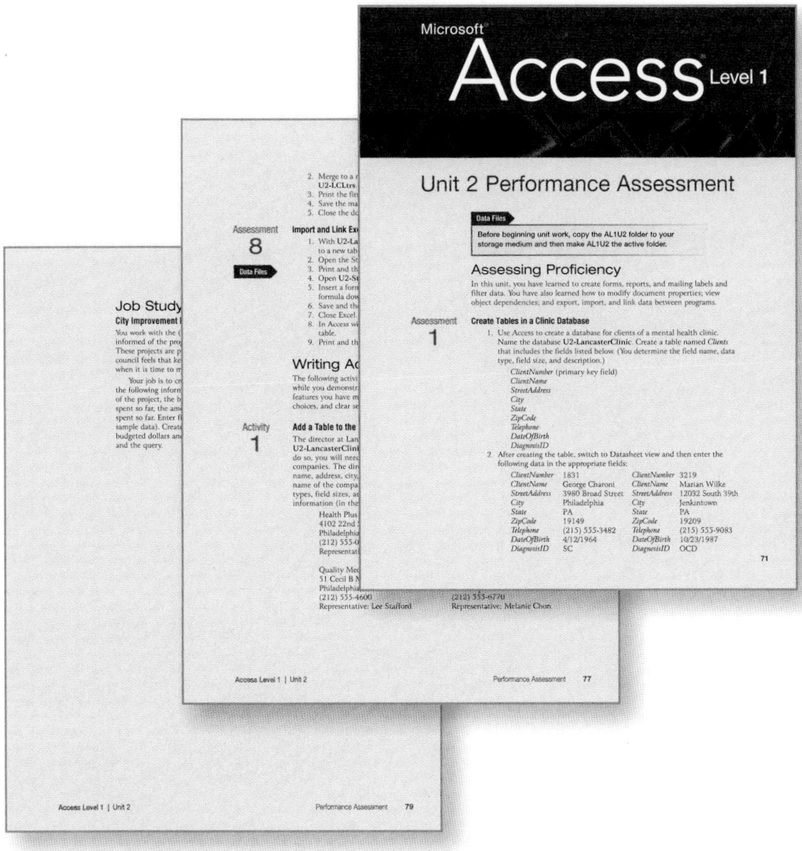

Microsoft® Access® Level 1

Unit 2 Performance Assessment

Data Files

Before beginning unit work, copy the AL1U2 folder to your storage medium and then make AL1U2 the active folder.

Assessing Proficiency

In this unit, you have learned to create forms, reports, and mailing labels and filter data. You have also learned how to modify document properties; view object dependencies; and export, import, and link data between programs.

Assessment 1

Create Tables in a Clinic Database

1. Use Access to create a database for clients of a mental health clinic. Name the database **U2-LancasterClinic**. Create a table named *Clients* that includes the fields listed below. (You determine the field name, data type, field size, and description.)

   ClientNumber (primary key field)
   ClientName
   StreetAddress
   City
   State
   ZipCode
   Telephone
   DateOfBirth
   DiagnosisID

2. After creating the table, switch to Datasheet view and then enter the following data in the appropriate fields:

ClientNumber	1831	*ClientNumber*	3219
ClientName	George Charoni	*ClientName*	Marian Wilke
StreetAddress	3980 Broad Street	*StreetAddress*	12032 South 39th
City	Philadelphia	*City*	Jenkintown
State	PA	*State*	PA
ZipCode	19149	*ZipCode*	19209
Telephone	(215) 555-3482	*Telephone*	(215) 555-9083
DateOfBirth	4/12/1964	*DateOfBirth*	10/23/1987
DiagnosisID	SC	*DiagnosisID*	OCD

71

Access Level 1 | Unit 2 Performance Assessment 77

Access Level 1 | Unit 2 Performance Assessment 79

Assessing Proficiency exercises check mastery of features.

Writing Activities involve applying application skills in a communication context.

Internet Research projects reinforce research and information processing skills.

Job Study at the end of each application's Unit 2 presents a capstone assessment requiring critical thinking and problem solving.

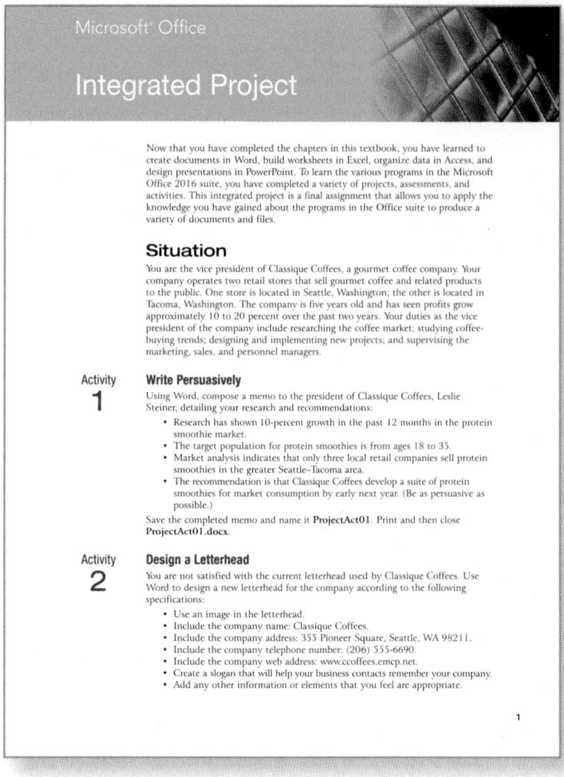

Microsoft® Office

Integrated Project

Now that you have completed the chapters in this textbook, you have learned to create documents in Word, build worksheets in Excel, organize data in Access, and design presentations in PowerPoint. To learn the various programs in the Microsoft Office 2016 suite, you have completed a variety of projects, assessments, and activities. This integrated project is a final assignment that allows you to apply the knowledge you have gained about the programs in the Office suite to produce a variety of documents and files.

Situation

You are the vice president of Classique Coffees, a gourmet coffee company. Your company operates two retail stores that sell gourmet coffee and related products to the public. One store is located in Seattle, Washington; the other is located in Tacoma, Washington. The company is five years old and has seen profits grow approximately 10 to 20 percent over the past two years. Your duties as the vice president of the company include researching the coffee market; studying coffee-buying trends; designing and implementing new projects; and supervising the marketing, sales, and personnel managers.

Activity 1

Write Persuasively

Using Word, compose a memo to the president of Classique Coffees, Leslie Steiner, detailing your research and recommendations:

- Research has shown 10-percent growth in the past 12 months in the protein smoothie market.
- The target population for protein smoothies is from ages 18 to 35.
- Market analysis indicates that only three local retail companies sell protein smoothies in the greater Seattle–Tacoma area.
- The recommendation is that Classique Coffees develop a suite of protein smoothies for market consumption by early next year. (Be as persuasive as possible.)

Save the completed memo and name it **ProjectAct01**. Print and then close **ProjectAct01.docx**.

Activity 2

Design a Letterhead

You are not satisfied with the current letterhead used by Classique Coffees. Use Word to design a new letterhead for the company according to the following specifications:

- Use an image in the letterhead.
- Include the company name: Classique Coffees.
- Include the company address: 355 Pioneer Square, Seattle, WA 98211.
- Include the company telephone number: (206) 555-6690.
- Include the company web address: www.ccoffees.emcp.net.
- Create a slogan that will help your business contacts remember your company.
- Add any other information or elements that you feel are appropriate.

1

Integrated Project at the end of the *Workbook* ebook offers students the opportunity to experience the power of the Office 2016 suite—importing and exporting data among the major applications to meet information processing needs most effectively.

SNAP Training and Assessment

SNAP

SNAP is a web-based training and assessment program and learning management system (LMS) for learning Microsoft Office 2016. SNAP is comprised of rich content, a sophisticated grade book, and robust scheduling and analytics tools. SNAP courseware supports the *Benchmark Series* content and delivers live-in-the-application assessments for students to demonstrate their skills mastery. Interactive tutorials increase skills-focused moments with guided training and measured practice. SNAP provides automatic scoring and detailed feedback on the many activities, exercises, and quizzes to help identify areas where additional support is needed, evaluating student performance both at an individual and course level. The *Benchmark Series* SNAP course content is also available to export into any LMS system that supports LTI tools.

Paradigm Education Solutions provides technical support for SNAP through 24-7 chat at ParadigmCollege.com. In addition, an online User Guide and other SNAP training tools for using SNAP are available.

Student eBook and *Workbook* eBook

The student ebook and *Workbook* ebook available through SNAP or online at Paradigm.bookshelf.emcp.com provide access to the *Benchmark Series* content from any device (desktop, tablet, and smartphone) anywhere, through a live Internet connection. The versatile ebook platform features dynamic navigation tools including a linked table of contents and the ability to jump to specific pages, search for terms, bookmark, highlight, and take notes. The ebooks offer live links to the interactive content and resources that support the print textbook, including the student data files, Precheck and Recheck quizzes, and interactive tutorials. The *Workbook* ebook also provides access to presentations with audio support and to end-of-section Concept Check, Skills Assessment, Visual Benchmark, Case Study, and end-of-unit Performance Assessment activities.

Instructor eResources eBook

All instructor resources are available digitally through a web-based ebook at Paradigm.bookshelf.emcp.com. The instructor materials include these items:

- Planning resources, such as lesson plans, teaching hints, and sample course syllabi
- Presentation resources, such as PowerPoint slide shows with lecture notes
- Assessment resources, including live and annotated PDF model answers for chapter work and workbook activities, rubrics for evaluating student work, and chapter-based exam banks

SNAP
Personalized. Powerful. Proven.
Welcome to a better way to teach Microsoft® Office.
SNAP 2016's Microsoft Office training and assessments give students real-world experience by working directly in the application. You have a suite of powerful tools at your fingertips, granting you instant access to performance metrics and reporting tools so you can focus on teaching.
Work live in Microsoft applications
One integrated system
Automatic grading
Instant performance insights
Call 800-535-6865 or visit snap2016.com to schedule a demo.

Microsoft®

Office

Getting Started in Office 2016

Several computer applications are combined to make the Microsoft Office 2016 application suite. The applications are known as *software*, and they contain instructions that tell the computer what to do. Some of the applications in the suite include Word, a word processing applicaton; Excel, a spreadsheet applicaton; Access, a database applicaton; and PowerPoint, a presentation applicaton.

Identifying Computer Hardware

The Microsoft Office suite can run on several types of computer equipment, referred to as *hardware*. You will need access to a laptop or a desktop computer system that includes a PC/tower, monitor, keyboard, printer, drives, and mouse. If you are not sure what equipment you will be operating, check with your instructor. The computer systems shown in Figure G.1 consists of six components. Each component is discussed separately in the material that follows.

Figure G.1 Computer System

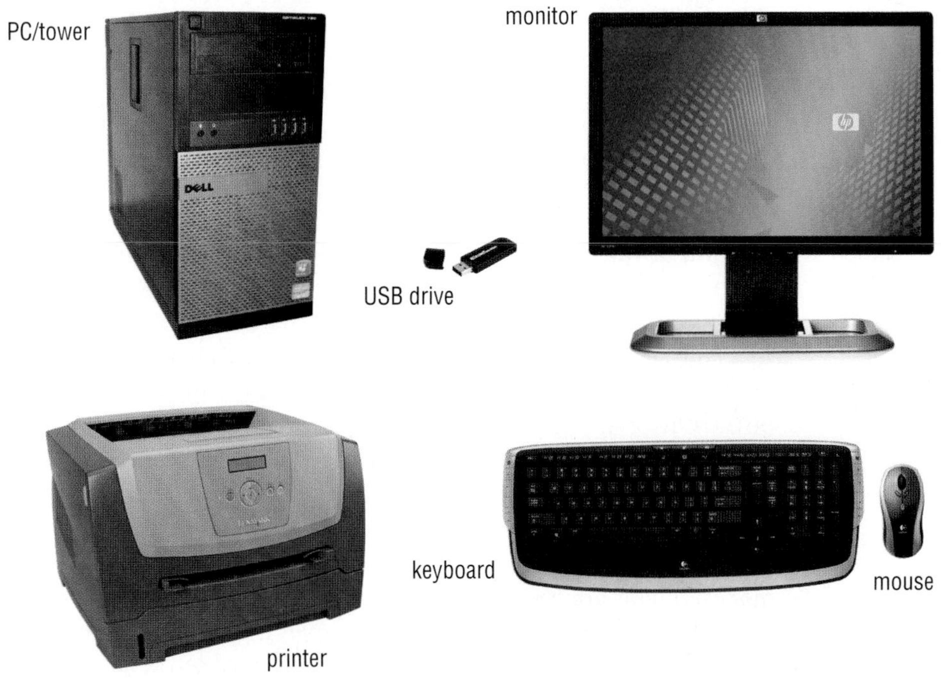

Figure G.2 PC/Tower

PC/Tower

The PC, also known as the *tower*, is the brain of the computer and is where all processing occurs. A PC/tower consists of components such as the Central Processing Unit (CPU), hard drives, and video cards plugged into a motherboard. The motherboard is mounted inside the case, which includes input and output ports for attaching external peripherals (as shown in Figure G.2). When a user provides input through the use of peripherals, the PC/tower computes that input and outputs the results. Similar hardware is included in a laptop, but the design is more compact to allow for mobility.

Monitor

Hint Monitor size is measured diagonally. For example, the distance from the bottom left corner to the top right corner of the monitor.

A computer monitor looks like a television screen. It displays the visual information that the computer is outputting. The quality of display for monitors varies depending on the type of monitor and the level of resolution. Monitors can also vary in size—generally from 13 inches to 26 inches or larger.

Keyboard

The keyboard is used to input information into the computer. The number and location of the keys on a keyboard can vary. In addition to letters, numbers, and symbols, most computer keyboards contain function keys, arrow keys, and a numeric keypad. Figure G.3 shows an enhanced keyboard.

The 12 keys at the top of the keyboard, labeled with the letter F followed by a number, are called *function keys*. Use these keys to perform functions within each of the Office applications. To the right of the regular keys is a group of special or dedicated keys. These keys are labeled with specific functions that will be performed when you press the key. Below the special keys are arrow keys. Use these keys to move the insertion point in the document screen.

Some keyboards include mode indicator lights. When you select certain modes, a light appears on the keyboard. For example, if you press the Caps Lock key, which disables the lowercase alphabet, a light appears next to Caps Lock. Similarly, pressing the Num Lock key will disable the special functions on the numeric keypad, which is located at the right side of the keyboard.

Figure G.3 Keyboard

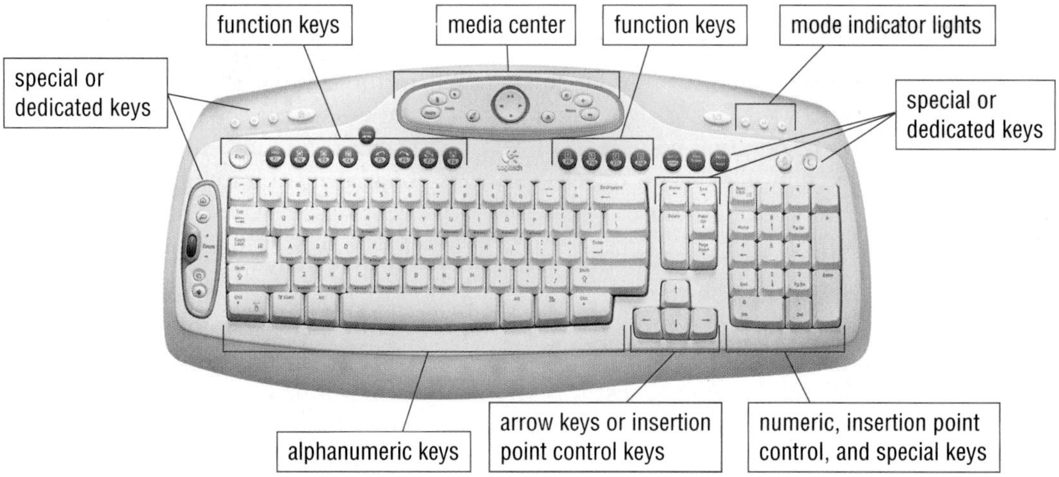

Drives and Ports

A PC includes drives and ports that allow you to input and output data. For example, a hard drive is a disk drive inside of the PC that stores data that may have been inputted or outputted. Other drives may include CD, DVD and BluRay disc drives, although newer computers may not include these drives, because USB flash drives are becoming the preferred technology. Ports are the "plugs" on the PC, and are used to connect devices to the computer, such as the keyboard and mouse, the monitor, speakers, a USB flash drive and so on. Most PCs will have a few USB ports, at least one display port, an audio cable port, and possibly an ethernet port (used to physically connect to the Internet or a network).

Printer

An electronic version of a file is known as a *soft copy*. If you want to create a hard copy of a file, you need to print it. To print documents you will need to access a printer (as shown in Figure G.4), which will probably be either a laser printer or an ink-jet printer. A laser printer uses a laser beam combined with heat and pressure to print documents, while an ink-jet printer prints a document by spraying a fine mist of ink on the page.

Figure G.4 Printer

Mouse

Most functions and commands in the Microsoft Office suite are designed to be performed using a mouse or a similar pointing device. A mouse is an input device that sits on a flat surface next to the computer. You can operate a mouse with your left or right hand. Moving the mouse on the flat surface causes a corresponding pointer to move on the screen, and clicking the left or right mouse buttons allows you to select various objects and commands. Figure G.5 shows an example of a mouse.

Using the Mouse The applications in the Microsoft Office suite can be operated with the keyboard and a mouse. The mouse generally has two buttons on top, which you press to execute specific functions and commands. A mouse may also contain a wheel, which can be used to scroll in a window or as a third button. To use the mouse, rest it on a flat surface or a mouse pad. Put your hand over it with your palm resting on top of the mouse and your index finger resting on the left mouse button. As you move your hand, and thus the mouse, a corresponding pointer moves on the screen.

When using the mouse, you should understand four terms — point, click, double-click, and drag. When operating the mouse, you may need to point to a specific command, button, or icon. To *point* means to position the mouse pointer on the desired item. With the mouse pointer positioned on the item, you may need to click a button on the mouse to select the item. To *click* means to quickly tap a button on the mouse once. To complete two steps at one time, such as choosing and then executing a function, double-click the mouse button. To *double-click* means to tap the left mouse button twice in quick succession. The term *drag* means to click and hold down the left mouse button, move the mouse pointer to a specific location, and then release the button.

Hint This textbook will use the verb *click* to refer to the mouse and the verb press to refer to a key on the keyboard.

Using the Mouse Pointer The mouse pointer will look different depending on where you have positioned it and what function you are performing. The following are some of the ways the mouse pointer can appear when you are working in the Office suite:

- The mouse pointer appears as an I-beam (called the *I-beam pointer*) when you are inserting text in a file. The I-beam pointer can be used to move the insertion point or to select text.

- The mouse pointer appears as an arrow pointing up and to the left (called the *arrow pointer*) when it is moved to the Title bar, Quick Access Toolbar, ribbon, or an option in a dialog box, among other locations.

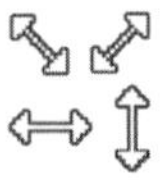

- The mouse pointer becomes a double-headed arrow (either pointing left and right, pointing up and down, or pointing diagonally) when you perform certain functions such as changing the size of an object.

Figure G.5 Mouse

- In certain situations, such as when you move an object or image, the mouse pointer displays with a four-headed arrow attached. The four-headed arrow means that you can move the object left, right, up, or down.

- When a request is being processed or when an application is being loaded, the mouse pointer may appear as a moving circle. The moving circle means "please wait." When the process is completed, the circle is replaced with a normal mouse pointer.

- When the mouse pointer displays as a hand with a pointing index finger, it indicates that more information is available about an item. The mouse pointer also displays as a hand with a pointing index finger when you hover the mouse over a hyperlink.

Touchpad

If you are working on a laptop computer, you may use a touchpad instead of a mouse. A *touchpad* allows you to move the mouse pointer by moving your finger across a surface at the base of the keyboard. You click and right-click by using your thumb to press the buttons located at the bottom of the touchpad. Some touchpads have special features such as scrolling or clicking something by tapping the surface of the touchpad instead of pressing a button with a thumb.

TouchScreen

Smartphones, tablets, and touch monitors all use TouchScreen technology (as shown in Figure G.6), which allows users to directly interact with the objects on the screen by touching them with fingers, thumbs, or a stylus. Multiple fingers or both thumbs can be used on most modern touchscreens, giving users the ability to zoom, rotate, and manipulate items on the screen. While a lot of activities in this textbook can be completed using a device with a touchscreen, a mouse or touchpad might be required to complete a few activities.

Figure G.6 Touchscreen

Choosing Commands

Once an application is open, you can use several methods in the application to choose commands. A command is an instruction that tells the application to do something. You can choose a command using the mouse or the keyboard. When an application such as Word or PowerPoint is open, the ribbon contains buttons and options for completing tasks, as well as tabs you can click to display additional buttons and options. To choose a button on the Quick Access Toolbar or on the ribbon, position the tip of the mouse arrow pointer on the button and then click the left mouse button.

The Office suite provides accelerator keys you can press to use a command in an application. Press the Alt key on the keyboard to display KeyTips that identify the accelerator key you can press to execute a command. For example, if you press the Alt key in a Word document with the Home tab active, KeyTips display as shown in Figure G.7. Continue pressing accelerator keys until you execute the desired command. For example, to begin checking the spelling in a document, press the Alt key, press the R key on the keyboard to display the Review tab, and then press the letter S on the keyboard.

Choosing Commands from Drop-Down Lists

To choose a command from a drop-down list with the mouse, position the mouse pointer on the option and then click the left mouse button. To make a selection from a drop-down list with the keyboard, type the underlined letter in the option.

Some options at a drop-down list may appear in gray (dimmed), indicating that the option is currently unavailable. If an option at a drop-down list displays preceded by a check mark, it means the option is currently active. If an option at a drop-down list displays followed by an ellipsis (…), clicking that option will display a dialog box.

Choosing Options from a Dialog Box

A dialog box contains options for applying formatting or otherwise modifying a file or data within a file. Some dialog boxes display with tabs along the top that provide additional options. For example, the Font dialog box shown in Figure G.8 contains two tabs—the Font tab and the Advanced tab. The tab that displays in the front is the active tab. To make a tab active using the mouse, position the arrow pointer on the tab and then click the left mouse button. If you are using the keyboard, press Ctrl + Tab or press Alt + the underlined letter on the tab.

To choose an option from a dialog box with the mouse, position the arrow pointer on the option and then click the left mouse button. If you are using the keyboard, press the Tab key to move the insertion point forward from option to option. Press Shift + Tab to move the insertion point backward from option to option. You can also press and hold down the Alt key and then press the

Figure G.7 Word Home Tab KeyTips

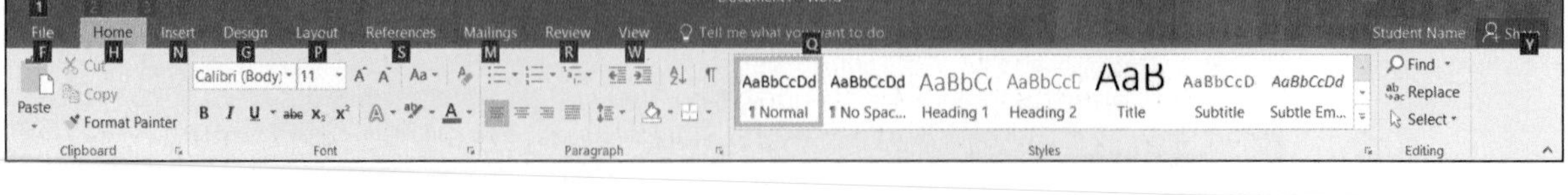

Figure G.8 Word Font Dialog Box

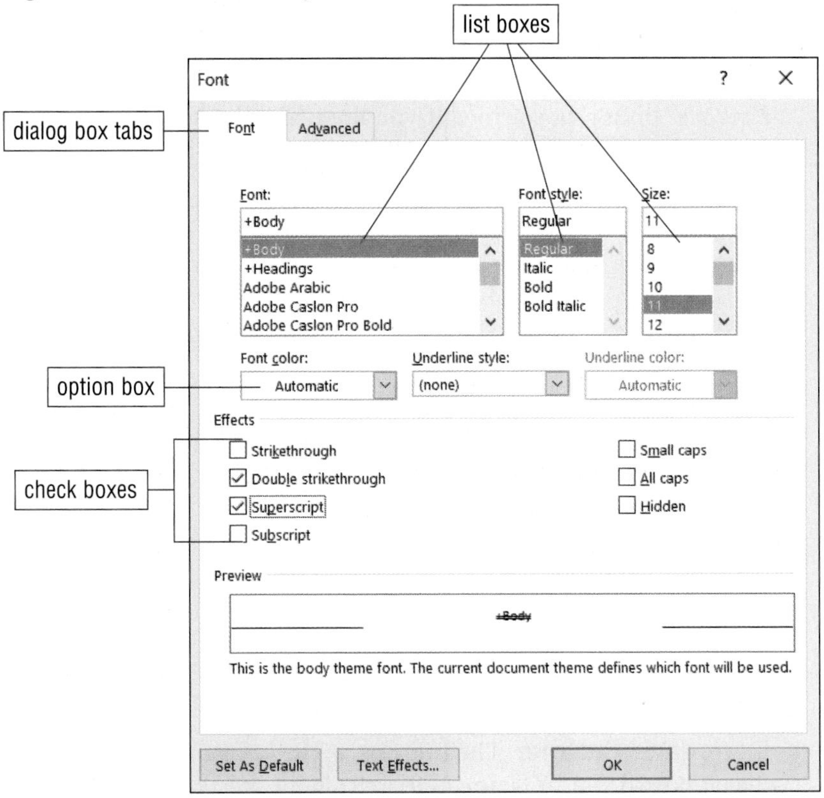

underlined letter of the option. When an option is selected, it displays with a blue background or surrounded by a dashed box called a *marquee*. A dialog box contains one or more of the following elements: list boxes, option boxes, check boxes, text boxes, option buttons, measurement boxes, and command buttons.

List Boxes and Option Boxes The fonts available in the Font dialog box, shown in Figure G.8, are contained in a list box. To make a selection from a list box with the mouse, move the arrow pointer to the option and then click the left mouse button.

Some list boxes may contain a scroll bar. This scroll bar will display at the right side of the list box (a vertical scroll bar) or at the bottom of the list box (a horizontal scroll bar). Use a vertical scroll bar or a horizontal scroll bar to move through the list if the list is longer (or wider) than the box. To move down a list using a vertical scroll bar, position the arrow pointer on the down arrow, and then click and hold down the left mouse button. To scroll up through the list, position the arrow pointer on the up arrow, and then click and hold down the left mouse button. You can also move the arrow pointer above the scroll box and click the left mouse button to scroll up the list or move the arrow pointer below the scroll box and click the left mouse button to move down the list. To navigate in a list with a horizontal scroll bar, click the left arrow to scroll to the left of the list or click the right arrow to scroll to the right of the list.

To use the keyboard to make a selection from a list box, move the insertion point into the box by holding down the Alt key and pressing the underlined letter of the desired option. Press the Up and/or Down Arrow keys on the keyboard to move through the list, and press the Enter key when the desired option is selected.

In some dialog boxes where there is not enough room for a list box, lists of options are contained in a drop-down list box called an *option box*. Option boxes display with a down arrow. For example, in Figure G.8, the font color options are contained in an option box. To display the different color options, click the *Font color* option box arrow. If you are using the keyboard, press Alt + C.

Hint This textbook will refer to the down arrow for an option box as an option box arrow.

Check Boxes Some dialog boxes contain options preceded by a box. A check mark may or may not appear in the box. The Word Font dialog box shown in Figure G.8 displays a variety of check boxes within the *Effects* section. If a check mark appears in the box, the option is active (turned on). If the check box does not contain a check mark, the option is inactive (turned off). Any number of check boxes can be active. For example, in the Word Font dialog box, you can insert a check mark in several of the boxes in the *Effects* section to activate the options.

To make a check box active or inactive with the mouse, position the tip of the arrow pointer in the check box and then click the left mouse button. If you are using the keyboard, press Alt + the underlined letter of the option.

Text Boxes Some options in a dialog box require you to enter text. For example, the boxes below the *Find what* and *Replace with* options at the Excel Find and Replace dialog box shown in Figure G.9 are text boxes. In a text box, type text or edit existing text. Edit text in a text box in the same manner as normal text. Use the Left and Right Arrow keys on the keyboard to move the insertion point without deleting text and use the Delete key or Backspace key to delete text.

Command Buttons The buttons at the bottom of the Excel Find and Replace dialog box shown in Figure G.9 are called *command buttons*. Use a command button to execute or cancel a command. Some command buttons display with an ellipsis (...), which means another dialog box will open if you click that button. To choose a command button with the mouse, position the arrow pointer on the button and then click the left mouse button. To choose a command button with the keyboard, press the Tab key until the command button is surrounded by a marquee and then press the Enter key.

Option Buttons The Word Insert Table dialog box shown in Figure G.10 contains options in the *AutoFit behavior* section preceded by option buttons. Only one option button can be selected at any time. When an option button is selected, a blue or black circle displays in the button. To select an option button with the mouse, position the tip of the arrow pointer inside the option button or on the option and then click the left mouse button. To make a selection with the keyboard, press and hold down the Alt key, press the underlined letter of the option, and then release the Alt key.

Figure G.9 Excel Find and Replace Dialog Box

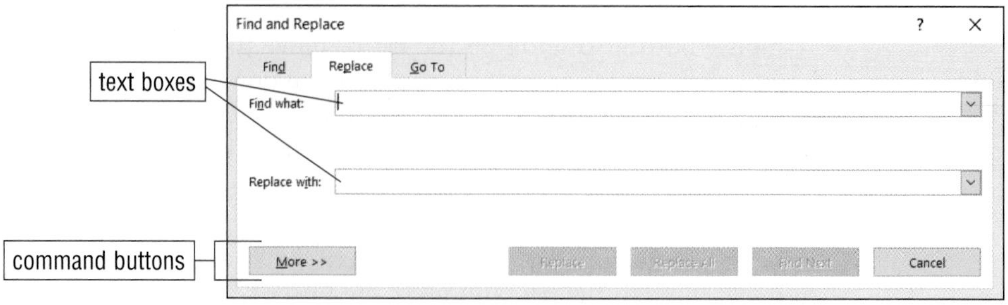

Figure G.10 Word Insert Table Dialog Box

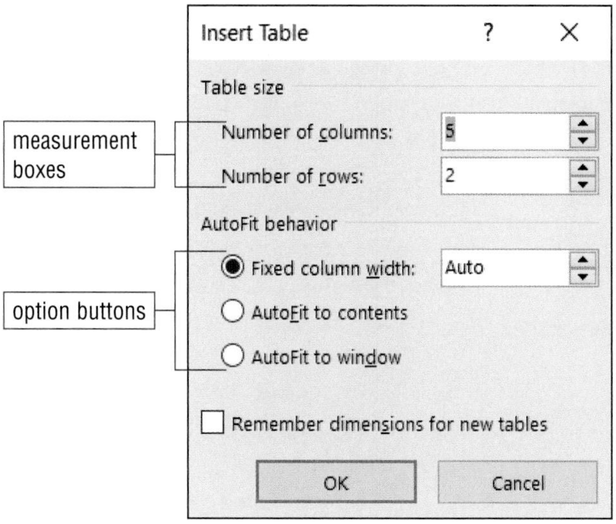

Hint In addition to using the up and down arrows, you can change the current measurement by selecting it and then typing the new measurement using the keyboard.

Measurement Boxes Some options in a dialog box contain measurements or amounts you can increase or decrease. These options are generally located in a measurement box. For example, the Word Insert Table dialog box shown in Figure G.10 contains the *Number of columns* and *Number of rows* measurement boxes. To increase a number in a measurement box, position the tip of the arrow pointer on the up arrow at the right of the measurement box and then click the left mouse button. To decrease the number, click the down arrow. If you are using the keyboard, press and hold down the Alt key and then press the underlined letter for the option, press the Up Arrow key to increase the number or the Down Arrow key to decrease the number, and then release the Alt key.

Choosing Commands with Keyboard Shortcuts

Applications in the Office suite offer a variety of keyboard shortcuts you can use to execute specific commands. Keyboard shortcuts generally require two or more keys. For example, the keyboard shortcut to display the Open dialog box in an application is Ctrl + F12. To use this keyboard shortcut, press and hold down the Ctrl key, press the F12 function on the keyboard, and then release the Ctrl key. For a list of keyboard shortcuts, refer to the Help files.

Choosing Commands with Shortcut Menus

The software applications in the Office suite include shortcut menus that contain commands related to different items. To display a shortcut menu, position the mouse pointer over the item for which you want to view more options, and then click the right mouse button or press Shift + F10. The shortcut menu will appear wherever the insertion point is positioned. For example, if the insertion point is positioned in a paragraph of text in a Word document, clicking the right mouse button or pressing Shift + F10 will cause the shortcut menu shown in Figure G.11 to display in the document screen (along with the Mini toolbar).

To select an option from a shortcut menu with the mouse, click the option. If you are using the keyboard, press the Up or Down Arrow key until the option is selected and then press the Enter key. To close a shortcut menu without choosing an option, click outside the shortcut menu or press the Esc key.

Figure G.11 Word Shortcut Menu

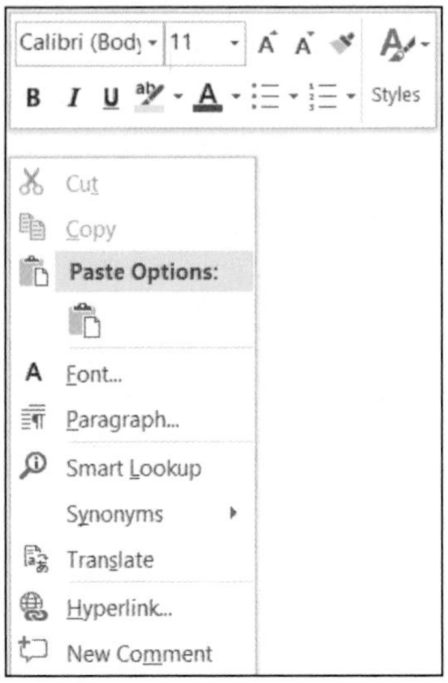

Working with Multiple Programs

As you learn the various applications in the Microsoft Office suite, you will notice many similarities between them. For example, the steps to save, close, and print are virtually the same whether you are working in Word, Excel, or PowerPoint. This consistency between applications greatly enhances your ability to transfer knowledge learned in one application to another within the suite. Another benefit to using Microsoft Office is the ability to have more than one application open at the same time and to integrate content from one program with another. For example, you can open Word and create a document, open Excel and create a spreadsheet, and then copy the Excel spreadsheet into Word.

When you open an application, a button containing an icon representing the application displays on the taskbar. If you open another application, a button containing an icon representing that application displays to the right of the first application button on the taskbar. Figure G.12 shows the taskbar with Word, Excel, Access, and PowerPoint open. To move from one program to another, click the taskbar button representing the desired application.

Customizing Settings

Before beginning computer projects in this textbook, you may need to customize your monitor's settings, change the DPI display setting, and turn on the display of file extensions. Projects in the chapters in this textbook assume that the monitor display is set at 1600 × 900 pixels, the DPI set at 125%, and that the display of file extensions is turned on. If you are unable to make changes to the monitor's resolution or the DPI settings, the projects can still be completed successfully. Some references in the text might not perfectly match what you see on your

Figure G.12 Taskbar with Word, Excel, Access, and PowerPoint Open

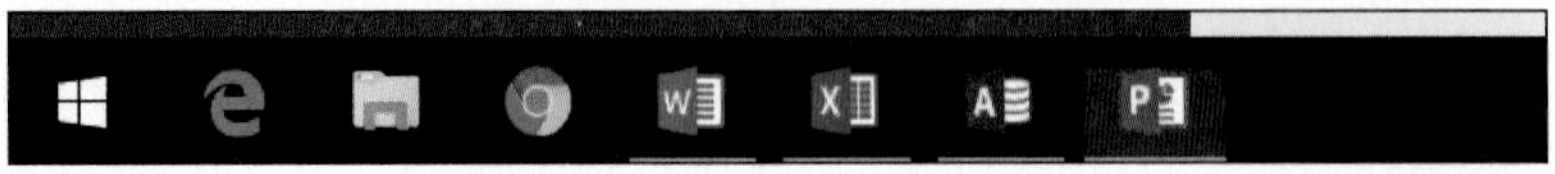

screen, so some mental adjustments may need to be made for certain steps. For example, an item in a drop-down gallery might appear in a different column or row than what is indicated in the step instructions.

Before you begin learning the applications in the Microsoft Office 2016 suite, take a moment to check the display settings on the computer you are using. Your monitor's display settings are important because the ribbon in the Microsoft Office suite adjusts to the screen resolution setting of your computer monitor. A computer monitor set at a high resolution will have the ability to show more buttons in the ribbon than will a monitor set to a low resolution. The illustrations in this textbook were created with a screen resolution display set at 1600 × 900 pixels. In Figure G.13, the Word ribbon is shown three ways: at a lower screen resolution (1366 × 768 pixels), at the screen resolution featured throughout this textbook, and at a higher screen resolution (1920 × 1080 pixels). Note the variances in the ribbon in all three examples. If possible, set your display to 1600 × 900 pixels to match the illustrations you will see in this textbook.

Figure G.13 The Home Tab Displayed on a Monitor Set at Different Screen Resolutions

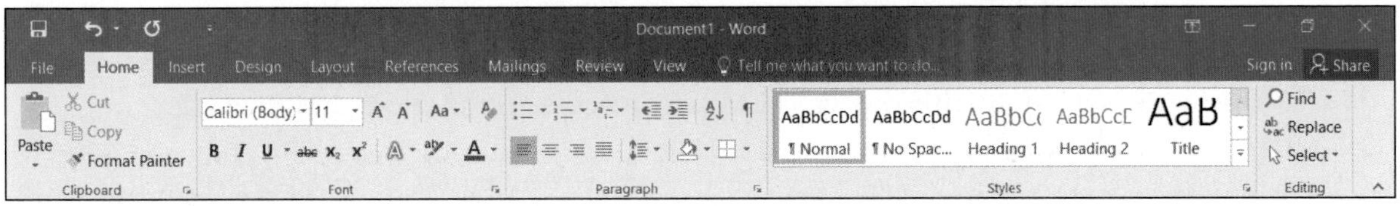

1366 × 768 screen resolution

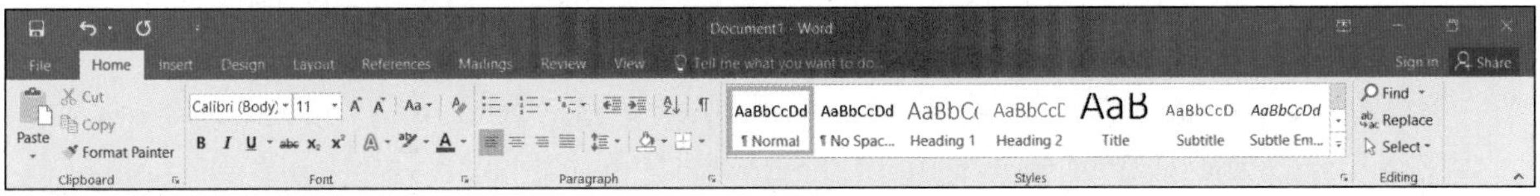

1600 × 900 screen resolution

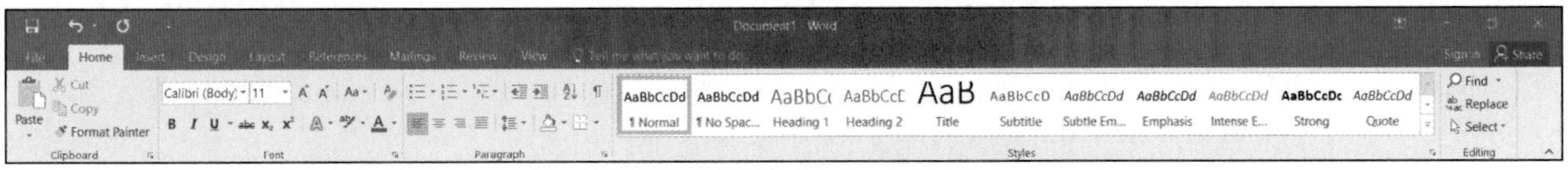

1920 × 1080 screen resolution

Project 1 Setting Monitor Display to 1600 × 900

Note: The resolution settings may be locked on lab computers. Also, some laptop screens and small monitors may not be able to display in a 1600 × 900 resolution.

1. At the Windows 10 desktop, right-click in a blank area of the screen.
2. At the shortcut menu, click the *Display settings* option.

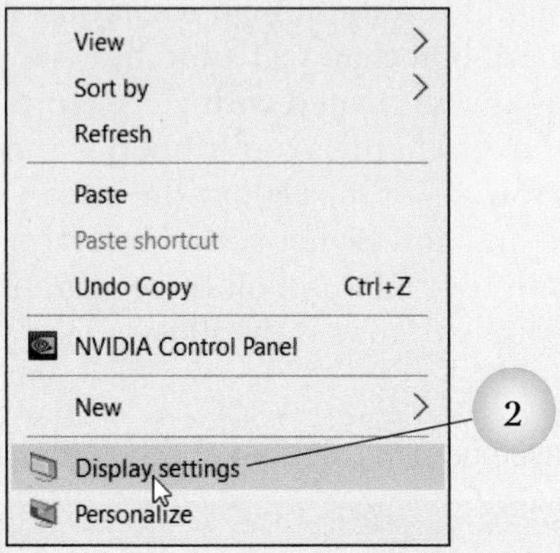

3. At the Settings window with the SYSTEM screen active, scroll down and then click *Advanced display settings*.

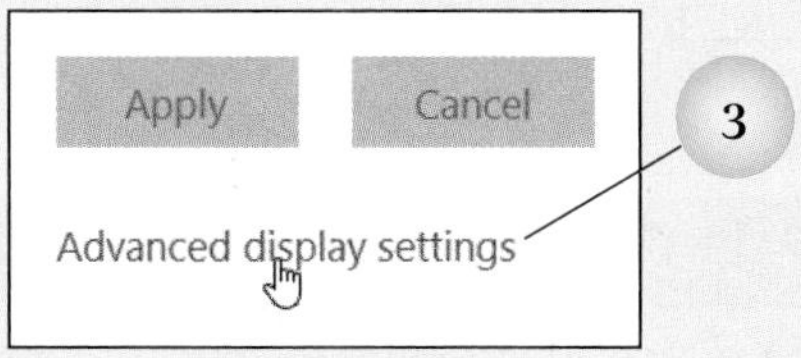

4. Scroll down the Settings window until the *Resolution* option box is visible and take note of the current resolution setting. If the current resolution is already set to 1600 × 900, skip ahead to Step 8.
5. Click in the Resolution option box and then click the 1600 × 900 option at the drop-down list.

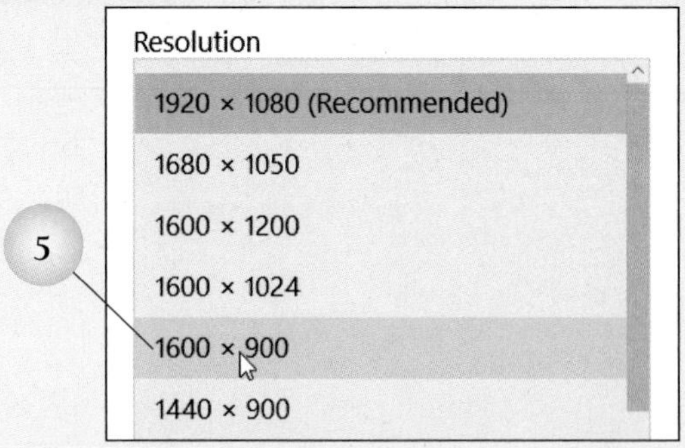

6. Click the Apply button.
7. Click the Keep Changes button.
8. Click the Close button.

Project 2 Changing the DPI Setting

Note: The DPI settings may be locked on lab computers. Also, some laptop screens and small monitors may not allow the DPI settings to be changed.

1. At the Windows 10 desktop, right-click in a blank area of the screen.
2. At the shortcut menu, click the *Display settings* option.
3. At the Settings window, take note of the current DPI percentage next to the text *Change the size of text, apps, and other items*. If the percentage is already set to 125%, skip to Step 5.
4. Click the slider bar below the text *Change the size of text, apps, and other items* and hold down the left mouse button, drag to the right until the DPI percentage is 125%, and then release the mouse button.

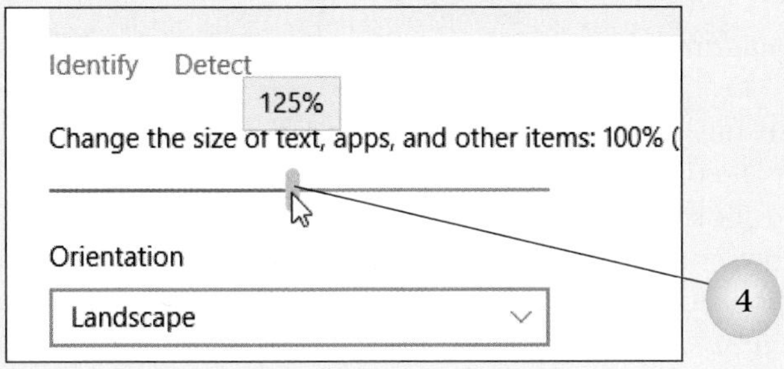

5. Close the computer window.

Project 3 Displaying File Extensions

1. At the Windows 10 desktop, click the File Explorer button on the taskbar.

2. At the File Explorer window, click the View tab.
3. Click the *File name extensions* check box in the Show/hide group to insert a check mark.

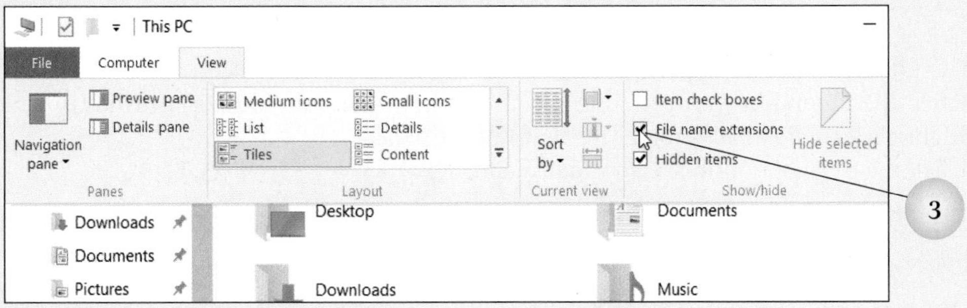

4. Close the computer window.

Data Files

Completing Computer Projects

Some projects in this textbook require that you open an existing file. Project files are saved on OneDrive in a zip file. Before beginning projects and assessments in this book and the accompanying ebook, copy the necessary folder from the zip file to your storage medium (such as a USB flash drive) using File Explorer. Begin downloading the files for this book by going to the ebook and clicking the Ancillary Links button that displays when the ebook displays this page or any chapter opener page with the Data Files tab on it.

Project 4 **Downloading Files to a USB Flash Drive**

Note: OneDrive is updated periodically, so the steps to download files may vary from the steps below.

1. Insert your USB flash drive into an available USB port.
2. Navigate to this textbook's ebook. If you are a SNAP user, navigate to the ebook by clicking the textbook ebook link on your Assignments page. If you are not a SNAP user, launch your browser and go to http://paradigm.bookshelf.emcp.com, log in, and then click the textbook ebook thumbnail. ***Note: The steps in this activity assume you are using the Microsoft Edge browser. If you are using a different browser, the following steps may vary.***
3. Navigate to the ebook page that corresponds to this textbook page.
4. Click the Ancillary Links button in the menu. The menu that appears may be at the top of the window or along the side of the window, depending on the size of the window.

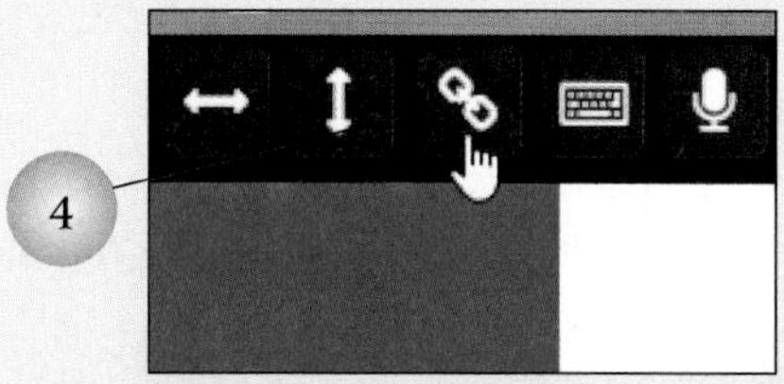

5. At the Ancillary Links dialog box, click the Data Files: All Files hyperlink.

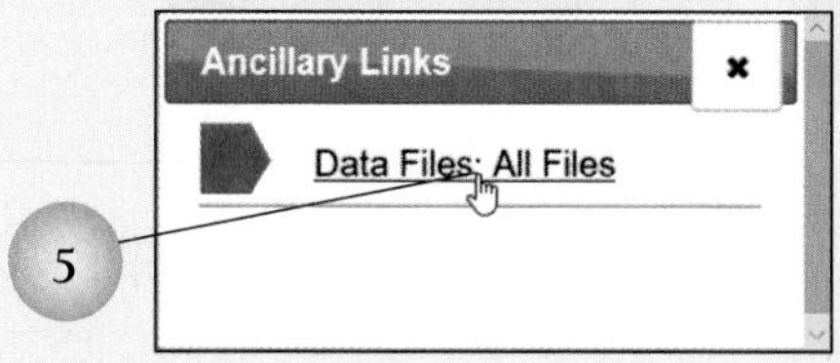

6. Click the Download hyperlink at the top of the window.
7. Click the Open button in the message box when the DataFiles.zip finishes downloading.
8. Right-click the DataFiles folder in the Content pane.
9. Click the *Copy* option in the shortcut menu.

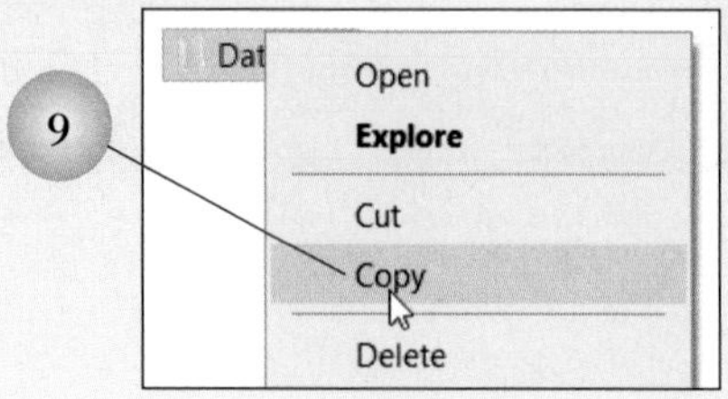

10. Click the USB flash drive that displays in the Navigation pane at the left side of the File Explorer window.
11. Click the Home tab in the File Explorer window.
12. Click the Paste button in the Clipboard group.

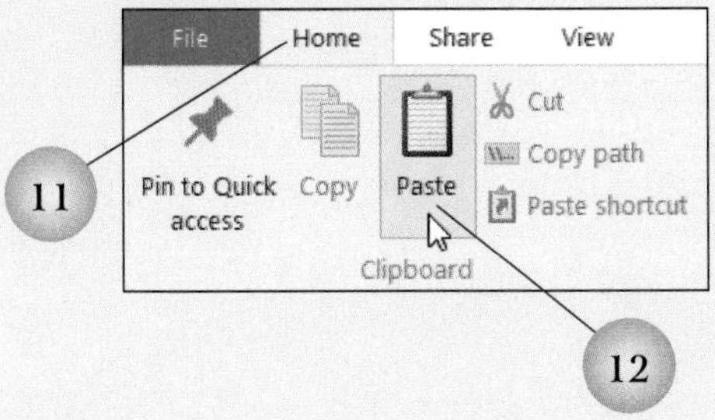

13. Close the File Explorer window by clicking the Close button in the upper right corner of the window.

Project 5 Deleting a File

Note: Check with your instructor before deleting a file.

1. At the Windows 10 desktop, open File Explorer by clicking the File Explorer button on the taskbar.
2. Click the *Downloads* folder in the navigation pane.
3. Right-click *DataFiles.zip*.
4. Click the *Delete* option at the shortcut menu.

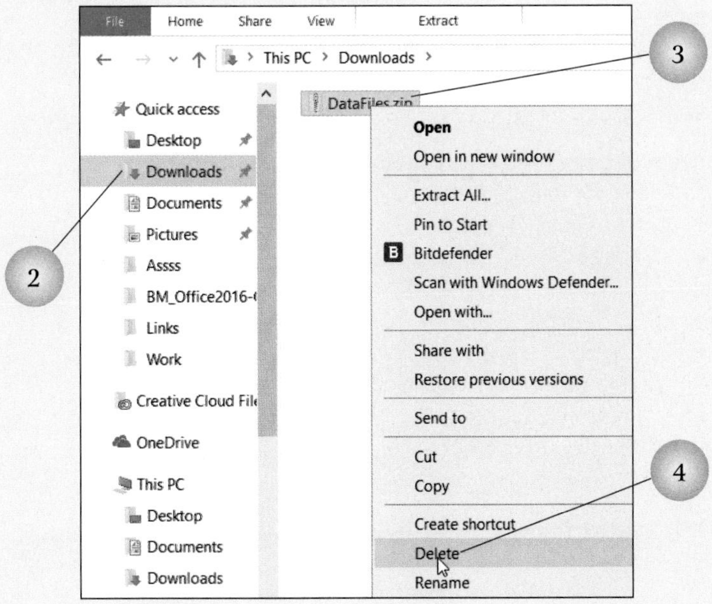

Microsoft®

Word Level 1

Unit 1

Editing and Formatting Documents

Microsoft®

Word

Preparing a Word Document

CHAPTER 1

Performance Objectives

Upon successful completion of Chapter 1, you will be able to:

1 Open Microsoft Word
2 Create, save, name, print, open, and close a Word document
3 Close Word
4 Open a document from and pin/unpin a document at the *Recent* Option list
5 Edit a document
6 Move the insertion point within a document
7 Scroll within a document
8 Select text
9 Use the Undo and Redo buttons
10 Check spelling and grammar
11 Use the Tell Me and Help features

Precheck

Check your current skills to help focus your study.

In this chapter, you will learn to create, save, name, print, open, close, and edit a Word document as well as complete a spelling and grammar check. You will also learn about the Tell Me feature, which provides information and guidance on how to complete a function, and the Help feature, which is an on-screen reference manual that provides information on features and commands for each program in the Microsoft Office suite. Before continuing, make sure you read the *Getting Started* section presented at the beginning of this book. It contains information about computer hardware and software, using the mouse, executing commands, and exploring Help files.

SNAP

If you are a SNAP user, launch the Precheck and Tutorials from your Assignments page.

Data Files

Before beginning chapter work, copy the WL1C1 folder to your storage medium and then make WL1C1 the active folder.

Project 1 **Prepare a Word Document** **2 Parts**

You will create a short document containing information on resumes and then save, print, and close the document.

Preview Finished Project

Tutorial

Opening a Blank Document

Opening Microsoft Word

Microsoft Office 2016 contains a word processing program named Word that can be used to create, save, edit, and print documents. The steps to open Word may vary but generally include clicking the Start button on the Windows 10 desktop and then clicking the Word 2016 tile at the Start menu. At the Word 2016 opening screen, click the *Blank document* template.

Tutorial

Exploring the Word Screen

Quick Steps

Open Word and Open a Blank Document

1. Click Word 2016 tile at Windows Start menu.
2. Click *Blank document* template.

Hint A book icon displays in the Status bar. A check mark on the book indicates no spelling errors have been detected by the spelling checker, while an X on the book indicates errors. Double-click the book icon to move to the next error. If the book icon is not visible, right-click the Status bar and then click the *Spelling and Grammar Check* option at the shortcut menu.

Creating, Saving, Printing, and Closing a Document

When the Blank document template is clicked, a blank document displays on the screen, as shown in Figure 1.1. The features of the document screen are described in Table 1.1.

At a blank document, type information to create a document. A document is a record containing information such as a letter, report, term paper, table, and so on. Here are some things to consider when typing text:

- **Word wrap:** As text is typed in the document, Word wraps text to the next line, so the Enter key does not need to be pressed at the end of each line. A word is wrapped to the next line if it begins before the right margin and continues past the right margin. The only times the Enter key needs to be pressed are to end a paragraph, create a blank line, and end a short line.
- **AutoCorrect:** Word contains a feature that automatically corrects certain words as they are typed. For example, if *adn* is typed instead of *and*, Word automatically corrects it when the spacebar is pressed after typing the word. AutoCorrect will also superscript the letters that follow an ordinal number (a number indicating a position in a series). For example, type *2nd* and then press the spacebar or Enter key, and Word will convert this ordinal number to 2nd.
- **Automatic spelling checker:** By default, Word automatically inserts a red wavy line below any word that is not contained in the Spelling dictionary or automatically corrected by AutoCorrect. This may include misspelled words, proper names, some terminology, and some foreign words. If a typed word is not recognized by the Spelling dictionary, leave it as written if the word is correct. However, if the word is incorrect, delete the word or position the I-beam pointer on the word, click the *right* mouse button, and then click the correct spelling at the shortcut menu.
- **Automatic grammar checker:** Word includes an automatic grammar checker. If the grammar checker detects a sentence containing a grammatical error, a blue wavy line is inserted below the error. The sentence can be left as written or corrected. To correct the sentence, position the I-beam pointer on the error, click the *right* mouse button, and choose from the shortcut menu of possible corrections.

Figure 1.1 Blank Document

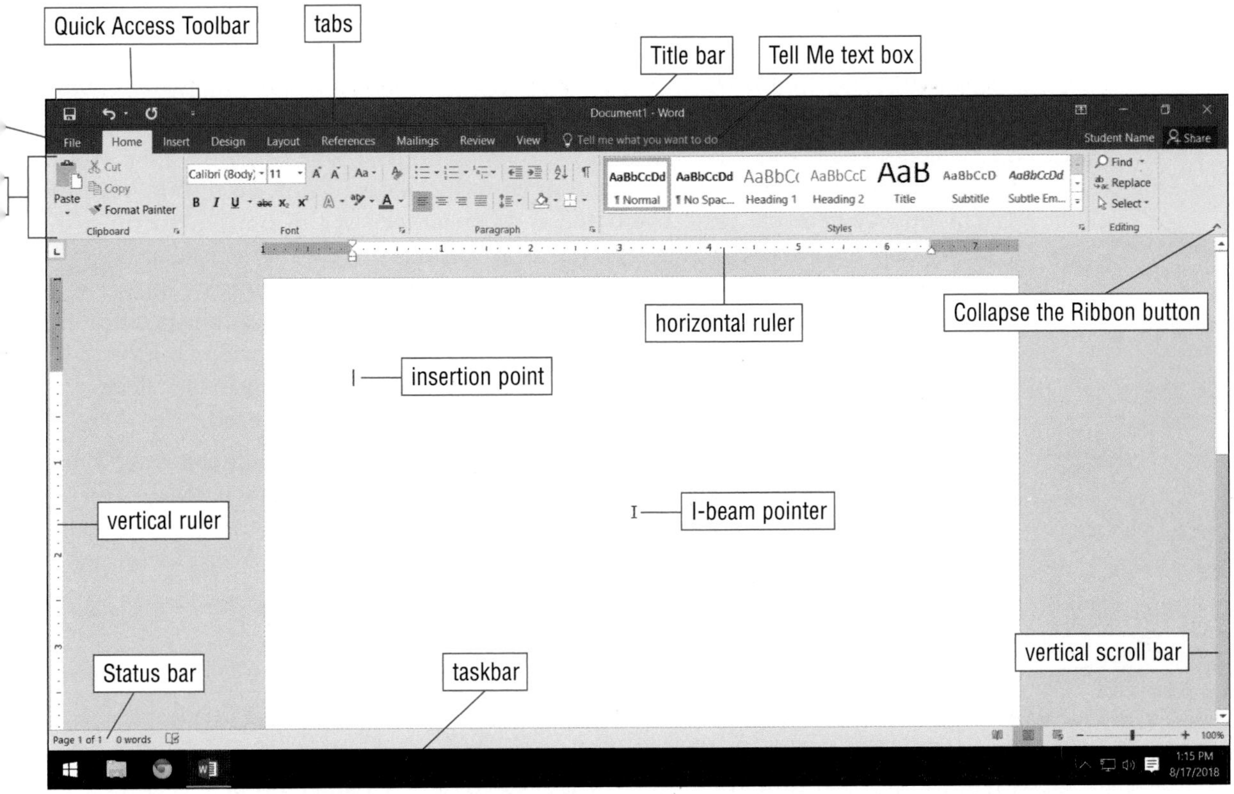

Table 1.1 Microsoft Word Screen Features

Feature	Description
Collapse the Ribbon button	when clicked, removes the ribbon from the screen
File tab	when clicked, displays backstage area, which contains options for working with and managing documents
horizontal ruler	used to set margins, indents, and tabs
I-beam pointer	used to move the insertion point or to select text
insertion point	indicates the location of the next character entered at the keyboard
Quick Access Toolbar	contains buttons for commonly used commands
ribbon	area containing tabs with options and buttons divided into groups
Status bar	displays the numbers of pages and words, plus the view buttons and Zoom slider bar
tabs	contain commands and features organized into groups
taskbar	contains icons for launching programs, buttons for active tasks, and a notification area
Tell Me feature	provides information and guidance on how to complete functions
Title bar	displays the document name followed by the program name
vertical ruler	used to set the top and bottom margins
vertical scroll bar	used to view various parts of the document beyond the screen

- **Spacing punctuation:** Typically, Word uses Calibri as the default typeface, which is a proportional typeface. (You will learn more about typefaces in Chapter 2.) When typing text in a proportional typeface, space once (rather than two times) after end-of-sentence punctuation such as a period, question mark, or exclamation point and after a colon. The characters in a proportional typeface are set closer together, and extra white space at the end of a sentence or after a colon is not needed.
- **Option buttons:** As text is inserted or edited in a document, an option button may display near the text. The name and appearance of this option button varies depending on the action. If a typed word is corrected by AutoCorrect, if an automatic list is created, or if autoformatting is applied to text, the AutoCorrect Options button appears. Click this button to undo the specific automatic action. If text is pasted in a document, the Paste Options button appears near the text. Click this button to display the Paste Options gallery, which has buttons for controlling how the pasted text is formatted.
- **AutoComplete:** Microsoft Word and other Office applications include an AutoComplete feature that inserts an entire item when a few identifying characters are typed. For example, type the letters *Mond* and *Monday* displays in a ScreenTip above the letters. Press the Enter key or press the F3 function key and Word inserts *Monday* in the document.

Tutorial

Entering Text

Using the New Line Command

A Word document is based on a template that applies default formatting. Some basic formatting includes 1.08 line spacing and 8 points of spacing after a paragraph. Each time the Enter key is pressed, a new paragraph begins and 8 points of spacing is inserted after the paragraph. To move the insertion point down to the next line without including the additional 8 points of spacing, use the New Line command, Shift + Enter.

Project 1a Creating a Document — Part 1 of 2

1. Open Word by clicking the Word 2016 tile at the Windows Start menu.
2. At the Word opening screen, click the *Blank document* template. (These steps may vary. Check with your instructor for specific instructions.)
3. At a blank document, type the information shown in Figure 1.2 with the following specifications:
   a. Correct any errors highlighted by the spelling checker or grammar checker as they occur.
   b. Press the spacebar once after end-of-sentence punctuation.
   c. After typing *Created:* press Shift + Enter to move the insertion point to the next line without adding 8 points of additional spacing.
   d. To insert the word *Thursday* at the end of the document, type Thur and then press F3. (This is an example of the AutoComplete feature.)
   e. To insert the word *December*, type Dece and then press the Enter key. (This is another example of the AutoComplete feature.)
   f. Press Shift + Enter after typing *December 6, 2018*.
   g. When typing the last line (the line containing the ordinal numbers), type the ordinal number text and AutoCorrect will automatically convert the letters in the ordinal numbers to a superscript.
4. When you are finished typing the text, press the Enter key. (Keep the document open for the next project.)

Check Your Work

Figure 1.2 Project 1a

> The traditional chronological resume lists your work experience in reverse-chronological order (starting with your current or most recent position). The functional style deemphasizes the "where" and "when" of your career and instead groups similar experiences, talents, and qualifications regardless of when they occurred.
>
> Like the chronological resume, the hybrid resume includes specifics about where you worked, when you worked there, and what your job titles were. Like a functional resume, a hybrid resume emphasizes your most relevant qualifications in an expanded summary section, in several "career highlights" bullet points at the top of your resume, or in project summaries.
>
> Created:
> Thursday, December 6, 2018
> Note: The two paragraphs will become the 2nd and 3rd paragraphs in the 5th section.

Tutorial

Saving with a New Name

Save

Quick Steps

Save a Document

1. Click File tab.
2. Click *Save As* option.
3. Click *Browse* option.
4. Type document name in *File name* text box.
5. Press Enter.

Saving a Document with a New Name

Save a document if it is going to be used in the future. Save a new document or save an existing document with a new name at the Save As dialog box.

To save a new document, click the Save button on the Quick Access Toolbar, click the File tab, and then click the *Save* option or the *Save As* option, or press the keyboard shortcut Ctrl + S and the Save As backstage area displays, as shown in Figure 1.3. Click the *Browse* option to display the Save As dialog box, as shown in Figure 1.4.

To save an existing document with a new name, click the File tab, click the *Save As* option to display the Save As backstage area, and then click the *Browse* option to display the Save As dialog box. Press the F12 function key to display the Save As dialog box without having to first display the Save As backstage area. At the Save As dialog box, type the name for the document in the *File name* text box and then press the Enter key or click the Save button.

Hint Save a document approximately every 15 minutes or when interrupted.

Figure 1.3 Save As Backstage Area

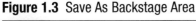

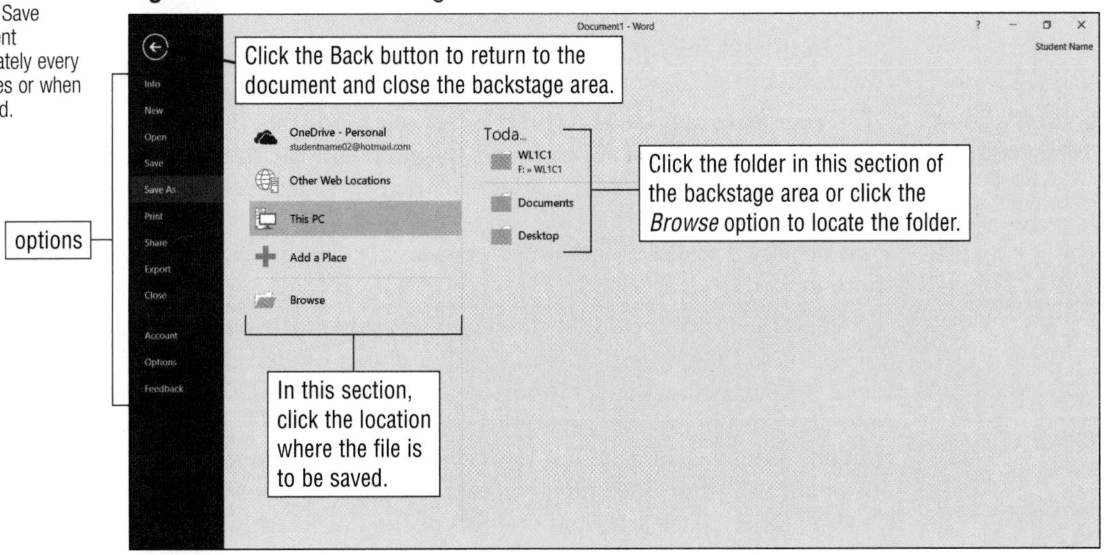

Figure 1.4 Save As Dialog Box

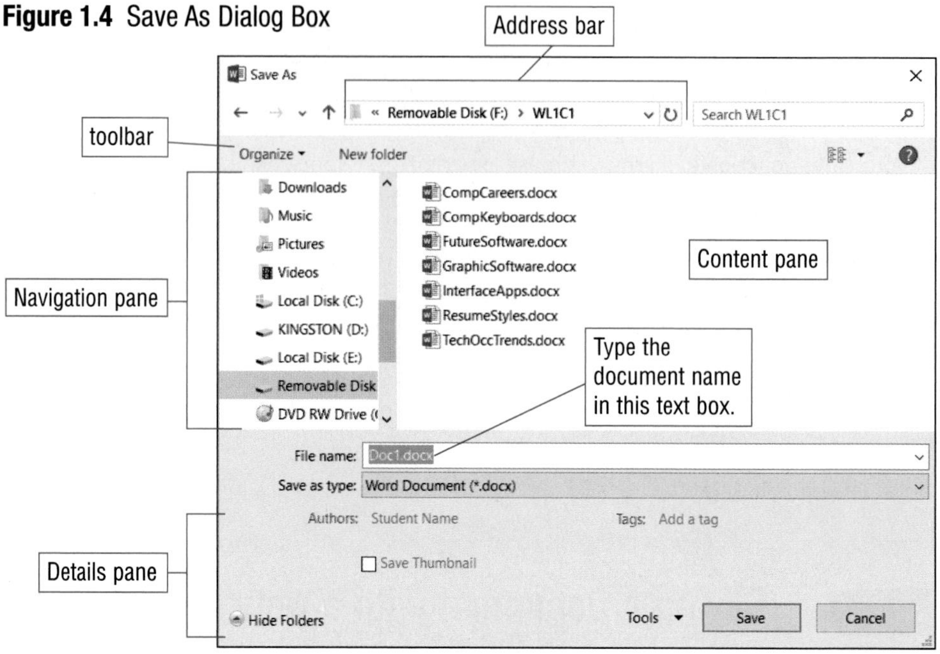

Naming a Document

Hint You cannot give a document the same name first in uppercase and then in lowercase letters.

Document names created in Word and other applications in the Microsoft Office suite can be up to 255 characters in length, including the drive letter and any folder names, and they may include spaces. File names cannot include any of the following characters:

forward slash (/)	less-than symbol (<)	quotation marks (" ")
backslash (\)	asterisk (*)	colon (:)
greater-than symbol (>)	question mark (?)	pipe symbol (|)

Printing a Document

Tutorial

Printing a Document

Click the File tab and the backstage area displays. The buttons and options at the backstage area change depending on the option selected at the left side of the backstage area. To leave the backstage area without completing an action, click the Back button in the upper left corner of the backstage area, or press the Esc key on the keyboard.

Quick Steps

Print a Document
1. Click File tab.
2. Click *Print* option.
3. Click Print button.

Documents may need to be printed and a printing of a document on paper is referred to as *hard copy*. A document displayed on the screen is referred to as *soft copy*. Print a document with options at the Print backstage area, shown in Figure 1.5. To display this backstage area, click the File tab and then click the *Print* option. The Print backstage area can also be displayed using the keyboard shortcut Ctrl + P.

Click the Print button, at the upper left side of the backstage area, to send the document to the printer and specify the number of copies to be printed with the *Copies* option. Below the Print button are two categories: *Printer* and *Settings*. Use the gallery in the *Printer* category to specify the desired printer. The *Settings* category contains a number of galleries. Each provides options for specifying how the document will print, including whether the pages are to be collated when printed; the orientation, page size, and margins of the document; and how many pages of the document are to print on a sheet of paper.

Figure 1.5 Print Backstage Area

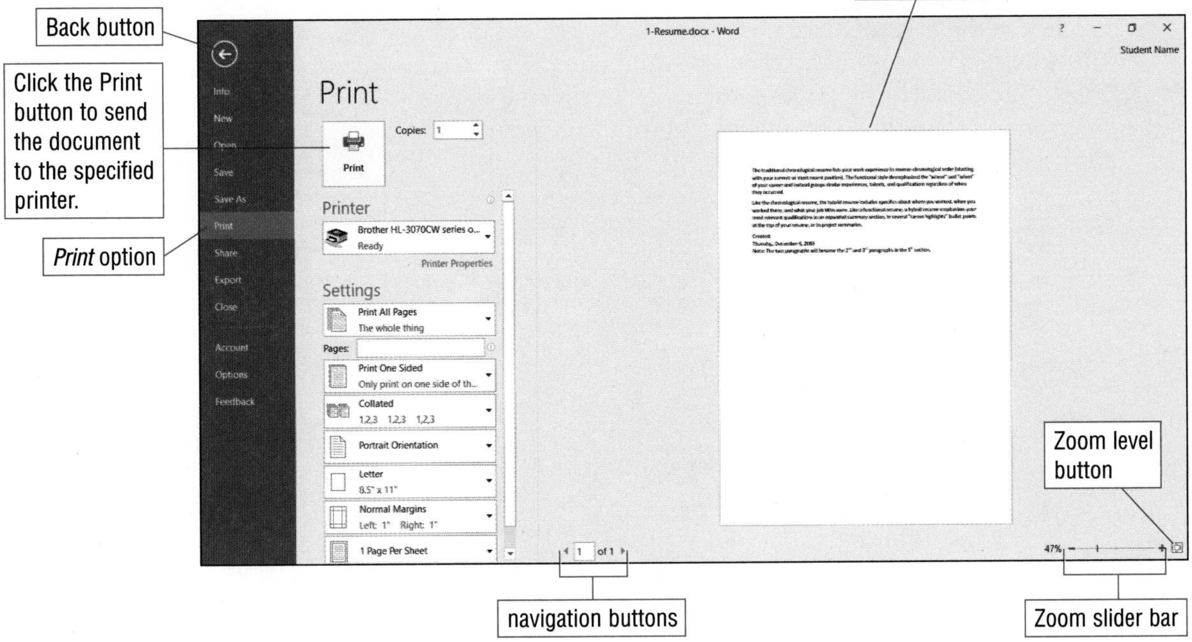

Quick Print

Quick Steps

Close a Document

1. Click File tab.
2. Click *Close* option.

Close Word

Click Close button.

Another method for printing a document is to insert the Quick Print button on the Quick Access Toolbar and then click the button. This sends the document directly to the printer without displaying the Print backstage area. To insert the button on the Quick Access Toolbar, click the Customize Quick Access Toolbar button at the right side of the toolbar and then click *Quick Print* at the drop-down list. To remove the Quick Print button from the Quick Access Toolbar, right-click the button and then click the *Remove from Quick Access Toolbar* option at the shortcut menu.

Tutorial

Closing a Document and Closing Word

Close

Closing a Document and Closing Word

When a document is saved, it is saved to the specified location and also remains on the screen. To remove the document from the screen, click the File tab and then click the *Close* option or use the keyboard shortcut Ctrl + F4. When a document is closed, it is removed and a blank screen displays. At this screen, open a previously saved document, create a new document, or close Word. To close Word, click the Close button in the upper right corner of the screen. The keyboard shortcut Alt + F4 also closes Word.

Project 1b Saving, Printing, and Closing a Document and Closing Word

Part 2 of 2

1. Save the document you created for Project 1a and name it **1-Resume** (*1-* for Chapter 1 and *Resume* because the document is about resumes) by completing the following steps:
   a. Click the File tab.
   b. Click the *Save As* option.
   c. At the Save As backstage area, click the *Browse* option.
   d. At the Save As dialog box, if necessary, navigate to the WL1C1 folder on your storage medium.

1a

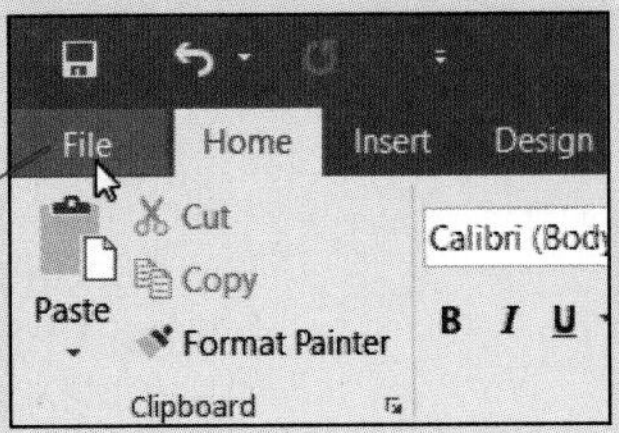

e. Click in the *File name* text box (this selects any text in the box), type 1-Resume, and then press the Enter key.

2. Print the document by clicking the File tab, clicking the *Print* option, and then clicking the Print button at the Print backstage area.

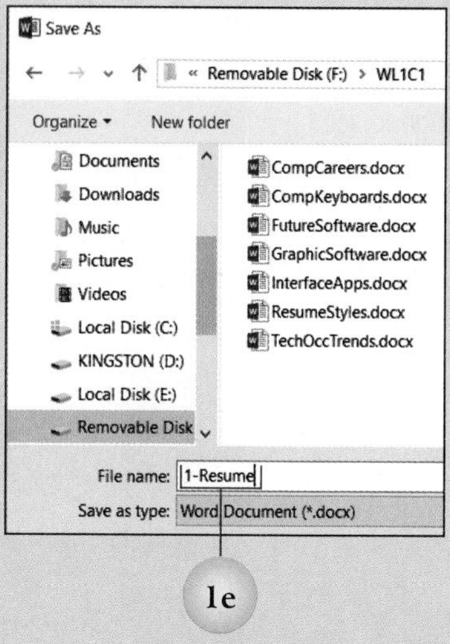

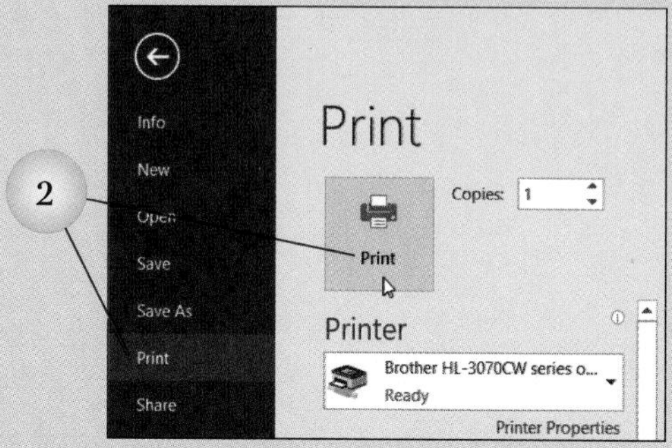

3. Close the document by clicking the File tab and then clicking the *Close* option.
4. Close Word by clicking the Close button in the upper right corner of the screen.

Check Your Work

Project 2 Save a Document with a New Name and the Same Name 2 Parts

You will open a document in the WL1C1 folder on your storage medium, save the document with a new name, add text, and then save the document with the same name. You will also print and then close the document.

Preview Finished Project

Creating a New Document

Quick Steps

Create a New Document
1. Click File tab.
2. Click *New* option.
3. Click *Blank document* template.

When a document is closed, a blank screen displays. To create a new document, display a blank document by clicking the File tab, clicking the *New* option, and then clicking the *Blank document* template. A new document can also be opened with the keyboard shortcut Ctrl + N or by inserting a New button on the Quick Access Toolbar. To insert the button, click the Customize Quick Access Toolbar button at the right side of the toolbar and then click *New* at the drop-down list.

The New backstage area also includes the *Single spaced (blank)* template. Click this template and a new document will open that contains single spacing and no spacing after paragraphs.

Opening a Document

Tutorial

Opening a Document from a Removable Disk

After a document is saved and closed, it can be opened at the Open dialog box, shown in Figure 1.6. To display this dialog box, display the Open backstage area and then click the *Browse* option. Display the Open backstage area by clicking the File tab. If a document is open, click the File tab and then click the *Open* option to display the Open backstage area. Other methods for displaying the Open backstage area include using the keyboard shortcut Ctrl + O, inserting an Open button on the Quick Access Toolbar, or clicking the Open Other Documents hyperlink in the lower left corner of the Word 2016 opening screen.

Figure 1.6 Open Dialog Box

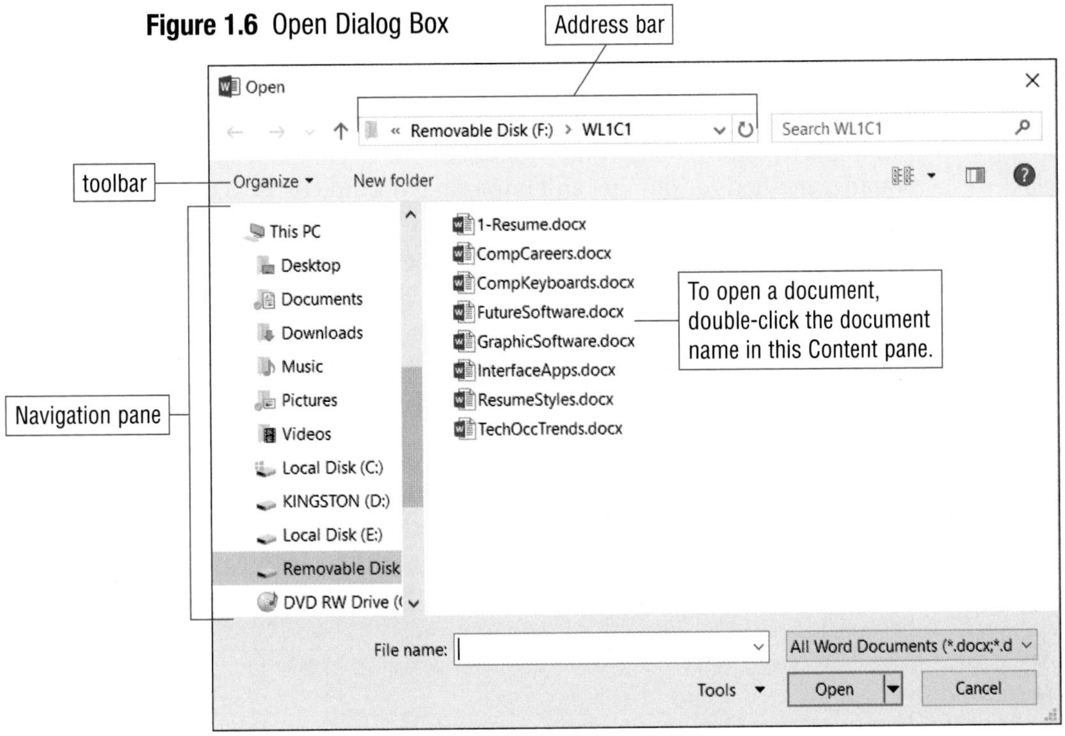

Quick Steps

Open a Document

1. Click File tab.
2. Click *Open* option.
3. Click *Browse* option.
4. Double-click document name.

At the Open backstage area, click the *Browse* option and the Open dialog box displays. Go directly to the Open dialog box without displaying the Open backstage area by pressing Ctrl + F12. At the Open dialog box, navigate to the desired location (such as the drive containing your storage medium), open the folder containing the document, and then double-click the document name in the Content pane.

Tutorial

Opening a Document from the *Recent* Option List

Opening a Document from the *Recent* Option List

At the Open backstage area with the *Recent* option selected, the names of the most recently opened documents display. By default, Word displays the names of 25 of the most recently opened documents and groups them into categories such as *Today*, *Yesterday*, and perhaps another category such as *Last Week*. To open a document from the *Recent* option list, scroll down the list and then click the document name. The Word 2016 opening screen also displays a list of the names of the most recently opened documents. Click a document name in the Recent list at the opening screen to open the document.

Tutorial

Pinning and Unpinning a Document at the *Recent* Option List

Pinning and Unpinning a Document at the *Recent* Option List

If a document is opened on a regular basis, consider pinning it to the *Recent* option list. To pin a document to the *Recent* option list at the Open backstage area, hover the mouse pointer over the document name and then click the small left-pointing push pin that displays to the right of the document name. The left-pointing push pin changes to a down-pointing push pin and the pinned document is inserted into a new category named *Pinned*. The *Pinned* category displays at the top of the *Recent* option list. The next time the Open backstage area displays, the pinned document displays in the *Pinned* category at the top of the *Recent* option list.

A document can also be pinned to the Recent list at the Word 2016 opening screen. When a document is pinned, it displays at the top of the Recent list and the *Recent* option list at the Open backstage area. To "unpin" a document from the Recent or *Recent* option list, click the pin to change it from a down-pointing push pin to a left-pointing push pin. More than one document can be pinned to a list. Another method for pinning and unpinning documents is to use the shortcut menu. Right-click a document name and then click the *Pin to list* or *Unpin from list* option.

In addition to documents, folders can be pinned to a list at the Save As backstage area. The third panel in the Save As backstage area displays a list of the most recently opened folders and groups them into categories such as *Today*, *Yesterday*, and *Last Week*. Pin a folder or folders to the list and a *Pinned* category is created; the folder names display in the category.

Project 2a Opening, Pinning, Unpinning, and Saving a Document — Part 1 of 2

1. Open Word and then open **CompCareers.docx** by completing the following steps:
   a. At the Word opening screen, click the Open Other Documents hyperlink.
   b. At the Open backstage area, click the *Browse* option.
   c. At the Open dialog box, navigate to the external drive containing your storage medium.
   d. Double-click the ***WL1C1*** folder in the Content pane.
   e. Double-click ***CompCareers.docx*** in the Content pane.

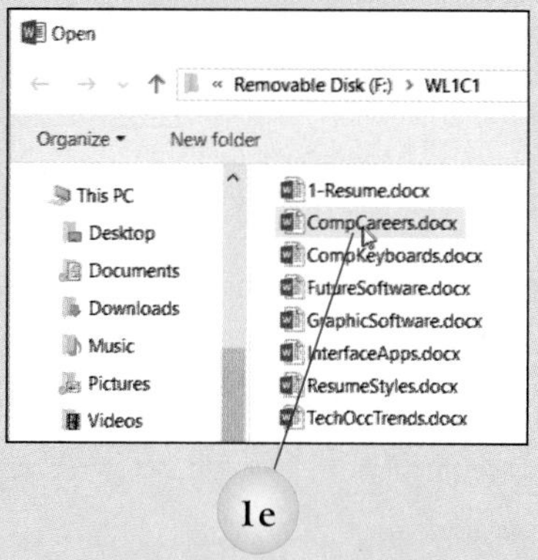

2. Close **CompCareers.docx**.
3. Press the F12 function key to display the Open dialog box and then double-click ***FutureSoftware.docx*** in the Content pane to open the document.
4. Close **FutureSoftware.docx**.
5. Pin **CompCareers.docx** to the *Recent* option list by completing the following steps:
   a. Click the File tab.
   b. At the Open backstage area, hover the mouse pointer over **CompCareers.docx** in the *Recent* option list and then click the left-pointing push pin that displays to the right of the document.

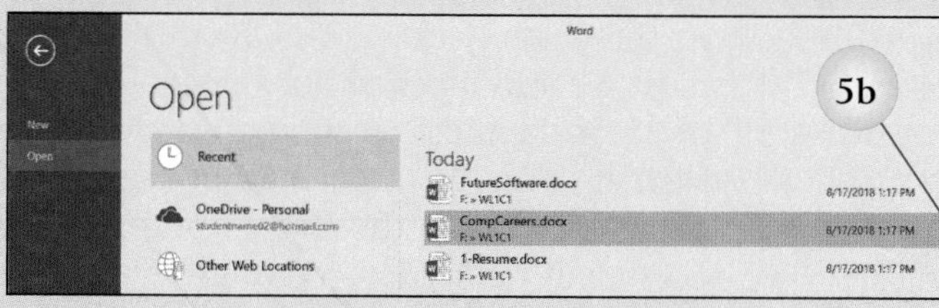

   (This creates a new category named *Pinned*, which displays at the top of the list. The **CompCareers.docx** file displays in the *Pinned* category and a down-pointing push pin displays to the right of the document name.)
6. Click ***CompCareers.docx*** in the *Pinned* category at the top of the *Recent* option list to open the document.
7. Unpin **CompCareers.docx** from the *Recent* option list by completing the following steps:
   a. Click the File tab and then click the *Open* option.
   b. At the Open backstage area, click the down-pointing push pin that displays to the right of **CompCareers.docx** in the *Pinned* category in the *Recent* option list. (This removes the *Pinned* category and changes the pin from a down-pointing push pin to a left-pointing push pin.)
   c. Click the Back button to return to the document.

8. With **CompCareers.docx** open, save the document with a new name by completing the following steps:
   a. Click the File tab and then click the *Save As* option.
   b. At the Save As backstage area, click the *Browse* option.
   c. At the Save As dialog box, if necessary, navigate to the WL1C1 folder on your storage medium.
   d. Press the Home key on your keyboard to move the insertion point to the beginning of the file name and then type 1-. (Pressing the Home key saves you from having to type the entire document name.)
   e. Press the Enter key.

8d

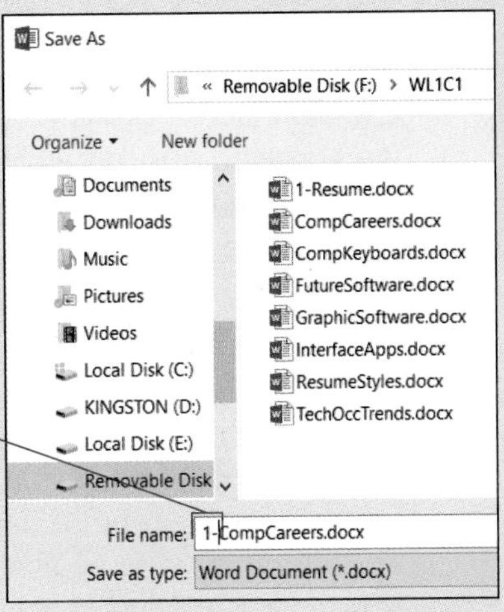

Tutorial

Saving with the Same Name

Saving a Document with the Same Name

If changes are made to an existing document, save the changes before closing the document. Consider saving changes to a document on a periodic basis to ensure that no changes are lost if the power is interrupted. Save a document with the same name using the Save button on the Quick Access Toolbar or the *Save* option at the backstage area.

Project 2b Saving a Document with the Same Name

Part 2 of 2

1. With **1-CompCareers.docx** open and the insertion point positioned at the beginning of the document, type the text shown in Figure 1.7.
2. Save the changes you just made by clicking the Save button on the Quick Access Toolbar.
3. Print the document by clicking the File tab, clicking the *Print* option, and then clicking the Print button at the Print backstage area. (If your Quick Access Toolbar contains the Quick Print button, you can click the button to send the document directly to the printer.)
4. Close the document by pressing Ctrl + F4.

2

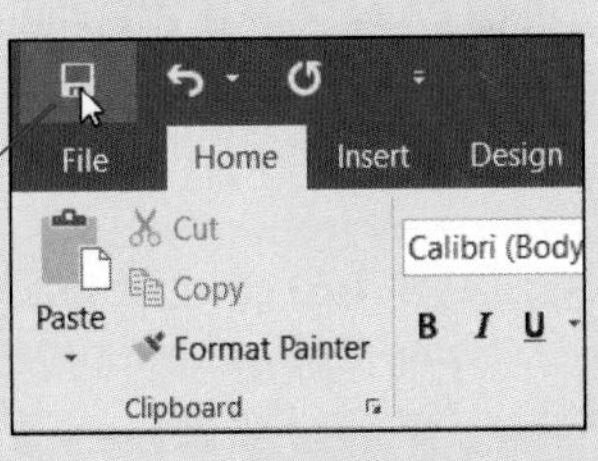

Check Your Work

Quick Steps

Save a Document with the Same Name

Click Save button on Quick Access Toolbar.

OR

1. Click File tab.
2. Click *Save* option.

Figure 1.7 Project 2b

The majority of new jobs being created in the United States today involve daily work with computers. Computer-related careers include technical support jobs, sales and training, programming and applications development, network and database administration, and computer engineering.

Project 3 Scroll and Browse in a Document

2 Parts

You will open a previously created document, save it with a new name, and then use scrolling and browsing techniques to move the insertion point to specific locations in the document.

Editing a Document

When a document is being edited, text may need to be inserted or deleted. To edit a document, use the mouse, the keyboard, or a combination of the two to move the insertion point to specific locations in the document. To move the insertion point using the mouse, position the I-beam pointer where the insertion point is to be positioned and then click the left mouse button.

Tutorial

Scrolling

Scrolling in a document changes the text display but does not move the insertion point. Use the mouse with the vertical scroll bar, at the right side of the screen, to scroll through text in a document. Click the up scroll arrow at the top of the vertical scroll bar to scroll up through the document and click the down scroll arrow to scroll down through the document.

The scroll bar contains a scroll box that indicates the location of the text in the document screen in relation to the remainder of the document. To scroll up one screen at a time, position the arrow pointer above the scroll box (but below the up scroll arrow) and then click the left mouse button. Position the arrow pointer below the scroll box and click the left button to scroll down a screen. Click and hold down the left mouse button and the action becomes continuous.

Another method for scrolling is to position the arrow pointer on the scroll box, click and hold down the left mouse button, and then drag the scroll box along the scroll bar to reposition text in the document screen. As the scroll box is dragged along the vertical scroll bar in a longer document, page numbers display in a box at the right side of the document screen.

Project 3a Scrolling in a Document

Part 1 of 2

1. Open **InterfaceApps.docx** (from the WL1C1 folder you copied to your storage medium).
2. Save the document with the new name **1-InterfaceApps** to the WL1C1 folder.
3. Position the I-beam pointer at the beginning of the first paragraph and then click the left mouse button.
4. Click the down scroll arrow on the vertical scroll bar several times. (This scrolls down lines of text in the document.) With the mouse pointer on the down scroll arrow, click and hold down the left mouse button and keep it down until the end of the document displays.
5. Position the mouse pointer on the up scroll arrow and click and hold down the left mouse button until the beginning of the document displays.
6. Position the mouse pointer below the scroll box and then click the left mouse button. Continue clicking the mouse button (with the mouse pointer positioned below the scroll box) until the end of the document displays.
7. Position the mouse pointer on the scroll box in the vertical scroll bar. Click and hold down the left mouse button, drag the scroll box to the top of the vertical scroll bar, and then release the mouse button. (Notice that the document page numbers display in a box at the right side of the document screen.)
8. Click in the title at the beginning of the document. (This moves the insertion point to the location of the mouse pointer.)

Moving the Insertion Point to a Specific Line or Page

Find

Word includes a Go To feature that moves the insertion point to a specific location in a document, such as a line or page. To use the feature, click the Find button arrow in the Editing group on the Home tab, and then click *Go To* at the drop-down list. At the Find and Replace dialog box with the Go To tab selected, move the insertion point to a specific page by typing the page number in the *Enter page number* text box and then pressing the Enter key. Move to a specific line by clicking the *Line* option in the *Go to what* list box, typing the line number in the *Enter line number* text box, and then pressing the Enter key. Click the Close button to close the dialog box.

Tutorial

Moving the Insertion Point and Inserting and Deleting Text

Moving the Insertion Point with the Keyboard

To move the insertion point with the keyboard, use the arrow keys to the right of the regular keyboard or use the arrow keys on the numeric keypad. When using the arrow keys on the numeric keypad, make sure Num Lock is off. Use the arrow keys together with other keys to move the insertion point to various locations in the document, as shown in Table 1.2.

When moving the insertion point, Word considers a word to be any series of characters between spaces. A paragraph is any text that is followed by a single press of the Enter key. A page is text that is separated by a soft or hard page break.

Table 1.2 Insertion Point Movement Commands

To move insertion point	Press
one character left	Left Arrow
one character right	Right Arrow
one line up	Up Arrow
one line down	Down Arrow
one word left	Ctrl + Left Arrow
one word right	Ctrl + Right Arrow
to beginning of line	Home
to end of line	End
to beginning of current paragraph	Ctrl + Up Arrow
to beginning of next paragraph	Ctrl + Down Arrow
up one screen	Page Up
down one screen	Page Down
to top of previous page	Ctrl + Page Up
to top of next page	Ctrl + Page Down
to beginning of document	Ctrl + Home
to end of document	Ctrl + End

Resuming Reading or Editing in a Document

If a previously saved document is opened, pressing Shift + F5 will move the insertion point to the position it was last located when the document was closed.

When opening a multiple-page document, Word remembers the page the insertion point was last positioned. When the document is reopened, Word displays a "Welcome back!" message at the right side of the screen near the vertical scroll bar. The message identifies the page where the insertion point was last located. Click the message and the insertion point is positioned at the top of that page.

Project 3b **Moving the Insertion Point in a Document** — Part 2 of 2

1. With **1-InterfaceApps.docx** open, move the insertion point to line 15 and then to page 3 by completing the following steps:
   a. Click the Find button arrow in the Editing group on the Home tab, and then click *Go To* at the drop-down list.
   b. At the Find and Replace dialog box with the Go To tab selected, click *Line* in the *Go to what* list box.
   c. Click in the *Enter line number* text box, type 15, and then press the Enter key.
   d. Click *Page* in the *Go to what* list box.
   e. Click in the *Enter page number* text box, type 3, and then press the Enter key.
   f. Click the Close button to close the Find and Replace dialog box.

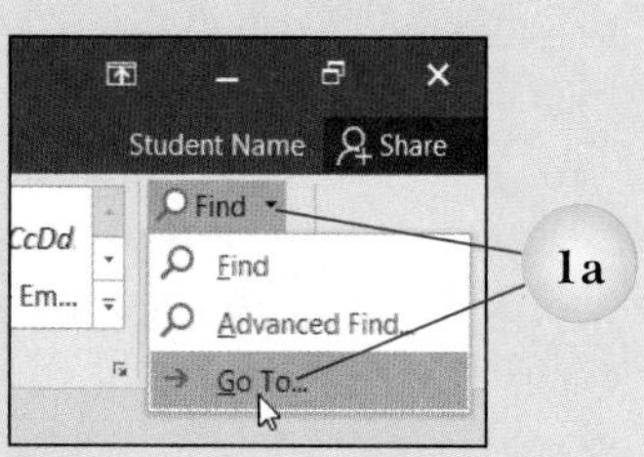

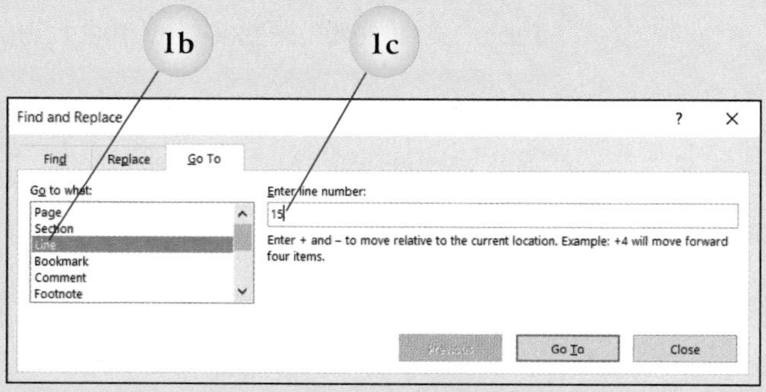

2. Close the document.
3. Open the document by clicking the File tab and then clicking the document name *1-InterfaceApps.docx* in the *Recent* option list in the *Today* category.
4. Move the mouse pointer to the right side of the screen to display the "Welcome back!" message. Hover the mouse pointer over the message and then click the left mouse button. (This positions the insertion point at the top of the third page—the page the insertion point was positioned when you closed the document.)

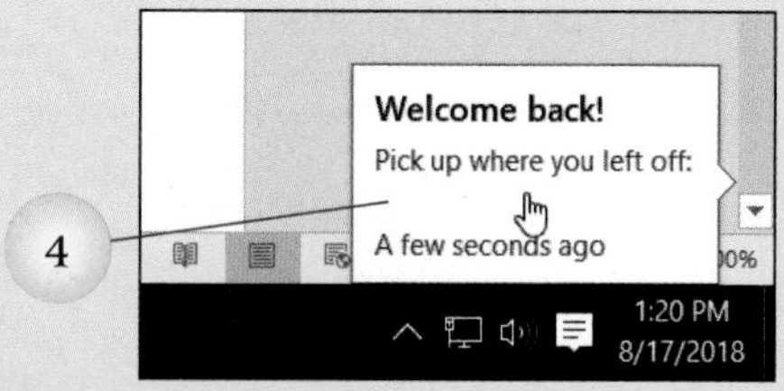

5. Press Ctrl + Home to move the insertion point to the beginning of the document.
6. Practice using the keyboard commands shown in Table 1.2 to move the insertion point within the document.
7. Close **1-InterfaceApps.docx**.

Project 4 Insert and Delete Text — 2 Parts

You will open a previously created document, save it with a new name, and then make editing changes to the document. The editing changes will include selecting, inserting, and deleting text and undoing and redoing edits.

Preview Finished Project

Inserting and Deleting Text

Editing a document may include inserting and/or deleting text. To insert text in a document, position the insertion point at the location text is to be typed and then type the text. Existing characters move to the right as text is typed. A number of options are available for deleting text. Some deletion commands are shown in Table 1.3.

Tutorial

Selecting, Replacing, and Deleting Text

Selecting Text

Use the mouse and/or keyboard to select a specific amount of text. Selected text can be deleted or other Word functions can be performed on it. When text is selected, it displays with a gray background, as shown in Figure 1.8, and the Mini toolbar displays. The Mini toolbar contains buttons for common tasks. (You will learn more about the Mini toolbar in Chapter 2.)

Table 1.3 Deletion Commands

To delete	Press
character right of insertion point	Delete key
character left of insertion point	Backspace key
text from insertion point to beginning of word	Ctrl + Backspace
text from insertion point to end of word	Ctrl + Delete

Figure 1.8 Selected Text and Mini Toolbar

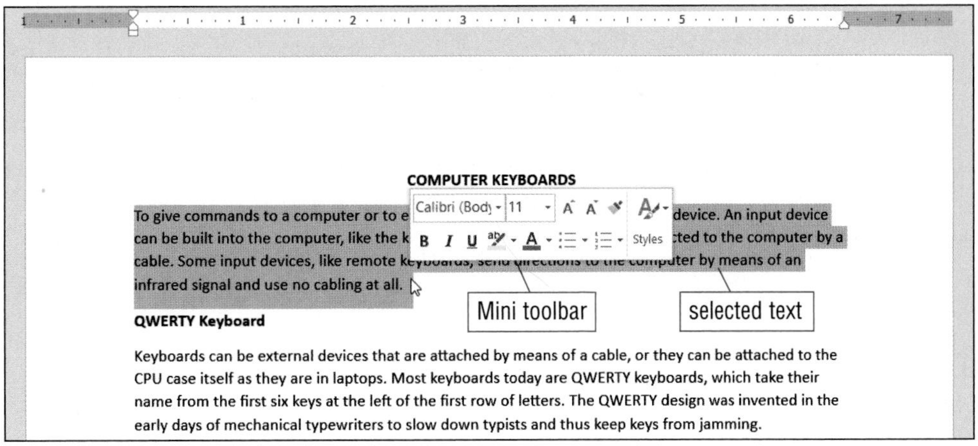

Selecting Text with the Mouse Use the mouse to select a word, line, sentence, paragraph, or entire document. Table 1.4 indicates the steps to follow to select various amounts of text.

To select a specific amount of text, such as a line or paragraph, click in the selection bar. The selection bar is the space at the left side of the document screen between the left edge of the page and the text. When the mouse pointer is positioned in the selection bar, the pointer turns into an arrow pointing up and to the right (instead of to the left).

To select an amount of text other than a word, sentence, or paragraph, position the I-beam pointer on the first character of the text to be selected, click and hold down the left mouse button, drag the I-beam pointer to the last character of the text to be selected, and then release the mouse button. All text between the current insertion point and the I-beam pointer can be selected. To do this, position the insertion point where the selection is to begin, press and hold down the Shift key, click the I-beam pointer at the end of the selection, and then release the Shift key. To cancel a selection using the mouse, click in the document screen.

Select text vertically in a document by holding down the Alt key while dragging with the mouse. This is especially useful when selecting a group of text, such as text set in columns.

Hint If text is selected, any character you type replaces the selected text.

Selecting Text with the Keyboard To select a specific amount of text using the keyboard, turn on the Selection mode by pressing the F8 function key. With the Selection mode activated, use the arrow keys to select the text. To cancel the selection, press the Esc key and then press any arrow key. The Status bar can be customized to indicate that the Selection mode is activated. To do this, right-click on the Status bar and then click *Selection Mode* at the pop-up list. When the F8 function key is pressed to turn on the Selection mode, the words *Extend Selection* display on the Status bar. Text can also be selected with the commands shown in Table 1.5.

Table 1.4 Selecting Text with the Mouse

To select	Complete these steps using the mouse
a word	Double-click the word.
a line of text	Click in the selection bar to the left of the line.
multiple lines of text	Drag in the selection bar to the left of the lines.
a sentence	Press and hold down the Ctrl key and then click in the sentence.
a paragraph	Double-click in the selection bar next to the paragraph, or triple-click in the paragraph.
multiple paragraphs	Drag in the selection bar.
an entire document	Triple-click in the selection bar.

Table 1.5 Selecting Text with the Keyboard

To select	Press
one character to right	Shift + Right Arrow
one character to left	Shift + Left Arrow
to end of word	Ctrl + Shift + Right Arrow
to beginning of word	Ctrl + Shift + Left Arrow
to end of line	Shift + End
to beginning of line	Shift + Home
one line up	Shift + Up Arrow
one line down	Shift + Down Arrow
to beginning of paragraph	Ctrl + Shift + Up Arrow
to end of paragraph	Ctrl + Shift + Down Arrow
one screen up	Shift + Page Up
one screen down	Shift + Page Down
to end of document	Ctrl + Shift + End
to beginning of document	Ctrl + Shift + Home
entire document	Ctrl + A or click Select button in Editing group and then click *Select All*

Project 4a **Editing a Document**

Part 1 of 2

1. Open **CompKeyboards.docx**. (This document is in the WL1C1 folder you copied to your storage medium.)
2. Save the document with the new name **1-CompKeyboards**.
3. Change the word *give* in the first sentence of the first paragraph to *enter* by double-clicking *give* and then typing enter.
4. Change the second *to* in the first sentence to *into* by double-clicking *to* and then typing into.

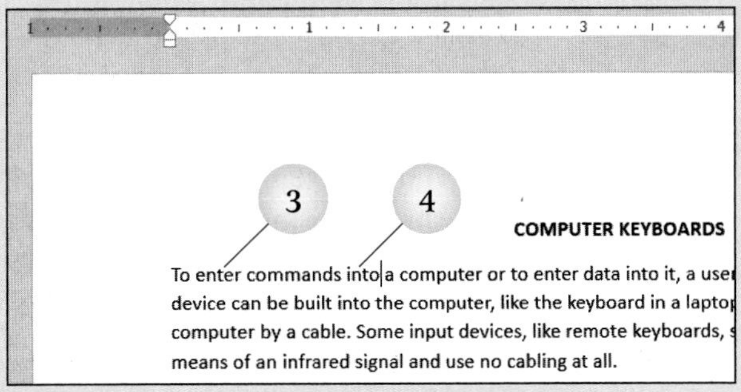

3
4
COMPUTER KEYBOARDS
To enter commands into a computer or to enter data into it, a
device can be built into the computer, like the keyboard in a
computer by a cable. Some input devices, like remote keyboards,
means of an infrared signal and use no cabling at all.

5. Delete the words *means of* (including the space after *of*) in the first sentence in the *QWERTY Keyboard* section.
6. Select the words *and use no cabling at all* and the period that follows at the end of the last sentence in the first paragraph and then press the Delete key.
7. Insert a period immediately following the word *signal*.

8. Delete the heading *QWERTY Keyboard* using the Selection mode by completing the following steps:
   a. Position the insertion point immediately left of the *Q* in *QWERTY*.
   b. Press F8 to turn on the Selection mode.
   c. Press the Down Arrow key.
   d. Press the Delete key.
9. Complete steps similar to those in Step 8 to delete the heading *DVORAK Keyboard*.
10. Begin a new paragraph with the sentence that reads *Keyboards have different physical appearances* by completing the following steps:
    a. Position the insertion point immediately left of the *K* in *Keyboards* (the first word of the fifth sentence in the last paragraph).
    b. Press the Enter key.
11. Save **1-CompKeyboards.docx**.

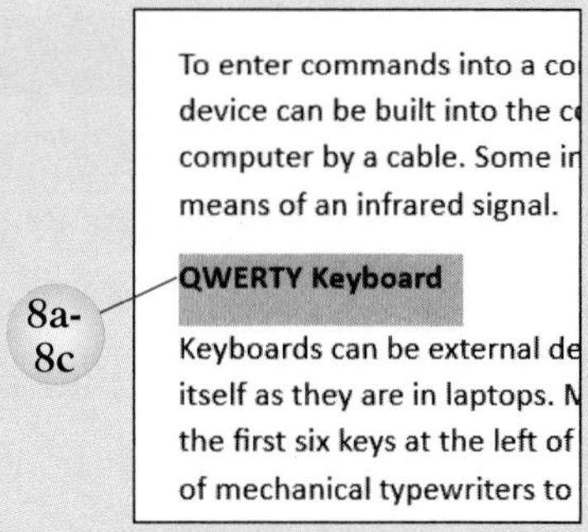

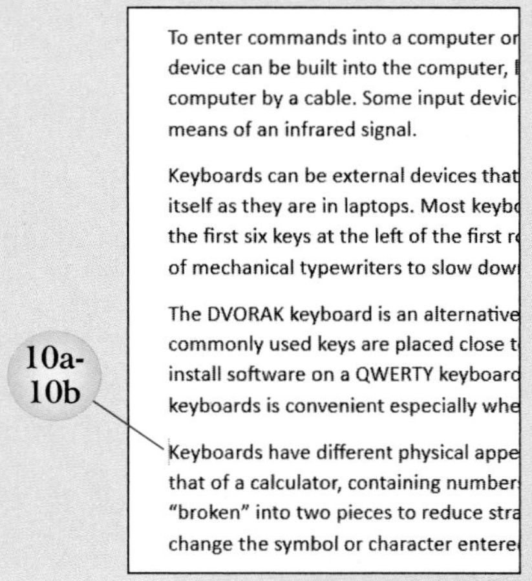

10a-
10b
To enter commands into a computer o
device can be built into the computer,
computer by a cable. Some input devic
means of an infrared signal.
Keyboards can be external devices tha
itself as they are in laptops. Most keyb
the first six keys at the left of the first r
of mechanical typewriters to slow dow
The DVORAK keyboard is an alternativ
commonly used keys are placed close t
install software on a QWERTY keyboar
keyboards is convenient especially wh
Keyboards have different physical app
that of a calculator, containing number
"broken" into two pieces to reduce str
change the symbol or character entere

Check Your Work

Tutorial

Using Undo and Redo

Undo

Redo

Hint You cannot undo a save.

Using the Undo and Redo Buttons

Undo typing, formatting, or another action by clicking the Undo button on the Quick Access Toolbar. For example, type text and then click the Undo button and the text is removed. Or, apply formatting to text and then click the Undo button and the formatting is removed.

Click the Redo button on the Quick Access Toolbar to reverse the original action. For example, apply formatting such as underlining to text and then click the Undo button and the underlining is removed. Click the Redo button and the underlining formatting is reapplied to the text. Many Word actions can be undone or redone. Some actions, however, such as printing and saving, cannot be undone or redone.

Word maintains actions in temporary memory. To undo an action performed earlier, click the Undo button arrow. This causes a drop-down list to display. To make a selection from this drop-down list, click the desired action; the action, along with any actions listed above it in the drop-down list, is undone.

Project 4b Undoing and Redoing Deletions

Part 2 of 2

1. With **1-CompKeyboards.docx** open, delete the last sentence in the last paragraph using the mouse by completing the following steps:
   a. Hover the I-beam pointer anywhere over the sentence that begins *All keyboards have modifier keys*.
   b. Press and hold down the Ctrl key, and then click the left mouse button, and then release the Ctrl key.

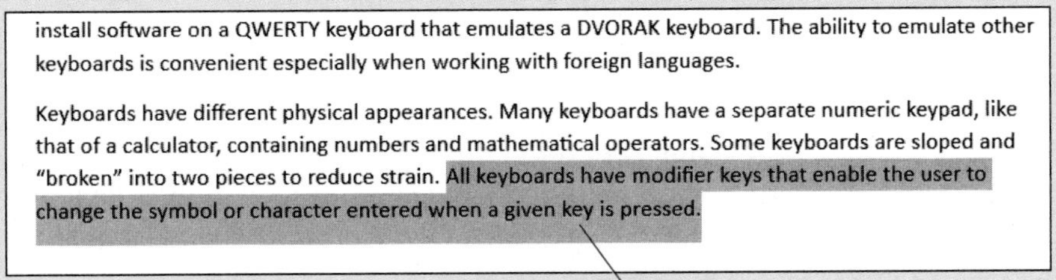

install software on a QWERTY keyboard that emulates a DVORAK keyboard. The ability to emulate other keyboards is convenient especially when working with foreign languages.

Keyboards have different physical appearances. Many keyboards have a separate numeric keypad, like that of a calculator, containing numbers and mathematical operators. Some keyboards are sloped and "broken" into two pieces to reduce strain. All keyboards have modifier keys that enable the user to change the symbol or character entered when a given key is pressed.

1a-1b

   c. Press the Delete key.
2. Delete the last paragraph by completing the following steps:
   a. Position the I-beam pointer anywhere in the last paragraph (the paragraph that begins *Keyboards have different physical appearances*).
   b. Triple-click the left mouse button.
   c. Press the Delete key.
3. Undo the deletion by clicking the Undo button on the Quick Access Toolbar.

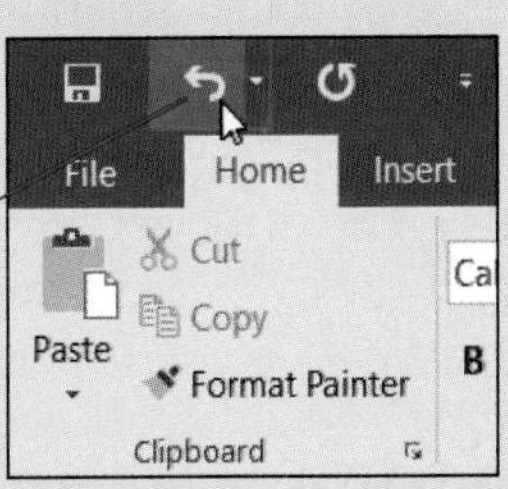

4. Redo the deletion by clicking the Redo button on the Quick Access Toolbar.
5. Select the first sentence in the second paragraph and then delete it.
6. Select the first paragraph in the document and then delete it.
7. Undo the two deletions by completing the following steps:
   a. Click the Undo button arrow.
   b. Click the second *Clear* listed in the drop-down list. (This will redisplay the first paragraph and the first sentence in the second paragraph. The sentence will be selected.)
8. Click outside the sentence to deselect it.
9. Save, print, and then close **1-CompKeyboards.docx**.

7a 7b

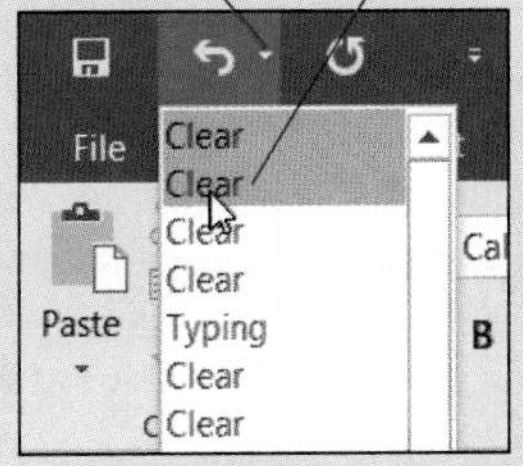

Check Your Work

Project 5 Complete a Spelling and Grammar Check

1 Part

You will open a previously created document, save it with a new name, and then check the spelling and grammar in the document.

Preview Finished Project

Tutorial

Checking Spelling and Grammar

Quick Steps

Check Spelling and Grammar

1. Click Review tab.
2. Click Spelling & Grammar button.
3. Change or ignore errors.
4. Click OK.

Spelling & Grammar

Hint Complete a spelling and grammar check on a portion of a document by selecting the text first and then clicking the Spelling & Grammar button.

Checking the Spelling and Grammar in a Document

Two tools for creating thoughtful and well-written documents are the spelling checker and the grammar checker. The spelling checker finds misspelled words and offers replacement words. It also finds duplicate words and irregular capitalizations. When spell checking a document, the spelling checker compares the words in the document with the words in its dictionary. If the spelling checker finds a match, it passes over the word. If the spelling checker does not find a match, it stops, selects the word, and offers possible corrections.

The grammar checker searches a document for errors in grammar, punctuation, and word usage. If the grammar checker finds an error, it stops and offers possible corrections. The spelling checker and the grammar checker can help create a well-written document but do not eliminate the need for proofreading.

To complete a spelling and grammar check, click the Review tab and then click the Spelling & Grammar button in the Proofing group or press the F7 function key. If Word detects a possible spelling error, the text containing the error is selected and the Spelling task pane displays. The Spelling task pane contains a list box with one or more possible corrections along with buttons to either change or ignore the spelling error, as described in Table 1.6. A definition of the selected word in the list box may display at the bottom of the Spelling task pane if a dictionary is installed.

If Word detects a grammar error, the word(s) or sentence is selected and possible corrections display in the Grammar task pane list box. Depending on the error selected, some or all of the buttons described in Table 1.6 may display in the Grammar task pane and a description of the grammar rule with suggestions may display at the bottom of the task pane. Use the buttons that display to ignore or change the grammar error.

When checking the spelling and grammar in a document, temporarily leave the Spelling task pane or Grammar task pane by clicking in the document. To resume the spelling and grammar check, click the Resume button in the Spelling task pane or Grammar task pane.

Table 1.6 Spelling Task Pane and Grammar Task Pane Buttons

Button	Function
Ignore	during spell checking, skips that occurrence of the word; during grammar checking, leaves currently selected text as written
Ignore All	during spell checking, skips that occurrence of the word and all other occurrences of the word in the document
Add	adds the selected word to the spelling checker dictionary
Delete	deletes the currently selected word(s)
Change	replaces the selected word with the selected word in the task pane list box
Change All	replaces the selected word and all other occurrences of it with the selected word in the task pane list box

Project 5 Checking the Spelling and Grammar in a Document

Part 1 of 1

1. Open **TechOccTrends.docx**.
2. Save the document with the name **1-TechOccTrends**.
3. Click the Review tab.
4. Click the Spelling & Grammar button in the Proofing group.
5. The spelling checker selects the word *tecnology* and displays the Spelling task pane. The proper spelling is selected in the Spelling task pane list box, so click the Change button (or Change All button).
6. The grammar checker selects the word *too* in the document and displays the Grammar task pane. The correct form of the word is selected in the list box. If definitions of *to* and *too* display at the bottom of the task pane, read the information. Click the Change button.
7. The grammar checker selects the sentence containing the words *downloaded* and *versus*, in which two spaces appear between the words. The Grammar task pane displays in the list box the two words with only one space between them. Read the information about spaces between words that displays at the bottom of the Grammar task pane and then click the Change button.
8. The spelling checker selects the word *sucessful* and offers *successful* in the Spelling task pane list box. Since this word is misspelled in another location in the document, click the Change All button.
9. The spelling checker selects the word *are*, which is used two times in a row. Click the Delete button in the Spelling task pane to delete the second *are*.
10. When the message displays stating that the spelling and grammar check is complete, click OK.
11. Save, print, and then close **1-TechOccTrends.docx**.

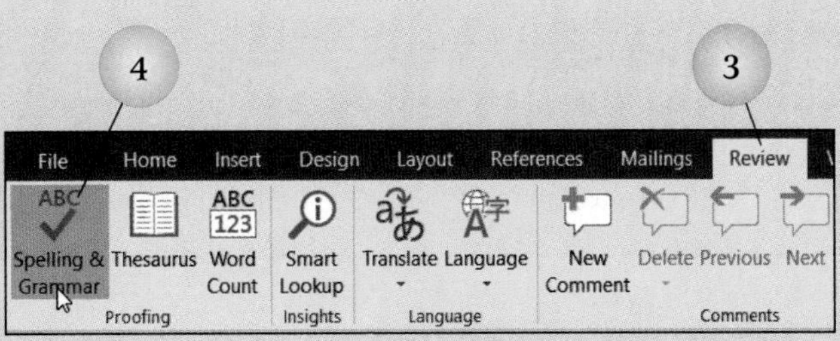

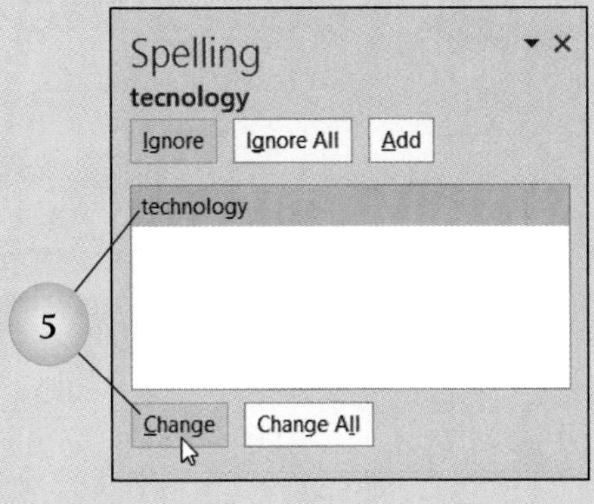

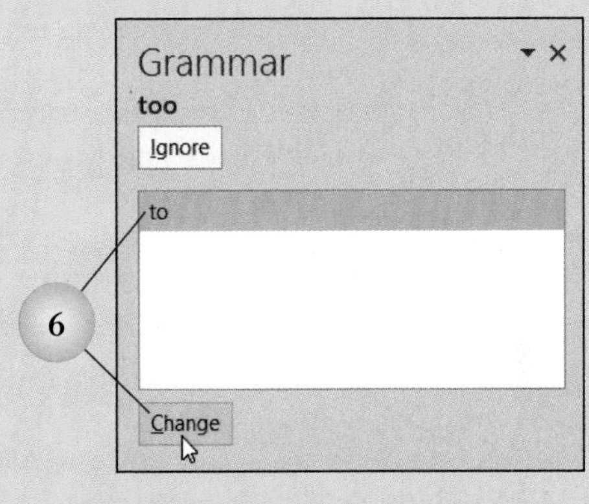

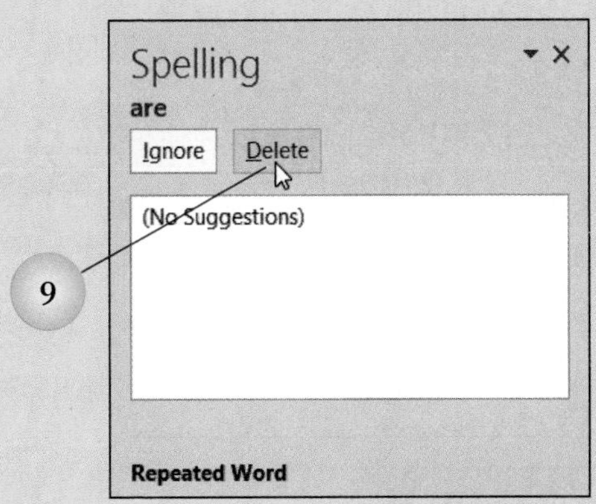

Check Your Work

Project 6 Use the Tell Me and Help Features

2 Parts

You will use the Tell Me feature to learn how to double-space text in a document, display the Word Help window with information on autocorrect, and display the Smart Lookup task pane with information on scrolling. You will also use the Help feature to learn more about printing documents.

Preview Finished Project

Tutorial

Using the Tell Me Feature

Using the Tell Me Feature

Word 2016 includes a Tell Me feature that provides information and guidance on how to complete a function. To use Tell Me, click in the *Tell Me* text box on the ribbon to the right of the View tab and then type the function. Type text in the *Tell Me* text box and a drop-down list displays with options that are refined as the text is typed; this is referred to as "word-wheeling." The drop-down list displays options for completing the function, displaying information on the function from sources on the Web, or displaying information on the function in the Word Help window.

The drop-down list also includes a *Smart Lookup* option. Clicking the *Smart Lookup* option will open the Smart Lookup task pane at the right side of the screen. This task pane provides information on the function from a variety of sources on the Internet. The *Smart Lookup* option can also be accessed with the Smart Lookup button on the Review tab or by selecting text, right-clicking the selected text, and then clicking *Smart Lookup* at the shortcut menu.

Project 6a Using the Tell Me Feature

Part 1 of 2

1. Open **GraphicSoftware.docx** and then save it with the name **1-GraphicSoftware**.
2. Press Ctrl + A to select the entire document.
3. Use the Tell Me feature to learn how to double-space the text in the document by completing the following steps:
   a. Click in the *Tell Me* text box.
   b. Type double space.
   c. Click the *Line and Paragraph Spacing* option.
   d. At the side menu, click the *2.0* option. (This double-spaces the selected text in the document.)
   e. Click in the document to deselect the text.

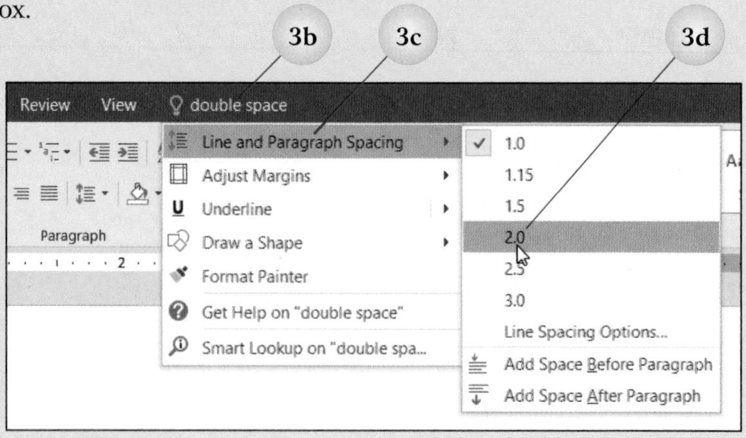

4. Use the Tell Me feature to display the Word Help window with information on AutoCorrect by completing the following steps:
   a. Click in the *Tell Me* text box.
   b. Type autocorrect.
   c. Click the *Get Help on "autocorrect"* option.
   d. At the Word Help window, click a hyperlink to an article that interests you.
   e. After reading the information about autocorrect, close the window by clicking the Close button in the upper right corner of the window.

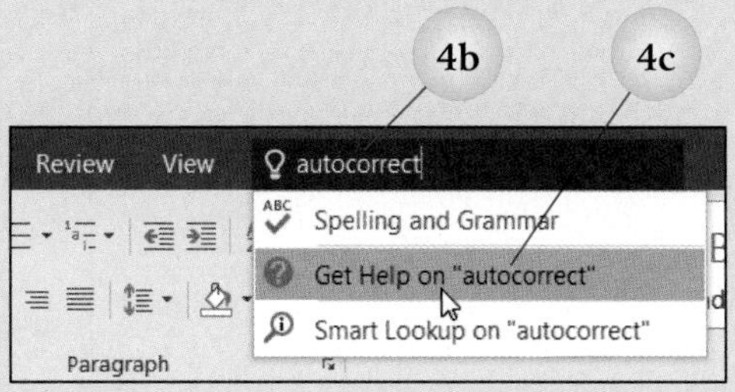

5. Display information on scrolling in the Smart Lookup task pane by completing the following steps:
   a. Click in the *Tell Me* text box.
   b. Type scrolling.
   c. Click the *Smart Lookup on "scrolling"* option. (The first time you use the Smart Lookup feature, the Smart Lookup task pane will display with a message stating that data will be sent to Bing and suggesting that you read the privacy statement for more details. At this message, click the Got it button.)

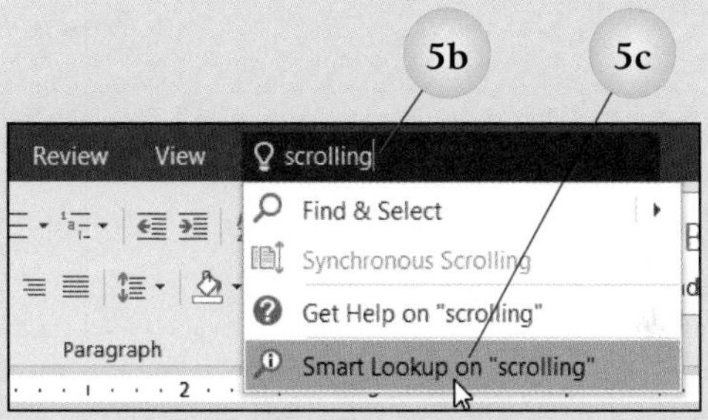

   d. Look at the information that displays in the Smart Lookup task pane on scrolling.
   e. If two options—*Explore* and *Define*—display at the top of the Smart Lookup task pane, click the *Define* option. This will display a definition of the term *scrolling* in the Smart Lookup task pane.
   f. Close the Smart Lookup task pane by clicking the Close button in the upper right corner of the task pane.
6. Save, print, then close **1-GraphicSoftware.docx**.

Check Your Work

Tutorial

Using the Help Feature

Using the Help Feature

Word's Help feature is an on-screen reference manual containing information about Word features and commands. Word's Help feature is similar to the Help features in Excel, PowerPoint, and Access. Get help by using the Tell Me feature or by pressing the F1 function key to display the Word Help window, shown in Figure 1.9.

Quick Steps

Use the Help Feature

1. Press F1.
2. Type search text in search text box.
3. Press Enter.
4. Click topic.

In this window, type a topic, feature, or question in the search text box and then press the Enter key. Articles related to the search text display in the Word Help window. Click an article to display it in the Word Help window. If the article window contains a Show All hyperlink in the upper right corner, click this hyperlink and the information expands to show all Help information related to the topic. Click the Show All hyperlink and it becomes the Hide All hyperlink.

The Word Help window contains five buttons, which display to the left of the search text box. Use the Back and Forward buttons to navigate within the window. Click the Home button to return to the Word Help window opening screen. To print information on a topic or feature, click the Print button and then click the Print button at the Print dialog box. Click the Use Large Text button in the Word Help window to increase the size of the text in the window.

Figure 1.9 Word Help Window

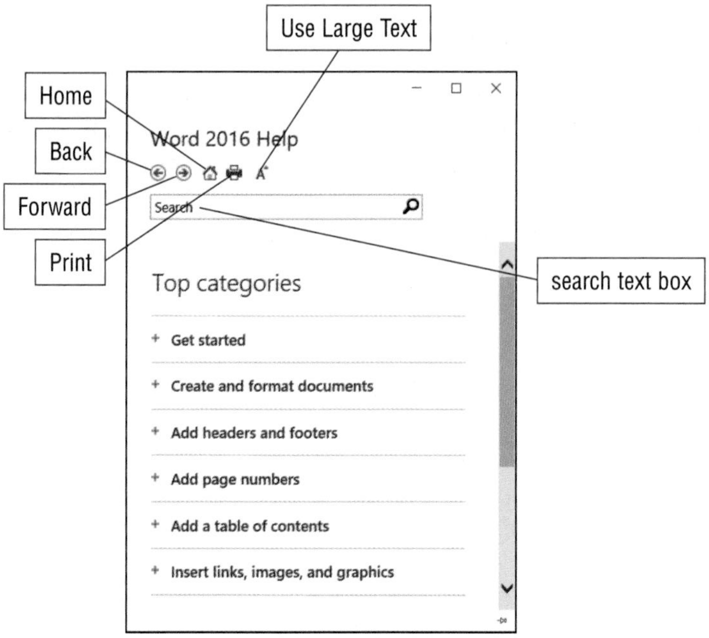

Getting Help from a ScreenTip

Hover the mouse pointer over a certain button such as the Format Painter button or Font Color button and the ScreenTip displays a Help icon and the Tell me more hyperlinked text. Click Tell me more or press the F1 function key and the Word Help window opens with information about the button feature.

Getting Help at the Backstage Area

The backstage area contains a Microsoft Word Help button in the upper right corner of the screen. Display a specific backstage area, click the Microsoft Word Help button, and information on the backstage area displays in the Word Help window.

Getting Help in a Dialog Box

Some dialog boxes contain a Help button. Open a dialog box and then click the Help button and information about the dialog box displays in the Word Help window. After reading and/or printing the information, close the Word Help window and then close the dialog box by clicking the Close button in the upper right corner.

Project 6b Using the Help Feature

1. Open a new blank document by completing the following steps:
   a. Click the File tab and then click the *New* option.
   b. At the New backstage area, double-click the *Single spaced (blank)* template.

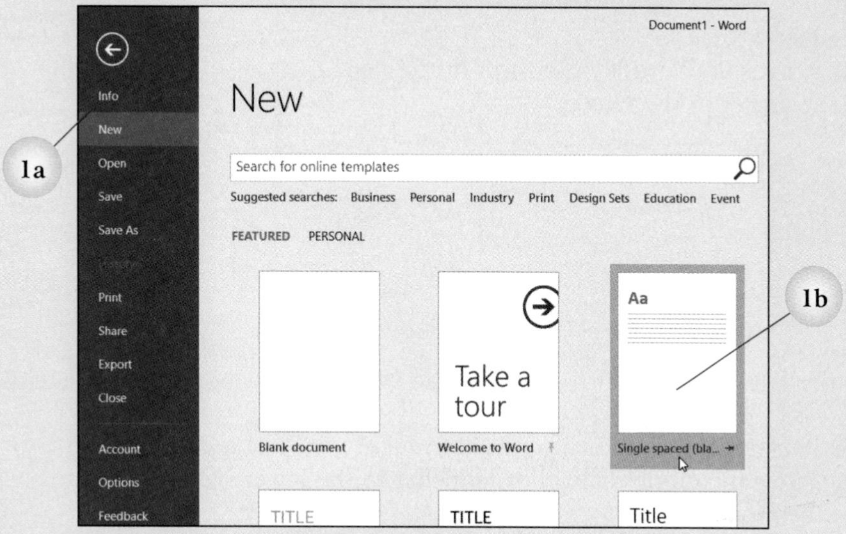

2. Press F1 to display the Microsoft Word Help window.
3. At the Word Help window, click in the search text box, type print preview, and then press the Enter key.
4. When the list of articles displays, click the Print a document in Word hyperlinked article. (You may need to scroll down the Word Help window to display this article.)
5. Scroll down the Word Help window and read the information about printing and previewing documents.
6. Click the Print button in the Word Help window. This displays the Print dialog box. If you want to print information about the topic, click the Print button; otherwise, click the Cancel button to close the dialog box.
7. At the Word Help window, click the Use Large Text button to increase the size of the text in the window.
8. Click the Use Large Text button again to return the text to the normal size.
9. Click the Back button to return to the previous window.
10. Click the Home button to return to the original Word Help window screen.
11. Click the Close button to close the Word Help window.
12. Hover your mouse over the Format Painter button in the Clipboard group on the Home tab.

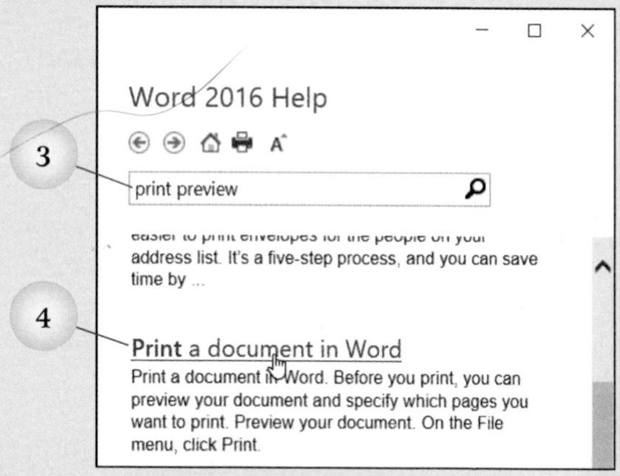

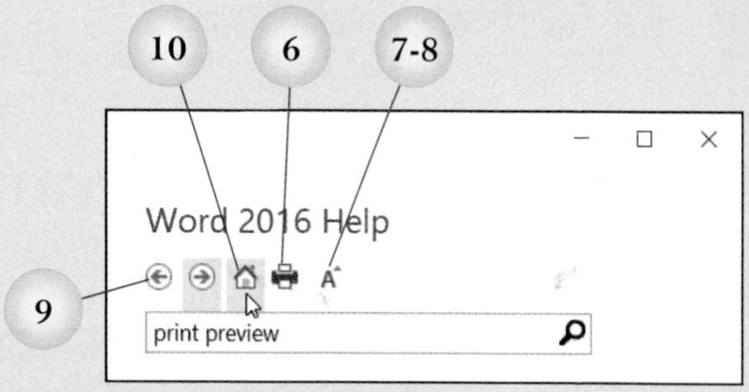

13. Click the Tell me more hyperlinked text at the bottom of the ScreenTip.
14. Read the information in the Word Help window about the Format Painter feature.
15. Click the Close button to close the Word Help window.
16. Click the File tab.
17. Click the Microsoft Word Help button in the upper right corner of the screen.

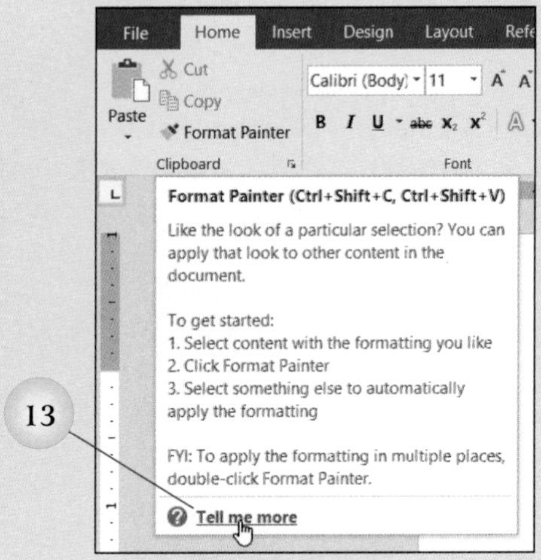

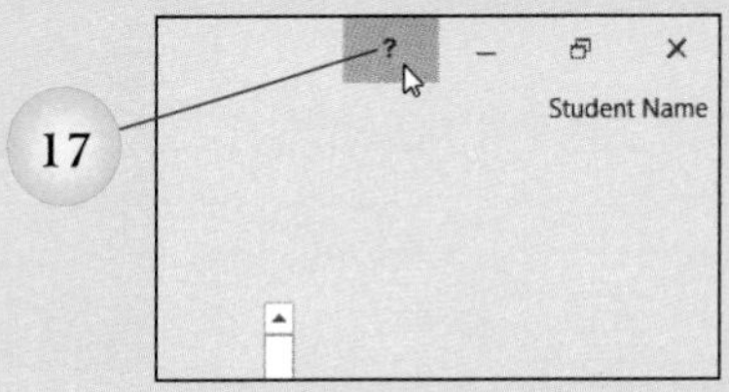

18. Look at the information that displays in the Word Help window and then close the window.
19. Click the Back button to return to the document.
20. Click the Paragraph group dialog box launcher in the lower right corner of the Pararaph group on the Home tab.

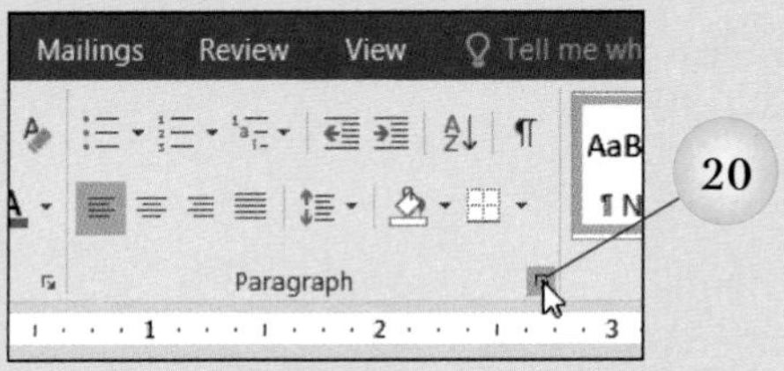

21. Click the Help button in the upper right corner of the Paragraph dialog box.

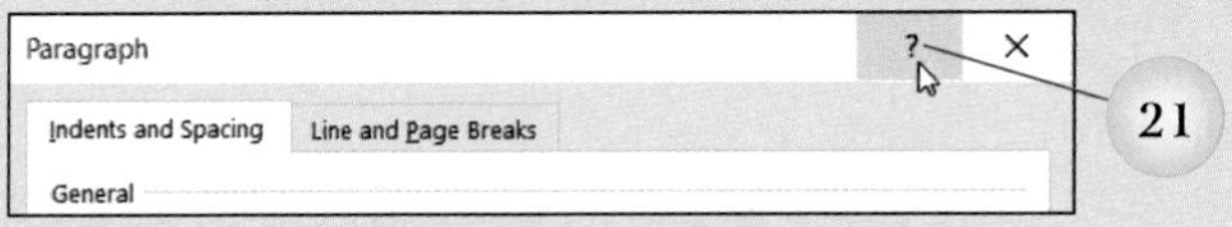

22. Read the information that displays in the Word Help window.
23. Close the Word Help window and then close the Paragraph dialog box.
24. Close the blank document.

Chapter Summary

- Refer to Figure 1.1 and Table 1.1 for an example and a list, respectively, of key Word screen features.
- Click the File tab and the backstage area displays, containing options for working with and managing documents.
- Document names can contain a maximum of 255 characters, including the drive letter and folder names, and may include spaces.
- The Quick Access Toolbar contains buttons for commonly used commands.

- The ribbon contains tabs with options and buttons divided into groups.
- The insertion point displays as a blinking vertical line and indicates the position of the next character to be entered in the document.
- The insertion point can be moved throughout the document without interfering with text by using the mouse, the keyboard, or the mouse combined with the keyboard.
- The scroll box on the vertical scroll bar indicates the location of the text in the document in relation to the remainder of the document.
- The insertion point can be moved by character, word, screen, or page and from the first to the last character in a document. Refer to Table 1.2 for keyboard insertion point movement commands.
- Delete text by character, word, line, several lines, or partial page using specific keys or by selecting text using the mouse or the keyboard. Refer to Table 1.3 for deletion commands.
- A specific amount of text can be selected using the mouse or the keyboard. Refer to Table 1.4 for information on selecting with the mouse, and refer to Table 1.5 for information on selecting with the keyboard.
- Use the Undo button on the Quick Access Toolbar to undo an action such as typing, deleting, or formatting text. Use the Redo button to redo something that has been undone with the Undo button.
- The spelling checker matches the words in a document with the words in its dictionary. If a match is not found, the word is selected and possible corrections are suggested in the Spelling task pane. The grammar checker searches a document for errors in grammar, punctuation, and word usage. When a grammar error is detected, possible corrections display in the Grammar task pane along with information about the grammar rule or error. Refer to Table 1.6 for Spelling task pane and Grammar task pane buttons.
- The Tell Me feature provides information and guidance on how to complete a function. The *Tell Me* text box is on the ribbon to the right of the View tab.
- Word's Help feature is an on-screen reference manual containing information about Word features and commands. Press the F1 function key to display the Word Help window.
- The Word Help window (Figure 1.9) contains five buttons, which are to the left of the search text box: the Back, Forward, Home, Print, and Use Large Text buttons.
- Hover the mouse pointer over a certain button and the ScreenTip displays a Help icon and the Tell me more hyperlinked text. Click this hyperlinked text to display the Word Help window, which contains information about the button feature.
- Some dialog boxes and the backstage area contain a help button that when clicked displays information about the dialog box or backstage area.

Commands Review

FEATURE	RIBBON TAB, GROUP	BUTTON, OPTION	KEYBOARD SHORTCUT
AutoComplete entry			F3
close document	File, *Close*		Ctrl + F4
close Word			Alt + F4
Find and Replace dialog box with Go To tab selected	Home, Editing	, *Go To*	Ctrl + G
Leave backstage area			Esc
Move insertion point to previous location when document was closed			Shift + F5
new blank document	File, *New*	*Blank document*	Ctrl + N
New Line command			Shift + Enter
Open backstage area	File, *Open*		Ctrl + O
Open dialog box	File, *Open*		Ctrl + F12
Print backstage area	File, *Print*		Ctrl + P
redo an action			Ctrl + Y
save	File, *Save*		Ctrl + S
Save As backstage area	File, *Save As*		
Save As dialog box	File, *Save As*		F12
Selection mode			F8
spelling and grammar checker	Review, Proofing		F7
Tell Me feature		Tell me what you want to do	Alt + Q
undo an action			Ctrl + Z
Word Help			F1

Workbook

Chapter study tools and assessment activities are available in the *Workbook* ebook. These resources are designed to help you further develop and demonstrate mastery of the skills learned in this chapter.

Microsoft®

Word

Formatting Characters and Paragraphs

CHAPTER 2

Performance Objectives

Upon successful completion of Chapter 2, you will be able to:

1. Change the font, font size, and choose font effects
2. Format selected text with buttons on the Mini toolbar
3. Apply styles from style sets
4. Apply themes
5. Customize style sets and themes.
6. Change the alignment of text in paragraphs
7. Indent text in paragraphs
8. Increase and decrease spacing before and after paragraphs
9. Repeat the last action
10. Automate formatting with Format Painter
11. Change line spacing
12. Reveal and compare formatting

Precheck

Check your current skills to help focus your study.

The appearance of a document in the document screen and when printed is called the *format*. A Word document is based on a template that applies default formatting. Some of the default formats include 11-point Calibri font, line spacing of 1.08, 8 points of spacing after each paragraph, and left-aligned text. In this chapter, you will learn about changing the typeface, type size, and typestyle as well as applying font effects such as bold and italic. The Paragraph group on the Home tab includes buttons for applying formatting to paragraphs of text. In Word, a paragraph is any amount of text followed by a press of the Enter key. In this chapter, you will learn to format paragraphs by changing text alignment, indenting text, applying formatting with Format Painter, and changing line spacing.

Data Files

Before beginning chapter work, copy the WL1C2 folder to your storage medium and then make WL1C2 the active folder.

SNAP

If you are a SNAP user, launch the Precheck and Tutorials from your Assignments page.

Project 1 Apply Character Formatting — 4 Parts

You will open a document containing a glossary of terms, add additional text, and then format the document by applying character formatting.

Preview Finished Project

Tutorial

Applying Font Formatting Using the Font Group

Applying Font Formatting

The Font group, shown in Figure 2.1, contains a number of options and buttons for applying character formatting to text in a document. The top row contains options for changing the font and font size as well as buttons for increasing and decreasing the size of the font, changing the text case, and clearing formatting. Remove character formatting (as well as paragraph formatting) applied to text by clicking the Clear All Formatting button in the Font group. Remove only character formatting from selected text by pressing the keyboard shortcut Ctrl + spacebar. The bottom row contains buttons for applying typestyles such as bold, italic, and underline and for applying text effects, highlighting, and color.

Hint Change the default font by selecting the font at the Font dialog box and then clicking the Set As Default button.

A Word document is based on a template that formats text in 11-point Calibri. This default may need to be changed to another font for such reasons as altering the mood of the document, enhancing its visual appeal, and increasing its readability. A font consists of three elements: typeface, type size, and typestyle.

Hint Use a serif typeface for text-intensive documents.

A typeface is a set of characters with a common design and shape and can be decorative or plain and either monospaced or proportional. Word refers to a typeface as a *font*. A monospaced typeface allots the same amount of horizontal space for each character, while a proportional typeface allots varying amounts of space for different characters. Typefaces are divided into two main categories: serif and sans serif. A serif is a small line at the end of a character stroke. Consider using a serif typeface for text-intensive documents because the serifs help move the reader's eyes across the page. Use a sans serif typeface for headings, headlines, and advertisements. Some popular typefaces are shown in Table 2.1.

Figure 2.1 Font Group Option Boxes and Buttons

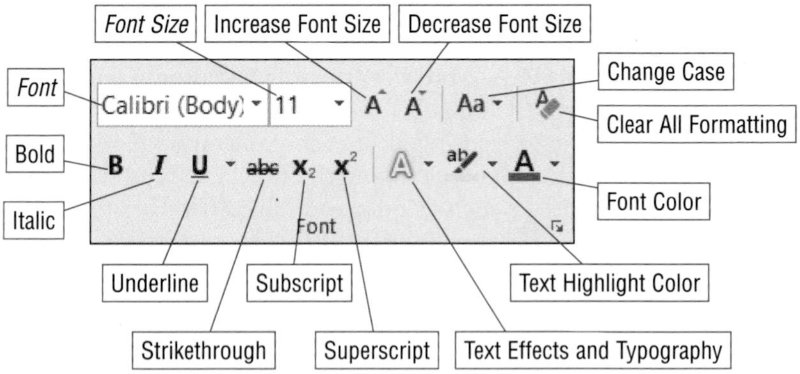

Table 2.1 Categories of Typefaces

Serif Typefaces	*Sans Serif Typefaces*	*Monospaced Typefaces*
Cambria	Calibri	Consolas
Constantia	Candara	Courier New
Times New Roman	Corbel	Lucida Console
Bookman Old Style	Arial	MS Gothic

Type is generally set in proportional size. The size of proportional type is measured vertically in units called *points*. A point is approximately 1/72 of an inch—the higher the point size, the larger the characters. Within a typeface, characters may have varying styles. Type styles are divided into four main categories: regular, bold, italic, and bold italic.

Hint Press Ctrl +] to increase font size by 1 point and press Ctrl + [to decrease font size by 1 point.

Use the *Font* option box arrow in the Font group to change the font. Select the text and then click the *Font* option box arrow and a drop-down gallery of font options displays. Hover the mouse pointer over a font option and the selected text in the document displays with the font applied. Continue hovering the mouse pointer over different font options to see how the selected text displays in each font.

The *Font* option drop-down gallery is an example of the live preview feature, which displays how the font formatting affects text without having to return to the document. The live preview feature is also available with the drop-down gallery of font sizes that displays when the *Font Size* option box arrow is clicked.

Project 1a Changing the Font and Font Size — Part 1 of 4

1. Open **CompTerms.docx** and then save it with the name **2-CompTerms**.
2. Change the typeface to Cambria by completing the following steps:
   a. Select the entire document by pressing Ctrl + A. (You can also select all text in the document by clicking the Select button in the Editing group and then clicking *Select All* at the drop-down list.)
   b. Click the *Font* option box arrow, scroll down the drop-down gallery until *Cambria* displays, and then hover the mouse pointer over *Cambria*. This displays a live preview of the text set in Cambria.
   c. Click the *Cambria* option.

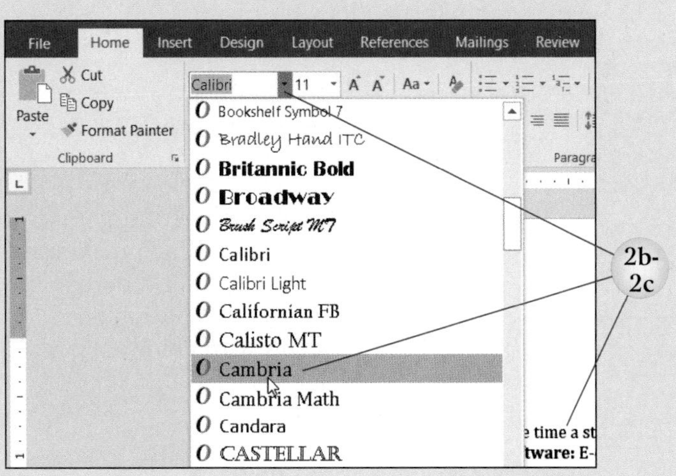

3. Change the type size to 14 points by completing the following steps:
   a. With the text in the document still selected, click the *Font Size* option box arrow.
   b. At the drop-down gallery, hover the mouse pointer over *14* and look at the live preview of the text with 14 points applied.
   c. Click the *14* option.

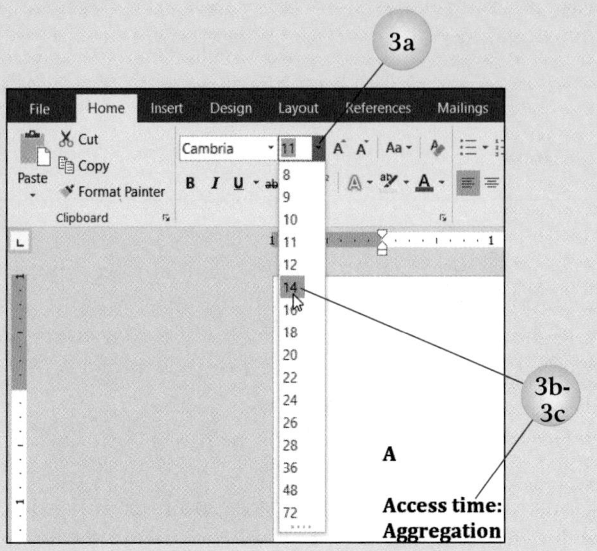

4. Change the type size and typeface by completing the following steps:
   a. Click the Decrease Font Size button in the Font group three times. (This decreases the size to 10 points.)
   b. Click the Increase Font Size button two times. (This increases the size to 12 points.)
   c. Click the *Font* option box arrow, scroll down the drop-down gallery, and then click *Constantia*. (The most recently used fonts display at the beginning of the gallery, followed by a listing of all fonts.)

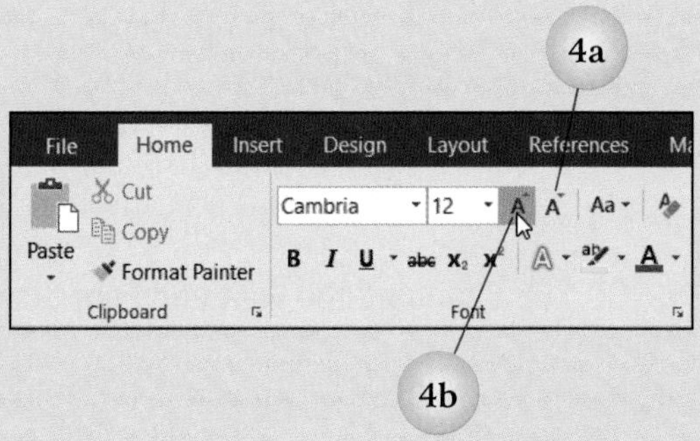

5. Deselect the text by clicking anywhere in the document.
6. Save **2-CompTerms.docx**.

Check Your Work

Choosing a Typestyle

B Bold

I Italic

U Underline

Apply a particular typestyle to text with the Bold, Italic, or Underline buttons in the bottom row in the Font group. More than one typestyle can be applied to text. Click the Underline button arrow and a drop-down gallery displays with underlining options such as a double line, dashed line, and thicker underline. Click the *Underline Color* option at the Underline button drop-down gallery and a side menu displays with color options.

1. With **2-CompTerms.docx** open, press Ctrl + Home to move the insertion point to the beginning of the document.
2. Type a heading for the document by completing the following steps:
   a. Click the Bold button in the Font group. (This turns on bold formatting.)
   b. Click the Underline button in the Font group. (This turns on underline formatting.)
   c. Type Glossary of Terms.

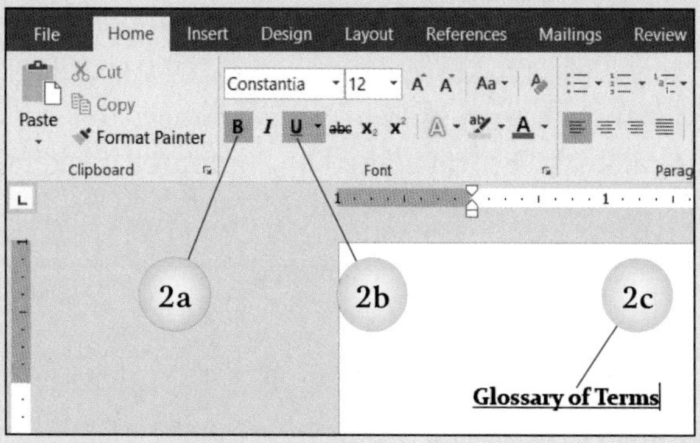

3. Press Ctrl + End to move the insertion point to the end of the document.
4. Type the text shown in Figure 2.2 with the following specifications:
   a. While typing, make the appropriate text bold, as shown in the figure, by completing the following steps:
      1) Click the Bold button in the Font group. (This turns on bold formatting.)
      2) Type the text.
      3) Click the Bold button in the Font group. (This turns off bold formatting.)
   b. Press the Enter key two times after typing the *C* heading.
   c. While typing, italicize the appropriate text, as shown in the figure, by completing the following steps:
      1) Click the Italic button in the Font group.
      2) Type the text.
      3) Click the Italic button in the Font group.
5. After typing the text, press the Enter key two times and then press Ctrl + Home to move the insertion point to the beginning of the document.
6. Change the underlining below the title by completing the following steps:
   a. Select the title *Glossary of Terms*.
   b. Click the Underline button arrow and then click the third underline option from the top of the drop-down gallery (*Thick underline*).
   c. Click the Underline button arrow, point to the *Underline Color* option, and then click the *Red* color (second color option in the *Standard Colors* section).

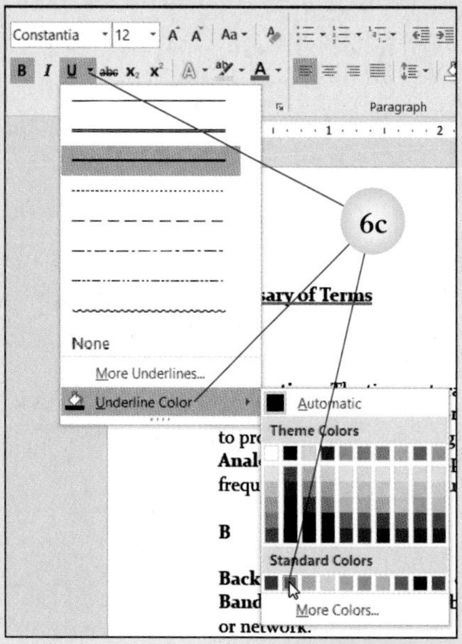

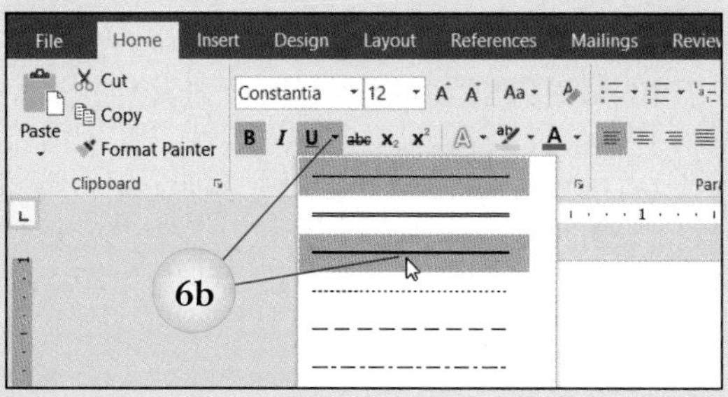

7. With the title still selected, change the font size to 14 points.
8. Save **2-CompTerms.docx**.

Check Your Work

Figure 2.2 Project 1b

> **C**
>
> **Chip:** A thin wafer of *silicon* containing electronic circuitry that performs various functions, such as mathematical calculations, storage, or controlling computer devices.
> **Cluster:** A group of two or more *sectors* on a disk, which is the smallest unit of storage space used to store data.
> **Coding:** A term used by programmers to refer to the act of writing source code.
> **Crackers:** A term coined by computer hackers for those who intentionally enter (or hack) computer systems to damage them.

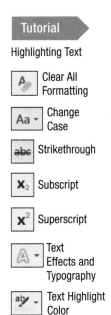

Tutorial

Highlighting Text

Clear All Formatting

Change Case

Strikethrough

Subscript

Superscript

Text Effects and Typography

Text Highlight Color

Font Color

Choosing a Font Effect

Apply font effects with some of the buttons in the top and bottom rows in the Font group, or clear all formatting from selected text with the Clear All Formatting button. Change the case of text with the Change Case button drop-down list. Click the Change Case button in the top row in the Font group and a drop-down list displays with the options *Sentence case*, *lowercase*, *UPPERCASE*, *Capitalize Each Word*, and *tOGGLE cASE*. The case of selected text can also be changed with the keyboard shortcut Shift + F3. Each time Shift + F3 is pressed, the selected text displays in the next case option in the list.

The bottom row in the Font group contains buttons for applying font effects. Use the Strikethrough button to draw a line through selected text. This has a practical application in some legal documents in which deleted text must be retained in the document. Use the Subscript button to create text that is lowered slightly below the line, as in the chemical formula H_2O. Use the Superscript button to create text that is raised slightly above the text line, as in the mathematical equation four to the third power (written as 4^3). Click the Text Effects and Typography button in the bottom row and a drop-down gallery displays with effect options. Use the Text Highlight Color button to highlight specific text in a document and use the Font Color button to change the color of text.

Applying Formatting Using Keyboard Shortcuts

Several of the options and buttons in the Font group have keyboard shortcuts. For example, press Ctrl + B to turn bold formatting on or off and press Ctrl + I to turn italic formatting on or off. Position the mouse pointer on an option or button and an enhanced ScreenTip displays with the name of the option or button; the keyboard shortcut, if any; a description of the action performed by the option or button; and sometimes, access to the Word Help window. Table 2.2 identifies the keyboard shortcuts available for options and buttons in the Font group.

Table 2.2 Font Group Option and Button Keyboard Shortcuts

Font Group Option/Button	Keyboard Shortcut
Font	Ctrl + Shift + F
Font Size	Ctrl + Shift + P
Increase Font Size	Ctrl + Shift + > OR Ctrl +]
Decrease Font Size	Ctrl + Shift + < OR Ctrl + [
Bold	Ctrl + B
Italic	Ctrl + I
Underline	Ctrl + U
Subscript	Ctrl + =
Superscript	Ctrl + Shift + +
Change Case	Shift + F3

Tutorial

Applying Font Formatting Using the Mini Toolbar

Formatting with the Mini Toolbar

When text is selected, the Mini toolbar displays above the selected text, as shown in Figure 2.3. Click a button on the Mini toolbar to apply formatting to the selected text. When the mouse pointer is moved away from the Mini toolbar, the toolbar disappears.

Figure 2.3 Mini Toolbar

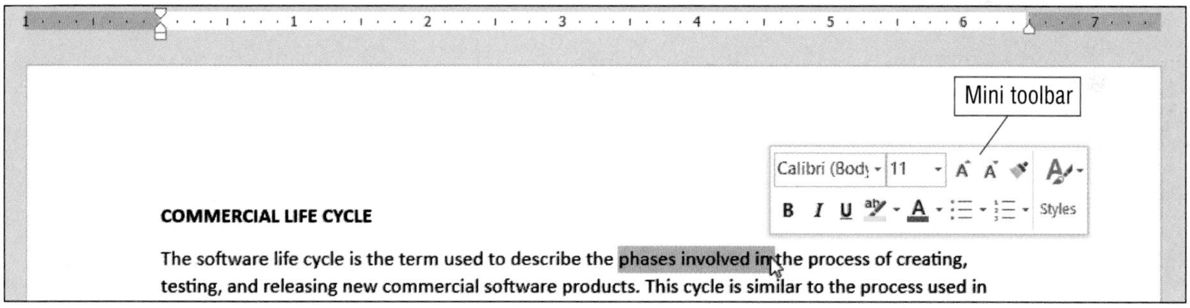

Project 1c Applying Font Effects

1. With **2-CompTerms.docx** open, move the insertion point to the beginning of the term *Chip*, press the Enter key, and then press the Up Arrow key.
2. Type the text shown in Figure 2.4. Create each superscript number by clicking the Superscript button, typing the number, and then clicking the Superscript button.
3. Remove underlining and change the case of the text in the title by completing the following steps:
   a. Select the title *Glossary of Terms*.
   b. Remove all formatting from the title by clicking the Clear All Formatting button in the Font group.
   c. Click the Change Case button in the Font group and then click *UPPERCASE* at the drop-down list.
   d. Click the Text Effects and Typography button in the Font group and then click the *Gradient Fill - Blue, Accent 1, Reflection* option (second column, second row) at the drop-down gallery.
   e. Change the font size to 14 points.
4. Strike through text by completing the following steps:
   a. Select the words and parentheses *(or hack)* in the *Crackers* definition.
   b. Click the Strikethrough button in the Font group.

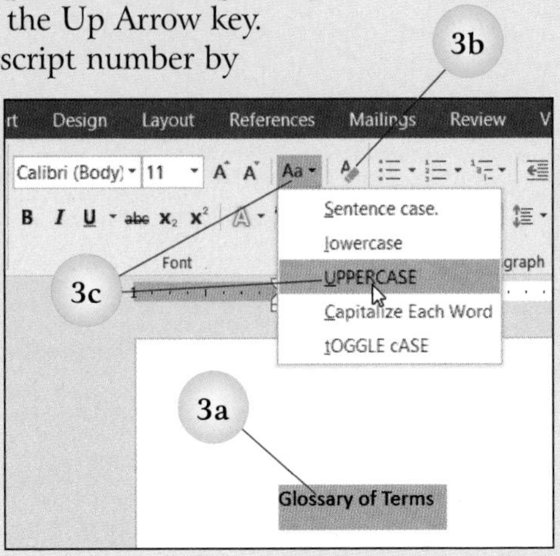

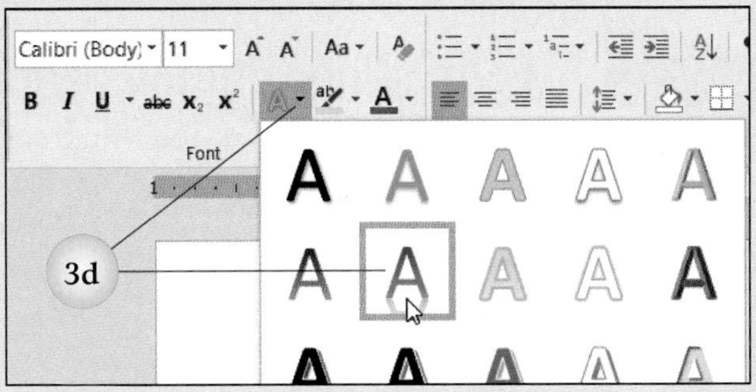

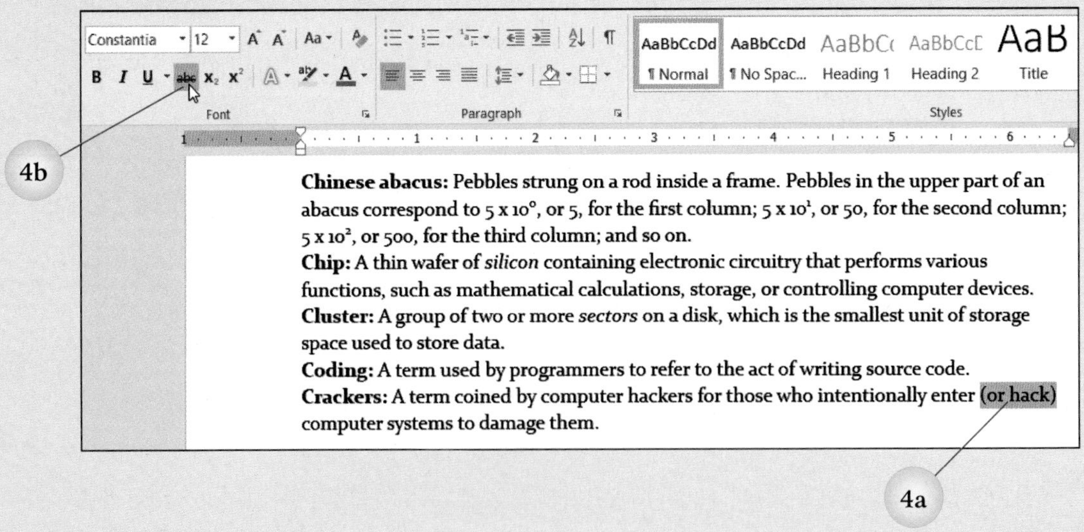
Constantia
12
AaBbCcDd
¶ Normal
AaBbCcDd
¶ No Spac...
AaBbC(
Heading 1
AaBbCcE
Heading 2
AaB
Title
Font
Paragraph
Styles
4b
Chinese abacus: Pebbles strung on a rod inside a frame. Pebbles in the upper part of an abacus correspond to 5×10^0, or 5, for the first column; 5×10^1, or 50, for the second column; 5×10^2, or 500, for the third column; and so on.
Chip: A thin wafer of silicon containing electronic circuitry that performs various functions, such as mathematical calculations, storage, or controlling computer devices.
Cluster: A group of two or more sectors on a disk, which is the smallest unit of storage space used to store data.
Coding: A term used by programmers to refer to the act of writing source code.
Crackers: A term coined by computer hackers for those who intentionally enter (or hack) computer systems to damage them.
4a

5. Change the font color by completing the following steps:
   a. Press Ctrl + A to select the entire document.
   b. Click the Font Color button arrow.
   c. Click the *Dark Red* color (first color option in the *Standard Colors* section) at the drop-down gallery.
   d. Click in the document to deselect text.

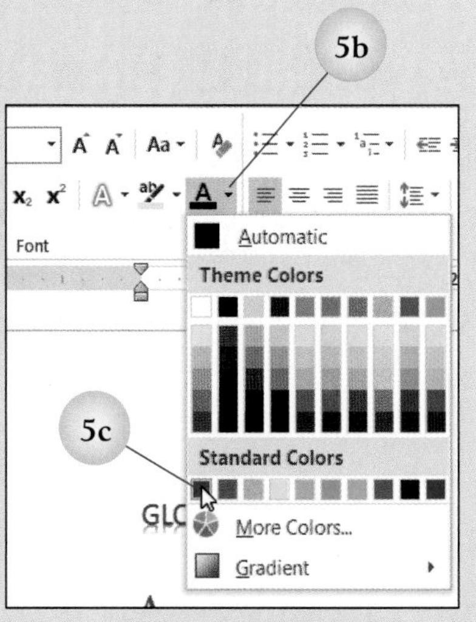

6. Highlight text in the document by completing the following steps:
   a. Click the Text Highlight Color button arrow in the Font group and then click the *Yellow* color (first column, first row) at the drop-down palette. (This causes the mouse pointer to display as an I-beam pointer with a highlighter pen attached.)
   b. Select the term *Beta-testing* and the definition that follows.
   c. Click the Text Highlight Color button arrow and then click the *Turquoise* color (third column, first row).
   d. Select the term *Cluster* and the definition that follows.
   e. Click the Text Highlight Color button arrow and then click the *Yellow* color at the drop-down gallery.
   f. Click the Text Highlight Color button to turn off highlighting.

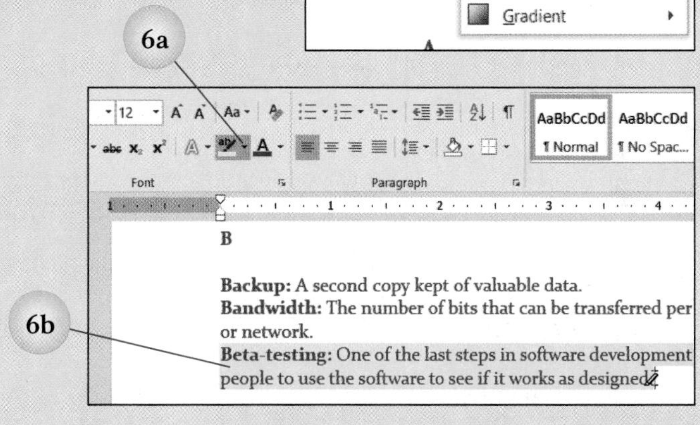

7. Apply italic formatting using the Mini toolbar by completing the following steps:
   a. Select the text *one-stop shopping* in the definition for the term *Aggregation software*. (When you select the text, the Mini toolbar displays.)
   b. Click the Italic button on the Mini toolbar.
   c. Select the word *bits* in the definition for the term *Bandwidth* and then click the Italic button on the Mini toolbar.
8. Save **2-CompTerms.docx**.

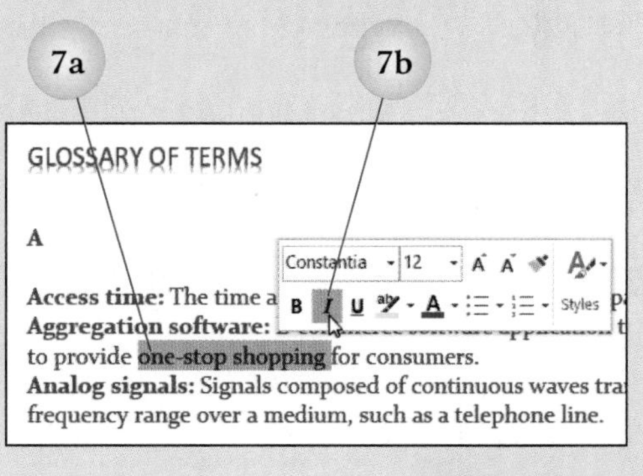

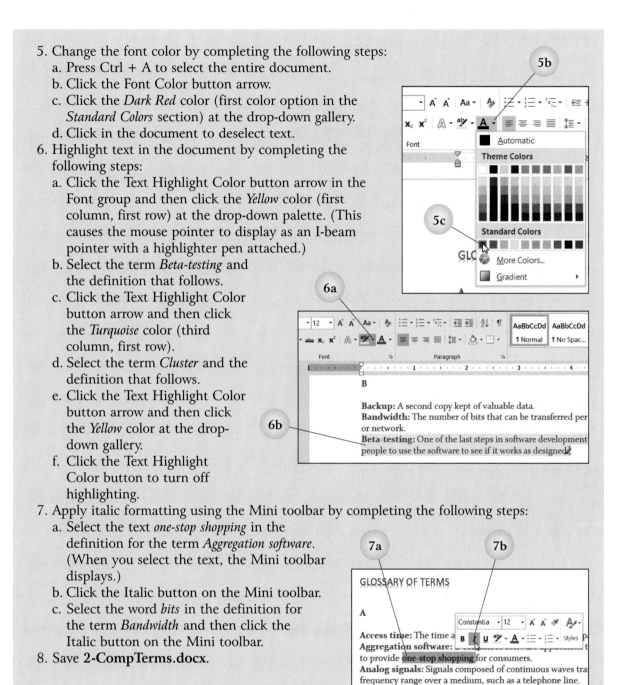

Check Your Work

Figure 2.4 Project 1c

Chinese abacus: Pebbles strung on a rod inside a frame. Pebbles in the upper part of an abacus correspond to 5×10^0, or 5, for the first column; 5×10^1, or 50, for the second column; 5×10^2, or 500, for the third column; and so on.

Figure 2.5 Font Dialog Box

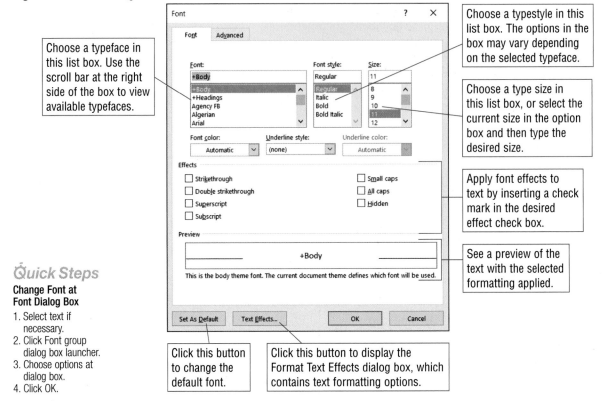

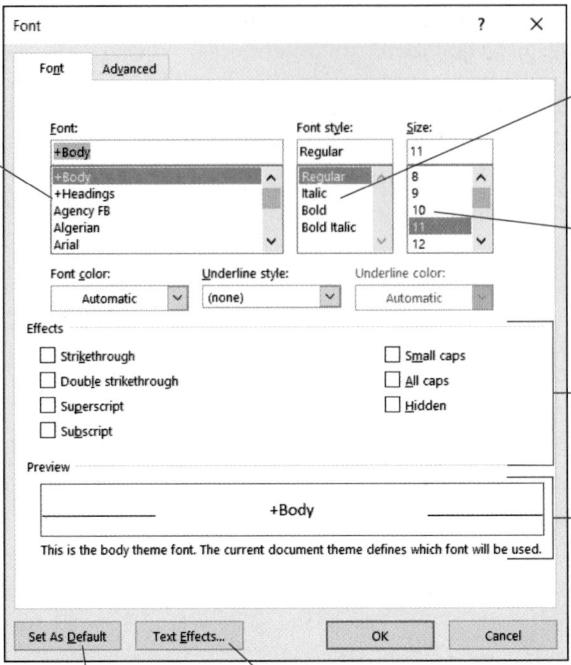

Quick Steps

Change Font at Font Dialog Box

1. Select text if necessary.
2. Click Font group dialog box launcher.
3. Choose options at dialog box.
4. Click OK.

Tutorial

Applying Font Formatting Using the Font Dialog Box

Applying Font Formatting Using the Font Dialog Box

In addition to options and buttons in the Font group, options at the Font dialog box, shown in Figure 2.5, can be used to change the typeface, type size, and typestyle of text as well as apply font effects. Display the Font dialog box by clicking the Font group dialog box launcher. The dialog box launcher is a small square containing a diagonal-pointing arrow in the lower right corner of the Font group.

Project 1d **Changing the Font at the Font Dialog Box** Part 4 of 4

1. With **2-CompTerms.docx** open, press Ctrl + End to move the insertion point to the end of the document. (Make sure the insertion point is positioned a double space below the last line of text.)
2. Type Created by Susan Ashby and then press the Enter key.
3. Type Wednesday, February 21, 2018.
4. Change the font to 13-point Candara and the color to standard dark blue for the entire document by completing the following steps:
   a. Press Ctrl + A to select the entire document.
   b. Click the Font group dialog box launcher.

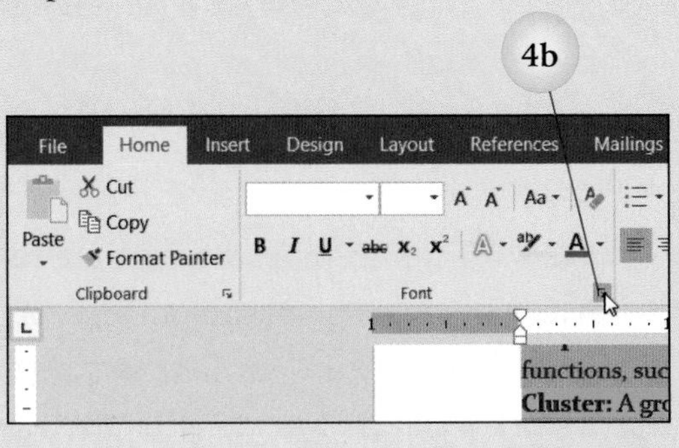

c. At the Font dialog box, type can in the *Font* option box (this displays fonts that begin with *can*) and then click *Candara* in the *Font* list box.
d. Click in the *Size* option box and then type 13.
e. Click the *Font color* option box arrow and then click the *Dark Blue* color option (ninth option in the *Standard Colors* section).
f. Click OK to close the dialog box.

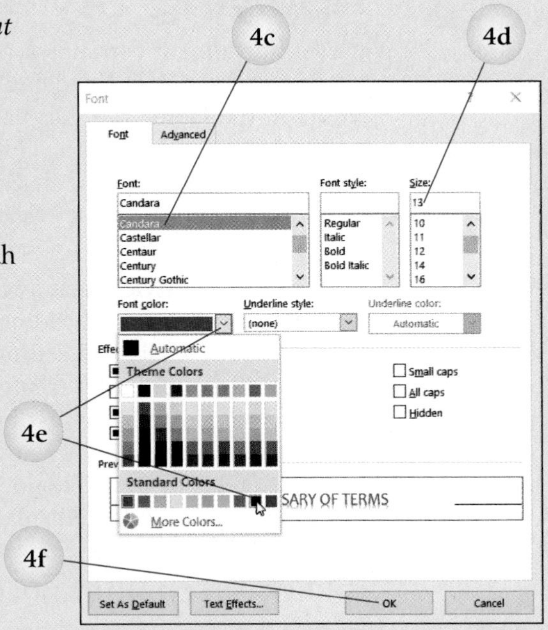

5. Double-underline text by completing the following steps:
   a. Select *Wednesday, February 21, 2018*.
   b. Click the Font group dialog box launcher.
   c. At the Font dialog box, click the *Underline style* option box arrow and then click the double-line option at the drop-down list.
   d. Click OK to close the dialog box.

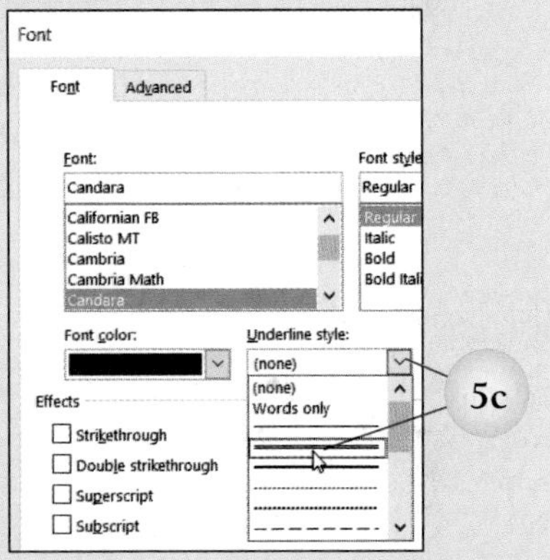

6. Change text to small caps by completing the following steps:
   a. Select the text *Created by Susan Ashby* and *Wednesday, February 21, 2018*.
   b. Display the Font dialog box.
   c. Click the *Small caps* check box in the *Effects* section. (This inserts a check mark in the check box.)
   d. Click OK to close the dialog box.

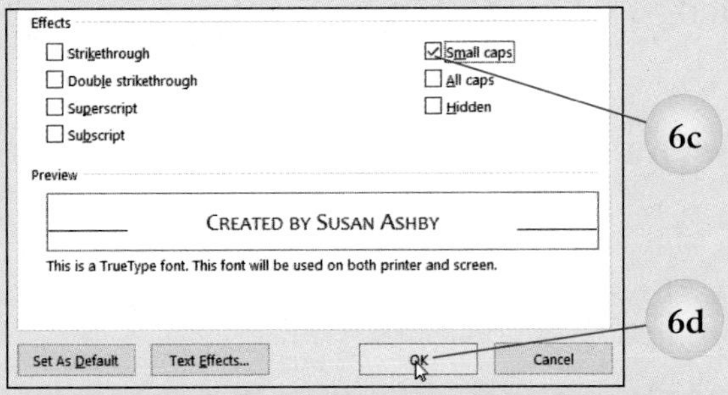

7. Save, print, and then close **2-CompTerms.docx**.

Check Your Work

Project 2 Apply Styles and Themes — 3 Parts

You will open a document containing information on the life cycle of software, apply styles to text, and then change the style set. You will also apply a theme and then change the theme colors and fonts.

Preview Finished Project

Tutorial

Applying Styles and Style Sets

Quick Steps

Apply a Style

1. Position insertion point in text or paragraph of text.
2. Click More Styles button in Styles group.
3. Click style.

Applying Styles from a Style Set

A Word document contains a number of predesigned formats grouped into style sets. Several styles in the default style set display in the styles gallery in the Styles group on the Home tab. Display additional styles by clicking the More Styles button in the Styles group. This displays a drop-down gallery of style options. To apply a style, position the insertion point in the text or paragraph of text, click the More Styles button in the Styles group, and then click the style at the drop-down gallery.

If a heading style (such as Heading 1, Heading 2, and so on) is applied to text, the text below the heading can be collapsed and expanded. Hover the mouse pointer over text with a heading style applied and a collapse triangle (solid, right- and down-pointing triangle) displays to the left of the heading. Click this collapse triangle and any text below the heading is collapsed (hidden). Redisplay the text below a heading by hovering the mouse over the heading text until an expand triangle displays (hollow, right-pointing triangle) and then click the expand triangle. This expands (redisplays) the text below the heading.

Removing Default Formatting

A Word document contains some default formatting, including 8 points of spacing after paragraphs and line spacing of 1.08. (You will learn more about these formatting options later in this chapter.) This default formatting, as well as any character formatting applied to text in the document, can be removed by applying the No Spacing style to the text. This style is in the styles gallery in the Styles group.

Quick Steps

Change Style Set

1. Click Design tab.
2. Click style set.

Changing the Style Set

Word provides a number of style sets containing styles that apply formatting to text in a document. To change the style set, click the Design tab and then click the style set in the style sets gallery in the Document Formatting group.

Project 2a Applying Styles and Changing the Style Set — Part 1 of 3

1. Open **SoftwareCycle.docx** and then save it with the name **2-SoftwareCycle**.
2. Position the insertion point anywhere in the title *COMMERCIAL LIFE CYCLE* and then click the *Heading 1* style in the Styles group.

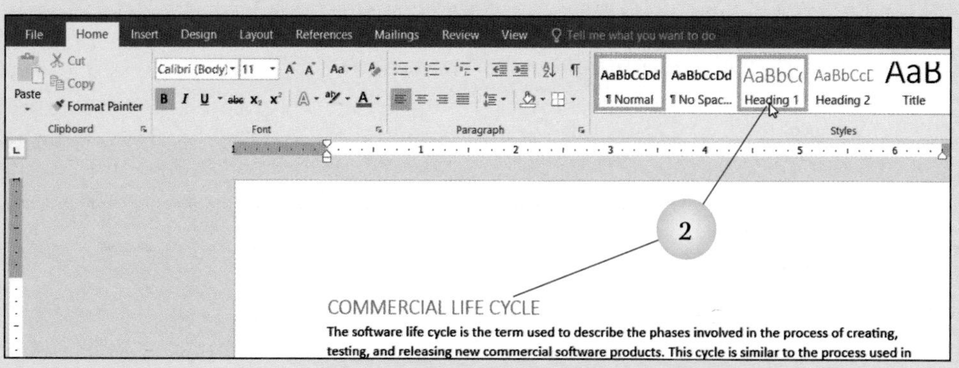

3. Position the insertion point anywhere in the heading *Proposal and Planning* and then click the *Heading 2* style in the styles gallery in the Styles group.

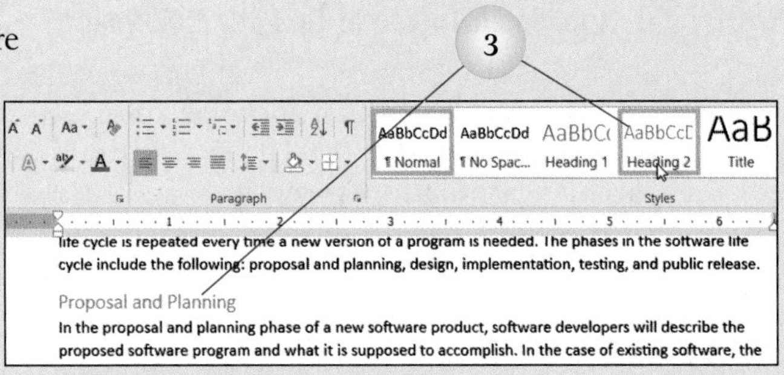

4. Position the insertion point anywhere in the heading *Design* and then click the *Heading 2* style in the styles gallery.
5. Apply the Heading 2 style to the remaining headings (*Implementation*, *Testing*, and *Public Release and Support*).
6. Collapse and expand text below the heading with the Heading 1 style applied by completing the following steps:
   a. Hover the mouse pointer over the heading *COMMERCIAL LIFE CYCLE* until a collapse triangle displays at the left side of the heading and then click the triangle. (This collapses all the text below the heading.)
   b. Click the expand triangle at the left side of the heading *COMMERCIAL LIFE CYCLE*. (This redisplays the text in the document.)

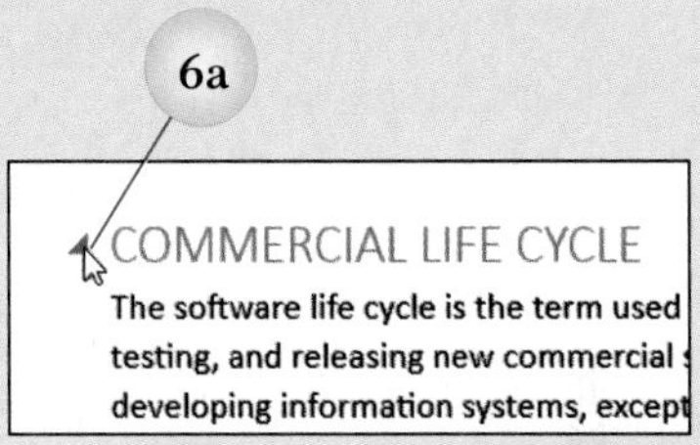

7. Click the Design tab.
8. Click the *Casual* style set in the style sets gallery in the Document Formatting group (the ninth option in the style set). (Notice how the Heading 1 and Heading 2 formatting changes.)

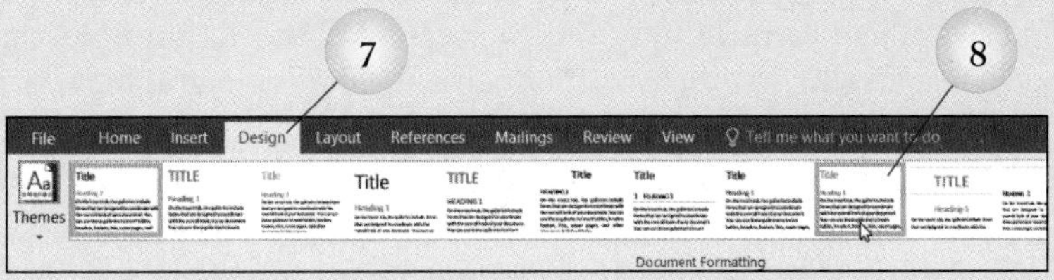

9. Save and then print **2-SoftwareCycle.docx**.

Check Your Work

Tutorial

Applying and Modifying a Theme

Themes

Quick Steps

Apply a Theme

1. Click Design tab.
2. Click Themes button.
3. Click theme.

Applying a Theme

Word provides a number of themes for formatting text in a document. A theme is a set of formatting choices that includes a color theme (a set of colors), a font theme (a set of heading and body text fonts), and an effects theme (a set of lines and fill effects). To apply a theme, click the Design tab and then click the Themes button in the Document Formatting group. At the drop-down gallery, click the theme. Hover the mouse pointer over a theme and the live preview feature will display the document with the theme formatting applied. Applying a theme is an easy way to give a document a professional look.

Project 2b Applying a Theme to Text in a Document

Part 2 of 3

1. With **2-SoftwareCycle.docx** open, click the Design tab and then click the Themes button in the Document Formatting group.
2. At the drop-down gallery, hover your mouse pointer over several different themes and notice how the text formatting changes in your document.
3. Click the *Organic* theme.
4. Save and then print **2-SoftwareCycle.docx**.

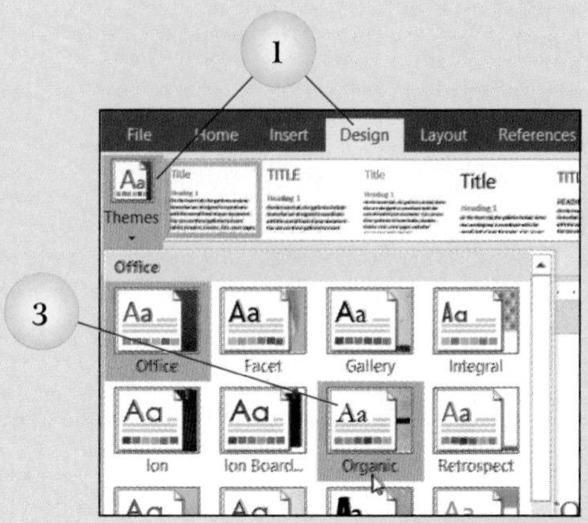

Check Your Work

Modifying a Theme

Quick Steps

Change Theme Color
1. Click Design tab.
2. Click Colors button.
3. Click theme color option.

Change Theme Fonts
1. Click Design tab.
2. Click Fonts button.
3. Click theme fonts option.

Change Paragraph Spacing
1. Click Design tab.
2. Click Paragraph Spacing button.
3. Click paragraph spacing option.

Theme Colors

Theme Fonts

Theme Effects

Paragraph Spacing

Modify the color applied by a style or theme with the Colors button in the Document Formatting group. Click the Colors button and a drop-down gallery displays with named color schemes. Modify the fonts applied to text in a document with the Fonts button in the Document Formatting group. Click this button and a drop-down gallery displays with font choices. Each font group in the drop-down gallery contains two choices. The first choice in the group is the font that is applied to headings, and the second choice is the font that is applied to body text in the document. If a document contains graphics with lines and fills, a specific theme effect can be applied with options at the Effects button drop-down gallery.

The buttons in the Document Formatting group display a visual representation of the current theme. If the theme colors are changed, the small color squares in the Themes button and the Colors button reflect the change. Change the theme fonts and the *A*s on the Themes button and the uppercase *A* on the Fonts button reflect the change. If the theme effects are changed, the circle in the Effects button reflects the change.

The Paragraph Spacing button in the Document Formatting group on the Design tab contains predesigned paragraph spacing options. To change paragraph spacing, click the Paragraph Spacing button and then click the option at the drop-down gallery. Hover the mouse pointer over an option at the drop-down gallery and after a moment a ScreenTip displays with information about the formatting applied by the option. For example, hover the mouse pointer over the *Compact* option at the side menu and a ScreenTip displays indicating that selecting the *Compact* option will change the spacing before paragraphs to 0 points, the spacing after paragraphs to 4 points, and the line spacing to single line spacing.

1. With **2-SoftwareCycle.docx** open, click the Colors button in the Document Formatting group on the Design tab and then click *Red Orange* at the drop-down gallery. (Notice how the colors in the title and headings change.)
2. Click the Fonts button and then click the *Corbel* option. (Notice how the document text font changes.)

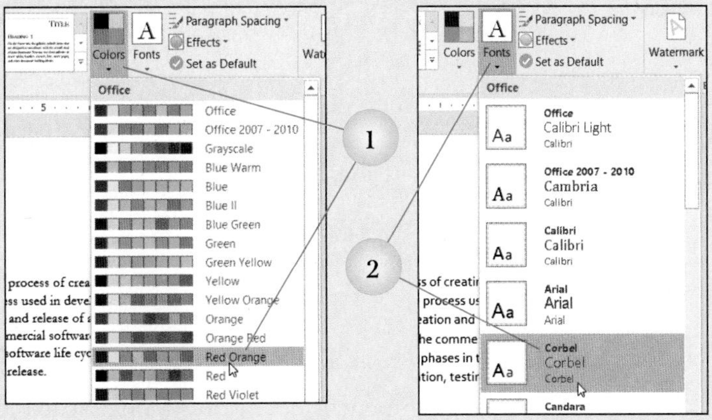

3. Click the Paragraph Spacing button and then, one at a time, hover the mouse pointer over each paragraph spacing option, beginning with *Compact*. For each option, read the ScreenTip that explains the paragraph spacing applied by the option.
4. Click the *Double* option.
5. Scroll through the document and notice the paragraph spacing.
6. Change the paragraph spacing by clicking the Paragraph Spacing button and then clicking *Compact*.
7. Save, print, and then close **2-SoftwareCycle.docx**.

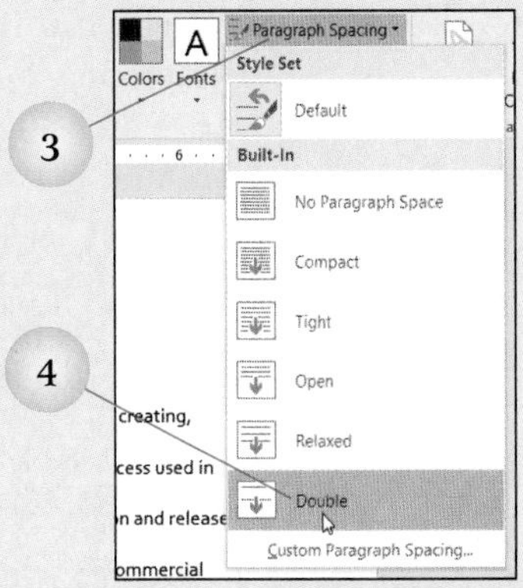

Check Your Work

Project 3 Apply Paragraph Formatting and Use Format Painter 6 Parts

You will open a report on intellectual property and fair use issues and then format the report by changing the alignment of text in paragraphs, applying spacing before and after paragraphs of text, and repeating the last formatting command.

Preview Finished Project

Tutorial

Changing Paragraph Alignment

Changing Paragraph Alignment

By default, paragraphs in a Word document are aligned at the left margin and are ragged at the right margin. Change this default alignment with buttons in the Paragraph group on the Home tab or with keyboard shortcuts, as shown in Table 2.3. The alignment of text in paragraphs can be changed before text is typed or the alignment of existing text can be changed.

Table 2.3 Paragraph Alignment Buttons and Keyboard Shortcuts

To align text	Paragraph Group Button	Keyboard Shortcut
At the left margin		Ctrl + L
Between margins		Ctrl + E
At the right margin		Ctrl + R
At the left and right margins		Ctrl + J

Changing Paragraph Alignment as Text Is Typed

Center

Show/Hide ¶

Align Right

Align Left

If the alignment is changed before text is typed, the alignment formatting is inserted in the paragraph mark. Type text and press the Enter key and the paragraph formatting is continued. For example, click the Center button in the Paragraph group, type text for the first paragraph, and then press the Enter key; the center alignment formatting is still active and the insertion point displays centered between the left and right margins. To display the paragraph symbols in a document, click the Show/Hide ¶ button in the Paragraph group. With the Show/Hide ¶ button active (displays with a gray background), nonprinting formatting symbols display, such as the paragraph symbol ¶ indicating a press of the Enter key or a dot indicating a press of the spacebar.

Changing Paragraph Alignment of Existing Text

Hint Align text to help the reader follow the message of a document and to make the layout look appealing.

To change the alignment of existing text in a paragraph, position the insertion point anywhere within the paragraph. The entire paragraph does not need to be selected. To change the alignment of several adjacent paragraphs in a document, select a portion of the first paragraph through a portion of the last paragraph. All the text in the paragraphs does not need to be selected.

To return paragraph alignment to the default (left-aligned), click the Align Left button in the Paragraph group. All paragraph formatting can also be returned to the default with the keyboard shortcut Ctrl + Q. This keyboard shortcut removes paragraph formatting from selected text. To remove all formatting from selected text, including character and paragraph formatting, click the Clear All Formatting button in the Font group.

Project 3a **Changing Paragraph Alignment** Part 1 of 6

1. Open **IntelProp.docx**. (Some of the default formatting in this document has been changed.)
2. Save the document with the name **2-IntelProp**.
3. Click the Show/Hide ¶ button in the Paragraph group on the Home tab to turn on the display of nonprinting characters.

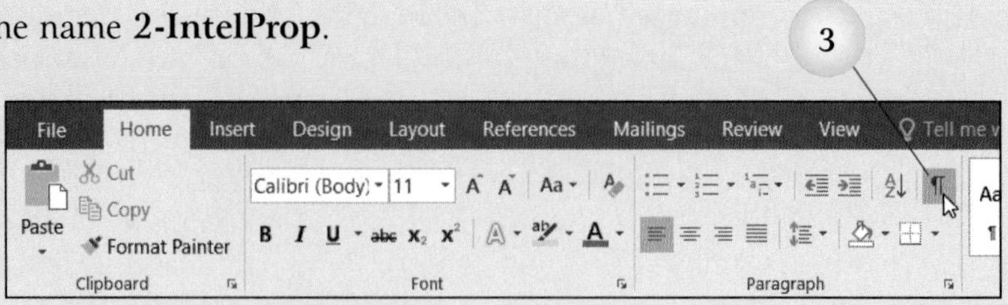

4. Press Ctrl + A to select the entire document and then change the paragraph alignment to justified alignment by clicking the Justify button in the Paragraph group.
5. Press Ctrl + End to move the insertion point to the end of the document.
6. Press the Enter key.
7. Press Ctrl + E to move the insertion point to the middle of the page.
8. Type Prepared by Clarissa Markham.
9. Press Shift + Enter and then type Edited by Joshua Streeter.

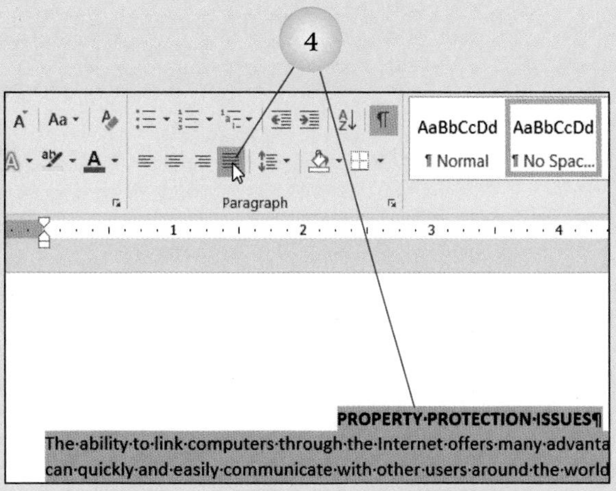

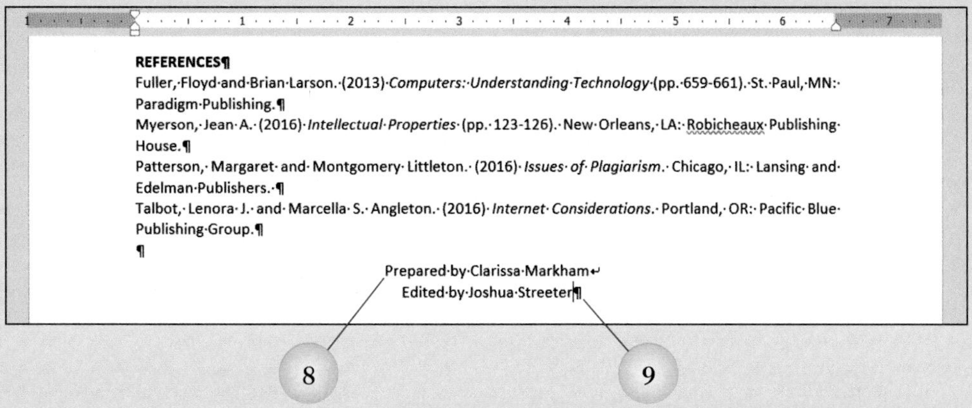

10. Click the Show/Hide ¶ button in the Paragraph group to turn off the display of nonprinting characters.
11. Save **2-IntelProp.docx**.

Check Your Work

Quick Steps

Change Paragraph Alignment

Click alignment button in Paragraph group on Home tab.

OR

1. Click Paragraph group dialog box launcher.
2. Click *Alignment* option box arrow.
3. Click alignment option.
4. Click OK.

Changing Alignment at the Paragraph Dialog Box

Along with buttons in the Paragraph group and keyboard shortcuts, paragraph alignment can be changed with the *Alignment* option box at the Paragraph dialog box, shown in Figure 2.6. Display this dialog box by clicking the Paragraph group dialog box launcher. At the Paragraph dialog box, click the *Alignment* option box arrow. At the drop-down list, click the alignment option and then click OK to close the dialog box.

Figure 2.6 Paragraph Dialog Box with Indents and Spacing Tab Selected

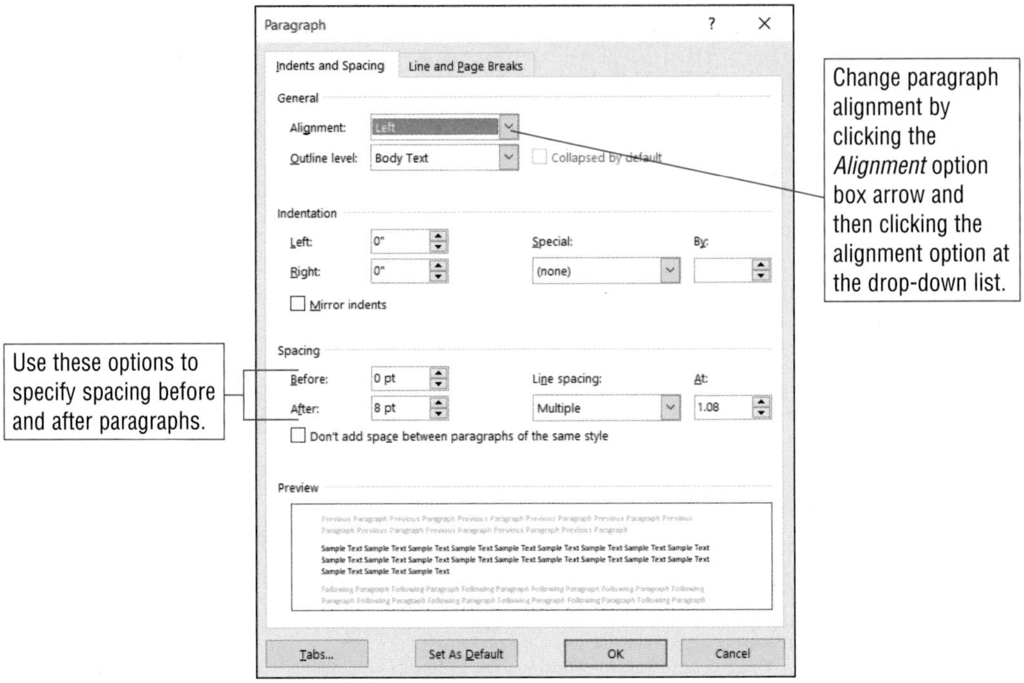

Project 3b Changing Paragraph Alignment at the Paragraph Dialog Box

Part 2 of 6

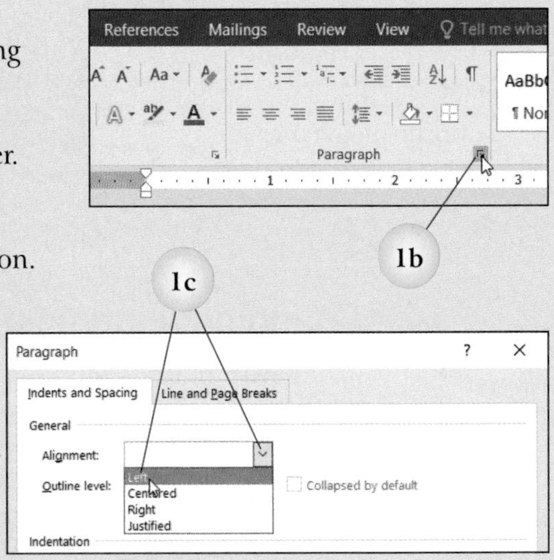

1. With **2-IntelProp.docx** open, change the paragraph alignment by completing the following steps:
   a. Select the entire document.
   b. Click the Paragraph group dialog box launcher.
   c. At the Paragraph dialog box with the Indents and Spacing tab selected, click the *Alignment* option box arrow and then click the *Left* option.
   d. Click OK to close the dialog box.
   e. Deselect the text.
2. Change the paragraph alignment by completing the following steps:
   a. Press Ctrl + End to move the insertion point to the end of the document.
   b. Position the insertion point anywhere in the text *Prepared by Clarissa Markham*.
   c. Click the Paragraph group dialog box launcher.
   d. At the Paragraph dialog box with the Indents and Spacing tab selected, click the *Alignment* option box arrow and then click the *Right* option.
   e. Click OK to close the dialog box. (The line of text containing the name *Clarissa Markham* and the line of text containing the name *Joshua Streeter* are both aligned at the right since you used the New Line command, Shift + Enter, to separate the lines of text without creating a new paragraph.)
3. Save and then print **2-IntelProp.docx**.

Check Your Work

Tutorial

Indenting Text

Quick Steps

Indent Text in Paragraph

Drag indent marker(s) on horizontal ruler.
OR
Press keyboard shortcut keys.
OR
1. Click Paragraph group dialog box launcher.
2. Insert measurement in *Left*, *Right*, and/or *By* text box.
3. Click OK.

Indenting Text in Paragraphs

To indent text from the left margin, the right margin, or both margins, use the indent buttons in the Paragraph group on the Layout tab, keyboard shortcuts, options from the Paragraph dialog box, markers on the horizontal ruler, or the Alignment button above the vertical ruler. Figure 2.7 identifies indent markers on the horizontal ruler and the Alignment button. Refer to Table 2.4 for methods for indenting text in a document. If the horizontal ruler is not visible, display the ruler by clicking the View tab and then clicking the *Ruler* check box in the Show group to insert a check mark.

Figure 2.7 Horizontal Ruler and Indent Markers

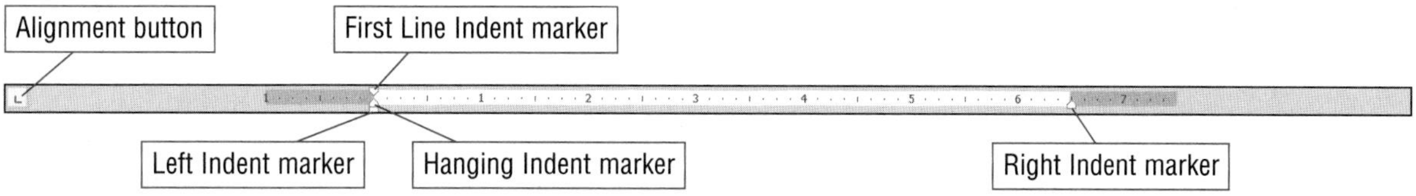

Table 2.4 Methods for Indenting Text

Indent	Methods for Indenting
First line of paragraph	• Press the Tab key. • Display the Paragraph dialog box, click the *Special* option box arrow, click *First line*, and then click OK. • Drag the First Line Indent marker on the horizontal ruler. • Click the Alignment button, until the First Line Indent symbol displays and then click the horizontal ruler at the desired location.
Text from left margin	• Click the Increase Indent button in the Paragraph group on the Home tab to increase the indent or click the Decrease Indent button to decrease the indent. • Insert a measurement in the *Indent Left* measurement box in the Paragraph group on the Layout tab. • Press Ctrl + M to increase the indent or press Ctrl + Shift + M to decrease the indent. • Display the Paragraph dialog box, type the indent measurement in the *Left* measurement box, and then click OK. • Drag the Left Indent marker on the horizontal ruler.

continues

Table 2.4 Methods for Indenting Text—*Continued*

Indent	Methods for Indenting
Text from right margin	• Insert a measurement in the *Indent Right* measurement box in the Paragraph group on the Layout tab. • Display the Paragraph dialog box, type the indent measurement in the *Right* measurement box, and then click OK. • Drag the Right Indent marker on the horizontal ruler.
All lines of text except the first (called a *hanging indent*)	• Press Ctrl + T. (Press Ctrl + Shift + T to remove a hanging indent.) • Display the Paragraph dialog box, click the *Special* option box arrow, click *Hanging*, and then click OK. • Click the Alignment button, left of the horizontal ruler and above the vertical ruler until the Hanging Indent symbol displays and then click the horizontal ruler at the desired location. • Drag the Hanging Indent marker on the horizontal ruler.
Text from both left and right margins	• Display the Paragraph dialog box, type the indent measurement in the *Left* measurement box, type the indent measurement in the *Right* measurement box, and then click OK. • Insert a measurements in the *Indent Right* and *Indent Left* measurement boxes in the Paragraph group on the Layout tab. • Drag the Left Indent marker on the horizontal ruler and then drag the Right Indent marker on the horizontal ruler.

Project 3c Indenting Text

Part 3 of 6

1. With **2-IntelProp.docx** open, indent the first line of text in each paragraph by completing the following steps:
   a. Select the first two paragraphs of text in the document (the text after the title *PROPERTY PROTECTION ISSUES* and before the heading *Intellectual Property*).
   b. Make sure the horizontal ruler displays. (If it does not display, click the View tab and then click the *Ruler* check box in the Show group to insert a check mark.)
   c. Position the mouse pointer on the First Line Indent marker on the horizontal ruler, click and hold down the left mouse button, drag the marker to the 0.5-inch mark, and then release the mouse button.

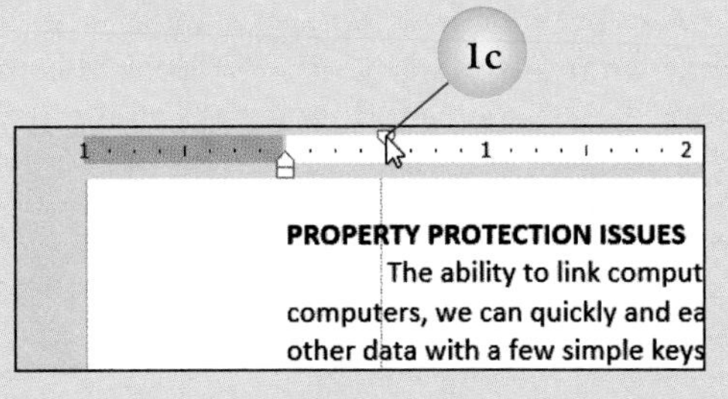

   d. Select the paragraphs of text in the *Intellectual Property* section and then drag the First Line Indent marker on the horizontal ruler to the 0.5-inch mark.

e. Select the paragraphs of text in the *Fair Use* section, click the Alignment button until the First Line Indent symbol displays, and then click the horizontal ruler at the 0.5-inch mark.

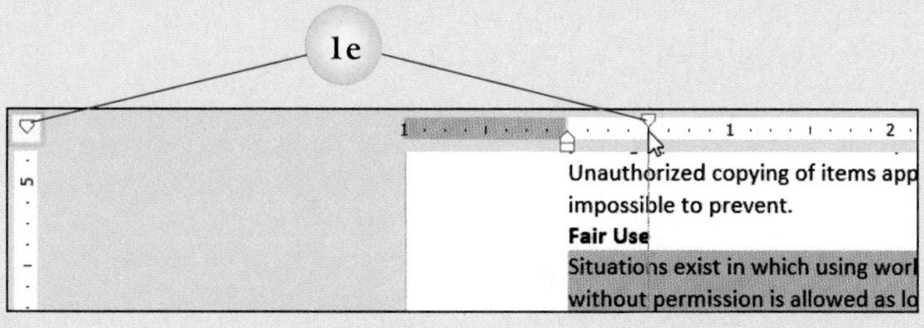

f. Position the insertion point anywhere in the paragraph of text below the heading *Intellectual Property Protection*, make sure the First Line Indent symbol displays on the Alignment button, and then click the 0.5-inch mark on the horizontal ruler.

2. Since the text in the second paragraph in the *Fair Use* section is a quote, indent the text from the left and right margins by completing the following steps:
   a. Position the insertion point anywhere in the second paragraph in the *Fair Use* section (the paragraph that begins *[A] copyrighted work, including such*).
   b. Click the Paragraph group dialog box launcher.
   c. At the Paragraph dialog box with the Indents and Spacing tab selected, select the current measurement in the *Left* measurement box and then type 0.5.
   d. Select the current measurement in the *Right* measurement box and then type 0.5.
   e. Click the *Special* option box arrow and then click *(none)* at the drop-down list.
   f. Click OK or press the Enter key.

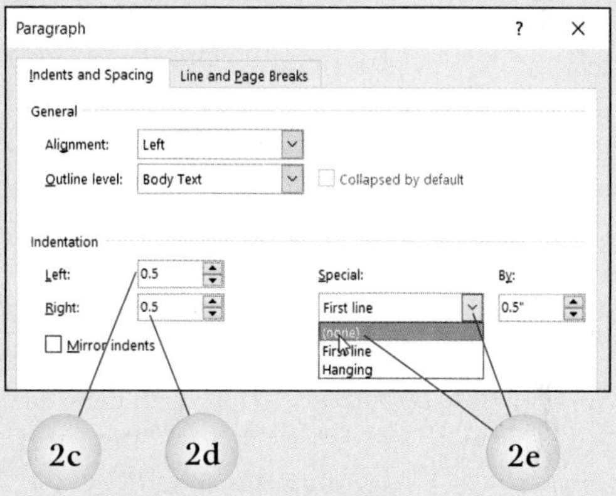

3. Create a hanging indent for the first paragraph in the *REFERENCES* section by positioning the insertion point anywhere in the first paragraph below the heading *REFERENCES* and then pressing Ctrl + T.
4. Create a hanging indent for the second paragraph in the *REFERENCES* section by completing the following steps:
   a. Position the insertion point anywhere in the second paragraph in the *REFERENCES* section.
   b. Click the Alignment button until the Hanging Indent symbol displays.
   c. Click the 0.5-inch mark on the horizontal ruler.

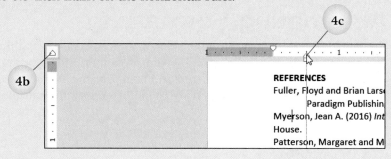

5. Create a hanging indent for the third and fourth paragraphs by completing the following steps:
   a. Select a portion of the third and fourth paragraphs.
   b. Click the Paragraph group dialog box launcher.
   c. At the Paragraph dialog box with the Indents and Spacing tab selected, click the *Special* option box arrow and then click *Hanging* at the drop-down list.
   d. Click OK or press the Enter key.
6. Save **2-IntelProp.docx**.

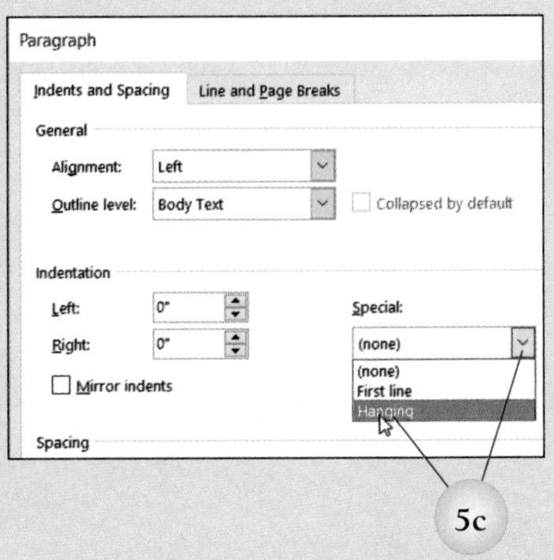

Check Your Work

Tutorial

Changing Spacing Before and After Paragraphs

Hint Line spacing determines the amount of vertical space between lines, while paragraph spacing determines the amount of space above or below paragraphs of text.

Spacing Before and After Paragraphs

By default, Word applies 8 points of additional spacing after a paragraph. This spacing can be removed or it can be increased or decreased, and spacing can be inserted above the paragraph. To change spacing before or after a paragraph, use the *Before* and *After* measurement boxes in the Paragraph group on the Layout tab, or the *Before* and *After* options at the Paragraph dialog box with the Indents and Spacing tab selected. Spacing can also be added before and after paragraphs at the Line and Paragraph Spacing button drop-down list.

Spacing before or after a paragraph is part of the paragraph and will be moved, copied, or deleted with the paragraph. If a paragraph, such as a heading, contains spacing before it and the paragraph falls at the top of a page, Word ignores the spacing.

Spacing before or after paragraphs is added in points and 1 vertical inch contains approximately 72 points. To add spacing before or after a paragraph, click the Layout tab, select the current measurement in the *Before* or *After* measurement box, and then type the number of points. The up or down arrows at the *Before* and *After* measurement boxes can also be clicked to increase or decrease the amount of spacing.

Automating Formatting

Applying consistent formatting in a document, especially a multiple-page document, can be time consuming. Word provides options for applying formatting automatically. Use the Repeat command to repeat the last action, such as applying formatting, or the Format Painter to apply formatting to multiple locations in a document.

Tutorial

Repeating the Last Command

Quick Steps

Repeat Last Action

Press F4.
OR
Press Ctrl + Y.

Repeating the Last Command

Formatting applied to text can be applied to other text in the document using the Repeat command. To use this command, apply the formatting, move the insertion point to the next location the formatting is to be applied, and then press the F4 function key or the keyboard shortcut Ctrl + Y. The Repeat command will repeat only the last command executed.

Project 3d Spacing Before and After Paragraphs and Repeating the Last Command — Part 4 of 6

1. With **2-IntelProp.docx** open, add 6 points of spacing before and after each paragraph in the document by completing the following steps:
   a. Select the entire document.
   b. Click the Layout tab.
   c. Click the *Before* measurement box up arrow. (This inserts *6 pt* in the box.)
   d. Click the *After* measurement box up arrow two times. (This inserts *6 pt* in the box.)

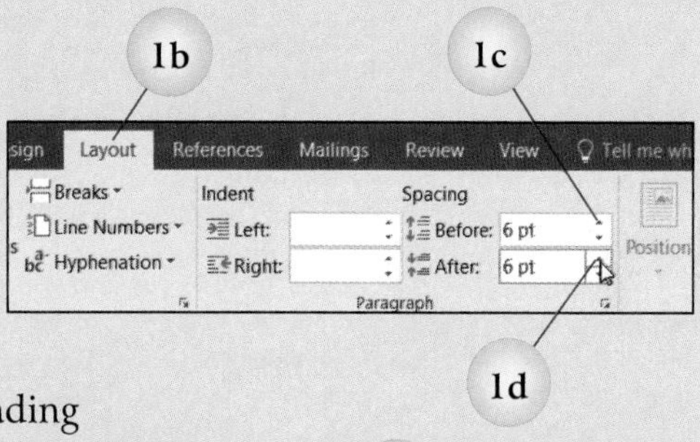

2. Add an additional 6 points of spacing above the headings by completing the following steps:
   a. Position the insertion point anywhere in the heading *Intellectual Property* and then click the *Before* measurement box up arrow. (This changes the measurement to *12 pt*.)
   b. Position the insertion point anywhere in the heading *Fair Use* and then press F4. (F4 is the Repeat command.)
   c. Position the insertion point anywhere in the heading *Intellectual Property Protection* and then press F4.
   d. Position the insertion point anywhere in the heading *REFERENCES* and then press Ctrl + Y. (Ctrl + Y is also the Repeat command.)

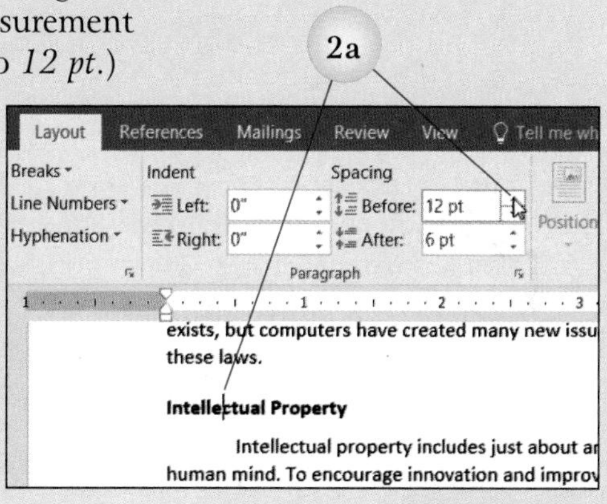

3. Save **2-IntelProp.docx**.

Check Your Work

Tutorial

Formatting with Format Painter

Format Painter

Quick Steps

Format with Format Painter

1. Format text then position insertion point within formatted text.
2. Double-click Format Painter button.
3. Select text to apply formatting.
4. Click Format Painter button.

Formatting with Format Painter

The Clipboard group on the Home tab contains a button for copying formatting and displays in the Clipboard group with a paintbrush. To use this button, called Format Painter, position the insertion point anywhere in text containing the desired formatting, click the Format Painter button, and then select the text to which the formatting is to be applied. When the Format Painter button is clicked, the I-beam pointer displays with a paintbrush attached. To apply the formatting a single time, click the Format Painter button. To apply the formatting in more than one location in the document, double-click the Format Painter button and then select the text to which the formatting is to be applied. When finished, click the Format Painter button to turn it off. The Format Painter button can also be turned off by pressing the Esc key.

Project 3e Formatting Headings with Format Painter

1. With **2-IntelProp.docx** open, click the Home tab.
2. Select the entire document and then change the font to 12-point Cambria.
3. Select the title *PROPERTY PROTECTION ISSUES*, click the Center button in the Paragraph group, and then change the font to 16-point Candara.
4. Apply 16-point Candara formatting to the heading *REFERENCES* by completing the following steps:
   a. Click anywhere in the title *PROPERTY PROTECTION ISSUES*.
   b. Click the Format Painter button in the Clipboard group.

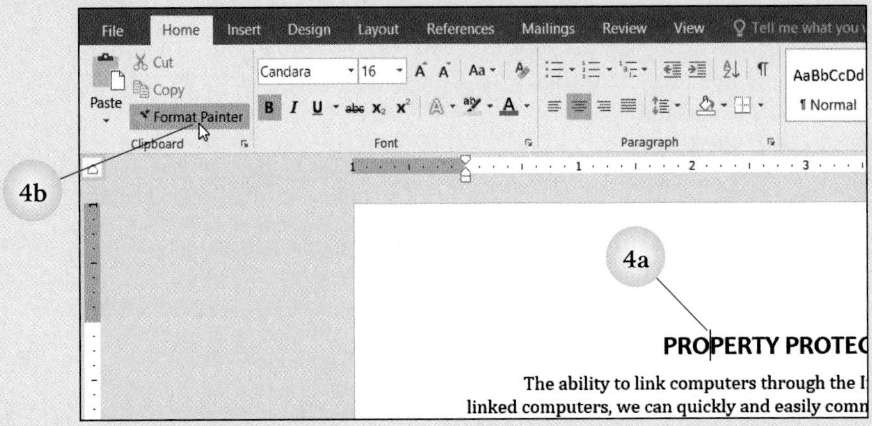

   c. Press Ctrl + End to move the insertion point to the end of the document and then click anywhere in the heading *REFERENCES*. (This applies the 16-point Candara formatting and centers the text.)
5. Select the heading *Intellectual Property* and then change the font to 14-point Candara.
6. Use the Format Painter button and apply 14-point Candara formatting to the other headings by completing the following steps:
   a. Position the insertion point anywhere in the heading *Intellectual Property*.
   b. Double-click the Format Painter button in the Clipboard group.
   c. Using the mouse, select the heading *Fair Use*.
   d. Using the mouse, select the heading *Intellectual Property Protection*.
   e. Click the Format Painter button in the Clipboard group. (This turns off the feature and deactivates the button.)
   f. Deselect the heading.
7. Save **2-IntelProp.docx**.

Check Your Work

Tutorial

Changing Line Spacing

Line and Paragraph Spacing

Changing Line Spacing

The default line spacing for a document is 1.08. (The line spacing for the IntelProp.docx file, which you opened at the beginning of Project 3, had been changed to single line spacing.) In certain situations, Word automatically adjusts the line spacing. For example, if a large character or object, such as a graphic, is inserted into a line, Word increases the line spacing of that line. The line spacing for a section or an entire document can also be changed.

Quick Steps

Change Line Spacing

1. Click Line and Paragraph Spacing button.
2. Click option.

OR

Press keyboard shortcut command.

OR

1. Click Paragraph group dialog box launcher.
2. Click *Line Spacing* option box arrow.
3. Click line spacing option.
4. Click OK.

OR

1. Click Paragraph group dialog box launcher.
2. Type line measurement in *At* measurement box.
3. Click OK.

Change line spacing using the Line and Paragraph Spacing button in the Paragraph group on the Home tab, keyboard shortcuts, or options from the Paragraph dialog box. Table 2.5 displays the keyboard shortcuts to change line spacing.

Line spacing can also be changed at the Paragraph dialog box with the *Line spacing* option or the *At* measurement box. Click the *Line spacing* option box arrow and a drop-down list displays with a variety of spacing options, such as *Single*, *1.5 lines*, and *Double*. A specific line spacing measurement can be entered in the *At* measurement box. For example, to change the line spacing to 1.75 lines, type *1.75* in the *At* measurement box.

Table 2.5 Line Spacing Keyboard Shortcuts

Press	To change line spacing to
Ctrl + 1	single line spacing
Ctrl + 2	double line spacing
Ctrl + 5	1.5 line spacing

Project 3f Changing Line Spacing

Part 6 of 6

1. With **2-IntelProp.docx** open, change the line spacing for all paragraphs to double spacing by completing the following steps:
   a. Select the entire document.
   b. Click the Line and Paragraph Spacing button in the Paragraph group on the Home tab.
   c. Click *2.0* at the drop-down list.
2. With the entire document still selected, press Ctrl + 5. (This changes the line spacing to 1.5 lines.)
3. Change the line spacing to 1.2 lines using the Paragraph dialog box by completing the following steps:
   a. With the entire document still selected, click the Paragraph group dialog box launcher.
   b. At the Paragraph dialog box, make sure the Indents and Spacing tab is selected, click in the *At* measurement box, and then type 1.2. (This measurement box is to the right of the *Line spacing* option box.)
   c. Click OK or press the Enter key.
   d. Deselect the text.
4. Save, print, and then close **2-IntelProp.docx**.

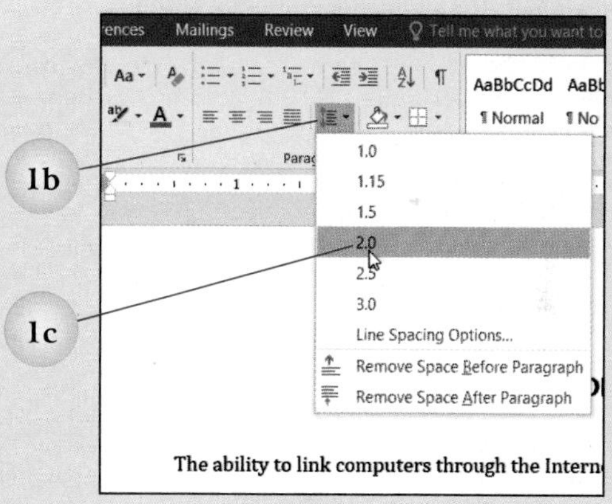

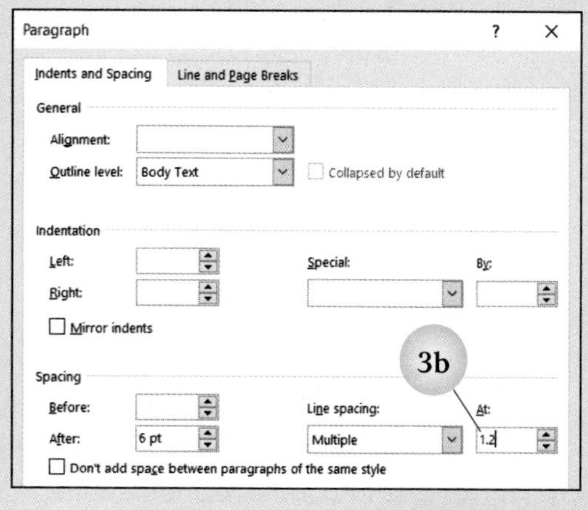

Check Your Work

Project 4 Format Computer Issues Document — 2 Parts

You will open a document containing two computer-related problems to solve, reveal the formatting, compare the formatting, and make formatting changes.

Preview Finished Project

Revealing and Comparing Formatting

Display formatting applied to specific text in a document at the Reveal Formatting task pane, shown in Figure 2.8. The Reveal Formatting task pane displays font, paragraph, and section formatting applied to text where the insertion point is positioned or to selected text. Display the Reveal Formatting task pane with the keyboard shortcut Shift + F1. Generally, a collapse triangle (a solid right-and-down-pointing triangle) precedes *Font* and *Paragraph* and an expand triangle (a hollow right-pointing triangle) precedes *Section* in the *Formatting of selected text* list box in the Reveal Formatting task pane. Click the collapse triangle to hide any items below a heading and click the expand triangle to reveal items. Some of the items below headings in the *Formatting of selected text* list box are hyperlinks. Click a hyperlink and a dialog box displays with the specific option.

Figure 2.8 Reveal Formatting Task Pane

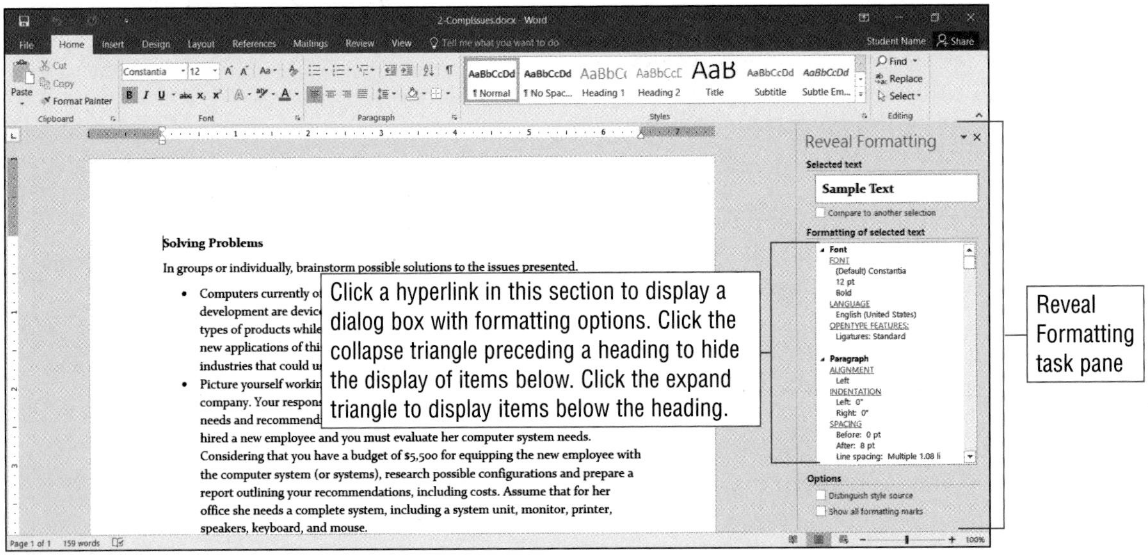

Project 4a Revealing Formatting — Part 1 of 2

1. Open **CompIssues.docx** and then save it with the name **2-CompIssues**.
2. Press Shift + F1 to display the Reveal Formatting task pane.
3. Click anywhere in the heading *Solving Problems* and then notice the formatting information in the Reveal Formatting task pane.
4. Click in the bulleted paragraph and notice the formatting information in the Reveal Formatting task pane.

Quick Steps

Compare Formatting

1. Press Shift + F1 to display Reveal Formatting task pane.
2. Click or select text.
3. Click *Compare to another selection* check box.
4. Click or select text.

Along with displaying formatting applied to text, the Reveal Formatting task pane can be used to compare formatting of two text selections to determine what is different. To compare formatting, select the first instance of formatting to be compared, click the *Compare to another selection* check box, and then select the second instance of formatting to be compared. Any differences between the two selections display in the *Formatting differences* list box.

Project 4b **Comparing Formatting** Part 2 of 2

1. With **2-CompIssues.docx** open, make sure the Reveal Formatting task pane displays. If it does not, turn it on by pressing Shift + F1.
2. Select the first bulleted paragraph (the paragraph that begins *Computers currently offer both*).
3. Click the *Compare to another selection* check box to insert a check mark.
4. Select the second bulleted paragraph (the paragraph that begins *Picture yourself working in the*).
5. Determine the formatting differences by reading the information in the *Formatting differences* list box. (The list box displays *12 pt -> 11 pt* below the FONT hyperlink, indicating that the difference is point size.)
6. Format the second bulleted paragraph so it is set in 12-point size.
7. Click the *Compare to another selection* check box to remove the check mark.
8. Select the word *visual*, which displays in the first sentence in the first bulleted paragraph.
9. Click the *Compare to another selection* check box to insert a check mark.
10. Select the word *audio*, which displays in the first sentence of the first bulleted paragraph.
11. Determine the formatting differences by reading the information in the *Formatting differences* list box.
12. Format the word *audio* so it matches the formatting of the word *visual*.
13. Click the *Compare to another selection* check box to remove the check mark.
14. Close the Reveal Formatting task pane by clicking the Close button in the upper right corner of the task pane.
15. Save, print, and then close **2-CompIssues.docx**.

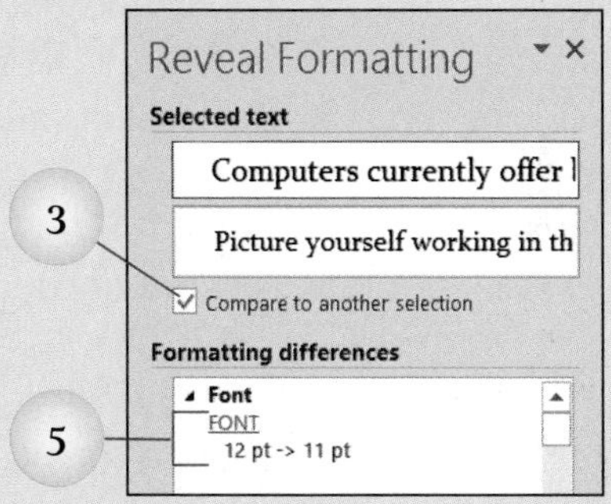

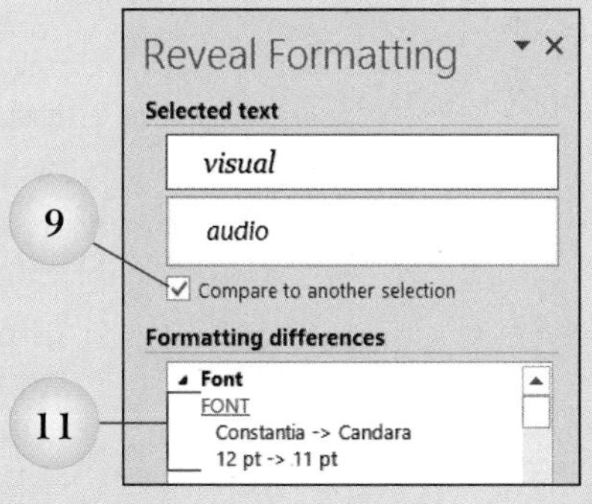

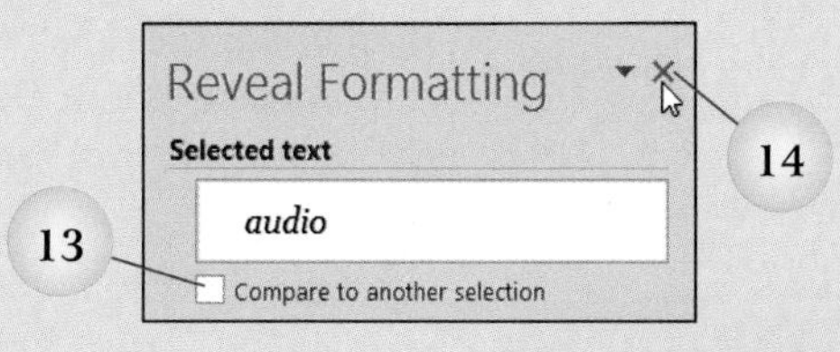

Check Your Work

Chapter Summary

- A font consists of three elements: typeface, type size, and typestyle.
- A typeface (font) is a set of characters with a common design and shape. Typefaces are either monospaced, allotting the same amount of horizontal space for each character, or proportional, allotting varying amounts of space for different characters. Proportional typefaces are divided into two main categories: serif and sans serif.
- Type size is measured in point size; the higher the point size, the larger the characters.
- A typestyle is a variation of style within a certain typeface, such as bold, italic, or underline. Apply typestyle formatting with some of the buttons in the Font group on the Home tab.
- Apply font effects with some of the buttons in the Font group on the Home tab, such as superscript, subscript, and strikethrough.
- The Mini toolbar automatically displays above selected text. Use options and buttons on this toolbar to apply formatting to selected text.
- Use options at the Font dialog box to change the font, font size, and font style and apply specific effects. Display this dialog box by clicking the Font group dialog box launcher.
- A Word document contains a number of predesigned formats grouped into style sets. Change to a different style set by clicking the Design tab and then clicking the style set in the styles set gallery in the Document Formatting group.
- Apply a theme and change theme colors, fonts, and effects with buttons in the Document Formatting group on the Design tab.
- Click the Paragraph Spacing button in the Document Formatting group on the Design tab to apply a predesigned paragraph spacing option to text in a document.
- By default, paragraphs in a Word document are aligned at the left margin and ragged at the right margin. Change this default alignment with buttons in the Paragraph group, at the Paragraph dialog box, or with keyboard shortcuts.
- To turn on or off the display of nonprinting characters, such as paragraph marks, click the Show/Hide ¶ button in the Paragraph group on the Home tab.
- Indent text in paragraphs with indent buttons in the Paragraph group on the Home tab, buttons in the Paragraph group on the Layout tab, keyboard shortcuts, options from the Paragraph dialog box, markers on the horizontal ruler, or the Alignment button above the vertical ruler.
- Increase and/or decrease spacing before and after paragraphs using the *Before* and *After* measurement boxes in the Paragraph group on the Layout tab or using the *Before* and/or *After* options at the Paragraph dialog box.
- Repeat the last command by pressing the F4 function key or the keyboard shortcut Ctrl + Y.
- Use the Format Painter button in the Clipboard group on the Home tab to copy formatting already applied to text to different locations in the document.
- Change line spacing with the Line and Paragraph Spacing button in the Paragraph group on the Home tab, keyboard shortcuts, or options from the Paragraph dialog box.
- Display the Reveal Formatting task pane to display formatting applied to text. Use the *Compare to another selection* option in the task pane to compare formatting of two text selections to determine what is different.

Commands Review

FEATURE	RIBBON TAB, GROUP	BUTTON	KEYBOARD SHORTCUT
bold text	Home, Font		Ctrl + B
center-align text	Home, Paragraph		Ctrl + E
change case of text	Home, Font		Shift + F3
clear all formatting	Home, Font		
clear character formatting			Ctrl + spacebar
clear paragraph formatting			Ctrl + Q
decrease font size	Home, Font		Ctrl + Shift + < OR Ctrl + [
display or hide nonprinting characters	Home, Paragraph		Ctrl + Shift + *
font	Home, Font		
font color	Home, Font		
Font dialog box	Home, Font		Ctrl + Shift + F
font size	Home, Font		
Format Painter	Home, Clipboard		Ctrl + Shift + C
Help			F1
highlight text	Home, Font		
increase font size	Home, Font		Ctrl + Shift + > OR Ctrl +]
italicize text	Home, Font		Ctrl + I
justify text	Home, Paragraph		Ctrl + J
left-align text	Home, Paragraph		Ctrl + L
line spacing	Home, Paragraph		Ctrl + 1 (single) Ctrl + 2 (double) Ctrl + 5 (1.5)
Paragraph dialog box	Home, Paragraph		
paragraph spacing	Design, Document Formatting		
repeat last action			F4 or Ctrl + Y
Reveal Formatting task pane			Shift + F1

FEATURE	RIBBON TAB, GROUP	BUTTON	KEYBOARD SHORTCUT
right-align text	Home, Paragraph		Ctrl + R
spacing after paragraph	Layout, Paragraph		
spacing before paragraph	Layout, Paragraph		
strikethrough text	Home, Font	abc	
subscript text	Home, Font	X_2	Ctrl + =
superscript text	Home, Font	X^2	Ctrl + Shift + +
text effects and typography	Home, Font		
theme colors	Design, Document Formatting		
theme effects	Design, Document Formatting		
theme fonts	Design, Document Formatting	A	
themes	Design, Document Formatting	Aa	
underline text	Home, Font	U	Ctrl + U

Workbook

Chapter study tools and assessment activities are available in the *Workbook* ebook. These resources are designed to help you further develop and demonstrate mastery of the skills learned in this chapter.

Microsoft®

Word

CHAPTER 3

Customizing Paragraphs

Performance Objectives

Upon successful completion of Chapter 3, you will be able to:

1 Apply numbering and bulleting formatting to text
2 Apply paragraph borders and shading
3 Sort paragraph text
4 Set, clear, and move tabs on the horizontal ruler and at the Tabs dialog box
5 Cut, copy, and paste text in a document
6 Use the Paste Options button to specify how text is pasted in a document
7 Use the Clipboard task pane to copy and paste text within and between documents

Precheck

Check your current skills to help focus your study.

As you learned in Chapter 2, Word contains a variety of options for formatting text in paragraphs. In this chapter you will learn how to apply numbering and bulleted formatting to text, how to apply borders and shading to paragraphs of text, how to sort paragraphs of text, and how to manipulate tabs on the horizontal ruler and at the Tabs dialog box. Editing some documents might include selecting and then deleting, moving, or copying text. You can perform this type of editing with buttons in the Clipboard group on the Home tab or with keyboard shortcuts.

Data Files

Before beginning chapter work, copy the WL1C3 folder to your storage medium and then make WL1C3 the active folder.

SNAP

If you are a SNAP user, launch the Precheck and Tutorials from your Assignments page.

Project 1 Format a Document on Computer Technology 3 Parts

You will open a document containing information on computer technology, type numbered text in the document, and apply numbering and bulleted formatting to paragraphs in the document.

Preview Finished Project

Applying Numbering and Bullets

Numbering

Bullets

Automatically number paragraphs or insert bullets before paragraphs using buttons in the Paragraph group on the Home tab. Use the Numbering button to insert numbers before specific paragraphs and use the Bullets button to insert bullets.

Tutorial

Creating Numbered Lists

Quick Steps

Type Numbered Paragraphs

1. Type 1.
2. Press spacebar.
3. Type text.
4. Press Enter.

Hint Define a new numbering format by clicking the Numbering button arrow and then clicking *Define New Number Format*.

Creating Numbered Lists

Type *1.* and then press the spacebar and Word indents the number 0.25 inch from the left margin and hang-indents the text in the paragraph 0.5 inch from the left margin. Additionally, when the Enter key is pressed to end the first item, *2.* is inserted 0.25 inch from the left margin at the beginning of the next paragraph. Continue typing items and Word inserts the next number in the list. To turn off numbering, press the Enter key two times or click the Numbering button in the Paragraph group on the Home tab. (Paragraph formatting can be removed from a paragraph, including automatic numbering, with the keyboard shortcut Ctrl + Q. Remove all formatting, including character and paragraph formatting from selected text, by clicking the Clear All Formatting button in the Font group on the Home tab.)

Press the Enter key two times between numbered paragraphs and the automatic numbering is removed. To turn it back on, type the next number in the list (and the period) followed by a space. Word will automatically indent the number and hang-indent the text. To insert a line break without inserting a bullet or number, press Shift + Enter.

When the AutoFormat feature inserts numbering and indents text, the AutoCorrect Options button displays. Click this button and a drop-down list displays with options for undoing and/or stopping the automatic numbering. An AutoCorrect Options button also displays when AutoFormat inserts automatic bulleting in a document.

Project 1a Creating a Numbered List Part 1 of 3

1. Open **TechInfo.docx** and then save it with the name **3-TechInfo**.
2. Press Ctrl + End to move the insertion point to the end of the document and then type the text shown in Figure 3.1. Apply bold formatting and center the title *Technology Career Questions*. When typing the numbered paragraphs, complete the following steps:
   a. Type 1. and then press the spacebar. (The *1.* is indented 0.25 inch from the left margin and the first paragraph of text is indented 0.5 inch from the left margin. Also, the AutoCorrect Options button displays. Use this button if you want to undo or stop automatic numbering.)
   b. Type the paragraph of text and then press the Enter key. (This moves the insertion point down to the next paragraph and inserts an indented number *2* followed by a period.)

c. Continue typing the remaining text. (Remember, you do not need to type the paragraph number and period—they are automatically inserted. The last numbered item will wrap differently on your screen than shown in Figure 3.1.)
d. After typing the last question, press the Enter key two times. (This turns off paragraph numbering.)
3. Save **3-TechInfo.docx**.

Check Your Work

Figure 3.1 Project 1a

Technology Career Questions

1. What is your ideal technical job?
2. Which job suits your personality?
3. Which is your first-choice certificate?
4. How does the technical job market look in your state right now? Is the job market wide open or are the information technology career positions limited?

Automatic numbering is turned on by default. Turn off automatic numbering at the AutoCorrect dialog box with the AutoFormat As You Type tab selected, as shown in Figure 3.2. To display this dialog box, click the File tab and then click *Options*. At the Word Options dialog box, click the *Proofing* option in the left panel and then click the AutoCorrect Options button in the *AutoCorrect options* section of the dialog box. At the AutoCorrect dialog box, click the AutoFormat As You Type tab and then click the *Automatic numbered lists* check box to remove the check mark. Click OK to close the AutoCorrect dialog box and then click OK to close the Word Options dialog box.

Figure 3.2 AutoCorrect Dialog Box with AutoFormat As You Type Tab Selected

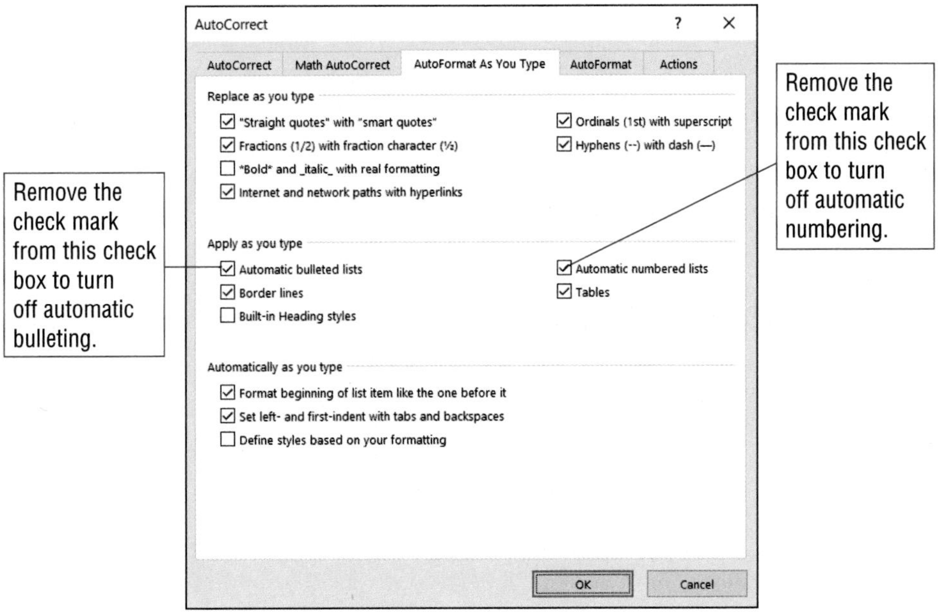

Quick Steps

Create a Numbered List

1. Select text.
2. Click Numbering button.

Numbering formatting can be turned on or applied to existing text with the Numbering button in the Paragraph group on the Home tab. Click the Numbering button to turn on numbering, type text, and then click the button again to turn off numbering, or select existing text and then click the Numbering button to apply numbering formatting.

Project 1b Applying Numbering Formatting

Part 2 of 3

1. With **3-TechInfo.docx** open, apply numbers to paragraphs by completing the following steps:
   a. Select the five paragraphs of text in the *Technology Information Questions* section.
   b. Click the Numbering button in the Paragraph group on the Home tab.

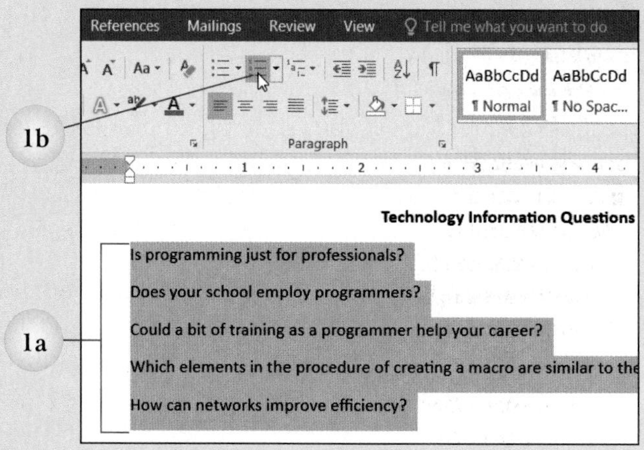

2. Add text between paragraphs 4 and 5 in the *Technology Information Questions* section by completing the following steps:
   a. Position the insertion point immediately right of the question mark at the end of the fourth paragraph.
   b. Press the Enter key.
   c. Type What kinds of networks are used in your local area?

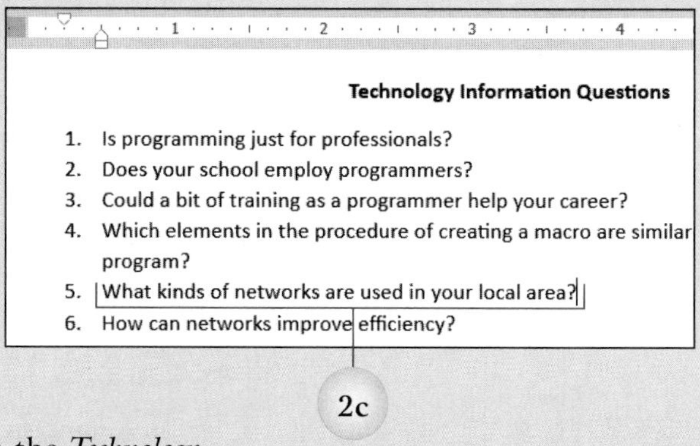

3. Delete the second question (paragraph) in the *Technology Information Questions* section by completing the following steps:
   a. Select the text of the second paragraph. (You will not be able to select the number.)
   b. Press the Delete key.
4. Save **3-TechInfo.docx**.

Check Your Work

Tutorial

Creating Bulleted Lists

Quick Steps

Type Bulleted List

1. Type *, >, or - symbol.
2. Press spacebar.
3. Type text.
4. Press Enter.

Create Bulleted List

1. Select text.
2. Click Bullets button.

Creating Bulleted Lists

In addition to automatically numbering paragraphs, Word's AutoFormat feature creates bulleted lists. A bulleted list with a hanging indent is automatically created when a paragraph begins with the symbol *, >, or -. Type one of the symbols and then press the spacebar and the AutoFormat feature inserts a bullet 0.25 inch from the left margin and indents the text following the bullet another 0.25 inch. Change the indent of bulleted text by pressing the Tab key to demote text or pressing Shift + Tab to promote text. Word uses different bullets for demoted text.

Bulleted formatting can be turned on or applied to existing text with the Bullets button in the Paragraph group on the Home tab. Click the Bullets button to turn on bulleting, type text, and then click the button again to turn off bulleting. Or, select existing text and then click the Bullets button to apply bulleted formatting. The automatic bulleting feature can be turned off at the AutoCorrect dialog box with the AutoFormat As You Type tab selected.

Project 1c Creating a Bulleted List and Applying Bulleted Formatting

Part 3 of 3

1. With **3-TechInfo.docx** open, press Ctrl + End to move the insertion point to the end of the document and then press the Enter key.
2. Type Technology Timeline: Computer Design bolded and centered, as shown in Figure 3.3, and then press the Enter key.
3. Turn off bold formatting and change to left alignment.
4. Type a greater-than symbol (>), press the spacebar, type the text of the first bulleted paragraph in Figure 3.3, and then press the Enter key.
5. Press the Tab key (which demotes the bullet to a hollow circle) and then type the bulleted text.
6. Press the Enter key (which displays another hollow circle bullet), type the bulleted text, and then press the Enter key.
7. Press Shift + Tab (which promotes the bullet to an arrow), type the bulleted text, and then press the Enter key two times (which turns off bullets).
8. Promote bulleted text by positioning the insertion point at the beginning of the text *1958: Jack Kilby, an engineer* and then pressing Shift + Tab. Promote the other hollow circle bullet to an arrow. (The four paragraphs of text should be preceded by arrow bullets.)
9. Format the paragraphs of text in the *Technology Timeline: Computers in the Workplace* section as a bulleted list by completing the following steps:
   a. Select the paragraphs of text in the *Technology Timeline: Computers in the Workplace* section.
   b. Click the Bullets button in the Paragraph group. (Word will insert the same arrow bullets that you inserted in Step 2. Word keeps the same bullet formatting until you choose a different bullet style.)
10. Save, print, and then close **3-TechInfo.docx**.

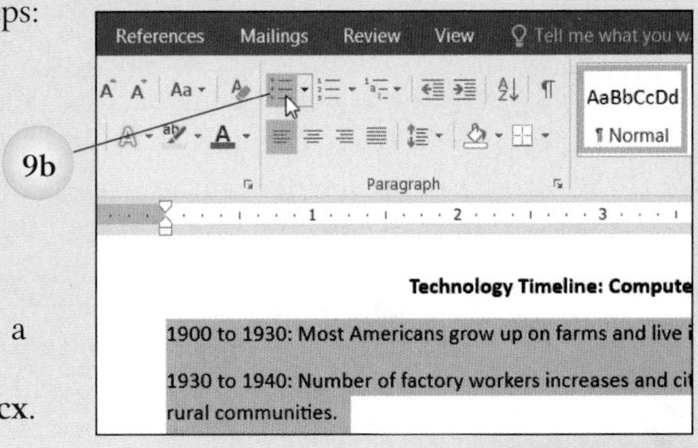

Check Your Work

Figure 3.3 Project 1c

Technology Timeline: Computer Design

- 1937: Dr. John Atanasoff and Clifford Berry design and build the first electronic digital computer.
    - 1958: Jack Kilby, an engineer at Texas Instruments, invents the integrated circuit, thereby laying the foundation for fast computers and large-capacity memory.
    - 1981: IBM enters the personal computer field by introducing the IBM-PC.
- 2004: Wireless computer devices, including keyboards, mice, and wireless home networks, become widely accepted among users.

Project 2 Customize a Document on Chapter Questions — 3 Parts

You will open a document containing chapter questions and then apply border and shading formatting to text.

Preview Finished Project

Adding Emphasis to Paragraphs

Borders

To call attention to or to highlight specific text in a paragraph, consider adding emphasis to the text by applying paragraph borders and/or shading. Apply borders with the Borders button on the Home tab and shading with the Shading button. Additional borders and shading options are available at the Borders and Shading dialog box.

Tutorial

Applying Borders

Applying Paragraph Borders

Every paragraph in a Word document contains an invisible frame and a border can be applied to the frame around the paragraph. Apply a border to specific sides of the paragraph frame or to all sides. Add borders to paragraphs using the Borders button in the Paragraph group on the Home tab or using options at the Borders and Shading dialog box.

When a border is added to a paragraph of text, the border expands and contracts as text is inserted or deleted from the paragraph. Insert a border around the active paragraph or around selected paragraphs.

Quick Steps

Apply Borders with Borders Button

1. Select text.
2. Click Borders button arrow.
3. Click border option at drop-down list.

One method for inserting a border is to use options from the Borders button in the Paragraph group. Click the Borders button arrow and a drop-down list displays. At the drop-down list, click the option that will insert the desired border. For example, to insert a border at the bottom of the paragraph, click the *Bottom Border* option. Clicking an option will add the border to the paragraph where the insertion point is located. To add a border to more than one paragraph, select the paragraphs first and then click the option.

Project 2a Applying Borders to Paragraphs of Text

Part 1 of 3

1. Open **Questions.docx** and then save it with the name **3-Questions**.
2. Insert an outside border to specific text by completing the following steps:
   a. Select text from the heading *Chapter 1 Questions* through the four bulleted paragraphs.
   b. In the Paragraph group, click the Borders button arrow.
   c. Click the *Outside Borders* option at the drop-down list.
3. Select text from the heading *Chapter 2 Questions* through the five bulleted paragraphs and then click the Borders button in the Paragraph group. (The button will apply the border option that was previously selected.)
4. Save **3-Questions.docx**.

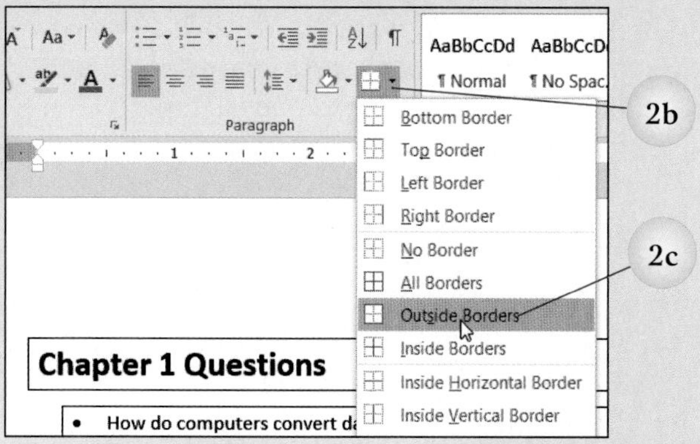

Check Your Work

Quick Steps

Apply Borders at the Borders and Shading Dialog Box

1. Select text.
2. Click Borders button arrow.
3. Click *Borders and Shading* option.
4. Choose options in dialog box.
5. Click OK.

To further customize paragraph borders, use options at the Borders and Shading dialog box shown in Figure 3.4. Display this dialog box by clicking the Borders button arrow and then clicking *Borders and Shading* at the drop-down list. At the Borders and Shading dialog box, specify the border setting, style, color, and width.

Figure 3.4 Borders and Shading Dialog Box with the Borders Tab Selected

Click the *Style* list box arrow to display additional line styles.

Click the *Color* option box arrow to display a drop-down list of color options.

Click the *Width* option box arrow to display a drop-down list of width options.

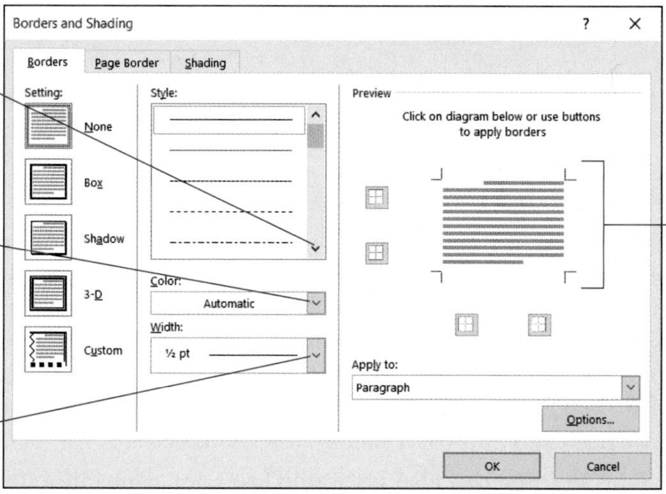

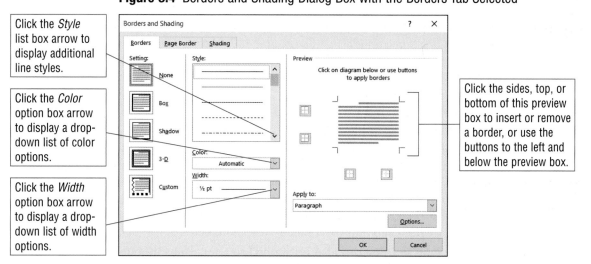

Click the sides, top, or bottom of this preview box to insert or remove a border, or use the buttons to the left and below the preview box.

Project 2b Applying Borders at the Borders and Shading Dialog Box

Part 2 of 3

1. With **3-Questions.docx** open, remove the paragraph borders around the heading *Chapter 1 Questions* by completing the following steps:
   a. Position the insertion point anywhere in the heading *Chapter 1 Questions*.
   b. Click the Borders button arrow and then click *No Border* at the drop-down list.
2. Apply a bottom border to the heading *Chapter 1 Questions* by completing the following steps:
   a. Click the Borders button arrow.
   b. Click the *Borders and Shading* option.
   c. At the Borders and Shading dialog box, click the *Style* list box down arrow two times. (This displays a double-line option.)
   d. Click the double-line option.
   e. Click the *Color* option box arrow.
   f. Click the *Blue* color option (eighth option in the *Standard Colors* section).
   g. Click the *Width* option box arrow.
   h. Click the *3/4 pt* option at the drop-down list.
   i. Click the *None* option in the *Setting* section.
   j. Click the bottom border of the box in the *Preview* section.
   k. Click the OK button to close the dialog box and apply the border.

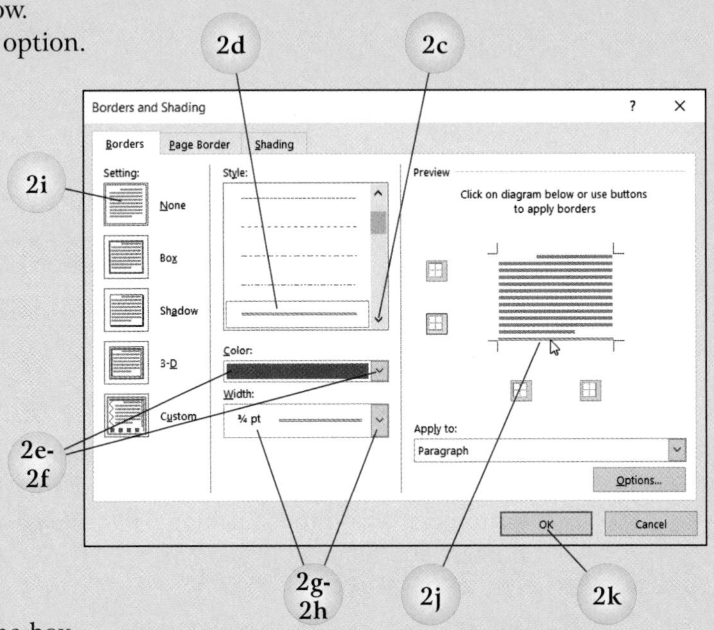

3. Apply the same border to the other heading by completing the following steps:
   a. With the insertion point positioned in the heading *Chapter 1 Questions*, click the Format Painter button.
   b. Click anywhere in the heading *Chapter 2 Questions*.
4. Save **3-Questions.docx**.

Check Your Work

Tutorial

Applying Shading

Shading

Quick Steps

Apply Shading

1. Select text.
2. Click Shading button.

OR

1. Click Borders button arrow.
2. Click *Borders and Shading* option.
3. Click Shading tab.
4. Choose options in dialog box.
5. Click OK.

Applying Paragraph Shading

Apply shading to text in a document with the Shading button in the Paragraph group. Select text and then click the Shading button arrow, and a drop-down gallery displays. Paragraph shading colors display in themes in the drop-down gallery. Use one of the theme colors or click one of the standard colors at the bottom of the gallery. Click the *More Colors* option and the Colors dialog box displays. At the Colors dialog box with the Standard tab selected, click a color or click the Custom tab and then specify a custom color.

Paragraph shading can also be applied to paragraphs in a document using options at the Borders and Shading dialog box with the Shading tab selected. Display this dialog box by clicking the Borders button arrow and then clicking the *Borders and Shading* option. At the Borders and Shading dialog box, click the Shading tab. Use options in the dialog box to specify a fill color, choose a pattern style, and specify a color for the dots that make up the pattern.

Project 2c Applying Paragraph Shading

1. With **3-Questions.docx** open, apply paragraph shading to the heading *Chapter 1 Questions* by completing the following steps:
   a. Click anywhere in the heading *Chapter 1 Questions*.
   b. Click the Shading button arrow.
   c. Click the *Blue, Accent 5, Lighter 80%* color option (ninth column, second row in the *Theme Colors* section).

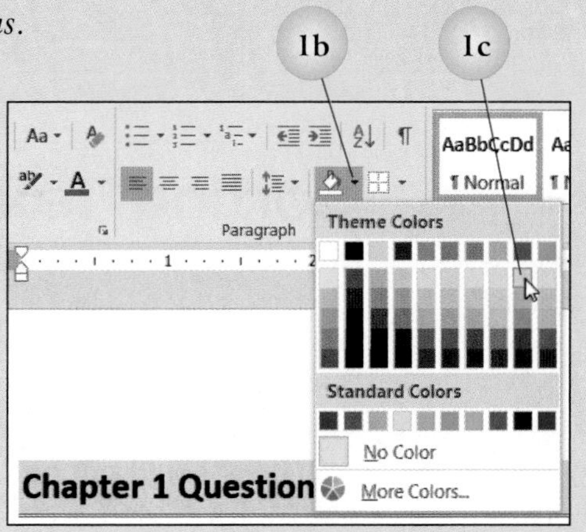

2. Apply the same blue shading to the other heading by completing the following steps:
   a. With the insertion point positioned in the heading *Chapter 1 Questions*, click the Format Painter button.
   b. Click anywhere in the heading *Chapter 2 Questions*.
3. Apply shading to text with options at the Borders and Shading dialog box by completing the following steps:
   a. Select the four bulleted paragraphs below the heading *Chapter 1 Questions*.
   b. Click the Borders button arrow.
   c. Click the *Borders and Shading* option.
   d. At the Borders and Shading dialog box, click the Shading tab.
   e. Click the *Fill* option box arrow.
   f. Click the *Gold, Accent 4, Lighter 80%* color option (eighth column, second row).
   g. Click the *Style* option box arrow.
   h. Click the *5%* option.
   i. Click the *Color* option box arrow.
   j. Click the *Blue, Accent 5, Lighter 60%* color option (ninth column, third row in the *Theme Colors* section).

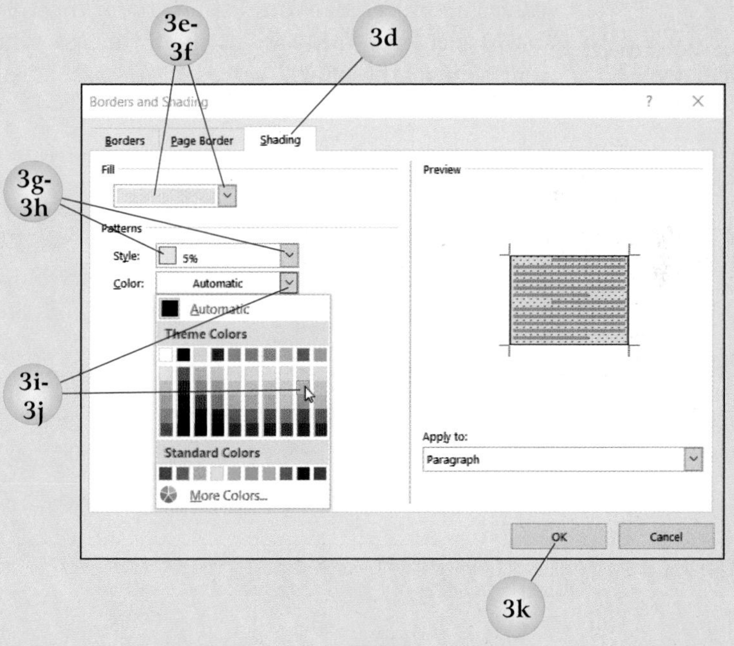

   k. Click OK to close the dialog box.
4. Apply the same shading to the bulleted paragraphs below the heading *Chapter 2 Questions* by completing the following steps:
   a. Click anywhere in the bulleted paragraphs below the heading *Chapter 1 Questions*.
   b. Click the Format Painter button.
   c. Select the five bulleted paragraphs below the heading *Chapter 2 Questions*.
5. Save, print, and then close **3-Questions.docx**.

Check Your Work

Project 3 Sort Text in a Document on Online Shopping — 1 Part

You will open a document on online shopping and then sort several different paragraphs of text.

Preview Finished Project

Tutorial

Sorting Text in Paragraphs

Sort

Quick Steps

Sort Paragraphs of Text

1. Click Sort button.
2. Make changes as needed at Sort Text dialog box.
3. Click OK.

Sorting Text in Paragraphs

Text arranged in paragraphs can be sorted alphabetically by the first character of each paragraph. The first character can be a number, symbol (such as $ or #), or letter. Type paragraphs to be sorted at the left margin or indented at a tab. Unless specific paragraphs are selected for sorting, Word sorts the entire document.

To sort text in paragraphs, open the document. If the document contains text that should not be included in the sort, select the specific paragraphs to be sorted. Click the Sort button in the Paragraph group and the Sort Text dialog box displays. At this dialog box, click OK.

The *Type* option at the Sort Text dialog box will display *Text*, *Number*, or *Date* depending on the text selected. Word attempts to determine the data type and chooses one of the three options. For example, if numbers with mathematical values are selected, Word assigns them the *Number* type. However, if a numbered list is selected, Word assigns them the *Text* type since the numbers do not represent mathematical values.

Project 3 Sorting Paragraphs Alphabetically — Part 1 of 1

1. Open **OnlineShop.docx** and then save it with the name **3-OnlineShop**.
2. Sort the bulleted paragraphs alphabetically by completing the following steps:
   a. Select the four bulleted paragraphs in the section *Advantages of Online Shopping*.
   b. Click the Sort button in the Paragraph group.
   c. At the Sort Text dialog box, make sure that *Paragraphs* displays in the *Sort by* option box and that the *Ascending* option is selected.
   d. Click OK.

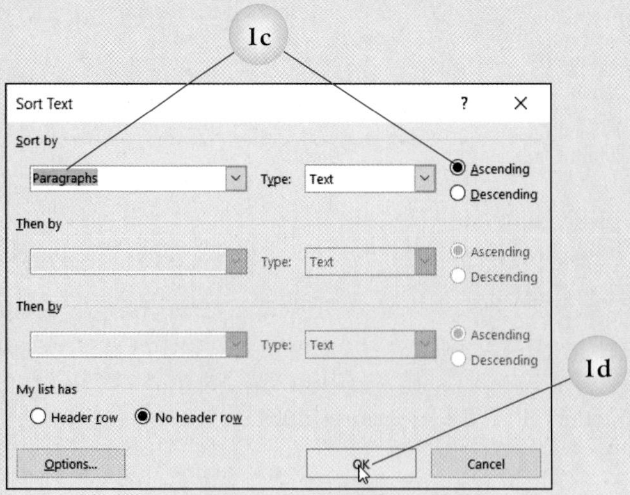

3. Sort the numbered paragraphs by completing the following steps:
   a. Select the six numbered paragraphs in the section *Online Shopping Safety Tips*.
   b. Click the Sort button in the Paragraph group.
   c. Click OK at the Sort Text dialog box.
4. Sort alphabetically the three paragraphs below the title *REFERENCES* by completing the following steps:
   a. Select the paragraphs below the title *REFERENCES*.
   b. Click the Sort button in the Paragraph group.
   c. Click the *Type* option box arrow and then click *Text* at the drop-down list.
   d. Click OK.
5. Save, print, and then close **3-OnlineShop.docx**.

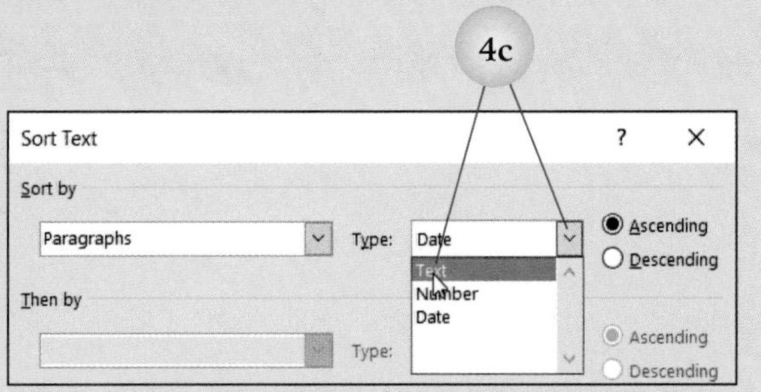

Check Your Work

Project 4 Prepare a Document on Workshops and Training Dates 4 Parts

You will set and move tabs on the horizontal ruler and at the Tabs dialog box and type tabbed text about workshops, training dates, and a table of contents.

Preview Finished Project

Setting and Modifying Tabs

A Word document includes a variety of default settings, such as margins and line spacing. One of these defaults is a left tab set every 0.5 inch. In some situations, these default tabs are appropriate; in others, custom tabs may be needed. Two methods are available for setting tabs: set tabs on the horizontal ruler or at the Tabs dialog box.

Setting and Modifying Tabs on the Horizontal Ruler

Tutorial

Setting and Modifying Tabs on the Horizontal Ruler

Quick Steps

Set Tabs on Horizontal Ruler

1. Click Alignment button above vertical ruler.
2. Click location on horizontal ruler.

Hint When setting tabs on the horizontal ruler, a dotted guideline displays to help align them.

Use the horizontal ruler to set, move, and delete tabs. If the ruler is not visible, click the View tab and then click the *Ruler* check box in the Show group to insert a check mark. By default, tabs are set every 0.5 inch on the horizontal ruler. With a left tab, text aligns at the left edge of the tab. The other types of tabs that can be set on the horizontal ruler are center, right, decimal, and bar. Use the Alignment button above the vertical ruler to specify types of tabs. Each time the Alignment button is clicked, a different tab or paragraph symbol displays. Table 3.1 shows the tab symbols and what type of tab each symbol will set.

To set a left tab on the horizontal ruler, make sure the left tab symbol (see Table 3.1) displays on the Alignment button. Position the arrow pointer on the tick mark (the vertical line on the ruler) where the tab is to be set and then click the left mouse button. When a tab is set on the horizontal ruler, any default tabs to the left are automatically deleted by Word. Set a center, right, decimal, or bar tab on the horizontal ruler in a similar manner.

Table 3.1 Alignment Button Tab Symbols

Alignment Button Symbol	Type of Tab
	left
	center
	right
	decimal
	bar

Hint Position the insertion point in any paragraph of text, and tabs for the paragraph appear on the horizontal ruler.

If the tab symbol on the Alignment button is changed, the symbol remains in place until it is changed again or Word is closed. If Word is closed and then reopened, the Alignment button displays with the left tab symbol.

To set a tab at a specific measurement on the horizontal ruler, press and hold down the Alt key, position the arrow pointer at the desired position, and then click and hold down the left mouse button. This displays two measurements in the white portion of the horizontal ruler. The first measurement is the location of the arrow pointer on the ruler in relation to the left margin. The second measurement is the distance from the arrow pointer to the right margin. With the left mouse button held down, position the tab symbol at the desired location and then release the mouse button followed by the Alt key.

Project 4a Setting Left, Center, and Right Tabs on the Horizontal Ruler — Part 1 of 4

1. Press Ctrl + N to open a new blank document.
2. Type WORKSHOPS centered and bolded, as shown in Figure 3.5.
3. Press the Enter key. In the new paragraph, change the paragraph alignment back to left and then turn off bold formatting.
4. Set a left tab at the 0.5-inch mark, a center tab at the 3.25-inch mark, and a right tab at the 6-inch mark by completing the following steps:
   a. Click the Show/Hide ¶ button in the Paragraph group on the Home tab to turn on the display of nonprinting characters.
   b. Make sure the horizontal ruler is displayed. (If it is not displayed, click the View tab and then click the *Ruler* check box in the Show group to insert a check mark.)
   c. Make sure the left tab symbol displays in the Alignment button.
   d. Position the arrow pointer on the 0.5-inch mark on the horizontal ruler and then click the left mouse button.

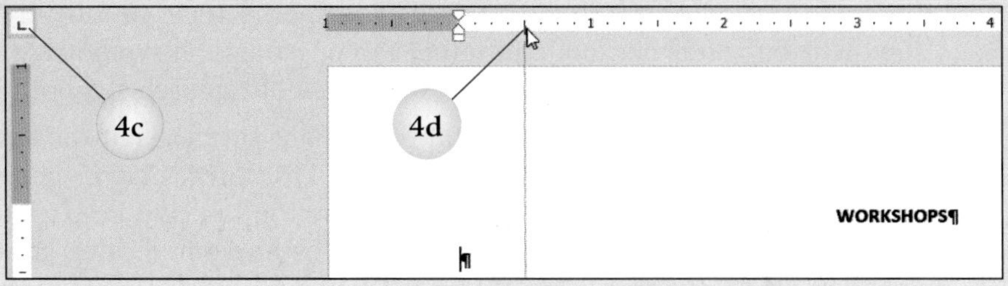

e. Position the arrow pointer on the Alignment button and then click the left mouse button until the center tab symbol displays (see Table 3.1).

f. Position the arrow pointer on the 3.25-inch mark on the horizontal ruler. Press and hold down the Alt key and then click and hold down the left mouse button. Make sure the first measurement on the horizontal ruler displays as *3.25"* and then release both the mouse button and the Alt key.

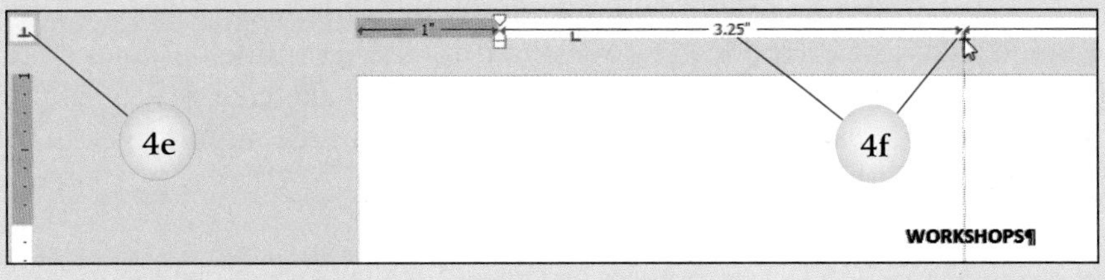

g. Position the arrow pointer on the Alignment button and then click the left mouse button until the right tab symbol displays (see Table 3.1).

h. Position the arrow pointer below the 6-inch mark on the horizontal ruler. Press and hold down the Alt key and then click and hold down the left mouse button. Make sure the first measurement on the horizontal ruler displays as *6"* and then release both the mouse button and the Alt key.

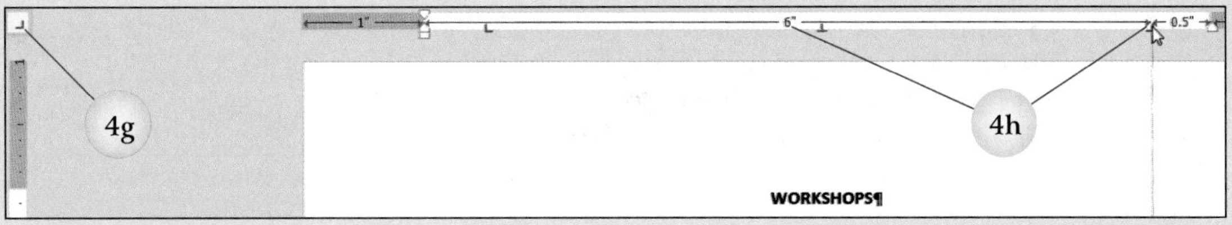

5. Type the text in columns, as shown in Figure 3.5. Press the Tab key before typing each column entry and press Shift + Enter after typing each entry in the third column. Bold the title and column headings as shown in the figure.
6. After typing the final entry in the last column entry, press the Enter key two times.
7. Press Ctrl + Q to remove paragraph formatting (tab settings) below the columns from the current paragraph.
8. Click the Show/Hide ¶ button to turn off the display of nonprinting characters.
9. Save the document and name it **3-Tabs**.

Check Your Work

Figure 3.5 Project 4a

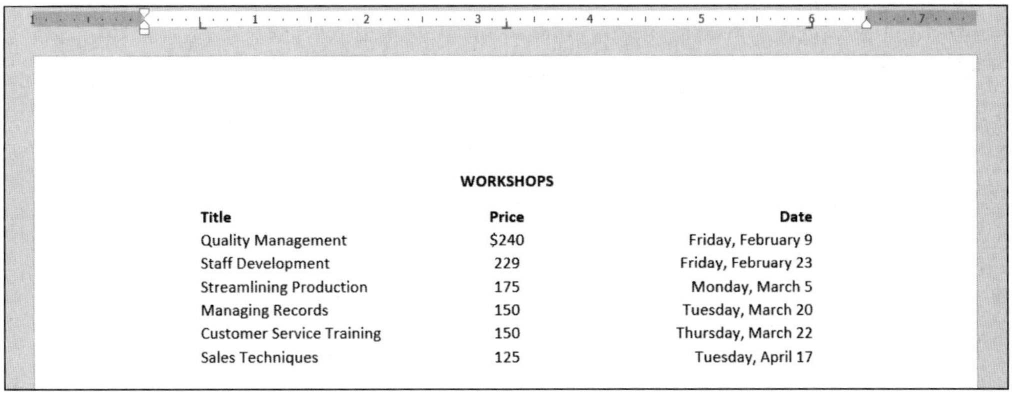

WORKSHOPS

Title	**Price**	**Date**
Quality Management	$240	Friday, February 9
Staff Development	229	Friday, February 23
Streamlining Production	175	Monday, March 5
Managing Records	150	Tuesday, March 20
Customer Service Training	150	Thursday, March 22
Sales Techniques	125	Tuesday, April 17

After a tab has been set on the horizontal ruler, it can be moved to a new location. To move a tab, position the arrow pointer on the tab symbol on the ruler, click and hold down the left mouse button, drag the symbol to the new location on the ruler, and then release the mouse button. To delete a tab from the ruler, position the arrow pointer on the tab symbol to be deleted, click and hold down the left mouse button, drag down into the document, and then release the mouse button.

When typing text in columns, press the Enter key or press Shift + Enter to end each line. If the Enter key is used to end each line, all lines of text in columns will need to be selected to make changes. To make changes to columns of text with line breaks inserted using Shift + Enter, the insertion point needs to be positioned only in one location in the columns of text.

Project 4b Moving Tabs

Part 2 of 4

1. With **3-Tabs.docx** open, position the insertion point anywhere in the first entry in the tabbed text.
2. Position the arrow pointer on the left tab symbol at the 0.5-inch mark on the horizontal ruler, click and hold down the left mouse button, drag the left tab symbol to the 1-inch mark on the ruler, and then release the mouse button. ***Hint: Use the Alt key to help you position the tab symbol precisely.***

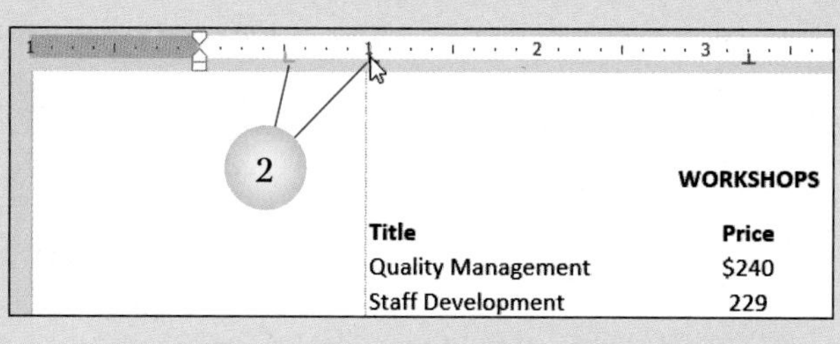

3. Position the arrow pointer on the right tab symbol at the 6-inch mark on the horizontal ruler, click and hold down the left mouse button, drag the right tab symbol to the 5.5-inch mark on the ruler, and then release the mouse button. ***Hint: Use the Alt key to help you position the tab symbol precisely.***
4. Save **3-Tabs.docx**.

Check Your Work

Tutorial

Setting and Clearing Tabs at the Tabs Dialog Box

Setting and Modifying Tabs at the Tabs Dialog Box

Use the Tabs dialog box, shown in Figure 3.6, to set tabs at specific measurements, set tabs with preceding leaders, and clear one tab or all tabs. To display the Tabs dialog box, click the Paragraph group dialog box launcher. At the Paragraph dialog box, click the Tabs button in the lower left corner of the dialog box.

Quick Steps

Set Tabs at Tabs Dialog Box

1. Click Paragraph group dialog box launcher.
2. Click Tabs button.
3. Specify tab positions, alignments, and leader options.
4. Click OK.

To clear an individual tab at the Tabs dialog box, specify the tab position and then click the Clear button. To clear all tabs, click the Clear All button. A left, right, center, decimal, or bar tab can be set at the Tabs dialog box. (For an example of a bar tab, refer to Figure 3.7.) A left, right, center, or decimal tab can be set with preceding leaders.

To change the type of tab at the Tabs dialog box, display the dialog box and then click the desired tab in the *Alignment* section. Type the measurement for the tab in the *Tab stop position* text box and then click the Set button.

Figure 3.6 Tabs Dialog Box

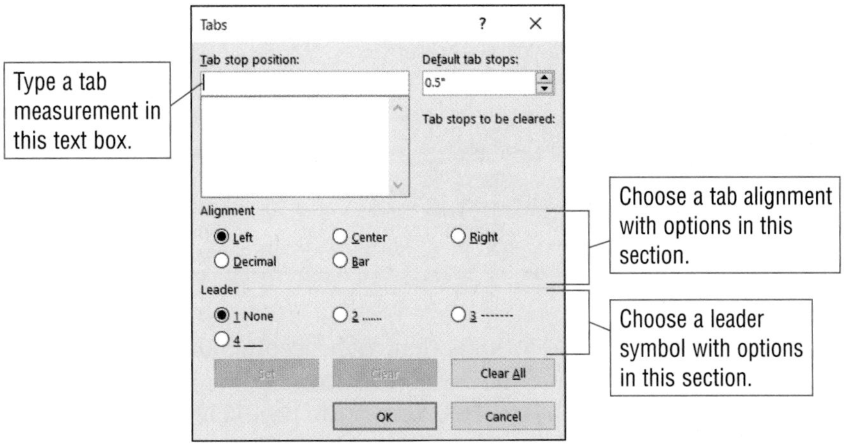

Project 4c Setting Left Tabs and a Bar Tab at the Tabs Dialog Box

Part 3 of 4

1. With **3-Tabs.docx** open, press Ctrl + End to move the insertion point to the end of the document.
2. Type the title TRAINING DATES bolded and centered (as shown in Figure 3.7), press the Enter key, return the paragraph alignment to left, and then turn off bold formatting.
3. Display the Tabs dialog box and then set left tabs and a bar tab by completing the following steps:
   a. Click the Paragraph group dialog box launcher.
   b. At the Paragraph dialog box, click the Tabs button in the lower left corner of the dialog box.
   c. Make sure *Left* is selected in the *Alignment* section of the dialog box.
   d. Type 1.75 in the *Tab stop position* text box.
   e. Click the Set button.
   f. Type 4 in the *Tab stop position* text box and then click the Set button.
   g. Type 3.25 in the *Tab stop position* text box, click *Bar* in the *Alignment* section, and then click the Set button.
   h. Click OK to close the Tabs dialog box.

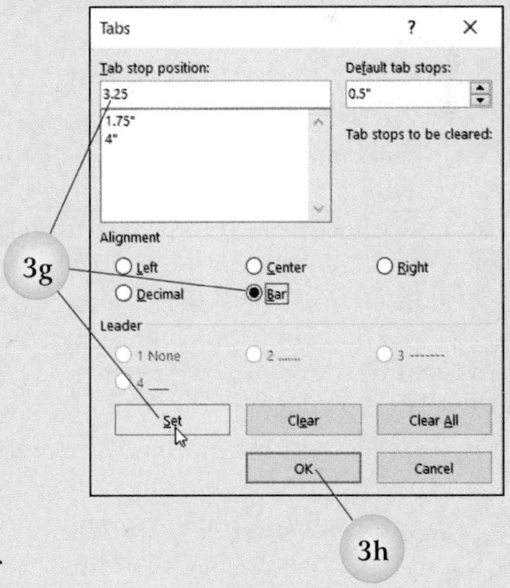

4. Type the text in columns, as shown in Figure 3.7. Press the Tab key before typing each column entry and press Shift + Enter to end each line. After typing *February 26*, press the Enter key.
5. Clear tabs below the columns from the current paragraph by completing the following steps:
   a. Click the Paragraph group dialog box launcher.
   b. At the Paragraph dialog box, click the Tabs button.
   c. At the Tabs dialog box, click the Clear All button.
   d. Click OK.
6. Press the Enter key.
7. Remove the 8 points of spacing after the last entry in the text by completing the following steps:
   a. Position the insertion point anywhere in the *January 24* entry.
   b. Click the Line and Paragraph Spacing button in the Paragraph group on the Home tab.
   c. Click the *Remove Space After Paragraph* option.
8. Save **3-Tabs.docx**.

Check Your Work

Figure 3.7 Project 4c

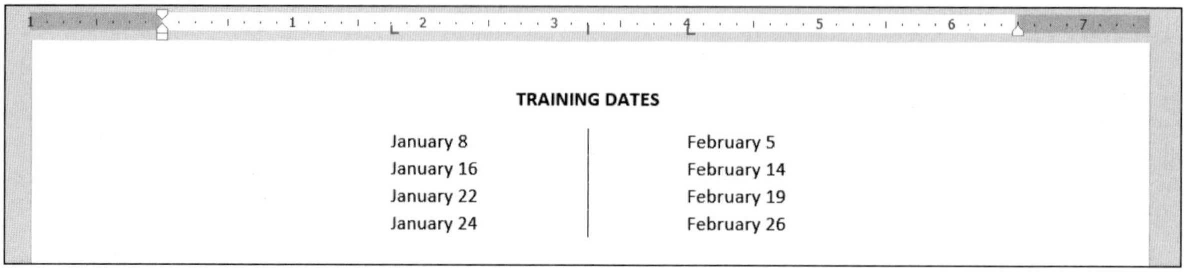

TRAINING DATES

January 8	February 5
January 16	February 14
January 22	February 19
January 24	February 26

Four types of tabs (left, right, center, and decimal) can be set with leaders. Leaders are useful in a table of contents or other material where the reader's eyes should be directed across the page. Figure 3.8 shows an example of leaders. Leaders can be periods (.), hyphens (-), or underlines (_). To add leaders to a tab, click the type of leader in the *Leader* section of the Tabs dialog box.

Project 4d Setting a Left Tab and a Right Tab with Period Leaders

Part 4 of 4

1. With **3-Tabs.docx** open, press Ctrl + End to move the insertion point to the end of the document.
2. Type the title TABLE OF CONTENTS bolded and centered, as shown in Figure 3.8.
3. Press the Enter key and then return the paragraph alignment to left and turn off bold formatting.
4. Set a left tab and then a right tab with period leaders by completing the following steps:
   a. Click the Paragraph group dialog box launcher.
   b. Click the Tabs button in the lower left corner of the Paragraph dialog box.
   c. At the Tabs dialog box, make sure *Left* is selected in the *Alignment* section of the dialog box.
   d. With the insertion point positioned in the *Tab stop position* text box, type 1 and then click the Set button.
   e. Type 5.5 in the *Tab stop position* text box.
   f. Click *Right* in the *Alignment* section of the dialog box.
   g. Click *2 ......* in the *Leader* section of the dialog box and then click the Set button.
   h. Click OK to close the dialog box.
5. Type the text in columns, as shown in Figure 3.8. Press the Tab key before typing each column entry and press Shift + Enter to end each line.
6. Save, print, and then close **3-Tabs.docx**.

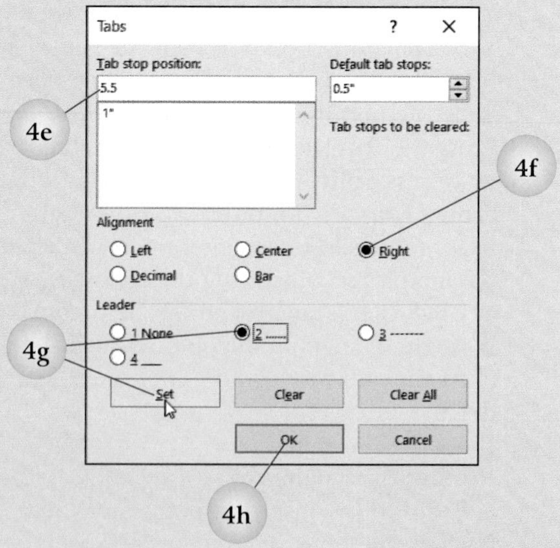

Check Your Work

Figure 3.8 Project 4d

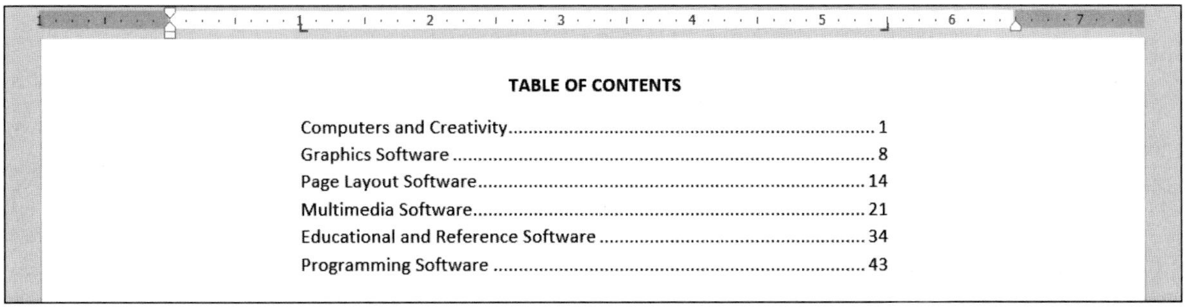

TABLE OF CONTENTS

Computers and Creativity	1
Graphics Software	8
Page Layout Software	14
Multimedia Software	21
Educational and Reference Software	34
Programming Software	43

Project 5 Move and Copy Text in a Document on Online Shopping Tips — 2 Parts

You will open a document containing information on online shopping safety tips and then cut, copy, and paste text in the document.

Preview Finished Project

Tutorial

Cutting, Copying, and Pasting Text

Cutting, Copying, and Pasting Text

When editing a document, specific text may need to be deleted, moved to a different location in the document, or copied to various locations in the document. These activites can be completed using buttons in the Clipboard group on the Home tab.

Deleting Selected Text

Hint The Clipboard content is deleted when the computer is turned off. Text you want to save permanently should be saved as a separate document.

Word offers several different methods for deleting text from a document. To delete a single character, use either the Delete key or the Backspace key. To delete more than a single character, select the text and then press the Delete key on the keyboard or click the Cut button in the Clipboard group. If the Delete key is used to delete selected text, the text is deleted permanently. (Deleted text can be restored with the Undo button on the Quick Access Toolbar.)

Using the Cut button in the Clipboard group will remove the selected text from the document and insert it in the Clipboard, which is a temporary area of memory. The Clipboard holds text while it is being moved or copied to a new location in the document or to a different document.

Cutting and Pasting Text

Cut

Paste

Quick Steps

Move Selected Text

1. Select text.
2. Click Cut button.
3. Position insertion point.
4. Click Paste button.

To move text to a different location in the document, select the text, click the Cut button in the Clipboard group, position the insertion point at the location the text is to be inserted, and then click the Paste button in the Clipboard group.

Selected text can also be moved using the shortcut menu. To do this, select the text and then position the insertion point inside the selected text until it turns into an arrow pointer. Click the right mouse button and then click *Cut* at the shortcut menu. Position the insertion point where the text is to be inserted, click the right mouse button, and then click *Paste* at the shortcut menu. Keyboard shortcuts are also available for cutting and pasting text. Use Ctrl + X to cut text and Ctrl + V to paste text.

Quick Steps

Move Text with the Mouse

1. Select text.
2. Position mouse pointer in selected text.
3. Click and hold down left mouse button and drag to new location.
4. Release left mouse button.

OR

1. Select text.
2. Press Ctrl + X.
3. Move to new location.
4. Click Ctrl + V.

When selected text is cut from a document and inserted in the Clipboard, it stays in the Clipboard until other text is inserted there. For this reason, text can be pasted from the Clipboard more than once.

Moving Text by Dragging with the Mouse

The mouse can be used to move text. To do this, select text to be moved and then position the I-beam pointer inside the selected text until it turns into an arrow pointer. Click and hold down the left mouse button, drag the arrow pointer (which displays with a gray box attached) to the location the selected text is to be inserted, and then release the button. If the selected text is inserted in the wrong location, click the Undo button immediately.

Project 5a Moving and Dragging Selected Text — Part 1 of 2

1. Open **ShoppingTips.docx** and then save it with the name **3-ShoppingTips**.
2. Move a paragraph by completing the following steps:
   a. Select the paragraph that begins with *Only buy at secure sites,* including the blank line below the paragraph.
   b. Click the Cut button in the Clipboard group on the Home tab.
   c. Position the insertion point at the beginning of the paragraph that begins with *Look for sites that follow*.
   d. Click the Paste button in the Clipboard group. (If the first and second paragraphs are not separated by a blank line, press the Enter key.)

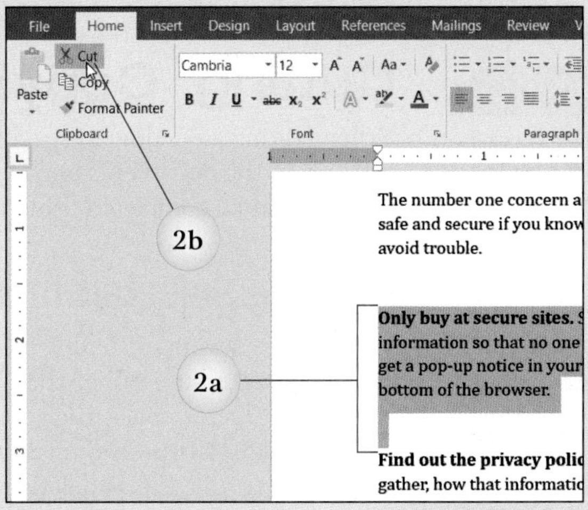

3. Following steps similar to those in Step 2, move the paragraph that begins with *Never provide your social* before the paragraph that begins *Look for sites that follow privacy* and after the paragraph that begins *Only buy at secure*.
4. Use the mouse to select the paragraph that begins with *Keep current with the latest Internet*, including one blank line below the paragraph.
5. Move the I-beam pointer inside the selected text until it displays as an arrow pointer.
6. Click and hold down the left mouse button, drag the arrow pointer (which displays with a small gray box attached) so that the insertion point (which displays as a black vertical bar) is positioned at the beginning of the paragraph that begins with *Never provide your social*, and then release the mouse button.
7. Deselect the text.
8. Save **3-ShoppingTips.docx**.

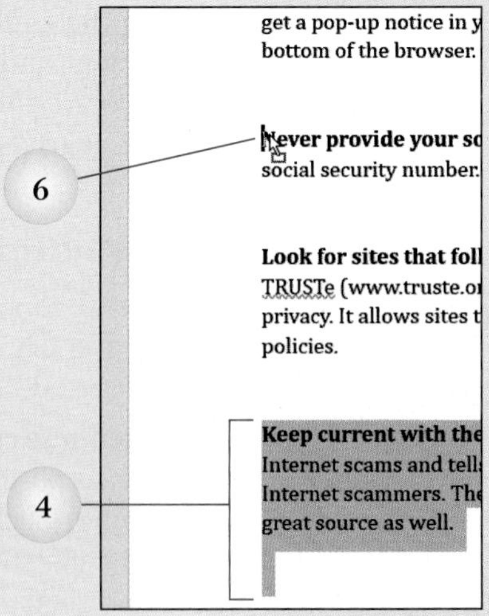

Check Your Work

Tutorial

Using the Paste Options Button

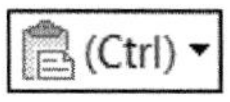

Paste Options

Using the Paste Options Button

When selected text is pasted, the Paste Options button displays in the lower right corner of the text. Click this button (or press the Ctrl key on the keyboard) and the *Paste Options* gallery displays, as shown in Figure 3.9. Use buttons in this gallery to specify how the text is pasted in the document. Hover the mouse pointer over a button in the gallery and the live preview displays the text in the document as it will appear when pasted.

By default, pasted text retains the formatting of the selected text. This can be changed to match the formatting of the pasted text with the formatting of where the text is pasted or to paste only the text without retaining formatting. To determine the function of any button in the *Paste Options* gallery, hover the mouse pointer over the button and a ScreenTip displays with an explanation of the function as well as the keyboard shortcut. For example, hover the mouse pointer over the first button from the left in the *Paste Options* gallery and the ScreenTip displays with *Keep Source Formatting (K)*. Click this button or press K on the keyboard and the pasted text keeps its original formatting.

Figure 3.9 Paste Options Button Drop-Down List

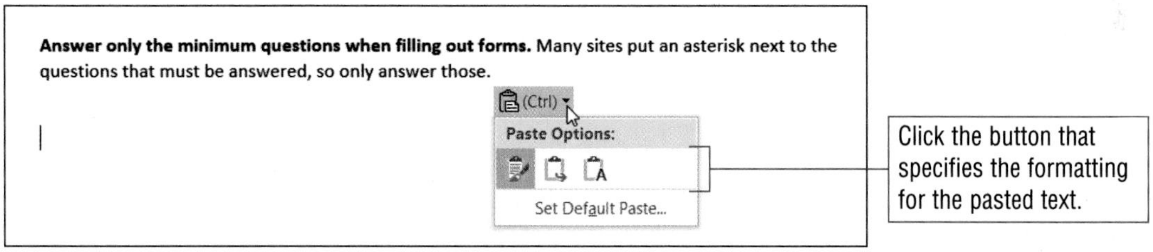

Project 5b Using the Paste Options Button

Part 2 of 2

1. With **3-ShoppingTips.docx** open, open **Tip.docx**.
2. Select the paragraph of text in the document, including the blank line below the paragraph, and then click the Copy button in the Clipboard group.
3. Close **Tip.docx**.
4. Press Ctrl + End to move the insertion point to the end of **3-ShoppingTips.docx**.
5. Click the Paste button in the Clipboard group.
6. Click the Paste Options button that displays at the end of the paragraph and then click the second button in the *Paste Options* gallery (Merge Formatting button). (This changes the font so it matches the font of the other paragraphs in the document.)
7. Save, print, and then close **3-ShoppingTips.docx**.

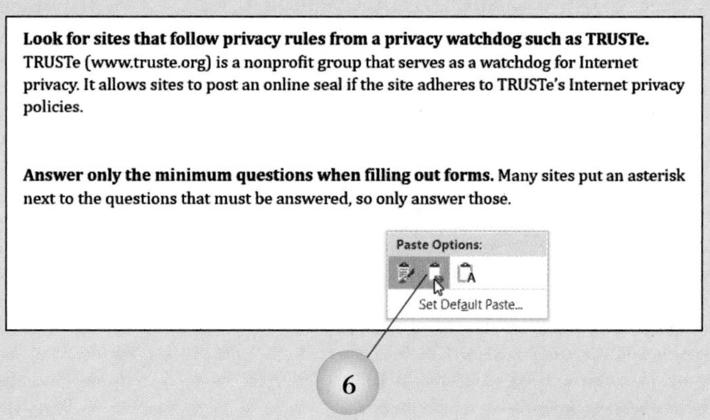

Check Your Work

Project 6 Copy Text in a Staff Meeting Announcement — 1 Part

You will copy and paste text in a document announcing a staff meeting for the Technical Support Team.

Preview Finished Project

Copy

Quick Steps

Copy Selected Text

1. Select text.
2. Click Copy button.
3. Position insertion point.
4. Click Paste button.

Copying and Pasting Text

Copying selected text can be useful in documents that contain repeated information. Use copy and paste to insert duplicate portions of text in a document instead of retyping them. Copy selected text to a different location using the Copy and Paste buttons in the Clipboard group on the Home tab, the mouse, or the keyboard shortcuts, Ctrl + C and Ctrl + V.

To use the mouse to copy text, select the text and then position the I-beam pointer inside the selected text until it becomes an arrow pointer. Click and hold down the left mouse button and also press and hold down the Ctrl key. Drag the arrow pointer (which displays with a small gray box and a box containing a plus [+] symbol) and a black vertical bar moves with the pointer. Position the black bar in the desired location, release the mouse button, and then release the Ctrl key.

Project 6 Copying Text — Part 1 of 1

1. Open **StaffMtg.docx** and then save it with the name **3-StaffMtg**.
2. Copy the text in the document to the end of the document by completing the following steps:
   a. Select all of the text in the document and include one blank line below the text. ***Hint: Click the Show/Hide ¶ button to turn on the display of nonprinting characters. When you select the text, select one of the paragraph markers below the text.***
   b. Click the Copy button in the Clipboard group.
   c. Move the insertion point to the end of the document.
   d. Click the Paste button in the Clipboard group.
3. Paste the text again at the end of the document. To do this, position the insertion point at the end of the document and then click the Paste button in the Clipboard group. (This inserts a copy of the text from the Clipboard.)
4. Select all the text in the document using the mouse and include one blank line below the text. (Consider turning on the display of nonprinting characters.)
5. Move the I-beam pointer inside the selected text until it becomes an arrow pointer.
6. Click and hold down the Ctrl key and then the left mouse button. Drag the arrow pointer (which displays with a box with a plus symbol inside) so the vertical black bar is positioned at the end of the document, release the mouse button, and then release the Ctrl key.

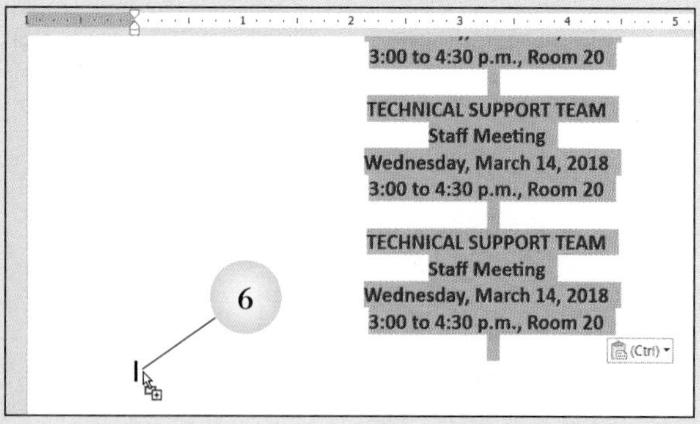

7. Deselect the text.
8. Make sure all the text fits on one page. If not, consider deleting any extra blank lines.
9. Save, print, and then close **3-StaffMtg.docx**.

Check Your Work

Project 7 Create a Contract Negotiations Document 1 Part

You will use the Clipboard task pane to copy and paste paragraphs to and from separate documents to create a contract negotiations document.

Preview Finished Project

Tutorial

Using the Clipboard Task Pane

Quick Steps

Use the Clipboard

1. Click Clipboard group task pane launcher.
2. Select and copy text.
3. Position insertion point.
4. Click option in Clipboard task pane.

Using the Clipboard Task Pane

Use the Clipboard task pane to collect and paste multiple items. Up to 24 different items can be collected and then pasted in various locations. To display the Clipboard task pane, click the Clipboard group task pane launcher in the lower right corner of the Clipboard group. The Clipboard task pane displays at the left side of the screen in a manner similar to what is shown in Figure 3.10.

Select the text or object to be copied and then click the Copy button in the Clipboard group. Continue selecting text or items and clicking the Copy button. To insert an item from the Clipboard task pane into the document, position the insertion point in the desired location and then click the option in the Clipboard task pane representing the item. Click the Paste All button to paste all of the items in the Clipboard task pane into the document. If the copied item is text, the first 50 characters display in the list box on the Clipboard task pane. When all the items are inserted, click the Clear All button to remove any remaining items.

Hint You can copy items to the Clipboard from various Microsoft Office applications and then paste them into any Office file.

Figure 3.10 Clipboard Task Pane

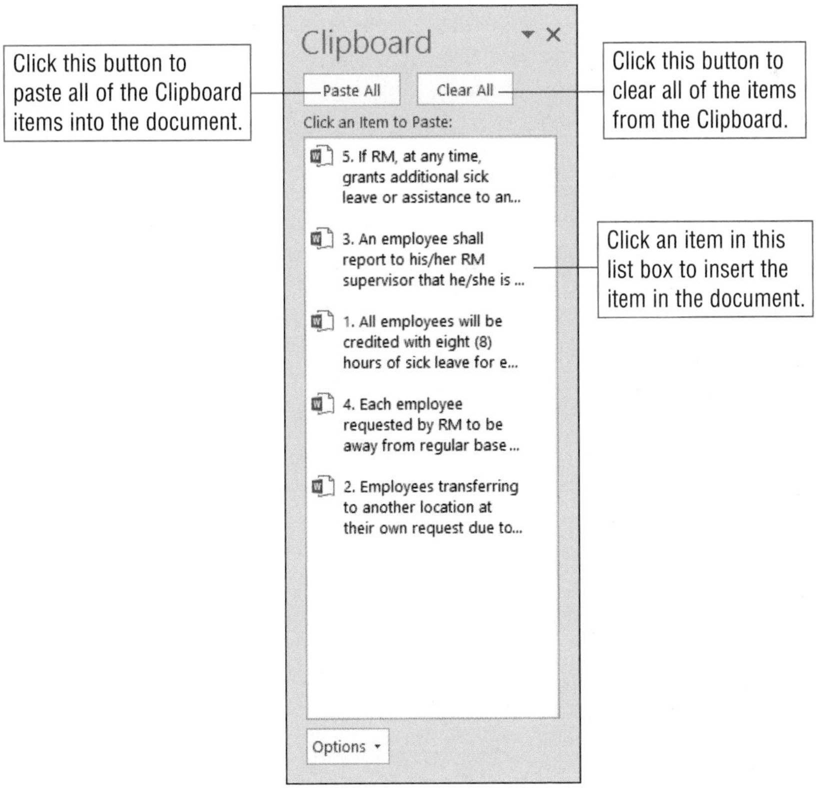

Project 7 Collecting and Pasting Paragraphs of Text

Part 1 of 1

1. Open **ContractItems.docx**.
2. Display the Clipboard task pane by clicking the Clipboard group task pane launcher in the bottom right corner of the Clipboard group. (If the Clipboard task pane list box contains any text, click the Clear All button in the upper right corner of the Clipboard task pane.)
3. Select paragraph 1 in the document (the *1.* is not selected) and then click the Copy button in the Clipboard group.
4. Select paragraph 3 in the document (the *3.* is not selected) and then click the Copy button in the Clipboard group.
5. Close **ContractItems.docx**.
6. Paste the paragraphs by completing the following steps:
   a. Press Ctrl + N to display a new blank document. (If the Clipboard task pane does not display, click the Clipboard group task pane launcher.)
   b. Type CONTRACT NEGOTIATION ITEMS centered and bolded.
   c. Press the Enter key, turn off bold formatting, and return the paragraph alignment to left alignment.
   d. Click the Paste All button in the Clipboard task pane to paste both paragraphs in the document.
   e. Click the Clear All button in the Clipboard task pane.
7. Open **UnionContract.docx**.
8. Select and then copy each of the following paragraphs:
   a. Paragraph 2 in the *Transfers and Moving Expenses* section.
   b. Paragraph 4 in the *Transfers and Moving Expenses* section.
   c. Paragraph 1 in the *Sick Leave* section.
   d. Paragraph 3 in the *Sick Leave* section.
   e. Paragraph 5 in the *Sick Leave* section.
9. Close **UnionContract.docx**.
10. Make sure the insertion point is positioned at the end of the document, on a new line, and then paste the paragraphs by completing the following steps:
    a. Click the button in the Clipboard task pane representing paragraph 2. (When the paragraph is inserted in the document, the paragraph number changes to *3.*)
    b. Click the button in the Clipboard task pane representing paragraph 4.
    c. Click the button in the Clipboard task pane representing paragraph 3.
    d. Click the button in the Clipboard task pane representing paragraph 5.
11. Click the Clear All button in the upper right corner of the Clipboard task pane.
12. Close the Clipboard task pane.
13. Save the document and name it **3-NegotiateItems**.
14. Print and then close **3-NegotiateItems.docx**.

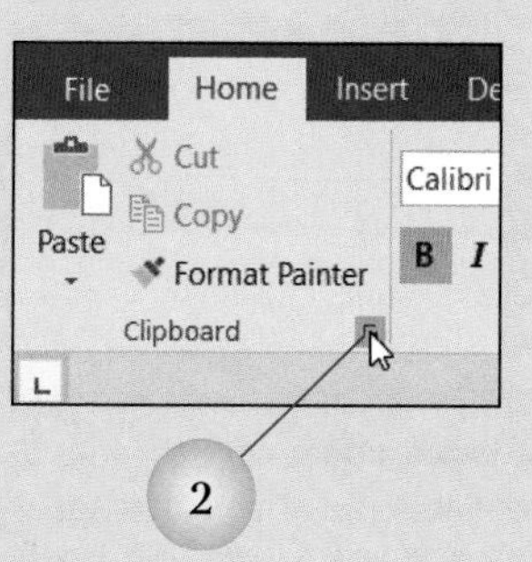

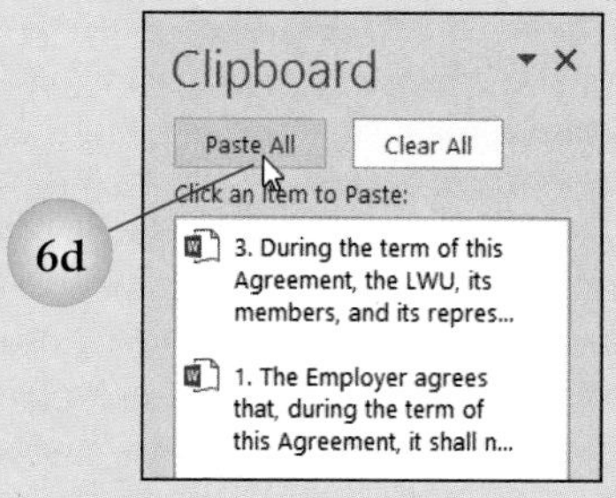

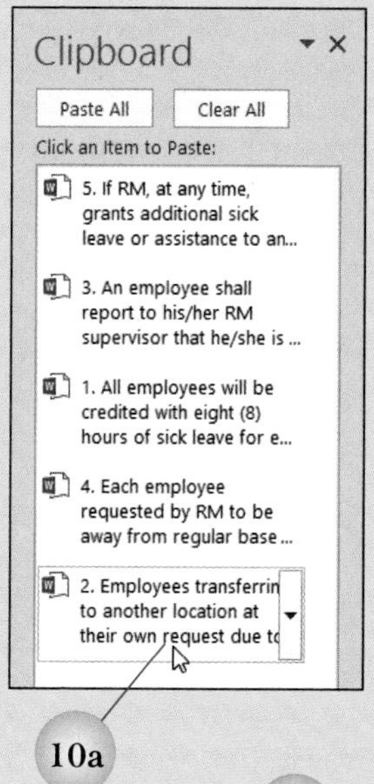

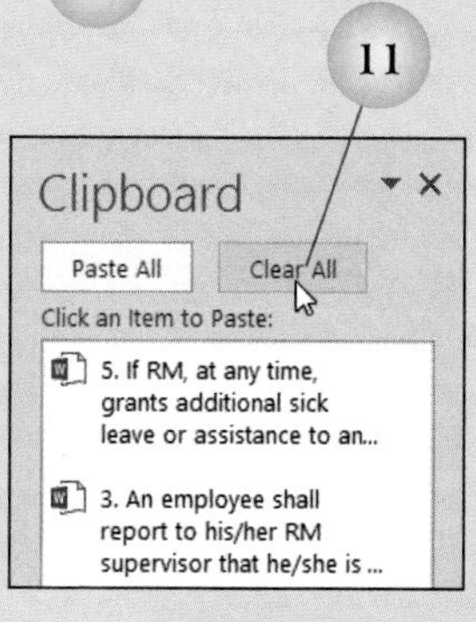

Check Your Work

Chapter Summary

- Number paragraphs using the Numbering button in the Paragraph group on the Home tab and insert bullets before paragraphs using the Bullets button.
- Remove all paragraph formatting from a paragraph by pressing the keyboard shortcut Ctrl + Q. Remove all character and paragraph formatting by clicking the Clear All Formatting button in the Font group.
- The AutoCorrect Options button displays when the AutoFormat feature inserts numbers. Click this button to display options for undoing and/or stopping automatic numbering.
- A bulleted list with a hanging indent is automatically created when a paragraph begins with *, >, or -. The type of bullet inserted depends on the type of character entered.
- Automatic numbering and bulleting can be turned off at the AutoCorrect dialog box with the AutoFormat As You Type tab selected.
- A paragraph created in Word contains an invisible frame and a border can be added to this frame. Click the Borders button arrow to display a drop-down list of border options.
- Use options at the Borders and Shading dialog box with the Borders tab selected to add a customized border to a paragraph or selected paragraphs.
- Apply shading to text by clicking the Shading button arrow and then clicking a color at the drop-down gallery. Use options at the Borders and Shading dialog box with the Shading tab selected to add shading or a pattern to a paragraph or selected paragraphs.
- Use the Sort button in the Paragraph group on the Home tab to sort text in paragraphs alphabetically by the first character of each paragraph, which can be a number, symbol, or letter.
- By default, tabs are set every 0.5 inch. Tab settings can be changed on the horizontal ruler or at the Tabs dialog box.
- Use the Alignment button above the vertical ruler to select a left, right, center, decimal, or bar tab. When a tab is set on the horizontal ruler, any default tabs to the left are automatically deleted.
- After a tab has been set on the horizontal ruler, it can be moved or deleted using the mouse pointer.
- At the Tabs dialog box, any of the five types of tabs can be set at a specific measurement. Tabs also can be set with preceding leaders, which can be periods, hyphens, or underlines. Individual tabs or all tabs can be cleared at the Tabs dialog box.
- Cut, copy, and paste text using buttons in the Clipboard group on the Home tab, with options at the shortcut menu, or with keyboard shortcuts.
- When selected text is pasted, the Paste Options button displays in the lower right corner of the text. Click the button and the *Paste Options* gallery displays with buttons for specifying how text is pasted in the document.
- With the Clipboard task pane, up to 24 items can be copied and then pasted in various locations in a document or other document.
- Display the Clipboard task pane by clicking the Clipboard group task pane launcher in the Clipboard group on the Home tab.

Commands Review

FEATURE	RIBBON TAB, GROUP	BUTTON, OPTION	KEYBOARD SHORTCUT
borders	Home, Paragraph		
Borders and Shading dialog box	Home, Paragraph	, *Borders and Shading*	
bullets	Home, Paragraph		
clear all formatting	Home, Font		
clear paragraph formatting			Ctrl + Q
Clipboard task pane	Home, Clipboard		
copy text	Home, Clipboard		Ctrl + C
cut text	Home, Clipboard		Ctrl + X
New Line command			Shift + Enter
numbering	Home, Paragraph		
Paragraph dialog box	Home, Paragraph		
paste text	Home, Clipboard		Ctrl + V
shading	Home, Paragraph		
Sort Text dialog box	Home, Paragraph		
Tabs dialog box	Home, Paragraph	, Tabs	

Workbook

Chapter study tools and assessment activities are available in the *Workbook* ebook. These resources are designed to help you further develop and demonstrate mastery of the skills learned in this chapter.

Microsoft®

Word

CHAPTER 4

Formatting Pages

Performance Objectives

Upon successful completion of Chapter 4, you will be able to:

1 Change document views
2 Navigate in a document with the Navigation pane
3 Change margins, page orientation, and paper size
4 Format pages at the Page Setup dialog box
5 Insert a page break, blank page, and cover page
6 Insert page numbering
7 Insert and edit predesigned headers and footers
8 Insert a watermark, page background color, and page border
9 Find and replace text and formatting

Precheck

Check your current skills to help focus your study.

A document generally displays in Print Layout view. This default view can be changed with buttons in the view area on the Status bar or with options on the View tab. The Navigation pane provides one method for navigating in a document. A Word document, by default, contains 1-inch top, bottom, left, and right margins. Change these default margins with the Margins button in the Page Setup group on the Layout tab or with options at the Page Setup dialog box. A variety of features can be inserted in a Word document, including a page break, blank page, and cover page, as well as page numbers, headers, footers, a watermark, page color, and page border. Use options at the Find and Replace dialog box to search for specific text or formatting and replace it with other text or formatting.

Data Files

Before beginning chapter work, copy the WL1C4 folder to your storage medium and then make WL1C4 the active folder.

SNAP

If you are a SNAP user, launch the Precheck and Tutorials from your Assignments page.

Project 1 **Change Views and Navigate in a Report on Navigating and Searching the Web** **2 Parts**

You will open a document containing information on navigating and searching the web, change document views, hide and show white space at the tops and bottoms of pages, and navigate in the document using the Navigation pane.

Tutorial

Changing Document Views

Changing Document Views

By default, a Word document displays in Print Layout view. This view displays the document on the screen as it will appear when printed. Other views are available, such as Draft and Read Mode. Change views with buttons in the view area on the Status bar (see Figure 4.1) or with options on the View tab.

Displaying a Document in Draft View

Draft

Change to Draft view and the document displays in a format for efficient editing and formatting. At this view, margins and other features, such as headers and footers, do not display on the screen. Change to Draft view by clicking the View tab and then clicking the Draft button in the Views group.

Displaying a Document in Read Mode View

Read Mode

Read Mode

Read Mode view displays a document in a format for easy viewing and reading. Change to Read Mode view by clicking the Read Mode button in the view area on the Status bar or by clicking the View tab and then clicking the Read Mode button in the Views group. Navigate in Read Mode view using the keys on the keyboard, as shown in Table 4.1. Other methods for navigating in Read Mode view include clicking at the right side of the screen or clicking the Next button (right-pointing arrow in a circle) to display the next pages and by clicking at the left side of the screen or clicking the Previous button (left-pointing arrow in a circle) to display the previous pages.

The File, Tools, and View tabs display in the upper left corner of the screen in Read Mode view. Click the File tab to display the backstage area. Click the Tools tab and a drop-down list displays options for finding specific text in the document and searching for information on the Internet using the Smart Lookup feature. Click the View tab and options display for customizing what appears in Read Mode view. Use View tab options to display the Navigation pane to navigate to specific locations in the document, show comments inserted in the document, change column widths or page layout, and change the page colors in Read Mode view.

Figure 4.1 View Buttons and Zoom Slider Bar

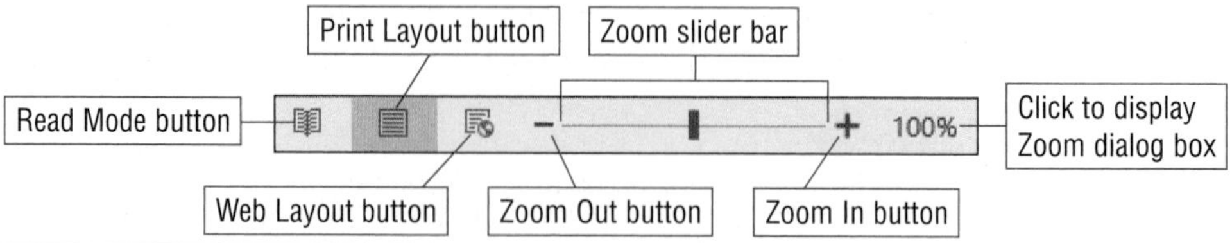

Table 4.1 Keyboard Commands in Read Mode View

Press this key	To complete this action
Page Down key, Right Arrow key, or spacebar	display next two pages
Page Up key, Left Arrow key, or Backspace key	display previous two pages
Home	display first page in document
End	display last page in document
Esc	return to previous view

If a document contains an object such as a table, SmartArt graphic, image, or shape, zoom in on the object in Read Mode view by double-clicking it. The display size of the object increases and a button containing a magnifying glass with a plus symbol inside ( ) displays just outside the upper right corner of the object. Click this button to zoom in even more on the object. Click the button again and the object returns to the original zoom size. Click outside the object to return it to its original display size. To close Read Mode view and return to the previous view, press the Esc key or click the View tab and then click *Edit Document* at the drop-down list.

Tutorial

Changing the Display Percentage

Zoom

Zoom Out

Zoom In

100%

Hint Click the 100% at the right side of the Zoom slider bar to display the Zoom dialog box.

Ribbon Display Options

Changing the Display Percentage

By default, a document displays at 100%. This display percentage can be changed with the Zoom slider bar at the right side of the Status bar (see Figure 4.1) and with options in the Zoom group on the View tab. To change the display percentage with the Zoom slider bar, drag the button on the bar to increase or decrease the percentage. Click the Zoom Out button at the left side of the slider bar to decrease the display percentage or click the Zoom In button to increase the display percentage.

Click the Zoom button in the Zoom group on the View tab to display the Zoom dialog box that contains options for changing the display percentage. If the display percentage has been changed, return to the default by clicking the 100% button in the Zoom group on the View tab. Click the One Page button to display the entire page on the screen and click the Multiple Pages button to display multiple pages on the screen. Click the Page Width button and the document expands across the screen.

Changing Ribbon Display Options

Use the Ribbon Display Options button in the upper right corner of the screen to view more of a document. Click the Ribbon Display Options button and a drop-down list displays with three options: *Auto-hide Ribbon*, *Show Tabs*, and *Show Tabs and Commands*. The default is Show Tabs and Commands, which displays the Quick Access Toolbar, ribbon, and Status bar on the screen. Click the first option, *Auto-hide Ribbon*, and the Quick Access Toolbar, ribbon, and Status bar are hidden, allowing more of the document to be visible on the screen. To temporarily redisplay these features, click at the top of the screen. Turn these features back on by clicking the Ribbon Display Options button and then clicking the *Show Tabs and Commands* option. Click the *Show Tabs* option at the drop-down list and the tabs display on the ribbon while the buttons and commands remain hidden.

Tutorial

Hiding and Showing White Space

Hide White Space

Show White Space

Hiding and Showing White Space

In Print Layout view, a page displays as it will appear when printed, including the white spaces at the top and the bottom of the page representing the document's margins. To save space on the screen in Print Layout view, the white space can be removed by positioning the mouse pointer at the top edge or bottom edge of a page or between pages until the pointer displays as the Hide White Space icon and then double-clicking the left mouse button. To redisplay the white space, position the mouse pointer on the thin gray line separating pages until the pointer turns into the Show White Space icon and then double-click the left mouse button.

Project 1a Changing Views and Hiding/Showing White Space — Part 1 of 2

1. Open **WebReport.docx** and then save it with the name **4-WebReport**.
2. Click the View tab and then click the Draft button in the Views group.
3. Click the Zoom Out button (to the left of the Zoom slider bar) three times. (This changes the display percentage and *70%* displays at the right side of the Zoom In button.)

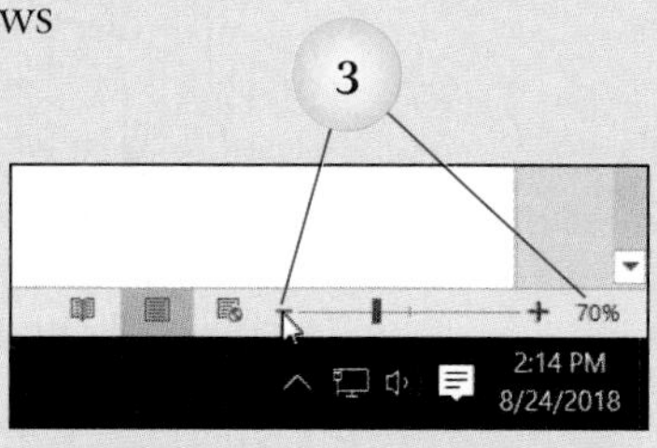

4. Using the mouse, drag the Zoom slider bar button to the middle until *100%* displays at the right side of the Zoom In button.
5. Click the Print Layout button in the view area on the Status bar.
6. Click the Zoom button in the Zoom group on the View tab.
7. At the Zoom dialog box, click the *75%* option and then click OK.

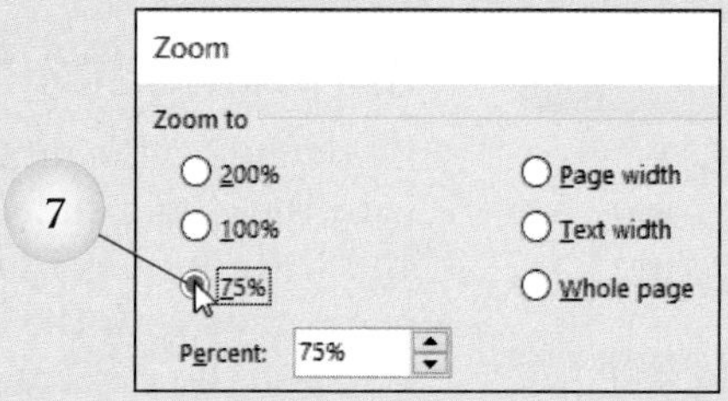

8. Return the display percentage to the default by clicking the 100% button in the Zoom group.
9. Click the Read Mode button in the view area on the Status bar.
10. Increase the display size of the table at the right side of the screen by double-clicking the table. (If the table is not visible, click the Next button at the right side of the screen to view the next page.)
11. Click the button containing a magnifying glass with a plus symbol that displays outside the upper right corner of the table. (This increases the zoom.)

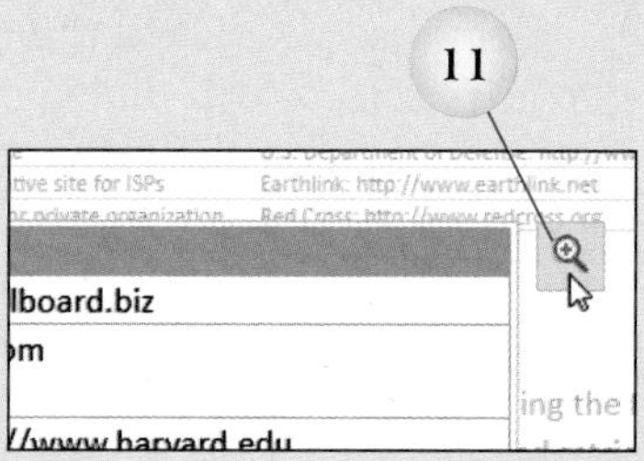

12. Click outside the table to return it to the original display size.
13. Practice navigating in Read Mode view using the actions shown in Table 4.1 (except the last action).
14. Press the Esc key to return to the Print Layout view.
15. Click the Ribbon Display Options button in the upper right corner of the screen and then click *Auto-hide Ribbon* at the drop-down list.

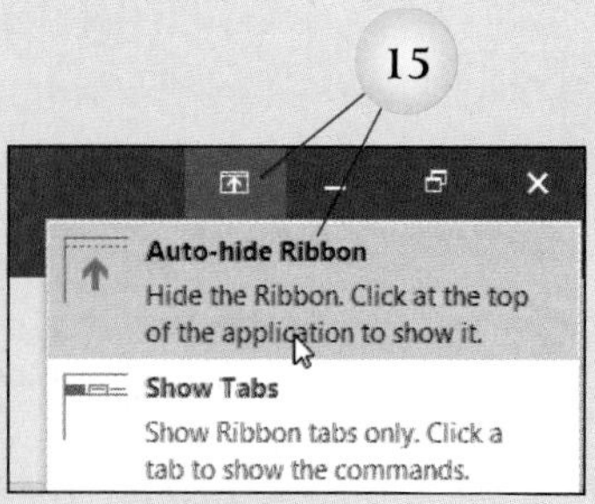

16. Press Ctrl + End to display the last page in the document and then press the Page Up key until the beginning of the document displays.
17. Click at the top of the screen to temporarily redisplay the Quick Access Toolbar, ribbon, and Status bar.
18. Click the Ribbon Display Options button and then click *Show Tabs* at the drop-down list.

19. Click the Ribbon Display Options button and then click *Show Tabs and Commands* at the drop-down list.
20. Press Ctrl + Home to move the insertion point to the beginning of the document.
21. Hide the white spaces at the tops and bottoms of pages by positioning the mouse pointer at the top edge of the page until the pointer turns into the Hide White Space icon and then double-clicking the left mouse button.

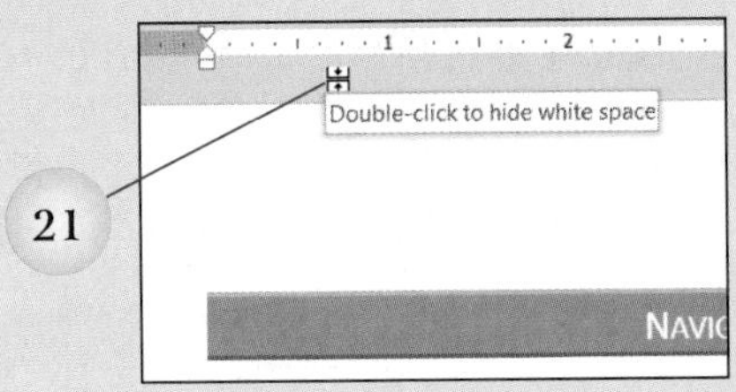

22. Scroll through the document and notice the display of pages.
23. Redisplay the white spaces at the tops and bottoms of pages by positioning the mouse pointer on any thin gray line separating pages until the pointer turns into the Show White Space icon and then double-clicking the left mouse button.

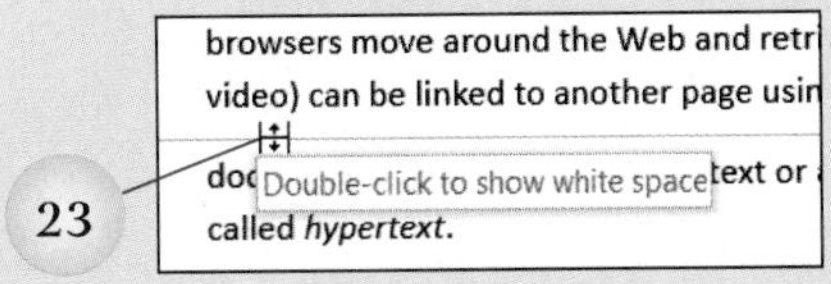

24. Save **4-WebReport.docx**.

Tutorial

Navigating Using the Navigation Pane

Navigating Using the Navigation Pane

Among the features that Word provides for navigating in a document is the Navigation pane, shown in Figure 4.2. Click the *Navigation Pane* check box in the Show group on the View tab to insert a check mark and the Navigation pane displays at the left side of the screen and includes a search text box and a pane with three tabs. Click the Headings tab to display titles and headings with styles applied. Click a title or heading in the pane to move the insertion point to that title or heading. Click the Pages tab to display a thumbnail of each page. Click a thumbnail to move the insertion point to the specific page. Click the Results tab to browse the current search results in the document. Close the Navigation pane by clicking the *Navigation Pane* check box in the Show group on the View tab to remove the check mark or by clicking the Close button in the upper right corner of the pane.

Quick Steps

Display Navigation Pane

1. Click View tab.
2. Click *Navigation Pane* check box.

Figure 4.2 Navigation Pane

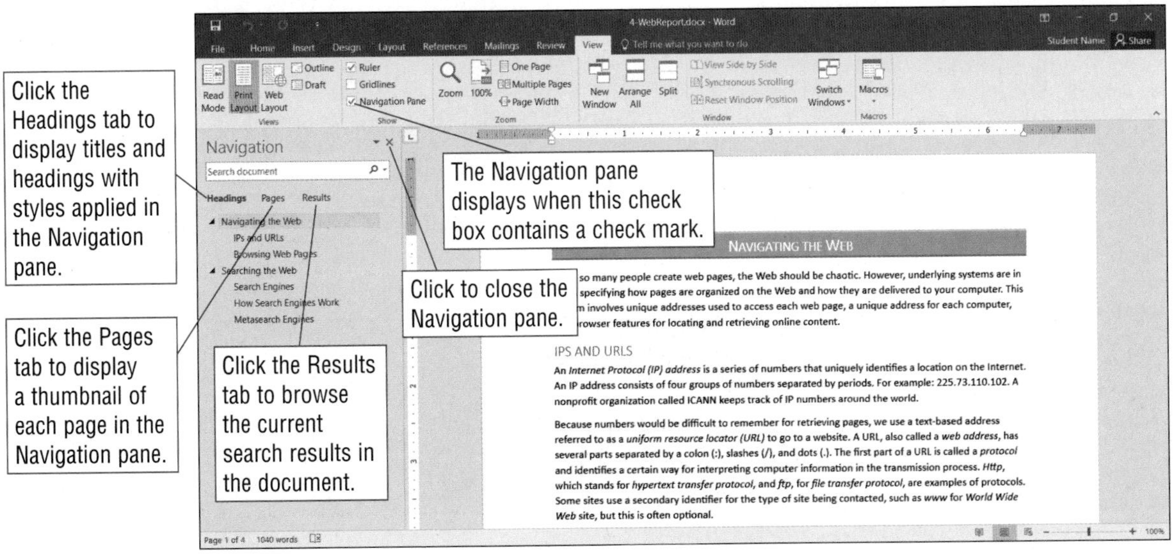

Project 1b Navigating Using the Navigation Pane

Part 2 of 2

1. With **4-WebReport.docx** open, make sure the document displays in Print Layout view.
2. Display the Navigation pane by clicking the View tab and then clicking the *Navigation Pane* check box in the Show group to insert a check mark.
3. Click the *Navigating the Web* heading in the Navigation pane.

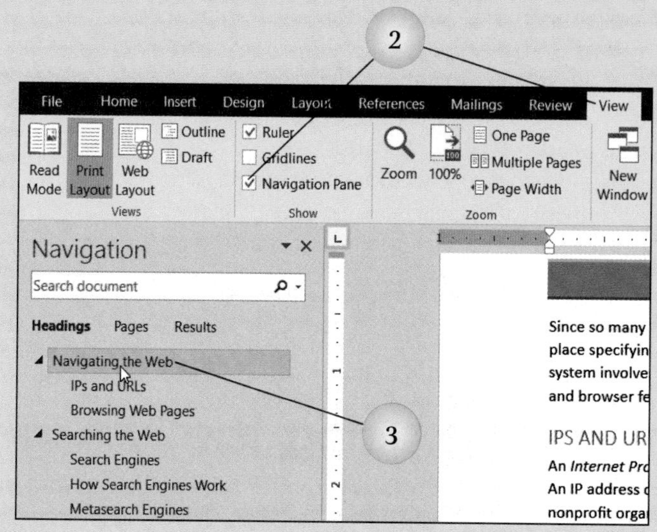

4. Click the *Searching the Web* heading in the Navigation pane.
5. Click the Pages tab in the Navigation pane to display the page thumbnails in the pane.
6. Click the page 4 thumbnail in the Navigation pane.
7. Scroll up the pane and then click the page 1 thumbnail.
8. Close the Navigation pane by clicking the Close button in the upper right corner of the pane.
9. Save and then close **4-WebReport.docx**.

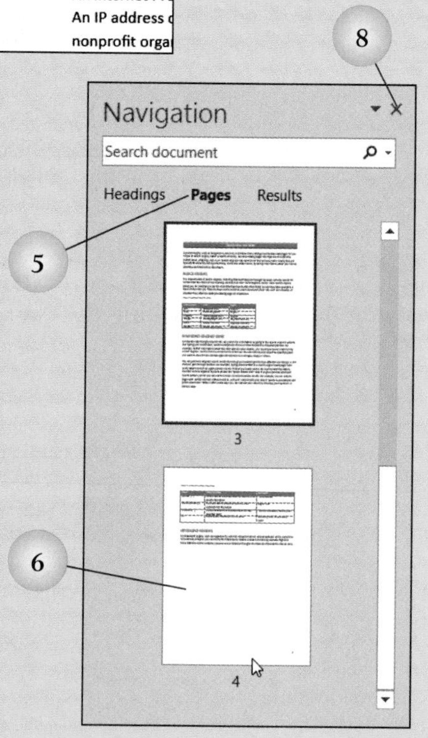

Project 2 Format a Document on Online Etiquette Guidelines

2 Parts

You will open a document containing information on guidelines for online etiquette and then change the margins, page orientation, and page size.

Preview Finished Project

Changing Page Setup

The Page Setup group on the Layout tab contains a number of options for changing pages in a document. Use options in the Page Setup group to perform such actions as changing margins, orientation, and page size and inserting page breaks. The Pages group on the Insert tab contains three buttons for inserting a cover page, blank page, and page break.

Tutorial

Changing Margins

Margins

Changing Margins

Change page margins with options at the Margins button drop-down list, as shown in Figure 4.3. To display this list, click the Layout tab and then click the Margins button in the Page Setup group. To change the margins, click one of the preset margins in the drop-down list. Be aware that most printers require a minimum margin (between ¼ and ⅜ inch) because they cannot print to the edge of the page.

Tutorial

Changing Page Orientation

Orientation

Changing Page Orientation

Click the Orientation button in the Page Setup group on the Layout tab and two options display: *Portrait* and *Landscape*. At the portrait orientation, which is the default, the page is 11 inches tall and 8.5 inches wide. At the landscape orientation, the page is 8.5 inches tall and 11 inches wide. Change the page orientation and the page margins automatically shift—the left and right margin measurements become the top and bottom margin measurements.

Tutorial

Changing Paper Size

Size

Changing Paper Size

By default, Word uses a paper size of 8.5 inches wide and 11 inches tall. Change this default setting with options at the Size button drop-down list. Display this drop-down list by clicking the Size button in the Page Setup group on the Layout tab.

Quick Steps

Change Margins
1. Click Layout tab.
2. Click Margins button.
3. Click margin option.

Change Page Orientation
1. Click Layout tab.
2. Click Orientation button.
3. Click orientation option.

Change Paper Size
1. Click Layout tab.
2. Click Size button.
3. Click size option.

Figure 4.3 Margins Button Drop-Down List

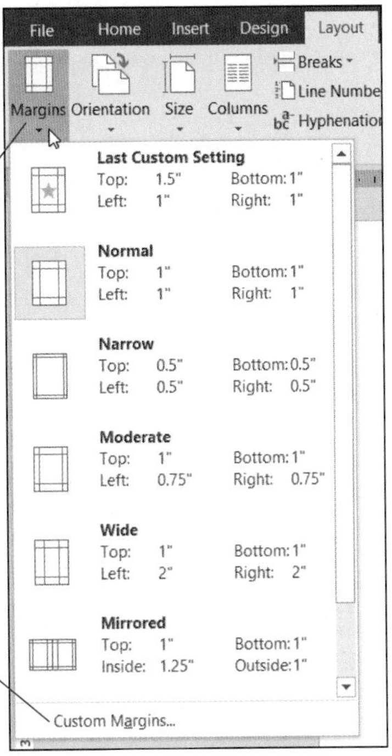

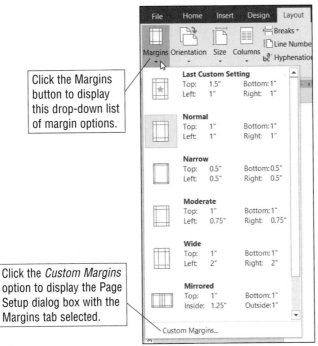

Click the Margins button to display this drop-down list of margin options.

Click the *Custom Margins* option to display the Page Setup dialog box with the Margins tab selected.

Project 2a Changing Margins, Page Orientation, and Size

Part 1 of 2

1. Open **Netiquette.docx** and then save it with the name **4-Netiquette**.
2. Click the Layout tab.
3. Click the Margins button in the Page Setup group and then click the *Narrow* option.
4. Click the Orientation button in the Page Setup group and then click *Landscape* at the drop-down list.

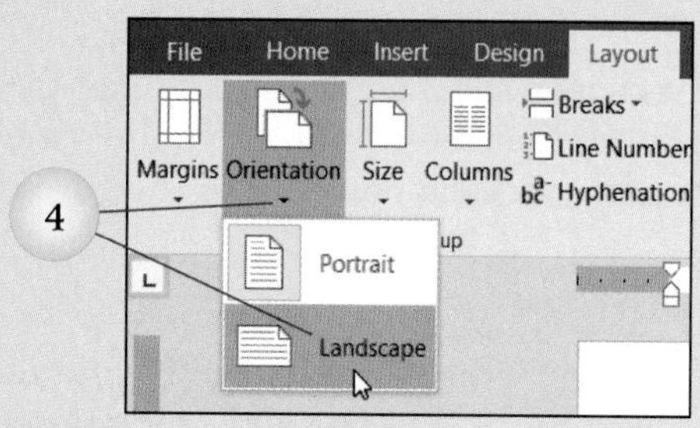

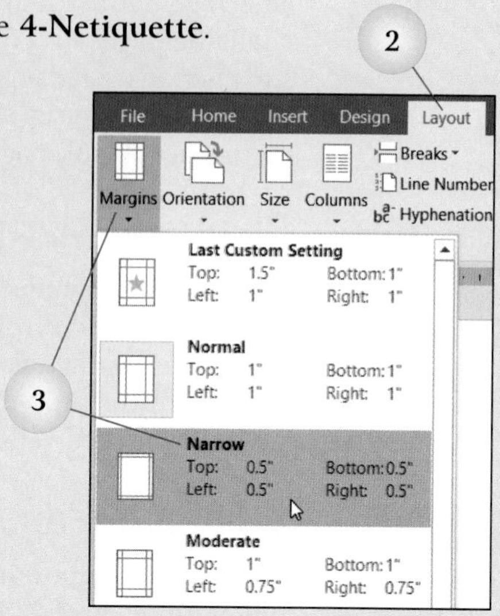

5. Scroll through the document and notice how the text displays on the page in landscape orientation.
6. Click the Orientation button in the Page Setup group and then click *Portrait* at the drop-down list. (This changes the orientation back to the default.)
7. Click the Size button in the Page Setup group and then click the *Executive* option (displays with *7.25" × 10.5"* below *Executive*). If this option is not available, choose an option with a similar paper size.

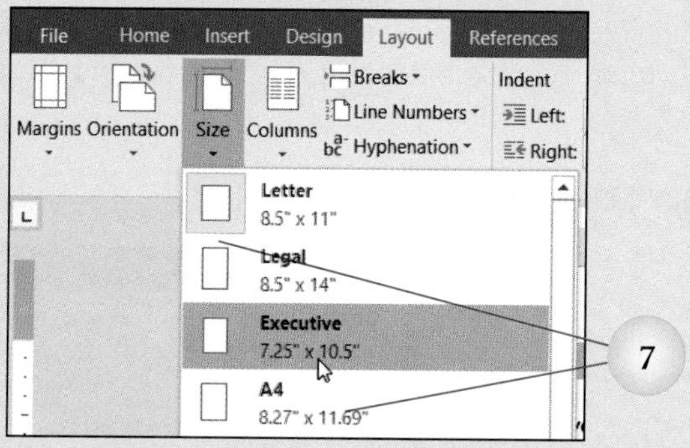

8. Scroll through the document and notice how the text displays on the page.
9. Click the Size button and then click *Legal* (displays with *8.5" × 14"* below *Legal*).
10. Scroll through the document and notice how the text displays on the page.
11. Click the Size button and then click *Letter* (displays with *8.5" × 11"* below *Letter*). (This returns the size back to the default.)
12. Save **4-Netiquette.docx**.

Check Your Work

Quick Steps

Change Margins at the Page Setup Dialog Box

1. Click Layout tab.
2. Click Page Setup group dialog box launcher.
3. Specify margins.
4. Click OK.

Change Paper Size at the Page Setup Dialog Box

1. Click Layout tab.
2. Click Size button.
3. Click *More Paper Sizes* at drop-down list.
4. Specify size.
5. Click OK.

Changing Margins at the Page Setup Dialog Box

The Margins button in the Page Setup group provides a number of preset margins. If these margins do not provide the desired margins, set specific margins at the Page Setup dialog box with the Margins tab selected, as shown in Figure 4.4. Display this dialog box by clicking the Page Setup group dialog box launcher or by clicking the Margins button and then clicking *Custom Margins* at the bottom of the drop-down list.

To change one of the margins, select the current measurement in the *Top*, *Bottom*, *Left*, or *Right* measurement box and then type the new measurement, or click the measurement box up arrow to increase the measurement or the measurement box down arrow to decrease the measurement. As the margin measurements change at the Page Setup dialog box, the sample page in the *Preview* section shows the effects of the changes.

Changing Paper Size at the Page Setup Dialog Box

The Size button drop-down list contains a number of preset paper sizes. If these sizes do not provide the desired paper size, specify a paper size at the Page Setup dialog box with the Paper tab selected. Display this dialog box by clicking the Size button in the Page Setup group and then clicking *More Paper Sizes* at the bottom of the drop-down list.

Figure 4.4 Page Setup Dialog Box with Margins Tab Selected

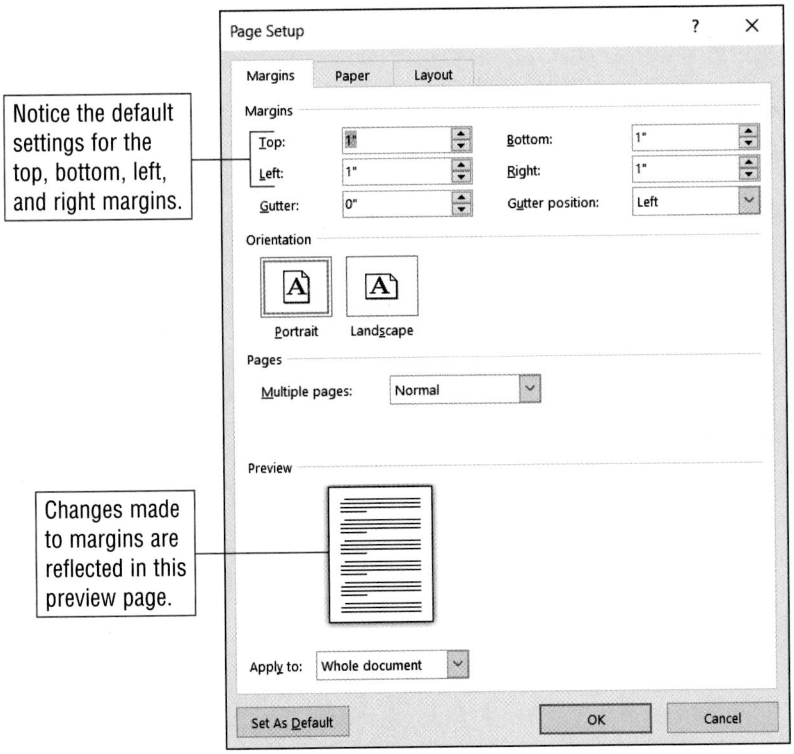

Project 2b Changing Margins at the Page Setup Dialog Box

Part 2 of 2

1. With **4-Netiquette.docx** open, make sure the Layout tab is selected.
2. Click the Page Setup group dialog box launcher.
3. At the Page Setup dialog box with the Margins tab selected, click the *Top* measurement box up arrow until *0.7"* displays.
4. Click the *Bottom* measurement box up arrow until *0.7"* displays.
5. Select the current measurement in the *Left* measurement box and then type 0.75.
6. Select the current measurement in the *Right* measurement box and then type 0.75.
7. Click OK to close the dialog box.
8. Click the Size button in the Page Setup group and then click *More Paper Sizes* at the drop-down list.
9. At the Page Setup dialog box with the Paper tab selected, click the *Paper size* option box arrow and then click *Legal* at the drop-down list.
10. Click OK to close the dialog box.
11. Scroll through the document and notice how the text displays on the page.
12. Click the Size button in the Page Setup group and then click *Letter* at the drop-down list.
13. Save, print, and then close **4-Netiquette.docx**.

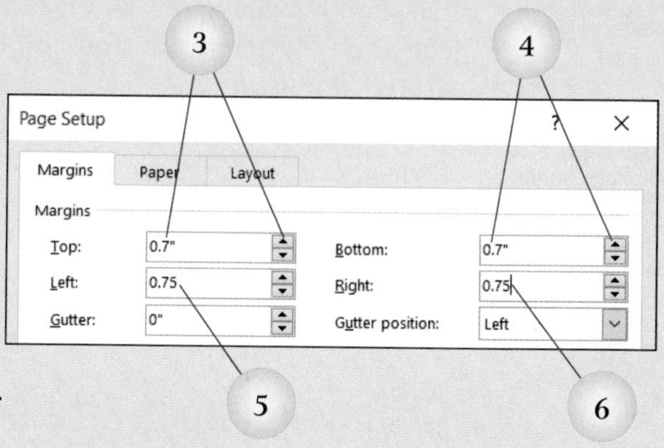

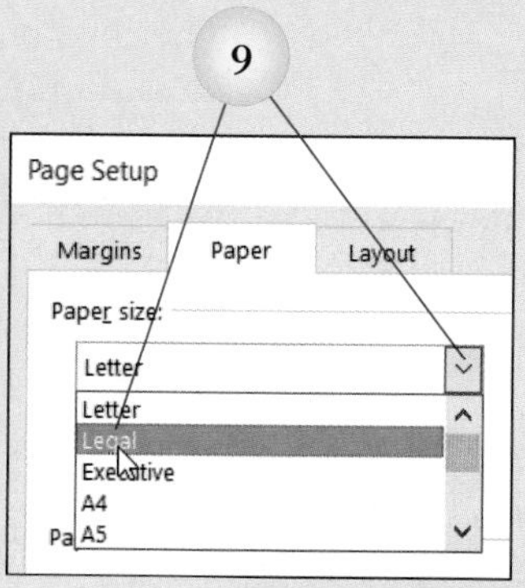

Check Your Work

Project 3 Customize a Report on Computer Input and Output Devices

3 Parts

You will open a document containing information on computer input and output devices and then insert page breaks, a blank page, a cover page, and page numbering.

Preview Finished Project

Tutorial

Inserting and Removing a Page Break

Page Break

Inserting and Removing a Page Break

With the default top and bottom margins set at 1 inch, approximately 9 inches of text prints on the page. At approximately the 10-inch mark, Word automatically inserts a page break. Insert a page break manually in a document with the keyboard shortcut Ctrl + Enter or with the Page Break button in the Pages group on the Insert tab.

A page break inserted by Word is considered a soft page break and a page break inserted manually is considered a hard page break. Soft page breaks automatically adjust if text is added to or deleted from a document. Hard page breaks do not adjust and are therefore less flexible than soft page breaks.

Quick Steps

Insert a Page Break
1. Click Insert tab.
2. Click Page Break button.

OR

Press Ctrl + Enter.

If text is added to or deleted from a document containing a hard page break, check the break to determine whether it is still in a desirable location. Display a hard page break, along with other nonprinting characters, by clicking the Show/Hide ¶ button in the Paragraph group on the Home tab. A hard page break displays as a row of dots with the words *Page Break* in the center. To delete a hard page break, position the insertion point at the beginning of the page break and then press the Delete key. If the display of nonprinting characters is turned off, delete a hard page break by positioning the insertion point immediately below the page break and then pressing the Backspace key.

Project 3a Inserting Page Breaks

Parts 1 of 3

1. Open **CompDevices.docx** and then save it with the name **4-CompDevices**.
2. Change the top margin by completing the following steps:
   a. Click the Layout tab.
   b. Click the Page Setup group dialog box launcher.
   c. At the Page Setup dialog box, click the Margins tab and then type 1.5 in the *Top* measurement box.
   d. Click OK to close the dialog box.

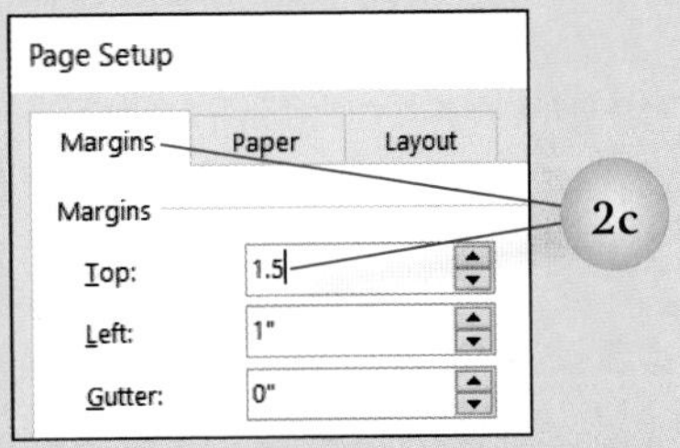

3. Insert a page break at the beginning of the heading *Mouse* by completing the following steps:
   a. Position the insertion point at the beginning of the heading *Mouse* (at the bottom of page 1).
   b. Click the Insert tab and then click the Page Break button in the Pages group.
4. Move the insertion point to the beginning of the title *COMPUTER OUTPUT DEVICES* (on the second page) and then insert a page break by pressing Ctrl + Enter.
5. Move the insertion point to the beginning of the heading *Printer* and then press Ctrl + Enter to insert a page break.

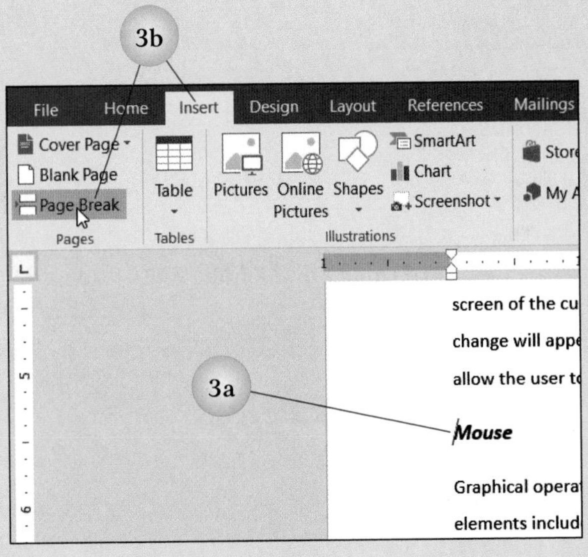

6. Delete a page break by completing the following steps:
   a. Click the Home tab.
   b. Click the Show/Hide ¶ button in the Paragraph group.
   c. Scroll up to display the bottom of the third page, position the insertion point at the beginning of the page break (displays with the words *Page Break*), and then press the Delete key.
   d. Press the Delete key again to remove the blank line.
   e. Turn off the display of nonprinting characters by clicking the Show/Hide ¶ button in the Paragraph group on the Home tab.
7. Save **4-CompDevices.docx**.

Check Your Work

Tutorial

Inserting and Removing a Blank Page

Blank Page

Inserting and Removing a Blank Page

Click the Blank Page button in the Pages group on the Insert tab to insert a blank page at the position of the insertion point. This might be useful in a document where a blank page is needed for an illustration, graphic, or figure. When a blank page is inserted, Word inserts a page break and then inserts another page break to create the blank page. To remove a blank page, turn on the display of nonprinting characters and then delete the page breaks.

Tutorial

Inserting and Removing a Cover Page

Cover Page

Quick Steps

Insert Blank Page

1. Click Insert tab.
2. Click Blank Page button.

Insert Cover Page

1. Click Insert tab.
2. Click Cover Page button.
3. Click cover page at drop-down list.

Hint Adding a cover page gives a document a polished and professional look.

Inserting and Removing a Cover Page

Consider inserting a cover page to improve the visual appeal of a document or to prepare it for distribution to others. Use the Cover Page button in the Pages group on the Insert tab to insert a predesigned cover page and then type personalized text in the placeholders on the page. Click the Cover Page button and a drop-down list displays with visual representations of the cover pages. Scroll through the list and then click a predesigned cover page option.

A predesigned cover page contains location placeholders, in which specific text is entered. For example, a cover page might contain the *[Document title]* placeholder. Click the placeholder to select it and then type personalized text. Delete a placeholder by clicking the placeholder to select it, clicking the placeholder tab, and then pressing the Delete key. Remove a cover page by clicking the Cover Page button and then clicking *Remove Current Cover Page* at the drop-down list.

Project 3b Inserting a Blank Page and a Cover Page

Part 2 of 3

1. With **4-CompDevices.docx** open, create a blank page by completing the following steps:
   a. Move the insertion point to the beginning of the heading *Touchpad and Touchscreen* on the second page.
   b. Click the Insert tab.
   c. Click the Blank Page button in the Pages group.
2. Insert a cover page by completing the following steps:
   a. Press Ctrl + Home to move the insertion point to the beginning of the document.
   b. Click the Cover Page button in the Pages group.
   c. Scroll down the drop-down list and then click the *Motion* cover page.

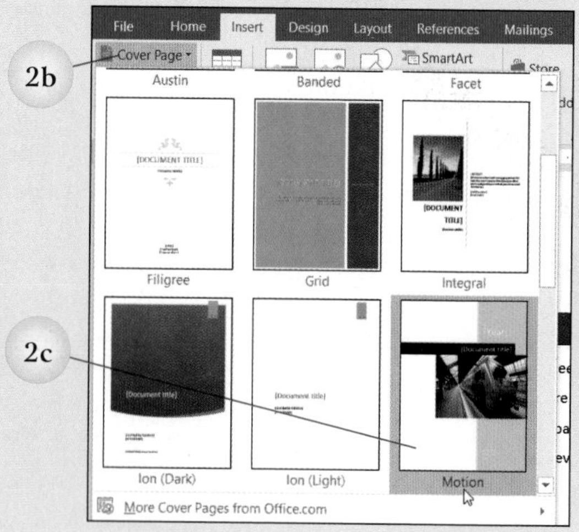

d. Click the *[Document title]* placeholder and then type Computer Devices.

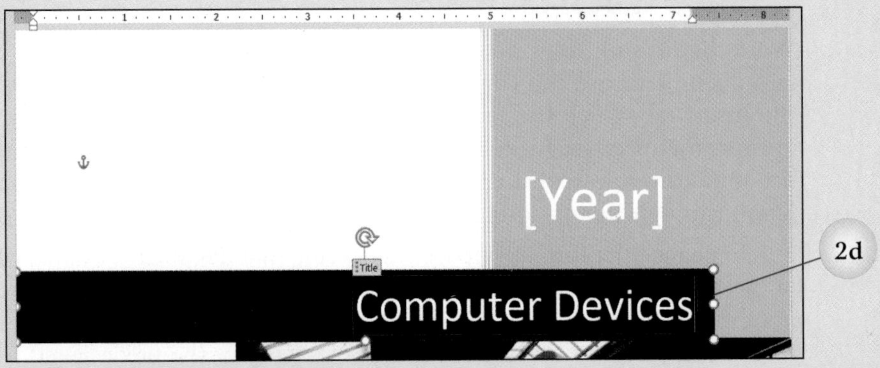

e. Click the *[Year]* placeholder. Click the placeholder down arrow and then click the Today button at the bottom of the drop-down calendar.

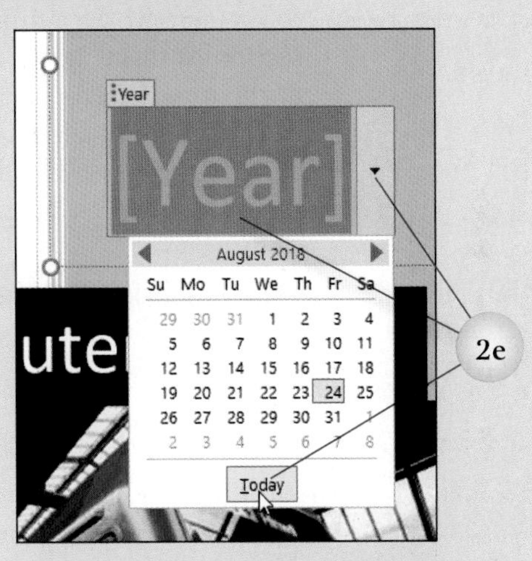

f. Click the *[Company name]* placeholder and then type Drake Computing. (If a name displays in the placeholder, select the name and then type Drake Computing.)

g. Select the name above the company name and then type your first and last names. If, instead of a name, the *[Author name]* placeholder displays above the company name, click the placeholder and then type your first and last names.

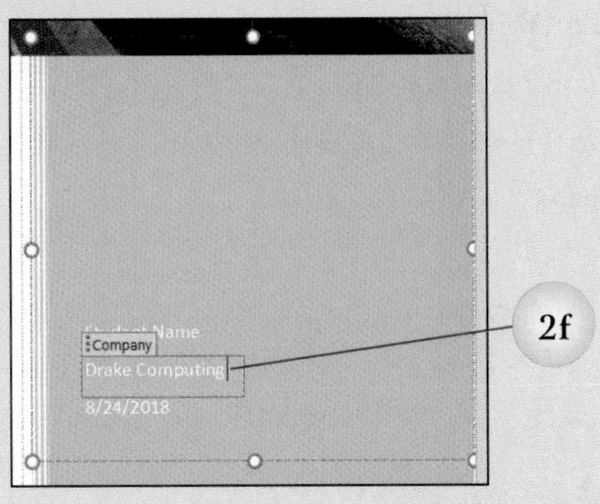

3. Remove the blank page you inserted in Step 1 by completing the following steps:
   a. Move the insertion point immediately right of the period that ends the last sentence in the paragraph of text in the *Trackball* section the bottom of page 3).
   b. Press the Delete key on the keyboard approximately six times until the heading *Touchpad and Touchscreen* displays on page 3.

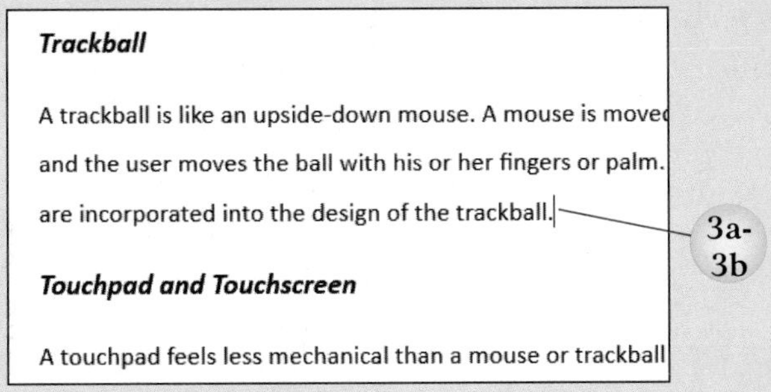

4. Save **4-CompDevices.docx**.

Check Your Work

Tutorial

Inserting and Removing Page Numbers

Page Number

Inserting and Removing Page Numbers

Word, by default, does not print page numbers on pages. To insert page numbers in a document, use the Page Number button in the Header & Footer group on the Insert tab. Click the Page Number button and a drop-down list displays with options for specifying the location of the page number. Point to an option in this list and a drop-down list displays a number of predesigned page number formats. Scroll through the options in the drop-down list and then click an option.

To change the format of page numbering in a document, double-click the page number, select the page number text, and then apply the formatting. Remove page numbers from a document by clicking the Page Number button and then clicking *Remove Page Numbers* at the drop-down list. Many of the predesigned page number formats insert page numbers in a header or footer pane. As explained in the next section of this chapter, a header pane contains text, such as a page number, that prints at the top of each page and a footer pane contains text that prints at the bottom of each page. If a page number is inserted in a header or footer pane, close the pane by clicking the Close Header and Footer button on the Header & Footer Tools Design tab or by double-clicking in the document, outside the header or footer pane.

Quick Steps

Insert Page Numbers

1. Click Insert tab.
2. Click Page Number button.
3. Click option at drop-down list.

Project 3c Inserting Predesigned Page Numbers — Part 3 of 3

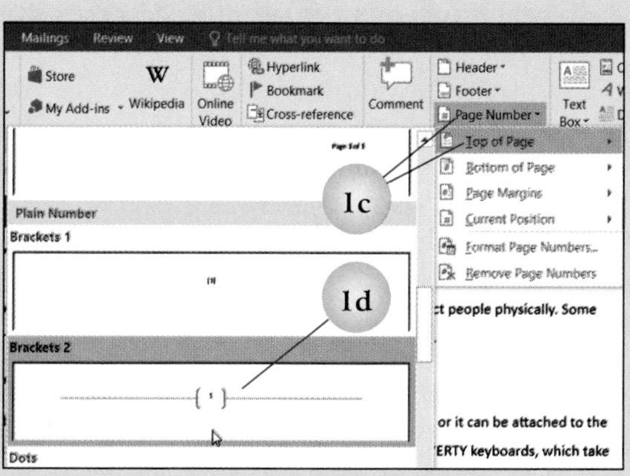

1. With **4-CompDevices.docx** open, insert page numbering by completing the following steps:
   a. Move the insertion point so it is positioned anywhere in the title *COMPUTER INPUT DEVICES*.
   b. Click the Insert tab.
   c. Click the Page Number button in the Header & Footer group and then point to *Top of Page*.
   d. Scroll through the drop-down list and then click the *Brackets 2* option.
2. Click the Close Header and Footer button on the Header & Footer Tools Design tab.
3. Scroll through the document and notice the page numbering that displays at the top of each page except the cover page. (The cover page and text are divided by a page break. Word does not include the cover page when numbering pages.)
4. Remove the page numbering by clicking the Insert tab, clicking the Page Number button, and then clicking *Remove Page Numbers* at the drop-down list.
5. Click the Page Number button, point to *Bottom of Page*, scroll down the drop-down list, and then click the *Accent Bar 2* option.
6. Click the Close Header and Footer button on the Header & Footer Tools Design tab.
7. Save, print, and then close **4-CompDevices.docx**.

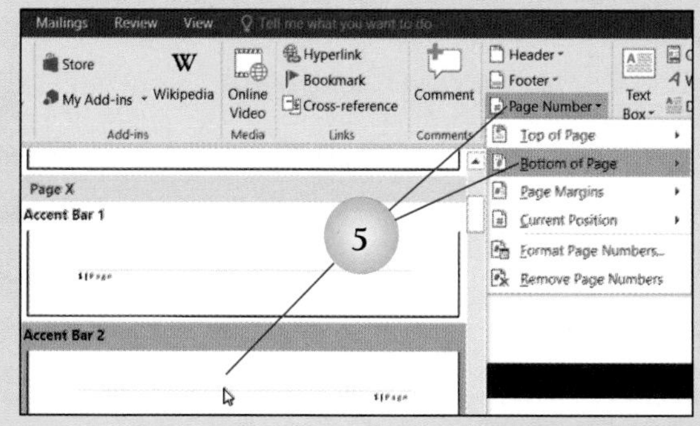

Check Your Work

Project 4 Add Elements to a Report on the Writing Process — 3 Parts

You will open a document containing information on the process of writing effectively, insert a predesigned header and footer, remove a header, and format and delete header and footer elements.

Preview Finished Project

Tutorial

Inserting and Removing a Predesigned Header and Footer

Header

Quick Steps

Insert Predesigned Header or Footer

1. Click Insert tab.
2. Click Header button or Footer button.
3. Click option at drop-down list.
4. Type text in specific placeholders in header or footer.
5. Click Close Header and Footer button.

Inserting Predesigned Headers and Footers

Text that appears in the top margin of a page is called a *header* and text that appears in the bottom margin of a page is referred to as a *footer*. Headers and footers are common in manuscripts, textbooks, reports, and other publications.

Insert a predesigned header in a document by clicking the Insert tab and then clicking the Header button in the Header & Footer group. This displays the Header button drop-down list. At this list, click a predesigned header option and the header is inserted in the document. Headers and footers are visible in Print Layout view but not Draft view.

A predesigned header or footer may contain location placeholders for entering specific information. For example, a header might contain the *[Document title]* placeholder. Click the placeholder and all the placeholder text is selected. With the placeholder text selected, type the personalized text. Delete a placeholder by clicking the placeholder to select it, clicking the placeholder tab, and then pressing the Delete key.

To return to the document after inserting a header or footer, double-click in the document outside the header or footer pane or click the Close Header and Footer button on the Header & Footer Tools Design tab.

Project 4a Inserting a Predesigned Header in a Document — Part 1 of 3

1. Open **WritingProcess.docx** and then save it with the name **4-WritingProcess**.
2. Press Ctrl + End to move the insertion point to the end of the document.
3. Move the insertion point to the beginning of the heading *REFERENCES* and then insert a page break by clicking the Insert tab and then clicking the Page Break button in the Pages group.

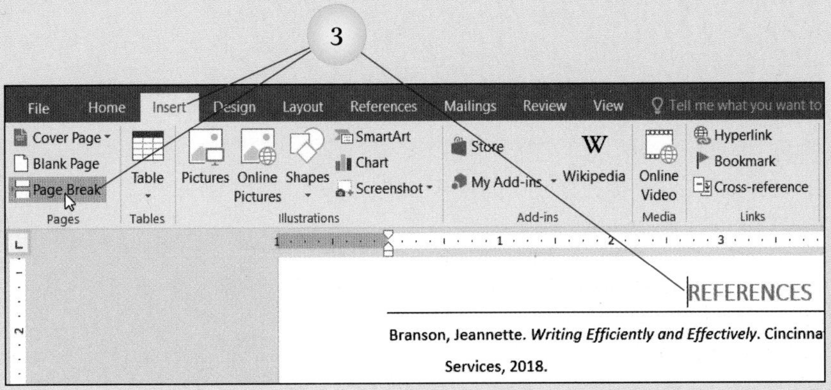

4. Press Ctrl + Home to move the insertion point to the beginning of the document and then insert a header by completing the following steps:
   a. If necessary, click the Insert tab.
   b. Click the Header button in the Header & Footer group.
   c. Scroll to the bottom of the drop-down list and then click the *Sideline* option.

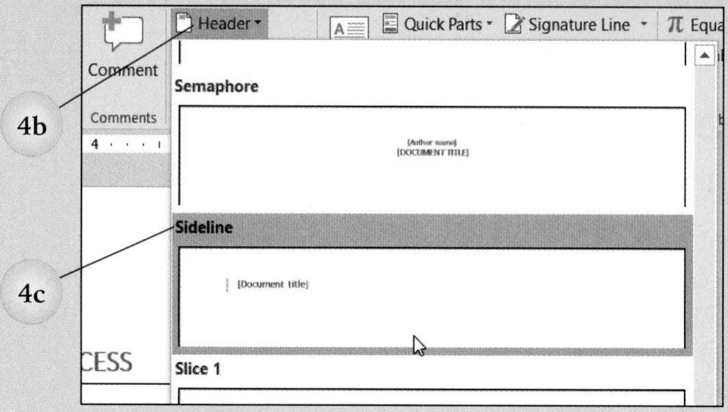

   d. Click the *[Document title]* placeholder and then type The Writing Process.
   e. Double-click in the document text. (This makes the document text active and dims the header.)
5. Scroll through the document to see how the header will print.
6. Save and then print **4-WritingProcess.docx**.

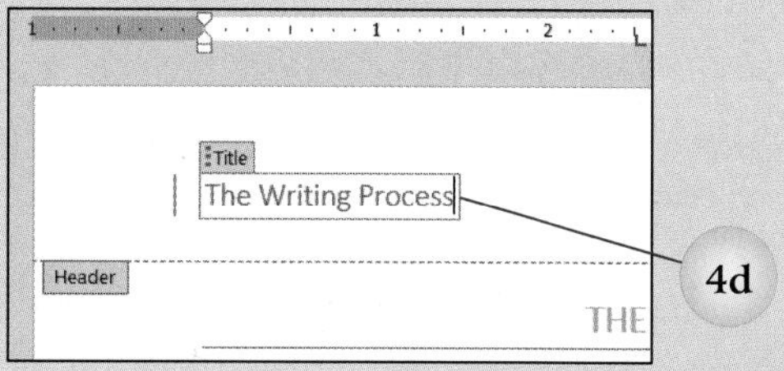

Check Your Work

Footer

Insert a predesigned footer in the same manner as inserting a header. Click the Footer button in the Header & Footer group on the Insert tab and a drop-down list displays that is similar to the Header button drop-down list. Click a footer and the predesigned footer is inserted in the document.

Removing a Header or Footer

Remove a header from a document by clicking the Insert tab and then clicking the Header button in the Header & Footer group. At the drop-down list, click the *Remove Header* option. Complete similar steps to remove a footer.

Project 4b Removing a Header and Inserting a Predesigned Footer

Part 2 of 3

1. With **4-WritingProcess.docx** open, press Ctrl + Home to move the insertion point to the beginning of the document.
2. Remove the header by clicking the Insert tab, clicking the Header button in the Header & Footer group, and then clicking the *Remove Header* option at the drop-down list.

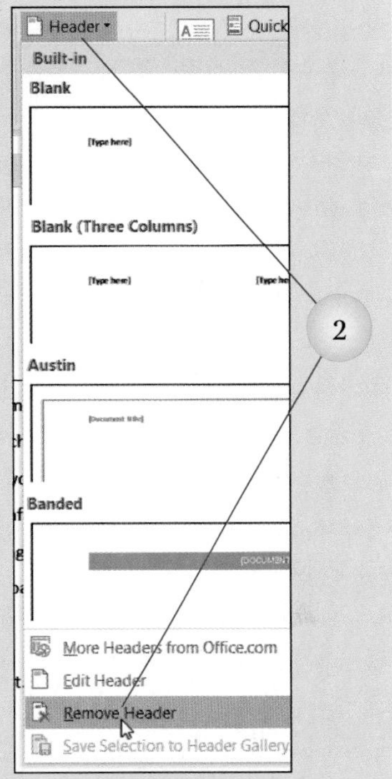

3. Insert a footer in the document by completing the following steps:
   a. Click the Footer button in the Header & Footer group.
   b. Scroll down the drop-down list and then click *Ion (Light)*.

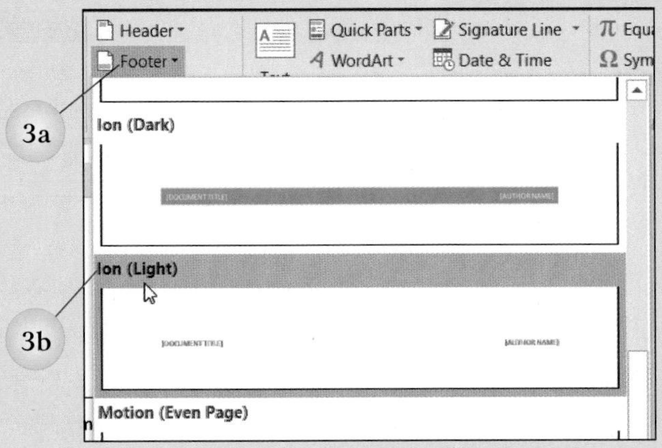

   c. Notice that Word inserted the document title at the left side of the footer. (Word remembered the document title you entered in the header.) Word also inserted your name at the right side of the footer. If the document title does not display, click the *[DOCUMENT TITLE]* placeholder and then type THE WRITING PROCESS. If your name does not display, click the *[AUTHOR NAME]* placeholder and then type your first and last names.
   d. Click the Close Header and Footer button on the Header & Footer Tools Design tab to close the Footer pane and return to the document.
4. Scroll through the document to see how the footer will print.
5. Save and then print **4-WritingProcess.docx**.

Check Your Work

Editing a Predesigned Header or Footer

Predesigned headers and footers contain elements such as page numbers, a title, and an author's name. The formatting of an element can be changed by clicking the element and then applying formatting. Delete an element from a header or footer by selecting the element and then pressing the Delete key.

Project 4c Formatting and Deleting Header and Footer Elements

Part 3 of 3

1. With **4-WritingProcess.docx** open, remove the footer by clicking the Insert tab, clicking the Footer button, and then clicking *Remove Footer* at the drop-down list.
2. Insert and then format a header by completing the following steps:
   a. Click the Header button in the Header & Footer group on the Insert tab, scroll down the drop-down list, and then click *Grid*. (This header inserts the document title and a date placeholder.)
   b. Delete the date placeholder by clicking the *[Date]* placeholder, clicking the placeholder tab, and then pressing the Delete key.
   c. Double-click in the document text.

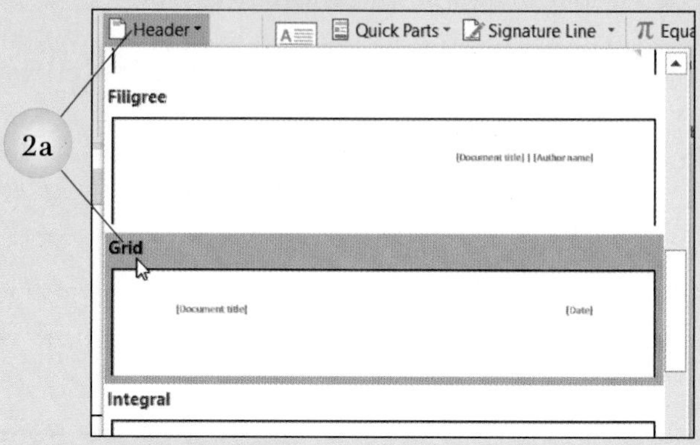

3. Insert and then format a footer by completing the following steps:
   a. Click the Insert tab.
   b. Click the Footer button, scroll down the drop-down list, and then click *Retrospect*.
   c. Select the name in the author placeholder at the left side of the footer and then type your first and last names.
   d. Select your name and the page number, apply bold formatting, and then change the font size to 10 point.
   e. Click the Close Header and Footer button.
4. Scroll through the document to see how the header and footer will print.
5. Save, print, and then close **4-WritingProcess.docx**.

Check Your Work

Project 5 Format a Report on Desirable Employee Qualities

2 Parts

You will open a document containing information on desirable employee qualities and then insert a watermark, change the page background color, and insert a page border.

Preview Finished Project

Quick Steps

Insert a Watermark

1. Click Design tab.
2. Click Watermark button.
3. Click option.

Quick Steps

Apply Page Background Color

1. Click Design tab.
2. Click Page Color button.
3. Click option.

Formatting the Page Background

The Page Background group on the Design tab contains three buttons for customizing the page background. Click the Watermark button and choose a predesigned watermark from options at the drop-down list. If a document is going to be viewed on-screen or on the Web, consider adding a page background color. Chapter 3 covered how to apply borders and shading to text at the Borders and Shading dialog box. This dialog box also contains options for inserting a page border. Display the Borders and Shading dialog box with the Page Border tab selected by clicking the Page Borders button in the Page Background group.

Tutorial

Inserting and Removing a Watermark

Watermark

Inserting a Watermark

A watermark is a lightened image that displays behind the text in a document. Use a watermark to add visual appeal or to identify a document as a draft, sample, or confidential document. Word provides a number of predesigned watermarks. Display these watermarks by clicking the Watermark button in the Page Background group on the Design tab. Scroll through the list of watermarks and then click an option.

Tutorial

Applying Page Background Color

Page Color

Applying Page Background Color

Use the Page Color button in the Page Background group to apply a background color to a document. This background color is intended for viewing a document on-screen or on the web. The color is visible on the screen but does not print. Insert a page color by clicking the Page Color button and then clicking a color at the drop-down color palette.

Project 5a Inserting a Watermark and Applying a Page Background Color

Part 1 of 2

1. Open **EmpQualities.docx** and then save it with the name **4-EmpQualities**.
2. Insert a watermark by completing the following steps:
   a. With the insertion point positioned at the beginning of the document, click the Design tab.
   b. Click the Watermark button in the Page Background group.
   c. At the drop-down list, click the *CONFIDENTIAL 1* option.
3. Scroll through the document and notice how the watermark displays behind the text.
4. Remove the watermark and insert a different one by completing the following steps:
   a. Click the Watermark button in the Page Background group and then click *Remove Watermark* at the drop-down list.
   b. Click the Watermark button and then click the *DO NOT COPY 1* option at the drop-down list.
5. Scroll through the document and notice how the watermark displays.
6. Move the insertion point to the beginning of the document.
7. Click the Page Color button in the Page Background group and then click the *Tan, Background 2* color option (third column, first row in the *Theme Colors* section).
8. Save **4-EmpQualities.docx**.

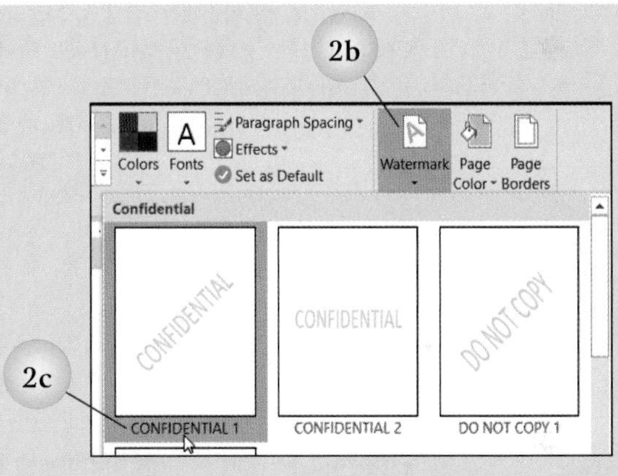

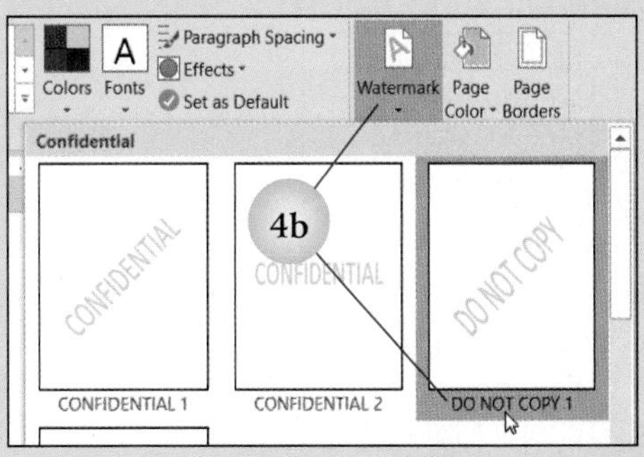

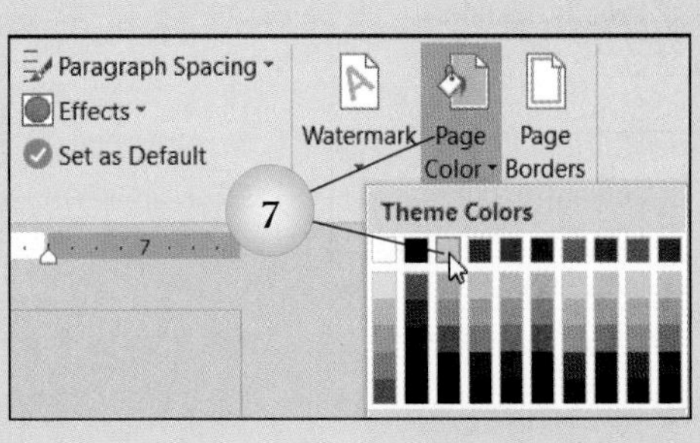

Check Your Work

Tutorial

Inserting a Page Border

Page Borders

Quick Steps

Insert Page Border
1. Click Design tab.
2. Click Page Borders button.
3. Specify options at dialog box.

Inserting a Page Border

To improve the visual appeal of a document, consider inserting a page border. When a page border is inserted in a multiple-page document, it prints on each page. To insert a page border, click the Page Borders button in the Page Background group on the Design tab. This displays the Borders and Shading dialog box with the Page Border tab selected, as shown in Figure 4.5. At this dialog box, specify the border style, color, and width.

The dialog box contains an option for inserting a page border containing an art image. To display the images available, click the *Art* option box arrow, scroll through the drop-down list, and then click an image.

Changing Page Border Options

By default, a page border displays and prints 24 points from the top, left, right, and bottom edges of the page. Some printers, particularly inkjet printers, have a nonprinting area around the outside edges of the page that can interfere with the printing of a border. Before printing a document with a page border, click the File tab and then click the *Print* option. Look at the preview of the page at the right side of the Print backstage area and determine whether the entire border is visible. If a portion of the border is not visible in the preview page (generally at the bottom and right sides of the page), consider changing measurements at the Border and Shading Options dialog box, shown in Figure 4.6.

Display the Border and Shading Options dialog box by clicking the Design tab and then clicking the Page Borders button. At the Borders and Shading dialog box with the Page Border tab selected, click the Options button in the lower right corner of the dialog box. The options at the Border and Shading Options dialog box change depending on whether the Borders tab or the Page Border tab is selected when the Options button is clicked.

Figure 4.5 Borders and Shading Dialog Box with Page Border Tab Selected

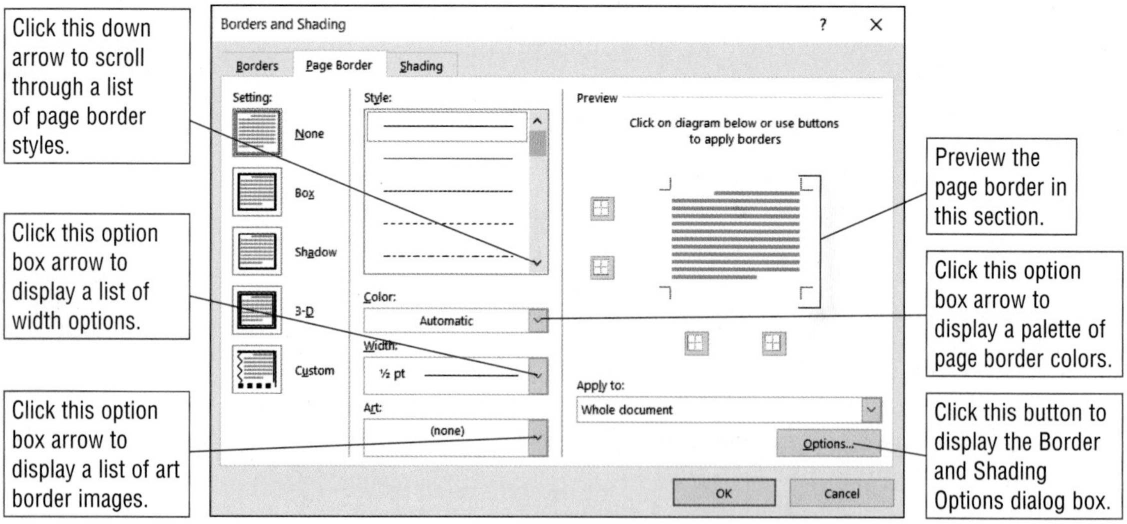

Figure 4.6 Border and Shading Options Dialog Box

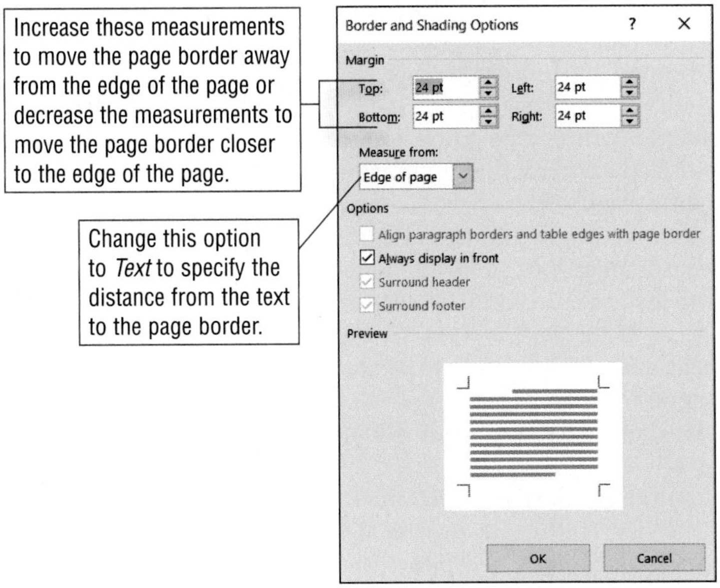

If a printer contains a nonprinting area and the entire page border will not print, consider increasing the spacing from the page border to the edge of the page. Do this with the *Top*, *Left*, *Bottom*, and/or *Right* measurement boxes. The *Measure from* option box has a default setting of *Edge of page*. This option can be changed to *Text*, which changes the top and bottom measurements to *1 pt* and the left and right measurements to *4 pt* and moves the page border into the page. Use the measurement boxes to specify the distances the page border should display and print from the edges of the text in the document.

Project 5b Inserting a Page Border

Part 2 of 2

1. With **4-EmpQualities.docx** open, remove the page color by clicking the Page Color button in the Page Background group on the Design tab and then clicking the *No Color* option.
2. Insert a page border by completing the following steps:
   a. Click the Page Borders button in the Page Background group on the Design tab.
   b. Click the *Box* option in the *Setting* section.
   c. Scroll down the list of line styles in the *Style* list box until the last line style displays and then click the third line from the end.
   d. Click the *Color* option box arrow and then click the *Dark Red, Accent 2* color option (sixth column, first row in the *Theme Colors* section).
   e. Click OK to close the dialog box.

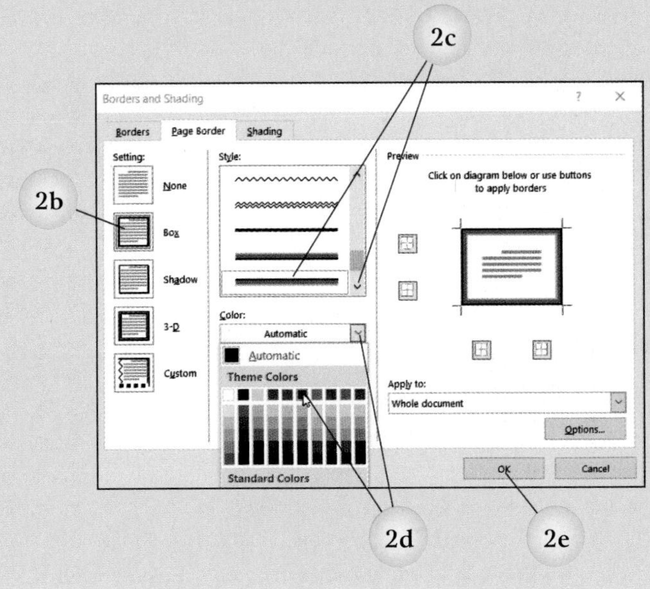

3. Increase the spacing from the page border to the edges of the page by completing the following steps:
   a. Click the Page Borders button in the Page Background group on the Design tab.
   b. At the Borders and Shading dialog box with the Page Border tab selected, click the Options button in the lower right corner.
   c. At the Border and Shading Options dialog box, click the *Top* measurement box up arrow until *31 pt* displays. (This is the maximum measurement allowed.)
   d. Increase the measurements in the *Left, Bottom,* and *Right* measurement boxes to *31 pt.*
   e. Click OK to close the Border and Shading Options dialog box.
   f. Click OK to close the Borders and Shading dialog box.

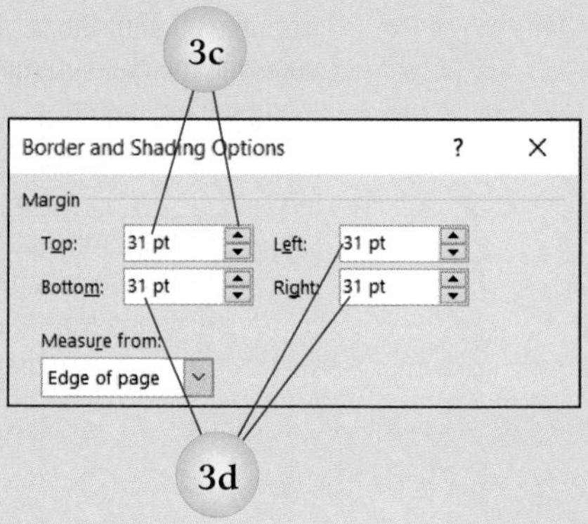

4. Save **4-EmpQualities.docx** and then print page 1.
5. Insert an image page border and change the page border spacing options by completing the following steps:
   a. Click the Page Borders button in the Page Background group on the Design tab.
   b. Click the *Art* option box arrow and then click the border image shown at the right (approximately one-third of the way down the drop-down list).
   c. Click the Options button in the lower right corner of the Borders and Shading dialog box.
   d. At the Border and Shading Options dialog box, click the *Measure from* option box arrow and then click *Text* at the drop-down list.
   e. Click the *Top* measurement box up arrow until *10 pt* displays.
   f. Increase the measurement in the *Bottom* measurement box to *10 pt* and the measurements in the *Left* and *Right* measurement boxes to *14 pt.*
   g. Click the *Surround header* check box to remove the check mark.
   h. Click the *Surround footer* check box to remove the check mark.
   i. Click OK to close the Border and Shading Options dialog box.
   j. Click OK to close the Borders and Shading dialog box.

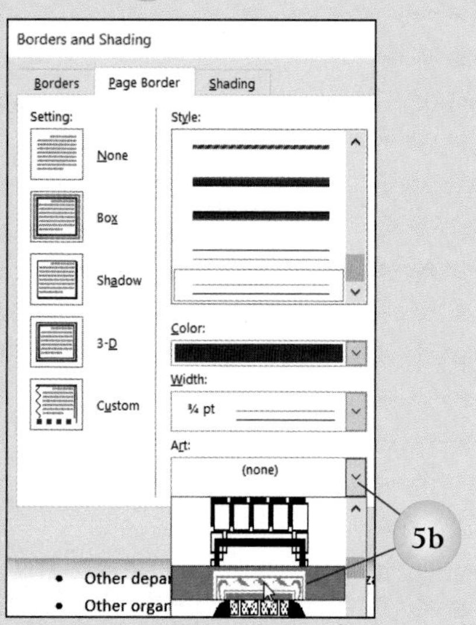

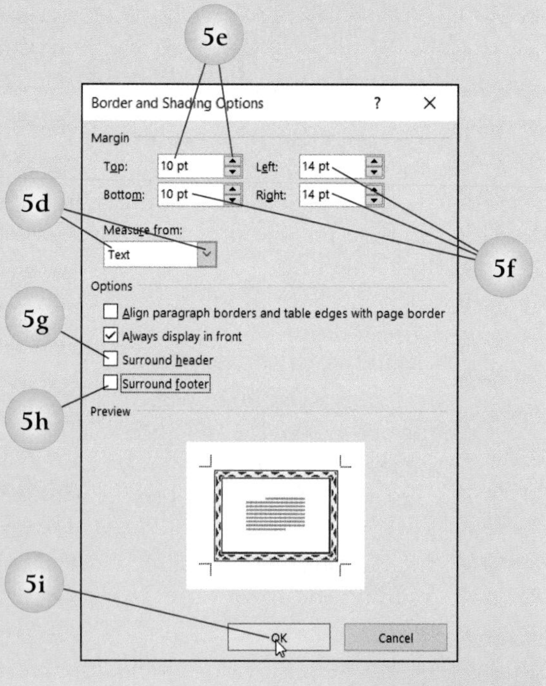

6. Save, print, and then close **4-EmpQualities.docx**.

Check Your Work

Project 6 **Format a Lease Agreement** **4 Parts**

You will open a lease agreement, search for specific text and replace it with other text, and then search for specific formatting and replace it with other formatting.

Preview Finished Project

Finding and Replacing Text and Formatting

Find

Replace

The Editing group on the Home tab contains the Find button and the Replace button. Use the Find button to search for specific text or formatting in a document and use the Replace button to search for and then replace specific text or formatting.

Tutorial

Finding Text

Finding Text

Quick Steps

Find Text

1. Click Find button.
2. Type search text.
3. Click Next button.

Click the Find button in the Editing group on the Home tab (or press the keyboard shortcut Ctrl + F) and the Navigation pane displays at the left side of the screen with the Results tab selected. With this tab selected, type search text in the search text box and any occurrence of the text in the document is highlighted. A fragment of the text surrounding the search text also displays in a thumbnail in the Navigation pane. For example, when searching for *Lessee* in **4-LeaseAgrmnt.docx** in Project 6a, the screen displays as shown in Figure 4.7. Any occurrence of *Lessee* displays highlighted in yellow in the document and the Navigation pane displays thumbnails of the text surrounding the occurrences of *Lessee*.

Figure 4.7 Navigation Pane Showing Search Results

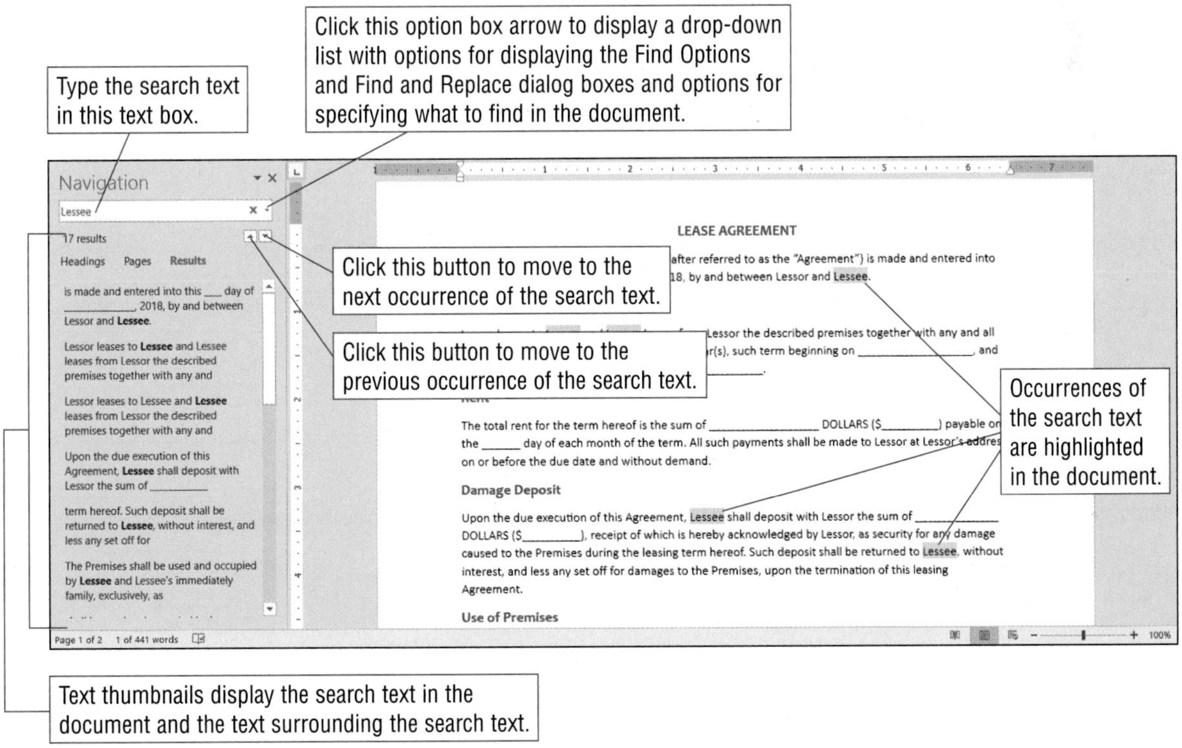

Click this option box arrow to display a drop-down list with options for displaying the Find Options and Find and Replace dialog boxes and options for specifying what to find in the document.
Type the search text in this text box.
Click this button to move to the next occurrence of the search text.
Click this button to move to the previous occurrence of the search text.
Occurrences of the search text are highlighted in the document.
Text thumbnails display the search text in the document and the text surrounding the search text.

Click a text thumbnail in the Navigation pane and the occurrence of the search text is selected in the document. Hover the mouse over a text thumbnail in the Navigation pane and the page number location displays in a small box near the mouse pointer. Move to the next occurrence of the search text by clicking the Next button (contains a down-pointing arrow) below and to the right of the search text box. Click the Previous button (contains an up-pointing arrow) to move to the previous occurrence of the search text.

Click the down arrow at the right side of the search text box and a drop-down list displays. It shows options for displaying dialog boxes, such as the Find Options dialog box and the Find and Replace dialog box. It also shows options for specifying what should be found in the document, such as figures, tables, and equations.

The search text in a document can be highlighted with options at the Find and Replace dialog box with the Find tab selected. Display this dialog box by clicking the Find button arrow in the Editing group on the Home tab and then clicking *Advanced Find* at the drop-down list. Another method for displaying the Find and Replace dialog box is to click the down arrow at the right side of the search text box in the Navigation pane and then click the *Advanced Find* option at the drop-down list. To highlight found text, type the search text in the *Find what* text box, click the Reading Highlight button, and then click *Highlight All* at the drop-down list. All occurrences of the text in the document are highlighted. To remove highlighting, click the Reading Highlight button and then click *Clear Highlighting* at the drop-down list.

Project 6a Finding and Highlighting Text **Part 1 of 4**

1. Open **LeaseAgrmnt.docx** and then save it with the name **4-LeaseAgrmnt.**
2. Find all occurrences of *lease* by completing the following steps:
   a. Click the Find button in the Editing group on the Home tab.
   b. If necessary, click the Results tab in the Navigation pane.
   c. Type lease in the search text box in the Navigation pane.
   d. After a moment, all occurrences of *lease* in the document are highlighted and text thumbnails display in the Navigation pane. Click a couple of the text thumbnails in the Navigation pane to select the text in the document.
   e. Click the Previous button (contains an up-pointing arrow) to select the previous occurrence of *lease* in the document.

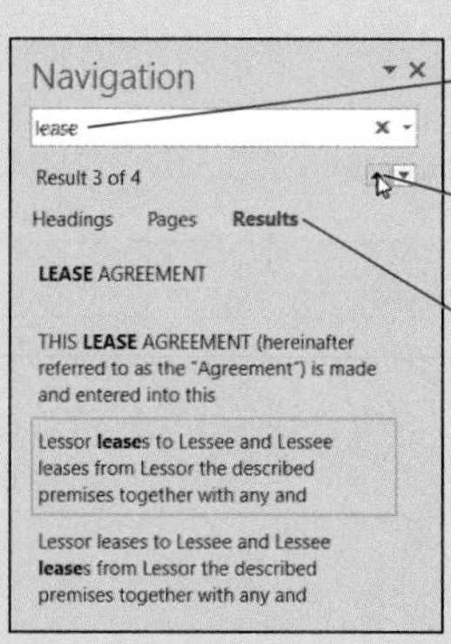

2c

2e

2b

3. Use the Find and Replace dialog box with the Find tab selected to highlight all occurrences of *Premises* in the document by completing the following steps:
   a. Click in the document and press Ctrl + Home to move the insertion point to the beginning of the document.
   b. Click the search option box arrow in the Navigation pane and then click *Advanced Find* at the drop-down list.

3b

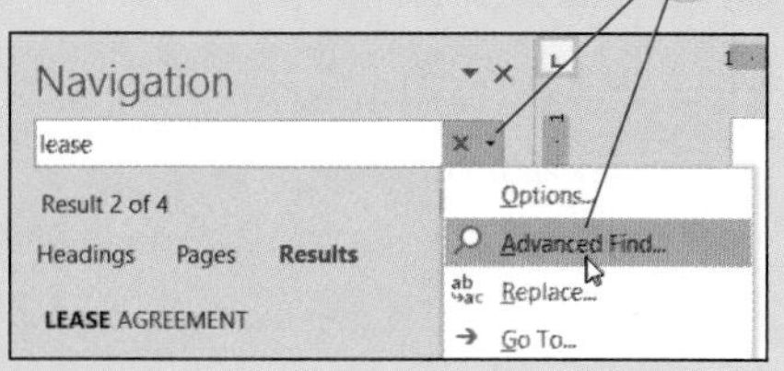

c. At the Find and Replace dialog box with the Find tab selected (and *lease* selected in the *Find what* text box), type Premises.
d. Click the Reading Highlight button and then click *Highlight All* at the drop-down list.
e. Click in the document to make it active and then scroll through the document and notice the occurrences of highlighted text.
f. Click in the dialog box to make it active.
g. Click the Reading Highlight button and then click *Clear Highlighting* at the drop-down list.
h. Click the Close button to close the Find and Replace dialog box.

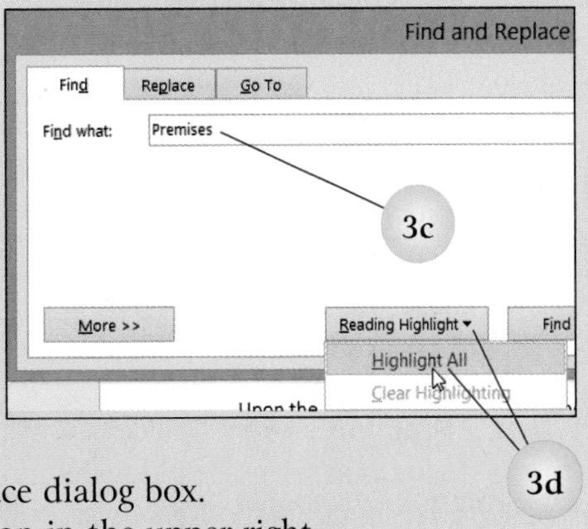

4. Close the Navigation pane by clicking the Close button in the upper right corner of the pane.

Tutorial

Finding and Replacing Text

Finding and Replacing Text

To find and replace text, click the Replace button in the Editing group on the Home tab or use the keyboard shortcut Ctrl + H. This displays the Find and Replace dialog box with the Replace tab selected, as shown in Figure 4.8. Type the search text in the *Find what* text box, press the Tab key, and then type the replacement text in the *Replace with* text box.

The Find and Replace dialog box contains several command buttons. Click the Find Next button to tell Word to find the next occurrence of the text. Click the Replace button to replace the text and find the next occurrence. If all occurrences of the text in the *Find what* text box are to be replaced with the text in the *Replace with* text box, click the Replace All button.

Quick Steps

Find and Replace Text

1. Click Replace button.
2. Type search text.
3. Press Tab key.
4. Type replacement text.
5. Click Replace or Replace All button.

Hint If the Find and Replace dialog box is in the way of specific text, drag it to a different location.

Figure 4.8 Find and Replace Dialog Box with the Replace Tab Selected

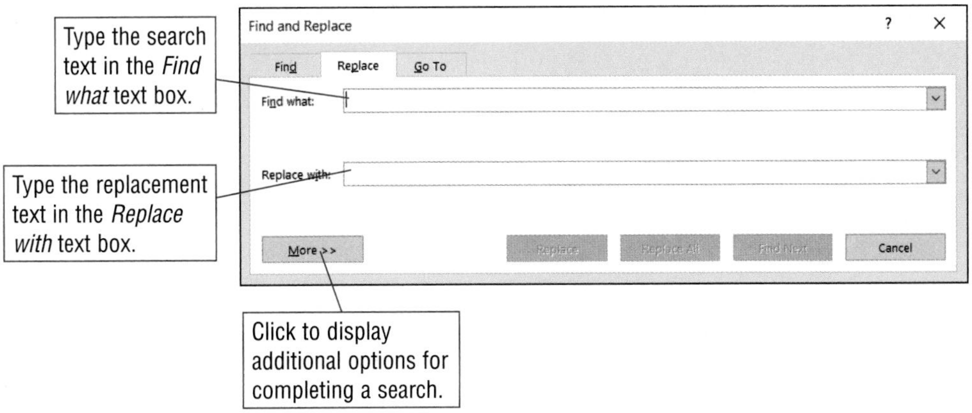

Project 6b Finding and Replacing Text

Part 2 of 4

1. With **4-LeaseAgrmnt.docx** open, make sure the insertion point is positioned at the beginning of the document.
2. Find all occurrences of *Lessor* and replace them with *Tracy Hartford* by completing the following steps:
   a. Click the Replace button in the Editing group on the Home tab.
   b. At the Find and Replace dialog box with the Replace tab selected, type Lessor in the *Find what* text box.
   c. Press the Tab key to move the insertion point to the *Replace with* text box.
   d. Type Tracy Hartford.
   e. Click the Replace All button.
   f. At the message stating that 11 replacements were made, click OK. (Do not close the Find and Replace dialog box.)

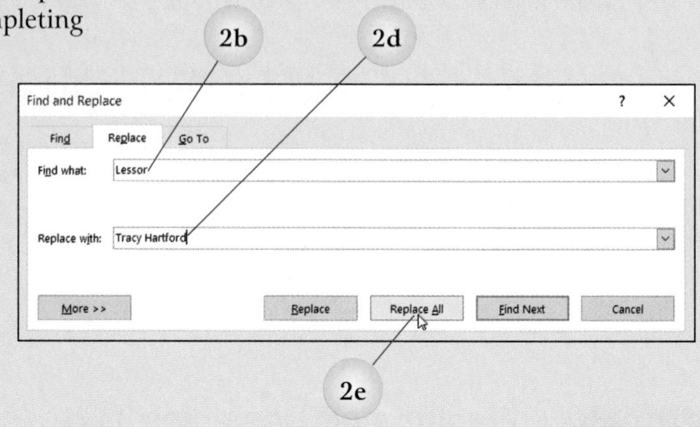

3. With the Find and Replace dialog box still open, complete steps similar to those in Step 2 to find all occurrences of *Lessee* and replace them with *Michael Iwami*.
4. Click the Close button to close the Find and Replace dialog box.
5. Save **4-LeaseAgrmnt.docx**.

Check Your Work

Defining Search Parameters

The Find and Replace dialog box contains a variety of check boxes with options for completing a search. To display these options, click the More button in the lower left corner of the dialog box. This causes the Find and Replace dialog box to expand, as shown in Figure 4.9. Each option and what will occur if it is selected

Figure 4.9 Expanded Find and Replace Dialog Box

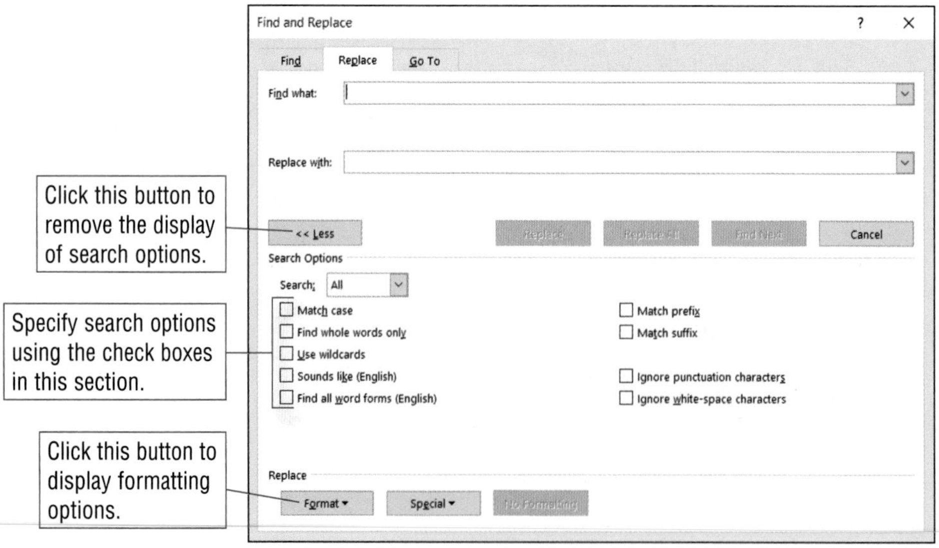

is described in Table 4.2. To remove the display of options, click the Less button. (The Less button was previously the More button.) If a mistake was made when replacing text, close the Find and Replace dialog box and then click the Undo button on the Quick Access Toolbar.

Table 4.2 Options at the Expanded Find and Replace Dialog Box

Choose this option	To
Match case	Exactly match the case of the search text. For example, search for *Book* and select the *Match case* option and Word will stop at *Book* but not *book* or *BOOK*.
Find whole words only	Find a whole word, not a part of a word. For example, search for *her* without selecting *Find whole words only* and Word will stop at *there*, *here*, *hers*, and so on.
Use wildcards	Use special characters as wildcards to search for specific text.
Sounds like (English)	Match words that sound alike but are spelled differently, such as *know* and *no*.
Find all word forms (English)	Find all forms of the word entered in the *Find what* text box. For example, enter *hold* and Word will stop at *held* and *holding*.
Match prefix	Find only those words that begin with the letters in the *Find what* text box. For example, enter *per* and Word will stop at words such as *perform* and *perfect* but skip words such as *super* and *hyperlink*.
Match suffix	Find only those words that end with the letters in the *Find what* text box. For example, enter *ly* and Word will stop at words such as *accurately* and *quietly* but skip words such as *catalyst* and *lyre*.
Ignore punctuation characters	Ignore punctuation within characters. For example, enter *US* in the *Find what* text box and Word will stop at *U.S.*
Ignore white-space characters	Ignore spaces between letters. For example, enter *F B I* in the *Find what* text box and Word will stop at *FBI*.

Project 6c Finding and Replacing Word Forms and Suffixes — Part 3 of 4

1. With **4-LeaseAgrmnt.docx** open, make sure the insertion point is positioned at the beginning of the document.
2. Find all word forms of the word *lease* and replace them with *rent* by completing the following steps:
   a. Click the Replace button in the Editing group on the Home tab.

b. At the Find and Replace dialog box with the Replace tab selected, type lease in the *Find what* text box.
c. Press the Tab key and then type rent in the *Replace with* text box.
d. Click the More button.
e. Click the *Find all word forms (English)* check box. (This inserts a check mark in the check box.)
f. Click the Replace All button.
g. At the message stating that Replace All is not recommended with Find All Word Forms, click OK.
h. At the message stating that six replacements were made, click OK.
i. Click the *Find all word forms* check box to remove the check mark.

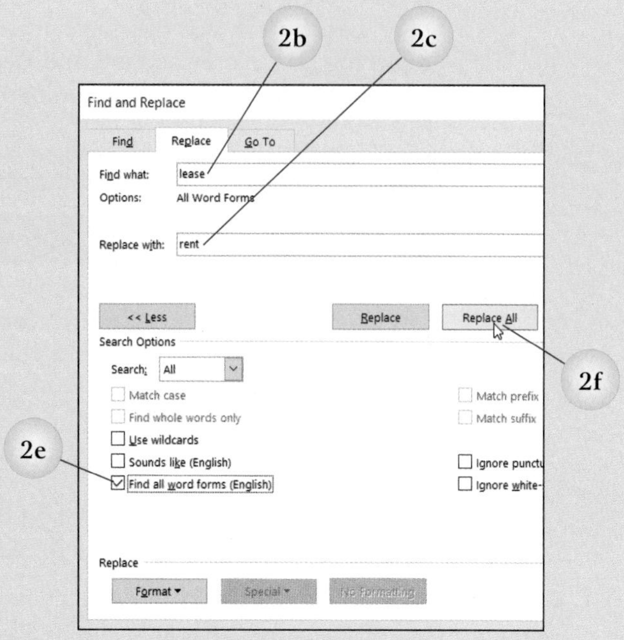

3. Find the word *less* and replace it with the word *minus* and specify that you want Word to find only those words that end in *less* by completing the following steps:
   a. At the expanded Find and Replace dialog box, select the text in the *Find what* text box and then type less.
   b. Select the text in the *Replace with* text box and then type minus.
   c. Click the *Match suffix* check box to insert a check mark (telling Word to find only words that end in *less*).
   d. Click the Replace All button.
   e. Click OK at the message stating that two replacements were made.
   f. Click the *Match suffix* check box to remove the check mark.
   g. Click the Less button.
   h. Close the Find and Replace dialog box.

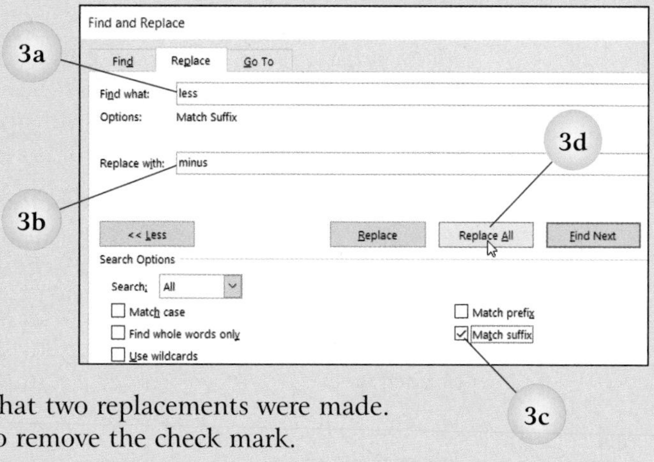

4. Save **4-LeaseAgrmnt.docx**.

Check Your Work

Tutorial

Finding and Replacing Formatting

Finding and Replacing Formatting

Use options at the Find and Replace dialog box with the Replace tab selected to search for characters containing specific formatting and replace them with other characters or formatting. With the insertion point positioned in the *Find what* text box, specify formatting to be found in the document by clicking the More button, clicking the Format button in the lower left corner of the dialog box, and then clicking the type of formatting at the pop-up list. Click in the *Replace with* text box and then complete similar steps.

Project 6d Finding and Replacing Fonts

1. With **4-LeaseAgrmnt.docx** open, make sure the insertion point displays at the beginning of the document.
2. Find text set in 12-point Candara bold, in the standard dark red color and replace it with text set in 14-point Calibri bold, in the standard dark blue color by completing the following steps:
   a. Click the Replace button in the Editing group on the Home tab.
   b. At the Find and Replace dialog box, press the Delete key. (This deletes any text in the *Find what* text box.)
   c. Click the More button. (If a check mark displays in any of the check boxes, click the option to remove it.)
   d. With the insertion point positioned in the *Find what* text box, click the Format button in the lower left corner of the dialog box and then click *Font* at the pop-up list.
   e. At the Find Font dialog box, choose the *Candara* font and change the font style to *Bold*, the size to *12*, and the font color to *Dark Red* (first color option in the *Standard Colors* section).

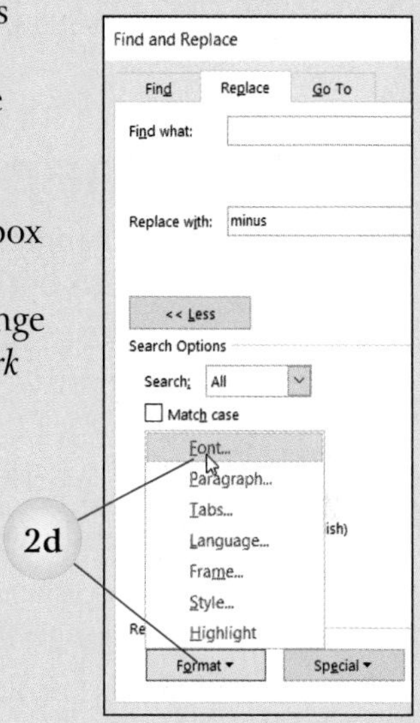

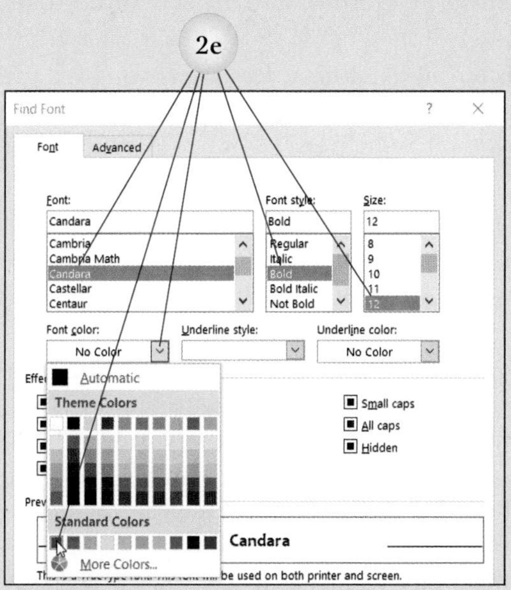

   f. Click OK to close the Find Font dialog box.
   g. At the Find and Replace dialog box, click in the *Replace with* text box and then delete any text that displays.
   h. Click the Format button in the lower left corner of the dialog box and then click *Font* at the pop-up list.
   i. At the Replace Font dialog box, choose the *Calibri* font and change the font style to *Bold*, the size to *14*, and the font color to *Dark Blue* (ninth color option in the *Standard Colors* section).
   j. Click OK to close the Replace Font dialog box.

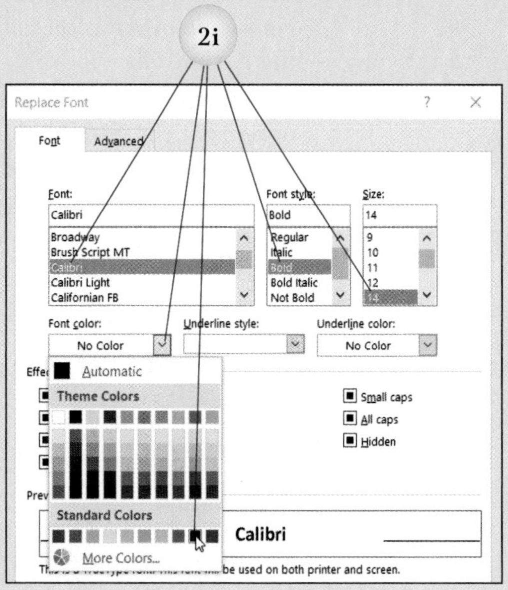

k. At the Find and Replace dialog box, click the Replace All button.
l. Click OK at the message stating that eight replacements were made.
m. Click in the *Find what* text box and then click the No Formatting button.
n. Click in the *Replace with* text box and then click the No Formatting button.
o. Click the Less button.
p. Close the Find and Replace dialog box.
3. Save, print, and then close **4-LeaseAgrmnt.docx**.

Check Your Work

Chapter Summary

- Change the document view with buttons in the view area on the Status bar or with options in the Views group on the View tab.
- Print Layout is the default view but this can be changed to other views, such as Draft view and Read Mode view.
- Draft view displays the document in a format for efficient editing and formatting.
- Read Mode view displays a document in a format for easy viewing and reading.
- Use the Zoom slider bar or buttons in the Zoom group on the View tab to change the display percentage.
- Use options at the Ribbon Display Options button drop-down list to specify if the Quick Access Toolbar, ribbon, and Status bar should be visible or hidden.
- Navigate in a document using the Navigation pane. Display the pane by inserting a check mark in the *Navigation Pane* check box in the Show group on the View tab.
- By default, a Word document contains 1-inch top, bottom, left, and right margins. Change margins with preset margin settings at the Margins button drop-down list or with options at the Page Setup dialog box with the Margins tab selected.
- The default page layout is portrait orientation, which can be changed to landscape orientation with the Orientation button in the Page Setup group on the Layout tab.
- The default page size is 8.5 inches by 11 inches, which can be changed with options at the Size button drop-down list or options at the Page Setup dialog box with the Paper tab selected.
- A page break that Word inserts automatically is a soft page break. A page break inserted manually is a hard page break. Insert a hard page break using the Page Break button in the Pages group on the Insert tab or by pressing Ctrl + Enter.
- Insert a predesigned and formatted cover page by clicking the Cover Page button in the Pages group on the Insert tab and then clicking an option at the drop-down list.
- Insert predesigned and formatted page numbering by clicking the Page Number button in the Header & Footer group on the Insert tab, specifying the location of the page number, and then clicking a page numbering option.
- Insert predesigned headers and footers in a document with the Header button and the Footer button in the Header & Footer group on the Insert tab.

- A watermark is a lightened image that displays behind the text in a document. Use the Watermark button in the Page Background group on the Design tab to insert a watermark.
- Insert a page background color in a document with the Page Color button in the Page Background group on the Design tab. The page background color is designed for viewing a document on screen and does not print.
- Click the Page Borders button in the Page Background group on the Design tab and the Borders and Shading dialog box with the Page Border tab selected displays. Use options at this dialog box to insert a page border or an art image page border in a document.
- Use the Find button in the Editing group on the Home tab to search for specific characters or formatting. Use the Replace button to search for specific characters or formatting and replace them with other characters or formatting.
- At the Find and Replace dialog box, click the Find Next button to find the next occurrence of the characters and/or formatting. Click the Replace button to replace the characters or formatting and find the next occurrence or click the Replace All button to replace all occurrences of the characters or formatting.
- Click the More button at the Find and Replace dialog box to display additional options for defining search parameters.

Commands Review

FEATURE	RIBBON TAB, GROUP	BUTTON, OPTION	KEYBOARD SHORTCUT
blank page	Insert, Pages		
Borders and Shading dialog box with Page Border tab selected	Design, Page Background		
Border and Shading Options dialog box	Design, Page Background	, Options	
cover page	Insert, Pages		
Draft view	View, Views		
Find and Replace dialog box with Find tab selected	Home, Editing	, *Advanced Find*	
Find and Replace dialog box with Replace tab selected	Home, Editing		Ctrl + H
footer	Insert, Header & Footer		
header	Insert, Header & Footer		
margins	Layout, Page Setup		
Navigation pane	View, Show	*Navigation Pane*	Ctrl + F
orientation	Layout, Page Setup		
page break	Insert, Pages		Ctrl + Enter

FEATURE	RIBBON TAB, GROUP	BUTTON, OPTION	KEYBOARD SHORTCUT
page background color	Design, Page Background		
page numbering	Insert, Header & Footer		
Page Setup dialog box with Margins tab selected	Layout, Page Setup	, *Custom Margins* OR	
Page Setup dialog box with Paper tab selected	Layout, Page Setup	, *More Paper Sizes*	
paper size	Layout, Page Setup		
Print Layout view	View, Views		
Read Mode view	View, Views		
ribbon display options			
watermark	Design, Page Background		

Workbook

Chapter study tools and assessment activities are available in the *Workbook* ebook. These resources are designed to help you further develop and demonstrate mastery of the skills learned in this chapter.

Unit assessment activities are also available in the *Workbook*. These activities are designed to help you demonstrate mastery of the skills learned in this unit.

Microsoft® Word Level 1

Unit 2

Enhancing and Customizing Documents

Microsoft®

Word

Applying Formatting and Inserting Objects

CHAPTER 5

Performance Objectives

Upon successful completion of Chapter 5, you will be able to:

1 Insert section breaks
2 Create and format text in columns
3 Hyphenate words automatically and manually
4 Create a drop cap
5 Insert symbols, special characters, and the date and time
6 Use the Click and Type feature
7 Vertically align text
8 Insert, format, and customize images, text boxes, shapes, and WordArt
9 Create and customize a screenshot

Precheck

Check your current skills to help focus your study.

To apply page or document formatting to only a portion of the document, insert a continuous section break or a section break that begins a new page. A section break is useful when formatting text in columns. The hyphenation feature hyphenates words at the ends of lines, creating a less ragged right margin. Use buttons in the Text and Symbols groups on the Insert tab to insert symbols, special characters, the date and time, text boxes, and WordArt. Word includes the Click and Type feature for positioning the insertion point at a particular location in the document and changing the paragraph alignment. Use the *Vertical alignment* option at the Page Setup dialog box with the Layout tab selected to specify how text is aligned vertically on the page. In addition to learning these features, you will learn how to increase the visual appeal of a document by inserting and customizing graphics, such as images, text boxes, shapes, WordArt, and screenshots.

Data Files

Before beginning chapter work, copy the WL1C5 folder to your storage medium and then make WL1C5 the active folder.

SNAP

If you are a SNAP user, launch the Precheck and Tutorials from your Assignments page.

Project 1 Format a Document on Computer Input Devices

8 Parts

In a document on computer input devices, you will format text into columns, improve the readability by hyphenating long words, and improve the visual appeal by inserting a drop cap, a special character, a symbol, and the date and time.

Preview Finished Project

Tutorial

Inserting and Deleting a Section Break

Breaks

Quick Steps

Insert a Section Break

1. Click Layout tab.
2. Click Breaks button.
3. Click section break type in drop-down list.

Hint When you delete a section break, the text that follows takes on the formatting of the text preceding the break.

Inserting a Section Break

Insert a section break in a document to change the layout and formatting of specific portions. For example, a section break can be inserted in the document and then the margins can be changed for the text between the section break and the end of the document or to the next section break.

Insert a section break in a document by clicking the Layout tab, clicking the Breaks button in the Page Setup group, and then clicking the desired option in the *Section Breaks* section of the drop-down list. A section break can be inserted that begins a new page or a continuous section break can be inserted. A continuous section break separates the document into sections but does not insert a page break.

A section break inserted in a document is not visible in Print Layout view. Change to Draft view or click the Show/Hide ¶ button on the Home tab to turn on the display of nonprinting characters and a section break displays in the document as a double row of dots with the words *Section Break* in the middle. Word will identify the type of section break. For example, if a continuous section break is inserted, the words *Section Break (Continuous)* display in the middle of the row of dots. To delete a section break, change to Draft view, click anywhere on the section break, and then press the Delete key. Another option is to click the Show/Hide ¶ button to turn on the display of nonprinting characters, click anywhere on the section break, and then press the Delete key.

Project 1a Inserting a Continuous Section Break

Part 1 of 8

1. Open **InputDevices.docx** and then save it with the name **5-InputDevices**.
2. Insert a continuous section break by completing the following steps:
   a. Move the insertion point to the beginning of the *Keyboard* heading.
   b. Click the Layout tab.
   c. Click the Breaks button in the Page Setup group and then click *Continuous* in the *Section Breaks* section of the drop-down list.
3. Click the Home tab, click the Show/Hide ¶ button in the Paragraph group, and then notice the section break at the end of the first paragraph of text.
4. Click the Show/Hide ¶ button to turn off the display of nonprinting characters.

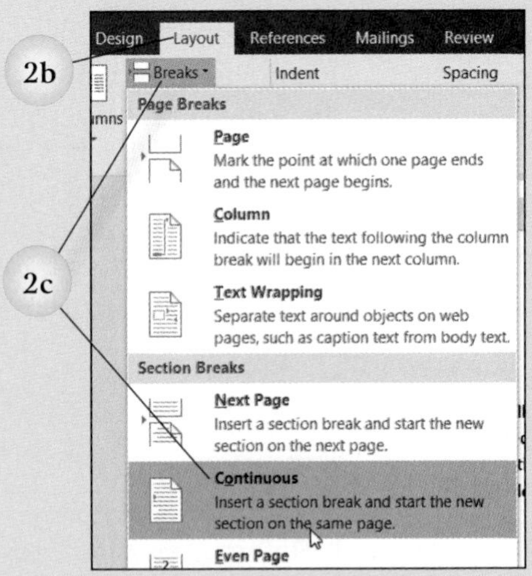

5. With the insertion point positioned at the beginning of the *Keyboard* heading, change the left and right margins to 1.5 inches. (The margin changes affect only the text after the continuous section break.)
6. Save and then print **5-InputDevices.docx**.

Check Your Work

Tutorial

Formatting Text into Columns

Formatting Text into Columns

When preparing a document containing text, an important point to consider is its readability. Readability refers to the ease with which a person can read and understand groups of words. The line length of text in a document can enhance or detract from its readability. If the line length is too long, the reader may lose his or her place and have a difficult time moving to the next line below.

To improve the readability of documents such as newsletters and reports, consider formatting the text in columns. One common type is the newspaper column, which is typically used for text in newspapers, newsletters, and magazines. Newspaper columns contain text in vertical columns.

Columns

Quick Steps

Create Columns

1. Click Layout tab.
2. Click Columns button.
3. Click number of columns.

Create newspaper columns with the Columns button in the Page Setup group on the Layout tab or with options at the Columns dialog box. Using the Columns button creates columns of equal width. Use the Columns dialog box to create columns with varying widths. A document can include as many columns as will fit the space available on the page. Word determines how many columns can be included on the page based on the page width, the margin widths, and the size and spacing of the columns. Columns must be at least 0.5 inch in width. Changing column widths affects the entire document or the section of the document in which the insertion point is positioned.

Project 1b Formatting Text into Columns

Part 2 of 8

1. With **5-InputDevices.docx** open, make sure the insertion point is positioned below the section break and then change the left and right margins back to 1 inch.
2. Delete the section break by completing the following steps:
   a. Click the Show/Hide ¶ button in the Paragraph group on the Home tab to turn on the display of nonprinting characters.
   b. Click anywhere on *Section Break (Continuous)* at the end of the first paragraph below the title in the document. (This moves the insertion point to the beginning of the section break.)

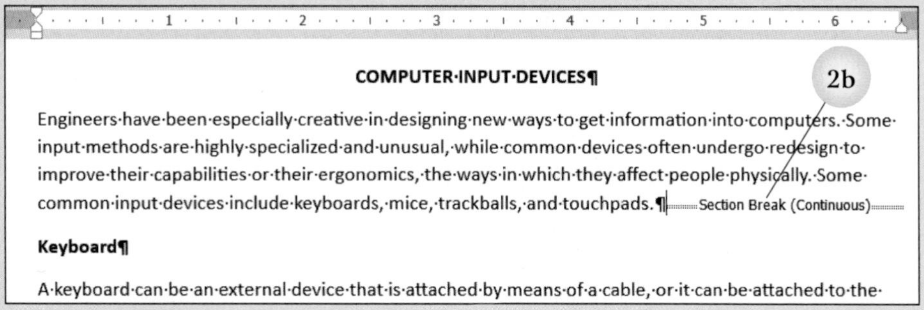

   c. Press the Delete key.
   d. Click the Show/Hide ¶ button to turn off the display of nonprinting characters.

3. Move the insertion point to the beginning of the first paragraph of text below the title and then insert a continuous section break.
4. Format the text into columns by completing the following steps:
   a. Make sure the insertion point is positioned below the section break.
   b. If necessary, click the Layout tab.
   c. Click the Columns button in the Page Setup group.
   d. Click *Two* at the drop-down list.
5. Save **5-InputDevices.docx**.

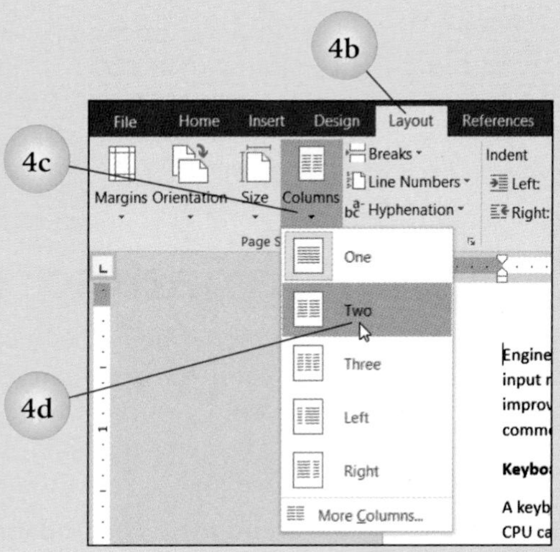

Check Your Work

Creating Columns with the Columns Dialog Box

Quick Steps

Create Columns with the Columns Dialog Box

1. Click Layout tab.
2. Click Columns button.
3. Click *More Columns*.
4. Specify column options.
5. Click OK.

Use the Columns dialog box to create newspaper columns that are equal or unequal in width. To display the Columns dialog box, shown in Figure 5.1, click the Columns button in the Page Setup group on the Layout tab and then click *More Columns* at the drop-down list.

With options at the Columns dialog box, specify the style and number of columns, enter specific column measurements, create unequal columns, and insert a line between columns. By default, column formatting is applied to the whole document. This can be changed to *This point forward* with the *Apply to* option box at the bottom of the Columns dialog box. With the *This point forward* option, a section break is inserted and the column formatting is applied to text from the location of the insertion point to the end of the document or until another column format is encountered. The *Preview* section of the dialog box displays an example of how the columns will appear in the document.

Figure 5.1 Columns Dialog Box

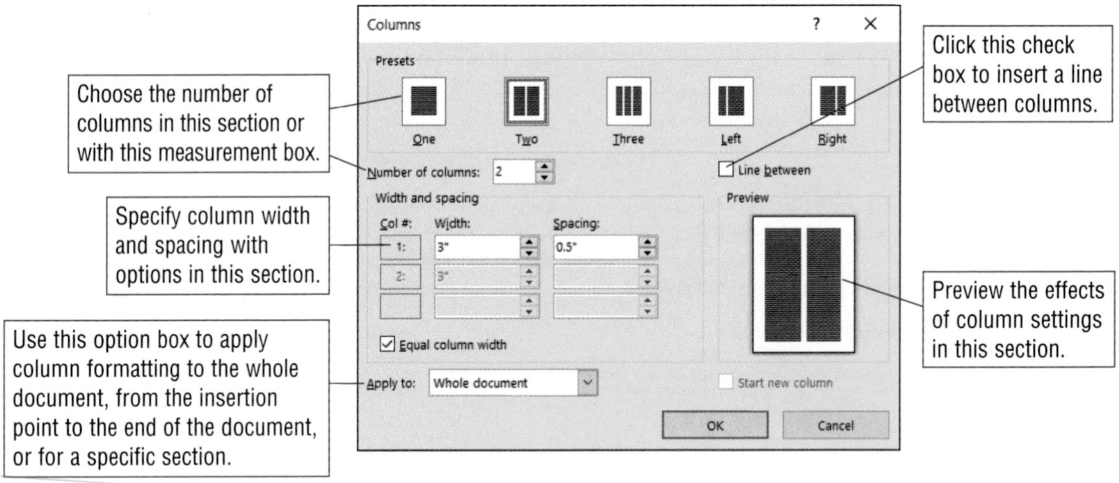

Removing Column Formatting

To remove column formatting using the Columns button, position the insertion point in the section containing columns, click the Layout tab, click the Columns button, and then click *One* at the drop-down list. Column formatting can also be removed at the Columns dialog box by selecting the *One* option in the *Presets* section.

Inserting a Column Break

Hint You can also insert a column break with the keyboard shortcut Ctrl + Shift + Enter.

When formatting text into columns, Word automatically breaks the columns to fit the page. At times, automatic column breaks may appear in undesirable locations. Insert a manual column break by positioning the insertion point where the column is to end, clicking the Layout tab, clicking the Breaks button, and then clicking *Column* at the drop-down list.

Project 1c Formatting Columns at the Columns Dialog Box — Part 3 of 8

1. With **5-InputDevices.docx** open, delete the section break by completing the following steps:
   a. Click the View tab and then click the Draft button in the Views group.
   b. Click anywhere on *Section Break (Continuous)* and then press the Delete key.
   c. Click the Print Layout button in the Views group on the View tab.
2. Remove column formatting by clicking the Layout tab, clicking the Columns button in the Page Setup group, and then clicking *One* at the drop-down list.
3. Format text in columns by completing the following steps:
   a. Position the insertion point at the beginning of the first paragraph of text below the title.
   b. Click the Columns button in the Page Setup group and then click *More Columns* at the drop-down list.
   c. At the Columns dialog box, click *Two* in the *Presets* section.
   d. Click the *Spacing* measurement box down arrow until *0.3"* displays.
   e. Click the *Line between* check box to insert a check mark.
   f. Click the *Apply to* option box arrow and then click *This point forward* at the drop-down list.
   g. Click OK to close the dialog box.

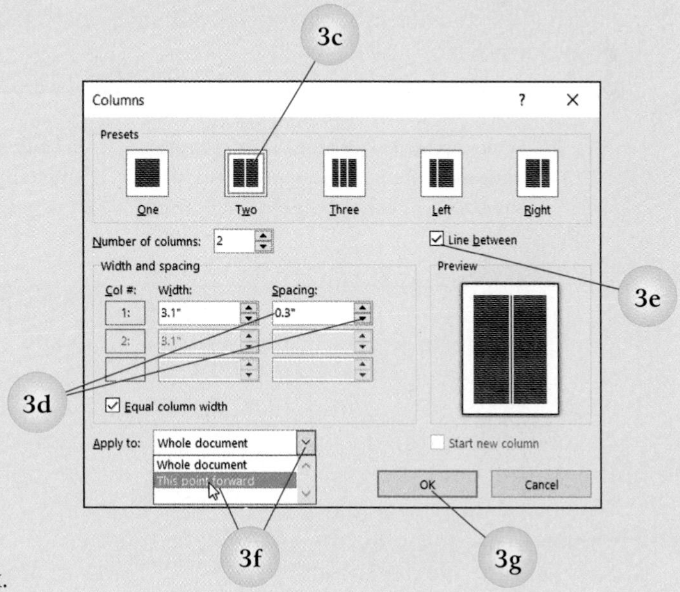

4. Insert a column break by completing the following steps:
   a. Position the insertion point at the beginning of the heading *Mouse*.
   b. Click the Breaks button in the Page Setup group and then click *Column* at the drop-down list.
5. Save and then print **5-InputDevices.docx**.

4b

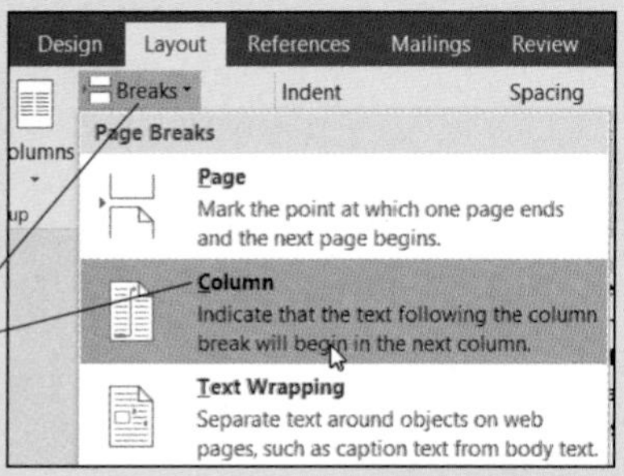

Check Your Work

Balancing Columns on a Page

In a document containing text formatted into columns, Word automatically lines up (balances) the last lines of text at the bottoms of the columns, except on the last page. Text in the first column of the last page may flow to the end of the page, while the text in the second column may end far short of the end of the page. Balance columns by inserting a continuous section break at the end of the text.

Project 1d Formatting and Balancing Columns of Text — Part 4 of 8

1. With **5-InputDevices.docx** open, delete the column break by positioning the insertion point at the beginning of the heading *Mouse* and then pressing the Backspace key.
2. Select the entire document and then change the font to 12-point Constantia.
3. Move the insertion point to the end of the document and then balance the columns by clicking the Layout tab, clicking the Breaks button, and then clicking *Continuous* at the drop-down list.

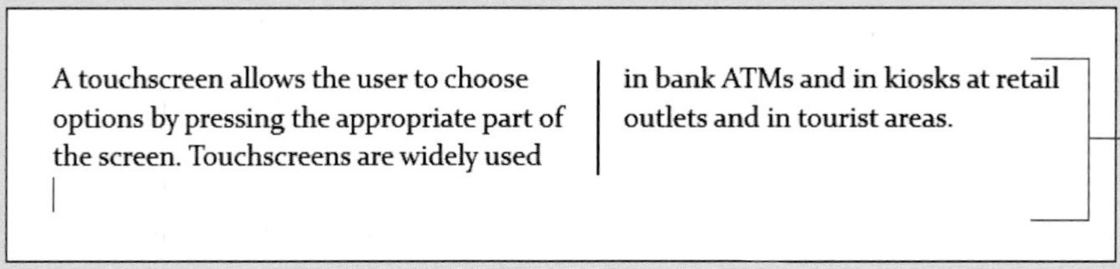

A touchscreen allows the user to choose options by pressing the appropriate part of the screen. Touchscreens are widely used
in bank ATMs and in kiosks at retail outlets and in tourist areas.

3

4. Apply the Green, Accent 6, Lighter 60% paragraph shading (last column, third row) to the title *COMPUTER INPUT DEVICES*.
5. Apply the Green, Accent 6, Lighter 80% paragraph shading (last column, second row) to each heading in the document.
6. Insert page numbering that prints at the bottom center of each page using the Plain Number 2 option.
7. Double-click in the document to make it active.
8. Save **5-InputDevices.docx**.

Check Your Work

Tutorial

Hyphenating Words

Hyphenating Words

In some Word documents, especially those with left and right margins wider than 1 inch or those with text set in columns, the right margin may appear quite ragged. Improve the display of the text by making line lengths more uniform using the hyphenation feature to hyphenate long words that fall at the ends of lines. Use the hyphenation feature to automatically or manually hyphenate words.

Automatically Hyphenating Words

Hyphenation

Hint Avoid dividing words at the ends of more than two consecutive lines.

To automatically hyphenate words in a document, click the Layout tab, click the Hyphenation button in the Page Setup group, and then click *Automatic* at the drop-down list. Scroll through the document and check to see if hyphens display in appropriate locations within the words. To remove all the hyphens after hyphenating words in a document, immediately click the Undo button on the Quick Access Toolbar.

Quick Steps

Automatically Hyphenate a Document

1. Click Layout tab.
2. Click Hyphenation button.
3. Click *Automatic*.

Manually Hyphenate a Document

1. Click Layout tab.
2. Click Hyphenation button.
3. Click *Manual*.
4. Click Yes or No to hyphenate indicated words.
5. When complete, click OK.

Manually Hyphenating Words

To control where hyphens appear in words during hyphenation, choose manual hyphenation. To do this, click the Layout tab, click the Hyphenation button in the Page Setup group, and then click *Manual* at the drop-down list. This displays the Manual Hyphenation dialog box, as shown in Figure 5.2. (The word in the *Hyphenate at* text box will vary.)

At this dialog box, click Yes to hyphenate the word as indicated in the *Hyphenate at* text box, click No if the word should not be hyphenated, or click Cancel to cancel hyphenation. The hyphenation can be repositioned in the *Hyphenate at* text box. Word displays the word with syllable breaks indicated by hyphens. Each place the word will be hyphenated displays as a blinking black bar. To hyphenate the word at a different place, position the blinking black bar where the word is to be hyphenated and then click Yes. Continue clicking Yes or No at the Manual Hyphenation dialog box.

Be careful with words ending in *-ed*. Several two-syllable words can be divided before that final syllable—for example, *noted*. However, one-syllable words ending in *-ed* should not be hyphenated. An example is *served*. Watch for this type of occurrence and click No to cancel the hyphenation. At the hyphenation complete message, click OK.

Figure 5.2 Manual Hyphenation Dialog Box

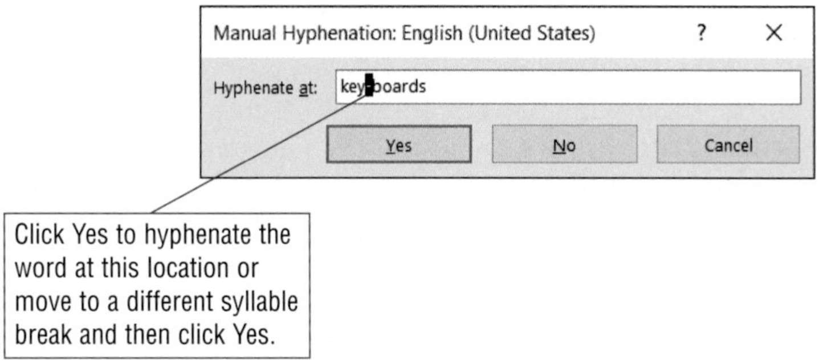

Remove all hyphens in a document by immediately clicking the Undo button on the Quick Access Toolbar. To delete a few but not all the optional hyphens inserted during hyphenation, use the Find and Replace dialog box. To do this, display the Find and Replace dialog box with the Replace tab selected, insert an optional hyphen symbol in the *Find what* text box (to do this, click the More button, click the Special button, and then click *Optional Hyphen* at the pop-up list), and make sure the *Replace with* text box is empty. Complete the find and replace, clicking the Replace button to replace the hyphen with nothing or clicking the Find Next button to leave the hyphen in the document.

Project 1e **Automatically and Manually Hyphenating Words** Part 5 of 8

1. With **5-InputDevices.docx** open, hyphenate words automatically by completing the following steps:
   a. Press Ctrl + Home.
   b. Click the Layout tab.
   c. Click the Hyphenation button in the Page Setup group and then click *Automatic* at the drop-down list.

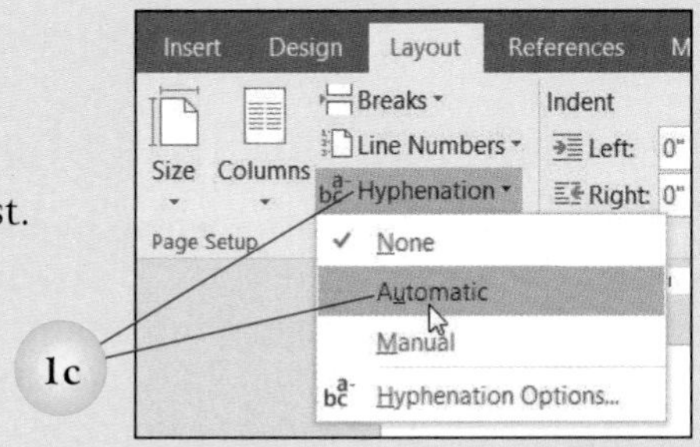

2. Scroll through the document and notice the hyphenation.
3. Click the Undo button to remove the hyphens.
4. Manually hyphenate words by completing the following steps:
   a. Click the Hyphenation button in the Page Setup group and then click *Manual* at the drop-down list.
   b. At the Manual Hyphenation dialog box, make one of the following choices:
      - Click Yes to hyphenate the word as indicated in the *Hyphenate at* text box.
      - Move the hyphen in the word to a more desirable location and then click Yes.
      - Click No if the word should not be hyphenated.
   c. Continue clicking Yes or No at the Manual Hyphenation dialog box.
   d. At the message indicating that hyphenation is complete, click OK.

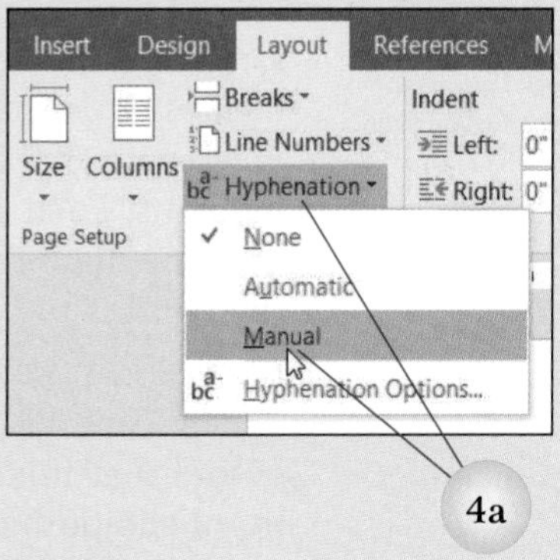

5. Save **5-InputDevices.docx**.

Check Your Work

Tutorial

Creating and Removing a Drop Cap

Drop Cap

Quick Steps

Create a Drop Cap
1. Click Insert tab.
2. Click Drop Cap button.
3. Click drop cap option.

Creating a Drop Cap

Use a drop cap to enhance the appearance of text. A drop cap is the first letter of the first word of a paragraph that is set into the paragraph with formatting that differentiates it from the rest of the paragraph. Drop caps can be used to identify the beginnings of major sections or parts of a document.

Create a drop cap with the Drop Cap button in the Text group on the Insert tab. The drop cap can be set in the paragraph or in the margin. At the Drop Cap dialog box, specify a font, the number of lines the letter should drop, and the distance the letter should be positioned from the text of the paragraph. Add a drop cap to the entire first word of a paragraph by selecting the word and then clicking the Drop Cap button.

Project 1f Inserting Drop Caps

Part 6 of 8

1. With **5-InputDevices.docx** open, create a drop cap by completing the following steps:
   a. Position the insertion point on the first word of the first paragraph below the title (*Engineers*).
   b. Click the Insert tab.
   c. Click the Drop Cap button in the Text group.
   d. Click *In margin* at the drop-down gallery.
2. Looking at the drop cap, you decide that you do not like it positioned in the margin and want it to be a little smaller. To change the drop cap, complete the following steps:
   a. With the *E* in the word *Engineers* selected, click the Drop Cap button in the Text group and then click *None* at the drop-down gallery.
   b. Click the Drop Cap button and then click *Drop Cap Options* at the drop-down gallery.
   c. At the Drop Cap dialog box, click *Dropped* in the *Position* section.
   d. Click the *Font* option box arrow, scroll up the drop-down list, and then click *Cambria*.
   e. Click the *Lines to drop* measurement box down arrow to change the number to *2*.
   f. Click OK to close the dialog box.
   g. Click outside the drop cap to deselect it.
3. Save **5-InputDevices.docx**.

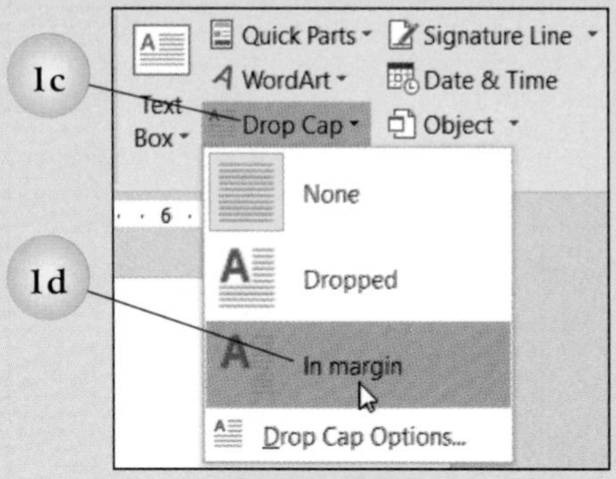

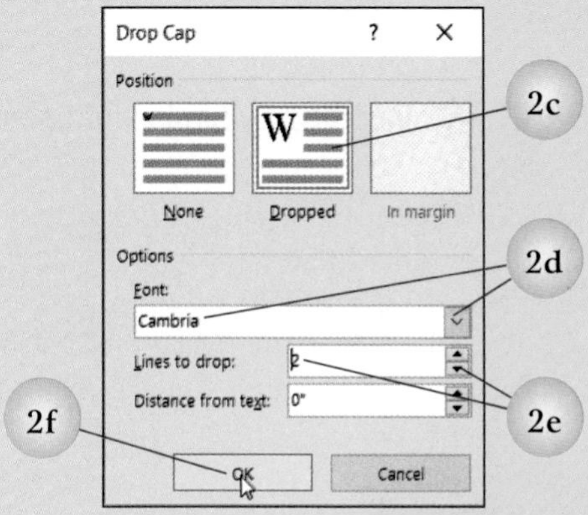

Check Your Work

Inserting Symbols and Special Characters

Tutorial

Inserting Symbols

Tutorial

Inserting Special Characters

Symbol

Use the Symbol button on the Insert tab to insert special symbols in a document. Click the Symbol button in the Symbols group on the Insert tab and a drop-down list displays the most recently inserted symbols along with a *More Symbols* option. Click one of the symbols in the list to insert it in the document or click the *More Symbols* option to display the Symbol dialog box, as shown in Figure 5.3. At the Symbol dialog box, double-click the desired symbol and then click Close or click the symbol, click the Insert button, and then click the Close button. Another method for selecting a symbol at the Symbol dialog box is to type the symbol code in the *Character code* text box.

At the Symbol dialog box with the Symbols tab selected, the font can be changed with the *Font* option box. When the font is changed, different symbols display in the dialog box. Click the Special Characters tab at the Symbol dialog box and a list of special characters displays along with keyboard shortcuts for creating them.

Quick Steps

Insert a Symbol
1. Click Insert tab.
2. Click Symbol button.
3. Click symbol.

OR
1. Click Insert tab.
2. Click Symbol button.
3. Click *More Symbols*.
4. Double-click symbol.
5. Click Close.

Figure 5.3 Symbol Dialog Box with Symbols Tab Selected

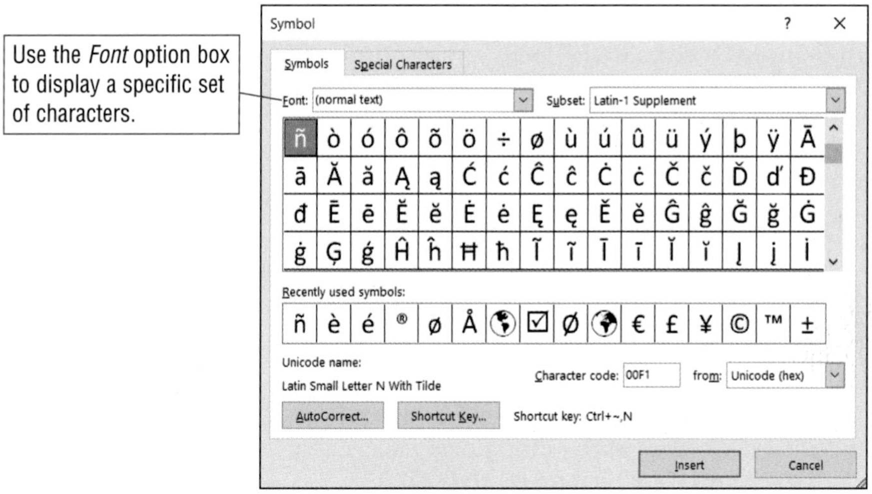

Project 1g Inserting Symbols and Special Characters

Part 7 of 8

1. With **5-InputDevices.docx** open, press Ctrl + End to move the insertion point to the end of the document.
2. Press the Enter key, type Prepared by:, and then press the spacebar.
3. Type the first name Matthew and then press the spacebar.
4. Insert the last name *Viña* by completing the following steps:
   a. Type Vi.
   b. If necessary, click the Insert tab.
   c. Click the Symbol button in the Symbols group.
   d. Click *More Symbols* at the drop-down list.
   e. At the Symbol dialog box, make sure the *Font* option box displays *(normal text)* and then double-click the *ñ* symbol (located in approximately the tenth through twelfth rows).
   f. Click the Close button.
   g. Type a.

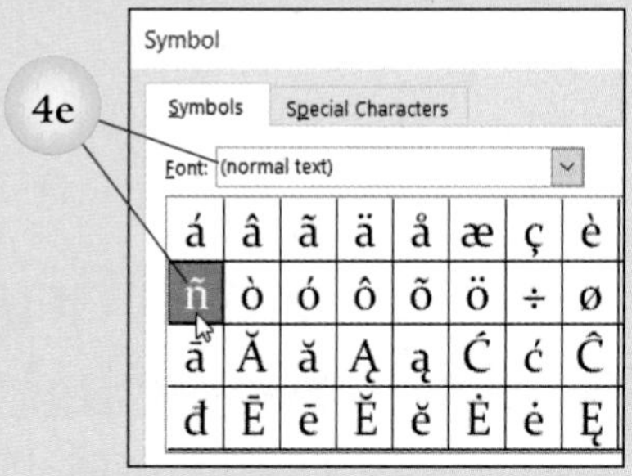

5. Press Shift + Enter.
6. Insert the keyboard symbol (🖮) by completing the following steps:
   a. Click the Symbol button and then click *More Symbols*.
   b. At the Symbol dialog box, click the *Font* option box arrow and then click *Wingdings* at the drop-down list. (You will need to scroll down the list to display this option.)
   c. Select the current number in the *Character code* text box and then type 55.
   d. Click the Insert button and then click the Close button.
7. Type SoftCell Technologies.

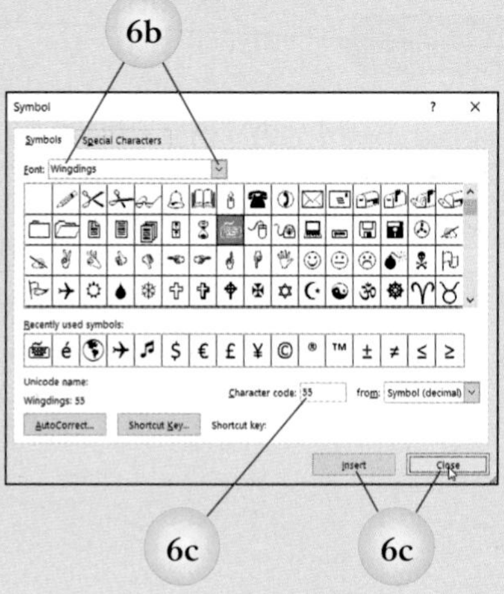

8. Insert the registered trademark symbol (®) by completing the following steps:
   a. Click the Symbol button and then click *More Symbols*.
   b. At the Symbol dialog box, click the Special Characters tab.
   c. Double-click the ® symbol (tenth option from the top).
   d. Click the Close button.
   e. Press Shift + Enter.
9. Select the keyboard symbol (⌨) and then change the font size to 18 points.
10. Save **5-InputDevices.docx**.

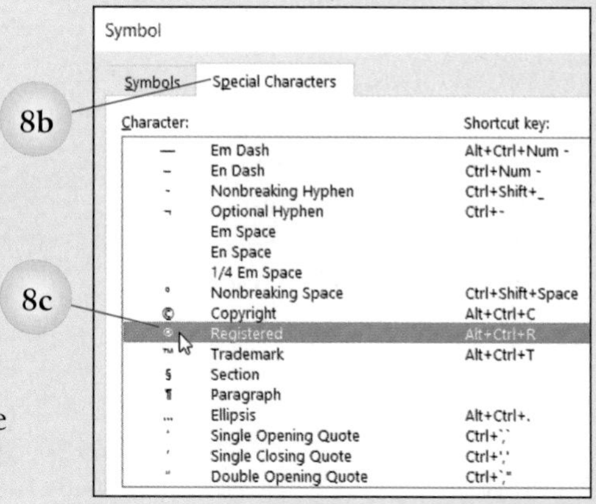

Check Your Work

Tutorial

Inserting the Date and Time

Date & Time

Quick Steps

Insert the Date and Time

1. Click Insert tab.
2. Click Date & Time button.
3. Click desired option in list box.
4. Click OK.

Inserting the Date and Time

Use the Date & Time button in the Text group on the Insert tab to insert the current date and time in a document. Click this button and the Date and Time dialog box displays, as shown in Figure 5.4. (Your date will vary from what you see in the figure.) At the Date and Time dialog box, click the desired date and/or time format in the *Available formats* list box.

If the *Update automatically* check box does not contain a check mark, the date and/or time are inserted in the document as text that can be edited in the normal manner. The date and/or time can also be inserted as a field. The advantage to using a field is that the date and time are updated when a document is reopened. Insert a check mark in the *Update automatically* check box to insert the date and/or time as a field. The date can also be inserted as a field using the keyboard shortcut Alt + Shift + D, and the time can be inserted as a field with the keyboard shortcut Alt + Shift + T.

A date or time field will automatically update when a document is reopened. The date and time can also be updated in the document by clicking the date or time field and then clicking the Update tab or pressing the F9 function key.

Figure 5.4 Date and Time Dialog Box

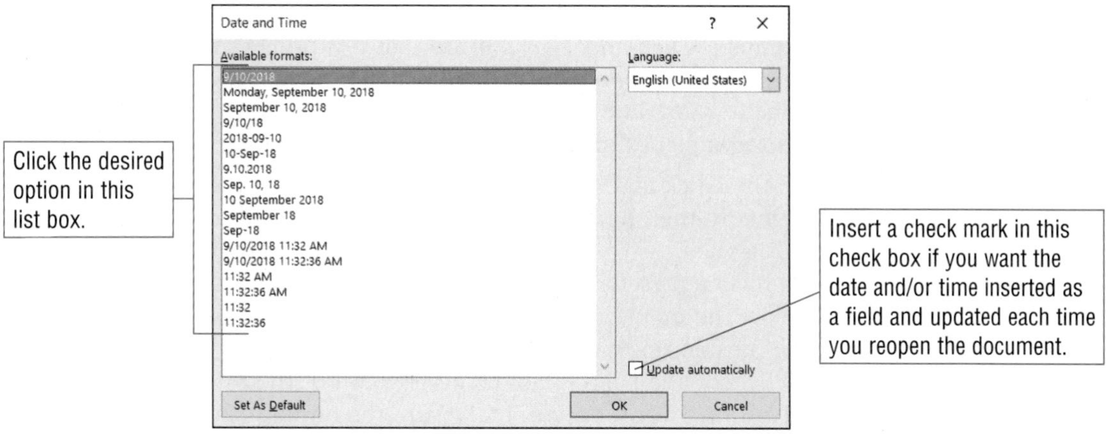

Project 1h Inserting the Date and Time

Part 8 of 8

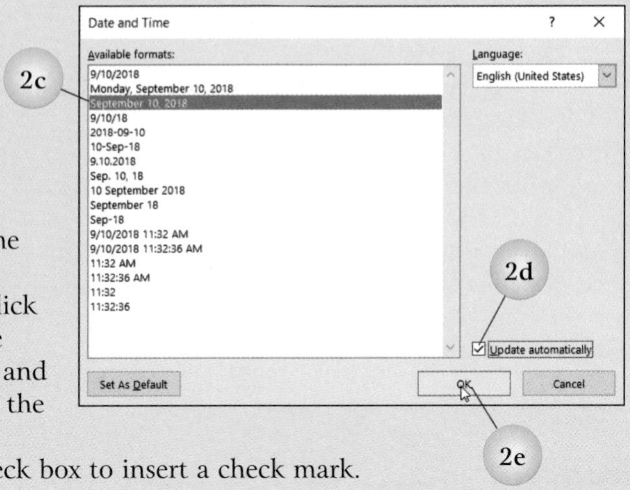

1. With **5-InputDevices.docx** open, press Ctrl + End and make sure the insertion point is positioned below the company name.
2. Insert the current date by completing the following steps:
   a. Click the Insert tab.
   b. Click the Date & Time button in the Text group.
   c. At the Date and Time dialog box, click the third option from the top in the *Available formats* list box. (Your date and time will vary from what you see in the image at the right.)
   d. Click in the *Update automatically* check box to insert a check mark.
   e. Click OK to close the dialog box.
3. Press Shift + Enter.
4. Insert the current time by pressing Alt + Shift + T.
5. Save **5-InputDevices.docx**.
6. Update the time by clicking the time and then pressing the F9 function key.
7. Save, print, and then close **5-InputDevices.docx**.

Check Your Work

Project 2 Create an Announcement about Supervisory Training

4 Parts

You will create an announcement about upcoming supervisory training in Australia and use the Click and Type feature to center and right-align text. You will vertically center the text on the page and insert and format an image and an online image to add visual appeal to the announcement.

Preview Finished Project

Tutorial

Using Click and Type

Quick Steps

Use Click and Type

1. Hover mouse at left margin, between left and right margins, or at right margin.
2. When horizontal lines display next to mouse pointer, double-click left mouse button.

Using the Click and Type Feature

Word contains a Click and Type feature that positions the insertion point at a specific location and alignment in the document. This feature can be used to position one or more lines of text as it is being typed rather than typing the text and then selecting and formatting the text, which requires multiple steps.

To use the Click and Type feature, make sure the document displays in Print Layout view and then hover the mouse pointer at the location the insertion point is to be positioned. As the mouse pointer moves, the pointer displays with varying horizontal lines representing the alignment. When the desired alignment lines display below the mouse pointer, double-click the left mouse button. If the horizontal lines do not display next to the mouse pointer when the mouse button is double-clicked, a left tab is set at the position of the insertion point. To change the alignment and not set a tab, make sure the horizontal lines display near the mouse pointer before double-clicking the mouse button.

Project 2a Using Click and Type

Part 1 of 4

1. At a blank document, create the centered text shown in Figure 5.5 by completing the following steps:
   a. Position the I-beam pointer between the left and right margins at about the 3.25-inch mark on the horizontal ruler and at the top of the vertical ruler.
   b. When the center alignment lines display below the I-beam pointer, double-click the left mouse button.
   c. Type the centered text shown in Figure 5.5. Press Shift + Enter to end each line except the last line.

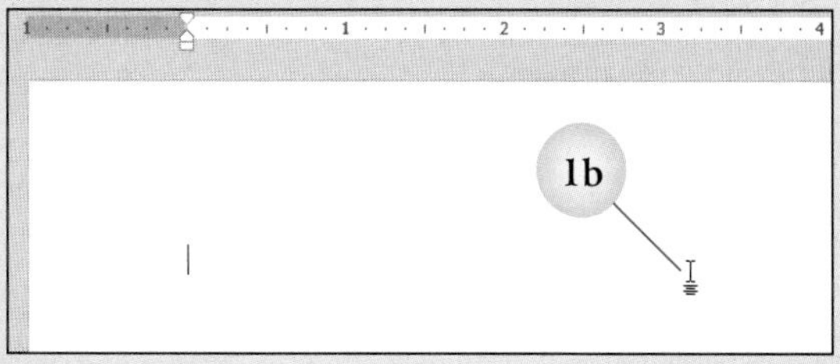

2. Change to right alignment by completing the following steps:
   a. Position the I-beam pointer near the right margin at approximately the 1-inch mark on the vertical ruler until the right alignment lines display at the left side of the I-beam pointer.
   b. Double-click the left mouse button.
   c. Type the right-aligned text shown in Figure 5.5. Press Shift + Enter to end the first line.

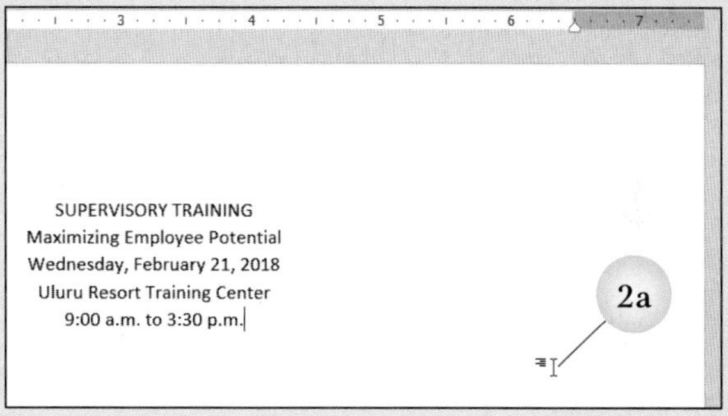

3. Select the centered text and then change the font to 14-point Candara bold and the line spacing to double spacing.
4. Select the right-aligned text, change the font to 10-point Candara bold, and then deselect the text.
5. Save the document and name it **5-Training**.

Check Your Work

Figure 5.5 Project 2a

SUPERVISORY TRAINING
Maximizing Employee Potential
Wednesday, February 21, 2018
Uluru Resort Training Center
9:00 a.m. to 3:30 p.m.

Sponsored by
Cell Systems

Tutorial

Vertically Aligning Data

Vertically Aligning Text

Text or items in a Word document are aligned at the top of the page by default. Change this alignment with the *Vertical alignment* option box at the Page Setup dialog box with the Layout tab selected, as shown in Figure 5.6. Display this dialog box by clicking the Layout tab, clicking the Page Setup group dialog box launcher, and then clicking the Layout tab at the Page Setup dialog box.

Figure 5.6 Page Setup Dialog Box with Layout Tab Selected

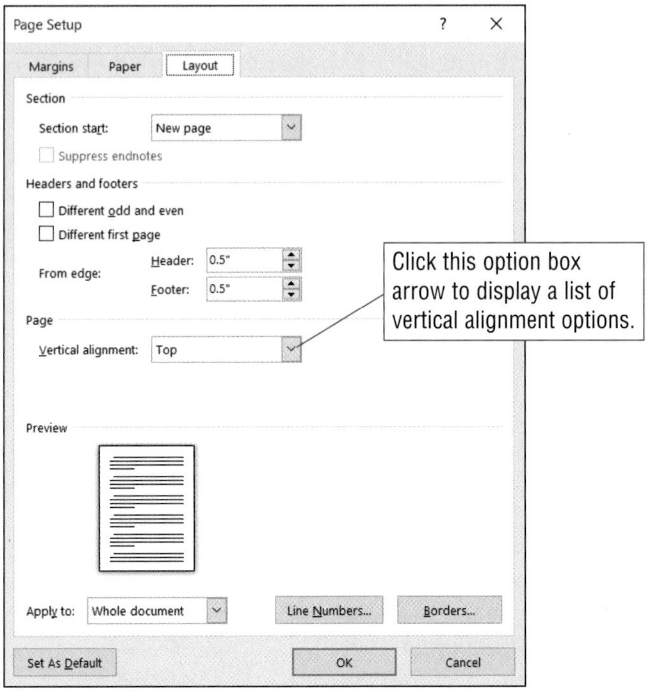

Quick Steps

Vertically Align Text

1. Click Layout tab.
2. Click Page Setup group dialog box launcher.
3. Click Layout tab.
4. Click *Vertical alignment* option box.
5. Click alignment.
6. Click OK.

The *Vertical alignment* option box in the *Page* section of the Page Setup dialog box contains four choices: *Top*, *Center*, *Justified*, and *Bottom*. The default setting is *Top*, which aligns text and items such as images at the top of the page. Choose *Center* to position the text in the middle of the page vertically. The *Justified* option aligns text between the top and bottom margins. The *Center* option positions text in the middle of the page vertically, while the *Justified* option adds space between paragraphs of text (not within) to fill the page from the top to the bottom margins. If the text is centered or justified, the text does not display centered or justified on the screen in Draft view but it does display centered or justified in Print Layout view. Choose the *Bottom* option to align text at the bottom of the page.

Project 2b Vertically Centering Text

Part 2 of 4

1. With **5-Training.docx** open, click the Layout tab and then click the Page Setup group dialog box launcher.
2. At the Page Setup dialog box, click the Layout tab.
3. Click the *Vertical alignment* option box arrow and then click *Center* at the drop-down list.
4. Click OK to close the dialog box.
5. Save and then print **5-Training.docx**.

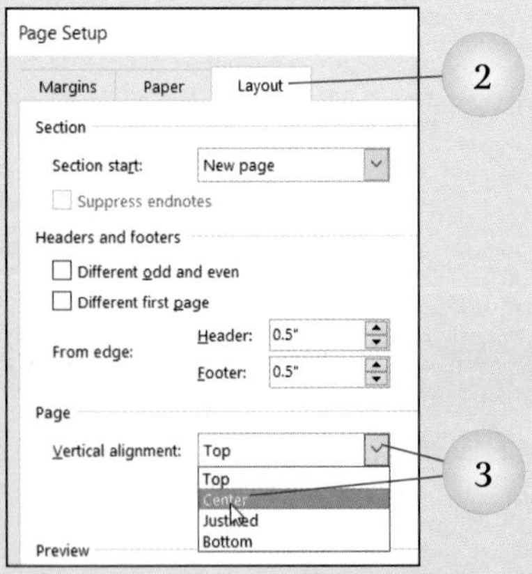

Check Your Work

Tutorial

Inserting, Sizing, and Positioning an Image

Inserting and Formatting Images

Insert an image, such as a picture or piece of clip art, in a Word document with buttons in the Illustrations group on the Insert tab. Click the Pictures button to display the Insert Picture dialog box containing the image file or click the Online Pictures button and search online for images, such as pictures and clip art.

Inserting an Image

Pictures

To insert an image in a document, click the Insert tab and then click the Pictures button in the Illustrations group. At the Insert Picture dialog box, navigate to the folder containing the image and then double-click the image file.

Tutorial

Formatting an Image

Quick Steps

Insert an Image

1. Click Insert tab.
2. Click Pictures button.
3. Double-click image file in Insert Picture dialog box.

Crop

Customizing and Formatting an Image

When an image is inserted in a document the Picture Tools Format tab is active. Use buttons on this tab to format and customize the image. Use options in the Adjust group on the Picture Tools Format tab to remove unwanted portions of the image, correct the brightness and contrast, change the image color, apply artistic effects, compress the size of the image file, change to a different image, and reset the image to the original formatting. Use buttons in the Picture Styles group to apply a predesigned style to the image, change the image border, and apply other picture effects to the image. With options in the Arrange group, position the image on the page, specify how text will wrap around it, align the image with other elements in the document, and rotate the image. Use the Crop button in the Size group to remove any unnecessary parts of the image and specify the image size with the *Shape Height* and *Shape Width* measurement boxes.

An image can also be customized and formatted with options at the shortcut menu. Display this menu by right-clicking the image. Use options at the shortcut menu to replace the image with another image, insert a caption, specify text wrapping, size and position the image, and display the Format Picture task pane.

Position

Wrap Text

Layout Options

To move an image, apply a text wrapping style with the Position button or the Wrap Text button on the Picture Tools Format tab and with options from the Layout Options button side menu. The Layout Options button displays just outside the upper right corner of the selected image. Click this button to display a side menu with wrapping options. Click the See more hyperlink text at the bottom of the side menu to display the Layout dialog box containing additional options for positioning the image on the page. Close the Layout Options button side menu by clicking the button or clicking the Close button in the upper right corner of the side menu.

Sizing an Image

Hint Size a selected image horizontally, vertically, or diagonally from the center outward by pressing and holding down the Ctrl key and then dragging a sizing handle.

Change the size of an image with the *Shape Height* and *Shape Width* measurement boxes in the Size group on the Picture Tools Format tab or with the sizing handles that display around a selected image. To change the image size with a sizing handle, position the mouse pointer on a sizing handle until the pointer turns into a double-headed arrow and then click and hold down the left mouse button. Drag the sizing handle in or out to decrease or increase the size of the image and then release the mouse button. Use the middle sizing handles at the left and right sides of the image to make the image wider or thinner. Use the middle sizing handles at the top and bottom of the image to make the image taller or shorter. Use the sizing handles at the corners of the image to change both the width and height at the same time.

Moving an Image

Move an image to a specific location on the page with options at the Position button drop-down gallery in the Arrange group on the Picture Tools Format tab. Choose an option from this gallery and the image is moved to the specified location and square text wrapping is applied to it.

The image can also be moved by dragging it to the new location. Before dragging an image, specify how the text will wrap around it by clicking the Wrap Text button in the Arrange group and then clicking the desired wrapping style at the drop-down list. After choosing a wrapping style, move the image by positioning the mouse pointer on the image border until the mouse pointer displays with a four-headed arrow attached. Click and hold down the left mouse button, drag the image to the new location, and then release the mouse button. As an image is moved to the top, left, right, or bottom margin or to the center of the document, green alignment guides display. Use these guides to help position the image on the page. Gridlines can be turned on to help position an image precisely. Do this by clicking the Align Objects button in the Arrange group on the Picture Tools Format tab and then clicking *View Gridlines*.

Align Objects

Rotate the image by positioning the mouse pointer on the round rotation handle (circular arrow) above the image until the pointer displays with a black circular arrow attached. Click and hold down the left mouse button, drag in the desired direction, and then release the mouse button. An image can also be rotated with options at the Rotate Objects button drop-down gallery. For example, the image can be rotated left or right or flipped horizontally or vertically.

Rotate Objects

Project 2c Inserting and Customizing an Image

Part 3 of 4

1. With **5-Training.docx** open, return the vertical alignment to top alignment by completing the following steps:
   a. Click the Layout tab.
   b. Click the Page Setup group dialog box launcher.
   c. At the Page Setup dialog box, make sure the Layout tab is selected.
   d. Click the *Vertical alignment* option box arrow and then click *Top* at the drop-down list.
   e. Click OK to close the dialog box.
2. Select and then delete the text *Sponsored by* and *Cell Systems*.
3. Select the remaining text and change the line spacing to single spacing.
4. Move the insertion point to the beginning of the document, press the Enter key, and then move the insertion point back to the beginning of the document.
5. Insert an image by completing the following steps:
   a. Click the Insert tab and then click the Pictures button in the Illustrations group.
   b. At the Insert Picture dialog box, navigate to your WL1C5 folder.
   c. Double-click ***Uluru.jpg*** in the Content pane.

5a

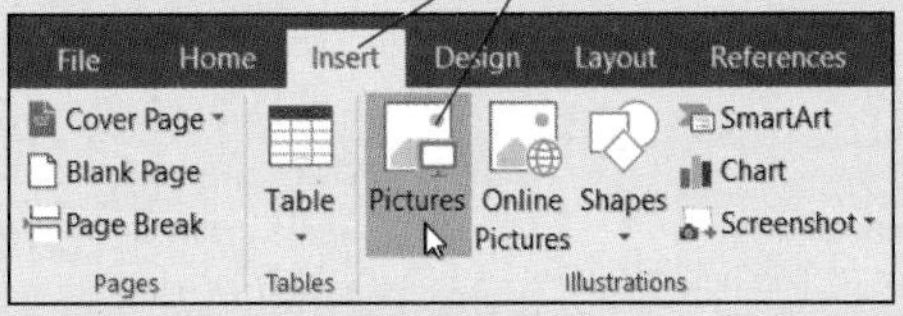

6. Crop the image by completing the following steps:
   a. Click the Crop button in the Size group on the Picture Tools Format tab.

b. Position the mouse pointer on the bottom middle crop handle (which displays as a short black line) until the pointer turns into the crop tool (which displays as a small black T).

c. Click and hold down the left mouse button, drag up to just below the rock (as shown at the right), and then release the mouse button.

d. Click the Crop button in the Size group to turn the feature off.

7. Change the size of the image by clicking in the *Shape Height* measurement box in the Size group, typing 3.1, and then pressing the Enter key.
8. Move the image behind the text by clicking the Layout Options button outside the upper right corner of the image and then clicking the *Behind Text* option at the side menu (second column, second row in the *With Text Wrapping* section). Close the side menu by clicking the Close button in the upper right corner of the side menu.

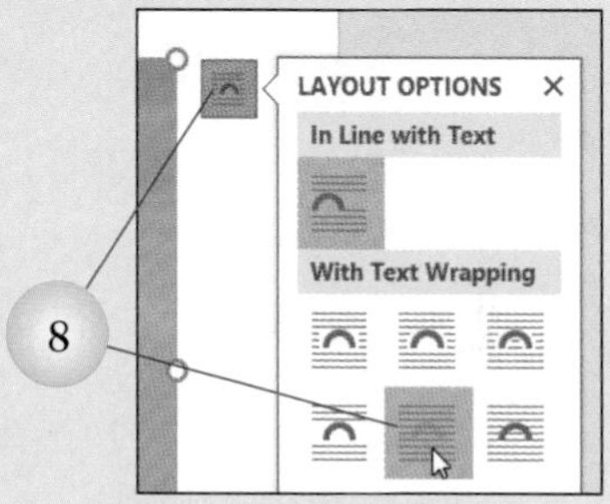

9. Rotate the image by clicking the Rotate Objects button in the Arrange group and then clicking *Flip Horizontal* at the drop-down gallery.
10. Change the image color by clicking the Color button in the Adjust group and then clicking *Saturation: 300%* (sixth option in the *Color Saturation* section).

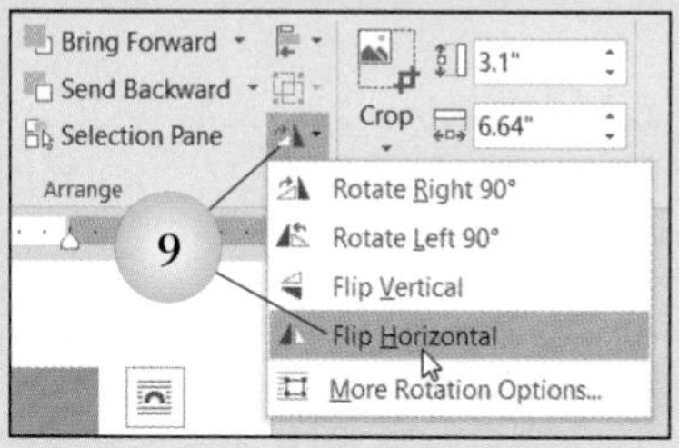

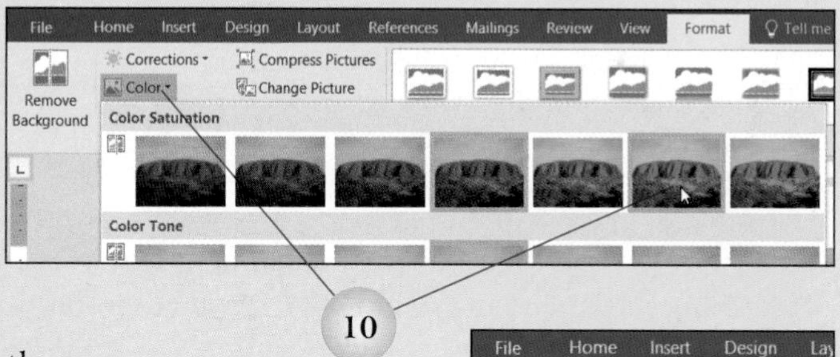

11. Apply an artistic effect by clicking the Artistic Effects button in the Adjust group and then clicking the *Watercolor Sponge* option (second column, third row).
12. Apply a picture effect by clicking the Picture Effects button in the Picture Styles group, pointing to Bevel, and then clicking the *Circle* option (first column, first row in the *Bevel* section).
13. After looking at the new color and artistic effect, you decide to return to the original color and artistic effect and remove the bevel effect by clicking the Reset Picture button in the Adjust group on the Picture Tools Format tab.

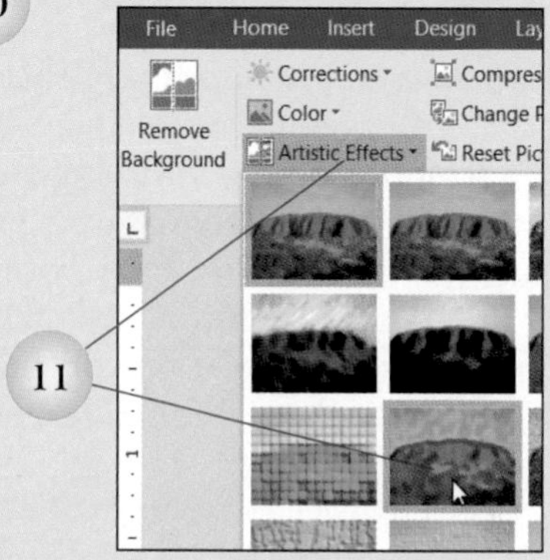

14. Sharpen the image by clicking the Corrections button in the Adjust group and then clicking the *Sharpen: 25%* option (fourth option in the *Sharpen/Soften* section).

15. Change the contrast of the image by clicking the Corrections button in the Adjust group and then clicking the *Brightness: 0% (Normal) Contrast: +40%* option (third column, bottom row in the *Brightness/Contrast* section).

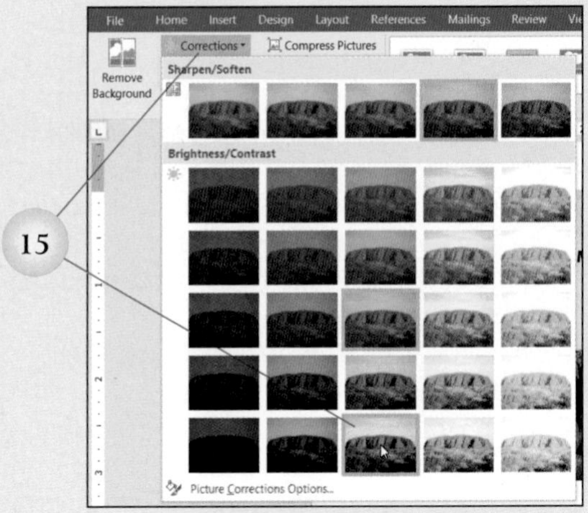

16. Apply a picture style by clicking the More Picture Styles button in the Picture Styles group and then clicking the *Simple Frame, Black* option.

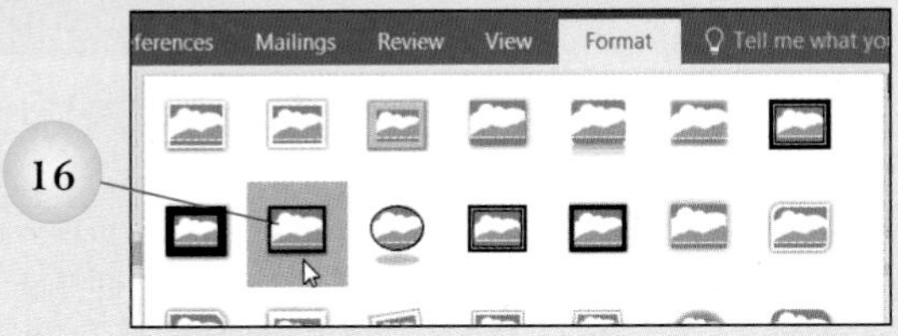

17. Compress the image file by completing the following steps:
    a. Click the Compress Pictures button in the Adjust group.
    b. At the Compress Pictures dialog box, make sure check marks display in both options in the *Compression options* section and then click OK.

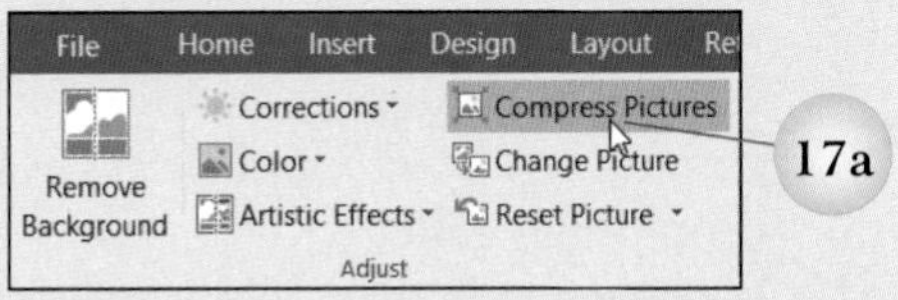

18. Position the mouse pointer on the border of the selected image until the pointer displays with a four-headed arrow attached. Click and hold down the left mouse button, drag the image up and slightly to the left until you see green alignment guides at the top margin and the center of the page, and then release the mouse button. If the green alignment guides do not display, turn on the guides by clicking the Align button in the Arrange group on the Picture Tools Format tab and then clicking the *Use Alignment Guides* option.

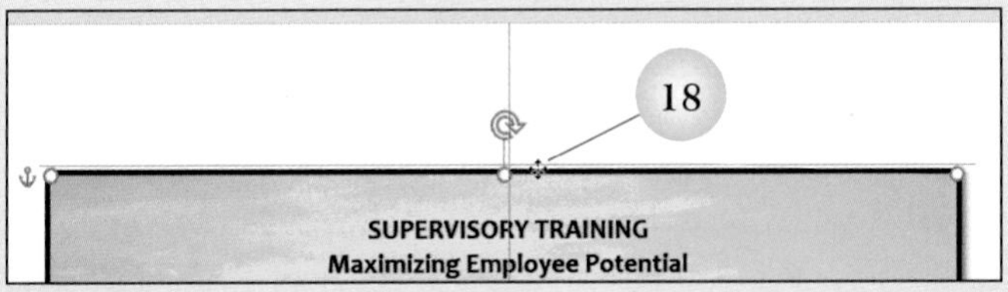

19. Save and then print **5-Training.docx**.
20. With the image selected, remove the background by completing the following steps:
    a. Click the Remove Background button in the Adjust group on the Picture Tools Format tab.
    b. Using the left middle sizing handle, drag the left border to the left border line of the image.
    c. Drag the right middle sizing handle to the right border line of the image.
    d. Drag the bottom middle sizing handle to the bottom border of the image, which displays as a dashed line.
    e. Drag the top middle sizing handle down to just above the top of the rock.

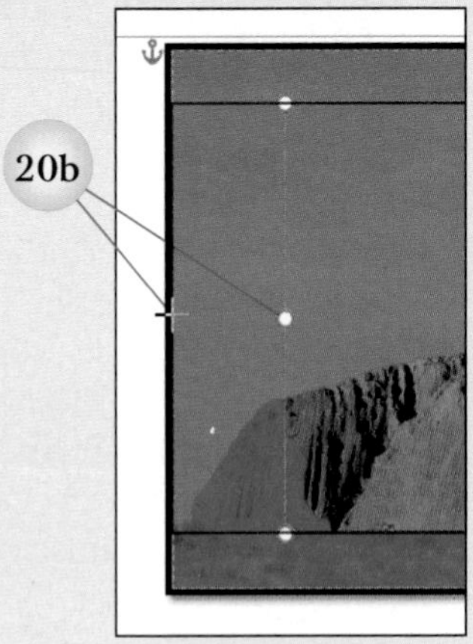

f. Click the Keep Changes button in the Close group on the Background Removal tab. (The image should now display with the sky removed.)

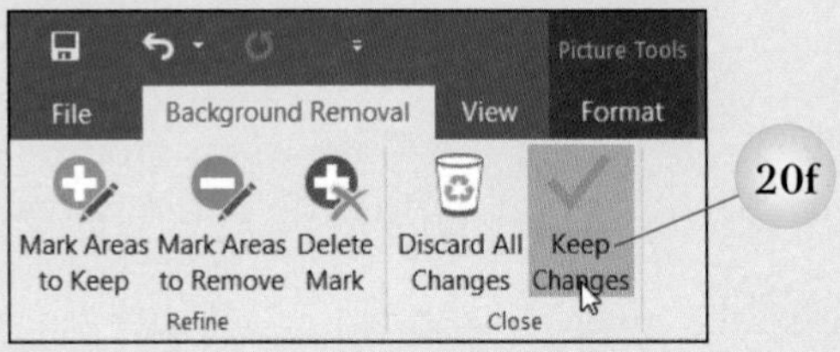

21. Save **5-Training.docx**.

Check Your Work

Inserting an Online Image

Online Pictures

Quick Steps

Insert an Online Image

1. Click Insert tab.
2. Click Online Pictures button.
3. Type search word or topic.
4. Press Enter.
5. Double-click image.

Use the Bing Image Search feature to search for specific images online. To use this feature, click the Insert tab and then click the Online Pictures button. This displays the Insert Pictures window, shown in Figure 5.7. Click in the search text box, type the search term or topic, and then press the Enter key. Images that match the search term or topic display in the window.

To insert an image, click the image and then click the Insert button or double-click the image. This downloads the image to the document. Customize the image with options and buttons on the Picture Tools Format tab.

When selecting online images to use in documents, be aware that many images are copyrighted and thus may not be available for use without permission. By default, Bing will limit search results to those licensed under Creative Commons. Usually, these images are free to use, but an image may have limitations for its use. For example, it may be necessary to credit the source. Always review the specific license for any image you want to use to ensure you can comply with the specific requirements for that image.

Figure 5.7 Insert Pictures Window

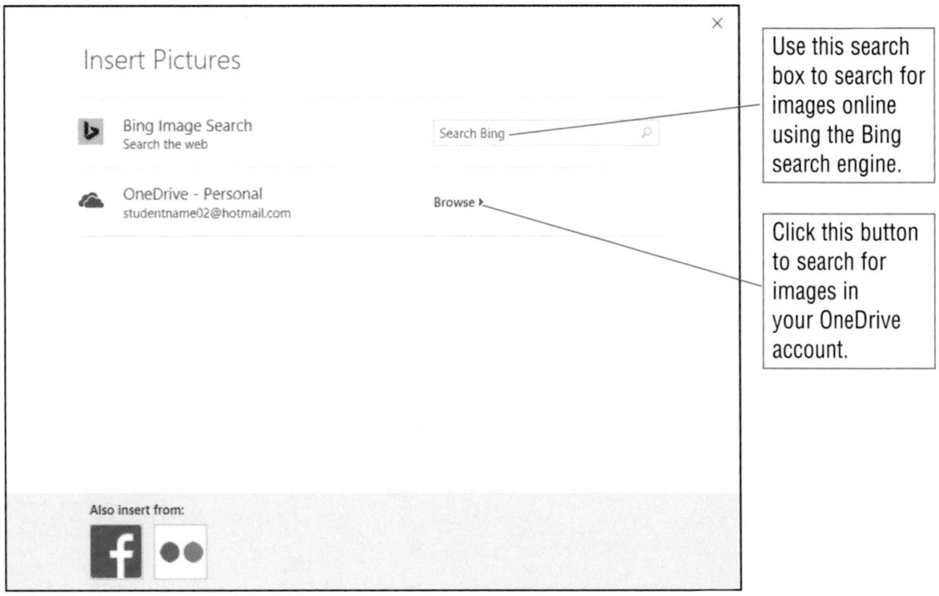

Project 2d Inserting an Online Image

Part 4 of 4

1. With **5-Training.docx** open, insert an image of Australia (with the Northern Territory highlighted) by completing the following steps:
   a. Click the Insert tab.
   b. Click the Online Pictures button in the Illustrations group.
   c. At the Insert Pictures window, type northern territory australia and then press the Enter key.
   d. Double-click the Australia image shown below. (If this image is not available online, click the Pictures button on the Insert tab. At the Insert Picture dialog box, navigate to your WL1C5 folder and then double-click the file ***NT-Australia.png***.)

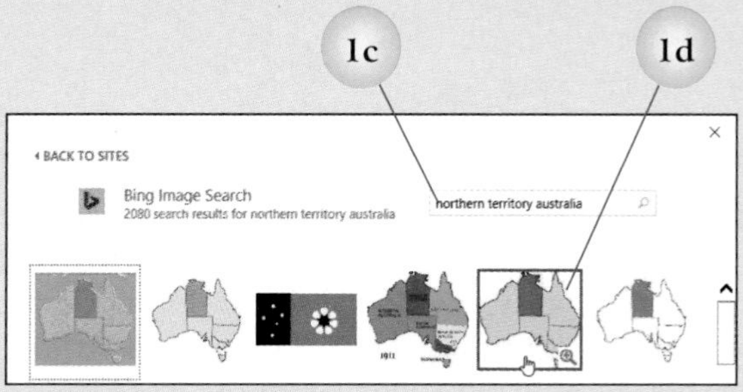

2. Size and position the image by completing the following steps:
   a. Click the Position button in the Arrange group.
   b. Click the *Position in Top Right with Square Text Wrapping* option (third column, first row in the *With Text Wrapping* section).
   c. Click the Wrap Text button.
   d. Click the *Behind Text* option at the drop-down gallery.
   e. Click in the *Shape Height* measurement box in the Size group, type 1, and then press the Enter key.

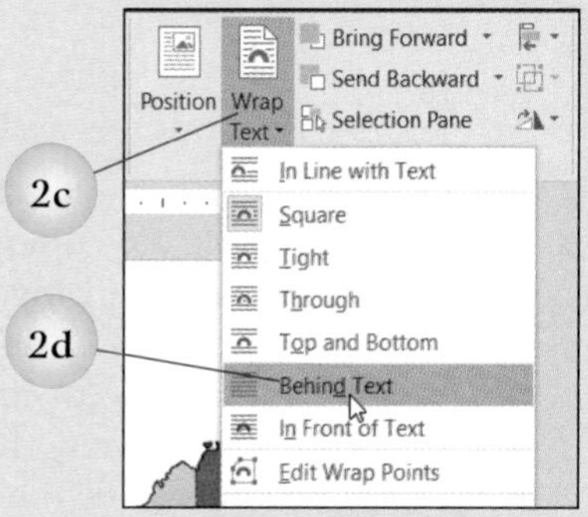

3. Make the white background of the image transparent by completing the following steps:
   a. Click the Color button in the Adjust group.
   b. Click the *Set Transparent Color* option at the bottom of the drop-down list. (The mouse pointer turns into a dropper tool.)
   c. Position the dropper tool on the white background of the image and then click the left mouse button.
4. Click the Color button in the Adjust group and then click the *Orange, Accent color 2 Light* option (third column, third row in the *Recolor* section).
5. Click outside the image to deselect it.
6. Save, print, and then close **5-Training.docx**.

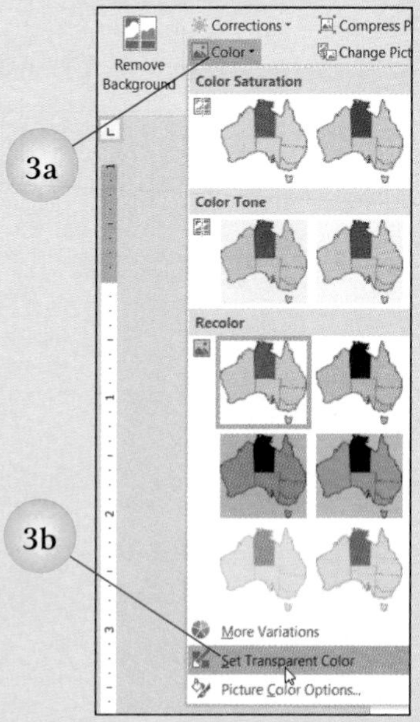

Check Your Work

Project 3 Customize a Report on Robots — 2 Parts

You will open a report on robots and then add a pull quote using a predesigned text box and insert a drawn text box with information about an upcoming conference.

Preview Finished Project

Tutorial

Inserting a Text Box

Text Box

Inserting a Text Box

Add interest or create a location in a document for text by inserting or drawing a text box. Click the Insert tab and then click the Text Box button and a drop-down list displays with predesigned text boxes and the *Draw Text Box* option. Choose one of the predesigned text boxes, which already contain formatting, or draw a text box and then customize or apply formatting to it with options and buttons on the Drawing Tools Format tab.

Quick Steps

Insert a Predesigned Text Box

1. Click Insert tab.
2. Click Text Box button.
3. Click option at drop-down list.

Inserting a Predesigned Text Box

One use for a text box in a document is to insert a pull quote. A pull quote is a quote from the text that is "pulled out" and enlarged and positioned in an attractive location on the page. Some advantages of using pull quotes are that they reinforce important concepts, summarize the message, and break up text blocks to make them easier to read. If a document contains multiple pull quotes, keep them in the order in which they appear in the text to ensure clear comprehension by readers.

A text box for a pull quote can be drawn in a document or a predesigned text box can be inserted in the document. To insert a predesigned text box, click the Insert tab, click the Text Box button, and then click the predesigned text box at the drop-down list.

Tutorial

Formatting a Text Box

Formatting a Text Box

When a text box is selected, the Drawing Tools Format tab is active. This tab contains buttons for formatting and customizing the text box. Use options in the Insert Shapes group on the Drawing Tools Format tab to insert a shape in the document. Click the Edit Shape button in the Insert Shapes group and a drop-down list displays. Click the *Change Shape* option to change the shape of the selected text box. Click the *Edit Points* option and small black squares display at points around the text box. Use the mouse to drag these points to increase or decrease specific points around the text box.

Apply predesigned styles to a text box and change the shape fill, outline, and effects with options in the Shape Styles group. Change the formatting of the text in the text box with options in the WordArt Styles group. Click the More WordArt Styles button in the WordArt Styles group and then click a style at the drop-down gallery. Customize text in the text box with the Text Fill, Text Outline, and Text Effects buttons in the Text group. Use options in the Arrange group to position the text box on the page, specify text wrapping in relation to the text box, align the text box with other objects in the document, and rotate the text box. Specify the text box size with the *Shape Height* and *Shape Width* measurement boxes in the Size group.

Project 3a **Inserting a Predesigned Text Box**

1. Open **Robots.docx** and then save it with the name **5-Robots**.
2. Insert a predesigned text box by completing the following steps:
   a. Click the Insert tab.
   b. Click the Text Box button in the Text group.
   c. Scroll down the drop-down list and then click the *Ion Quote (Dark)* option.
3. Type the following text in the text box: "The task of creating a humanlike body has proven incredibly difficult."
4. Delete the line and the source placeholder in the text box by pressing the F8 function key (which turns on the Selection Mode), pressing Ctrl + End (which selects text from the location of the insertion point to the end of the text box), and then pressing the Delete key.

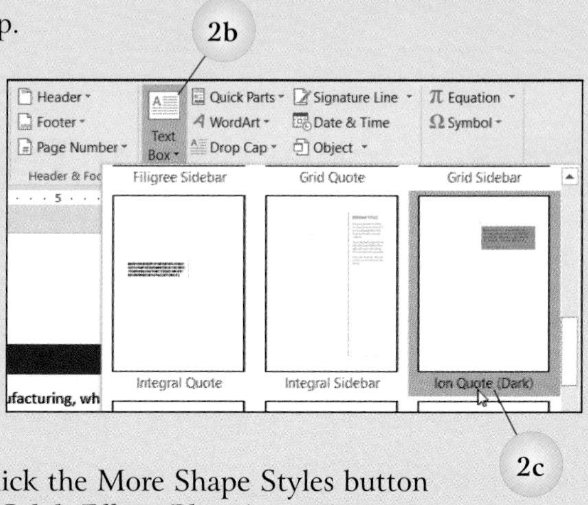

5. With the Drawing Tools Format tab active, click the More Shape Styles button in the Shape Styles group and then click the *Subtle Effect - Blue, Accent 5* option (sixth column, fourth row in the *Theme Styles* section).
6. Click the Shape Effects button in the Shape Styles group, point to *Shadow*, and then click the *Offset Diagonal Bottom Right* option (first column, first row in the *Outer* section).

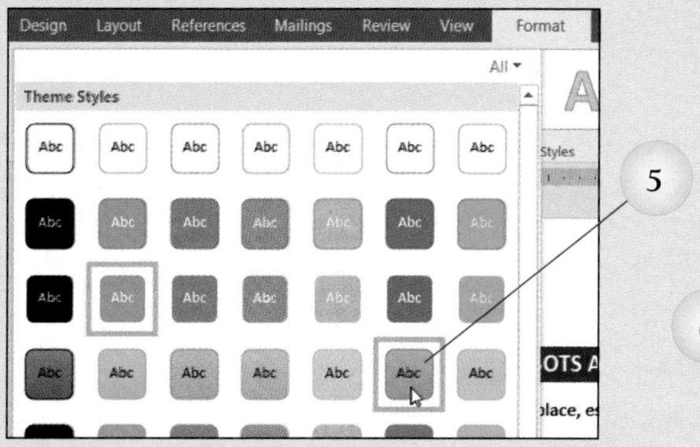

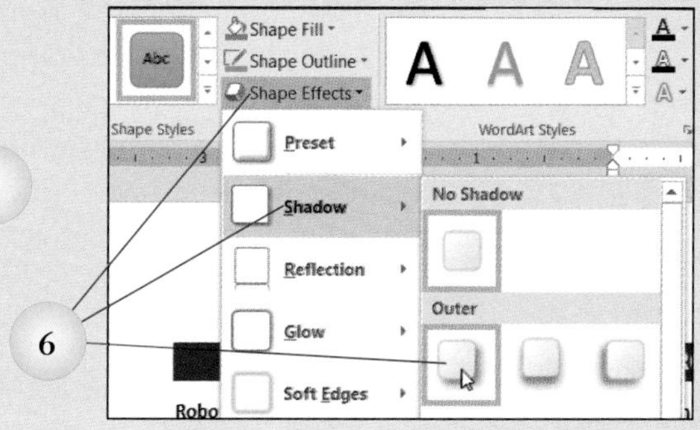

7. Position the mouse pointer on the border of the selected text box until the pointer turns into a four-headed arrow and then drag the text box so it is positioned as shown at the right.
8. Click outside the text box to deselect it.
9. Save **5-Robots.docx**.

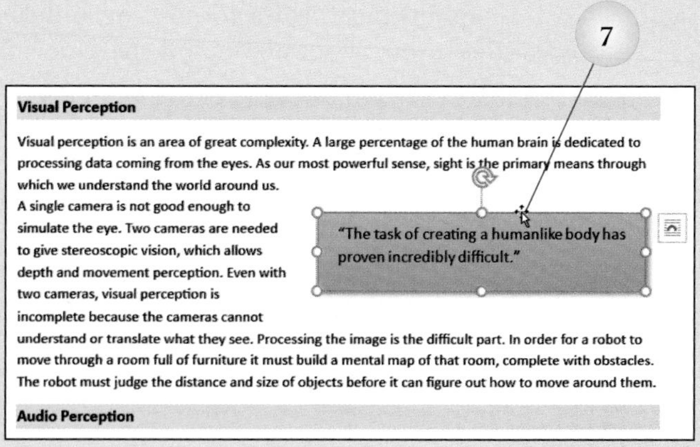

Check Your Work

Drawing and Formatting a Text Box

Quick Steps

Draw a Text Box

1. Click Insert tab.
2. Click Text Box button.
3. Click *Draw Text Box.*
4. Click or drag in document to create box.

In addition to the built-in text boxes provided by Word, a text box can be drawn in a document. To draw a text box, click the Insert tab, click the Text Box button in the Text group, and then click *Draw Text Box* at the drop-down list. With the mouse pointer displaying as crosshairs (a plus [+] symbol), click in the document to insert the text box or position the crosshairs in the document and then drag to create the text box. When a text box is selected, the Drawing Tools Format tab is active. Use buttons on this tab to format drawn text boxes in the same manner as built-in text boxes.

Project 3b Inserting and Formatting a Text Box

Part 2 of 2

1. With **5-Robots.docx** open, press Ctrl + End to move the insertion point to the end of the document.
2. Insert a text box by completing the following steps:
   a. Click the Insert tab.
   b. Click the Text Box button and then click the *Draw Text Box* option.
   c. Position the mouse pointer (displays as crosshairs) immediately right of the insertion point and then click the left mouse button. (This inserts the text box in the document.)
3. Change the text box height and width by completing the following steps:
   a. Click in the *Shape Height* measurement box in the Size group, type 1.2, and then press the Enter key.
   b. Click in the *Shape Width* measurement box in the Size group, type 4.5, and then press the Enter key.
4. Center the text box by clicking the Align button and then clicking *Align Center* at the drop-down list.
5. Apply a shape style by clicking the More Shape Styles button in the Shape Styles group and then clicking the *Subtle Effect - Blue, Accent 1* option (second column, fourth row in the *Theme Styles* section).
6. Apply a bevel shape effect by clicking the Shape Effects button, pointing to the *Bevel* option, and then clicking the *Soft Round* option at the side menu (second column, second row in the *Bevel* section).
7. Apply a 3-D shape effect by clicking the Shape Effects button, pointing to *3-D Rotation*, and then clicking the *Perspective Above* option (first column, second row in the *Perspective* section).
8. Insert and format text in the text box by completing the following steps:
   a. Press the Enter key two times. (The insertion point should be positioned in the text box.)
   b. Click the Home tab.
   c. Change the font size to 14 points, apply bold formatting, and change the font color to standard *Dark Blue*.
   d. Click the Center button in the Paragraph group.
   e. Type International Conference on Artifical Intelligence Summer 2019.
   f. Click outside the text box to deselect it. (Your text box should appear as shown at the right.)
9. Save, print, and then close **5-Robots.docx**.

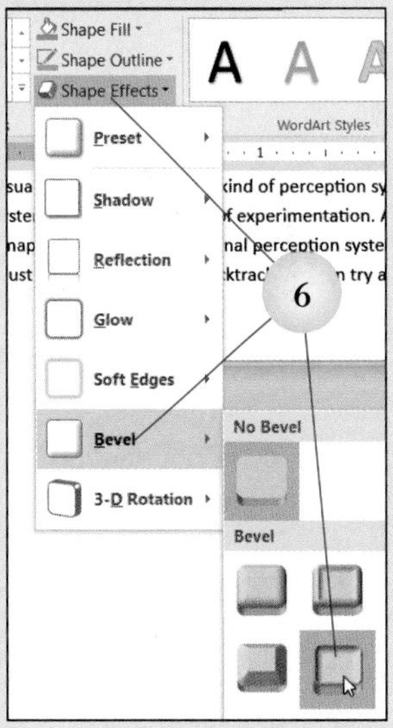

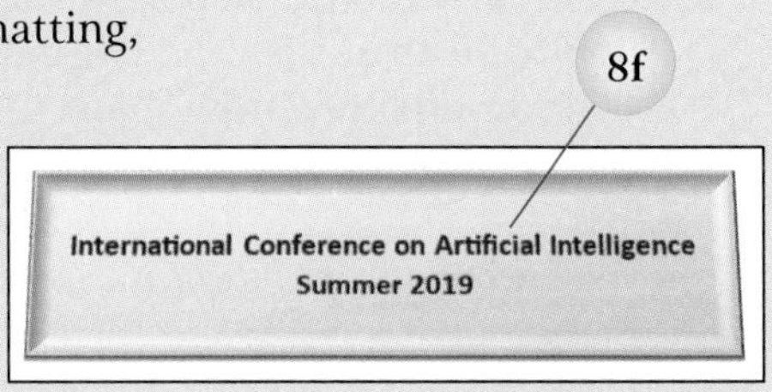

Check Your Work

Project 4 Prepare a Company Flyer — 2 Parts

You will prepare a company flyer by inserting and customizing shapes and WordArt.

Preview Finished Project

Tutorial

Inserting, Sizing, and Positioning a Shape and Line

Tutorial

Formatting a Shape and Line

Shapes

Quick Steps

Draw a Shape

1. Click Insert tab.
2. Click Shapes button.
3. Click shape.
4. Click or drag in document to create shape.

Hint To draw a square, choose the Rectangle shape and then press and hold down the Shift key while drawing.

Drawing Shapes

Use the Shapes button on the Insert tab to draw shapes in a document, including lines, basic shapes, block arrows, flow chart shapes, stars and banners, and callouts. Click a shape and the mouse pointer displays as crosshairs. Position the crosshairs in the document where the shape is to be inserted and then click the left mouse button or click and hold down the left mouse button, drag to create the shape, and then release the mouse button. The shape is inserted in the document and the Drawing Tools Format tab is active.

A shape selected from the *Lines* section of the drop-down list and then drawn in the document is considered a line drawing. A shape selected from another section of the drop-down list and then drawn in the document is considered an enclosed object. When drawing an enclosed object, maintain the proportions of the shape by pressing and holding down the Shift key while dragging with the mouse to create the shape.

Copying Shapes

To copy a shape, select the shape and then click the Copy button in the Clipboard group on the Home tab. Position the insertion point at the location where the copied shape is to be inserted and then click the Paste button. A selected shape can also be copied by pressing and holding down the Ctrl key while dragging a copy of the shape to the new location.

Project 4a Drawing Arrow Shapes — Part 1 of 2

1. At a blank document, press the Enter key two times and then draw an arrow shape by completing the following steps:
   a. Click the Insert tab.
   b. Click the Shapes button in the Illustrations group and then click the *Striped Right Arrow* shape (fifth column, second row) in the *Block Arrows* section.
   c. Position the mouse pointer (which displays as crosshairs) immediately right of the insertion point and then click the left mouse button. (This inserts the arrow shape in the document.)

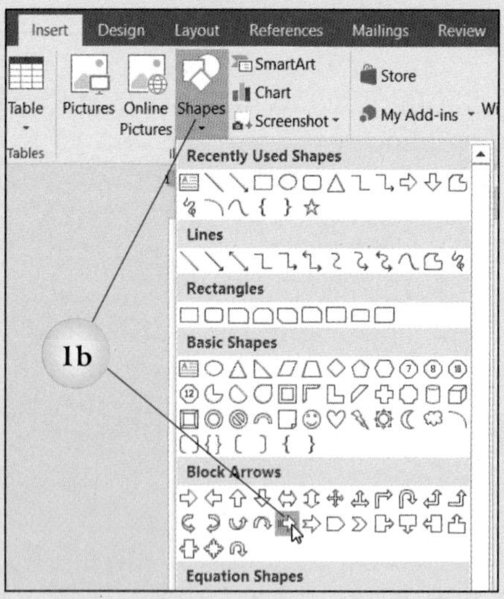

2. Format the arrow by completing the following steps:
   a. Click in the *Shape Height* measurement box in the Size group, type 2.4, and then press the Enter key.
   b. Click in the *Shape Width* measurement box in the Size group, type 4.5, and then press the Enter key.

c. Horizontally align the arrow by clicking the Align button in the Arrange group and then clicking *Distribute Horizontally* at the drop-down list.
d. Click the More Shape Styles button in the Shape Styles group and then click the *Intense Effect - Green, Accent 6* option (last option at the drop-down gallery).

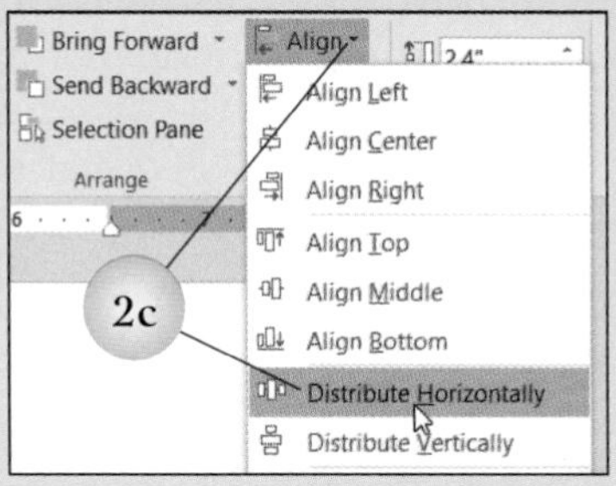

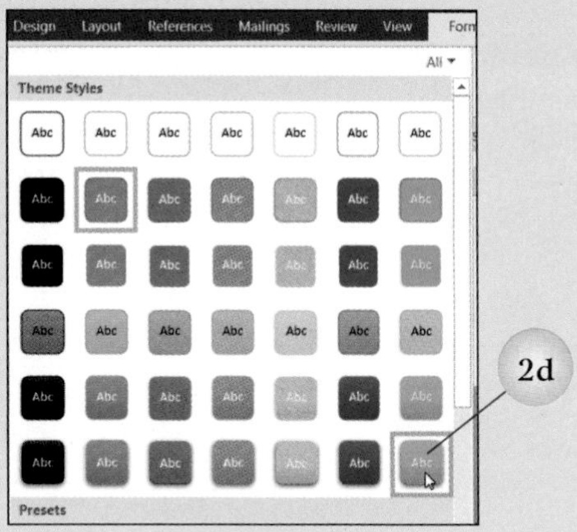

e. Click the Shape Effects button in the Shape Styles group, point to *Bevel*, and then click the *Angle* option (first column, second row in the *Bevel* section).
f. Click the Shape Outline button arrow in the Shape Styles group and then click the *Dark Blue* option (ninth option in the *Standard Colors* section).

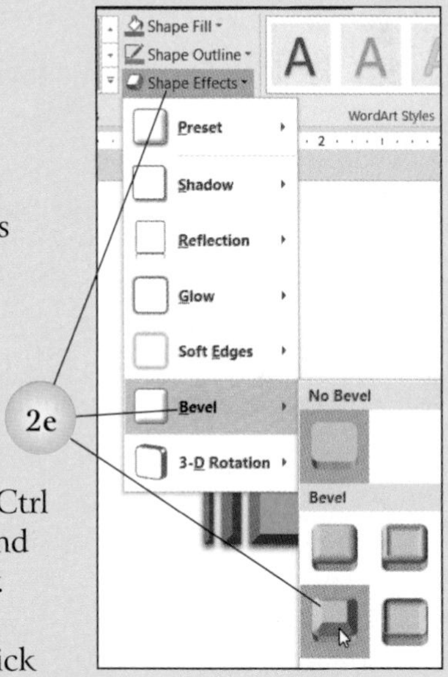

3. Copy the arrow by completing the following steps:
   a. With the mouse pointer positioned in the arrow (mouse pointer displays with a four-headed arrow attached), press and hold down the Ctrl key and click and hold down the left mouse button. Drag down until the copied arrow displays just below the top arrow, release the mouse button, and then release the Ctrl key.
   b. Click in the document to deselect the arrows and then click the second arrow to select it.
   c. Copy the selected arrow by pressing and holding down the Ctrl key and clicking and holding down the left mouse button and then dragging the copied arrow just below the second arrow.
4. Flip the middle arrow by completing the following steps:
   a. Click in the document to deselect the arrows and then click the middle arrow to select it.
   b. Click the Rotate button in the Arrange group on the Drawing Tools Format tab and then click the *Flip Horizontal* option at the drop-down gallery.

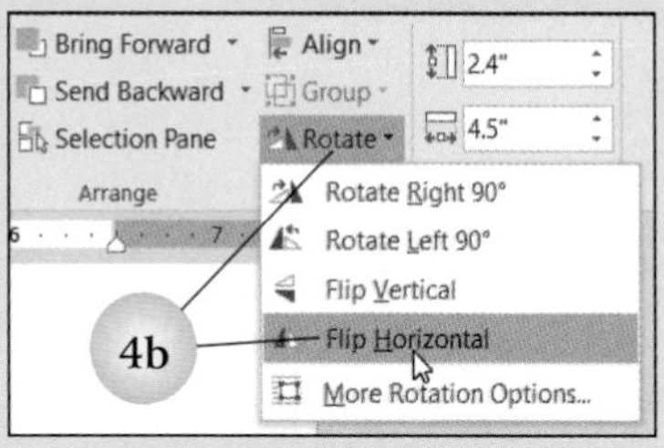

5. Insert the text *Financial* in the top arrow by completing the following steps:
   a. Click the top arrow to select it.
   b. Type Financial.
   c. Select *Financial*.
   d. Click the Home tab.
   e. Change the font size to 16 points, apply bold formatting, and change the font color to standard *Dark Blue* (ninth option in the *Standard Colors* section).
6. Complete steps similar to those in Step 5 to insert the word *Direction* in the middle arrow.
7. Complete steps similar to those in Step 5 to insert the word *Retirement* in the bottom arrow.
8. Save the document and name it **5-FinConsult**.
9. Print the document.

Check Your Work

Tutorial

Inserting, Sizing, and Positioning WordArt

Tutorial

Formatting WordArt

WordArt

Quick Steps

Create WordArt Text

1. Click Insert tab.
2. Click WordArt button.
3. Click option.
4. Type WordArt text.

Creating and Formatting WordArt

Use the WordArt feature to distort or modify text to conform to a variety of shapes. This is useful for creating company logos, letterheads, flyer titles, and headings.

To insert WordArt in a document, click the Insert tab and then click the WordArt button in the Text group. At the drop-down list, click the desired option and a WordArt text box is inserted in the document containing the words *Your text here* and the Drawing Tools Format tab is active. Type the WordArt text and then format the WordArt with options on the Drawing Tools Format tab. Existing text can also be formatted as WordArt. To do this, select the text, click the WordArt button on the Insert tab and then click the WordArt option at the drop-down list.

Project 4b Inserting and Modifying WordArt

Part 2 of 2

1. With **5-FinConsult.docx** open, press Ctrl + Home to move the insertion point to the beginning of the document.
2. Insert WordArt text by completing the following steps:
   a. Type Miller Financial Services and then select *Miller Financial Services*.
   b. Click the Insert tab.
   c. Click the WordArt button in the Text group and then click the *Fill - Orange, Accent 2, Outline - Accent 2* option (third column, first row).

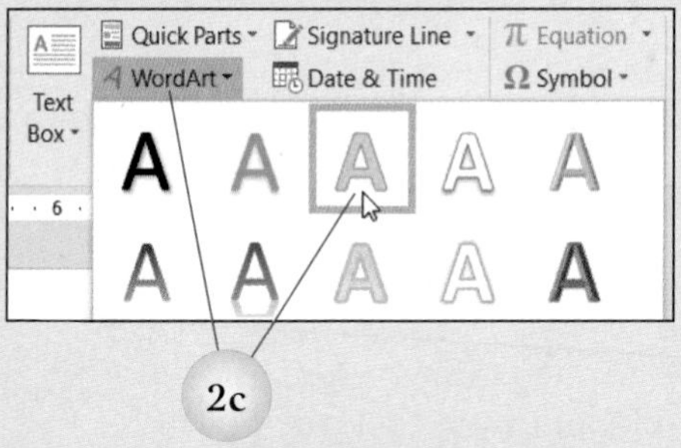

3. Format the WordArt text by completing the following steps:
   a. Make sure the WordArt text border displays as a solid line.
   b. Click the Text Fill button arrow in the WordArt Styles group on the Drawing Tools Format tab and then click the *Light Green* color option (fifth option in the *Standard Colors* section).
   c. Click the Text Outline button arrow in the WordArt Styles group and then click the *Green, Accent 6, Darker 50%* option (last option in *Theme Colors* section).

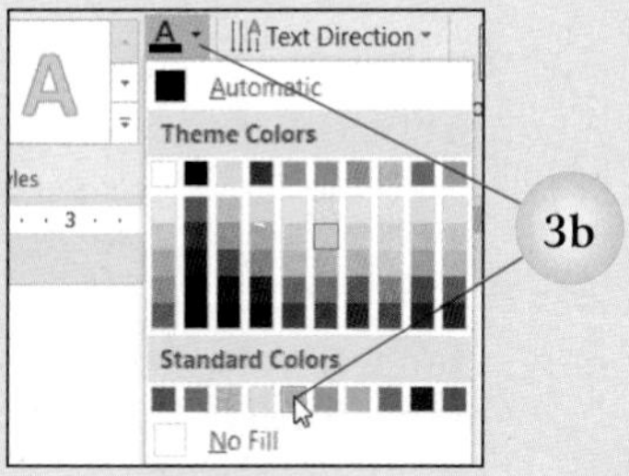

d. Click the Text Effects button in the WordArt Styles group, point to *Glow*, and then click the *Blue, 5 pt glow, Accent color 1* option (first option in the *Glow Variations* section).

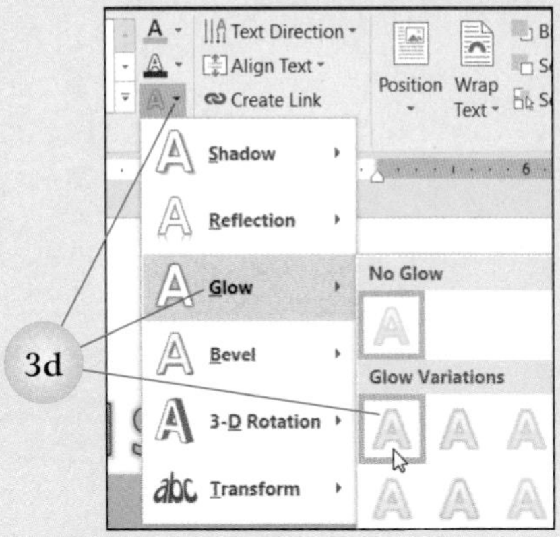

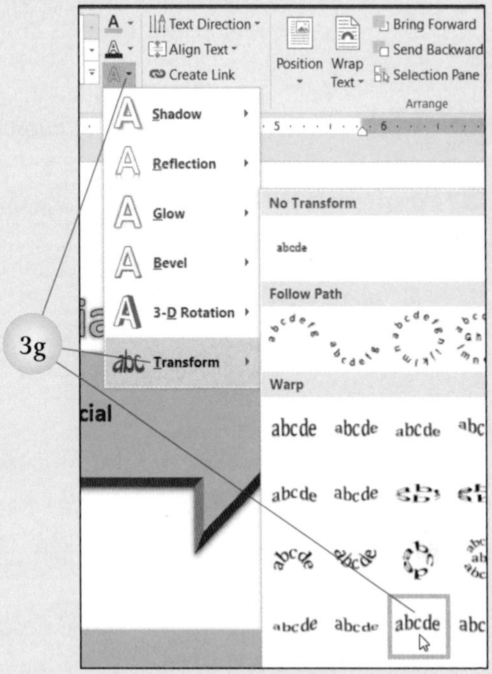

e. Click in the *Shape Height* measurement box in the Size group and then type 1.
f. Click in the *Shape Width* measurement box in the Size group, type 6, and then press the Enter key.
g. Click the Text Effects button in the WordArt Styles group, point to *Transform*, and then click the *Can Up* option (third column, fourth row in the *Warp* section).
h. Click the Position button in the Arrange group and then click the *Position in Top Center with Square Text Wrapping* option (second column, first row in the *With Text Wrapping* section).

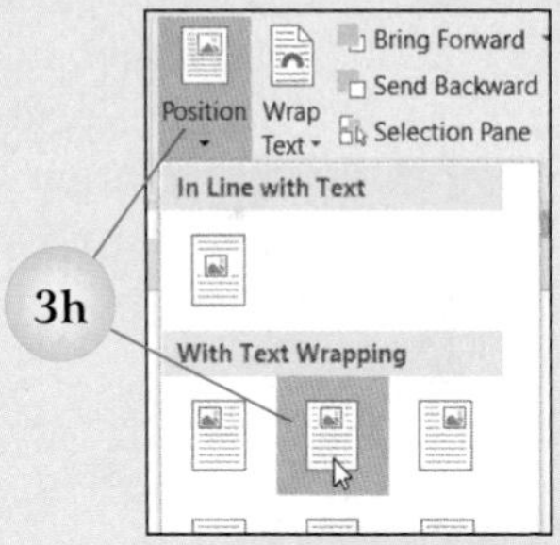

4. Click outside the WordArt to deselect it.
5. Move the arrows as needed to ensure they do not overlap the WordArt or each other and that they all fit on one page.
6. Save, print, and then close **5-FinConsult.docx**.

Check Your Work

Project 5 Create and Format Screenshots — 2 Parts

You will create screenshots of the Print and Export backstage areas, screen clippings of cover pages, and a sample cover page document.

Preview Finished Project

Tutorial

Inserting and Formatting Screenshot and Screen Clipping Images

Creating and Inserting a Screenshot

The Illustrations group on the Insert tab contains a Screenshot button, which captures the contents of a screen as an image or captures a portion of a screen. To capture the entire screen, open a new document, click the Insert tab, click the Screenshot button in the Illustrations group, and then click the desired screen thumbnail at the drop-down list. The currently active document does not display

Screenshot

as a thumbnail at the drop-down list—only other documents or files that are open. Click the specific thumbnail in the drop-down list and a screenshot of the screen is inserted as an image in the open document. The screenshot image is selected and the Picture Tools Format tab is active. Use buttons on this tab to customize the screenshot image.

Project 5a Inserting and Formatting Screenshots

Part 1 of 2

1. Press Ctrl + N to open a blank document.
2. Press Ctrl + N to open a second blank document, type Print Backstage Area at the left margin, and then press the Enter key.
3. Save the document and name it **5-BackstageAreas**.
4. Point to the Word button on the taskbar and then click the thumbnail representing the blank document.

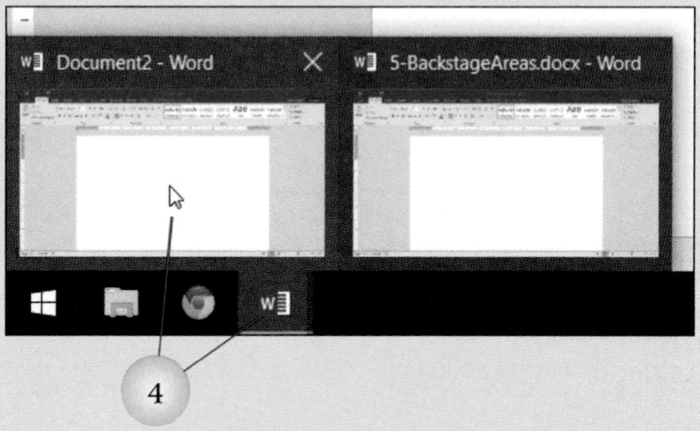

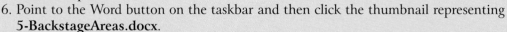

5. Display the Print backstage area by clicking the File tab and then clicking the *Print* option.
6. Point to the Word button on the taskbar and then click the thumbnail representing **5-BackstageAreas.docx**.
7. Insert and format a screenshot of the Print backstage area by completing the following steps:
   a. Click the Insert tab.
   b. Click the Screenshot button in the Illustrations group and then click the thumbnail in the drop-down list. (This inserts a screenshot of the Print backstage area in the document.)
   c. With the screenshot image selected, click the *Drop Shadow Rectangle* picture style option (fourth option in the picture styles gallery).
   d. Select the measurement in the *Shape Width* measurement box in the Size group, type 5.5, and then press the Enter key.

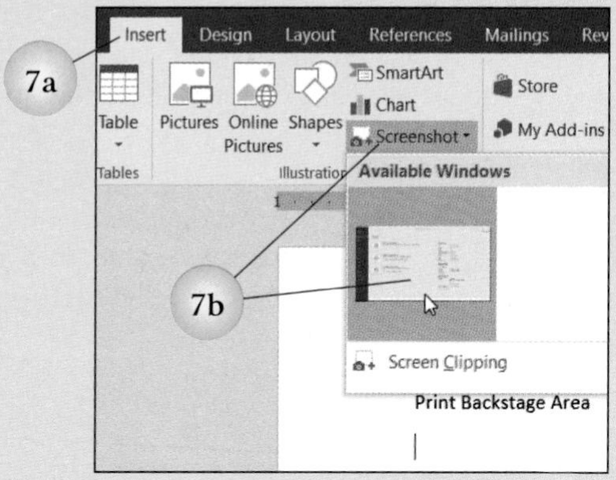

8. Press Ctrl + End and then press the Enter key. (The insertion point should be positioned below the screenshot image.)
9. Type Export Backstage Area at the left margin and then press the Enter key.
10. Point to the Word button on the taskbar and then click the thumbnail representing the blank document.
11. At the backstage area, click the *Export* option. (This displays the Export backstage area.)
12. Point to the Word button on the taskbar and then click the thumbnail representing **5-BackstageAreas.docx**.
13. Insert and format a screenshot of the Export backstage area by completing steps similar to those in Step 7.
14. Press Ctrl + Home to move the insertion point to the beginning of the document.
15. Save, print, and then close **5-BackstageAreas.docx**.
16. At the Export backstage area, press the Esc key to redisplay the blank document.
17. Close the blank document.

Check Your Work

Not only can a screenshot be made of an entire screen, but a screenshot can also be made of a specific portion of a screen by clicking the *Screen Clipping* option at the Screenshot button drop-down list. Click this option and the other open document, file, or Windows Start screen or desktop displays in a dimmed manner and the mouse pointer displays as crosshairs. Using the mouse, draw a border around the specific area of the screen to be captured. The area identified is inserted in the other document as an image, the image is selected, and the Picture Tools Format tab is active.

Project 5b Creating and Formatting a Screen Clipping

Part 2 of 2

1. Open **NSSLtrhd.docx** and then save it with the name **5-NSSCoverPages**.
2. Type the text Sample Cover Pages and then press the Enter key two times.
3. Select the text you just typed, change the font to 18-point Copperplate Gothic Bold, and then center the text.
4. Press Ctrl + End to move the insertion point below the text.
5. Open **NSSCoverPg01.docx** and then change the zoom to 40% by clicking six times on the Zoom Out button at the left side of the Zoom slider bar on the Status bar.
6. Point to the Word button on the taskbar and then click the thumbnail representing **5-NSSCoverPages.docx**.
7. Insert and format a screen clipping image by completing the following steps:
   a. Click the Insert tab.
   b. Click the Screenshot button in the Illustrations group and then click the *Screen Clipping* option.
   c. When **NSSCoverPg01.docx** displays in a dimmed manner, position the mouse crosshairs in the upper left corner of the cover page, click and hold down the left mouse button, drag down to the lower right corner of the cover page, and then release the mouse button. (See the image below and to the right.)
   d. With the cover page screen clipping image inserted in **5-NSSCoverPages.docx**, make sure the image is selected. (The sizing handles should display around the cover page image.)
   e. Click the Wrap Text button in the Arrange group on the Picture Tools Format tab and then click *Square* at the drop-down gallery.
   f. Select the current measurement in the *Shape Width* measurement box in the Size group, type 3, and then press the Enter key.
8. Point to the Word button on the Taskbar and then click the thumbnail representing **NSSCoverPg01.docx**.
9. Close **NSSCoverPg01.docx**.
10. Open **NSSCoverPg02.docx** and then, if necessary, change the zoom to 40%.

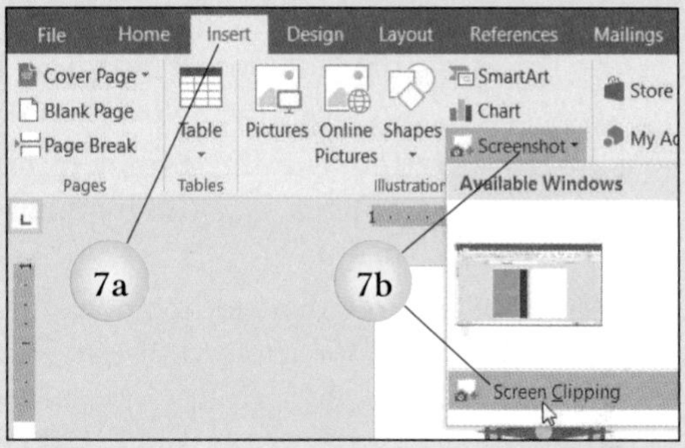

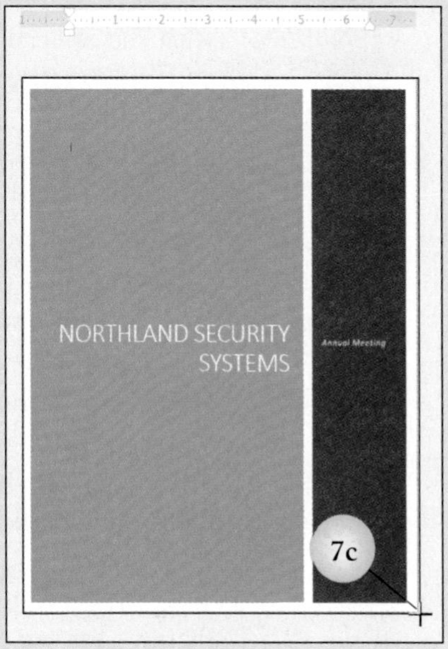

11. Point to the Word button on the Taskbar and then click the thumbnail representing **5-NSSCoverPages.docx**.
12. Insert and format a screen clipping image of the cover page by completing steps similar to those in Step 7.
13. If necessary, position the two cover page screenshot images side by side in the document.
14. Save, print, and then close **5-NSSCoverPages.docx**.
15. Close **NSSCoverPg02.docx**.

Check Your Work

Chapter Summary

- Apply formatting to a portion of a document by inserting a continuous section break or a section break that begins a new page. Turn on the display of nonprinting characters or change to Draft view to display section breaks; they are not visible in Print Layout view.
- Set text in columns to improve the readability of documents such as newsletters and reports. Format text in columns using the Columns button in the Page Setup group on the Layout tab or with options at the Columns dialog box.
- Remove column formatting with the Columns button on the Layout tab or at the Columns dialog box. Balance column text on the last page of a document by inserting a continuous section break at the end of the text.
- Improve the display of text by hyphenating long words that fall at the ends of lines. Use the hyphenation feature to hyphenate words automatically or manually.
- To enhance the appearance of text, use drop caps to identify the beginnings of major sections or paragraphs. Create drop caps with the Drop Cap button in the Text group on the Insert tab.
- Insert symbols with options at the Symbol dialog box with the Symbols tab selected, and insert special characters with options at the Symbol dialog box with the Special Characters tab selected.
- Click the Date & Time button in the Text group on the Insert tab to display the Date and Time dialog box. Insert the date or time with options at this dialog box or with keyboard shortcuts. If the date or time is inserted as a field, update the field with the Update tab or the F9 function key.
- Use the Click and Type feature to center, right-align, and left-align text.
- Vertically align text in a document with the *Vertical alignment* option at the Page Setup dialog box with the Layout tab selected.
- Insert an image such as a picture or clip art with buttons in the Illustrations group on the Insert tab.
- To insert an image from a folder on the computer's hard drive or removable drive, click the Insert tab and then click the Pictures button. At the Insert Picture dialog box, navigate to the specific folder and then double-click the image file.
- To insert an online image, click the Insert tab and then click the Online Pictures button. At the Insert Pictures window, type the search text or topic, press the Enter key, and then double-click the image.

- Customize and format an image with options and buttons on the Picture Tools Format tab. Size an image with the *Shape Height* and *Shape Width* measurement boxes in the Size group or with the sizing handles that display around a selected image.
- Move an image using options from the Position button drop-down gallery on the Picture Tools Format tab, or by choosing a text wrapping style and then moving the image by dragging it with the mouse.
- Insert a predesigned text box using options from the Text Box button drop-down gallery on the Insert tab. A predesigned text box or drawn text box can be used to create a pull quote, which is a quote that is pulled from the document text.
- Draw a text box by clicking the Text Box button in the Text group on the Insert tab, clicking the *Draw Text Box* option at the drop-down list, and then clicking or dragging in the document.
- Customize a text box with buttons on the Drawing Tools Format tab.
- Draw shapes in a document by clicking the Shapes button in the Illustrations group on the Insert tab, clicking a shape at the drop-down list, and then clicking or dragging in the document to draw the shape. Customize a shape with options the Drawing Tools Format tab.
- Copy a shape by pressing and holding down the Ctrl key while dragging the selected shape.
- Use WordArt to distort or modify text to conform to a variety of shapes. Customize WordArt with options on the Drawing Tools Format tab.
- Use the Screenshot button in the Illustrations group on the Insert tab to capture the contents of a screen or a portion of a screen. Use buttons on the Picture Tools Format tab to customize a screenshot image.

Commands Review

FEATURE	RIBBON TAB, GROUP	BUTTON, OPTION	KEYBOARD SHORTCUT
Column break	Layout, Page Setup	, *Columns*	Ctrl + Shift + Enter
columns	Layout, Page Setup		
Columns dialog box	Layout, Page Setup	, *More Columns*	
continuous section break	Layout, Page Setup	, *Continuous*	
Date and Time dialog box	Insert, Text		
drop cap	Insert, Text		
hyphenate words automatically	Layout, Page Setup	, *Automatic*	
insert date as field			Alt + Shift + D
Insert Picture dialog box	Insert, Illustrations		
Insert Pictures window	Insert, Illustrations		
insert time as field			Alt + Shift + T
Manual Hyphenation dialog box	Layout, Page Setup	, *Manual*	
Page Setup dialog box	Layout, Page Setup		
predesigned text box	Insert, Text		
screenshot	Insert, Illustrations		
shapes	Insert, Illustrations		
Symbol dialog box	Insert, Symbols	, *More Symbols*	
text box	Insert, Text		
update field			F9
WordArt	Insert, Text		

Workbook

Chapter study tools and assessment activities are available in the *Workbook* ebook. These resources are designed to help you further develop and demonstrate mastery of the skills learned in this chapter.

Microsoft®

Word

CHAPTER 6

Maintaining Documents and Printing Envelopes and Labels

Performance Objectives

Upon successful completion of Chapter 6, you will be able to:

1 Create and rename a folder

2 Select, delete, copy, move, rename, and print documents

3 Save documents in different file formats

4 Open, close, arrange, maximize, minimize, and restore documents

5 Split a window, view documents side by side, and open a new window

6 Insert a file into an open document

7 Preview and print specific text and pages in a document

8 Print envelopes and labels

9 Create a document using a template

Precheck

Check your current skills to help focus your study.

Almost every company that conducts business maintains a filing system. The system may consist of documents, folders, and cabinets or it may be a computerized filing system, where information is stored on the computer's hard drive or another storage medium. Whatever type of filing system a business uses, daily maintenance of files is important to its operation. In this chapter, you will learn to maintain files (documents) in Word, performing such activities as creating additional folders and copying, moving, and renaming documents. You will also learn how to create and print documents, envelopes, and labels and create a document using a Word template.

Data Files

Before beginning chapter work, copy the WL1C6 folder to your storage medium and then make WL1C6 the active folder.

SNAP

If you are a SNAP user, launch the Precheck and Tutorials from your Assignments page.

Project 1 **Manage Documents** **8 Parts**

You will perform a variety of file management tasks, including creating and renaming a folder; selecting and then deleting, copying, cutting, pasting, and renaming documents; deleting a folder; opening multiple documents; and saving a document in a different format.

Preview Finished Project

Maintaining Documents

Hint Display the Open dialog box with the keyboard shortcut Ctrl + F12.

Many file (document) management tasks can be completed at the Open dialog box (and some at the Save As dialog box). These tasks can include copying, moving, printing, and renaming documents; opening multiple documents; and creating new folders and renaming existing folders.

Directions and projects in this chapter assume that you are managing documents and folders on a USB flash drive or your computer's hard drive. If you are using your OneDrive account, some of the document and folder management tasks may vary.

Using Print Screen

Keyboards contain a Print Screen key that will capture the contents of the screen and insert the image in temporary memory. The image can then be inserted in a Word document. Press the Print Screen key to capture the entire screen as an image or press Alt + Print Screen to capture only the dialog box or window open on the screen. The Print Screen feature is useful for file management because the folder contents can be printed to help keep track of documents and folders.

To use the Print Screen key, display the desired information on the screen and then press the Print Screen key on the keyboard (generally located in the top row) or press Alt + Print Screen to capture the dialog box or window open on the screen. When the Print Screen key or Alt + Print Screen is pressed, nothing seems to happen, but in fact, the screen image is captured and inserted in the Clipboard. To insert this image in a document, display a blank document and then click the Paste button in the Clipboard group on the Home tab. The image can also be pasted by right-clicking in a blank location in a document and then clicking the *Paste* option at the shortcut menu.

Tutorial

Managing Folders

Creating a Folder

Word documents, like paper documents, should be grouped logically and placed in folders. The main folder on a storage medium is called the *root folder* and additional folders can be created within it. At the Open or Save As dialog box, documents display in the Content pane preceded by document icons and folders display preceded by folder icons.

New folder

New folder

Create a new folder by clicking the New folder button on the dialog box toolbar. This inserts a folder in the Content pane that contains the text *New folder*. Type a name for the folder (the typed name replaces *New folder*) and then press the Enter key. A folder name can contain a maximum of 255 characters. Folder names can use numbers, spaces, and symbols, except those symbols explained in the *Naming a Document* section on page 8 in Chapter 1.

Quick Steps

Create a Folder

1. Display Open dialog box.
2. Click New folder button.
3. Type folder name.
4. Press Enter.

To make the new folder active, double-click the folder name in the Open dialog box Content pane. The current folder path displays in the Address bar and includes the current folder and any previous folders. If the folder is located on an external storage device, the drive letter and name may display in the path. A right-pointing triangle displays to the right of each folder name in the Address bar. Click this right-pointing triangle and a drop-down list displays the names of any subfolders within the folder.

Project 1a Creating a Folder

Part 1 of 8

1. Open a blank document and then press Ctrl + F12 to display the Open dialog box.
2. In the *This PC* list in the Navigation pane, click the drive containing your storage medium. (You may need to scroll down the list to display the drive.)
3. Double-click the *WL1C6* folder in the Content pane.
4. Click the New folder button on the dialog box toolbar.
5. Type Correspondence and then press the Enter key.
6. Capture the Open dialog box as an image and insert the image in a document by completing the following steps:
   a. With the Open dialog box displayed, hold down the Alt key and then press the Print Screen key on your keyboard (generally located in the top row).
   b. Close the Open dialog box.
   c. At the blank document, click the Paste button in the Clipboard group on the Home tab. (If a blank document does not display on your screen, press Ctrl + N to open a blank document.)
   d. With the print screen image inserted in the document, print the document by clicking the File tab, clicking the *Print* option, and then clicking the Print button at the Print backstage area.
7. Close the document without saving it.
8. Display the Open dialog box and make WL1C6 the active folder.

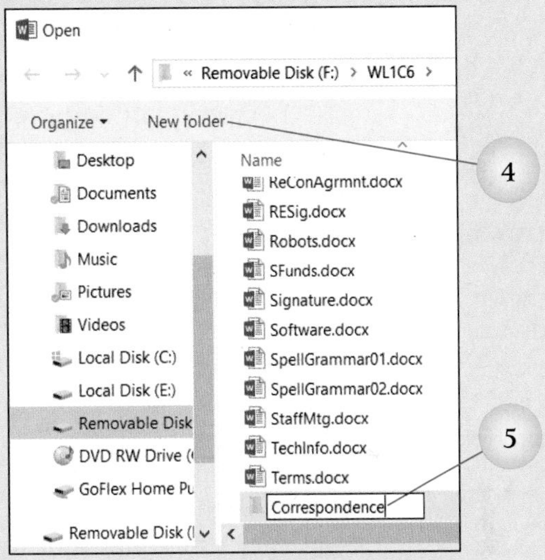

Check Your Work

Renaming a Folder

Organize

Quick Steps

Rename a Folder

1. Display Open dialog box.
2. Right-click folder.
3. Click *Rename*.
4. Type new name.
5. Press Enter.

When organizing files and folders, a folder may need to be renamed. Rename a folder using the Organize button on the toolbar in the Open or Save As dialog box or using a shortcut menu. To rename a folder using the Organize button, display the Open or Save As dialog box, click the folder to be renamed, click the Organize button on the toolbar in the dialog box, and then click *Rename* at the drop-down list. This selects the folder name and inserts a border around it. Type the new name for the folder and then press the Enter key. To rename a folder using a shortcut menu, display the Open dialog box, right-click the folder name in the Content pane, and then click *Rename* at the shortcut menu. Type a new name for the folder and then press the Enter key.

Project 1b Renaming a Folder

Part 2 of 8

1. With the Open dialog box open, right-click the *Correspondence* folder name in the Content pane.
2. Click *Rename* at the shortcut menu.
3. Type ComputerDocs and then press the Enter key.

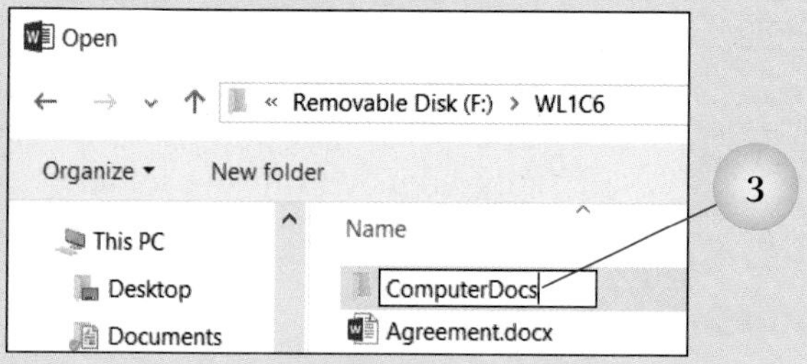

Selecting Documents

Complete document management tasks on one document or selected documents. To select one document, display the Open dialog box and then click the desired document. To select several adjacent documents (documents that display next to each other), click the first document, hold down the Shift key, and then click the last document. To select documents that are not adjacent, click the first document, hold down the Ctrl key, click any other documents, and then release the Ctrl key.

Deleting Documents

Tutorial

Managing Documents

Quick Steps

Delete a Folder or Document

1. Display Open dialog box.
2. Click folder or document name.
3. Click Organize button.
4. Click *Delete*.
5. Click Yes.

Hint Remember to empty the Recycle Bin on a regular basis.

Deleting documents is part of document maintenance. To delete a document, display the Open or Save As dialog box, select the document, click the Organize button on the toolbar, and then click *Delete* at the drop-down list. If documents are being deleted from an external drive, such as a USB flash drive, click the Yes button at the confirmation message. This message does not display if a document is being deleted from the computer's hard drive. To delete a document using the shortcut menu, right-click the document name in the Content pane and then click *Delete* at the shortcut menu. If a confirmation message displays, click Yes.

Documents deleted from the hard drive are automatically sent to the Recycle Bin. If a document is accidentally sent to the Recycle Bin, it can be easily restored. To free space on the drive, empty the Recycle Bin on a periodic basis. Restoring a document from or emptying the contents of the Recycle Bin is completed at the Windows desktop (not in Word). To display the Recycle Bin, minimize the Word window, display the Windows desktop, and then double-click the *Recycle Bin* icon on the Windows desktop. At the Recycle Bin, files can be restored and the Recycle Bin can be emptied.

Project 1c Selecting and Deleting Documents

Part 3 of 8

1. Open **FutureHardware.docx** and save it with the name **6-FutureHardware**.
2. Close **6-FutureHardware.docx**.
3. Delete **6-FutureHardware.docx** by completing the following steps:
   a. Display the Open dialog box.
   b. Click ***6-FutureHardware.docx*** to select it.
   c. Click the Organize button on the toolbar and then click *Delete* at the drop-down list.
   d. At the question asking if you want to delete **6-FutureHardware.docx**, click Yes. (This question will not display if you are deleting the file from your computer's hard drive.)

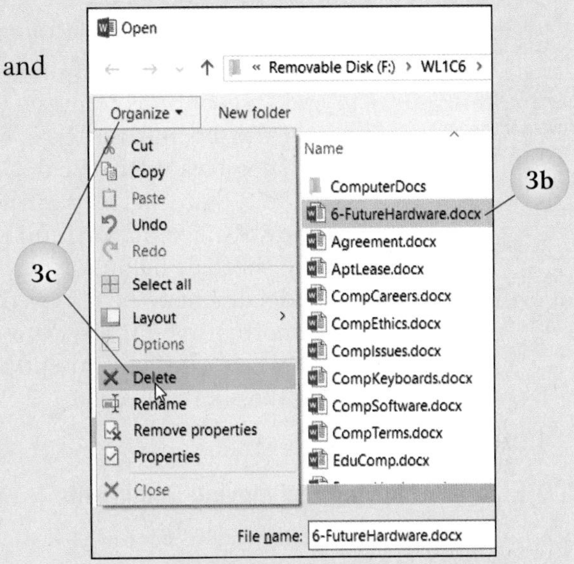

4. Delete selected documents by completing the following steps:
   a. At the Open dialog box, click ***CompCareers.docx***.
   b. Hold down the Shift key and then click ***CompEthics.docx***.
   c. Position the mouse pointer on a selected document and then click the right mouse button.
   d. At the shortcut menu, click *Delete*.
   e. At the question asking if you want to delete the items, click Yes.
5. Open **CompKeyboards.docx** and save it with the name **6-CompKeyboards**.
6. Save a copy of the **6-CompKeyboards.docx** file in the ComputerDocs folder by completing the following steps:
   a. With **6-CompKeyboards.docx** open, press the function key F12 to display the Save As dialog box.
   b. At the Save As dialog box, double-click the *ComputerDocs* folder at the top of the Content pane. (Folders are listed before documents.)
   c. Click the Save button in the lower right corner of the dialog box.
7. Close **6-CompKeyboards.docx**.
8. Press Ctrl + F12 to display the Open dialog box and then click *WL1C6* in the Address bar.

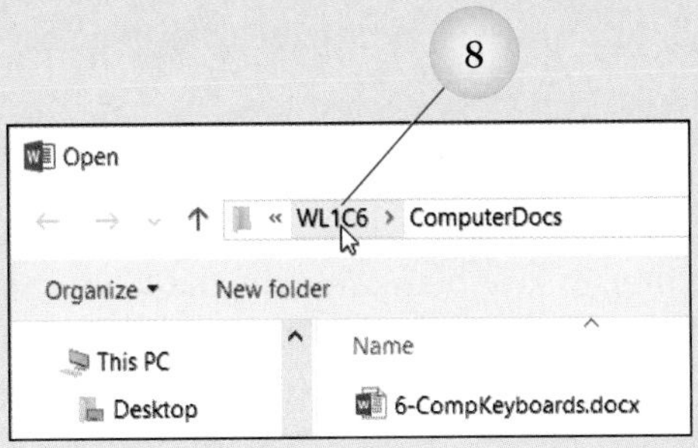

Copying and Moving Documents

Quick Steps

Copy a Document
1. Display Open dialog box.
2. Right-click document name.
3. Click *Copy*.
4. Navigate to folder.
5. Right-click blank area in Content pane.
6. Click *Paste*.

Move a Document
1. Display Open dialog box.
2. Right-click document name.
3. Click *Cut*.
4. Navigate to folder.
5. Right-click blank area in Content pane.
6. Click *Paste*.

A document can be copied to another folder without opening the document first. To do this, use the *Copy* and *Paste* options from the Organize button drop-down list or the shortcut menu at the Open dialog box or the Save As dialog box. A document or selected documents also can be copied into the same folder. When a document is copied a second time into the same folder, Word adds to the document name a hyphen followed by the word *Copy*.

Remove a document from one folder and insert it in another folder using the *Cut* and *Paste* options from the Organize button drop-down list or the shortcut menu at the Open dialog box. To do this with the Organize button, display the Open dialog box, select the document to be removed (cut), click the Organize button, and then click *Cut* at the drop-down list. Navigate to the desired folder, click the Organize button, and then click *Paste* at the drop-down list. To do this with the shortcut menu, display the Open dialog box, position the arrow pointer on the document to be removed, click the right mouse button, and then click *Cut* at the shortcut menu. Navigate to the desired folder, position the arrow pointer in a blank area in the Content pane, click the right mouse button, and then click *Paste* at the shortcut menu.

Project 1d Copying and Moving Documents — Part 4 of 8

Note: If you are using your OneDrive account, the steps for copying and moving files will vary from the steps in this project. Check with your instructor.

1. At the Open dialog box with WL1C6 the active folder, copy a document to another folder by completing the following steps:
   a. Click ***CompTerms.docx*** in the Content pane, click the Organize button, and then click *Copy* at the drop-down list.
   b. Navigate to the ComputerDocs folder by double-clicking *ComputerDocs* at the top of the Content pane.
   c. Click the Organize button and then click *Paste* at the drop-down list.
2. Change back to the WL1C6 folder by clicking *WL1C6* in the Address bar.
3. Copy several documents to the ComputerDocs folder by completing the following steps:
   a. Click ***IntelProp.docx***. (This selects the document.)
   b. Hold down the Ctrl key, click ***Robots.docx***, click ***TechInfo.docx***, and then release the Ctrl key. (You may need to scroll down the Content pane to display the three documents and then select the documents.)
   c. Position the arrow pointer on one of the selected documents, click the right mouse button, and then click *Copy* at the shortcut menu.
   d. Double-click the *ComputerDocs* folder.
   e. Position the arrow pointer in any blank area in the Content pane, click the right mouse button, and then click *Paste* at the shortcut menu.
4. Click *WL1C6* in the Address bar.

5. Move **CompIssues.docx** to the ComputerDocs folder by completing the following steps:
   a. Position the arrow pointer on ***CompIssues.docx***, click the right mouse button, and then click *Cut* at the shortcut menu.
   b. Double-click *ComputerDocs* to make it the active folder.
   c. Position the arrow pointer in any blank area in the Content pane, click the right mouse button, and then click *Paste* at the shortcut menu.
6. Capture the Open dialog box as an image and insert the image in a document by completing the following steps:
   a. With the Open dialog box displayed, press Alt + Print Screen.
   b. Close the Open dialog box.
   c. At a blank document, click the Paste button in the Clipboard group on the Home tab. (If a blank document does not display on your screen, press Ctrl + N to open a blank document.)
   d. With the print screen image inserted in the document, print the document.
7. Close the document without saving it.
8. Display the Open dialog box and make WL1C6 the active folder.

Check Your Work

Renaming Documents

Quick Steps

Rename a Document
1. Display Open dialog box.
2. Click document name.
3. Click Organize button and then click *Rename*.
4. Type new name.
5. Press Enter.

At the Open dialog box, use the *Rename* option from the Organize button drop-down list to give a document a different name. The *Rename* option changes the name of the document and keeps it in the same folder. To rename a document, display the Open dialog box, click the document to be renamed, click the Organize button, and then click *Rename* at the drop-down list. This selects the name and displays a black border around the document name. Type the new name and then press the Enter key. A document can also be renamed by right-clicking the document name at the Open dialog box and then clicking *Rename* at the shortcut menu. Type the new name for the document and then press the Enter key.

Deleting a Folder

As explained earlier in this chapter, a document or selected documents can be deleted. Delete a folder and all of its contents in the same manner as deleting a document.

Opening Multiple Documents

Hint Open a recently opened document by clicking the File tab, clicking the *Open* option, and then clicking the document in the *Recent* option list.

To open more than one document, select the documents in the Open dialog box and then click the Open button. Multiple documents can also be opened by positioning the arrow pointer on one of the selected documents, clicking the right mouse button, and then clicking *Open* at the shortcut menu.

Changing Dialog Box View

Use options in the Change your view button drop-down list at the Open or Save As dialog box to customize the display of folders and documents in the Content pane. Click the Change your view button arrow and a drop-down list displays with options for displaying folders and documents as icons, a list, with specific details, as tiles, or in content form. Change the view by clicking an option at the drop-down list or by clicking the Change your view button until the dialog box displays in the desired view.

Project 1e Renaming and Opening Documents and Deleting a Folder

Part 5 of 8

1. Rename a document in the ComputerDocs folder by completing the following steps:
   a. At the Open dialog box with the WL1C6 folder open, double-click the *ComputerDocs* folder to make it active.
   b. Click ***Robots.docx*** to select it.
   c. Click the Organize button.
   d. Click *Rename* at the drop-down list.
   e. Type Androids and then press the Enter key.

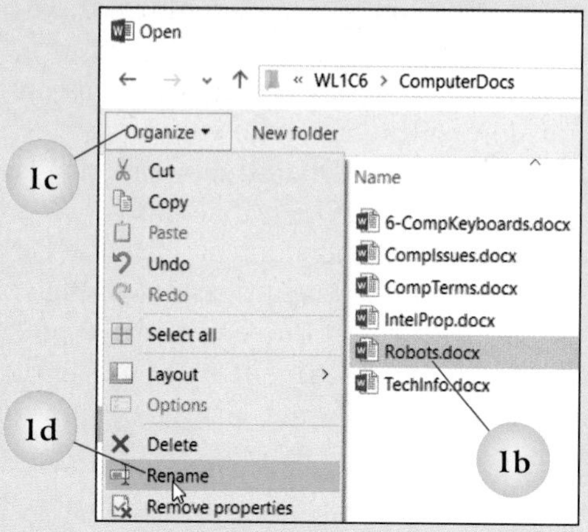

2. Capture the Open dialog box as an image and insert the image in a document by completing the following steps:
   a. Press Alt + Print Screen.
   b. Close the Open dialog box.
   c. At a blank document, click the Paste button in the Clipboard group on the Home tab. (If a blank document does not display on your screen, press Ctrl + N to open a blank document.)
   d. With the print screen image inserted in the document, print the document.
3. Close the document without saving it.
4. Display the Open dialog box and make WL1C6 the active folder.
5. Change the dialog box view by clicking the Change your view button arrow and then clicking *Large icons* at the drop-down list.
6. Change the view again by clicking the Change your view button arrow and then clicking *Content* at the drop-down list.
7. Change the view back to a list by clicking the Change your view button and then clicking *List* at the drop-down list.
8. At the Open dialog box, click the *ComputerDocs* folder to select it.
9. Click the Organize button and then click *Delete* at the drop-down list.
10. If a message displays asking if you want to remove the folder and its contents, click Yes.
11. Select ***CompKeyboards.docx***,***CompSoftware.docx***, and ***CompTerms.docx***.
12. Click the Open button in the lower right corner of the dialog box.
13. Close the open documents.

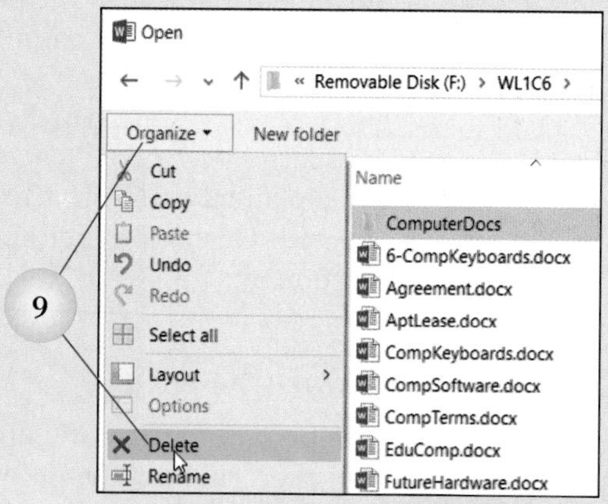

Check Your Work

Tutorial

Saving in a Different Format

Saving in a Different Format

When a document is saved, it is saved as a Word document with the .docx file extension. If the document is to be shared with someone who is using a different word processing program or a different version of Word, consider saving the document in another format. At the Export backstage area, click the *Change File Type* option and the backstage area displays, as shown in Figure 6.1.

Quick Steps

Save in a Different Format

1. Click File tab.
2. Click *Export* option.
3. Click *Change File Type* option.
4. Click format in *Document File Types* or *Other File Types* section.
5. Click Save As button.

Saving in Different Document File Types Use options in the *Document File Types* section, which is below the *Change File Type* heading, to save the Word document with the default file format, in a previous version of Word, in the OpenDocument Text format, or as a template. The OpenDocument Text format is an XML-based file format for displaying, storing, and editing files, such as word processing, spreadsheet, and presentation files. OpenDocument Text format is free from any licensing, royalty payments, or other restrictions. Since technology changes at a rapid pace, saving a document in the OpenDocument Text format ensures that the information in it can be accessed, retrieved, and used now and in the future.

Saving in Other File Types Additional file types are available in the *Other File Types* section. If a document is being sent to a user who does not have access to Microsoft Word, consider saving the document in plain text or rich text file format. Use the *Plain Text (*.txt)* option to save the document with all the formatting stripped, which is good for universal file exchange. Use the *Rich Text Format (*.rtf)* option to save the document with most of the character formatting applied to the text in the document, such as bold, italic, underline, bullets, and fonts, as well as some paragraph formatting. Before the widespread use of Adobe's portable document format (PDF), rich text format was the most portable file format used to exchange files. With the *Single File Web Page (*.mht, *.mhtml)* option, a document can be saved as a single-page web document. Click the *Save as Another File Type* option and the Save As dialog box displays. Click the *Save as type* option box and a drop-down list displays with a variety of available file type options.

Figure 6.1 Export Backstage Area with *Change File Type* Option Selected

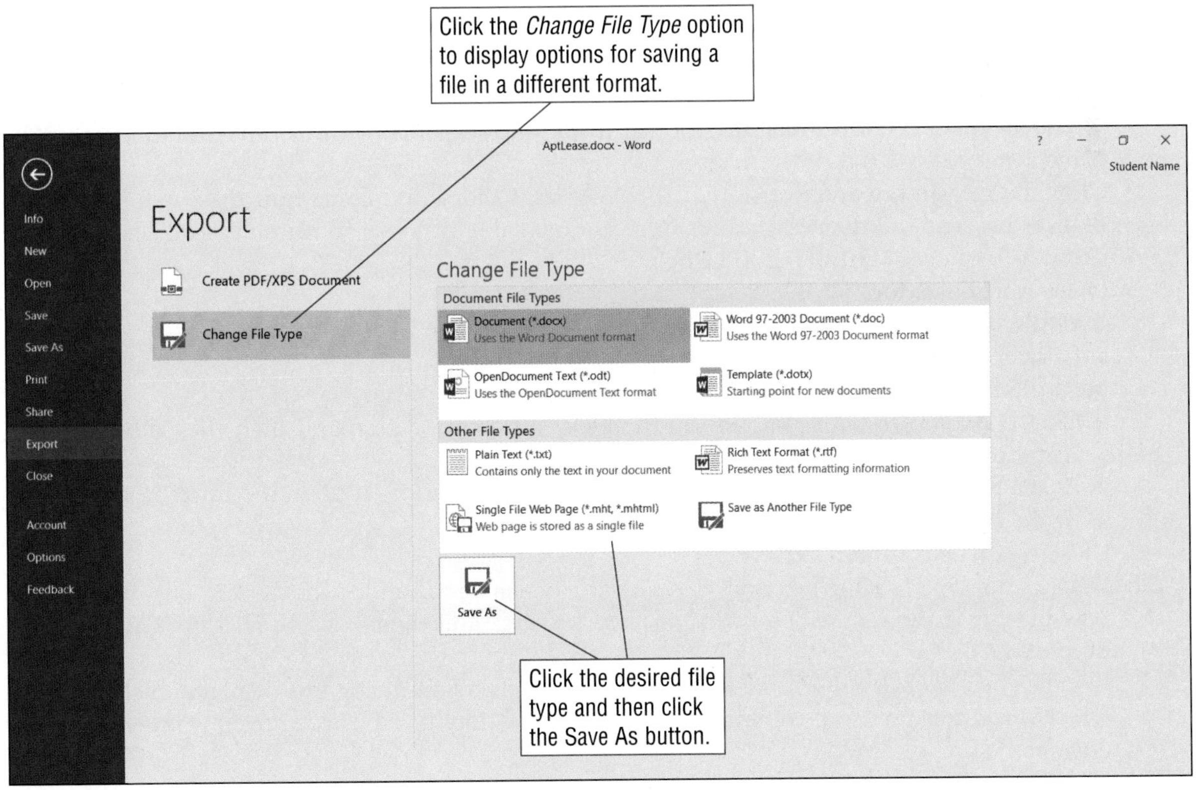

Project 1f **Saving in Different File Formats**

Part 6 of 8

1. Open **AptLease.docx** and then save it in Word 97-2003 format by completing the following steps:
   a. Click the File tab and then click the *Export* option.
   b. At the Export backstage area, click the *Change File Type* option.
   c. Click the *Word 97-2003 Document (*.doc)* option in the *Document File Types* section and then click the Save As button.

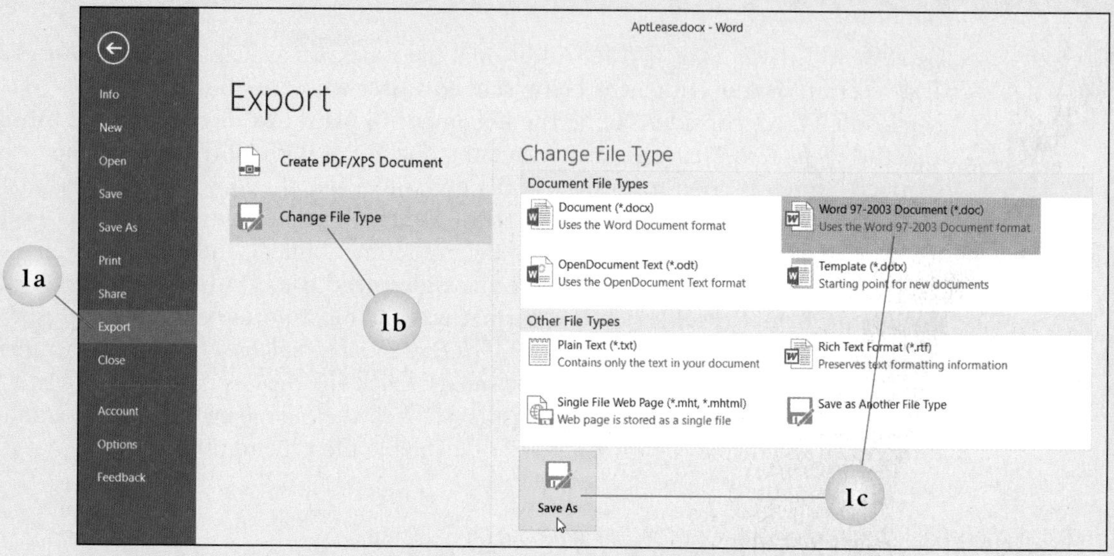

   d. At the Save As dialog box with the *Save as type* option changed to *Word 97-2003 Document (*.doc)*, type 6-AptLease-Word97-2003 in the *File name* text box and then press the Enter key.
2. At the document, notice that the title bar displays *[Compatibility Mode]* after the document name.
3. Click the Design tab and notice that the Themes, Colors, and Fonts buttons are dimmed. (This is because the themes features were not available in Word 97 through 2003.)
4. Close **6-AptLease-Word97-2003.doc**.
5. Open **AptLease.docx**.
6. Save the document in plain text format by completing the following steps:
   a. Click the File tab and then click the *Export* option.
   b. At the Export backstage area, click the *Change File Type* option.
   c. Click the *Plain Text (*.txt)* option in the *Other File Types* section and then click the Save As button.
   d. At the Save As dialog box, type 6-AptLease-PlainTxt and then press the Enter key.
   e. At the File Conversion dialog box, click OK.
7. Close **6-AptLease-PlainTxt.txt**.
8. Display the Open dialog box and, if necessary, display all the files. To do this, click the file type button at the right side of the *File name* text box and then click *All Files (*.*)* at the drop-down list.
9. Double-click ***6-AptLease-PlainTxt.txt***. (If a File Conversion dialog box displays, click OK. Notice that the character and paragraph formatting have been removed from the document.)
10. Close **6-AptLease-PlainTxt.txt**.

Check Your Work

Quick Steps

Save in a Different Format at the Save As Dialog Box

1. Press F12 to display Save As dialog box.
2. Type document name.
3. Click *Save as type* option box.
4. Click format.
5. Click Save button.

Saving in a Different File Type at the Save As Dialog Box In addition to saving a document using options in the Export backstage area with the *Change File Type* option selected, a document can be saved in a different format using the *Save as type* option box at the Save As dialog box. Click the *Save as type* option box and a drop-down list displays containing all the available file formats for saving a document. Click the desired format and then click the Save button.

Project 1g Saving in a Different Format at the Save As Dialog Box — Part 7 of 8

1. Open **AptLease.docx**.
2. Save the document in rich text format by completing the following steps:
   a. Press the function key F12 to display the Save As dialog box.
   b. At the Save As dialog box, type 6-AptLease-RichTxt in the *File name* text box.
   c. Click the *Save as type* option box.
   d. Click *Rich Text Format (*.rtf)* at the drop-down list.
   e. Click the Save button.
3. Close the document.
4. Display the Open dialog box and, if necessary, display all the files.
5. Double-click ***6-AptLease-RichTxt.rtf***. (Notice that the formatting has been retained in the document.)
6. Close the document.

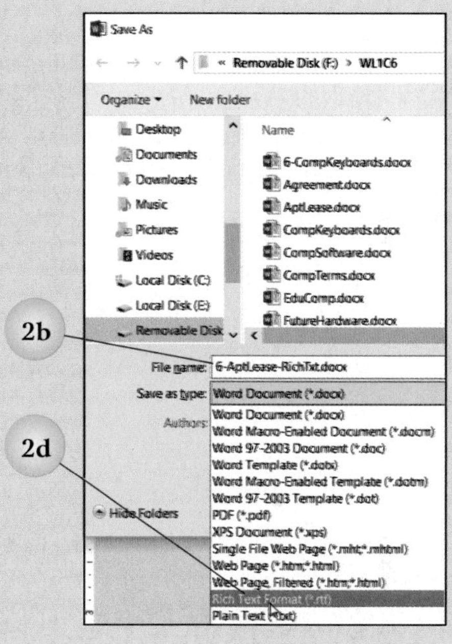

Tutorial

Saving and Opening a Document in PDF Format

Saving in PDF/XPS Format A Word document can be saved in PDF or XPS file format. PDF stands for *portable document format* and is a file format that preserves fonts, formatting, and images in a printer-friendly version that looks the same on most computers. A person who receives a Word file saved in PDF format does not need to have the Word application on his or her computer to open, read, and print the file. Exchanging PDF files is a popular method for collaborating, since this file type has cross-platform compatibility, allowing users to open PDF files on Windows-based personal computers, Macintosh computers, tablets, and smartphones. The XML paper specification (XPS) format, which was developed by Microsoft, is a fixed-layout format with all the formatting preserved (similar to PDF).

To save a document in PDF or XPS format, click the File tab, click the *Export* option, and then click the Create PDF/XPS button. This displays the Publish as PDF or XPS dialog box with the *PDF (*.pdf)* option selected in the *Save as type* option box. To save the document in XPS format, click the *Save as type* option box and then click *XPS Document (*.xps)* at the drop-down list. At the Save As dialog box, type a name in the *File name* text box and then click the Publish button.

Quick Steps

Save in PDF/XPS Format

1. Click File tab.
2. Click *Export* option.
3. Click Create PDF/XPS button.
4. At Publish as PDF or XPS dialog box, specify PDF or XPS format.
5. Click Publish button.

A PDF file will open in Adobe Acrobat Reader, Microsoft Edge, and Word 2016. An XPS file will open in Internet Explorer and XPS Viewer. One method for opening a PDF or XPS file is to open File Explorer navigate, to the folder containing the file, right-click the file, and then point to *Open with*. This displays a side menu with the programs that can be used to open the file. A PDF file can be opened and edited in Word but an XPS file cannot.

Project 1h Saving in PDF Format and Editing a PDF File in Word

Part 8 of 8

1. Open **NSS.docx** and then save the document in PDF format by completing the following steps:
   a. Click the File tab and then click the *Export* option.
   b. At the Export backstage area, click the Create PDF/XPS button.
   c. At the Publish as PDF or XPS dialog box, make sure that *PDF (*.pdf)* is selected in the *Save as type* option box and that the *Open file after publishing* check box contains a check mark. After confirming both selections, click the Publish button.

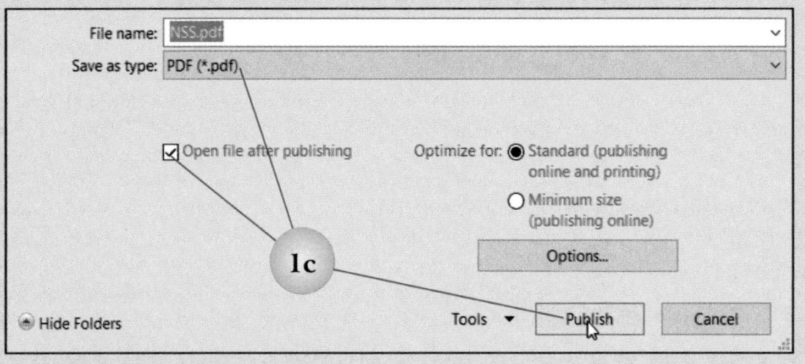

2. Scroll through the document in Adobe Acrobat Reader and then close Acrobat Reader by clicking the Close button in the upper right corner of the window.
3. Close **NSS.docx**.
4. In Word, open the **NSS.pdf** file you saved to your WL1C6 folder. At the message telling you that Word will convert the file to an editable Word document, click the OK button.
5. Notice that the formatting of the text is slightly different from the original formatting and that the graphic has been moved to the second page. Edit the file by completing the following steps:
   a. Click the Design tab and then click the *Lines (Distinctive)* style set.
   b. Delete the text *We are* in the text below the first heading and replace it with Northland Security Systems is.
6. Save the file with Save As and name it **6-NSS**. (The file will be saved in the .docx file format.)
7. Print and then close **6-NSS.docx**.
8. Display the Open dialog box, capture the Open dialog box as an image, and then close the Open dialog box. Press Ctrl + N to open a blank document, paste the image in the document, print the document, and then close the document without saving it.

Check Your Work

Project 2 Manage Multiple Documents 7 Parts

You will arrange, maximize, restore, and minimize windows; move selected text between split windows; compare formatting of documents side by side; and print specific text, pages, and multiple copies.

Preview Finished Project

Tutorial

Working with Windows

Working with Windows

Multiple documents can be opened in Word. The insertion point can be moved between the documents and information can be moved or copied from one document and pasted into another. When a new document is opened, it displays on top of any previously opened document. With multiple documents open, the window containing each document can be resized to see all or a portion of it on the screen.

Hint Press Ctrl + F6 to switch between open documents.

When a document is open, a Word button displays on the taskbar. Hover the mouse pointer over this button and a thumbnail of the document displays above the button. If more than one document is open, another Word button displays behind the first button in a cascading manner with only a portion of the button displaying at the right side of the first button. If multiple documents are open, hovering the mouse pointer on the Word button or clicking the Word button on the taskbar will display thumbnails of all the documents above the buttons. To make a change to a document, click the thumbnail that represents the document.

Hint Press Ctrl + W or Ctrl + F4 to close the active document window.

Switch Windows

Another method for determining what documents are open is to click the View tab and then click the Switch Windows button in the Window group. The document name in the list with the check mark in front of it is the active document. The active document contains the insertion point. To make a different document active, click the document name. To switch to another document using the keyboard, type the number shown in front of the desired document.

Arranging Windows

Quick Steps

Arrange Windows

1. Open documents.
2. Click View tab.
3. Click Arrange All button.

Arrange All

If several documents are open, they can be arranged so a portion of each displays. The portion that displays includes the title (if present) and the opening paragraph of each document. To arrange a group of open documents, click the View tab and then click the Arrange All button in the Window group.

Maximizing, Restoring, and Minimizing Documents

Use the Maximize and Minimize buttons in the upper right corner of the active document to change the size of the window. The two buttons are at the left of the Close button. (The Close button is in the upper right corner of the screen and contains an X.)

Maximize

Minimize

Restore

If all of the open documents are arranged on the screen, clicking the Maximize button in the active document causes that document to expand to fill the screen. In addition, the Maximize button changes to the Restore button. To return the active document back to its original size, click the Restore button. Click the Minimize button in the active document and the document is reduced and a button displays on the taskbar representing it. To maximize a document that has been minimized, click the button on the taskbar representing it.

Project 2a Arranging, Maximizing, Restoring, and Minimizing Windows — Part 1 of 7

Note: If you are using Word on a network system that contains a virus checker, you may not be able to open multiple documents at once. Continue by opening each document individually.

1. Open the following documents: **AptLease.docx**, **CompSoftware.docx**, **IntelProp.docx**, and **NSS.docx**.
2. Arrange the windows by clicking the View tab and then clicking the Arrange All button in the Window group.

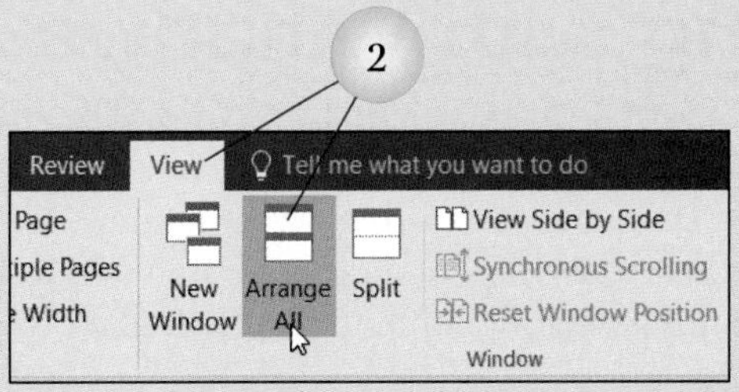

3. Make **AptLease.docx** the active document by clicking the Switch Windows button in the Window group on the View tab of the document at the top of your screen and then clicking ***AptLease.docx*** at the drop-down list.
4. Close **AptLease.docx**.
5. Make **IntelProp.docx** active and then close it.
6. Make **CompSoftware.docx** active and minimize it by clicking the Minimize button in the upper right corner of the active window.

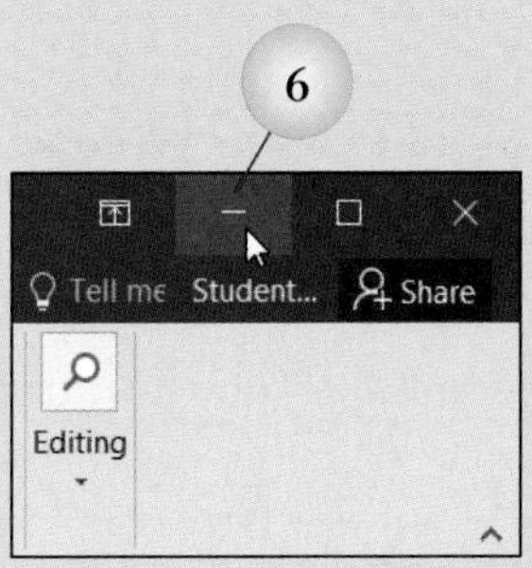

7. Maximize **NSS.docx** by clicking the Maximize button immediately left of the Close button.
8. Close **NSS.docx**.
9. Restore **CompSoftware.docx** by clicking the button on the taskbar that represents the document.
10. Maximize **CompSoftware.docx**.

Splitting a Window

Quick Steps
Split a Window
1. Open document.
2. Click View tab.
3. Click Split button.

Split

A window can be split into two panes, which is helpful for viewing different parts of a document at one time. For example, display an outline for a report in one pane and the part of the report to be edited in the other pane. The original window is split into two panes that extend horizontally across the screen.

Split a window by clicking the View tab and then clicking the Split button in the Window group. This splits the window in two with a split bar and another horizontal ruler. The location of the split bar can be changed by positioning the mouse pointer on the split bar until it displays as an up-and-down-pointing arrow with two small lines in the middle, holding down the left mouse button, dragging to the new location, and then releasing the mouse button.

When a window is split, the insertion point is positioned in the bottom pane. To move the insertion point to the other pane with the mouse, position the I-beam pointer in the other pane and then click the left mouse button. To remove the split bar from the document, click the View tab and then click the Remove Split button in the Window group. The split bar can also be double-clicked or dragged to the top or bottom of the screen.

Project 2b Moving Selected Text between Split Windows Part 2 of 7

1. With **CompSoftware.docx** open, save the document and name it **6-CompSoftware**.
2. Click the View tab and then click the Split button in the Window group.

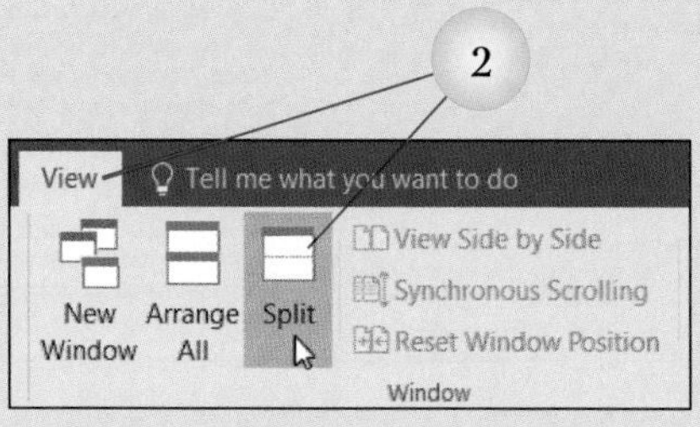

3. Move the first section below the second section by completing the following steps:
   a. Click in the top pane and then click the Home tab.
   b. Select the section *SECTION 1: PERSONAL-USE SOFTWARE* from the title to right above *SECTION 2: GRAPHICS AND MULTIMEDIA SOFTWARE*.
   c. Click the Cut button in the Clipboard group in the Home tab.
   d. Click in the bottom pane and then move the insertion point to the end of the document.
   e. Click the Paste button in the Clipboard group on the Home tab.
   f. Reverse the numbers in the two titles to *SECTION 1: GRAPHICS AND MULTIMEDIA SOFTWARE* and *SECTION 2: PERSONAL-USE SOFTWARE*.
4. Remove the split from the window by clicking the View tab and then clicking the Remove Split button in the Window group.
5. Press Ctrl + Home to move the insertion point to the beginning of the document.
6. Save **6-CompSoftware.docx**.

Check Your Work

Viewing Documents Side by Side

View Side by Side

Synchronous Scrolling

Quick Steps

View Documents Side by Side

1. Open two documents.
2. Click View tab.
3. Click View Side by Side button.

The contents of two documents can be compared on screen by opening both documents, clicking the View tab, and then clicking the View Side by Side button in the Window group. Both documents are arranged on the screen side by side, as shown in Figure 6.2. By default, synchronous scrolling is active. With this feature active, scrolling in one document causes the same scrolling in the other document. This feature is useful for comparing the text, formatting, or another feature between documents. To scroll in one document and not the other, click the Synchronous Scrolling button in the Window group to turn it off.

Figure 6.2 Viewing Documents Side by Side

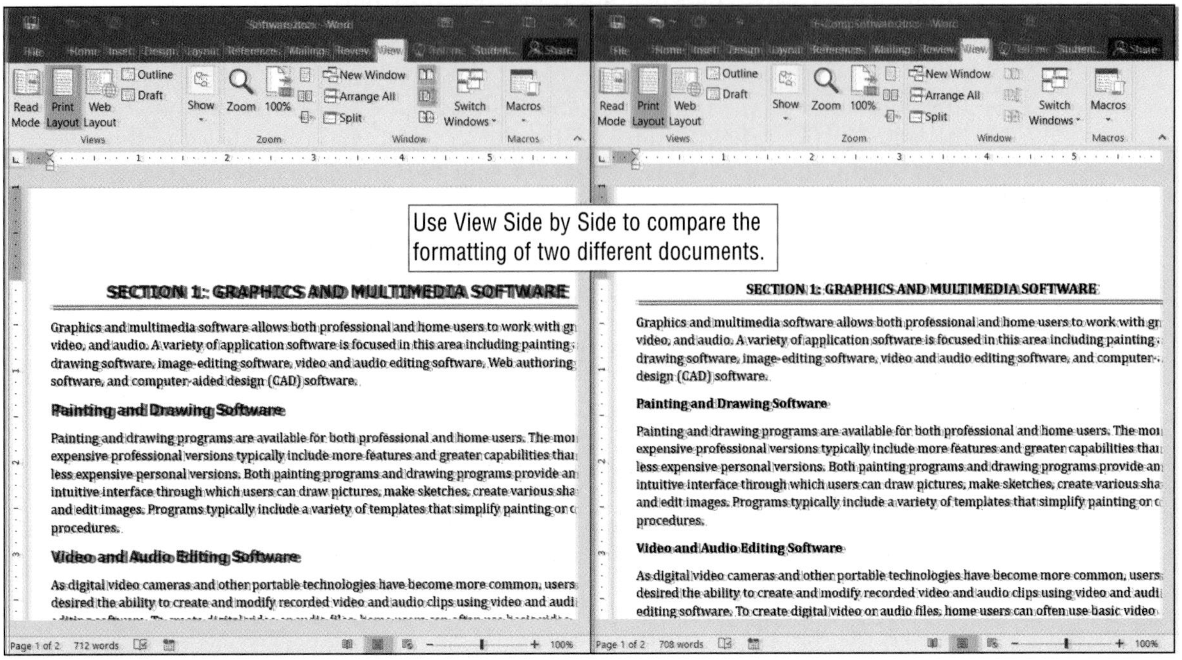

Project 2c Viewing Documents Side by Side

Part 3 of 7

1. With **6-CompSoftware.docx** open, open **Software.docx**.
2. Click the View tab and then click the View Side by Side button in the Window group.
3. Scroll through both documents simultaneously. Notice the difference between the two documents. (The titles and headings are set in different fonts and colors.) Select and then format the title and headings in **6-CompSoftware.docx** so they match the formatting in **Software.docx**. ***Hint: Use the Format Painter button to copy the formats.***
4. Turn off synchronous scrolling by clicking the Synchronous Scrolling button in the Window group on the View tab.
5. Scroll through the document and notice that no scrolling occurs in the other document.
6. Make **Software.docx** the active document and then close it.
7. Save **6-CompSoftware.docx**.

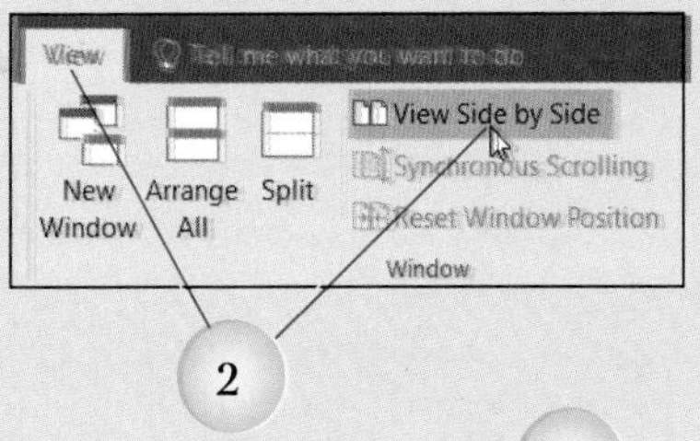

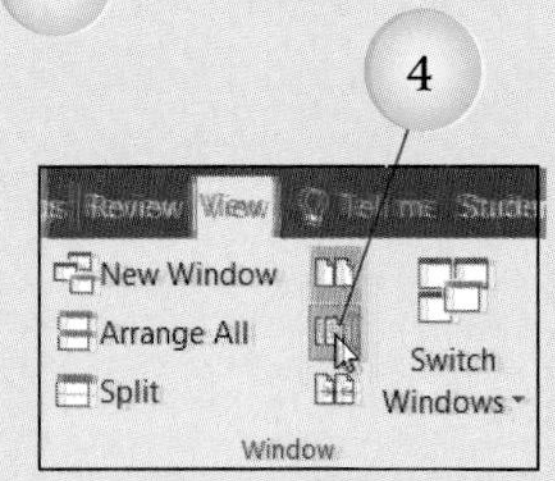

Check Your Work

Quick Steps

Open a New Window
1. Open document.
2. Click View tab.
3. Click New Window button.

New Window

Opening a New Window

In addition to splitting a document to view two locations of the same document, a new window can be opened that contains the same document. When a new window is opened, the document name in the Title bar displays followed by *:2*. The document name in the original window displays followed by *:1*. Any change made to the document in one window is reflected in the document in the other window.

Project 2d Opening a New Window

Part 4 of 7

1. With **6-CompSoftware.docx** open, open a new window by clicking the New Window button in the Window group on the View tab. (Notice that the document name in the Title bar displays followed by *:2*.)
2. Click the View tab and then click the View Side by Side button in the Window group.
3. Click the Synchronous Scrolling button to turn off synchronous scrolling.
4. With the **6-CompSoftware.docx:2** window active, look at the first paragraph of text and notice the order in which the software is listed in the last sentence (painting and drawing software, image-editing software, video and audio editing software, and computer-aided design [CAD] software).
5. Click in the **6-CompSoftware.docx:1** window and then cut and paste the headings and text so the software displays in the order listed in the paragraph.
6. Click the Save button on the Quick Access Toolbar.
7. Close the second version of the document by clicking the Word buttons on the taskbar and then clicking the Close button in the upper right corner of the **6-CompSoftware.docx:2** thumbnail (above the Word button on the taskbar).

Check Your Work

Tutorial

Inserting a File

Object

Quick Steps

Insert a File

1. Click Insert tab.
2. Click Object button arrow.
3. Click *Text from File.*
4. Navigate to folder.
5. Double-click document.

Inserting a File

The contents of one document can be inserted into another using the Object button in the Text group on the Insert tab. Click the Object button arrow and then click *Text from File* and the Insert File dialog box displays. This dialog box contains similar features as the Open dialog box. Navigate to the desired folder and then double-click the document to be inserted in the open document.

Project 2e Inserting a File

Part 5 of 7

1. With **6-CompSoftware.docx** open, move the insertion point to the end of the document.
2. Insert a file into the open document by completing the following steps:
   a. Click the Insert tab.
   b. Click the Object button arrow in the Text group and then click *Text from File* at the drop-down list.
   c. At the Insert File dialog box, navigate to the WL1C6 folder and then double-click ***EduComp.docx***.
3. Save **6-CompSoftware.docx**.

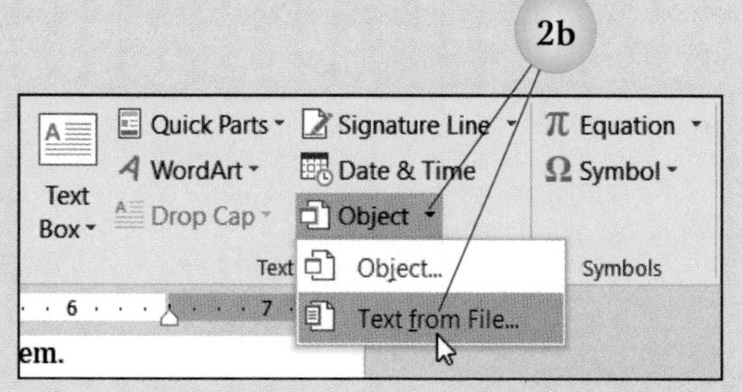

Check Your Work

Tutorial

Previewing and Printing

Previewing and Printing

Use options at the Print backstage area, shown in Figure 6.3, to specify what is to be printed and to preview pages before printing them. To display the Print backstage area, click the File tab and then click the *Print* option.

Previewing Pages

Hint Display the Print backstage area with the keyboard shortcut Ctrl + P.

Zoom to Page

At the Print backstage area, a preview of the page where the insertion point is positioned displays at the right side (see Figure 6.3). Click the Next Page button (right-pointing triangle) below and to the left of the page, to view the next page in the document and click the Previous Page button (left-pointing triangle) to display the previous page in the document. Use the Zoom slider bar to increase or decrease the size of the page and click the Zoom to Page button to fit the page in the viewing area in the Print backstage area.

Figure 6.3 Print Backstage Area

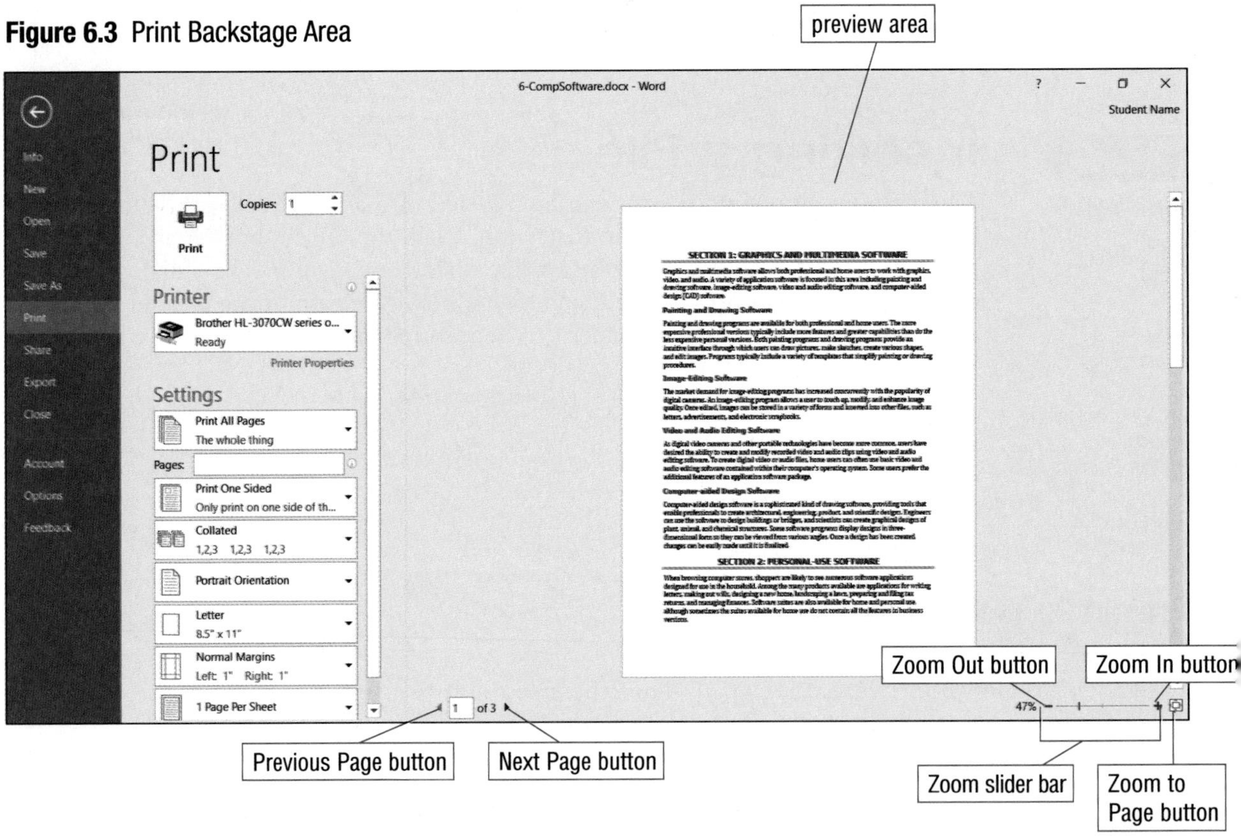

Project 2f Previewing Pages

1. With **6-CompSoftware.docx** open, press Ctrl + Home to move the insertion point to the beginning of the document.
2. Preview the document by clicking the File tab and then clicking the *Print* option.
3. Click the Zoom In button (plus symbol) at the right side of the Zoom slider bar two times. (This increases the size of the preview page.)
4. At the Print backstage area, click the Next Page button below and to the left of the preview page. (This displays page 2 in the preview area.)
5. Click the Zoom Out button (minus [-] symbol) at the left side of the Zoom slider bar, until two pages of the document display in the preview area.
6. Change the zoom at the Zoom dialog box by completing the following steps:
   a. Click the percentage number at the left side of the Zoom slider bar.
   b. At the Zoom dialog box, click the *Many pages* option in the *Zoom to* section.
   c. Click OK to close the dialog box. (Notice that all pages in the document display as thumbnails in the preview area.)
7. Click the Zoom to Page button at the right side of the Zoom slider bar. (This returns the page to the default size.)
8. Click the Back button to return to the document.

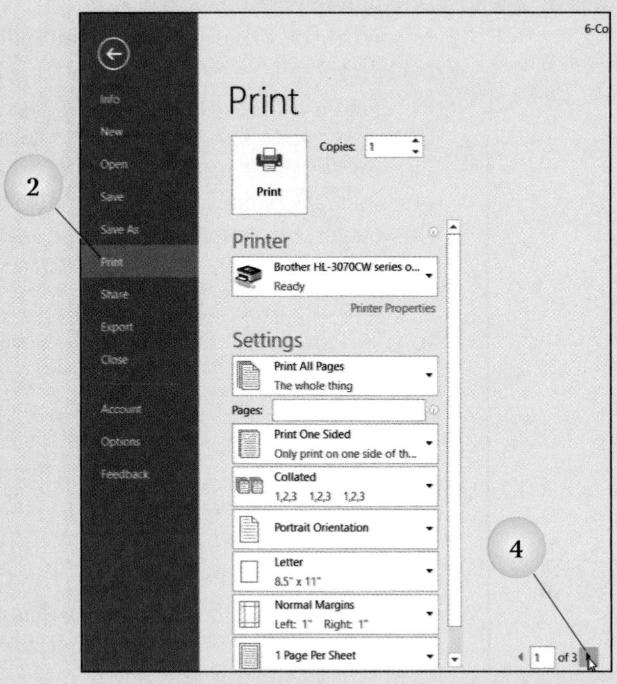

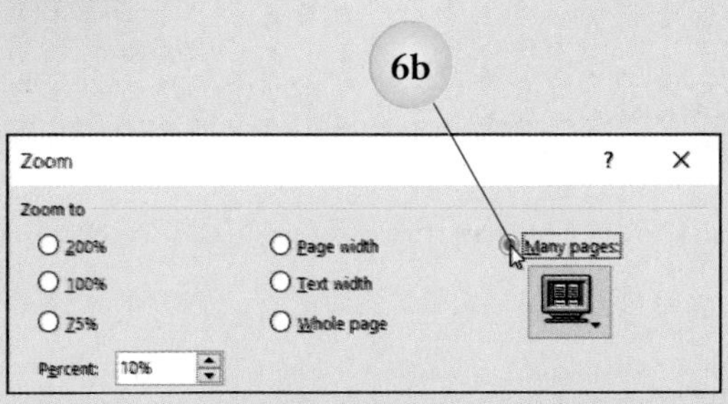

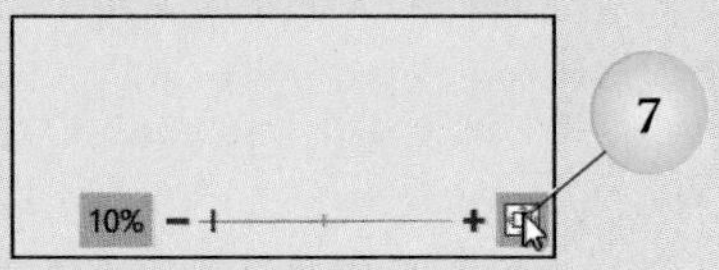

Printing Specific Text and Pages

Hint Save a document before printing it.

Control what prints in a document with options at the Print backstage area. Click the first gallery in the *Settings* category and a drop-down list displays with options for printing all the pages in the document, selected text, the current page, or a custom range of pages.

Print a portion of a document by selecting the text and then choosing the *Print Selection* option at the Print backstage area. With this option, only the selected text in the document prints. (This option is dimmed unless text is selected in the document.) Click the *Print Current Page* option to print only the page on which the insertion point is located. Use the *Custom Print* option to identify a specific page, multiple pages, or a range of pages to print. To print specific pages, use a comma (,) to indicate *and* and use a hyphen (-) to indicate *through*. For example, to print pages 2 and 5, type 2,5 in the *Pages* text box and to print pages 6 through 10, type 6-10.

With the other galleries available in the *Settings* category of the Print backstage area, specify whether to print on one or both sides of the page, change the page orientation (portrait or landscape), specify how the pages are collated, choose a paper size, and specify margins of a document. The last gallery contains options for printing 1, 2, 4, 6, 8, or 16 pages of a multiple-page document on one sheet of paper. This gallery also contains the *Scale to Paper Size* option. Click this option and then use the side menu to choose the paper size to scale the document.

To print more than one copy of a document, use the *Copies* measurement box to the right of the Print button. If several copies of a multiple-page document are printed, Word collates the pages as they print. For example, if two copies of a three-page document are printed, pages 1, 2, and 3 print and then the pages print a second time. Printing collated pages is helpful for assembling them but takes more printing time. To reduce printing time, tell Word *not* to print collated pages by clicking the *Collated* gallery in the *Settings* category and then clicking *Uncollated*.

To send a document directly to the printer without displaying the Print backstage area, consider adding the Quick Print button to the Quick Access Toolbar. To do this, click the Customize Quick Access Toolbar button at the right side of the toolbar, and then click *Quick Print* at the drop-down gallery. Click the Quick Print button and all the pages of the active document print.

Project 2g **Printing Specific Text and Pages** — Part 7 of 7

1. With **6-CompSoftware.docx** open, print selected text by completing the following steps:
   a. Select the heading *Painting and Drawing Software* and the paragraph of text that follows it.
   b. Click the File tab and then click the *Print* option.
   c. At the Print backstage area, click the first gallery in the *Settings* category (displays with *Print All Pages*) and then click *Print Selection* at the drop-down list.
   d. Click the Print button.

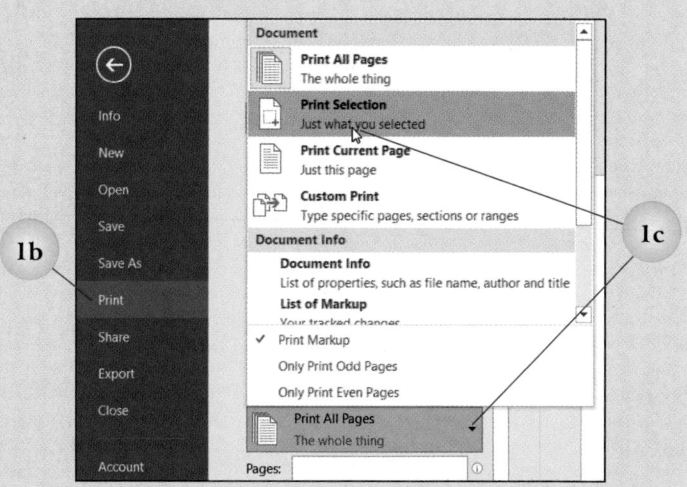

2. Change the margins and page orientation and then print only the first page by completing the following steps:
   a. Press Ctrl + Home to move the insertion point to the beginning of the document.

b. Click the File tab and then click the *Print* option.
c. At the Print backstage area, click the fourth gallery (displays with *Portrait Orientation)* in the *Settings* category and then click *Landscape Orientation* at the drop-down list.
d. Click the sixth gallery (displays with *Normal Margins*) in the *Settings* category and then click *Narrow* at the drop-down list.
e. Click the first gallery (displays with *Print All Pages*) in the *Settings* category and then click *Print Current Page* at the drop-down list.
f. Click the Print button. (The first page of the document prints in landscape orientation with 0.5-inch margins.)

3. Print all the pages as thumbnails on one page by completing the following steps:
   a. Click the File tab and then click the *Print* option.
   b. At the Print backstage area, click the bottom gallery (displays with *1 Page Per Sheet*) in the *Settings* category and then click *4 Pages Per Sheet* at the drop-down list.
   c. Click the first gallery (displays with *Print Current Page*) in the *Settings* category and then click *Print All Pages* at the drop-down list.
   d. Click the Print button.
4. Select the entire document, change the line spacing to 1.5 lines, and then deselect the text.

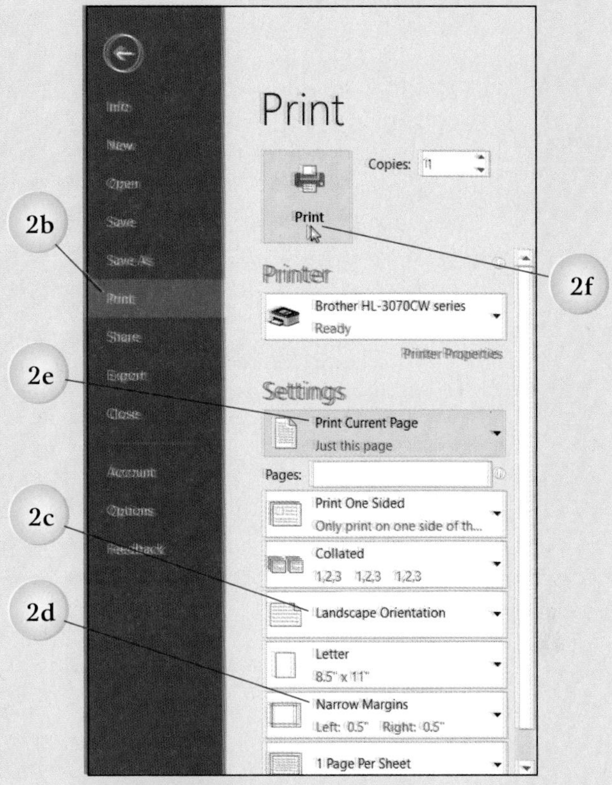

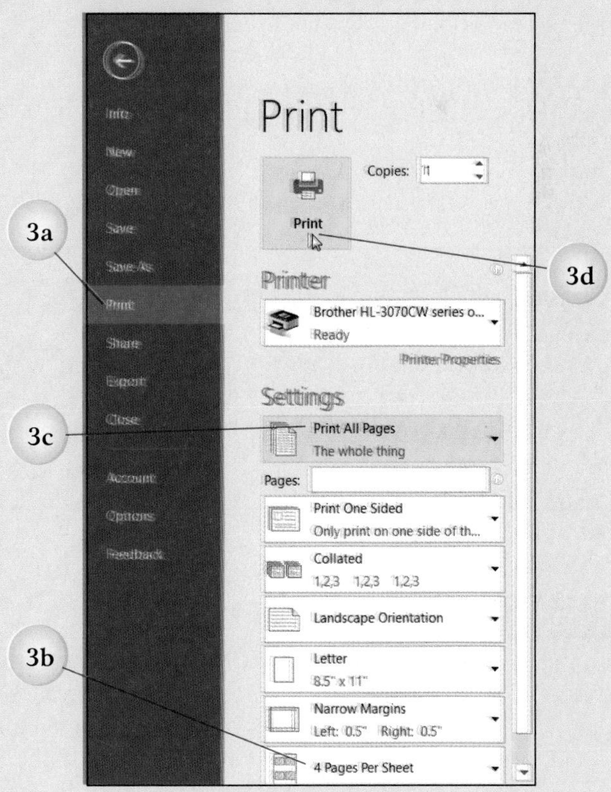

5. Print two copies of specific pages by completing the following steps:
   a. Click the File tab and then click the *Print* option.
   b. Click the fourth gallery (displays with *Landscape Orientation*) at the *Settings* category and then click *Portrait Orientation* in the drop-down list.
   c. Click in the *Pages* text box below the first gallery in the *Settings* category, and then type 1,3.
   d. Click the *Copies* measurement box up arrow (located to the right of the Print button) to display *2*.
   e. Click the third gallery (displays with *Collated*) in the *Settings* category and then click *Uncollated* at the drop-down list.
   f. Click the bottom gallery (displays with *4 Pages Per Sheet*) in the *Settings* category and then click *1 Page Per Sheet* at the drop-down list.
   g. Click the Print button. (The first page of the document will print two times and then the third page will print two times.)
6. Save and then close **6-CompSoftware.docx**.

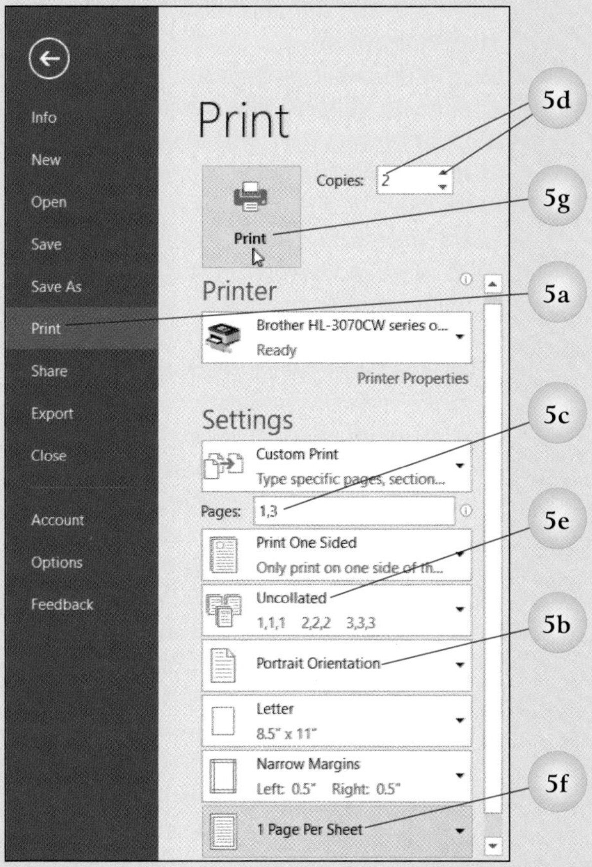

Check Your Work

Project 3 Create and Print Envelopes — 2 Parts

You will create an envelope document and type the return address and delivery address using envelope addressing guidelines issued by the United States Postal Service. You will also open a letter document and then create an envelope using the inside address.

Preview Finished Project

Tutorial

Preparing an Envelope

Envelopes

Creating and Printing Envelopes

Word automates the creation of envelopes with options at the Envelopes and Labels dialog box with the Envelopes tab selected, as shown in Figure 6.4. Display this dialog box by clicking the Mailings tab and then clicking the Envelopes button in the Create group. At the dialog box, type the delivery address in the *Delivery address* text box and the return address in the *Return address* text box. Send the envelope directly to the printer by clicking the Print button or insert the envelope in the current document by clicking the Add to Document button.

Figure 6.4 Envelopes and Labels Dialog Box with Envelopes Tab Selected

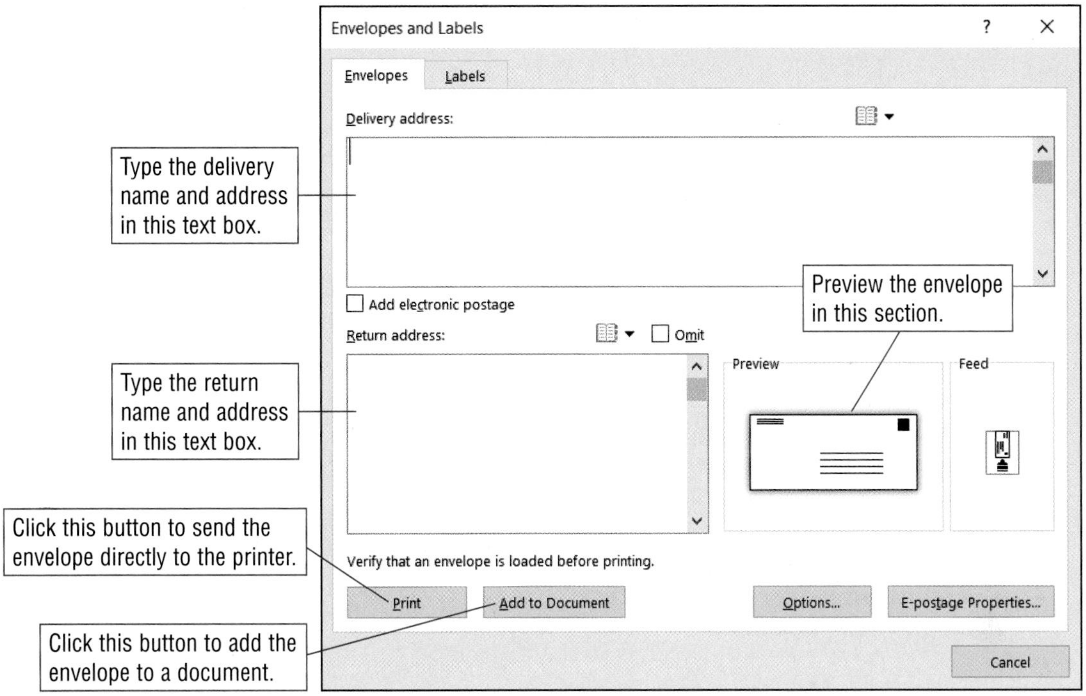

Quick Steps

Create an Envelope

1. Click Mailings tab.
2. Click Envelopes button.
3. Type delivery address.
4. Click in *Return address* text box.
5. Type return address.
6. Click Add to Document button or Print button.

If a return address is entered before printing the envelope, Word will display the question *Do you want to save the new return address as the default return address?* At this question, click Yes to save the current return address for future envelopes or click No if the return address should not be used as the default. By default, the return address in the *Return address* text box will print on the envelope. To omit the printing of the return address, insert a check mark in the *Omit* check box.

The Envelopes and Labels dialog box contains a *Preview* sample box and a *Feed* sample box. The *Preview* sample box shows how the envelope will appear when printed and the *Feed* sample box shows how the envelope should be inserted into the printer.

When addressing envelopes, consider following general guidelines issued by the United States Postal Service (USPS). The USPS guidelines suggest using all capital letters with no commas or periods for return and delivery addresses. Figure 6.5 shows envelope addresses that follow the USPS guidelines. Use abbreviations for street suffixes (such as *ST* for *Street* and *AVE* for *Avenue*). For a complete list of address abbreviations, visit the USPS.com website and then search for *Official USPS Abbreviations*.

Project 3a Printing an Envelope

Part 1 of 2

1. At a blank document, create an envelope that prints the delivery address and return address shown in Figure 6.5. Begin by clicking the Mailings tab.
2. Click the Envelopes button in the Create group.

3. At the Envelopes and Labels dialog box with the Envelopes tab selected, type the delivery address shown in Figure 6.5 (the one containing the name *GREGORY LINCOLN*). (Press the Enter key to end each line in the name and address.)
4. Click in the *Return address* text box. (If any text displays in the *Return address* text box, select and then delete it.)
5. Type the return address shown in Figure 6.5 (the one containing the name *WENDY STEINBERG*). (Press the Enter key to end each line in the name and address.)
6. Click the Add to Document button.
7. At the message *Do you want to save the new return address as the default return address?*, click No.
8. Save the document and name it **6-Env**.
9. Print and then close **6-Env.docx**. ***Note: Manual feed of the envelope may be required. Please check with your instructor.***

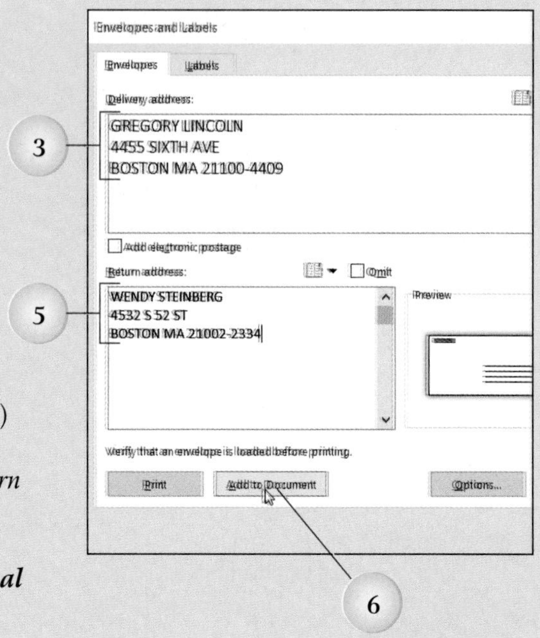

Check Your Work

Figure 6.5 Project 3a

WENDY STEINBERG
4532 S 52 ST
BOSTON MA 21002-2334

GREGORY LINCOLN
4455 SIXTH AVE
BOSTON MA 21100-4409

If the Envelopes and Labels dialog box opens in a document containing a name and address (each name and address line must end with a press of the Enter key and not Shift + Enter), the name and address are automatically inserted in the *Delivery address* text box in the dialog box. The name and address are inserted in the *Delivery address* text box as they appear in the document and may not conform to the USPS guidelines. The USPS guidelines for addressing envelopes are only suggestions, not requirements. Word automatically inserts the first name and address in a document in the *Delivery address* text box if the name and address lines end with a press of the Enter key. A different name and address in a document with each line ending in a press of the Enter key can be inserted in the *Delivery address* text box by selecting the name and address and then displaying the Envelopes and Labels dialog box.

Project 3b Creating an Envelope in an Existing Document Part 2 of 2

1. Open **LAProg.docx**.
2. Click the Mailings tab.
3. Click the Envelopes button in the Create group.
4. At the Envelopes and Labels dialog box (with the Envelopes tab selected), make sure the delivery address displays properly in the *Delivery address* text box.
5. If any text displays in the *Return address* text box, insert a check mark in the *Omit* check box (located to the right of the *Return address* option). (This tells Word not to print the return address on the envelope.)
6. Click the Print button.
7. Close **LAProg.docx** without saving the changes.

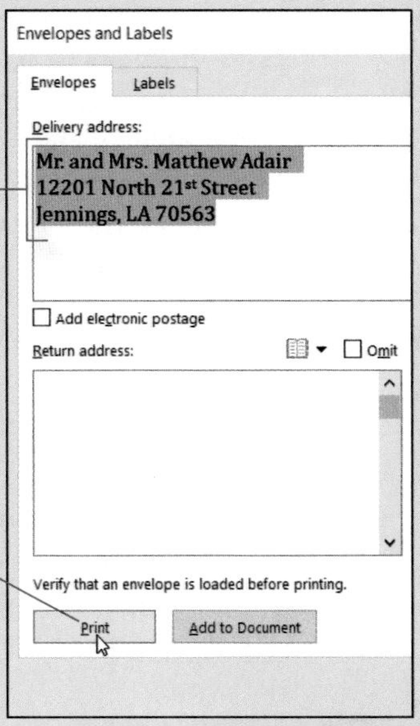

Check Your Work

Project 4 Create Labels 2 Parts

You will create mailing labels containing different names and addresses, labels with the same name and address, and labels with an image.

Preview Finished Project

Creating and Printing Labels

Use Word's labels feature to print text on mailing labels, file labels, disc labels, and other types of labels. Word includes a variety of predefined formats for the brands and sizes of labels that can be purchased at most office supply stores. Use the Labels feature to create a sheet of mailing labels with different names and addresses on each label or the same name and address or image on each label.

Tutorial

Creating Mailing Labels with Different Names and Addresses

Labels

Creating Mailing Labels with Different Names and Addresses

To create a sheet of mailing labels with different names and addresses on each label, click the Labels button in the Create group on the Mailings tab. At the Envelopes and Labels dialog box with the Labels tab selected, as shown in Figure 6.6, leave the *Address* text box empty and then click the New Document button to insert the labels in a new document. The insertion point is positioned in the first label. Type the name and address in the label and then press the Tab key one or two times (depending on the label) to move the insertion point to the next label. Pressing Shift + Tab will move the insertion point to the preceding label.

Changing Label Options

Click the Options button at the Envelopes and Labels dialog box with the Labels tab selected and the Label Options dialog box displays, as shown in Figure 6.7. At the Label Options dialog box, choose the type of printer, the label product, and the product number. This dialog box also displays information about the selected label, such as type, height, width, and paper size. When a label is selected, Word automatically determines the label margins. To customize these default settings, click the Details button at the Label Options dialog box.

Figure 6.6 Envelopes and Labels Dialog Box with Labels Tab Selected

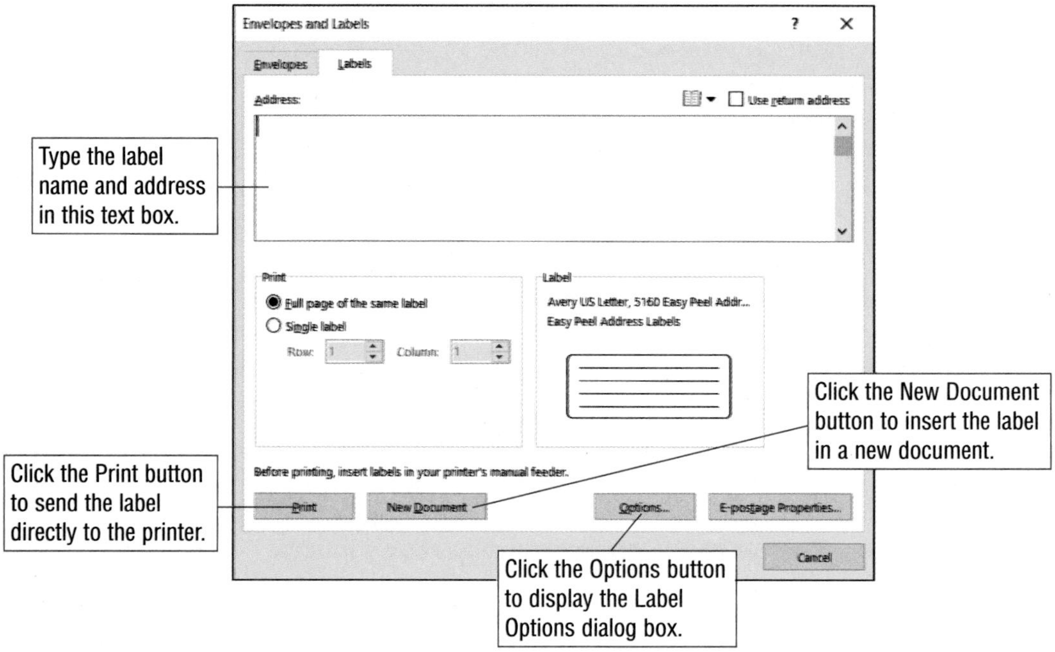

Figure 6.7 Label Options Dialog Box

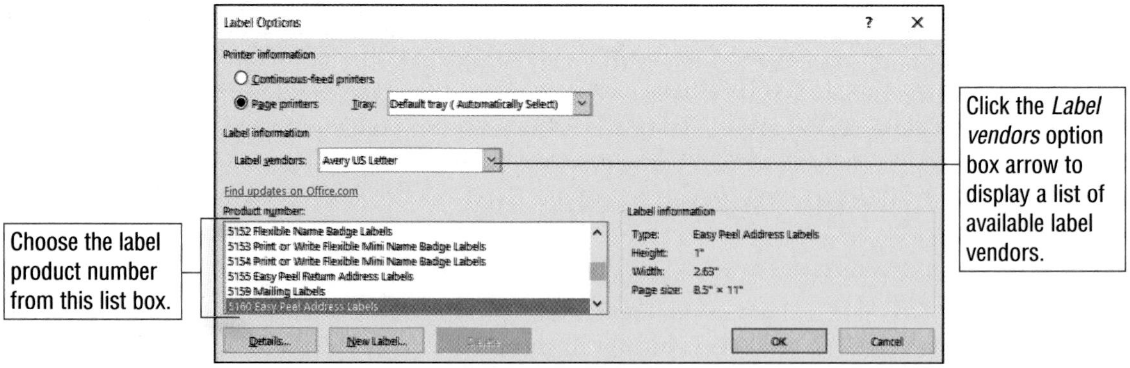

Project 4a Creating Mailing Labels with Different Names and Addresses

1. At a blank document, click the Mailings tab.
2. Click the Labels button in the Create group.
3. At the Envelopes and Labels dialog box with the Labels tab selected, click the Options button.
4. At the Label Options dialog box, click the *Label vendors* option box arrow and then click *Avery US Letter* at the drop-down list.
5. Scroll down the *Product number* list box and then click *5160 Easy Peel Address Labels*.
6. Click OK or press the Enter key.
7. At the Envelopes and Labels dialog box, click the New Document button.
8. At the document screen, type the first name and address shown in Figure 6.8 in the first label.
9. Press the Tab key two times to move the insertion point to the next label and then type the second name and address shown in Figure 6.8.
10. Continue in this manner until all the names and addresses shown in Figure 6.8 have been typed. (After typing the third name and address, you only need to press the Tab key once to move the insertion point to the first label in the second row.)
11. Save the document and name it **6-Labels**.
12. Print and then close **6-Labels.docx**.
13. Close the blank document without saving changes.

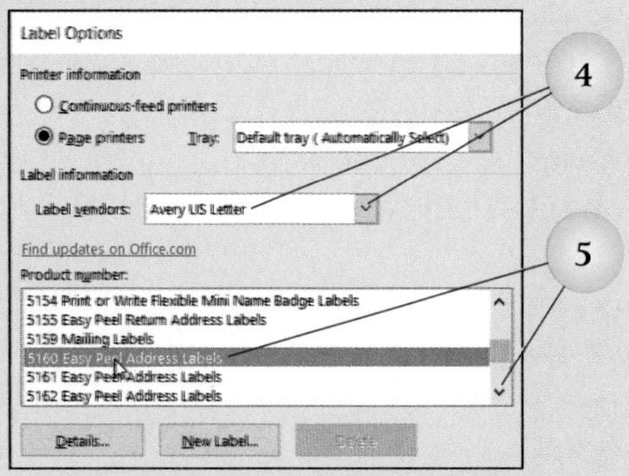

Check Your Work

Tutorial

Creating Mailing Labels with the Same Name and Address and an Image

Creating Mailing Labels with the Same Name and Address

To create labels with the same name and address on each label, open a document containing the desired name and address, click the Mailings tab, and then click the Labels button. At the Envelopes and Labels dialog box, make sure the desired label vendor and product number are selected and then click the New Document button. Another method for creating labels with the same name and address is to display the Envelopes and Labels dialog box with the Labels tab selected, type the name and address in the *Address* text box, and then click the New Document button.

Creating Mailing Labels with an Image

Labels can be created with a graphic image, such as a company's logo and address or a company's slogan. To create labels with an image, insert the image in a

Figure 6.8 Project 4a

DAVID LOWRY 12033 S 152 ST HOUSTON TX 77340	MARCELLA SANTOS 394 APPLE BLOSSOM FRIENDSWOOD TX 77533	KEVIN DORSEY 26302 PRAIRIE DR HOUSTON TX 77316
AL AND DONNA SASAKI 1392 PIONEER DR BAYTOWN TX 77903	JACKIE RHYNER 29039 107 AVE E HOUSTON TX 77302	MARK AND TINA ELLIS 607 FORD AVE HOUSTON TX 77307

document, select the image, click the Mailings tab. and then click the Labels button. At the Envelopes and Labels dialog box, make sure the desired label vendor and product number are selected and then click the New Document button.

Project 4b Creating Mailing Labels with the Same Name and Address and an Image — Part 2 of 2

1. Open **LAProg.docx** and create mailing labels with the delivery address. Begin by clicking the Mailings tab.
2. Click the Labels button in the Create group.
3. At the Envelopes and Labels dialog box with the Labels tab selected, make sure the delivery address displays properly in the *Address* text box as shown at the right.
4. Make sure *Avery US Letter, 5160 Easy Peel Address Labels* displays in the *Label* section; if not, refer to Steps 3 through 6 of Project 4a to select the label type.
5. Click the New Document button.
6. Save the mailing label document and name it **6-LAProg.docx**.
7. Print and then close **6-LAProg.docx**.
8. Close **LAProg.docx**.
9. At a blank document, insert an image by completing the following steps:
   a. Click the Insert tab and then click the Pictures button in the Illustrations group.
   b. At the Insert Picture dialog box, make sure the WL1C6 folder on your storage medium is active and then double-click ***BGCLabels.png***.
10. With the image selected in the document, click the Mailings tab and then click the Labels button.
11. At the Envelopes and Labels dialog box, make sure *Avery US Letter, 5160 Easy Peel Address Labels* displays in the *Label* section and then click the New Document button.
12. Save the document and name it **6-BGCLabels**.
13. Print and then close **6-BGCLabels.docx**.
14. Close the document containing the image without saving changes.

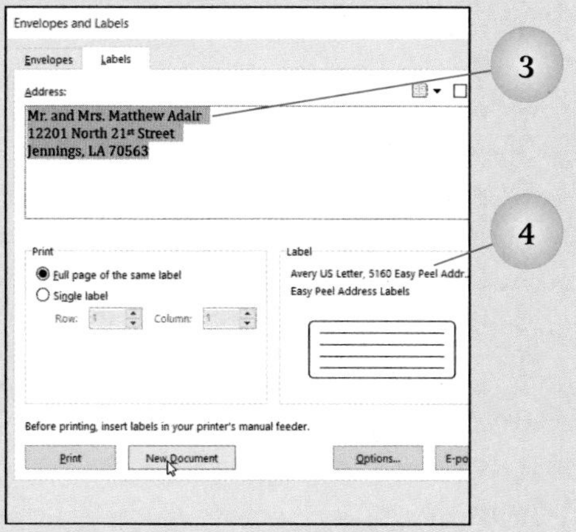

Check Your Work

Project 5 Use a Template to Create a Business Letter — 1 Part

You will use a letter template provided by Word to create a business letter.

Preview Finished Project

Tutorial

Creating a Document Using a Template

Creating a Document Using a Template

Word includes a number of template documents that are formatted for specific uses. Each Word document is based on a template document and the Normal template is the default. Use Word templates to create a variety of documents with special formatting, such as letters, calendars, and awards.

Figure 6.9 New Backstage Area

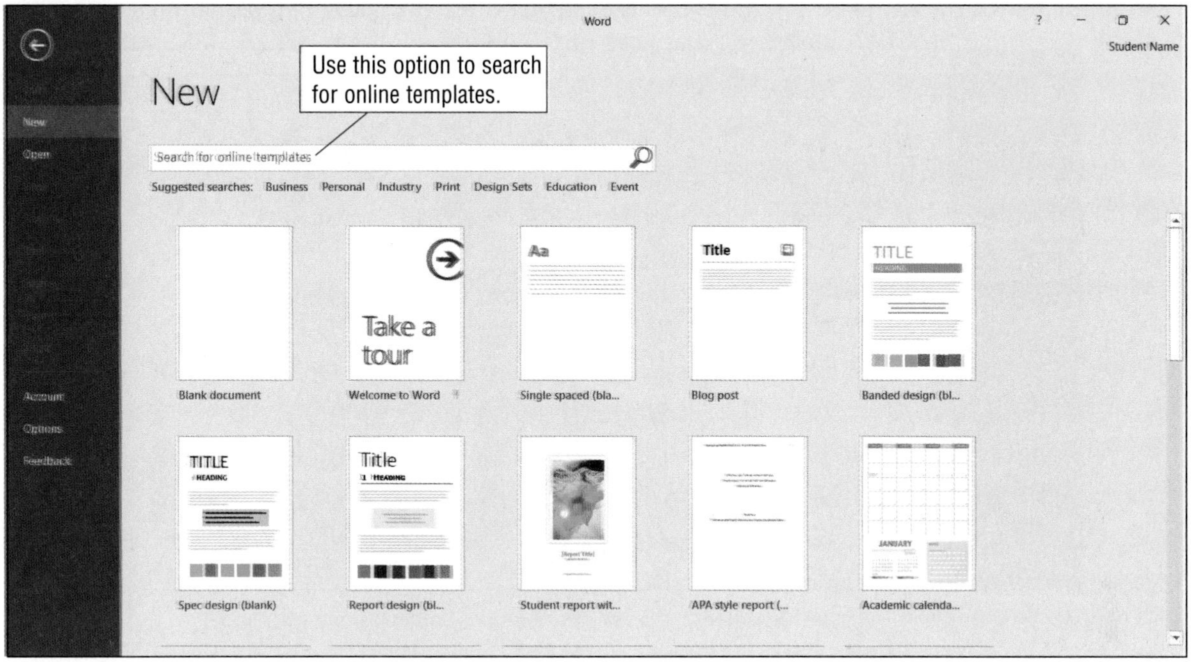

Quick Steps

Create a Document Using a Template

1. Click File tab.
2. Click *New* option.
3. Click template.

OR

1. Click File tab.
2. Click *New* option.
3. Click in search text box.
4. Type search text.
5. Press Enter.
6. Double-click template.

Display templates by clicking the File tab and then clicking the *New* option. This displays the New backstage area, as shown in Figure 6.9. Open one of the templates in the New backstage area by clicking the template. This opens a document based on the template, not the template file.

In addition to the templates that display at the New backstage area, templates can be downloaded from the Internet. To do this, click in the search text box, type the search text or category, and then press the Enter key. Templates that match the search text or category display in the New backstage area. Click the desired template and then click the Create button or double-click the template. This downloads the template and opens a document based on it. Locations for personalized text may display in placeholders in the document. Click the placeholder text and then type the personalized text.

If a template is used on a regular basis, consider pinning it to the New backstage area. To do this, search for the template, hover the mouse pointer over it, and then click the left-pointing stick pin (Pin to list) to the right of the template name. To unpin a template, click the down-pointing stick pin (Unpin from list).

Project 5 Creating a Letter Using a Template Part 1 of 1

1. Click the File tab and then click the *New* option.
2. At the New backstage area, click in the search text box, type letter, and then press the Enter key.
3. When templates display that match *letter*, notice the *Category* list box at the right side of the New backstage area.
4. Click the *Business* option in the *Category* list box. (This displays only business letter templates.)

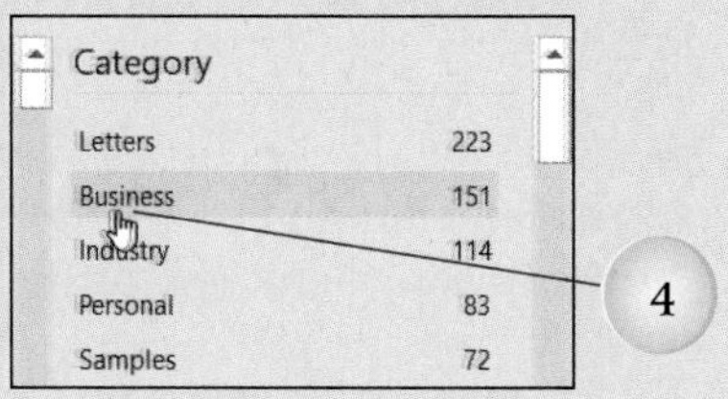

5. Scroll down the template list and then double-click the *Letter (Equity theme)* template.

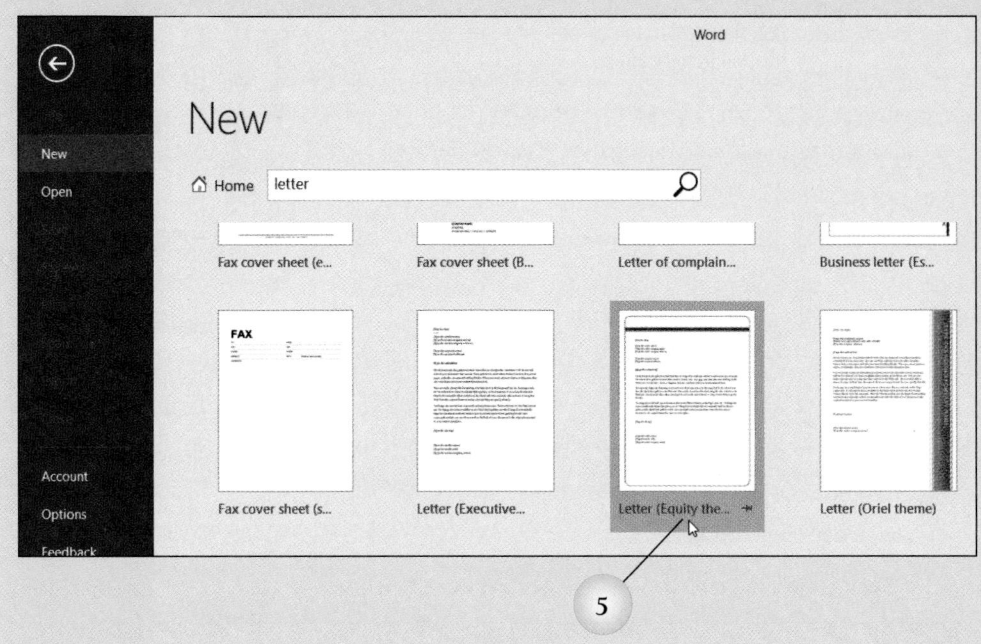

6. When the letter document displays on the screen, click the *[Pick the date]* placeholder, click the placeholder down arrow, and then click the Today button at the bottom of the calendar.
7. Click in the name below the date, select the name, and then type your first and last names.
8. Click the *[Type the sender company name]* placeholder and then type Sorenson Funds.
9. Click the *[Type the sender company address]* placeholder, type 6250 Aurora Boulevard, press the Enter key, and then type Baltimore, MD 20372.
10. Click the *[Type the recipient name]* placeholder and then type Ms. Jennifer Gonzalez.
11. Click the *[Type the recipient address]* placeholder, type 12990 Boyd Street, press the Enter key, and then type Baltimore, MD 20375.
12. Click the *[Type the salutation]* placeholder and then type Dear Ms. Gonzalez:.
13. Insert a file in the document by completing the following steps:
    a. Click anywhere in the three paragraphs of text in the body of the letter and then press the Delete key.
    b. Click the Insert tab.
    c. Click the Object button arrow in the Text group and then click *Text from File* at the drop-down list.
    d. At the Insert File dialog box, navigate to the WL1C6 folder on your storage medium and then double-click ***SFunds.docx***.
    e. Press the Backspace key to delete a blank line.
14. Click the *[Type the closing]* placeholder and then type Sincerely,.
15. If your name does not display above the *[Type the sender title]* placeholder, select the name and then type your first and last names.
16. Click the *[Type the sender title]* placeholder and then type Financial Consultant.
17. Save the document and name it **6-SFunds**. (If a message displays notifying you that the document will be upgraded to the newest file format, click OK.)
18. Print and then close **6-SFunds.docx**.

Check Your Work

Chapter Summary

- Group Word documents logically into folders. Create a new folder at the Open or Save As dialog box.
- One document or several documents can be selected at the Open dialog box. Copy, move, rename, delete, or open a document or selected documents.
- Use the *Cut*, *Copy*, and *Paste* options from the Organize button drop-down list or the Open dialog box shortcut menu to move or copy a document from one folder to another.
- Delete documents and/or folders with the *Delete* option from the Organize button drop-down list or shortcut menu.
- Click the *Change File Type* option at the Export backstage area and options display for saving the document in a different file format. Documents can also be saved in different file formats with the *Save as type* option box at the Save As dialog box.
- Move among open documents by hovering the mouse pointer over the Word button on the taskbar and then clicking the thumbnail of the document or by clicking the View tab, clicking the Switch Windows button in the Window group, and then clicking the document name.
- View portions of all open documents by clicking the View tab and then clicking the Arrange All button in the Window group.
- Use the Minimize, Restore, and Maximize buttons in the upper right corner of the window to reduce or increase the size of the active window.
- Divide a window into two panes by clicking the View tab and then clicking the Split button in the Window group.
- View the contents of two open documents side by side by clicking the View tab and then clicking the View Side by Side button in the Window group.
- Open a new window containing the same document by clicking the View tab and then clicking the New Window button in the Window group.
- Insert a document into the open document by clicking the Insert tab, clicking the Object button arrow, and then clicking *Text from File* at the drop-down list. At the Insert File dialog box, double-click the document.
- Preview a document at the Print backstage area. Scroll through the pages in the document with the Next Page and the Previous Page buttons, which display below the preview page. Use the Zoom slider bar to increase or decrease the display size of the preview page.
- Use options at the Print backstage area to customize the print job by changing the page orientation, size, and margins; specify how many pages to print on one page; indicate the number of copies and whether to collate the pages; and specify the printer.
- Create and print an envelope at the Envelopes and Labels dialog box with the Envelopes tab selected.
- If the Envelopes and Labels dialog box is opened in a document containing a name and address (with each line ending with a press of the Enter key), that information is automatically inserted in the *Delivery address* text box in the dialog box.
- Use Word's labels feature to print text on mailing labels, file labels, disc labels, and other types of labels. Create labels at the Envelopes and Labels dialog box with the Labels tab selected.

- Available templates display in the New backstage area. Double-click a template to open a document based on it. Search for templates online by typing in the search text or category in the search text box and then pressing the Enter key.

Commands Review

FEATURE	RIBBON TAB, GROUP	BUTTON, OPTION	KEYBOARD SHORTCUT
arrange documents	View, Window		
Envelopes and Labels dialog box with Envelopes tab selected	Mailings, Create		
Envelopes and Labels dialog box with Labels tab selected	Mailings, Create		
Export backstage area	File, *Export*		
Insert File dialog box	Insert, Text	, *Text from File*	
maximize document			Ctrl + F10
minimize document			
New backstage area	File, *New*		
new window	View, Window		
Open dialog box	File, *Open*	*Browse*	Ctrl + F12
Print backstage area	File, *Print*		Ctrl + P
restore document to previous size			
Save As dialog box	File, *Save As*	*Browse*	F12
split window	View, Window		Alt + Ctrl + S
switch windows	View, Window		
synchronous scrolling	View, Window		
view documents side by side	View, Window		

Workbook

Chapter study tools and assessment activities are available in the *Workbook* ebook. These resources are designed to help you further develop and demonstrate mastery of the skills learned in this chapter.

Microsoft®

Word

Creating Tables and SmartArt

CHAPTER 7

Performance Objectives

Upon successful completion of Chapter 7, you will be able to:

1 Create a table
2 Change the table design and layout
3 Convert text to a table and a table to text
4 Draw a table
5 Insert a Quick Table
6 Perform calculations on data in a table
7 Insert an Excel spreadsheet
8 Create, format, and modify a SmartArt graphic

Precheck

Check your current skills to help focus your study.

Some Word data can be organized in a table, which is a combination of columns and rows. Use the Tables feature to insert data in columns and rows. This data can consist of text, values, and formulas. In this chapter, you will learn how to create and format a table and insert and format data in it. Word also includes a SmartArt feature that provides a number of predesigned graphics. In this chapter, you will learn how to use these graphics to create diagrams and organizational charts.

Data Files

Before beginning chapter work, copy the WL1C7 folder to your storage medium and then make WL1C7 the active folder.

SNAP

If you are a SNAP user, launch the Precheck and Tutorials from your Assignments page.

Project 1 Create and Format Tables with Company Information — 8 Parts

You will create one table containing contact information and another containing information on plans offered by the company. You will then change the design and layout of each table.

Preview Finished Project

Tutorial

Creating a Table

Table

Quick Steps

Create a Table
1. Click Insert tab.
2. Click Table button.
3. Point to create number of columns and rows.
4. Click mouse button.

OR
1. Click Insert tab.
2. Click Table button.
3. Click *Insert Table.*
4. Specify number of columns and rows.
5. Click OK.

Creating a Table

Use the Tables feature to create boxes of information called *cells*. A cell is the intersection between a row and a column. A cell can contain text, characters, numbers, data, graphics, or formulas. Create a table by clicking the Insert tab, clicking the Table button, moving the mouse pointer down and to the right in the drop-down grid until the correct numbers of rows and columns display, and then clicking the mouse button. A table can also be created with options at the Insert Table dialog box. Display this dialog box by clicking the Table button in the Tables group on the Insert tab and then clicking *Insert Table* at the drop-down list.

Figure 7.1 shows an example of a table with four columns and four rows. Various parts of the table are identified in Figure 7.1, such as the gridlines, move table column marker, end-of-cell marker, end-of-row marker, table move handle, and resize handle. In a table, nonprinting characters identify the ends of cells and the ends of rows. To view these characters, click the Show/Hide ¶ button in the Paragraph group on the Home tab. The end-of-cell marker displays inside each cell and the end-of-row marker displays at the end of each row of cells. These markers are identified in Figure 7.1.

When a table is created, the insertion point is positioned in the cell in the upper left corner of the table. Each cell in a table has a cell designation. Columns in a table are lettered from left to right beginning with *A*. Rows in a table are numbered from top to bottom beginning with *1*. The cell in the upper left corner of the table is cell A1. The cell to the right of A1 is B1, the cell to the right of B1 is C1, and so on.

When the insertion point is positioned in a cell in the table, move table column markers display on the horizontal ruler. These markers represent the ends of columns and are useful in changing the widths of columns. Figure 7.1 identifies a move table column marker.

Hint You can create a table within a table, creating a *nested* table.

Figure 7.1 Table with Nonprinting Characters Displayed

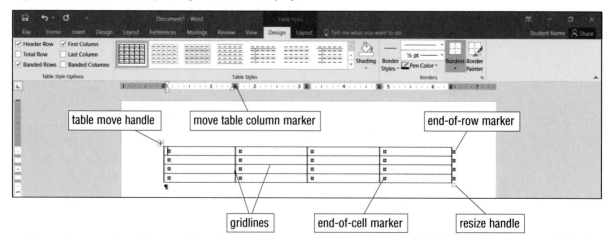

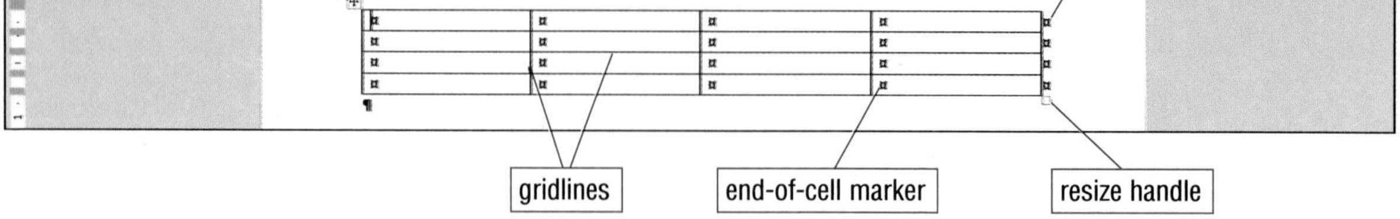

Entering Text in Cells

Hint Pressing the Tab key in a table moves the insertion point to the next cell. Pressing Ctrl + Tab moves the insertion point to the next tab within a cell.

With the insertion point positioned in a cell, type or edit text. Move the insertion point to another cell with the mouse by clicking in the cell. To move the insertion point to another cell using the keyboard, press the Tab key to move to the next cell or press Shift + Tab to move to the preceding cell.

If the text typed in a cell does not fit on one line, it wraps to the next line within the same cell, or if the Enter key is pressed within a cell, the insertion point moves to the next line within the same cell. The cell vertically lengthens to accommodate the text and all cells in that row also lengthen. Pressing the Tab key in a table causes the insertion point to move to the next cell in the table. To move the insertion point to a tab within a cell, press Ctrl + Tab. If the insertion point is in the last cell of the table, pressing the Tab key adds another row to the table. Insert a page break within a table by pressing Ctrl + Enter. The page break is inserted between rows, not within a row.

Moving the Insertion Point within a Table

To use the mouse to move the insertion point to a different cell within the table, click in the specific cell. To use the keyboard to move the insertion point to a different cell within the table, refer to the information shown in Table 7.1.

Table 7.1 Insertion Point Movement within a Table Using the Keyboard

To move the insertion point	Press
to next cell	Tab
to preceding cell	Shift + Tab
forward one character	Right Arrow key
backward one character	Left Arrow key
to previous row	Up Arrow key
to next row	Down Arrow key
to first cell in row	Alt + Home
to last cell in row	Alt + End
to top cell in column	Alt + Page Up
to bottom cell in column	Alt + Page Down

Project 1a Creating a Table

Part 1 of 8

1. At a blank document, turn on bold formatting and then type the title CONTACT INFORMATION, as shown in Figure 7.2.
2. Turn off bold formatting and then press the Enter key.
3. Create the table shown in Figure 7.2 by completing the following steps:
   a. Click the Insert tab.
   b. Click the Table button in the Tables group.
   c. Move the mouse pointer down and to the right in the drop-down grid until the label above the grid displays as *3x5 Table* and then click the left mouse button.

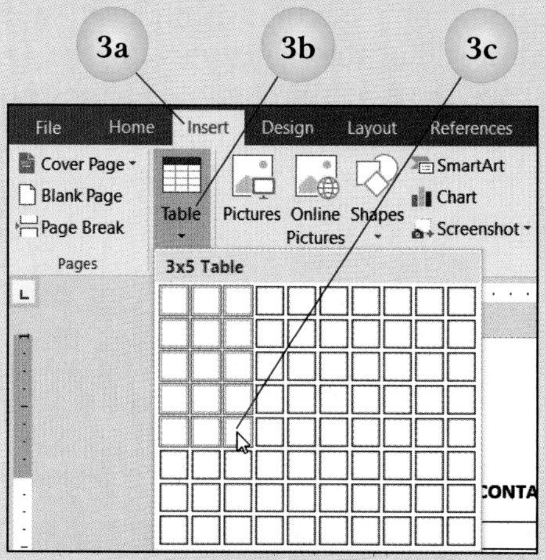

4. Type the text in the cells as indicated in Figure 7.2. Press the Tab key to move to the next cell and press Shift + Tab to move to the preceding cell. (If you accidentally press the Enter key within a cell, immediately press the Backspace key. Do not press the Tab key after typing the text in the last cell. If you do, another row is inserted in the table. If this happens, immediately click the Undo button on the Quick Access Toolbar.)
5. Save the table and name it **7-Tables**.

Check Your Work

Figure 7.2 Project 1a

CONTACT INFORMATION

Maggie Rivera	First Trust Bank	(203) 555-3440
Les Cromwell	Madison Trust	(602) 555-4900
Cecilia Nordyke	American Financial	(509) 555-3995
Regina Stahl	United Fidelity	(301) 555-1201
Justin White	Key One Savings	(360) 555-8963

Using the Insert Table Dialog Box

A table can also be created with options at the Insert Table dialog box, shown in Figure 7.3. To display this dialog box, click the Insert tab, click the Table button in the Tables group, and then click *Insert Table*. At the Insert Table dialog box, enter the numbers of columns and rows and then click OK.

Figure 7.3 Insert Table Dialog Box

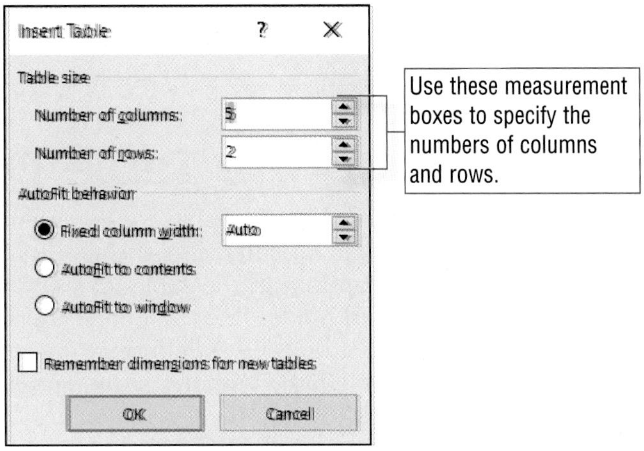

Project 1b Creating a Table with the Insert Table Dialog Box — Part 2 of 8

1. With **7-Tables.docx** open, press Ctrl + End to move the insertion point below the table.
2. Press the Enter key two times.
3. Turn on bold formatting and then type the title OPTIONAL PLAN PREMIUM RATES, as shown in Figure 7.4.
4. Turn off bold formatting and then press the Enter key.
5. Click the Insert tab, click the Table button in the Tables group, and then click *Insert Table* at the drop-down list.
6. At the Insert Table dialog box, type 3 in the *Number of columns* measurement box. (The insertion point is automatically positioned in this measurement box.)
7. Press the Tab key (this moves the insertion point to the *Number of rows* measurement box) and then type 5.
8. Click OK.
9. Type the text in the cells as indicated in Figure 7.4. Press the Tab key to move to the next cell and press Shift + Tab to move to the preceding cell. To indent the text in cells B2 through B5 and cells C2 through C5, press Ctrl + Tab to move the insertion point to a tab within a cell and then type the text.
10. Save **7-Tables.docx**.

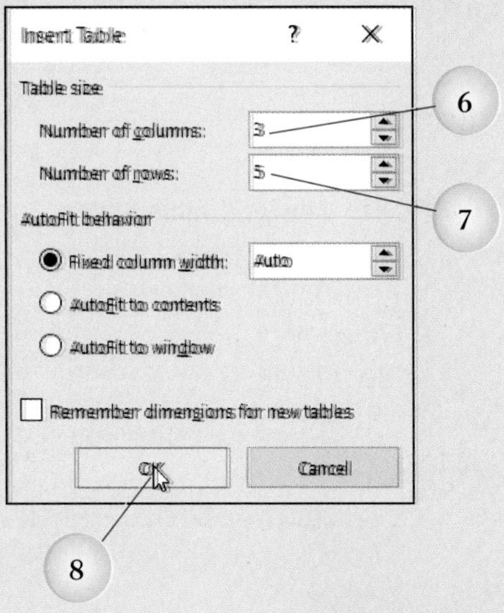

Check Your Work

Figure 7.4 Project 1b

OPTIONAL PLAN PREMIUM RATES

Waiting Period	Basic Plan Employees	Plan 2018 Employees
60 days	0.67%	0.79%
90 days	0.49%	0.59%
120 days	0.30%	0.35%
180 days	0.23%	0.26%

Tutorial

Changing the Table Design

Changing the Table Design

When a table is created, the Table Tools Design tab is active. This tab contains a number of options for enhancing the appearance of the table, as shown in Figure 7.5. With options in the Table Styles group, apply a predesigned style that adds color and border lines to a table and shading to cells. Maintain further control over the predesigned style formatting applied to columns and rows with options in the Table Style Options group. For example, if the table contains a total row, insert a check mark in the *Total Row* check box. Apply a predesigned table style with options in the Table Styles group.

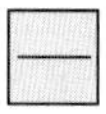
Border Styles

Border Painter

Use options in the Borders group to customize the borders of cells in a table. Click the Border Styles button to display a drop-down list of predesigned border lines. Use other buttons in the Borders group to change the line style, width, and color; add or remove borders; and apply the same border style to other cells with the Border Painter button.

Figure 7.5 Table Tools Design Tab

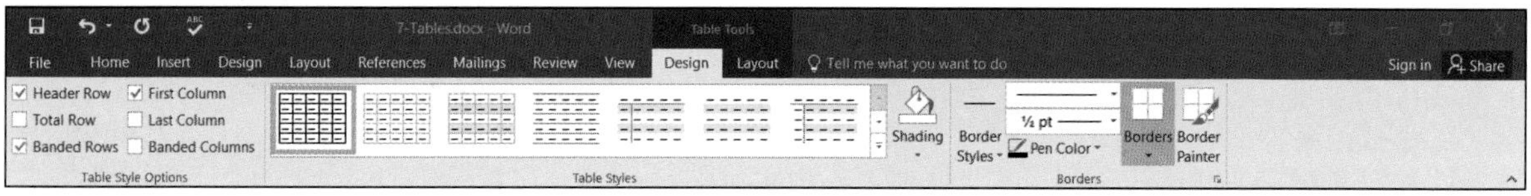

Project 1c Applying Table Styles

Part 3 of 8

1. With **7-Tables.docx** open, click in any cell in the top table.
2. Apply a table style by completing the following steps:
   a. Make sure the Table Tools Design tab is active.
   b. Click the More Table Styles button in the table styles gallery in the Table Styles group.
   c. Click the *Grid Table 5 Dark - Accent 5* table style (sixth column, fifth row in the *Grid Tables* section).

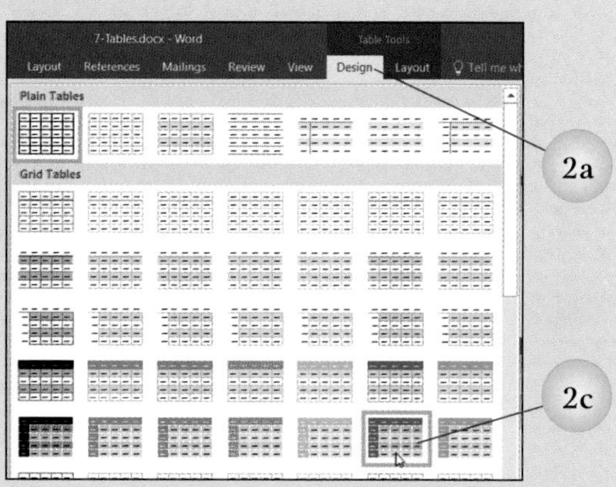

3. After looking at the table, you realize that the first row is not a header row and the first column should not be formatted differently from the other columns. To format the first row and the first column in the same manner as the other rows and columns, click the *Header Row* check box and the *First Column* check box in the Table Style Options group to remove the check marks.

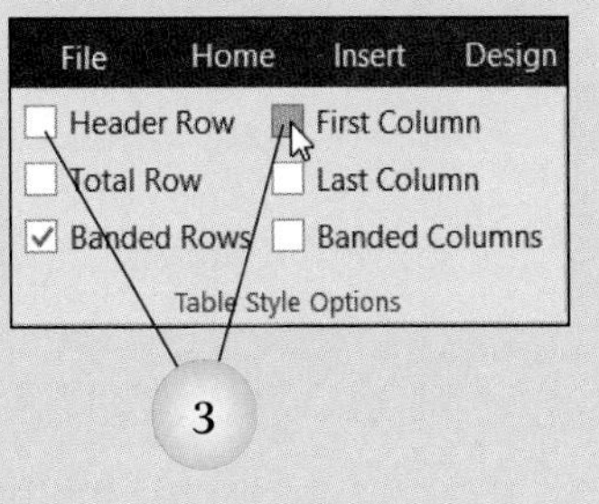

4. Click in any cell in the bottom table and then apply the List Table 6 Colorful - Accent 5 table style (sixth column, sixth row in the *List Tables* section).
5. Add color borders to the top table by completing the following steps:
   a. Click in any cell in the top table.
   b. Click the Pen Color button arrow in the Borders group on the Table Tools Design tab and then click the *Orange, Accent 2, Darker 50%* color option (sixth column, bottom row in the *Theme Colors* section).
   c. Click the *Line Weight* option box arrow in the Borders group and then click *1½ pt* at the drop-down list. (When you choose a line weight, the Border Painter button is automatically activated.)

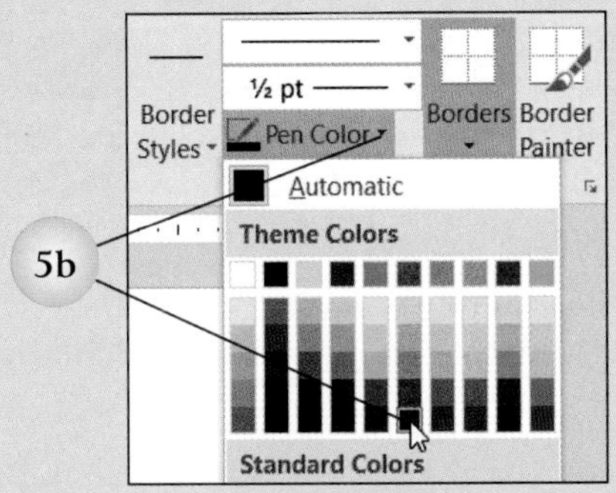

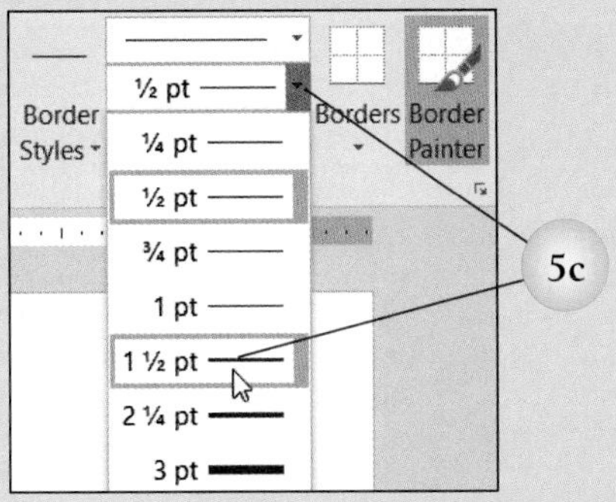

   d. Using the mouse (the mouse pointer displays as a pen), drag along all four sides of the table. (As you drag with the mouse, a thick brown line is inserted. If you make a mistake or the line does not display as you intended, click the Undo button and then continue drawing along each side of the table.)
6. Click the Border Styles button arrow and then click the *Double solid lines, 1/2 pt, Accent 2* option (third column, third row in the *Theme Borders* section).

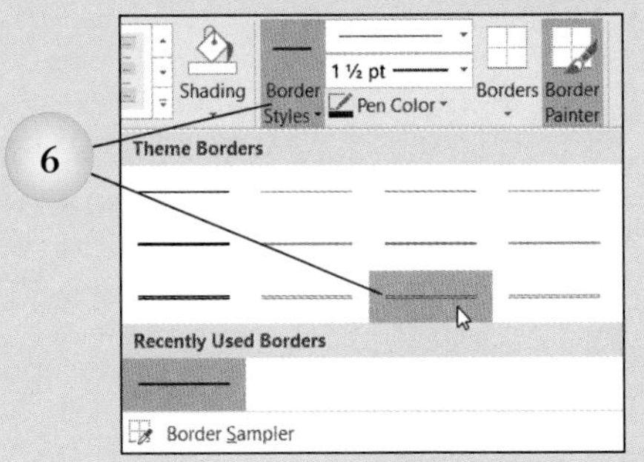

7. Drag along all four sides of the bottom table.
8. Click the Border Painter button to turn off the feature.
9. Save **7-Tables.docx**.

Check Your Work

Selecting Cells

Data within a table can be formatted in several ways. For example, the alignment of text within cells or rows can be changed, rows or columns can be selected and then moved or copied, and character formatting can be applied to text, such as bold, italic, and underlining. To format specific cells, rows, or columns, select the cells.

Selecting in a Table with the Mouse

Use the mouse pointer to select a cell, row, or column or to select an entire table. Table 7.2 describes methods for selecting in a table with the mouse. The left edge of each cell, between the left column border and the end-of-cell marker or first character in the cell, is called the cell selection bar. Position the mouse pointer in the cell selection bar and it turns into a small black arrow that points up and to the right. Each row in a table contains a row selection bar, which is the space just left of the left edge of the table. Position the mouse pointer in the row selection bar and the mouse pointer turns into a white arrow that points up and to the right.

Table 7.2 Selecting in a Table with the Mouse

To select this	Do this
cell	Position the mouse pointer in the cell selection bar at the left edge of the cell until it turns into a small black arrow that points up and to the right and then click the left mouse button.
row	Position the mouse pointer in the row selection bar at the left edge of the table until it turns into an arrow that points up and to the right and then click the left mouse button.
column	Position the mouse pointer on the uppermost horizontal gridline of the table in the appropriate column until it turns into a small black arrow that points down and then click the left mouse button.
adjacent cells	Position the mouse pointer in the first cell to be selected, click and hold down the left mouse button, drag the mouse pointer to the last cell to be selected, and then release the mouse button.
all cells in a table	Click the table move handle or position the mouse pointer in the row selection bar for the first row at the left edge of the table until it turns into an arrow that points up and to the right, click and hold down the left mouse button, drag down to select all the rows in the table, and then release the left mouse button.
text within a cell	Position the mouse pointer at the beginning of the text, click and hold down the left mouse button, and then drag the mouse across the text. (When a cell is selected, its background color changes to gray. When the text within a cell is selected, only those lines containing text are selected.)

Selecting in a Table with the Keyboard

In addition to the mouse, the keyboard can be used to select specific cells within a table. Table 7.3 displays the commands for selecting specific elements of a table.

To select only the text within a cell, rather than the entire cell, press the F8 function key to turn on the Extend mode and then move the insertion point with an arrow key. When a cell is selected, its background color changes to gray. When the text within a cell is selected, only those lines containing text are selected.

Table 7.3 Selecting in a Table with the Keyboard

To select	Press
next cell's contents	Tab
preceding cell's contents	Shift + Tab
entire table	Alt + 5 (on numeric keypad with Num Lock off)
adjacent cells	Press and hold down the Shift key and then press an arrow key repeatedly.
column	Position the insertion point in the top cell of the column, click and hold down the Shift key, and then press the Down Arrow key until the column is selected.

Project 1d Selecting, Moving, and Formatting Cells in a Table

Part 4 of 8

1. With **7-Tables.docx** open, move two rows in the top table by completing the following steps:
   a. Position the mouse pointer in the row selection bar at the left side of the row containing the name *Cecilia Nordyke*, click and hold down the left mouse button, and then drag down to select two rows (the *Cecilia Nordyke* row and the *Regina Stahl* row).

1a

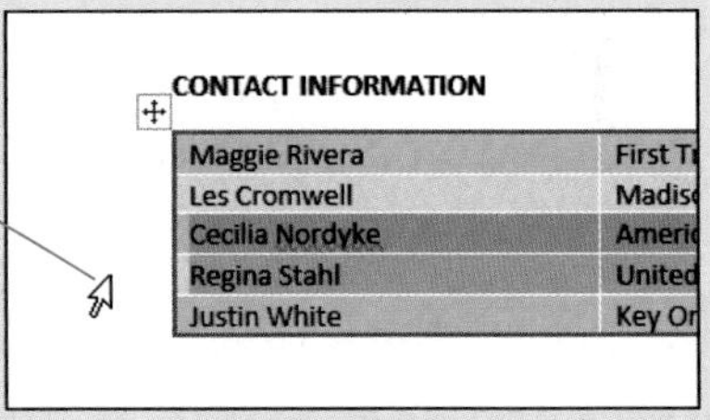

   b. Click the Home tab and then click the Cut button in the Clipboard group.
   c. Move the insertion point so it is positioned at the beginning of the name *Les Cromwell* and then click the Paste button in the Clipboard group.
2. Move the third column in the bottom table by completing the following steps:
   a. Position the mouse pointer on the top border of the third column in the bottom table until the pointer turns into a short black arrow that points down and then click the left mouse button. (This selects the entire column.)

2a

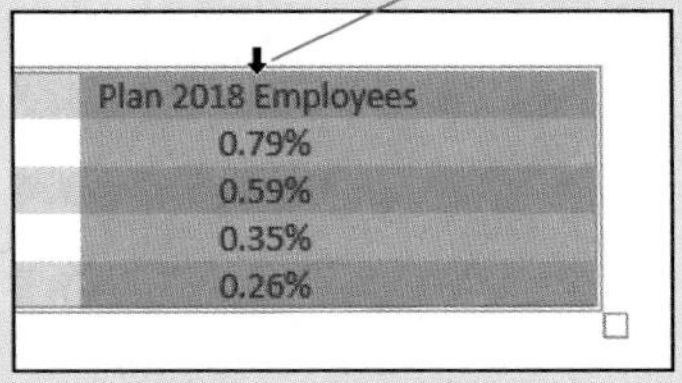

   b. Click the Cut button in the Clipboard group on the Home tab.
   c. With the insertion point positioned at the beginning of the text *Basic Plan Employees*, click the Paste button in the Clipboard group. (Moving the column removed the right border.)
   d. Insert the right border by clicking the Table Tools Design tab, clicking the Border Styles button arrow, and then clicking the *Double solid lines, 1/2 pt, Accent 2* option at the drop-down list (third column, third row in the *Theme Borders* section).

e. Drag along the right border of the bottom table.
f. Click the Border Painter button to turn off the feature.

3. Apply shading to a row by completing the following steps:
   a. Position the mouse pointer in the row selection bar at the left edge of the first row in the bottom table until the pointer turns into an arrow that points up and to the right and then click the left mouse button. (This selects the entire first row of the bottom table.)
   b. Click the Shading button arrow in the Table Styles group and then click the *Orange, Accent 2, Lighter 80%* color option (sixth column, second row in the *Theme Colors* section).

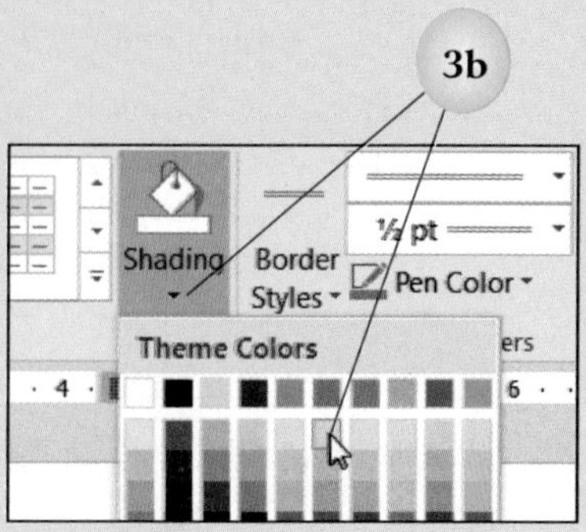

4. Apply a border line to the right sides of two columns by completing the following steps:
   a. Position the mouse pointer on the top border of the first column in the bottom table until the pointer turns into a short black arrow that points down and then click the left mouse button.
   b. Click the *Line Style* option box arrow and then click the top line option (a single line).
   c. Click the Borders button arrow and then click *Right Border* at the drop-down list.
   d. Select the second column in the bottom table.
   e. Click the Borders button arrow and then click *Right Border* at the drop-down list.

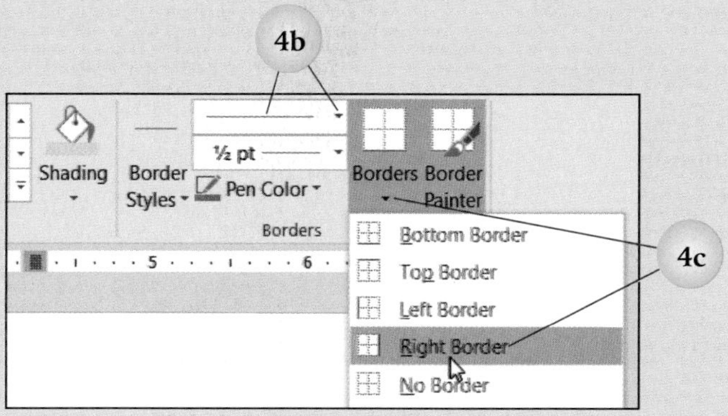

5. Apply italic formatting to a column by completing the following steps:
   a. Click in the first cell of the first row in the top table.
   b. Press and hold down the Shift key and then press the Down Arrow key four times. (This should select all the cells in the first column.)
   c. Press Ctrl + I.
6. Save **7-Tables.docx**.

Check Your Work

Tutorial

Changing the Table Layout

Changing the Table Layout

To further customize a table, consider changing the layout by inserting or deleting columns and rows and specifying cell alignments. Change the table layout with options at the Table Tools Layout tab, shown in Figure 7.6. Use options and buttons on the tab to select specific cells, delete and insert rows and columns, merge and split cells, specify cell height and width, sort data in cells, and insert formulas.

Figure 7.6 Table Tools Layout Tab

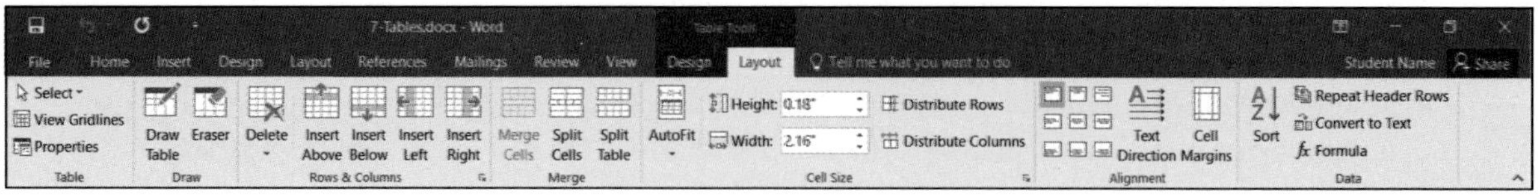

Selecting with the Select Button

Select

Along with selecting cells with the keyboard and mouse, specific cells can be selected with the Select button in the Table group on the Table Tools Layout tab. To select with this button, position the insertion point in the specific cell, column, or row and then click the Select button. At the drop-down list, specify what is to be selected: the entire table or a column, row, or cell.

Hint Some table layout options are available at a shortcut menu that can be viewed by right-clicking in a table.

Viewing Gridlines

View Gridlines

In a table, cell borders are identified by horizontal and vertical thin black gridlines. A cell border gridline can be removed but the cell border is maintained. If cell border gridlines are removed or a table style is applied that removes gridlines, the display of nonprinting gridlines can be turned on to help visually determine cell borders. These nonprinting gridlines display as dashed lines. Turn on or off the display of nonprinting dashed gridlines with the View Gridlines button in the Table group on the Table Tools Layout tab.

Inserting and Deleting Rows and Columns

Insert Above

Insert Below

Insert Left

Insert Right

Delete

Insert a row or column and delete a row or column with buttons in the Rows & Columns group on the Table Tools Layout tab. Click the button in the group that inserts the row or column in the desired location, such as above, below, to the left, or to the right. To delete a table, row, or column, click the Delete button and then click the option identifying what is to be deleted.

In addition to using options on the Table Tools Layout tab, rows or columns can be inserted using icons. Display the insert row icon by positioning the mouse pointer just outside the left border of the table at the left of the row border. When the insert row icon displays (a plus symbol in a circle and a border line), click the icon and a row is inserted below the insert icon border line. To insert a column, position the mouse pointer above the column border line until the insert column icon displays and then click the icon. This inserts a new column immediately left of the insert column icon border line.

Project 1e Selecting, Inserting, and Deleting Columns and Rows — Part 5 of 8

1. Make sure **7-Tables.docx** is open.
2. The table style applied to the bottom table removed row border gridlines. If you do not see dashed row border gridlines in the bottom table, turn on the display of nonprinting gridlines by positioning your insertion point in the table, clicking the Table Tools Layout tab, and then clicking the View Gridlines button in the Table group. (The button should display with a gray background, indicating it is active.)
3. Select a column and apply formatting by completing the following steps:
   a. Click in any cell in the first column in the top table.
   b. Make sure the Table Tools Layout tab is active, click the Select button in the Table group, and then click *Select Column* at the drop-down list.
   c. With the first column selected, press Ctrl + I to remove italic formatting and then press Ctrl + B to apply bold formatting.

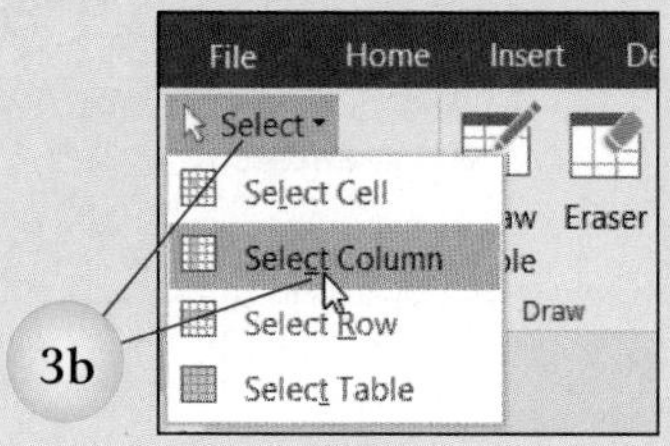

4. Select a row and apply formatting by completing the following steps:
   a. Click in any cell in the first row in the bottom table.
   b. Click the Select button in the Table group and then click *Select Row* at the drop-down list.
   c. With the first row selected in the bottom table, press Ctrl + I to apply italic formatting.
5. Insert a new row in the bottom table and type text in the new cells by completing the following steps:
   a. Click in the cell containing the text *60 days*.
   b. Click the Insert Above button in the Rows & Columns group.
   c. Type 30 days in the first cell of the new row. Press the Tab key, press Ctrl + Tab, and then type 0.85% in the second cell of the new row. Press the Tab key, press Ctrl + Tab, and then type 0.81% in the third cell of the new row.

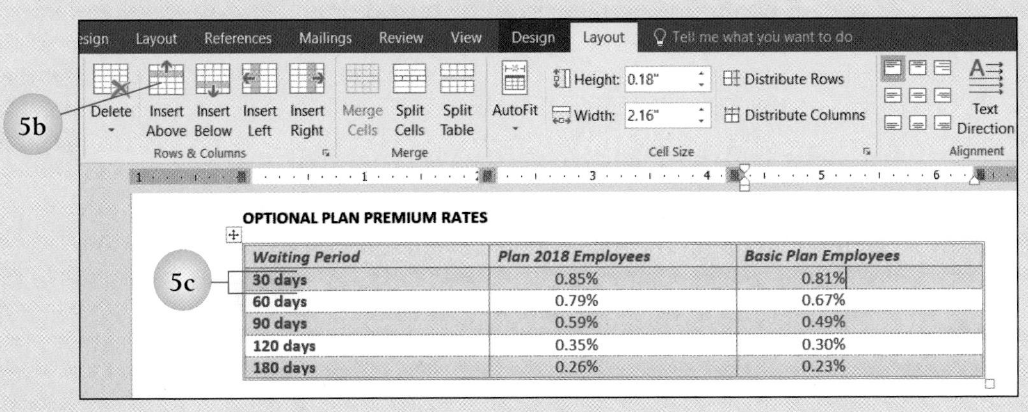

Waiting Period	Plan 2018 Employees	Basic Plan Employees
30 days	0.85%	0.81%
60 days	0.79%	0.67%
90 days	0.59%	0.49%
120 days	0.35%	0.30%
180 days	0.26%	0.23%

6. Insert two new rows in the top table by completing the following steps:
   a. Select the two rows of cells that begin with the names *Cecilia Nordyke* and *Regina Stahl*.
   b. Click the Insert Below button in the Rows & Columns group.
   c. Click in any cell of the top table to deselect the new rows.
7. Insert a new row in the top table by positioning the mouse pointer at the left side of the table next to the border line below *Regina Stahl* until the insert row icon displays and then clicking the icon.

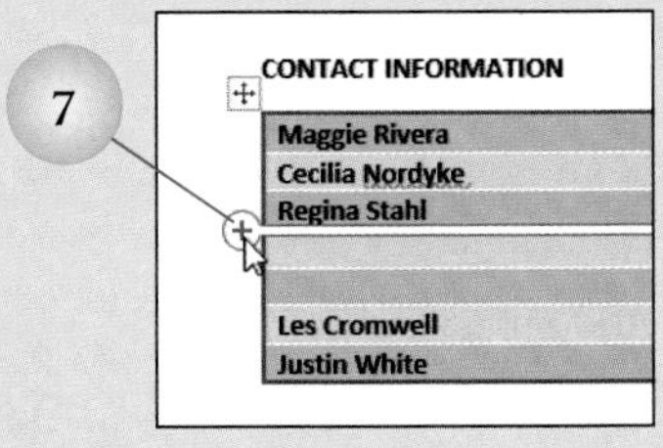

8. Type the following text in the new cells:

Teresa Getty	Meridian Bank	(503) 555-9800
Michael Vazquez	New Horizon Bank	(702) 555-2435
Samantha Roth	Cascade Mutual	(206) 555-6788

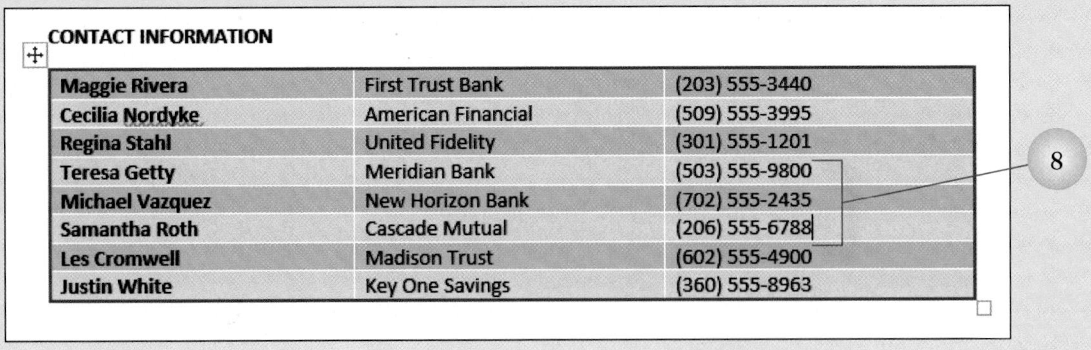

Maggie Rivera	First Trust Bank	(203) 555-3440
Cecilia Nordyke	American Financial	(509) 555-3995
Regina Stahl	United Fidelity	(301) 555-1201
Teresa Getty	Meridian Bank	(503) 555-9800
Michael Vazquez	New Horizon Bank	(702) 555-2435
Samantha Roth	Cascade Mutual	(206) 555-6788
Les Cromwell	Madison Trust	(602) 555-4900
Justin White	Key One Savings	(360) 555-8963

9. Delete a row by completing the following steps:
   a. Click in the cell containing the name *Les Cromwell*.
   b. Click the Delete button in the Rows & Columns group and then click *Delete Rows* at the drop-down list.
10. Insert a new column in the top table by completing the following steps:
   a. Position the mouse pointer immediately above the border line between the first and second columns in the top table until the insert column icon displays.
   b. Click the insert column icon.
11. Type the following text in the new cells:
   B1 = Vice President
   B2 = Loan Officer
   B3 = Account Manager
   B4 = Branch Manager
   B5 = President
   B6 = Vice President
   B7 = Regional Manager
12. Save **7-Tables.docx**.

9b

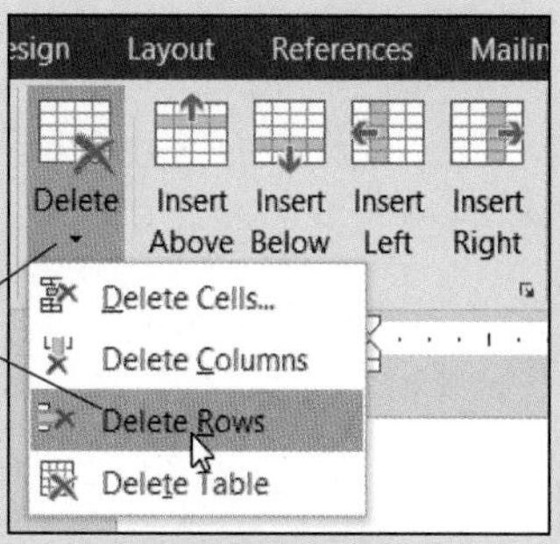

10b

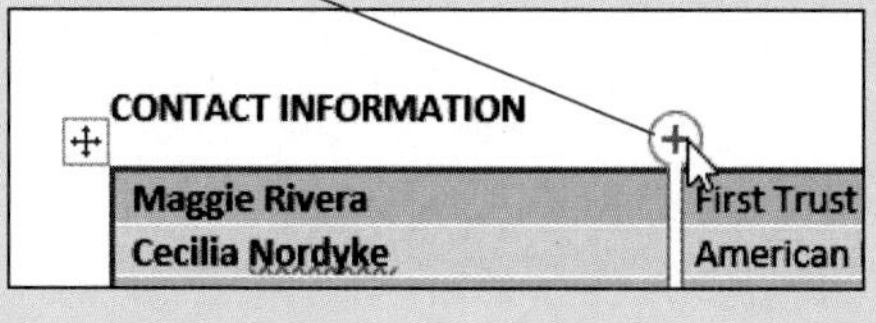

11

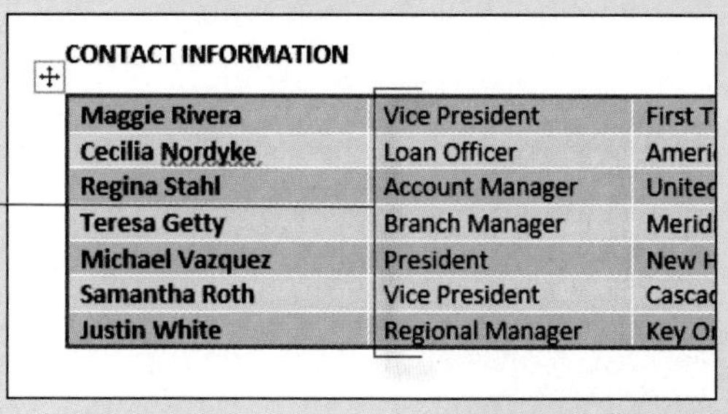

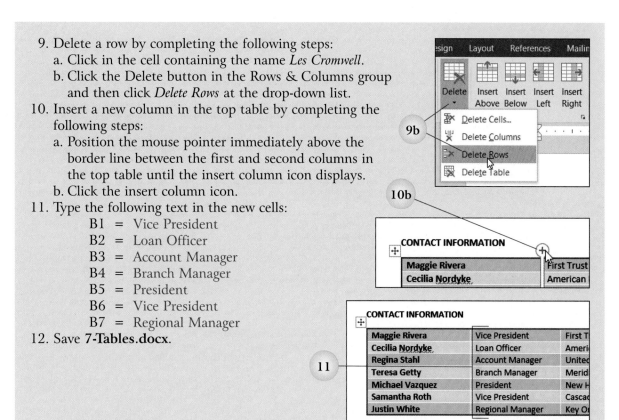

Check Your Work

Merging and Splitting Cells and Tables

Merge Cells

Split Cells

Split Table

Click the Merge Cells button in the Merge group on the Table Tools Layout tab to merge selected cells and click the Split Cells button to split the currently active cell. Click the Split Cells button and the Split Cells dialog box displays with options for specifying the number of columns or rows into which the active cell should be split. To split one table into two tables, position the insertion point in a cell in the row that will be the first row in the new table and then click the Split Table button.

Project 1f Merging and Splitting Cells and Splitting a Table

Part 6 of 8

1. With **7-Tables.docx** open, insert a new row and merge cells in the row by completing the following steps:
   a. Click in the cell containing the text *Waiting Period* (in the bottom table).

b. Click the Insert Above button in the Rows & Columns group on the Table Tools Layout tab.
c. With all of the cells in the new row selected, click the Merge Cells button in the Merge group.
d. Type OPTIONAL PLAN PREMIUM RATES and then press Ctrl + E to center-align the text in the cell. (The text you type will be italicized.)

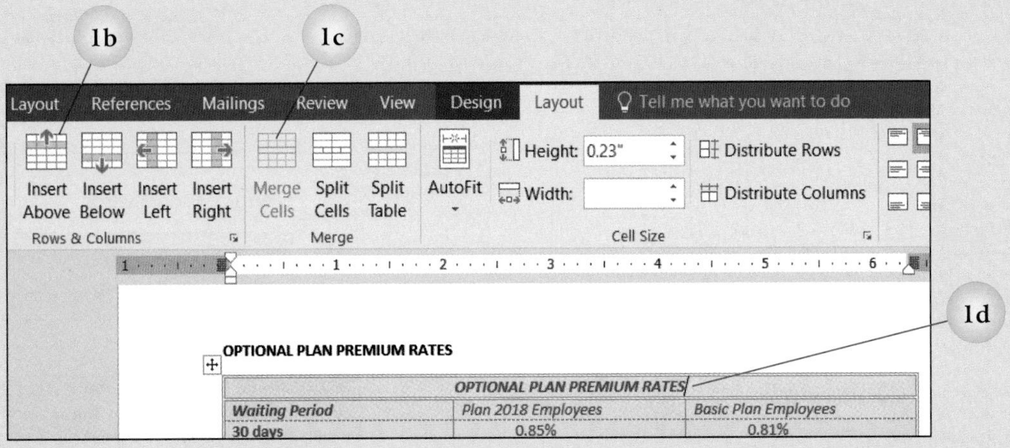

2. Select and then delete the text *OPTIONAL PLAN PREMIUM RATES* above the bottom table.
3. Insert rows and text in the top table and merge cells by completing the following steps:
   a. Click in the cell containing the text *Maggie Rivera*.
   b. Click the Table Tools Layout tab.
   c. Click the Insert Above button two times. (This inserts two rows at the top of the table.)
   d. With the cells in the top row selected, click the Merge Cells button in the Merge group.
   e. Type CONTACT INFORMATION, NORTH and then press Ctrl + E to center-align the text in the cell.
   f. Type the following text in the four cells in the new second row.
      Name Title Company Telephone

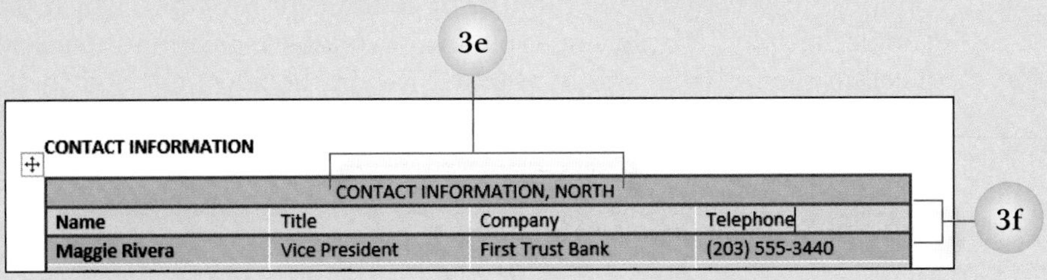

4. Apply heading formatting to the new top row by completing the following steps:
   a. Click the Table Tools Design tab.
   b. Click the *Header Row* check box in the Table Style Options group to insert a check mark.
5. Select and then delete the text *CONTACT INFORMATION* above the top table.
6. Split a cell by completing the following steps:
   a. Click in the cell containing the telephone number *(301) 555-1201*.
   b. Click the Table Tools Layout tab.
   c. Click the Split Cells button in the Merge group.
   d. At the Split Cells dialog box, click OK. (The telephone number will wrap to a new line. You will change this in the next project.)
   e. Click in the new cell.

f. Type x453 in the new cell. If AutoCorrect automatically capitalizes the *x*, hover the mouse pointer over the *X* until the AutoCorrect Options button displays. Click the AutoCorrect Options button and then click *Undo Automatic Capitalization* or click *Stop Auto-capitalizing First Letter of Table Cells*.

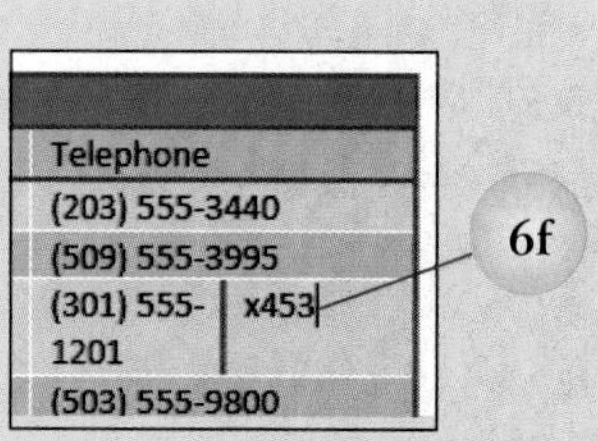

7. Split the cell containing the telephone number *(206) 555-6788* and then type x2310 in the new cell. (If necessary, make the *x* lowercase.)
8. Split the top table into two tables by completing the following steps:
   a. Click in the cell containing the name *Teresa Getty*.
   b. Click the Split Table button in the Merge group.
   c. Click in the cell containing the name *Teresa Getty* (in the first row of the new table).
   d. Click the Insert Above button in the Rows and Columns group on the Table Tools Layout tab.
   e. With the new row selected, click the Merge Cells button.
   f. Type CONTACT INFORMATION, SOUTH in the new row and then press Ctrl + E to center-align the text.
9. Save and then print **7-Tables.docx**.
10. Delete the middle table by completing the following steps:
    a. Click in any cell in the middle table.
    b. Click the Table Tools Layout tab.
    c. Click the Delete button in the Rows & Columns group and then click *Delete Table* at the drop-down list.
11. Draw a dark-orange border at the bottom of the top table by completing the following steps:
    a. Click in any cell in the top table and then click the Table Tools Design tab.
    b. Click the *Line Weight* option box arrow in the Borders group and then click *1½ pt* at the drop-down list. (This activates the Border Painter button.)
    c. Click the Pen Color button and then click the *Orange, Accent 2, Darker, 50%* color option (sixth column, bottom row in the *Theme Colors* section).
    d. Using the mouse, drag along the bottom border of the top table.
    e. Click the Border Painter button to turn off the feature.
12. Save **7-Tables.docx**.

Check Your Work

Tutorial

Customizing Cells in a Table

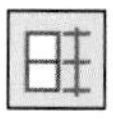
Distribute Rows

Distribute Columns

Customizing Cell Size

When a table is created, the column width and row height are equal. Both can be customized with buttons in the Cell Size group on the Table Tools Layout tab. Use the *Table Row Height* measurement box to increase or decrease the heights of rows and use the *Table Column Width* measurement box to increase or decrease the widths of columns. The Distribute Rows button will make all the selected rows the same height and the Distribute Columns button will make all the selected columns the same width.

Column width can also be changed using the move table column markers on the horizontal ruler or using the table gridlines. To change column width using the horizontal ruler, position the mouse pointer on a move table column marker until it turns into a left-and-right-pointing arrow and then drag the marker on the horizontal ruler to the desired position. Press and hold down the Shift key while dragging a table column marker and the horizontal ruler remains stationary while the table column marker moves. Press and hold down the Alt key while dragging a table column marker and measurements display on the horizontal ruler. To change column width using gridlines, position the arrow pointer on the gridline separating columns until the insertion point turns into a left-and-right-pointing arrow with a vertical double-line in the middle and then drag the gridline to the desired position. Press and hold down the Alt key while dragging the gridline and column measurements display on the horizontal ruler.

Adjust row height in a manner similar to adjusting column width. Drag the adjust table row marker on the vertical ruler or drag the gridline separating rows. Press and hold down the Alt key while dragging the adjust table row marker or the row gridline and measurements display on the vertical ruler.

AutoFit

Use the AutoFit button in the Cell Size group to make the column widths in a table automatically fit the contents. To do this, position the insertion point in any cell in the table, click the AutoFit button in the Cell Size group, and then click *AutoFit Contents* at the drop-down list.

Project 1g Changing Column Width and Row Height — Part 7 of 8

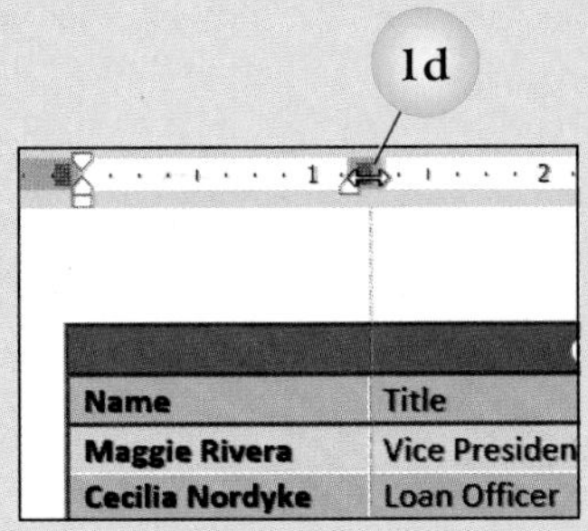

1. With **7-Tables.docx** open, change the width of the first column in the top table by completing the following steps:
   a. Click in the cell containing the name *Maggie Rivera*.
   b. Position the mouse pointer on the move table column marker just right of the 1.5-inch mark on the horizontal ruler until the pointer turns into a left-and-right-pointing arrow.
   c. Press and hold down the Shift key and then click and hold down the left mouse button.
   d. Drag the marker to the 1.25-inch mark, release the mouse button, and then release the Shift key.
2. Complete steps similar to those in Step 1 to drag the move table column marker just right of the 3-inch mark on the horizontal ruler to the 2.75-inch mark. (Make sure the text *Account Manager* in the second column does not wrap to the next line. If it does, slightly increase the width of the column.)
3. Change the width of the third column in the top table by completing the following steps:
   a. Position the mouse pointer on the gridline separating the third and fourth columns until the pointer turns into a left-and-right-pointing arrow with a vertical double-line in the middle.
   b. Press and hold down the Alt key and then click and hold down the left mouse button, drag the gridline to the left until the measurement for the third column on the horizontal ruler displays as *1.31"*, and then release the Alt key followed by the mouse button.

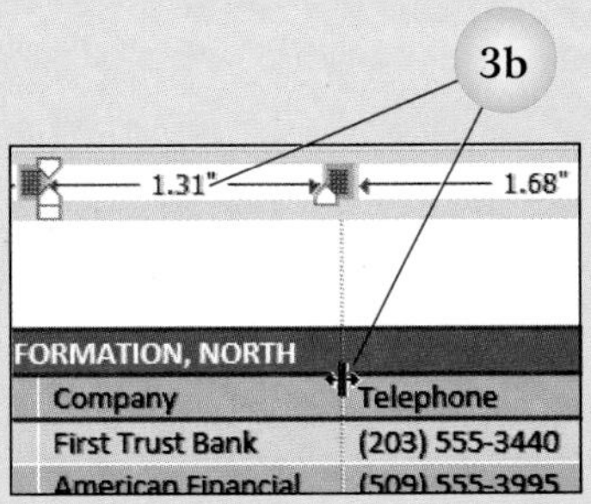

4. Position the mouse pointer on the gridline that separates the telephone number *(301) 555-1201* from the extension *x453* and then drag the gridline to the 5.25-inch mark on the horizontal ruler. (Make sure the phone number does not wrap down to the next line.)
5. Drag the right border of the top table to the 5.75-inch mark on the horizontal ruler.

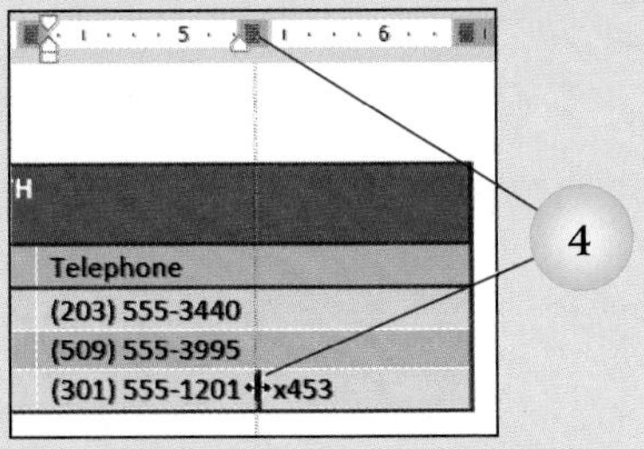

6. Automatically fit the columns in the bottom table by completing the following steps:
   a. Click in any cell in the bottom table.
   b. Click the AutoFit button in the Cell Size group on the Table Tools Layout tab and then click *AutoFit Contents* at the drop-down list.

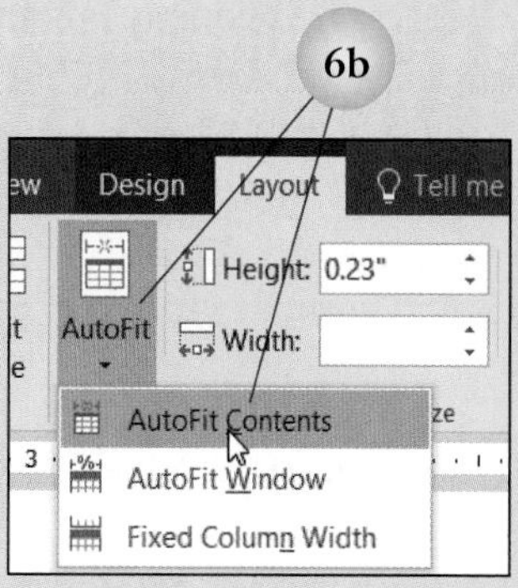

7. Increase the height of the first row in the bottom table by completing the following steps:
   a. Make sure the insertion point is positioned in one of the cells in the bottom table.
   b. Position the mouse pointer on the top adjust table row marker on the vertical ruler.
   c. Press and hold down the Alt key and then click and hold down the left mouse button.
   d. Drag the adjust table row marker down until the first row measurement on the vertical ruler displays as *0.39"*, release the mouse button, and then release the Alt key.

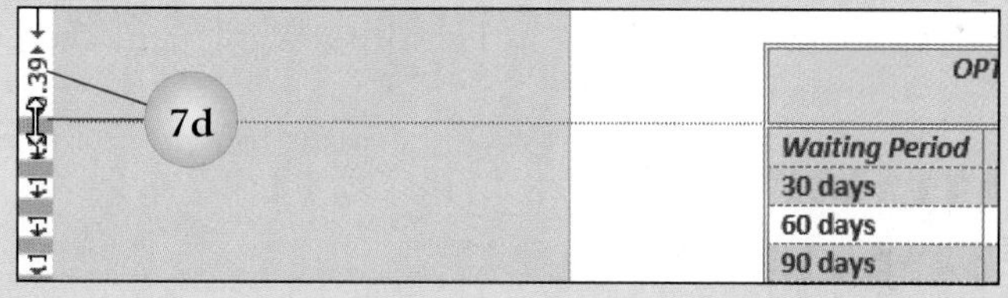

8. Increase the height of the first row in the top table by completing the following steps:
   a. Click in any cell in the top table.
   b. Position the arrow pointer on the gridline at the bottom of the top row until the arrow pointer turns into an up-and-down-pointing arrow with a vertical double-line in the middle.
   c. Click and hold down the left mouse button and then press and hold down the Alt key.
   d. Drag the gridline down until the first row measurement on the vertical ruler displays as *0.39"*, release the mouse button, and then release the Alt key.

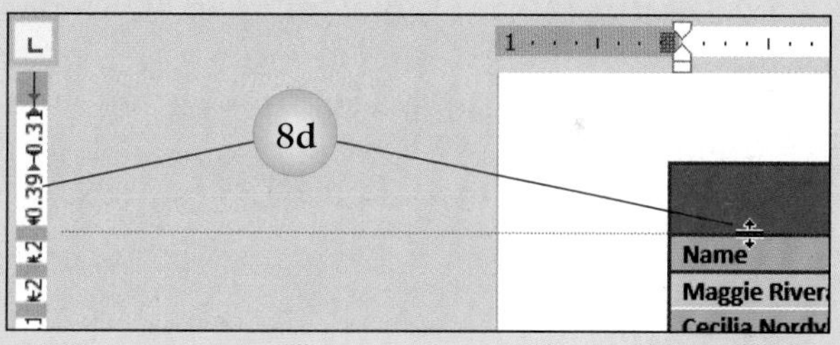

9. Save **7-Tables.docx**.

Check Your Work

Changing Cell Alignment

The Alignment group on the Table Tools Layout tab contains a number of buttons for specifying the horizontal and vertical alignment of text in cells. Each button contains a visual representation of the alignment. Hover the mouse pointer over a button to display a ScreenTip with the button name and description.

Quick Steps

Repeat a Header Row
1. Click in header row or select rows.
2. Click Table Tools Layout tab.
3. Click Repeat Header Rows button.

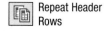

Repeat Header Rows

Repeating a Header Row

If a table is divided between two pages, consider adding the header row at the beginning of the table that continues on the second page. This helps the reader understand the data in each column. To repeat a header row, click in the first row (header row) and then click the Repeat Header Rows button in the Data group on the Table Tools Layout tab. To repeat more than one header row, select the rows and then click the Repeat Header Rows button.

Project 1h Aligning Text in Cells and Repeating Header Rows

Part 8 of 8

1. With **7-Tables.docx** open, click in the top cell in the top table (the cell containing the title *CONTACT INFORMATION, NORTH*).
2. Click the Align Center button in the Alignment group on the Table Tools Layout tab.

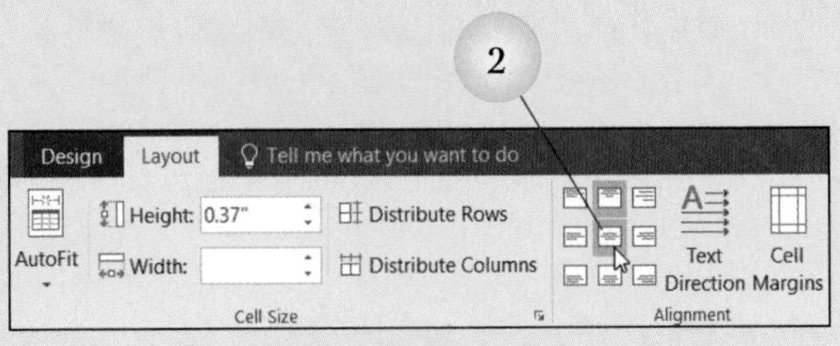

3. Format and align the text in the second row in the top table by completing the following steps:
   a. Select the second row.
   b. Press Ctrl + B to turn off bold formatting for the entry in the first cell and then press Ctrl + B again to turn on bold formatting for all the entries in the second row.
   c. Click the Align Top Center button in the Alignment group.
4. Click in the top cell in the bottom table and then click the Align Center button in the Alignment group.
5. Press Ctrl + End to move the insertion point to the end of the document, press the Enter key four times, and then insert a table into the current document by completing the following steps:
   a. Click the Insert tab.
   b. Click the Object button arrow in the Text group and then click *Text from File* at the drop-down list.
   c. At the Insert File dialog box, navigate to the WL1C7 folder on your storage medium and then double-click ***ContactsWest.docx***.
6. Repeat the header row by completing the following steps:
   a. Select the first two rows in the table you just inserted.
   b. Click the Table Tools Layout tab.
   c. Click the Repeat Header Rows button in the Data group.

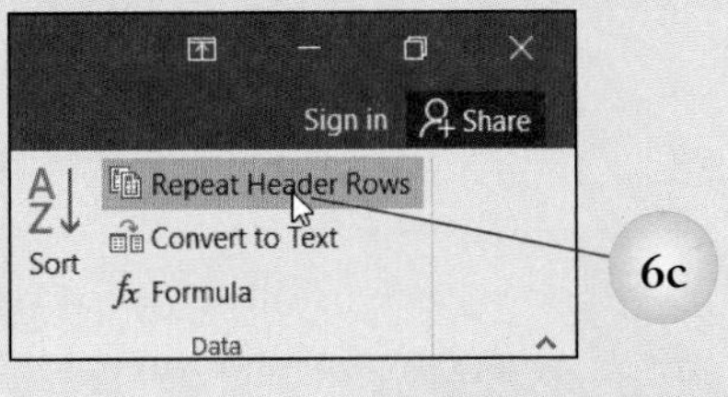

7. Save, print, and then close **7-Tables.docx**.

Check Your Work

Project 2 Create and Format Tables with Employee Information

6 Parts

You will create and format a table containing information on the names and departments of employees of Tri-State Products, a table containing additional information on employees, and a calendar quick table.

Preview Finished Project

Changing Cell Margin Measurements

Cell Margins

By default, the cells in a table contain specific margin measurements. The top and bottom margins in a cell have a default measurement of 0 inch and the left and right margins have a default measurement of 0.08 inch. Change these default measurements with options at the Table Options dialog box, shown in Figure 7.7. Display this dialog box by clicking the Cell Margins button in the Alignment group on the Table Tools Layout tab. Use the measurement boxes in the *Default cell margins* section to change the top, bottom, left, and/or right cell margin measurements.

Figure 7.7 Table Options Dialog Box

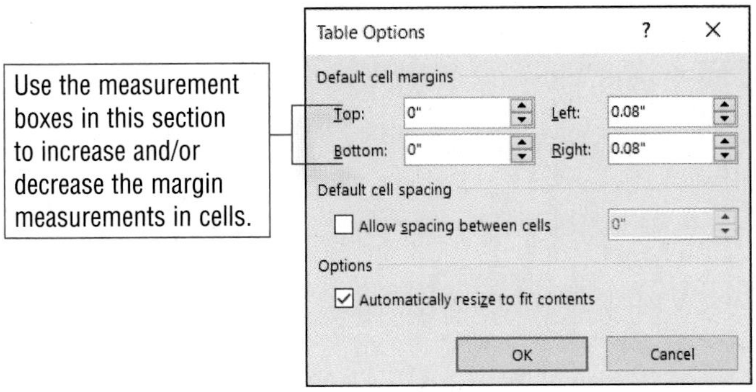

Properties

Changes to cell margins will affect all the cells in a table. To change the cell margin measurements for one cell or selected cells, position the insertion point in the cell or select the cells and then click the Properties button in the Table group on the Table Tools Layout tab (or click the Cell Size group dialog box launcher). At the Table Properties dialog box, click the Cell tab and then the Options button in the lower right corner of the dialog box. This displays the Cell Options dialog box, shown in Figure 7.8.

Before setting the new cell margin measurements, remove the check mark from the *Same as the whole table* check box. With the check mark removed, the cell margin options become available. Specify the new cell margin measurements and then click OK to close the dialog box.

Figure 7.8 Cell Options Dialog Box

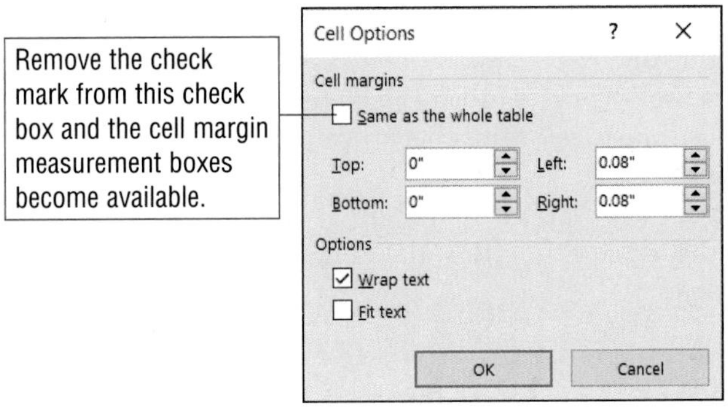

Project 2a Changing Cell Margin Measurements

Part 1 of 6

1. Open **TSPTables.docx** and then save it with the name **7-TSPTables**.
2. Change the top and bottom cell margin measurements for all the cells in the table by completing the following steps:
   a. Position the insertion point in any cell in the table and then click the Table Tools Layout tab.
   b. Click the Cell Margins button in the Alignment group.

c. At the Table Options dialog box, change the *Top* and *Bottom* measurements to 0.05 inch.
d. Click OK to close the Table Options dialog box.

3. Change the top and bottom cell margin measurements for the first row of cells by completing the following steps:
   a. Select the first row of cells (the cells containing *Name* and *Department*).
   b. Click the Properties button in the Table group.
   c. At the Table Properties dialog box, click the Cell tab.
   d. Click the Options button in the lower right corner of the dialog box.
   e. At the Cell Options dialog box, click the *Same as the whole table* check box to remove the check mark.
   f. Change the *Top* and *Bottom* measurements to 0.1 inch.
   g. Click OK to close the Cell Options dialog box.
   h. Click OK to close the Table Properties dialog box.
4. Change the left cell margin measurement for specific cells by completing the following steps:
   a. Select all of the rows in the table *except* the top row.
   b. Click the Cell Size group dialog box launcher.
   c. At the Table Properties dialog box, make sure the Cell tab is active.
   d. Click the Options button.
   e. At the Cell Options dialog box, remove the check mark from the *Same as the whole table* check box.
   f. Change the *Left* measurement to 0.3 inch.
   g. Click OK to close the Cell Options dialog box.
   h. Click OK to close the Table Properties dialog box.
5. Save **7-TSPTables.docx**.

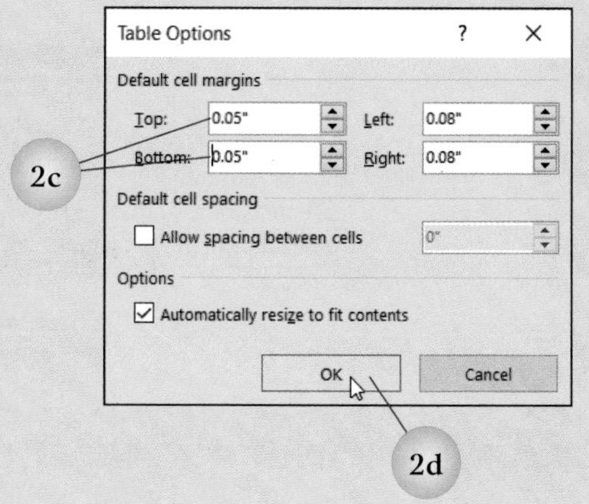

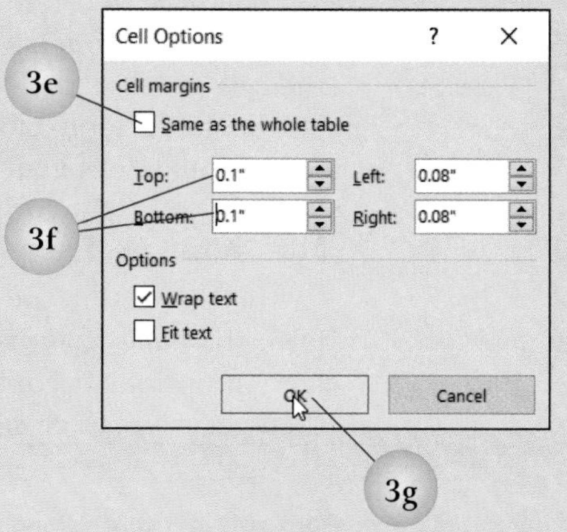

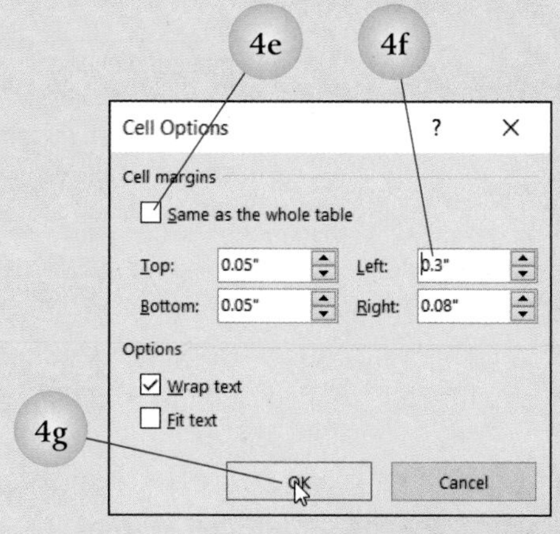

Check Your Work

Changing Cell Direction

Text Direction

Change the direction of text in a cell using the Text Direction button in the Alignment group on the Table Tools Layout tab. Each time the Text Direction button is clicked, the text in the cell rotates 90 degrees.

Changing Table Alignment and Dimensions

By default, a table aligns at the left margin. Change this alignment with options at the Table Properties dialog box with the Table tab selected, as shown in Figure 7.9. To change the alignment, click the desired alignment option in the *Alignment* section of the dialog box. Change table dimensions by clicking the *Preferred width* check box to insert a check mark. This makes active both the width measurement box and the *Measure in* option box. Type a width measurement in the measurement box and specify whether the measurement type is inches or a percentage with the *Measurement in* option box.

Figure 7.9 Table Properties Dialog Box with Table Tab Selected

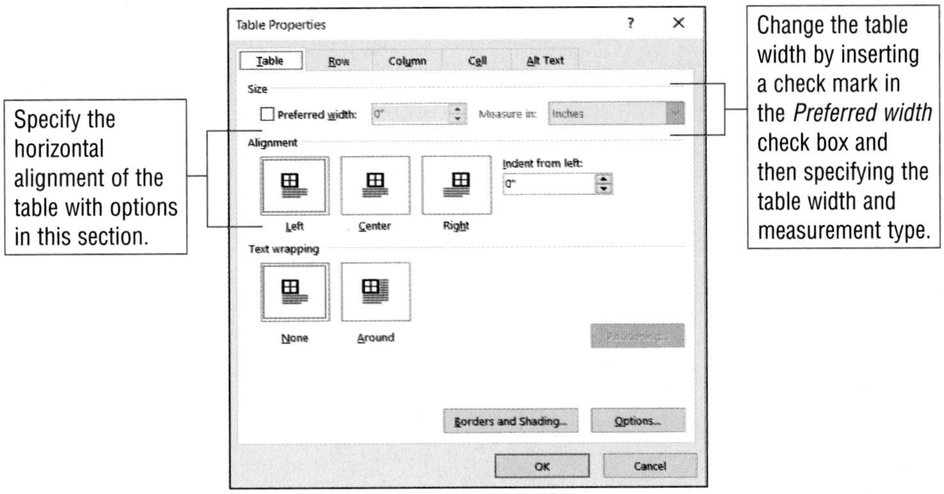

Project 2b Changing Table Alignment and Dimensions

Part 2 of 6

1. With **7-TSPTables.docx** open, insert a new column and change text direction by completing the following steps:
   a. Click in any cell in the first column.
   b. Click the Insert Left button in the Rows & Columns group.
   c. With the cells in the new column selected, click the Merge Cells button in the Merge group.
   d. Type Tri-State Products.
   e. Click the Align Center button in the Alignment group.
   f. Click two times on the Text Direction button in the Alignment group.
   g. With *Tri-State Products* selected, click the Home tab and then increase the font size to 16 points.

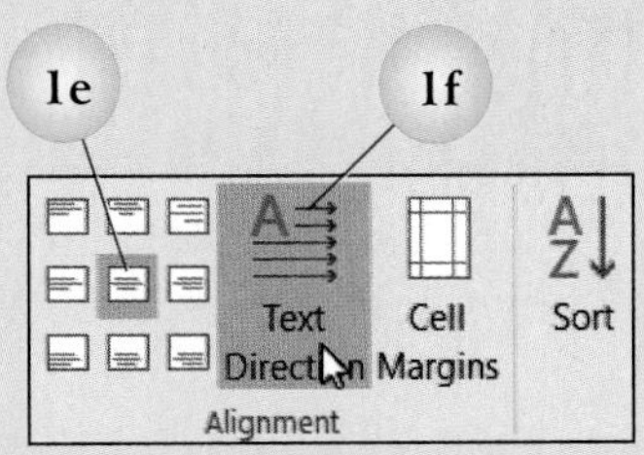

2. Automatically fit the contents by completing the following steps:
   a. Click in any cell in the table.
   b. Click the Table Tools Layout tab.
   c. Click the AutoFit button in the Cell Size group and then click *AutoFit Contents* at the drop-down list.

3. Change the table width and alignment by completing the following steps:
   a. Click the Properties button in the Table group on the Table Tools Layout tab.
   b. At the Table Properties dialog box, click the Table tab.
   c. Click the *Preferred width* check box to insert a check mark.
   d. Select the measurement in the measurement box and then type 4.5.
   e. Click the *Center* option in the *Alignment* section.
   f. Click OK.

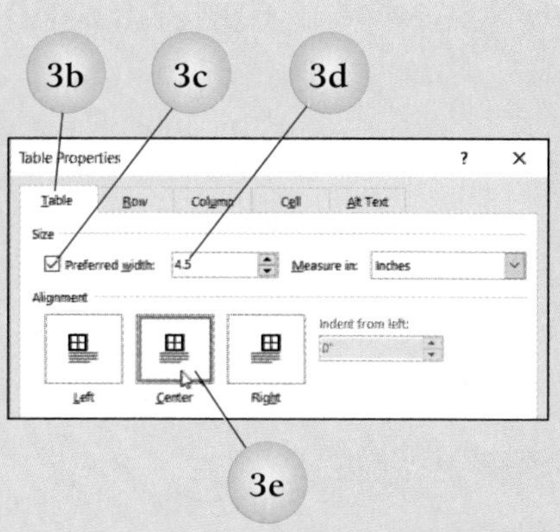

4. Select the two cells containing the text *Name* and *Department* and then click the Align Center button in the Alignment group.
5. Save **7-TSPTables.docx**.

Check Your Work

Quick Steps

Move a Table

1. Position mouse pointer on table move handle until pointer displays with four-headed arrow attached.
2. Click and hold down left mouse button.
3. Drag table to new location.
4. Release mouse button.

Changing Table Size with the Resize Handle

Hover the mouse pointer over a table and a resize handle displays in the lower right corner. The resize handle displays as a small white square. Drag this resize handle to increase and/or decrease the size and proportion of the table.

Moving a Table

Position the mouse pointer in a table and a table move handle displays in the upper left corner. Use this handle to move the table in the document. To move a table, position the mouse pointer on the table move handle until the pointer displays with a four-headed arrow attached, click and hold down the left mouse button, drag the table to the new location, and then release the mouse button.

Project 2c Resizing and Moving Tables — Part 3 of 6

1. With **7-TSPTables.docx** open, insert a table into the current document by completing the following steps:
   a. Press Ctrl + End to move the insertion point to the end of the document and then press the Enter key.
   b. Click the Insert tab.
   c. Click the Object button arrow in the Text group and then click *Text from File* at the drop-down list.
   d. At the Insert File dialog box, navigate to the WL1C7 folder and then double-click ***TSPEmps.docx***.
2. Automatically fit the bottom table by completing the following steps:
   a. Click in any cell in the bottom table.
   b. Click the Table Tools Layout tab.
   c. Click the AutoFit button in the Cell Size group and then click *AutoFit Contents* at the drop-down list.

3. Format the bottom table by completing the following steps:
   a. Click the Table Tools Design tab.
   b. Click the More Table Styles button in the table styles gallery and then click the *List Table 4 - Accent 6* table style (last column, fourth row in the *List Tables* section).
   c. Click the *First Column* check box in the Table Style Options group to remove the check mark.
   d. Select the first and second rows, click the Table Tools Layout tab, and then click the Align Center button in the Alignment group.
   e. Select the second row and then press Ctrl + B to turn on bold formatting.

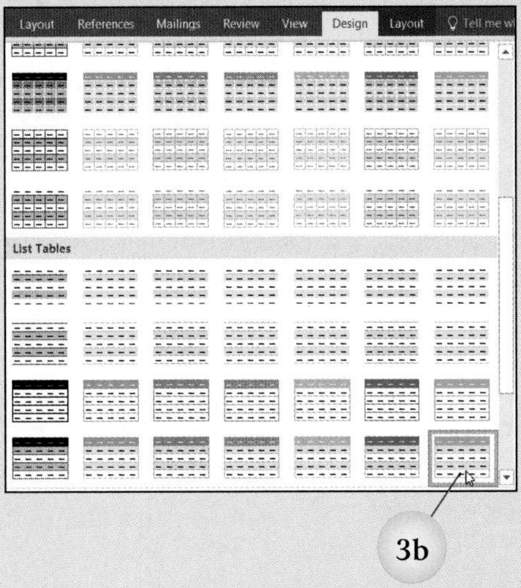

4. Resize the bottom table by completing the following steps:
   a. Position the mouse pointer on the resize handle in the lower right corner of the bottom table.
   b. Click and hold down the left mouse button, drag down and to the right until the width and height of the table increase approximately 1 inch, and then release the mouse button.

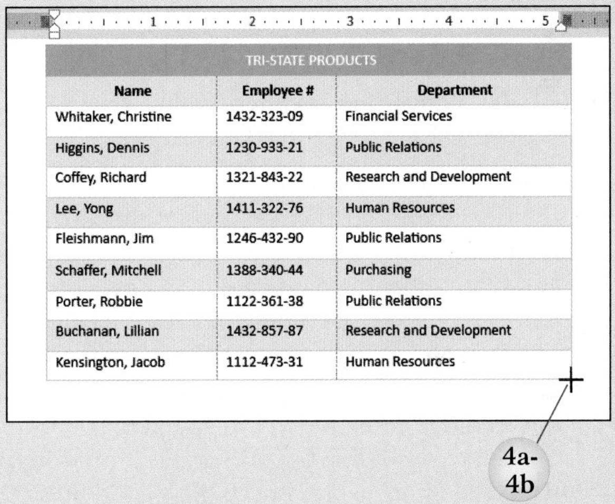

TRI-STATE PRODUCTS
Name
Employee #
Department
Whitaker, Christine
1432-323-09
Financial Services
Higgins, Dennis
1230-933-21
Public Relations
Coffey, Richard
1321-843-22
Research and Development
Lee, Yong
1411-322-76
Human Resources
Fleishmann, Jim
1246-432-90
Public Relations
Schaffer, Mitchell
1388-340-44
Purchasing
Porter, Robbie
1122-361-38
Public Relations
Buchanan, Lillian
1432-857-87
Research and Development
Kensington, Jacob
1112-473-31
Human Resources
4a-4b

5. Move the bottom table by completing the following steps:
   a. Move the mouse pointer over the bottom table and then position the mouse pointer on the table move handle until the pointer displays with a four-headed arrow attached.
   b. Click and hold down the left mouse button, drag the table so it is positioned equally between the left and right margins, and then release the mouse button.

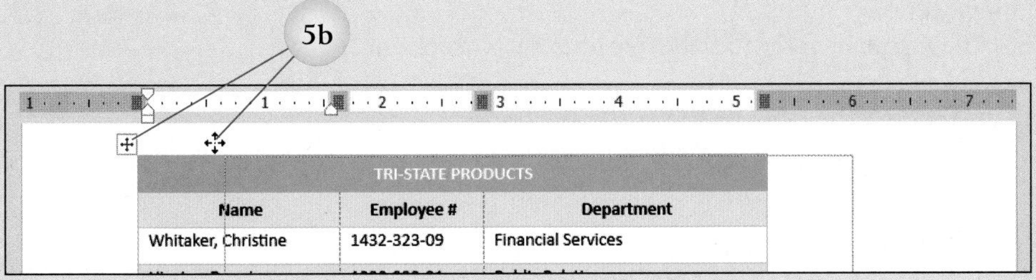

5b
TRI-STATE PRODUCTS
Name
Employee #
Department
Whitaker, Christine
1432-323-09
Financial Services

6. Select the cells in the column below the heading *Employee #* and then click the Align Top Center button in the Alignment group.
7. Save **7-TSPTables.docx**.

Check Your Work

Tutorial

Converting Text to a Table and a Table to Text

Quick Steps

Convert Text to Table

1. Select text.
2. Click Insert tab.
3. Click Table button.
4. Click *Convert Text to Table.*
5. Click OK.

Convert Table to Text

1. Click Table Tools Layout tab.
2. Click Convert to Text button.
3. Specify separator.
4. Click OK.

Convert to Text

Converting Text to a Table and a Table to Text

Create a table and then enter text in the cells or create the text and then convert it to a table. Converting text to a table provides formatting and layout options available on the Table Tools Design tab and the Table Tools Layout tab. When typing the text to be converted to a table, separate units of information using separator characters, such as commas or tabs. These characters identify where the text is divided into columns. To convert text, select the text, click the Insert tab, click the Table button in the Tables group, and then click *Convert Text to Table* at the drop-down list. At the Convert Text to Table dialog box, specify the separator and then click OK.

Convert a table to text by positioning the insertion point in any cell of the table, clicking the Table Tools Layout tab, and then clicking the Convert to Text button in the Data group. At the Convert Table To dialog box, specify the separator and then click OK.

Project 2d Converting Text to a Table

Part 4 of 6

1. With **7-TSPTables.docx** open, press Ctrl + End to move the insertion point to the end of the document. (If the insertion point does not display below the second table, press the Enter key until the insertion point displays there.)
2. Insert the document named **TSPExecs.docx** into the current document.
3. Convert the text to a table by completing the following steps:
   a. Select the text you just inserted.
   b. Make sure the Insert tab is active.
   c. Click the Table button in the Tables group and then click *Convert Text to Table* at the drop-down list.
   d. At the Convert Text to Table dialog box, type 2 in the *Number of columns* measurement box.
   e. Click the *AutoFit to contents* option in the *AutoFit behavior* section.
   f. Click the *Commas* option in the *Separate text at* section.
   g. Click OK.

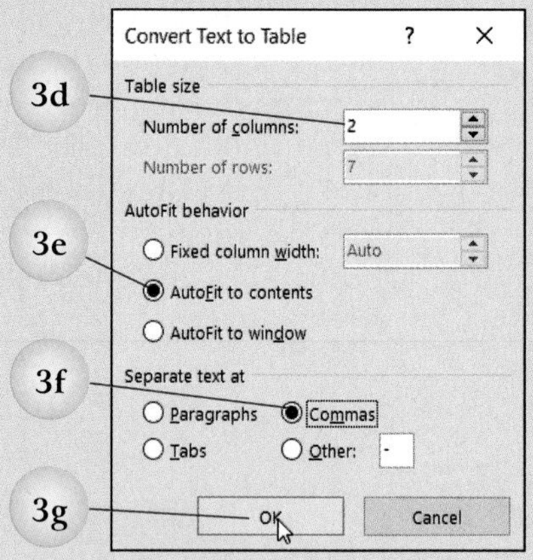

4. Select and merge the cells in the top row (the row containing the title *TRI-STATE PRODUCTS*) and then center-align the text in the merged cell.
5. Apply the List Table 4 - Accent 6 style (last column, fourth row in the *List Tables* section) and remove the check mark from the *First Column* check box in the Table Style Options group on the Table Tools Design tab.
6. Drag the table so it is centered below the table above it.
7. Apply the List Table 4 - Accent 6 style to the top table. Increase the widths of the columns so the text *Tri-State Products* is visible and the text in the second and third columns displays on one line.
8. Drag the table so it is centered above the middle table. Make sure the three tables fit on one page.

9. Click in the middle table and then convert the table to text by completing the following steps:
   a. Click the Table Tools Layout tab and then click the Convert to Text button in the Data group.
   b. At the Convert Table To dialog box, make sure *Tabs* is selected and then click OK.
10. Print **7-TSPTables.docx**.
11. Click the Undo button to return the text to a table.
12. Save **7-TSPTables.docx**.

Check Your Work

Drawing a Table

Eraser

In Project 1, options in the Borders group on the Table Tools Design tab were used to draw borders around an existing table. These options can also be used to draw an entire table. To draw a table, click the Insert tab, click the Table button in the Tables group, and then click *Draw Table* at the drop-down list. Or click the Draw Table button in the Draw group on the Table Tools Layout tab; this turns the mouse pointer into a pen. Drag the pen pointer in the document to create the table. To correct an error when drawing a table, click the Eraser button in the Draw group on the Table Tools Layout tab (which changes the mouse pointer to an eraser) and then drag over any border lines to be erased. Clicking the Undo button will also undo the most recent action.

Project 2e Drawing and Formatting a Table — Part 5 of 6

1. With **7-TSPTables.docx** open, select and then delete three rows in the middle table from the row that begins with the name *Lee, Yong* through the row that begins with the name *Schaffer, Mitchell*.
2. Move the insertion point to the end of the document (outside any table) and then press the Enter key. (Make sure the insertion point is positioned below the third table.)
3. Click the Insert tab, click the Table button, and then click the *Draw Table* option at the drop-down list. (This turns the insertion point into a pen.)
4. Using the mouse, drag in the document (below the bottom table) to create the table shown at the right, drawing the outside border first. If you make a mistake, click the Undo button. You can also click the Eraser button in the Draw group on the Table Tools Layout tab and drag over a border line to erase it. Click the Draw Table button in the Draw group to turn off the pen feature.

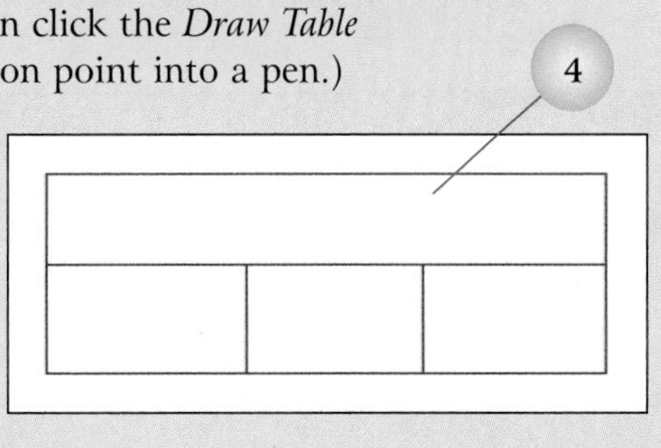

5. After drawing the table, type Tri-State Products in the top cell, Washington Division in the cell at the left, Oregon Division in the middle bottom cell, and California Division in the cell at the right.
6. Apply the Grid Table 4 - Accent 6 table style (last column, fourth row in the *Grid Tables* section).
7. Select the table, change the font size to 12 points, apply bold formatting, and then center-align the text in the cells using the Align Center button in the Alignment group.
8. Make any adjustments needed to the border lines so the text in each cell displays on one line.
9. Drag the table so it is centered and positioned below the bottom table.
10. Save **7-TSPTables.docx**.

Check Your Work

Inserting a Quick Table

Quick Steps
Insert a Quick Table
1. Click Insert tab.
2. Click Table button.
3. Point to *Quick Tables*.
4. Click table.

Word includes a Quick Tables feature for inserting predesigned tables in a document. To insert a quick table, click the Insert tab, click the Table button, point to *Quick Tables*, and then click a table at the side menu. A quick table has formatting applied but additional formatting can be applied with options on the Table Tools Design tab and the Table Tools Layout tab.

Project 2f Inserting a Quick Table — Part 6 of 6

1. With **7-TSPTables.docx** open, press Ctrl + End to move the insertion point to the end of the document and then press Ctrl + Enter to insert a page break.
2. Insert a quick table by clicking the Insert tab, clicking the Table button, pointing to *Quick Tables*, and then clicking the *Calendar 3* option at the side menu.

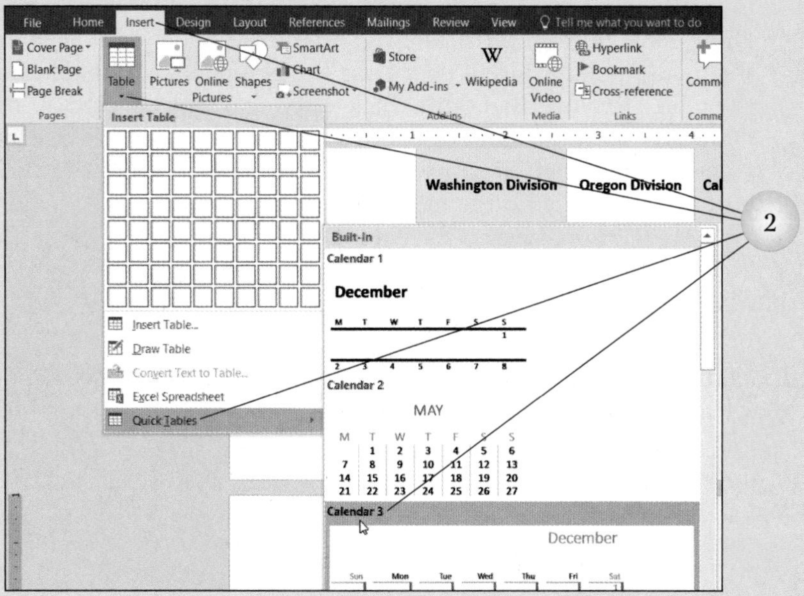

3. Edit the text in each cell so the calendar reflects the current month. (If the bottom row is empty, select and then delete the row.)
4. Select the entire table by clicking the Table Tools Layout tab, clicking the Select button in the Table group, and then clicking the *Select Table* option. With the table selected, change the font to Copperplate Gothic Light.
5. Save, print, and then close **7-TSPTables.docx**.

Check Your Work

Project 3 Calculate Sales Data — 1 Part

You will insert formulas in a Tri-State Products sales table to calculate total sales, average sales, and top sales.

Preview Finished Project

Tutorial

Performing Calculations in a Table

Performing Calculations in a Table

Use the Formula button in the Data group on the Table Tools Layout tab to insert formulas that perform calculations on the data in a table. The numbers in cells can be added, subtracted, multiplied, and divided. In addition, other calculations can be performed, such as determining averages, counting items, and identifying minimum and maximum values. Data can be calculated in a Word table, but for complex calculations consider using an Excel worksheet.

Formula

Quick Steps

Insert a Formula in a Table
1. Click in cell.
2. Click Table Tools Layout tab.
3. Click Formula button.
4. Type formula in Formula dialog box.
5. Click OK.

To perform a calculation on the data in a table, position the insertion point in the cell where the result of the calculation is to be inserted and then click the Formula button in the Data group on the Table Tools Layout tab. This displays the Formula dialog box, as shown in Figure 7.10. At this dialog box, accept the default formula in the *Formula* text box or type a calculation and then click OK.

Figure 7.10 Formula Dialog Box

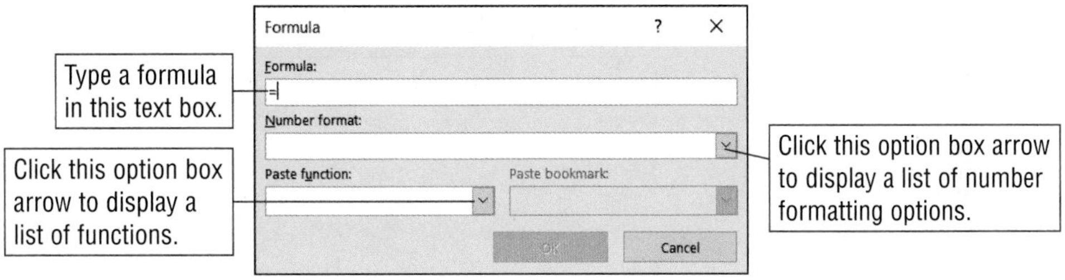

Four basic operators are available for writing a formula, including the plus symbol (+) for addition, the minus symbol (–) for subtraction, the asterisk (*) for multiplication, and the forward slash (/) for division. If a calculation contains two or more operators, Word performs the operations from left to right. To change the order of operations, put parentheses around the part of the calculation to be performed first.

In the default formula, the SUM part of the formula is called a *function*. Word also provides other functions for inserting formulas. These functions are available in the *Paste function* option box in the Formula dialog box. For example, use the AVERAGE function to average numbers in cells.

Specify the numbering format with the *Number format* option box in the Formula dialog box. For example, when calculating amounts of money, specify that the numbers display with no numbers or two numbers following the decimal point.

Hint Use the Update Field keyboard shortcut, F9, to update the selected field.

If changes are made to the values in a formula, the result of the formula needs to be updated. To do this, right-click the formula result and then click *Update Field* at the shortcut menu. Or click the formula result and then press the F9 function key, which is the Update Field keyboard shortcut. To update the results of all the formulas in a table, select the entire table and then press the F9 function key.

1. Open **TSPSalesTable.docx** and then save it with the name **7-TSPSalesTable**.
2. Insert a formula in the table by completing the following steps:
   a. Click in cell B9. (Cell B9 is the empty cell immediately below the cell containing the amount *$375,630.*)
   b. Click the Table Tools Layout tab.
   c. Click the Formula button in the Data group.
   d. At the Formula dialog box, make sure *=SUM(ABOVE)* displays in the *Formula* text box.
   e. Click the *Number format* option box arrow and then click *#,##0* at the drop-down list (the top option in the list).
   f. Click OK to close the Formula dialog box.

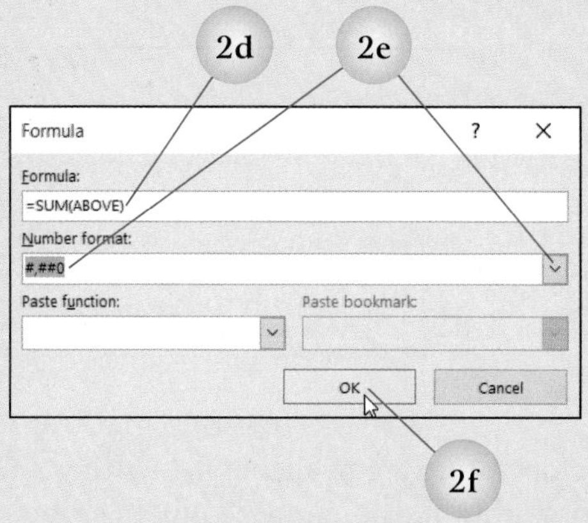

   g. In the table, type a dollar symbol ($) before the number just inserted in cell B9.
3. Complete steps similar to those in Steps 2c through 2g to insert a formula in cell C9. (Cell C9 is the empty cell immediately below the cell containing the amount *$399,120.*)
4. Insert a formula that calculates the average of amounts by completing the following steps:
   a. Click in cell B10. (Cell B10 is the empty cell immediately right of the cell containing the word *Average*.)
   b. Click the Formula button in the Data group.
   c. At the Formula dialog box, delete the formula in the *Formula* text box *except* for the equals (=) sign.
   d. With the insertion point positioned immediately right of the equals sign, click the *Paste function* option box arrow and then click *AVERAGE* at the drop-down list.
   e. With the insertion point positioned between the left and right parentheses, type B2:B8. (When typing cell designations in a formula, you can type either uppercase or lowercase letters.)

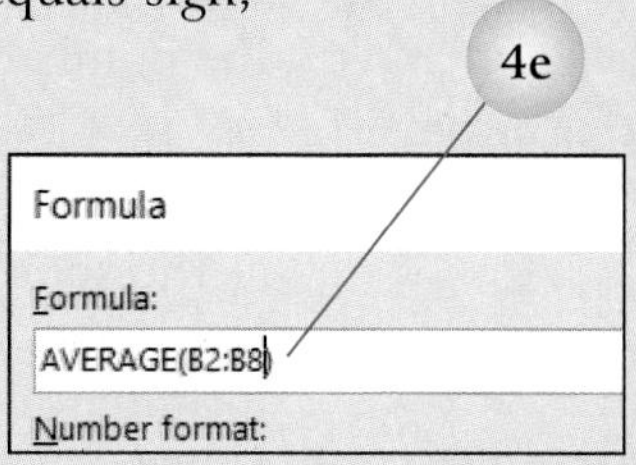

   f. Click the *Number format* option box arrow and then click *#,##0* at the drop-down list (the top option in the list).
   g. Click OK to close the Formula dialog box.
   h. Type a dollar symbol ($) before the number just inserted in cell B10.
5. Complete steps similar to those in Steps 4b through 4h to insert a formula in cell C10 that calculates the average of the amounts in cells C2 through C8.

6. Insert a formula that calculates the maximum number by completing the following steps:
   a. Click in cell B11. (Cell B11 is the empty cell immediately right of the cell containing the words *Top Sales*.)
   b. Click the Formula button in the Data group.
   c. At the Formula dialog box, delete the formula in the *Formula* text box *except* for the equals sign.
   d. With the insertion point positioned immediately right of the equals sign, click the *Paste function* option box arrow and then click *MAX* at the drop-down list. (You will need to scroll down the list to display the *MAX* option.)
   e. With the insertion point positioned between the left and right parentheses, type B2:B8.
   f. Click the *Number format* option box arrow and then click *#,##0* at the drop-down list (the top option in the list).
   g. Click OK to close the Formula dialog box.
   h. Type a dollar symbol ($) before the number just inserted in cell B11.

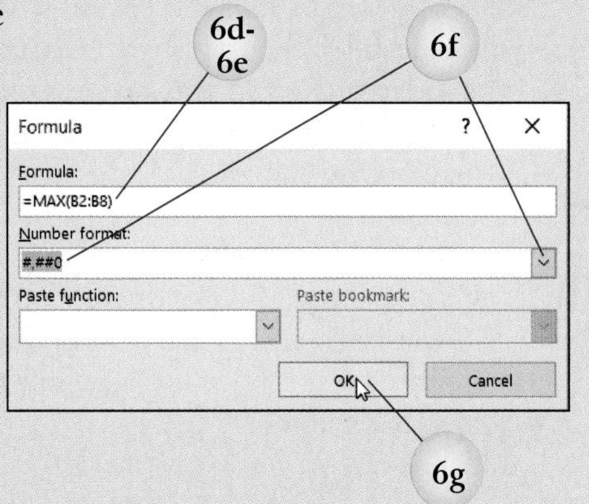

7. Complete steps similar to those in Steps 6b through 6h to insert the maximum number in cell C11.
8. Save and then print **7-TSPSalesTable.docx**.
9. Change the amount in cell B2 from *$543,241* to *$765,700*.
10. Recalculate all the formulas in the table by completing the following steps:
    a. Make sure the Table Tools Layout tab is active and then click the Select button in the Table group.
    b. Click the *Select Table* option.
    c. Press the F9 function key.
11. Save, print, and then close **7-TSPSalesTable.docx**.

Check Your Work

Project 4 Insert an Excel Worksheet 1 Part

You will insert an Excel worksheet in a blank document, decrease the number of rows and columns in the worksheet, insert data on sales increases in the worksheet from a Word document, and calculate data in the worksheet.

Preview Finished Project

Inserting an Excel Spreadsheet

An Excel spreadsheet (usually referred to as a *worksheet*) can be inserted into a Word document, which provides some Excel functions for modifying and formatting the data. To insert an Excel worksheet, click the Insert tab, click the Table button in the Tables group, and then click the *Excel Spreadsheet* option at the drop-down list. This inserts a worksheet in the document with seven columns and ten rows visible. Increase or decrease the number of visible cells by dragging the sizing handles that display around the worksheet. Use buttons on the Excel ribbon tabs to format the worksheet. Click outside the worksheet and the Excel ribbon tabs are removed. Double-click the table to redisplay the Excel ribbon tabs.

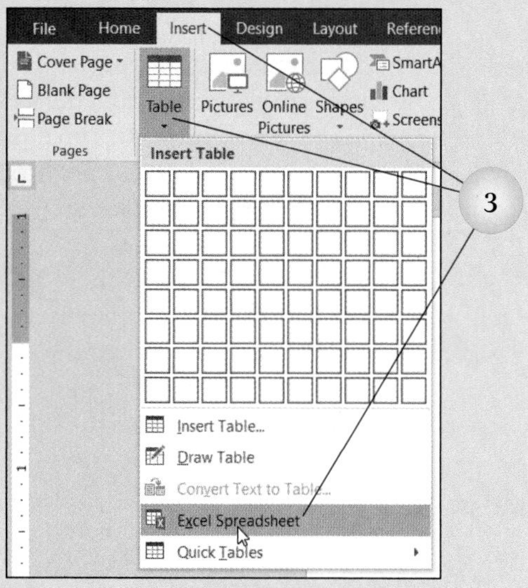

1. Open **SalesIncrease.docx**.
2. Press Ctrl + N to open a blank document.
3. Insert an Excel spreadsheet into the blank document by clicking the Insert tab, clicking the Table button in the Tables group, and then clicking *Excel Spreadsheet* at the drop-down list.
4. Decrease the size of the worksheet by completing the following steps:
   a. Position the mouse pointer on the sizing handle (small black square) located in the lower right corner of the worksheet until the pointer displays as a black, diagonal, two-headed arrow.
   b. Click and hold down the left mouse button, drag up and to the left, and release the mouse button. Continue dragging the sizing handles until columns A, B, and C and rows 1 through 7 are visible.
5. Copy a table into the Excel worksheet by completing the following steps:
   a. Position the mouse pointer on the Word button on the taskbar and then click the *SalesIncrease.docx* thumbnail.
   b. Position the mouse pointer over the table and then click the table move handle (small square containing a four-headed arrow) that displays in the upper left corner of the table. (This selects all of the cells in the table.)
   c. Click the Copy button in the Clipboard group on the Home tab.
   d. Close **SalesIncrease.docx**.
   e. With the first cell in the worksheet active, click the Paste button in the Clipboard group.

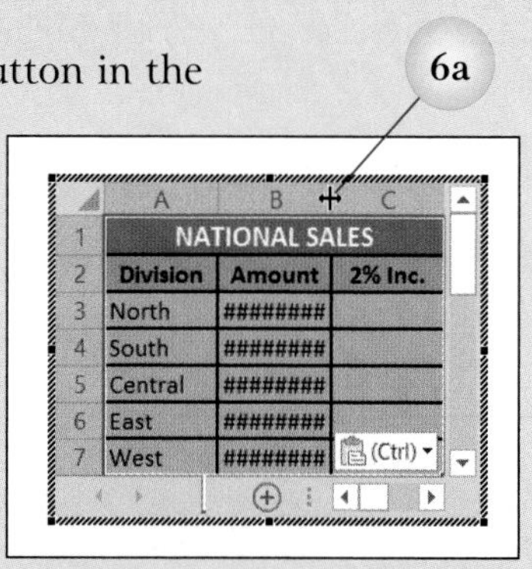

6. Format the worksheet and insert a formula by completing the following steps:
   a. Increase the width of the second column by positioning the mouse pointer on the column boundary between columns B and C and double-clicking the left mouse button.
   b. Click in cell C3, type the formula =B3*102, and then press the Enter key.
7. Copy the formula in cell C3 to the range C4:C7 by completing the following steps:
   a. Position the mouse pointer (white plus symbol) in cell C3, click and hold down the left mouse button, drag down into cell C7, and then release the mouse button.
   b. Click the Fill button in the Editing group on the Home tab and then click *Down* at the drop-down list.

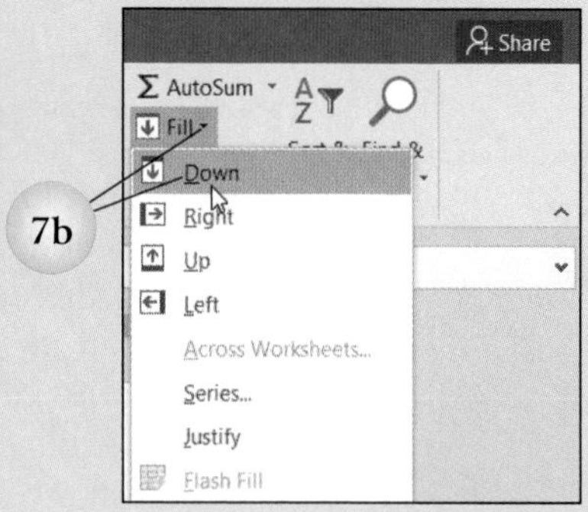

8. Click outside the worksheet to remove the Excel ribbon tabs.
9. Save the document and name it **7-Worksheet**.
10. Print and then close **7-Worksheet.docx**.

Check Your Work

Project 5 Prepare and Format a SmartArt Graphic **2 Parts**

You will prepare a SmartArt process graphic that identifies steps in the production process and then apply formatting to enhance the graphic.

Preview Finished Project

Tutorial

Inserting, Sizing, and Positioning SmartArt

Tutorial

Formatting SmartArt

SmartArt

Hint Use SmartArt to communicate your message and ideas in a visual manner.

Quick Steps

Insert a SmartArt Graphic

1. Click Insert tab.
2. Click SmartArt button.
3. Double-click graphic.

Creating SmartArt

Use Word's SmartArt feature to insert graphics such as diagrams and organizational charts in a document. SmartArt offers a variety of predesigned graphics that are available at the Choose a SmartArt Graphic dialog box, as shown in Figure 7.11. At this dialog box, *All* is selected by default in the left panel and all of the available predesigned SmartArt graphics display in the middle panel.

Inserting and Formatting a SmartArt Graphic

To insert a SmartArt graphic, click the Insert tab and then click the SmartArt button in the Illustrations group to open the Choose a SmartArt Graphic dialog box. Predesigned SmartArt graphics display in the middle panel of the dialog box. Use the scroll bar at the right side of the middle panel to scroll down the list of choices. Click a graphic in the middle panel and its name displays in the right panel along with a description. SmartArt includes graphics for presenting a list of data; showing data processes, cycles, and relationships; and presenting data in a matrix or pyramid. Double-click a graphic in the middle panel of the dialog box and the graphic is inserted in the document.

When a SmartArt graphic is inserted in a document, a text pane displays at the left side of the graphic. Type text in the text pane or type directly in the graphic. Apply formatting to a graphic with options on the SmartArt Tools Design tab. This

Figure 7.11 Choose a SmartArt Graphic Dialog Box

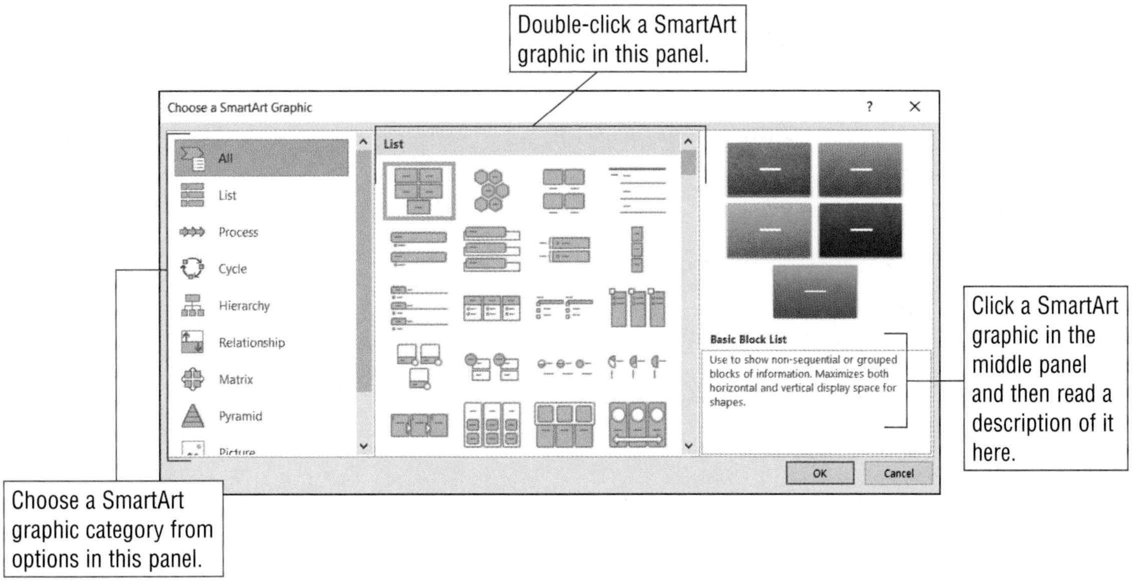

Hint Limit the number of shapes and amount of text in your SmartArt graphic.

tab becomes active when the graphic is inserted in the document. Use options and buttons on this tab to add objects, change the graphic layout, apply a style to the graphic, and reset the graphic to the original formatting.

Apply formatting to a SmartArt graphic with options on the SmartArt Tools Format tab. Use options and buttons on this tab to change the sizes and shapes of objects in the graphic; apply shape styles and WordArt styles; change the shape fill, outline, and effects; and arrange and size the graphic.

Project 5a Inserting and Formatting a SmartArt Graphic

Part 1 of 2

1. At a blank document, insert the SmartArt graphic shown in Figure 7.12 by completing the following steps:
   a. Click the Insert tab.
   b. Click the SmartArt button in the Illustrations group.
   c. At the Choose a SmartArt Graphic dialog box, click *Process* in the left panel and then double-click the *Alternating Flow* graphic.

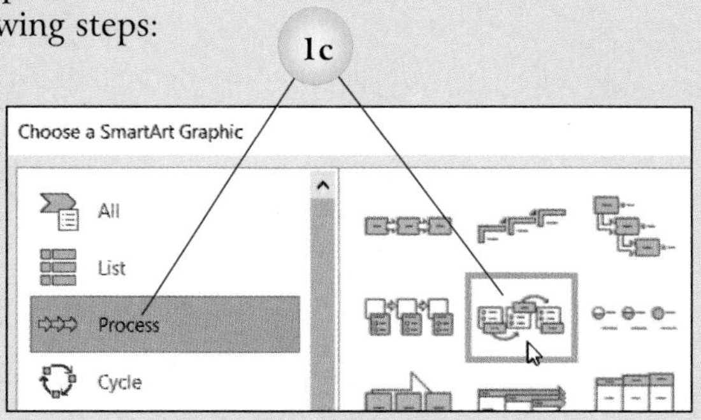

   d. If a *Type your text here* text pane does not display at the left side of the graphic, click the Text Pane button in the Create Graphic group to display it.
   e. With the insertion point positioned after the top bullet in the *Type your text here* text pane, type Design.
   f. Click the *[Text]* placeholder below *Design* and then type Mock-up.
   g. Continue clicking occurrences of the *[Text]* placeholder and typing text so the text pane displays as shown at the right.
   h. Close the text pane by clicking the Close button in the upper right corner of the pane. (You can also click the Text Pane button in the Create Graphic group.)

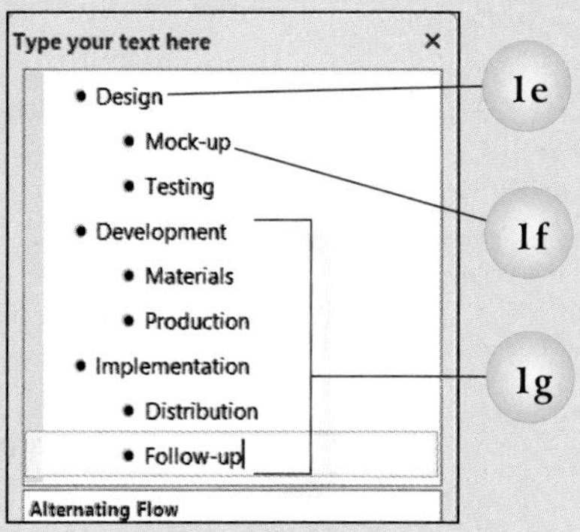

2. Change the graphic colors by clicking the Change Colors button in the SmartArt Styles group and then clicking the *Colorful Range - Accent Colors 5 to 6* option (last option in the *Colorful* section).

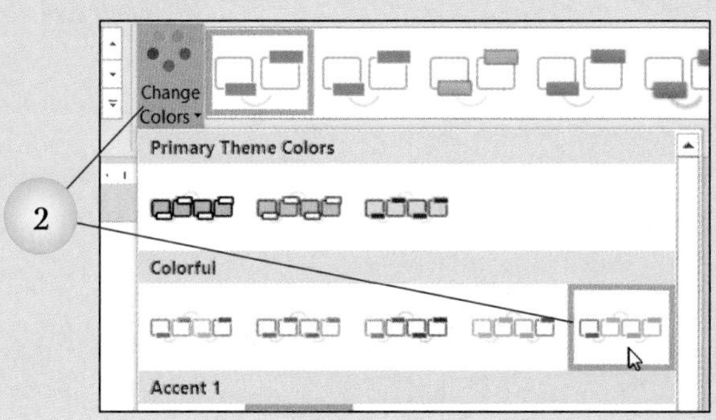

3. Apply a style by clicking the More SmartArt Styles button in the gallery in the SmartArt Styles group and then clicking the *Inset* option (second column, first row in the *3-D* section).
4. Copy the graphic and then change the layout by completing the following steps:
   a. Click inside the SmartArt graphic border but outside any shapes.
   b. Click the Home tab and then click the Copy button in the Clipboard group.
   c. Press Ctrl + End, press the Enter key, and then press Ctrl + Enter to insert a page break.
   d. Click the Paste button in the Clipboard group.
   e. Click inside the SmartArt graphic border but outside any shapes.
   f. Click the SmartArt Tools Design tab.
   g. Click the More Layouts button in the Layouts gallery and then click the *Continuous Block Process* layout (second column, second row).
   h. Click outside the graphic to deselect it.
5. Save the document and name it **7-SAGraphics**.

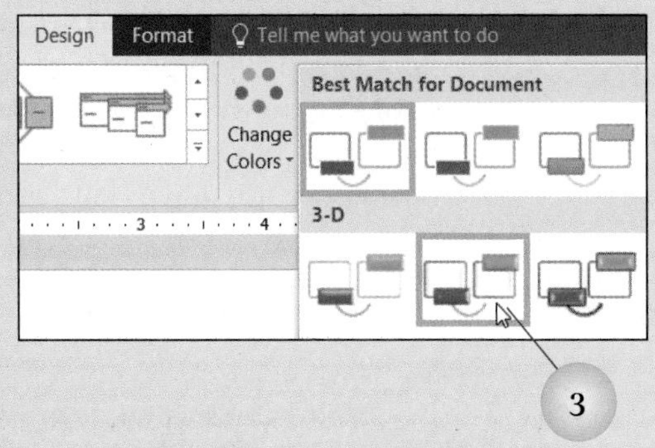

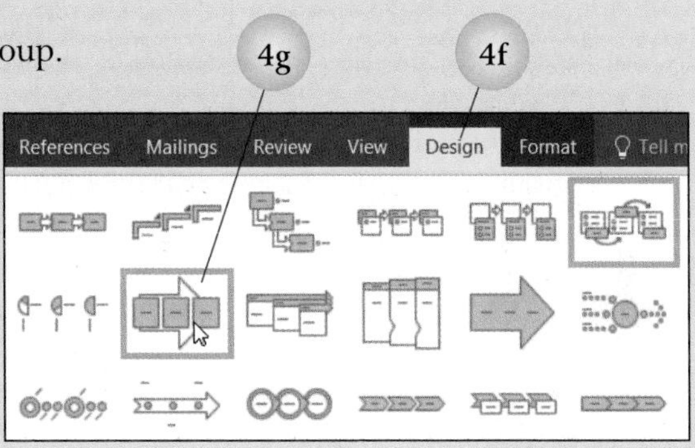

Check Your Work

Figure 7.12 Project 5a

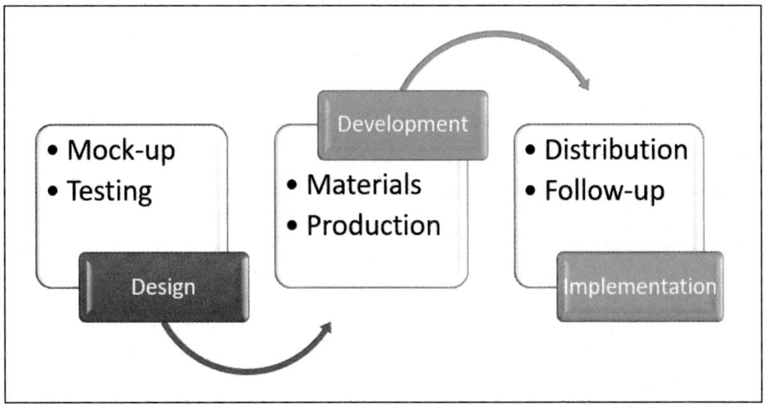

Arranging and Moving a SmartArt Graphic

Position

Arrange

Wrap Text

Position a SmartArt graphic by clicking the Arrange button on the SmartArt Tools Format tab, clicking the Position button, and then clicking the desired position option at the drop-down gallery. Along with positioning the SmartArt graphic, the options at the Position button drop-down gallery apply square text wrapping, which means text wraps around the border of an object. Text wrapping can also be applied by clicking the Arrange button, clicking the Wrap Text button, and then clicking a wrapping style at the drop-down gallery. Or it can be applied with options from the Layout Options button outside the upper right corner of the selected SmartArt graphic. Move a SmartArt graphic by positioning the arrow pointer on the graphic border until the pointer displays with a four-headed arrow attached, clicking and holding down the left mouse button, and then dragging the graphic to the new location. Nudge the SmartArt graphic or a shape or selected shapes in the graphic using the up, down, left, and right arrow keys on the keyboard.

Project 5b Formatting SmartArt Graphics

Part 2 of 2

1. With **7-SAGraphics.docx** open, format shapes by completing the following steps:
   a. Click the graphic on the first page to select it (a border surrounds the graphic).
   b. Click the SmartArt Tools Format tab.
   c. In the graphic, click the rectangle shape containing the word *Design*.
   d. Press and hold down the Shift key and then click the shape containing the word *Development*.
   e. With the Shift key still held down, click the shape containing the word *Implementation*. (All three shapes should now be selected.)
   f. Click the Change Shape button in the Shapes group.
   g. Click the *Pentagon* shape (seventh column, second row in the *Block Arrows* section).
   h. With the shapes still selected, click the Larger button in the Shapes group.
   i. With the shapes still selected, click the Shape Outline button arrow in the Shape Styles group and then click the *Dark Blue* color option (ninth option in the *Standard Colors* section).
   j. Click inside the graphic border but outside any shape. (This deselects the shapes but keeps the graphic selected.)

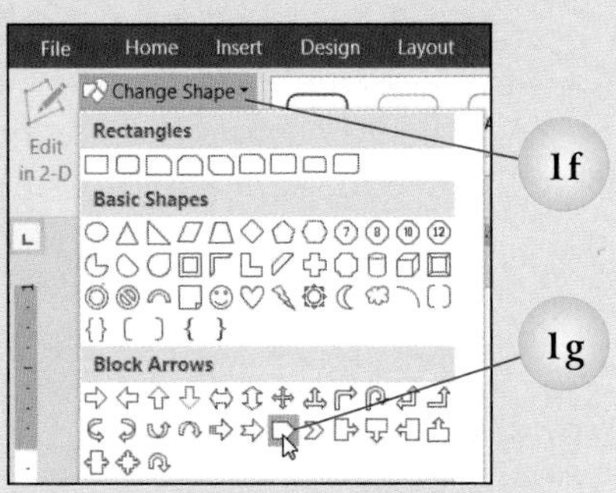

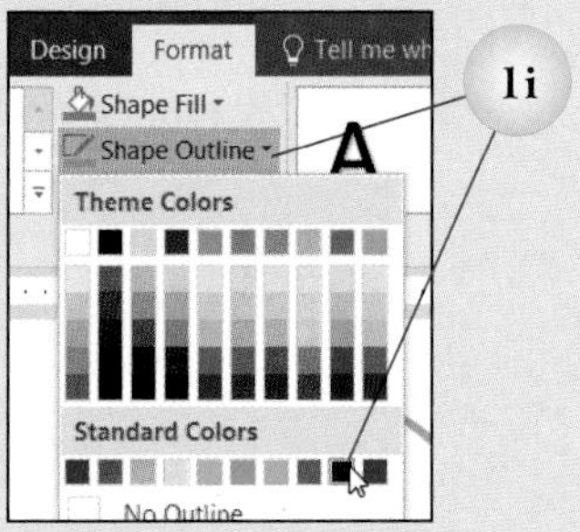

2. Change the size of the graphic by completing the following steps:
   a. Click the Size button at the right side of the SmartArt Tools Format tab.
   b. Click in the *Shape Height* measurement box, type 4, and then press the Enter key.
3. Position the graphic by completing the following steps:
   a. Click the Arrange button on the SmartArt Tools Format tab and then click the Position button at the drop-down list.
   b. Click the *Position in Middle Center with Square Text Wrapping* option (second column, second row in the *With Text Wrapping* section).
   c. Click outside the graphic to deselect it.
4. Format the bottom SmartArt graphic by completing the following steps:
   a. Press Ctrl + End to move to the end of the document and then click in the bottom SmartArt graphic to select it.

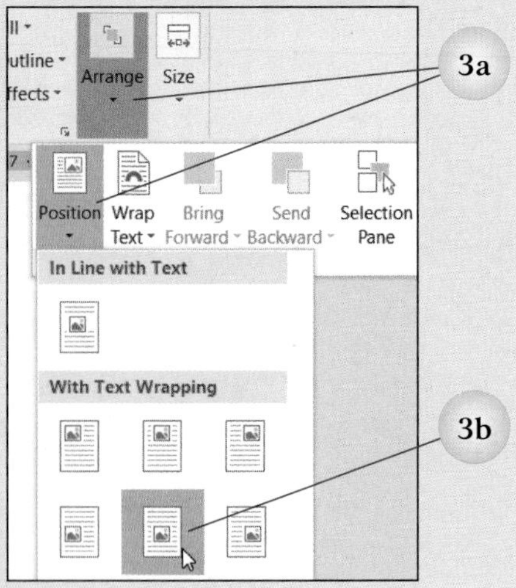

b. Press and hold down the Shift key and then click each of the three shapes.

c. Click the More WordArt Styles button in the WordArt styles gallery on the SmartArt Tools Format tab.

d. Click the *Fill - Black, Text 1, Shadow* option (first column, first row).

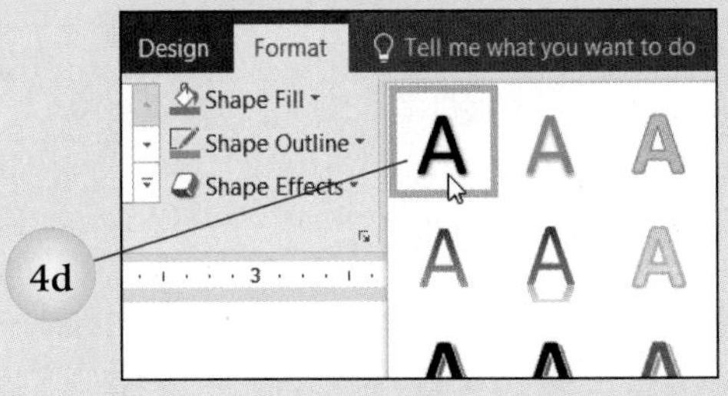

e. Click the Text Outline button arrow in the WordArt Styles group and then click the *Dark Blue* color option (ninth color in the *Standard Colors* section).

f. Click the Text Effects button in the WordArt Styles group, point to *Glow* at the drop-down list, and then click the *Orange, 5 pt glow, Accent color 2* option (second column, first row in the *Glow Variations* section).

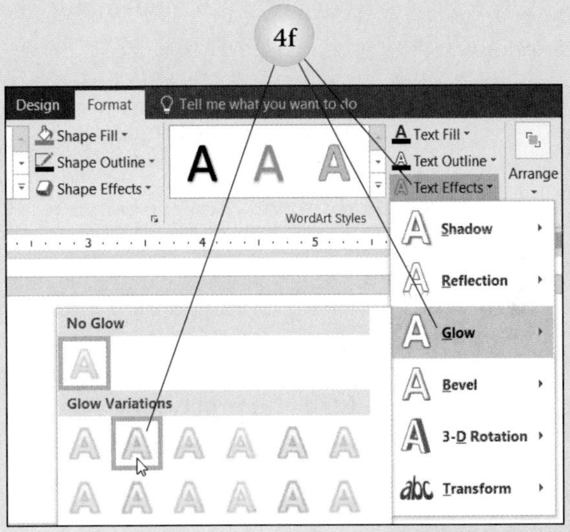

g. Click inside the SmartArt graphic border but outside any shape.

5. Arrange the graphic by clicking the Arrange button, clicking the Position button, and then clicking the *Position in Middle Center with Square Text Wrapping* option (second column, second row in the *With Text Wrapping* section).
6. Click outside the graphic to deselect it.
7. Save, print, and then close **7-SAGraphics.docx**.

Check Your Work

Project 6 Prepare and Format a Company Organizational Chart 1 Part

You will prepare an organizational chart for a company and then apply formatting to enhance the visual appeal of the chart.

Preview Finished Project

Creating an Organizational Chart with SmartArt

Quick Steps

Insert an Organizational Chart

1. Click Insert tab.
2. Click SmartArt button.
3. Click *Hierarchy*.
4. Double-click organizational chart.

To visually illustrate hierarchical data, consider creating an organizational chart with a SmartArt option. To display organizational chart SmartArt options, click the Insert tab and then click the SmartArt button in the Illustrations group. At the Choose a SmartArt Graphic dialog box, click *Hierarchy* in the left panel. Organizational chart options display in the middle panel of the dialog box. Double-click an organizational chart and the chart is inserted in the document. Type text in a SmartArt graphic by selecting the shape and then typing text in it or type text in the *Type your text here* window at the left side of the graphic. Format a SmartArt organizational chart with options and buttons on the SmartArt Tools Design tab, the SmartArt Tools Format tab, and the Layout Options button.

Project 6 Creating and Formatting a SmartArt Organizational Chart

Part 1 of 1

1. At a blank document, create the organizational chart shown in Figure 7.13. To begin, click the Insert tab.
2. Click the SmartArt button in the Illustrations group.
3. At the Choose a SmartArt Graphic dialog box, click *Hierarchy* in the left panel of the dialog box and then double-click the *Organization Chart* option (first option in the middle panel).

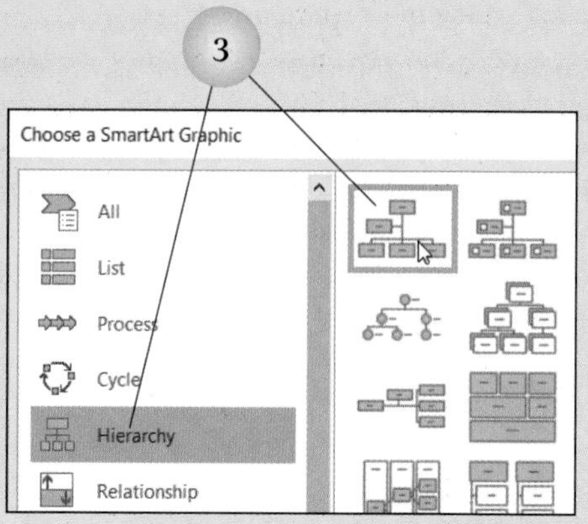

4. If a *Type your text here* pane displays at the left side of the organizational chart, close it by clicking the Text Pane button in the Create Graphic group.
5. Delete one of the boxes in the organizational chart by clicking the border of the box in the lower right corner to select it and then pressing the Delete key. (Make sure that the selection border surrounding the box is a solid line and not a dashed line. If a dashed line displays, click the box border again. This should change the border to a solid line.)
6. With the bottom right box selected, click the Add Shape button arrow in the Create Graphic group and then click the *Add Shape Below* option.

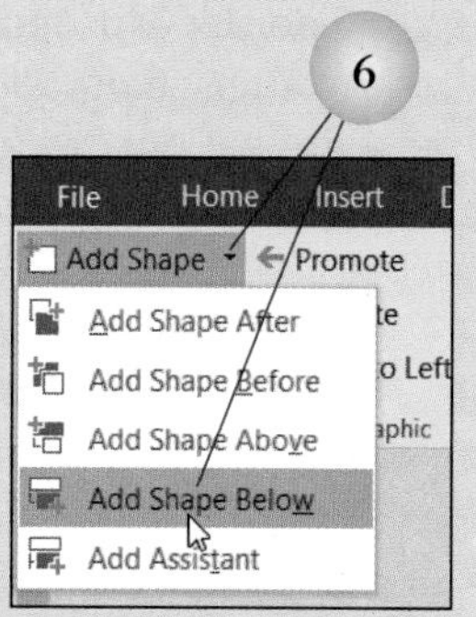

7. Click the *[Text]* placeholder in the top box, type Blaine Willis, press Shift + Enter, and then type President. Click in each of the remaining boxes and type the text as shown in Figure 7.13. (Press Shift + Enter after typing the name.)
8. Click the More SmartArt Styles button in the gallery in the SmartArt Styles group and then click the *Inset* style (second column, first row in the *3-D* section).
9. Click the Change Colors button in the SmartArt Styles group and then click the *Colorful Range - Accent Colors 4 to 5* option (fourth option in the *Colorful* section).

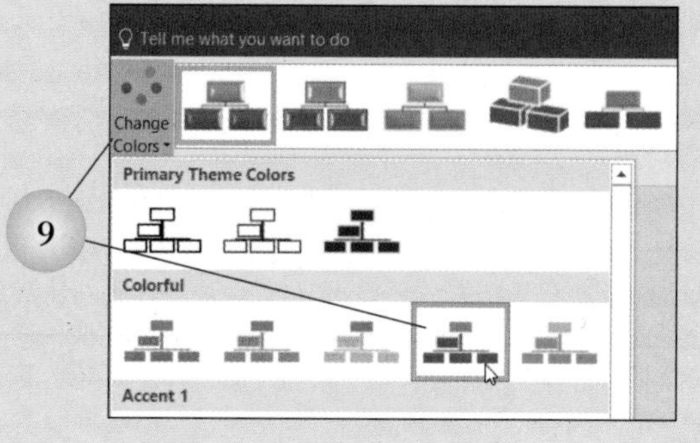

10. Click the SmartArt Tools Format tab.
11. Click the text pane control (displays with a left-pointing arrow) at the left side of the graphic border. (This displays the *Type your text here* window.)
12. Using the mouse, select all the text in the *Type your text here* window.
13. Click the Change Shape button in the Shapes group and then click the *Round Same Side Corner Rectangle* option (eighth option in the *Rectangles* section).

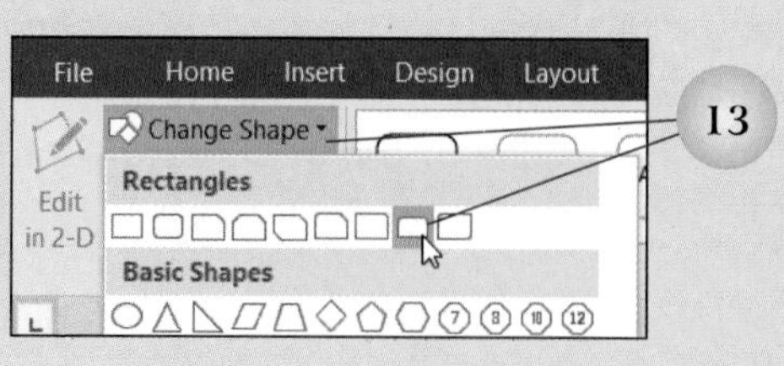

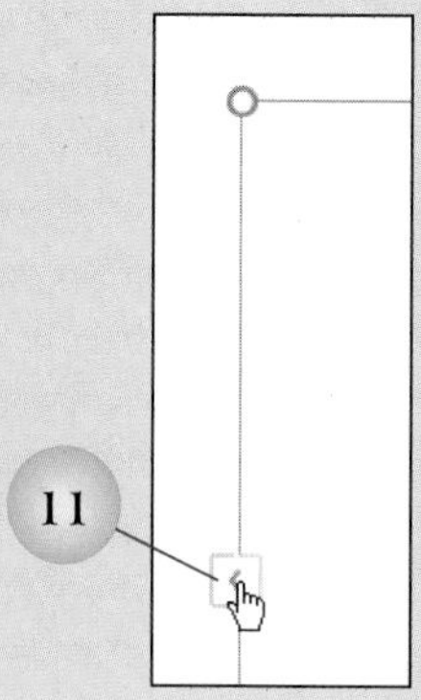

14. Click the Shape Outline button arrow in the Shape Styles group and then click the *Dark Blue* color option (ninth option in the *Standard Colors* section).
15. Close the *Type your text here* window by clicking the Close button in the upper right corner of the window.
16. Click inside the organizational chart border but outside any shape.
17. Click the Size button at the right side of the SmartArt Tools Format tab, click in the *Shape Height* measurement box, and then type 4. Click in the *Shape Width* measurement box, type 6.5, and then press the Enter key.
18. Click outside the chart to deselect it.
19. Save the document and name it **7-OrgChart**.
20. Print and then close the document.

Check Your Work

Figure 7.13 Project 6

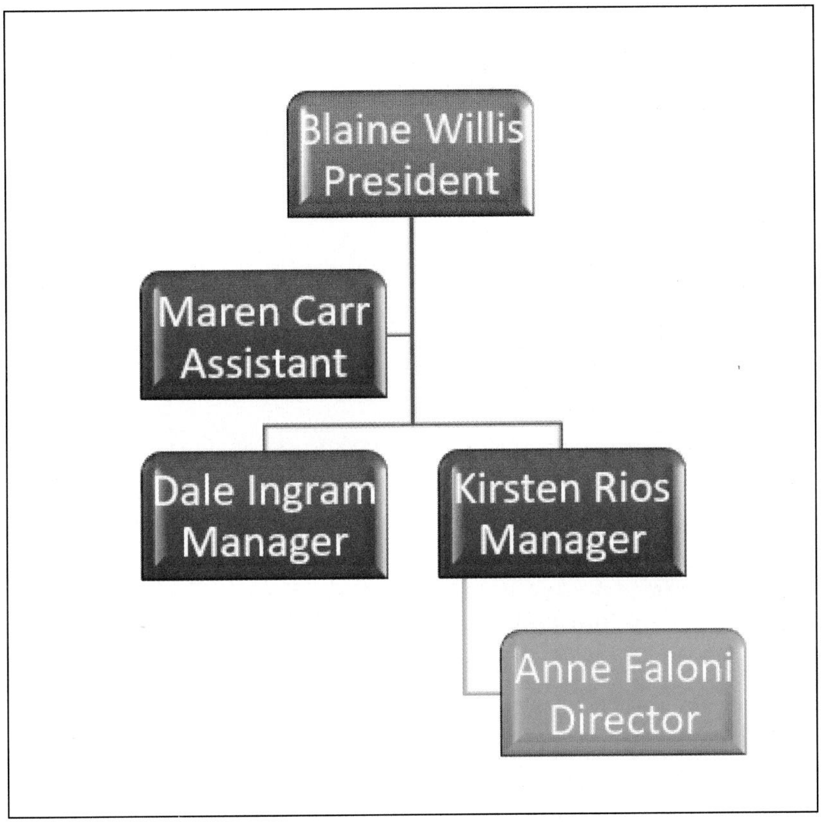

Chapter Summary

- Use the Tables feature to create columns and rows of information. Create a table with the Table button in the Tables group on the Insert tab or with options at the Insert Table dialog box.
- A cell is the intersection between a row and a column. The lines that form the cells of the table are called *gridlines*.
- Move the insertion point to cells in a table using the mouse by clicking in a cell or using the keyboard commands shown in Table 7.1.
- Change the table design with options and buttons on the Table Tools Design tab.
- Refer to Table 7.2 for a list of mouse commands for selecting specific cells in a table and Table 7.3 for a list of keyboard commands for selecting specific cells in a table.
- Change the layout of a table with options and buttons on the Table Tools Layout tab.
- Select a table, column, row, or cell using the Select button in the Table group on the Table Tools Layout tab.
- Turn on and off the display of gridlines by clicking the View Gridlines button in the Table group on the Table Tools Layout tab.
- Insert and delete columns and rows with buttons in the Rows & Columns group on the Table Tools Layout tab.
- Merge selected cells with the Merge Cells button and split cells with the Split Cells button, both in the Merge group on the Table Tools Layout tab.
- Change the column width and row height using the height and width measurement boxes in the Cell Size group on the Table Tools Layout tab; by dragging move table column markers on the horizontal ruler, adjust table row markers on the vertical ruler, or gridlines in the table; or using the AutoFit button in the Cell Size group.
- Change the alignment of text in cells with buttons in the Alignment group on the Table Tools Layout tab.
- If a table spans two pages, a header row can be inserted at the beginning of the rows that extend to the second page. To do this, click in the header row or select the header rows and then click the Repeat Header Rows button in the Data group on the Table Tools Layout tab.
- Change cell margins with options in the Table Options dialog box.
- Change text direction in a cell with the Text Direction button in the Alignment group on the Table Tools Layout tab.
- Change the table dimensions and alignment with options at the Table Properties dialog box with the Table tab selected.
- Use the resize handle to change the size of the table and the table move handle to move the table.
- Convert text to a table with the *Convert Text to Table* option at the Table button drop-down list. Convert a table to text with the Convert to Text button in the Data group on the Table Tools Layout tab.
- Draw a table in a document by clicking the Insert tab, clicking the Table button, and then clicking *Draw Table*. Using the mouse, drag in the document to create the table.

- Quick tables are predesigned tables that can be inserted in a document by clicking the Insert tab, clicking the Table button, pointing to *Quick Tables*, and then clicking a table at the side menu.
- Perform calculations on data in a table by clicking the Formula button in the Data group on the Table Tools Layout tab and then specifying the formula and number format at the Formula dialog box.
- Insert an Excel spreadsheet (worksheet) into a Word document to provide Excel functions by clicking the Insert tab, clicking the Table button in the Tables group, and then clicking Excel Spreadsheet at the drop-down list.
- Use the SmartArt feature to insert predesigned graphics and organizational charts in a document. Click the SmartArt button on the Insert tab to display the Choose a SmartArt Graphic dialog box.
- Format a SmartArt graphic with options and buttons on the SmartArt Tools Design tab and the SmartArt Tools Format tab.
- Choose a position or a text wrapping style for a SmartArt graphic with the Arrange button on the SmartArt Tools Format tab or the Layout Options button outside the upper right corner of the selected SmartArt graphic.

Commands Review

FEATURE	RIBBON TAB, GROUP	BUTTON, OPTION
AutoFit table contents	Table Tools Layout, Cell Size	
cell alignment	Table Tools Layout, Alignment	
Choose a SmartArt Graphic dialog box	Insert, Illustrations	
convert table to text	Table Tools Layout, Data	
convert text to table	Insert, Tables	, *Convert Text to Table*
delete column	Table Tools Layout, Rows & Columns	, *Delete Columns*
delete row	Table Tools Layout, Rows & Columns	, *Delete Rows*
delete table	Table Tools Layout, Rows & Columns	, *Delete Table*
draw table	Insert, Tables	, *Draw Table*
Formula dialog box	Table Tools Layout, Data	*fx*
insert column left	Table Tools Layout, Rows & Columns	
insert column right	Table Tools Layout, Rows & Columns	
Insert Excel spreadsheet	Insert, Tables	, *Excel Spreadsheet*
insert row above	Table Tools Layout, Rows & Columns	

FEATURE	RIBBON TAB, GROUP	BUTTON, OPTION
insert row below	Table Tools Layout, Rows & Columns	
Insert Table dialog box	Insert, Tables	, *Insert Table*
merge cells	Table Tools Layout, Merge	
Quick Table	Insert, Tables	, *Quick Tables*
repeat header row	Table Tools Layout, Data	
Split Cells dialog box	Table Tools Layout, Merge	
table	Insert, Tables	
Table Options dialog box	Table Tools Layout, Alignment	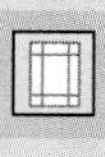
text direction	Table Tools Layout, Alignment	
view gridlines	Table Tools Layout, Table	

Workbook

Chapter study tools and assessment activities are available in the *Workbook* ebook. These resources are designed to help you further develop and demonstrate mastery of the skills learned in this chapter.

Microsoft®

Word

CHAPTER 8

Merging Documents

Performance Objectives

Upon successful completion of Chapter 8, you will be able to:

1 Create a data source file

2 Create a main document and merge it with a data source file

3 Preview a merge and check for errors before merging

4 Create an envelope, a labels, and a directory main document and then merge it with a data source file

5 Edit a data source file

6 Select specific records for merging

7 Input text during a merge

8 Use the Mail Merge wizard to merge a letter main document with a data source file

Precheck

Check your current skills to help focus your study.

Word includes a Mail Merge feature for creating customized letters, envelopes, labels, directories, email messages, and faxes. The Mail Merge feature is useful for situations where the same letter is to be sent to a number of people and an envelope needs to be created for each letter. Use Mail Merge to create a main document that contains a letter, an envelope, or other data and then merge it with a data source file. In this chapter, you will use Mail Merge to create letters, envelopes, labels, and directories.

Data Files

Before beginning chapter work, copy the WL1C8 folder to your storage medium and then make WL1C8 the active folder.

SNAP

If you are a SNAP user, launch the Precheck and Tutorials from your Assignments page.

Project 1 **Merge Letters to Customers** **3 Parts**

You will create a data source file and a letter main document and then merge the main document with the records in the data source file.

Preview Finished Project

Completing a Merge

Use buttons and options on the Mailings tab to complete a merge. A merge generally takes two files: the data source file and the main document. The main document contains the standard text along with fields identifying where variable information is inserted during the merge. The data source file contains the variable information that will be inserted in the main document.

Start Mail Merge

Select Recipients

Use the Start Mail Merge button on the Mailings tab to identify the type of main document to be created and use the Select Recipients button to create a data source file or specify an existing data source file. The Mail Merge Wizard is also available to provide guidance on the merge process.

Tutorial

Creating a Data Source File

Quick Steps

Create a Data Source File

1. Click Mailings tab.
2. Click Select Recipients button.
3. Click *Type a New List* at drop-down list.
4. Type data in predesigned or custom fields.
5. Click OK.

Creating a Data Source File

Before creating a data source file, determine what type of correspondence will be created and what type of information is needed to insert in the correspondence. Word provides predesigned field names when creating the data source file. Use these field names if they represent the desired data. Variable information in a data source file is saved as a record. A record contains all the information for one unit (for example, a person, family, customer, client, or business). A series of fields makes one record and a series of records makes a data source file.

Create a data source file by clicking the Select Recipients button in the Start Mail Merge group on the Mailings tab and then clicking *Type a New List* at the drop-down list. At the New Address List dialog box, shown in Figure 8.1, use the predesigned fields offered by Word or edit the fields by clicking the Customize Columns button. At the Customize Address List dialog box, insert new fields or delete existing fields and then click OK. With the fields established, type the required data. Note that fields in the main document correspond to the column headings in the data source file. When all the records have been entered, click OK.

Figure 8.1 New Address List Dialog Box

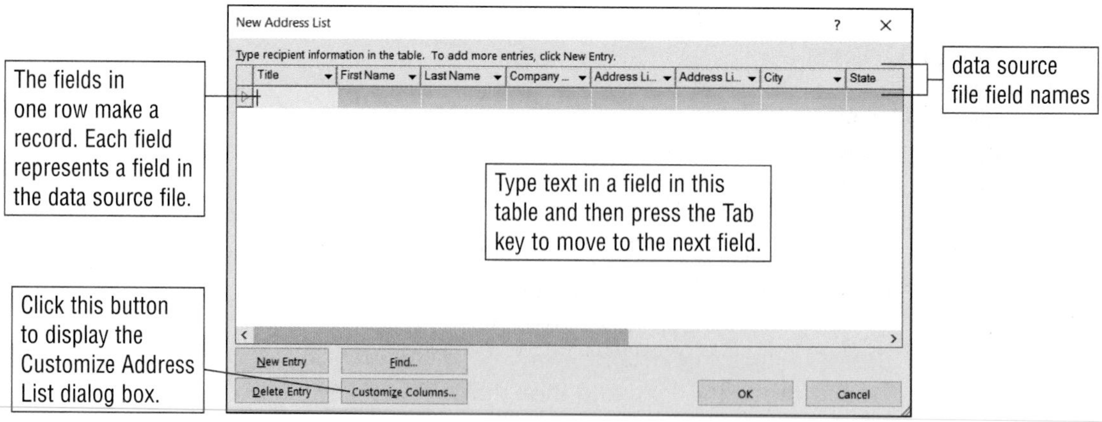
New Address List
Type recipient information in the table. To add more entries, click New Entry.
Title
First Name
Last Name
Company ...
Address Li...
Address Li...
City
State
New Entry
Find...
Delete Entry
Customize Columns...
OK
Cancel
The fields in one row make a record. Each field represents a field in the data source file.
data source file field names
Type text in a field in this table and then press the Tab key to move to the next field.
Click this button to display the Customize Address List dialog box.

At the Save Address List dialog box, navigate to the desired folder, type a name for the data source file, and then click OK. Word saves a data source file as an Access database. Having Access is not required on the computer to complete a merge with a data source file.

Project 1a **Creating a Data Source File** **Part 1 of 3**

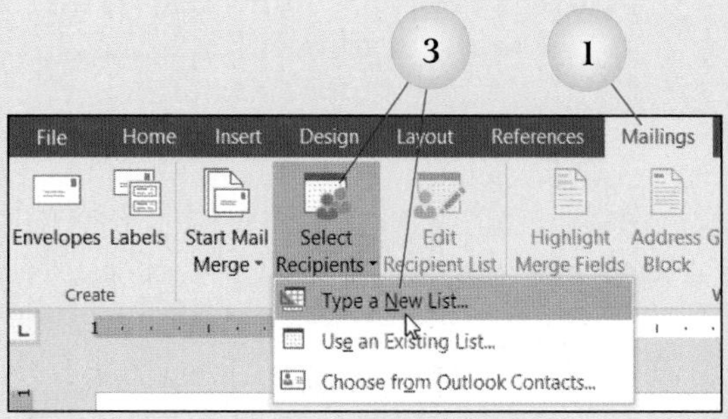

1. At a blank document, click the Mailings tab.
2. Click the Start Mail Merge button in the Start Mail Merge group and then click *Letters* at the drop-down list.
3. Click the Select Recipients button in the Start Mail Merge group and then click *Type a New List* at the drop-down list.
4. At the New Address List dialog box, Word provides a number of predesigned fields. Delete the fields you do not need by completing the following steps:
   a. Click the Customize Columns button.
   b. At the Customize Address List dialog box, click *Company Name* to select it and then click the Delete button.
   c. At the message that displays, click Yes.
   d. Complete steps similar to those in 4b and 4c to delete the following fields:
      Country or Region
      Home Phone
      Work Phone
      E-mail Address

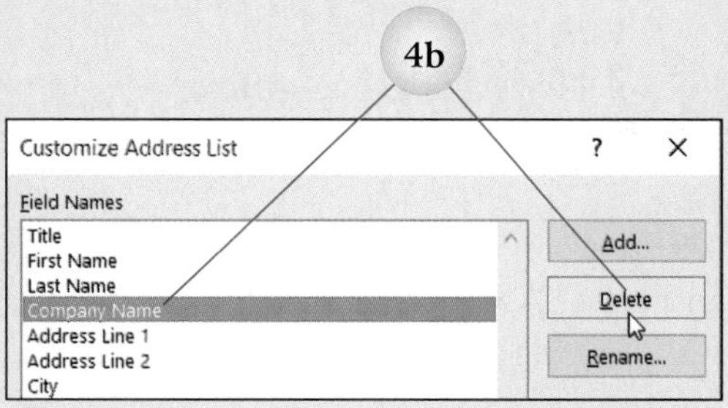

5. Insert a custom field by completing the following steps:
   a. With the *ZIP Code* field selected in the *Field Names* list in the Customize Address List dialog box, click the Add button.
   b. At the Add Field dialog box, type Fund and then click OK.
   c. Click OK to close the Customize Address List dialog box.

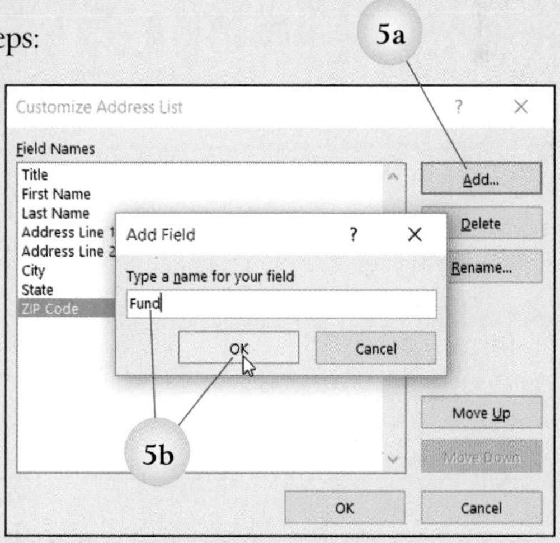

6. At the New Address List dialog box, enter the information for the first client shown in Figure 8.2 by completing the following steps:
   a. Type Mr. in the field in the *Title* column and then press the Tab key. (This moves the insertion point to the field in the *First Name* column. Pressing Shift + Tab will move the insertion point to the previous field. When typing text, do not press the spacebar after the last word in the field and proofread all entries to ensure that the data is accurate.)
   b. Type Kenneth and then press the Tab key.
   c. Type Porter and then press the Tab key.
   d. Type 7645 Tenth Street and then press the Tab key.
   e. Type Apt. 314 and then press the Tab key.

f. Type New York and then press the Tab key.
g. Type NY and then press the Tab key.
h. Type 10192 and then press the Tab key.
i. Type Mutual Investment Fund and then press the Tab key. (This makes the field in the *Title* column active in the next row.)
j. With the insertion point positioned in the field in the *Title* column, complete steps similar to those in 6a through 6i to enter the information for the three other clients shown in Figure 8.2 (reading the records from left to right).

7. After entering all the information for the last client in Figure 8.2 (Mrs. Wanda Houston), click OK in the bottom right corner of the New Address List dialog box.
8. At the Save Address List dialog box, navigate to the WL1C8 folder on your storage medium, type 8-MFDS in the *File name* text box, and then click the Save button.

Figure 8.2 Project 1a

Title	=	Mr.	Title	=	Ms.
First Name	=	Kenneth	First Name	=	Carolyn
Last Name	=	Porter	Last Name	=	Renquist
Address Line 1	=	7645 Tenth Street	Address Line 1	=	13255 Meridian Street
Address Line 2	=	Apt. 314	Address Line 2	=	(leave this blank)
City	=	New York	City	=	New York
State	=	NY	State	=	NY
Zip Code	=	10192	Zip Code	=	10435
Fund	=	Mutual Investment Fund	Fund	=	Quality Care Fund
Title	=	Dr.	Title	=	Mrs.
First Name	=	Amil	First Name	=	Wanda
Last Name	=	Ranna	Last Name	=	Houston
Address Line 1	=	433 South 17th Street	Address Line 1	=	566 North 22nd Avenue
Address Line 2	=	Apt. 17-D	Address Line 2	=	(leave this blank)
City	=	New York	City	=	New York
State	=	NY	State	=	NY
Zip Code	=	10322	Zip Code	=	10634
Fund	=	Priority One Fund	Fund	=	Quality Care Fund

Tutorial

Creating a Main Document

Creating a Main Document

After creating and typing the records in the data source file, type the main document. Insert in the main document fields that identify where variable information is to be inserted when the document is merged with the data source file. Use buttons in the Write & Insert Fields group to insert fields in the main document.

Quick Steps

Create a Main Document

1. Click Mailings tab.
2. Click Start Mail Merge button.
3. Click document type at drop-down list.
4. Type main document text and insert fields as needed.

Address Block

Greeting Line

Insert Merge Field

Insert all of the fields required for the inside address of a letter with the Address Block button in the Write & Insert Fields group. Click this button and the Insert Address Block dialog box displays with a preview of how the fields will be inserted in the document to create the inside address; the dialog box also contains buttons and options for customizing the fields. Click OK and the «AddressBlock» field is inserted in the document. The «AddressBlock» field is an example of a composite field, which groups a number of fields (such as *Title*, *First Name*, *Last Name*, *Address Line 1*, and so on).

Click the Greeting Line button and the Insert Greeting Line dialog box displays with options for customizing how the fields are inserted in the document to create the greeting line. Click OK at the dialog box and the «GreetingLine» composite field is inserted in the document.

To insert an individual field from the data source file, click the Insert Merge Field button. This displays the Insert Merge Field dialog box with a list of fields from the data source file. Click the Insert Merge Field button arrow and a drop-down list displays containing the fields in the data source file.

A field or composite field is inserted in the main document surrounded by chevrons (« and »). The chevrons distinguish fields in the main document and do not display in the merged document. Formatting can be applied to merged data by formatting the merge field in the main document.

Project 1b Creating a Main Document

Part 2 of 3

1. At a blank document, create the letter shown in Figure 8.3. Begin by clicking the *No Spacing* style in the styles gallery on the Home tab.
2. Press the Enter key six times and then type February 23, 2018.
3. Press the Enter key four times and then insert the «AddressBlock» composite field by completing the following steps:
   a. Click the Mailings tab and then click the Address Block button in the Write & Insert Fields group.
   b. At the Insert Address Block dialog box, click OK.
   c. Press the Enter key two times.
4. Insert the «GreetingLine» composite field by completing the following steps:
   a. Click the Greeting Line button in the Write & Insert Fields group.
   b. At the Insert Greeting Line dialog box, click the option box arrow for the option box containing the comma (the box to the right of the box containing *Mr. Randall*).
   c. At the drop-down list, click the colon.
   d. Click OK to close the Insert Greeting Line dialog box.
   e. Press the Enter key two times.

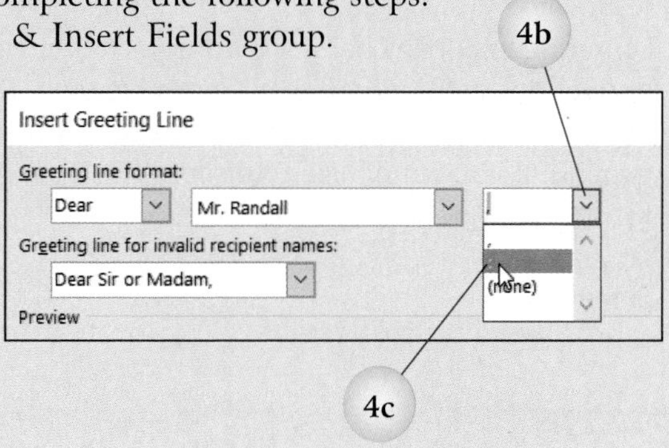

5. Type the letter shown in Figure 8.3 to the point where «Fund» displays and then insert the «Fund» field by clicking the Insert Merge Field button arrow and then clicking *Fund* at the drop-down list.
6. Type the letter to the point where the «Title» field displays and then insert the «Title» field by clicking the Insert Merge Field button arrow and then clicking *Title* at the drop-down list.
7. Press the spacebar and then insert the «Last_Name» field by clicking the Insert Merge Field button arrow and then clicking *Last_Name* at the drop-down list.
8. Type the remainder of the letter shown in Figure 8.3. (Insert your initials instead of *XX* at the end of the letter.)
9. Save the document and name it **8-MFMD**.

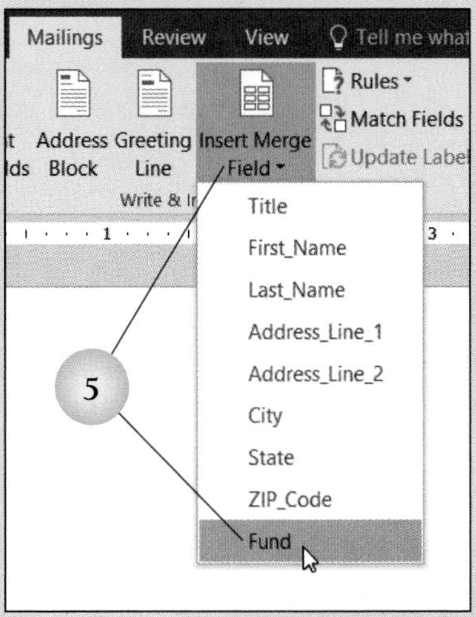

Check Your Work

Figure 8.3 Project 1b

February 23, 2018

«AddressBlock»

«GreetingLine»

McCormack Funds is lowering its expense charges beginning May 1, 2018. The reduction in expense charges means that more of your account investment performance in the «Fund» is returned to you, «Title» «Last_Name». The reductions are worth your attention because most of our competitors' fees have gone up.

Lowering expense charges is noteworthy because before the reduction, McCormack expense deductions were already among the lowest, far below most mutual funds and variable annuity accounts with similar objectives. At the same time, services for you, our client, will continue to expand. If you would like to discuss this change, please call us at (212) 555-2277. Your financial future is our main concern at McCormack.

Sincerely,

Jodie Langstrom
Director, Financial Services

XX
8-MFMD.docx

Tutorial

Previewing and Merging Documents

Preview Results

First Record

Previous Record

Next Record

Last Record

Find Recipient

Previewing a Merge

To view how the main document will appear when merged with the first record in the data source file, click the Preview Results button on the Mailings tab. View the main document merged with other records by using the navigation buttons in the Preview Results group. This group contains the First Record, Previous Record, Next Record, and Last Record buttons and the *Go to Record* text box. Click the button that will display the main document merged with the desired record. Viewing the merged document before printing is helpful to ensure that the merged data is correct. To use the *Go to Record* text box, click in the text box, type the number of the record, and then press the Enter key. Turn off the preview feature by clicking the Preview Results button.

The Preview Results group on the Mailings tab also includes a Find Recipient button. To search for and preview merged documents with specific entries, click the Preview Results button and then click the Find Recipient button. At the Find Entry dialog box, type the specific field entry in the *Find* text box and then click the Find Next button. Continue clicking the Find Next button until Word displays a message indicating that there are no more entries that contain the typed text.

Check for Errors

Checking for Errors

Before merging documents, check for errors using the Check for Errors button in the Preview Results group on the Mailings tab. Click this button and the Checking and Reporting Errors dialog box, shown in Figure 8.4, displays containing three options. Click the first option, *Simulate the merge and report errors in a new document,* and Word will test the merge, not make any changes, and report errors in a new document. Choose the second option, *Complete the merge, pausing to report each error as it occurs,* and Word will merge the documents and display errors as they occur during the merge. Choose the third option, *Complete the merge without pausing. Report errors in a new document,* and Word will complete the merge without pausing and insert any errors in a new document.

Finish & Merge

Merging Documents

To complete the merge, click the Finish & Merge button in the Finish group on the Mailings tab. At the drop-down list, merge the records and create a new document, send the merged documents directly to the printer, or send the merged documents by email.

Figure 8.4 Checking and Reporting Errors Dialog Box

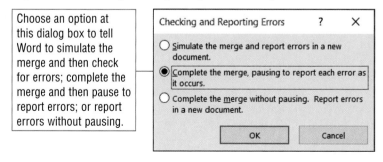

Choose an option at this dialog box to tell Word to simulate the merge and then check for errors; complete the merge and then pause to report errors; or report errors without pausing.

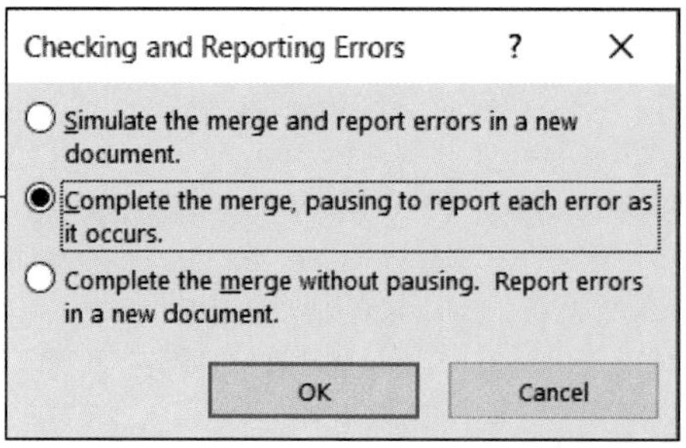

Quick Steps

Merge Documents

1. Click Finish & Merge button.
2. Click *Edit Individual Documents* at drop-down list.
3. Make sure *All* is selected in Merge to New Document dialog box.
4. Click OK.

Hint Press Alt + Shift + N to display the Merge to New Document dialog box and press Alt + Shift + M to display the Merge to Printer dialog box.

To merge the documents and create a new document with the merged records, click the Finish & Merge button and then click *Edit Individual Documents* at the drop-down list. At the Merge to New Document dialog box, make sure *All* is selected in the *Merge records* section and then click OK. This merges the records in the data source file with the main document and inserts the merged documents in a new document.

Identify specific records to be merged with options at the Merge to New Document dialog box. Display this dialog box by clicking the Finish & Merge button on the Mailings tab and then clicking the *Edit Individual Documents* option at the drop-down list. Click the *All* option in the Merge to New Document dialog box to merge all the records in the data source file and click the *Current record* option to merge only the current record. To merge specific adjacent records, click in the *From* text box, type the beginning record number, press the Tab key, and then type the ending record number in the *To* text box.

Project 1c Merging the Main Document with the Data Source File — Part 3 of 3

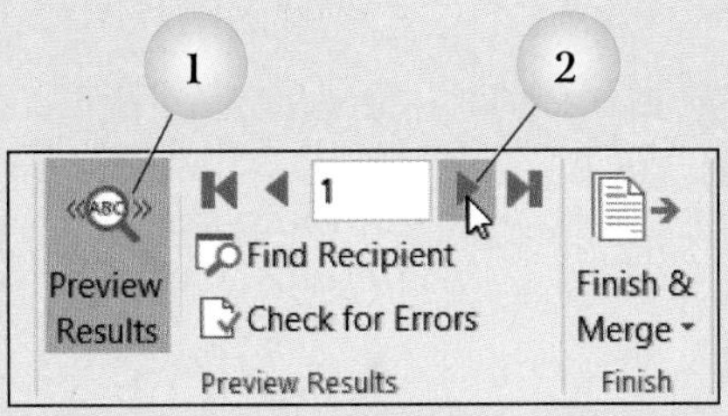

1. With **8-MFMD.docx** open, preview the main document merged with the first record in the data source file by clicking the Preview Results button on the Mailings tab.
2. Click the Next Record button to view the main document merged with the second record in the data source file.
3. Click the Preview Results button to turn off the preview feature.
4. Automatically check for errors by completing the following steps:
   a. Click the Check for Errors button in the Preview Results group on the Mailings tab.
   b. At the Checking and Reporting Errors dialog box, click the first option, *Simulate the merge and report errors in a new document.*
   c. Click OK.
   d. If a new document displays with any errors, print the document and then close it without saving it. If a message displays that no errors were found, click OK.

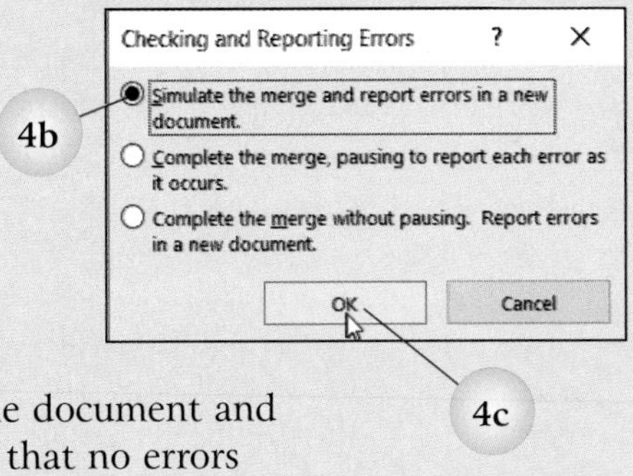

5. Click the Finish & Merge button in the Finish group and then click *Edit Individual Documents* at the drop-down list.
6. At the Merge to New Document dialog box, make sure *All* is selected and then click OK.
7. Save the merged letters and name the document **8-MFLtrs**.
8. Print **8-MFLtrs.docx**. (This document will print four letters.)
9. Close **8-MFLtrs.docx**.
10. Save and then close **8-MFMD.docx**.

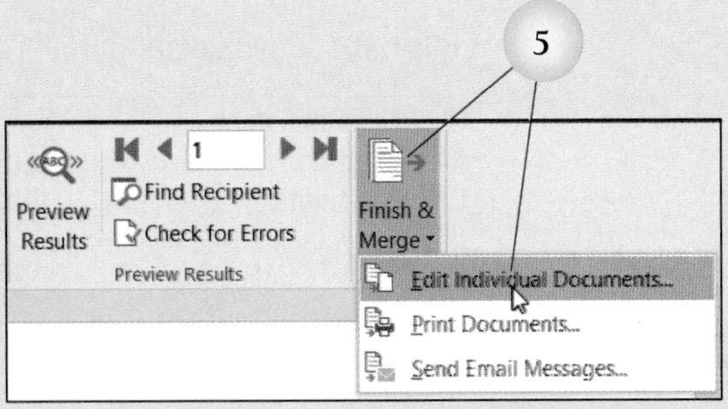

Check Your Work

Project 2 **Merge Envelopes** **1 Part**

You will use Mail Merge to prepare envelopes with customer names and addresses.

Preview Finished Project

Tutorial

Merging Labels

Merging with Other Main Documents

In addition to merging letters, a data source file can be merged with an envelope, label, or directory main document. Create an envelope main document with the *Envelopes* option at the Start Mail Merge button drop-down list and create a label main document with the *Labels* option. Create a directory, which merges fields to the same page, with the *Directory* option at the Start Mail Merge button drop-down list.

Tutorial

Merging Envelopes

Merging Envelopes

A letter created as a main document and then merged with a data source file will more than likely need properly addressed envelopes in which to send the letters. To prepare an envelope main document that is merged with a data source file, click the Mailings tab, click the Start Mail Merge button, and then click *Envelopes* at the drop-down list. This displays the Envelope Options dialog box, as shown in Figure 8.5. At this dialog box, specify the envelope size, make any other changes, and then click OK.

The next step in the envelope merge process is to create the data source file or identify an existing data source file. To identify an existing data source file, click the Select Recipients button in the Start Mail Merge group and then click *Use an Existing List* at the drop-down list. At the Select Data Source dialog box, navigate to the folder containing the data source file and then double-click the file.

With the data source file attached to the envelope main document, the next step is to insert the appropriate fields. Click in the envelope in the approximate location the recipient's address will appear and a box with a dashed gray border displays. Click the Address Block button in the Write & Insert Fields group and then click OK at the Insert Address Block dialog box.

Figure 8.5 Envelope Options Dialog Box

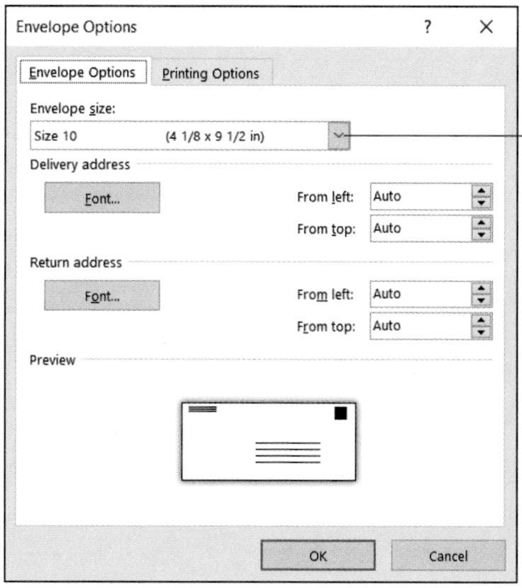

Click the *Envelope size* option box arrow to display a list of available envelope sizes.

Project 2 Merging Envelopes

Part 1 of 1

1. At a blank document, click the Mailings tab.
2. Click the Start Mail Merge button in the Start Mail Merge group and then click *Envelopes* at the drop-down list.

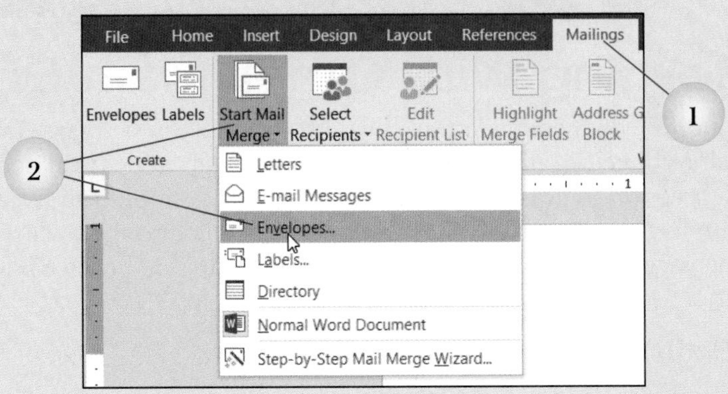

3. At the Envelope Options dialog box, make sure the envelope size is Size 10 and then click OK.
4. Click the Select Recipients button in the Start Mail Merge group and then click *Use an Existing List* at the drop-down list.
5. At the Select Data Source dialog box, navigate to the WL1C8 folder on your storage medium and then double-click the data source file named ***8-MFDS.mdb***.

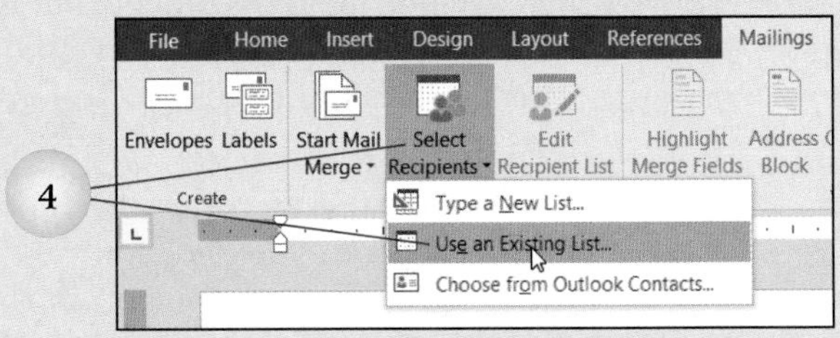

6. Click in the approximate location in the envelope document where the recipient's address will appear. (This causes a box with a dashed gray border to display. If you do not see this box, try clicking in a different location on the envelope.)

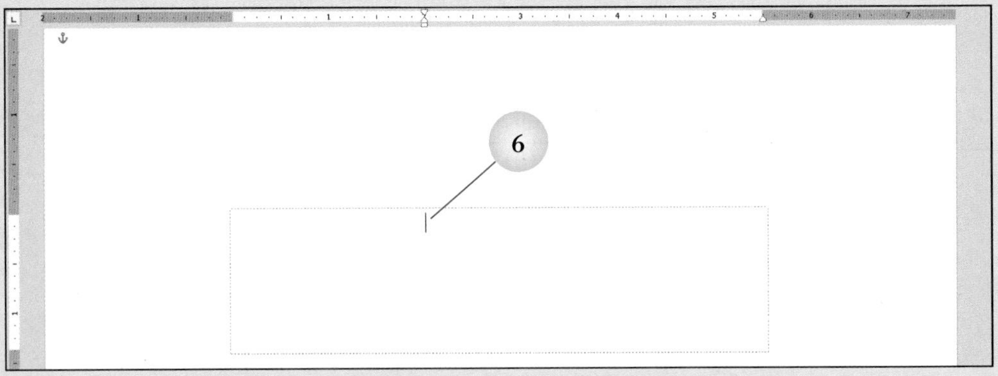

7. Click the Address Block button in the Write & Insert Fields group.
8. At the Insert Address Block dialog box, click OK.
9. Click the Preview Results button to see how the envelope appears merged with the first record in the data source file.
10. Click the Preview Results button to turn off the preview feature.
11. Click the Finish & Merge button in the Finish group and then click *Edit Individual Documents* at the drop-down list.

12. At the Merge to New Document dialog box, specify that you want only the first two records to merge by completing the following steps:
   a. Click in the *From* text box and then type 1.
   b. Click in the *To* text box and then type 2.
   c. Click OK. (This merges only the first two records and opens a document with two merged envelopes.)
13. Save the merged envelopes and name the document **8-MFEnvs**.
14. Print **8-MFEnvs.docx**. (This document will print two envelopes. Manual feeding of the envelopes may be required. Please check with your instructor.)
15. Close **8-MFEnvs.docx**.
16. Save the envelope main document and name it **8-EnvMD**.
17. Close **8-EnvMD.docx**.

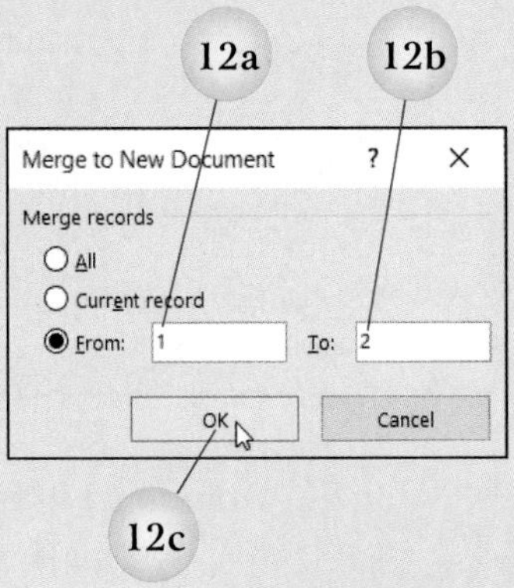

Check Your Work

Project 3 Merge Mailing Labels — 1 Part

You will use Mail Merge to prepare mailing labels with customer names and addresses.

Preview Finished Project

Merging Labels

Mailing labels for records in a data source file are created in much the same way that envelopes are created. Click the Start Mail Merge button and then click *Labels* at the drop-down list. This displays the Label Options dialog box, as shown in Figure 8.6. Make sure the desired label is selected and then click OK to close the dialog box. The next step is to create the data source file or identify an existing data source file. With the data source file attached to the label main document, insert the appropriate fields and then complete the merge.

Figure 8.6 Label Options Dialog Box

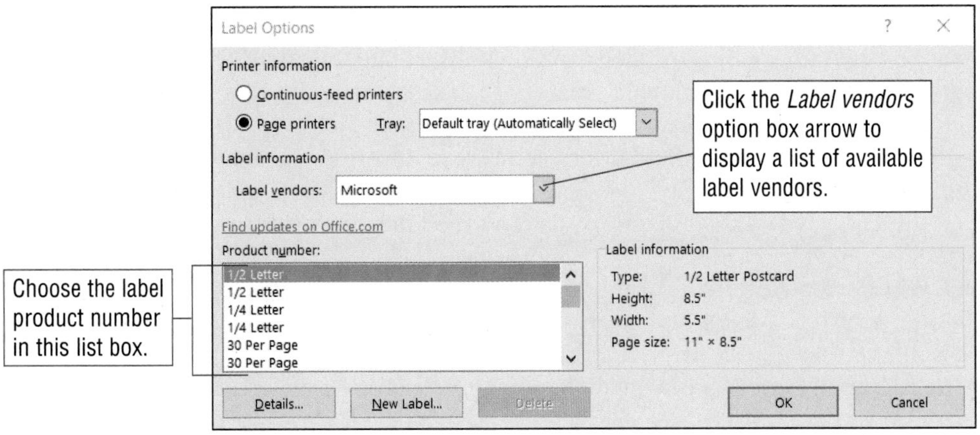

Project 3 Merging Mailing Labels

Part 1 of 1

1. At a blank document, change the document zoom to 100% and then click the Mailings tab.
2. Click the Start Mail Merge button in the Start Mail Merge group and then click *Labels* at the drop-down list.
3. At the Label Options dialog box, complete the following steps:
   a. If necessary, click the *Label vendors* option box arrow and then click *Avery US Letter* at the drop-down list. (If this option is not available, choose a vendor that offers labels that print on a full page.)
   b. Scroll in the *Product number* list box and then, if necessary, click *5160 Easy Peel Address Labels*. (If this option is not available, choose a label number that prints labels in two or three columns down a full page.)
   c. Click OK to close the dialog box.

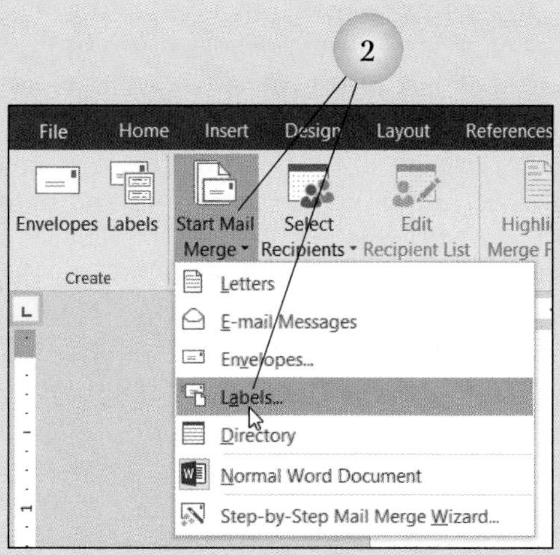

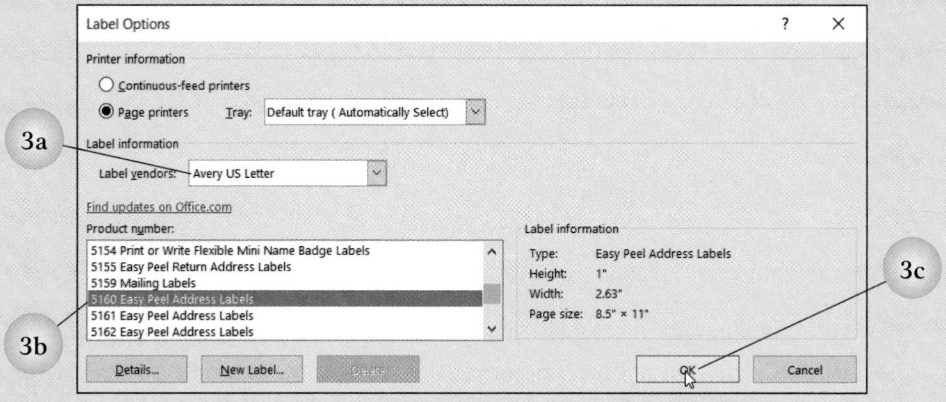

4. Click the Select Recipients button in the Start Mail Merge group and then click *Use an Existing List* at the drop-down list.
5. At the Select Data Source dialog box, navigate to the WL1C8 folder on your storage medium and then double-click the data source file named ***8-MFDS.mdb***.
6. At the labels document, click the Address Block button in the Write & Insert Fields group.
7. At the Insert Address Block dialog box, click OK. (This inserts the «AddressBlock» composite field in the first label. The other labels contain the «Next Record» field.)
8. Click the Update Labels button in the Write & Insert Fields group. (This adds the «AddressBlock» composite field after each «Next Record» field in the second and subsequent labels.)
9. Click the Preview Results button to see how the labels appear merged with the records in the data source file.
10. Click the Preview Results button to turn off the preview feature.
11. Click the Finish & Merge button in the Finish group and then click *Edit Individual Documents* at the drop-down list.
12. At the Merge to New Document dialog box, make sure *All* is selected and then click OK.

13. Format the labels by completing the following steps:
    a. Click the Table Tools Layout tab.
    b. Click the Select button in the Table group and then click the *Select Table* option.
    c. Click the Align Center Left button in the Alignment group.
    d. Click the Home tab and then click the Paragraph group dialog box launcher.
    e. At the Paragraph dialog box, click the *Before* measurement box up arrow to change the measurement to 0 points.
    f. Click the *After* measurement box up arrow to change the measurement to 0 points.
    g. Click the *Inside* measurement box up arrow three times to change the measurement to 0.3 inch.
    h. Click OK.

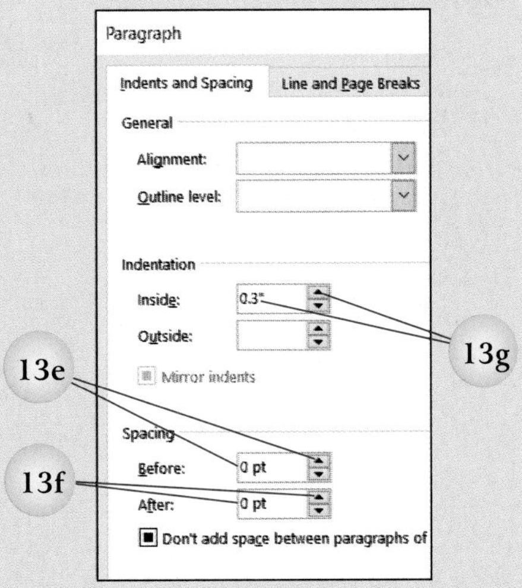

14. Save the merged labels and name the document **8-MFLabels**.
15. Print and then close **8-MFLabels.docx**.
16. Save the label main document and name it **8-LabelsMD**.
17. Close **8-LabelsMD.docx**.

Check Your Work

Project 4 Merge a Directory — 1 Part

You will use Mail Merge to prepare a directory list containing customer names and types of financial investment funds.

Preview Finished Project

Tutorial

Merging a Directory

Merging a Directory

When merging letters, envelopes, or mailing labels, a new form is created for each record. For example, if the data source file merged with the letter contains eight records, eight letters are created, each on a separate page. If the data source file merged with a mailing label contains 20 records, 20 labels are created. In some situations, merged information should remain on the same page. This is useful, for example, when creating a list such as a directory or address list.

Begin creating a merged directory by clicking the Start Mail Merge button and then clicking *Directory* at the drop-down list. Create or identify an existing data source file and then insert the desired fields in the directory document. To display the merged data in columns, set tabs for all of the columns.

Project 4 Merging a Directory

1. At a blank document, click the Mailings tab.
2. Click the Start Mail Merge button in the Start Mail Merge group and then click *Directory* at the drop-down list.

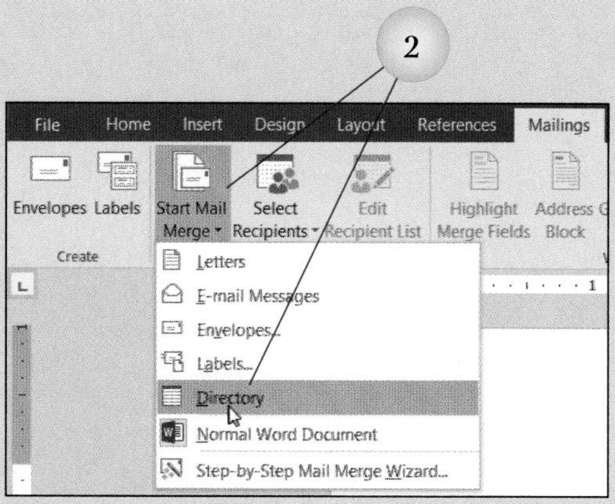

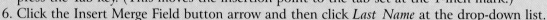

3. Click the Select Recipients button in the Start Mail Merge group and then click *Use an Existing List* at the drop-down list.
4. At the Select Data Source dialog box, navigate to the WL1C8 folder on your storage medium and then double-click the data source file named ***8-MFDS.mdb***.
5. At the document screen, set left tabs at the 1-inch mark, the 2.5-inch mark, and the 4-inch mark on the horizontal ruler and then press the Tab key. (This moves the insertion point to the tab set at the 1-inch mark.)
6. Click the Insert Merge Field button arrow and then click *Last_Name* at the drop-down list.
7. Press the Tab key to move the insertion point to the tab set at the 2.5-inch mark.
8. Click the Insert Merge Field button arrow and then click *First_Name* at the drop-down list.
9. Press the Tab key to move the insertion point to the tab set at the 4-inch mark.
10. Click the Insert Merge Field button arrow and then click *Fund* at the drop-down list.
11. Press the Enter key.
12. Click the Finish & Merge button in the Finish group and then click *Edit Individual Documents* at the drop-down list.
13. At the Merge to New Document dialog box, make sure *All* is selected and then click OK. (This merges the fields in the document.)
14. Press Ctrl + Home, press the Enter key, and then press the Up Arrow key.
15. Press the Tab key, turn on bold formatting, and then type Last Name.
16. Press the Tab key and then type First Name.
17. Press the Tab key and then type Fund.

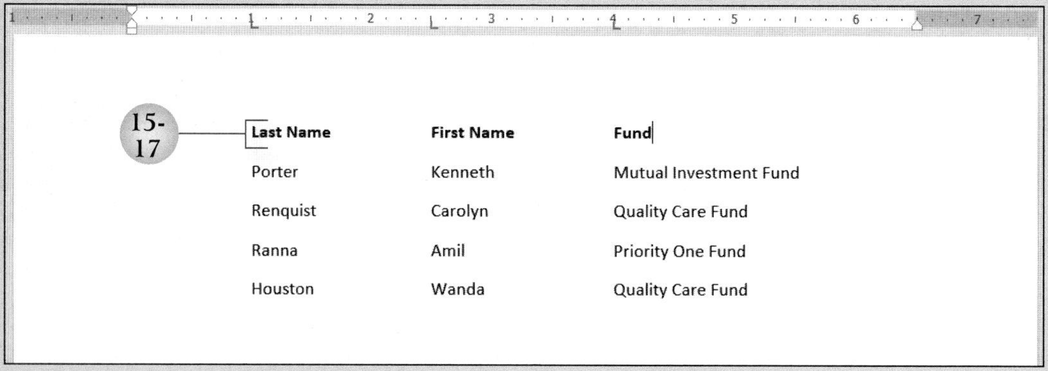

18. Save the directory document and name it **8-Directory**.
19. Print and then close the document.
20. Close the directory main document without saving it.

Check Your Work

Project 5 Select Records and Merge Mailing Labels — 1 Part

You will use Mail Merge to prepare mailing labels with the names and addresses of customers living in Baltimore.

Preview Finished Project

Tutorial

Editing a Data Source File

Edit Recipient List

Editing a Data Source File

Edit a main document in the normal manner. Open the document, make the required changes, and then save the document. Since a data source file is actually an Access database file, it cannot be opened in the normal manner. Open a data source file for editing using the Edit Recipient List button in the Start Mail Merge group on the Mailings tab. Click the Edit Recipient List button and the Mail Merge Recipients dialog box displays, as shown in Figure 8.7. Select or edit records at this dialog box.

Selecting Specific Records

Each record in the Mail Merge Recipients dialog box contains a check mark before the first field. To select specific records, remove the check marks from those records that should not be included in a merge. This way, only certain records in the data source file will be merged with the main document.

Figure 8.7 Mail Merge Recipients Dialog Box

Select specific records by removing the check marks from those records that should not be included in the merge.

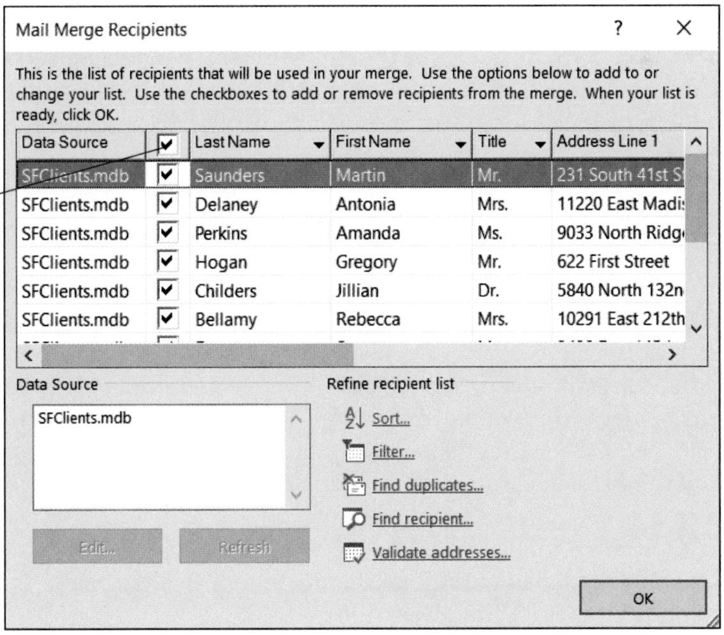

Project 5 Selecting Records and Merging Mailing Labels

Part 1 of 1

1. At a blank document, create mailing labels for customers living in Baltimore. Begin by clicking the Mailings tab.
2. Click the Start Mail Merge button in the Start Mail Merge group and then click *Labels* at the drop-down list.
3. At the Label Options dialog box, make sure *Avery US Letter* displays in the *Label vendors* option box and *5160 Easy Peel Address Labels* displays in the *Product number* list box and then click OK.
4. Click the Select Recipients button in the Start Mail Merge group and then click *Use an Existing List* at the drop-down list.
5. At the Select Data Source dialog box, navigate to the WL1C8 folder on your storage medium and then double-click the data source file named ***SFClients.mdb***.
6. Click the Edit Recipient List button in the Start Mail Merge group.
7. At the Mail Merge Recipients dialog box, complete the following steps:
   a. Click the check box immediately left of the *Last Name* field column heading to remove the check mark. (This removes all the check marks from the check boxes.)
   b. Click the check box immediately left of each of the following last names: *Saunders*, *Perkins*, *Dutton*, *Fernandez*, and *Stahl*. (These are the customers who live in Baltimore.)
   c. Click OK to close the dialog box.

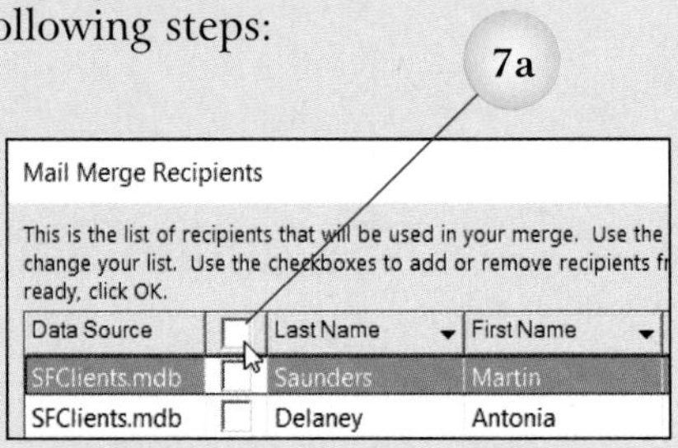

8. At the labels document, click the Address Block button in the Write & Insert Fields group.
9. At the Insert Address Block dialog box, click OK.
10. Click the Update Labels button in the Write & Insert Fields group.
11. Click the Preview Results button and then click the Previous Record button to display each label. Make sure only labels for those customers living in Baltimore display.
12. Click the Preview Results button to turn off the preview feature.
13. Click the Finish & Merge button in the Finish group and then click *Edit Individual Documents* at the drop-down list.
14. At the Merge to New Document dialog box, make sure *All* is selected and then click OK.
15. Format the labels by completing the following steps:
    a. Click the Table Tools Layout tab.
    b. Click the Select button in the Table group and then click *Select Table*.
    c. Click the Align Center Left button in the Alignment group.
    d. Click the Home tab and then click the Paragraph group dialog box launcher.
    e. At the Paragraph dialog box, click the *Before* measurement box up arrow to change the measurement to 0 points.
    f. Click the *After* measurement box up arrow to change the measurement to 0 points.
    g. Click the *Inside* measurement box up arrow three times to change the measurement to 0.3 inch.
    h. Click OK.
16. Save the merged labels and name the document **8-SFLabels**.
17. Print and then close **8-SFLabels.docx**.
18. Close the main labels document without saving it.

Check Your Work

Project 6 Edit Records in a Data Source File 1 Part

You will edit records in a data source file and then use Mail Merge to prepare a directory with the edited records that contains customer names, telephone numbers, and cell phone numbers.

Preview Finished Project

Editing Records

Quick Steps

Edit a Data Source File

1. Open main document.
2. Click Mailings tab.
3. Click Edit Recipient List button.
4. Click data source file name in *Data Source* list box.
5. Click Edit button.
6. Make changes at Edit Data Source dialog box.
7. Click OK.
8. Click OK.

A data source file may need editing on a periodic basis to add or delete customer names, update fields, insert new fields, or delete existing fields. To edit a data source file, click the Edit Recipient List button in the Start Mail Merge group. At the Mail Merge Recipients dialog box, click the data source file name in the *Data Source* list box and then click the Edit button below the list box. This displays the Edit Data Source dialog box, as shown in Figure 8.8. At this dialog box, add a new entry, delete an entry, find a particular entry, and customize columns.

Figure 8.8 Edit Data Source Dialog Box

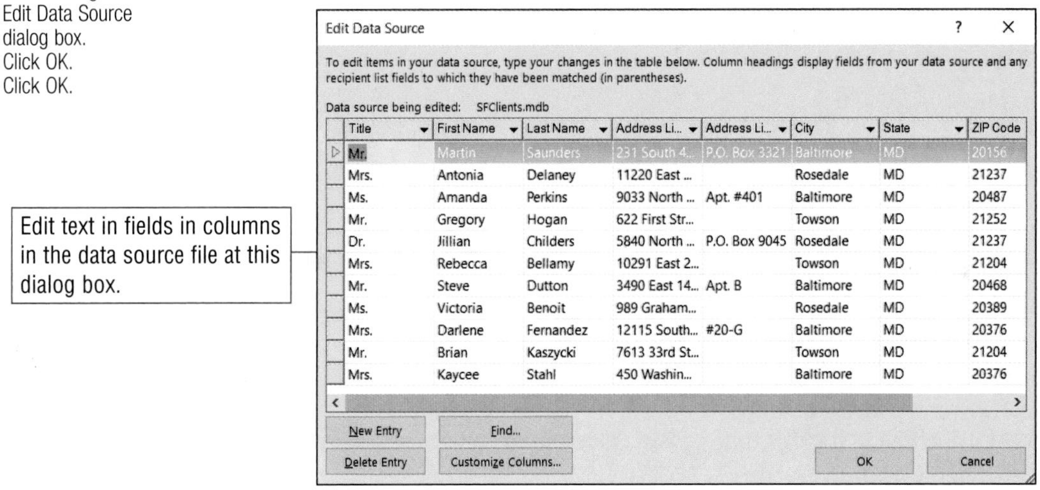

Project 6 Editing Records in a Data Source File Part 1 of 1

1. Make a copy of the **SFClients.mdb** file by completing the following steps:
   a. Display the Open dialog box and make WL1C8 the active folder.
   b. If necessary, change the file type option to *All Files (*.*)*.
   c. Right-click ***SFClients.mdb*** and then click *Copy* at the shortcut menu.
   d. Position the mouse pointer in a white portion of the Open dialog box Content pane (outside any file name), click the right mouse button, and then click *Paste* at the shortcut menu. (This inserts a copy of the file in the dialog box Content pane and names the file **SFClients - Copy.mdb**.)
   e. Right-click ***SFClients - Copy.mdb*** and then click *Rename* at the shortcut menu.
   f. Type 8-DS and then press the Enter key.
   g. Close the Open dialog box.

2. At a blank document, click the Mailings tab.
3. Click the Select Recipients button and then click *Use an Existing List* from the drop-down list.
4. At the Select Data Source dialog box, navigate to the WL1C8 folder on your storage medium and then double-click the data source file named ***8-DS.mdb***.
5. Click the Edit Recipient List button in the Start Mail Merge group.
6. At the Mail Merge Recipients dialog box, click *8-DS.mdb* in the *Data Source* list box and then click the Edit button.
7. Delete the record for Steve Dutton by completing the following steps:
    a. Click the square at the beginning of the row for *Mr. Steve Dutton*.
    b. Click the Delete Entry button.
    c. At the message asking if you want to delete the entry, click Yes.
8. Insert a new record by completing the following steps:
    a. Click the New Entry button in the dialog box.
    b. Type the following text in the new record in the specified fields:

Title	Ms.
First Name	Jennae
Last Name	Davis
Address Line 1	3120 South 21st
Address Line 2	(none)
City	Rosedale
State	MD
ZIP Code	20389
Home Phone	410-555-5774

9. Insert a new field and type text in the field by completing the following steps:
    a. At the Edit Data Source dialog box, click the Customize Columns button.
    b. At the message asking if you want to save the changes made to the data source file, click Yes.
    c. At the Customize Address List dialog box, click *ZIP Code* in the *Field Names* list box. (A new field is inserted below the selected field.)
    d. Click the Add button.
    e. At the Add Field dialog box, type Cell Phone and then click OK.
    f. You decide that you want the *Cell Phone* field to display after the *Home Phone* field. To move the *Cell Phone* field, make sure it is selected and then click the Move Down button.
    g. Click OK to close the Customize Address List dialog box.

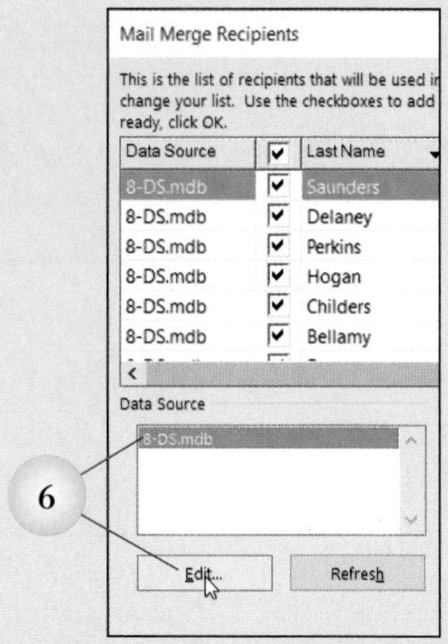

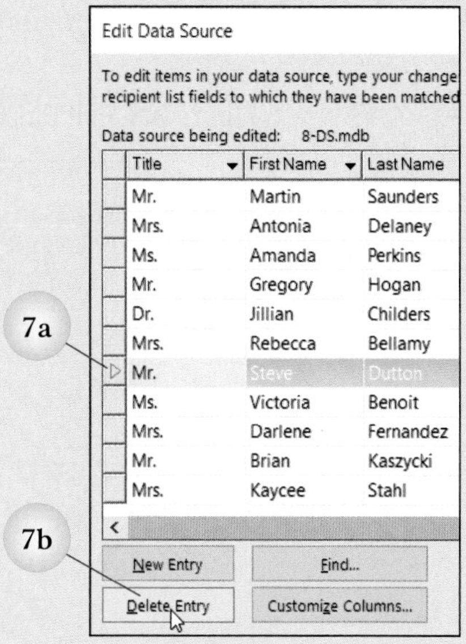

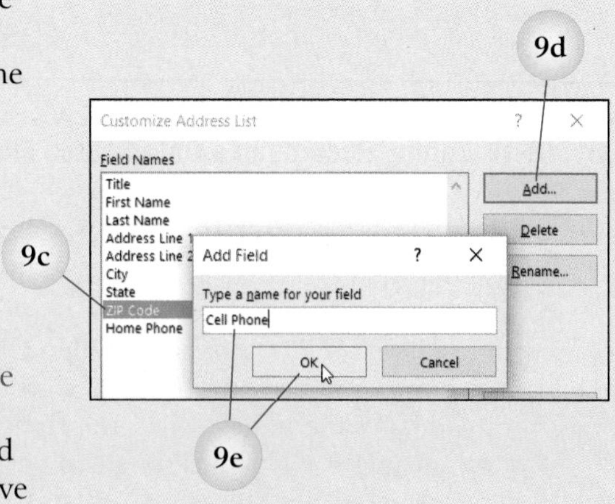

h. At the Edit Data Source dialog box, scroll to the right to display the *Cell Phone* field (last field in the file) and then type the following cell phone numbers (after typing each cell phone number except the last number, press the Down Arrow key to make the next field below active):

Record 1	410-555-1249
Record 2	410-555-3443
Record 3	410-555-0695
Record 4	410-555-9488
Record 5	410-555-1200
Record 6	410-555-7522
Record 7	410-555-8833
Record 8	410-555-9378
Record 9	410-555-4261
Record 10	410-555-9944
Record 11	410-555-2321

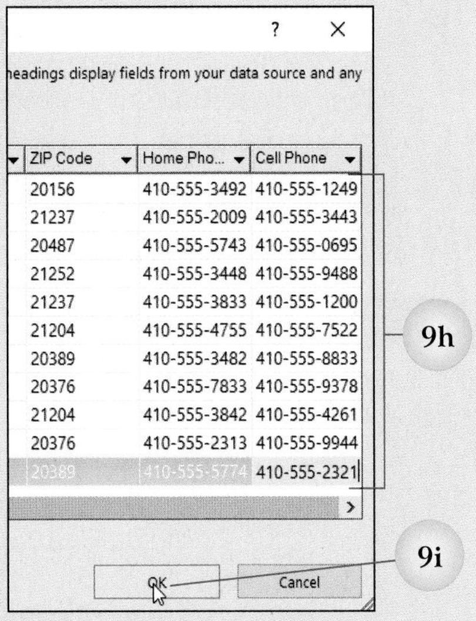

i. Click OK to close the Edit Data Source dialog box.
j. At the message asking if you want to update the recipient list and save changes, click Yes.
k. At the Mail Merge Recipients dialog box, click OK.

10. Create a directory by completing the following steps:
   a. Click the Start Mail Merge button and then click *Directory* at the drop-down list.
   b. At the blank document, set left tabs on the horizontal ruler at the 1-inch mark, the 3-inch mark, and the 4.5-inch mark.
   c. Press the Tab key. (This moves the insertion point to the first tab set at the 1-inch mark.)
   d. Click the Insert Merge Field button arrow and then click *Last_Name* at the drop-down list.
   e. Type a comma and then press the spacebar.
   f. Click the Insert Merge Field button arrow and then click *First_Name* at the drop-down list.
   g. Press the Tab key, click the Insert Merge Field button arrow, and then click *Home_Phone* at the drop-down list.
   h. Press the Tab key, click the Insert Merge Field button arrow, and then click *Cell_Phone* at the drop-down list.
   i. Press the Enter key.
   j. Click the Finish & Merge button in the Finish group and then click *Edit Individual Documents* at the drop-down list.
   k. At the Merge to New Document dialog box, make sure *All* is selected and then click OK. (This merges the fields in the document.)
11. Press Ctrl + Home, press the Enter key, and then press the Up Arrow key.
12. Press the Tab key, turn on bold formatting, and then type Name.
13. Press the Tab key and then type Home Phone.
14. Press the Tab key and then type Cell Phone.

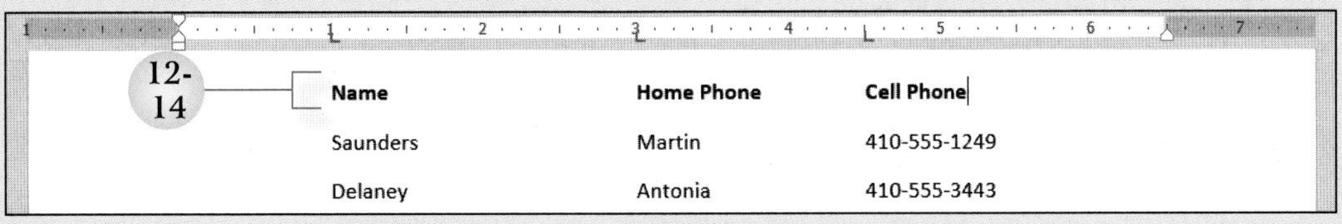

12-
14
Name
Home Phone
Cell Phone
Saunders
Martin
410-555-1249
Delaney
Antonia
410-555-3443

15. Save the directory document and name it **8-Directory-P6**.
16. Print and then close the document.
17. Close the directory main document without saving it.

Check Your Work

Project 7 Add Fill-in Fields to a Main Document — 1 Part

You will edit a form letter and insert sales representative contact information during a merge.

Preview Finished Project

Tutorial

Inputting Text during a Merge

Inputting Text during a Merge

Word's Merge feature contains a large number of merge fields that can be inserted in a main document. The fill-in field is used to identify information that will be entered at the keyboard during a merge. For more information on the other merge fields, please refer to the on-screen help.

In some situations, keeping all the variable information in a data source file may not be necessary. For example, variable information that changes on a regular basis might include a customer's monthly balance, a product price, and so on. Insert a fill-in field in the main document and when the main document is merged with the data source file, variable information can be inserted in the document using the keyboard. Insert a fill-in field in a main document by clicking the Rules button in the Write & Insert Fields group on the Mailings tab and then clicking *Fill-in* at the drop-down list. This displays the Insert Word Field: fill-in dialog box, shown in Figure 8.9. At this dialog box, type a short message indicating what should be entered at the keyboard and then click OK. At the Microsoft Word dialog box with the message entered displayed in the upper left corner, type the text to display in the document and then click OK. When the fill-in field or fields are added, save the main document in the normal manner. A document can contain any number of fill-in fields.

Rules

Quick Steps

Insert a Fill-in Field in a Main Document

1. Click Mailings tab.
2. Click Rules button.
3. Click *Fill-in*.
4. Type prompt text.
5. Click OK.
6. Type text to be inserted.
7. Click OK.

When the main document is merged with the data source file, the first record is merged with the main document and the Microsoft Word dialog box displays with the message entered displayed in the upper left corner. Type the required information for the first record in the data source file and then click OK. Word displays the dialog box again. Type the required information for the second record in the data source file and then click OK. Continue in this manner until the required information has been entered for each record in the data source file. Word then completes the merge.

Figure 8.9 Insert Word Field: Fill-in Dialog Box

In this text box, type a short message indicating what should be entered at the keyboard.

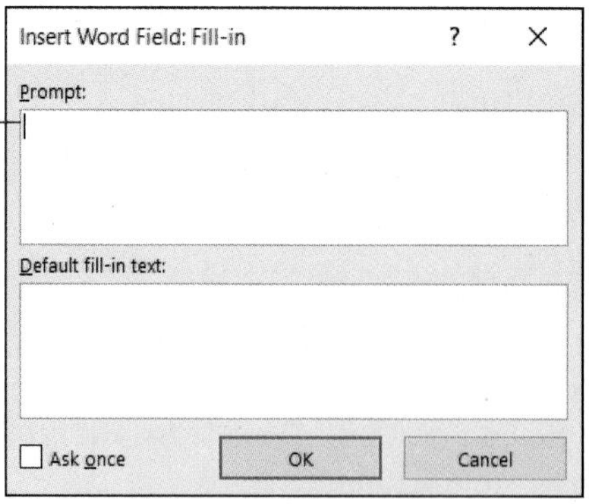

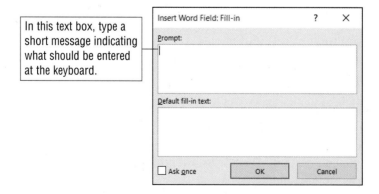

1. Open the document **8-MFMD.docx**. (At the message asking if you want to continue, click Yes.) Save the document with the name **8-MFMD-P7**.
2. Edit the second paragraph in the body of the letter to the paragraph shown in Figure 8.10. Insert the first fill-in field (representative's name) by completing the following steps:
   a. Click the Mailings tab.
   b. Click the Rules button in the Write & Insert Fields group and then click *Fill-in* at the drop-down list.
   c. At the Insert Word Field: Fill-in dialog box, type Insert rep name in the *Prompt* text box and then click OK.
   d. At the Microsoft Word dialog box with *Insert rep name* displayed in the upper left corner, type (representative's name) and then click OK.

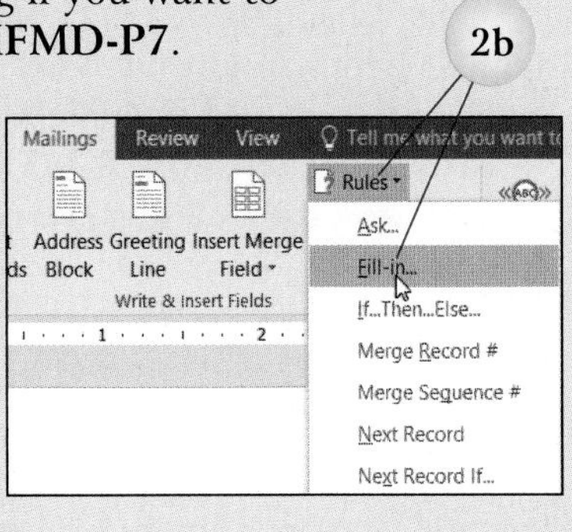

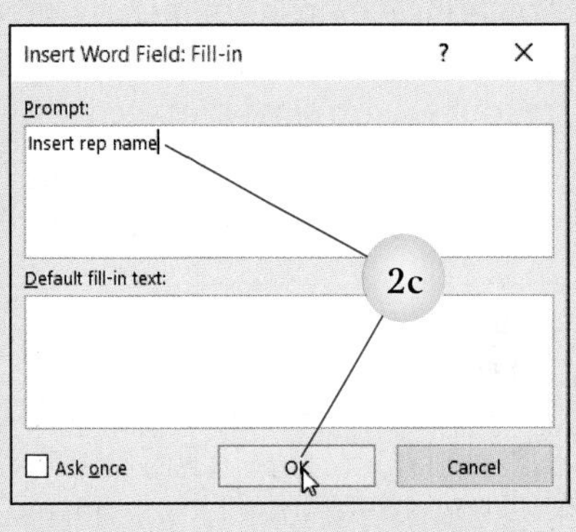

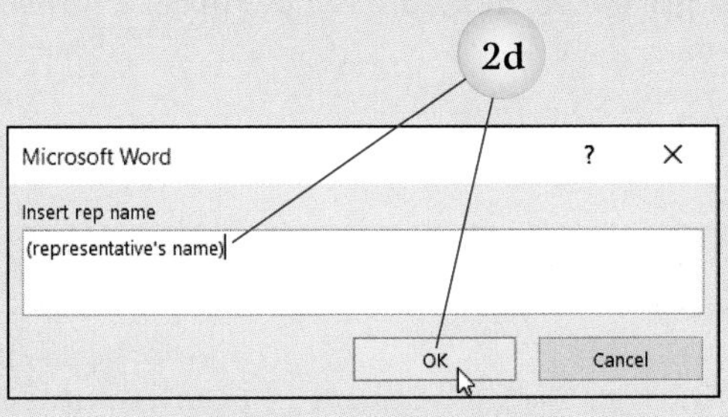

3. Complete steps similar to those in Step 2 to insert the second fill-in field (phone number), except type Insert phone number in the *Prompt* text box at the Insert Word Field: Fill-in dialog box and type (phone number) at the Microsoft Word dialog box.
4. Save **8-MFMD-P7.docx**.
5. Merge the main document with the data source file by completing the following steps:
   a. Click the Finish & Merge button and then click *Edit Individual Documents* at the drop-down list.
   b. At the Merge to New Document dialog box, make sure *All* is selected and then click OK.
   c. When Word merges the main document with the first record, a dialog box displays with the message *Insert rep name* and the text *(representative's name)* selected. At this dialog box, type Marilyn Smythe and then click OK.

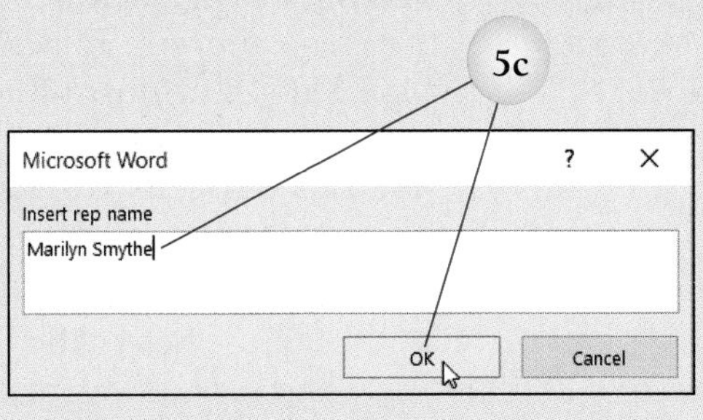

   d. At the dialog box with the message *Insert phone number* and *(phone number)* selected, type (646) 555-8944 and then click OK.
   e. At the dialog box with the message *Insert rep name*, type Anthony Mason (over *Marilyn Smythe*) and then click OK.
   f. At the dialog box with the message *Insert phone number*, type (646) 555-8901 (over the previous number) and then click OK.
   g. At the dialog box with the message *Insert rep name*, type Faith Ostrom (over *Anthony Mason*) and then click OK.
   h. At the dialog box with the message *Insert phone number*, type (646) 555-8967 (over the previous number) and then click OK.

i. At the dialog box with the message *Insert rep name*, type Thomas Rivers (over *Faith Ostrom*) and then click OK.

j. At the dialog box with the message *Insert phone number*, type (646) 555-0793 (over the previous number) and then click OK.

6. Save the merged document and name it **8-MFLtrs**.
7. Print and then close **8-MFLtrs.docx**.
8. Save and then close **8-MFMD-P7.docx**.

Check Your Work

Figure 8.10 Project 7

Lowering expense charges is noteworthy because before the reduction, McCormack expense deductions were already among the lowest, far below most mutual funds and variable annuity accounts with similar objectives. At the same time, services for you, our client, will continue to expand. If you would like to discuss this change, please call our service representative, **(representative's name)**, at **(phone number)**.

Project 8 Use Mail Merge Wizard — 1 Part

You will use the Mail Merge wizard to merge a main document with a data source file and create letters for clients of Sorenson Funds.

Preview Finished Project

Tutorial

Using the Mail Merge Wizard

Merging Using the Mail Merge Wizard

The Mail Merge feature includes a Mail Merge wizard with steps for completing the merge process. To access the wizard, click the Mailings tab, click the Start Mail Merge button, and then click the *Step-by-Step Mail Merge Wizard* option at the drop-down list. The first of six Mail Merge task panes displays at the right side of the screen. The options in each task pane may vary depending on the type of merge being performed. Generally, one of the following steps is completed at each task pane:

- Step 1: Select the type of document to be created, such as a letter, email message, envelope, label, or directory.
- Step 2: Specify whether the current document is to be used to create the main document, a template, or an existing document.
- Step 3: Specify whether a new list will be created or an existing list or Outlook contacts list will be used.
- Step 4: Use the items in this task pane to help prepare the main document by performing tasks such as inserting fields.
- Step 5: Preview the merged documents.
- Step 6: Complete the merge.

1. At a blank document, click the Mailings tab, click the Start Mail Merge button in the Start Mail Merge group, and then click *Step-by-Step Mail Merge Wizard* at the drop-down list.
2. At the first Mail Merge task pane, make sure *Letters* is selected in the *Select document type* section and then click the Next: Starting document hyperlink at the bottom of the task pane.
3. At the second Mail Merge task pane, click the *Start from existing document* option in the *Select starting document* section.
4. Click the Open button in the *Start from existing* section of the task pane.
5. At the Open dialog box, navigate to the WL1C8 folder on your storage medium and then double-click ***SFLtrMD.docx***.
6. Click the Next: Select recipients hyperlink at the bottom of the task pane.
7. At the third Mail Merge task pane, click the Browse hyperlink in the *Use an existing list* section of the task pane.
8. At the Select Data Source dialog box, navigate to the WL1C8 folder on your storage medium and then double-click ***SFClients.mdb***.
9. At the Mail Merge Recipients dialog box, click OK.
10. Click the Next: Write your letter hyperlink at the bottom of the task pane.
11. At the fourth Mail Merge task pane, enter fields in the form letter by completing the following steps:
    a. Position the insertion point a double space above the first paragraph of text in the letter.
    b. Click the Address block hyperlink in the *Write your letter* section of the task pane.
    c. At the Insert Address Block dialog box, click OK.
    d. Press the Enter key two times and then click the Greeting line hyperlink in the *Write your letter* section of the task pane.
    e. At the Insert Greeting Line dialog box, click the option box arrow at the right of the option box containing the comma (the box to the right of the box containing *Mr. Randall*).
    f. At the drop-down list, click the colon.
    g. Click OK to close the Insert Greeting Line dialog box.
12. Click the Next: Preview your letters hyperlink at the bottom of the task pane.
13. At the fifth Mail Merge task pane, look over the letter in the document window and make sure the information merged properly. If you want to see the letters for the other recipients, click the Next button (button containing two right-pointing arrows) in the Mail Merge task pane.
14. Click the Preview Results button in the Preview Results group to turn off the preview feature.
15. Click the Next: Complete the merge hyperlink at the bottom of the task pane.

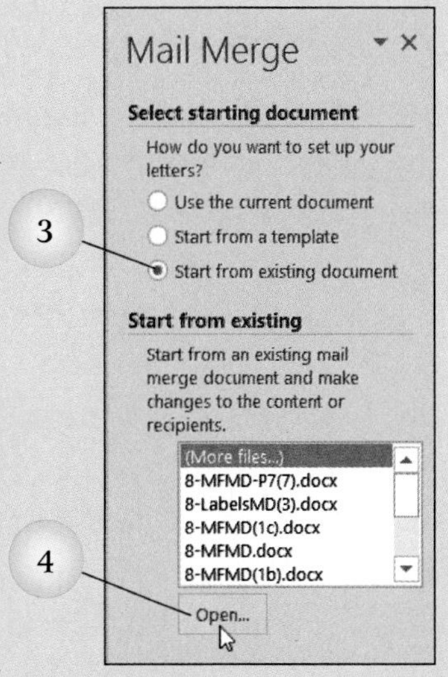

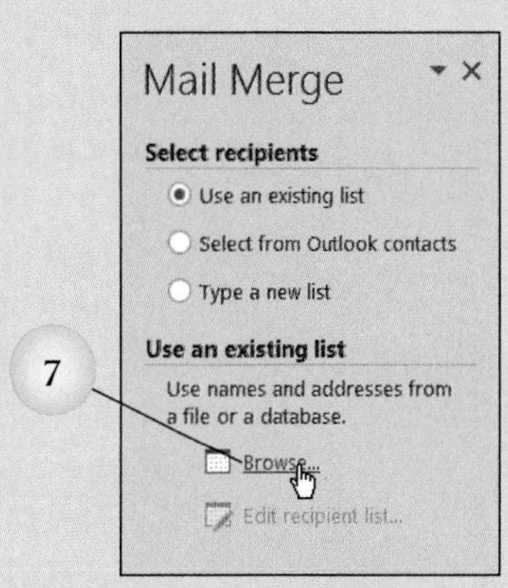

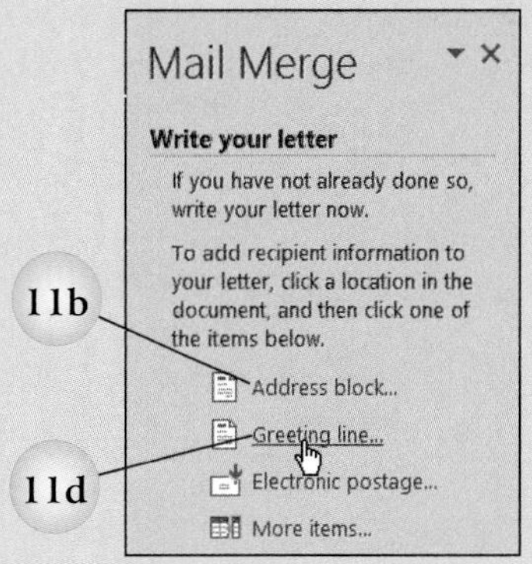

16. At the sixth Mail Merge task pane, click the Edit individual letters hyperlink in the *Merge* section of the task pane.
17. At the Merge to New Document dialog box, make sure *All* is selected and then click OK.
18. Save the merged letters document with the name **8-SFLtrs**.
19. Print only the first two pages of **8-SFLtrs.docx**.
20. Close the document.
21. Close the letter main document without saving it.

Check Your Work

Chapter Summary

- Use the Mail Merge feature to create documents such as letters, envelopes, labels, and directories with personalized information.
- Generally, a merge takes two documents: the data source file containing the variable information and the main document containing standard text along with fields identifying where variable information is inserted during the merge process.
- Variable information in a data source file is saved as a record. A record contains all the information for one unit. A series of fields makes a record and a series of records makes a data source file.
- A data source file is saved as an Access database but having Access on the computer is not required to complete a merge with a data source file.
- Use predesigned fields when creating a data source file or create custom fields at the Customize Address List dialog box.
- Use the Address Block button in the Write & Insert Fields group on the Mailings tab to insert all of the fields required for the inside address of a letter. This inserts the «AddressBlock» field, which is considered a composite field because it groups together a number of fields.
- Click the Greeting Line button in the Write & Insert Fields group on the Mailings tab to insert the «GreetingLine» composite field in the document.
- Click the Insert Merge Field button arrow in the Write & Insert Fields group on the Mailings tab to display a drop-down list of the fields contained in the data source file.
- Click the Preview Results button on the Mailings tab to view the main document merged with the first record in the data source file. Use the navigation buttons in the Preview Results group on the Mailings tab to display the main document merged with the desired record.
- Before merging documents, check for errors by clicking the Check for Errors button in the Preview Results group on the Mailings tab. This displays the Checking and Reporting Errors dialog box with three options for checking errors.
- Click the Finish & Merge button on the Mailings tab to complete the merge.
- Select specific records for merging by inserting or removing check marks from the records in the Mail Merge Recipients dialog box. Display this dialog box by clicking the Edit Recipient List button on the Mailings tab.
- Edit specific records in a data source file at the Edit Data Source dialog box. Display this dialog box by clicking the Edit Recipient List button on the Mailings tab, clicking the data source file name in the *Data Source* list box, and then clicking the Edit button.

- Use the fill-in field in a main document to insert variable information at the keyboard during a merge.
- Word includes a Mail Merge wizard that provides guidance through the process of creating letters, envelopes, labels, directories, and email messages with personalized information.

Commands Review

FEATURE	RIBBON TAB, GROUP	BUTTON, OPTION
Address Block field	Mailings, Write & Insert Fields	
Checking and Reporting Errors dialog box	Mailings, Preview Results	
directory main document	Mailings, Start Mail Merge	, *Directory*
envelopes main document	Mailings, Start Mail Merge	, *Envelopes*
fill-in merge field	Mailings, Write & Insert Fields	, *Fill-in*
Greeting Line field	Mailings, Write & Insert Fields	
insert merge fields	Mailings, Write & Insert Fields	
labels main document	Mailings, Start Mail Merge	, *Labels*
letter main document	Mailings, Start Mail Merge	, *Letters*
Mail Merge Recipients dialog box	Mailings, Start Mail Merge	
Mail Merge wizard	Mailings, Start Mail Merge	, *Step-by-Step Mail Merge Wizard*
New Address List dialog box	Mailings, Start Mail Merge	, *Type a New List*
preview merge results	Mailings, Preview Results	

Workbook

Chapter study tools and assessment activities are available in the *Workbook* ebook. These resources are designed to help you further develop and demonstrate mastery of the skills learned in this chapter.

Unit assessment activities are also available in the *Workbook*. These activities are designed to help you demonstrate mastery of the skills learned in this unit.

Index

G

H

I

O

P

T

U

V

W

X

Z

Microsoft®

Excel® Level 1

Unit 1

Preparing and Formatting Worksheets

Chapter 1 Preparing an Excel Workbook

Chapter 2 Inserting Formulas in a Worksheet

Chapter 3 Formatting a Worksheet

Chapter 4 Enhancing a Worksheet

Microsoft®

Excel®

Preparing an Excel Workbook

CHAPTER 1

Performance Objectives

Upon successful completion of Chapter 1, you will be able to:

1 Identify the various elements of an Excel workbook
2 Create a workbook
3 Enter data in a worksheet
4 Save a workbook
5 Edit data in a worksheet
6 Print a worksheet
7 Close a workbook and close Excel
8 Use the AutoComplete, AutoCorrect, and AutoFill features
9 Open a workbook
10 Pin and unpin a workbook and folder to and from the *Recent* option list
11 Insert a formula using the AutoSum button
12 Select cells and data within cells
13 Apply basic formatting to cells in a workbook
14 Use the Tell Me feature
15 Use the Help feature

Precheck

Check your current skills to help focus your study.

Many companies use spreadsheets to organize numerical and financial data and to analyze and evaluate information. An Excel spreadsheet can be used for such activities as creating financial statements, preparing budgets, managing inventory, and analyzing cash flow. In addition, numbers and values can be easily manipulated to create "What if?" situations. For example, using a spreadsheet, a person in a company can ask questions such as "What if the value in this category is decreased? How will that change affect the department budget?" Questions like these can be easily answered using the information in an Excel spreadsheet. Change the value in a category and Excel will recalculate formulas for the other values. In this way, a spreadsheet can be used not only for creating financial statements or budgets but also as a planning tool.

SNAP

If you are a SNAP user, launch the Precheck and Tutorials from your Assignments page.

Data Files

Before beginning the chapter work, copy the EL1C1 folder to your storage medium and then make EL1C1 the active folder.

Project 1 **Prepare a Worksheet with Employee Information** **3 Parts**

You will create a worksheet containing employee information, edit the contents, and then save and close the workbook.

Preview Finished Project

Tutorial

Opening a Blank Workbook

Creating a Worksheet

Open Excel by clicking the *Excel 2016* tile at the Windows Start menu.(Depending on your operating system, these steps may vary.) At the Excel 2016 opening screen, click the *Blank workbook* template. This displays a workbook with a blank worksheet, as shown in Figure 1.1. The elements of a blank Excel worksheet are described in Table 1.1.

A file created in Excel is referred to as a *workbook*. An Excel workbook consists of an individual worksheet (or *sheet*) by default but it can contain multiple worksheets, like the sheets of paper in a notebook. Notice the tab named *Sheet1*, at the bottom of the Excel window. The area containing the gridlines in the Excel window is called the *worksheet area*. Figure 1.2 identifies the elements of the worksheet area. Create a worksheet in the worksheet area that will be saved as part of a workbook. Columns in a worksheet are labeled with letters of the alphabet and rows are labeled with numbers. The intersection of columns and rows create a box, which is referred to as a *cell*. A cell is where data and formulas are entered.

Figure 1.1 Blank Excel Worksheet

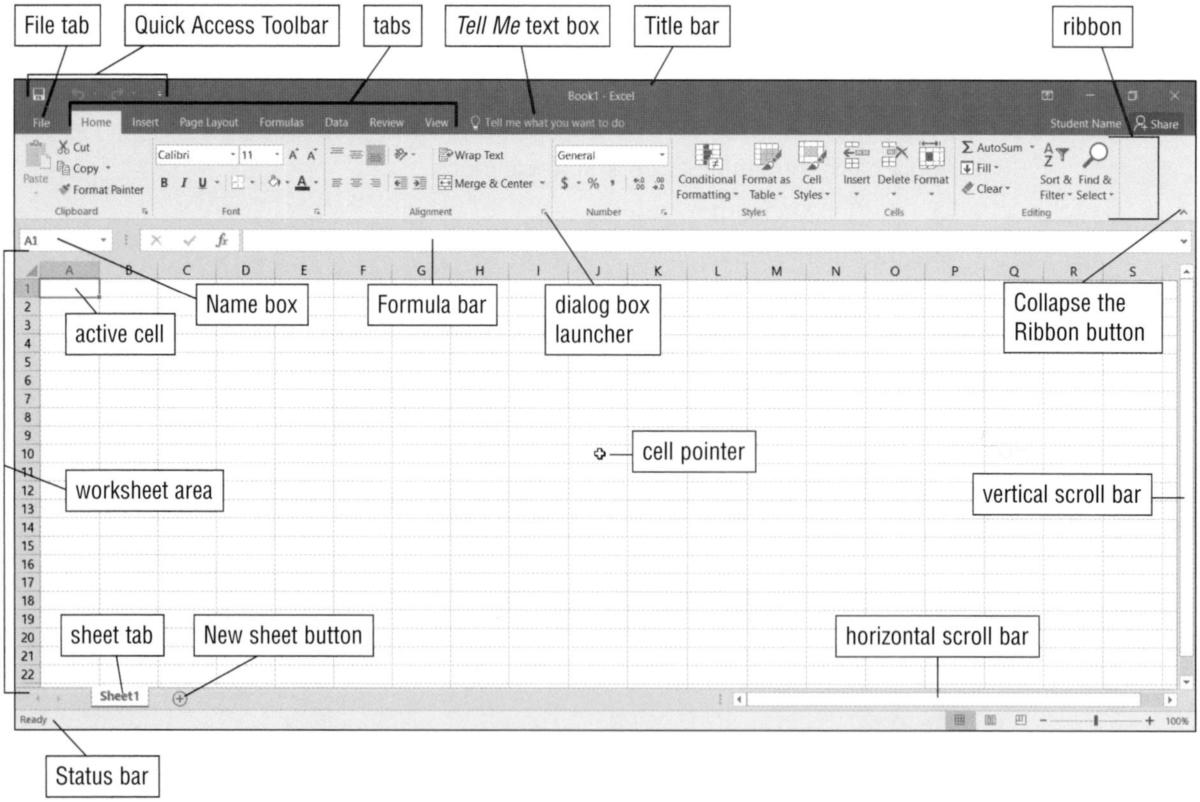

Table 1.1 Elements of an Excel Worksheet

Feature	Description
active cell	location in the worksheet that displays typed data or is affected by a command
cell pointer	when this icon appears, select cells by clicking or dragging the mouse
Collapse the Ribbon button	when clicked, removes the ribbon from the screen (Redisplay the ribbon by double-clicking a tab, except the File tab.)
dialog box launcher	click to open a dialog box with more options for that group
File tab	displays the backstage area that contains options for working with and managing files
Formula bar	displays the contents stored in the active cell
horizontal and vertical scroll bars	used to view various parts of the worksheet beyond the current screen
Name box	displays the active cell address or name assigned to the active cell
New sheet button	click to insert a new worksheet in the workbook
Quick Access Toolbar	contains buttons for commonly used commands that can be executed with a single mouse click
ribbon	contains the tabs with commands and buttons
sheet tab	identifies the current worksheet in the workbook
Status bar	displays the current mode, action messages, view buttons, and Zoom slider bar
tab	contains commands and buttons organized into groups
Tell Me text box	provides information and guidance on how to perform a function
Title bar	displays the workbook name followed by the application name
worksheet area	contains the cells used to create a worksheet

Figure 1.2 Elements of the Worksheet Area

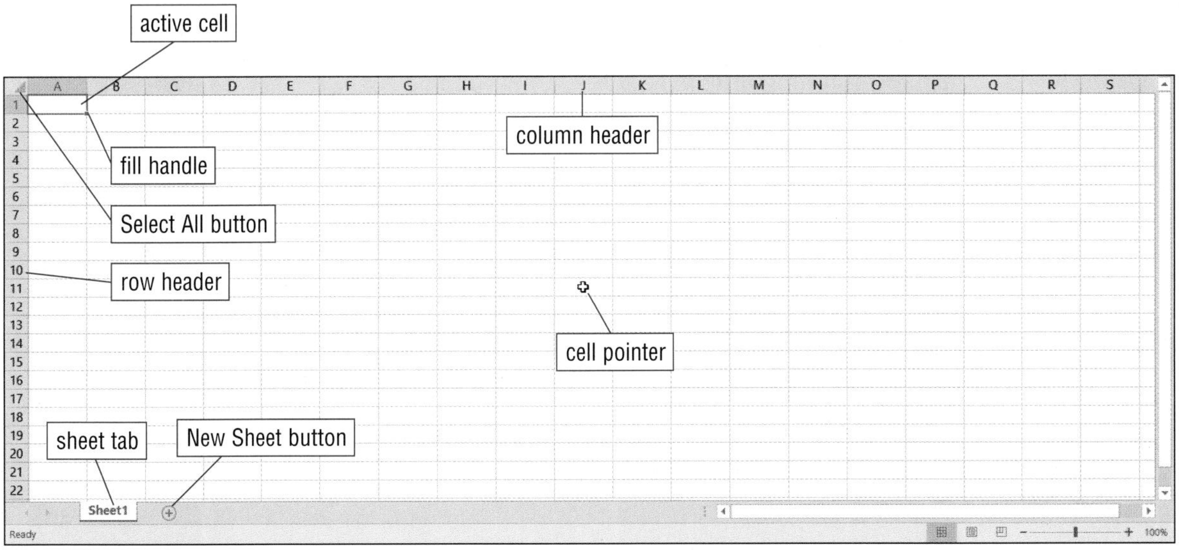

The horizontal and vertical lines that define the cells in the worksheet area are called *gridlines*. When a cell is active (displays with a green border), the cell address, also called the *cell reference*, displays in the Name box. The cell reference includes the column letter and row number. For example, if the first cell of the worksheet is active, the cell reference *A1* displays in the Name box. A green border surrounds the active cell. Any number of adjacent cells can be made active and form a range. A range is typically identified by the first cell reference and last cell reference separated by a colon. For example, the range A1:C1 contains the cells A1, B1, and C1.

Tutorial

Entering Data

Entering Data in a Worksheet

Enter data such as text, a number, or a value in a cell. To enter data in a cell, make the cell active and then type the data. To make the next cell active, press the Tab key. Table 1.2 displays additional commands for making a specific cell active.

Find & Select

Hint To make a cell active, position the cell pointer in the cell and then click the left mouse button.

Hint Ctrl + G is the keyboard shortcut to display the Go To dialog box.

Another method for making a cell active is to use the Go To feature. To use this feature, click the Find & Select button in the Editing group on the Home tab and then click *Go To*. At the Go To dialog box, type the cell reference in the *Reference* text box and then click OK.

Before typing data into the active cell, check the Status bar. The word *Ready* should display at the left side. As data is typed in a cell, the word *Ready* changes to *Enter*. Data typed in a cell displays in the cell and in the Formula bar. If the data entered in a cell is longer than the cell can accommodate, the data overlaps the next cell to the right. (It does not become a part of the next cell—it simply overlaps it. How to change column widths to accommodate data is explained later in this chapter.)

Table 1.2 Commands for Making a Specific Cell Active

To make this cell active	Press
cell below current cell	Enter
cell above current cell	Shift + Enter
next cell	Tab
previous cell	Shift + Tab
cell at beginning of row	Home
next cell in direction of arrow	Up, Down, Left, or Right Arrow key
last cell in worksheet	Ctrl + End
first cell in worksheet	Ctrl + Home
cell in next window	Page Down
cell in previous window	Page Up
cell in window to right	Alt + Page Down
cell in window to left	Alt + Page Up

If data entered in a cell consists of text and the text does not fit into the cell, it overlaps the next cell. If, however, a number is entered in a cell and the number is too long to fit in the cell, Excel changes the display of the number to number symbols *(###)*. This change is made because Excel does not want to mislead users by a number when only a portion of it displays in the cell.

Along with the keyboard, the mouse can be used to make a specific cell active. To make a specific cell active with the mouse, position the mouse pointer, which displays as a white plus symbol (+) (called the *cell pointer*), in the cell and then click the left mouse button. The cell pointer displays as a white plus sign when positioned in a cell in the worksheet and displays as an arrow pointer when positioned on other elements of the Excel window, such as options and buttons on tabs and scroll bars.

Scroll through a worksheet using the horizontal and/or vertical scroll bars. Scrolling shifts the display of cells in the worksheet area but does not change the active cell. Scroll through a worksheet until the desired cell is visible and then click in the cell.

Tutorial

Saving with the Same Name

Tutorial

Saving with a New Name

Save

Quick Steps

Save a Workbook

1. Click Save button on Quick Access Toolbar.
2. At Save As backstage area, click *Browse* option.
3. At Save As dialog box, navigate to folder.
4. Type workbook name.
5. Press Enter.

Hint Ctrl + S is the keyboard shortcut to save a workbook.

Saving a Workbook

Save an Excel workbook, which consists of one or more worksheets, by clicking the Save button on the Quick Access Toolbar or by clicking the File tab and then clicking the *Save As* option at the backstage area. At the Save As backstage area, click the *Browse* option and the Save As dialog box displays. At the Save As dialog box, click the desired location in the Navigation pane, type a name for the workbook in the *File name* text box, and then press the Enter key or click the Save button. Bypass the Save As backstage area and go directly to the Save As dialog box by using the keyboard shortcut F12.

To save an Excel workbook in the EL1C1 folder on your storage medium, display the Save As dialog box, click the drive representing your storage medium in the Navigation pane, and then double-click *EL1C1* in the Content pane.

A workbook file name can contain up to 255 characters, including the drive letter and any folder names, and it can include spaces. A workbook cannot have the same name first in uppercase and then in lowercase letters. Also, some symbols cannot be used in a file name, such as the following:

forward slash (/)	question mark (?)
backslash (\)	quotation mark (")
greater-than symbol (>)	colon (:)
less-than symbol (<)	asterisk (*)
pipe symbol (|)	

Project 1a Creating and Saving a Workbook

1. Open Excel by clicking the *Excel 2016* tile at the Windows Start menu. (Depending on your operating system, these steps may vary.)
2. At the Excel 2016 opening screen, click the *Blank workbook* template. (This opens a workbook with a blank worksheet.)
3. At the blank Excel worksheet, create the worksheet shown in Figure 1.3 by completing the following steps:
   a. Press the Enter key to make cell A2 the active cell.
   b. Type Employee in cell A2.
   c. Press the Tab key. (This makes cell B2 active.)
   d. Type Location and then press the Tab key. (This makes cell C2 active.)
   e. Type Benefits and then press the Enter key to move the insertion point to cell A3.
   f. Type Avery in cell A3.
   g. Continue typing the data shown in Figure 1.3. (For commands that make specific cells active, refer to Table 1.2.)

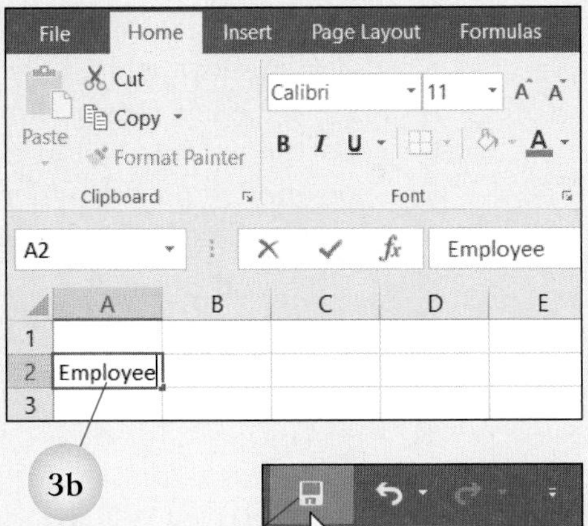

4. After typing the data shown in the cells in Figure 1.3, save the workbook by completing the following steps:
   a. Click the Save button on the Quick Access Toolbar.
   b. At the Save As backstage area, click the *Browse* option.
   c. At the Save As dialog box, navigate to the EL1C1 folder in the Navigation pane and then double-click the *EL1C1* folder in the Content pane.
   d. Select the text in the *File name* text box and then type 1-EmpBene.
   e. Press the Enter key or click the Save button.

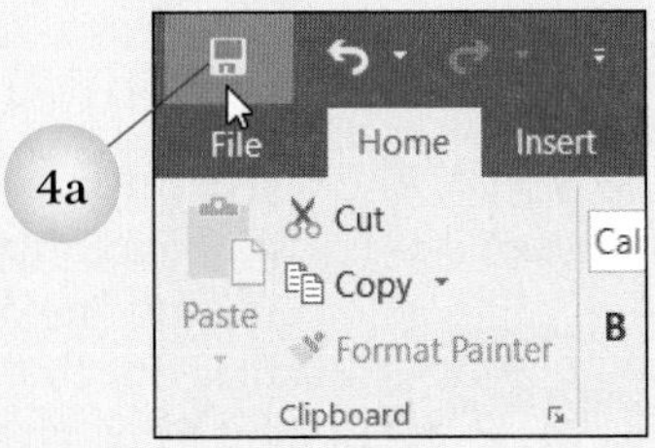

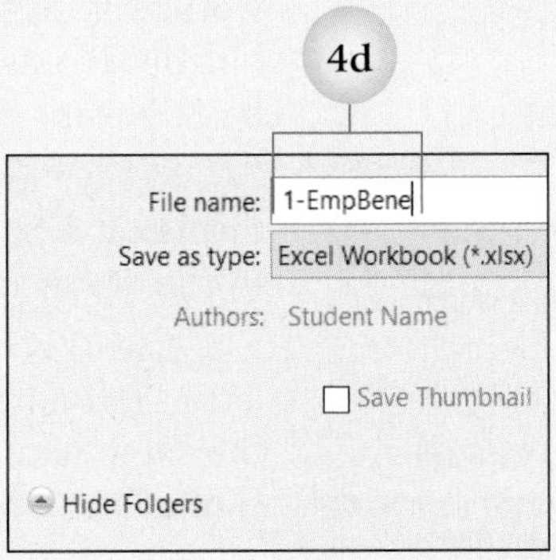

Check Your Work

Figure 1.3 Project 1a

	A	B	C	D
1				
2	Employee	Location	Benefits	
3	Avery			
4	Connors			
5	Estrada			
6	Juergens			
7	Mikulich			
8	Talbot			
9				

Tutorial

Editing Data

Editing Data in a Cell

Edit data being typed in a cell by pressing the Backspace key to delete the character to the left of the insertion point or pressing the Delete key to delete the character to the right of the insertion point. To change the data in a cell, click in the cell to make it active and then type the new data. When a cell containing data is active, anything typed will take the place of the existing data.

If only a portion of the data in a cell needs to be edited, double-click in the cell. This makes the cell active, moves the insertion point inside the cell, and displays the word *Edit* at the left side of the Status bar. Move the insertion point using the arrow keys or the mouse and then make the needed corrections. Press the Home key to move the insertion point to the first character in the cell or Formula bar or press the End key to move the insertion point to the last character.

When the editing of data in a cell is complete, be sure to change out of the Edit mode. To do this, make another cell active by pressing the Enter key, the Tab key, or Shift + Tab. Another way to change out of the Edit mode and return to the Ready mode is clicking in another cell or clicking the Enter button on the Formula bar.

Cancel

Enter

If the active cell does not contain data, the Formula bar displays only the cell reference (by column letter and row number). As data is typed, two buttons become active on the Formula bar to the right of the Name box, as shown in Figure 1.4. Click the Cancel button to delete the current cell entry. (A cell entry can also be deleted by pressing the Delete key.) Click the Enter button when finished typing or editing the cell entry. Click the Enter button on the Formula bar and the word *Enter* (or *Edit*) at the left side of the Status bar changes to *Ready*.

Figure 1.4 Buttons on the Formula Bar

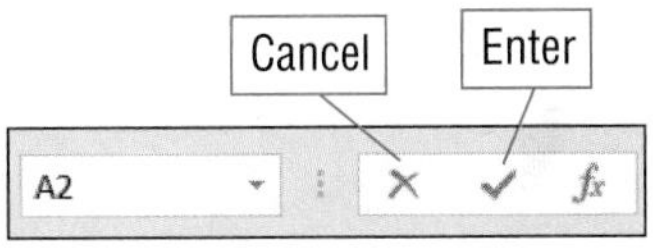

Project 1b **Editing Data in a Cell**

Part 2 of 3

1. With **1-EmpBene.xlsx** open, double-click in cell A7 (contains *Mikulich*).
2. Move the insertion point immediately left of the *k* and then type c. (This changes the spelling to *Mickulich*.)
3. Click in cell A4 (contains *Connors*), type Bryant, and then press the Tab key. (Clicking only once allows you to type over the existing data.)
4. Edit cell C2 by completing the following steps:
   a. Click the Find & Select button in the Editing group on the Home tab and then click *Go To* at the drop-down list.

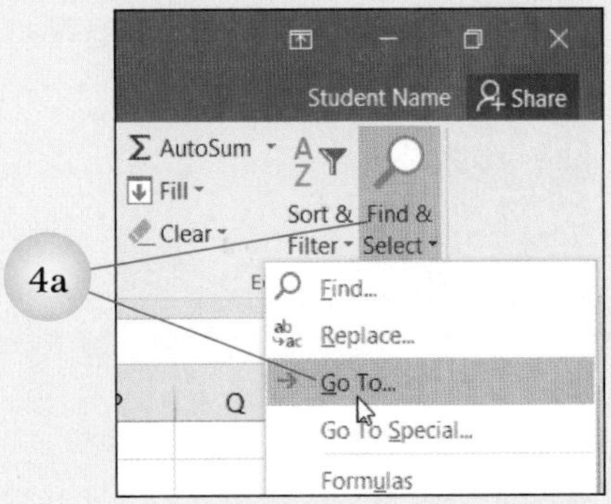

b. At the Go To dialog box, type c2 in the *Reference* text box and then click OK.
c. Type Classification (over *Benefits*).
5. Click in any other cell.
6. Click the Save button on the Quick Access Toolbar to save the workbook again.

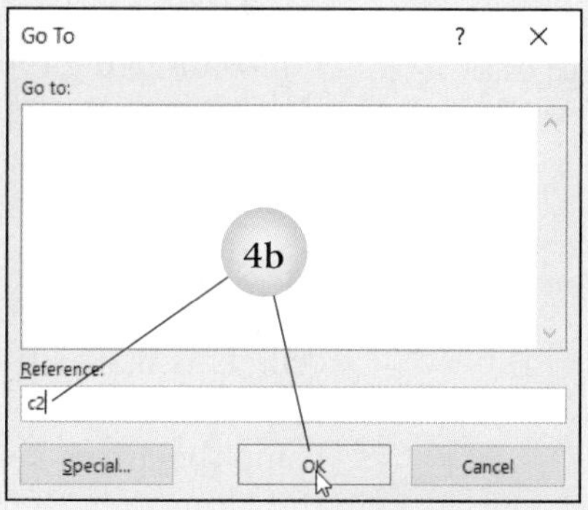

Check Your Work

Tutorial

Printing a Worksheet

Hint Ctrl + P is the keyboard shortcut to display the Print backstage area.

Printing a Worksheet

With a workbook open, click the File tab and the Info backstage area displays, as shown in Figure 1.5. Use buttons and options at the backstage area to perform functions such as opening, closing, saving, and printing a workbook. Click the Back button (in the upper left corner of the backstage area) to exit the backstage area without completing an action or press the Esc key on the keyboard.

Print a worksheet from the Print backstage area, as shown in Figure 1.6. To display this backstage area, click the File tab and then click the *Print* option. The Print backstage area can also be displayed with the keyboard shortcut Ctrl + P.

Figure 1.5 Info Backstage Area

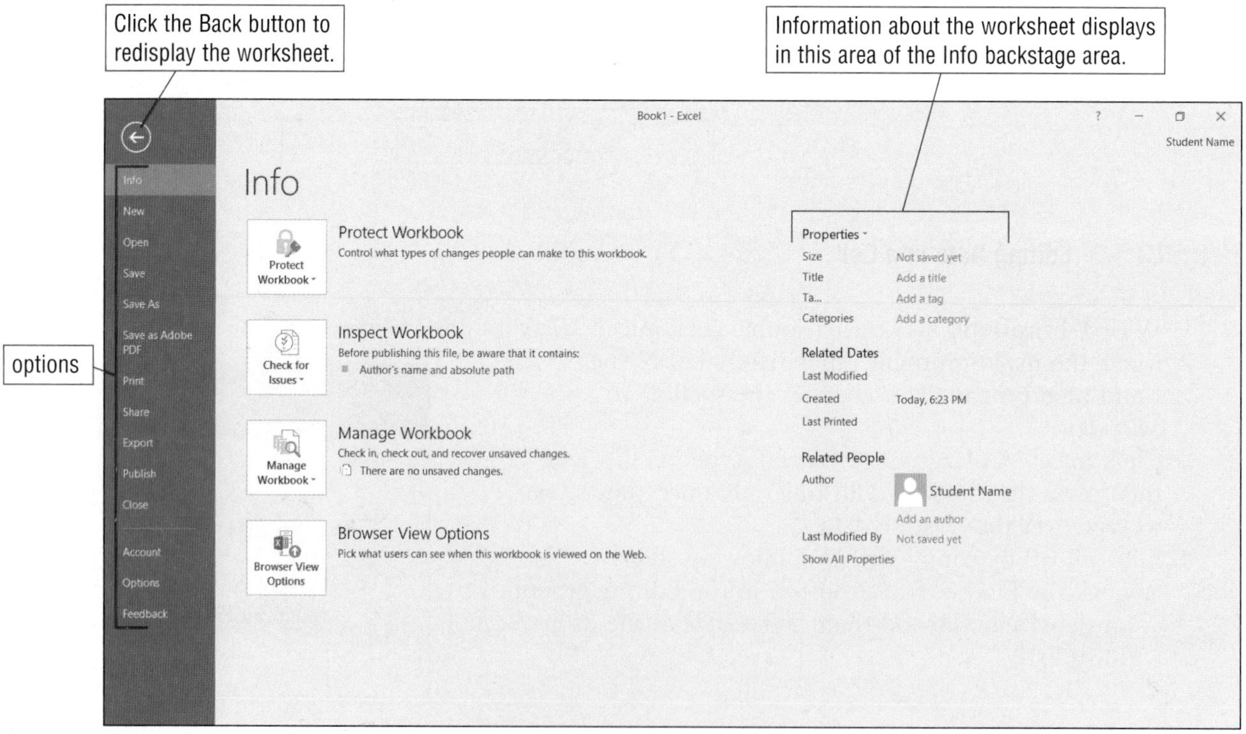

Figure 1.6 Print Backstage Area

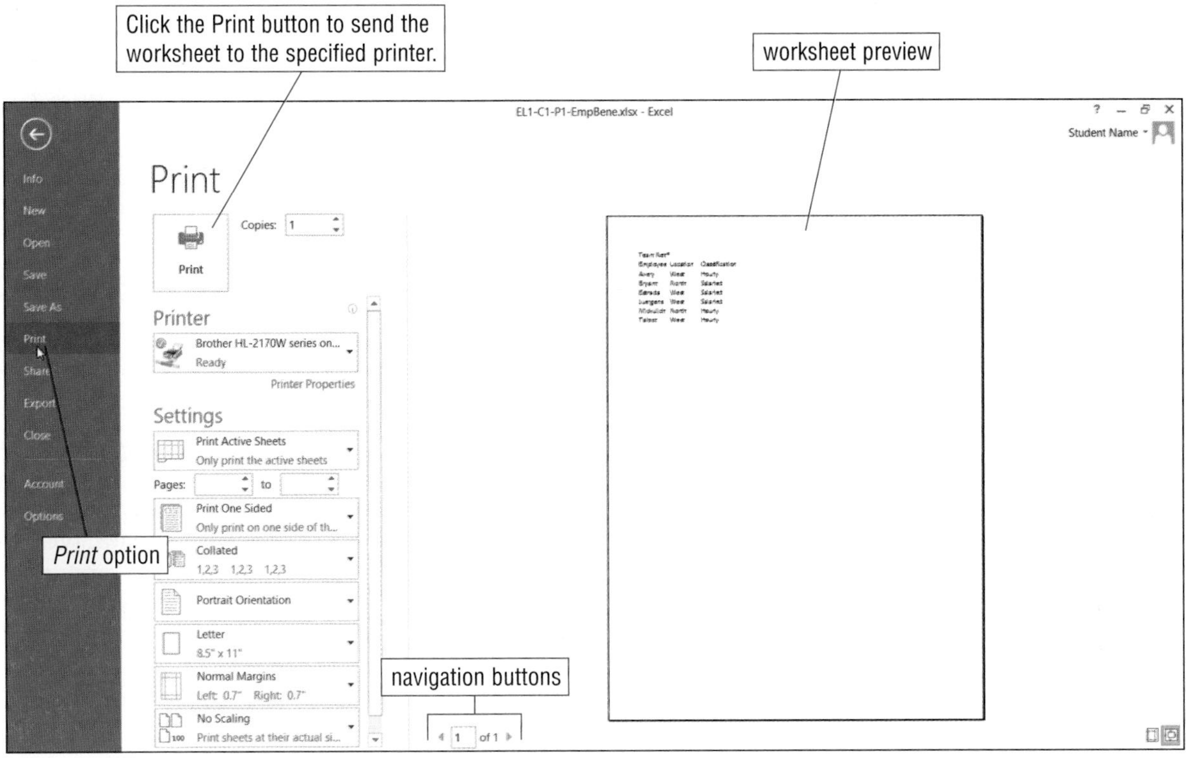

Quick Steps

Print a Worksheet

1. Click File tab.
2. Click *Print* option.
3. Click Print button.

Click the Print button in the Print backstage area to send the worksheet to the printer and use the *Copies* measurement box to specify the number of copies to be printed. Below the Print button are two categories: *Printer* and *Settings*. Use the gallery in the *Printer* category to specify the printer. The *Settings* category contains a number of galleries, each with options for specifying how the workbook will be printed. Use the galleries to specify whether the pages are collated when printed; what page orientation, page size, and margins the workbook should have; and whether the worksheet will be scaled to print all rows and columns of data on one page.

Another method for printing a workbook is to add the Quick Print button on the Quick Access Toolbar and then click the button. This sends the workbook directly to the printer without displaying the Print backstage area. To insert this button on the Quick Access Toolbar, click the Customize Quick Access Toolbar button at the right side of the toolbar and then click *Quick Print* at the drop-down list. To remove the Quick Print button from the Quick Access Toolbar, right-click the button and then click *Remove from Quick Access Toolbar* at the drop-down list.

Tutorial

Closing a Workbook and Closing Excel

Closing a Workbook

To close an Excel workbook without closing Excel, click the File tab and then click the *Close* option. Using the keyboard shortcut Ctrl + F4 will also close a workbook.

Quick Steps

Close a Workbook

1. Click File tab.
2. Click *Close* option.

Close

Quick Steps
Close Excel
Click Close button.

Closing Excel

To close Excel, click the Close button in the upper right corner of the screen. The Close button contains an *X* and, if the mouse pointer is positioned on the button, a ScreenTip displays with the name *Close*. Pressing the keyboard shortcut Alt + F4 will also close Excel.

Using Automatic Entering Features

Excel contains several features that help enter data into cells quickly and efficiently. These features include AutoComplete, which automatically inserts data in a cell that begins the same as a previous entry; AutoCorrect, which automatically corrects many common typographical errors; and AutoFill, which automatically inserts words, numbers, or formulas in a series.

Using AutoComplete

The AutoComplete feature automatically inserts data in a cell that begins the same as a previous entry. If the data inserted by AutoComplete is the correct data, press the Tab key or the Enter key. If it is not the correct data, simply continue typing the correct data. This feature can be very useful in a worksheet that contains repetitive data entries. For example, consider a worksheet that repeats the word *Payroll*. The second and subsequent times this word is to be inserted in a cell, simply typing the letter *P* will cause AutoComplete to insert the entire word.

Using AutoCorrect

The AutoCorrect feature automatically corrects many common typing errors. To see what symbols and words are included in AutoCorrect, click the File tab and then click *Options*. At the Excel Options dialog box, click *Proofing* in the left panel and then click the AutoCorrect Options button in the right panel. This displays the AutoCorrect dialog box with the AutoCorrect tab selected, as shown in Figure 1.7, with a list box containing the replacement data.

Figure 1.7 AutoCorrect Dialog Box with AutoCorrect Tab Selected

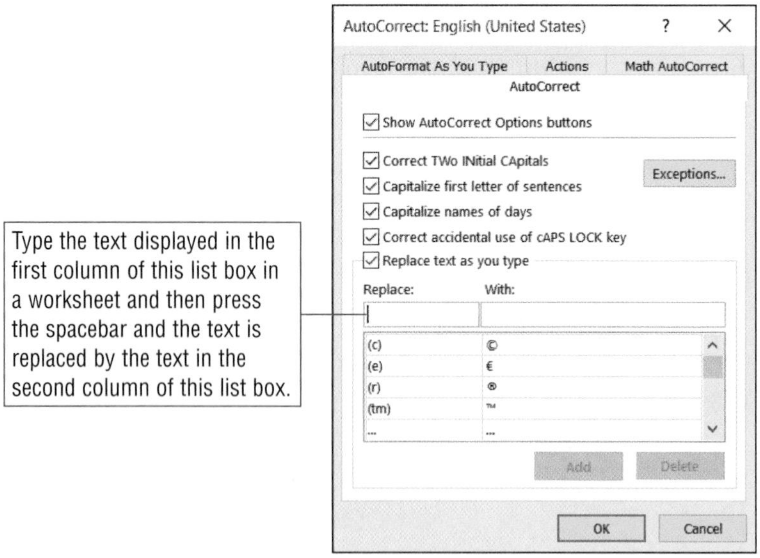

At the AutoCorrect dialog box, type the text shown in the first column in the list box and then press the spacebar and the text in the second column is inserted in the cell. Along with symbols, the AutoCorrect dialog box contains commonly misspelled words and common typographical errors.

Project 1c Inserting Data in Cells with AutoCorrect and AutoComplete

Part 3 of 3

1. With **1-EmpBene.xlsx** open, make cell A1 active.
2. Type the text in cell A1, as shown in Figure 1.8. Insert the ® symbol by typing (r) and then pressing the Enter key. (AutoCorrect will change (r) to ®.)
3. Type the remaining text in the cells. When you type the *W* in *West* in cell B5, the AutoComplete feature will insert *West*. Accept this by pressing the Tab key. (Pressing the Tab key accepts *West* and also makes the cell to the right active.) Use the AutoComplete feature to enter *West* in cells B6 and B8 and *North* in cell B7. Use AutoComplete to enter the second and subsequent occurrences of *Salaried* and *Hourly*.
4. Click the Save button on the Quick Access Toolbar.
5. Print **1-EmpBene.xlsx** by clicking the File tab, clicking the *Print* option, and then clicking the Print button at the Print backstage area. (The gridlines will not print.)

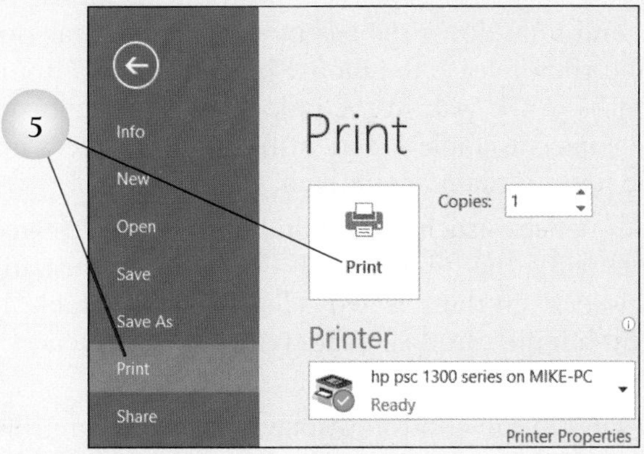

6. Close the workbook by clicking the File tab and then clicking the *Close* option at the backstage area.

Check Your Work

Figure 1.8 Project 1c

	A	B	C	D
1	Team Net®			
2	Employee	Location	Classification	
3	Avery	West	Hourly	
4	Bryant	North	Salaried	
5	Estrada	West	Salaried	
6	Juergens	West	Salaried	
7	Mickulich	North	Hourly	
8	Talbot	West	Hourly	
9				

Project 2 Open and Format a Workbook and Insert Formulas — 3 Parts

You will open an existing workbook and insert formulas to find the sums and averages of numbers.

Preview Finished Project

Tutorial

Entering Data Using the Fill Handle

Using AutoFill

When a cell is active, a thick green border surrounds it and a small green square displays in the bottom right corner of the border. This green square is called the AutoFill *fill handle* (see Figure 1.2 on page 5). Use the fill handle to fill a range of cells with the same data or with consecutive data. For example, suppose the year 2018 is to be inserted in a row or column of cells. To do this quickly, type *2018* in the first cell, position the mouse pointer on the fill handle, click and hold down the left mouse button, drag across or down into the cells in which the year is to be inserted, and then release the mouse button.

Hint When filling cells with the fill handle, press and hold down the Ctrl key if you want to copy the same data instead of displaying the next instance in the series.

The fill handle can also be used to insert a series in a row or column of cells. For example, suppose a worksheet is being created with data for all the months in the year. Type *January* in the first cell, position the mouse pointer on the fill handle, click and hold down the left mouse button, drag down or across into 11 more cells, and then release the mouse button. Excel automatically inserts the other 11 months in the year in the proper order. When using the fill handle, the cells must be adjacent. Table 1.3 identifies the sequences inserted in cells by Excel when specific types of data are entered.

Certain sequences—such as *2, 4* and *Jan 12, Jan 13*—require that both cells be selected before using the fill handle. If only the cell containing *2* is active, the fill handle will insert *2*s in the selected cells. The list in Table 1.3 is only a sampling of what the fill handle can do. A variety of other sequences can be inserted in a worksheet using the fill handle.

Auto Fill Options

An Auto Fill Options button displays when cells are filled with data using the fill handle. Click this button and a list of options displays for filling the cells. By default, data and formatting are filled in each cell. Use the Auto Fill Options button to choose to fill only the formatting in the cells or fill only the data without the formatting. Other fill options include choosing to copy data into the selected cells or to fill the data as a series.

Table 1.3 AutoFill Fill Handle Series

Enter this data*	And the fill handle will insert this sequence in adjacent cells*
January	February, March, April, and so on
Jan	Feb, Mar, Apr, and so on
Jan 15, Jan 16	17-Jan, 18-Jan, 19-Jan, and so on
Monday	Tuesday, Wednesday, Thursday, and so on
Product 1	Product 2, Product 3, Product 4, and so on
Qtr 1	Qtr 2, Qtr 3, Qtr 4
2, 4	6, 8, 10, and so on

* Commas represent data in separate cells.

Tutorial

Opening a Workbook from a Removable Disk

Opening a Workbook

Open an Excel workbook at the Open dialog box. To display this dialog box, click the File tab and then click the *Open* option. This displays the Open backstage area. Other methods of displaying the Open backstage area include using the keyboard shortcut Ctrl + O and inserting an Open button on the Quick Access Toolbar. At the Open backstage area, click the *Browse* option. At the Open dialog box, navigate to the desired folder and then double-click the workbook name in the Content pane. Bypass the Open backstage area and go directly to the Open dialog box by using the keyboard shortcut Ctrl + F12.

Tutorial

Opening from the *Recent* Option List

Opening a Workbook from the *Recent* Option List

With the *Recent* option selected in the middle panel at the Open backstage area, a list displays with the most recently opened workbooks. Up to 25 workbook names display in the list by default. Open a workbook from this list by clicking the workbook name.

Quick Steps

Open a Workbook

1. Click File tab.
2. Click *Open* option.
3. Click *Browse* option.
4. Navigate to folder.
5. Double-click workbook name.

Pin a Workbook to *Recent* Option List

1. Click File tab.
2. Click *Open* option.
3. Position mouse pointer over workbook name.
4. Click left-pointing push pin.

Unpin a Workbook from *Recent* Option List

1. Click File tab.
2. Click *Open* option.
3. Position mouse pointer over workbook name.
4. Click down-pointing push pin.

Pinning and Unpinning Workbooks and Folders

If a workbook is opened on a regular basis, consider pinning it to the *Recent* option list. To pin a workbook, position the mouse pointer over the workbook name and then click the left-pointing push pin at the right of the workbook name. The left-pointing push pin changes to a down-pointing push pin and the pinned workbook is inserted into a new category named *Pinned*. The *Pinned* category displays at the top of the *Recent* option list. The next time the Open backstage area displays, the pinned workbook displays in the *Pinned* category at the top of the *Recent* option list.

A workbook can also be pinned to the Recent list at the Excel 2016 opening screen. When a workbook is pinned, it displays at the top of the Recent list and the *Recent* option list at the Open backstage area. To "unpin" a workbook from the Recent or *Recent* option list, click the pin to change it from a down-pointing push pin to a left-pointing push pin. More than one workbook can be pinned to a list. Another method for pinning and unpinning documents is to use the shortcut menu. Right-click a workbook name and then click the option *Pin to list* or *Unpin from list*.

In addition to workbooks, folders can be pinned to a list at the Save As backstage area. The third panel in the Save As backstage area displays a list of the most recently opened folders and groups them into categories such as *Today*, *Yesterday*, and *Last Week*. Pin a folder or folders to the list and a *Pinned* category is created; the folder names display in the category.

Project 2a Inserting Data in Cells with the Fill Handle — Part 1 of 3

1. Open **FillCells.xlsx** by completing the following steps:
   a. Click the File tab and then click the *Open* option.
   b. With the *This PC* option selected, click the *Browse* option.
   c. Navigate to the to the EL1C1 folder on your storage medium and then double-click **FillCells.xlsx**.
2. Save the workbook with the name **1-FillCells** by completing the following steps:
   a. Press F12 to display the Save As dialog box.
   b. Press the Home key on the keyboard to position the insertion point at the beginning of the name in the *File name* text box and then type 1-.
   c. Click the Save button.

3. Add data to cells as shown in Figure 1.9. Begin by making cell B1 active and then typing January.
4. Position the mouse pointer on the fill handle for cell B1, click and hold down the left mouse button, drag across into cell G1, and then release the mouse button.

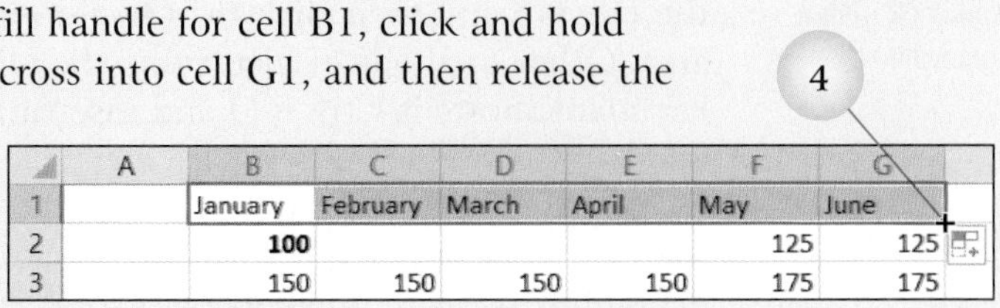

5. Type a sequence and then use the fill handle to fill the remaining cells by completing the following steps:
   a. Make cell A2 active and then type Year 1.
   b. Make cell A3 active and then type Year 3.
   c. Select cells A2 and A3 by clicking in cell A2 and holding down the left mouse button, dragging into cell A3, and then releasing the mouse button.
   d. Drag the fill handle for cell A3 down into cell A5. (This inserts *Year 5* in cell A4 and *Year 7* in cell A5.)
6. Use the fill handle to fill adjacent cells with a number but not the formatting by completing the following steps:
   a. Make cell B2 active. (This cell contains *100* with bold formatting.)
   b. Drag the fill handle for cell B2 to the right into cell E2. (This inserts *100* in cells C2, D2, and E2.)
   c. Click the Auto Fill Options button at the bottom right of the selected cells.
   d. Click the *Fill Without Formatting* option at the drop-down list.

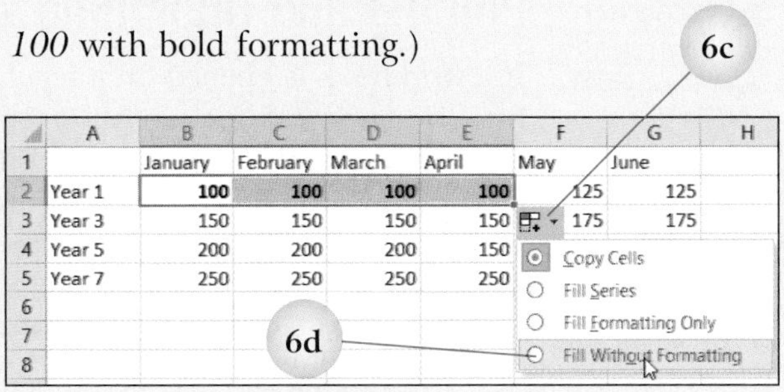

7. Use the fill handle to apply formatting only by completing the following steps:
   a. Make cell B2 active.
   b. Drag the fill handle down into cell B5.
   c. Click the Auto Fill Options button and then click *Fill Formatting Only* at the drop-down list.
8. Make cell A10 active and then type Qtr 1.
9. Drag the fill handle for cell A10 into cell A13.
10. Save **1-FillCells.xlsx**.

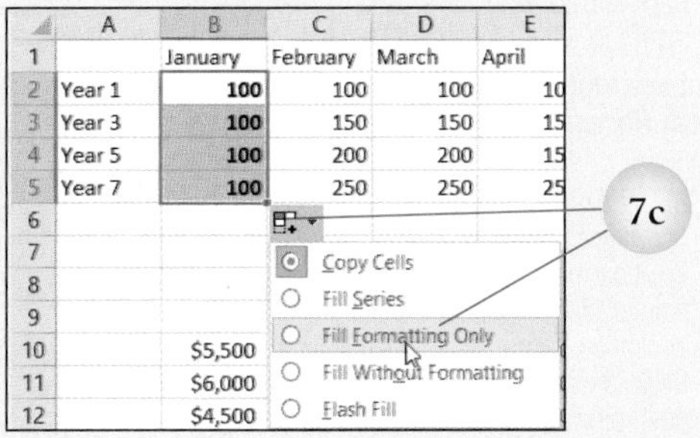

Check Your Work

Figure 1.9 Project 2a

	A	B	C	D	E	F	G
1		January	February	March	April	May	June
2	Year 1	**100**	100	100	100	125	125
3	Year 3	**150**	150	150	150	175	175
4	Year 5	**200**	200	200	150	150	150
5	Year 7	**250**	250	250	250	250	250
6							
7							
8							
9							
10	Qtr1	$5,500	$6,250	$7,000	$8,500	$5,500	$4,500
11	Qtr2	$6,000	$7,250	$6,500	$9,000	$4,000	$5,000
12	Qtr3	$4,500	$8,000	$6,000	$7,500	$6,000	$5,000
13	Qtr4	$6,500	$8,500	$7,000	$8,000	$5,500	$6,000
14							

Entering Formulas

Quick Steps

Enter a Formula Using the AutoSum button

1. Click in cell.
2. Click AutoSum button.
3. Check range identified and make changes if necessary.
4. Press Enter.

Excel is a powerful decision-making tool for manipulating data to answer questions in "What if?" situations. Insert a formula in a worksheet and then manipulate the data to make projections, answer specific questions, and plan for the future. For example, the manager of a department might use an Excel worksheet to prepare a department budget and then determine how hiring a new employee or increasing the volume of production will affect the budget.

Insert a formula in a worksheet to perform calculations on values. A formula contains a mathematical operator, value, cell reference, cell range, and function. Formulas can be written that add, subtract, multiply, and/or divide values. Formulas can also be written that calculate averages, percentages, minimum and maximum values, and much more. The AutoSum button in the Editing group on the Home tab inserts a formula to calculate the total of a range of cells.

Tutorial

Entering Formulas Using the AutoSum Button

Σ AutoSum

Hint You can use the keyboard shortcut Alt + = to insert the SUM function in a cell.

Using the AutoSum Button to Add Numbers

Use the AutoSum button in the Editing group on the Home tab to insert a formula. The AutoSum button adds numbers automatically with the SUM function. Make active the cell in which the formula will be inserted (this cell should be empty) and then click the AutoSum button. Excel looks for a range of cells containing numbers above the active cell. If no cell above contains numbers, then Excel looks to the left of the active cell. Excel suggests the range of cells to be added. If the suggested range is not correct, drag through the range of cells with the mouse and then press the Enter key. Double-click the AutoSum button to automatically insert the SUM function with the range Excel chooses.

Project 2b Adding Values with the AutoSum Button Part 2 of 3

1. With **1-FillCells.xlsx** open, make cell A6 active and then type Total.
2. Make cell B6 active and then calculate the sum of the cells by clicking the AutoSum button in the Editing group on the Home tab.
3. Excel inserts the formula *=SUM(B2:B5)* in cell B6. This is the correct range of cells, so press the Enter key.

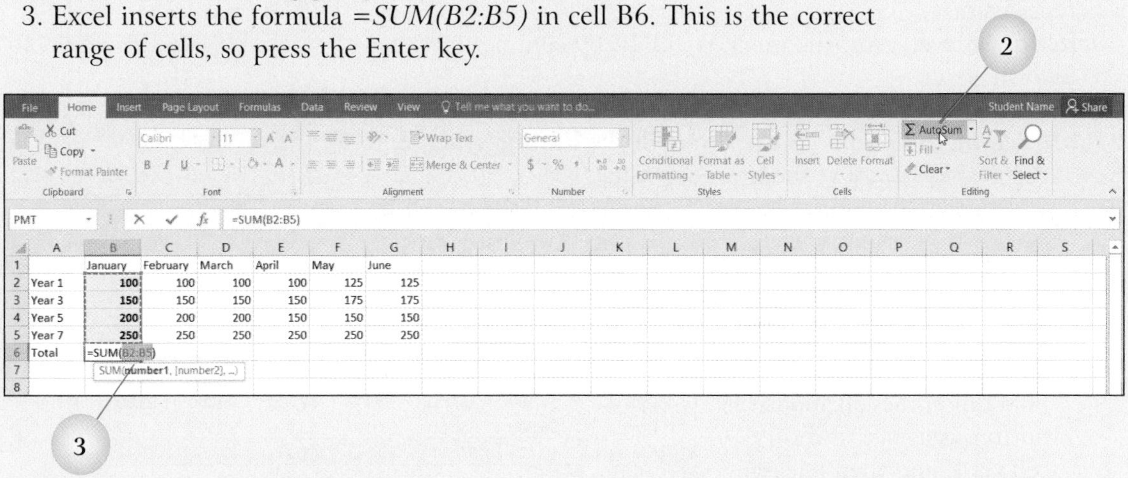

4. Make cell C6 active and then click the AutoSum button in the Editing group.
5. Excel inserts the formula *=SUM(C2:C5)* in cell C6. This is the correct range of cells, so press the Enter key.

6. Make cell D6 active.
7. Double-click the AutoSum button. This inserts the formula *=SUM(D2:D5)* in cell D6 and inserts the sum *700*.
8. Insert the sum in cells E6, F6, and G6.
9. Save **1-FillCells.xlsx**.

Check Your Work

Quick Steps

Insert an Average Formula Using the AutoSum Button
1. Click in cell.
2. Click AutoSum button arrow.
3. Click *Average*.
4. Specify range.
5. Press Enter.

Using the AutoSum Button to Average Numbers

A common function in a formula is the AVERAGE function. With this function, a range of cells are added together and then the total is divided by the number of cell entries. The AVERAGE function is available on the AutoSum button. Click the AutoSum button arrow and a drop-down list displays with a number of common functions.

Tutorial

Copying Formulas

Quick Steps

Copy a Formula Using the Fill Handle
1. Insert formula in cell.
2. Make active cell containing formula.
3. Using fill handle, drag into cells to contain formula.

Using the Fill Handle to Copy a Formula

The same basic formula can be inserted in other cells in a worksheet. When copying a formula to other locations in a worksheet, use a relative cell reference. Copy a formula containing relative cell references and the cell references change. For example, insert the formula *=SUM(A2:C2)* in cell D2 and then copy it relatively to cell D3 and the formula in cell D3 displays as *=SUM(A3:C3)*. Use the fill handle to copy a formula relatively in a worksheet. To do this, position the mouse pointer on the fill handle until the mouse pointer turns into a thin black cross, click and hold down the left mouse button, drag and select the cells, and then release the mouse button.

Project 2c **Inserting the AVERAGE Function and Copying a Formula Relatively** Part 3 of 3

1. With **1-FillCells.xlsx** open, make cell A14 active and then type Average.
2. Insert the average of the range B10:B13 by completing the following steps:
   a. Make cell B14 active.
   b. Click the AutoSum button arrow in the Editing group and then click *Average* at the drop-down list.
   c. Excel inserts the formula *=AVERAGE(B10:B13)* in cell B14. This is the correct range of cells, so press the Enter key.

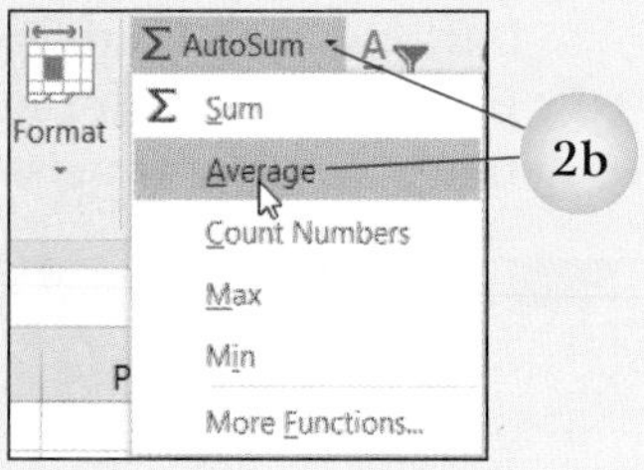

3. Copy the formula relatively to the range C14:G14 by completing the following steps:
   a. Make cell B14 active.
   b. Position the mouse pointer on the fill handle, click and hold down the left mouse button, drag across into cell G14, and then release the mouse button.

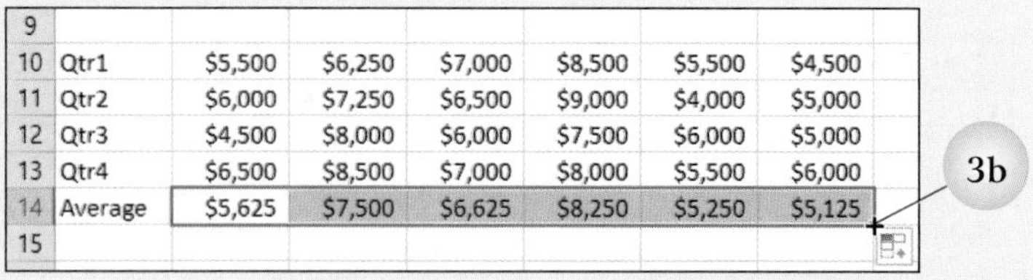

10 Qtr1 $5,500 $6,250 $7,000 $8,500 $5,500 $4,500
11 Qtr2 $6,000 $7,250 $6,500 $9,000 $4,000 $5,000
12 Qtr3 $4,500 $8,000 $6,000 $7,500 $6,000 $5,000
13 Qtr4 $6,500 $8,500 $7,000 $8,000 $5,500 $6,000
14 Average $5,625 $7,500 $6,625 $8,250 $5,250 $5,125
3b

4. Save, print, and then close **1-FillCells.xlsx**.

Check Your Work

Project 3 Format a Monthly Expenses Worksheet — 2 Parts

You will open a workbook containing a monthly expenses worksheet and then change the column width, merge and center cells, and apply number formatting to numbers in cells.

Preview Finished Project

Tutorial

Selecting Cells

Selecting Cells

Use a variety of methods for formatting cells in a worksheet. For example, change the alignment of data in cells or rows or add character formatting. To identify the cells that are to be affected by the formatting, select the specific cells.

Selecting Cells Using the Mouse

Select specific cells, columns, or rows in a worksheet using the mouse. Table 1.4 displays the methods for selecting cells using the mouse.

Hint The first cell in a range displays with a white background and is the active cell.

Selected cells, except the active cell, display with a gray background (this may vary) rather than a white background. The active cell is the first cell in the selection block and displays in the normal manner (white background with black data). Selected cells remain selected until another cell is clicked with the mouse or an arrow key is pressed on the keyboard.

Selecting Cells Using the Keyboard

Keys on the keyboard can be used to select specific cells within a worksheet. Table 1.5 displays the commands for selecting specific cells. If a worksheet contains data, Ctrl + A selects all cells containing data. If a worksheet contains groups of data separated by empty cells, Ctrl + A or Ctrl + Shift + spacebar selects a group of cells rather than all the cells.

Selecting Data within Cells

The selection commands presented in Table 1.4 and Table 1.5 select the entire cell. Specific characters within a cell can also be selected. To do this with the

Table 1.4 Selecting with the Mouse

To select this	Do this
column	Position the cell pointer on the column header (a letter) and then click the left mouse button.
row	Position the cell pointer on the row header (a number) and then click the left mouse button.
adjacent cells	Drag with the mouse into specific cells to select them.
nonadjacent cells	Press and hold down the Ctrl key while clicking the column header, row header, or specific cells.
all cells in worksheet	Click the Select All button. (Refer to Figure 1.2 on page 5.)

Table 1.5 Selecting Cells Using the Keyboard

To select	Press
cells in direction of arrow key	Shift + arrow key
from active cell to beginning of row	Shift + Home
from active cell to beginning of worksheet	Shift + Ctrl + Home
from active cell to last cell in worksheet containing data	Shift + Ctrl + End
entire column	Ctrl + spacebar
entire row	Shift + spacebar
cells containing data	Ctrl + A
groups of data separated by empty cells	Ctrl + Shift + spacebar

Hint Select nonadjacent columns or rows by holding down the Ctrl key while selecting cells.

mouse, position the cell pointer in a cell and then double-click the left mouse button. Drag with the I-beam pointer through the data to be selected. Data selected within a cell displays with a gray background. To select data in a cell using the keyboard, press and hold down the Shift key and then press the arrow key that moves the insertion point in the desired direction. All the data the insertion point passes through will be selected. Press the F8 function key to turn on the Extend Selection mode, move the insertion point in the desired direction to select the data, and then press F8 to turn off the Extend Selection mode. When the Extend Selection mode is on, the words *Extend Selection* display at the left side of the Status bar.

Applying Basic Formatting

Quick Steps

Change Column Width

Drag column boundary line.
OR
Double-click column boundary line.

Merge and Center Cells

1. Select cells.
2. Click Merge & Center button on Home tab.

Excel provides a wide range of formatting options that can be applied to cells in a worksheet. Some basic formatting options that are helpful when creating a worksheet include changing the column width, merging and centering cells, and formatting numbers.

Changing Column Width

If data such as text or numbers overlaps in a cell, increase the width of the column to accommodate the data. To do this, position the mouse pointer on the gray boundary line between columns in the column header (Figure 1.2 identifies the column header) until the pointer turns into a double-headed arrow pointing left and right and then drag the boundary to the new location. If the column contains data, double-click the column boundary line at the right side to automatically adjust the width of the column to accommodate the longest entry.

Tutorial

Merging and Centering Cells

Merge & Center

Merging and Centering Cells

As explained earlier in this chapter, if the typed text is longer than the cell can accommodate, the text overlaps the next cell to the right (unless the text typed is numbers). Merge cells to accommodate the text and also center the text within the merged cells. To merge cells and center the text, select the cells and then click the Merge & Center button in the Alignment group on the Home tab.

Project 3a Changing Column Width and Merging and Centering Cells — Part 1 of 2

1. Open **MoExps.xlsx** and then save it with the name **1-MoExps**.
2. Change column widths by completing the following steps:
   a. Position the mouse pointer in the column header on the boundary line between columns A and B until the pointer turns into a double-headed arrow pointing left and right.

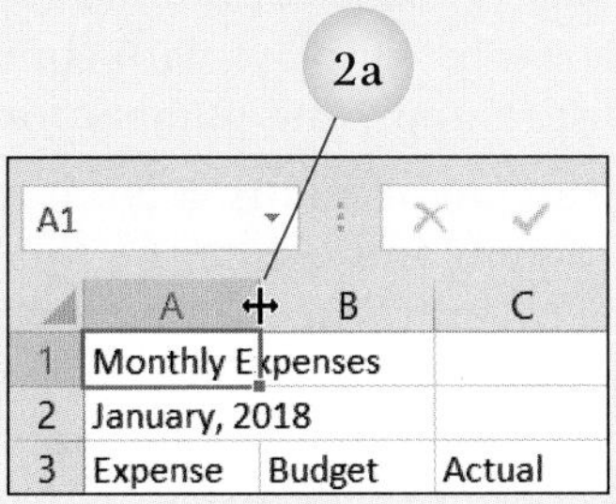

   b. Double-click the left mouse button.
   c. Position the mouse pointer in the column header on the boundary line between columns E and F and then double-click the left mouse button.
   d. Position the mouse pointer in the column header on the boundary line between columns F and G and then double-click the left mouse button.
3. Merge and center cells by completing the following steps:
   a. Select the range A1:C1.
   b. Click the Merge & Center button in the Alignment group on the Home tab.

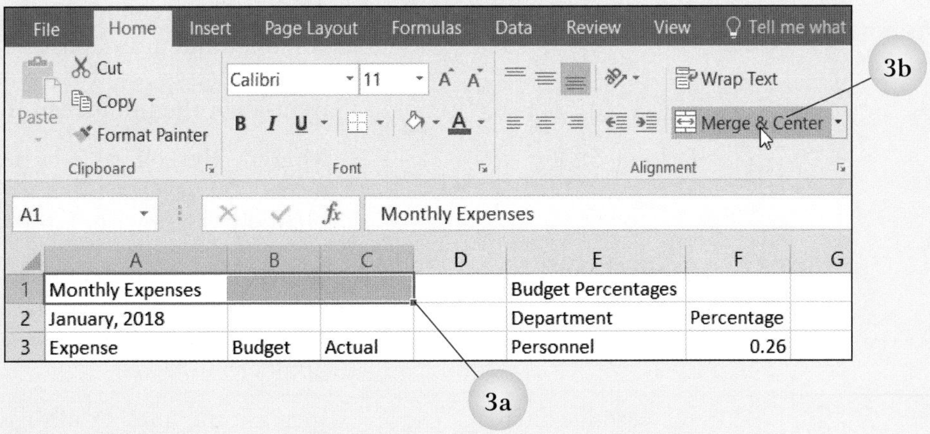

   c. Select the range A2:C2.
   d. Click the Merge & Center button.
   e. Select cells E1 and F1 and then click the Merge & Center button.
4. Save **1-MoExps.xlsx**.

Check Your Work

Tutorial

Applying Number Formatting

Formatting Numbers

Numbers in a cell by default align at the right and decimals and commas do not display unless they are typed in the cell. Change the format of numbers with buttons in the Number group on the Home tab. Symbols that can be added when a number is formatted include a percent symbol (%), a comma (,), and a dollar symbol ($). For example, if the number *$45.50* is typed in a cell, Excel automatically applies the Currency format to the number. If *45%* is entered in a cell, Excel automatically applies the Percentage format to the number. The Number group on the Home tab contains five buttons that are used to format numbers in cells. The five buttons are shown and described in Table 1.6.

Specify the formatting for numbers in cells in a worksheet before typing the numbers or format existing numbers in a worksheet. The Increase Decimal and Decrease Decimal buttons in the Number group on the Home tab change how many digits display after the decimal point. The Number group on the Home tab also contains the *Number Format* option box. Click the *Number Format* option box arrow and a drop-down list displays with common number formats. Click a format at the drop-down list to apply the number format to the cell or selected cells.

A general guideline in accounting is to insert a dollar symbol before the first amount in a column and before the total amount but not before the number amounts between them. Format a worksheet following this guideline by applying the Accounting format to the first amount and total amount using the Accounting Number Format button and applying the Accounting format to the number amounts between them using the Comma Style button. To differentiate between the two Accounting formats, steps in this textbook will use the term *Accounting format* when the Accounting Number Format button in the Number group on the Home tab is to be clicked. The term *Comma format* will be used when the Comma Style button is to be clicked.

Table 1.6 Number Formatting Buttons

Click this button		To do this
$ ▾	Accounting Number Format	Add a dollar symbol, any necessary commas, and a decimal point followed by two digits even if none are typed; right-align the number in the cell.
%	Percent Style	Multiply the cell value by 100 and display the result with a percent symbol; right-align the number in the cell.
,	Comma Style	Add any necessary commas and a decimal point followed by two digits even if none are typed; right-align the number in the cell.
←.0 .00	Increase Decimal	Increase the number of digits displayed after the decimal point in the selected cell.
.00 →.0	Decrease Decimal	Decrease the number of digits displayed after the decimal point in the selected cell.

Project 3b **Formatting Numbers**

Part 2 of 2

1. With **1-MoExps.xlsx** open, make cell B13 active and then double-click the AutoSum button. (This inserts the total of the numbers in the range B4:B12.)
2. Make cell C13 active and then double-click the AutoSum button.
3. Apply the Accounting format to cells by completing the following steps:
   a. Select cells B4 and C4.
   b. Click the Accounting Number Format button in the Number group on the Home tab.
   c. Decrease the number of digits displayed after the decimal point to none by clicking the Decrease Decimal button in the Number group two times.

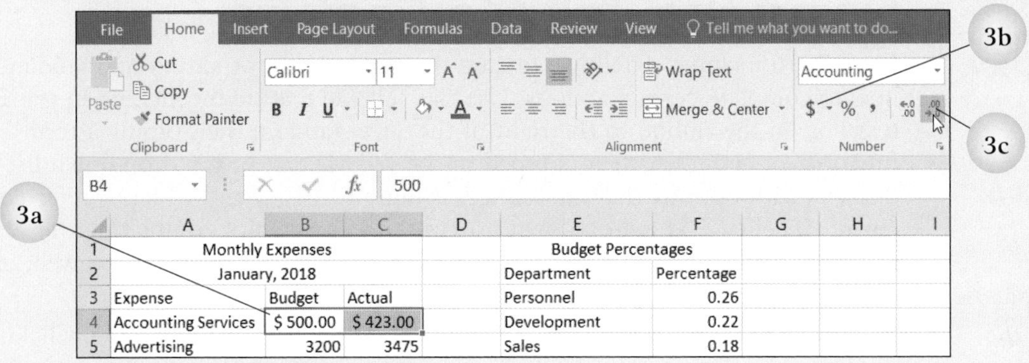

   d. Select cells B13 and C13.
   e. Click the Accounting Number Format button.
   f. Click the Decrease Decimal button two times.
4. Apply the Comma format to numbers by completing the following steps:
   a. Select the range B5:C12.
   b. Click the Comma Style button in the Number group.
   c. Click the Decrease Decimal button two times.

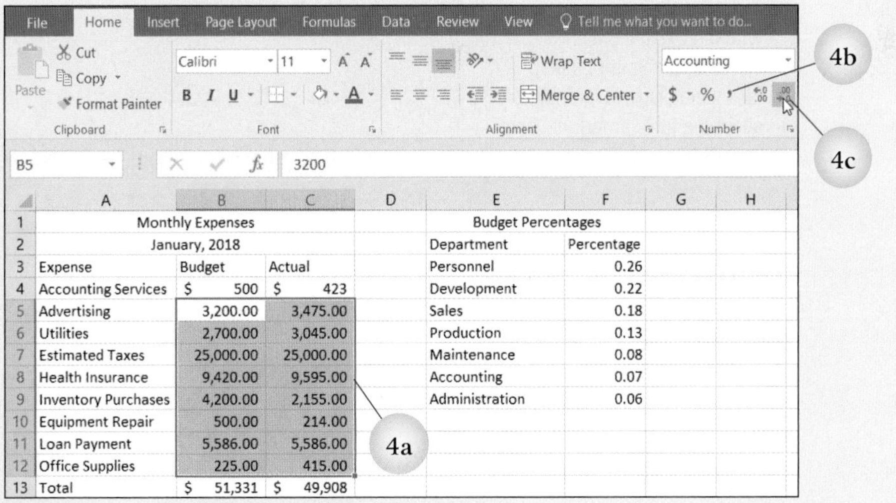

5. Apply the Percentage format to numbers by completing the following steps:
   a. Select the range F3:F9.
   b. Click the Percent Style button in the Number group on the Home tab.
6. Click in cell A1.
7. Save **1-MoExps.xlsx**.

Check Your Work

Project 4 **Use the Tell Me and Help Features** **3 Parts**

You will use the Tell Me feature to learn how to change the font size of text and display the Excel Help window with information about wrapping text. You will use the Help feature to learn more about entering data in cells, changing the font color, and printing a workbook.

Preview Finished Project

Tutorial

Using the Tell Me Feature

Quick Steps

Use the Tell Me Feature

1. Click in *Tell Me* text box.
2. Type topic or feature.
3. Click option at drop-down list.

Using the Tell Me Feature

Excel 2016 includes a Tell Me feature that provides information and guidance on how to complete certain actions. Use the Tell Me feature by clicking in the *Tell Me* text box on the ribbon to the right of the View tab and then typing a term, function, or action. As text is typed in the *Tell Me* text box, a drop-down list displays with options that are refined as more text is typed, which is referred to as "word-wheeling." The drop-down list contains options for completing the function, displaying information on the function from sources on the web, or displaying information on the action in the Excel Help window.

The Tell Me drop-down list also includes a Smart Lookup option. Clicking the Smart Lookup option opens the Smart Lookup task pane, as shown in Figure 1.10, at the right side of the screen with information on the typed text from a variety of Internet sources. Smart Lookup can also be accessed using the Smart Lookup button on the Review tab or by selecting a cell, right-clicking in the selected cell, and then clicking the *Smart Lookup* option at the shortcut menu.

Figure 1.10 Smart Lookup Task Pane

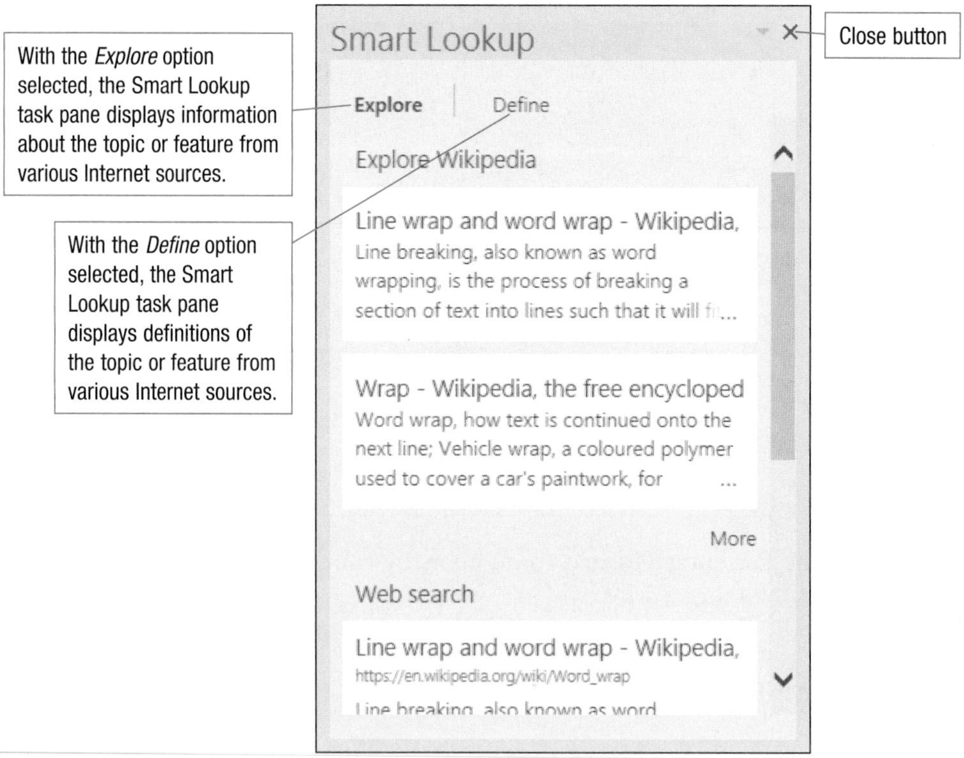

Project 4a Using the Tell Me Feature

Part 1 of 3

1. With **1-MoExps.xlsx** open, select the range A1:E1.
2. Click in the *Tell Me* text box and then type font size.
3. At the drop-down list, click the *Font Size* option.
4. At the side menu, click the *14* option. (This increases the font size of the text in the range A1:E1, and the height of row 1 automatically adjusts to accommodate the larger text.)
5. Use the Tell Me feature to display the Excel Help window with information on wrapping text by completing the following steps:
   a. Click in the *Tell Me* text box and then type wrap text.
   b. Click the *Get Help on "wrap text"* option.

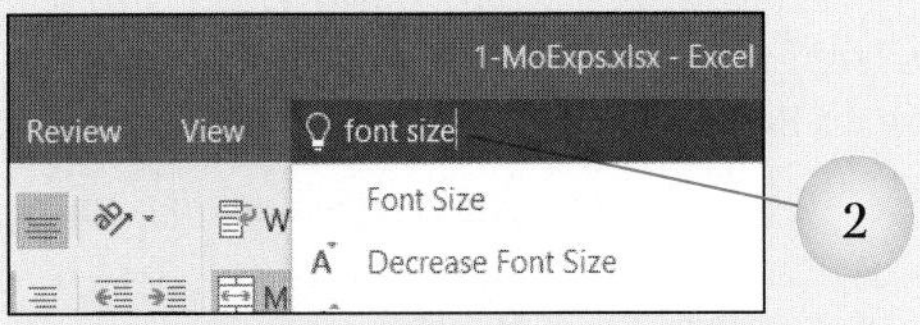

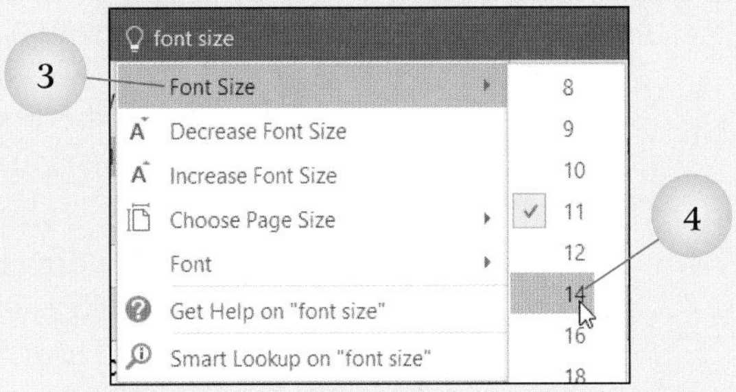

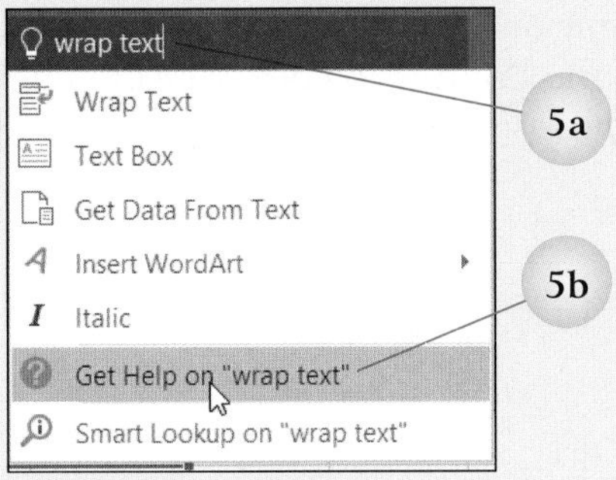

   c. At the Excel Help window, click a hyperlink to an article that interests you.
   d. After reading the information on wrapping text, close the Excel Help window by clicking the Close button in the upper right corner of the window.
6. Display information on scrolling in a workbook in the Smart Lookup task pane by completing the following steps:
   a. Click in the *Tell Me* text box and then type scrolling.
   b. Click the *Smart Lookup on "scrolling"* option. (The first time you use the Smart Lookup feature, the Smart Lookup task pane displays a message indicating that data will be sent to Bing and suggesting that you read the privacy statement for more details. At this message, click the Got it button.)
   c. If two options—*Explore* and *Define*—display at the top of the Smart Lookup task pane, click the *Define* option. This will display a definition of the word *scrolling* in the Smart Lookup task pane.
   d. Close the Smart Lookup task pane by clicking the Close button in the upper right corner of the task pane.
7. Save, print, and then close **1-MoExps.xlsx**.

Check Your Work

Tutorial

Using the Help Feature

Quick Steps

Use the Help Feature

1. Press F1.
2. Click in search text box.
3. Type term, function, or action.
4. Press Enter.

OR

1. Click in *Tell Me* text box.
2. Type term, function, or action.
3. Click *Get Help on* option.

Using Help

Microsoft Excel includes a Help feature that contains information about Excel features and commands. This on-screen reference manual is similar to Windows Help and the Help features in Word, PowerPoint, and Access. Press the keyboard shortcut F1 to display the Excel Help window, as shown in Figure 1.11.

Alternatively, type a term, function, or action in the *Tell Me* text box and then click the *Get Help on* option to open the Excel Help file with articles related to the typed text. In the Excel Help window, type a topic, feature, or question in the search text box and then press the Enter key or click the Search help button. Articles related to the search text display in the Excel Help window. Click an article and the article information displays in the Excel Help window. If the article contains a Show All hyperlink, click the hyperlink and the article expands to show additional information related to the topic. When the Show All hyperlink is clicked, it becomes the Hide All hyperlink.

The Excel Help window contains five buttons to the left of the search text box, as identified in Figure 1.11. Use the Back and Forward buttons to navigate in the window. Click the Home button to return to the Excel Help window opening screen. Print information on a topic or feature by clicking the Print button and then clicking the Print button at the Print dialog box. Make the text in the Excel Help window larger by clicking the Use Large Text button.

Figure 1.11 Excel Help Window

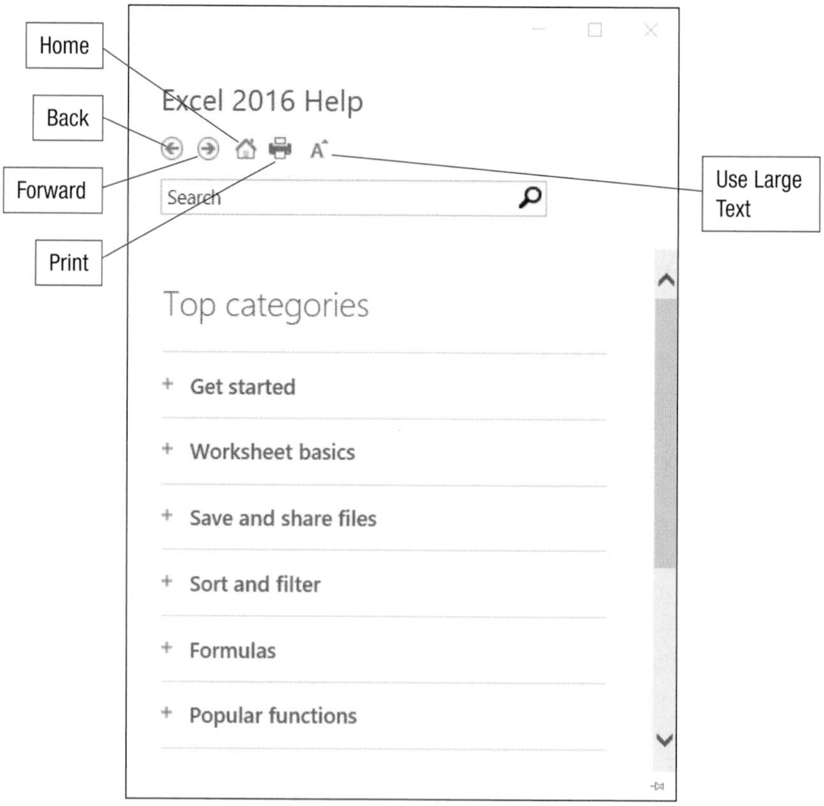

Getting Help from a ScreenTip

Hover the mouse pointer over a button and a ScreenTip displays with information about the button. Some button ScreenTips display with a Help icon and the Tell me more hyperlink. Click the Tell me more hyperlink text or press the F1 function key and the Excel Help window opens with information about the button feature.

Project 4b Using the Help Feature

Part 2 of 3

1. At the blank screen, press Ctrl + N to display a blank workbook. (Ctrl + N is the keyboard shortcut to open a blank workbook.)
2. Click in the *Tell Me* text box and then type enter data.
3. Click the *Get Help on "enter data"* option.
4. When the Excel Help window displays with a list of articles, click the article Enter data manually in worksheet cells hyperlink.
5. When the article displays, read the information about entering data in cells.
6. Click the Print button in the Excel Help window to display the Print dialog box. If you want to print the information about the topic, click the Print button; otherwise, click the Cancel button to close the dialog box.
7. Click the Use Large Text button in the Excel Help window to increase the size of the text.
8. Click the Use Large Text button again to return the text to the normal size.
9. Click the Back button to return to the previous window.
10. Click the Forward button to return to the article on entering data manually in worksheet cells.
11. Click the Home button to return to the original Excel Help window screen.
12. Click the Close button to close the Excel Help window.
13. Hover the mouse pointer over the Font Color button in the Alignment group on the Home tab until the ScreenTip displays and then click the Tell me more hyperlink at the bottom of the ScreenTip.
14. At the Excel Help window, read the information and then close the window.

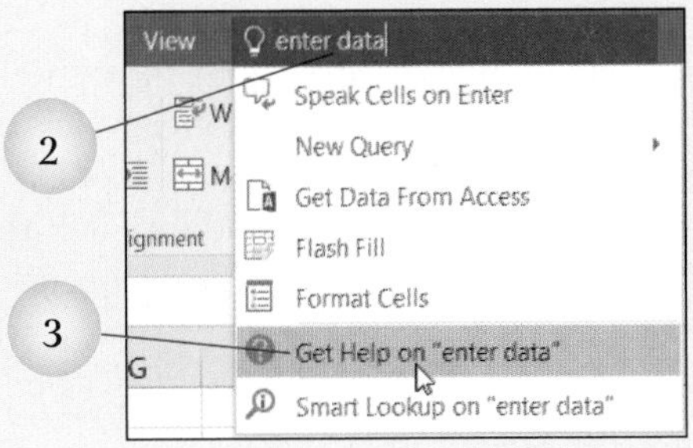

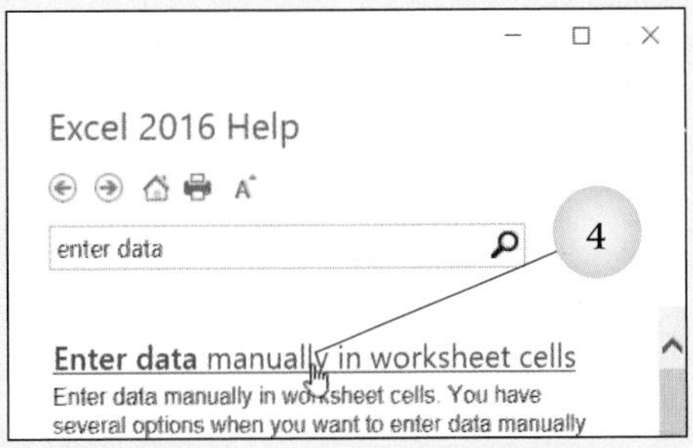

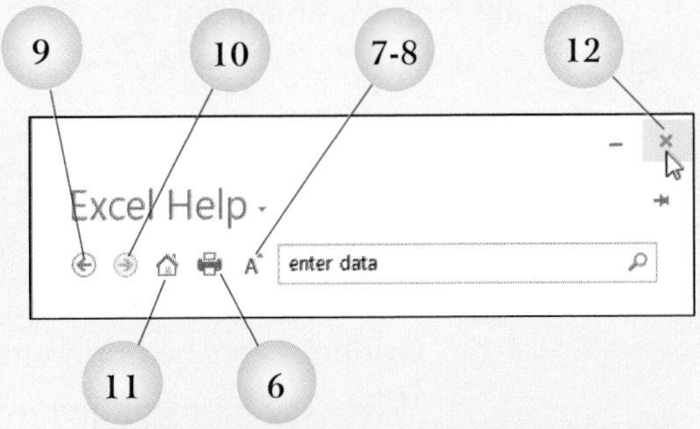

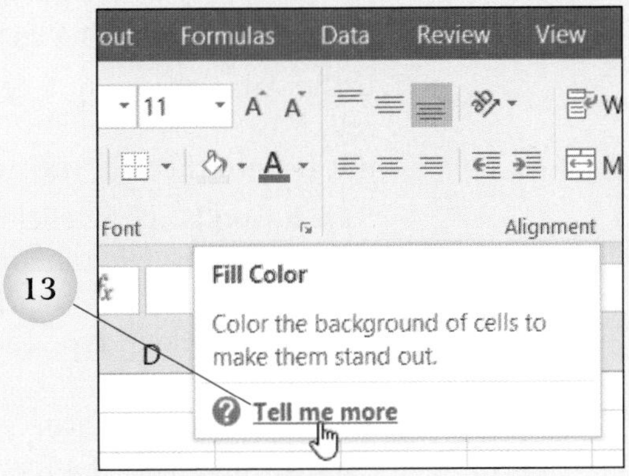

Getting Help in a Dialog Box or at the Backstage Area

Some dialog boxes and the backstage area contain a Help button that, when clicked, displays the Excel Help window with specific information about the dialog box or backstage area. After reading and/or printing the information, close the dialog box by clicking the Close button in the upper right corner of the dialog box or close the backstage area by clicking the Back button or pressing the Esc key.

Project 4c Getting Help in a Dialog Box and Backstage Area **Part 3 of 3**

1. At the blank workbook, click the File tab and then click the *Print* option.
2. At the Print backstage area, click the Microsoft Excel Help button in the upper right corner of the backstage area.
3. At the Excel Help window, click the hyperlink to an article on printing that interests you. Read the article and then close the Excel Help window.
4. Click the Back button to return to the blank workbook.
5. At the blank workbook, click the Number group dialog box launcher.
6. At the Format Cells dialog box with the Number tab selected, click the Help button in the upper right corner of the dialog box.

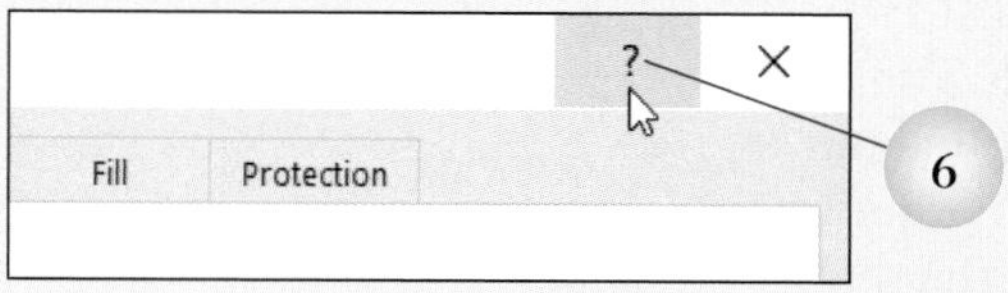

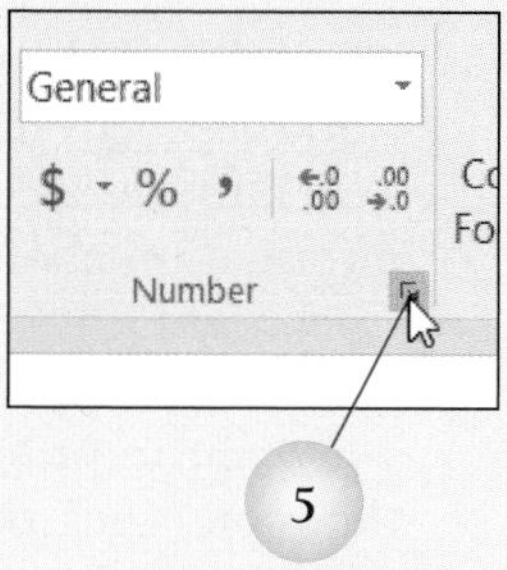

7. Click the hyperlink to the article on available number formats.
8. Read the article, close the Excel Help window, and then close the Format Cells dialog box.
9. Close the blank workbook.

Chapter Summary

- A file created in Excel is called a *workbook* and consists of individual worksheets.
- The intersection of a column and a row in a worksheet is referred to as a *cell*. Gridlines are the horizontal and vertical lines that define cells.
- When the insertion point is positioned in a cell, the cell name (also called the *cell reference*) displays in the Name box at the left side of the Formula bar. The cell name includes the column letter and row number.
- If the data entered in a cell consists of text (letters) and does not fit into the cell, it overlaps the cell to the right. If the data consists of numbers and does not fit into the cell, the numbers change to number symbols (###).
- Save a workbook by clicking the Save button on the Quick Access Toolbar or by clicking the File tab and then clicking the *Save As* option. At the Save As backstage area, click the *Browse* option. At the Save As dialog box, navigate to the desired folder, type the workbook name in the *File name* text box, and then press the Enter key.
- To replace data in a cell, click in the cell and then type the new data. To edit data within a cell, double-click in the cell and then make the necessary changes.
- Print a workbook by clicking the File tab, clicking the *Print* option, and then clicking the Print button.

- Close a workbook by clicking the File tab and then clicking the *Close* option or by using the keyboard shortcut Ctrl + F4.
- Close Excel by clicking the Close button in the upper right corner of the screen or using the keyboard shortcut Alt + F4.
- The AutoComplete feature automatically inserts a previous entry if the character or characters being typed in a cell match a previous entry. The AutoCorrect feature corrects many common typographical errors. The AutoFill fill handle adds the same or consecutive data into a range of cells.
- Open a workbook by clicking the File tab and then clicking the *Open* option. At the Open backstage area, click the *Browse* option. At the Open dialog box, double-click the workbook.
- Use the AutoSum button in the Editing group on the Home tab to find the total or average of data in columns or rows.
- Select all the cells in a column by clicking the column header. Select all the cells in a row by clicking the row header. Select all the cells in a worksheet by clicking the Select All button immediately to the left of the column headers.
- Change the column width by dragging or double-clicking the column boundary line.
- Merge and center adjacent cells by selecting them and then clicking the Merge & Center button in the Alignment group on the Home tab.
- Format numbers in cells with buttons in the Number group on the Home tab.
- The Tell Me feature provides information and guidance on how to complete actions. The *Tell Me* text box is located on the ribbon to the right of the View tab.
- Use the Tell Me feature, click a hyperlink in a button ScreenTip, or press F1 to display the Excel Help window. At this window, type a topic in the search text box and then press the Enter key.
- Some dialog boxes and the backstage area contain a Help button that, when clicked, displays information specific to the dialog box or backstage area.

Commands Review

FEATURE	RIBBON TAB, GROUP/OPTION	BUTTON	KEYBOARD SHORTCUT
Accounting format	Home, Number	$	
AutoSum	Home, Editing	Σ	Alt + =
close Excel			Alt + F4
close workbook	File, *Close*		Ctrl + F4
Comma format	Home, Number	,	
decrease decimal place	Home, Number	.00 →.0	
Excel Help window			F1
Go To dialog box	Home, Editing		Ctrl + G
increase decimal place	Home, Number	←.0 .00	
merge and center cells	Home, Alignment		
Open backstage area	File, *Open*		Ctrl + O
Percentage format	Home, Number	%	Ctrl + Shift + %
Print backstage area	File, *Print*		Ctrl + P
Save As backstage area	File, *Save As*		Ctrl + S

Workbook

Chapter study tools and assessment activities are available in the *Workbook* ebook. These resources are designed to help you further develop and demonstrate mastery of the skills learned in this chapter.

Microsoft®

Excel®

CHAPTER 2

Inserting Formulas in a Worksheet

Performance Objectives

Upon successful completion of Chapter 2, you will be able to:

1 Write formulas with mathematical operators
2 Type a formula in the Formula bar
3 Copy a formula
4 Identify common formula and function errors
5 Use the Insert Function dialog box to insert a formula in a cell
6 Write formulas with the AVERAGE, MAX, MIN, COUNT, COUNTA, NOW, and TODAY functions
7 Display formulas
8 Use absolute and mixed cell references in formulas

Precheck

Check your current skills to help focus your study.

Excel is a powerful decision-making tool that contains data that can be manipulated in "What if?" situations. Insert a formula in a worksheet and then manipulate the data to make projections, answer specific questions, and plan for the future. For example, the owner of a company might prepare a worksheet on production costs and then determine the impact on company revenues if production is increased or decreased. Insert a formula in a worksheet to perform calculations on values. A formula contains a mathematical operator, value, cell reference, cell range, and function. Formulas can be written that add, subtract, multiply, and/or divide values. Formulas can also be written that calculate averages, percentages, minimum and maximum values, and much more. As you learned in Chapter 1, Excel includes an AutoSum button in the Editing group on the Home tab that inserts a formula to calculate the total of a range of cells, along with some other commonly used formulas. Along with the AutoSum button, Excel includes a Formulas tab that offers a variety of functions, which are built-in formulas, to create formulas.

Data Files

Before beginning chapter work, copy the EL1C2 folder to your storage medium and then make EL1C2 the active folder.

SNAP

If you are a SNAP user, launch the Precheck and Tutorials from your Assignments page.

Project 1 Insert Formulas in a Worksheet 4 Parts

You will open a worksheet containing data and then insert formulas to calculate differences, salaries, and percentages of budgets.

Preview Finished Project

Tutorial

Entering Formulas Using the Keyboard

Hint After typing a formula in a cell, press the Enter key, the Tab key, Shift + Tab, or click the Formula bar.

Writing Formulas with Mathematical Operators

As explained in Chapter 1, the AutoSum button in the Editing group on the Home tab creates a formula. A formula can also be written using mathematical operators. Commonly used mathematical operators and their purposes are displayed in Table 2.1. When writing a formula, begin it with the equals sign (=). For example, to create a formula that divides the contents of cell B2 by the contents of cell C2 and inserts the result in cell D2, make D2 the active cell and then type *=b2/c2*. The column reference letters used in formulas can be entered as either lowercase or uppercase letters. If the column reference letters are entered in a formula in lowercase, Excel will automatically convert the column reference letters to uppercase.

Table 2.1 Mathematical Operators

Operator	Purpose	Operator	Purpose
+	addition	/	division
-	subtraction	%	percentage
*	multiplication	^	exponentiation

Tutorial

Copying Formulas

Copying a Formula with Relative Cell References

In many worksheets, the same basic formula is used repetitively. In a situation where a formula is copied to other locations in a worksheet, use a relative cell reference. Copy a formula containing relative cell references and the cell references change. For example, if the formula *=SUM(A2:C2)* is entered in cell D2 and then copied relatively into cell D3, the formula in cell D3 displays as *=SUM(A3:C3)*. (Additional information on cell references is provided later in this chapter in the section "Using an Absolute Cell Reference in a Formula.")

Fill

Quick Steps

Copy a Formula Relatively

1. Insert formula in cell.
2. Select cell containing formula and all cells to which the formula is to be copied.
3. Click Fill button.
4. Click direction option.

To copy a formula relatively in a worksheet, use the Fill button or the fill handle. (You used the fill handle to copy a formula in Chapter 1.) To use the Fill button, select the cell containing the formula and all the cells to which the formula is to be copied and then click the Fill button in the Editing group on the Home tab. At the Fill button drop-down list, click the direction. For example, click the *Down* option if the formula is being copied down the worksheet.

Project 1a Finding Differences by Inserting and Copying a Formula

Part 1 of 4

1. Open **HCReports.xlsx** and then save it with the name **2-HCReports**.
2. Insert a formula by completing the following steps:
   a. Make cell D3 active.
   b. Type the formula =c3-b3.
   c. Press the Enter key.
3. Copy the formula into the range D4:D10 by completing the following steps:
   a. Select the range D3:D10.
   b. Click the Fill button in the Editing group on the Home tab and then click *Down* at the drop-down list.

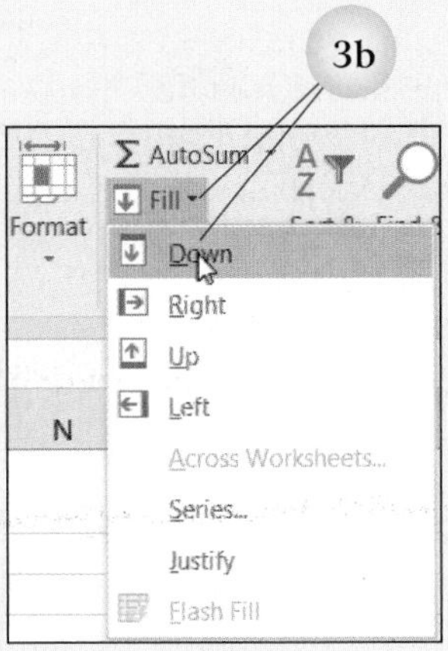

4. Save **2-HCReports.xlsx**.
5. With the worksheet open, make the following changes to cell contents:
   B4: Change *48,290* to *46425*
   C6: Change *61,220* to *60000*
   B8: Change *55,309* to *57415*
   B9: Change *12,398* to *14115*
6. Make cell D3 active, apply the Accounting format by clicking the Accounting Number Format button in the Number group on the Home tab, and then click the Decrease Decimal button two times to decrease the digits past the decimal point to none.
7. Save **2-HCReports.xlsx**.

Check Your Work

As explained in Chapter 1, the fill handle can be used to copy a formula up, down, left, or right within a worksheet. To use the fill handle, insert the data in the cell (text, value, formula, etc.). With the cell active, position the mouse pointer on the fill handle until the mouse pointer turns into a thin black cross. Click and hold down the left mouse button, drag and select the cells, and then release the mouse button. When dragging a cell containing a formula, a relative version of the formula is copied to the selected cells.

Checking Cell References in a Formula

Hint Use the fill handle to copy a relative version of a formula.

To verify if a formula is using the correct cell references, double-click in a cell containing a formula and the cells referenced in the formula display with a colored border and shading in the worksheet. This feature makes it easy to identify which cells are being referenced in a formula and is helpful when trying to identify errors that may occur in a formula.

Project 1b Calculating Salaries by Inserting and Copying a Formula with the Fill Handle

Part 2 of 4

1. With **2-HCReports.xlsx** open, insert a formula by completing the following steps:
   a. Make cell D15 active.
   b. Click in the Formula bar text box and then type =c15*b15.
   c. Click the Enter button on the Formula bar.
2. Copy the formula into the range D16:D20 by completing the following steps:
   a. Make sure cell D15 is still the active cell.
   b. Position the mouse pointer on the fill handle at the lower right corner of cell D15 until the pointer turns into a thin black cross.
   c. Click and hold down the left mouse button, drag into cell D20, and then release the mouse button.
3. Save **2-HCReports.xlsx**.
4. Double-click in cell D20 to display the formula with cell references color coded to ensure the formula was copied relatively and then press the Enter key to exit Edit mode.
5. Make the following changes to cell contents in the worksheet:
   B16: Change *20* to *28*
   C17: Change *18.75* to *19.10*
   B19: Change *15* to *24*
6. Select the range D16:D20 and then apply the Comma format by clicking the Comma Style button in the Number group on the Home tab.
7. Save **2-HCReports.xlsx**.

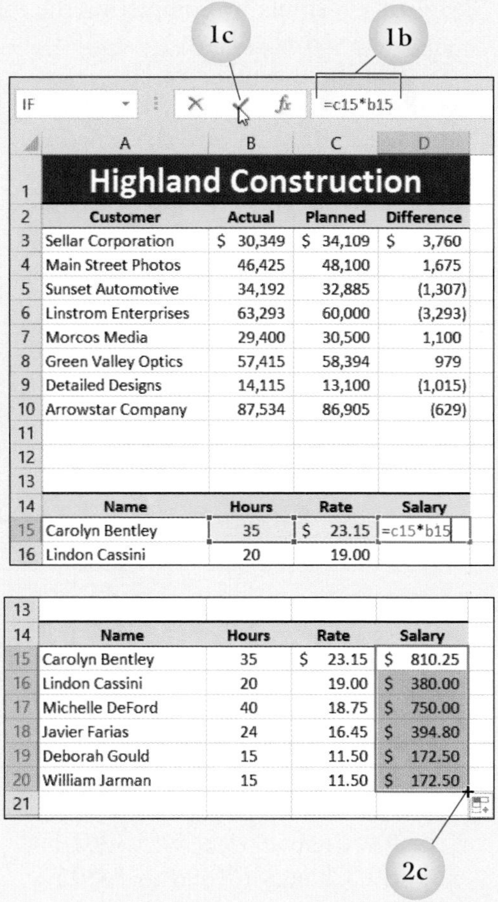

Check Your Work

Tutorial

Entering Formulas Using the Mouse

Writing a Formula by Pointing

Quick Steps

Write a Formula by Pointing
1. Click in cell that will contain formula.
2. Type equals sign.
3. Click in cell to be referenced in formula.
4. Type mathematical operator.
5. Click in next cell reference.
6. Press Enter.

The formulas written in Projects 1a and Project 1b used cell references such as *=c3-b3*. Another method for writing a formula is to "point" to the specific cells that are to be part of the formula. Creating a formula by pointing is more accurate than typing the cell reference because a mistake can be made when the cell reference is typed.

To write a formula by pointing, click in the cell that will contain the formula, type the equals sign to begin the formula, and then click in the cell to be referenced in the formula. This inserts a moving border around the cell and changes the mode from Enter to Point. (The word *Point* displays at the left side of the Status bar.) Type the mathematical operator and then click in the next cell reference. Continue in this manner until all the cell references are specified and then press the Enter key. This ends the formula and inserts the result of the calculation in the active cell. When a formula is written by pointing, the range of cells to be included in the formula can be selected.

Project 1c Writing a Formula by Pointing That Calculates Percentage of Actual Budget

Part 3 of 4

1. With **2-HCReports.xlsx** open, enter a formula by pointing that calculates the percentage of actual budget by completing the following steps:
   a. Make cell D25 active.
   b. Type the equals sign (=).
   c. Click in cell B25. (This inserts a moving border around the cell and changes the mode from Enter to Point.)
   d. Type the forward slash symbol (/).
   e. Click in cell C25.
   f. Make sure the formula in D25 is *=B25/C25* and then press the Enter key.

23				
24	Expense	Actual	Budget	% of Actual
25	Salaries	$ 126,000	$ 124,000	=B25/C25
26	Commissions	58,000	54,500	
27	Media space	8,250	10,100	
28	Travel expenses	6,350	6,000	
29	Dealer display	4,140	4,500	
30	Payroll taxes	2,430	2,200	
31	Telephone	1,450	1,500	
32				

1a-1f

2. Make cell D25 active, click the fill handle and hold down the left mouse button, drag into cell D31, and then release the mouse button.
3. Save **2-HCReports.xlsx**.

Budget	% of Actual
$ 124,000	102%
54,500	106%
10,100	82%
6,000	106%
4,500	92%
2,200	110%
1,500	97%

2

Check Your Work

Tutorial

Determining the Order of Operations

Determining the Order of Operations

If a formula contains two or more operators, Excel uses the same order of operations used in algebra. From left to right in a formula, this order is negations (negative number—a number preceded by -) first, then percentages (%), then exponentiations (^), followed by multiplications (*), divisions (/), additions (+), and subtractions (-). To change the order of operations, put parentheses around the part of the formula that is to be calculated first. For example, if cells A1, B1, and C1 all contain the value 5, the result of the formula *=a1+b1*c1* will be 30 (because 5*5=25 and 5+25=30). However, if parentheses are placed around the first two cell references so the formula displays as *=(a1+b1)*c1*, the result will be 50 (because 5+5=10 and 10*5=50).

Excel requires each left parenthesis to be paired with a right parenthesis. If a formula is missing a left or right parenthesis, a message box will display explaining that an error exists in the formula and providing a possible correction, which can be accepted or declined. This feature is useful when creating a formula that contains multiple layers of parentheses (called *nested parentheses*) because it will identify any missing left or right parentheses in the formula. Parentheses can also be used in various functions to further determine the order of operations.

Using the Trace Error Button

Trace Error

When typing or editing data in a worksheet, a button may display near the active cell. The general term for this button is *smart tag*. The display of the smart tag button varies depending on the action performed. In Project 1d, you will insert a formula that causes a smart tag button named the Trace Error button to appear. When the Trace Error button appears, a small dark-green triangle also displays in the upper left corner of the cell. Click the Trace Error button and a drop-down list displays with options for updating the formula to include specific cells, getting help with the error, ignoring the error, editing the error in the Formula bar, and completing an error check. In Project 1d, two of the formulas you insert return the correct results. You will click the Trace Error button, read about what Excel perceives to be the error, and then tell Excel to ignore the error.

Identifying Common Formula Errors

Excel is a sophisticated program that requires data input and formula creation to follow strict guidelines in order to function properly. When guidelines that specify how data or formulas are entered are not followed, Excel will display one of many error codes. When an error is identified with a code, determining and then fixing the problem is easier than if no information is provided. Table 2.2 lists some common error codes.

Most errors in Excel result from the user incorrectly inputting data into a worksheet. However, most error messages will not display until the data is used in a formula or function. Common mistakes made while inputting data include placing text in a cell that requires a number, entering data in the wrong location, and entering numbers in an incorrect format. Other errors result from entering a formula or function improperly. A formula will often display an error message if it is trying to divide a number by 0 or contains a circular reference (that is, when a formula within a cell uses the results of that formula in the same cell).

Table 2.2 Common Error Codes

Error Code	Meaning
#DIV/O	A formula is attempting to divide a number by 0.
#N/A	An argument parameter has been left out of a function.
#NAME?	A function name is not entered correctly.
#NUM!	An argument parameter does not meet a function's requirements.
#REF!	A referenced cell no longer exists within a worksheet.
#VALUE	The data entered is the wrong type (for example, text instead of numbers).

Project 1d Writing a Formula by Pointing That Calculates Percentage of Down Time

Part 4 of 4

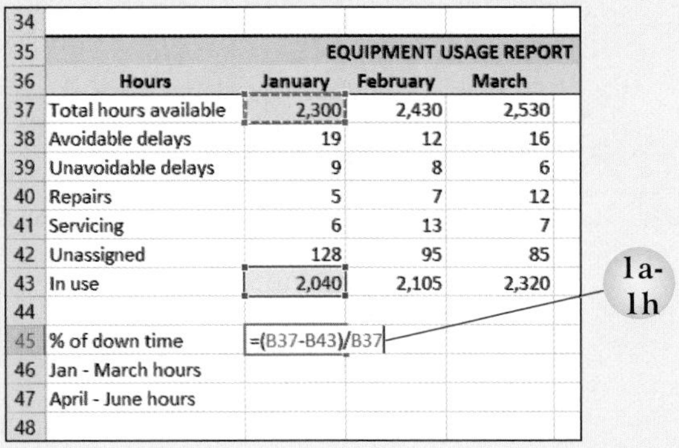

1. With **2-HCReports.xlsx** open, enter a formula by pointing that calculates the percentage of equipment down time by completing the following steps:
   a. Make cell B45 active.
   b. Type the equals sign followed by the left parenthesis (=().
   c. Click in cell B37. (This inserts a moving border around the cell and changes the mode from Enter to Point.)
   d. Type the minus symbol (-).
   e. Click in cell B43.
   f. Type the right parenthesis followed by the forward slash ()/).
   g. Click in cell B37.
   h. Make sure the formula in cell B45 is *=(B37-B43)/B37* and then press the Enter key.
2. Make cell B45 active, click the fill handle and hold down the left mouse button, drag into cell G45, and then release the mouse button.

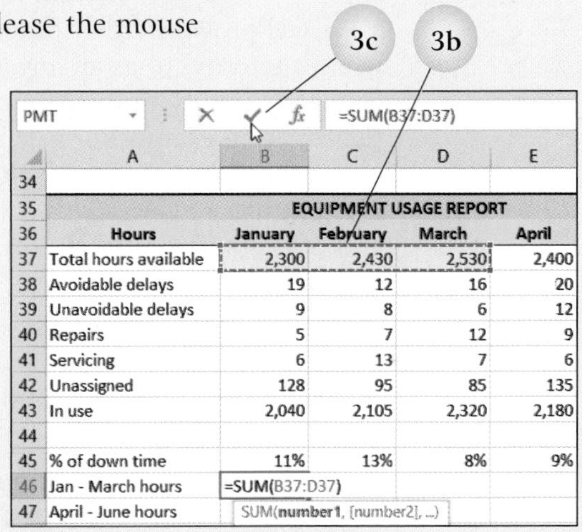

3. Enter a formula by dragging into a range of cells by completing the following steps:
   a. Click in cell B46 and then click the AutoSum button in the Editing group on the Home tab.
   b. Select the range B37:D37.
   c. Click the Enter button on the Formula bar. (This inserts *7,260* in cell B46.)
4. Click in cell B47 and then complete steps similar to those in Step 3 to create a formula that totals hours available from April through June (the range E37:G37). (This inserts *7,080* in cell B47.)
5. Click in cell B46 and notice the Trace Error button. Complete the following steps to read about the error and then tell Excel to ignore it:
   a. Click the Trace Error button.
   b. At the drop-down list, click the *Help on this error* option.
   c. Read the information in the Excel Help window and then close the window.
   d. Click the Trace Error button again and then click *Ignore Error* at the drop-down list.

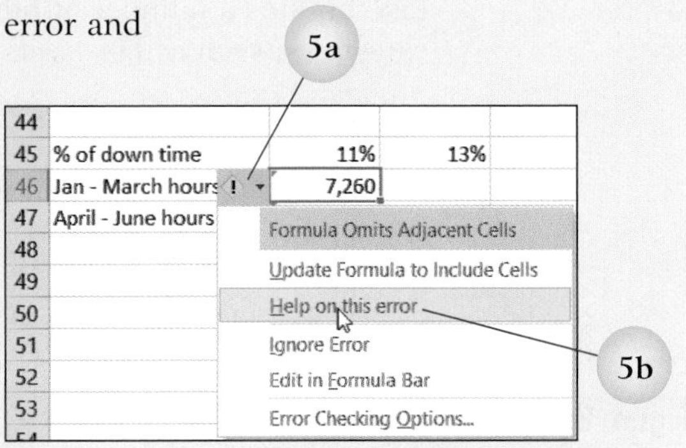

6. Remove the dark-green triangle from cell B47 by completing the following steps:
   a. Click in cell B47.
   b. Click the Trace Error button and then click *Ignore Error* at the drop-down list.
7. Save, print, and then close **2-HCReports.xlsx**.

Check Your Work

Project 2 Insert Formulas with Statistical Functions **4 Parts**

You will use the AVERAGE function to determine average test scores, use the MINIMUM and MAXIMUM functions to determine lowest and highest averages, use the COUNT function to count the number of students taking a test, use the COUNTA function to determine the number of tests administered, and display a formula in a cell rather than the result of a formula.

Preview Finished Project

Inserting Formulas with Functions

In Project 2b in Chapter 1, the AutoSum button was used to insert the formula *=SUM(b2:b5)* in a cell. The beginning section of the formula, *=SUM*, is called a *function*, and it is a built-in formula. Using a function takes fewer keystrokes when creating a formula. For example, using the *=SUM* function made it unnecessary to type each cell to be included in the formula with the plus symbol (+) between cell entries.

Excel provides other functions for writing formulas. A function operates on what is referred to as an *argument*. An argument may consist of a constant, a cell reference, or another function. In the formula *=SUM(b2:b5)*, the cell range *(b2:b5)* is an example of a cell reference argument. An argument may also contain a *constant*. A constant is a value entered directly into the formula. For example, in the formula *=SUM(b3:b9,100)*, the cell range *b3:b9* is a cell reference argument and *100* is a constant. In this formula, 100 is always added to the sum of the cells.

The phrase *returning the result* is used to describe when a value calculated by the formula is inserted in a cell. The term *returning* refers to the process of calculating the formula and the term *result* refers to the value inserted in the cell.

Insert Function

Type a function in a cell in a worksheet or use the Insert Function button on the Formula bar or the Formulas tab to write the formula. Figure 2.1 displays the Formulas tab, which provides the Insert Function button and other buttons for inserting functions in a worksheet. The Function Library group on the Formulas tab contains a number of buttons for inserting functions from a variety of categories, such as *Financial*, *Logical*, *Text*, and *Date & Time*.

Click the Insert Function button on the Formula bar or the Formulas tab and the Insert Function dialog box displays, as shown in Figure 2.2. At the Insert Function dialog box, the most recently used functions display in the *Select a function* list box. Choose a function category by clicking the *Or select a category* option box arrow and then clicking the category at the drop-down list. Use the *Search for a function* search box to locate a specific function.

Figure 2.1 Formulas Tab

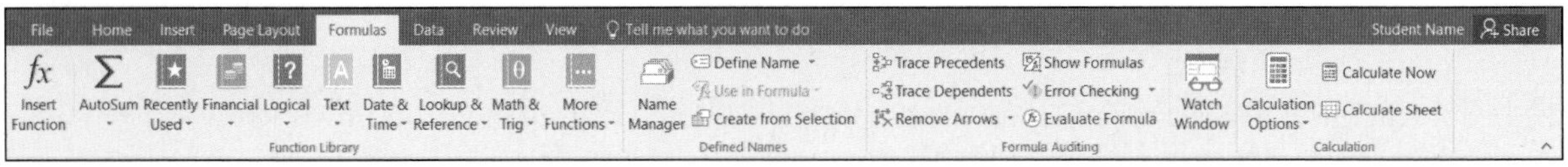

Figure 2.2 Insert Function Dialog Box

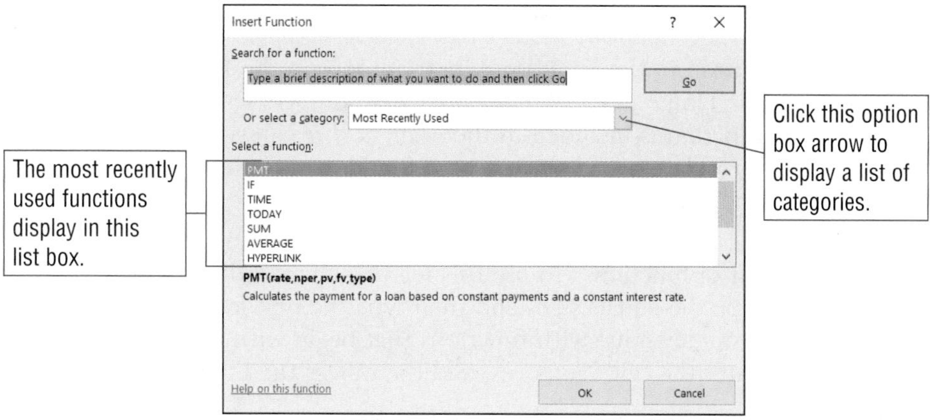

Hint You can also display the Insert Function dialog box by clicking the AutoSum button arrow and then clicking *More Functions.*

With the function category selected, choose a function in the *Select a function* list box and then click OK. This displays a Function Arguments dialog box, like the one shown in Figure 2.3. At this dialog box, enter in the *Number1* text box the range of cells to be included in the formula, any constants to be included as part of the formula, or another function.

Type a cell reference or a range of cells in an argument text box or point to a cell or select a range of cells with the mouse pointer. Pointing to cells or selecting a range of cells using the mouse pointer is the preferred method of entering data into an argument text box because there is less chance of making errors. After entering a range of cells, a constant, or another function, click OK.

More than one argument can be included in a function. If the function contains more than one argument, press the Tab key to move the insertion point to the *Number2* text box and then enter the second argument. If the function dialog box covers a specific cell or cells, move the dialog box by positioning the mouse pointer on the dialog box title bar, clicking and holding down the left mouse button, dragging the dialog box to a different location, and then releasing the mouse button.

Figure 2.3 Example of a Function Arguments Dialog Box

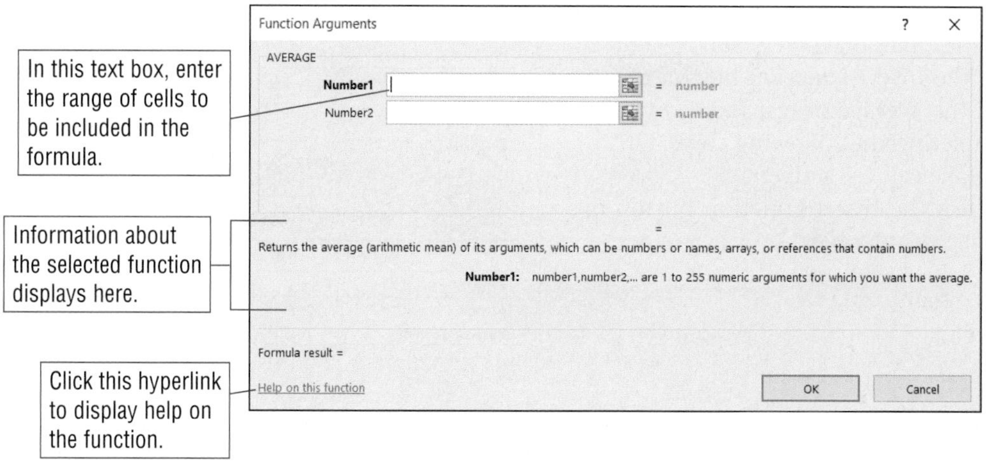

Hint Click the AutoSum button arrow on the Formulas tab and common functions display in a drop-down list.

Excel performs over 300 functions that are divided into these 13 categories: *Financial*, *Date & Time*, *Math & Trig*, *Statistical*, *Lookup & Reference*, *Database*, *Text*, *Logical*, *Information*, *Engineering*, *Cube*, *Compatibility*, and *Web*. Clicking the AutoSum button in the Function Library group on the Formulas tab or the Editing group on the Home tab automatically adds numbers with the SUM function. The SUM function is included in the *Math & Trig* category. In some projects in this chapter, formulas will be written with functions in other categories, including *Statistical* and *Date & Time*.

Excel includes the Formula AutoComplete feature that displays a drop-down list of functions. To use this feature, click in the cell or in the Formula bar text box, type the equals sign, and then type the first letter of the function. This displays a drop-down list with functions that begin with the letter. Double-click the function, enter the cell references, and then press the Enter key.

Tutorial

Using Statistical Functions

Writing Formulas with Statistical Functions

Write formulas with statistical functions such as AVERAGE, MAX, MIN, and COUNT. The AVERAGE function returns the average (arithmetic mean) of the arguments. The MAX function returns the largest value in a set of values and the MIN function returns the smallest value in a set of values. Use the COUNT or COUNTA functions to count the number of cells that contain numbers or letters within the specified range.

Finding Averages A common function in a formula is the AVERAGE function. With this function, a range of cells are added together and then divided by the number of cells. In Project 2a, you will use the AVERAGE function, to add all the test scores for a student and then divide that number by the total number of scores. You will use the Insert Function button to simplify the creation of the formula containing an AVERAGE function.

One of the advantages to using formulas in a worksheet is that the data can be easily manipulated to answer certain questions. In Project 2a, you will learn the impact of retaking certain tests on the final average score.

Project 2a Averaging Test Scores in a Worksheet

Part 1 of 4

1. Open **DWTests.xlsx** and then save it with the name **2-DWTests**.
2. Use the Insert Function button to find the average of test scores by completing the following steps:
   a. Make cell E4 active.
   b. Click the Insert Function button on the Formula bar.

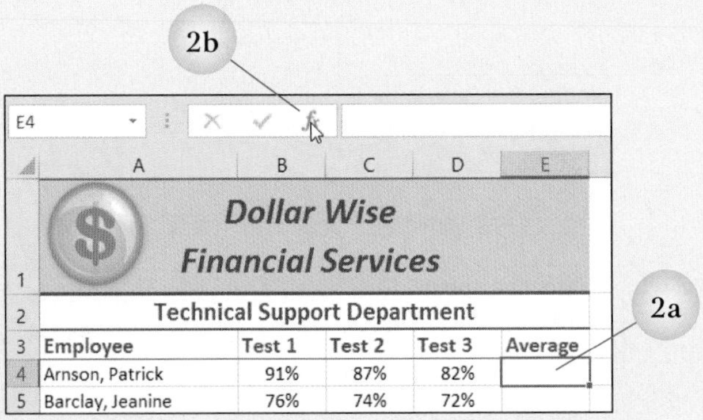

c. At the Insert Function dialog box, click the *Or select a category* option box arrow and then click *Statistical* at the drop-down list.

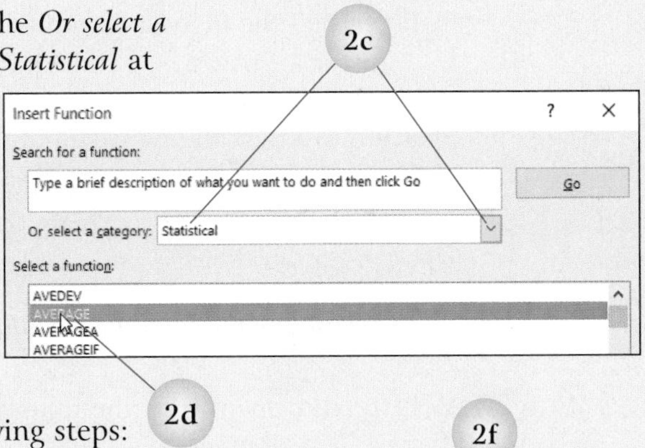

d. Click *AVERAGE* in the *Select a function* list box.

e. Click OK.

f. At the Function Arguments dialog box, make sure *B4:D4* displays in the *Number1* text box. (If not, type b4:d4 in the *Number1* text box.)

g. Click OK.

3. Copy the formula by completing the following steps:

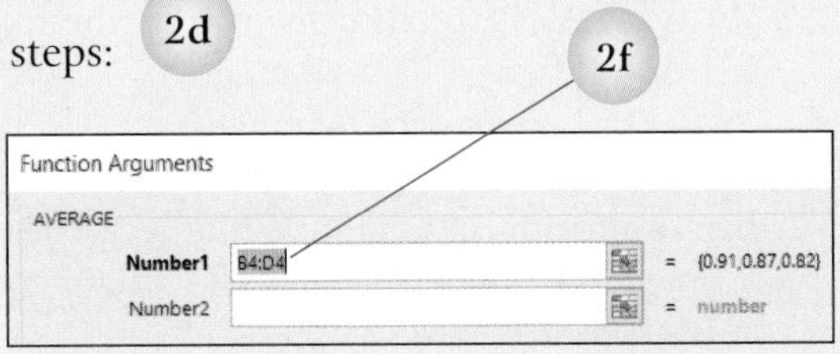

a. Make sure cell E4 is still active.

b. Position the mouse pointer on the fill handle until the pointer turns into a thin black cross.

c. Click and hold down the left mouse button, drag into cell E16, and then release the mouse button.

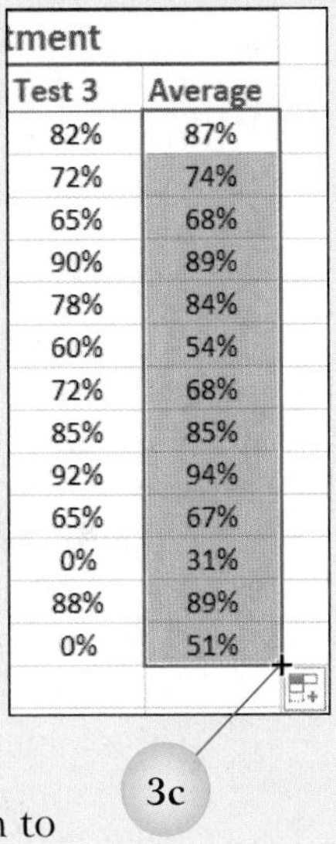

4. Save and then print **2-DWTests.xlsx**.
5. After viewing the averages of test scores, you notice that a couple of students have low averages. You decide to see what happens to these average scores if students retake the tests on which they scored the lowest. You decide that a student can score a maximum of 70% on a retake of the test. Make the following changes to test scores to see how the changes affect the test averages:

   B9: Change *50* to *70*
   C9: Change *52* to *70*
   D9: Change *60* to *70*
   B10: Change *62* to *70*
   B14: Change *0* to *70*
   D14: Change *0* to *70*
   D16: Change *0* to *70*

6. Save and then print **2-DWTests.xlsx**. (Compare the test averages of Teri Fisher-Edwards, Stephanie Flanery, Claude Markovits, and Douglas Pherson to see how retaking the tests affects their final test averages.)

Check Your Work

When a function such as the AVERAGE function calculates cell entries, it ignores certain cell entries. The AVERAGE function will ignore text in cells and blank cells (not zeros). For example, in the worksheet containing test scores, a couple of cells contained *0%*. This entry was included in the averaging of the test scores. To prevent including that particular test in the average, enter text in the cell such as *N/A* (for *not applicable*) or leave the cell blank.

Finding Maximum and Minimum Values The MAX function in a formula returns the maximum value in a cell range and the MIN function returns the minimum value in a cell range. For example, the MAX and MIN functions in a worksheet containing employee hours can be used to determine which employee worked the most hours and which worked the least. In a worksheet containing sales commissions, the MAX and MIN functions can be used to identify the salesperson who earned the highest commission and the one who earned the lowest.

Insert a MAX or a MIN function into a formula in the same manner as an AVERAGE function. In Project 2b, you will use the Formula AutoComplete feature to insert the MAX function in cells to determine the highest test score average and the Insert Function button to insert the MIN function to determine the lowest test score average.

Project 2b Finding Maximum and Minimum Values in a Worksheet

Part 2 of 4

1. With **2-DWTests.xlsx** open, type the following in the specified cells:
   A19: Highest Test Average
   A20: Lowest Test Average
   A21: Average of Completed Tests
2. Insert a formula to identify the highest test score average by completing the following steps:
   a. Make cell B19 active.
   b. Type =m. (This displays the Formula AutoComplete list.)
   c. Double-click *MAX* in the Formula AutoComplete list.
   d. Type e4:e16) and then press the Enter key.

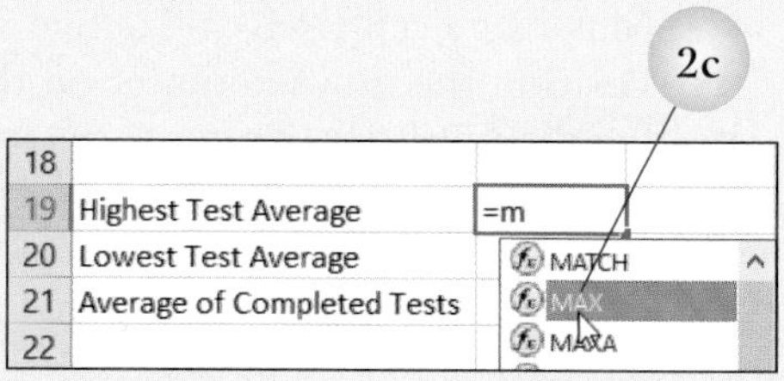

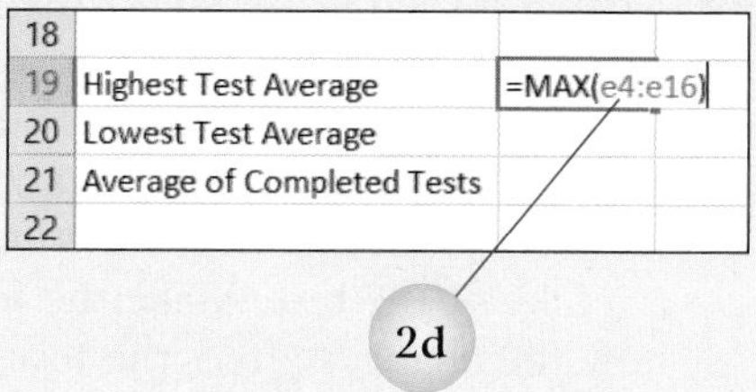

3. Insert a formula to identify the lowest test score average by completing the following steps:
   a. Make sure cell B20 is active.
   b. Click the Insert Function button on the Formula bar.
   c. At the Insert Function dialog box, make sure *Statistical* is selected in the *Or select a category* option box and then click *MIN* in the *Select a function* list box. (You will need to scroll down the list to display *MIN*.)
   d. Click OK.
   e. At the Function Arguments dialog box, type e4:e16 in the *Number1* text box.
   f. Click OK.

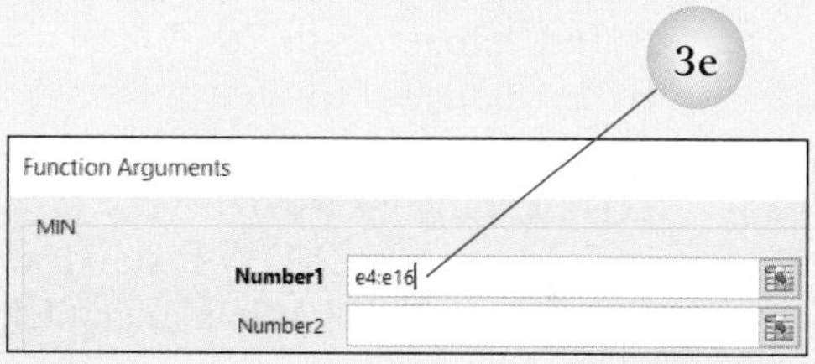

4. Insert a formula to determine the average of the completed test scores by completing the following steps:
   a. Make cell B21 active.
   b. Click the Formulas tab.
   c. Click the Insert Function button in the Function Library group.
   d. At the Insert Function dialog box, make sure *Statistical* is selected in the *Or select a category* option box and then click *AVERAGE* in the *Select a function* list box.
   e. Click OK.
   f. At the Function Arguments dialog box, make sure the insertion point is positioned in the *Number1* text box with existing text selected, use the mouse pointer to select the range E4:E16 in the worksheet (you may need to move the dialog box to display the cells), and then click OK.

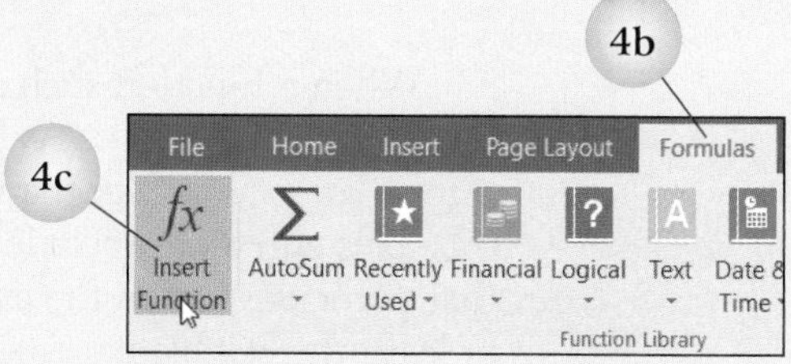

5. Save and then print **2-DWTests.xlsx**.
6. Change the *70%* values (which were previously *0%*) in cells B14, D14, and D16 to *N/A*. (This will cause the average test scores for Claude Markovits and Douglas Pherson to increase and will change the average of completed tests.)
7. Save and then print **2-DWTests.xlsx**.

Check Your Work

Counting Numbers in a Range Use the COUNT function to count the numeric values in a range and use the COUNTA function to count the cells in a range containing any characters. In Project 2c, you will use the COUNT function to specify the number of students who have completed Test 3. In the worksheet, the cells containing the text *N/A* are not counted by the COUNT function. Additionally, you will use the COUNTA function to determine how many students should have completed Test 3 by counting the cells that contain test scores and the text N/A.

Project 2c Counting the Number of Students Taking Tests

Part 3 of 4

1. With **2-DWTests.xlsx** open, make cell A22 active.
2. Type Test 3 Completed.
3. Make cell B22 active.
4. Insert a formula counting the number of students who have completed Test 3 by completing the following steps:
   a. With cell B22 active, click in the Formula bar text box.
   b. Type =c.
   c. At the Formula AutoComplete list, scroll down the list until *COUNT* displays and then double-click *COUNT*.
   d. Type d4:d16) and then press the Enter key.

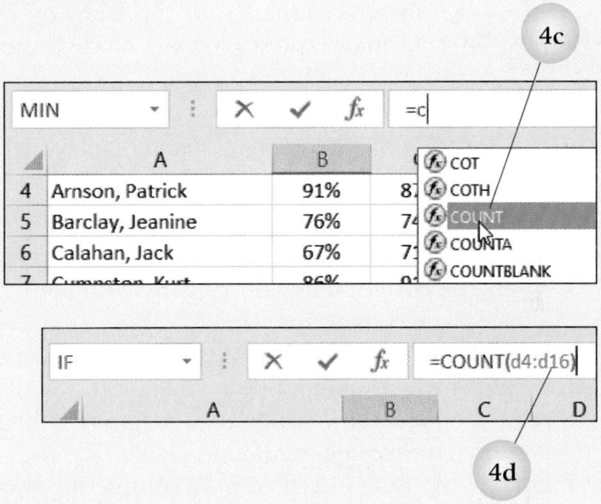

5. Count the number of students who have completed Test 3 by completing the following steps:
   a. Make cell A23 active.
   b. Type Test 3 Administered.
   c. Make cell B23 active.
   d. Click the Insert Function button on the Formula bar.
   e. At the Insert Function dialog box, make sure *Statistical* is selected in the *Or select a category* option box.
   f. Scroll down the list of functions in the *Select a function* list box until *COUNTA* is visible and then double-click *COUNTA*.
   g. At the Function Arguments dialog box, type d4:d16 in the *Value1* text box and then click OK.
6. Save and then print **2-DWTests.xlsx**.

Check Your Work

Tutorial

Using Date and Time Functions

Date & Time

Calculate Now

Writing Formulas with the NOW and TODAY Functions

The NOW and TODAY functions are part of the *Date & Time* category of functions. The NOW function returns the current date and time in a date-and-time format. The TODAY function returns the current date in a date format. Both the NOW and TODAY functions automatically update when a workbook is opened. To access the NOW and TODAY functions, click the Date & Time button in the Function Library group on the Formulas tab. The formulas can also be accessed at the Insert Function dialog box.

The NOW and TODAY functions can also be updated without closing and then reopening the workbook. To update a workbook that contains a NOW or TODAY function, click the Calculate Now button in the Calculation group on the Formulas tab or press the F9 function key.

Tutorial

Displaying Formulas

Show Formulas

Hint Press Ctrl + ` to display the formulas in a worksheet rather than the results.

Displaying Formulas

In some situations, displaying the formulas in a worksheet, rather than the results, may be useful—for example, to display formulas for auditing purposes or to check formulas for accuracy. Display all the formulas in a worksheet, rather than the results, by clicking the Formulas tab and then clicking the Show Formulas button in the Formula Auditing group. The display of formulas can also be turned on with the keyboard shortcut Ctrl + `. (This symbol is the grave accent, generally located to the left of the 1 key on the keyboard.) To turn off the display of formulas, press Ctrl + ` or click the Show Formulas button on the Formulas tab.

Project 2d Using the NOW Function and Displaying Formulas — Part 4 of 4

1. With **2-DWTests.xlsx** open, make cell A26 active and then type Prepared by:.
2. Make cell A27 active and then type your first and last names.
3. Insert the current date and time by completing the following steps:
   a. Make cell A28 active.
   b. Click the Date & Time button in the Function Library group on the Formulas tab and then click *NOW* at the drop-down list.
   c. At the Function Arguments dialog box telling you that the function takes no argument, click OK.
4. Update the time in cell A28 by completing the following steps:
   a. Wait for 1 minute.
   b. Click the Calculate Now button in the Calculation group on the Formulas tab.
5. Click the Show Formulas button in the Formula Auditing group to turn on the display of formulas.
6. Print the worksheet with the formulas. (The worksheet will print on two pages.)
7. Press Ctrl + ` to turn off the display of formulas.
8. Save, print, and then close **2-DWTests.xlsx**.

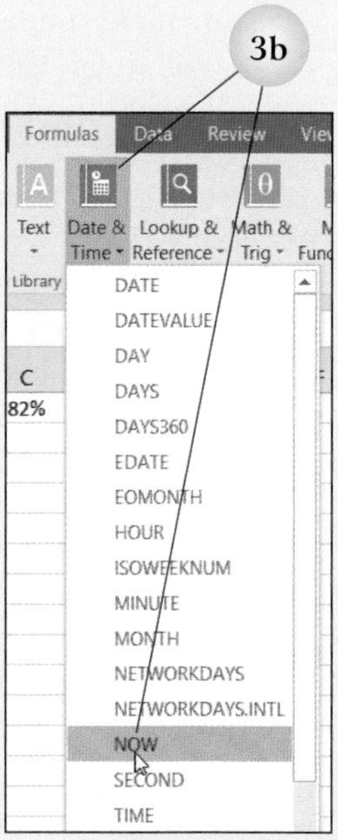

Check Your Work

Project 3 Insert Formulas Using Absolute and Mixed Cell References — 4 Parts

You will insert a formula containing an absolute cell reference that determines the effect on earnings with specific increases, insert a formula with multiple absolute cell references that determines the weighted average of scores, and use mixed cell references to determine simple interest.

Preview Finished Project

Tutorial

Absolute Addressing

Using Absolute and Mixed Cell References in Formulas

A reference identifies a cell or range of cells in a worksheet and can be relative, absolute, or mixed. A relative cell reference refers to a cell relative to a position in a formula. An absolute cell reference refers to a cell in a specific location. When a formula is copied, a relative cell reference adjusts while an absolute cell reference remains constant. A mixed cell reference does both: either the column remains absolute and the row is relative or the column is relative and the row remains absolute. Distinguish among relative, absolute, and mixed cell references using the dollar symbol ($). Type a dollar symbol before the column and/or row cell reference in a formula to specify that the column or row is an absolute cell reference.

Using an Absolute Cell Reference in a Formula

In this chapter, you have learned to copy a relative formula. For example, if the formula *=SUM(A2:C2)* in cell D2 is copied relatively into cell D3, it changes to *=SUM(A3:C3)*. In some situations, a formula may contain an absolute cell reference, which always refers to a cell in a specific location. In Project 3a, you will add a column for projected job earnings and then consider "What if?" situations using a formula with an absolute cell reference. To identify an absolute cell reference, insert a dollar symbol before the row and the column. For example, the absolute cell reference *C12* is typed as *c12* in a formula.

Project 3a Inserting and Copying a Formula with an Absolute Cell Reference — Part 1 of 4

1. Open **CCReports.xlsx** and then save it with the name **2-CCReports**.
2. Determine the effect of a 10% pay increase on actual job earnings by completing the following steps:
   a. Make cell C3 active, type the formula =b3*b12, and then press the Enter key.
   b. Make cell C3 active and then use the fill handle to copy the formula into the range C4:C10.
   c. Make cell C3 active, click the Accounting Number Format button on the Home tab, and then click the Decrease Decimal button two times.

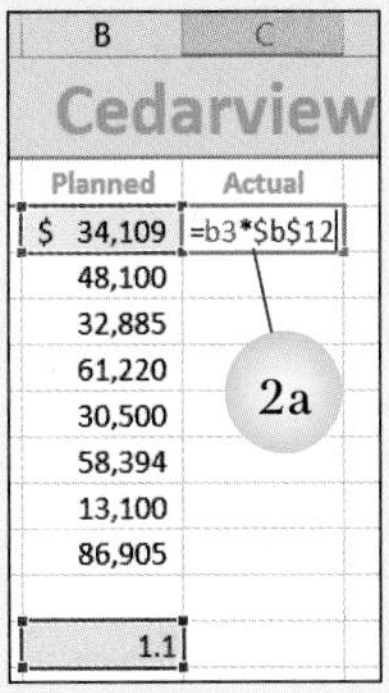
B
C
Cedarview
Planned
Actual
$ 34,109
=b3*b12
48,100
32,885
61,220
30,500
58,394
13,100
86,905
1.1
2a

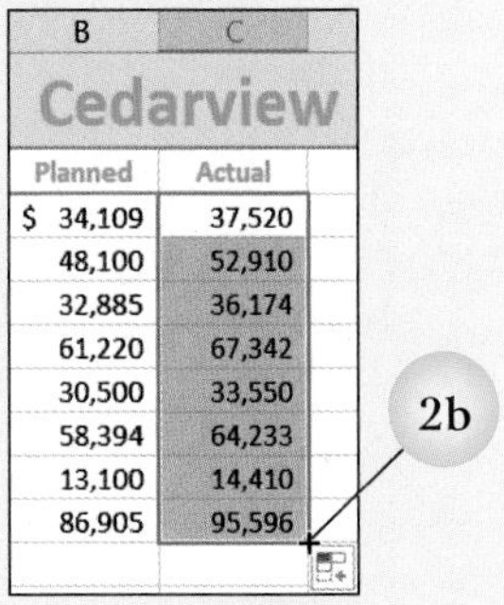
B
C
Cedarview
Planned
Actual
$ 34,109
37,520
48,100
52,910
32,885
36,174
61,220
67,342
30,500
33,550
58,394
64,233
13,100
14,410
86,905
95,596
2b

3. Save and then print **2-CCReports.xlsx**.
4. With the worksheet still open, determine the effect of a 10% pay decrease on actual job earnings by completing the following steps:
   a. Make cell B12 active.
   b. Type 0.9 and then press the Enter key.
5. Save and then print the **2-CCReports.xlsx**.
6. Determine the effect of a 20% pay increase on actual job earnings. (To do this, type 1.2 in cell B12 and then press the Enter key.)
7. Save and then print **2-CCReports.xlsx**.

B	C
Cedarview	
Planned	Actual
$ 34,109	$ 30,698
48,100	43,290
32,885	29,597
61,220	55,098
30,500	27,450
58,394	52,555
13,100	11,790
86,905	78,215
0.9	

4b

Check Your Work

In Project 3a, you created a formula with one absolute cell reference. A formula also can be created with multiple absolute cell references. For example, in Project 3b, you will create a formula that contains both relative and absolute cell references to determine the average of training scores based on specific weight percentages. In a weighted average, some scores have more value (weight) than others. For example, in Project 3b, you will create a formula that determines the weighted average of training scores that gives more weight to the *Carpentry* percentages than the *Plumbing* or *Electrical* percentages.

Project 3b Inserting and Copying a Formula with Multiple Absolute Cell References

Part 2 of 4

1. With **2-CCReports.xlsx** open, insert the following formulas:
   a. Insert a formula in cell B23 that averages the percentages in the range B17:B22.
   b. Copy the formula in cell B23 into cells C23 and D23.
2. Insert a formula that determines the weighted average of training scores by completing the following steps:
   a. Make cell E17 active.
   b. Type the following formula:
      =b24*b17+c24*c17+d24*d17
   c. Press the Enter key.
   d. Copy the formula in cell E17 into the range E18:E22.
   e. With the range E17:E22 selected, click the Decrease Decimal button three times.
3. Save and then print **2-CCReports.xlsx**.
4. With the worksheet still open, determine the effect on weighted training scores if the weighted values change by completing the following steps:
   a. Make cell B24 active, type 30, and then press the Enter key.
   b. Make cell D24 active, type 40, and then press the Enter key.
5. Save and then print **2-CCReports.xlsx**.

Employee Training				
Name	Plumbing	Electrical	Carpentry	Weighted Average
Allesandro	76%	80%	84%	80%
Ellington	66%	72%	64%	67%
Goodman	90%	88%	94%	91%
Huntington	76%	82%	88%	83%
Kaplan-Downing	90%	84%	92%	89%
Larimore	58%	62%	60%	60%
Training Averages	76%	78%	80%	
Training Weights	30%	30%	40%	

4a 4b

Check Your Work

Using a Mixed Cell Reference in a Formula

The formula you created in Step 2a in Project 3a contained a relative cell reference (b3) and an absolute cell reference (b12). A formula can also contain a mixed cell reference. As stated earlier, in a mixed cell reference, either the column remains absolute and the row is relative or the column is relative and the row remains absolute. In Project 3c, you will insert a number of formulas—two of which will contain mixed cell references. You will insert the formula *=e29*e$26* to calculate withholding tax and *=e29*h$36* to calculate social security tax. The dollar symbol before each row number indicates that the row is an absolute cell reference.

Project 3c Determining Payroll Using Formulas with Absolute and Mixed Cell References

Part 3 of 4

1. With **2-CCReports.xlsx** open, make cell E29 active and then type the following formula that calculates the gross pay, including overtime (press the Enter key after typing each formula):
   =(b29*c29+(b29*b36*d29))
2. Copy the formula in cell E29 into the range E30:E34.
3. Make cell F29 active and then type the following formula that calculates the amount of withholding tax:
   =e29*e$36
4. Copy the formula in cell F29 into the range F30:F34.
5. Make cell G29 active and then type the following formula that calculates the amount of social security tax:
   =e29*h$36
6. Copy the formula in cell G29 into the range G30:G34.
7. Make cell H29 active and then type the following formula that calculates net pay:
   =e29-(f29+g29)
8. Copy the formula in cell H29 into the range H30:H34.
9. Select the range E29:H29 and then click the Accounting Number Format button.
10. Save **2-CCReports.xlsx**.

Check Your Work

As you learned in Project 3c, a formula can contain a mixed cell reference. In Project 3d, you will create the formula *=$a41*b$40*. In the first cell reference in the formula, *$a41*, the column is absolute and the row is relative. In the second cell reference, *b$40*, the column is relative and the row is absolute. The formula containing the mixed cell reference allows you to fill in the column and row data using only one formula.

Identify an absolute or mixed cell reference by typing a dollar symbol before the column and/or row reference or press the F4 function key to cycle through the various cell references. For example, type *=a41* in a cell, press the F4 function key, and the cell reference changes to *=a41*. Press F4 again and the cell reference changes to *=a$41*. Press F4 a third time and the cell reference changes to *=$a41* and press F4 a fourth time and the cell reference changes back to *=a41*.

Project 3d Determining Simple Interest Using a Formula with Mixed Cell References

Part 4 of 4

1. With **2-CCReports.xlsx** open, make cell B41 the active cell and then insert a formula containing mixed cell references by completing the following steps:
   a. Type =a41 and then press the F4 function key three times. (This changes the cell reference to *$A41*.)
   b. Type *b40 and then press the F4 function key two times. (This changes the cell reference to *B$40*.)
   c. Make sure the formula displays as =*$A41*B$40* and then press the Enter key.

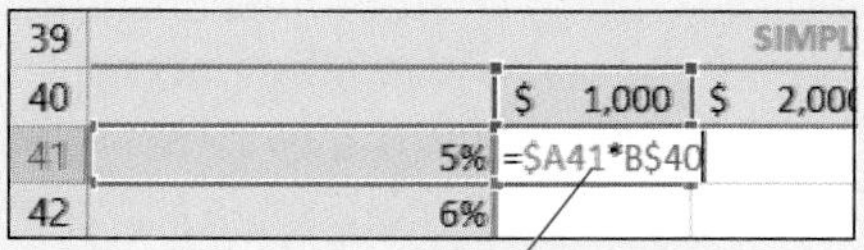

2. Copy the formula to the right by completing the following steps:
   a. Make cell B41 active and then use the fill handle to copy the formula into cell F41.
   b. With the range B41:F41 selected, use the fill handle to copy the formula into cell F51.

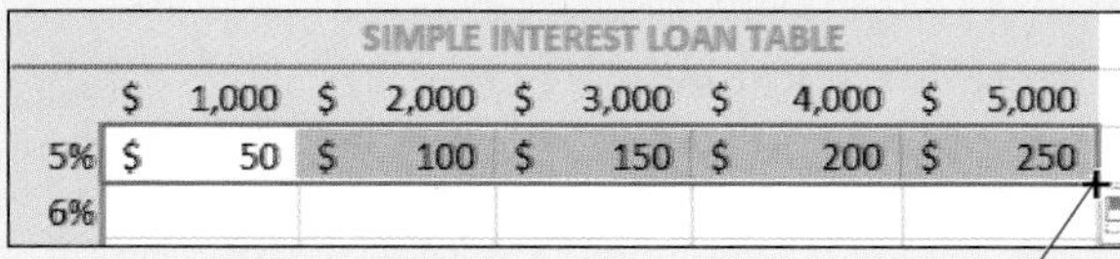

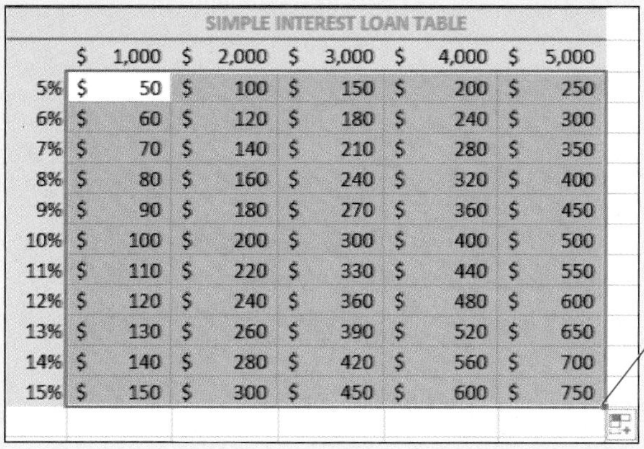

SIMPLE INTEREST LOAN TABLE					
	$ 1,000	$ 2,000	$ 3,000	$ 4,000	$ 5,000
5%	$ 50	$ 100	$ 150	$ 200	$ 250
6%	$ 60	$ 120	$ 180	$ 240	$ 300
7%	$ 70	$ 140	$ 210	$ 280	$ 350
8%	$ 80	$ 160	$ 240	$ 320	$ 400
9%	$ 90	$ 180	$ 270	$ 360	$ 450
10%	$ 100	$ 200	$ 300	$ 400	$ 500
11%	$ 110	$ 220	$ 330	$ 440	$ 550
12%	$ 120	$ 240	$ 360	$ 480	$ 600
13%	$ 130	$ 260	$ 390	$ 520	$ 650
14%	$ 140	$ 280	$ 420	$ 560	$ 700
15%	$ 150	$ 300	$ 450	$ 600	$ 750

2b

3. Save, print, and then close **2-CCReports.xlsx**.

Check Your Work

Chapter Summary

- Type a formula in a cell and the formula displays in the cell and in the Formula bar. If cell entries are changed, a formula automatically recalculates the values and inserts the result in the cell.
- Write a formula using commonly used operators, such as addition (+), subtraction (-), multiplication (*), division (/), percentage (%), and exponentiation (^). When writing a formula, begin with the equals sign (=).
- Copy a formula to other cells in a row or column with the Fill button in the Editing group on the Home tab or with the fill handle in the bottom right corner of the active cell.
- Double-click in a cell containing a formula and the cell references displays with a colored border and cell shading.

- Another method for writing a formula is to point to specific cells that are part of the formula as the formula is being built.
- Excel uses the same order of operations as algebra and that order can be modified by adding parentheses around certain parts of a formula.
- If Excel detects an error in a formula, a Trace Error button appears and a dark-green triangle displays in the upper left corner of the cell containing the formula.
- Excel displays different error codes for different formula errors. An error code helps identify an error in a formula by providing information on the specific issue.
- Excel performs over 300 functions that are divided into 13 categories.
- A function operates on an argument, which may consist of a cell reference, a constant, or another function. When a value calculated by a formula is inserted in a cell, this is referred to as *returning the result*.
- The AVERAGE function returns the average (arithmetic mean) of the arguments. The MAX function returns the largest value in a set of values and the MIN function returns the smallest value in a set of values. The COUNT function counts the number of cells containing numbers within the list of arguments. The COUNTA function counts the number of cells containing any data, numerical or alphabetical.
- The NOW function returns the current date and time and the TODAY function returns the current date.
- Turn on the display of formulas in a worksheet with the Show Formulas button on the Formulas tab or with the keyboard shortcut Ctrl + ` (grave accent).
- A reference identifies a cell or a range of cells in a worksheet and can be relative, absolute, or mixed. Identify an absolute cell reference by inserting a dollar symbol ($) before the column and row. Cycle through the various cell reference options by typing the cell reference and then pressing the F4 function key.

Commands Review

FEATURE	RIBBON TAB, GROUP	BUTTON	KEYBOARD SHORTCUT
cycle through cell references			F4
display formulas	Formulas, Formula Auditing		Ctrl + `
Insert Function dialog box	Formulas, Function Library	*fx*	Shift + F3
SUM function	Home, Editing OR Formulas, Function Library	Σ	Alt + =
update formulas	Formulas, Calculation		F9

Workbook

Chapter study tools and assessment activities are available in the *Workbook* ebook. These resources are designed to help you further develop and demonstrate mastery of the skills learned in this chapter.

Microsoft®

Excel®

CHAPTER 3

Formatting a Worksheet

Performance Objectives

Upon successful completion of Chapter 3, you will be able to:

1 Change column widths and row heights
2 Insert rows and columns
3 Delete cells, rows, and columns
4 Clear data in cells
5 Apply formatting to data in cells
6 Apply formatting to selected data using the Mini toolbar
7 Apply a theme and customize the theme font and colors
8 Format numbers
9 Apply formatting at the Format Cells dialog box
10 Repeat the last action
11 Automate formatting with Format Painter
12 Hide and unhide rows and columns

Precheck

Check your current skills to help focus your study.

The appearance of a worksheet on screen and how it looks when printed is called the *format*. In Chapter 1, you learned how to apply basic formatting to cells in a worksheet. Additional types of formatting include changing column width and row height; applying character formatting such as bold, italic, and underlining; specifying number formatting; inserting and deleting rows and columns; and applying borders, shading, and patterns to cells. You can also apply formatting to a worksheet with a theme. A theme is a set of formatting choices that include colors and fonts.

Data Files

Before beginning chapter work, copy the EL1C3 folder to your storage medium and then make EL1C3 the active folder.

SNAP

If you are a SNAP user, launch the Precheck and Tutorials from your Assignments page.

Project 1 Format a Product Pricing Worksheet — 7 Parts

You will open a workbook containing a worksheet with product pricing data and then format it by changing column widths and row heights, inserting and deleting rows and columns, and clearing data in cells. You will also apply font and alignment formatting to data in cells.

Preview Finished Project

Tutorial

Adjusting Column Width and Row Height

Changing Column Width

The columns in a worksheet are the same width by default. In some worksheets, column widths may need to be changed to accommodate more or less data. Change column widths using the mouse on column boundary lines or at a dialog box.

Changing Column Width Using Column Boundaries

Hint To change the width of all the columns in a worksheet, click the Select All button and then drag a column boundary line to the desired position.

As explained in Chapter 1, column width can be adjusted by dragging the column boundary line or adjusted to the longest entry by double-clicking the boundary line. When dragging a column boundary line, the column width displays in a box above the mouse pointer. The number that displays represents the average number of characters in the standard font that can fit in a cell.

The width of selected adjacent columns can be changed at the same time. To do this, select the columns and then drag one of the column boundary lines within the selected columns. When dragging the boundary line, the column width changes for all the selected columns. To select adjacent columns, position the cell pointer on the first column header to be selected (the mouse pointer turns into a black down-pointing arrow), click and hold down the left mouse button, drag the cell pointer into the last column header, and then release the mouse button.

Project 1a Changing Column Width Using a Column Boundary Line — Part 1 of 7

1. Open **CMProducts.xlsx** and then save it with the name **3-CMProducts**.
2. Insert a formula in cell D2 that multiplies the price in cell B2 with the number in cell C2. Copy the formula in cell D2 down into the range D3:D14.
3. Change the width of column D by completing the following steps:
   a. Position the mouse pointer on the column boundary line in the column header between columns D and E until it turns into a double-headed arrow pointing left and right.
   b. Click and hold down the left mouse button, drag the column boundary line to the right until *Width: 11.00* displays in the box, and then release the mouse button.

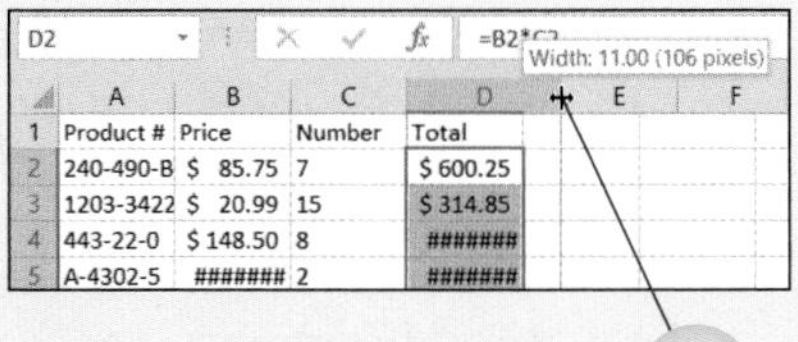

3a

4. Make cell D15 active and then insert the sum of the range D2:D14.
5. Change the width of columns A and B by completing the following steps:
   a. Select columns A and B. To do this, position the cell pointer on the column A header, click and hold down the left mouse button, drag the cell pointer into the column B header, and then release the mouse button.
   b. Position the cell pointer on the column boundary line between columns A and B until it turns into a double-headed arrow pointing left and right.

c. Click and hold down the left mouse button, drag the column boundary line to the right until *Width: 10.33* displays in the box, and then release the mouse button.
6. Adjust the width of column C to accommodate the longest entry by double-clicking on the column boundary line between columns C and D.
7. Save **3-CMProducts.xlsx**.

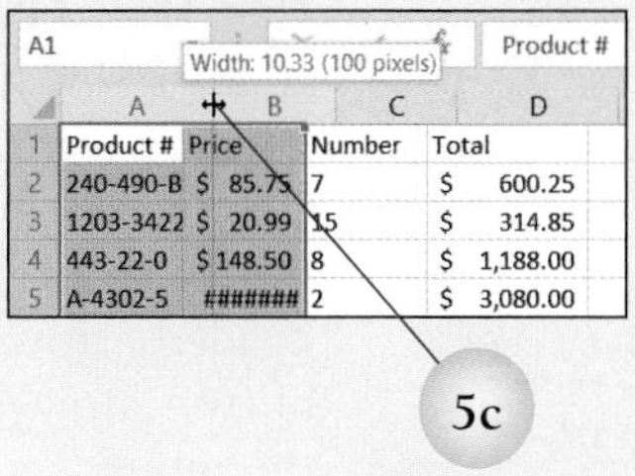

Check Your Work

Changing Column Width at the Column Width Dialog Box

Use the *Column width* measurement box in the Column Width dialog box, shown in Figure 3.1, to specify a column width number. Increase the number to make the column wider and decrease the number to make the column narrower.

Format

Quick Steps

Change Column Width

Drag column boundary line.
OR
Double-click column boundary line.
OR
1. Click Format button.
2. Click *Column Width*.
3. Type width.
4. Click OK.

Display the Column Width dialog box by clicking the Format button in the Cells group on the Home tab and then clicking *Column Width* at the drop-down list. At the Column Width dialog box, type a measurement number (the number represents the number of characters in the standard font that can fit in the column) and then press the Enter key or click OK.

Figure 3.1 Column Width Dialog Box

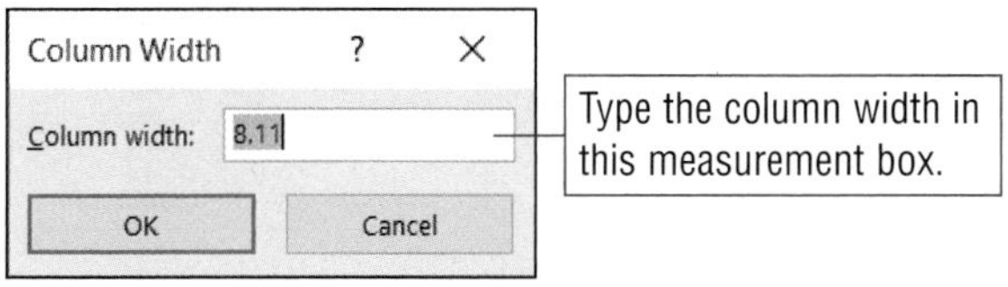

Project 1b Changing Column Width at the Column Width Dialog Box Part 2 of 7

1. With **3-CMProducts.xlsx** open, change the width of column A by completing the following steps:
   a. Make any cell in column A active.
   b. Click the Format button in the Cells group on the Home tab and then click *Column Width* at the drop-down list.
   c. At the Column Width dialog box, type 12.7 in the *Column width* measurement box.
   d. Click OK to close the dialog box.
2. Make any cell in column B active and then change the width of column B to 12.5 characters by completing steps similar to those in Step 1.
3. Make any cell in column C active and then change the width of column C to 8 characters by completing steps similar to those in Step 1.
4. Save **3-CMProducts.xlsx**.

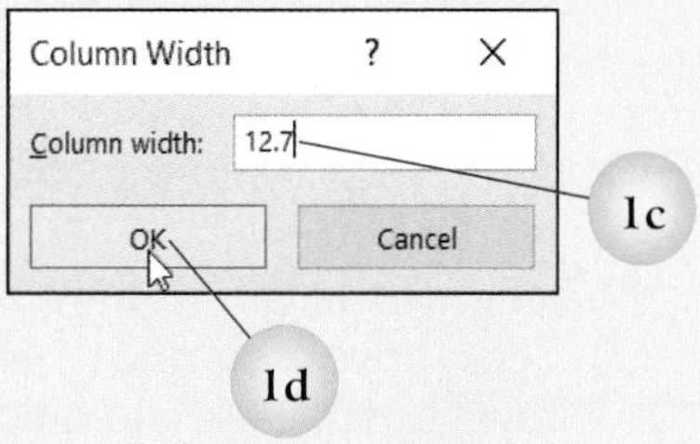

Check Your Work

Changing Row Height

Quick Steps

Change Row Height

Drag row boundary line.
OR
1. Click Format button.
2. Click *Row Height.*
3. Type height.
4. Click OK.

Hint To change the height of all the rows in a worksheet, click the Select All button and then drag a row boundary line to the desired position.

Hint Excel measures row height in points and column width in characters.

Change row height in much the same manner as column width. Change row height using the mouse on a row boundary line or at the Row Height dialog box. Change row height using a row boundary line by positioning the cell pointer on the boundary line between rows in the row header until it turns into a double-headed arrow pointing up and down, clicking and holding down the left mouse button, dragging up or down until the row is the desired height, and then releasing the mouse button.

Change the height of adjacent rows by selecting the rows and then dragging one of the row boundary lines within the selected rows. As the boundary line is being dragged, the row height changes for all the selected rows.

As a row boundary line is being dragged, the row height displays in a box above the mouse pointer. The number that displays represents a point measurement. Increase the point size to increase the row height; decrease the point size to decrease the row height.

Another method for changing row height is to use the *Row height* measurement box at the Row Height dialog box, shown in Figure 3.2. Display this dialog box by clicking the Format button in the Cells group on the Home tab and then clicking *Row Height* at the drop-down list.

Figure 3.2 Row Height Dialog Box

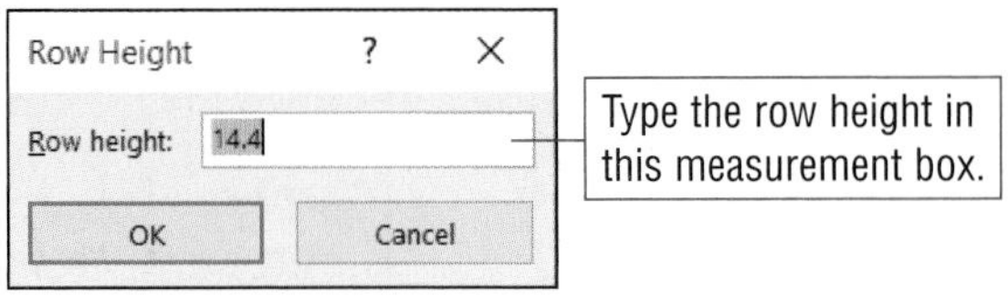

Project 1c Changing Row Height — Part 3 of 7

1. With **3-CMProducts.xlsx** open, change the height of row 1 by completing the following steps:
   a. Position the cell pointer in the row header on the row boundary line between rows 1 and 2 until it turns into a double-headed arrow pointing up and down.
   b. Click and hold down the left mouse button, drag the row boundary line down until *Height: 19.80* displays in the box, and then release the mouse button.

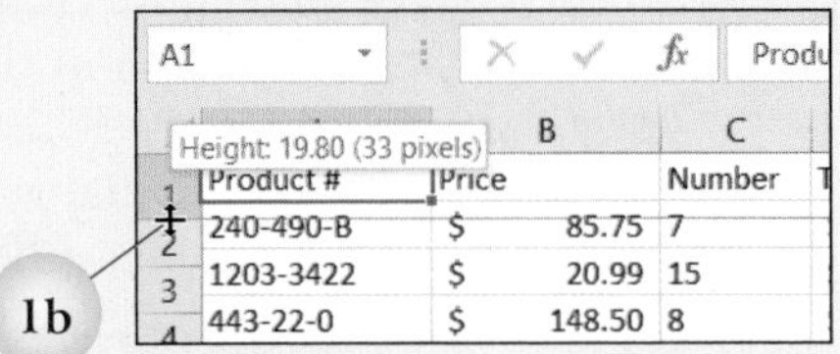

2. Change the height of rows 2 through 14 by completing the following steps:
   a. Select rows 2 through 14. To do this, position the cell pointer on the number *2* in the row header, click and hold down the left mouse button, drag the cell pointer to the number *14* in the row header, and then release the mouse button.
   b. Position the cell pointer on the row boundary line between rows 2 and 3 until it turns into a double-headed arrow pointing up and down.

c. Click and hold down the left mouse button, drag the row boundary line down until *Height: 16.80* displays in the box, and then release the mouse button.

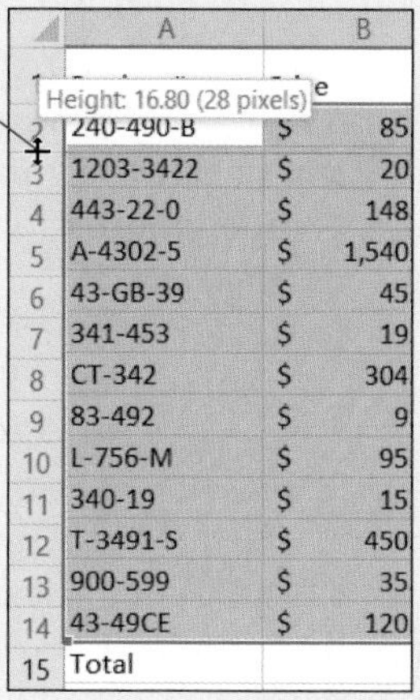

3. Change the height of row 15 by completing the following steps:
   a. Make cell A15 active.
   b. Click the Format button in the Cells group on the Home tab and then click *Row Height* at the drop-down list.
   c. At the Row Height dialog box, type 20 in the *Row height* measurement box and then click OK.

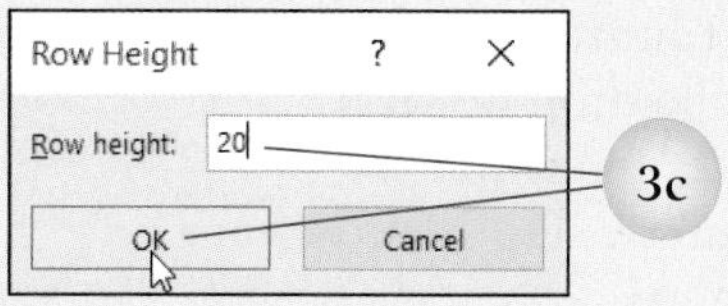

4. Save **3-CMProducts.xlsx**.

Check Your Work

Tutorial

Inserting Columns and Rows

Inserting and Deleting Cells, Rows, and Columns

New data may need to be included in an existing worksheet. For example, a row or several rows of new data may need to be inserted into a worksheet or data may need to be removed from a worksheet.

Inserting Rows

Hint When you insert cells, rows, or columns in a worksheet, all the references affected by the insertion automatically adjust.

A row or rows can be inserted in an existing worksheet. Insert a row with the Insert button in the Cells group on the Home tab or with options at the Insert dialog box. By default, a row is inserted above the row containing the active cell. To insert a row in a worksheet, select the row below where the row is to be inserted and then click the Insert button. To insert more than one row, select the number of rows to be inserted in the worksheet and then click the Insert button.

Insert

Quick Steps

Insert a Row

Click Insert button.

OR

1. Click Insert button arrow.
2. Click *Insert Sheet Rows.*

OR

1. Click Insert button arrow.
2. Click *Insert Cells.*
3. Click *Entire row.*
4. Click OK.

Another method for inserting a row is to make a cell active in the row below where the row is to be inserted, click the Insert button arrow, and then click *Insert Sheet Rows*. A row also can be inserted by clicking the Insert button arrow and then clicking *Insert Cells*. This displays the Insert dialog box, as shown in Figure 3.3. At the Insert dialog box, click *Entire row* and then click OK. This inserts a row above the active cell.

Figure 3.3 Insert Dialog Box

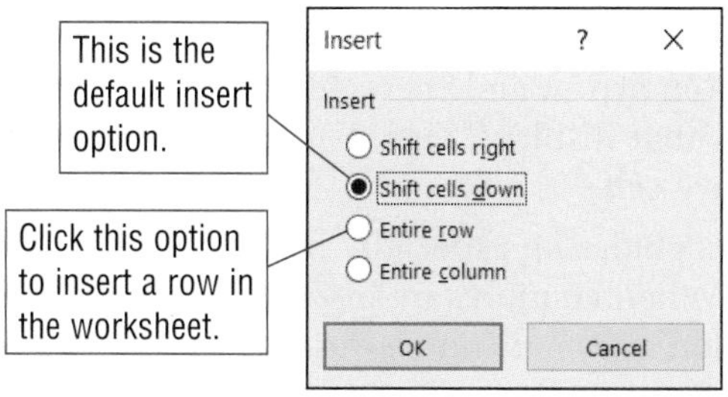

Project 1d Inserting Rows

Part 4 of 7

1. With **3-CMProducts.xlsx** open, insert two rows at the beginning of the worksheet by completing the following steps:
   a. Make cell A1 active.
   b. Click the Insert button arrow in the Cells group on the Home tab.
   c. At the drop-down list that displays, click *Insert Sheet Rows*.
   d. With cell A1 active, click the Insert button arrow and then click *Insert Sheet Rows* at the drop-down list.

1b

1c

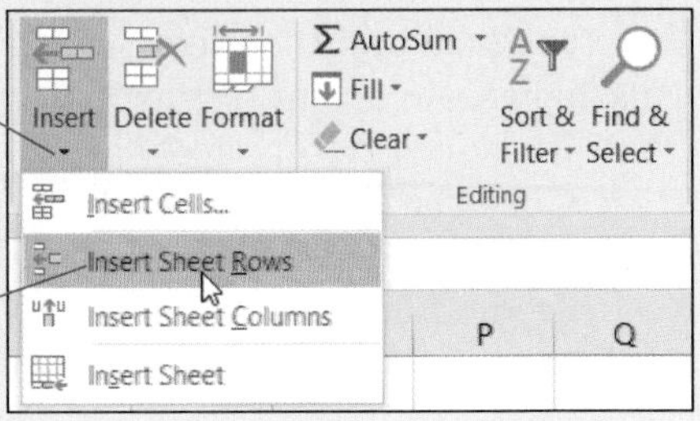

2. Type the text Capstan Marine Products in cell A1.
3. Make cell A2 active and then type Purchasing Department.
4. Change the height of row 1 to 42 points.
5. Change the height of row 2 to 21 points.
6. Insert two rows by completing the following steps:
   a. Select rows 7 and 8 in the worksheet.
   b. Click the Insert button in the Cells group on the Home tab.

6b

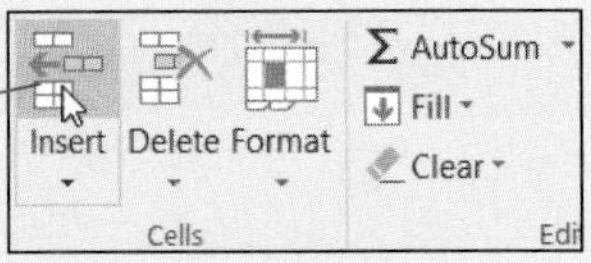

7. Type the following data in the specified cells. For the cells that contain money amounts, you do not need to type the dollar symbols:
   A7: 855-495
   B7: 42.75
   C7: 5
   A8: ST039
   B8: 12.99
   C8: 25
8. Make cell D6 active and then use the fill handle to copy the formula down into cells D7 and D8.
9. Save **3-CMProducts.xlsx**.

Check Your Work

Inserting Columns

Quick Steps

Insert a Column
Click Insert button.
OR
1. Click Insert button arrow.
2. Click *Insert Sheet Columns.*
OR
1. Click Insert button arrow.
2. Click *Insert Cells.*
3. Click *Entire column.*
4. Click OK.

Insert columns in a worksheet in much the same way as rows. Insert a column with options from the Insert button drop-down list or with options at the Insert dialog box. By default, a column is inserted immediately to the left of the column containing the active cell. To insert a column in a worksheet, make a cell active in the column immediately to the right of where the new column is to be inserted, click the Insert button arrow, and then click *Insert Sheet Columns* at the drop-down list. To insert more than one column, select the number of columns to be inserted in the worksheet, click the Insert button arrow, and then click *Insert Sheet Columns*.

Another method for inserting a column is to make a cell active in the column immediately to the right of where the new column is to be inserted, click the Insert button arrow, and then click *Insert Cells* at the drop-down list. At the Insert dialog box that displays, click *Entire column*. This inserts a column immediately left of the active cell.

Excel includes an especially helpful and time-saving feature related to inserting columns. When columns are inserted in a worksheet, all the references affected by the insertion automatically adjust.

1. With **3-CMProducts.xlsx** open, insert a column to the left of column A by completing the following steps:
   a. Click in any cell in column A.
   b. Click the Insert button arrow in the Cells group on the Home tab and then click *Insert Sheet Columns* at the drop-down list.
2. Type the following data in each specified cell:
   A3: Company
   A4: RD Manufacturing
   A8: Smithco, Inc.
   A11: Sunrise Corporation
   A15: Geneva Systems
3. Make cell A1 active and then adjust the width of column A to accommodate the longest entry.
4. Insert another column to the left of column B by completing the following steps:
   a. Make cell B1 active.
   b. Click the Insert button arrow and then click *Insert Cells* at the drop-down list.
   c. At the Insert dialog box, click *Entire column*.
   d. Click OK.
5. Type Date in cell B3 and then press the Enter key.
6. Save **3-CMProducts.xlsx**.

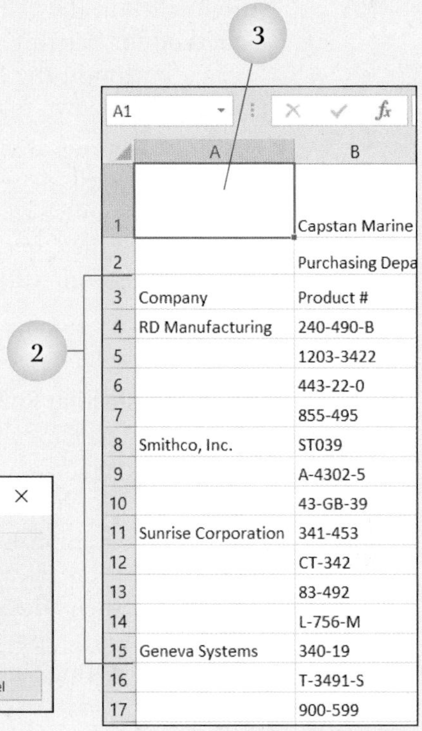

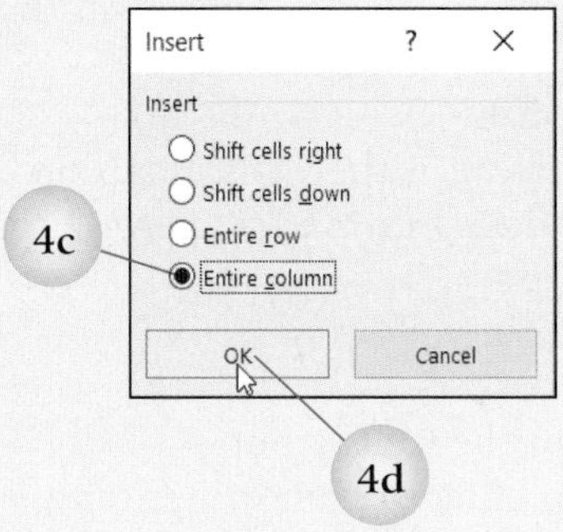

Check Your Work

Tutorial

Deleting Columns and Rows

Delete

Hint Display the Delete dialog box by positioning the cell pointer in the worksheet, clicking the right mouse button, and then clicking *Delete* at the shortcut menu.

Deleting Cells, Rows, or Columns

Specific cells in a worksheet or rows or columns in a worksheet can be deleted. To delete a row, select it and then click the Delete button in the Cells group on the Home tab. To delete a column, select it and then click the Delete button. Delete a specific cell by making it active, clicking the Delete button arrow, and then clicking *Delete Cells* at the drop-down list. This displays the Delete dialog box, shown in Figure 3.4. At the Delete dialog box, specify what is to be deleted and then click OK. Delete adjacent cells by selecting them and then displaying the Delete dialog box.

Figure 3.4 Delete Dialog Box

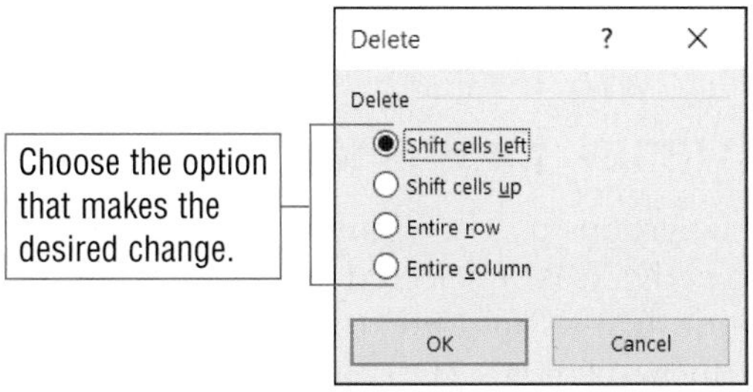

Tutorial

Clearing Cell Contents and Formatting

Clear

Quick Steps

Clear Data in Cells

1. Select cells.
2. Press Delete key.

OR

1. Select cells.
2. Click Clear button.
3. Click *Clear Contents.*

Clearing Data in Cells

To delete the cell contents but not the cell, make the cell active or select cells and then press the Delete key. A quick method for clearing the contents of a cell is to right-click in the cell and then click *Clear Contents* at the shortcut menu. Another method for deleting cell content is to make the cell active or select cells, click the Clear button in the Editing group on the Home tab, and then click *Clear Contents* at the drop-down list.

Use options at the Clear button drop-down list to clear the contents of the cell or selected cells as well as the formatting and comments. Click the *Clear Formats* option to remove the formatting from the cell or selected cells while leaving the data. Click the *Clear All* option to clear the contents of the cell or selected cells as well as the formatting.

Project 1f Deleting and Clearing Rows in a Worksheet

Part 6 of 7

1. With **3-CMProducts.xlsx** open, delete column B in the worksheet by completing the following steps:
   a. Click in any cell in column B.
   b. Click the Delete button arrow in the Cells group on the Home tab and then click *Delete Sheet Columns* at the drop-down list.
2. Delete row 5 by completing the following steps:
   a. Select row 5.
   b. Click the Delete button in the Cells group.
3. Clear row contents by completing the following steps:
   a. Select rows 7 and 8.
   b. Click the Clear button in the Editing group on the Home tab and then click *Clear Contents* at the drop-down list.
4. Type the following data in each specified cell:
   A7: Ray Enterprises
   B7: S894-T
   C7: 4.99
   D7: 30
   B8: B-3448
   C8: 25.50
   D8: 12
5. Make cell E6 active and then copy the formula down into cells E7 and E8.
6. Save **3-CMProducts.xlsx**.

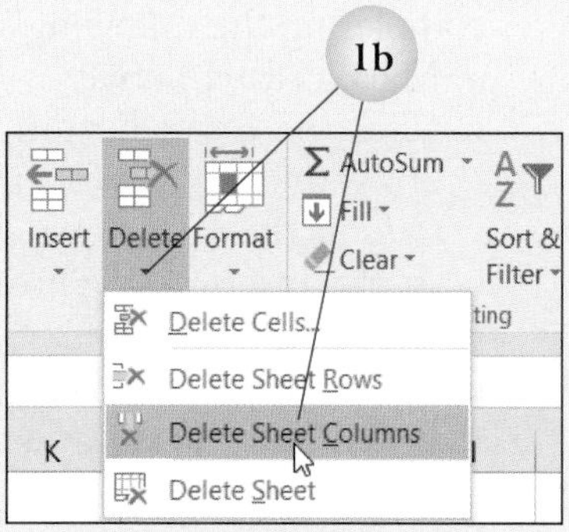

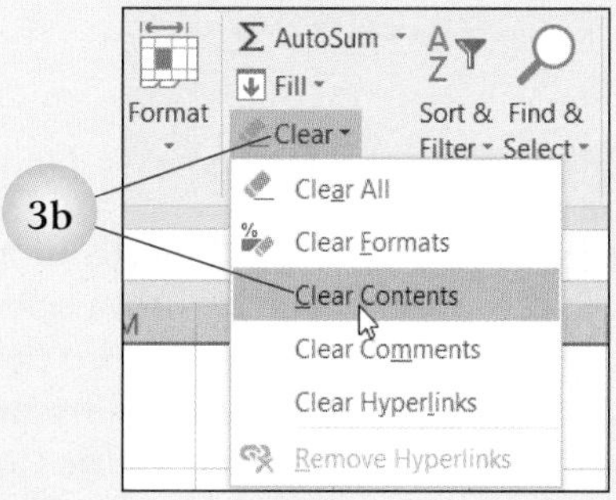

4
6 855-495 $ 42.75 5 $ 213.75
7 Ray Enterprises S894-T $ 4.99 30
8 B-3448 $ 25.50 12
9 43-GB-39 $ 45.00 20 $ 900.00

Check Your Work

Applying Formatting

Many of the groups on the Home tab contain options for applying formatting to text in the active cell or selected cells. Use buttons and options in the Font group to apply font formatting to text and use buttons in the Alignment group to apply alignment formatting.

Figure 3.5 Font Group

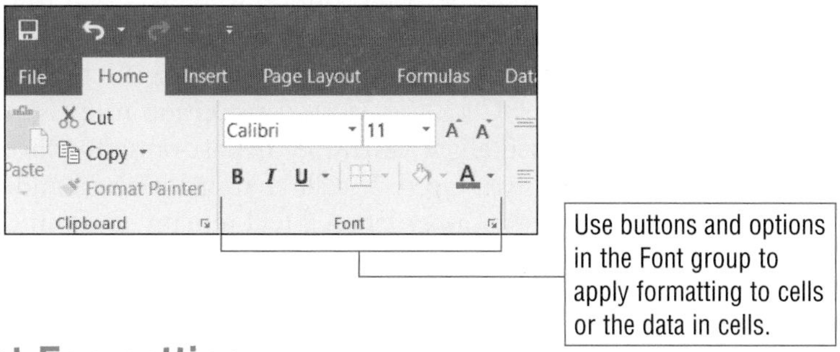

Tutorial

Applying Font Formatting

Applying Font Formatting

Apply a variety of formatting to cells in a worksheet with buttons and options in the Font group on the Home tab. Use buttons and options in the Font group, shown in Figure 3.5, to change the font, font size, and font color; to bold, italicize, and underline data in cells; to change the text color; and to apply a border or add fill to cells.

Bold

Italic

Underline

Increase Font Size

Decrease Font Size

Borders

Fill Color

Font Color

Use the *Font* option box in the Font group to change the font of the text in a cell and use the *Font Size* option box to specify the size of the text. Apply bold formatting to text in a cell with the Bold button, italic formatting with the Italic button, and underlining with the Underline button.

Click the Increase Font Size button and the text in the active cell or selected cells increases to the next font size in the *Font Size* option box drop-down gallery. Click the Decrease Font Size button and the text in the active cell or selected cells decreases to the next point size.

Use the Borders button in the Font group to insert a border on any or all sides of the active cell or any or all sides of selected cells. The name of the button changes depending on the most recent border applied to a cell or selected cells. Use the Fill Color button to insert color in the active cell or in selected cells. Change the color of the text within a cell with the Font Color button.

Formatting with the Mini Toolbar

Double-click in a cell and then select the data within it and the Mini toolbar displays above the selected data. The Mini toolbar also displays when right-clicking in a cell. The Mini toolbar contains buttons and options for applying font formatting such as font, font size, and font color, as well as bold and italic formatting. Click a button or option on the Mini toolbar to apply formatting to selected text.

Tutorial

Applying Alignment Formatting

Applying Alignment Formatting

The alignment of data in cells depends on the type of data entered. Enter words or text combined with numbers in a cell and the text aligns at the left edge of the cell. Enter numbers in a cell and the numbers align at the right side of the cell. Use options in the Alignment group to align data at the left, center, or right side of the cell; align data at the top, center, or bottom of the cell; increase and/or decrease the indent of data in a cell; and change the orientation of data in a cell.

Merge & Center

As explained in Chapter 1, selected cells can be merged by clicking the Merge & Center button. If cells are merged, the merged cell can be split into the original cells by selecting the cell and then clicking the Merge & Center button. Click the Merge & Center button arrow and a drop-down list of options displays. Click the *Merge &*

Center option to merge all of the selected cells and to apply center cell alignment. Click the *Merge Across* option to merge each row of selected cells. For example, if three cells and two rows are selected, clicking the *Merge Across* option will merge the three cells in the first row and merge the three cells in the second row, resulting in two cells. Click the *Merge Cells* option to merge all the selected cells but not apply center cell alignment. Use the last option, *Unmerge Cells*, to split cells that were previously merged. If cells that are selected and then merged contain data, only the data in the upper left cell will remain. Data in the other merged cells is deleted.

Orientation

Wrap Text

Click the Orientation button in the Alignment group and a drop-down list displays with options for rotating data in a cell. If the data typed in a cell is longer than the cell, it overlaps the next cell to the right. To wrap the data to the next line within the cell, click the Wrap Text button in the Alignment group.

Project 1g Applying Font and Alignment Formatting — Part 7 of 7

1. With **3-CMProducts.xlsx** open, make cell B1 active and then click the Wrap Text button in the Alignment group on the Home tab. (This wraps the company name within the cell.)
2. Select the range B1:C2, click the Merge & Center button arrow in the Alignment group on the Home tab, and then click *Merge Across* at the drop-down list.
3. After looking at the merged cells, you decide to merge additional cells and horizontally and vertically center the text in the cells by completing the following steps:
   a. With the range B1:C2 selected, click the Merge & Center button arrow and then click *Unmerge Cells* at the drop-down list.
   b. Select the range A1:E2.
   c. Click the Merge & Center button arrow and then click the *Merge Across* option at the drop-down list.
   d. Click the Middle Align button in the Alignment group and then click the Center button.

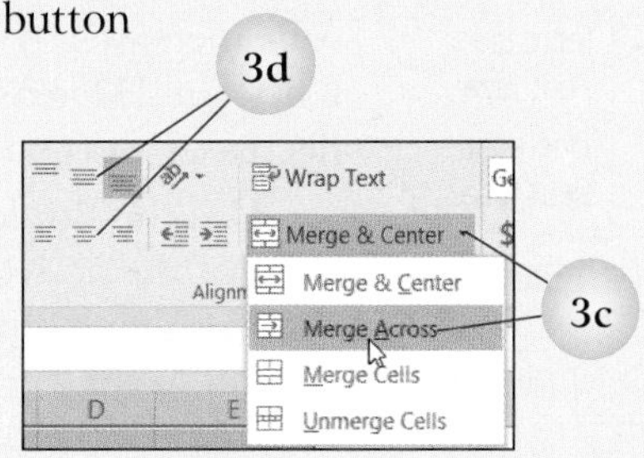

4. Rotate the text in the third row by completing the following steps:
   a. Select the range A3:E3.
   b. Click the Orientation button in the Alignment group and then click *Angle Counterclockwise* at the drop-down list.
   c. After looking at the rotated text, you decide to return the orientation to horizontal by clicking the Undo button on the Quick Access Toolbar.

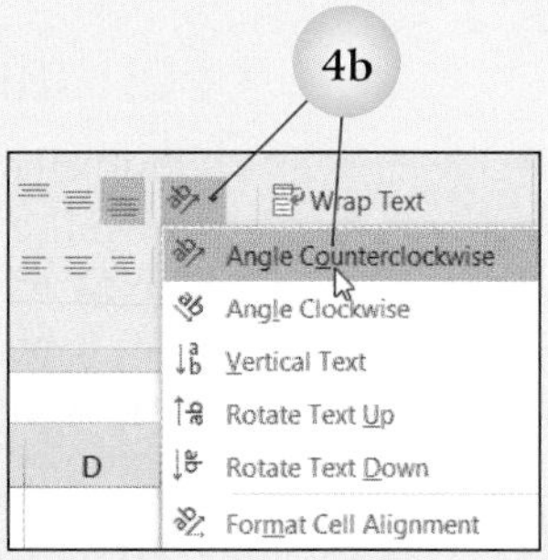

5. Change the font, font size, and font color for the text in specific cells by completing the following steps:
   a. Make cell A1 active.
   b. Click the *Font* option box arrow in the Font group, scroll down the drop-down gallery, and then click *Bookman Old Style*.
   c. Click the *Font Size* option box arrow in the Font group and then click *22* at the drop-down gallery.

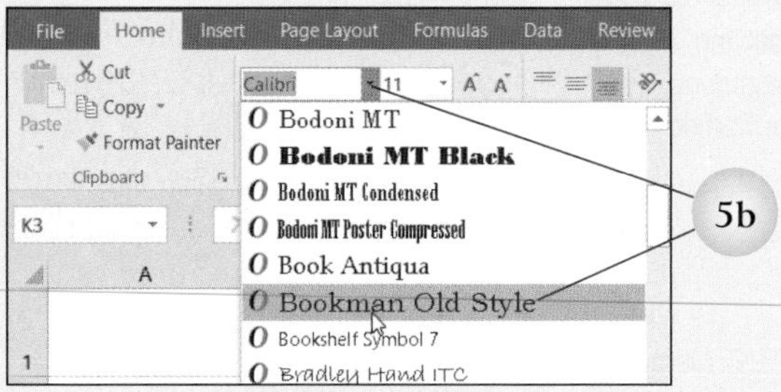

d. Click the Font Color button arrow and then click the *Dark Blue* option (ninth option in the *Standard Colors* section).

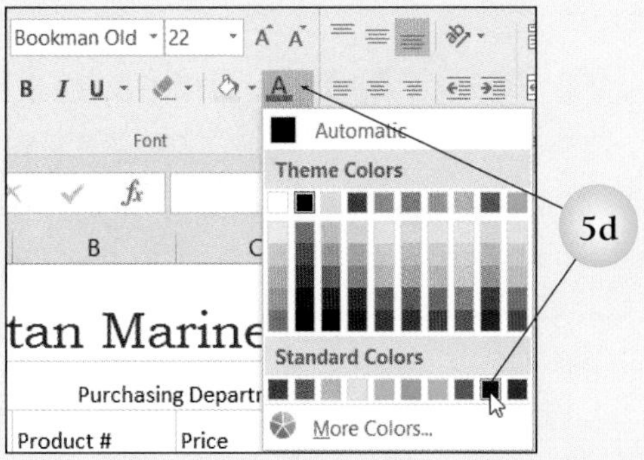

6. Make cell A2 active and then complete steps similar to those in Step 5 to change the font to Bookman Old Style, the font size to 16 points, and the font color to standard dark blue.
7. Select the range A3:E3 and then click the Center button in the Alignment group.
8. With the range A3:E3 still selected, click the Bold button in the Font group and then click the Italic button.
9. Select the range A3:E18 and then change the font to Bookman Old Style.
10. Use the Mini toolbar to apply formatting to selected data by completing the following steps:
    a. Double-click in cell A4.
    b. Select the letters *RD*. (This displays the Mini toolbar above the selected word.)
    c. Click the Increase Font Size button on the Mini toolbar.
    d. Double-click in cell A14.
    e. Select the word *Geneva* and then click the Italic button on the Mini toolbar.

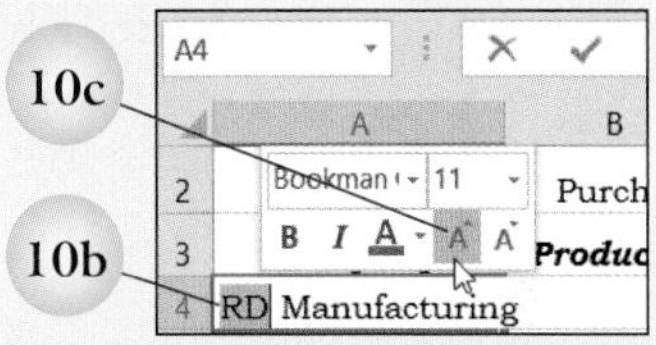

11. Adjust columns A through E to accommodate the longest entry in each column. To do this, select columns A through E and then double-click any selected column boundary line.
12. Select the range D4:D17 and then click the Center button in the Alignment group.
13. Add a double-line bottom border to cell A2 by completing the following steps:
    a. Make cell A2 active.
    b. Click the Borders button arrow in the Font group. (The name of this button varies depending on the last option selected.)
    c. Click the *Bottom Double Border* option at the drop-down list.

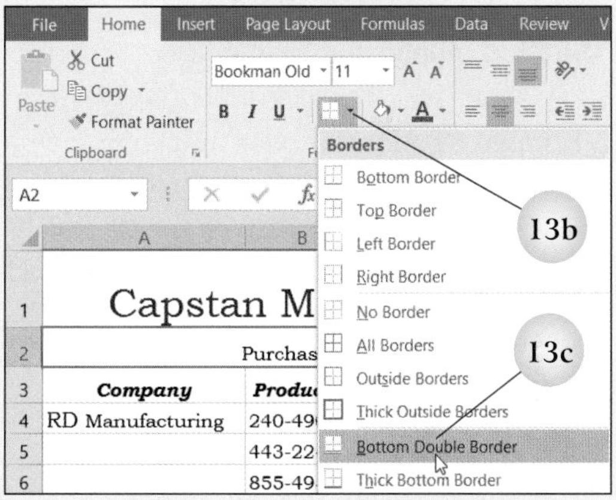

14. Add a single-line bottom border to the range A3:E3 by completing the following steps:
    a. Select the range A3:E3.
    b. Click the Borders button arrow and then click the *Bottom Border* option.
15. Apply a fill color to specific cells by completing the following steps:
    a. Select the range A1:E3.
    b. Click the Fill Color button arrow in the Font group.
    c. Click the *Blue, Accent 5, Lighter 80%* color option (ninth column, second row in the *Theme Colors* section).

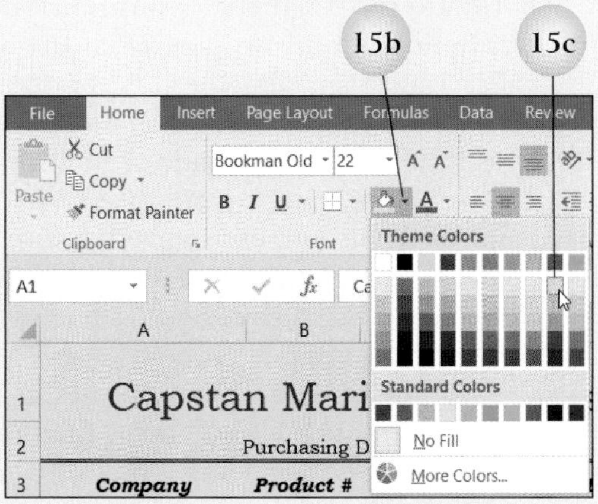

16. Select the range C5:C17 and then click the Comma Style button.
17. Select the range E5:E17 and then click the Comma Style button.
18. Save, print, and then close **3-CMProducts.xlsx**.

Check Your Work

Project 2 Apply a Theme to a Payroll Worksheet — 1 Part

You will open a workbook containing a worksheet with payroll information and then insert text in cells, apply formatting to the cells and cell contents, apply a theme, and then change the theme font and colors.

Preview Finished Project

Tutorial

Applying and Modifying Themes

Themes

Hint Apply a theme to give your worksheet a professional look.

Applying a Theme

Excel provides a number of themes that can be used to format text and cells in a worksheet. A theme is a set of formatting choices that includes a color theme (a set of colors), a font theme (a set of heading and body text fonts), and an effects theme (a set of lines and fill effects). To apply a theme, click the Page Layout tab and then click the Themes button in the Themes group. At the drop-down gallery that displays, click the desired theme. Position the mouse pointer over a theme and the live preview feature displays the worksheet with the theme formatting applied.

Project 2 Applying a Theme — Part 1 of 1

1. Open **SBAPayroll.xlsx** and then save it with the name **3-SBAPayroll**.
2. Make cell G4 active and then insert a formula that calculates the amount of social security tax. (Multiply the gross pay amount in cell E4 with the social security rate in cell H11; you will need to use the mixed cell reference H$11 when writing the formula.)
3. Copy the formula in cell G4 down into the range G5:G9.
4. Make H4 the active cell and then insert a formula that calculates the net pay (gross pay minus withholding and social security tax).
5. Copy the formula in cell H4 down into the range H5:H9.
6. Increase the height of row 1 to 36.00 points.
7. Make cell A1 active, click the Middle Align button in the Alignment group, click the *Font Size* option box arrow, click *18* at the drop-down gallery, and then click the Bold button.
8. Type Stanton & Barnett Associates in cell A1.
9. Select the range A2:H3 and then click the Bold button in the Font group.
10. Apply a theme and customize the font and colors by completing the following steps:
    a. Make cell A1 active.
    b. Click the Page Layout tab.
    c. Click the Themes button in the Themes group and then click *Wisp* at the drop-down gallery. (You might want to point the mouse to individual themes to see how they affect the formatting of the worksheet.)

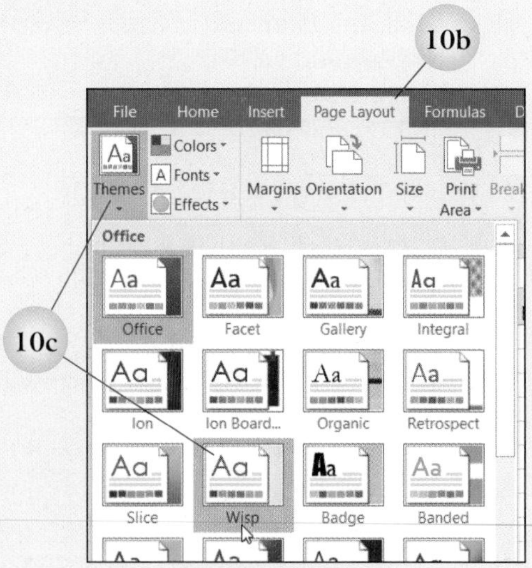

d. Click the Colors button in the Themes group and then click *Red Orange* at the drop-down gallery.
e. Click the Fonts button in the Themes group, scroll down the drop-down gallery, and then click *Trebuchet MS*.

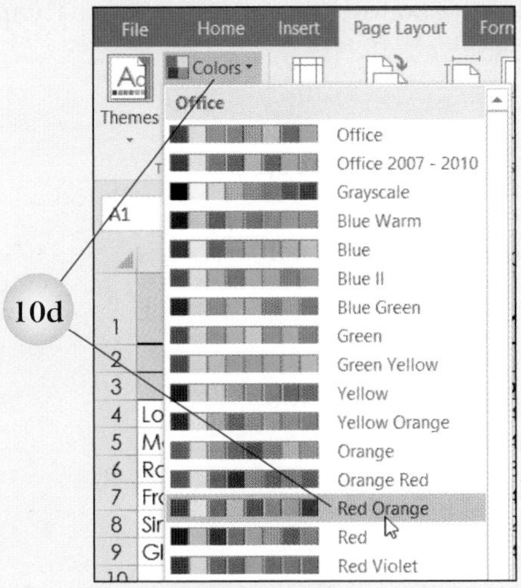

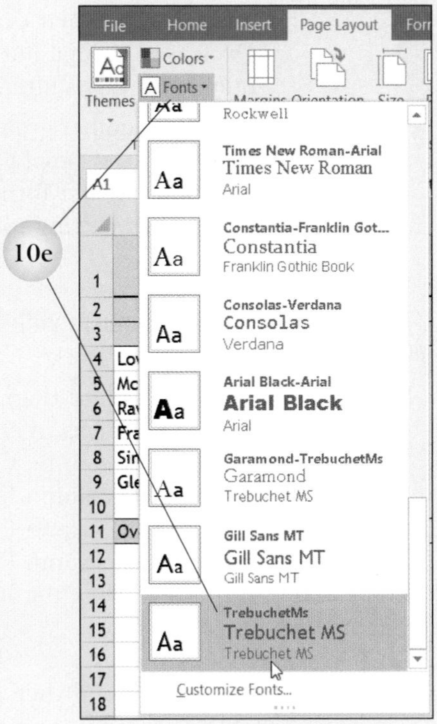

11. Select columns A through H and adjust the width of the columns to accommodate the longest entries.
12. Save, print, and then close **3-SBAPayroll.xlsx**.

Check Your Work

Project 3 Format an Invoices Worksheet **2 Parts**

You will open a workbook containing an invoice worksheet and apply number formatting to the numbers in the cells.

Preview Finished Project

Tutorial

Applying Number Formatting

Formatting Numbers

By default, the numbers in a cell align at the right and decimals and commas do not display unless they are typed in the cell. Change the format of numbers with buttons in the Number group on the Home tab or with options at the Format Cells dialog box with the Number tab selected.

Formatting Numbers Using Number Group Buttons

The format symbols available for formatting numbers include a percent symbol (%), comma (,), and dollar symbol ($). For example, type *$45.50* in a cell and Excel automatically applies the Currency format to the number. Type *45%* in a cell and Excel automatically applies the Percentage format to the number. The Number group on the Home tab contains five buttons for formatting numbers in cells. (These buttons were explained in Chapter 1.)

Specify the formatting for numbers in cells in a worksheet before typing the numbers or format existing numbers in a worksheet. Use the Increase Decimal and Decrease Decimal buttons in the Number group on the Home tab to change the number of digits after the decimal point for existing numbers only.

The Number group on the Home tab also contains the *Number Format* option box. Click the *Number Format* option box arrow and a drop-down list displays common number formats. Click a format at the drop-down list to apply the number formatting to the cell or selected cells.

Project 3a Formatting Numbers with Buttons in the Number Group — Part 1 of 2

1. Open **RPInvoices.xlsx** and then save it with the name **3-RPInvoices**.
2. Make the following changes to column widths:
   a. Change the width of column C to 17.00 characters.
   b. Change the width of column D to 10.00 characters.
   c. Change the width of column E to 7.00 characters.
   d. Change the width of column F to 12.00 characters.
3. Select row 1 and then click the Insert button in the Cells group on the Home tab.
4. Change the height of row 1 to 42.00 points.
5. Select the range A1:F1 and then make the following changes:
   a. Click the Merge & Center button in the Alignment group on the Home tab.
   b. With cell A1 active, change the font size to 24 points and the font color to Green, Accent 6, Darker 50% (last column, sixth row in the *Theme Colors* section).
   c. Click the Fill Color button arrow in the Font group and then click *Gray-50%, Accent 3, Lighter 60%* (seventh column, third row in the *Theme Colors* section).
   d. Click the Borders button arrow in the Font group and then click the *Top and Thick Bottom Border* option.
   e. With cell A1 active, type REAL PHOTOGRAPHY and then press the Enter key.
6. Change the height of row 2 to 24.00 points.
7. Select the range A2:F2 and then make the following changes:
   a. Click the Merge & Center button in the Alignment group.
   b. With cell A2 active, change the font size to 18 points.
   c. Click the Fill Color button in the Font group. (This will fill the cell with the gray color applied in Step 5c.)
   d. Click the Borders button arrow in the Font group and then click the *Bottom Border* option.
8. Make the following changes to row 3:
   a. Change the height of row 3 to 18.00 points.
   b. Select the range A3:F3, click the Bold button in the Font group, and then click the Center button in the Alignment group.
   c. With the cells still selected, click the Borders button.

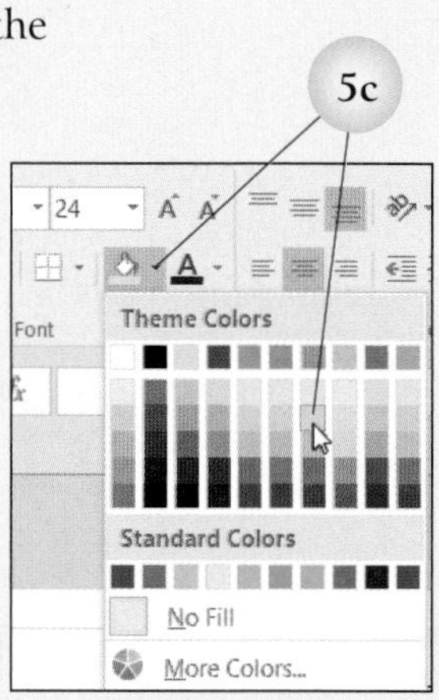

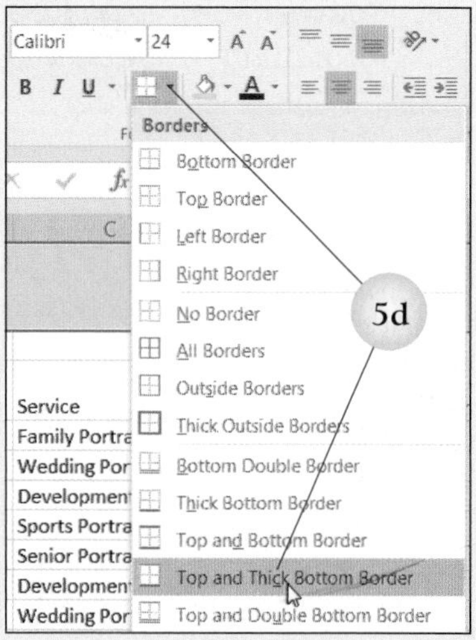

9. Make the following number formatting changes:
   a. Select the range E4:E16 and then click the Percent Style button in the Number group on the Home tab.
   b. With the cells still selected, click the Increase Decimal button in the Number group. (The percentages should include one digit after the decimal point.)

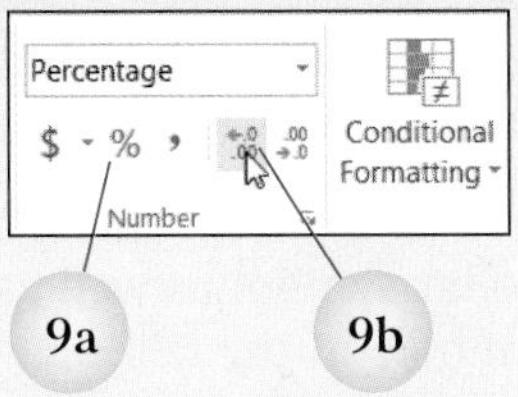

   c. Select the range A4:B16.
   d. Click the *Number Format* option box arrow, scroll down the drop-down list, and then click *Text*.
   e. With the range A4:B16 still selected, click the Center button in the Alignment group.

10. Save **3-RPInvoices.xlsx**.

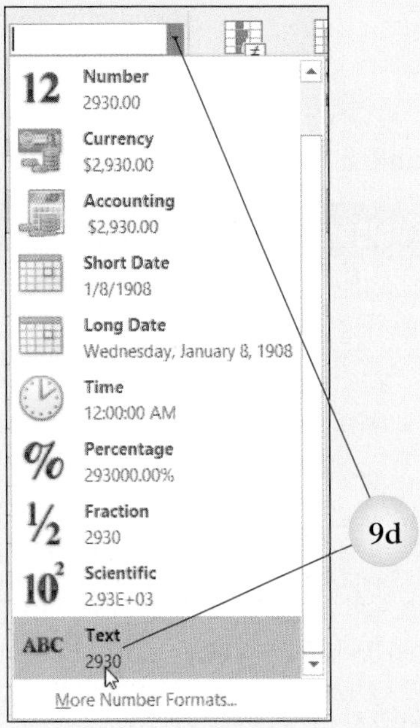

Check Your Work

Applying Number Formatting at the Format Cells Dialog Box

In addition to using buttons in the Number group, numbers can be formatted with options at the Format Cells dialog box with the Number tab selected, as shown in Figure 3.6. Display this dialog box by clicking the Number group dialog box launcher or by clicking the *Number Format* option box arrow and then clicking *More Number Formats* at the drop-down list. The left side of the dialog

Figure 3.6 Format Cells Dialog Box with Number Tab Selected

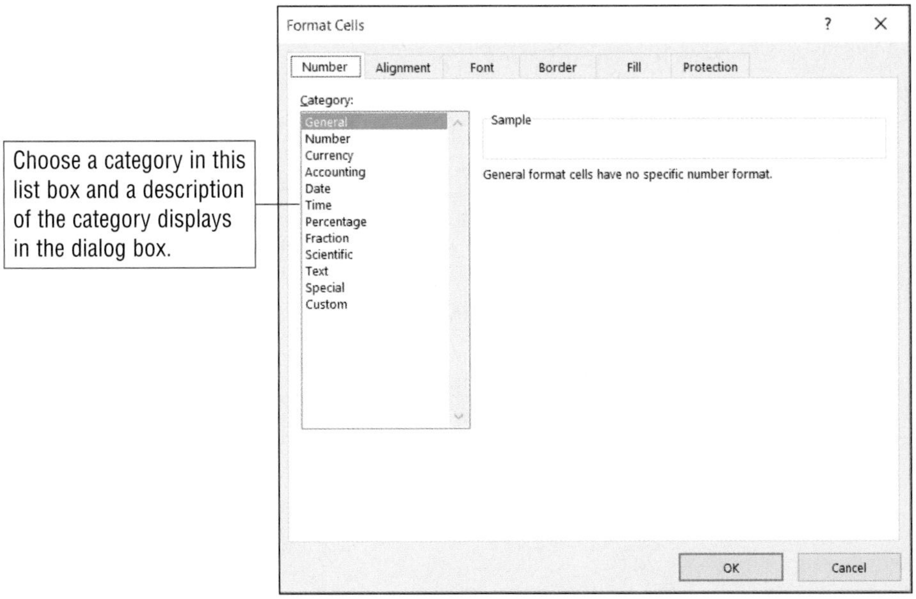

box displays number categories; the default category is *General*. At this setting, no specific formatting is applied to numbers except right alignment in cells. The other number categories are described in Table 3.1.

Table 3.1 Number Formatting Options at the Format Cells Dialog Box

Category	Formatting
Number	Specify the number of digits after the decimal point and whether a "thousand" separator should be used; choose the display of negative numbers; right-align numbers in the cell.
Currency	Apply general monetary values; add a dollar symbol as well as commas and decimal points, if needed; right-align numbers in the cell.
Accounting	Line up the currency symbols and decimal points in a column; add a dollar symbol and two digits after the decimal point; right-align numbers in the cell.
Date	Display the date as a date value; specify the type of formatting desired by clicking an option in the *Type* list box; right-align the date in the cell.
Time	Display the time as a time value; specify the type of formatting desired by clicking an option in the *Type* list box; right-align the time in the cell.
Percentage	Multiply the cell value by 100 and display the result with a percent symbol; add a decimal point followed by two digits by default; change the number of digits with the *Decimal places* option; right-align numbers in the cell.
Fraction	Specify how a fraction displays in the cell by clicking an option in the *Type* list box; right-align a fraction in the cell.
Scientific	Use for very large or very small numbers; use the letter *E* to have Excel move the decimal point a specified number of digits.
Text	Treat a number in the cell as text; the number is displayed in the cell exactly as typed.
Special	Choose a number type, such as *Zip Code*, *Phone Number*, or *Social Security Number*, in the *Type* option list box; useful for tracking list and database values.
Custom	Specify a numbering type by choosing an option in the *Type* list box.

Project 3b Formatting Numbers at the Format Cells Dialog Box

Part 2 of 2

1. With **3-RPInvoices.xlsx** open, make cell F4 active, type the formula =(d4*e4)+d4, and then press the Enter key.
2. Make cell F4 active and then copy the formula down into the range F5:F16.
3. Apply the Accounting format by completing the following steps:
   a. Select the range D4:D16.
   b. Click the Number group dialog box launcher.

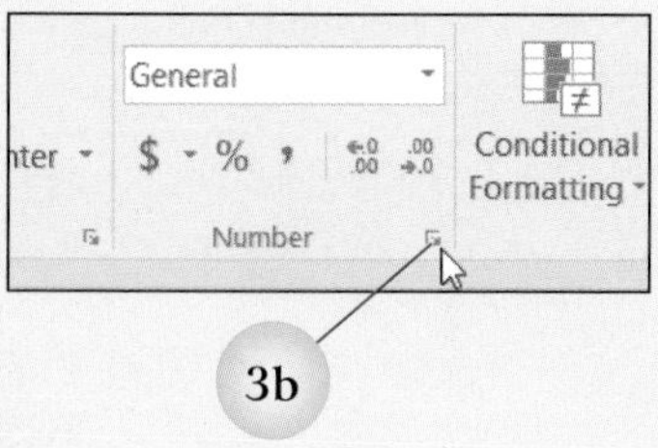

3b

c. At the Format Cells dialog box with the Number tab selected, click *Accounting* in the *Category* list box.
d. Make sure a *2* displays in the *Decimal places* option box and a *$* (dollar symbol) displays in the *Symbol* option box.
e. Click OK.

4. Apply the Accounting format to the range F4:F16 by completing actions similar to those in Step 3.
5. Save, print, and then close **3-RPInvoices.xlsx**.

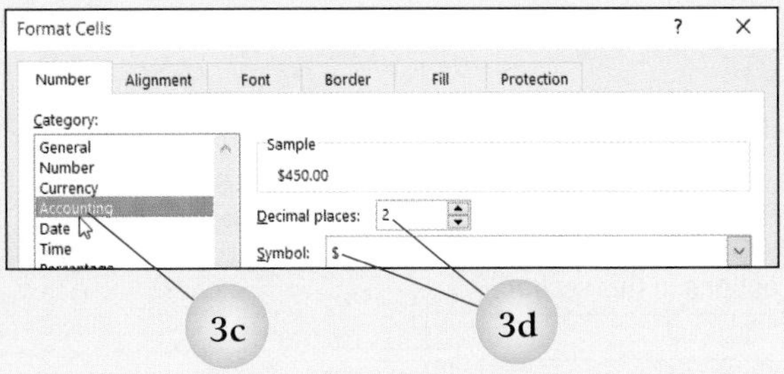

Check Your Work

Project 4 **Format a Company Budget Worksheet** **6 Parts**

You will open a workbook containing a company budget worksheet and then apply formatting to cells with options at the Format Cells dialog box, use Format Painter to apply formatting, and hide and unhide rows and columns.

Preview Finished Project

Tutorial

Applying Formatting at the Format Cells Dialog Box

Applying Formatting at the Format Cells Dialog Box

As explained earlier in this chapter, the Format Cells dialog box with the Number tab selected provides options for formatting numbers. This dialog box also contains other tabs with options for formatting cells.

Aligning and Indenting Data

Align and indent data in cells using buttons in the Alignment group on the Home tab or using options at the Format Cells dialog box with the Alignment tab selected, as shown in Figure 3.7. Display this dialog box by clicking the Alignment group dialog box launcher.

Use options in the *Orientation* section to rotate data. A portion of the *Orientation* section shows points on an arc. Click a point on the arc to rotate the text along that point. Or type a rotation degree in the *Degrees* measurement box. Type a positive number to rotate selected text from the lower left to the upper right of the cell. Type a negative number to rotate selected text from the upper left to the lower right of the cell.

If the data typed in a cell is longer than the cell, it overlaps the next cell to the right. To wrap text to the next line within a cell, insert a check mark in the *Wrap text* check box in the *Text control* section of the dialog box. Insert a check mark in the *Shrink to fit* check box to reduce the size of the text font so all the data fits within the cell. Insert a check mark in the *Merge cells* check box to combine two or more selected cells into a single cell. To enter data on more than one line within a cell, enter the data on the first line and then press Alt + Enter. Pressing Alt + Enter moves the insertion point to the next line within the same cell.

Figure 3.7 Format Cells Dialog Box with Alignment Tab Selected

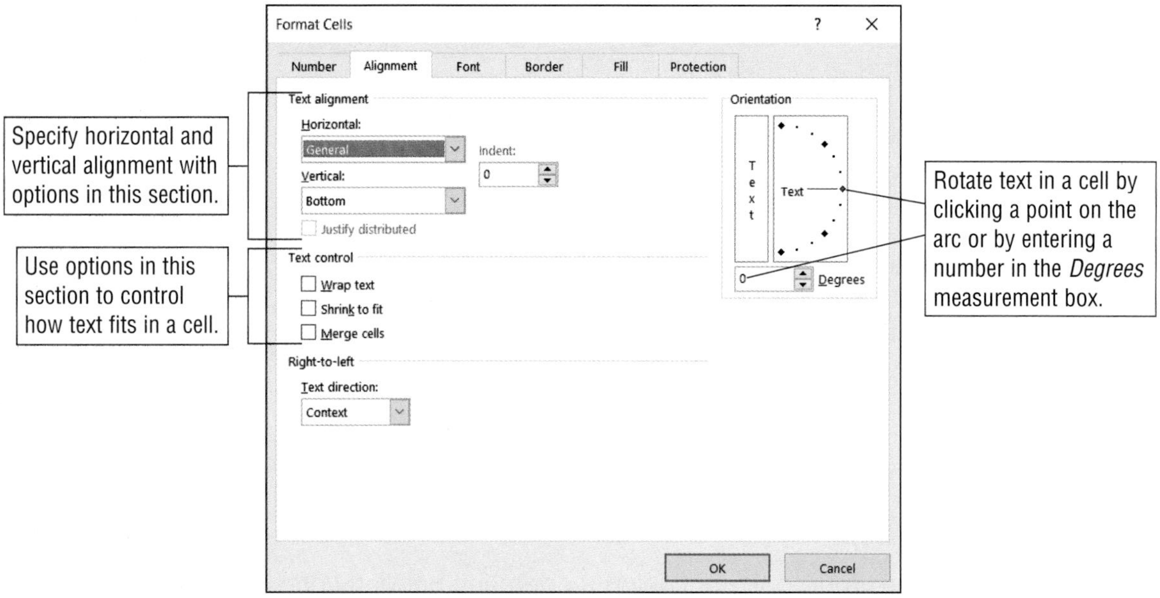

Project 4a **Aligning and Rotating Data in Cells** — Part 1 of 6

1. Open **HBCJobs.xlsx** and then save it with the name **3-HBCJobs**.
2. Make the following changes to the worksheet:
   a. Insert a new row at the beginning of the worksheet.
   b. Change the height of row 1 to 66.00 points.
   c. Merge and center the range A1:E1.
   d. Type Harris & Briggs in cell A1 and then press Alt + Enter. (This moves the insertion point down to the next line in the same cell.)
   e. Type Construction and then press the Enter key.
   f. With cell A2 active, type Preferred, press Alt + Enter, type Customer, and then press the Enter key.
   g. Change the width of column A to 22.00 characters.
   h. Change the width of column B to 7.00 characters.
   i. Change the widths of columns C, D, and E to 10.00 characters.
3. Make cell E3 active and then type the formula =d3-c3. Copy this formula down into the range E4:E11.
4. Change the number formatting for specific cells by completing the following steps:
   a. Select the range C3:E3.
   b. Click the Number group dialog box launcher.
   c. At the Format Cells dialog box with the Number tab selected, click *Accounting* in the *Category* list box.

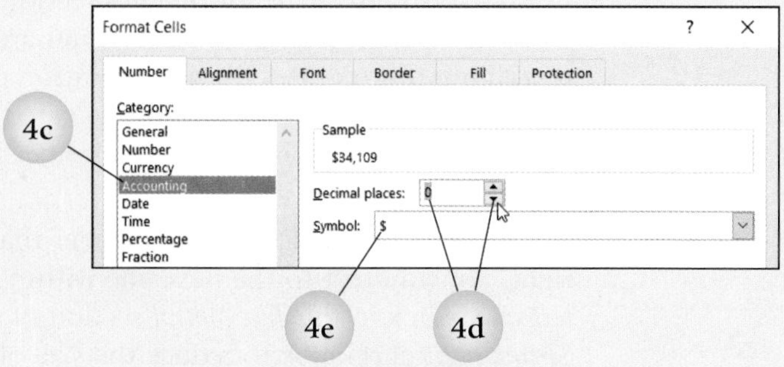

   d. Click the *Decimal places* measurement box down arrow until *0* displays.
   e. Make sure a *$* (dollar symbol) displays in the *Symbol* option box.
   f. Click OK.

5. Select the range C4:E11, click the Comma Style button in the Number group on the Home tab, and then decrease the number of digits that display after the decimal point to 0.

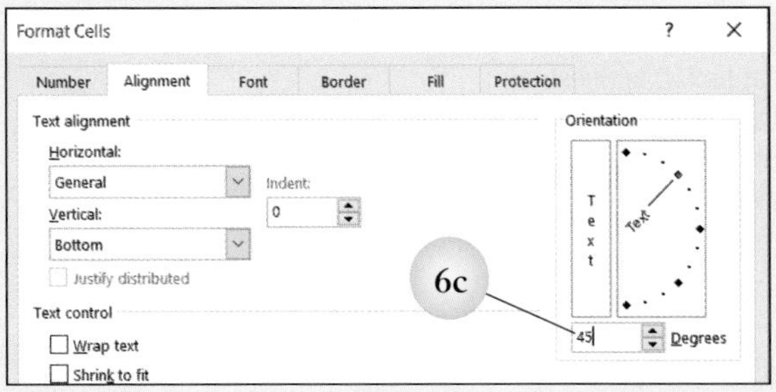

6. Change the orientation of data in cells by completing the following steps:
   a. Select the range B2:E2.
   b. Click the Alignment group dialog box launcher.
   c. At the Format Cells dialog box with the Alignment tab selected, select *0* in the *Degrees* measurement box and then type 45.
   d. Click OK.

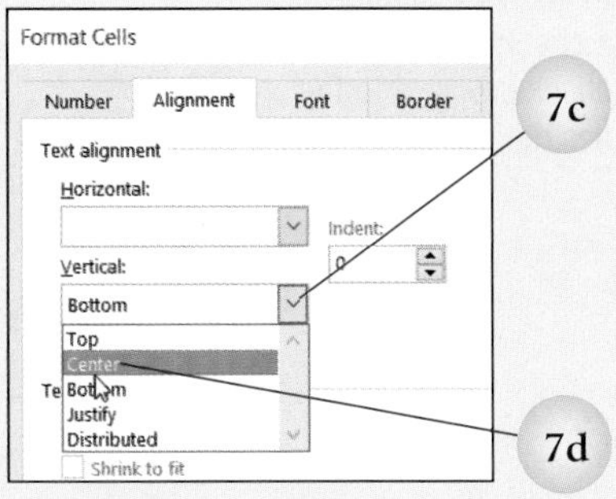

7. Change the vertical alignment of text in cells by completing the following steps:
   a. Select the range A1:E2.
   b. Click the Alignment group dialog box launcher.
   c. At the Format Cells dialog box with the Alignment tab selected, click the *Vertical* option box arrow.
   d. Click *Center* at the drop-down list.
   e. Click OK.

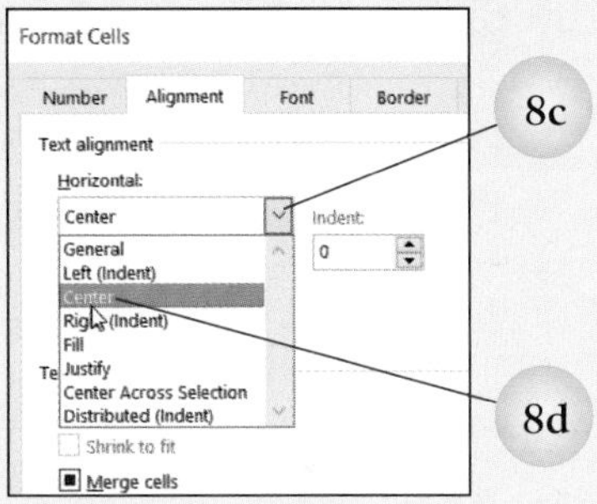

8. Change the horizontal alignment of text in cells by completing the following steps:
   a. Select the range A2:E2.
   b. Click the Alignment group dialog box launcher.
   c. At the Format Cells dialog box with the Alignment tab selected, click the *Horizontal* option box arrow.
   d. Click *Center* at the drop-down list.
   e. Click OK.

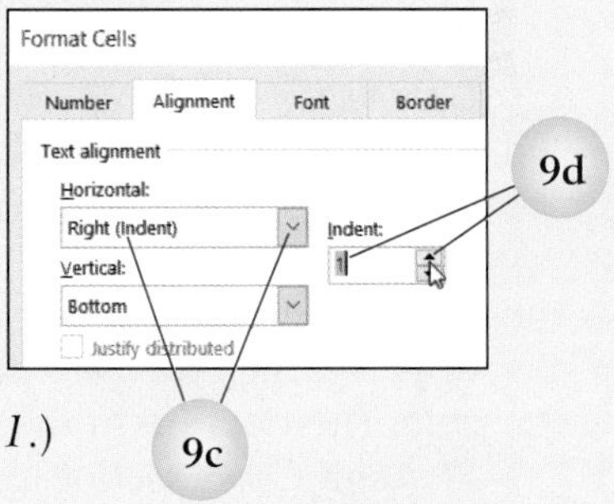

9. Change the horizontal alignment and indent of text in cells by completing the following steps:
   a. Select the range B3:B11.
   b. Click the Alignment group dialog box launcher.
   c. At the Format Cells dialog box with the Alignment tab selected, click the *Horizontal* option box arrow and then click *Right (Indent)* at the drop-down list.
   d. Click the *Indent* measurement box up arrow. (This displays *1*.)
   e. Click OK.
10. Save **3-HBCJobs.xlsx**.

Check Your Work

Changing the Font

As explained earlier in this chapter, the Font group on the Home tab contains buttons and options for applying font formatting to data in cells. The font for data in cells can also be changed with options at the Format Cells dialog box with the Font tab selected, as shown in Figure 3.8. Use options at the Format Cells dialog box with the Font tab selected to change the font, font style, font size, and font color; to change the underlining method; and to add effects such as superscript and subscript. Click the Font group dialog box launcher to display this dialog box.

Figure 3.8 Format Cells Dialog Box with Font Tab Selected

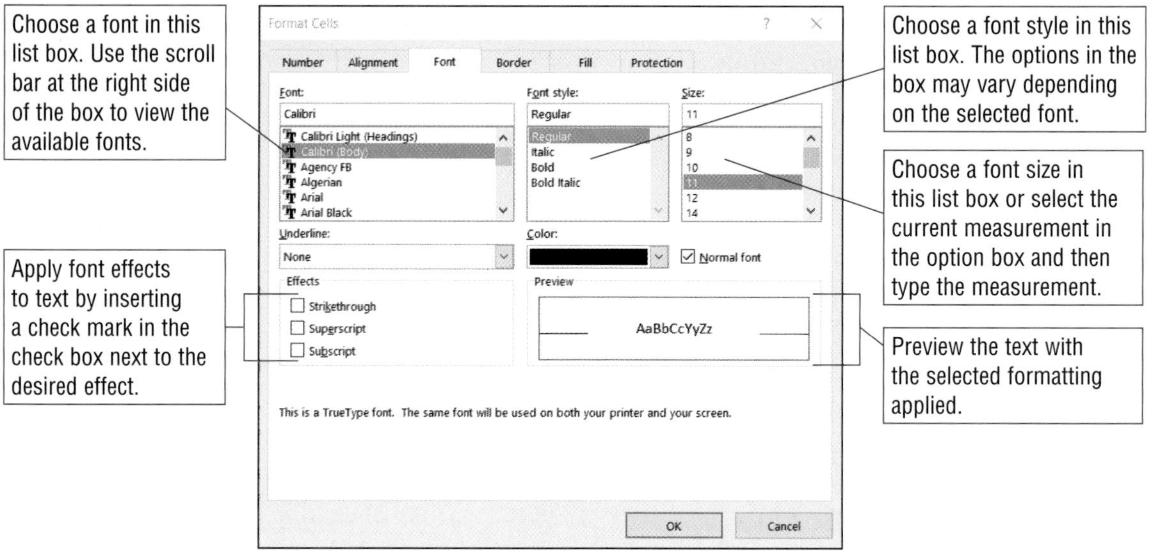

Project 4b Applying Font Formatting at the Format Cells Dialog Box

Part 2 of 6

1. With **3-HBCJobs.xlsx** open, change the font and font color by completing the following steps:
   a. Select the range A1:E11.
   b. Click the Font group dialog box launcher.
   c. At the Format Cells dialog box with the Font tab selected, scroll down the *Font* option list box and then click *Garamond*.
   d. Click *12* in the *Size* list box.
   e. Click the *Color* option box arrow.
   f. At the color palette that displays, click the *Dark Red* color (first option in the *Standard Colors* section).
   g. Click OK to close the dialog box.
2. Make cell A1 active and then change the font size to 24 points and apply bold formatting.
3. Select the range A2:E2 and then apply bold formatting.
4. Save and then print **3-HBCJobs.xlsx**.

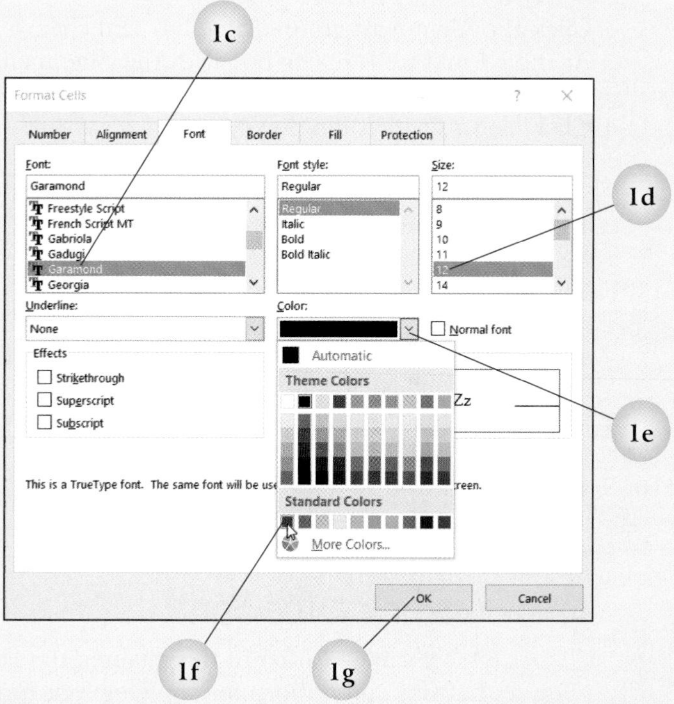

Check Your Work

Tutorial

Adding Borders to Cells

Quick Steps

Add Borders to Cells

1. Select cells.
2. Click Borders button arrow.
3. Click border.

OR

1. Select cells.
2. Click Borders button arrow.
3. Click *More Borders*.
4. Use options in dialog box to apply border.
5. Click OK.

Adding Borders to Cells

The gridlines that display in a worksheet do not print. As explained earlier in this chapter, use the Borders button in the Font group to add borders to cells that will print. Borders can also be added to cells with options at the Format Cells dialog box with the Border tab selected, as shown in Figure 3.9. Display this dialog box by clicking the Borders button arrow in the Font group and then clicking *More Borders* at the drop-down list.

With options in the *Presets* section, remove borders with the *None* option, add only outside borders with the *Outline* option, and add borders to the insides of selected cells with the *Inside* option. In the *Border* section of the dialog box, specify the side of the cell or selected cells to which the border is to be applied. Choose the line style for the border with options in the *Style* list box. Add color to border lines by clicking the *Color* option box arrow and then clicking a color at the color palette that displays.

Figure 3.9 Format Cells Dialog Box with Border Tab Selected

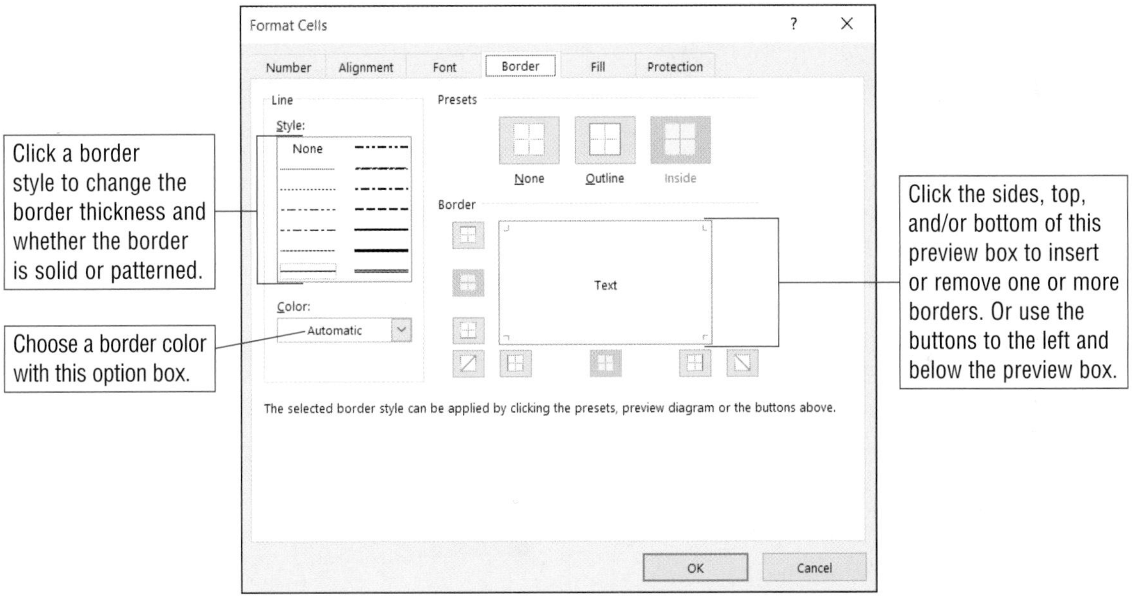

Format Cells
Number
Alignment
Font
Border
Fill
Protection
Line
Style:
None
Color:
Automatic
Presets
None
Outline
Inside
Border
Text
The selected border style can be applied by clicking the presets, preview diagram or the buttons above.
OK
Cancel
Click a border style to change the border thickness and whether the border is solid or patterned.
Choose a border color with this option box.
Click the sides, top, and/or bottom of this preview box to insert or remove one or more borders. Or use the buttons to the left and below the preview box.

Project 4c **Adding Borders to Cells**

Part 3 of 6

1. With **3-HBCJobs.xlsx** open, remove the 45-degree orientation you applied in Project 4a by completing the following steps:
   a. Select the range B2:E2.
   b. Click the Alignment group dialog box launcher.
   c. At the Format Cells dialog box with the Alignment tab selected, select *45* in the *Degrees* measurement box and then type 0.
   d. Click OK.
2. Change the height of row 2 to 33.00 points.

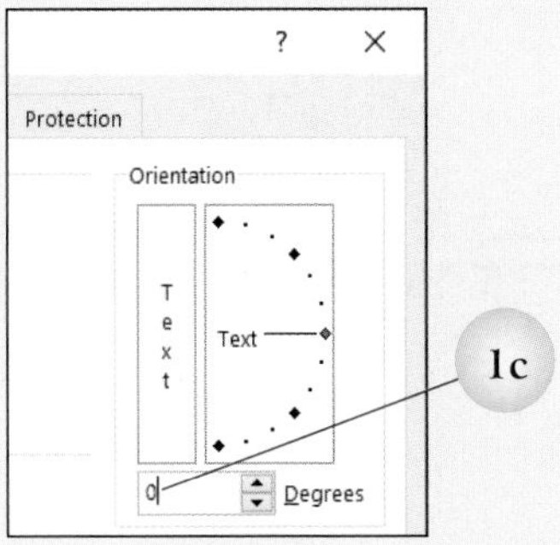

Protection
Orientation
Text
Degrees
1c

3. Add a thick, standard dark red border line to cells by completing the following steps:
   a. Select the range A1:E11.
   b. Click the Borders button arrow in the Font group and then click the *More Borders* option at the drop-down list.
   c. At the Format Cells dialog box with the Border tab selected, click the *Color* option box arrow and then click the *Dark Red* color (first option in the *Standard Colors* section).
   d. Click the thick single-line option in the *Style* list box in the *Line* section (sixth option in the second column).
   e. Click the *Outline* option in the *Presets* section.
   f. Click OK.

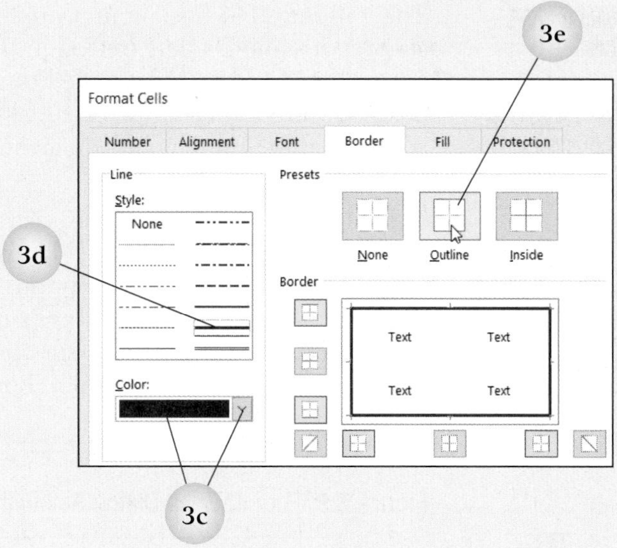

4. Add borders above and below cells by completing the following steps:
   a. Select the range A2:E2.
   b. Click the Borders button arrow in the Font group and then click *More Borders* at the drop-down list.
   c. At the Format Cells dialog box with the Border tab selected, make sure the color is still standard dark red.
   d. Make sure the thick single-line option is still selected in the *Style* list box in the *Line* section.
   e. Click the top border of the sample cell in the *Border* section of the dialog box.
   f. Click the double-line option in the *Style* list box (last option in the second column).
   g. Click the bottom border of the sample cell in the *Border* section of the dialog box.
   h. Click OK.

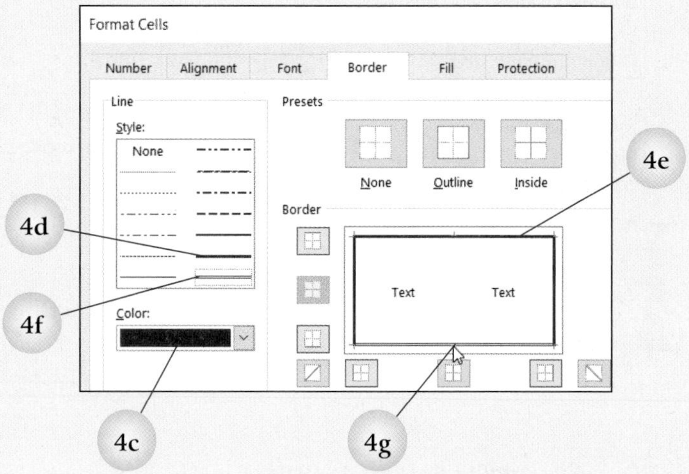

5. Save **3-HBCJobs.xlsx**.

Check Your Work

Tutorial

Adding Fill Color to Cells

Quick Steps

Add Fill and Shading

1. Select cells.
2. Click Fill Color button arrow.
3. Click color.

OR

1. Select cells.
2. Click Format button.
3. Click *Format Cells*.
4. Click Fill tab.
5. Use options in dialog box to apply shading.
6. Click OK.

Adding Fill and Shading to Cells

To enhance the appearance of cells and data within cells, consider adding fill color. As explained earlier in this chapter, fill color can be added to cells with the Fill Color button in the Font group. Fill color can also be added to cells in a worksheet with options at the Format Cells dialog box with the Fill tab selected, as shown in Figure 3.10. Display the Format Cells dialog box by clicking the Format button in the Cells group and then clicking *Format Cells* at the drop-down list. The dialog box can also be displayed by clicking the Font group, Alignment group, or Number group dialog box launcher. At the Format Cells dialog box, click the Fill tab or right-click in a cell and then click *Format Cells* at the shortcut menu. Choose a fill color for a cell or selected cells by clicking a color choice in the *Background Color* section. To add gradient fill to a cell or selected cells, click the Fill Effects button and then click a style at the Fill Effects dialog box.

Tutorial

Using Format Painter and the Repeat Command

Quick Steps

Repeat Last Action

1. Apply formatting.
2. Move to location.
3. Press F4 or Ctrl + Y.

Repeating the Last Action

To apply the same formatting to other cells in a worksheet, use the Repeat command by pressing the F4 function key or the keyboard shortcut Ctrl + Y. The Repeat command repeats the last action performed.

Figure 3.10 Format Cells Dialog Box with Fill Tab Selected

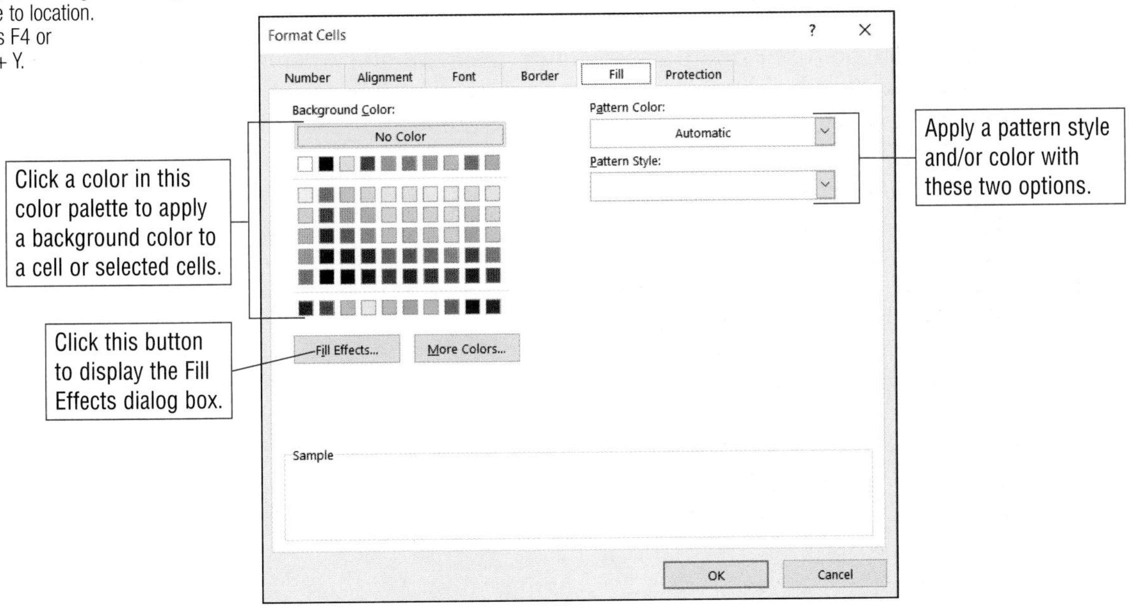
Click a color in this color palette to apply a background color to a cell or selected cells.
Click this button to display the Fill Effects dialog box.
Format Cells
Number
Alignment
Font
Border
Fill
Protection
Background Color:
No Color
Fill Effects...
More Colors...
Pattern Color:
Automatic
Pattern Style:
Sample
OK
Cancel
Apply a pattern style and/or color with these two options.

1. With **3-HBCJobs.xlsx** open, add a fill color to cell A1 and repeat the formatting by completing the following steps:
   a. Make cell A1 active.
   b. Click the Format button in the Cells group and then click *Format Cells* at the drop-down list.
   c. At the Format Cells dialog box, click the Fill tab.
   d. Click the light gold color in the *Background Color* section (eighth column, second row).

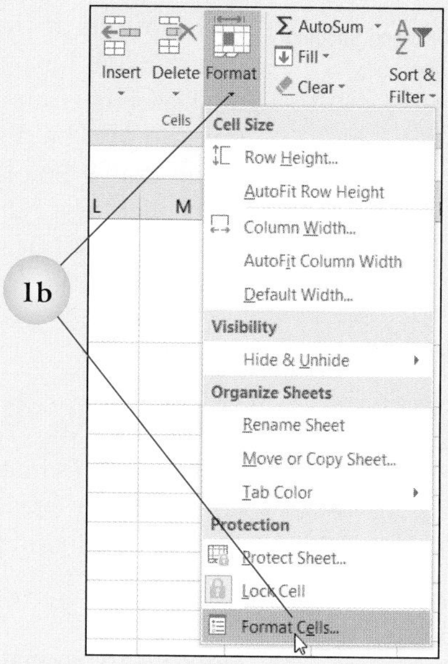

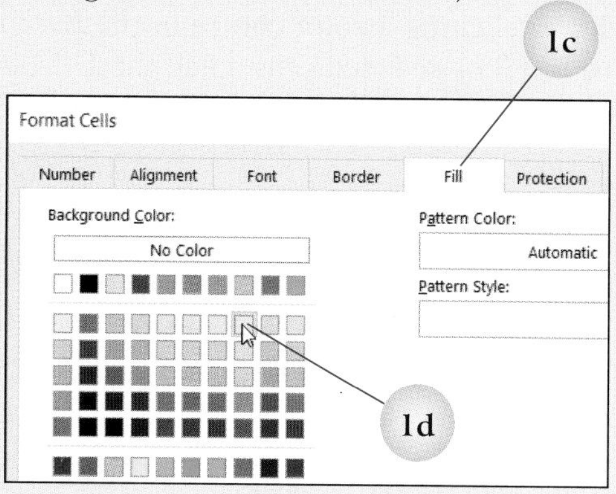

   e. Click OK.
   f. Select the range A2:E2 and then press the F4 function key. (This repeats the application of the light gold fill.)
2. Select row 2, insert a new row, and then change the height of the new row to 12.00 points.
3. Add gradient fill to cells by completing the following steps:
   a. Select the range A2:E2.
   b. Click the Format button in the Cells group and then click *Format Cells* at the drop-down list.
   c. At the Format Cells dialog box, click the Fill tab, if necessary.
   d. Click the Fill Effects button.
   e. At the Fill Effects dialog box, click the *Color 2* option box arrow and then click the *Gold, Accent 4* option (eighth column, first row in the *Theme Colors* section).
   f. Click OK to close the Fill Effects dialog box.
   g. Click OK to close the Format Cells dialog box.
4. Save **3-HBCJobs.xlsx**.

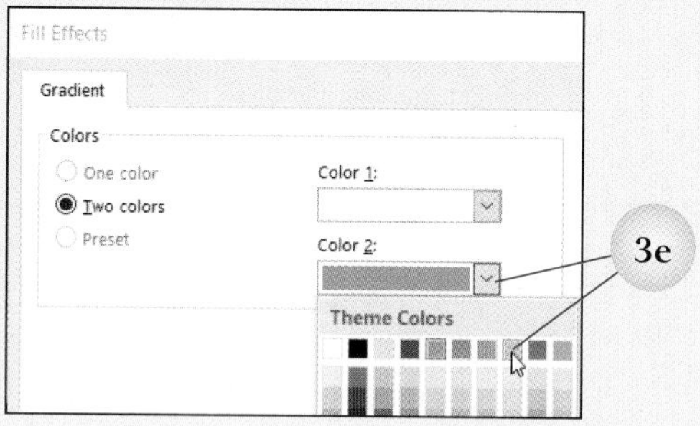

Check Your Work

Quick Steps

Format with Format Painter
1. Select cells with formatting.
2. Double-click Format Painter button.
3. Select cells.
4. Click Format Painter button.

Formatting with Format Painter

Use the Format Painter button in the Clipboard group on the Home tab to copy formatting to different locations in the worksheet. To use the Format Painter button, make active a cell or selected cells that contain the desired formatting, click the Format Painter button, and then click in the cell or selected cells to which the formatting is to be applied.

Format Painter

Click the Format Painter button and the mouse pointer displays with a paintbrush attached. To apply formatting in a single location, click the Format Painter button. To apply formatting in more than one location, double-click the Format Painter button, selected the desired cells, and then click the Format Painter button to turn off the feature.

Project 4e Formatting with Format Painter

Part 5 of 6

1. With **3-HBCJobs.xlsx** open, select the range A5:E5.
2. Click the Font group dialog box launcher.
3. At the Format Cells dialog box, click the Fill tab.
4. Click the light green color in the *Background Color* section (last column, second row).
5. Click OK to close the dialog box.
6. Use Format Painter to apply the light green color to rows by completing the following steps:
   a. With the range A5:E5 selected, double-click the Format Painter button in the Clipboard group.
   b. Select the range A7:E7.
   c. Select the range A9:E9.
   d. Select the range A11:E11.
   e. Turn off Format Painter by clicking the Format Painter button.
7. Save and then print **3-HBCJobs.xlsx**.

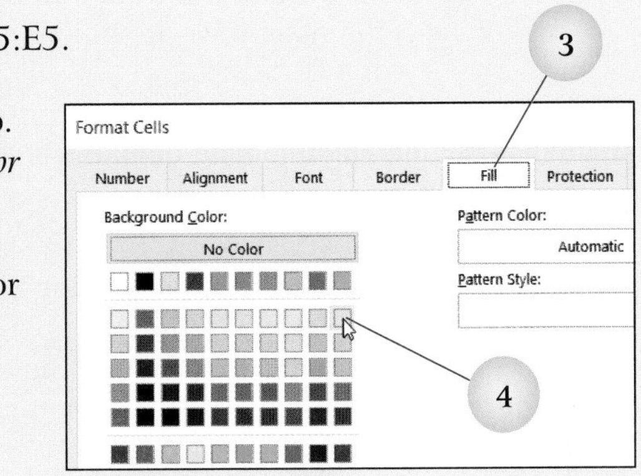

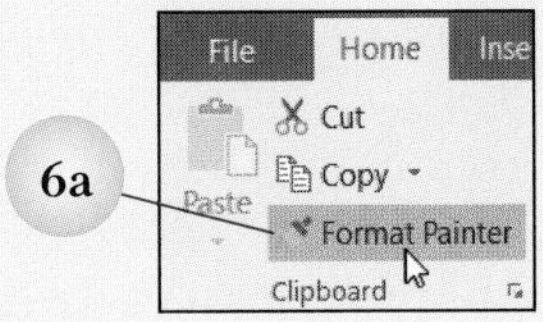

Check Your Work

Tutorial

Hiding and Unhiding Columns and Rows

Quick Steps

Hide Columns
1. Select columns.
2. Click Format button.
3. Point to *Hide & Unhide*.
4. Click *Hide Columns*.

Hide Rows
1. Select rows.
2. Click Format button.
3. Point to *Hide & Unhide*.
4. Click *Hide Rows*.

Hint Set the column width to 0 and the column is hidden. Set the row height to 0 and the row is hidden.

Hiding and Unhiding Columns and Rows

If a worksheet contains columns and/or rows of data that is not being used or should not be viewed, consider hiding the columns and/or rows. To hide columns in a worksheet, select the columns, click the Format button in the Cells group on the Home tab, point to *Hide & Unhide*, and then click *Hide Columns*. To hide rows, select the rows, click the Format button in the Cells group, point to *Hide & Unhide*, and then click *Hide Rows*. To make a hidden column visible, select the columns to the left and the right of the hidden column, click the Format button in the Cells group, point to *Hide & Unhide*, and then click *Unhide Columns*. To make a hidden row visible, select the rows above and below the hidden row, click the Format button in the Cells group, point to *Hide & Unhide*, and then click *Unhide Rows*.

If the first row or column is hidden, use the Go To feature to make it visible. To do this, click the Find & Select button in the Editing group on the Home tab and then click *Go To* at the drop-down list. At the Go To dialog box, type *A1* in the *Reference* text box and then click OK. At the worksheet, click the Format button in the Cells group, point to *Hide & Unhide*, and then click *Unhide Columns* or click *Unhide Rows*.

The mouse also can be used to unhide columns or rows. If a column or row is hidden, the light-gray boundary line in the column or row header displays as a slightly thicker gray line. To unhide a column, position the mouse pointer on the slightly thicker gray line in the column header until the mouse pointer changes into a left-and-right-pointing arrow with a double line in the middle. (Make sure the mouse pointer displays with two lines between the arrows. If a single line displays, only the size of the visible column will change.) Click and hold down the left mouse button, drag to the right until the column displays at the desired width, and then release the mouse button. Unhide a row in a similar manner. Position the mouse pointer on the slightly thicker gray line in the row header until the mouse pointer changes into an up-and-down-pointing arrow with a double line in the middle. Drag down to display the row and then release the mouse button. If two or more adjacent columns or rows are hidden, unhide each column or row separately.

Project 4f Hiding and Unhiding Columns and Rows

Part 6 of 6

1. With **3-HBCJobs.xlsx** open, hide the row for Linstrom Enterprises and the row for Summit Services by completing the following steps:
   a. Click the row 7 header to select the entire row.
   b. Press and hold down the Ctrl key and then click the row 11 header to select the entire row.
   c. Click the Format button in the Cells group on the Home tab, point to *Hide & Unhide*, and then click *Hide Rows*.

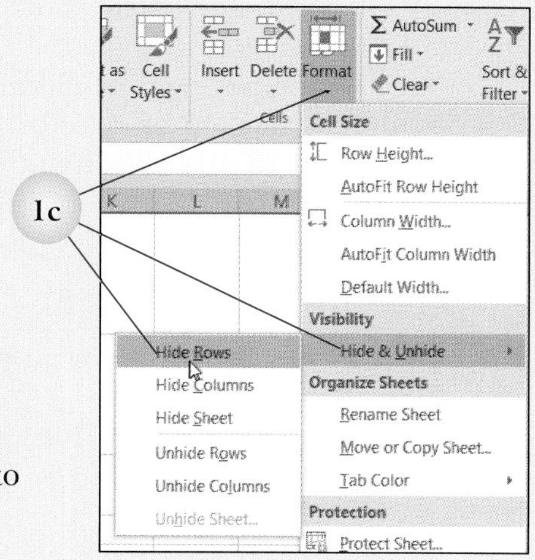

2. Hide the column containing the dollar amounts by completing the following steps:
   a. Click in cell D3 to make it the active cell.
   b. Click the Format button in the Cells group, point to *Hide & Unhide*, and then click *Hide Columns*.
3. Save and then print **3-HBCJobs.xlsx**.
4. Unhide the rows by completing the following steps:
   a. Select rows 6 through 12.
   b. Click the Format button in the Cells group, point to *Hide & Unhide*, and then click *Unhide Rows*.
   c. Click in cell A4.
5. Unhide column D by completing the following steps:
   a. Position the mouse pointer on the thicker gray line between columns C and E in the column header until the pointer turns into a left-and-right-pointing arrow with a double line in the middle.
   b. Click and hold down the left mouse button, drag to the right until *Width: 9.56* displays in a box above the mouse pointer, and then release the mouse button.

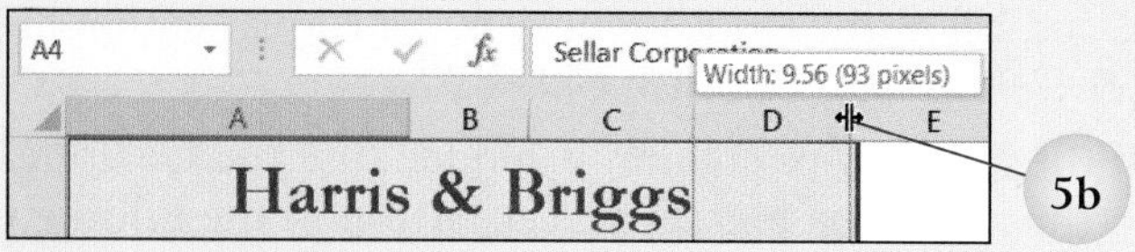

6. Save, print, and then close **3-HBCJobs.xlsx**.

Check Your Work

Chapter Summary

- Change column width using the mouse on column boundary lines or using options at the Column Width dialog box. Change row height using the mouse on row boundary lines or using options at the Row Height dialog box.
- Insert a row or column in a worksheet with the Insert button in the Cells group on the Home tab or with options at the Insert dialog box.
- Delete a specific cell by clicking the Delete button arrow and then clicking *Delete Cells* at the drop-down list. At the Delete dialog box, specify if only the cell should be deleted or an entire row or column.
- Delete a selected row or column or multiple rows or columns by clicking the Delete button in the Cells group.
- Delete the cell contents by pressing the Delete key or clicking the Clear button in the Editing group on the Home tab and then clicking *Clear Contents*.
- Apply font formatting with buttons and options in the Font group on the Home tab. Use the Mini toolbar to apply font formatting to selected data in a cell.
- Apply alignment formatting with buttons in the Alignment group on the Home tab. Use the Themes button in the Themes group on the Page Layout tab to apply a theme to cells in a worksheet, which includes formatting such as color, font, and effects. Use the other buttons in the Themes group to customize the theme.
- Format numbers in cells with buttons in the Number group on the Home tab or with options at the Format Cells dialog box with the Number tab selected.
- Apply formatting to cells in a worksheet with options at the Format Cells dialog box, which includes the Number, Alignment, Font, Border, and Fill tabs.
- Press the F4 function key or the keyboard shortcut Ctrl + Y to repeat the last action performed.
- Use the Format Painter button in the Clipboard group on the Home tab to apply formatting to several locations in a worksheet.
- Hide selected columns or rows in a worksheet by clicking the Format button in the Cells group on the Home tab, pointing to *Hide & Unhide*, and then clicking *Hide Columns* or *Hide Rows*.
- To make a hidden column visible, select the columns to the left and right, click the Format button in the Cells group, point to *Hide & Unhide*, and then click *Unhide Columns*.
- To make a hidden row visible, select the rows above and below, click the Format button in the Cells group, point to *Hide & Unhide*, and then click *Unhide Rows*.

Commands Review

FEATURE	RIBBON TAB, GROUP	BUTTON	KEYBOARD SHORTCUT
bold text	Home, Font		Ctrl + B
borders	Home, Font	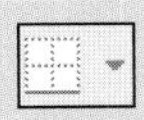	
bottom-align (in row)	Home, Alignment		
center-align (in column)	Home, Alignment		
clear cell or cell contents	Home, Editing		

FEATURE	RIBBON TAB, GROUP	BUTTON	KEYBOARD SHORTCUT
decrease font size	Home, Font		
decrease indent	Home, Alignment		
delete cells, rows, or columns	Home, Cells		
fill color	Home, Font		
font	Home, Font		
font color	Home, Font		
font size	Home, Font		
format	Home, Cells		
Format Painter	Home, Clipboard		
increase font size	Home, Font		
increase indent	Home, Alignment		
insert cells, rows, or columns	Home, Cells		
italicize text	Home, Font		Ctrl + I
left-align (in column)	Home, Alignment		
merge and center cells	Home, Alignment		
middle-align (in row)	Home, Alignment		
number format	Home, Number		
orientation	Home, Alignment		
repeat last action			F4 or Ctrl + Y
right-align (in column)	Home, Alignment		
themes	Page Layout, Themes		
top-align (in row)	Home, Alignment		
underline text	Home, Font		Ctrl + U
wrap text	Home, Alignment		

Workbook

Chapter study tools and assessment activities are available in the *Workbook* ebook. These resources are designed to help you further develop and demonstrate mastery of the skills learned in this chapter.

Microsoft®

Excel®

CHAPTER

4

Enhancing a Worksheet

Performance Objectives

Upon successful completion of Chapter 4, you will be able to:

1. Change the margins in a worksheet
2. Center a worksheet horizontally and vertically on the page
3. Change page orientation and size
4. Insert and remove a page break in a worksheet
5. Print column and row titles on multiple pages
6. Scale data
7. Insert a background picture
8. Print gridlines and row and column headings
9. Set and clear a print area
10. Insert headers and footers
11. Customize a print job
12. Complete a spelling check
13. Use the Undo and Redo
14. Find and replace data and cell formatting
15. Sort data in cells in ascending and descending order
16. Filter data

Precheck

Check your current skills to help focus your study.

Excel contains features you can use to enhance and control the formatting of a worksheet. In this chapter, you will learn how to change worksheet margins, orientation, size, and scale; print column and row titles; print gridlines; and center a worksheet horizontally and vertically on the page. You will also learn how to complete a spelling check on the text in a worksheet, find and replace specific data and formatting in a worksheet, sort and filter data, and plan and create a worksheet.

Data Files

Before beginning chapter work, copy the EL1C4 folder to your storage medium and then make EL1C4 the active folder.

SNAP

If you are a SNAP user, launch the Precheck and Tutorials from your Assignments page.

Project 1 Format a Yearly Budget Worksheet

12 Parts

You will format a yearly budget worksheet by inserting formulas; changing margins, page orientation, and page size; inserting a page break; printing column headings on multiple pages; scaling data to print on one page; inserting a background picture; inserting headers and footers; and identifying a print area and customizing a print job.

Preview Finished Project

Tutorial

Changing Page Layout Options

Formatting a Worksheet Page

An Excel worksheet has default page formatting. For example, a worksheet has left and right margins of 0.7 inch and top and bottom margins of 0.75 inch. In addition, a worksheet prints in portrait orientation and its page size is 8.5 inches by 11 inches. These defaults, along with additional settings, can be changed and/or controlled with options on the Page Layout tab.

Changing Margins

The Page Setup group on the Page Layout tab contains buttons for changing the margins and the page orientation and size. In addition, it contains buttons for establishing a print area, inserting a page break, applying a picture background, and printing titles.

Margins

Quick Steps

Change Worksheet Margins

1. Click Page Layout tab.
2. Click Margins button.
3. Click predesigned margin.

OR

1. Click Page Layout tab.
2. Click Margins button.
3. Click *Custom Margins* at drop-down list.
4. Change the top, left, right, and/or bottom measurements.
5. Click OK.

Change the worksheet margins by clicking the Margins button in the Page Setup group on the Page Layout tab. This displays a drop-down list of predesigned margin choices. If one of the predesigned choices applies the desired margins, click that option. To customize the margins, click the *Custom Margins* option at the bottom of the Margins button drop-down list. This displays the Page Setup dialog box with the Margins tab selected, as shown in Figure 4.1.

Figure 4.1 Page Setup Dialog Box with Margins Tab Selected

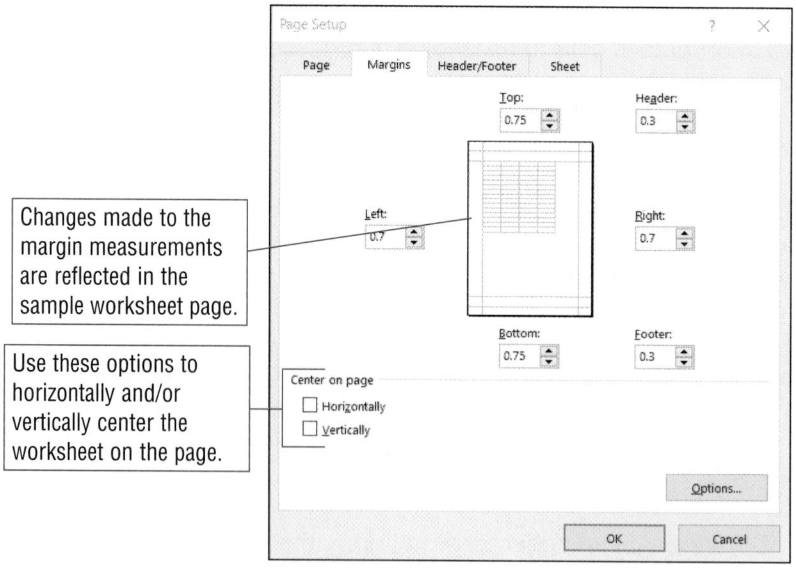

A worksheet page showing the cells and margins displays in the dialog box. As the top, bottom, left, or right margin measurements are increased or decreased, the sample worksheet page reflects the change. The measurement from the top of the page to the header can be increased or decreased with the *Header* measurement box and the measurement from the footer to the bottom of the page can be changed with the *Footer* measurement box. (Headers and footers are covered later in this chapter.)

Quick Steps

Center a Worksheet Horizontally and/or Vertically

1. Click Page Layout tab.
2. Click Margins button.
3. Click *Custom Margins.*
4. Click *Horizontally* option and/or click *Vertically* check box.
5. Click OK.

Centering a Worksheet Horizontally and/or Vertically

By default, a worksheet prints in the upper left corner of the page. A worksheet can be centered on the page by changing the margins. However, an easier method for centering a worksheet is to use the *Horizontally* and/or *Vertically* check boxes that display in the Page Setup dialog box with the Margins tab selected. Choose one or both of these check boxes and the worksheet page in the preview section displays how the worksheet will print on the page.

Project 1a Changing Margins and Horizontally and Vertically Centering a Worksheet

Part 1 of 12

1. Open **RPBudget.xlsx** and then save it with the name **4-RPBudget.**
2. Insert the following formulas in the worksheet:
   a. Insert formulas in column N, rows 5 through 10 that sum the totals for all the income items.
   b. Insert formulas in row 11, columns B through N that sum the income amounts and the totals for all the income items.
   c. Insert formulas in column N, rows 14 through 19 that sum the totals for all the expense items.
   d. Insert formulas in row 20, columns B through N that sum the expenses and the totals for all the expense items.
   e. Insert formulas in row 21, columns B through N that subtract the total expenses from the income. (Make cell B21 active and then type the formula =b11-b20. Copy this formula to columns C through N.)
   f. Apply the Accounting format with no digits past the decimal point to cell N5 and cell N14.
3. Click the Page Layout tab.
4. Click the Margins button in the Page Setup group and then click *Custom Margins* at the drop-down list.

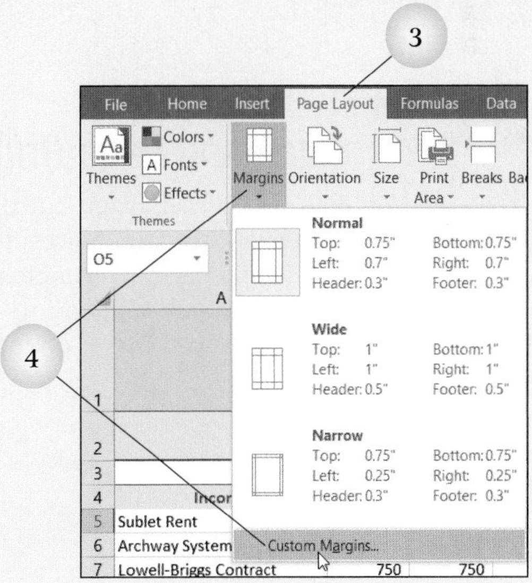

5. At the Page Setup dialog box with the Margins tab selected, click the *Top* measurement box up arrow until *3.5* displays.
6. Click the *Bottom* measurement box up arrow until *1.5* displays.
7. Preview the worksheet by clicking the Print Preview button at the bottom of the Page Setup dialog box. The worksheet appears to be a little low on the page so you decide to horizontally and vertically center it by completing the following steps:
   a. Click the Page Setup hyperlink below the galleries in the *Settings* category in the Print backstage area.
   b. Click the Margins tab at the Page Setup dialog box.
   c. Change the *Top* and *Bottom* measurements to *1*.
   d. Click the *Horizontally* check box to insert a check mark.
   e. Click the *Vertically* check box to insert a check mark.
   f. Click OK to close the dialog box.
   g. Look at the preview of the worksheet and then click the Back button to return to the worksheet.
8. Save **4-RPBudget.xlsx**.

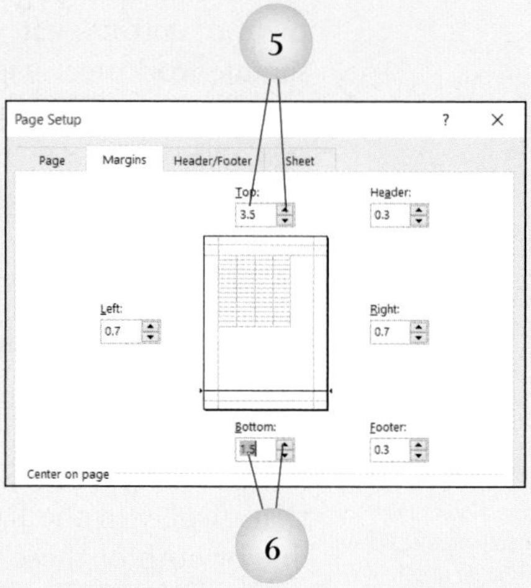

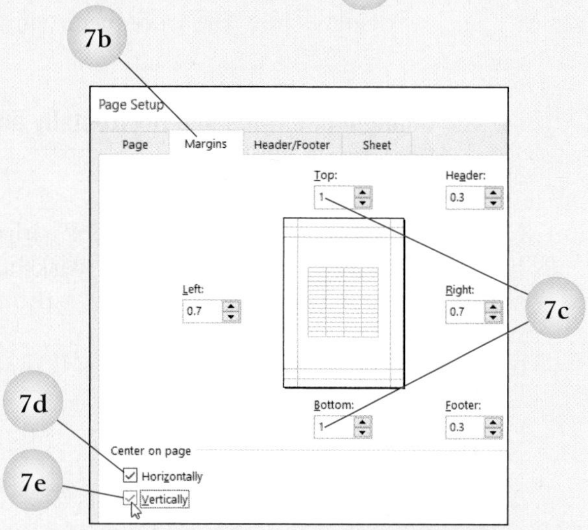

Check Your Work

Changing Page Orientation

Orientation

Quick Steps

Change Page Orientation

1. Click Page Layout tab.
2. Click Orientation button.
3. Click orientation at drop-down list.

Click the Orientation button in the Page Setup group and a drop-down list displays with two choices: *Portrait* and *Landscape*. The two choices are represented by sample pages. A sample page that is taller than it is wide shows how the default orientation (*Portrait*) prints data on the page. The other choice, *Landscape*, rotates the data and prints it on a page that is wider than it is tall.

Changing the Page Size

Quick Steps

Change Page Size
1. Click Page Layout tab.
2. Click Size button.
3. Click size at drop-down list.

Size

By default, an Excel worksheet page size is 8.5 inches by 11 inches. Change this default page size by clicking the Size button in the Page Setup group. At the drop-down list that displays, notice that the default setting is *Letter* and that the measurement *8.5" × 11"* displays below *Letter*. This drop-down list also contains a number of page sizes, such as *Executive* and *Legal*, and a number of envelope sizes.

Project 1b Changing Page Orientation and Size

Part 2 of 12

1. With **4-RPBudget.xlsx** open, click the Orientation button in the Page Setup group on the Page Layout tab and then click *Landscape* at the drop-down list.
2. Click the Size button in the Page Setup group and then click *Legal* at the drop-down list.
3. Preview the worksheet by clicking the File tab and then clicking the *Print* option. After viewing the worksheet in the Print backstage area, press the Esc key to return to the worksheet.
4. Save **4-RPBudget.xlsx**.

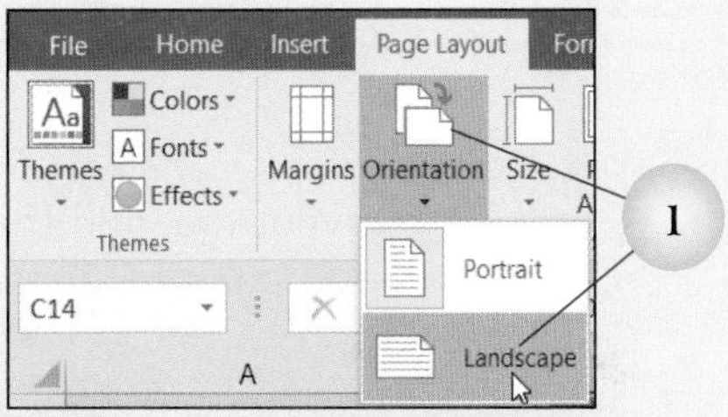

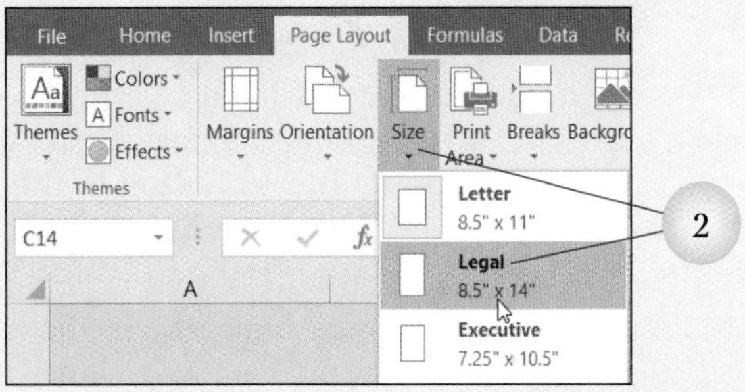

Check Your Work

Inserting and Removing Page Breaks

Tutorial

Using Page Break Preview

Quick Steps

Insert a Page Break
1. Select column or row.
2. Click Page Layout tab.
3. Click Breaks button.
4. Click *Insert Page Break*.

Breaks

The default left and right margins of 0.7 inch allow approximately 7 inches of cells across the page (8.5 inches minus 1.4 inches equals 7.1 inches). If a worksheet contains more than 7 inches of cells across the page, a page break is inserted and the remaining columns are moved to the next page. A page break displays as a dashed line along cell borders. Figure 4.2 shows the page break in **4-RPBudget.xlsx** when the paper size is set to *Letter*.

A page break also displays horizontally in a worksheet. By default, a worksheet can contain approximately 9.5 inches of cells down the page. This is because the paper size is set by default at 11 inches. With the default top and bottom margins of 0.75 inch, this allows 9.5 inches of cells to print vertically on one page.

Excel automatically inserts page breaks in a worksheet. To have more control over what cells print on a page, insert a page break. To insert a page break, select a column or row, click the Breaks button in the Page Setup group on the Page

Figure 4.2 Page Break

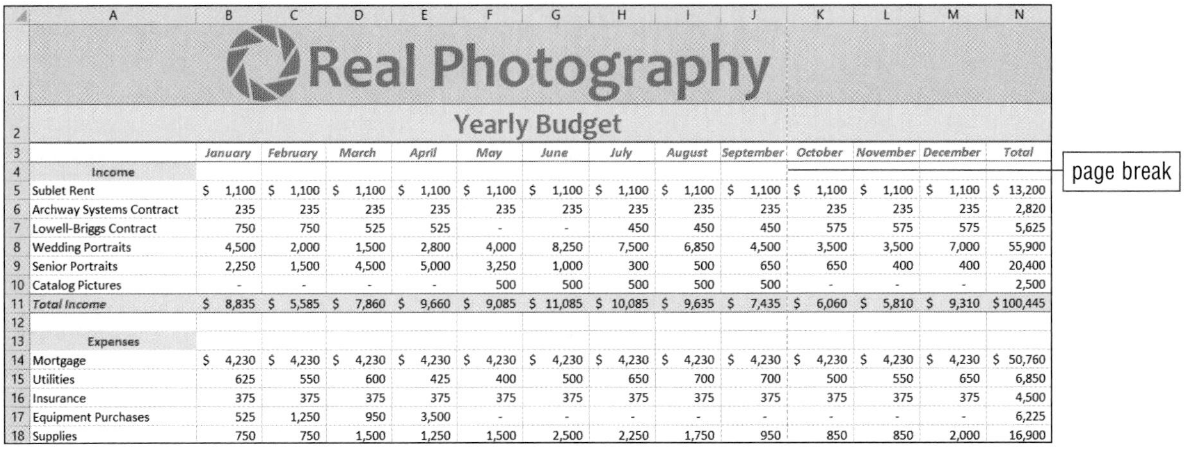

	A	B	C	D	E	F	G	H	I	J	K	L	M	N
1	Real Photography													
2	Yearly Budget													
3		*January*	*February*	*March*	*April*	*May*	*June*	*July*	*August*	*September*	*October*	*November*	*December*	*Total*
4	Income													
5	Sublet Rent	$ 1,100	$ 1,100	$ 1,100	$ 1,100	$ 1,100	$ 1,100	$ 1,100	$ 1,100	$ 1,100	$ 1,100	$ 1,100	$ 1,100	$ 13,200
6	Archway Systems Contract	235	235	235	235	235	235	235	235	235	235	235	235	2,820
7	Lowell-Briggs Contract	750	750	525	525	-	-	450	450	450	575	575	575	5,625
8	Wedding Portraits	4,500	2,000	1,500	2,800	4,000	8,250	7,500	6,850	4,500	3,500	3,500	7,000	55,900
9	Senior Portraits	2,250	1,500	4,500	5,000	3,250	1,000	300	500	650	650	400	400	20,400
10	Catalog Pictures	-	-	-	-	500	500	500	500	500	-	-	-	2,500
11	*Total Income*	$ 8,835	$ 5,585	$ 7,860	$ 9,660	$ 9,085	$ 11,085	$ 10,085	$ 9,635	$ 7,435	$ 6,060	$ 5,810	$ 9,310	$ 100,445
12														
13	Expenses													
14	Mortgage	$ 4,230	$ 4,230	$ 4,230	$ 4,230	$ 4,230	$ 4,230	$ 4,230	$ 4,230	$ 4,230	$ 4,230	$ 4,230	$ 4,230	$ 50,760
15	Utilities	625	550	600	425	400	500	650	700	700	500	550	650	6,850
16	Insurance	375	375	375	375	375	375	375	375	375	375	375	375	4,500
17	Equipment Purchases	525	1,250	950	3,500	-	-	-	-	-	-	-	-	6,225
18	Supplies	750	750	1,500	1,250	1,500	2,500	2,250	1,750	950	850	850	2,000	16,900

Layout tab, and then click *Insert Page Break* at the drop-down list. A page break is inserted immediately left of the selected column or immediately above the selected row.

To insert both horizontal and vertical page breaks at the same time, make a cell active, click the Breaks button in the Page Setup group, and then click *Insert Page Break*. This causes a horizontal page break to be inserted immediately above the active cell and a vertical page break to be inserted at the left side of the active cell. To remove a page break, select the column or row or make the cell active, click the Breaks button in the Page Setup group, and then click *Remove Page Break* at the drop-down list.

A page break that is automatically inserted by Excel may not be visible in a worksheet. One way to display the page break is to display the worksheet in the Print backstage area. Return to the worksheet and the page break will display in the worksheet.

Page Break Preview

Hint You can edit a worksheet in Page Break Preview.

Normal

Excel provides a page break view that displays worksheet pages and page breaks. To display this view, click the Page Break Preview button in the view area at the right side of the Status bar or click the View tab and then click the Page Break Preview button in the Workbook Views group. This causes the worksheet to display similarly to the worksheet shown in Figure 4.3. The word *Page* along with the page number displays in gray behind the cells in the worksheet. A dashed blue line indicates a page break inserted automatically by Excel and a solid blue line indicates a page break inserted manually.

Move a page break by positioning the arrow pointer on the blue line, holding down the left mouse button, dragging the line to the desired location, and then releasing the mouse button. To return to Normal view, click the Normal button in the view area on the Status bar or click the View tab and then click the Normal button in the Workbook Views group.

Figure 4.3 Worksheet in Page Break Preview

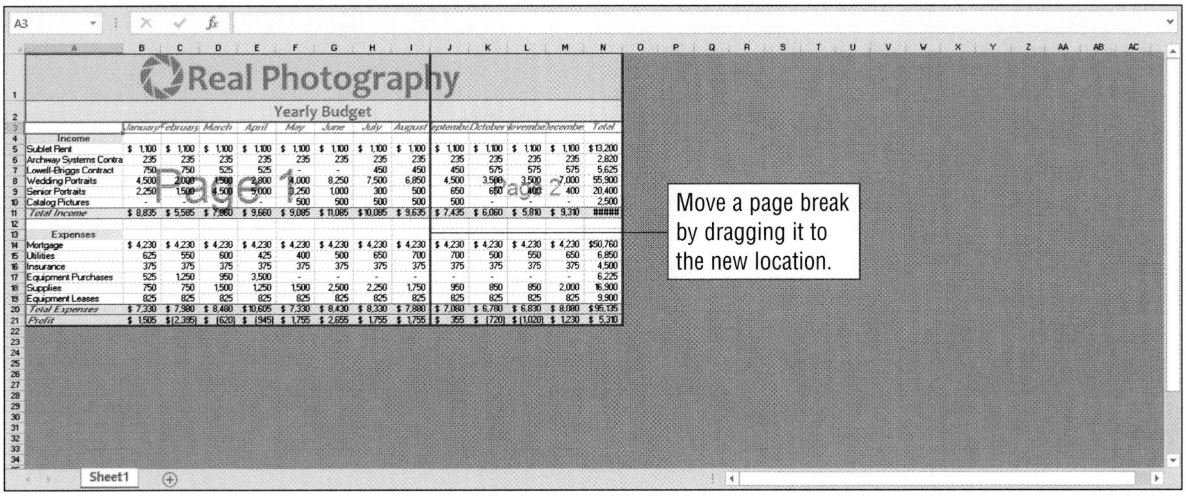

Project 1c Inserting a Page Break in a Worksheet

Part 3 of 12

1. With **4-RPBudget.xlsx** open, click the Size button in the Page Setup group on the Page Layout tab and then click *Letter* at the drop-down list.
2. Click the Margins button and then click *Custom Margins* at the drop-down list.
3. At the Page Setup dialog box with the Margins tab selected, click in the *Horizontally* check box to remove the check mark, click in the *Vertically* check box to remove the check mark, and then click OK to close the dialog box.
4. Insert a page break between columns I and J by completing the following steps:
   a. Select column J.
   b. Click the Breaks button in the Page Setup group and then click *Insert Page Break* at the drop-down list. Click in any cell in column I.
5. View the worksheet in Page Break Preview by completing the following steps:
   a. Click the Page Break Preview button in the view area at the right side of the Status bar.
   b. View the pages and page breaks in the worksheet.
   c. You decide to include the first six months of the year on one page. To do this, position the arrow pointer on the vertical blue line until the arrow pointer displays as a left-and-right-pointing arrow, click and hold down the left mouse button, drag the line to the left so it is positioned between columns G and H, and then release the mouse button.

4b

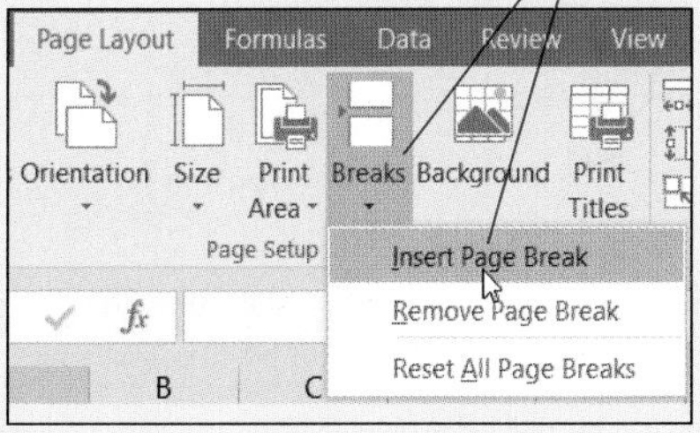

5a

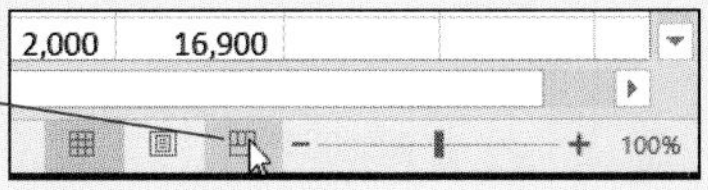

5c

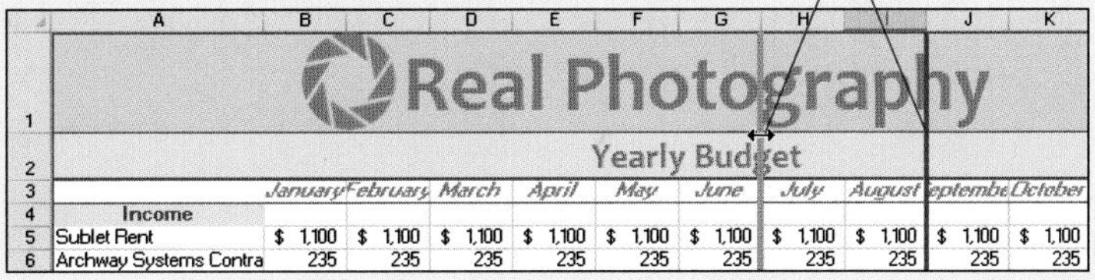

d. Click the Normal button in the view area on the Status bar.

6. Save **4-RPBudget.xlsx**.

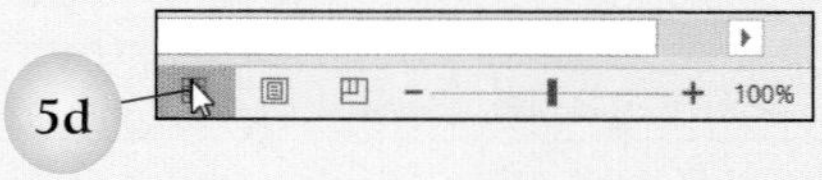

Check Your Work

Printing Column and Row Titles on Multiple Pages

The columns and rows in a worksheet are usually titled. For example, in 4-RPBudget.xlsx, the column titles include *Income*, *Expenses*, *January*, *February*, *March*, and so on. The row titles include the income and expenses categories. If a worksheet prints on more than one page, having column and/or row titles print on each page provides context for understanding the text and values in columns and rows. To do this, click the Print Titles button in the Page Setup group on the Page Layout tab. This displays the Page Setup dialog box with the Sheet tab selected, as shown in Figure 4.4.

Print Titles

Quick Steps

Print Column and Row Titles

1. Click Page Layout tab.
2. Click Print Titles button.
3. Type row range in *Rows to repeat at top* option.
4. Type column range in *Columns to repeat at left* option.
5. Click OK.

At the Page Setup dialog box with the Sheet tab selected, specify the range of row cells to print on every page in the *Rows to repeat at top* text box. Type a cell range using a colon. For example, to print the range A1:J1 on every page, type *a1:j1* in the *Rows to repeat at top* text box. Type the range of column cells to print on every page in the *Columns to repeat at left* text box. To make rows and columns easy to identify on the printed page, specify that row and/or column headings print on each page.

Figure 4.4 Page Setup Dialog Box with Sheet Tab Selected

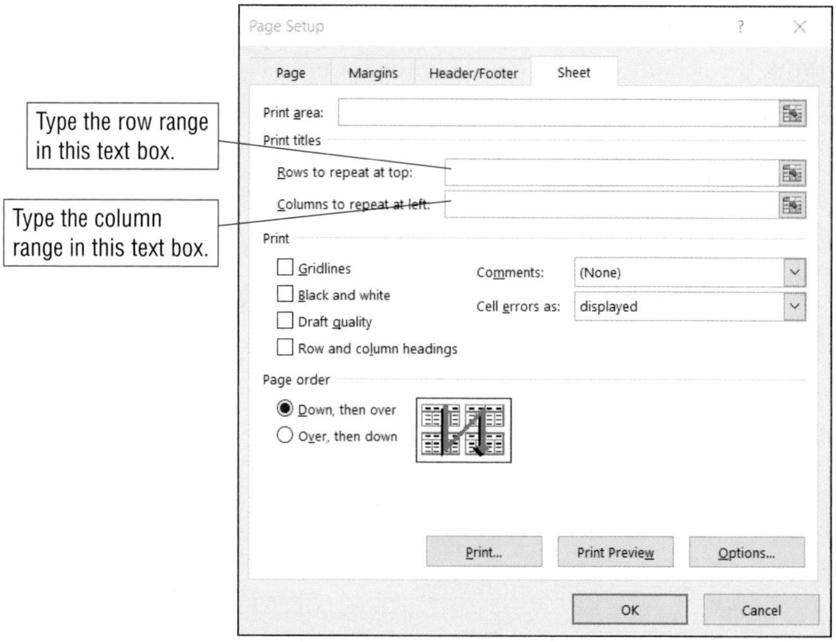

Project 1d **Printing Column Titles on Each Page of a Worksheet** Part 4 of 12

1. With **4-RPBudget.xlsx** open, click the Page Layout tab and then click the Print Titles button in the Page Setup group.
2. At the Page Setup dialog box with the Sheet tab selected, click in the *Columns to repeat at left* text box.
3. Type a1:a21.
4. Click OK to close the dialog box.
5. Save and then print **4-RPBudget.xlsx**.

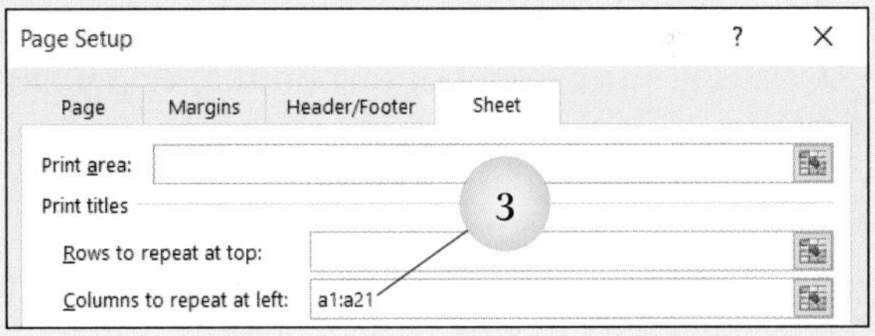

Check Your Work

Scaling Data

Width

Use buttons in the Scale to Fit group on the Page Layout tab to adjust the printed output by a percentage to fit the number of pages specified. For example, if a worksheet contains too many columns to print on one page, click the *Width* option box arrow in the Scale to Fit group on the Page Layout tab and then click *1 page*. This reduces the size of the data so all the columns display and print on one page. Manually adjust the scale of a worksheet by clicking the up or down arrows in the *Scale* measurement box, or by typing a percentage into the *Scale* measurement box and pressing the Enter key.

Project 1e **Scaling Data to Fit on One Page and Printing Row Titles on Each Page** Part 5 of 12

1. With **4-RPBudget.xlsx** open, display the Page Setup dialog box with the Sheet tab selected.
2. Select and then delete the text that displays in the *Columns to repeat at left* text box and then click the OK button.
3. Click the *Width* option box arrow in the Scale to Fit group on the Page Layout tab and then click the *1 page* option at the drop-down list.

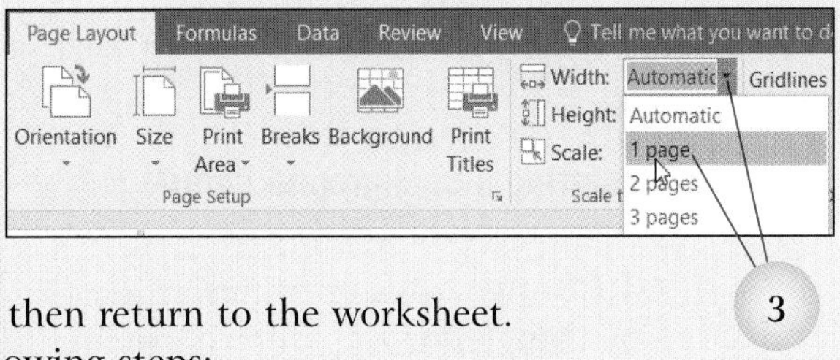

4. Display the Print backstage area, notice that all the cells that contain data display on one page in the worksheet, and then return to the worksheet.
5. Change the margins by completing the following steps:
   a. Click the Margins button in the Page Setup group and then click *Custom Margins* at the drop-down list.
   b. At the Page Setup dialog box with the Margins tab selected, select the current number in the *Top* measurement box and then type 3.5.
   c. Select the current number in the *Left* measurement box and then type 0.3.
   d. Select the current number in the *Right* measurement box and then type 0.3.
   e. Click OK to close the Page Setup dialog box.
6. Specify that you want row titles to print on each page by completing the following steps:
   a. Click the Print Titles button in the Page Setup group on the Page Layout tab.
   b. Click in the *Rows to repeat at top* text box and then type a3:n3.
   c. Click OK to close the dialog box.

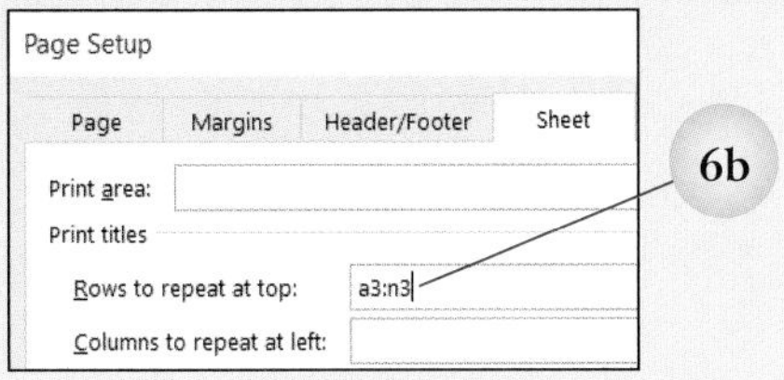

7. Save and then print **4-RPBudget.xlsx**. (The worksheet prints on two pages and the row titles are repeated on the second page.)
8. At the worksheet, return to the default margins by clicking the Page Layout tab, clicking the Margins button, and then clicking the *Normal* option at the drop-down list.
9. Prevent titles from printing on the second and subsequent pages by completing the following steps:
   a. Click the Print Titles button in the Page Setup group.
   b. At the Page Setup dialog box with the Sheet tab selected, select and then delete the text in the *Rows to repeat at top* text box.
   c. Click OK to close the dialog box.
10. Change the scaling back to the default by completing the following steps:
   a. Click the *Width* option box arrow in the Scale to Fit group and then click *Automatic* at the drop-down list.
   b. Click the *Scale* measurement box up arrow until *100%* displays in the box.
11. Save **4-RPBudget.xlsx**.

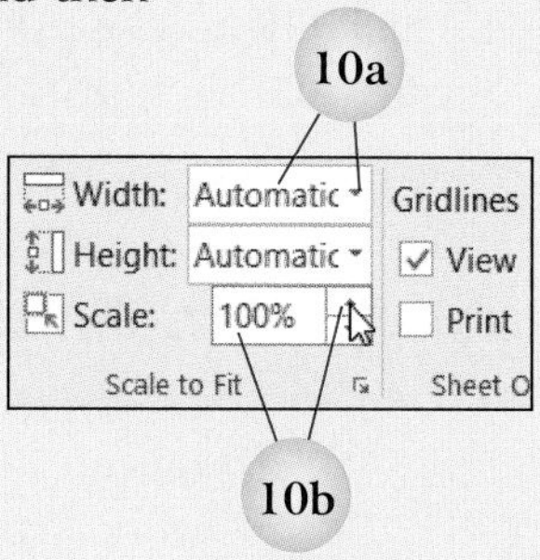

Check Your Work

Inserting a Background Picture

Quick Steps
Insert a Background Picture
1. Click Page Layout tab.
2. Click Background button.
3. Navigate to picture and double-click picture.

Background

Insert a picture as a background for a worksheet with the Background button in the Page Setup group on the Page Layout tab. The picture displays only on the screen and does not print. To insert a picture, click the Background button in the Page Setup group and then click the Browse button at the Insert Pictures window. At the Sheet Background dialog box, navigate to the folder containing the picture and then double-click the picture. To remove the picture from the worksheet, click the Delete Background button.

Project 1f Inserting a Background Picture — Part 6 of 12

1. With **4-RPBudget.xlsx** open, insert a background picture by completing the following steps:
   a. Click the Background button in the Page Setup group on the Page Layout tab.
   b. At the Insert Pictures window, click the Browse button.
   c. At the Sheet Background dialog box, navigate to your EL1C4 folder and then double-click ***Ship.jpg***.
   d. Scroll down the worksheet to display the ship.
2. Display the Print backstage area, notice that the picture does not display in the preview worksheet, and then return to the worksheet.
3. Remove the picture by clicking the Delete Background button in the Page Setup group on the Page Layout tab.
4. Save **4-RPBudget.xlsx**.

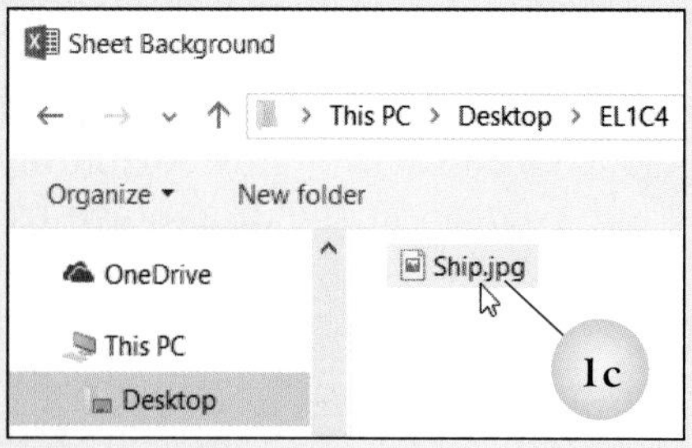

Check Your Work

Printing Gridlines and Row and Column Headings

Quick Steps

Print Gridlines and/or Row and Column Headings
1. Click Page Layout tab.
2. Click *Print* check boxes in *Gridlines* and/ or *Headings* section in Sheet Options group.

OR
1. Click Page Layout tab.
2. Click Sheet Options dialog box launcher.
3. Click *Gridlines* and/ or *Row and column headings* check boxes.
4. Click OK.

By default, the gridlines that create the cells in a worksheet and the row numbers and column letters that label the cells do not print. The Sheet Options group on the Page Layout tab contains check boxes for gridlines and headings. The *View* check boxes for gridlines and headings contain check marks. At these settings, gridlines and row and column headings display on the screen but do not print. To print gridlines and headings, insert check marks in the *Print* check boxes. Complex worksheets may be easier to read with the gridlines printed.

The display and printing of gridlines and headings can also be controlled with options at the Page Setup dialog box with the Sheet tab selected. Display this dialog box by clicking the Sheet Options group dialog box launcher. To print gridlines and headings, insert check marks in the check boxes in the *Print* section of the dialog box. The *Print* section contains two additional options: *Black and white* and *Draft quality*. When printing with a color printer, insert a check mark in the *Black and white* check box to print the worksheet in black and white. Insert a check mark in the *Draft quality* option to print a draft of the worksheet. With this option checked, some types of formatting, such as shading and fill, do not print.

Project 1g Printing Gridlines and Row and Column Headings — Part 7 of 12

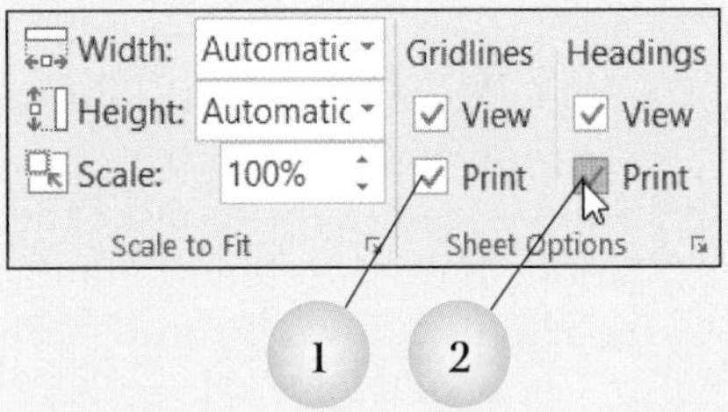

1. With **4-RPBudget.xlsx** open, click in the *Print* check box below *Gridlines* in the Sheet Options group on the Page Layout tab to insert a check mark.
2. Click in the *Print* check box below *Headings* in the Sheet Options group to insert a check mark.
3. Click the Margins button in the Page Setup group and then click *Custom Margins* at the drop-down list.
4. At the Page Setup dialog box with the Margins tab selected, click in the *Horizontally* check box to insert a check mark.
5. Click in the *Vertically* check box to insert a check mark.
6. Click OK to close the dialog box.
7. Save and then print **4-RPBudget.xlsx**.
8. Click in the *Print* check box below *Headings* in the Sheet Options group to remove the check mark.
9. Click in the *Print* check box below *Gridlines* in the Sheet Options group to remove the check mark.
10. Save **4-RPBudget.xlsx**.

Check Your Work

Printing a Specific Area of a Worksheet

Print Area

Use the Print Area button in the Page Setup group on the Page Layout tab to select and print specific areas of a worksheet. To do this, select the cells to print, click the Print Area button in the Page Setup group, and then click *Set Print Area* at the drop-down list. This inserts a border around the selected cells. Display the Print backstage area and click the Print button to print the cells within the border.

More than one print area can be specified in a worksheet. To do this, select the first group of cells, click the Print Area button in the Page Setup group, and then click *Set Print Area*. Select the next group of cells, click the Print Area button, and then click *Add to Print Area*. Clear a print area by clicking the Print Area button in the Page Setup group and then clicking *Clear Print Area* at the drop-down list.

Each area specified as a print area prints on a separate page. To print nonadjacent print areas on the same page, consider hiding columns and/or rows in the worksheet to bring the areas together.

Project 1h Printing Specific Areas

Part 8 of 12

1. With **4-RPBudget.xlsx** open, print the first half of the year's income and expenses by completing the following steps:
   a. Select the range A3:G21.
   b. Click the Print Area button in the Page Setup group on the Page Layout tab and then click *Set Print Area* at the drop-down list.
   c. With the border surrounding the range A3:G21, click the File tab, click the *Print* option, and then click the Print button at the Print backstage area.
   d. Clear the print area by clicking the Print Area button in the Page Setup group and then clicking *Clear Print Area* at the drop-down list.

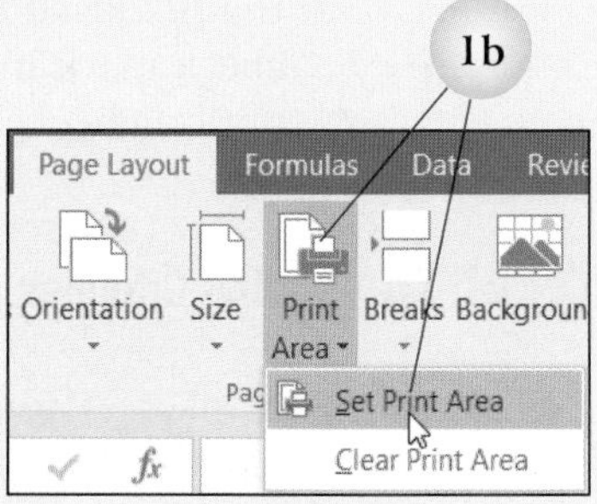

2. Suppose you want to print the income and expenses information as well as the totals for April. To do this, hide columns and select a print area by completing the following steps:
   a. Select columns B through D.
   b. Click the Home tab.
   c. Click the Format button in the Cells group, point to *Hide & Unhide*, and then click *Hide Columns*.
   d. Click the Page Layout tab.
   e. Select the range A3:E21. (Columns A and E are now adjacent.)
   f. Click the Print Area button in the Page Setup group and then click *Set Print Area* at the drop-down list.
3. Click the File tab, click the *Print* option, and then click the Print button.
4. Clear the print area by ensuring that the range A3:E21 is selected, clicking the Print Area button in the Page Setup group, and then clicking *Clear Print Area* at the drop-down list.
5. Unhide the columns by completing the following steps:
   a. Click the Home tab.
   b. Select columns A and E. (These columns are adjacent.)
   c. Click the Format button in the Cells group, point to *Hide & Unhide*, and then click *Unhide Columns*.
   d. Deselect the text by clicking in any cell containing data in the worksheet.
6. Save **4-RPBudget.xlsx**.

Check Your Work

Tutorial

Inserting Headers and Footers

Header & Footer

Quick Steps

Insert a Header or Footer

1. Click Insert tab.
2. Click Header & Footer button.
3. Click Header button and then click predesigned header or click Footer button and then click predesigned footer.

OR

1. Click Insert tab.
2. Click Header & Footer button.
3. Click header or footer elements.

Inserting Headers and Footers

Text that prints at the top of each worksheet page is called a *header* and text that prints at the bottom of each worksheet page is called a *footer*. Create a header and/or footer with the Header & Footer button in the Text group on the Insert tab in Page Layout view or with options at the Page Setup dialog box with the Header/Footer tab selected.

To create a header with the Header & Footer button, click the Insert tab and then click the Header & Footer button in the Text group. This displays the worksheet in Page Layout view and displays the Header & Footer Tools Design tab. Use buttons on this tab, shown in Figure 4.5, to insert predesigned headers and/or footers or to insert header and footer elements such as page numbers, date, time, path name, and file name. A different header or footer can be created on the first page of the worksheet or one header or footer can be created for even pages and another for odd pages.

At the Print backstage area, preview headers and footers before printing. Click the File tab and then click the *Print* option to display the Print backstage area. A preview of the worksheet displays at the right side of the backstage area. If the worksheet will print on more than one page, view the different pages by clicking the Next Page button or the Previous Page button. These buttons are below and to the left of the preview worksheet at the Print backstage area. Two buttons display in the bottom right corner of the Print backstage area. Click the Zoom to Page button to zoom in or out of the preview of the worksheet. Click the Show Margins button to display margin guidelines and handles on the preview page. The handles, which display as black squares, can be used to increase or decrease the page margins and column widths. To do this, position the mouse pointer on the desired handle, click and hold down the left mouse button, drag to the new position, and then release the mouse button.

Figure 4.5 Header & Footer Tools Design Tab

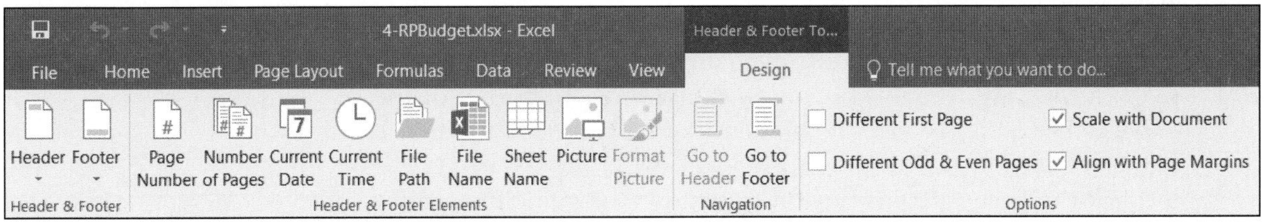

Project 1i **Inserting a Header in a Worksheet** Part 9 of 12

1. With **4-RPBudget.xlsx** open, create a header by completing the following steps:
   a. Click the Insert tab.
   b. Click the Header & Footer button in the Text group.

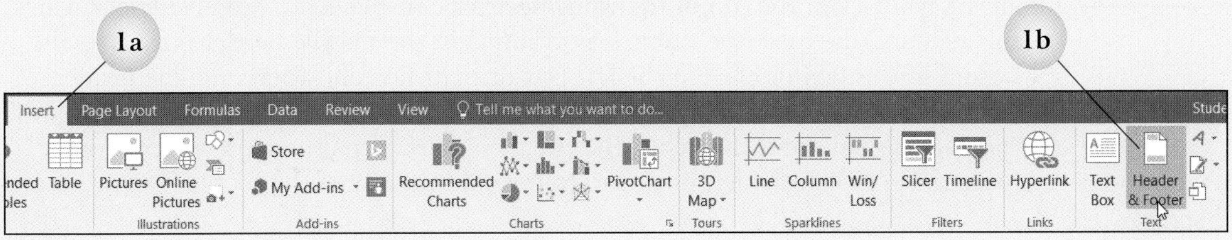

c. Click the Header button at the left side of the Header & Footer Tools Design tab and then click *Page 1, 4-RPBudget.xlsx* at the drop-down list. (This inserts the page number in the middle header box and the workbook name in the right header box.)

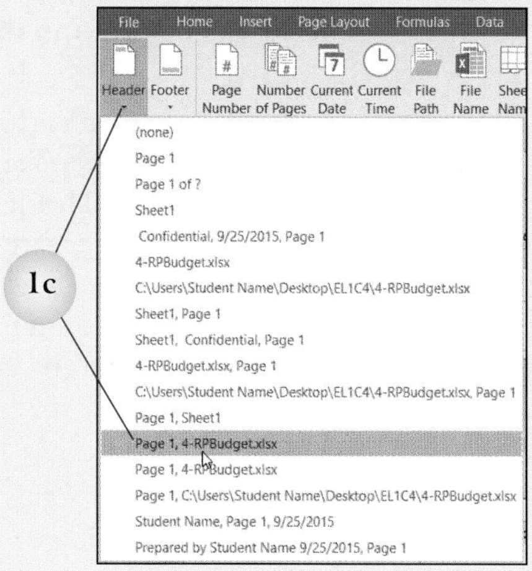

2. Preview the worksheet by completing the following steps:
   a. Click the File tab and then click the *Print* option.
   b. At the Print backstage area, look at the preview worksheet at the right side of the backstage area.
   c. View the next page of the worksheet by clicking the Next Page button below and to the left of the preview worksheet.
   d. View the first page by clicking the Previous Page button left of the Next Page button.
   e. Click the Zoom to Page button in the lower right corner of the backstage area. (Notice that the preview page has zoomed in on the worksheet.)
   f. Click the Zoom to Page button again.
   g. Click the Page Margins button in the lower right corner of the backstage area. (Notice the guidelines and handles that display on the preview page.)
   h. Click the Page Margins button to remove the guidelines and handles.
   i. Click the Back button to return to the worksheet.

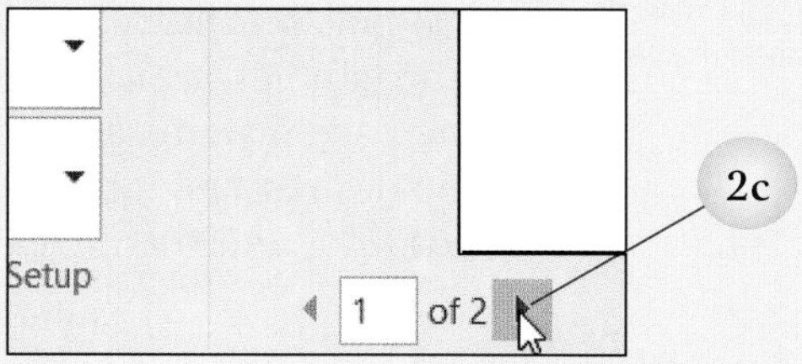

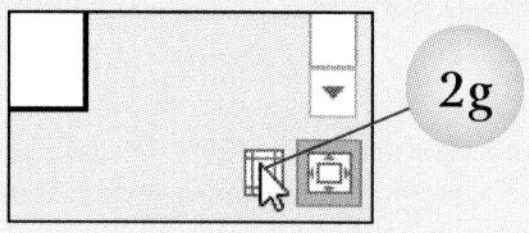

3. Save **4-RPBudget.xlsx**.

Check Your Work

A header and/or footer can also be inserted by working in Page Layout view. In Page Layout view, the top of the worksheet page displays the text *Add header*. Click this text and the insertion point is positioned in the middle header box. Type the header in this box or click in the left box or right box and then type the header. Create a footer in a similar manner. Scroll down the worksheet until the bottom of the page displays and then click the text *Add footer*. Type the footer in the center footer box or click the left box or right box and then type the footer.

Project 1j Inserting a Footer and Modifying a Header in a Worksheet

Part 10 of 12

1. With **4-RPBudget.xlsx** open, make sure the workbook displays in Page Layout view.
2. Scroll down the worksheet until the text *Add footer* displays and then click the text.

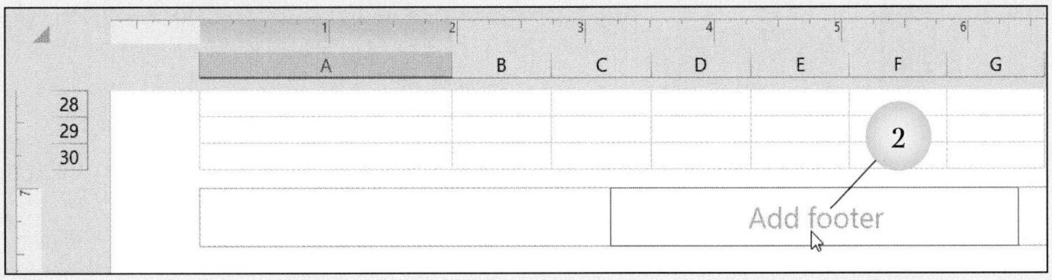

3. Type your first and last names.
4. Click in the left footer box, click the Header & Footer Tools Design tab, and then click the Current Date button in the Header & Footer Elements group. (This inserts a date code. The date will display when you click outside the footer box.)
5. Click in the right footer box and then click the Current Time button in the Header & Footer Elements group. (This inserts the time as a code. The time will display when you click outside the footer box.)
6. View the header and footer at the Print backstage area and then return to the worksheet.
7. Modify the header by completing the following steps:
   a. Scroll to the beginning of the worksheet and display the header text.
   b. Click the page number in the middle header box. (This displays the Header & Footer Tools Design tab, changes the header to a field, and selects the field.)
   c. Press the Delete key to delete the header.
   d. Click the header text in the right header box and then press the Delete key.
   e. With the insertion point positioned in the right header box, insert the page number by clicking the Header & Footer Tools Design tab and then clicking the Page Number button in the Header & Footer Elements group.
   f. Click in the left header box and then click the File Name button in the Header & Footer Elements group.
8. Click in any cell in the worksheet that contains data.
9. View the header and footer at the Print backstage area and then return to the worksheet.
10. Save **4-RPBudget.xlsx**.

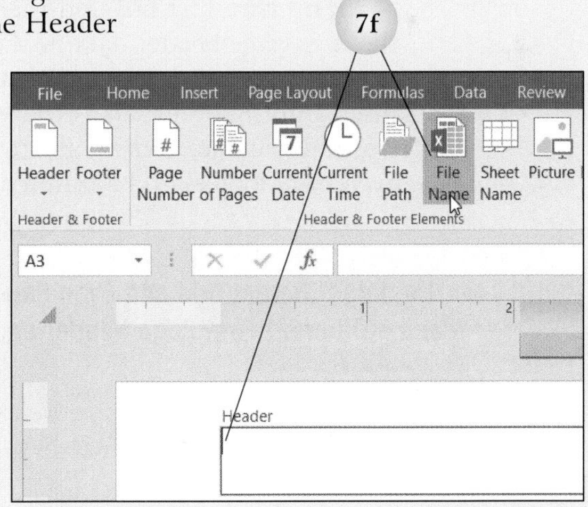

Check Your Work

Headers and footers can also be inserted and customized using options at the Page Setup dialog box with the Header/Footer tab selected, as shown in Figure 4.6. Display this dialog box by clicking the Page Layout tab and then clicking the Page Setup group dialog box launcher. At the Page Setup dialog box, click the Header/Footer tab. If a worksheet contains headers or footers, they will display in the dialog box. Use the check box options in the lower left corner of the dialog box to

Figure 4.6 Page Setup Dialog Box with Header/Footer Tab Selected

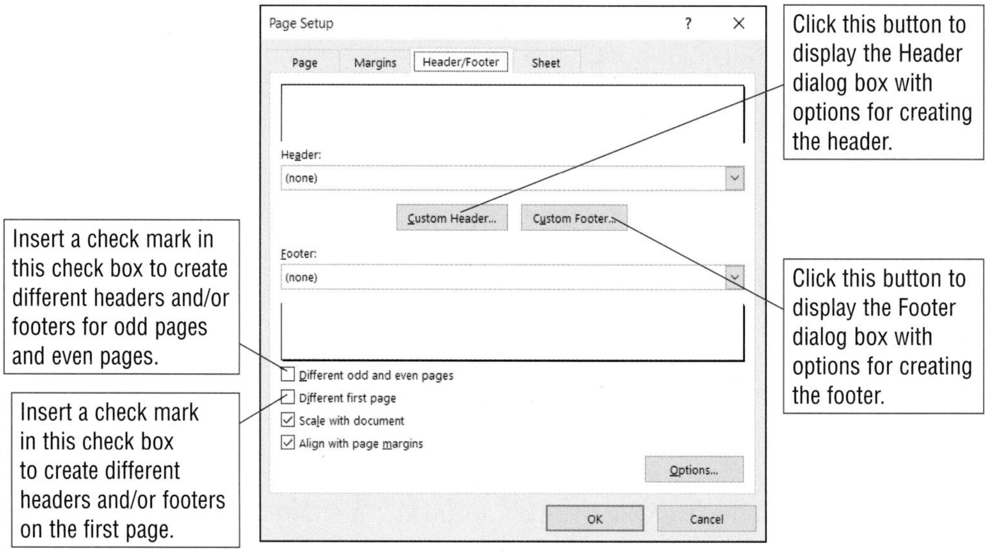

Page Setup
Page
Margins
Header/Footer
Sheet
Header:
(none)
Custom Header...
Custom Footer...
Footer:
(none)
Different odd and even pages
Different first page
Scale with document
Align with page margins
Options...
OK
Cancel
Click this button to display the Header dialog box with options for creating the header.
Click this button to display the Footer dialog box with options for creating the footer.
Insert a check mark in this check box to create different headers and/or footers for odd pages and even pages.
Insert a check mark in this check box to create different headers and/or footers on the first page.

insert different odd and even page headers and/or footers or to insert a different first page header and/or footer. The bottom two check box options are active by default. These defaults scale the header and footer text with the worksheet text and align the header and footer with the page margins.

To create different odd and even page headers, click the *Different odd and even pages* check box to insert a check mark and then click the Custom Header button. This displays the Header dialog box with the Odd Page Header tab selected. Type or insert the odd page header data in the *Left section*, *Center section*, or *Right section* text box and then click the Even Page Header tab. Type or insert the even page header data in the desired section text box and then click OK. Use the buttons that display above the section boxes to format the header text and insert information such as the page number, current date, current time, file name, worksheet name, and so on. Complete similar steps to create different odd and even page footers and a different first page header or footer.

Project 1k Creating Different Odd and Even Page Headers and Footers and a Different First Page Header and Footer

Part 11 of 12

1. With **4-RPBudget.xlsx** open, remove the page break by clicking the Page Layout tab, clicking the Breaks button in the Page Setup group, and then clicking *Reset All Page Breaks* at the drop-down list.
2. Change the margins by completing the following steps:
   a. Click the Margins button in the Page Setup group on the Page Layout tab and then click *Custom Margins* at the drop-down list.
   b. At the Page Setup dialog box with the Margins tab selected, select the current number in the *Left* measurement box and then type 3.
   c. Select the current number in the *Right* measurement box and then type 3.
   d. Click OK to close the dialog box.

3. Click the Page Setup group dialog box launcher on the Page Layout tab.
4. At the Page Setup dialog box, click the Header/Footer tab.
5. At the Page Setup dialog box with the Header/Footer tab selected, click the *Different odd and even pages* check box to insert a check mark and then click the Custom Header button.
6. At the Header dialog box with the Odd Page Header tab selected, click the Format Text button (above the *Left section* text box).
7. At the Font dialog box, click *12* in the *Size* list box and then click OK.
8. At the Header dialog box with the file name code (&[File]) highlighted, type Yearly Budget in the *Left section* text box.

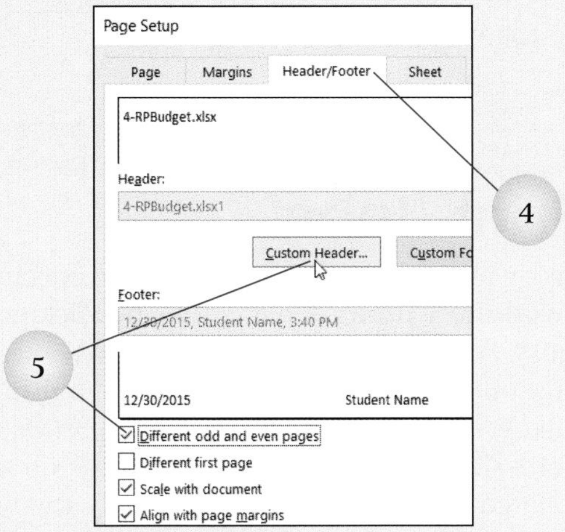

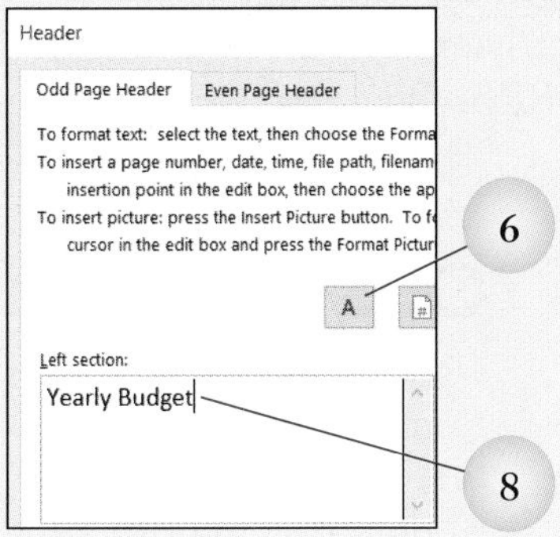

9. Click the Even Page Header tab, click in the *Left section* text box, and then click the Insert Page Number button.
10. Click in the *Right section* text box and then type Yearly Budget.
11. Select the text *Yearly Budget*, click the Format Text button, click *12* in the *Size* list box, and then click OK.
12. Click OK to close the Header dialog box.

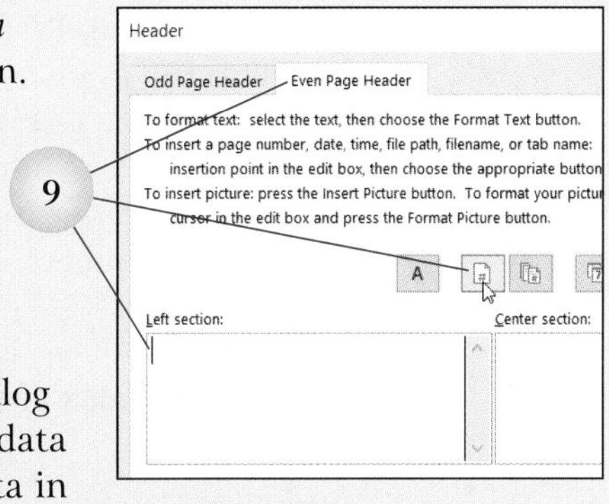

13. Click the Custom Footer button and, at the Footer dialog box with the Odd Page Footer tab selected, delete the data in the *Left section* text box and select and delete the data in the *Right section* text box. (The footer should contain only your name.)
14. Select your name, click the Format Text button, click *12* in the *Size* list box, and then click OK.
15. Click the Even Page Footer tab, type your name in the *Center section* text box, select your name, and then change the font size to 12 points.
16. Click OK to close the Footer dialog box and then click OK to close the Page Setup dialog box. (View the header and footer in the Print backstage area and then return to the worksheet.)
17. Click the Page Setup group dialog box launcher on the Page Layout tab.
18. At the Page Setup dialog box, click the Header/Footer tab.
19. At the Page Setup dialog box with the Header/Footer tab selected, click the *Different odd and even pages* check box to remove the check mark.
20. Click the *Different first page* check box to insert a check mark and then click the Custom Header button.

21. At the Header dialog box with the Header tab selected, click the First Page Header tab.
22. Click in the *Right section* text box and then click the Insert Page Number button.
23. Click OK to close the Header dialog box and then click OK to close the Page Setup dialog box.
24. View the header and footer in the Print backstage area and then return to the worksheet.
25. Save **4-RPBudget.xlsx**.

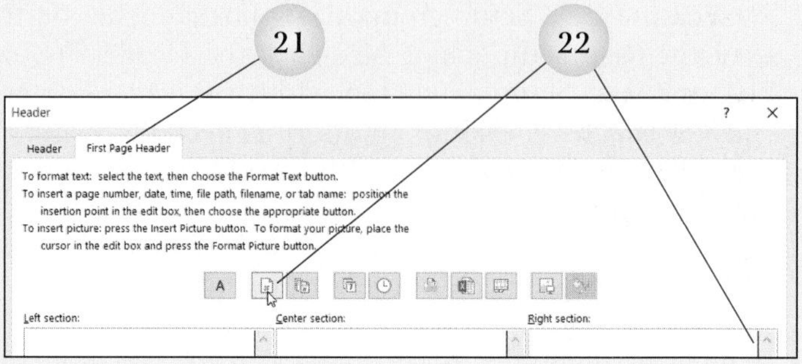

Check Your Work

Customizing Print Jobs

Use options in the *Settings* category at the Print backstage area to specify what to print. By default, the active worksheet prints. Change this by clicking the first gallery in the *Settings* category. At the drop-down list, specify if the entire workbook is to print (which is useful when a workbook contains multiple worksheets) or only selected cells. With the other galleries in the *Settings* category, specify if pages are to print on one side or both sides (this depends on the printer) and if they are to be collated. With other options, specify the worksheet orientation, size, and margins and whether the worksheet is to be scaled to fit all the columns or rows on one page.

With the *Pages* text boxes in the *Settings* category, specify the pages of the worksheet to be printed. For example, to print pages 2 and 3 of the active worksheet, type *2* in the *Pages* measurement box in the *Settings* category and then type *3* in the *to* measurement box. Or click the up- and down-pointing arrows to insert page numbers.

Project 1l Printing Specific Pages of a Worksheet

Part 12 of 12

1. With **4-RPBudget.xlsx** open, print the first two pages of the worksheet by completing the following steps:
   a. Click the File tab and then click the *Print* option.
   b. At the Print backstage area, click in the *Pages* measurement box below the first gallery in the *Settings* category and then type 1.
   c. Click in the *to* measurement box in the *Settings* category and then type 2.
   d. Click the Print button.

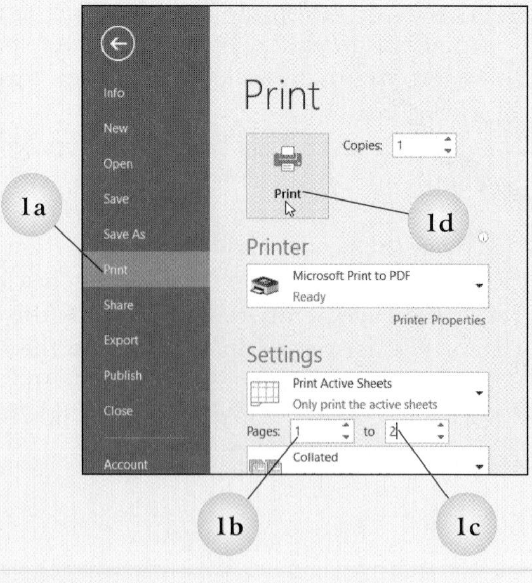

2. Print selected cells by completing the following steps:
   a. Display the worksheet in Normal view.
   b. Select the range A3:D11.
   c. Click the File tab and then click the *Print* option.
   d. At the Print backstage area, select and then delete the number in the *Pages* measurement box and the number in the *to* measurement box. (These are the numbers you inserted in Steps 1b and 1c.)
   e. Click the first gallery in the *Settings* category (displays with *Print Active Sheets*) and then click *Print Selection* at the drop-down list.
   f. Click the Print button.
3. Save and then close **4-RPBudget.xlsx**.

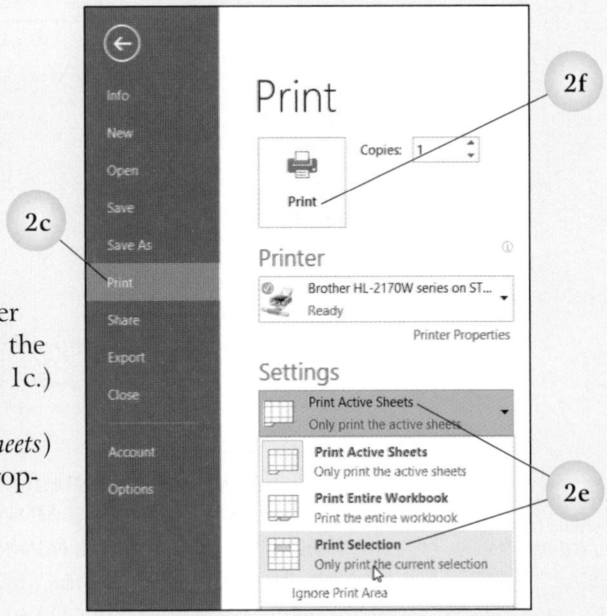

Check Your Work

Project 2 Format a Sales and Commissions Worksheet — 3 Parts

You will format a sales commission worksheet by inserting a formula, completing a spelling check, and finding and replacing data and cell formatting.

Preview Finished Project

Tutorial

Checking Spelling

Spelling

Quick Steps

Checking Spelling
1. Click Review tab.
2. Click Spelling button.
3. Replace or ignore selected words.

Checking Spelling

Excel provides a spelling check feature that verifies the spelling of text in a worksheet. The spelling check uses an electronic dictionary to identify misspelled words and suggest alternatives. Before checking the spelling in a worksheet, make the first cell active. The spelling check reviews the worksheet from the active cell to the last cell in the worksheet that contains data.

To use the spelling check, click the Review tab and then click the Spelling button. Figure 4.7 displays the Spelling dialog box. At this dialog box, tell Excel to ignore a word or to replace a misspelled word with a word from the *Suggestions* list box using one of the available buttons.

Tutorial

Using Undo and Redo

Undo

Redo

Using Undo and Redo

Excel includes an Undo button on the Quick Access Toolbar that reverses certain commands or deletes the last data typed in a cell. For example, apply formatting to cells in a worksheet and then click the Undo button on the Quick Access Toolbar and the formatting is removed. To reapply the formatting, click the Redo button on the Quick Access Toolbar.

Figure 4.7 Spelling Dialog Box

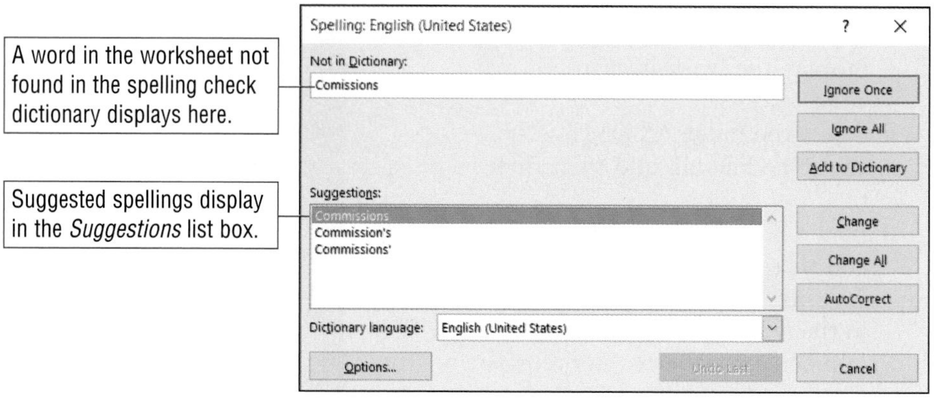

Hint Ctrl + Z is the keyboard shortcut to undo a command.

Excel maintains actions in temporary memory. To undo an action, click the Undo button arrow and a drop-down list displays containing the actions performed on the worksheet. Click a specific action at the drop-down list and that action along with any preceding actions are undone. Click the Redo button and click a specific action at the drop-down list and that action along with any preceding actions are redone. Multiple actions must be undone or redone in sequence.

Project 2a Spell Checking and Formatting a Worksheet

Part 1 of 3

1. Open **MRSales.xlsx** and then save it with the name **4-MRSales**.
2. Complete a spelling check on the worksheet by completing the following steps:
   a. If necessary, make cell A1 active.
   b. Click the Review tab.
   c. Click the Spelling button in the Proofing group.
   d. Click the Change button as needed to correct misspelled words in the worksheet. (When the spelling check stops at the proper names *Pirozzi* and *Yonemoto*, click the Ignore All button.)
   e. At the message stating the spelling check is complete, click OK.

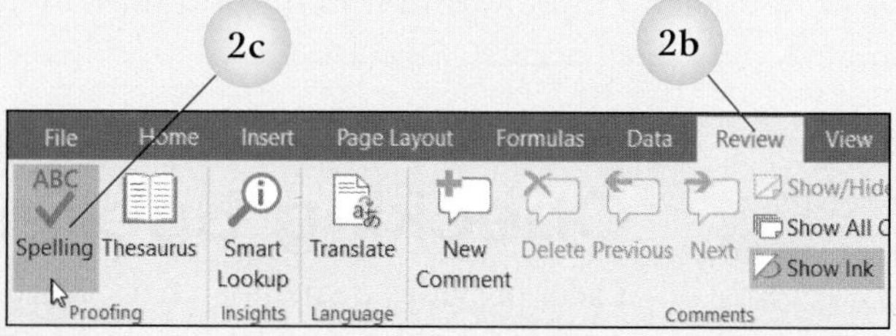

3. Insert a formula and then copy the formula without the formatting by completing the following steps:
   a. Make cell G4 active and then insert a formula that multiplies the sale price by the commission percentage.
   b. Copy the formula down into the range G5:G26.
   c. Some of the cells contain shading that you do not want removed, so click the Auto Fill Options button at the bottom right of the selected cells and then click the *Fill Without Formatting* option at the drop-down list.

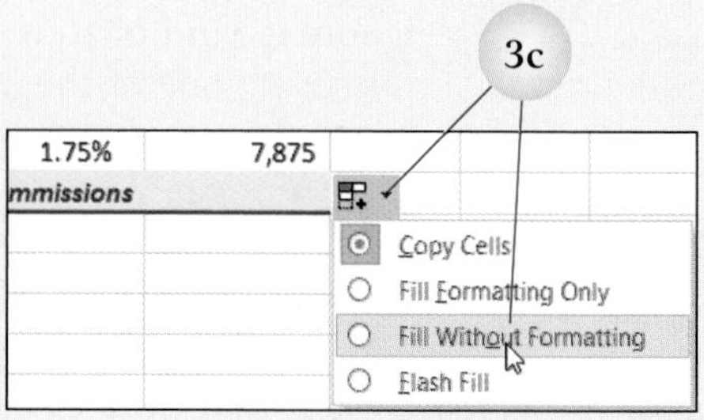

4. Make cell G27 active and then insert the sum of the range G4:G26.
5. Apply the Accounting format with no digits displayed after the decimal point to cell G4 and cell G27.

6. Apply a theme by clicking the Page Layout tab, clicking the Themes button, and then clicking *Ion* at the drop-down gallery.

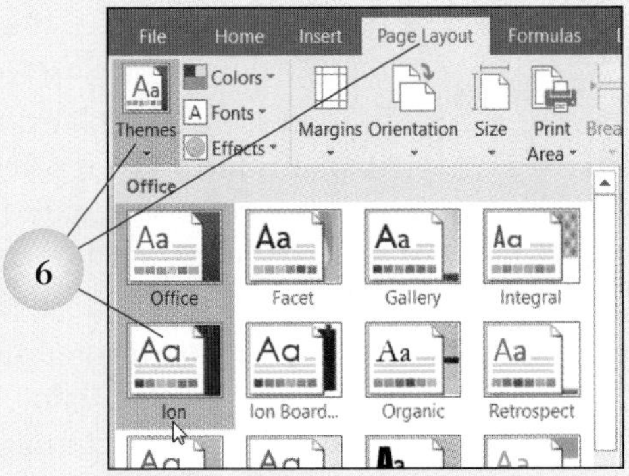

7. After looking at the worksheet with the Ion theme applied, you decide that you want to return to the original formatting. To do this, click the Undo button on the Quick Access Toolbar.

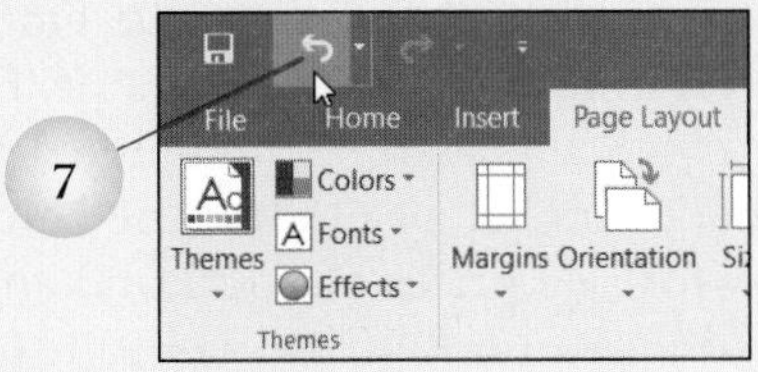

8. Save **4-MRSales.xlsx**.

Check Your Work

Tutorial

Finding Data

Tutorial

Replacing Data

Tutorial

Replacing Formatting

Finding and Replacing Data and Cell Formatting

Quick Steps

Find Data

1. Click Find & Select button.
2. Click *Find*.
3. Type data in *Find what* text box.
4. Click Find Next button.

Find & Select

Use Excel's find feature to look for specific data and either replace it with nothing or replace it with other data. This feature is particularly helpful for finding data quickly in a large worksheet. Excel also includes a find and replace feature. Use this feature to look for specific data in a worksheet and replace it with other data.

To find specific data in a worksheet, click the Find & Select button in the Editing group on the Home tab and then click *Find* at the drop-down list. This displays the Find and Replace dialog box with the Find tab selected, as shown in Figure 4.8. Type the find data in the *Find what* text box and then click the Find Next button. Continue clicking the Find Next button to move to the next occurrence of the data. If the Find and Replace dialog box obstructs the worksheet, use the mouse pointer on the title bar to drag the dialog box to a different location.

To find specific data in a worksheet and replace it with other data, click the Find & Select button in the Editing group on the Home tab and then click *Replace* at the drop-down list. This displays the Find and Replace dialog box with the

Figure 4.8 Find and Replace Dialog Box with Find Tab Selected

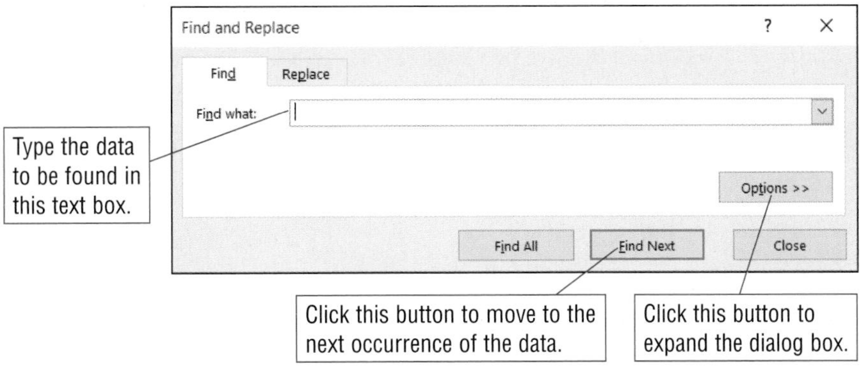

Quick Steps

Find and Replace Data

1. Click Find & Select button.
2. Click *Replace*.
3. Type data in *Find what* text box.
4. Type data in *Replace with* text box.
5. Click Replace button or Replace All button.

Replace tab selected, as shown in Figure 4.9. Enter the find data in the *Find what* text box. Press the Tab key or click in the *Replace with* text box and then enter the replace data in the *Replace with* text box.

Click the Find Next button to find the next occurrence of the data. Click the Replace button to replace the data and find the next occurrence. To replace all the occurrences of the data in the *Find what* text box with the data in the *Replace with* text box, click the Replace All button. Click the Close button to close the Replace dialog box.

Display additional find and replace options by clicking the Options button. This expands the dialog box, as shown in Figure 4.10. By default, Excel will look for any data that contains the same characters as the data entered in the *Find what* text box, without concern for the characters before or after the entered data. For example, in Project 2b, you will look for sale prices of $450,000 and replace them with sale prices of $475,000. If you do not specify that you want to find only cells that contain *450000,* Excel will stop at any cell containing *450000.* For example, Excel will stop at a cell containing *$1,450,000* and a cell containing *$2,450,000.* To specify that the only data to be contained in the cell is what is entered in the *Find what* text box, click the Options button to expand the dialog box and then insert a check mark in the *Match entire cell contents* check box.

If the *Match case* option is active (contains a check mark), Excel will look for only that data that matches the case of the data entered in the *Find what* text box. Remove the check mark from this check box and Excel will find the data entered in the *Find what* text box in any case. By default, Excel will search in the current worksheet. If the workbook contains more than one worksheet, change the *Within* option to *Workbook*. By default, Excel searches by rows in a worksheet. This can be changed to by columns with the *Search* option.

Figure 4.9 Find and Replace Dialog Box with Replace Tab Selected

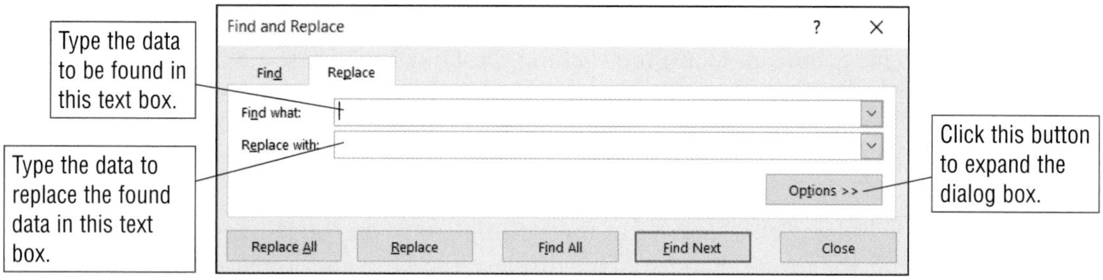

Figure 4.10 Expanded Find and Replace Dialog Box

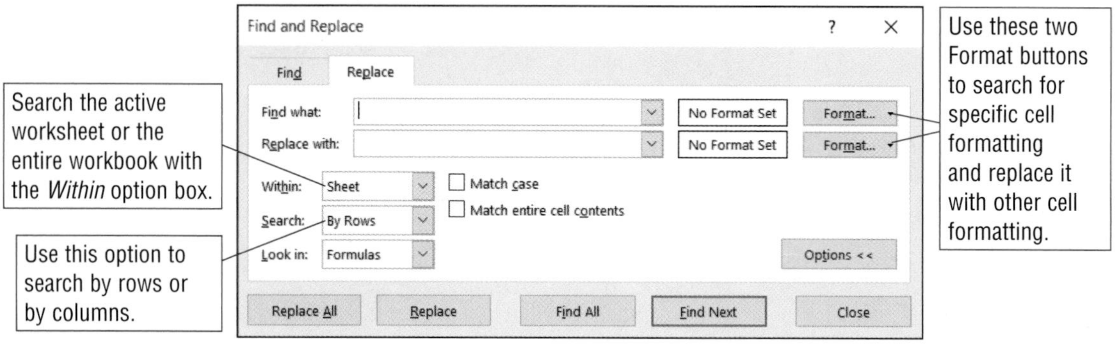

1. With **4-MRSales.xlsx** open, find all occurrences of *Land* in the worksheet and replace them with *Acreage* by completing the following steps:
   a. Click the Find & Select button in the Editing group on the Home tab and then click *Replace* at the drop-down list.
   b. At the Find and Replace dialog box with the Replace tab selected, type Land in the *Find what* text box.
   c. Press the Tab key. (This moves the insertion point to the *Replace with* text box.)
   d. Type Acreage.
   e. Click the Replace All button.
   f. At the message stating that four replacements were made, click OK.
   g. Click the Close button to close the Find and Replace dialog box.

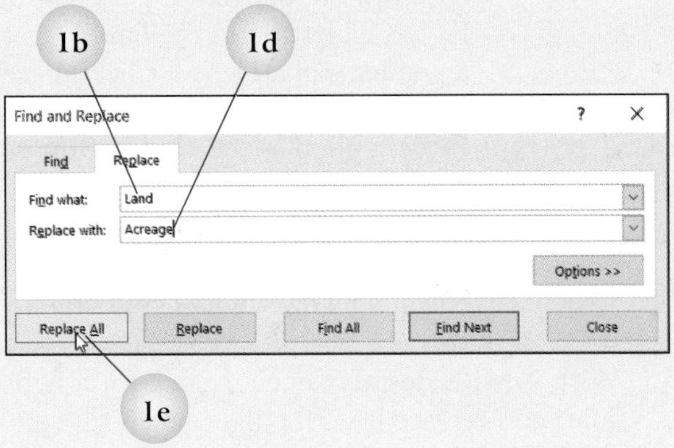

2. Find all occurrences of *$450,000* and replace them with *$475,000* by completing the following steps:
   a. Click the Find & Select button in the Editing group and then click *Replace* at the drop-down list.
   b. At the Find and Replace dialog box with the Replace tab selected, select any text that displays in the *Find what* box and then type 450000.
   c. Press the Tab key.
   d. Type 475000.
   e. Click the Options button to display additional options. (If additional options already display, skip this step.)
   f. Click the *Match entire cell contents* check box to insert a check mark.
   g. Click the Replace All button.
   h. At the message stating that two replacements were made, click OK.
   i. At the Find and Replace dialog box, click the *Match entire cell contents* check box to remove the check mark.
   j. Click the Close button to close the Find and Replace dialog box.

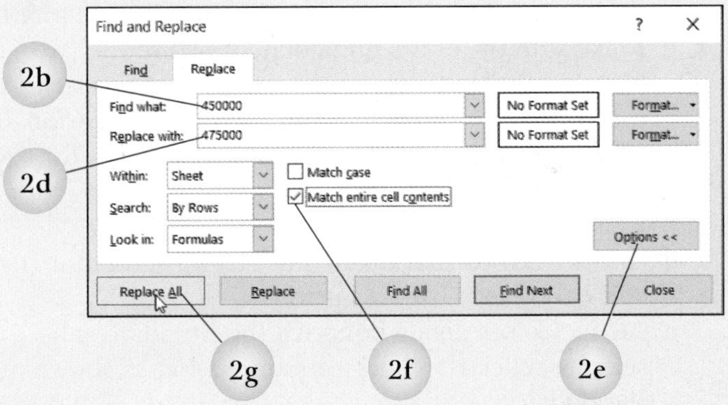

3. Save **4-MRSales.xlsx**.

Check Your Work

Use the Format buttons at the expanded Find and Replace dialog box (see Figure 4.10) to search for specific cell formatting and replace it with other formatting. Click the Format button arrow and a drop-down list displays. Click the *Format* option and the Find Format dialog box displays with the Number, Alignment, Font, Border, Fill, and Protection tabs. Specify formatting at this dialog box. Click the *Choose Format From Cell* option from the Format button drop-down list or click the Choose Format From Cell button in the Find Format dialog box and the mouse pointer displays with a pointer tool attached. Click in the cell containing the desired formatting and the formatting displays in the *Preview* box left of the Format button. Click the *Clear Find Format* option at the Find button drop-down list and any formatting in the *Preview* box is removed.

Project 2c **Finding and Replacing Cell Formatting** Part 3 of 3

1. With **4-MRSales.xlsx** open, search for a light-turquoise fill color and replace it with a light-green fill color by completing the following steps:
   a. Click the Find & Select button in the Editing group on the Home tab and then click *Replace* at the drop-down list.
   b. At the Find and Replace dialog box with the Replace tab selected, make sure the dialog box is expanded. (If not, click the Options button.)
   c. Select and then delete any text in the *Find what* text box.
   d. Select and then delete any text in the *Replace with* text box.
   e. Make sure the boxes immediately before the two Format buttons display with the text *No Format Set*. (If not, click the Format button arrow and then click the *Clear Find Format* option at the drop-down list. Do this for each Format button.)
   f. Click the top Format button.
   g. At the Find Format dialog box, click the Fill tab.
   h. Click the More Colors button.
   i. At the Colors dialog box with the Standard tab selected, click the light turquoise color, as shown at the right.
   j. Click OK to close the Colors dialog box.
   k. Click OK to close the Find Format dialog box.
   l. Click the bottom Format button.
   m. At the Replace Format dialog box with the Fill tab selected, click the light green color (last column, second row), as shown at the right.
   n. Click OK to close the dialog box.
   o. At the Find and Replace dialog box, click the Replace All button.
   p. At the message stating that 10 replacements were made, click OK.

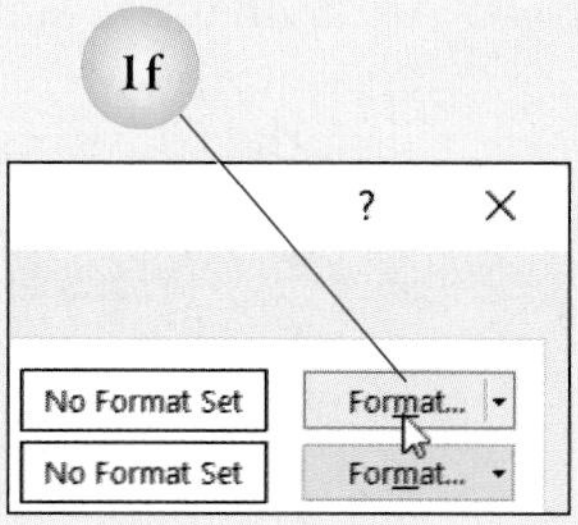

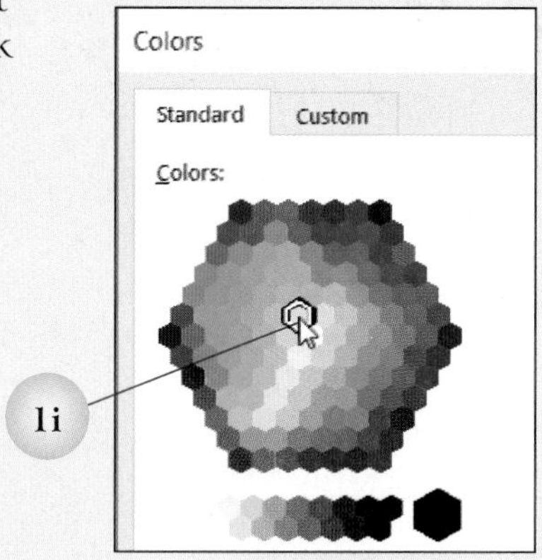

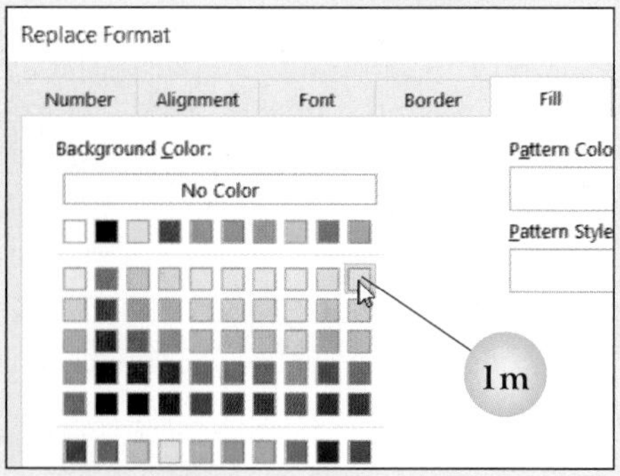

2. Search for a light-gray fill color and replace it with a light-yellow fill color by completing the following steps:
   a. At the Find and Replace dialog box, click the top Format button.
   b. At the Find Format dialog box with the Fill tab selected, click the light gray color (fourth column, second row), as shown at the right.
   c. Click OK to close the Find Format dialog box.
   d. Click the bottom Format button.
   e. At the Replace Format dialog box with the Fill tab selected, click the yellow color (eighth column, second row), as shown below and to the right.
   f. Click OK to close the dialog box.
   g. At the Find and Replace dialog box, click the Replace All button.
   h. At the message stating that 78 replacements were made, click OK.

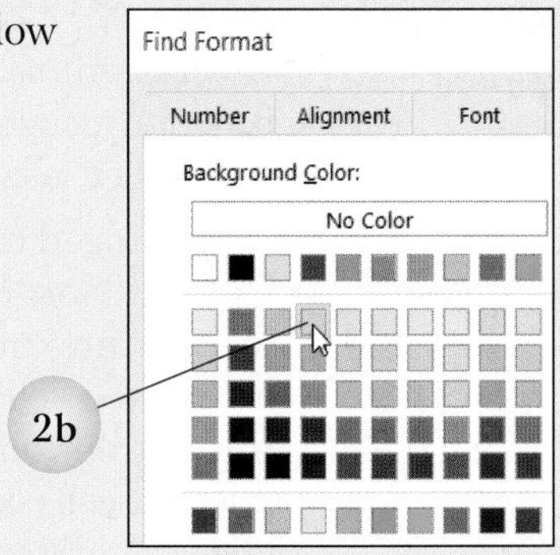

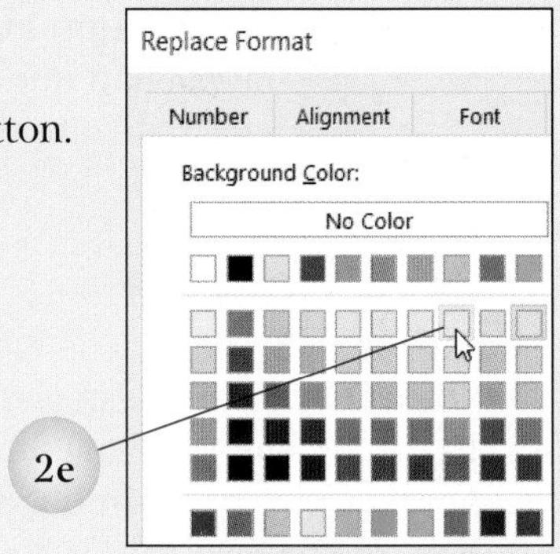

3. Search for 11-point Calibri formatting and replace it with 10-point Arial formatting by completing the following steps:
   a. With the Find and Replace dialog box open, clear formatting from the top Format button by clicking the top Format button arrow and then clicking the *Clear Find Format* option at the drop-down list.
   b. Clear formatting from the bottom Format button by clicking the bottom Format button arrow and then clicking *Clear Replace Format.*
   c. Click the top Format button.
   d. At the Find Format dialog box, click the Font tab.
   e. Scroll down the *Font* list box and then click *Calibri.*
   f. Click *11* in the *Size* list box.
   g. Click OK to close the dialog box.
   h. Click the bottom Format button.
   i. At the Replace Format dialog box with the Font tab selected, scroll down the *Font* list box and then click *Arial.*
   j. Click *10* in the *Size* list box.
   k. Click OK to close the dialog box.
   l. At the Find and Replace dialog box, click the Replace All button.
   m. At the message stating that 174 replacements were made, click OK.
   n. At the Find and Replace dialog box, remove formatting from both Format buttons.
   o. Click the Close button to close the Find and Replace dialog box.

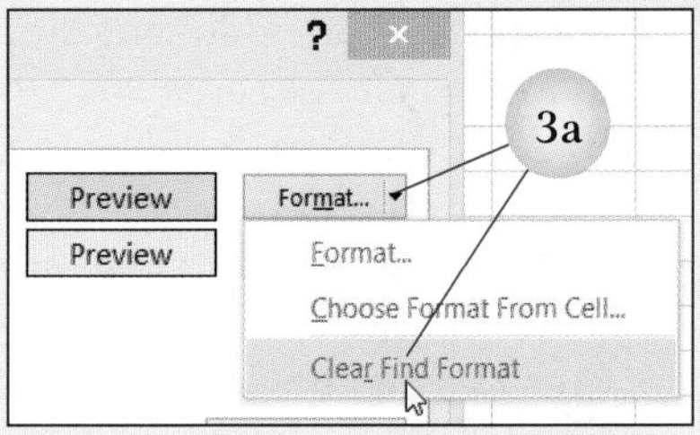

4. Save, print, and then close **4-MRSales.xlsx**.

Check Your Work

Project 3 Insert a Formula and Sort and Filter Data in a Billing Worksheet — 4 Parts

You will insert a formula in a weekly billing worksheet and then sort and filter specific data in the worksheet.

Preview Finished Project

Tutorial

Sorting Data

Sort & Filter

Quick Steps

Sort Data

1. Select cells.
2. Click Sort & Filter button.
3. Click sort option at drop-down list.

Sorting Data

Excel is primarily a spreadsheet program but it also includes some basic database functions, such as sorting data in alphabetic or numeric order. To sort data in a worksheet, use the Sort & Filter button in the Editing group on the Home tab.

To sort data in a worksheet, select the cells containing the data to be sorted, click the Sort & Filter button in the Editing group, and then click the option representing the desired sort. The sort option names vary depending on the data in selected cells. For example, if the first column of selected cells contains text, the sort options in the drop-down list display as *Sort A to Z* and *Sort Z to A*. If the selected cells contain dates, the sort options in the drop-down list display as *Sort Oldest to Newest* and *Sort Newest to Oldest*. If the cells contain numbers or values, the sort options display as *Sort Smallest to Largest* and *Sort Largest to Smallest*. If more than one column is selected in a worksheet, Excel sorts the data in the first selected column.

Project 3a **Sorting Data**

Part 1 of 4

1. Open **APTBilling.xlsx** and then save it with the name **4-APTBilling**.
2. Insert a formula in cell F4 that multiplies the rate by the hours. Copy the formula down into the range F5:F29.
3. Sort the data in the first column in descending order by completing the following steps:
   a. Make cell A4 active.
   b. Click the Sort & Filter button in the Editing group on the Home tab.
   c. Click the *Sort Largest to Smallest* option at the drop-down list.
4. Sort in ascending order by clicking the Sort & Filter button and then clicking *Sort Smallest to Largest* at the drop-down list.
5. Save **4-APTBilling.xlsx**.

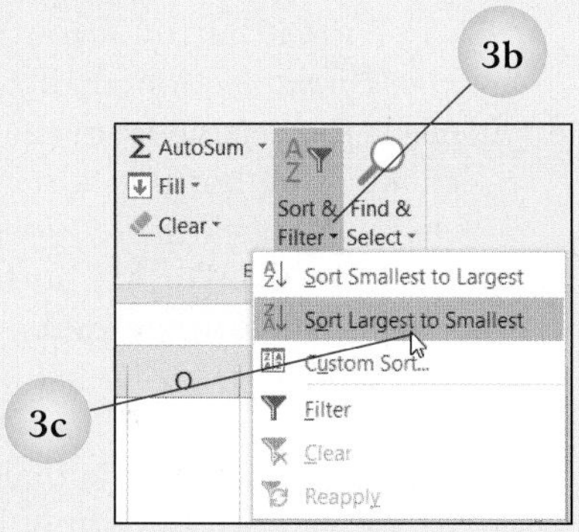

Check Your Work

Quick Steps

Complete a Custom Sort

1. Select cells.
2. Click Sort & Filter button.
3. Click *Custom Sort* at drop-down list.
4. Specify options at Sort dialog box.
5. Click OK.

Completing a Custom Sort

To sort data in a column other than the first column, use options at the Sort dialog box. Select one column in a worksheet, click the Sort & Filter button, and then click the desired sort option; only the data in that column is sorted. If this data is related to data to the left or right of the data in the sorted column, that relationship is broken. For example, after sorting the range C4:C29 in 4-APTBilling.xlsx, the client number, treatment, hours, and total no longer match the date.

Use options at the Sort dialog box to sort data and maintain the relationship among all the cells. To sort using the Sort dialog box, select the cells to be sorted, click the Sort & Filter button, and then click *Custom Sort*. This displays the Sort dialog box, shown in Figure 4.11.

Figure 4.11 Sort Dialog Box

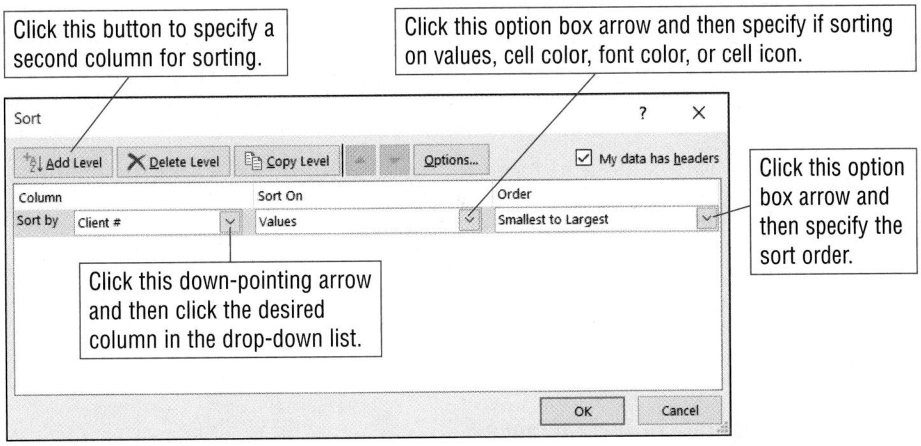

The data displayed in the *Sort by* option box will vary depending on what is selected. Generally, the data that displays is the title of the first column of selected cells. If the selected cells do not have a title, the data may display as *Column A*. Use this option to specify what column is to be sorted. Using the Sort dialog box to sort data in a column maintains the relationship among the data.

Project 3b Sorting Data Using the Sort Dialog Box

Part 2 of 4

1. With **4-APTBilling.xlsx** open, sort the rates in the range E4:E29 in descending order and maintain the relationship to the other data by completing the following steps:
   a. Select the range A3:F29.
   b. Click the Sort & Filter button and then click *Custom Sort*.
   c. At the Sort dialog box, click the *Sort by* option box arrow and then click *Rate* at the drop-down list.
   d. Click the *Order* option box arrow and then click *Largest to Smallest* at the drop-down list.

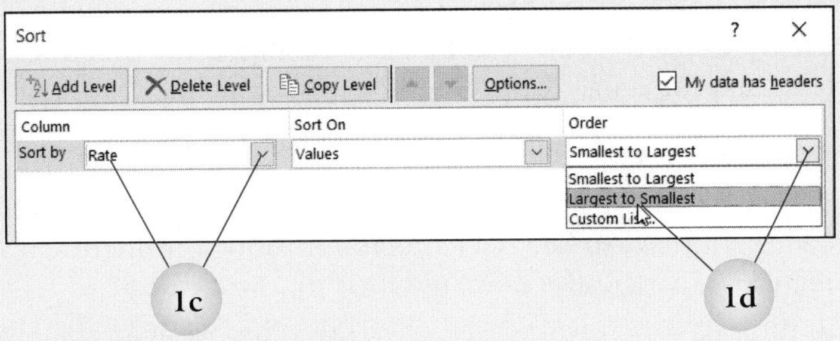

   e. Click OK to close the Sort dialog box.
   f. Deselect the cells.
2. Sort the dates in ascending order (oldest to newest) by completing steps similar to those in Step 1.
3. Save and then print **4-APTBilling.xlsx**.

Check Your Work

Sorting More Than One Column

When sorting data in cells, data in more than one column can be sorted. For example, in Project 3c, you will sort the dates from oldest to newest and the client numbers from lowest to highest. In this sort, the dates are sorted first and then the client numbers are sorted in ascending order within the same date.

To sort data in more than one column, select all the columns in the worksheet that need to remain relative and then display the Sort dialog box. At the Sort dialog box, specify the first column to be sorted in the *Sort by* option box, click the *Add Level* button, and then specify the second column in the first *Then by* option box. To sort multiple columns, add additional *Then by* option boxes by clicking the *Add Level* button.

Project 3c Sorting Data in Two Columns

Part 3 of 4

1. With **4-APTBilling.xlsx** open, select the range A3:F29.
2. Click the Sort & Filter button and then click *Custom Sort*.
3. At the Sort dialog box, click the *Sort by* option box arrow and then click *Date* in the drop-down list. (Skip this step if *Date* already displays in the *Sort by* option box.)
4. Make sure *Oldest to Newest* displays in the *Order* option box.
5. Click the Add Level button.
6. Click the *Then by* option box arrow and then click *Client #* in the drop-down list.
7. Click OK to close the dialog box.
8. Deselect the cells.
9. Save and then print **4-APTBilling.xlsx**.

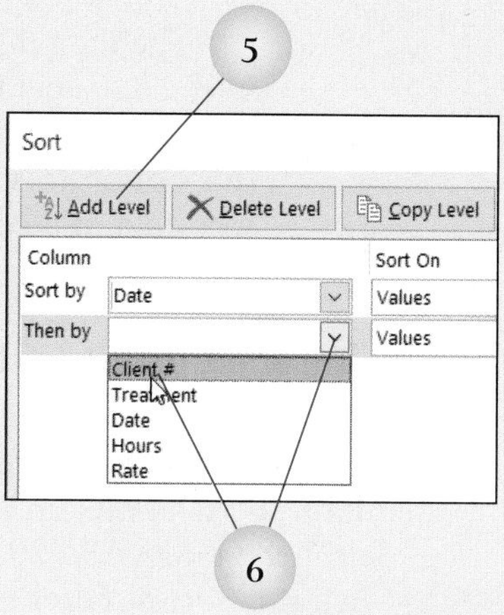

Check Your Work

Tutorial

Filtering Data

Quick Steps

Filter a List

1. Select cells.
2. Click Sort & Filter button.
3. Click *Filter* at drop-down list.
4. Click filter arrow in heading to filter.
5. Click option at drop-down list.

Filtering Data

A restriction, called a *filter*, can be placed temporarily on data in a worksheet to isolate specific data. To turn on filtering, make a cell containing data active, click the Sort & Filter button in the Editing group on the Home tab, and then click *Filter* at the drop-down list. This turns on filtering and causes a filter arrow to appear with each column label in the worksheet, as shown in Figure 4.12. Data does not need to be selected before turning on filtering because Excel automatically searches for column labels in a worksheet.

To filter data in a worksheet, click the filter arrow in the heading to be filtered. This causes a drop-down list to display with options to filter all the records, create a custom filter, or select an entry that appears in one or more of the cells in the column. When data is filtered, the filter arrow changes to a funnel icon. The funnel icon indicates that rows in the worksheet have been filtered. To turn off filtering, click the Sort & Filter button and then click *Filter*.

If a column contains numbers, click the filter arrow and point to *Number Filters* and a side menu displays with options for filtering numbers. For example, numbers can be filtered that are equal to, greater than, or less than a specified number; the top 10 numbers can be filtered; and numbers can be filtered that are above or below a specified number.

Figure 4.12 Filtering Data

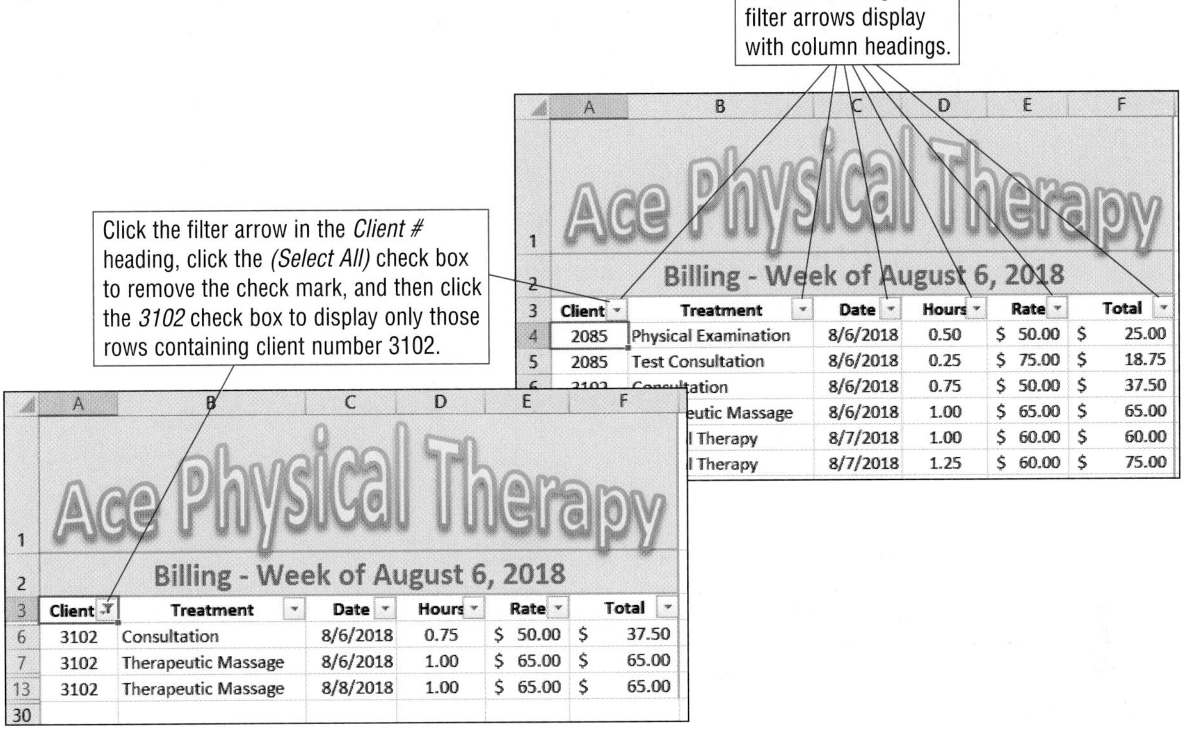

Project 3d Filtering Data

Part 4 of 4

1. With **4-APTBilling.xlsx** open, click in cell A4.
2. Turn on filtering by clicking the Sort & Filter button in the Editing group on the Home tab and then clicking *Filter* at the drop-down list.
3. Filter rows for client number 3102 by completing the following steps:
   a. Click the filter arrow in the *Client #* heading.
   b. Click the *(Select All)* check box to remove the check mark.
   c. Scroll down the list box and then click *3102* to insert a check mark in the check box.
   d. Click OK.
4. Redisplay all the rows containing data by completing the following steps:
   a. Click the funnel icon in the *Client #* heading.
   b. Click the *(Select All)* check box to insert a check mark. (This also inserts check marks for all the items in the list.)
   c. Click OK.

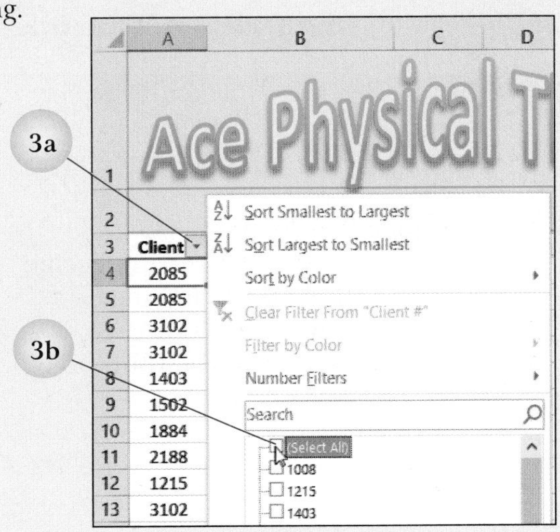

5. Filter a list of clients who receive physical therapy by completing the following steps:
   a. Click the filter arrow in the *Treatment* heading.
   b. Click the *(Select All)* check box to remove the check mark.
   c. Click the *Physical Therapy* check box to insert a check mark.
   d. Click OK.
6. Redisplay all the rows containing data by completing the following steps:
   a. Click the funnel icon in the *Treatment* heading.
   b. Click the *Clear Filter From "Treatment"* option.
7. Display the two highest rates by completing the following steps:
   a. Click the filter arrow in the *Rate* heading.
   b. Point to *Number Filters* and then click *Top 10* at the side menu.
   c. At the Top 10 AutoFilter dialog box, select the *10* in the middle measurement box and then type 2.
   d. Click OK to close the dialog box.

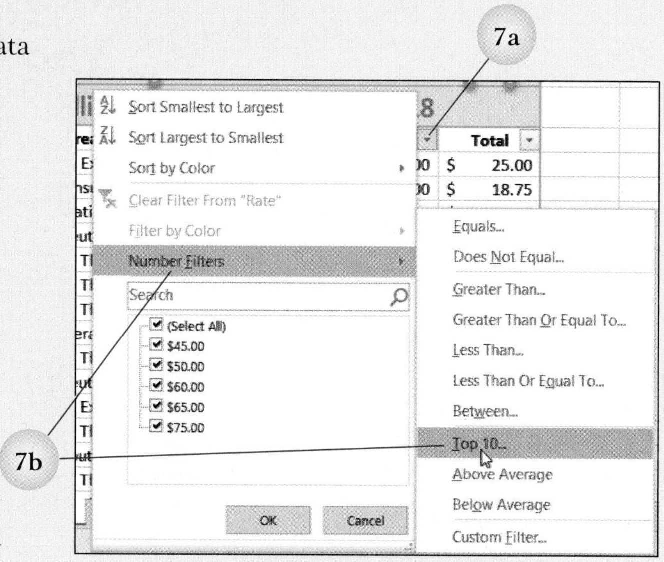

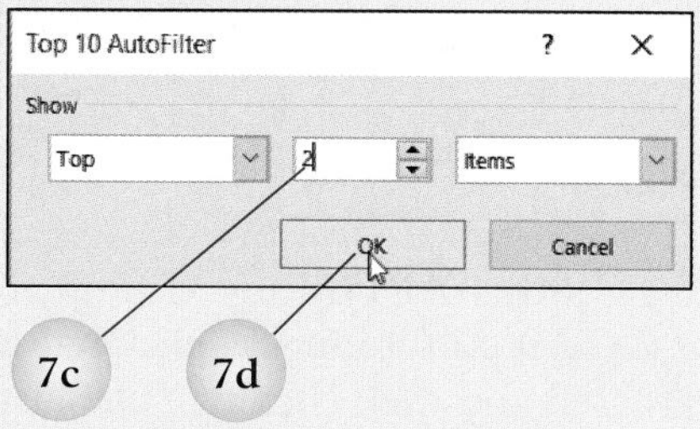

8. Redisplay all the rows that contain data by completing the following steps:
   a. Click the funnel icon in the *Rate* heading.
   b. Click the *Clear Filter From "Rate"* option.
9. Display totals greater than $60 by completing the following steps:
   a. Click the filter arrow in the *Total* heading.
   b. Point to *Number Filters* and then click *Greater Than*.
   c. At the Custom AutoFilter dialog box, type 60 and then click OK.

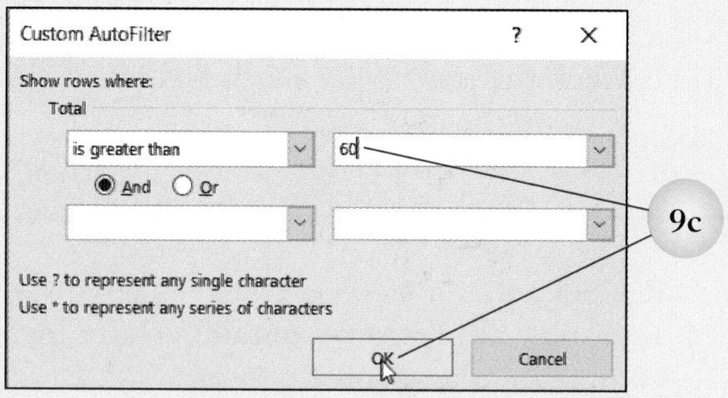

10. Print the worksheet by clicking the File tab, clicking the *Print* option, and then clicking the Print button.
11. Turn off the filtering feature by clicking the Sort & Filter button and then clicking *Filter* at the drop-down list.
12. Save and then close **4-APTBilling.xlsx**.

Check Your Work

Chapter Summary

- The Page Setup group on the Page Layout tab contains buttons for changing the margins and page orientation and size, as well as buttons for establishing the print area, inserting a page break, applying a picture background, and printing titles.
- The default left and right margins are 0.7 inch and the default top and bottom margins are 0.75 inch. Change these default margins with the Margins button in the Page Setup group on the Page Layout tab.
- Display the Page Setup dialog box with the Margins tab selected by clicking the Margins button in the Page Setup group on the Page Layout tab and then clicking *Custom Margins* at the drop-down list.
- Center a worksheet on the page with the *Horizontally* and *Vertically* check boxes at the Page Setup dialog box with the Margins tab selected.
- Click the Orientation button in the Page Setup group on the Page Layout tab to display the two orientation choices: *Portrait* and *Landscape*.
- Insert a page break by selecting the column or row, clicking the Breaks button in the Page Setup group on the Page Layout tab, and then clicking *Insert Page Break* at the drop-down list.
- To insert both horizontal and vertical page breaks at the same time, make a cell active, click the Breaks button, and then click *Insert Page Break* at the drop-down list.
- Preview the page breaks in a worksheet by clicking the Page Break Preview button in the view area on the Status bar or clicking the View tab and then clicking the Page Break Preview button in the Workbook Views group.
- Use options at the Page Setup dialog box with the Sheet tab selected to specify printing column and/or row titles on each page. Display this dialog box by clicking the Print Titles button in the Page Setup group on the Page Layout tab.
- Use options in the Scale to Fit group on the Page Layout tab to scale data to fit on a specific number of pages.
- Use the Background button in the Page Setup group on the Page Layout tab to insert a worksheet background picture. A background picture displays on the screen but does not print.
- Use options in the Sheet Options group on the Page Layout tab to specify whether to view and/or print gridlines and headings.
- Specify the print area by selecting cells, clicking the Print Area button in the Page Setup group on the Page Layout tab, and then clicking *Set Print Area* at the drop-down list. Add another print area by selecting the cells, clicking the Print Area button, and then clicking *Add to Print Area* at the drop-down list.
- Create a header and/or footer with the Header & Footer button in the Text group on the Insert tab, in Page Layout view, or with options at the Page Setup dialog box with the Header/Footer tab selected.
- Customize a print job with options at the Print backstage area.
- To check spelling in a worksheet, click the Review tab and then click the Spelling button.
- Click the Undo button on the Quick Access Toolbar to reverse the most recent action and click the Redo button to redo a previously reversed action.

- Use options at the Find and Replace dialog box with the Find tab selected to find specific data and/or formatting in a worksheet.
- Use options at the Find and Replace dialog box with the Replace tab selected to find specific data and/or formatting and replace it with other data and/or formatting.
- Sort data in a worksheet with options from the Sort & Filter button in the Editing group on the Home tab.
- Create a custom sort with options at the Sort dialog box. Display this dialog box by clicking the Sort & Filter button and then clicking *Custom Sort* at the drop-down list.
- Temporarily isolate data by filtering it. Turn on the filter feature by clicking the Sort & Filter button in the Editing group on the Home tab and then clicking *Filter* at the drop-down list. This inserts a filter arrow with each column label. Click a filter arrow and then use options at the drop-down list to specify the filter data.

Commands Review

FEATURE	RIBBON TAB, GROUP	BUTTON, OPTION	KEYBOARD SHORTCUT
background picture	Page Layout, Page Setup		
filter data	Home, Editing		
Find and Replace dialog box with Find tab selected	Home, Editing	, *Find*	Ctrl + F
Find and Replace dialog box with Replace tab selected	Home, Editing	, *Replace*	Ctrl + H
header and footer	Insert, Text		
insert page break	Page Layout, Page Setup	, *Insert Page Break*	
margins	Page Layout, Page Setup		
orientation	Page Layout, Page Setup		
Page Layout view	View, Workbook Views		
Page Setup dialog box with Margins tab selected	Page Layout, Page Setup	, *Custom Margins*	
Page Setup dialog box with Sheet tab selected	Page Layout, Page Setup		
preview page break	View, Workbook Views		
print area	Page Layout, Page Setup		
remove page break	Page Layout, Page Setup	, *Remove Page Break*	

FEATURE	RIBBON TAB, GROUP	BUTTON, OPTION	KEYBOARD SHORTCUT
scale height	Page Layout, Scale to Fit		
scale to fit	Page Layout, Scale to Fit		
scale width	Page Layout, Scale to Fit		
size	Page Layout, Page Setup		
sort data	Home, Editing		
spelling check	Review, Proofing		F7

Workbook

Chapter study tools and assessment activities are available in the *Workbook* ebook. These resources are designed to help you further develop and demonstrate mastery of the skills learned in this chapter.

Unit assessment activities are also available in the *Workbook*. These activities are designed to help you demonstrate mastery of the skills learned in this unit.

Microsoft®

Excel® Level 1

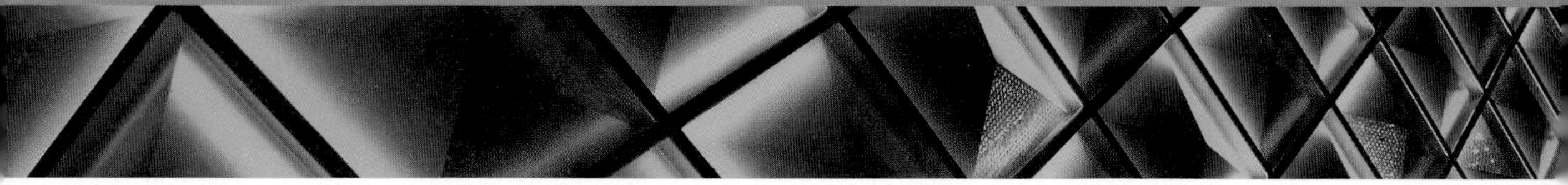

Unit 2

Enhancing the Display of Workbooks

Microsoft®

Excel®

CHAPTER 5

Moving Data within and between Workbooks

Performance Objectives

Upon successful completion of Chapter 5, you will be able to:

1 Insert and delete worksheets
2 Move, copy, and paste cells within and between worksheets
3 Move, rename, format worksheet tabs
4 Hide/unhide worksheets
5 Print a workbook containing multiple worksheets
6 Change the zoom
7 Split a worksheet into windows and freeze/unfreeze panes
8 Name a range of cells and use a range in a formula
9 Open multiple workbooks
10 Arrange, size, and move workbooks
11 Copy and paste data between workbooks
12 Link data between worksheets

Precheck

Check your current skills to help focus your study.

Up to this point, the workbooks you have worked in have consisted of single worksheets. In this chapter, you will learn to create a workbook with several worksheets and complete tasks such as copying and pasting data within and between worksheets. Moving and pasting or copying and pasting selected cells within and between worksheets is useful for rearranging data and saving time. You will also work with multiple workbooks and complete tasks such as arranging, sizing, and moving workbooks and opening and closing multiple workbooks.

Data Files

Before beginning chapter work, copy the EL1C5 folder to your storage medium and then make EL1C5 the active folder.

SNAP

If you are a SNAP user, launch the Precheck and Tutorials from your Assignments page.

Project 1 **Manage Data in a Multiple-Worksheet Account Workbook** **7 Parts**

You will open an account workbook containing multiple worksheets and then insert and delete worksheets and move, copy, and paste data between worksheets. You will also hide and unhide worksheets and format and print multiple worksheets in the workbook.

Preview Finished Project

Creating a Workbook with Multiple Worksheets

Hint Creating multiple worksheets within a workbook is helpful for saving related data.

An Excel workbook contains one worksheet by default but additional worksheets can be added. Add additional worksheets to a workbook to store related data, such as a worksheet for expenses for individual salespeople in the company and another worksheet for the monthly payroll for all the departments within the company. Another example is to record quarterly sales statistics in individual worksheets within a workbook.

Tutorial

Inserting and Renaming Worksheets

New sheet

Quick Steps

Insert a Worksheet

Click New sheet button.
OR
Press Shift + F11.

Delete a Worksheet

1. Click worksheet tab.
2. Click Delete button arrow.
3. Click *Delete Sheet.*
4. Click Delete button.

Inserting a New Worksheet

Insert a new worksheet in a workbook by clicking the New sheet button to the right of the Sheet1 tab at the bottom of the worksheet area. A new worksheet can also be inserted in a workbook with the keyboard shortcut Shift + F11. A new worksheet tab is inserted to the right of the active tab. To move between worksheets, click the desired tab. The active worksheet tab displays with a white background and the worksheet name displays in green. Any inactive tabs display with a light-gray background and gray text.

Deleting a Worksheet

If a worksheet is no longer needed in a workbook, delete it by clicking the worksheet tab, clicking the Delete button arrow in the Cells group on the Home tab, and then clicking *Delete Sheet* at the drop-down list. Another method for deleting a worksheet is to right-click the worksheet tab and then click *Delete* at the shortcut menu. When deleting a worksheet, Excel displays a deletion confirmation message. At this message, click the Delete button.

Selecting Multiple Worksheets

To work with more than one worksheet at a time, select the worksheets. With multiple worksheets selected, the same formatting can be applied to cells or the selected worksheets can be deleted. To select adjacent worksheet tabs, click the first tab, press and hold down the Shift key, click the last tab, and then release the Shift key. To select nonadjacent worksheet tabs, click the first tab, press and hold down the Ctrl key, click any other tabs to be selected, and then release the Ctrl key.

Tutorial

Copying and Pasting Cells between Worksheets

Copy

Cut

Paste

Quick Steps

Copy and Paste Cells
1. Select cells.
2. Click Copy button.
3. Click cell.
4. Click Paste button.

Hint Ctrl + C is the keyboard shortcut to copy selected data.

Copying, Cutting, and Pasting Cells

Cells in a workbook may need to be copied or moved to different locations within a worksheet or to another worksheet in the workbook. Move or copy cells in a worksheet or between worksheets or workbooks by selecting the cells and then using the Cut, Copy, and/or Paste buttons in the Clipboard group on the Home tab.

Copying and Pasting Selected Cells

Copying selected cells can be useful in worksheets that contain repetitive data. To copy cells, select the cells and then click the Copy button in the Clipboard group on the Home tab. This causes a moving dashed line border (called a *marquee*) to display around the selected cells. To copy cells to another worksheet, click the worksheet tab, click in the cell where the first selected cell is to be pasted, and then click the Paste button in the Clipboard group. Remove the moving marquee from selected cells by pressing the Esc key or double-clicking in any cell.

Selected cells in the same worksheet can be copied using the mouse and the Ctrl key. To do this, select the cells to be copied and then position the mouse pointer on any border around the selected cells until the pointer turns into an arrow pointer. Press and hold down the Ctrl key, click and hold down the left mouse button, drag the outline of the selected cells to the new location, release the left mouse button, and then release the Ctrl key.

Project 1a **Inserting, Deleting, Selecting, Copying, Pasting, and Formatting Worksheets**

Part 1 of 7

1. Open **RPFacAccts.xlsx** and then save it with the name **5-RPFacAccts**.
2. Insert a new worksheet in the workbook by completing the following steps:
   a. Click the 2ndHalfSales worksheet tab to make it active.
   b. Click the New sheet button to the right of the 2ndHalfSales worksheet tab. (This inserts a new worksheet to the right of the 2ndHalfSales worksheet with the name Sheet4.)

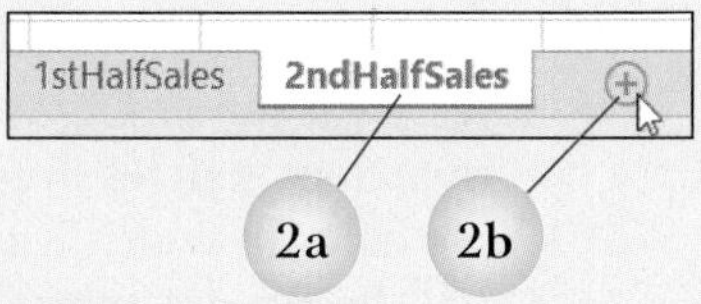

3. Delete two worksheet tabs by completing the following steps:
   a. Click the 1stHalfSales worksheet tab.
   b. Press and hold down the Shift key, click the 2ndHalfSales worksheet tab, and then release the Shift key. (These tabs must be adjacent. If they are not, press and hold down the Ctrl key when clicking the 2ndHalfSales worksheet tab.)

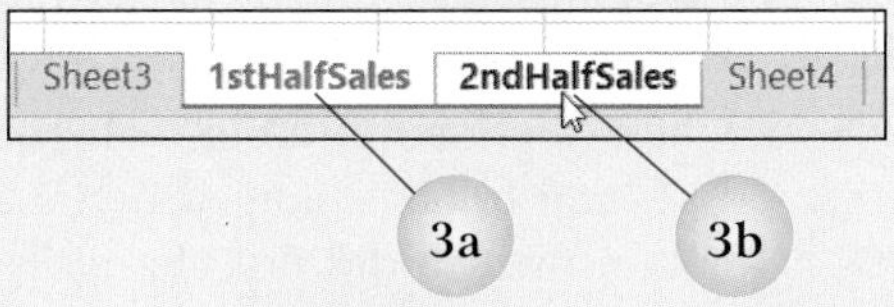

   c. With the two worksheet tabs selected, click the Delete button arrow in the Cells group on the Home tab and then click *Delete Sheet* at the drop-down list.
   d. At the message stating that you cannot undo deleting sheets, click the Delete button.

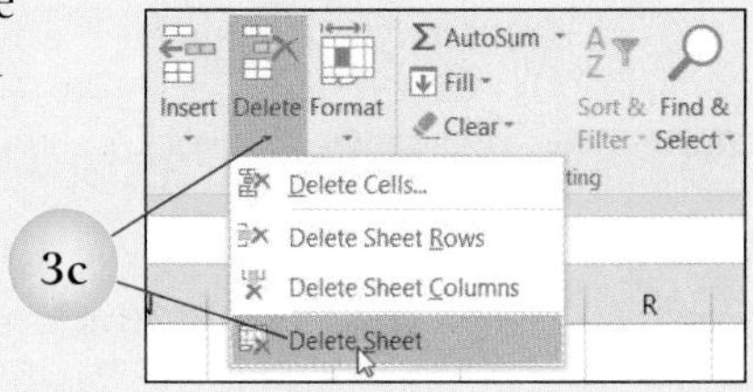

4. Copy cells from Sheet1 to Sheet4 by completing the following steps:
   a. Click the Sheet1 tab to make it the active worksheet.
   b. Select the range A1:A3 (the first three rows of data).
   c. Click the Copy button in the Clipboard group on the Home tab.
   d. Click the Sheet4 tab to make it the active tab.
   e. With A1 the active cell, click the Paste button in the Clipboard group on the Home tab.

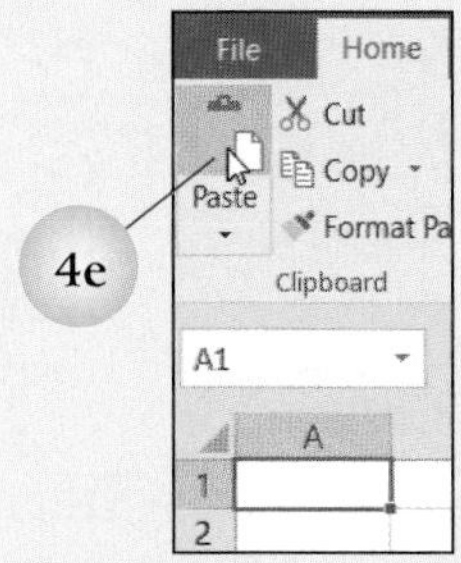

5. Make the following changes to the new worksheet:
   a. Click in cell A3 and then type First Quarter Summary 2018.
   b. Change the width of column A to 20.00 characters.
   c. Change the width of columns B, C, and D to 12.00 characters.
   d. Type the following text in the specified cells:
      B4: January
      C4: February
      D4: March
      A5: Checks amount
      A6: Deposit amount
      A7: End-of-month balance
   e. Select the range B4:D4, click the Bold button in the Font group on the Home tab, and then click the Center button in the Alignment group.
   f. Select the range B5:D7 and then apply the Comma format (using the Comma Style button in the Number group on the Home tab) with two digits after the decimal point.
6. Apply formatting to the cells in all four worksheets by completing the following steps:
   a. Click the Sheet1 tab to make it active and then click in cell A1 to make it the active cell.
   b. Press and hold down the Shift key, click the Sheet4 tab, and then release the Shift key. (This selects all four worksheets.)
   c. With cell A1 active, change the row height to 51.00 points.
   d. Click in cell A3.
   e. Change the font size to 14 points.
   f. Click each remaining worksheet tab (Sheet2, Sheet3, and Sheet4) and notice the formatting changes applied to all the cells.

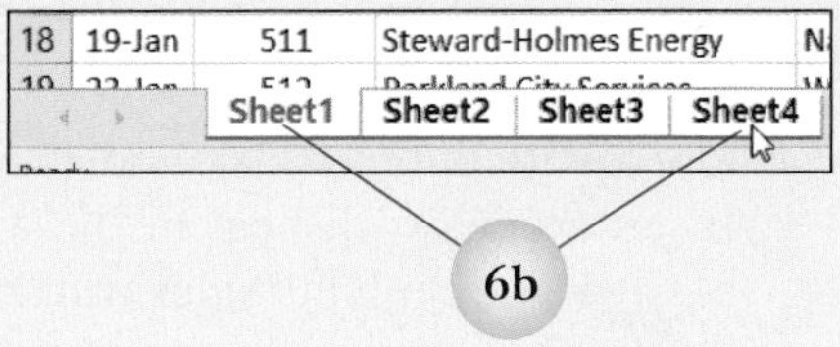

7. Change column width for the three worksheets by completing the following steps:
   a. Click the Sheet1 tab to make it active.
   b. Press and hold down the Shift key, click the Sheet3 tab, and then release the Shift key.
   c. Select columns E, F, and G and then change the column width to 10.00 characters.
   d. Click the Sheet2 tab and then click the Sheet3 tab. Notice that the width of columns E, F, and G has changed to 10.00 characters. Click the Sheet4 tab and notice that the column width did not change.
8. Save **5-RPFacAccts.xlsx**.

Check Your Work

Tutorial

Using Paste Options

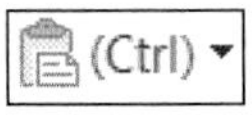

Paste Options

Using Paste Options

When pasting cells in a worksheet, specify how the cells are pasted by clicking the Paste button arrow and then clicking a paste option button at the drop-down list. Click the Paste button (not the button arrow) and a Paste Options button displays in the lower right corner of the pasted cell(s). Display a list of paste options by clicking the button or pressing the Ctrl key. This causes a drop-down list to display, as shown in Figure 5.1. The same option buttons display when the

Figure 5.1 Paste Options Buttons

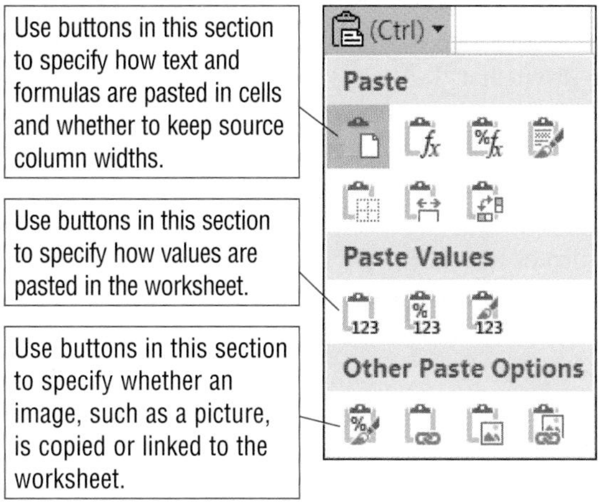
Use buttons in this section to specify how text and formulas are pasted in cells and whether to keep source column widths.
Use buttons in this section to specify how values are pasted in the worksheet.
Use buttons in this section to specify whether an image, such as a picture, is copied or linked to the worksheet.
(Ctrl)
Paste
Paste Values
123
123
123
Other Paste Options

Paste button arrow is clicked. Hover the mouse pointer over a button in the drop-down list and the descriptive name of the button displays along with the keyboard shortcut. Use buttons in this drop-down list to specify what is pasted.

Tutorial

Moving Cells

Quick Steps

Move and Paste Cells
1. Select cells.
2. Click Cut button.
3. Click cell.
4. Click Paste button.

Hint Ctrl + X is the keyboard shortcut to cut selected data. Ctrl + V is the keyboard shortcut to paste data.

Moving Selected Cells

Selected cells and cell contents can be moved within and between worksheets. Move selected cells with the Cut and Paste buttons in the Clipboard group on the Home tab or by dragging with the mouse.

To move selected cells with buttons on the Home tab, select the cells and then click the Cut button in the Clipboard group. Click in the cell where the first selected cell is to be inserted and then click the Paste button in the Clipboard group.

To move selected cells with the mouse, select the cells and then position the mouse pointer on any border of the selected cells until the pointer turns into an arrow pointer with a four-headed arrow attached. Click and hold down the left mouse button, drag the outline of the selected cells to the new location, and then release the mouse button.

Project 1b **Copying and Moving Cells and Pasting Cells Using Paste Options** Part 2 of 7

1. With **5-RPFacAccts.xlsx** open, copy cells from Sheet2 to Sheet3 using the Paste Options button by completing the following steps:
   a. Click the Sheet2 tab to make it active.
   b. Select the range C7:E9.
   c. Click the Copy button in the Clipboard group.
   d. Click the Sheet3 tab.
   e. Click in cell C7.
   f. Click the Paste button in the Clipboard group.

g. Click the Paste Options button in the lower right corner of the pasted cells and then click the Keep Source Column Widths button at the drop-down list.
h. Make Sheet2 active and then press the Esc key to remove the moving marquee.

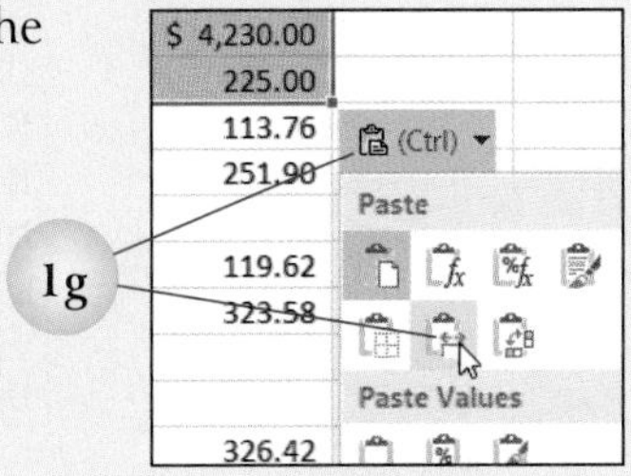

2. Click the Sheet1 tab.
3. You realize that the sublet rent deposit was recorded on the wrong day. The correct day is January 9. To move the cells containing information on the deposit, complete the following steps:
   a. Click in cell A13 and then insert a row. (The new row should display above the row containing *Rainier Suppliers*.)
   b. Select the range A7:F7.
   c. Click the Cut button in the Clipboard group on the Home tab.
   d. Click in cell A13.
   e. Click the Paste button in the Clipboard group.
   f. Change the date of the deposit from January 1 to January 9.
   g. Select row 7 and then delete it.

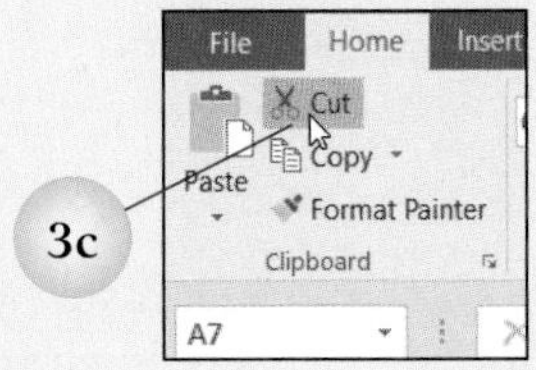

4. Move cells using the mouse by completing the following steps:
   a. Click the Sheet2 tab.
   b. Click in cell A13 and then insert a new row.
   c. Using the mouse, select the range A7:F7.
   d. Position the mouse pointer on any boundary of the selected cells until it turns into an arrow pointer with a four-headed arrow attached. Click and hold down the left mouse button, drag the outline of the selected cells to row 13, and then release the mouse button.

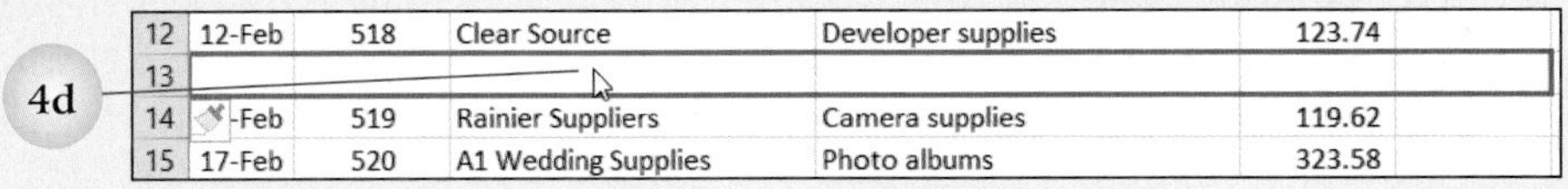
4d
12 12-Feb 518 Clear Source Developer supplies 123.74
13
14 -Feb 519 Rainier Suppliers Camera supplies 119.62
15 17-Feb 520 A1 Wedding Supplies Photo albums 323.58

   e. Change the date of the deposit to February 13.
   f. Delete row 7.
5. Save **5-RPFacAccts.xlsx**.

Check Your Work

Copying and Pasting Using the Clipboard Task Pane

Quick Steps

Copy and Paste Multiple Items

1. Click Clipboard group task pane launcher.
2. Select cells.
3. Click Copy button.
4. Repeat Steps 2 and 3 as desired.
5. Make cell active.
6. Click item in Clipboard task pane to be inserted in worksheet.
7. Repeat Step 6 as desired.

Use the Clipboard task pane to copy and paste multiple items. To use the task pane, click the Clipboard group task pane launcher in the lower right corner of the Clipboard group on the Home tab. The Clipboard task pane displays at the left side of the screen similarly to what is shown in Figure 5.2.

Select data or an object to be copied and then click the Copy button in the Clipboard group. Continue selecting cells, text, or other items and clicking the Copy button. To paste an item into a worksheet, make the desired cell active and then click the item in the Clipboard task pane. If the copied item is text, the first 50 characters display in the task pane. To paste all the selected items into a single location, make the desired cell active and then click the Paste All button in the task pane. When all the items have been pasted into the worksheet, click the Clear All button to remove any remaining items from the task pane.

Figure 5.2 Clipboard Task Pane

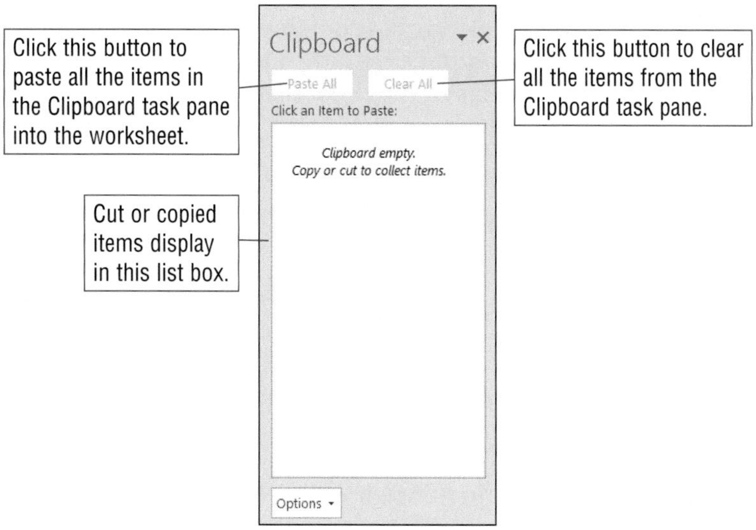

Project 1c Copying and Pasting Cells Using the Clipboard Task Pane

Part 3 of 7

1. With **5-RPFacAccts.xlsx** open, select cells for copying by completing the following steps:
   a. Display the Clipboard task pane by clicking the Clipboard group task pane launcher. (If the Clipboard task pane contains any copied data, click the Clear All button.)
   b. Click the Sheet1 tab.
   c. Select the range C15:E16.
   d. Click the Copy button in the Clipboard group.
   e. Select the range C19:E19.
   f. Click the Copy button in the Clipboard group.

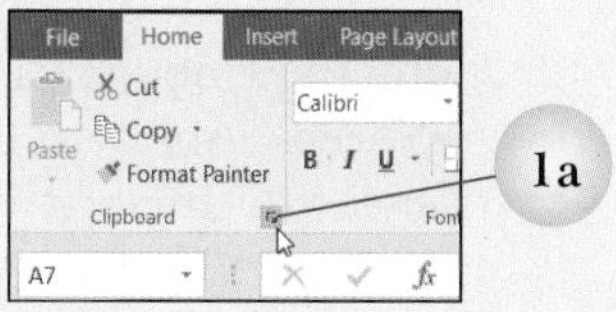

2. Paste the copied cells by completing the following steps:
   a. Click the Sheet2 tab.
   b. Click in cell C15.
   c. Click the item in the Clipboard task pane representing *General Systems Developer*.
   d. Click the Sheet3 tab.
   e. Click in cell C15.
   f. Click the item in the Clipboard task pane representing *General Systems Developer*.
   g. Click in cell C19.
   h. Click the item in the Clipboard task pane representing *Parkland City Services*.

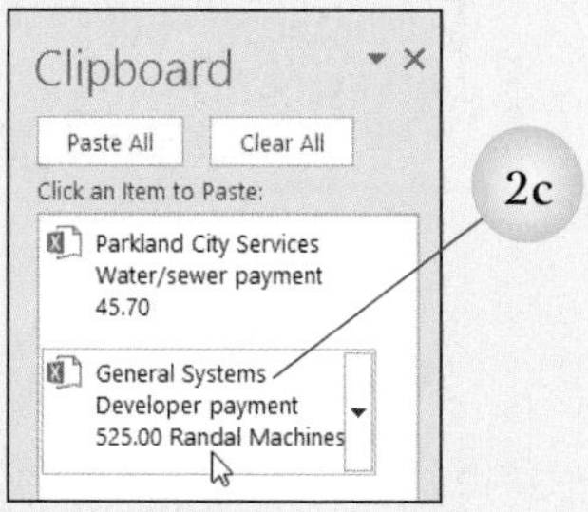

3. Click the Clear All button at the top of the Clipboard task pane.
4. Close the Clipboard task pane by clicking the Close button (contains an *X*) in the upper right corner of the task pane.
5. Save **5-RPFacAccts.xlsx**.

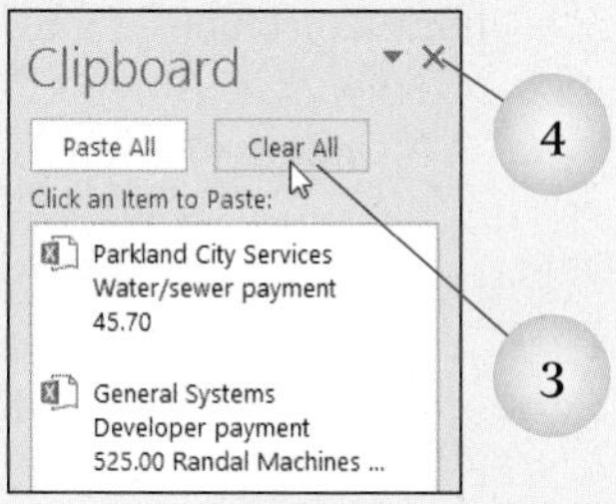

Check Your Work

Pasting Values Only

When pasting cells that contain a value and a formula, specify what is to be pasted using button options from the Paste button or Paste Options button drop-down list. Use the buttons in the *Paste Values* section of the drop-down list to insert only the value, the value with numbering formatting, or the value with source formatting.

Project 1d Copying and Pasting Values

Part 4 of 7

1. With **5-RPFacAccts.xlsx** open, make Sheet1 the active tab.
2. Click in cell G6, type the formula =(f6-e6)+g5, and then press the Enter key.
3. Copy the formula in cell G6 down into the range G7:G20.
4. Copy as a value (and not a formula) the final balance amount from Sheet1 to Sheet2 by completing the following steps:
   a. Click in cell G20.
   b. Click the Copy button in the Clipboard group.
   c. Click the Sheet2 tab.
   d. Click in cell G5 and then click the Paste button arrow.
   e. At the drop-down list, click the Values button in the *Paste Values* section of the drop-down list. (This inserts the value and not the formula.)

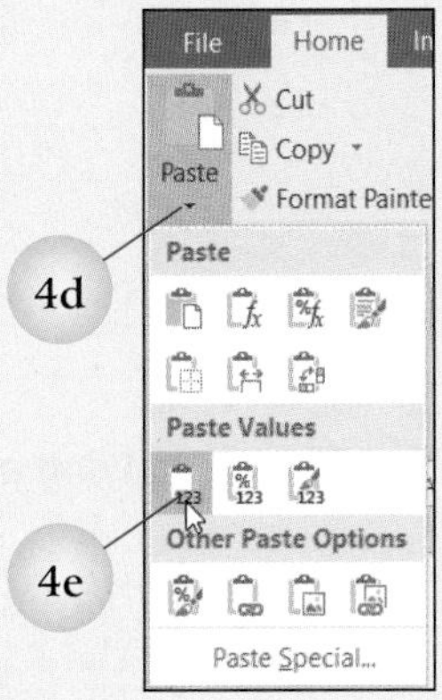

5. Click in cell G6, insert a formula that determines the balance (see Step 2), and then copy the formula down into the range G7:G20.
6. Copy the amount in cell G20 and then paste the value only in cell G5 in Sheet3. Apply to the cell the Accounting format with a dollar symbol and two digits past the decimal point.
7. With Sheet3 active, make cell G6 active, insert a formula that determines the balance (see Step 2), and then copy the formula down into the range G7:G20.
8. Insert formulas and apply formatting to cells in the three worksheets by completing the following steps:
   a. Click the Sheet1 tab.
   b. Press and hold down the Shift key, click the Sheet3 tab, and then release the Shift key.
   c. Click in cell D21, click the Bold button in the Font group on the Home tab, and then type Total.
   d. Click in cell E21 and then click the AutoSum button in the Editing group on the Home tab. (This inserts the formula *=SUM(E13:E20)*.)
   e. Change the formula to *=SUM(E7:E20)* and then press the Enter key.
   f. Click in cell F21 and then click the AutoSum button. (This inserts the formula *=SUM(F12:F20)*.)
   g. Change the formula to *=SUM(F6:F20)* and then press the Enter key.
   h. Select cells E21 and F21 and then click the Accounting Number Format button. Click in cell G5 and then click the Accounting Number Format button. (Cell G5 in Sheet1 already contains the Accounting format but cells G5 in Sheet2 and Sheet3 do not.)
   i. Click the Sheet2 tab and notice the text and formulas inserted in the worksheet, click the Sheet3 tab and notice the text and formulas, and then click the Sheet4 tab (to deselect the tabs).

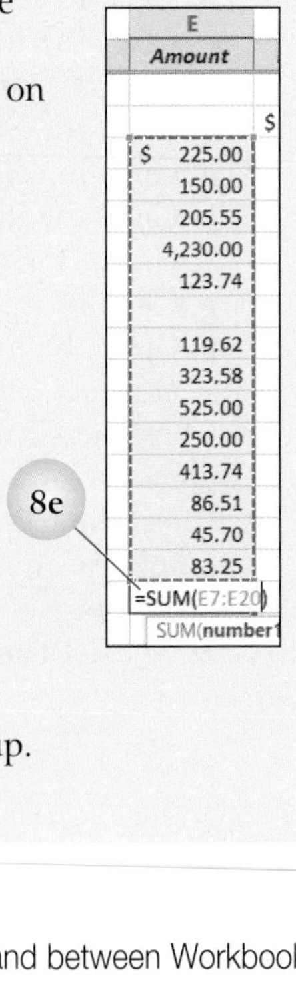

9. Copy values from Sheet1 to Sheet4 by completing the following steps:
   a. Click the Sheet1 tab.
   b. Click in cell E21 and then click the Copy button in the Clipboard group.
   c. Click the Sheet4 tab.

d. Click in cell B5 and then click the Paste button in the Clipboard group.
e. Click the Paste Options button and then click the Values button in the *Paste Values* section of the drop-down list.

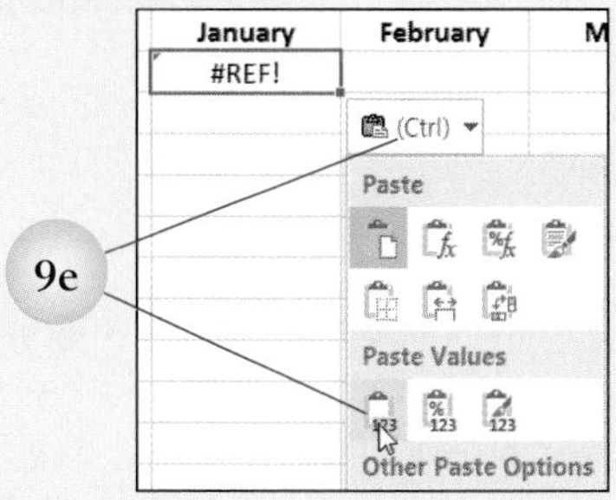

f. Click the Sheet1 tab.
g. Click in cell F21 and then click the Copy button.
h. Click the Sheet4 tab.
i. Click in cell B6, click the Paste button arrow, and then click the Values button at the drop-down list.
j. Click the Sheet1 tab.
k. Click in cell G20 and then click the Copy button.
l. Click the Sheet4 tab.
m. Click in cell B7, click the Paste button arrow, and then click the Values button at the drop-down list.

10. Complete steps similar to those in Step 9 to insert amounts and balances for February and March.
11. Select the range B5:D5 and then click the Accounting Number Format button.
12. Save **5-RPFacAccts.xlsx**.

Check Your Work

Tutorial

Moving, Copying, and Deleting a Worksheet

Quick Steps

Move or Copy a Worksheet
1. Right-click sheet tab.
2. Click *Move or Copy*.
3. At Move or Copy dialog box, click worksheet name in *Before sheet* list box.
4. Click OK.

OR

Drag worksheet tab to new position. (To copy, press and hold down Ctrl key while dragging.)

Managing Worksheets

Right-click a sheet tab and a shortcut menu displays with options for managing worksheets, as shown in Figure 5.3. For example, remove a worksheet by clicking the *Delete* option. Move or copy a worksheet by clicking the *Move or Copy* option. Clicking this option causes a Move or Copy dialog box to display with options for specifying where to move or copy the selected sheet. By default, Excel names worksheets in a workbook *Sheet1, Sheet2, Sheet3,* and so on. To rename a worksheet, click the *Rename* option (which selects the default sheet name) and then type the new name.

In addition to the shortcut menu options, the mouse can be used to move or copy worksheets. To move a worksheet, position the mouse pointer on the worksheet tab, click and hold down the left mouse button (a page icon displays next to the mouse pointer), drag the page icon to the new position, and then release the mouse button. For example, to move the Sheet2 tab after the Sheet3 tab, position the mouse pointer on the Sheet2 tab, click and hold down the left mouse button, drag the page icon after the Sheet3 tab, and then release the mouse button. To copy a worksheet, press and hold down the Ctrl key while dragging the sheet tab.

Figure 5.3 Sheet Tab Shortcut Menu

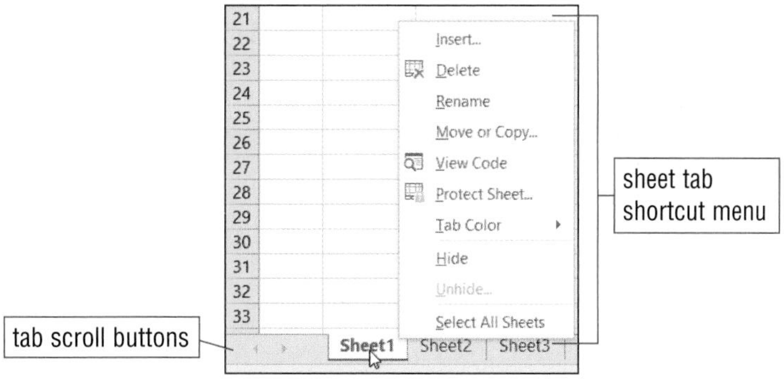

Quick Steps
Apply Color to a Sheet Tab
1. Right-click sheet tab.
2. Point to *Tab Color*.
3. Click color at color palette.

Use the *Tab Color* option at the shortcut menu to apply a color to a worksheet tab. Right-click a worksheet tab, point to *Tab Color* at the shortcut menu, and then click a color at the color palette.

Project 1e Selecting, Moving, Renaming, and Changing the Color of Worksheet Tabs — Part 5 of 7

1. With **5-RPFacAccts.xlsx** open, move Sheet4 by completing the following steps:
   a. Right-click the Sheet4 tab and then click *Move or Copy* at the shortcut menu.
   b. At the Move or Copy dialog box, make sure *Sheet1* is selected in the *Before sheet* list box and then click OK.

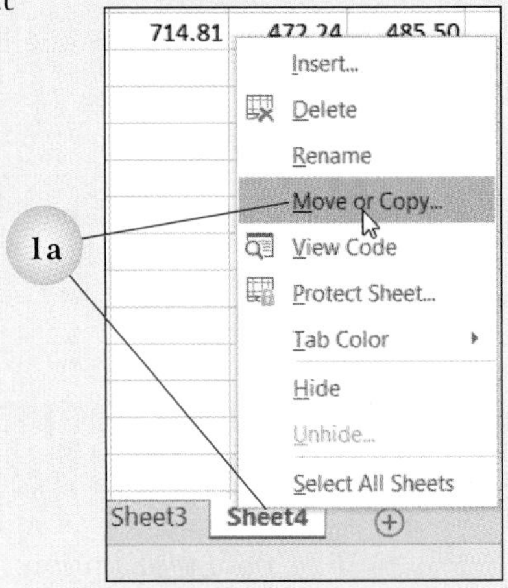

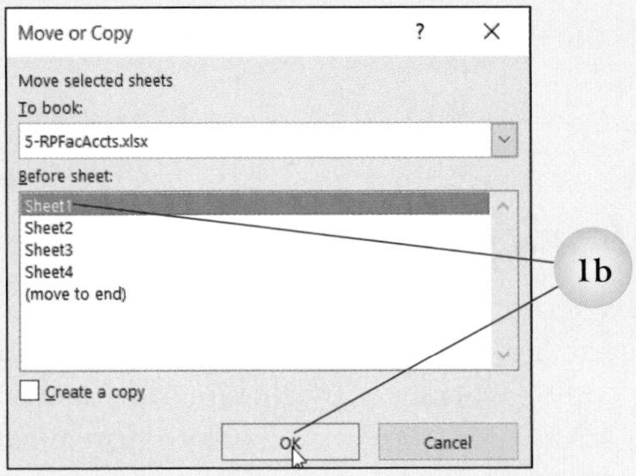

2. Rename Sheet4 by completing the following steps:
   a. Right-click the Sheet4 tab and then click *Rename*.
   b. Type Summary and then press the Enter key.
3. Complete steps similar to those in Step 2 to rename Sheet1 to *January*, Sheet2 to *February*, and Sheet3 to *March*.

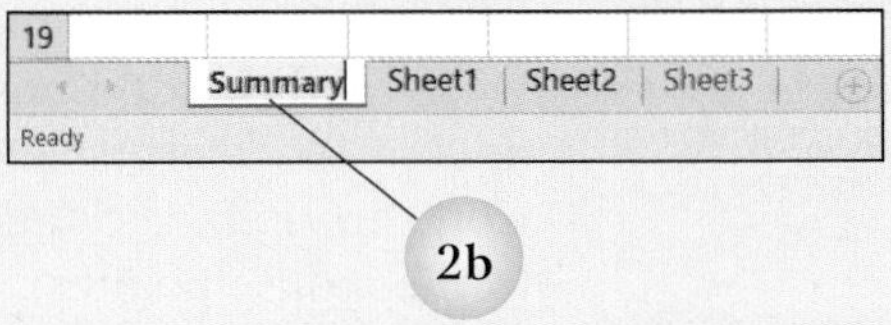

4. Change the color of the Summary sheet tab by completing the following steps:
   a. Right-click the Summary sheet tab.
   b. Point to *Tab Color* at the shortcut menu.
   c. Click the *Red* color option (second option in the *Standard Colors* section).
5. Follow steps similar to those in Step 4 to change the January sheet tab to standard blue (eighth option in the *Standard Colors* section), the February sheet tab to standard purple (last option in the *Standard Colors* section), and the March sheet tab to standard green (sixth option in the *Standard Colors* section).
6. Save **5-RPFacAccts.xlsx**.

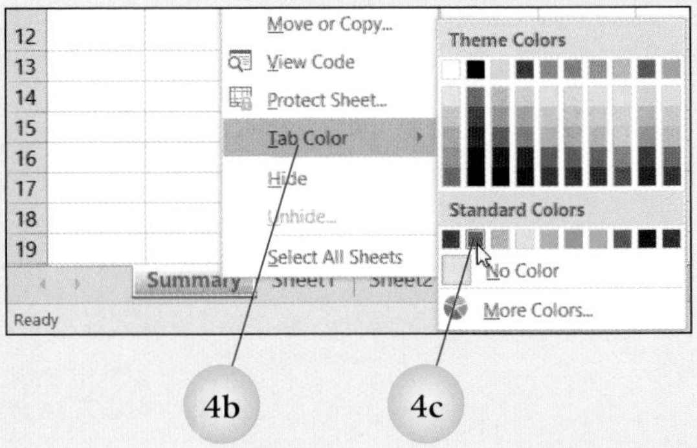

Check Your Work

Hiding a Worksheet in a Workbook

Quick Steps

Hide a Worksheet
1. Click Format button.
2. Point to *Hide & Unhide*.
3. Click *Hide Sheet*.

OR
1. Right-click worksheet tab.
2. Click *Hide* at shortcut menu.

Unhide a Worksheet
1. Click Format button.
2. Point to *Hide & Unhide*.
3. Click *Unhide Sheet*.
4. Double-click hidden worksheet in Unhide dialog box.

OR
1. Right-click worksheet tab.
2. Click *Unhide* at shortcut menu.
3. Double-click hidden worksheet in Unhide dialog box.

In a workbook with multiple worksheets, a worksheet can be hidden that contains data that should not display or print with the workbook. To hide a worksheet in a workbook, click the Format button in the Cells group on the Home tab, point to *Hide & Unhide*, and then click *Hide Sheet*. A worksheet can also be hidden by right-clicking a worksheet tab and then clicking the *Hide* option at the shortcut menu.

To make a hidden worksheet visible, click the Format button in the Cells group, point to *Hide & Unhide* and then click *Unhide Sheet*, or right-click a worksheet tab and then click *Unhide* at the shortcut menu. At the Unhide dialog box, shown in Figure 5.4, double-click the name of the worksheet to be unhidden.

Figure 5.4 Unhide Dialog Box

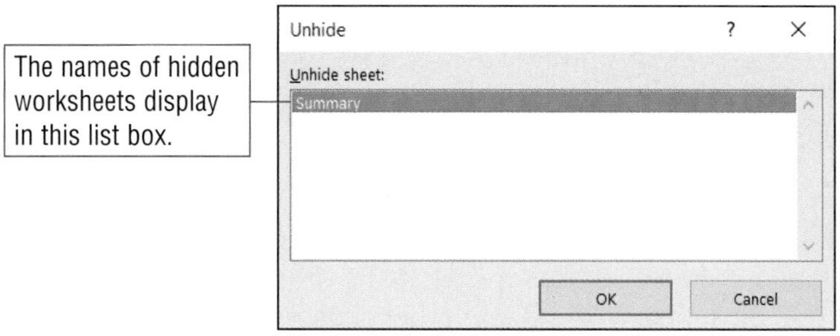

Project 1f **Hiding a Worksheet and Formatting Multiple Worksheets** Part 6 of 7

1. With **5-RPFacAccts.xlsx** open, hide the Summary worksheet by completing the following steps:
   a. Click the Summary tab.
   b. Click the Format button in the Cells group on the Home tab, point to *Hide & Unhide*, and then click *Hide Sheet*.

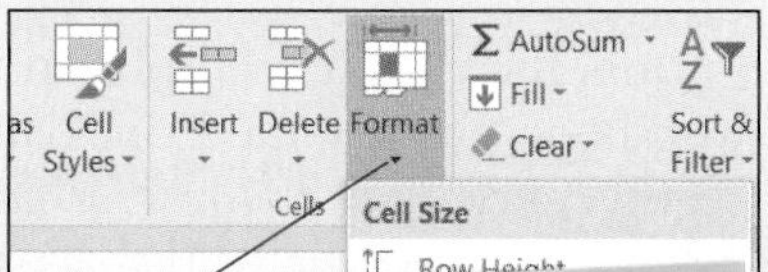

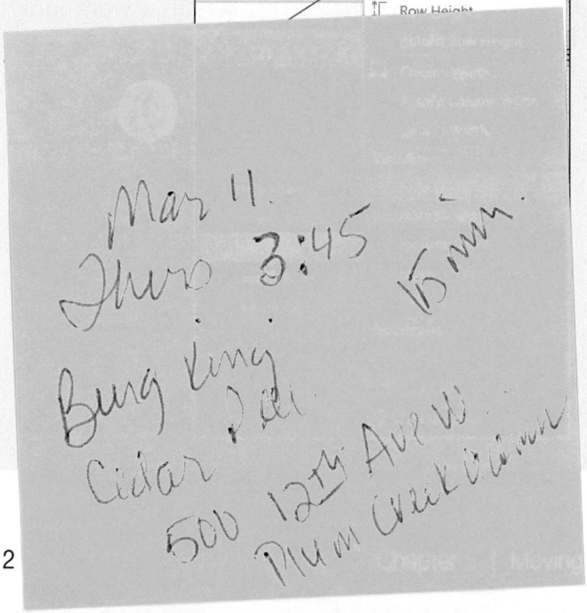

2. Unhide the worksheet by completing the following steps:
   a. Click the Format button in the Cells group, point to *Hide & Unhide*, and then click *Unhide Sheet*.
   b. At the Unhide dialog box, make sure *Summary* is selected and then click OK.

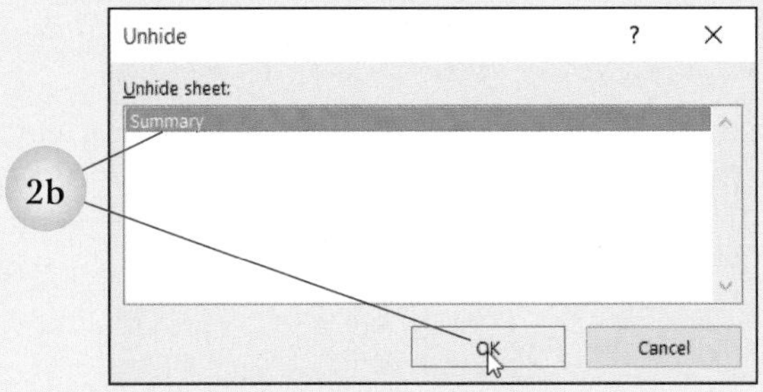

3. Insert a header for each worksheet by completing the following steps:
   a. With the Summary tab active, press and hold down the Shift key, click the March tab, and then release the Shift key. (This selects all four tabs.)
   b. Click the Insert tab.
   c. Click the Header & Footer button in the Text group.
   d. Click the Header button in the Header & Footer group on the Header & Footer Tools Design tab and then click the option at the drop-down list that prints your name at the left side of the page (if a name other than your own displays at the left side of the page, select the name and then type your first and last names), the page number in the middle, and the date at the right side.
4. With all the sheet tabs selected, center each worksheet horizontally and vertically on the page. ***Hint: Do this at the Page Setup dialog box with the Margins tab selected.***
5. With all the sheet tabs still selected, change to landscape orientation. ***Hint: Do this with the Orientation button on the Page Layout tab.***
6. Save **5-RPFacAccts.xlsx**.

Check Your Work

Tutorial

Printing Multiple Worksheets

Printing a Workbook Containing Multiple Worksheets

By default, Excel prints the currently displayed worksheet. To print all the worksheets in a workbook, display the Print backstage area, click the first gallery in the *Settings* category, click *Print Entire Workbook* at the drop-down list, and then click the Print button. Print specific worksheets in a workbook by selecting the tabs of the worksheets to be printed. With the worksheet tabs selected, display the Print backstage area and then click the Print button.

Quick Steps

Print All Worksheets in a Workbook
1. Click File tab.
2. Click *Print* option.
3. Click first gallery in *Settings* category.
4. Click *Print Entire Workbook*.
5. Click Print button.

Project 1g Printing All Worksheets in a Workbook

Part 7 of 7

1. With **5-RPFacAccts.xlsx** open, click the File tab and then click the *Print* option.
2. At the Print backstage area, click the first gallery in the *Settings* category and then click *Print Entire Workbook* at the drop-down list.
3. Click the Print button.
4. Save and then close **5-RPFacAccts.xlsx**.

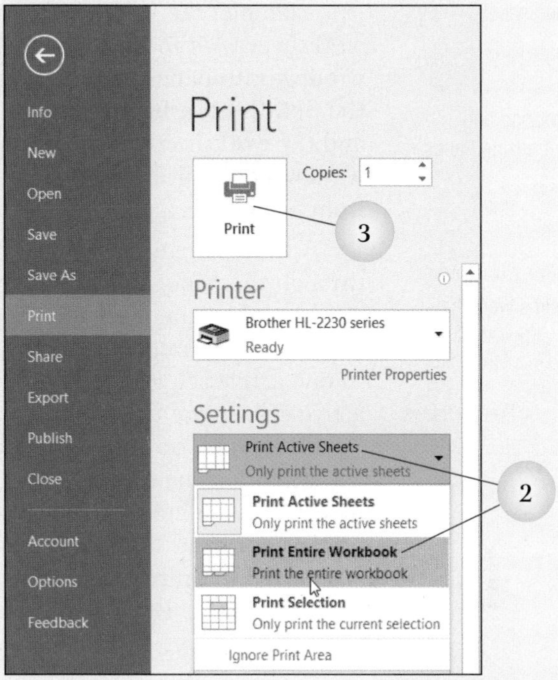

Check Your Work

Project 2 Write Formulas Using Ranges in an Equipment Usage Workbook

2 Parts

You will open an equipment usage workbook, view the document at different zoom percentages, and then split the window and edit cells. You will also name ranges and then use the range names to write formulas in the workbook.

Preview Finished Project

Tutorial

Changing the Zoom

Zoom

100%

Zoom to Selection

Changing the Zoom

The View tab contains a Zoom group with three buttons for changing zoom settings. Click the Zoom button in the Zoom group to open the Zoom dialog box, which contains options for changing the zoom percentage. Click the 100% button in the Zoom group to return the view to 100%, which is the default. Select a range of cells and then click the Zoom to Selection button to scale the zoom setting so the selected range fills the worksheet area.

Use the zoom slider bar at the right side of the Status bar to change the zoom percentage. Click the Zoom Out button (displays with a minus symbol [–]) to decrease the zoom percentage or click the Zoom In button (displays with a plus symbol [+]) to increase the zoom percentage. Another method for increasing or decreasing zoom percentage is to click and drag the zoom slider bar button on the slider bar.

Tutorial

Splitting a Worksheet

Tutorial

Freezing and Unfreezing Panes

Split

Quick Steps

Split a Worksheet

1. Click View tab.
2. Click Split button.

Freeze Panes

Hint Remove a split line by double-clicking anywhere on the split line that divides the panes.

Splitting a Worksheet and Freezing and Unfreezing Panes

In some worksheets, not all the cells display at one time in the worksheet area (for example, the worksheet that will be used in Project 2a). When working in a worksheet with more cells than can display at one time, splitting the worksheet window into panes may be helpful. Split the worksheet window into panes with the Split button in the Window group on the View tab. Click the Split button and the worksheet splits into four window panes, as shown in Figure 5.5. The windows are split by thick light-gray lines called *split lines*. To remove split lines from a worksheet, click the Split button to deactivate it.

A window pane will display the active cell. As the insertion point is moved through the pane, another active cell may display. This additional active cell displays when the insertion point passes over one of the split lines that creates the pane. Move through a worksheet and both active cells may display. Make a change to one active cell and the change is made in the other as well. To display only one active cell, freeze the window panes by clicking the Freeze Panes button in the Window group on the View tab and then clicking *Freeze Panes* at the drop-down list. Maintain the display of column headings while editing or typing text in cells by clicking the Freeze Panes button and then clicking *Freeze Top Row*. Maintain the display of row headings by clicking the Freeze Panes button and then clicking *Freeze First Column*. Unfreeze window panes by clicking the Freeze Panes button and then clicking *Unfreeze Panes* at the drop-down list.

The split lines that divide the window can be moved using the mouse. To do this, position the mouse pointer on a split line until the pointer turns into a left-and-right-pointing arrow with a double line in the middle. Click and hold down the left mouse button, drag the outline of the split line to the desired location, and then release the mouse button. To move both the horizontal and vertical split lines at the same time, position the mouse pointer on the intersection of the split lines until the pointer turns into a four-headed arrow. Click and hold down the left mouse button, drag the split lines to the desired location, and then release the mouse button.

Figure 5.5 Split Window

split lines

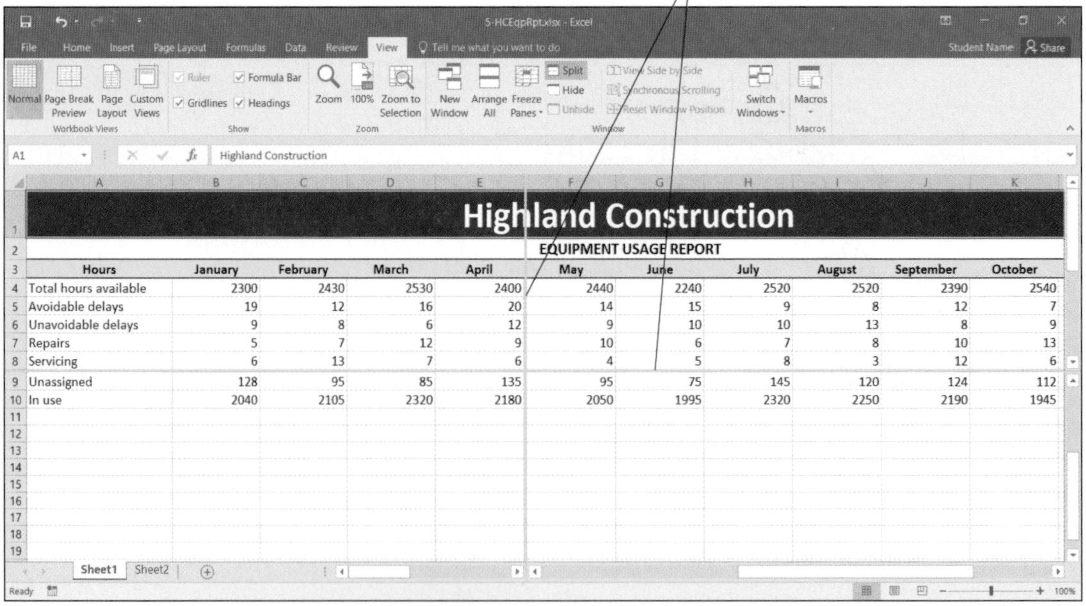

Project 2a Using Zoom, Splitting Windows, and Editing Cells
Part 1 of 2

1. Open **HCEqpRpt.xlsx** and then save it with the name **5-HCEqpRpt**.
2. Increase the Zoom percentage by clicking the Zoom In button at the right side of the zoom slider bar two times.
3. Select the range G3:I10, click the View tab, and then click the Zoom to Selection button in the Zoom group.
4. Click the Zoom button in the Zoom group, click the *75%* option at the Zoom dialog box, and then click OK.
5. Click the 100% button in the Zoom group.
6. Make cell A1 active and then split the window by clicking the Split button in the Window group on the View tab. (This splits the window into four panes.)
7. Drag the vertical split line by completing the following steps:
   a. Position the mouse pointer on the vertical split line until the pointer turns into a left-and-right-pointing arrow with a double line in the middle.
   b. Click and hold down the left mouse button, drag to the left until the vertical split line is immediately to the right of the first column, and then release the mouse button.

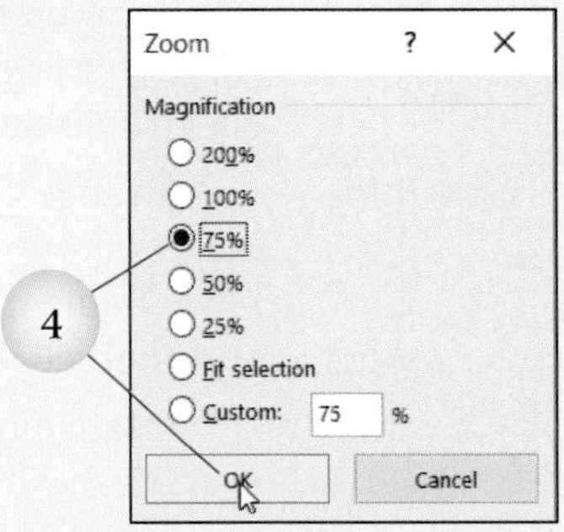

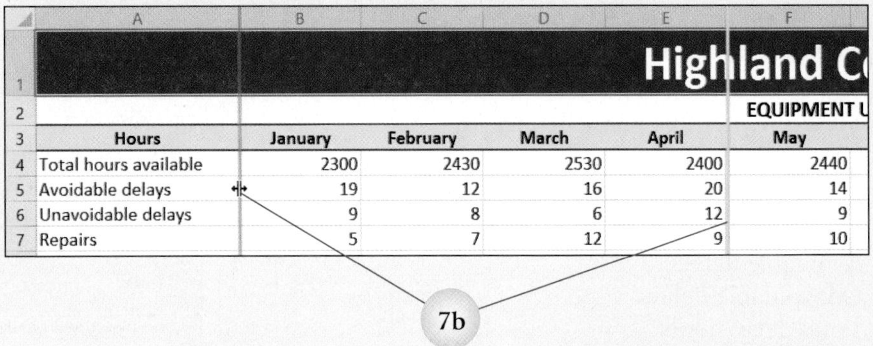

A
B
C
D
E
F
Highland C
EQUIPMENT U
Hours
January
February
March
April
May
Total hours available
2300
2430
2530
2400
2440
Avoidable delays
19
12
16
20
14
Unavoidable delays
9
8
6
12
9
Repairs
5
7
12
9
10
7b

8. Freeze the window panes by clicking the Freeze Panes button in the Window group on the View tab and then clicking *Freeze Panes* at the drop-down list.
9. Make cell L4 active and then type the following data in the specified cells:

L4	2310	M4	2210
L5	12	M5	5
L6	5	M6	7
L7	9	M7	8
L8	11	M8	12
L9	95	M9	120
L10	2005	M10	1830

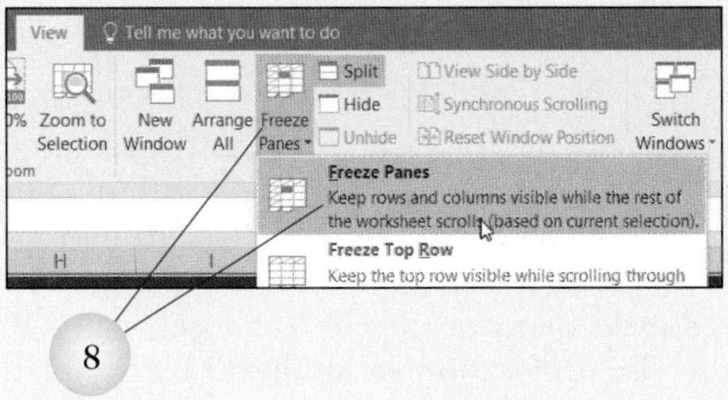

10. Unfreeze the window panes by clicking the Freeze Panes button and then clicking *Unfreeze Panes* at the drop-down list.
11. Remove the panes by clicking the Split button in the Window group to deactivate it.
12. Save **5-HCEqpRpt.xlsx**.

Check Your Work

Tutorial

Naming and Using a Range

Quick Steps

Name a Range
1. Select cells.
2. Click in Name box.
3. Type range name.
4. Press Enter.

Define Name

Hint Another method for moving to a range is to click the Find & Select button in the Editing group on the Home tab and then click *Go To*. At the Go To dialog box, double-click the range name.

Naming and Using a Range

A selected group of cells is referred to as a *range*. A range of cells can be formatted, moved, copied, or deleted. A range can also be named and then the insertion point can be moved to the range or the named range can be used as part of a formula.

To name a range, select the cells and then click in the Name box at the left of the Formula bar. Type a name for the range (do not use a space) and then press the Enter key. To move the insertion point to a specific range and select the range, click the Name box arrow and then click the range name at the drop-down list.

A range can also be named using the Define Name button in the Defined Names group on the Formulas tab. Clicking the Define Name button displays the New Name dialog box. At the New Name dialog box, type a name for the range and then click OK.

A range name can be used in a formula. For example, to insert in a cell the average of all the cells in a range named *Profit*, make the cell active and then type the formula =*AVERAGE(Profit)*. Use a named range in the current worksheet or in another worksheet within the workbook.

Project 2b Naming a Range and Using a Range in a Formula

Part 2 of 2

1. With **5-HCEqpRpt.xlsx** open, click the Sheet2 tab and then type the following text in the specified cells:

   A1 EQUIPMENT USAGE REPORT
   A2 Yearly hours
   A3 Avoidable delays
   A4 Unavoidable delays
   A5 Total delay hours
   A6 (leave blank)
   A7 Repairs
   A8 Servicing
   A9 Total repair/servicing hours

1

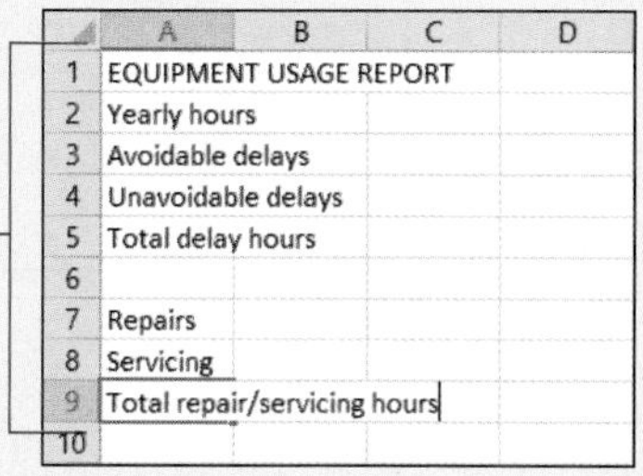

A
B
C
D
EQUIPMENT USAGE REPORT
Yearly hours
Avoidable delays
Unavoidable delays
Total delay hours
Repairs
Servicing
Total repair/servicing hours

2. Make the following formatting changes to the worksheet:
   a. Automatically adjust the width of column A.
   b. Center and apply bold formatting to the text in cells A1 and A2.
3. Select a range of cells in Sheet1, name the range, and use it in a formula in Sheet2 by completing the following steps:
   a. Click the Sheet1 tab.
   b. Select the range B5:M5.
   c. Click in the Name box to the left of the Formula bar.
   d. Type adhours (for Avoidable Delays Hours) and then press the Enter key.
   e. Click the Sheet2 tab.
   f. Click in cell B3.
   g. Type the equation =sum(adhours) and then press the Enter key.

3d

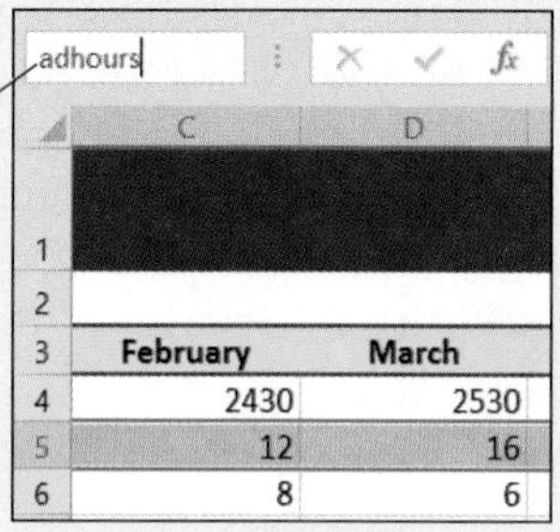

3g

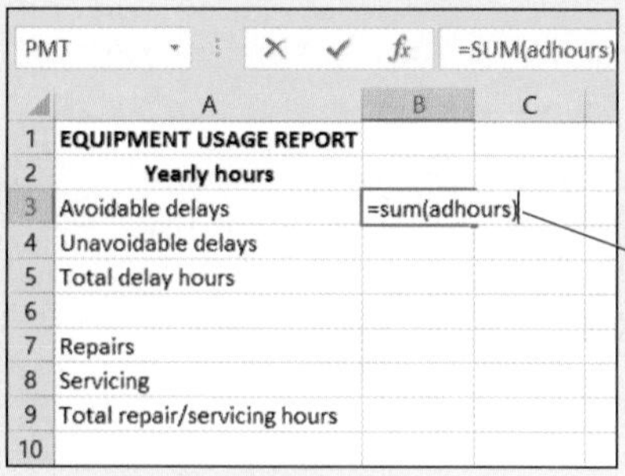

4. Click the Sheet1 tab and then complete the following steps:
   a. Select the range B6:M6.
   b. Click the Formulas tab.
   c. Click the Define Name button in the Defined Names group.
   d. At the New Name dialog box, type udhours and then click OK.
   e. Click the Sheet2 tab, make sure cell B4 is active, type the equation =sum(udhours), and then press the Enter key.

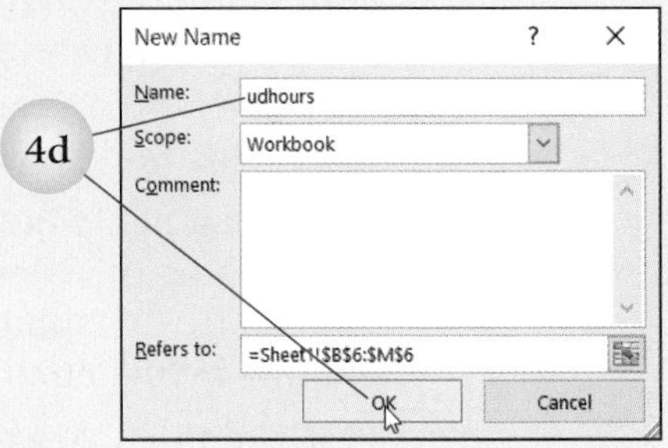

5. Click the Sheet1 tab and then complete the following steps:
   a. Select the range B7:M7 and then name the range *rhours*.
   b. Click the Sheet2 tab, make cell B7 active, type the equation =sum(rhours), and then press the Enter key.
   c. Click the Sheet1 tab.
   d. Select the range B8:M8 and then name the range *shours*.
   e. Click the Sheet2 tab, make sure cell B8 is active, type the equation =sum(shours), and then press the Enter key.
6. With Sheet2 still active, make the following changes:
   a. Make cell B5 active.
   b. Double-click the AutoSum button in the Editing group on the Home tab.
   c. Make cell B9 active.
   d. Double-click the AutoSum button in the Editing group.
7. Click the Sheet1 tab and then move to the adhours range by clicking the Name box arrow and then clicking *adhours* at the drop-down list.
8. Select both sheet tabs, change to landscape orientation, scale the contents to fit on one page (by changing the width to *1 page* on the Page Layout tab), and then insert a custom footer with your name, the page number, and the date.
9. With both worksheet tabs selected, print both worksheets in the workbook.
10. Save and then close **5-HCEqpRpt.xlsx**.

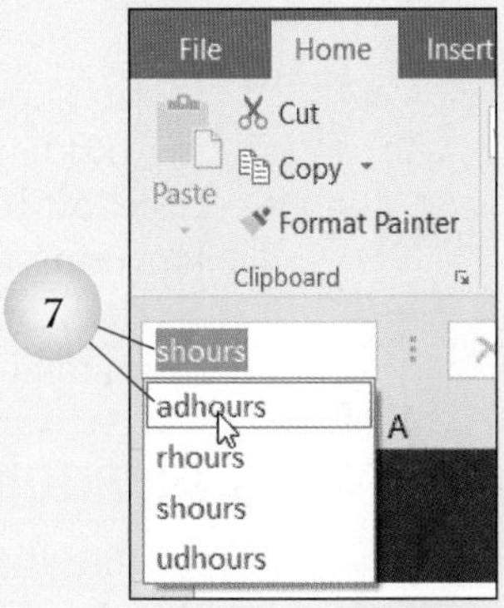

Check Your Work

Project 3 Arrange, Size, and Copy Data between Workbooks — 3 Parts

You will open, arrange, hide, unhide, size, and move multiple workbooks. You will also copy cells from one workbook and paste them in another workbook.

Preview Finished Project

Tutorial

Working with Windows and Hiding and Unhiding Workbooks

Working with Windows

In Excel, multiple workbooks can be opened, a new window with the current workbook can be opened, and the open workbooks can be arranged in the Excel window. With multiple workbooks open, cell entries can be cut and pasted or copied and pasted from one workbook to another using the techniques discussed earlier in this chapter. The exception is that the destination workbook must be active before using the Paste command.

Opening Multiple Workbooks

With multiple workbooks or more than one version of the current workbook open, data can be moved or copied between workbooks and the contents of several workbooks can be compared. When a new workbook or a new window of the current workbook is opened, it is placed on top of the original workbook.

New Window

Open a new window of the current workbook by clicking the View tab and then clicking the New Window button in the Window group. Excel adds a colon followed by the number *2* to the end of the workbook title and adds a colon followed by the number *1* to the end of the originating workbook name.

Open multiple workbooks at one time at the Open dialog box. Select adjacent workbooks by clicking the name of the first workbook to be opened, pressing and holding down the Shift key, clicking the name of the last workbook to be opened, releasing the Shift key, and then clicking the Open button. If the workbooks are nonadjacent, click the name of the first workbook to be opened, press and hold down the Ctrl key, and then click the names of any other workbooks to be opened.

Switch Windows

To see what workbooks are currently open, click the View tab and then click the Switch Windows button in the Window group. The names of the open workbooks display in a drop-down list and the workbook name preceded by a check mark is the active workbook. To make another workbook active, click the workbook name at the drop-down list.

Another method for determining which workbooks are open is to hover the mouse over the Excel button on the taskbar. This causes a thumbnail to display of each open workbook. If more than one workbook is open, the Excel button on the taskbar displays additional layers in a cascaded manner. The layer behind the Excel button displays only a portion of the edge at the right side of the button. Hovering the mouse over the Excel button on the taskbar displays thumbnails of all the workbooks above the button. To make another workbook active, click the thumbnail that represents the workbook.

Arranging Workbooks

If more than one workbook is open, arrange the workbooks at the Arrange Windows dialog box, shown in Figure 5.6. To display this dialog box, click the Arrange All button in the Window group on the View tab. At the Arrange Windows dialog box, click *Tiled* to display a portion of each open workbook. Figure 5.7 displays four tiled workbooks.

Arrange All

Quick Steps

Arrange Workbooks

1. Click View tab.
2. Click Arrange All button.
3. At Arrange Windows dialog box, click arrangement.
4. Click OK.

Figure 5.6 Arrange Windows Dialog Box

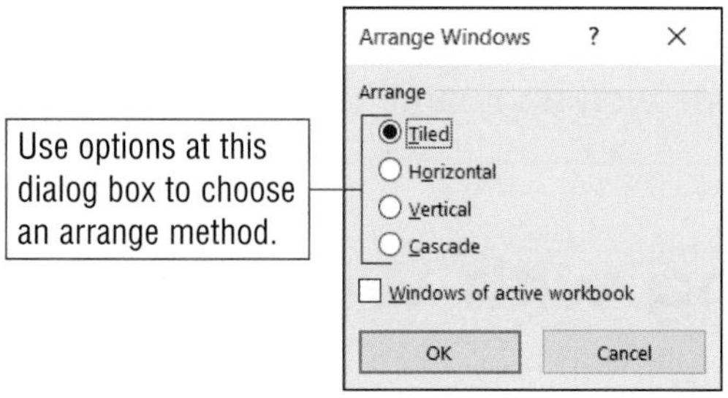

Choose the *Horizontal* option at the Arrange Windows dialog box to display the open workbooks across the screen. Choose the *Vertical* option to display the open workbooks up and down the screen. Choose the last option, *Cascade*, to display the Title bar of each open workbook. Figure 5.8 shows four cascaded workbooks.

Select the arrange option for displaying multiple workbooks based on which parts of the workbooks are most important to view simultaneously. For example, the tiled workbooks in Figure 5.7 display the company names of each workbook.

Figure 5.7 Tiled Workbooks

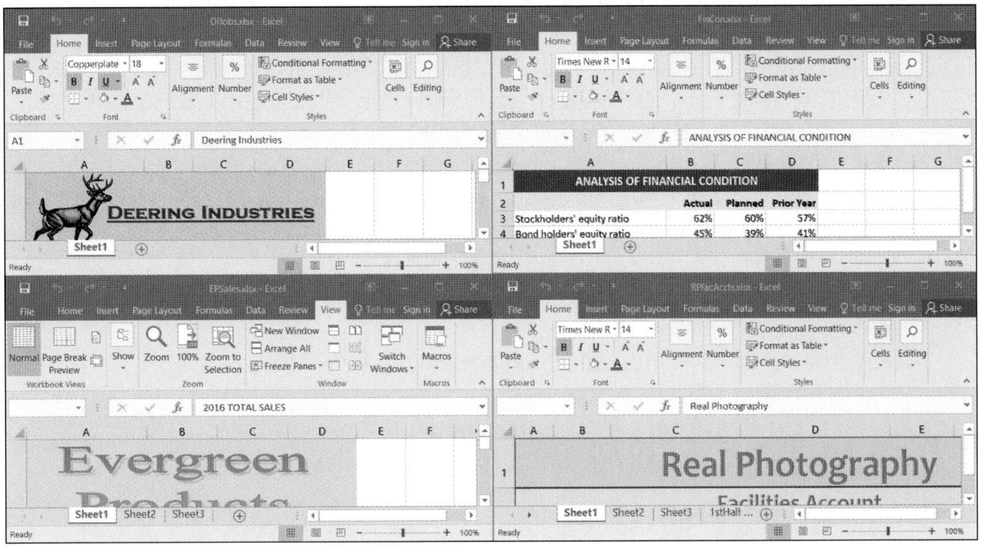

Figure 5.8 Cascaded Workbooks

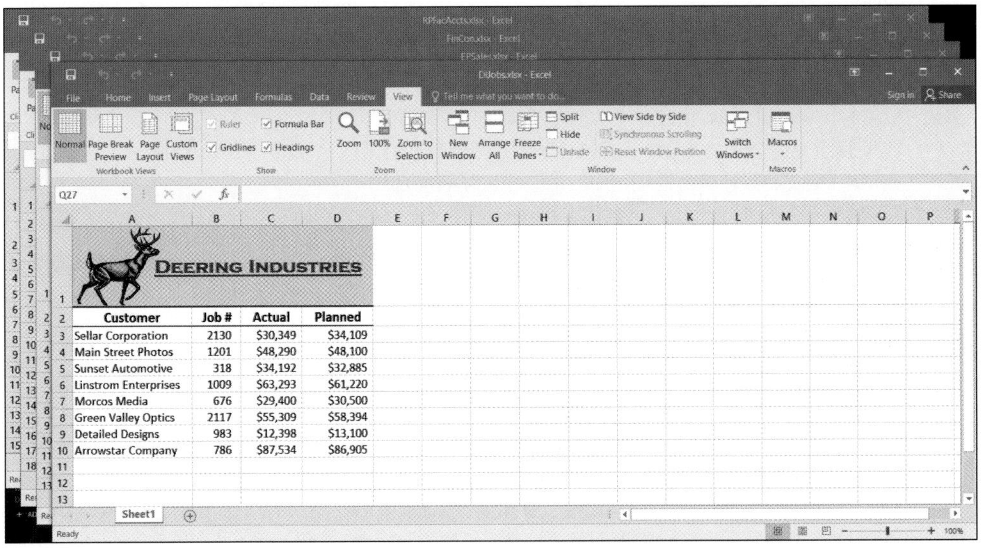

Hiding and Unhiding Workbooks

Hide

Unhide

Use the Hide button in the Window group on the View tab to hide the active workbook. If a workbook has been hidden, redisplay it by clicking the Unhide button in the Window group. At the Unhide dialog box, make sure the specific workbook is selected in the list box and then click OK.

Project 3a Opening, Arranging, and Hiding and Unhiding Workbooks — Part 1 of 3

1. Open several workbooks at the same time by completing the following steps:
   a. Display the Open dialog box with EL1C5 the active folder.
   b. Click the workbook named ***DIJobs.xlsx***.
   c. Press and hold down the Ctrl key, click ***EPSales.xlsx***, click ***FinCon.xlsx***, click ***RPFacAccts.xlsx***, and then release the Ctrl key.
   d. Click the Open button in the dialog box.
2. Make **DIJobs.xlsx** the active workbook by clicking the View tab, clicking the Switch Windows button, and then clicking ***DIJobs.xlsx*** at the drop-down list.

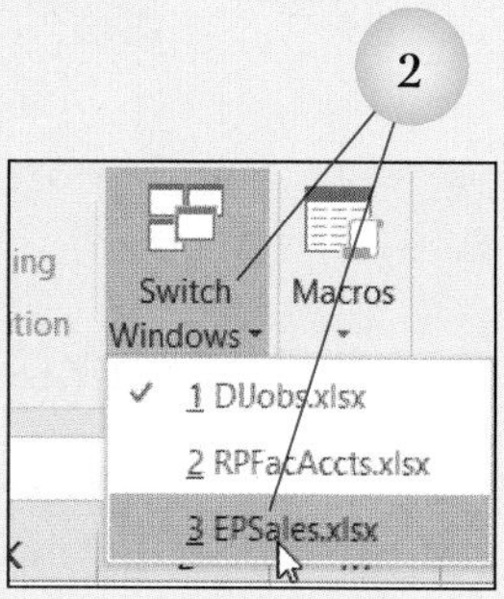

3. Tile the workbooks by completing the following steps:
   a. Click the View tab and then click the Arrange All button in the Window group.
   b. At the Arrange Windows dialog box, make sure *Tiled* is selected and then click OK.

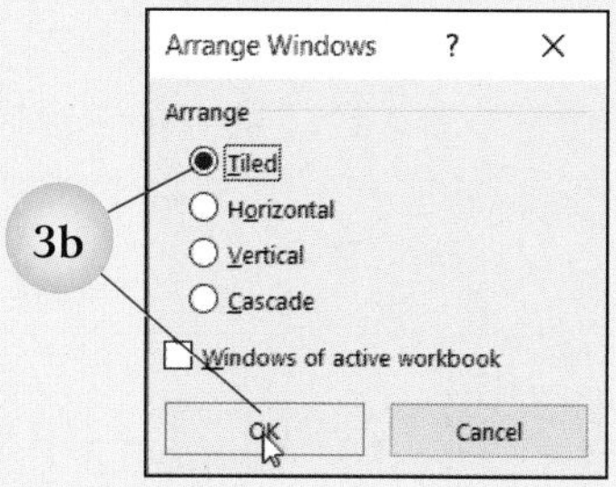

4. Cascade the workbooks by completing the following steps:
   a. Click the Arrange All button in the **DIJobs.xlsx** workbook.
   b. At the Arrange Windows dialog box, click *Cascade* and then click OK.
5. Hide and unhide workbooks by completing the following steps:
   a. Make sure **DIJobs.xlsx** is the active workbook. (The file name displays on top of each workbook file.)
   b. Click the Hide button in the Window group on the View tab.
   c. Make sure **RPFacAccts.xlsx** is the active workbook. (The file name displays at the top of each workbook file.)
   d. Click the Hide button in the Window group on the View tab.
   e. At the active workbook, click the View tab and then click the Unhide button.
   f. At the Unhide dialog box, click *RPFacAccts.xlsx* in the list box and then click OK.
   g. Click the Unhide button.
   h. At the Unhide dialog box, make sure **DIJobs.xlsx** is selected in the list box and then click OK.

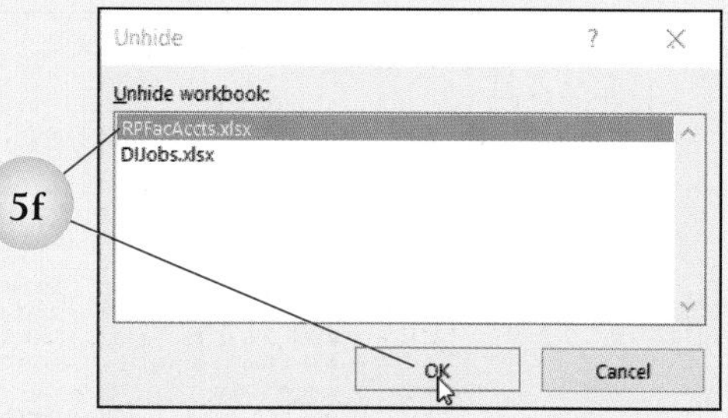

6. Close all the open workbooks (without saving changes) except **DIJobs.xlsx**.
7. Open a new window with the current workbook by clicking the New Window button in the Window group on the View tab. (Notice that the new window contains the workbook name followed by a colon and the number *2*.)
8. Switch back and forth between the two versions of the workbook.
9. Make **DIJobs.xlsx:2** the active window and then close the workbook.

Sizing and Moving Workbooks

Maximize

Minimize

Close

Restore Down

Change the size of the window using the Maximize and Minimize buttons in the upper right corner of the active workbook. The Maximize button is in the upper right corner of the active workbook immediately to the left of the Close button. (The Close button is the button containing the *X*.) The Minimize button is immediately to the left of the Maximize button.

If all the open workbooks are arranged, clicking the Maximize button causes the active workbook to expand to fill the screen. In addition, the Maximize button changes to the Restore Down button. To return the active workbook back to its original size, click the Restore Down button.

Click the Minimize button in the active workbook and the workbook is reduced and displays as a layer behind the Excel button on the taskbar. To maximize a workbook that has been minimized, click the Excel button on the taskbar and then click the thumbnail representing the workbook.

Project 3b Minimizing, Maximizing, and Restoring Workbooks

Part 2 of 3

1. Make sure **DIJobs.xlsx** is open.
2. Maximize **DIJobs.xlsx** by clicking the Maximize button in the upper right corner of the screen immediately left of the Close button.

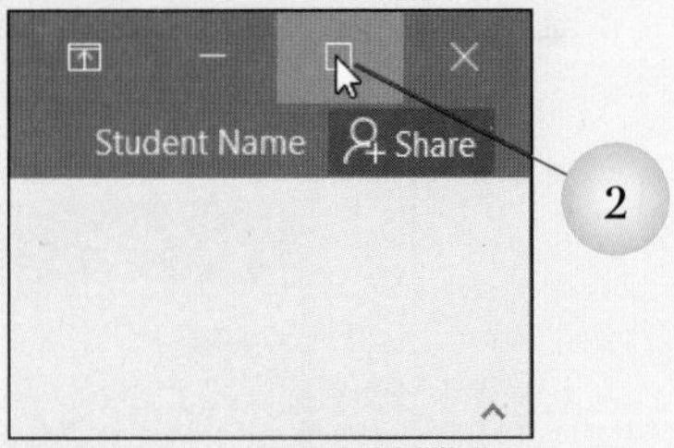

3. Open **EPSales.xlsx** and **FinCon.xlsx**.
4. Make the following changes to the open workbooks:
   a. Tile the workbooks.
   b. Click the **DIJobs.xlsx** Title bar to make it the active workbook.
   c. Minimize **DIJobs.xlsx** by clicking the Minimize button at the right side of the Title bar.
   d. Make **EPSales.xlsx** the active workbook and then minimize it.
   e. Minimize **FinCon.xlsx**.

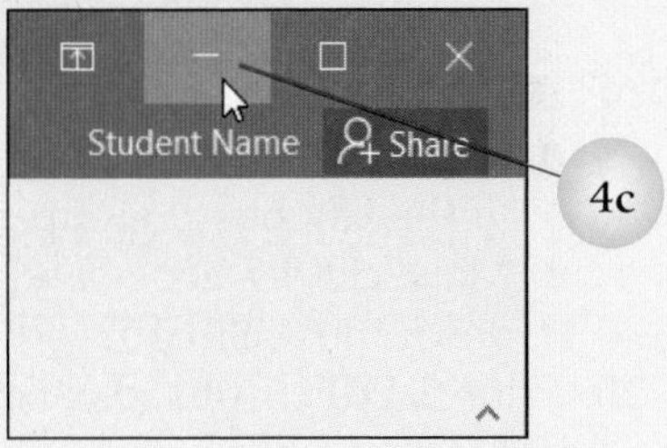

5. Click the Excel button on the taskbar, click the **DIJobs.xlsx** thumbnail, and then close the workbook without saving changes.
6. Complete steps similar to Step 5 to close the other two workbooks.

Moving, Linking, Copying, and Pasting Data between Workbooks

With more than one workbook open, data can be moved, linked, copied, and/or pasted from one workbook to another. To move, link, copy, and/or paste data between workbooks, use the cutting and pasting options discussed earlier in this chapter together with the information about windows.

Moving and Copying Data

Data can be moved or copied within a worksheet, between worksheets, and between workbooks and documents created in other programs, such as Word, PowerPoint, and Access. The Paste Options button provides a variety of options for pasting data in a worksheet, another workbook, or a document created in another program. In addition to being pasted, data can be linked and data can be pasted as an object or a picture object.

Project 3c **Copying Selected Cells from One Open Worksheet to Another** Part 3 of 3

1. Open **DIFebJobs.xlsx**.
2. If you just completed Project 3b, click the Maximize button so the worksheet fills the entire worksheet window.
3. Save the workbook and name it **5-DIFebJobs**.
4. With **5-DIFebJobs.xlsx** open, open **DIJobs.xlsx**.
5. Select and then copy text from **DIJobs.xlsx** to **5-DIFebJobs.xlsx** by completing the following steps:
   a. With **DIJobs.xlsx** the active workbook, select the range A3:D10.
   b. Click the Copy button in the Clipboard group on the Home tab.
   c. Click the Excel button on the taskbar and then click the **5-DIFebJobs.xlsx** thumbnail.

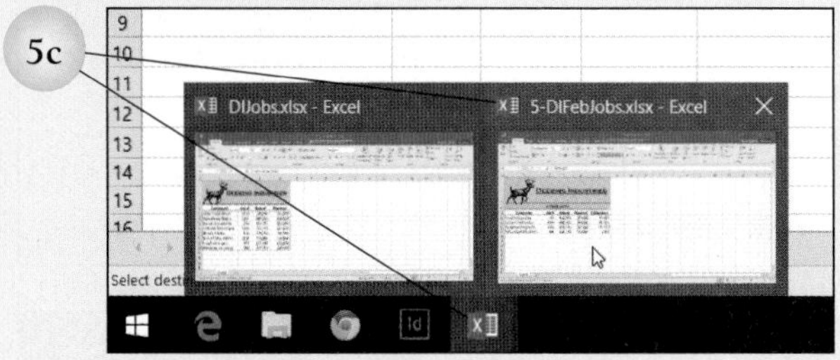

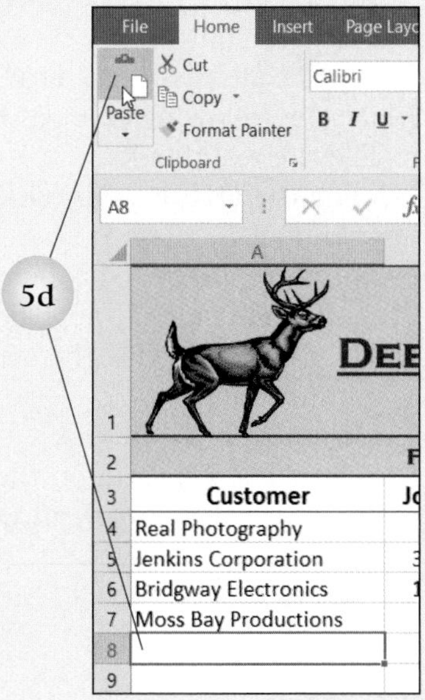

   d. Make cell A8 active and then click the Paste button in the Clipboard group.
   e. Make cell E7 active and then drag the fill handle down into cell E15.
6. Print **5-DIFebJobs.xlsx** centered horizontally and vertically on the page.
7. Save and then close **5-DIFebJobs.xlsx**.
8. Close **DIJobs.xlsx**.

Check Your Work

Project 4 **Linking and Copying Data within and between Worksheets and Word** 2 Parts

You will open a workbook containing four worksheets with quarterly expenses data, copy and link cells between the worksheets, and then copy and paste the worksheets into Word as picture objects.

Preview Finished Project

Tutorial

Linking Data

Quick Steps

Link Data between Worksheets

1. Select cells.
2. Click Copy button.
3. Click worksheet tab.
4. Click in cell.
5. Click Paste button arrow.
6. Click Paste Link button.

Linking Data

In addition to being copied and pasted, data can be copied and then linked within or between worksheets or workbooks. Linking data is useful for maintaining consistency and control over critical data in worksheets or workbooks. When data is linked, a change made in a linked cell is automatically made to the other cells in the link. Links can be made with individual cells or with a range of cells. When linking data, the worksheet that contains the original data is called the *source worksheet* and the worksheet that relies on the source worksheet for the data in the link is called the *dependent worksheet*.

To create a link, make active the cell containing the data to be linked (or select the cells) and then click the Copy button in the Clipboard group on the Home tab. Make active the worksheet where the cells are to be linked, click the Paste button arrow, and then click the Paste Link button in the *Other Paste Options* section in the drop-down list. Another method for creating a link is to click the Paste button, click the Paste Options button, and then click the Paste Link button in the *Other Paste Options* section in the drop-down list.

Project 4a **Linking Cells between Worksheets**

Part 1 of 2

1. Open **DWQtrlyExp.xlsx** and then save it with the name **5-DWQtrlyExp**.
2. Link cells in the first-quarter worksheet to the other three worksheets by completing the following steps:
   a. With the 1st Qtr tab active, select the range C4:C10.
   b. Click the Copy button in the Clipboard group on the Home tab.
   c. Click the 2nd Qtr tab.
   d. Make cell C4 active.
   e. Click the Paste button arrow and then click the Paste Link button in the *Other Paste Options* section in the drop-down list.
   f. Click the 3rd Qtr tab and then make cell C4 active.
   g. Click the Paste button arrow and then click the Paste Link button.
   h. Click the 4th Qtr tab and then make cell C4 active.
   i. Click the Paste button.
   j. Click the Paste Options button and then click the Paste Link button in the *Other Paste Options* section in the drop-down list.

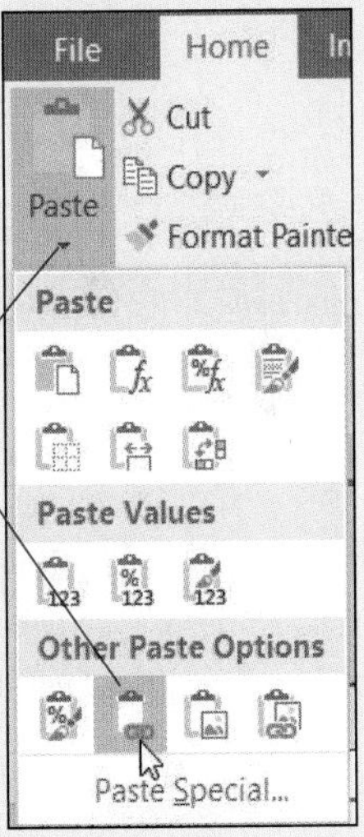

2e

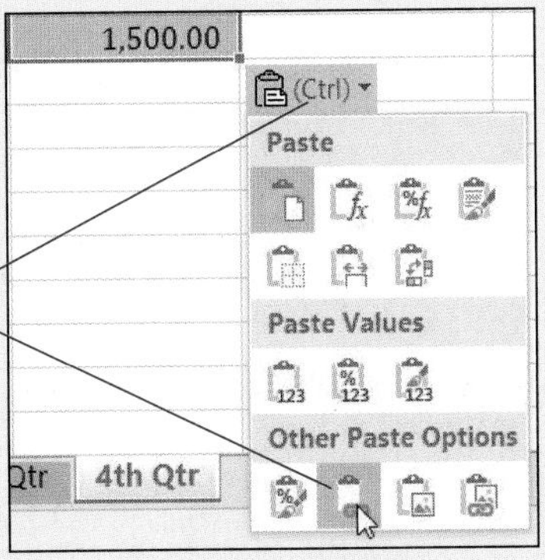

2j

3. Click the 1st Qtr tab and then press the Esc key to remove the moving marquee.

4. Insert a formula in each worksheet that subtracts the budget amount from the variance amount by completing the following steps:
   a. Make sure the first-quarter worksheet displays.
   b. Press and hold down the Shift key, click the 4th Qtr tab. (This selects all four tabs.)
   c. Make cell D4 active, type the formula =c4-b4, and then press the Enter key.
   d. Copy the formula in cell D4 down into the range D5:D10.
   e. Make cell D4 active and then apply the Accounting format with two digits after the decimal point and a dollar symbol.
   f. Click the 2nd Qtr tab and notice that the formula was inserted and copied in this worksheet.
   g. Click the other worksheet tabs and notice the amounts in column D.
   h. Click the 1st Qtr tab.

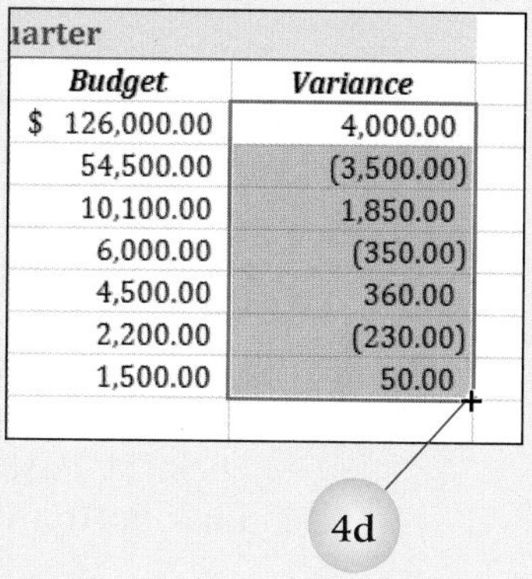

arter
Budget
Variance
$ 126,000.00
4,000.00
54,500.00
(3,500.00)
10,100.00
1,850.00
6,000.00
(350.00)
4,500.00
360.00
2,200.00
(230.00)
1,500.00
50.00
4d

5. With the first-quarter worksheet active, make the following changes to the specified linked cells:

   C4: Change *$126,000* to *$128,000*

   C5: Change *54,500* to *56,000*

   C9: Change *2,200* to *2,400*
6. Click the 2nd Qtr tab and notice that the values in cells C4, C5, and C9 automatically changed (because they were linked to the first-quarter worksheet).
7. Click the other tabs and notice that the values changed.
8. Save **5-DWQtrlyExp.xlsx** and then print all four worksheets in the workbook.

Check Your Work

Tutorial

Copying and Pasting Data between Programs

Copying and Pasting Data between Programs

Microsoft Office is a suite that allows *integration*, which is the combining of data from files created by two or more programs into one file. Integration can occur by copying and pasting data between files created in different programs. For example, a worksheet can be created in Excel and specific data can be selected in the worksheet and then copied to a Word document. When pasting Excel data in a Word document, choose from among these formatting options: keep the source formatting, use destination styles, link the data, insert the data as a picture, or keep the text only.

Project 4b Copying and Pasting Excel Data into a Word Document

Part 2 of 2

1. With **5-DWQtrlyExp.xlsx** open, open the Word program.
2. In Word, open the document named **DWQtrlyRpt.docx** in the EL1C5 folder on your storage medium.
3. Save the Word document with the name **5-DWQtrlyRpt**.
4. Click the Excel button on the taskbar.
5. Copy the first-quarter data into the Word document by completing the following steps:
   a. Click the 1st Qtr tab.
   b. Select the range A2:D10.
   c. Click the Copy button in the Clipboard group on the Home tab.
   d. Click the Word button on the taskbar.

e. In the **5-DWQtrlyRpt.docx** document, press Ctrl + End to move the insertion point below the heading.
f. Click the Paste button arrow. (This displays a drop-down list of paste option buttons.)
g. Move the mouse over the various buttons in the drop-down list to see how each option inserts the data in the document.
h. Click the Picture button. (This inserts the data as a picture object.)
i. Press Ctrl + End and then press the Enter key two times. (This moves the insertion point below the data.)
j. Click the Excel button on the taskbar.

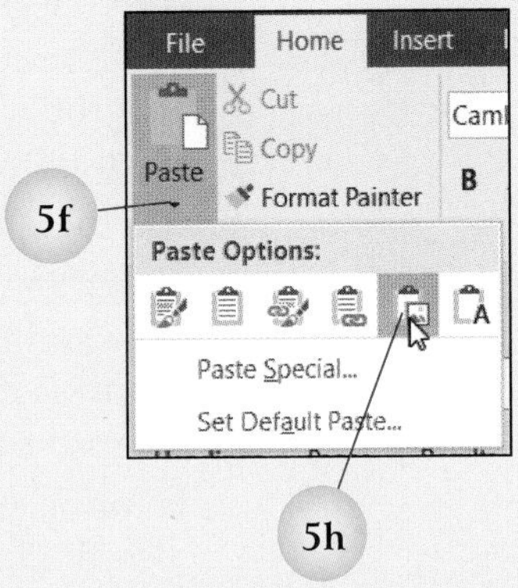

6. Click the 2nd Qtr tab and then complete steps similar to those in Step 5 to copy and paste the second-quarter data into the Word document.
7. Click the 3rd Qtr tab and then complete steps similar to those in Step 5 to copy and paste the third-quarter data to the Word document.
8. Click the 4th Qtr tab and then complete steps similar to those in Step 5 to copy and paste the fourth-quarter data to the Word document. (The data will display on two pages.)
9. Print the document by clicking the File tab, clicking the *Print* option, and then clicking the Print button at the Print backstage area.
10. Save and close **5-DWQtrlyRpt.docx** and then close Word.
11. In Excel, press the Esc key to remove the moving marquee and then make cell A1 active.
12. Save and then close **5-DWQtrlyExp.xlsx**.

Check Your Work

Chapter Summary

- By default, an Excel workbook contains one worksheet. Add a new worksheet to a workbook by clicking the New sheet button or using the keyboard shortcut Shift + F11.
- Delete a worksheet with the Delete button in the Cells group on the Home tab or by right-clicking a worksheet tab and then clicking *Delete* at the shortcut menu.
- To manage more than one worksheet at a time, first select the worksheets. Use the mouse together with the Shift key to select adjacent worksheet tabs and use the mouse together with the Ctrl key to select nonadjacent worksheet tabs.
- Copy or move selected cells and cell contents in and between worksheets using the Cut, Copy, and Paste buttons in the Clipboard group on the Home tab or by dragging with the mouse.
- Move selected cells with the mouse by dragging the outline of the selected cells to the new position.
- Copy selected cells with the mouse by pressing and holding down the Ctrl key while dragging the cells to the new position.
- When pasting data, specify how cells are to be pasted by clicking the Paste button arrow or pasting the cells and then clicking the Paste Options button. Clicking either button displays a drop-down list of paste option buttons. Click a button at the drop-down list.
- Use the Clipboard task pane to copy and paste data within and between worksheets and workbooks. Display the Clipboard task pane by clicking the Clipboard group task pane launcher.

- Perform maintenance activities, such as deleting and renaming, on worksheets within a workbook by right-clicking a worksheet tab and then clicking an option at the shortcut menu.
- The mouse can be used to move or copy worksheets. To move a worksheet, drag the worksheet tab with the mouse. To copy a worksheet, press and hold down the Ctrl key and then drag the worksheet tab with the mouse.
- Use the *Tab Color* option at the worksheet tab shortcut menu to apply a color to a worksheet tab.
- Hide and unhide a worksheet by clicking the Format button in the Cells group and then clicking the desired option at the drop-down list or by right-clicking the worksheet tab and then clicking the desired option at the shortcut menu.
- To print all the worksheets in a workbook, display the Print backstage area, click the first gallery in the *Settings* category, and then click *Print Entire Workbook* at the drop-down list. Print specific worksheets by selecting their tabs.
- Use buttons in the Zoom group on the View tab or the zoom slider bar at the right side of the Status bar to change the display zoom percentage.
- Split the worksheet window into panes with the Split button in the Window group on the View tab. To remove a split from a worksheet, click the Split button to deactivate it.
- Freeze window panes by clicking the Freeze Panes button in the Window group on the View tab and then clicking *Freeze Panes* at the drop-down list. Unfreeze window panes by clicking the Freeze Panes button and then clicking *Unfreeze Panes* at the drop-down list.
- A selected group of cells is referred to as a *range*. A range can be named and used in a formula. Name a range by typing the name in the Name box to the left of the Formula bar or at the New Name dialog box.
- To open multiple workbooks that are adjacent, display the Open dialog box, click the first workbook, press and hold down the Shift key, click the last workbook, release the Shift key, and then click the Open button. To open workbooks that are nonadjacent, click the first workbook, press and hold down the Ctrl key, click the desired workbooks, release the Ctrl key, and then click the Open button.
- To see a list of open workbooks, click the View tab and then click the Switch Windows button in the Window group.
- Arrange multiple workbooks in a window with options at the Arrange Windows dialog box.
- Hide the active workbook by clicking the Hide button and unhide a workbook by clicking the Unhide button in the Window group on the View tab.
- Click the Maximize button in the upper right corner of the active workbook to make the workbook fill the entire window area. Click the Minimize button to shrink the active workbook to a button on the taskbar. Click the Restore Down button to return the workbook to its previous size.
- Data can be moved, copied, linked, and/or pasted between workbooks. Also, a workbook can be pasted as a link in a different Microsoft Office application, such a Word or PowerPoint. Changing the data in one application will change linked data that exists in a different application.

Commands Review

FEATURE	RIBBON TAB, GROUP	BUTTON, OPTION	KEYBOARD SHORTCUT
Arrange Windows dialog box	View, Window		
Clipboard task pane	Home, Clipboard		
copy selected cells	Home, Clipboard		Ctrl + C
cut selected cells	Home, Clipboard		Ctrl + X
freeze window panes	View, Window	, *Freeze Panes*	
hide worksheet	Home, Cells	, *Hide & Unhide, Hide Sheet*	
insert new worksheet			Shift + F11
maximize window			
minimize window			
New Name dialog box	Formulas, Defined Names		
paste selected cells	Home, Clipboard		Ctrl + V
restore down			
split window into panes	View, Window		
unfreeze window panes	View, Window	, *Unfreeze Panes*	
unhide worksheet	Home, Cells	, *Hide & Unhide, Unhide Sheet*	

Workbook

Chapter study tools and assessment activities are available in the *Workbook* ebook. These resources are designed to help you further develop and demonstrate mastery of the skills learned in this chapter.

Microsoft®

Excel®

CHAPTER 6

Maintaining Workbooks

Performance Objectives

Upon successful completion of Chapter 6, you will be able to:

1. Create and rename a folder
2. Delete workbooks and folders
3. Copy and move workbooks within and between folders
4. Copy and move worksheets between workbooks
5. Maintain consistent formatting with cell styles
6. Insert, modify, and remove hyperlinks
7. Create financial forms using templates

Precheck

Check your current skills to help focus your study.

After you have worked with Excel for a period of time, you will have accumulated several workbook files. You should organize your workbooks into folders to facilitate the fast retrieval of information. Occasionally, you should perform file maintenance tasks, such as copying, moving, renaming, and deleting workbooks, to ensure the workbook lists in your folders are manageable. You will learn these tasks in this chapter, along with how to create and apply styles to a workbook, insert hyperlinks in a workbook, and use an Excel template to create a workbook.

Data Files

Before beginning the projects, copy the EL1C6 folder to your storage medium and then make EL1C6 the active folder.

SNAP

If you are a SNAP user, launch the Precheck and Tutorials from your Assignments page.

Project 1 **Manage Workbooks** **8 Parts**

You will perform a variety of file management tasks, including creating and renaming a folder; selecting and then deleting, copying, cutting, pasting, and renaming a workbook; deleting a folder; and opening, printing, and closing a workbook.

Maintaining Workbooks

Many workbook management tasks can be completed at the Open dialog box and Save As dialog box. These tasks include copying, moving, printing, and renaming workbooks; opening multiple workbooks; and creating and renaming new folders. Perform some file maintenance tasks, such as creating a folder and deleting files, with options from the Organize button drop-down list or the shortcut menu and navigate to folders using the Address bar. The elements of the Open dialog box are identified in Figure 6.1.

Figure 6.1 Open Dialog Box

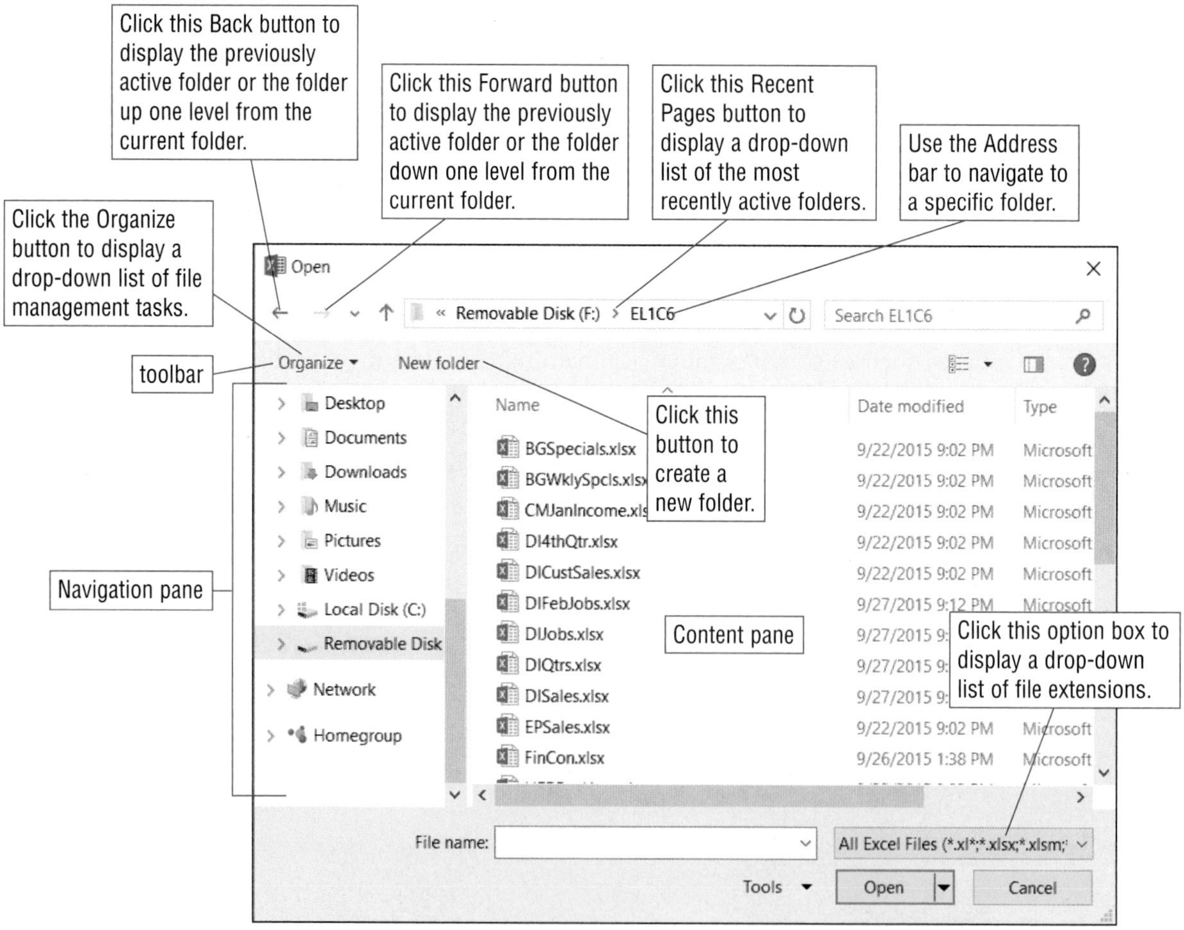

Click this Back button to display the previously active folder or the folder up one level from the current folder.
Click this Forward button to display the previously active folder or the folder down one level from the current folder.
Click this Recent Pages button to display a drop-down list of the most recently active folders.
Use the Address bar to navigate to a specific folder.
Click the Organize button to display a drop-down list of file management tasks.
toolbar
Click this button to create a new folder.
Navigation pane
Content pane
Click this option box to display a drop-down list of file extensions.
Open
Removable Disk (F:) > EL1C6
Search EL1C6
Organize
New folder
Desktop
Documents
Downloads
Music
Pictures
Videos
Local Disk (C:)
Removable Disk
Network
Homegroup
Name
Date modified
Type
BGSpecials.xlsx
DI4thQtr.xlsx
DICustSales.xlsx
DIFebJobs.xlsx
DIJobs.xlsx
DIQtrs.xlsx
DISales.xlsx
EPSales.xlsx
FinCon.xlsx
File name:
All Excel Files (*.xl*;*.xlsx;*.xlsm;
Tools
Open
Cancel

Hint Change the default folder with the *Default local file location* option at the Excel Options dialog box with *Save* selected.

Directions and projects in this chapter assume that you are managing workbooks and folders on a USB flash drive or your computer's hard drive. If you are using your OneDrive account, some of the workbook and folder management tasks may vary.

Creating a Folder

Tutorial

Managing Folders

Quick Steps

Create a Folder

1. Press Ctrl + F12.
2. Click New folder button.
3. Type folder name.
4. Press Enter.

New folder

New folder

In Excel, workbooks should be grouped logically and stored in folders. For example, all the workbooks related to one department can be stored in one folder that is named the department name. A folder can also be created within a folder (called a *subfolder*). The main folder on a disk or drive is called the *root folder*. Additional folders can be created as branches of this root folder.

At the Open dialog box and Save As dialog box, workbook file names display in the Content pane preceded by workbook icons and folder names display preceded by folder icons. Create a new folder by clicking the New folder button on the toolbar at the Open dialog box or Save As dialog box. This inserts a new folder in the Content pane. Type the name for the folder and then press the Enter key.

A folder name can contain a maximum of 255 characters. The characters can include numbers, spaces, and symbols, except those symbols identified in the Saving a Workbook section in Chapter 1.

Project 1a **Creating a Folder** Part 1 of 8

1. With Excel open, create a folder named *Payroll* on your storage medium by completing the following steps:
   a. Press Ctrl + F12 to display the Open dialog box.
   b. At the Open dialog box, navigate to your storage medium.
   c. Click the View button arrow on the toolbar.
   d. Click the *Details* option in the drop-down list.
2. Double-click the *EL1C6* folder name to make it the active folder.
3. Click the New folder button on the toolbar.
4. Type Payroll and then press the Enter key.
5. Close the Open dialog box.

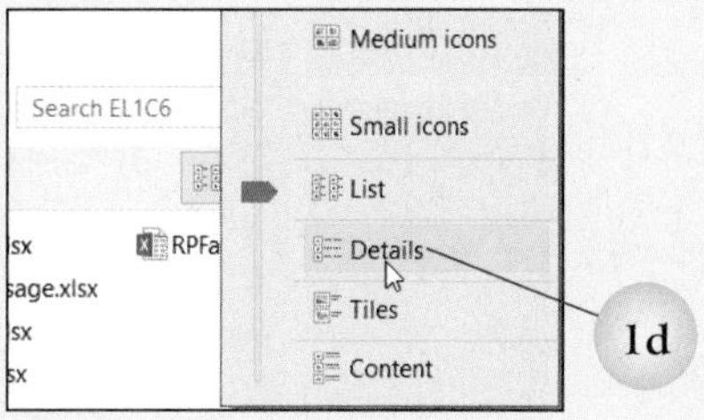

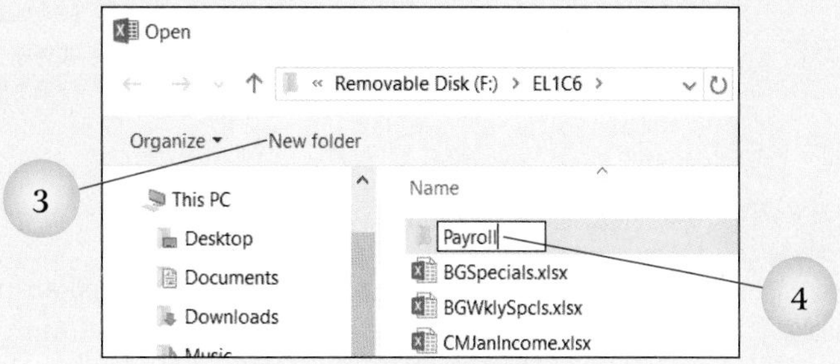

Renaming a Folder

Organize

Quick Steps

Rename a Folder

1. Display Open dialog box.
2. Click folder.
3. Click Organize button.
4. Click *Rename*.
5. Type new name.
6. Press Enter.

OR

1. Display Open dialog box.
2. Right-click folder name.
3. Click *Rename*.
4. Type new name.
5. Press Enter.

Managing folders may include renaming them. Rename a folder using the Organize button in the Open dialog box or using the shortcut menu. To rename a folder using the Organize button, display the Open dialog box, click in the Content pane the folder to be renamed, click the Organize button on the toolbar, and then click *Rename* at the drop-down list. This selects the folder name and inserts a border around it. Type the new name for the folder and then press the Enter key. To rename a folder using the shortcut menu, display the Open dialog box, right-click the folder name in the Content pane, and then click *Rename* at the shortcut menu. Type a new name for the folder and then press the Enter key.

When organizing files and folders, make sure the computer is set to display all the files in a particular folder and not just the Excel files, for example. Display all the files in a folder in the Open dialog box by clicking the button to the right of the *File name* text box and then clicking *All Files (*.*)* at the drop-down list.

Project 1b **Renaming a Folder** Part 2 of 8

1. Press Ctrl + F12 to display the Open dialog box and make sure EL1C6 is the active folder.
2. Right-click the *Payroll* folder name in the Content pane.
3. Click *Rename* at the shortcut menu.
4. Type Finances and then press the Enter key.

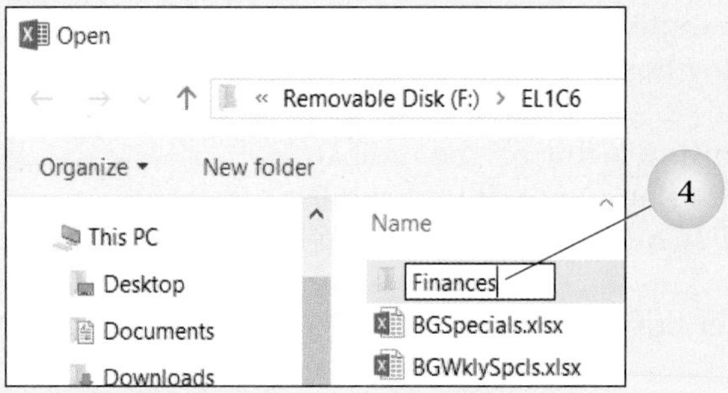

Selecting Workbooks

Tutorial

Maintaining Workbooks

Complete workbook management tasks on one workbook or selected workbooks. To select one workbook, display the Open dialog box and then click the workbook name. To select several adjacent workbooks, click the first workbook name, press and hold down the Shift key, click the last workbook name, and then release the Shift key. To select workbooks that are not adjacent, click the first workbook name, press and hold down the Ctrl key, click any other workbook names, and then release the Ctrl key.

Deleting Workbooks and Folders

Quick Steps

Delete a Workbook or Folder

1. Display Open dialog box.
2. Right-click workbook or folder name.
3. Click *Delete*.
4. If deleting from a removable drive, click Yes.

At some point, certain workbooks may need to be deleted from a storage medium or any other drive or folder in which workbooks are located. To delete a workbook, display the Open dialog box or the Save As dialog box, click the workbook name in the Content pane, click the Organize button, and then click *Delete* at the drop-down list. If the workbook is being deleted from a removable storage medium, such as a USB drive, a message will display asking to confirm the deletion. At this message, click Yes. To delete a workbook using the shortcut menu, display the Open dialog box, right-click the workbook name in the Content pane, and then click *Delete* at the shortcut menu.

Deleting to the Recycle Bin

Workbooks deleted from a removable drive are deleted permanently while workbooks deleted from the hard drive are automatically sent to the Windows Recycle Bin. A deleted workbook can be restored from the Recycle Bin. To free space on the drive, empty the Recycle Bin on a periodic basis. Restore a workbook from or empty the contents of the Recycle Bin at the Windows desktop (not in Excel). To display the Recycle Bin, minimize the Excel window and then double-click the Recycle Bin icon on the Windows desktop. At the Recycle Bin, restore file(s) and empty the Recycle Bin.

Project 1c Selecting and Deleting Workbooks — Part 3 of 8

1. At the Open dialog box, open **RPFacAccts.xlsx** and then save it with the name **6-RPFacAccts**.
2. Close **6-RPFacAccts.xlsx**.
3. Delete **6-RPFacAccts.xlsx** by completing the following steps:
   a. Display the Open dialog box with EL1C6 the active folder.
   b. Click ***6-RPFacAccts.xlsx*** to select it.
   c. Click the Organize button and then click *Delete* at the drop-down list.

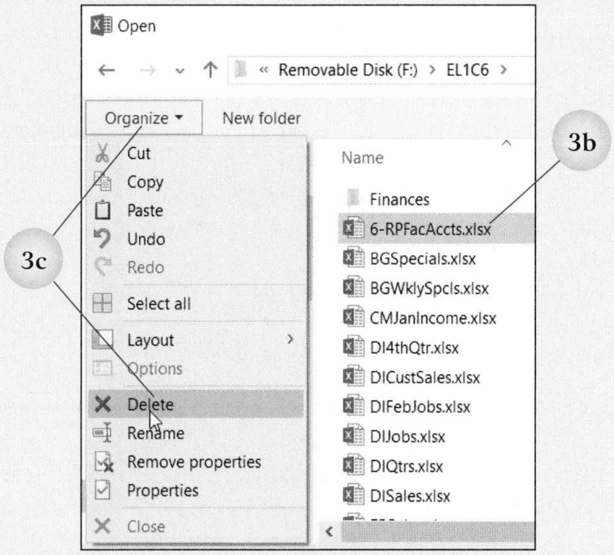

   d. If a message displays asking if you are sure you want to delete the worksheet, click Yes.

4. Delete selected workbooks by completing the following steps:
   a. Click ***DICustSales.xlsx*** in the Content pane.
   b. Press and hold down the Shift key, click ***DIJobs.xlsx***, and then release the Shift key.
   c. Position the mouse pointer on one of the selected workbook names and then click the right mouse button.
   d. At the shortcut menu that displays, click *Delete*.
   e. If a message displays asking if you are sure you want to delete the items, click Yes.
5. Close the Open dialog box.

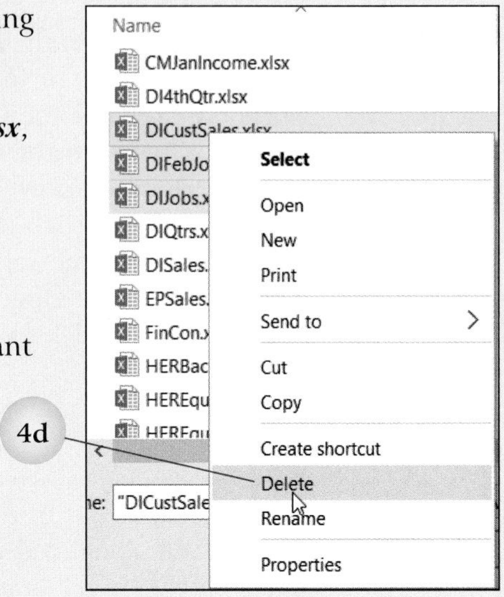

Copying Workbooks

In previous chapters, a workbook has been opened and then saved with a new name in the same location. This makes an exact copy of the workbook, preserving the original file. A workbook can also be copied into another folder.

Project 1d Saving a Copy of an Open Workbook to Another Folder — Part 4 of 8

1. Open **EPSales.xlsx**.
2. Save the workbook with Save As and name it **TotalSales**. (Make sure EL1C6 is the active folder.)
3. Save a copy of **TotalSales.xlsx** in the Finances folder you created in Project 1a (and renamed in Project 1b) by completing the following steps:
   a. With **TotalSales.xlsx** open, press the F12 function key to display the Save As dialog box.
   b. At the Save As dialog box, change to the Finances folder. To do this, double-click *Finances* at the beginning of the Content pane. (Folders are listed before workbooks.)
   c. Click the Save button in the lower right corner of the dialog box.
4. Close **TotalSales.xlsx**.
5. Change back to the EL1C6 folder by completing the following steps:
   a. Press Ctrl + F12 to display the Open dialog box.
   b. Click *EL1C6* that displays in the Address bar.
6. Close the Open dialog box.

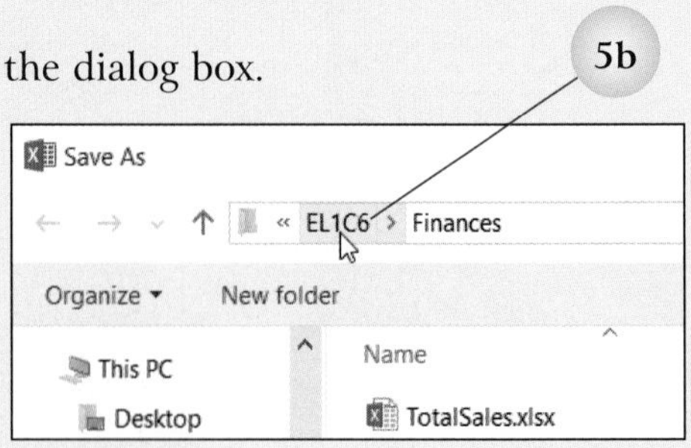

Quick Steps
Copy a Workbook
1. Display Open or Save As dialog box.
2. Right-click workbook name.
3. Click *Copy*.
4. Navigate to folder.
5. Right-click blank area in Content pane.
6. Click *Paste*.

A workbook can be copied to another folder without opening the workbook first. To do this, use the *Copy* and *Paste* options from the shortcut menu at the Open dialog box or the Save As dialog box. A workbook or selected workbooks can also be copied into the same folder. When copied into the same folder, Excel adds a hyphen followed by the word *Copy* to the end of the workbook name.

To move or copy files or folders in your OneDrive account, go to onedrive.com, make sure you are logged into your account, and then use the onedrive.com toolbar to move a workbook or folder to another location. Or copy and then move a workbook or folder to another location.

Project 1e **Copying a Workbook at the Open Dialog Box** Part 5 of 8

Note: If you are using your OneDrive account, the steps for copying, cutting, and pasting workbooks will vary from the steps in Project 1e and 1f. Please check with your instructor.

1. Copy **CMJanIncome.xlsx** to the Finances folder. To begin, display the Open dialog box with the EL1C6 folder active.
2. Position the mouse pointer on **CMJanIncome.xlsx**, click the right mouse button, and then click *Copy* at the shortcut menu.
3. Change to the Finances folder by double-clicking *Finances* at the beginning of the Content pane.
4. Position the mouse pointer in any blank area in the Content pane, click the right mouse button, and then click *Paste* at the shortcut menu.
5. Change back to the EL1C6 folder by clicking *EL1C6* in the Address bar.
6. Close the Open dialog box.

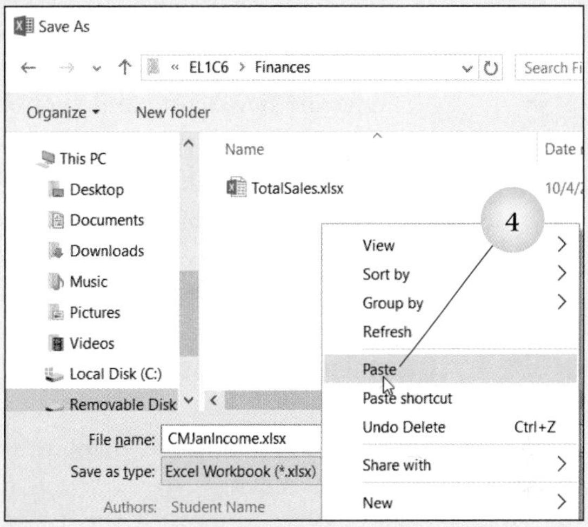

Sending Workbooks to a Different Drive or Folder

Quick Steps
Move a Workbook
1. Display Open dialog box.
2. Right-click workbook name.
3. Click *Cut*.
4. Navigate to folder.
5. Right-click in blank area in Content pane.
6. Click *Paste*.

Use the *Send to* option to copy a workbook to another folder or drive without having to navigate to the new location. To use this option, position the mouse pointer on the name of the workbook to be copied, click the right mouse button, point to *Send to* (which causes a side menu to display), and then click the specific drive or folder.

Cutting and Pasting a Workbook

Remove a workbook from one folder and insert it in another folder using the *Cut* and *Paste* options from the shortcut menu at the Open dialog box. To do this, display the Open dialog box, position the mouse pointer on the workbook to be removed (cut), click the right mouse button, and then click *Cut* at the shortcut menu. Change to the specific folder or drive, position the mouse pointer in any blank area in the Content pane, click the right mouse button, and then click *Paste* at the shortcut menu.

Project 1f Cutting and Pasting a Workbook

Part 6 of 8

1. Display the Open dialog box with the EL1C6 folder active.
2. Position the mouse pointer on **FinCon.xlsx**, click the right mouse button, and then click *Cut* at the shortcut menu.
3. Double-click *Finances* to make it the active folder.
4. Position the mouse pointer in any blank area in the Content pane, click the right mouse button, and then click *Paste* at the shortcut menu.
5. Click *EL1C6* in the Address bar.

Quick Steps

Rename a Workbook

1. Display Open dialog box.
2. Click workbook.
3. Click Organize button.
4. Click *Rename*.
5. Type new name.
6. Press Enter.

OR

1. Display Open dialog box.
2. Right-click workbook name.
3. Click *Rename*.
4. Type new name.
5. Press Enter.

Renaming Workbooks

At the Open dialog box, use the *Rename* option from the Organize button drop-down list or the shortcut menu to give a workbook a different name. The *Rename* option changes the name of the workbook and keeps the workbook in the same folder. To use *Rename*, display the Open dialog box, click the workbook to be renamed, click the Organize button, and then click *Rename* at the drop-down list. This puts a thin black border around the workbook name and selects the name. Type the new name and then press the Enter key.

Another method for renaming a workbook is to right-click the workbook name at the Open dialog box and then click *Rename* at the shortcut menu. Type the new name for the workbook and then press the Enter key.

Project 1g Renaming a Workbook

Part 7 of 8

1. Make sure the Open dialog box displays with EL1C6 the active folder.
2. Double-click *Finances* to make it the active folder.
3. Click ***FinCon.xlsx*** to select it.
4. Click the Organize button on the toolbar.
5. Click *Rename* at the drop-down list.
6. Type Analysis and then press the Enter key.

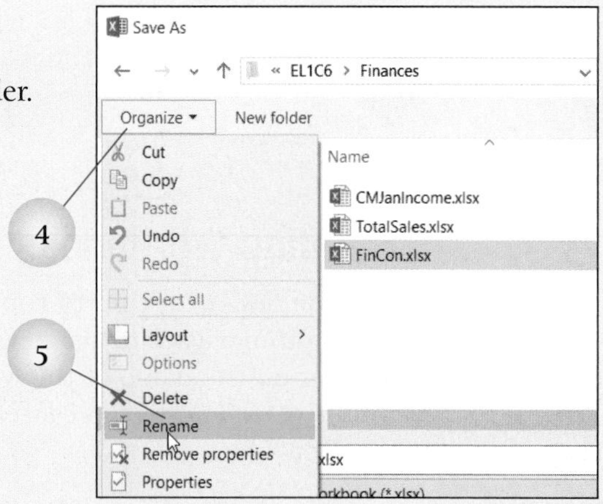

7. Complete steps similar to those in Steps 3 through 6 to rename **CMJanIncome.xlsx** to **CMJanProfits**.
8. Click the Back button (displays as *Back to EL1C6*) at the left side of the Address bar.

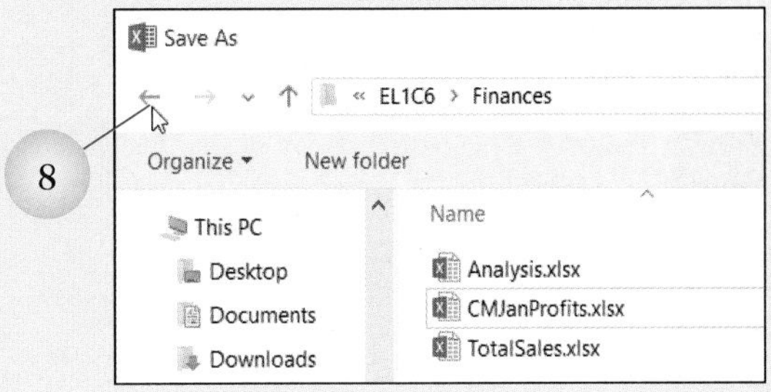

Deleting a Folder and Its Contents

As explained earlier in this chapter, a workbook or selected workbooks can be deleted. In addition, a folder and all of its contents can be deleted. Delete a folder in the same manner as a workbook.

Project 1h Deleting a Folder and Its Contents — Part 8 of 8

1. Make sure the Open dialog box displays with the EL1C6 folder active.
2. Right-click *Finances* in the Content pane.
3. Click *Delete* at the shortcut menu.
4. If you are deleting the folder from a removable drive, click Yes at the message that displays asking if you want to delete the folder.
5. Close the Open dialog box.

Project 2 Copy and Move Worksheets into an Equipment Rental Workbook — 3 Parts

You will manage workbooks at the Open backstage area and then open multiple workbooks and copy and move worksheets between the workbooks.

Preview Finished Project

Tutorial

Managing the *Recent* Option List

Managing the *Recent* Option List

As workbooks are opened and closed, Excel keeps a list of the most recently opened workbooks. To view this list, click the File tab and then click the *Open* option. This displays the Open backstage area, similar to what is shown in Figure 6.2. (The workbook names you see may vary from those in the figure.) Generally, the names of the 25 most recently opened workbooks display in the *Recent* option list and are organized in categories such as *Today*, *Yesterday*, and *Last Week*. To open a workbook, scroll down the list and then click the workbook name. The Excel 2016 opening screen also displays a list of the most recently opened workbooks. The workbook names in the Recent list are the same as those in the *Recent* option list at the Open backstage area.

Figure 6.2 Open Backstage Area

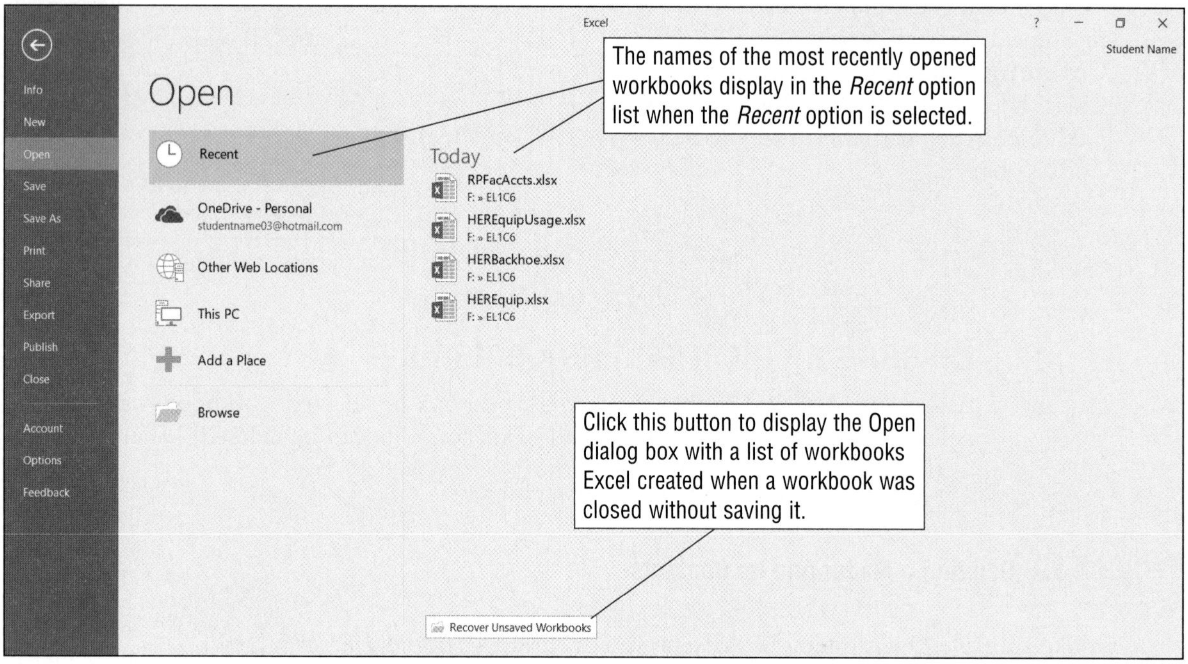

Pinning and Unpinning a Workbook

A workbook that is opened on a regular basis can be pinned to the *Recent* option list. To pin a workbook to the *Recent* option list at the Open backstage area, hover the mouse pointer over the workbook name and then click the small left-pointing push pin to the right of the workbook name. The left-pointing push pin changes to a down-pointing push pin and the pinned workbook is inserted into a new category named *Pinned*. The *Pinned* category displays at the top of the *Recent* option list. The next time the Open backstage area displays, the pinned workbook displays in the *Pinned* category at the top of the *Recent* option list. A workbook can also be pinned to the Recent list at the Excel 2016 opening screen. When a workbook is pinned, it displays at the tops of both the Recent list and the *Recent* option list at the Open backstage area.

To "unpin" a workbook from the Recent list or the *Recent* option list, click the push pin to change it from a down-pointing pin to a left-pointing pin. More than one workbook can be pinned to a list. Another method for pinning and unpinning a workbook is to use the shortcut menu. Right-click a workbook name and then click the *Pin to list* or *Unpin from list* option.

Like workbooks, folders can be pinned to a list at the Save As backstage area. The third panel in the Save As backstage area displays a list of the most recently opened folders and organizes them into categories such as *Today*, *Yesterday*, and *Last Week*. Pin a folder or folders to the list and a *Pinned* category is created and the folder names display in the category.

Recovering an Unsaved Workbook

If a workbook is closed without saving it, it can be recovered with the Recover Unsaved Workbooks button below the *Recent* option list. Click this button and the Open dialog box displays with the names of the workbooks that Excel automatically saved. At this dialog box, double-click the workbook name to open it.

Clearing the *Recent* Option List and the Recent List

Clear the contents (except pinned workbooks) of the *Recent* option list or Recent list by right-clicking a workbook name in the list and then clicking *Clear unpinned Workbooks* at the shortcut menu. At the message asking to confirm removal of the items, click Yes. To clear a folder from the Save As backstage area, right-click a folder in the list and then click *Remove from list* at the shortcut menu.

Project 2a **Managing Workbooks at the Open Backstage Area** — Part 1 of 3

1. Close any open workbooks.
2. Click the File tab and then click the *Open* option.
3. Make sure the *Recent* option below the heading *Open* is selected. Notice the workbook names that display in the *Recent* option list.
4. Navigate to the EL1C6 folder on your storage medium, open **HEREquip.xlsx**, and then save it with the name **6-HEREquip**.
5. Close **6-HEREquip.xlsx**.
6. Open **HEREquipUsage.xlsx** and then close it.
7. Open **HERBackhoe.xlsx** and then close it.
8. Pin the three workbooks to the *Recent* option list (you will use them in Project 2b) by completing the following steps:
   a. Click the File tab and then make sure the *Open* option is selected. (This displays the Open backstage area with the *Recent* option selected.)
   b. Click the left-pointing push pin at the right side of **6-HEREquip.xlsx**. (This changes the pin from left pointing to down pointing.)

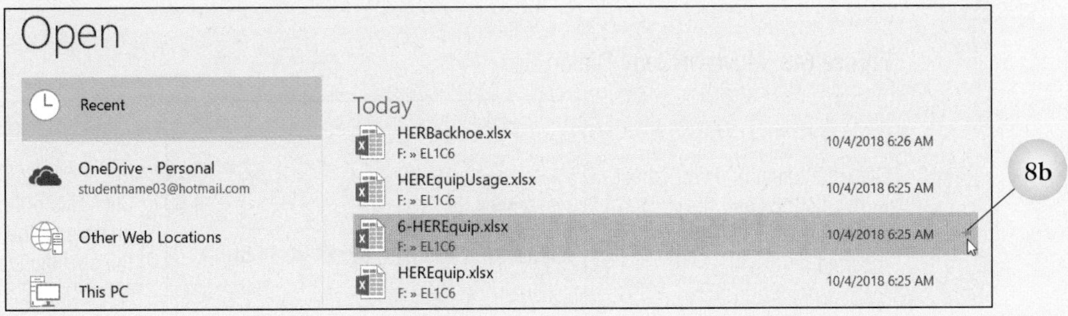

   c. Click the left-pointing push pin at the right side of **HEREquipUsage.xlsx**.

d. Right-click ***HERBackhoe.xlsx*** and then click *Pin to list* at the shortcut menu.

e. Click the Back button to exit the Open backstage area.

9. Open **6-HEREquip.xlsx** by clicking the File tab and then clicking ***6-HEREquip.xlsx*** in the *Recent* option list. (After clicking the File tab, make sure the *Open* option is selected. This displays the Open backstage area with the *Recent* option selected.)

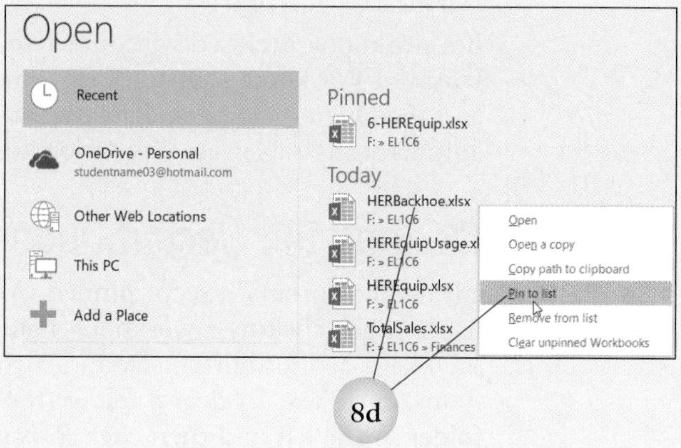

Managing Worksheets

Quick Steps

Copy a Worksheet to Another Workbook

1. Right-click sheet tab.
2. Click *Move or Copy.*
3. Select destination workbook.
4. Select worksheet location.
5. Click *Create a copy* check box.
6. Click OK.

Individual worksheets can be moved or copied within the same workbook or to another existing workbook. Exercise caution when moving sheets, because the calculations and charts based on the data in a worksheet might become inaccurate. To duplicate a worksheet in the same workbook, press and hold down the Ctrl key, click the worksheet tab and hold down the left mouse button, drag to the new location, and then release the mouse button and the Ctrl key.

Copying a Worksheet to Another Workbook

To copy a worksheet to another workbook, open both the source and the destination workbooks. Right-click the worksheet tab and then click *Move or Copy* at the shortcut menu. At the Move or Copy dialog box, shown in Figure 6.3, select the name of the destination workbook in the *To book* option drop-down list, select the name of the worksheet the copied worksheet will be placed before in the *Before sheet* list box, click the *Create a copy* check box, and then click OK.

Figure 6.3 Move or Copy Dialog Box

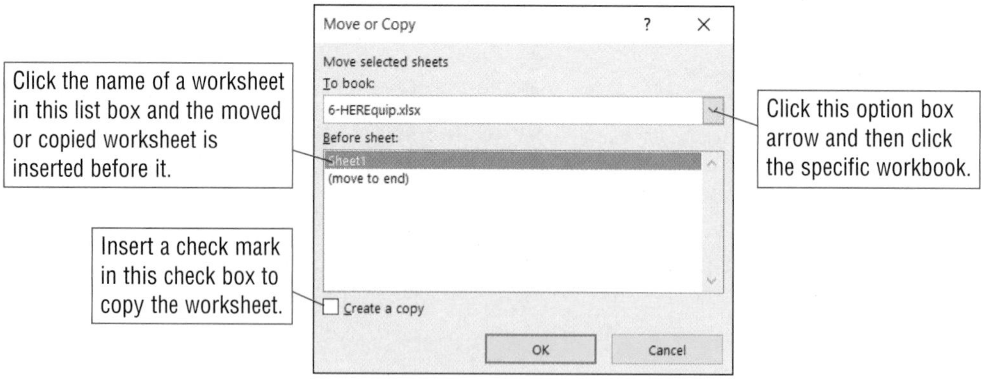

Project 2b **Copying a Worksheet to Another Workbook** Part 2 of 3

1. With **6-HEREquip.xlsx** open, open **HEREquipUsage.xlsx**.
2. Copy the Front Loader worksheet by completing the following steps:
   a. With **HEREquipUsage.xlsx** the active workbook, right-click the Front Loader tab and then click *Move or Copy* at the shortcut menu.
   b. Click the *To book* option box arrow and then click ***6-HEREquip.xlsx*** at the drop-down list.
   c. Click *(move to end)* in the *Before sheet* list box.
   d. Click the *Create a copy* check box to insert a check mark.
   e. Click OK. (Excel switches to the **6-HEREquip.xlsx** workbook and inserts the copied Front Loader worksheet after Sheet1.)
3. Complete steps similar to those in Step 2 to copy the Tractor worksheet to the **6-HEREquip.xlsx** workbook.
4. Complete steps similar to those in Step 2 to copy the Forklift worksheet to the **6-HEREquip.xlsx** workbook and insert the Forklift worksheet before the Tractor worksheet.
5. Save **6-HEREquip.xlsx**.
6. Make **HEREquipUsage.xlsx** the active workbook and then close it.

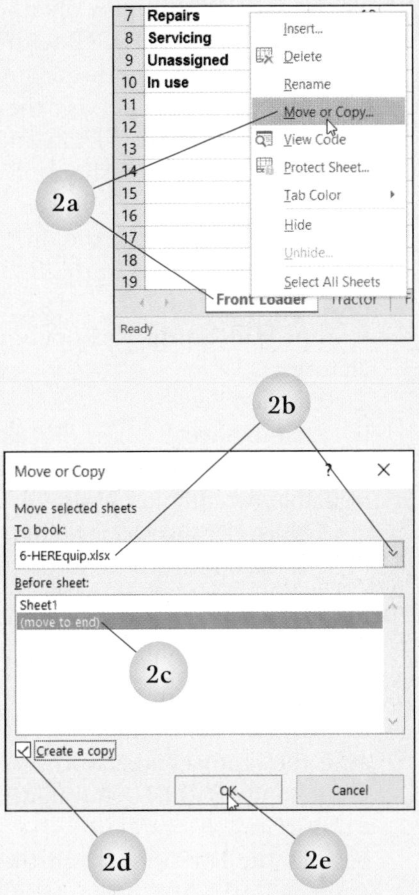

Check Your Work

Moving a Worksheet to Another Workbook

Quick Steps

Move a Worksheet to Another Workbook

1. Right-click worksheet tab.
2. Click *Move or Copy*.
3. Select destination workbook.
4. Select worksheet location.
5. Click OK.

To move a worksheet to another workbook, open both the source and the destination workbooks. Make active the worksheet to be moved in the source workbook, right-click the worksheet tab, and then click *Move or Copy* at the shortcut menu. At the Move or Copy dialog box, shown in Figure 6.3, select the name of the destination workbook in the *To book* drop-down list, select the name of the worksheet the moved worksheet will be placed before in the *Before sheet* list box, and then click OK. To reposition a worksheet tab, drag the tab to the new position.

Be careful when moving a worksheet to another workbook file. If formulas in the source workbook depend on the contents of the cells in the worksheet that is moved, they will no longer work properly.

Project 2c Moving a Worksheet to Another Workbook

1. With **6-HEREquip.xlsx** open, open **HERBackhoe.xlsx**.
2. Move Sheet1 from **HERBackhoe.xlsx** to **6-HEREquip.xlsx** by completing the following steps:
   a. With **HERBackhoe.xlsx** the active workbook, right-click the Sheet1 tab and then click *Move or Copy* at the shortcut menu.
   b. Click the *To book* option box arrow and then click ***6-HEREquip.xlsx*** at the drop-down list.
   c. Click *(move to end)* in the *Before sheet* list box.
   d. Click OK.

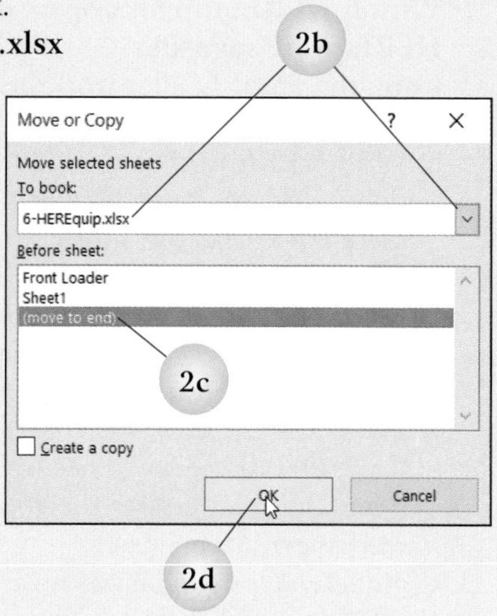

3. With **6-HEREquip.xlsx** open, make the following changes:
   a. Rename Sheet1 as *Equipment Hours*.
   b. Rename Sheet1 (2) as *Backhoe*.
4. Create a range for the front loader total hours available by completing the following steps:
   a. Click the Front Loader tab.
   b. Select the range B4:E4.
   c. Click in the Name box.
   d. Type FrontLoaderHours.
   e. Press the Enter key.

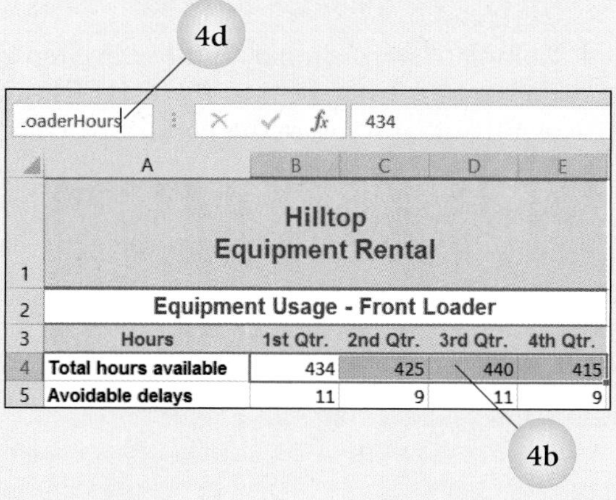

5. Complete steps similar to those in Step 4 to create the following ranges:
   a. In the Front Loader worksheet, select the range B10:E10 and name it *FrontLoaderHoursInUse*.
   b. Click the Forklift tab and then select the range B4:E4 and name it *ForkliftHours*. Also select the range B10:E10 and name it *ForkliftHoursInUse*.
   c. Click the Tractor tab and then select the range B4:E4 and name it *TractorHours*. Also select the range B10:E10 and name it *TractorHoursInUse*.
   d. Click the Backhoe tab and then select the range B4:E4 and name it *BackhoeHours*. Also select the range B10:E10 and name it *BackhoeHoursInUse*.

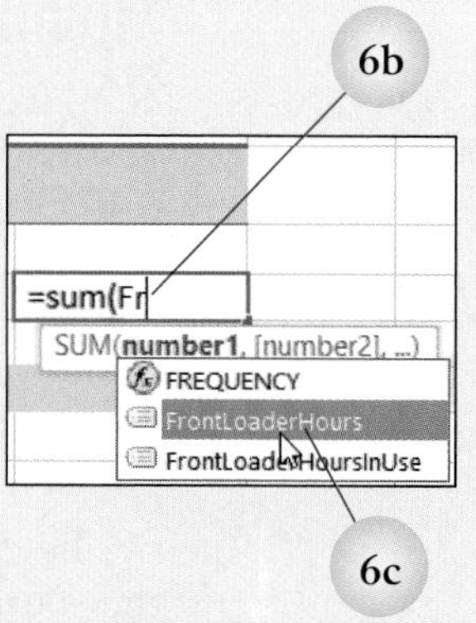

6. Click the Equipment Hours tab to make it the active worksheet and then insert a formula that calculates the total hours for the front loader by completing the following steps:
   a. Make cell C4 active.
   b. Type =sum(Fr.
   c. When you type *Fr*, a drop-down list displays with the front loader ranges. Double-click *FrontLoaderHours*.
   d. Type) (the closing parenthesis).
   e. Press the Enter key.

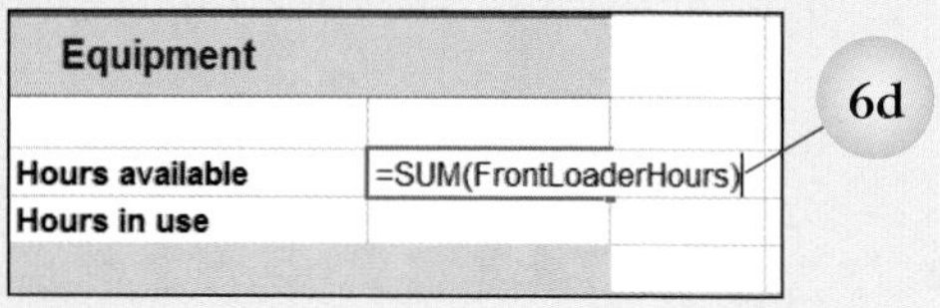

7. Complete steps similar to those in Step 6 to insert ranges in the following cells:
   a. Make cell C5 active and then insert a formula that calculates the total in-use hours for the front loader.
   b. Make cell C8 active and then insert a formula that calculates the total hours available for the forklift.
   c. Make cell C9 active and then insert a formula that calculates the total in-use hours for the forklift.
   d. Make cell C12 active and then insert a formula that calculates the total hours available for the tractor.
   e. Make cell C13 active and then insert a formula that calculates the total in-use hours for the tractor.
   f. Make cell C16 active and then insert a formula that calculates the total hours available for the backhoe.
   g. Make cell C17 active and then insert a formula that calculates the total in-use hours for the backhoe.
8. Make the following changes to specific worksheets:
   a. Click the Front Loader tab and then change the number in cell E4 from *415* to *426* and the number in cell C6 from *6* to *14*.
   b. Click the Forklift tab and then change the number in cell E4 from *415* to *426* and the number in cell D8 from *4* to *12*.
9. Select all the worksheet tabs and then create a header that prints your name at the left side of each worksheet, the page number in the middle, and the current date at the right side.
10. Save and then print all the worksheets in **6-HEREquip.xlsx**.
11. Close the workbook. (Make sure all the workbooks are closed.)
12. Make the following changes to the Open backstage area:
   a. Click the File tab.
   b. Make sure the *Open* option is selected and the *Recent* option is selected.
   c. Unpin **6-HEREquip.xlsx** from the *Recent* option list by clicking the down-pointing push pin at the right side of **6-HEREquip.xlsx**. (This changes the down-pointing push pin to a left-pointing push pin and moves the workbook down the list.)
   d. Unpin **HERBackhoe.xlsx** and **HEREquipUsage.xlsx**.
13. Click the Back button to exit the Open backstage area.

Check Your Work

Project 3 Create and Apply Styles to a Payroll Workbook — 5 Parts

You will open a payroll workbook, define and apply styles, and then modify the styles. You will also copy the styles to another workbook and then apply the styles in that new workbook.

Preview Finished Project

Formatting with Cell Styles

Formatting can be applied in a worksheet to highlight or accentuate certain cells. Apply formatting to a cell or selected cells with a cell style, which is a predefined set of formatting attributes, such as font, font size, alignment, borders, shading, and so forth. Excel provides predesigned styles at the Cell Styles drop-down gallery.

Tutorial

Applying Cell Styles

Quick Steps

Apply a Cell Style

1. Select cell(s).
2. Click Cell Styles button.
3. Click style.

Cell Styles

Applying a Cell Style

To apply a style, select the cell(s), click the Cell Styles button in the Styles group on the Home tab, and then click the style at the drop-down gallery, shown in Figure 6.4. Hover the mouse pointer over a style in the drop-down gallery and the cell or selected cells display with the formatting applied.

Figure 6.4 Cell Styles Drop-Down Gallery

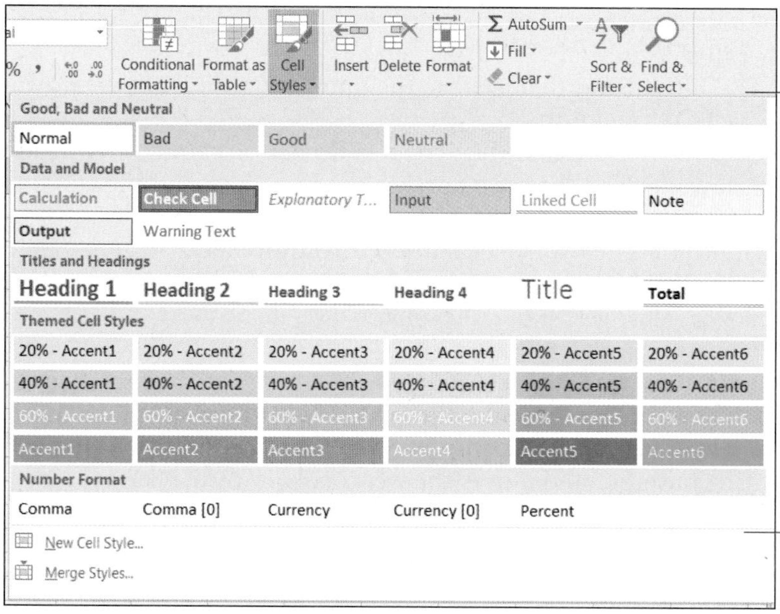

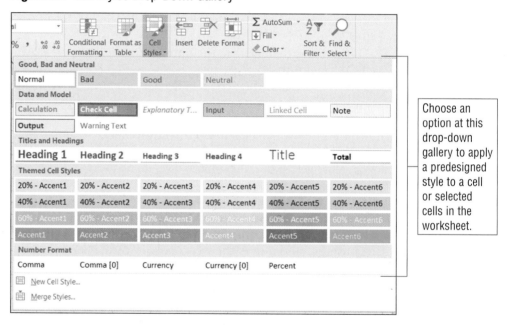

Choose an option at this drop-down gallery to apply a predesigned style to a cell or selected cells in the worksheet.

Project 3a Formatting with Cell Styles

Part 1 of 5

1. Open **OEPayroll.xlsx** and then save it with the name **6-OEPayroll**.
2. With Sheet1 the active worksheet, insert the necessary formulas to calculate gross pay, withholding tax amount, social security tax amount, and net pay. ***Hint: Refer to Project 3c in Chapter 2 for assistance.*** Select the range D4:G4 and then click the Accounting Number Format button to insert dollar symbols.
3. Make Sheet2 active and then insert a formula that calculates the amount due. ***Hint: The formula in cell F4 will be =D4*(1+E4).*** Make cell F4 active and then click the Accounting Number Format button to insert a dollar symbol.

4. Make Sheet3 active and then insert a formula in the *Due Date* column that calculates the purchase date plus the number of days in the *Terms* column. ***Hint: The formula in cell F4 will be*** **=D4+E4**.
5. Apply cell styles to cells by completing the following steps:
   a. Make Sheet1 active and then select cells A11 and A12.
   b. Click the Cell Styles button in the Styles group on the Home tab.
   c. At the drop-down gallery, hover the mouse pointer over different styles to see how the formatting affects the selected cells.
   d. Click the *Check Cell* option (second column, first row in the *Data and Model* section).
6. Select cells B11 and B12, click the Cell Styles button, and then click the *Output* option (first column, second row in the *Data and Model* section).

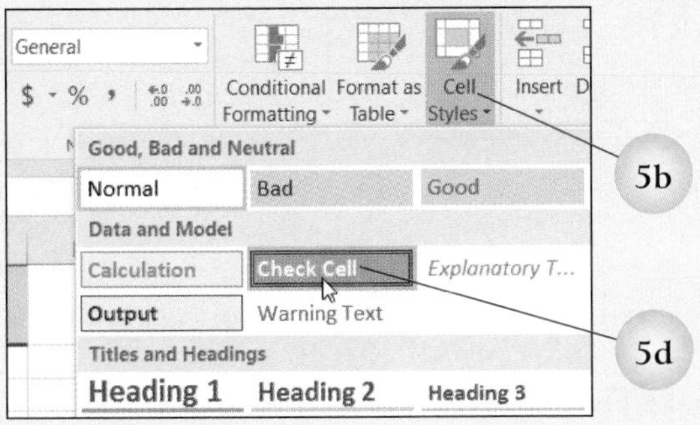

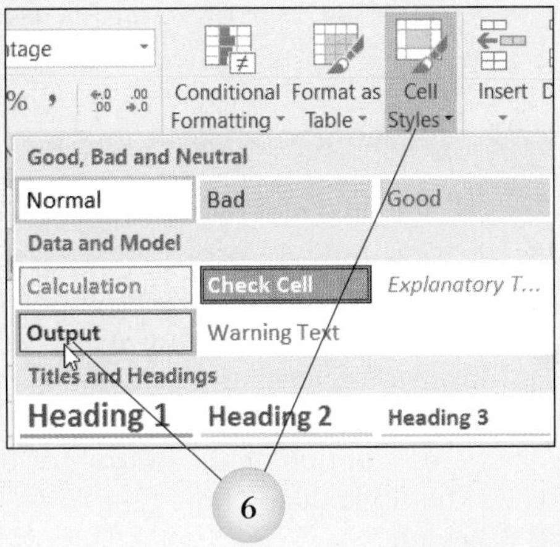

7. Save **6-OEPayroll.xlsx**.

Check Your Work

Tutorial

Defining a Cell Style

Hint Cell styles are based on the workbook theme.

Quick Steps

Define a Cell Style with Existing Formatting

1. Select cell containing formatting.
2. Click Cell Styles button.
3. Click *New Cell Style*.
4. Type name for new style.
5. Click OK.

Defining a Cell Style

Apply a style from the Cell Styles drop-down gallery or create a new style. Using a style to apply formatting has several advantages. One key advantage is that it helps to ensure consistent formatting from one worksheet to another. To change the formatting, change the style and all the cells formatted with that style automatically reflect the change.

Two basic methods are available for defining a cell style. Define a style with formats already applied to a cell or display the Style dialog box, click the Format button, and then choose formatting options at the Format Cells dialog box. New styles are available only in the workbook in which they are created.

To define a style with existing formatting, select the cell or cells containing the formatting, click the Cell Styles button in the Styles group on the Home tab, and then click the *New Cell Style* option at the bottom of the drop-down gallery. At the Style dialog box, shown in Figure 6.5, type a name for the new style in the *Style name* text box and then click OK to close the dialog box. Custom styles display at the top of the Cell Styles button drop-down gallery in the *Custom* section.

Figure 6.5 Style Dialog Box

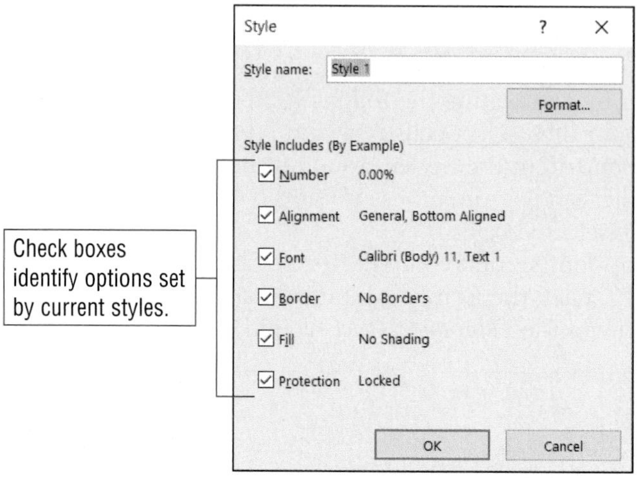

Project 3b Defining and Applying a Cell Style

Part 2 of 5

1. With **6-OEPayroll.xlsx** open, define a style named *C06Title* with the formatting in cell A1 by completing the following steps:
   a. Make sure Sheet1 is active and then make cell A1 active.
   b. Click the Cell Styles button in the Styles group on the Home tab and then click the *New Cell Style* option at the bottom of the drop-down gallery.
   c. At the Style dialog box, type C06Title in the *Style name* text box.
   d. Click OK.

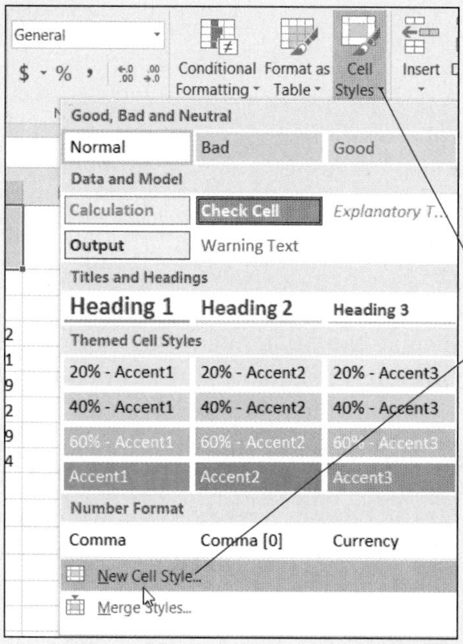

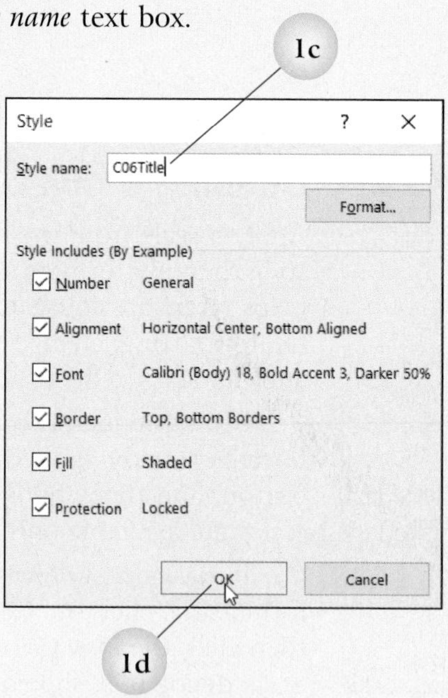

2. Even though cell A1 is already formatted, the style has not been applied to it. (Later, you will modify the style and the style must be applied to the cell for the change to affect it.) Apply the C06Title style to cell A1 by completing the following steps:
   a. Make sure cell A1 is the active cell.

b. Click the Cell Styles button in the Styles group on the Home tab.
c. Click the *C06Title* style in the *Custom* section at the top of the drop-down gallery.

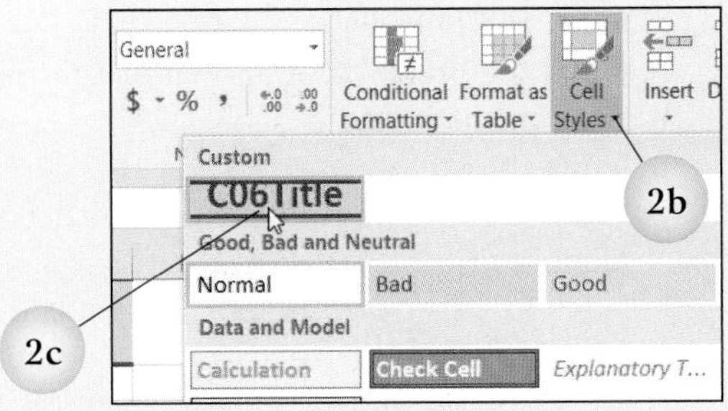

3. Apply the C06Title style to other cells by completing the following steps:
   a. Click the Sheet2 tab.
   b. Make cell A1 active.
   c. Click the Cell Styles button in the Styles group and then click the *C06Title* style at the drop-down gallery. (Notice that the style does not apply row height formatting. The style applies only cell formatting.)
   d. Click the Sheet3 tab.
   e. Make cell A1 active.
   f. Click the Cell Styles button and then click the *C06Title* style at the drop-down gallery.
   g. Click the Sheet1 tab.
4. Save **6-OEPayroll.xlsx**.

Check Your Work

Quick Steps
Define a Cell Style
1. Click in blank cell.
2. Click Cell Styles button.
3. Click *New Cell Style*.
4. Type style name.
5. Click Format button.
6. Choose formatting options.
7. Click OK.
8. Click OK.

In addition to defining a style based on cell formatting, a custom style can be defined without first applying the formatting. To do this, display the Style dialog box, type a name for the custom style, and then click the Format button. At the Format Cells dialog box, apply the formatting and then click OK to close the dialog box. At the Style dialog box, remove the check mark from any formatting that should not be included in the style and then click OK to close the Style dialog box.

Project 3c Defining a Cell Style without First Applying Formatting

Part 3 of 5

1. With **6-OEPayroll.xlsx** open, define a custom style named *C06Subtitle* without first applying the formatting by completing the following steps:
   a. With Sheet1 active, click in any empty cell.
   b. Click the Cell Styles button in the Styles group and then click *New Cell Style* at the drop-down gallery.
   c. At the Style dialog box, type C06Subtitle in the *Style name* text box.
   d. Click the Format button in the Style dialog box.
   e. At the Format Cells dialog box, click the Font tab.
   f. At the Format Cells dialog box with the Font tab selected, change the font to Candara, the font style to bold, the size to 12 points, and the color to White, Background 1.

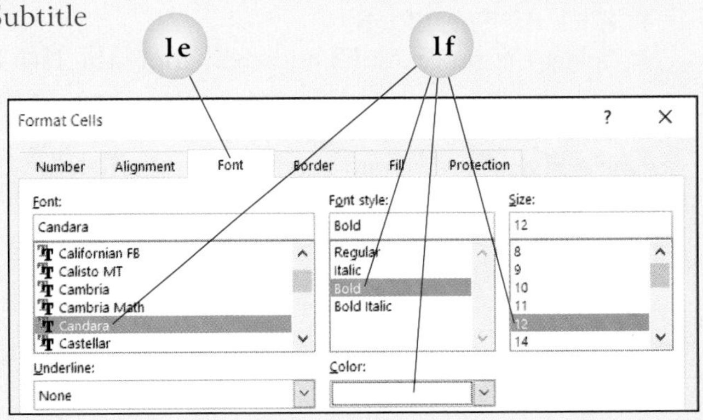

g. Click the Fill tab.
h. Click the green color shown at the right (last column, fifth row).
i. Click the Alignment tab.
j. Change the horizontal alignment to center alignment.
k. Click OK to close the Format Cells dialog box.
l. Click OK to close the Style dialog box.

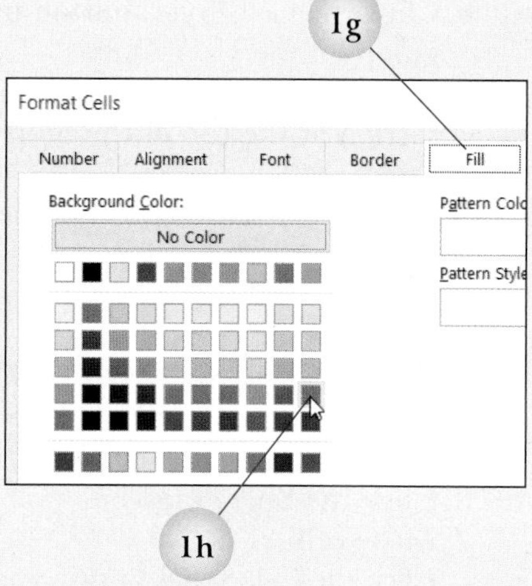

2. Apply the C06Subtitle custom style by completing the following steps:
   a. Make cell A2 active.
   b. Click the Cell Styles button and then click the *C06Subtitle* style in the *Custom* section at the top of the drop-down gallery.
   c. Click the Sheet2 tab.
   d. Make cell A2 active.
   e. Click the Cell Styles button and then click the *C06Subtitle* style.
   f. Click the Sheet3 tab.
   g. Make cell A2 active.
   h. Click the Cell Styles button and then click the *C06Subtitle* style.
   i. Click the Sheet1 tab.
3. Apply the following predesigned cell styles:
   a. With Sheet1 the active tab, select the range A3:G3.
   b. Click the Cell Styles button and then click the *Heading 3* style in the *Titles and Headings* section at the drop-down gallery.
   c. Select the range A5:G5.
   d. Click the Cell Styles button and then click the *20% - Accent3* style.
   e. Apply the 20% - Accent3 style to the range A7:G7 and the range A9:G9.
   f. Click the Sheet2 tab.
   g. Select the range A3:F3 and then apply the Heading 3 style.

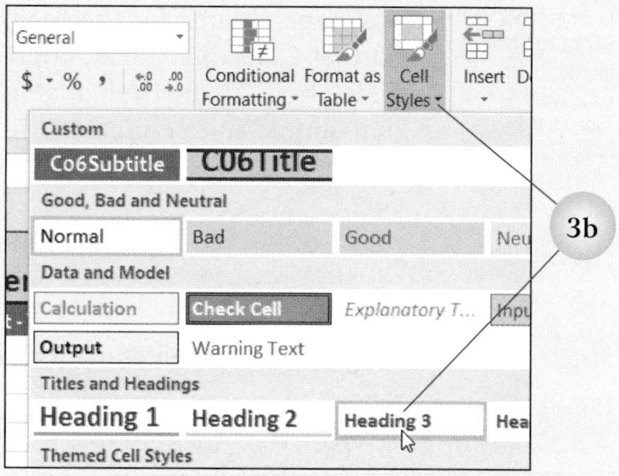

   h. Select the range A5:F5 and then apply the 20% - Accent3 style.
   i. Apply the 20% - Accent3 style to every other row of cells (the range A7:F7, A9:F9, and so on, finishing with the range A17:F17).
   j. Click the Sheet3 tab.
   k. Select the range A3:F3 and then apply the Heading 3 style.
   l. Apply the 20% - Accent3 style to the ranges A5:F5, A7:F7, and A9:F9.
4. With Sheet3 active, change the height of row 1 to 36.00 points.
5. Make Sheet2 active and then change the height of row 1 to 36.00 points.
6. Make Sheet1 active.
7. Save **6-OEPayroll.xlsx** and then print only the first worksheet.

Check Your Work

Tutorial

Modifying a Cell Style

Quick Steps

Modify a Cell Style

1. Click Cell Styles button.
2. Right-click style.
3. Click *Modify.*
4. Click Format button.
5. Make formatting changes.
6. Click OK.
7. Click OK.

Modifying a Cell Style

One of the advantages to formatting cells with a style is that the formatting can be modified and all the cells formatted with that style update automatically. Modify a predesigned style and only the style in the current workbook is affected. Open a blank workbook and the cell styles available are the default styles.

To modify a style, click the Cell Styles button in the Styles group on the Home tab and then right-click the style at the drop-down gallery. At the shortcut menu that displays, click *Modify*. At the Style dialog box, click the Format button. Make the formatting changes at the Format Cells dialog box and then click OK. Click OK to close the Style dialog box and any cells formatted with the style are automatically updated.

Project 3d **Modifying Cell Styles**

Part 4 of 5

1. With **6-OEPayroll.xlsx** open, modify the C06Title custom style by completing the following steps:
   a. Click in any empty cell.
   b. Click the Cell Styles button in the Styles group.
   c. At the drop-down gallery, right-click the *C06Title* style in the *Custom* section and then click *Modify* at the drop-down gallery.
   d. At the Style dialog box, click the Format button.
   e. At the Format Cells dialog box, click the Font tab and then change the font to Candara.
   f. Click the Alignment tab.
   g. Click the *Vertical* option box arrow and then click *Center* at the drop-down list.
   h. Click the Fill tab.
   i. Click the light blue fill color (fifth column, third row) as shown at the right.
   j. Click OK to close the Format Cells dialog box.
   k. Click OK to close the Style dialog box.

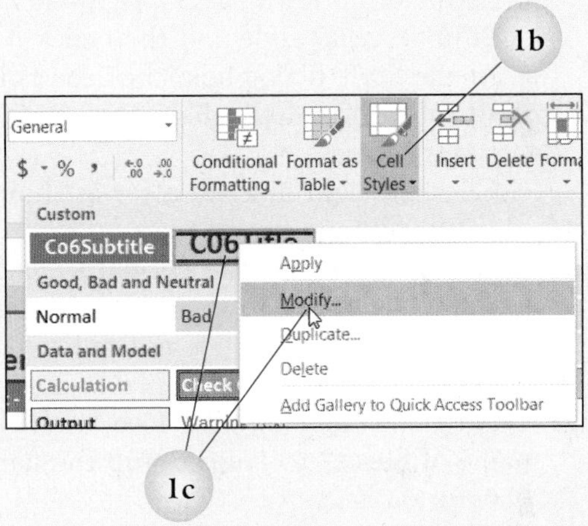

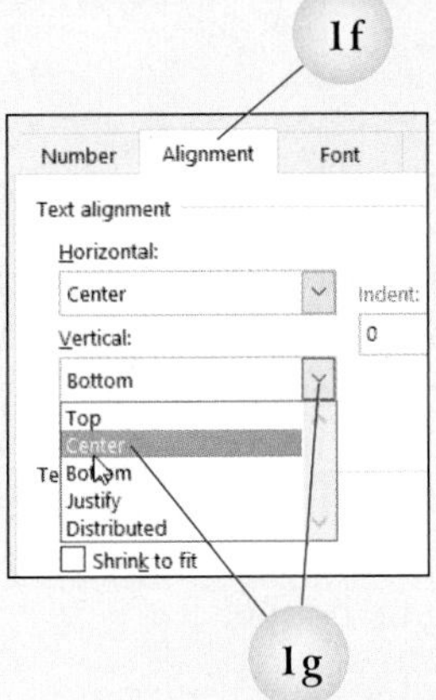

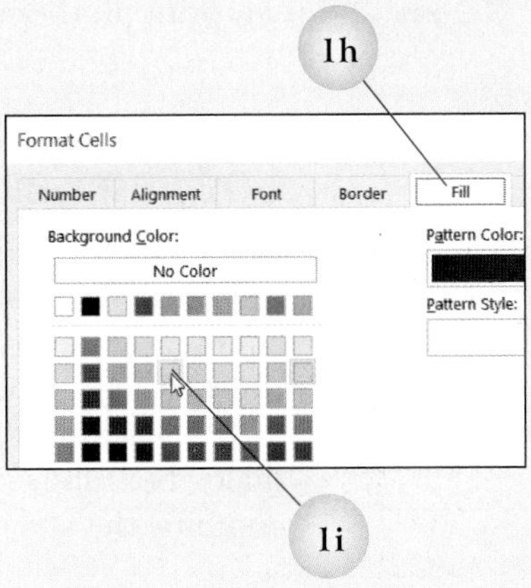

2. Modify the C06Subtitle style by completing the following steps:
   a. Click in any empty cell.
   b. Click the Cell Styles button in the Styles group.
   c. At the drop-down gallery, right-click the *C06Subtitle* style in the *Custom* section and then click *Modify*.
   d. At the Style dialog box, click the Format button.
   e. At the Format Cells dialog box, click the Font tab and then change the font to Calibri.
   f. Click the Fill tab.
   g. Click the dark blue fill color as shown at the right (fifth column, sixth row).
   h. Click OK to close the Format Cells dialog box.
   i. Click OK to close the Style dialog box.

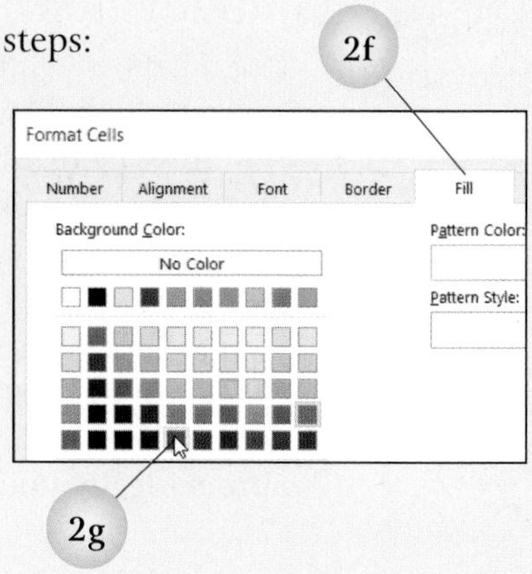

3. Modify the predefined 20% - Accent3 style by completing the following steps:
   a. Click the Cell Styles button in the Styles group.
   b. At the drop-down gallery, right-click the *20% - Accent3* style and then click *Modify*.
   c. At the Style dialog box, click the Format button.
   d. At the Format Cells dialog box, make sure the Fill tab is active.
   e. Click the light blue fill color as shown at the right (fifth column, second row).
   f. Click OK to close the Format Cells dialog box.
   g. Click OK to close the Style dialog box.

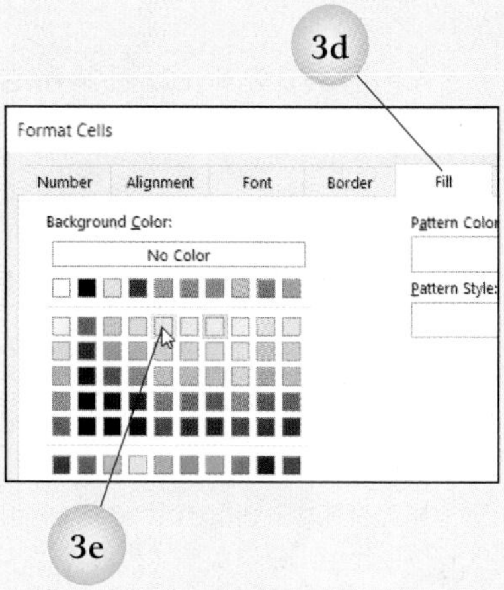

4. Click each worksheet tab and notice the formatting changes made by the modified styles.
5. Change the name of Sheet1 to *Weekly Payroll*, the name of Sheet2 to *Invoices*, and the name of Sheet3 to *Overdue Accounts*.
6. Apply a different color to each of the three worksheet tabs.
7. Save and then print all the worksheets in **6-OEPayroll.xlsx**.

Check Your Work

Copying Cell Styles to Another Workbook

Quick Steps

Copy Cell Styles to Another Workbook

1. Open workbook containing styles.
2. Open workbook to be modified.
3. Click Cell Styles button.
4. Click *Merge Styles* option.
5. Double-click name of workbook that contains styles.

Custom styles are saved with the workbook they are created in. However, styles can be copied from one workbook to another. To do this, open the workbook containing the styles and open the workbook the styles will be copied into. Click the Cell Styles button in the Styles group on the Home tab and then click the *Merge Styles* option at the bottom of the drop-down gallery. At the Merge Styles dialog box, shown in Figure 6.6, double-click the name of the workbook that contains the styles to be copied.

Hint The Undo command will not reverse the merging of styles at the Merge Styles dialog box.

Figure 6.6 Merge Styles Dialog Box

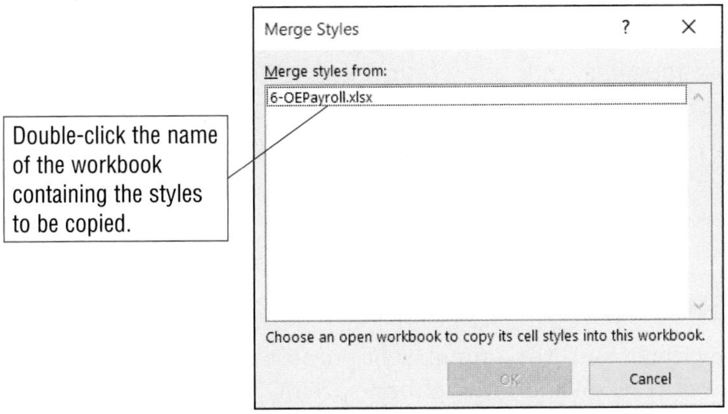

Removing a Cell Style

Quick Steps

Remove a Cell Style
1. Select cells formatted with style to be removed.
2. Click Cell Styles button.
3. Click *Normal*.

Delete a Cell Style
1. Click Cell Styles button.
2. Right-click style.
3. Click *Delete*.

Remove formatting applied by a style by applying the Normal style, which is the default. To do this, select the cells, click the Cell Styles button, and then click *Normal* at the drop-down gallery.

Deleting a Cell Style

To delete a style, click the Cell Styles button in the Styles group on the Home tab. At the drop-down gallery that displays, right-click the style to be deleted and then click *Delete* at the shortcut menu. Formatting applied by the deleted style is removed from cells in the workbook. The Normal cell style cannot be deleted.

Project 3e **Copying Cell Styles to Another Workbook**

Part 5 of 5

1. With **6-OEPayroll.xlsx** open, open **OEPlans.xlsx**.
2. Save the workbook and name it **6-OEPlans**.
3. Copy the styles in **6-OEPayroll.xlsx** into **6-OEPlans.xlsx** by completing the following steps:
   a. Click the Cell Styles button in the Styles group on the Home tab.
   b. Click the *Merge Styles* option at the bottom of the drop-down gallery.
   c. At the Merge Styles dialog box, double-click ***6-OEPayroll.xlsx*** in the *Merge styles from* list box.
   d. At the message that displays asking if you want to merge styles that have the same names, click Yes.

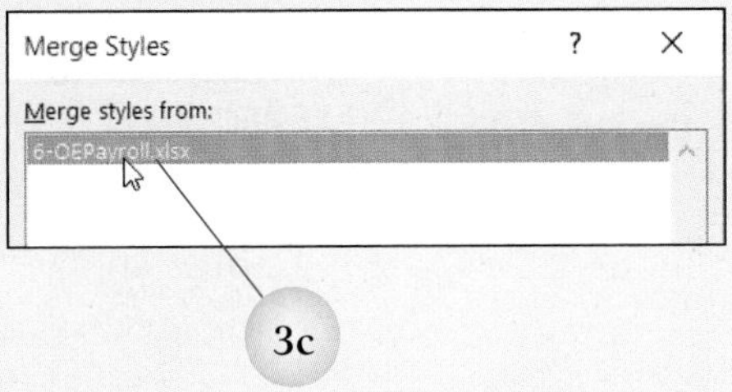

4. Apply the C06Title custom style to cell A1 and the C06Subtitle custom style to cell A2.
5. Increase the height of row 1 to 36.00 points.
6. Save, print, and then close **6-OEPlans.xlsx**.
7. Close **6-OEPayroll.xlsx**.

Check Your Work

Project 4 Insert, Modify, and Remove Hyperlinks

3 Parts

You will open a facilities account workbook and then insert hyperlinks to a website, to cells in other worksheets in the workbook, and to another workbook. You will modify and edit hyperlinks and then remove a hyperlink from the workbook.

Preview Finished Project

Tutorial

Inserting Hyperlinks

Quick Steps

Insert Hyperlink

1. Click Insert tab.
2. Click Hyperlink button.
3. Make changes at Insert Hyperlink dialog box.
4. Click OK.

Hyperlink

Inserting Hyperlinks

A hyperlink can serve a number of purposes in a workbook: Click it to navigate to a web page on the Internet or a specific location in the workbook, to display a different workbook, to open a file in a different program, to create a new document, or to link to an email address. Create a customized hyperlink by clicking in a cell in a workbook, clicking the Insert tab, and then clicking the Hyperlink button in the Links group. This displays the Insert Hyperlink dialog box, shown in Figure 6.7. At this dialog box, identify what is to be linked and the location of the link. Click the ScreenTip button to customize the hyperlink ScreenTip.

Linking to an Existing Web Page or File

Link to a web page on the Internet by typing a web address or by using the Existing File or Web Page button in the *Link to* section. To link to an existing web page, type the address of the web page, such as *www.paradigmcollege.com*.

By default, the automatic formatting of hyperlinks is turned on and the web address is formatted as a hyperlink. (The text is underlined and the color changes to blue.) Turn off the automatic formatting of hyperlinks at the AutoCorrect dialog box. Display this dialog box by clicking the File tab, clicking *Options*, and then clicking *Proofing* in the left panel of the Excel Options dialog box. Click the AutoCorrect Options button to display the AutoCorrect dialog box. At this dialog

Figure 6.7 Insert Hyperlink Dialog Box

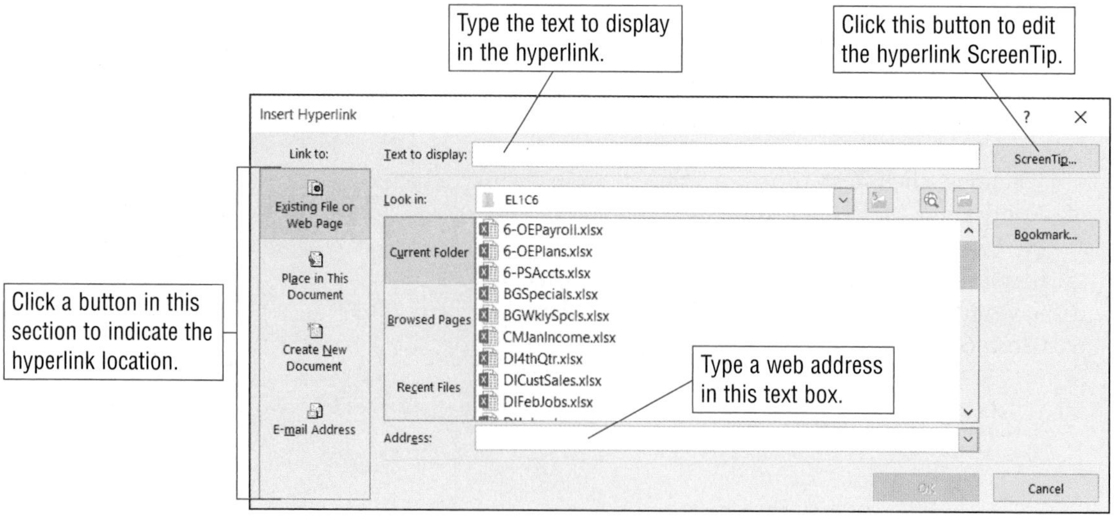

box, click the AutoFormat As You Type tab and then remove the check mark from the *Internet and network paths with hyperlinks* check box.

A hyperlink can be inserted that links to any of several sources, such as another Excel workbook, a Word document, or a PowerPoint presentation. To link an Excel workbook to a workbook or file in another application, display the Insert Hyperlink dialog box and then click the Existing File or Web Page button in the *Link to* section. Use buttons in the *Look in* section to navigate to the folder containing the file and then click the file name. Make other changes in the Insert Hyperlink dialog box as needed and then click OK.

Navigating Using Hyperlinks

Navigate to a hyperlinked location by clicking the hyperlink in the worksheet. Hover the mouse pointer over the hyperlink and a ScreenTip displays with the address of the hyperlinked location. To display specific information in the ScreenTip, click the ScreenTip button at the Insert Hyperlink dialog box, type the text in the Set Hyperlink ScreenTip dialog box, and then click OK.

Project 4a **Linking to a Website and Another Workbook** Part 1 of 3

1. Open **PSAccts.xlsx** and then save it with the name **6-PSAccts**.
2. Insert a hyperlink to information about Pyramid Sales, a fictitious company (the hyperlink will connect to the publishing company website), by completing the following steps:
   a. Make cell A13 active.
   b. Click the Insert tab and then click the Hyperlink button in the Links group.
   c. At the Insert Hyperlink dialog box, if necessary, click the Existing File or Web Page button in the *Link to* section.
   d. Type www.paradigmcollege.com in the *Address* text box.
   e. Select the text that displays in the *Text to display* text box and then type Company information.
   f. Click the ScreenTip button in the upper right corner of the dialog box.

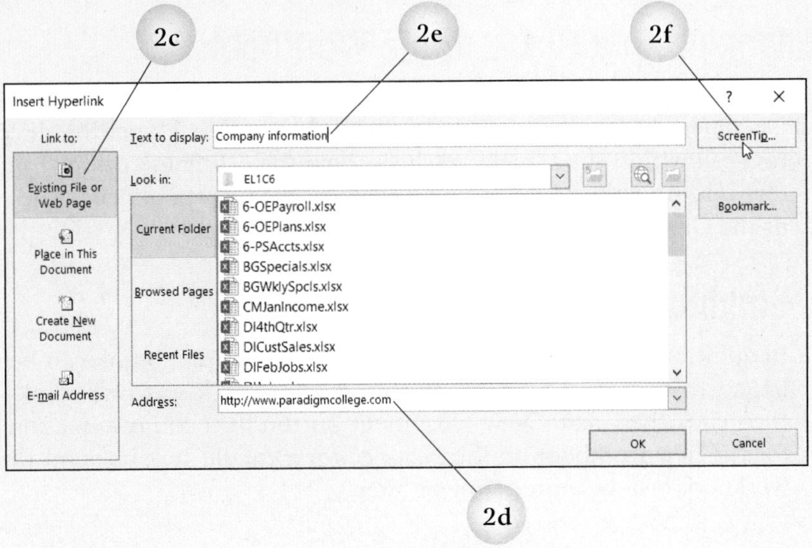

g. At the Set Hyperlink ScreenTip dialog box, type View the company website. and then click OK.

h. Click OK to close the Insert Hyperlink dialog box.

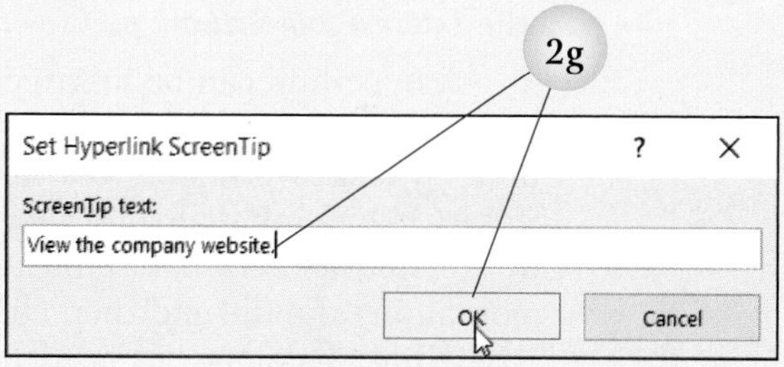

3. Navigate to the company website (in this case, the publishing company website) by clicking the Company information hyperlink in cell A13.

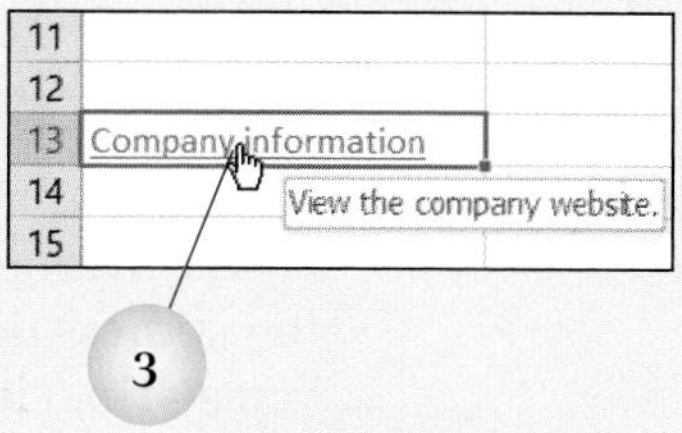

4. Close the web browser.
5. Create a link to another workbook by completing the following steps:
   a. Make cell A11 active, type Semiannual sales, and then press the Enter key.
   b. Make cell A11 active and then click the Hyperlink button in the Links group on the Insert tab.
   c. At the Insert Hyperlink dialog box, make sure the Existing File or Web Page button is selected.
   d. If necessary, click the *Look in* option box arrow and then navigate to the EL1C6 folder on your storage medium.
   e. Double-click ***PSSalesAnalysis.xlsx***.

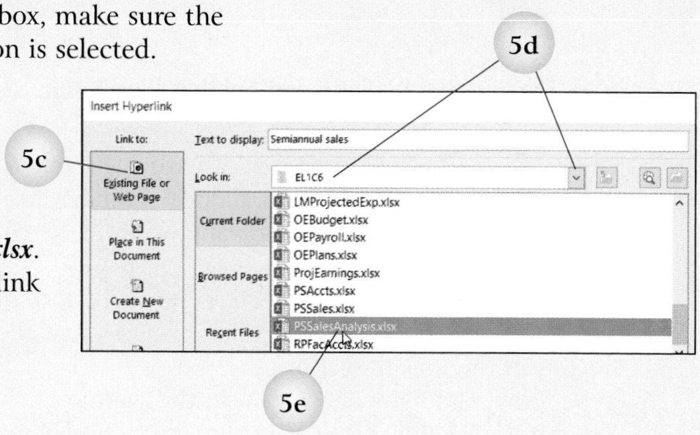

6. Click the Semiannual sales hyperlink to open **PSSalesAnalysis.xlsx**.
7. Look at the information in the workbook and then close it.
8. Save **6-PSAccts.xlsx**.

Check Your Work

Linking to a Place in the Workbook

To create a hyperlink to another location in the workbook, click the Place in This Document button in the *Link to* section in the Edit Hyperlink dialog box. To link to a cell within the same worksheet, type the cell name in the *Type the cell reference* text box. To link to another worksheet in the workbook, click the worksheet name in the *Or select a place in this document* list box.

Linking to a New Workbook

In addition to linking to an existing workbook, a hyperlink can be inserted that links to a new workbook. To do this, display the Insert Hyperlink dialog box and then click the Create New Document button in the *Link to* section. Type a name for the new workbook in the *Name of new document* text box and then specify if the workbook will be edited now or later.

Linking Using a Graphic

A graphic—such as a clip art image, picture, or text box—can be used to create a hyperlink to a file or website. To create a hyperlink with a graphic, select the graphic, click the Insert tab, and then click the Hyperlink button. Or right-click the graphic and then click *Hyperlink* at the shortcut menu. At the Insert Hyperlink dialog box, specify the location to be linked to and the text to display in the hyperlink.

Linking to an Email Address

At the Insert Hyperlink dialog box, a hyperlink can be inserted that links to an email address. To do this, click the E-mail Address button in the *Link to* section, type the address in the *E-mail address* text box, and then type a subject for the email in the *Subject* text box. Click in the *Text to display* text box and then type the text to display in the worksheet.

Project 4b Linking to a Place in a Workbook, to Another Workbook, and Using a Graphic

Part 2 of 3

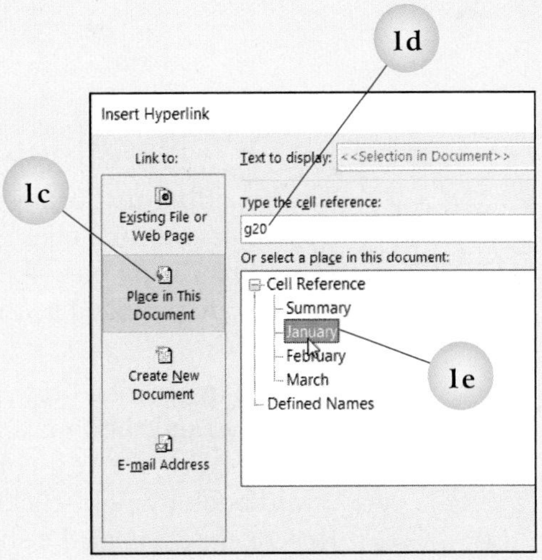

1. With **6-PSAccts.xlsx** open, create a link from the balance in cell B8 to the balance in cell G20 in the January worksheet by completing the following steps:
   a. Make cell B8 active.
   b. Click the Hyperlink button in the Links group on the Insert tab.
   c. At the Insert Hyperlink dialog box, click the Place in This Document button in the *Link to* section.
   d. Select the text in the *Type the cell reference* text box and then type g20.
   e. Click *January* in the *Or select a place in this document* list box.
   f. Click OK to close the Insert Hyperlink dialog box.
2. Make cell C8 active and then complete steps similar to those in Steps 1b through 1f except click *February* in the *Or select a place in this document* list box.
3. Make cell D8 active and then complete steps similar to those in Steps 1b through 1f except click *March* in the *Or select a place in this document* list box.
4. Click the hyperlinked amount in cell B8. (This makes cell G20 active in the January worksheet.)
5. Click the Summary worksheet tab.
6. Click the hyperlinked amount in cell C8. (This makes cell G20 active in the February worksheet.)
7. Click the Summary worksheet tab.
8. Click the hyperlinked amount in cell D8. (This makes cell G20 active in the March worksheet.)
9. Click the Summary worksheet tab.

10. Use the first pyramid graphic image in cell A1 to create a link to the company web page by completing the following steps:
    a. Right-click the first pyramid graphic image in cell A1 and then click *Hyperlink* at the shortcut menu.
    b. At the Insert Hyperlink dialog box, if necessary, click the Existing File or Web Page button in the *Link to* section.
    c. Type www.paradigmcollege.com in the *Address* text box.
    d. Click the ScreenTip button in the upper right corner of the dialog box.
    e. At the Set Hyperlink ScreenTip dialog box, type View the company website. and then click OK.
    f. Click OK to close the Insert Hyperlink dialog box.
11. Make cell A5 active.
12. Navigate to the company website (the publishing company website) by clicking the first pyramid graphic image.
13. Close the Web browser.
14. Save **6-PSAccts.xlsx**.

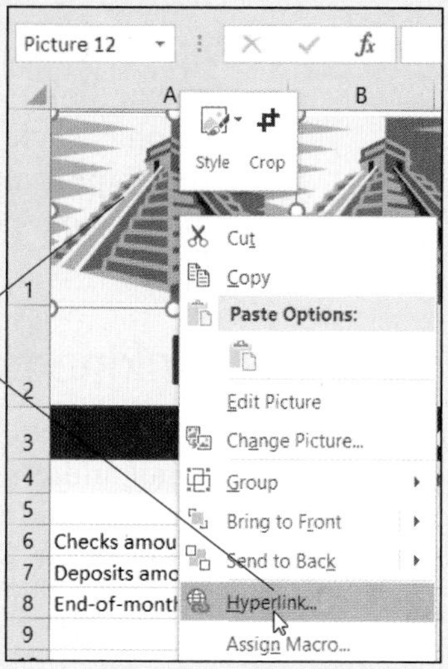

Check Your Work

Modifying, Editing, and Removing a Hyperlink

The hyperlink text or destination can be modified. To do this, right-click the hyperlink and then click *Edit Hyperlink* at the shortcut menu. At the Edit Hyperlink dialog box, make changes and then close the dialog box. The same options are provided at the Edit Hyperlink dialog box as the Insert Hyperlink dialog box.

The hyperlinked text in a cell can also be modified. To do this, make the cell active and then make the changes, such as applying a different font or font size, changing the text color, and adding a text effect. Remove a hyperlink from a workbook by right-clicking the cell containing the hyperlink and then clicking *Remove Hyperlink* at the shortcut menu.

Project 4c **Modifying, Editing, and Removing a Hyperlink** Part 3 of 3

1. With **6-PSAccts.xlsx** open, modify the Semiannual sales hyperlink by completing the following steps:
    a. Position the mouse pointer on the Semiannual sales hyperlink in cell A11, click the right mouse button, and then click *Edit Hyperlink* at the shortcut menu.
    b. At the Edit Hyperlink dialog box, select the text *Semiannual sales* in the *Text to display* text box and then type Customer sales analysis.

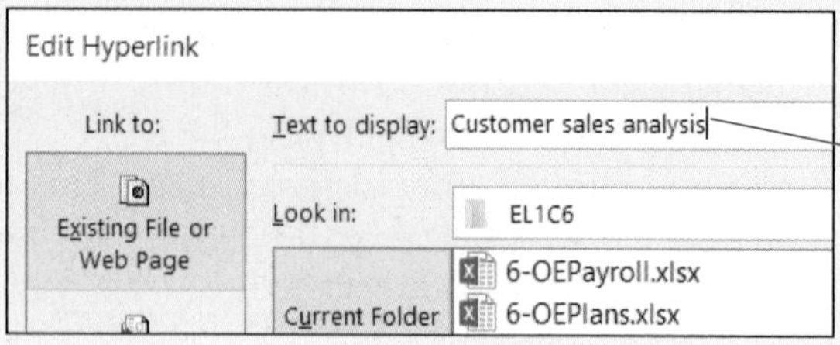

c. Click the ScreenTip button in the upper right corner of the dialog box.
d. At the Set Hyperlink ScreenTip dialog box, type Click this hyperlink to display the workbook containing customer sales analysis.
e. Click OK to close the Set Hyperlink ScreenTip dialog box.
f. Click OK to close the Edit Hyperlink dialog box.
2. Click the Customer sales analysis hyperlink.
3. After looking at the **PSSalesAnalysis.xlsx** workbook, close it.
4. With cell A11 active, edit the Customer sales analysis hyperlink text by completing the following steps:
   a. Click the Home tab.
   b. Click the Font Color button arrow in the Font group and then click the *Dark Red* color option (first option in the *Standard Colors* section).
   c. Click the Bold button.
   d. Click the Underline button. (This removes underlining from the text.)
5. Remove the Company information hyperlink by right-clicking in cell A13 and then clicking *Remove Hyperlink* at the shortcut menu.
6. Press the Delete key to remove the contents of cell A13.
7. Save, print only the first worksheet (the Summary worksheet), and then close **6-PSAccts.xlsx**.

Check Your Work

Project 5 Create a Billing Statement Workbook Using a Template **1 Part**

You will open a Billing Statement template provided by Excel, add data, save the template as an Excel workbook, and then print the workbook.

Preview Finished Project

Tutorial

Using Templates

Using Excel Templates

Excel provides a number of template worksheet forms for specific uses. Use Excel templates to create a variety of worksheets with specialized formatting, such as balance sheets, billing statements, loan amortizations, sales invoices, and time cards. Display installed templates by clicking the File tab and then clicking the *New* option. This displays the New backstage area, as shown in Figure 6.8.

Quick Steps

Use an Excel Template
1. Click File tab.
2. Click *New* option.
3. Double-click template.

Click a template in the New backstage area and a preview of the template displays in a window. Click the Create button in the template window and a workbook based on the template opens and displays on the screen.

Locations for personalized text display in placeholders in the worksheet. To enter information in the worksheet, position the mouse pointer (white plus symbol) in the location the data is to be typed and then click the left mouse button. After typing the data, click the next location. The insertion point can also be moved to another cell using the commands learned in Chapter 1. For example, press the Tab key to make the next cell active or press Shift + Tab to make the previous cell active. If the computer is connected to the Internet, a number of templates offered by Microsoft can be downloaded.

Figure 6.8 New Backstage Area

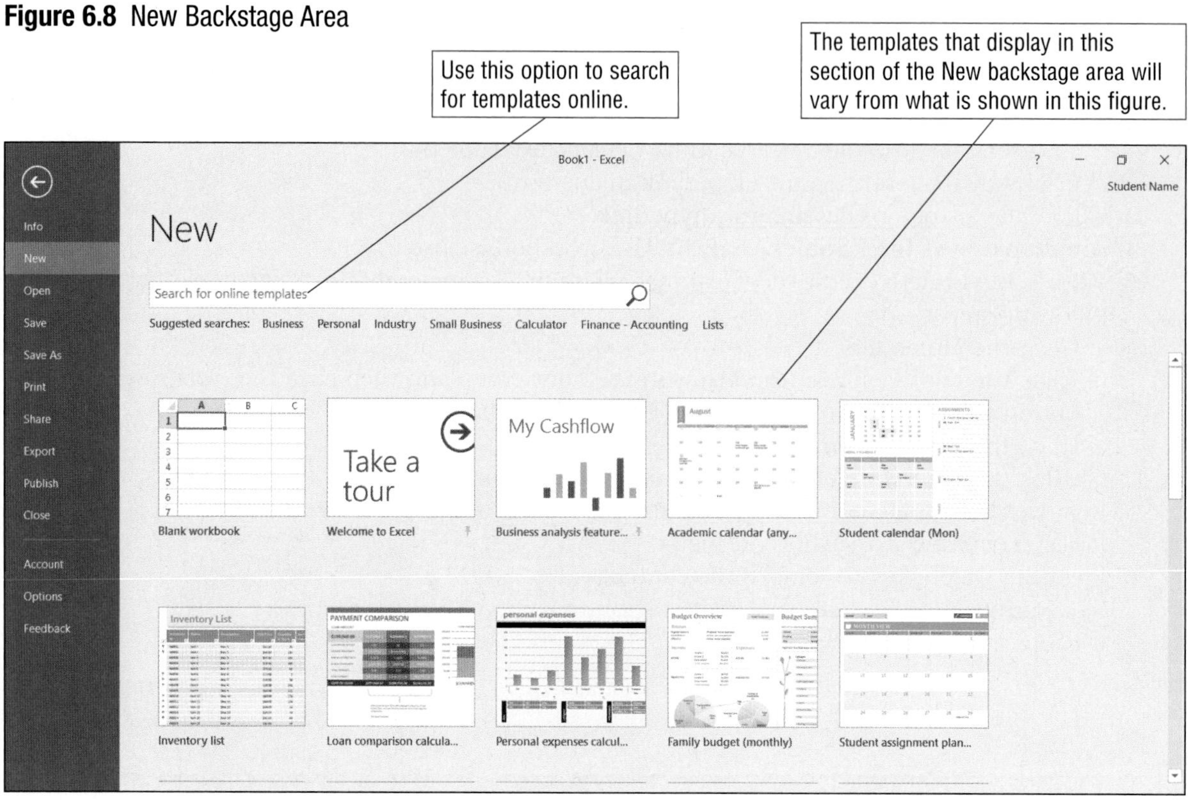

Project 5 Preparing a Billing Statement Using a Template

Part 1 of 1

1. Click the File tab and then click the *New* option.
2. At the New backstage area, click in the search text box, type billing statement, and then press the Enter key.
3. Double-click the *Billing statement* template (see image below).

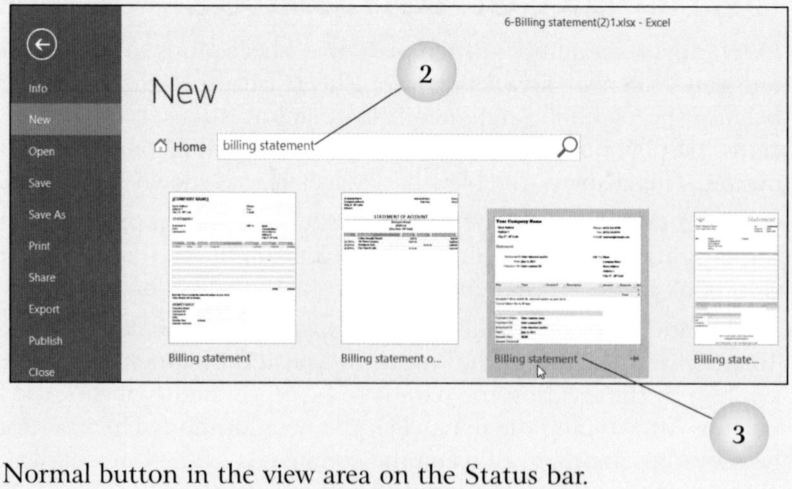

4. Click the Normal button in the view area on the Status bar.
5. With cell B1 active, type IN-FLOW SYSTEMS.
6. Click the text *Street Address* (cell B2) and then type 320 Milander Way.

7. Click in each specified location (cell) and then type the text indicated:
   Address 2 (cell B3): P.O. Box 2300
   City, ST ZIP Code (cell B4): Boston, MA 02188
   Phone (cell F2): (617) 555-3900
   Fax (cell F3): (617) 555-3945
   E-mail (cell F3): inflow@emcp.net
   Statement # (cell C8): 5432
   Customer ID (cell C10): 25-345
   Name (cell F8): Aidan Mackenzie
   Company Name (cell F9): Stanfield Enterprises
   Street Address (cell F10): 9921 South 42nd Avenue
   Address 2 (cell F11): P.O. Box 5540
   City, ST ZIP Code (cell F12): Boston, MA 02193
   Date (cell B15): (insert current date in numbers as ##/##/#### and if necessary, adjust the width of the column)
   Type (cell C15): System Unit
   Invoice # (cell D15): 7452
   Description (cell E15): Calibration Unit
   Amount (cell F15): 950
   Payment (cell G15): 200
   Customer Name (cell C21): Stanfield Enterprises
   Amount Enclosed (cell C26): 750

5-7

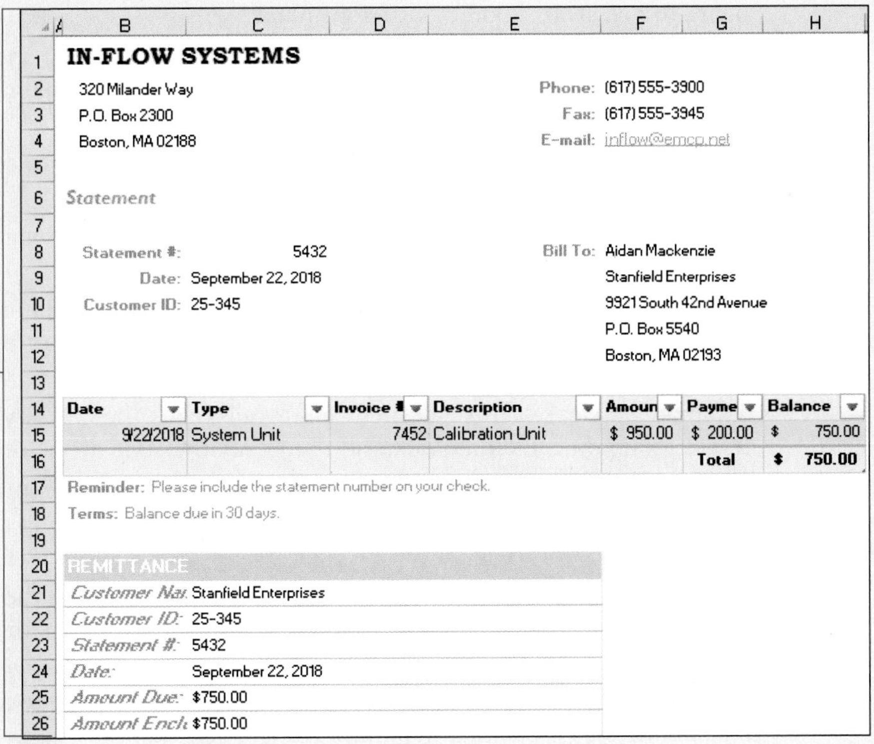

8. Save the completed invoice and name it **6-Billing**.
9. Print and then close **6-Billing.xlsx**.

Check Your Work

Chapter Summary

- Perform file management tasks—such as copying, moving, printing, and renaming workbooks and creating and renaming folders—at the Open dialog box or Save As dialog box.
- Create a new folder by clicking the New folder button on the toolbar at the Open dialog box or Save As dialog box.
- Rename a folder with the *Rename* option from the Organize button drop-down list or with the shortcut menu.
- Use the Shift key to select adjacent workbooks in the Open dialog box and use the Ctrl key to select nonadjacent workbooks.
- To delete a workbook, use the *Delete* option from the Organize button drop-down list or use the *Delete* option at the shortcut menu. Workbooks deleted from the hard drive are automatically sent to the Windows Recycle Bin, where they can be restored or permanently deleted.
- Use the *Copy* and *Paste* options from the shortcut menu at the Open dialog box or Save As dialog box to copy a workbook from one folder to another folder or drive.
- Use the *Send to* option from the shortcut menu to send a copy of a workbook to another drive or folder.
- Remove a workbook from a folder or drive and insert it in another folder or drive using the *Cut* and *Paste* options from the shortcut menu.
- Use the *Rename* option from the Organize button drop-down list or the shortcut menu to give a workbook a different name.
- To move or copy a worksheet to another existing workbook, open both the source workbook and the destination workbook and then open the Move or Copy dialog box.
- Use options from the Cell Styles button drop-down gallery to apply predesigned styles to a cell or selected cells.
- Automate the formatting of cells in a workbook by defining and then applying styles. A style is a predefined set of formatting attributes.
- Define a style with formats already applied to a cell or display the Style dialog box, click the Format button, and then choose formatting options at the Format Cells dialog box.
- To apply a style, select the desired cell or cells, click the Cell Styles button in the Styles group on the Home tab, and then click the style at the drop-down gallery.
- Modify a style and all the cells to which it is applied update automatically. To modify a style, click the Cell Styles button in the Styles group on the Home tab, right-click the style, and then click *Modify* at the shortcut menu.
- Styles are saved in the workbook they are created in but can be copied to another workbook. Do this with options at the Merge Styles dialog box.
- With options at the Insert Hyperlink dialog box, create a hyperlink to a web page, another workbook, a location within a workbook, a new workbook, or an email address. Or create a hyperlink using a graphic.
- Hyperlinks can be modified, edited, and removed.
- Excel provides templates for creating forms. Search for and download templates at the New backstage area.
- Templates contain unique areas where information is entered at the keyboard. These areas vary depending on the template.

Commands Review

FEATURE	RIBBON TAB, GROUP/OPTION	BUTTON, OPTION	KEYBOARD SHORTCUT
cell styles	Home, Styles		
Insert Hyperlink dialog box	Insert, Links		Ctrl + K
Merge Styles dialog box	Home, Styles	, *Merge Styles*	
New backstage area	File, *New*		
new folder	File, *Open*, *Browse*	New folder	
Open backstage area	File, *Open*		Ctrl + O
Open dialog box	File, *Open*, *Browse*		Ctrl + F12
Save As backstage area	File, *Save As*		Ctrl + S
Save As dialog box	File, *Save As*, *Browse*		F12
Style dialog box	Home, Styles	, *New Cell Style*	

Workbook

Chapter study tools and assessment activities are available in the *Workbook* ebook. These resources are designed to help you further develop and demonstrate mastery of the skills learned in this chapter.

Microsoft®

Excel®

CHAPTER

7

Creating Charts and Inserting Formulas

Performance Objectives

Upon successful completion of Chapter 7, you will be able to:

1 Create a chart with data in an Excel worksheet
2 Size, move, edit, format, and delete charts
3 Print a selected chart and print a worksheet containing a chart
4 Change a chart location
5 Insert, move, size, and delete chart elements and shapes
6 Using the Quick Analysis feature
7 Write formulas with the PMT and FV financial functions
8 Write formulas with the IF logical function

Precheck

Check your current skills to help focus your study.

In the previous Excel chapters, you learned how to create data in worksheets. While a worksheet does an adequate job of representing data, some data are better represented visually with a chart. A chart, which is sometimes referred to as a *graph*, is a picture of numeric data. In this chapter, you will learn to create and customize charts in Excel. You will also learn how to write formulas using financial and logical functions.

Data Files

Before beginning the projects, copy the EL1C7 folder to your storage medium and then make EL1C7 the active folder.

SNAP

If you are a SNAP user, launch the Precheck and Tutorials from your Assignments page.

Project 1 Create a Quarterly Sales Column Chart 3 Parts

You will open a workbook containing quarterly sales data and then use the data to create a column chart. You will decrease the size of the chart, move it to a different location in the worksheet, and then make changes to sales numbers. You will also use buttons to customize and filter chart elements.

Preview Finished Project

Tutorial

Creating Charts

Quick Steps

Create a Chart

1. Select cells.
2. Click Insert tab.
3. Click chart button.
4. Click chart style.

Quick Steps

Create a Recommended Chart

1. Select cells.
2. Click Insert tab.
3. Click Recommended Charts button.
4. Click OK at Insert Chart dialog box.

OR

1. Select cells.
2. Press Alt + F1.

Creating a Chart

To provide a visual representation of data, consider inserting data in a chart. Use buttons in the Charts group on the Insert tab to create a variety of charts, such as a column chart, line chart, pie chart, and much more. Excel provides 15 basic chart types, as described in Table 7.1.

Table 7.1 Types of Charts

Chart	Description
Area	Emphasizes the magnitude of change rather than time and the rate of change. Also shows the relationship of the parts to the whole by displaying the sum of the plotted values.
Bar	Shows individual figures at a specific time or shows variations between components but not in relationship to the whole.
Box & Whisker	Displays medians, quartiles, and extremes of a data set on a number line to show the distribution of data. Lines extending vertically are called whiskers and indicate variability outside the upper and lower quartiles.
Column	Compares separate (noncontinuous) items as they vary over time.
Combo	Combines two or more chart types to make data easy to understand.
Histogram	Condenses a data series into a visual representation by grouping data points into logical ranges called *bins*.
Line	Shows trends and overall change across time at even intervals. Emphasizes the rate of change across time rather than the magnitude of change.
Pie	Shows proportions and the relationship of the parts to the whole.
Radar	Emphasizes differences and amounts of change over time as well as variations and trends. Each category has a value axis radiating from the center point. Lines connect all values in the same series.
Stock	Shows four values for a stock: open, high, low, and close.
Sunburst	Displays hierarchical data. Each level is represented by one ring, with the innermost ring as the top of the hierarchy.
Surface	Shows trends in values across two dimensions in a continuous curve.
Treemap	Provides a hierarchical view of data and compares proportions within the hierarchy.

continues

Table 7.1 Types of Charts—*Continued*

Chart	Description
X Y (Scatter)	Shows the relationships among numeric values in several data series or plots the interception points between *x* and *y* values. Shows uneven intervals of data and is commonly used for scientific data.
Waterfall	Determines how an initial value is affected by a series of positive and negative values.

To create a chart, select the cells in the worksheet to be charted, click the Insert tab, and then click a specific chart button in the Charts group. At the drop-down gallery that displays, click a specific chart style. Excel will make a recommendation on the type of chart that will best illustrate the data. To let Excel recommend a chart, select the data, click the Insert tab, and then click the Recommended Charts button. This displays the data in a chart in the Insert Chart dialog box. Customize the recommended chart with options in the left panel of the dialog box. Click the OK button to insert the recommended chart in the worksheet. Another method for inserting a recommended chart is to use the keyboard shortcut Alt + F1.

Recommended Charts

Sizing and Moving a Chart

Hint Hide rows or columns you do not want to chart.

By default, a chart is inserted in the same worksheet as the selected cells. Figure 7.1 displays the worksheet and chart that will be created in Project 1a. The chart is inserted in a box, which can be sized or moved within the worksheet.

Change the size of the chart using the sizing handles (white circles) on the chart borders. Drag the top-middle and bottom-middle sizing handles to increase or decrease the height of the chart; use the left-middle and right-middle sizing

Figure 7.1 Project 1a Chart

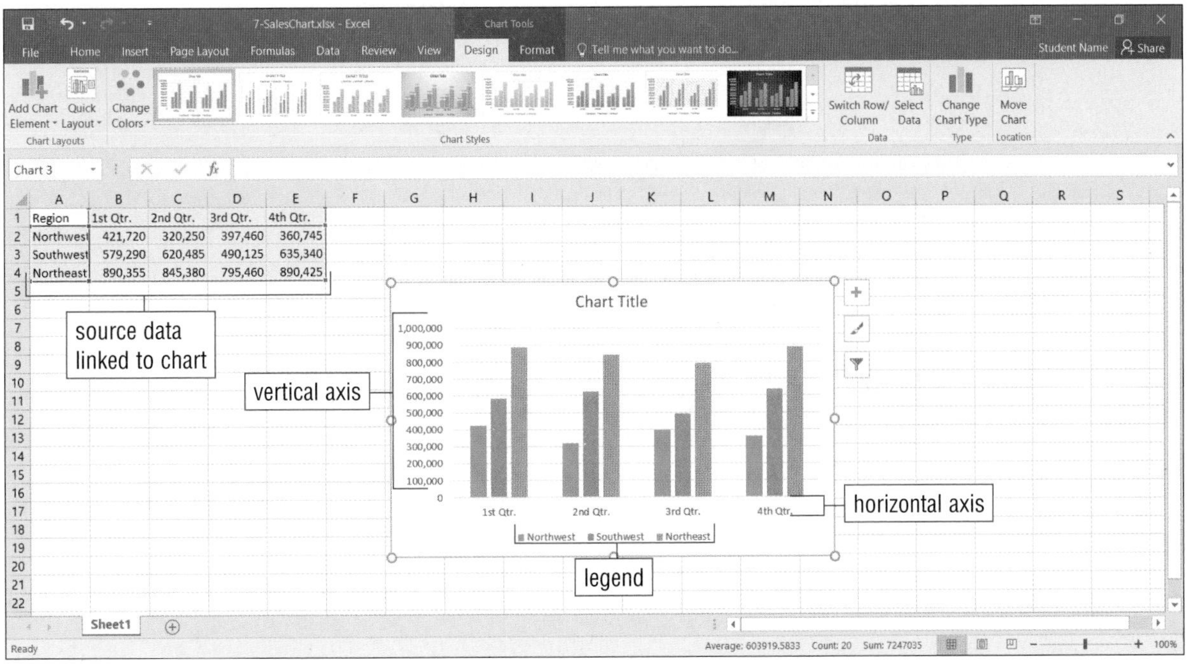

handles to increase or decrease the width; and use the corner sizing handles to increase or decrease the height and width at the same time. To increase or decrease the size of the chart but maintain its proportions, press and hold down the Shift key while dragging one of the chart's corner borders.

To move the chart, make sure it is selected (a border with sizing handles displays around the chart), position the mouse pointer on a border until the pointer displays with a four-headed arrow attached, click and hold down the left mouse button, drag to the new position, and then release the mouse button.

Tutorial

Editing Chart Data

Editing Data and Adding a Data Series

The cells selected to create a chart are linked to it. To change the data for a chart, edit the data in the specific cells and the corresponding sections of the chart will update automatically. If data is added to cells within the range of cells used for the chart, called the *source data*, the new data will be included in the chart. If a data series is added in cells next to or below the source data, click in the chart to display the source data with sizing handles and then drag with a sizing handle to include the new data.

Project 1a **Creating a Chart** Part 1 of 3

1. Open **SalesChart.xlsx** and then save it with the name **7-SalesChart**.
2. Select the range A1:E4.
3. Let Excel recommend a chart type by completing the following steps:
   a. Click the Insert tab.
   b. Click the Recommended Charts button in the Charts group.

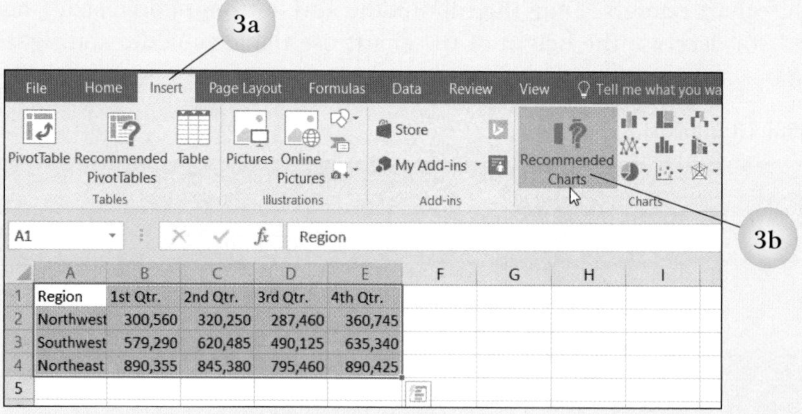

   c. At the Insert Chart dialog box, look at the options that display in the left panel and then click OK.
4. Slightly increase the size of the chart and maintain its proportions by completing the following steps:
   a. Position the mouse pointer on the sizing handle in the lower right corner of the chart border until the pointer turns into a two-headed arrow pointing diagonally.

b. Press and hold down the Shift key and then click and hold down the left mouse button.
c. Drag out approximately 0.5 inch. Release the mouse button and then release the Shift key.

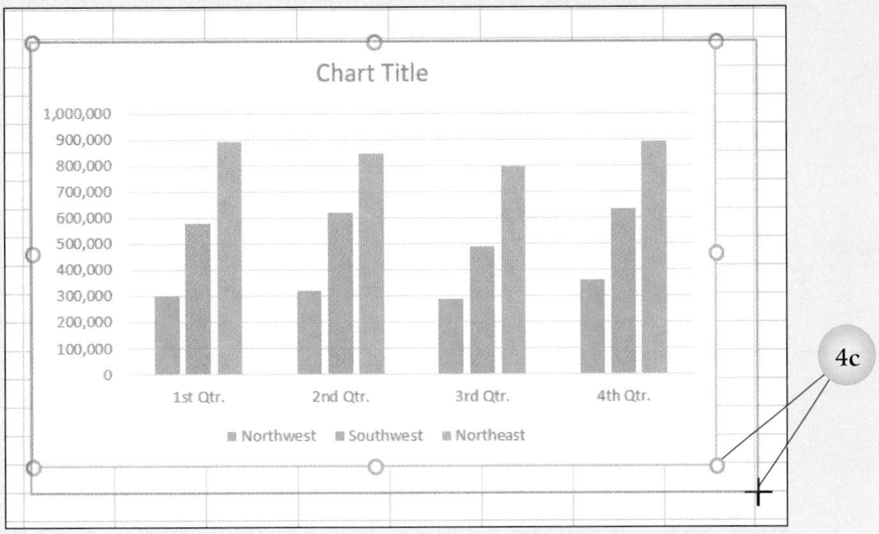

5. Move the chart below the cells containing data by completing the following steps:
   a. Make sure the chart is selected. (When the chart is selected, the border surrounding it displays with sizing handles.)
   b. Position the mouse pointer on the chart border until the pointer displays with a four-headed arrow attached.
   c. Click and hold down the left mouse button, drag the chart to row 6 below the cells containing data, and then release the mouse button.

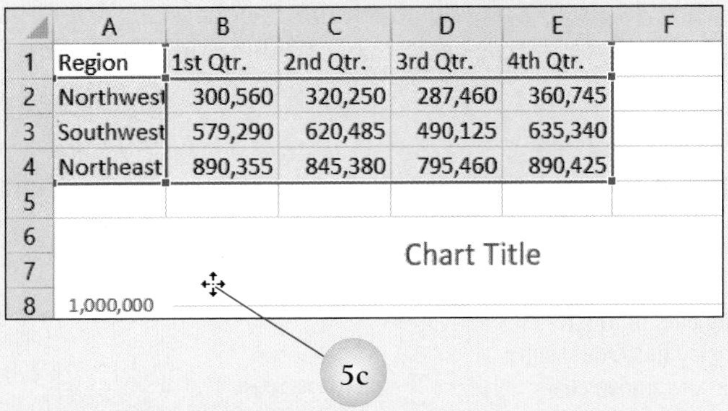

6. Make the following changes to the specified cells:
   a. Make cell B2 active and then change *300,560* to *421,720*.
   b. Make cell D2 active and then change *287,460* to *397,460*.
7. Add a new data series by typing data in the following cells:

   A5 Southeast
   B5 290,450
   C5 320,765
   D5 270,450
   E5 300,455

8. Add the new data series to the chart by completing the following steps:
   a. Click in the chart. (This selects the data source, which is the range A1:E4.)
   b. Position the mouse pointer on the sizing handle in the lower right corner of cell E4 until the pointer displays as a two-headed diagonally pointing arrow.
   c. Click and hold down the left mouse button, drag down into cell E5, and then release the mouse button. (This incorporates data row 5 in the chart.)
9. Save **7-SalesChart.xlsx**.

Check Your Work

Tutorial

Formatting with Chart Buttons

Chart Elements

Formatting with Chart Buttons

When a chart is inserted in a worksheet, three buttons display at the right side of the chart border. Click the top button, Chart Elements, and a side menu displays chart elements, as shown in Figure 7.2. The check boxes containing check marks indicate the elements that are currently part of the chart. Add a new element to the chart by inserting a check mark in the check box for that element and remove an element by removing the check mark. Remove the Chart Elements side menu by clicking one of the other chart buttons or by clicking the Chart Elements button.

Chart Styles

Excel offers a variety of chart styles that can be applied to a chart. Click the Chart Styles button at the right side of the chart and a side menu gallery of styles displays, as shown in Figure 7.3. Scroll down the gallery, hover the mouse pointer over a style option, and the style formatting is applied to the chart. Click the chart style that applies the desired formatting. Remove the Chart Styles side menu gallery by clicking one of the other chart buttons or by clicking the Chart Styles button.

In addition to offering a variety of chart styles, the Chart Styles button side menu gallery offers a variety of chart colors. Click the Chart Styles button and then click the Color tab to the right of the Style tab. Click a color option at the color palette that displays. Hover the mouse pointer over a color option to view how the color change affects the elements in the chart.

Chart Filters

Use the bottom button, Chart Filters, to isolate specific data in the chart. Click the button and a side menu displays, as shown in Figure 7.4. Specify the series or categories to display in the chart. To do this, remove the check marks from those elements that should not appear in the chart. After removing the specific check marks, click the Apply button at the bottom of the side menu. Click the Names tab at the Chart Filters button side menu and options display for turning on/off the display of column and row names.

Figure 7.2 Chart Elements Button Side Menu

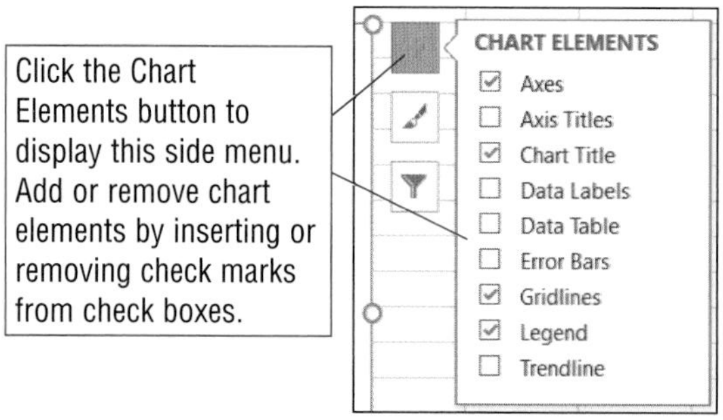
Click the Chart Elements button to display this side menu. Add or remove chart elements by inserting or removing check marks from check boxes.
CHART ELEMENTS
Axes
Axis Titles
Chart Title
Data Labels
Data Table
Error Bars
Gridlines
Legend
Trendline

Figure 7.3 Chart Styles Button Side Menu Gallery

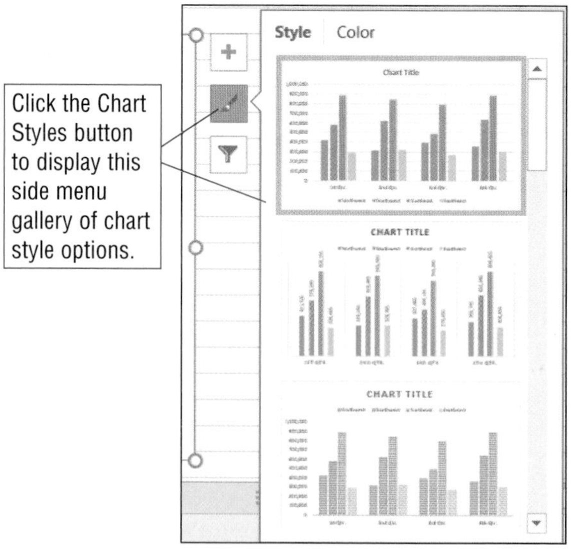
Style
Color
Click the Chart Styles button to display this side menu gallery of chart style options.
CHART TITLE
CHART TITLE

Figure 7.4 Chart Filters Button Side Menu

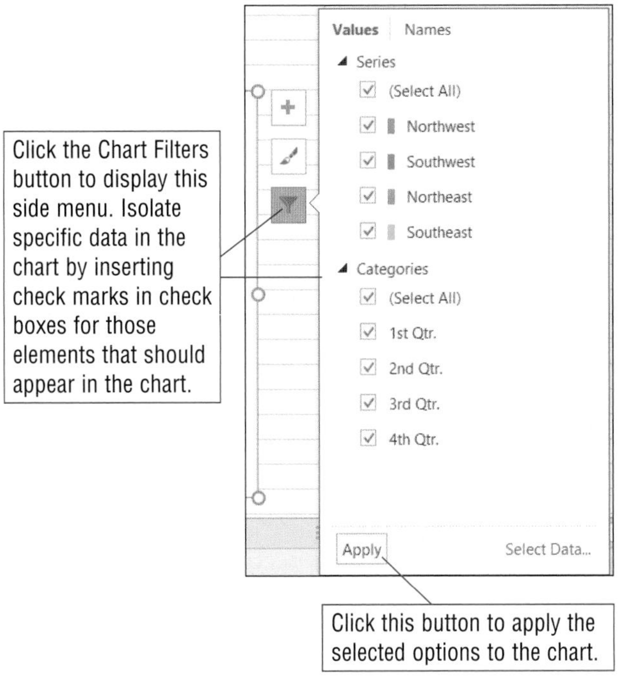

Project 1b **Formatting with Chart Buttons**

Part 2 of 3

1. With **7-SalesChart.xlsx** open, make the chart active by clicking inside it but outside any elements.
2. Insert and remove chart elements by completing the following steps:
   a. Click the Chart Elements button outside the upper right side of the chart.
   b. At the side menu that displays, click the *Chart Title* check box to remove the check mark.
   c. Click the *Data Table* check box to insert a check mark.
   d. Hover the mouse pointer over *Gridlines* in the Chart Elements button side menu and then click the right-pointing triangle that displays.
   e. At the side menu that displays, click the *Primary Major Vertical* check box to insert a check mark.

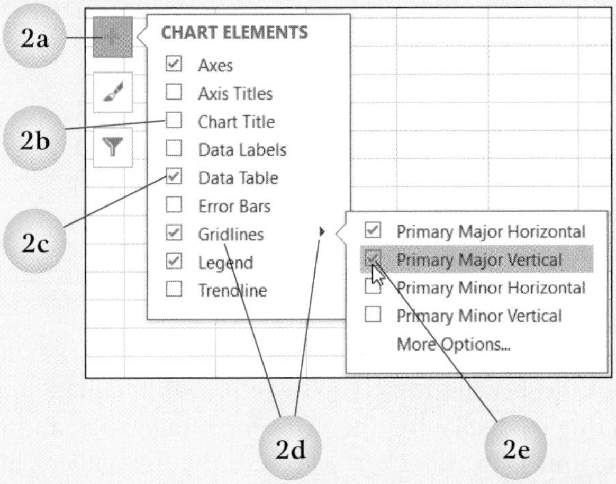

   f. Click the *Legend* check box to remove the check mark.

3. Apply a different chart style by completing the following steps:
   a. Click the Chart Styles button outside the upper right side of the chart (immediately below the Chart Elements button). (Clicking the Chart Styles button removes the Chart Elements button side menu.)
   b. At the side menu gallery, click the *Style 3* option (third option in the gallery).

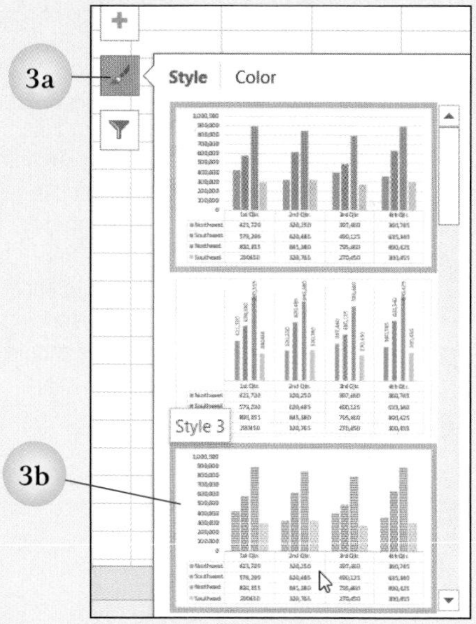

4. Display only the first-quarter and second-quarter sales by completing the following steps:
   a. Click the Chart Filters button outside the upper right corner of the chart (immediately below the Chart Styles button). (Clicking the Chart Filters button removes the Chart Styles side menu gallery.)
   b. Click the *3rd Qtr.* check box in the *Categories* section to remove the check mark.
   c. Click the *4th Qtr.* check box in the *Categories* section to remove the check mark.
   d. Click the Apply button at the bottom of the side menu.
   e. Click the Chart Filters button to remove the side menu.

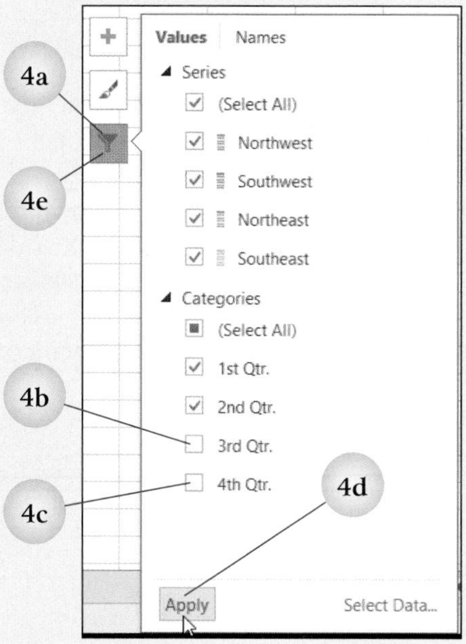

5. Save **7-SalesChart.xlsx**.

Check Your Work

Printing a Chart

In a worksheet containing data in cells and in a chart, print only the chart by selecting it, displaying the Print backstage area, and then clicking the Print button. With the chart selected, the first gallery in the *Settings* category automatically changes to *Print Selected Chart*. A preview of the chart displays at the right side of the Print backstage area.

Project 1c Printing a Chart

Part 3 of 3

1. With **7-SalesChart.xlsx** open, make sure the chart is selected.
2. Click the File tab and then click the *Print* option.
3. At the Print backstage area, look at the preview of the chart in the preview area and notice that the first gallery in the *Settings* category is set to *Print Selected Chart*.
4. Click the Print button.
5. Save and then close **7-SalesChart.xlsx**.

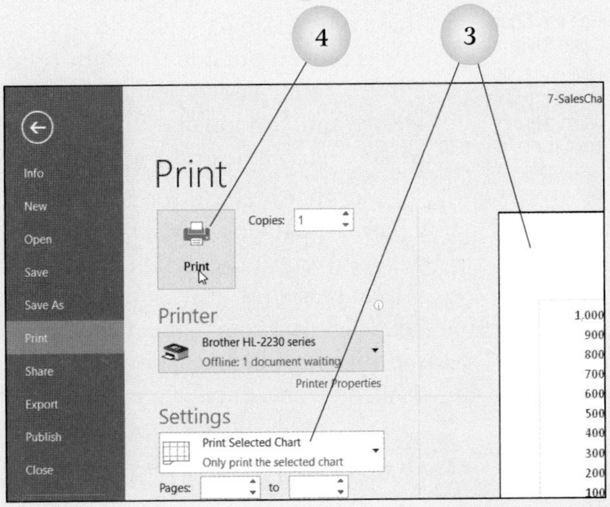

Check Your Work

Project 2 Create a Department Expenditures Bar Chart and Column Chart

2 Parts

You will open a workbook containing expenditure data by department and then create a bar chart with the data. You will then change the chart type, layout, and style; add chart elements; and move the chart to a new worksheet.

Preview Finished Project

Tutorial

Changing Chart Design

Changing the Chart Design

Along with the buttons outside the upper right side of the chart, buttons and options on the Chart Tools Design tab can be used to apply formatting to change the chart design. This tab, shown in Figure 7.5, displays when a chart is inserted in a worksheet or a chart is selected. Use buttons and options on the tab to add chart elements, change the chart type, specify a different layout or style for the chart, and change the location of the chart so it displays in a separate worksheet.

Figure 7.5 Chart Tools Design Tab

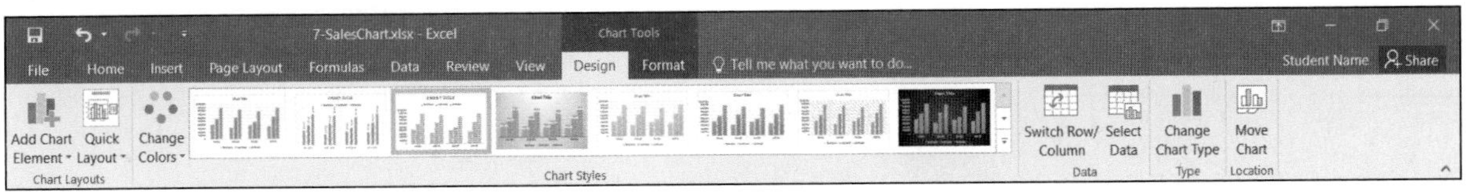

Changing the Chart Style

Quick Steps

Change the Chart Type and Style

1. Make chart active.
2. Click Chart Tools Design tab.
3. Click Change Chart Type button.
4. Click chart type.
5. Click chart style.
6. Click OK.

Change Chart Type

Excel offers a variety of preformatted custom charts and varying styles for each chart type. A chart style was applied to a chart in Project 1b using the Chart Styles button outside the right border of the chart. A chart style can also be applied to a chart with options in the Chart Styles group on the Chart Tools Design tab. To do this, click a chart style in the Chart Styles group or click the More Chart Styles button and then click the desired chart style.

Another method for applying a chart style is to use options at the Change Chart Type dialog box. Display this dialog box by clicking the Change Chart Type button in the Type group. The dialog box displays with the All Charts tab selected, as shown in Figure 7.6. Click a chart type in the left panel of the dialog box, click the chart style in the row of options at the top right, and then click a specific chart layout below the row of styles. Click the Recommended Charts tab to display chart styles recommended for the data by Excel.

Switching Rows and Columns

Switch Row/Column

Quick Steps

Switch Rows and Columns

1. Make chart active.
2. Click Chart Tools Design tab.
3. Click Switch Row/Column button.

When creating a chart, Excel uses row headings for grouping data along the bottom of the chart (the horizontal axis) and column headings for the legend (the area of a chart that identifies the data in the chart). Change this order by clicking the Switch Row/Column button in the Data group on the Chart Tools Design tab. Click this button and Excel uses the column headings to group data along the horizontal axis and the row headings for the legend.

Figure 7.6 Change Chart Type Dialog Box

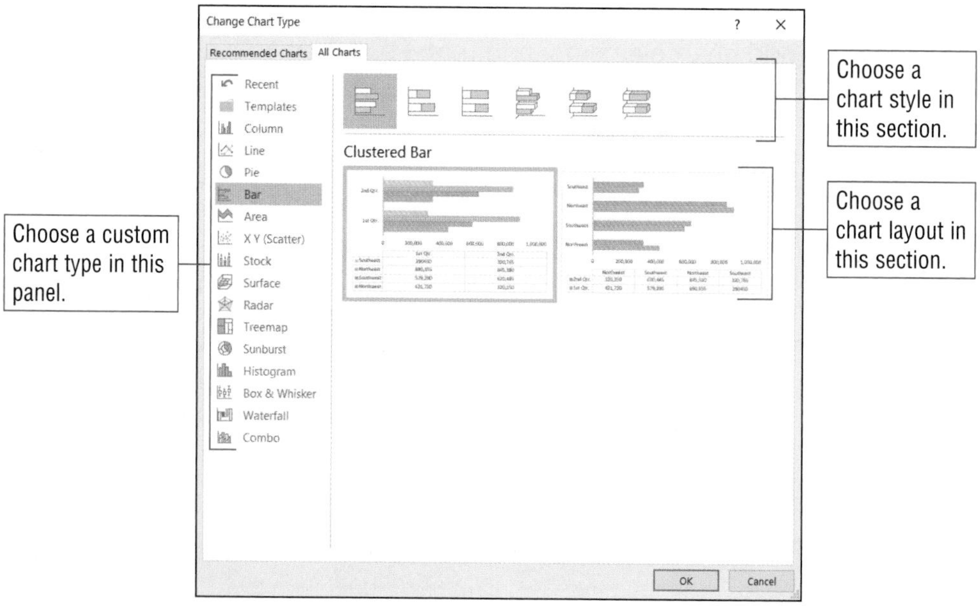

Project 2a Creating a Chart and Changing the Design

1. Open **DIDeptExp.xlsx** and then save it with the name **7-DIDeptExp**.
2. Create a bar chart by completing the following steps:
   a. Select the range A3:G9.
   b. Click the Insert tab.
   c. Click the Insert Column or Bar Chart button in the Charts group.
   d. Click the *3-D Clustered Bar* option (first option in the *3-D Bar* section).

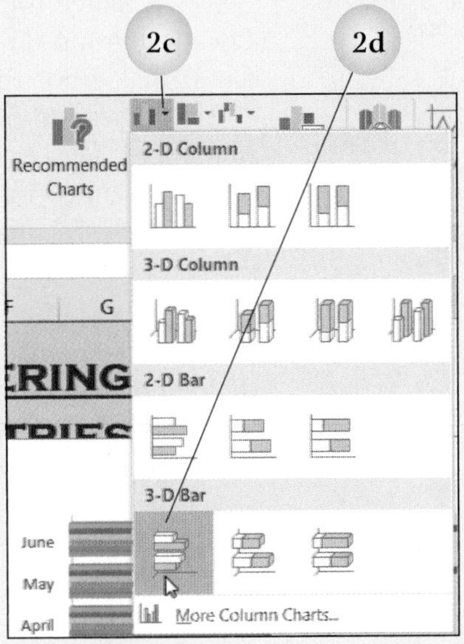

3. With the Chart Tools Design tab active, change the chart type by completing the following steps:
   a. Click the Change Chart Type button in the Type group.
   b. At the Change Chart Type dialog box, click the *Column* option in the left panel.
   c. Click the *3-D Clustered Column* option in the top row (fourth option from left).
   d. Click OK to close the Change Chart Type dialog box.

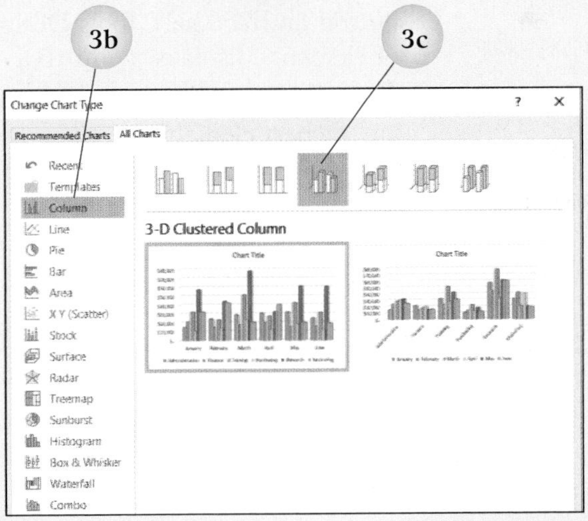

4. With the chart selected and the Chart Tools Design tab active, click the Switch Row/Column button in the Data group.

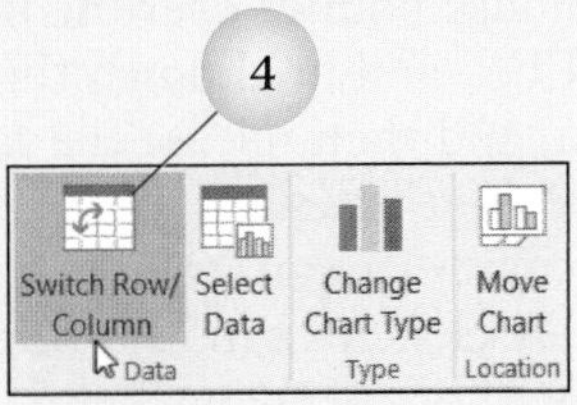

5. Save **7-DIDeptExp.xlsx**.

Check Your Work

Changing Chart Layout and Colors

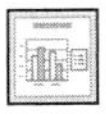
Quick Layout

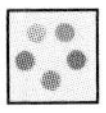
Change Colors

The Chart Tools Design tab contains options for changing the chart layout and chart colors. Click the Quick Layout button in the Chart Layouts group and a drop-down gallery of layout options displays. Hover the mouse pointer over a layout option and the chart reflects the layout. Change the colors used in the chart by clicking the Change Colors button in the Chart Styles group and then clicking a color option at the drop-down gallery.

Changing the Chart Location

Quick Steps

Change the Chart Location

1. Make chart active.
2. Click Chart Tools Design tab.
3. Click Move Chart button.
4. Click *New Sheet* option.
5. Click OK.

Move Chart

Create a chart and it is inserted in the currently open worksheet as an embedded object. Change the location of a chart with the Move Chart button in the Location group on the Chart Tools Design tab. Click this button and the Move Chart dialog box displays, as shown in Figure 7.7. To move the chart to a new sheet in the workbook, click the *New sheet* option; Excel automatically names the new sheet *Chart1*. As explained earlier in the chapter, pressing Alt + F1 will insert a recommended chart in the active worksheet. To insert a recommended chart into a separate worksheet, press the F11 function key.

A chart that is moved to a separate sheet can be moved back to the original sheet or to a different sheet within the workbook. To move a chart to a different sheet, click the Move Chart button in the Location group. At the Move Chart dialog box, click the *Object in* option box arrow and then click the sheet at the drop-down list. Click OK and the chart is inserted in the specified sheet as an object that can be moved, sized, and formatted.

Adding, Moving, and Deleting Chart Elements

Add Chart Element

In addition to adding chart elements with the Chart Elements button at the right side of a selected chart, chart elements can be added with the Add Chart Element button on the Chart Tools Design tab. Click this button and a drop-down list of elements displays. Point to a category of elements and then click the desired element at the side menu.

Quick Steps

Delete a Chart Element

1. Click chart element.
2. Press Delete key.

OR

1. Right-click chart element.
2. Click *Delete*.

A chart element can be moved and/or sized. To move a chart element, click the element to select it and then move the mouse pointer over the border until the pointer turns into a four-headed arrow. Click and hold down the left mouse button, drag the element to the new location, and then release the mouse button. To size a chart element, click to select the element and then use the sizing handles to increase or decrease the size. To delete a chart element, click the element to select it and then press the Delete key. A chart element can also be deleted by right-clicking it and then clicking *Delete* at the shortcut menu.

Figure 7.7 Move Chart Dialog Box

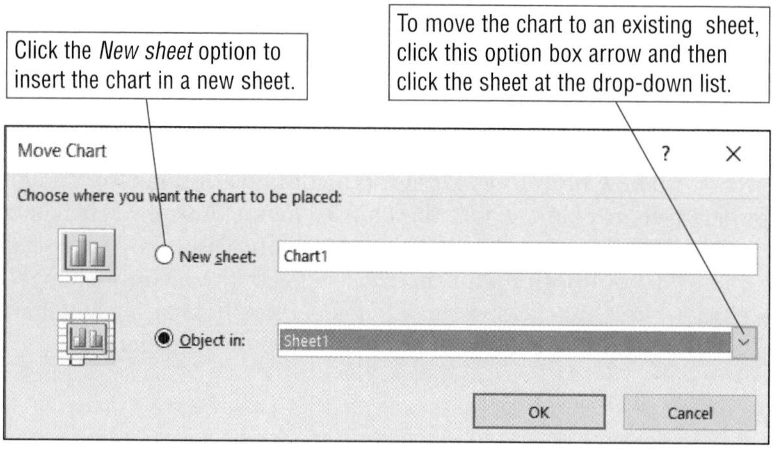
Click the New sheet option to insert the chart in a new sheet.
To move the chart to an existing sheet, click this option box arrow and then click the sheet at the drop-down list.
Move Chart
?
Choose where you want the chart to be placed:
New sheet:
Chart1
Object in:
Sheet1
OK
Cancel

Project 2b Changing Chart Layout and Location and Adding Chart Elements

1. With **7-DIDeptExp.xlsx** open, make sure the Chart Tools Design tab is active. (If it is not, make sure the chart is selected and then click the Chart Tools Design tab.)
2. Change the chart style by clicking the *Style 5* option in the Chart Styles group (fifth option from the left).

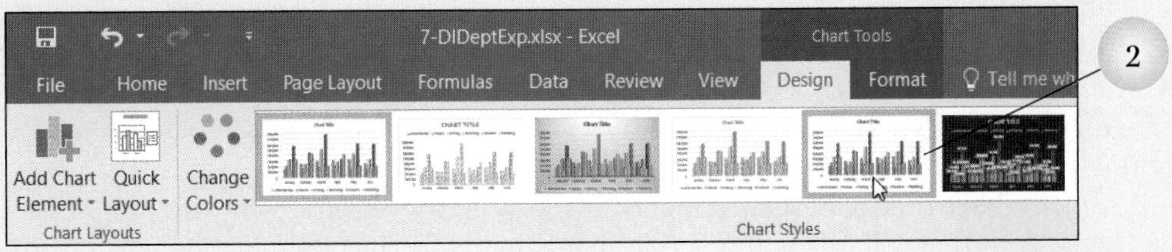

3. Change the chart colors by clicking the Change Colors button in the Chart Styles group and then clicking the *Color 3* option (third row in the *Colorful* group).
4. Change the chart layout by clicking the Quick Layout button in the Chart Layouts group and then clicking the *Layout 1* option (first option in the drop-down gallery).
5. Add axis titles by completing the following steps:
   a. Click the Add Chart Element button in the Chart Layouts group on the Chart Tools Design tab.
   b. Point to *Axis Titles* and then click *Primary Horizontal* at the side menu.
   c. Type Department and then press the Enter key. (The word *Department* will display in the Formula bar.)
   d. Click the Add Chart Element button, point to *Axis Titles*, and then click *Primary Vertical* at the side menu.
   e. Type Expenditure Amounts and then press the Enter key.
6. Click in the *Chart Title* placeholder text at the top of the chart, type Half-Yearly Expenditures, and then press the Enter key.
7. Delete the *Expenditure Amounts* axis title by clicking anywhere in it and then pressing the Delete key.
8. Move the legend by completing the following steps:
   a. Click in the legend to select it.
   b. Move the mouse pointer over the border until the pointer turns into a four-headed arrow.
   c. Click and hold down the left mouse button, drag up until the top border of the legend aligns with the top gridline in the chart, and then release the mouse button.

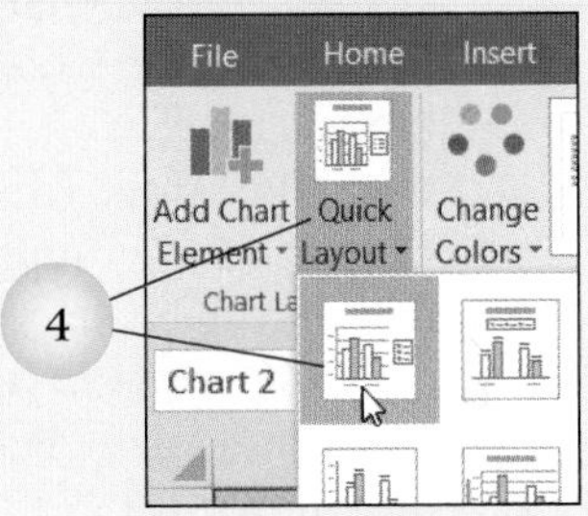

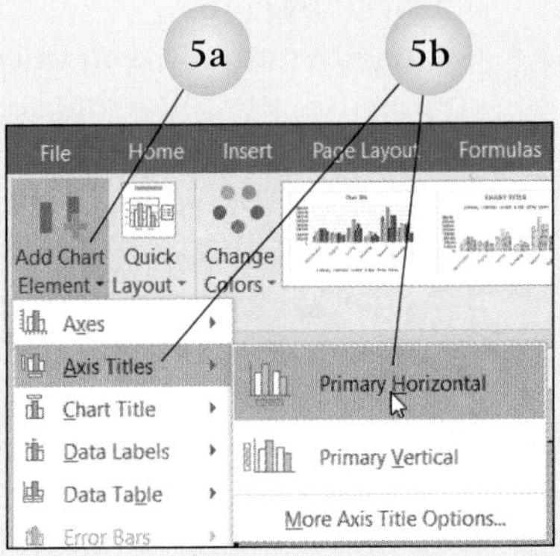

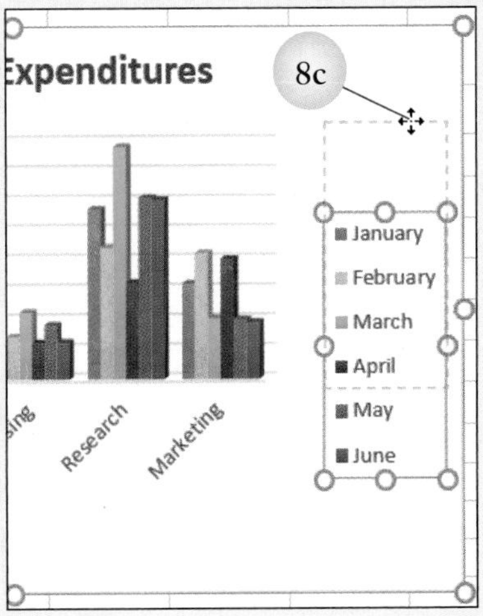

9. Move the chart to a new location by completing the following steps:
   a. Click the Move Chart button in the Location group.
   b. At the Move Chart dialog box, click the *New sheet* option and then click OK. (The chart is inserted in a worksheet named *Chart1*.)

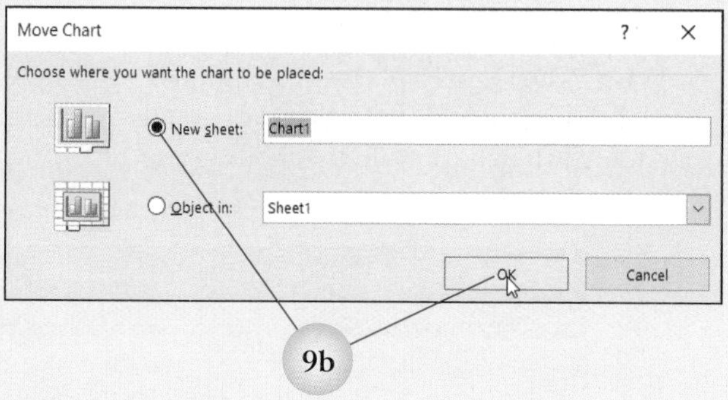

10. Save **7-DIDeptExp.xlsx**.
11. Print the Chart1 worksheet.
12. Move the chart from Chart1 to Sheet2 by completing the following steps:
    a. Make sure that Chart1 is the active worksheet and that the chart is selected (not just an element in the chart).
    b. Make sure the Chart Tools Design tab is active.
    c. Click the Move Chart button in the Location group.
    d. At the Move Chart dialog box, click the *Object in* option box arrow and then click *Sheet2* at the drop-down list.
    e. Click OK.

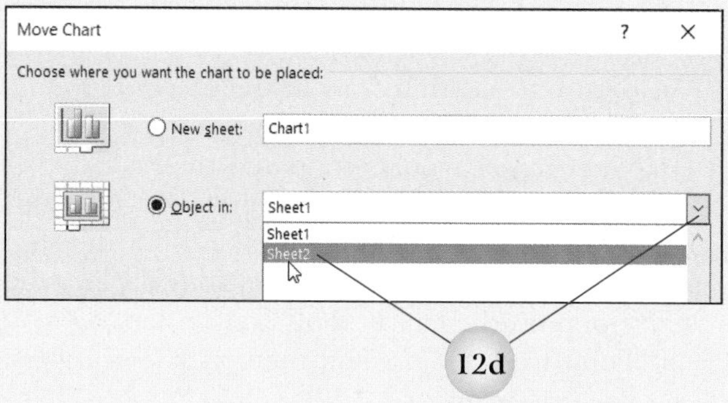

13. Change the amounts in Sheet1 by completing the following steps:
    a. Click the Sheet1 tab.
    b. Make cell B7 active and then change the amount from *10,540* to *19,750*.
    c. Make cell D8 active and then change the amount from *78,320* to *63,320*.
    d. Make cell G8 active and then change the amount from *60,570* to *75,570*.
    e. Make cell A2 active.
    f. Click the Sheet2 tab and notice that the chart displays the updated amounts.
14. Click outside the chart to deselect it.
15. Insert a header in the Sheet2 worksheet that prints your name at the left side, the current date in the middle, and the workbook file name at the right side.
16. Display the worksheet at the Print backstage area and make sure it will print on one page. If the chart does not fit on the page, return to the worksheet and then move and/or decrease the size of the chart until it fits on one page.
17. Print the active worksheet (Sheet2).
18. Save and then close **7-DIDeptExp.xlsx**.

Check Your Work

Project 3 Create a Population Comparison Line Chart — 2 Parts

You will open a workbook containing population comparison data for Seattle and Portland and then create a line chart with the data. You will move the chart to a new worksheet, format the chart elements, and insert a shape in the chart.

Preview Finished Project

Tutorial

Changing Chart Formatting

Changing Chart Formatting

Customize the formatting of a chart and its elements with options on the Chart Tools Format tab, as shown in Figure 7.8. Use buttons in the Current Selection group to identify specific elements in the chart and then apply formatting. Insert a shape in a chart with options in the Insert Shapes group and format shapes with options in the Shape Styles group. Apply WordArt formatting to data in a chart with options in the WordArt Styles group. Arrange, align, and size a chart with options in the Arrange and Size groups.

Formatting a Selection

Identify a specific element in a chart for formatting by clicking the *Chart Elements* option box arrow in the Current Selection group on the Chart Tools Format tab and then clicking the element at the drop-down list. This selects the specific element in the chart. Click the Reset to Match Style button to return the formatting of the element back to the original style. Use buttons in the Shapes Styles group to apply formatting to a selected object and use buttons in the WordArt Styles group to apply formatting to selected data.

Figure 7.8 Chart Tools Format Tab

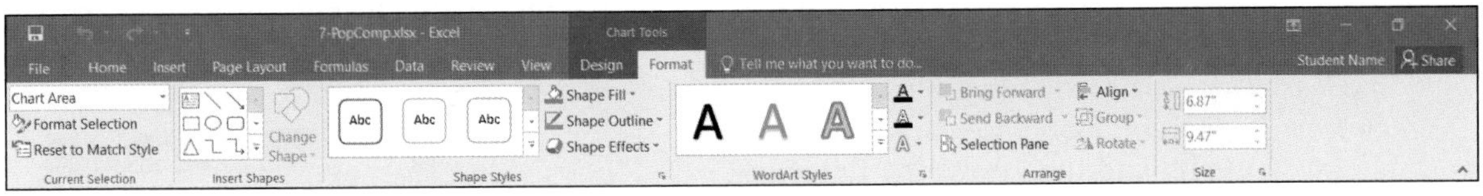

Project 3a **Creating and Formatting a Line Chart** **Part 1 of 2**

1. Open **PopComp.xlsx** and then save it with the name **7-PopComp**.
2. Create a line chart and add a chart element by completing the following steps:
   a. Select the range A2:I4.
   b. Click the Insert tab.
   c. Click the Insert Line or Area Chart button in the Charts group.
   d. Click the *Line with Markers* option at the drop-down list (fourth column, first row in the *2-D Line* section).
   e. Click the Chart Elements button outside the upper right side of the chart.
   f. Hover the mouse pointer over the *Data Table* option at the side menu, click the right-pointing triangle, and then click *No Legend Keys* at the side menu.
   g. Click the Chart Elements button to remove the side menu.
3. Move the chart to a new sheet by completing the following steps:
   a. Click the Move Chart button in the Location group on the Chart Tools Design tab.
   b. At the Move Chart dialog box, click the *New sheet* option.
   c. Click OK.
4. Format the *Portland* line by completing the following steps:
   a. Click the Chart Tools Format tab.

b. Click the *Chart Elements* option box arrow in the Current Selection group and then click *Series "Portland"* at the drop-down list.

c. Click the Shape Fill button arrow in the Shape Styles group and then click the *Green* color (sixth color in the *Standard Colors* section).

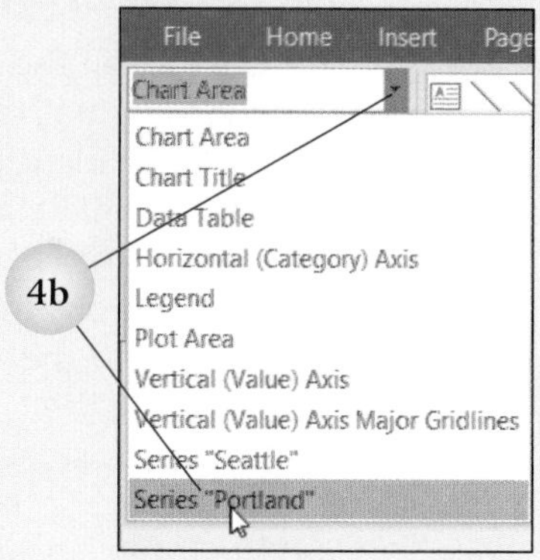

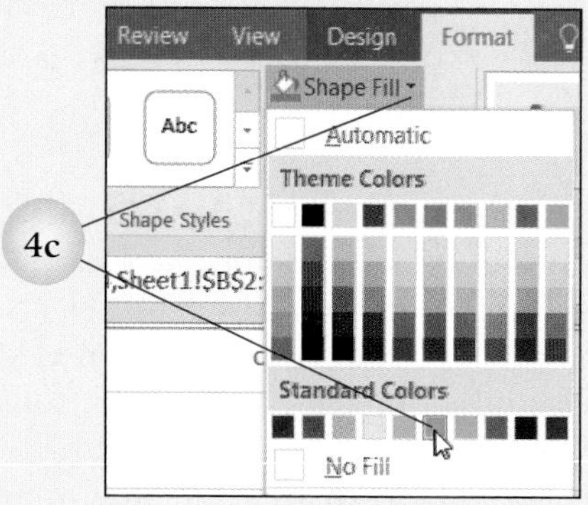

d. Click the Shape Outline button arrow in the Shape Styles group and then click the *Green* color.

5. Type a title for the chart and format the title by completing the following steps:

a. Click the *Chart Elements* option box arrow in the Current Selection group and then click *Chart Title* at the drop-down list.

b. Type Population Comparison between Seattle and Portland and then press the Enter key.

c. Click the *Fill - Black, Text 1, Shadow* WordArt style in the WordArt Styles group (first style in the WordArt Styles gallery).

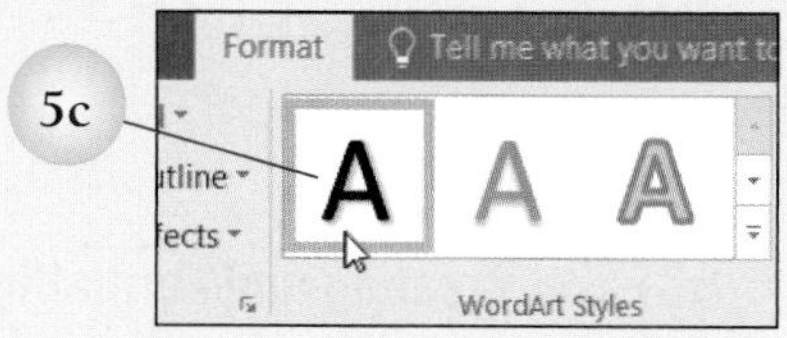

6. Format the legend by completing the following steps:

a. Click the *Chart Elements* option box arrow in the Current Selection group and then click *Legend* at the drop-down list.

b. Click the *Colored Outline - Blue, Accent 1* shape style in the Shape Styles group (second shape style).

7. Save **7-PopComp.xlsx**.

Check Your Work

Inserting a Shape

Quick Steps

Insert a Shape

1. Make chart active.
2. Click Chart Tools Format tab.
3. Click More Shapes button.
4. Click shape at drop-down list.
5. Click or drag to create shape.

The Insert Shapes group on the Chart Tools Format tab contains options for inserting shapes in a chart. Click a shape option and the mouse pointer turns into crosshairs (thin black plus symbol). Click in the chart or drag with the mouse to create the shape in the chart. The shape is inserted in the chart and the Drawing Tools Format tab is active. This tab contains many of the same options as the Chart Tools Format tab. For example, a shape style or WordArt style can be applied to the shape and the shape can be arranged and sized. Size a shape by clicking the up and down arrows at the right sides of the *Shape Height* and *Shape Width* measurement boxes in the Size group on the Drawing Tools Format tab. Or select the current measurement in the *Shape Height* or *Shape Width* measurement box and then type a specific measurement.

Project 3b Inserting and Customizing a Shape

1. With **7-PopComp.xlsx** open, create a shape similar to the one shown in Figure 7.9 by completing the following steps:
   a. Click the More Shapes button in the Insert Shapes group on the Chart Tools Format tab.
   b. Click the *Up Arrow Callout* shape (last column, second row in the *Block Arrows* section).
   c. Click in the chart to insert the shape.
   d. Click in the *Shape Height* measurement box in the Size group on the Drawing Tools Format tab, type 1.5, and then press the Enter key.
   e. Click in the *Shape Width* measurement box, type 1.5, and then press the Enter key.
   f. Apply a shape style by clicking the More Shape Styles button in the Shape Styles group and then clicking the *Subtle Effect - Blue, Accent 1* option (second column, fourth row in the *Theme Styles* section).

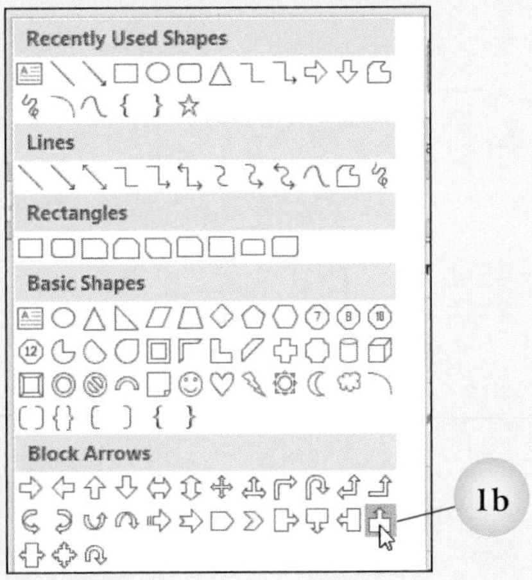

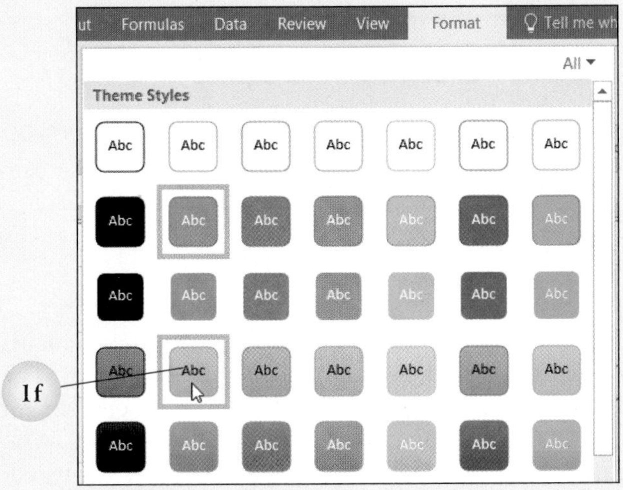

   g. Type Largest disparity in the shape, press the Enter key, and then type (184,411).
   h. Select the text you just typed.
   i. Click the Home tab.
   j. Click the Bold button in the Font group.
   k. Click the *Font Size* option box arrow and then click *14*.
   l. Click the Center button in the Alignment group.
2. With the shape selected, drag the shape so it is positioned as shown in Figure 7.9.
3. Save **7-PopComp.xlsx**, print the Chart1 worksheet, and then close the workbook.

Check Your Work

Figure 7.9 Project 3 Chart

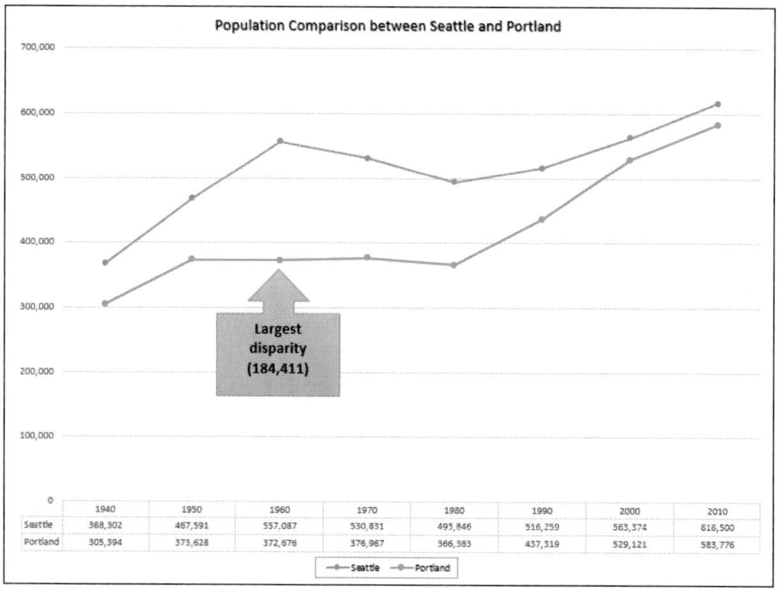

Project 4 Create a Costs Percentage Pie Chart — 2 Parts

You will create a pie chart, add data labels, apply a style, format chart elements, and then size and move the pie chart.

Preview Finished Project

Using the Quick Analysis Feature

A variety of methods are available for adding visual elements to a worksheet, including charts, sparklines, and conditional formatting. The Quick Analysis feature consists of a toolbar that has buttons and options for inserting all of these visual elements plus common formulas in one location. When a range is selected, Excel determines how the data in the range can be analyzed and then provides buttons and options for inserting relevant visual elements or formulas. When a range of data that is used to create a pie chart is selected, the Quick Analysis Toolbar provides buttons and options for inserting many different visual elements or formulas, but also specifically including a pie chart.

A Quick Analysis button appears at the bottom right corner of the selected range and when clicked, displays the Quick Analysis Toolbar as shown in Figure 7.10. The Quick Analysis Toolbar includes the *Formatting*, *Charts*, *Totals*, *Tables*, and *Sparklines* options. Each option displays buttons that relate to how the data can be analyzed. Click a button to insert an element or formula into the worksheet.

Figure 7.10 Quick Analysis Toolbar

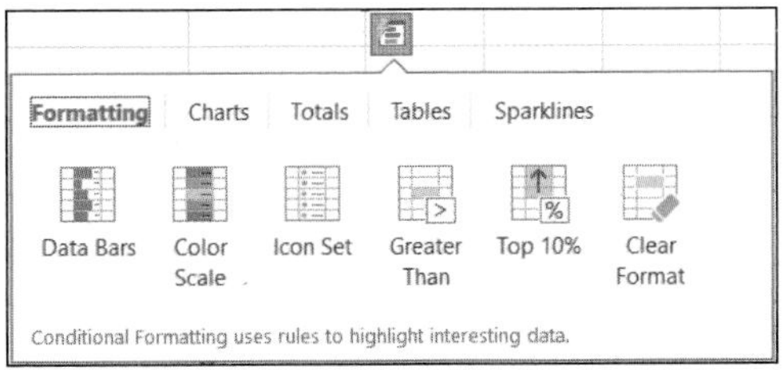

Applying Formatting at a Task Pane

Quick Steps

Display a Task Pane

1. Select chart or specific element.
2. Click Chart Tools Format tab.
3. Click Format Selection button.

Format Selection

To view and apply more formatting options for charts, display the formatting task pane by clicking the Format Selection button in the Current Selection group on the Chart Tools Format tab. The task pane displays at the right side of the screen and the name of and contents in the task pane vary depending on what is selected. If the entire chart is selected, the Format Chart Area task pane displays, as shown in Figure 7.11. Format the chart by clicking formatting options in the task pane. Display additional formatting options by clicking the icons toward the top of the task pane. For example, click the Effects icon in the Format Chart Area task pane and options display for applying shadow, glow, soft edges, and three-dimensional formatting.

Click a chart element and then click the Format Selection button and the task pane name and options change. Another method for displaying the task pane is to right-click a chart or chart element and then click the format option at the shortcut menu. The name of the format option varies depending on the selected element.

Figure 7.11 Format Chart Area Task Pane

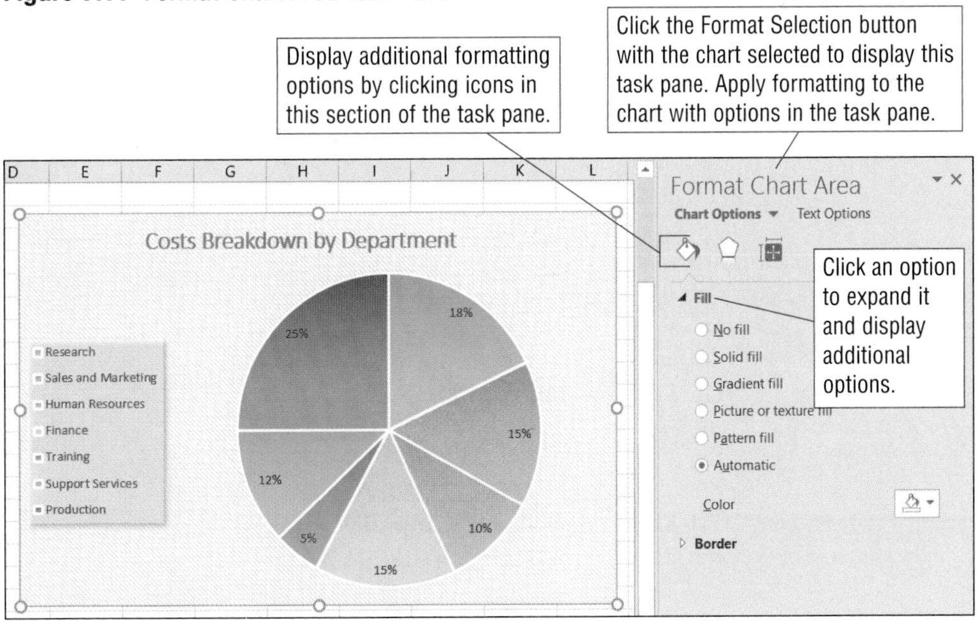

Changing Chart Height and Width Measurements

Quick Steps

Change Chart Height and/or Width
1. Make chart active.
2. Click Chart Tools Format tab.
3. Insert height and/or width with *Shape Height* and/or *Shape Width* measurement boxes.

A chart that is inserted into the current worksheet (not a separate new worksheet) can be sized by selecting it and dragging a sizing handle. A chart can also be sized with the *Shape Height* and *Shape Width* measurement boxes in the Size group on the Chart Tools Format tab. Click the up or down arrow at the right side of the measurement box to increase or decrease the size or click in the measurement box and then type a specific measurement. Another method for changing a chart size is to use options at the Format Chart Area task pane. Display this task pane by clicking the Size group task pane launcher on the Chart Tools Format tab.

Project 4a **Deleting a Chart and Creating and Formatting a Pie Chart** Part 1 of 2

1. Open **DIDeptCosts.xlsx** and then save it with the name **7-DIDeptCosts**.
2. Create the pie chart shown in Figure 7.11 by completing the following steps:
   a. Select the range A3:B10.
   b. Click the Quick Analysis button below and to the right of the selected range.
   c. Click the *Charts* option.
   d. Click the Pie button.

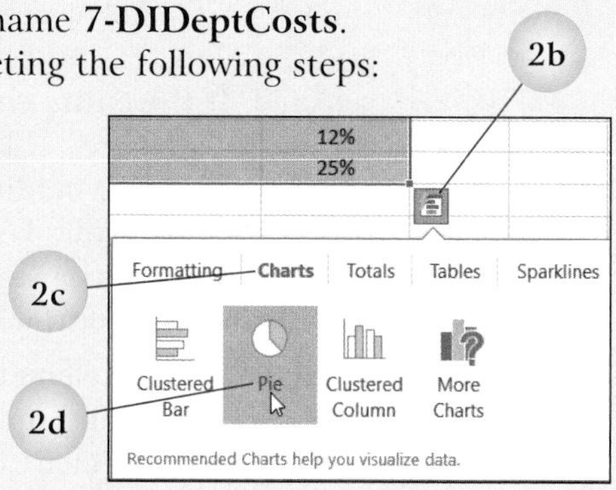

3. Insert data labels in the chart by completing the following steps:
   a. Click the Chart Elements button outside the upper right border of the chart.
   b. Hover the mouse pointer over the *Data Labels* option and then click the right-pointing triangle that displays.
   c. Click *Inside End* at the side menu.
   d. Click the Chart Elements button to hide the side menu.

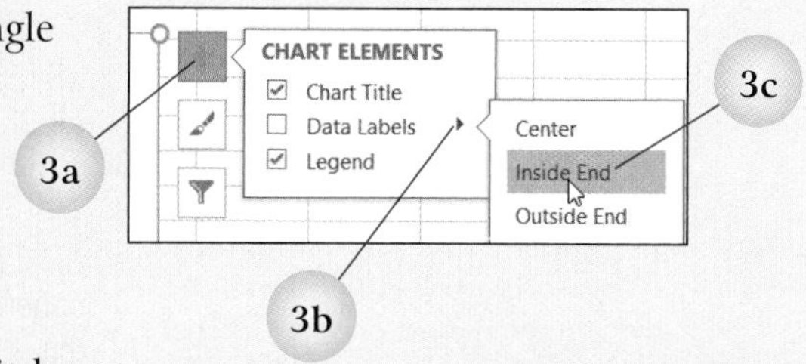

4. Click the *Style 6* option in the Chart Styles group on the Chart Tools Design tab.
5. Type a title and then apply a WordArt style to it by completing the following steps:
   a. Click the Chart Tools Format tab.
   b. Click the *Chart Elements* option box arrow in the Current Selection group.
   c. Click *Chart Title* at the drop-down list.
   d. Type C and Excel's AutoComplete feature inserts the entire title, *Costs Breakdown by Department*, in the Formula bar. Accept this name by pressing the Enter key.
   e. Click the More WordArt Styles button in the WordArt Styles group.
   f. Click the *Pattern Fill - Gray-50%, Accent 3, Narrow Horizontal, Inner Shadow* style at the drop-down gallery (second column, fourth row).

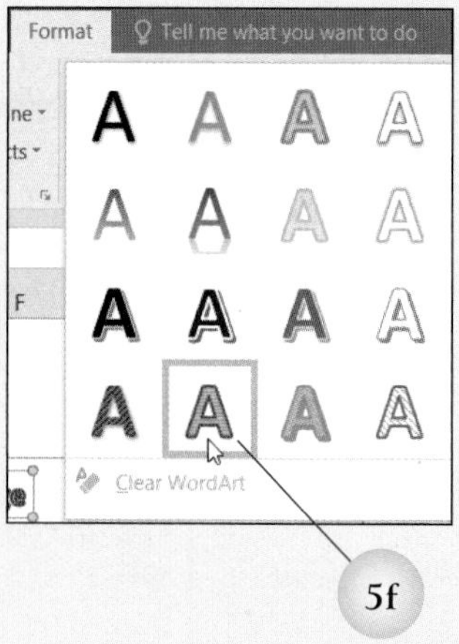

6. Use the Format Legend task pane to apply formatting to the legend by completing the following steps:
   a. Click the *Chart Elements* option box arrow and then click *Legend* at the drop-down list.
   b. Click the Format Selection button in the Current Selection group.
   c. At the Format Legend task pane, click the *Left* option in the *Legend Options* section to select it.

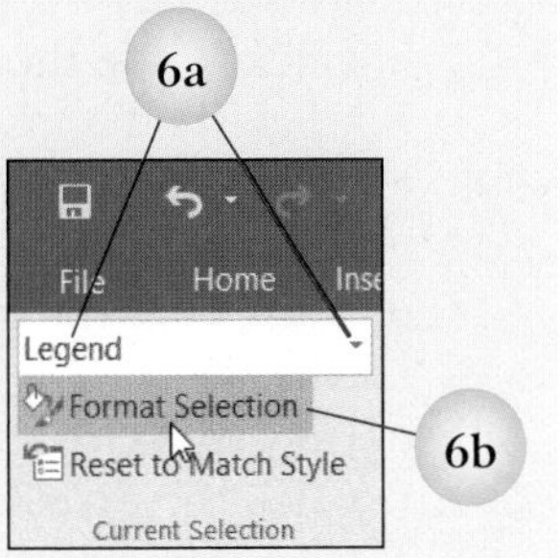

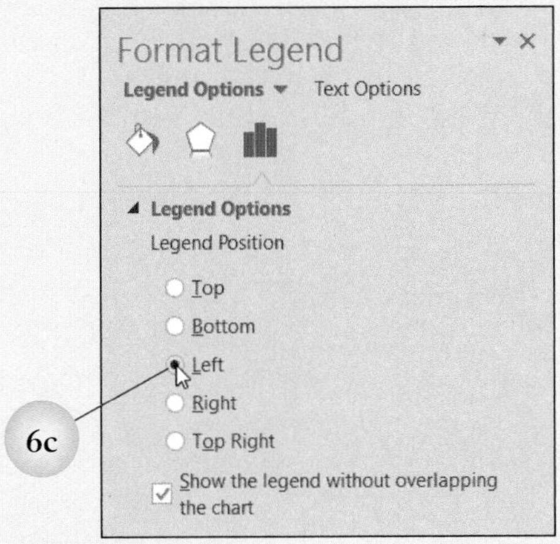

   d. Click the Effects icon in the task pane. (This changes the options in the task pane.)
   e. Click *Shadow* to expand the shadow options in the task pane.
   f. Click the Shadow button to the right of *Presets* and then click the *Offset Diagonal Bottom Right* option (first option in the *Outer* section).

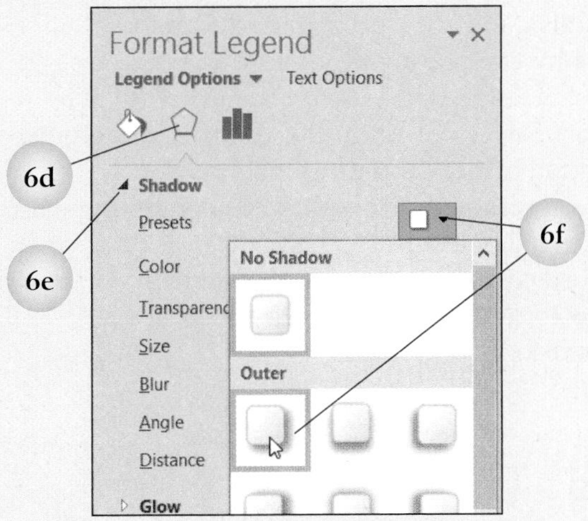

   g. Click the Fill & Line icon in the task pane.
   h. Click *Fill* to expand the fill options in the task pane.
   i. Click the *Gradient fill* option.
   j. Close the task pane by clicking the Close button in the upper right corner of the task pane.

7. Use the Format Chart Area task pane to apply formatting to the chart by completing the following steps:
   a. Click inside the chart but outside any chart elements.
   b. Click the Format Selection button in the Current Selection group.
   c. Make sure the Fill & Line icon in the Format Chart Area task pane is selected. (If not, click the icon.)
   d. Make sure the *Fill* option is expanded. (If not, click *Fill*.)
   e. Click the *Gradient fill* option.
   f. Click the Size & Properties icon in the task pane.
   g. Click *Size* to expand the size options in the task pane.
   h. Select the current measurement in the *Height* measurement box, type 3.5, and then press the Enter key.
   i. Select the current measurement in the *Width* measurement box, type 5.5, and then press the Enter key.

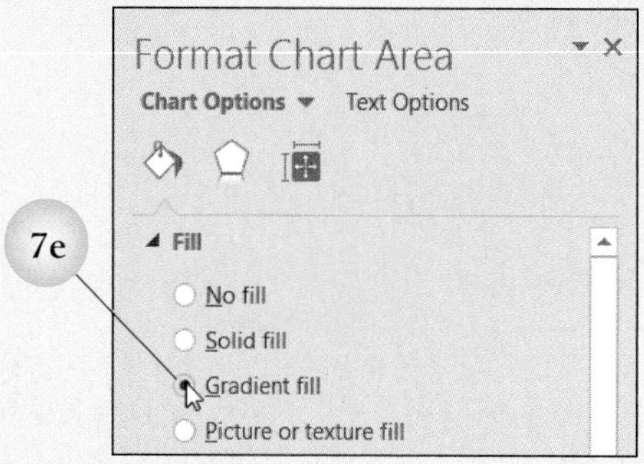

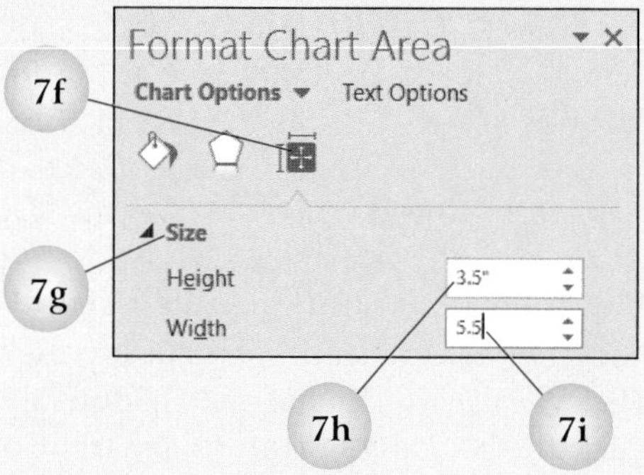

   j. Close the task pane.
8. Save **7-DIDeptCosts.xlsx** and then print only the chart.
9. Change the chart style by completing the following steps:
   a. Click the Chart Tools Design tab.
   b. Click the More Chart Styles button in the Chart Styles group.
   c. Click the *Style 9* option at the drop-down gallery.
10. Move the chart so it is positioned below the cells containing data.
11. Click outside the chart to deselect it.
12. Display the Print backstage area, make sure the chart fits on one page with the data, and then click the Print button.
13. Save **7-DIDeptCosts.xlsx**.

Check Your Work

Deleting a Chart

Quick Steps

Delete a Chart
1. Click chart.
2. Press Delete key.

OR
1. Right-click chart tab.
2. Click *Delete*.

Delete a chart created in Excel by clicking the chart to select it and then pressing the Delete key. If a chart has been moved to a different worksheet in the workbook, deleting the chart will delete the chart but not the worksheet. To delete the worksheet and the chart, position the mouse pointer on the sheet tab, click the right mouse button, and then click *Delete* at the shortcut menu. At the message box indicating that the selected sheet will be permanently deleted, click the Delete button.

Project 4b Deleting a Chart and Creating and Formatting a Treemap Chart

Part 2 of 2

1. With **7-DIDeptCosts.xlsx** open, click the Sheet2 tab.
2. Delete the column chart by completing the following steps:
   a. Click the column chart to select it. (Make sure the chart is selected, not a specific element in the chart.)
   b. Press the Delete key.
3. Create a treemap chart by completing the following steps:
   a. Select the range A2:C8.
   b. Click the Insert tab.
   c. Click the Insert Hierarchy Chart button.
   d. Click the *Treemap* option (first option).
4. Click the *Style 4* option in the Chart Styles group on the Chart Tools Design tab.
5. Click the Change Colors button in the Chart Styles group and then click the *Color 3* option in the *Colorful* section of the drop-down gallery.
6. Click the Add Chart Element button, position the mouse pointer over the *Legend* option, click the right-pointing triangle that displays, and then click the *None* option.
7. Click in the *Chart Title* placeholder text and then type Proportionate Departmental Expenses.
8. Change the chart height and width by completing the following steps:
   a. Make the entire chart active and then click the Chart Tools Format tab.
   b. Click in the *Shape Height* measurement box, type 5, and then press the Enter key.
   c. Click in the *Shape Width* measurement box, type 4, and then press the Enter key.
9. Move the chart so it is positioned below the cells containing data.
10. Click outside the chart to deselect it.
11. Center the worksheet horizontally and vertically.
12. Save, print, and then close **7-DIDeptCosts.xlsx**.

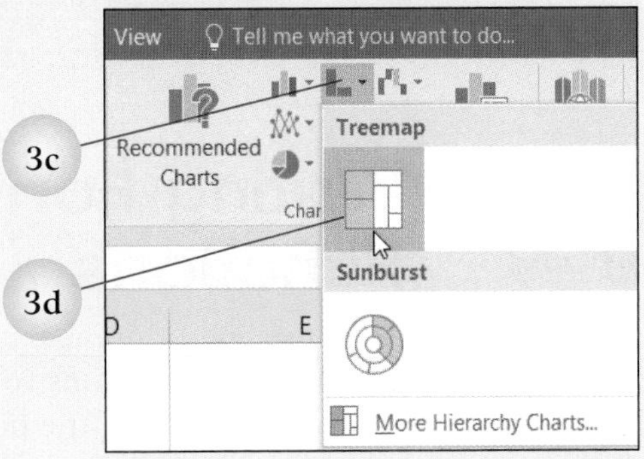

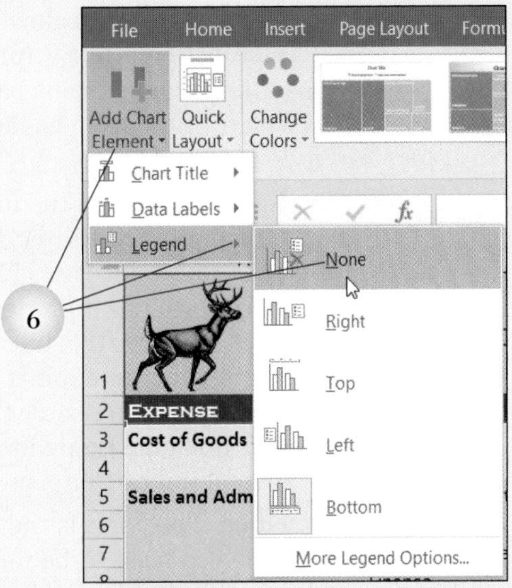

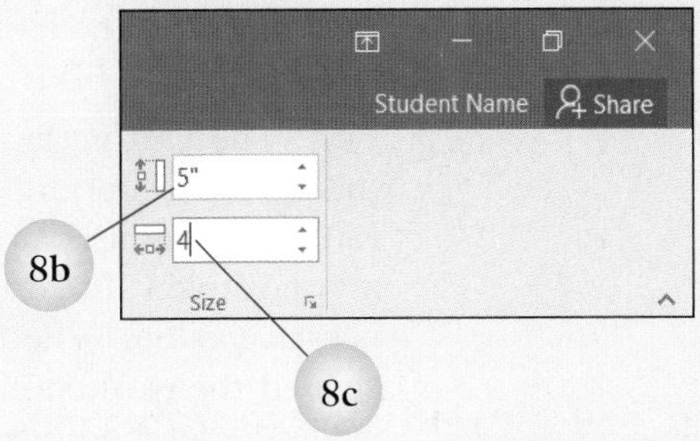

Check Your Work

Project 5 **Calculate Payments and the Future Value of an Investment** **2 Parts**

You will use the PMT financial function to calculate payments and the FV financial function to find the future value of an investment.

Preview Finished Project

Tutorial

Using Financial Functions

Writing Formulas with Financial Functions

Excel provides a number of financial functions that can be used in formulas. Use financial functions to determine different aspects of a financial loan or investment, such as the payment amount, present value, future value, interest rate, and number of payment periods. Each financial function requires some of the variables listed below to return a result. Two such financial functions are the PMT function and FV function. The PMT function calculates the payment for a loan based on constant payments and a constant interest rate. The FV function calculates the future value of an investment. Financial functions use some of the following arguments:

- **Rate:** The rate is the interest rate for a payment period. The rate may need to be modified for the function to display the desired results. For example, most rate values are given as an APR (annual percentage rate), which is the percentage rate for one year, not a payment period. So a percentage rate may be given as 12% APR but if the payment period is a month, then the percentage rate for the function is 1%, not 12%. If a worksheet contains the annual percentage rate, enter the cell reference in the function argument and specify that it should be divided by 12 months. For example, if cell B6 contains the annual interest rate, enter *b6/12* as the Rate argument.
- **Nper:** The Nper is the number of payment periods in an investment. The Nper may also need to be modified depending on what information is provided. For example, if a loan duration is expressed in years but the payments are made each month, the Nper value needs to be adjusted accordingly. A five-year loan has an Nper of 60 (five years times 12 months in each year).
- **Pmt:** The Pmt is the payment amount for each period. This argument describes the payment amount for a period and is commonly expressed as a negative value because it is an outflow of cash. However, the Pmt value can be entered as a positive value if the present value (Pv) or future value (Fv) is entered as a negative value. Whether the Pmt value is positive or negative depends on who created the workbook. For example, a home owner lists the variable as outflow, while the lending institution lists it as inflow.
- **Pv:** The Pv is the present value of an investment, expressed in a lump sum. The Pv argument is generally the initial loan amount. For example, if a person is purchasing a new home, the Pv is the amount of money he or she borrowed to buy the home. Pv can be expressed as a negative value, which denotes it as an investment instead of a loan. For example, if a bank issues a loan to a home buyer, it enters the Pv value as negative because it is an outflow of cash.

- **Fv:** The Fv is the future value of an investment, expressed in a lump sum amount. The Fv argument is generally the loan amount plus the amount of interest paid during the loan. In the example of a home buyer, the Fv is the sum of payments, which includes both the principle and interest paid on the loan. In the example of a bank, the Fv is the total amount received after a loan has been paid off. Fv can also be expressed as either a positive or negative value depending on which side of the transaction is being reviewed.

Finding the Periodic Payments for a Loan

The PMT function finds the payment for a loan based on constant payments and a constant interest rate. In Project 5a, the PMT function will be used to determine monthly payments for equipment and a used van as well as monthly income from selling equipment. The formulas created with the PMT function will include Rate, Nper, and Pv arguments. The Nper argument is the number of payments that will be made on the loan or investment, Pv is the current value of amounts to be received or paid in the future, and Fv is the value of the loan or investment at the end of all periods.

Financial

To write the PMT function, click the Formulas tab, click the Financial button in the Function Library group, and then click the PMT function at the drop-down list. This displays the Function Arguments dialog box with options for inserting cell designations for Rate, Nper, and Pv. (These are the arguments displayed in bold formatting in the Function Arguments dialog box. The dialog box also contains the Fv and Type functions, which are dimmed.)

Project 5a Calculating Payments

Part 1 of 2

1. Open **RPReports.xlsx** and then save it with the name **7-RPReports**.
2. The owner of Real Photography is interested in purchasing a new developer and needs to determine monthly payments on three different models. Insert a formula that calculates monthly payments and then copy that formula by completing the following steps:
   a. Make cell E5 active.
   b. Click the Formulas tab.
   c. Click the Financial button in the Function Library group, scroll down the drop-down list, and then click *PMT*.

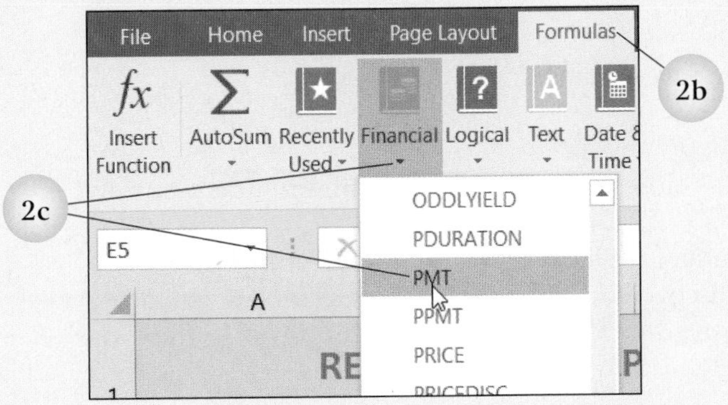

d. At the Function Arguments dialog box, type c5/12 in the *Rate* text box. (This tells Excel to divide the interest rate by 12 months.)
e. Press the Tab key. (This moves the insertion point to the *Nper* text box.)
f. Type d5. (This is the total number of months for the investment.)
g. Press the Tab key. (This moves the insertion point to the *Pv* text box.)
h. Type b5. (This is the purchase price of the developer.)
i. Click OK. (This closes the dialog box and inserts the monthly payment of *($316.98)* in cell E5. Excel displays the result of the PMT function as a negative number since the loan represents money going out of the company—a negative cash flow.)

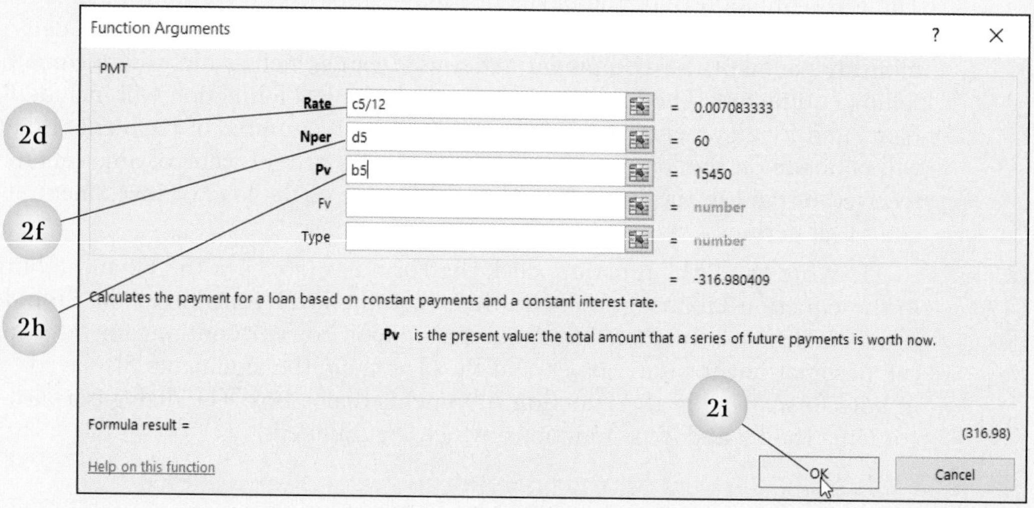

j. Copy the formula in cell E5 down into cells E6 and E7.

3. The owner is interested in purchasing a used van for the company and wants an idea of what monthly payments would be at various terms and rates. Insert a formula that calculates monthly payments for a three-year loan at 5% interest by completing the following steps:
   a. Make cell E12 active.
   b. Make sure the Formulas tab is active.
   c. Click the Financial button in the Function Library group, scroll down the drop-down list, and then click *PMT*.
   d. At the Function Arguments dialog box, type c12/12 in the *Rate* text box. (This tells Excel to divide the interest rate by 12 months.)
   e. Press the Tab key.
   f. Type d12 in the *Nper* text box. (This is the total number of months for the investment.)
   g. Press the Tab key.
   h. Type b12 in the *Pv* text box.
   i. Click OK. (This closes the dialog box and inserts the monthly payment of *($299.71)* in cell E12.)
   j. Copy the formula in cell E12 down into the range E13:E15.

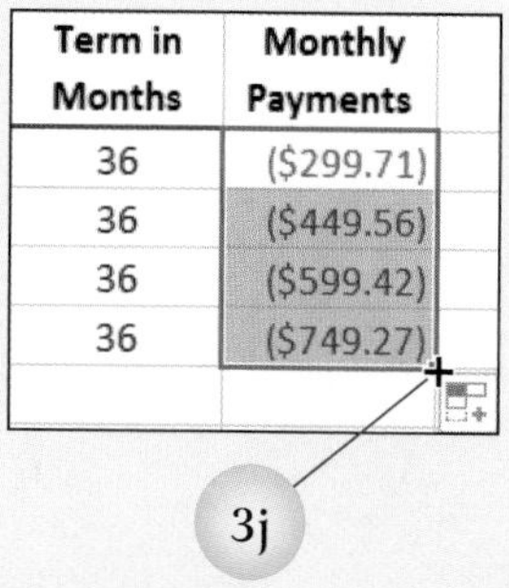

Term in Months
Monthly Payments
36
($299.71)
36
($449.56)
36
($599.42)
36
($749.27)
3j

4. The owner has discovered that the interest rate for a used van will be 6.25% instead of 5%. Change the percentages in the range C12:C15 to 6.25%.

5. The owner is selling a camera and wants to determine the monthly payments for a two-year loan at 4.5% interest. Determine monthly payments on the camera (income to Real Photography) by completing the following steps:
   a. Make cell E20 active.
   b. Make sure the Formulas tab is active.
   c. Click the Financial button in the Function Library group, scroll down the drop-down list, and then click *PMT*.
   d. At the Function Arguments dialog box, type c20/12 in the *Rate* text box.
   e. Press the Tab key.
   f. Type d20 in the *Nper* text box.
   g. Press the Tab key.
   h. Type -b20 in the *Pv* text box. (Enter the *Pv* cell reference preceded by a hyphen because the sale of the camera represents an outflow of an asset. Excel displays the result of the PMT function as a positive number since the camera payments represent a positive cash inflow.)
   i. Click OK. (This closes the dialog box and inserts the monthly income of *$185.92* in cell E20.)
6. Save, print, and then close **7-RPReports.xlsx**.

Check Your Work

Finding the Future Value of a Series of Payments

The FV function calculates the future value of a series of equal payments or an annuity. Use this function to determine information such as how much money can be earned in an investment account with a specific interest rate and over a specific period of time.

Project 5b Finding the Future Value of an Investment

Part 2 of 2

1. Open **RPInvest.xlsx** and then save it with the name **7-RPInvest**.
2. The owner of Real Photography has decided to save the money needed to purchase a new developer and wants to compute how much money can be earned by investing in an investment account that returns 7.5% annual interest. The owner determines that $1,200 per month can be invested in the account for three years. Complete the following steps to determine the future value of the investment account:
   a. Make cell B6 active.
   b. Make sure the Formulas tab is active.
   c. Click the Financial button in the Function Library group.
   d. At the drop-down list that displays, scroll down the list and then click *FV*.
   e. At the Function Arguments dialog box, type b3/12 in the *Rate* text box.
   f. Press the Tab key.
   g. Type b4 in the *Nper* text box.
   h. Press the Tab key.
   i. Type b5 in the *Pmt* text box.
   j. Click OK. (This closes the dialog box and also inserts the future value of *$48,277.66* in cell B6.)
3. Save and then print **7-RPInvest.xlsx**.
4. The owner decides to determine the future return after two years. To do this, change the amount in cell B4 from *36* to *24* and then press the Enter key. (This recalculates the future investment amount in cell B6.)
5. Save, print, and then close **7-RPInvest.xlsx**.

Check Your Work

Project 6 Insert Formulas with the IF Logical Function — 3 Parts

You will use the IF logical function to calculate sales bonuses, determine pass/fail grades based on averages, and identify discounts and discount amounts.

Preview Finished Project

Tutorial

Using Logical IF Functions

Writing Formulas with the Logical IF Function

A question that can be answered true or false is considered a ***logical test***. The ***IF function*** can be used to create a logical test that performs a particular action if the answer is true (condition met) and another action if the answer is false (condition not met).

For example, an IF function can be used to write a formula that calculates a salesperson's bonus as 10% if he or she sells more than $99,999 worth of product and 0% if he or she does not sell more than $99,999 worth of product. When writing a formula with an IF function, think about the words *if* and *then*. For example, the formula written out for the bonus example would look like this:

> ***If*** the salesperson sells more than $99,999 of product, ***then*** the salesperson receives a bonus of 10%.
>
> ***If*** the salesperson does not sell more than $99,999 of product, ***then*** the salesperson receives a bonus of 0%.

When writing a formula with an IF function, use commas to separate the condition and the action. The formula for the bonus example would look like this: ***=IF(sales>99999,sales*0.1,0)***. The formula contains three parts:

- the condition or logical test: ***IF(sales>99999***
- the action taken if the condition or logical test is true: ***sales*0.1***
- the action taken if the condition or logical test is false: ***0***

In Project 6a, you will write a formula with cell references rather than cell data. You will write a formula with an IF function that determines the following:

> ***If*** the sales amount is greater than the quota amount, ***then*** the salesperson will receive a 15% bonus.
>
> ***If*** the sales amount is not greater than the quota amount, ***then*** the salesperson will not receive a bonus.

Written with cell references in the project, the formula looks like this: ***=IF(C4>B4,C4*0.15,0)***. In this formula, the condition or logical test is whether the number in cell C4 is greater than the number in cell B4. If the condition is true and the number is greater, then the number in cell C4 is multiplied by 0.15 (providing a 15% bonus). If the condition is false and the number in cell C4 is less than the number in cell B4, then nothing happens (no bonus). Notice how commas are used to separate the logical test from the action.

Project 6a Writing a Formula with an IF Function

Part 1 of 3

1. Open **CMPReports.xlsx** and then save it with the name **7-CMPReports**.
2. Write a formula with the IF function that determines if a sales quota has been met and if it has, inserts the bonus of 15% of actual sales. (If the quota has not been met, the formula will insert a 0.) Write the formula by completing the following steps:
   a. Make cell D4 active.
   b. Type =if(c4>b4,c4*0.15,0) and then press the Enter key.

	A	B	C	D
1	Capstan Marine Products			
2	Sales Department			
3	Salesperson	Quota	Actual Sales	Bonus
4	Allejandro	$ 95,500.00	$	=if(c4>b4,c4*0.15,0)
5	Crispin	137,000.00	129,890.00	

2b

   c. Make cell D4 active and then use the fill handle to copy the formula into the range D5:D9.
3. Print the worksheet.
4. Revise the formula so it inserts a 20% bonus if the quota has been met by completing the following steps:
   a. Make cell D4 active.
   b. Click in the Formula bar, edit the formula so it displays as *=IF(C4>B4,C4*0.2,0)*, and then click the Enter button on the Formula bar.
   c. Copy the formula in cell D4 down into the range D5:D9.
   d. Make cell D4 active and then apply the Accounting format with a dollar symbol and two digits after the decimal point.
5. Save **7-CMPReports.xlsx**.

Check Your Work

Writing Formulas with an IF Function Using the Function Arguments Dialog Box

? Logical

A formula containing an IF function can be typed directly into a cell or the Function Arguments dialog box can be used to help write the formula. To use the Function Arguments dialog box to write a formula with the IF function, click the Formulas tab, click the Logical button in the Function Library group, and then click *IF* at the drop-down list. This displays the Function Arguments dialog box, shown in Figure 7.12. The Function Arguments dialog box displays the information you will type in the three argument text boxes for Project 6b.

At the Function Arguments dialog box, click in the *Logical_test* text box and information about the Logical_test argument displays in the dialog box. In this text box, type the cell designation followed by what is evaluated. In the figure, the *Logical_test* text box contains *b14>599*, indicating that what is being evaluated is whether the amount in cell B14 is greater than $599. The *Value_if_true* text box contains *b14*0.95*, indicating that if the logical test is true, then the amount in cell B14 is multiplied by 0.95. (The discount for any product price greater than $599

Figure 7.12 Function Arguments Dialog Box

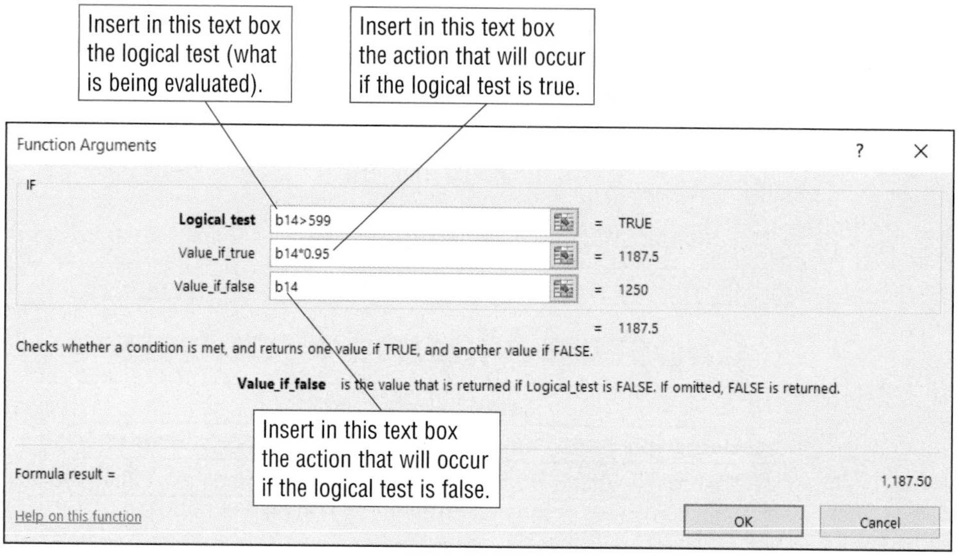
Insert in this text box the logical test (what is being evaluated).
Insert in this text box the action that will occur if the logical test is true.
Function Arguments
IF
Logical_test
b14>599
= TRUE
Value_if_true
b14*0.95
= 1187.5
Value_if_false
b14
= 1250
= 1187.5
Checks whether a condition is met, and returns one value if TRUE, and another value if FALSE.
Value_if_false is the value that is returned if Logical_test is FALSE. If omitted, FALSE is returned.
Insert in this text box the action that will occur if the logical test is false.
Formula result =
1,187.50
Help on this function
OK
Cancel

is 5% and multiplying the product price by 0.95 determines the price after the 5% discount is applied.) The *Value_if_false* text box contains *b14,* indicating that if the logical test is false (the product price is not greater than $599), then the amount from cell B14 is simply inserted.

Project 6b Writing a Formula with an IF Function Using the Function Arguments Dialog Box

Part 2 of 3

1. With **7-CMPReports.xlsx** open, insert a formula with an IF function using the Function Arguments dialog box by completing the following steps:
   a. Make cell C14 active.
   b. Click the Formulas tab.
   c. Click the Logical button in the Function Library group.
   d. Click *IF* at the drop-down list.
   e. At the Function Arguments dialog box, type b14>599 in the *Logical_test* text box and then press the Tab key.
   f. Type b14*0.95 in the *Value_if_true* text box and then press the Tab key.
   g. Type b14 in the *Value_if_false* text box.

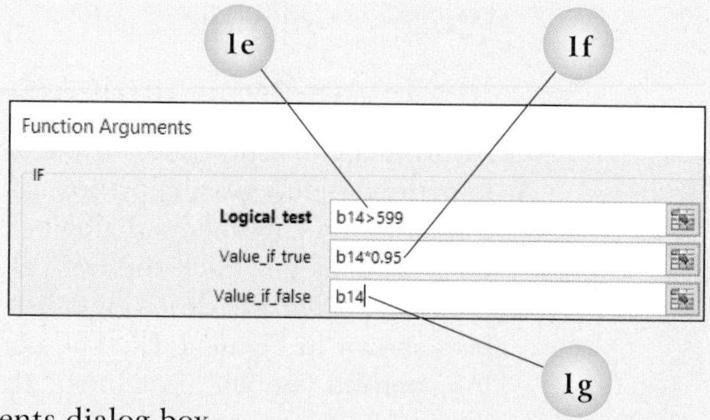
1e
1f
Function Arguments
IF
Logical_test
b14>599
Value_if_true
b14*0.95
Value_if_false
b14
1g

   h. Click OK to close the Function Arguments dialog box.
2. Copy the formula in cell C14 down into the range C15:C26.
3. Apply the Accounting format with a dollar symbol and two digits after the decimal point to cell C14.
4. Save **7-CMPReports.xlsx**.

Check Your Work

Writing IF Statements Containing Text

When writing a formula with an IF statement, if text is to be inserted in a cell rather than a value, insert quotation marks around the text. For example, in Step 2 of Project 6c, you will write a formula with an IF function that looks like this when written out:

> ***If*** the student averages more than 79 on the quizzes, ***then*** the student passes.
>
> ***If*** the student does not average more than 79 on the quizzes, ***then*** the student fails.

In Project 6c, you will write the formula so the word *PASS* is inserted in a cell if the average of the new employee quizzes is greater than 79 and the word *FAIL* is inserted if the condition is not met. The formula would be ***=IF(E31>79, "PASS", "FAIL")***. The quotation marks before and after *PASS* and *FAIL* identify the data as text rather than values.

The Function Arguments dialog box can be used to write a formula with an IF function that contains text. For example, in Step 3 of Project 6c, you will write a formula with an IF function using the Function Arguments dialog box that looks like this when written out:

> ***If*** the product price is greater than $599, ***then*** insert *YES*.
>
> ***If*** the product price is not greater than $599, ***then*** insert *NO*.

To create the formula in Step 3 using the Function Arguments dialog box, display the dialog box and then type *b14>599* in the *Logical_test* text box, *YES* in the *Value_if_true* text box, and *NO* in the *Value_if_false* text box. When you press the Enter key after typing *YES* in the *Value_if_true* text box, Excel automatically inserts quotation marks around the text. Excel will do the same thing for *NO* in the *Value_if_false* text box.

Project 6c Writing IF Statements Containing Text

Part 3 of 3

1. With **7-CMPReports.xlsx** open, insert quiz averages by completing the following steps:
   a. Make cell E31 active and then insert a formula that calculates the average of the test scores in the range B31:D31.
   b. Copy the formula in cell E31 down into the range E32:E35.
2. Write a formula with an IF function that inserts the word *PASS* if the quiz average is greater than 79 and inserts the word *FAIL* if the quiz average is not greater than 79. Write the formula by completing the following steps:
   a. Make cell F31 active.
   b. Type =if(e31>79,"PASS","FAIL") and then press the Enter key.

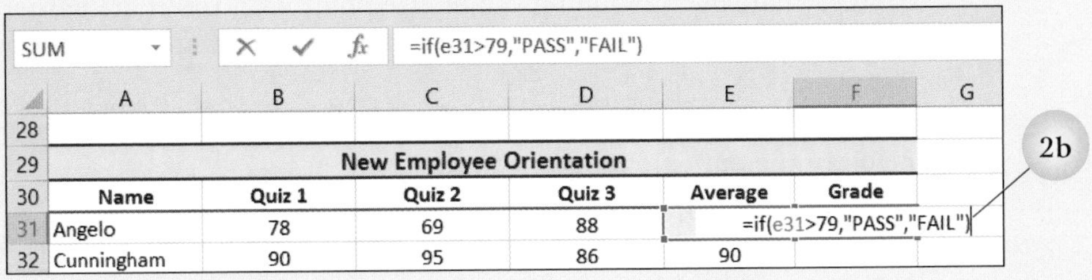

   c. Copy the formula in cell F31 down into the range F32:F35.

3. Write a formula with an IF function using the Function Arguments dialog box that inserts the word *YES* in the cell if the product price is greater than $599 and inserts the word *NO* if the price is not greater than $599. Write the formula by completing the following steps:
   a. Make cell D14 active.
   b. Click the Formulas tab.
   c. Click the Logical button in the Function Library group.
   d. Click *IF* at the drop-down list.
   e. Type b14>599 in the *Logical_test* text box and then press the Tab key.
   f. Type YES in the *Value_if_true* text box and then press the Tab key.
   g. Type NO in the *Value_if_false* text box.
   h. Click OK to close the Function Arguments dialog box.
   i. Copy the formula in cell D14 down into the range D15:D26.

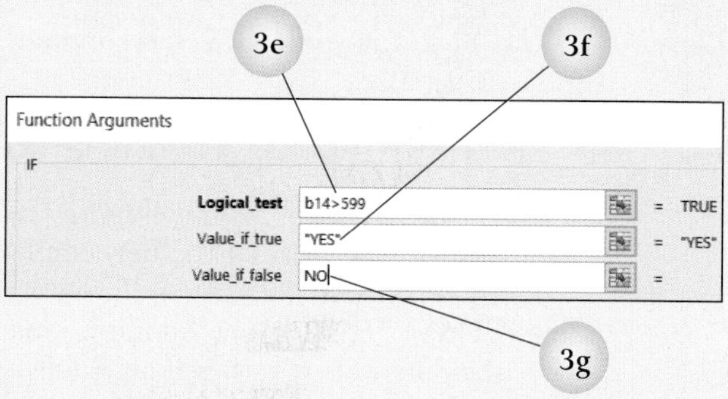

4. Save and then print **7-CMPReports.xlsx**.
5. Press Ctrl + ` to turn on the display of formulas.
6. Print the worksheet again. (The worksheet will print on two pages.)
7. Press Ctrl + ` to turn off the display of formulas.
8. Save and then close **7-CMPReports.xlsx**.

Check Your Work

Chapter Summary

- A chart is a visual presentation of data. Excel provides 15 basic chart types: Area, Bar, Box & Whisker, Column, Combo, Histogram, Line, Pie, Radar, Stock, Sunburst, Surface, Treemap, X Y (Scatter), and Waterfall.
- To create a chart, select the cells, click the Insert tab, and then click the chart button in the Charts group. Click the Recommended Charts button in the Charts group and Excel will recommend a type of chart for the data.
- A chart is inserted in the same worksheet as the selected cells by default.
- Change the size of a chart using the mouse by dragging one of the sizing handles that display around the border of the chart. When changing the chart size, maintain the proportions of the chart by pressing and holding down the Shift key while dragging a sizing handle.
- Move a chart by positioning the mouse pointer on the chart border until the pointer displays with a four-headed arrow attached and then dragging with the mouse.
- The data in the cells used to create the chart are linked to the chart. Changes made to the data are reflected in the chart.
- Three buttons appear outside the right border of a selected chart. Use the Chart Elements button to insert or remove chart elements, use the Chart Styles button to apply chart styles, and use the Chart Filters button to isolate specific data in the chart.

- Print a chart by selecting it, displaying the Print backstage area, and then clicking the Print button.
- When a chart is inserted in a worksheet, the Chart Tools Design tab is active. Use options on this tab to add chart elements, change the chart type, specify a different layout or style, and change the location of the chart.
- Choose a chart style with options in the Chart Styles group on the Chart Tools Design tab or at the Change Chart Type dialog box.
- Click the Switch Row/Column button in the Data group to change what Excel uses to determine the grouping of data along the horizontal axis and legend.
- Use the Quick Layout button in the Chart Layouts group to change the chart layout.
- Use the Change Colors button to apply different colors to a chart.
- By default, a chart is inserted in the active worksheet. The chart can be moved to a new worksheet within the workbook with the *New sheet* option at the Move Chart dialog box.
- Add chart elements with the Add Chart Element button arrow in the Chart Layouts group on the Chart Tools Design tab.
- Move a chart element by selecting it and then dragging it with the mouse. Use the sizing handles that display around a chart element to change its size. Delete a chart element by selecting it and then pressing the Delete key or by right-clicking the selected element and then clicking *Delete* at the shortcut menu.
- Customize the formatting of a chart and chart elements with options on the Chart Tools Format tab. Use these options to identify specific elements in the chart for formatting, insert a shape, apply formatting to a shape, apply WordArt formatting to data in a chart, and arrange, align, and size a chart.
- Insert a shape by clicking it in the Insert Shapes group on the Chart Tools Format tab and then clicking or dragging in the chart.
- Excel provides additional formatting options at a formatting task pane. A formatting task pane displays at the right side of the screen; the name and the contents in the task pane vary depending on whether the entire chart or an element in the chart is selected. Display a task pane by clicking the chart or element in the chart and then clicking the Format Selection button in the Current Selection group on the Chart Tools Format tab.
- Change the size of a chart with the *Shape Height* and *Shape Width* measurement boxes on the Chart Tools Format tab or at the Format Chart Area task pane.
- To delete a chart in a worksheet, click the chart to select it and then press the Delete key. To delete a chart created in a separate sheet, position the mouse pointer on the chart sheet tab, click the right mouse button, and then click *Delete*.
- Write a formula with the PMT function to calculate the payment for a loan based on constant payments and a constant interest rate. Write a formula with the FV function to calculate the future value of an investment based on periodic constant payments and a constant interest rate.
- A logical test is a question that can be answered true or false. Use the IF function to create a logical test that performs one action if the answer is true (condition met) or another action if the answer is false (condition not met).

Commands Review

FEATURE	RIBBON TAB, GROUP	BUTTON	KEYBOARD SHORTCUT
Change Chart Type dialog box	Chart Tools Design, Type		
chart or chart element task pane	Chart Tools Format, Current Selection		
financial functions	Formulas, Function Library		
logical functions	Formulas, Function Library		
Move Chart dialog box	Chart Tools Design, Location		
recommended chart	Insert, Charts		Alt + F1
recommended chart in separate sheet			F11

Workbook

Chapter study tools and assessment activities are available in the *Workbook* ebook. These resources are designed to help you further develop and demonstrate mastery of the skills learned in this chapter.

Microsoft®

Excel®

Adding Visual Interest to Workbooks

CHAPTER 8

Performance Objectives

Upon successful completion of Chapter 8, you will be able to:

1 Insert symbols and special characters
2 Insert, size, move, and format images
3 Insert screenshots
4 Draw, format, and copy shapes
5 Insert, format, and type text in text boxes
6 Insert and format SmartArt graphics
7 Insert and format WordArt

Precheck

Check your current skills to help focus your study.

Microsoft Excel includes a variety of features that you can use to enhance the appearance of a workbook. Some methods for adding visual appeal that you will learn in this chapter include inserting and modifying images, screenshots, shapes, text boxes, SmartArt, and WordArt.

Data Files

Before beginning the projects, copy the EL1C8 folder to your storage medium and then make EL1C8 the active folder.

SNAP

If you are a SNAP user, launch the Precheck and Tutorials from your Assignments page.

Project 1 **Insert Symbols, Images, and Shapes in a Financial Analysis Workbook** **5 Parts**

You will open a financial analysis workbook and then insert symbols and move, size, and format an image in the workbook. You will also insert an arrow shape, type and format text in the shape, and then copy the shape.

Preview Finished Project

Tutorial

Inserting Symbols and Special Characters

Symbol

Quick Steps

Insert a Symbol
1. Click in cell.
2. Click Insert tab.
3. Click Symbol button.
4. Double-click symbol.
5. Click Close.

Insert a Special Character
1. Click in cell.
2. Click Insert tab.
3. Click Symbol button.
4. Click Special Characters tab.
5. Double-click special character.
6. Click Close.

Hint Increase or decrease the size of the Symbol dialog box by positioning the mouse pointer on the lower right corner until the pointer displays as a two-headed arrow and then dragging with the mouse.

Inserting Symbols and Special Characters

Use the Symbol button on the Insert tab to insert symbols in a worksheet. Click the Symbol button in the Symbols group and the Symbol dialog box displays, as shown in Figure 8.1. At the Symbol dialog box, double-click a symbol and then click the Close button or click the symbol, click the Insert button, and then click the Close button. At the Symbol dialog box with the Symbols tab selected, additional symbols are available with different fonts. Change the font by clicking the *Font* option box arrow and then clicking a font at the drop-down list. Click the Special Characters tab at the Symbol dialog box and a list of special characters displays. Insert a special character by double-clicking a character and then clicking the Close button or by clicking the character, clicking the Insert button, and then clicking the Close button.

Figure 8.1 Symbol Dialog Box with Symbols Tab Selected

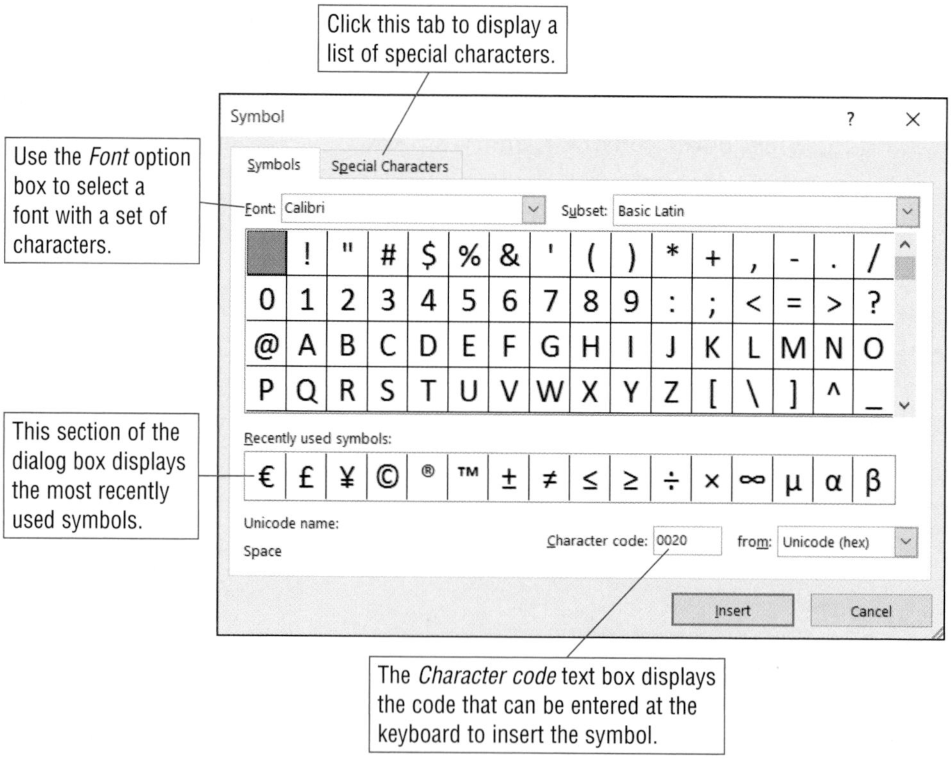
Click this tab to display a list of special characters.
Use the *Font* option box to select a font with a set of characters.
This section of the dialog box displays the most recently used symbols.
The *Character code* text box displays the code that can be entered at the keyboard to insert the symbol.
Symbol
Symbols
Special Characters
Font: Calibri
Subset: Basic Latin
Recently used symbols:
Unicode name:
Space
Character code: 0020
from: Unicode (hex)
Insert
Cancel

Project 1a Inserting Symbols and Special Characters

Part 1 of 5

1. Open **SMFFinCon.xlsx** and then save it with the name **8-SMFFinCon**.
2. Insert a symbol by completing the following steps:
   a. Double-click in cell A2.
   b. Delete the *e* that displays at the end of *Qualite*.
   c. With the insertion point positioned immediately right of the *t* in *Qualit*, click the Insert tab.
   d. Click the Symbol button in the Symbols group.
   e. At the Symbol dialog box, scroll down the list box and then click the *é* symbol (located in approximately the ninth through eleventh rows). (You can also type *00E9* in the *Character code* text box to select the symbol.)
   f. Click the Insert button and then click the Close button.

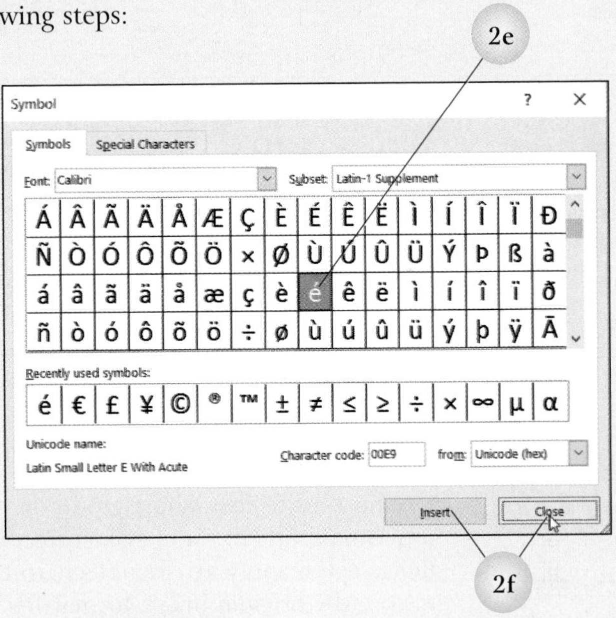

3. Insert a special character by completing the following steps:
   a. With cell A2 selected and in Edit mode, move the insertion point so it is positioned immediately right of *Group*.
   b. Click the Symbol button in the Symbols group.
   c. At the Symbol dialog box, click the Special Characters tab.
   d. Double-click the ® *Registered* symbol (tenth option from the top).
   e. Click the Close button.

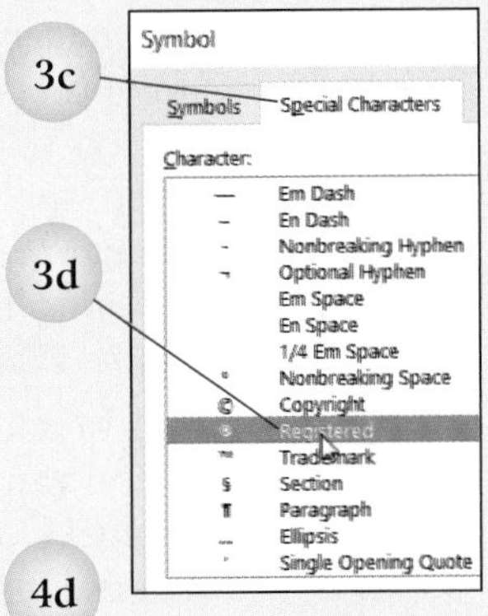

4. Insert a symbol by completing the following steps:
   a. With cell A2 selected and in Edit mode, move the insertion point so it is positioned immediately left of the *Q* in *Qualité*.
   b. Click the Symbol button in the Symbols group.
   c. At the Symbol dialog box, click the *Font* option box arrow and then click *Wingdings* at the drop-down list. (You will need to scroll down the list to display this option.)
   d. Click the ❖ symbol (located in approximately the fifth or sixth row). (You can also type *118* in the *Character code* text box to select the symbol.)
   e. Click the Insert button and then click the Close button.
5. Click in cell A3.
6. Save **8-SMFFinCon.xlsx**.

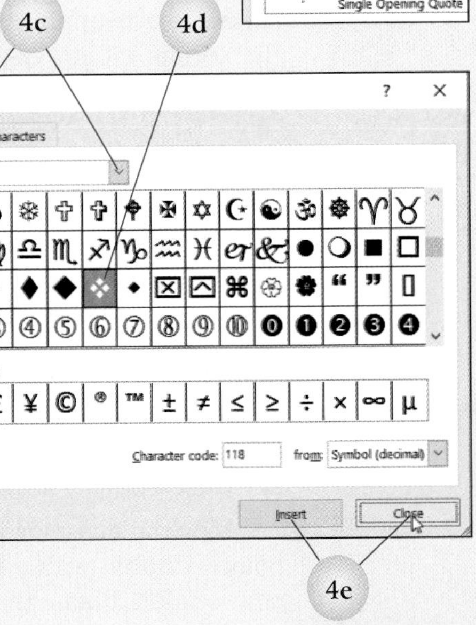

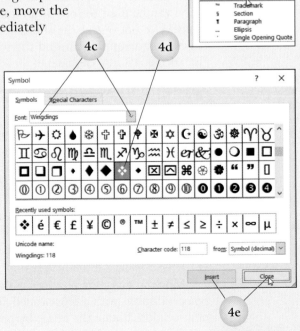

Check Your Work

Figure 8.2 Picture Tools Format Tab

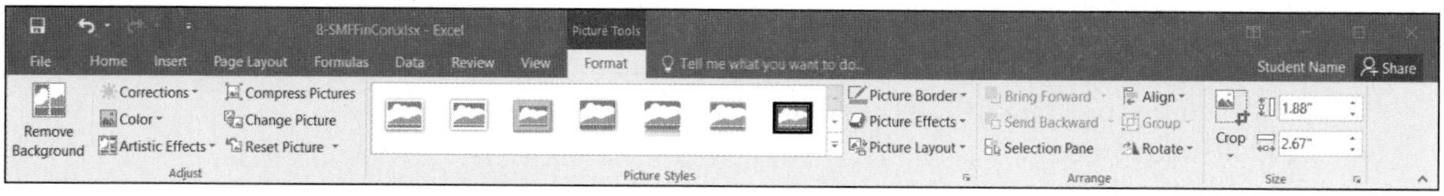

Tutorial

Inserting an Image

Pictures

Inserting an Image

Insert an image, such as a picture or clip art image, in an Excel workbook with buttons in the Illustrations group on the Insert tab. Click the Pictures button to display the Insert Picture dialog box with options for inserting an image from a folder on the computer or a removable drive. Or click the Online Pictures button and search for images online. When an image is inserted in a worksheet, the Picture Tools Format tab displays, as shown in Figure 8.2.

Tutorial

Modifying Images

Compress Pictures

Quick Steps

Insert an Image

1. Click Insert tab.
2. Click Pictures button.
3. Navigate to folder.
4. Double-click image.

Customizing and Formatting an Image

Use buttons in the Adjust group on the Picture Tools Format tab to remove unwanted parts of an image, correct the image brightness and contrast, change the image color, apply artistic effects to the image, change to a different image, and restore the original image formatting. Use the Compress Pictures button in the Adjust group to compress the size of an image file and reduce the amount of space the image requires on the storage medium. Use buttons in the Picture Styles group to apply a predesigned style to the image, change the image border, or apply other effects to the image. With options in the Arrange group, position the image on the page, specify how text will wrap around the image, align the image with other elements in the worksheet, and rotate the image. Use the Crop button in the Size group to remove any unwanted parts of the image and use the *Shape Height* and *Shape Width* measurement boxes to specify the image size.

In addition to options at the Picture Tools Format tab, options at the shortcut menu can be used to format an image. Display this menu by right-clicking the image. Use options at the shortcut menu to change the image, insert a caption, choose text wrapping around the image, size and position the image, and display the Format Picture task pane.

Sizing and Moving an Image

Change the size of an image with the *Shape Height* and *Shape Width* measurement boxes in the Size group on the Picture Tools Format tab or with the sizing handles that display around the selected image. To change size with a sizing handle, position the mouse pointer on a sizing handle until the pointer turns into a double-headed arrow and then drag in or out to decrease or increase the size of the image. Use the middle sizing handles at the left and right sides of the image to make the image wider or thinner. Use the middle sizing handles at the top and bottom of the image to make the image taller or shorter. Use the sizing handles at the corners of the image to change both the width and height at the same time. Press and hold down the Shift key while dragging a sizing handle to maintain the proportions of the image.

Move an image by positioning the mouse pointer on the image border until the pointer displays with a four-headed arrow attached and then dragging the image to the new location. Rotate the image by positioning the mouse pointer on the white round rotation handle until the pointer displays as a circular arrow. Click and hold down the left mouse button, drag in the desired direction, and then release the mouse button.

Project 1b Formatting an Image

Part 2 of 5

1. With **8-SMFFinCon.xlsx** open, insert an image by completing the following steps:
   a. Click the Insert tab and then click the Pictures button in the Illustrations group.
   b. At the Insert Picture dialog box, navigate to the EL1C8 folder on your storage medium and then double-click ***WallStreet.jpg***.
2. Change the size of the image by clicking in the *Shape Height* measurement box in the Size group on the Picture Tools Format tab, typing 2, and then pressing the Enter key.
3. Remove the yellow background from the image by completing the following steps:
   a. Click the Remove Background button in the Adjust group.
   b. Position the mouse pointer on the middle sizing handle at the top of the image until the pointer displays as an up-and-down-pointing arrow.
   c. Click and hold down the left mouse button, drag the border up to the top of the image, and then release the mouse button.
   d. Position the mouse pointer on the middle sizing handle at the bottom of the image until the pointer displays as an up-and-down-pointing arrow.
   e. Click and hold down the left mouse button, drag the border up 0.25 inch, and then release the mouse button.
   f. Click the Keep Changes button in the Close group on the Background Removal tab.

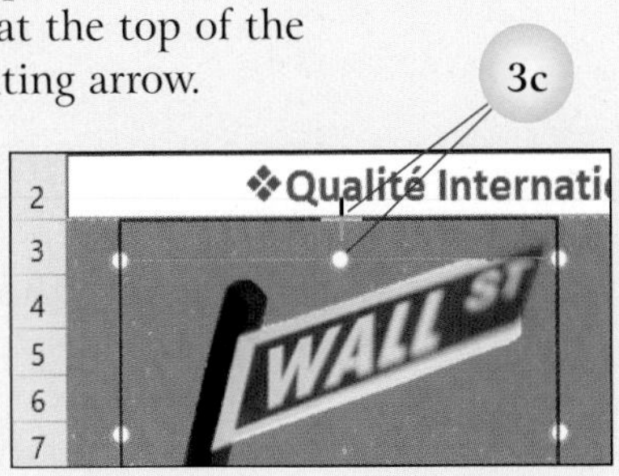

4. Change the color by clicking the Color button in the Adjust group and then clicking the *Blue, Accent color 1 Light* option (second column, third row in the *Recolor* section).
5. Apply a correction by clicking the Corrections button and then clicking the *Brightness: +20% Contrast: +20%* option (fourth column, fourth row in the *Brightness/Contrast* section).
6. Apply an artistic effect by clicking the Artistic Effects button and then clicking the *Glow Edges* option (last option in the drop-down gallery).

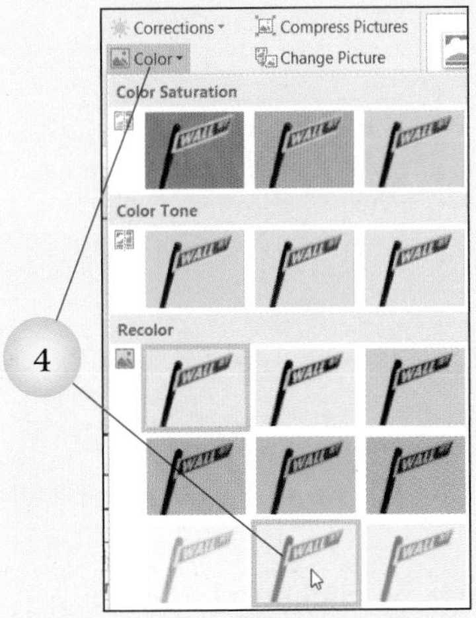

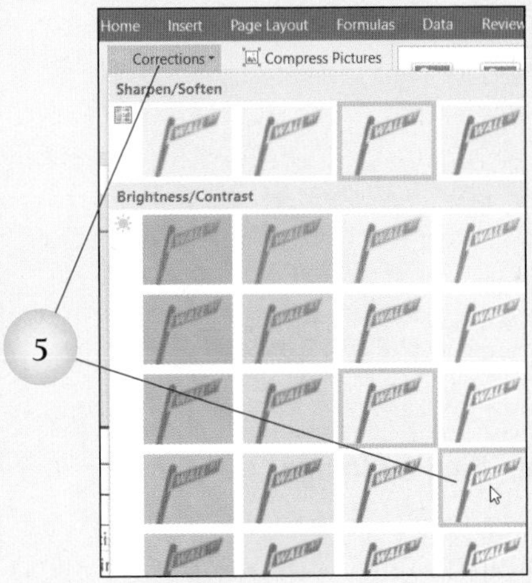

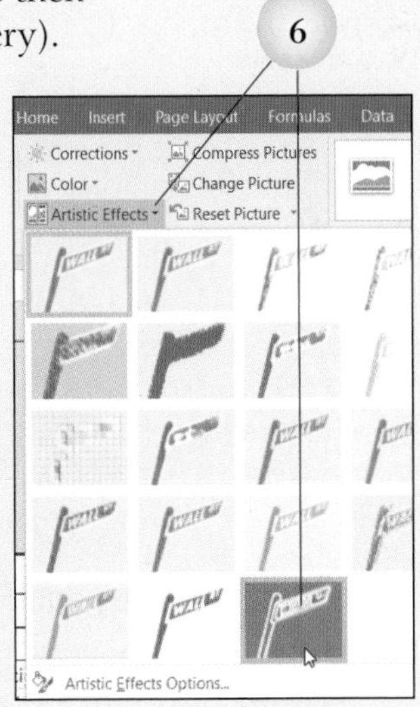

7. Move the image by completing the following steps:
   a. Position the mouse pointer on the image (displays with a four-headed arrow attached).
   b. Click and hold down the left mouse button, drag the image to the upper left corner of the worksheet, and then release the mouse button.
8. Save and then print **8-SMFFinCon.xlsx**.

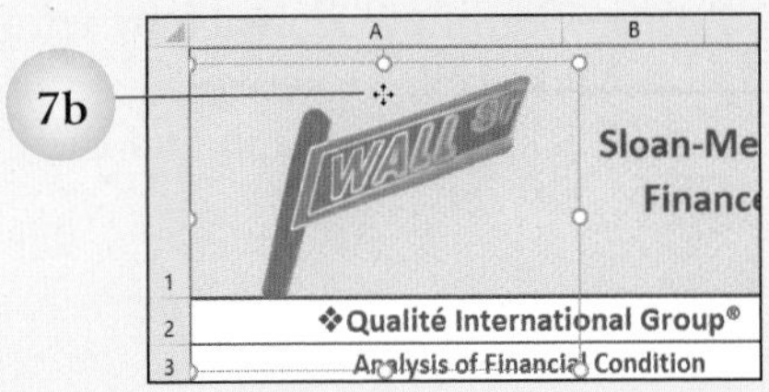

Check Your Work

Formatting an Image at the Format Picture Task Pane

In addition to the Picture Tools Format tab, the Format Picture task pane provides options for formatting an image. Click the Picture Styles group task pane launcher or the Size group task pane launcher and the Format Picture task pane displays at the right side of the screen. Click the Picture Styles group task pane launcher and the task pane displays with the Effects icon selected; click the Size group task pane launcher and the Size & Properties icon is selected. Two other icons are also available in this task pane: the Fill & Line icon and the Picture icon. The formatting options may need to be expanded. For example, click *Size* with the Size & Properties icon selected and options for changing the size of the image display. Close the task pane by clicking the Close button in the upper right corner.

Tutorial

Inserting an Online Image

Online Pictures

Quick Steps

Insert an Online Image
1. Click Insert tab.
2. Click Online Pictures button.
3. Type search word or topic.
4. Press Enter.
5. Double-click image.

Inserting an Online Image

Use the Bing Image Search feature to search for images online. To use this feature, click the Insert tab and then click the Online Pictures button in the Illustrations group. This displays the Insert Pictures window, shown in Figure 8.3. Click in the search text box, type the search term or topic, and then press the Enter key. Images that match the search term or topic display in the window. To insert an image, click the image and then click the Insert button or double-click the image. This downloads the image to the document. Customize the image with options and buttons on the Picture Tools Format tab.

Figure 8.3 Insert Pictures Window

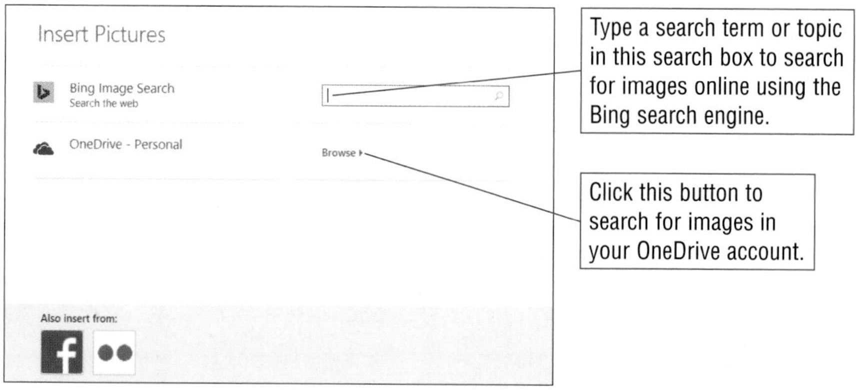
Insert Pictures
Bing Image Search
Search the web
OneDrive - Personal
Browse
Also insert from:
Type a search term or topic in this search box to search for images online using the Bing search engine.
Click this button to search for images in your OneDrive account.

Project 1c Inserting and Formatting an Image — Part 3 of 5

1. With **8-SMFFinCon.xlsx** open, delete the Wall Street sign image by clicking the image and then pressing the Delete key.
2. Insert a different image by completing the following steps:
   a. Make cell A1 active.
   b. Click the Insert tab and then click the Online Pictures button in the Illustrations group.

c. At the Insert Pictures window, type stock market clip art in the search box and then press the Enter key.

d. Double-click the graph image shown below and to the right. (If this image is not available online, click the Pictures button on the Insert tab. At the Insert Picture dialog box, navigate to your EL1C8 folder and then double-click ***StockMarket.png***.)

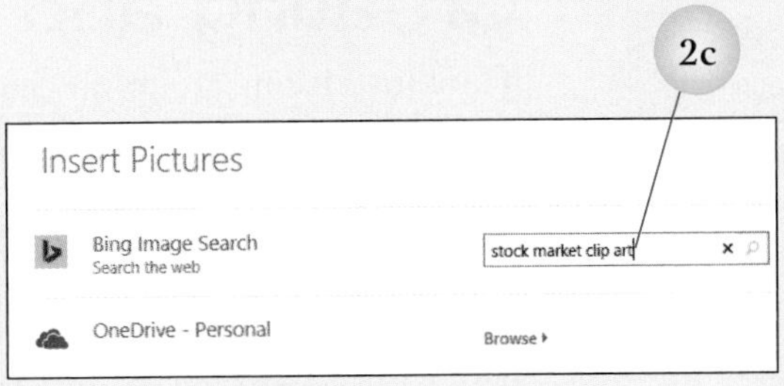

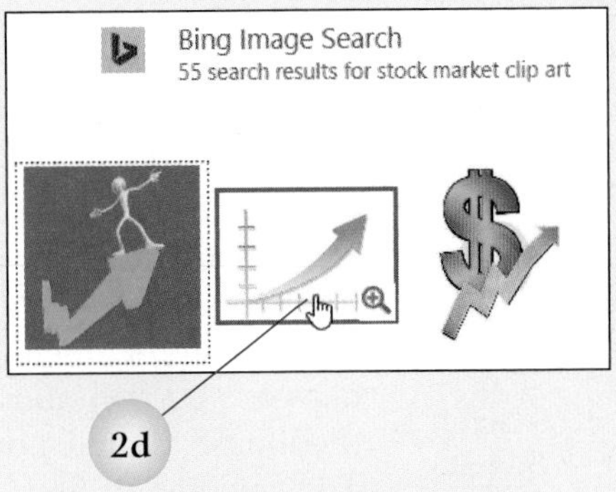

3. Display the Format Picture task pane with the Size & Properties icon selected by clicking the Size group task pane launcher on the Picture Tools Format tab.
4. If necessary, click *Size* in the task pane to display the sizing options.
5. Change the height of the image by selecting the current measurement in the *Height* measurement box, typing 1.65, and then pressing the Enter key. (The width automatically changes to maintain the proportions of the image.)
6. Change the properties of the image by clicking *Properties* to expand the options and then clicking the *Move and size with cells* option. (With this option selected, changing the size of the row also changes the size of the image.)

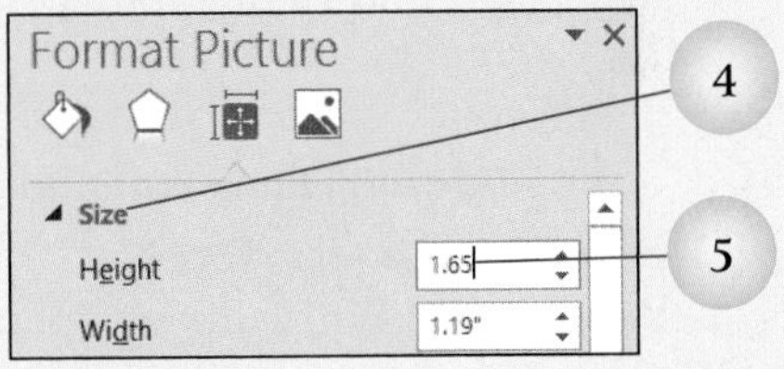

7. Make a correction to the image by completing the following steps:
   a. Click the Picture icon at the top of the task pane.
   b. Click *Picture Corrections* to expand the options.
   c. Select the current percentage in the *Brightness* text box and then type -25.
   d. Select the current percentage in the *Contrast* text box, type 45, and then press the Enter key.
8. Close the Format Picture task pane by clicking the Close button in the upper right corner.
9. Click outside the image to deselect it.
10. Increase the height of row 1 to 126.00 points and notice that the image size increases with the row height.
11. Save **8-SMFFinCon.xlsx**.

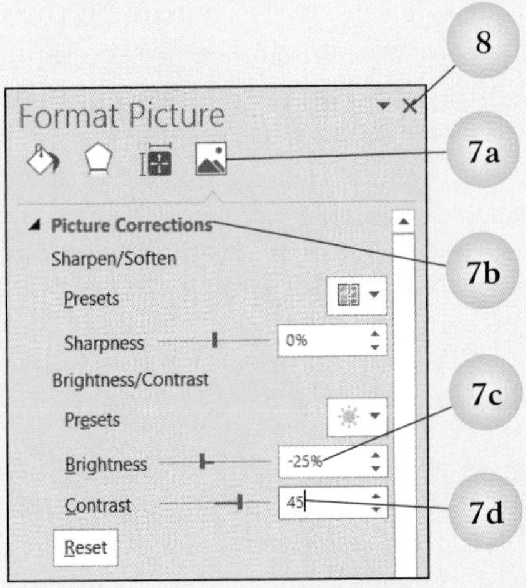

Check Your Work

Tutorial

Creating and Inserting a Screenshot

 Screenshot

Quick Steps

Insert a Screenshot

1. Open workbook.
2. Open another file.
3. Display information.
4. Make workbook active.
5. Click Insert tab.
6. Click Screenshot button.
7. Click window at drop-down list.

OR

1. Click Screenshot button and then *Screen Clipping*.
2. Drag to specify capture area.

Creating and Inserting a Screenshot

The Illustrations group on the Insert tab contains a Screenshot button that can be used to capture all or part of the contents of a screen as an image. This is useful for capturing information from a web page or a file in another program. To capture the entire screen, display a web page or open a file from a program, make Excel active, and then open a workbook or blank workbook. Click the Insert tab, click the Screenshot button, and then click the screen thumbnail at the drop-down list. The currently active worksheet does not display as a thumbnail at the drop-down list—only any other open file or program displays. If no other file or program is open, the Windows desktop displays. Click the thumbnail at the drop-down list and the screenshot is inserted as an image in the open workbook, the image is selected, and the Picture Tools Format tab is active. Use buttons on this tab to customize the screenshot image.

A screenshot can also be made of a specific portion of the screen by clicking the *Screen Clipping* option at the Screenshot button drop-down list. Click this option and the open web page, file, or Windows desktop displays in a dimmed manner and the mouse pointer displays as crosshairs (a plus symbol [+]). Using the mouse, draw a border around the specific area of the screen to be captured. The area identified is inserted in the workbook as an image, the image is selected, and the Picture Tools Format tab is active.

Project 1d **Inserting and Formatting a Screenshot** Part 4 of 5

1. With **8-SMFFinCon.xlsx** open, make sure that no other programs are open.
2. Open Word and then open **SMFProfile.docx** from your EL1C8 folder.
3. Click the Excel button on the taskbar.
4. Insert a screenshot of the table in the Word document by completing the following steps:
   a. Click the Insert tab.
   b. Click the Screenshot button in the Illustrations group and then click *Screen Clipping* at the drop-down list.
   c. When **SMFProfile.docx** displays in a dimmed manner, position the mouse crosshairs in the upper left corner of the table, click and hold down the left mouse button, drag down to the lower right corner of the table, and then release the mouse button. (This creates a screenshot of the entire table.)

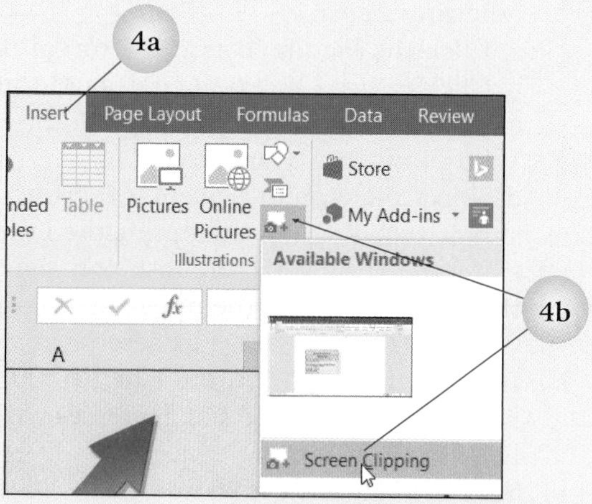

5. With the screenshot image inserted in **8-SMFFinCon.xlsx**, make the following changes:
   a. Click in the *Shape Width* measurement box in the Size group on the Picture Tools Format tab, type 3.7, and then press the Enter key.

b. Click the Corrections button and then click the *Sharpen: 25%* option (fourth option in the *Sharpen/Soften* section).
c. Click the Corrections button and then click the *Brightness: 0% (Normal) Contrast: -40%* (third column, first row in the *Brightness/Contrast* section).
d. Using the mouse, drag the screenshot image one row below the data in row 10.

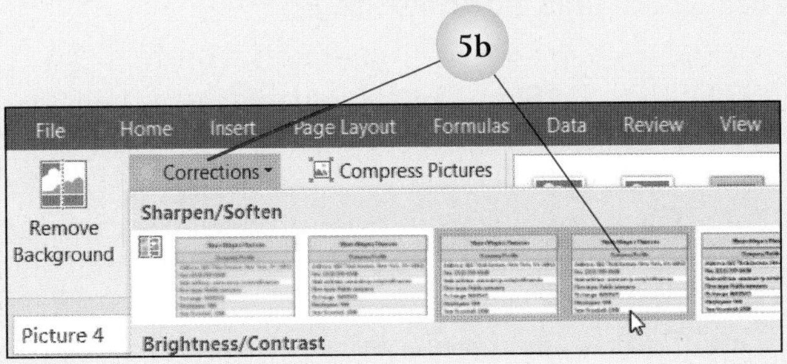

6. Make cell A4 active.
7. Save **8-SMFFinCon.xlsx**.
8. Click the Word button on the taskbar, close **SMFProfile.docx**, and then close Word.

Check Your Work

Tutorial
Inserting a Shape

Tutorial
Formatting a Shape

Shapes

Quick Steps

Insert a Shape
1. Click Insert tab.
2. Click Shapes button.
3. Click desired shape at drop-down list.
4. Click or drag in worksheet.

Copy a Shape
1. Select shape.
2. Click Copy button.
3. Position insertion point in new location.
4. Click Paste button.

OR
1. Select shape.
2. Press and hold down Ctrl key.
3. Drag shape to new location.

Inserting and Formatting a Shape

Chapter 7 covered how to insert shapes in a chart with options on the Chart Tools Format tab. Shapes can also be inserted in a worksheet with the Shapes button in the Illustrations group on the Insert tab. Use the Shapes button to draw shapes in a worksheet, including lines, basic shapes, block arrows, flow chart symbols, callouts, stars, and banners. Click a shape and the mouse pointer displays as crosshairs. Click in the worksheet or position the crosshairs where the shape is to begin, click and hold down the left mouse button, drag to create the shape, and then release the mouse button. Click or drag in the worksheet and the shape is inserted and the Drawing Tools Format tab, shown in Figure 8.4, becomes active. Use options and buttons on this tab to choose a shape, apply a style to a shape, arrange a shape, and change the size of a shape.

Choose a shape in the *Lines* section of the Shapes button drop-down list and the shape that is drawn is considered a line drawing. Choose an option in another section of the drop-down list and the shape drawn is considered an enclosed object. When drawing an enclosed object, maintain the proportions of the shape by pressing and holding down the Shift key while dragging with the mouse. Text can be typed in an enclosed object and then formatted using buttons in the WordArt Styles group (or options on the Home tab).

Copy a shape in a worksheet by selecting the shape and then clicking the Copy button in the Clipboard group on the Home tab. Make active the cell where the shape is to be copied and then click the Paste button. A shape can also be copied by pressing and holding down the Ctrl key while dragging the shape to the new location.

Figure 8.4 Drawing Tools Format Tab

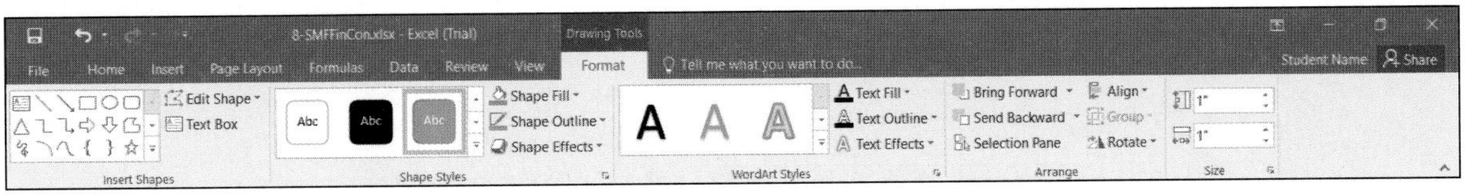

1. With **8-SMFFinCon.xlsx** open, create the larger arrow shown in Figure 8.5 by completing the following steps:
   a. Click the Insert tab.
   b. Click the Shapes button in the Illustrations group and then click the *Up Arrow* shape (third column, first row in the *Block Arrows* section).
   c. Position the mouse pointer (displays as crosshairs) near the upper left corner of cell D1 and then click the left mouse button. (This inserts the arrow in the worksheet.)

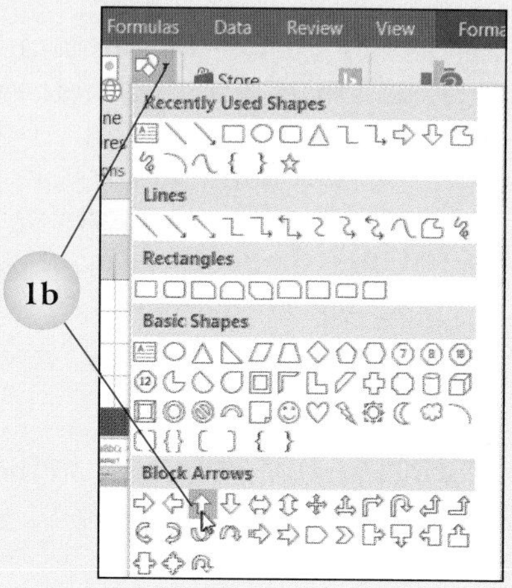

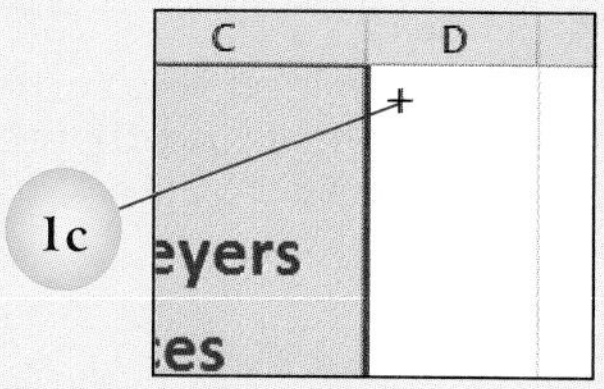

   d. Click in the *Shape Height* measurement box and then type 3.7.
   e. Click in the *Shape Width* measurement box, type 2.1, and then press the Enter key.
   f. If necessary, drag the arrow so it is positioned as shown in Figure 8.5. (To drag the arrow, position the mouse pointer on the border of the selected arrow until the pointer displays with a four-headed arrow attached, click and hold down the left mouse button, drag the arrow to the new position, and then release the mouse button.)
   g. Click the More Shape Styles button in the Shape Styles group on the Drawing Tools Format tab and then click the *Intense Effect - Blue, Accent 1* option (second column, last row in the *Theme Styles* section).
   h. Click the Shape Effects button in the Shape Styles group, point to *Glow*, and then click the *Orange, 11 pt glow, Accent color 2* option (second column, third row in the *Glow Variations* section).

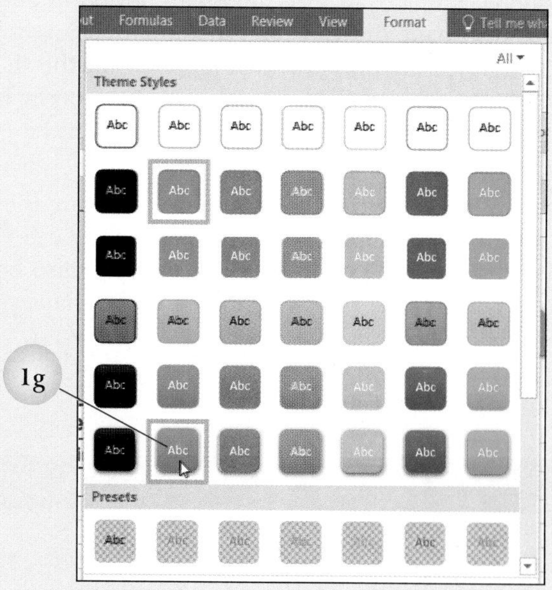

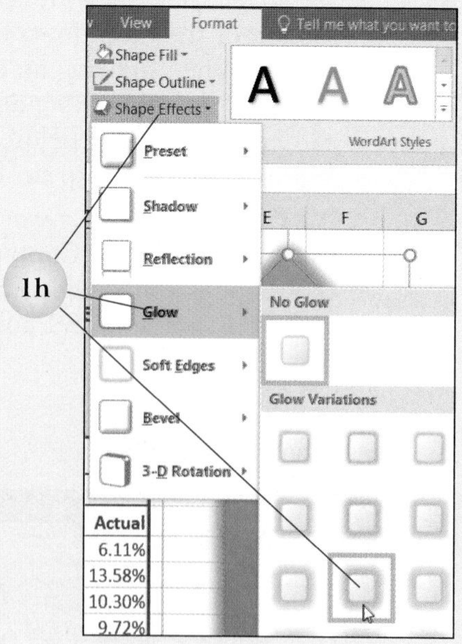

2. Insert text in the arrow by completing the following steps:
   a. With the arrow selected, type McGuire Mutual Shares 5.33%.
   b. Select the text you just typed (*McGuire Mutual Shares 5.33%*).
   c. Click the More WordArt Styles button in the WordArt Styles group and then click the *Fill - White, Outline - Accent 2, Hard Shadow - Accent 2* option (fourth column, third row).
   d. Press Ctrl + E to center the text.

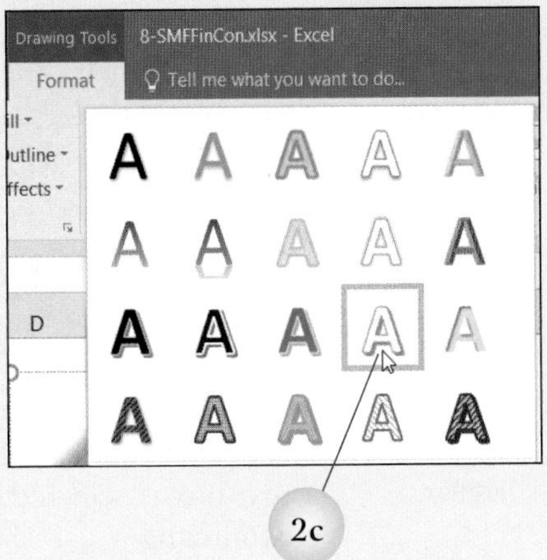

3. With the arrow selected, copy it by completing the following steps:
   a. Press and hold down the Ctrl key.
   b. Position the mouse pointer on the arrow border until the pointer displays with a square box and plus symbol attached.
   c. Click and hold down the left mouse button and drag to the right so the outline of the arrow is positioned at the right side of the existing arrow.
   d. Release the mouse button and then release the Ctrl key.
4. Format the second arrow by completing the following steps:
   a. With the second arrow selected, click in the *Shape Height* measurement box on the Drawing Tools Format tab and then type 2.
   b. Click in the *Shape Width* measurement box, type 1.6, and then press the Enter key.
   c. Select the text *McGuire Mutual Shares 5.33%* and then type SR Linus Fund 0.22%.
   d. Drag the arrow so it is positioned as shown in Figure 8.5.
5. Change to landscape orientation. (Make sure the cells containing the data, screenshot image, and arrows will print on the same page.)
6. Save, print, and then close **8-SMFFinCon.xlsx**.

Check Your Work

Figure 8.5 Project 1e

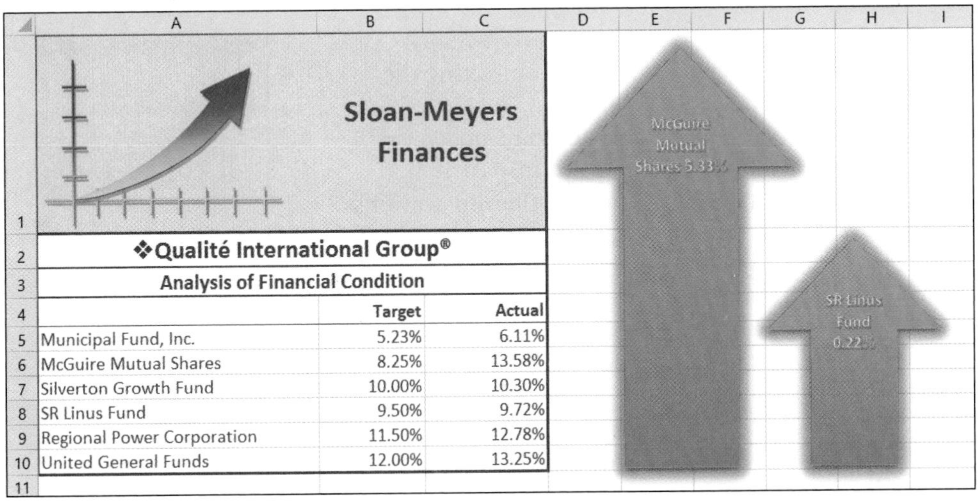

Sloan-Meyers Finances		
❖Qualité International Group®		
Analysis of Financial Condition		
	Target	Actual
Municipal Fund, Inc.	5.23%	6.11%
McGuire Mutual Shares	8.25%	13.58%
Silverton Growth Fund	10.00%	10.30%
SR Linus Fund	9.50%	9.72%
Regional Power Corporation	11.50%	12.78%
United General Funds	12.00%	13.25%

Project 2 **Insert an Image and Text Box in a Division Sales Workbook** **1 Part**

You will open a division sales workbook and then insert, move, and size an image. You will also insert a text box and then format the text.

Preview Finished Project

Tutorial

Inserting and Modifying Text Boxes

Text Box

Quick Steps

Draw a Text Box
1. Click Insert tab.
2. Click Text Box button.
3. Click or drag in worksheet to create text box.

Inserting and Modifying Text Boxes

Use the Text Box button on the Insert tab to draw a text box in a worksheet. To draw a text box, click the Insert tab and then click the Text Box button in the Text group. This causes the mouse pointer to display as a long, thin, crosslike pointer. Position the pointer in the worksheet and then drag to create the text box. When a text box is selected, the Drawing Tools Format tab displays with options for customizing it.

Click a text box to select it and a dashed border and sizing handles display around it. To delete the text box, click the border again to change the dashed lines to solid lines and then press the Delete key.

Project 2 Inserting and Customizing an Image and a Text Box

Part 1 of 1

1. Open **SPDivSales.xlsx** and then save it with the name **8-SPDivSales**.
2. Make the following changes to the bird image:
   a. Click the image to select it.
   b. Click the Picture Tools Format tab.
   c. Click the Rotate button in the Arrange group and then click *Flip Horizontal* at the drop-down list.

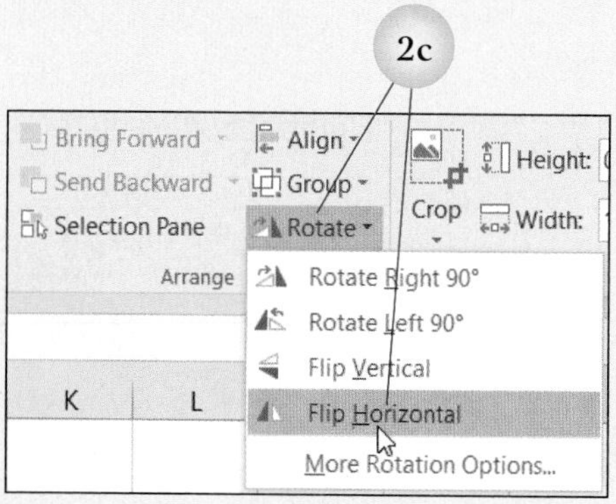

3. Insert and format an image by completing the following steps:
   a. Click in cell A1 outside the bird image.
   b. Click the Insert tab.
   c. Click the Pictures button in the Illustrations group.
   d. At the Insert Picture dialog box, navigate to the EL1C8 folder on your storage medium and then double-click ***Ocean.jpg***.
   e. With the image selected, click the Send Backward button in the Arrange group on the Picture Tools Format tab.
   f. Use the sizing handles that display around the image to move and size it so it fills cell A1, as shown in Figure 8.6.
   g. If necessary, click the bird image and then drag it so it is positioned as shown in Figure 8.6.

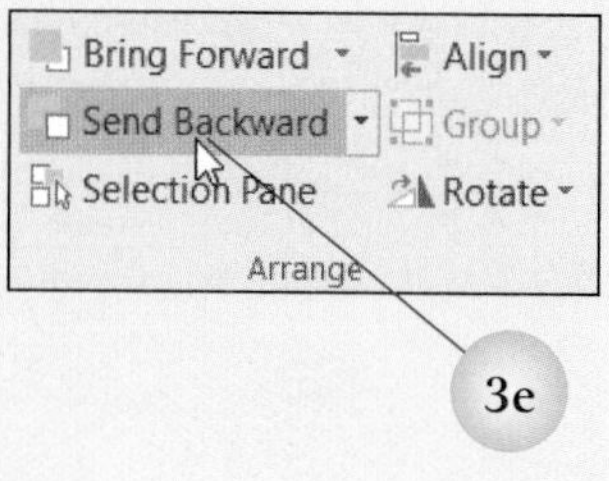

4. Save **8-SPDivSales.xlsx**.

5. Draw a text box by completing the following steps:
   a. Click the Insert tab.
   b. Click the Text Box button in the Text group.
   c. Drag into cell A1 to draw a text box the approximate size and shape shown at the right.

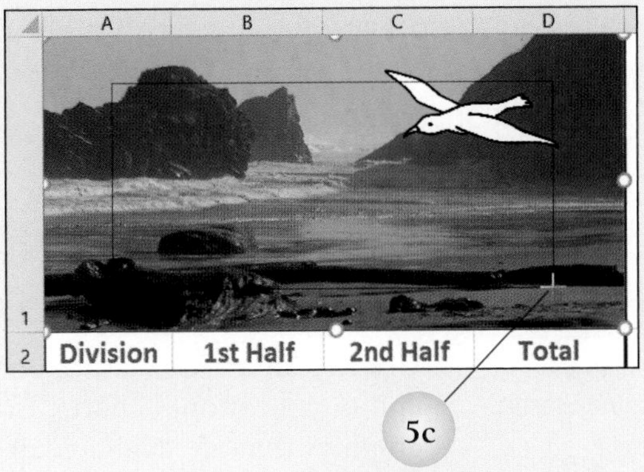

6. Format the text box by completing the following steps:
   a. Click the Drawing Tools Format tab.
   b. Click the Shape Fill button arrow in the Shape Styles group and then click *No Fill* at the drop-down gallery.
   c. Click the Shape Outline button arrow in the Shape Styles group and then click *No Outline* at the drop-down gallery.

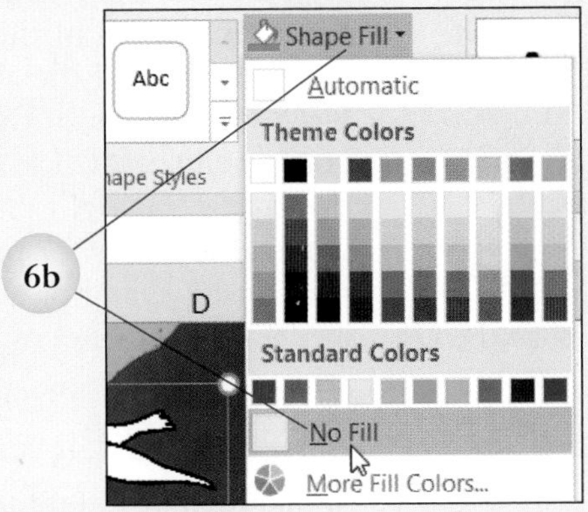

7. Insert text in the text box by completing the following steps:
   a. With the text box selected, click the Home tab.
   b. Click the *Font* option box arrow and then click *Lucida Calligraphy* at the drop-down gallery. (Scroll down the gallery to display this font.)
   c. Click the *Font Size* option box arrow and then click *32* at the drop-down gallery.
   d. Click the Font Color button arrow and then click *White, Background 1* (first column, first row in the *Theme Colors* section).
   e. Type Seabird Productions.
8. Move the text box so the text is positioned in cell A1 as shown in Figure 8.6.
9. Save, print, and then close **8-SPDivSales.xlsx**.

Check Your Work

Figure 8.6 Project 2

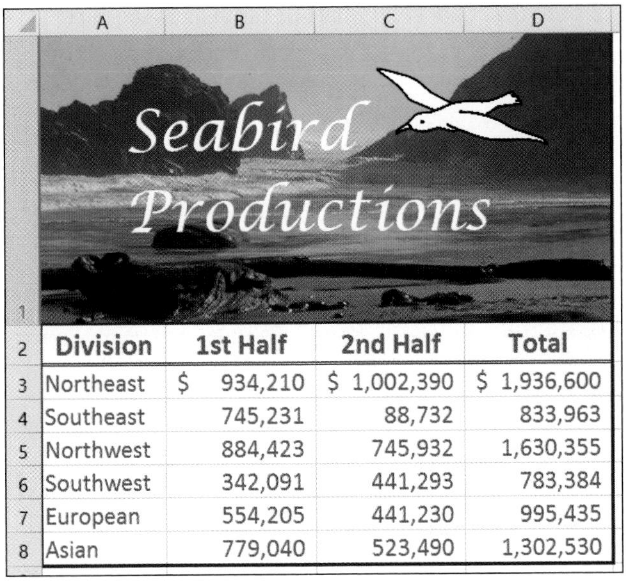

Division	1st Half	2nd Half	Total
Northeast	$ 934,210	$ 1,002,390	$ 1,936,600
Southeast	745,231	88,732	833,963
Northwest	884,423	745,932	1,630,355
Southwest	342,091	441,293	783,384
European	554,205	441,230	995,435
Asian	779,040	523,490	1,302,530

Project 3 Insert and Format SmartArt Graphics in a Company Sales Workbook **4 Parts**

You will open a workbook that contains two company sales worksheets. You will insert and format a SmartArt cycle graphic in one worksheet and a SmartArt relationship graphic in the other. You will also create and format WordArt text.

Preview Finished Project

Tutorial

Inserting a SmartArt Graphic

SmartArt

Quick Steps

Insert a SmartArt Graphic

1. Click Insert tab.
2. Click SmartArt button.
3. Double-click graphic.

Inserting a SmartArt Graphic

Use the SmartArt feature included in Excel to insert graphics, such as diagrams and organizational charts, in a worksheet. SmartArt offers a variety of predesigned graphics that are available at the Choose a SmartArt Graphic dialog box, shown in Figure 8.7. Display this dialog box by clicking the Insert tab and then clicking the SmartArt button in the Illustrations group. At the dialog box, *All* is selected in the left panel and all the available predesigned graphics display in the middle panel. Use the scroll bar at the right side of the middle panel to scroll down the list of graphic choices. Click a graphic in the middle panel and the name of the graphic displays in the right panel along with a description of the graphic type. SmartArt includes graphics for presenting lists of data; showing data processes, cycles, and relationships; and presenting data in a matrix or pyramid. Double-click a graphic in the middle panel of the dialog box and the graphic is inserted in the worksheet.

Entering Data in a SmartArt Graphic

Text Pane

Hint Generally, you would use a SmartArt graphic to represent text and a chart to represent numbers.

Some SmartArt graphics are designed to include text. Type text in a graphic by selecting a shape in the graphic and then typing text in the shape or display a text pane and then type text in the pane. Display the text pane by clicking the Text Pane button in the Create Graphic group on the SmartArt Tools Design tab. Turn off the display of the pane by clicking the Text Pane button or clicking the Close button in the upper right corner of the pane.

Figure 8.7 Choose a SmartArt Graphic Dialog Box

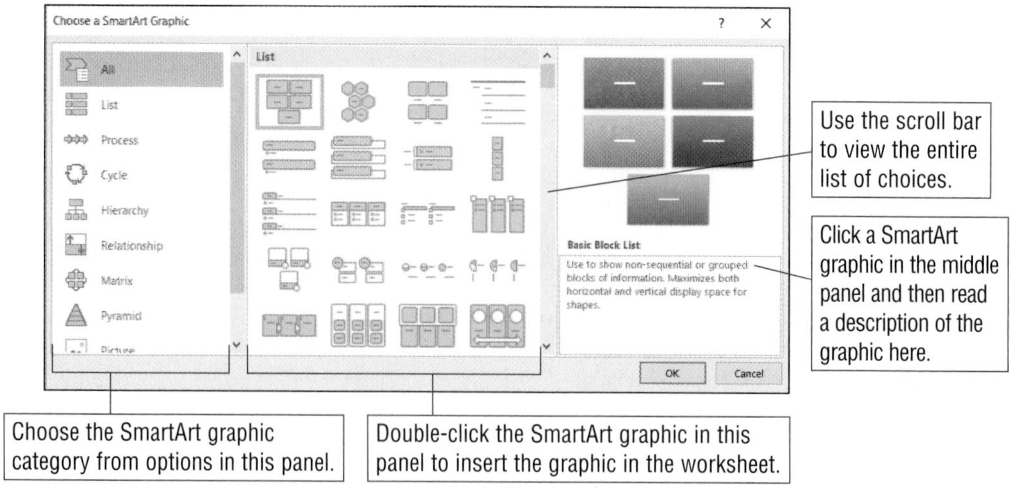
Choose a SmartArt Graphic
All
List
Process
Cycle
Hierarchy
Relationship
Matrix
Pyramid
Picture
List
Basic Block List
Use to show non-sequential or grouped blocks of information. Maximizes both horizontal and vertical display space for shapes.
OK
Cancel
Use the scroll bar to view the entire list of choices.
Click a SmartArt graphic in the middle panel and then read a description of the graphic here.
Choose the SmartArt graphic category from options in this panel.
Double-click the SmartArt graphic in this panel to insert the graphic in the worksheet.

Tutorial

Modifying a SmartArt Graphic

Sizing, Moving, and Deleting a SmartArt Graphic

Increase or decrease the size of a SmartArt graphic by dragging one of the sizing handles that display around the selected graphic. Use the corner sizing handles to increase or decrease the height and width at the same time. Use the middle sizing handles to increase or decrease the height or width of the SmartArt graphic.

To move a SmartArt graphic, select it and then position the mouse pointer on the graphic border until the pointer displays with a four-headed arrow attached. Click and hold down the left mouse button, drag the graphic to the new position, and then release the mouse button. Delete a graphic by selecting it and then pressing the Delete key.

Project 3a Inserting, Moving, and Sizing a SmartArt Graphic in a Worksheet — Part 1 of 4

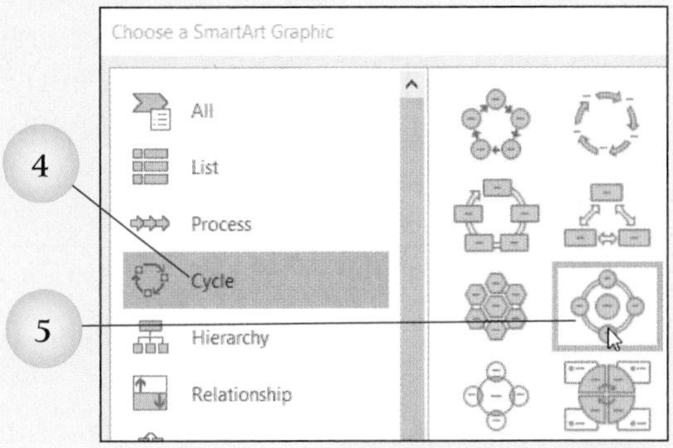

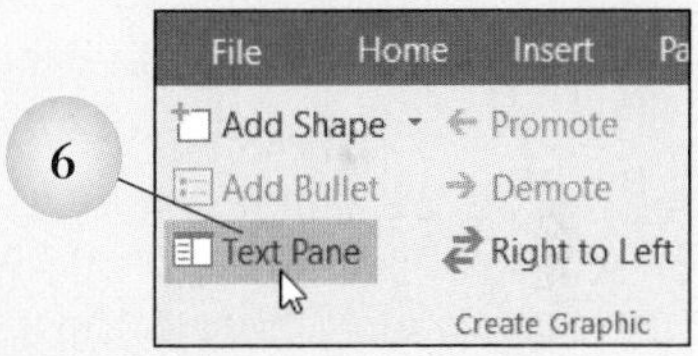

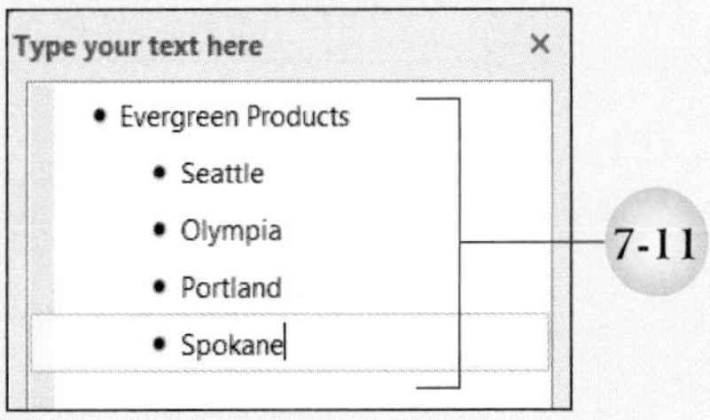

1. Open **EPCoSales.xlsx** and then save it with the name **8-EPCoSales**.
2. Create the SmartArt graphic shown in Figure 8.8. To begin, click the Insert tab.
3. Click the SmartArt button in the Illustrations group.
4. At the Choose a SmartArt Graphic dialog box, click *Cycle* in the left panel.
5. Double-click *Radial Cycle* in the middle panel.
6. If the text pane is not open, click the Text Pane button in the Create Graphic group. (The text pane will display at the left side of the SmartArt graphic.)
7. With the insertion point positioned after the top bullet in the text pane, type Evergreen Products.
8. Click in the *[Text]* placeholder below *Evergreen Products* and then type Seattle.
9. Click in the next *[Text]* placeholder and then type Olympia.
10. Click in the next *[Text]* placeholder and then type Portland.
11. Click in the next *[Text]* placeholder and then type Spokane.
12. Click the Text Pane button to turn off the display of the text pane.
13. Drag the SmartArt graphic so it is positioned as shown in Figure 8.8. To drag the graphic, position the mouse pointer on the graphic border until the pointer displays with a four-headed arrow attached. Click and hold down the left mouse button, drag the graphic to the new position, and then release the mouse button.
14. Use the sizing handles that display around the SmartArt graphic to increase or decrease the size so it displays as shown in Figure 8.8. Note: The color of the graphic will be changed in Project 3b.
15. Save **8-EPCoSales.xlsx**.

Check Your Work

Figure 8.8 Projects 3a and 3b

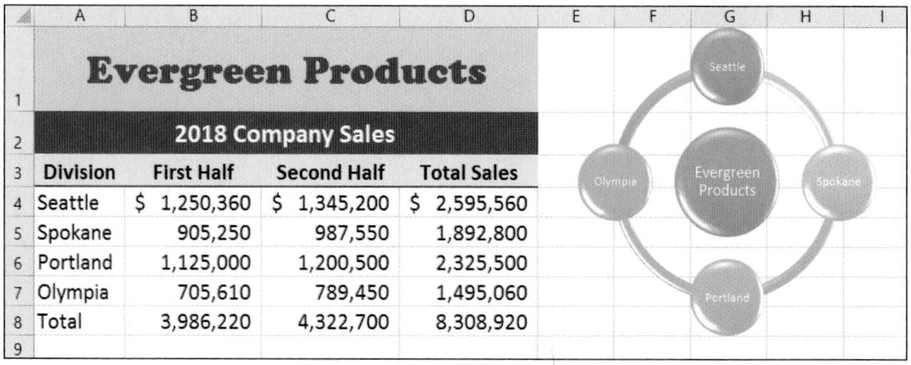

	A	B	C	D
1	Evergreen Products			
2	2018 Company Sales			
3	Division	First Half	Second Half	Total Sales
4	Seattle	$ 1,250,360	$ 1,345,200	$ 2,595,560
5	Spokane	905,250	987,550	1,892,800
6	Portland	1,125,000	1,200,500	2,325,500
7	Olympia	705,610	789,450	1,495,060
8	Total	3,986,220	4,322,700	8,308,920
9				

Changing the SmartArt Graphic Design

Hint To restore the SmartArt default layout and color, click the Reset Graphic button in the Reset group on the SmartArt Tools Design tab.

Double-click a SmartArt graphic at the Choose a SmartArt Graphic dialog box and the graphic is inserted in the worksheet and the SmartArt Tools Design tab is active. Use options and buttons on this tab to add objects, change the graphic layout, apply a style to the graphic, and reset the original formatting of the graphic.

Project 3b Changing the SmartArt Graphic Design

Part 2 of 4

1. With **8-EPCoSales.xlsx** open, make sure the SmartArt Tools Design tab is active and then click the *Spokane* circle shape in the graphic to select it.
2. Click the Right to Left button in the Create Graphic group. (This switches *Olympia* and *Spokane*.)
3. Click the More SmartArt Styles button in the SmartArt Styles group and then click the *Polished* option at the drop-down list (first column, first row in the *3-D* section).

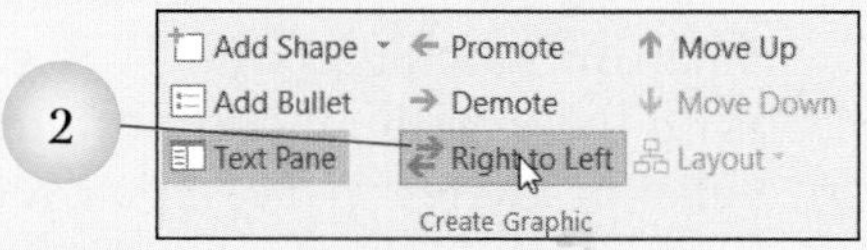

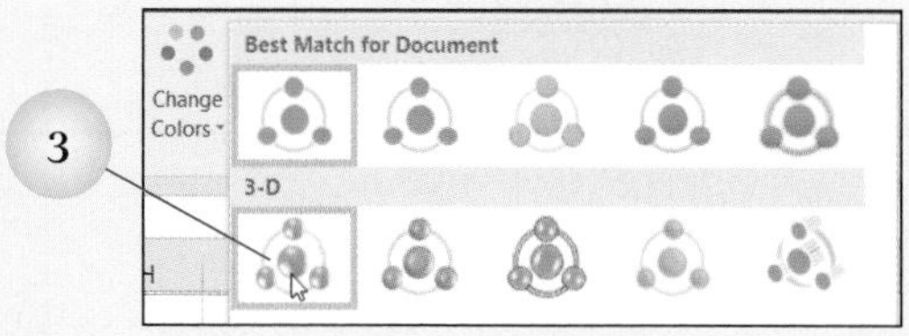

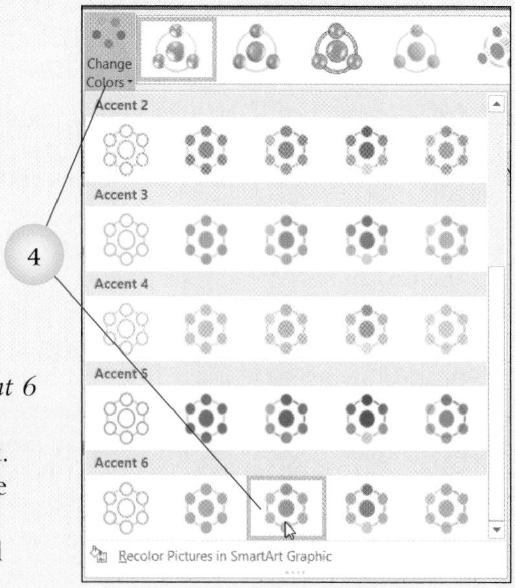

4. Click the Change Colors button in the SmartArt Styles group, scroll down the drop-down gallery, and then click the *Gradient Range - Accent 6* option (third option in the *Accent 6* section).
5. Click outside the SmartArt graphic to deselect it.
6. Change to landscape orientation. (Make sure the graphic fits on the first page.)
7. Save **8-EPCoSales.xlsx** and then print the Total Sales worksheet.

Check Your Work

Changing the SmartArt Graphic Formatting

Click the SmartArt Tools Format tab and options display for formatting a SmartArt graphic. Use buttons on this tab to insert and customize shapes; apply a shape style; apply WordArt styles; and specify the position, alignment, rotation, wrapping style, height, and width of a graphic.

Project 3c Changing the SmartArt Graphic Formatting

Part 3 of 4

1. With **8-EPCoSales.xlsx** open, click the Seattle Sales worksheet tab.
2. Create the SmartArt graphic shown in Figure 8.9. To begin, click the Insert tab and then click the SmartArt button in the Illustrations group.
3. At the Choose a SmartArt Graphic dialog box, click *Relationship* in the left panel and then double-click *Gear* in the middle panel.

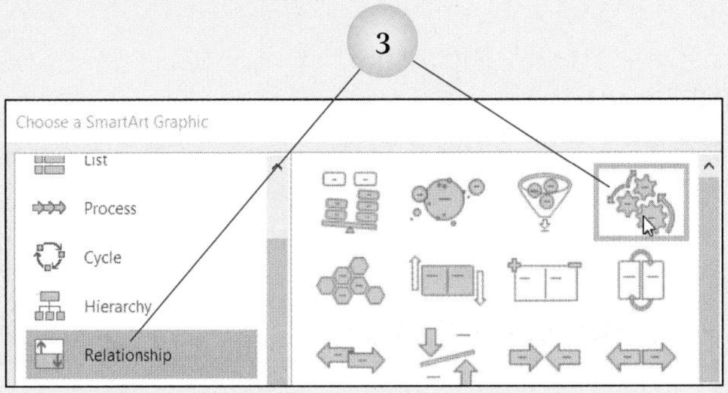

4. Click in the *[Text]* placeholder in the bottom gear and then type Quality Products.
5. Click in the *[Text]* placeholder in the left gear and then type Customized Plans.
6. Click in the *[Text]* placeholder in the top gear and then type Exemplary Service.
7. Click inside the SmartArt graphic border but outside any specific shape.
8. Click the More SmartArt Styles button in the SmartArt Styles group and then click the *Inset* option (second column, first row in the *3-D* section).
9. Click the Change Colors button in the SmartArt Styles group and then click the *Gradient Loop - Accent 6* option (fourth option in the *Accent 6* section).
10. Click the SmartArt Tools Format tab.
11. Click in the *Shape Height* measurement box in the Size group and then type 4.
12. Click in the *Shape Width* measurement box, type 4.5, and then press the Enter key.

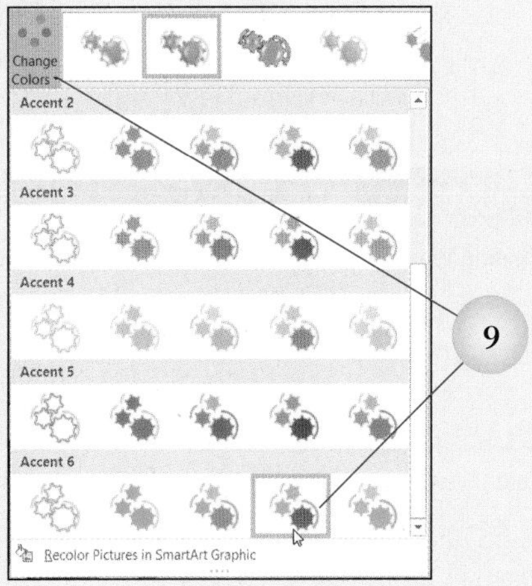

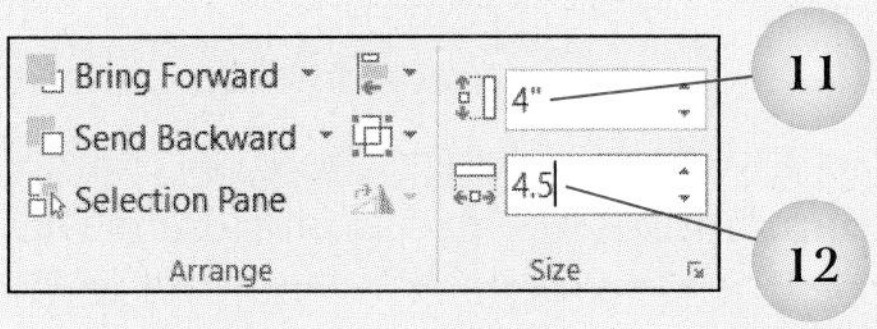

13. Click the bottom gear to select it.

14. Click the Shape Fill button arrow in the Shape Styles group and then click the *Green, Accent 6, Darker 50%* option (last column, last row in the *Theme Colors* section).
15. Click the top gear to select it.
16. Click the Shape Fill button arrow and then click the *Green, Accent 6, Darker 25%* option (last column, fifth row in the *Theme Colors* section).
17. Change to landscape orientation.
18. Move the SmartArt graphic so it fits on the first page and displays as shown in Figure 8.9.
19. Click outside the SmartArt graphic to deselect it.
20. Save **8-EPCoSales.xlsx** and then print the Seattle Sales worksheet.

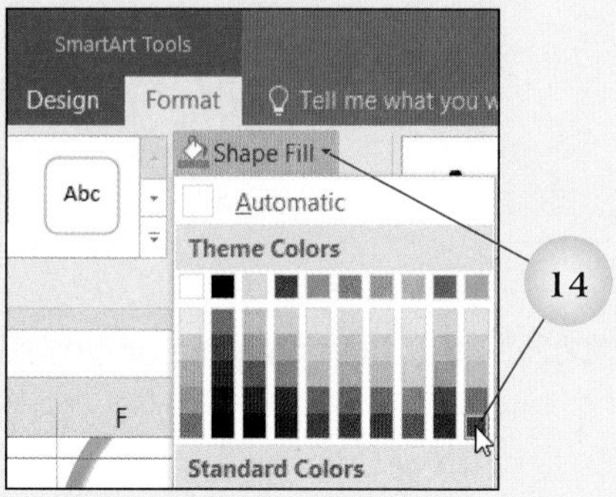

Check Your Work

Figure 8.9 Project 3c

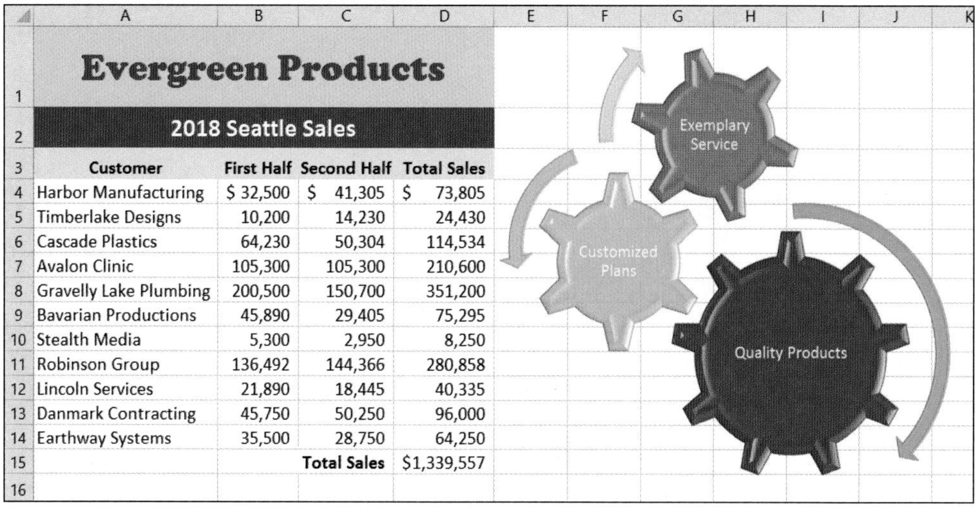

1	**Evergreen Products**			
2	**2018 Seattle Sales**			
3	**Customer**	**First Half**	**Second Half**	**Total Sales**
4	Harbor Manufacturing	$ 32,500	$ 41,305	$ 73,805
5	Timberlake Designs	10,200	14,230	24,430
6	Cascade Plastics	64,230	50,304	114,534
7	Avalon Clinic	105,300	105,300	210,600
8	Gravelly Lake Plumbing	200,500	150,700	351,200
9	Bavarian Productions	45,890	29,405	75,295
10	Stealth Media	5,300	2,950	8,250
11	Robinson Group	136,492	144,366	280,858
12	Lincoln Services	21,890	18,445	40,335
13	Danmark Contracting	45,750	50,250	96,000
14	Earthway Systems	35,500	28,750	64,250
15			**Total Sales**	$1,339,557
16				

Tutorial

Creating WordArt

Insert WordArt

Quick Steps

Create WordArt

1. Click Insert tab.
2. Click Insert WordArt button.
3. Click WordArt style at drop-down list.
4. Type text.

Creating, Sizing, and Moving WordArt

Use the WordArt feature to distort or modify text so it conforms to a variety of shapes. This is useful for creating company logos and headings. Change the font, style, and alignment of text with WordArt and use fill patterns and colors, customize border lines, and add shadow and three-dimensional effects.

To insert WordArt in an Excel worksheet, click the Insert tab, click the Insert WordArt button in the Text group, and then click an option at the drop-down list. This inserts the text *Your text here* in the worksheet, formatted in the WordArt option selected at the drop-down list. Type text and then use the options and buttons on the Drawing Tools Format tab to format the WordArt.

WordArt text inserted in a worksheet is surrounded by white sizing handles. Use these sizing handles to change the height and width of the WordArt text. To move WordArt text, position the mouse pointer on the border of the WordArt text box until the pointer displays with a four-headed arrow attached and then drag the outline of the text box to the new location.

Hint To remove a WordArt style from text and retain the text, click the More Styles button in the WordArt Styles group on the Drawing Tools Format tab and then click *Clear WordArt.*

Make WordArt text conform to a variety of shapes using the *Transform* option from the Text Effects button drop-down list. Apply a transform shape and a small yellow circle displays below the WordArt text. Use this circle to change the slant of the WordArt text.

Project 3d Inserting and Formatting WordArt

Part 4 of 4

1. With **8-EPCoSales.xlsx** open, click the Total Sales worksheet tab.
2. Make cell A1 active and then press the Delete key. (This removes the text from the cell.)
3. Increase the height of row 1 to 138 points.
4. Click the Insert tab.
5. Click the Insert WordArt button in the Text group and then click the *Fill - Black, Text 1, Outline - Background 1, Hard Shadow - Background 1* option (first column, third row).

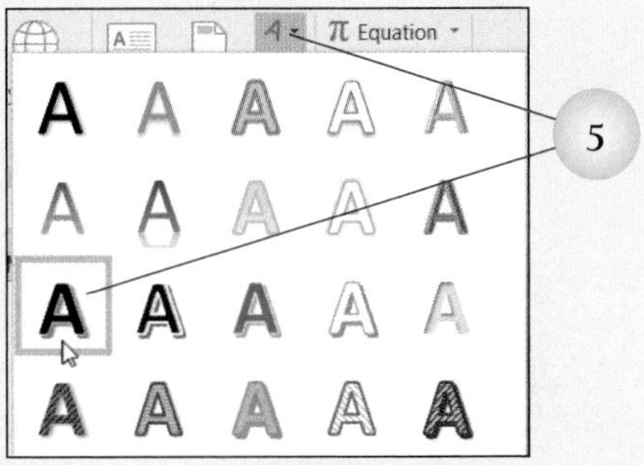

6. Type Evergreen, press the Enter key, and then type Products.
7. Click the WordArt border to change it to a solid line (not a dashed line).
8. Click the Text Fill button arrow in the WordArt Styles group and then click the *Green, Accent 6, Darker 50%* option (last column, last row in the *Theme Colors* section).

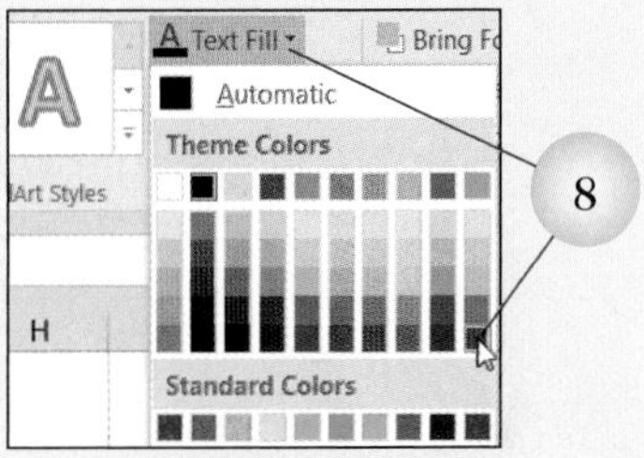

9. Click the Text Effects button in the WordArt Styles group, point to *Transform*, and then click the *Can Up* option (third column, fourth row in the *Warp* section).
10. Position the mouse pointer (turns into a white arrow) on the small yellow circle immediately below the *d* in *Products*, click and hold down the left mouse button, drag up approximately 0.25 inch, and then release the mouse button. (This changes the slant of the text.)
11. Drag the WordArt text so it is positioned in cell A1.
12. If necessary, size the SmartArt graphic and position it so it prints on one page with the data.
13. Click the Seattle Sales worksheet tab and then complete steps similar to those in Steps 2 through 11 to insert *Evergreen Products* as WordArt in cell A1.
14. Make sure the SmartArt graphic fits on one page with the data. If necessary, decrease the size of the graphic.

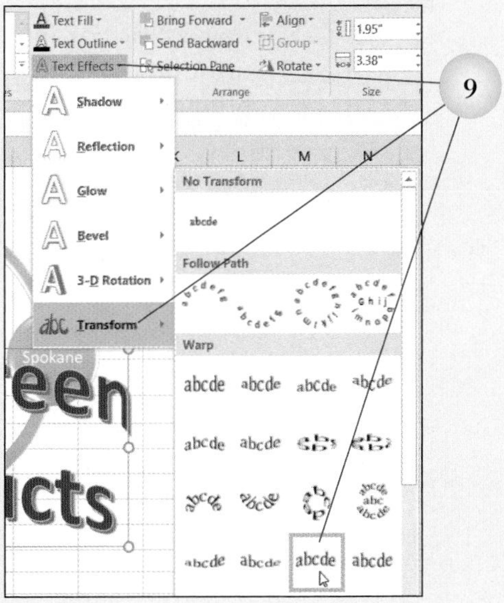

15. Save **8-EPCoSales.xlsx** and then print both worksheets.
16. Close **8-EPCoSales.xlsx**.

Check Your Work

Chapter Summary

- Insert symbols with options at the Symbol dialog box with the Symbols tab or Special Characters tab selected.
- Use buttons in the Illustrations group on the Insert tab to insert an image such as a picture, clip art image, screenshot, shape, or SmartArt graphic.
- Insert an image by clicking the Insert tab, clicking the Pictures button in the Illustrations group, and then double-clicking an image at the Insert Picture dialog box.
- Insert an image in a worksheet and the Picture Tools Format tab is active. It provides options for adjusting the image, applying preformatted styles to the image, and arranging and sizing the image.
- Change the size of an image with the *Shape Height* and *Shape Width* measurement boxes in the Size group on the Picture Tools Format tab or with the sizing handles that display around a selected image.
- Move an image by positioning the mouse pointer on the image border until the pointer displays with a four-headed arrow attached and then dragging the image to the new location.
- Insert an online image with options at the Insert Pictures window. Display this window by clicking the Insert tab and then clicking the Online Pictures button in the Illustrations group.
- Use the Screenshot button in the Illustrations group on the Insert tab to capture all or part of the contents of a screen.
- To draw a shape in a workbook, click the Insert tab, click the Shapes button in the Illustrations group, and then click a shape at the drop-down list. Click or drag in the worksheet to insert the shape. To maintain the proportions of the shape, press and hold down the Shift key while dragging in the worksheet.
- Copy a shape by using the Copy and Paste buttons in the Clipboard group on the Home tab or by pressing and holding down the Ctrl key while dragging the shape.
- Draw a text box in a worksheet by clicking the Insert tab, clicking the Text Box button in the Text group, and then clicking or dragging in the worksheet. Use options on the Drawing Tools Format tab to format and customize the text box.
- Insert a SmartArt graphic in a worksheet by clicking the Insert tab, clicking the SmartArt button in the Illustrations group, and then double-clicking a graphic at the Choose a SmartArt Graphic dialog box. Customize a SmartArt graphic with options on the SmartArt Tools Design tab and SmartArt Tools Format tab.
- Use WordArt to create, distort, and modify text and to make it conform to a variety of shapes. Insert WordArt in a worksheet with the WordArt button in the Text group on the Insert tab. Customize WordArt text with options on the Drawing Tools Format tab.

Commands Review

FEATURE	RIBBON TAB, GROUP	BUTTON
Choose a SmartArt Graphic dialog box	Insert, Illustrations	
Insert Picture dialog box	Insert, Illustrations	
Insert Pictures window	Insert, Illustrations	
Insert WordArt button drop-down list	Insert, Text	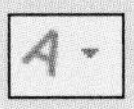
screenshot	Insert, Illustrations	
Shapes button drop-down list	Insert, Illustrations	
Symbol dialog box	Insert, Symbols	
text box	Insert, Text	

Workbook

Chapter study tools and assessment activities are available in the *Workbook* ebook. These resources are designed to help you further develop and demonstrate mastery of the skills learned in this chapter

Unit assessment activities are also available in the *Workbook*. These activities are designed to help you demonstrate mastery of the skills learned in this unit.

Index

D

G

H

I

T

U

V

W

X

Z

Microsoft® Access® Level 1

Unit 1

Creating Tables and Queries

Microsoft®

Access®

Managing and Creating Access Tables

CHAPTER 1

Performance Objectives

Upon successful completion of Chapter 1, you will be able to:

1. Open and close objects in a database
2. Insert, delete, and move fields in a table
3. Hide, unhide, freeze, and unfreeze fields
4. Adjust table column width
5. Preview and print a table
6. Design and create a table
7. Rename fields
8. Insert a field name, caption, and description
9. Insert Quick Start fields
10. Assign a default value and field size

Precheck

Check your current skills to help focus your study.

Managing information is an integral part of operating a business. Information can come in a variety of forms, such as data about customers, including names, addresses, and telephone numbers; product data; and purchasing and buying data. Most companies today manage data using system software. Microsoft Office Professional Plus includes a database management system software program named *Access*. With Access, you can organize, store, maintain, retrieve, sort, and print all types of business data.

This chapter contains just a few ideas on how to manage data with Access. A properly designed and maintained database management system can help a company operate smoothly.

Data Files

Before beginning chapter work, copy the AL1C1 folder to your storage medium and then make AL1C1 the active folder.

SNAP

If you are a SNAP user, launch the Precheck and Tutorials from your Assignments page.

Project 1 Explore an Access Database **1 Part**

You will open a database and open and close objects in the database, including tables, queries, forms, and reports.

Tutorial

Opening a Blank Database

Exploring a Database

A database is comprised of a series of objects (such as tables, queries, forms, and reports) used to enter, manage, view, and print data. Data in a database is organized into tables, which contain information for related items (such as customers, employees, orders, and products).

Quick Steps

Create a New Database

1. Open Access.
2. Click *Blank desktop database* template.
3. Type database name.
4. Click Create button.

Create

To create a new database or open a previously created database, click the Windows 10 Start button and then click the Access 2016 tile. (These steps may vary depending on your system configuration.) This displays the Access 2016 opening screen, as shown in Figure 1.1. At this screen, open a recently opened database, a blank database, a database from the Open backstage area, or a database based on a template.

To create a new blank database, click the *Blank desktop database* template. At the Blank desktop database window, type a name for the database in the *File Name* text box, and then click the Create button. To save the database in a particular location, click the Browse button at the right side of the *File Name* text box. At the File New Database dialog box, navigate to the desired location or folder, type the database name in the *File name* text box, and then click OK.

Tutorial

Opening an Existing Database

Opening a Database

A previously saved database can be opened at the Open dialog box. To display this dialog box, display the Open backstage area and then click the *Browse* option.

Figure 1.1 Access 2016 Opening Screen

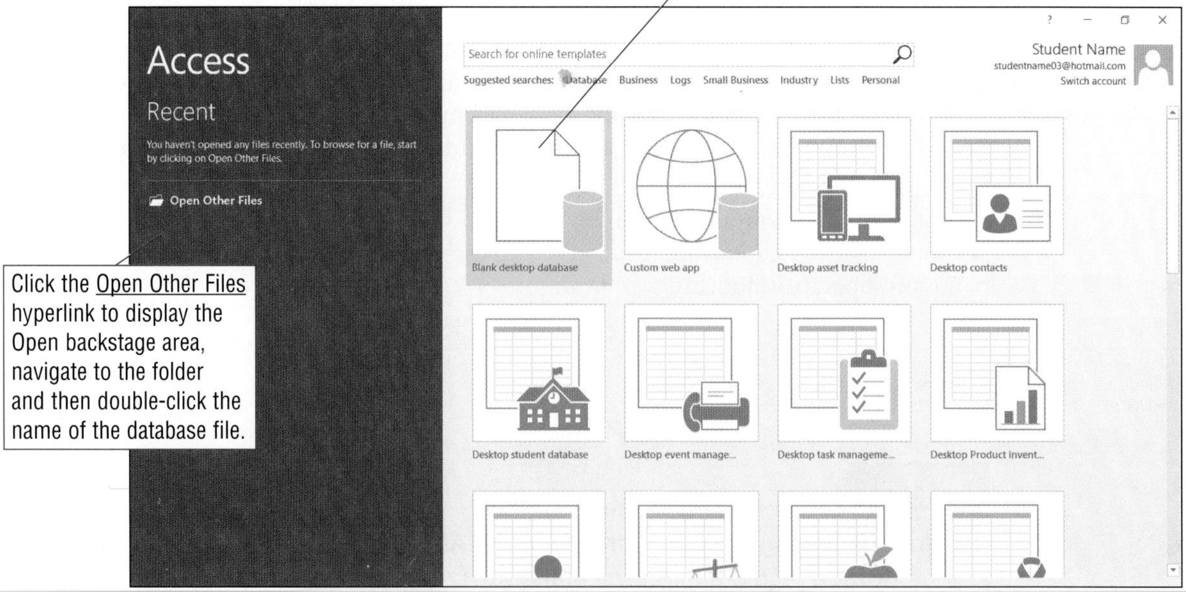

Quick Steps

Open a Database

1. Open Access.
2. Click Open Other Files hyperlink.
3. Click *Browse* option.
4. Navigate to location.
5. Double-click database.

Display the Open backstage area by clicking the Open Other Files hyperlink at the Access 2016 opening screen. Or, click the File tab at the blank Access screen and then click the *Open* option. Other methods for displaying the Open backstage area include using the keyboard shortcut, Ctrl + O, or inserting an Open button on the Quick Access Toolbar.

At the Open backstage area, click the *Browse* option and the Open dialog box displays. At the Open dialog box, navigate to the desired location, such as the drive containing your storage medium, open the folder containing the database, and then double-click the database name in the Content pane. When a database is open, the Access screen looks similar to what is shown in Figure 1.2. Refer to Table 1.1 for descriptions of the Access screen elements.

Hint The active database is saved automatically on a periodic basis and when you make another record active, close the table, or close the database.

Only one Access database can be open at a time. If a new database is opened in the current Access window, the existing database closes. However, multiple instances of Access can be opened and a database can be opened in each instance. In other applications in the Microsoft Office suite, a revised file must be saved after changes are made to the file. In an Access database, any changes made to data are saved automatically when moving to a new record, closing a table, or closing the database.

Enabling Content

A security warning message bar may appear below the ribbon if Access determines the file being opened did not originate from a trusted location on the computer and may contain viruses or other security hazards. This often occurs when an Access database is copied from another medium (such as a CD or the web). Active content in the file is disabled until the Enable Content button is clicked. The message bar closes when the database is identified as a trusted source. Before making any changes to the database, the Enable Content button must be clicked.

Figure 1.2 Access Screen

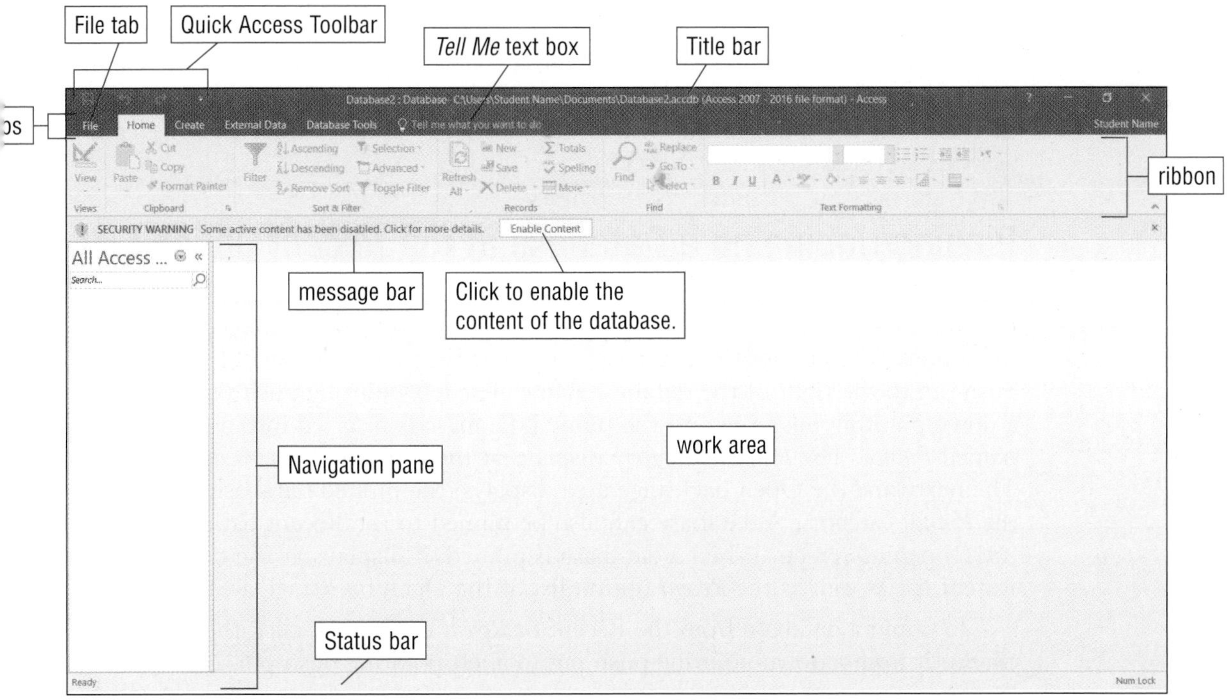

Table 1.1 Access Screen Elements

Feature	Description
File tab	when clicked, displays the backstage area that contains options for working with and managing databases
message bar	displays security alerts if the database being opened contains potentially unsafe content
Navigation pane	displays the names of objects within the database grouped by categories
Quick Access Toolbar	contains buttons for commonly used commands
ribbon	contains tabs with commands and buttons divided into groups
Status bar	displays messages, the current view, and view buttons
tabs	contain commands and features organized into groups
Tell Me text box	provides information as well as guidance on how to perform a function
Title bar	displays the database name followed by the program name
work area	displays opened objects

Tutorial

Managing the *Recent* Option List

Opening a Database from the *Recent* Option List

At the Open backstage area with the *Recent* option selected, a list of the most recently opened databases displays. Access displays 25 of the most recently opened databases and groups them into categories such as *Today*, *Yesterday*, and perhaps another category such as *Last Week*. Click the database name in the *Recent* option list to open the database.

(Note: If opening a database from a OneDrive account, Access requires that a copy of the database be saved to a location such as the computer's hard drive or a USB flash drive. Any changes made to the database will be saved to the local copy of the database but not the database in the OneDrive account. To save a database back to the OneDrive account, the database will need to be uploaded by opening a web browser, going to onedrive.com, logging in to the OneDrive account, and then clicking the Upload link. Microsoft constantly updates the OneDrive.com website, so these steps may vary.)

Pinning/Unpinning a Database at the *Recent* Option List

If a database is opened on a regular basis, consider pinning it to the *Recent* option list. To pin a database to the *Recent* option list at the Open backstage area, hover the mouse pointer over the database name and then click the small left-pointing push pin to the right of the database name. The left-pointing push pin changes to a down-pointing push pin and the pinned database is inserted into a new category named *Pinned*. The *Pinned* category displays at the top of the *Recent* option list. The next time the Open backstage area displays, the pinned database displays in the *Pinned* category. A database can also be pinned to the Recent list at the Access 2016 opening screen. When a database is pinned, it displays at the top of the Recent list as well as the *Recent* option list at the Open backstage area.

To unpin a database from the Recent or *Recent* option list, click the pin to change it from a down-pointing push pin to a left-pointing push pin. More than one database can be pinned to a list. Another method for pinning and unpinning databases is to use the shortcut menu. Right-click a database name and then click the *Pin to list* or *Unpin from list* option.

Tutorial

Opening and Closing an Object

Opening and Closing Objects

The Navigation pane at the left side of the Access screen displays the objects contained in the database. Some common objects found in a database include tables, queries, forms, and reports. Refer to Table 1.2 for descriptions of these four types of objects.

Control what displays in the pane by clicking the menu bar at the top of the Navigation pane and then clicking an option at the drop-down list or by clicking the button on the menu bar containing the down arrow. (The name of this button changes depending on what is selected.) For example, to display a list of all saved objects in the database, click the *Object Type* option at the drop-down list. This view displays the objects grouped by type: *Tables*, *Queries*, *Forms*, and *Reports*. To open an object, double-click the object in the Navigation pane. The object opens in the work area and a tab displays with the object name at the left side of the object. An object can also be opened with the shortcut menu by right-clicking the object in the Navigation pane and then clicking the *Open* option at the shortcut menu.

Shutter Bar Open/Close Button

To view more of an object, consider closing the Navigation pane by clicking the Shutter Bar Open/Close Button in the upper right corner of the Navigation pane or by pressing the F11 function key. Click the button or press F11 again to reopen the Navigation pane. More than one object can be opened in the work area. Each object opens with a visible tab. Navigate to objects by clicking the object tab.

Hint Hide the Navigation pane by clicking the Shutter Bar Open/Close Button or by pressing F11.

To close an object, click the Close button in the upper right corner of the work area or use the keyboard shortcut Ctrl + F4. The shortcut menu can also be used to close an object by right-clicking the object and then clicking *Close* at the shortcut menu. Close multiple objects by right-clicking an object tab and then clicking *Close All* at the shortcut menu.

Tutorial

Closing a Database and Closing Access

Close

Closing a Database

To close a database, click the File tab and then click the *Close* option. Close Access by clicking the Close button in the upper right corner of the screen or with the keyboard shortcut Alt + F4.

Table 1.2 Database Objects

Object Type	Description
table	Organizes data in fields (columns) and records (rows). A database must contain at least one table. The table is the base upon which other objects are created.
query	Displays data from a table or related tables that meets a conditional statement and/or performs calculations. For example, all records from a specific month can be displayed or only those records containing a specific city.
form	Allows fields and records to be presented in a layout different from the datasheet. Used to facilitate data entry and maintenance.
report	Prints data from tables or queries.

Project 1 Opening and Closing a Database and Objects in a Database

1. Open Access by clicking the Windows Start button and then clicking the Access 2016 tile in the Start menu.
2. At the Access 2016 opening screen, click the Open Other Files hyperlink.
3. At the Open backstage area, click the *Browse* option.
4. At the Open dialog box, navigate to the AL1C1 folder on your storage medium and then double-click ***1-SampleDatabase.accdb***. (This database contains data on orders, products, and suppliers for a specialty hiking and backpacking outfitters store named Pacific Trek.)
5. Click the Enable Content button in the message bar if a security warning message appears. (The message bar will display immediately below the ribbon.)
6. With the database open, click the Navigation pane menu bar and then click *Object Type* at the drop-down list. (This option displays the objects grouped by type: *Tables*, *Queries*, *Forms*, and *Reports*.)
7. Double-click *Suppliers* in the Tables group in the Navigation pane. This opens the Suppliers table in the work area, as shown in Figure 1.3.
8. Close the Suppliers table by clicking the Close button in the upper right corner of the work area.

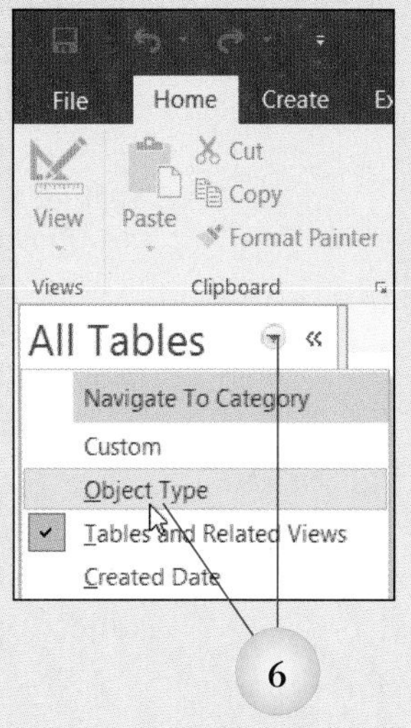

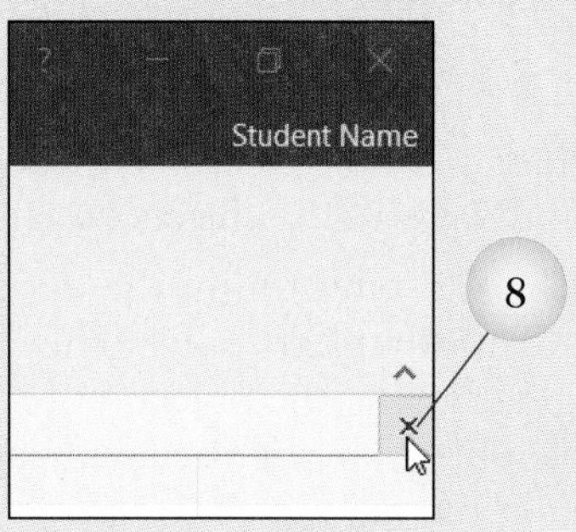

9. Double-click *OrdersOver$500* in the Queries group in the Navigation pane. A query displays data that meets a conditional statement. This query displays orders that meet the criterion of being more than $500.
10. Close the query by clicking the Close button in the upper right corner of the work area.
11. Right-click *SuppliersNotVancouver* in the Queries group in the Navigation pane and then click *Open* at the shortcut menu. This query displays information about suppliers but excludes those in Vancouver.
12. Right-click the SuppliersNotVancouver tab in the work area and then click *Close* at the shortcut menu.
13. Double-click *Orders* in the Forms group in the Navigation pane. This displays an order form. A form is used to view and edit data in a table one record at a time.
14. Double-click *Orders* in the Reports group in the Navigation pane. The Orders form is still open and the report opens in the work area over the Orders form. The Orders report displays information about orders and order amounts.

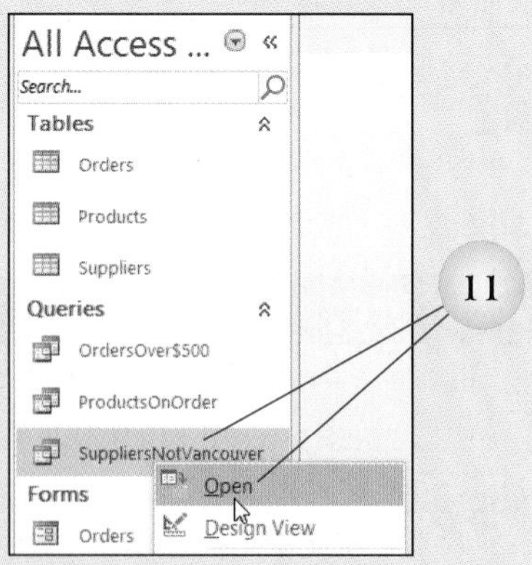

15. Close the Navigation pane by clicking the Shutter Bar Open/Close Button in the upper right corner of the pane.
16. After viewing the report, click the Shutter Bar Open/Close Button again to open the Navigation pane.
17. Right-click the Orders tab and then click *Close All* at the shortcut menu. (This closes both open objects.)
18. Close the database by clicking the File tab and then clicking the *Close* option.
19. Close Access by clicking the Close button in the upper right corner of the screen.

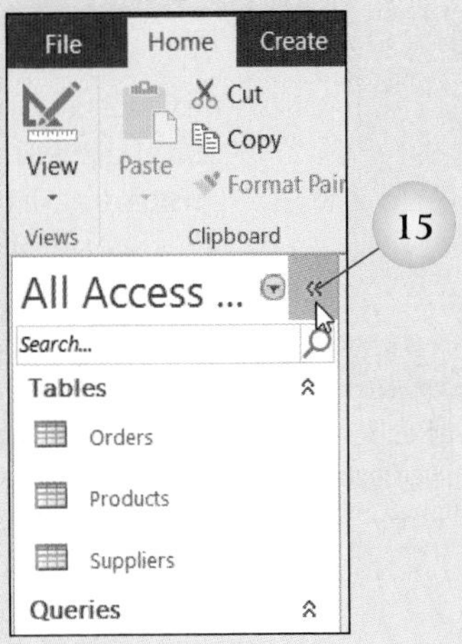

Figure 1.3 Suppliers Table

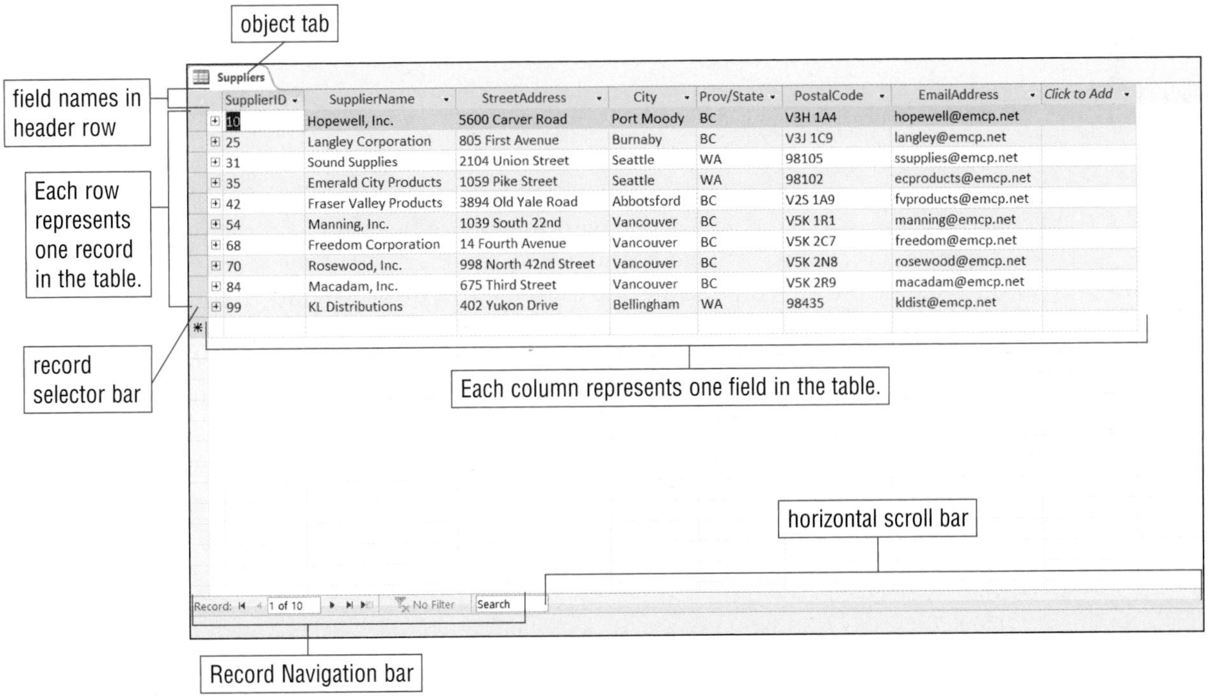

Project 2 Manage Tables in a Database

7 Parts

Pacific Trek is an outfitting store specializing in hiking and backpacking gear. Information about the store, including suppliers and products, is contained in a database. You will open the database and then insert and delete records; insert, move, and delete fields; preview and print tables; rename and delete a table; and create two new tables for the database.

Preview Finished Project

Managing Tables

In a new database, tables are the first objects created, since all other database objects rely on a table as the source for their data. Managing the tables in the database is important for keeping the database up to date and may include inserting or deleting records, inserting or deleting fields, renaming fields, creating a hard copy of the table by printing the table, and renaming and deleting tables.

Adding and Deleting Records

Tutorial

Adding and Deleting Records in a Table

When a table is opened, it displays in Datasheet view in the work area. The Datasheet view displays the contents of a table in a column and row format similar to an Excel worksheet. Columns contain field data, with the field names in the header row at the top of the table, and rows contain records. A Record Navigation bar displays at the bottom of the screen just above the Status bar and contains buttons to navigate in the table. Figure 1.4 identifies the buttons and other elements on the Record Navigation bar.

New

Quick Steps

Add a New Record

1. Open table.
2. Click New button on Home tab.
3. Type data.

OR

1. Open table.
2. Click New (blank) record button on Record Navigation bar.
3. Type data.

To add a new record to the open table, make sure the Home tab is active and then click the New button in the Records group. This moves the insertion point to the first field in the blank row at the bottom of the table and the *Current Record* box on the Record Navigation bar indicates what record is being created (or edited). A new record can also be added by clicking the New (blank) record button on the Record Navigation bar.

When working in a table, press the Tab key to make the next field in the current record active or press Shift + Tab to make the previous field in the current record active. Make a field active with the mouse by clicking in the field. When typing data for the first field in the record, another row of cells is automatically inserted below the current row and a pencil icon displays in the record selector bar at the beginning of the current record. The pencil icon indicates that the record is being edited and that the changes to the data have not been saved. When data is entered in the last field and the insertion point is moved out of the field, the pencil icon is removed, indicating that the data has been saved.

Delete

Quick Steps

Delete a Record

1. Click a field in the record.
2. Click Delete button arrow.
3. Click *Delete Record*.
4. Click Yes.

To delete a record, click in one of the fields in the record, make sure the Home tab is active, click the Delete button arrow, and then click *Delete Record* at the drop-down list. At the message asking to confirm the deletion, click Yes. Click in a field in a record and the Delete button displays in a dimmed manner unless specific data is selected.

Data entered in a table is automatically saved, however, changes to the layout of a table are not automatically saved. For example, if a column is deleted in a table, a deletion confirmation message will display when the table is closed.

Figure 1.4 Record Navigation Bar

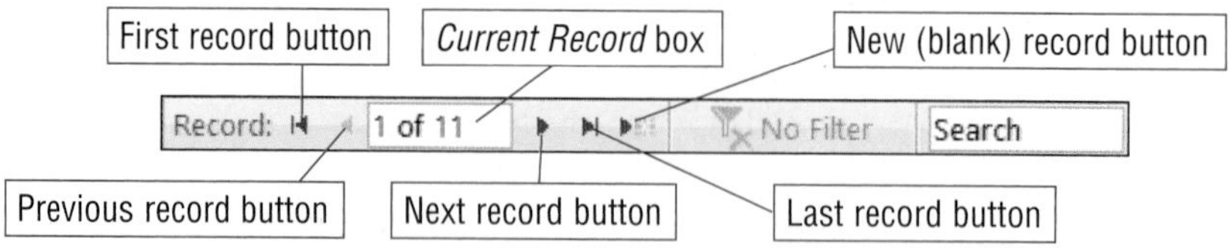

Project 2a Inserting and Deleting Records in a Table

1. Open Access.
2. At the Access 2016 opening screen, click the Open Other Files hyperlink.
3. At the Open backstage area, click the *Browse* option.
4. At the Open dialog box, navigate to the AL1C1 folder on your storage medium and then double-click ***1-PacTrek.accdb***.
5. Click the Enable Content button in the message bar if a security warning message appears. (The message bar will display immediately below the ribbon.)
6. With the database open, make sure the Navigation pane displays object types. (If it does not, click the Navigation pane menu bar and then click *Object Type* at the drop-down list.)
7. Double-click *Suppliers* in the Tables group in the Navigation pane. (This opens the table in Datasheet view.)

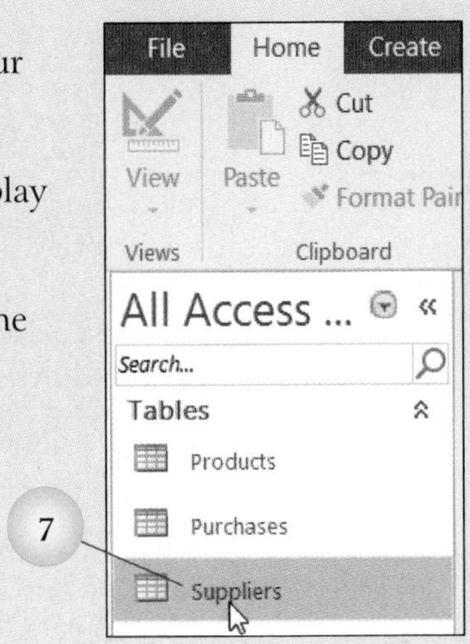

8. With the Suppliers table open and the Home tab active, add a new record by completing the following steps:
   a. Click the New button in the Records group on the Home tab. (This moves the insertion point to the first field in the blank record at the bottom of the table and the *Current Record* box in the Record Navigation bar indicates what record you are creating or editing.)
   b. Type 38. (This inserts *38* in the field immediately below *99*.)
   c. Press the Tab key (to make the next field in the current record active) and then type Hadley Company.
   d. Press the Tab key and then type 5845 Jefferson Street.
   e. Press the Tab key and then type Seattle.
   f. Press the Tab key and then type WA.
   g. Press the Tab key and then type 98107.
   h. Press the Tab key and then type hcompany@emcp.net.
   i. Press the Tab key and then type Jurene Miller.

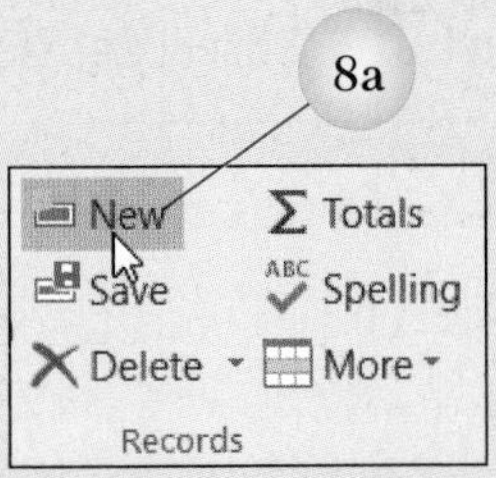

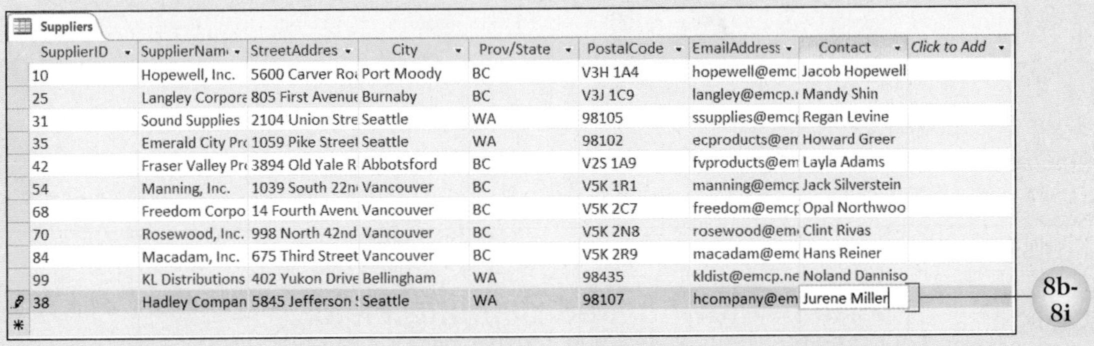

SupplierID	SupplierName	StreetAddres	City	Prov/State	PostalCode	EmailAddress	Contact	Click to Add
10	Hopewell, Inc.	5600 Carver Ro	Port Moody	BC	V3H 1A4	hopewell@emc	Jacob Hopewell	
25	Langley Corpor	805 First Avenu	Burnaby	BC	V3J 1C9	langley@emcp.i	Mandy Shin	
31	Sound Supplies	2104 Union Stre	Seattle	WA	98105	ssupplies@emc	Regan Levine	
35	Emerald City Pr	1059 Pike Street	Seattle	WA	98102	ecproducts@en	Howard Greer	
42	Fraser Valley Pr	3894 Old Yale R	Abbotsford	BC	V2S 1A9	fvproducts@em	Layla Adams	
54	Manning, Inc.	1039 South 22n	Vancouver	BC	V5K 1R1	manning@emcp	Jack Silverstein	
68	Freedom Corpo	14 Fourth Aven	Vancouver	BC	V5K 2C7	freedom@emcp	Opal Northwoo	
70	Rosewood, Inc.	998 North 42nd	Vancouver	BC	V5K 2N8	rosewood@em	Clint Rivas	
84	Macadam, Inc.	675 Third Street	Vancouver	BC	V5K 2R9	macadam@emc	Hans Reiner	
99	KL Distributions	402 Yukon Drive	Bellingham	WA	98435	kldist@emcp.ne	Noland Danniso	
38	Hadley Compan	5845 Jefferson	Seattle	WA	98107	hcompany@em	Jurene Miller	
*								

9. Close the Suppliers table by clicking the Close button in the work area.
10. Open the Products table by double-clicking *Products* in the Tables group in the Navigation pane. (This opens the table in Datasheet view.)
11. Insert two new records by completing the following steps:
    a. Click the New button in the Records group and then enter the data for a new record as shown in Figure 1.5. (See the record that begins with *901-S*.)

b. After typing the last field entry in the record for product number 901-S, press the Tab key. This moves the insertion point to the blank field below *901-S*.
c. Type the new record as shown in Figure 1.5. (See the record that begins with *917-S*.)

12. With the Products table open, delete a record by completing the following steps:
    a. Click in the field containing the data *780-2*.
    b. Click the Delete button arrow in the Records group (notice that the button displays in a dimmed manner) and then click *Delete Record* at the drop-down list.
    c. At the message asking if you want to delete the record, click Yes.

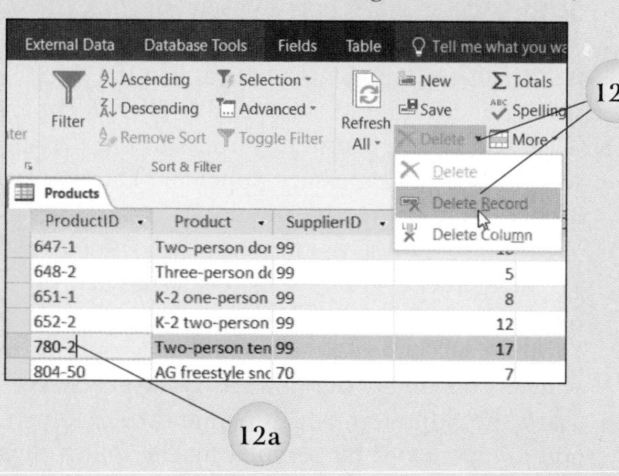

13. Close the Products table by clicking the Close button in the work area.

Check Your Work

Figure 1.5 Project 2a, Step 11

Products

ProductID	Product	SupplierID	UnitsInStock	UnitsOnOrde	ReorderLevel	*Click to Add*
559-B	ICE snow goggles, bronze	68	22	0	20	
602-XR	Binoculars, 8 x 42	35	3	5	5	
602-XT	Binoculars, 10.5 x 45	35	5	0	4	
602-XX	Binoculars, 10 x 50	35	7	0	5	
647-1	Two-person dome tent	99	10	15	15	
648-2	Three-person dome tent	99	5	0	10	
651-1	K-2 one-person tent	99	8	0	10	
652-2	K-2 two-person tent	99	12	0	10	
780-2	Two-person tent	99	17	10	20	
804-50	AG freestyle snowboard, X50	70	7	0	10	
804-60	AG freestyle snowboard, X60	70	8	0	5	
897-L	Lang blunt snowboard	70	8	0	7	
897-W	Lang blunt snowboard, wide	70	4	0	3	
901-S	Solar battery pack	38	16	0	15	
917-S	Silo portable power pack	38	8	0	10	
*						

Step 11

Tutorial

Managing Fields in Datasheet View

Quick Steps

Insert a New Field
1. Open table.
2. Click in first cell below *Click to Add*.
3. Type data.

Inserting, Moving, and Deleting Fields

When managing a database, an additional field may need to be added to a table. For example, a field column may need to be added for contact information, one for cell phone numbers, or for the number of items in stock. To insert a new field column in a table, open the table in Datasheet view and then click in the first cell below *Click to Add* in the header row. Type the data in the cell, press the Down Arrow key, and then type the data for the second row. Continue in this manner until all data has been entered for the new field. In addition to pressing the Down Arrow key to move the insertion point down to the next cell, click in the desired cell using the mouse or press the Tab key until the desired cell is active.

Move a Field
1. Select column.
2. Position mouse pointer on field name in header row.
3. Click and hold down left mouse button.
4. Drag to new location.
5. Release mouse button.

Delete a Field
1. Click in field.
2. Click Delete button arrow.
3. Click *Delete Column*.
4. Click Yes.

A new field column is added to the right of existing field columns. Move a field column by positioning the mouse pointer on the field name in the header row until the pointer displays as a down-pointing black arrow and then click the left mouse button. This selects the entire field column. With the field column selected, position the mouse pointer on the field name; click and hold down the left mouse button; drag to the left or right until a thick, black vertical line displays in the desired location; and then release the mouse button. The thick, black vertical line indicates where the field column will be positioned when the mouse button is released. In addition, the pointer displays with the outline of a gray box attached to it, indicating that a move operation is being performed.

Delete a field column in a manner similar to deleting a row. Click in one of the fields in the column, make sure the Home tab is active, click the Delete button arrow, and then click *Delete Column* at the drop-down list. At the message asking to confirm the deletion, click Yes.

Project 2b Inserting, Moving, and Deleting Fields

Part 2 of 7

1. With **1-PacTrek.accdb** open, add a new field to the Suppliers table by completing the following steps:
   a. Double-click *Suppliers* in the Tables group in the Navigation pane.
   b. Click in the field immediately below *Click to Add* in the header row.
   c. Type (604) 555-3843 and then press the Down Arrow key on the keyboard.
   d. Type the remaining telephone numbers as shown below and at the right.

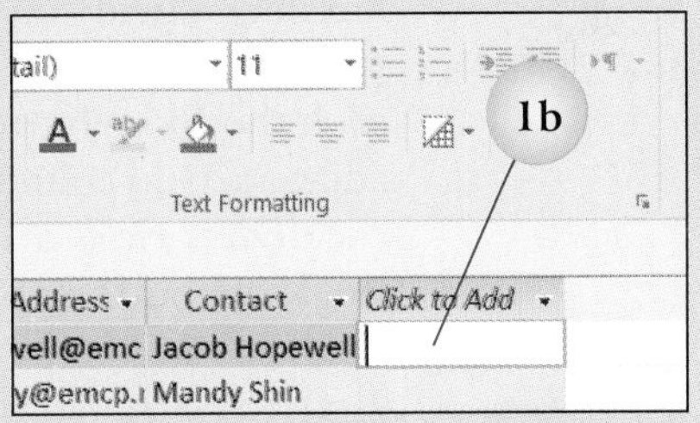

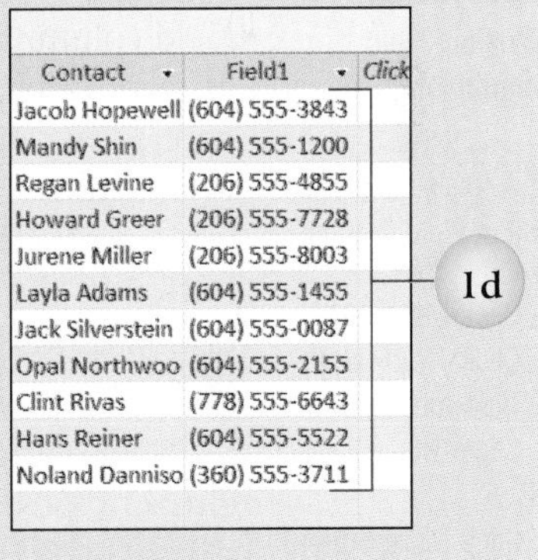

2. Move the *Field1* field column so it is positioned immediately left of the *EmailAddress* field column by completing the following steps:
   a. Position the mouse pointer on the *Field1* field name in the header row until the pointer displays as a down-pointing black arrow and then click the left mouse button. (This selects the field column.)
   b. Position the mouse pointer on the *Field1* field name. (The pointer displays as the normal, white arrow pointer.) Click and hold down the left mouse button; drag to the left until the thick, black vertical line displays immediately left of the *EmailAddress* field column; and then release the mouse button.

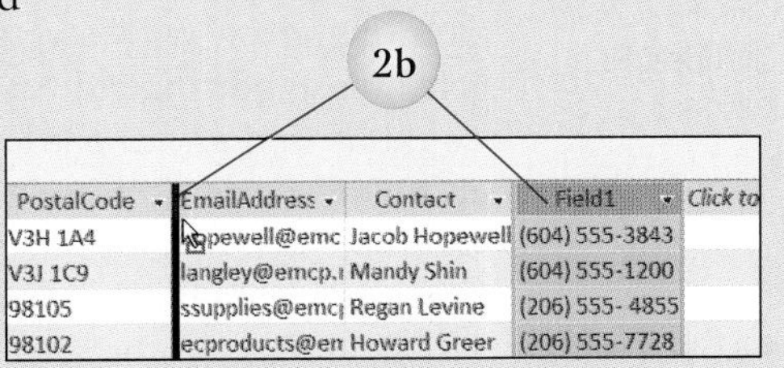

3. Delete the *Contact* field by completing the following steps:
   a. Position the mouse pointer on the *Contact* field name in the header row until the pointer displays as a down-pointing black arrow and then click the left mouse button. (This selects the field column.)
   b. Click the Delete button arrow in the Records group and then click *Delete Column* at the drop-down list.

c. At the message asking if you want to permanently delete the selected field(s) click Yes.

4. Close the Suppliers table. At the message asking if you want to save the changes to the layout of the table, click Yes.

Check Your Work

More

Hiding, Unhiding, Freezing, and Unfreezing Field Columns

A field column in a table can be hidden if the column is not needed for data entry or editing purposes or to make viewing easier for two nonadjacent field columns containing data to be compared. To hide a field column, click in any field in the column, click the More button in the Records group on the Home tab, and then click *Hide Fields* at the drop-down list. Hide adjacent field columns by selecting the columns, clicking the More button in the Records group, and then clicking *Hide Fields* at the drop-down list. To unhide field columns, click the More button and then click *Unhide Fields*. At the Unhide Columns dialog box insert a check mark in the check boxes for those field columns that should remain visible.

Another method for comparing field columns side by side is to freeze a column. Freezing a field column is also helpful when not all of the columns of data are visible at one time. To freeze a field column, click in any field in the column, click the More button, and then click *Freeze Fields* at the drop-down list. To freeze adjacent field columns, select the columns first, click the More button, and then click *Freeze Fields* at the drop-down list. To unfreeze all field columns in a table, click the More button and then click *Unfreeze All Fields* at the drop-down list.

Tutorial

Adjusting Field Column Width

Quick Steps

Adjust Field Column Width

1. Click More button.
2. Click *Field Width.*
3. Type measurement
4. Click OK.

OR

1. Click More button.
2. Click *Field Width.*
3. Click Best Fit button.

OR

Double-click column boundary line.

OR

Select field columns and then double-click column boundary line.

OR

Drag column boundary line to new position.

Adjusting Field Column Width

Field columns have a default width of 13.111 characters, which is the approximate number of characters that will display in a field in the column. Depending on the data entered in a field in a field column, not all of the data will be visible. Or, data entered in a field may take up only a portion of the field. Change a field's column width with options at the Column Width dialog box. Display the dialog box by clicking the More button in the Records group on the Home tab and then clicking the *Field Width* option. Enter a measurement in the *Column Width* measurement box or click the Best Fit button to adjust the column width to accommodate the longest entry.

The width of a field column also can be adjusted to accommodate the longest entry by positioning the arrow pointer on the column boundary line at the right side of the column in the header row until the pointer turns into a left-and-right-pointing arrow with a vertical line in the middle and then double-clicking the left mouse button. Adjust the widths of adjacent field columns by selecting the columns first and then double-clicking one of the selected column boundary lines in the header row. To select adjacent field columns, position the arrow pointer on the first field name to be selected in the header row until the pointer turns into a down-pointing black arrow, click and hold down the left mouse button, drag to the last field name to be selected, and then release the mouse button. With the field columns selected, double-click one of the field column boundary lines.

Another method for adjusting the width of a field column is to drag a boundary line to the desired position. To do this, position the arrow pointer on the column boundary line (until the pointer turns into a left-and-right-pointing arrow with a vertical line in the middle), click and hold down the left mouse button, drag until the field column is the desired width, and then release the mouse button.

Project 2c Hiding, Unhiding, Freezing, and Unfreezing Field Columns and Changing Field Column Widths

Part 3 of 7

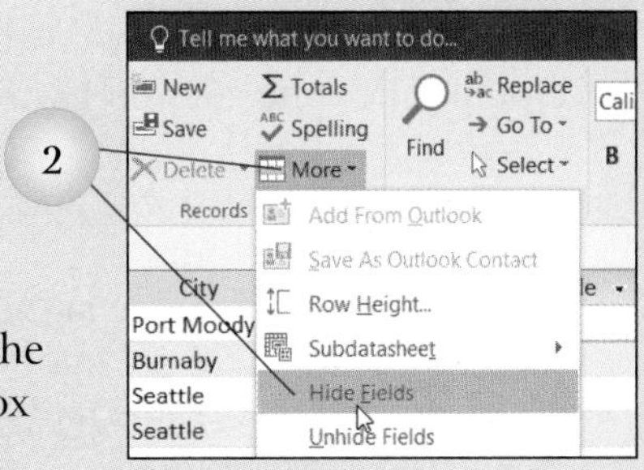

1. With **1-PacTrek.accdb** open, open the Suppliers table.
2. Hide the *PostalCode* field column by clicking the *PostalCode* field name in the header row, clicking the More button in the Records group on the Home tab, and then clicking *Hide Fields* at the drop-down list.
3. Unhide the field column by clicking the More button and then clicking *Unhide Fields* at the drop-down list. At the Unhide Columns dialog box, click the *PostalCode* check box to insert a check mark, and then click the Close button.

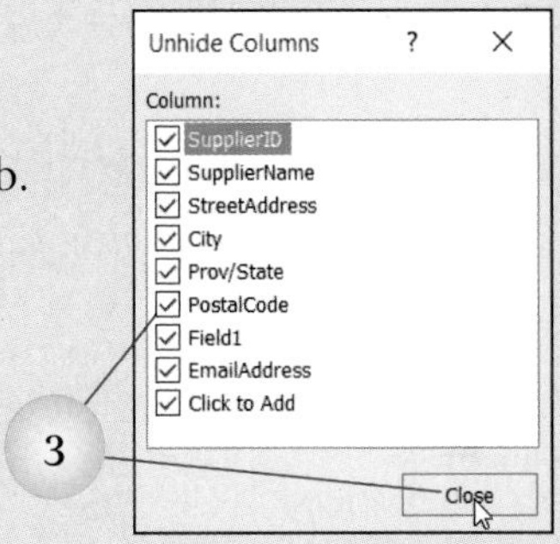

4. Adjust the width of the *SupplierID* field column by completing the following steps:
   a. Click the *SupplierID* field name in the header row.
   b. Click the More button in the Records group on the Home tab.
   c. Click the *Field Width* option.
   d. Type 11 in the *Column Width* measurement box.
   e. Click OK.
5. Adjust the *SupplierName* field column by completing the following steps:
   a. Click the *SupplierName* field name in the header row.
   b. Click the More button in the Records group.
   c. Click the *Field Width* option.
   d. Click the Best Fit button.

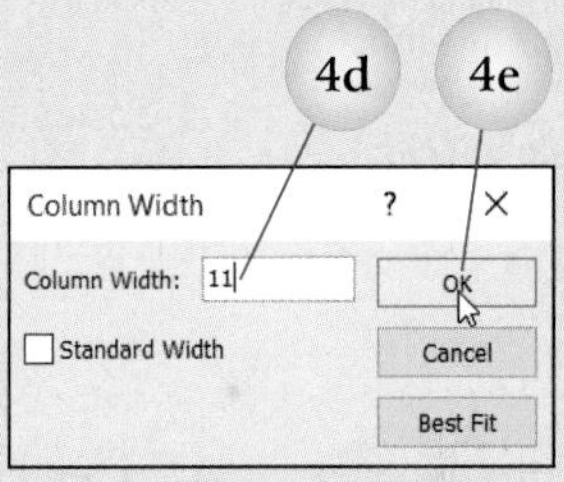

6. Adjust the width of the remaining columns by completing the following steps:
   a. Position the arrow pointer on the *StreetAddress* field name in the header row until the pointer turns into a down-pointing black arrow, click and hold down the left mouse button, drag to the *EmailAddress* field name, and then release the mouse button.
   b. With the columns selected, double-click one of the column boundary lines in the header row.
   c. Click in any field in the table to deselect the field columns.
7. Increase the width of the *EmailAddress* field column by positioning the arrow pointer on the column boundary line in the header row at the right side of the *EmailAddress* field column until it turns into a left-and-right-pointing arrow with a vertical line in the middle, clicking and holding down the left mouse button, dragging all of the way to the right side of the screen, and then releasing the mouse button. (Check the horizontal scroll bar at the bottom of the table and notice that the scroll bar contains a scroll box.)
8. Position the mouse pointer on the scroll box on the horizontal scroll bar and then drag to the left until the *SupplierID* field is visible.
9. Freeze the *SupplierID* field column by clicking in any field in the *SupplierID* field column, clicking the More button in the Records group, and then clicking *Freeze Fields* at the drop-down list.

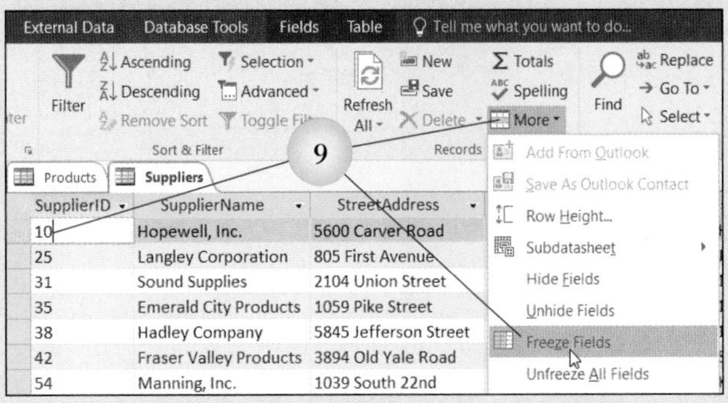

10. Using the mouse, drag the scroll box along the horizontal scroll to the right and left to view that the *SupplierID* field column remains visible on the screen.
11. Unfreeze the field column by clicking the More button in the Records group and then clicking *Unfreeze All Fields* at the drop-down list.
12. Double-click the column boundary line in the header row at the right side of the *EmailAddress* field column.
13. Close the Suppliers table and click Yes at the message that asks if you want to save the changes to the layout.
14. Open the Products table and then complete steps similar to those in Step 6 to select and then adjust the field column widths.
15. Close the Products table and click Yes at the message that asks if you want to save the changes to the layout.

Check Your Work

Tutorial

Renaming and Deleting Objects

Quick Steps

Rename a Table

1. Right-click table name in Navigation pane.
2. Click *Rename*.
3. Type new name.
4. Press Enter.

Delete a Table

1. Right-click table name in Navigation pane.
2. Click *Delete*.
3. Click Yes, if necessary.

Renaming and Deleting a Table

Managing tables might include actions such as renaming and deleting a table. Rename a table by right-clicking the table name in the Navigation pane, clicking *Rename* at the shortcut menu, typing the new name, and then pressing the Enter key. Delete a table from a database by clicking the table name in the Navigation pane, clicking the Delete button in the Records group on the Home tab, and then clicking Yes at the message asking to confirm the deletion. Another method is to right-click the table in the Navigation pane, click *Delete* at the shortcut menu, and then click Yes at the message. If a table is deleted from the computer's hard drive, the message asking to confirm the deletion does not display. This is because Access automatically sends the deleted table to the Recycle Bin, where it can be retrieved if necessary.

Tutorial

Previewing and Printing a Table

Quick Steps

Print a Table

1. Click File tab.
2. Click *Print*.
3. Click *Quick Print*.

OR

1. Click File tab.
2. Click *Print*.
3. Click *Print*.
4. Click OK.

Printing Tables

Click the File tab and then click the *Print* option to display the Print backstage area as shown in Figure 1.6. Click the *Quick Print* option to send the table directly to the printer without making any changes to the printer setup or the table formatting. Click the *Print* option to display the Print dialog box, with options for specifying the printer, page range, and specific records to print. Click OK to close the dialog box and send the table to the printer. By default, Access prints a table on letter-size paper in portrait orientation.

Figure 1.6 Print Backstage Area

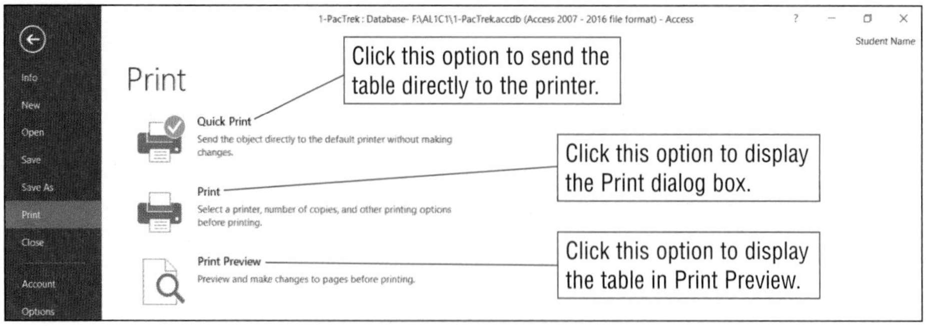

Previewing a Table

Quick Steps

Preview a Table

1. Click File tab.
2. Click *Print* option.
3. Click *Print Preview* option.

Print Preview

Print

Close Print Preview

Before printing a table, consider displaying the table in Print Preview to see how the table will print on the page. To display a table in Print Preview, as shown in Figure 1.7, click the *Print Preview* option at the Print backstage area.

Use options in the Zoom group on the Print Preview tab to increase or decrease the size of the page display. The size of the page display can also be changed using the Zoom slider bar at the right side of the Status bar. If a table spans more than one page, use buttons on the Navigation bar to display the next or previous page.

Print a table from Print Preview by clicking the Print button at the left side of the Print Preview tab. Click the Close Print Preview button to close Print Preview and continue working in the table without printing it.

Changing Page Size and Margins

Size

Margins

By default, Access prints a table in standard letter size (8.5 inches wide and 11 inches tall). Click the Size button in the Page Size group on the Print Preview tab and a drop-down list displays with options for changing the page size to legal, executive, envelope, and so on. Access uses default top, bottom, left, and right margins of 1 inch. Change these default margins by clicking the Margins button in the Page Size group and then clicking one of the predesigned margin options.

Figure 1.7 Print Preview

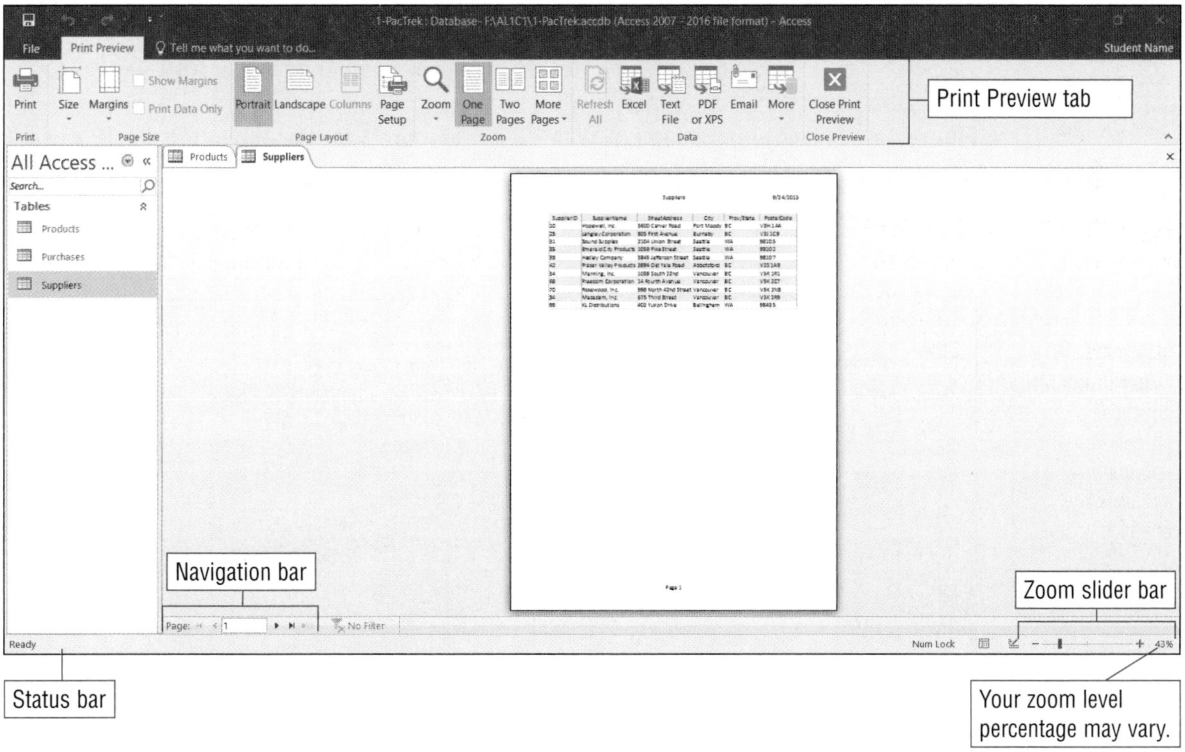

Changing Page Layout

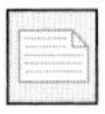
Landscape

Page Setup

Quick Steps

Display Page Setup Dialog Box

1. Click File tab.
2. Click *Print* option.
3. Click *Print Preview* option.
4. Click Page Setup button.

The Print Preview tab contains the Page Layout group with buttons for controlling how data is printed on the page. By default, Access prints a table in portrait orientation, which prints the text on the page so that it is taller than it is wide (like a page in this textbook). If a table contains a number of columns, changing to landscape orientation allows more columns to fit on a page. Landscape orientation rotates the printout to be wider than it is tall. To change from the default portrait orientation to landscape orientation, click the Landscape button in the Page Layout group on the Print Preview tab.

Click the Page Setup button in the Page Layout group and the Page Setup dialog box displays as shown in Figure 1.8. At the Page Setup dialog box with the Print Options tab selected, notice that the default margins are 1 inch. Change these defaults by typing different numbers in the margin measurement boxes. By default, the table name prints at the top center of the page and the current date prints in the upper right corner of the page. In addition, the word *Page* followed by the page number prints at the bottom of the page. To specify that the name of the table, date, and page number should not print, remove the check mark from the *Print Headings* option at the Page Setup dialog box with the Print Options tab selected.

Click the Page tab at the Page Setup dialog box and the dialog box displays as shown in Figure 1.9. Change the orientation with options in the *Orientation* section and change the paper size with options in the *Paper* section. Click the *Size* option box arrow and a drop-down list displays with paper sizes similar to the options available at the *Size* button drop-down list in the Page Size group on the Print Preview tab. Specify the printer with options in the *Printer for (table name)* section of the dialog box.

Figure 1.8 Page Setup Dialog Box with Print Options Tab Selected

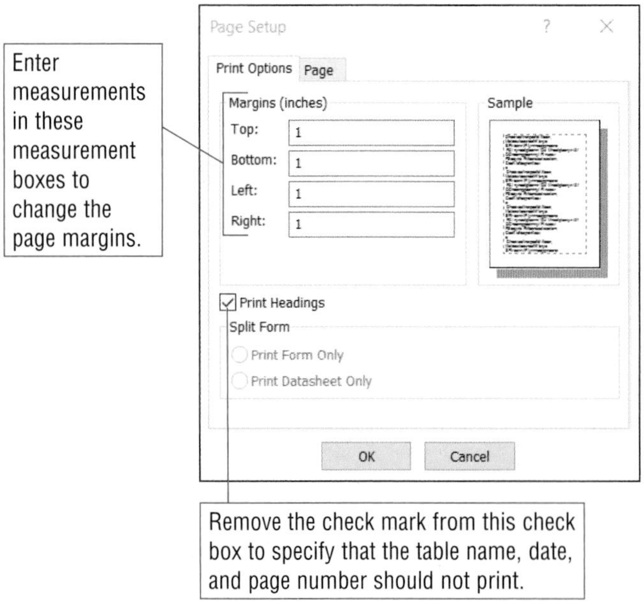

Figure 1.9 Page Setup Dialog Box with Page Tab Selected

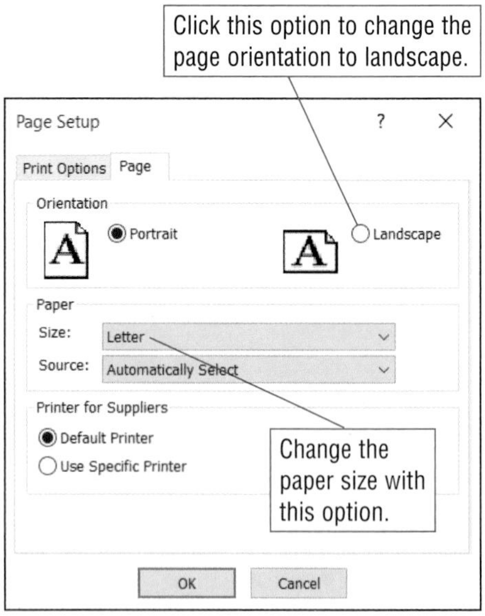

Project 2d Previewing, Changing Page Layout, Renaming, Deleting, and Printing Tables Part 4 of 7

1. With **1-PacTrek.accdb** open, open the Suppliers table.
2. Preview and then print the Suppliers table in landscape orientation by completing the following steps:
   a. Click the File tab and then click the *Print* option.
   b. At the Print backstage area, click the *Print Preview* option.
   c. Click the Two Pages button in the Zoom group on the Print Preview tab. (This displays two pages of the table.)
   d. Click the Zoom button arrow in the Zoom group on the Print Preview tab and then click *75%* at the drop-down list.

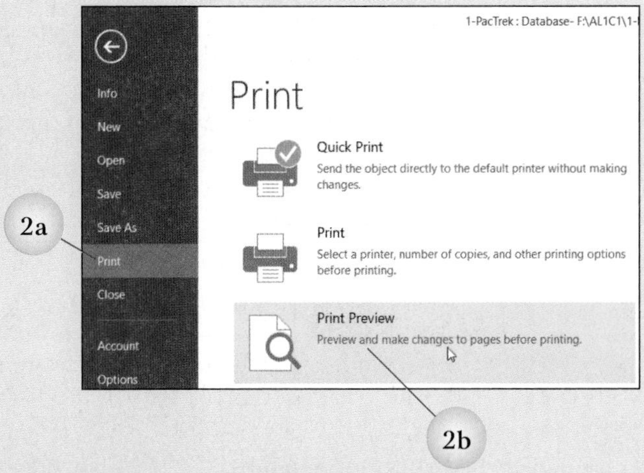

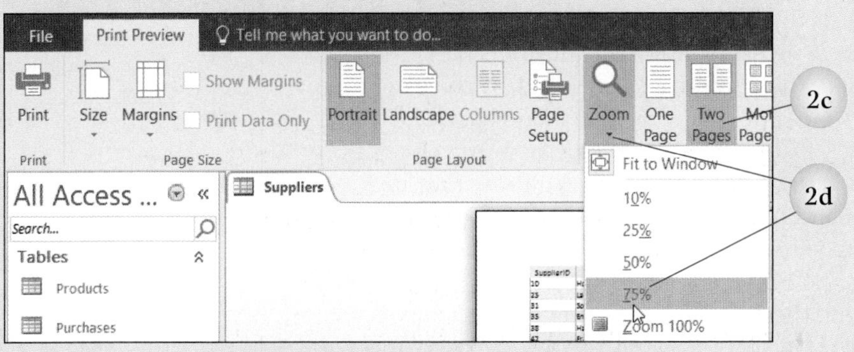

   e. Position the arrow pointer on the Zoom slider bar button at the right side of the Status bar, click and hold down the left mouse button, drag to the right until *100%* displays at the right of the Zoom slider bar, and then release the mouse button.

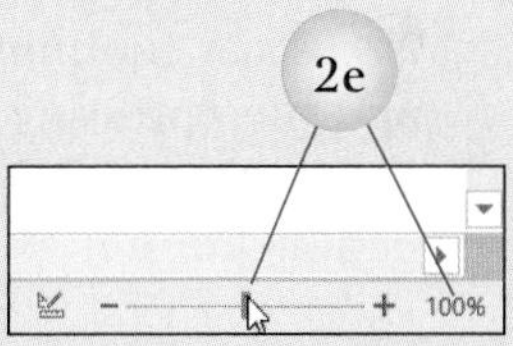

   f. Return the display to a full page by clicking the One Page button in the Zoom group on the Print Preview tab.
   g. Click the Margins button in the Page Size group on the Print Preview tab and then click the *Narrow* option at the drop-down list. (Notice how the data will print on the page with the narrow margins.)
   h. Change the margins back to the default by clicking the Margins button in the Page Size group and then clicking the *Normal* option at the drop-down list.
   i. Change to landscape orientation by clicking the Landscape button in the Page Layout group. (Check the Next Page button on the Record Navigation bar and notice that it is dimmed. This indicates that the table will print on only one page.)
   j. Print the table by clicking the Print button at the left side of the Print Preview tab and then clicking OK at the Print dialog box.

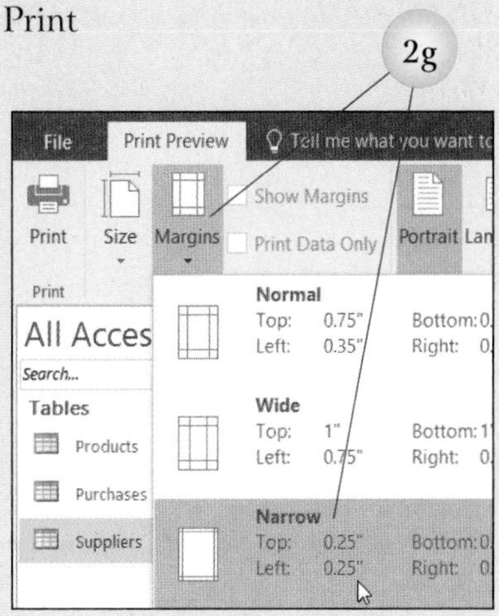

3. Close the Suppliers table.
4. Open the Products table and then print the table by completing the following steps:
   a. Click the File tab and then click the *Print* option.
   b. At the Print backstage area, click the *Print Preview* option.
   c. Click the Page Setup button in the Page Layout group on the Print Preview tab. (This displays the Page Setup dialog box with the Print Options tab selected.)
   d. At the Page Setup dialog box, click the Page tab.
   e. Click the *Landscape* option.

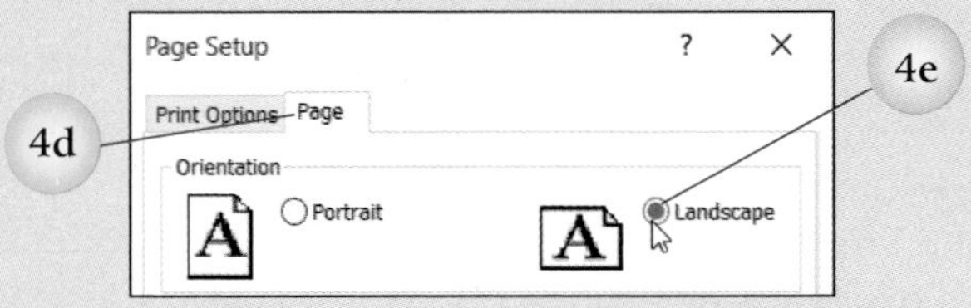

   f. Click the Print Options tab.
   g. Select the current measurement in the *Top* measurement box and then type 0.5.
   h. Select the current measurement in the *Bottom* measurement box and then type 0.5.
   i. Select the current measurement in the *Left* measurement box and then type 1.5.
   j. Click OK to close the dialog box.
   k. Click the Print button on the Print Preview tab and then click OK at the Print dialog box. (This table will print on two pages.)

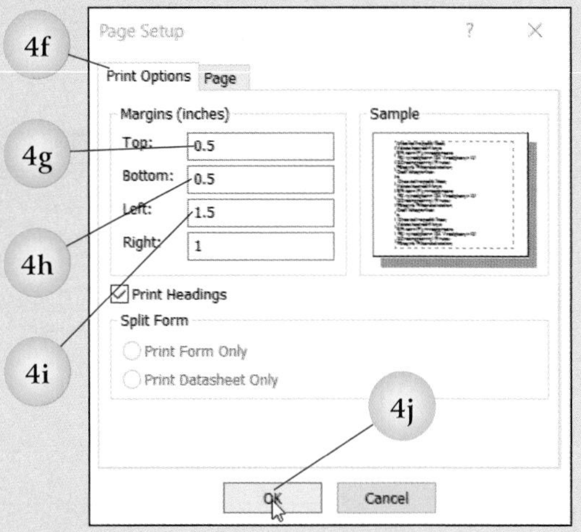

5. Close the Products table.
6. Rename the Purchases table by right-clicking *Purchases* in the Navigation pane, clicking *Rename* at the shortcut menu, typing Orders, and then pressing the Enter key.
7. Delete the Orders table by right-clicking *Orders* in the Tables group in the Navigation pane and then clicking *Delete* at the shortcut menu. If a message displays asking if you want to permanently delete the table, click Yes.

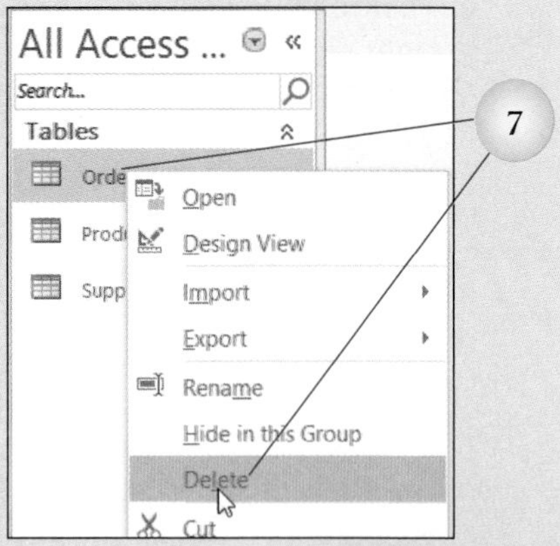

Check Your Work

Designing a Table

Tables are the first objects created in a new database and all other objects in a database rely on tables for data. Designing a database involves planning the number of tables needed and the fields that will be included in each table. Each table in a database should contain information about only one subject. For example, the Suppliers table in the 1-PacTrek.accdb database contains data only about suppliers and the Products table contains data only about products.

Database designers often create a visual representation of the database's structure in a diagram similar to the one shown in Figure 1.10. Each table is represented by a box with the table name at the top. Within each box, the fields that will be stored in the table are listed with the field names that will be used when the table is created.

Notice that one field in each table has an asterisk next to its name. The field with the asterisk is called the *primary key field*. A primary key field holds data that uniquely identifies each record in a table and is usually an identification number. The lines drawn between each table in Figure 1.10 are called *join lines,* and they represent links established between tables (called *relationships*) so that data can be extracted from one or more tables. The join lines point to a common field name included in each table that is to be linked. (Joining tables is covered in Chapter 2.) A database with related tables is called a *relational database*.

The join line in the database diagram connects the *SupplierID* field in the Suppliers table with the *SupplierID* field in the Products table and another join line connects the *SupplierID* field in the Suppliers table with the *SupplierID* field in the Orders table. A join line connects the *ProductID* field in the Products table with the *ProductID* field in the Orders table.

Hint Join tables to minimize or eliminate data duplication.

Consider certain design principles when designing a database. The first principle is to reduce redundant (duplicate) data. Redundant data increases the amount of data entry required, increases the chances for errors and inconsistencies, and takes up additional storage space. The Products table contains a *SupplierID* field and that field reduces the duplicate data needed in the table by keeping the data in one table instead of two and then joining the tables by a common field.

Figure 1.10 Database Diagram

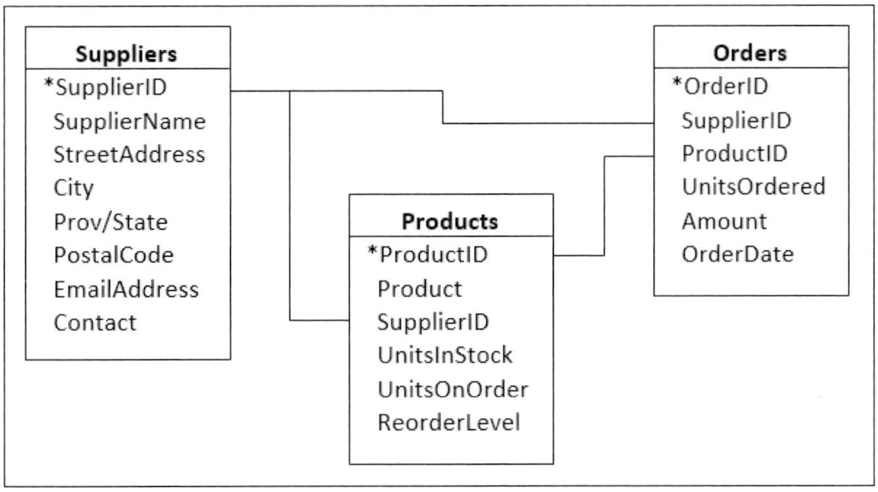

For example, rather than typing the supplier information in the Suppliers table *and* the Products table, type the information once in the Suppliers table and then join the tables with the connecting field *SupplierID*. If information is needed on suppliers as well as specific information about products, the information can be drawn into one object, such as a query or report using data from both tables. When creating the Orders table, the *SupplierID* field and the *ProductID* field will be used rather than typing all of the information for the suppliers and the product description. Typing a two-letter unique identifier number for a supplier greatly reduces the amount of typing required to create the Orders table. Inserting the *ProductID* field in the Orders table eliminates the need to type the product description for each order; instead, a unique five-, six-, or seven-digit identifier number is typed.

Tutorial

Creating a Table in Datasheet View

Hint A database table contains fields that can describe a person, customer, client, object, place, idea, or event.

Creating a Table

Creating a new table generally involves determining fields, assigning a data type to each field, modifying properties, designating the primary key field, and naming the table. This process is referred to as defining the table structure.

The first step in creating a table is to determine the fields. A field, commonly called a column, is one piece of information about a person, place, or item. Each field contains data about one aspect of the table subject, such as a company name or product number. All fields for one unit, such as a customer or product, are considered a record. For example, in the Suppliers table in the 1-PacTrek.accdb database, a record is all of the information pertaining to one supplier. A collection of records becomes a table.

When designing a table, determine the fields to be included based on how the information will be used. When organizing fields be sure to consider not only the current needs for the data but also any future needs. For example, a company may need to keep track of customer names, addresses, and telephone numbers for current mailing lists. In the future, the company may want to promote a new product to customers who purchase a specific type of product. For this information to be available at a later date, a field that identifies product type must be included in the database. When organizing fields, consider all potential needs for the data but also try to keep the fields logical and manageable.

Table

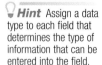

A table can be created in Datasheet view or Design view. To create a table in Datasheet view, open the desired database (or create a new database), click the Create tab, and then click the Table button in the Tables group. This inserts a blank table in the work area with the tab labeled *Table1*, as shown in Figure 1.11. Notice the column with the field name *ID* has been created automatically. Access creates *ID* as an AutoNumber data type field in which the field value is assigned automatically by Access as each record is entered in the table. In many tables, this AutoNumber data type field is used to create the unique identifier for the table. For example, in Project 2e, you will create an Orders table and use the *ID* AutoNumber data type field to assign automatically a number to each order, since each order must contain a unique number.

Hint Assign a data type to each field that determines the type of information that can be entered into the field.

When creating a new field (column), determine the type of data to be inserted in the field. For example, one field might contain text such as a name or product description, another field might contain an amount of money, and another might contain a date. The data type defines the type of information Access will allow to be entered into the field. For example, Access will not allow alphabetic characters to be entered into a field with a data type set to Date & Time.

Figure 1.11 Blank Table in Datasheet View

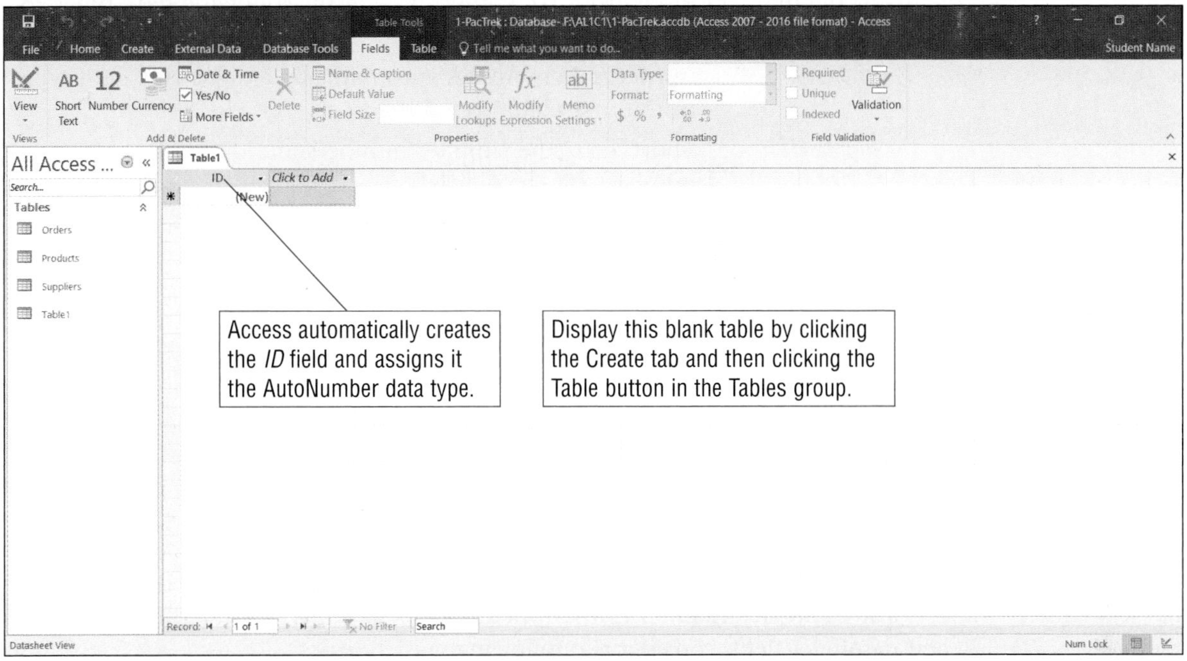
Access automatically creates the *ID* field and assigns it the AutoNumber data type.
Display this blank table by clicking the Create tab and then clicking the Table button in the Tables group.

More Fields

The Add & Delete group on the Table Tools Fields tab contains five buttons for assigning data types plus a More Fields button. Descriptions of the five data types assigned by the buttons are provided in Table 1.3.

Table 1.3 Data Types

Button	Description
Short Text	Alphanumeric data up to 255 characters in length—for example, a name, an address, or a value such as a telephone number or social security number that is used as an identifier and not for calculating.
Number	Positive or negative values that can be used in calculations; not to be used for values that will calculate monetary amounts (see Currency).
Currency	Values that involve money; Access will not round off during calculations.
Date & Time	Used to ensure dates and times are entered and sorted properly.
Yes/No	Data in the field will be either *Yes* or *No*; *True* or *False*, *On* or *Off*.

In Project 2e, you will create the Orders table, as shown in Figure 1.12. Looking at the diagram in Figure 1.10, you will assign the following data types to the columns:

OrderID:	AutoNumber (Access automatically assigns this data type to the first column)
SupplierID:	Short Text (the supplier numbers are identifiers, not numbers for calculating)
ProductID:	Short Text (the product numbers are identifiers, not numbers for calculating)
UnitsOrdered:	Number (the unit numbers are values for calculating)
Amount:	Currency
OrderDate:	Date & Time

Click a data type button and Access inserts a field to the right of the *ID* field and selects the field heading *Field1*. Type a name for the field; press the Enter key; and Access selects the next field heading, named *Click to Add,* and displays a drop-down list of data types. This drop-down list contains the same five data types as the buttons in the Add & Delete group as well as additional data types. Click the data type at the drop-down list, type the field name, and then press the Enter key. Continue in this manner until all field names have been entered for the table. When naming a field, consider the following guidelines:

- Each field must have a unique name.
- The name should describe the contents of the field.
- A field name can contain up to 64 characters.
- A field name can contain letters and numbers. Some symbols are permitted but others are excluded, so avoid using symbols other than the underscore (to separate words) and the number symbol (to indicate an identifier number).
- Do not use spaces in field names. Although a space is an accepted character, most database designers avoid using spaces in field names and object names. Use field compound words for field names or the underscore character as a word separator. For example, a field name for a person's last name could be named *LastName*, *Last_Name*, or *LName*.
- Abbreviate field names so that they are as short as possible but still easily understood. For example, a field such as *CompanyName* could be shortened to *CoName* and a field such as *EmailAddress* could be shortened to *Email*.

Hint Avoid using spaces in field names.

Project 2e Creating a Table and Entering Data

Part 5 of 7

1. With **1-PacTrek.accdb** open, create a new table and specify data types and field names by completing the following steps:
   a. Click the Create tab.
   b. Click the Table button in the Tables group.
   c. Click the Short Text button in the Add & Delete group.

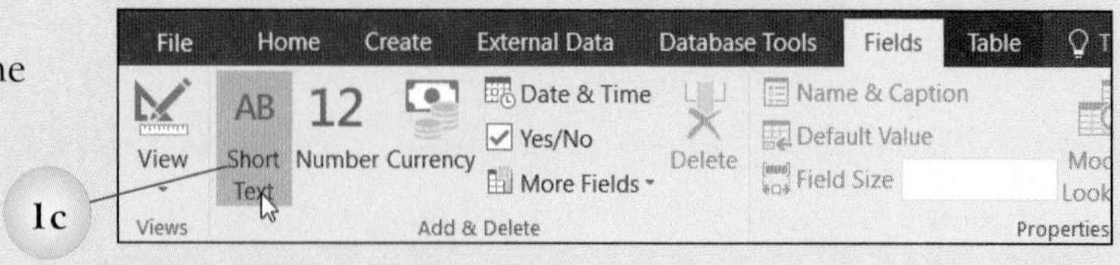

d. With the *Field1* field name selected, type SupplierID and then press the Enter key. (This displays a drop-down list of data types below the *Click to Add* heading.)
e. Click the *Short Text* option at the drop-down list.
f. Type ProductID in the next field name and then press the Enter key.

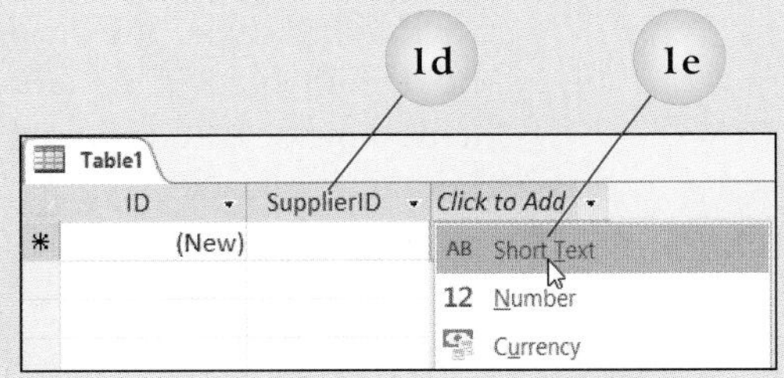

g. Click *Number* at the drop-down list, type UnitsOrdered in the next field name, and then press the Enter key.
h. Click *Currency* at the drop-down list, type Amount for the next field, and then press the Enter key.
i. Click *Date & Time* at the drop-down list and then type OrderDate. (Do not press the Enter key since this is the last field in the table.)

2. Enter the first record in the table, as shown in Figure 1.12, by completing the following steps:
   a. Click two times in the first field below the *SupplierID* field name. (The first time you click the mouse button, the row is selected. Clicking the second time makes only the field below *SupplierID* active.)
   b. Type the data in the fields as shown in Figure 1.12. Press the Tab key to move to the next field or press Shift + Tab to move to the previous field. Access will automatically insert the next number in the sequence in the first field column (the *ID* field column). When typing the money amounts in the *Amount* field column, you do not need to type the dollar symbol or the comma. Access will automatically insert them when you make the next field active. Make sure to proofread the data after you type it to ensure it is accurate.
3. When the 14 records have been entered, click the Save button on the Quick Access Toolbar.
4. At the Save As dialog box, type Orders and then press the Enter key. (This saves the table with the name *Orders*.)
5. Close the Orders table by clicking the Close button in the upper right corner of the work area.

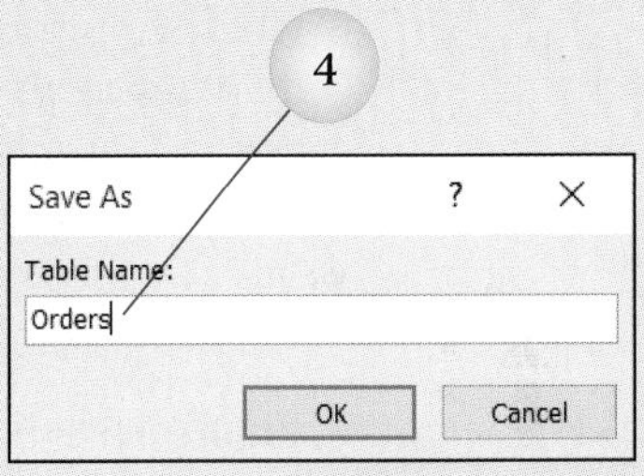

Check Your Work

Figure 1.12 Project 2e

Orders

ID	SupplierID	ProductID	UnitsOrderec	Amount	OrderDate	Click to Add
1	54	101-S3	10	$1,137.50	1/5/2018	
2	68	209-L	25	$173.75	1/5/2018	
3	68	209-XL	25	$180.00	1/5/2018	
4	68	209-XXL	20	$145.80	1/5/2018	
5	68	210-M	15	$97.35	1/5/2018	
6	68	210-L	25	$162.25	1/5/2018	
7	31	299-M2	10	$887.90	1/19/2018	
8	31	299-M3	10	$887.90	1/19/2018	
9	31	299-M5	10	$887.90	1/19/2018	
10	31	299-W1	8	$602.32	1/19/2018	
11	31	299-W3	10	$752.90	1/19/2018	
12	31	299-W4	10	$752.90	1/19/2018	
13	31	299-W5	10	$752.90	1/19/2018	
14	35	602-XR	5	$2,145.00	1/19/2018	
(New)			0	$0.00		

Renaming a Field

Click a data type button or click a data type at the data type drop-down list and the default field name (such as *Field1*) is automatically selected. With the default field name selected, type a name for the field. To change a field name, right-click the name, click *Rename Field* at the shortcut menu (which selects the current field name), and then type the new name.

Tutorial

Modifying Field Properties in Datasheet View

Name & Caption

Inserting a Name, Caption, and Description

When creating a table that others will use, consider providing additional information so users understand the fields in the table and what should be entered in each one. Along with the field name, provide a caption and description for each field with options at the Enter Field Properties dialog box, shown in Figure 1.13. Display this dialog box by clicking the Name & Caption button in the Properties group on the Table Tools Fields tab.

At the Enter Field Properties dialog box, type the desired name for the field in the *Name* text box. To provide a more descriptive name for the field, type the descriptive name in the *Caption* text box. The text typed will display as the field caption but the actual field name will still be part of the table structure. Creating a caption is useful if the field name is abbreviated or to show spaces between words in a field name. The field name is what Access uses for the table and the caption is what displays to users.

The *Description* text box is another source for providing information about the field to others using the database. Type information in the text box that specifies what should be entered in the field. The text typed in the *Description* text box displays at the left side of the Status bar when a field in a column is active. For example, type *Enter the total amount of the order* in the *Description* text box for the *Amount* field and that text will display at the left side of the Status bar when a field in the column is active.

Figure 1.13 Enter Field Properties Dialog Box

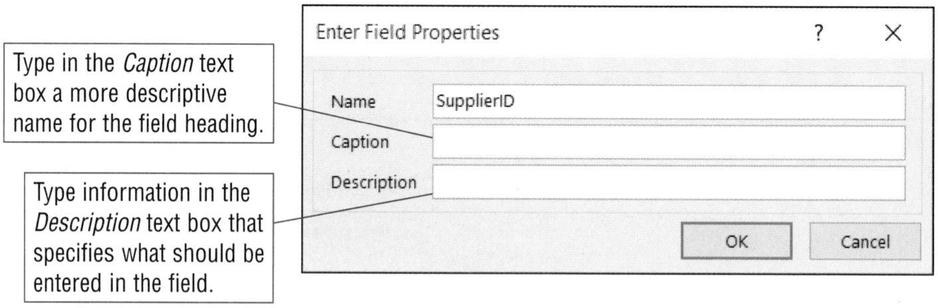
Type in the Caption text box a more descriptive name for the field heading.
Type information in the Description text box that specifies what should be entered in the field.
Enter Field Properties
?
X
Name
SupplierID
Caption
Description
OK
Cancel

Project 2f Inserting a Name, Caption, and Description

1. With **1-PacTrek.accdb** open, open the Orders table.
2. Access automatically named the first field *ID*. You want to make the field name more descriptive so you decide to rename it. To do this, right-click the *ID* field name and then click *Rename Field* at the drop-down list.

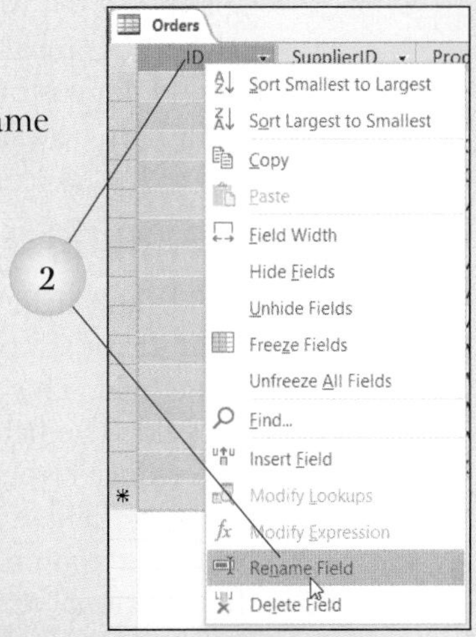

3. Type OrderID and then press the Enter key.
4. To provide more information for others using the table, you decide to add information for the *SupplierID* field by creating a caption and description. To do this, complete the following steps:
   a. Click the *SupplierID* field name in the header row. (This selects the entire column.)
   b. Click the Table Tools Fields tab.
   c. Click the Name & Caption button in the Properties group. (At the Enter Field Properties dialog box, notice that *SupplierID* is already inserted in the *Name* text box.)

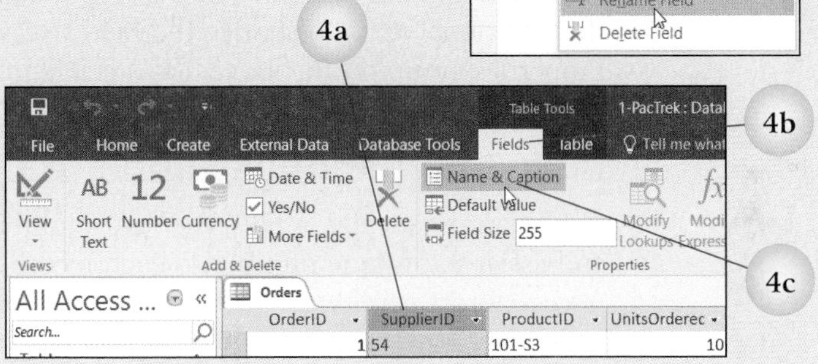

   d. At the Enter Field Properties dialog box, click in the *Caption* text box and then type Supplier Number.
   e. Click in the *Description* text box and then type Supplier identification number.
   f. Click OK to close the dialog box. (Notice that the field name now displays as *Supplier Number*. The field name is still *SupplierID* but what displays is *Supplier Number*.)

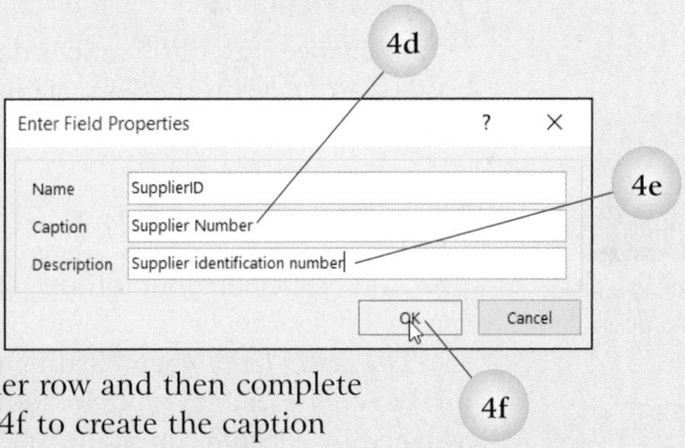

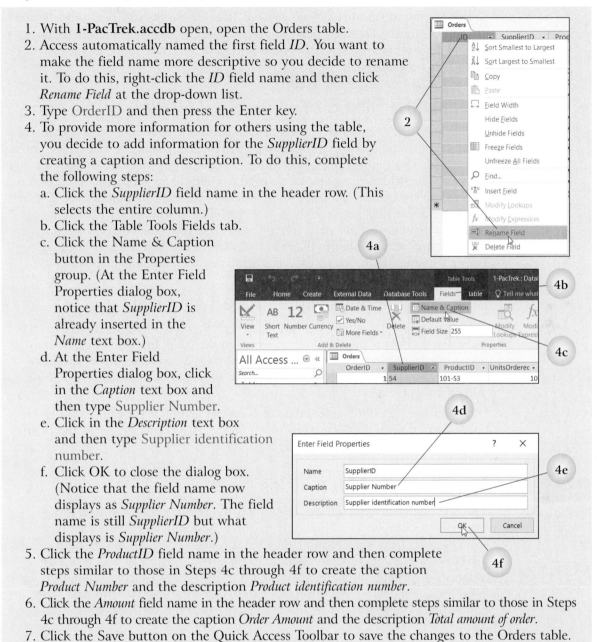

5. Click the *ProductID* field name in the header row and then complete steps similar to those in Steps 4c through 4f to create the caption *Product Number* and the description *Product identification number*.
6. Click the *Amount* field name in the header row and then complete steps similar to those in Steps 4c through 4f to create the caption *Order Amount* and the description *Total amount of order*.
7. Click the Save button on the Quick Access Toolbar to save the changes to the Orders table.
8. Close the Orders table.

Check Your Work

Assigning a Default Value

Default Value

The Properties group on the Table Tools Fields tab contains additional buttons for defining field properties in a table. If most records in a table are likely to contain the same field value in a column, consider inserting that value by default. Do this by clicking the Default Value button in the Properties group. At the Expression Builder dialog box, type the default value and then click OK.

For example, in Project 2g, you will create a new table in the 1-PacTrek database containing information on customers, most of whom live in Vancouver, British Columbia. You will create a default value of *Vancouver* for the *City* field and a default value of *BC* for the *Prov/State* field. You can replace the default value with different text, so if a customer lives in Abbotsford instead of Vancouver, simply type *Abbotsford* in the *City* field instead.

Assigning a Field Size

The default field size property varies depending on the data type. For example, the Short Text data type assigns a maximum length of 255 characters that can be entered in the field. This number can be decreased depending on what data will be entered in the field. The field size can also be changed to control how much data is entered to help reduce errors. For example, if the two-letter state abbreviation is to be inserted in a state field, a field size of 2 characters can be assigned to the field. If someone entering data into the table tries to type more than two letters, Access will not accept the additional text. To change the field size, click in the *Field Size* text box in the Properties group on the Table Tools Fields tab and then type the number.

Changing the AutoNumber Data Type Field

Access automatically applies the AutoNumber data type to the first field in a table and assigns a unique number to each record in the table. In many cases, letting Access automatically assign a number to a record is a good idea. Some situations may arise, however, when the unique value in the first field should be something other than a number.

To change the AutoNumber data type for the first field, click the *Data Type* option box arrow in the Formatting group on the Table Tools Fields tab and then click the data type at the drop-down list.

Tutorial

Creating a Table Using Quick Start Fields

AB Short Text

Inserting Quick Start Fields

The Add & Delete group on the Table Tools Fields tab contains buttons for specifying data types. The Short Text button was used to specify the data type for the *SupplierID* field when creating the Orders table. The field drop-down list was also used to choose a data type. In addition to these two methods, a data type can be assigned by clicking the More Fields button in the Add & Delete group on the Table Tools Fields tab. Click this button and a drop-down list displays with data types grouped into categories such as *Basic Types*, *Number*, *Date and Time*, *Yes/No*, and *Quick Start*.

The options in the *Quick Start* category not only define a data type but also assign a field name. Additionally, with options in the *Quick Start* category, a group of related fields can be added in one step. For example, click the *Name* option in the *Quick Start* category and Access inserts the *LastName* field in one column and the *FirstName* field in the next column. Both fields are automatically assigned a Short Text data type. Click the *Address* option in the *Quick Start* category and Access inserts five fields, including *Address*, *City*, *StateProvince*, *ZIPPostal*, and *CountryRegion*—all with the Short Text data type assigned.

Project 2g Creating a Customers Table

Part 7 of 7

1. The owners of Pacific Trek have decided to publish a semiannual product catalog and have asked customers who want to receive the catalog to fill out a form and include on the form whether or not they want to receive notices of upcoming sales in addition to the catalog. Create a table to store the data for customers by completing the following steps:
   a. With **1-PacTrek.accdb** open, click the Create tab.
   b. Click the Table button in the Tables group.
   c. With the *Click to Add* field active, click the More Fields button in the Add & Delete group on the Table Tools Fields tab.
   d. Scroll down the drop-down list and then click *Name* in the *Quick Start* category. (This inserts the captions *Last Name* and *First Name* in the table. The actual field names are *LastName* and *FirstName*.)

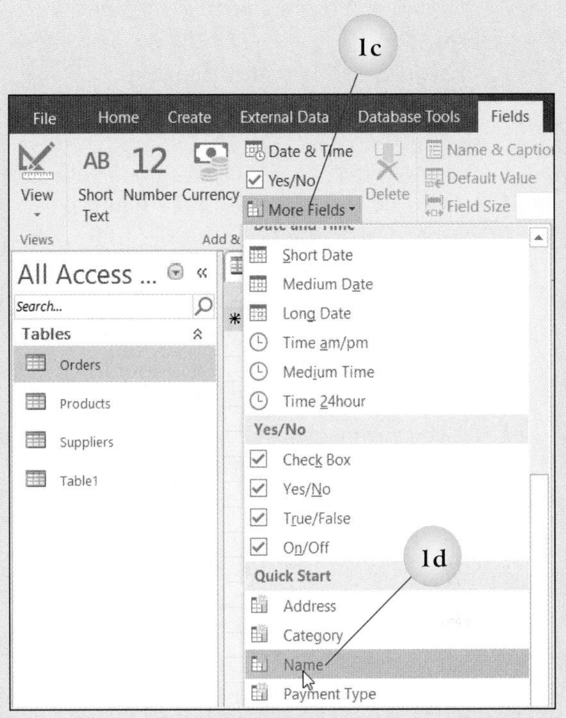

   e. Click *Click to Add* immediately right of the *First Name* field name in the header row. (Although the data type drop-down list displays, you are going to use the More Fields button rather than the drop-down list to create the next fields.)
   f. Click the More Fields button, scroll down the drop-down list, and then click *Address* in the *Quick Start* category. (This inserts five more fields in the table.)
   g. Scroll to the right in the table to display *Click to Add* that follows the *Country Region* field name in the header row. (You can scroll in the table using the horizontal scroll bar to the right of the Record Navigation bar.)
   h. Click *Click to Add* and then click *Yes/No* at the drop-down list.

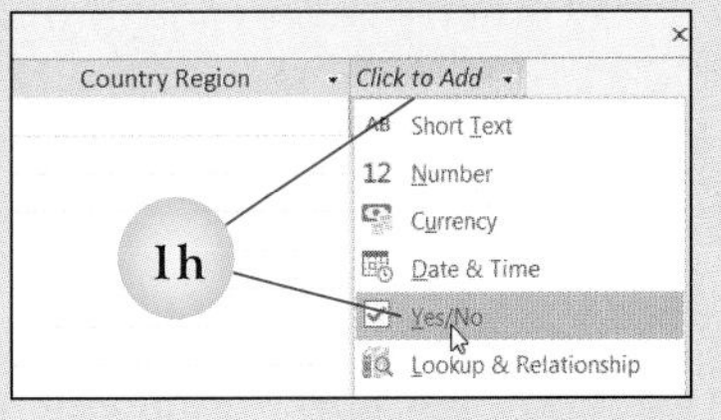

   i. With the name *Field1* selected, type Mailers. (When entering records in the table, you will insert a check mark in the field check box if a customer wants to receive sales promotion mailers. If a customer does not want to receive the mailers, you will leave the check box blank.)

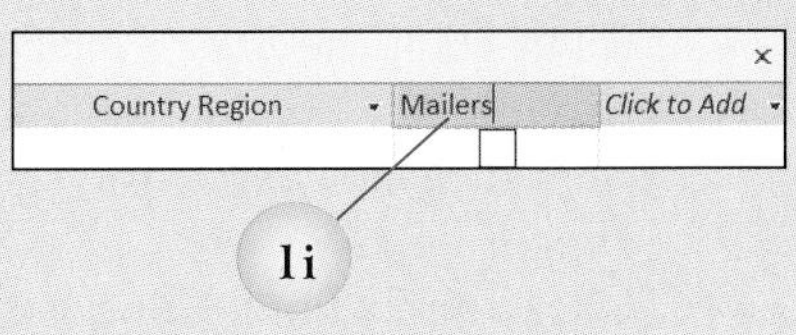

2. Rename and create a caption and description for the *ID* field by completing the following steps:
   a. Scroll to the beginning of the table and then click the *ID* field name in the header row. (You can scroll in the table using the horizontal scroll bar to the right of the Record Navigation bar.)
   b. Click the Name & Caption button in the Properties group on the Table Tools Fields tab.
   c. At the Enter Field Properties dialog box, select the text *ID* in the *Name* text box and then type CustomerID.

d. Press the Tab key and then type Customer Number in the *Caption* text box.
e. Press the Tab key and then type Access will automatically assign the record the next number in the sequence.
f. Click OK to close the Enter Field Properties dialog box. (Notice the description at the left side of the Status bar.)

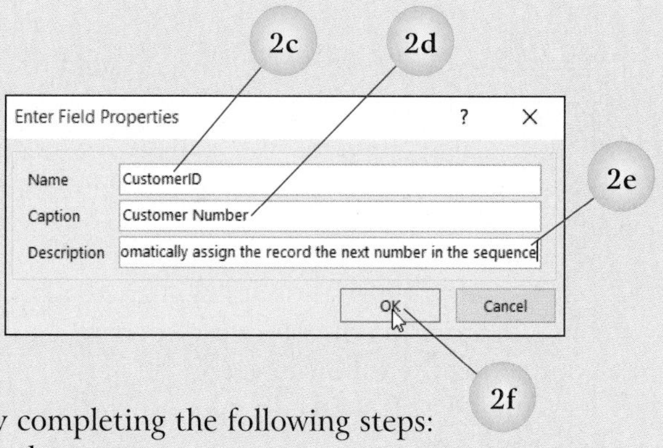

3. Add a description to the *Last Name* field by completing the following steps:
   a. Click the *Last Name* field name in the header row.
   b. Click the Name & Caption button in the Properties group.
   c. At the Enter Field Properties dialog box notice that Access named the field *LastName* but provided the caption *Last Name*. You do not want to change the name and caption so press the Tab key two times to make the *Description* text box active and then type Customer last name.
   d. Click OK to close the dialog box.
4. You know that a customer's last name will not likely exceed 30 characters, so you decide to limit the field size. To do this, click in the *Field Size* text box in the Properties group (this selects *255*), type 30, and then press the Enter key.

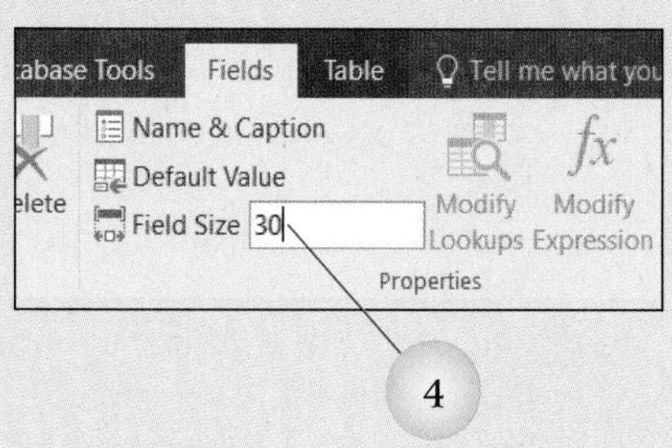

5. Click the *First Name* field name in the header row and then complete steps similar to those in Steps 3 and 4 to create the description *Customer first name* and change the field size to 30 characters.
6. Since most of Pacific Trek's customers live in the city of Vancouver, you decide to make it the default field value. To do this, complete the following steps:
   a. Click the *City* field name in the header row.
   b. Click the Default Value button in the Properties group.
   c. At the Expression Builder dialog box, type Vancouver.
   d. Click the OK button to close the dialog box.

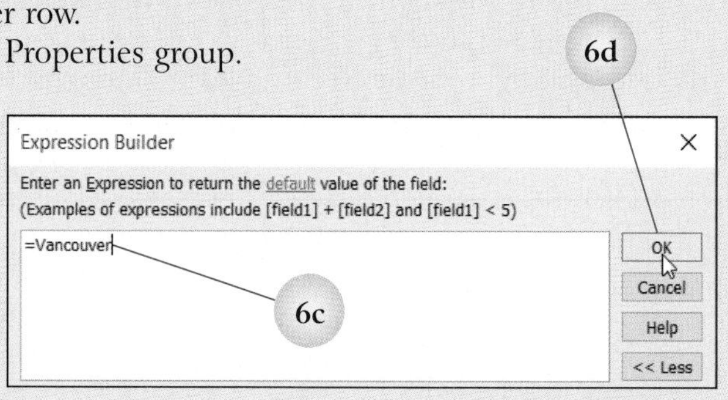

7. Change the *State Province* field name and insert a default value by completing the following steps:
   a. Right-click the *State Province* field name in the header row and then click *Rename Field* at the shortcut menu.
   b. Type Province.
   c. Click the Default Value button in the Properties group.
   d. Type BC in the Expression Builder dialog box and then click the OK button.
8. Click the *ZIP Postal* field name in the header row and then limit the field size to 7 characters by clicking in the *Field Size* text box (which selects *255*), typing 7, and then pressing the Enter key.

9. Since most customers want to be sent the sales promotional mailers, you decide to insert a check mark as the default value in the check boxes in the *Yes/No* column. To do this, complete the following steps:
   a. Click the *Mailers* field name in the header row.
   b. Click the Default Value button in the Properties group.
   c. At the Expression Builder dialog box, press the Backspace key two times to delete *No* and then type Yes.
   d. Click OK to close the dialog box.
10. Delete the *Country Region* field by clicking the *Country Region* field name in the header row and then clicking the Delete button in the Add & Delete group.
11. Save the table by completing the following steps:
   a. Click the Save button on the Quick Access Toolbar.
   b. At the Save As dialog box, type Customers and then press the Enter key.
12. Enter the six records in the table shown in Figure 1.14. To remove a check mark in the *Mailers* column, press the spacebar.
13. Adjust the field column widths to accommodate the longest entry in each column by completing the following steps:
   a. Position the arrow pointer on the *Customer Number* field name in the header row until the pointer turns into a down-pointing black arrow, click and hold down the left mouse button, drag to the *Mailers* field name, and then release the mouse button.
   b. With the columns selected, double-click one of the column boundary lines in the header row.
14. Click the Save button on the Quick Access Toolbar to save the Customers table.
15. Print the Customers table by completing the following steps:
   a. Click the File tab and then click the *Print* option.
   b. At the Print backstage area, click the *Print Preview* option.
   c. Click the Landscape button in the Page Layout group on the Print Preview tab.
   d. Click the Print button at the left side of the Print Preview tab.
   e. At the Print dialog box, click OK.
16. Close the Customers table.
17. Open the Orders table.
18. Automatically adjust the field column widths to accommodate the longest entry in each column.
19. Click the Save button to save the Orders table.
20. Print the table in landscape orientation (refer to Step 15) and then close the table.
21. Close **1-PacTrek.accdb**.

Check Your Work

Figure 1.14 Project 2g

Customers

	Customer Number	Last Name	First Name	Address	City	Province	ZIP Postal	Mailers
	1	Blakely	Mathias	7433 224th Ave. E	Vancouver	BC	V5K 2M7	☑
	2	Donato	Antonio	18225 Victoria Dr.	Vancouver	BC	V5K 1H4	☐
	3	Girard	Stephanie	430 Deer Lake Pl.	Burnaby	BC	V3J 1E4	☑
	4	Hernandez	Angelica	1233 E. 59th Ave.	Vancouver	BC	V5K 3H3	☑
	5	Ives-Keller	Shane	9055 Gilbert Rd.	Richmond	BC	V6Y 1B2	☐
	6	Kim	Keung	730 West Broadway	Vancouver	BC	V5K 5B2	☑
*	(New)				Vancouver	BC		☑

Chapter Summary

- Microsoft Access is a database management system software program that can organize, store, maintain, retrieve, sort, and print all types of business data.
- In Access, open an existing database by clicking the Open Other Files hyperlink at the Access 2016 opening screen. At the Open backstage area, click the *Browse* option. At the Open dialog box, navigate to the location of the database and then double-click the database.
- Some common objects found in a database include tables, queries, forms, and reports.
- The Navigation pane displays at the left side of the Access screen and displays the objects that are contained in the database.
- Open a database object by double-clicking the object in the Navigation pane or by right-clicking the object and then clicking *Open* at the shortcut menu.
- Close an object by clicking the Close button in the upper right corner of the work area or right-clicking the object tab and then clicking *Close* at the shortcut menu.
- When a table is open, the Record Navigation bar displays at the bottom of the screen and contains buttons for displaying records in the table.
- Insert a new record in a table by clicking the New button in the Records group on the Home tab or by clicking the New (blank) record button in the Record Navigation bar.
- Delete a record by clicking in a field in the record to be deleted, clicking the Delete button arrow on the Home tab, and then clicking *Delete Record* at the drop-down list.
- Add a field column to a table by clicking in the first field below *Click to Add* and then typing the data.
- Move a field column by selecting the column and then using the mouse to drag a thick, black, vertical line (representing the column) to the desired location.
- Delete a field column by clicking in any field in the column, clicking the Delete button arrow, and then clicking *Delete Column* at the drop-down list.
- Data entered in a table is automatically saved while changes to the layout of a table are not automatically saved.
- Hide, unhide, freeze, and unfreeze field columns with options at the More button drop-down list. Display this list by clicking the More button in the Records group on the Home tab.
- Adjust the width of a field column with options at the Column Width dialog box. Display the dialog box by clicking the More button and then clicking *Field Width* at the drop-down list. Enter a column measurement in the *Column Width* measurement box or click the Best Fit button.
- Adjust the width of a field column by dragging the column boundary line in the header row. Or, adjust the width of a column (or selected columns) to accommodate the longest entry by double-clicking the column boundary line.
- Rename a table by right-clicking the table name in the Navigation pane, clicking *Rename*, and then typing the new name. Delete a table by right-clicking the table name in the Navigation pane and then clicking *Delete*.
- Print a table by clicking the File tab, clicking the *Print* option, and then clicking the *Quick Print* option. Preview a table before printing by clicking the *Print Preview* option at the Print backstage area.

- Use buttons and options on the Print Preview tab to change the page size, orientation, and margins.
- The first principle in database design is to reduce redundant data, because redundant data increases the amount of data entry required and the potential for errors, as well as takes up additional storage space.
- A data type defines the type of data Access will allow in the field. Assign a data type to a field with buttons in the Add & Delete group on the Table Tools Fields tab, by clicking an option from the field drop-down list, or with options at the More Fields button drop-down list.
- Rename a field by right-clicking the field name, clicking *Rename Field* at the shortcut menu, and then typing the new name.
- Type a name, caption, and description for a field with options at the Enter Field Properties dialog box.
- Use options in the *Quick Start* category in the More Fields button drop-down list to define a data type and assign a field name to a group of related fields.
- Insert a default value in a field with the Default Value button and assign a field size with the *Field Size* text box in the Properties group on the Table Tools Fields tab.
- Use the *Data Type* option box in the Formatting group on the Table Tools Fields tab to change the AutoNumber data type for the first column in a table.

Commands Review

FEATURE	RIBBON TAB, GROUP/OPTION	BUTTON, OPTION	KEYBOARD SHORTCUT
close Access			Alt + F4
close database	File, *Close*		
create table	Create, Tables		
Currency data type	Table Tools Fields, Add & Delete		
Date & Time data type	Table Tools Fields, Add & Delete		
delete column	Home, Records	, *Delete Column*	
delete record	Home, Records	, *Delete Record*	
Enter Field Properties dialog box	Table Tools Fields, Properties		
Expression Builder dialog box	Table Tools Fields, Properties		
freeze column	Home, Records	, *Freeze Fields*	
hide column	Home, Records	, *Hide Fields*	

FEATURE	RIBBON TAB, GROUP/OPTION	BUTTON, OPTION	KEYBOARD SHORTCUT
landscape orientation	File, *Print*	*Print Preview*,	
new record	Home, Records		Ctrl + +
next field			Tab
Number data type	Table Tools Fields, Add & Delete	12	
Page Setup dialog box	File, *Print*	*Print Preview*,	
page size	File, *Print*	*Print Preview*,	
page margins	File, *Print*	*Print Preview*,	
portrait orientation	File, *Print*	*Print Preview*,	
previous field			Shift + Tab
Print backstage area	File, *Print*		
Print dialog box	File, *Print*	*Print*	Ctrl + P
Print Preview	File, *Print*	*Print Preview*	
Short Text data type	Table Tools Fields, Add & Delete	AB	
unfreeze column	Home, Records	, *Unfreeze Fields*	
unhide column	Home, Records	, *Unhide Fields*	
Yes/No data type	Table Tools Fields, Add & Delete		

Workbook

Chapter study tools and assessment activities are available in the *Workbook* ebook. These resources are designed to help you further develop and demonstrate mastery of the skills learned in this chapter.

Microsoft®

Access®

Creating Relationships between Tables

CHAPTER 2

Performance Objectives

Upon successful completion of Chapter 2, you will be able to:

1 Define a primary key field in a table
2 Create a one-to-many relationship
3 Specify referential integrity
4 Print, edit, and delete relationships
5 Create a one-to-one relationship
6 View and edit a subdatasheet

Precheck

Check your current skills to help focus your study.

Access is a relational database program you can use to create tables that are related or connected within the same database. When a relationship is established between tables, you can view and edit records in related tables with a subdatasheet. In this chapter, you will learn how to identify a primary key field in a table that is unique to that table, how to join tables by creating a relationship between them, and how to view and edit subdatasheets.

Data Files

Before beginning chapter work, copy the AL1C2 folder to your storage medium and then make AL1C2 the active folder.

SNAP

If you are a SNAP user, launch the Precheck and Tutorials from your Assignments page.

Project 1 **Establish Relationships between Tables** **4 Parts**

You will specify the primary keys field in tables, establish one-to-many relationships between tables, specify referential integrity, and print the relationships. You will also edit and delete a relationship.

Preview Finished Project

Relating Tables

Hint Defining a relationship between tables is one of the most powerful features of a relational database management system.

Generally, a database management system fits into one of two categories: a file management system (also sometimes referred to as a *flat file database*) or a relational database management system. A flat file management system stores all data in a single directory and cannot contain multiple tables. This type of management system is a simple way to store data but becomes inefficient as more data is added. In a relational database management system, like Access, relationships are defined between sets of data, allowing greater flexibility in manipulating data and eliminating data redundancy (entering the same data in more than one place).

In Project 1, you will define relationships between tables in the Pacific Trek database. Because the tables in the database will be related, information on the same product does not need to be repeated in multiple tables. If you used a flat file management system to maintain product information, you would need to repeat that product description each time.

Determining Relationships

Taking time to plan a database is extremely important. Creating a database with related tables takes even more consideration. Determine how to break down the required data and what tables to create to eliminate redundancies. One idea to help determine what tables are necessary in a database is to think of the word *about*. For example, the Pacific Trek store needs a table *about* products, another *about* suppliers, and another *about* orders. A table should be about only one subject, such as products, suppliers, or orders.

Along with determining the necessary tables for a database, determine the relationship between those tables. The ability to relate, or "join," tables is what makes Access a relational database management system. As explained in Chapter 1, database designers often create a visual representation of the database's structure in a diagram. Figure 2.1 displays the database diagram for the Pacific Trek database. (Some of the fields in tables have been modified slightly from the database used in Chapter 1.)

Tutorial

Setting the Primary Key Field

Setting the Primary Key Field

A database table can contain two different types of key fields: a primary key field and a foreign key field. In the database diagram in Figure 2.1, notice that one field in each table contains an asterisk. The asterisk indicates a primary key field, which is a field that holds data that uniquely identifies each record in a table. For example, the *SupplierID* field in the Suppliers table contains a unique supplier number for each record in the table and the *ProductID* field in the Products table contains a unique product number for each product. A table can have only one primary key field and it is the field by which the table is sorted whenever the table is opened.

Figure 2.1 Pacific Trek Database Diagram

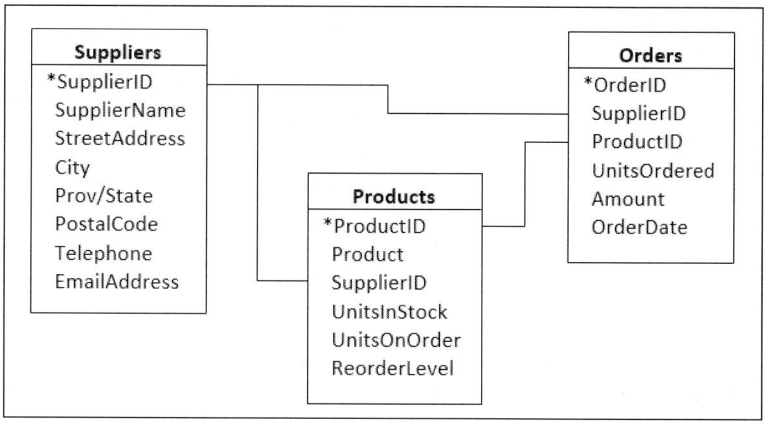

Quick Steps

Define a Primary Key Field

1. Open table.
2. Click View button.
3. Click field.
4. Click Primary Key button.
5. Click Save button

When a new record is added to a table, Access checks to ensure that there is no existing record with the same data in the primary key field. If there is, Access displays an error message indicating there are duplicate values and does not allow the record to be saved. When adding a new record to a table, the primary key field cannot be left blank. Access expects a value in each record in the table and this is referred to as *entity integrity*. If a value is not entered in a field, Access actually enters a null value. A null value cannot be given to a primary key field. Access will not allow a database to be closed that contains a primary key field with a null value.

Primary Key

Hint Access uses a primary key field to associate data from multiple tables.

By default, Access includes the *ID* field as the first field in a table, assigns the AutoNumber data type, and identifies the field as the primary key field. The AutoNumber data type assigns the first record a field value of *1* and each new record is assigned the next sequential number. Use this default field as the primary key field or define a different primary key field. To determine what field is the primary key field or to define a primary key field, display the table in Design view. To do this, open the table and then click the View button at the left side of the Home tab. A table also can be opened in Design view by clicking the View button arrow and then clicking *Design View* at the drop-down list. To add or remove a primary key designation from a field, click the desired field in the *Field Name* column and then click the Primary Key button in the Tools group on the Table Tools Design tab. A key icon is inserted in the field selector bar (the blank column to the left of the field names) for the desired field. Figure 2.2 displays the Products table in Design view with the *ProductID* field identified as the primary key field.

Typically, a primary key field in one table becomes the foreign key field in a related table. For example, the primary key field *SupplierID* in the Suppliers table is considered the foreign key field in the Orders table. In the Suppliers table, each entry in the *SupplierID* field must be unique since it is the primary key field but the same supplier number may appear more than once in the *SupplierID* field in the Orders table (for instance, in a situation when more than one product is ordered from the same supplier).

Hint You must enter a value in the primary key field in every record.

Data in the foreign key field must match data in the primary key field of the related table. For example, any supplier number entered in the *SupplierID* field in the Orders table must also be contained in the Suppliers table. In other words, an order would not be placed by a supplier that does not exist in the Suppliers table. Figure 2.3 identifies the primary and foreign key fields in the tables in the Pacific Trek database. Primary key fields are identified with *(PK)* and foreign key fields are identified with *(FK)* in the figure.

Figure 2.2 Products Table in Design View

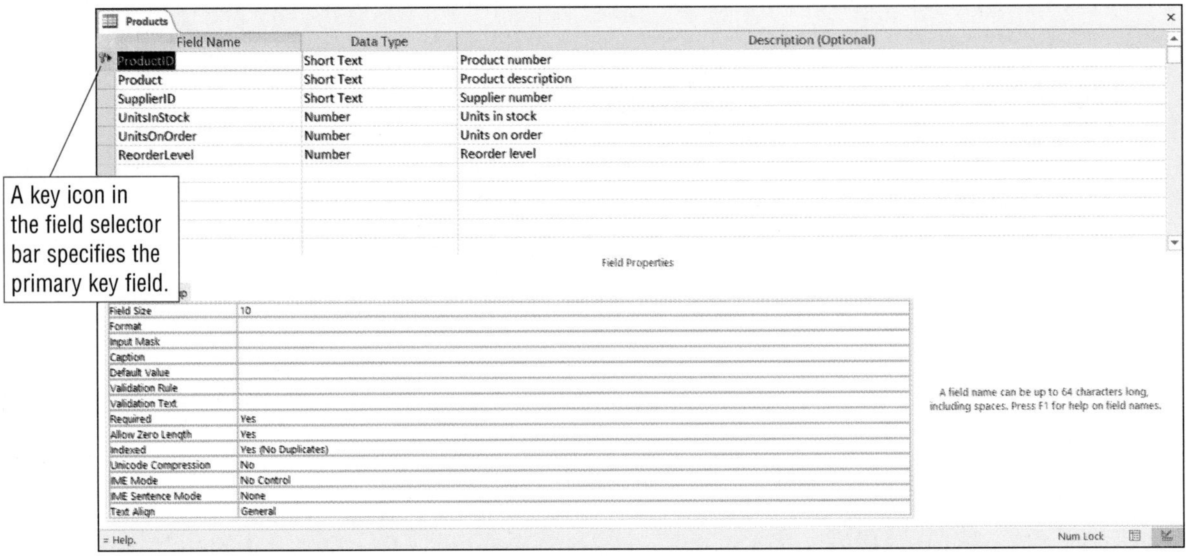

Figure 2.3 Pacific Trek Database Diagram with Primary and Foreign Key Fields Identified

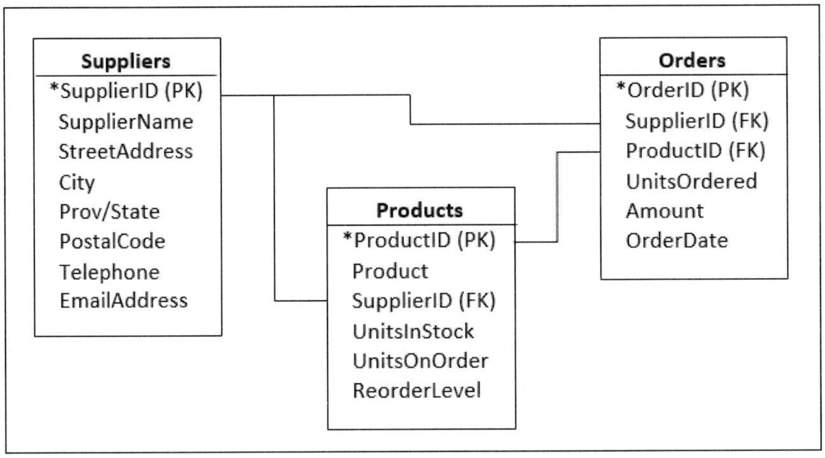

Project 1a Defining a Primary Key Field

Part 1 of 4

1. Open Access.
2. At the Access 2016 opening screen, click the Open Other Files hyperlink at the left side of the screen.
3. At the Open backstage area, click the *Browse* option.
4. At the Open dialog box, navigate to the AL1C2 folder on your storage medium and then double-click the database ***2-PacTrek.accdb***.
5. Click the Enable Content button in the message bar if the security warning message appears. (The message bar will display immediately below the ribbon.)
6. Open the Products table.

7. View the primary key field by completing the following steps:
   a. Click the View button at the left side of the Home tab. (This displays the table in Design view.)

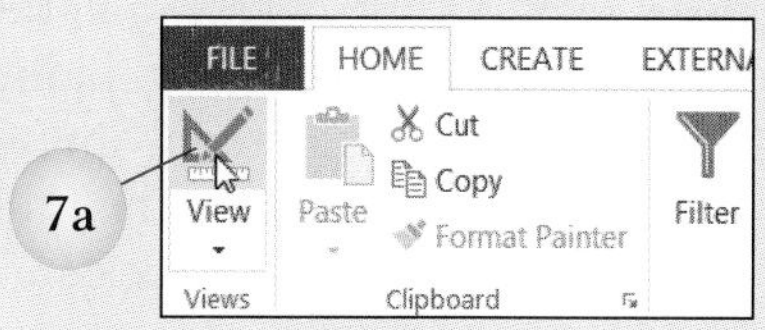

   b. In Design view, notice the *Field Name*, *Data Type*, and *Description* columns and the information that displays for each field. The first field, *ProductID*, is the primary key field and is identified by the key icon in the field selector bar.
   c. Click the View button to return to the Datasheet view.
   d. Close the Products table.
8. Open the Suppliers table, click the View button to display the table in Design view, and then notice the *SupplierID* field is defined as the primary key field.
9. Click the View button to return to Datasheet view and then close the table.
10. Open the Orders table. (The first field in the Orders table has been changed from the AutoNumber data type field automatically assigned by Access, to a Short Text data type field.)
11. Define the *OrderID* field as the primary key field by completing the following steps:
    a. Click the View button at the left side of the Home tab.
    b. With the table in Design view and the *OrderID* field selected in the *Field Name* column, click the Primary Key button in the Tools group on the Table Tools Design tab.

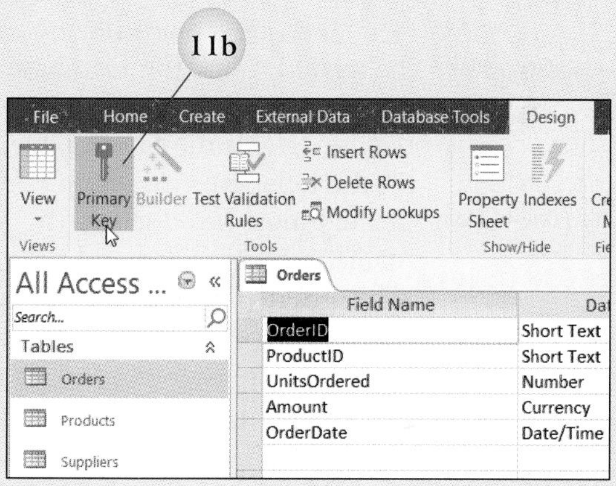

    c. Click the Save button on the Quick Access Toolbar.
    d. Click the View button to return the table to Datasheet view.
12. Move the *OrderDate* field by completing the following steps:
    a. Click the *OrderDate* field name in the header row. (This selects the column.)
    b. Position the mouse pointer on the field name in the header row; click and hold down the left mouse button; drag to the left until the thick, black vertical line displays immediately left of the *ProductID* field; and then release the mouse button.

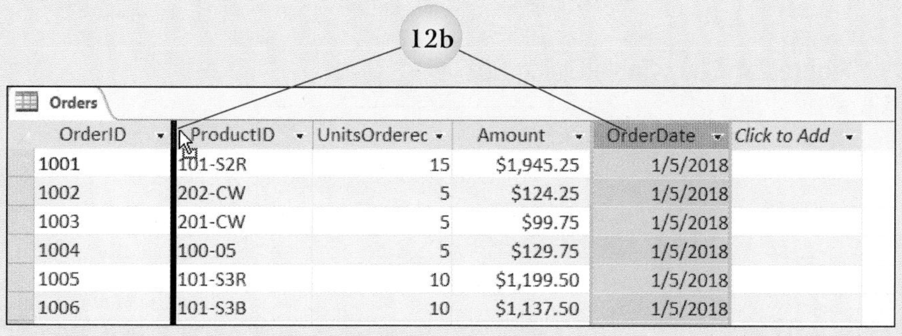
12b
Orders
OrderID
ProductID
UnitsOrderec
Amount
OrderDate
Click to Add
1001 101-S2R 15 $1,945.25 1/5/2018
1002 202-CW 5 $124.25 1/5/2018
1003 201-CW 5 $99.75 1/5/2018
1004 100-05 5 $129.75 1/5/2018
1005 101-S3R 10 $1,199.50 1/5/2018
1006 101-S3B 10 $1,137.50 1/5/2018

13. Automatically adjust the column widths.
14. Save and then close the Orders table.

Check Your Work

Tutorial

Creating a One-to-Many Relationship

Relating Tables in a One-to-Many Relationship

In Access, one table can be related to another, which is generally referred to as performing a join. When tables with a common field are joined, data can be extracted from both tables as if they were one large table. Relating tables helps to ensure the integrity of the data by avoiding entering the same data in multiple tables. For example, in Project 1b, a relationship will be established between the Suppliers table and the Products table. The relationship will ensure that a supplier number cannot be entered in the Products table without first being entered in the Suppliers table. This type of relationship is called a *one-to-many relationship*, which means that one record in the Suppliers table will match zero, one, or many records in the Products table.

In a one-to-many relationship, the table containing the "one" is referred to as the *primary table* and the table containing the "many" is referred to as the *related table*. Access follows a set of rules that provide referential integrity, which enforces consistency between related tables. These rules are enforced when data is updated in related tables. The referential integrity rules ensure that a record added to a related table has a matching record in the primary table.

Relationships

Quick Steps

Create a One-to-Many Relationship

1. Click Database Tools tab.
2. Click Relationships button.
3. Add tables.
4. Drag "one" field from primary table to "many" field in related table.
5. At Edit Relationships dialog box, click Create button.
6. Click Save button.

To create a one-to-many relationship, open the database containing the tables to be related. Click the Database Tools tab and then click the Relationships button in the Relationships group. This displays the Show Table dialog box, as shown in Figure 2.4. (If the Show Table dialog box is not visible, click the Show Table button in the Relationships group.) At the Show Table dialog box, each table that will be related must be added to the Relationships window. To do this, click the first table name to be included and then click the Add button (or double-click the table name). This inserts the fields of the table in a table field list box. Continue in this manner until all necessary tables (in table field list boxes) have been added to the Relationships window and then click the Close button.

At the Relationships window, such as the one shown in Figure 2.5, use the mouse to drag the common field from the primary table's table field list box (the "one") to the related table's table field list box (the "many"). This causes the Edit Relationships dialog box to display, as shown in Figure 2.6. At the Edit Relationships dialog box, check to make sure the correct field name displays in the *Table/Query* and *Related Table/Query* list boxes and the relationship type at the bottom of the dialog box displays as *One-To-Many*.

Figure 2.4 Show Table Dialog Box

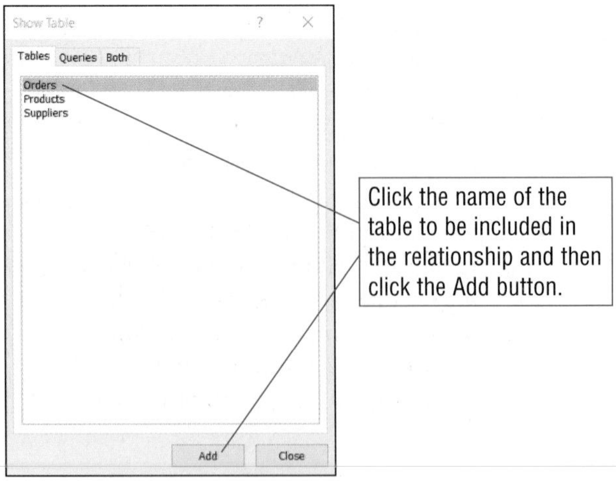

Figure 2.5 Relationships Window

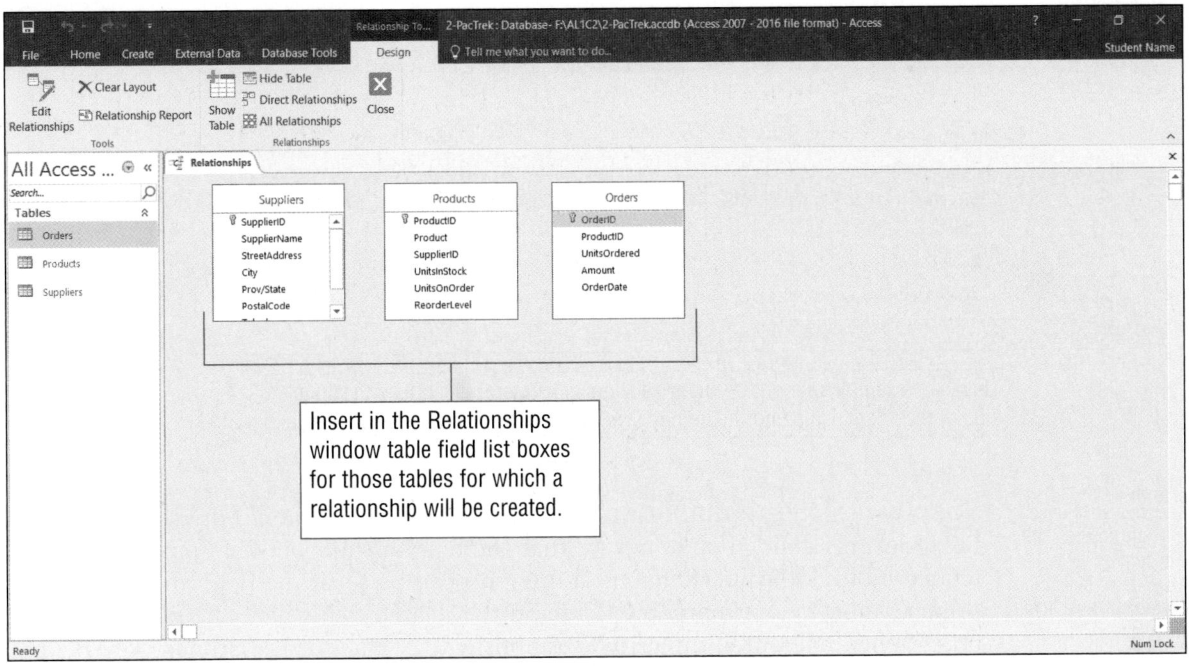

Figure 2.6 Edit Relationships Dialog Box

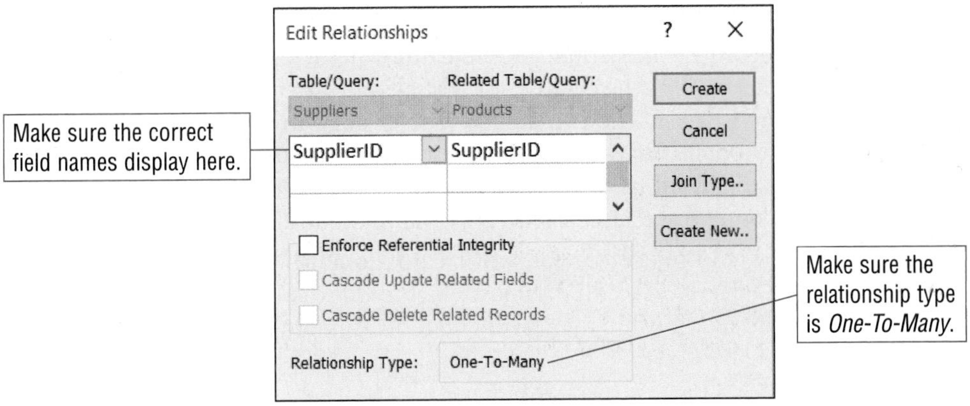

Specify the relationship options by choosing *Enforce Referential Integrity*, as well as *Cascade Update Related Fields* and/or *Cascade Delete Related Records*, and then click the Create button. This causes the Edit Relationships dialog box to close and the Relationships window to display showing the relationship between the tables.

In Figure 2.7, the Suppliers table field list box displays with a black line attached along with the number *1* (signifying the "one" side of the relationship). The black line is connected to the Products table field list box along with the infinity symbol, ∞ (signifying the "many" side of the relationship). The black line, called the *join line*, is thick at both ends if the *Enforce Referential Integrity* option is chosen. If this option is not chosen, the line is thin at both ends. Click the Save button on the Quick Access Toolbar to save the relationship. Close the Relationships window by clicking the Close button in the upper right corner of the window.

Figure 2.7 One-to-Many Relationship

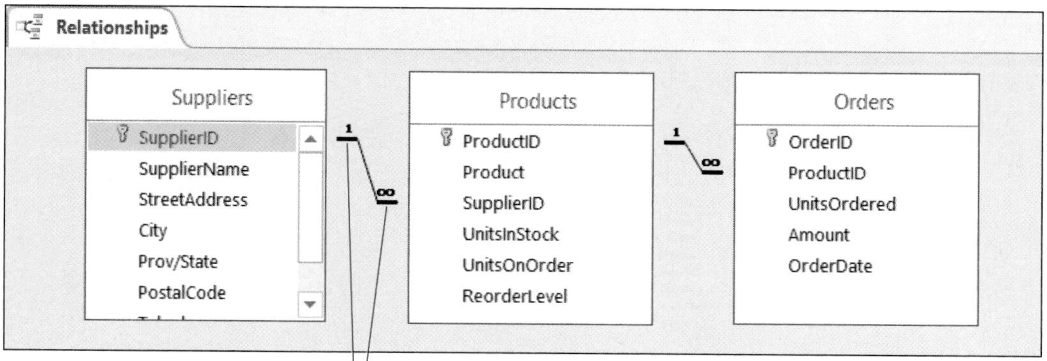

This is an example of a one-to-many relationship, where 1 identifies the "one" side of the relationship and the infinity symbol (∞) identifies the "many" side.

Hint Referential integrity ensures that a record exists in the "one" table before the record can be entered in the "many" table.

Specifying Referential Integrity Choose *Enforce Referential Integrity* at the Edit Relationships dialog box to ensure that the relationships between records in related tables are valid. Referential integrity can be set if the field from the primary table is a primary key field and the related fields have the same data type. When referential integrity is established, a value for the primary key field must first be entered in the primary table before it can be entered in the related table.

If only *Enforce Referential Integrity* is selected and the related table contains a record, a primary key field value in the primary table cannot be changed. A record in the primary table cannot be deleted if its key value equals a foreign key field in the related table. Select *Cascade Update Related Fields* and, if changes are made to the primary key field value in the primary table, Access will automatically update the matching value in the related table. Choose *Cascade Delete Related Records* and, if a record is deleted in the primary table, Access will delete any related records in the related table.

In Project 1b, you will create a one-to-many relationship between tables in the C2-PacTrek.accdb database. Figure 2.8 displays the Relationships window showing the relationships you will create in this project.

Figure 2.8 Relationships in the 2-PacTrek Database

A one-to-many relationship with referential integrity and cascade updated and deleted records selected.

A one-to-many relationship with referential integrity selected. (Notice the join line is thick in the middle, indicating that cascade updated and cascade deleted records are not selected.)

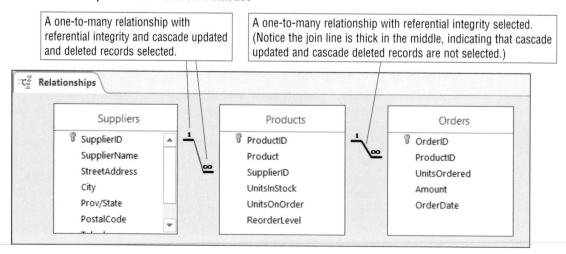

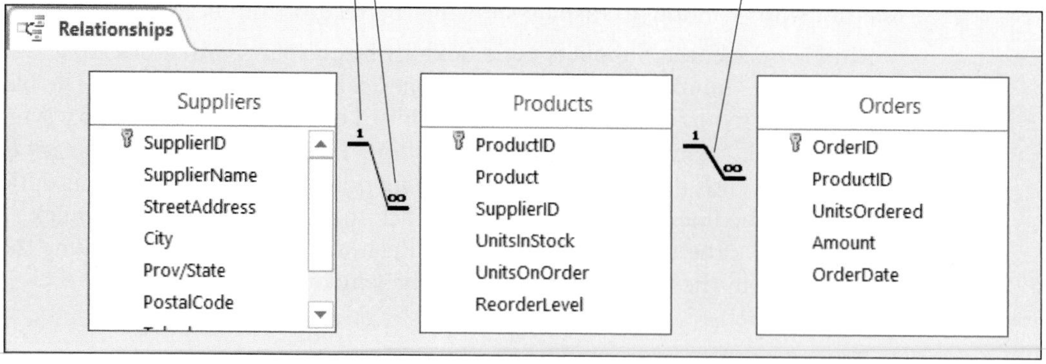

Tutorial

Creating a Relationship Report

Relationship Report

Quick Steps

Create a Relationship Report

1. Click Database Tools tab.
2. Click Relationships button.
3. Click Relationship Report button.

Creating and Printing a Relationship Report Once all relationships have been created in a database, printing a hard copy of the relationships is a good idea. The documentation is a quick reference of all of the table names, fields within each table, and relationships between tables. To print a relationship report, display the Relationships window and then click the Relationship Report button in the Tools group. This displays a relationship report in Print Preview. Click the Print button in the Print group on the Print Preview tab and then click OK at the Print dialog box. After printing the relationship report, click the Close button to close the relationship report.

Project 1b Relating Tables

Part 2 of 4

1. With **2-PacTrek.accdb** open, click the Database Tools tab and then click the Relationships button in the Relationships group. (The Show Table dialog box should display in the Relationships window. If it does not display, click the Show Table button in the Relationships group on the Relationship Tools Design tab.)

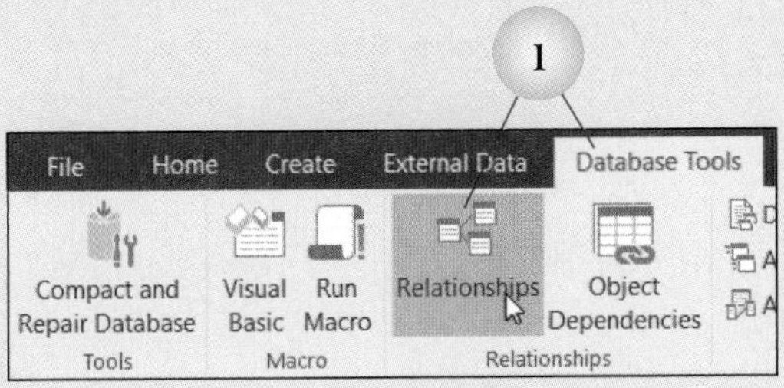

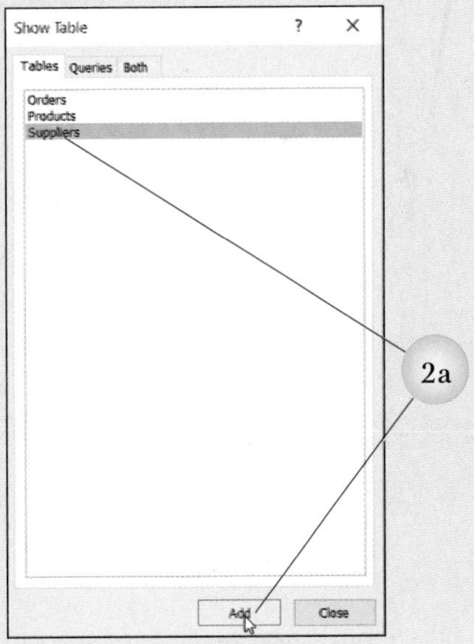

2. At the Show Table dialog box with the Tables tab selected, add the Suppliers, Products, and Orders tables to the Relationships window by completing the following steps:
   a. Click *Suppliers* in the list box and then click the Add button.
   b. Click *Products* in the list box and then click the Add button.
   c. Double-click *Orders* in the list box.
3. Click the Close button to close the Show Table dialog box.

4. At the Relationships window, drag the *SupplierID* field from the Suppliers table field list box to the Products table field list box by completing the following steps:
   a. Position the arrow pointer on the *SupplierID* field in the Suppliers table field list box.
   b. Click and hold down the left mouse button, drag the arrow pointer (with a field icon attached) to the *SupplierID* field in the Products table field list box, and then release the mouse button. (This causes the Edit Relationships dialog box to display.)

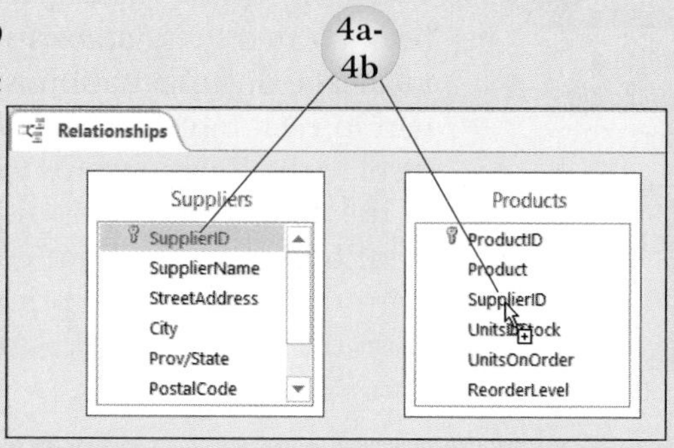

5. At the Edit Relationships dialog box, make sure *SupplierID* displays in the *Table/Query* and *Related Table/Query* list boxes and the relationship type at the bottom of the dialog box displays as *One-To-Many*.
6. Enforce the referential integrity of the relationship by completing the following steps:
   a. Click the *Enforce Referential Integrity* check box to insert a check mark. (This makes the other two options available.)
   b. Click the *Cascade Update Related Fields* check box to insert a check mark.
   c. Click the *Cascade Delete Related Records* check box to insert a check mark.

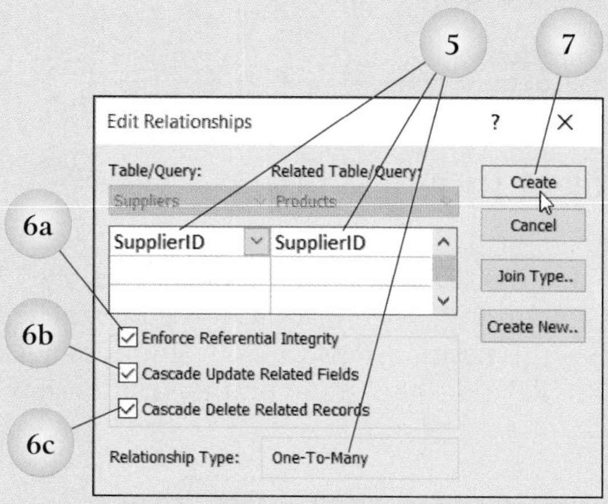

7. Click the Create button. (This causes the Edit Relationships dialog box to close and the Relationships window to display, showing a black join line [thick on the ends and thin in the middle] connecting the *SupplierID* field in the Suppliers table field list box to the *SupplierID* field in the Products table field list box. A *1* appears on the join line on the Suppliers table side and an infinity symbol [∞] appears on the join line on the Products table side.)
8. Click the Save button on the Quick Access Toolbar to save the relationship.
9. Create a one-to-many relationship between the Products table and the Orders table with the *ProductID* field by completing the following steps:
   a. Position the arrow pointer on the *ProductID* field in the Products table field list box.
   b. Click and hold down the left mouse button, drag the arrow pointer (with a field icon attached) to the *ProductID* field in the Orders table field list box, and then release the mouse button.

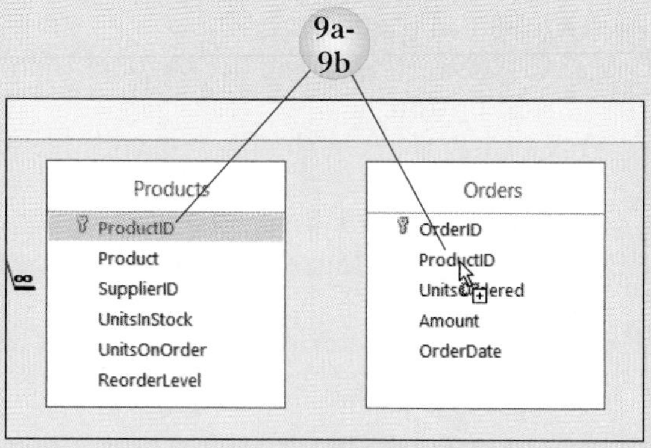

c. At the Edit Relationships dialog box, make sure *ProductID* displays in the *Table/Query* and *Related Table/Query* list boxes and the relationship type displays as *One-To-Many*.

d. Click the *Enforce Referential Integrity* check box to insert a check mark. (Do not insert check marks in the other two check boxes.)

e. Click the Create button.

10. Click the Save button on the Quick Access Toolbar to save the relationships.

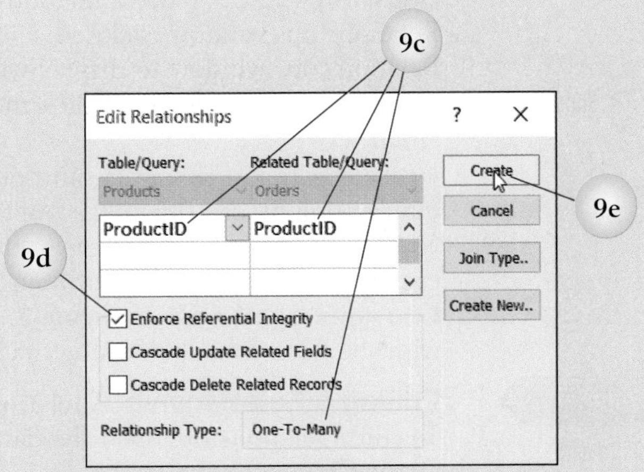

11. Print the relationships by completing the following steps:

a. At the Relationships window, click the Relationship Report button in the Tools group. This displays the relationship report in Print Preview. (If a security notice displays, click the Open button.)

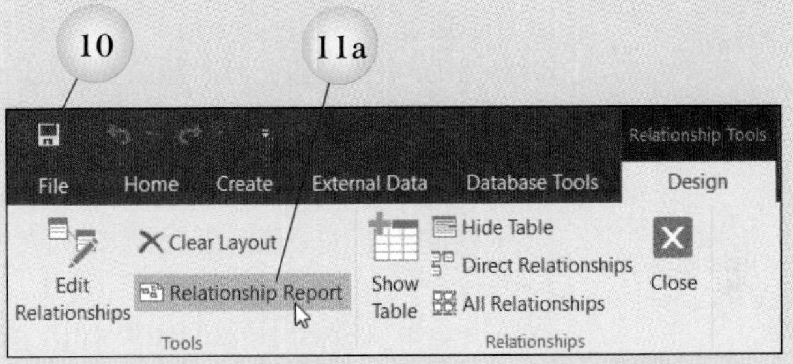

b. Click the Print button in the Print group at the left side of the Print Preview tab.

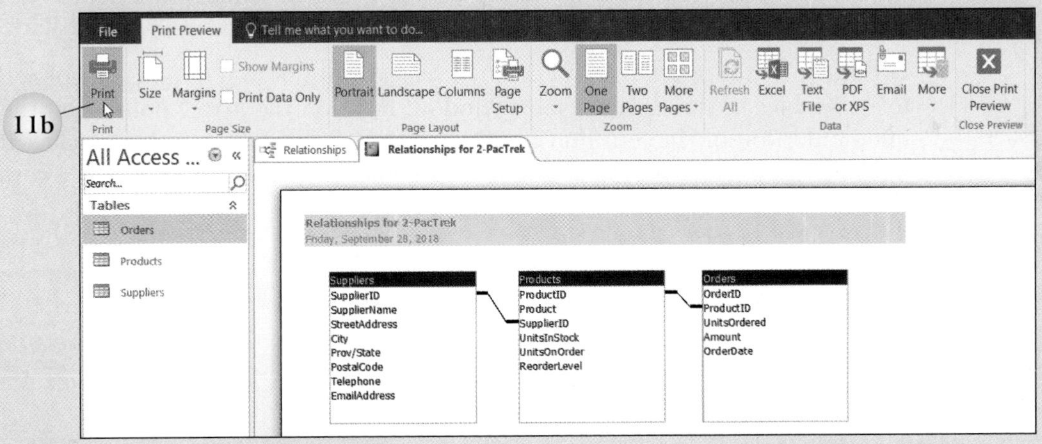

c. Click OK at the Print dialog box.

d. Close the report by clicking the Close button in the upper right corner of the work area.

e. At the message asking if you want to save changes to the design of the report, click No.

12. Close the Relationships window by clicking the Close button in the upper right corner of the work area.

Check Your Work

Show Table

Showing Tables Once a relationship is established between tables and the Relationships window is closed, clicking the Relationships button causes the Relationships window to display without the Show Table dialog box. To display the Show Table dialog box, click the Show Table button in the Relationships group.

Pacific Trek offers a discount on one product each week. Keep track of this information by creating a Discounts table that includes the discount item for each week of the first three months of the year. A new record will be added to this field each week when the discount item is chosen. (In Project 1c, you will create the Discounts table shown in Figure 2.9 on page 49 and then relate the Products table with the Discounts table using the *ProductID* field.)

Tutorial

Editing and Deleting a Relationship

Edit Relationships

Quick Steps

Edit a Relationship

1. Click Database Tools tab.
2. Click Relationships button.
3. Click Edit Relationships button.
4. Make changes at Edit Relationships dialog box.
5. Click OK.

Editing a Relationship A relationship between tables can be edited or deleted. To edit a relationship, open the database containing the tables with the relationship, click the Database Tools tab, and then click the Relationships button in the Relationships group. This displays the Relationships window with the related tables. Click the Edit Relationships button in the Tools group to display the Edit Relationships dialog box. The dialog box will be similar to the one shown in Figure 2.6 on page 41. Identify the relationship to be edited by clicking the *Table/Query* option box arrow and then clicking the table name containing the "one" field. Click the *Related Table/Query* option box arrow and then click the table name containing the "many" field.

To edit a specific relationship, position the arrow pointer on the middle portion of the join line that connects the related tables and then click the right mouse button. At the shortcut menu, click the *Edit Relationship* option. This displays the Edit Relationships dialog box with the specific related field in both list boxes.

Deleting a Relationship To delete a relationship between tables, display the related tables in the Relationships window. Position the arrow pointer on the middle portion of the join line connecting the related tables and then click the right mouse button. At the shortcut menu, click *Delete*. At the message asking to confirm the deletion, click Yes.

Project 1c Creating a Table and Creating and Editing Relationships Part 3 of 4

1. With **2-PacTrek.accdb** open, create the Discounts table shown in Figure 2.9 on page 49 by completing the following steps:
   a. Click the Create tab.
   b. Click the Table button in the Tables group.
   c. Click the Short Text button in the Add & Delete group. (This creates and then selects *Field1* at the right of the *ID* column.)

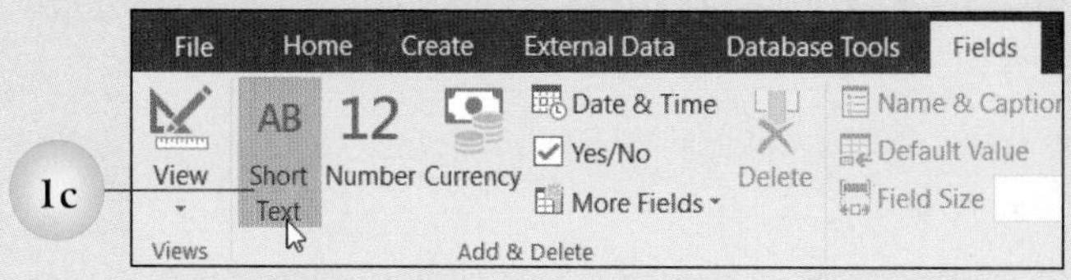

d. Type ProductID and then press the Enter key.
e. Click the *Short Text* option at the drop-down list and then type Discount.
f. Click the *ID* field name (in the first column), click the *Data Type* option box arrow in the Formatting group, and then click *Date/Time* at the drop-down list.

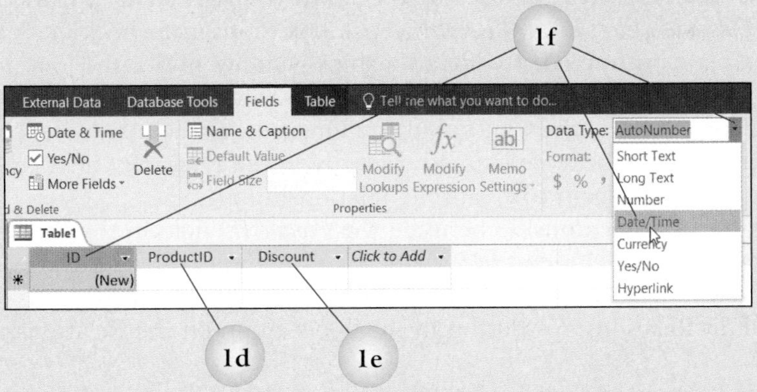

g. Right-click the *ID* field name, click *Rename Field* at the shortcut menu, type Week, and then press the Enter key.
h. Type the 13 records in the Discounts table shown in Figure 2.9 on page 49.
2. After typing the records, save the table by completing the following steps:
a. Click the Save button on the Quick Access Toolbar.
b. At the Save As dialog box, type Discounts and then press the Enter key.
3. Close the Discounts table.
4. Display the Relationships window and add the Discounts table to the window by completing the following steps:
a. Click the Database Tools tab and then click the Relationships button in the Relationships group.
b. Display the Show Table dialog box by clicking the Show Table button in the Relationships group.
c. At the Show Table dialog box, double-click the *Discounts* table.
d. Click the Close button to close the Show Table dialog box.

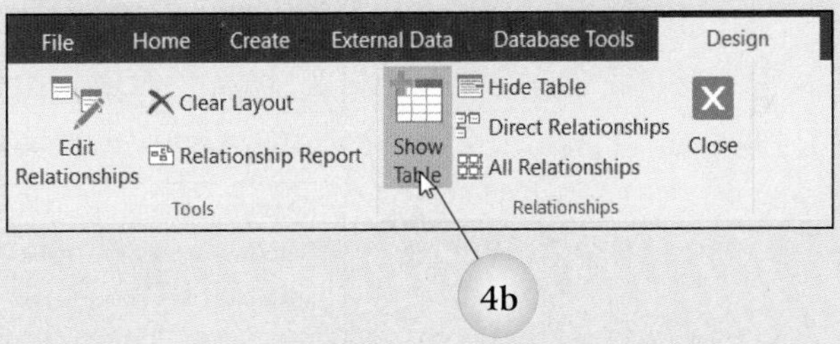

5. At the Relationships window, create a one-to-many relationship between the Products table and the Discounts table with the *ProductID* field by completing the following steps:
a. Drag the *ProductID* field from the Products table field list box to the *ProductID* field in the Discounts table field list box.

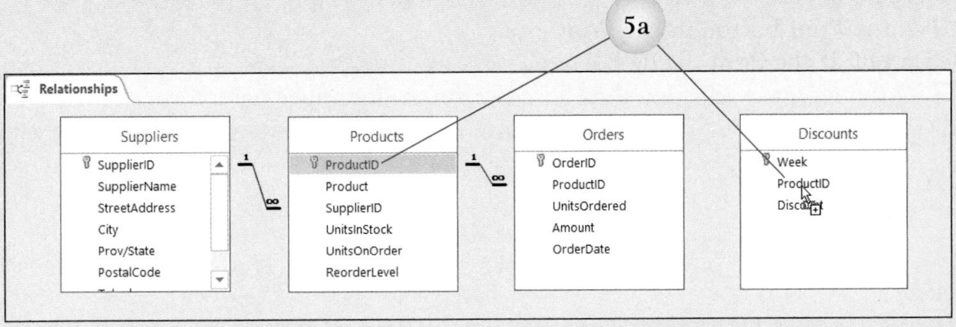

b. At the Edit Relationships dialog box, make sure *ProductID* displays in the *Table/Query* and *Related Table/Query* list boxes and the relationship type at the bottom of the dialog box displays as *One-To-Many*.
c. Click the *Enforce Referential Integrity* check box to insert a check mark.
d. Click the *Cascade Update Related Fields* check box to insert a check mark.
e. Click the *Cascade Delete Related Records* check box to insert a check mark.
f. Click the Create button. (At the Relationships window, notice the join line between the Products table and the Discounts table. If a message occurs stating that the relationship cannot be created, click the Cancel button. Open the Discounts table, check to make sure the product numbers are entered correctly in the *ProductID* field, and then close the Discounts table. Try again to create the relationship.)

6. Edit the one-to-many relationship between the *ProductID* field in the Products table and the Orders table and specify that you want to cascade updated and related fields and cascade and delete related records by completing the following steps:
   a. Click the Edit Relationships button in the Tools group on the Relationship Tools Design tab.
   b. At the Edit Relationships dialog box, click the *Table/Query* option box arrow and then click *Products* at the drop-down list.
   c. Click the *Related Table/Query* option box arrow and then click *Orders* at the drop-down list.
   d. Click the *Cascade Update Related Fields* check box to insert a check mark.
   e. Click the *Cascade Delete Related Records* check box to insert a check mark.
   f. Click the OK button.

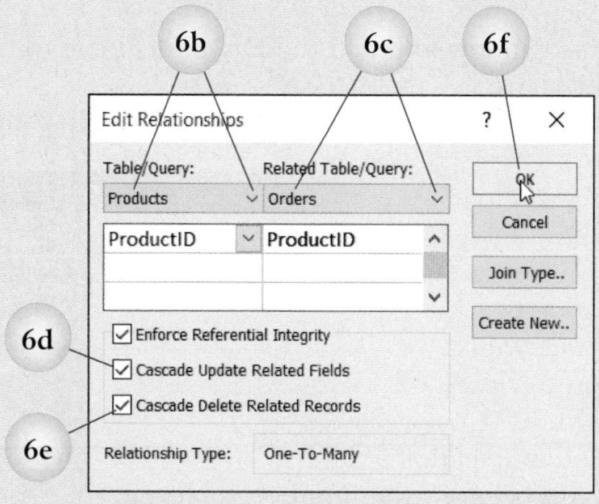

7. Click the Save button on the Quick Access Toolbar to save the relationship.
8. Print the relationships by completing the following steps:
   a. Click the Relationship Report button in the Tools group.
   b. Click the Print button in the Print group.
   c. Click OK at the Print dialog box.
   d. Close the report by clicking the Close button in the upper right corner of the work area.
   e. At the message asking if you want to save changes to the design of the report, click No.

9. Delete the relationship between the Products table and the Discounts table by completing the following steps:
   a. Position the arrow pointer on the thin portion of the join line connecting the *ProductID* field in the Products table field list box with the *ProductID* field in the Discounts table field list box and then click the right mouse button.
   b. Click the *Delete* option at the shortcut menu.

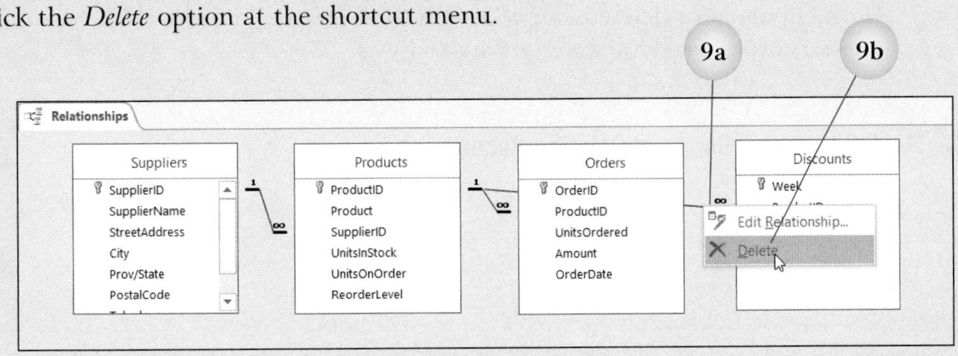

   c. At the message asking if you are sure you want to permanently delete the selected relationship from your database, click Yes.
10. Click the Save button on the Quick Access Toolbar to save the relationship.
11. Print the relationships by completing the following steps:
   a. Click the Relationship Tools Design tab and then click the Relationship Report button in the Tools group.
   b. Click the Print button in the Print group.
   c. Click OK at the Print dialog box.
   d. Close the report by clicking the Close button in the upper right corner of the work area.
   e. At the message asking if you want to save changes to the design of the report, click No.
12. Close the Relationships window by clicking the Close button in the upper right corner of the work area.

Check Your Work

Figure 2.9 Discounts Table in Datasheet View

Discounts

Week	ProductID	Discount	*Click to Add*
1/7/2018	155-45	20%	
1/14/2018	652-2	15%	
1/21/2018	443-1A	20%	
1/28/2018	202-CW	15%	
2/4/2018	804-60	10%	
2/11/2018	652-2	15%	
2/18/2018	101-S1B	5%	
2/25/2018	560-TL	20%	
3/4/2018	652-2	20%	
3/11/2018	602-XX	15%	
3/18/2018	100-05	10%	
3/25/2018	652-2	15%	
4/1/2018	202-CW	15%	

Inserting and Deleting Records in Related Tables In the relationship established in Project 1b, a record must first be added to the Suppliers table before a related record can be added to the Products table. This is because the *Enforce Referential Integrity* option was selected at the Edit Relationships dialog box. Because the two options, *Cascade Update Related Fields* and *Cascade Delete Related Records*, were also selected, records in the Suppliers table (the primary table) can be updated or deleted and related records in the Products table (the related table) are automatically updated or deleted.

Project 1d Editing, Inserting, and Deleting Records

Part 4 of 4

1. With **2-PacTrek.accdb** open, open the Suppliers table.
2. Change two supplier numbers in the Suppliers table (Access will automatically change them in the Products table and the Orders table) by completing the following steps:
   a. Double-click the field value *15* in the *SupplierID* field.
   b. Type 33.
   c. Double-click the field value *42* in the *SupplierID* field.
   d. Type 51.
   e. Click the Save button on the Quick Access Toolbar.
   f. Close the Suppliers table.
   g. Open the Products table and notice that supplier number *15* changed to *33* and supplier number *42* changed to *51*.
   h. Close the Products table.

Suppliers

SupplierID	SupplierName
10	Hopewell, Inc.
33	Bayside Supplies
25	Langley Corporati
31	Sound Supplies
35	Emerald City Prod
38	Hadley Company
51	Fraser Valley Proc
54	Manning, Inc.
68	Freedom Corpora
70	Rosewood, Inc.
84	Macadam, Inc.
99	KL Distributions

2b

2d

3. Open the Suppliers table and then add the following records:

SupplierID	16	*SupplierID*	28
SupplierName	Olympic Suppliers	*SupplierName*	Gorman Company
StreetAddress	1773 50th Avenue	*StreetAddress*	543 26th Street
City	Seattle	*City*	Vancouver
Prov/State	WA	*Prov/State*	BC
PostalCode	98101	*PostalCode*	V5K 3C5
Telephone	(206) 555-9488	*Telephone*	(778) 555-4550
EmailAddress	olysuppliers@emcp.net	*EmailAddress*	gormanco@emcp.net

Suppliers

SupplierID	SupplierName	StreetAddress	City	Prov/State	PostalCode	Telephone	EmailAddress	Click to Add
10	Hopewell, Inc.	5600 Carver Road	Port Moody	BC	V3H 1A4	(604) 555-3843	hopewell@emcp.net	
25	Langley Corporatio	805 First Avenue	Burnaby	BC	V3J 1C9	(604) 555-1200	langley@emcp.net	
31	Sound Supplies	2104 Union Street	Seattle	WA	98105	(206) 555-4855	ssupplies@emcp.net	
33	Bayside Supplies	6705 North Street	Bellingham	WA	98432	(360) 555-6005	bside@emcp.net	
35	Emerald City Produ	1059 Pike Street	Seattle	WA	98102	(206) 555-7728	ecproducts@emcp.ne	
38	Hadley Company	5845 Jefferson Stre	Seattle	WA	98107	(206) 555-8003	hcompany@emcp.net	
51	Fraser Valley Produ	3894 Old Yale Roa	Abbotsford	BC	V2S 1A9	(604) 555-1455	fvproducts@emcp.ne	
54	Manning, Inc.	1039 South 22nd	Vancouver	BC	V5K 1R1	(604) 555-0087	manning@emcp.net	
68	Freedom Corporati	14 Fourth Avenue	Vancouver	BC	V5K 2C7	(604) 555-2155	freedom@emcp.net	
70	Rosewood, Inc.	998 North 42nd Str	Vancouver	BC	V5K 2N8	(778) 555-6643	rosewood@emcp.net	
84	Macadam, Inc.	675 Third Street	Vancouver	BC	V5K 2R9	(604) 555-5522	macadam@emcp.net	
99	KL Distributions	402 Yukon Drive	Bellingham	WA	98435	(360) 555-3711	kldist@emcp.net	
16	Olympic Suppliers	1773 50th Avenue	Seattle	WA	98101	(206) 555-9488	olysuppliers@emcp.n	
28	Gorman Company	543 26th Street	Vancouver	BC	V5K 3C5	(778) 555-4550	gormanco@emcp.net	
*								

3

4. Delete the record for supplier number 38 (Hadley Company). At the message stating that relationships that specify cascading deletes are about to cause records in this table and related tables to be deleted, click Yes.

5. Display the table in Print Preview, change to landscape orientation, and then print the table.
6. Close the Suppliers table.
7. Open the Products table and then add the following records to the table:

ProductID	701-BK	*ProductID*	703-SP
Product	Basic first aid kit	*Product*	Medical survival pack
SupplierID	33	*SupplierID*	33
UnitsInStock	8	*UnitsInStock*	8
UnitsOnOrder	0	*UnitsOnOrder*	0
ReorderLevel	5	*ReorderLevel*	5

ProductID	185-10	*ProductID*	185-50
Product	Trail water filter	*Product*	Trail filter replacement cartridge
SupplierID	51	*SupplierID*	51
UnitsInStock	4	*UnitsInStock*	14
UnitsOnOrder	10	*UnitsOnOrder*	0
ReorderLevel	10	*ReorderLevel*	10

8. Display the Products table in Print Preview, change to landscape orientation, change the top and bottom margins to 0.5 inch and then print the table. (The table will print on two pages.)
9. Close the Products table.
10. Open the Orders table and then add the following record:

OrderID	1033
OrderDate	2/15/2018
ProductID	185-10
UnitsOrdered	10
Amount	$310.90

11. Print and then close the Orders table.
12. Close **2-PacTrek.accdb**.

Check Your Work

Project 2 Create Relationships and Display Subdatasheets in a Database — 2 Parts

You will open a company database and then create one-to-many relationships between tables, as well as a one-to-one relationship. You will also display and edit subdatasheets.

Preview Finished Project

Tutorial

Creating a One-to-One Relationship

Creating a One-to-One Relationship

A one-to-one relationship can be created between tables in which each record in the first table matches only one record in the second table and one record in the second table matches only one record in the first table. (One-to-one relationships exist between primary key fields.) A one-to-one relationship is not as common as a one-to-many relationship, since the type of information used to create the relationship can be stored in one table. A one-to-one relationship is generally used to break a large table with many fields into two smaller tables.

Hint The Relationships window displays any relationship you have defined between tables.

In Project 2a, you will create a one-to-one relationship between the Employees table and the Benefits table in the Griffin database. Each record in the Employees table and each record in the Benefits table pertains to one employee. These two tables could be merged into one but the data in each table is easier to manage when separated. Figure 2.10 shows the relationships you will define between the tables in the Griffin database. The Benefits table and the Departments table have been moved down so you can more easily see the relationships.

Figure 2.10 Griffin Database Table Relationships

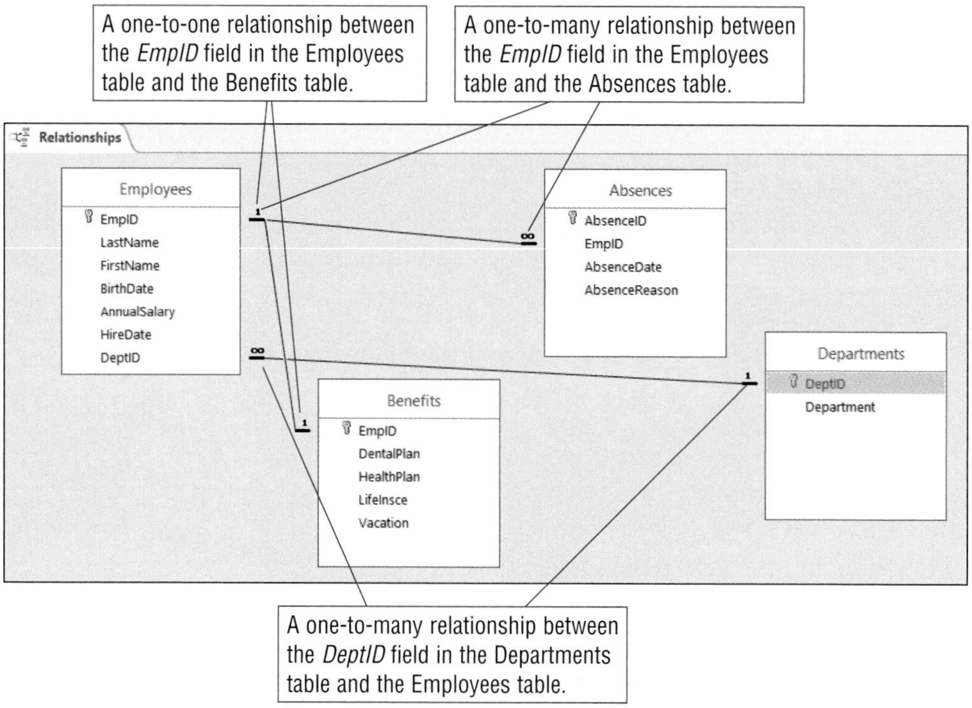

A one-to-one relationship between the *EmpID* field in the Employees table and the Benefits table.
A one-to-many relationship between the *EmpID* field in the Employees table and the Absences table.
Relationships
Employees
EmpID
LastName
FirstName
BirthDate
AnnualSalary
HireDate
DeptID
Absences
AbsenceID
EmpID
AbsenceDate
AbsenceReason
Departments
DeptID
Department
Benefits
EmpID
DentalPlan
HealthPlan
LifeInsce
Vacation
A one-to-many relationship between the *DeptID* field in the Departments table and the Employees table.

Project 2a Creating One-to-Many and One-to-One Relationships — Part 1 of 2

1. Open **2-Griffin.accdb** and enable the content.
2. Click the Database Tools tab.
3. Click the Relationships button in the Relationships group.
4. At the Show Table dialog box with the Tables tab selected, add all of the tables to the Relationships window by completing the following steps:
   a. Double-click *Employees* in the list box. (This inserts the table in the Relationships window.)
   b. Double-click *Benefits* in the list box.
   c. Double-click *Absences* in the list box.
   d. Double-click *Departments* in the list box.
   e. Click the Close button to close the Show Table dialog box.
5. At the Relationships window, create a one-to-many relationship with the *EmpID* field in the Employees table as the "one" and the *EmpID* field in the Absences table the "many" by completing the following steps:
   a. Position the arrow pointer on the *EmpID* field in the Employees table field list box.

b. Click and hold down the left mouse button, drag the arrow pointer (with a field icon attached) to the *EmpID* field in the Absences table field list box, and then release the mouse button. (This causes the Edit Relationships dialog box to display.)

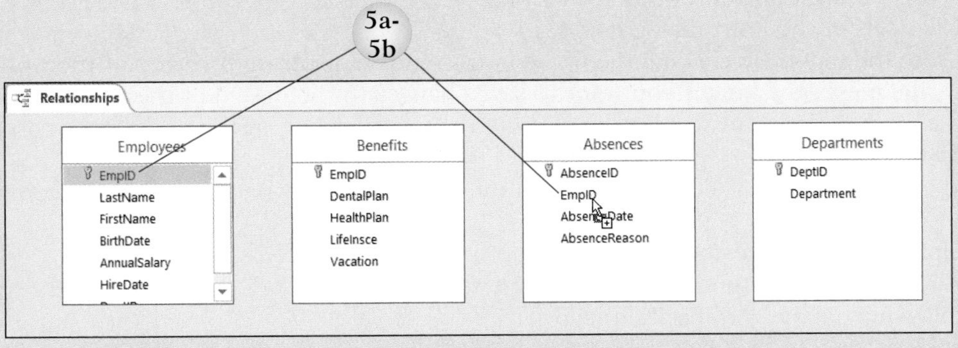

c. At the Edit Relationships dialog box, make sure *EmpID* displays in the *Table/Query* and *Related Table/Query* list boxes and the relationship type at the bottom of the dialog box displays as *One-To-Many*.
d. Click the *Enforce Referential Integrity* check box to insert a check mark.
e. Click the *Cascade Update Related Fields* check box to insert a check mark.
f. Click the *Cascade Delete Related Records* check box to insert a check mark.
g. Click the Create button. (A *1* appears at the Employees table field list box side and an infinity symbol (∞) appears at the Absences table field list box side of the black line.)

6. Complete steps similar to those in Step 5 to create a one-to-many relationship with the *DeptID* field in the Departments table the "one" and the *DeptID* field in the Employees table the "many." (You may need to scroll down the Employees table field list box to display the *DeptID* field.)
7. Create a one-to-one relationship with the *EmpID* field in the Employees table and the *EmpID* field in the Benefits table by completing the following steps:
   a. Position the arrow pointer on the *EmpID* field in the Employees table field list box.
   b. Click and hold down the left mouse button, drag the arrow pointer to the *EmpID* field in the Benefits table field list box, and then release the mouse button. (This displays the Edit Relationships dialog box; notice at the bottom of the dialog box that the relationship type displays as *One-To-One*.)
   c. Click the *Enforce Referential Integrity* check box to insert a check mark.
   d. Click the *Cascade Update Related Fields* check box to insert a check mark.
   e. Click the *Cascade Delete Related Records* check box to insert a check mark.
   f. Click the Create button. (Notice that a *1* appears at both the side of the Employees table field list box and at the side of the *Benefits* field list box, indicating a one-to-one relationship.)

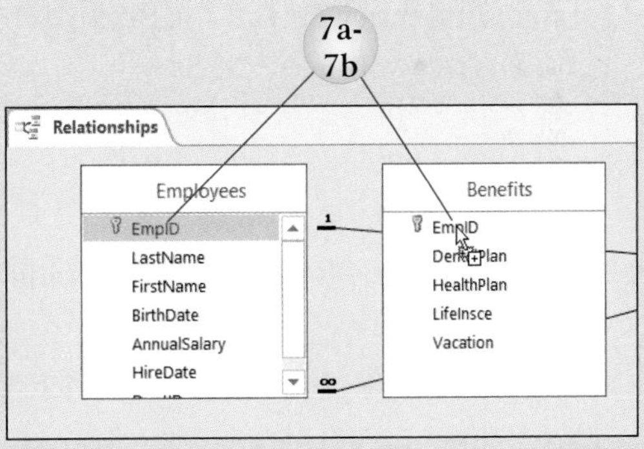

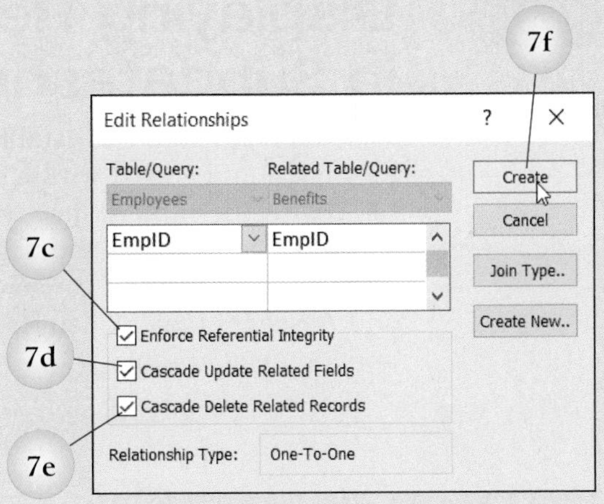

8. Click the Save button on the Quick Access Toolbar to save the relationships.
9. Print the relationships by completing the following steps:
   a. Click the Relationship Report button in the Tools group.
   b. Click the Print button in the Print group.
   c. Click OK at the Print dialog box.
   d. Close the report by clicking the Close button in the upper right corner of the work area.
   e. At the message asking if you want to save changes to the design of the report, click No.
10. Close the Relationships window by clicking the Close button in the upper right corner of the work area.
11. Add a record to and delete a record from the Employees and Benefits tables by completing the following steps:
    a. Open the Employees table.
    b. Click the New button in the Records group on the Home tab and then type the following data in the specified field:

EmpID	1096
LastName	Schwartz
FirstName	Bryan
BirthDate	5/21/1983
DeptID	IT
AnnualSalary	$45,000.00
HireDate	1/15/2010

    c. Delete the record for Trevor Sargent (employee number 1005). At the message stating that relationships that specify cascading deletes are about to cause records in this table and related tables to be deleted, click Yes.
    d. Print and then close the Employees table.
12. Open the Benefits table and notice that the record for Trevor Sargent is deleted but the new employee record you entered in the Employees table is not reflected in the Benefits table. Add a new record for Bryan Schwartz with the following information:

EmpID	1096
Dental Plan	(Press spacebar to remove check mark.)
Health Plan	(Leave check mark.)
Life Insurance	$100,000.00
Vacation	2 weeks

13. Print and then close the Benefits table.

Check Your Work

Tutorial

Viewing a Subdatasheet

Displaying Related Records in Subdatasheets

When a relationship is established between tables, records in related tables can be viewed and edited with a subdatasheet. Figure 2.11 displays the Employees table with the subdatasheet displayed for employee Kate Navarro. The subdatasheet displays the fields in the Benefits table related to Kate Navarro. Use this subdatasheet to view and edit information in both the Employees table and Absences table. Changes made to fields in a subdatasheet affect the table and any related tables.

Quick Steps

Display a Subdatasheet

1. Open table.
2. Click expand indicator at left side of record.
3. Click table at Insert Subdatasheet dialog box.
4. Click OK.

Access automatically inserts a plus symbol (referred to as an *expand indicator*) before each record in a table that is joined to another table by a one-to-many relationship. Click the expand indicator and, if the table is related to only one other table, a subdatasheet containing fields from the related table displays below the record, as shown in Figure 2.11. To close the subdatasheet, click the minus symbol (referred to as a *collapse indicator*) preceding the record. (The plus symbol turns into the minus symbol when a subdatasheet displays.)

If a table has more than one relationship defined, clicking the expand indicator will display the Insert Subdatasheet dialog box, as shown in Figure 2.12. At this dialog box, click the desired table in the Tables list box and then click OK. The Insert Subdatasheet dialog box can also be displayed by clicking the More button in the Records group on the Home tab, pointing to *Subdatasheet*, and then clicking *Subdatasheet*. Display subdatasheets for all records by clicking the More button, pointing to *Subdatasheet*, and then clicking *Expand All*. Close all subdatasheets by clicking the More button, pointing to *Subdatasheet*, and then clicking *Collapse All*.

If a table is related to two or more tables, specify the subdatasheet at the Insert Subdatasheet dialog box. To display a different subdatasheet, remove the subdatasheet first, before selecting the next subdatasheet. Do this by clicking the More button, pointing to *Subdatasheet*, and then clicking *Remove*.

Figure 2.11 Table with Subdatasheet Displayed in Datasheet View

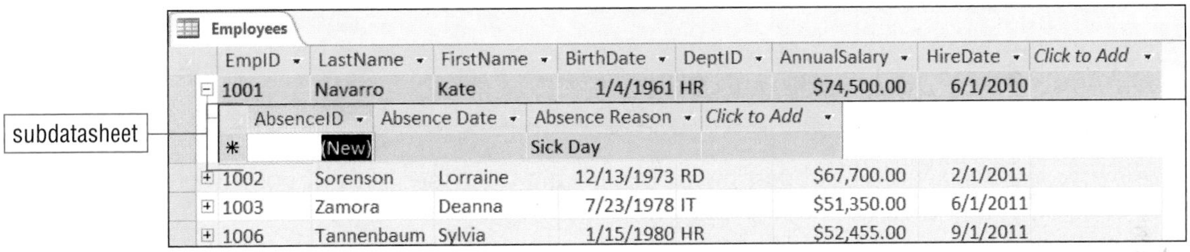

Figure 2.12 Insert Subdatasheet Dialog Box

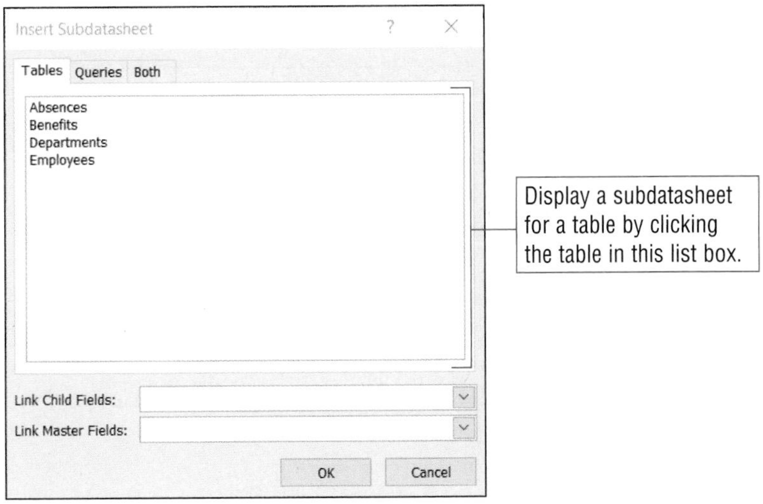

Project 2b Viewing and Editing a Subdatasheet

1. With **2-Griffin.accdb** open, open the Employees table.
2. Display a subdatasheet by clicking the expand indicator (plus symbol) at the left side of the first row (the row for Kate Navarro).
3. Close the subdatasheet by clicking the collapse indicator (minus symbol) at the left side of the record for Kate Navarro.
4. Display subdatasheets for all of the records by clicking the More button in the Records group, pointing to *Subdatasheet*, and then clicking *Expand All*.

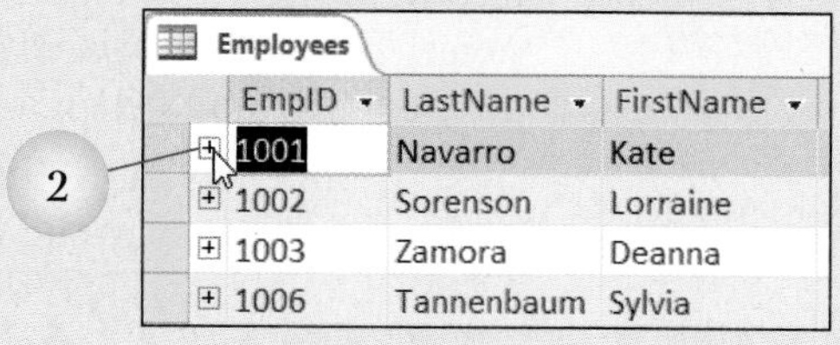

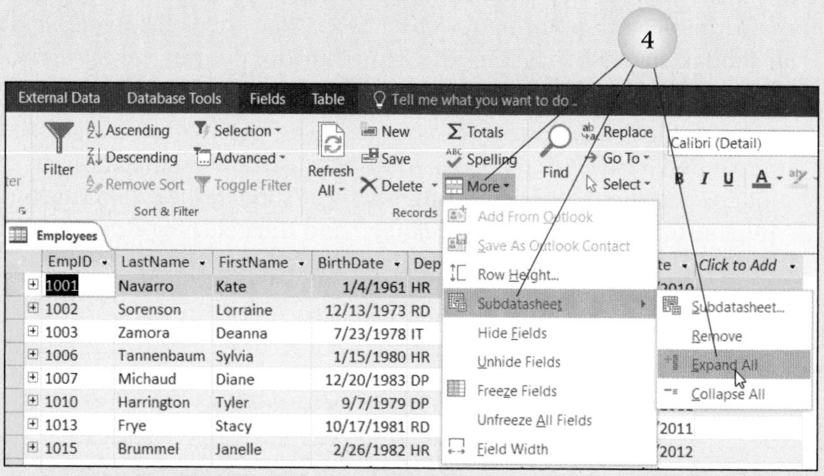

5. Remove the display of all subdatasheets by clicking the More button, pointing to *Subdatasheet*, and then clicking *Collapse All*.
6. Remove the connection between the Employees table and Absences table by clicking the More button, pointing to *Subdatasheet*, and then clicking *Remove*. (Notice that the expand indicators [plus symbols] no longer display before each record.)

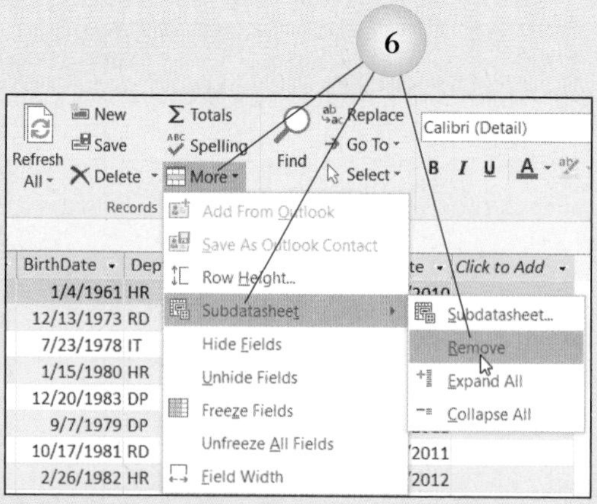

7. Suppose that the employee, Diane Michaud, has moved to a different department and has had an increase in salary. You would like to update her record in the tables. Display the Benefits subdatasheet and make changes to fields in the Employees table and Benefits table by completing the following steps:
   a. Click the More button in the Records group, point to *Subdatasheet*, and then click *Subdatasheet* at the side menu.
   b. At the Insert Subdatasheet dialog box, click *Benefits* in the list box and then click OK.
   c. Change the department ID for the record for *Diane Michaud* from *DP* to *A*.
   d. Change the salary from *$56,250.00* to *$57,500.00*.

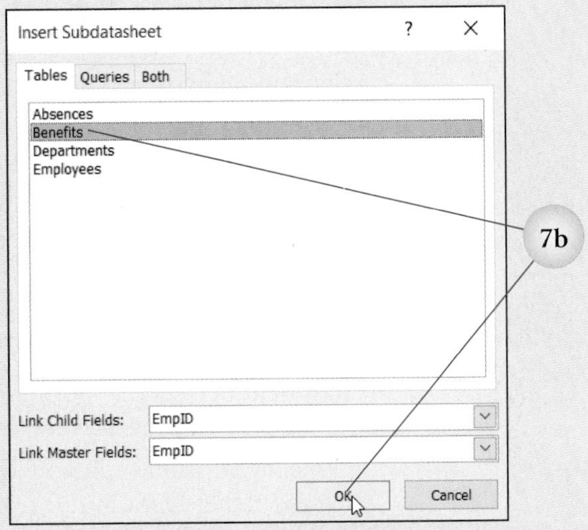

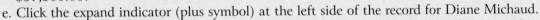

   e. Click the expand indicator (plus symbol) at the left side of the record for Diane Michaud.
   f. Insert a check mark in the *Dental Plan* check box and change the vacation from 3 weeks to 4 weeks.
   g. Click the collapse indicator (minus symbol) at the left side of the record for Diane Michaud.

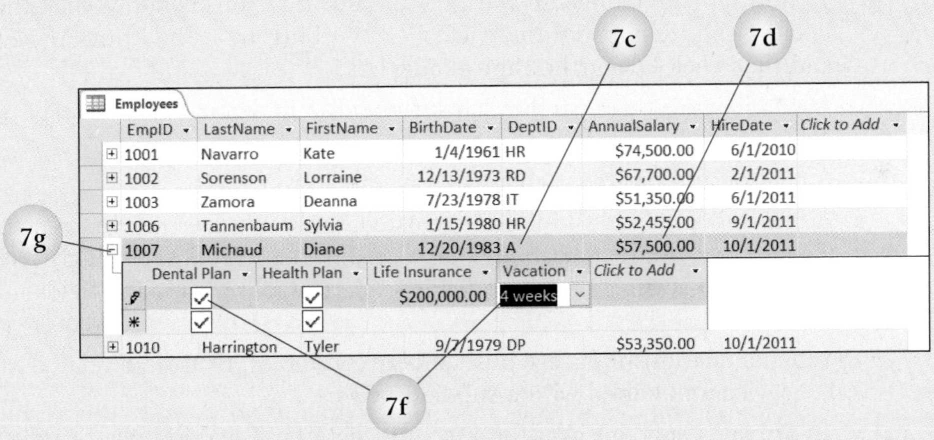

8. Click the Save button on the Quick Access Toolbar.
9. Print and then close the Employees table.
10. Open, print, and then close the Benefits table.
11. Close **2-Griffin.accdb**.

Check Your Work

Chapter Summary

- Access is a relational database software program in which tables can be created that are related or connected.
- When planning a table, take time to determine how to break down the required data and what relationships need to be defined to eliminate data redundancies.
- Generally, one field in a table must be unique so that one record can be distinguished from another. A field with a unique value is considered a primary key field.
- A table can have only one primary key field and it is the field by which the table is sorted whenever it is opened.
- In a field defined as a primary key field, duplicate values are not allowed. Access also expects a value in each record in the primary key field.
- Typically, a primary key field in one table becomes the foreign key field in a related table. Data in a foreign key field must match data in the primary key field of the related tables.
- Tables are related by performing a join. When tables that have a common field are joined, data can be extracted from both tables as if they were one large table.
- A one-to-many relationship can be created between tables. In this relationship, a record must be added to the "one" table before it can be added to the "many" table.
- To print table relationships, display the Relationships window, click the Relationship Report button, click the Print button on the Print Preview tab, and then click OK at the Print dialog box.
- At the Relationships window, click the Show Table button to display the Show Table dialog box.
- A relationship between tables can be edited or deleted.
- A one-to-one relationship can be created between tables in which each record in the first table matches only one record in the related table. This type of relationship is generally used to break a large table with many fields into two smaller tables.
- When a relationship is established between tables, fields in a related table can be viewed and edited with a subdatasheet.
- To display a subdatasheet for a record, click the expand indicator (plus symbol) at the left of the record in Datasheet view. To display subdatasheets for all records, click the More button in the Records group on the Home tab, point to *Subdatasheet*, and then click *Expand All*.
- Display the Insert Subdatasheet dialog box by clicking the More button in the Reports group on the Home tab, pointing to *Subdatasheet*, and then clicking *Subdatasheet*.
- Turn off the display of a subdatasheet by clicking the collapse indicator (minus symbol) at the left of the record. To turn off the display of subdatasheets for all records, click the More button, point to *Subdatasheet*, and then click *Collapse All*.

Commands Review

FEATURE	RIBBON, GROUP	BUTTON, OPTION
Edit Relationships dialog box	Relationship Tools Design, Tools	
Insert Subdatasheet dialog box	Home, Records	*Subdatasheet, Subdatasheet*
primary key field	Table Tools Design, Tools	
print relationships report	Relationship Tools Design, Tools	
Relationships window	Database Tools, Relationships	
Show Table dialog box	Relationship Tools Design, Relationships	

Workbook

Chapter study tools and assessment activities are available in the *Workbook* ebook. These resources are designed to help you further develop and demonstrate mastery of the skills learned in this chapter.

Microsoft®

Access®

CHAPTER 3

Performing Queries

Performance Objectives

Upon successful completion of Chapter 3, you will be able to:

1 Design queries to extract specific data from tables
2 Modify queries
3 Design queries with *Or* and *And* criteria
4 Use the Simple Query Wizard to create queries
5 Create and format a calculated field
6 Use aggregate functions in queries
7 Create crosstab, duplicate, and unmatched queries

Precheck

Check your current skills to help focus your study.

One of the primary uses of a database is to extract the specific information needed to answer questions and make decisions. A company might need to know how much inventory is currently on hand, which products have been ordered, which accounts are past due, or which customers live in a particular city. You can extract specific information from a table or multiple tables by creating and running a query. You will learn how to perform a variety of queries on information in tables in this chapter.

Data Files

Before beginning chapter work, copy the AL1C3 folder to your storage medium and then make AL1C3 the active folder.

SNAP

If you are a SNAP user, launch the Precheck and Tutorials from your Assignments page.

Project 1 Design Queries — 8 Parts

You will design and run a number of queries including queries with fields from one table and queries with fields from more than one table. You will also use the Simple Query Wizard to design queries and create and format a calculated field.

Preview Finished Project

Tutorial

Creating a Query in Design View and Showing/Hiding Query Columns

Hint The first step in designing a query is to choose the fields that you want to display in the query results datasheet.

Designing Queries

Being able to extract (pull out) specific data from a table is one of the most important functions of a database. Extracting data in Access is referred to as performing a query. The word *query* means "question" and to perform a query means to ask a question. Access provides several methods for designing a query. In this chapter, you will learn how to design your own query; use the Simple Query Wizard; create a calculated field; use aggregate functions in a query; and use the Crosstab Query Wizard, Find Duplicates Query Wizard, and Find Unmatched Query Wizard.

Designing a query consists of identifying the table or tables containing the data to be extracted, the field or fields from which the data will be drawn, and the criteria for selecting the data.

Specifying Tables and Fields for a Query

Query Design

To design a query, open a database, click the Create tab, and then click the Query Design button in the Queries group. This displays a query window in the work area and also displays the Show Table dialog box, as shown in Figure 3.1.

Quick Steps

Design a Query

1. Click Create tab.
2. Click Query Design button.
3. Click table at Show Table dialog box.
4. Click Add button.
5. Add any additional tables.
6. In query design grid, click down arrow in field in *Field* row.
7. Click field at drop-down list.
8. Insert criterion.
9. Click Run button.
10. Save query.

Figure 3.1 Query Window with Show Table Dialog Box

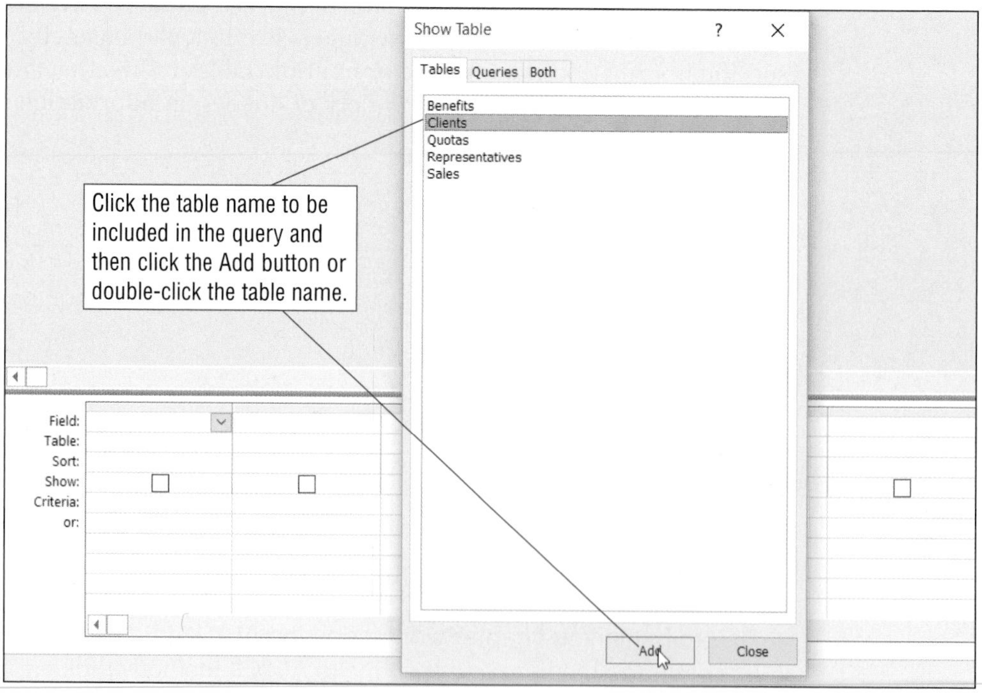

Click the table name in the Show Table dialog box to be included in the query and then click the Add button or double-click the table. This inserts a field list box for the table. Add any other tables required for the query. When all tables have been added, click the Close button. Figure 3.2 displays a sample query window.

To insert a field in the query design grid, click the down arrow that displays in the field in the *Field* row and then click the specific field at the drop-down list. Or, double-click a field in a table field list box to insert the field in the first available field in the *Field* row in the query design grid.

A third method for inserting a field in the query design grid is to drag a field from the table field list box to the desired field in the query design grid. To do this, position the mouse pointer on the field in the table field list box, click and hold down the left mouse button, drag to the specific field in the *Field* row in the query design grid, and then release the mouse button.

Tutorial

Adding a Criteria Statement to a Query

Quick Steps

Establish a Query Criterion

1. At query window, click in field in the *Criteria* row in query design grid.
2. Type criterion and then press Enter key.
3. Click Run button.

! Run

Adding a Criteria Statement to a Query

Unless a criterion statement is added to a query in the *Criteria* row, the query will return (*return* is the term used for the query results) all records with the fields specified in the query design grid. While returning this information may be helpful, the information could easily be found in the table or tables. The value of performing a query is to extract specific information from a table or tables. To extract specific information, add a criterion statement to the query. To do this, click in the field in the *Criteria* row in the column containing the field name in the query design grid and then type the criterion. With the fields and criterion established, click the Run button in the Results group on the Query Tools Design tab. Access searches the specified tables for records that match the criterion and then displays those records in the query results datasheet.

Figure 3.2 Query Window

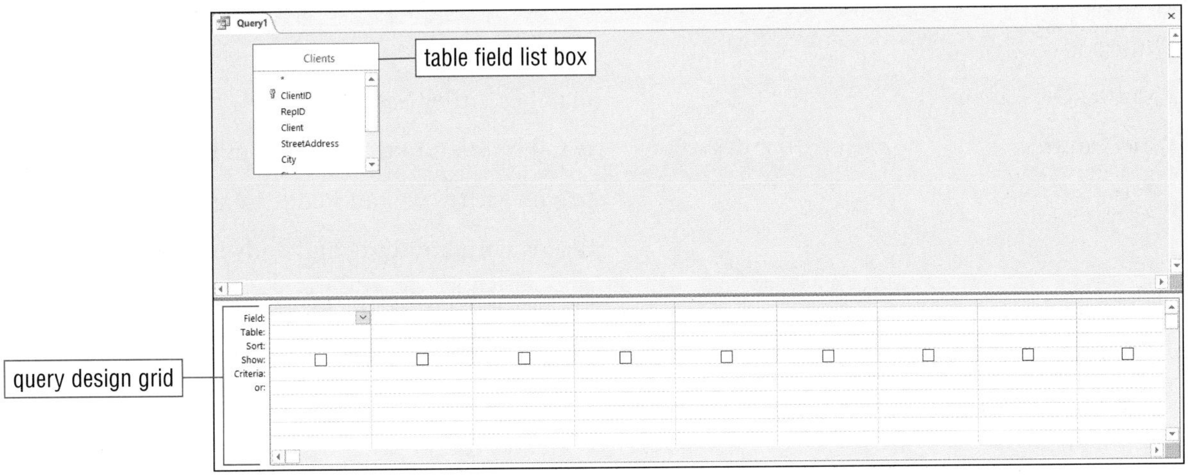

For example, to determine how many purchase orders were issued on a specific date, double-click the *PurchaseOrderID* field in the table field list box (which inserts *PurchaseOrderID* in the first field in the *Field* row in the query design grid) and then double-click the *OrderDate* field in the table field list box (which inserts *OrderDate* in the second field in the *Field* row in the query design grid). In this example, both fields are needed, so the purchase order ID is displayed along with the specific order date. After inserting the fields, add the criterion statement. The criterion statement for this example would be something like *#1/15/2018#*. After inserting the criterion, click the Run button in the Results group and the query returns only purchase orders for 1/15/2018 in the query results datasheet. If the criterion statement for the date was not added to the query, the query would return all purchase orders for all of the dates.

Hint Insert fields in the *Field* row in the query design grid in the order in which you want the fields to display in the query results datasheet.

Access makes writing a criterion statement fairly simple by inserting the necessary symbols in the criterion. Type a city name, such as *Indianapolis*, in the *Criteria* row for a *City* field and then press the Enter key and Access changes the criterion to "*Indianapolis*". The quotation marks are inserted by Access and are necessary for the query to run properly. Let Access put the proper symbols around the criterion data in the field in the *Criteria* row or type the criterion with the symbols. Table 3.1 shows some examples of criteria statements, including what is typed and what is returned.

Hint Access inserts quotation marks around text criteria and pound symbols around date criteria.

In the criteria examples, the asterisk is used as a wildcard character, which is a symbol that can be used to indicate any character. This is consistent with many other software applications. Two of the criteria examples in Table 3.1 use less-than and greater-than symbols. These symbols can be used for fields containing numbers, values, dates, amounts, and so forth. In the next several projects, you will design queries to extract specific information from different tables in databases.

Table 3.1 Criteria Examples

Typing This Criterion	Returns a Field Value Result That
"Smith"	matches *Smith*
"Smith" Or "Larson"	matches either *Smith* or *Larson*
Not "Smith"	is not *Smith* (anything but "Smith")
"s*"	begins with *S* or *s* and ends in anything
"*s"	begins with anything and ends in *S* or *s*
"[A-D]*"	begins with *A*, *B*, *C*, or *D* and ends in anything
#01/01/2018#	matches the date 01/01/2018
<#04/01/2018#	is less than (before) 04/01/2018
>#04/01/2018#	is greater than (after) 04/01/2018
Between #01/01/2018# And #03/31/2018#	is between 01/01/2018 and 03/31/2018

Project 1a Performing Queries on Tables

Part 1 of 8

1. Open **3-Dearborn.accdb** from the AL1C3 folder on your storage medium and enable the content.
2. Create the following relationships and enforce referential integrity and cascade fields and records for each relationship:
   a. Create a one-to-many relationship with the *ClientID* field in the Clients table field list box the "one" and the *ClientID* field in the Sales table field list box the "many."
   b. Create a one-to-one relationship with the *RepID* field in the Representatives table field list box the "one" and the *RepID* field in the Benefits table field list box the "one."
   c. Create a one-to-many relationship with the *RepID* field in the Representatives table field list box the "one" and the *RepID* field in the Clients table field list box the "many."
   d. Create a one-to-many relationship with the *QuotaID* field in the Quotas table field list box the "one" and the *QuotaID* field in the Representatives table field list box the "many."
3. Click the Save button on the Quick Access Toolbar.
4. Print the relationships by completing the following steps:
   a. Click the Relationship Report button in the Tools group on the Relationship Tools Design tab.
   b. At the relationship report window, click the Landscape button in the Page Layout group on the Print Preview tab.
   c. Click the Print button at the left side of the Print Preview tab.
   d. At the Print dialog box, click OK.
5. Close the relationship report window without saving the report.
6. Close the Relationships window.
7. Extract records of those clients in Indianapolis by completing the following steps:
   a. Click the Create tab.
   b. Click the Query Design button in the Queries group.
   c. At the Show Table dialog box with the Tables tab selected (see Figure 3.1 on page 62), click *Clients* in the list box, click the Add button, and then click the Close button.
   d. Insert fields from the Clients table field list box to the *Field* row in the query design grid by completing the following steps:
      1) Click the down arrow at the right of the first field in the *Field* row in the query design grid and then click *Client* at the drop-down list.
      2) Click in the next field in the *Field* row (to the right of *Client*) in the query design grid, click the down arrow, and then click *StreetAddress* at the drop-down list.
      3) Click in the next field in the *Field* row (to the right of *StreetAddress*), click the down arrow, and then click *City* at the drop-down list.
      4) Click in the next field in the *Field* row (to the right of *City*), click the down arrow, and then click *State* at the drop-down list.

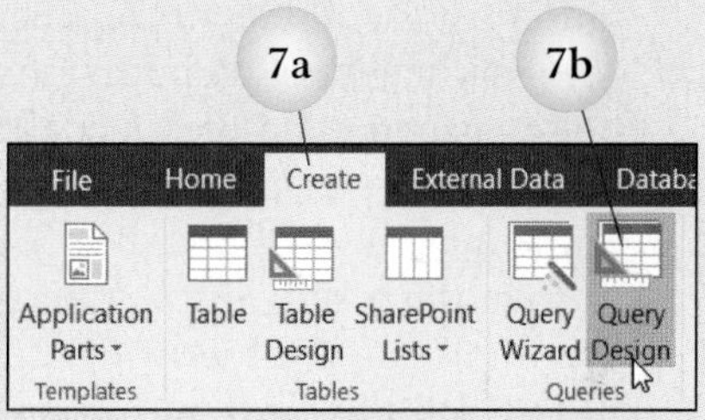

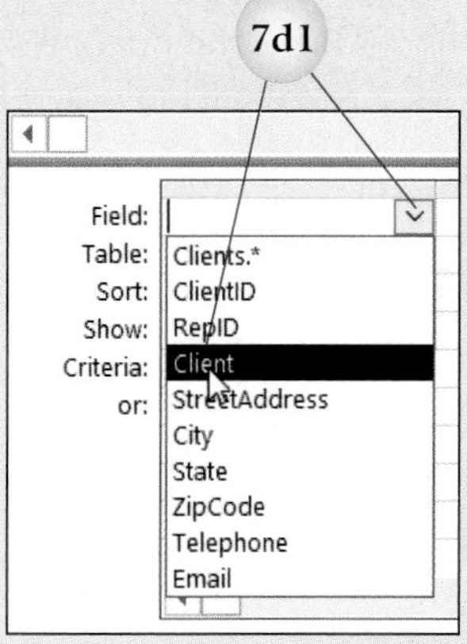

5) Click in the next field in the *Field* row (to the right of *State*), click the down arrow, and then click *ZipCode* at the drop-down list.

e. Insert the query criterion statement telling Access to display only those suppliers in Indianapolis by completing the following steps:
   1) Click in the *City* field in the *Criteria* row in the query design grid. (This positions the insertion point in the field.)
   2) Type Indianapolis and then press the Enter key. (This changes the criterion to "*Indianapolis*".)

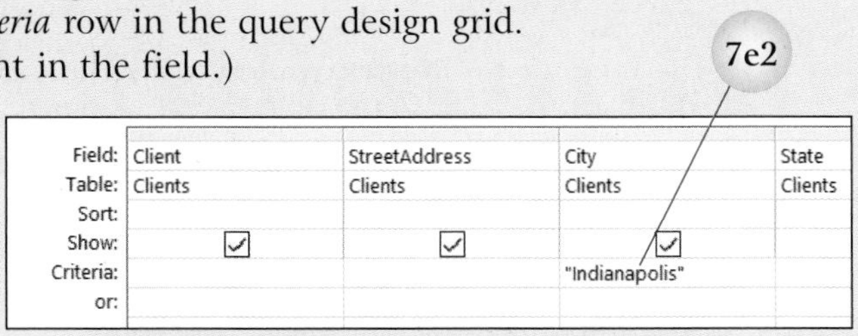

f. Return the results of the query by clicking the Run button in the Results group on the Query Tools Design tab. (This displays the results in the query results datasheet.)

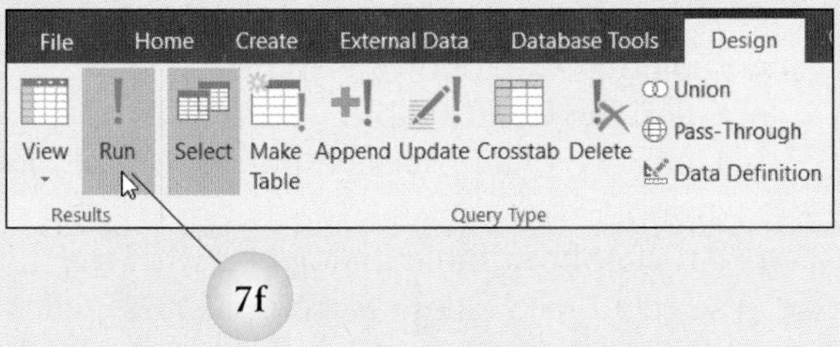

g. Save the results of the query by completing the following steps:
   1) Click the Save button on the Quick Access Toolbar.
   2) At the Save As dialog box, type ClientsIndianapolisQuery and then press the Enter key or click OK.
h. Print the query results datasheet by clicking the File tab, clicking the *Print* option, and then clicking the *Quick Print* option.
i. Close ClientsIndianapolisQuery.

8. Extract those records with quota identification numbers greater than 2 by completing the following steps:
   a. Click the Create tab and then click the Query Design button in the Queries group.
   b. Double-click *Representatives* in the Show Table dialog box and then click the Close button.
   c. In the query window, double-click *RepName*. (This inserts the field in the first field in the *Field* row in the query design grid.)
   d. Double-click *QuotaID*. (This inserts the field in the second field in the *Field* row in the query design grid.)

e. Insert the query criterion by completing the following steps:
   1) Click in the *QuotaID* field in the *Criteria* row in the query design grid.
   2) Type >2 and then press the Enter key. (Access will automatically insert quotation marks around *2* since the data type for the field is identified as *Short Text* [rather than *Number*].)

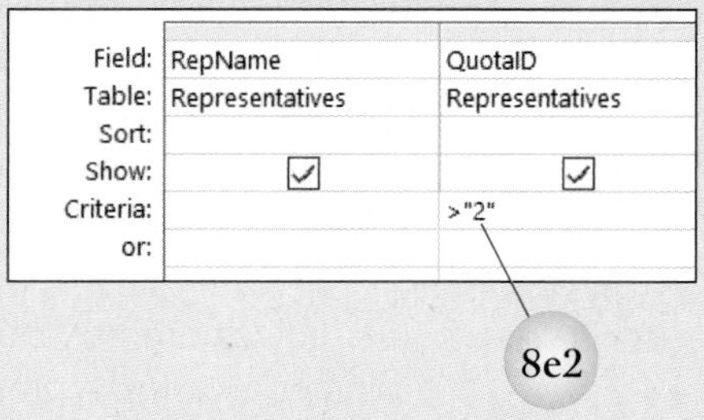

f. Return the results of the query by clicking the Run button in the Results group.
g. Save the query and name it *QuotaIDGreaterThanTwoQuery*.
h. Print and then close the query.

9. Extract those sales greater than $99,999 by completing the following steps:
   a. Click the Create tab and then click the Query Design button.
   b. Double-click *Sales* in the Show Table dialog box and then click the Close button.
   c. At the query window, double-click *ClientID*. (This inserts the field in the first field in the *Field* row in the query design grid.)
   d. Insert the *Sales* field in the second field in the *Field* row.
   e. Insert the query criterion by completing the following steps:
      1) Click in the *Sales* field in the *Criteria* row in the query design grid.
      2) Type >99999 and then press the Enter key. (Access will not insert quotation marks around *99999* since the field is identified as *Currency*.)

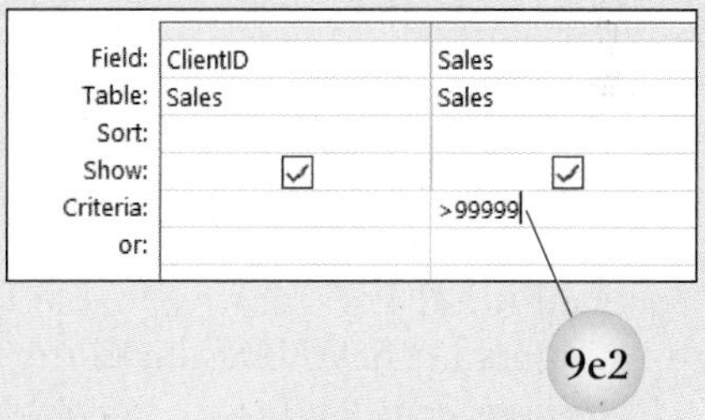

   f. Return the results of the query by clicking the Run button in the Results group.
   g. Save the query and name it *SalesOver$99999Query*.
   h. Print and then close the query.

10. Extract records of those representatives with a telephone number that begins with the 765 area code by completing the following steps:
   a. Click the Create tab and then click the Query Design button.
   b. Double-click *Representatives* in the Show Table dialog box and then click the Close button.
   c. Insert the *RepName* field in the first field in the *Field* row.
   d. Insert the *Telephone* field in the second field in the *Field* row.
   e. Insert the query criterion by completing the following steps:
      1) Click in the *Telephone* field in the *Criteria* row.
      2) Type "(765*" and then press the Enter key. (You need to type the quotation marks in this criterion because the criterion contains a left parenthesis.)

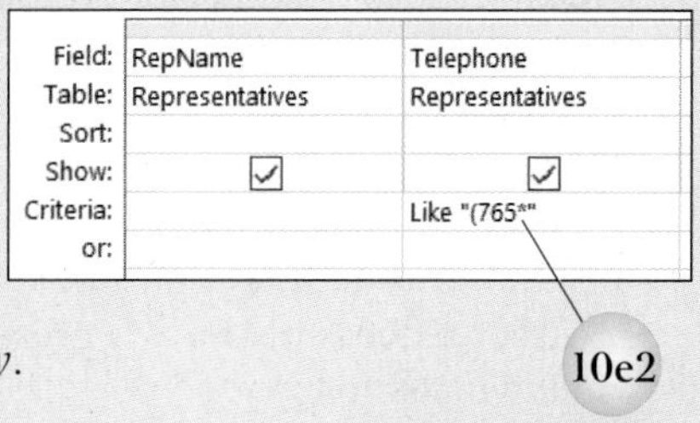

   f. Return the results of the query by clicking the Run button in the Results group.
   g. Save the query and name it *RepsWith765AreaCodeQuery*.
   h. Print and then close the query.

Check Your Work

Tutorial

Creating a Query in Design View Using Multiple Tables

In Project 1a, each query was performed on fields from one table. Queries can also be performed on fields from multiple tables. In Project 1b, queries will be performed on tables containing yes/no check boxes. When designing a query, both records that contain a check mark and records that do not contain a check mark can be extracted. To extract records that contain a check mark, click in the desired field in the *Criteria* row in the query design grid, type a *1*, press the Enter key, and Access changes the *1* to *True*. To extract records that do not contain a check mark, type *0* in the field in the *Criteria* row, press the Enter key, and Access changes the *0* to *False*.

The Zoom box can be used when entering a criterion in a query to provide a larger area for typing. To display the Zoom box, press Shift + F2 or right-click in the specific field in the *Criteria* row and then click *Zoom* at the shortcut menu. Type the criterion in the Zoom box and then click OK.

Project 1b Performing Queries on Related Tables

Part 2 of 8

1. With **3-Dearborn.accdb** open, extract information on representatives hired between January 2016 and June 2016 and include the representatives' names by completing the following steps:
   a. Click the Create tab and then click the Query Design button.
   b. Double-click *Representatives* in the Show Table dialog box.
   c. Double-click *Benefits* in the Show Table dialog box and then click the Close button.
   d. At the query window, double-click *RepName* in the Representatives table field list box.
   e. Double-click *HireDate* in the Benefits table field list box.
   f. Insert the query criterion in the Zoom box by completing the following steps:
      1) Click in the *HireDate* field in the *Criteria* row.
      2) Press Shift + F2 to display the Zoom box.
      3) Type Between 1/1/2016 And 6/30/2016.
      4) Click OK.
   g. Return the results of the query by clicking the Run button in the Results group.
   h. Save the query and name it *JanToJun2016HiresQuery*.
   i. Print and then close the query.

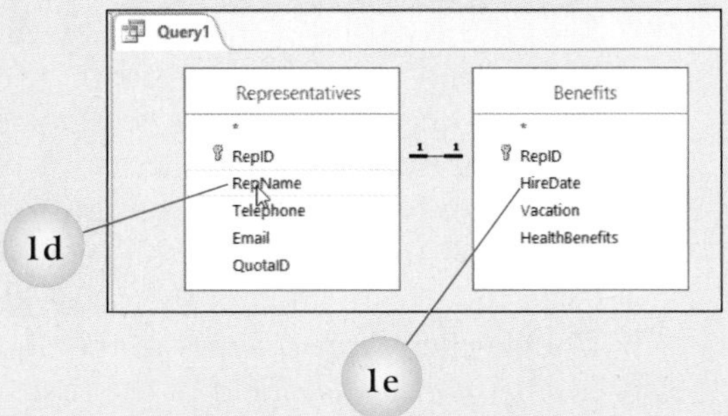

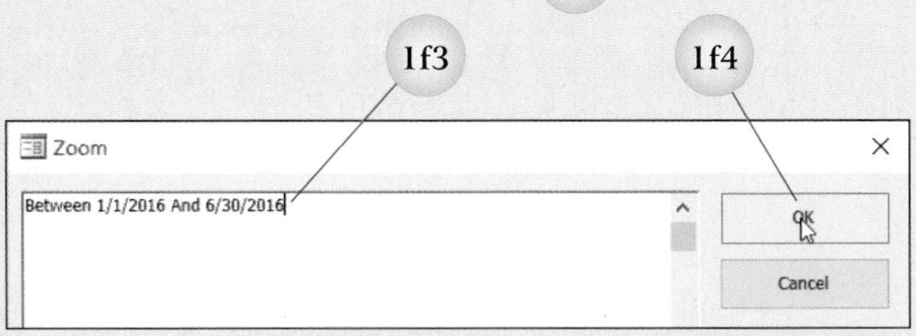

2. Extract records of those representatives who were hired in 2015 by completing the following steps:
   a. Click the Create tab and then click the Query Design button.
   b. Double-click *Representatives* in the Show Table dialog box.
   c. Double-click *Benefits* in the Show Table dialog box and then click the Close button.
   d. Double-click *RepID* in the Representatives table field list box.
   e. Double-click *RepName* in the Representatives table field list box.
   f. Double-click *HireDate* in the Benefits table field list box.

g. Insert the query criterion by completing the following steps:
   1) Click in the *HireDate* field in the *Criteria* row.
   2) Type *2015 and then press the Enter key.
h. Return the results of the query by clicking the Run button in the Results group.
i. Save the query and name it *RepsHiredIn2015Query*.
j. Print and then close the query.

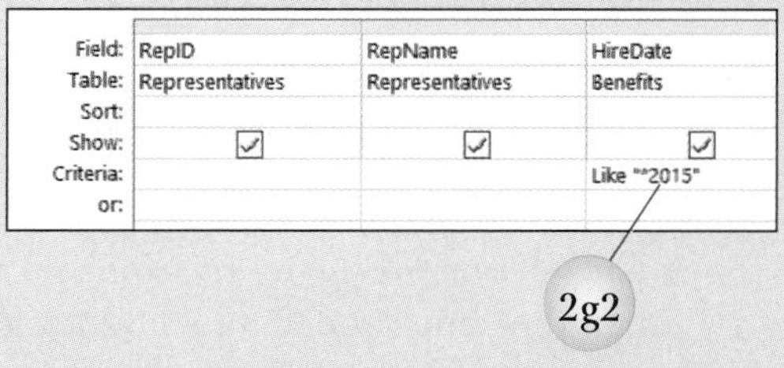

3. Suppose you need to determine sales for a company but you can only remember that the company name begins with *Blue*. Create a query that finds the company and identifies the sales by completing the following steps:
   a. Click the Create tab and then click the Query Design button.
   b. Double-click *Clients* in the Show Table dialog box.
   c. Double-click *Sales* in the Show Table dialog box and then click the Close button.
   d. Insert the *ClientID* field from the Clients table field list box in the first field in the *Field* row in the query design grid.
   e. Insert the *Client* field from the Clients table field list box in the second field in the *Field* row.
   f. Insert the *Sales* field from the Sales table field list box in the third field in the *Field* row.
   g. Insert the query criterion by completing the following steps:
      1) Click in the *Client* field in the *Criteria* row.
      2) Type Blue* and then press the Enter key.
   h. Return the results of the query by clicking the Run button in the Results group.
   i. Save the query and name it *BlueRidgeSalesQuery*.
   j. Print and then close the query.

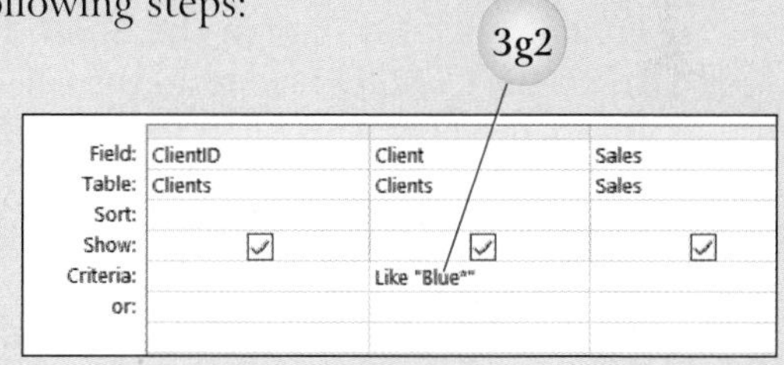

4. Close **3-Dearborn.accdb**.
5. Display the Open dialog box with the AL1C3 folder on your storage medium active.
6. Open **3-PacTrek.accdb** and enable the content.
7. Extract information on products ordered between February 1, 2018, and February 28, 2018, by completing the following steps:
   a. Click the Create tab and then click the Query Design button.
   b. Double-click *Products* in the Show Table dialog box.
   c. Double-click *Orders* in the Show Table dialog box and then click the Close button.
   d. Insert the *ProductID* field from the Products table field list box in the first field in the *Field* row.
   e. Insert the *Product* field from the Products table field list box in the second field in the *Field* row.
   f. Insert the *OrderDate* field from the Orders table field list box in the third field in the *Field* row.
   g. Insert the query criterion by completing the following steps:
      1) Click in the *OrderDate* field in the *Criteria* row.
      2) Type Between 2/1/2018 And 2/28/2018 and then press the Enter key.

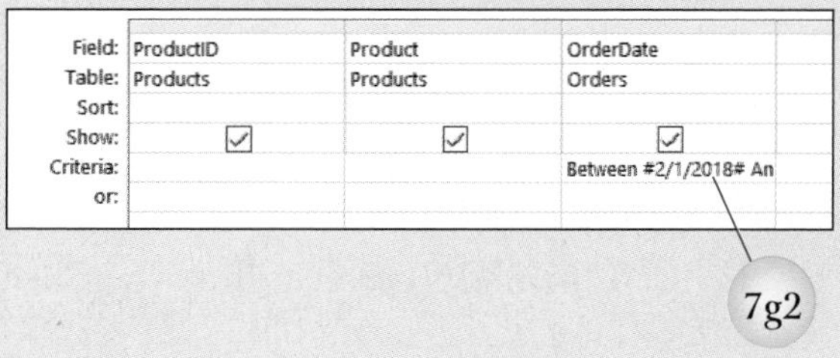

h. Return the results of the query by clicking the Run button in the Results group.
i. Save the query and name it *Feb1-28OrdersQuery*.
j. Print and then close the query.

8. Close **3-PacTrek.accdb**.
9. Open **3-CopperState.accdb** and enable the content.
10. Display the Relationships window and create the following additional relationships (enforce referential integrity and cascade fields and records):
    a. Create a one-to-many relationship with the *AgentID* field in the Agents table field list box the "one" and the *AgentID* field in the Assignments table field list box the "many."
    b. Create a one-to-many relationship with the *OfficeID* field in the Offices table field list box the "one" and the *OfficeID* field in the Assignments table field list box the "many."
    c. Create a one-to-many relationship with the *OfficeID* field in the Offices table field list box the "one" and the *OfficeID* field in the Agents table field list box the "many."
11. Save and then print the relationships.
12. Close the relationship report without saving it and then close the Relationships window.
13. Extract records of clients that have uninsured motorist coverage by completing the following steps:
    a. Click the Create tab and then click the Query Design button.
    b. Double-click *Clients* in the Show Table dialog box.
    c. Double-click *Coverage* in the Show Table dialog box and then click the Close button.
    d. Insert the *ClientID* field from the Clients table field list box in the first field in the *Field* row.
    e. Insert the *FirstName* field from the Clients table field list box in the second field in the *Field* row.
    f. Insert the *LastName* field from the Clients table field list box in the third field in the *Field* row.
    g. Insert the *UninsMotorist* field from the Coverage table field list box in the fourth field in the *Field* row. (You may need to scroll down the Coverage table field list box to display the *UninsMotorist* field.)
    h. Insert the query criterion by clicking in the *UninsMotorist* field in the *Criteria* row, typing *1*, and then pressing the Enter key. (Access changes the *1* to *True*.)

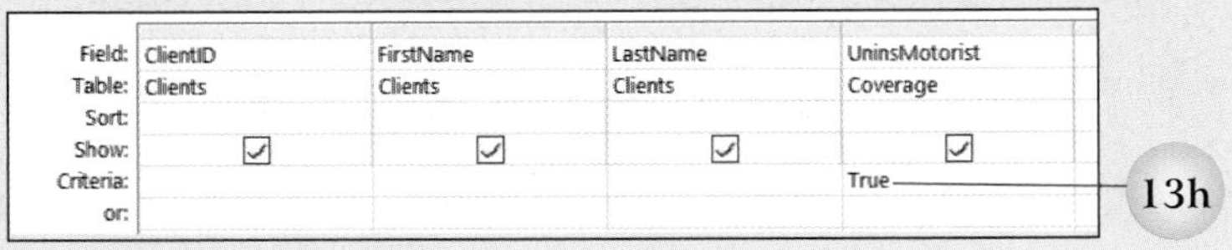

    i. Click the Run button in the Results group.
    j. Save the query and name it *UninsMotoristCoverageQuery*.
    k. Print and then close the query.
14. Extract records of claims in January over $999 by completing the following steps:
    a. Click the Create tab and then click the Query Design button.
    b. Double-click *Clients* in the Show Table dialog box.
    c. Double-click *Claims* in the Show Table dialog box and then click the Close button.
    d. Insert the *ClientID* field from the *Clients* table field list box in the first field in the *Field* row.
    e. Insert the *FirstName* field from the Clients table field list box in the second field in the *Field* row.
    f. Insert the *LastName* field from the Clients table field list box in the third field in the *Field* row.
    g. Insert the *ClaimID* field from the Claims table field list box in the fourth field in the *Field* row.
    h. Insert the *DateOfClaim* field from the Claims table field list box in the fifth field in the *Field* row.

i. Insert the *AmountOfClaim* field from the Claims table field list box in the sixth field in the *Field* row.
j. Click in the *DateOfClaim* field in the *Criteria* row, type Between 1/1/2018 And 1/31/2018, and then press the Enter key.
k. With the insertion point positioned in the *AmountOfClaim* field in the *Criteria* row, type >999 and then press the Enter key.

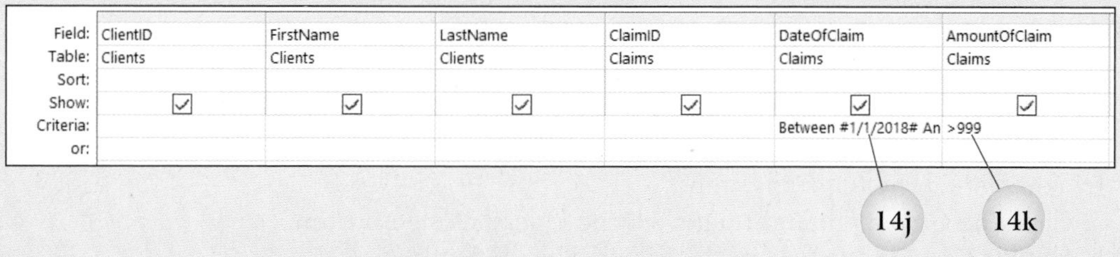

l. Click the Run button in the Results group.
m. Save the query and name it *JanClaimsOver$999Query*.
n. Print and then close the query.

Check Your Work

Tutorial

Sorting Data and Hiding Fields in Query Results

Sorting in a Query

When designing a query, the sort order of a field or fields can be specified. Click in a field in the *Sort* row and a down arrow displays at the right of the field. Click this down arrow and a drop-down list displays with the choices *Ascending*, *Descending*, and *(not sorted)*. Click *Ascending* to sort from lowest to highest or click *Descending* to sort from highest to lowest.

Quick Steps

Sort Fields in a Query
1. At query window, click in field in *Sort* row in query design grid.
2. Click down arrow in field.
3. Click *Ascending* or *Descending*.

Hiding Fields in a Query

By default, each check box in the fields in the *Show* row in the query design grid contains a check mark, indicating that the column will be displayed in the query results datasheet. If a specific field is needed for the query but not needed when viewing the query results, remove the check mark from the field in the *Show* row to hide the field in the query results datasheet.

Arranging Fields in a Query

Insert Columns

Delete Columns

Use buttons in the Query Setup group on the Query Design Tools tab to insert a new field column in or delete an existing field column from the query design grid. To insert a field column, click in a field in the column that will display immediately to the right of the new column and then click the Insert Columns button in the Query Setup group on the Query Design Tools tab. To remove a column, click in a field in the column to be deleted and then click the Delete Columns button in the Query Setup group. Complete similar steps to insert or delete a row in the query design grid.

Columns in the query design grid can be rearranged by selecting the field column and then dragging the column to the desired position. To select a column in the query design grid, position the mouse pointer at the top of the column until the pointer turns into a small, black, down-pointing arrow and then click the left mouse button. Position the mouse pointer at the top of the selected column until the mouse displays as a pointer, click and hold down the left mouse button, drag to the desired position in the query design grid, and then release the mouse button. When dragging the column, a thick, black, vertical line displays identifying the location where the column will be inserted.

Project 1c Performing Queries on Related Tables and Sorting in Field Values — Part 3 of 8

1. With **3-CopperState.accdb** open, extract information on clients with agents from the West Bell Road Glendale office and sort the information alphabetically by client last name by completing the following steps:
   a. Click the Create tab and then click the Query Design button.
   b. Double-click *Assignments* in the Show Table dialog box.
   c. Double-click *Clients* in the Show Table dialog box and then click the Close button.
   d. Insert the *OfficeID* field from the Assignments table field list box in the first field in the *Field* row.
   e. Insert the *AgentID* field from the Assignments table field list box in the second field in the *Field* row.
   f. Insert the *FirstName* field from the Clients table field list box in the third field in the *Field* row.
   g. Insert the *LastName* field from the Clients table field list box in the fourth field in the *Field* row.
   h. Click in the *OfficeID* field in the *Criteria* row, type GW, and then press the Enter key.
   i. Sort the *LastName* field column in ascending alphabetical order (A–Z) by completing the following steps:
      1) Click in the *LastName* field in the *Sort* row. (This causes a down arrow to display in the field.)
      2) Click the down arrow that displays in the field in the *Sort* row and then click *Ascending*.

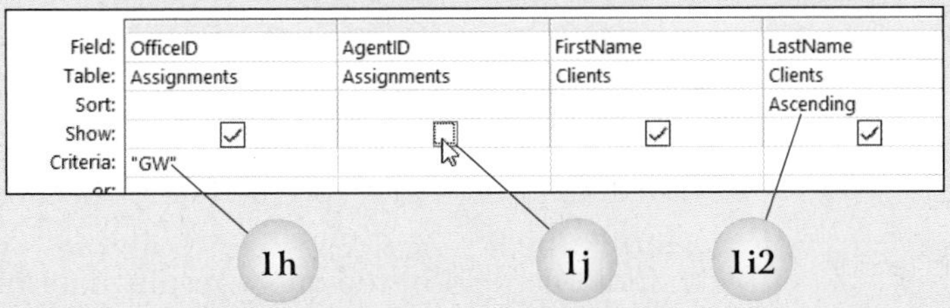

   j. Specify that you do not want the *AgentID* field to show in the query results by clicking in the check box in the *AgentID* field in the *Show* row to remove the check mark.
   k. Click the Run button in the Results group.
   l. Save the query and name it *GWClientsQuery*.
   m. Print and then close the query.
2. Close **3-CopperState.accdb**.
3. Open **3-PacTrek.accdb**.
4. Extract information on orders less than $1,500 by completing the following steps:
   a. Click the Create tab and then click the Query Design button.
   b. Double-click *Products* in the Show Table dialog box.
   c. Double-click *Orders* in the Show Table dialog box and then click the Close button.
   d. Insert the *ProductID* field from the Products table field list box in the first field in the *Field* row.
   e. Insert the *SupplierID* field from the Products table field list box in the second field in the *Field* row.

f. Insert the *UnitsOrdered* field from the Orders table field list box in the third field in the *Field* row.

g. Insert the *Amount* field from the Orders table field list box in the fourth field in the *Field* row.

h. Insert the query criterion by completing the following steps:

   1) Click in the *Amount* field in the *Criteria* row.

   2) Type <1500 and then press the Enter key.

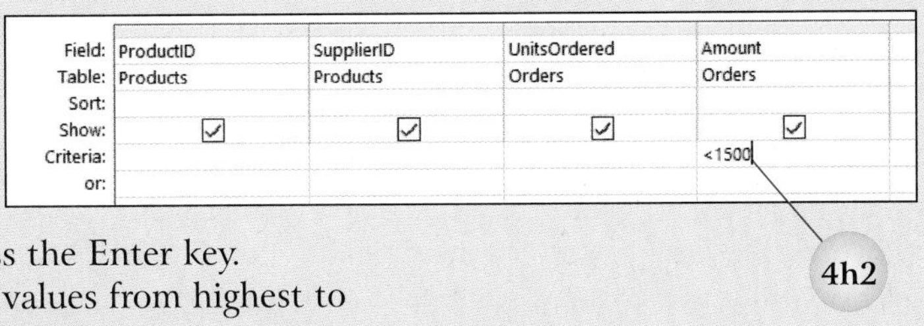

i. Sort the *Amount* field column values from highest to lowest by completing the following steps:

   1) Click in the *Amount* field in the *Sort* row. (This causes a down arrow to display in the field.)

   2) Click the down arrow that displays in the field in the *Sort* row and then click *Descending*.

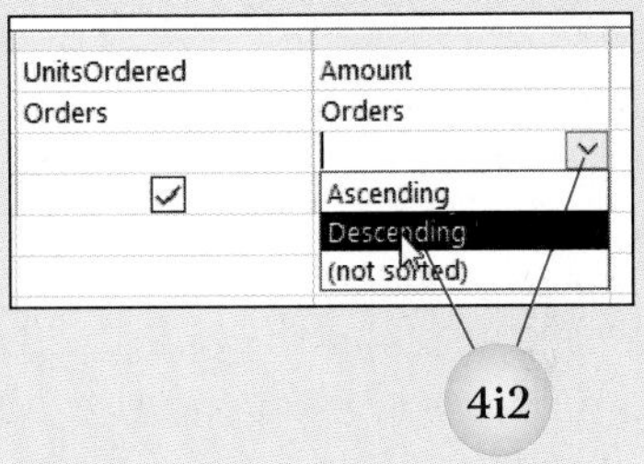

j. Return the results of the query by clicking the Run button in the Results group.

k. Save the query and name it *OrdersLessThan$1500Query*.

l. Print and then close the query.

5. Close **3-PacTrek.accdb**.
6. Open **3-Dearborn.accdb**.
7. Design a query by completing the following steps:

   a. Click the Create tab and then click the Query Design button.

   b. Double-click *Representatives* in the Show Table dialog box.

   c. Double-click *Clients* in the Show Table dialog box.

   d. Double-click *Sales* in the Show Table dialog box and then click the Close button.

   e. Insert the *RepID* field from the Representatives table field list box in the first field in the *Field* row.

   f. Insert the *RepName* field from the Representatives table field list box in the second field in the *Field* row.

   g. Insert the *ClientID* field from the Clients table field list box in the third field in the *Field* row.

   h. Insert the *Sales* field from the Sales table field list box in the fourth field in the *Field* row.

8. Move the *RepName* field column by completing the following steps:

   a. Position the mouse pointer at the top of the *RepName* field column until the pointer turns into a small, black, down-pointing arrow and then click the left mouse button. (This selects the entire column.)

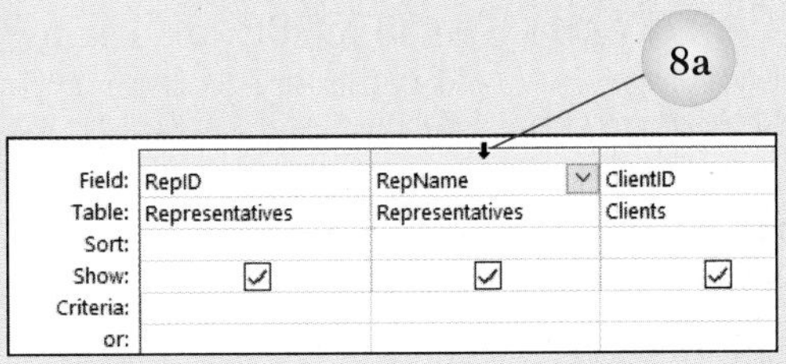

   b. Position the mouse pointer at the top of the selected column until the pointer turns into a white arrow.

   c. Click and hold down the left mouse button; drag to the right until a thick, black horizontal line displays between the *ClientID* field column and the *Sales* field column; and then release the mouse button.

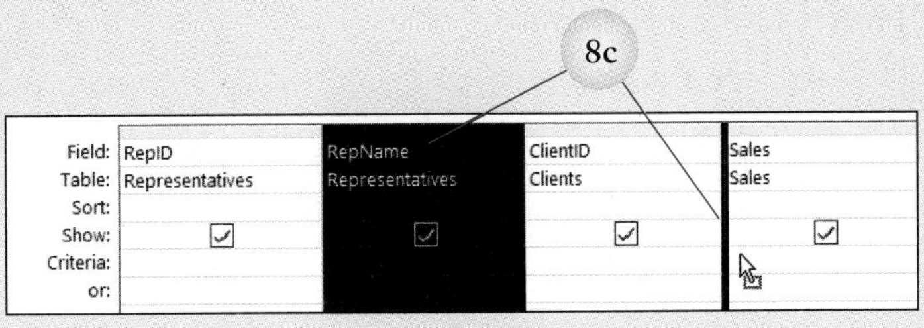

9. Delete the *RepID* field column by clicking in a field in the column and then clicking the Delete Columns button in the Query Setup group.
10. Insert a new field column and insert a new field in the column by completing the following steps:
    a. Click in a field in the *Sales* field column and then click the Insert Columns button in the Query Setup group.
    b. Click the down arrow that displays in the *Field* row in the new field column and then click *Clients.Client* at the drop-down list.

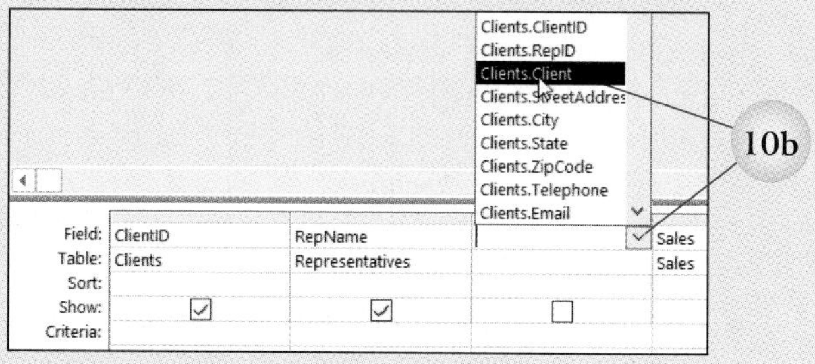

11. Hide the *ClientID* field so it does not display in the query results by clicking the *Show* check box in the *ClientID* field in the *Show* row to remove the check mark.
12. Insert the query criterion that extracts information on sales over $100,000 by completing the following steps:
    a. Click in the *Sales* field in the *Criteria* row.
    b. Type >100000 and then press the Enter key.
13. Sort the *Sales* field column values from highest to lowest by completing the following steps:
    a. Click in the *Sales* field in the *Sort* row.
    b. Click the down arrow that displays in the field in the *Sort* row and then click *Descending*.
14. Return the results of the query by clicking the Run button in the Results group.
15. Save the query and name it *SalesMoreThan$100000Query*.
16. Print and then close the query.

Check Your Work

Modifying a Query

A query can be modified and used for a new purpose rather than designing a new query. For example, if a query is designed that displays sales of more than $100,000, the query can be used to find sales that are less than $100,000. Rather than design a new query, open the existing query, make any needed changes, and then run the query.

Quick Steps

Modify a Query

1. Double-click query in Navigation pane.
2. Click View button.
3. Make changes to query.
4. Click Run button.
5. Click Save button.

To modify an existing query, double-click the query in the Navigation pane. (This displays the query in Datasheet view.) Click the View button to display the query in Design view. A query can also be opened in Design view by right-clicking the query in the Navigation pane and then clicking *Design View* at the shortcut menu. Make changes to the query and then click the Run button in the Results group. Click the Save button on the Quick Access Toolbar to save the query with the same name. To save the query with a new name, click the File tab, click the *Save As* option, click the *Save Object As* option, and then click the Save As button. At the Save As dialog box, type a name for the query and then press the Enter key.

Hint Save time designing a new query by modifying an existing query.

If a database contains a number of queries, the queries can be grouped and displayed in the Navigation pane. To do this, click the down arrow in the Navigation pane menu bar and then click *Object Type* at the drop-down list. This displays objects grouped in categories, such as *Tables* and *Queries*.

Tutorial

Renaming and Deleting Objects

Renaming and Deleting a Query

If a query has been modified, consider renaming it. To do this, right-click the query name in the Navigation pane, click *Rename* at the shortcut menu, type the new name, and then press the Enter key. If a query is no longer needed in the database, delete it by clicking the query name in the Navigation pane, clicking the Delete button in the Records group on the Home tab, and then clicking the Yes button at the deletion message. Another method is to right-click the query in the Navigation pane, click *Delete* at the shortcut menu, and then click Yes at the deletion message. If a query is being deleted from a file on the computer's hard drive, the deletion message will not display. This is because Access automatically sends the deleted query to the Recycle Bin, where it can be retrieved if necessary.

Project 1d Modifying Queries

Part 4 of 8

1. With **3-Dearborn.accdb** open, find sales less than $100,000 by completing the following steps:
   a. Double-click *SalesMoreThan$100000Query* in the Queries group in the Navigation pane.
   b. Click the View button in the Views group to switch to Design view.
   c. Click in the field in the *Criteria* row containing the text *>100000* and then edit the text so it displays as *<100000*.

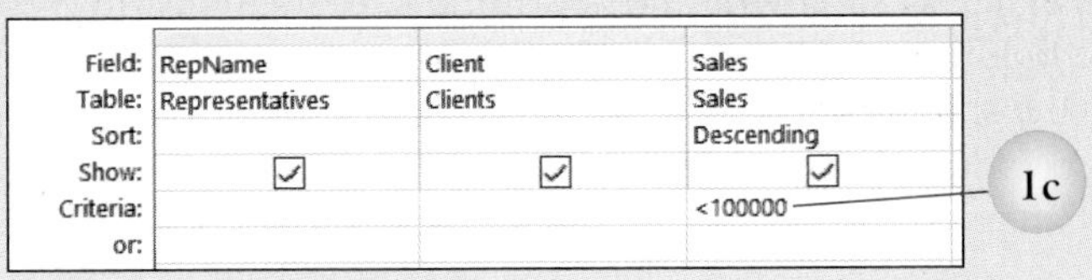

   d. Click the Run button in the Results group.
2. Save the query with a new name by completing the following steps:
   a. Click the File tab, click the *Save As* option, click the *Save Object As* option, and then click the Save As button.
   b. At the Save As dialog box, type SalesLessThan$100000Query and then press the Enter key.
   c. Print and then close the query.

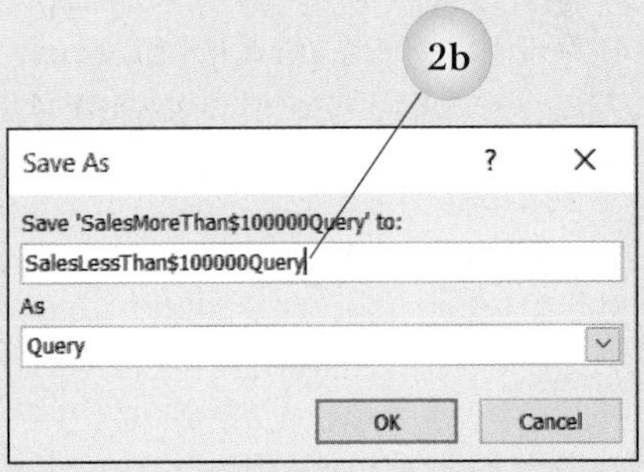

3. Modify an existing query and find employees with three weeks of vacation by completing the following steps:
   a. Right-click *JanToJun2016HiresQuery* in the Queries group in the Navigation pane and then click *Design View* at the shortcut menu.
   b. Click in the *HireDate* field in the *Field* row.
   c. Click the down arrow that displays in the field and then click *Vacation* at the drop-down list.
   d. Select the current text in the *Vacation* field in the *Criteria* row, type 3 weeks, and then press the Enter key.
   e. Click the Run button in the Results group.
   f. Save and then close the query.

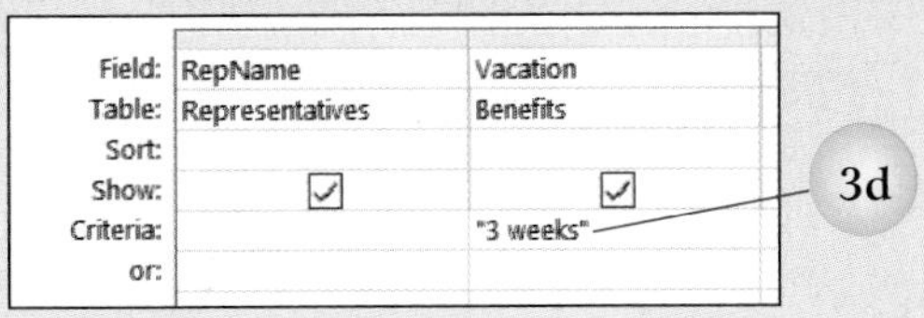

4. Rename the query by completing the following steps:
   a. Right-click *JanToJun2016HiresQuery* in the Navigation pane and then click *Rename* at the shortcut menu.
   b. Type RepsWith3WeekVacationsQuery and then press the Enter key.
   c. Open, print, and then close the query.
5. Delete the *SalesOver$99999Query* by right-clicking the query name in the Navigation pane and then clicking *Delete* at the shortcut menu. If a deletion message displays, click Yes.

Check Your Work

Designing Queries with *Or* and *And* Criteria

Tutorial

Designing a Query with *Or* Criteria

Tutorial

Designing a Query with *And* Criteria

Hint A query can be designed that combines *And* and *Or* statements.

The query design grid contains an *or* row for designing a query that instructs Access to display records matching any of the criteria. Multiple criterion statements on different rows in a query become an *Or* statement, which means that any of the criterion can be met for a record to be displayed in the query results datasheet. For example, to display a list of employees with three weeks of vacation *or* four weeks of vacation, type *3 weeks* in the *Vacation* field in the *Criteria* row and then type *4 weeks* in the field immediately below *3 weeks* in the *or* row. Other examples include finding clients that live in *Muncie* or *Lafayette* and finding representatives with quotas of *1* or *2*.

When designing a query, criteria statements can be entered into more than one field in the *Criteria* row. Multiple criteria all entered in the same row become an *And* statement, for which each criterion must be met for Access to select the record. For example, a query can be designed that displays clients in the Indianapolis area with sales greater than $100,000.

Project 1e Designing Queries with *Or* and *And* Criteria — Part 5 of 8

1. With **3-Dearborn.accdb** open, modify an existing query and find employees with three weeks or four weeks of vacation by completing the following steps:
   a. Double-click the *RepsWith3WeekVacationsQuery*.
   b. Click the View button in the Views group to switch to Design view.
   c. Click in the empty field below *"3 weeks"* in the *or* row, type 4 weeks, and then press the Enter key.
   d. Click the Run button in the Results group.

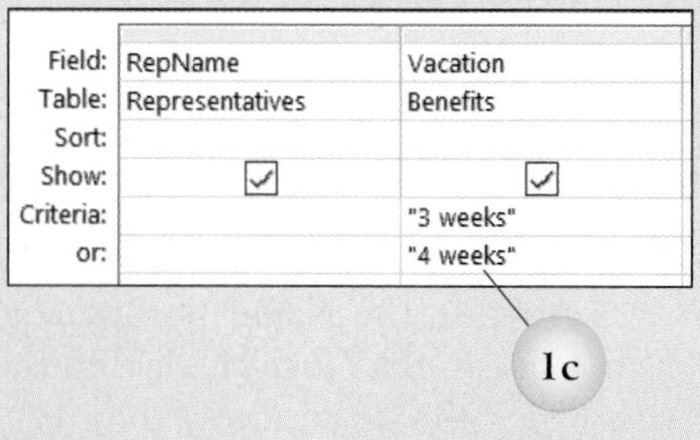

2. Save the query with a new name by completing the following steps:
   a. Click the File tab, click the *Save As* option, click the *Save Object As* option, and then click the Save As button.
   b. At the Save As dialog box, type RepsWith3Or4WeekVacationsQuery and then press the Enter key.
   c. Print and then close the query.
3. Design a query that finds records of clients in the Indianapolis area with sales over $100,000 by completing the following steps:
   a. Click the Create tab and then click the Query Design button.
   b. Double-click *Clients* in the Show Table dialog box.

c. Double-click *Sales* in the Show Table dialog box and then click the Close button.
d. Insert the *Client* field from the Clients table field list box in the first field in the *Field* row.
e. Insert the *City* field from the Clients table field list box in the second field in the *Field* row.
f. Insert the *Sales* field from the Sales table field list box in the third field in the *Field* row.
g. Insert the query criteria by completing the following steps:
   1) Click in the *City* field in the *Criteria* row.
   2) Type Indianapolis and then press the Enter key.
   3) With the insertion point positioned in the *Sales* field in the *Criteria* row, type >100000 and then press the Enter key.

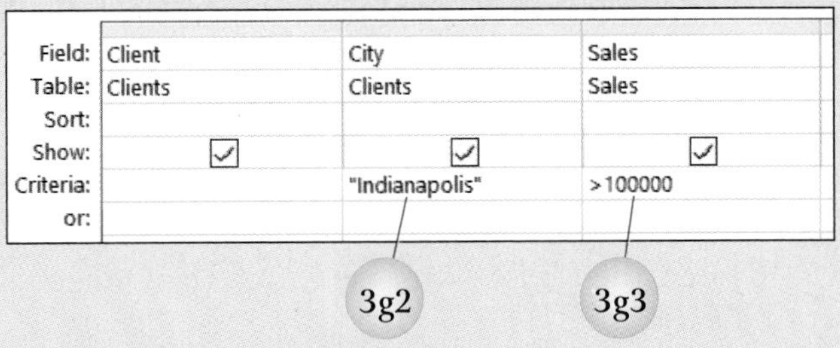

h. Click the Run button in the Results group.
i. Save the query and name it *SalesOver$100000IndianapolisQuery*.
j. Print and then close the query.

4. Close **3-Dearborn.accdb**.
5. Open **3-PacTrek.accdb**.
6. Design a query that finds products available from supplier numbers 25, 31, and 42 by completing the following steps:
   a. Click the Create tab and then click the Query Design button.
   b. Double-click *Suppliers* in the Show Table dialog box.
   c. Double-click *Products* in the Show Table dialog box and then click the Close button.
   d. Insert the *SupplierID* field from the Suppliers table field list box in the first field in the *Field* row.
   e. Insert the *SupplierName* field from the Suppliers table field list box in the second field in the *Field* row.
   f. Insert the *Product* field from the Products table field list box in the third field in the *Field* row.
   g. Insert the query criteria by completing the following steps:
      1) Click in the *SupplierID* field in the *Criteria* row.
      2) Type 25 and then press the Down Arrow key. (This makes the field below *25* active.)
      3) Type 31 and then press the Down Arrow key. (This makes the field below *31* active.)
      4) Type 42 and then press the Enter key.

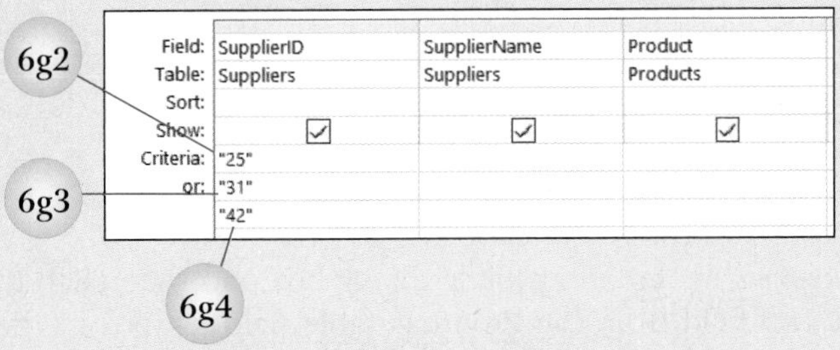

   h. Click the Run button in the Results group.
   i. Save the query and name it *Suppliers25-31-42Query*.
   j. Print and then close the query.

7. Design a query that finds the number of ski hats or gloves on order by completing the following steps:
   a. Click the Create tab and then click the Query Design button.
   b. Double-click *Orders* in the Show Table dialog box.
   c. Double-click *Suppliers* in the Show Table dialog box.
   d. Double-click *Products* in the Show Table dialog box and then click the Close button.
   e. Insert the *OrderID* field from the Orders table field list box in the first field in the *Field* row.
   f. Insert the *SupplierName* field from the Suppliers table field list box in the second field in the *Field* row.
   g. Insert the *Product* field from the Products table field list box in the third field in the *Field* row.
   h. Insert the *UnitsOrdered* field from the Orders table field list box in the fourth field in the *Field* row.
   i. Insert the query criteria by completing the following steps:
      1) Click in the *Product* field in the *Criteria* row.
      2) Type *ski hat* and then press the Down Arrow key. (You need to type the asterisk before and after *ski hat* so the query will find any product that includes the words *ski hat* in the description, no matter what text comes before or after the words. When you press the Down Arrow key, Access changes the criteria to *Like "*ski hat*"*.)
      3) Type *gloves* and then press the Enter key.

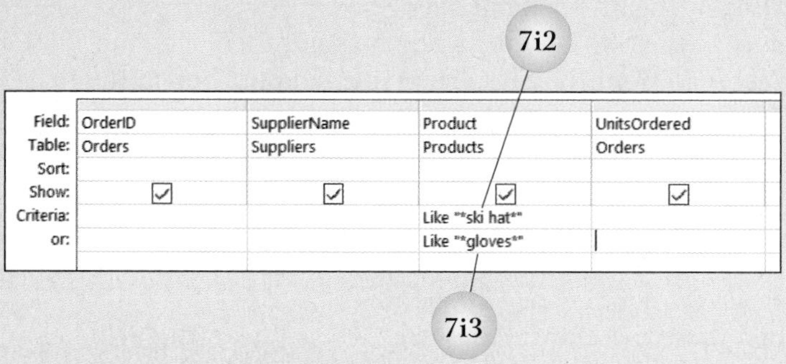

   j. Click the Run button in the Results group.
   k. Save the query and name it *SkiHatsGlovesOnOrderQuery*.
   l. Print and then close the query.
8. Design a query that finds boots, sleeping bags, or backpacks and the suppliers that produce them by completing the following steps:
   a. Click the Create tab and then click the Query Design button.
   b. Double-click *Products* in the Show Table dialog box.
   c. Double-click *Suppliers* in the Show Table dialog box and then click the Close button.
   d. Insert the *ProductID* field from the Products table field list box in the first field in the *Field* row.
   e. Insert the *Product* field from the Products table field list box in the second field in the *Field* row.
   f. Insert the *SupplierName* field from the Suppliers table field list box in the third field in the *Field* row.
   g. Insert the query criteria by completing the following steps:
      1) Click in the *Product* field in the *Criteria* row.

2) Type *boots* and then press the Down Arrow key on your keyboard.

3) Type *sleeping bag* and then press the Down Arrow key on your keyboard.

4) Type *backpack* and then press the Enter key.

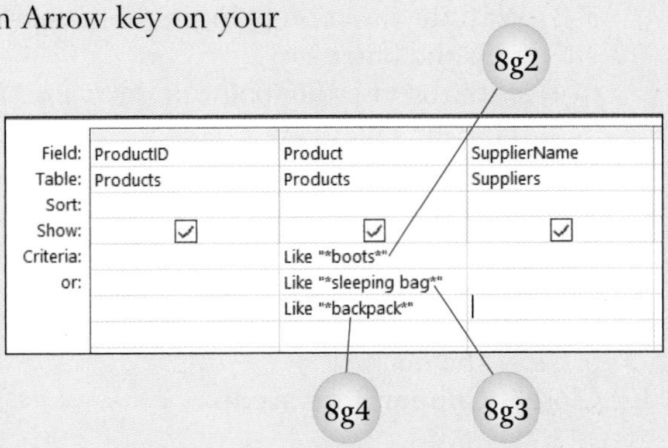

h. Click the Run button in the Results group.

i. Save the query and name it *BootsSleepingBagsBackpacksQuery*.

j. Print and then close the query.

9. Close **3-PacTrek.accdb**.

10. Open **3-CopperState.accdb**.

11. Design a query that finds clients who have only liability auto coverage by completing the following steps:

a. Click the Create tab and then click the Query Design button.

b. Double-click *Clients* in the Show Table dialog box.

c. Double-click *Coverage* in the Show Table dialog box and then click the Close button.

d. Insert the *ClientID* field from the Clients table field list box in the first field in the *Field* row.

e. Insert the *FirstName* field from the Clients table field list box in the second field in the *Field* row.

f. Insert the *LastName* field from the Clients table field list box in the third field in the *Field* row.

g. Insert the *Medical* field from the Coverage table field list box in the fourth field in the *Field* row.

h. Insert the *Liability* field from the Coverage table field list box in the fifth field in the *Field* row.

i. Insert the *Comprehensive* field from the Coverage table field list box in the sixth field in the *Field* row.

j. Insert the *UninsMotorist* field from the Coverage table field list box in the seventh field in the *Field* row. (You may need to scroll down the Coverage table field list box to display the *UninsMotorist* field.)

k. Insert the *Collision* field from the Coverage table field list box in the eighth field in the *Field* row. (You may need to scroll down the Coverage table field list box to display the *Collision* field.)

l. Insert the query criteria by completing the following steps:

1) Click in the *Medical* field in the *Criteria* row, type 0, and then press the Enter key. (Access changes the *0* to *False*.)

2) With the insertion point in the *Liability* field in the *Criteria* row, type 1 and then press the Enter key. (Access changes the *1* to *True*.)

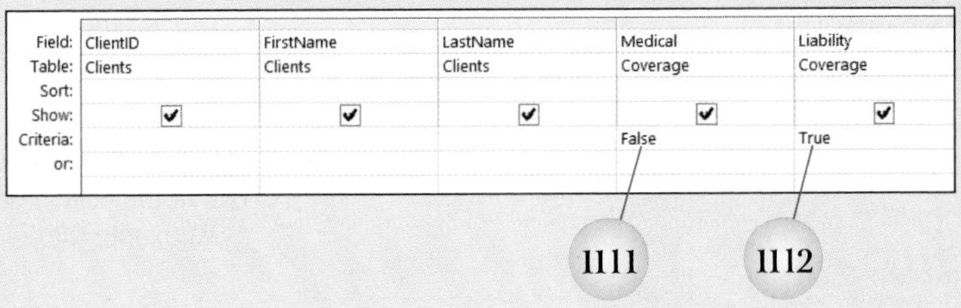

Field: ClientID | FirstName | LastName | Medical | Liability
Table: Clients | Clients | Clients | Coverage | Coverage
Sort:
Show:
Criteria: False | True
or:
11l1
11l2

3) With the insertion point in the *Comprehensive* field in the *Criteria* row, type 0 and then press the Enter key.
4) With the insertion point in the *UninsMotorist* field in the *Criteria* row, type 0 and then press the Enter key.
5) With the insertion point in the *Collision* field in the *Criteria* row, type 0 and then press the Enter key.

m. Click the Run button in the Results group.
n. Save the query and name it *ClientsWithOnlyLiabilityQuery*.
o. Print the query in landscape orientation.
p. Close the query.

12. Close **3-CopperState.accdb**.

Check Your Work

Tutorial

Creating a Query Using the Simple Query Wizard

Query Wizard

Creating a Query Using the Simple Query Wizard

The Simple Query Wizard provided by Access provides steps for preparing a query. To use this wizard, open the database, click the Create tab, and then click the Query Wizard button in the Queries group. At the New Query dialog box, make sure *Simple Query Wizard* is selected in the list box and then click the OK button. At the first Simple Query Wizard dialog box, shown in Figure 3.3, specify the table(s) in the *Tables/Queries* option box. After specifying the table(s), insert the fields to be included in the query in the *Selected Fields* list box and then click the Next button.

At the second Simple Query Wizard dialog box, specify a detail or summary query and then click the Next button. At the third (and last) Simple Query Wizard dialog box, shown in Figure 3.4, type a name for the completed query or accept the name provided by the wizard. The third Simple Query Wizard dialog box also includes options for choosing to open the query to view the information or to modify the query design. To extract specific information, be sure to choose the *Modify the query design* option. After making any necessary changes, click the Finish button.

If the query design is not modified in the last Simple Query Wizard dialog box, the query displays all records for the fields identified in the first Simple Query Wizard dialog box.

Quick Steps

Create a Query Using the Simple Query Wizard

1. Click Create tab.
2. Click Query Wizard button.
3. Make sure *Simple Query Wizard* is selected in list box and then click OK.
4. Follow query steps.
5. Click Finish button.

Figure 3.3 First Simple Query Wizard Dialog Box

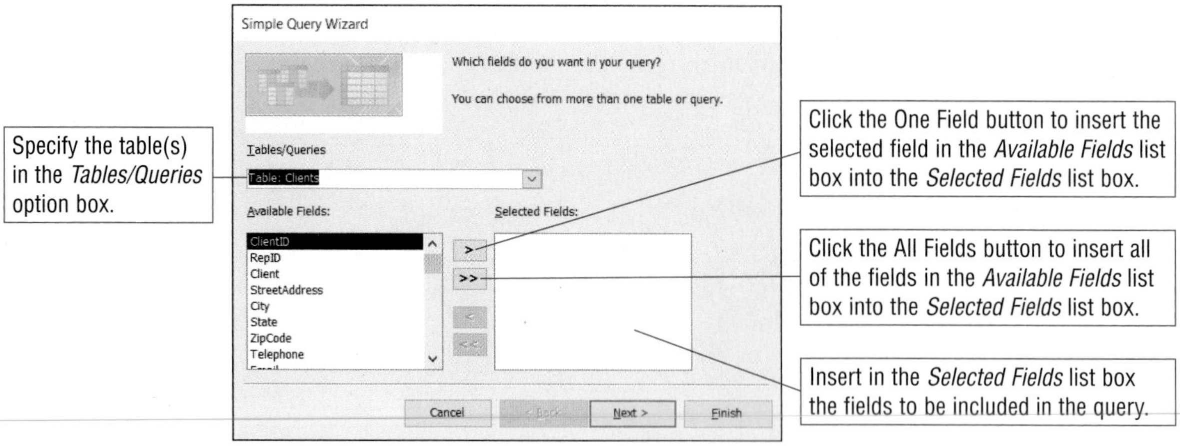
Simple Query Wizard
Which fields do you want in your query?
You can choose from more than one table or query.
Tables/Queries
Table: Clients
Available Fields:
Selected Fields:
ClientID
RepID
Client
StreetAddress
City
State
ZipCode
Telephone
Cancel
< Back
Next >
Finish
Specify the table(s) in the *Tables/Queries* option box.
Click the One Field button to insert the selected field in the *Available Fields* list box into the *Selected Fields* list box.
Click the All Fields button to insert all of the fields in the *Available Fields* list box into the *Selected Fields* list box.
Insert in the *Selected Fields* list box the fields to be included in the query.

Figure 3.4 Last Simple Query Wizard Dialog Box

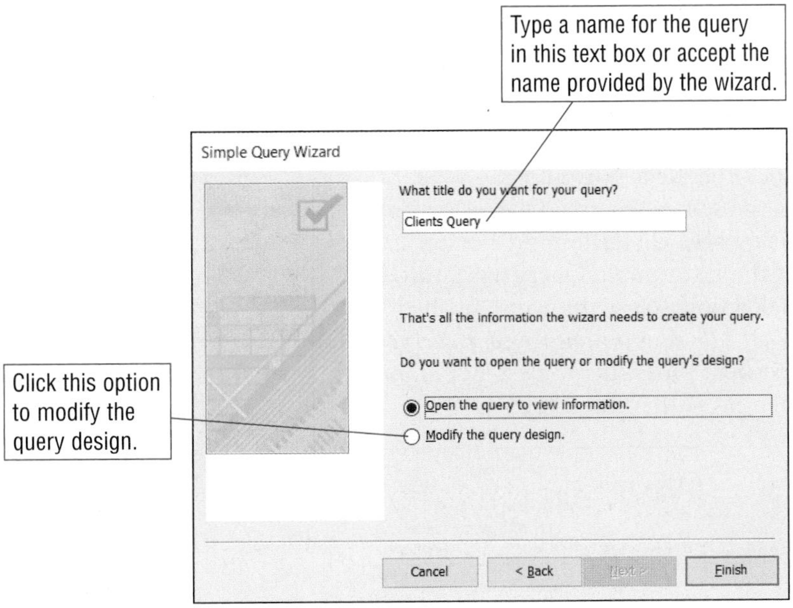

Project 1f Creating Queries Using the Simple Query Wizard

Part 6 of 8

1. Open **3-Dearborn.accdb** and then use the Simple Query Wizard to create a query that displays client names along with sales by completing the following steps:
   a. Click the Create tab and then click the Query Wizard button in the Queries group.
   b. At the New Query dialog box, make sure *Simple Query Wizard* is selected in the list box and then click OK.
   c. At the first Simple Query Wizard dialog box, click the *Tables/Queries* option box arrow and then click *Table: Clients*.
   d. With *ClientID* selected in the *Available Fields* list box, click the One Field button (the button containing the greater-than symbol, >). This inserts the *ClientID* field in the *Selected Fields* list box.
   e. Click *Client* in the *Available Fields* list box and then click the One Field button.

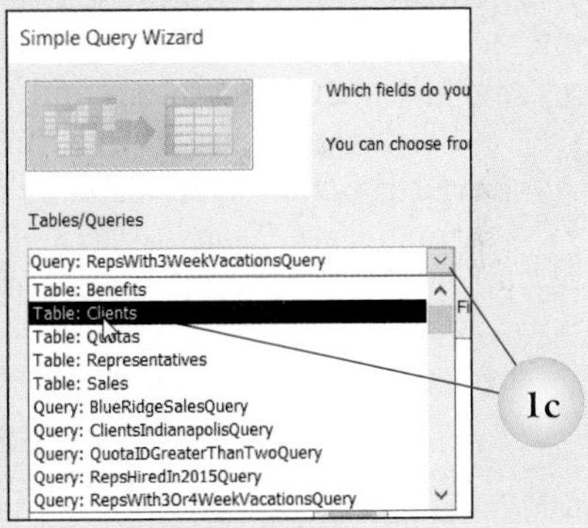

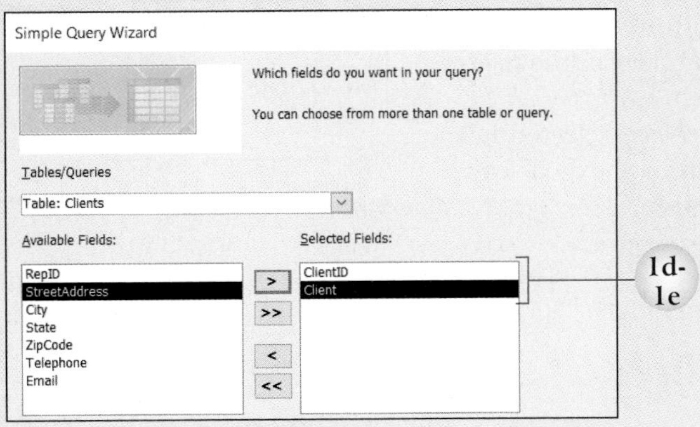

f. Click the *Tables/Queries* option box arrow and then click *Table: Sales*.
g. Click *Sales* in the *Available Fields* list box and then click the One Field button.
h. Click the Next button.
i. At the second Simple Query Wizard dialog box, click the Next button.
j. At the last Simple Query Wizard dialog box, select the name in the *What title do you want for your query?* text box, type ClientSalesQuery, and then press the Enter key.

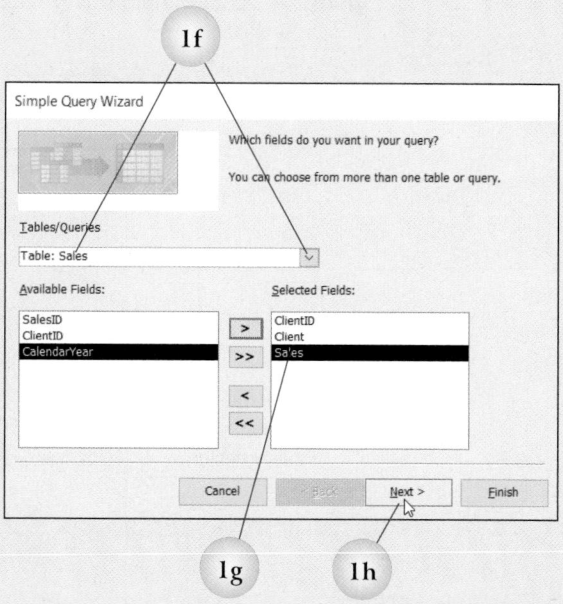

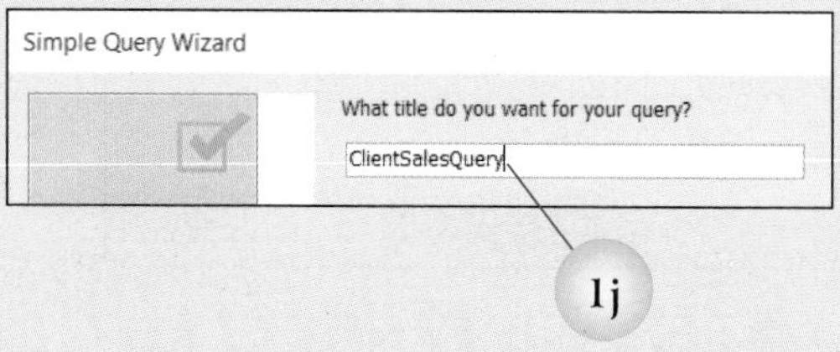

k. When the results of the query display, print the results.
2. Close the query.
3. Close **3-Dearborn.accdb**.
4. Open **3-PacTrek.accdb**.
5. Create a query that displays the products on order, order amounts, and supplier names by completing the following steps:
   a. Click the Create tab and then click the Query Wizard button.
   b. At the New Query dialog box, make sure *Simple Query Wizard* is selected in the list box and then click OK.
   c. At the first Simple Query Wizard dialog box, click the *Tables/Queries* option box arrow and then click *Table: Suppliers*.
   d. With *SupplierID* selected in the *Available Fields* list box, click the One Field button. (This inserts the *SupplierID* field in the *Selected Fields* list box.)
   e. With *SupplierName* selected in the *Available Fields* list box, click the One Field button.

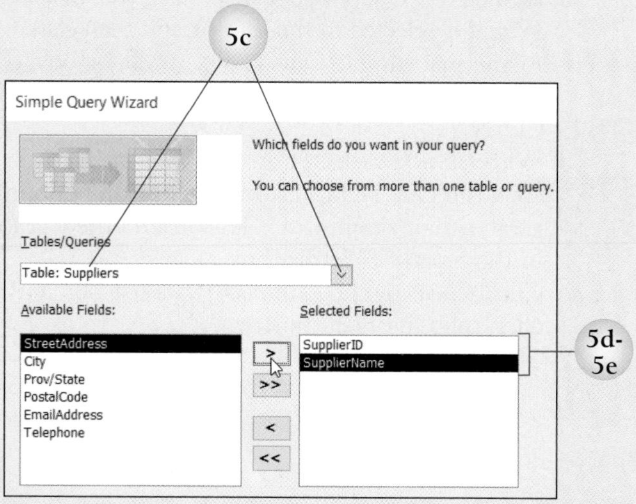

f. Click the *Tables/Queries* option box arrow and then click *Table: Orders*.
g. Click *ProductID* in the *Available Fields* list box and then click the One Field button.
h. Click *Amount* in the *Available Fields* list box and then click the One Field button.
i. Click the Next button.

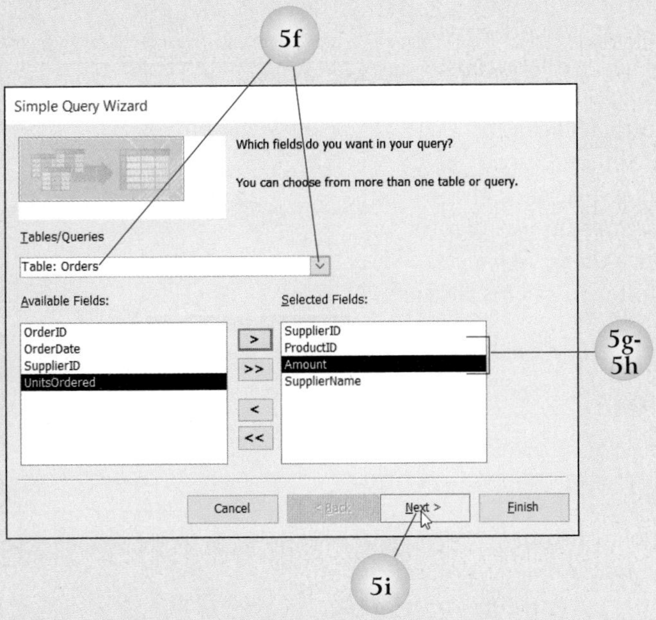

j. At the second Simple Query Wizard dialog box, click the Next button.
k. At the last Simple Query Wizard dialog box, select the text in the *What title do you want for your query?* text box, type ProductOrderAmountsQuery, and then press the Enter key.

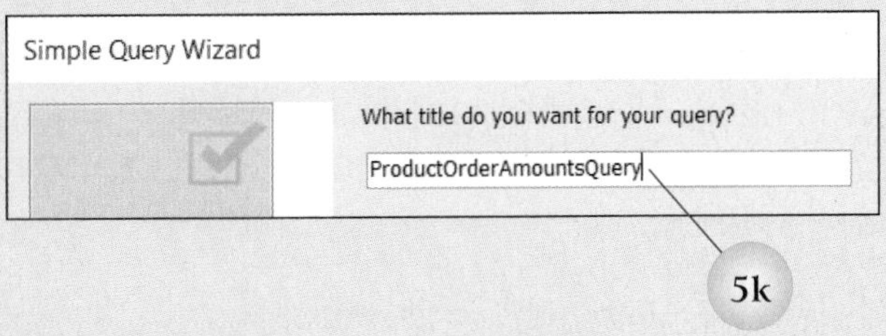

l. When the results of the query display, print the results.
m. Close the query.

Check Your Work

To extract specific information when using the Simple Query Wizard, tell the wizard that the query design is to be modified. This displays the query window with the query design grid, where query criteria can be entered.

1. With **3-PacTrek.accdb** open, use the Simple Query Wizard to create a query that displays suppliers outside British Columbia by completing the following steps:
   a. Click the Create tab and then click the Query Wizard button.
   b. At the New Query dialog box, make sure *Simple Query Wizard* is selected and then click OK.
   c. At the first Simple Query Wizard dialog box, click the *Tables/Queries* option box arrow and then click *Table: Suppliers*.
   d. Insert the following fields in the *Selected Fields* list box:

      SupplierName
      StreetAddress
      City
      Prov/State
      PostalCode

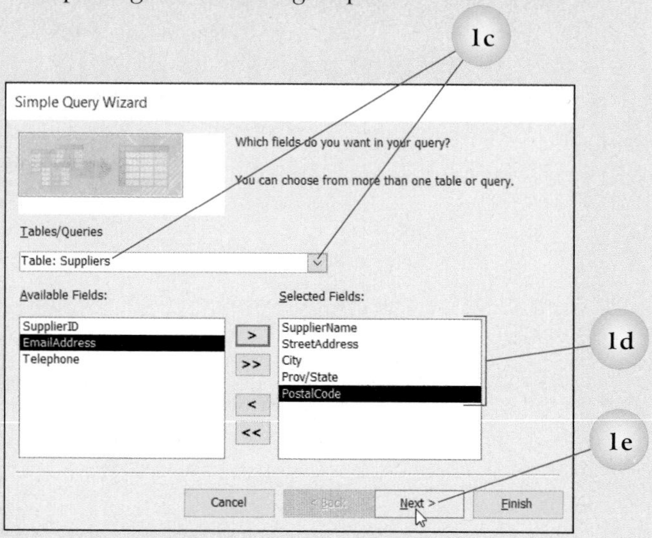

   e. Click the Next button.
   f. At the last Simple Query Wizard dialog box, select the current text in the *What title do you want for your query?* text box and then type SuppliersNotBCQuery.
   g. Click the *Modify the query design* option and then click the Finish button.
   h. At the query window, complete the following steps:
      1) Click in the *Prov/State field* field in the *Criteria* row in the query design grid.
      2) Type Not BC and then press the Enter key.
   i. Specify that the fields are to be sorted in descending order by postal code by completing the following steps:
      1) Click in the *PostalCode* field in the *Sort* row.
      2) Click the down arrow that displays in the field and then click *Descending*.

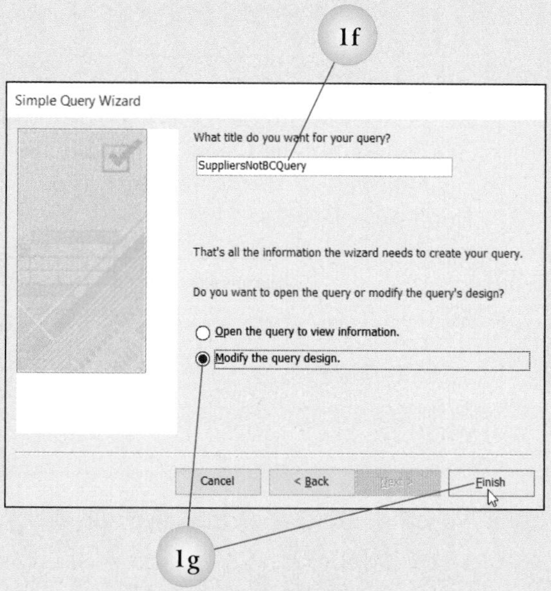

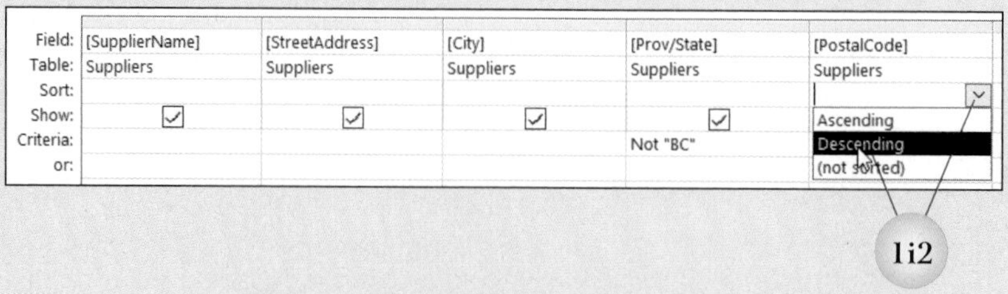

   j. Click the Run button in the Results group. (This displays suppliers that are not in British Columbia and displays the records sorted by postal code in descending order.)
   k. Save, print, and then close the query.

2. Close **3-PacTrek.accdb**.
3. Open **3-Dearborn.accdb**.
4. Use the Simple Query Wizard to create a query that displays clients in Muncie by completing the following steps:
   a. Click the Create tab and then click the Query Wizard button.
   b. At the New Query dialog box, make sure *Simple Query Wizard* is selected and then click OK.
   c. At the first Simple Query Wizard dialog box, click the *Tables/Queries* option box arrow and then click *Table: Clients*. (You may need to scroll up the list to display this table.)
   d. Insert the following fields in the *Selected Fields* list box:

      Client
      StreetAddress
      City
      State
      ZipCode

   e. Click the Next button.
   f. At the last Simple Query Wizard dialog box, select the current text in the *What title do you want for your query?* text box and then type ClientsMuncieQuery.
   g. Click the *Modify the query design* option and then click the Finish button.
   h. At the query window, complete the following steps:
      1) Click in the *City* field in the *Criteria* row in the query design grid.
      2) Type Muncie and then press the Enter key.

Field:	[Client]	[StreetAddress]	[City]	[State]	[ZipCode]
Table:	Clients	Clients	Clients	Clients	Clients
Sort:					
Show:	☑	☑	☑	☑	☑
Criteria:			"Muncie"		
or:					

4h2

   i. Click the Run button in the Results group. (This displays clients in Muncie.)
   j. Save, print, and then close the query.
5. Close **3-Dearborn.accdb**.
6. Open **3-CopperState.accdb**.
7. Use the Simple Query Wizard to display clients that live in Phoenix with claims over $500 by completing the following steps:
   a. Click the Create tab and then click the Query Wizard button in the Queries group.
   b. At the New Query dialog box, make sure *Simple Query Wizard* is selected in the list box and then click OK.
   c. At the first Simple Query Wizard dialog box, click the *Tables/Queries* option box arrow and then click *Table: Clients*.
   d. Insert the following fields in the *Selected Fields* list box:

      ClientID
      FirstName
      LastName
      StreetAddress
      City
      State
      ZIP

   e. Click the *Tables/Queries* option box arrow and then click *Table: Claims*.

f. With *ClaimID* selected in the *Available Fields* list box, click the One Field button.
g. Click *AmountOfClaim* in the *Available Fields* list box and then click the One Field button.
h. Click the Next button.
i. At the second Simple Query Wizard dialog box, click the Next button.
j. At the last Simple Query Wizard dialog box, select the current text in the *What title do you want for your query?* text box and then type PhoenixClientClaimsOver$500Query.
k. Click the *Modify the query design* option and then click the Finish button.
l. At the query window, complete the following steps:
  1) Click in the *City* field in the *Criteria* row in the query design grid.
  2) Type "Phoenix" and then press the Enter key. (Type the quotation marks to tell Access that this is a criterion, otherwise Access will insert the query name *PhoenixClientClaimsOver$500Query* in the field in the *Criteria* row.)
  3) Click in the *AmountOfClaim* field in the *Criteria* row. (You may need to scroll to the right to display this field.)
  4) Type >500 and then press the Enter key.

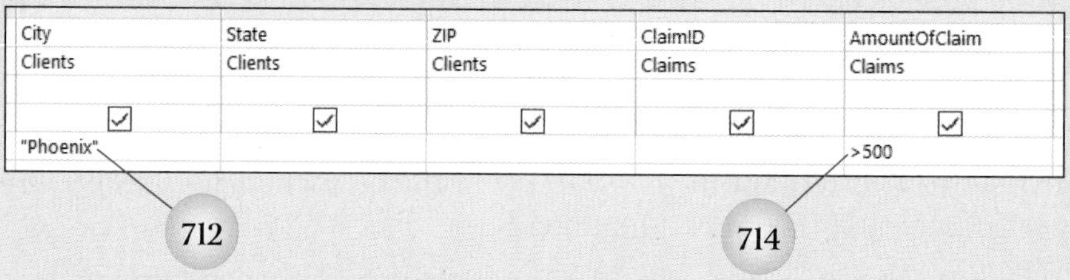

m. Click the Run button in the Results group. (This displays clients in Phoenix with claims greater than $500.)
n. Save the query, print the query in landscape orientation, and then close the query.
8. Close **3-CopperState.accdb**.

Check Your Work

Tutorial

Performing Calculations in a Query

Performing Calculations in a Query

In a query, values from a field can be calculated by inserting a calculated field in a field in the *Field* row in the query design grid. To insert a calculated field, click in a field in the *Field* row, type a field name followed by a colon, and then type the equation. For example, to determine pension contributions as 3% of an employee's annual salary, type *PensionContribution:[AnnualSalary]*0.03* in the field in the *Field* row. Use brackets to specify field names and use mathematical operators to perform the equation. Some basic operators include the plus (+) for addition, the hyphen (-) for subtraction, the asterisk (*) for multiplication, and the forward slash (/) for division.

Type a calculation in a field in the *Field* row or in the Expression Builder dialog box. To display the Expression Builder dialog box, display the query in Design view, click in the field where the calculated field expression is to be inserted, and then click the Builder button in the Query Setup group on the Query Tools Design tab. Type field names in the Expression Builder and click OK and the equation is inserted in the field with the correct symbols. For example, type *AnnualSalary*0.03* in the Expression Builder and *Expr1: [AnnualSalary]*0.03* is inserted in the field in the *Field* row when OK is clicked. If a name is not typed for the field, Access creates the alias *Expr1* for the field name. Provide a specific name for the field, such as *PensionContribution*, by typing the name in the Expression Builder, followed by a colon, and then typing the expression.

Builder

If the results of the calculation should display as currency, apply numeric formatting and define the number of digits past the decimal point using the Property Sheet task pane. In Design view, click the Property Sheet button in the Show/Hide group on the Query Tools Design tab and the Property Sheet task pane displays at the right side of the screen. Click in the *Format* property box, click the down arrow, and then click *Currency* at the drop-down list.

Project 1h Creating and Formatting a Calculated Field in a Query — Part 8 of 8

1. Open **3-MRInvestments.accdb** and enable the content.
2. Create a query that displays employer pension contributions at 3% of employees' annual salary by completing the following steps:
   a. Click the Create tab and then click the Query Design button.
   b. Double-click *Employees* in the Show Table dialog box and then click the Close button.
   c. Insert the *EmpID* field from the Employees table field list box in the first field in the *Field* row.
   d. Insert the *FirstName* field in the second field in the *Field* row.
   e. Insert the *LastName* field in the third field in the *Field* row.
   f. Insert the *AnnualSalary* field in the fourth field in the *Field* row.
   g. Click in the fifth field in the *Field* row.
   h. Type PensionContribution:[AnnualSalary]*0.03 and then press the Enter key.
   i. Click in the *PensionContribution* field and then click the Property Sheet button in the Show/Hide group.
   j. Click in the *Format* property box, click the down arrow, and then click *Currency* at the drop-down list.
   k. Click the Close button in the upper right corner of the Property Sheet task pane.
   l. Click the Run button in the Results group.
   m. Save the query and name it *PensionContributionsQuery*.
   n. Print and then close the query.

2h

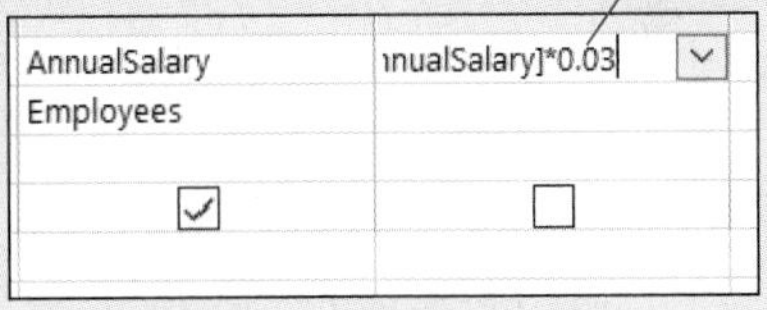

3. Modify *PensionContributionsQuery* and use the Expression Builder to write an equation finding the total amount of annual salary plus a 3% employer pension contribution by completing the following steps:
   a. Right-click *PensionContributionsQuery* in the Queries group in the Navigation pane and then click *Design View* at the shortcut menu.
   b. Click in the field in the *Field* row containing *PensionContribution:[AnnualSalary]*0.03*.
   c. Click the Builder button in the Query Setup group on the Query Tools Design tab.
   d. In the Expression Builder, select the existing expression *PensionContribution: [AnnualSalary]*0.03*.
   e. Type Salary&Pension:[AnnualSalary]*1.03 and then click OK.

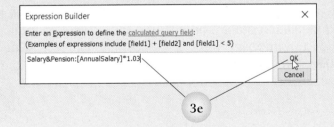

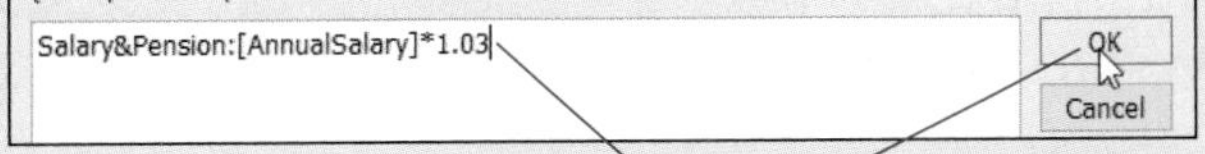

3e

4. Click the Run button in the Results group.
5. Save the query by completing the following steps:
   a. Click the File tab, click the *Save As* option, click the *Save Object As* option, and then click the Save As button.
   b. At the Save As dialog box, type Salary&PensionQuery and then click OK.
6. Print and then close the query.
7. Close **3-MRInvestments.accdb**.
8. Open **3-PacTrek.accdb**.
9. Create a query that displays orders and total order amounts by completing the following steps:
   a. Click the Create tab and then click the Query Design button.
   b. Double-click *Products* in the Show Table dialog box.
   c. Double-click *Orders* in the Show Table dialog box and then click the Close button.
   d. Insert the *Product* field from the Products table field list box in the first field in the *Field* row.
   e. Insert the *OrderID* field from the Orders table field list box in the second field in the *Field* row.
   f. Insert the *UnitsOrdered* field from the Orders table field list box in the third field in the *Field* row.
   g. Insert the *Amount* field from the Orders table field list box in the fourth field in the *Field* row.
   h. Click in the fifth field in the *Field* row.
   i. Click the Builder button in the Query Setup group on the Query Tools Design tab.
   j. Type Total:Amount*UnitsOrdered in the Expression Builder and then click OK.
   k. Click the Run button in the Results group.
   l. Adjust the width of the columns to fit the longest entries.
   m. Save the query and name it *UnitsOrderedTotalQuery*.
   n. Print and then close the query.
10. Close **3-PacTrek.accdb**.

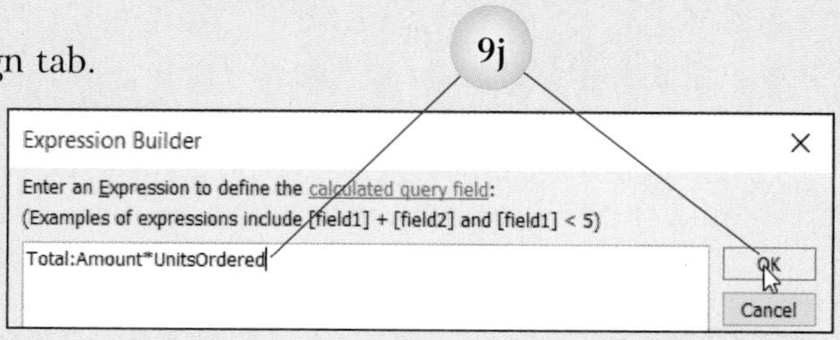

Check Your Work

Project 2 Create Aggregate Functions, Crosstab, Find Duplicates, and Find Unmatched Queries — 6 Parts

You will create an aggregate functions query that determines the total, average, minimum, and maximum order amounts and then calculate total and average order amounts grouped by supplier. You will also use the Crosstab Query Wizard, Find Duplicates Query Wizard, and Find Unmatched Query Wizard to design queries.

Preview Finished Project

Tutorial

Using Aggregate Functions

Designing Queries with Aggregate Functions

An *aggregate function*—such as Sum, Avg, Min, Max, or Count—can be included in a query to calculate statistics from numeric field values of all the records in the table. When an aggregate function is used, Access displays one row in the query results datasheet with the formula result for the function used. For example, in a table with a numeric field containing annual salary amounts, the Sum function can be used to calculate the total of all salary amount values.

Σ Totals

Quick Steps

Design a Query with an Aggregate Function
1. At query window, click Totals button.
2. Click down arrow in field in the *Total* row.
3. Click aggregate function.

To use aggregate functions, click the Totals button in the Show/Hide group on the Query Tools Design tab. Access adds a *Total* row to the query design grid with a drop-down list of functions. Access also inserts the words *Group By* in the field in the *Total* row. Click the down arrow and then click an aggregate function at the drop-down list. In Project 2a, Step 1, you will create a query in Design view and use aggregate functions to find the total of all sales, average sales amount, maximum and minimum sales, and total number of sales. The completed query will display as shown in Figure 3.5. Access automatically determines the column heading names.

Figure 3.5 Query Results for Project 2a, Step 1

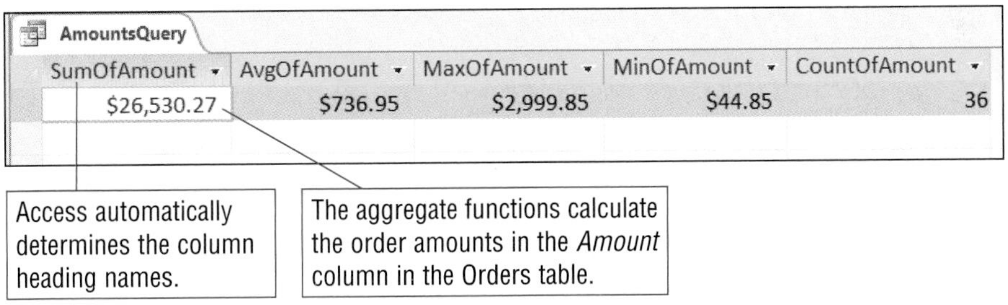

Project 2a Using Aggregate Functions in Queries

Part 1 of 6

1. Open **3-PacTrek.accdb** and then create a query with aggregate functions that determines total, average, maximum, and minimum order amounts, as well as the total number of orders, by completing the following steps:
   a. Click the Create tab and then click the Query Design button.
   b. At the Show Table dialog box, make sure *Orders* is selected in the list box, click the Add button, and then click the Close button.
   c. Insert the *Amount* field in the first, second, third, fourth, and fifth fields in the *Field* row. (You may need to scroll down the Orders table field list box to display the *Amount* field.)

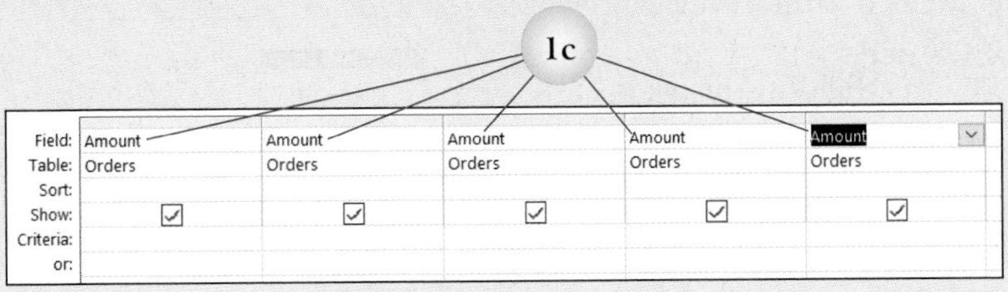

d. Click the Totals button in the Show/Hide group on the Query Tools Design tab. (This adds a *Total* row to the query design grid between *Table* and *Sort* with the default option of *Group By*.)

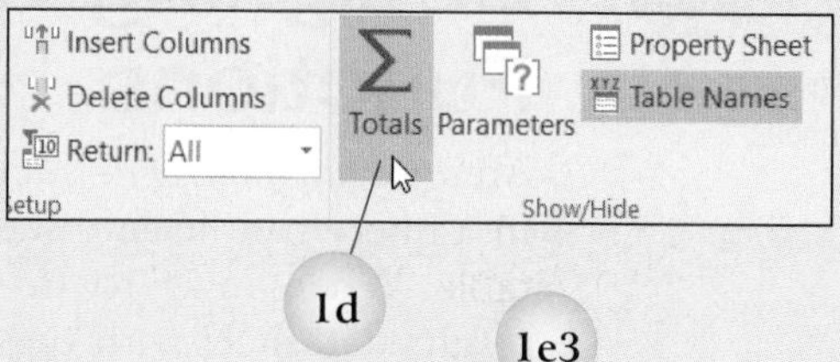

e. Specify a Sum function for the first field in the *Total* row by completing the following steps:
   1) Click in the first field in the *Total* row.
   2) Click the down arrow that displays in the field.
   3) Click *Sum* at the drop-down list.

f. Complete steps similar to those in Step 1e to insert *Avg* in the second field in the *Total* row.

g. Complete steps similar to those in Step 1e to insert *Max* in the third field in the *Total* row.

h. Complete steps similar to those in Step 1e to insert *Min* in the fourth field in the *Total* row.

i. Complete steps similar to those in Step 1e to insert *Count* in the fifth field in the *Total* row.

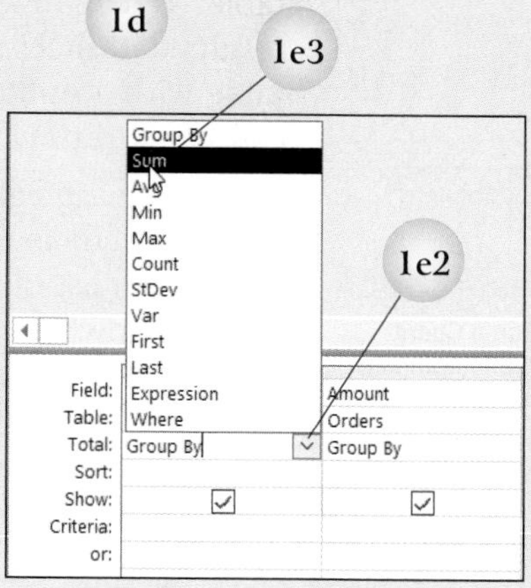

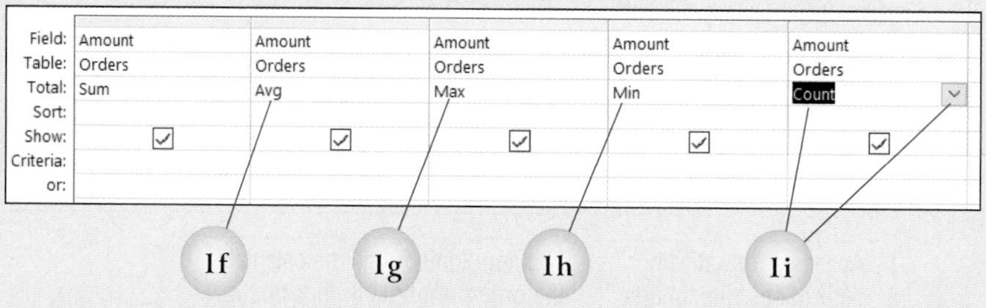

j. Click the Run button in the Results group. (Notice the headings that Access assigns to the columns.)

k. Automatically adjust the widths of the columns.

l. Save the query and name it *AmountsQuery*.

m. Print and then close the query.

2. Close **3-PacTrek.accdb**.
3. Open **3-CopperState.accdb**.
4. Create a query with aggregate functions that determines total, average, maximum, and minimum claim amounts by completing the following steps:

a. Click the Create tab and then click the Query Design button.

b. At the Show Table dialog box, double-click *Claims*.

c. Click the Close button to close the Show Table dialog box.

d. Insert the *AmountOfClaim* field in the first, second, third, and fourth fields in the *Field* row.

e. Click the Totals button in the Show/Hide group.

f. Click in the first field in the *Total* row, click the down arrow that displays in the field, and then click *Sum* at the drop-down list.

g. Click in the second field in the *Total* row, click the down arrow, and then click *Avg* at the drop-down list.

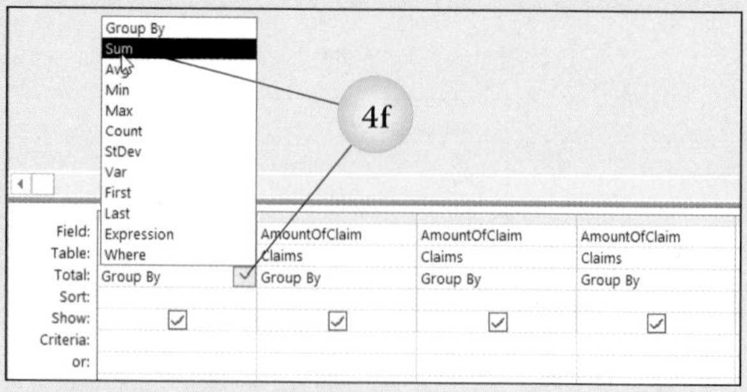

h. Click in the third field in the *Total* row, click the down arrow, and then click *Max* at the drop-down list.
i. Click in the fourth field in the *Total* row, click the down arrow, and then click *Min* at the drop-down list.
j. Click the Run button in the Results group. (Notice the headings that Access chooses for the columns.)
k. Automatically adjust the widths of the columns.
l. Save the query and name it *ClaimAmountsQuery*.
m. Print the query in landscape orientation and then close the query.

Check Your Work

Use the *Group By* field in the *Total* row to add a field to the query that groups records for statistical calculations. For example, to calculate the total of all orders for a specific supplier, add the *SupplierID* field to the query design grid with the *Total* row set to *Group By*. In Project 2b, Step 1, you will create a query in Design view and use aggregate functions to find the total of all order amounts and the average order amounts grouped by supplier number.

Project 2b Using Aggregate Functions and Grouping Records — Part 2 of 6

1. With **3-CopperState.accdb** open, determine the sum and average of client claims by completing the following steps:
   a. Click the Create tab and then click the Query Design button.
   b. At the Show Table dialog box, double-click *Clients* in the list box.
   c. Double-click *Claims* in the list box and then click the Close button.
   d. Insert the *ClientID* field from the Clients table field list box to the first field in the *Field* row.
   e. Insert the *AmountOfClaim* field from the Claims table field list box to the second field in the *Field* row.
   f. Insert the *AmountOfClaim* field from the Claims table field list box to the third field in the *Field* row.
   g. Click the Totals button in the Show/Hide group.
   h. Click in the second field in the *Total* row, click the down arrow, and then click *Sum* at the drop-down list.
   i. Click in the third field in the *Total* row, click the down arrow, and then click *Avg* at the drop-down list.

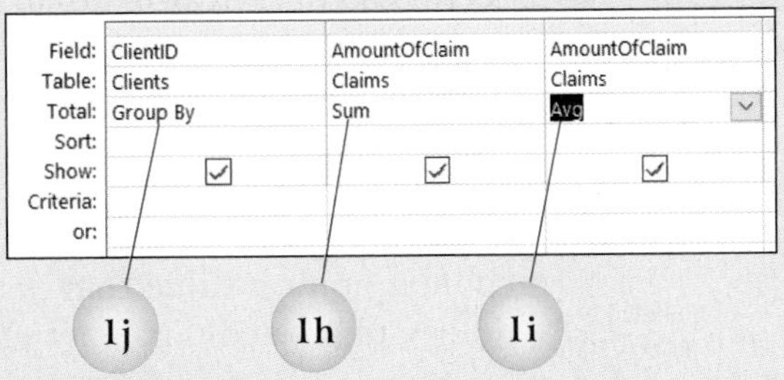

   j. Make sure *Group By* displays in the first field in the *Total* row.
   k. Click the Run button in the Results group.
   l. Automatically adjust column widths.
   m. Save the query and name it *SumAvgClaimAmountsQuery*.
   n. Print and then close the query.
2. Close **3-CopperState.accdb**.
3. Open **3-PacTrek.accdb**.
4. Determine the total and average order amounts for each supplier by completing the following steps:
   a. Click the Create tab and then click the Query Design button.

b. At the Show Table dialog box, make sure *Orders* is selected in the list box and then click the Add button.
c. Click *Suppliers* in the list box, click the Add button, and then click the Close button.
d. Insert the *Amount* field from the Orders table field list box to the first field in the *Field* row. (You may need to scroll down the Orders table field list box to display the *Amount* field.)
e. Insert the *Amount* field from the Orders table field list box to the second field in the *Field* row.
f. Insert the *SupplierID* field from the Suppliers table field list box to the third field in the *Field* row.
g. Insert the *SupplierName* field from the Suppliers table field list box to the fourth field in the *Field* row.
h. Click the Totals button in the Show/Hide group.
i. Click in the first field in the *Total* row, click the down arrow, and then click *Sum* at the drop-down list.
j. Click in the second field in the *Total* row, click the down arrow, and then click *Avg* at the drop-down list.
k. Make sure *Group By* displays in the third and fourth fields in the *Total* row.
l. Click the Run button in the Results group.
m. Automatically adjust column widths.
n. Save the query and name it *SupplierAmountsQuery*.
o. Print and then close the query.

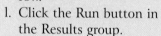

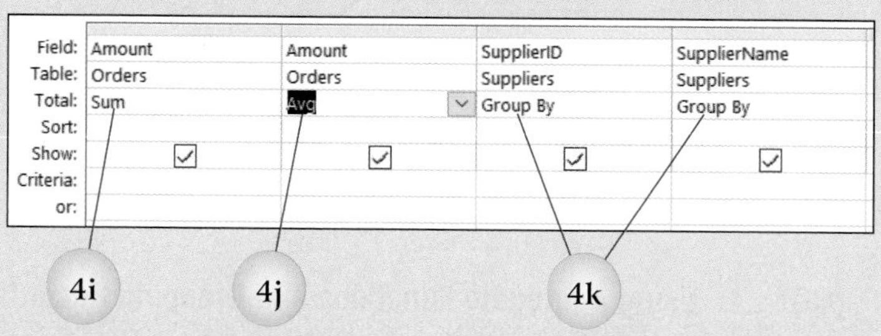

Check Your Work

Tutorial

Creating a Crosstab Query

Quick Steps

Create a Crosstab Query
1. Click Create tab.
2. Click Query Wizard button.
3. Double-click *Crosstab Query Wizard.*
4. Complete wizard steps.

Creating a Crosstab Query

A crosstab query calculates aggregate functions, such as Sum and Avg, in which field values are grouped by two fields. A wizard is included that provides the steps to create the query. The first field selected causes one row to display in the query results datasheet for each group. The second field selected displays one column in the query results datasheet for each group. A third field is specified that is the numeric field to be summarized. The cell at the intersection of each row and column holds a value that is the result of the specified aggregate function for the designated row and column group.

Create a crosstab query from fields in one table. To include fields from more than one table, first create a query containing the fields, and then create the crosstab query. For example, in Project 2c, Step 2, you will create a new query that contains fields from each of the three tables in the Pacific Trek database. Using this query, you will use the Crosstab Query Wizard to create a query that summarizes the order amounts by supplier name and product ordered. Figure 3.6 displays the results of that crosstab query. The first column displays the supplier names, the second column displays the total amounts for each supplier, and the remaining columns display the amounts by suppliers for specific items.

Figure 3.6 Crosstab Query Results for Project 2c, Step 2

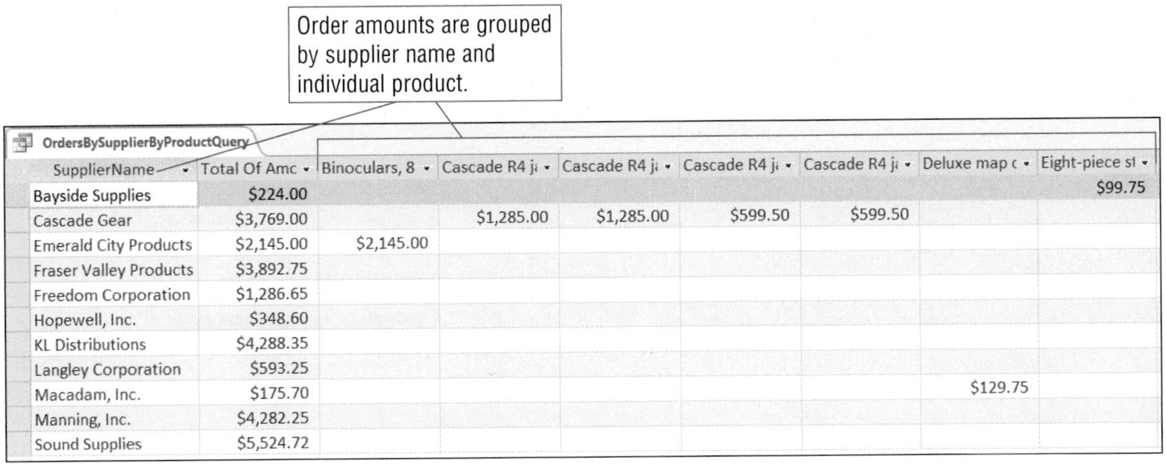
Order amounts are grouped by supplier name and individual product.
OrdersBySupplierByProductQuery

SupplierName	Total Of Amc	Binoculars, 8	Cascade R4 ja	Cascade R4 ja	Cascade R4 ja	Cascade R4 ja	Deluxe map c	Eight-piece st
Bayside Supplies	$224.00							$99.75
Cascade Gear	$3,769.00		$1,285.00	$1,285.00	$599.50	$599.50		
Emerald City Products	$2,145.00	$2,145.00						
Fraser Valley Products	$3,892.75							
Freedom Corporation	$1,286.65							
Hopewell, Inc.	$348.60							
KL Distributions	$4,288.35							
Langley Corporation	$593.25							
Macadam, Inc.	$175.70						$129.75	
Manning, Inc.	$4,282.25							
Sound Supplies	$5,524.72							

Project 2c Creating Crosstab Queries

Part 3 of 6

1. With **3-PacTrek.accdb** open, create a query containing fields from the three tables by completing the following steps:
   a. Click the Create tab and then click the Query Design button.
   b. At the Show Table dialog box with *Orders* selected in the list box, click the Add button.
   c. Double-click *Products* in the list box.
   d. Double-click *Suppliers* in the list box and then click the Close button.
   e. Insert the following fields to the specified fields in the *Field* row:
      1) From the Orders table field list box, insert the *ProductID* field in the first field in the *Field* row.
      2) From the Products table field list box, insert the *Product* field in the second field in the *Field* row.
      3) From the Orders table field list box, insert the *UnitsOrdered* field in the third field in the *Field* row.
      4) From the Orders table field list box, insert the *Amount* field in the fourth field in the *Field* row.
      5) From the Suppliers table field list box, insert the *SupplierName* field in the fifth field in the *Field* row.
      6) From the Orders table field list box, insert the *OrderDate* field in the sixth field in the *Field* row.

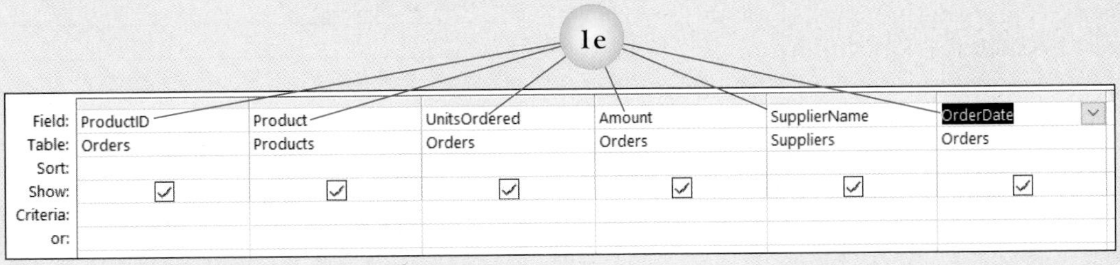
1e

Field:	ProductID	Product	UnitsOrdered	Amount	SupplierName	OrderDate
Table:	Orders	Products	Orders	Orders	Suppliers	Orders
Sort:						
Show:	☑	☑	☑	☑	☑	☑
Criteria:						
or:						

   f. Click the Run button to run the query.
   g. Save the query and name it *ItemsOrderedQuery*.
   h. Close the query.

2. Create a crosstab query that summarizes the orders by supplier name and by product ordered by completing the following steps:
   a. Click the Create tab and then click the Query Wizard button.
   b. At the New Query dialog box, double-click *Crosstab Query Wizard* in the list box.
   c. At the first Crosstab Query Wizard dialog box, click the *Queries* option in the *View* section and then click *Query: ItemsOrderedQuery* in the list box.
   d. Click the Next button.
   e. At the second Crosstab Query Wizard dialog box, click *SupplierName* in the *Available Fields* list box and then click the One Field button. (This inserts *SupplierName* in the *Selected Fields* list box and specifies that you want the *SupplierName* field for the row headings.)
   f. Click the Next button.
   g. At the third Crosstab Query Wizard dialog box, click *Product* in the list box. (This specifies that you want the *Product* field for the column headings.)
   h. Click the Next button.
   i. At the fourth Crosstab Query Wizard dialog box, click *Amount* in the *Fields* list box and then click *Sum* in the *Functions* list box.
   j. Click the Next button.
   k. At the fifth Crosstab Query Wizard dialog box, select the current text in the *What do you want to name your query?* text box and then type OrdersBySupplierByProductQuery.
   l. Click the Finish button.
3. Display the query in Print Preview, change to landscape orientation, change the left margin to 0.4 inch and the right margin to 0.5 inch, and then print the query. (The query will print on four pages.)
4. Close the query.
5. Close **3-PacTrek.accdb**.

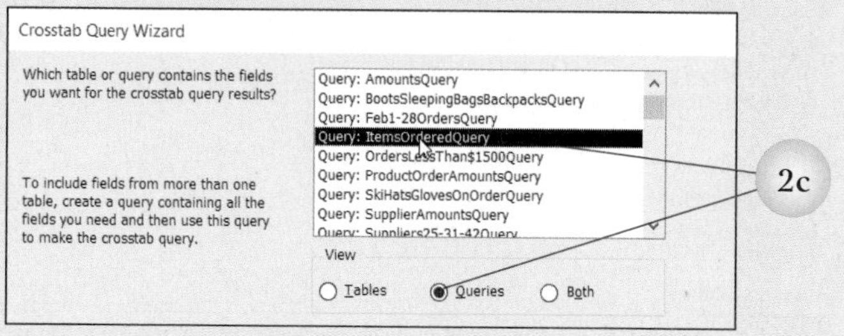

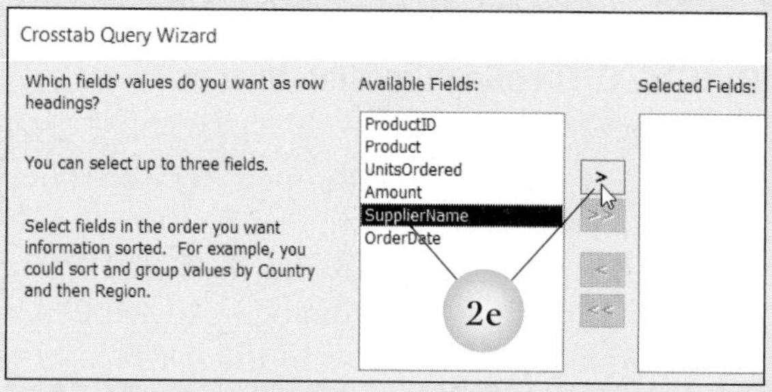

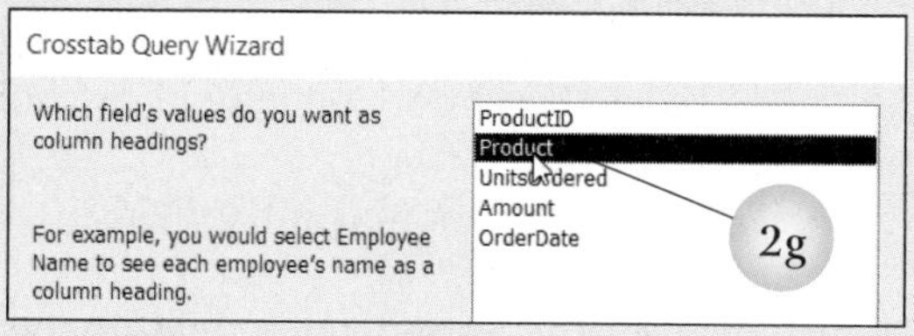

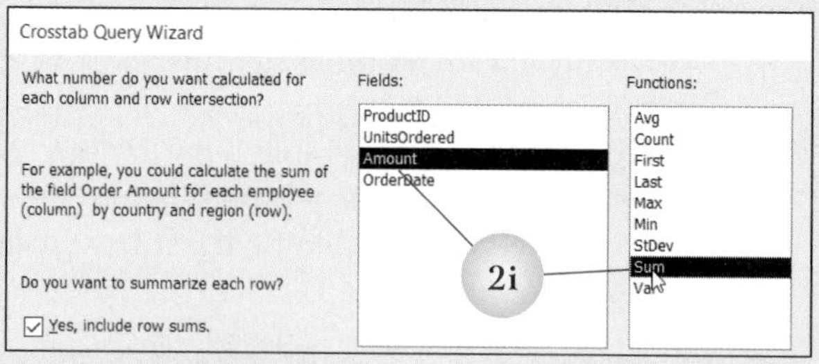

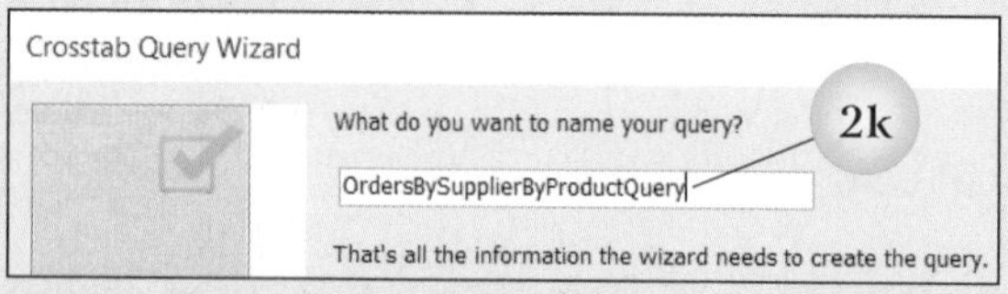

6. Open **3-CopperState.accdb**.
7. Create a crosstab query from fields in one table that summarizes clients' claims by completing the following steps:
   a. Click the Create tab and then click the Query Wizard button.
   b. At the New Query dialog box, double-click *Crosstab Query Wizard* in the list box.
   c. At the first Crosstab Query Wizard dialog box, click *Table: Claims* in the list box.
   d. Click the Next button.
   e. At the second Crosstab Query Wizard dialog box, click the One Field button. (This inserts the *ClaimID* field in the *Selected Fields* list box.)
   f. Click the Next button.
   g. At the third Crosstab Query Wizard dialog, make sure *ClientID* is selected in the list box and then click the Next button.
   h. At the fourth Crosstab Query Wizard dialog box, click *AmountOfClaim* in the *Fields* list box and click *Sum* in the *Functions* list box.
   i. Click the Next button.
   j. At the fifth Crosstab Query Wizard dialog box, select the current text in the *What do you want to name your query?* text box and then type ClaimsByClaimIDByClientIDQuery.
   k. Click the Finish button.
8. Change to landscape orientation and then print the query. The query will print on two pages.
9. Close the query.
10. Close **3-CopperState.accdb**.

Check Your Work

Tutorial

Creating a Find Duplicates Query

Quick Steps

Create a Find Duplicates Query
1. Click Create tab.
2. Click Query Wizard button.
3. Double-click *Find Duplicates Query Wizard*.
4. Complete wizard steps.

Creating a Find Duplicates Query

Use a find duplicates query to search a specified table or query for duplicate field values within a designated field or fields. Create this type of query, for example, if a record (such as a product record) may have been entered two times inadvertently (perhaps under two different product numbers). A find duplicates query has many applications. Here are a few other examples of how to use a find duplicates query:

- In an orders table, find records with the same customer number to identify loyal customers.
- In a customers table, find records with the same last name and mailing address so only one mailing will be sent to a household to save on printing and postage costs.
- In an employee expenses table, find records with the same employee number to determine which employee is submitting the most claims.

Access provides the Find Duplicates Query Wizard to build the query based on the selections made in a series of dialog boxes. To use this wizard, open a database, click the Create tab, and then click the Query Wizard button. At the New Query dialog box, double-click *Find Duplicates Query Wizard* in the list box and then complete the steps provided by the wizard.

In Project 2d, you will assume that you have been asked to update the address for a supplier in the Pacific Trek database. Instead of updating the address, you create a new record. You will then use the Find Duplicates Query Wizard to find duplicate field values in the Suppliers table.

Project 2d Creating a Find Duplicates Query

Part 4 of 6

1. Open **3-PacTrek.accdb** and then open the Suppliers table.
2. Add the following record to the table:

SupplierID#	29
SupplierName	Langley Corporation
StreetAddress	1248 Larson Avenue
City	Burnaby
Prov/State	BC
PostalCode	V5V 9K2
EmailAddress	lc@emcp.net
Telephone	(604) 555-1200

3. Close the Suppliers table.
4. Use the Find Duplicates Query Wizard to find any duplicate supplier names by completing the following steps:
   a. Click the Create tab and then click the Query Wizard button.
   b. At the New Query dialog box, double-click *Find Duplicates Query Wizard*.
   c. At the first wizard dialog box, click *Table: Suppliers* in the list box.
   d. Click the Next button.
   e. At the second wizard dialog box, click *SupplierName* in the *Available fields* list box and then click the One Field button. (This moves the *SupplierName* field to the *Duplicate-value fields* list box.)
   f. Click the Next button.
   g. At the third wizard dialog box, click the All Fields button (the button containing the two greater-than symbols, >>). This moves all the fields to the *Additional query fields* list box. You are doing this because if you find a duplicate supplier name, you want to view all the fields to determine which record is accurate.
   h. Click the Next button.
   i. At the fourth (and last) wizard dialog box, type DuplicateSuppliersQuery in the *What do you want to name your query?* text box.

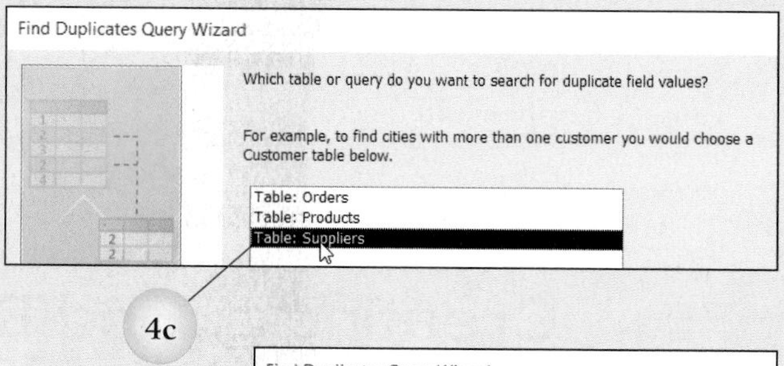

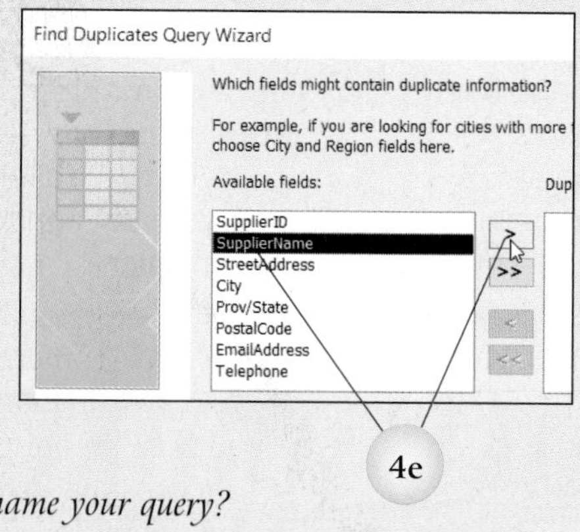

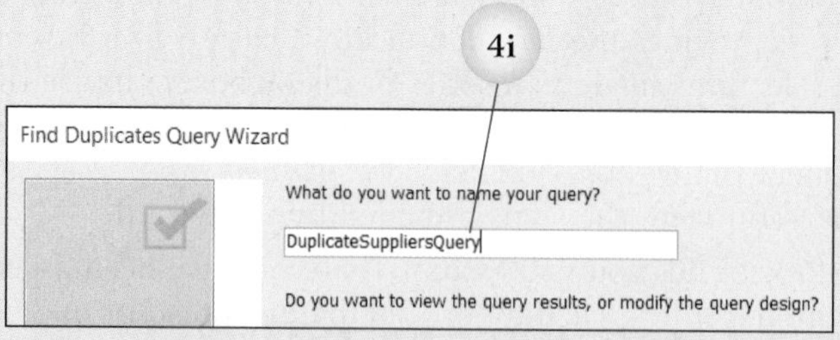

   j. Click the Finish button.
   k. Change to landscape orientation and then print the query.

5. As you look at the query results, you realize that an inaccurate record was entered for the Langley Corporation, so you decide to delete one of the records. To do this, complete the following steps:
   a. Select the row with a supplier ID of *29*.
   b. Click the Home tab and then click the Delete button in the Records group.
   c. At the message asking you to confirm the deletion, click Yes.
   d. Close the query.

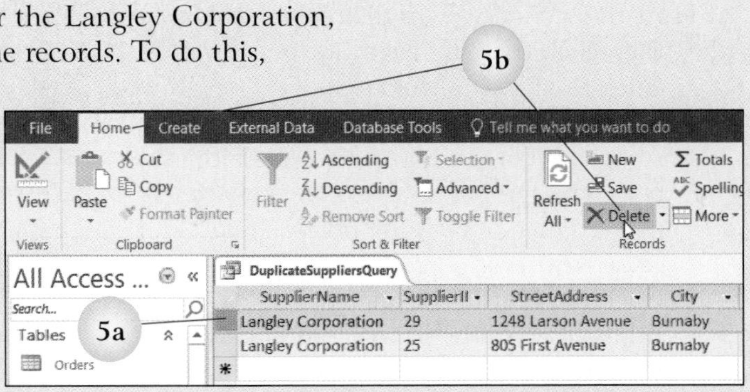

6. Change the street address for Langley Corporation by completing the following steps:
   a. Open the Suppliers table in Datasheet view.
   b. Change the address for Langley Corporation from *805 First Avenue* to *1248 Larson Avenue*. Leave the other fields as displayed.
   c. Close the Suppliers table.

Check Your Work

In Project 2d, you used the Find Duplicates Query Wizard to find records containing the same field. In Project 2e, you will use the Find Duplicates Query Wizard to find information on the suppliers you order from the most. You could use this information to negotiate for better prices or to ask for discounts.

Project 2e Finding Duplicate Orders

Part 5 of 6

1. With **3-PacTrek.accdb** open, create a query with the following fields (in the order shown) from the specified tables:

SupplierID	Suppliers table
SupplierName	Suppliers table
ProductID	Orders table
Product	Products table

2. Run the query.
3. Save the query with the name *SupplierOrdersQuery* and then close the query.
4. Use the Find Duplicates Query Wizard to find the suppliers you order from the most by completing the following steps:
   a. Click the Create tab and then click the Query Wizard button.
   b. At the New Query dialog box, double-click *Find Duplicates Query Wizard*.
   c. At the first wizard dialog box, click the *Queries* option in the *View* section and then click *Query: SupplierOrdersQuery*. (You may need to scroll down the list to display this query.)

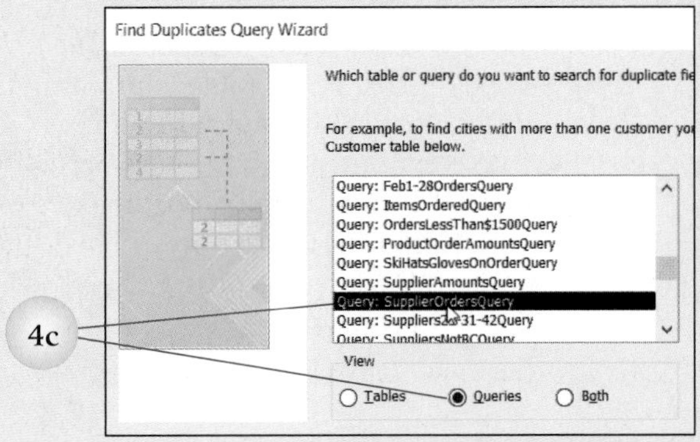

d. Click the Next button.
e. At the second wizard dialog box, click *SupplierName* in the *Available fields* list box and then click the One Field button.
f. Click the Next button.
g. At the third wizard dialog box, click the Next button.
h. At the fourth (and last) wizard dialog box, type SupplierOrdersCountQuery in the *What do you want to name your query?* text box.

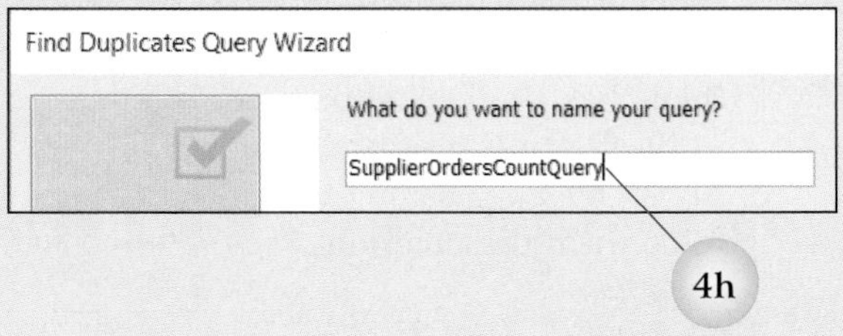

i. Click the Finish button.
j. Adjust the widths of the columns to fit the longest entries.
k. Save and then print the query.

5. Close the query.

Check Your Work

Tutorial

Creating a Find Unmatched Query

Quick Steps

Create a Find Unmatched Query

1. Click Create tab.
2. Click Query Wizard button.
3. Double-click *Find Unmatched Query Wizard*.
4. Complete wizard steps.

Creating a Find Unmatched Query

Create a find unmatched query to compare two tables and produce a list of the records in one table that have no matching record in the other table. This type of query is useful to produce lists such as customers who have never placed orders and invoices that have no records of payment. Access provides the Find Unmatched Query Wizard to build the query.

In Project 2f, you will use the Find Unmatched Query Wizard to find all of the products that have no units on order. This information is helpful in identifying which products are not selling and might need to be discontinued or returned. To use the Find Unmatched Query Wizard, click the Create tab and then click the Query Wizard button in the Queries group. At the New Query dialog box, double-click *Find Unmatched Query Wizard* in the list box and then follow the wizard steps.

Project 2f Creating a Find Unmatched Query

Part 6 of 6

1. With **3-PacTrek.accdb** open, use the Find Unmatched Query Wizard to find all products that do not have units on order by completing the following steps:
   a. Click the Create tab and then click the Query Wizard button.
   b. At the New Query dialog box, double-click *Find Unmatched Query Wizard*.
   c. At the first wizard dialog box, click *Table: Products* in the list box. (This is the table containing the fields you want to see in the query results.)

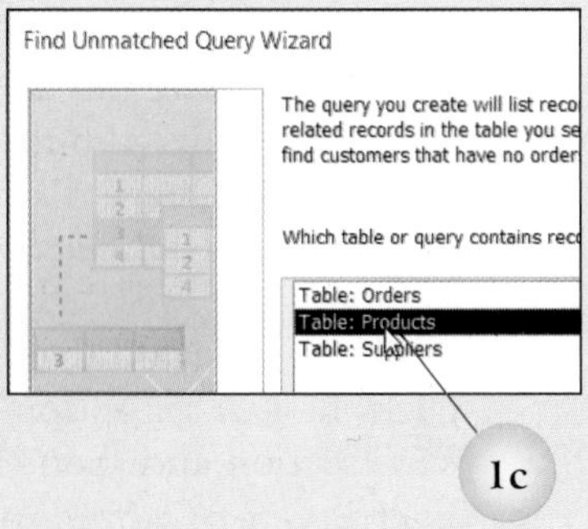

   d. Click the Next button.
   e. At the second wizard dialog box, make sure *Table: Orders* is selected in the list box. (This is the table containing the related records.)
   f. Click the Next button.

g. At the third wizard dialog box, make sure *ProductID* is selected in both the *Fields in 'Products'* list box and in the *Fields in 'Orders'* list box.
h. Click the Next button.
i. At the fourth wizard dialog box, click the All Fields button to move all of the fields from the *Available fields* list box to the *Selected fields* list box.
j. Click the Next button.
k. At the fifth wizard dialog box, click the Finish button. (Let the wizard determine the query name: *Products Without Matching Orders*.)

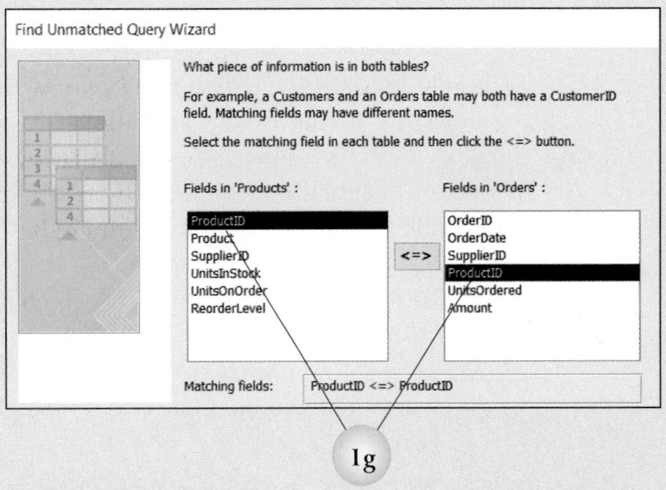

2. Print the query in landscape orientation and then close the query.
3. Close **3-PacTrek.accdb**.

Check Your Work

Chapter Summary

- One of the most important uses of a database is to select the information needed to answer questions and make decisions. Data can be extracted from an Access database by performing a query, which can be accomplished by designing a query or using a query wizard.
- Designing a query consists of identifying the table, the field or fields from which the data will be drawn, and the criterion or criteria for selecting the data.
- In designing a query, type the criterion (or criteria) statement for extracting the specific data. Access inserts any necessary symbols in the criterion when the Enter key is pressed.
- In a criterion, quotation marks surround field values and pound symbols (#) surround dates. Use the asterisk (*) as a wildcard character.
- A query can be performed on fields within one table or on fields from related tables.
- When designing a query, the sort order of a field or fields can be specified.
- An existing query can be modified and used for a new purpose rather than creating a new one from scratch.
- Enter a criterion in the *or* row in the query design grid to instruct Access to display records that match any of the criteria.
- Multiple criteria entered in the *Criteria* row in the query design grid become an *And* statement, where each criterion must be met for Access to select the record.
- The Simple Query Wizard provides the steps for preparing a query.
- A calculated field can be inserted in a field in the *Field* row when designing a query. If the results of the calculation should display as currency, apply numeric formatting and decimal places using the Format property box at the Property Sheet task pane. Display the task pane by clicking the Property Sheet button in the Show/Hide group on the Query Tools Design tab.

- Include an aggregate function (such as Sum, Avg, Min, Max, or Count) to calculate statistics from numeric field values. Click the Totals button in the Show/Hide group on the Query Tools Design tab to display the aggregate function list.
- Use a *Group By* field in the *Total* row to add a field to a query for grouping records for statistical calculations.
- Create a crosstab query to calculate aggregate functions (such as Sum and Avg), in which fields are grouped by two. Create a crosstab query from fields in one table. To include fields from more than one table, create a query first and then create the crosstab query.
- Use a find duplicates query to search a specified table for duplicate field values within a designated field or fields.
- Create a find unmatched query to compare two tables and produce a list of the records in one table that have no matching records in the other related table.

Commands Review

FEATURE	RIBBON TAB, GROUP	BUTTON, OPTION
add *Total* row to query design	Query Tools Design, Show/Hide	Σ
Crosstab Query Wizard	Create, Queries	, *Crosstab Query Wizard*
Expression Builder dialog box	Query Tools Design, Query Setup	
Find Duplicates Query Wizard	Create, Queries	, *Find Duplicates Query Wizard*
Find Unmatched Query Wizard	Create, Queries	, *Find Unmatched Query Wizard*
New Query dialog box	Create, Queries	
Property Sheet task pane	Query Tools Design, Show/Hide	
query results	Query Tools Design, Results	!
query window	Create, Queries	
Simple Query Wizard	Create, Queries	, *Simple Query Wizard*

Workbook

Chapter study tools and assessment activities are available in the *Workbook* ebook. These resources are designed to help you further develop and demonstrate mastery of the skills learned in this chapter.

Microsoft®

Access®

Creating and Modifying Tables in Design View

CHAPTER 4

Performance Objectives

Upon successful completion of Chapter 4, you will be able to:

1 Create a table in Design view
2 Assign a default value
3 Use the Input Mask Wizard and the Lookup Wizard
4 Validate field entries
5 Insert, move, and delete fields in Design view
6 Insert a *Total* row
7 Sort records in a table
8 Print selected records in a table
9 Complete a spelling check
10 Find and replace data in records in a table
11 Apply text formatting
12 Use the Help and Tell Me features

Precheck

Check your current skills to help focus your study.

In Chapter 1, you learned how to create a table in Datasheet view. A table can also be created in Design view, where the table's structure and properties are established before entering data. In this chapter, you will learn how to create a table in Design view and use the Input Mask Wizard and Lookup Wizards; insert, move, and delete fields in Design view; sort records; check spelling in a table; find and replace data; apply text formatting to a table; and use the Help and Tell Me features.

Data Files

Before beginning chapter work, copy the AL1C4 folder to your storage medium and then make AL1C4 the active folder.

SNAP

If you are a SNAP user, launch the Precheck and Tutorials from your Assignments page.

Project 1 Create and Modify Tables in a Property Management Database — 9 Parts

You will open the Sun Properties database, create two new tables in Design view, modify existing tables, and sort data in tables. You will also complete a spelling check on data in tables, find data in a table and replace it with other data, create relationships and perform queries, and use the Help and Tell Me features.

Preview Finished Project

Tutorial

Creating a Table in Design View

Table

View

Quick Steps

Create a Table in Design View

1. Open database.
2. Click Create tab.
3. Click Table button.
4. Click View button.
5. Type name for table.
6. Press Enter or click OK.
7. Type field names, specify data types, and include descriptions.
8. Click Save button.

Creating a Table in Design View

In Datasheet view, a table is created by assigning each column a data type and typing the field name. Once the columns are defined, the data is entered into records. A table can also be created in Design view, where field properties can be set before entering data.

To display a table in Design view, open the database, click the Create tab, and then click the Table button. This opens a new blank table in Datasheet view. Display the table in Design view by clicking the View button at the left side of the Table Tools Fields tab in the Views group. Click the View button in a new table and Access displays the Save As dialog box. Type a name for the table and then press the Enter key or click OK. Figure 4.1 displays the Properties table in Design view in the SunProperties database.

In Design view, each row in the top section of the work area represents one field in the table and is used to define the field name, the field data type, and a description. The *Field Properties* section in the lower half of the work area displays the properties for the active field. The properties vary depending on the active field. In the lower right corner of Design view, Help information displays about the active field or property in the Design window. In Figure 4.1, the *PropID* field name is active in Design view, so Access displays information on field names in the Help area.

Define each field in the table in the rows in the top section of Design view. When a table is created in Design view, Access automatically assigns the first field the name *ID* and assigns the AutoNumber data type. Leave this field name as *ID* or type a new name and accept the AutoNumber data type or change to a different data type. To create a new field in the table, click in a field in the *Field Name* column, type the field name, and then press the Tab key or Enter key. This makes the field in the *Data Type* column active. Click the down arrow in the field in the *Data Type* column and then click the data type at the drop-down list. In Chapter 1, you created tables in Datasheet view and assigned data types of Short Text, Date/Time, Currency, and Yes/No. The drop-down list in the *Data Type* column includes these data types plus additional types, as described in Table 4.1.

Click the specific data type at the drop-down list and then press the Tab key and the field in the *Description* column becomes active. In the field, type a description that provides useful information to someone entering data in the table. For example, consider identifying the field's purpose or contents or providing instructional information for data entry. The description typed in the field in the *Description* column displays in the Status bar when the table's field is active in the table in Datasheet view.

Figure 4.1 Properties Table in Design View

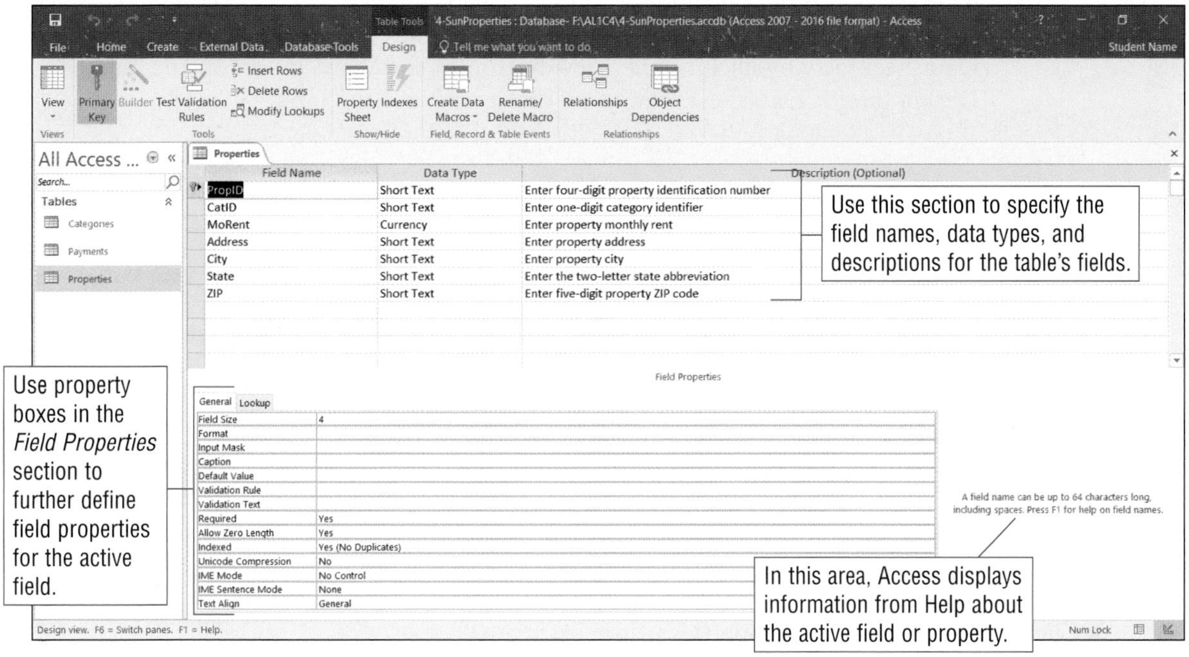
Use this section to specify the field names, data types, and descriptions for the table's fields.
Use property boxes in the *Field Properties* section to further define field properties for the active field.
In this area, Access displays information from Help about the active field or property.

Table 4.1 Data Types

Data Type	Description
Short Text	Used for alphanumeric data up to 255 characters in length—for example, a name, address, or value (such as a telephone number or social security number) that is used as an identifier and not for calculating.
Long Text	Used for alphanumeric data up to 65,535 characters in length.
Number	Used for positive and negative values that can be used in calculations. Do not use for values that will calculate monetary amounts (see Currency).
Date/Time	Used to ensure dates and times are entered and sorted properly.
Currency	Used for values that involve money. Access will not round off during calculations.
AutoNumber	Used to automatically number records sequentially (increments of 1); each new record is numbered as it is typed.
Yes/No	Used for values of *Yes* or *No*, *True* or *False*, or *On* or *Off*.
OLE Object	Used to embed or link objects created in other Office applications.
Hyperlink	Used to store a hyperlink, such as a URL.
Attachment	Used to add file attachments to a record such as a Word document or Excel workbook.
Calculated	Used to display the Expression Builder dialog box, where an expression is entered to calculate the value of the calculated column.
Lookup Wizard	Used to enter data in the field from another existing table or to display a list of values in a drop-down list from which the user chooses.

Save

When creating the table, continue typing field names, assigning data types to fields, and typing field descriptions. When the table design is completed, save the table by clicking the Save button on the Quick Access Toolbar. Return to Datasheet view by clicking the View button in the Views group on the Table Tools Design tab. In Datasheet view, type the records for the table.

Project 1a Creating a Renters Table in Design View — Part 1 of 9

1. Open Access and then open **4-SunProperties.accdb** from the AL1C4 folder on your storage medium.
2. Click the Enable Content button in the message bar. (The message bar will display immediately below the ribbon.)
3. View the Properties table in Design view by completing the following steps:
   a. Open the Properties table.
   b. Click the View button in the Views group on the Home tab.
   c. Click each field name and then look at the information that displays in the *Field Properties* section.
   d. Click in various fields or properties in the work area and then read the information that displays in the Help area in the lower right corner of Design view.
   e. Click the View button to return the table to Datasheet view.
   f. Close the Properties table.

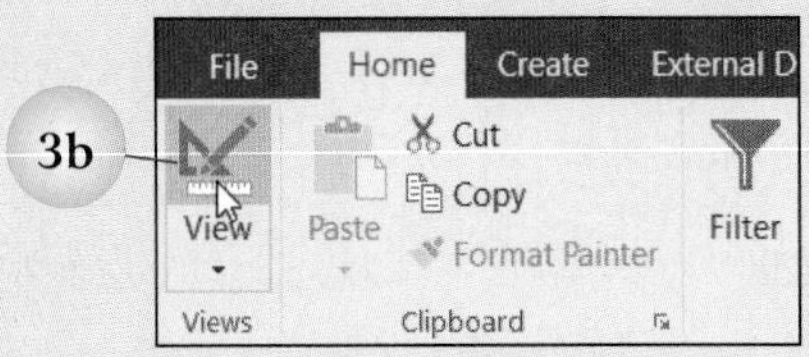

4. Create a new table in Design view, as shown in Figure 4.2, by completing the following steps:
   a. Click the Create tab and then click the Table button in the Tables group.
   b. Click the View button in the Views group on the Table Tools Fields tab.
   c. At the Save As dialog box, type Renters and then press the Enter key.
   d. Type RenterID in the first field in the *Field Name* column and then press the Tab key.
   e. Change to the Short Text data type by clicking the down arrow in the field in the *Data Type* column and then clicking *Short Text* at the drop-down list.
   f. Change the field size from the default of 255 characters to 3 characters by selecting *255* in the *Field Size* property box in the *Field Properties* section and then typing 3.

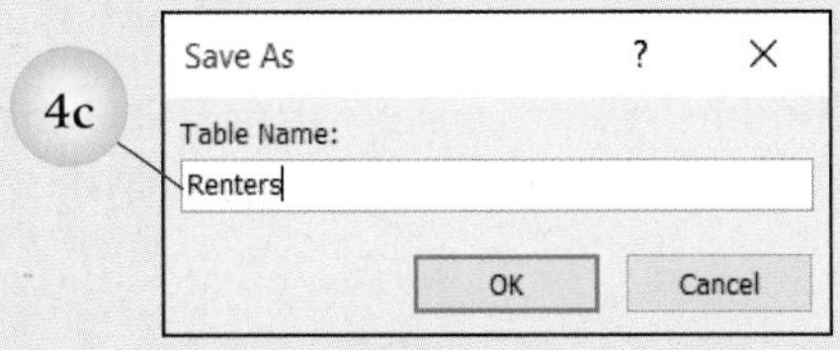

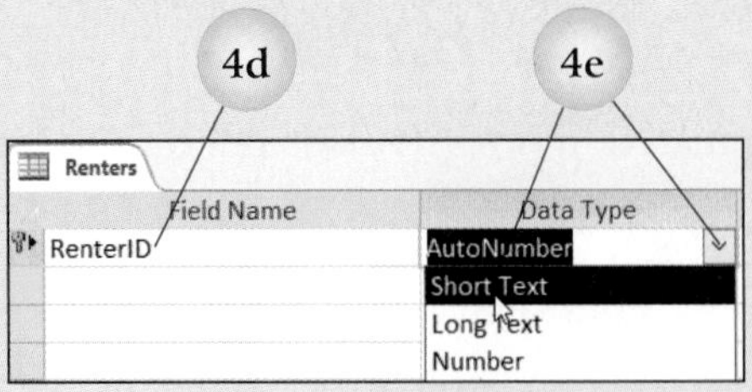

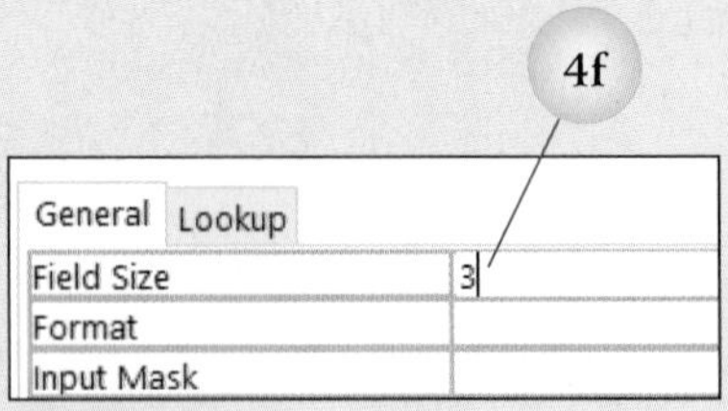

g. Click in the *Description* column for the *RenterID* field, type Enter three-digit renter identification number, and then press the Tab key.

Renters

Field Name	Data Type	Description (Optional)
RenterID	Short Text	Enter three-digit renter identification number

4g

h. Type FirstName in the second field in the *Field Name* column and then press the Tab key.
i. Select *255* in the *Field Size* property box in the *Field Properties* section and then type 20.
j. Click in the *Description* column for the *FirstName* field, type Enter renter's first name, and then press the Tab key.
k. Type LastName in the third field in the *Field Name* column and then press the Tab key.
l. Change the field size to 30 characters (at the *Field Size* property box).
m. Click in the *Description* column for the *LastName* field, type Enter renter's last name, and then press the Tab key.
n. Enter the remaining field names, data types, and descriptions as shown in Figure 4.2. (Change the field size to 4 characters for the *PropID* field, 5 characters for the *EmpID* field, and 3 characters for the *CreditScore* field.)
o. After all of the fields are entered, click the Save button on the Quick Access Toolbar.
p. Make sure the *RenterID* field is identified as the primary key field. (A key icon displays in the *RenterID* field selector bar.)
q. Click the View button to return the table to Datasheet view.

5. Enter the records in the Renters table as shown in Figure 4.3.
6. After all of the records are entered, automatically adjust the column widths.
7. Save and then close the Renters table.

Check Your Work

Figure 4.2 Project 1a Renters Table in Design View

Renters

Field Name	Data Type	Desc
RenterID	Short Text	Enter three-digit renter identification number
FirstName	Short Text	Enter renter's first name
LastName	Short Text	Enter renter's last name
PropID	Short Text	Enter four-digit property identification number
EmpID	Short Text	Enter five-digit employee identification number
CreditScore	Short Text	Enter renter's current credit score
LeaseBegDate	Date/Time	Enter beginning date of lease
LeaseEndDate	Date/Time	Enter ending date of lease

Figure 4.3 Project 1a Renters Table in Datasheet View

Renters

RenterID	FirstName	LastName	PropID	EmpID	CreditScore	LeaseBegDate	LeaseEndDate	Click t
110	Greg	Hamilton	1029	04-14	624	1/1/2018	12/31/2018	
111	Julia	Perez	1013	07-20	711	1/1/2018	12/31/2018	
115	Dana	Rozinski	1026	02-59	538	2/1/2018	1/31/2019	
117	Miguel	Villegas	1007	07-20	695	2/1/2018	1/31/2019	
118	Mason	Ahn	1004	07-23	538	3/1/2018	2/28/2019	
119	Michelle	Bertram	1001	03-23	621	3/1/2018	2/28/2019	
121	Travis	Jorgenson	1010	04-14	590	3/1/2018	2/28/2019	
123	Richard	Terrell	1014	07-20	687	3/1/2018	2/28/2019	
125	Rose	Wagoner	1015	07-23	734	4/1/2018	3/31/2019	
127	William	Young	1023	05-31	478	4/1/2018	3/31/2019	
129	Susan	Lowrey	1002	04-14	634	4/1/2018	3/31/2019	
130	Ross	Molaski	1027	03-23	588	5/1/2018	4/30/2019	
131	Danielle	Rubio	1020	07-20	722	5/1/2018	4/30/2019	
133	Katie	Smith	1018	07-23	596	5/1/2018	4/30/2019	
134	Carl	Weston	1009	03-23	655	6/1/2018	5/31/2019	
135	Marty	Lobdell	1006	04-14	510	6/1/2018	5/31/2019	
136	Nadine	Paschal	1022	05-31	702	6/1/2018	5/31/2019	
*								

Assigning a Default Value

Chapter 1 covered how to specify a default value for a field in a table in Datasheet view using the Default Value button in the Properties group on the Table Tools Fields tab. In addition to this method, a default value for a field can be specified in Design view with the *Default Value* property box in the *Field Properties* section. Click in the *Default Value* property box and then type the field value.

In Project 1b, a health insurance field will be created with a Yes/No data type. Since most of the agents of Sun Properties have signed up for health insurance benefits, the default value for the field will be set to *Yes*. If a new field containing a default value is added to an existing table, the existing records do not reflect the default value. Only new records entered in the table reflect the default value.

Tutorial

Creating an Input Mask

Creating an Input Mask

Hint An input mask is a set of characters that control what can and cannot be entered in a field.

To maintain consistency and control data entered in a field, consider using the *Input Mask* property box to set a pattern for how data is entered in the field. For example, a pattern can be set for a zip code field that requires that the nine-digit zip code is entered in the field rather than the five-digit zip code. Or, a pattern can be set for a telephone field that requires that the three-digit area code is entered with the telephone number. Use the *Input Mask* field property to set a pattern for how data is entered in a field. Access includes an Input Mask Wizard that provides the steps for creating an input mask. The Input Mask is available for fields with a data type of Short Text or Date/Time.

... Build

Use the Input Mask Wizard when assigning a data type to a field. In Design view, click in the *Input Mask* property box in the *Field Properties* section and then run the Input Mask Wizard by clicking the Build button (contains three black dots) that appears at the right side of the *Input Mask* property box. This displays the first Input Mask Wizard dialog box, as shown in Figure 4.4. In the *Input Mask*

Quick Steps

Use the Input Mask Wizard

1. Open table in Design view.
2. Type text in *Field Name* column.
3. Press Tab.
4. Change data type to *Short Text* or *Date/Time*.
5. Click Save button.
6. Click in *Input Mask* property box.
7. Click Build button.
8. Complete wizard steps.

list box, choose which input mask the data should look like and then click the Next button. At the second Input Mask Wizard dialog box, as shown in Figure 4.5, specify the appearance of the input mask and the placeholder character and then click the Next button. At the third Input Mask Wizard dialog box, specify if the data should be stored with or without the symbol in the mask and then click the Next button. At the fourth dialog box, click the Finish button.

The input mask controls how data is entered into a field. In some situations, such as establishing an input mask to enter the date in the Medium Date format, what is entered will not match what Access displays. An input mask with the Medium Date data type format will require that the date be entered as *12-Sep-18* but, after the date is entered, Access will change the display to *09/12/2018*. Use the *Format* property box to match how Access displays the date with the input mask. Click in the *Format* property box, click the down arrow in the property box and then click *Medium Date* at the drop-down list.

Figure 4.4 First Input Mask Wizard Dialog Box

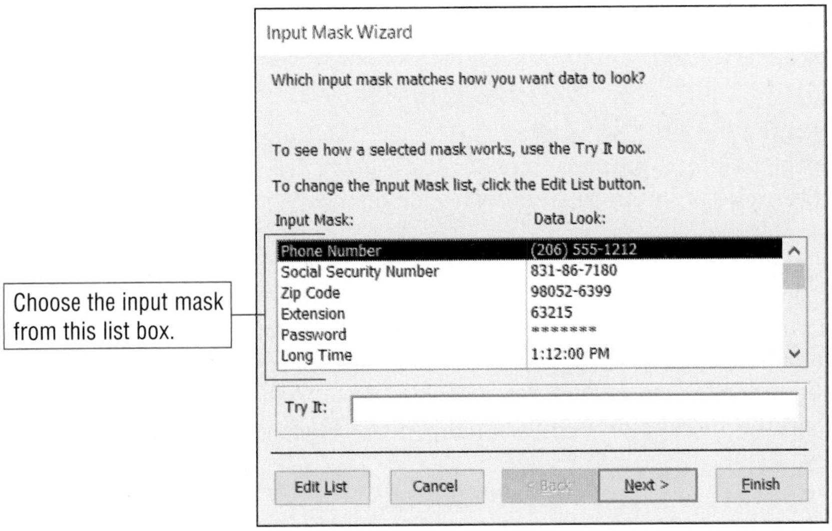

Figure 4.5 Second Input Mask Wizard Dialog Box

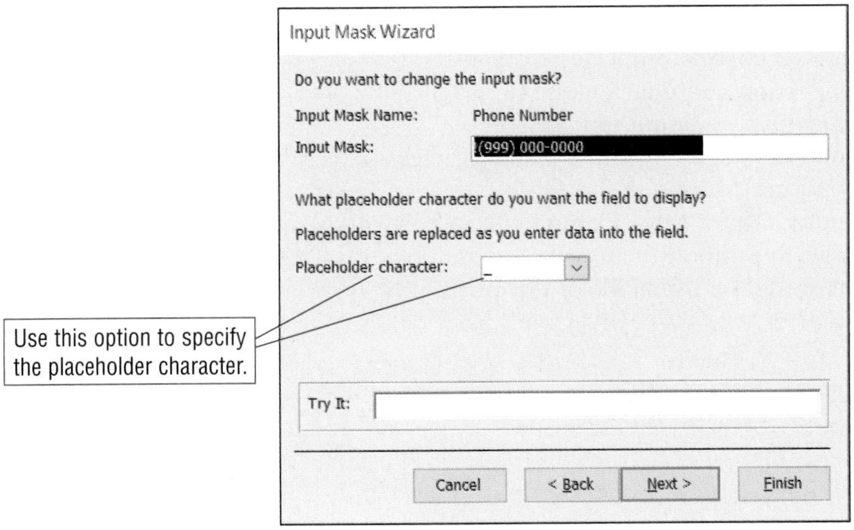

Project 1b Creating an Employees Table in Design View

Part 2 of 9

1. With **4-SunProperties.accdb** open, create the Employees table in Design view as shown in Figure 4.6. Begin by clicking the Create tab and then clicking the Table button.
2. Click the View button to switch to Design view.
3. At the Save As dialog box, type Employees and then press the Enter key.
4. Type EmpID in the first field in the *Field Name* column and then press the Tab key.
5. Change to the Short Text data type by clicking the down arrow in the *Data Type* column and then clicking *Short Text* at the drop-down list.
6. Change the field size from the default of 255 characters to 5 characters by selecting *255* in the *Field Size* property box in the *Field Properties* section and then typing 5.
7. Click in the *Description* column for the *EmpID* field, type Enter five-digit employee identification number, and then press the Tab key.

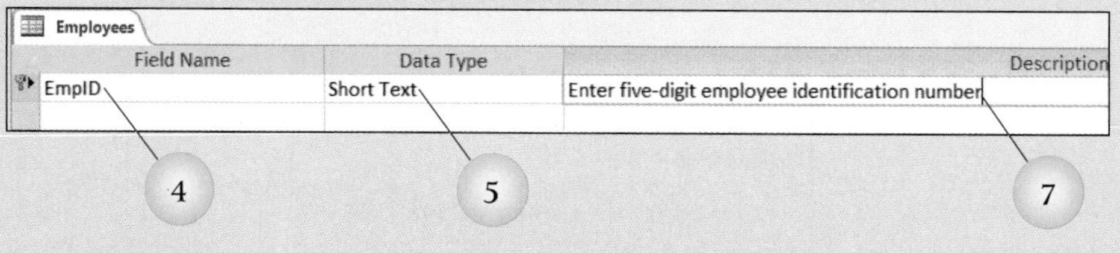

8. Type FName in the second field in the *Field Name* column and then press the Tab key.
9. Select *255* in the *Field Size* property box in the *Field Properties* section and then type 20.
10. Click in the *Description* column for the *FName* field, type Enter employee's first name, and then press the Tab key.
11. Complete steps similar to those in Steps 8 through 10 to create the *LName*, *Address*, and *City* fields as shown in Figure 4.6. Change the field size for the *LName* field and *Address* field to 30 characters and change the *City* field to 20 characters.
12. Create the *State* field with a default value of *CA,* since all employees live in California, by completing the following steps:
    a. Type State in the field below the *City* field in the *Field Name* column and then press the Tab key.
    b. Click in the *Default Value* property box in the *Field Properties* section and then type CA.
    c. Click in the *Description* column for the *State* field, type CA automatically entered as state, and then press the Tab key.

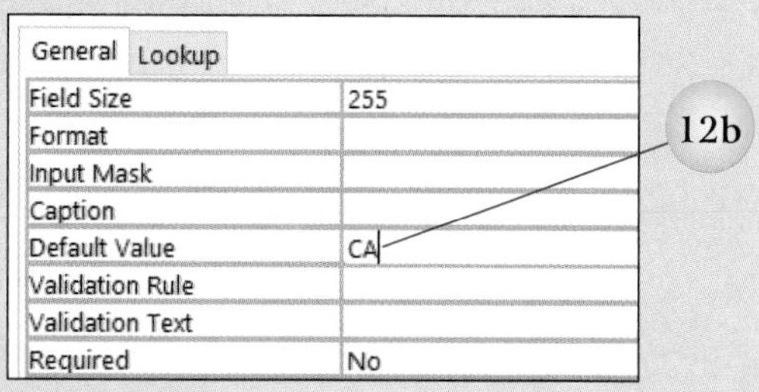

13. Type ZIP and then press the Tab key.
14. Select *255* in the *Field Size* property box in the *Field Properties* section and then type 5.
15. Click in the *Description* column for the *ZIP* field, type Enter five-digit ZIP code, and then press the Tab key.
16. Type Telephone and then press the Tab key.
17. Create an input mask for the telephone number by completing the following steps:
    a. Click the Save button on the Quick Access Toolbar to save the table. (You must save the table before using the Input Mask Wizard.)

b. Click in the *Input Mask* property box in the *Field Properties* section.
c. Click the Build button (contains three black dots) that displays at the right side of the *Input Mask* property box.

d. At the first Input Mask Wizard dialog box, make sure *Phone Number* is selected in the *Input Mask* list box and then click the Next button.
e. At the second Input Mask Wizard dialog box, click the *Placeholder character* option box arrow and then click # at the drop-down list.

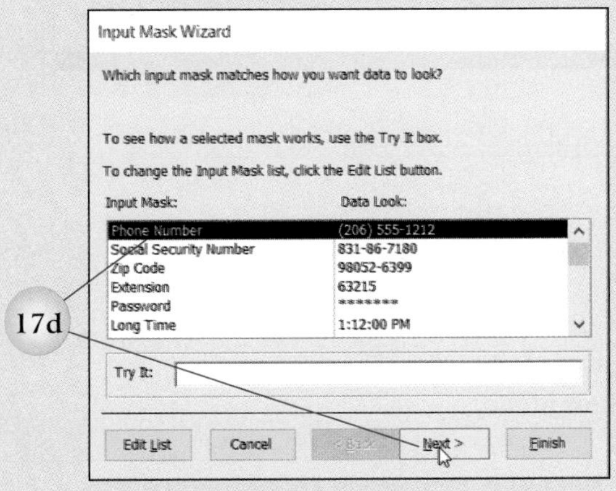

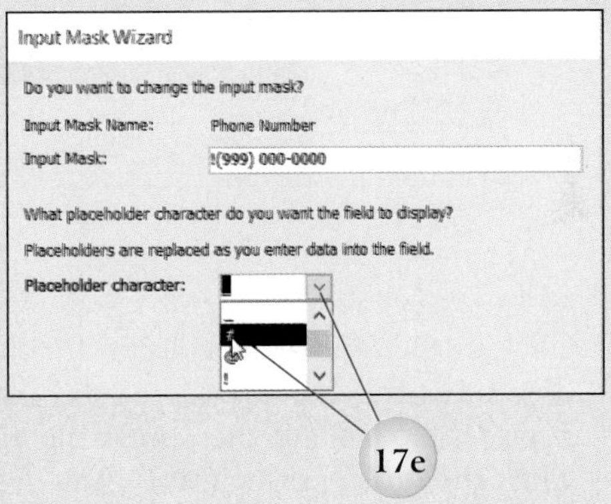

f. Click the Next button.
g. At the third Input Mask Wizard dialog box, click the *With the symbols in the mask, like this* option.
h. Click the Next button.
i. At the fourth Input Mask Wizard dialog box, click the Finish button.

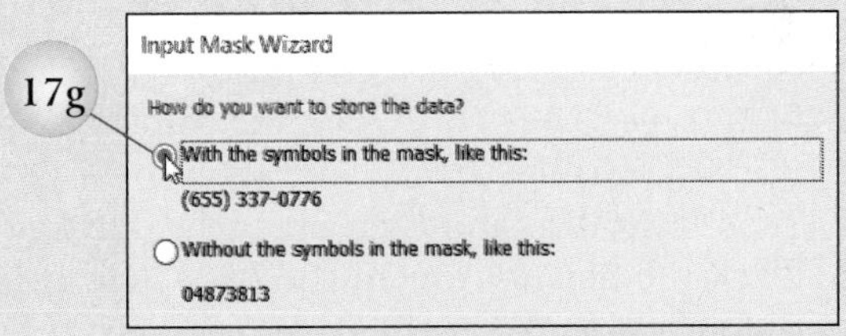

18. Click in the *Description* column for the *Telephone* field, type Enter employee's telephone number, and then press the Tab key.
19. Type HireDate and then press the Tab key.
20. Click the down arrow in the *Date Type* column and then click *Date/Time*.
21. Create an input mask for the date by completing the following steps:
a. Click the Save button on the Quick Access Toolbar to save the table.
b. Click in the *Input Mask* property box in the *Field Properties* section.
c. Click the Build button (contains three black dots) at the right side of the *Input Mask* property box.

d. At the first Input Mask Wizard dialog box, click *Medium Date* in the list box and then click the Next button.
e. At the second Input Mask Wizard dialog box, click the Next button.
f. At the third Input Mask Wizard dialog box, click the Finish button.
g. Click in the *Format* property box.
h. Click the down arrow in the *Format* property box and then click *Medium Date* at the drop-down list.

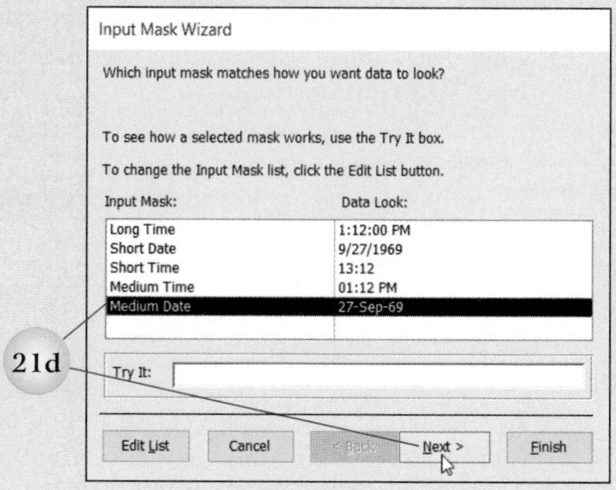

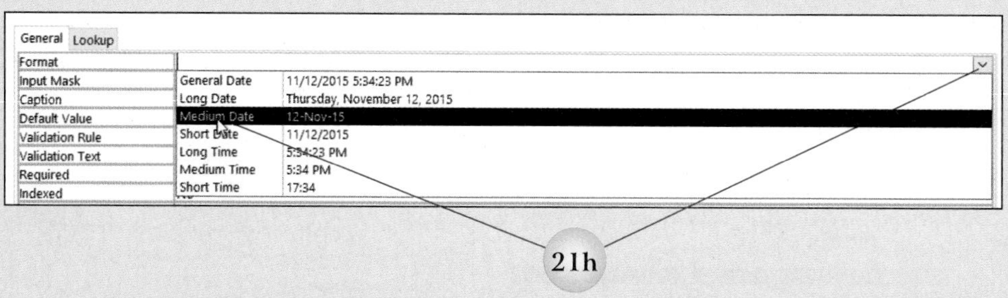

22. Click in the *Description* column for the *HireDate* field, type Enter employee's hire date and then press the Tab key.
23. Type HealthIns and then press the Tab key.
24. Click the down arrow in the *Data Type* column and then click *Yes/No* at the drop-down list.
25. Click in the *Default Value* property box in the *Field Properties* section, delete the text *No*, and then type Yes.
26. Click in the *Description* column for the *HealthIns* field, type Leave check mark if employee is signed up for health insurance, and then press the Tab key.
27. Type DentalIns and then press the Tab key.
28. Click the down arrow in the *Data Type* column and then click *Yes/No* at the drop-down list. (The text in the *Default Value* property box will remain as *No*.)

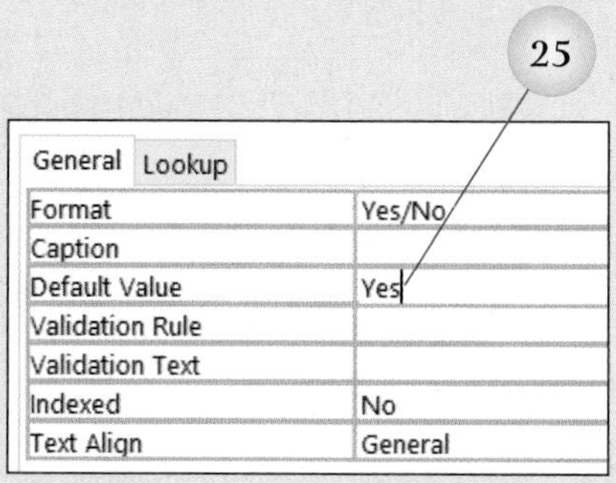

29. Click in the *Description* column for the *DentalIns* field, type Insert check mark if employee is signed up for dental insurance, and then press the Tab key.
30. After all of the fields are entered, click the Save button on the Quick Access Toolbar.
31. Click the View button to return the table to Datasheet view.
32. Enter the records in the Employees table as shown in Figure 4.7.
33. After all of the records are entered, automatically adjust the widths of the columns in the table as shown in Figure 4.7.
34. Save and then close the Employees table.

Check Your Work

Figure 4.6 Project 1b Employees Table in Design View

Employees

	Field Name	Data Type	Description (Optional)
🔑	EmpID	Short Text	Enter five-digit employee identification number
	FName	Short Text	Enter employee's first name
	LName	Short Text	Enter employee's last name
	Address	Short Text	Enter employee's address
	City	Short Text	Enter employee's city
	State	Short Text	CA automatically entered as state
	ZIP	Short Text	Enter five-digit ZIP code
	Telephone	Short Text	Enter employee's telephone number
	HireDate	Date/Time	Enter employee's hire date
	HealthIns	Yes/No	Leave check mark if employee is signed up for health insurance
	DentalIns	Yes/No	Insert check mark if employee is signed up for dental insurance

Figure 4.7 Project 1b Employees Table in Datasheet View

Employees

	EmpID	FName	LName	Address	City	State	ZIP	Telephone	HireDate	HealthIns	DentalIns
	02-59	Christina	Solomon	12241 East 51st	Citrus Heights	CA	95611	(916) 555-8844	01-Feb-08	☑	☑
	03-23	Douglas	Ricci	903 Mission Road	Roseville	CA	95678	(916) 555-4125	01-Mar-08	☑	☐
	03-55	Tatiana	Kasadev	6558 Orchard Drive	Citrus Heights	CA	95610	(916) 555-8534	15-Nov-10	☑	☐
	04-14	Brian	West	12232 142nd Avenue East	Citrus Heights	CA	95611	(916) 555-0967	01-Apr-12	☑	☑
	04-32	Kathleen	Addison	21229 19th Street	Citrus Heights	CA	95621	(916) 555-3408	01-Feb-13	☑	☑
	05-20	Teresa	Villanueva	19453 North 42nd Street	Citrus Heights	CA	95611	(916) 555-2302	15-Jul-14	☑	☑
	05-31	Marcia	Griswold	211 Haven Road	North Highlands	CA	95660	(916) 555-1449	01-May-14	☐	☐
	06-24	Tiffany	Gentry	12312 North 20th	Roseville	CA	95661	(916) 555-0043	15-Apr-16	☑	☑
	06-33	Joanna	Gallegos	6850 York Street	Roseville	CA	95747	(916) 555-7446	01-Jul-17	☐	☐
	07-20	Jesse	Scholtz	3412 South 21st Street	Fair Oaks	CA	95628	(916) 555-4204	15-Feb-17	☑	☐
	07-23	Eugene	Bond	530 Laurel Road	Orangevale	CA	95662	(916) 555-9412	01-Mar-18	☑	☐
*						CA				☑	☐

Tutorial

Applying a Validation Rule in Design View

Hint Enter a validation rule in a field to control what is entered in the field. Create validation text that displays when someone enters invalid data.

Validating Field Entries

Use the *Validation Rule* property box in the *Field Properties* section in Design view to enter a statement containing a conditional test that is checked each time data is entered into a field. If data is entered that fails to satisfy the conditional test, Access does not accept the entry and displays an error message. Entering a conditional statement in the *Validation Rule* property box that checks each entry against the acceptable range reduces errors. Customize the error message that will display if incorrect data is entered in the field by typing that message in the *Validation Text* property box.

Tutorial

Creating a Lookup Field

Using the Lookup Wizard

Like the Input Mask Wizard, the Lookup Wizard can be used to control data entered in a field. Use the Lookup Wizard to confine data entered into a field to a specific list of items. For example, in Project 1c, the Lookup Wizard will be used to restrict the new *EmpCategory* field to one of three choices: *Salaried*, *Hourly*, and *Temporary*. When entering data, clicking in the field displays a down arrow. Click the down arrow and then click an option at the drop-down list.

Use the Lookup Wizard when assigning a data type to a field. Click in the field in the *Data Type* column, click the down arrow, and then click *Lookup Wizard* at the drop-down list. This displays the first Lookup Wizard dialog box, as shown in Figure 4.8. At this dialog box, indicate that specific field choices will be entered

Quick Steps

Use the Lookup Wizard

1. Open table in Design view.
2. Type text in *Field Name* column.
3. Press Tab.
4. Click down arrow.
5. Click *Lookup Wizard.*
6. Complete wizard steps.

Figure 4.8 First Lookup Wizard Dialog Box

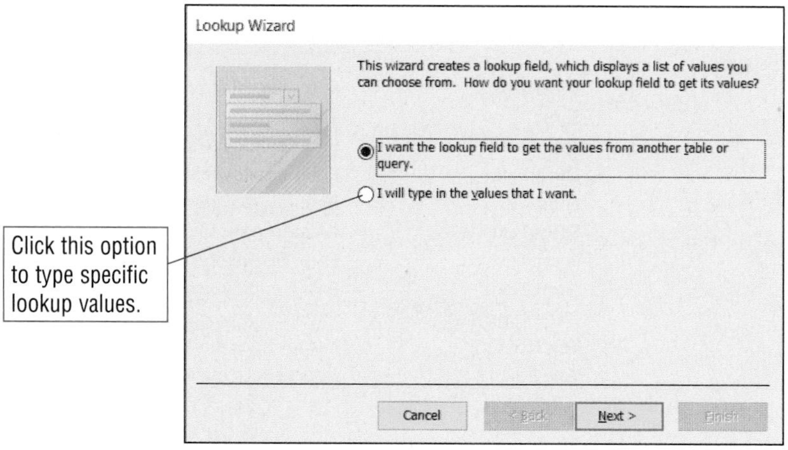

Figure 4.9 Second Lookup Wizard Dialog Box

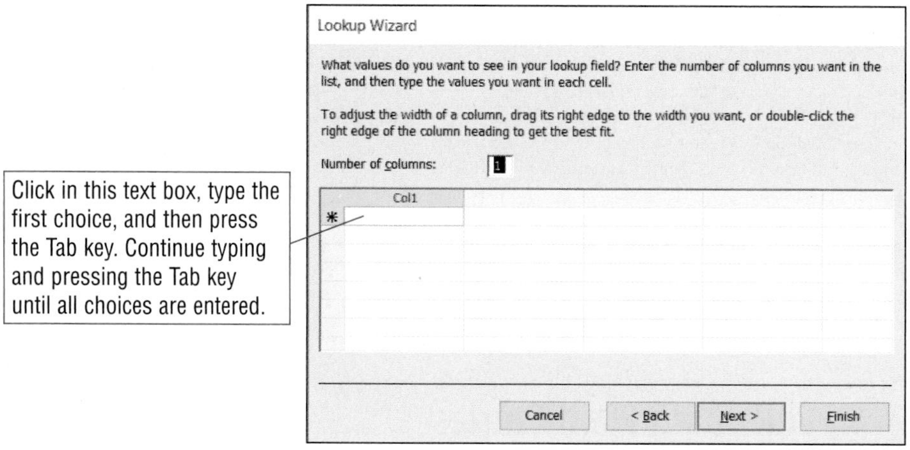

by clicking the *I will type in the values that I want* option and then click the Next button. At the second Lookup Wizard dialog box, shown in Figure 4.9, click in the blank text box below *Col1* and then type the first choice. Press the Tab key and then type the second choice. Continue in this manner until all choices have been entered and then click the Next button. At the third Lookup Wizard dialog box, make sure the proper name displays in the *What label would you like for your lookup column?* text box and then click the Finish button.

Tutorial

Managing Fields in Design View

Insert Rows

Quick Steps

Insert a Field in Design View

1. Open table in Design view.
2. Click in row that will follow new field.
3. Click Insert Rows button.

Inserting, Moving, and Deleting Fields in Design View

As shown in Chapter 1, field management tasks such as inserting, moving, and deleting fields can be completed in Datasheet view. These tasks can also be completed in Design view.

To insert a new field in a table in Design view, position the insertion point in a field in the row that will be immediately *below* the new field and then click the Insert Rows button in the Tools group on the Table Tools Design tab. Another option is to position the insertion point in text in the row that will display immediately *below* the new field, click the right mouse button, and then click *Insert Rows* at the shortcut menu. A row in the Design view creates a field in the table.

Quick Steps

Delete a Field in Design View

1. Open table in Design view.
2. Click in row to be deleted.
3. Click Delete Rows button.
4. Click Yes.

Delete Rows

A field in a table can be moved to a different location in Datasheet view or Design view. To move a field in Design view, click the field selector bar at the left side of the row to be moved. With the row selected, position the arrow pointer in the field selector bar at the left side of the selected row, click and hold down the left mouse button, drag the arrow pointer with a gray square attached until a thick black line displays in the desired position, and then release the mouse button.

Delete a field in a table and all data entered in that field is also deleted. When a field is deleted, the deletion cannot be undone with the Undo button. Delete a field only if all data associated with it should be removed from the table. To delete a field in Design view, click in the field selector bar at the left side of the row to be deleted and then click the Delete Rows button in the Tools group. At the confirmation message, click Yes. A row can also be deleted by positioning the mouse pointer in the row to be deleted, clicking the right mouse button, and then clicking *Delete Rows* at the shortcut menu.

Tutorial

Inserting a *Total* Row

Totals

Inserting a *Total* Row

A *Total* row can be added to a table in Datasheet view and then used to perform functions such as finding the sum, average, maximum, minimum, count, standard deviation, or variance results in a numeric column. To insert a *Total* row, click the Totals button in the Records group on the Home tab. Access adds a row to the bottom of the table with the label *Total*. Click in the *Total* row, click the down arrow that displays, and then click a specific function at the drop-down list.

Project 1c Validating Field Entries; Using the Lookup Wizard; and Inserting, Moving, and Deleting a Field

Part 3 of 9

1. With **4-SunProperties.accdb** open, open the Employees table.
2. Insert a new field in the Employees table and apply a validation rule by completing the following steps:
   a. Click the View button to switch to Design view.
   b. Click in the empty field immediately below the *DentalIns* field in the *Field Name* column and then type LifeIns.
   c. Press the Tab key.
   d. Click the down arrow in the field in the *Data Type* column and then click *Currency* at the drop-down list.
   e. Click in the *Validation Rule* property box, type <=100000, and then press the Enter key.
   f. With the insertion point positioned in the *Validation Text* property box, type Enter a value that is equal to or less than $100,000.

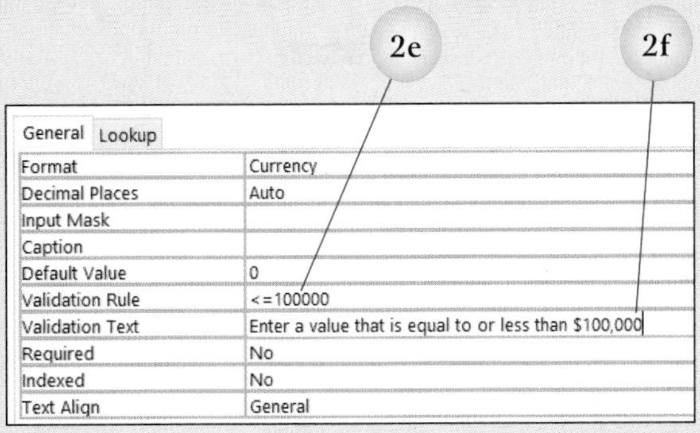

   g. Click in the *LifeIns* field in the *Description* column and then type Enter optional life insurance amount.
   h. Click the Save button on the Quick Access Toolbar. Since the validation rule was created *after* data was entered into the table, Access displays a warning message indicating that some data may not be valid. At this message, click No.
   i. Click the View button to switch to Datasheet view.

3. Click in the first empty field in the *LifeIns* column, type 200000, and then press the Down Arrow key on the keyboard.
4. Access displays the error message prompting you to enter an amount that is equal to or less than $100,000. At this error message, click OK.
5. Edit the amount in the field so it displays as *100000* and then press the Down Arrow key.
6. Type the following entries in the remaining fields in the *LifeIns* column:

Record 2	25000	Record 7	100000
Record 3	0	Record 8	50000
Record 4	50000	Record 9	25000
Record 5	50000	Record 10	0
Record 6	0	Record 11	100000

7. Insert the *EmpCategory* field in the Employees table and use the Lookup Wizard to specify field choices by completing the following steps:
   a. Click the View button to change to Design view.
   b. Click in the *FName* field in the *Field Name* column.
   c. Click the Insert Rows button in the Tools group.
   d. With the insertion point positioned in the new empty field in the *Field Name* column, type EmpCategory.
   e. Press the Tab key. (This moves the insertion point to the *Data Type* column.)
   f. Click the down arrow in the field in the *Data Type* column and then click *Lookup Wizard* at the drop-down list.
   g. At the first Lookup Wizard dialog box, click the *I will type in the values that I want* option and then click the Next button.

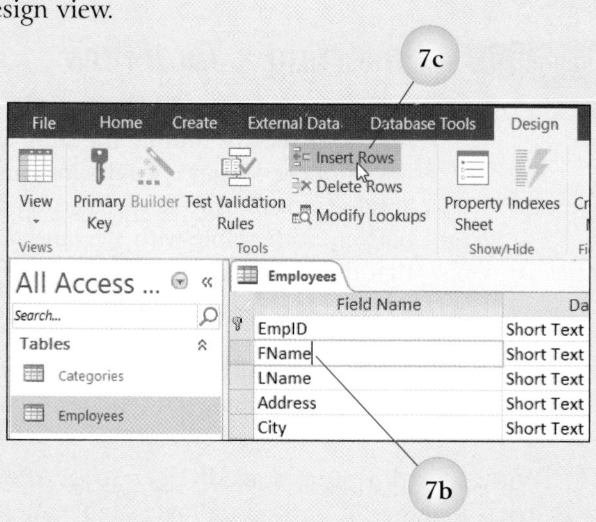

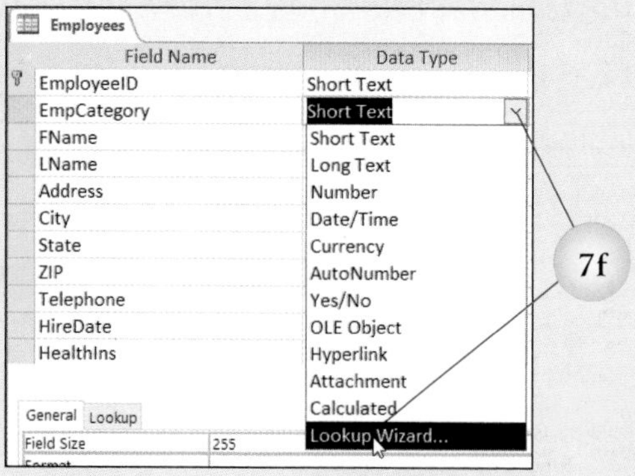

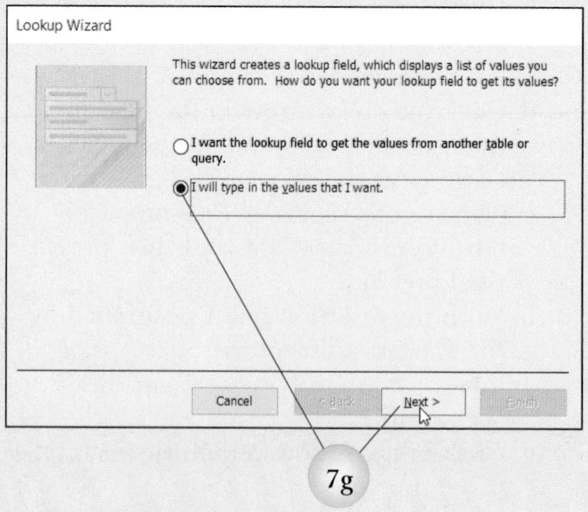

h. At the second Lookup Wizard dialog box, click in the blank text box below *Col1*, type Salaried, and then press the Tab key.
i. Type Hourly and then press the Tab key.
j. Type Temporary.
k. Click the Next button.
l. At the third Lookup Wizard dialog box, click the Finish button.
m. Press the Tab key and then type Click down arrow and then click employee category in the *Description* column.

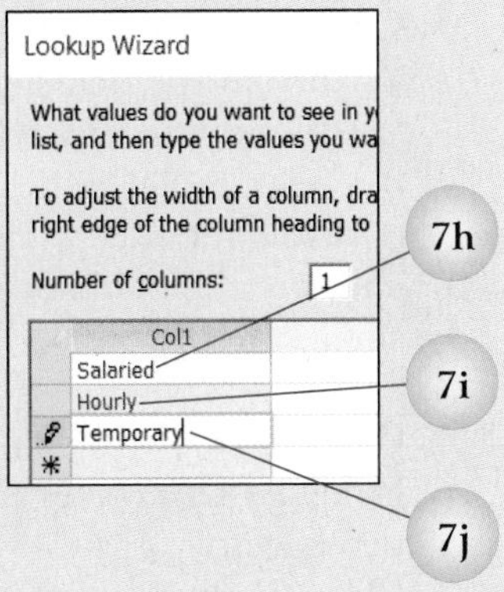

8. Click the Save button on the Quick Access Toolbar.
9. Click the View button to switch to Datasheet view.
10. Insert information in the *EmpCategory* column by completing the following steps:
    a. Click in the first empty field in the new *EmpCategory* column.
    b. Click the down arrow in the field and then click *Hourly* at the drop-down list.
    c. Click in the next empty field in the *EmpCategory* column, click the down arrow, and then click *Salaried* at the drop-down list.
    d. Continue entering information in the *EmpCategory* column by completing similar steps. Choose the following in the specified record:

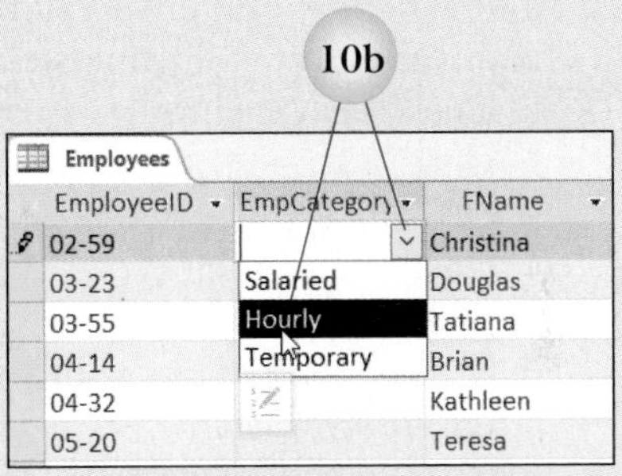

Third record: *Hourly*
Fourth record: *Salaried*
Fifth record: *Temporary*
Sixth record: *Hourly*
Seventh record: *Salaried*
Eighth record: *Temporary*
Ninth record: *Hourly*
Tenth record: *Salaried*
Eleventh record: *Salaried*

11. Print the Employees table. (The table will print on two pages.)
12. After looking at the printed table, you decide to move the *EmpCategory* field. Move the *EmpCatgory* field in Design view by completing the following steps:
    a. With the Employees table open, click the View button to switch to Design view.
    b. Click in the field selector bar at the left side of the *EmpCategory* field to select the row.
    c. Position the arrow pointer in the *EmpCategory* field selector bar, click and hold down the left mouse button, drag down until a thick black line displays below the *Telephone* field, and then release the mouse button.

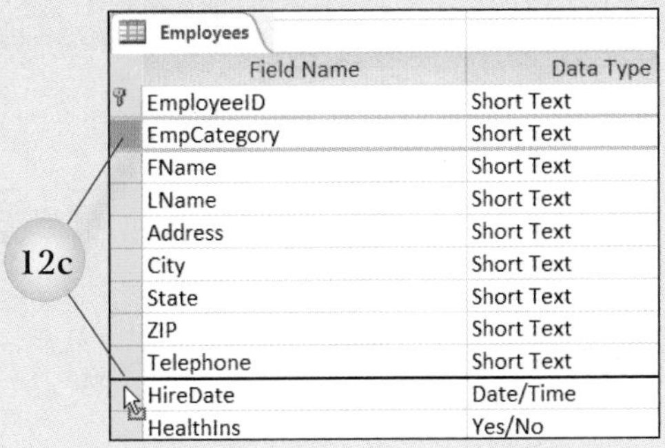

13. Delete the *DentalIns* field by completing the following steps:
    a. Click in the field selector bar at the left side of the *DentalIns* field. (This selects the row.)
    b. Click the Delete Rows button in the Tools group.
    c. At the message asking if you want to permanently delete the field and all of the data in the field, click Yes.
14. Click the Save button on the Quick Access Toolbar.
15. Click the View button to switch to Datasheet view.
16. Print the Employees table. (The table will print on two pages.)
17. Close the Employees table.
18. Open the Payments table and then insert a new field and apply a validation rule by completing the following steps:
    a. Click the View button to switch to Design view.

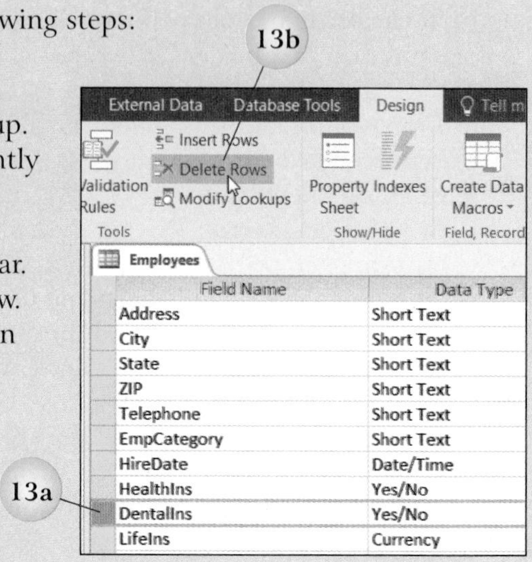

    b. Click in the empty field immediately below the *PymntAmount* field in the *Field Name* column and then type LateFee.
    c. Press the Tab key.
    d. Click the down arrow in the field in the *Data Type* column and then click *Currency* at the drop-down list.
    e. Click in the *Validation Rule* property box, type <=50, and then press the Enter key.
    f. With the insertion point positioned in the *Validation Text* property box, type Late fee must be $50 or less.
    g. Click in the box in the *Description* column for the *LateFee* field and then type Enter a late fee amount if applicable.

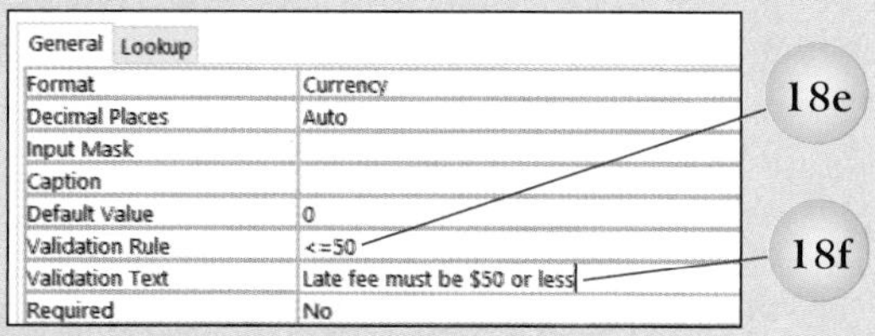

    h. Click the Save button on the Quick Access Toolbar. Since the validation rule was created *after* data was entered into the table, Access displays a warning message indicating that some data may not be valid. At this message, click No.
    i. Click the View button to switch to Datasheet view.
19. Insert late fees for the last three records by completing the following steps:
    a. Click in the *LateFee* field for record 15, type 25, and then press the Down Arrow key.
    b. With the *LateFee* field for record 16 active, type 25 and then press the Down Arrow key.
    c. With the *LateFee* field for record 17 active, type 50 and then press the Up Arrow key.

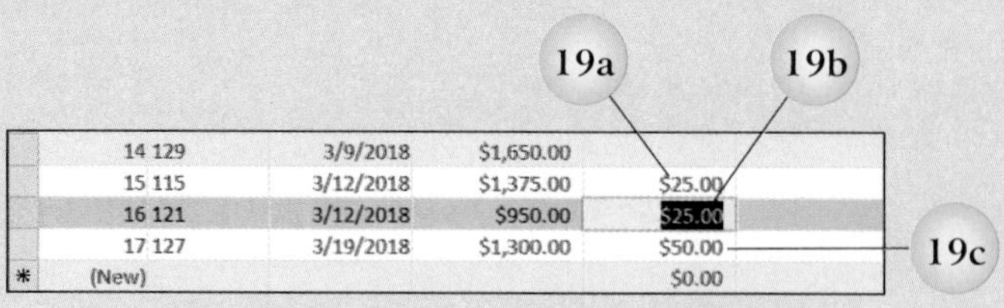

19a
19b
14 129 3/9/2018 $1,650.00
15 115 3/12/2018 $1,375.00 $25.00
16 121 3/12/2018 $950.00 $25.00
17 127 3/19/2018 $1,300.00 $50.00
(New) $0.00
19c

20. Insert a *Total* row by completing the following steps:
    a. In Datasheet view, click the Totals button in the Records group on the Home tab.
    b. Click in the empty field in the *PymntAmount* column in the *Total* row.
    c. Click the down arrow in the field and then click *Sum* at the drop-down list.
    d. Click in the empty field in the *LateFee* column in the *Total* row.
    e. Click the down arrow in the field and then click *Sum* at the drop-down list.
    f. Click in any other field.
21. Save, print, and then close the Payments table.

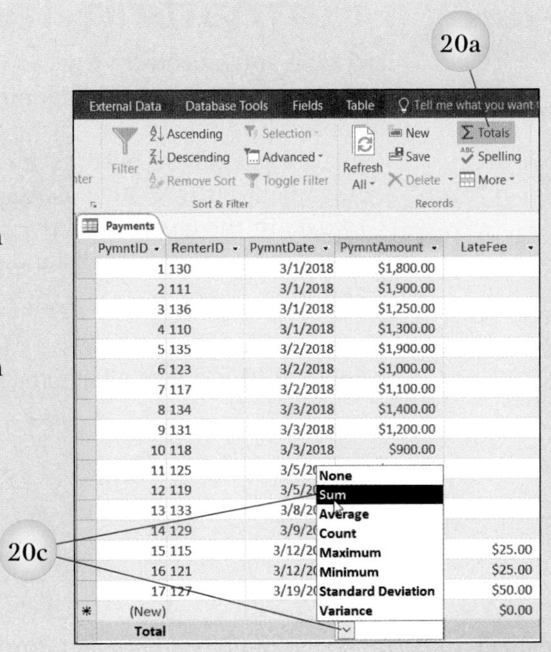

Check Your Work

Tutorial

Sorting Records in a Table

Ascending

Descending

Quick Steps

Sort Records

1. Open table in Datasheet view.
2. Click field in specific column.
3. Click Ascending button or Descending button.

Quick Steps

Print Selected Records

1. Open table and select records.
2. Click File tab.
3. Click *Print* option.
4. Click next *Print* option.
5. Click *Selected Record(s)*.
6. Click OK.

Sorting Records

The Sort & Filter group on the Home tab contains two buttons for sorting data in records. Click the Ascending button to sort data in the active field and text is sorted in alphabetical order from A to Z, numbers are sorted from lowest to highest, and dates are sorted from earliest to latest. Click the Descending button to sort data in the active field and text is sorted in alphabetical order from Z to A, numbers from highest to lowest, and dates from latest to earliest.

Printing Specific Records

Specific records in a table can be printed by seleting the records and then displaying the Print dialog box. Display this dialog box by clicking the File tab, clicking the *Print* option, and then clicking the next *Print* option. At the Print dialog box, click the *Selected Record(s)* option in the *Print Range* section and then click OK.

To select specific records, display the table in Datasheet view, click the record selector for the first record, click and hold the left mouse button, drag to select the specific records, and then release the mouse button. The record selector is the light gray square at the left side of the record. When the mouse pointer is positioned on the record selector, the pointer turns into a right-pointing black arrow.

Tutorial

Formatting Table Data

Formatting Table Data

A table in Datasheet view can be formatted with options available in the Text Formatting group on the Home tab as shown in Figure 4.10 and described in Table 4.2 (Some of the buttons in the Text Formatting group are dimmed and unavailable. These buttons are only available for fields formatted as rich text.) Alignment buttons such as Align Left, Center, or Align Right, apply formatting to data in the currently active column. Click one of the other options or buttons in the Text Formatting group and the formatting is applied to data in all columns and rows.

Figure 4.10 Text Formatting Group on the Home Tab

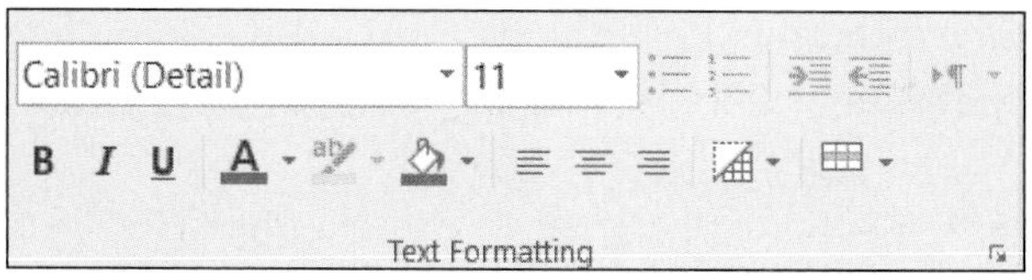

Table 4.2 Text Formatting Buttons and Option Boxes

Button/Option Box	Name	Description
Calibri (Detail)	*Font*	Change the text font.
11	*Font Size*	Change the text size.
B	Bold	Bold the text.
I	Italic	Italicize the text.
U	Underline	Underline the text.
A	Font Color	Change the text color.
	Background Color	Apply a background color to all fields.
	Align Left	Align all text in the currently active column at the left side of the fields.
	Center	Center all text in the currently active column in the center of the fields.
	Align Right	Align all text in the currently active column at the right side of the fields.
	Gridlines	Specify whether to display vertical and/or horizontal gridlines.
	Alternate Row Color	Apply a specified color to alternating rows in the table.

When creating a table, a data type is specified for a field, such as the Short Text, Date/Time, or Currency data type. To format text in a field rather than all of the fields in a column or the entire table, choose the Long Text data type and then specify rich text formatting. For example, in Project 1d, specific credit scores will be formatted in the *CreditScore* column. To be able to format specific scores, the data type will be changed to Long Text with rich text formatting. Use the Long Text data type only for fields containing text—not for fields containing currency amounts, numbers, or dates.

By default, the Long Text data type uses plain text formatting. To change to rich text, click in the *Text Format* property box in the *Field Properties* section (displays with the text *Plain Text*), click the down arrow that displays at the right side of the property box, and then click *Rich Text* at the drop-down list.

Project 1d Sorting, Printing, and Formatting Records and Fields in Tables — Part 4 of 9

1. With **4-SunProperties.accdb** open, open the Renters table.
2. With the table in Datasheet view, sort records in ascending alphabetical order by last name by completing the following steps:
   a. Click in any last name in the *LastName* column in the table.
   b. Click the Ascending button in the Sort & Filter group on the Home tab.
   c. Print the Renters table in landscape orientation.

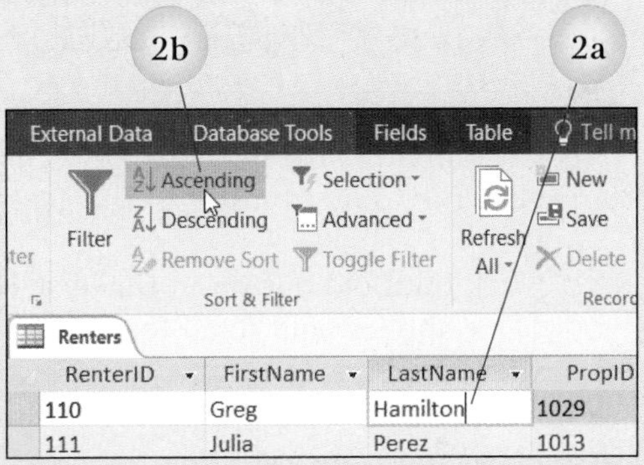

3. Sort records in descending order (highest to lowest) by credit score number by completing the following steps:
   a. Click in any number in the *CreditScore* column.
   b. Click the Descending button in the Sort & Filter group.
   c. Print the Renters table in landscape orientation.
4. Close the Renters table without saving the changes.
5. Open the Properties table.
6. Sort and then print selected records with a specific apartment property type by completing the following steps:
   a. Click in any entry in the *CatID* column.
   b. Click the Ascending button in the Sort & Filter group.
   c. Position the mouse pointer on the record selector of the first record with a category ID of *A*, click and hold down the left mouse button, drag to select the four records with a category ID of *A*, and then release the mouse button.
   d. Click the File tab and then click the *Print* option.
   e. Click the next *Print* option.

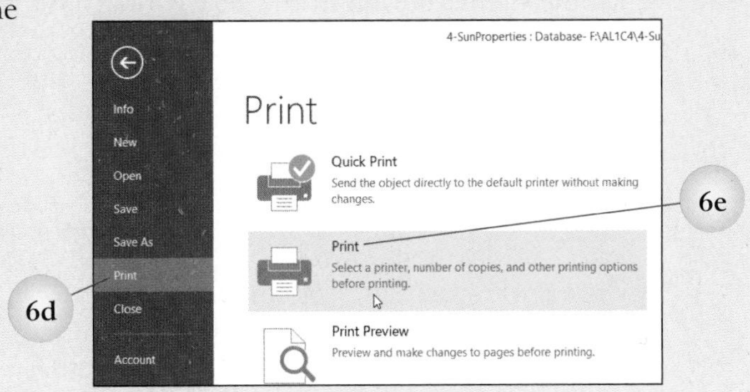

f. At the Print dialog box, click the *Selected Record(s)* option in the *Print Range* section.

g. Click OK.

7. With the Properties table open, apply the following text formatting:

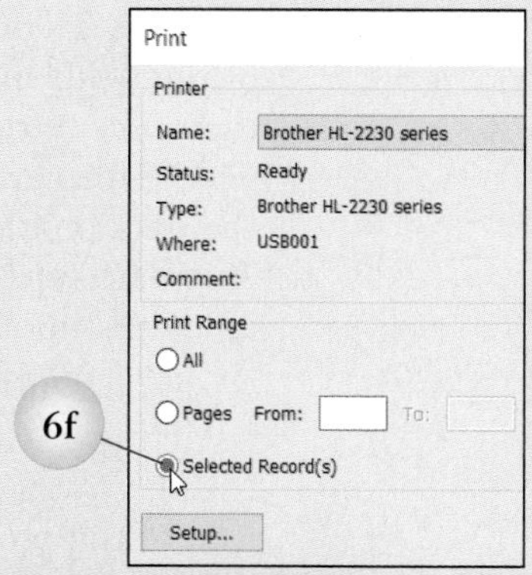

a. Click in any field in the *CatID* column and then click the Center button in the Text Formatting group on the Home tab.

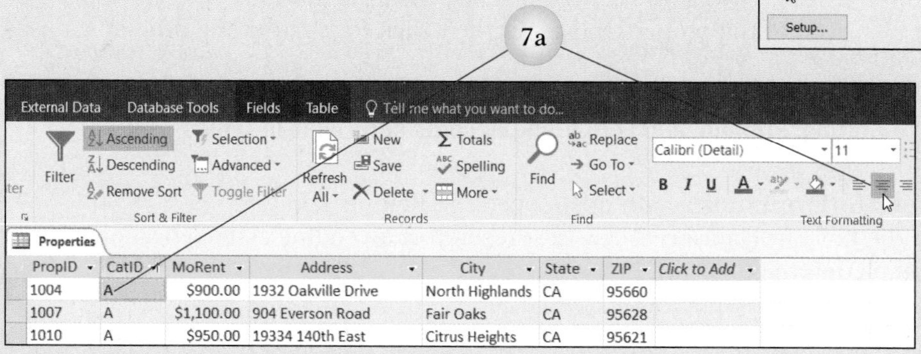

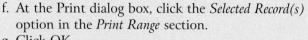

b. Click in any field in the *PropID* column and then click the Center button in the Text Formatting group.

c. Click the Bold button in the Text Formatting group. (This applies bold to all text in the table.)

d. Click the Font Color button arrow and then click the *Dark Blue* color option (fourth column, first row in the *Standard Colors* section).

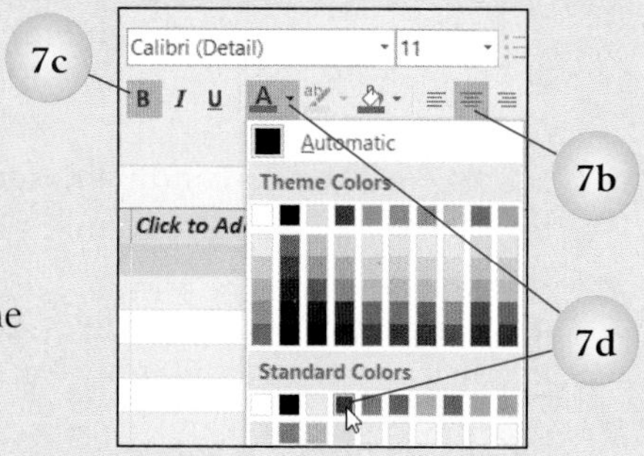

e. Adjust the column widths.

f. Save, print, and then close the Properties table.

8. Open the Payments table and apply the following text formatting:

a. With the first field active in the *PymntID* column, click the Center button in the Text Formatting group on the Home tab

b. Click in any field in the *RenterID* column and then click the Center button in the Text Formatting group.

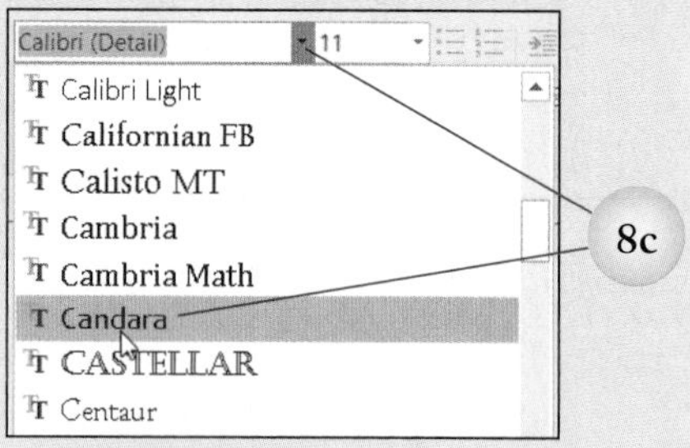

c. Click the *Font* option box arrow, scroll down the drop-down list, and then click *Candara*. (Fonts are listed in alphabetical order in the drop-down list.)

d. Click the *Font Size* option box arrow and then click *12* at the drop-down list.

e. Click the Alternate Row Color button arrow and then click the *Green 2* color option (seventh column, third row in the *Standard Colors* section).

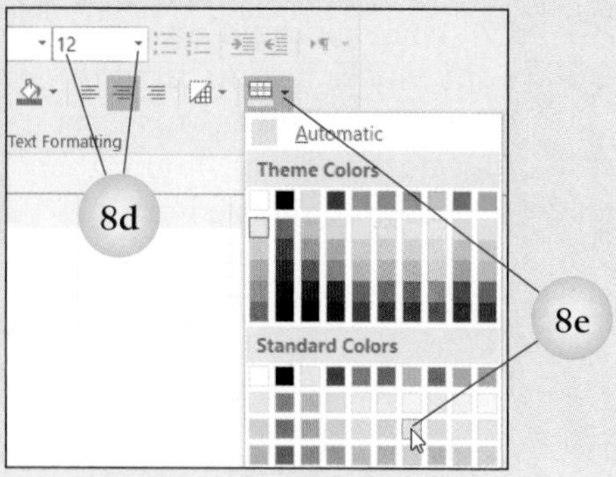

f. Adjust the column widths.

g. Save, print, and then close the Payments table.

9. Open the Renters table and then apply the following formatting to columns in the table:
   a. With the first field active in the *RenterID* column, click the Center button in the Text Formatting group on the Home tab.
   b. Click in any field in the *PropID* column and then click the Center button.
   c. Click in any field in the *EmpID* column and then click the Center button
   d. Click in any field in the *CreditScore* column and then click the Center button.
10. Change the data type for the *CreditScore* field to Long Text with rich text formatting and apply formatting by completing the following steps:
    a. Click the View button to switch to Design view.
    b. Click in the *CreditScore* field in the *Data Type* column, click the down arrow that displays in the field, and then click *Long Text* at the drop-down list.
    c. Click in the *Text Format* property box in the *Field Properties* section (displays with the words *Plain Text*), click the down arrow that displays in the property box, and then click *Rich Text* at the drop-down list.

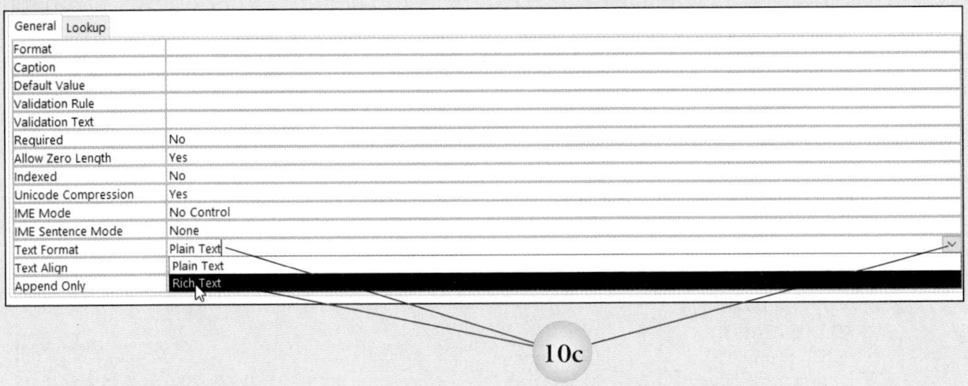

    d. At the message stating that the field will be converted to rich text, click the Yes button.
    e. Click the Save button on the Quick Access Toolbar.
    f. Click the View button to switch to Datasheet view.
    g. Double-click the field value *538* in the *CreditScore* column in the row for Dana Rozinski. (Double-clicking in the field selects the field value *538*.)
    h. With *538* selected, click the Font Color button in the Text Formatting group. (This changes the number to standard red. If the font color does not change to red, click the Font Color button arrow and then click the *Red* option [second column, bottom row in the *Standard Colors* section].)
    i. Change the font to standard red for any credit scores below 600.
    j. Save and print the Renters table in landscape orientation and then close the table.

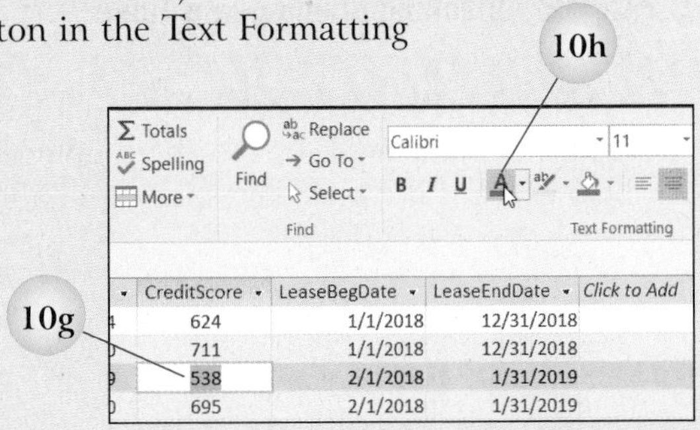

Check Your Work

Tutorial

Completing a Spelling Check

Hint Begin a spelling check with the keyboard shortcut F7.

Spelling

Quick Steps

Complete a Spelling Check

1. Open table in Datasheet view.
2. Click Spelling button.
3. Change or ignore spelling.
4. Click OK.

Completing a Spelling Check

The spelling feature in Access finds misspelled words and suggests replacement words. It also finds duplicate words and irregular capitalizations. When checking the spelling of an object in a database, such as a table, the words in a table are compared with the words in the spelling dictionary. If a match is found, the word is passed over. If no match is found, then the word is selected and possible replacements are suggested.

To complete a spelling check, open a table in Datasheet view and then click the Spelling button in the Records group on the Home tab. If no match is found for a word in the table, the Spelling dialog box displays with replacement options. Figure 4.11 displays the Spelling dialog box with the word *Citruis* selected and possible replacements display in the *Suggestions* list box. Use options in the Spelling dialog box, to ignore the word (for example, if a proper name is selected), change to one of the replacement options, or add the word to the dictionary or AutoCorrect feature. A spelling check also can be completed on other objects in a database, such as a query, form, and report. (Forms and reports are covered in future chapters.)

Figure 4.11 Spelling Dialog Box

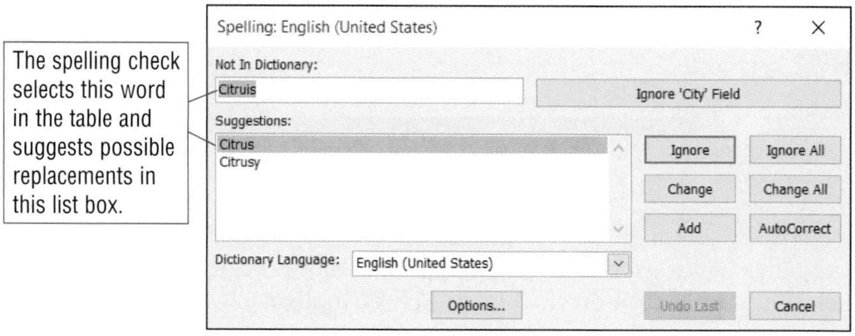

Project 1e **Checking Spelling in a Table** — Part 5 of 9

1. With **4-SunProperties.accdb** open, open the Employees table.
2. Add the following record to the Employees table. (Type the misspelled words as shown below. You will correct the spelling in a later step.)

EmpID	02-72
FName	Roben
LName	Wildre
Address	9945 Valley Avenue
City	Citruis Heights
State	(CA automatically inserted)
ZIP	95610
Telephone	9165556522
EmpCategory	(choose *Salaried*)
HireDate	01may18
HealthIns	No (Remove check mark)
LifeIns	50000

3. Save the Employees table.

4. Click in the first field in the *EmpID* column.
5. Click the Spelling button in the Records group on the Home tab.
6. The name *Kasadev* is selected. This is a proper name, so click the Ignore button to leave the name as written.

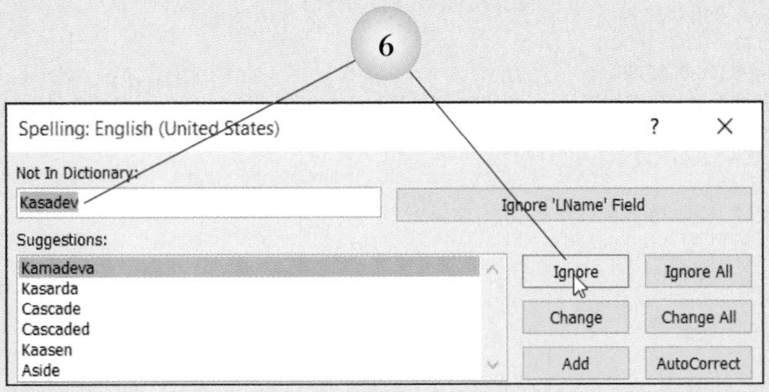

7. The name *Scholtz* is selected. This is a proper name, so click the Ignore button to leave the name as written.
8. The name *Roben* is selected. Although this is a proper name, it is spelled incorrectly. Click *Robin* (the proper spelling) in the *Suggestions* list box and then click the Change button.

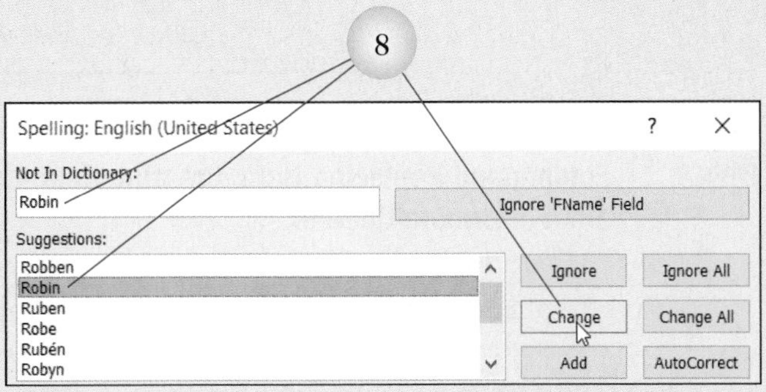

9. The name *Wildre* is selected. Although this is a proper name, it is spelled incorrectly. The proper spelling *(Wilder)* is selected in the *Suggestions* list box, so click the Change button.
10. The word *Citruis* is selected. The proper spelling *(Citrus)* is selected in the *Suggestions* list box, so click the Change button.
11. At the message stating that the spelling check is complete, click OK.
12. Print the Employees table and then close the table.

Check Your Work

Tutorial

Finding Data

Tutorial

Finding and Replacing Data

Find

Quick Steps

Find Data in Table

1. Click Find button.
2. Type data in *Find What* text box.
3. Click Find Next button.

Finding and Replacing Data

To find a specific entry in a field in a table, consider using options at the Find and Replace dialog box with the Find tab selected, as shown in Figure 4.12. Display this dialog box by clicking the Find button in the Find group on the Home tab or with the keyboard shortcut Ctrl + F. At the Find and Replace dialog box, enter the data to be found in the *Find What* text box. By default, Access looks only in the specific column where the insertion point is positioned. Click the Find Next button to find the next occurrence of the data or click the Cancel button to close the Find and Replace dialog box.

The *Look In* option defaults to the column where the insertion point is positioned. This can be changed to search the entire table by clicking the *Look In* option box arrow and then clicking the table name at the drop-down list. The *Match* option has a default setting of *Whole Field*. This can be changed to *Any Part of Field* or *Start of Field*. The *Search* option has a default setting of *All*, which means that Access will search all of the data in a specific column. This can be changed to *Up* or *Down*. To find data that contains specific uppercase and lowercase letters, insert a check mark in the *Match Case* check box and Access will return results that match the case formatting of the text entered in the *Find What* text box.

Quick Steps

Find and Replace Data in Table

1. Click Replace button.
2. Type find data in *Find What* text box.
3. Type replacement data in *Replace With* text box.
4. Click Find Next button.
5. Click Replace button or Find Next button.

ab→ac Replace

Use the Find and Replace dialog box with the Replace tab selected to search for specific data and replace it with other data. Display this dialog box by clicking the Replace button in the Find group on the Home tab or with the keyboard shortcut Ctrl + H.

Figure 4.12 Find and Replace Dialog Box with Find Tab Selected

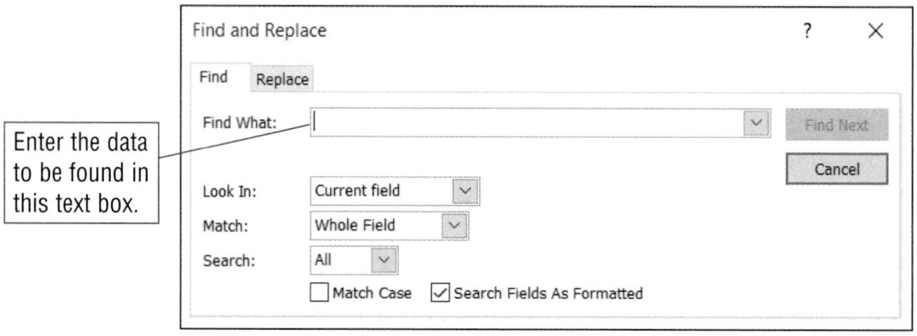

Project 1f Finding and Replacing Data, Creating Relationships, and Performing Queries

Part 6 of 9

1. With **4-SunProperties.accdb** open, open the Properties table.
2. Find records containing the zip code *95610* by completing the following steps:
   a. Click in the first field in the *ZIP* column.
   b. Click the Find button in the Find group on the Home tab.
   c. At the Find and Replace dialog box with the Find tab selected, type 95610 in the *Find What* text box.
   d. Click the Find Next button. (Access finds and selects the first occurrence of *95610*. If the Find and Replace dialog box covers the data, position the mouse pointer on the dialog box title bar, click and hold down the left mouse button, and then drag the dialog box to a different location on the screen.)

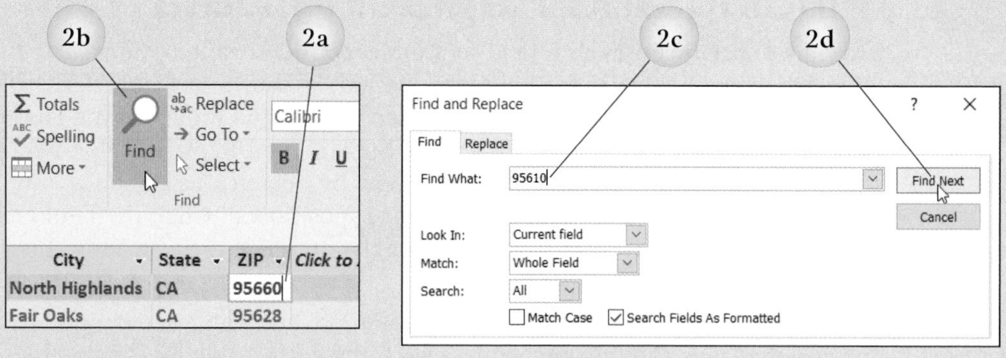

   e. Continue clicking the Find Next button until a message displays stating that Access has finished searching the records. At this message, click OK.
   f. Click the Cancel button to close the Find and Replace dialog box.
3. Suppose a new zip code has been added to the city of North Highlands and you need to change to this new zip code for some of the North Highlands properties. Complete the following steps to find *95660* and replace it with *95668*:
   a. Click in the first field in the *ZIP* column.
   b. Click the Replace button in the Find group.

c. At the Find and Replace dialog box with the Replace tab selected, delete the existing text in the *Find what* text box, and then type 95660 in the *Find What* text box.

d. Press the Tab key. (This moves the insertion point to the *Replace With* text box.)

e. Type 95668 in the *Replace With* text box.

f. Click the Find Next button.

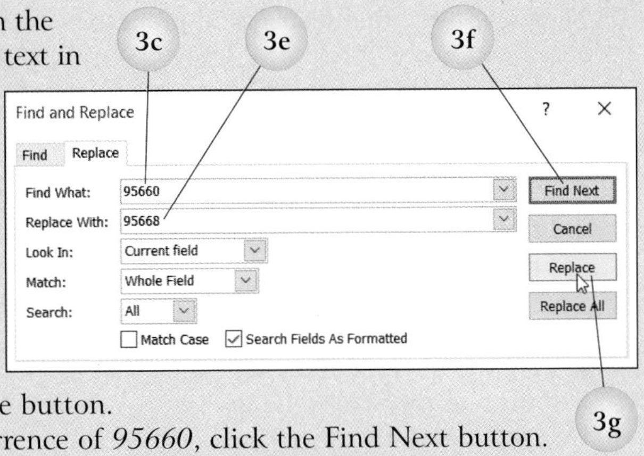

g. When Access selects the first occurrence of *95660*, click the Replace button.

h. When Access selects the second occurrence of *95660*, click the Find Next button.

i. When Access selects the third occurrence of *95660*, click the Replace button.

j. When Access selects the fourth occurrence of *95660*, click the Find Next button.

k. When Access selects the fifth occurrence of *95660*, click the Find Next button.

l. When Access selects the sixth occurrence of *95660*, click the Replace button.

m. Access goes back and selects the first occurrence of *95660* (record 1003) in the table. Click the Cancel button to close the Find and Replace dialog box.

4. Print and then close the Properties table.

5. Display the Relationships window and then create the following relationships (enforce referential integrity and cascade fields and records):

   a. Create a one-to-many relationship with the *CatID* field in the Categories table field list box the "one" and the *CatID* field in the Properties table field list box the "many."

   b. Create a one-to-many relationship with the *EmpID* field in the Employees table field list box the "one" and the *EmpID* field in the Renters table field list box the "many."

   c. Create a one-to-many relationship with the *PropID* field in the Properties table field list box the "one" and the *PropID* field in the Renters table field list box the "many."

   d. Create a one-to-many relationship with the *RenterID* field in the Renters table field list box the "one" and the *RenterID* field in the Payments table field list box the "many."

   e. Save the relationships and then print the relationships in landscape orientation.

   f. Close the relationship report without saving it and then close the Relationships window.

6. Design a query that displays employees with health insurance benefits with the following specifications:

   a. Insert the Employees table in the query window.

   b. Insert the *EmpID* field in the first field in the *Field* row.

   c. Insert the *FName* field in the second field in the *Field* row.

   d. Insert the *LName* field in the third field in the *Field* row.

   e. Insert the *HealthIns* field in the fourth field in the *Field* row.

   f. Click in the check box in the *EmpID* field in the *Show* row to remove the check mark. (This hides the EmpID numbers in the query results.)

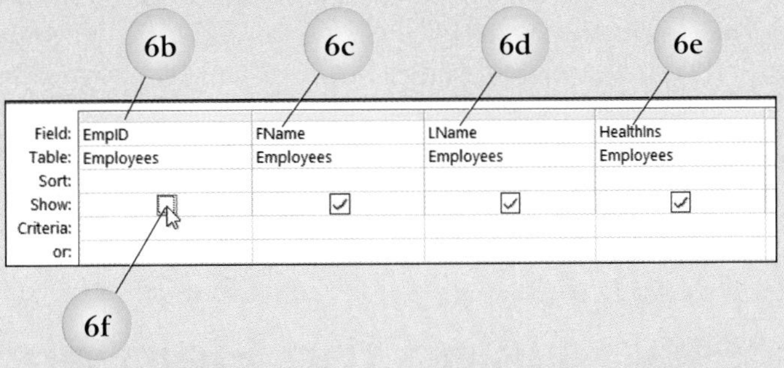

   g. Extract those employees with health benefits. (Type 1 in the *HealthIns* field in the *Criteria* row.)

   h. Run the query.

   i. Save the query and name it *EmpsWithHealthInsQuery*.

   j. Print and then close the query.

7. Design a query that displays all properties in the city of Citrus Heights with the following specifications:
   a. Insert the Properties table and the Categories table field list box in the query window.
   b. Insert the *PropID* field from the Properties table field list box in the first field in the *Field* row.
   c. Insert the *Category* field from the Categories table in the second field in the *Field* row.
   d. Insert the *Address*, *City*, *State*, and *ZIP* fields from the Properties table field list box to the third, fourth, fifth, and sixth fields in the *Field* row, respectively.
   e. Extract those properties in the city of Citrus Heights.
   f. Run the query.
   g. Save the query and name it *CitrusHeightsPropsQuery*.
   h. Print and then close the query.
8. Design a query that displays rent payments made between 3/1/2018 and 3/5/2018 with the following specifications:
   a. Insert the Payments table and the Renters table in the query window.
   b. Insert the *PymntID*, *PymntDate*, and *PymntAmount* fields from the Payments table field list box in the first, second, and third fields in the *Field* row fields, respectively.
   c. Insert the *FirstName* and *LastName* fields from the Renters table field list box in the fourth and fifth fields in the *Field* row, respectively.
   d. Extract those payments made between 3/1/2018 and 3/5/2018.
   e. Run the query.
   f. Save the query and name it *Pymnts3/1To3/5Query*.
   g. Print and then close the query.
9. Design a query that displays properties in Citrus Heights or Orangevale that rent for less than $1,501 a month as well as the type of property with the following specifications:
   a. Insert the Categories table and the Properties table in the query window.
   b. Insert the *Category* field from the Categories table field list box.
   c. Insert the *PropID*, *MoRent*, *Address*, *City*, *State*, and *ZIP* fields from the Properties table field list box.
   d. Extract those properties in Citrus Heights or Orangevale that rent for less than $1,501.
   e. Run the query.
   f. Save the query and name it *RentLessThan$1501InCHAndOVQuery*.
   g. Print the query in landscape orientation and then close the query.
10. Design a query that displays properties in Citrus Heights assigned to employee identification number *07-20* with the following specifications:
    a. Insert the Employees table and Properties table in the query window.
    b. Insert the *EmpID*, *FName*, and *LName* fields from the Employees table field list box.
    c. Insert the *Address*, *City*, *State*, and *ZIP* fields from the Properties table field list box.
    d. Extract those properties in Citrus Heights assigned to employee identification number 07-20.
    e. Run the query.
    f. Save the query and name it *Emp07-20CHPropsQuery*.
    g. Print and then close the query.

Check Your Work

Tutorial

Using the Help and Tell Me Features

Using the Help and Tell Me Features

Microsoft Access includes a Help feature that contains information about Access features and commands. This on-screen reference manual is similar to Windows Help and the Help features in Word, PowerPoint, and Excel. The Tell Me feature provides information and guidance on how to complete a function.

Help

Hint Press the F1 function key to display the Access Help window.

Quick Steps

Use the Help Feature

1. Click Microsoft Access Help button.
2. Type topic or feature.
3. Press Enter.
4. Click article.

Getting Help at the Access Help Window

Click the Microsoft Access Help button (the question mark) in the upper right corner of the screen or press the keyboard shortcut F1 to display the Access Help window, as shown in Figure 4.13. In this window, type a topic, feature, or question in the search text box and then press the Enter key. Articles related to the search text display in the Access Help window. Open an article by clicking the article's hyperlink.

The Access Help window contains five buttons, which display above the search text box. Use the Back and Forward buttons to navigate within the window. Click the Home button to return to the Access Help window opening screen. Print information by clicking the Print button and then clicking the Print button at the Print dialog box. Click the Use Large Text button to increase the size of the text in the window.

Getting Help on a Button

Position the mouse pointer on a button and a ScreenTip displays with information about the button. Some button ScreenTips display with a Help icon and the text *Tell me more*. Click this hyperlinked text or press the F1 function key and the Access Help window opens with information about the button feature.

Figure 4.13 Access Help Window

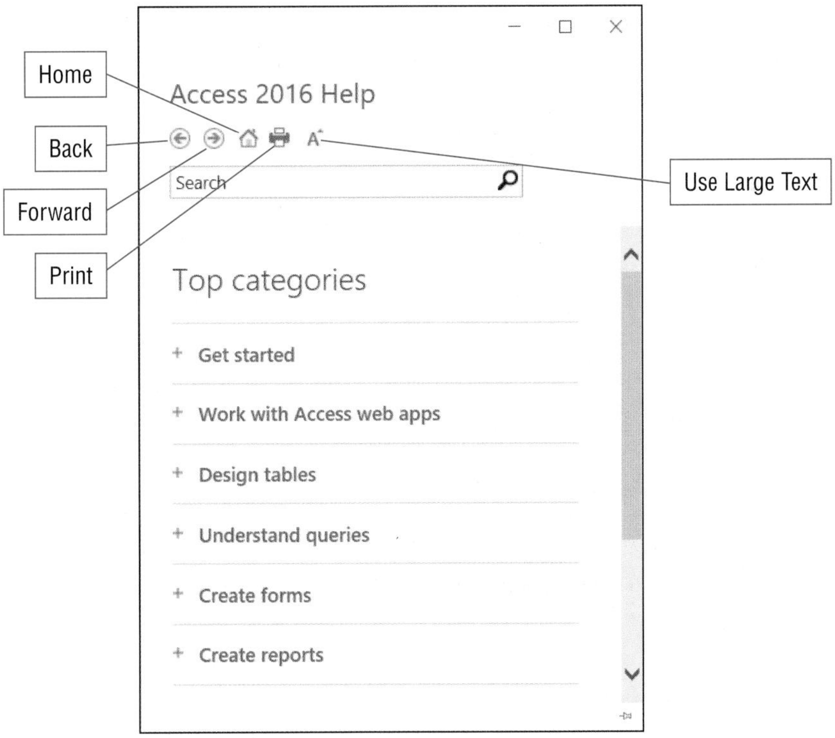

Project 1g Using the Help Feature

Part 7 of 9

1. With **4-SunProperties.accdb** open, click the Microsoft Access Help button in the upper right corner of the screen.
2. At the Access Help window, type input mask in the search text box and then press the Enter key.
3. When the list of articles displays, click the Guide data entry in Access by using input masks hyperlink. (If this article is not available, choose a similar article.)
4. Read the information on creating an input mask. (If you want a printout of the information, click the Print button in the Access Help window and then click the Print button at the Print dialog box.)
5. Close the Access Help window by clicking the Close button in the upper right corner of the window.
6. Click the Create tab.
7. Hover the mouse over the Table button and then click the Tell me more hyperlink at the bottom of the ScreenTip.
8. At the Access Help window, read the information on tables and then click the Close button in the upper right corner of the Access Help window.

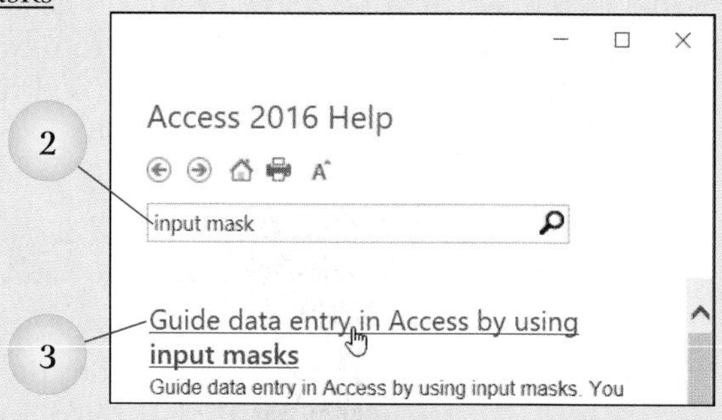

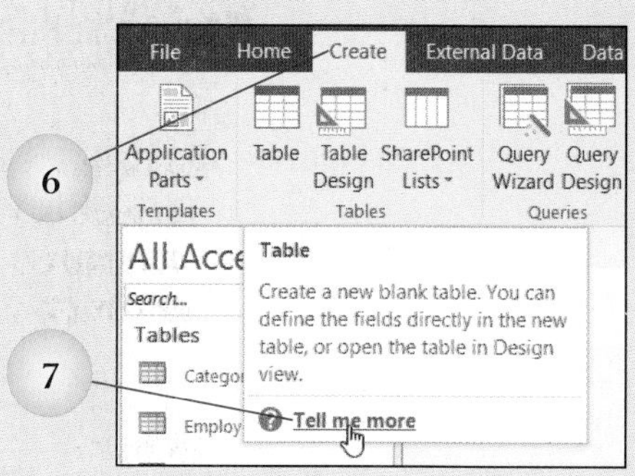

Getting Help in a Dialog Box or Backstage Area

Some dialog boxes and backstage areas provide a Help button that, when clicked, displays the Access Help window with specific information about the dialog box or backstage area. After reading and/or printing the information, close the dialog box by clicking the Close button in the upper right corner of the dialog box or close the backstage area by clicking the Back button or pressing the Esc key.

Project 1h Getting Help in a Dialog Box and Backstage Area

Part 8 of 9

1. With **4-SunProperties.accdb** open, click the Database Tools tab.
2. Click the Relationships button. (Make sure the Show Table dialog box displays. If it does not, click the Show Table button in the Relationships group.)
3. Click the Help button in the upper right corner of the Show Table dialog box.
4. Click the Guide to table relationships hyperlink. (If this article is not available, choose a similar article.)

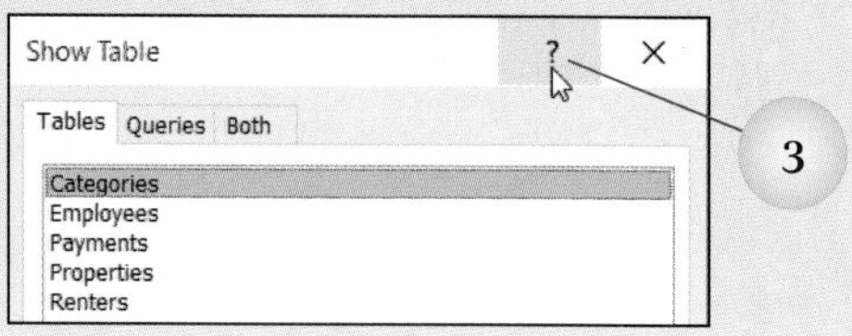

5. Read the information about table relationships and then close the Access Help window.
6. Close the Show Table dialog box and then close the Relationships window.
7. Click the File tab and then click the *Open* option.
8. At the Open backstage area, click the Microsoft Access Help button in the upper right corner.
9. Read the information in the Access Help window.
10. Close the Access Help window and then press the Esc key to return to the database.

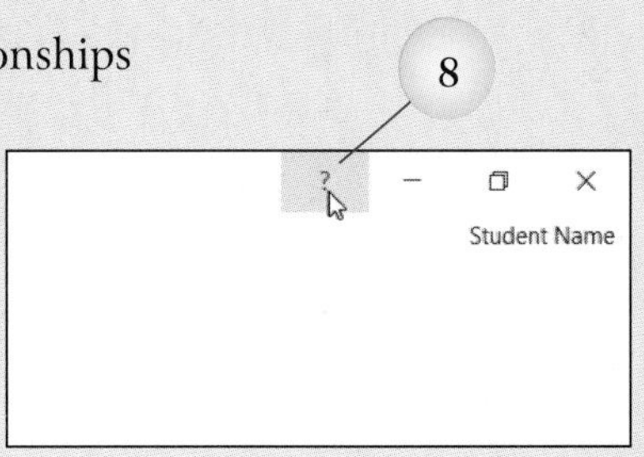

Using the Tell Me Feature

Hint Alt + Q is the keybord shortcut to make the *Tell Me* text box active.

Access 2016 includes a Tell Me feature that provides information as well as guidance on how to complete a function. To use Tell Me, click in the *Tell Me* text box on the ribbon to the right of the View tab and then type the function. Type text in the *Tell Me* text box and a drop-down list displays with options that are refined as the text is typed, which is referred to as "word-wheeling." The drop-down list displays options for completing the function or for displaying information on the function in the Access Help window.

Project 1i Using the Tell Me Feature — Part 9 of 9

1. With **4-SunProperties.accdb** open, open the query named *CitrusHeightsPropsQuery*.
2. Use the Tell Me feature to display the Find and Replace dialog box with the Replace tab selected and apply vertical gridlines by completing the following steps:
   a. Click in the *Tell Me* text box.
   b. Type replace.
   c. Click the *Replace* option at the drop-down list. (This displays the Find and Replace dialog box with the Replace tab selected.)
   d. Click the Cancel button to close the Find and Replace dialog box.
   e. Click in the *Tell Me* text box.
   f. Type gridlines.
   g. Click the right arrow at the right side of the *Gridlines* option at the drop-down list.
   h. Click the *Gridlines: Vertical* option at the side menu.
3. Save, print, and then close the CitrusHeightsPropsQuery query.
4. Close the **4-SunProperties.accdb** database.

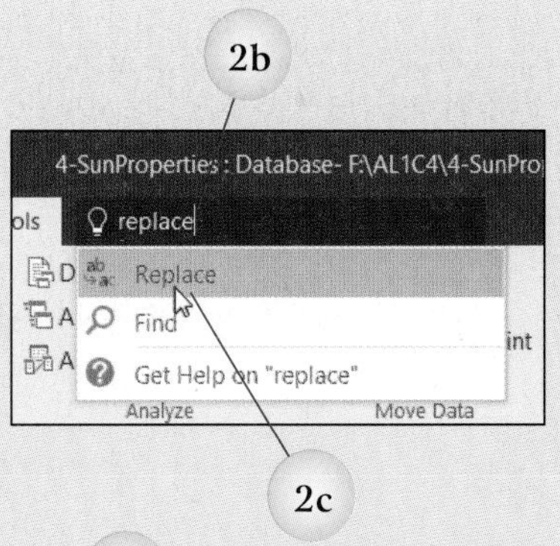

Check Your Work

Chapter Summary

- A table can be created in Datasheet view or Design view. Click the View button on the Table Tools Fields tab or the Home tab to switch between Datasheet view and Design view.
- Define each field in a table in the rows in the top section of Design view. Access automatically assigns the first field the name *ID* and assigns the AutoNumber data type.
- In Design view, specify a field name, data type, and description for each field.
- Assign a data type in Design view by clicking in a specific field in the *Data Type* column, clicking the down arrow at the right side of the field, and then clicking the data type at the drop-down list.
- Create a default value for a field in Design view with the *Default Value* property box in the *Field Properties* section.
- Use the Input Mask Wizard to set a pattern for how data is entered in a field. Use the *Format* property box to control what displays in a field.
- Use the *Validation Rule* property box in the *Field Properties* section in Design view to enter a statement containing a conditional test. Customize the error message that displays if the data entered violates the validation rule by typing that message in the *Validation Text* property box.
- Use the Lookup Wizard to confine data entered in a field to a specific list of items.
- Insert a field in Design view by clicking in the row immediately below where the new field is to be inserted and then clicking the Insert Rows button.
- Move a field in Design view by clicking in the field selector bar of the field to be moved and then dragging to the new position.
- Delete a field in Design view by clicking in the field selector bar at the left side of the field to be deleted and then clicking the Delete Rows button.
- Insert a *Total* row in a table in Datasheet view by clicking the Totals button in the Records group on the Home tab, clicking the down arrow in the *Total* row field, and then clicking a function at the drop-down list.
- Click the Ascending button in the Sort & Filter group on the Home tab to sort records in ascending order and click the Descending button to sort records in descending order.
- To print specific records in a table, select the records, display the Print dialog box, make sure *Selected Record(s)* is selected, and then click OK.
- Apply formatting to a table in Datasheet view with options and buttons in the Text Formatting group on the Home tab. Depending on the option or button selected, formatting is applied to all of the data in a table or data in a specific column in the table.
- To format text in a specific field, change the data type to Long Text and then specify rich text formatting. Do this in Design view with the *Text Format* property box in the *Field Properties* section.
- Use the spelling feature to find misspelled words in a table and consider possible replacement words. Begin checking the spelling in a table by clicking the Spelling button in the Records group on the Home tab.

- Use options at the Find and Replace dialog box with the Find tab selected to search for specific field entries in a table. Use options at the Find and Replace dialog box with the Replace tab selected to search for specific data and replace it with other data.
- Click the Microsoft Access Help button or press the F1 function key to display the Access Help window. At this window, type a topic in the search text box and then press the Enter key.
- The ScreenTip for some buttons displays with a Help icon and the text *Tell me more*. Click this hyperlinked text or press the F1 function key and the Access Help window opens with information about the button.
- Some dialog boxes and backstage areas contain a Help button that, when clicked, displays information specific to the dialog box or backstage area.
- The Tell Me feature provides information and guidance on how to complete a function. The *Tell Me* text box is on the ribbon to the right of the View tab.

Commands Review

FEATURE	RIBBON TAB, GROUP	BUTTON	KEYBOARD SHORTCUT
Access Help window		?	F1
align text left	Home, Text Formatting		
align text right	Home, Text Formatting		
alternate row color	Home, Text Formatting		
background color	Home, Text Formatting		
bold formatting	Home, Text Formatting	B	
center text	Home, Text Formatting		
delete field	Table Tools Design, Tools		
Design view	Home, Views OR Table Tools Fields, Views		
Find and Replace dialog box with Find tab selected	Home, Find		Ctrl + F
Find and Replace dialog box with Replace tab selected	Home, Find	ab ac	Ctrl + H
font	Home, Text Formatting	Calibri (Detail)	
font color	Home, Text Formatting	A	
font size	Home, Text Formatting	11	
gridlines	Home, Text Formatting		
insert field	Table Tools Design, Tools		

FEATURE	RIBBON TAB, GROUP	BUTTON	KEYBOARD SHORTCUT
italic formatting	Home, Text Formatting		
sort records ascending	Home, Sort & Filter		
sort records descending	Home, Sort & Filter		
spelling check	Home, Records		F7
Tell Me feature			Alt + Q
Total row	Home, Records		
underline formatting	Home, Text Formatting		

Workbook

Chapter study tools and assessment activities are available in the *Workbook* ebook. These resources are designed to help you further develop and demonstrate mastery of the skills learned in this chapter.

Unit assessment activities are also available in the *Workbook*. These activities are designed to help you demonstrate mastery of the skills learned in this unit.

Microsoft®

Access® Level 1

Unit 2

Creating Forms and Reports

Microsoft®

Access®

CHAPTER 5

Creating Forms

Performance Objectives

Upon successful completion of Chapter 5, you will be able to:

1 Create a form using the Form button
2 Change views in a form
3 Print a form
4 Navigate in a form
5 Delete a form
6 Add records to and delete records from a form
7 Sort records in a form
8 Create a form with a related table
9 Manage control objects in a form
10 Format a form
11 Apply conditional formatting to data in a form
12 Add an existing field to a form
13 Insert a calculation in a form
14 Create a split form and multiple items form
15 Create a form using the Form Wizard

Precheck

Check your current skills to help focus your study.

In this chapter, you will learn how to create forms from database tables, improving the data display and making data entry easier. Access offers several methods for presenting data on the screen for easier data entry. You will create a form using the Form button, create a split form and multiple items form, and use the Form Wizard to create a form. You will also learn how to customize control objects, insert control objects and fields, and apply formatting to a form.

SNAP

If you are a SNAP user, launch the Precheck and Tutorials from your Assignments page.

Data Files

Before beginning chapter work, copy the AL1C5 folder to your storage medium and then make AL1C5 the active folder.

Project 1 **Create Forms with the Form Button** **7 Parts**

You will use the Form button to create forms with fields in the Clients, Representatives, and Sales tables. You will also add, delete, and print records and use buttons on the Form Layout Tools Format tab to apply formatting to control objects in the forms.

Preview Finished Project

Creating a Form

Hint A form allows you to focus on a single record at a time.

Hint Save a form before making changes or applying formatting to it.

Access offers a variety of options for presenting data in a clear and attractive format. For instance, data can be viewed, added, or edited in a table in Datasheet view. When data is entered in a table in Datasheet view, multiple records display at the same time. If a record contains several fields, not all of the fields in the record may be visible at the same time. Create a form, however, and all of the fields for a record are generally visible on the screen.

A form is an object used to enter and edit data in a table or query. It is a user-friendly interface for viewing, adding, editing, and deleting records. A form is also useful in helping to prevent incorrect data from being entered and it can be used to control access to specific data. Several methods are available for creating forms. This chapter covers creating forms using the Form, Split Form, and Multiple Items buttons, as well as the Form Wizard.

Tutorial

Creating a Form Using the Form Button

Creating a Form Using the Form Button

The simplest method for creating a form is to click a table in the Navigation pane, click the Create tab, and then click the Form button in the Forms groups. Figure 5.1 shows the form that will be created in Project 1a with the Sales table in 5-Dearborn.accdb. Access creates the form using all fields in the table in a vertical layout and displays the form in Layout view with the Form Layout Tools Design tab active.

Form

Form View

Layout View

Quick Steps

Create a Form with the Form Button

1. Click table in Navigation pane.
2. Click Create tab.
3. Click Form button.

Changing Views

Click the Form button to create a form and the form displays in Layout view. This is one of three views for working with forms. Use the Form view to enter and manage records. Use the Layout view to view the data and modify the appearance and contents of the form. Use the Design view to view the form's structure and modify it. Change views with the View button in the Views group on the Form Layout Tools Design tab or with buttons in the view area at the right side of the Status bar. An existing form can be opened in Layout view by right-clicking the form name in the Navigation pane and then clicking *Layout View* at the shortcut menu.

Printing a Form

Print all of the records in a form by clicking the File tab, clicking the *Print* option, and then clicking the *Quick Print* option. To print a specific record in a form, click the File tab, click the *Print* option, and then click the next *Print* option. At the Print dialog box, click the *Selected Record(s)* option and then click OK. Print a range of records by clicking the *Pages* option in the *Print Range* section of the Print dialog

Figure 5.1 Form Created with the Sales Table

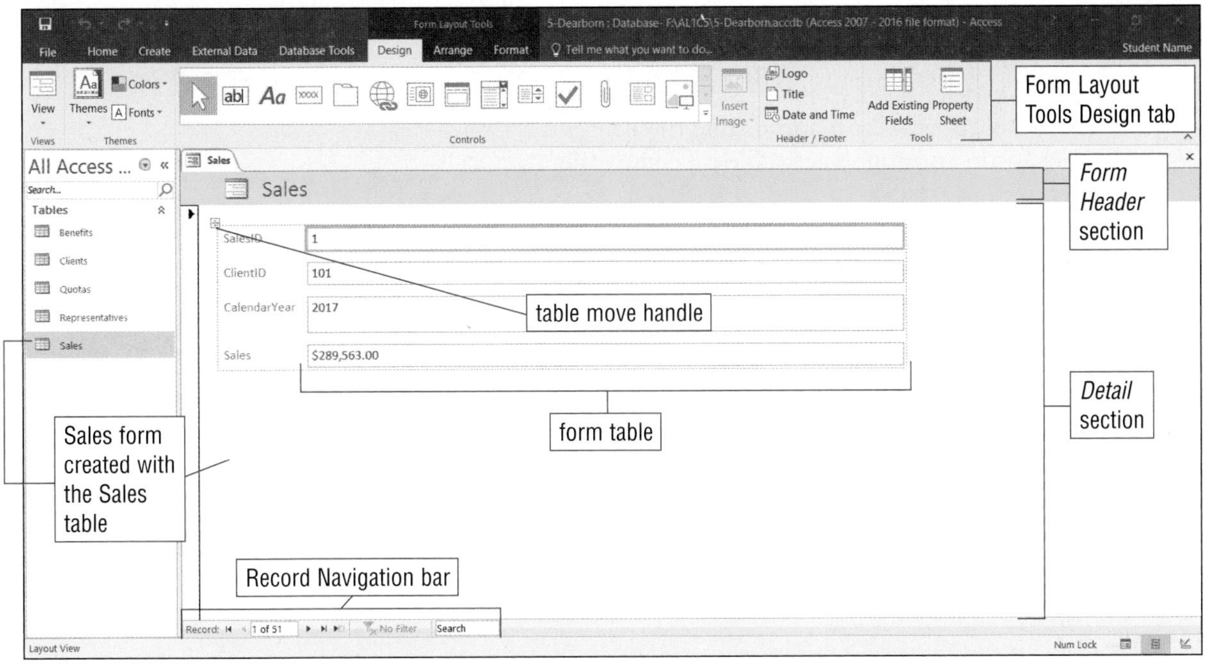

Quick Steps

Print a Specific Record

1. Click File tab.
2. Click *Print* option.
3. Click next *Print* option.
4. Click *Selected Record(s).*
5. Click OK.

box and then entering the beginning record number in the *From* text box and the ending record number in the *To* text box.

Before printing a form, display the form in Print Preview. If column shading displays on the second page without any other data, decrease the width of the column. To do this, click the Columns button in the Page Layout group on the Print Preview tab. At the Page Setup dialog box with the Columns tab selected, decrease the measurement in the *Width* measurement box, and then click OK.

Deleting a Form

If a form is no longer needed in a database, delete the form. Delete a form by clicking the form name in the Navigation pane, clicking the Delete button in the Records group on the Home tab, and then clicking the Yes button at the confirmation message. Another method is to right-click the form name in the Navigation pane, click *Delete* at the shortcut menu, and then click Yes at the message. If a form is being deleted from a computer's hard drive, the confirmation message will not display. This is because Access automatically sends the deleted form to the Recycle Bin, where it can be retrieved if necessary.

Tutorial

Navigating in Objects

Navigating in a Form

When a form displays in Form view or Layout view, navigation buttons display along the bottom of the form in the Record Navigation bar, as identified in Figure 5.1. Use these navigation buttons to display the first, previous, next, or last record in the form or add a new record. Navigate to a specific record by clicking in the *Current Record* box, selecting the current number, typing the number of the record to view, and then pressing Enter. The keyboard also can be used to navigate in a form. Press the Page Down key to move forward or the Page Up key to move back a single record. Press Ctrl + Home to display the first record or press Ctrl + End to display the last record.

Project 1a Creating a Form with the Sales Table and Deleting a Form

1. Display the Open dialog box with AL1C5 folder the active folder.
2. Open **5-Dearborn.accdb** and enable the content.
3. Create a form with the Sales table by completing the following steps:
   a. Click *Sales* in the Tables group in the Navigation pane.
   b. Click the Create tab.
   c. Click the Form button in the Forms group.

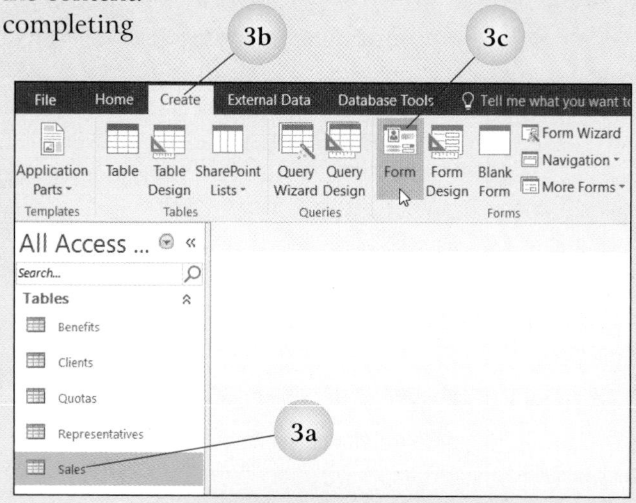

4. Switch to Form view by clicking the View button in the Views group on the Form Layout Tools Design tab.
5. Navigate in the form by completing the following steps:
   a. Click the Next record button in the Record Navigation bar to display the next record.
   b. Click in the *Current Record* box, select any numbers that display, type 15, and then press the Enter key.
   c. Click the First record button in the Record Navigation bar to display the first record.

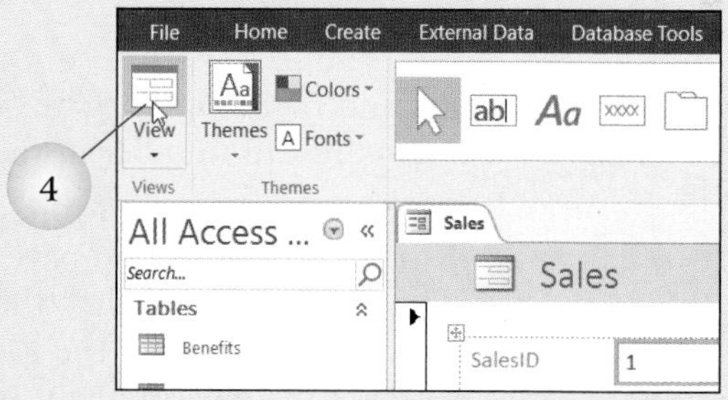

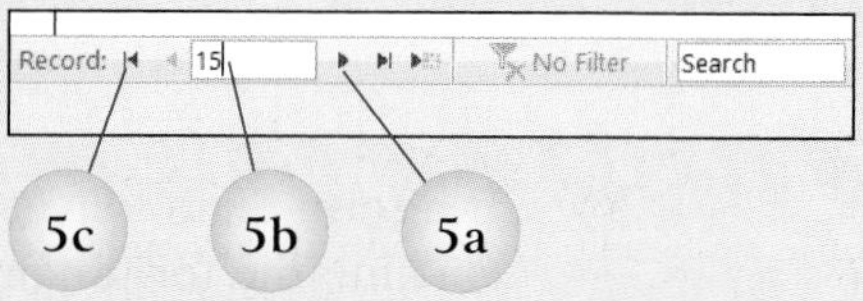

6. Save the form by completing the following steps:
   a. Click the Save button on the Quick Access Toolbar.
   b. At the Save As dialog box, with *Sales* inserted in the *Form Name* text box, click OK.
7. Print the current record in the form by completing the following steps:
   a. Click the File tab and then click the *Print* option.
   b. Click the next *Print* option.
   c. At the Print dialog box, click the *Selected Record(s)* option in the *Print Range* section and then click OK.

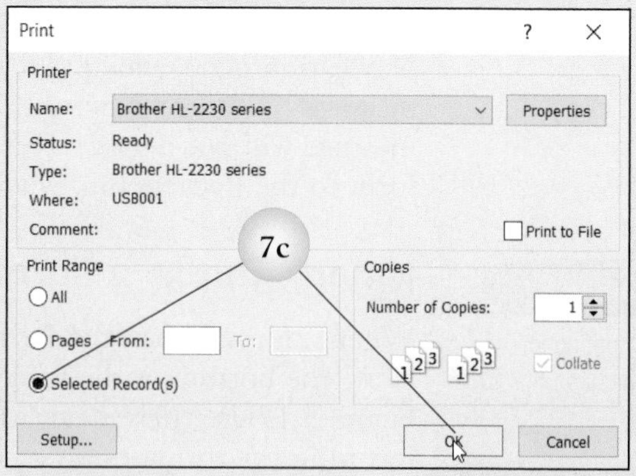

8. Close the Sales form.
9. Delete the RepBenefits form by right-clicking *RepBenefits* in the Navigation pane, clicking *Delete* at the shortcut menu, and then clicking Yes at the confirmation message.

Check Your Work

Tutorial

Adding and Deleting Records in a Form

New (blank) record

Delete

Quick Steps

Add a Record
Click New (blank) record button on Record Navigation bar.
OR
1. Click Home tab.
2. Click New button.

Delete a Record
1. Click Home tab.
2. Click Delete button arrow.
3. Click *Delete Record*.
4. Click Yes.

Adding and Deleting Records

Add a new record to the form by clicking the New (blank) record button (contains a right-pointing arrow and a yellow asterisk) on the Record Navigation bar along the bottom of the form. A new record also can be added to a form by clicking the Home tab and then clicking the New button in the Records group.

To delete a record, display the record, click the Home tab, click the Delete button arrow in the Records group, and then click *Delete Record* at the drop-down list. At the confirmation message, click the Yes button. Add records to or delete records from the table from which the form was created and the form will reflect the additions or deletions. Also, if additions or deletions are made to the form, the changes are reflected in the table from which the form was created.

Sorting Records

Sort data in a form by clicking in the field containing data on which to sort and then clicking the Ascending button or Descending button in the Sort & Filter group on the Home tab. Click the Ascending button to sort text in alphabetic order from A to Z, numbers from lowest to highest, and dates from earliest to latest. Click the Descending button to sort text in alphabetic order from Z to A, numbers from highest to lowest, and dates from latest to earliest.

Project 1b Adding, Deleting, and Sorting Records in a Form

Part 2 of 7

1. With **5-Dearborn.accdb** open, open the Sales table (not the form) and add a new record by completing the following steps:
   a. Click the New (blank) record button in the Record Navigation bar.

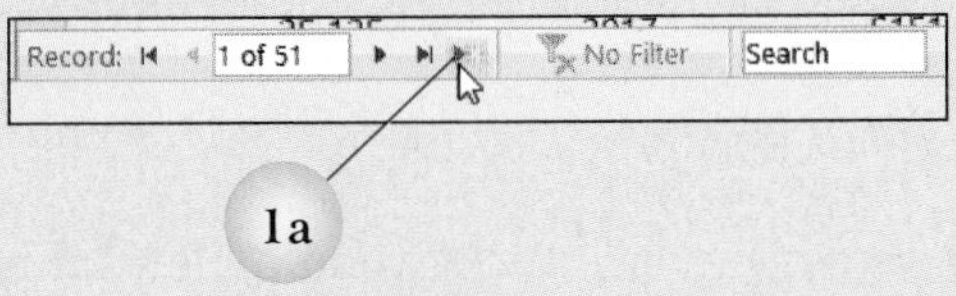

   b. At the new blank record, type the following information in the specified fields. (Move to the next field by pressing the Tab key or the Enter key; move to the previous field by pressing Shift + Tab.)

SalesID	(This is an AutoNumber field, so press the Tab key.)
ClientID	*127*
CalendarYear	*2018*
Sales	*176420*

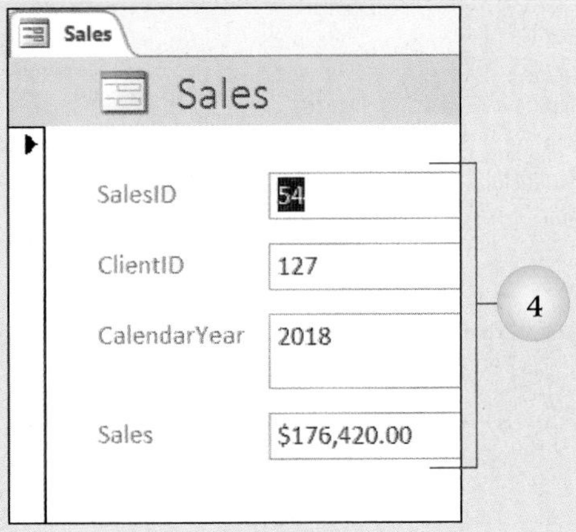

2. Close the Sales table.
3. Open the Sales form.
4. Click the Last record button on the Record Navigation bar and notice that the new record you added to the table also has been added to the form.

5. Delete the second record (*SalesID 3*) in the form by completing the following steps:
   a. Click the First record button in the Record Navigation bar.
   b. Click the Next record button in the Record Navigation bar.
   c. With Record 2 active, click the Delete button arrow in the Records group on the Home tab and then click *Delete Record* at the drop-down list.

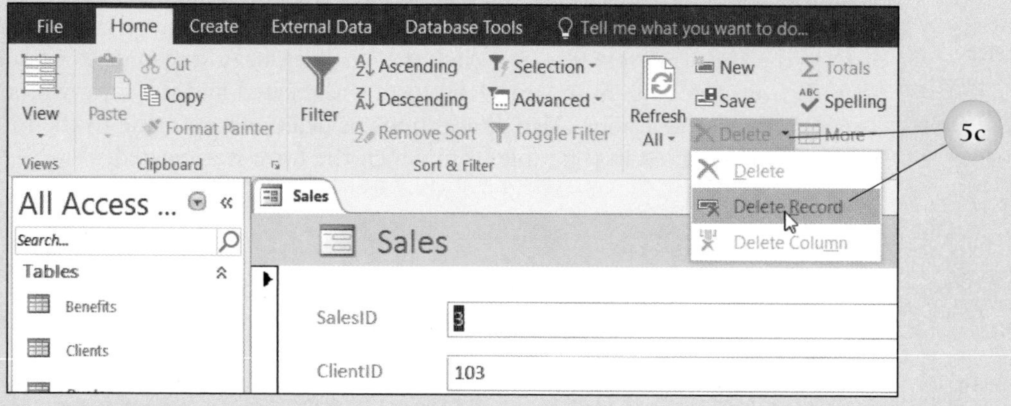

   d. At the confirmation message, click the Yes button.
6. Click the New (blank) record button in the Record Navigation bar and then type the following information in the specified fields:

SalesID	(Press the Tab key.)
ClientID	*103*
CalendarYear	*2018*
Sales	*110775*

7. Sort the records in the form by completing the following steps:
   a. Click in the field containing *103* and then click the Ascending button in the Sort & Filter group on the Home tab.
   b. Click in the field containing *$289,563.00* and then click the Descending button in the Sort & Filter group.
   c. Click in the field containing *36* and then click the Ascending button in the Sort & Filter group.
8. Close the Sales form.

Check Your Work

Tutorial

Creating a Form with a Related Table

Creating a Form with a Related Table

When the form was created with the Sales table, only the Sales table fields displayed in the form. If a form is created with a table that has a one-to-many relationship established, Access adds a datasheet to the form that is based on the related table.

For example, in Project 1c, a form will be created from the Representatives table and, since it is related to the Clients table by a one-to-many relationship, Access inserts a datasheet at the bottom of the form containing all of the records in the Clients table. Figure 5.2 displays the form that will be created in Project 1c. Notice the datasheet at the bottom of the form.

If only a single one-to-many relationship has been created in a database, the datasheet for the related table displays in the form. If multiple one-to-many relationships have been created in a table, Access will not display any datasheets when a form is created with that table.

Figure 5.2 Representatives Form with Clients Datasheet

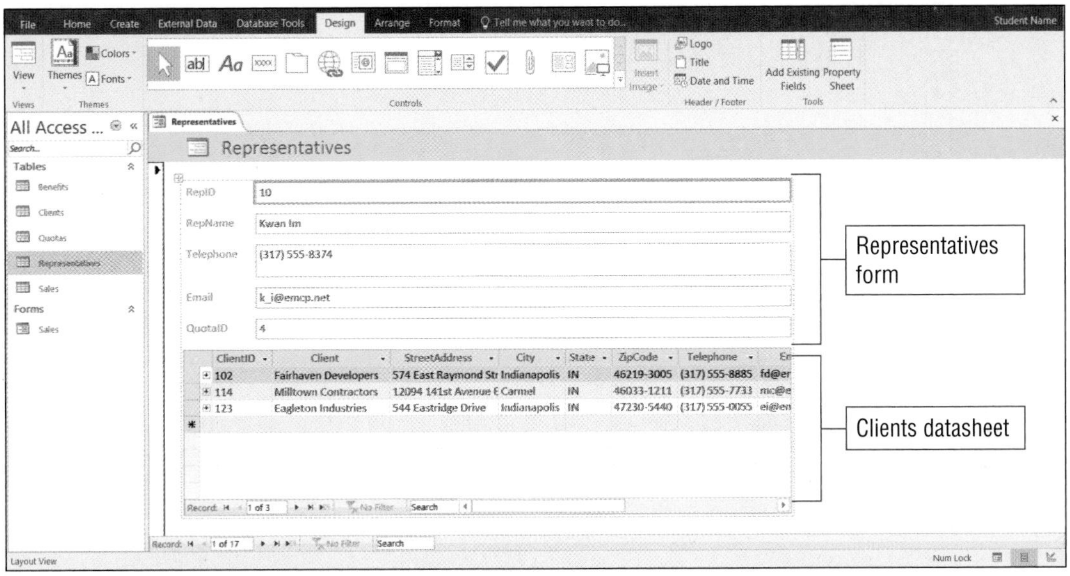

Project 1c Creating a Form with a Related Table

Part 3 of 7

1. With **5-Dearborn.accdb** open, create a form with the Representatives table by completing the following steps:
   a. Click *Representatives* in the Tables group in the Navigation pane.
   b. Click the Create tab.
   c. Click the Form button in the Forms group.
2. Insert a new record in the Clients table for representative *12* (Catherine Singleton) by completing the following steps:
   a. Click two times on the Next record button in the Record Navigation bar at the bottom of the form window (not the Record Navigation bar in the Clients datasheet) to display the record for Catherine Singleton.
   b. Click in the cell immediately below *127* in the *ClientID* field in the Clients datasheet.

c. Type the following information in the specified fields:

ClientID	*129*	*State*	*IN*
Client	*Dan-Built Construction*	*ZipCode*	*460339050*
StreetAddress	*903 James Street*	*Telephone*	*3175551122*
City	*Carmel*	*Email*	*dc@emcp.net*

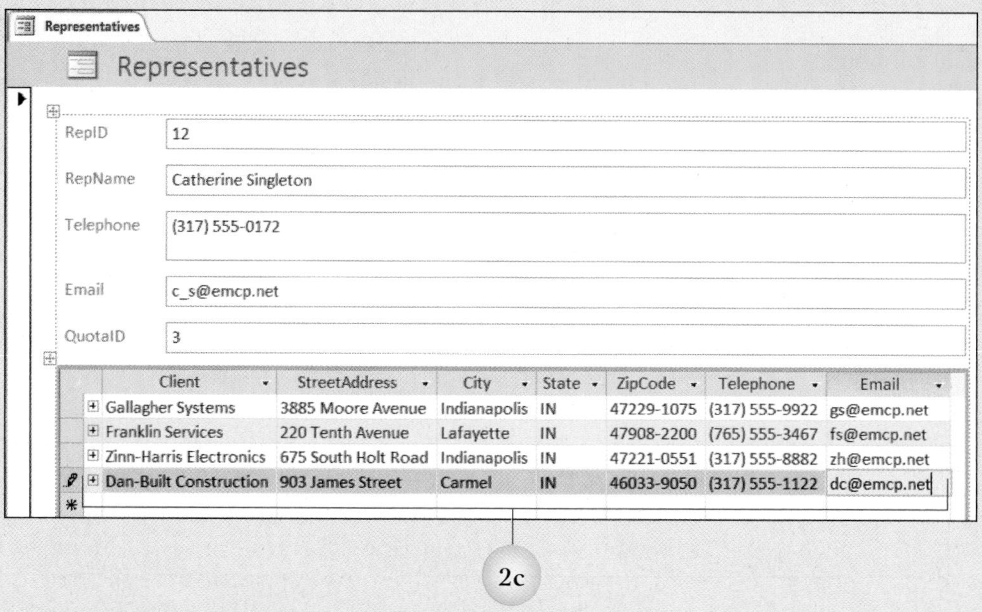

3. Click the Save button on the Quick Access Toolbar and then, at the Save As dialog box with *Representatives* in the *Form Name* text box, click OK.
4. Print the current record in the form by completing the following steps:
   a. Click the File tab and then click the *Print* option.
   b. Click the next *Print* option.
   c. At the Print dialog box, click the *Selected Record(s)* option in the *Print Range* section and then click OK.
5. Close the Representatives form.

Check Your Work

Tutorial

Managing Control Objects in a Form

Hint Almost all changes can be made to a form in Layout view.

Managing Control Objects

A form, like a table in a Word document, is made up of cells that are arranged in rows and columns. Each cell in a form can contain one control object, which is an object that displays a title or description, accepts data, or performs an action. For example, a cell can contain a label control object that displays a field name from the table used to create the form, a text box control that displays and accepts data, or a logo control object that will display a logo image. Control objects are contained in the *Form Header* and *Detail* sections of the form. (Refer to Figure 5.1 on page 137.) The control objects in the *Detail* section are contained within a form table.

Manage control objects with buttons on the Form Layout Tools ribbon with the Design tab, Arrange tab, or Format tab selected. When a form is opened in Layout view, the Form Layout Tools Design tab is active.

Inserting Data in a Control Object

Logo

Title

Date and Time

Use buttons in the Header/Footer group on the Form Layout Tools Design tab to insert a logo, form title, or date and time. Click the Logo button and the Insert Picture dialog box displays. Browse to the folder containing the image and then double-click the image file. Click the Title button and the current title is selected. Type the new title and then press the Enter key. Click the Date and Time button in the Header/Footer group and the Date and Time dialog box displays. At this dialog box, choose a date and time format and then click OK. The date and time are inserted at the right side of the *Form Header* section.

Resizing Control Objects

When Access creates a form from a table, the cells in the first column in the *Detail* section of the form contain the label control objects and displays the field names from the table. The second column of cells contains the text box control objects that display the field values entered in the table. The control objects in the *Form Header* section and the columns in the *Detail* section can be resized by dragging the border of a selected control object or with the *Width* property box on the Format tab in the Property Sheet task pane.

To resize a control object by dragging, select the object (displays with an orange border) and then position the mouse pointer on the left or right border of the object until the pointer displays as a left-and-right pointing arrow. Click and hold down the left mouse button, drag left or right to change the width of the column, and then release the mouse button. Complete similar steps to change the height of a control object. When dragging a border, a line and character count displays at the left side of the Status bar. Use the line and character count numbers to move the border to a precise location. When dragging the border of a label control or text box control object, the entire column width is resized.

In addition to dragging a control object border, the column width can be adjusted with the *Width* property box on the Format tab in the Property Sheet task pane and the height can be adjusted with the *Height* property box. Display this task pane by clicking the Property Sheet button in the Tools group. In the Property Sheet task pane with the Format tab selected, select the current measurement in the *Width* or *Height* property box, type the new measurement, and then press the Enter key. Close the Property Sheet task pane by clicking the Close button in the upper right corner of the task pane.

Deleting a Control Object

To delete a control object from the form, click the object and then press the Delete key. Or, right-click the object and then click *Delete* at the shortcut menu. To delete a form row, right-click an object in the row to be deleted and then click *Delete Row* at the shortcut menu. To delete a column, right-click one of the objects in the column to be deleted and then click *Delete Column* at the shortcut menu.

Tutorial

Inserting Control Objects

Inserting Control Objects

The Controls group on the Form Layout Tools Design tab contains a number of control objects that can be inserted in a form. By default, the Select button is active. With this button active, use the mouse pointer to select control objects.

Select

Text Box

A new label control and text box control object can be inserted in a form by clicking the Text Box button in the Controls group and then clicking in the desired position in the form. Click the label control object, select the default text, and then type the label text.

Text can be entered in a label control object in Layout view, but not in a text box control object. In Form view, data can be entered in a text box control object but text in a label control object cannot be edited. The Controls group contains a number of additional buttons for inserting control objects in a form, such as a hyperlink, combo box, or image.

Project 1d Creating a Form and Customizing the Design of a Form — Part 4 of 7

1. With **5-Dearborn.accdb** open, create a form with the Clients table and delete the accompanying datasheet by completing the following steps:
   a. Click *Clients* in the Tables group in the Navigation pane.
   b. Click the Create tab.
   c. Click the Form button in the Forms group.
   d. Click in the *SalesID* field in the datasheet that displays below the form.
   e. Click the table move handle in the upper left corner of the datasheet (see image at right).
   f. Press the Delete key.

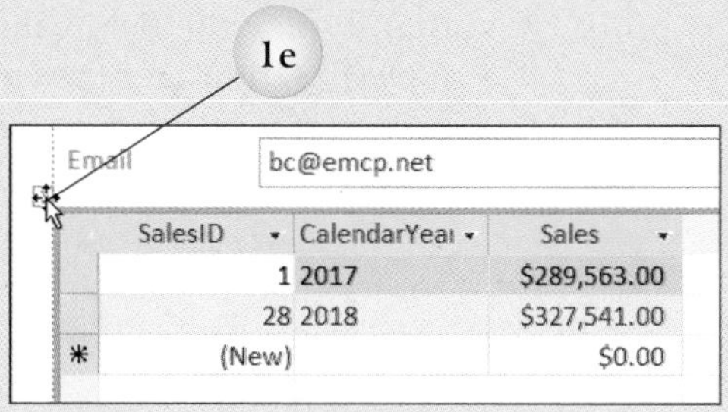

2. Insert a logo image in the *Form Header* section by completing the following steps:
   a. Right-click the logo object that displays in the *Form Header* section (to the left of the title *Clients*) and then click *Delete* at the shortcut menu.
   b. Click the Logo button in the Header/Footer group.
   c. At the Insert Picture dialog box, navigate to the AL1C5 folder on your storage medium and then double-click the file named ***DearbornLogo.jpg***.

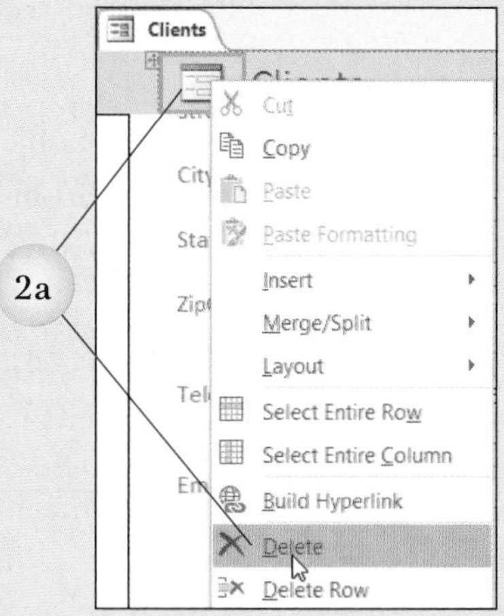

3. Change the title by completing the following steps:
   a. Click the Title button in the Header/Footer group. (This selects *Clients* in the *Form Header* section.)
   b. Type Dearborn Clients Form and then press the Enter key.
4. Insert the date and time in the *Form Header* section by completing the following steps:
   a. Click the Date and Time button in the Header/Footer group.
   b. At the Date and Time dialog box, click OK.

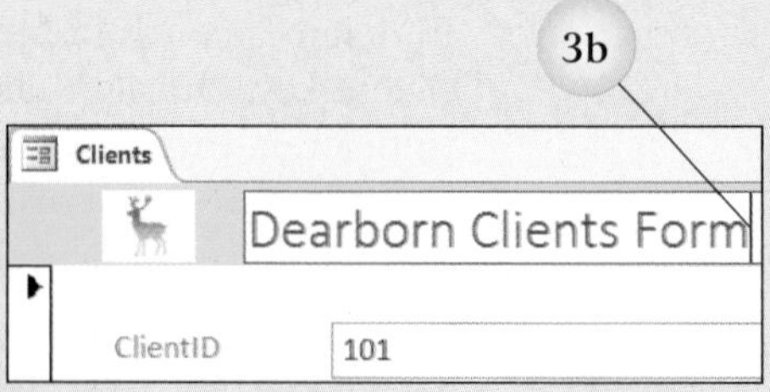

5. Size the control object containing the title by completing the following steps:
   a. Click any field outside the title and then click the title to select the control object.
   b. Position the mouse pointer on the right border of the selected object until the pointer displays as a black left-and-right-pointing arrow.

c. Click and hold down the left mouse button, drag to the left until the right border is immediately right of the title, and then release the mouse button.

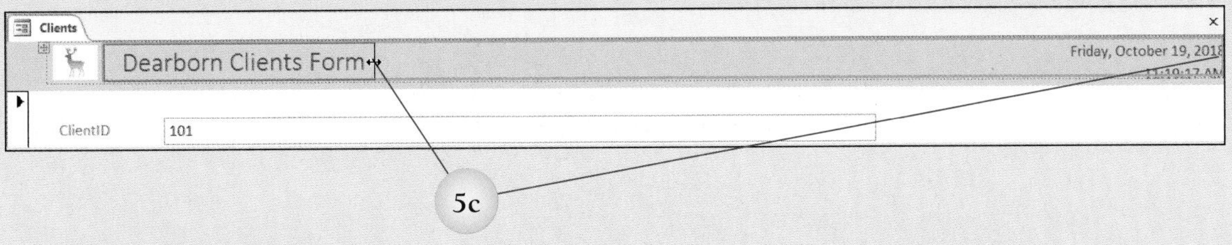

6. Size and move the control objects containing the date and time by completing the following steps:
   a. Click the date to select the control object.
   b. Press and hold down the Shift key, click the time, and then release the Shift key. (Both control objects should be selected.)
   c. Position the mouse pointer on the left border of the selected objects until the pointer displays as a black left-and-right-pointing arrow.
   d. Click and hold down the left mouse button, drag to the right until the border is immediately left of the date, and then release the mouse button.

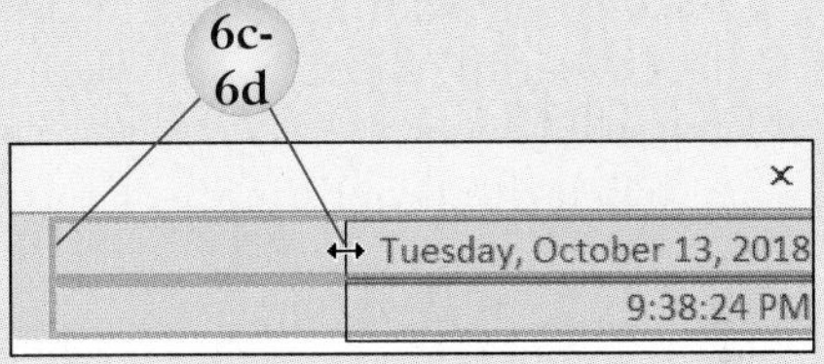

   e. Position the mouse pointer in the selected objects until the pointer displays with a four-headed arrow attached.
   f. Click and hold down the left mouse button, drag the outline of the date and time objects to the left until the outline displays near the title, and then release the mouse button.
7. Decrease the size of the second column of cells containing control objects in the *Detail* section by completing the following steps:
   a. Click the text box control object containing the client number *101*. (This selects and inserts an orange border around the object.)
   b. Position the mouse pointer on the right border of the selected object until the pointer displays as a black left-and-right-pointing arrow.
   c. Click and hold down the left mouse button, drag to the left until *Lines: 1 Characters: 30* displays at the left side of the Status bar, and then release the mouse button.

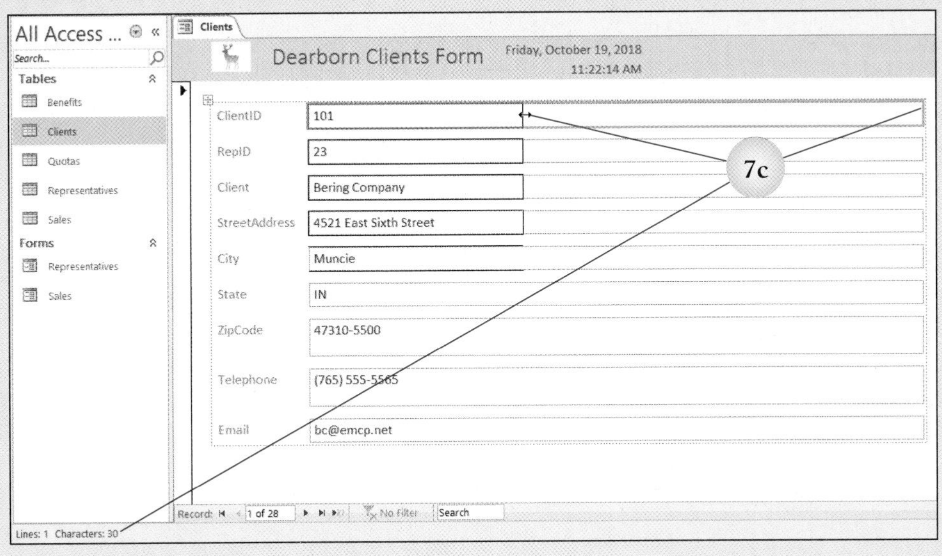

8. Insert a label control object by completing the following steps:
   a. Click the Label button in the Controls group.
   b. Click immediately right of the text box control object containing the telephone number *(765) 555-5565*. (This inserts the label to the right of the *Telephone* text box control object.)
   c. With the insertion point positioned inside the label, type Type the telephone number without symbols or spaces and then press the Enter key.

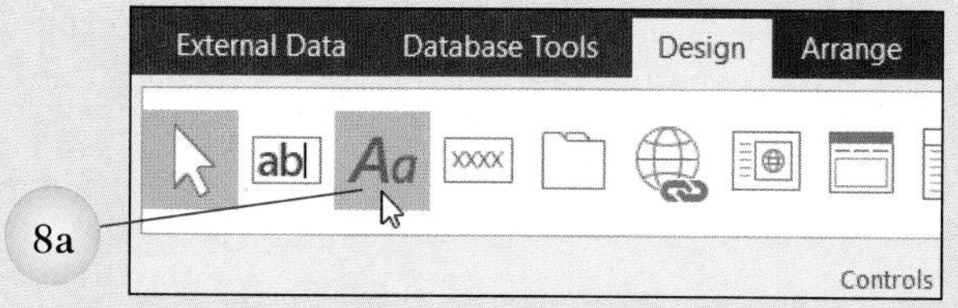

9. Change the width and height of the new label control object by completing the following steps:
   a. Click the Property Sheet button in the Tools group.
   b. In the Property Sheet task pane that displays, if necessary, click the Format tab.
   c. Select the current measurement in the *Width* property box, type 2, and then press the Enter key.
   d. With the current measurement selected in the *Height* property box, type 0.4.
   e. Close the Property Sheet task pane by clicking the Close button in the upper right corner of the task pane.

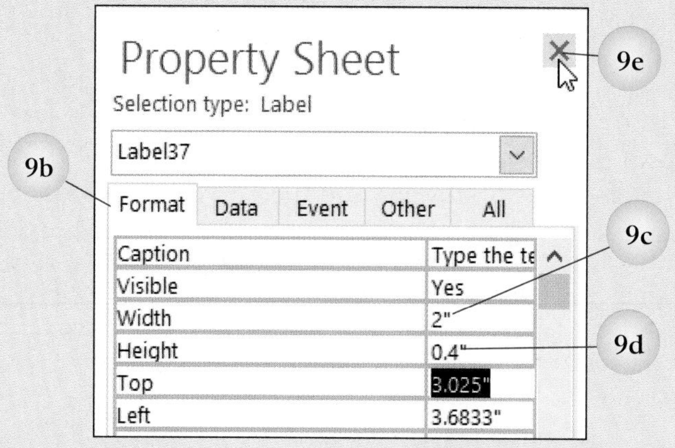

10. Delete the control object containing the time by clicking the time to select the object and then pressing the Delete key.
11. Click the Save button on the Quick Access Toolbar.
12. At the Save As dialog box with *Clients* in the *Form Name* text box, click OK.

Check Your Work

Moving a Form Table

Hint You can move a control object by dragging it to a new location.

The control objects in the *Detail* section in a form in Layout view are contained in cells within the form table. Click in a control object and the table move handle is visible. The table move handle is a small square with a four-headed arrow inside that displays in the upper left corner of the table. (Refer to Figure 5.1 on page 137.) To move the table, position the mouse pointer on the table move handle, click and hold down the left mouse button, drag the table to the new position, and then release the mouse button.

Arranging a Control Object

The Form Layout Tools Arrange tab contains options for selecting, inserting, deleting, arranging, merging, and splitting cells. When a label control object was inserted to the right of the *Telephone* text box control object in Project 1d, empty cells were inserted in the form above and below the new label control object. Select a control object or cell by clicking in the object or cell. Select adjacent control objects or cells by pressing and holding down the Shift key while clicking in each of the objects or cells. To select nonadjacent control objects or cells, press and hold down the Ctrl key while clicking in each of the objects or cells.

Select Row

Select Column

Select a row of cells by clicking the Select Row button in the Rows & Columns group or by right-clicking in a cell and then clicking *Select Entire Row* at the shortcut menu. To select a column of cells, click the Select Column button in the Rows & Columns group or right-click an object or cell and then click *Select Entire Column* at the shortcut menu. A column of cells can also be selected by positioning the mouse pointer at the top of the column until the pointer displays as a small black arrow that points down and then clicking the left mouse button.

The Rows & Columns group contains buttons for inserting a row or column of blank cells. To insert a new row, select a cell in a row and then click the Insert Above button to insert a row of blank cells above the current row or click the Insert Below button to insert a row of blank cells below the current row. Complete similar steps to insert a new column of blank cells to the left or right of the current column.

Insert Above

Insert Below

Merge

Split Vertically

Split Horizontally

Merge adjacent selected cells by clicking the Merge button in the Merge/Split group on the Form Layout Tools Arrange tab. A cell can contain only one control object. So, merging two cells, each containing a control object, is not possible. A cell containing a control object can be merged with an empty cell or cells. Split a cell by clicking in the cell to make it active and then clicking the Split Vertically button or Split Horizontally button in the Merge/Split group. When a cell is split, an empty cell is created to the right of the cell or below the cell.

Control Margins

Control Padding

A row of cells can be moved up or down by selecting the row and then clicking the Move Up button in the Move group or the Move Down button. Use the Control Margins button in the Position group to increase or decrease margins within cells. The Position group also contains a Control Padding button for increasing or decreasing spacing between cells.

The Table group at the left side of the Form Layout Tools Arrange tab contains buttons for applying gridlines to cells and changing the layout of the cells to a stacked or columnar layout.

Project 1e Arranging Control Objects in a Form

Part 5 of 7

1. With the Clients form in **5-Dearborn.accdb** open in Design view, select and merge cells by completing the following steps:
   a. Click to the right of the text box control object containing the text *101*. (This selects the empty cell.)
   b. Press and hold down the Shift key, click to the right of the text box control object containing the text *Muncie*, and then release the Shift key. (This selects five adjacent cells.)
   c. Click the Form Layout Tools Arrange tab.
   d. Click the Merge button in the Merge/Split group.

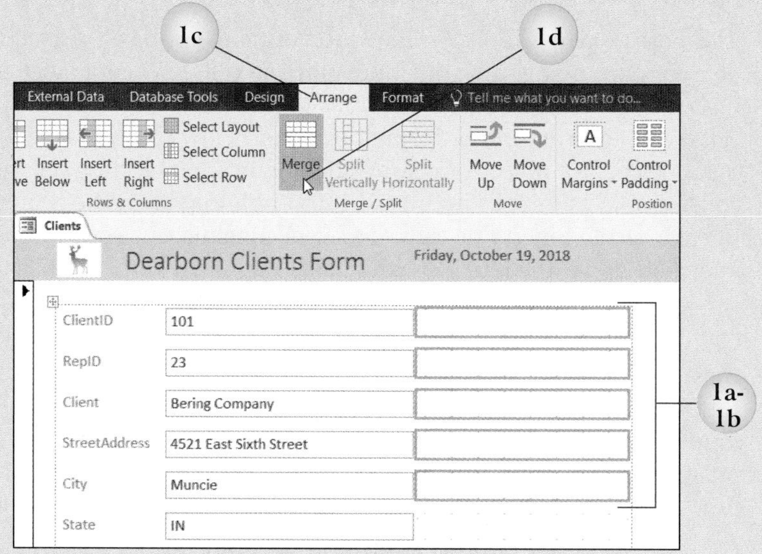

2. With the cells merged, insert an image control object and then insert an image by completing the following steps:
   a. Click the Form Layout Tools Design tab.
   b. Click the Image button in the Controls group.
   c. Move the mouse pointer (which displays as crosshairs with an image icon next to the crosshairs) to the location of the merged cell until the cell displays with pink fill color and then click the left mouse button.

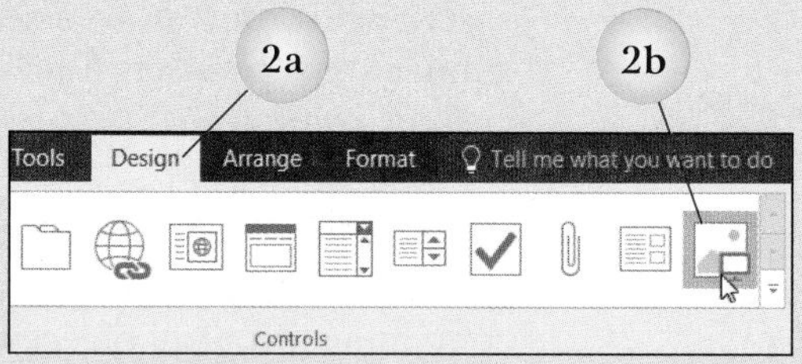

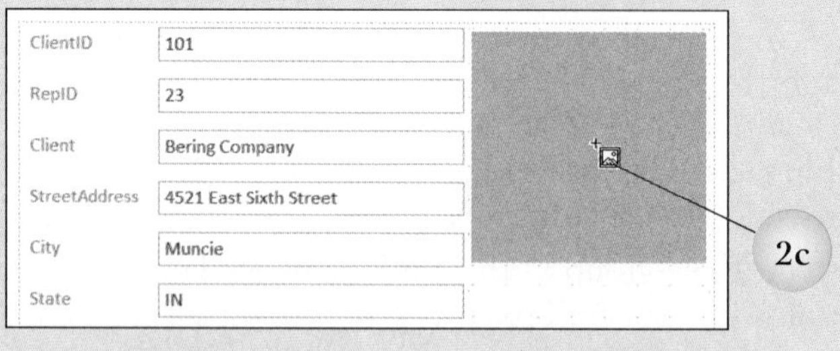

   d. At the Insert Picture dialog box, navigate to the AL1C5 folder on your storage medium and then double-click ***Dearborn.jpg***.

3. Move down a row of cells by completing the following steps:
   a. Click the Form Layout Tools Arrange tab.
   b. Click in the control object containing the text *Telephone*.
   c. Click the Select Row button in the Rows & Columns group.
   d. Click the Move Down button in the Move group.
4. Decrease the margins within cells, increase the spacing (padding) between cells in the form, and apply gridlines by completing the following steps:
   a. If necessary, click the Form Layout Tools Arrange tab.
   b. Click the Select Layout button in the Rows & Columns group. (This selects all cells in the form table.)
   c. Click the Control Margins button in the Position group and then click *Narrow* at the drop-down list.

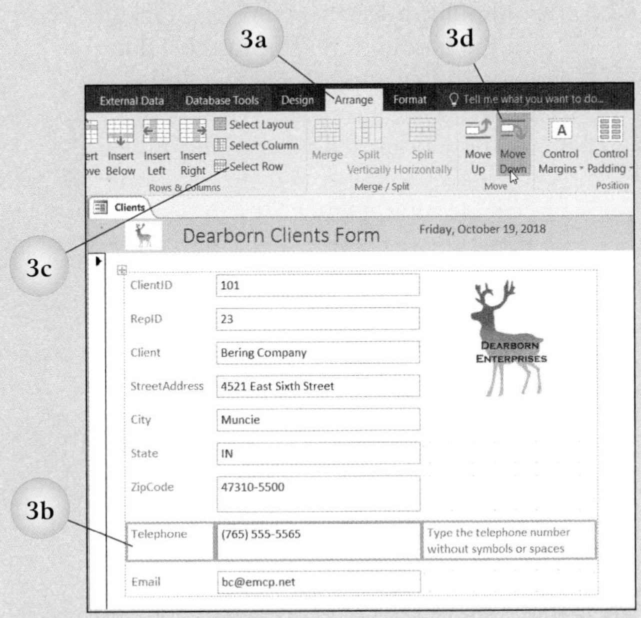

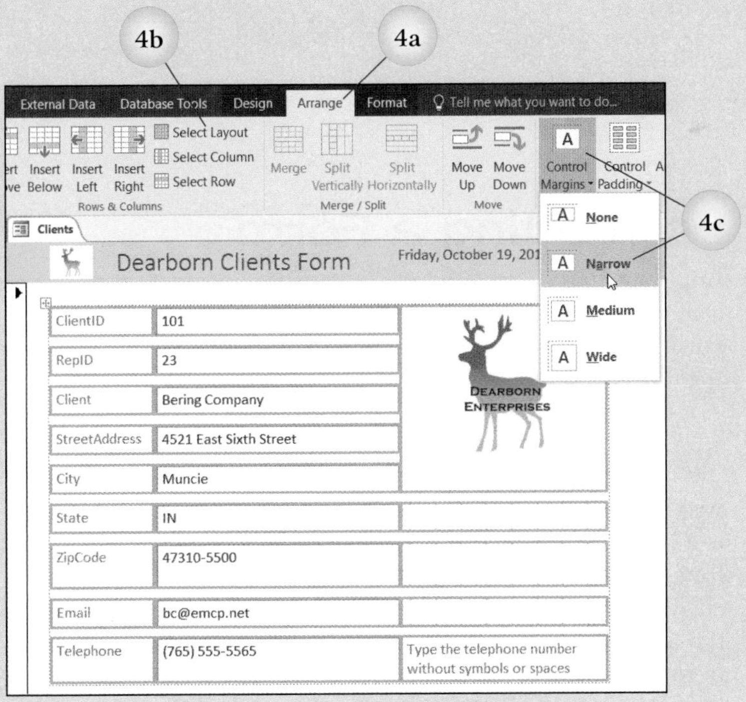

d. Click the Control Padding button in the Position group and then click *Medium* at the drop-down list.
e. Click the Gridlines button in the Table group and then click *Top* at the drop-down list.
f. Click the Gridlines button in the Table group, point to *Color*, and then click the *Orange, Accent 2, Darker 50%* option (sixth column, bottom row in the *Theme Colors* section).

5. Move the form table by completing the following steps:
   a. Position the mouse pointer on the table move handle (which displays as a small square with a four-headed arrow inside in the upper left corner of the table).
   b. Click and hold down the left mouse button, drag the form table up and to the left so it is positioned close to the top left border of the *Detail* section, and then release the mouse button.
6. Click in the control object containing the field name *ClientID*.
7. Save the Clients form.

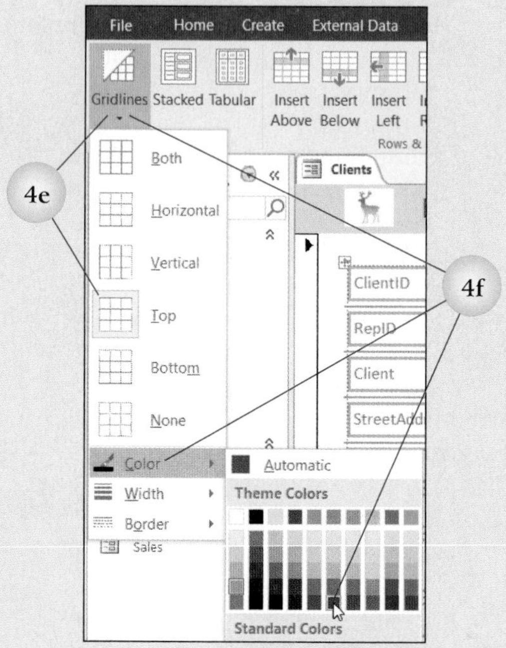

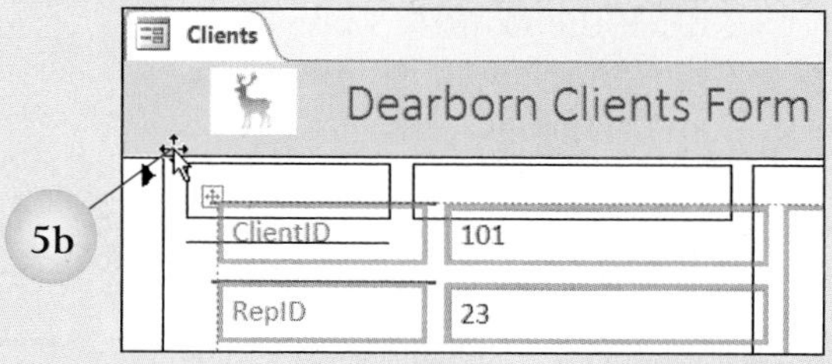

Check Your Work

Tutorial

Formatting a Form

Hint Themes available in Access are the same as the themes available in Word, Excel, and PowerPoint.

Themes

Colors

Fonts

Formatting a Form

Apply formatting to enhance the appearance of a form. Format a form by applying a theme, theme colors, and theme fonts; applying formatting with options on the Form Layout Tools Format tab; and applying conditional formatting that meets a specific criterion.

Applying Themes

Access provides a number of themes for formatting objects in a database. A theme is a set of formatting choices that include a color theme (a set of colors) and a font theme (a set of heading and body text fonts). To apply a theme to a form, click the Themes button in the Themes group on the Form Layout Tools Design tab and then click a theme at the drop-down gallery. Position the mouse pointer over a theme and the live preview feature will display the form with the theme formatting applied. When a theme is applied, any new objects created in the database will be formatted with that theme.

Further customize the formatting of a form with the Colors button and the Fonts button in the Themes group on the Form Layout Tools Design tab. To customize the theme colors, click the Colors button in the Themes group and then click an option at the drop-down list. Change the theme fonts by clicking the Fonts button in the Themes group and then clicking an option at the drop-down list.

Formatting with the Form Layout Tools Format Tab

Object

Select All

Background Image

Click the Form Layout Tools Format tab and buttons and options display for applying formatting to a form or specific cells in a form. To apply formatting to a specific cell, click the cell in the form or click the Object button arrow in the Selection group and then click the control object at the drop-down list. To format all cells in the form, click the Select All button in the Selection group. This selects all cells in the form, including cells in the *Form Header* section. To select all of the cells in the *Detail* section (and not the *Form Header* section), click in a cell in the *Detail* section and then click the table move handle.

Use buttons in the Font, Number, Background, and Control Formatting groups to apply formatting to a cell or selected cells in a form. Use options and buttons in the Font group to change the font, change the font size, apply text effects (such as bold and underline), and change the alignment of data in cells. If the form contains data with a Number or Currency data type, use buttons in the Number group to apply specific formatting to numbers. Insert a background image in the form using the Background Image button and apply formatting to cells with buttons in the Control Formatting group. Depending on what is selected in the form, some of the buttons may not be active.

Project 1f Formatting a Form **Part 6 of 7**

1. With the Clients form in **5-Dearborn.accdb** open and in Layout view, apply a theme by completing the following steps:
   a. Click the Form Layout Tools Design tab.
   b. Click the Themes button and then click the *Facet* option (second column, first row in the *Office* section).
2. Change the theme fonts by clicking the Fonts button in the Themes group and then clicking *Gill Sans MT* at the drop-down gallery. (You will need to scroll down the list to display *Gill Sans MT*.)
3. Change the theme colors by clicking the Colors button in the Themes group and then clicking *Orange* at the drop-down gallery.

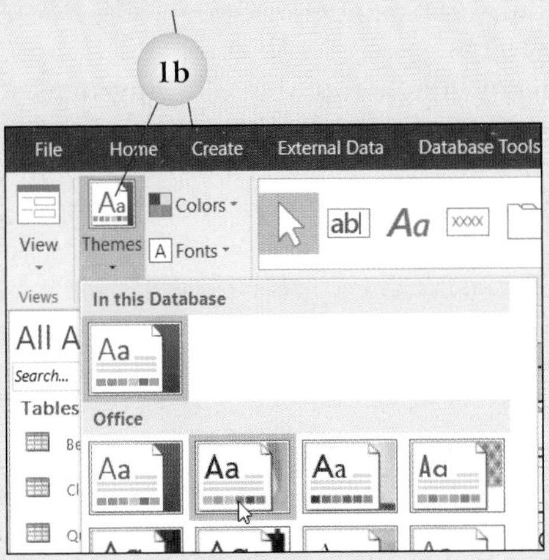

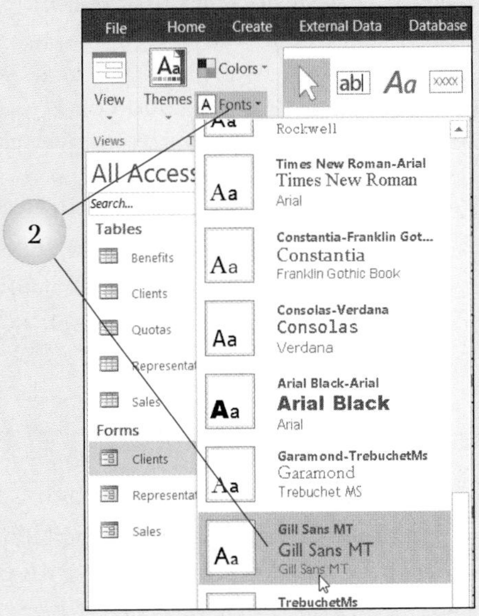

4. Change the font and font size of text in the form table by completing the following steps:
   a. Click in any cell containing a control object in the form table.
   b. Select all cells in the form table by clicking the table move handle in the upper left corner of the *Detail* section.
   c. Click the Form Layout Tools Format tab.
   d. Click the *Font* option box arrow, scroll down the drop-down list, and then click *Tahoma*. (Fonts are alphabetized in the drop-down list.)
   e. Click the *Font Size* option box arrow and then click *10* at the drop-down list.

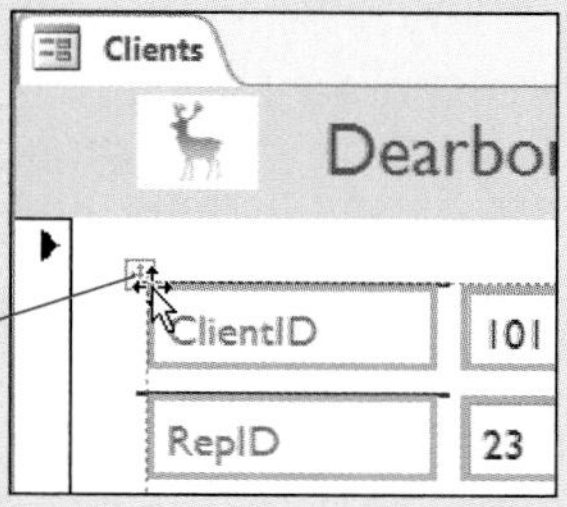

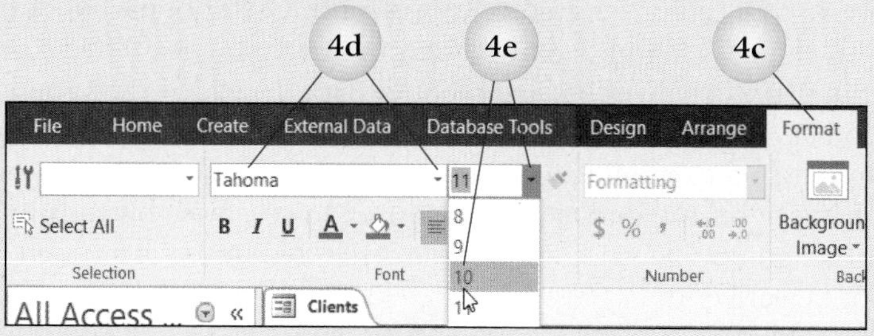

5. Apply formatting and change the alignment of the first column of cells by completing the following steps:
   a. Click in the control object containing the field name *ClientID*, press and hold down the Shift key, click in the bottom control object containing the field name *Telephone*, and then release the Shift key.
   b. Click the Bold button in the Font group.
   c. Click the Shape Fill button in the Control Formatting group and then click the *Brown, Accent 3, Lighter 60%* option (seventh column, third row in the *Theme Colors* section).
   d. Click the Shape Outline button in the Control Formatting group and then click the *Brown, Accent 3, Darker 50%* option (seventh column, bottom row in the *Theme Colors* section).
   e. Click the Align Right button in the Font group.

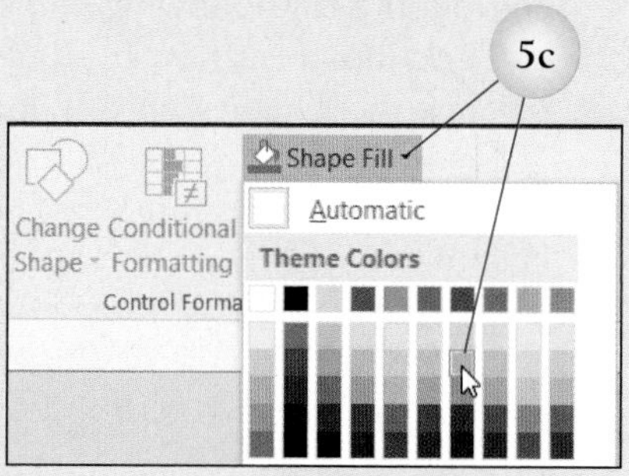

6. Apply shape fill to the second column of cells by completing the following steps:
   a. Click in the text box control object containing the text *101*.
   b. Position the mouse pointer at the top border of the selected cell until the pointer displays as a small black arrow that points down and then click the left mouse button. (Make sure all of the cells in the second column are selected.)

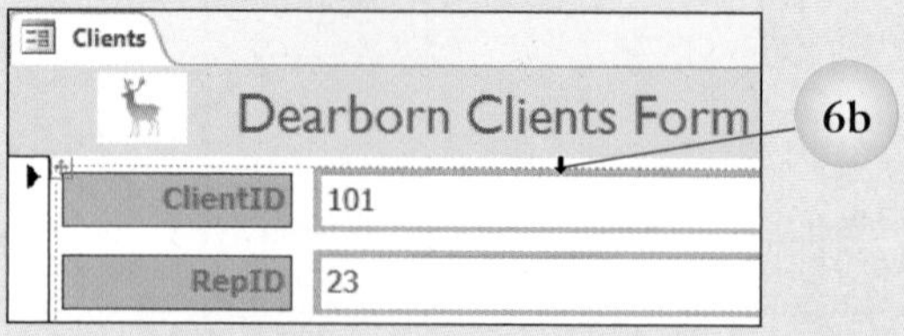

   c. Click the Shape Fill button in the Control Formatting group and then click the *Brown, Accent 3, Lighter 80%* option (seventh column, second row in the *Theme Colors* section).

7. Remove the gridlines by completing the following steps:
   a. Click the Form Layout Tools Arrange tab.
   b. Click the Select Layout button in the Rows & Columns group.
   c. Click the Gridlines button in the Table group and then click *None* at the drop-down list.
8. Click the Save button on the Quick Access Toolbar to save the Clients form.
9. Insert a background image by completing the following steps:
   a. Click the Form Layout Tools Format tab.
   b. Click the Background Image button in the Background group and then click *Browse* at the drop-down list.
   c. Navigate to the AL1C5 folder on your storage medium and then double-click ***Mountain.jpg***.
   d. View the form and background image in Print Preview. (To display Print Preview, click the File tab, click the *Print* option, and then click the *Print Preview* option.)
   e. After viewing the form in Print Preview, return to the form by clicking the Close Print Preview button.
10. Click the Undo button on the Quick Access Toolbar to remove the background image. (If this does not remove the image, close the form without saving it and then reopen the form.)
11. Save the Clients form.

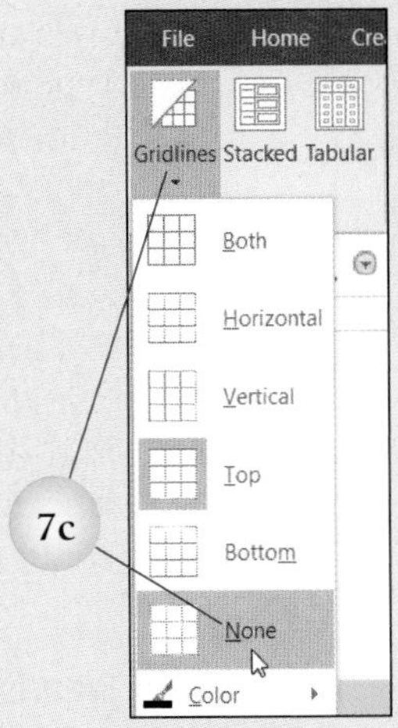

Check Your Work

Tutorial

Applying Conditional Formatting to a Form

Conditional Formatting

Quick Steps

Apply Conditional Formatting

1. Click Form Layout Tools Format tab.
2. Click Conditional Formatting button.
3. Click New Rule button.
4. Specify formatting.
5. Click OK.
6. Click OK.

Applying Conditional Formatting

Use the Conditional Formatting button in the Control Formatting group on the Form Layout Tools Format tab to apply formatting to data that meets a specific criterion. For example, conditional formatting can be applied to display sales amounts higher than a certain number in a different color, or to display certain state names in a specific color. Conditional formatting also can be applied that inserts data bars that visually compare data among records. The data bars provide a visual representation of the comparison. For example, in Project 1g, data bars will be inserted in the *Sales* field that provide a visual representation of how the sales amount in one record compares to the sales amounts in other records.

To apply conditional formatting, click the Conditional Formatting button in the Control Formatting group and the Conditional Formatting Rules Manager dialog box displays. At this dialog box, click the New Rule button and the New Formatting Rule dialog box displays, as shown in Figure 5.3. In the *Select a rule type* list box, choose the *Check values in the current record or use an expression* option if the conditional formatting is applied to a field in the record that matches a specific condition. Click the *Compare to other records* option to insert data bars in a field in all records that compare the data among the records.

Apply conditional formatting to a field by specifying the field and field condition with options in the *Edit the rule description* section of the dialog box. Specify the type of formatting to be applied to data in a field that meets the specific criterion. For example, in Project 1g, conditional formatting will be applied that changes the shape fill to a light green for all *City* fields containing the text *Indianapolis*. When all changes have been made at the dialog box, click OK to close the dialog box and then click OK to close the Conditional Formatting Rules Manager dialog box.

To insert data bars in a field, click the Conditional Formatting button, click the New Rule button at the Conditional Formatting Rules Manager dialog box, and then click the *Compare to other records* option in the *Select a rule type* list box. This changes the options in the dialog box, as shown in Figure 5.4. Make specific changes in the *Edit the rule description* section.

Figure 5.3 New Formatting Rule Dialog Box with the *Check values in the current record or use an expression* Option Selected

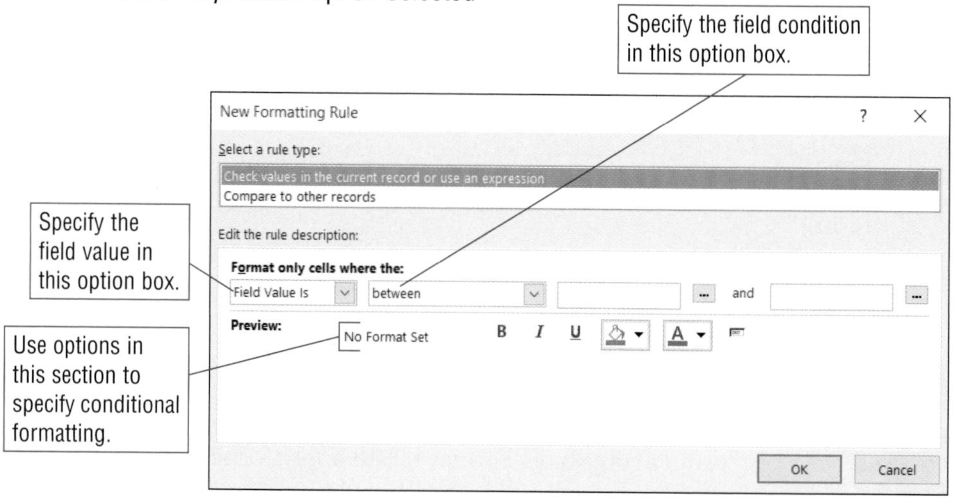

Figure 5.4 New Formatting Rule Dialog Box with the *Compare to other records* Option Selected

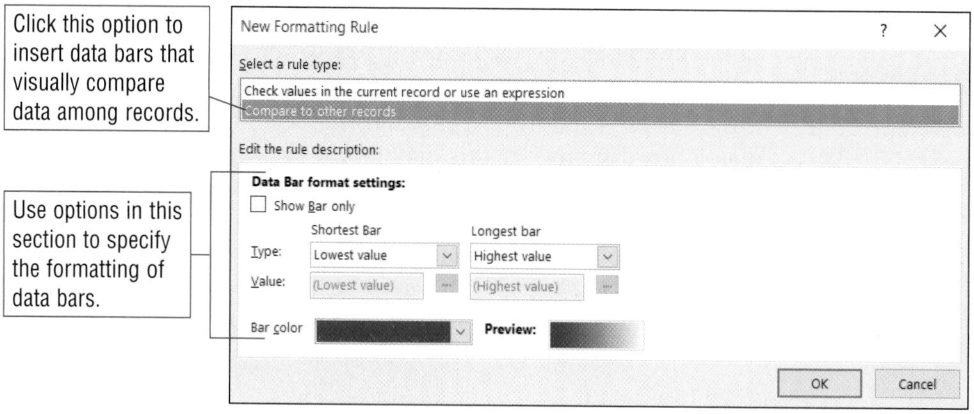

Project 1g Applying Conditional Formatting to Fields in Forms

Part 7 of 7

1. With the Clients form in **5-Dearborn.accdb** open and in Layout view, apply conditional formatting so that the *City* field displays all Indianapolis entries with a light green shape fill by completing the following steps:
   a. Click in the text box control object containing the text *Muncie*.
   b. Click the Form Layout Tools Format tab.
   c. Click the Conditional Formatting button in the Control Formatting group.
   d. At the Conditional Formatting Rules Manager dialog box, click the New Rule button.

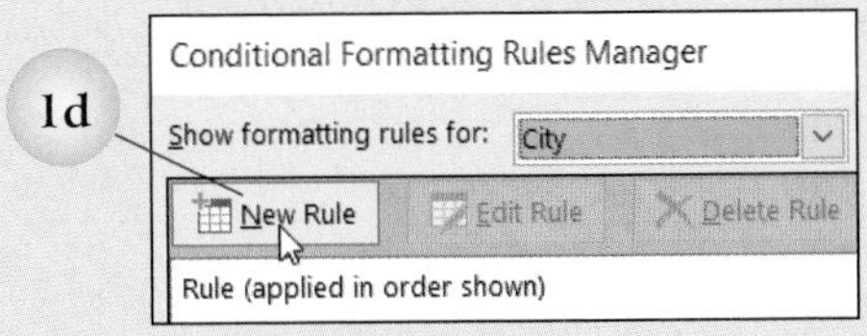

   e. At the New Formatting Rule dialog box, click the option box arrow for the option box containing the word *between* and then click *equal to* at the drop-down list.
   f. Click in the text box to the right of the *equal to* option box and then type Indianapolis.
   g. Click the Background color button arrow and then click the *Green 3* option (seventh column, fourth row).
   h. Click OK to close the New Formatting Rule dialog box.
   i. Click OK to close the Conditional Formatting Rules Manager dialog box.

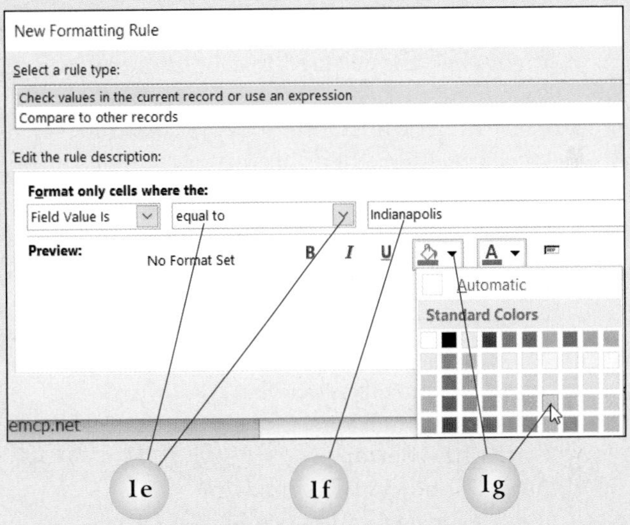

2. Click the Home tab and then click the View button to switch to Form view.
3. Click the Next record button to display the next record in the form. Continue clicking the Next record button to view records and notice that *Indianapolis* entries display with a light green shape fill.
4. Click the First record button in the Record Navigation bar.
5. Click the Save button on the Quick Access Toolbar.
6. Print page 1 of the form by completing the following steps:
   a. Click the File tab and then click the *Print* option.
   b. Click the next *Print* option.
   c. At the Print dialog box, click the *Pages* option in the *Print Range* section, type 1 in the *From* text box, press the Tab key, and then type 1 in the *To* text box.
   d. Click OK.
7. Close the Clients form.
8. Open the Sales form and switch to Layout View by clicking the View button in the Views group on the Home tab.

9. With the text box control object containing the sales ID number *1* selected, drag the right border to the left until *Lines: 1 Characters: 21* displays at the left side of the Status bar.

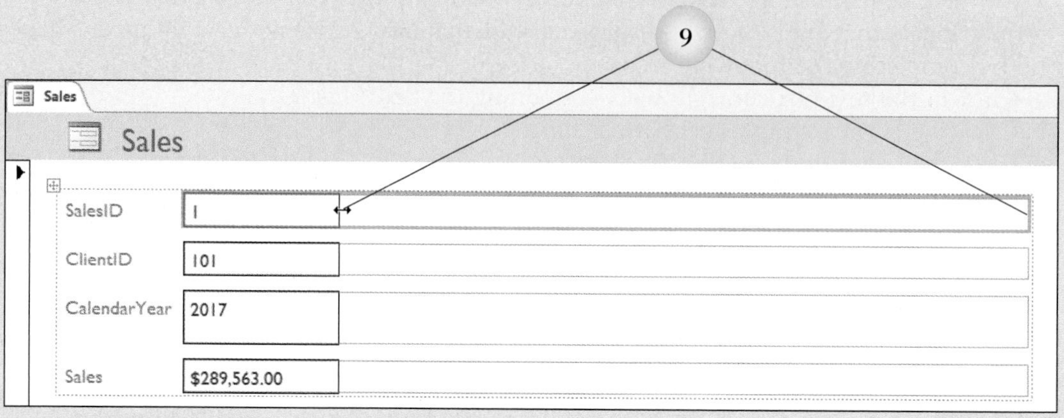

10. Change the alignment of text by completing the following steps:
    a. Right-click the selected text box control object (the object containing *1*) and then click *Select Entire Column* at the shortcut menu.
    b. Click the Form Layout Tools Format tab.
    c. Click the Align Right button in the Font group.
11. Apply data bars to the *Sales* field by completing the following steps:
    a. Click in the text box control object containing the amount *$289,563.00*.
    b. Make sure the Form Layout Tools Format tab is active.
    c. Click the Conditional Formatting button.
    d. At the Conditional Formatting Rules Manager dialog box, click the New Rule button.
    e. At the New Formatting Rule dialog box, click the *Compare to other records* option in the *Select a rule type* list box.
    f. Click the *Bar color* option box arrow and then click the *Green 4* option (seventh column, fifth row).
    g. Click OK to close the New Formatting Rule dialog box and then click OK to close the Conditional Formatting Rules Manager dialog box.

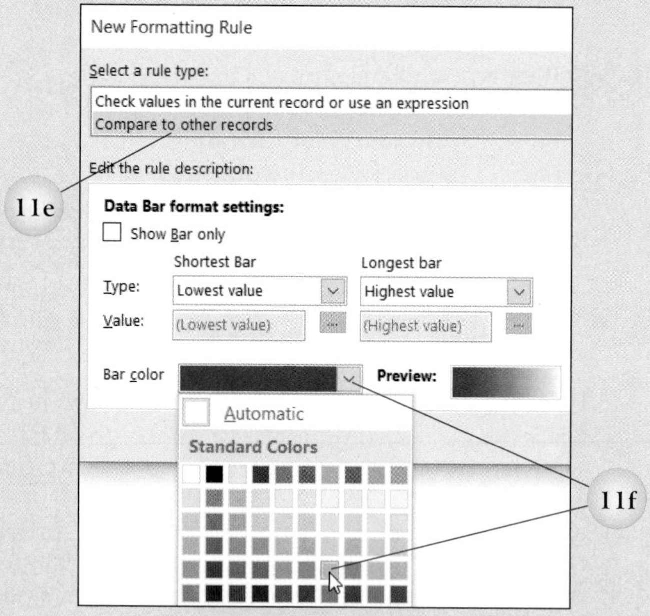

12. Click the Next record button in the Record Navigation bar to display the next record. Continue clicking the Next record button and notice the data bars that display in the *Sales* field.
13. Click the First record button in the Record Navigation bar.
14. Click the Save button on the Quick Access Toolbar.

15. Print page 1 of the form by completing the following steps:
    a. Click the File tab and then click the *Print* option.
    b. Click the next *Print* option.
    c. At the Print dialog box, click the *Selected Record(s)* option in the *Print Range* section and then click OK.
16. Close the Sales form.
17. Close **5-Dearborn.accdb**.

Check Your Work

Project 2 Add Fields, Create a Split Form and Multiple Items Form, and Use the Form Wizard — 6 Parts

You will open the Skyline database, create a form and add related fields and a calculation to the form, create a split and multiple items form, and create a form using the Form Wizard.

Preview Finished Project

Tutorial

Adding an Existing Field to a Form

Add Existing Fields

Adding an Existing Field

A field can be inserted into an existing form by opening the form in Layout view and then clicking the Add Existing Fields button in the Tools group on the Form Layout Tools Design tab. Clicking the Add Existing Field button displays the Field List task pane at the right side of the screen. This task pane displays the fields available in the current view, fields available in related tables, and fields available in other tables. Figure 5.5 displays the Field List task pane that will be opened in Project 2a.

In the *Fields available for this view* section, Access displays all fields in any tables used to create the form. So far, forms in projects have been created using all fields in one table. In the *Fields available in related tables* section, Access displays tables that are related to the table(s) used to create the form. To display the fields in the related table, click the expand button (plus symbol in a square) that displays before the table name in the Field List task pane and the list expands to display all of the field names.

Hint Alt + F8 is the keyboard shortcut to display the Field List task pane.

To add a field to the form, double-click the field in the Field List task pane. This inserts the field below the active control object in the form. Another method for inserting a field is to drag the field from the Field List task pane into the form. To do this, position the mouse pointer on the field in the Field List task pane, click and hold down the left mouse button, drag into the form, and then release the mouse button. A pink insert indicator bar displays when dragging the field into the existing fields in the form. Drag over an empty cell and the cell displays with pink fill. When the pink insert indicator bar is in the desired position or the cell is selected, release the mouse button.

Hint Use the Field List task pane to add fields from a table or query to a form.

Quick Steps

Add Existing Field to Form
1. Click Add Existing Fields button on Form Layout Tools Design tab.
2. Drag field from Field List task pane to specific location in form.

Multiple fields can be inserted in a form from the Field List task pane. To do this, press and hold down the Ctrl key while clicking specific fields and then drag the fields into the form. Trying to drag a field from a table in the *Fields available in other tables* section will cause the Specify Relationship dialog box to display. To move a field from the Field List task pane to the form, the field must be in a table that is related to the table(s) used to create the form.

Figure 5.5 Field List Task Pane

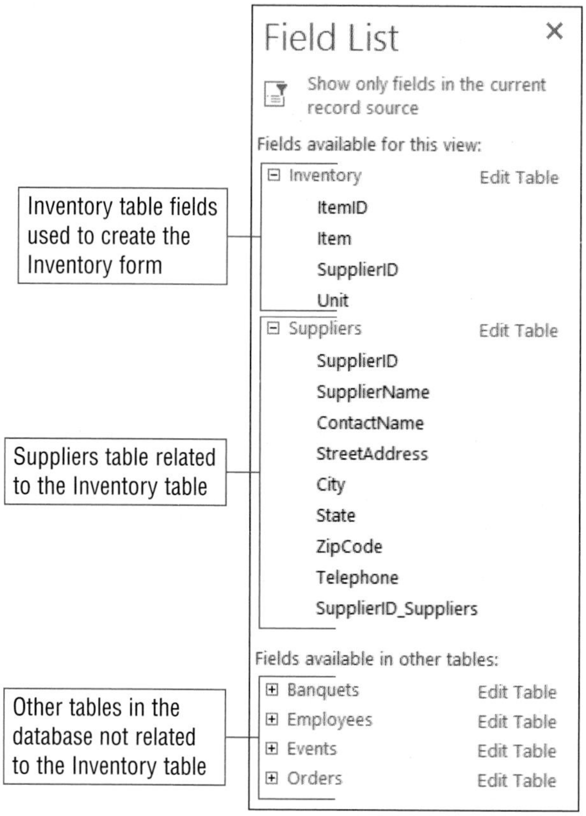

Project 2a Adding Existing Fields to a Form

Part 1 of 6

1. Open **5-Skyline.accdb** from the AL1C5 folder on your storage medium and enable the content.
2. Create a form with the Inventory table by clicking *Inventory* in the Tables group in the Navigation pane, clicking the Create tab, and then clicking the Form button in the Forms group.
3. With the text box control object containing the text *001* selected, drag the right border to the left until the selected object is approximately one-half the original width.

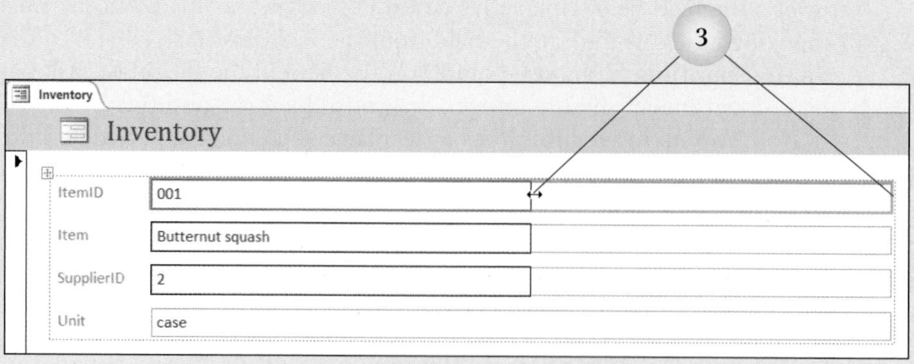

4. With the text box control object still selected, click the Form Layout Tools Arrange tab and then click the Split Horizontally button in the Merge/Split group. (This splits the text box control object into one object and one empty cell.)
5. You decide that you want to add the supplier name to the form so the name displays when entering data in the form. Add the *SupplierName* field by completing the following steps:
   a. Click the Form Layout Tools Design tab.
   b. Click the Add Existing Fields button in the Tools group.
   c. Click the Show all tables hyperlink that displays in the Field List task pane.
   d. Click the expand button immediately left of the Suppliers table name in the *Fields available in related tables* section of the Field List task pane.

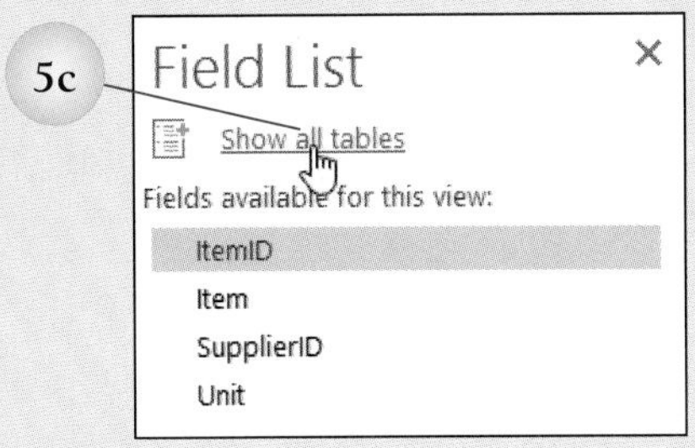

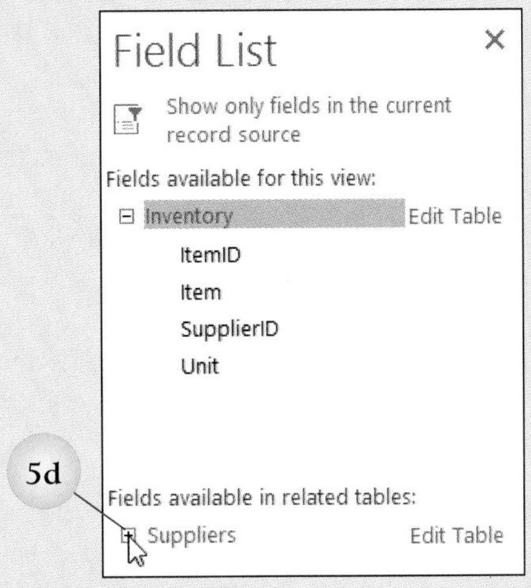

   e. Position the mouse pointer on the *SupplierName* field, click and hold down the left mouse button, drag into the form until the pink insert indicator bar displays immediately right of the text box control containing the *2* (the text box control at the right side of the *SupplierID* label control), and then release the mouse button. Access inserts the field as a Lookup field (a down arrow displays at the right side of the field).

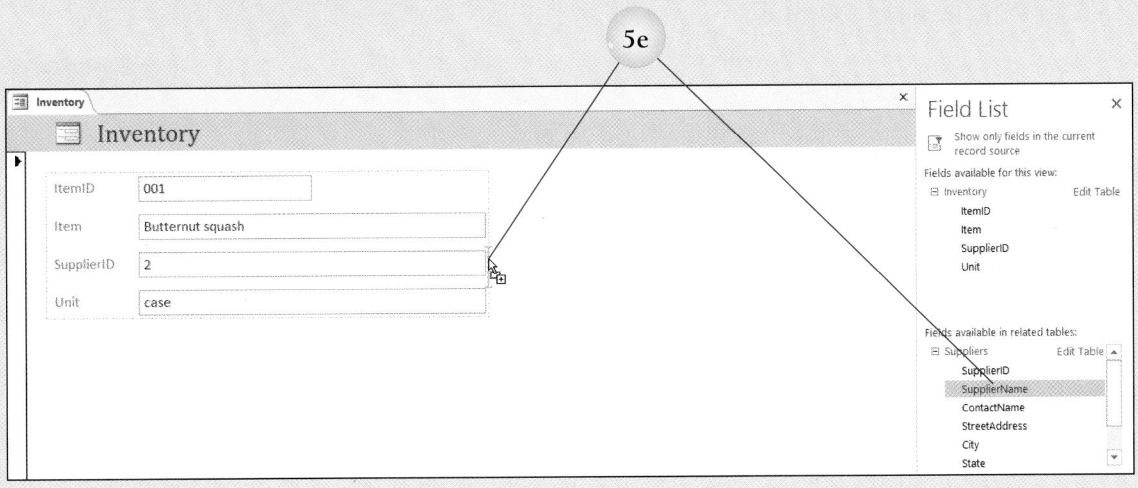

f. Change the *SupplierName* field from a Lookup field to a text box by clicking the Options button that displays below the field and then clicking *Change to Text Box* at the drop-down list. (This removes the down arrow at the right side of the field.)

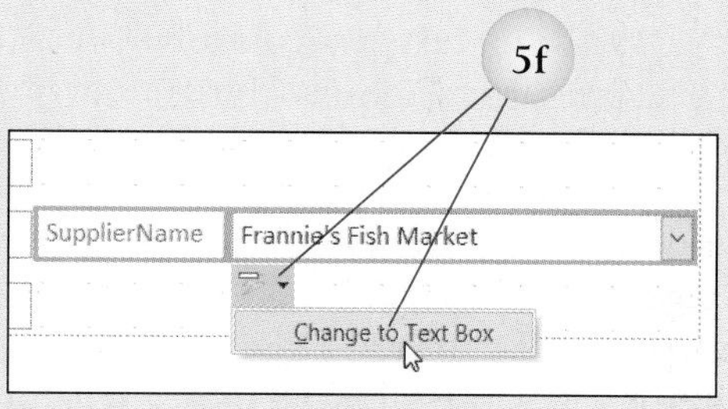

g. Close the Field List task pane by clicking the Close button in the upper right corner of the task pane.

6. Insert a logo image in the *Form Header* section by completing the following steps:
   a. Right-click the logo object that displays in the *Form Header* section (to the left of the title *Inventory*) and then click *Delete* at the shortcut menu.
   b. Click the Logo button in the Header/Footer group.
   c. At the Insert Picture dialog box, navigate to the AL1C5 folder on your storage medium and then double-click the file named ***Cityscape.jpg***.
7. Change the title by completing the following steps:
   a. Click the Title button in the Header/Footer group. (This selects *Inventory* in the *Form Header* section.)
   b. Type Skyline Inventory Input Form and then press the Enter key.
8. Insert the date and time in the *Form Header* section by clicking the Date and Time button in the Header/Footer group and then clicking OK at the Date and Time dialog box.
9. Click in any field outside the title, click the title to select the control object, and then drag the right border of the title control object to the left until the border displays near the title.
10. Select the date and time control objects, drag in the left border until the border displays near the date and time, and then drag the objects so they are positioned near the title.
11. Scroll through the records in the form.
12. Click the First record button in the Record Navigation bar.
13. Click the Save button on the Quick Access Toolbar and save the form with the name *Inventory*.
14. Print the current record.
15. Close the Inventory form.

Check Your Work

Tutorial

Inserting a Calculation in a Form

Inserting a Calculation in a Form

A calculation can be inserted in a form in a text box control object. To insert a text box control object as well as a label control object, click the Text Box button in the gallery in the Controls group on the Form Layout Tools Design tab, and then click in the location in the form where the two objects are to display. Click in the label control box and then type a label for the calculated field.

Insert a calculation by clicking in the text box control object and then clicking the Property Sheet button in the Tools group on the Form Layout Tools Design tab. This displays the Property Sheet task pane at the right side of the screen. The Property Sheet task pane contains options for setting the form's properties. To insert a calculation in the text box, click the Data tab in the Property Sheet task pane, click in the *Control Source* property box, and then type the calculation.

Quick Steps

Insert Calculation in Form

1. Click Text Box button on Form Layout Tools Design tab.
2. Click in form to insert label and text box control objects.
3. Click in text box control object.
4. Click Property Sheet button in Tools group.
5. Click Data tab.
6. Click in *Control Source* property box.
7. Type calculation.
8. Click Close button.

Type a calculation in the *Control Source* property box using mathematical operators such as the plus symbol (+) for addition, hyphen (-) for subtraction, the asterisk (*) for multiplication, and the forward slash symbol (/) for division. Type field names in the calculation inside square brackets. A field name must be typed in the calculation as it appears in the source object. For example, in Project 2b the calculation *=[AmountTotal]-[AmountPaid]* will be inserted in a text box control object to determine the amount due on banquet reservations. Notice that the calculation begins with the equals sign, the field names are typed inside brackets, and the hyphen is used to indicate subtraction. This calculation will subtract the amount paid for a banquet event from the banquet event total amount.

If a calculation result is currency, apply currency formatting to the text box control object. Apply currency formatting by clicking the Form Layout Tools Format tab and then clicking the Apply Currency Format button in the Number group.

Project 2b Inserting a Calculation in a Form — Part 2 of 6

1. With **5-Skyline.accdb** open, create a form with the AmountDue query using the Form button in the Forms group on the Create tab.
2. With the form open in Layout view, insert a text box control by completing the following steps:
   a. Click the Text Box button in the gallery in the Controls group on the Form Layout Tools Design tab.
   b. Position the crosshair below the *AmountPaid* field (the pink insert indicator bar displays below the field) and then click the left mouse button. (This inserts a label control object and a text box control object in the form.)

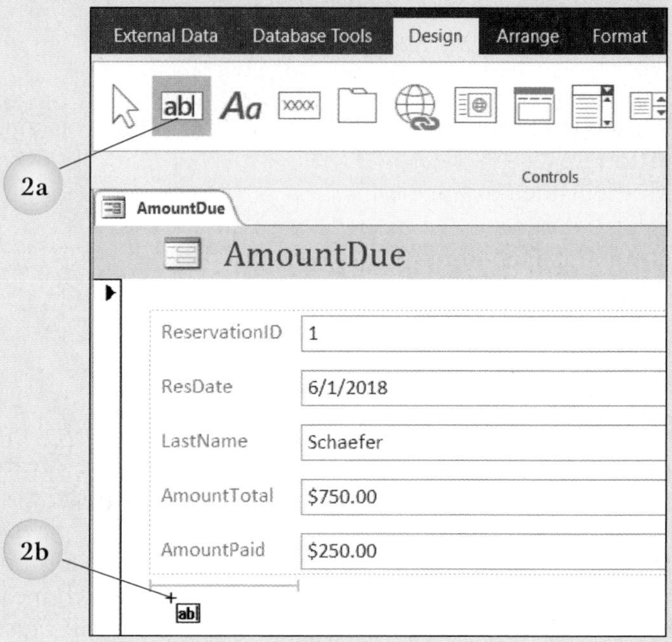

3. Name the new field by clicking in the label control object, double-clicking the text in the label control object, and then typing AmountDue.
4. Click in the text box control object and then insert a calculation by completing the following steps:
   a. Click the Property Sheet button in the Tools group on the Form Layout Tools Design tab.
   b. At the Property Sheet task pane, click the Data tab.
   c. Click in the *Control Source* property box.
   d. Type =[AmountTotal]-[AmountPaid] and then press the Enter key.
   e. Close the Property Sheet task pane by clicking the Close button in the upper right corner of the task pane.

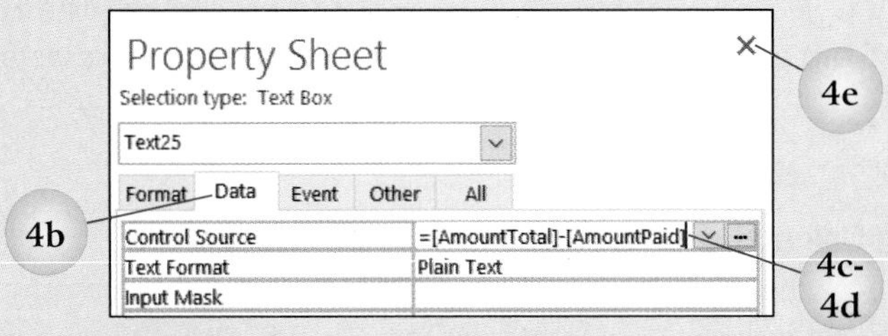

5. With the text box control object still selected, apply currency formatting by completing the following steps:
   a. Click the Form Layout Tools Format tab.
   b. Click the Apply Currency Format button in the Number group.

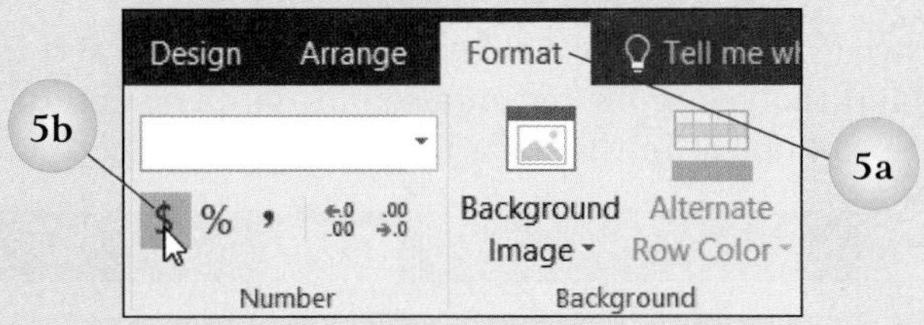

6. Scroll through the records in the form by clicking the Next record button and then click the First record button.
7. Save the form with the name *BanquetAmountsDue*.
8. Print the first page of the form.
9. Close the BanquetAmountsDue form.

Check Your Work

Tutorial

Creating a Split Form and Multiple Items Form

More Forms

Quick Steps

Create a Split Form

1. Click table.
2. Click Create tab.
3. Click More Forms button.
4. Click *Split Form*.

Creating a Split Form

Another method for creating a form is to use the *Split Form* option at the More Forms button drop-down list in the Forms group on the Create tab. Use this option to create a form and Access splits the screen in the work area and provides two views of the form. The top half of the work area displays the form in Layout view and the bottom half of the work area displays the form in Datasheet view. The two views are connected and are synchronous, which means that displaying or modifying a specific field in the Layout view portion will cause the same action to occur in the field in the Datasheet view portion. Figure 5.6 displays the split form that will be created in Project 2c.

Figure 5.6 Split Form

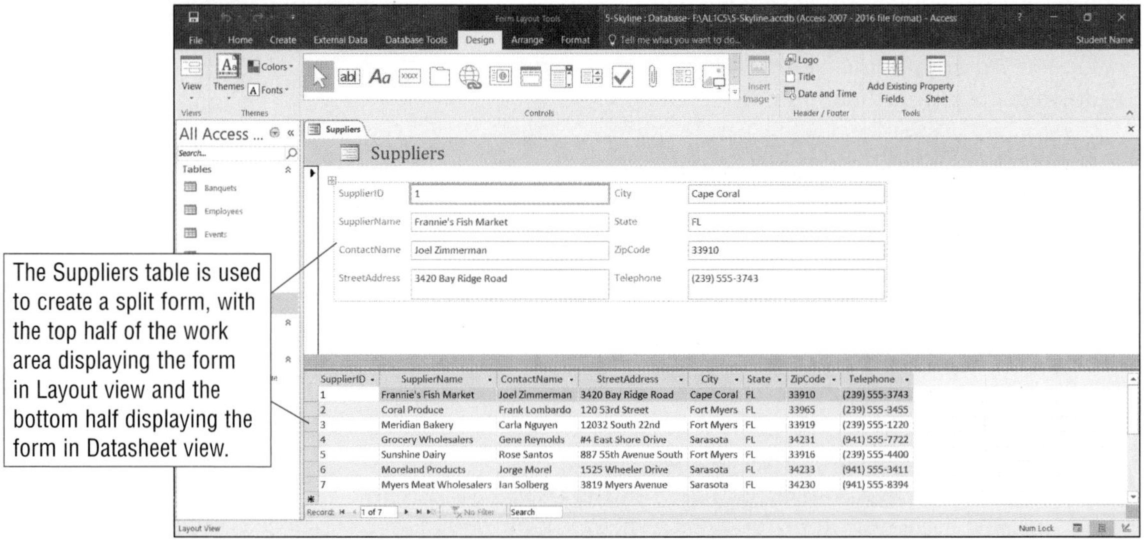

Project 2c Creating a Split Form

Part 3 of 6

1. With **5-Skyline.accdb** open, create a split form with the Suppliers table by completing the following steps:
   a. Click *Suppliers* in the Tables group in the Navigation pane.
   b. Click the Create tab.
   c. Click the More Forms button in the Forms group and then click *Split Form* at the drop-down list.

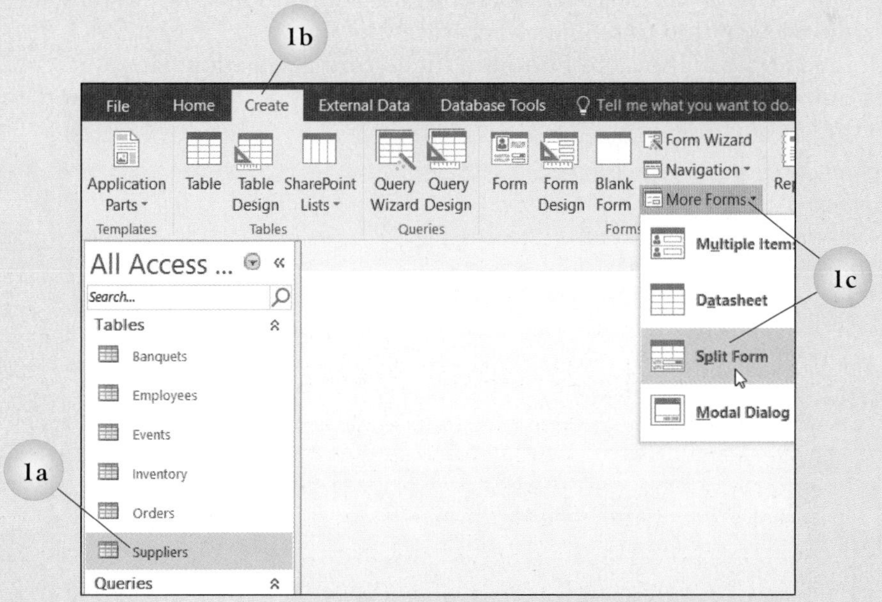

   d. Click several times on the Next record button in the Record Navigation bar. (As you display records, notice that the current record in the Form view in the top portion of the window is the same record selected in Datasheet view in the lower portion of the window.)
   e. Click the First record button.

2. Apply a theme by clicking the Themes button in the Themes group on the Form Layout Tools Design tab and then clicking *Integral* at the drop-down gallery (fourth column, first row in the *Office* section).

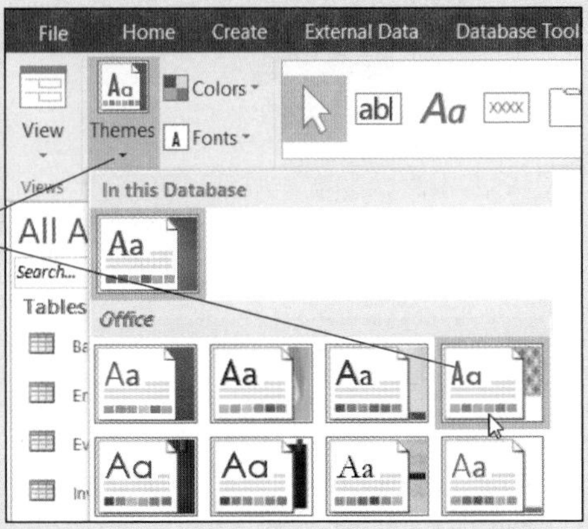

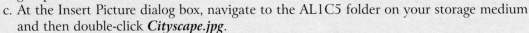

3. Insert a logo image in the *Form Header* section by completing the following steps:
   a. Right-click the logo object that displays in the *Form Header* section (to the left of the title *Suppliers*) and then click *Delete* at the shortcut menu.
   b. Click the Logo button in the Header/Footer group.
   c. At the Insert Picture dialog box, navigate to the AL1C5 folder on your storage medium and then double-click ***Cityscape.jpg***.
4. Change the title by completing the following steps:
   a. Click the Title button in the Header/Footer group. (This selects *Suppliers* in the *Form Header* section.)
   b. Type Skyline Suppliers Input Form and then press the Enter key.
   c. Click in any field outside the title, click the title again to select the control object, and then drag the right border to the left until the border displays near the title.
5. Click the text box control object containing the supplier identification number *1*, and then drag the right border of the text box control object to the left until *Lines: 1 Characters: 25* displays at the left side of the Status bar.
6. Click the text box control object containing the city *Cape Coral* and drag the right border of the text box control object to the left until *Lines: 1 Characters: 25* displays at the left side of the Status bar.
7. Insert a new record in the Suppliers form by completing the following steps:
   a. Click the View button to switch to Form view.
   b. Click the New (blank) record button in the Record Navigation bar.
   c. Click in the *SupplierID* field in the Form view portion of the window and then type the following information in the specified fields:

SupplierID	8
SupplierName	Jackson Produce
ContactName	Marshall Jackson
StreetAddress	5790 Cypress Avenue
City	Fort Myers
State	FL
ZipCode	33917
Telephone	2395555002

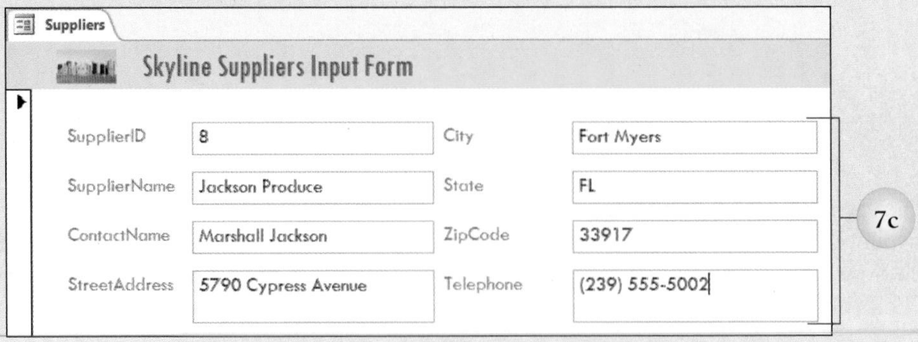

8. Click the Save button on the Quick Access Toolbar and save the form with the name *Suppliers*.
9. Print the current form by completing the following steps:
   a. Click the File tab and then click the *Print* option.
   b. Click the next *Print* option.
   c. At the Print dialog box, click the Setup button.
   d. At the Page Setup dialog box, click the *Print Form Only* option in the *Split Form* section of the dialog box and then click OK.
   e. At the Print dialog box, click the *Selected Record(s)* option and then click OK.
10. Close the Suppliers form.

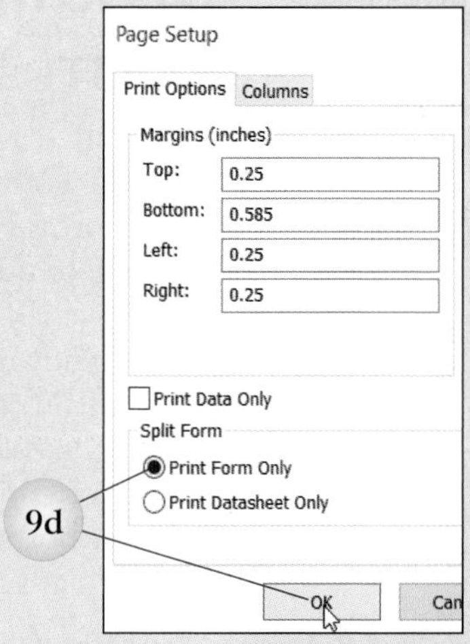

Check Your Work

Creating a Multiple Items Form

Quick Steps

Create a Multiple Items Form
1. Click table.
2. Click Create tab.
3. Click More Forms button.
4. Click *Multiple Items*.

When a form is created with the Form button, a single record displays. Use the *Multiple Items* option at the More Forms button drop-down list to create a form that displays multiple records. The advantage to creating a multiple items form over displaying the table in Datasheet view is that the form can be customized using buttons on the Form Layout Tools ribbon with the Design, Arrange, or Format tab selected.

Project 2d Creating a Multiple Items Form

Part 4 of 6

1. With **5-Skyline.accdb** open, create a multiple items form by completing the following steps:
   a. Click *Orders* in the Tables group in the Navigation pane.
   b. Click the Create tab.
   c. Click the More Forms button in the Forms group and then click *Multiple Items* at the drop-down list.
2. Delete the existing logo and then insert the **Cityscape.jpg** image as the logo.
3. Type Skyline Orders as the title.
4. Click in any field outside the title, click the title again to select the control object, and then drag the right border to the left until the border displays near the title.
5. Save the form with the name *Orders*.
6. Print the first page of the form by completing the following steps:
   a. Click the File tab and then click the *Print* option.
   b. Click the next *Print* option.
   c. At the Print dialog box, click the *Pages* option in the *Print Range* section.
   d. Type 1 in the *From* text box, press the Tab key, and then type 1 in the *To* text box.
   e. Click OK.
7. Close the Orders form.

Check Your Work

Tutorial

Creating a Form Using the Form Wizard

Form Wizard

Quick Steps

Create a Form Using the Form Wizard

1. Click Create tab.
2. Click Form Wizard button.
3. Choose options at each Form Wizard dialog box.

Hint With the Form Wizard, you can be more selective about which fields you insert in a form.

Creating a Form Using the Form Wizard

Access offers a Form Wizard that provides steps for creating a form. To create a form using the Form Wizard, click the Create tab and then click the Form Wizard button in the Forms group. At the first Form Wizard dialog box, shown in Figure 5.7, specify the table or query and then the fields to be included in the form. To select the table or query, click the *Table/Queries* option box arrow and then click the table or query at the drop-down list. Select a field in the *Available Fields* list box and then click the One Field button (the button containing the greater-than [>] symbol). This inserts the field in the *Selected Fields* list box. Continue in this manner until all of the fields have been inserted in the *Selected Fields* list box. To insert all of the fields into the *Selected Fields* list box at one time, click the All Fields button (the button containing two greater-than symbols). After specifying the fields, click the Next button.

At the second Form Wizard dialog box, specify the layout for the records. Choose from these layout type options: *Columnar*, *Tabular*, *Datasheet*, and *Justified*. Click the Next button and the third and final Form Wizard dialog box displays. It offers a title for the form and also provides the option *Open the form to view or enter information*. Make any necessary changes in this dialog box and then click the Finish button.

Figure 5.7 First Form Wizard Dialog Box

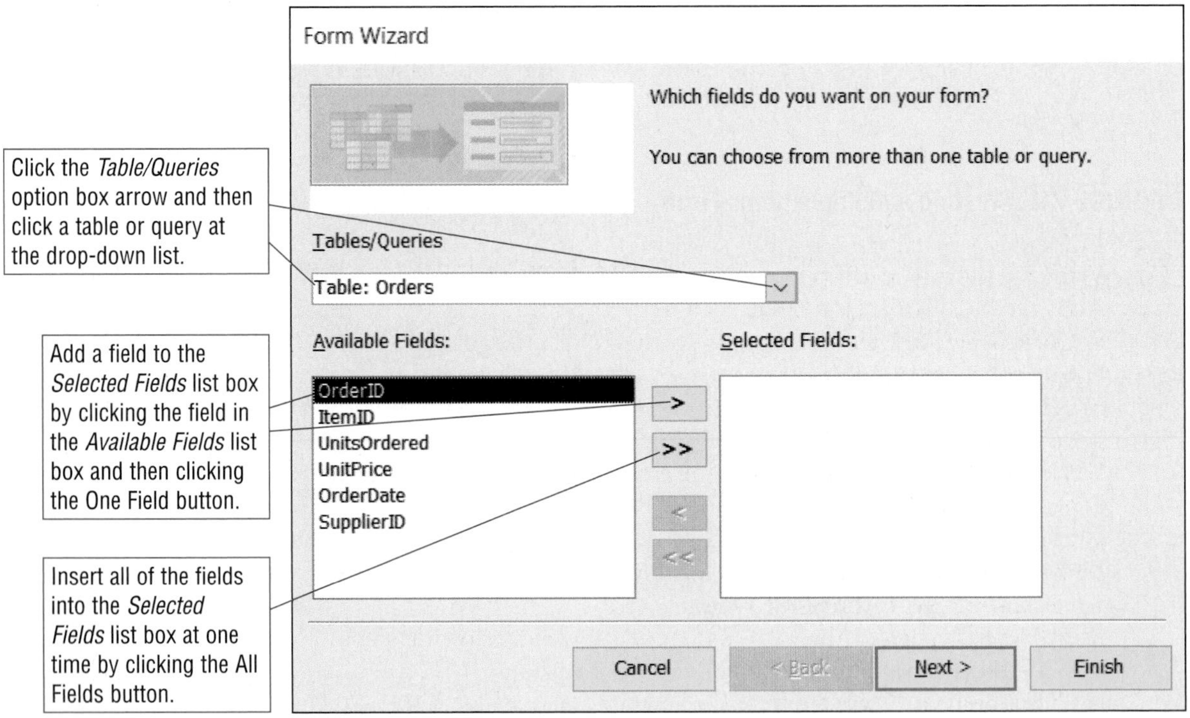

Project 2e Creating a Form Using the Form Wizard

Part 5 of 6

1. With **5-Skyline.accdb** open, create a form with the Form Wizard by completing the following steps:
   a. Click the Create tab.
   b. Click the Form Wizard button in the Forms group.
   c. At the first Form Wizard dialog box, click the *Tables/Queries* option box arrow and then click *Table: Employees* at the drop-down list.
   d. Specify that you want all of the fields included in the form by clicking the All Fields button (the button containing the two greater-than symbols).

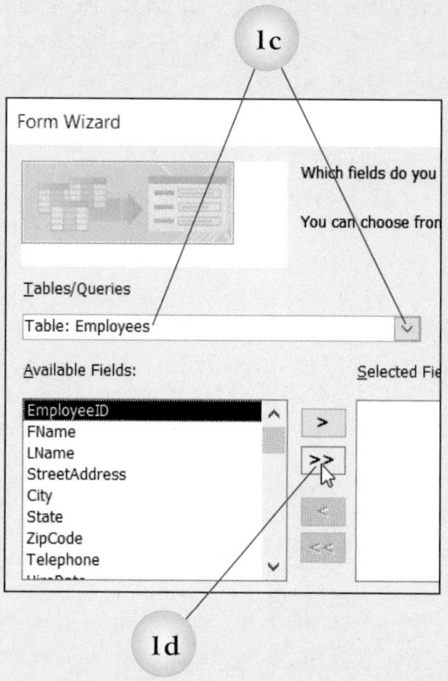

   e. Click the Next button.
   f. At the second Form Wizard dialog box, click the *Justified* option and then click the Next button.
   g. At the third and final Form Wizard dialog box, click the Finish button.
2. Format the field headings by completing the following steps:
   a. Click the View button to switch to Layout view.
   b. Click the *EmployeeID* label control object. (This selects the object.)

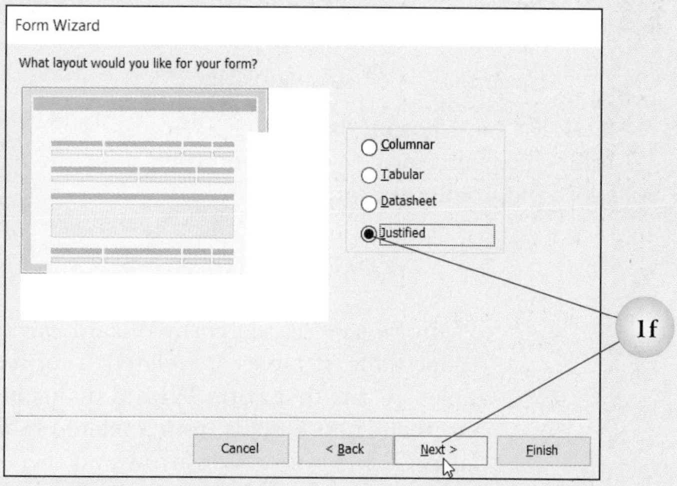

c. Press and hold down the Ctrl key and then click each of the following label control objects: *FName*, *LName*, *StreetAddress*, *City*, *State*, *ZipCode*, *Telephone*, *HireDate*, and *HealthIns*.
d. With all of the label control objects selected, release the Ctrl key.
e. Click the Form Layout Tools Format tab.
f. Click the Shape Fill button and then click the *Aqua Blue 2* option (ninth column, third row in the *Standard Colors* section).
g. Click the Form Layout Tools Design tab and then click the View button to switch to Form view.

3. In Form view, click the New (blank) record button and then add the following records:

EmployeeID	13
FName	Carol
LName	Thompson
StreetAddress	6554 Willow Drive, Apt. B
City	Fort Myers
State	FL
ZipCode	33915
Telephone	2395553719
HireDate	10/1/2018
HealthIns	(Click the check box to insert a check mark.)

EmployeeID	14
FName	Eric
LName	Hahn
StreetAddress	331 South 152nd Street
City	Cape Coral
State	FL
ZipCode	33906
Telephone	2395558107
HireDate	10/1/2018
HealthIns	(Leave blank.)

4. Click the Save button on the Quick Access Toolbar.
5. Print the record for Eric Hahn and then print the record for Carol Thompson.
6. Close the Employees form.

Check Your Work

In Project 2e, the Form Wizard was used to create a form with all of the fields in one table. If tables are related, a form can be created using fields from related tables. At the first Form Wizard dialog box, choose fields from the selected table and then choose fields from a related table. To change to a related table, click the *Tables/Queries* option box arrow and then click the name of the related table.

Project 2f Creating a Form with Related Tables

Part 6 of 6

1. With **5-Skyline.accdb** open, create a form with related tables by completing the following steps:
   a. Click the Create tab.
   b. Click the Form Wizard button in the Forms group.
   c. At the first Form Wizard dialog box, click the *Tables/Queries* option box arrow and then click *Table: Banquets*.
   d. Click *ResDate* in the *Available Fields* list box and then click the One Field button. (This inserts *ResDate* in the *Selected Fields* list box.)
   e. Click *AmountTotal* in the *Available Fields* list box and then click the One Field button.
   f. With *AmountPaid* selected in the *Available Fields* list box, click the One Field button.
   g. Click the *Tables/Queries* option box arrow and then click *Table: Events* at the drop-down list.
   h. Click *Event* in the *Available Fields* list box and then click the One Field button.
   i. Click the *Tables/Queries* option box arrow and then click *Table: Employees* at the drop-down list.
   j. Click *LName* in the *Available Fields* list box and then click the One Field button.
   k. Click the Next button.
   l. At the second Form Wizard dialog box, click the Next button.
   m. At the third Form Wizard dialog box, click the Next button.
   n. At the fourth Form Wizard dialog box, select the text in the *What title do you want for your form?* text box, type Upcoming Banquets, and then click the Finish button.
2. When the first record displays, print the record.
3. Save and then close the form.
4. Close **5-Skyline.accdb**.

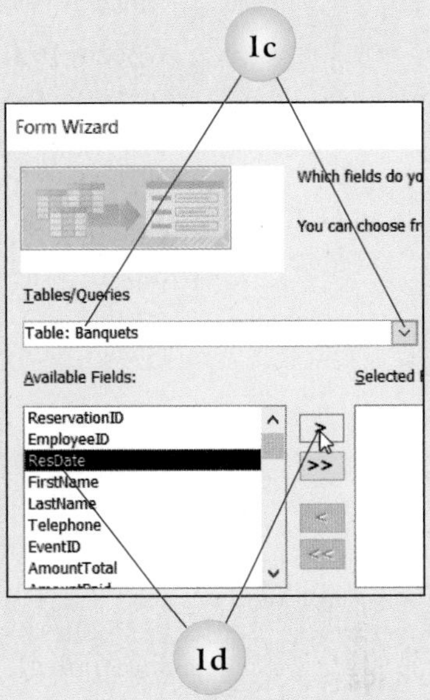

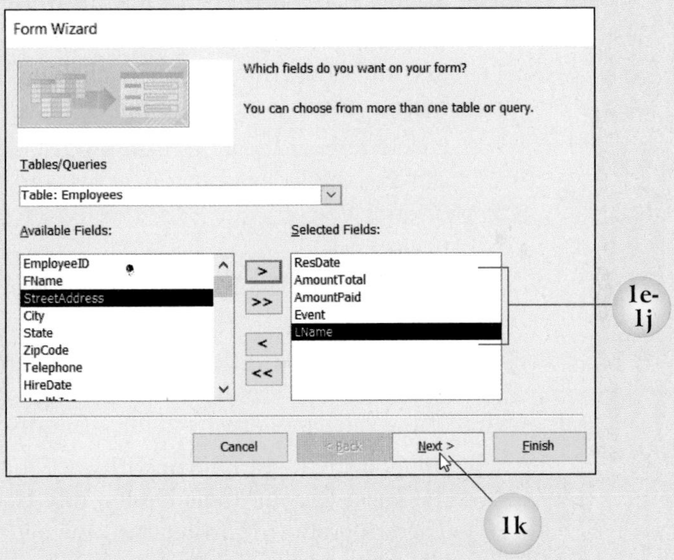

Check Your Work

Chapter Summary

- Creating a form generally improves the ease of entering data into a table. Some methods for creating a form include using the Form, Split Form, and Multiple Items buttons or the Form Wizard.
- A form is an object used to enter and edit data in a table or query and to help prevent incorrect data from being entered in a database.
- The simplest method for creating a form is to click a table in the Navigation pane, click the Create button, and then click the Form button in the Forms group.
- Create a form and it displays in Layout view. Use this view to display data and modify the appearance and contents of the form. Other form views include Form view and Design view. Use Form view to enter and manage records and use Design view to view and modify the structure of the form.
- Open an existing form in Layout view by right-clicking the form in the Navigation pane and then clicking *Layout View* at the shortcut menu.
- Print a form with options at the Print dialog box. To print an individual record, display the Print dialog box, click the *Selected Record(s)* option, and then click OK.
- Delete a form with the Delete button in the Records group on the Home tab or by right-clicking the form in the Navigation pane and then clicking *Delete* at the shortcut menu. A message may display asking to confirm the deletion.
- Navigate in a form with buttons in the Record Navigation bar.
- Add a new record to a form by clicking the New (blank) record button in the Record Navigation bar or by clicking the Home tab and then clicking the New button in the Records group.
- Delete a record from a form by displaying the record, clicking the Home tab, clicking the Delete button arrow, and then clicking *Delete Record* at the drop-down list.
- If a form is created with a table that has a one-to-many relationship established, Access adds a datasheet at the bottom of the form.
- A form is made up of cells arranged in rows and columns and each cell can contain one control object. Customize control objects with buttons on the Form Layout Tools ribbon with the Design tab, Arrange tab, or Format tab selected. These tabs are active when a form displays in Layout view.
- Apply a theme to a form with the Themes button in the Themes group on the Form Layout Tools Design tab. Use the Colors and Fonts buttons in the Themes group to further customize a theme.
- Use buttons in the Header/Footer group on the Form Layout Tools Design tab to insert a logo, form title, and the date and time.
- Control objects can be resized, deleted, and inserted in Layout view.
- Use buttons in the Rows & Columns group on the Form Layout Tools Arrange tab to select or insert rows or columns of cells.
- The Controls group on the Form Layout Tools Design tab contains control objects that can be inserted in a form.
- Merge cells in a form by selecting cells and then clicking the Merge button in the Merge/Split group on the Form Layout Tools Arrange tab. Split selected cells by clicking the Split Vertically or Split Horizontally button.

- Format cells in a form with buttons on the Form Layout Tools Format tab.
- Use the Conditional Formatting button in the Control Formatting group on the Form Layout Tools Format tab to apply formatting to data that matches a specific criterion.
- Click the Add Existing Fields button in the Tools group on the Form Layout Tools Design tab to display the Field List task pane. Add fields to the form by double-clicking a field or dragging the field from the task pane to the form.
- Insert a calculation in a form by inserting a text box control object, displaying the Property Sheet task pane with the Data tab selected, and then typing the calculation in the *Control Source* property box. If a calculation result is currency, apply currency formatting with the Apply Currency Format button on the Form Layout Tools Format tab.
- Create a split form by clicking the More Forms button on the Create tab and then clicking *Split Form* in the drop-down list. Access displays the form in Layout view in the top portion of the work area and in Datasheet view in the bottom portion of the work area. The two views are connected and synchronous.
- Create a Multiple Items form by clicking the More Forms button on the Create tab and then clicking *Multiple Items* in the drop-down list.
- The Form Wizard provides steps for creating a form such as specifying the fields to be included in the form, a layout for the records, and a name for the form.
- A form can be created with the Form Wizard that contains fields from tables connected by a one-to-many relationship.

Commands Review

FEATURE	RIBBON TAB, GROUP	BUTTON, OPTION	KEYBOARD SHORTCUT
Conditional Formatting Rules Manager dialog box	Form Layout Tools Format, Control Formatting		
Field List task pane	Form Layout Tools Design, Tools		
form	Create, Forms		
Form Wizard	Create, Forms		
multiple items form	Create, Forms	, *Multiple Items*	
Property Sheet task pane	Form Layout Tools Design, Tools		Alt + Enter
split form	Create, Forms	, *Split Form*	

Workbook

Chapter study tools and assessment activities are available in the *Workbook* ebook. These resources are designed to help you further develop and demonstrate mastery of the skills learned in this chapter.

Microsoft®

Access®

Creating Reports and Mailing Labels

CHAPTER 6

Performance Objectives

Upon successful completion of Chapter 6, you will be able to:

1 Create a report using the Report button
2 Modify the record source
3 Select, edit, size, move, and delete control objects
4 Sort records
5 Find data
6 Display and customize a report in Print Preview
7 Delete a report
8 Format a report
9 Apply conditional formatting to data in a report
10 Group and sort records in a report
11 Insert a calculation in a report
12 Create a report using the Report Wizard
13 Create mailing labels using the Label Wizard

Precheck

Check your current skills to help focus your study.

In this chapter, you will learn how to prepare reports from data in a table or query using the Report button in the Reports group on the Create tab and using the Report Wizard. You will also learn how to manage control objects, format, and insert a calculation in a report and create mailing labels using the Label Wizard.

Data Files

Before beginning chapter work, copy the AL1C6 folder to your storage medium and then make AL1C6 the active folder.

SNAP

If you are a SNAP user, launch the Precheck and Tutorials from your Assignments page.

Project 1 Create and Customize Reports Using Tables and Queries 5 Parts

You will create reports with the Report button using tables and queries. You will change the report views; select, move, and size control objects; sort records; customize reports; apply conditional formatting; group and sort fields; and insert a calculation in a report.

Preview Finished Project

Tutorial

Creating a Report

Quick Steps

Create a Report

1. Click table or query in Navigation pane.
2. Click Create tab.
3. Click Report button.

Report

Hint Create a report to control what data appears on the page when printed.

Creating a Report

Create a report in a database to control what data appears on the page when printed and how the data is formatted. Reports generally answer specific questions (queries). For example, a report could answer the question *What customers have submitted claims?* or *What products do we currently have on order?* The record source for a report can be a table or query. Create a report with the Report button in the Reports group or use the Report Wizard that provides steps for creating a report.

Creating a Report with the Report Button

To create a report with the Report button, click a table or query in the Navigation pane, click the Create tab, and then click the Report button in the Reports group. This displays the report in columnar style in Layout view with the Report Layout Tools Design tab active, as shown in Figure 6.1. Access creates the report using all of the fields in the table or query.

Figure 6.1 Report Created with Sales Table

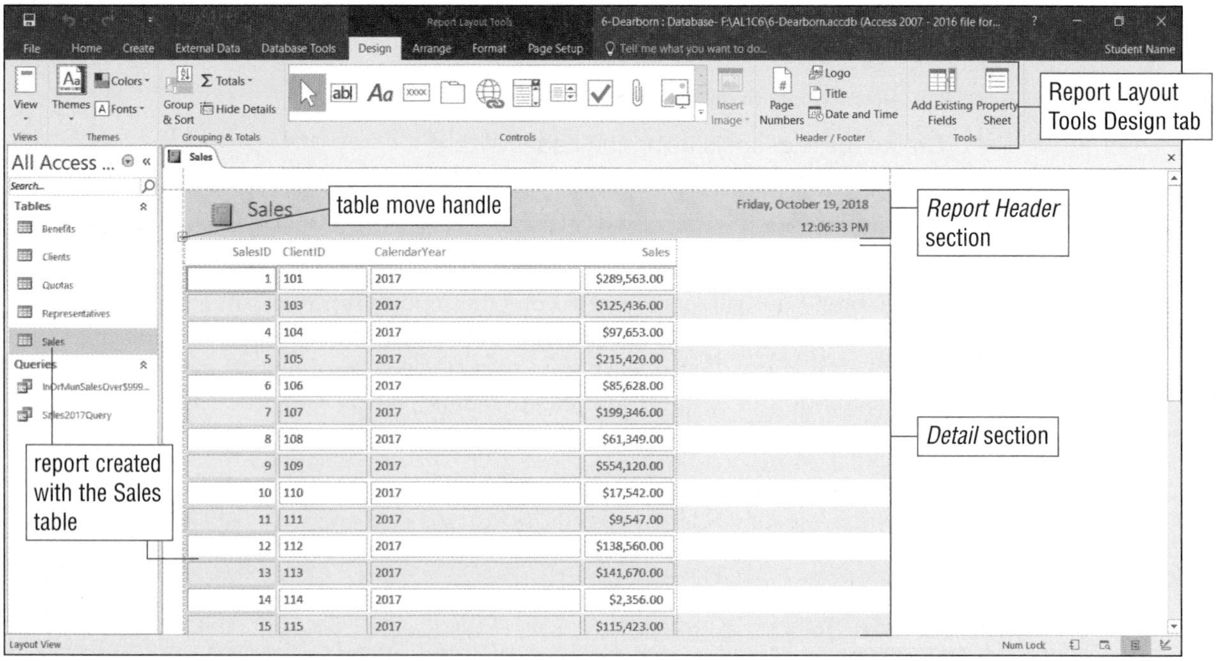

Modifying the Record Source

The record source for a report is the table or query used to create the report. If changes are made to the record source, such as adding or deleting records, those changes are reflected in the report. For example, in Project 1a, a report will be created based on the Sales table. A record will be added to the Sales table (the record source for the report) and the added record will display in the Sales report.

Project 1a Creating a Report with the Report Button

Part 1 of 5

1. Open **6-Dearborn.accdb** from the AL1C6 folder on your storage medium and enable the content.
2. Create a report based on the Sales table by completing the following steps:
   a. Click *Sales* in the Tables group in the Navigation pane.
   b. Click the Create tab.
   c. Click the Report button in the Reports group.

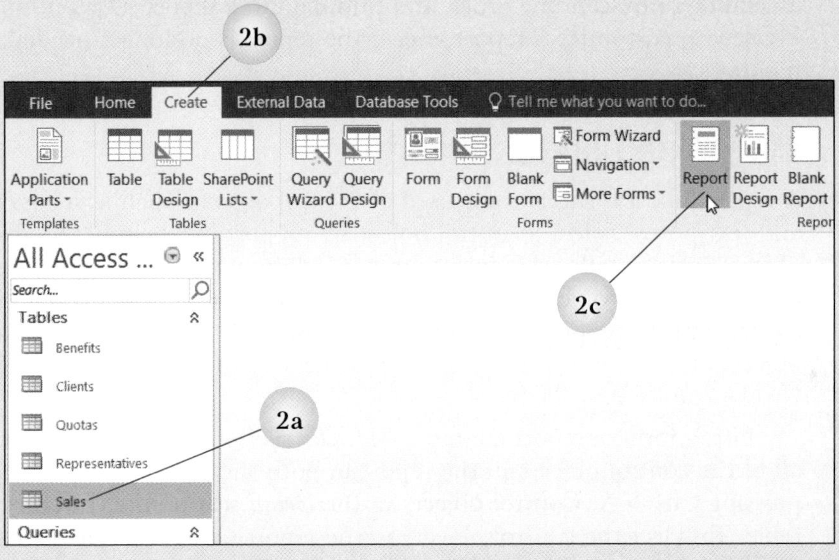

   d. Save the report by clicking the Save button on the Quick Access Toolbar and then clicking OK at the Save As dialog box. (This saves the report with the default name *Sales*.)
   e. Close the Sales report.
3. Add a record to the Sales table by completing the following steps:
   a. Double-click *Sales* in the Tables group in the Navigation pane. (Make sure you open the Sales table and not the Sales report.)
   b. Click the New button in the Records group on the Home tab.
   c. Press the Tab key to accept the default number in the *SalesID* field.
   d. Type 127 in the *ClientID* field and then press the Tab key.
   e. Type 2018 in the *CalendarYear* field and then press the Tab key.
   f. Type 176420 in the *Sales* field.
   g. Close the Sales table.
4. Open the Sales report and then scroll down to the bottom. Notice that the new record you added to the Sales table displays in the report.
5. Close the Sales report.

6. Use the Sales2017Query query to create a report by completing the following steps:
   a. Click *Sales2017Query* in the Queries group in the Navigation pane.
   b. Click the Create tab.
   c. Click the Report button in the Reports group.
7. Access automatically inserted a total amount for the *Sales* column of the report. Delete this amount by scrolling down to the bottom of the report, clicking the total amount at the bottom of the *Sales* column, and then pressing the Delete key. (This deletes the total amount but not the underline above the amount.)
8. Save the report by clicking the Save button on the Quick Access Toolbar, typing 2017Sales in the *Report Name* text box in the Save As dialog box, and then clicking OK.

Check Your Work

Modifying a Report

Make modifications to a report as needed to address specific needs. For example, select, size, move, edit, or delete control objects in a report; sort records in ascending or descending order, and find data in a report. Use options in Print Preview to customize a report and, if the report is no longer needed, delete the report.

Tutorial

Managing Control Objects in a Report

Managing Control Objects

A report, like a form, is comprised of control objects, such as logos, titles, labels, and text boxes. Select a control object in a report by clicking the object and the object displays with an orange border. Click in a cell in the report and Access selects all of the objects in the column except the column heading. Select adjacent control objects by pressing and holding down the Shift key and then clicking objects or select nonadjacent control objects by pressing and holding down the Ctrl key and then clicking objects.

Like a form, a report contains a *Header* section and a *Detail* section. Select all of the control objects in the report in both the *Header* and *Detail* sections by pressing Ctrl + A. Control objects in the *Detail* section are contained in a report table. To select the control objects in the report table, click in any cell in the report and then click the table move handle. The table move handle is a small square with a four-headed arrow inside that displays in the upper left corner of the table (see Figure 6.1). Move the table and all of the control objects within the table by dragging the table move handle using the mouse.

Change the size of control objects by dragging the border of a selected control object or with the *Width* and *Height* property boxes in the Property Sheet task pane with the Data tab selected. To change the size of a control object by dragging, select the object (displays with an orange border) and then, using the mouse, drag a left or right border to increase or decrease the width or drag a top or bottom border to increase or decrease the height of the control object. When dragging the border of a control object, a line and character count displays at the left side of the Status bar. Use the line and character count numbers to adjust the width and/or height of the object by a precise line and character count number.

The width and height of a control object or column of control objects can be adjusted with the *Width* and *Height* property boxes in the Property Sheet task pane. Display this task pane by clicking the Property Sheet button in the Tools group. In the Property Sheet task pane, click the Data tab, select the current measurement in the *Width* or *Height* property box, type the new measurement, and then press the Enter key.

A selected control object can be moved by positioning the mouse pointer in the object until the pointer displays with a four-headed arrow attached. Click and hold down the left mouse button, drag to the new location, and then release the mouse button. To move a column of selected control objects, position the mouse pointer in the column heading until the pointer displays with a four-headed arrow attached and then click and drag to the new location. While dragging a control object(s), a pink insert indicator bar displays indicating where the control object(s) will be positioned when the mouse button is released.

Some control objects in a report, such as a column heading or title, are label control objects. Edit a label control by double-clicking in the label control object and then making the specific changes. For example, to rename a label control, double-click in the label control and then type the new name.

Sorting Records

Ascending

Descending

Quick Steps

Sort Records

1. Click in field containing data.
2. Click Ascending button or Descending button.

Sort data in a report by clicking in the field containing the data to be sorted and then clicking the Ascending button or the Descending button in the Sort & Filter group on the Home tab. Click the Ascending button to sort text in alphabetic order from A to Z, numbers from lowest to highest, and dates from earliest to latest. Click the Descending button to sort text in alphabetic order from Z to A, numbers from highest to lowest, and dates from latest to earliest.

Finding Data in a Report

Find

Find specific data in a report with options at the Find dialog box. Display this dialog box by clicking the Find button in the Find group on the Home tab. At the Find dialog box, enter the search data in the *Find What* text box.

The *Match* option at the Find dialog box is set at *Whole Field* by default. At this setting, the data entered must match the entire entry in a field. To search for partial data in a field, change the *Match* option to *Any Part of Field* or *Start of Field*. If the text entered in the *Find What* text box needs to match the case in a field entry, click the *Match Case* check box to insert a check mark.

Access searches the entire report by default. This can be changed to *Up* to tell Access to search from the currently active field to the beginning of the report or *Down* to search from the currently active field to the end of the report. Click the Find Next button to find data that matches the data in the *Find What* text box.

Displaying and Customizing a Report in Print Preview

Tutorial

Customizing a Report in Print Preview

Print Preview

When a report is created, the report displays in the work area in Layout view. In addition to Layout view, three other views are available: Report, Print Preview, and Design. Use Print Preview to display the report as it will appear when printed. To change to Print Preview, click the Print Preview button in the view area at the right side of the Status bar. Another method for displaying the report in Print Preview is to click the View button arrow in the Views group on the Home tab or Report Layout Tools Design tab and then click *Print Preview* at the drop-down list.

In Print Preview, send the report to the printer by clicking the Print button on the Print Preview tab. Use options in the Page Size group to change the page size and margins. To print only the report data and not the column headings, report title, shading, and gridlines, insert a check mark in the *Print Data Only* check box. Use options in the Page Layout group to specify the page orientation, specify the number and size of columns, and display the Page Setup dialog box. Click the Page Setup button and the Page Setup dialog box displays with options for customizing margins, orientation, size, and columns. The Zoom group contains options and buttons for specifying a zoom percentage and for displaying one, two, or multiples pages of the report.

Deleting a Report

Quick Steps

Delete a Report

1. Click report name in Navigation pane.
2. Click Delete button on Home tab.
3. Click Yes.

OR

1. Right-click report name in Navigation pane.
2. Click *Delete.*
3. Click Yes.

If a report is no longer needed in a database, delete the report. Delete a report by clicking the report name in the Navigation pane, clicking the Delete button in the Records group on the Home tab, and then clicking the Yes button at the confirmation message. Another method is to right-click the report in the Navigation pane, click *Delete* at the shortcut menu, and then click the Yes at the message. If a report is being deleted from the computer's hard drive, the confirmation message will not display. This is because Access automatically sends the deleted report to the Recycle Bin, where it can be retrieved at a later time, if necessary.

Project 1b Adjusting Control Objects, Renaming Labels, Finding and Sorting Data, Displaying a Report in Print Preview, and Deleting a Report

Part 2 of 5

1. With the 2017Sales report open, reverse the order of the *RepName* and *Client* columns by completing the following steps:
   a. Make sure the report displays in Layout view.
   b. Click the *RepName* column heading.
   c. Press and hold down the Shift key, click in the first control object below the *RepName* column heading (the control object containing *Linda Foster*), and then release the Shift key.
   d. Position the mouse pointer inside the *RepName* column heading until the pointer displays with a four-headed arrow attached.
   e. Click and hold down the left mouse button, drag to the left until the vertical pink insert indicator bar displays to the left of the *Client* column, and then release the mouse button.

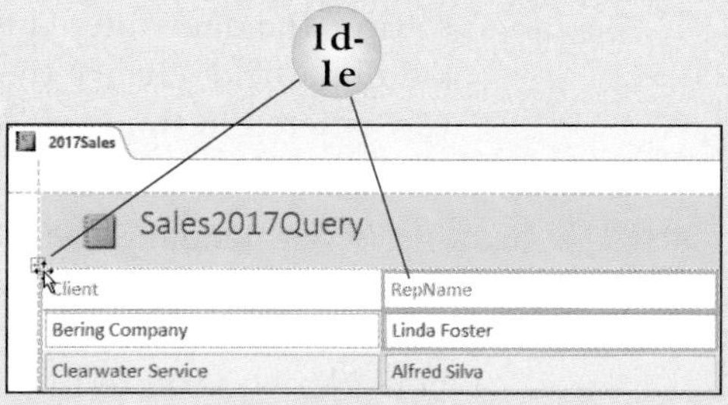

2. Sort the data in the *Sales* column in descending order by completing the following steps:
   a. Click the Home tab.
   b. Click in any field in the *Sales* column.
   c. Click the Descending button in the Sort & Filter group.
3. Rename the *RepName* label control as *Representative* by double-clicking in the label control object containing the text *RepName*, selecting *RepName*, and then typing Representative.

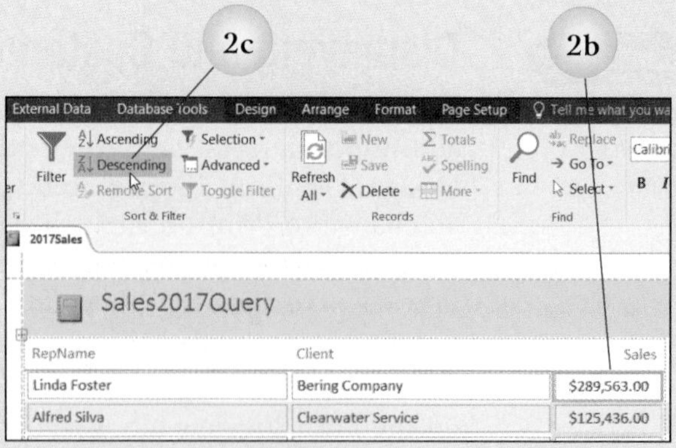

4. Double-click in the *Sales* label control and then rename it *Sales 2017*.
5. Move the report table by completing the following steps:
   a. Click in a cell in the report.
   b. Position the mouse pointer on the table move handle (a small square with a four-headed arrow inside that displays in the upper left corner of the table).
   c. Click and hold down the left mouse button, drag the report table to the right until it is centered between the left and right sides of the *Detail* section, and then release the mouse button. (When you drag with the mouse, you will see only outlines of some of the control objects.)

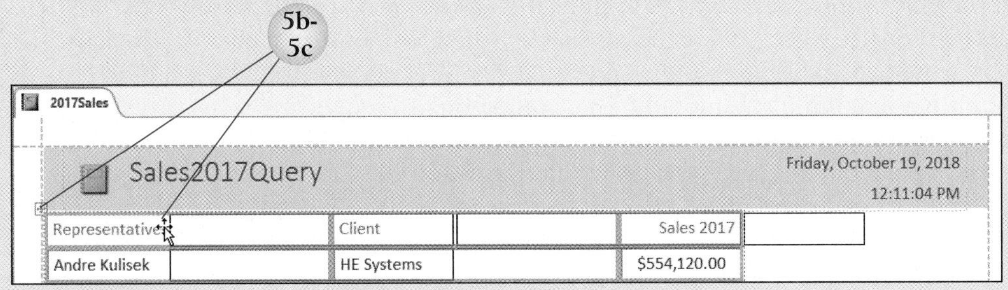

6. Display the report in Print Preview by clicking the Print Preview button in the view area at the right side of the Status bar.

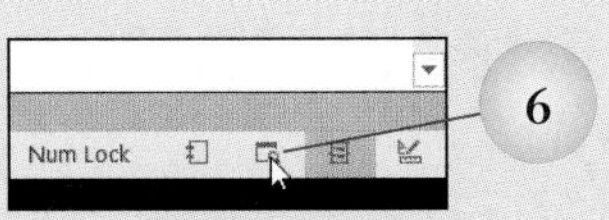

7. Click the One Page button (already active) in the Zoom group to display the entire page.
8. Click the Zoom button arrow in the Zoom group and then click *50%* at the drop-down list.
9. Click the One Page button in the Zoom group.
10. Print the report by clicking the Print button on the Print Preview tab and then clicking OK at the Print dialog box.

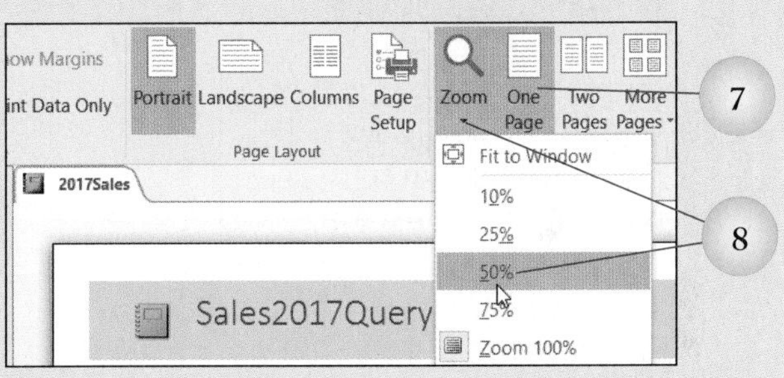

11. Close Print Preview by clicking the Close Print Preview button at the right side of the Print Preview tab.
12. Save and then close the 2017Sales report.
13. Create a report with the Representatives table by completing the following steps:
   a. Click *Representatives* in the Tables group in the Navigation pane.
   b. Click the Create tab.
   c. Click the Report button in the Reports group.
14. Adjust the width of the second column by completing the following steps:
   a. Click in the *RepName* column heading.
   b. Drag the right border of the selected column heading to the left until *Lines: 1 Characters: 16* displays at the left side of the Status bar, and then release the mouse button.
15. Complete steps similar to those in Step 14 to decrease the width of the third column (*Telephone*) to *Lines: 1 Characters: 12* and the fourth column (*Email*) to *Lines: 1 Characters: 13*.

16. Adjust the width of the *QuotaID* column and the width and height of the title control object by completing the following steps:
    a. Click in the *QuotaID* column heading.
    b. Click the Property Sheet button in the Tools group and, if necessary, click the Format tab.
    c. Select the current measurement in the *Width* property box, type 0.8, and then press the Enter key.
    d. Click *Representatives* in the title control object.
    e. Select the current measurement in the *Width* property box, type 2, and then press the Enter key.
    f. With the current measurement selected in the *Height* property box, type 0.6.
    g. Close the Property Sheet task pane by clicking the Close button in the upper right corner of the task pane.
17. Search for fields containing a quota of *2* by completing the following steps:
    a. Click in the *RepID* column heading.
    b. Click the Home tab and then click the Find button in the Find group.
    c. At the Find dialog box, type 2 in the *Find What* text box.
    d. Make sure the *Match* option is set to *Whole Field*. (If not, click the *Match* option box arrow and then click *Whole Field* at the drop-down list.)
    e. Click the Find Next button.
    f. Continue clicking the Find Next button until a message displays stating that Access has finished searching the records. Click OK at the message.
    g. Click the Cancel button to close the Find dialog box.

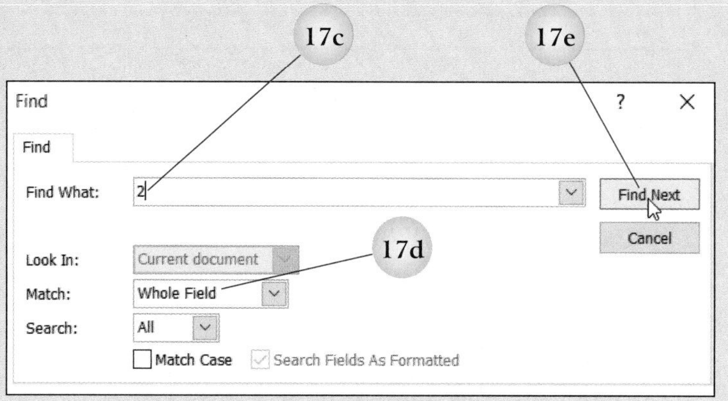

18. Suppose you want to find information on a representative and you remember the first name but not the last name. Search for a field containing the first name *Lydia* by completing the following steps:
    a. Click in the *RepID* column heading.
    b. Click the Find button in the Find group.
    c. At the Find dialog box, type Lydia in the *Find What* text box.
    d. Click the *Match* option box arrow and then click *Any Part of Field* at the drop-down list.
    e. Click the Find Next button. (Access will find and select the representative name *Lydia Alvarado*.)
    f. Click the Cancel button to close the Find dialog box.

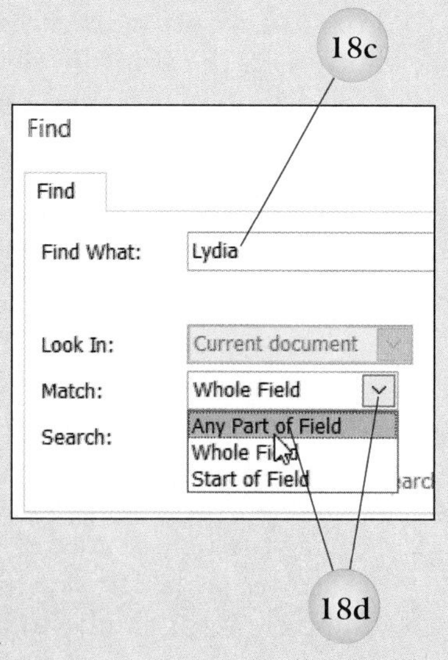

19. Click the control object at the bottom of the *RepID* column containing the number *17* and then press the Delete key. (This does not delete the underline above the amount.)

20. Switch to Print Preview by clicking the View button arrow in the Views group on the Home tab and then clicking *Print Preview* at the drop-down list.
21. Click the Margins button in the Page Size group and then click *Normal* at the drop-down list.

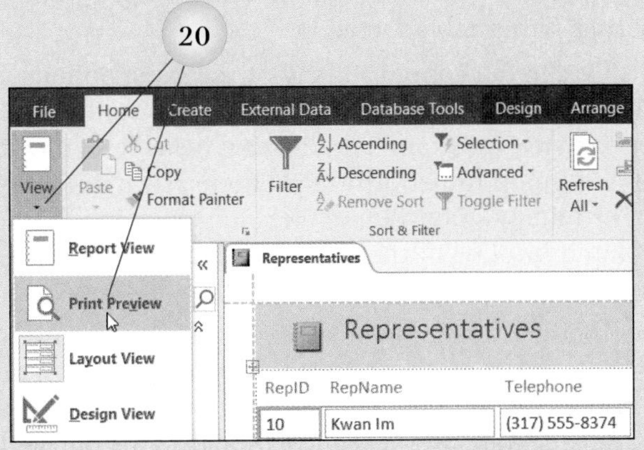

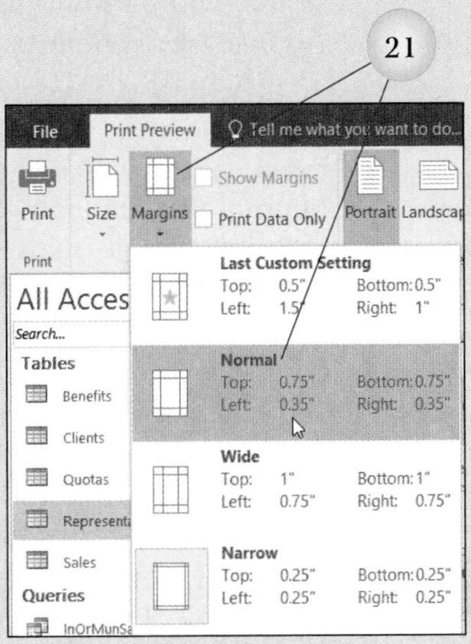

22. Decrease column width (so gray shading does not print on a second page) by completing the following steps:
    a. Click the Columns button in the Page Layout group on the Print Preview tab.
    b. Select the current measurement in the *Width* measurement box in the *Column Size* section of the dialog box and then type 8.
    c. Click OK to close the dialog box.

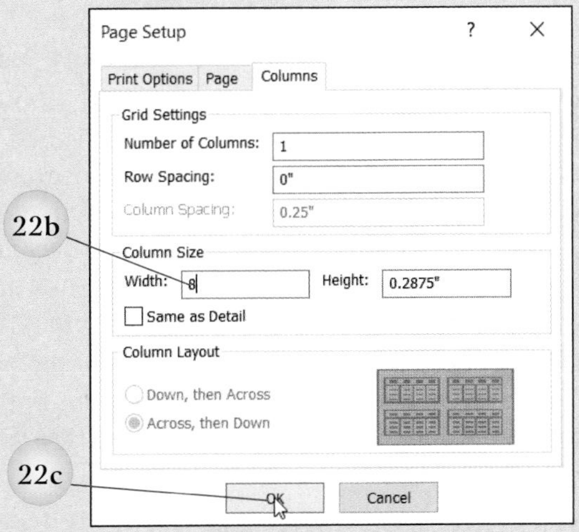

23. Print the report by clicking the Print button at the left side of the Print Preview tab and then clicking OK at the Print dialog box.
24. Close Print Preview by clicking the Close Print Preview button.
25. Save the report with the name *Representatives*.
26. Close the Representatives report.
27. Delete the Sales report by right-clicking *Sales* in the Reports group in the Navigation pane, clicking *Delete* at the shortcut menu, and then cicking Yes at the confirmation message.

Check Your Work

Tutorial

Formatting a Report

Totals

Hint The themes available in Access are the same as the themes available in Word, Excel, and PowerPoint.

Background

Formatting a Report

Customize a report in much the same manner as customizing a form. When a report is created, the report displays in Layout view and the Report Layout Tools Design tab is active. Customize control objects in the *Detail* section and the *Header* section with buttons on the Report Layout Tools ribbon with the Design tab, Arrange tab, Format tab, or Page Setup tab selected.

The Report Layout Tools Design tab contains many of the same options as the Form Layout Tools Design tab. Use options on this tab to apply a theme, insert controls, insert header or footer data, and add existing fields. Use the Totals button in the Grouping & Totals group to perform calculations, such as finding the sum, average, maximum, or minimum of the numbers in a column. To use the Totals button, click in the column heading of the column containing the data to be totaled, click the Totals button, and then click a function at the drop-down list.

Click the Report Layout Tools Arrange tab and options display for inserting and selecting rows, splitting cells horizontally and vertically, moving data up or down, controlling margins, and changing the padding between cells. The options on the Report Layout Tools Arrange tab are the same as the options on the Form Layout Tools Arrange tab.

Select and format data in a report with options on the Report Layout Tools Format tab. The options on this tab are the same as the options on the Form Layout Tools Format tab. Use options to apply formatting to a report or specific objects in a report. To apply formatting to a specific object, click the object in the report or click the Object button arrow in the Selection group on the Report Layout Tools Format tab and then click the object at the drop-down list. To format all objects in the report, click the Select All button in the Selection group. This selects all objects in the report, including objects in the *Header* section. To select all of the objects in the report table, click the table move handle.

Use buttons in the Font, Number, Background, and Control Formatting groups to apply formatting to a cell or selected cells in a report. Use buttons in the Font group to change the font, apply a different font size, apply text effects (such as bold and underline), and change the alignment of data in objects. Insert a background image in the report using the Background button and apply formatting to cells with buttons in the Control Formatting group. Depending on what is selected in the report, some of the buttons may not be active.

Click the Report Layout Tools Page Setup tab and the buttons that display are also available in Print Preview. For example, the tab contains buttons for changing the page size and page layout of the report and displaying the Page Setup dialog box.

Tutorial

Applying Conditional Formatting to a Report

Conditional Formatting

Applying Conditional Formatting to a Report

Apply conditional formatting to a report in the same manner as applying conditional formatting to a form (covered in Chapter 5). Click the Conditional Formatting button in the Control Formatting group on the Report Layout Tools Format tab and the Conditional Formatting Rules Manager dialog box displays. Click the New Rule button and then use options in the New Formatting Rule dialog box to specify the conditional formatting.

Project 1c Applying Formatting to a Report

Part 3 of 5

1. With **6-Dearborn.accdb** open, open the 2017Sales report.
2. Display the report in Layout view.
3. Click the Themes button in the Themes group on the Report Layout Tools Design tab and then click *Ion* at the drop-down gallery.
4. Click the Title button in the Header/Footer group (which selects the current title), type 2017 Sales, and then press the Enter key.
5. Insert a row of empty cells in the report by completing the following steps:
   a. Click in the *Representative* cell.
   b. Click the Report Layout Tools Arrange tab.
   c. Click the Insert Above button in the Rows & Columns group.
6. Merge the cells in the new row by completing the following steps:
   a. Click in the empty cell immediately above the *Representative* cell.
   b. Press and hold down the Shift key, click immediately above the *Sales 2017* cell, and then release the Shift key. (This selects three cells.)
   c. Click the Merge button in the Merge/Split group.
   d. Type Dearborn 2017 Sales in the new cell.
7. Split a cell by completing the following steps:
   a. Click in the *2017 Sales* title in the *Header* section.
   b. Split the cell containing the title by clicking the Split Horizontally button in the Merge/Split group.
   c. Click in the empty cell immediately right of the cell containing the title *Sales 2017* and then press the Delete key. (Deleting the empty cell causes the date and time to move to the left in the *Header* section.)
8. Change the report table margins and padding by completing the following steps:
   a. Click in any cell in the *Detail* section and then click the table move handle in the upper left corner of the *Dearborn 2017 Sales* cell. (This selects all of the control objects in the report table in the *Detail* section.)
   b. Click the Control Margins button in the Position group and then click *Narrow* at the drop-down list.
   c. Click the Control Padding button in the Position group and then click *Medium* at the drop-down list.

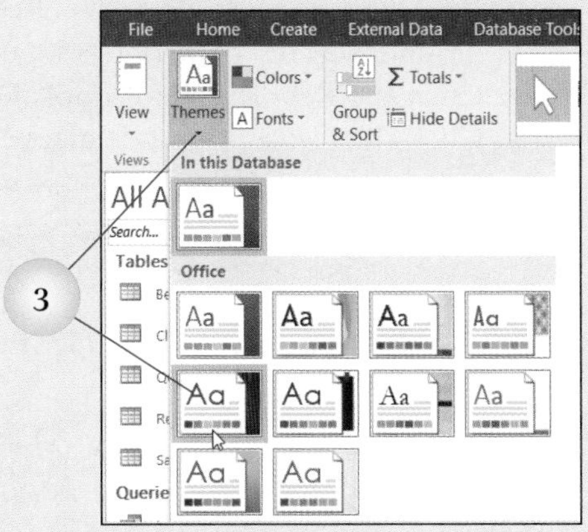

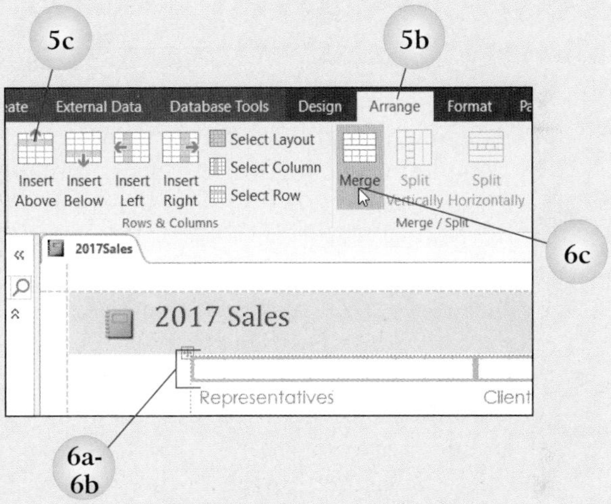

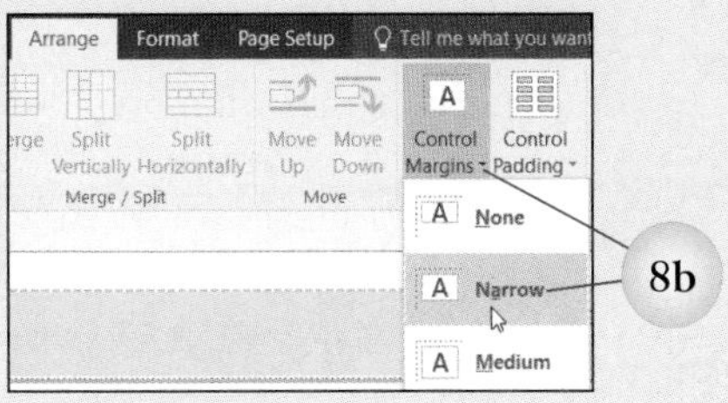

9. Click in the *Dearborn 2017 Sales* cell and then drag down the bottom border so all of the text in the cell is visible.
10. Change the font for all of the data in the report by completing the following steps:
   a. Press Ctrl + A to select all control objects in the report. (An orange border displays around selected objects.)
   b. Click the Report Layout Tools Format tab.
   c. Click the *Font* option box arrow in the Font group and then click *Cambria* at the drop-down list. (You may need to scroll down the list to display *Cambria*.)

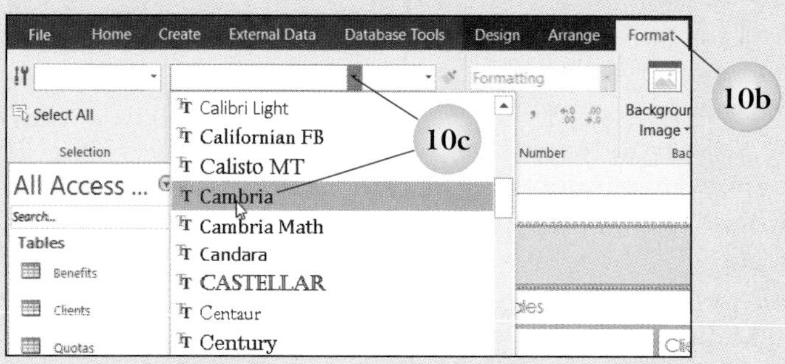

11. Apply bold formatting and change the alignment of the column headings by completing the following steps:
   a. Click *Dearborn 2017 Sales* to select the control object.
   b. Press and hold down the Shift key, click *Sales 2017*, and then release the Shift key. (This selects four cells.)
   c. Click the Bold button in the Font group.
   d. Click the Center button in the Font group.

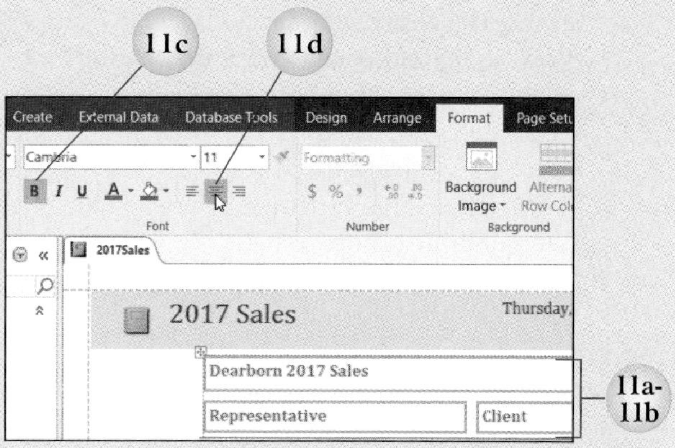

12. Format and apply conditional formatting to the amounts by completing the following steps:
   a. Click the first field value below the *Sales 2017* column heading. (This selects all of the amounts in the column.)
   b. Click the Decrease Decimals button in the Number group two times.

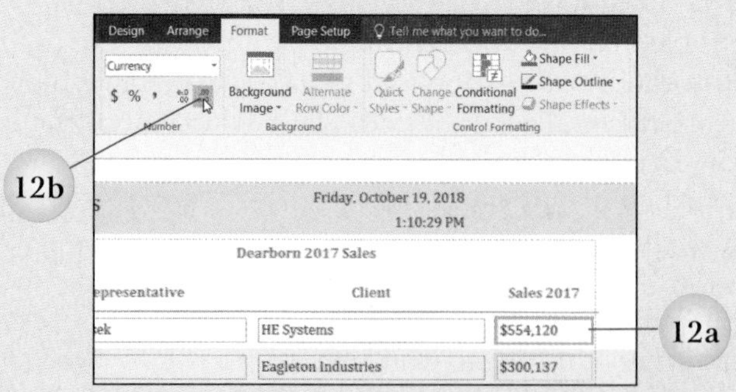

   c. Click the Conditional Formatting button in the Control Formatting group.
   d. At the Conditional Formatting Rules Manager dialog box, click the New Rule button.

e. At the New Formatting Rule dialog box, click the option box arrow for the second option box in the *Edit the rule description* section and then click *greater than* at the drop-down list.
f. Click in the text box immediately right of the option box containing *greater than* and then type 199999.
g. Click the Background color button arrow and then click the *Green 2* color option (seventh column, third row).
h. Click OK.
i. At the Conditional Formatting Rules Manager dialog box, click the New Rule button.
j. At the New Formatting Rule dialog box, click the option box arrow for the second option box in the *Edit the rule description* section and then click *less than* at the drop-down list.
k. Click in the text box immediately right of the option box containing *less than* and then type 200000.
l. Click the Background color button arrow and then click the *Maroon 2* color option (sixth column, third row).
m. Click OK to close the New Formatting Rule dialog box.
n. Click OK to close the Conditional Formatting Rules Manager dialog box.

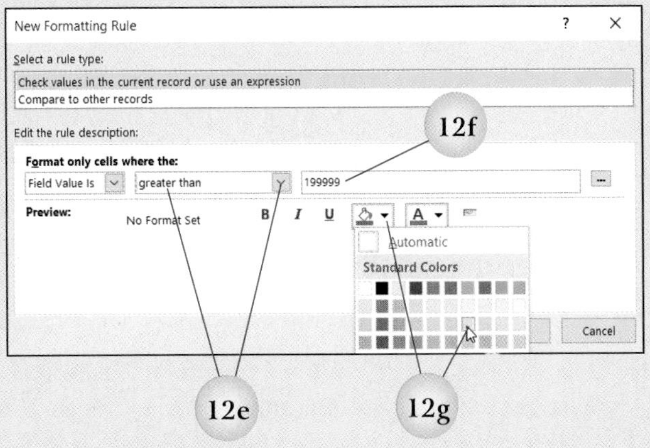

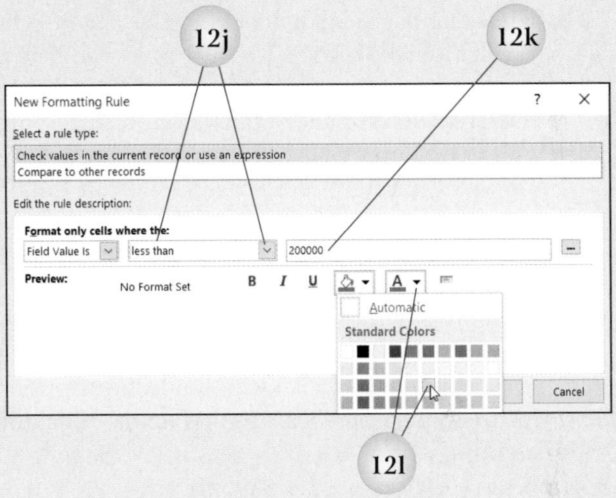

13. Sum the totals in the *Sales 2017* column by completing the following steps:
a. Click in the *Sales 2017* column heading.
b. Click the Report Layout Tools Design tab.
c. Click the Totals button in the Grouping & Totals group and then click *Sum* at the drop-down list.

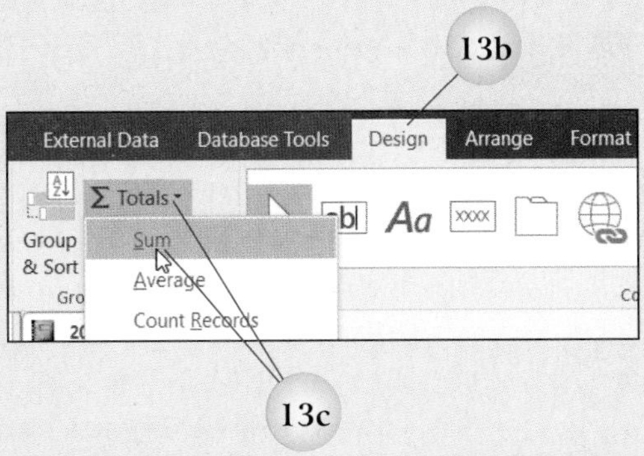

14. Click in the *Sales 2017* sum amount (at the bottom of the *Sales 2017* column) and then drag down the bottom border so the entire amount is visible in the cell.
15. Change the top margin by completing the following steps:
a. Click in the *Representative* column heading and then click the Report Layout Tools Page Setup tab.

b. Click the Page Setup button in the Page Layout group.

c. At the Page Setup dialog box with the Print Options tab selected, select the current measurement in the *Top* measurement box and then type 0.5.

d. Click OK to close the Page Setup dialog box.

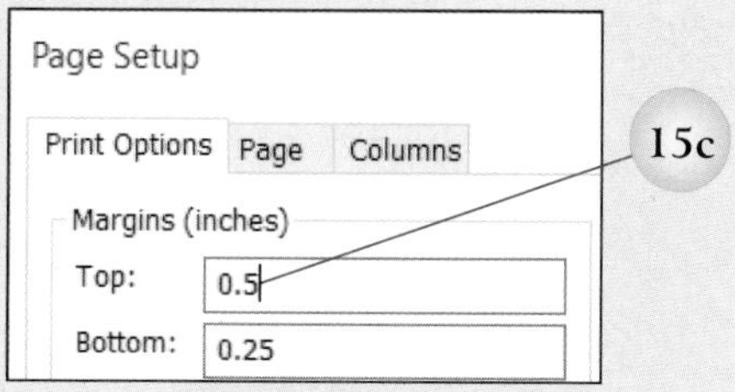

16. Change the page size by clicking the Size button in the Page Size group and and then clicking *Legal* at the drop-down list.
17. Display the report in Print Preview by clicking the File tab, clicking the *Print* option, and then clicking the *Print Preview* option.
18. Click the One Page button in the Zoom group and notice that the entire report will print on one legal-sized page.
19. Click the Close Print Preview button to return to the report.
20. Change the page size by clicking the Page Layout Tools Page Setup tab, clicking the Size button in the Page Size group, and then clicking *Letter* at the drop-down list.

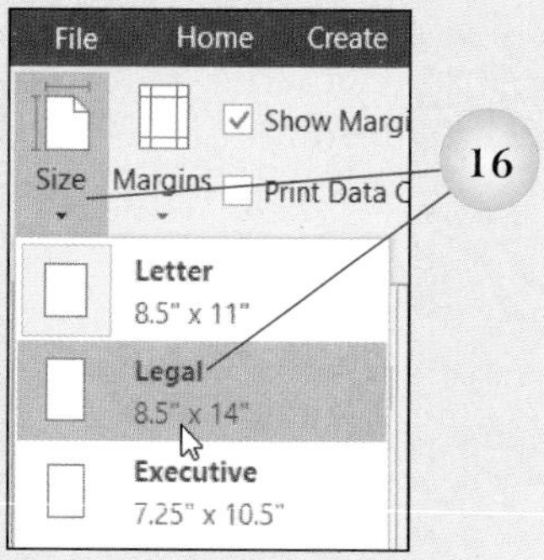

21. Insert and then remove a background image by completing the following steps:
    a. Click the Report Layout Tools Format tab.
    b. Click the Background Image button in the Background group and then click *Browse* at the drop-down list.
    c. At the Insert Picture dialog box, navigate to the AL1C6 folder on your storage medium and then double-click ***Mountain.jpg***.
    d. Scroll through the report and notice how the image displays in the report.
    e. Click the Undo button on the Quick Access Toolbar to remove the background image. (You may need to click the Undo button more than once.)
22. Print the report by clicking the File tab, clicking the *Print* option, and then clicking the *Quick Print* option.
23. Save and then close the report.

Check Your Work

Tutorial

Grouping and Sorting Records in a Report

Group & Sort

Add a group

Quick Steps

Group and Sort Records

1. Open report in Layout view.
2. Click Group & Sort button.
3. Click Add a group button.
4. Click group field.

Grouping and Sorting Records in a Report

A report presents database information in a printed form and generally displays data that answers a specific question. To make the data in a report easy to understand, divide the data into groups. For example, data can be divided in a report by regions, sales, dates, or any other division that helps clarify the data for the reader. Access contains a group and sort feature for dividing data into groups and sorting the data.

Click the Group & Sort button in the Grouping & Totals group on the Report Layout Tools Design tab and the Group, Sort, and Total pane displays at the bottom of the work area, as shown in Figure 6.2. Click the Add a group button in the Group, Sort, and Total pane and Access adds a new grouping level row to the pane, along with a list of available fields. Click the field by which data is to be grouped in the report and Access adds the grouping level in the report. With options in the grouping level row, change the group, specify the sort order, and expand the row to display additional options.

Figure 6.2 Group, Sort, and Total Pane

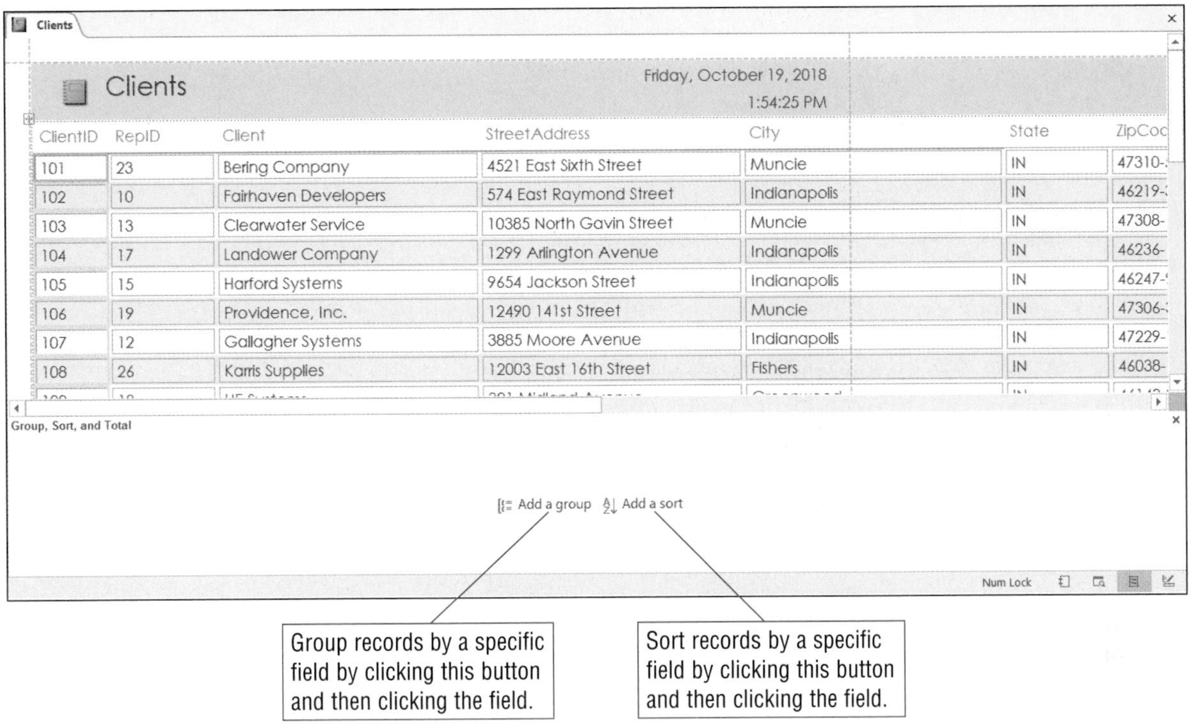

Add a sort

Hint Grouping allows you to separate groups of records visually.

When a grouping level is specified, Access automatically sorts that level in ascending order (from A to Z or lowest to highest). Additional data can be sorted within the report by clicking the Add a sort button in the Group, Sort, and Total pane. This inserts a sorting row in the pane below the grouping level row, along with a list of available fields. At this list, click the field by which to sort. For example, in Project 1d, one of the reports will be grouped by city (which will display in ascending order) and then the client names will display in alphabetic order within the city.

To delete a grouping or sorting level in the Group, Sort, and Total pane, click the Delete button at the right side of the level row. After specifying the grouping and sorting levels, close the Group, Sort, and Total pane by clicking the Close button in the upper right corner of the pane or by clicking the Group & Sort button in the Grouping & Totals group.

Project 1d Grouping and Sorting Records in a Report

Part 4 of 5

1. With **6-Dearborn.accdb** open, create a report with the Clients table using the Report button on the Create tab.
2. Click in each column heading individually and then decrease the size of each column so the right border is just right of the longest entry.
3. Change to landscape orientation by completing the following steps:
   a. Click the Report Layout Tools Page Setup tab.
   b. Click the Landscape button in the Page Layout group.
4. Group the report by representative ID and then sort by clients by completing the following steps:
   a. Click the Report Layout Tools Design tab.
   b. Click the Group & Sort button in the Grouping & Totals group.

c. Click the Add a group button in the Group, Sort, and Total pane.

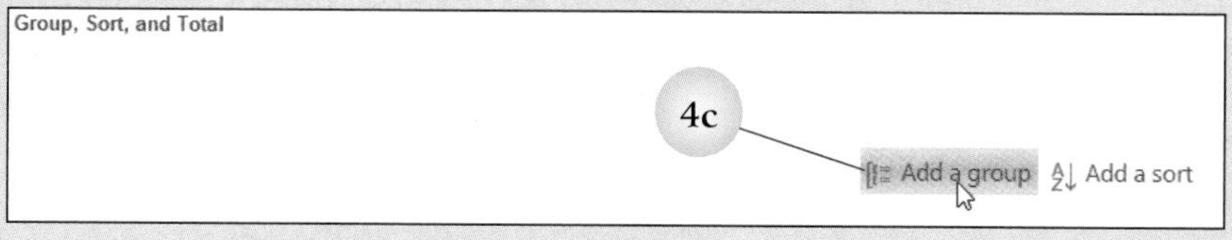

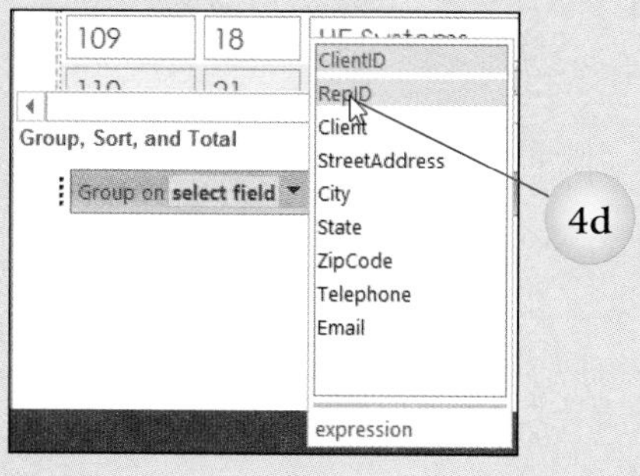

d. Click the *RepID* field in the list box.
e. Scroll through the report and notice that the records are grouped by the *RepID* field. Also, notice that the client names within each *RepID* field group are not in alphabetic order.
f. Click the Add a sort button in the Group, Sort, and Total pane.
g. Click the *Client* field in the list box.
h. Scroll through the report and notice that client names are now alphabetized within *RepID* field groups.

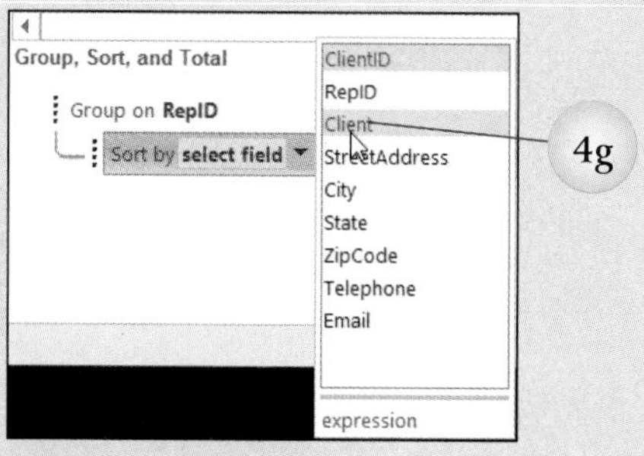

i. Close the Group, Sort, and Total pane by clicking the Group & Sort button in the Grouping & Totals group.

5. Save the report with the name *RepIDGroupedRpt*.
6. Change column width and print the first page of the report by completing the following steps:
   a. Click the File tab, click the *Print* option, and then click the *Print Preview* option.
   b. Click the Columns button on the Print Preview tab, select the current measurement in the *Width* measurement box, type 10, and then click OK.
   c. Click the Print button on the Print Preview tab.
   d. At the Print dialog box, click the *Pages* option in the *Print Range* section.
   e. Type 1 in the *From* text box, press the Tab key, and then type 1 in the *To* text box.
   f. Click OK.
7. Close the RepIDGroupedRpt report.
8. Create a report with the InOrMunSalesOver$99999Query query using the Report button on the Create tab. Make sure the report displays in Layout view.
9. Group the report by city and then sort by clients by completing the following steps:
   a. Click the Group & Sort button in the Grouping & Totals group on the Report Layout Tools Design tab.
   b. Click the Add a group button in the Group, Sort, and Total pane.
   c. Click the *City* field in the list box.
   d. Click the Add a sort button in the Group, Sort, and Total pane.
   e. Click the *Client* field in the list box.
   f. Close the Group, Sort, and Total pane by clicking the Group & Sort button in the Grouping & Totals group.
10. Print the first page of the report. (Refer to Step 6.)
11. Save the report, name it *InMunSalesOver$99999*, and then close the report.
12. Close **6-Dearborn.accdb**.
13. Open **6-WarrenLegal.accdb** from the AL1C6 folder on your storage medium and enable the content.

14. Design a query that extracts records from three tables with the following specifications:
    a. Add the Billing, Clients, and Rates tables to the query window.
    b. Insert the *LastName* field from the Clients table field list box in the first field in the *Field* row.
    c. Insert the *Date* field from the Billing table field list box in the second field in the *Field* row.
    d. Insert the *Hours* field from the Billing table field list box in the third field in the *Field* row.
    e. Insert the *Rate* field from the Rates table field list box in the fourth field in the *Field* row.
    f. Click in the fifth field in the *Field* row, type Total: [Hours]*[Rate], and then press the Enter key.

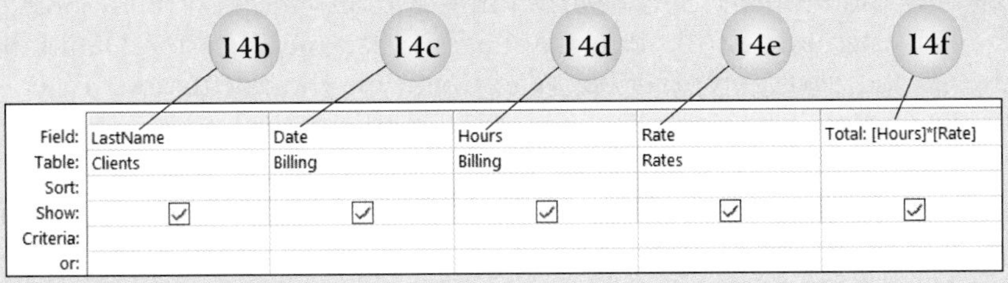

    g. Run the query.
    h. Save the query with the name *ClientBilling*.
    i. Close the query.
15. Create a report with the ClientBilling query using the Report button on the Create tab.
16. Click in each column heading individually and then decrease the size of each column so the right border is near the longest entry.
17. Apply currency formatting to the numbers in the *Total* column by completing the following steps:
    a. Click the Report Layout Tools Format tab.
    b. Click in the first field below the *Total* column (the field containing the number *350*).
    c. Click the Apply Currency Format button in the Number group.
    d. If necessary, increase the size of the *Total* column so the entire amounts (including the dollar symbols ($)) are visible.

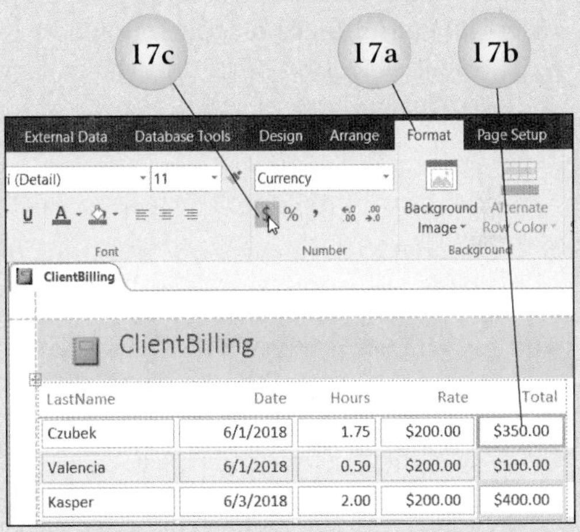

18. Group the report by last name and then sort by date by completing the following steps:
    a. Click the Report Layout Tools Design tab.
    b. Click the Group & Sort button in the Grouping & Totals group.
    c. Click the Add a group button in the Group, Sort, and Total pane.
    d. Click the *LastName* field in the list box.
    e. Click the Add a sort button in the Group, Sort, and Total pane.
    f. Click the *Date* field in the list box.
    g. Close the Group, Sort, and Total pane by clicking the Close button in the upper right corner of the pane.
19. Scroll to the bottom of the report and delete the total amount in the *Rate* column and the line above the total. (Click the line and then press the Delete key.)
20. Save the report with the name *ClientBillingRpt*.
21. Close the report.

Check Your Work

Tutorial

Inserting a Calculation in a Report

Quick Steps

Insert Calculation in Report

1. Click Text Box button on Report Layout Tools Design tab.
2. Click in report to insert label and text box control objects.
3. Click in text box control object.
4. Click Property Sheet button in Tools group.
5. Click Data tab.
6. Click in *Control Source* property box.
7. Type calculation.
8. Click Close button.

Inserting a Calculation in a Report

Like a form, a calculation can be inserted in a report in a text box control object. To insert a text box control object as well as a label control object, click the Text Box button in the gallery in the Controls group on the Report Layout Tools Design tab, and then click in a location in the report where the two objects are to display. Click in the label control box and then type a label for the calculated field.

Insert a calculation by clicking in the text box control object and then clicking the Property Sheet button in the Tools group on the Report Layout Tools Design tab. At the Property Sheet task pane, click the Data tab, click in the *Control Source* property box, and then type the calculation. Type a calculation in the *Control Source* property box using mathematical operators and type field names in the calculation inside square brackets. Begin the calculation with an equals sign (=). A field name must be typed in the calculation as it appears in the source object.

If a calculation result is currency, apply currency formatting to the text box control object. Apply currency formatting by clicking the Report Layout Tools Format tab and then clicking the Apply Currency Format button in the Number group.

Project 1e Inserting a Calculation in a Report

Part 5 of 5

1. With **6-WarrenLegal.accdb** open, open the ClientBillingRpt report in Layout view.
2. Insert label and text box control objects by completing the following steps:
   a. Click the Text Box button in the gallery in the Controls group on the Report Layout Tools Design tab.
   b. Position the crosshairs to the right of the *Total* field name and then click the left mouse button. (This inserts a label control object and text box object in the report.)

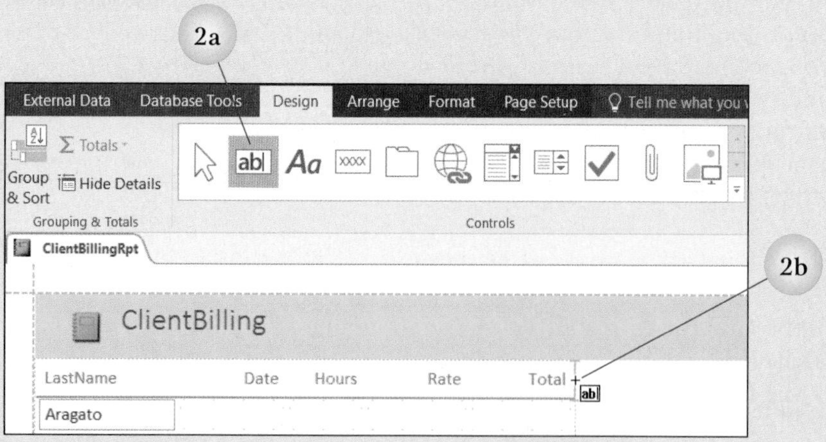

3. Name the new field by clicking in the label control object, double-clicking the text in the label control object, and then typing Total + 9% Tax.

4. Click in the text box control object and then insert a calculation by completing the following steps:
   a. Click the Property Sheet button in the Tools group on the Report Layout Tools Design tab.
   b. At the Property Sheet task pane, click the Data tab.
   c. Click in the *Control Source* property box.
   d. Type =[Total]*1.09 and then press the Enter key.

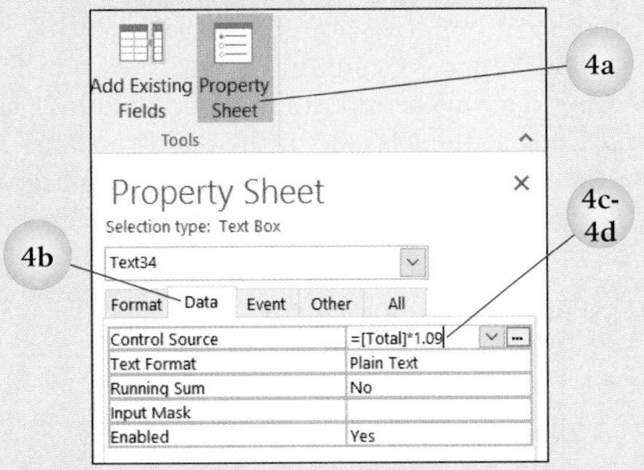

   e. Close the Property Sheet task pane by clicking the Close button in the upper right corner of the task pane.
5. With the text box control object still selected, apply currency formatting by clicking the Report Layout Tools Format tab and then clicking the Apply Currency Format button in the Number group.
6. Save and then print the report. (The report will print on three pages.).
7. Close the ClientBillingRpt report and then close **6-WarrenLegal.accdb**.

Check Your Work

Project 2 Use Wizards to Create Reports and Labels — 3 Parts

You will create reports using the Report Wizard and prepare mailing labels using the Label Wizard.

Preview Finished Project

Tutorial

Creating a Report Using the Report Wizard

Report Wizard

Quick Steps

Create a Report Using the Report Wizard

1. Click Create tab.
2. Click Report Wizard button.
3. Choose options at each Report Wizard dialog box.

Hint Use the Report Wizard to select specific fields and specify how data is grouped and sorted.

Creating a Report Using the Report Wizard

Access offers a Report Wizard that provides the steps for creating a report. To create a report using the wizard, click the Create tab and then click the Report Wizard button in the Reports group. At the first Report Wizard dialog box, shown in Figure 6.3, choose a table or query with options from the *Tables/Queries* option box. Specify the fields to be included in the report by inserting them in the *Selected Fields* list box and then clicking the Next button.

At the second Report Wizard dialog box, shown in Figure 6.4, specify the grouping level of data in the report. To group data by a specific field, click the field in the list box at the left side of the dialog box and then click the One Field button. Use the button containing the left-pointing arrow to remove an option as a grouping level. Use the up and down arrows to change the priority of the field.

Figure 6.3 First Report Wizard Dialog Box

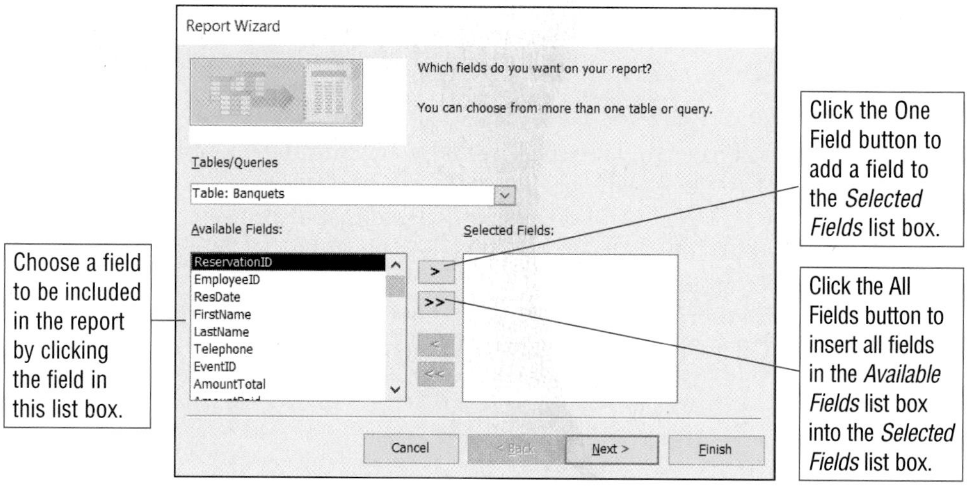

Figure 6.4 Second Report Wizard Dialog Box

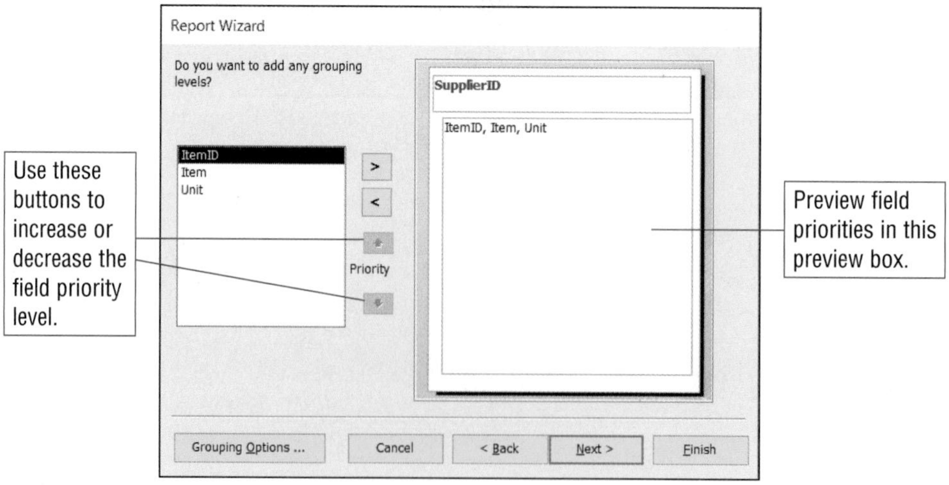

Specify a sort order with options at the third Report Wizard dialog box, shown in Figure 6.5. To specify a sort order, click the option box arrow for the option box preceded by the number *1* and then click the field name. The default sort order is ascending. This can be changed to descending by clicking the button at the right side of the option box. After identifying the sort order, click the Next button.

Use options at the fourth Report Wizard dialog box, shown in Figure 6.6, to specify the layout and orientation of the report. The *Layout* section has the default setting of *Stepped*, which can be changed to *Block* or *Outline*. By default, the report will print in portrait orientation. Change to landscape orientation by clicking the *Landscape* option in the *Orientation* section of the dialog box. Access will adjust field widths in the report so all of the fields fit on one page. To specify that field widths should not be adjusted, remove the check mark from the *Adjust the field width so all fields fit on a page* option.

At the fifth and final Report Wizard dialog box, type a name for the report and then click the Finish button.

Figure 6.5 Third Report Wizard Dialog Box

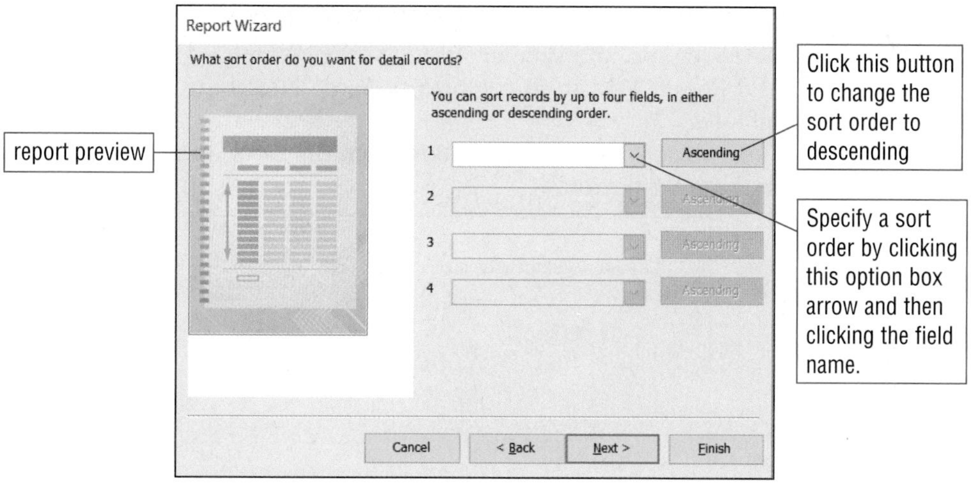

Figure 6.6 Fourth Report Wizard Dialog Box

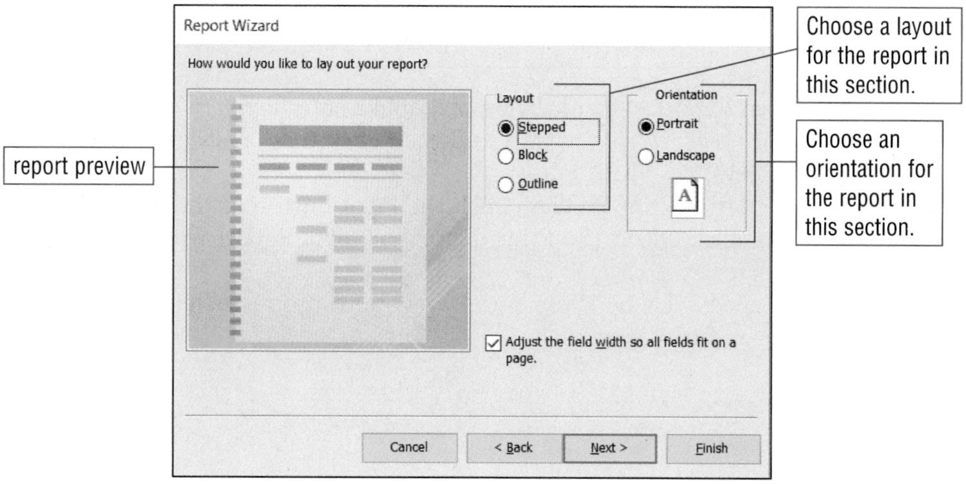

Project 2a Creating a Report Using the Report Wizard

1. Open **6-Skyline.accdb** from the AL1C6 folder on your storage medium and enable the content.
2. Create a report using the Report Wizard by completing the following steps:
   a. Click the Create tab.
   b. Click the Report Wizard button in the Reports group.
   c. At the first Report Wizard dialog box, click the *Tables/Queries* option box arrow and then click *Table: Inventory* at the drop-down list.
   d. Click the All Fields button to insert all of the Inventory table fields in the *Selected Fields* list box.
   e. Click the Next button.
   f. At the second Report Wizard dialog box, make sure *SupplierID* displays in blue at the top of the preview page at the right side of the dialog box and then click the Next button.
   g. At the third Report Wizard dialog box, click the Next button. (You want to use the sorting defaults.)
   h. At the fourth Report Wizard dialog box, click the *Block* option in the *Layout* section and then click the Next button.

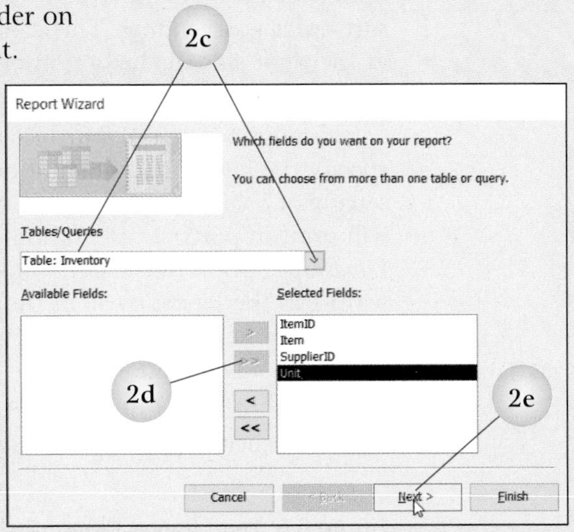

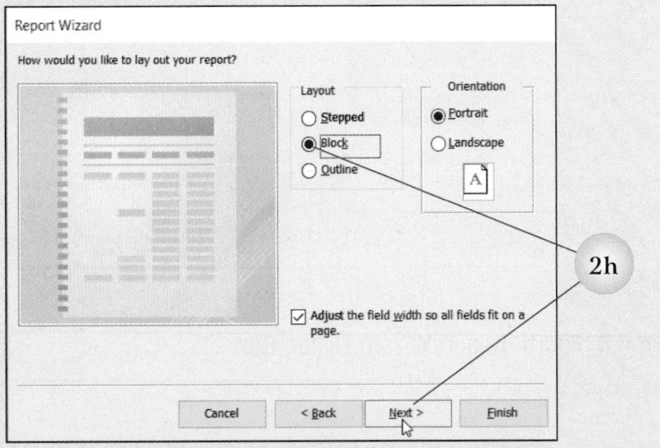

   i. At the fifth Report Wizard dialog box, make sure *Inventory* displays in the *What title do you want for your report?* text box and then click the Finish button. (The report displays in Print Preview.)
3. With the report in Print Preview, click the Print button at the left side of the Print Preview tab and then click OK at the Print dialog box. (The report will print on two pages.)
4. Close Print Preview.
5. Switch to Report view by clicking the View button on the Report Design Tools Design tab.
6. Close the Inventory report.

Check Your Work

If a report is created with fields from only one table, options are specified in five Report Wizard dialog boxes. If a report is created with fields from more than one table, options are specified in six Report Wizard dialog boxes. After choosing the tables and fields at the first dialog box, the second dialog box that displays asks how the data will be viewed. For example, if fields are selected from a Suppliers table and an Orders table, the second Report Wizard dialog box will ask if the data is to be viewed "by Suppliers" or "by Orders."

Project 2b Creating a Report with Fields from Two Tables

Part 2 of 3

1. With **6-Skyline.accdb** open, create a report with the Report Wizard by completing the following steps:
   a. Click the Create tab.
   b. Click the Report Wizard button in the Reports group.
   c. At the first Report Wizard dialog box, click the *Tables/Queries* option box arrow and then click *Table: Events* at the drop-down list.
   d. Click the *Event* field in the *Available Fields* list box and then click the One Field button.

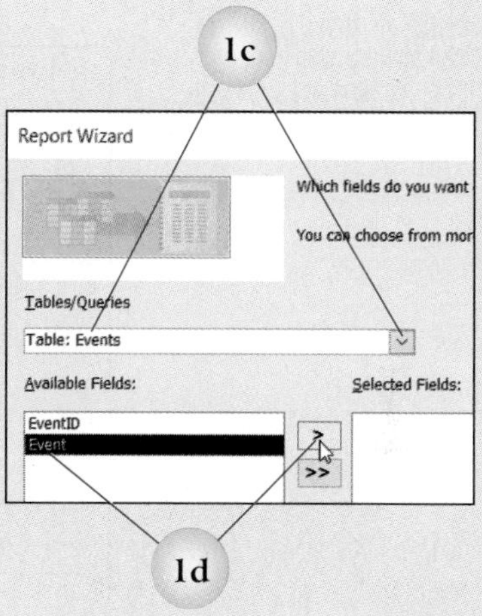

   e. Click the *Tables/Queries* option box arrow and then click *Table: Banquets* at the drop-down list.
   f. Insert the following fields in the *Selected Fields* list box:
      ResDate
      FirstName
      LastName
      AmountTotal
      AmountPaid
   g. After inserting the fields, click the Next button.
   h. At the second Report Wizard dialog box, make sure *by Events* is selected and then click the Next button.
   i. At the third Report Wizard dialog box, click the Next button. (The report preview shows that the report will be grouped by event.)

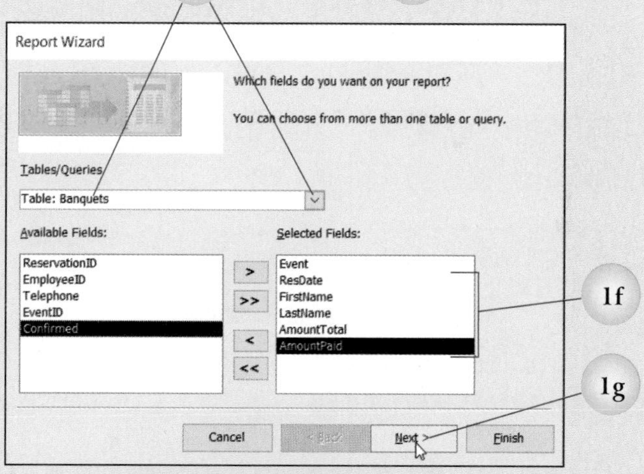

   j. At the fourth Report Wizard dialog box, click the Next button. (You want to use the sorting defaults.)
   k. At the fifth Report Wizard dialog box, click the *Block* option in the *Layout* section, click *Landscape* in the *Orientation* section, and then click the Next button.
   l. At the sixth Report Wizard dialog box, select the current name in the *What title do you want for your report?* text box and then type BanquetEvents.
   m. Click the Finish button.

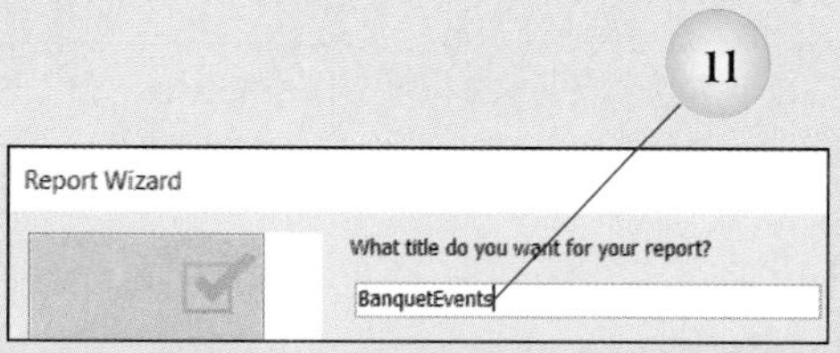

2. Close Print Preview and then change to Layout view.
3. Print and then close the BanquetEvents report.
4. Close **6-Skyline.accdb**.

Check Your Work

Tutorial

Creating Mailing Labels

Labels

Quick Steps

Create Mailing Labels Using the Label Wizard

1. Click table.
2. Click Create tab.
3. Click Labels button.
4. Choose options at each Label Wizard dialog box.

Creating Mailing Labels

Access includes a mailing label wizard that provides the steps for creating mailing labels with fields in a table. To create mailing labels, click a table, click the Create tab, and then click the Labels button in the Reports group. At the first Label Wizard dialog box, shown in Figure 6.7, specify the label size, unit of measure, and label type and then click the Next button. At the second Label Wizard dialog box, shown in Figure 6.8, specify the font name, size, weight, and color and then click the Next button.

Figure 6.7 First Label Wizard Dialog Box

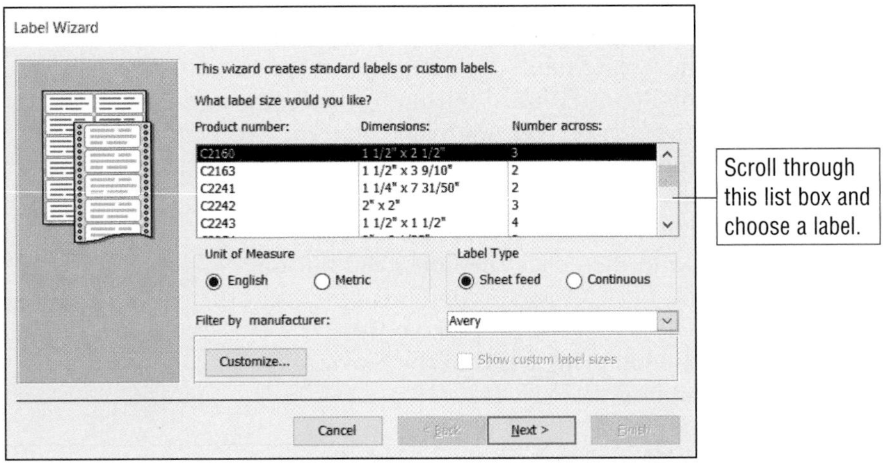

Figure 6.8 Second Label Wizard Dialog Box

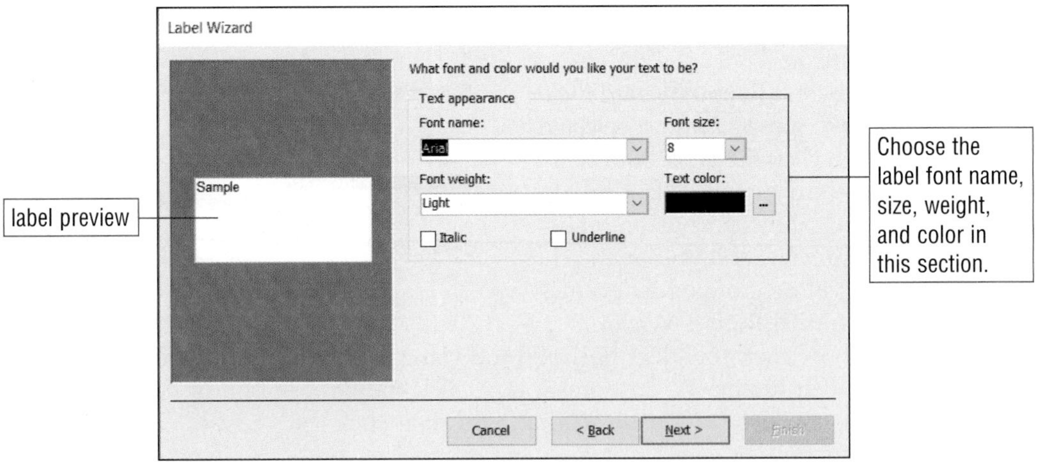

Specify the fields to be included in the mailing labels at the third Label Wizard dialog box, shown in Figure 6.9. To do this, click the field in the *Available fields* list box and then click the One Field button. This moves the field to the *Prototype label* box. Insert the fields in the *Prototype label* box as the text should display on the label. After inserting the fields in the *Prototype label* box, click the Next button.

At the fourth Label Wizard dialog box, shown in Figure 6.10, specify a field from the database by which the labels will be sorted. To sort labels (for example, by last name, postal code, etc.), insert that field in the *Sort by* list box and then click the Next button.

At the last Label Wizard dialog box, type a name for the label report and then click the Finish button. After a few moments, the labels display on the screen in Print Preview. Print the labels and/or close Print Preview.

Figure 6.9 Third Label Wizard Dialog Box

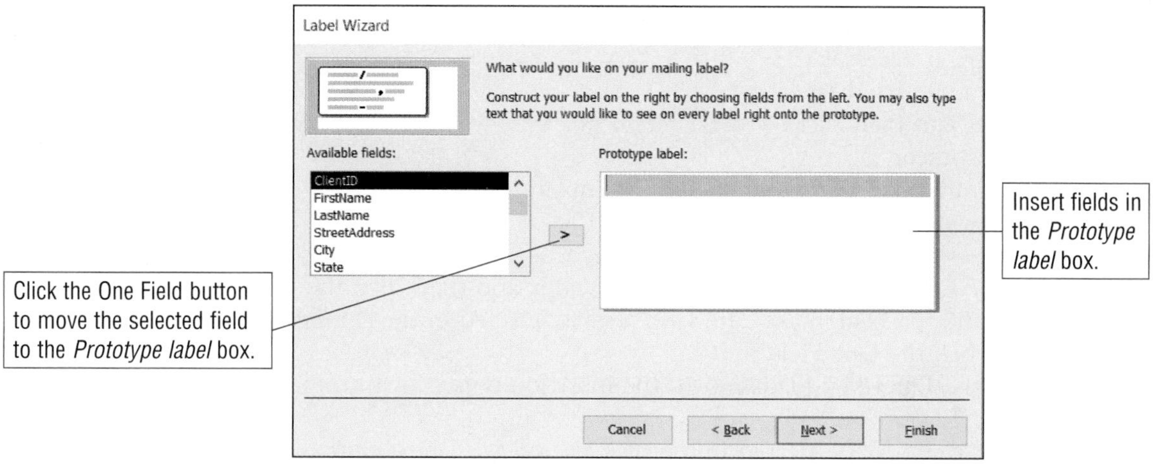

Figure 6.10 Fourth Label Wizard Dialog Box

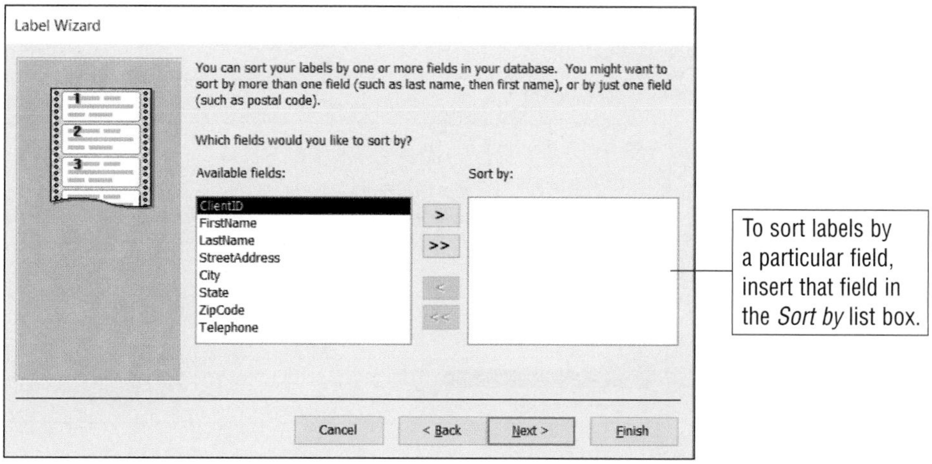

Project 2c Creating Mailing Labels

Part 3 of 3

1. Open **6-WarrenLegal.accdb** and enable the content.
2. Click *Clients* in the Tables group in the Navigation pane.
3. Click the Create tab and then click the Labels button in the Reports group.
4. At the first Label Wizard dialog box, make sure *English* is selected in the *Unit of Measure* section, *Avery* is selected in the *Filter by manufacturer* list box, *Sheet feed* is selected in the *Label Type* section, and *C2160* is selected in the *Product number* list box and then click the Next button.

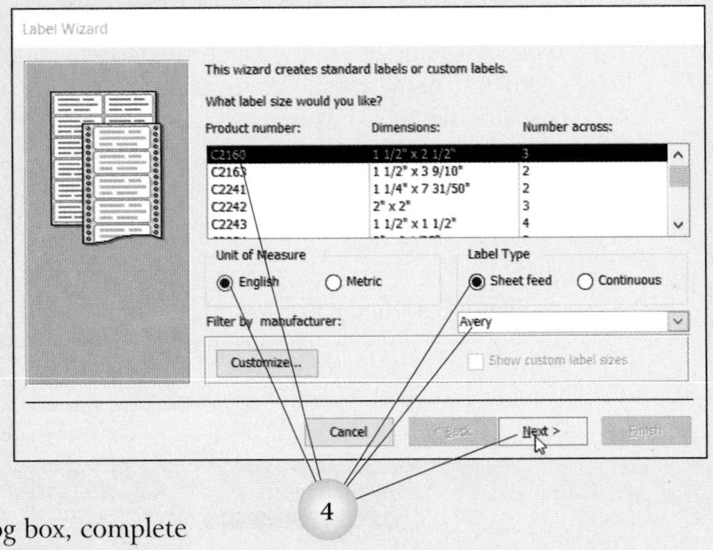

5. At the second Label Wizard dialog box, if necessary, change the font size to 10 points and then click the Next button.
6. At the third Label Wizard dialog box, complete the following steps to insert the fields in the *Prototype label* box:
   a. Click *FirstName* in the *Available fields* list box and then click the One Field button.
   b. Press the spacebar, make sure *LastName* is selected in the *Available fields* list box, and then click the One Field button.
   c. Press the Enter key. (This moves the insertion point down to the next line in the *Prototype label* box.)
   d. With *StreetAddress* selected in the *Available fields* list box, click the One Field button.
   e. Press the Enter key.
   f. With *City* selected in the *Available fields* list box, click the One Field button.
   g. Type a comma (,) and then press the spacebar.
   h. With *State* selected in the *Available fields* list box, click the One Field button.
   i. Press the spacebar.
   j. With *ZipCode* selected in the *Available fields* list box, click the One Field button.

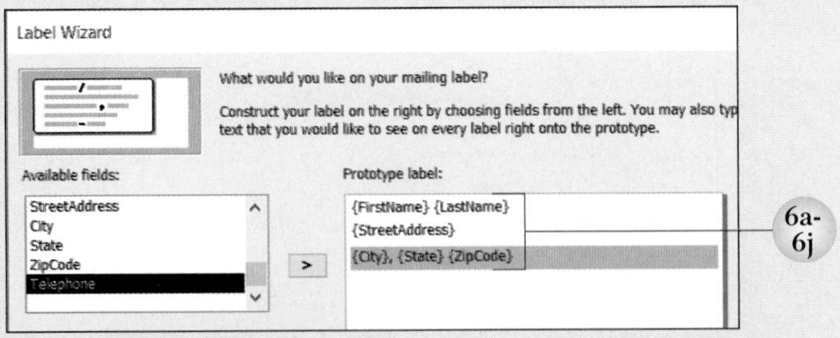

   k. Click the Next button.

7. At the fourth Label Wizard dialog box, sort by zip code. To do this, click *ZipCode* in the *Available fields* list box and then click the One Field button.
8. Click the Next button.
9. At the last Label Wizard dialog box, click the Finish button. (The Label Wizard automatically names the label report *Labels Clients*.)
10. Print the labels by clicking the Print button at the left side of the Print Preview tab and then click OK at the Print dialog box.
11. Close Print Preview.
12. Switch to Report view by clicking the View button on the Report Design Tools Design tab.
13. Close the labels report and then close **6-WarrenLegal.accdb**.

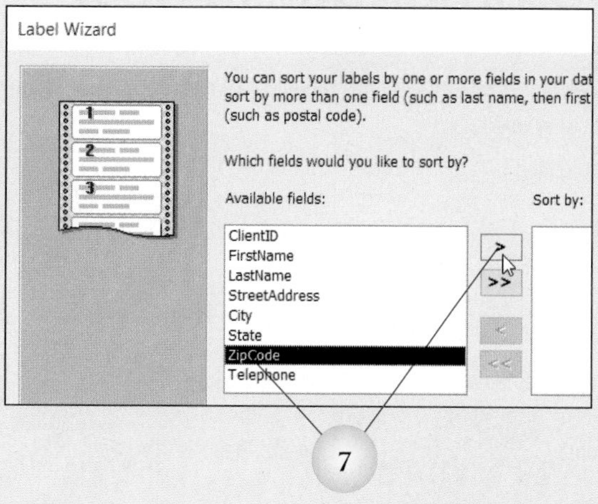

Check Your Work

Chapter Summary

- Create a report with data in a table or query to control how data appears on the page and how the data is formatted when printed.
- Create a report with the Report button in the Reports group on the Create tab.
- Four views are available for viewing a report: Report view, Print Preview, Layout view, and Design view.
- Use options on the Print Preview tab to specify how a report prints.
- In Layout view, a report control object can be selected and then sized or moved.
- One method for changing column width in a report is to click a column heading and then drag the border to the desired width.
- Sort data in a record using the Ascending button or Descending button in the Sort & Filter group on the Home tab.
- Customize a report with options on the Report Layout Tools ribbon with the Design tab, Arrange tab, Format tab, or Page Setup tab selected.
- To make data in a report easier to understand, divide the data into groups using the Group, Sort, and Total pane. Display this pane by clicking the Group & Sort button in the Grouping & Totals group on the Report Layout Tools Design tab.
- Insert a calculation in a report by inserting a text box object, displaying the Property Sheet task pane with the Data tab selected, and then typing the calculation in the *Control Source* property box. If a calculation result is currency, apply currency formatting with the Apply Currency Format button on the Report Layout Tools Format tab.
- Use the Report Wizard to provide the steps for creating a report. Begin the wizard by clicking the Create tab and then clicking the Report Wizard button in the Reports group.
- Create mailing labels with data in a table using the Label Wizard. Begin the wizard by clicking a table, clicking the Create tab, and then clicking the Labels button in the Reports group.

Commands Review

FEATURE	RIBBON TAB, GROUP	BUTTON	KEYBOARD SHORTCUT
Conditional Formatting Rules Manager dialog box	Report Layout Tools Format, Control Formatting		
Find dialog box	Home, Find		Ctrl + F
Group, Sort, and Total pane	Report Layout Tools Design, Grouping & Totals		
Labels Wizard	Create, Reports		
Property Sheet task pane	Report Layout Tools Design, Tools		Alt + Enter
report	Create, Reports		
Report Wizard	Create, Reports		
Sort data in ascending order	Home, Sort & Filter		
Sort data in descending order	Home, Sort & Filter		

Workbook

Chapter study tools and assessment activities are available in the *Workbook* ebook. These resources are designed to help you further develop and demonstrate mastery of the skills learned in this chapter.

Microsoft®

Access®

Modifying, Filtering, and Viewing Data

CHAPTER 7

Performance Objectives

Upon successful completion of Chapter 7, you will be able to:

1. Filter records using the Filter button
2. Remove a filter
3. Filter on specific values, by selection, by shortcut menu, and using the *Filter By Form* option
4. View object dependencies
5. Compact and repair a database
6. Encrypt a database with a password
7. View and customize document properties
8. Save a database in an earlier version of Access
9. Save a database object as a PDF or XPS file
10. Backup a database

Precheck

Check your current skills to help focus your study.

Data in a database object can be filtered to view specific records without having to change the design of the object. In this chapter, you will learn how to filter data by selection, by shortcut menu, by form, and how to remove a filter. You will also learn how to view object dependencies, compact and repair a database, encrypt a database with a password, view and customize database properties, save a database in an earlier version of Access, save a database object as a PDF or XPS file, and back up a database.

Data Files

Before beginning chapter work, copy the AL1C7 folder to your storage medium and then make AL1C7 the active folder.

SNAP

If you are a SNAP user, launch the Precheck and Tutorials from your Assignments page.

Project 1 Filter Records

4 Parts

You will filter records in a table, query, and report in the Skyline database using the Filter button, Selection button, Toggle Filter button, and shortcut menu. You will also remove filters and filter by form.

Preview Finished Project

Tutorial

Filtering Records

Quick Steps

Filter Records

1. Open object.
2. Click in entry in field to filter.
3. Click Filter button.
4. Select sorting option at drop-down list.

Filtering Records

A set of restrictions, called a *filter*, can be set on records in a table, query, form, or report to isolate temporarily specific records. A filter, like a query, displays specific records without having to change the design of the table, query, form, or report. Access provides a number of buttons and options for filtering data. Filter data using the Filter button in the Sort & Filter group on the Home tab, right-click specific data in a record and then specify a filter, and use the Selection and Advanced buttons in the Sort & Filter group.

Filtering Using the Filter Button

Filter

Use the Filter button in the Sort & Filter group on the Home tab to filter records in an object (a table, query, form, or report). To use this button, open the object, click in any entry in the field column to be filtered, and then click the Filter button. This displays a drop-down list with sorting options and a list of all of the field entries. In a table, display this drop-down list by clicking the filter arrow at the right side of a column heading. Figure 7.1 shows the drop-down list that displays when clicking in an entry in the *City* field and then clicking the Filter

Figure 7.1 *City* Field Drop-down List

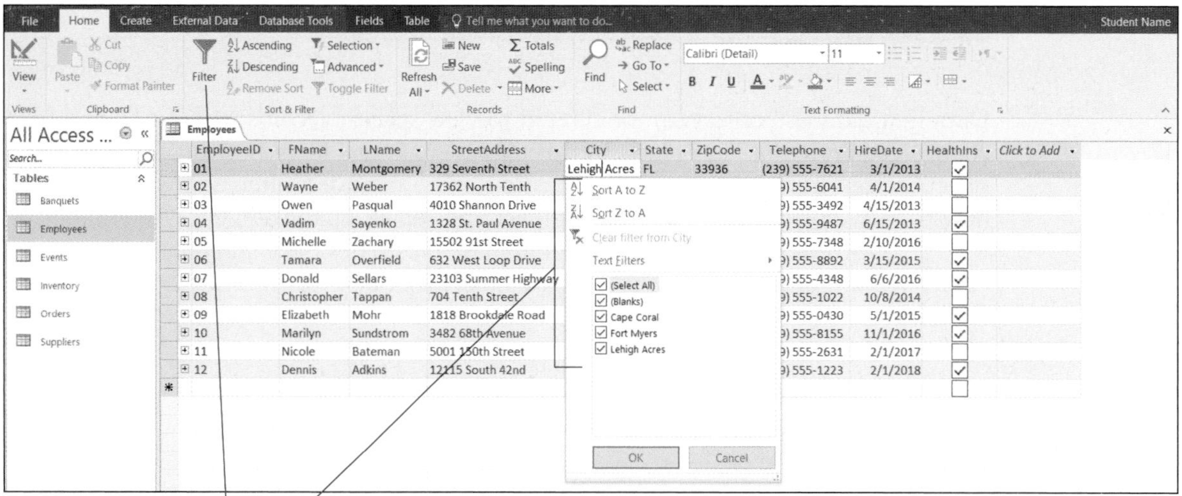

To filter on the *City* field, click in any entry in the field and then click the Filter button. This displays a drop-down list with sorting options and a list of all field entries.

Hint The availability of filters depends on the type of data selected in a column.

button. To filter on a specific criterion, click the *(Select All)* check box to remove all check marks from the list of field entries. Click the item to filter by in the list box and then click OK.

Open a table, query, or form and the Record Navigation bar contains the dimmed words *No Filter* preceded by a filter icon with a delete symbol (X). If records are filtered, *Filtered* displays in place of *No Filter*, the delete symbol is removed, and the text and filter icon display with an orange background. In a report, apply a filter to records and the word *Filtered* displays at the right side of the Status bar.

Removing a Filter

Toggle Filter

Quick Steps

Remove a Filter

1. Click in an entry in field containing filter.
2. Click Filter button.
3. Click *Clear filter from (name of field).*

OR

1. Click Advanced button.
2. Click *Clear All Filters* at drop-down list.

When data is filtered, the underlying data in the object is not deleted. Switch back and forth between the data and filtered data by clicking the Toggle Filter button in the Sort & Filter group on the Home tab. Click the Toggle Filter button to turn off the filter and all of the data in the table, query, or form displays and the message *Filtered* in the Record Navigation bar changes to *Unfiltered*.

Clicking the Toggle Filter button may redisplay all of the data in an object, but it does not remove the filter. To remove the filter, click in the field column containing the filter and then click the Filter button in the Sort & Filter group on the Home tab. At the drop-down list that displays, click *Clear filter from xxx* (where *xxx* is the name of the field). Remove all of the filters from an object by clicking the Advanced button in the Sort & Filter group and then clicking the *Clear All Filters* option. When all filters are removed (cleared) from an object, the *Unfiltered* message in the Record Navigation bar changes to *No Filter*.

Project 1a Filtering Records in a Table, Form, and Report — Part 1 of 4

1. Open **7-Skyline.accdb** from the AL1C7 folder on your storage medium and enable the content.
2. Filter records in the Employees table by completing the following steps:
   a. Open the Employees table.
   b. Click in any entry in the *City* field.
   c. Click the Filter button in the Sort & Filter group on the Home tab. (This displays a drop-down list of options for sorting and filtering the *City* field.)

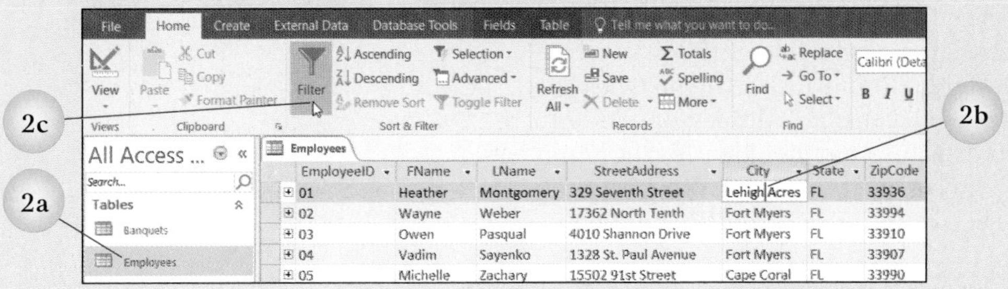

d. Click the *(Select All)* check box in the filter drop-down list box. (This removes all check marks from the list options.)
e. Click the *Fort Myers* check box in the list box. (This inserts a check mark in the check box.)
f. Click OK. (Access displays only those records with a city field entry of *Fort Myers* and also displays *Filtered* and the filter icon with an orange background in the Record Navigation bar.)
g. Print the filtered records by pressing Ctrl + P (the keyboard shortcut to display the print dialog box) and then clicking OK at the Print dialog box.

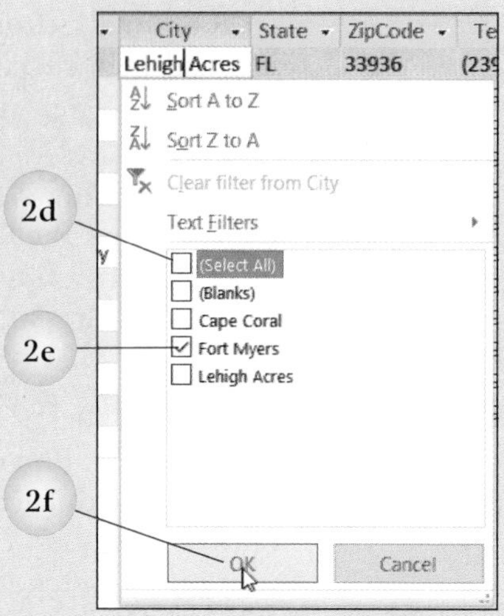

3. Toggle the display of filtered data by clicking the Toggle Filter button in the Sort & Filter group on the Home tab. (This redisplays all of the data in the table.)
4. Remove the filter by completing the following steps:
   a. Click in any entry in the *City* field.
   b. Click the Filter button in the Sort & Filter group.
   c. Click the *Clear filter from City* option at the drop-down list. (Notice that the message on the Record Navigation bar changes to *No Filter* and dims the words.)

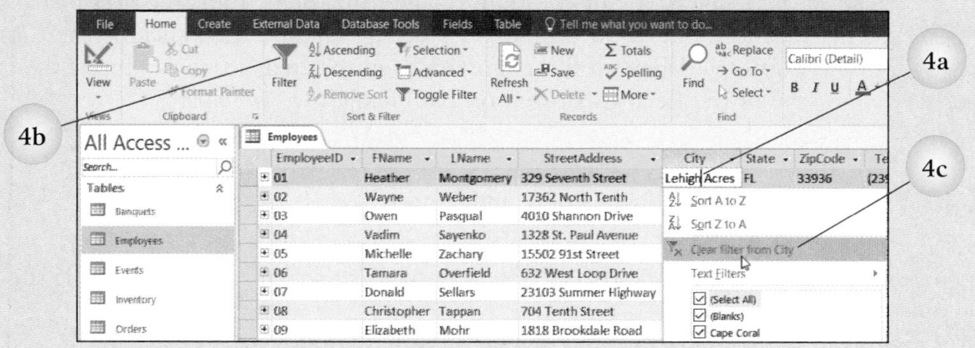

5. Save and then close the Employees table.
6. Create a form by completing the following steps:
   a. Click *Orders* in the Tables group in the Navigation pane.
   b. Click the Create tab and then click the Form button in the Forms group.
   c. Click the Form View button in the view area at the right side of the Status bar.
   d. Save the form with the name *Orders*.
7. Filter the records and display only those records with a supplier identification number of 2 by completing the following steps:
   a. Click in the *SupplierID* field containing the text *2*.
   b. Click the Filter button in the Sort & Filter group.
   c. At the filter drop-down list, click *(Select All)* to remove all of the check marks from the list options.
   d. Click the *2* option to insert a check mark.
   e. Click OK.

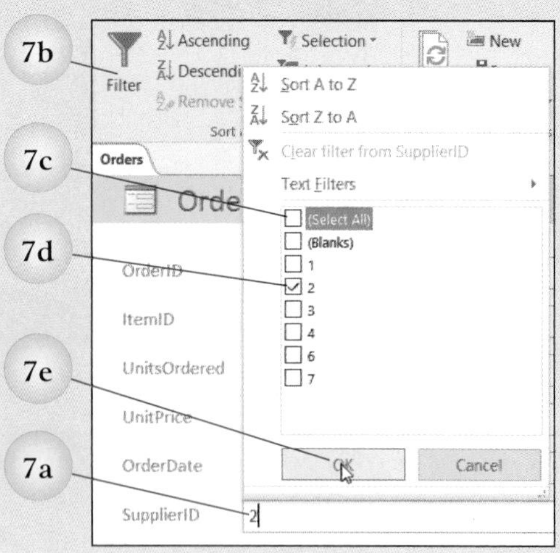

f. Navigate through the records and notice that only the records with a supplier identification number of 2 display.

8. Close the Orders form.

Check Your Work

Filtering on Specific Values

Quick Steps

Filter on Specific Value

1. Click in entry in field.
2. Click Filter button on Home tab.
3. Point to filter option.
4. Click specific value.

When filtering on a specific field, a list of unique values for that field can be displayed. Click the Filter button for a field containing text and the drop-down list for the specific field will contain a *Text Filters* option. Click this option and a values list displays next to the drop-down list. The options in the values list vary depending on the type of data in the field. Click the Filter button for a field containing number values and the option in the drop-down list displays as *Number Filters*. If filtering dates, the Filter button's drop-down list displays as *Date Filters*. Use the options in the values list to refine a filter for a specific field. For example, the values list can be used to display money amounts within a specific range or order dates from a certain time period. The values list can also be used to find fields that are "equal to" or "not equal to" data in the current field.

Project 1b Filtering Records in a Query and Report

Part 2 of 4

1. With **7-Skyline.accdb** open, create a query in Design view with the following specifications:
   a. Add the Banquets and Events tables to the query window.
   b. Insert the *ResDate* field from the Banquets table field list box in the first field in the *Field* row.
   c. Insert the *FirstName* field from the Banquets table field list box in the second field in the *Field* row.
   d. Insert the *LastName* field from the Banquets table field list box in the third field in the *Field* row.
   e. Insert the *Telephone* field from the Banquets table field list box in the fourth field in the *Field* row.
   f. Insert the *Event* field from the Events table field list box in the fifth field in the *Field* row.
   g. Insert the *EmployeeID* field from the Banquets table field list box in the sixth field in the *Field* row.
   h. Run the query.
   i. Save the query with the name *BanquetReservations*.
2. Filter records of reservations on or before June 15, 2018, in the query by completing the following steps:
   a. With the BanquetReservations query open, make sure the first entry is selected in the *ResDate* field.
   b. Click the Filter button in the Sort & Filter group on the Home tab.
   c. Point to the *Date Filters* option in the drop-down list box.
   d. Click *Before* in the values list.

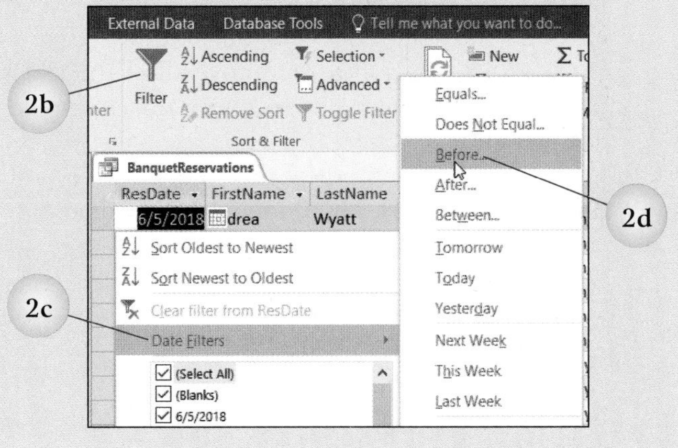

e. At the Custom Filter dialog box, type 6/15/2018 and then click OK.
f. Print the filtered query by pressing Ctrl + P and then clicking OK at the Print dialog box.

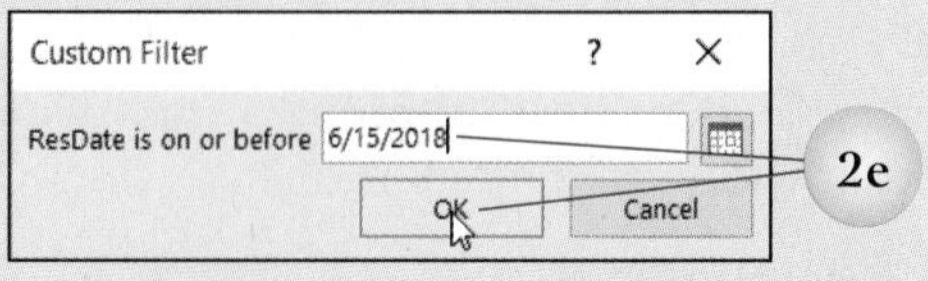

3. Remove the filter by clicking the filter icon at the right side of the *ResDate* column heading and then clicking *Clear filter from ResDate* at the drop-down list.

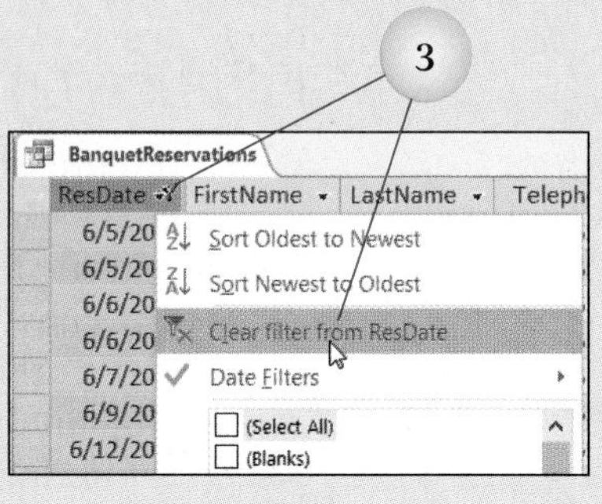

4. Save and then close the BanquetReservations query.
5. Create and format a report by completing the following steps:
   a. Click *BanquetReservations* in the Queries group in the Navigation pane.
   b. Click the Create tab and then click the Report button in the Reports group.
   c. Delete the total amount and line at the bottom of the *ResDate* column.
   d. Delete the page number control object.
   e. With the report in Layout view, decrease the column widths so the right column border displays near the longest entry in each column.
   f. Move the date and time control objects so they align with the last column in the report.
   g. Click the Report Layout Tools Page Setup tab and then click the Columns button in the Page Layout group.
   h. Click the Report View button in the view area at the right side of the Status bar.
   i Save the report with the name *BanquetReport*.
6. Filter the records and display all records of events except *Other* events by completing the following steps:
   a. Click in the first entry in the *Event* field.
   b. Click the Filter button in the Sort & Filter group.
   c. Point to the *Text Filters* option in the drop-down list box and then click *Does Not Equal* at the values list.
   d. At the Custom Filter dialog box, type Other and then click OK.

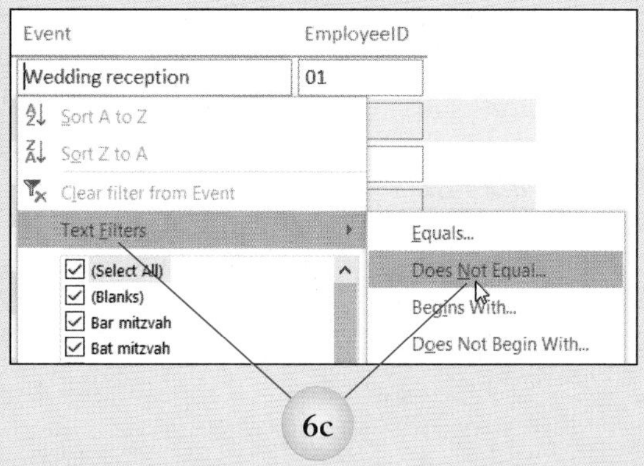

7. Further refine the filter by completing the following steps:
   a. Click in the first entry in the *EmployeeID* field.
   b. Click the Filter button.
   c. At the filter drop-down list, click the *(Select All)* check box to remove all of the check marks from the list options.
   d. Click the *03* check box to insert a check mark.
   e. Click OK.
8. Print the filtered report by pressing Ctrl + P and then clicking OK at the Print dialog box.
9. Save and then close the BanquetReport report.

Check Your Work

Filtering by Selection

Selection

Click in a field in an object and then click the Selection button in the Sort & Filter group on the Home tab and a drop-down list displays below the button with options for filtering on the data in the field. For example, click in a field containing the city name *Fort Myers* and then click the Selection button and a drop-down list will display as shown in Figure 7.2. Click one of the options at the drop-down list to filter records.

Specific data can be selected in an object and then filtered by the selected data. For example, in Project 1c, the word *peppers* will be selected in the entry *Green peppers* and then records will be filtered containing the word *peppers*.

Quick Steps

Filter by Selection
1. Click in entry in field.
2. Click Selection button.
3. Click filtering option.

Filter by Shortcut Menu
1. Right-click in entry in field.
2. Click filtering option at shortcut menu.

Filtering by Shortcut Menu

Right-click in a field entry, and a shortcut menu displays with options to sort the text, display a values list, or filter on a specific value. For example, right-click in the field entry *Birthday* in the *Event* field and the shortcut menu displays, as shown in Figure 7.3. Click a sort option to sort text in the field in ascending or descending order, point to the *Text Filters* option to display a values list, or click one of the values filters at the bottom of the menu. The shortcut menu can also be displayed by selecting specific text within a field entry and then right-clicking the selection.

Figure 7.2 Selection Button Drop-Down List

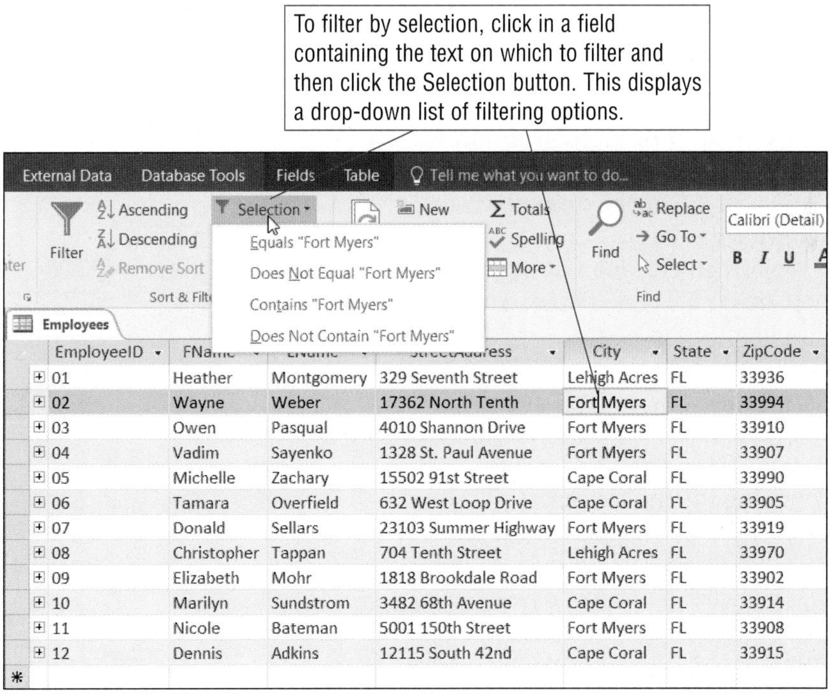

Figure 7.3 Filtering Shortcut Menu

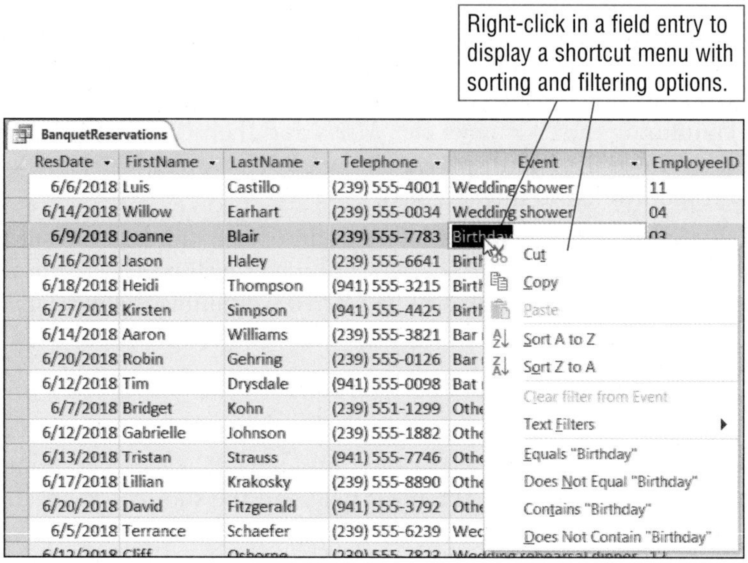

Project 1c Filtering Records by Selection

Part 3 of 4

1. With **7-Skyline.accdb** open, open the Inventory table.
2. Filter only those records with a supplier number of 6 by completing the following steps:
   a. Click in the first entry containing *6* in the *SupplierID* field.
   b. Click the Selection button in the Sort & Filter group on the Home tab and then click *Equals "6"* at the drop-down list.
   c. Print the filtered table by pressing Ctrl + P and then clicking OK at the Print dialog box.
   d. Click the Toggle Filter button in the Sort & Filter group.

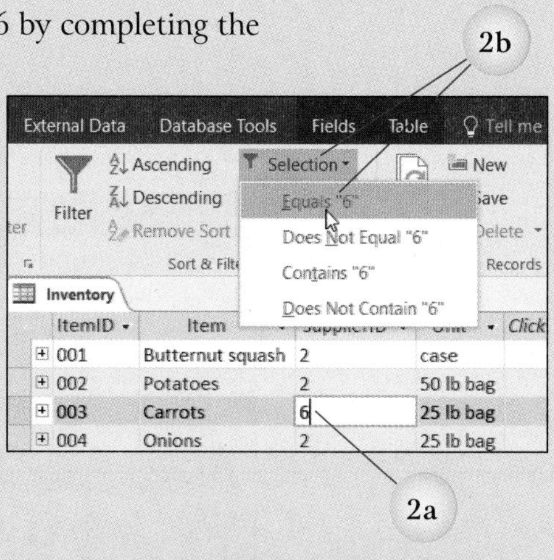

3. Filter any records in the *Item* field containing the word *peppers* by completing the following steps:
   a. Click in an entry in the *Item* field containing the text *Green peppers*.
   b. Using the mouse, select the word *peppers*.
   c. Click the Selection button and then click *Contains "peppers"* at the drop-down list.
   d. Print the filtered table by pressing Ctrl + P and then clicking OK at the Print dialog box.
4. Close the Inventory table without saving the changes.

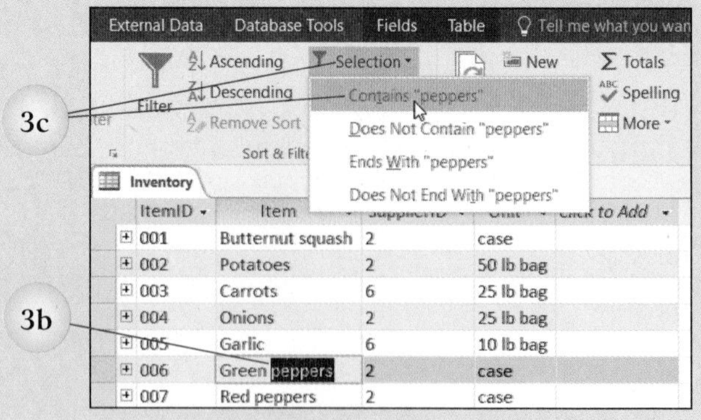

5. Open the BanquetReservations query.
6. Filter the records so that all but those containing *Wedding reception* in the *Event* field display by completing the following steps:
   a. Right-click in the first *Wedding reception* entry in the *Event* field.
   b. Click *Does Not Equal "Wedding reception"* at the shortcut menu.

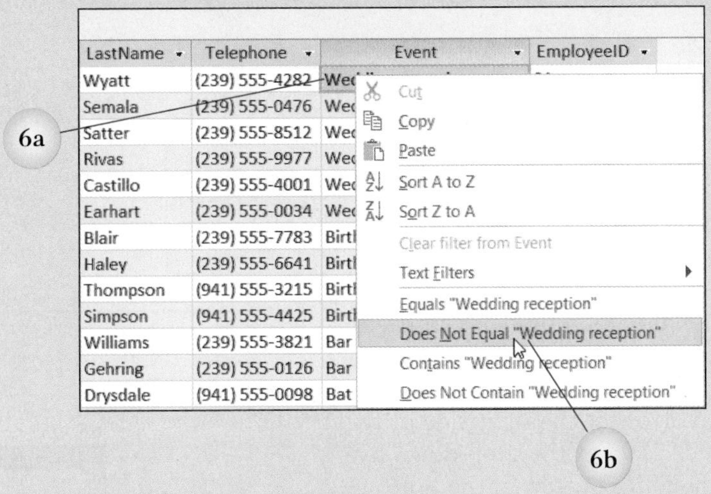

   c. Print the filtered query.
   d. Click the Toggle Filter button in the Sort & Filter group.
7. Filter the records so that only those containing the word *mitzvah* in the *Event* field display by completing the following steps:
   a. Click in an entry in the *Event* field containing the entry *Bar mitzvah*.
   b. Using the mouse, select the word *mitzvah*.
   c. Right-click in the selected word and then click *Contains "mitzvah"* at the shortcut menu.
   d. Print the filtered query.
8. Close the BanquetReservations query without saving the changes.

Check Your Work

Using the *Filter By Form* Option

Advanced

Quick Steps

Use the *Filter By Form* Option
1. Click Advanced button.
2. Click *Filter By Form*.
3. Click in empty field below column to filter.
4. Click down arrow.
5. Click item to filter.

One of the options from the Advanced button drop-down list is *Filter By Form*. Click this option and a blank record displays in a Filter by Form window in the work area. In the Filter by Form window, the Look for tab and the Or tab display at the bottom of the form. The Look for tab is active by default and tells Access to look for whatever data is inserted in a field. Click in the empty field below the column and a down arrow displays at the right side of the field. Click the down arrow and then click the item by which to filter. Click the Toggle Filter button to display the desired records. Add an additional value to a filter by clicking the Or tab at the bottom of the form.

Project 1d Using the *Filter By Form* Option to Display Specific Records — Part 4 of 4

1. With **7-Skyline.accdb** open, open the Banquets table.
2. Filter records by a specific employee ID number by completing the following steps:
   a. Click the Advanced button in the Sort & Filter group on the Home tab and then click *Filter By Form* at the drop-down list.

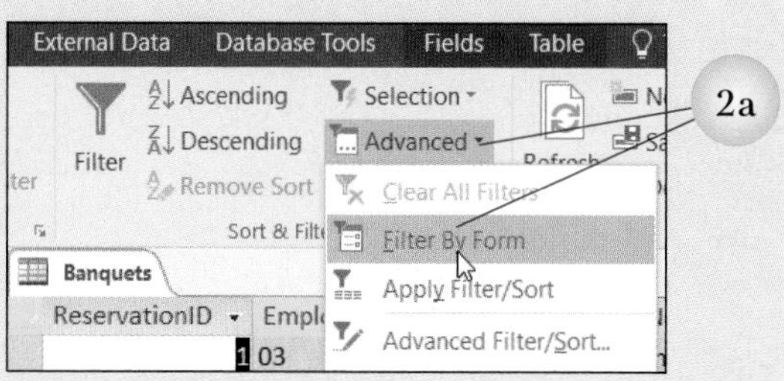

   b. At the Filter by Form window, click in the empty field below the *EmployeeID* column heading.
   c. Click the down arrow at the right side of the field and then click *03* at the drop-down list.
   d. Click the Toggle Filter button in the Sort & Filter group.

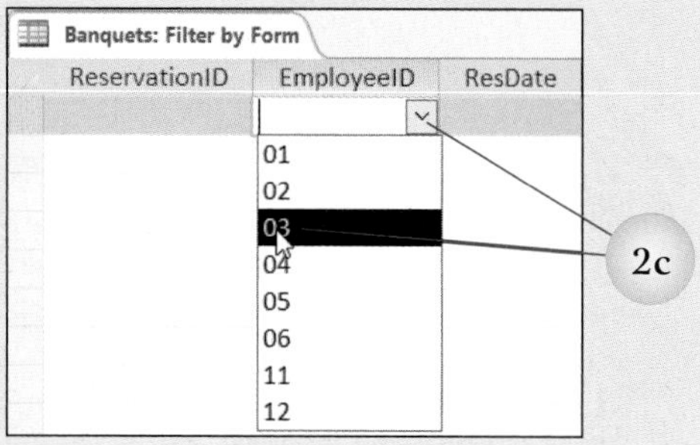

3. Print the filtered table by completing the following steps:
   a. Click the File tab, click the *Print* option, and then click the *Print Preview* option.
   b. Change the orientation to landscape and the left and right margins to 0.5 inch.
   c. Click the Print button and then click OK at the Print dialog box.
   d. Click the Close Print Preview button.
4. Close the Banquets table without saving the changes.
5. Open the Inventory table.
6. Filter records by the supplier number 2 or 7 by completing the following steps:
   a. Click the Advanced button in the Sort & Filter group on the Home tab and then click *Filter By Form* at the drop-down list.
   b. At the Filter by Form window, click in the empty field below the *SupplierID* column heading.
   c. Click the down arrow at the right side of the field and then click *2* at the drop-down list.
   d. Click the Or tab at the bottom of the form.
   e. If necessary, click in the empty field below the *SupplierID* column heading.
   f. Click the down arrow at the right side of the field and then click *7* at the drop-down list.

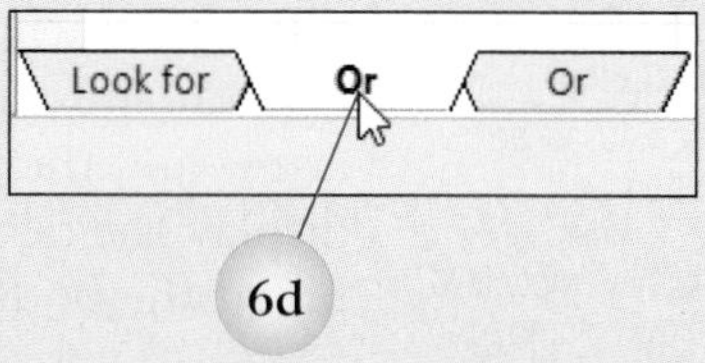

   g. Click the Toggle Filter button in the Sort & Filter group.
   h. Print the filtered table.
   i. Click the Toggle Filter button to redisplay all records in the table.
   j. Click the Advanced button and then click *Clear All Filters* at the drop-down list.
7. Close the Inventory table without saving the changes.

Check Your Work

Project 2 View Object Dependencies, Manage a Database, and Save a Database in a Different File Format

4 Parts

You will display object dependencies in the Skyline database, compact and repair the database, encrypt it with a password, view and customize database properties, save an object in the database in PDF file format, and save the database in a previous version of Access.

Preview Finished Project

Tutorial

Viewing Object Dependencies

Quick Steps

View Object Dependencies

1. Open database.
2. Click object in Navigation pane.
3. Click Database Tools tab.
4. Click Object Dependencies button.

Object Dependencies

Viewing Object Dependencies

The structure of a database is comprised of table, query, form, and report objects. Tables are related to other tables by the relationships that have been created. Queries, forms, and reports draw the source data from the records in the tables to which they have been associated, and forms and reports can include subforms and subreports, which further expand the associations between objects. A database with a large number of interdependent objects is more complex to work with than a simpler database. Viewing a list of the objects within a database and viewing the dependencies between objects can be beneficial to ensure an object is not deleted or otherwise modified, causing an unforeseen effect on another object.

Display the structure of a database—including tables, queries, forms, and reports, as well as relationships—at the Object Dependencies task pane. Display this task pane by opening the database, clicking an object in the Navigation pane, clicking the Database Tools tab, and then clicking the Object Dependencies button in the Relationships group. The Object Dependencies task pane, shown in Figure 7.4, displays the objects in the Skyline database that depend on the Banquets table.

Figure 7.4 Object Dependencies Task Pane

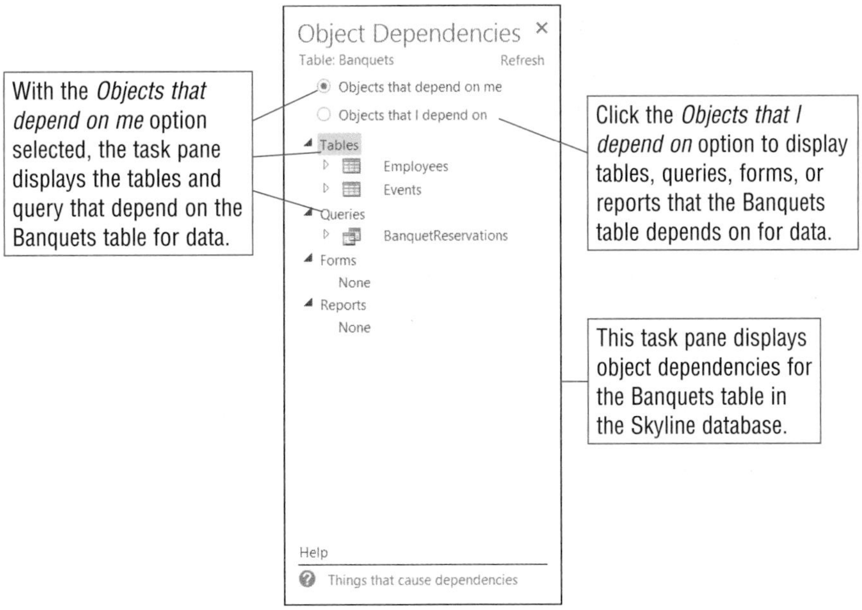

With the *Objects that depend on me* option selected, the task pane displays the tables and query that depend on the Banquets table for data.
Object Dependencies
Table: Banquets
Refresh
Objects that depend on me
Objects that I depend on
Tables
Employees
Events
Queries
BanquetReservations
Forms
None
Reports
None
Help
Things that cause dependencies
Click the *Objects that I depend on* option to display tables, queries, forms, or reports that the Banquets table depends on for data.
This task pane displays object dependencies for the Banquets table in the Skyline database.

By default, *Objects that depend on me* is selected in the Object Dependencies task pane and the list box displays the names of the objects for which the selected object is the source. Next to each object in the task pane list box is an expand button (a right-pointing, white triangle). Clicking the expand button next to an object shows the other objects that depend on it. For example, if a query is based on the Banquets and Events tables and the query is used to generate a report, clicking the expand button next to the query name will show the report name. Clicking an object name in the Object Dependencies task pane opens the object in Design view.

Project 2a Viewing Object Dependencies — Part 1 of 4

1. With **7-Skyline.accdb** open, display the structure of the database by completing the following steps:
   a. Click *Banquets* in the Tables group in the Navigation pane.
   b. Click the Database Tools tab and then click the Object Dependencies button in the Relationships group. (This displays the Object Dependencies task pane. By default, *Objects that depend on me* is selected and the task pane lists the names of the objects for which the Banquets table is the source.)

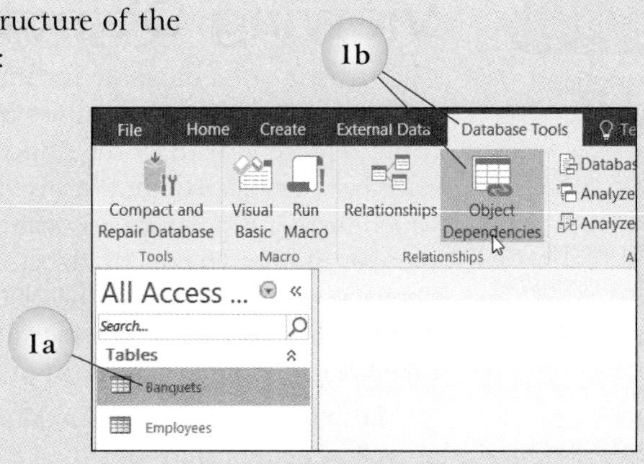

   c. Click the expand button (the right-pointing, white triangle that turns pink when you hover your mouse pointer over it) to the left of *Employees* in the *Tables* section. (This displays all of the objects that depend on the Employees table.)
   d. Click the *Objects that I depend on* option near the top of the Object Dependencies task pane.

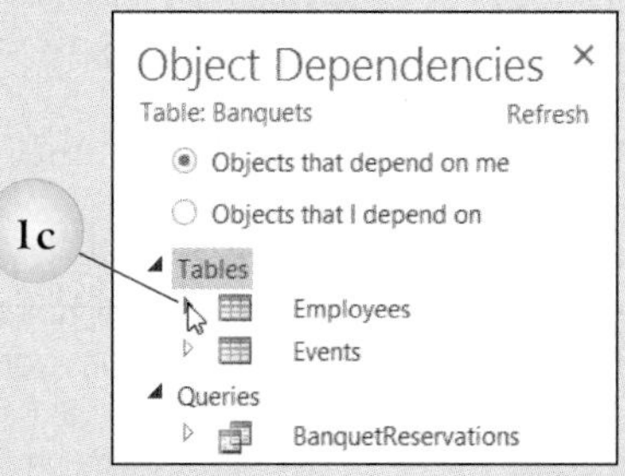

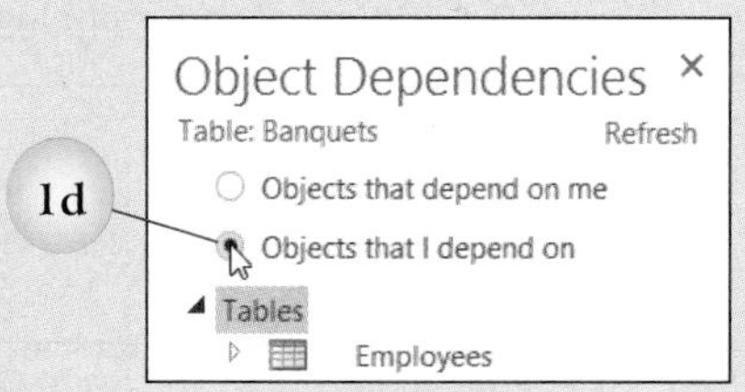

   e. Click *Events* in the Tables group in the Navigation pane. (Make sure to click *Events* in the Navigation pane and not the Object Dependencies task pane.)
   f. Click the Refresh hyperlink in the upper right corner of the Object Dependencies task pane.
   g. Click the *Objects that depend on me* option near the top of the Object Dependencies task pane.

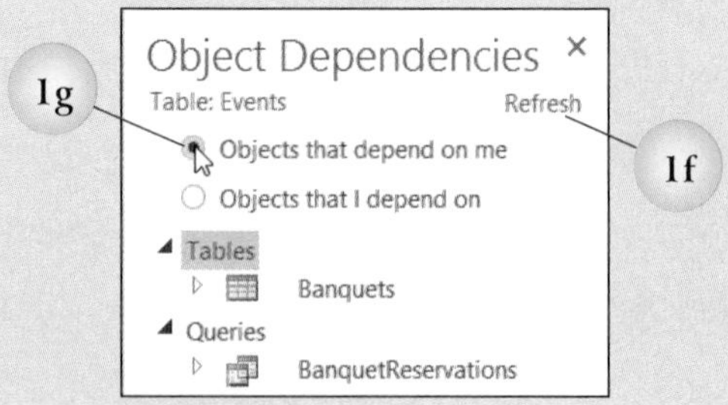

2. Close the Object Dependencies task pane.

Using Options at the Info Backstage Area

The Info backstage area contains options for compacting and repairing a database, encrypting a database with a password, and displaying and customizing database properties. Display the Info backstage area, shown in Figure 7.5, by opening a database and then clicking the File tab.

Tutorial

Compacting and Repairing a Database

Compact & Repair Database

Quick Steps

Compact and Repair a Database

1. Open database.
2. Click File tab.
3. Click Compact & Repair Database button.

Compacting and Repairing a Database

To optimize the performance of a database, compact and repair it on a regular basis. When working in a database on an ongoing basis, data in it can become fragmented, causing the amount of space the database takes on the storage medium or in the folder to be larger than necessary. To compact and repair a database, open the database, click the File tab and then click the Compact & Repair Database button or click the Compact and Repair Database button in the Tools group on the Database Tools tab.

A database can be compacted and repaired each time it is closed. To do this, click the File tab and then click *Options*. At the Access Options dialog box, click the *Current Database* option in the left panel. Click the *Compact on Close* option to insert a check mark and then click OK to close the dialog box. Before compacting and repairing a database in a multi-user environment, make sure that no other user has the database open.

Figure 7.5 Info Backstage Area

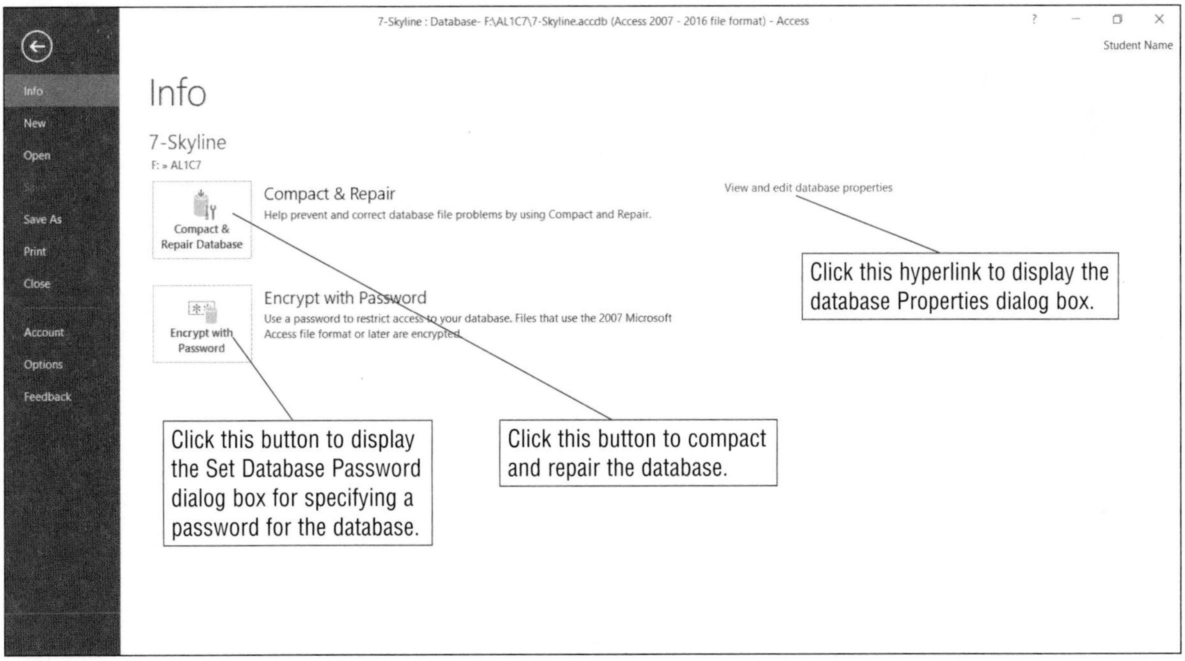

Tutorial

Encrypting a Database with a Password

Encrypt with Password

Decrypt Database

Quick Steps

Open a Database in Exclusive Mode

1. Display Open dialog box.
2. Click database.
3. Click Open button arrow.
4. Click *Open Exclusive*.

Encrypt a Database with a Password

1. Open database in Exclusive mode.
2. Click File tab.
3. Click Encrypt with Password button.
4. Type password, press Tab, and type password again.
5. Click OK.

Hint When encrypting a database with a password, use a password that combines uppercase and lowercase letters, numbers, and symbols.

Encrypting a Database with a Password

To prevent unauthorized access to a database, encrypt the database with a password to ensure that it can be opened only by someone who knows the password. Be careful when encrypting a database with a password because if the password is lost, the database will not open.

To encrypt a database with a password, the database must be opened in Exclusive mode. To do this, display the Open dialog box, navigate to the folder containing the database, and then click the database to select it. Click the Open button arrow (in the lower right corner of the dialog box) and then click *Open Exclusive* at the drop-down list. When the database opens, click the File tab and then click the Encrypt with Password button in the Info backstage area. This displays the Set Database Password dialog box, as shown in Figure 7.6. At this dialog box, type a password in the *Password* text box, press the Tab key, and then type the password again. The typed text will display as asterisks. Click OK to close the Set Database Password dialog box.

To remove a password from a database, open the database in Exclusive mode, click the File tab, and then click the Decrypt Database button. At the Unset Database Password dialog box, type the password and then click OK.

Figure 7.6 Set Database Password Dialog Box

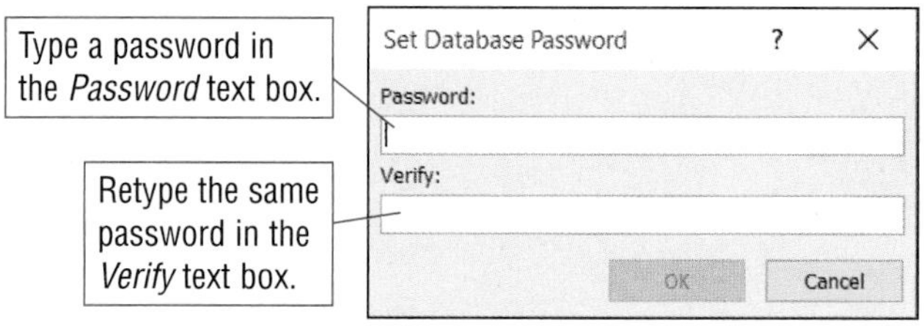

Project 2b Compacting and Repairing a Database and Encrypting with a Password — Part 2 of 4

1. With **7-Skyline.accdb** open, compact and repair the database by completing the following steps:
   a. Click the File tab. (This displays the Info backstage area.)
   b. Click the Compact & Repair Database button.
2. Close **7-Skyline.accdb**.
3. Open the database in Exclusive mode by completing the following steps:
   a. Display the Open dialog box and make AL1C7 the active folder.
   b. Click **7-Skyline.accdb** in the Content pane to select it.

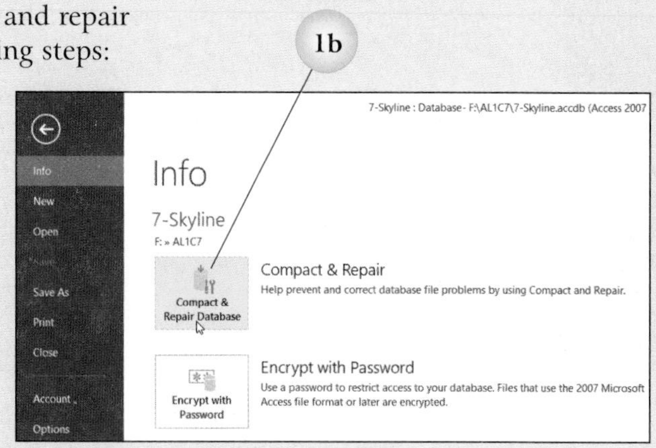

c. Click the Open button arrow (in the lower right corner of the dialog box) and then click *Open Exclusive* at the drop-down list.

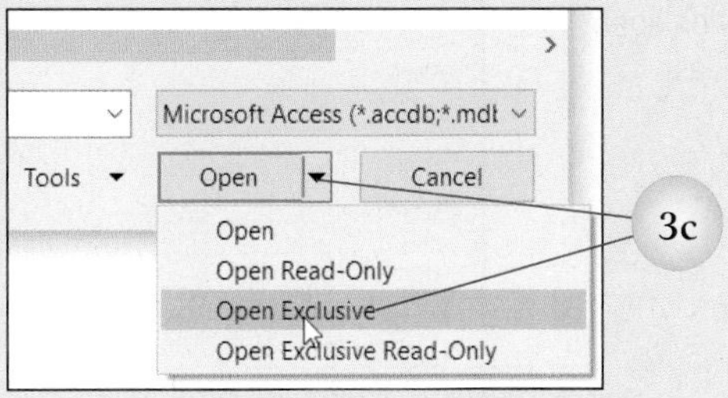

4. Encrypt the database with a password by completing the following steps:
   a. Click the File tab.
   b. At the Info backstage area, click the Encrypt with Password button.
   c. At the Set Database Password dialog box, type your first and last names in all lowercase letters with no space, press the Tab key, and then type your first and last names again in lowercase letters.
   d. Click OK to close the dialog box.
   e. If a message displays with information about encrypting with a block cipher, click OK.

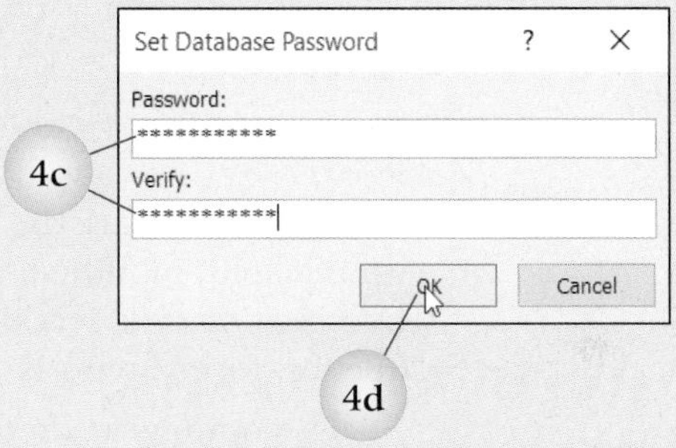

5. Close **7-Skyline.accdb**.
6. Display the Open dialog box with AL1C7 as the active folder and then open **7-Skyline.accdb** in Exclusive mode.
7. At the Password Required dialog box, type your password and then click OK.
8. Remove the password by completing the following steps:
   a. Click the File tab.
   b. Click the Decrypt Database button.
   c. At the Unset Database Password dialog box, type your first and last names in lowercase letters and then press the Enter key.

Tutorial

Viewing and Customizing Database Properties

Quick Steps

View Database Properties

1. Click File tab.
2. Click View and edit database properties.

Viewing and Customizing Database Properties

Each database has associated properties, such as the type of file; its location; and when it was created, accessed, and modified. These properties can be viewed and modified at the Properties dialog box. To view properties for the currently open database, click the File tab to display the Info backstage area and then click the View and edit database properties hyperlink at the right side of the backstage area. This displays the Properties dialog box, similar to what is shown in Figure 7.7.

The Properties dialog box for an open database contains tabs with information about the database. With the General tab selected, the dialog box displays information about the database type, size, and location. Click the Summary tab to display fields such as *Title*, *Subject*, *Author*, *Category*, *Keywords*, and *Comments*. Some fields contain data and others are blank. Text can be inserted, edited, or deleted in the fields. Move the insertion point to a field by clicking in the field or by pressing the Tab key until the insertion point is positioned in the field.

Figure 7.7 Properties Dialog Box

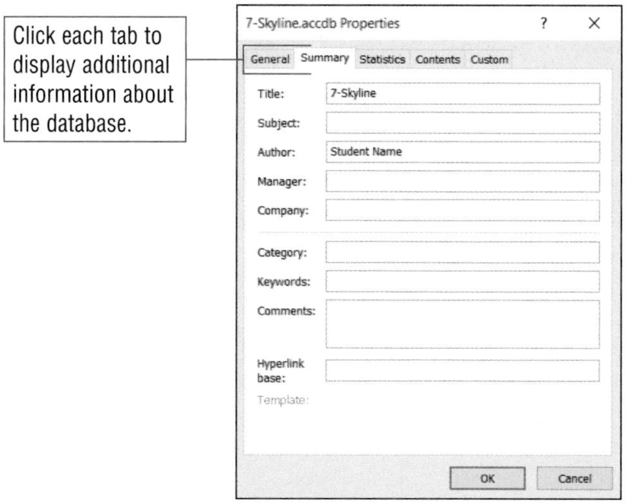

Click the Statistics tab to display information such as the dates the database was created, modified, accessed, and printed. Click the Contents tab and the *Document contents* section displays the objects in the database, including tables, queries, forms, reports, macros, and modules.

Use options at the Properties dialog box with the Custom tab selected to add custom properties to the database. For example, a property can be added that displays the date the database was completed, information on the department in which the database was created, and much more. The list box below the *Name* option box displays the predesigned properties provided by Access. Choose a predesigned property from this list box or create a custom property.

To choose a predesigned property, click a predesigned property in the list box, specify what type of property it is (such as value, date, number, yes/no), and then type a value. For example, to specify the department in which the database was created, click *Department* in the list box, make sure the *Type* displays as *Text*, click in the *Value* text box, and then type the name of the department.

Project 2c Viewing and Customizing Database Properties

Part 3 of 4

1. With **7-Skyline.accdb** open, click the File tab and then click the View and edit database properties hyperlink at the right side of the backstage area.

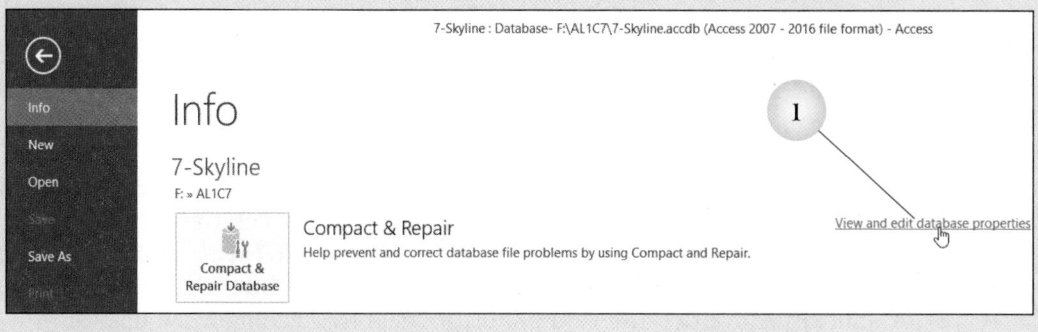

2. At the 7-Skyline.accdb Properties dialog box, click the General tab and then read the information that displays in the dialog box.
3. Click the Summary tab and then type the following text in the specified text boxes:

Title	7-Skyline database
Subject	Restaurant and banquet facilities
Author	(*Type your first and last names.*)
Category	restaurant
Keywords	restaurant, banquet, event, Fort Myers
Comments	This database contains information on Skyline Restaurant employees, banquets, inventory, and orders.

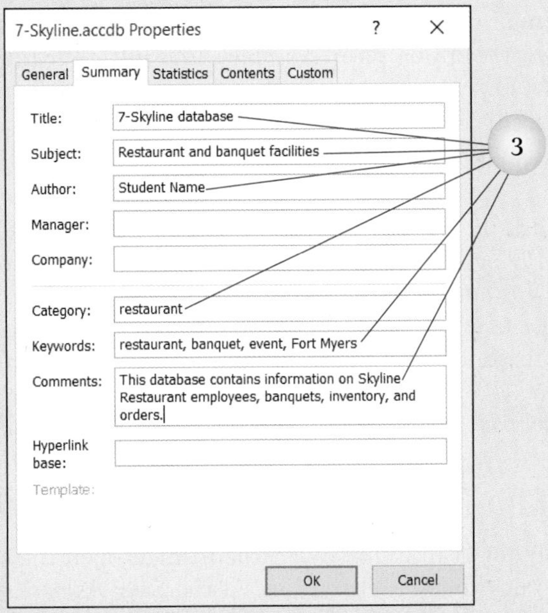

4. Click the Statistics tab and read the information that displays in the dialog box.
5. Click the Contents tab and notice that the *Document contents* section of the dialog box displays the objects in the database.
6. Click the Custom tab and then create custom properties by completing the following steps:
   a. Click the *Date completed* option in the *Name* list box.
   b. Click the *Type* option box arrow and then click *Date* at the drop-down list.
   c. Click in the *Value* text box and then type the current date in this format: *dd/mm/yyyy*.
   d. Click the Add button.
   e. With the insertion point positioned in the *Name* text box, type Course.
   f. Click the *Type* option box arrow and then click *Text* at the drop-down list.
   g. Click in the *Value* text box, type your current course number, and then press the Enter key.
   h. Click OK to close the dialog box.

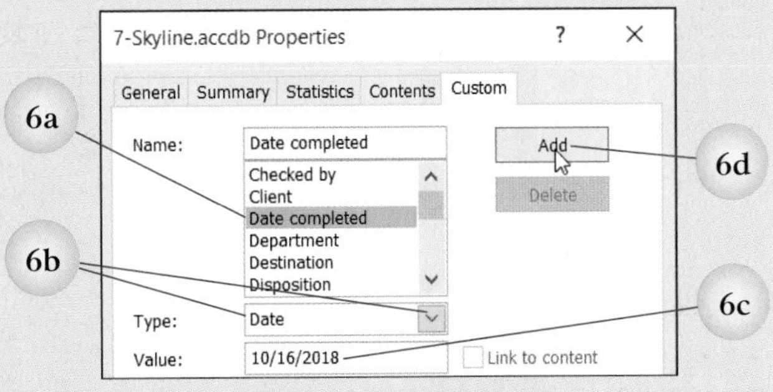

7. Click the Back button to return to the database.

Check Your Work

Tutorial

Saving a Database and Database Object in Different Formats

Saving a Database and Database Object in Different Formats

An Access 2016, Access 2013, Access 2010, or Access 2007 database is saved with the file extension *.accdb*. Earlier versions of Access (such as 2003, 2002, and 2000) use the file extension *.mdb*. To open an Access 2016, 2013, 2010, or 2007 database in an earlier version of Access, the database must be saved in the .mdb file format.

Quick Steps

Save a Database in an Earlier Version

1. Open database.
2. Click File tab.
3. Click *Save As* option.
4. Click version in *Save Database As* section.
5. Click Save As button.
6. Click Save button.

To save an Access database in the Access 2002 and 2003 file format, open the database, click the File tab, and then click the *Save As* option. This displays the Save As backstage area, as shown in Figure 7.9. Click the *Access 2002-2003 Database (*.mdb)* option in the *Save Database As* section and then click the Save As button at the bottom of the *Save Database As* section. This displays the Save As dialog box with the *Save as type* option set to *Microsoft Access Database (2002-2003) (*.mdb)* and the current database file name with the file extension *.mdb* inserted in the *File name* text box. At this dialog box, click the Save button.

With an object open in a database, clicking the *Save Object As* option in the *File Types* section of the Save As backstage area displays options for saving the object. Click the *Save Object As* option to save the selected object in the database or click the *PDF or XPS* option to save the object in PDF or XPS file format. The letters *PDF* stand for *portable document format*, a file format developed by Adobe Systems that captures all of the elements of a file as an electronic image. An XPS file is a Microsoft file format for publishing content in an easily viewable format. The letters *XPS* stand for *XML paper specification* and the letters *XML* stand for *extensible markup language*, which is a set of rules for encoding files electronically.

Hint An Access 2007, 2010, 2013, or 2016 database cannot be opened with an earlier version of Access.

Saving an Object in PDF or XPS File Format

Quick Steps

Save an Object in PDF or XPS File Format

1. Open object.
2. Click File tab.
3. Click *Save As* option.
4. Click *Save Object As* option.
5. Click *PDF or XPS* option.
6. Click Save As button.

To save an object in PDF or XPS file format, open the object, click the File tab, and then click the *Save As* option. At the Save As backstage area, click the *Save Object As* option in the *File Types* section, click the *PDF or XPS* option in the *Save the current database object* section, and then click the Save As button. This displays the Publish as PDF or XPS dialog box with the name of the object inserted in the

Figure 7.9 Save As Backstage Area with *Save Database As* Option Selected

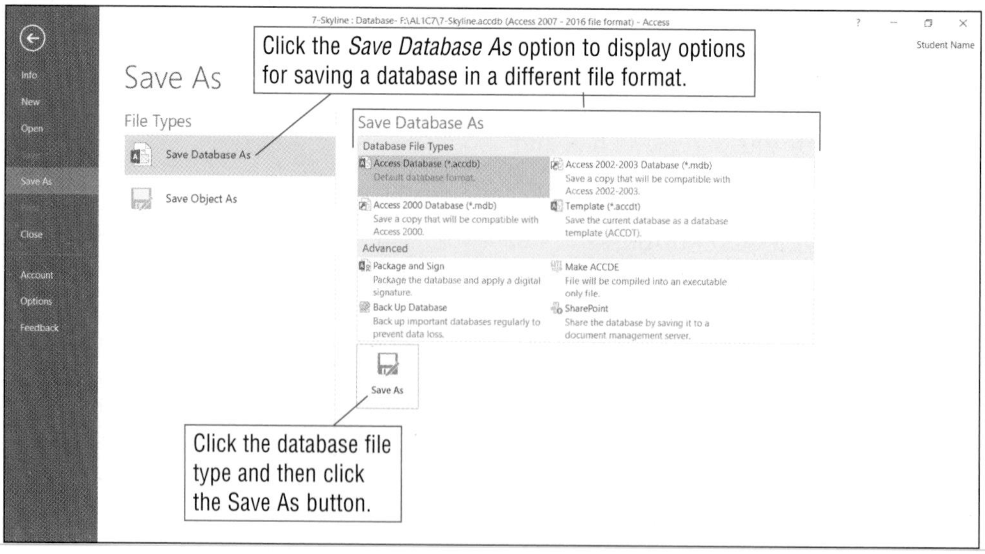

File name text box followed by the file extension *.pdf*, and the *Save as type* option set at *PDF (*.pdf)*. Click the Publish button and the object is saved in PDF file format. To specify that the object should open in Adobe Acrobat Reader, click the *Open file after publishing* check box to insert a check box. With this check box active, the object will open in Adobe Acrobat Reader when the Publish button is clicked.

A PDF file can be opened in Adobe Acrobat Reader, Microsoft Edge, or Word 2016. An XPS file can be opened in Adobe Acrobat Reader, Internet Explorer, or XPS Viewer. One method for opening a PDF or XPS file is to open File Explorer, navigate to the folder containing the file, right-click on the file, and then point to *Open with*. This displays a side menu with the programs that will open the file.

Tutorial

Backing Up a Database

Quick Steps

Backup Database

1. Click File tab.
2. Click *Save As* option.
3. Click *Back Up Database* option.
4. Click Save As button.
5. Click Save button.

Backing Up a Database

Databases often contain important company information, and loss of this information can cause major problems. Backing up a database is important to minimize the chances of losing critical company data and is especially important when several people update and manage a database.

To back up a database, open the database, click the File tab, and then click the *Save As* option. At the Save As backstage area, click the *Back Up Database* option in the *Advanced* section and then click the Save As button. This displays the Save As dialog box with a default database file name, which is the original database name followed by the current date, in the *File name* text box. Click the Save button to save the backup database while keeping the original database open.

Project 2d Saving a Database in a Previous Version, Saving an Object as a PDF File, and Backing Up a Database

Part 4 of 4

1. With **7-Skyline.accdb** open, save the Orders table as a PDF file by completing the following steps:
   a. Open the Orders table.
   b. Click the File tab and then click the *Save As* option.
   c. At the Save As backstage area, click the *Save Object As* option in the *File Types* section.
   d. Click the *PDF or XPS* option in the *Save the current database object* section.
   e. Click the Save As button.

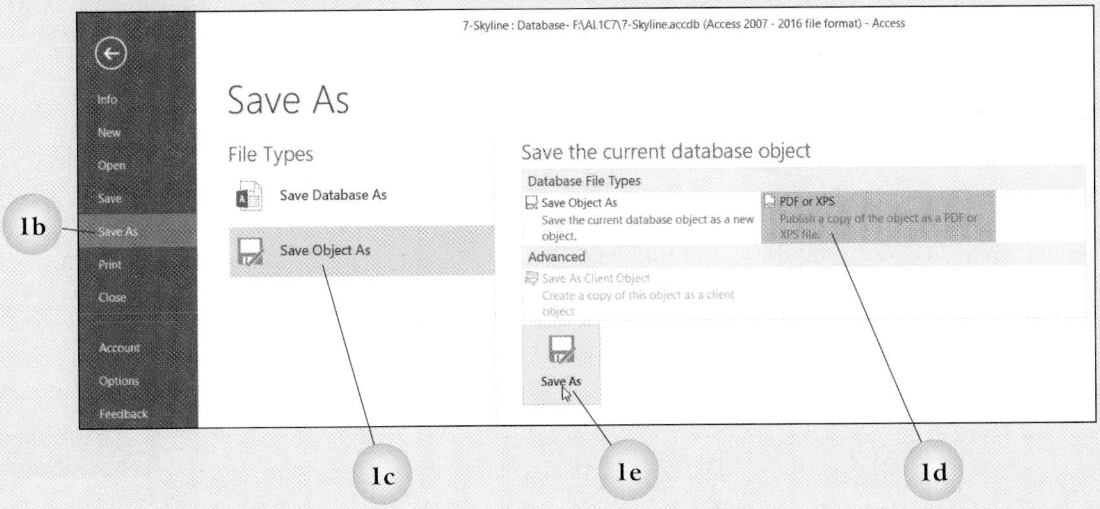

f. At the Publish as PDF or XPS dialog box, make sure the AL1C7 folder on your storage medium is the active folder and then click the *Open file after publishing* check box to insert a check mark. (Skip this step if the check box already contains a check mark.)
g. Click the Publish button.
h. When the Orders table opens in Adobe Acrobat Reader, scroll through the file and then close the file by clicking the Close button in the upper right corner of the screen.

2. Close the Orders table.
3. Save the database in a previous version of Access by completing the following steps:
   a. Click the File tab and then click the *Save As* option.
   b. At the Save As backstage area, click the *Access 2002-2003 Database (*.mdb)* option in the *Save Database As* section.
   c. Click the Save As button.

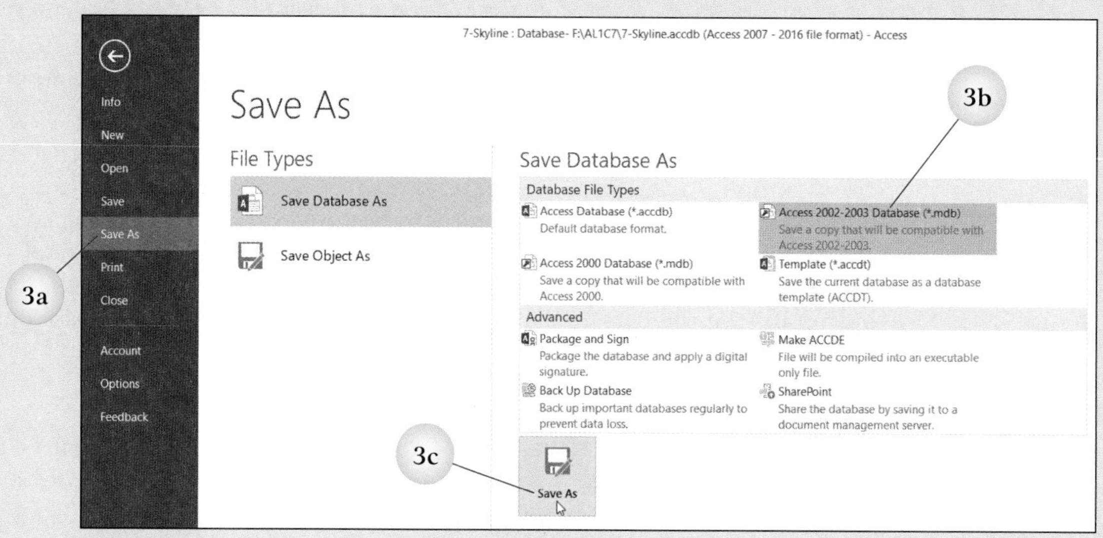

   d. At the Save As dialog box, make sure the AL1C7 folder on your storage medium is the active folder and then click the Save button. This saves the database with the same name (**7-Skyline**) but with the file extension *.mdb*.
   e. Notice that the Title bar displays the database file name *7-Skyline : Database (Access 2002 - 2003 file format)*.
4. Close the database.
5. Open **7-Skyline.accdb**. (Make sure you open the 7-Skyline database with the .accdb file extension.)
6. Create a backup of the database by completing the following steps:
   a. Click the File tab and then click the *Save As* option.
   b. At the Save As backstage area, click the *Back Up Database* option in the *Advanced* section and then click the Save As button.
   c. At the Save As dialog box, notice that the database name in the *File name* text box displays the original file name followed by the current date (year, month, day).
   d. Make sure the AL1C7 folder on your storage medium is the active folder and then click the Save button. (This saves the backup copy of the database to your folder and the original database remains open.)
7. Close **7-Skyline.accdb**.

Check Your Work

Chapter Summary

- A set of restrictions called a filter can be set on records in a table or form. A filter is used to select specific field values.
- Filter records with the Filter button in the Sort & Filter group on the Home tab.
- Click the Toggle Filter button in the Sort & Filter group to switch back and forth between data and filtered data.
- Remove a filter by clicking the Filter button in the Sort & Filter group and then clicking the *Clear filter from xxx* (where *xxx* is the name of the field).
- Another method for removing a filter is to click the Advanced button in the Sort & Filter group and then click *Clear All Filters*.
- Display a list of filter values by clicking the Filter button and then pointing to *Text Filters* (if the data is text), *Number Filters* (if the data is numbers), or *Date Filters* (if the data is dates).
- Filter by selection by clicking the Selection button in the Sort & Filter group.
- Right-click in a field entry to display a shortcut menu with filtering options.
- Filter by form by clicking the Advanced button in the Sort & Filter group and then clicking *Filter By Form* at the drop-down list. This displays a blank record with two tabs: Look for and Or.
- Display the structure of a database and relationships between objects at the Object Dependencies task pane. Display this task pane by clicking the Database Tools tab and then clicking the Object Dependencies button in the Relationships group.
- Click the Compact & Repair Database button in the Info backstage area to optimize database performance.
- To prevent unauthorized access to a database, encrypt the database with a password. To encrypt a database, the database must be opened in Exclusive mode using the Open button drop-down list in the Open dialog box. While in Exclusive mode, encrypt a database with a password using the Encrypt with Password button in the Info backstage area.
- To view properties for the current database, click the View and edit database properties hyperlink in the Info backstage area. The Properties dialog box contains a number of tabs containing information about the database.
- Save a database in a previous version of Access using options in the *Save Database As* section of the Save As backstage area.
- To save a database object in PDF or XPS file format, display the Save As backstage area, click the *Save Object As* option, click the *PDF or XPS* option, and then click the Save As button.
- Backup a database to maintain critical data. Backup a database with the *Back Up Database* option at the Save As backstage area.

Commands Review

FEATURE	RIBBON TAB, GROUP/OPTION	BUTTON, OPTION
filter	Home, Sort & Filter	
filter by form	Home, Sort & Filter	, *Filter By Form*
filter by selection	Home, Sort & Filter	
Info backstage area	File, *Info*	
Object Dependencies task pane	Database Tools, Relationships	
remove filter	Home, Sort & Filter	, *Clear filter from xxx* OR , *Clear All Filters*
toggle filter	Home, Sort & Filter	

Workbook

Chapter study tools and assessment activities are available in the *Workbook* ebook. These resources are designed to help you further develop and demonstrate mastery of the skills learned in this chapter.

Microsoft®

Access®

Exporting and Importing Data

CHAPTER 8

Performance Objectives

Upon successful completion of Chapter 8, you will be able to:

1 Export Access data to Excel
2 Export Access data to Word
3 Merge Access data with a Word document
4 Export an Access object to a PDF or XPS file
5 Import data to a new table
6 Link data to a new table
7 Use the Office Clipboard

Precheck

Check your current skills to help focus your study.

Microsoft Office 2016 is a suite of programs that allows for easy data exchange between programs. In this chapter, you will learn how to export data from Access to Excel and Word, merge Access data with a Word document, export an Access object to a PDF or XPS file, import and link Excel data to a new table, and copy and paste data between applications and programs.

Data Files

Before beginning chapter work, copy the AL1C8 folder to your storage medium and then make AL1C8 the active folder.

SNAP

If you are a SNAP user, launch the Precheck and Tutorials from your Assignments page.

Project 1 **Export Data to Excel and Export and Merge Data to Word** **5 Parts**

You will export a table and query to Excel and export a table and report to Word. You will also merge data in an Access table and query with a Word document.

Preview Finished Project

Exporting Data

One of the advantages of using the Microsoft Office suite is the ability to exchange data between programs. Access, like other programs in the suite, offers a feature to export data from Access into Excel and/or Word. The Export group on the External Data tab contains buttons for exporting a table, query, form, or report to other programs, such as Excel and Word.

Tutorial

Exporting Access Data to Excel

Excel

Quick Steps

Export Access Data to Excel

1. Click table, query, or form.
2. Click External Data tab.
3. Click Excel button in Export group.
4. Make changes at Export - Excel Spreadsheet dialog box.
5. Click OK.

Exporting Access Data to Excel

Use the Excel button in the Export group on the External Data tab to export data in a table, query, or form to an Excel worksheet. Click the object containing the data to be exported to Excel, click the External Data tab, and then click the Excel button in the Export group. The Export - Excel Spreadsheet dialog box displays, as shown in Figure 8.1.

Figure 8.1 Export - Excel Spreadsheet Dialog Box

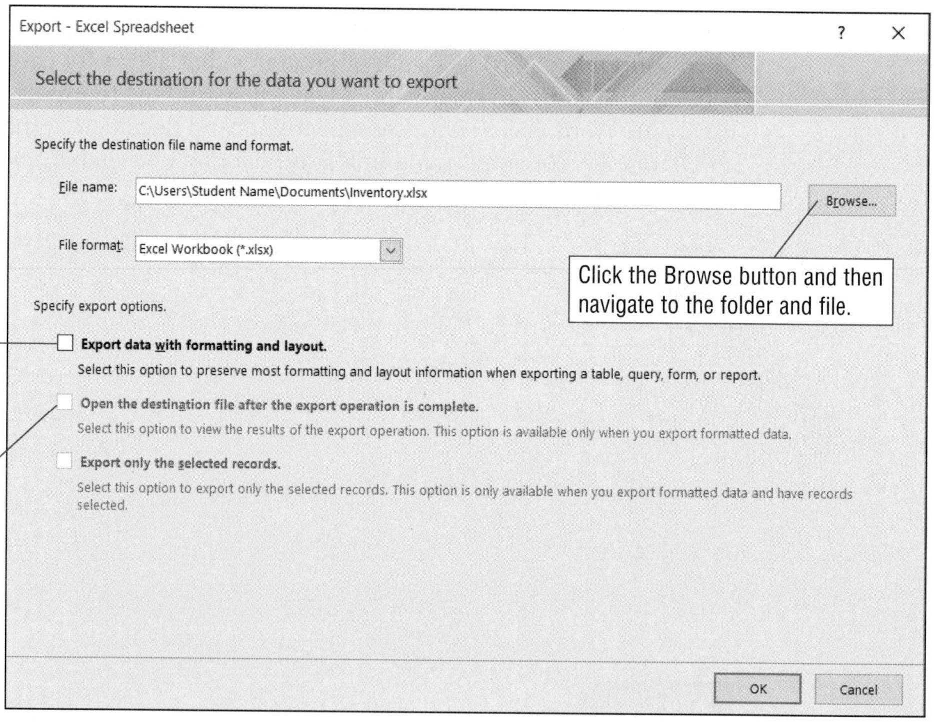

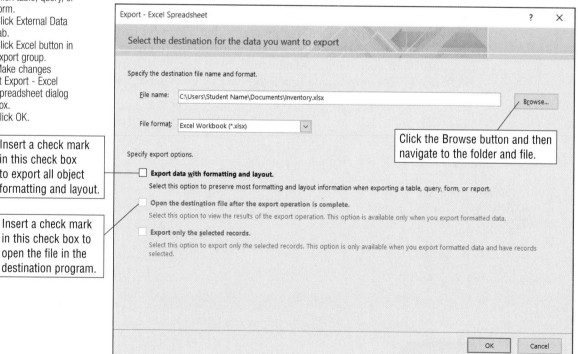

Hint Data exported from Access to Excel is saved as an Excel workbook with the .xlsx file extension.

Hint You can export only one database object at a time.

At the dialog box, Access uses the name of the object as the Excel workbook name. This can be changed by selecting the current name and then typing a new name. The file format also can be changed with the *File format* option. Click the *Export data with formatting and layout* check box to insert a check mark. This exports all data formatting to the Excel workbook. To open Excel with the exported data, click the *Open the destination file after the export operation is complete* option to insert a check mark.

When all changes have been made, click OK. This opens Excel with the data in a workbook. Make changes to the workbook and then save, print, and close the workbook. When Excel is closed, Access displays with a dialog box, asking if the export step should be saved. At this dialog box, insert a check mark in the *Save export steps* check box to save the export steps or leave the check box blank and then click the Close button.

Project 1a Exporting a Table and Query to Excel **Part 1 of 5**

1. Open **8-Hilltop.accdb** from the AL1C8 folder on your storage medium and enable the content.
2. Save the Inventory table as an Excel workbook by completing the following steps:
   a. Click *Inventory* in the Tables group in the Navigation pane.
   b. Click the External Data tab and then click the Excel button in the Export group.
   c. At the Export - Excel Spreadsheet dialog box, click the Browse button.
   d. At the File Save dialog box, navigate to the AL1C8 folder on your storage medium and then click the Save button.
   e. Click the *Export data with formatting and layout* option to insert a check mark in the check box.
   f. Click the *Open the destination file after the export operation is complete* option to insert a check mark in the check box.

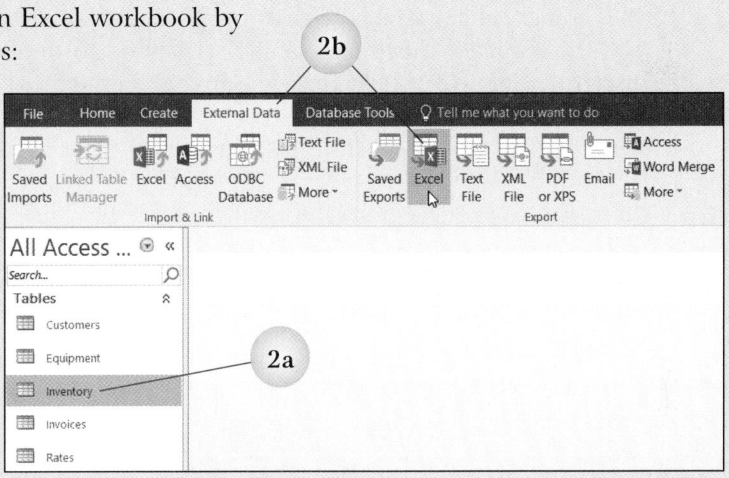

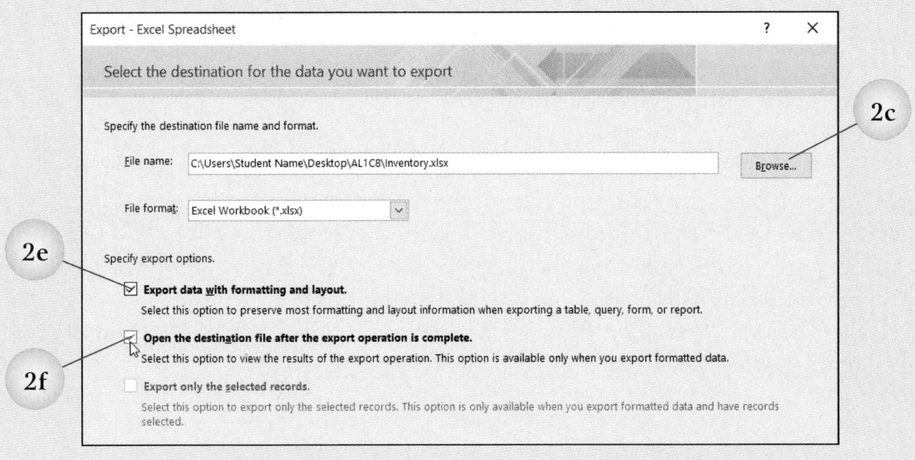

g. Click OK.

h. When the data displays on the screen in Excel as a worksheet, select the range A2:A11 and then click the Center button in the Alignment group on the Home tab.

i. Select the range D2:F11 and then click the Center button.

j. Click the Save button on the Quick Access Toolbar.

k. Print the worksheet by pressing Ctrl + P and then clicking the Print button at the Print backstage area.

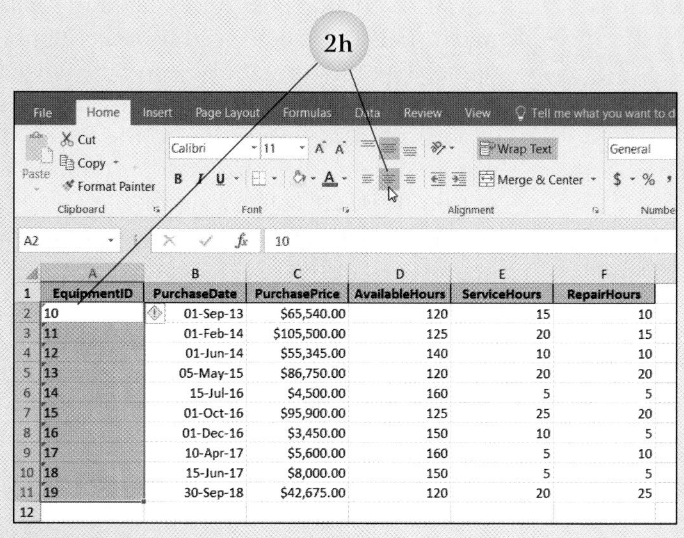

l. Close the worksheet and then close Excel.

3. In Access, click the Close button to close the dialog box.
4. Design a query that extracts records from three tables with the following specifications:
   a. Add the Invoices, Customers, and Rates tables to the query window.
   b. Insert the *BillingDate* field from the Invoices table field list box in the first field in the *Field* row.
   c. Insert the *Customer* field from the Customers table field list box in the second field in the *Field* row.
   d. Insert the *Hours* field from the Invoices table field list box in the third field in the *Field* row.
   e. Insert the *Rate* field from the Rates table field list box in the fourth field in the *Field* row.
   f. Click in the fifth field in the *Field* row, type Total: [Hours]*[Rate], and then press the Enter key.

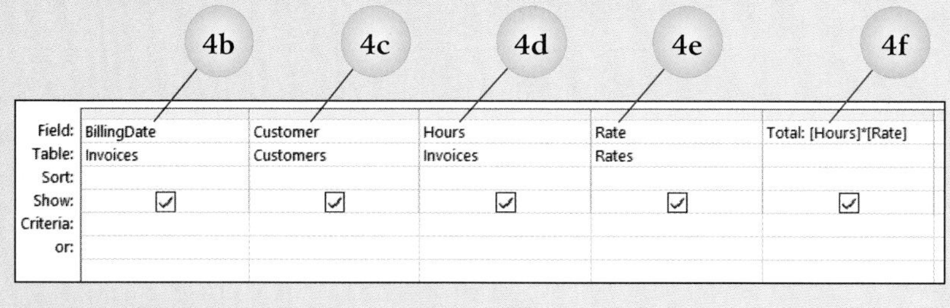

   g. Run the query.
   h. If necessary, automatically adjust the column width of the *Customer* field.
   i. Save the query with the name *CustomerInvoices*.
   j. Close the query.
5. Export the CustomerInvoices query to Excel by completing the following steps:
   a. Click *CustomerInvoices* in the Queries group in the Navigation pane.
   b. Click the External Data tab and then click the Excel button in the Export group.
   c. At the Export - Excel Spreadsheet dialog box, click the *Export data with formatting and layout* option to insert a check mark in the check box.
   d. Click the *Open the destination file after the export operation is complete* option to insert a check mark in the check box.
   e. Click OK.

f. When the data displays on the screen in Excel as a worksheet, select the range C2:C31 and then click the Center button in the Alignment group on the Home tab.
g. Click the Save button on the Quick Access Toolbar.
h. Print the worksheet by pressing Ctrl + P and then clicking the Print button at the Print backstage area.
i. Close the worksheet and then close Excel.

6. In Access, click the Close button to close the dialog box.

Check Your Work

Tutorial

Exporting Access Data to Word

More

Quick Steps

Export Data to Word

1. Click table, query, form, or report.
2. Click External Data tab.
3. Click More button in Export group.
4. Click *Word.*
5. Make changes at Export - RTF File dialog box.
6. Click OK.

Exporting Access Data to Word

Export data from Access to Word in a similar manner as exporting to Excel. To export data to Word, click the object in the Navigation pane, click the External Data tab, click the More button in the Export group, and then click *Word* at the drop-down list. At the Export - RTF File dialog box, make changes and then click OK. Word automatically opens and the data displays in a Word document that is saved automatically with the same name as the database object. The difference is that the file extension *.rtf* is added to the name. An RTF file is saved in rich-text format, which preserves formatting such as fonts and styles. A document saved with the .rtf extension can be exported in Word and other Windows word processing or desktop publishing programs.

Project 1b Exporting a Table and Report to Word — Part 2 of 5

1. With **8-Hilltop.accdb** open, click *Invoices* in the Tables group in the Navigation pane.
2. Click the External Data tab, click the More button in the Export group, and then click *Word* at the drop-down list.

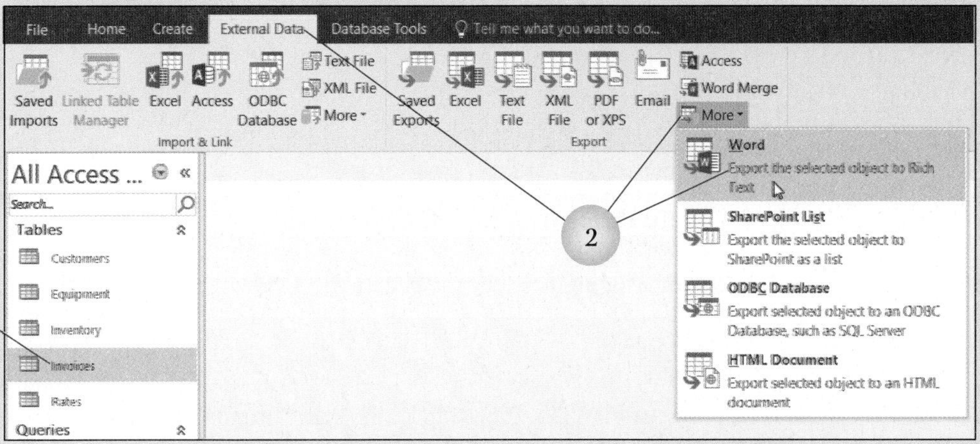

3. At the Export - RTF File dialog box, click the Browse button.
4. At the File Save dialog box, make sure the AL1C8 folder on your storage medium is active and then click the Save button.
5. At the Export - RTF File dialog box, click the *Open the destination file after the export operation is complete* check box to insert a check mark.

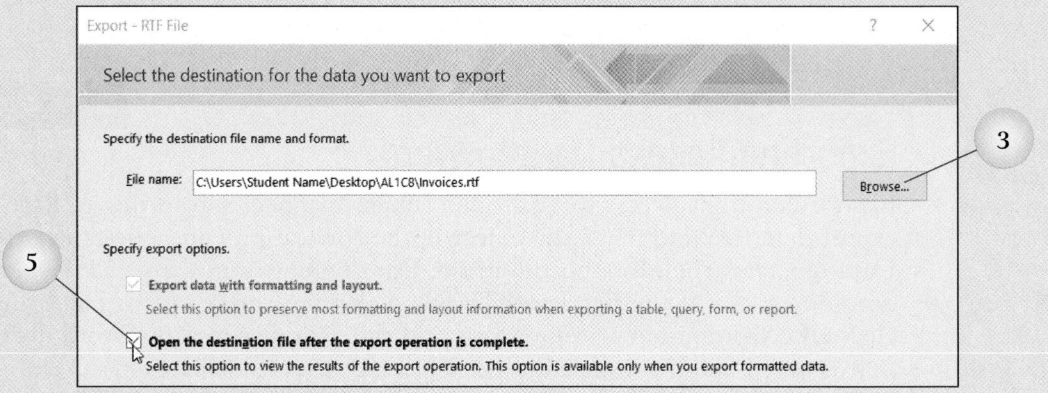

6. Click OK.
7. With **Invoices.rtf** open in Word, print the file by pressing Ctrl + P and then clicking the Print button at the Print backstage area.
8. Close **Invoices.rtf** and then close Word.
9. In Access, click the Close button to close the dialog box.
10. Create a report with the Report Wizard by completing the following steps:
    a. Click the Create tab and then click the Report Wizard button in the Reports group.
    b. At the first Report Wizard dialog box, insert the following fields in the *Selected Fields* list box:
       From the Customers table:
          Customer
       From the Equipment table:
          Equipment
       From the Invoices table:
          BillingDate
          Hours
    c. After inserting the fields, click the Next button.
    d. At the second Report Wizard dialog box, make sure *by Customers* is selected in the list box in the upper left corner and then click the Next button.

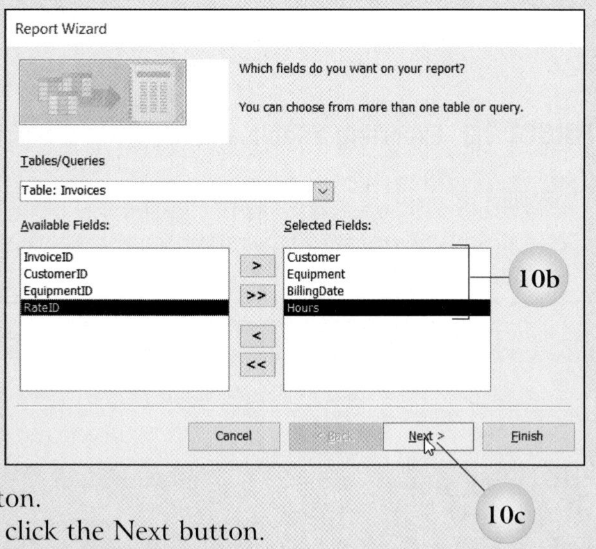

    e. At the third Report Wizard dialog box, click the Next button.
    f. At the fourth Report Wizard dialog box, click the Next button.
    g. At the fifth Report Wizard dialog box, click *Block* in the *Layout* section and then click the Next button.
    h. At the sixth and final Report Wizard dialog box, select the current name in the *What title do you want for your report?* text box, type CustomerReport, and then click the Finish button.
    i. When the report displays in Print Preview, click the Print button at the left side of the Print Preview tab and then click OK at the Print dialog box.
    j. Save and then close the CustomerReport report.

11. Export the CustomerReport report to Word by completing the following steps:
    a. Click *CustomerReport* in the Reports group in the Navigation pane.
    b. Click the External Data tab, click the More button in the Export group, and then click *Word* at the drop-down list.
    c. At the Export - RTF File dialog box, click the *Open the destination file after export operation is complete* option to insert a check mark in the check box and then click OK.
    d. When the data displays on the screen in Word, print the document by pressing Ctrl + P and then clicking the Print button at the Print backstage area.
    e. Save and then close the CustomerReport document.
    f. Close Word.
12. In Access, click the Close button to close the dialog box.

Check Your Work

Tutorial

Merging Access Data with a Word Document

Merging Access Data with a Word Document

Data from an Access table or query can be merged with a Word document. When merging data, the data in the Access table is considered the data source and the Word document is considered the main document. When the merge is completed, the merged documents display in Word.

Word Merge

To merge data in a table, click the table in the Navigation pane, click the External Data tab, and then click the Word Merge button. When merging Access data, either type the text in the main document or merge Access data with an existing Word document.

Project 1c Merging Access Table Data with a Word Document

Part 3 of 5

1. With **8-Hilltop.accdb** open, click *Customers* in the Tables group in the Navigation pane.
2. Click the External Data tab.
3. Click the Word Merge button in the Export group.

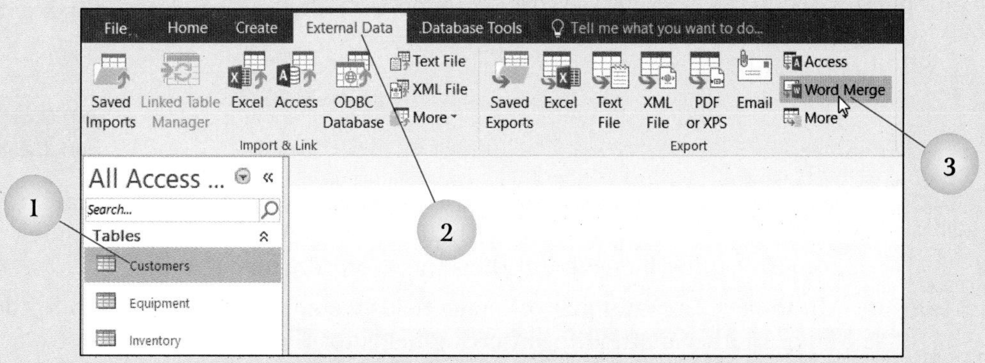

4. At the Microsoft Word Mail Merge Wizard dialog box, make sure *Link your data to an existing Microsoft Word document* is selected and then click OK.
5. At the Select Microsoft Word Document dialog box, make sure the AL1C8 folder on your storage medium is the active folder and then double-click the document named ***8-HilltopLetter.docx***.
6. Click the Word button on the taskbar.

7. Click the Maximize button that displays in the *8-HilltopLetter.docx* Title bar and then close the Mail Merge task pane.
8. Press the Down Arrow key six times (not the Enter key) and then type the current date.
9. Press the Down Arrow key four times and then insert fields for merging from the Customers table by completing the following steps:
   a. Click the Insert Merge Field button arrow in the Write & Insert Fields group and then click *Customer* in the drop-down list. (This inserts the «Customer» field in the document.)

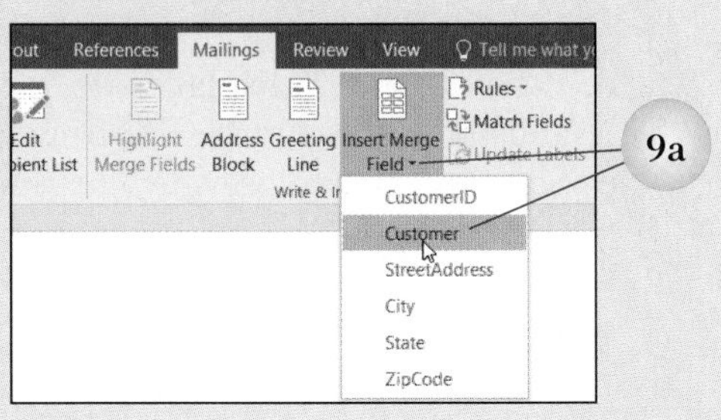

   b. Press the Enter key, click the Insert Merge Field button arrow, and then click *StreetAddress* in the drop-down list.
   c. Press the Enter key, click the Insert Merge Field button arrow, and then click *City* in the drop-down list.
   d. Type a comma (,) and then press the spacebar.
   e. Click the Insert Merge Field button arrow and then click *State* in the drop-down list.

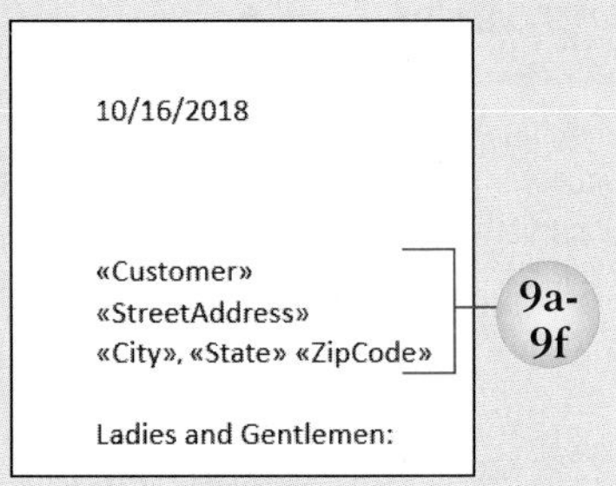

   f. Press the spacebar, click the Insert Merge Field button arrow, and then click *ZipCode* in the drop-down list.
   g. Replace the letters *XX* at the bottom of the letter with your initials.
   h. Click the Finish & Merge button in the Finish group and then click *Edit Individual Documents* in the drop-down list.
   i. At the Merge to New Document dialog box, make sure *All* is selected and then click OK.
   j. When the merge is completed, save the new document and name it **8-HilltopLtrs** in the AL1C8 folder on your storage medium.

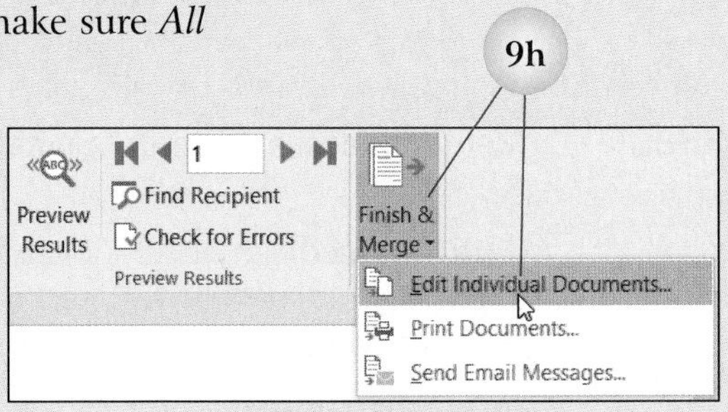

10. Print just the first two pages (two letters) of **8-HilltopLtrs.docx**.
11. Close **8-HilltopLtrs.docx** and then close **8-HilltopLetter.docx** without saving the changes.
12. Close Word.
13. Close **8-Hilltop.accdb**.

Check Your Work

Quick Steps

Merge Data with Word

1. Click table or query.
2. Click External Data tab.
3. Click Word Merge button.
4. Make choices at each dialog box.

Address Block

A query in a database can be used to merge with a Word document. In Project 1c, a table was merged with an existing Word document. A table or query also can be merged and then the Word document typed.

In Project 1c, a number of merge fields were inserted for the inside address of a letter. Another method for inserting fields for the inside address is to insert the «AddressBlock» field, which inserts all of the fields required for the inside address. Insert the «AddressBlock» composite field by clicking the Address Block button in the Write & Insert Fields group on the Mailings tab. Clicking the button displays the Insert Address Block dialog box with a preview of how the fields will be inserted in the document to create the inside address. The dialog box also contains buttons and options for customizing the fields. Click OK and the «AddressBlock» field is inserted in the document. The «AddressBlock» field is an example of a composite field, which groups a number of fields together.

In Project 1c, the «AddressBlock» composite field could not be used because the *Customer* field was not recognized by Word as a field for the inside address. In Project 1d, a query will be created that contains the *FirstName* and *LastName* fields, which Word recognizes and uses for the «AddressBlock» composite field.

Project 1d Performing a Query and then Merging with a Word Document — Part 4 of 5

1. Open **8-CopperState.accdb** from the AL1C8 folder on your storage medium and enable the content.
2. Perform a query with the Query Wizard and modify the query by completing the following steps:
   a. Click the Create tab and then click the Query Wizard button in the Queries group.
   b. At the New Query dialog box, make sure Simple Query Wizard is selected and then click OK.
   c. At the first Simple Query Wizard dialog box, click the *Tables/Queries* option box arrow and then click *Table: Clients*.
   d. Click the All Fields button to insert all of the fields in the *Selected Fields* list box.
   e. Click the Next button.
   f. At the second Simple Query Wizard dialog box, make the following changes:
      1) Select the current name in the *What title do you want for your query?* text box and then type ClientsPhoenix.
      2) Click the *Modify the query design* option.
      3) Click the Finish button.
   g. At the query window, click in the *City* field in the *Criteria* row, type Phoenix, and then press the Enter key.
   h. Click the Run button in the Results group. (Only clients living in Phoenix will display.)
   i. Save and then close the query.

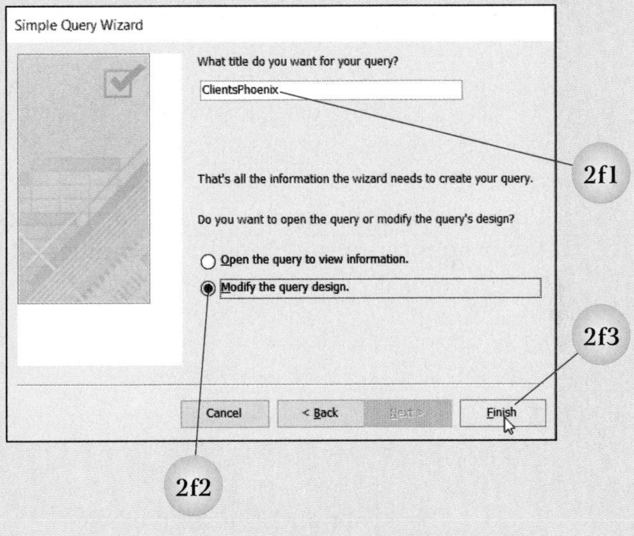

3. Click *ClientsPhoenix* in the Queries group in the Navigation pane.
4. Click the External Data tab and then click the Word Merge button in the Export group.
5. At the Microsoft Word Mail Merge Wizard dialog box, click the *Create a new document and then link the data to it* option and then click OK.
6. Click the Word button on the taskbar.

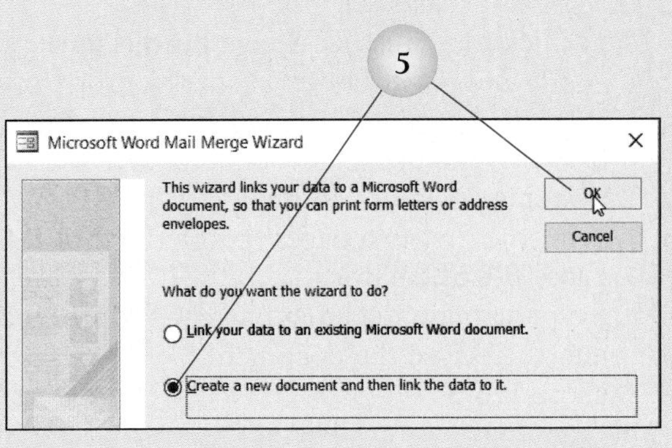

7. Click the Maximize button that displays in the Document1 Title bar and then close the Mail Merge task pane.
8. Complete the following steps to type text and insert the «AddressBlock» composite field in the blank Word document:
   a. Click the Home tab and then click the *No Spacing* style in the Styles group.
   b. Press the Enter key six times.
   c. Type the current date.
   d. Press the Enter key four times.
   e. Click the Mailings tab.
   f. Insert the «AddressBlock» composite field by clicking the Address Block button in the Write & Insert Fields group on the Mailings tab and then clicking OK at the Insert Address Block dialog box. (This inserts the «AddressBlock» composite field in the document.)
   g. Press the Enter key two times and then type the salutation Ladies and Gentlemen:.
   h. Press the Enter key two times and then type the following paragraphs of text (press the Enter key two times after typing the first paragraph):

      At the Grant Street West office of Copper State Insurance, we have hired two additional insurance representatives as well as one support staff member to ensure that we meet all your insurance needs. To accommodate the new staff, we have moved to a larger office just a few blocks away. Our new address is 3450 Grant Street West, Suite 110, Phoenix AZ 85003. Our telephone number, (602) 555-6300, has remained the same.

      If you have any questions or concerns about your insurance policies or want to discuss adding or changing current coverage, please stop by or give us a call. We are committed to providing our clients with the most comprehensive automobile insurance coverage in the county.

   i. Press the Enter key two times and then type the following complimentary close at the left margin (press the Enter key four times after typing *Sincerely,*):

      Sincerely,

      Lou Galloway
      Manager

      XX (Type your initials instead of XX.)
      8-CSLtrs.docx

   j. Click the Finish & Merge button in the Finish group on the Mailings tab and then click *Edit Individual Documents* in the drop-down menu.
   k. At the Merge to New Document dialog box, make sure *All* is selected, and then click OK.
   l. When the merge is complete, save the new document in the AL1C8 folder on your storage medium and name it **8-CSLtrs**.
9. Print the first two pages (two letters) of **8-CSLtrs.docx**.
10. Close **8-CSLtrs.docx**.
11. Save the main document as **8-CSMainDoc** in the AL1C8 folder on your storage medium and then close the document.
12. Close Word.

Check Your Work

Quick Steps

Export an Access Object to a PDF or XPS File

1. Click object in the Navigation pane.
2. Click External Data tab.
3. Click PDF or XPS button.
4. Navigate to folder.
5. Click Publish button.

PDF or XPS

Exporting an Access Object to a PDF or XPS File

With the PDF or XPS button in the Export group on the External Data tab, an Access object can be exported to a PDF or XPS file. As explained in Chapter 7, the letters *PDF* stand for *portable document format*, which is a file format that captures all of the elements of a file as an electronic image. The letters *XPS* stand for *XML paper specification* and the letters *XML* stand for *extensible markup language*, which is a set of rules for encoding files electronically.

To export an Access object to the PDF or XPS file format, click the object, click the External Data tab, and then click the PDF or XPS button in the Export group. This displays the Publish as PDF or XPS dialog box with the *PDF (*.pdf)* option selected in the *Save as type* option box. To save the Access object in XPS file format, click the *Save as type* option box and then click *XPS Document (*.xps)* at the drop-down list. At the Save As dialog box, type a name in the *File name* text box and then click the Publish button.

To open a PDF or XPS file in a web browser, open the browser and then press Ctrl + O to display the Open dialog box. At the Open dialog box, change the *Files of type* to *All Files (*.*)*, navigate to the folder containing the file, and then double-click the file.

Project 1e Exporting an Access Object to a PDF File

Part 5 of 5

1. With **8-CopperState.accdb** open, export the Coverage table to a PDF file by completing the following steps:
   a. Click *Coverage* in the Tables group in the Navigation pane.
   b. Click the External Data tab.
   c. Click the PDF or XPS button in the Export group.
   d. At the Publish as PDF or XPS dialog box, navigate to the AL1C8 folder on your storage medium, click the *Open file after publishing* check box to insert a check mark, and then click the Publish button.
   e. When the Coverage table data displays in Adobe Acrobat Reader, scroll through the file to see how it looks.

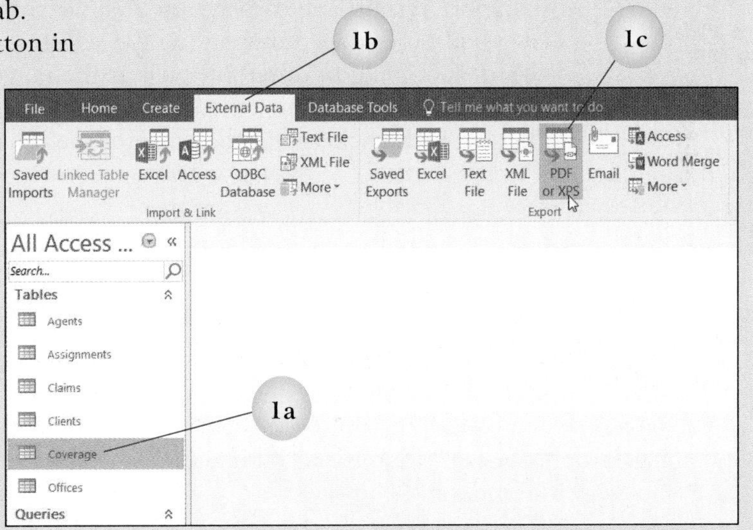

   f. Print the PDF file by clicking the Print button on the menu bar and then clicking the Print button at the Print dialog box.
   g. Close Adobe Acrobat Reader by clicking the Close button in the upper right corner of the window.
2. In Access, click the Close button to close the dialog box.

Check Your Work

Project 2 Import and Link Excel Worksheets with an Access Table — 2 Parts

You will import an Excel worksheet into an Access table. You will also link an Excel worksheet to an Access table and then add a new record to the Access table.

Preview Finished Project

Importing and Linking Data to a New Table

Hint Store data in Access and analyze it using Excel.

In addition to exporting Access data to Excel or Word, data from other programs can be imported into an Access table. For example, data from an Excel worksheet can be imported to create a new table in a database. Data in the original program is not connected to the data imported into an Access table. If changes are made to data in the original program, those changes are not reflected in the Access table. To connect the imported data with the data in the original program, link the data.

Tutorial

Importing Data to a New Table

Quick Steps

Import Data into a New Table

1. Click External Data tab.
2. Click application in Import & Link group.
3. Click Browse button.
4. Double-click file name.
5. Make choices at each wizard dialog box.

Importing Data to a New Table

To import data, click the External Data tab and then determine where to retrieve data with options in the Import & Link group. At the Import dialog box that displays, click the Browse button and then double-click the file name. This activates the Import Wizard and displays the first wizard dialog box. The appearance of the dialog box varies depending on the file selected. Complete the steps of the Import Wizard, specifying information such as the range of data, whether the first row contains column headings, whether to store the data in a new table or existing table, the primary key, and the name of the table.

Project 2a Importing an Excel Worksheet to an Access Table — Part 1 of 2

1. With **8-CopperState.accdb** open, import an Excel worksheet into a new table in the database by completing the following steps:
   a. Click the External Data tab and then click the Excel button in the Import & Link group.

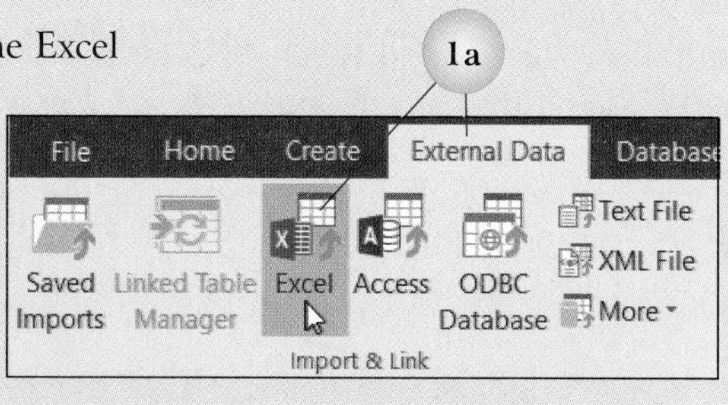

   b. At the Get External Data - Excel Spreadsheet dialog box, click the Browse button and then make the AL1C8 folder on your storage medium the active folder.
   c. Double-click *8-Policies.xlsx* in the list box.
   d. Click OK at the Get External Data - Excel Spreadsheet dialog box.
   e. At the first Import Spreadsheet Wizard dialog box, make sure the *First Row Contains Column Headings* check box contains a check mark and then click the Next button.

f. At the second Import Spreadsheet Wizard dialog box, click the Next button.

g. At the third Import Spreadsheet Wizard dialog box, click the *Choose my own primary key* option (which inserts *PolicyID* in the option box to the right of the option) and then click the Next button.

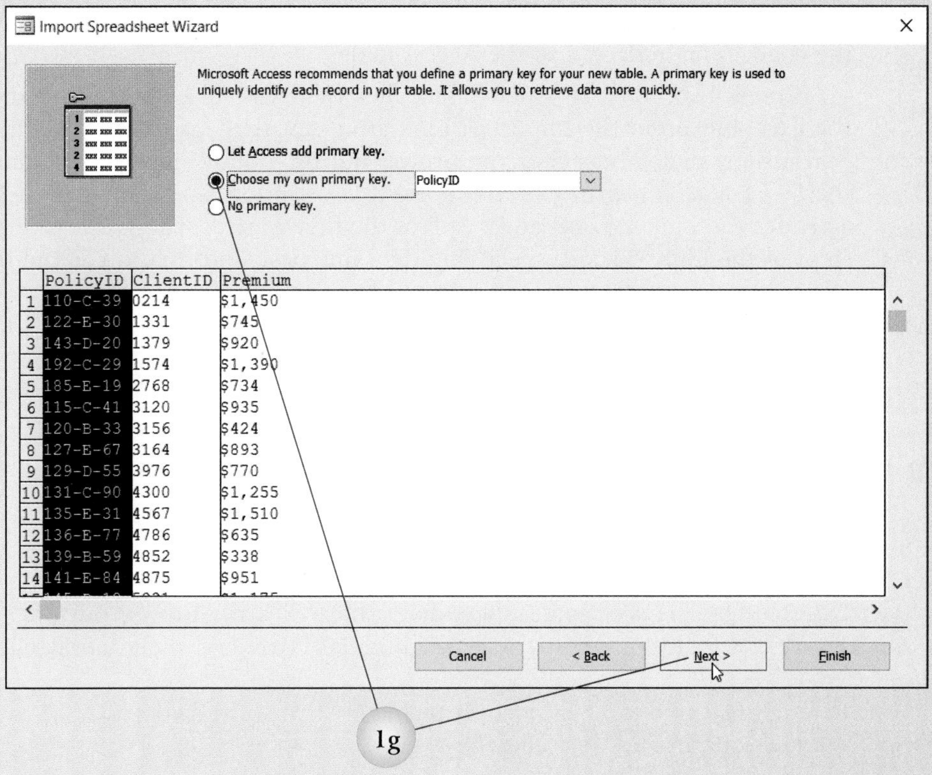

h. At the fourth Import Spreadsheet Wizard dialog box, type Policies in the *Import to Table* text box and then click the Finish button.

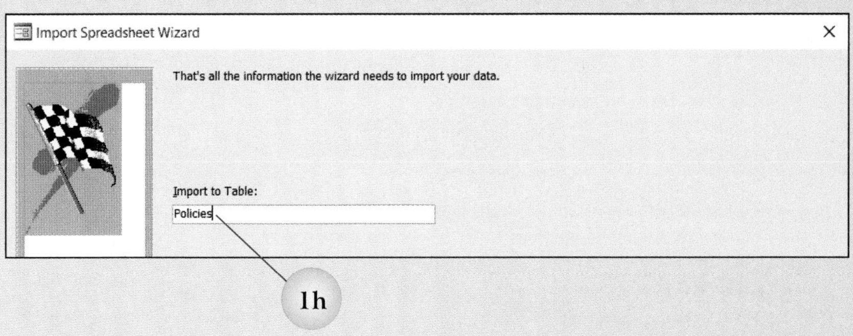

i. At the Get External Data - Excel Spreadsheet dialog box, click the Close button.

2. Open the new Policies table in Datasheet view.
3. Print and then close the Policies table.

Check Your Work

Tutorial

Linking Data to a New Table

Quick Steps

Link Data to an Excel Worksheet

1. Click External Data tab.
2. Click Excel button in Import & Link group.
3. Click Browse button.
4. Double-click file name.
5. Click *Link to a data source by creating a linked table.*
6. Make choices at each wizard dialog box.

Excel

Linking Data to an Excel Worksheet

Imported data is not connected to the source program. If the data will only be used in Access, import it. However, to update the data in a program other than Access, link the data. Changes made to linked data in the source program file are reflected in the destination program file. For example, an Excel worksheet can be linked with an Access table and, when changes are made to the Excel worksheet, the changes are reflected in the Access table.

To link Excel data to a new table, click the External Data tab and then click the Excel button in the Import & Link group. At the Get External Data - Excel Spreadsheet dialog box, click the Browse button, double-click the file name, click the *Link to a data source by creating a linked table* option, and then click OK. This activates the Link Wizard and displays the first wizard dialog box. Complete the steps of the Link Wizard, specifying the same basic information as the Import Wizard.

Project 2b Linking an Excel Worksheet to an Access Table — Part 2 of 2

1. With **8-CopperState.accdb** open, click the External Data tab and then click the Excel button in the Import & Link group.
2. At the Get External Data - Excel Spreadsheet dialog box, click the Browse button, make sure the AL1C8 folder on your storage medium is active, and then double-click ***8-Policies.xlsx***.
3. At the Get External Data - Excel Spreadsheet dialog box, click the *Link to the data source by creating a linked table* option and then click OK.

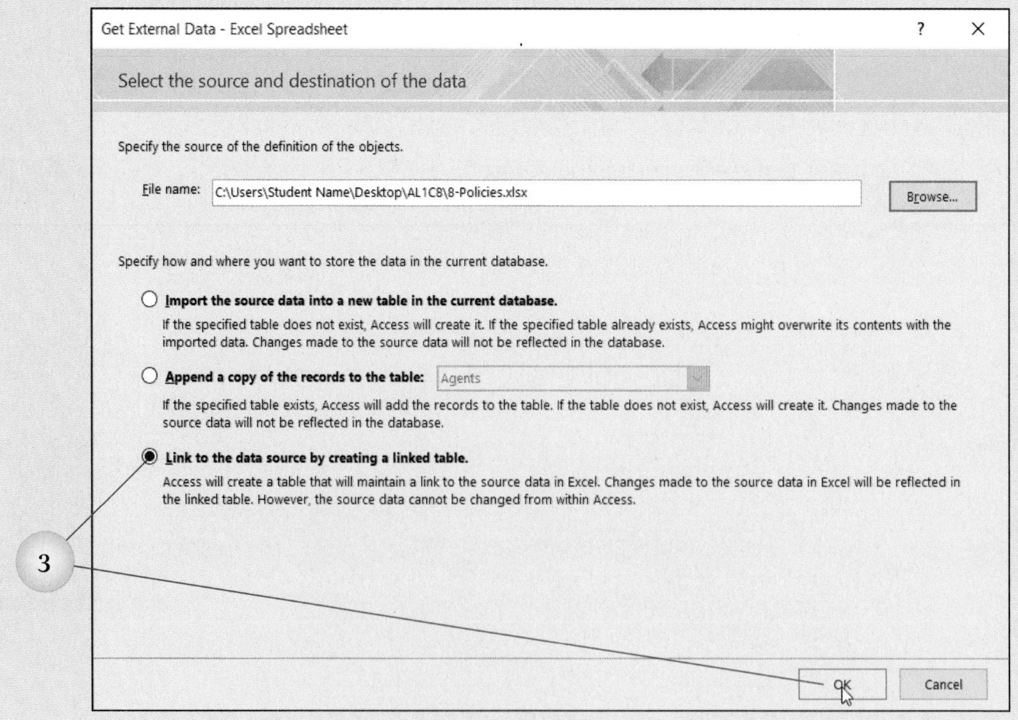

4. At the first Link Spreadsheet Wizard dialog box, make sure the *First Row Contains Column Headings* option contains a check mark and then click the Next button.
5. At the second Link Spreadsheet Wizard dialog box, type LinkedPolicies in the *Linked Table Name* text box and then click the Finish button.
6. At the message stating the linking is finished, click OK.
7. Open the new LinkedPolicies table in Datasheet view.
8. Close the LinkedPolicies table.
9. Open Excel, open the **8-Policies.xlsx** workbook, and then make the following changes:
   a. Change the amount *$745* in cell C3 to *$850*.
   b. Add the following information in the specified cells:
      A26: 190-C-28
      B26: 3120
      C26: 685

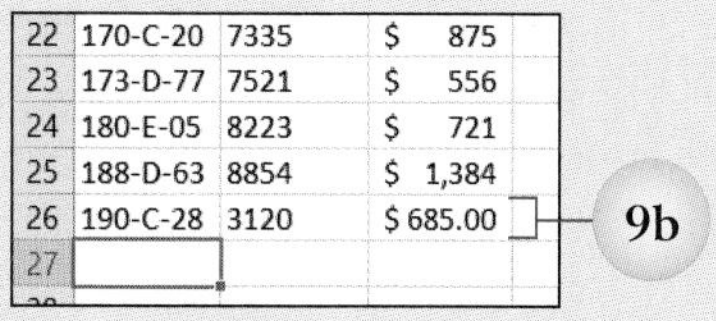

22	170-C-20	7335	$ 875
23	173-D-77	7521	$ 556
24	180-E-05	8223	$ 721
25	188-D-63	8854	$ 1,384
26	190-C-28	3120	$ 685.00
27			

10. Save, print, and then close **8-Policies.xlsx**.
11. Close Excel.
12. With Access as the active program and **8-CopperState.accdb** open, open the LinkedPolicies table. Notice the changes you just made in Excel are reflected in the table.
13. Close the LinkedPolicies table.
14. Close **8-CopperState.accdb**.

Check Your Work

Project 3 Collect Data in Word and Paste It into an Access Table — 1 Part

You will open a Word document containing Hilltop customer names and addresses and then copy the data and paste it into an Access table.

Preview Finished Project

Tutorial

Using the Office Clipboard

Using the Office Clipboard

Use the Office Clipboard to collect and paste multiple items. Up to 24 different items can be collected and pasted in Access or other programs in the Office suite. To copy and paste multiple items, display the Clipboard task pane, shown in Figure 8.2, by clicking the Clipboard group task pane launcher on the Home tab.

Quick Steps

Display the Clipboard Task Pane

Click Clipboard group task pane launcher.

Select the data or object to be copied and then click the Copy button in the Clipboard group on the Home tab. Continue selecting text or items and clicking the Copy button. To insert an item from the Clipboard task pane to a field in an Access table, make the destination field active and then click the button in the task pane representing the item. If the copied item is text, the first 50 characters display in the Clipboard task pane. After items have been inserted, click the Clear All button to remove any remaining items from the Clipboard task pane.

Data can be copied from one object to another in an Access database or from a file in another program to an Access database. In Project 3, data from a Word document will be copied and then pasted into an Access table. Data also can be collected from other programs, such as PowerPoint and Excel.

Figure 8.2 Office Clipboard Task Pane

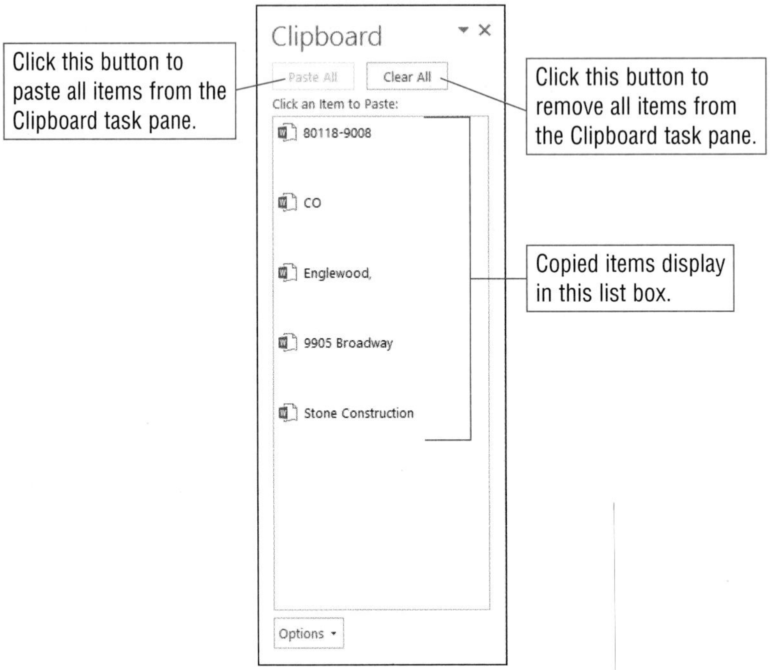

Project 3 Collecting Data in Word and Pasting It into an Access Table

Part 1 of 1

1. Open **8-Hilltop.accdb** and then open the Customers table.
2. Copy data from Word and paste it into the Customers table by completing the following steps:
   a. Open Word, make AL1C8 the active folder, and then open **8-HilltopCustomers.docx**.
   b. Make sure the Home tab is active.
   c. Click the Clipboard group task pane launcher to display the Clipboard task pane.
   d. Select the first company name, *Stone Construction*, and then click the Copy button in the Clipboard group.

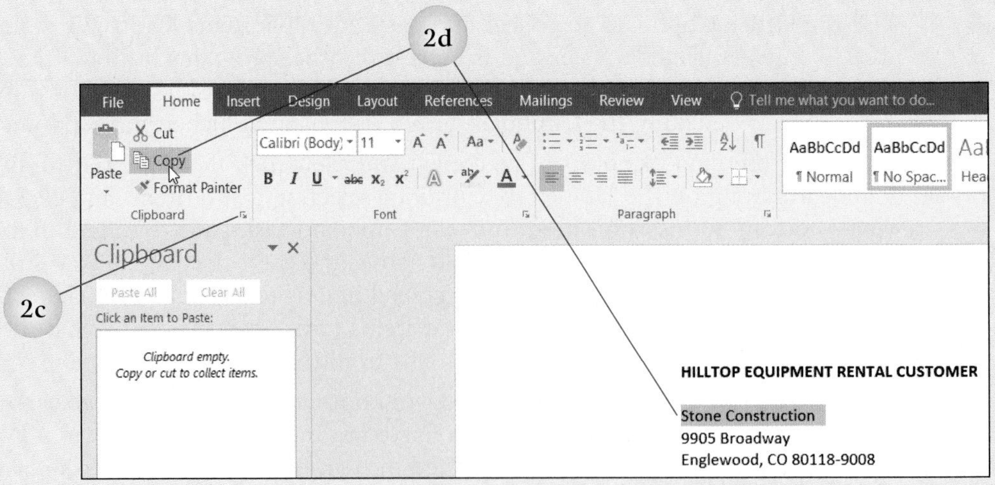

e. Select the street address, *9905 Broadway*, and then click the Copy button.
f. Select the city, *Englewood* (selecting only the city and not the comma after the city), and then click the Copy button.
g. Select the state, *CO* (selecting only the two letters and not the space after the letters), and then click the Copy button.
h. Select the zip code, *80118-9008*, and then click the Copy button.
i. Click the button on the taskbar representing Access. (Make sure the Customers table is open and displays in Datasheet view.)
j. Click in the first empty field in the *CustomerID* field column and then type 178.
k. Display the Clipboard task pane by clicking the Home tab and then clicking the Clipboard group task pane launcher.
l. Close the Navigation pane by clicking the Shutter Bar Open/Close Button.
m. Click in the first empty field in the *Customer* field column and then click *Stone Construction* in the Clipboard task pane.

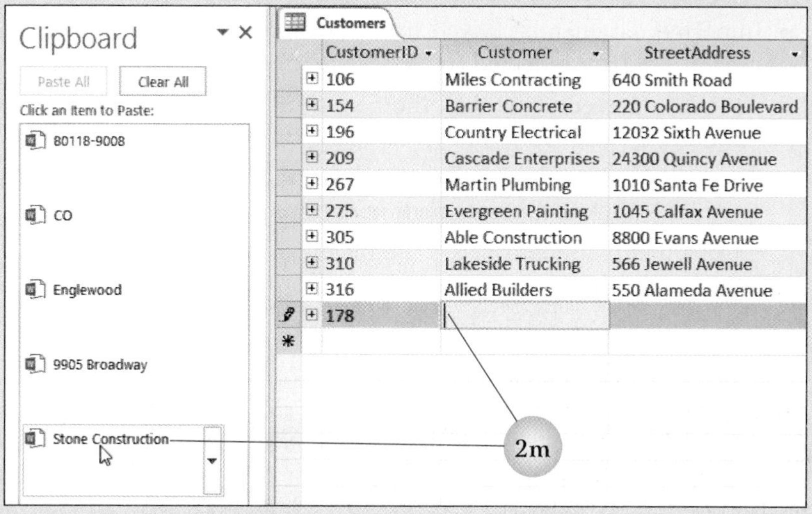

n. Click in the *StreetAddress* field and then click *9905 Broadway* in the Clipboard task pane.
o. Click in the *City* field and then click *Englewood* in the Clipboard task pane.
p. Click in the *State* field and then click *CO* in the Clipboard task pane.
q. Click in the *ZipCode* field, make sure the insertion point is positioned at the left side of the field, and then click *80118-9008* in the Clipboard task pane.
r. Click the Clear All button in the Clipboard task pane. (This removes all entries from the Clipboard.)

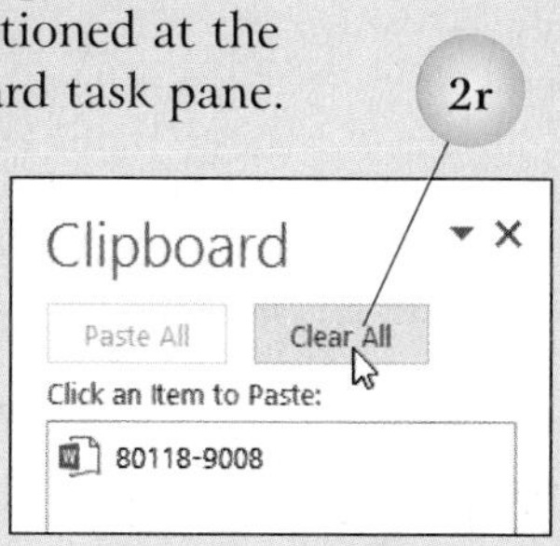

3. Complete steps similar to those in 2d through 2q to copy the information for Laughlin Products and paste it into the Customers table. (The customer ID number is 225.)
4. Click the Clear All button in the Clipboard task pane.
5. Close the Clipboard task pane by clicking the Close button (which contains an *X*) in the upper right corner of the task pane.
6. Save, print, and then close the Customers table.
7. Open the Navigation pane by clicking the Shutter Bar Open/Close Button.
8. Make Word the active program, close **8-HilltopCustomers.docx** without saving changes, and then close Word.
9. Close **8-Hilltop.accdb**.

Check Your Work

Chapter Summary

- Use the Excel button in the Export group on the External Data tab to export data in a table, query, or form to an Excel worksheet.
- Export data in a table, query, form, or report to a Word document by clicking the More button and then clicking *Word* at the drop-down list. Access exports the data to an RTF (rich-text format) file.
- Access data can be merged with a Word document. The Access data is the data source and the Word document is the main document. To merge data, click the table or query, click the External Data tab, and then click the Word Merge button in the Export group.
- Export an Access object to a PDF or XPS file with the PDF or XPS button in the Export group on the External Data tab.
- Use the Excel button in the Import group on the External Data tab to import Excel data to an Access table.
- Imported data can be linked so that changes made to the data in the source program file are reflected in the destination source file.
- To link imported data, click the *Link to the data source by creating a linked table* option at the Get External Data dialog box.
- Use the Clipboard task pane to collect up to 24 different items in Access or other programs and paste them in various locations.
- Display the Clipboard task pane by clicking the Clipboard group task pane launcher on the Home tab.

Commands Review

FEATURE	RIBBON TAB, GROUP	BUTTON, OPTION
Clipboard task pane	Home, Clipboard	
export object to Excel	External Data, Export	
export object to PDF or XPS	External Data, Export	
export object to Word	External Data, Export	, *Word*
import Excel data	External Data, Import & Link	
merge Access data with Word	External Data, Export	

Workbook

Chapter study tools and assessment activities are available in the *Workbook* ebook. These resources are designed to help you further develop and demonstrate mastery of the skills learned in this chapter.

Unit assessment activities are also available in the *Workbook*. These activities are designed to help you demonstrate mastery of the skills learned in this unit.

Index

E

F

G

H

I

J

K

L

M

N

O

P

Q

R

S

T

U

V

W

X

Y

Z

Microsoft®

PowerPoint®

Unit 1

Creating and Formatting Presentations

Microsoft®

PowerPoint®

Preparing a PowerPoint Presentation

CHAPTER 1

Performance Objectives

Upon successful completion of Chapter 1, you will be able to:

1. Open a presentation
2. Pin and unpin presentations and folders
3. Run a slide show
4. Plan a presentation
5. Close a presentation
6. Create a presentation using a design theme template
7. Insert slides, insert text in slides, and change slide layouts
8. Change presentation views
9. Save a presentation
10. Navigate and edit slides
11. Preview and print a presentation
12. Apply a design theme and a color variant to a presentation
13. Delete a presentation
14. Prepare a presentation from a blank presentation
15. Prepare a presentation in Outline view
16. Add transitions, transition sounds, and timings to a presentation

Precheck

Check your current skills to help focus your study.

During a presentation, the presenter may use visual aids to strengthen the impact of his or her message as well as help organize the presented information. Visual aids may include transparencies, slides, photographs, or an on-screen slide show. With Microsoft's PowerPoint program, you can easily create visual aids for a presentation and then print copies of the aids as well as run the slide show. PowerPoint is a presentation graphics program that you can use to organize and present information.

SNAP

If you are a SNAP user, launch the Precheck and Tutorials from your Assignments page.

Data Files

Before beginning the projects, copy the PC1 folder to your storage medium and then make PC1 the active folder.

Project 1 Open a Presentation, Run a Slide Show, and Close a Presentation

1 Part

You will open a presentation on using color in publications, run the slide show, and then close the presentation.

Tutorial

Opening a Presentation Based on a Template

Tutorial

Exploring the PowerPoint Screen

Creating a Presentation

PowerPoint provides several methods for creating a presentation. Create a presentation using a theme template or starting with a blank presentation. The steps to follow when creating a presentation will vary depending on the chosen method, but will often follow these basic steps:

1. Open PowerPoint.
2. Choose the theme template or start with a blank presentation.
3. Type the text for each slide, adding additional elements, such as images, as needed.
4. If necessary, apply a design theme.
5. Save the presentation.
6. Print the presentation as slides, handouts, notes pages, or an outline.
7. Run the slide show.
8. Close the presentation.
9. Close PowerPoint.

After choosing the specific type of presentation to be created, the PowerPoint window displays in Normal view. The window displayed will vary depending on the type of presentation being created. However, the PowerPoint window contains some consistent elements, as shown in Figure 1.1. Many of these elements are similar to those in other Microsoft Office programs, such as Word and Excel. For example, the PowerPoint window, like the Word and Excel windows, contains a File tab, Quick Access Toolbar, tabs, ribbon, vertical and horizontal scroll bars, and Status bar. The PowerPoint window elements are described in Table 1.1.

PowerPoint, like other Microsoft Office programs, provides enhanced ScreenTips for buttons and options. Hover the mouse pointer over a button or option and, after approximately one second, an enhanced ScreenTip will display the name of the button or option, any shortcut command if one is available, and a description of that button or option.

Figure 1.1 PowerPoint Window

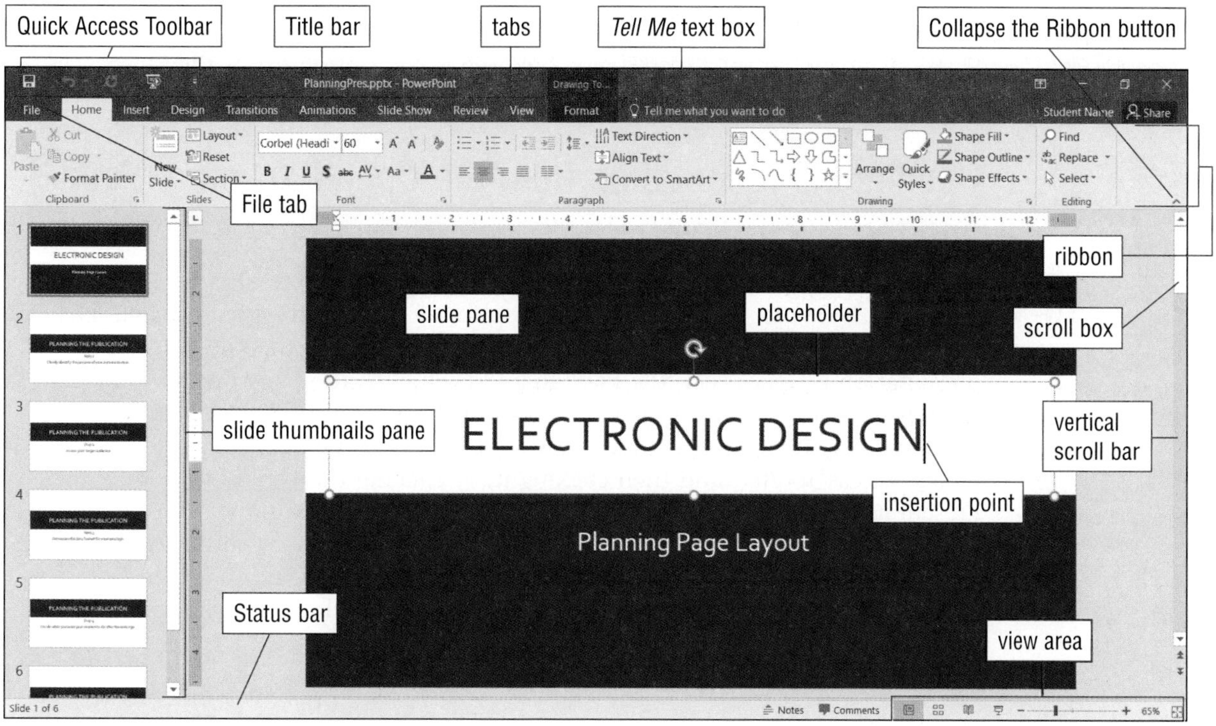

Table 1.1 PowerPoint Window Elements

Feature	Description
Collapse the Ribbon button	when clicked, removes the ribbon from the screen (To redisplay the ribbon, click any tab [except the File tab] and then click the Pin the Ribbon button [previously the Collapse the Ribbon button])
File tab	when clicked, displays the backstage area with options for working with and managing presentations
horizontal scroll bar	used to shift the slide in the slide pane left or right
I-beam pointer	used to move the insertion point or to select text
insertion point	indicates the location of the next character entered at the keyboard
placeholder	location on a slide that holds text or objects
Quick Access Toolbar	contains buttons for commonly used commands
ribbon	area containing the tabs with options and buttons divided into groups
slide pane	displays the slide and slide contents
slide thumbnails pane	area on the left side of the screen that displays slide thumbnails
Status bar	displays the slide number and number of slides, buttons for inserting notes and comments, and the view area
tabs	contain commands and features organized into groups
Tell Me feature	provides information as well as guidance on how to complete a function
Title bar	displays presentation name followed by the program name
vertical scroll bar	displays specific slides
view area	a feature of the Status bar that contains buttons for changing the presentation view or slide display percentage

Tutorial

Opening from a Removable Disk

Opening a Presentation

After a presentation is saved and closed, it can be opened from a variety of locations including the Open dialog box, the *Recent* option list at the Open backstage area, or from the PowerPoint opening screen.

Quick Steps

Open a Presentation

1. Click File tab.
2. Click *Open* option.
3. Click *Browse* option.
4. Navigate to folder or drive.
5. Double-click presentation name.

Hint To display the Open dialog box without displaying the Open backstage area, press Ctrl + F12.

Opening a Presentation from the Open Backstage Area and the Open Dialog Box

The Open dialog box provides one method for opening a presentation. Display the Open dialog box by clicking the *Browse* option at the Open backstage area. Display the Open backstage area, shown in Figure 1.2, by clicking the File tab. If a presentation is open, click the File tab and then click the *Open* option to display the Open backstage area. Other methods for displaying the Open backstage area include using the keyboard shortcut, Ctrl + O, inserting an Open button on the Quick Access Toolbar and then clicking it, or clicking the Open Other Presentations hyperlink in the lower left corner of the PowerPoint 2016 opening screen. Go directly to the Open dialog box without displaying the Open backstage area by pressing Ctrl + F12. At the Open dialog box, navigate to a specific location, open the folder containing the file, and then double-click the file name in the Content pane.

Figure 1.2 Open Backstage Area

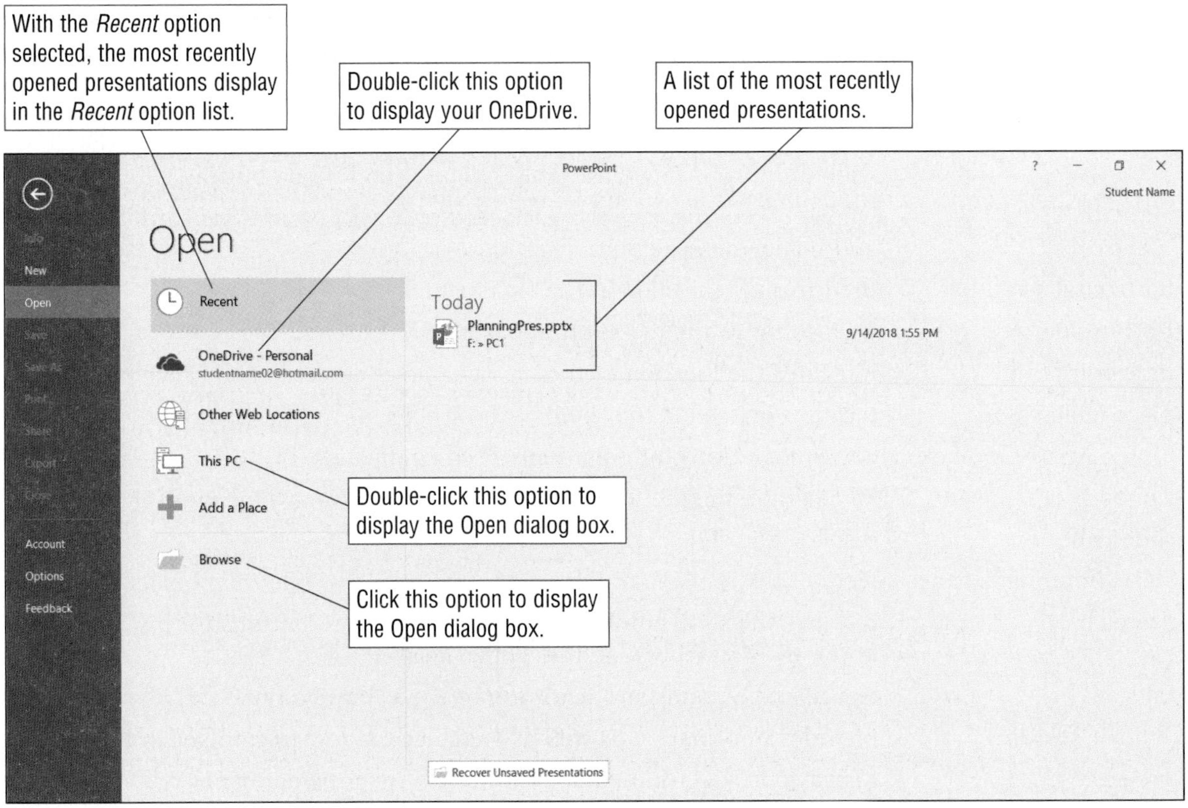

With the *Recent* option selected, the most recently opened presentations display in the *Recent* option list.
Double-click this option to display your OneDrive.
A list of the most recently opened presentations.
PowerPoint
Student Name
New
Open
Account
Options
Feedback
Open
Recent
OneDrive - Personal
studentname02@hotmail.com
Other Web Locations
This PC
Add a Place
Browse
Today
PlanningPres.pptx
F: » PC1
9/14/2018 1:55 PM
Double-click this option to display the Open dialog box.
Click this option to display the Open dialog box.
Recover Unsaved Presentations

Tutorial

Opening from the *Recent* Option List

Opening a Presentation from the *Recent* Option List

At the Open backstage area with *Recent* option selected, the names of the most recently opened presentations display. By default, PowerPoint displays 25 of the most recently opened presentations and groups them into categories such as *Today*, *Yesterday*, and sometimes *Last Week*. The PowerPoint 2016 opening screen also contains a list of the most recently opened presentations. Click a presentation name in the *Recent* option list at the Open backstage area or the Recent list at the opening screen to open the presentation.

Tutorial

Pinning and Unpinning a File to the *Recent* Option List

Quick Steps

Pin a Presentation to the *Recent* Option List

1. Display PowerPoint 2016 opening screen or Open backstage area.
2. Hover mouse over presentation in list.
3. Click left-pointing push pin.

Pinning and Unpinning Presentations and Folders

If a presentation is opened on a regular basis, consider pinning it to the *Recent* option list at the Open backstage area. To pin a presentation, hover the mouse pointer over the presentation name in the *Recent* option list and then click the left-pointing push pin at the right of the presentation name. This turns the push pin into a down-pointing push pin and inserts the presentation into a new category named *Pinned*. The *Pinned* category displays at the top of the *Recent* option list, and the next time the Open backstage area displays, the presentation will display in the *Pinned* category of the *Recent* option list.

A presentation can also be pinned to the Recent list at the PowerPoint 2016 opening screen. When a presentation is pinned, it displays at the top of the Recent list as well as the *Recent* option list at the Open backstage area. To "unpin" a document from the Recent list or *Recent* option list, click the pin to change it from a down-pointing push pin to a left-pointing push pin. More than one presentation can be pinned to a list. Another method for pinning and unpinning presentations is to right-click a presentation name in the Recent list or *Recent* option list and then click the *Pin to list* or *Unpin from list* option.

In addition to presentations, folders can be pinned to a list at the Save As backstage area. The third panel in the Save As backstage area displays a list of the most recently opened folders and groups them into categories such as *Today*, *Yesterday*, and *Last Week*. When you pin a folder or folders to the list, a *Pinned* category is created and the folder names display in that category.

Tutorial

Running a Slide Show

Start from Beginning

Running a Slide Show

When a presentation is opened, the presentation displays in Normal view. A presentation can be edited and customized in this view. To run the slide show, click the Start From Beginning button on the Quick Access Toolbar, click the Slide Show button in the view area on the Status bar, or click the Slide Show tab and then click the From Beginning button in the Start Slide Show group. Navigate through the slides in the slide show by clicking the left mouse button.

Tutorial

Closing a Presentation and Closing PowerPoint

Quick Steps

Close a Presentation

1. Click File tab.
2. Click *Close* option.

Closing a Presentation

To remove a presentation from the screen, close the presentation. Close a presentation by clicking the File tab and then clicking the *Close* option or with the keyboard shortcut Ctrl + F4. If any changes are made to the presentation, a message will display asking if the presentation should be saved.

1. Open PowerPoint by clicking the PowerPoint 2016 tile at the Windows Start menu. (Depending on your operating system, these steps may vary.)
2. At the PowerPoint opening screen, click the Open Other Presentations hyperlink in the lower left corner of the screen.
3. At the Open backstage area, click the *Browse* option.

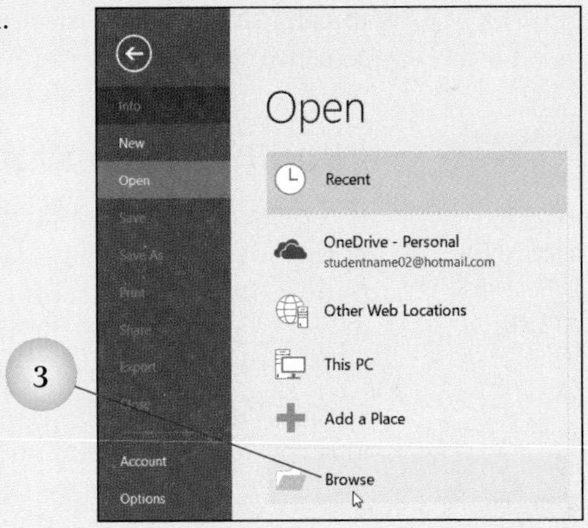

4. At the Open dialog box, navigate to the PC1 folder on your storage medium and then double-click ***ColorInfo.pptx***.
5. Run the slide show by completing the following steps:
   a. Click the Start From Beginning button on the Quick Access Toolbar.

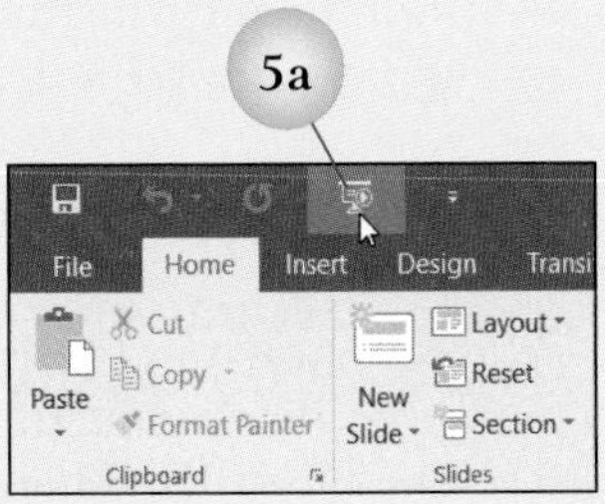

   b. Read the information in the first slide in the presentation and then click the left mouse button.
   c. Continue reading the information in the slides and clicking the left mouse button to advance the slides.
   d. At the black screen with the *End of slide show* message, click the left mouse button. (This returns the presentation to Normal view.)
6. Close the presentation by clicking the File tab and then clicking the *Close* option. (If a message displays asking if you want to save changes, click the No button.)
7. Pin **ColorInfo.pptx** to the *Recent* option list by completing the following steps:
   a. Click the File tab.
   b. At the Open backstage area with the *Recent* option selected, hover your mouse over the **ColorInfo.pptx** presentation name at the top of the *Recent* option list and then click the push pin to the right of the presentation name.

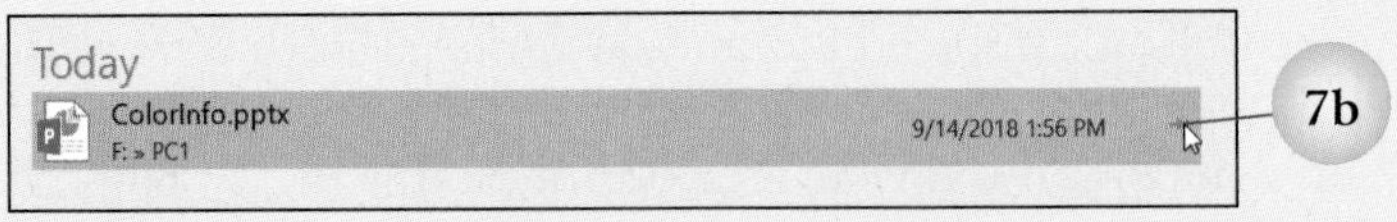

   c. Click the Back button to return to the blank presentation screen. (The Back button is in the upper left corner of the backstage area and displays as a circle with a left-pointing arrow.)
8. Close PowerPoint by clicking the Close button in the upper right corner of the screen.
9. Open PowerPoint by clicking the PowerPoint 2016 tile at the Windows Start menu. (These steps may vary; check with your instructor.)
10. At the PowerPoint 2016 opening screen, notice that **ColorInfo.pptx** is pinned in the *Pinned* section of the Recent list. Open the presentation by clicking ***ColorInfo.pptx*** at the top of the list.
11. Close **ColorInfo.pptx**.
12. Unpin **ColorInfo.pptx** from the *Recent* option list by completing steps 7a through 7c.

Project 2 Create a Resume Style Presentation Using a Design Theme Template — 3 Parts

You will use a design theme template to create a presentation, insert text in slides in the presentation, choose a slide layout, insert new slides, change views, navigate through the presentation, edit text in slides, and then print the presentation.

Preview Finished Project

Planning a Presentation

When planning a presentation, first define the purpose of the presentation. Is the intent to inform, educate, sell, motivate, and/or entertain? Also consider the audience who will be listening to and watching the slide show. Determine the content of the presentation and the medium that will be used to convey the message. Will a computer monitor be used to display the presentation or will the presentation be projected onto a screen? Consider these guidelines when preparing the content of a presentation:

- **Determine the main purpose of the presentation.** Do not try to cover too many topics — this may strain the audience's attention or cause confusion. Identifying the main point of the presentation will help to stay focused and convey a clear message to the audience.
- **Show one idea per slide.** Each slide in a presentation should convey only one main idea. Too many thoughts or ideas on a slide may confuse the audience and cause you to stray from the purpose of the slide. Determine the specific message you want to convey and then outline the message to organize your ideas.
- **Determine the display medium.** Is the presentation going to be presented on a computer or will the slides be projected onto a screen? To help determine which type of output to use, consider the availability of equipment, the size of the room where the presentation will be given, and the number of people who will be attending the presentation.
- **Maintain a consistent layout.** Using a consistent layout and color scheme for slides in a presentation will create continuity and cohesiveness. Do not get carried away by using too many colors, pictures, and/or other graphic elements.
- **Keep slides simple.** Keep slides uncluttered so that they are easy for the audience to read. Keep words and other items, such as bullets, to a minimum.
- **Determine the output needed.** Will you be providing audience members with handouts? If so, what format will the handouts take? Will they show the slides either with or without space for taking notes or an outline of the slide content?

Quick Steps

Create a Presentation Using a Design Theme Template

1. Click File tab.
2. Click *New* option.
3. Click design theme template.
4. Click color variant.
5. Click Create button.

Creating a Presentation Using a Design Theme Template

PowerPoint provides built-in design theme templates for creating slides for a presentation. These design theme templates include formatting options such as color, background, fonts, and so on. Choose a design theme template at the New backstage area shown in Figure 1.3. Display the New backstage area by clicking the File tab and then clicking the *New* option. At this backstage area, click the design theme template or search for a template online by typing a category in the

Figure 1.3 New Backstage Area

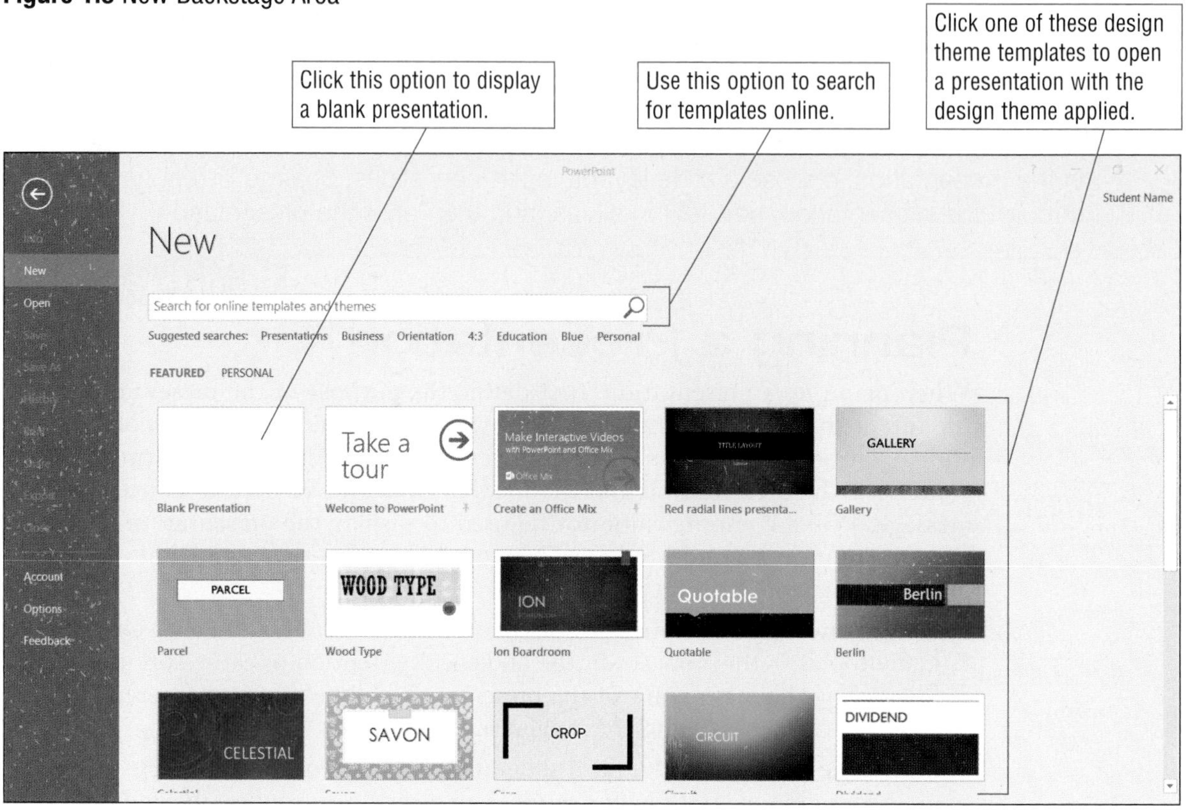

search text box or clicking one of the categories listed next to *Suggested searches* below the search text box.

Click a design theme template at the New backstage area and a window opens containing a slide with the design theme applied as well as theme color variants. The color variants display at the right side of the window and provide color options for the theme. To change the color of the theme, click the color variant and then click the Create button. This opens a presentation with the design theme and the new theme colors applied.

Inserting Text in a Placeholder

Choose a blank presentation template or design theme template at the New backstage area and a slide displays in the slide pane in Normal view. The slide displays with the default Title Slide layout. This layout contains placeholders for entering the slide title and subtitle. To insert text in a placeholder, click in the placeholder. This moves the insertion point inside the placeholder, removes the placeholder label (the text inside the placeholder), and makes the placeholder active. An active placeholder displays surrounded by a dashed border with sizing handles and a white rotation handle, as shown in Figure 1.4.

With the insertion point positioned in a placeholder, type the text. Edit text in a placeholder in the same manner as editing text in a Word document. Press the Backspace key to delete the character immediately left of the insertion point and press the Delete key to delete the character immediately right of the insertion point. Use the arrow keys on the keyboard to move the insertion point in a specific direction.

Figure 1.4 Slide Placeholders

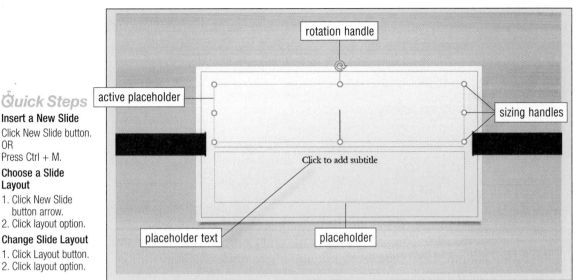

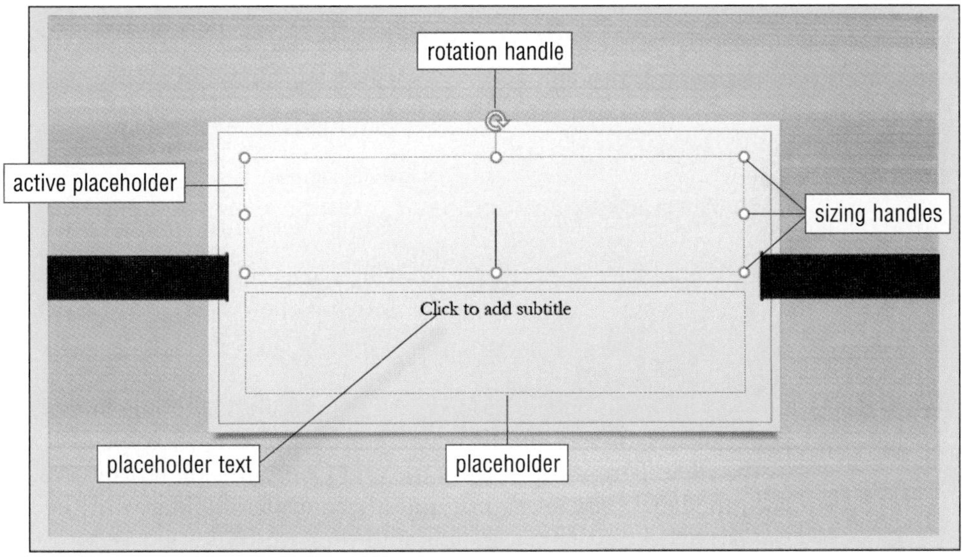

Quick Steps

Insert a New Slide
Click New Slide button.
OR
Press Ctrl + M.

Choose a Slide Layout
1. Click New Slide button arrow.
2. Click layout option.

Change Slide Layout
1. Click Layout button.
2. Click layout option.

Tutorial
Inserting a New Slide

Tutorial
Choosing a Slide Layout

New Slide

Inserting Slides

Create a new slide in a presentation by clicking the New Slide button in the Slides group on the Home tab or by pressing Ctrl + M. By default, PowerPoint inserts a new slide with the Title and Content layout. However, if a slide with a different layout is selected in the slide thumbnails pane, the layout of the selected slide is applied to the new slide. Choose a different slide layout for a new slide by clicking the New Slide button arrow and then clicking the layout option at the drop-down list.

Tutorial
Changing Slide Layout

Layout

Changing a Slide Layout

Choose a blank presentation template or design theme template to create a presentation and the slide displays in the Title Slide layout. Change the slide layout with the Layout button in the Slides group on the Home tab. Click the Layout button and a drop-down list of layout options displays. Click a layout at the drop-down list and that layout is applied to the current slide.

Tutorial
Inserting and Deleting Text in Slides

Tutorial
Selecting Text

Inserting, Selecting, and Deleting Text in Slides

Text in a slide may need to be edited, moved, copied, or deleted. Specific text in a slide may need to be replaced with other text. Text is generally inserted in a slide placeholder. Placeholders can be moved, sized, and/or deleted.

To insert or delete text in an individual slide, open the presentation, edit the text as needed, and then save the presentation. To delete more than one character, consider selecting the text first. This will help reduce the number of times the Delete key or Backspace key needs to be pressed. Several methods can be used for selecting text, as described in Table 1.2.

Table 1.2 Selecting Text

To select	Perform this action
text the mouse pointer passes through	Click and drag the mouse.
an entire word	Double-click in the word.
an entire bulleted item	Click the bullet.
an entire paragraph	Triple-click in the paragraph.
all text in a selected placeholder	Click Select button in Editing group on Home tab and then click *Select All*, or press Ctrl + A.

Text in a slide is positioned inside a placeholder. Slide layouts provide placeholders for text and display a label suggesting the type of text to be entered in the slide. For example, the Title and Content slide layout contains a placeholder with the label *Click to add title* and a second placeholder with the label *Click to add text*. Click in the placeholder and the insertion point is positioned inside the placeholder, the default label is removed, and the placeholder is selected.

Saving a Presentation

Save

After creating or editing a presentation, save it for future use by clicking the Save button on the Quick Access Toolbar, by clicking the File tab and then clicking the *Save* or *Save As* option, or with the keyboard shortcut Ctrl + S. A presentation file name can contain up to 255 characters, including the drive letter and any folder names, and can include spaces. A presentation cannot contain the same name in first uppercase and then lowercase letters. For example, one presentation cannot be named Planning.pptx and another presentation named planning.pptx. Also, some symbols cannot be used in a file name, including /, ?, \, ", >, :, <, ;, *, and |.

Tutorial

Saving to a Removable Disk

Quick Steps

Save a Presentation with a New Name

1. Click File tab.
2. Click *Save As*.
3. Click *Browse*.
4. Navigate to folder.
5. Type name in *File name* text box.
6. Click Save.

Saving a Presentation with a New Name

Save a presentation with a new name using options at the Save As dialog box. Display the Save As dialog box by clicking the File tab and then clicking the *Save As* option. At this backstage area, click the *Browse* option and the Save As dialog box displays. At the Save As dialog box, navigate to a specific folder, type a name for the presentation in the *File name* text box and then press the Enter key or click the Save button. Press the F12 function key to go directly to the Save As dialog box without displaying the Save As backstage area.

Click the OneDrive or *This PC* option at the Save As backstage area and the names of the most recently accessed folders display in the third panel of the backstage area. Open a folder by clicking the folder name.

Tutorial

Saving with the Same Name

Quick Steps

Save a Presentation with the Same Name

1. Click File tab.
2. Click *Save*.

Saving a Presentation with the Same Name

If changes are made to an existing presentation, save the changes before closing the presentation. Consider saving changes to a presentation on a periodic basis to ensure that no changes are lost if the power is interrupted. Save a presentation with the same name using the Save button on the Quick Access Toolbar or the *Save* option at the backstage area.

Project 2a Creating a Presentation Using a Design Theme Template

Part 1 of 3

1. With PowerPoint open, click the File tab and then click the *New* option.
2. At the New backstage area, click the *Organic* design theme template.
3. At the window, click the Create button.

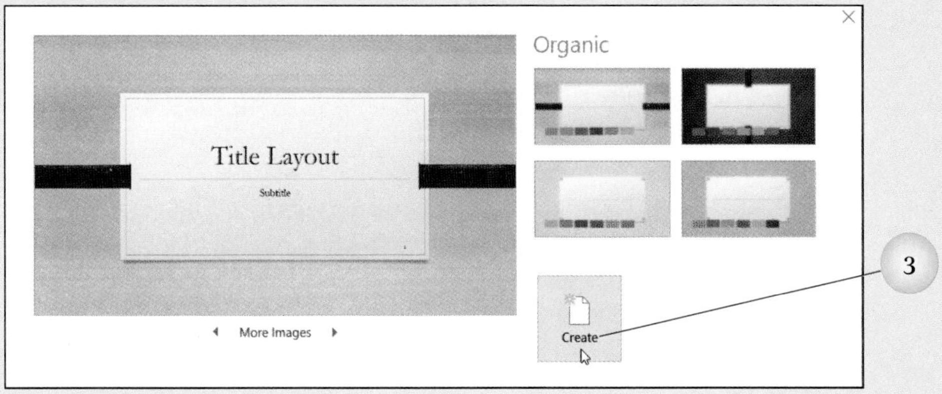

4. Click anywhere in the *Click to add title* placeholder and then type Career Finders.
5. Click anywhere in the *Click to add subtitle* placeholder and then type Resume Writing.

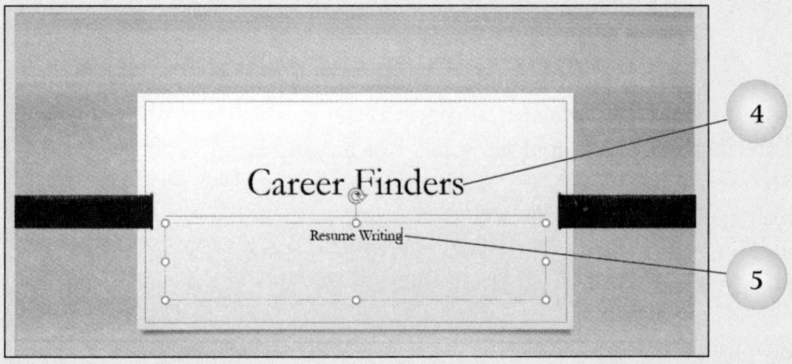

6. Click the New Slide button in the Slides group on the Home tab. (This inserts a slide with the Title and Content slide layout.)

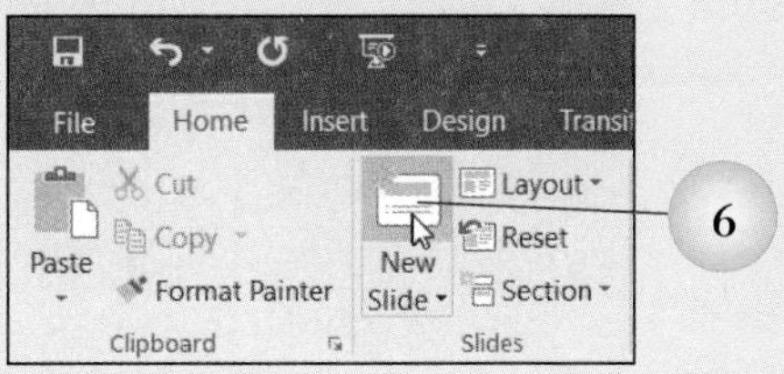

7. Click anywhere in the *Click to add title* placeholder and then type Resume Styles.
8. Click anywhere in the *Click to add text* placeholder and then type Chronological resume.
9. Press the Enter key (this moves the insertion point to the next line and inserts a bullet) and then type Functional resume.
10. Press the Enter key and then type Hybrid resume.

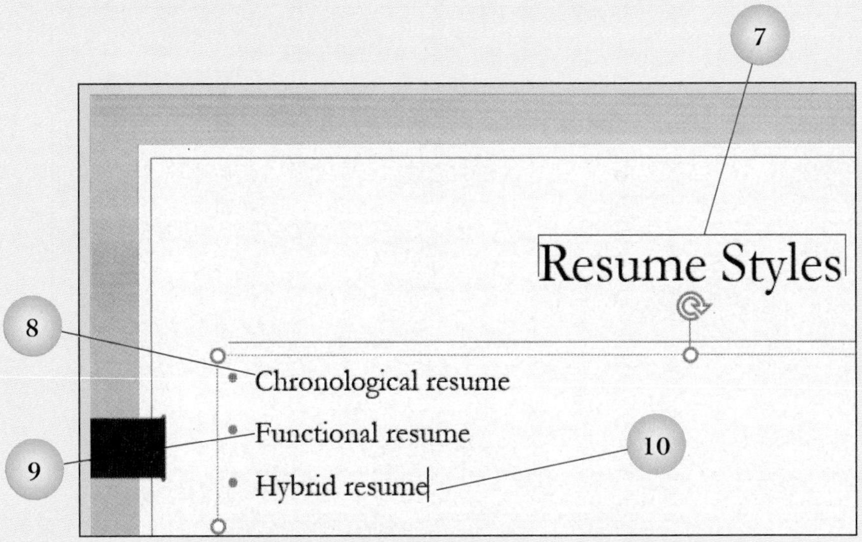

11. Click the New Slide button in the Slides group.
12. Click anywhere in the *Click to add title* placeholder and then type Resume Sections.
13. Click anywhere in the *Click to add text* placeholder and then type Contact information.
14. Press the Enter key and then type Summary or job objective statement.
15. Press the Enter key and then type Work history.
16. Press the Enter key and then type Education details.
17. Press the Enter key and then type References.

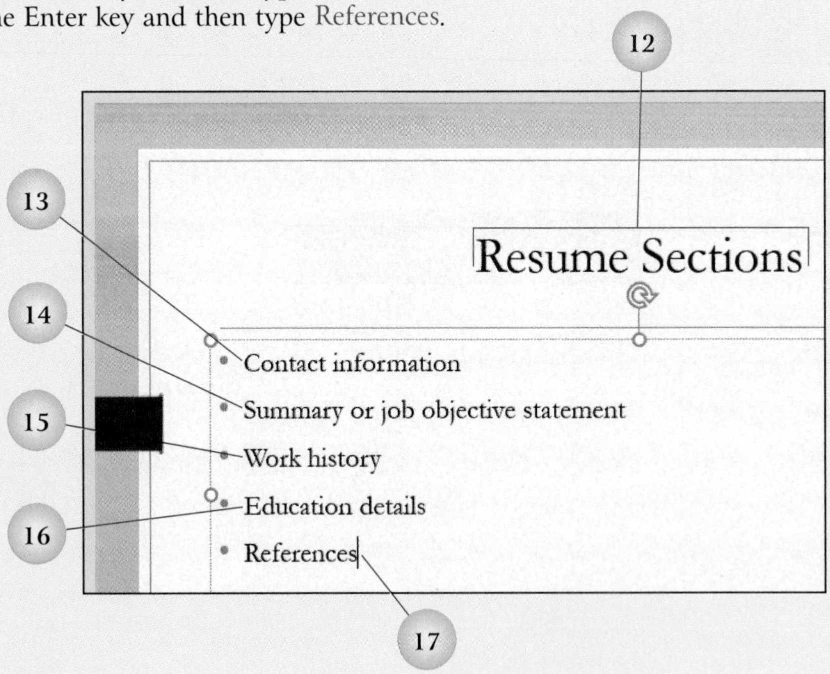

18. Click the New Slide button arrow and then click the *Title Only* layout option.

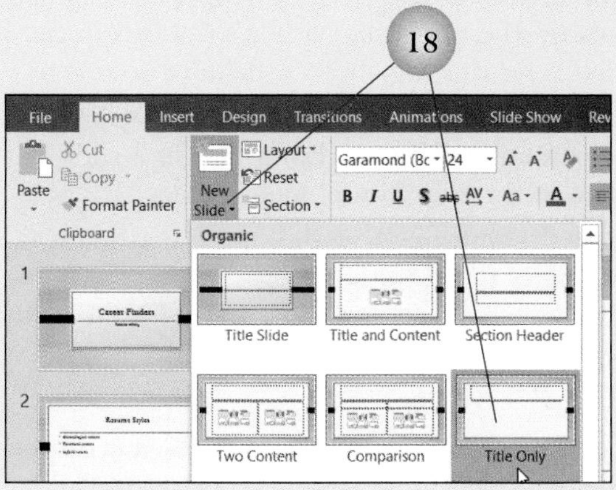

19. Click anywhere in the *Click to add title* placeholder and then type Career Finders.
20. Click the Layout button in the Slides group on the Home tab and then click the *Title Slide* layout option.

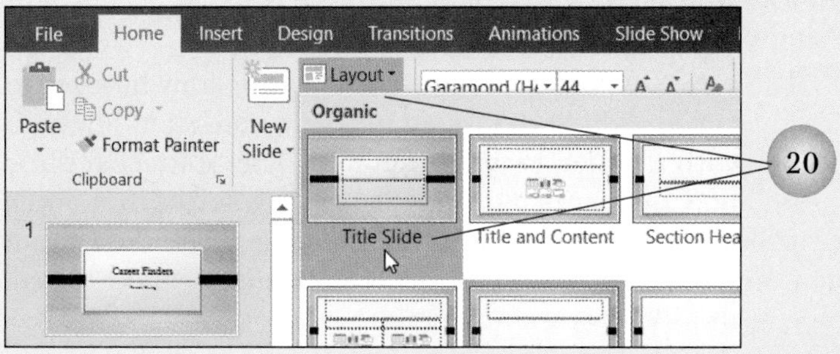

21. Click anywhere in the *Click to add subtitle* placeholder and then type Contact us by calling 1-800-555-2255.
22. Click in the slide pane, but outside the slide. (This deselects the placeholder.)
23. Save the presentation by completing the following steps:
    a. Click the Save button on the Quick Access Toolbar.
    b. At the Save As backstage area, click the *Browse* option.
    c. At the Save As dialog box, navigate to the PC1 folder on your storage medium.
    d. Select the text in the *File name* text box and then type 1-Resumes (*1* for Chapter 1 and *Resumes* because that is the topic of the presentation).
    e. Press the Enter key or click the Save button.

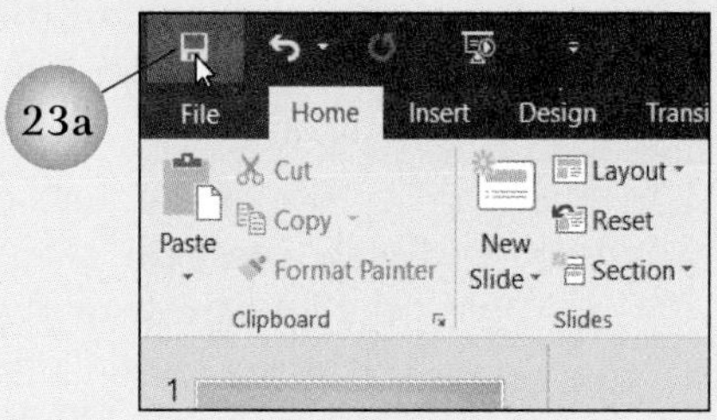

Check Your Work

Tutorial

Changing Views

Normal

Outline View

Slide Sorter

Notes Page

Reading View

Slide Sorter

Reading View

Normal

Slide Show

Hint In Normal view, you can increase or decrease the size of the slide thumbnails pane.

Changing Views

PowerPoint provides a variety of viewing options. Change the view with buttons in the view area on the Status bar or with options in the Presentation Views group on the View tab. The viewing choices include:

- **Normal view.** This is the default view and displays two panes: The slide pane and the slide thumbnails pane. Enter text in a slide in the slide pane and manage slides in the slide thumbnails pane.
- **Outline view.** In Outline view, the slide thumbnails pane changes to an outline pane where text is typed for slides.
- **Slide Sorter view.** Choosing Slide Sorter view displays all slides in the presentation as thumbnails. In this view, add, move, rearrange, and delete slides.
- **Notes Page view.** Changing to Notes Page view displays an individual slide on a page with any added notes displayed below the slide.
- **Reading view.** Use Reading view to deliver a presentation to people viewing the presentation on their own computers. In this view, a slide show can be played in the PowerPoint window without switching to a full-screen slide show.
- **Slide Show view.** Use Slide Show view to run a slide show. Choose this view and each slide fills the entire screen.

The view area on the Status bar contains four buttons for changing the view: Normal, Slide Sorter, Reading View, and Slide Show. The active button displays with a darker gray background. The Status bar also contains a Notes button and Comments button. Click the Notes button and a notes pane displays at the bottom of the slide in the slide pane. Click the Comments button to display the Comments task pane, in which a comment can be typed.

Tutorial

Navigating to Slides

Previous Slide

Next Slide

Navigating in a Presentation

In Normal view, change slides by clicking the Previous Slide or Next Slide buttons at the bottom of the vertical scroll bar. Or, change to a different slide using the mouse pointer on the vertical scroll bar. To do this, position the mouse pointer on the scroll box on the vertical scroll bar, hold down the left mouse button, drag up or down until a box displays with the desired slide number, and then release the button.

Keyboard keys can also be used to display slides in a presentation. In Normal view, press the Down Arrow or Page Down key to display the next slide or press the Up Arrow or Page Up key to display the previous slide in the presentation. Press the Home key to display the first slide in the presentation and press the End key to display the last slide in the presentation. Navigate in the slide thumbnails pane by clicking the slide thumbnail. Navigate in Slide Sorter view by clicking the slide or using the arrow keys on the keyboard.

Project 2b Navigating and Editing Slides in a Presentation — Part 2 of 3

1. With **1-Resumes.pptx** open, navigate within the presentation by completing the following steps:
   a. Make sure no placeholders are selected.
   b. Press the Home key to display Slide 1 in the slide pane.
   c. Click the Next Slide button at the bottom of the vertical scroll bar.
   d. Press the End key to display the last slide in the slide pane.
   e. Click the Slide Sorter button in the view area on the Status bar.

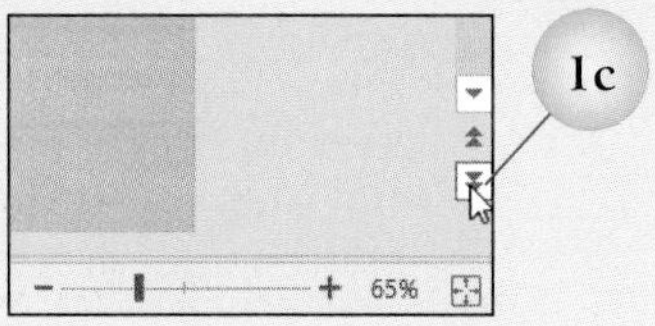

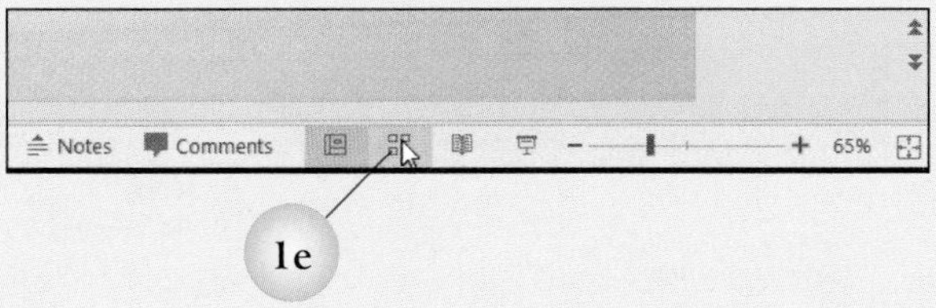

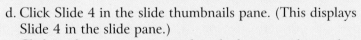

   f. Click Slide 1. (Notice that the active slide displays with an orange border.)
   g. Double-click Slide 3. (This closes Slide Sorter view and displays the presentation in Normal view with Slide 3 active.)
2. Insert text in slides by completing the following steps:
   a. Click in the bulleted text. (This positions the insertion point inside the placeholder.)
   b. Move the insertion point so it is positioned immediately right of *Education details*.
   c. Press the Enter key and then type Professional affiliations.

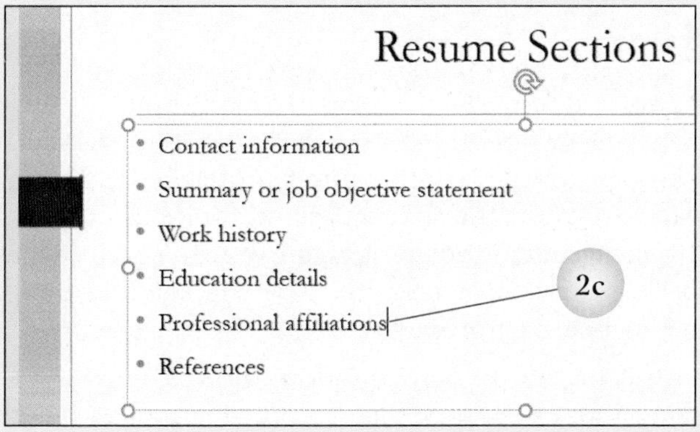

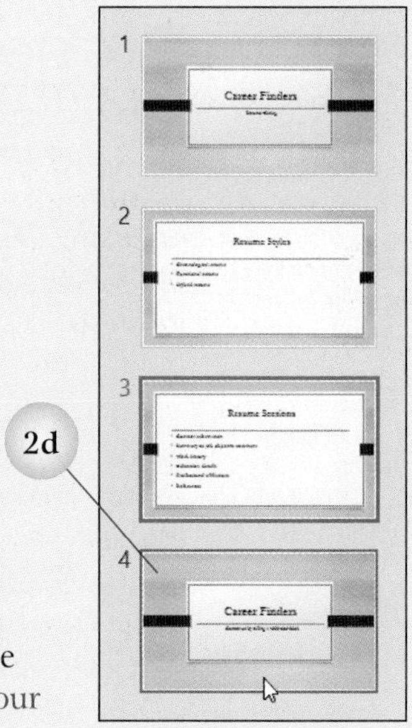

   d. Click Slide 4 in the slide thumbnails pane. (This displays Slide 4 in the slide pane.)
   e. Click in the text containing the telephone number and move the insertion point so it is positioned immediately right of the telephone number. Press the spacebar and then type or visit our website at emcp.net/careerfinders.
3. Type a note in the notes pane by completing the following steps:
   a. Click Slide 2 in the slide thumbnails pane.
   b. Click the Notes button on the Status bar.
   c. Click in the *Click to add notes* placeholder in the notes pane.

d. Type Distribute resume examples to the audience.

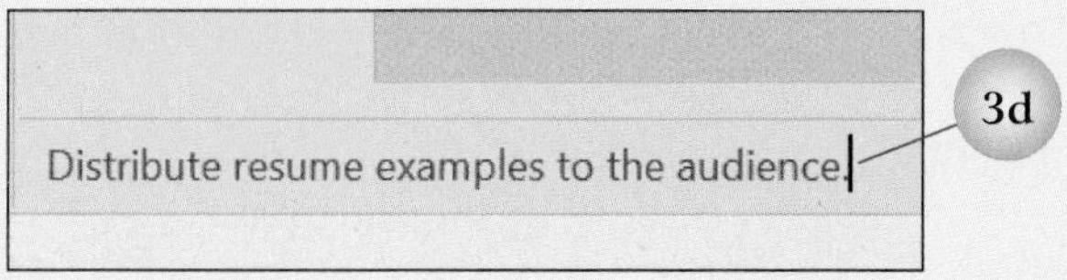

e. Display the slide in Notes Page view by clicking the View tab and then clicking the Notes Page button in the Presentation Views group. (Notice the note you typed displays below the slide in this view.)

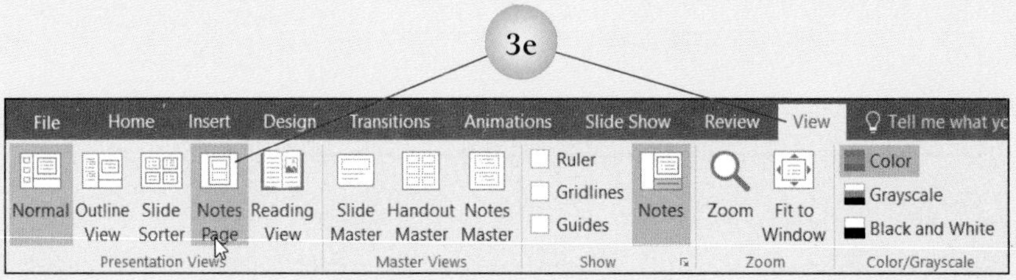

f. Return to Normal view by clicking the Normal button in the view area on the Status bar.
g. Click the Notes button on the Status bar to close the notes pane.
h. Press the Home key to make Slide 1 the active slide.

4. Save the presentation by clicking the Save button on the Quick Access Toolbar.

Check Your Work

Tutorial

Previewing Slides and Printing

Quick Steps

Print a Presentation

1. Click File tab.
2. Click *Print* option.
3. Click Print button.

Hint Printing a hard copy of your presentation and distributing it to your audience helps reinforce your message.

Printing and Previewing a Presentation

A PowerPoint presentation can be printed in a variety of formats. Print each slide on a separate piece of paper; print each slide at the top of the page, leaving the bottom of the page for notes; print a specific number of slides (up to nine slides) on a single piece of paper; or print the slide titles and topics in outline form. Use options in the Print backstage area, shown in Figure 1.5, to specify what is to be printed. To display the Print backstage area, click the File tab and then click the *Print* option or use the keyboard shortcut Ctrl + P.

Click the Print button to send the presentation to the printer and specify the number of copies to be printed with the *Copies* measurement box. Below the Print button are two categories: *Printer* and *Settings*. Use the gallery in the *Printer* category to specify the printer. Click the first gallery in the *Settings* category and options display for specifying what is to be printed, such as all of the presentation or specific slides in the presentation. The *Settings* category also contains a number of galleries that describe how the slides will print.

In the *Settings* category, print a range of slides using the hyphen and print specific slides using a comma. For example, to print Slides 2 through 6, type *2-6* in the *Slides* text box. To print Slides 1, 3, and 7, type *1,3,7*. A hyphen and comma can be combined. For example, to print Slides 1 through 5 and Slide 8, type *1-5,8* in the *Slides* text box.

Figure 1.5 Print Backstage Area

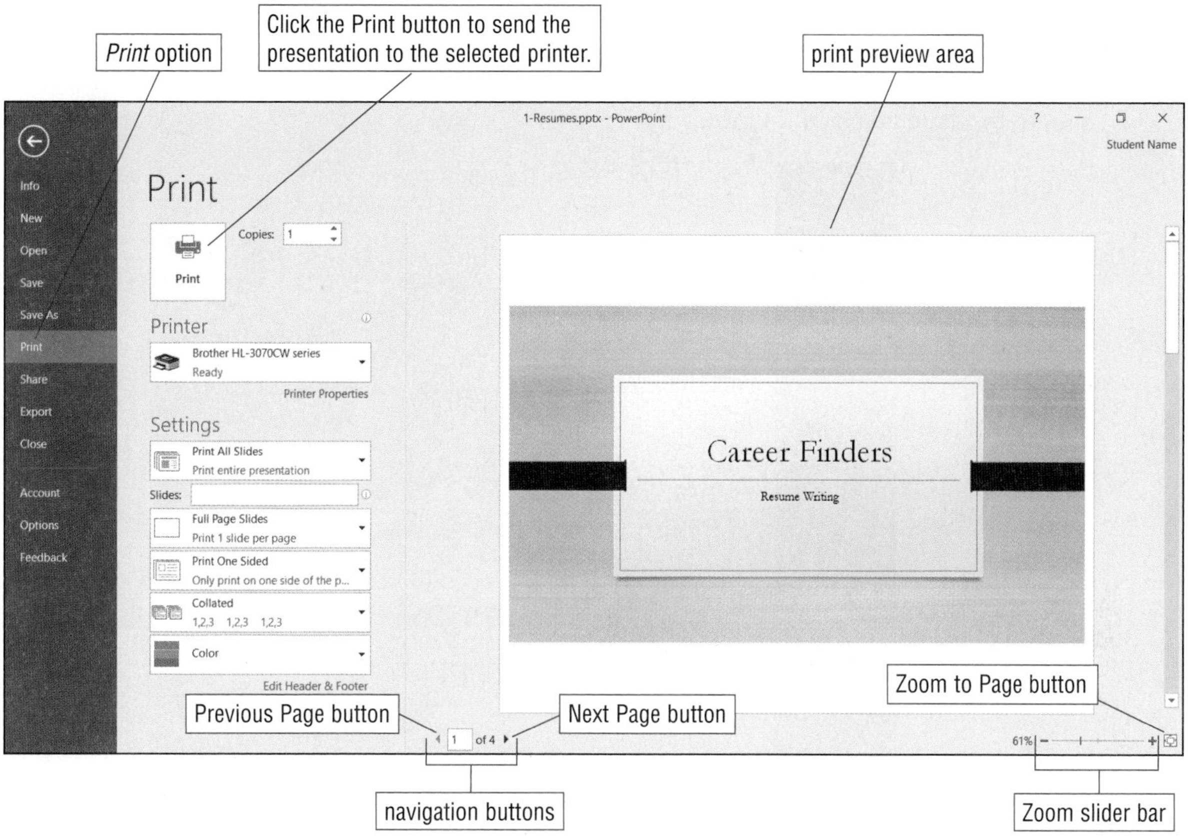

A preview of how a slide or slides will print displays at the right side of the Print backstage area. If a color printer is selected, the slide or slides at the right side of the Print backstage area display in color, and if a black-and-white printer is selected, the slide or slides will display in grayscale. Use the Next Page button (right-pointing arrow) below and to the left of the page to view the next slide in the presentation; click the Previous Page button (left-pointing arrow) to display the previous slide in the presentation; use the Zoom slider bar to increase or decrease the size of the slide; and click the Zoom to Page button to fit the slide in the viewing area in the Print backstage area.

A presentation can be printed as individual slides, handouts, notes pages, or an outline. If a presentation is printed as handouts or an outline, PowerPoint will automatically print the current date in the upper right corner of the page and the page number in the lower right corner. If the presentation is printed as notes pages, PowerPoint will automatically print the page number in the lower right corner. PowerPoint does not insert the date or page number when individual slides are printed.

Project 2c Printing a Presentation

Part 3 of 3

1. With **1-Resumes.pptx** open, click the File tab and then click the *Print* option.
2. Click the Next Page button (below and to the left of the slide in the viewing area) two times to display Slide 3 in the print preview area.

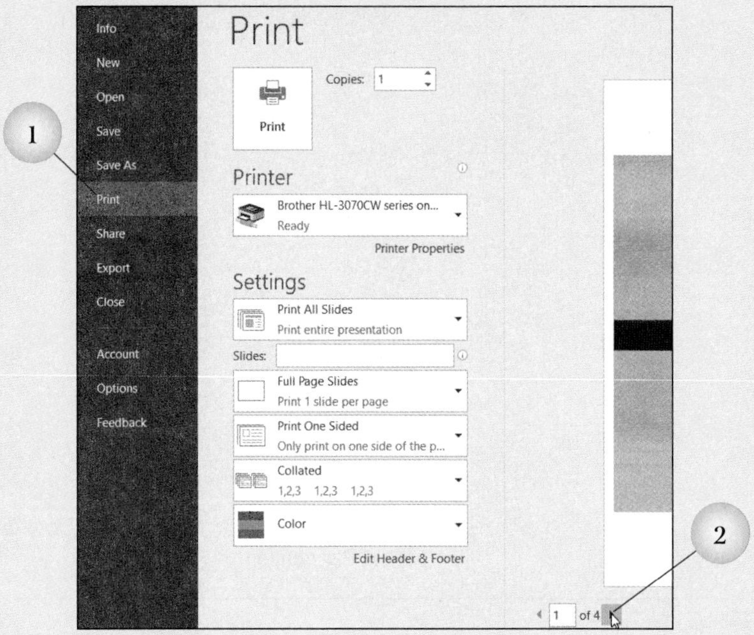

3. Click the Previous Page button two times to display Slide 1.
4. Change the zoom by completing the following steps:
   a. Position the mouse pointer on the Zoom slider bar button (at the bottom right of the Print backstage area), drag the button to the right to increase the size of the slide in the print preview area of the Print backstage area, and then to the left to decrease the size of the slide.
   b. Click the percentage at the left side of the Zoom slider bar. (This displays the Zoom dialog box.)
   c. Click the *50%* option in the Zoom dialog box and then click OK.
   d. Click the Zoom to Page button to the right of the Zoom slider bar. (This changes the size of the slide to fill the print preview area.)

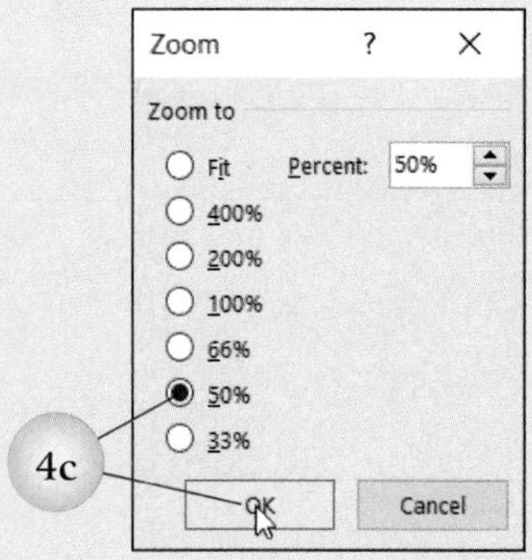

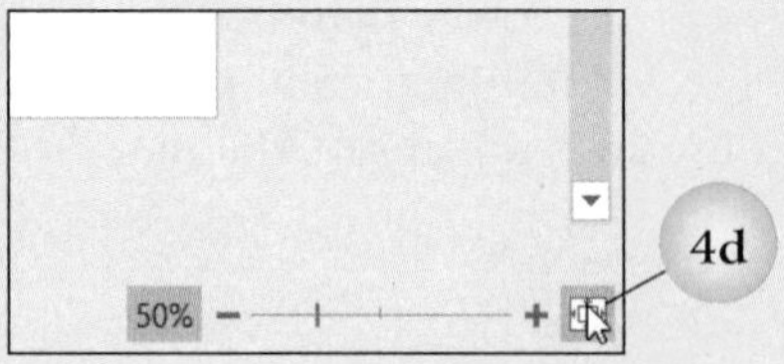

5. Print the presentation as a handout with four slides displayed horizontally on the page by completing the following steps:
   a. At the Print backstage area, click the second gallery (displays with *Full Page Slides*) in the *Settings* category and then click *4 Slides Horizontal* in the *Handouts* section.

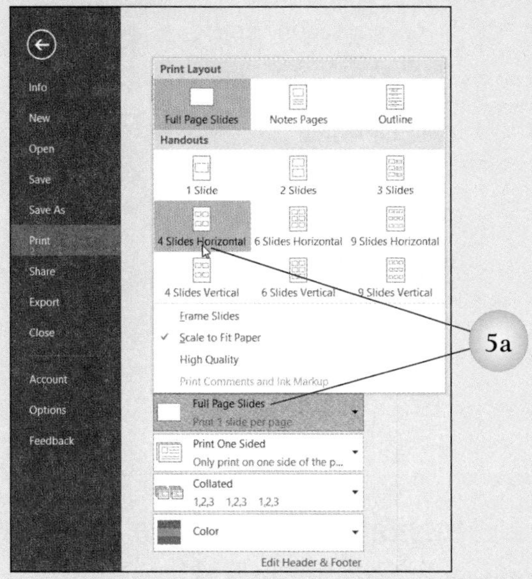

   b. Click the Print button.
6. Print Slide 2 as a notes page by completing the following steps:
   a. Click the File tab and then click the *Print* option.
   b. At the Print backstage area, click in the *Slides* text box in the *Settings* category, and then type 2.
   c. Click the second gallery (displays with *4 Slides Horizontal*) in the *Settings* category and then click *Notes Pages* in the *Print Layout* section.
   d. Click the Print button.

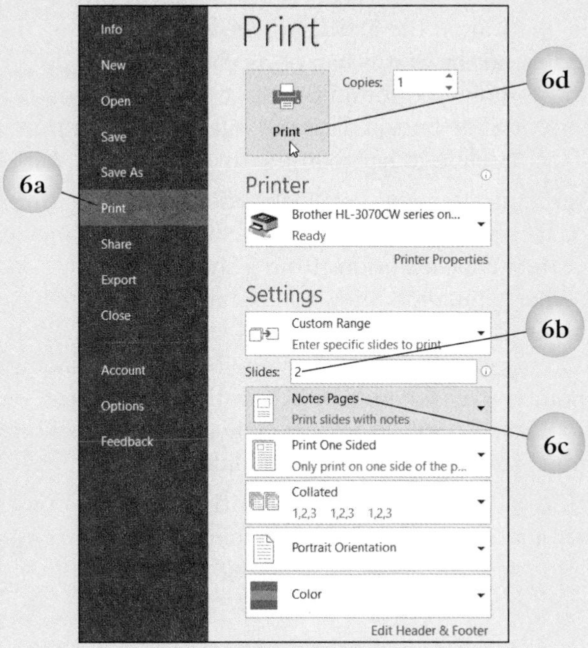

7. Print Slides 1, 2, and 4 by completing the following steps:
   a. Click the File tab and then click the *Print* option.
   b. At the Print backstage area, click in the *Slides* text box in the *Settings* category and then type 1-2,4.
   c. Click the second gallery (displays with *Notes Pages*) in the *Settings* category and then click *4 Slides Horizontal* in the *Handouts* section.
   d. Click the Print button.
8. Close the presentation by clicking the File tab and then clicking the *Close* option.

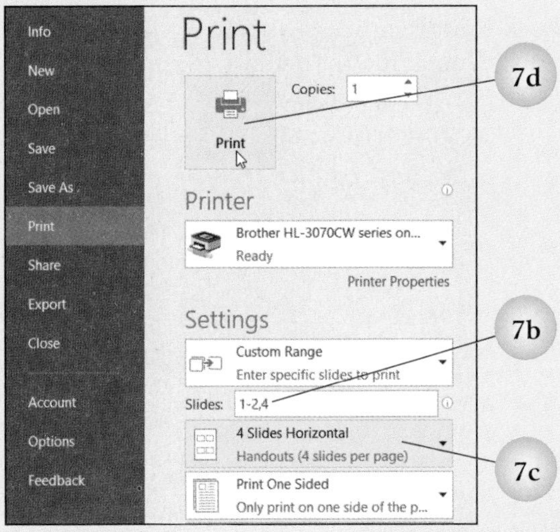

Check Your Work

Project 3 Open a Presentation, Run a Slide Show, and Change the Presentation Design Theme — 3 Parts

You will open a presentation, run the slide show using buttons on the Slide Show toolbar, apply a different design theme and color variant to the presentation, and then delete the presentation.

Preview Finished Project

Tutorial

Running a Slide Show

Tutorial

Changing the Display when Running a Slide Show

Tutorial

Displaying Slide Show Help and Hiding Slides during a Slide Show

Tutorial

Using the Pen Tool during a Slide Show

From Beginning

From Current Slide

Using the Slide Show Toolbar

As discussed earlier in this chapter, run a slide show by clicking the Start From Beginning button on the Quick Access Toolbar, clicking the Slide Show button in the view area on the Status bar, or by clicking the Slide Show tab and then clicking the From Beginning button in the Start Slide Show group. This group also contains a From Current Slide button. Use this button to begin running the slide show with the currently active slide rather than the first slide in the presentation.

PowerPoint offers a number of options for navigating through slides in a slide show. Click the left mouse button to advance slides in a slide show, right-click in a slide and then choose options from a shortcut menu, or use buttons on the Slide Show toolbar. The Slide Show toolbar displays in the lower left corner of a slide when running the slide show. Figure 1.6 identifies the buttons on the Slide Show toolbar. To display the Slide Show toolbar, run the slide show and then hover the mouse pointer over the buttons. Click the Next button (displays with a right arrow) on the toolbar to display the next slide and click the Previous button (displays with a left arrow) to display the previous slide.

Click the Pen button (displays with a pen icon) on the Slide Show toolbar and a pop-up list displays with the following options: *Laser Pointer*, *Pen*, *Highlighter*, *Eraser*, and *Erase All Ink on Slide*, along with a row of color options. Click the *Laser Pointer* option and the pointer displays as a red, glowing circle, which can be used

Quick Steps

Run a Slide Show

1. Click Start From Beginning button on Quick Access Toolbar.
2. Click left mouse button to advance slides.

OR

1. Click Slide Show button on Status bar.
2. Click left mouse button to advance slides.

OR

1. Click Slide Show tab.
2. Click From Beginning button.
3. Click left mouse button to advance slides.

Figure 1.6 Slide Show Toolbar

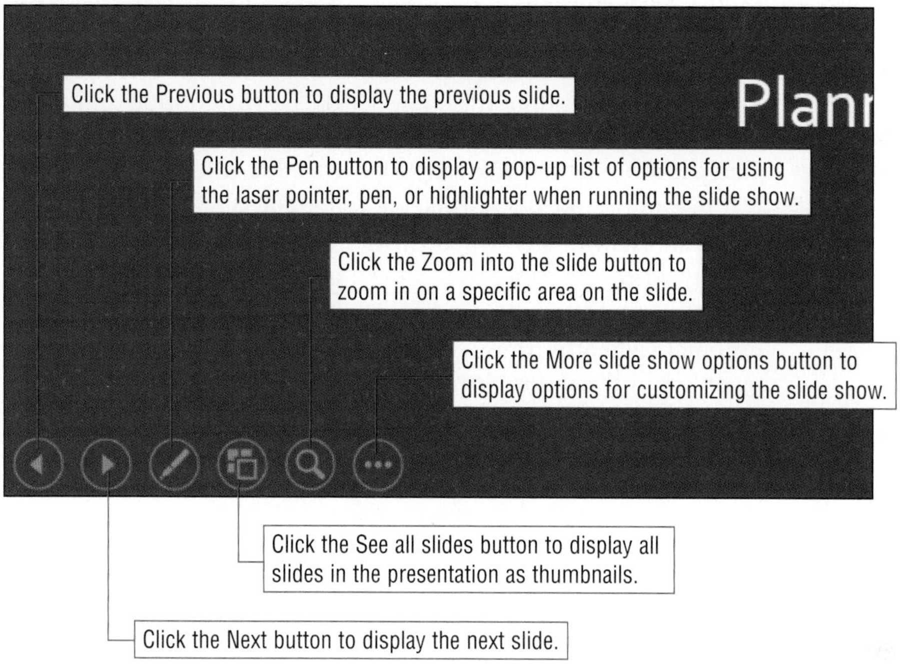

Plan
Click the Previous button to display the previous slide.
Click the Pen button to display a pop-up list of options for using the laser pointer, pen, or highlighter when running the slide show.
Click the Zoom into the slide button to zoom in on a specific area on the slide.
Click the More slide show options button to display options for customizing the slide show.
Click the See all slides button to display all slides in the presentation as thumbnails.
Click the Next button to display the next slide.

to point to specific locations on the slide. Use the *Pen* option to draw in the slide, and use the *Highlighter* option to highlight specific items in the slide. Select the *Pen* or *Highlighter* option and then drag the mouse in the slide to draw or highlight items. Erase the drawing or highlighting in a slide by clicking the Pen button on the Slide Show toolbar, clicking the *Eraser* option, and then dragging the mouse to erase the drawing or highlighting. To erase all drawing or highlighting on the slide, click the Pen button and then click the *Erase All Ink on Slide* option.

Quick Steps

Use the Pen or Highlighter During a Slide Show

1. Run slide show.
2. Display slide.
3. Click Pen button on Slide Show toolbar.
4. Click *Pen* or *Highlighter* option.
5. Drag to draw line or highlight text.

Hint If you use the pen or highlighter on a slide when running a slide show, choose an ink color that the audience can see easily.

Change the pen or highlighter color by clicking the Pen button and then clicking a color option in the color row. Draw in a slide with the pen or highlighter and PowerPoint will ask if the ink annotations are to be kept or discarded. Reply to this message, and return the laser pointer, pen, or highlighter option back to the mouse pointer by pressing the Esc key on the keyboard.

Click the See all slides button on the Slide Show toolbar and all slides in the slide show display on the screen. Use this feature to display all of the slides in the slide show and/or move to a different slide by clicking the slide.

Zoom in on a portion of a slide by clicking the Zoom into the slide button (contains an image of a magnifying glass) on the Slide Show toolbar. Clicking this button creates a magnification area and dims the remainder of the slide. Drag the magnification area with the mouse to specify what is to be magnified and then click the left mouse button. Return to the normal zoom by pressing the Esc key or right-clicking the slide.

Click the More slide show options button (the last button on the Slide Show toolbar; depicting three dots) and a pop-up list displays with a variety of options. The pop-up list contains options for displaying a custom show or switching to Presenter view; changing the screen display, display settings, and arrow options; and pausing or ending the show. Click the *Help* option and the Slide Show Help dialog box displays, as shown in Figure 1.7. This dialog box contains various tabs that describe the keyboard options available when running a slide show.

In addition to the options on the Slide Show toolbar, right-click in a slide and a shortcut menu displays with many of the same options as the options that display when the More slide show options button is clicked.

When running a slide show, the mouse pointer is set, by default, to be hidden automatically after three seconds of inactivity. The mouse pointer will appear again when the mouse is moved. Change this default setting by clicking the More slide show options button on the Slide Show toolbar, clicking *Arrow Options*, and then clicking *Visible* to make the mouse pointer always visible or *Hidden* if the mouse pointer should not display at all when running the slide show. The *Automatic* option is the default setting.

If the mouse pointer displays as the pen or highlighter, return to the regular pointer by pressing the Esc key or clicking the More slide show options button on the Slide Show toolbar, clicking *Arrow Options* at the pop-up list, and then clicking *Visible*.

Figure 1.7 Slide Show Help Dialog Box

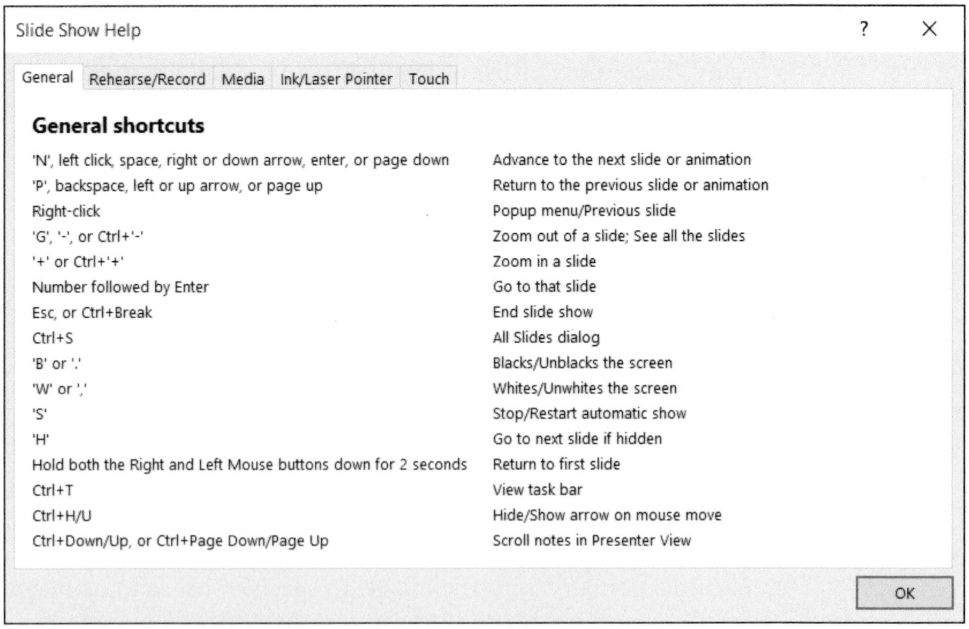

Slide Show Help
?
X
General
Rehearse/Record
Media
Ink/Laser Pointer
Touch
General shortcuts
'N', left click, space, right or down arrow, enter, or page down
Advance to the next slide or animation
'P', backspace, left or up arrow, or page up
Return to the previous slide or animation
Right-click
Popup menu/Previous slide
'G', '-', or Ctrl+'-'
Zoom out of a slide; See all the slides
'+' or Ctrl+'+'
Zoom in a slide
Number followed by Enter
Go to that slide
Esc, or Ctrl+Break
End slide show
Ctrl+S
All Slides dialog
'B' or '.'
Blacks/Unblacks the screen
'W' or ','
Whites/Unwhites the screen
'S'
Stop/Restart automatic show
'H'
Go to next slide if hidden
Hold both the Right and Left Mouse buttons down for 2 seconds
Return to first slide
Ctrl+T
View task bar
Ctrl+H/U
Hide/Show arrow on mouse move
Ctrl+Down/Up, or Ctrl+Page Down/Page Up
Scroll notes in Presenter View
OK

Project 3a Opening a Presentation and Running a Slide Show

1. Click the File tab and then click the *Open* option.
2. At the Open backstage area, click the *Browse* option.
3. At the Open dialog box, navigate to the PC1 folder on your storage medium and then double-click ***PlanningPres.pptx***.
4. Save the presentation by completing the following steps:
   a. Click the File tab and then click the *Save As* option.
   b. At the Save As backstage area, click the *Browse* option.
   c. At the Save As dialog box, make sure the PC1 folder on your storage medium is active and then type 1-PlanningPres in the *File name* text box.
   d. Press the Enter key or click the Save button.
5. Run the slide show by completing the following steps:
   a. Click the Slide Show button in the view area on the Status bar.
   b. When Slide 1 fills the screen, move the mouse to display the Slide Show toolbar. (This toolbar displays in a dimmed manner in the lower left corner of the slide.)
   c. Click the Next button (contains a right arrow) to display the next slide.
   d. Continue clicking the Next button until a black screen displays.
   e. Click the left mouse button. (This displays the presentation in Normal view.)

6. Run the slide show from the current slide by completing the following steps:
   a. Click Slide 4 in the slide thumbnails pane. (This makes Slide 4 active.)
   b. Click the Slide Show tab.
   c. Click the From Current Slide button in the Start Slide Show group.

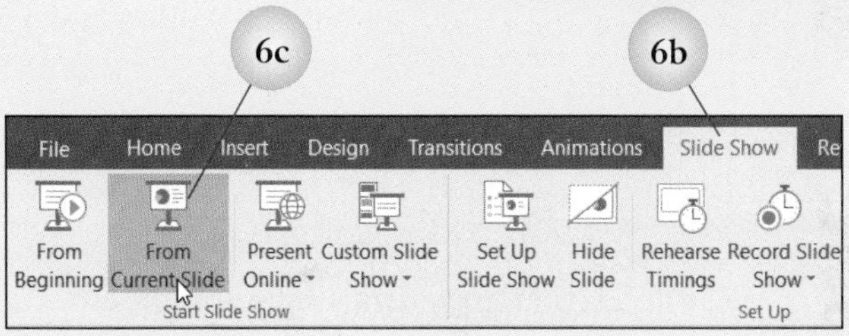

7. With Slide 4 active, zoom in on the step text by completing these steps:
   a. Move the mouse to display the Slide Show toolbar.
   b. Click the Zoom into the slide button on the Slide Show toolbar.
   c. Using the mouse, drag the magnification area so it displays the step text and then click the left mouse button.
   d. Press the Esc key to return to the normal zoom.
8. Click the See all slides button on the Slide Show toolbar and then click the Slide 2 thumbnail.
9. With Slide 2 active, use the pen to draw in the slide by completing the following steps:
   a. Move the mouse to display the Slide Show toolbar.
   b. Click the Pen button on the Slide Show toolbar and then click *Pen* at the pop-up list. (This changes the mouse pointer to a small circle.)

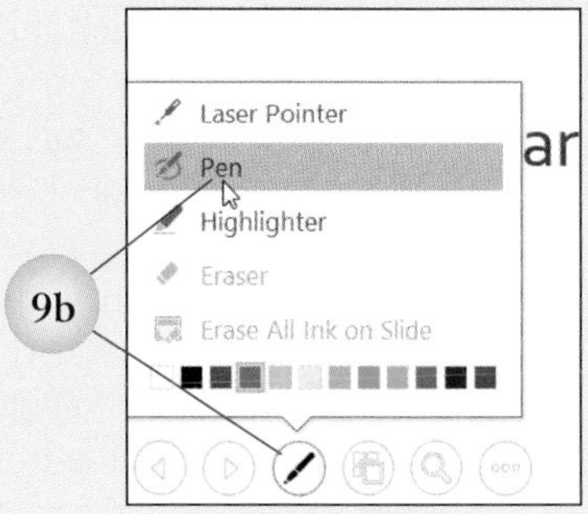

c. Using the mouse, draw a circle around the text *Step 1*.
d. Draw a line below the word *identify*.

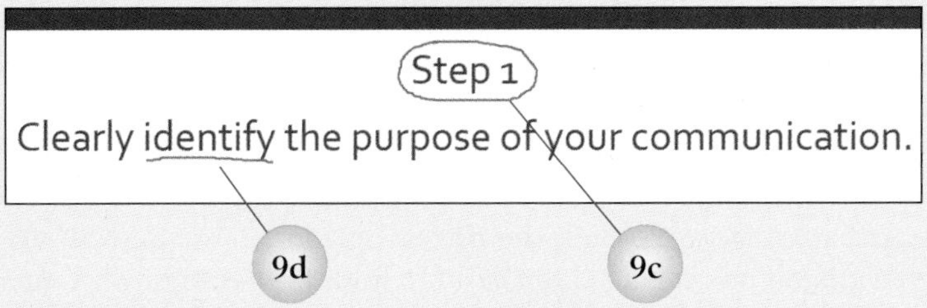

e. Press the Esc key to return the mouse pointer to an arrow.

10. Erase the pen markings by clicking the Pen button on the Slide Show toolbar and then clicking *Erase All Ink on Slide* at the pop-up list.
11. Click the Next button to display Slide 3.
12. Click the Pen button and then click *Highlighter*.
13. Click the Pen button and then click the *Light Green* color (seventh option).
14. Drag through the text *Assess your target audience.*

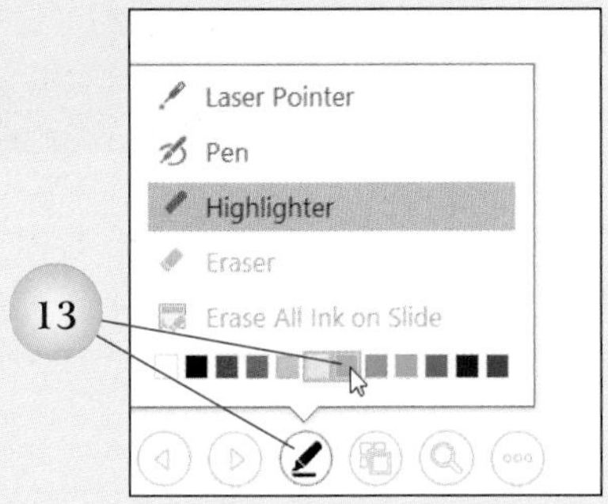

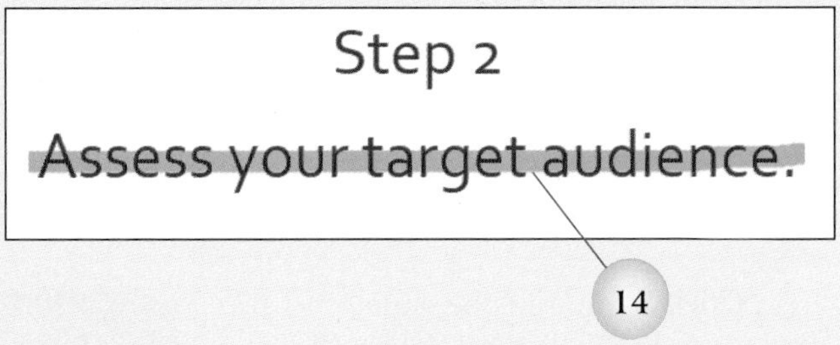

15. Press the Esc key to return the mouse pointer to an arrow.
16. Press the Esc key to end the slide show. Click the Discard button at the message asking if you want to keep or discard the ink annotations.
17. With Slide 3 active, click the Slide Show button on the Status bar to start the slide show.
18. Click the Pen button on the Slide Show toolbar and then click *Laser Pointer* at the pop-up list.
19. Use the laser pointer to point to various locations on the slide.
20. Press the Esc key to return to the mouse pointer to an arrow.
21. Click the Next button on the Slide Show toolbar. (This displays Slide 4.)
22. Turn on the highlighter and then drag through the words *best format* to highlight them.
23. Press the Esc key to return the mouse pointer to an arrow.
24. Continue clicking the left mouse button to move through the presentation.
25. At the black screen, click the left mouse button.
26. At the message asking if you want to keep your ink annotations, click the Keep button.
27. Save the presentation with a new name by completing the following steps:
    a. Click the File tab and then click the *Save As* option.
    b. At the Save As backstage area, click the *Browse* option.
    c. At the Save As dialog box, make sure the PC1 folder on your storage medium is the active folder, type 1-PlanningPres-Ink in the *File name* text box, and then press the Enter key.
28. Print Slide 4 as a handout.
29. Close **1-PlanningPres-Ink.pptx**.

Check Your Work

Tutorial

Applying a Design Theme

More Themes

Quick Steps

Apply a Design Theme

1. Click Design tab.
2. Click theme in themes gallery.

Hint Design themes were designed by professional graphic artists who understand the use of color, space, and design.

Applying a Design Theme and Color Variant

PowerPoint provides a variety of built-in design theme templates that can be used when creating slides for a presentation. Choose a design theme template at the New backstage area or with options in the Themes group on the Design tab. Click the Design tab and themes display in the themes gallery in the Themes group. Click one of these themes to apply it to the current presentation. Click the More Themes button at the right side of the themes gallery to display any additional themes. Click the up arrow or down arrow at the right side of the themes gallery to scroll through the list. Hover the mouse pointer over a theme and the active slide in the presentation displays with the theme formatting applied. This is an example of the live preview feature, which displays how theme formatting will affect the presentation.

Each design theme contains color variations that display in the Variants group on the Design tab. These are the same theme color variants that display when applying a theme template at the New backstage area. Click a color variant in the Variants group to apply the colors to the slides in the presentation.

Hover the mouse pointer over a theme in the theme gallery and a ScreenTip displays (after approximately a second) containing the theme name. Theme names in PowerPoint are similar to those in Word, Excel, Access, and Outlook and apply similar formatting. With the availability of the themes across these applications, business files such as documents, workbooks, and presentations can be "branded" with a consistent and uniform appearance.

Project 3b Applying a Design Theme and Color Variant

Part 2 of 3

1. Open **1-PlanningPres.pptx**.
2. Make sure Slide 1 is active and that the presentation displays in Normal view.
3. Apply a different design theme to the presentation by completing the following steps:
   a. Click the Design tab.
   b. Hover the mouse pointer over the *Ion* theme in the themes gallery in the Themes group and notice the theme formatting applied to the slide in the slide pane.
   c. Click the *Ion* theme.

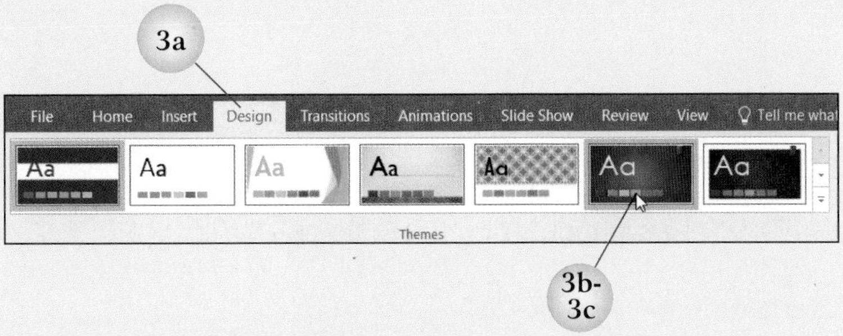

4. Run the slide show and notice the formatting applied by the theme.
5. With the presentation displayed in Normal view, apply a different design theme by clicking the *Facet* theme in the themes gallery in the Themes group on the Design tab.

6. Apply a color variant by clicking the fourth option in the Variants group.
7. Run the slide show.
8. Print the presentation as a handout by completing the following steps:
   a. Click the File tab and then click the *Print* option.
   b. At the Print backstage area, click the second gallery (displays with *Full Page Slides*) in the *Settings* category and then click *6 Slides Horizontal* in the *Handouts* section.
   c. Click the Print button.
9. Save and then close **1-PlanningPres.pptx**.

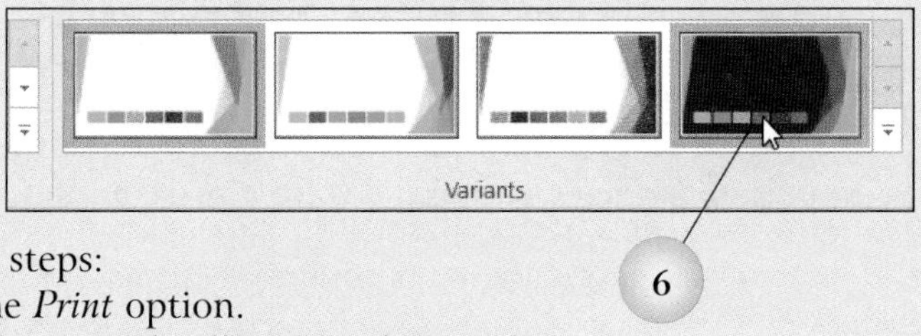

Check Your Work

Deleting a Presentation

Quick Steps

Delete a Presentation
1. Display Open dialog box.
2. Navigate to folder or drive.
3. Click presentation.
4. Click Organize button.
5. Click *Delete*.
6. Click Yes.

File management tasks in PowerPoint can be performed at the Open dialog box or Save As dialog box. To delete a PowerPoint presentation, display the Open dialog box, click the presentation to be deleted, click the Organize button on the toolbar, and then click *Delete* at the drop-down list. At the message asking to confirm the deletion, click the Yes button. The presentation file must be closed to be deleted.

If a presentation is deleted from a folder on the computer's hard drive, the confirmation message does not display. This is because the deleted presentation is sent to the Recycle Bin where it can be restored, if needed.

Project 3c Deleting a PowerPoint Presentation

Part 3 of 3

1. Click the File tab and then, if necessary, click the *Open* option.
2. At the Open backstage area, click the *Browse* option.
3. At the Open dialog box, make sure the PC1 folder on your storage medium is the active folder and then click ***PlanningPres.pptx*** in the Content pane.
4. Click the Organize button on the toolbar and then click *Delete* at the drop-down list.
5. At the message asking if you are sure you want to delete the presentation, click Yes. (If you are deleting the presentation from a folder on your computer's hard drive, the confirmation message will not display because the presentation is sent automatically to the Recycle Bin.)
6. Click the Cancel button to close the Open dialog box.

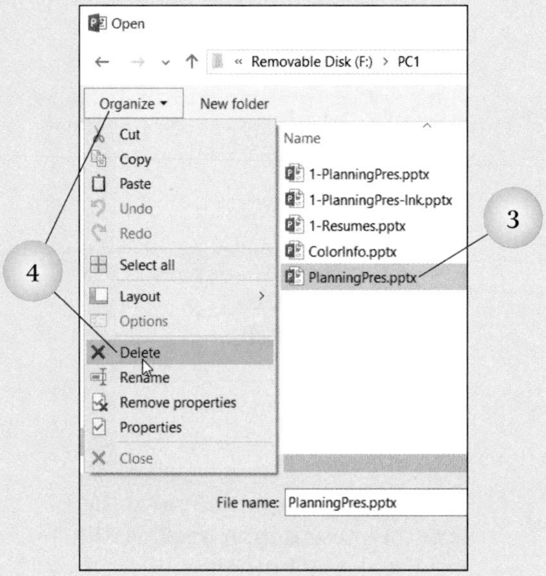

Project 4 Create a Technology Presentation in the Outline Pane — 3 Parts

You will create a computer technology presentation in the outline pane, add and remove transitions and sounds to the presentation, and set up the presentation to advance slides automatically after a specified amount of time.

Tutorial

Opening a Blank Presentation

Preparing a Presentation from a Blank Presentation

To create a presentation without a design theme applied, open a blank presentation. Open a blank presentation at the PowerPoint opening screen or at the New backstage area by clicking the *Blank Presentation* template. Another method for opening a blank presentation is to use the keyboard shortcut Ctrl + N.

Tutorial

Entering Text in the Outline Pane

Quick Steps

Prepare a Presentation from a Blank Presentation

1. Click File tab.
2. Click *New* option.
3. Click *Blank Presentation.*

OR

Press Ctrl + N.

Preparing a Presentation in Outline View

Text can be inserted in a slide by typing the text in the outline pane. Display this pane by clicking the View tab and then clicking the Outline View button in the Presentation Views group. The outline pane replaces the slide thumbnails pane at the left side of the screen. A slide number displays in the pane followed by a small slide icon. When typing text in the outline pane, press the Tab key to move the insertion point to the next tab. This moves the insertion point and also changes the formatting. The formatting will vary depending on the theme applied. Press Shift + Tab to move the insertion point to the previous tab. Moving the insertion point back to the left margin will create a new slide.

Project 4a Preparing a Presentation in Outline View — Part 1 of 3

1. At a blank screen, click the File tab and then click the *New* option.
2. At the New backstage area, click the *Blank Presentation* template.
3. At the blank presentation, click the View tab and then click the Outline View button in the Presentation Views group.

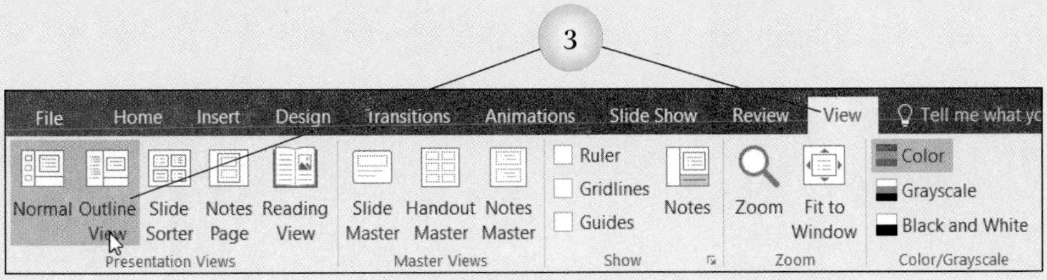

4. Click in the outline pane immediately right of the slide icon.
5. Type the first slide title shown in Figure 1.8 (*Computer Technology*) and then press the Enter key. (The text you type displays immediately right of the small orange slide icon in the outline pane.)
6. Type the second slide title shown in Figure 1.8 (*The Motherboard*) and then press the Enter key.
7. Press the Tab key, type the text after the first bullet in Figure 1.8 (*Buses*), and then press the Enter key.
8. Continue typing the text as it displays in Figure 1.8. Press the Tab key to move the insertion point to the next tab or press Shift + Tab to move the insertion point back to a previous tab.

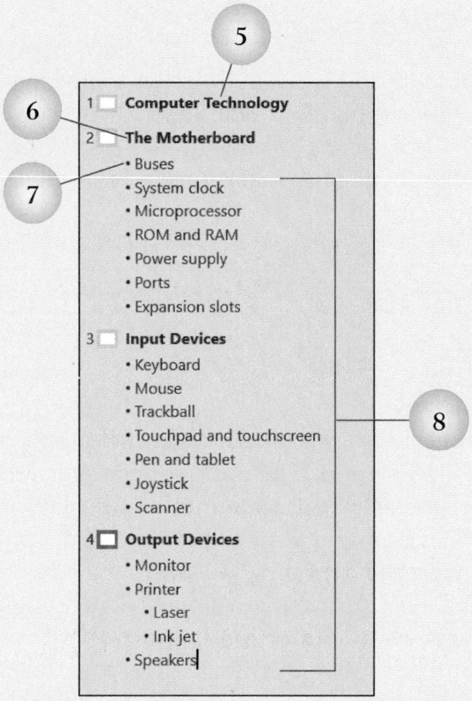

9. After typing all of the information as shown in Figure 1.8, click the Normal button in the Presentation Views group on the View tab.
10. Click the Notes button on the Status bar to close the notes pane.
11. Click Slide 1 in the slide thumbnails pane. (This displays Slide 1 in the slide pane.)
12. Apply a design theme by completing the following steps:
    a. Click the Design tab.
    b. Click the *Ion* theme in the themes gallery in the Themes group.
    c. Click the fourth option in the Variants group (the orange color variant).
13. Save the presentation and name it **1-Computers**.
14. Run the slide show.

Check Your Work

Figure 1.8 Project 4a

1 Computer Technology
2 The Motherboard
- Buses
- System clock
- Microprocessor
- ROM and RAM
- Power supply
- Ports
- Expansion slots

3 Input Devices
- Keyboard
- Mouse
- Trackball
- Touchpad and touchscreen
- Pen and tablet
- Joystick
- Scanner

4 Output Devices
- Monitor
- Printer
  - Laser
  - Ink jet
- Speakers

Adding Transitions and Transition Sounds

Interesting transitions and transition sounds can be applied to a presentation. A transition is how one slide is removed from the screen during a slide show and the next slide is displayed. Transitions such as cut, fade, push, wipe, split, reveal, and random bars can be applied to a presentation. To add transitions and transition sounds, open a presentation, and then click the Transitions tab. This displays transition buttons and options, as shown in Figure 1.9.

Apply To All

Transitions and transition sounds apply by default to the active slide. To apply transitions and transition sounds to all slides in the presentation, click the Apply To All button in the Timing group. In Slide Sorter view, select all slides by pressing Ctrl + A (or by clicking the Home tab, clicking the Select button, and then clicking *Select All* at the drop-down list) and then apply the transition and/or transition sounds.

Figure 1.9 Transitions Tab

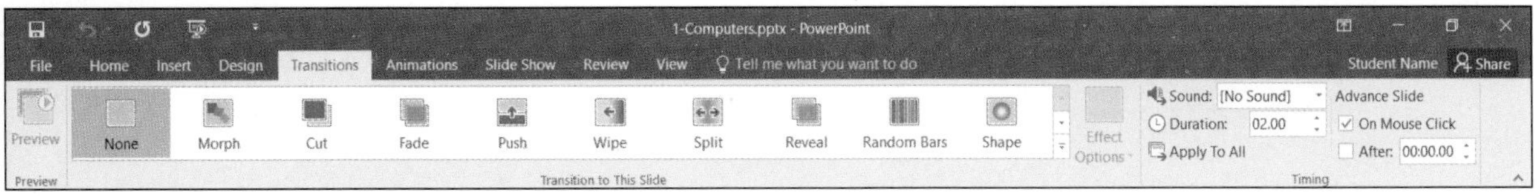

Tutorial

Adding Transitions

Quick Steps

Apply a Transition to All Slides

1. Click Transitions tab.
2. Click transition in transitions gallery in Transition to This Slide group.
3. Click Apply To All button.

Adding Transitions

To add a transition, click an option in the gallery in the Transition to This Slide group on the Transitions tab and the transition displays in the slide in the slide pane. Use the down and up arrows at the right side of the transitions gallery to display additional transitions. Click the More Transitions button at the right side of the transitions gallery and a drop-down list displays with additional options. Use the *Duration* measurement box to specify the duration of slide transitions when running the slide show. Click the *Duration* measurement box up or down arrows to change the duration time. Or, select the current time in the measurement box and then type the specific time.

Use options in the Effect Options button drop-down gallery to change transition effects. The options in the drop-down gallery vary depending on the transition applied. The Effect Options button is located in the Transition to This Slide group on the Transitions tab.

When a transition is applied to slides in a presentation, animation icons display below the slide numbers in the slide thumbnails pane and in Slide Sorter view. Click an animation icon for a particular slide and the slide will display the transition effect.

Tutorial

Adding Sound to Slide Transitions

Quick Steps

Apply Transition Sound to All Slides

1. Click Transitions tab.
2. Click *Sound* option box arrow.
3. Click sound.
4. Click Apply To All button.

Adding Sound to Slide Transitions

To add a sound effect to slide transitions in a presentation, click the *Sound* option box arrow and then click a sound at the drop-down list. Preview a transition and/or transition sound applied to a slide by clicking the Preview button at the left side of the Transitions tab.

Removing Transitions and Transition Sounds

Remove a transition from a slide by clicking the *None* option in the transitions gallery in the Transition to This Slide group. To remove transitions from all slides, click the Apply To All button in the Timing group. To remove a transition sound from a slide, click the *Sound* option box arrow and then click *[No Sound]* at the drop-down gallery. To remove sound from all slides, click the Apply To All button.

Project 4b **Adding Transitions and Transition Sounds to a Presentation** Part 2 of 3

1. With **1-Computers.pptx** open, click the Transitions tab.
2. Apply transitions and a transition sound to all slides in the presentation by completing the following steps:
   a. Click the More Transitions button at the right side of the transitions gallery in the Transition to This Slide group.

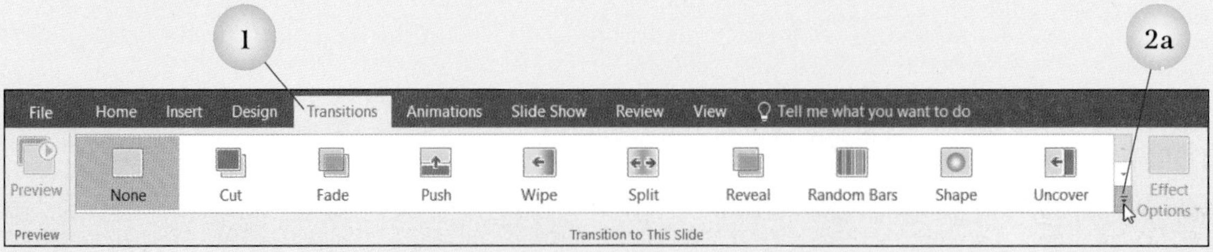

b. Click the *Fall Over* option in the *Exciting* section.

c. Click the Effect Options button in the Transition to This Slide group and then click *Right* at the drop-down list.

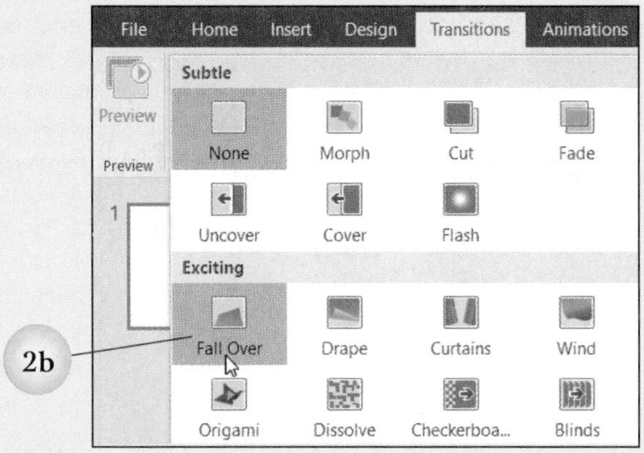

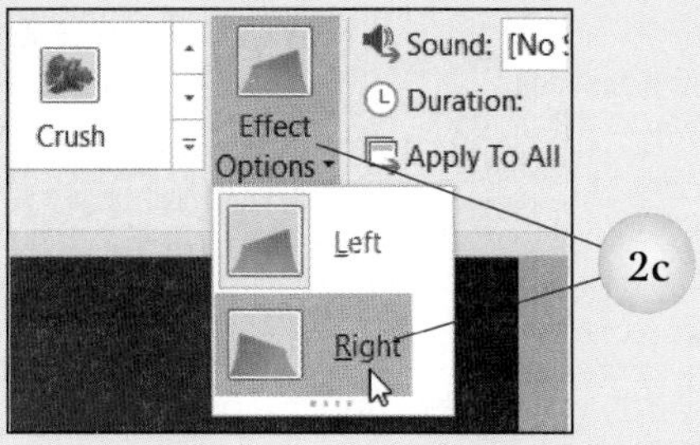

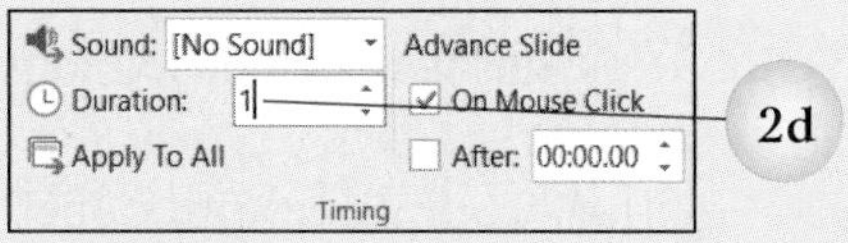

d. Click in the *Duration* measurement box in the Timing group, type 1, and then press the Enter key.

e. Click the *Sound* option box arrow in the Timing group and then click *Chime* at the drop-down list.

f. Click the Apply To All button in the Timing group.

3. Run the slide show. (Notice the transitions and transition sound as you move from slide to slide.)
4. With the presentation in Normal view and the Transitions tab active, remove the transitions and transition sound by completing the following steps:

   a. Click the More Transitions button in the Transition to This Slide group and then click the *None* option in the *Subtle* section.

   b. Click the *Sound* option box arrow and then click *[No Sound]* at the drop-down list.

   c. Click the Apply To All button.

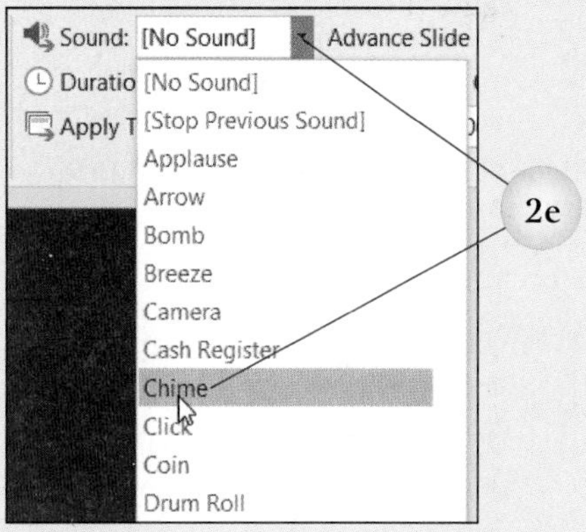

5. Apply transitions and transition sounds to specific slides by completing the following steps:

   a. Make sure the presentation displays in Normal view.

   b. Click Slide 1 in the slide thumbnails pane.

   c. Hold down the Shift key and then click Slide 2. (Slides 1 and 2 will display with orange backgrounds.)

   d. Click the More Transitions button at the right side of the transitions gallery and then click the *Ferris Wheel* option in the *Dynamic Content* section.

   e. Click the *Sound* option box arrow and then click the *Breeze* option.

   f. Click Slide 3 in the slide pane.

   g. Hold down the Shift key and then click Slide 4.

   h. Click the More Transitions button at the right side of the transitions gallery and then click the *Glitter* option in the *Exciting* section.

   i. Click the *Sound* option box arrow and then click the *Wind* option.
6. Run the slide show from the beginning.
7. Remove the transitions and transition sounds from all slides. (Refer to Step 4.)
8. Save **1-Computers.pptx**.

Tutorial

Advancing Slides Automatically

Quick Steps

Advance Slides Automatically

1. Click Transitions tab.
2. Click *After* check box.
3. Insert number of seconds in measurement box.
4. Click *On Mouse Click* check box.
5. Click Apply To All button.

Advancing Slides Automatically

Slides in a slide show can be advanced after a specific number of seconds by selecting options in the Timing group on the Transitions tab. To advance slides automatically, click the *After* check box and then insert the number of seconds in the measurement box. Or, select the current time in the measurement box and then type the time, or click the up or down arrows to increase or decrease the time. Click the *On Mouse Click* check box to remove the check mark. To apply the transition time to all slides in the presentation, click the Apply To All button. In Slide Sorter view, the transition time displays below each affected slide.

Project 4c Advancing Slides Automatically — Part 3 of 3

1. With **1-Computers.pptx** open, make sure the Transitions tab is active.
2. Click the *On Mouse Click* check box to remove the check mark.
3. Click in the *After* check box in the Timing group to insert a check mark.
4. Click the *After* measurement box up arrow until *00:04.00* displays in the box.
5. Click the Apply To All button.
6. Run the slide show from the beginning. (Each slide will advance automatically after four seconds.)
7. At the black screen, click the left mouse button.
8. Print the presentation as an outline by completing the following steps:
   a. Click the File tab and then click the *Print* option.
   b. At the Print backstage area, click the second gallery (displays with *Full Page Slides*) in the *Settings* category and then click *Outline* in the *Print Layout* section.
   c. Click the Print button.
9. Save and then close **1-Computers.pptx**.

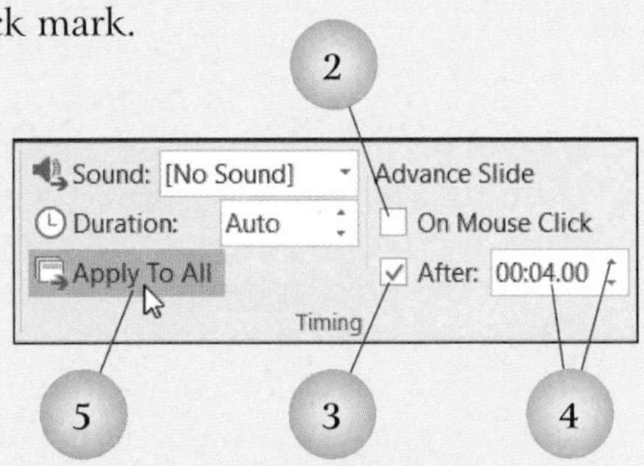

Check Your Work

Chapter Summary

- PowerPoint is a presentation graphics program used for creating slides for an on-screen presentation.
- Open a presentation at the Open dialog box. Display this dialog box by clicking the File tab and then clicking the *Open* option. At the Open backstage area, click the *Browse* option.
- A presentation can be pinned to or unpinned from the Recent list at the PowerPoint opening screen and the *Recent* option list at the Open backstage area.
- Start running a slide show by clicking the Start From Beginning button on the Quick Access Toolbar, clicking the Slide Show button in the view area on the Status bar, or by clicking the View tab and then clicking the From Beginning button.
- Close a presentation by clicking the File tab and then clicking the *Close* option or with the keyboard shortcut Ctrl + F4.
- Before creating a presentation in PowerPoint, plan the presentation by defining the purpose and determining the content and display medium.
- Built-in presentation design theme templates are available at the New backstage area. Display this backstage area by clicking the File tab and then clicking the *New* option.
- To insert text in a slide, click in a placeholder and then type the text.
- Insert a new slide in a presentation with the Title and Content layout by clicking the New Slide button in the Slides group on the Home tab. Insert a new slide with a specific layout by clicking the New Slide button arrow and then clicking the layout at the drop-down list.
- A slide layout provides placeholders for specific data in a slide. Choose a slide layout by clicking the Layout button in the Slides group on the Home tab and then clicking a layout at the drop-down list.
- Save a presentation by clicking the Save button on the Quick Access Toolbar or clicking the File tab and then clicking the *Save As* option. At the Save As backstage area, click the *Browse* option. At the Save As dialog box, navigate to the location where the presentation is to be saved and then type a name for the presentation.
- View a presentation in one of the following six views: Normal view, which is the default view and displays two panes—the slide thumbnails pane and the slide pane; Outline view, which displays the outline pane for typing text in slides; Slide Sorter view, which displays all slides in the presentation in slide thumbnails; Reading view, which delivers a presentation to people viewing it on their computers; Notes Page view, which displays an individual slide with any added notes displayed below the slide; and Slide Show view, which runs the slide show.
- Navigate to various slides in a presentation using the mouse and/or keyboard. Navigate in the presentation using the Previous Slide and Next Slide buttons at the bottom of the vertical scroll bar, the scroll box on the vertical scroll bar, arrow keys on the keyboard, or the Page Up and Page Down keys on the keyboard.
- Click the File tab and the backstage area displays options for working with and managing presentations.

- Use options at the Print backstage area to print presentations with each slide on a separate piece of paper; each slide at the top of the page, leaving room for notes; all or a specific number of slides on a single piece of paper; or slide titles and topics in outline form.
- When running a slide show, the Slide Show toolbar displays in the lower left corner of the slide. This toolbar contains buttons and options for running a slide show. Use the buttons to navigate to slides, make ink notations on slides, display slide thumbnails, zoom in on a specific location in a slide, and display a Help menu.
- Apply a design theme to a presentation by clicking the Design tab and then clicking the theme in the themes gallery in the Themes group. Apply a color variation to a theme by clicking an option in the Variants group on the Design tab.
- Delete a presentation at the Open dialog box by clicking the presentation file name, clicking the Organize button on the toolbar, and then clicking *Delete* at the drop-down list.
- Open a blank presentation by displaying the New backstage area and then clicking the *Blank Presentation* template or with the keyboard shortcut Ctrl + N.
- Type text in a slide in the slide pane or in the outline pane. Display the outline pane by clicking the View tab and then clicking the Outline View button.
- Enhance a presentation by adding transitions (how one slide is removed from the screen and replaced with the next slide) and transition sounds. Add transitions and transition sounds to a presentation with options on the Transitions tab.
- Advance slides automatically in a slide show by removing the check mark from the *On Mouse Click* check box on the Transitions tab, inserting a check mark in the *After* check box, and then specifying the time in the *After* measurement box.
- Click the Apply To All button to apply transitions, transition sounds, and/or time settings to all slides in a presentation.

Commands Review

FEATURE	RIBBON TAB, GROUP/OPTION	BUTTON	KEYBOARD SHORTCUT
close presentation	File, *Close*		Ctrl + F4
design theme	Design, Themes		
New backstage area	File, *New*		
new slide	Home, Slides		Ctrl + M
Normal view	View, Presentation Views		
Notes Page view	View, Presentation Views		
Open backstage area	File, *Open*		Ctrl + O
Outline view	View, Presentation Views		
Print backstage area	File, *Print*		Ctrl + P
run slide show	Slide Show, Start Slide Show OR Quick Access Toolbar		F5
Save As backstage area	File, *Save* OR *Save As*		Ctrl + S
slide layout	Home, Slides		
Slide Sorter view	View, Presentation Views		
transition	Transitions, Transition to This Slide		
transition duration	Transitions, Timing		
transition sound	Transitions, Timing		

Workbook

Chapter study tools and assessment activities are available in the *Workbook* ebook. These resources are designed to help you further develop and demonstrate mastery of the skills learned in this chapter.

Microsoft®

PowerPoint®

Modifying a Presentation and Using Help and Tell Me

CHAPTER 2

Performance Objectives

Upon successful completion of Chapter 2, you will be able to:

1 Check spelling
2 Use the Thesaurus
3 Find and replace text in slides
4 Cut, copy, and paste text in slides
5 Rearrange text in the outline pane
6 Size and rearrange placeholders
7 Insert, delete, move, and copy slides
8 Copy slides between presentations
9 Duplicate slides
10 Reuse slides
11 Create and manage sections
12 Customize the Quick Access Toolbar
13 Use the Help and Tell Me features

Precheck

Check your current skills to help focus your study.

When preparing a presentation, you may need to modify the contents by finding and replacing specific text or copying and pasting text in slides. Improve the quality of your presentation by completing a spelling check to ensure that the words in your presentation are spelled correctly and use the Thesaurus to find synonyms and antonyms. Additional modifications you may need to make to a presentation could include sizing and rearranging placeholders and rearranging, inserting, deleting, or copying slides. In this chapter, you will learn how to make these modifications to a presentation as well as how to create sections within a presentation and use the Help and Tell Me features.

Data Files

Before beginning the projects, copy the PC2 folder to your storage medium and then make PC2 the active folder.

SNAP

If you are a SNAP user, launch the Precheck and Tutorials from your Assignments page.

Project 1 Check Spelling, Use the Thesaurus, and Manage Text in a Design Presentation

2 Parts

You will open a presentation on steps for planning a design publication, complete a spelling check on the text in the presentation, use the Thesaurus to find synonyms, and find and replace specific text in slides.

Preview Finished Project

Tutorial

Checking Spelling

Checking Spelling

When preparing a presentation, perform a spelling check on text in slides using PowerPoint's spelling checker feature. The spelling checker feature compares words in slides in a presentation with words in its dictionary. If a match is found, the word is passed over. If a match is not found, the Spelling task pane displays replacement suggestions. At this task pane, choose to change the word or ignore it and leave it as written. To perform a spelling check, click the Review tab and then click the Spelling button in the Proofing group. Pressing the F7 function key will also start the spelling checker.

Spelling

Quick Steps

Complete a Spelling Check

1. Click Review tab.
2. Click Spelling button.
3. Change or ignore errors.
4. Click OK.

When checking the spelling in the presentation in Project 1a, the spelling checker will stop at the misspelled word *Layuot* and display the Spelling task pane as shown in Figure 2.1. The buttons available in the Spelling task pane are described in Table 2.1.

Figure 2.1 Spelling Task Pane

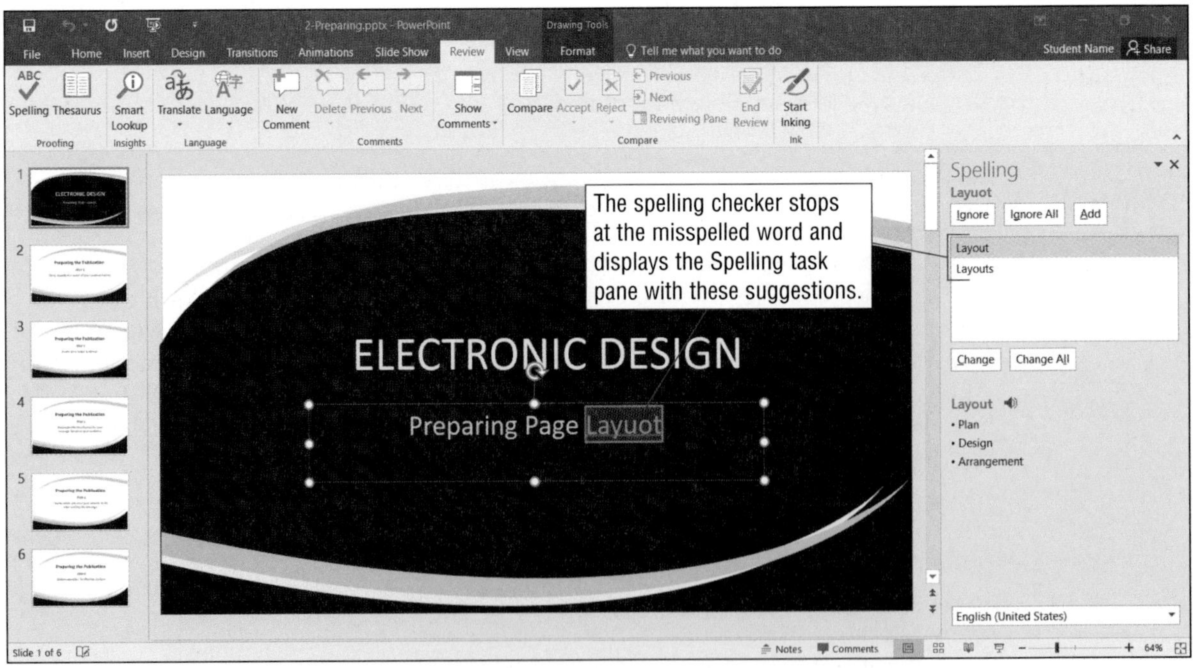

Table 2.1 Spelling Task Pane Options

Button	Function
Ignore	skips that occurrence of the word
Ignore All	skips that occurrence of the word and all other occurrences of the word in the presentation
Add	adds the selected word to the main spelling check dictionary
Delete	deletes the currently selected word(s)
Change	replaces the selected word with the word selected in the task pane list box
Change All	replaces the selected word and all other occurrences of it in the presentation with the word selected in the task pane list box

Tutorial

Using the Thesaurus

Thesaurus

Quick Steps

Use the Thesaurus

1. Click word.
2. Click Review tab.
3. Click Thesaurus button.
4. Position mouse pointer on replacement word in Thesaurus task pane.
5. Click down-pointing arrow at right of word.
6. Click *Insert*.

Using the Thesaurus

Use the Thesaurus to find synonyms, antonyms, and related words for a particular word. Synonyms are words that have the same or nearly the same meaning and antonyms are words with the opposite meanings.

To use the Thesaurus, click in the word, click the Review tab, and then click the Thesaurus button in the Proofing group. This displays the Thesaurus task pane with information about the word where the insertion point is positioned. Hover the mouse over the synonym or antonym, click the down-pointing arrow at the right of the word, and then click *Insert* at the drop-down list. Another method for displaying and inserting a synonym for a word is to right-click the word, point to *Synonyms*, and then click the replacement word at the side menu.

Project 1a Checking the Spelling in a Presentation — Part 1 of 2

1. Open **Preparing.pptx** and then save it with the name **2-Preparing**.
2. With the presentation in Normal view, run a spelling check by completing the following steps:
    a. Click the Review tab.
    b. Click the Spelling button in the Proofing group.
    c. The spelling checker selects the misspelled word *Layuot* and displays the Spelling task pane. The proper spelling (*Layout*) is selected in the Spelling task pane list box, so click the Change button (or the Change All button) to correct the misspelling.

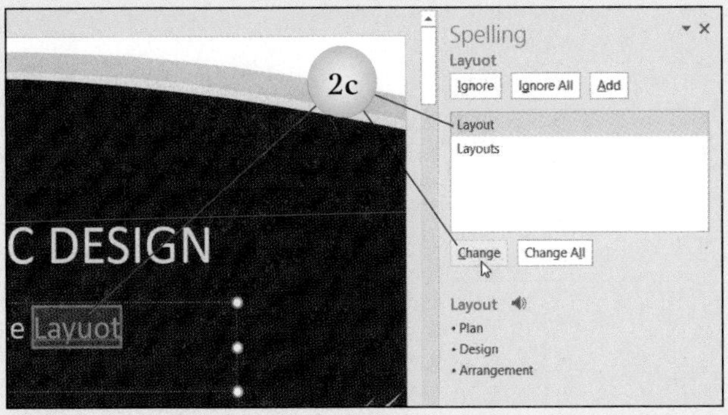

d. The spelling checker selects the misspelled word *Clerly*. The correct spelling is selected in the Spelling task pane list box, so click the Change button (or the Change All button).
e. When the spelling checker selects the misspelled word *massege*, click *message* in the Spelling task pane list box and then click the Change button (or the Change All button).

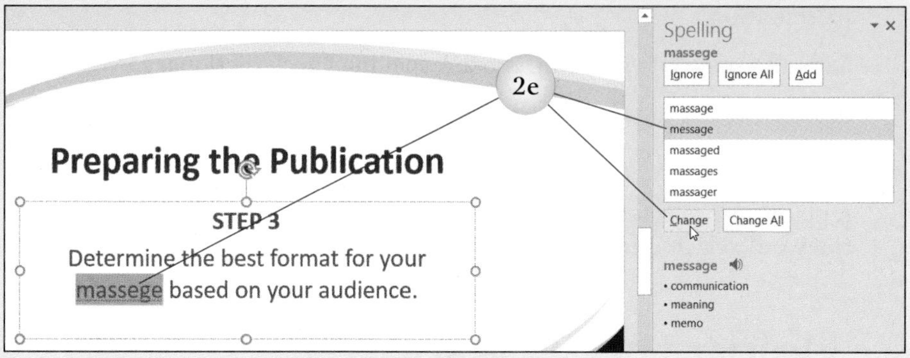

f. The spelling checker selects the misspelled word *fo*. The correct spelling is selected in the Spelling task pane list box, so click the Change button (or the Change All button).
g. At the message stating that the spelling check is complete, click the OK button.

3. Make Slide 2 active and then use the Thesaurus to find a synonym for *point* by completing the following steps:
   a. Click in the word *point*.
   b. Click the Review tab, if necessary, and then click the Thesaurus button.
   c. At the Thesaurus task pane, scroll down the task pane list box to display *purpose* (below *purpose (n.)*).
   d. Hover your mouse pointer over the word *purpose* in the task pane, click the down-pointing arrow, and then click *Insert* at the drop-down list.
   e. Close the Thesaurus task pane by clicking the Close button (contains an *X*) in the upper right corner of the task pane.

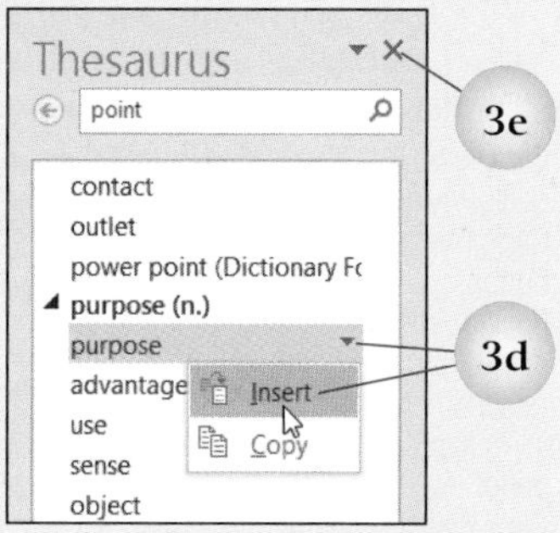

4. Make Slide 6 active and right-click in the word *Gather*.
5. Point to *Synonyms* at the short-cut menu and then click *Collect* at the side menu.
6. Save **2-Preparing.pptx**.

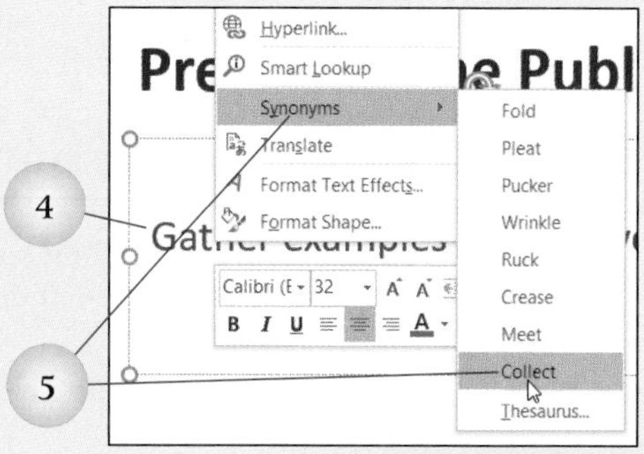

Check Your Work

Managing Text and Placeholders

Text in a placeholder in a slide can be edited, modified, and rearranged. For example, text can be replaced with other text and text can be cut, copied, and pasted to other locations. The placeholder containing text or other objects can be modified by resizing it or moving it to another location.

Tutorial

Finding and Replacing Text

Find

Replace

Quick Steps

Find Text

1. Click Find button.
2. Type search text.
3. Click Find Next button.

Replace Text

1. Click Replace button.
2. Type search text.
3. Press Tab key.
4. Type replacement text.
5. Click Replace All button.

Finding and Replacing Text in Slides

Use the Find feature to look for specific text in slides in a presentation and use the Find and Replace feature to look for specific text in slides in a presentation and replace it with other text. Begin a search by clicking the Find button in the Editing group on the Home tab. This displays the Find dialog box, as shown in Figure 2.2. In the *Find what* text box, type the text to be found and then click the Find Next button. Continue clicking this button until a message displays indicating that the search is complete. At this message, click OK.

Use options at the Replace dialog box, shown in Figure 2.3, to search for text and replace it with other text. Display this dialog box by clicking the Replace button in the Editing group on the Home tab. Type the text to be found in the *Find what* text box, press the Tab key, and then type the replacement text in the *Replace with* text box. Click the Find Next button to find the next occurrence of the text and then click the Replace button to replace it with the new text, or click the Replace All button to replace all occurrences in the presentation.

Both the Find dialog box and the Replace dialog box contain two additional options. Insert a check mark in the *Match case* check box to specify that the text in the presentation should exactly match the case of the text in the *Find what* text box. For example, search for *Planning* and PowerPoint will stop at *Planning* but not *planning* or *PLANNING*. Insert a check mark in the *Find whole words only* check box to specify that the text to be found is a whole word only and not part of a word. For example, if you search for *plan* and do not check the *Find whole words only* option, PowerPoint will stop at ex*plan*ation, *plan*ned, *plan*ning, and so on.

Figure 2.2 Find Dialog Box

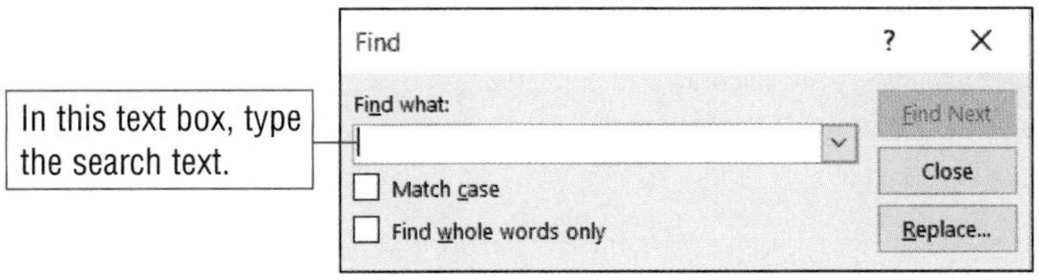

Figure 2.3 Replace Dialog Box

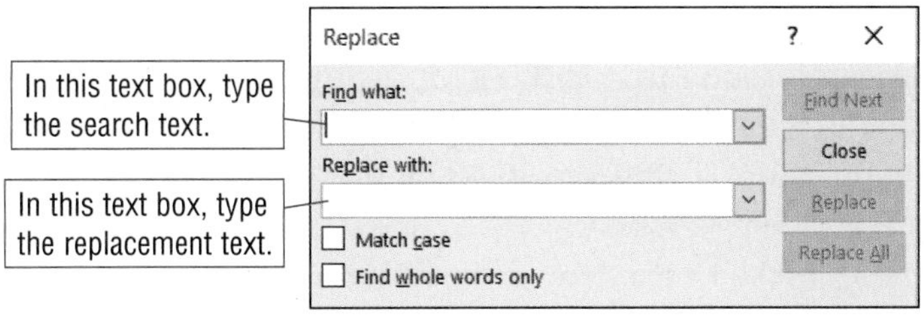

Project 1b Finding and Replacing Text

Part 2 of 2

1. With **2-Preparing.pptx** open, make Slide 1 active.
2. Find all occurrences of *Preparing* in the presentation and replace them with *Planning* by completing the following steps:
   a. With Slide 1 active, click the Replace button in the Editing group on the Home tab.
   b. At the Replace dialog box, type Preparing in the *Find what* text box.
   c. Press the Tab key.
   d. Type Planning in the *Replace with* text box.
   e. Click the Replace All button.

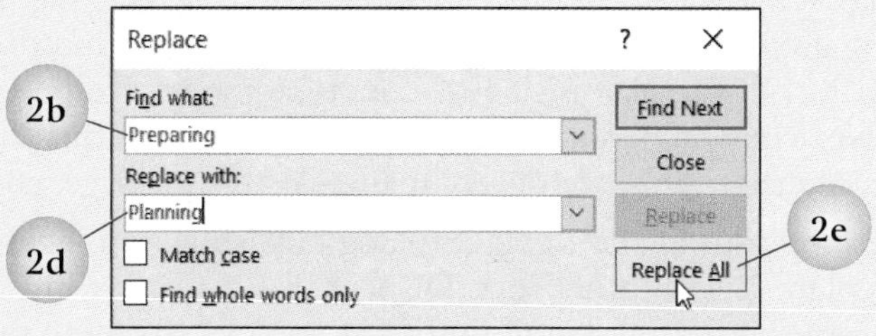

   f. At the message stating that six replacements were made, click the OK button.
   g. Click the Close button to close the Replace dialog box.
3. Find all occurrences of *Publication* and replace them with *Newsletter* by completing steps similar to those in Step 2.
4. Save the presentation.
5. Apply a transition and transition sound of your choosing to all slides in the presentation.
6. Run the slide show.
7. Print Slide 1 by completing the following steps:
   a. Click the File tab and then click the *Print* option.
   b. At the Print backstage area, click in the *Slides* text box in the *Settings* category and then type 1.
   c. Click the Print button.
8. Print the presentation as a handout with six slides displayed horizontally on the page. (Change the second gallery in the *Settings* category to *6 Slides Horizontal* and delete the *1* in the *Slides* text box.)
9. Save and then close **2-Preparing.pptx**.

Check Your Work

Project 2 Cut, Copy, Paste, Rearrange, and Manage Slides in a Network Presentation

5 Parts

You will open a network evaluation presentation and then cut, copy, and paste text in slides; rearrange text in the slide thumbnails pane; size and rearrange placeholders in slides; and manage slides by inserting, deleting, moving, and copying them. You will also create sections within a presentation and copy slides between presentations.

Preview Finished Project

Tutorial

Cutting, Copying, and Pasting Text

Cut

Copy

Paste

Cutting, Copying, and Pasting Text in Slides

Use buttons in the Clipboard group on the Home tab and/or shortcut menu options to cut, copy, and paste text in slides. For example, to move text in a slide, click in the placeholder containing the text to be moved, select the text, and then click the Cut button in the Clipboard group or use the keyboard shortcut Ctrl + X. Position the insertion point where the text is to be inserted and then click the Paste button in the Clipboard group or use the keyboard shortcut Ctrl + V.

To cut and paste with the shortcut menu, select the text to be moved, right-click in the selected text, and then click *Cut* at the shortcut menu. Position the insertion point where the text is to be inserted, right-click in the placeholder, and then click *Paste* at the shortcut menu. Complete similar steps to copy and paste text, except click the Copy button instead of the Cut button, use the keyboard shortcut Ctrl + C, or click the *Copy* option at the shortcut menu instead of the *Cut* option.

Project 2a **Cutting, Copying, and Pasting Text in Slides** Part 1 of 5

1. Open **NetworkSystem.pptx** and then save it with the name **2-NetworkSystem.**
2. Insert a new slide by completing the following steps:
   a. Make Slide 4 active.
   b. Click the New Slide button in the Slides group on the Home tab.
   c. Click in the title placeholder and then type TIME.
3. Cut text from Slide 3 and paste it into Slide 5 by completing the following steps:
   a. Make Slide 3 active.
   b. Click in the bulleted text in the slide pane.
   c. Using the mouse, select the bottom three lines of bulleted text. (The bullets will not be selected.)
   d. With the text selected, click the Cut button in the Clipboard group on the Home tab.

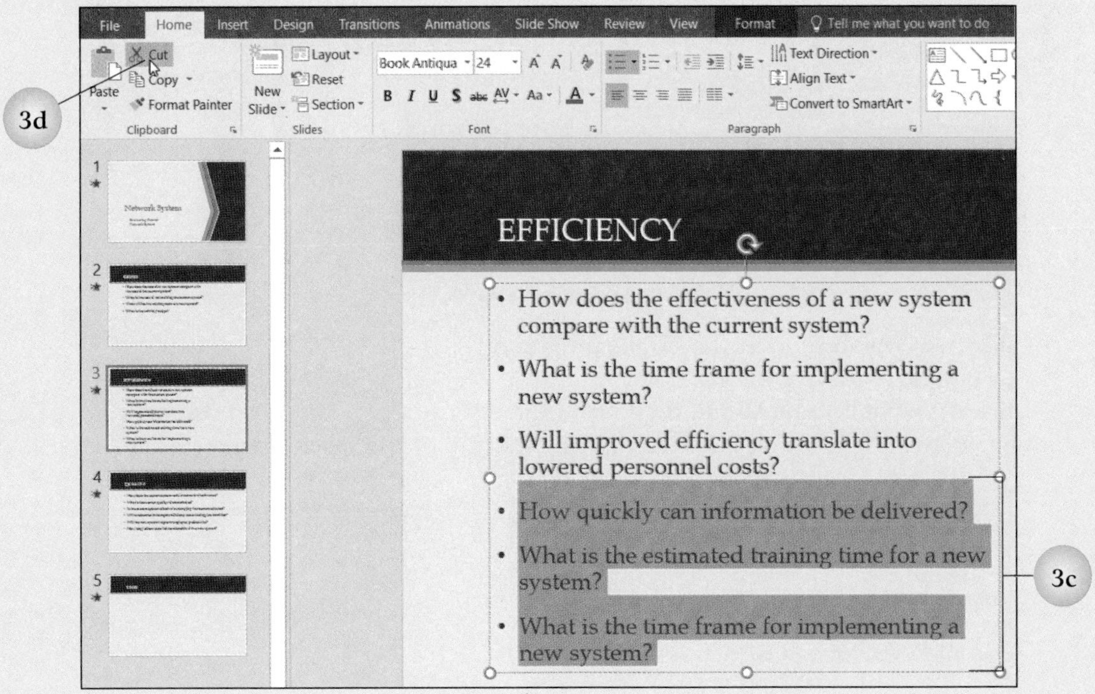

e. Make Slide 5 the active slide (contains the title *TIME*).
f. Click in the text placeholder.
g. Click the Paste button in the Clipboard group.
h. With the insertion point positioned below the third bulleted item following a bullet, press the Backspace key two times. (This removes the bullet and deletes the blank line below that bullet.)

4. Insert a new slide by completing the following steps:
   a. With Slide 5 the active slide, click the New Slide button in the Slides group on the Home tab.
   b. Click in the title placeholder and then type EASE OF USE.
5. Cut text from Slide 4 and paste it into Slide 6 by completing the following steps:
   a. Make Slide 4 active.
   b. Click in the bulleted text.
   c. Select the bottom three bulleted items.
   d. Click the Cut button in the Clipboard group on the Home tab.
   e. Make Slide 6 active (contains the title *EASE OF USE*).
   f. Click in the text placeholder.
   g. Click the Paste button in the Clipboard group.
   h. With the insertion point positioned below the third bulleted item following a bullet, press the Backspace key two times.
6. Copy text from Slide 3 to Slide 5 by completing the following steps:
   a. Make Slide 3 active.
   b. Click in the bulleted text.
   c. Position the mouse pointer over the last bullet until the pointer turns into a four-headed arrow and then click the left mouse button. (This selects the text following the bullet.)

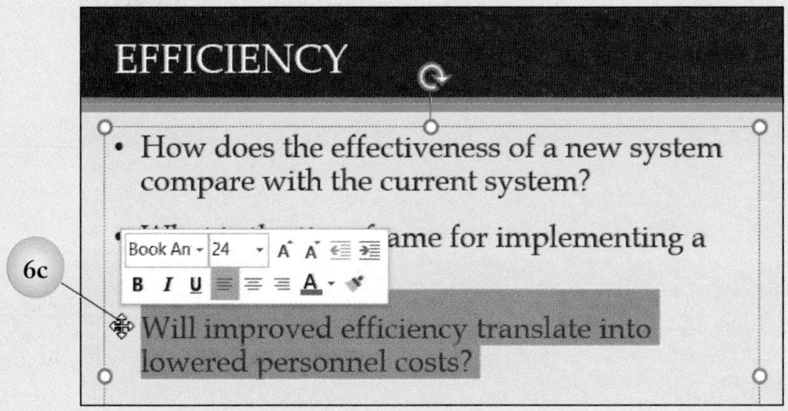

   d. Click the Copy button in the Clipboard group.
   e. Make Slide 5 active.
   f. Click in the bulleted text and then move the insertion point so it is positioned immediately right of the question mark at the end of the second bulleted item.

g. Press the Enter key. (This moves the insertion point down to the next line and inserts another bullet.)
h. Click the Paste button in the Clipboard group.

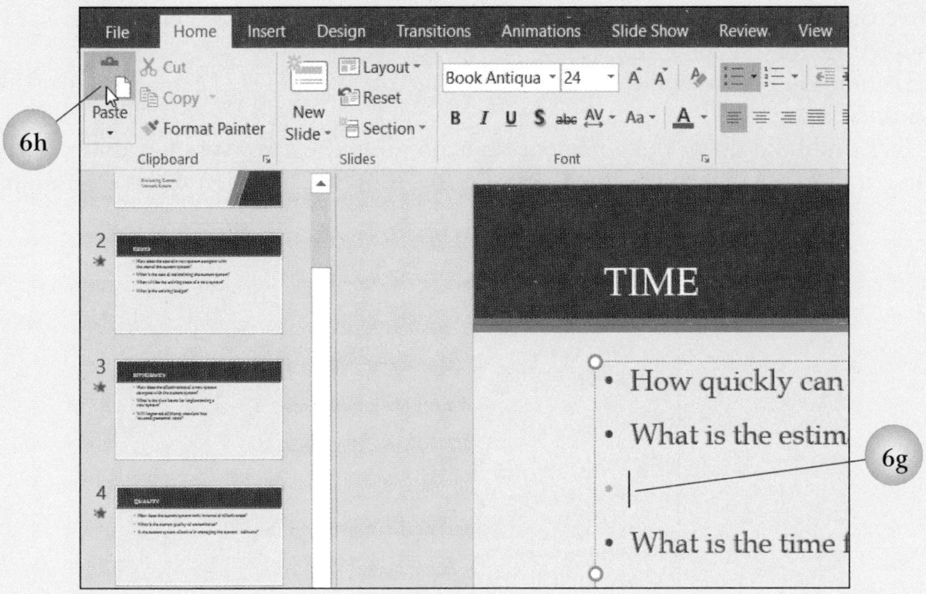

i. If there is a blank line between the third and fourth bullets, press the Backspace key two times to remove it.

7. Save **2-NetworkSystem.pptx**.

Check Your Work

Rearranging Text Using the Outline Pane

Text in slides can be moved and copied in the outline pane. Display the outline pane by clicking the View tab and then clicking the Outline View button in the Presentation Views group or with the keyboard shortcut Ctrl + Shift + Tab. To move text in the outline pane, position the mouse pointer on the slide icon or bullet at the left side of the text until the arrow pointer turns into a four-headed arrow. Click and hold down the left mouse button, drag the arrow pointer (a thin horizontal line displays) to the new location, and then release the mouse button.

Position the arrow pointer on the slide icon and then click the left mouse button and all of the text in the slide is selected. Click a bullet and all text following that bullet is selected.

Dragging selected text with the mouse moves the selected text to a new location in the presentation. Selected text can also be copied. To do this, click the slide icon or the bullet to select the text. Position the arrow pointer in the selected text, press and hold down the Ctrl key, and then click and hold down the left mouse button. Drag the arrow pointer (displays with a light gray box and a plus symbol attached) to the new location, release the mouse button, and then release the Ctrl key.

Project 2b Rearranging Text Using the Slide Thumbnails Pane

1. With **2-NetworkSystem.pptx** open, make Slide 1 active.
2. Press Ctrl + Shift + Tab to display the outline pane.
3. Move the first bulleted item in Slide 4 in the outline pane to the end of the list by completing the following steps:
   a. Position the mouse pointer on the first bullet below *QUALITY* until it turns into a four-headed arrow.
   b. Click and hold down the left mouse button, drag the arrow pointer down until a thin horizontal line displays below the last bulleted item, and then release the mouse button.

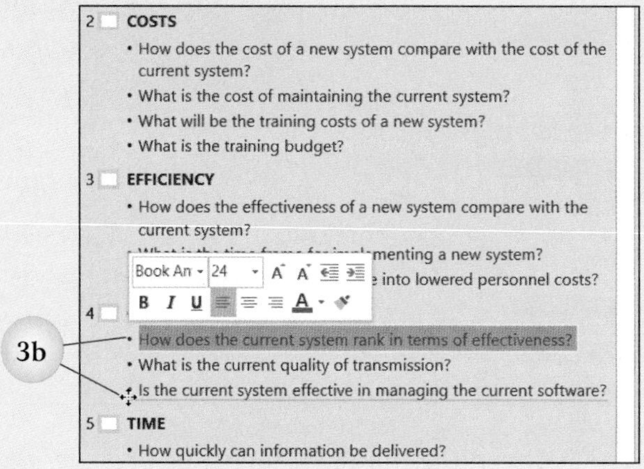

4. Copy and paste text by completing the following steps:
   a. In the outline pane, move the insertion point to the end of the text in Slide 6 and then press the Enter key. (This inserts a new bullet in the slide.)
   b. Scroll up the outline pane until the last bulleted item in Slide 2 is visible in the outline pane as well as the last bullet in Slide 6. (You may need to increase the width of the outline pane to display both bulleted items.)
   c. Position the mouse pointer near the last bulleted item in Slide 2 until it turns into a four-headed arrow and then click the left mouse button. (This selects the text.)
   d. Position the mouse pointer in the selected text, click and hold down the left mouse button, press and hold down the Ctrl key, and then drag down until the arrow pointer and light gray vertical line display on the blank line below the text in Slide 6.
   e. Release the mouse button and then release the Ctrl key.

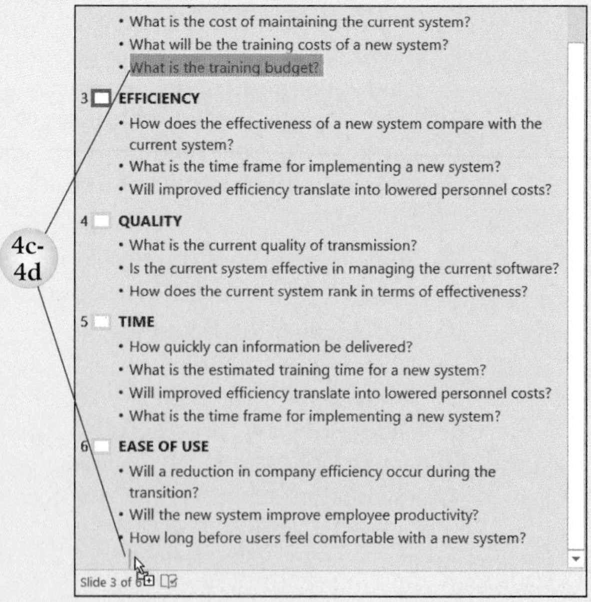

5. Press Ctrl + Shift + Tab to return to the slide thumbnails pane.
6. Click the Notes button on the Status bar to close the notes pane.
7. Save **2-NetworkSystem.pptx**.

Check Your Work

Tutorial

Modifying Placeholders

Modifying Placeholders

Clicking in a placeholder selects the placeholder and displays white sizing handles and a white rotation handle around the placeholder border. Use the sizing handles to increase or decrease the size of the placeholder by positioning the arrow pointer on a sizing handle until the pointer turns into a double-headed arrow and then dragging the placeholder border to the desired size. To move a placeholder, position the arrow pointer on the placeholder border until the arrow pointer displays with a four-headed arrow attached. Click and hold down the left mouse button, drag the placeholder to the new position, and then release the mouse button.

Dragging a selected placeholder with the mouse moves the placeholder. To copy a placeholder, press and hold down the Ctrl key while dragging the placeholder. When the placeholder is in position, release the mouse button, and then release the Ctrl key. If an unwanted change is made to the size and/or location of a placeholder, click the Reset button in the Slides group on the Home tab to return the formatting of the placeholder back to the default.

When dragging a placeholder on a slide, guidelines may display. Use the guidelines to help position placeholders. For example, use the guidelines to help align a title placeholder with a subtitle placeholder.

If a placeholder is no longer necessary, delete the placeholder. To delete a placeholder, click in the placeholder, click the border to change it to a solid line border, and then press the Delete key.

Project 2c Sizing and Rearranging Placeholders

Part 3 of 5

1. With **2-NetworkSystem.pptx** open, make Slide 1 active.
2. Size and move a placeholder by completing the following steps:
   a. Click in the subtitle *Evaluating Current Network System*.
   b. Position the arrow pointer on the sizing handle in the middle of the right border until the pointer turns into a left-and-right-pointing arrow.
   c. Click and hold down the left mouse button, drag to the right until the subtitle text appears on one line, and then release the mouse button.

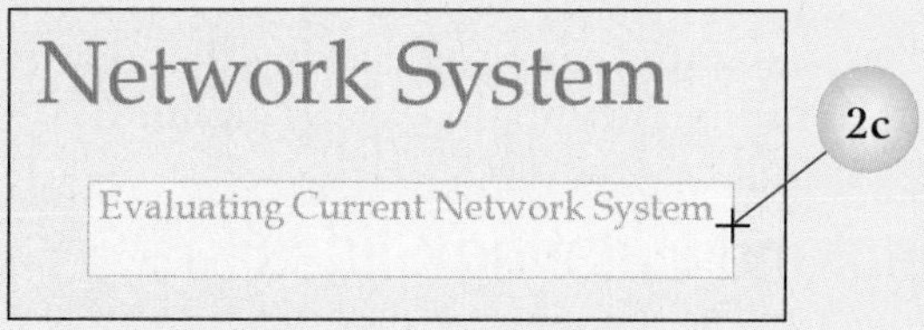

   d. Position the arrow pointer on the border of the placeholder until the pointer turns into a four-headed arrow.
   e. Click and hold down the left mouse button, drag the placeholder up and to the left so the placeholder is positioned as shown at the right, and then release the mouse button. Use the guideline to the left and above the placeholder to align the subtitle placeholder with the title placeholder.

3. Make Slide 4 active.

4. Size and move a placeholder by completing the following steps:
   a. Click in the bulleted text.
   b. Position the arrow pointer on the sizing handle in the middle of the right border until the pointer turns into a left-and-right-pointing arrow.
   c. Click and hold down the left mouse button and then drag to the left until the right border is positioned just to the right of the question mark in the first bulleted item.
   d. Drag the middle sizing handle on the bottom border up until the bottom border of the placeholder is positioned just below the last bulleted item.
   e. Position the arrow pointer on the border of the placeholder until the pointer turns into a four-headed arrow.
   f. Click and hold down the left mouse button and then drag the placeholder to the left until the vertical guideline displays left of the title and then release the mouse button.
5. Save **2-NetworkSystem.pptx**.

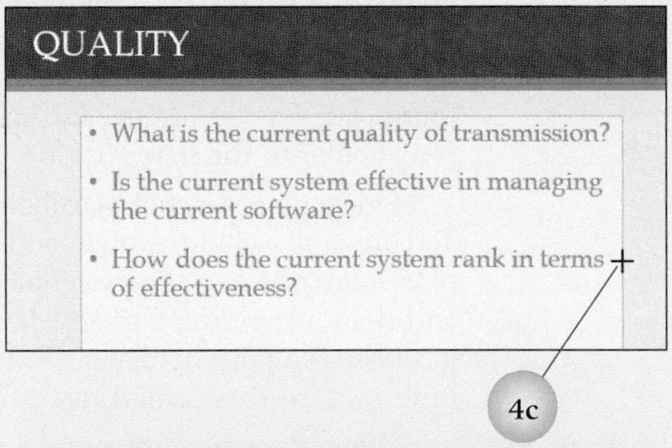

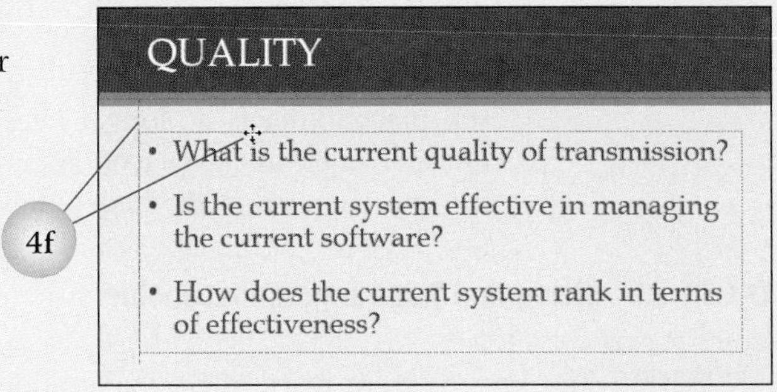

Check Your Work

Managing Slides

Editing a presentation may require reorganizing slides, inserting new slides, or deleting existing slides. Manage slides in the slide thumbnails pane or in Slide Sorter view. Switch to Slide Sorter view by clicking the Slide Sorter button in the view area on the Status bar or by clicking the View tab and then clicking the Slide Sorter button in the Presentation Views group.

Tutorial

Deleting Slides

Quick Steps

Insert a Slide
1. Click Home Tab.
2. Click New Slide Button.

Delete a Slide
1. Click slide in slide thumbnails pane.
2. Press Delete key.

Inserting and Deleting Slides

As explained in Chapter 1, clicking the New Slide button in the Slides group on the Home tab inserts a new slide in the presentation immediately following the currently active slide. A new slide can also be inserted in Slide Sorter view. To do this, click the slide that should immediately precede the new slide and then click the New Slide button in the Slides group. Delete a slide in Normal view by clicking the slide thumbnail in the slide thumbnails pane and then pressing the Delete key. A slide can also be deleted by switching to Slide Sorter view, clicking the slide thumbnail, and then pressing the Delete key.

Tutorial

Rearranging Slides

Rearranging Slides

Rearrange slides in a presentation in Normal view or Slide Sorter view. In Normal view, click a slide in the slide thumbnails pane and then position the mouse pointer on the selected slide. Click and hold down the left mouse button, drag the pointer up or down until the slide thumbnail is in the new location, and then release the mouse button. Complete similar steps to move a slide in Slide Sorter view. Click the desired slide and hold down the left mouse button, drag the slide to the new location, and then release the mouse button.

Tutorial

Copying a Slide

Hint Press Ctrl + X to cut the selected slide and then press Ctrl + V to paste the cut slide.

Hint Press Ctrl + C to copy the selected slide and then press Ctrl + V to paste the copied slide.

Copying a Slide

When creating slides in a presentation, some slides may contain similar text, objects, and/or formatting. Rather than creating new slides in these presentations, consider copying an existing slide. To do this, display the presentation in Slide Sorter view, position the mouse on the slide to be copied, press and hold down the Ctrl key, and then click and hold down the left mouse button. Drag the copy of the slide thumbnail to the location where it is to be inserted, release the mouse button, and then release the Ctrl key. Slides can also be copied using the Ctrl key in the slide thumbnails pane in Normal view.

Slides can also be copied in Normal view or Slide Sorter view with buttons in the Clipboard group on the Home tab. To copy a slide, click the slide thumbnail and then click the Copy button in the Clipboard group. Click the slide thumbnail of the slide that will precede the copied slide and then click the Paste button in the Clipboard group.

Project 2d Moving and Copying Slides — Part 4 of 5

1. With **2-NetworkSystem.pptx** open in Normal view, move slides by completing the following steps:
   a. Click Slide 3 (*EFFICIENCY*) in the slide thumbnails pane.
   b. Position the mouse pointer on Slide 3, click and hold down the left mouse button, drag the slide thumbnail up between Slides 1 and 2, and then release the mouse button.
   c. Click Slide 4 (*QUALITY*) in the slide thumbnails pane.
   d. Position the mouse pointer on Slide 4, click and hold down the left mouse button, drag the slide thumbnail down below Slide 6, and then release the mouse button.
2. Move and copy slides in Slide Sorter view by completing the following steps:
   a. Click the Slide Sorter button in the view area on the Status bar.
   b. Click Slide 4 (*TIME*) to make it the active slide. (The slide thumbnail displays with an orange border.)

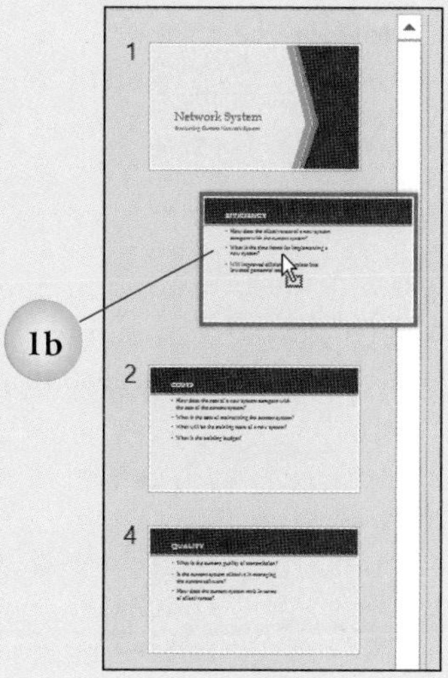

c. Position the mouse pointer on Slide 4, click and hold down the left mouse button, drag the slide thumbnail between Slides 1 and 2, and then release the mouse button.

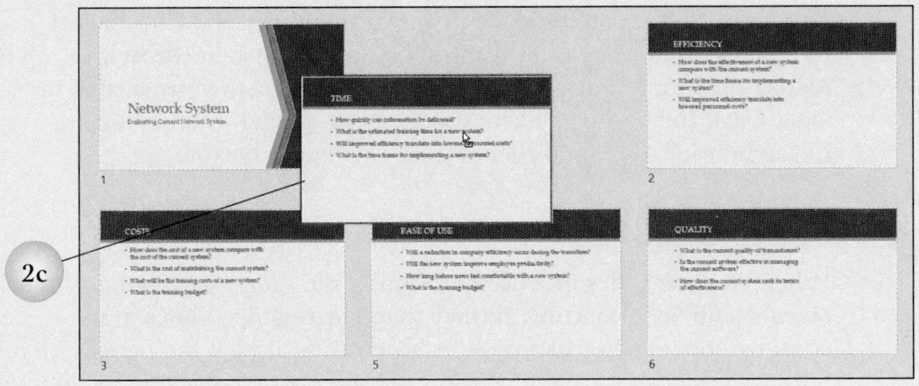

d. Click Slide 1 to make it the active slide.
e. Position the mouse pointer on Slide 1 (*Network System*), click and hold down the left mouse button, and then press and hold down the Ctrl key.
f. Drag the slide thumbnail down and to the right of Slide 6.

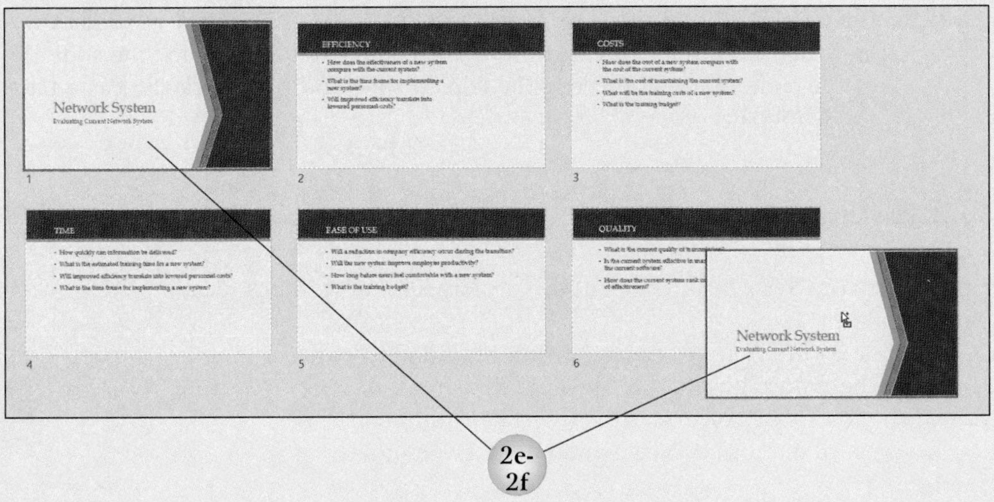

g. Release the mouse button and then release the Ctrl key.
3. Click the Normal button in the view area on the Status bar.
4. Save **2-NetworkSystem.pptx**.

Check Your Work

Copying a Slide between Presentations

Slides can be copied between presentations as well as within them. To copy a slide, click the slide thumbnail of the slide to be copied (either in Slide Sorter view or in the slide thumbnails pane in Normal view) and then click the Copy button in the Clipboard group on the Home tab. Open the presentation into which the slide is to be copied (in either Normal view or Slide Sorter view). Click in the location where the slide is to be positioned and then click the Paste button. The copied slide will take on the design theme of the presentation into which it is copied.

Project 2e Copying Slides between Presentations

Part 5 of 5

1. With **2-NetworkSystem.pptx** open, open the file named **EvalNetwork.pptx** in the PC2 folder on your storage medium.
2. Copy Slide 2 from **EvalNetwork.pptx** to the **2-NetworkSystem.pptx** file by completing the following steps:
   a. Click Slide 2 in the slide thumbnails pane to make it the active slide.
   b. Click the Copy button in the Clipboard group on the Home tab.
   c. Position the mouse pointer on the PowerPoint button on the taskbar and then click the ***2-NetworkSystem.pptx*** thumbnail.
   d. Click Slide 4 (*COSTS*) in the slide thumbnails pane.
   e. Click the Paste button in the Clipboard group.
   f. Position the mouse pointer on the PowerPoint button on the taskbar and then click the ***EvalNetwork.pptx*** thumbnail.
3. Copy Slide 3 from the **EvalNetwork.pptx** to **2-NetworkSystem.pptx** by completing the following steps:
   a. With **EvalNetwork.pptx** active, click Slide 3 in the slide thumbnails pane.
   b. Position the mouse pointer on Slide 3 and then click the right mouse button. (This displays a shortcut menu.)
   c. Click *Copy* at the shortcut menu.
   d. Position the mouse pointer on the PowerPoint button on the taskbar and then click the ***2-NetworkSystem.pptx*** thumbnail.
   e. Right-click Slide 3 in the slide thumbnails pane.
   f. Click the Use Destination Theme button in the *Paste Options* section.

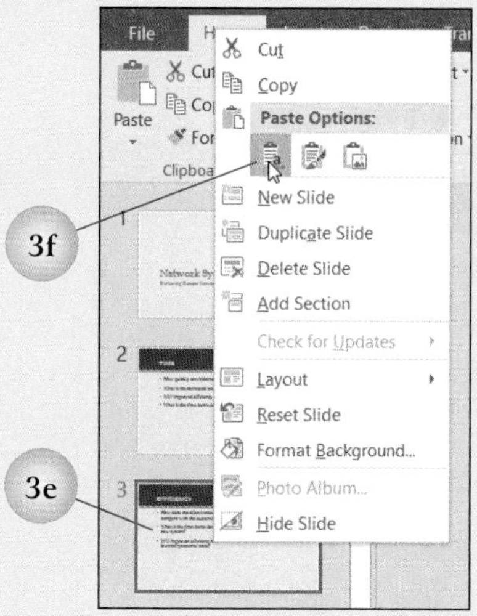

4. Position the mouse pointer on the PowerPoint button on the taskbar and then click the **EvalNetwork.pptx** thumbnail.
5. Close the presentation.
6. With **2-NetworkSystem.pptx** open, delete Slide 9 by completing the following steps:
   a. If necessary, scroll down the slide thumbnails pane until Slide 9 is visible.
   b. Click to select Slide 9.
   c. Press the Delete key.
7. Save the presentation.
8. Print the presentation as a handout with four slides displayed horizontally per page.
9. Close **2-NetworkSystem.pptx**.

Check Your Work

Project 3 Insert and Manage Slides in an Adventure Tours Presentation

4 Parts

You will open a presentation on Adventure Tours and then insert additional slides by duplicating existing slides in the presentation and reusing slides from another presentation. You will also divide the presentation into sections, rearrange sections, and print a section.

Preview Finished Project

Tutorial

Duplicating Slides

Quick Steps

Duplicate Slides

1. Select slides in slide thumbnails pane.
2. Click New Slide button arrow.
3. Click *Duplicate Selected Slides* at drop-down list.

Duplicating Slides

In Project 2, the Copy and Paste buttons in the Clipboard group and options from a shortcut menu were used to copy slides in a presentation. Slides can also be copied in a presentation using the *Duplicate Selected Slides* option from the New Slide button drop-down list or by clicking the Copy button arrow and then clicking *Duplicate* at the drop-down list. In addition to duplicating slides, the *Duplicate* option from the Copy button drop-down list can be used to duplicate a selected object in a slide, such as a placeholder.

A single slide or multiple selected slides can be duplicated. To select adjacent (sequential) slides, click the first slide in the slide thumbnails pane, press and hold down the Shift key, and then click the last slide. This will select all slides between that first slide and the last slide. To select nonadjacent (nonsequential) slides, press and hold down the Ctrl key while clicking each slide.

Project 3a Duplicating Selected Slides

Part 1 of 4

1. Open **AdvTours.pptx** and then save it with the name **2-AdvTours**.
2. Make sure the presentation displays in Normal view.
3. Select and then duplicate slides by completing the following steps:
   a. Click Slide 1 in the slide thumbnails pane.
   b. Press and hold down the Ctrl key.
   c. Click Slide 3, Slide 4, and then Slide 5.
   d. Release the Ctrl key.

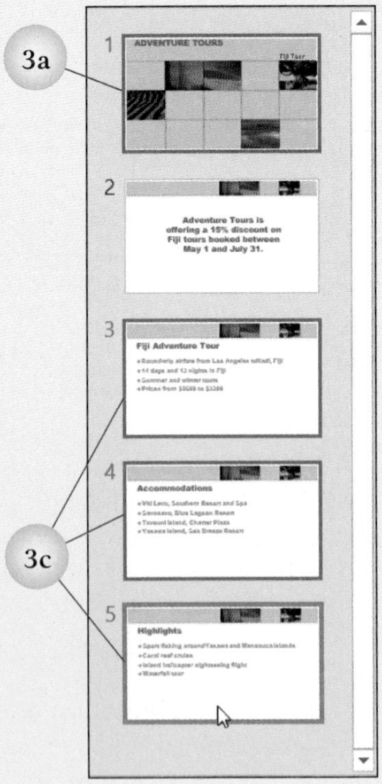

e. Click the New Slide button arrow in the Slides group on the Home tab and then click *Duplicate Selected Slides* at the drop-down list.

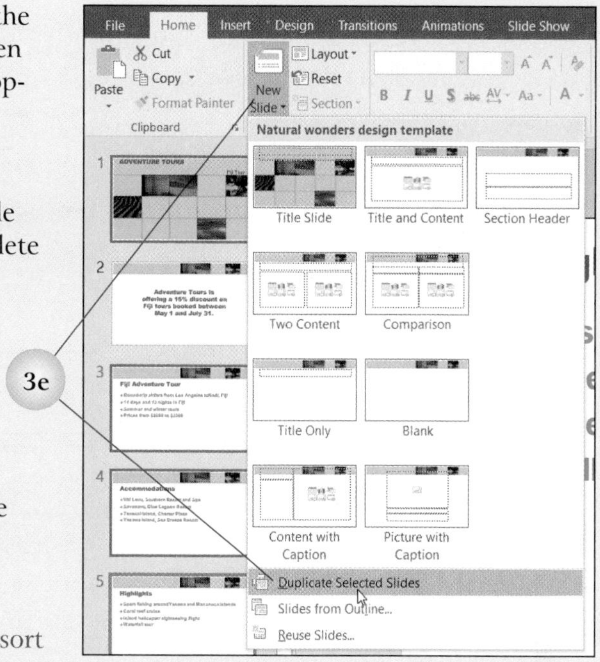

4. With Slide 6 active in the slide pane, change *Fiji Tour* to *Costa Rica Tour*.
5. Make Slide 7 active, select *Fiji* in the title and then type Costa Rica. Select and delete the existing bulleted text and then type the following bulleted text:
   - Round-trip airfare from Los Angeles to San Jose, Costa Rica
   - 8 days and 7 nights in Costa Rica
   - Monthly tours
   - Prices from $1099 to $1599
6. Make Slide 8 active, select and delete the existing bulleted text, and then type the following bulleted text:
   - San Jose, Emerald Suites
   - Tortuguero, Plantation Spa and Resort
   - Fortuna, Pacific Resort
   - Jaco, Monteverde Cabanas
7. Make Slide 9 active, select and delete the existing bulleted text, and then type the following bulleted text:
   - San Jose city tour
   - Rainforest tram
   - Canal cruise
   - Forest hike
8. Save **2-AdvTours.pptx**.

Check Your Work

Tutorial

Reusing Slides

Quick Steps

Reuse Slides

1. Click New Slide button arrow.
2. Click *Reuse Slides.*
3. Click Browse button.
4. Click *Browse File.*
5. Navigate to folder.
6. Double-click presentation.
7. Click slide in Reuse Slides task pane.

Reusing Slides

Reusing slides is another method for copying slides from one presentation to another. Click the New Slide button arrow and then click the *Reuse Slides* option at the drop-down list to display the Reuse Slides task pane at the right side of the screen, as shown in Figure 2.4. At this task pane, click the Browse button and then click *Browse File* at the drop-down list and the Browse dialog box displays. At this dialog box, navigate to the desired folder and then double-click the presentation. This inserts the presentation slides in the Reuse Slides task pane. Click a slide in the Reuse Slides task pane to insert it into the currently open presentation.

Slides can also be shared and used from a Slide Library on a server running SharePoint Server. Add slides to a Slide Library and then insert slides from a Slide Library into a presentation. Before reusing slides from a Slide Library, the Slide Library must first be created. Refer to the SharePoint help files to learn how to create a Slide Library. To reuse slides from a Slide Library in a presentation, click the Open a Slide Library hyperlink in the Reuse Slides task pane. Or, click the Browse button in the Reuse Slides task pane and then click *Browse Slide Library* at the drop-down list. This displays the Select a Slide Library dialog box. At this dialog box, navigate to the location of the library and then double-click the library.

Figure 2.4 Reuse Slides Task Pane

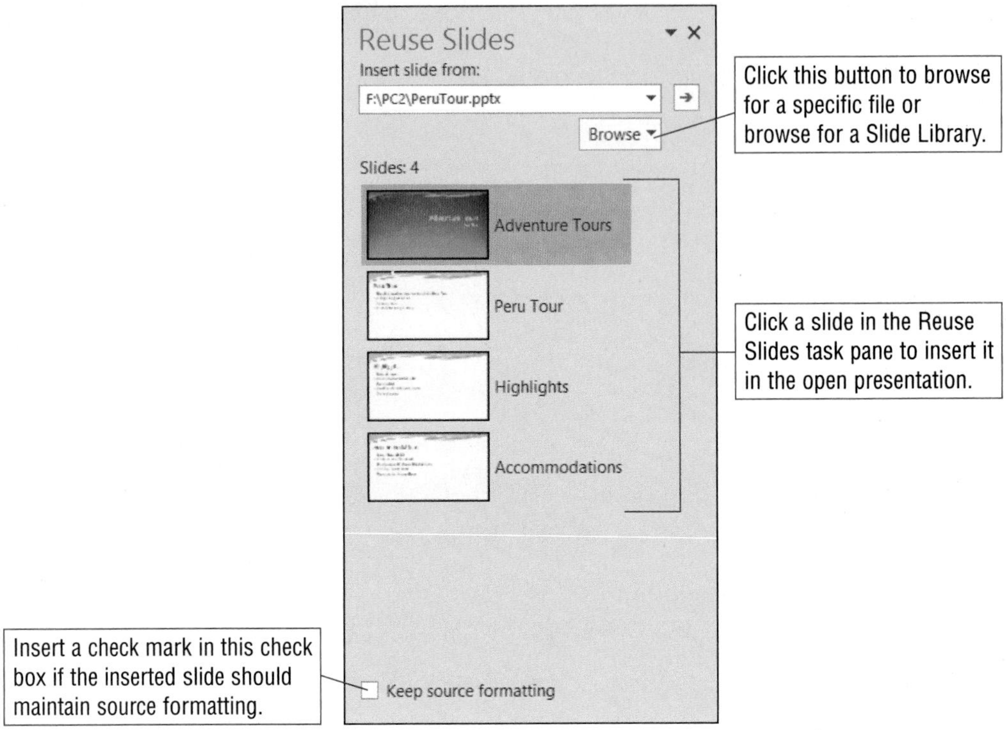
Reuse Slides
Insert slide from:
F:\PC2\PeruTour.pptx
Browse
Slides: 4
Adventure Tours
Peru Tour
Highlights
Accommodations
Keep source formatting
Click this button to browse for a specific file or browse for a Slide Library.
Click a slide in the Reuse Slides task pane to insert it in the open presentation.
Insert a check mark in this check box if the inserted slide should maintain source formatting.

By default, the slides inserted from the Reuse Slides task pane will take on the formatting of the current presentation. To retain the original formatting of the slides when inserted into the current presentation, insert a check mark in the *Keep source formatting* check box at the bottom of the Reuse Slides task pane.

Project 3b **Reusing Slides** — Part 2 of 4

1. With **2-AdvTours.pptx** open, click the New Slide button arrow in the Slides group on the Home tab and then click *Reuse Slides* at the drop-down list. (This displays the Reuse Slides task pane at the right side of the screen.)
2. Click the Browse button in the Reuse Slides task pane and then click *Browse File* at the drop-down list.
3. At the Browse dialog box, navigate to the PC2 folder on your storage medium and then double-click ***PeruTour.pptx***.
4. In the slide thumbnails pane, scroll down the slide thumbnails until Slide 9 displays and then click below Slide 9. (This inserts a thin, horizontal line below the Slide 9 thumbnail in the slide thumbnails pane.)

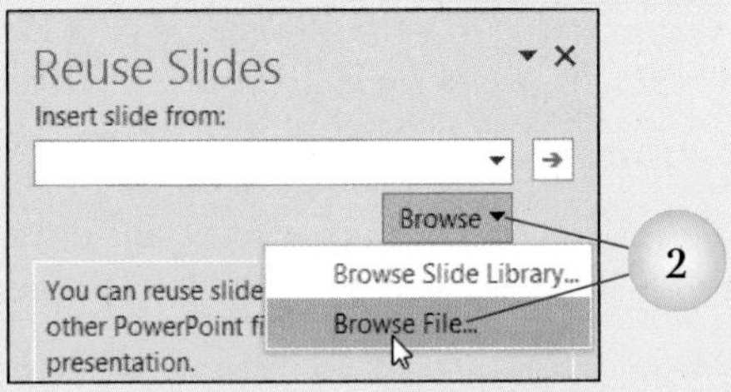
Reuse Slides
Insert slide from:
Browse
Browse Slide Library...
Browse File...
You can reuse slide
other PowerPoint fi
presentation.
2

5. Click the first slide thumbnail (*Adventure Tours*) in the Reuse Slides task pane. (This inserts the slide in the open presentation immediately below Slide 9.)

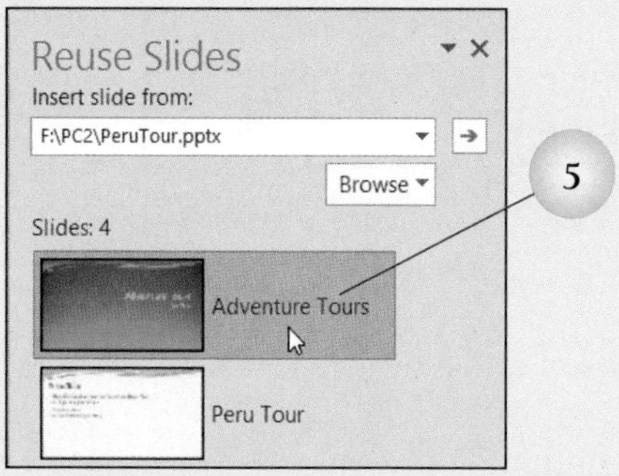

6. Click the second slide thumbnail (*Peru Tour*) in the Reuse Slides task pane.
7. Click the fourth slide thumbnail (*Accommodations*) in the Reuse Slides task pane.
8. Click the third slide thumbnail (*Highlights*) in the Reuse Slides task pane.
9. Close the Reuse Slides task pane by clicking the Close button (contains an *X*) in the upper right corner of the task pane.
10. Save **2-AdvTours.pptx**.

Check Your Work

Tutorial

Creating Sections within a Presentation

Creating Sections within a Presentation

When working on a presentation with others in a group or working in a presentation containing numerous slides, consider dividing related slides in the presentation into sections. Dividing a presentation into sections allows for easy navigating and editing of slides within the presentation.

Section

Create a section by selecting the first slide in the slide thumbnails pane, clicking the Section button in the Slides group on the Home tab, and then clicking *Add Section* at the drop-down list. A section title bar displays in the slide thumbnails pane. By default, the section title is *Untitled Section*. Rename a section by clicking the Section button in the Slides group on the Home tab and then clicking *Rename Section* at the drop-down list. A section can also be renamed by right-clicking the section title bar in the slide thumbnails pane and then clicking *Rename Section* at the shortcut menu.

Quick Steps

Create Section

1. Select first slide for new section.
2. Click Section button.
3. Click *Add Section.*

Remove, move, collapse, and expand sections with options in the Section button drop-down list or by right-clicking the section title bar and then clicking an option at the shortcut menu. Different formatting can be applied to an individual section by clicking the section title bar to select that section and then applying the formatting.

Creating sections within a presentation provides the option to print only certain sections of the presentation. To print a section of a presentation, click the File tab, click the *Print* option, click the first gallery in the *Settings* category, click the section in the drop-down list, and then click the Print button.

1. With **2-AdvTours.pptx** open, create a section for slides about Fiji by completing the following steps:
   a. Click Slide 1 in the slide thumbnails pane.
   b. Click the Section button in the Slides group on the Home tab and then click *Add Section* at the drop-down list.
2. Rename the new section by completing the following steps:
   a. Click the Section button and then click *Rename Section* at the drop-down list.
   b. At the Rename Section dialog box, type Fiji Tour and then click the Rename button.
3. Create a section for slides about Costa Rica by completing the following steps:
   a. Click Slide 6 in the slide thumbnails pane.
   b. Click the Section button in the Slides group and then click *Add Section* at the drop-down list.
   c. Right-click in the section title bar (contains the text *Untitled Section*) and then click *Rename Section* at the shortcut menu.
   d. At the Rename Section dialog box, type Costa Rica Tour and then press the Enter key.
4. Complete steps similar to those in Step 3 to create a section beginning with Slide 10 and rename the section *Peru Tour*.
5. Change the design theme of a section by completing the following steps:
   a. Click the *Fiji Tour* section title bar at the top of the slide thumbnails pane. (This selects all five slides in the *Fiji Tour* section.)
   b. Click the Design tab.
   c. Click the More Themes button in the themes gallery.
   d. Click *Wisp* at the drop-down gallery.
6. Complete steps similar to those in Steps 5a through 5d to apply the Ion design theme to the *Costa Rica Tour* section.
7. Move the Peru Tour section above the *Costa Rica Tour* section by completing the following steps:
   a. Click the Home tab, click the Section button in the Slides group, and then click *Collapse All* at the drop-down list.

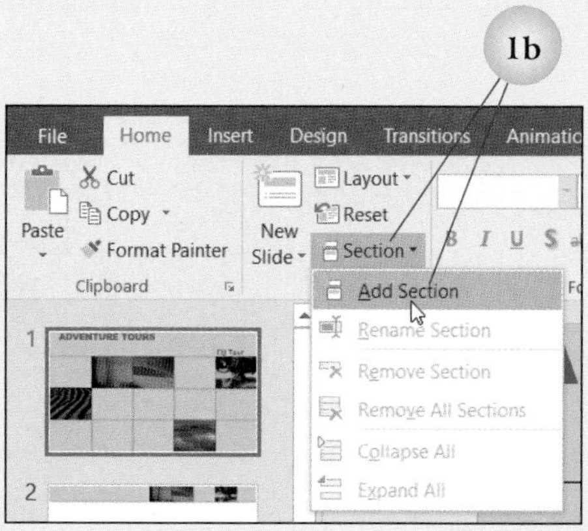

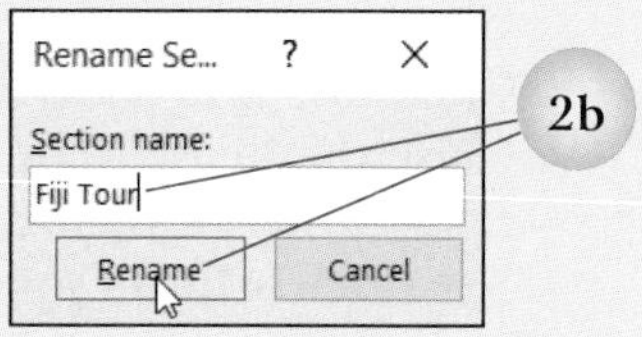

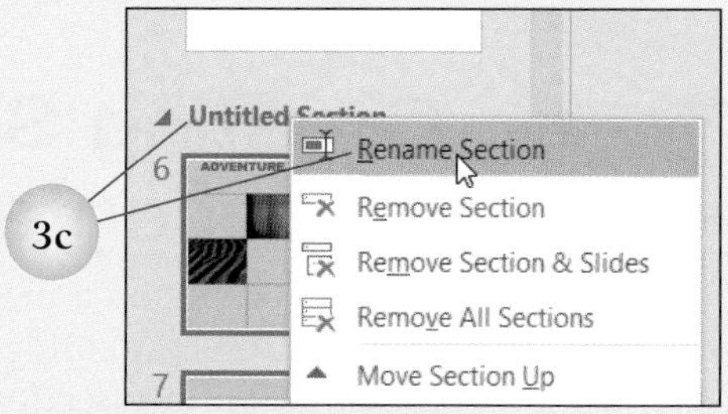

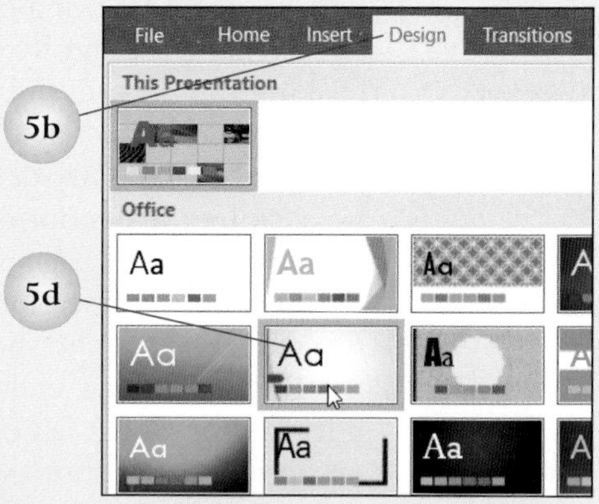

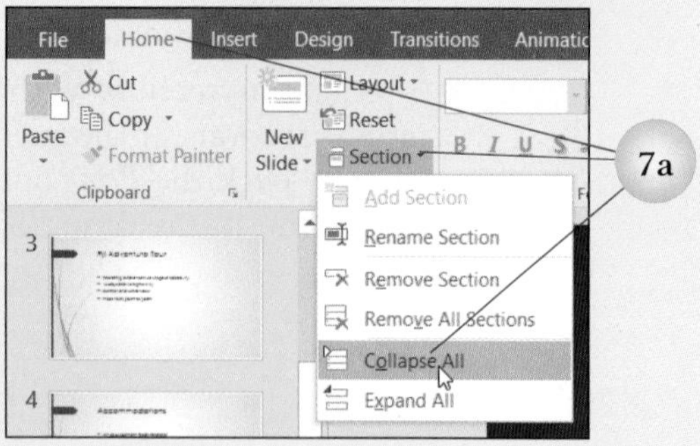

b. Position the mouse pointer on the *Peru Tour* section title bar, click and hold down the left mouse button, drag the title bar up until the title displays above the *Costa Rica* Tour section title bar, and then release the mouse button.

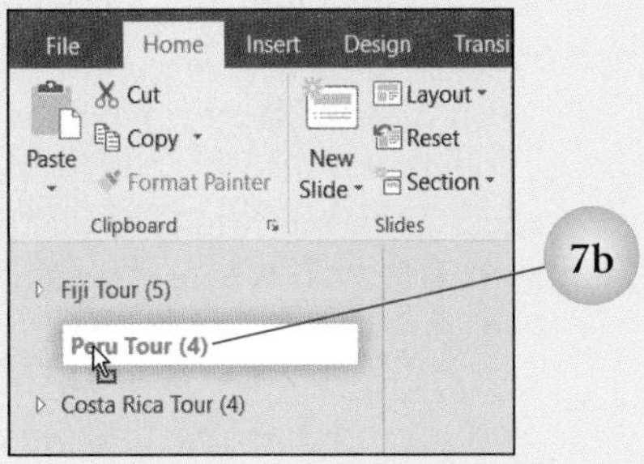

8. Display only slides in the *Costa Rica Tour* section by double-clicking the *Costa Rica Tour* section title bar in the slide thumbnails pane. (Notice that only Slides 10 through 13 display in the slide thumbnails pane and that the slides in the *Fiji Tour* and *Peru Tour* sections are hidden.)
9. Redisplay the *Fiji Tour* section slides by double-clicking the *Fiji Tour* section title bar in the slide thumbnails pane.
10. Display all sections by clicking the Section button in the Slides group and then clicking *Expand All* at the drop-down list.
11. Print only the *Costa Rica Tour* section by completing the following steps:
    a. Click the File tab and then click the *Print* option.
    b. At the Print backstage area, click the first gallery in the *Settings* category and then click *Costa Rica Tour* in the *Sections* section (at the bottom of the drop-down list).
    c. Click the second gallery (contains the text *Full Page Slides*) in the *Settings* category and then click *4 Slides Horizontal* in the *Handouts* section.
    d. Click the Print button.

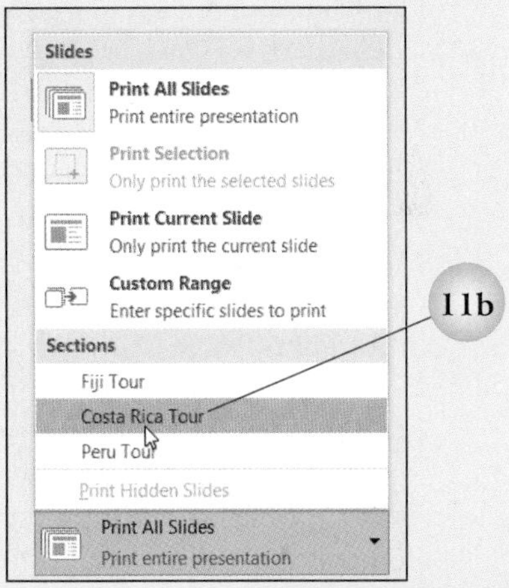

12. Complete steps similar to those in Step 11 to print only the *Peru Tour* section.
13. Save **2-AdvTours.pptx**.

Check Your Work

Tutorial

Customizing the Quick Access Toolbar

Save

Undo

Redo

Start from Beginning

Customize Quick Access Toolbar

Customizing the Quick Access Toolbar

The Quick Access Toolbar contains buttons for some of the most commonly performed tasks. By default, the toolbar contains the Save, Undo, Redo, and Start From Beginning buttons. Buttons can be added to or deleted from the Quick Access Toolbar. To add or delete a button, click the Customize Quick Access Toolbar button at the right side of the toolbar. At the drop-down list, click an option to insert a check mark next to those buttons that should display on the toolbar and click an option to remove the check mark from those that should not.

Click the *More Commands* option at the drop-down list and the PowerPoint Options dialog box displays with *Quick Access Toolbar* selected in the left panel. Use options at this dialog box to add buttons from a list of PowerPoint commands. Click the Reset button at the dialog box to reset the Quick Access Toolbar back to the default.

By default, the Quick Access Toolbar displays above the ribbon tabs. Display the Quick Access Toolbar below the ribbon by clicking the Customize Quick Access Toolbar button at the right side of the toolbar and then clicking the *Show Below the Ribbon* option at the drop-down list.

Project 3d Customizing the Quick Access Toolbar Part 4 of 4

1. With **2-AdvTours.pptx** open, add a New button to the Quick Access Toolbar by clicking the Customize Quick Access Toolbar button and then clicking *New* at the drop-down list.

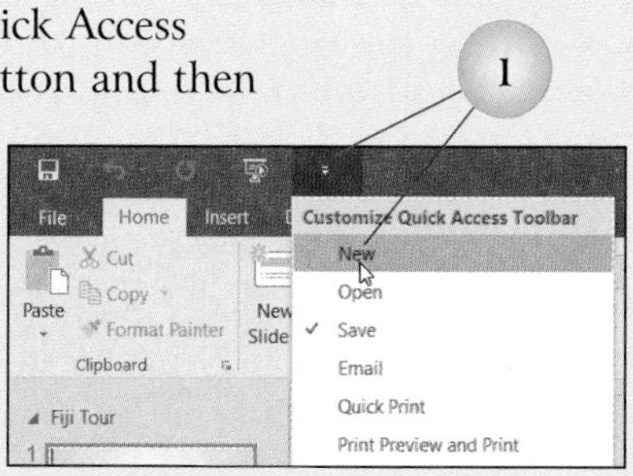

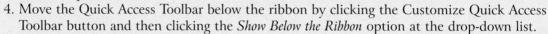

2. Add an Open button to the Quick Access Toolbar by clicking the Customize Quick Access Toolbar button and then clicking *Open* at the drop-down list.
3. Add a Print Preview and Print button to the Quick Access Toolbar by clicking the Customize Quick Access Toolbar button and then clicking *Print Preview and Print* at the drop-down list.
4. Move the Quick Access Toolbar below the ribbon by clicking the Customize Quick Access Toolbar button and then clicking the *Show Below the Ribbon* option at the drop-down list.
5. Click the Print Preview and Print button on the Quick Access Toolbar. (This displays the Print backstage area.)
6. Click the Back button to close the Print backstage area and return to the presentation.
7. Close **2-AdvTours.pptx**.
8. Click the New button to open a new blank presentation.
9. Click the Open button to display the Open backstage area.
10. Press the Esc key to return to the blank presentation and then close the presentation.
11. Move the Quick Access Toolbar back to the original position by clicking the Customize Quick Access Toolbar button and then clicking the *Show Above the Ribbon* option at the drop-down list.
12. Remove the New button by clicking the Customize Quick Access Toolbar button and then clicking *New* at the drop-down list.
13. Remove the Open button by right-clicking the button and then clicking *Remove from Quick Access Toolbar* at the drop-down list.
14. Remove the Print Preview and Print button from the Quick Access Toolbar.

Project 4 Use the PowerPoint Help and Tell Me Features and Create a Presentation 2 Parts

You will use the Help feature to learn more about PowerPoint features. You will also use the Help feature to find information on keyboard shortcuts and then use that information to create a presentation. You will use the Tell Me feature to change the font color for the presentation title.

Preview Finished Project

Tutorial

Using the Help Feature

Using the Help Feature

Microsoft PowerPoint includes a Help feature that contains information about PowerPoint features and commands. This on-screen reference manual is similar to Windows Help and the Help features in Word, Excel, and Access.

Quick Steps

Use the Help Feature

1. Press F1.
2. Click in search text box.
3. Type topic or feature name.
4. Press the Enter key.
5. Click article.

Display the PowerPoint Help window, shown in Figure 2.5, by pressing the F1 function key. In this window, click in the search text box, type a topic, feature name, or question, and then press the Enter key. Articles related to the search text display in the PowerPoint Help window. Click an article hyperlink and the article information displays in the window. If the article contains a Show All hyperlink, click this hyperlink to expand the article options to show additional related information. Click the Show All hyperlink and it becomes the Hide All hyperlink.

Getting Help on a Button

Position the mouse pointer on a button and a ScreenTip displays with information about the button. Some button ScreenTips display with a Help icon and the text *Tell me more*. Click this hyperlinked text or press the F1 function key and the PowerPoint Help window opens with information about the button feature.

Getting Help in a Dialog Box or Backstage Area

Some dialog boxes and the backstage area contain a help button. Click this button to display the PowerPoint Help window with specific information about the dialog box or backstage area. After reading and/or printing the information, close a dialog box by clicking the Close button in the upper right corner of the dialog box or close the backstage area by clicking the Back button or pressing the Esc key.

Figure 2.5 PowerPoint Help Window

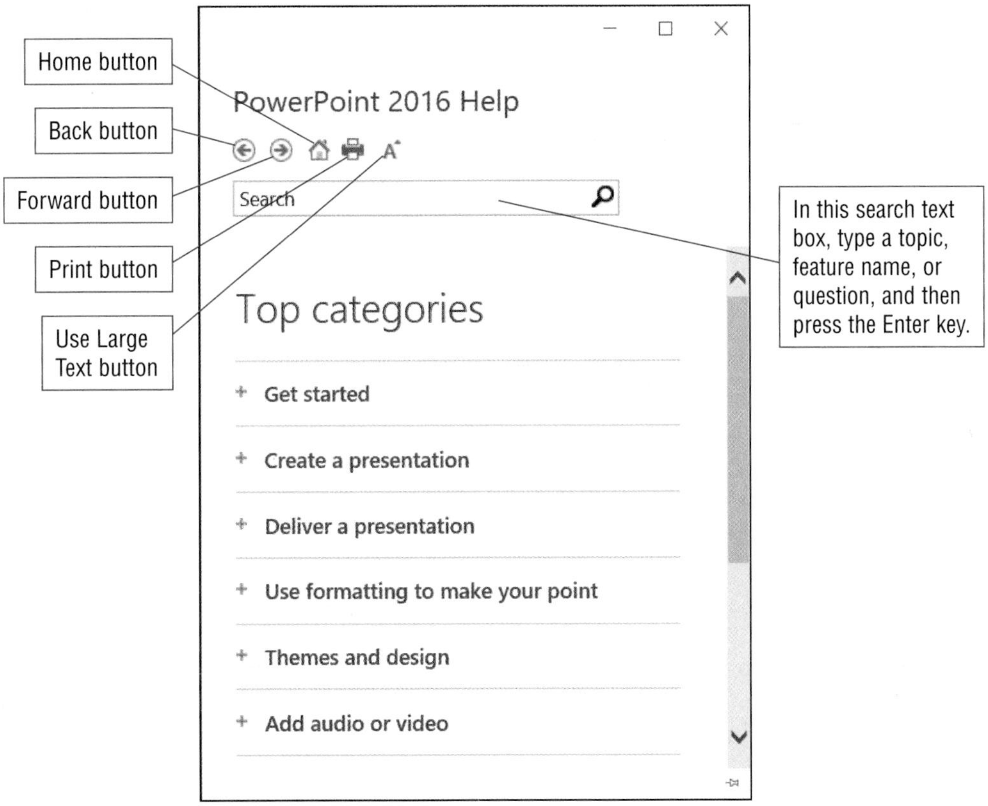

Project 4a Using the Help Feature and Creating a Presentation Part 1 of 2

1. At the blank PowerPoint screen, press Ctrl + N to display a blank presentation. (Ctrl + N is the keyboard shortcut to open a blank presentation.)
2. Press the F1 function key.
3. At the PowerPoint Help window, click in the search text box, type basic tasks for creating a presentation, and then press the Enter key.
4. When the list of articles displays, click the Basic tasks for creating a PowerPoint presentation hyperlink. (If your PowerPoint Help window does not display this hyperlink, click a similar hyperlink.)
5. Read the information in the article. (If you want a hard copy of the information, you can click the Print button above the search text box in the PowerPoint Help window and then click the Print button at the Print dialog box.)
6. Close the PowerPoint Help window by clicking the Close button in the upper right corner of the window.
7. Hover the mouse over the New Slide button in the Slides group on the Home tab and then click the Tell me more hyperlinked text at the bottom of the ScreenTip.
8. At the PowerPoint Help window, read the information on adding, rearranging, and deleting slides and then click the Close button in the upper right corner of the PowerPoint Help window.
9. Click the File tab and then click the *Open* option.
10. At the Open backstage area, click the Microsoft PowerPoint Help button in the upper right corner of the backstage area.
11. Read the information in the PowerPoint Help window.
12. Click in the search text box, type keyboard shortcuts, and then press the Enter key.
13. When the list of articles displays, click the Use keyboard shortcuts to create your presentation hyperlink.
14. Click the Common tasks in PowerPoint hyperlink.
15. Scroll down the *Common tasks in PowerPoint* section to the *Delete and copy text and objects* section. (This section displays a list of keyboard shortcuts for deleting and copying text and objects.)

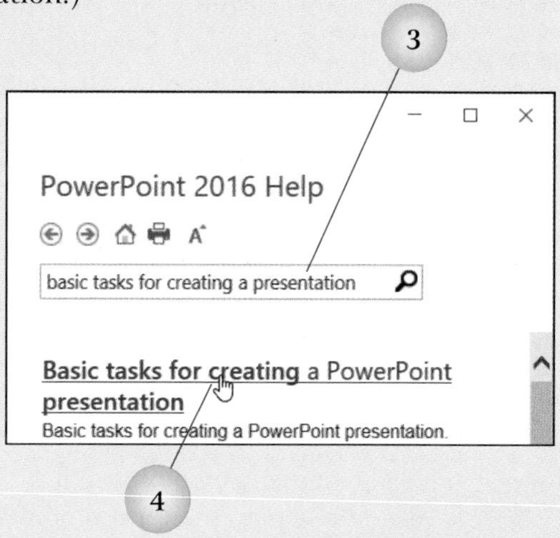

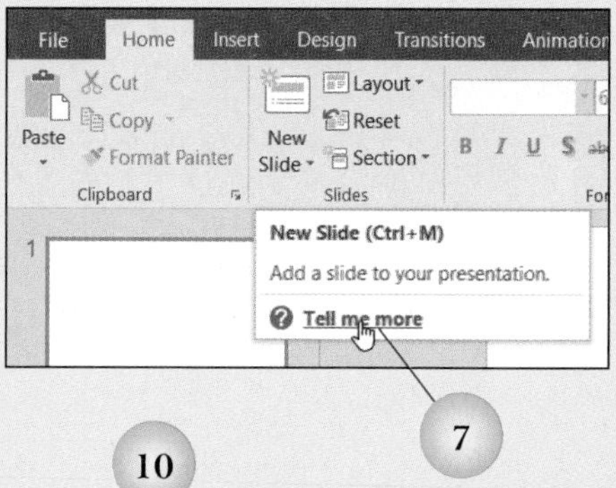

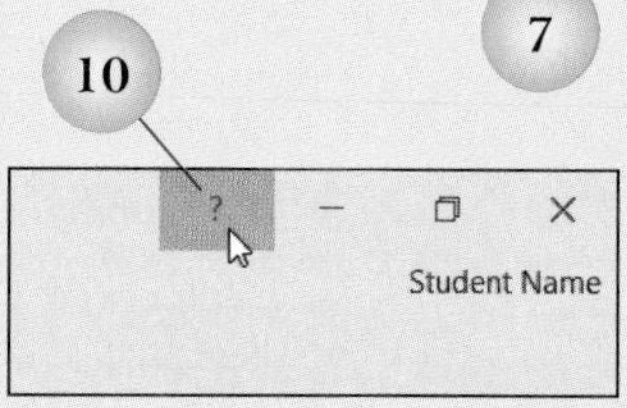

16. Select the list of keyboard shortcuts for deleting and copying text and objects by positioning the mouse pointer at the left side of the heading *To do this*, Click and hold down the left mouse button, drag down to the lower right corner of the list of keyboard shortcuts, and then release the mouse button.
17. With the information selected, click the Print button above the search text box in the PowerPoint Help window.
18. At the Print dialog box, click the *Selection* option in the *Page Range* section and then click the Print button.
19. Close the PowerPoint Help window.
20. Press the Esc key to return to the blank presentation.

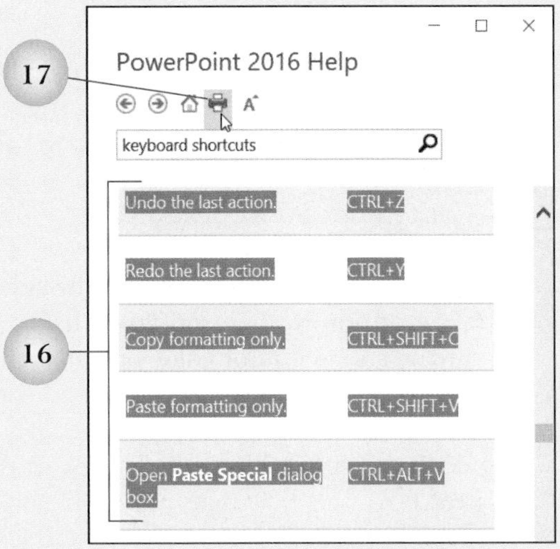

21. At the blank presentation, click in the title placeholder and then type PowerPoint Help.
22. Click in the subtitle placeholder and then type Keyboard Shortcuts.
23. Using the information you printed, create slides with the following information:
    - Slide 2: Type the text Delete Text as the title and then insert the four delete keyboard shortcuts as bulleted text. (For each keyboard shortcut, type the description followed by a colon and then the keyboard shortcut. For example, type Delete one character to the left: Backspace as the first bulleted item in the slide.)
    - Slide 3: Type the text Cut, Copy, Paste Text as the title and then insert the three cut, copy, and paste keyboard shortcuts as bulleted text.
    - Slide 4: Type the text Undo and Redo as the title and then insert the two undo and redo keyboard shortcuts as bulleted text.
    - Slide 5: Type the text Copy and Paste Formatting as the title and then insert the three copy and paste formatting keyboard shortcuts as bulleted text.
24. Apply the Facet design theme with the blue variant to the presentation.
25. Apply a transition and transition sound of your choosing to all slides in the presentation.
26. Save the presentation and name it **2-Shortcuts.pptx**.

Check Your Work

Tutorial

Using the Tell Me Feature

Using the Tell Me Feature

PowerPoint 2016 includes a Tell Me feature that provides information as well as guidance on how to complete a function. To use Tell Me, click in the *Tell Me* text box on the ribbon to the right of the View tab and then type the function. Type text in the *Tell Me* text box and a drop-down list displays with options that are refined as the text is typed, which is referred to as "word-wheeling." The drop-down list displays options for completing the function, displaying information on the function from sources on the web, or displaying information on the function in the PowerPoint help window.

The drop-down list also includes a Smart Lookup option. Clicking the Smart Lookup option will open the Smart Lookup task pane at the right side of the screen with information on the function from a variety of sources on the Internet. Smart Lookup can also be accessed with the Smart Lookup button in the Insights group on the Review tab or by selecting text, right-clicking the selected text, and then clicking *Smart Lookup* at the shortcut menu.

Project 4b **Using the Tell Me Feature** Part 2 of 2

1. With **2-Shortcuts.pptx** open, make Slide 1 active.
2. Select the title *PowerPoint Help* by triple-clicking in the title.
3. Use the Tell Me feature to change the font color and increase the font size for the title by completing the following steps:
   a. Click in the *Tell Me* text box.
   b. Type font color.
   c. Click the right arrow at the right side of the *Font Color* option in the drop-down list.
   d. At the side menu of color options, click the *Dark Blue* color option (ninth option in the *Standard Colors* section).
   e. With the title still selected, click in the *Tell Me* text box.
   f. Type font size.
   g. Click the *Increase Font Size* option at the drop-down list.
   h. Click in the slide to deselect the text.

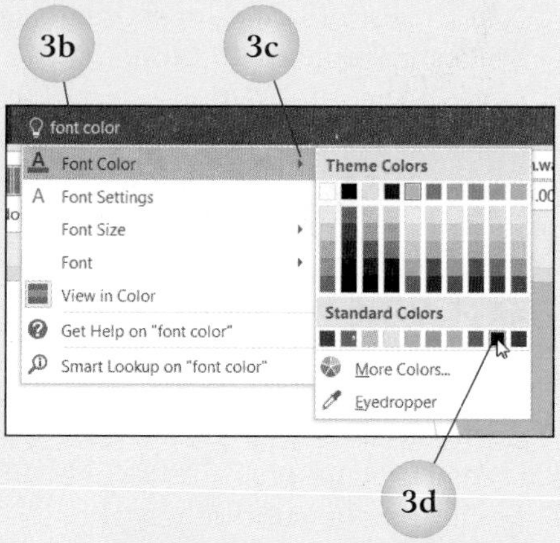

4. Use the Tell Me feature to display the PowerPoint Help window with information on the Quick Access Toolbar by completing the following steps:
   a. Click in the *Tell Me* text box.
   b. Type Quick Access Toolbar.
   c. Click the *Get Help on "Quick Access Toolbar"* option.
   d. At the PowerPoint help window, click the <u>Customize the Quick Access Toolbar</u> hyperlink.
   e. Look at the information in the article on customizing the Quick Access Toolbar and then close the PowerPoint help window by clicking the Close button in the upper right corner of the window.

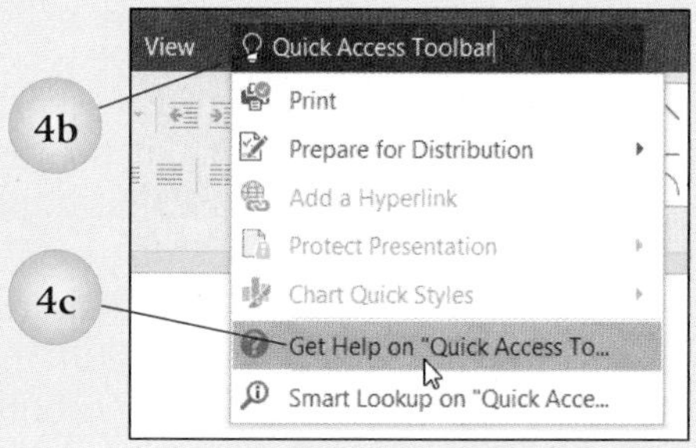

5. Display information in the Smart Lookup task pane on tips for preparing a presentation by completing the following steps:
   a. Click in the *Tell Me* text box.
   b. Type tips for preparing a presentation.
   c. Click the *Smart Lookup on "tips for preparing a presentation"* option (not all of the text is visible). The first time you use the Smart Lookup feature, the Smart Lookup task pane will display with a message indicating that data will be sent to Bing and suggesting that you read the privacy statement for more details. At this message, click the Got it button.
   d. Look at the information in the Smart Lookup task pane on tips for preparing a presentation.
   e. Close the Smart Lookup task pane by clicking the Close button in the upper right corner of the task pane.

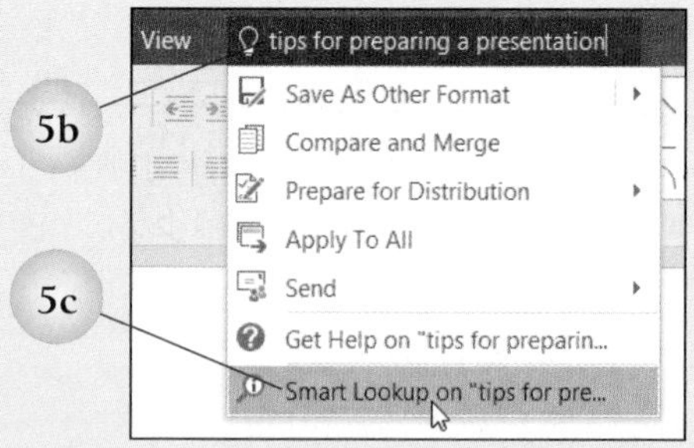

6. Print the presentation as a handout with six slides displayed horizontally per page.
7. Save and then close **2-Shortcuts.pptx**.

Check Your Work

Chapter Summary

- Use the spelling checker feature to check the spelling of the text in a presentation. Begin a spelling check by clicking the Review tab and then clicking the Spelling button in the Proofing group.
- Use the Thesaurus to find synonyms and antonyms for words in a presentation. Display synonyms in the Thesaurus task pane or by right-clicking a word and then pointing to *Synonyms* at the shortcut menu.
- Display the Find dialog box by clicking the Find button in the Editing group on the Home tab.
- Display the Replace dialog box by clicking the Replace button in the Editing group on the Home tab.
- Click in a placeholder to select that placeholder and position the insertion point inside the placeholder.
- Cut and paste or copy and paste text in slides using buttons in the Clipboard group or with options from the shortcut menu.
- Use the mouse to move text in the slide thumbnails pane by selecting and then dragging text to a new location. To copy text to a new location, press and hold down the Ctrl key while dragging.
- Use the sizing handles that display around a selected placeholder to increase or decrease the size of the placeholder. Use the mouse to drag a selected placeholder to a new location in the slide.
- Use the New Slide button on the Home tab or Insert tab to insert a slide in a presentation.
- Delete a selected slide by pressing the Delete key.
- Move or delete a selected slide in Normal view in the slide thumbnails pane or in Slide Sorter view.
- Copy a selected slide by pressing and holding down the Ctrl key while dragging the slide to the new location.
- Use the Copy and Paste buttons in the Clipboard group on the Home tab to copy a slide between presentations.
- Select adjacent slides in the slide thumbnails pane or in Slide Sorter view by clicking the first slide, pressing and holding down the Shift key, and then clicking the last slide. Select nonadjacent slides by pressing and holding down the Ctrl key while clicking each slide.
- Duplicate slides in a presentation by selecting the slides in the slide thumbnails pane, clicking the New Slide button arrow, and then clicking the *Duplicate Selected Slides* option or clicking the Copy button arrow and then clicking *Duplicate* at the drop-down list.
- Copy slides from a presentation into the open presentation with options at the Reuse Slides task pane. Display this task pane by clicking the New Slide button arrow and then clicking *Reuse Slides* at the drop-down list.
- Divide a presentation into sections to easily navigate and edit slides in a presentation.
- Customize the Quick Access Toolbar by clicking the Customize Quick Access Toolbar button at the right side of the toolbar and then clicking the button or option at the drop-down list. Buttons can be added to or deleted from the Quick Access Toolbar and the toolbar can be displayed below the ribbon.

- Press the F1 function key to display the PowerPoint Help window.
- Some dialog boxes and the backstage area contain a Help button that, when clicked, will display information specific to the dialog box or backstage area.
- Use the Tell Me feature to provide information and guidance on how to complete a function.

Commands Review

FEATURE	RIBBON TAB, GROUP	BUTTON,OPTION	KEYBOARD SHORTCUT
copy text or slide	Home, Clipboard		Ctrl + C
create section	Home, Slides		
cut text or slide	Home, Clipboard		Ctrl + X
duplicate slide	Home, Slides	, *Duplicate Selected Slides*	
Find dialog box	Home, Editing		Ctrl + F
paste text or slide	Home, Clipboard		Ctrl + V
PowerPoint Help window			F1
Replace dialog box	Home, Editing		Ctrl + H
Reuse Slides task pane	Home, Slides	, *Reuse Slides*	
spelling checker	Review, Proofing		F7
Tell Me feature	*Tell Me* text box		Alt + Q
Thesaurus task pane	Review, Proofing		Shift + F7

Workbook

Chapter study tools and assessment activities are available in the *Workbook* ebook. These resources are designed to help you further develop and demonstrate mastery of the skills learned in this chapter.

Microsoft®

PowerPoint®

CHAPTER 3

Formatting Slides

Performance Objectives

Upon successful completion of Chapter 3, you will be able to:

1. Apply font and paragraph formatting to text in slides
2. Apply formatting with the Mini toolbar and Format Painter
3. Replace fonts
4. Customize columns
5. Customize bullets and numbers
6. Customize placeholders
7. Change slide size and page setup
8. Modify design themes
9. Customize slide backgrounds
10. Create custom design themes including custom theme colors and theme fonts
11. Delete custom design themes

Precheck

Check your current skills to help focus your study.

The Font and Paragraph groups on the Home tab contain a number of buttons and options for formatting text in slides. PowerPoint also provides a Mini toolbar and the Format Painter feature to format text. The design theme colors and fonts provided by PowerPoint can be modified and custom design themes can be created. You will learn to use these features in this chapter along with how to change slide size and page setup options.

Data Files

Before beginning chapter work, copy the PC3 folder to your storage medium and then make PC3 the active folder.

SNAP

If you are a SNAP user, launch the Precheck and Tutorials from your Assignments page.

Project 1 **Format an E-Commerce Presentation** **6 Parts**

You will open an e-commerce presentation, apply font and paragraph formatting, apply formatting with Format Painter, apply column formatting to text in placeholders, and rotate text in placeholders.

Preview Finished Project

Formatting a Presentation

PowerPoint provides a variety of design themes that can be applied to a presentation. These themes contain formatting options such as font, color, and graphics effect. In some situations, the formatting provided by a theme is appropriate; in other situations, specific formatting can be applied to enhance the presentation.

Tutorial

Applying Font Formatting

Tutorial

Applying Font Formatting at the Font Dialog Box

Applying Font Formatting

The Font group on the Home tab contains a number of buttons and options for applying font formatting to text in a slide. Use these buttons and options to change the font, font size, and font color, as well as apply font effects. Table 3.1 describes the buttons and options in the Font group along with any keyboard shortcuts for applying font formatting.

Changing Fonts Design themes apply a certain font (or fonts) to text in slides. A different font or font size can be applied to text to change the mood of a presentation, enhance the visual appearance of slides, or increase the readability of the text. Change the font with the *Font* and *Font Size* option boxes in the Font group on the Home tab.

Select text and then click the *Font* option box arrow and a drop-down gallery displays with font options. Hover the mouse pointer over a font option and the selected text in the slide displays with the font applied. Continue hovering the mouse pointer over different font options to see how the selected text displays in the specified font. The *Font* option drop-down gallery is an example of the live preview feature, which displays text with different formatting before actually applying the formatting. The live preview feature is also available at the *Font Size* option drop-down gallery and the Font Color button drop-down gallery.

Hint Consider using a sans serif font for titles and headings and a serif font for body text.

Fonts may be decorative or plain and generally fall into one of two categories: serif fonts or sans serif fonts. A serif is a small line at the end of a character stroke. A serif font is easier to read and is generally used for large blocks of text. A sans serif font does not have serifs (*sans* is French for *without*). Sans serif fonts are generally used for titles and headings.

Hint Use options at the Font dialog box with the Character Spacing tab selected to increase or decrease spacing between characters and to apply kerning to text.

In addition to option boxes and buttons in the Font group on the Home tab, use options at the Font dialog box, shown in Figure 3.1, to apply character formatting to text. Display the Font dialog box by clicking the Font group dialog box launcher or with the keyboard shortcut Ctrl + Shift + F. (The dialog box launcher is the small button containing a diagonal arrow in the lower right corner of the group.) Use options at the Font dialog box to choose a font, font style, and font size and to apply special text effects in slides such as superscript, subscript, and double strikethrough.

Figure 3.1 Font Dialog Box

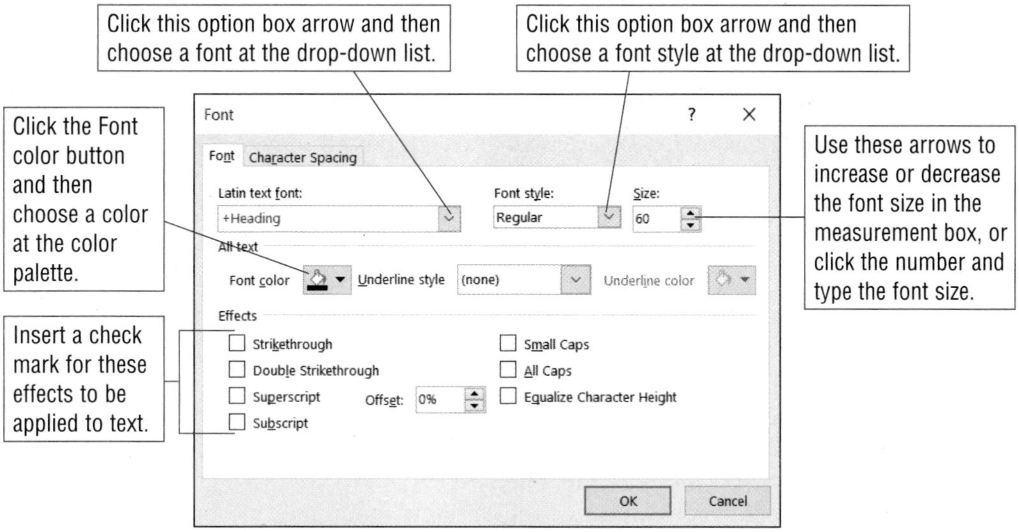

Click this option box arrow and then choose a font at the drop-down list.
Click this option box arrow and then choose a font style at the drop-down list.
Click the Font color button and then choose a color at the color palette.
Use these arrows to increase or decrease the font size in the measurement box, or click the number and type the font size.
Insert a check mark for these effects to be applied to text.
Font
Font
Character Spacing
Latin text font:
+Heading
Font style:
Regular
Size:
60
All text
Font color
Underline style
(none)
Underline color
Effects
Strikethrough
Double Strikethrough
Superscript
Offset:
0%
Subscript
Small Caps
All Caps
Equalize Character Height
OK
Cancel

Table 3.1 PowerPoint Home Tab Font Group Option Boxes and Buttons

Button/ Option Box	Name	Function	Keyboard Shortcut
B	Bold	Applies or removes bold formatting to or from selected text.	Ctrl + B
Aa	Change Case	Changes the case of selected text.	Shift + F3
AV	Character Spacing	Adjusts spacing between selected characters.	
A	Clear All Formatting	Clears all character formatting from selected text.	Ctrl + Spacebar
A	Decrease Font Size	Decreases font size of selected text to next smaller size.	Ctrl + Shift + <
Calibri Light (H	*Font*	Changes selected text to a different font.	
A	Font Color	Changes the font color for selected text.	
32	*Font Size*	Changes selected text to a different font size.	
A	Increase Font Size	Increases font size of selected text to next larger size.	Ctrl + Shift + >
I	Italic	Applies or removes italic formatting to or from selected text.	Ctrl + I
~~abc~~	Strikethrough	Inserts or removes a line through the middle of selected text.	
S	Text Shadow	Applies or removes shadow formatting to or from selected text.	
U	Underline	Applies or removes underline formatting to or from selected text.	Ctrl + U

Tutorial

Formatting with the Mini Toolbar

Formatting with the Mini Toolbar When text is selected, the Mini toolbar displays above the selected text. Click a button or option on the Mini toolbar to apply formatting to selected text. The option to display the Mini toolbar can be turned off. To do this, click the File tab and then click *Options*. At the PowerPoint Options dialog box with the *General* option selected in the left panel, click the *Show Mini Toolbar on selection* check box to remove the check mark.

Project 1a Applying Font Formatting to Text

Part 1 of 6

1. Open **EComm.pptx** and then save it with the name **3-EComm**.
2. Apply the Ion Boardroom design theme with the green variant by completing the following steps:
   a. Click the Design tab.
   b. Click the More Themes button at the right side of the themes gallery.
   c. Click the *Ion Boardroom* theme.
   d. Click the green color variant in the Variants group (second option).
3. Change the font formatting of the Slide 1 subtitle by completing the following steps:
   a. With Slide 1 active, click in the subtitle and then select *ONLINE SERVICES*.
   b. Click the Home tab.
   c. Click the *Font* option box arrow, scroll down the drop-down gallery, and then click *Cambria*.
   d. Click the *Font Size* option box arrow and then click *40* at the drop-down gallery.
   e. Click the Bold button in the Font group.
   f. Click the Text Shadow button.
   g. Click the Font Color button arrow and then click the *Dark Red, Accent 1, Darker 25%* option (fifth column, fifth row) in the *Theme Colors* section.

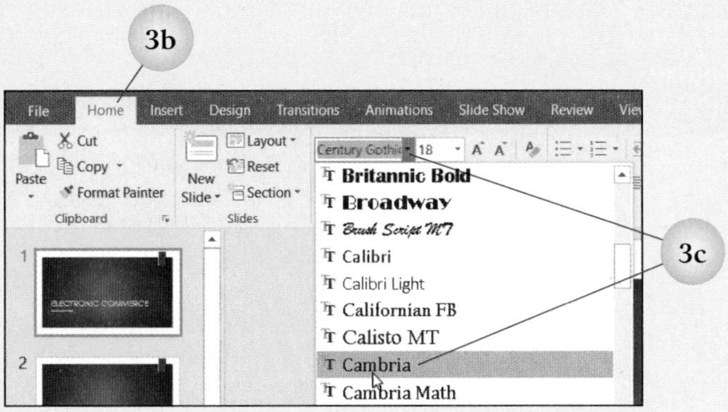

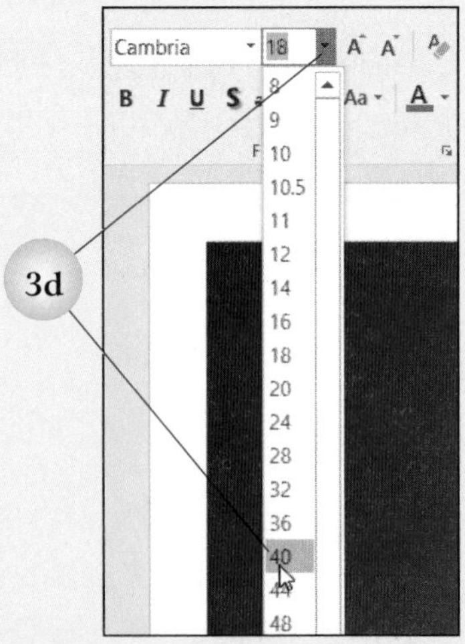

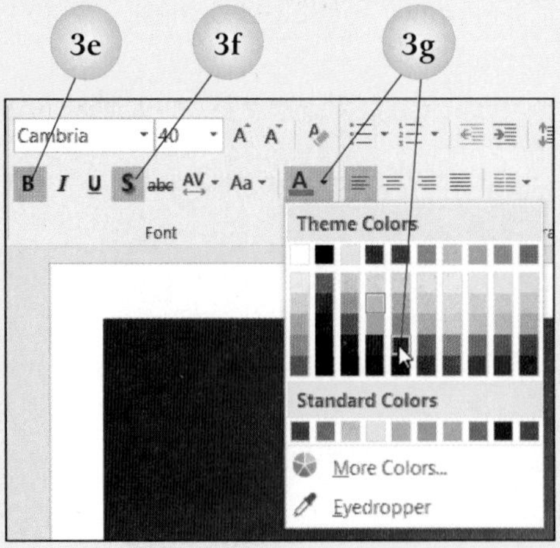

4. Change the size of the title text by completing the following steps:
   a. Click in the title *ELECTRONIC COMMERCE* and then click the placeholder border to change the border line to a solid line.
   b. Click the Decrease Font Size button in the Font group.
5. Change the case of the title text in Slide 2 by completing the following steps:
   a. Make Slide 2 active.
   b. Click in the title *ELECTRONIC COMMERCE* and then click the placeholder border to change the border line to a solid line.
   c. Click the Change Case button in the Font group and then click *Capitalize Each Word* at the drop-down list.

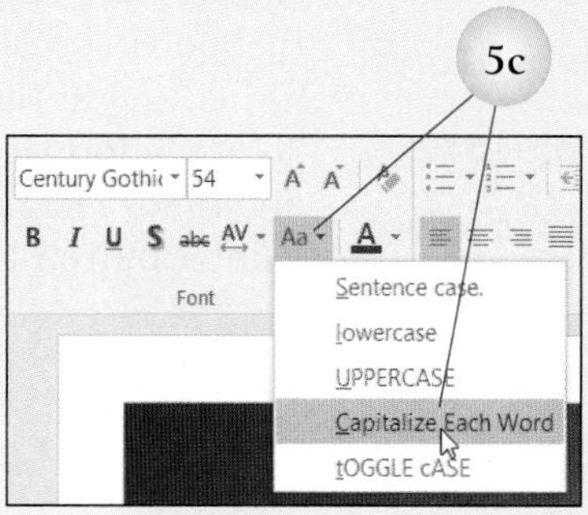

6. Apply and then clear formatting from text by completing the following steps:
   a. Make Slide 3 active.
   b. Click in the bulleted text.
   c. Select the text *m-commerce* (in parentheses).
   d. Click the Underline button in the Font group on the Home tab.
   e. Click the Bold button in the Font group.
   f. After applying underlining and bold formatting, remove the formatting by clicking the Clear All Formatting button in the Font group.
   g. With the text still selected, click the Italic button in the Font group on the Home tab.

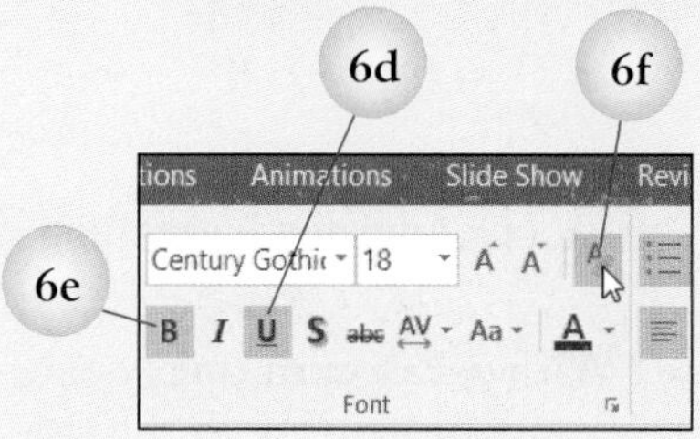

7. Apply italic formatting with the Mini toolbar by completing the following steps:
   a. Select *B2C* in the second bulleted item and then click the Italic button on the Mini toolbar.

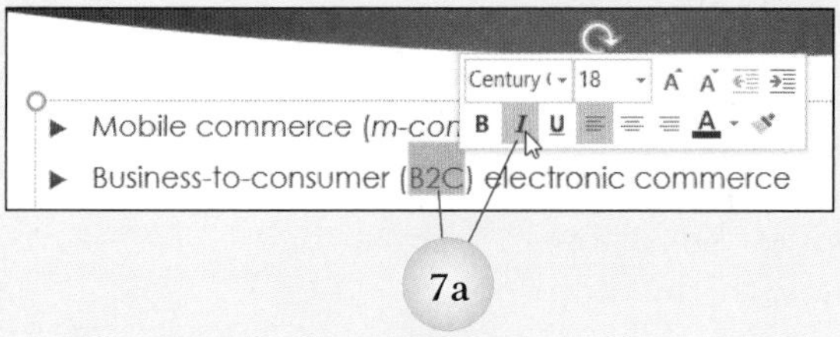

   b. Select *B2B* in the third bulleted item and then click the Italic button on the Mini toolbar.
8. Save **3-EComm.pptx**.

Check Your Work

Tutorial

Formatting with Format Painter

Format Painter

Quick Steps

Format with Format Painter

1. Click text containing formatting.
2. Double-click Format Painter button.
3. Select or click text.
4. Click Format Painter button.

Hint You can also turn off the Format Painter by pressing the Esc key.

Formatting with Format Painter

If character and/or paragraph formatting is applied to text in a slide and the same formatting should be applied to other text in the presentation, use Format Painter. With Format Painter, the same formatting can be applied in more than one location in a slide or slides. To use Format Painter, apply specific formatting to text, position the insertion point anywhere in the formatted text, and then double-click the Format Painter button in the Clipboard group on the Home tab. Using the mouse, select the additional text to apply the formatting. After applying the formatting in the new locations, click the Format Painter button to deactivate it. To apply formatting in only one other location, click the Format Painter button one time. The first time text is selected and the formatting is applied, the Format Painter button is deactivated.

Project 1b Applying Formatting with Format Painter

Part 2 of 6

1. With **3-EComm.pptx** open, make sure Slide 3 is active.
2. Apply formatting to the title by completing the following steps:
   a. Click in the title and then click the title placeholder border to change the border line to a solid line.
   b. Click the Font group dialog box launcher on the Home tab.
   c. At the Font dialog box, click the *Latin text font* option box arrow, scroll down the drop-down list, and then click *Candara*.
   d. Click the *Font style* option box arrow and then click *Bold Italic* at the drop-down list.
   e. Select the current measurement in the *Size* measurement box and then type 40.
   f. Click OK to close the dialog box.

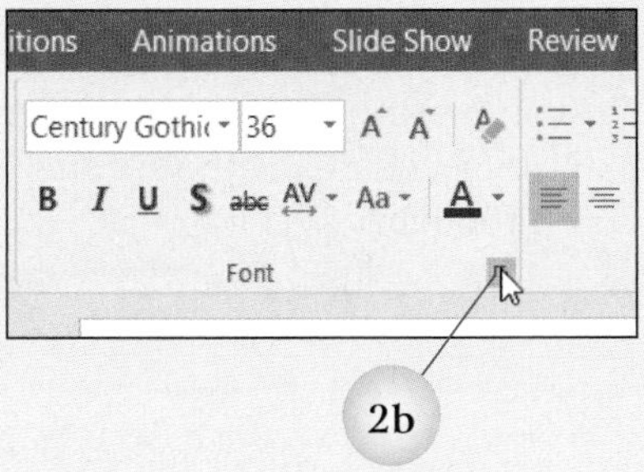

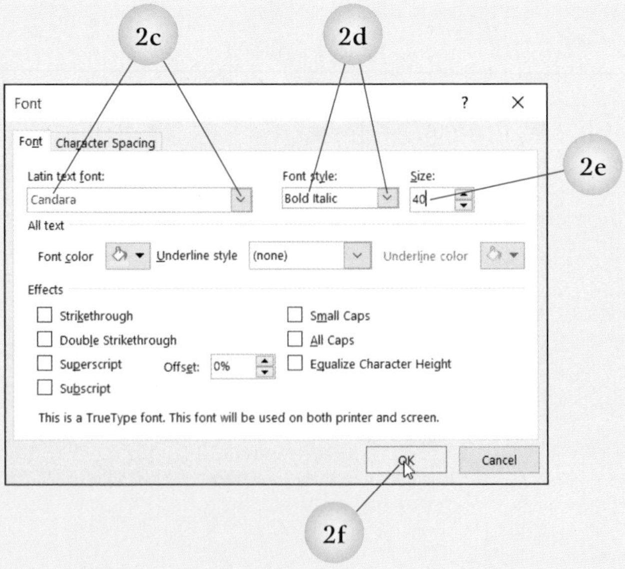

3. Click in the title.
4. Double-click the Format Painter button in the Clipboard group on the Home tab.

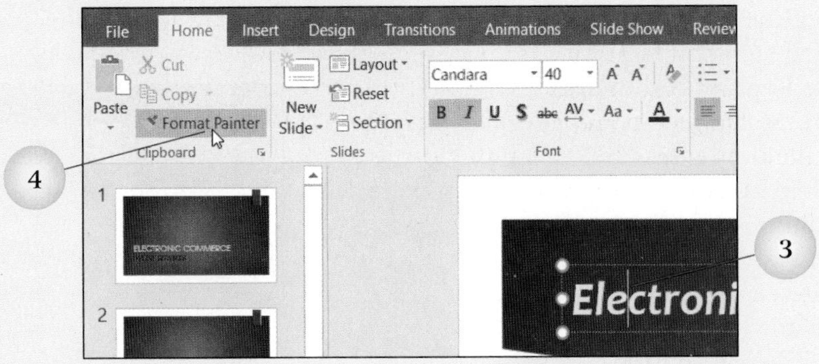

5. Make Slide 8 active.
6. Using the mouse, select the title *Advantages of Online Shopping*. (The mouse pointer displays as an I-beam with a paintbrush attached. Instead of selecting the whole title, you can also click each word in the title to apply the formatting. However, clicking individual words will not format the spaces between the words in multiple-word titles.)
7. Make Slide 9 active and then select the title.
8. Make Slide 10 active and then select the title.
9. Click the Format Painter button to deactivate it.
10. If necessary, deselect the text.
11. Save **3-EComm.pptx**.

Check Your Work

Tutorial

Replacing Fonts

Replace

Quick Steps

Replace Fonts

1. Click Replace button arrow.
2. Click *Replace Fonts*.
3. At Replace Font dialog box, make sure font displays in *Replace* text box.
4. Press Tab.
5. Click *With* option box arrow and click font.
6. Click Replace button.
7. Click Close button.

Replacing Fonts

Search for a specific font in the presentation and replace all occurrences of that font with a different font using options at the Replace Font dialog box. Display the Replace Font dialog box by clicking the Replace button arrow in the Editing group on the Home tab and then clicking the *Replace Fonts* option at the drop-down list. At the Replace Font dialog box, click the *Replace* option box arrow and then click a font to replace at the drop-down list. Click the *With* option box arrow and then click a font with which to replace the existing font at the drop-down list. Click the Replace button to replace all the fonts and then click the Close button to close the Replace Font dialog box.

Project 1c Replacing Fonts

Part 3 of 6

1. With **3-EComm.pptx** open, make Slide 1 active.
2. Replace the Century Gothic font with Candara in the entire presentation by completing the following steps:
   a. Click the Replace button arrow in the Editing group on the Home tab and then click *Replace Fonts* at the drop-down list.
   b. At the Replace Font dialog box, click the *Replace* option box arrow and then click *Century Gothic* at the drop-down list.
   c. Click the *With* option box arrow, scroll down the drop-down list, and then click *Candara*.
   d. Click the Replace button.
   e. Click the Close button.
3. Scroll through the slides to view the Candara font that has been applied to titles and bulleted text in each slide.
4. Save **3-EComm.pptx**.

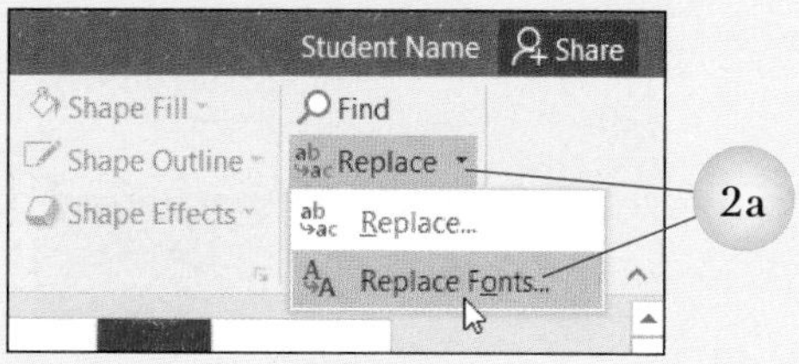

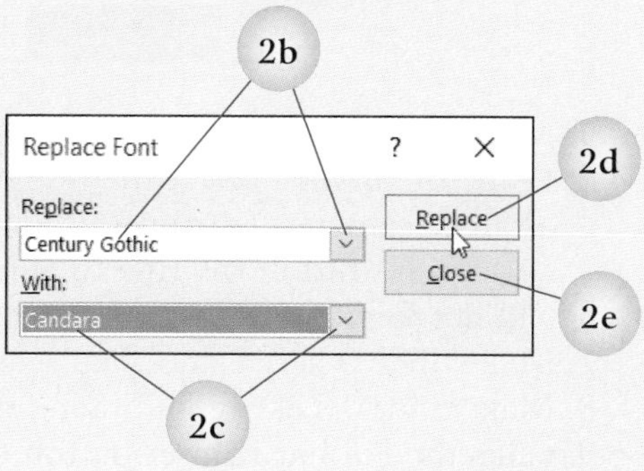

Check Your Work

Tutorial

Changing Alignment

Tutorial

Changing Line Spacing

AutoFit Options

Formatting Paragraphs

The Paragraph group on the Home tab contains a number of buttons for applying paragraph formatting to text in a slide, such as applying bullets and numbers, increasing and decreasing list levels, changing the horizontal and vertical alignment of text, changing line spacing, and rotating text in a placeholder. Table 3.2 describes the buttons in the Paragraph group along with any keyboard shortcuts.

Fitting Contents in a Placeholder

If text in a placeholder exceeds the size of the placeholder, use the AutoFit Options button to decrease the spacing between bulleted items or decrease the font size to ensure that all the text fits in the placeholder. The AutoFit Options button displays in the lower left corner of the placeholder when text no longer fits inside the placeholder. Click the AutoFit Options button to display a list of options such as *Autofit Text to Placeholder*, *Stop Fitting Text to This Placeholder*, *Split Between Two Slides*, *Continue on a New Slide*, *Change to Two Columns*, and *Control AutoCorrect Options*.

Tutorial

Creating and Customizing Columns

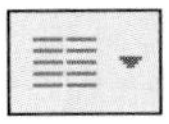
Add or Remove Columns

Hint Format text into columns to make it attractive and easy to read.

Creating and Customizing Columns

Click the Add or Remove Columns button in the Paragraph group to specify one-, two-, or three-column formatting for text. To format text into more than three columns or to control spacing between columns, click the *More Columns* option at the drop-down list. This displays the Columns dialog box, as shown in Figure 3.2. With options at this dialog box, specify the number of columns and the amount of spacing between them.

Figure 3.2 Columns Dialog Box

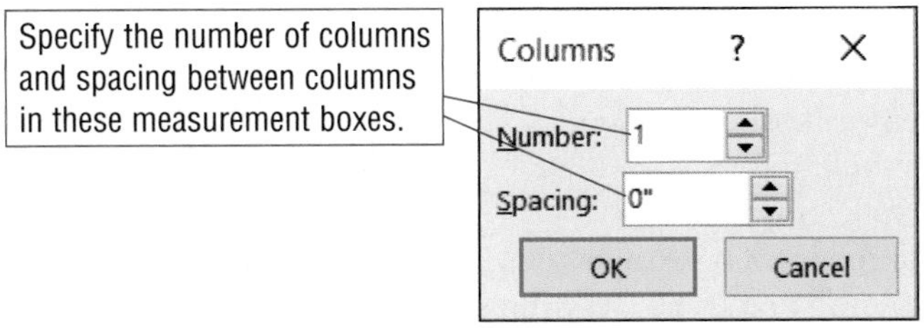

Table 3.2 Buttons in the Paragraph Group on the Home Tab

Button	Name	Function	Keyboard Shortcut
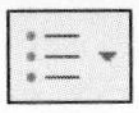	Bullets	Adds or removes bullets to or from selected text.	
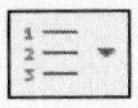	Numbering	Adds or removes numbers to or from selected text.	
	Decrease List Level	Moves text to the previous tab (level).	Shift + Tab
	Increase List Level	Moves text to the next tab (level).	Tab
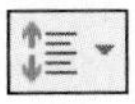	Line Spacing	Increases or reduces spacing between lines of text.	
	Align Left	Left-aligns text.	Ctrl + L
	Center	Center-aligns text.	Ctrl + E
	Align Right	Right-aligns text.	Ctrl + R
	Justify	Justifies text.	
	Add or Remove Columns	Splits text into two or more columns.	
	Text Direction	Rotates or stacks text.	
	Align Text	Changes the alignment of text within a text box.	
	Convert to SmartArt Graphic	Converts selected text to a SmartArt graphic.	

Project 1d Applying Paragraph Formatting to Text

1. With **3-EComm.pptx** open, change bullets by completing the following steps:
   a. Make Slide 3 active.
   b. Click in the bulleted text.
   c. Select the bulleted text.
   d. Click the Bullets button arrow in the Paragraph group on the Home tab and then click the *Filled Square Bullets* option at the drop-down gallery.

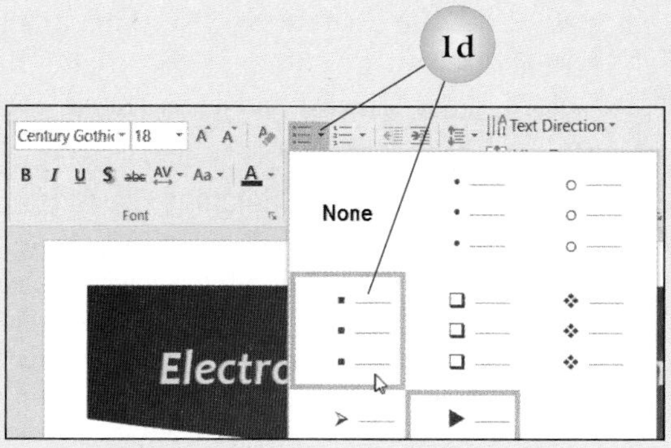

2. Change bullets to letters by completing the following steps:
   a. Make Slide 8 active.
   b. Click in the bulleted text.
   c. Select the bulleted text.
   d. Click the Numbering button arrow in the Paragraph group on the Home tab and then click the *A. B. C.* option at the drop-down gallery.

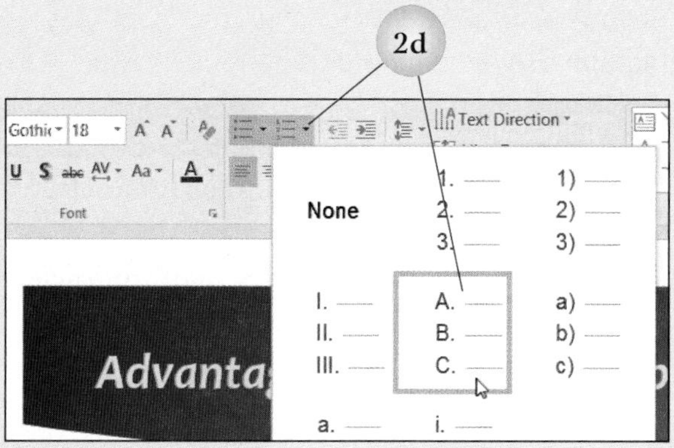

   e. With the lettered text selected, change to numbers by clicking the Numbering button arrow and then clicking the *1. 2. 3.* option at the drop-down gallery.
3. Decrease and increase list levels by completing the following steps:
   a. With Slide 8 active and the numbered text selected, click the Increase List Level button in the Paragraph group.
   b. With the text still selected, click the Font Color button arrow in the Font group on the Home tab and then click *Teal, Accent 5, Darker 50%* at the drop-down gallery (ninth column, last row in the *Theme Colors* section).
   c. Make Slide 10 active.
   d. Click in the bulleted text.

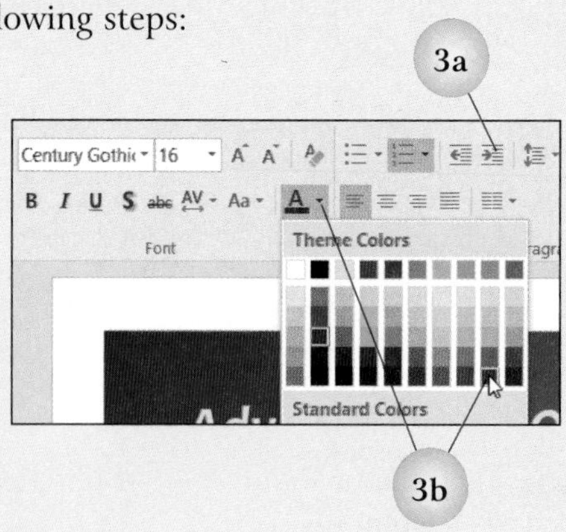

e. Move the insertion point so it is positioned immediately left of the *N* in *Nordstrom*.
f. Click the Decrease List Level button in the Paragraph group.
g. Move the insertion point so it is positioned immediately left of the *M* in *Macy's*.
h. Press Shift + Tab.
i. Move the insertion point so it is positioned immediately left of the first *L.* in *L.L. Bean.*
j. Click the Increase List Level button in the Paragraph group.
k. Move the insertion point so it is positioned immediately left of the *T* in *The Gap*.
l. Press the Tab key.
m. Use the Increase List Level button or Tab key to indent *Bloomingdale's, Expedia, Travelocity,* and *Orbitz* to the next level.

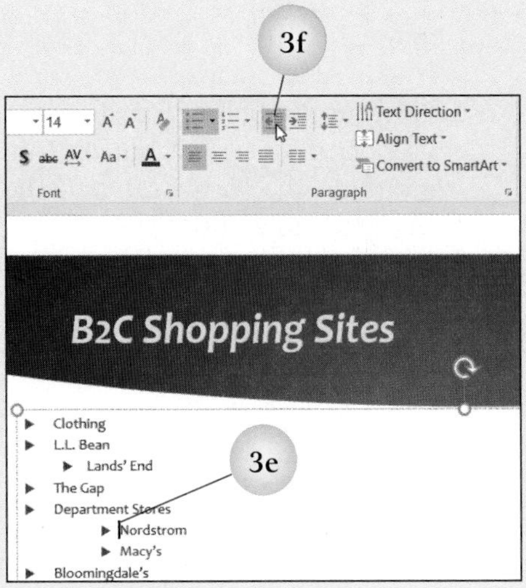

4. Increase the size of the text and make sure the content fits within the Slide 10 placeholder by completing the following steps:
   a. With Slide 10 active, select all the bulleted items and then change the font size to 16 points.
   b. Click in the bulleted text to deselect the text.
   c. Click the AutoFit Options button that displays in the lower left corner of the placeholder and then click *AutoFit Text to Placeholder* at the drop-down list. (This decreases the spacing between the bulleted items to ensure all items fit in the placeholder.)

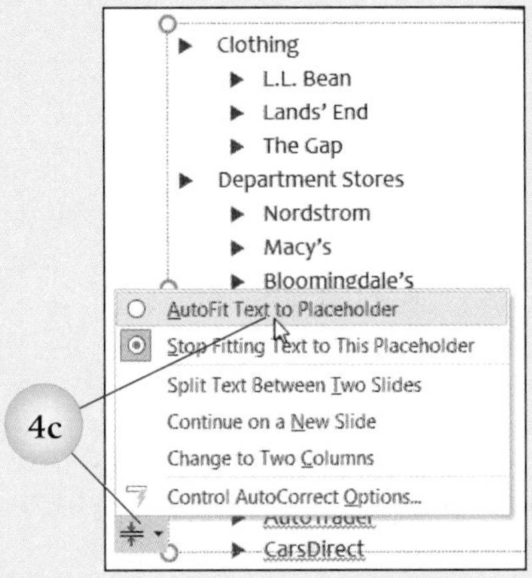

5. Change the line spacing of text by completing the following steps:
   a. Make Slide 3 active.
   b. Click in the bulleted text and then select the bulleted text.
   c. Click the Line Spacing button in the Paragraph group and then click *1.5* at the drop-down list.
   d. Make Slide 8 active.
   e. Click in the numbered text and then select the numbered text.
   f. Click the Line Spacing button and then click *2.0* at the drop-down list.

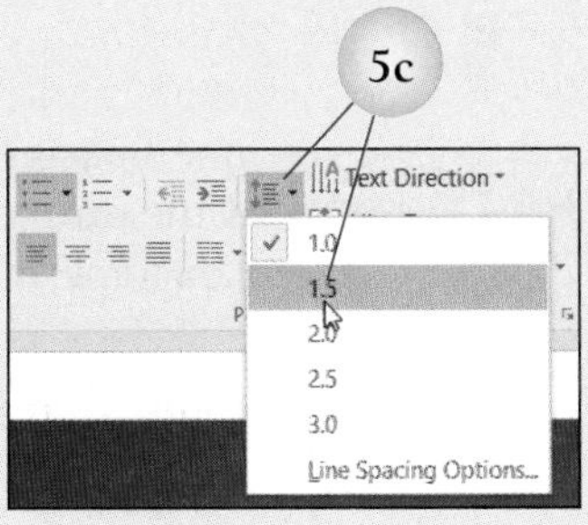

6. Change paragraph alignment by completing the following steps:
   a. Make Slide 3 active, click in the title, and then click the Center button in the Paragraph group.
   b. Make Slide 8 active, click in the title, and then click the Center button.
   c. Make Slide 9 active, click in the title, and then click the Center button.
   d. Make Slide 10 active, click in the title, and then click the Center button.

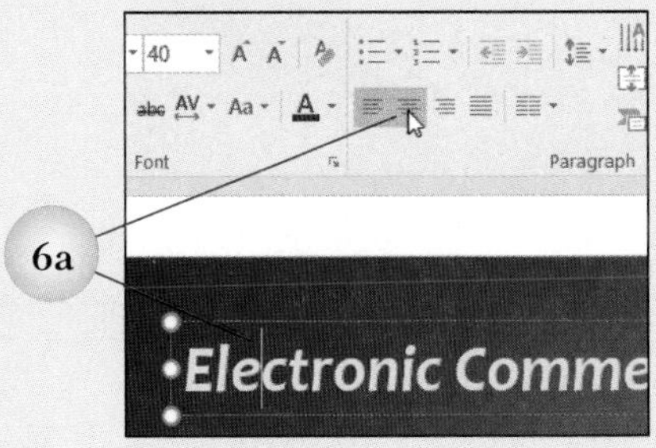

7. Change the vertical alignment of text by completing the following steps:
   a. Make Slide 3 active.
   b. Click in the bulleted text.
   c. Click the Align Text button in the Paragraph group on the Home tab and then click *Middle* at the drop-down list.

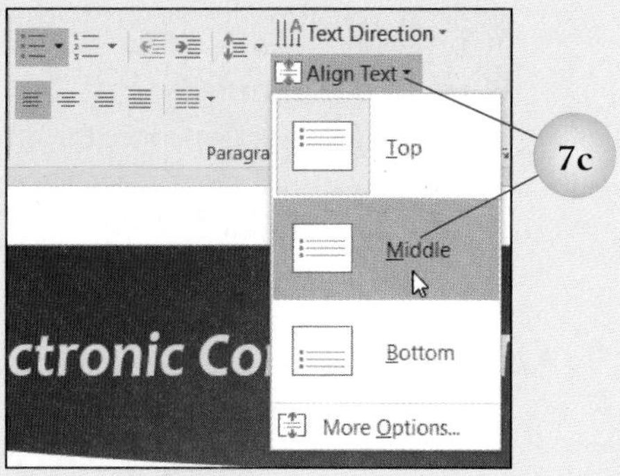

8. Split text into two columns by completing the following steps:
   a. Make Slide 9 active.
   b. Click in the bulleted text and then select the bulleted text.
   c. Click the Add or Remove Columns button in the Paragraph group and then click *Two Columns* at the drop-down list.
   d. Select the first sentence in the first bulleted paragraph (*Clear selling terms.*) and then click the Bold button.
   e. Select and then bold the first sentence in each of the remaining bulleted paragraphs in Slide 9.
   f. Drag the bottom border of the bulleted text placeholder up until two bulleted items display in each column.

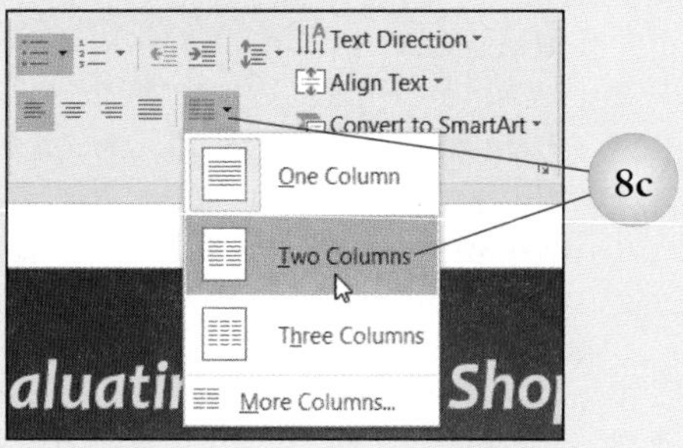

9. Save **3-EComm.pptx**.

Check Your Work

Tutorial

Changing Paragraph Spacing

Line Spacing

Customizing Paragraphs

Control paragraph alignment, indenting, and spacing with options at the Paragraph dialog box. Display the dialog box, shown in Figure 3.3, by clicking the Paragraph group dialog box launcher. The dialog box can also be displayed by clicking the Line Spacing button in the Paragraph group and then clicking *Line Spacing Options* at the drop-down list. Use options at this dialog box to specify text alignment, paragraph indentation, spacing before and after paragraphs, and line spacing.

Figure 3.3 Paragraph Dialog Box

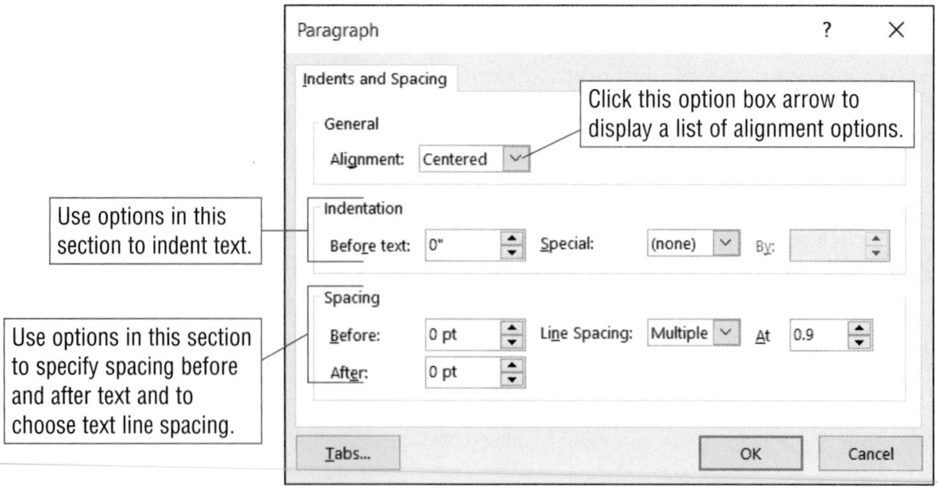

Project 1e Customizing Paragraph and Column Formatting

1. With **3-EComm.pptx** open, change line and paragraph spacing by completing the following steps:
   a. Make Slide 3 active.
   b. Click in the bulleted text and then select the text.
   c. Click the Paragraph group dialog box launcher.
   d. In the *Indentation* section at the Paragraph dialog box, click the *Before text* measurement box up arrow three times. (This inserts *0.6"* in the measurement box.)
   e. In the *Spacing* section, click the *After* measurement box up arrow two times. (This inserts *12 pt* in the box.)
   f. Click the *Line Spacing* option box arrow and then click *Multiple* at the drop-down list.
   g. Select the current measurement in the *At* measurement box and then type 1.8.
   h. Click OK.
2. Format text into columns by completing the following steps:

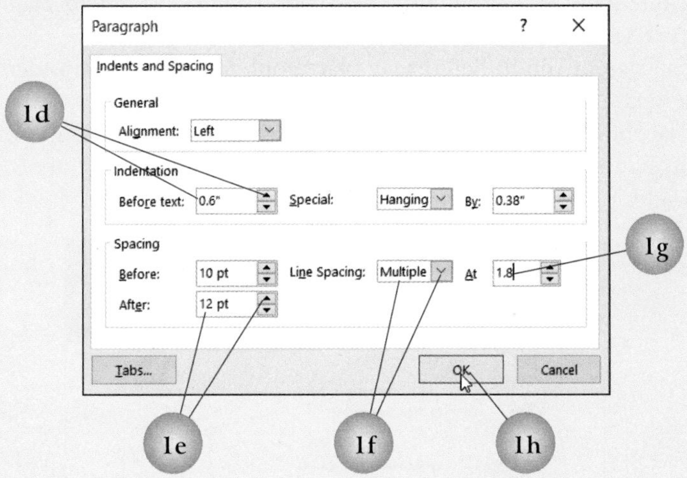

   a. Make Slide 10 active.
   b. Click in the bulleted text and then select the text.
   c. Click the Add or Remove Columns button in the Paragraph group and then click *More Columns* at the drop-down list.
   d. At the Columns dialog box, click the *Number* measurement box up arrow. (This inserts a *2* in the measurement box.)
   e. Click the *Spacing* measurement box up arrow until *0.5"* displays in the measurement box.
   f. Click OK.
   g. With the text still selected, click the Paragraph group dialog box launcher.
   h. In the *Spacing* section at the Paragraph dialog box, click the *After* measurement box up arrow three times. (This inserts *18 pt* in the measurement box.)
   i. Click OK.

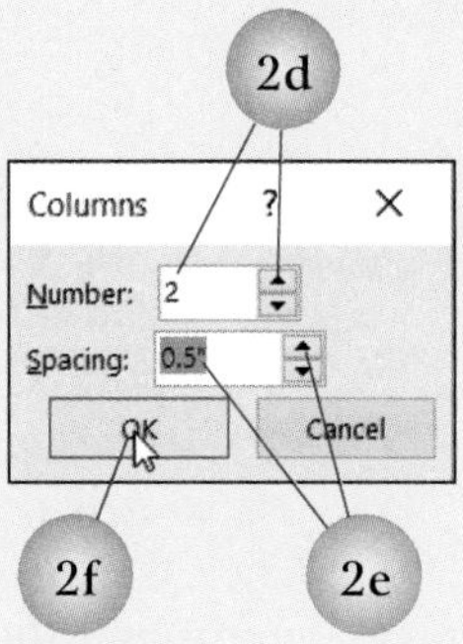

3. With the bulleted text selected, change the font size to 20 points.
4. Save **3-EComm.pptx**.

Check Your Work

Tutorial

Rotating Text

Text Direction

Rotating Text

To make specific text stand out or to enhance the appearance of text, consider rotating or stacking text by changing the text direction. For example, text can be rotated so that it displays vertically in the placeholder. Rotate text in a placeholder using the Text Direction button. Click the Text Direction button in the Paragraph group on the Home tab and then click an option at the drop-down gallery.

Project 1f **Rotating Text** Part 6 of 6

1. With **3-EComm.pptx** open, make Slide 8 active.
2. Modify the slide so it displays as shown in Figure 3.4 on page 81 by completing the following steps:
   a. Click in the numbered text and then select the text.
   b. Click the Bullets button arrow and then click the *Hollow Square Bullets* option.
   c. With the text selected, change the font size to 20 points.
   d. Decrease the size of the bulleted text placeholder so the placeholder borders display just outside the text.
   e. Drag the placeholder to the middle of the slide until the guideline (a vertical dashed line) displays and then release the mouse button. (Refer to Figure 3.4 for the position of the placeholder.)

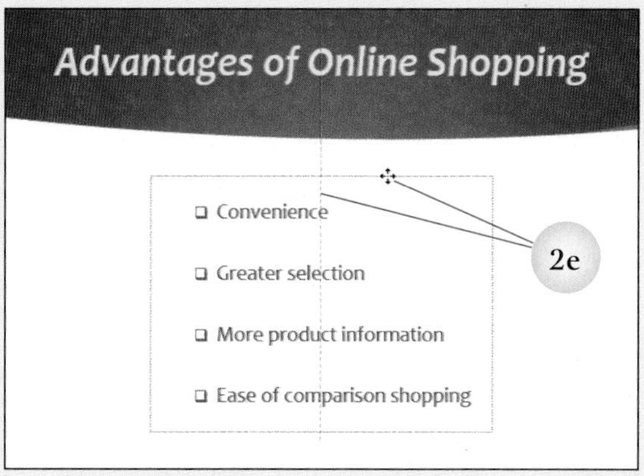

   f. Click in the title *Advantages of Online Shopping*.
   g. Delete the text *of Online Shopping*.
   h. Select *Advantages* and then change the font size to 54 points.
   i. Drag the right border of the placeholder to the left so it is positioned just outside the text.
   j. Click the Text Direction button in the Paragraph group and then click *Rotate all text 270°*.

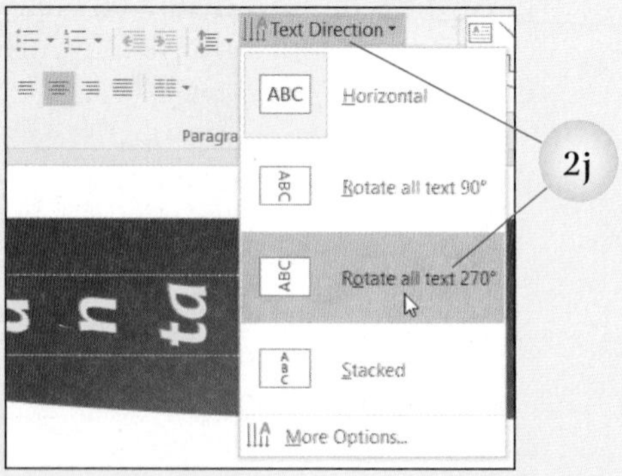

k. Using the sizing handles around the title placeholder, increase the height and decrease the width of the placeholder and then drag the placeholder so the title displays as shown in Figure 3.4. Use the horizontal guideline (a dashed line) to help you vertically center the placeholder on the slide.

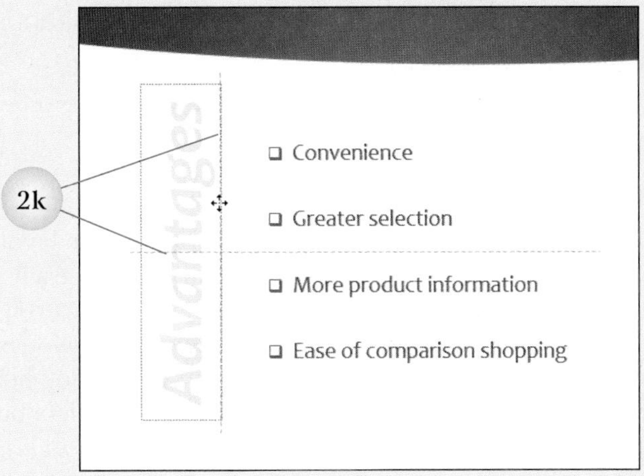

l. With the title placeholder selected, click the Font Color button arrow in the Font group and then click *Dark Red, Accent 1, Darker 25%* at the drop-down gallery (fifth column, fifth row in the *Theme Colors* section).

3. Apply a transition and transition sound to all slides in the presentation.
4. Print the presentation as a handout with six slides displayed horizontally per page.
5. Save and then close **3-EComm.pptx**.

Check Your Work

Figure 3.4 Project 1f, Slide 8

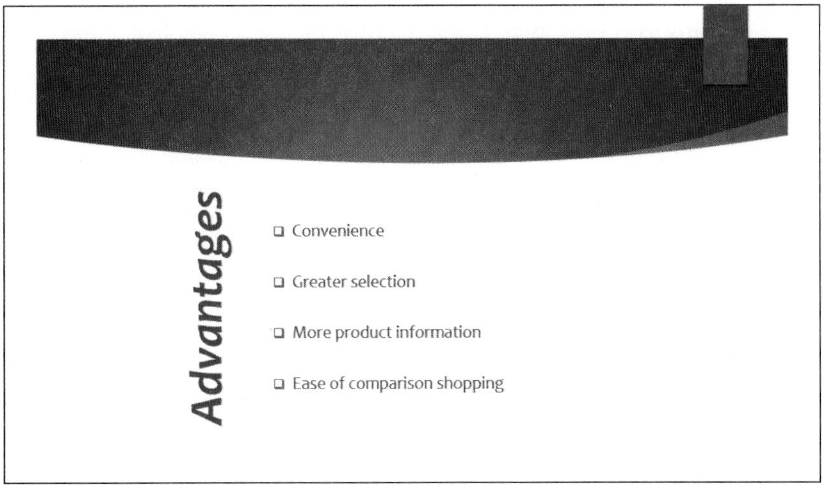

Project 2 Customize Bullets and Numbers, Change Slide Size, and Page Setup in a Color Presentation

4 Parts

You will open a presentation on using colors in publications, create and apply custom bullets and numbering, customize placeholders, change slide size, and change the page setup.

Preview Finished Project

Tutorial

Customizing Bullets

Bullets

Quick Steps

Customize Bullets

1. Click in bulleted text.
2. Click Bullets button arrow.
3. Click *Bullets and Numbering.*
4. Make changes.
5. Click OK.

Hint Choose a custom bullet that matches the theme or mood of the presentation.

Customizing Bullets

Each design theme contains a Title and Content slide layout with bullets. The appearance and formatting of the bullets vary within each design theme. Use the bullet style provided by the design theme or create custom bullets. Customize bullets with options at the Bullets and Numbering dialog box with the Bulleted tab selected, as shown in Figure 3.5. Display this dialog box by clicking in a placeholder containing bulleted text, clicking the Bullets button arrow in the Paragraph group on the Home tab, and then clicking *Bullets and Numbering* at the drop-down gallery.

At the Bullets and Numbering dialog box, choose one of the predesigned bullets from the list box, change the size of the bullets (measured by percentage in relation to the size of the text), change the bullet color, and/or specify an image or symbol to use as a bullet. Click the Picture button at the bottom of the dialog box and the Insert Pictures window displays. Click the Browse button to the right of the *From a file* option, navigate to the desired folder in the Insert Picture dialog box, and then double-click the image. Use the Bing Image Search text box to search for images online. Click the Customize button at the bottom of the Bullets and Numbering dialog box and the Symbol dialog box displays. Choose a symbol bullet option at the Symbol dialog box and then click OK. Image or symbol bullets are particularly effective for adding visual interest to a presentation.

To insert a new, blank bullet point in a bulleted list, press the Enter key. To move the insertion point down to the next line without inserting a new bullet, press Shift + Enter. A new bullet will be inserted the next time the Enter key is pressed.

Figure 3.5 Bullets and Numbering Dialog Box with Bulleted Tab Selected

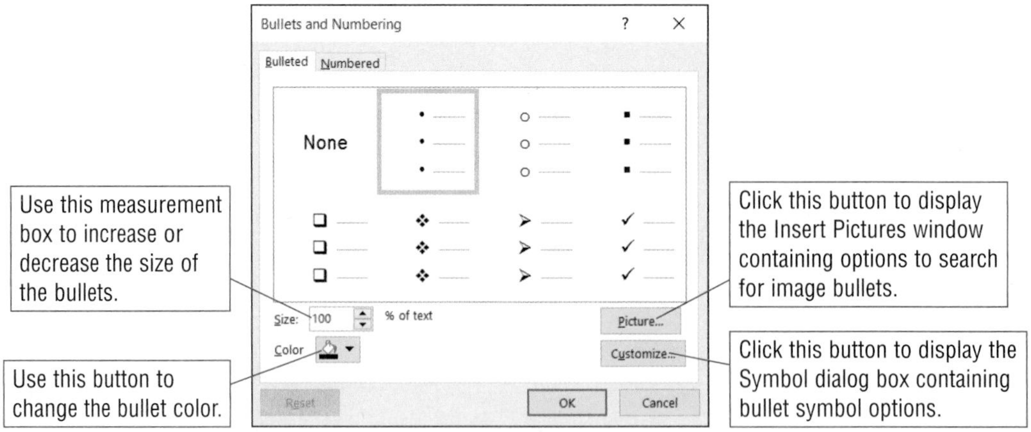

Project 2a **Customizing Bullets**

Part 1 of 4

1. Open **ColorPres.pptx** and then save it with the name **3-ColorPres**.
2. Increase the list level of text and create custom bullets by completing the following steps:
   a. Make Slide 2 active.
   b. Select the second, third, and fourth bulleted paragraphs.
   c. Click the Increase List Level button in the Paragraph group on the Home tab.
   d. With the three bulleted paragraphs still selected, click the Bullets button arrow and then click *Bullets and Numbering* at the drop-down list.
   e. At the Bullets and Numbering dialog box with the Bulleted tab selected, select the current number (*100*) in the *Size* measurement box and then type 75.
   f. Click the Picture button in the bottom right corner of the dialog box.
   g. At the Insert Pictures window, click the Browse button to the right of the *From a file* option.
   h. At the Insert Picture dialog box, navigate to the PC3 folder on your storage medium and then double-click ***Bullet.png***.

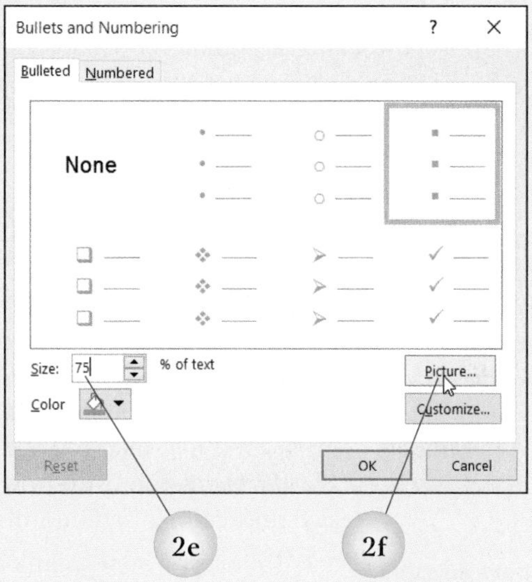

3. Insert symbol bullets by completing the following steps:
   a. Make Slide 3 active.
   b. Select all of the bulleted text.
   c. Click the Bullets button arrow and then click *Bullets and Numbering* at the drop-down list.
   d. At the Bullets and Numbering dialog box with the Bulleted tab selected, click the *Size* measurement box down arrow until *90* displays.
   e. Click the Customize button in the bottom right corner of the dialog box.
   f. At the Symbol dialog box, scroll down almost to the bottom of the list box and then click the infinity symbol in the eighth row from the bottom of the list box. (The location may vary.)
   g. Click OK.

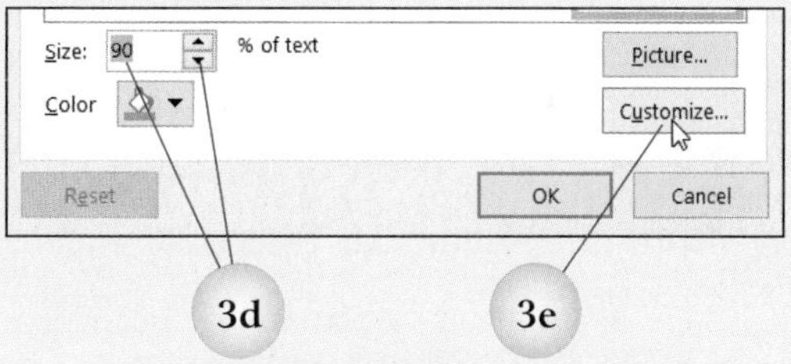

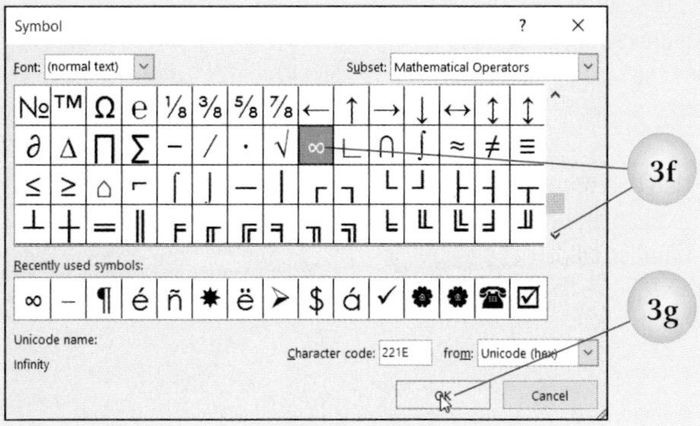

h. At the Bullets and Numbering dialog box, click the Color button and then click *Blue, Accent 5* (ninth column, first row in the *Theme Colors* section).
i. Click OK to close the Bullets and Numbering dialog box. (This applies the blue infinity symbol bullets to the selected text.)

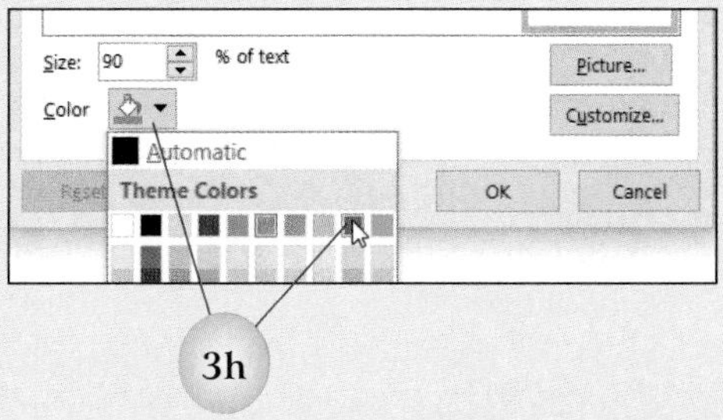

4. Increase the spacing between the bullets and the text by completing these steps:
   a. With the bulleted text selected, click the Paragraph group dialog box launcher.
   b. At the Paragraph dialog box, select the current measurement in the *By* measurement box (in the *Indentation* section), type 0.5, and then press the Enter key.
5. Save **3-ColorPres.pptx**.

Check Your Work

Tutorial

Customizing Numbers

 Numbering

Quick Steps

Customize Numbers

1. Click in numbered text.
2. Click Numbering button arrow.
3. Click *Bullets and Numbering*.
4. Make changes.
5. Click OK.

Customizing Numbers

Click the Numbering button arrow in the Paragraph group and several numbering options display in a drop-down gallery. Customize numbers with options at the Bullets and Numbering dialog box with the Numbered tab selected, as shown in Figure 3.6. Display this dialog box by clicking in a placeholder containing a numbered list, clicking the Numbering button arrow and then clicking *Bullets and Numbering* at the drop-down gallery. Use options at this dialog box to change the size and color of the numbers as well as the starting number.

To insert a new, blank numbered item in a numbered list, press the Enter key. To move the insertion point down to the next line without inserting the next number, press Shift + Enter. The next number will be inserted the next time the Enter key is pressed.

Figure 3.6 Bullets and Numbering Dialog Box with Numbered Tab Selected

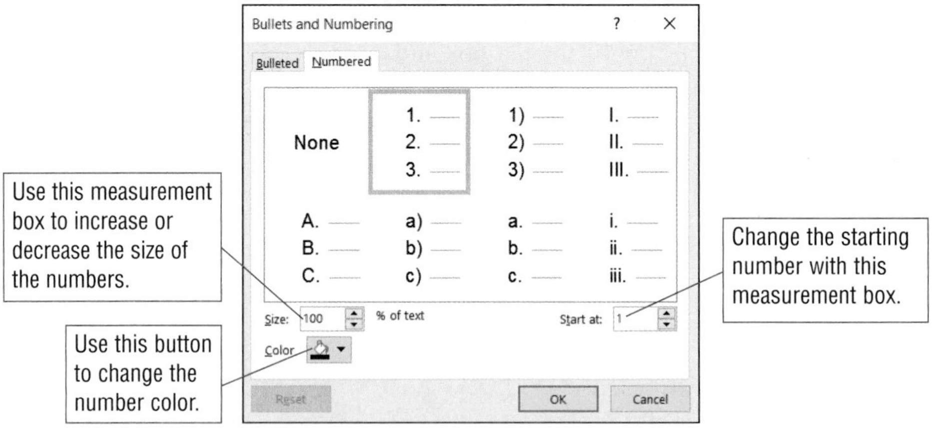

Project 2b Customizing Numbers

Part 2 of 4

1. With **3-ColorPres.pptx** open, create and insert custom numbers by completing the following steps:
   a. Make Slide 4 active.
   b. Select the bulleted text in the slide.
   c. Click the Numbering button arrow in the Paragraph group on the Home tab and then click the *Bullets and Numbering* option at the drop-down list.
   d. At the Bullets and Numbering dialog box with the Numbered tab selected, click the *1. 2. 3.* option (second column, first row).
   e. Select the measurement in the *Size* measurement box and then type 80.
   f. Click the Color button and then click *Blue, Accent 5* (ninth column, first row in the *Theme Colors* section).
   g. Click OK.

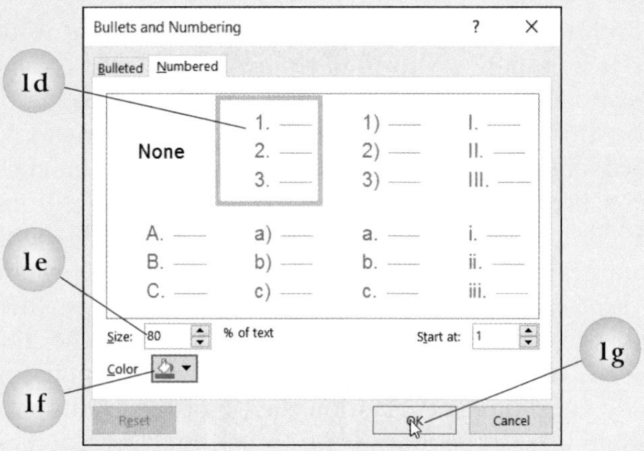

   h. Make Slide 5 active.
   i. Select the bulleted text in the slide.
   j. Click the Numbering button arrow and then click the *Bullets and Numbering* option at the drop-down list.
   k. At the Bullets and Numbering dialog box with the Numbered tab selected, click the *1. 2. 3.* option (second column, first row).
   l. Select the number in the *Size* measurement box and then type 80.
   m. Click the Color button and then click *Blue, Accent 5* (ninth column, first row in the *Theme Colors* section).
   n. Click the *Start at* measurement box up arrow until *6* displays.
   o. Click OK.

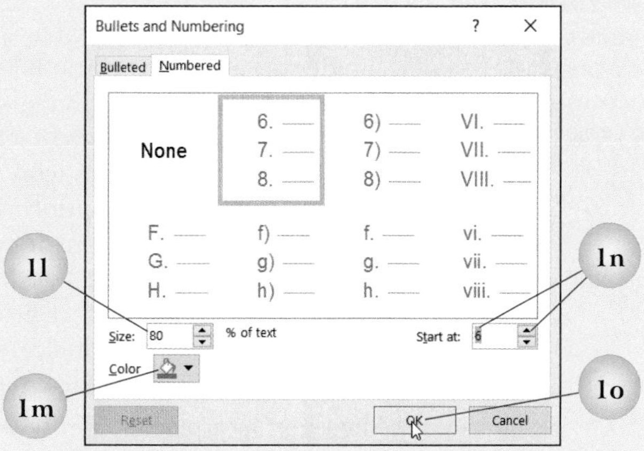

2. Add a transition and transition sound to all slides in the presentation.
3. Run the slide show.
4. Save **3-ColorPres.pptx**.

Check Your Work

Tutorial

Customizing Placeholders Using the Ribbon

Customizing Placeholders

Customize a placeholder in a slide with buttons in the Drawing group on the Home tab. Use options in the Drawing group to choose a shape, arrange the placeholder, apply a quick style, change the shape fill and outline colors, and apply a shape effect.

Quick Styles

Arrange

Shape Fill

Shape Outline

Shape Effects

Click the Quick Styles button in the Drawing group and a drop-down gallery of styles displays. Choose a quick style from this gallery or click the *Other Theme Fills* option to display a side menu with additional fills. Arrange, align, and rotate a placeholder with options at the Arrange button drop-down list. Use the Shape Fill button to apply a fill to a placeholder. Click the Shape Fill button arrow and a drop-down gallery displays with options for applying a color, picture, gradient, or texture to the placeholder. Use the Shape Outline button to apply an outline to a placeholder and specify the outline color, weight, and style. Use the Shape Effects button to choose from a variety of effects such as shadow, reflection, glow, and soft edges.

Hint You can also use options on the Drawing Tools Format tab to customize a placeholder.

Quick Steps

Apply Color with the Eyedropper

1. Click object.
2. Click Shape Fill button arrow.
3. Click *Eyedropper.*
4. Click color.

Both the Shape Fill and Shape Outline buttons in the Drawing group contain drop-down galleries with the *Eyedropper* option. Use the eyedropper to capture an exact color from one object and apply it to another object in the slide. To use the eyedropper to apply a fill color, click the object to which the fill color is to be applied, click the Shape Fill button arrow, and then click *Eyedropper* at the drop-down gallery. The mouse pointer displays as an eyedropper. Position the tip of the eyedropper on the desired color and then click the mouse button. The color clicked is applied to the selected object. Move the eyedropper and a live preview box displays above and right of the eyedropper. Use this live preview box to help choose the specific color. To pick a color outside the slide pane, press and hold down the Ctrl key, click and hold down the left mouse button, and then drag outside the slide pane. Position the tip of the eyedropper on the desired color and then release the mouse button and the Ctrl key. The *Eyedropper* option is also available with the Shape Outline and Font Color buttons on the Home tab as well as with buttons on other tabs that apply color.

Tutorial

Customizing Placeholders at the Format Shape Task Pane

Customizing Placeholders at the Format Shape Task Pane

With options in the Format Shape task pane, apply shape options to a placeholder or apply text options to the text within a placeholder. The Shape Options tab in the Format Shape task pane displays three icons: Fill & Line, Effects, and Size & Properties, each with different options for formatting a placeholder. After clicking an icon, the icon options may need to be expanded. For example, click the *Fill* option with the Fill & Line icon selected on the Shape Options tab to display options for applying a fill to a placeholder, as shown in Figure 3.7. The Text Options tab in the Format Shape task pane displays three icons: Text Fill & Outline, Text Effects, and Textbox, each with different options for formatting text within a placeholder. Display the Format Shape task pane by clicking the Drawing group task pane launcher on the Home tab.

Align text in a placeholder with options at the Format Shape task pane with the Size & Properties icon selected and options in the *Text Box* section displayed. (If necessary, click the *Text Box* option to expand the list.) Use options in the *Text Box* section to align text in a placeholder as well as change text direction, autofit contents, and change internal margins.

Figure 3.7 Format Shape Task Pane with Shape Options Tab Selected

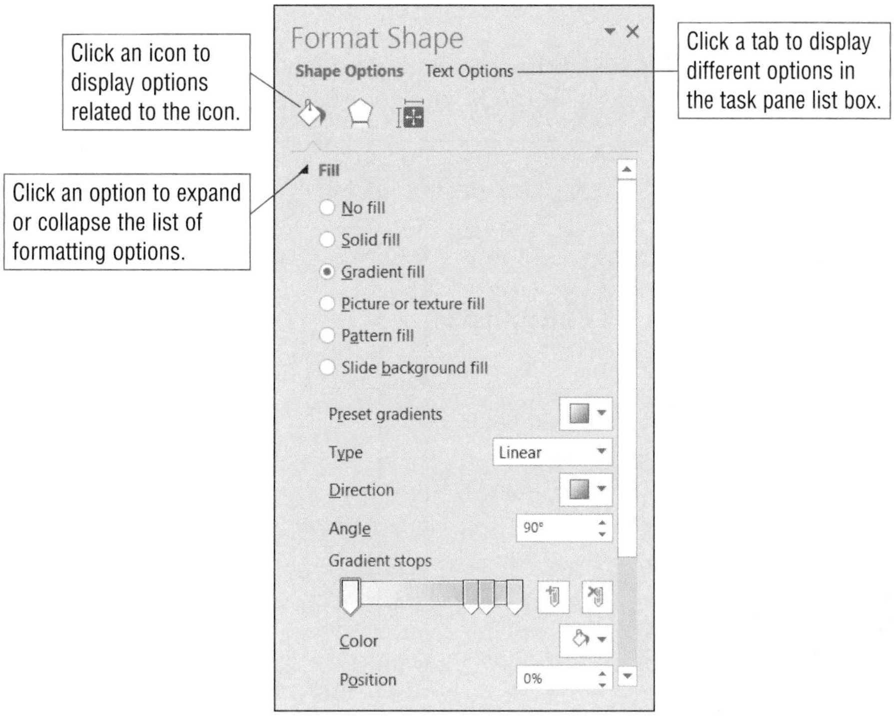

Text can be moved within a placeholder with the margin measurements in the Format Shape task pane. Display the margin measurements by clicking the Size & Properties icon and then scrolling down the task pane list box to the *Text Box* section. Use the *Left margin*, *Right margin*, *Top margin*, and *Bottom margin* measurement boxes to specify internal margins for text inside a placeholder.

Project 2c **Customizing Placeholders** Part 3 of 4

1. With **3-ColorPres.pptx** open, customize the title placeholder in Slide 1 by completing the following steps:
   a. If necessary, make Slide 1 active.
   b. Click in the title to make the title placeholder active.
   c. If necessary, click the Home tab.
   d. Click the Quick Styles button in the Drawing group.
   e. Click the *Subtle Effect - Gold, Accent 4* option at the drop-down gallery (fifth column, fourth row).
   f. Click the Shape Outline button arrow in the Drawing group and then click *Green, Accent 6* (last column, first row in the *Theme Colors* section).

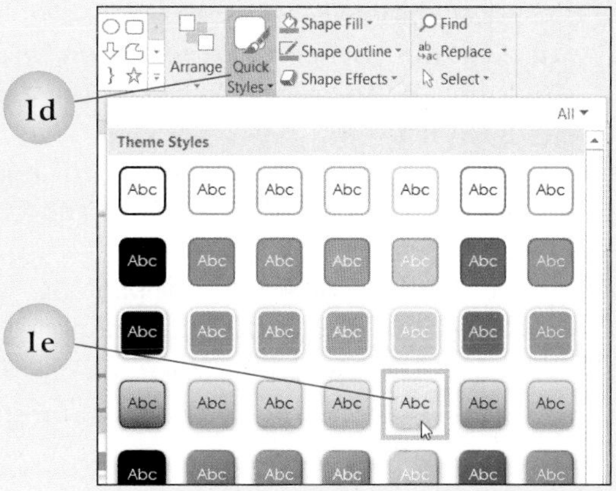

g. Click the Shape Outline button arrow, point to *Weight*, and then click *3 pt* at the side menu.

h. Click the Shape Effects button, point to *Bevel*, and then click *Cool Slant* at the side menu (fourth column, first row in the *Bevel* section).

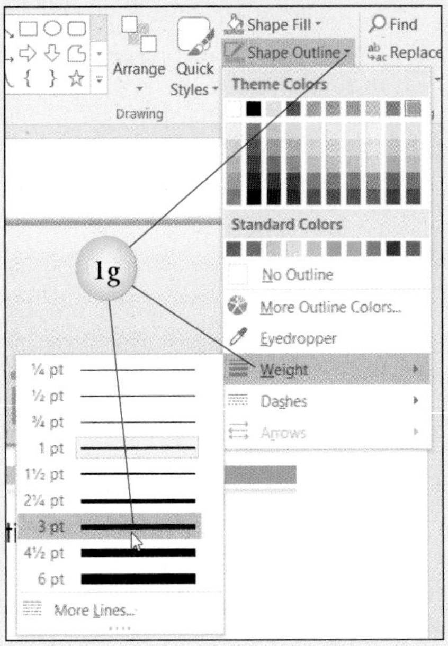

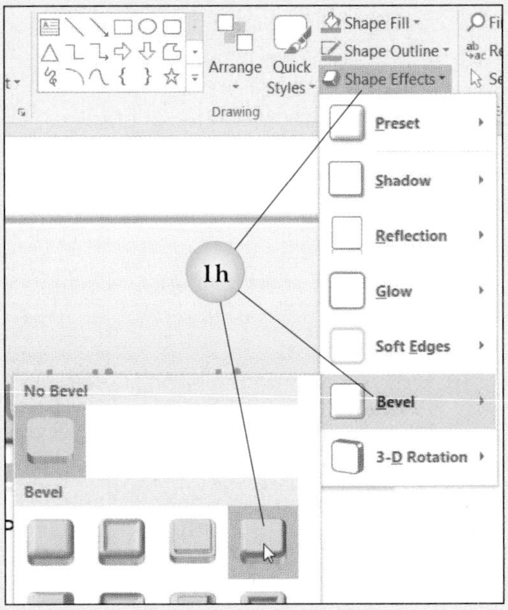

i. Change the fill color by clicking the Quick Styles button in the Drawing group, pointing to *Other Theme Fills* at the bottom of the drop-down gallery, and then clicking *Style 9* at the side menu (first column, third row).

2. Change the alignment of the text within the placeholder by completing the following steps:
   a. With the title placeholder active, click the Drawing group task pane launcher.
   b. At the Format Shape task pane, make sure the Shape Options tab is selected, and then click the Size & Properties icon.
   c. Click the *Text Box* option to display the list of options.
   d. Click the *Vertical alignment* option box arrow and then click *Middle* at the drop-down list.
   e. Click the *Top margin* measurement box up arrow until *0.3″* displays in the measurement box.
3. Close the Format Shape task pane by clicking the Close button in the upper right corner of the task pane.

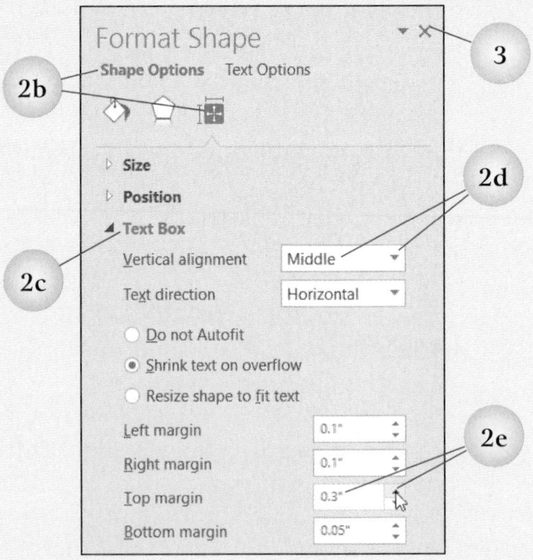

4. Customize the subtitle placeholder by completing the following steps:
   a. Click in the subtitle text to make the subtitle placeholder active.
   b. Click the Shape Fill button arrow in the Drawing group, point to *Texture*, and then click *Blue tissue paper* at the drop-down gallery (first column, fifth row).
   c. Click the Shape Effects button, point to *Bevel*, and then click *Cool Slant* at the side menu (fourth column, first row in the *Bevel* section).

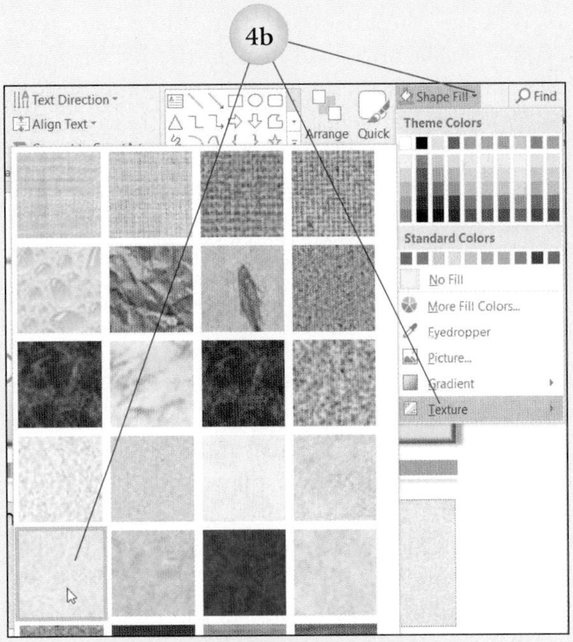

5. You decide the texture fill does not match the theme of the presentation. Change the subtitle placeholder fill by completing the following steps:
   a. With the subtitle placeholder active, click the Drawing group task pane launcher.
   b. At the Format Shape task pane, make sure the Shape Options tab is selected, click the Fill & Line icon, and then click the *Fill* option to display the list of options.
   c. Click *Gradient fill*.
   d. Click the Preset gradients button and then click *Light Gradient, Accent 6* (sixth column, first row).

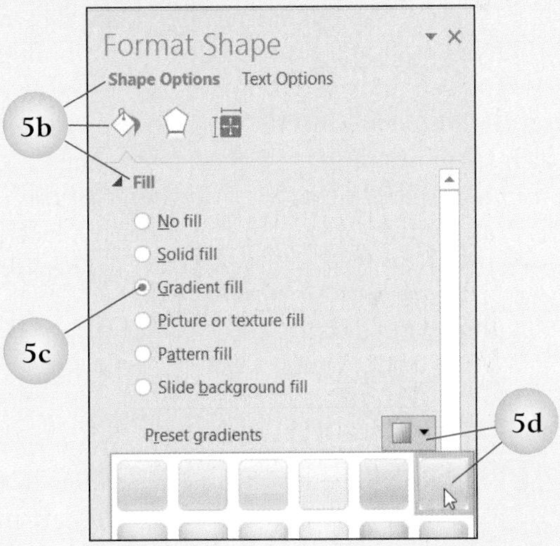

6. At the Format Shape task pane, click the Size & Properties icon, make sure the options in the *Text Box* section are displayed, click the *Vertical alignment* option box arrow, and then click *Middle* at the drop-down list.
7. Make Slide 3 active and then change the spacing after paragraphs by completing the following steps:
   a. Select the bulleted text.
   b. Click the Paragraph group dialog box launcher.
   c. In the *Spacing* section at the Paragraph dialog box, click the *After* measurement box up arrow two times to display *12 pt* in the measurement box.
   d. Click OK to close the dialog box.

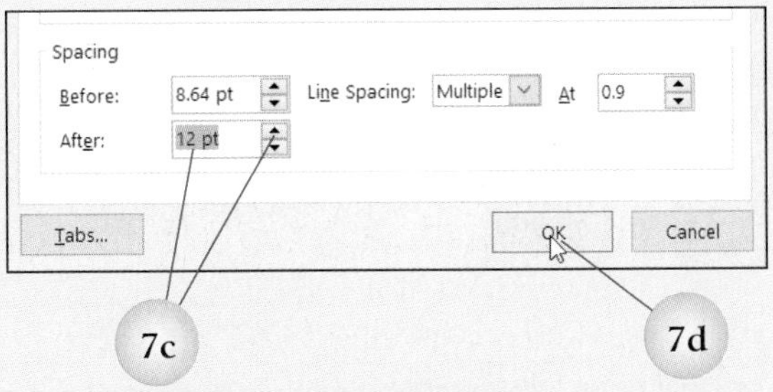

8. Customize and arrange the placeholder by completing the following steps:
   a. With the bulleted text placeholder selected and the Format Shape task pane open, click the Fill & Line icon, make sure the options in the *Fill* section are displayed, and then click *Solid fill*.
   b. Click the Color button and then click *Blue, Accent 5, Lighter 80%* (ninth column, second row in the *Theme Colors* section).

c. Click the Effects icon and then click the *Shadow* option to display the list of options.
d. Click the Presets button and then click *Offset Diagonal Bottom Right* (first column, first row in *Outer* section).
e. Click the Color button and then click *Blue, Accent 5, Darker 50%* (ninth column, bottom row in *Theme Colors* section).
f. Click the *Distance* measurement box up arrow until *15 pt* displays.
g. Click the Size & Properties icon.
h. Click the *Size* option to display the list of options.
i. Click the *Height* measurement box down arrow until *2.8″* displays in the measurement box.

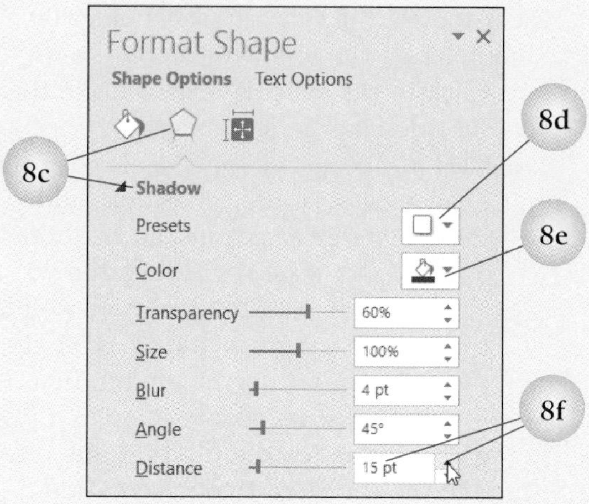

j. Scroll down the task pane and, if necessary, click the *Text Box* option to display the list of options.
k. Change the left and top margin measurements to 0.2 inches.
l. Click the Arrange button in the Drawing group on the Home tab, point to *Align* in the drop-down list, and then click *Distribute Vertically* at the side menu.

9. Make Slide 2 active, click in the bulleted text, and then customize and arrange the placeholder by completing the steps in Step 8. Change the height of the placeholder in Slide 2 to 3 inches.
10. Close the Format Shape task pane.
11. Make Slide 1 active and then use the eyedropper to apply fill color from the subtitle placeholder to the title placeholder by completing the following steps:
    a. Click in the title placeholder.
    b. Click the Shape Fill button arrow in the Drawing group on the Home tab, and then click the *Eyedropper* option at the drop-down gallery.
    c. Position the tip of the eyedropper on the green color above the word *Publications* in the subtitle placeholder and then click the left mouse button.
12. Run the slide show.
13. Print the presentation as a handout with six slides displayed horizontally per page.
14. Save **3-ColorPres.pptx**.

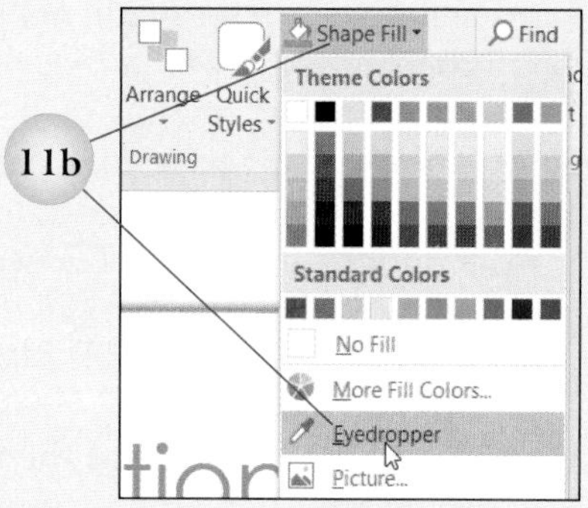

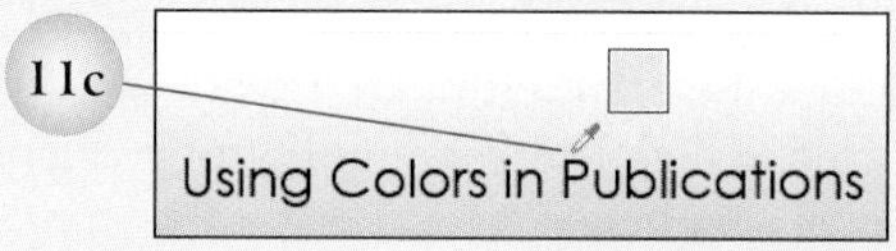

Check Your Work

Tutorial

Changing Slide Size

Slide Size

Changing Slide Size and Page Setup

Control the page setup and the size and orientation of slides using options in the Slide Size dialog box, as shown in Figure 3.8. Display the Slide Size dialog box by clicking the Slide Size button in the Customize group on the Design tab and then clicking *Custom Slide Size* at the drop-down list. With options in the dialog box, change the slide orientation, specify how slides are sized, change the slide size ratio, and change the starting slide number. By default, slides are sized for an on-screen show with a widescreen 16:9 ratio. If a widescreen size (16:9) presentation is changed to a standard size (4:3) presentation, the slide content will need to be maximized or scaled down to fit in the new slide size. Click the *Slides sized for* option box arrow and a drop-down list displays with options for changing the slide size ratio and choosing other paper sizes. The Slide Size dialog box also contains options for changing the orientation of notes, handouts, and outline pages.

Figure 3.8 Slide Size Dialog Box

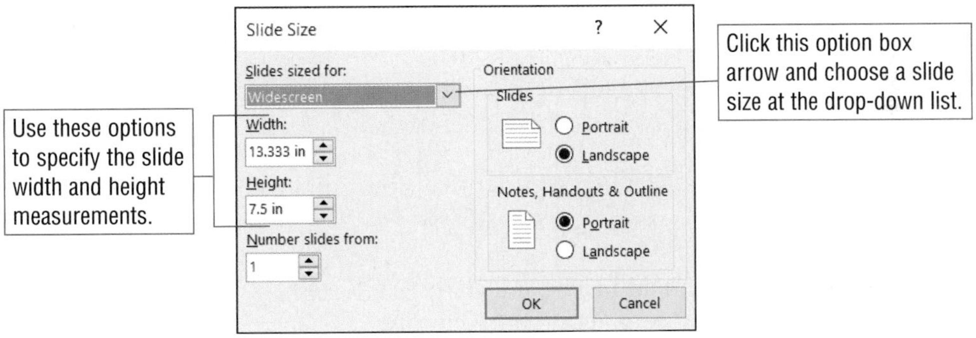

Project 2d **Changing Slide Orientation and Page Setup** Part 4 of 4

1. With **3-ColorPres.pptx** open, change the slide size by completing the following steps:
   a. Click the Design tab.
   b. Click the Slide Size button in the Customize group and then click *Standard (4:3)* at the drop-down list.

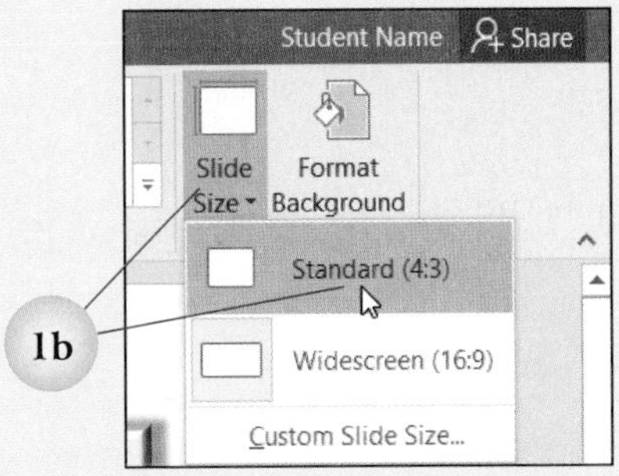

   c. At the Microsoft PowerPoint dialog box, click the Ensure Fit button.
2. Run the slide show to view how the slides appear in the standard size.

3. Change the slide orientation by completing the following steps:
   a. Click the Slide Size button in the Customize group and then click *Custom Slide Size* at the drop-down list.
   b. At the Slide Size dialog box, click the *Portrait* option in the *Slides* section, and then click OK.
   c. Click the Ensure Fit button at the Microsoft PowerPoint dialog box.

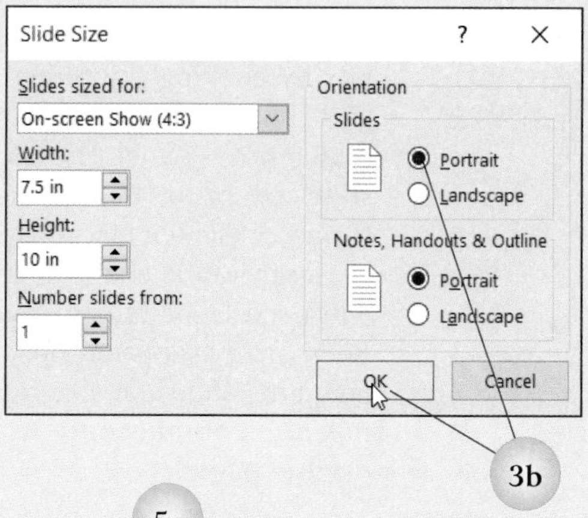

4. Run the slide show to view how the slides appear in portrait orientation.
5. After running the slide show, change the page setup by completing the following steps:
   a. Click the Slide Size button and then click *Custom Slide Size* at the drop-down list.
   b. At the Slide Size dialog box, click the *Landscape* option in the *Slides* section.
   c. Click the *Slides sized for* option box arrow and then click *On-screen Show (16:10)*. (Notice that the slide height changed from *10* to *6.25* in the *Height* measurement box.)
   d. Click OK.
   e. Click the Maximize button at the Microsoft PowerPoint dialog box.

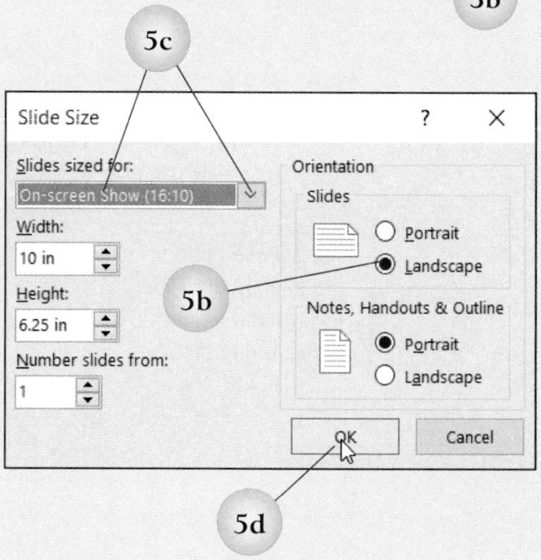

6. Run the slide show.
7. Specify slide width and height and change slide numbering by completing the following steps:
   a. Click the Slide Size button and then click *Custom Slide Size* at the drop-down list.
   b. At the Slide Size dialog box, click the *Width* measurement box down arrow until *9 in* displays.
   c. Click the *Height* measurement box down arrow until *6 in* displays.
   d. Click the *Number slides from* measurement box up arrow until *6* displays.
   e. Click OK.
   f. Click the Ensure Fit button at the Microsoft PowerPoint dialog box.

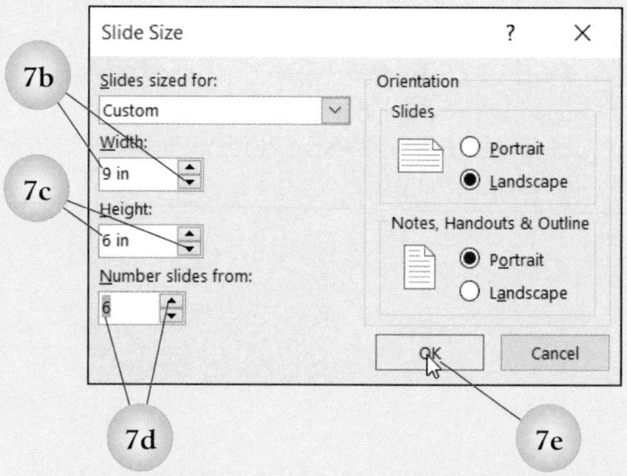

8. Notice that the slide numbering in the slide thumbnails pane begins with Slide 6.
9. Run the slide show.
10. Save and then close **3-ColorPres.pptx**.

Check Your Work

Project 3 Modify the Design Theme and Slide Background of a Network Presentation — 1 Part

You will open a network presentation, apply a design theme, and then change the theme colors and fonts. You will also apply and customize a background style.

Preview Finished Project

Tutorial

Changing and Modifying Design Themes

Hint Themes are shared across Office programs such as PowerPoint, Word, Excel, and Access.

Changing and Modifying Design Themes

A design theme is a set of formatting choices that includes a color theme (a set of colors), a font theme (heading and text fonts), and an effects theme (a set of lines and fill effects). Click the More Variants button in the Variants group on the Design tab to display options for changing design theme colors, fonts, and effects.

A theme contains specific color formatting that can be changed with color options. Change color options by clicking the More Variants button in the Variants group, pointing to the *Colors* option, and then clicking a color option in the side menu. Each theme applies specific fonts and these fonts can be changed by pointing to the *Fonts* option at the More Variants button drop-down gallery and then choosing an option at the side menu. Each font group in the side menu contains two choices: The first choice is the font that is applied to slide titles and the second choice is the font that is applied to slide subtitles and text. If a presentation contains graphic elements such as illustrations, images, or text boxes, specify theme effects by pointing to the *Effects* option at the More Variants button drop-down gallery and then choosing an option at the side menu.

Tutorial

Formatting the Slide Background

Format Background

Quick Steps

Change the Slide Background

1. Click Design tab.
2. Click Format Background button.
3. Make changes at Format Background task pane.

Formatting the Slide Background

Format the slide background with background styles or with options at the Format Background task pane. Display background styles by clicking the More Variants button in the Variants group on the Design tab and then pointing to the *Background Styles* option. Apply a background style by clicking an option at the side menu.

Click the Format Background button in the Customize group on the Design tab to display the Format Background task pane, as shown in Figure 3.9. Use options in the Format Background task pane to apply fill, effects, or a picture to the slide background. Apply the slide background to all slides in the presentation by clicking the Apply to All button at the bottom of the task pane. If changes are made to the slide background, reset the background to the default by clicking the Reset Background button at the bottom of the Format Background task pane.

Some of the design themes provided by PowerPoint contain a background graphic. The background graphic can be removed from slides by inserting a check mark in the *Hide background graphics* check box in the *Fill* section of the Format Background task pane with the Fill icon selected and then clicking the Apply to All button.

Figure 3.9 Format Background Task Pane

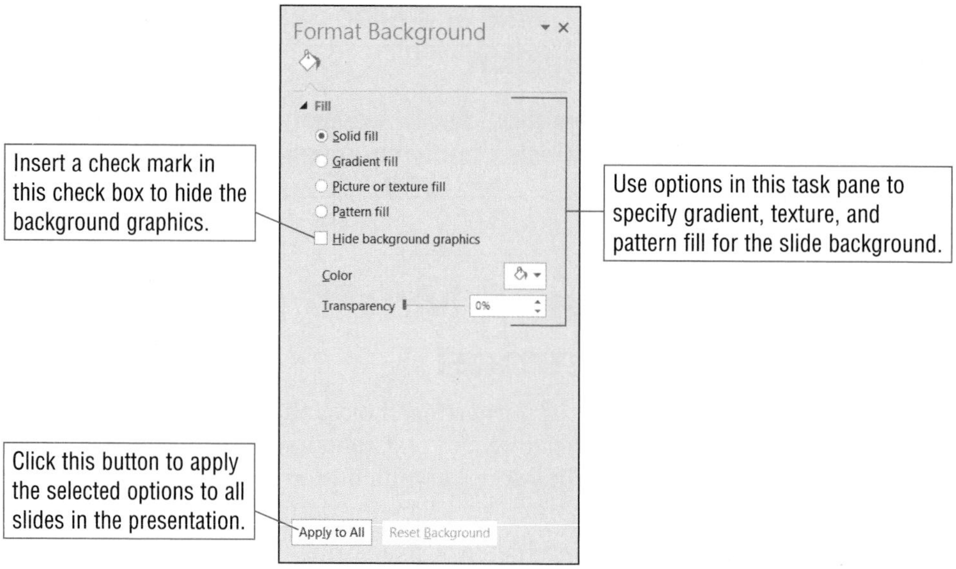

Project 3 Changing Theme Colors, Theme Fonts, and Slide Backgrounds

Part 1 of 1

1. Open **NetworkPres.pptx** and then save it with the name **3-NetworkPres.pptx**.
2. Apply a design theme by completing the following steps:
   a. Click the Design tab.
   b. Click the More Themes button at the right side of the themes gallery in the Themes group and then click *Dividend* at the drop-down gallery.
3. Change the theme colors by clicking the More Variants button in the Variants group, pointing to *Colors*, scrolling down the color options in the side menu, and then clicking *Marquee*.

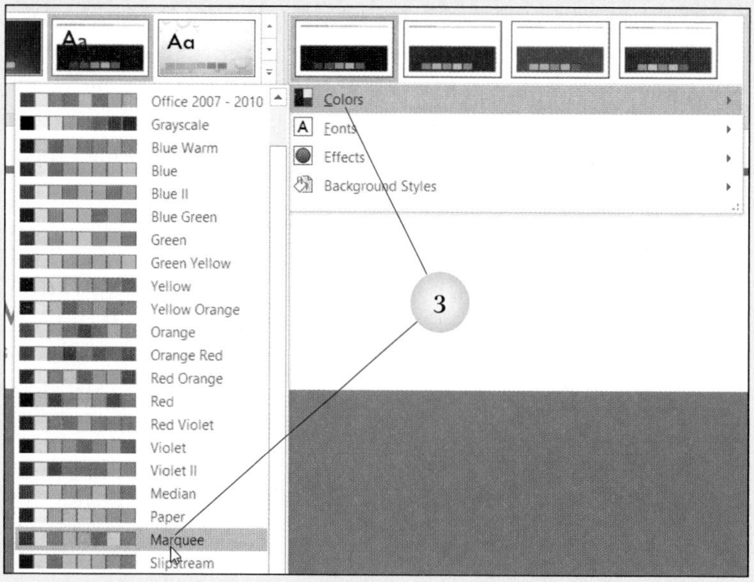

4. Change the theme fonts by clicking the More Variants button, pointing to *Fonts*, scrolling down the side menu, and then clicking *Calibri-Cambria*.

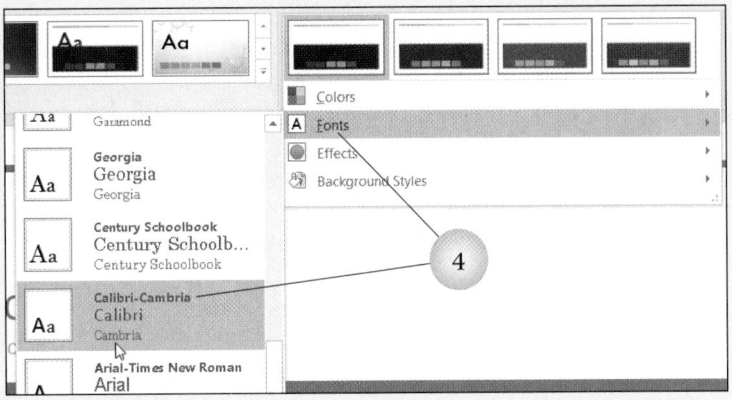

5. Change the background style by clicking the More Variants button, pointing to *Background Styles*, and then clicking *Style 5* at the side menu (first column, second row).
6. With Slide 1 active, run the slide show to view the formatting applied by the design theme, theme colors, theme fonts, and background style.
7. With Slide 1 still active, apply and customize the background style of all slides by completing the following steps:
   a. Click the Format Background button in the Customize group on the Design tab.
   b. At the Format Background task pane with the Fill icon selected and the fill options displayed in the *Fill* section, click the *Picture or texture fill* option.
   c. Click the Texture button (below the Online button) and then click the *Stationery* option (first column, fourth row).
   d. Click the *Transparency* measurement box up arrow until *25%* displays.
   e. Click the Apply to All button at the bottom of the task pane.
   f. Close the Format Background task pane.

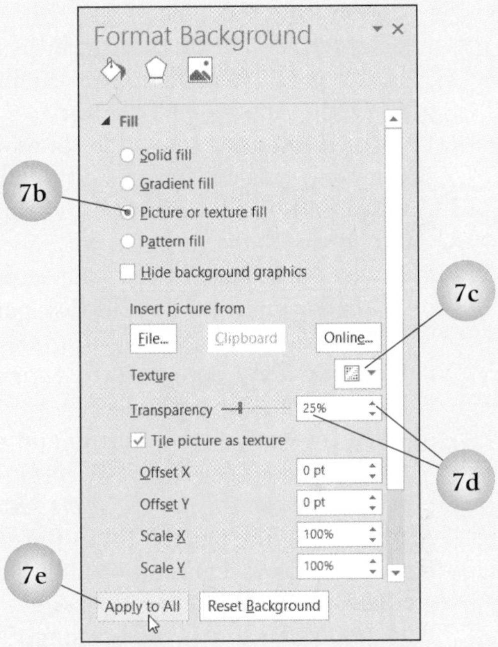

8. Run the slide show to view the background formatting.
9. Apply an artistic effect to all slides in the presentation by completing the following steps:
   a. Make Slide 2 active.
   b. Click the Format Background button in the Customize group on the Design tab.
   c. Click the Effects icon in the Format Background task pane.
   d. Click the Artistic Effects button and then click the *Paint Brush* option (third column, second row).
   e. Click the Apply to All button.
10. Run the slide show to view the artistic effect applied to all slides in the presentation.

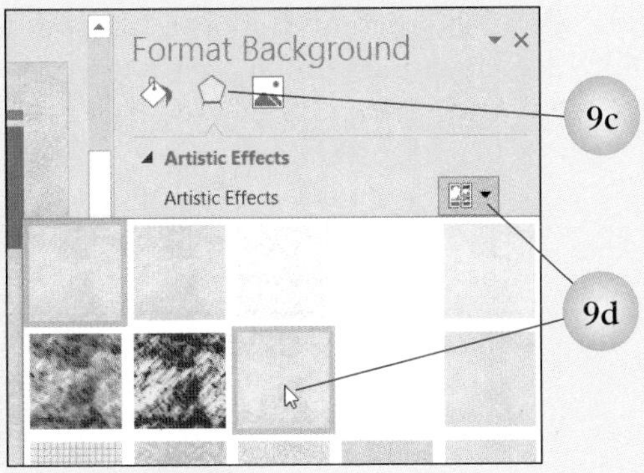

11. Change the background to a gradient fill rather than an artistic effect by completing the following steps:
    a. Click the Fill icon in the Format Background task pane.
    b. Click the *Gradient fill* option.
    c. Click the Preset gradients button and then click *Light Gradient - Accent 2* (second column, first row).
    d. Click the *Type* option box arrow and then click *Radial* at the drop-down list.
    e. Click the Direction button and then click the *From Bottom Left Corner* option (second option from the left).
    f. Select the *0%* in the *Position* measurement box, type 25, and then press the Enter key.
    g. Click the Apply to All button.
12. Look at the slides in the slide thumbnails pane to view the gradient fill applied to all slides.
13. Apply a pattern fill to Slide 1 by completing the following steps:
    a. If necessary, make Slide 1 the active slide.
    b. At the Format Background task pane, click the *Pattern fill* option.
    c. Click the *Divot* option in the *Pattern* section (first column, seventh row).
    d. Click the Background button and then click the *Green, Accent 2, Lighter 80%* option (sixth column, second row in the *Theme Colors* section).
14. After viewing the pattern fill in the slide pane, reset the slide background of Slide 1 to the gradient fill background by clicking the Reset Background button at the bottom of the Format Background task pane.
15. Close the Format Background task pane.
16. Run the slide show to view the background formatting.
17. Print the presentation as a handout with six slides displayed horizontally per page.
18. Save and then close **3-NetworkPres.pptx**.

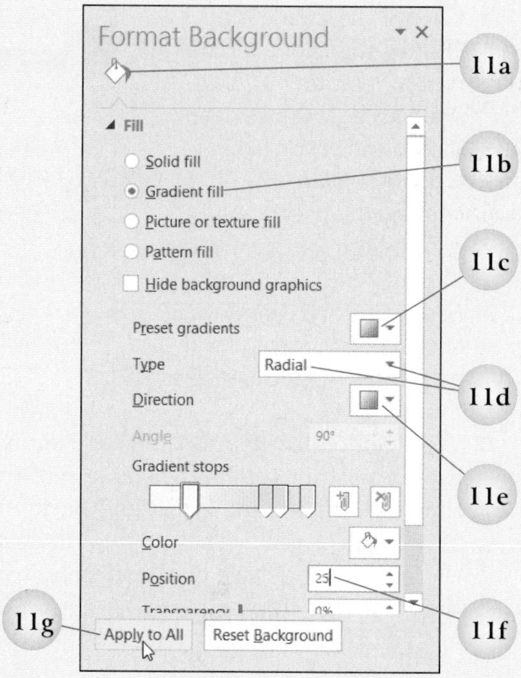

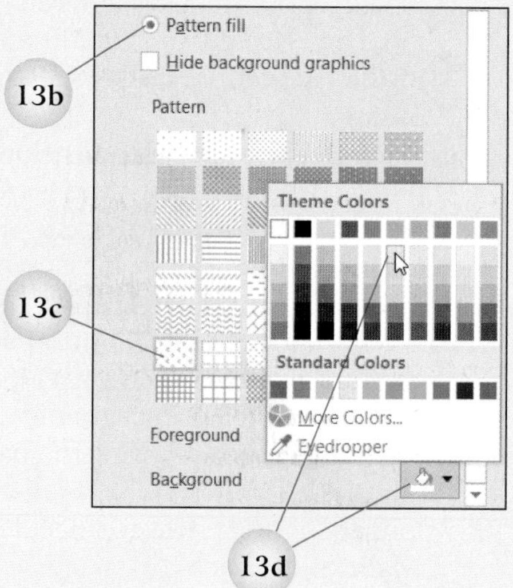

Check Your Work

Project 4 **Create and Apply Custom Design Themes to Presentations** **4 Parts**

You will create custom theme colors and custom theme fonts and then save the changes as a custom design theme. You will then apply the custom design theme to a job search presentation and a resume writing presentation.

Preview Finished Project

Creating Custom Design Themes

If the default themes, theme colors, and theme fonts do not provide the necessary formatting for a presentation, create custom theme colors, custom theme fonts, and a custom design theme. A custom design theme will display in the *Custom* section of the Themes drop-down gallery. To create a custom design theme, change the theme colors, theme fonts, and/or theme effects.

Click the More Variants button in the Variants group on the Design tab and the options at the drop-down gallery display a visual representation of the current theme. If the theme colors are changed, the colors are reflected in the small color squares on the *Colors* option. If the theme fonts are changed, the *A* on the *Fonts* option reflects the change.

Tutorial

Creating Custom Theme Colors

Quick Steps

Create Custom Theme Colors

1. Click Design tab.
2. Click More Variants button.
3. Point to *Colors*.
4. Click *Customize Colors*.
5. Change background, accent, and hyperlink colors.
6. Type name for custom theme colors.
7. Click Save button.

Creating Custom Theme Colors

To create custom theme colors, click the Design tab, click the More Variants button, point to the *Colors* option, and then click *Customize Colors* at the side menu. This displays the Create New Theme Colors dialog box, similar to the one shown in Figure 3.10. Theme colors contain four text and background colors, six accent colors, and two hyperlink colors, as shown in the *Themes colors* section of the dialog box. Change a theme color by clicking the color button at the right side of the color option and then clicking the desired color at the color palette. If changes are made to colors at the Create New Theme Colors dialog box, clicking the Reset button in the lower left corner of the dialog box will change the colors back to the default.

Figure 3.10 Create New Theme Colors Dialog Box

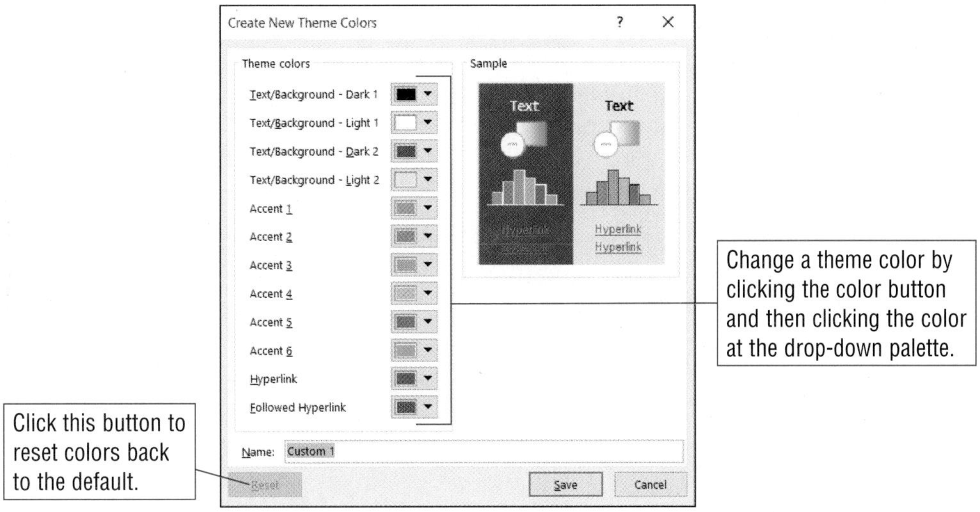

After making color changes, click in the *Name* text box, type a name for the custom theme colors, and then click the Save button. This saves the custom theme colors and applies the color changes to the currently open presentation.

Apply custom theme colors to a presentation by clicking the More Variants button in the Variants group, pointing to the *Colors* option, and then clicking the custom theme colors at the top of the drop-down gallery in the *Custom* section.

Project 4a Creating Custom Theme Colors

Part 1 of 4

Note: If you are running PowerPoint 2016 on a computer connected to a network in a public environment such as a school, you may need to complete all four parts of Project 4 during the same session. Network system software may delete your custom themes when you close PowerPoint. Check with your instructor.

1. At a blank presentation, click the Design tab, click the More Themes button in the Themes group, and then click *Wisp* at the drop-down gallery.
2. Click the third option in the Variants group (light blue color).
3. Create custom theme colors by completing the following steps:
   a. Click the More Variants button in the Variants group, point to the *Colors* option, and then click the *Customize Colors* option at the side menu.
   b. At the Create New Theme Colors dialog box, click the color button at the right side of the *Text/Background - Dark 2* option and then click the *Dark Blue, Accent 3, Darker 25%* option (seventh column, fifth row in the *Theme Colors* section).
   c. Click the color button at the right side of the *Text/Background - Light 2* option and then click the *Purple, Accent 4, Lighter 80%* option (eighth column, second row in the *Theme Colors* section).
   d. Click the color button at the right side of the *Accent 1* option and then click the *Purple, Accent 4, Darker 50%* option (eighth column, last row in the *Theme Colors* section).
4. Save the custom colors by completing the following steps:
   a. Select the text in the *Name* text box.
   b. Type your first and last names.
   c. Click the Save button.
5. Save the presentation and name it **3-CustomTheme**.

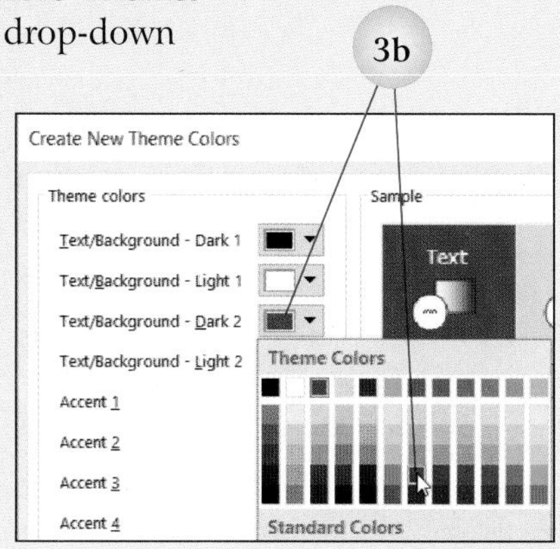

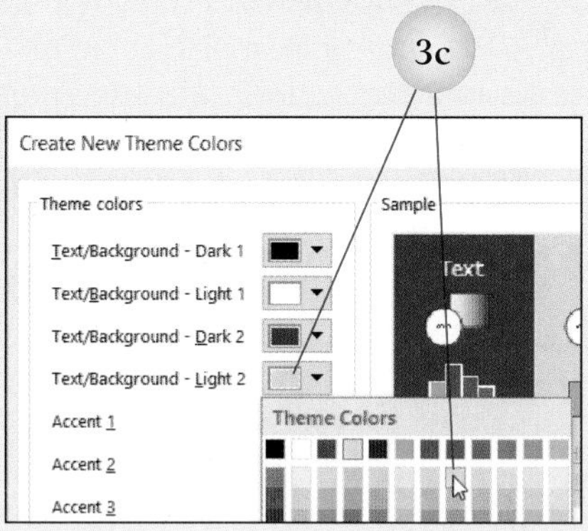

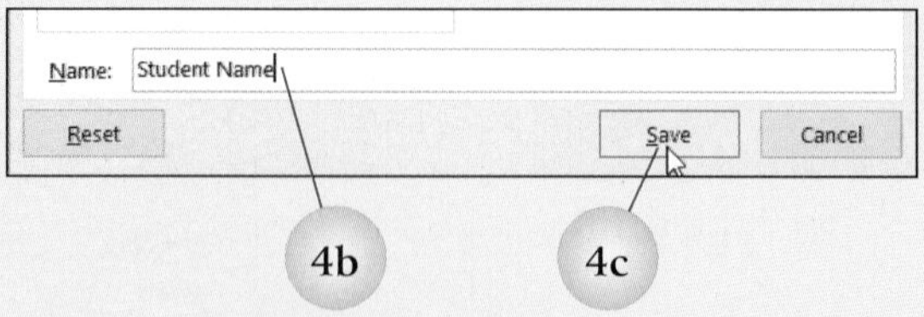

Tutorial

Creating Custom Theme Fonts

Quick Steps

Create Custom Fonts

1. Click Design tab.
2. Click More Variants button.
3. Point to *Fonts*.
4. Click *Customize Fonts*.
5. Choose fonts.
6. Type name for custom theme fonts.
7. Click Save button.

Creating Custom Theme Fonts

To create custom theme fonts, click the Design tab, click the More Variants button in the Variants group, point to the *Fonts* option, and then click *Customize Fonts* at the side menu. This displays the Create New Theme Fonts dialog box, similar to the one shown in Figure 3.11. At this dialog box, choose a heading font and body font. Type the name of the custom theme fonts in the *Name* box and then click the Save button.

Figure 3.11 Create New Theme Fonts Dialog Box

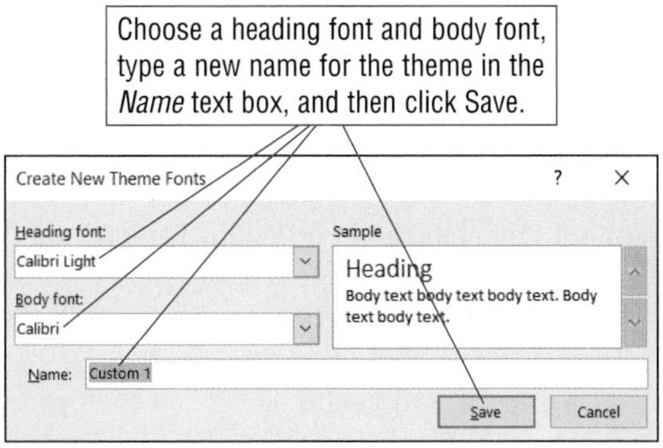

Project 4b **Creating Custom Theme Fonts**

Part 2 of 4

1. With **3-CustomTheme.pptx** open, create custom theme fonts by completing the following steps:
   a. If necessary, click the Design tab.
   b. Click the More Variants button in the Variants group, point to the *Fonts* option, and then click the *Customize Fonts* option at the side menu.
   c. At the Create New Theme Fonts dialog box, click the *Heading font* option box arrow and then click *Candara*.
   d. Click the *Body font* option box arrow, scroll down the drop-down list, and then click *Constantia*.
2. Save the custom theme fonts by completing the following steps:
   a. Select the current text in the *Name* text box.
   b. Type your first and last names.
   c. Click the Save button.
3. Save **3-CustomTheme.pptx**.

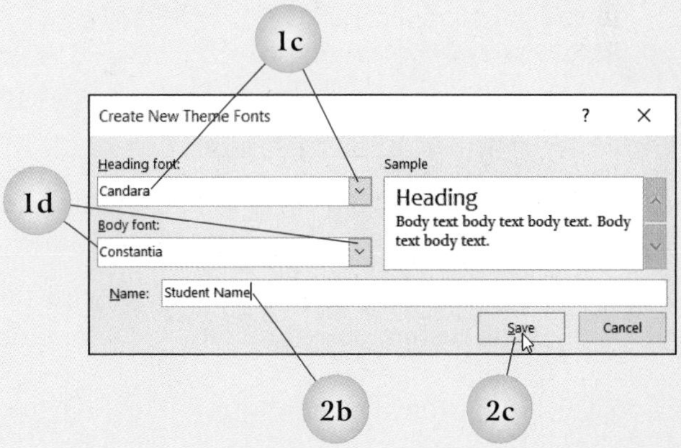

Tutorial

Saving and Deleting a Custom Design Theme

Quick Steps

Save a Custom Design Theme

1. Click Design tab.
2. Click More Themes button.
3. Click *Save Current Theme.*
4. Type name for custom theme.
5. Click Save button.

Saving a Custom Design Theme

When theme colors and fonts have been customized, save these as a custom design theme. To do this, click the More Themes button in the Themes group on the Design tab and then click *Save Current Theme*. This displays the Save Current Theme dialog box with the Document Themes folder active on the computer's hard drive, which contains many of the same options as the Save As dialog box. Type a name for the custom design theme in the *File name* text box and then click the Save button. To apply a custom design theme, click the More Themes button in the Themes group, and then click the theme in the *Custom* section of the drop-down gallery.

Project 4c Saving and Applying a Custom Design Theme

Part 3 of 4

1. With **3-CustomTheme.pptx** open, save the custom theme colors and fonts as a custom design theme by completing the following steps:
   a. If necessary, click the Design tab.
   b. Click the More Themes button in the Themes group.
   c. Click the *Save Current Theme* option at the bottom of the drop-down gallery.
   d. At the Save Current Theme dialog box with the Document Themes folder active on the computer's hard drive, type C3 and then type your last name in the *File name* text box.
   e. Click the Save button.

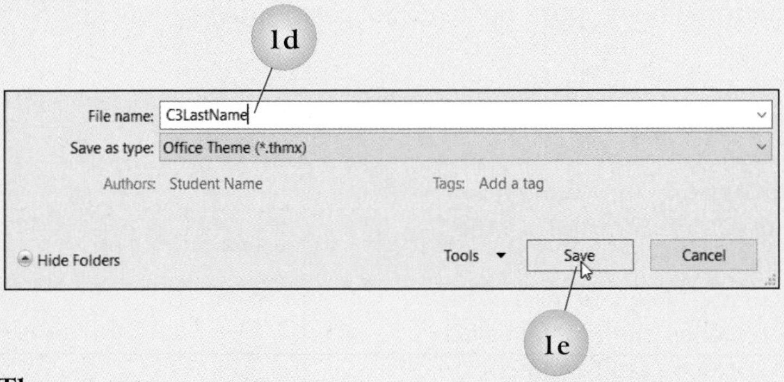

2. Close **3-CustomTheme.pptx**.
3. Open **JobSearch.pptx** and then save it with the name **3-JobSearch**.
4. Apply your custom design theme by completing the following steps:
   a. Click the Design tab.
   b. Click the More Themes button in the Themes group.
   c. Click the custom design theme that begins with *C3* followed by your last name. (The theme will display in the *Custom* section of the drop-down gallery.)

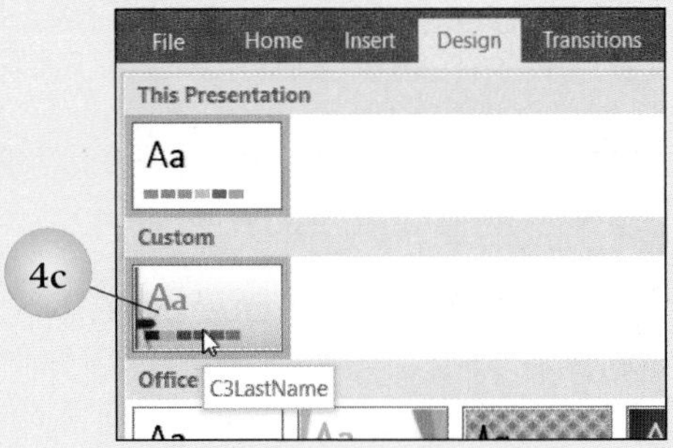

5. Run the slide show to view how the slides display with the custom design theme applied.
6. Print Slide 1 of the presentation.
7. Save and then close **3-JobSearch.pptx**.
8. Open **ResumePres.pptx** and then save it with the name **3-ResumePres**.

9. Apply your custom design theme (the theme beginning with *C3* followed by your last name) to the presentation.
10. Run the slide show.
11. Print Slide 1 of the presentation.
12. Save and then close **3-ResumePres.pptx**.

Check Your Work

Editing Custom Themes

Custom theme colors and custom theme fonts can be edited. To edit the custom theme colors, click the More Variants button in the Variants group on the Design tab and then point to the *Colors* option. At the side menu of custom and built-in themes, right-click the custom theme and then click *Edit* at the shortcut menu. This displays the Edit Theme Colors dialog box, which contains the same options as the Create New Theme Colors dialog box shown in Figure 3.10 on page 97. Make the changes to theme colors and then click the Save button.

To edit custom theme fonts, click the More Variants button in the Variants group on the Design tab, point to the *Fonts* option, right-click the custom theme fonts, and then click *Edit* at the shortcut menu. This displays the Edit Theme Fonts dialog box that contains the same options as the Create New Theme Fonts dialog box shown in Figure 3.11 on page 99. Make the changes and then click the Save button.

Deleting Custom Themes

Delete custom theme colors from the *Colors* option side menu, delete custom theme fonts from the *Fonts* option side menu, and delete custom design themes from the More Themes button drop-down gallery or the Save Current Theme dialog box. To delete custom theme colors, click the More Variants button in the Variants group, point to the *Colors* option, right-click the theme to be deleted, and then click *Delete* at the shortcut menu. At the message asking to confirm the deletion, click the Yes button. Complete similar steps to delete custom theme fonts.

Delete a custom design theme by clicking the More Themes button in the Themes group on the Design tab, right-clicking the custom design theme, and then clicking *Delete* at the shortcut menu. A custom design theme can also be deleted at the Save Current Theme dialog box. To display this dialog box, click the More Themes button in the Themes group on the Design tab and then click *Save Current Theme* at the drop-down gallery. At the Save Current Theme dialog box, click the custom design theme file name, click the Organize button on the toolbar, and then click *Delete* at the drop-down list. At the message asking to confirm the deletion, click the Yes button.

Quick Steps

Edit Custom Theme Colors
1. Click Design tab.
2. Click More Variants button.
3. Point to *Colors* option.
4. Right-click custom theme.
5. Click *Edit*.
6. Make changes.
7. Click Save button.

Edit Custom Theme Fonts
1. Click Design tab.
2. Click More Variants button.
3. Point to *Fonts* option.
4. Right-click custom theme.
5. Click *Edit*.
6. Make changes.
7. Click Save button.

Delete Custom Theme Colors
1. Click Design tab.
2. Click More Variants button.
3. Point to *Colors* option.
4. Right-click custom theme.
5. Click *Delete*.
6. Click Yes.

Delete Custom Theme Fonts
1. Click Design tab.
2. Click More Variants button.
3. Point to *Fonts* option.
4. Right-click custom theme.
5. Click *Delete*.
6. Click Yes.

Delete Custom Design Theme
1. Click Design tab.
2. Click More Themes button.
3. Right-click custom theme.
4. Click *Delete*.
5. Click Yes.

Project 4d Deleting Custom Themes

Part 4 of 4

1. Open a new, blank presentation and delete the custom theme colors by completing the following steps:
   a. Click the Design tab.
   b. Click the More Variants button in the Variants group and then point to the *Colors* option.
   c. Right-click the custom theme colors named with your first and last names.
   d. Click *Delete* at the shortcut menu.
   e. At the message asking if you want to delete the theme colors, click Yes.

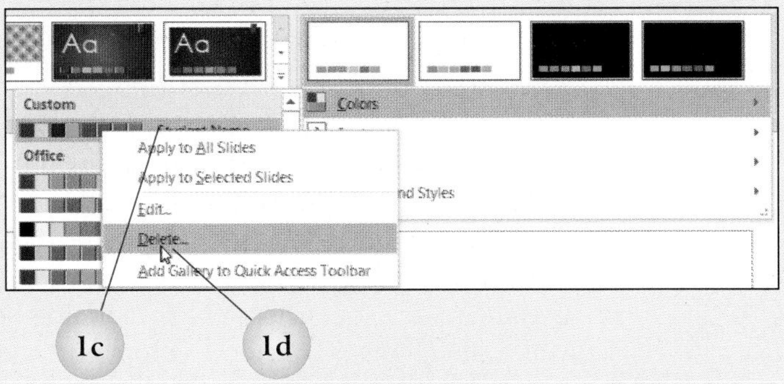

2. Complete steps similar to those in Step 1 to delete the custom theme fonts you created named with your first and last names.
3. Delete the custom design theme by completing the following steps:
   a. Click the More Themes button in the Themes group.
   b. Right-click the custom design theme that begins with *C3* followed by your last name.
   c. Click *Delete* at the shortcut menu.
   d. At the message asking if you want to delete the theme, click Yes.
4. Close the presentation without saving it.

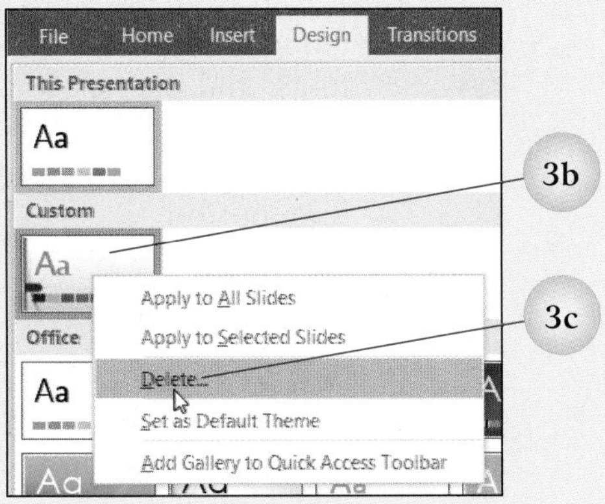

Chapter Summary

- The Font group on the Home tab contains buttons and options for applying character formatting to text in slides.
- Change the default font with the *Font* option box and the *Font Size* option box in the Font group.
- Some options, such as the *Font* and *Font Size* options, contain the live preview feature, which displays how the formatting affects selected text without having to return to the presentation.
- Character formatting can also be applied with options at the Font dialog box. Display this dialog box by clicking the Font group dialog box launcher.
- Select text in a slide and the Mini toolbar displays above the selected text. Apply formatting using the buttons and options on this toolbar.
- Use the Format Painter feature to apply formatting to more than one location in a slide or slides.
- The Paragraph group on the Home tab contains a number of buttons for applying paragraph formatting to text in slides.

- Customize paragraph formatting with options at the Paragraph dialog box with the Indents and Spacing tab selected. Display this dialog box by clicking the Paragraph group dialog box launcher or by clicking the Line Spacing button in the Paragraph group and then clicking *Line Spacing Options* at the drop-down list.
- Use the Add or Remove Columns button in the Paragraph group or options at the Columns dialog box to format selected text into columns. Display the Columns dialog box by clicking the Add or Remove Columns button and then clicking *More Columns* at the drop-down list.
- Use the Text Direction button or options at the Format Shape task pane to rotate or stack text in a slide. Display the Format Shape task pane by clicking the Drawing group task pane launcher on the Home tab.
- The Shape Options tab in the Format Shape task pane displays four icons: Fill & Line, Effects, Size & Properties, and Picture, each with different options for formatting a placeholder.
- Customize bullets with options at the Bullets and Numbering dialog box with the Bulleted tab selected. Display this dialog box by clicking the Bullets button arrow and then clicking *Bullets and Numbering* at the drop-down list.
- Customize numbering with options at the Bullets and Numbering dialog box with the Numbered tab selected. Display this dialog box by clicking the Numbering button arrow and then clicking *Bullets and Numbering* at the drop-down list.
- Click the Quick Styles button in the Drawing group on the Home tab to apply formatting to a placeholder. The Drawing group also contains the Shape Fill, Shape Outline, and Shape Effects buttons for customizing a placeholder, and the Arrange button for arranging slide elements.
- Click the Slide Size button and then click *Custom Slide Size* at the drop-down list to display the Slide Size dialog box. Use options at this dialog box to change the slide size and ratio, the start slide number, and the orientation of slides, notes, handouts, and outline pages.
- Use the Format Background task pane to customize the background of slides. Display the task pane by clicking the Format Background button in the Customize group on the Design tab.
- Create custom theme colors with options at the Create New Theme Colors dialog box. Display this dialog box by clicking the More Variants button in the Variants group on the Design tab, pointing to the *Colors* option, and then clicking *Customize Colors* at the side menu.
- Create custom theme fonts with options at the Create New Theme Fonts dialog box. Display this dialog box by clicking the More Variants button in the Variants group on the Design tab, pointing to the *Fonts* option, and then clicking *Customize Fonts* at the side menu.
- Save a custom design theme at the Save Current Theme dialog box. Display this dialog box by clicking the More Themes button in the Themes group on the Design tab and then clicking *Save Current Theme*.
- Edit custom theme colors with options at the Edit Theme Colors dialog box and edit custom theme fonts with options at the Edit Theme Fonts dialog box.
- Delete custom theme colors by clicking the More Variants button in the Variants group, pointing to the *Colors* option, right-clicking the custom theme, and then clicking the *Delete* option.

- Delete custom theme fonts by clicking the More Variants button in the Variants group, pointing to the *Fonts* option, right-clicking the custom theme, and then clicking the *Delete* option.
- Delete a custom design theme by clicking the More Themes button in the Themes group, right-clicking the custom theme, and then clicking *Delete* at the shortcut menu. A custom design theme also can be deleted at the Save Current Theme dialog box. Display this dialog box by clicking the Themes button and then clicking *Save Current Theme* at the drop-down gallery.

Commands Review

FEATURE	RIBBON TAB, GROUP	BUTTON, OPTION	KEYBOARD SHORTCUT
Bullets and Numbering dialog box with Bulleted tab selected	Home, Paragraph	, *Bullets and Numbering*	
Bullets and Numbering dialog box with Numbered tab selected	Home, Paragraph	, *Bullets and Numbering*	
Columns dialog box	Home, Paragraph	, *More Columns*	
Create New Theme Colors dialog box	Design, Variants	, *Colors, Customize Colors*	
Create New Theme Fonts dialog box	Design, Variants	, *Fonts, Customize Fonts*	
Font dialog box	Home, Font		Ctrl + Shift + F
Format Background task pane	Design, Customize		
Format Painter	Home, Clipboard		
Format Shape task pane	Home, Drawing		
Paragraph dialog box	Home, Paragraph		
Save Current Theme dialog box	Design, Themes	, *Save Current Theme*	
slide size	Design, Customize		

Workbook

Chapter study tools and assessment activities are available in the *Workbook* ebook. These resources are designed to help you further develop and demonstrate mastery of the skills learned in this chapter.

Microsoft®

PowerPoint®

Inserting Elements in Slides

CHAPTER 4

Performance Objectives

Upon successful completion of Chapter 4, you will be able to:

1 Insert, format, select, and align a text box
2 Set the default text box format
3 Set tabs in a text box
4 Insert, format, and copy shapes
5 Display rulers, gridlines, and guides
6 Merge, group, and ungroup objects
7 Insert, crop, size, move, and format an image
8 Insert an image as a slide background
9 Insert, size, scale, rotate, and position an online image
10 Copy objects within and between presentations
11 Create and insert a screenshot
12 Create and format WordArt text
13 Insert symbols, headers, footers, the current date, and slide numbers

Precheck

Check your current skills to help focus your study.

An audience may overlook a presentation consisting only of text-heavy slides. Adding visual elements, where appropriate, can help by adding interest and impact to the information. In this chapter, you will learn how to create and add visual elements on slides such as text boxes, shapes, images, screenshots, and WordArt text. These elements will make the delivery of your presentation a dynamic experience for your audience.

Data Files

Before beginning chapter work, copy the PC4 folder to your storage medium and then make PC4 the active folder.

SNAP

If you are a SNAP user, launch the Precheck and Tutorials from your Assignments page.

Project 1 Create a Company Presentation Containing Text Boxes, Shapes, and Images — 14 Parts

You will create a company presentation that includes slides with text boxes, a slide with tabbed text in a text box, slides with shapes and text, and slides with images. You will also insert elements in slides such as slide numbers, headers, footers, the date, and symbols.

Preview Finished Project

Tutorial

Inserting and Formatting Text Boxes

Text Box

Inserting and Formatting Text Boxes

Many slide layouts contain placeholders for entering text and other elements in a slide. Along with placeholders, a text box can be inserted and formatted in a slide. To insert a text box in a slide, click the Insert tab, click the Text Box button in the Text group, and the mouse pointer displays as a thin, down-pointing arrow. Using the mouse, click and drag in the slide to create the text box. Or, click in a slide to insert a small text box at that location.

Quick Steps

Draw a Text Box
1. Click Insert tab.
2. Click Text Box button.
3. Click or drag in slide to create box.

Formatting a Text Box

When a text box is inserted in a slide, the Home tab displays. Use options in the Drawing group to format the text box by applying a Quick Style or adding a shape fill, outline, or effect. Format a text box in a manner similar to formatting a placeholder. Formatting can also be applied to a text box with options on the Drawing Tools Format tab. Click this tab and the ribbon displays as shown in Figure 4.1. The Shape Styles group contains the same options as the Drawing group on the Home tab. Use other options on the tab to apply WordArt formatting to text and arrange and size the text box.

Move a text box in the same way as a placeholder. Click the text box to select it, position the mouse pointer on the text box border until the pointer displays with a four-headed arrow, and then click and drag the text box to the desired position. Change the size of a selected text box using the sizing handles that display around the box. Use the *Shape Height* and *Shape Width* measurement boxes in the Size group on the Drawing Tools Format tab to adjust the size of the text box to a specific height and width measurement.

Hint Use a text box to place text anywhere in a slide. Text in inserted text boxes does not appear in the Outline view.

PowerPoint provides a task pane with a variety of options for formatting a placeholder. The same task pane is available with options for formatting and customizing a text box. Click the Shape Styles group task pane launcher and the Format Shape task pane displays at the right side of the screen with options for formatting the text box fill, effects, and size; options for formatting an image in the text box; and options for formatting text in a text box. Click the WordArt

Figure 4.1 Drawing Tools Format Tab

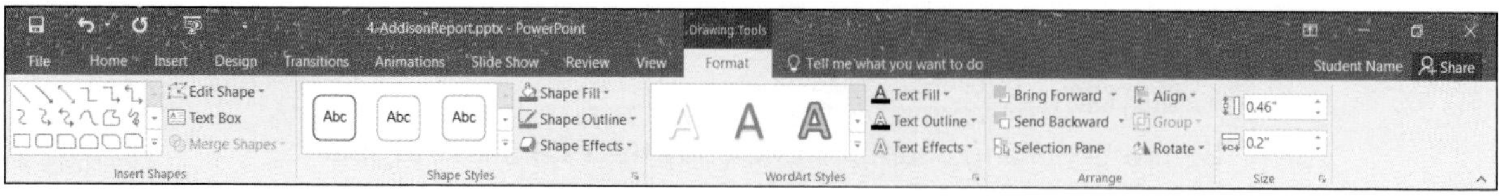

Styles group task pane launcher and the Format Shape task pane displays text formatting options. Click the Size group task pane launcher and the Format Shape task pane displays size and position options.

The same formatting applied to a placeholder can also be applied to a text box. For example, use the buttons in the Paragraph group on the Home tab to align text horizontally and vertically in a text box, change text direction, set text in columns, and set internal margins for the text in the text box.

Quick Steps

Select All Text Boxes

1. Click Select button.
2. Click *Select All*.

OR

Press Ctrl + A.

Select

Selecting Multiple Objects

Multiple text boxes and other objects can be selected in a slide and then the objects can be formatted, aligned, and arranged in the slide. To select all objects in a slide, click the Select button in the Editing group on the Home tab and then click *Select All* at the drop-down list. Or, select all objects in a slide with the keyboard shortcut Ctrl + A. To select specific text boxes or objects in a slide, click the first object, press and hold down the Shift key, and then click each of the other objects.

Align

Hint To select an object that is behind another object, select the top object and then press the Tab key to cycle through and select the other objects.

Aligning Text Boxes

Use the Align button in the Arrange group on the Drawing Tools Format tab to align the edges of multiple objects in a slide. Click the Align button and a drop-down list of alignment options displays, including options for aligning objects vertically and horizontally and distributing objects in the slide.

Project 1a Inserting and Formatting Text Boxes

Part 1 of 14

1. Open **AddisonReport.pptx** and then save it with the name **4-AddisonReport**.
2. Insert a new slide with the Blank layout by completing the following steps:
   a. Click the New Slide button arrow in the Slides group on the Home tab.
   b. Click *Blank* at the drop-down list.
3. Insert and format the *Safety* text box shown in Figure 4.2 (on page 110) by completing the following steps:
   a. Click the Insert tab.
   b. Click the Text Box button in the Text group.
   c. Click anywhere in the slide. (This inserts a small text box in the slide.)
   d. Type Safety.
   e. Select the text and then change the font to Copperplate Gothic Bold and the font size to 36 points.

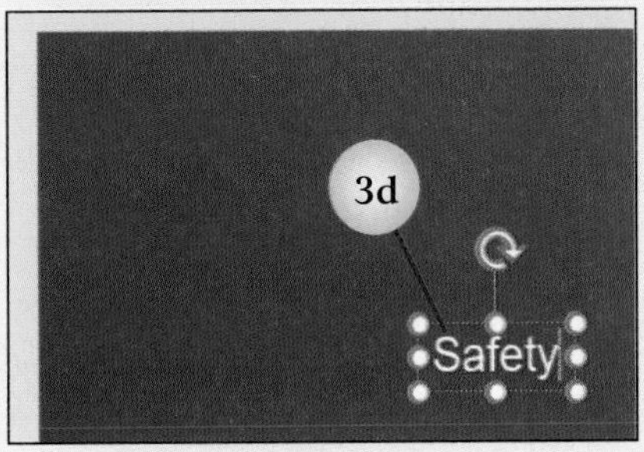

f. Click the Text Direction button in the Paragraph group on the Home tab and then click *Stacked* at the drop-down list.
g. Click the Drawing Tools Format tab.
h. Click the More Shape Styles button in the Shape Styles group and then click the *Moderate Effect - Aqua, Accent 5* option (sixth column, fifth row).

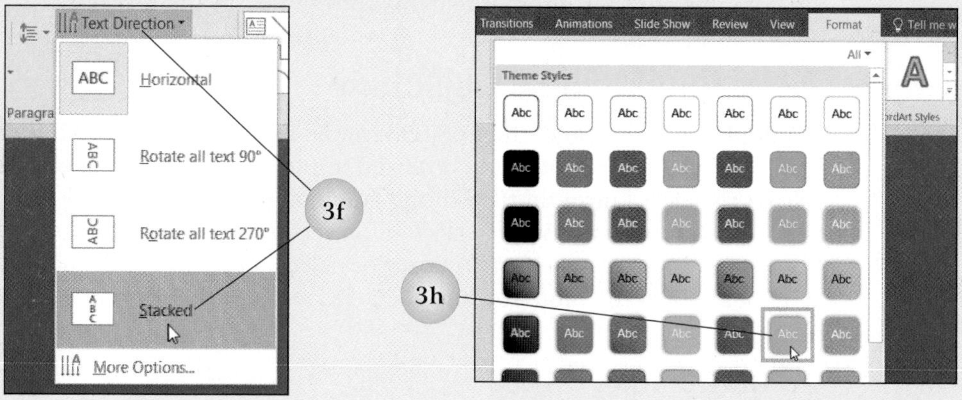

i. Click the Shape Outline button arrow in the Shape Styles group and then click the *Blue* color (eighth option in the *Standard Colors* section).
j. Click the Shape Outline button arrow, point to *Weight*, and then click the *1½ pt* option.
k. Click the Shape Effects button, point to *Bevel*, and then click the *Circle* option (first option in the *Bevel* section).
l. Click the More WordArt Styles button in the WordArt Styles group and then click the *Fill - White, Text 1, Outline - Background 1, Hard Shadow - Background 1* option (first column, third row).
m. Click in the *Shape Height* measurement box, type 4, and then press the Enter key.
n. Drag the text box so it is positioned as shown in Figure 4.2 (on page 110).

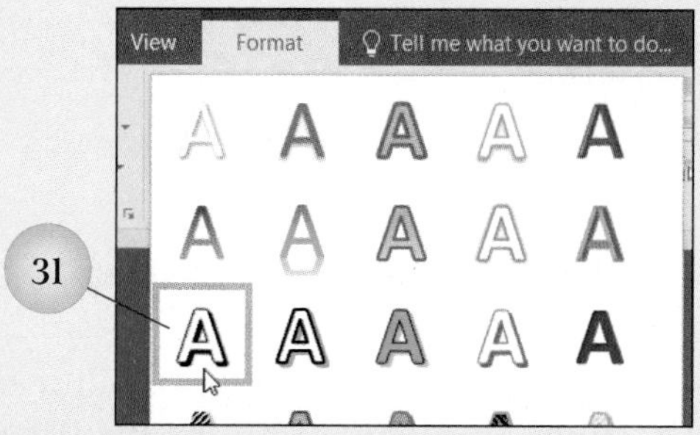

4. Insert and size the other text box shown in Figure 4.2 by completing the following steps:
a. Click the Insert tab.
b. Click the Text Box button in the Text group.
c. Drag in the slide to create a text box. (Drag to the approximate width of the text box in Figure 4.2.)
d. Type the text shown in the text box in Figure 4.2 in a single column. Type the text in the first column and then type the text in the second column. (Your text will display as shown at the right in one column, in a smaller font, and with different line spacing than in Figure 4.2.)

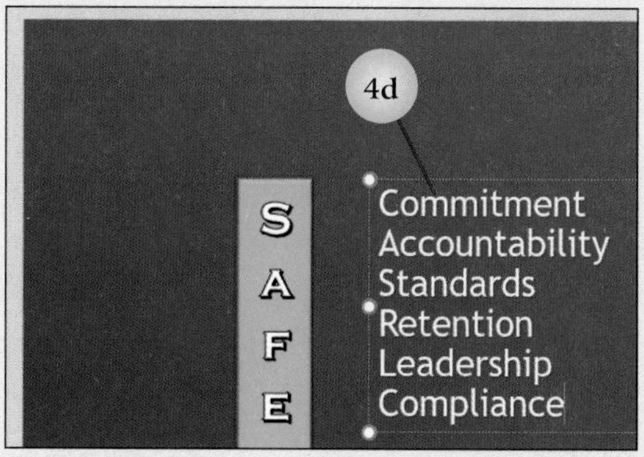

e. Select the text and then change the font size to 32 points.
f. Click the Line Spacing button in the Paragraph group and then click *2.0* at the drop-down list. (The text will flow off the slide.)

g. Click the Add or Remove Columns button in the Paragraph group and then click *Two Columns* at the drop-down list. (The text in the slide will not display in two columns until you complete steps 7i and 7j.)

5. Click the Drawing Tools Format tab.
6. Apply a WordArt style by completing the following steps:
   a. Click the More WordArt Styles button in the WordArt Styles group.
   b. Click the *Fill - White, Text 1, Outline - Background 1, Hard Shadow - Background 1* option (first column, third row).
7. Change the height, width, and internal margin measurements of the text box and turn off Autofit in the Format Shape task pane by completing the following steps:
   a. Click the Size group task pane launcher.
   b. At the Format Shape task pane, click the Size & Properties icon if it is not selected.
   c. If necessary, click *Text Box* in the task pane to display the text box options.
   d. Scroll down the task pane list box and click the *Do not Autofit* option.
   e. Select the current measurement in the *Left margin* measurement box and then type 0.8.
   f. Select the current measurement in the *Right margin* measurement box and then type 0.
   g. Select the current measurement in the *Top margin* measurement box, type 0.2, and then press the Enter key.
   h. Scroll up to the top of the task pane list box and, if necessary, click *Size* to display the size options.
   i. Select the current measurement in the *Height* measurement box and then type 4.
   j. Select the current measurement in the *Width* measurement box, type 8, and then press the Enter key.

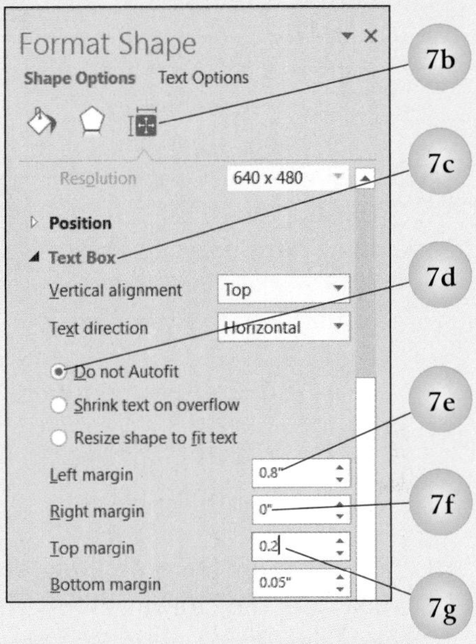

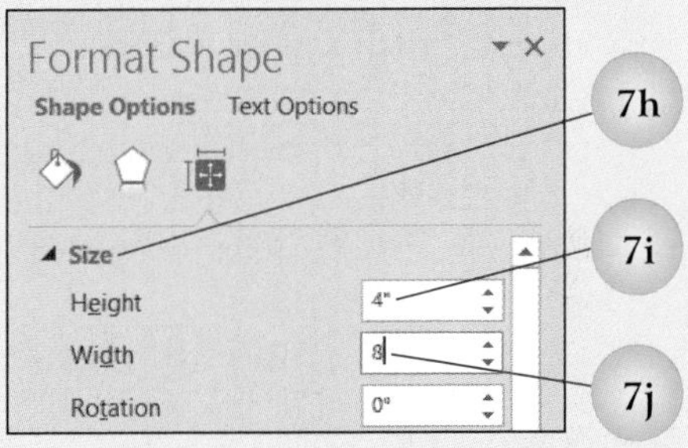

8. Apply fill formatting with options in the Format Shape task pane by completing the following steps:
   a. Click the Fill & Line icon in the task pane.
   b. If necessary, click *Fill* to display the fill options.
   c. Click the *Gradient fill* option to select it. (Notice the options available for customizing the gradient fill.)
   d. Click the *Pattern fill* option to select it. (Notice the options available for applying a pattern fill.)
   e. Click the *Picture or texture fill* option to select it.
   f. Click the File button in the *Insert picture from* section.
   g. At the Insert Picture dialog box, navigate to the PC4 folder on your storage medium and then double-click ***Ship.jpg***.

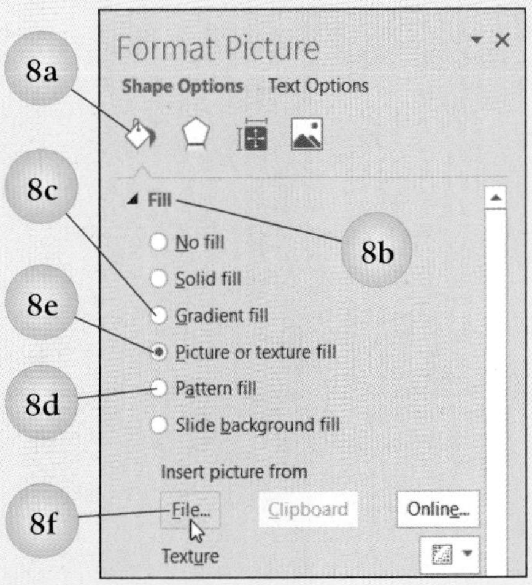

h. Select *0%* in the *Transparency* measurement box, type 10, and then press the Enter key.
i. Close the task pane by clicking the Close button in the upper right corner of the task pane.

9. Click in the slide outside the text box.
10. Arrange the text boxes by completing the following steps:
    a. Press Ctrl + A to select both text boxes.
    b. Click the Drawing Tools Format tab.
    c. Click the Align button in the Arrange group and then click *Align Bottom* at the drop-down list.
    d. Drag both boxes to the approximate location in the slide as shown in Figure 4.2.

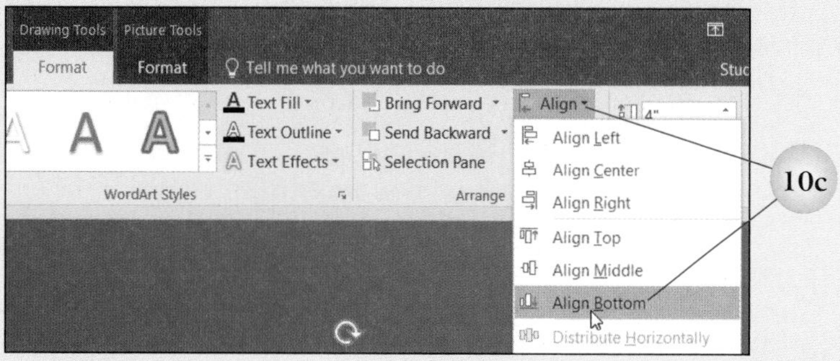

11. Save **4-AddisonReport.pptx**.
12. Print only Slide 2 by completing the following steps:
    a. Press Ctrl + P to display the Print backstage area.
    b. Click in the *Slides* text box in the *Settings* category and then type 2.
    c. Click the Print button.
13. Select the text box containing the image of the ship.
14. Make sure the Drawing Tools Format tab is active, click the More Shape Styles button in the Shape Styles group, and then click the *Moderate Effect - Aqua, Accent 5* option (sixth column, fifth row).
15. Click the Shape Outline button arrow in the Shape Styles group, and then click the *Blue* color (eighth option in the *Standard Colors* section).
16. Click the Shape Outline button arrow, point to *Weight*, and then click the *1½ pt* option.
17. Click the Shape Effects button, point to *Bevel*, and then click the *Circle* option (first option in the *Bevel* section).
18. Save **4-AddisonReport.pptx**.

Check Your Work

Figure 4.2 Project 1a, Slide 2

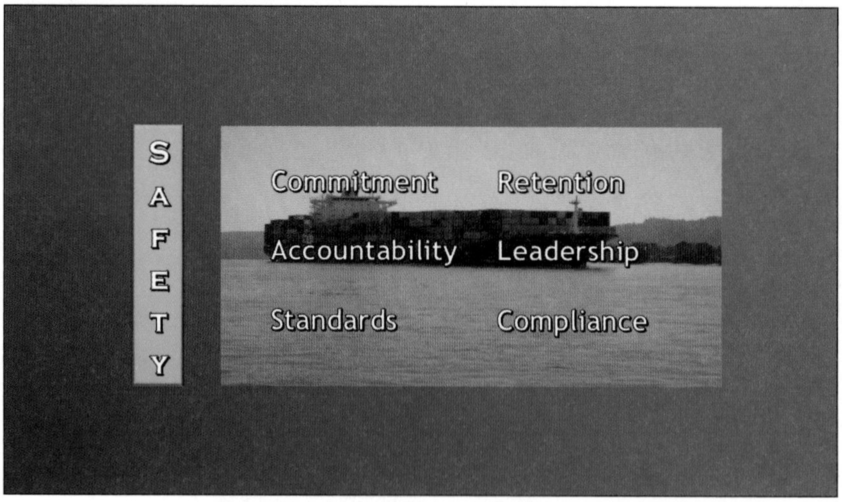

Setting the Default Text Box Format

The Format Shape task pane can be displayed using the shortcut menu. To do this, position the mouse pointer on the border of the text box until the pointer displays with a four-headed arrow and then click the right mouse button. At the shortcut menu, click the *Size and Position* option to display the Format Shape task pane with the Size & Properties icon active. Click the *Format Shape* option at the shortcut menu and the Format Shape task pane displays with the Fill & Line icon active. Formatting applied to a text box can become the default for other text boxes in the current presentation by clicking the *Set as Default Text Box* option at the shortcut menu.

Project 1b Formatting a Text Box and Setting the Default Text Box — Part 2 of 14

1. With **4-AddisonReport.pptx** open, make sure Slide 2 is the active slide and then complete the following steps:
   a. Click the Insert tab, click the Text Box button, and then click in the lower right corner of the slide.
   b. Type Default text box. (In the next step you will change the default text box. You will then use the text box you just inserted to return to the original default text box.)
2. Set as default the text box containing the word *SAFETY* by completing the following steps:
   a. Position the mouse pointer on the border of the text box containing the word *SAFETY* until the pointer displays with a four-headed arrow and then click the right mouse button.
   b. Click the *Set as Default Text Box* option at the shortcut menu.

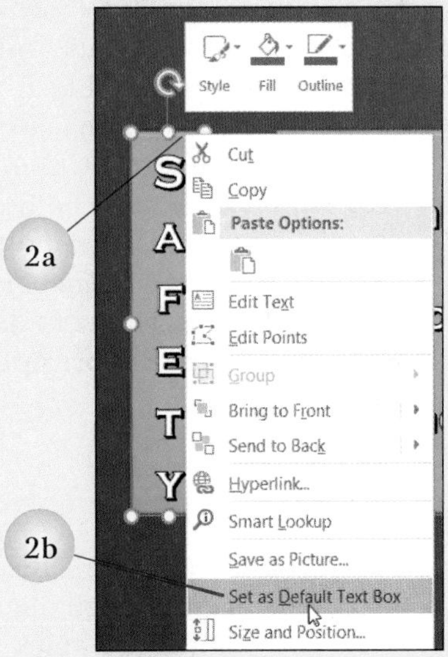

3. Make Slide 1 active.
4. Insert a text box by clicking the Insert tab, clicking the Text Box button, and then clicking between the company name and the left side of the slide.
5. Type 2018 in the text box.
6. Change the *Autofit* option, wrap text in the text box, and change the size of the text box by completing the following steps:
   a. Position the mouse pointer on the border of the text box until the pointer displays with a four-headed arrow and then click the right mouse button.
   b. Click the *Size and Position* option at the shortcut menu.
   c. At the Format Shape task pane with the Size & Properties icon selected, click *Text Box* to display the options, scroll to the bottom of the task pane list box, and then click in the *Wrap text in shape* check box to insert a check mark.
   d. Click the *Shrink text on overflow* option to select it.
   e. Scroll up to the top of the task pane and then click *Size* if the section is not displayed.

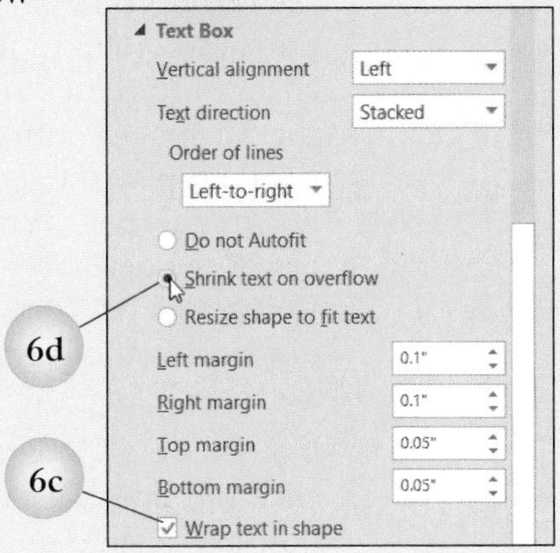

f. Select the current measurement in the *Height* measurement box in the *Size* section and then type 2.4.
g. Select the current measurement in the *Width* measurement box, type 0.8, and then press the Enter key.

7. With the text box selected, change the shape of the text box by completing the following steps:
   a. Click the Drawing Tools Format tab.
   b. Click the Edit Shape button in the Insert Shapes group, point to *Change Shape*, and then click the *Bevel* option (last option, second row in the *Basic Shapes* section).

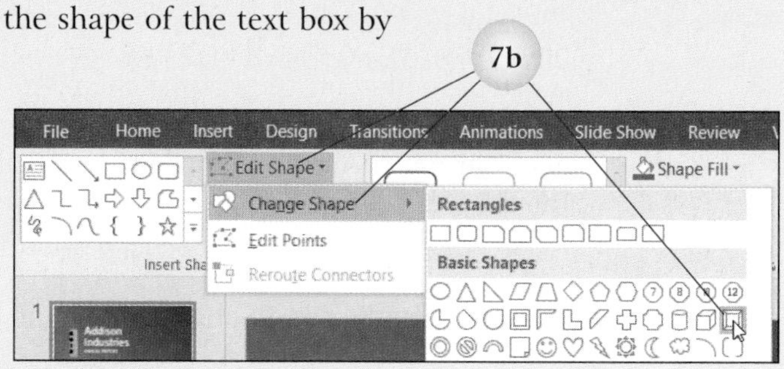

8. Precisely position the text box by completing the following steps:
   a. If necessary, scroll down the Format Shape task pane list box to the *Position* section and then click *Position* to display the options.
   b. Select the current measurement in the *Horizontal position* measurement box and then type 1.8.
   c. Select the current measurement in the *Vertical position* measurement box, type 2, and then press the Enter key.
9. Close the Format Shape task pane.
10. Return to the original text box by completing the following steps:
    a. Make Slide 2 active.
    b. Click in the text box containing the words *Default text box*.
    c. Position the mouse pointer on the border of the text box until the pointer displays with a four-headed arrow and then click the right mouse button.
    d. Click the *Set as Default Text Box* option at the shortcut menu.
    e. Press the Delete key to delete the text box.
11. Save **4-AddisonReport.pptx**.

Check Your Work

Setting Tabs in a Text Box

Hint Setting tabs helps you align text in a slide.

Left Tab

Center Tab

Right Tab

Decimal Tab

Text inside a text box can be aligned in columns using tabs. A text box, by default, contains left alignment tabs that display as gray marks along the bottom of the horizontal ruler. (If the ruler is not visible, display the horizontal ruler as well as the vertical ruler by clicking the View tab and then clicking the *Ruler* check box in the Show group to insert a check mark.) These default left alignment tabs can be changed to center, right, or decimal. To change to a different tab alignment, click the Alignment button above the vertical ruler and at the left side of the horizontal ruler. Display the desired tab alignment symbol and then click a location on the horizontal ruler. When a tab is set on the horizontal ruler, any default tabs to the left of the new tab are deleted. Move tabs on the horizontal ruler using the mouse to drag the tab to the new position. To delete a tab, use the mouse to drag the tab down and off of the ruler.

Tabs can also be set with option at the Tabs dialog box. To display this dialog box, click the Paragraph group dialog box launcher. At the Paragraph dialog box, click the Tabs button in the lower left corner. At the Tabs dialog box, type a tab position in the *Tab stop position* measurement box, choose a tab alignment with options in the *Alignment* section, and then click the Set button. Clear a specific tab by typing the tab position in the *Tab stop position* measurement box and then clicking the Clear button. Clear all tabs from the horizontal ruler by clicking the Clear All button. When all changes have been made, click OK to close the Tabs dialog box and then click OK to close the Paragraph dialog box.

Project 1c Creating a Text Box and Setting Tabs — Part 3 of 14

1. With **4-AddisonReport.pptx** open, make Slide 1 active and then click the Home tab.
2. Click the New Slide button arrow and then click the *Title Only* layout.
3. Click in the title placeholder and then type Executive Officers.
4. Draw a text box by completing the following steps:
   a. Click the Insert tab.
   b. Click the Text Box button in the Text group.
   c. Draw a text box in the slide that is approximately 10 inches wide and 0.5 inch tall.
5. Change tabs in the text box by completing the following steps:
   a. If necessary, display the horizontal ruler by clicking the View tab and then clicking the *Ruler* check box in the Show group to insert a check mark.
   b. With the insertion point inside the text box, check the Alignment button above the vertical ruler and at the left side of the horizontal ruler and make sure the left tab symbol displays.
   c. Position the tip of the mouse pointer on the horizontal ruler below the 0.5-inch mark and then click the left mouse button.

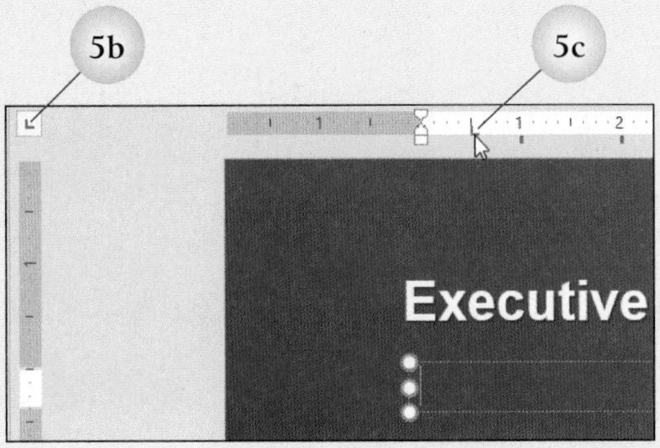

   d. Click the Alignment button to display the Center alignment symbol.
   e. Click immediately below the 5-inch mark on the horizontal ruler.
   f. Click the Alignment button to display the Right alignment symbol.

   g. Click the horizontal ruler immediately below the 9.5-inch mark. (You may need to expand the size of the text box to set the tab at the 9.5-inch mark.)
6. Type the text in the text box as shown in Figure 4.3. Make sure you press the Tab key before typing text in the first column. (This moves the insertion point to the first tab, which is a left alignment tab.) Bold the three column headings—*Name*, *Title*, and *Number*.
7. When you are finished typing the text in the text box, press Ctrl + A to select all of the text in the text box and then change the font size to 24 points.
8. With the text in the text box still selected, drag the left alignment marker on the horizontal ruler from the 0.5-inch mark to the 0.25-inch mark and then drag the center alignment marker on the horizontal ruler from the 5-inch mark on the ruler to the 5.5-inch mark.

9. Click the Line Spacing button in the Paragraph group on the Home tab and then click the *1.5* option.
10. Position the text box as shown in Figure 4.3.
11. Save **4-AddisonReport.pptx**.

Check Your Work

Figure 4.3 Project 1c, Slide 2

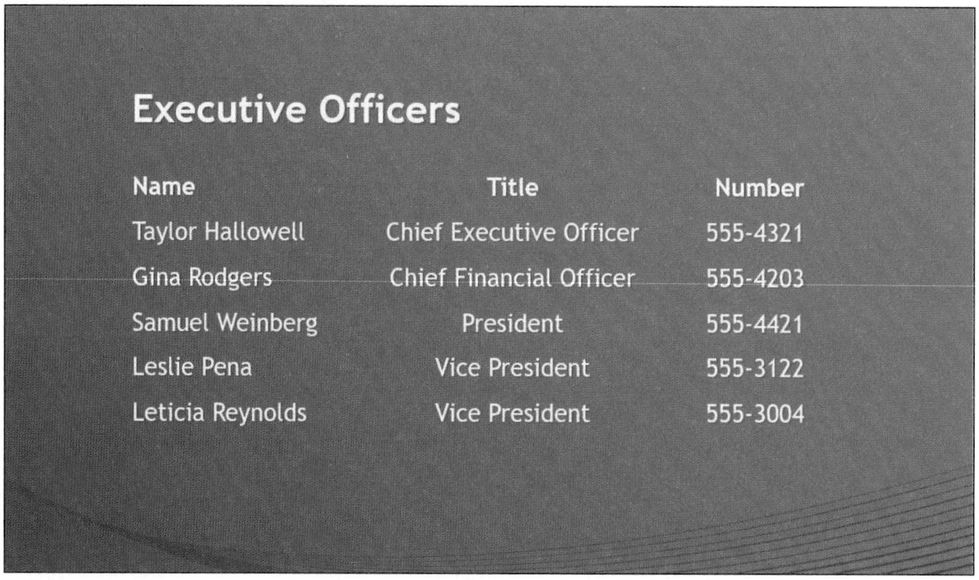

Executive Officers
Name
Title
Number
Taylor Hallowell
Chief Executive Officer
555-4321
Gina Rodgers
Chief Financial Officer
555-4203
Samuel Weinberg
President
555-4421
Leslie Pena
Vice President
555-3122
Leticia Reynolds
Vice President
555-3004

Tutorial

Inserting, Sizing, and Positioning Shapes

Tutorial

Formatting Shapes

Shapes

Quick Steps

Insert a Shape

1. Click Insert tab.
2. Click Shapes button.
3. Choose shape at drop-down list.
4. Click or drag in slide to create shape.

Quick Steps

Copy a Shape

1. Select shape.
2. Click Copy button.
3. Position insertion point at new location.
4. Click Paste button.

Inserting, Formatting, and Copying Shapes

Draw shapes in a slide with shapes in the Drawing group or with the Shapes button in the Illustrations group on the Insert tab. Use the Shapes button drop-down list to draw shapes including lines, basic shapes, block arrows, flow chart symbols, callouts, stars, and banners. Click a shape and the mouse pointer displays as crosshairs (plus sign). Click in the slide to insert the shape, or position the crosshairs in the slide and then click and drag to create the shape.

Apply formatting to a shape in a manner similar to formatting a text box. Format a shape with buttons in the Drawing group on the Home tab, with buttons on the Drawing Tools Format tab, using options in the Format Shape task pane, or with options at the shortcut menu. When drawing an enclosed object, maintain the proportions of the shape by holding down the Shift key while dragging with the mouse to create the shape. The formatting applied to a shape can be saved as the default formatting. To do this, right-click the border of the shape and then click *Set as Default Shape*.

To copy a shape, select the shape and then click the Copy button in the Clipboard group on the Home tab. Position the insertion point and then click the Paste button. A selected shape can also be copied by pressing and holding down the Ctrl key while dragging the shape to the new location.

Tutorial

Displaying Rulers, Gridlines, and Guides; Copying and Rotating Shapes

Displaying Rulers, Gridlines, and Guides

PowerPoint provides a number of features for positioning objects such as placeholders, text boxes, and shapes. Display horizontal and vertical rulers, gridlines, and/or drawing guides and use Smart Guides as shown in Figure 4.4. Turn the horizontal and vertical rulers on and off with the *Ruler* check box in the Show group on the View tab as you did in Project 1c. The Show group also contains a *Gridlines* check box. Insert a check mark in this check box and gridlines display in the active slide. Gridlines are intersecting lines that create a grid on the slide and are useful for aligning objects. Turn the gridlines on and off with the keyboard shortcut, Shift + F9.

Turn on drawing guides to help position objects on a slide. Drawing guides are a horizontal dashed line and a vertical dashed line that display on the slide in the slide pane as shown in Figure 4.4. To turn on the drawing guides, display the Grid and Guides dialog box shown in Figure 4.5. Display this dialog box by clicking the Show group dialog box launcher on the View tab. At the dialog box, insert a check mark in the *Display drawing guides on screen* check box. By default, the horizontal and vertical drawing guides intersect in the middle of the slide. Move these guides by dragging the guide with the mouse. Drag a guide and a measurement displays next to the mouse pointer. Drawing guides and gridlines display on the slide but do not print.

Figure 4.4 Rulers, Gridlines, Drawing Guides, and Smart Guides

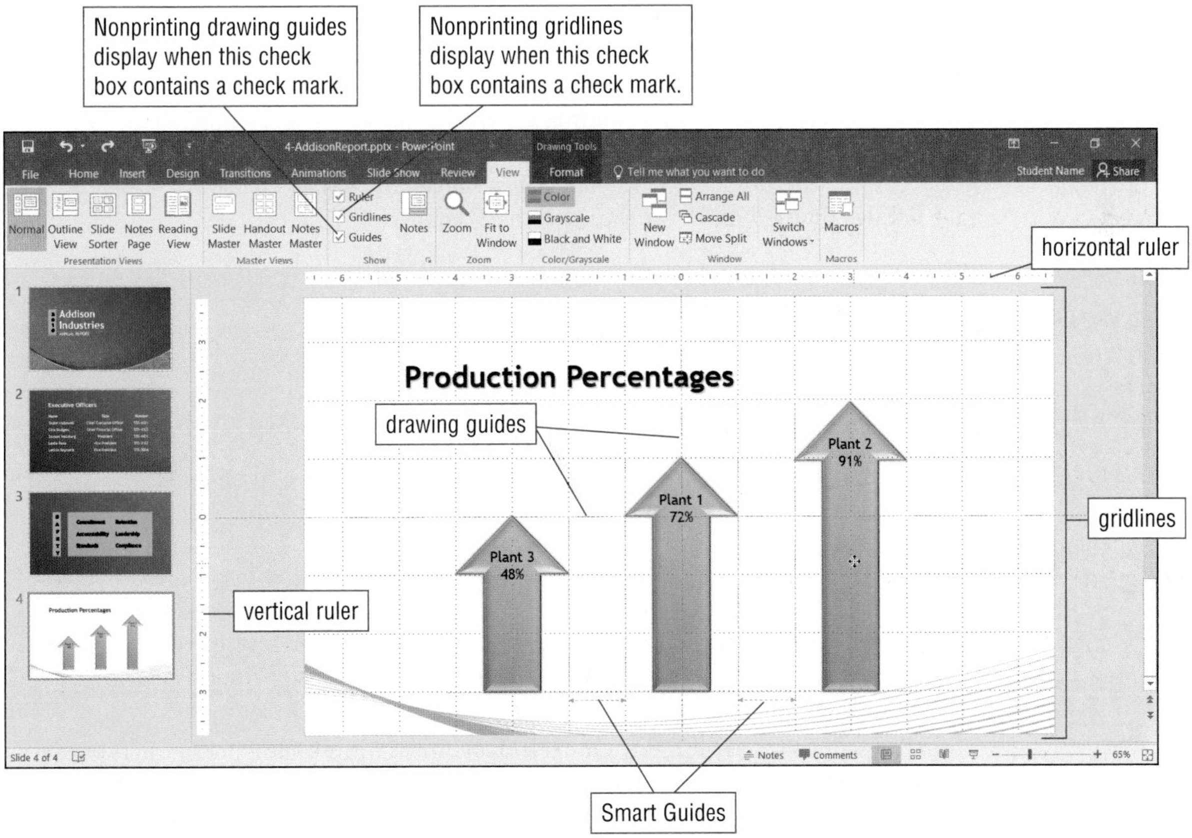

Figure 4.5 Grid and Guides Dialog Box

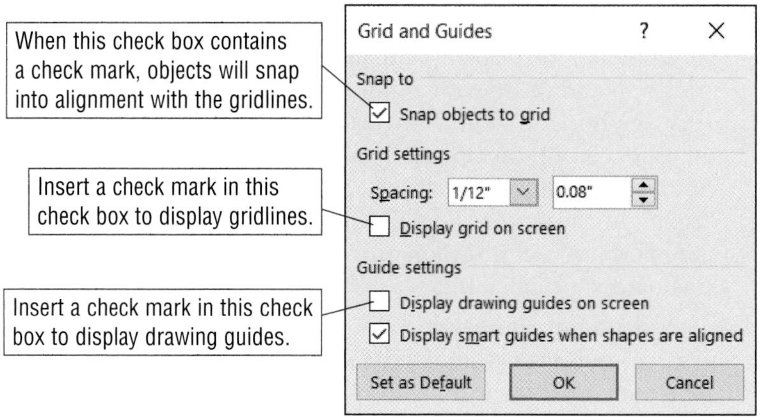

PowerPoint includes Smart Guides, which appear when objects that are close together are moved on a slide. Use these guides to help align and evenly space the objects on the slide. Turn on gridlines by inserting a check mark in the *Gridlines* check box on the View tab or by inserting a check mark in the *Display grid on screen* check box at the Grid and Guides dialog box. The horizontal and vertical spacing between the gridlines is 0.08 inch by default. This measurement can be changed with the *Spacing* option at the Grid and Guides dialog box.

As an object is moved on the slide, it is pulled into alignment with the nearest intersection of gridlines. This is because the *Snap objects to grid* check box at the Grid and Guides dialog box contains a check mark by default. To position an object precisely, turn off this option by removing the check mark from the *Snap objects to grid* check box or by holding down the Alt key while dragging an object. Smart Guides display when shapes are aligned. To turn off the display of Smart Guides, click the *Display smart guides when shapes are aligned* check box in the Grid and Guides dialog box to remove the check mark.

Project 1d Drawing and Formatting Shapes — Part 4 of 14

1. With **4-AddisonReport.pptx** open, make Slide 3 active and then insert a new slide by clicking the New Slide button arrow in the Slides group on the Home tab and then clicking the *White Background* layout at the drop-down list.
2. Turn on the display of gridlines by clicking the View tab and then clicking *Gridlines* to insert a check mark in the check box.

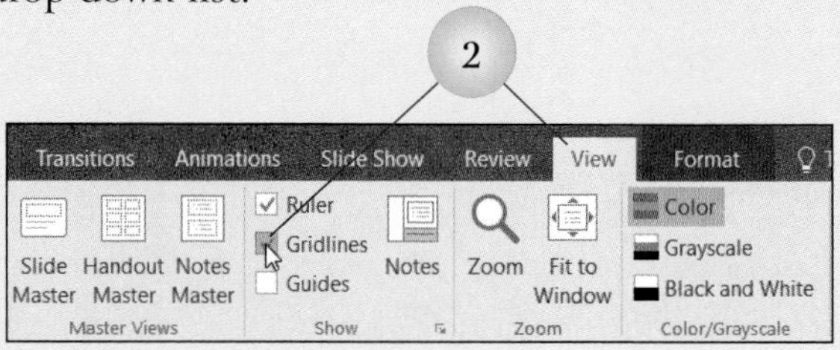

3. Click in the title placeholder and then type Production Percentages.
4. Turn on the drawing guides and turn off the snap-to-grid feature by completing the following steps:
   a. Make sure the View tab is active and then click the Show group dialog box launcher.

b. At the Grid and Guides dialog box, click the *Snap objects to grid* check box to remove the check mark.
c. Make sure the *Display grid on screen* check box contains a check mark.
d. Click the *Display drawing guides on screen* check box to insert a check mark.
e. Click OK.

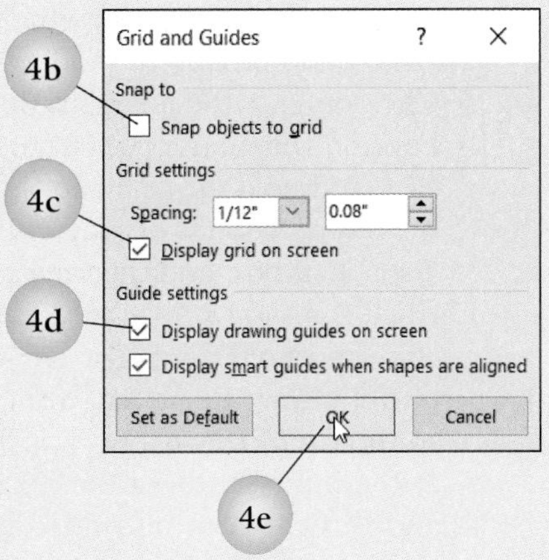

5. Insert the left-most arrow in the slide, as shown in Figure 4.6 (on page 119), by completing the following steps:
   a. Click outside the title placeholder to deselect it.
   b. Click the Insert tab.
   c. Click the Shapes button in the Illustrations group and then click the *Up Arrow* shape (third column, first row in the *Block Arrows* section).
   d. Position the crosshairs at the intersection of the horizontal drawing guide and the third vertical gridline from the left.
   e. Click and hold down the left mouse button, drag down and to the right until the crosshairs are positioned on the intersection of the fifth vertical line from the left and the first horizontal line from the bottom, and then release the mouse button. (Your arrow should be the approximate size shown in Figure 4.6.)

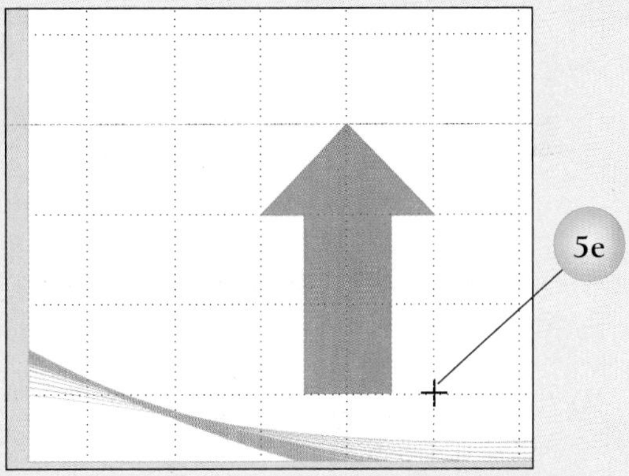

   f. With the arrow selected and the Drawing Tools Format tab active, click the Shape Fill button arrow in the Shape Styles group, and then click *Aqua, Accent 5* at the drop-down gallery (ninth column, first row in the *Theme Colors* section).
   g. Click the Shape Outline button arrow and then click *Dark Blue* at the drop-down gallery (ninth option in the *Standard Colors* section).
   h. Apply a shape style to the arrow by clicking the More Shape Styles button in the Shapes Styles group and then clicking the *Subtle Effect - Blue, Accent 1* option (second column, fourth row).
   i. Click the Shape Effects button in the Shape Styles group, point to *Bevel*, and then click the *Soft Round* option (second column, second row in the *Bevel* section).
6. Insert text in the arrow by completing the following steps:
   a. With the arrow selected, type Plant 3, press the Enter key, and then type 48%.
   b. Click the Home tab, click the Align Text button in the Paragraph group, and then click the *Top* option at the drop-down list.
7. Copy the arrow by completing the following steps:
   a. Position the mouse pointer on the border of the selected arrow until the mouse pointer displays with a four-headed arrow.
   b. Press and hold down the Ctrl key, click and hold down the left mouse button, drag the arrow to the intersection of the horizontal and vertical drawing guides, and then release the Ctrl key and the mouse button.

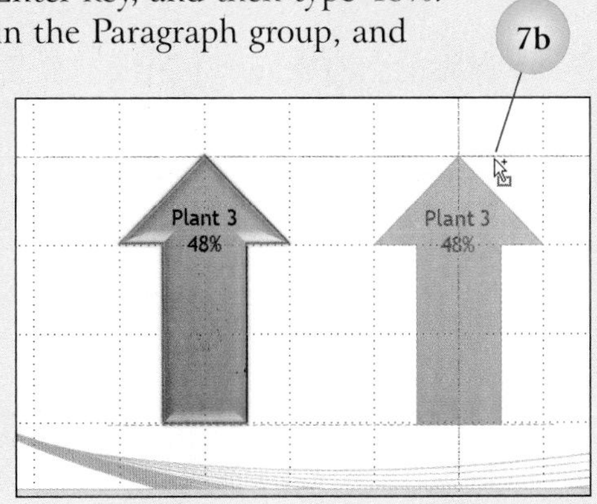

8. Move the vertical drawing guide and then copy the right arrow by completing the following steps:
   a. Click outside the arrow to deselect the arrow.
   b. Position the mouse pointer on the vertical drawing guide, click and hold down the left mouse button, drag right until the mouse pointer displays with *3.00* and a right-pointing arrow in a box, and then release the mouse button.

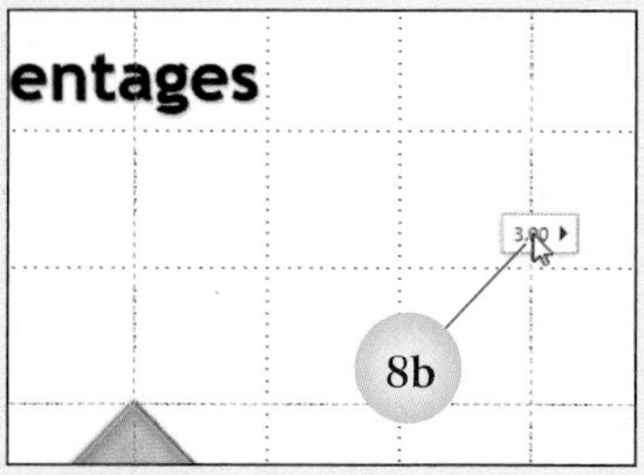

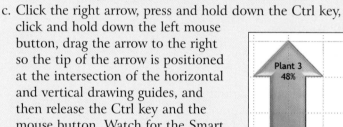

   c. Click the right arrow, press and hold down the Ctrl key, click and hold down the left mouse button, drag the arrow to the right so the tip of the arrow is positioned at the intersection of the horizontal and vertical drawing guides, and then release the Ctrl key and the mouse button. Watch for the Smart Guides to display indicating that the arrows are aligned and evenly spaced (see image at the right).

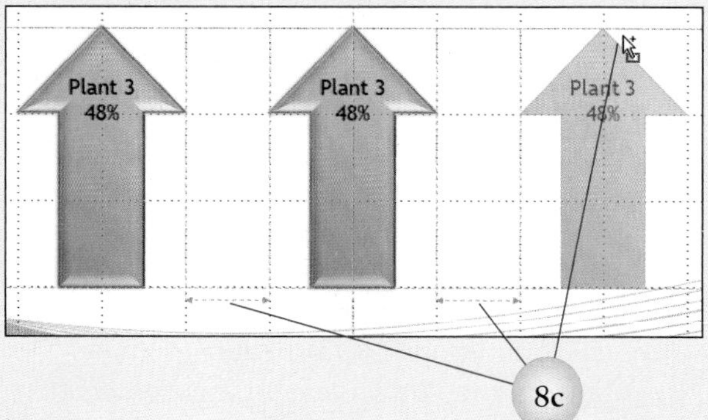

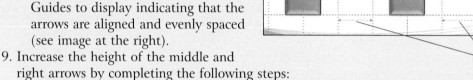

9. Increase the height of the middle and right arrows by completing the following steps:
   a. Click the middle arrow to select it.
   b. Use the mouse to drag the top middle sizing handle up to the next horizontal gridline.
   c. Click the right arrow and then drag the top middle sizing handle up to the second horizontal gridline (see Figure 4.6).
   d. Change the text in the middle arrow to *Plant 1 72%* and change the text in the right arrow to *Plant 2 91%* (see Figure 4.6).
10. Turn on the snap-to-grid feature and turn off the gridlines and drawing guides by completing the following steps:
    a. Click the View tab.
    b. Click the Show group dialog box launcher.
    c. At the Grid and Guides dialog box, click the *Snap objects to grid* check box to insert a check mark.
    d. Click the *Display grid on screen* option to remove the check mark.
    e. Click the *Display drawing guides on screen* check box to remove the check mark.
    f. Click OK.
11. Change the slide layout by clicking the Home tab, clicking the Layout button in the Slides group, and then clicking the *Title Only* layout.
12. Set the formatting of the arrow shape as the default by completing the following steps:
    a. Click the left arrow shape.
    b. Position the mouse pointer on the arrow shape border until the pointer displays with a four-headed arrow and then click the right mouse button.
    c. Click the *Set as Default Shape* option at the shortcut menu.
13. Draw a shape by completing the following steps:
    a. Click the Insert tab, click the Shapes button, and then click the *Bevel* option (first column, third row in the *Basic Shapes* section).
    b. Click in the lower right corner of the slide.
    c. Change the height and width of the shape to 0.6 inch.
    d. Type AI in the shape.
    e. Position the shape in the slide as shown in Figure 4.6.
14. Save **4-AddisonReport.pptx**.

Check Your Work

Figure 4.6 Project 1d, Slide 4

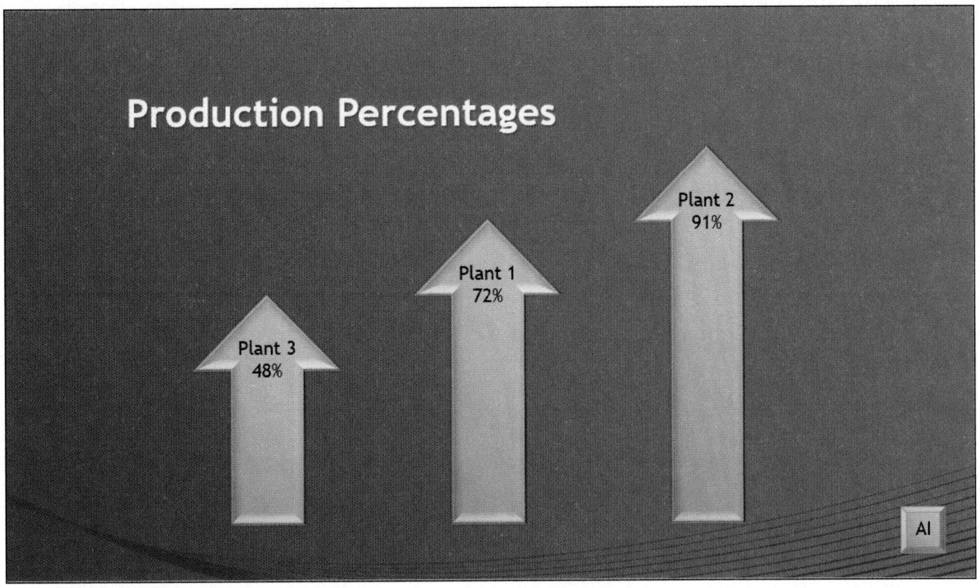

Merging Shapes

Merge Shapes

Use the Merge Shapes button on the Drawing Tools Format tab to merge shapes to create custom shapes that are not available with the default shapes. To merge shapes, draw the shapes in the slide, select the shapes, and then click the Merge Shapes button in the Insert Shapes group on the Drawing Tools Format tab. At the drop-down list, choose one of the following options: *Union*, *Combine*, *Fragment*, *Intersect*, and *Subtract*. Each option merges the shapes in a different manner.

Project 1e **Merging Shapes** — **Part 5 of 14**

1. With **4-AddisonReport.pptx** open, make Slide 4 active and then insert a slide from another presentation by completing the following steps:
   a. Click the Home tab.
   b. Click the New Slide button arrow and then click *Reuse Slides* at the drop-down list.
   c. At the Reuse Slides task pane, click the Browse button and then click *Browse File* at the drop-down list.
   d. At the Browse dialog box, navigate to the PC4 folder on your storage medium and then double-click ***IEC.pptx***.
   e. Click the second slide thumbnail in the Reuse Slides task pane.
   f. Close the Reuse Slides task pane by clicking the Close button in the upper right corner of the task pane.

2. The slide you inserted contains a circle shape and four rectangle shapes. Merge the shapes to create an image for the International Energy Consortium by completing the following steps:
   a. Click the slide in the slide pane and then press Ctrl + A to select all of the shapes in the slide.
   b. Click the Drawing Tools Format tab.
   c. Click the Merge Shapes button in the Insert Shapes group.
   d. Hover your mouse over each option in the drop-down list to view how the option merges the shapes in the slide, and then click the *Subtract* option. (This merges the shapes into one shape.)

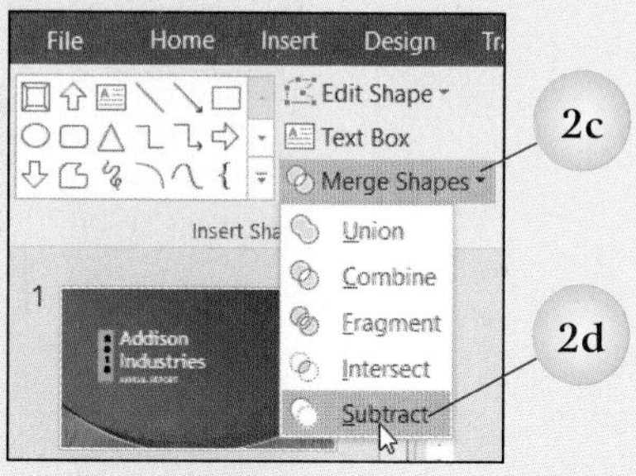

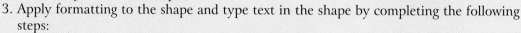

3. Apply formatting to the shape and type text in the shape by completing the following steps:
   a. Click the Shape Fill button arrow in the Shape Styles group and then click the *White, Text 1* option (second column, first row in the *Theme Colors* section).
   b. Click the Text Fill button arrow in the WordArt Styles group and then click the *Black, Background 1* option (first column, first row in the *Theme Colors* section).
   c. Type the following in the shape pressing the Enter key to end each line as shown:

      International Energy
      Consortium
      Global Summit
      March 7 to 9, 2018
      Paris, France

   d. Select the text you just typed and then change the font size to 20 points.
4. Save **4-AddisonReport.pptx**.

Check Your Work

Tutorial

Grouping and Ungrouping Objects

Quick Steps

Group Objects
1. Select objects.
2. Click Drawing Tools Format tab.
3. Click Group button.
4. Click *Group*.

Group

Hint Group objects so you can move, size, flip, or rotate objects at the same time.

Grouping and Ungrouping Objects

To apply the same formatting or make the same adjustments to the size or rotation of objects, group the objects. When objects are grouped, any formatting applied such as a shape fill, effect, or shape style, is applied to each object within the group. To group objects, select the objects to be included in the group by clicking each object while holding down the Shift key or, using the mouse, click and drag a border around all the objects. With the objects selected, click the Drawing Tools Format tab, click the Group button in the Arrange group, and then click *Group* at the drop-down list.

An individual object within a group can be formatted. To do this, click any object in the group and the group border displays around the objects. Click the individual object and then apply the desired formatting. To ungroup objects, click the group to select it, click the Drawing Tools Format tab, click the Group button in the Arrange group, and then click *Ungroup* at the drop-down list.

1. With **4-AddisonReport.pptx** open, make Slide 3 active.
2. Group the objects and apply formatting by completing the following steps:
   a. Using the mouse, click and drag a border around the two text boxes in the slide to select them.
   b. Click the Drawing Tools Format tab.
   c. Click the Group button in the Arrange group and then click *Group* at the drop-down list.
   d. Click the More Shape Styles button in the Shape Styles group and then click the *Subtle Effect - Blue, Accent 1* option (second column, fourth row).

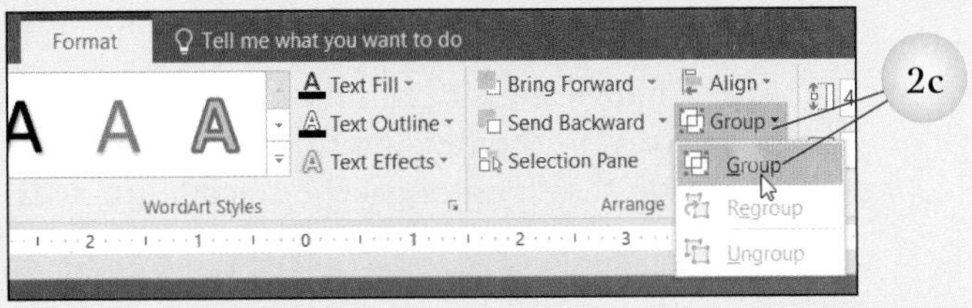

   e. Click the Shape Outline button arrow and then click the *Dark Blue* color (ninth color in the *Standard Colors* section).
   f. Click the Shape Outline button arrow, point to *Weight*, and then click *4½ pt*.
3. With the text boxes selected, ungroup the text boxes by clicking the Group button in the Arrange group and then clicking *Ungroup* at the drop-down list.
4. Click the text box containing the columns of text, click the More WordArt Styles button in the WordArt Styles group, and then click the *Fill - White, Text 1, Outline - Background 1, Hard Shadow - Background 1* option (first column, third row).
5. Make Slide 1 active, click the text box containing the text *2018*, click the Quick Styles button in the Drawing group on the Home tab, and then click the *Subtle Effect - Blue, Accent 1* option (second column, fourth row).
6. Save **4-AddisonReport.pptx**.

Check Your Work

Tutorial

Inserting, Sizing, and Moving an Image

Pictures

Inserting an Image

Insert an image such as a picture or clip art in a slide using the buttons in the Images group on the Insert tab. To insert an image in a presentation, click the Insert tab and then click the Pictures button in the Images group. At the Insert Picture dialog box, navigate to the folder containing the image and then double-click the image. Use buttons on the Picture Tools Format tab to format and customize the image.

Tutorial

Formatting an Image

Quick Steps

Insert an Image

1. Click Insert tab.
2. Click Pictures button.
3. Navigate to folder.
4. Double-click image.

Customizing and Formatting an Image

When an image that has been inserted in a slide is selected, the Picture Tools Format tab becomes active, as shown in Figure 4.7. Use buttons on this tab to apply formatting to the image. Use options in the Adjust group on the Picture Tools Format tab to crop or remove unwanted portions of the image, correct the brightness and contrast, change the image color, apply artistic effects, compress the size of the image file, change to a different image, and reset the image back to its original formatting.

Use buttons in the Picture Styles group to apply a predesigned style to the image, change the image border, or apply other effects to the image. The Arrange group contains options for positioning the image, specifying how text will wrap around it, aligning the image with other elements in the document, and rotating the image. Use options in the Size group to crop the image and change the image size.

Figure 4.7 Picture Tools Format Tab

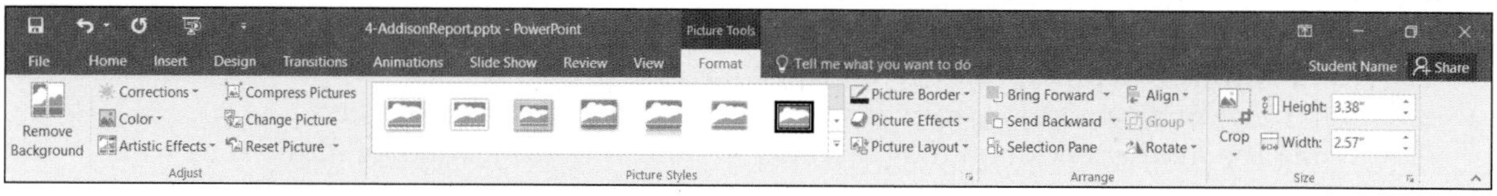

Sizing, Cropping, and Moving an Image

Change the size of an image with the *Shape Height* and *Shape Width* measurement boxes in the Size group on the Picture Tools Format tab or with the sizing handles that display around the selected image. To change the size with a sizing handle, position the mouse pointer on a sizing handle until the pointer turns into a double-headed arrow and then click and hold down the left mouse button. Drag the sizing handle in or out to decrease or increase the size of the image and then release the mouse button. Use the middle sizing handles at the left or right side of the image to make the image wider or thinner. Use the middle sizing handles at the top or bottom of the image to make the image taller or shorter. Use the sizing handles at the corners of the image to change both the width and height at the same time.

Crop

Hint Insert a picture from your camera by downloading the picture to your computer and then copying or inserting the picture into PowerPoint.

The Size group on the Picture Tools Format tab contains a Crop button. Use this button to remove portions of an image. Click the Crop button and the mouse pointer displays with the crop tool attached, which is a black square with overlapping lines, and the image displays with cropping handles around the border. Drag a cropping handle to remove a portion of the image.

Move a selected image by dragging it to the new location. Move the image by positioning the mouse pointer on the image border until the arrow pointer turns into a four-headed arrow. Click and hold down the left mouse button, drag the image to the new position, and then release the mouse button. The arrow keys on the keyboard can be used to move the image in the desired direction. To move the image in small increments (called *nudging*), press and hold down the Ctrl key while pressing an arrow key.

Use the rotation handle to rotate an image by positioning the mouse pointer on the white, round rotation handle until the pointer displays as a circular arrow. Click and hold down the left mouse button, drag in the desired direction, and then release the mouse button.

Arranging Images

Bring Forward

Send Backward

Use the Bring Forward and Send Backward buttons in the Arrange group on the Drawing Tools Format tab or the Picture Tools Format tab to layer one object on top of another. Click the Bring Forward button and the selected object is moved forward one layer. For example, if three objects are layered on top of each other, select the object at the bottom of the layers and then click the Bring Forward button to move the object in front of the second object (but not the first object). To move an object to the top layer, select the object, click the Bring Forward button arrow, and then click the *Bring to Front* option at the drop-down list. To move the selected object back one layer, click the Send Backward button. To move the selected object behind all other objects, click the Send Backward button arrow and then click the *Send to Back* option at the drop-down list.

Project 1g Inserting and Formatting Images

Part 7 of 14

1. With **4-AddisonReport.pptx** open, make Slide 4 active and click the Insert tab.
2. Insert a new slide by clicking the New Slide button arrow in the Slides group and then clicking *Blank* at the drop-down list.
3. Insert a text box by completing the following steps:
   a. Click the Text Box button in the Text group on the Insert tab.
   b. Click in the middle of the slide.
   c. Change the font to Arial Black and the font size to 36 points.
   d. Click the Center button in the Paragraph group.
   e. Type Alternative, press the Enter key, and then type Energy Resources.
   f. With the text box selected, click the Drawing Tools Format tab.
   g. Click the Align button in the Arrange group and then click *Distribute Horizontally* at the drop-down list.
   h. Click the Align button and then click *Distribute Vertically* at the drop-down list.

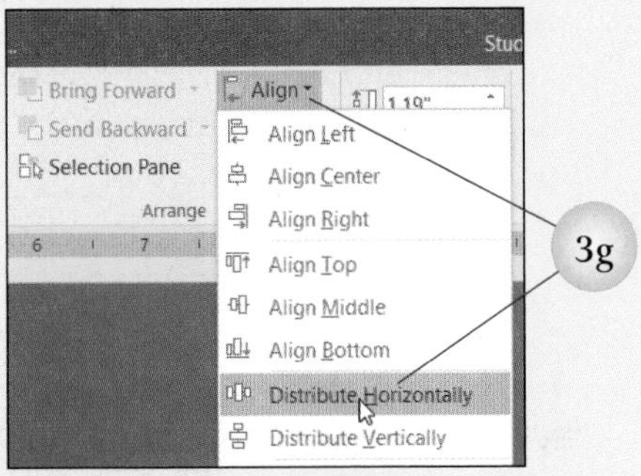

4. Insert an image by completing the following steps:
   a. Click the Insert tab.
   b. Click the Pictures button in the Images group.
   c. At the Insert Picture dialog box, navigate to the PC4 folder on your storage medium and then double-click ***Mountain.jpg***.
5. You decide to insert an image of the ocean rather than a mountain. Change the image by completing the following steps:
   a. With the image of the mountain selected, click the Change Picture button in the Adjust group.
   b. At the Insert Pictures window, click the Browse button at the right of the *From a file* option.
   c. At the Insert Picture dialog box, make sure the PC4 folder on your storage medium is selected and then double-click ***Ocean.jpg***.

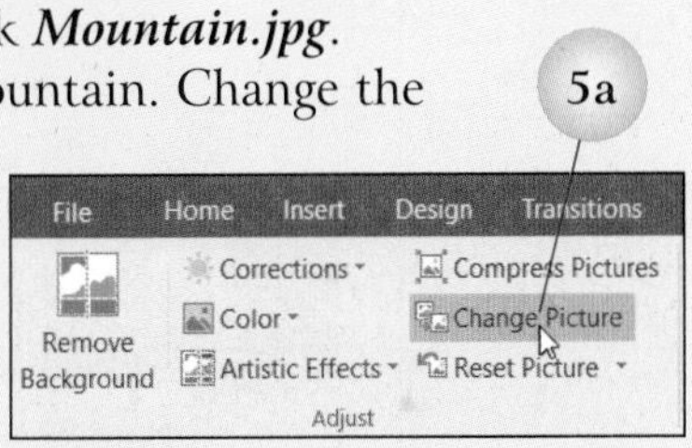

6. Crop the image by completing the following steps:
   a. With the image selected, click the Crop button in the Size group on the Picture Tools Format tab.
   b. Position the mouse pointer (displays with the crop tool attached) on the cropping handle in the middle of the right side of the image.
   c. Click and hold down the left mouse button and then drag to the left approximately 0.25 inch. (Use the guideline on the horizontal ruler to crop the image 0.25 inch.)
   d. Click the Crop button to turn off cropping.

e. Click the Crop button arrow, point to the *Crop to Shape* option at the drop-down list, and then click the *Oval* shape (first option) in the *Basic Shapes* section of the side menu.

7. Click in the *Shape Height* measurement box in the Size group, type 5, and then press the Enter key.
8. Click the Send Backward button in the Arrange group. (This moves the image behind the text in the text box.)

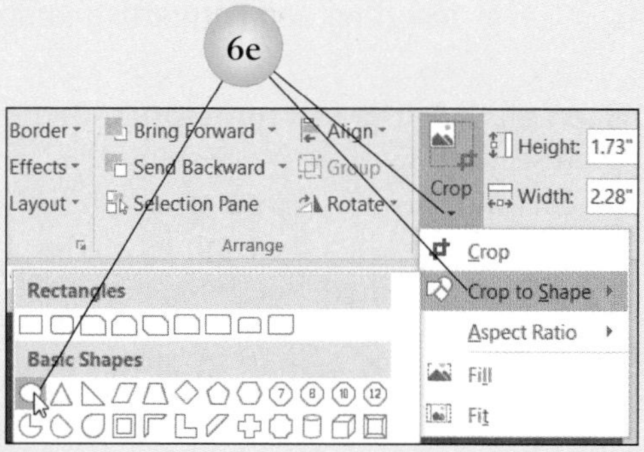

9. Align the image by completing the following steps:
   a. Click the Align button in the Arrange group on the Picture Tools Format tab and then click the *Distribute Horizontally* option.
   b. Click the Align button and then click the *Distribute Vertically* option.
10. Format the image by completing the following steps:
    a. Click the Artistic Effects button in the Adjust group and then click the *Cutout* option (first column, bottom row).
    b. Click the Corrections button in the Adjust group and then click the *Soften: 25%* option (second option in the *Sharpen/Soften* section).

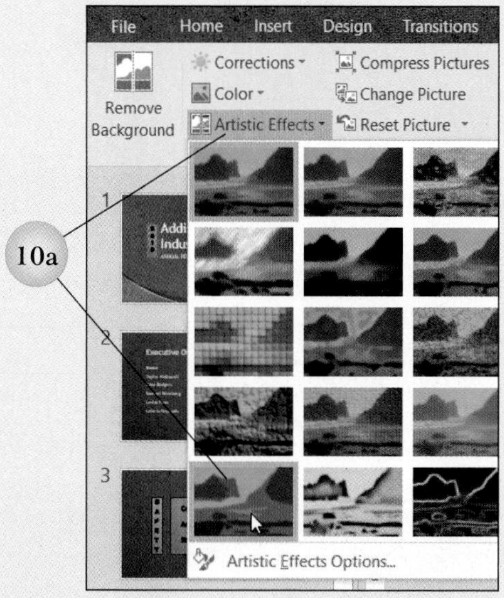

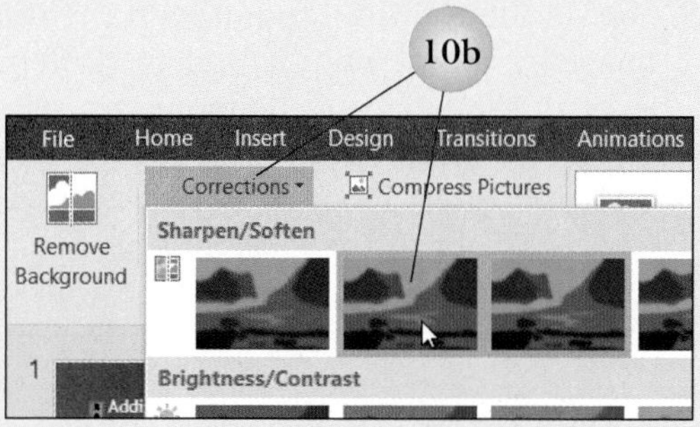

    c. Click the Picture Border button arrow in the Picture Styles group and then click the *Dark Blue* color (ninth option in the *Standard Colors* section).
11. After viewing the effects applied to the image, reset the image to the original formatting by clicking the Reset Picture button arrow in the Adjust group and then clicking *Reset Picture* at the drop-down list.

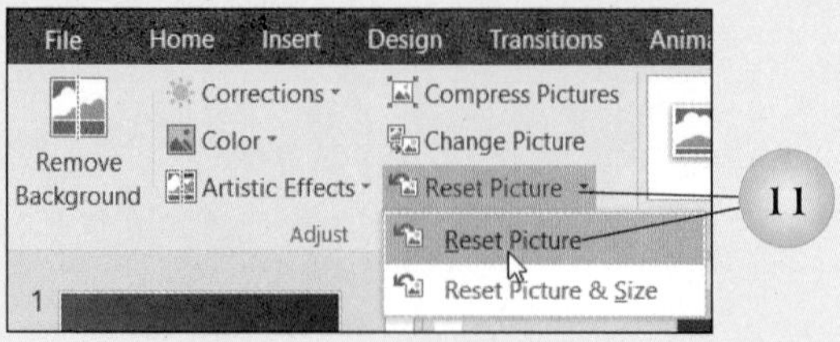

12. Format the image by completing the following steps:
   a. Click the Corrections button in the Adjust group and then click the *Brightness: -20% Contrast: +40%* option (second column, last row in the *Brightness/Contrast* section).
   b. Click the Corrections button and then click the *Sharpen: 25%* option (fourth option in the *Sharpen/Soften* section).
   c. Click the More Picture Styles button in the Picture Styles group and then click the *Soft Edge Oval* option at the drop-down gallery (sixth column, third row).

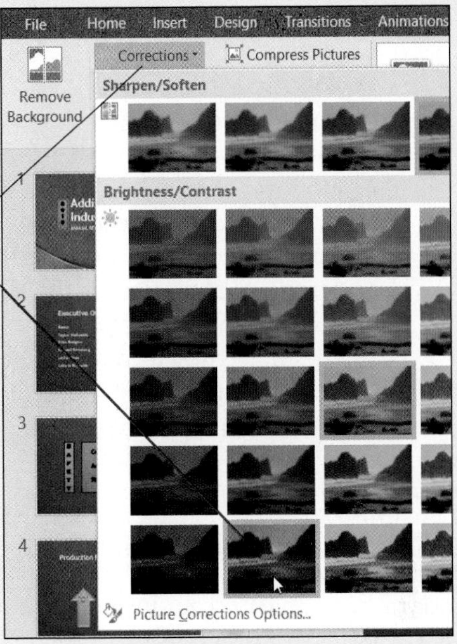

12a

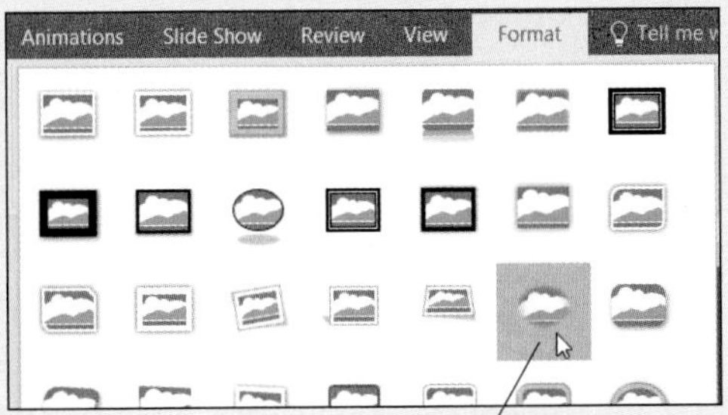

12c

   d. Click the Compress Pictures button in the Adjust group. At the Compress Pictures dialog box, click OK.
13. Make Slide 6 active and then insert a new slide by clicking the Home tab, clicking the New Slide button arrow in the Slides group, and then clicking *Title Only* at the drop-down list.
14. Click in the title placeholder and then type Shipping Contracts.
15. Insert an image by completing the following steps:
   a. Click the Insert tab and then click the Pictures button in the Images group.
   b. At the Insert Picture dialog box, make sure the PC4 folder on your storage medium is active and then double-click ***Ship.jpg***.
16. With the image selected, remove some of the background by completing the following steps:
   a. Click the Remove Background button in the Adjust group on the Picture Tools Format tab.
   b. Using the left middle sizing handle, drag the border to the left to include the back of the ship (see image at the right).
   c. Click the Mark Areas to Remove button in the Refine group on the Background Removal tab.
   d. Click anywhere in the water below the ship. (This removes the water from the image. If all of the water is not removed, you will need to click again in the remaining water.)
   e. Using the right middle sizing handle, drag the border to the left so the border is near the front of the ship.
   f. If part of the structure above the front of the ship has been removed, include it in the image. To begin, click the Mark Areas to Keep button in the Refine group. (The mouse pointer displays as a pencil.)

16b

g. Using the mouse, position the pencil at the top of the structure (as shown at the right), drag down to the top of the containers on the ship, and then release the mouse button.
h. Click the Keep Changes button in the Close group on the Background Removal tab.

17. Click the Corrections button in the Adjust group on the Picture Tools Format tab and then click the *Brightness: +40% Contrast: +40%* option at the drop-down gallery (last column, last row in the *Brightness/Contrast* section).
18. Click the Corrections button in the Adjust group and then click the *Sharpen: 50%* option at the drop-down gallery (last option in the *Sharpen/Soften* section).
19. Drag the image down to the middle of the slide.
20. Click outside the image to deselect it.
21. Save **4-AddisonReport.pptx**.

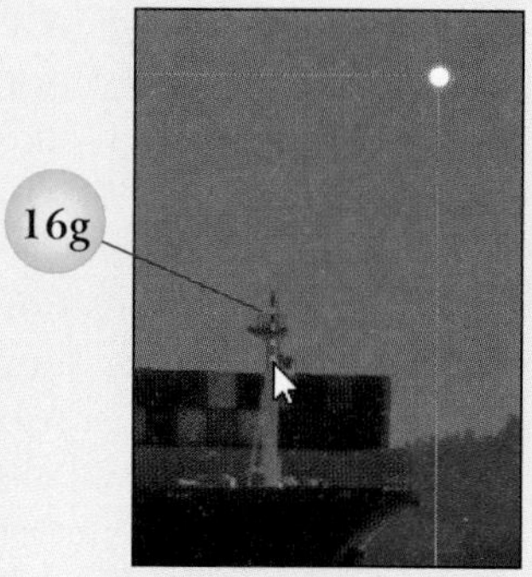

Check Your Work

Tutorial

Inserting an Image as a Slide Background

Inserting an Image as a Slide Background

Insert an image, such as a picture or clip art, as a slide background by clicking the Design tab and then clicking the Format Background button in the Customize group. This displays the Format Background task pane with the Fill icon selected. Click the *Picture or texture fill* option in the *Fill* section of the task pane and then click the File button. At the Insert Picture dialog box, navigate to the desired folder and then double-click the image. To display the image background on all slides, click the Apply to All button at the Format Background task pane.

Use options in the Format Background task pane to apply formatting to the background image. When an image is inserted in a slide, the Format Background task pane (with the Fill icon selected) includes options for hiding background graphics, applying a texture, changing the image transparency, and offsetting the image on the slide either at the left, right, top, or bottom. Click the Effects icon and then click the Artistic Effects button and a drop-down palette of artistic options displays. Click the Picture icon and options display in the task pane for correcting the sharpness, softness, brightness, and contrast of the image and for changing the color saturation and tone of the image.

Quick Steps

Insert an Image as a Slide Background
1. Click Design tab.
2. Click Format Background button.
3. Click *Picture or texture fill* option.
4. Click File button.
5. Navigate to folder.
6. Double-click image.
7. Click Close button.

Project 1h Inserting an Image as a Slide Background — Part 8 of 14

1. With **4-AddisonReport.pptx** open, make sure both Slide 7 and the Home tab are active.
2. Click the New Slide button arrow in the Slides group and then click the *Title Only* layout at the drop-down list.
3. Insert an image background on Slide 8 by completing the following steps:
   a. Click the Design tab.
   b. Click the Format Background button in the Customize group.

c. At the Format Background task pane, click the *Picture or texture fill* option in the *Fill* section to select it.
d. Click the File button in the task pane below the text *Insert picture from*.
e. At the Insert Picture dialog box, navigate to the PC4 folder on your storage medium and then double-click ***EiffelTower.jpg***.

4. Apply formatting to the image background by completing these steps:
   a. Click the *Hide background graphics* check box to insert a check mark.
   b. Select the current percentage in the *Transparency* measurement box, type 5, and then press the Enter key.
   c. Select the current number in the *Offset top* measurement box, type -50, and then press the Enter key. (Decreasing the negative number displays more of the top of the Eiffel Tower.)
   d. Click the Effects icon in the task pane and then, if necessary, click *Articist Effects* to display the formatting options.
   e. Click the Artistic Effects button and then click the *Glow Diffused* option (fourth column, second row).
   f. Click the Picture icon and, if necessary, expand the *Picture Corrections* section.
   g. Select the current number in the *Contrast* measurement box, type 25, and then press the Enter key.
   h. If necessary, expand the *Picture Color* section.
   i. Select the current number in the *Saturation* measurement box, type 80, and then press the Enter key.
5. Remove the artistic effect by clicking the Effects icon, clicking the Artistic Effects button, and then clicking the *None* option (first option).
6. Close the Format Background task pane.
7. Click in the title placeholder, type European, press the Enter key, and then type Division 2020. Drag the placeholder so it is positioned attractively on the slide in the upper left corner.
8. Save **4-AddisonReport.pptx**.

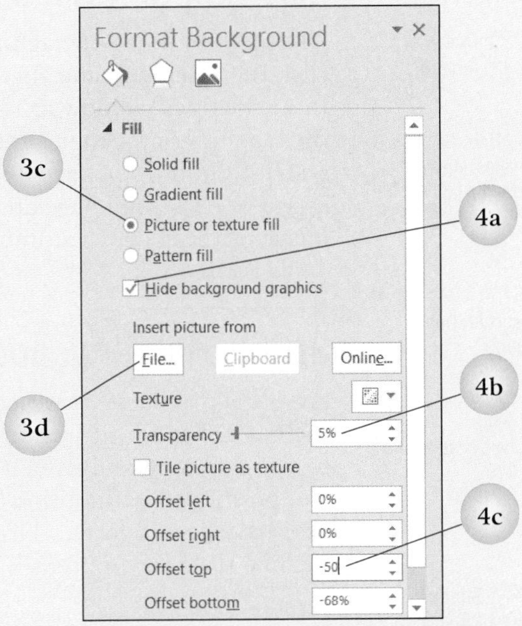

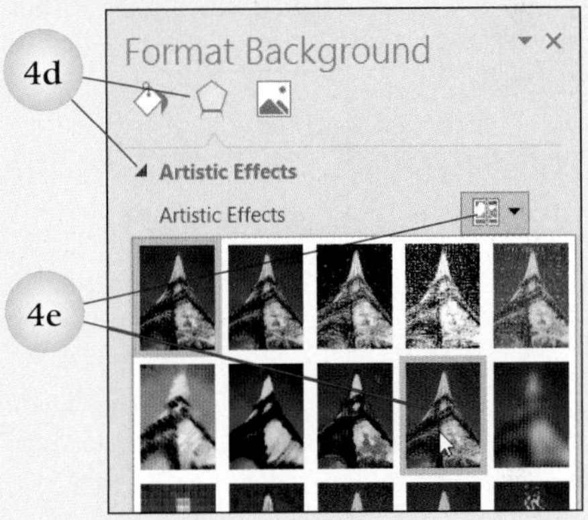

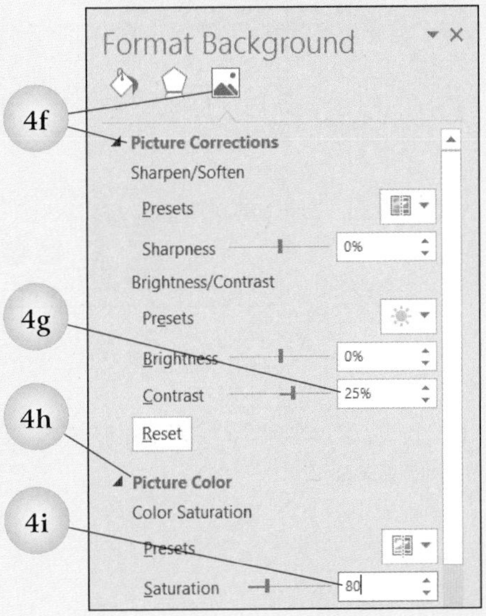

Check Your Work

Online Pictures

Hint For additional images, consider buying a commercial package of images.

Quick Steps

Insert an Online Image

1. Click Insert tab.
2. Click Online Pictures button.
3. Type search term or topic.
4. Press Enter.
5. Double-click image.

Shape Height

Shape Width

Inserting an Online Image

Use the Bing Image Search feature to search for images online. To use this feature, click the Insert tab and then click the Online Pictures button. This displays the Insert Pictures window as shown in Figure 4.8. Click in the search text box, type the search term or topic, and then press the Enter key. Images that match the search term or topic display in the window. To insert an image, double-click the image or click the image and then click the Insert button. This downloads the image to the slide. Customize the image with options and buttons on the Picture Tools Format tab.

Sizing, Rotating, and Positioning Objects

PowerPoint provides a variety of methods for sizing and positioning an object such as a shape, text box, or image on a slide. In addition to using sizing handles to size an image and using the mouse to drag an image, an object can be sized and positioned with options at the Format Picture task pane with the Size & Properties icon selected. Display this task pane by selecting an object and then clicking the Size group task pane launcher on the Picture Tools Format tab.

Figure 4.8 Insert Pictures Window

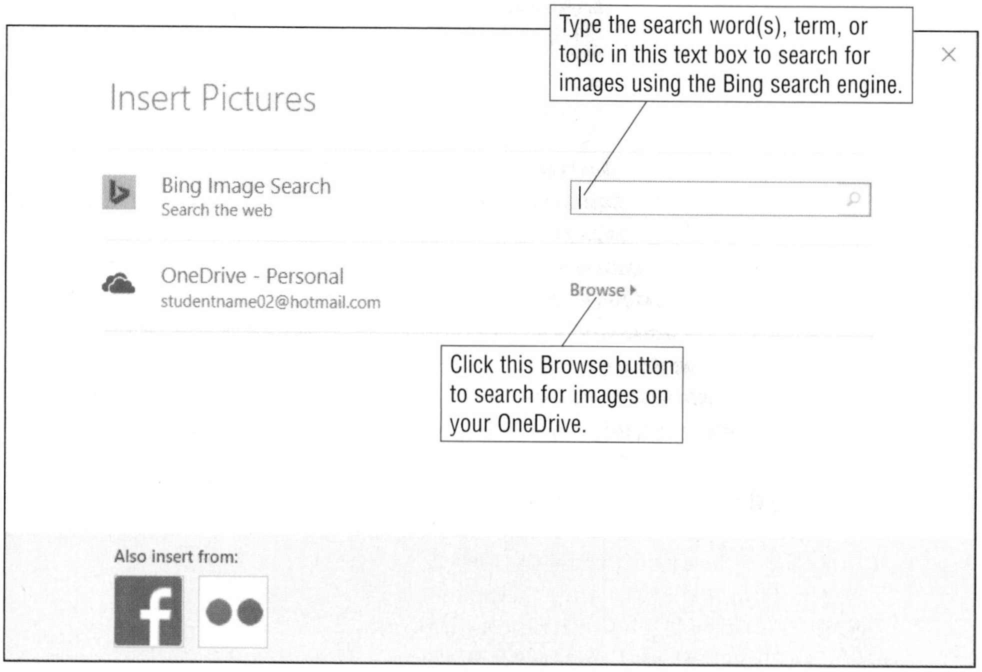

Project 1i Inserting and Formatting an Image

Part 9 of 14

1. With **4-AddisonReport.pptx** open, make Slide 4 active.
2. Click the New Slide button arrow in the Slides group on the Home tab and then click the *Two Content* layout at the drop-down list.
3. Click in the title placeholder and then type Technology.
4. Click in the content placeholder at the right side of the slide.
5. Click the Bullets button in the Paragraph group to turn off bullets.
6. Change the font size to 24 points and turn on bold formatting.
7. Type Equipment and then press the Enter key two times.
8. Type Software and then press the Enter key two times.
9. Type Personnel.

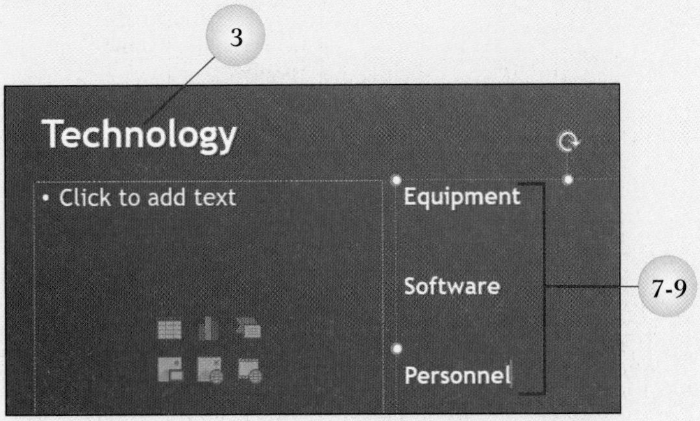

10. Insert an image by completing the following steps:
    a. Click the Online Pictures button in the middle of the placeholder at the left side of the slide.
    b. At the Insert Pictures window, type computer in the search text box and then press the Enter key.
    c. Double-click the image in the window as shown below. If this image is not available online, click the Pictures button on the Insert tab. At the Insert Picture dialog box, navigate to the PC4 folder and then double-click ***Computer.png***.

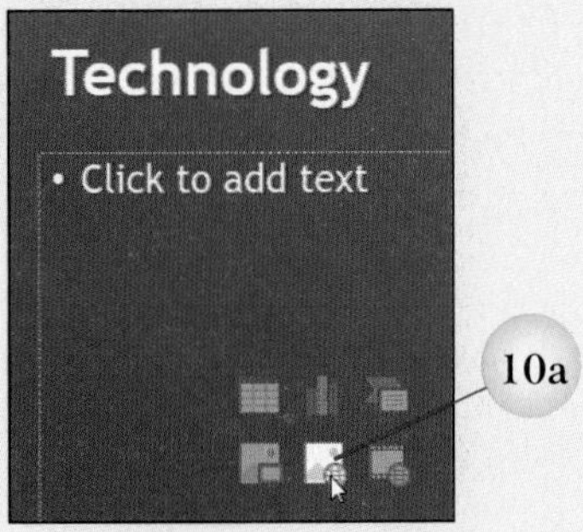

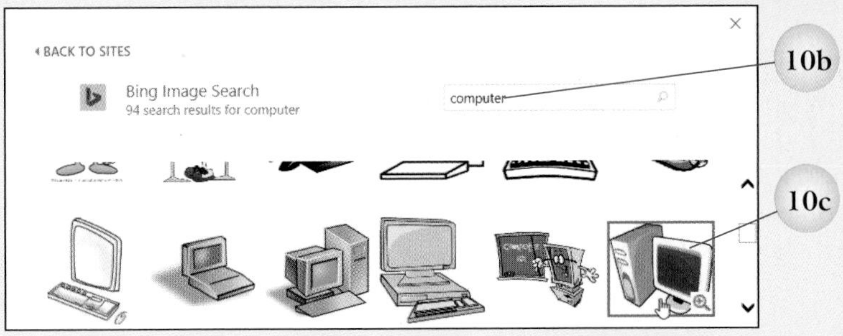

11. Scale, rotate, and position the computer image by completing the following steps:
    a. With the image selected, click the Rotate button in the Arrange group on the Picture Tools Format tab and then click *Flip Horizontal* at the drop-down list.
    b. Click the Size group task pane launcher.

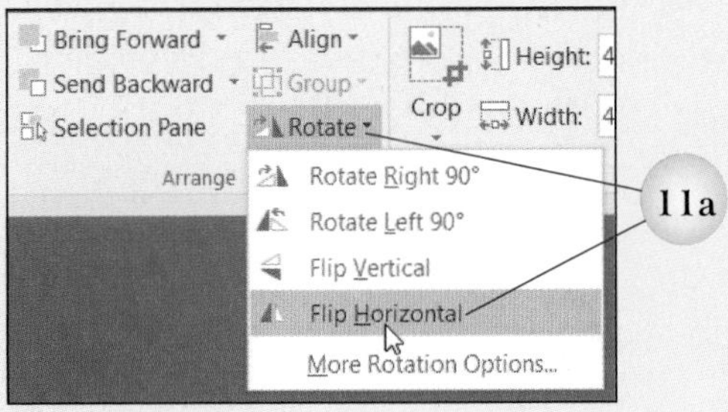

c. At the Format Picture task pane with the Size & Properties icon selected, if necessary, click *Size* to expand the options.
d. Select *0°* in the *Rotation* measurement box and then type -10.
e. Select the current percentage in the *Scale Height* measurement box and then type 50.

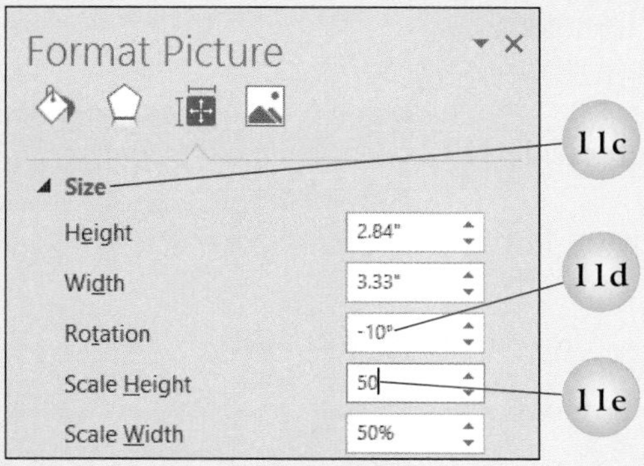

f. If necessary, click *Position* to expand the options.
g. Select the current measurement in the *Horizontal position* measurement box and then type 2.9.
h. Select the current measurement in the *Vertical position* measurement box, type 2.2, and then press the Enter key.
i. Close the Format Picture task pane.

12. Save **4-AddisonReport.pptx**.

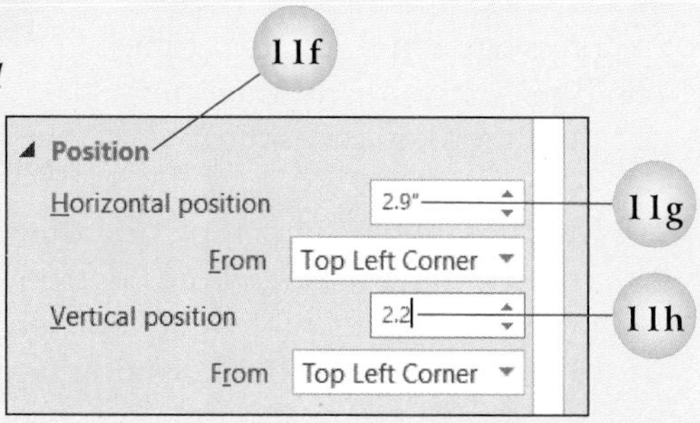

Check Your Work

Copying Objects within and between Presentations

Hint An object pasted to a different slide is positioned in the same location as the copied object.

Objects can be copied within a presentation and also between presentations. To copy an object, select the object and then click the Copy button in the Clipboard group on the Home tab. Make the slide in which the object is to be pasted active or open another presentation and then click the Paste button in the Clipboard group. Another method for copying an object is to right-click the object and then click *Copy* at the shortcut menu. To paste the object, make the slide in which the object is to be pasted active, click the right mouse button, and then click *Paste* at the shortcut menu.

Project 1j Copying an Object within and between Presentations — Part 10 of 14

1. With **4-AddisonReport.pptx** open, make Slide 1 active.
2. Open **Addison.pptx**.
3. Click the image in Slide 1, click the Copy button in the Clipboard group, and then close **Addison.pptx**.
4. With **4-AddisonReport.pptx** open, click the Paste button. (This inserts the image in Slide 1.)
5. With the image selected, make Slide 2 active and then click the Paste button.

6. Decrease the size and position of the image by completing the following steps:
   a. Click the Picture Tools Format tab.
   b. Click in the *Shape Height* measurement box, type 0.8, and then press the Enter key.

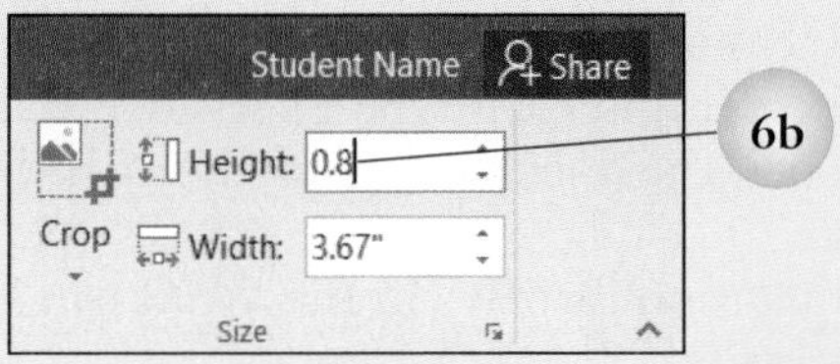

   c. Drag the image so that it is positioned in the upper right corner of the slide.

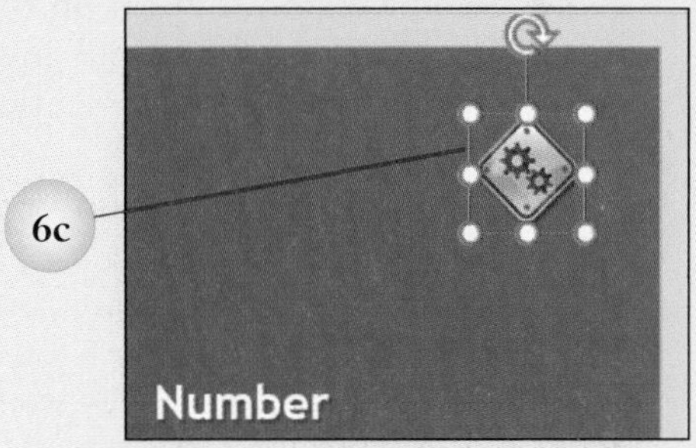

7. Copy the image to other slides by completing the following steps:
   a. With the image selected in Slide 2, click the Home tab and then click the Copy button in the Clipboard group.
   b. Make Slide 3 active and then click the Paste button in the Clipboard group.
   c. Paste the image in Slide 5 and Slide 7.
8. Save **4-AddisonReport.pptx**.

Check Your Work

Tutorial

Inserting and Formatting Screenshot and Screen Clipping Images

Screenshot

Quick Steps

Insert a Screenshot Image

1. Open presentation.
2. Open another file.
3. Display information.
4. Make presentation active.
5. Click Insert tab.
6. Click Screenshot button.
7. Click window at drop-down list.

OR

6. Click Screenshot button.
7. Click *Screen Clipping*.
8. Drag to specify capture area.

Creating Screenshot Images

The Images group on the Insert tab contains a Screenshot button for capturing the contents or a portion of a screen as an image. This is useful for capturing information from a web page or from a file in another program. To capture the entire screen, display a web page, or open a file, make PowerPoint active, and then open a presentation. Click the Insert tab, click the Screenshot button, and then click the specific screen thumbnail at the drop-down list. The currently active presentation does not display as a thumbnail at the drop-down list. Instead, any other open file or program displays. If no other file or program is open, the Windows desktop displays. Click a thumbnail at the drop-down list and a screenshot of the screen is inserted as an image in the active slide in the open presentation, the image is selected, and the Picture Tools Format tab is active. Use options and buttons on this tab to customize the screenshot image.

In addition to making a screenshot of an entire screen, make a screenshot of a specific portion of the screen by clicking the *Screen Clipping* option at the Screenshot button drop-down list. Click this option and the open web page, file, or Windows desktop displays in a dimmed manner and the mouse pointer displays as crosshairs. Using the mouse, draw a border around a specific area of the screen. The identified area is inserted in the active slide in the presentation as an image, the image is selected, and the Picture Tools Format tab is active.

Project 1k Inserting and Formatting a Screenshot

1. With **4-AddisonReport.pptx** open, make sure that no other programs are open.
2. Make Slide 9 active and then insert a new slide by clicking the New Slide button arrow in the Slides group on the Home tab and then clicking the *Title Only* layout.
3. Click in the title placeholder and then type Draft Invitation.
4. Open Word and then open the document named **AddIndInvite.docx** from the PC4 folder on your storage medium.
5. Make sure the entire invitation displays in the Word window. If necessary, decrease the size of the invitation using the Zoom Out button on the Status bar.
6. Click the PowerPoint button on the taskbar.
7. Insert a screenshot of the draft invitation in the Word document by completing the following steps:
   a. Click the Insert tab.
   b. Click the Screenshot button in the Images group and then click *Screen Clipping* at the drop-down list.
   c. When the invitation displays in a dimmed manner, position the mouse crosshairs in the upper left corner of the invitation, click and hold down the left mouse button, drag down to the lower right corner of the invitation, and then release the mouse button.

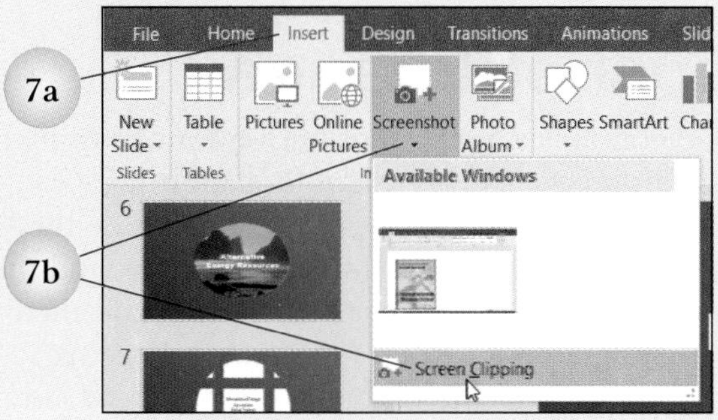

8. With the screenshot image inserted in the slide in the presentation, make the following changes:
   a. Click in the *Shape Width* measurement box in the Size group on the Picture Tools Format tab, type 4.5, and then press the Enter key.
   b. Click the Corrections button in the Adjust group and then click the *Sharpen: 25%* option (fourth option in the *Sharpen/Soften* section).
   c. Using the mouse, drag the screenshot image so it is centered on the slide.
9. Click outside the screenshot image to deselect it.
10. Save **4-AddisonReport.pptx**.
11. Click the Word button, close **AddIndInvite.docx**, and then close Word.

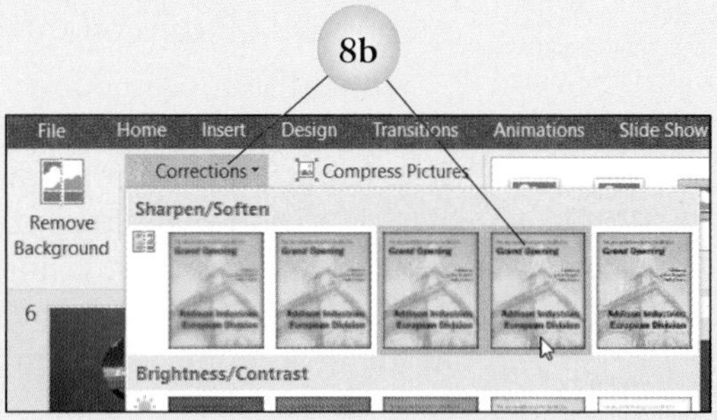

Check Your Work

Tutorial

Inserting and Formatting WordArt

Quick Steps

Create WordArt Text

1. Click Insert tab.
2. Click WordArt button.
3. Click WordArt style.
4. Type WordArt text.

WordArt

Text Fill

Text Outline

Text Effects

Creating and Formatting WordArt Text

Use the WordArt feature to insert preformatted, decorative text in a slide and to modify text to conform to a variety of shapes. Consider using WordArt to create a company logo, letterhead, flyer title, or heading. Insert WordArt in a slide by clicking the Insert tab and then clicking the WordArt button in the Text group. This displays the WordArt drop-down list as shown in Figure 4.10. Click a WordArt style at the drop-down list and a text box is inserted in the slide containing the text *Your Text Here*. Type the WordArt text and then use the options and buttons on the Drawing Tools Format tab to customize the WordArt text.

Apply predesigned formatting to WordArt text with a WordArt style. Customize the text with the Text Fill, Text Outline, and Text Effects buttons in the WordArt Styles group. Use the Text Fill button to change the fill color; the Text Outline button to change the text outline color, width, and style; and the Text Effects button to apply a variety of text effects and shapes.

Click the Text Effects button and then point to *Transform* and a side menu displays with shaping and warping options as shown in Figure 4.11. Use these options to conform the WordArt text to a specific shape.

Figure 4.10 WordArt Drop-down List

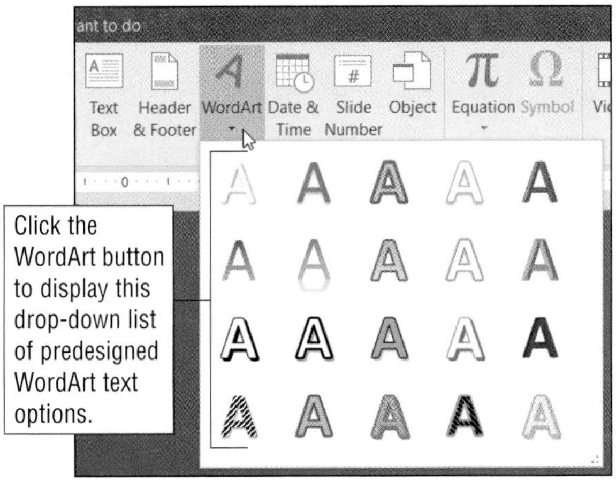

Figure 4.11 Text Effects *Transform* Side Menu

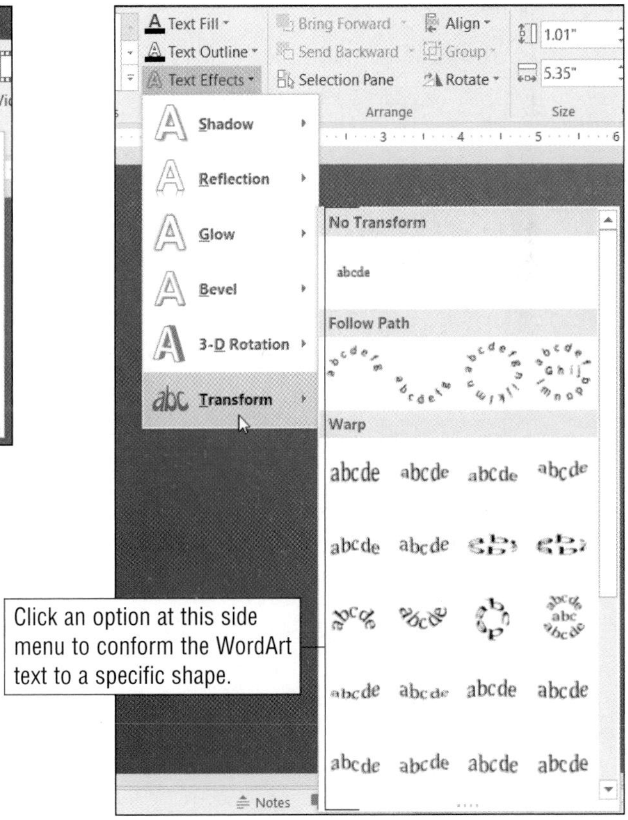

Hint Use WordArt to create interesting text effects in slides.

Hint Edit WordArt by double-clicking the WordArt text.

Project 1I Inserting and Formatting WordArt Part 12 of 14

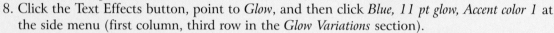

1. With **4-AddisonReport.pptx** open, make sure Slide 10 and the Home tab are active.
2. Click the New Slide button arrow in the Slides group and then click the *Blank* layout.
3. Click the Insert tab.
4. Click the WordArt button in the Text group and then click the *Fill - White, Text 1, Outline - Background 1, Hard Shadow - Accent 1* option (second column, third row).
5. Type Addison Industries, press the Enter key, and then type 2018.
6. Click the WordArt text border to change the border from a dashed line to a solid line. (This selects the text box.)
7. Click the Text Outline button arrow in the WordArt Styles group and then click the *Dark Blue* color (ninth option in the *Standard Colors* section).

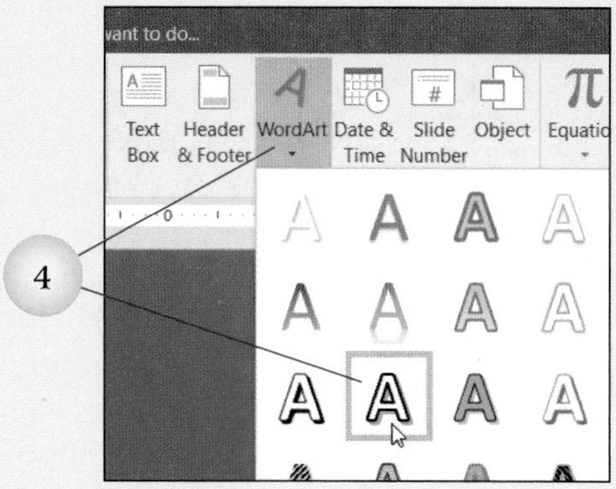

8. Click the Text Effects button, point to *Glow*, and then click *Blue, 11 pt glow, Accent color 1* at the side menu (first column, third row in the *Glow Variations* section).
9. Click the Text Effects button, point to *Transform*, and then click the *Triangle Up* option (third column, first row in the *Warp* section).

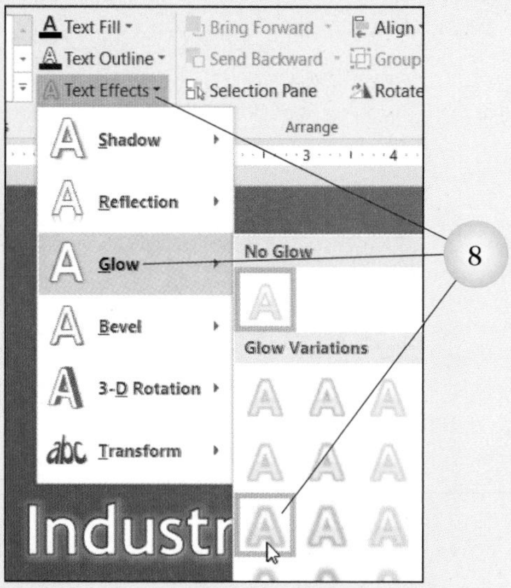

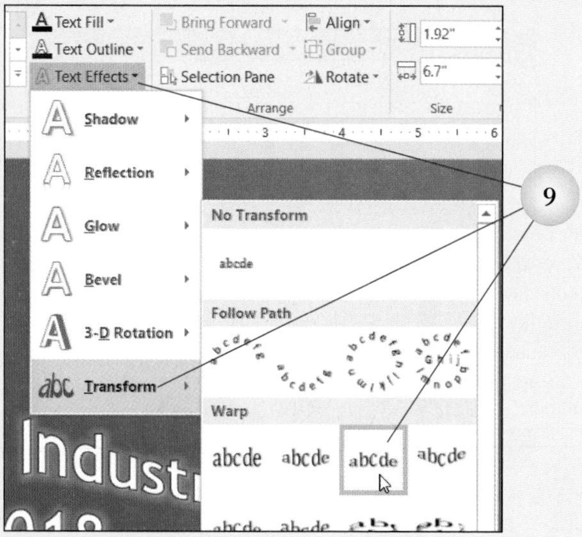

10. Click in the *Shape Height* measurement box, type 5, and then press the Enter key.
11. Click in the *Shape Width* measurement box, type 10, and then press the Enter key.
12. Click the Align button in the Arrange group and then click *Distribute Horizontally*.
13. Click the Align button and then click *Distribute Vertically*.
14. Save **4-AddisonReport.pptx**.

Check Your Work

Tutorial: Inserting Symbols

Symbol

Inserting Symbols

Insert symbols in a slide using options at the Symbol dialog box. Display this dialog box by clicking the Symbol button in the Symbols group on the Insert tab. At the Symbol dialog box, choose a symbol font with the *Font* option in the dialog box, click a symbol in the list box, click the Insert button, and then click the Close button. The symbol is inserted in the slide at the location of the insertion point.

Project 1m Inserting Symbols in a Presentation **Part 13 of 14**

1. With **4-AddisonReport.pptx** open, insert a symbol by completing the following steps:
   a. Make Slide 2 active.
   b. Click in the text box containing the names, titles, and telephone numbers.
   c. Delete the *n* in *Pena* (the last name of the fourth person).
   d. Click the Insert tab and then click the Symbol button in the Symbols group.
   e. At the Symbol dialog box, click the *Font* option box arrow, scroll down the drop-down list to the *Trebuchet MS* option, and then click that option.
   f. Scroll down the symbol list box and then click the *ñ* symbol (in approximately the twelfth row).
   g. Click the Insert button and then click the Close button.
2. Save **4-AddisonReport.pptx**.

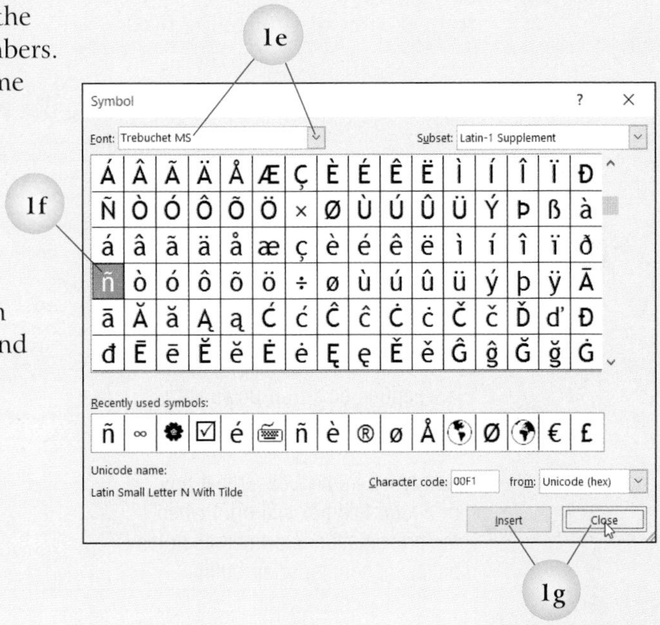

Check Your Work

Tutorial: Inserting Headers and Footers

Header & Footer

Date & Time

Slide Number

Inserting Headers and Footers

If a presentation is printed as a handout or an outline, PowerPoint automatically prints the current date in the upper right corner of the page and the page number in the lower right corner. Print the presentation as notes pages and PowerPoint automatically prints the page number on individual slides. The date and page numbers are considered header and footer elements. These existing header and footer elements can be modified or additional elements can be inserted using options in the Header and Footer dialog box. Display the Header and Footer dialog box shown in Figure 4.12 by clicking the Header & Footer button in the Text group on the Insert tab, clicking the Date & Time button in the Text group, or clicking the Slide Number button in the Text group. Another method for displaying the Header and Footer dialog box is to display the Print backstage area and then click the Edit Header & Footer hyperlink below the galleries in the *Settings* category.

The Header and Footer dialog box has two tabs, the Slide tab and the Notes and Handouts tab, and the options in the dialog box are similar with either tab selected. Use options in the dialog box to insert the date and time, a header, a footer, and page numbers. Insert the date and time in a presentation and then choose the *Update automatically* option to update the date and time when the presentation is opened. Choose the date and time formatting by clicking the *Update automatically* option box arrow and then clicking the desired formatting at the drop-down list. Choose the *Fixed* option and then type the desired date and/or time in the *Fixed* text box. Type header text in the *Header* text box and type footer text in the *Footer* text box.

To print the slide number on slides, insert a check mark in the *Slide number* check box in the Header and Footer dialog box with the Slide tab selected. To include page numbers on handouts, notes pages, or outline pages, insert a check mark in the *Page number* check box in the Header and Footer dialog box with the Notes and Handouts tab selected. Apply changes to all slides or all handouts, notes pages, and outline pages, by clicking the Apply to All button in the lower right corner of the dialog box.

Figure 4.12 Header and Footer Dialog Box with the Notes and Handouts Tab Selected

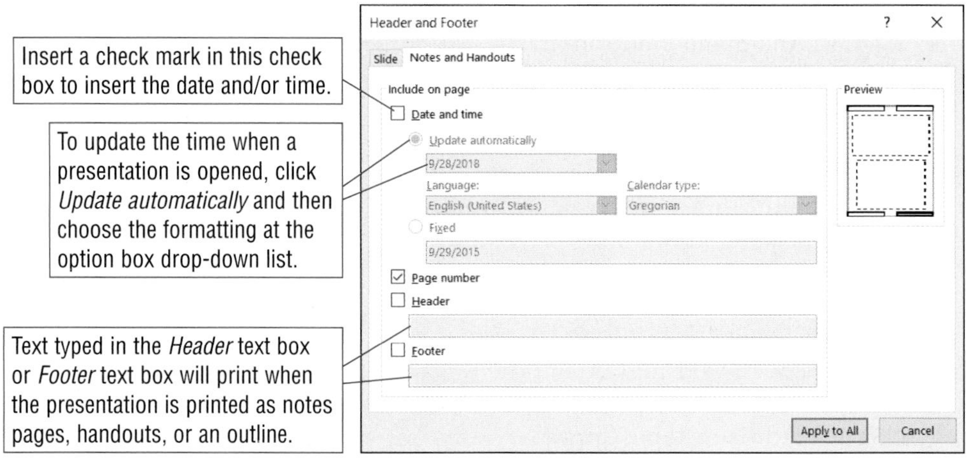

Project 1n Inserting Headers and Footers

Part 14 of 14

1. With **4-AddisonReport.pptx** open, insert slide numbers on each slide in the presentation by completing the following steps:
   a. Make Slide 1 active.
   b. Click the Insert tab.
   c. Click the Slide Number button in the Text group.
   d. At the Header and Footer dialog box with the Slide tab selected, click the *Slide number* check box to insert a check mark.
   e. Click the Apply to All button.
   f. Scroll through the slides to view the slide number in the lower right corner of each slide, except for the first slide.

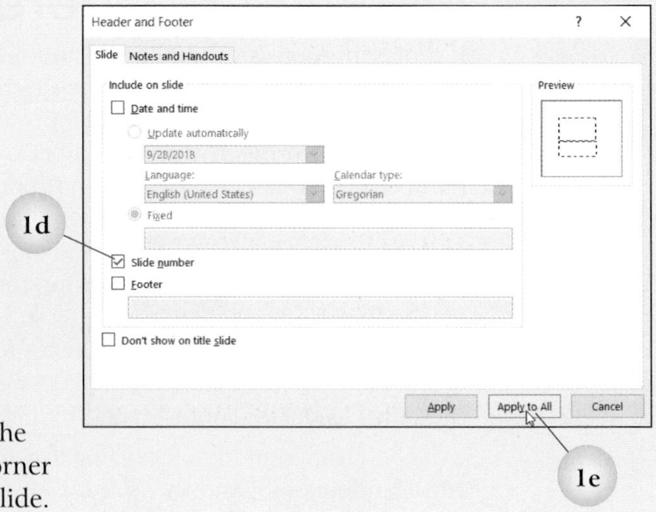

2. Insert your name as a footer on each slide (except the first slide) in the presentation by completing the following steps:
   a. Click the Header & Footer button in the Text group.
   b. Click the *Footer* check box to insert a check mark, click in the *Footer* text box, and then type your first and last names.
   c. Make sure a check mark displays in the *Slide number* check box.
   d. Click the Apply to All button.
   e. Run the slide show to confirm that your name displays at the bottom left side of each slide (except the first slide).
3. You decide that you also want your name to print as a footer on handouts pages. To do this, complete the following steps:
   a. Click the Header & Footer button in the Text group.
   b. At the Header and Footer dialog box, click the Notes and Handouts tab.
   c. Click the *Footer* check box to insert a check mark, click in the *Footer* text box, and then type your first and last names.
   d. Click the Apply to All button.
4. Insert the current date as a header that prints on handouts pages by completing the following steps:
   a. Click the Date & Time button in the Text group.
   b. At the Header and Footer dialog box, click the Notes and Handouts tab.
   c. Click the *Date and time* check box to insert a check mark.
   d. Click the Apply to All button.
5. Insert the presentation name as a header that prints on handouts pages by completing the following steps:
   a. Click the File tab and then click the *Print* option.
   b. At the Print backstage area, click the Edit Header & Footer hyperlink below the galleries in the *Settings* category.

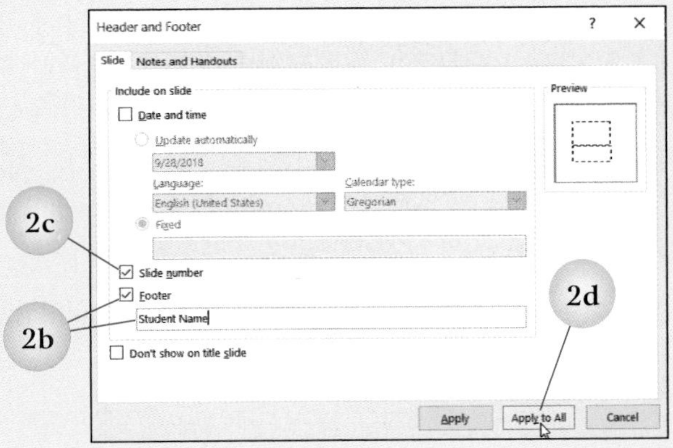

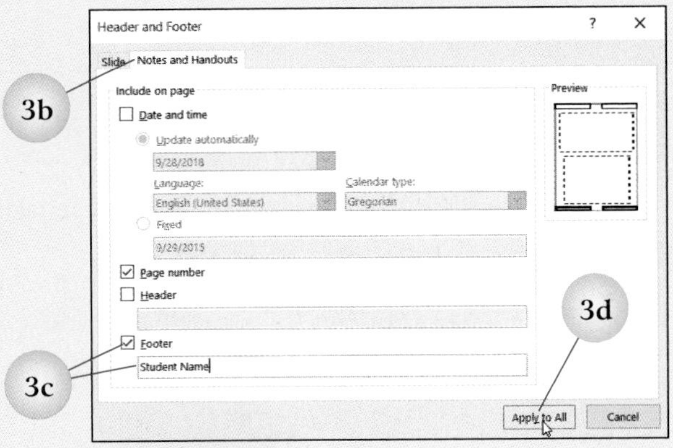

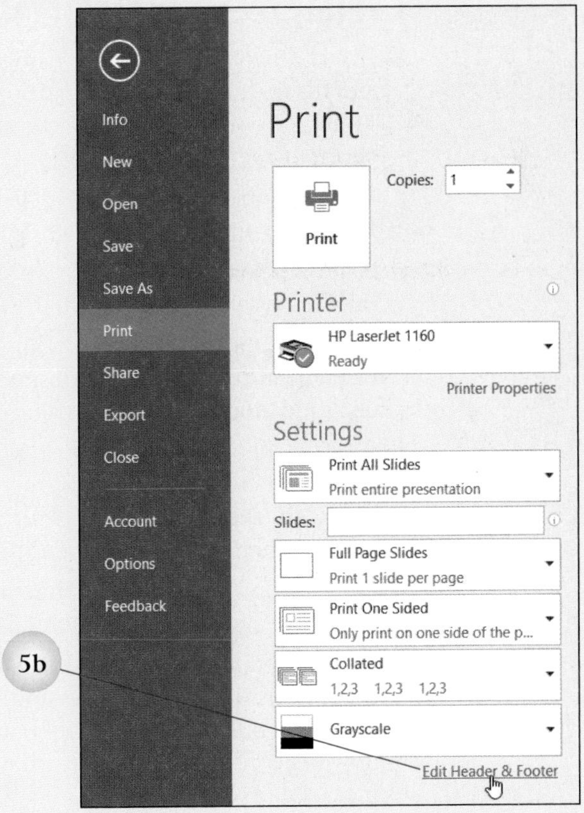

c. At the Header and Footer dialog box, click the Notes and Handouts tab.
d. Click the *Header* check box to insert a check mark, click in the *Header* text box, and then type 4-AddisonReport.pptx.
e. Click the Apply to All button.
f. Click the second gallery in the *Settings* category and then click *6 Slides Horizontal* at the drop-down list. (If a number apears in the *Slides* text box, delete the number.)
g. Display the next handout page by clicking the Next Page button at the bottom of the Print backstage area.
h. Click the Previous page button to display the first handout page.

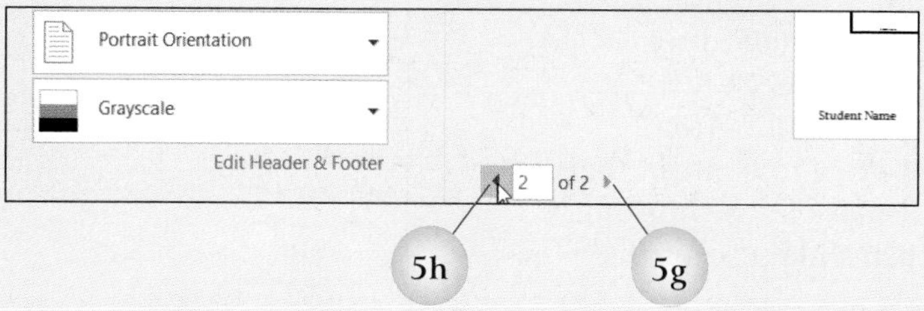

i. Click the Print button to print the presentation as a handout with six slides displayed horizontally per page.

6. Save and then close **4-AddisonReport.pptx**.

Check Your Work

Chapter Summary

- Insert a text box in a slide using the Text Box button in the Text group on the Insert tab. Format a text box with options in the Drawing group on the Home tab, with options on the Drawing Tools Format tab, with options at the shortcut menu, or with options at the Format Shape task pane.
- Select all objects in a slide by clicking the Select button in the Editing group on the Home tab and then clicking *Select All* or by using the keyboard shortcut, Ctrl + A.
- Align selected objects using options from the Align button in the Arrange group on the Drawing Tools Format tab.
- Set tabs in a text box by clicking the Alignment button at the left side of the horizontal ruler until the desired tab alignment symbol displays and then clicking a location on the ruler. Set left, center, right, and/or decimal tabs.
- Insert a shape in a slide by clicking a shape in the Drawing group on the Home tab and then clicking or clicking and dragging in the slide. Or, click the Shapes button in the Illustrations group on the Insert tab, click a shape at the drop-down list and then click or click and drag in the slide.
- Use options in the Shapes button drop-down list to draw a line, basic shapes, block arrows, flow chart symbols, callouts, stars, and banners.
- Copy a shape by selecting the shape, clicking the Copy button in the Clipboard group, positioning the insertion point in the new position, and then clicking the Paste button in the Clipboard group. A shape can also be copied by holding down the Ctrl key and then dragging the shape to the new location.

- Turn the horizontal and vertical rulers on and off with the *Ruler* check box in the Show group on the View tab and turn gridlines on and off with the *Gridlines* check box. Turn gridlines as well as drawing guides and the snap-to-grid feature on and off with options at the Grid and Guides dialog box.
- Group objects together to apply the same formatting to all the objects in that group. To group objects, select the objects, click the Group button in the Arrange group on the Drawing Tools Format tab, and then click *Group* at the drop-down list.
- Size images with the *Shape Height* and *Shape Width* measurement boxes on the Picture Tools Format tab or with the sizing handles that display around a selected image.
- Use the Crop button in the Size group on the Picture Tools Format tab to remove portions of an image.
- Move an image by dragging it to a new location. Move an image in small increments, called *nudging*, by holding down the Ctrl key while pressing an arrow key on the keyboard.
- Specify the order in which objects are to be layered with the Bring Forward and Send Backward buttons in the Adjust group on the Drawing Tools Format tab or the Picture Tools Format tab.
- Insert an image in a slide with the Pictures button in the Images group on the Insert tab.
- Insert an image as a slide background using options at the Format Background task pane. Display this task pane by clicking the Format Background button in the Customize group on the Design tab.
- Insert an online image using the Insert Pictures window. Display this window by clicking the Online Pictures button in the Images group on the Insert tab or clicking the Online Pictures button in a layout content placeholder.
- Size objects with options at the Format Shape or Format Picture task pane with the Size & Properties icon selected.
- Use the Screenshot button in the Images group on the Insert tab to capture the contents of a screen or a portion of a screen.
- Use the WordArt feature to distort or modify text to conform to a variety of shapes. Insert WordArt with the WordArt button in the Text group on the Insert tab. Format WordArt using options and buttons on the Drawing Tools Format tab.
- Insert symbols in a slide with options at the Symbol dialog box. Display this dialog box by clicking the Symbol button in the Symbols group on the Insert tab.
- Click the Header & Footer button, the Date & Time button, or the Slide Number button in the Text group on the Insert tab to display the Header and Footer dialog box. Another method for displaying this dialog box is to click the Edit Header & Footer hyperlink at the Print backstage area.

Commands Review

FEATURE	RIBBON TAB, GROUP	BUTTON, OPTION	KEYBOARD SHORTCUT
date and time	Insert, Text		
Format Background task pane	Design, Customize		
Format Picture task pane	Picture Tools Format, Picture Styles OR Size		
Grid and Guides dialog box	View, Show		
gridlines	View, Show	*Gridlines*	Shift + F9
guides	View, Show	*Guides*	
header and footer	Insert, Text		
Insert Picture dialog box	Insert, Images		
Insert Pictures window	Insert, Images		
rulers	View, Show	*Ruler*	
screenshot	Insert, Images		
shape	Insert, Illustrations OR Home, Drawing		
slide number	Insert, Text		
Symbol dialog box	Insert, Symbols		
text box	Insert, Text		
WordArt	Insert, Text		

Workbook

Chapter study tools and assessment activities are available in the *Workbook* ebook. These resources are designed to help you further develop and demonstrate mastery of the skills learned in this chapter.

Unit assessment activities are also available in the *Workbook*. These activities are designed to help you demonstrate mastery of the skills learned in this unit.

Microsoft®

PowerPoint®

Unit 2

Customizing and Enhancing Presentations

Microsoft®

PowerPoint®

Creating Tables, Charts, and SmartArt Graphics

CHAPTER 5

Performance Objectives

Upon successful completion of Chapter 5, you will be able to:

1 Create a table
2 Modify the design and layout of a table
3 Insert an image in a table
4 Insert an Excel spreadsheet
5 Draw a table
6 Create SmartArt graphics
7 Modify the design and layout of SmartArt
8 Convert text and WordArt to a SmartArt graphic
9 Convert a SmartArt graphic to text and shapes
10 Create and format charts
11 Modify the design and layout of charts
12 Select and format chart elements
13 Create, edit, and format a photo album

Precheck

Check your current skills to focus your study.

PowerPoint allows you to present information using different formats. Use the Tables feature to present numbers and lists in a slide in columns and rows in a manner similar to a spreadsheet. Use the SmartArt feature to present data in a more visual way by creating a SmartArt graphic. While a table does an adequate job of representing data, create a chart from data to provide a more visual representation. Use the Photo Album feature to attractively display personal or business photographs and then format the appearance of the images in the presentation.

Data Files

Before beginning chapter work, copy the PC5 folder to your storage medium and then make PC5 the active folder.

SNAP

If you are a SNAP user, launch the Precheck and Tutorials from your Assignments page.

Project 1 Create a Company Sales Conference Presentation — 14 Parts

You will create a sales conference presentation for Nature's Way that includes a table, a column chart, a pie chart, and four SmartArt graphics.

Preview Finished Project

Tutorial

Creating a Table

Table

Quick Steps

Insert a Table
1. Click Insert Table button in content placeholder.
2. Type number of columns.
3. Press Tab.
4. Type number of rows.
5. Click OK.

OR
1. Click Insert tab.
2. Click Table button.
3. Position mouse pointer in grid until correct number for columns and rows displays above grid and then click left mouse button.

Hint Add a row to the bottom of a table by positioning the insertion point in the last cell and then pressing the Tab key.

Creating a Table

Use the Tables feature to create boxes of information called *cells*. A cell is the intersection between a row and a column. A cell can contain text, characters, numbers, data, graphics, or formulas. To arrange the content of a slide in columns and rows, insert a new slide with a slide layout that includes a content placeholder. Click the Insert Table button in the content placeholder and the Insert Table dialog box displays. At the Insert Table dialog box, type the number of columns, press the Tab key, type the number of rows, and then press the Enter key or click OK. A table can also be inserted using the Table button in the Tables group on the Insert tab. Click the Table button, position the mouse pointer in the grid until the correct number for columns and rows displays above the grid, and then click the left mouse button.

When a table is inserted in a slide, the insertion point is in the cell in the upper left corner of the table. Cells in a table contain a cell designation. Columns in a table are lettered from left to right, beginning with *A*. Rows in a table are numbered from top to bottom beginning with *1*. The cell in the upper left corner of the table is cell A1. The cell to the right of A1 is B1, the cell to the right of B1 is C1, and so on.

Entering Text in Cells

With the insertion point positioned in a cell, type or edit text. Move the insertion point to other cells by clicking in the cell, or press the Tab key to move the insertion point to the next cell or press Shift + Tab to move the insertion point to the previous cell.

If the text typed does not fit on one line, it wraps to the next line within the same cell. Press the Enter key in a cell and the insertion point is moved to the next line within the same cell. The cell vertically lengthens to accommodate the text, and all cells in that row also lengthen. Pressing the Tab key in a table causes the insertion point to move to the next cell. To move the insertion point to a tab position within a cell, press Ctrl + Tab. If the insertion point is in the last cell of a table pressing the Tab key will add another row to the bottom of the table.

Selecting Cells

Formatting can be applied to an entire table or to specific cells, rows, or columns in a table. To identify cells for formatting, select the specific cells using the mouse or the keyboard. Press the Tab key to select the next cell or press Shift + Tab to select the previous cell. Refer to Table 5.1 for additional methods for selecting in a table.

Table 5.1 Selecting in a Table

To select this	Do this
A cell	Position the mouse pointer at the left side of the cell until the pointer turns into a small, black, diagonally pointing arrow and then click the left mouse button.
A column	Position the mouse pointer outside the table at the top of the column until the pointer turns into a small, black, down-pointing arrow and then click the left mouse button. Drag to select multiple columns.
A row	Position the mouse pointer outside the table at the left edge of the row until the pointer turns into a small, black, right-pointing arrow and then click the left mouse button. Drag to select multiple rows.
All cells in a table	With the insertion point positioned in the table, drag to select all cells or press Ctrl + A.
Text within a cell	Position the mouse pointer at the beginning of the text, click and hold down the left mouse button, drag the mouse across the text, and then release the mouse button. (When a cell is selected, the cell background color changes to gray. When text within a cell is selected, only those lines containing text are highlighted in gray.)

Project 1a **Creating a Table**

Part 1 of 14

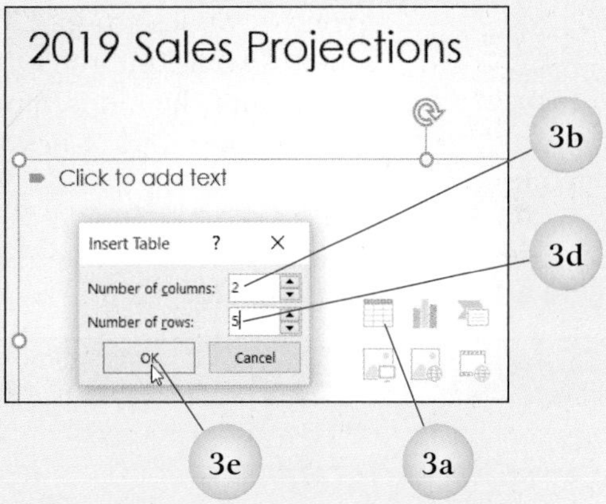

1. Open **Conference.pptx** and then save it with the name **5-Conference**.
2. Make Slide 3 active.
3. Insert a table in the slide and enter text into the cells by completing the following steps:
   a. Click the Insert Table button in the middle of the slide in the content placeholder.
   b. At the Insert Table dialog box, select the current number in the *Number of columns* measurement box and then type 2.
   c. Press the Tab key.
   d. Type 5 in the *Number of rows* measurement box.
   e. Click OK or press the Enter key.
   f. Type the text as displayed in the table below. Press the Tab key to move the insertion point to the next cell or press Shift + Tab to move the insertion point to the previous cell. Do not press the Tab key after typing the last cell entry.

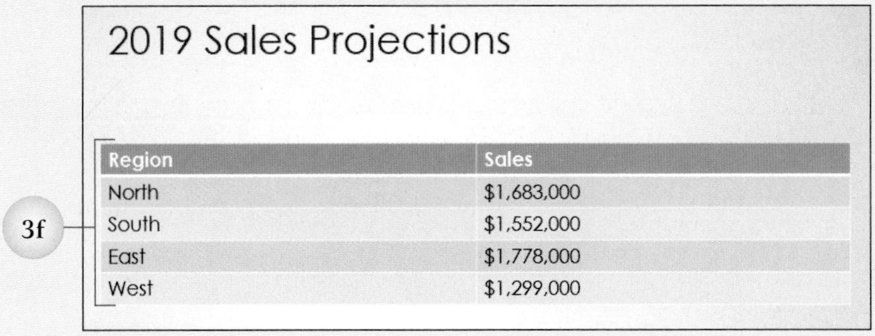
2019 Sales Projections
Region
Sales
North
$1,683,000
South
$1,552,000
East
$1,778,000
West
$1,299,000
3f

4. Apply formatting to text in specific cells by completing the following steps:
   a. With the insertion point positioned in the table, press Ctrl + A to select all of the text in the table.
   b. Click the Home tab and then change the font size to 32 points.
   c. Set the text below the headings in a smaller point size by positioning the mouse pointer at the left edge of the second row (to the left of the cell containing *North*) until the pointer turns into a small, black, right-pointing arrow. Click and hold down the left mouse button, drag down so the remaining rows are selected, and then release the mouse button. Change the font size to 28 points.
   d. Click outside the table to deselect it.
5. Save **5-Conference.pptx**.

Check Your Work

Tutorial

Changing the Table Design

Shading

Borders

Effects

Draw Table

Eraser

Changing the Table Design

When a table is inserted in a slide, the Table Tools Design tab is active. This tab contains a number of options for enhancing the appearance of the table, as shown in Figure 5.1. With options in the Table Styles group, select a predesigned style that applies color and border lines to a table. Maintain further control over the predesigned style formatting applied to columns and rows with options in the Table Style Options group. For example, to format the first column differently than the other columns in a table, insert a check mark in the *First Column* check box. Apply additional design formatting to cells in a table with the Shading, Borders, and Effects buttons in the Table Styles group and the options in the WordArt Styles group. Draw a table or draw additional rows and/or columns in a table by clicking the Draw Table button in the Draw Borders group. Click this button and the mouse pointer turns into a pencil. Drag in the table to create the columns and rows. Click the Eraser button and the mouse pointer turns into an eraser. Drag through the column and/or row lines to erase the lines.

Figure 5.1 Table Tools Design Tab

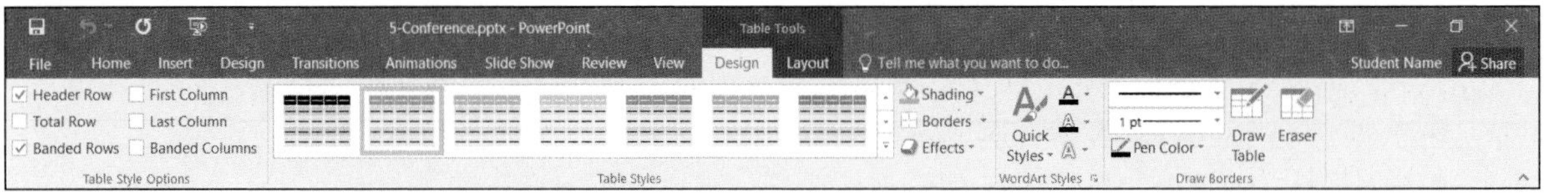

Project 1b **Modifying the Table Design**

1. With **5-Conference.pptx** open, make sure Slide 3 is active, click in a cell in the table, and then click the Table Tools Design tab.
2. Click the *First Column* check box in the Table Style Options group to insert a check mark. (This applies bold formatting to the text in the first column and applies darker shading to the cells.)
3. Click the More Table Styles button in the Table Styles group and then click the *Themed Style 1 - Accent 1* option (second column, first row in the *Best Match for Document* section).

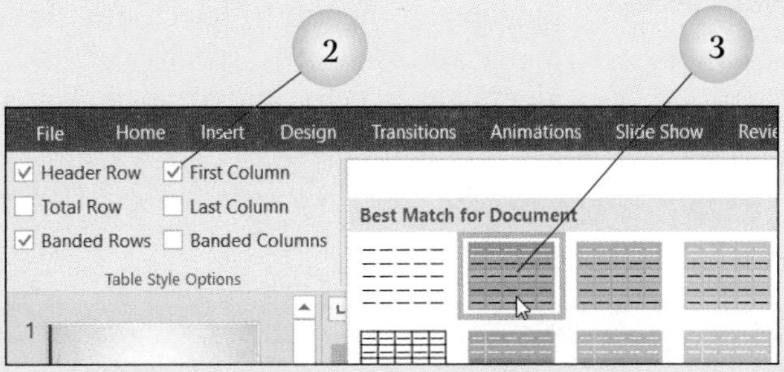

4. Select the first row of the table and then apply the following formatting options:
   a. Click the Quick Styles button in the WordArt Styles group and then click the *Fill - White, Outline - Accent 2, Hard Shadow - Accent 2* option (fourth column, third row).
   b. Click the Text Fill button arrow in the WordArt Styles group and then click the *Lime, Accent 3, Lighter 80%* option (seventh column, second row in the *Theme Colors* section).
   c. Click the Text Outline button arrow in the WordArt Styles group and then click the *Green, Accent 1, Lighter 80%* option (fifth column, second row in the *Theme Colors* section).

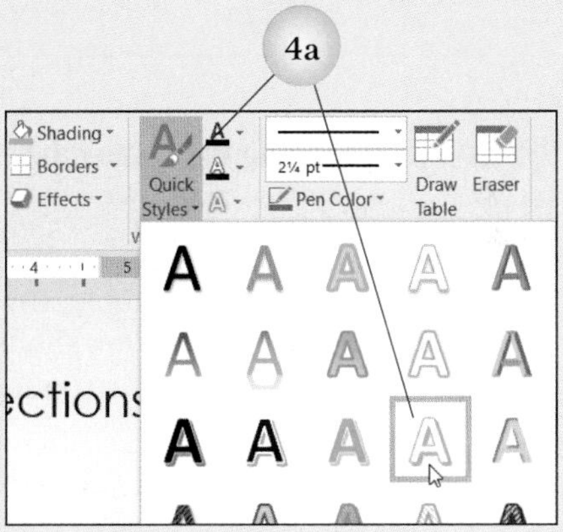

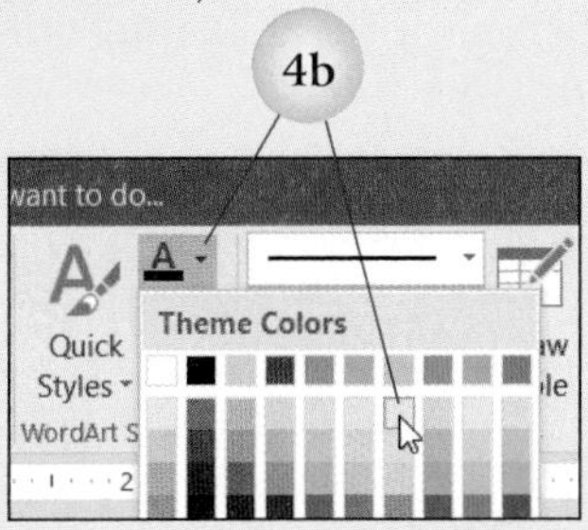

5. Click the *Pen Weight* option box arrow in the Draw Borders group and then click the *2¼ pt* option. (This activates the Draw Table button.)
6. Click the Pen Color button in the Draw Borders group and then click the *Green, Accent 1, Darker 25%* option (fifth column, fifth row in the *Theme Colors* section).

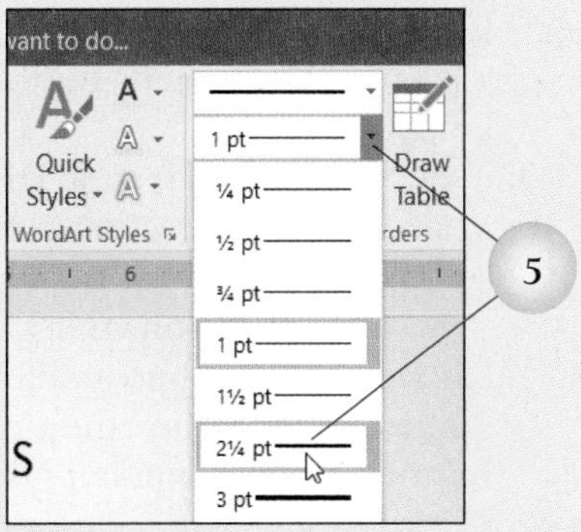

7. Draw along the border that separates the two columns from the top of the first row to the bottom of the last row.
8. Draw along the border that separates the first row from the second row.
9. Click the Draw Table button to deactivate the tool.
10. Save **5-Conference.pptx**.

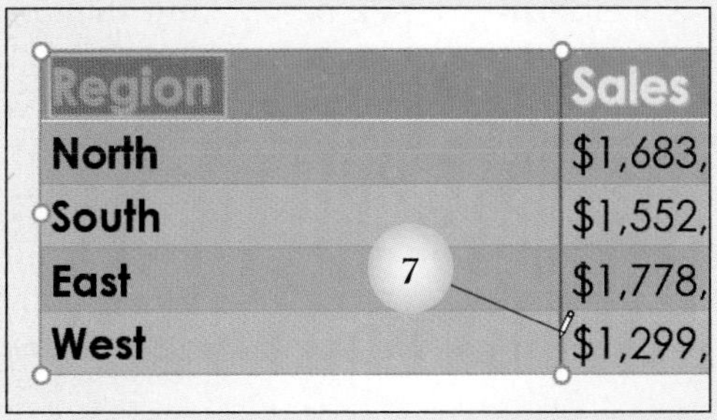
Region
Sales
North
$1,683,
South
$1,552,
East
$1,778,
West
$1,299,
7

Check Your Work

Tutorial

Changing the Table Layout

Hint If you make a mistake while formatting a table, immediately click the Undo button on the Quick Access Toolbar.

Changing the Table Layout

To further customize a table, consider changing the table layout by inserting or deleting columns or rows and specifying cell alignments. Change the table layout with options on the Table Tools Layout tab, shown in Figure 5.2. Use options and buttons on the tab to select specific cells, delete and insert rows and columns, merge and split cells, specify cell and table height and width, specify text alignment in cells, and arrange elements in a slide.

Figure 5.2 Table Tools Layout Tab

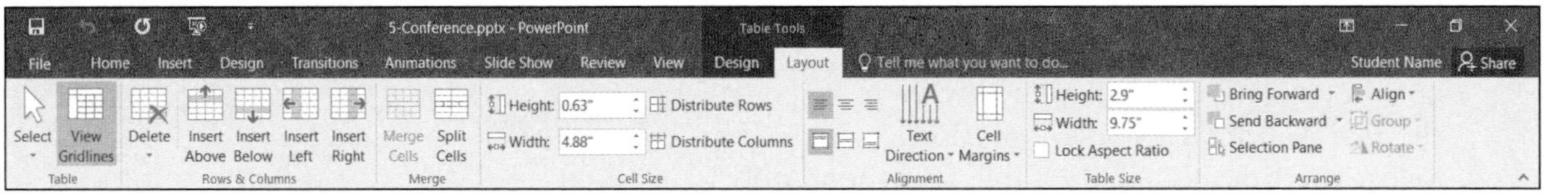

Project 1c **Modifying the Table Layout**

Part 3 of 14

1. With **5-Conference.pptx** open, make sure Slide 3 is active.
2. Click in any cell in the table and then click the Table Tools Layout tab.
3. Click in the cell containing the word *East*.
4. Click the Insert Above button in the Rows & Columns group.
5. Type Central in the new cell at the left, press the Tab key, and then type $1,024,000 in the new cell at the right.
6. Click in the cell containing the word *Region*.
7. Click the Insert Left button in the Rows & Columns group.
8. Click the Merge Cells button in the Merge group.
9. Type Sales Projections in the new cell.
10. Click the Text Direction button in the Alignment group and then click *Rotate all text 270°* at the drop-down list.
11. Click the Center button in the Alignment group and then click the Center Vertically button in the Alignment group.
12. Click in the *Width* measurement box in the Cell Size group, type 1.2, and then press the Enter key.

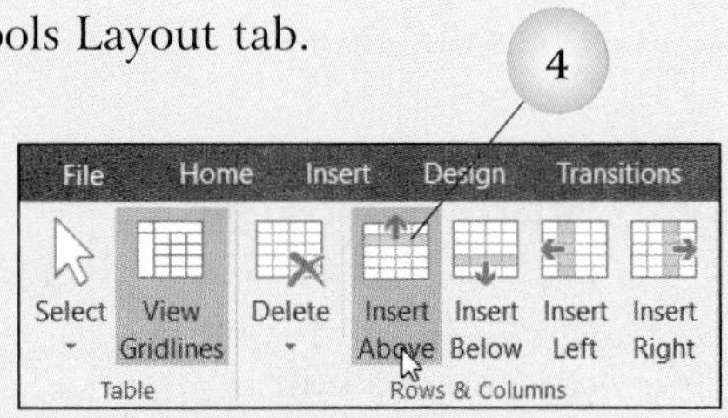

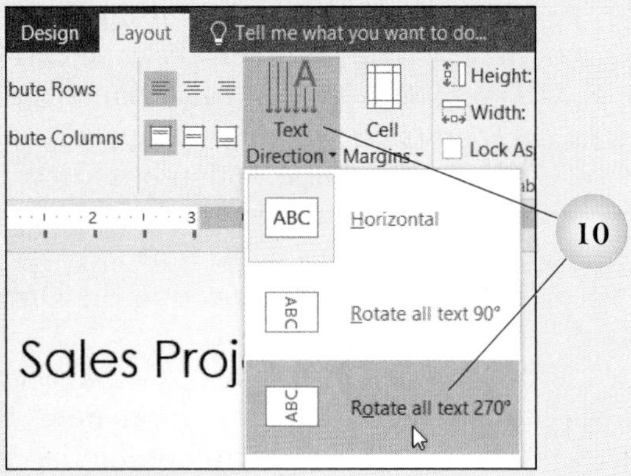

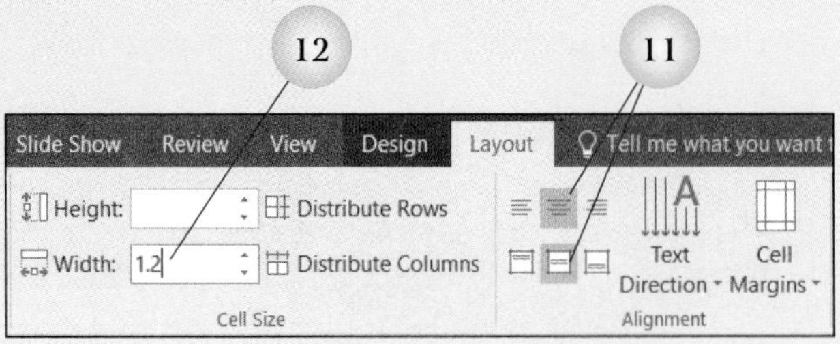

13. Click the Table Tools Design tab.
14. With the insertion point positioned in the cell containing the text *Sales Projections*, click the Borders button arrow in the Table Styles group and then click *Bottom Border* at the drop-down list.
15. Click in the cell containing the text *Sales* and then click the Table Tools Layout tab.
16. Click in the *Height* measurement box in the Cell Size group and then type 0.7.
17. Click in the *Width* measurement box in the Cell Size group, type 2.5, and then press the Enter key.
18. Click in the cell containing the text *Region*.
19. Click in the *Width* measurement box in the Cell Size group, type 4, and then press the Enter key.
20. Click in the *Height* measurement box in the Table Size group, type 4.2, and then press the Enter key.
21. Click the Select button in the Table group and then click *Select Table* at the drop-down list.
22. Click the Center button and then click the Center Vertically button in the Alignment group.
23. After looking at the text in cells, you decide that you want the text in the second column left-aligned. To do this, complete the following steps:
    a. Click in the cell containing the text *Region*.
    b. Click the Select button in the Table group and then click *Select Column* at the drop-down list.
    c. Click the Align Left button in the Alignment group.
    d. Click in any cell in the table.

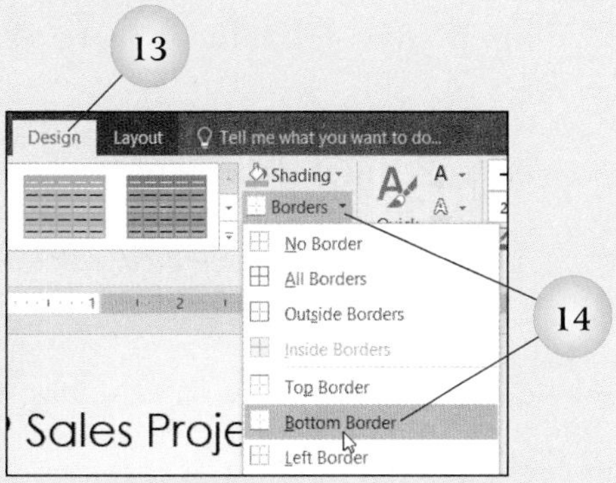

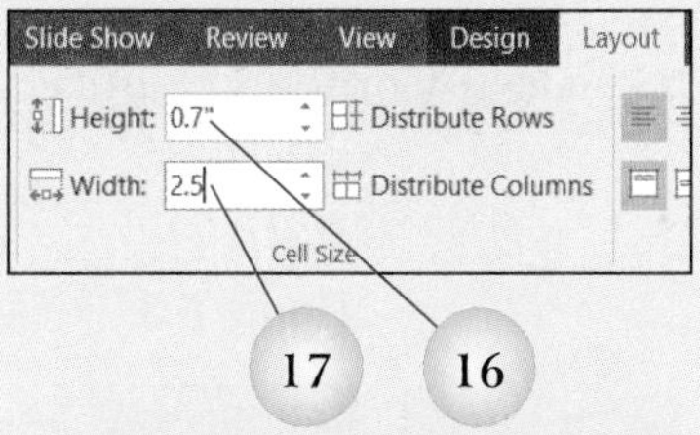

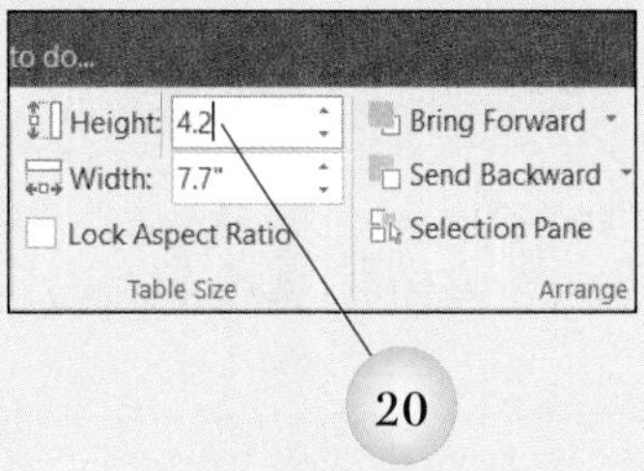

24. Align the table by completing the following steps:
    a. Click the Align button in the Arrange group on the Table Tools Layout tab and then click *Distribute Horizontally* at the drop-down list.

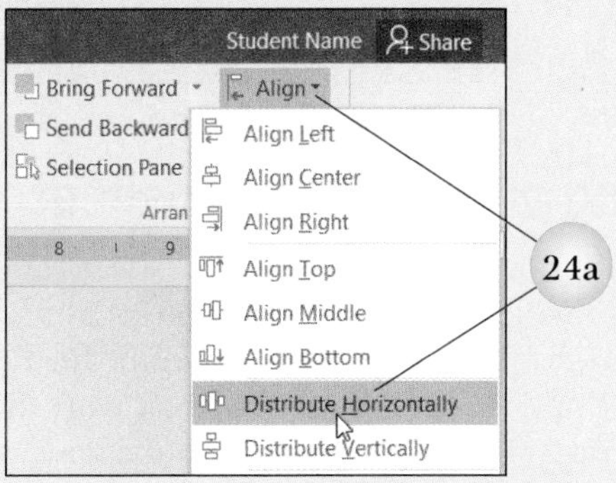

    b. Click the Align button and then click *Distribute Vertically* at the drop-down list.
    c. Looking at the table, you decide that it should be moved down in the slide. To do this, position the mouse pointer on the table border until the pointer displays with a four-headed arrow attached. Click and hold down the left mouse button, drag down approximately 0.5 inch, and then release the mouse button.

25. Insert an image in the table by completing the following steps:
    a. Click the Insert tab.
    b. Click the Pictures button in the Images group.
    c. At the Insert Picture dialog box, navigate to the PC5 folder on your storage medium and then double-click **Sales.png**.
    d. With the image selected, click the Color button on the Pictures Tools Format tab and then click the *Green Accent color 1 Dark* option (second column, second row in the *Recolor* section).
    e. Click in the *Shape Height* measurement box in the Size group, type 2.5, and then press the Enter key.
    f. Drag the image so it is positioned in the table as shown in Figure 5.3.
    g. Click outside the image to deselect it.
26. Save **5-Conference.pptx**.

Check Your Work

Figure 5.3 Project 1c, Slide 3

Inserting an Excel Spreadsheet

In addition to a table, an Excel worksheet can be inserted in a slide, which provides some Excel functions in PowerPoint. To insert an Excel worksheet, click the Insert tab, click the Table button in the Tables group, and then click the *Excel Spreadsheet* option. This inserts a small worksheet in the slide with two columns and two rows visible and the ribbon displays with Excel tabs. Increase the number of visible cells by dragging the sizing handles that display around the selected worksheet. Click outside the worksheet and the cells display as an object that can be formatted with options on the Drawing Tools Format tab. To format the worksheet with Excel options, double-click the worksheet and the Excel tabs display.

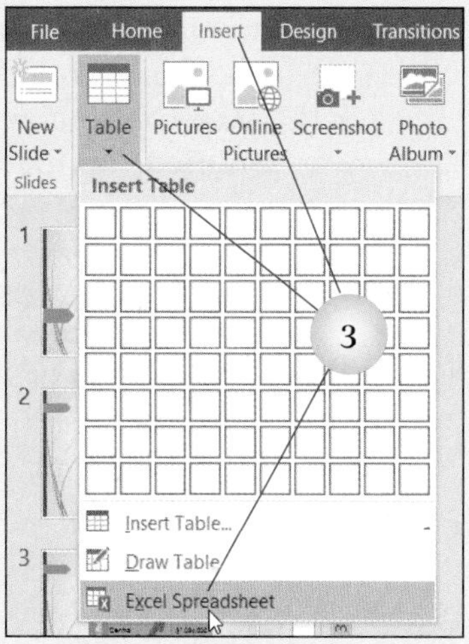

1. With **5-Conference.pptx** open, make sure Slide 3 is active and then insert a new slide with the Title Only layout.
2. Click in the title placeholder and then type Projected Increase.
3. Insert an Excel worksheet by clicking the Insert tab, clicking the Table button in the Tables group, and then clicking *Excel Spreadsheet*.
4. Increase the size of the worksheet by completing the following steps:
   a. Position the mouse pointer on the sizing handle (small black square) in the lower right corner of the worksheet until the pointer displays as a black, diagonal, two-headed arrow.
   b. Click and hold down the left mouse button; drag down and to the right and then release the mouse button. Continue dragging the small black square and releasing the mouse button until columns A, B, and C and rows 1 through 6 are visible.
5. Copy a Word table into the Excel worksheet by completing the following steps:
   a. Open Word and then open **NWSalesInc.docx** from the PC5 folder on your storage medium.
   b. Hover your mouse pointer over the table and then click the table move handle (small square containing a four-headed arrow) in the upper left corner of the table. (This selects all cells in the table.)
   c. Click the Copy button in the Clipboard group on the Home tab.
   d. Click the PowerPoint button on the taskbar.
   e. With Slide 4 and the first cell in the worksheet active, click the Paste button in the Clipboard group on the Home tab.
6. Size and position the worksheet object by completing the following steps:
   a. Click outside the worksheet to remove the Excel ribbon tabs.
   b. With the worksheet object selected, click the Drawing Tools Format tab.
   c. Click in the *Shape Width* measurement box, type 7, and then press the Enter key.
   d. Using the mouse, drag the worksheet object so it is centered on the slide.
7. Format the worksheet and insert a formula by completing the following steps:
   a. Double-click in the worksheet. (This displays the Excel ribbon tabs.)
   b. Click in cell C2, type the formula =b2*1.02, and then press the Enter key.

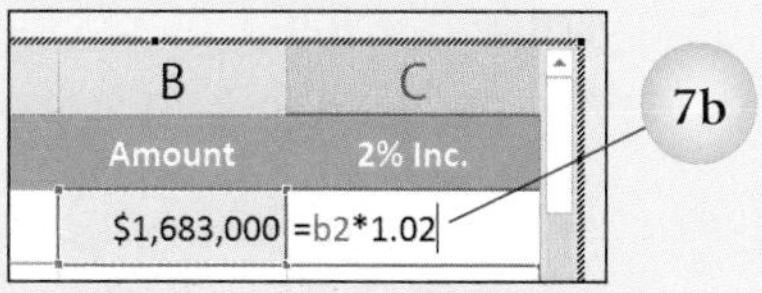

8. Copy the formula in C2 to cells C3 through C6 by completing the following steps:
   a. Position the mouse pointer (white plus symbol) in cell C2, click and hold down the left mouse button, drag down to cell C6, and then release the mouse button.
   b. Click the Fill button in the Editing group on the Home tab and then click *Down* at the drop-down list.
   c. With cells C2 through C6 selected, click the Decrease Decimal button in the Number group two times.
9. Click outside the worksheet to remove the Excel ribbon tabs.

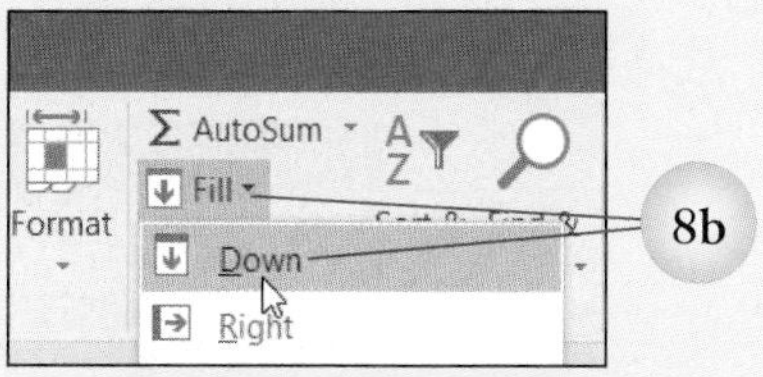

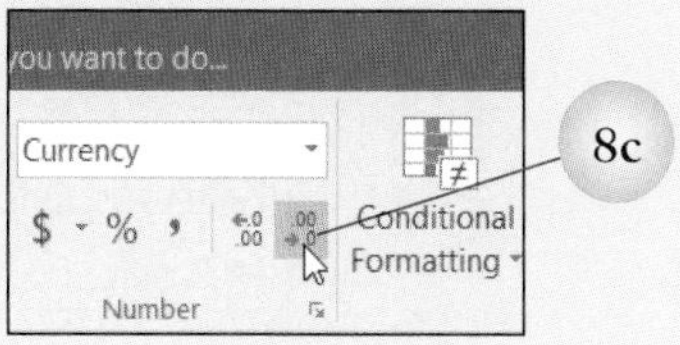

10. Make the following changes to the table:
    a. Click the Drawing Tools Format tab.
    b. Click the Align button and then click *Distribute Horizontally* at the drop-down list.
    c. Click the Align button and then click *Distribute Vertically* at the drop-down list.
11. Click the Word button on the taskbar, close the document, and then close Word.
12. Save **5-Conference.pptx**.

Check Your Work

Drawing a Table

A table can be drawn in a slide using the *Draw Table* option at the Table button drop-down list. Click the Table button and then click the *Draw Table* option and the mouse pointer displays as a pen. Drag in the slide to create the table. Use buttons on the Table Tools Design tab and Table Tools Format tab to format the table.

Project 1e Drawing a Table

Part 5 of 14

1. With **5-Conference.pptx** open, make sure Slide 4 is active.
2. Draw a table and then split the table into two columns and two rows by completing the following steps:
    a. Click the Insert tab, click the Table button in the Tables group, and then click the *Draw Table* option at the drop-down list.
    b. Position the mouse pointer (displays as a pen) below the worksheet and then drag to create a table that is approximately 7 inches wide and 1 inch tall.
    c. Click the Table Tools Layout tab and then click the Split Cells button in the Merge group.
    d. At the Split Cells dialog box, press the Tab key, type 2, and then click OK. (This splits the table into two columns and two rows.)
    e. Select the current measurement in the *Height* measurement box in the Table Size group and then type 1.
    f. Select the current measurement in the *Width* measurement box in the Table Size group, type 7, and then press the Enter key.

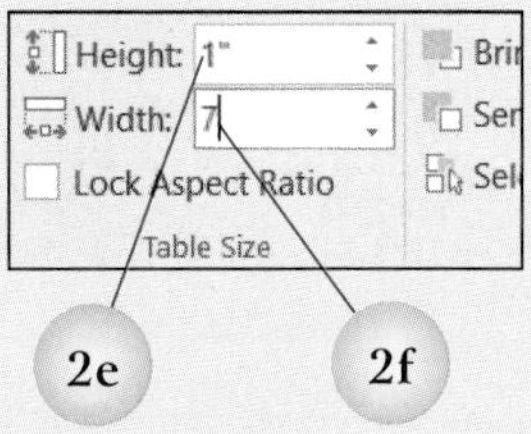

3. With the table selected, make the following formatting changes:
    a. Click the Table Tools Design tab.
    b. Click the More Table Styles button in the Table Styles group and then click the *Themed Style 2 - Accent 1* option (second column, second row in the *Best Match for Document* section).
    c. Click the Effects button in the Table Styles group, point to *Cell Bevel*, and then click the *Relaxed Inset* option (second column, first row in the *Bevel* section).

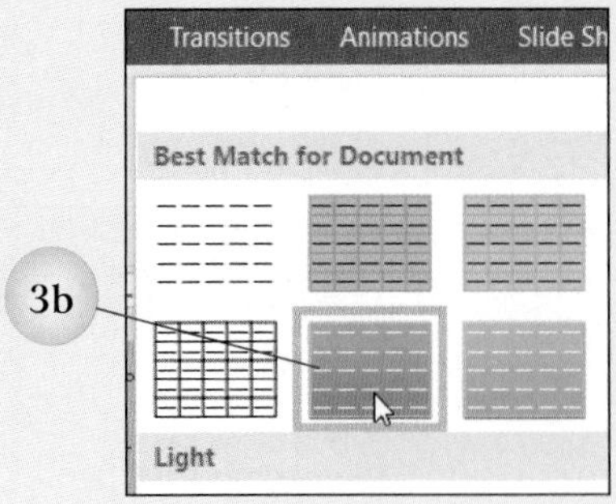

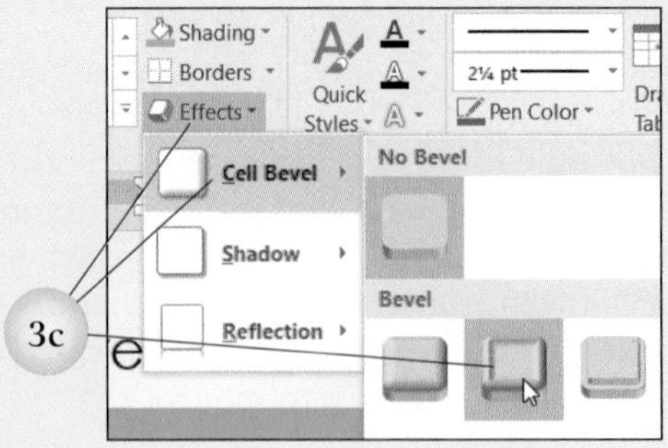

d. Click the Home tab, click the Bold button, and then click the Center button.
e. Click the Align Text button and then click *Middle* at the drop-down list.
f. Make sure the table is positioned evenly between the bottom of the top table and the bottom of the slide.
g. Click the Arrange button in the Drawing group, point to *Align*, and then click *Distribute Horizontally* at the side menu.

4. Type Maximum in the first cell in the table, press the Tab key, and then type $1,813,560.
5. Press the Tab key and then type Minimum.
6. Press the Tab key and then type $1,044,480.
7. Click outside the table to deselect it.
8. Save **5-Conference.pptx**.

Check Your Work

Tutorial

Inserting, Sizing, and Moving SmartArt

SmartArt

Quick Steps

Insert a SmartArt Graphic

1. Click Insert a SmartArt Graphic button in content placeholder.
2. Double-click graphic.

OR

1. Click Insert tab.
2. Click SmartArt button.
3. Double-click graphic.

Creating SmartArt

Use the SmartArt feature to insert graphics such as diagrams and organizational charts in a slide. SmartArt offers a variety of predesigned graphics that are available at the Choose a SmartArt Graphic dialog box, shown in Figure 5.4. Display the Choose a SmartArt Graphic dialog box by clicking the Insert a SmartArt Graphic button in a content placeholder or by clicking the Insert tab and then clicking the SmartArt button in the Illustrations group. At the dialog box, *All* is selected in the left panel and all available predesigned graphics display in the middle panel.

Predesigned graphics display in the middle panel of the Choose a SmartArt Graphic dialog box. Use the scroll bar at the right side of the middle panel to scroll down the list of graphic choices.

Figure 5.4 Choose a SmartArt Graphic Dialog Box

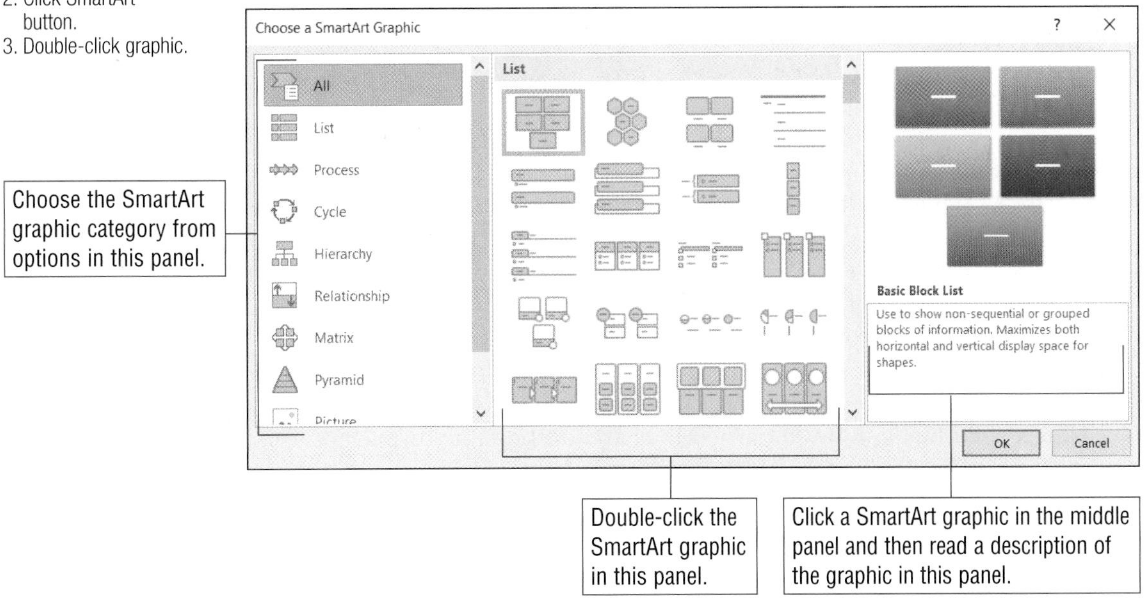
Choose a SmartArt Graphic
All
List
Process
Cycle
Hierarchy
Relationship
Matrix
Pyramid
List
Basic Block List
Use to show non-sequential or grouped blocks of information. Maximizes both horizontal and vertical display space for shapes.
OK
Cancel
Choose the SmartArt graphic category from options in this panel.
Double-click the SmartArt graphic in this panel.
Click a SmartArt graphic in the middle panel and then read a description of the graphic in this panel.

Hint Use SmartArt to communicate your message and ideas in a visual manner.

Hint Limit the number of shapes and the amount of text in a slide to key points.

Click a graphic in the middle panel and the name of the graphic displays in the right panel along with a description of the graphic type. SmartArt includes graphics for presenting a list of data; showing data processes, cycles, and relationships; and presenting data in a matrix or pyramid. Double-click a graphic in the middle panel of the dialog box and the graphic is inserted in the slide.

When a graphic is inserted in the slide, a text pane may display at the left side of the graphic. Type text in the text pane or directly in the graphic. Apply design formatting to a graphic with options on the SmartArt Tools Design tab, shown in Figure 5.5. This tab is active when the graphic is selected in the slide. Use options and buttons on this tab to change the graphic layout, apply a style to the graphic, and reset the graphic back to the original formatting.

Figure 5.5 SmartArt Tools Design Tab

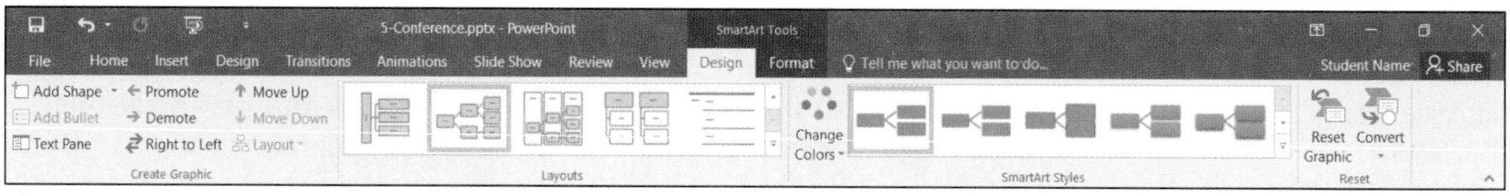

Project 1f Inserting and Modifying a SmartArt Graphic

Part 6 of 14

1. With **5-Conference.pptx** open, make sure Slide 4 is active and then insert a new slide with the Title and Content layout.
2. Click in the title placeholder and then type Division Reorganization.
3. Click the Insert a SmartArt Graphic button in the middle of the slide in the content placeholder.
4. At the Choose a SmartArt Graphic dialog box, click *Hierarchy* in the left panel of the dialog box.
5. Double-click the *Horizontal Hierarchy* option (as shown at the right).

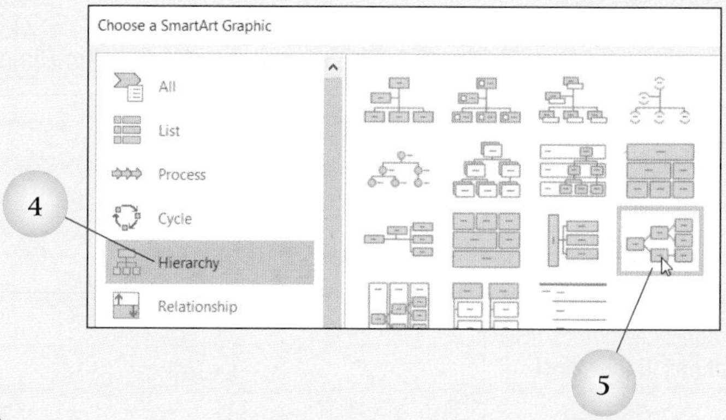

6. If a *Type your text here* pane displays at the left side of the organizational chart, close the pane by clicking the Text Pane button in the Create Graphic group.
7. Delete one of the boxes in the organizational chart by clicking the border of the top box at the right side of the slide (the top box of the three stacked boxes) and then pressing the Delete key. (Make sure that the selection border that surrounds the box is a solid line and not a dashed line. If a dashed line displays, click the box border again. This should change it to a solid line.)

8. Click the *[Text]* placeholder in the first box at the left, type Andrew Singh, press Shift + Enter, and then type Director. Click in each of the remaining box placeholders and type the text as shown below. (Press Shift + Enter after each name.)

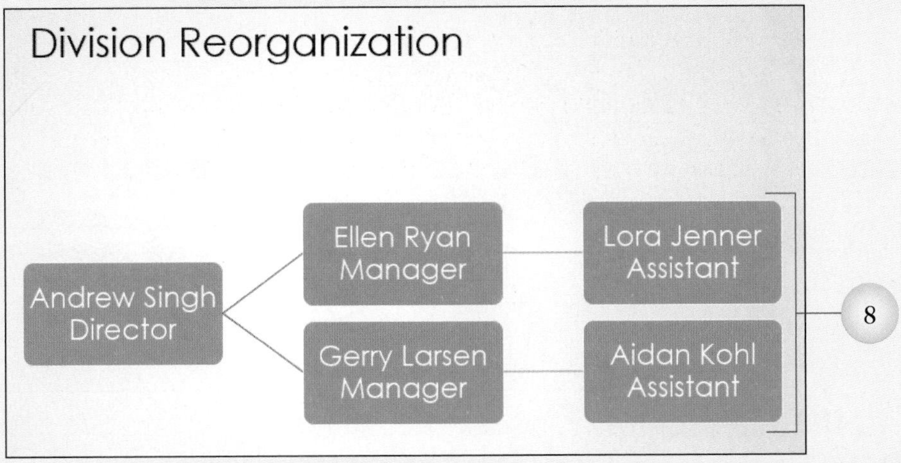

9. Click inside the SmartArt border, but outside of any shape, and then click the SmartArt Tools Design tab.
10. Click the More SmartArt Styles button in the SmartArt Styles group and then click the *Polished* option (first column, first row in the *3-D* section).
11. Click the Change Colors button in the SmartArt Styles group and then click the *Colorful Range - Accent Colors 3 to 4* option (third option in the *Colorful* section).
12. Change the layout of the organizational chart by clicking the More Layouts button in the Layouts group and then clicking *Table Hierarchy*. Your slide should now look like the slide shown in Figure 5.6.

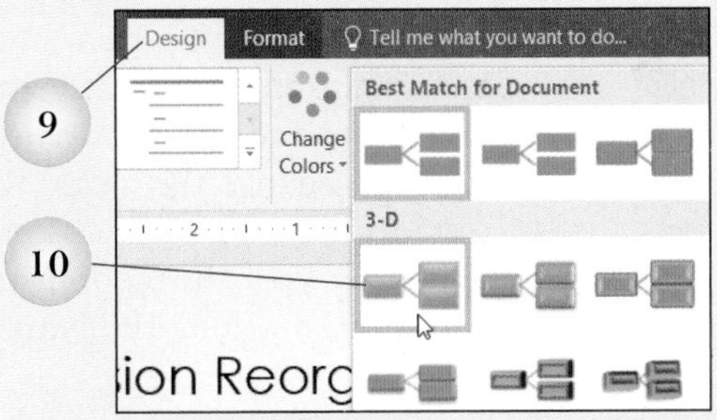

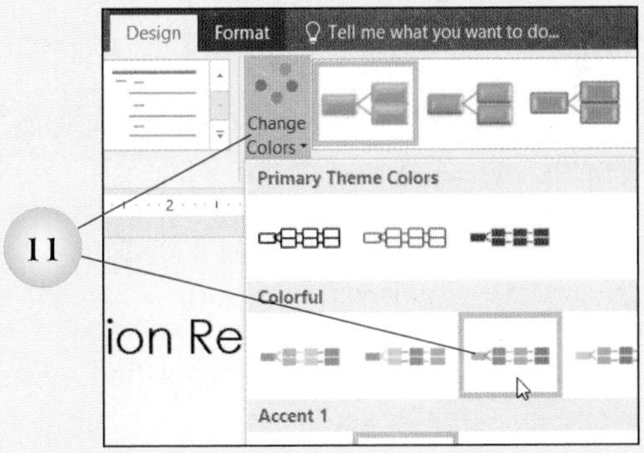

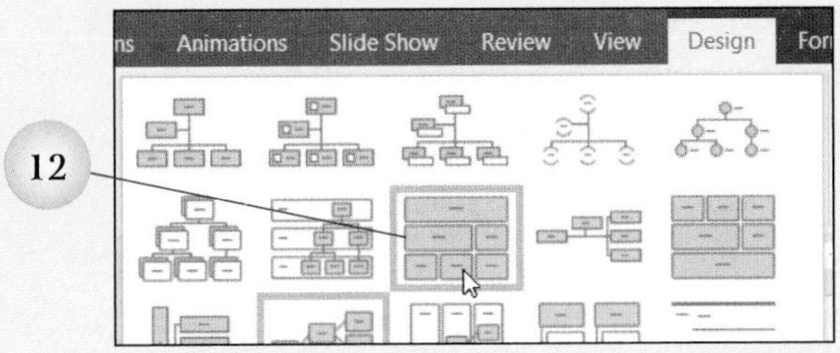

13. Save **5-Conference.pptx**.

Check Your Work

Figure 5.6 Project 1f, Slide 5

Tutorial

Formatting SmartArt

Hint Nudge selected shape(s) with the up, down, left, or right arrow keys on the keyboard.

Formatting SmartArt

Apply formatting to a SmartArt graphic with options on the SmartArt Tools Format tab, shown in Figure 5.7. Use options and buttons on this tab to change the size and shape of objects in the graphic; apply shape styles and WordArt styles; change the shape fill, outline, and effects; and arrange and size the graphic. Move the graphic by positioning the arrow pointer on the graphic border until the pointer turns into a four-headed arrow, clicking and holding down the left mouse button, dragging the graphic to the new location, and then releasing the mouse button.

Figure 5.7 SmartArt Tools Format Tab

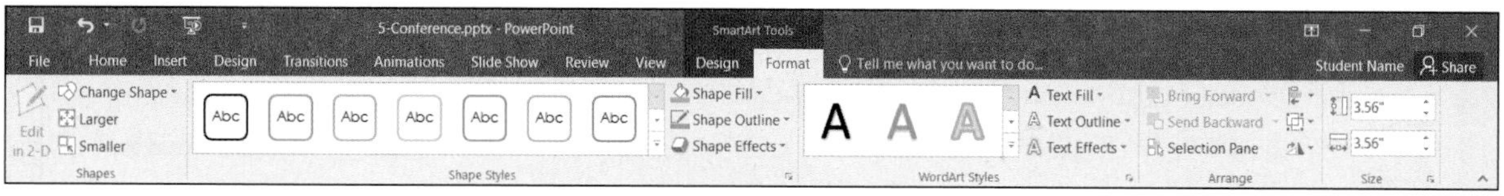

Project 1g **Inserting and Formatting a SmartArt Graphic**

Part 7 of 14

1. With **5-Conference.pptx** open, make Slide 1 active and then insert a new slide with the Blank layout.
2. Click the Insert tab and then click the SmartArt button in the Illustrations group.
3. At the Choose a SmartArt Graphic dialog box, click *Relationship* in the left panel.
4. Double-click the *Basic Venn* option shown at the right. (You will need to scroll down the list to display this graphic.)
5. Click in the top shape and type Health.

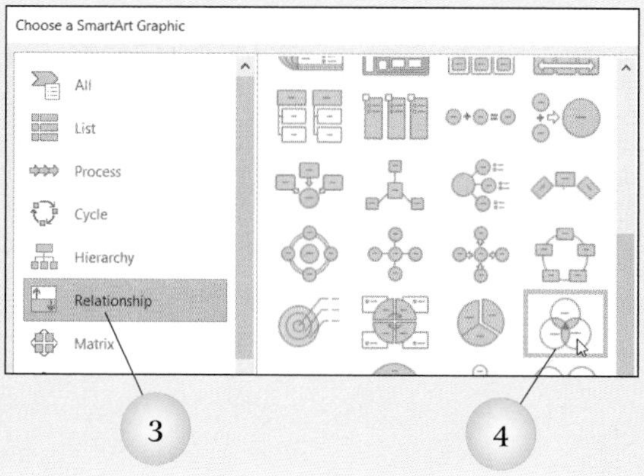

6. Click in the shape at the left and type Happiness.
7. Click in the shape at the right and type Harmony.
8. Click inside the SmartArt border but outside of any shape.
9. Click the Change Colors button in the SmartArt Styles group and then click the *Colorful Range - Accent Colors 3 to 4* option (third option in the *Colorful* section).
10. Click the More SmartArt Styles button in the SmartArt Styles group and then click the *Cartoon* option (third column, first row in the *3-D* section).

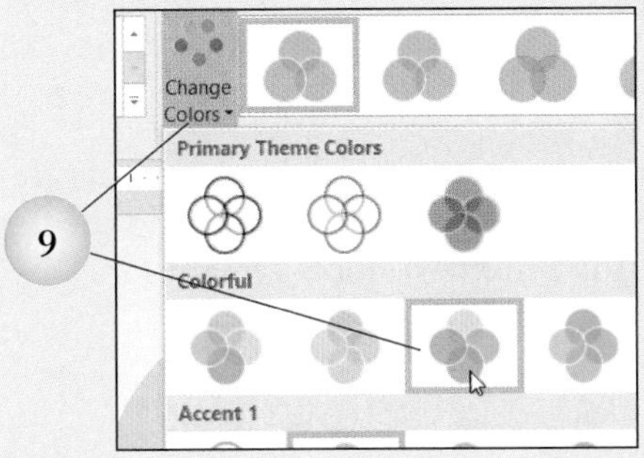

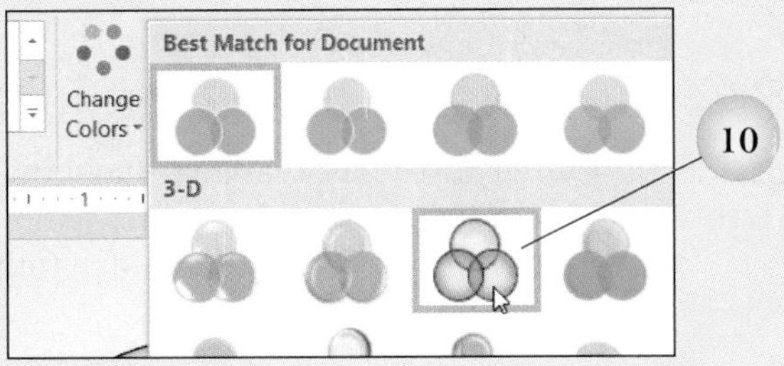

11. Click the SmartArt Tools Format tab.
12. Click the More WordArt Styles button in the WordArt Styles group and then click the *Pattern Fill - Green, Accent 1, 50%, Hard Shadow - Accent 1* option (third column, bottom row).

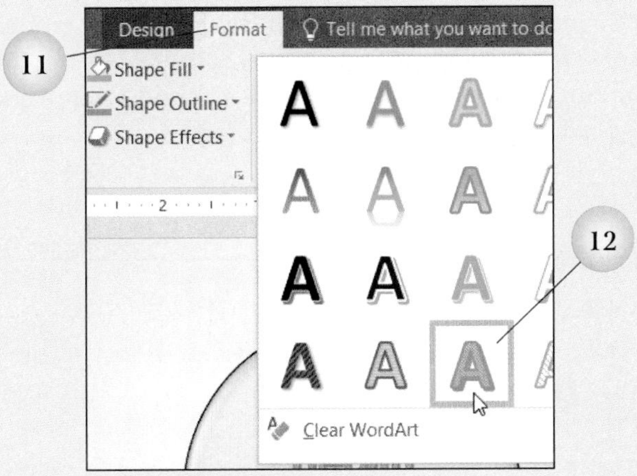

13. Click the Text Outline button arrow in the WordArt Styles group and then click the *Green, Accent 1, Darker 50%* option (fifth column, bottom row in the *Theme Colors* section).
14. Click in the *Shape Height* measurement box in the Size group and then type 6.
15. Click in the *Shape Width* measurement box in the Size group, type 9, and then press the Enter key.
16. Save **5-Conference.pptx**.

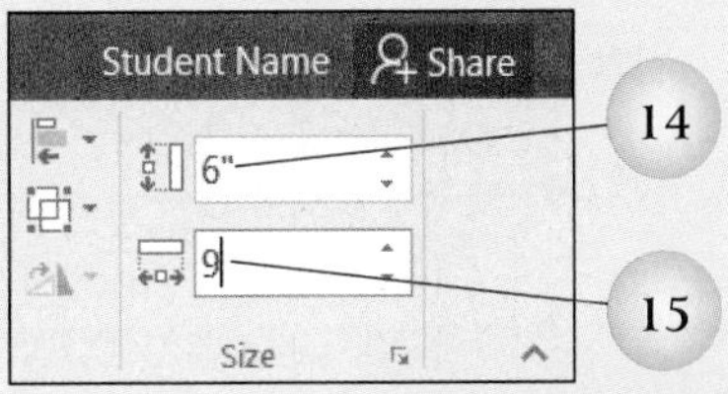

Check Your Work

Converting Text and WordArt to a SmartArt Graphic

Tutorial

Converting Text and WordArt to a SmartArt Graphic

Convert to SmartArt Graphic

To improve the visual display of text or WordArt and to create a professionally designed image, consider converting text or WordArt to a SmartArt graphic. To do this, select the placeholder containing the text or WordArt and then click the Convert to SmartArt Graphic button in the Paragraph group on the Home tab. Click the SmartArt graphic at the drop-down gallery or click the *More SmartArt Graphics* option and then choose a SmartArt graphic at the Choose a SmartArt Graphic dialog box.

Inserting Text in the Text Pane

Tutorial

Inserting Text in the Text Pane

Text Pane

Enter text in a SmartArt shape by clicking in the shape and then typing the text or by typing text in the Text pane. Display the Text pane by clicking the Text Pane button in the Create Graphic group on the SmartArt Tools Design tab.

Project 1h Creating a SmartArt Graphic with Text and WordArt — Part 8 of 14

1. With **5-Conference.pptx** open, make Slide 7 active. (This slide contains WordArt text.)
2. Click anywhere in the WordArt text.
3. If necessary, click the Home tab.
4. Click the Convert to SmartArt Graphic button in the Paragraph group.
5. Click the *More SmartArt Graphics* option.
6. At the Choose a SmartArt Graphic dialog box, click *Cycle* in the left panel and then double-click *Diverging Radial* in the middle panel.

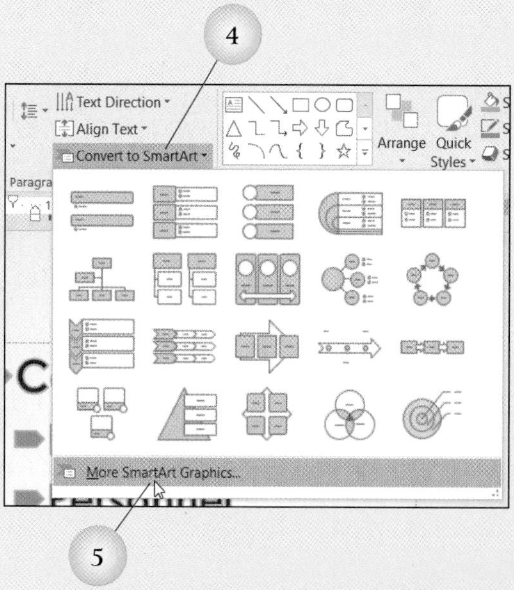

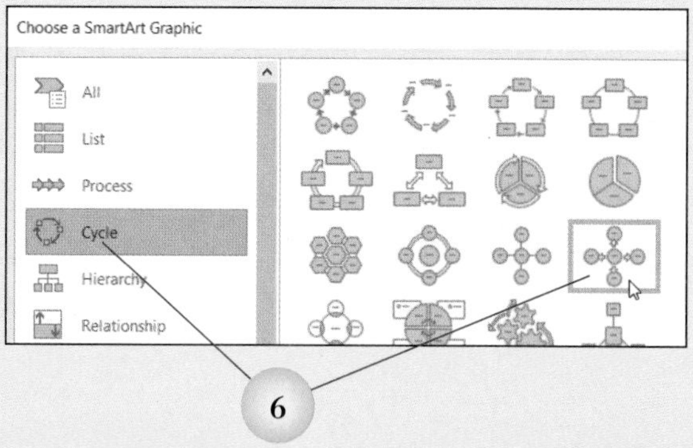

7. Click the Add Shape button in the Create Graphic group on the SmartArt Tools Design tab and then type Supplies in the new shape.
8. Change the order of the text in the shapes at the left and right sides of the graphic by clicking the Right to Left button in the Create Graphic group.

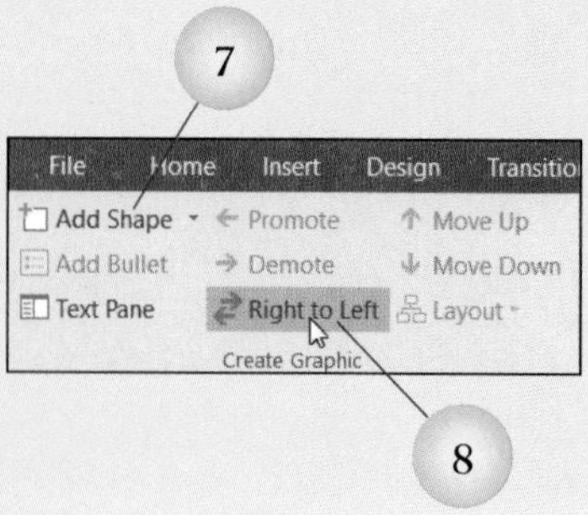

9. Click the Change Colors button in the SmartArt Styles group and then click the *Colorful - Accent Colors* option (first option in the *Colorful* section).
10. Click the More SmartArt Styles button in the SmartArt Styles group and then click the *Inset* option (second column, first row in the *3-D* section).
11. Click the SmartArt Tools Format tab.
12. Click the middle circle (contains the text *Central Division*).
13. Click the Larger button in the Shapes group three times.
14. Click inside the SmartArt border but outside of any shape.
15. Click in the *Shape Height* measurement box in the Size group and then type 6.6.
16. Click in the *Shape Width* measurement box, type 8.2, and then press the Enter key.
17. With the SmartArt graphic selected, click the Align button in the Arrange group and then click *Distribute Horizontally*.
18. Click the Align button in the Arrange group and then click *Distribute Vertically*.
19. Click the Home tab.
20. Click the Bold button in the Font group.
21. Make Slide 9 active.
22. Click anywhere in the bulleted text and, if necessary, click the Home tab.
23. Click the Convert to SmartArt Graphic button in the Paragraph group and then click the *Vertical Block List* option (second column, first row).
24. Click the shape containing the text *Sales over $2 million* and then click the Demote button in the Create Graphic group on the SmartArt Tools Design tab.

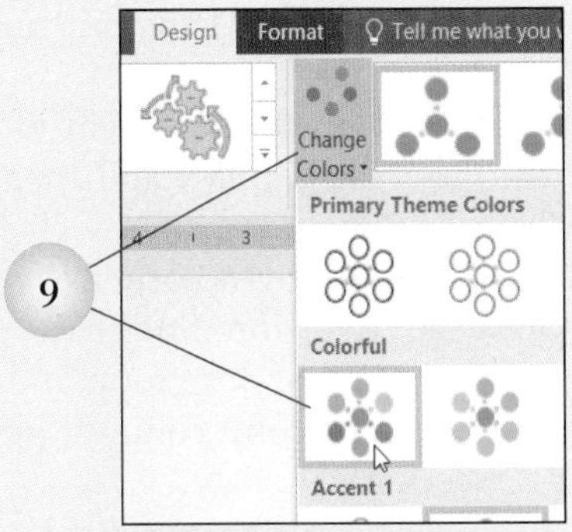

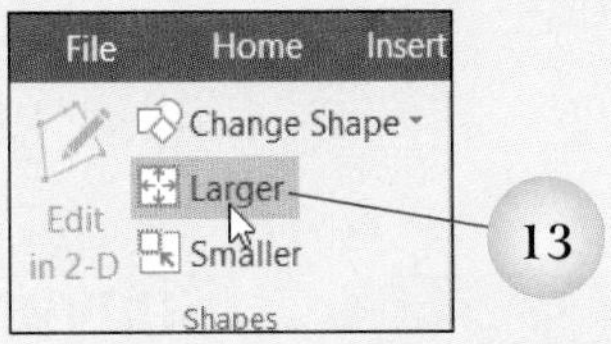

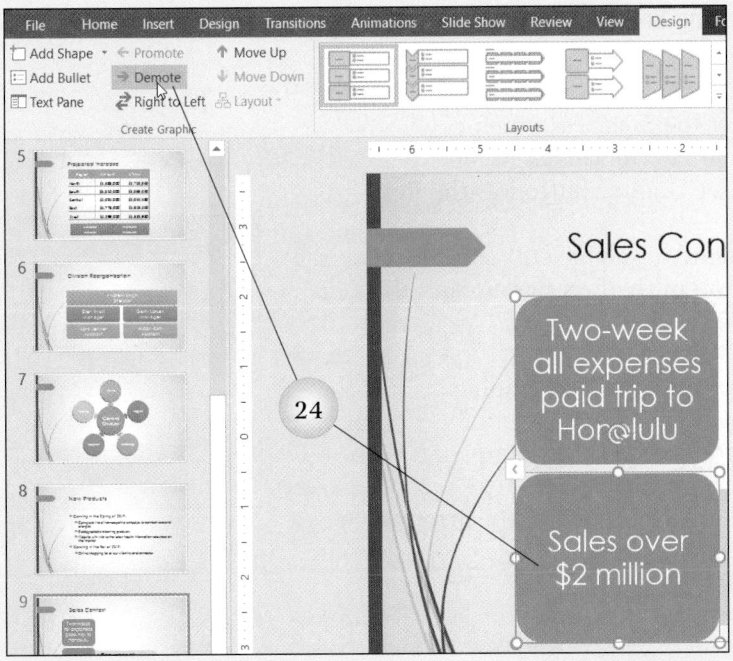

25. Click anywhere in the text *One-week all expenses paid trip to Las Vegas* and then click the Promote button in the Create Graphic group.

26. Click the Text Pane button in the Create Graphic group to display the *Type your text here* text pane.
27. Click immediately right of the *s* in *Vegas* in the text pane and then press the Enter key.
28. Press the Tab key and then type Sales over $1 million.
29. Close the text pane by clicking the Close button in the upper right corner of the pane.
30. Click the More SmartArt Styles button in the SmartArt Styles group and then click the *Inset* option (second column, first row in the *3-D* section).
31. Save **5-Conference.pptx**.
32. Print Slides 7 and 9.

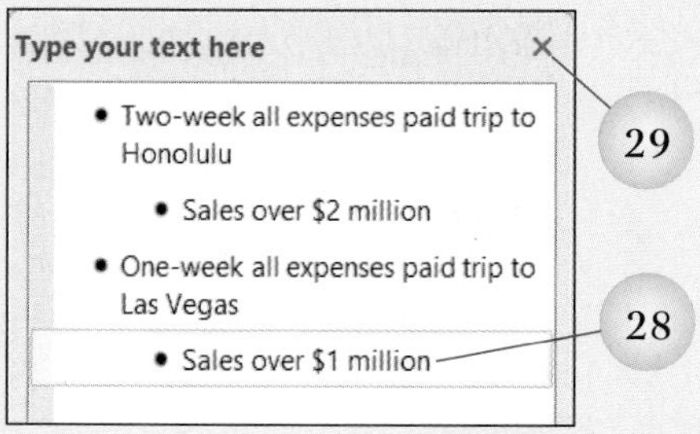

Check Your Work

Tutorial

Converting SmartArt to Text and to Shapes

Reset Graphic

Convert

Converting SmartArt Graphic to Text and to Shapes

To remove all formatting from a SmartArt graphic, click the Reset Graphic button in the Reset group on the SmartArt Tools Design tab. Use the Convert button to convert a SmartArt graphic to text or shapes. Click the Convert button and then click the *Convert to Text* option to convert the SmartArt graphic to bulleted text or click the *Convert to Shapes* option to convert a SmartArt graphic to shapes. Once the SmartArt graphic has been converted to shapes, those shapes can be moved, sized, or deleted independently from the other shapes.

Project 1i Converting SmartArt to Text and to Shapes

Part 9 of 14

1. With **5-Conference.pptx** open, make sure Slide 9 is active.
2. Click to select the SmartArt graphic.
3. Click the SmartArt Tools Design tab.
4. Click the Reset Graphic button in the Reset group.
5. With the SmartArt graphic still selected, click the Convert button in the Reset group and then click *Convert to Text*.
6. Make Slide 7 active.
7. Click to select the SmartArt graphic.
8. Click the SmartArt Tools Design tab, click the Convert button in the Reset group, and then click *Convert to Shapes*.
9. Select and then delete each of the arrows that points from the middle circle to each of the outer circles.
10. Save **5-Conference.pptx**.

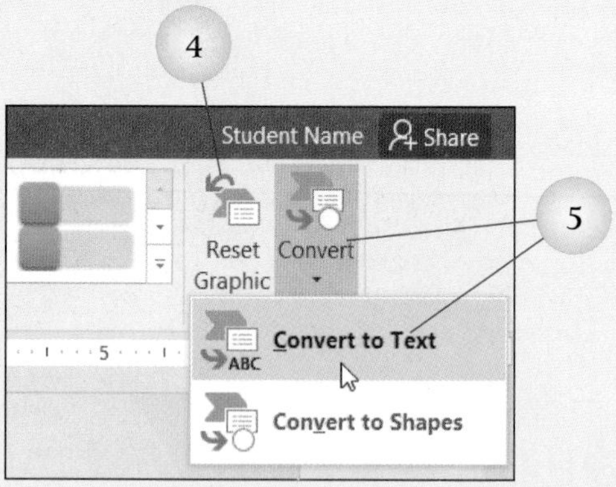

Check Your Work

Tutorial

Creating a Chart

Chart

Quick Steps

Insert a Chart

1. Click Insert Chart button in content placeholder.
2. Click chart style and type.
3. Enter data in Excel worksheet.
4. Close Excel.

OR

1. Click Insert tab.
2. Click Chart button.
3. Click chart type and style.
4. Enter data in Excel worksheet.
5. Close Excel.

Creating a Chart

A variety of charts can be created in a slide including bar and column charts, pie charts, area charts, and much more. To create a chart, click the Insert Chart button in a content placeholder or click the Insert tab and then click the Chart button in the Illustrations group. This displays the Insert Chart dialog box, as shown in Figure 5.8. At this dialog box, choose the chart type in the list at the left side, click the chart style, and then click OK. Table 5.2 describes the fifteen basic chart types that can be created.

Click OK at the Insert Chart dialog box and a sample chart is inserted in the slide and an Excel window opens with a worksheet containing sample data, as shown in Figure 5.9. Type the data in the Excel worksheet cells over the existing data. As data is typed, the chart in the slide reflects the new data. To type data in the Excel worksheet, click in the cell, type the data, and then press the Tab key to make the next cell active, press Shift + Tab to make the previous cell active, or press the Enter key to make the cell below active.

The sample worksheet contains a data range of four columns and five rows and the cells in the data range display with a light fill color. Excel uses the data in the range to create the chart in the slide. The data is not limited to four columns and five rows. Simply type data in cells outside the data range and Excel will expand the data range and incorporate the new data in the chart. This is because the table AutoExpansion feature is on by default. If data is typed in a cell outside the data range, an AutoCorrect Options button displays in the lower right corner of the cell. This button can be used to turn off AutoExpansion. If data is not entered in the four columns and five rows, decrease the size of the data range. To do this, position the mouse pointer on the small, square, blue icon in the lower right corner of cell E5 until the pointer displays as a diagonally pointing two-headed arrow and then drag up to decrease the number of rows in the range and/or drag left to decrease the number of columns.

Once all data is entered in the worksheet, click the Close button in the upper right corner of the Excel window. This closes the Excel window and displays the chart in the slide.

Figure 5.8 Insert Chart Dialog Box

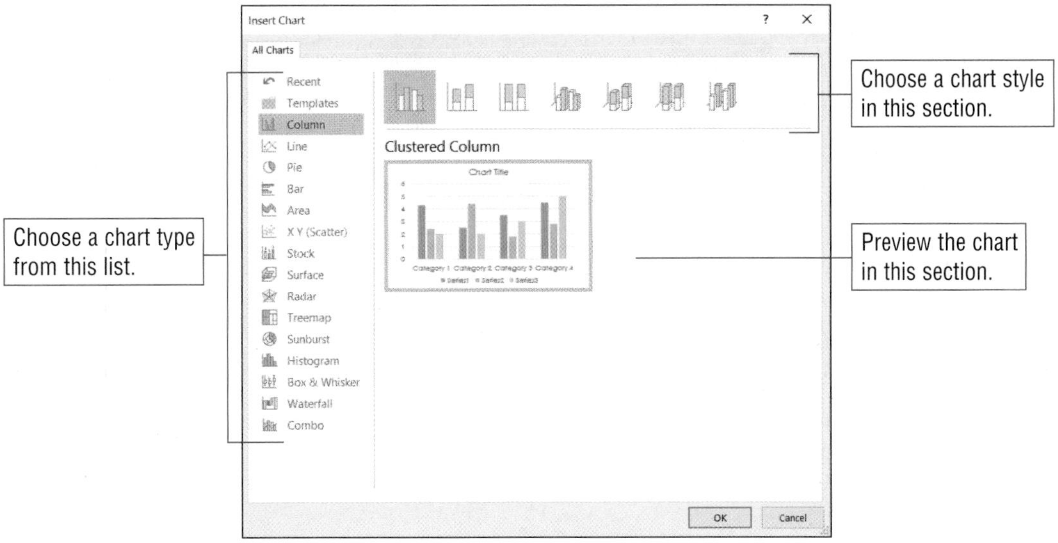

Table 5.2 Types of Charts

Type	Description
Area	Emphasizes the magnitude of change, rather than time and rate of change. It also shows the relationship of parts to a whole by displaying the sum of the plotted values.
Bar	Shows individual figures at a specific time, or shows variations between components but not in relationship to the whole.
Box & Whisker	Displays median, quartiles, and extremes of a data set on a number line to show distribution of data. Lines extending vertically are called whiskers and indicate variability outside the upper and lower quartiles.
Column	Compares separate (noncontinuous) items as they vary over time.
Combo	Combines two or more chart types to make data easier to understand.
Histogram	Condenses a data series into a visual representation by grouping data points into logical ranges called *bins*.
Line	Shows trends and changes over time at even intervals. It emphasizes the rate of change over time rather than the magnitude of change.
Pie	Shows proportions and relationships of parts to the whole.
Radar	Emphasizes differences and amounts of change over time, and variations and trends. Each category has its own value axis radiating from the center point. Lines connect all values in the same series.
Stock	Shows four values for a stock—open, high, low, and close.
Sunburst	Displays hierarchical data with each level represented by one ring with the innermost ring as the top of the hierarchy.
Surface	Shows trends in values across two dimensions in a continuous curve.
Treemap	Provides a hierarchical view of data and compares proportions within the hierarchy.
X Y (Scatter)	Either shows the relationships among numeric values in several data series or plots the interception points between x and y values. It shows uneven intervals of data and is commonly used in scientific data.
Waterfall	Determines how an initial value is affected by a series of positive and negative values.

Figure 5.9 Sample Chart

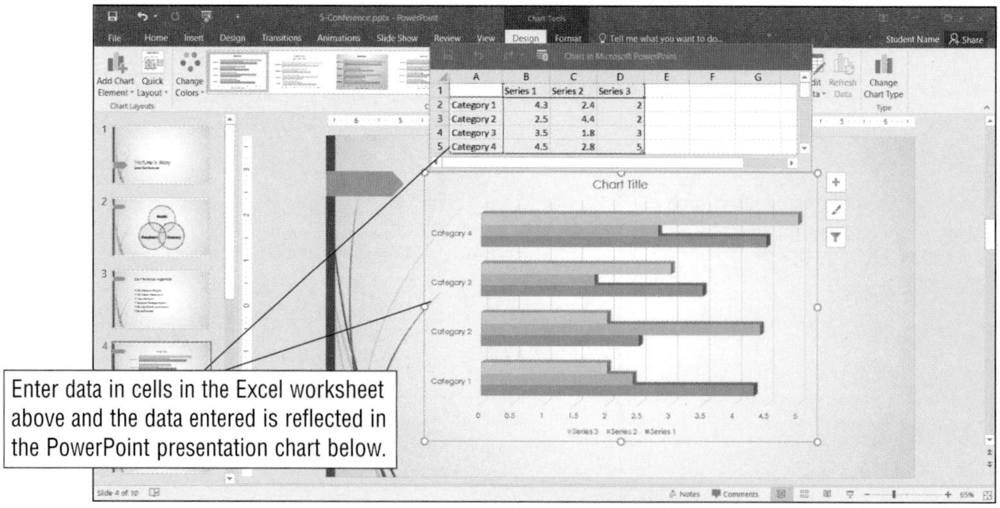
Chart Title
Category 4
Category 3
Category 2
Category 1
Enter data in cells in the Excel worksheet above and the data entered is reflected in the PowerPoint presentation chart below.

Project 1j Creating a Chart

Part 10 of 14

1. With **5-Conference.pptx** open, make Slide 3 active and then insert a new slide with the Blank layout.
2. Click the Insert tab and then click the Chart button in the Illustrations group.
3. At the Insert Chart dialog box, click *Bar* in the left panel.
4. Double-click the *3-D Clustered Bar* option at the top of the dialog box (fourth option).
5. In the Excel worksheet, position the mouse pointer in the bottom right corner of the cell D5 border until the mouse pointer displays as a diagonally pointing two-headed arrow. Click and hold down the left mouse button, drag to the left until the border displays at the right side of column C, and then release the mouse button.
6. Type the text in cells as shown below and to the right by completing the following steps:
   a. Click in cell B1 in the Excel worksheet, type 1st Half, and then press the Tab key.
   b. With cell C1 active, type 2nd Half and then press the Tab key.
   c. Click in cell A2, type North, and then press the Tab key.
   d. Type $853,000 and then press the Tab key.
   e. Type $970,000 and then press the Enter key.
   f. Continue typing the remaining data in cells as indicated at the right. (The data range will automatically expand to include row 6.)
7. Click the Close button in the upper right corner of the Excel window.
8. Save **5-Conference.pptx**.

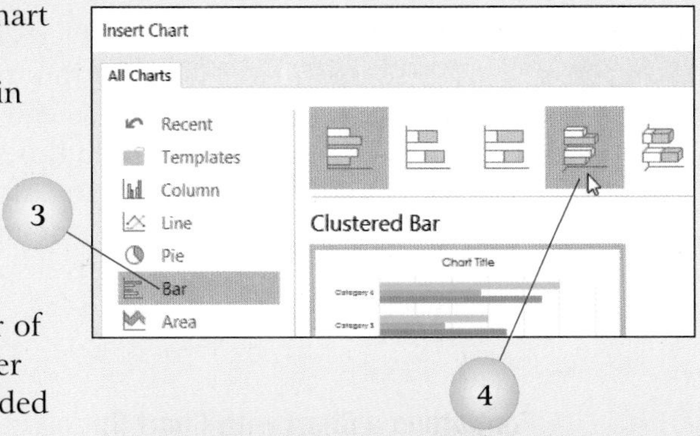

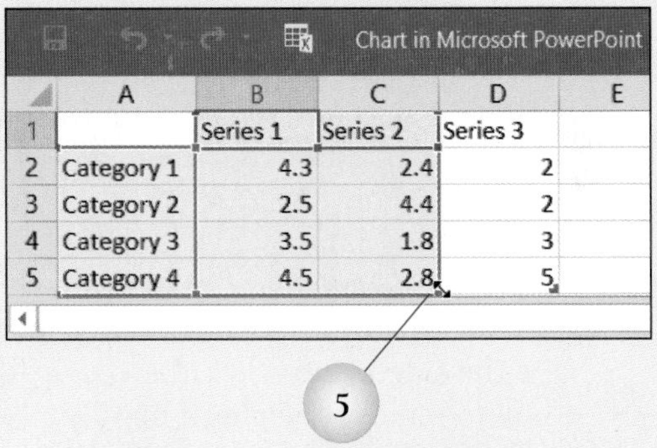

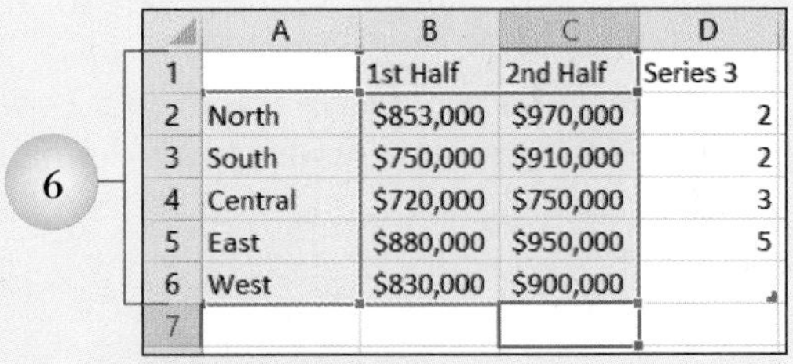

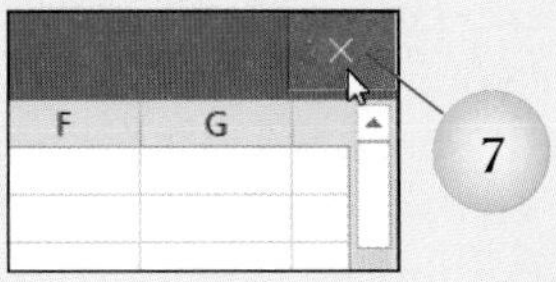

Check Your Work

Tutorial

Formatting with Chart Buttons

Chart Elements

Formatting with Chart Buttons

When a chart is inserted in a slide, three buttons display at the right side of the chart border. Click the top button, Chart Elements, and a side menu displays with chart elements such as axis title, chart title, data labels, data table, gridlines, and a legend. Elements containing a check mark in the check box are included in the chart. Include other elements in the chart by inserting a check mark in the check boxes.

Chart Styles

Chart Filters

Apply a chart style to a chart by clicking the Chart Styles button that displays at the right side of the chart. At the side menu that displays, scroll down the gallery and then click an option. In addition to applying a chart style, use the Chart Styles button side menu to change the chart colors. Click the Chart Styles button and then click the Color tab to the right of the Style tab. Click a color option at the color palette that displays.

Use the Chart Filters button to isolate specific data in a chart. Click the button and then, at the side menu that displays, specify the series or categories to include in the chart. To do this, remove check marks from those elements that should not appear in the chart. After removing the check marks, click the Apply button at the bottom of the side menu. Click the Names tab at the Chart Filters button side menu and options display for turning the display of column and row names on or off.

Project 1k Formatting a Chart with Chart Buttons

Part 11 of 14

1. With **5-Conference.pptx** open, make sure Slide 4 is the active slide and that the chart in the slide is selected. (Make sure the entire chart is selected and not just an element in the chart.)
2. Insert and remove chart elements by completing the following steps:
   a. Click the Chart Elements button that displays outside the upper right side of the chart.
   b. At the side menu, click the *Chart Title* check box to remove the check mark.
   c. Click the *Data Table* check box to insert a check mark.
   d. Hover your mouse pointer over *Gridlines* in the Chart Elements button side menu and then click the right-pointing arrow that displays.
   e. At the other side menu, click the *Primary Major Horizontal* check box to insert a check mark.
   f. Click the *Legend* check box to remove the check mark.
   g. Hover your mouse pointer over *Axis Titles* in the Chart Elements button side menu and then click the right-pointing arrow that displays.
   h. At the other side menu, click the *Primary Vertical* check box to insert a check mark.
   i. With *Axis Title* selected in the rotated box at the left side of the chart, type Region.

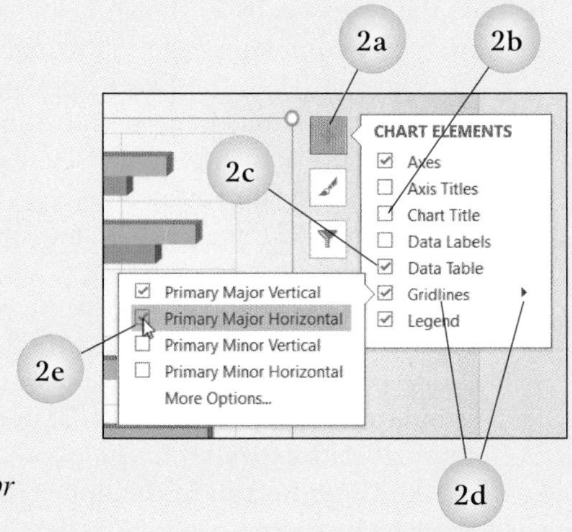

3. Apply a different chart style by completing the following steps:
   a. Click the chart border to redisplay the chart buttons.
   b. Click the Chart Styles button that displays to the right of the chart below the Chart Elements button.
   c. At the side menu gallery, click the *Style 3* option (third option in the gallery).

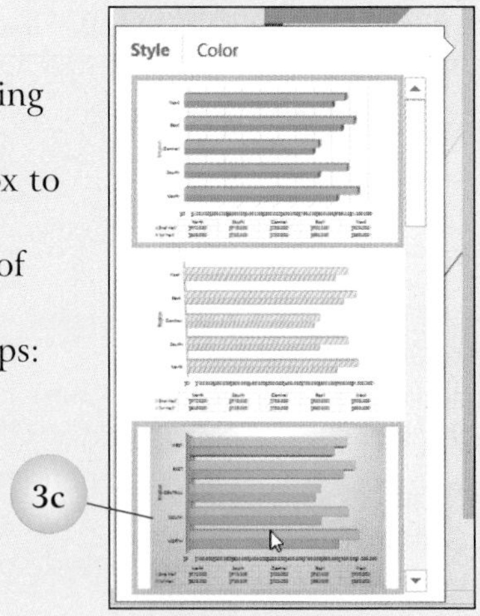

d. Click the Color tab at the top of the side menu and then click the *Color 2* option (second row in the *Colorful* section).

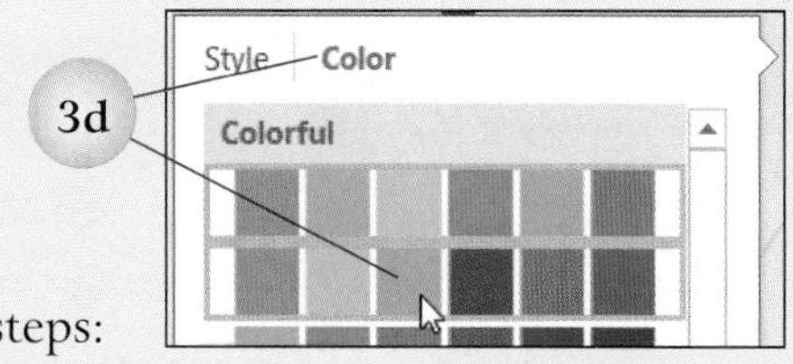

e. Click the Chart Styles button to remove the side menu.

4. Remove the horizontal axis title by completing these steps:
   a. Click the Chart Elements button.
   b. Hover your mouse pointer over *Axes* in the Chart Elements button side menu and then click the right-pointing arrow that displays.
   c. At the other side menu that displays, click the *Primary Horizontal* check box to remove the check mark.
   d. Click the Chart Elements button to remove the side menu.
5. Display only the North and South sales by completing the following steps:
   a. Click the Chart Filters button that displays below the Chart Styles button.
   b. Click the *Central* check box in the *Categories* section to remove the check mark.
   c. Click the *East* check box in the *Categories* section to remove the check mark.
   d. Click the *West* check box in the *Categories* section to remove the check mark.
   e. Click the Apply button at the bottom of the side menu.
   f. Click the Chart Filters button to remove the side menu.
   g. After viewing only the *North* and *South* sales, redisplay the other regions by clicking the Chart Filters button, clicking the *Central*, *East*, and *West* check boxes to insert check marks, and then clicking the Apply button.
   h. Click the Chart Filters button to remove the side menu.
6. Save **5-Conference.pptx**.

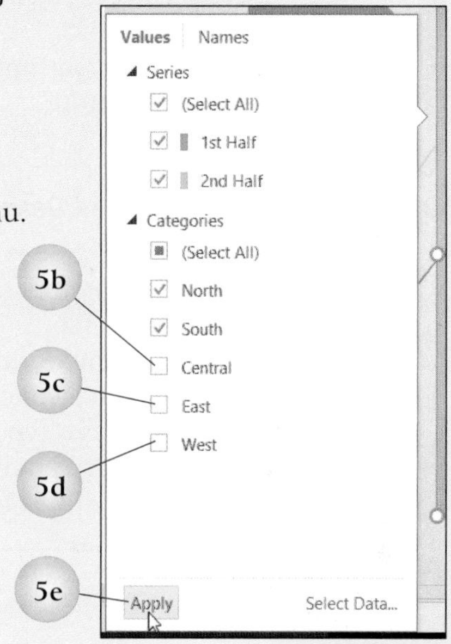

Check Your Work

Tutorial

Changing Chart Design

Quick Steps

Change the Chart Type and Style
1. Make the chart active.
2. Click Chart Tools Design tab.
3. Click Change Chart Type button.
4. Click chart type.
5. Click chart style.
6. Click OK.

Change Chart Type

Changing Chart Design

In addition to the buttons that display outside the chart border, a chart can be customized with options on the Chart Tools Design tab, shown in Figure 5.10. Use options on this tab to add a chart element, change the chart layout and colors, apply a chart style, select data and switch rows and columns, and change the chart type.

After creating a chart, the chart type can be changed by clicking the Change Chart Type button in the Type group on the Chart Tools Design tab. This displays the Change Chart Type dialog box. This dialog box contains the same options as the Insert Chart dialog box shown in Figure 5.8. At the Change Chart Type dialog box, click the chart type in the left panel and click the chart style in the right panel.

Use options in the Data group on the Chart Tools Design tab to change the grouping of the data in the chart, select specific data, edit data, and refresh the data. When a chart is created, the cells in the Excel worksheet are linked to the chart in the slide. Click the Select Data button in the Data group and Excel opens

Figure 5.10 Chart Tools Design Tab

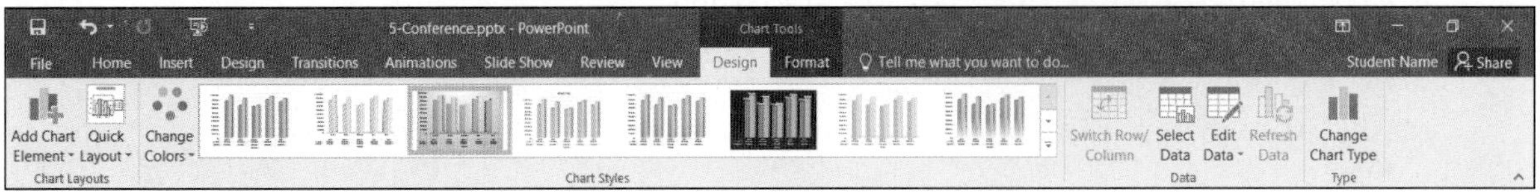

Select Data

Switch Row/ Column

Edit Data

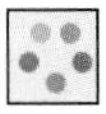
Change Colors

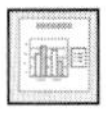
Quick Layout

and the Select Data Source dialog box displays. At the Select Data Source dialog box, click the Switch Row/Column button to change the grouping of the selected data. Filter data at the dialog box by removing the check mark from those items that should not appear in the chart. To edit data in the chart, click the Edit Data button and the Excel worksheet opens. Make edits to cells in the Excel worksheet and then click the Close button.

Apply predesigned chart styles with options in the Chart Styles group and use the Change Colors button to change the color of the selected element or chart. Click the Quick Layout button in the Chart Layouts group to display a drop-down gallery of layout options and add an element to the chart with the Add Chart Element button.

Project 1l Changing the Chart Design

Part 12 of 14

1. With **5-Conference.pptx** open, make sure Slide 4 is active and the chart is selected. Click the Chart Tools Design tab to make it active.
2. Looking at the chart, you decide that the bar chart was not the best choice for the data and decide to change to a column chart. Do this by completing the following steps:
   a. Click the Change Chart Type button in the Type group on the Chart Tools Design tab.
   b. At the Change Chart Type dialog box, click the *Column* option in the left panel.
   c. Click the *3-D Clustered Column* option (fourth option at the top of the dialog box).

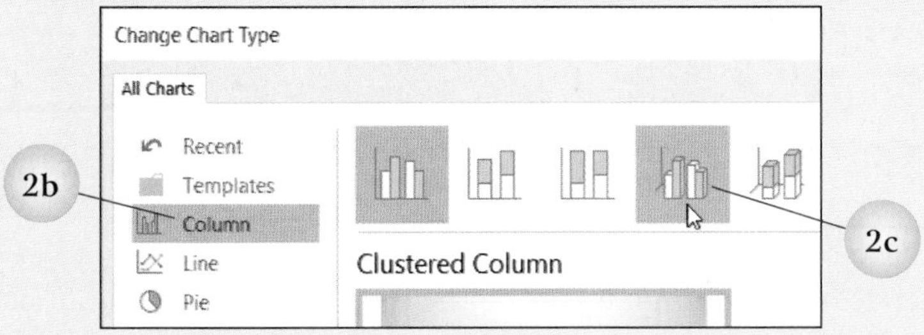

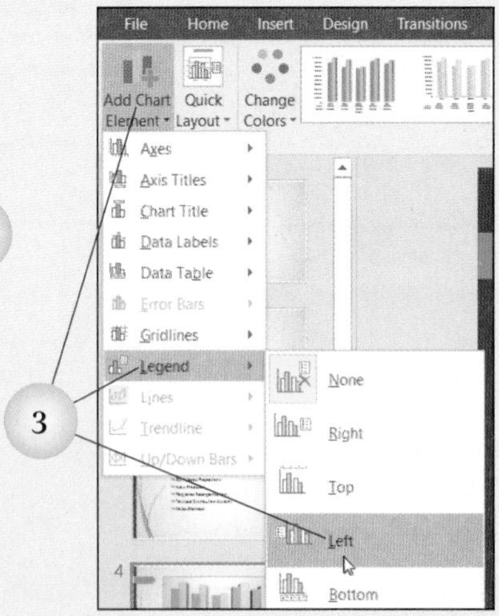

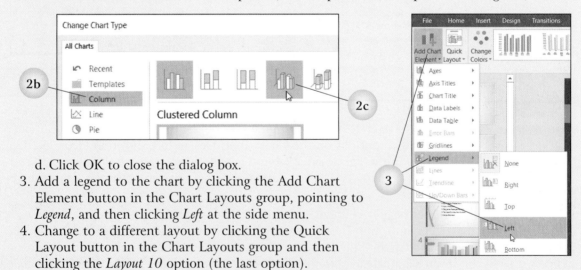

   d. Click OK to close the dialog box.
3. Add a legend to the chart by clicking the Add Chart Element button in the Chart Layouts group, pointing to *Legend*, and then clicking *Left* at the side menu.
4. Change to a different layout by clicking the Quick Layout button in the Chart Layouts group and then clicking the *Layout 10* option (the last option).

5. Click the Add Chart Element button in the Chart Layouts group, point to *Chart Title* at the drop-down list, and then click *Above Chart* at the side menu.
6. Type 2018 Regional Sales as the chart title.
7. Click the chart border to deselect the chart title.
8. Click the *Style 1* option in the chart styles gallery in the Chart Styles group (first option).
9. Select data and switch rows and columns by completing the following steps:
   a. Click the Select Data button in the Data group. (This opens Excel and displays the Select Data Source dialog box.)
   b. Click the Switch Row/Column button in the Select Data Source dialog box.
   c. Click OK. (This switches the grouping of the data from *Region* to *Half Yearly Sales*.)
10. After viewing the chart, switch the rows and columns back to the original groupings by dragging the Excel window so the Switch Row/Column button is visible in the Data group on the Chart Tools Design tab, clicking in the chart, and then clicking the Switch Row/Column button.
11. Close the Excel window by clicking the Close button in the upper right corner of the Excel window.
12. Click the Edit Data button in the Data group.
13. Click in cell B4 (the cell containing the amount *$720,000*), type 650000, and then press the Enter key. (When you press the Enter key, a dollar symbol is automatically inserted in front of the number and a thousand separator comma is inserted.)
14. Click in cell B6 (the cell containing the amount *$830,000*), type 730000, and then press the Enter key.
15. Click the Close button in the upper right corner of the Excel window.
16. Save **5-Conference.pptx**.

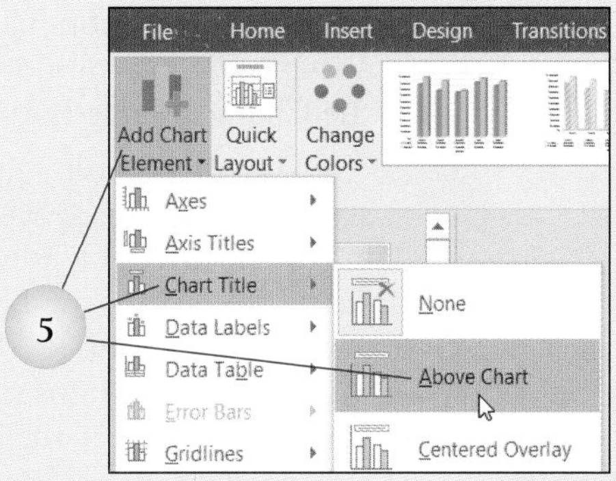

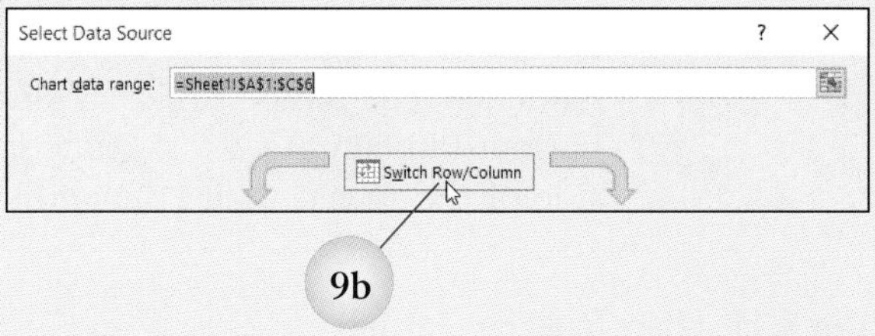

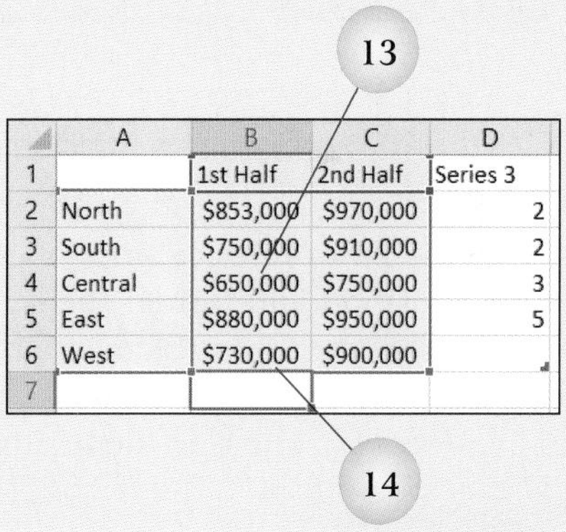

	A	B	C	D
1		1st Half	2nd Half	Series 3
2	North	$853,000	$970,000	2
3	South	$750,000	$910,000	2
4	Central	$650,000	$750,000	3
5	East	$880,000	$950,000	5
6	West	$730,000	$900,000	
7				

Check Your Work

Tutorial

Changing Chart Format

Hint Right-click text in a chart element to display the Mini toolbar.

Format Selection

Formatting a Chart and Chart Elements

Apply formatting to a chart or chart elements using options in the Drawing group on the Home tab. Apply a predesigned style to a chart or chart element with the Quick Styles button. Use other buttons in the group to add fill and outline color and apply effects.

In addition to the buttons in the Drawing group on the Home tab, a chart and chart elements can be formatted using options on the Chart Tools Format tab, as shown in Figure 5.11. To format or modify a specific element in a chart, select the element. Do this by clicking the element or by clicking the *Chart Elements* option box arrow in the Current Selection group and then clicking the element at the drop-down list. With the element selected, apply the formatting. Click the Format Selection button in the Current Selection group and a task pane displays with

Hint Chart elements can be repositioned for easier viewing.

options for formatting the selected element. Insert shapes with options in the Insert Shapes group. Click a shape, or click the More Shapes button and then click a shape at the drop-down list, and then drag in the chart to create the shape. Click the Change Shape button to change the shape to a different shape.

The Shape Styles group on the Chart Tools Format tab contains predesigned styles that can be applied to elements in the chart. Click the More Shape Styles button at the right side of the shape styles gallery and a drop-down gallery displays shape styles. Use the buttons that display at the right side of the Shape Styles group to apply fill, an outline, and an effect to a selected element. The WordArt Styles group contains predesigned styles for applying formatting to text in a chart. Use the buttons at the right side of the WordArt Styles group to apply fill color, an outline color, or an effect to text in a chart. Use options in the Arrange group to specify the layering, alignment, rotation, and size of a chart or chart element.

Additional formatting options are available at various task panes. Display a task pane by the clicking Format Selection button or by clicking a group task pane launcher. The Shape Styles, WordArt Styles, and Size groups on the Chart Tools Format tab contain a task pane launcher. The task pane that opens at the right side of the screen varies depending on the chart or chart element selected.

Figure 5.11 Chart Tools Format Tab

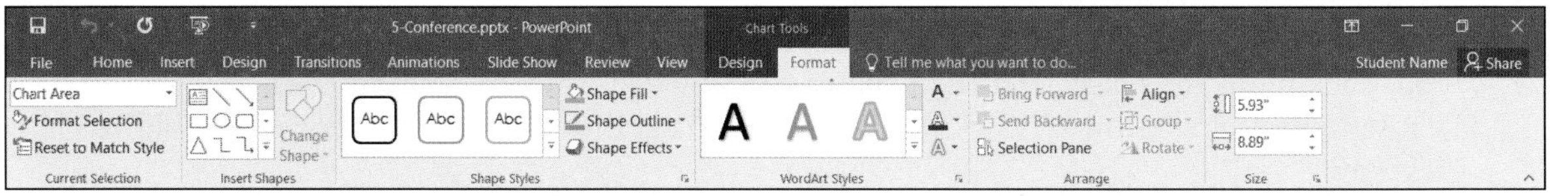

Project 1m Formatting a Chart and Chart Elements

Part 13 of 14

1. With **5-Conference.pptx** open, make sure Slide 4 is active and the chart is selected.
2. Reposition and format the legend by completing the following steps:
   a. Click the Chart Elements button that displays at the right side of the chart.
   b. Hover your mouse pointer over *Legend*, click the right-pointing arrow at the right side of *Legend* in the side menu, and then click the *Right* option at the other side menu.

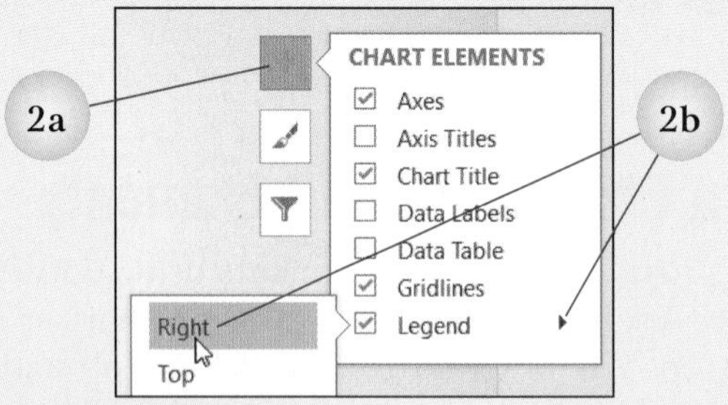

   c. Click the Chart Elements button again to remove the side menu.
   d. Click the legend to select it.
   e. If necessary, click the Home tab.

f. Click the Quick Styles button in the Drawing group and then click the *Subtle Effect - Lime, Accent 3* option (fourth column, fourth row).
g. Click the Shape Outline button arrow in the Drawing group and then click the *Green, Accent 1, Darker 50%* option (fifth column, bottom row in the *Theme Colors* section).
h. Increase the size of the legend by dragging down the bottom middle sizing handle about 0.25 inch.

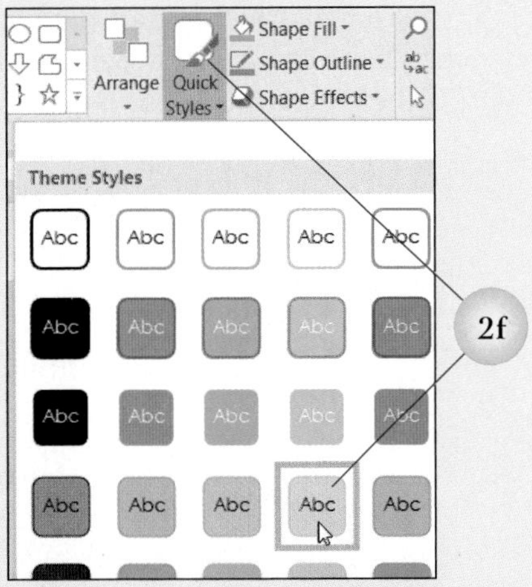

3. Format the title by completing the following steps:
a. Click the Chart Tools Format tab.
b. Click the *Chart Elements* option box arrow in the Current Selection group and then click *Chart Title* at the drop-down list.
c. Click the More Shape Styles button at the right side of the gallery in the Shape Styles group and then click the *Intense Effect - Green, Accent 1* option (second column, bottom row).
d. Click the Shape Effects button, point to *Bevel*, and then click the *Cross* option (third column, first row in the *Bevel* section).

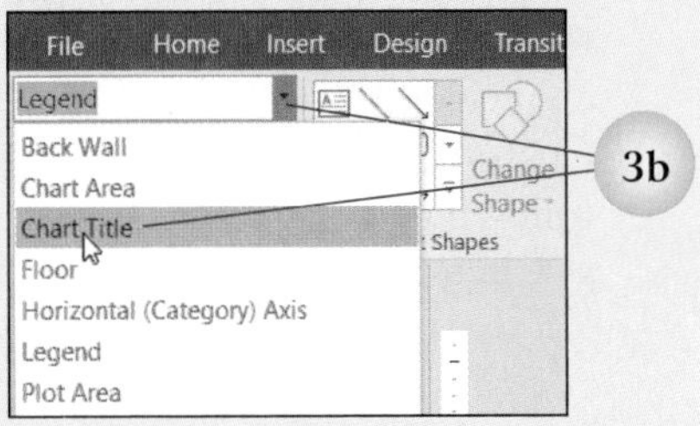

4. Customize the chart wall and floor by completing the following steps:
a. Click the *Chart Elements* option box arrow in the Current Selection group and then click *Back Wall* at the drop-down list.
b. Click the Format Selection button in the Current Selection group. (This displays the Format Wall task pane with the Fill & Line icon selected.)

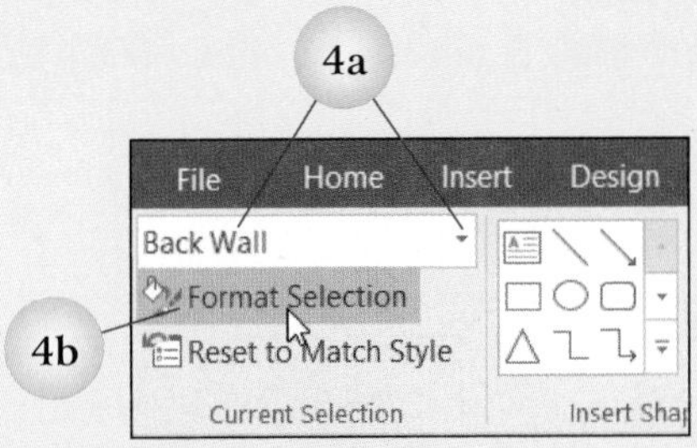

c. If necessary, click *Fill* to display the options.
d. Click the *Gradient fill* option.
e. Click the Preset gradients button and then click the *Light Gradient - Accent 3* option (third column, first row).
f. Click the *Chart Elements* option box arrow and then click *Floor*. (This displays the Format Floor task pane.)
g. Click the *Solid fill* option.

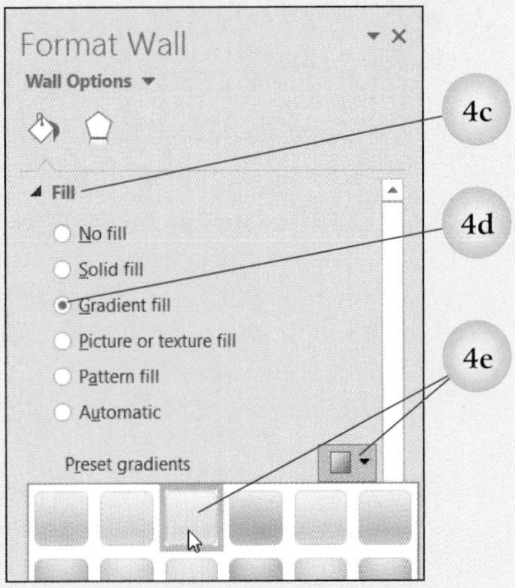

5. Customize the 1st Half data series by completing the following steps:
   a. Click the *Chart Elements* option box arrow in the Current Selection group and then click *Series "1st Half"* at the drop-down list.
   b. Click the Effects icon in the Format Data Series task pane.
   c. Click *3-D Format* to display the options.
   d. Click the Material button in the task pane.
   e. At the gallery that displays, click the *Dark Edge* option (first option in the *Special Effect* section).
   f. Click the Bottom bevel button and then click the *Hard Edge* option (third column, third row in the *Bevel* section).

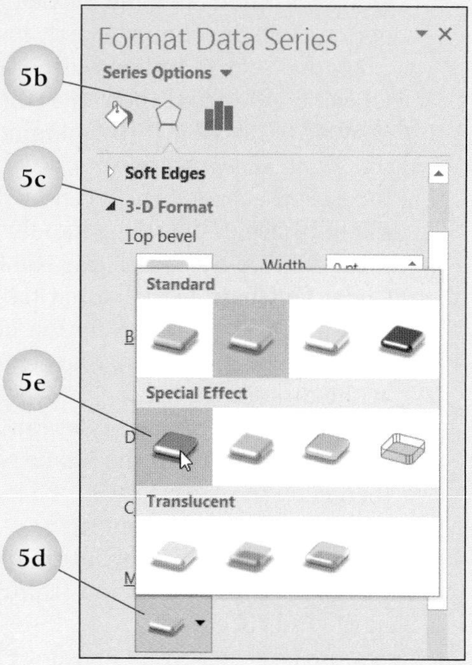

6. Complete steps similar to those in Step 5a through Step 5f to format the *Series "2nd Half"* chart element.
7. Customize the chart by completing the following steps:
   a. Click the *Chart Elements* option box arrow in the Current Selection group and then click *Chart Area* at the drop-down list.
   b. Click the Fill & Line icon and make sure fill options display in the Format Chart Area task pane. (If necessary, click *Fill* to expand the options.)
   c. Click the *Picture or texture fill* option.
   d. Click the Texture button (located below the Online button)
   e. Click the *Parchment* option (last column, third row).
   f. Scroll down the task pane to the *Border* section and, if necessary, click *Border* to expand the options.
   g. Click the *Solid line* option in the *Border* section.
   h. Click the Size & Properties icon.
   i. If necessary, click *Size* to display the options.
   j. Select the current measurement in the *Height* measurement box and then type 6.
   k. Select the current measurement in the *Width* measurement box, type 9, and then press the Enter key.
   l. Click *Position* to display the options.
   m. Select the current measurement in the *Horizontal position* measurement box and then type 2.5.
   n. Select the current measurement in the *Vertical position* measurement box, type 0.8, and then press the Enter key.

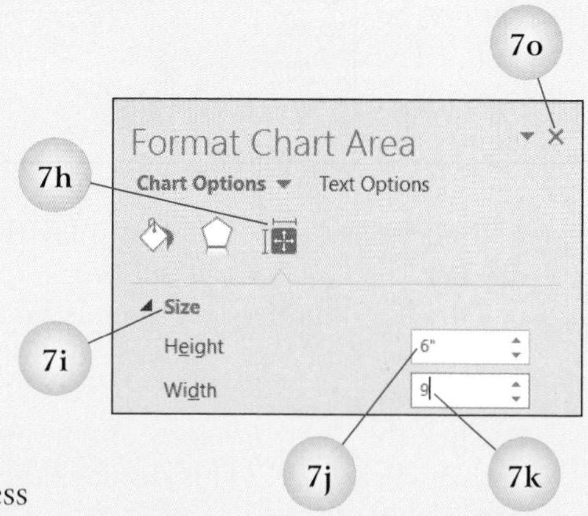

   o. Close the task pane by clicking the Close button in the upper right corner of the task pane.
8. Save **5-Conference.pptx**.

Check Your Work

Another method for formatting a chart or chart elements is to use options at the shortcut menu. Some of the options on the shortcut menu vary depending on the chart or chart element selected. Some common options include deleting the element, editing data, rotating the element, and adding data labels. To display the shortcut menu, right-click the element or the chart. In addition to the shortcut menu, the Mini toolbar also displays. The Mini toolbar contains options for applying fill color and outline color.

Project 1n **Creating and Formatting a Pie Chart** Part 14 of 14

1. With **5-Conference.pptx** open, make Slide 6 active and then insert a new slide with the Blank layout.
2. Click the Insert tab and then click the Chart button in the Illustrations group.
3. At the Insert Chart dialog box, click *Pie* in the left panel.
4. Double-click the *3-D Pie* option at the top of the dialog box (second option).
5. Type the text in cells in the Excel worksheet as shown at the right.

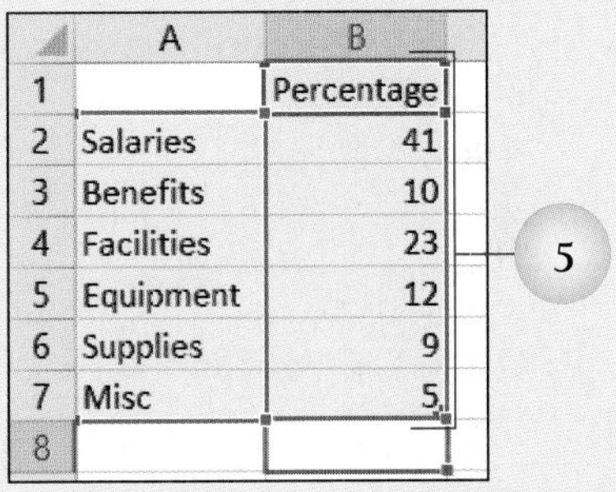

6. When all data is entered, click the Close button in the upper right corner of the Excel window.
7. Click the Chart Styles button that displays at the right side of the pie chart, click the *Style 3* chart style, and then click the Chart Styles button again to remove the side menu.
8. Move the data labels to the outside of the pie by completing the following steps:
   a. Click the Chart Elements button that displays at the right side of the chart.
   b. Hover your mouse pointer over the *Data Labels* option in the side menu and then click the right-pointing arrow that displays.
   c. Click the *Outside End* option.
   d. Click the Chart Elements button to remove the side menu.

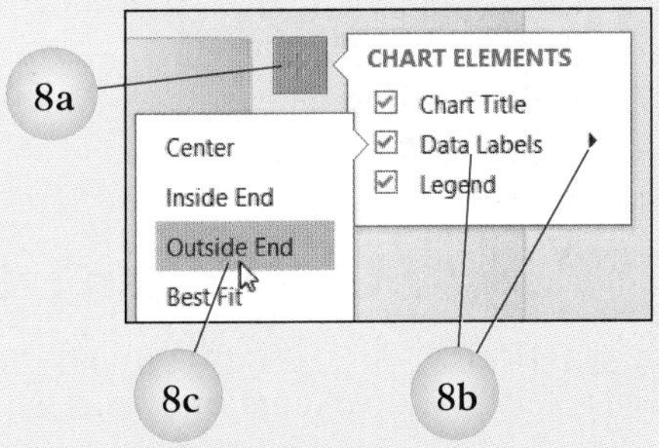

9. Apply formatting to the legend by completing the following steps:
   a. Hover your mouse just above the word *Salaries* in the legend until the mouse pointer displays with a four-headed arrow attached and then click the right mouse button.
   b. Click the Fill button on the Mini toolbar and then click *Tan, Background 2* (third column, first row in the *Theme Colors* section).
   c. Click the Outline button on the Mini toolbar and then click the *Green, Accent 1, Darker 50%* option (fifth column, bottom row in the *Theme Colors* section).
   d. Increase the size of the legend by dragging the bottom middle sizing handle down about 0.25 inch.

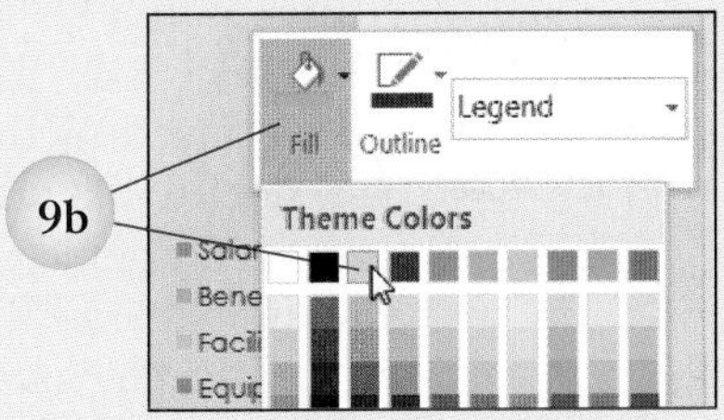

10. Edit the title by completing the following steps:
    a. Right-click the title *Percentage* and then click *Edit Text* in the shortcut menu.
    b. With the insertion point positioned in the title, press the End key to move the insertion point to the right of *Percentage*, press the spacebar, and then type of 100k Division Budget.

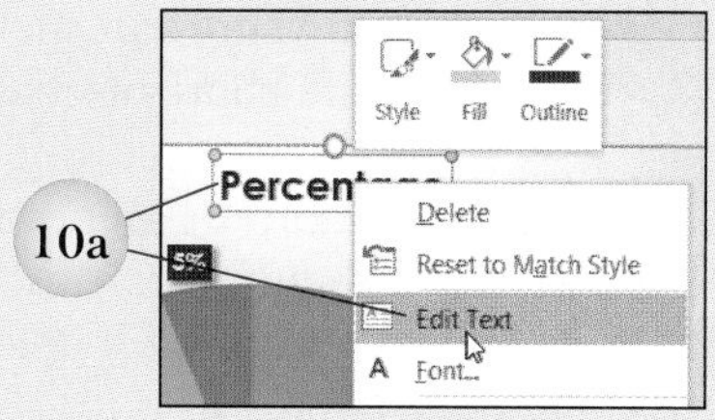

11. Click outside the title but inside the chart to select the chart.
12. Click the Chart Tools Format tab.
13. Change the chart height to 6.5 inches and the chart width to 9 inches.
14. Click the Align button in the Arrange group and then click *Distribute Horizontally*.
15. Click the Align button in the Arrange group and then click *Distribute Vertically*.
16. Apply a transition and transition sound of your choosing to all slides in the presentation.
17. Save **5-Conference.pptx**.
18. Run the slide show.
19. Print the presentation as a handout with six slides displayed horizontally per page.
20. Close **5-Conference.pptx**.

Check Your Work

Project 2 Create and Format a Travel Photo Album — 3 Parts

You will use the photo album feature to create a presentation containing travel photographs. You will also apply formatting and insert elements in the presentation.

Preview Finished Project

Tutorial

Creating a Photo Album

Photo Album

Quick Steps

Create a Photo Album
1. Click Insert tab.
2. Click Photo Album button arrow.
3. Click *New Photo Album*.
4. Click File/Disk button.
5. Double-click picture.
6. Repeat Steps 4 and 5 for all pictures.
7. Make changes at Photo Album dialog box.
8. Click Create button.

Creating a Photo Album

Use PowerPoint's photo album feature to create a presentation containing personal or business pictures. Customize and format the appearance of pictures by applying interesting layouts, frame shapes, and themes and insert elements such as captions and text boxes. To create a photo album, click the Insert tab, click the Photo Album button arrow in the Images group, and then click *New Photo Album* at the drop-down list. This displays the Photo Album dialog box, as shown in Figure 5.12.

To insert pictures in the photo album, click the File/Disk button to display the Insert New Pictures dialog box. At this dialog box, navigate to the desired folder and then double-click the picture to be inserted in the album. This inserts the picture name in the *Pictures in album* list box in the dialog box and also displays the picture in the *Preview* section. As pictures are inserted in the photo album, the picture names display in the *Pictures in album* list box in the order in which they will appear in the presentation. When all pictures have been inserted into the photo album, click the Create button. This creates the photo album as a presentation and displays the first slide. The photo album feature creates the first slide with the title *Photo Album* and the user's name.

Figure 5.12 Photo Album Dialog Box

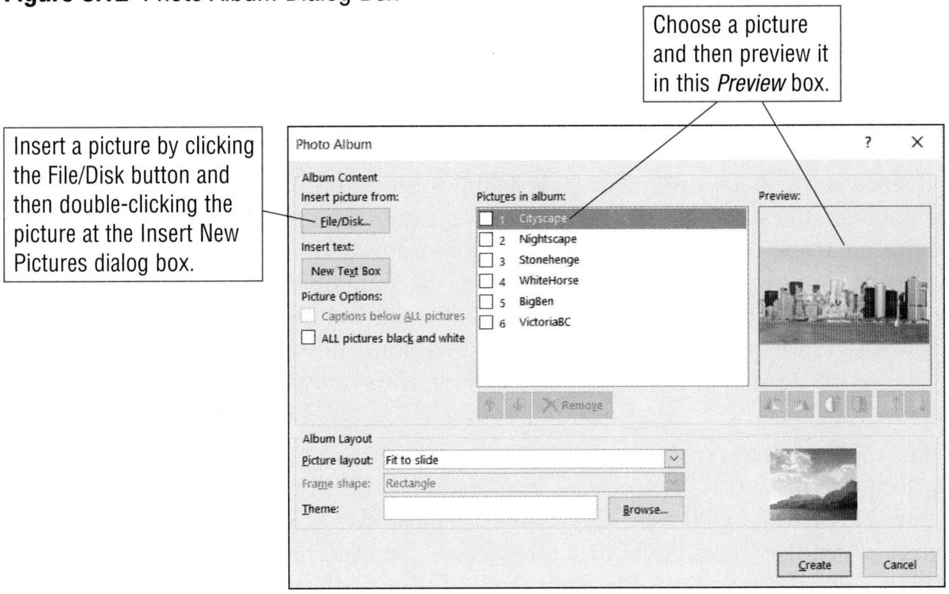

Project 2a Creating a Travel Photo Album

Part 1 of 3

1. At a blank screen, click the Insert tab, click the Photo Album button arrow in the Images group and then click *New Photo Album* at the drop-down list.
2. At the Photo Album dialog box, click the File/Disk button.
3. At the Insert New Pictures dialog box, navigate to the PC5 folder on your storage medium and then double-click ***Cityscape.jpg***.
4. At the Photo Album dialog box, click the File/Disk button, and then double-click ***Nightscape.jpg*** at the Insert New Pictures dialog box.
5. Insert the following additional pictures: **Stonehenge.jpg**, **WhiteHorse.jpg**, **BigBen.jpg**, and **VictoriaBC.jpg**.
6. Click the Create button. (This opens a presentation with each image in a separate slide. The first slide contains the default text *Photo Album* followed by your name (or the user name for the computer).
7. Save the presentation and name it **5-Album.pptx**.
8. Run the slide show.

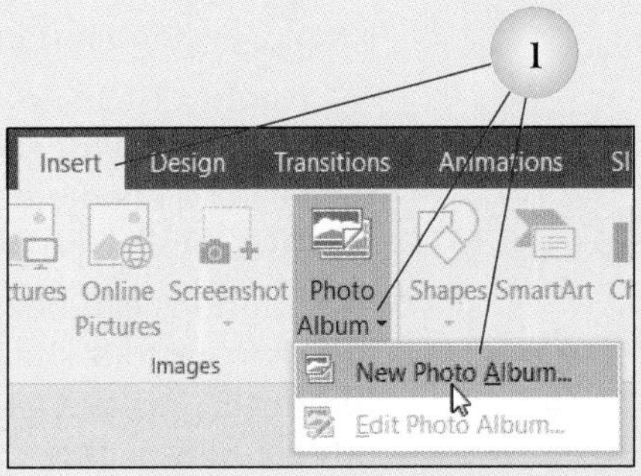

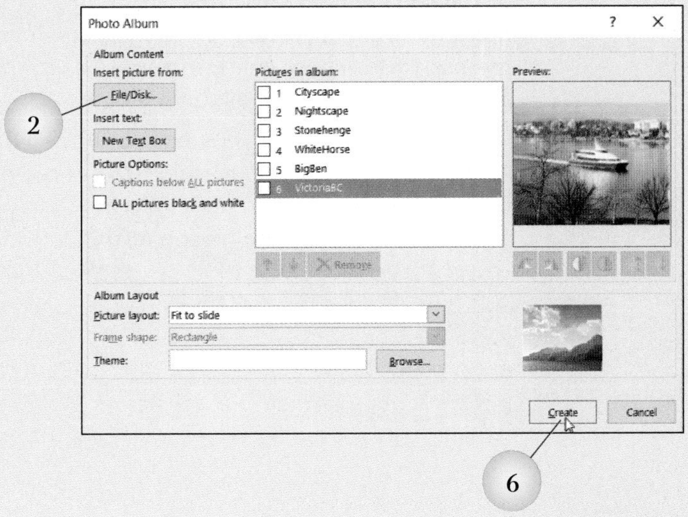

Check Your Work

Tutorial

Editing and Formatting a Photo Album

Quick Steps

Edit a Photo Album
1. Click Insert tab.
2. Click Photo Album button arrow.
3. Click *Edit Photo Album.*
4. Make changes at Edit Photo Album dialog box.
5. Click Update button.

Hint Search for predesigned photo album templates using the search text box at the New backstage area.

Editing and Formatting a Photo Album

To make changes to a photo album presentation, open the presentation, click the Insert tab, click the Photo Album button arrow in the Images group, and then click *Edit Photo Album* at the drop-down list. This displays the Edit Photo Album dialog box, which contains the same options as the Photo Album dialog box.

Rearrange the slide order in a photo album presentation by clicking a slide in the *Pictures in album* list box and then clicking the button containing the up-pointing arrow to move the slide up in the order or clicking the button containing the down-pointing arrow to move the slide down in the order. Remove a slide by clicking the slide in the list box and then clicking the Remove button. Use buttons below the *Preview* box in the Edit Photo Album dialog box to rotate the picture in the slide and increase or decrease the contrast or brightness of the picture.

The *Picture layout* option in the *Album Layout* section has a default setting of *Fit to slide*. At this setting the picture in each slide will fill most of the slide. Change this setting by clicking the *Picture layout* option box arrow. With options at the drop-down list, specify whether one picture, two pictures, or four pictures should be inserted into the slide and whether or not titles should be included with the pictures.

Change the *Picture layout* option to something other than the default of *Fit to slide* and the *Frame shape* option becomes available. Click the *Frame shape* option box arrow and a drop-down list displays with options for applying a rounded, simple, or double frame around the picture, or a soft or shadow effect frame.

Apply a theme to the photo album presentation by clicking the Browse button at the right side of the *Theme* option box and then double-clicking the theme in the Choose Theme dialog box. This dialog box contains the predesigned themes provided by PowerPoint.

Captions can be included with the pictures by changing the *Picture layout* to one, two, or four slides and then clicking the *Captions below ALL pictures* check box in the *Picture Options* section. When the *Captions below ALL pictures* check box contains a check mark, PowerPoint will insert a caption containing the name of the picture below each picture. The caption can be edited in the slide in the presentation. All pictures in the photo album can be displayed in black and white by inserting a check mark in the *ALL pictures black and white* check box in the *Picture Options* section of the dialog box.

Click the New Text Box button in the Edit Photo Album dialog box and a new slide containing a text box is inserted in the presentation. The information in the text box can be edited in the presentation. Once all changes have been made to the photo album, click the Update button at the bottom right side of the dialog box.

Project 2b Editing and Formatting a Photo Album

1. With **5-Album.pptx** open, make sure the Insert tab is active, click the Photo Album button arrow in the Images group, and then click *Edit Photo Album* at the drop-down list.
2. At the Edit Photo Album dialog box, make the following changes:
   a. Click the *ALL pictures black and white* check box to insert a check mark.
   b. Click in the *VictoriaBC* check box in the *Pictures in album* list box to insert a check mark and then click the up-pointing arrow button below the list box three times. (This moves *VictoriaBC* so it is positioned between *Nightscape* and *Stonehenge*).

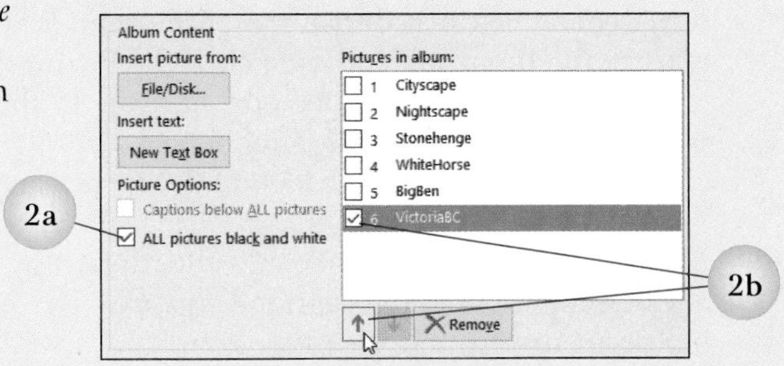

   c. Click the Rotate button below the *Preview* box (the first button from the left below the picture). Click the Rotate button three times to return the image to the original orientation.
   d. Click the *VictoriaBC* check box in the *Pictures in album* list box to remove the check mark.
   e. Click the *Cityscape* check box in the *Pictures in album* list box to insert a check mark and then click the Increase Contrast button below the *Preview* box two times (the third button from the left below the picture preview).

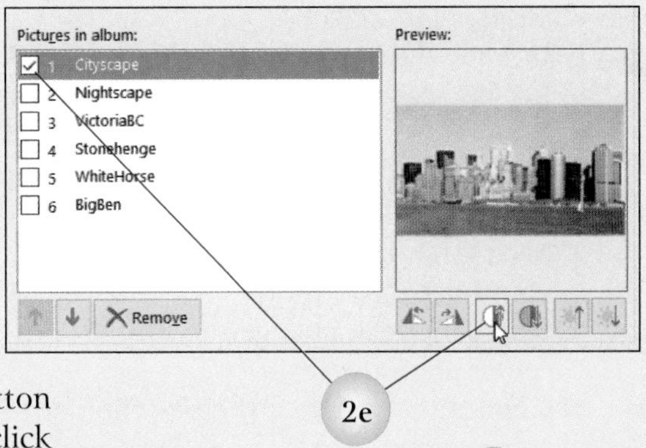

   f. Click the *Cityscape* check box to remove the check mark.
   g. Click the *Stonehenge* check box in the *Pictures in album* list box to insert a check mark, click the Increase Contrast button below the *Preview* box two times and then click the Increase Brightness button (fifth button to the right of the Remove button) two times.
   h. Click the *Picture layout* option box arrow and then click *1 picture* at the drop-down list.

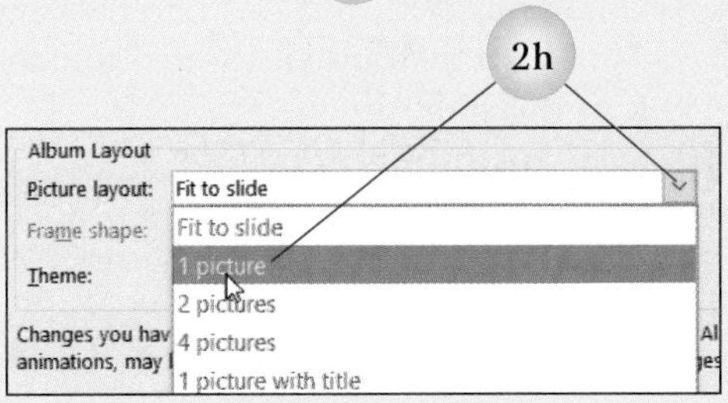

   i. Click the *Frame shape* option box arrow and then click *Center Shadow Rectangle* at the drop-down list.
   j. Click the Browse button at the right side of the *Theme* option box. At the Choose Theme dialog box, double-click ***Facet.thmx***.
   k. Click the *Captions below ALL pictures* check box to insert a check mark.
   l. Click the *Stonehenge* check box in the *Pictures in album* list box to remove the check mark and then click the *BigBen* check box in the *Pictures in album* list box to insert a check mark.

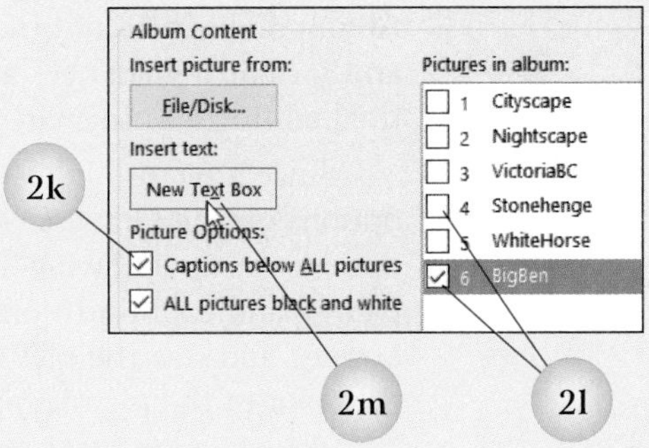

   m. Click the New Text Box button at the left side of the list box. (This inserts a new slide containing a text box at the end of the presentation.)
   n. Click the Update button in the lower right corner of the dialog box.

3. At the presentation, make the following formatting changes:
   a. Click the Design tab.
   b. Click the blue variant in the Variants group (second variant).
4. With Slide 1 active, make the following changes:
   a. Select the text *Photo Album* and then type Travel Album.
   b. Select any text that displays after the word *by* and then type your first and last names.
   c. Click the Insert tab and then click the Pictures button.
   d. At the Insert Picture dialog box, navigate to the PC5 folder on your storage medium and then double-click ***FCTLogo.jpg***.
   e. Change the height of the logo to 2.0 inches and then position the logo attractively in the slide.
5. Make Slide 2 active and then edit the caption by completing the following steps:
   a. Click anywhere in the caption *Cityscape*.
   b. Select *Cityscape* and then type New York City Skyline.

6. Complete steps similar to those in Step 5 to change the following captions:
   a. In Slide 3, change *Nightscape* to *New York City at Night*.
   b. In Slide 4, change *VictoriaBC* to *Victoria, British Columbia*.
   c. In Slide 5, change *Stonehenge* to *Stonehenge, Wiltshire County*.
   d. In Slide 6, change *WhiteHorse* to *White Horse, Wiltshire County*.
   e. In Slide 7, change *BigBen* to *Big Ben, London*.
7. Make Slide 8 active and then make the following changes:
   a. Select the text *Text Box* and then type Call First Choice Travel at 213-555-4500 to book your next travel tour.
   b. Select the text, change the font size to 48 points, apply the standard blue font color, and center align the text.
   c. Change the width of the placeholder to 9 inches. (Do this with the *Shape Width* measurement box on the Drawing Tools Format tab.)
8. Apply a transition and transition sound of your choosing to all slides.
9. Run the slide show.
10. Save **5-Album.pptx**.

Check Your Work

Formatting Pictures

If slides are formatted in the presentation instead of using the Edit Photo Album dialog box, some of those changes may be lost if changes are made at the Edit Photo Album dialog box and the Update button is clicked. Consider making initial editing and formatting changes at the Edit Photo Album dialog box and then make any final editing and formatting changes in the presentation slides.

Since a picture in a slide in a photo album is an object, it can be formatted with options on the Drawing Tools Format tab and the Picture Tools Format tab. With options on the Drawing Tools Format tab, insert shapes, apply a shape style to the picture and caption (if one is displayed), apply a WordArt style to caption text, and arrange and size the picture. Use options on the Picture Tools Format tab to adjust the color of the picture, apply a picture style, and arrange and size the picture.

Project 2c Formatting Pictures in a Presentation Part 3 of 3

1. With **5-Album.pptx** open, make Slide 2 active.
2. Change the pictures back to color by completing the following steps:
   a. Click the Insert tab.
   b. Click the Photo Album button arrow in the Images group and then click *Edit Photo Album* at the drop-down list.
   c. Click the *ALL pictures black and white* check box to remove the check mark.
   d. Click the Update button.
3. Format the picture in Slide 2 by completing the following steps:
   a. Click the picture to select it.
   b. Click the Drawing Tools Format tab.
   c. Click the More Shape Styles button in the Shape Styles group and then click the *Subtle Effect - Turquoise, Accent 1* option (second column, fourth row).

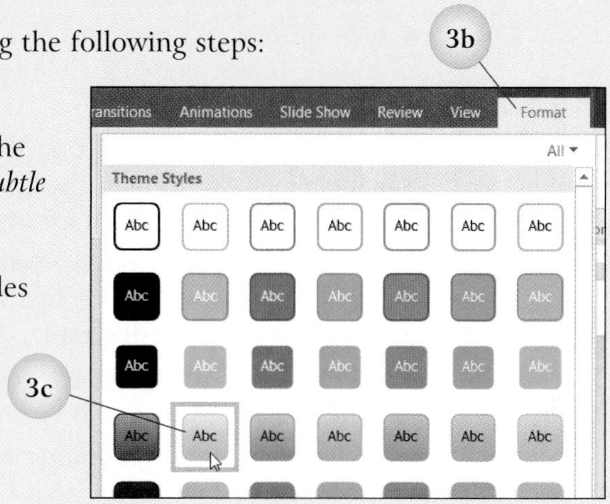

4. Apply the same style to the pictures in Slides 3 through 7 by making each slide active, clicking the picture, and then pressing the F4 function key. (Pressing F4 repeats the style formatting.)
5. Make Slide 2 active and then apply a WordArt style to the caption text by completing the following steps:
   a. With Slide 2 active, click the picture to select it.
   b. Click the Drawing Tools Format tab.
   c. Click the More WordArt Styles button in the WordArt Styles group and then click the *Fill - Blue, Accent 2, Outline - Accent 2* option (third column, first row).

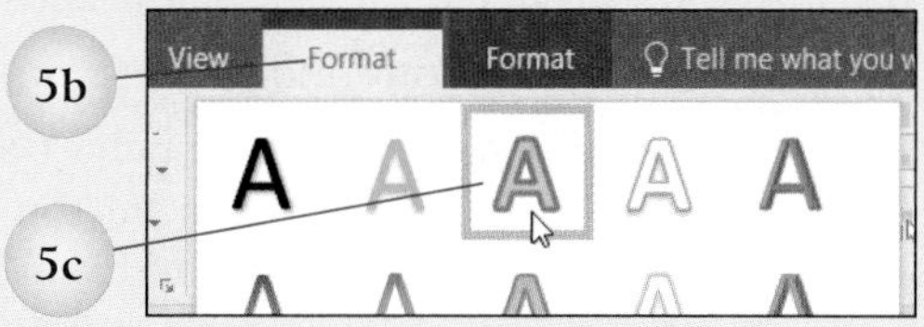

6. Apply the same WordArt style to the caption text in Slides 3 through 7 by making each slide active, clicking the picture, and then pressing the F4 function key.
7. Make Slide 8 active and then change the width of the placeholder to 9 inches.
8. Run the slide show.
9. Print the presentation as a handout with four slides displayed horizontally per page.
10. Save and then close **5-Album.pptx**.

Check Your Work

Chapter Summary

- Use the Table button in the Tables group on the Insert tab to create a table, insert an Excel worksheet, and draw a table in a slide.
- Change the table design with options and buttons on the Table Tools Design tab. Change the table layout with options and buttons on the Table Tools Layout tab.
- Use the SmartArt feature to insert predesigned graphics, such as diagrams and organizational charts, in a slide.
- Use options and buttons on the SmartArt Tools Design tab to change the graphic layout, apply a style to the graphic, and reset the graphic back to the original formatting.
- Use options and buttons on the SmartArt Tools Format tab to change the size and shape of objects in the graphic; apply shape styles; change the shape fill, outline, and effects; and arrange and size the graphic.
- Insert text directly into a SmartArt graphic shape or at the Text pane. Display this pane by clicking the Text Pane button in the Create Graphic group on the SmartArt Tools Design tab.
- Text or WordArt can be converted to a SmartArt graphic and a SmartArt graphic can be converted to text or shapes.
- A chart is a visual presentation of data. A variety of charts can be created as described in Table 5.2.
- To create a chart, display the Insert Chart dialog box by clicking the Insert Chart button in a content placeholder or clicking the Chart button in the Illustrations group on the Insert tab.
- Enter chart data in an Excel worksheet. When entering data, press the Tab key to make the next cell active, press Shift + Tab to make the previous cell active, and press the Enter key to make the cell below active.
- Modify a chart design with options and buttons on the Chart Tools Design tab.
- Cells in the Excel worksheet used to create a chart are linked to the chart in the slide. To edit chart data, click the Edit Data button on the Chart Tools Design tab and then make changes to the text in the Excel worksheet.
- Customize the format of a chart and chart elements with options and buttons on the Chart Tools Format tab. A style can be applied to a shape in a chart, a WordArt style can be applied to text in a chart, and a chart can be sized and arranged in the slide.
- Use the Photo Album feature in the Images group on the Insert tab to create a presentation containing pictures and then edit and format the pictures.
- At the Photo Album dialog box (or the Edit Photo Album dialog box), insert pictures and then use options to customize the photo album.
- Use options on the Drawing Tools Format tab and the Picture Tools Format tab to format pictures in a photo album presentation.

Commands Review

FEATURE	RIBBON TAB, GROUP	BUTTON, OPTION
Choose a SmartArt Graphic dialog box	Insert, Illustrations	
convert bulleted text to SmartArt	Home, Paragraph	
convert SmartArt to text or shapes	SmartArt Tools Design, Reset	
create photo album	Insert, Images	, *New Photo Album*
edit photo album	Insert, Images	, *Edit Photo Album*
Insert Chart dialog box	Insert, Illustrations	
Insert Table dialog box	Insert, Tables	, *Insert Table*
Text pane	SmartArt Tools Design, Create Graphic	

Workbook

Chapter study tools and assessment activities are available in the *Workbook* ebook. These resources are designed to help you further develop and demonstrate mastery of the skills learned in this chapter.

Microsoft®

PowerPoint®

CHAPTER 6

Using Slide Masters and Action Buttons

Performance Objectives

Upon successful completion of Chapter 6, you will be able to:

1 Format slides in Slide Master view
2 Apply themes and backgrounds in Slide Master view
3 Delete placeholders and slide master layouts
4 Insert elements in Slide Master view
5 Create and rename a custom slide layout
6 Insert placeholders and custom prompts in Slide Master view
7 Insert a new slide master
8 Preserve a slide master
9 Save a presentation as a template
10 Customize handouts pages in Handout Master view
11 Customize notes pages in Notes Master view
12 Change zoom, manage windows, and view presentations in color and grayscale
13 Insert action buttons
14 Apply actions to objects
15 Insert hyperlinks

Precheck

Check your current skills to focus your study.

To make design or formatting changes that affect all slides in the presentation, consider making the changes in a slide master in the Slide Master view. Along with the Slide Master view, changes can be made to all handouts pages with options in the Handout Master view and all notes pages in the Notes Master view. Action buttons can be inserted in a presentation to connect to slides within the same presentation, another presentation, a website, or to another program. Insert a hyperlink to connect to a website.

Data Files

Before beginning chapter work, copy the PC6 folder to your storage medium and then make PC6 the active folder.

SNAP

If you are a SNAP user, launch the Precheck and Tutorials from your Assignments page.

Project 1 **Create a Travel Presentation and Apply Formatting in Slide Master View** **6 Parts**

You will apply formatting to a blank presentation in Slide Master view, insert slides in the presentation, insert elements in Slide Master view, insert a custom slide layout, and insert a new slide master.

Preview Finished Project

Tutorial

Formatting with a Slide Master

Quick Steps

Display Slide Master View

1. Click View tab.
2. Click Slide Master button.

Slide Master

Hint Create a consistent look for your slides by customizing them in Slide Master view.

Close Master View

Customizing Slide Masters

To apply formatting or other changes to multiple slides in a presentation, make the changes in a slide master. Customize a slide master by changing the theme, theme colors, or theme fonts; inserting or changing the location of placeholders; applying a background style; and changing the page setup and slide orientation.

If formatting or other changes are made to an individual slide in Normal view, that slide's link to the slide master is broken. Changes made in Slide Master view will not affect the individually formatted slide. For this reason, make global formatting changes in Slide Master view before editing individual slides in a presentation.

To display Slide Master view, click the View tab and then click the Slide Master button in the Master Views group. This makes the Slide Master tab active, displays a blank slide master in the slide pane, and inserts slide master thumbnails in the slide thumbnails pane. The largest thumbnail in the pane is the slide master, and the other thumbnails represent associated layouts. Position the mouse pointer on a slide thumbnail and the name of the thumbnail displays in a ScreenTip by the thumbnail along with information on what slides in the presentation use the slide master. Figure 6.1 shows a blank presentation in Slide Master view. To specify the slide master or layout that will be customized, click the specific thumbnail in the slide thumbnails pane. With the slide master layout displayed in the slide pane, make the changes and then click the Close Master View button.

Figure 6.1 Slide Master View

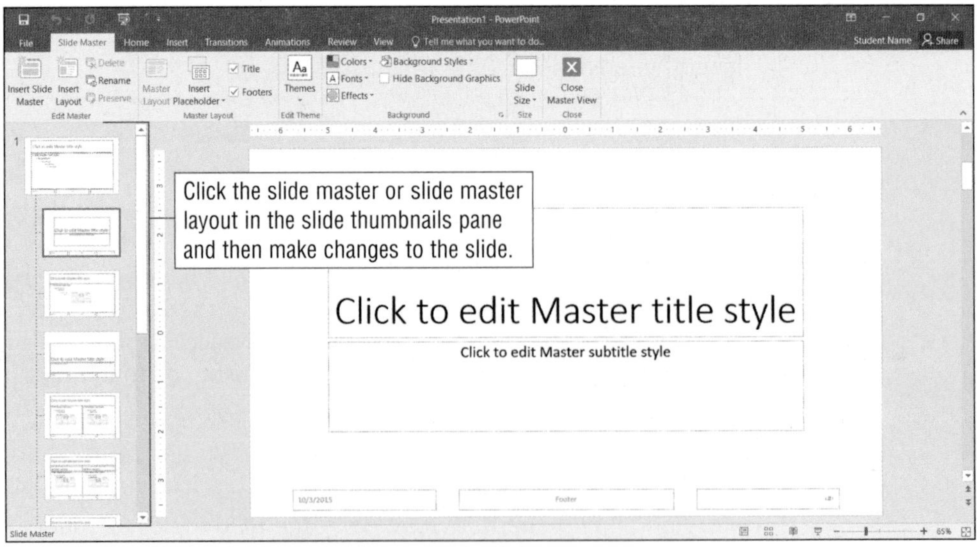

Applying Themes to Slide Masters

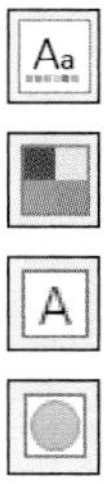

Themes

Colors

Fonts

Effects

Apply themes, theme colors, theme fonts, and theme effects to a slide master using buttons in the Edit Theme group and the Background group on the Slide Master tab. Click the Themes button and a drop-down gallery displays with available predesigned themes as well as any custom themes. Click a theme and the theme formatting is applied to the slide master. Use the Colors button in the Background group to change theme colors, use the Fonts button to change theme fonts, and apply a theme effect using the Effects button.

Project 1a **Formatting a Slide Master** Part 1 of 6

1. Open a blank presentation.
2. Click the View tab and then click the Slide Master button in the Master Views group.

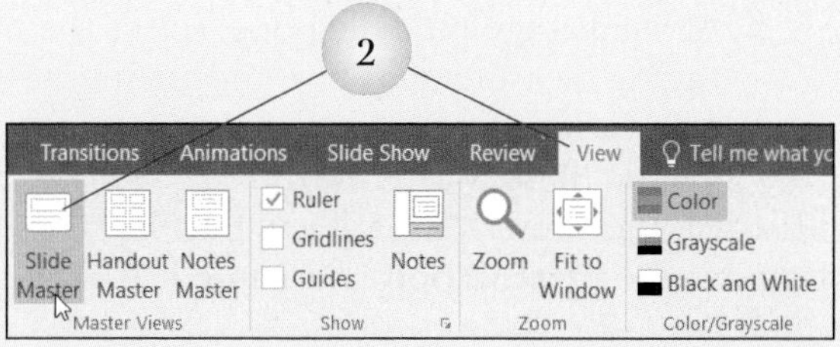

3. Scroll up the slide thumbnails pane and then click the top (and largest) slide master thumbnail in the slide thumbnails pane (*Office Theme Slide Master*). This displays the slide master layout in the slide pane.
4. Click the Themes button in the Edit Theme group on the Slide Master tab.
5. Click the *Retrospect* option.
6. Click the Colors button in the Background group and then click the *Blue* option at the drop-down gallery.
7. Click the Fonts button in the Background group, scroll down the drop-down gallery, and then click the *Arial Black-Arial* option.

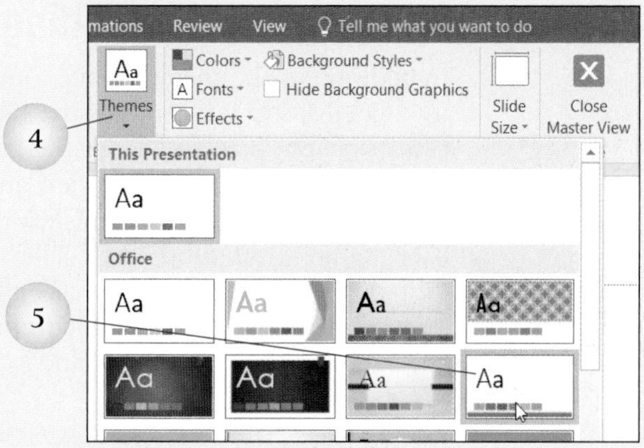

8. Change the font color for the title style by completing the following steps:
   a. Click the *Click to edit Master title style* placeholder border in the slide master in the slide pane.
   b. Click the Home tab.
   c. Click the Font Color button arrow in the Font group and then click the *Black, Text 1* option (second column, first row in the *Theme Colors* section).

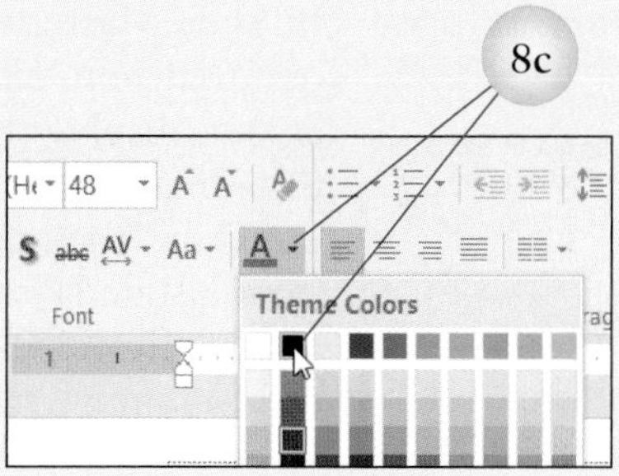

9. Change the font size and color and apply custom bullets by completing the following steps:
   a. Select the text *Edit Master text styles*.
   b. With the Home tab selected, click the *Font Size* option box arrow and then click *24* at the drop-down gallery.
   c. Click the Font Color button arrow and then click the *Light Blue, Background 2, Darker 50%* option (third column, fourth row in the *Theme Colors* section).

d. Click the Bullets button arrow in the Paragraph group and then click *Bullets and Numbering* at the drop-down gallery.
e. At the Bullets and Numbering dialog box, click the *Hollow Square Bullets* option.
f. Click the Color button and then click the *Light Blue, Background 2, Darker 50%* option (third column, fourth row in the *Theme Colors* section).
g. Select *100* in the *Size* measurement box and then type 80.
h. Click OK to close the dialog box.
i. Click the Paragraph group dialog box launcher.
j. At the Paragraph dialog box, select the measurement in the *By* measurement box and then type 0.4.
k. Click OK to close the dialog box.

10. Click the Slide Master tab.
11. Click the Close Master View button.
12. Save the presentation and name it **6-TravelMaster.pptx**.

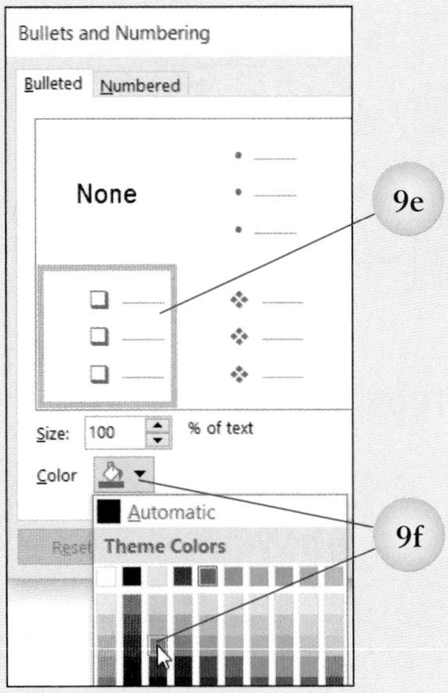

Applying and Formatting Backgrounds

In addition to the theme colors, fonts, and effects buttons, the Background group on the Slide Master tab contains the Background Styles button and the *Hide Background Graphics* check box. To change the background graphic for all slides, display the presentation in Slide Master view and then click the specific slide master layout in the slide thumbnails pane. Click the Background Styles button and then click a background at the drop-down gallery. Or, click the *Format Background* option at the drop-down gallery and then make changes at the Format Background task pane. To remove the background graphic from all slides, click the *Hide Background Graphics* check box to insert a check mark.

Deleting Placeholders

Hint You can also delete a slide master layout by right-clicking the layout in the slide thumbnails pane and then clicking *Delete Layout* at the shortcut menu.

In Slide Master view, if a placeholder is removed from a slide layout it is then removed from all slides based on that layout. To remove a placeholder from a layout, display the presentation in Slide Master view, click the specific slide layout thumbnail, click the placeholder border (make sure the border displays as a solid line), and then press the Delete key. The title placeholder can also be removed from a slide layout by clicking the *Title* check box in the Master Layout group to remove the check mark. Remove footer placeholders by clicking the *Footer* check box to remove the check mark.

Quick Steps

Delete a Slide Master Layout

1. Display presentation in Slide Master view.
2. Click slide layout thumbnail.
3. Click Delete button.

Delete

Deleting Slide Master Layouts

In Slide Master view, a slide master displays for each available layout. If a particular layout will not be used in the presentation, the slide layout can be deleted. To do this, display the presentation in Slide Master view, click the specific slide layout thumbnail in the slide thumbnails pane, and then click the Delete button in the Edit Master group.

Project 1b Applying and Formatting Background Graphics

1. With **6-TravelMaster.pptx** open, click the View tab and then click the Slide Master button in the Master Views group.
2. Apply a picture to the background of the title slide layout (the picture will appear only on slides with this layout applied) by completing the following steps:
   a. Make sure the second slide layout thumbnail (*Title Slide Layout*) is selected in the slide thumbnails pane.
   b. Click the *Click to edit Master title style* placeholder border, click the Home tab, change the font size to 48 points, apply the Black, Text 1 font color (second column, first row in the *Theme Colors* section), and click the Center button in the Paragraph group.
   c. Click the Slide Master tab and then make sure the *Hide Background Graphics* check box in the Background group contains a check mark.
   d. Click the Background Styles button in the Background group and then click *Format Background* at the drop-down list.
   e. At the Format Background task pane, click the *Picture or texture fill* option.
   f. Click the File button.
   g. At the Insert Picture dialog box, navigate to the PC6 folder on your storage medium and then double-click ***Stonehenge.jpg***.
   h. Close the Format Background task pane.
   i. Drag the master title placeholder so it is positioned above the stones and centered horizontally. (Make sure the bottom border of the placeholder is positioned above the stones.)

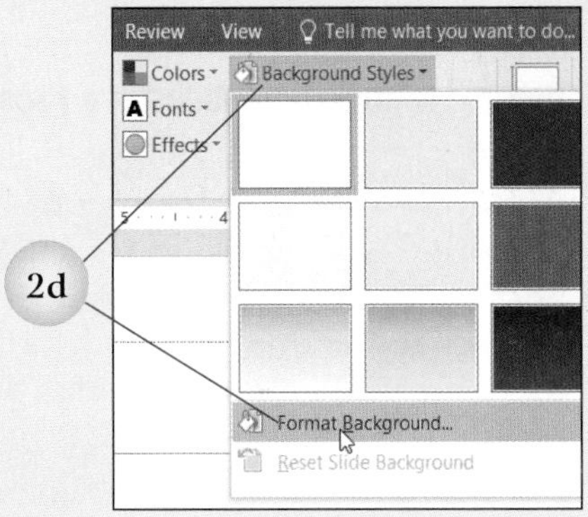

   j. Delete the master subtitle placeholder by clicking the placeholder border (make sure the border displays as a solid line) and then pressing the Delete key.
   k. Click the thin horizontal line that displays below the stones and then press the Delete key.
3. Delete slide layouts that you will not be using in the presentation by completing the following steps:
   a. Click the fourth slide layout thumbnail (*Section Header Layout*) in the slide thumbnails pane.
   b. Scroll down the pane until the last slide layout thumbnail is visible.
   c. Press and hold down the Shift key, click the last slide layout thumbnail, and then release the Shift key.
   d. Click the Delete button in the Edit Master group. (The slide thumbnails pane should now contain only one slide master and two associated layouts.)

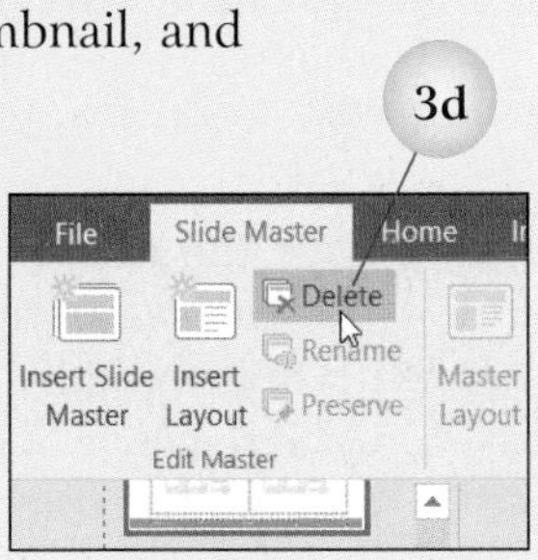

4. Click the Close Master View button.
5. Delete the slide that currently displays in the slide pane. (This displays a gray background with the text *Click to add first slide*. The presentation does not contain any slides, just formatting.)
6. Save **6-TravelMaster.pptx**.

Inserting Slides in a Customized Presentation

If slides in a presentation have been customized in Slide Master view, the presentation formatting can be used in other presentations. To do this, either save the formatted presentation as a template or save the presentation in the normal manner, open the presentation, save it with a new name, and then type text in slides. Slides can also be inserted into the current presentation using the Reuse Slides task pane. (You learned about this task pane in Chapter 2.) To use this task pane, click the Home tab, click the New Slide button arrow, and then click *Reuse Slides* at the drop-down list. This displays the Reuse Slides task pane at the right side of the screen. Click the Browse button and then click the *Browse File* option at the drop-down list. At the Browse dialog box, navigate to the desired folder and then double-click the presentation. Insert slides into the current presentation by clicking specific slides in the task pane.

Project 1c **Inserting Slides in a Presentation** Part 3 of 6

1. With **6-TravelMaster.pptx** open, save it with the name **6-England**.
2. With the Home tab active, click the New Slide button arrow, and then click the *Title Slide* option.

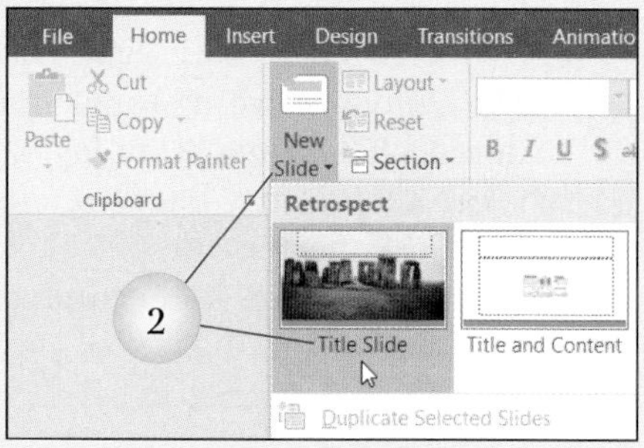

3. Click in the title placeholder and then type Wiltshire, England.
4. Insert slides into the current presentation from an existing presentation by completing the following steps:
   a. Click the New Slide button arrow and then click the *Reuse Slides* option.
   b. Click the Browse button in the Reuse Slides task pane and then click *Browse File* at the drop-down list.
   c. At the Browse dialog box, navigate to the PC6 folder on your storage medium and then double-click ***TravelEngland.pptx***.
   d. Click the *Wiltshire* slide in the Reuse Slides task pane. (This inserts the slide in the presentation and applies the custom formatting to the slide.)

   e. Click the *Ancient Stone Circles* slide in the Reuse Slides task pane.
   f. Click the *Ancient Wiltshire* slide in the Reuse Slides task pane.
   g. Click the *White Horses* slide in the Reuse Slides task pane.
   h. Click the Close button in the upper right corner of the Reuse Slides task pane.
5. With Slide 5 active, format the bulleted text into two columns by completing the following steps:
   a. Click anywhere in the bulleted text.
   b. Press Ctrl + A to select all of the bulleted text.
   c. Click the Line Spacing button in the Paragraph group and then click the *2.0* option.
   d. Click the Add or Remove Columns button in the Paragraph group and then click the *Two Columns* option.
6. With Slide 5 active, insert a new slide by completing the following steps:
   a. Click the New Slide button arrow and then click the *Title Slide* option.
   b. Click in the title placeholder and then type Call Lucy at 213-555-4500.
7. Save **6-England.pptx**.

Check Your Work

Inserting Elements in a Slide Master

A header, footer, or the date and time can be inserted in a presentation that will print on every slide in the presentation. These elements can also be inserted in a slide master. To insert a header or footer in a slide master, display the presentation in Slide Master view, click the Insert tab, and then click the Header & Footer button in the Text group. At the Header and Footer dialog box with the Slide tab selected, make the changes, click the Notes and Handouts tab, make the changes, and then click the Apply to All button. A picture, clip art image, shape, SmartArt graphic, or chart can also be inserted in Slide Master view. These elements are inserted in Slide Master view in the same manner as inserting them in Normal view.

Project 1d **Inserting Elements in Slide Master View** Part 4 of 6

1. With **6-England.pptx** open, display the presentation in Slide Master view by clicking the View tab and then clicking the Slide Master button in the Master Views group.
2. Insert a header, a footer, and the date and time by completing the following steps:
   a. Click the slide master thumbnail (the top slide thumbnail in the slide thumbnails pane).
   b. Click the Insert tab.
   c. Click the Header & Footer button in the Text group.
   d. At the Header and Footer dialog box with the Slide tab selected, click the *Date and time* check box to insert a check mark.
   e. Make sure the *Update automatically* option is selected. (With this option selected, the date and/or time will automatically update each time you open the presentation.)
   f. Click the *Slide number* check box to insert a check mark.
   g. Click the *Footer* check box to insert a check mark, click in the *Footer* text box, and then type your first and last names.
   h. Click the Notes and Handouts tab.
   i. Click the *Date and time* check box to insert a check mark.
   j. Make sure the *Update automatically* option is selected.
   k. Click the *Header* check box to insert a check mark, click in the *Header* text box, and then type the name of your school.
   l. Click the *Footer* check box to insert a check mark, click in the *Footer* text box, and then type your first and last names.
   m. Click the Apply to All button.

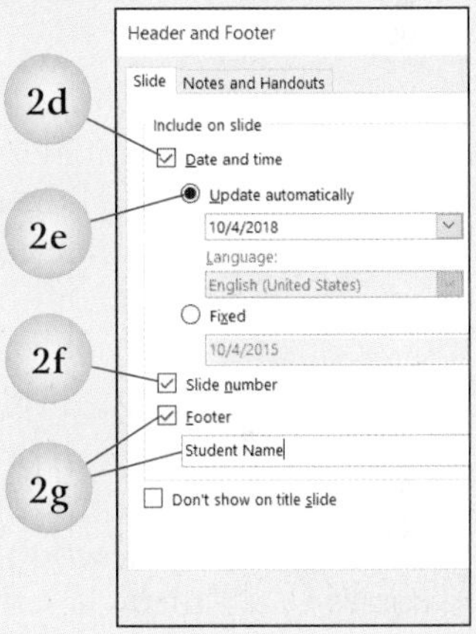

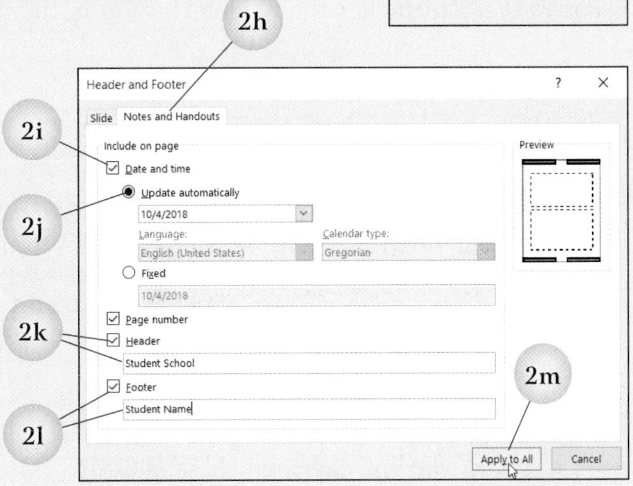

3. Insert the First Choice Travel logo in the upper right corner of the slide master by completing the following steps:
   a. Click the Pictures button in the Images group.
   b. At the Insert Picture dialog box, navigate to the PC6 folder on your storage medium and then double-click ***FCTLogo.jpg***.
   c. Click in the *Shape Height* measurement box in the Size group on the Picture Tools Format tab, type 0.6, and then press the Enter key.
   d. Drag the logo to position it in the upper right corner of the slide as shown at the right.
   e. Click outside the logo to deselect it.
4. If necessary, click the Slide Master tab.
5. Click the Close Master View button.
6. Run the slide show to view the logo and other elements in the slides.
7. Save **6-England.pptx**.

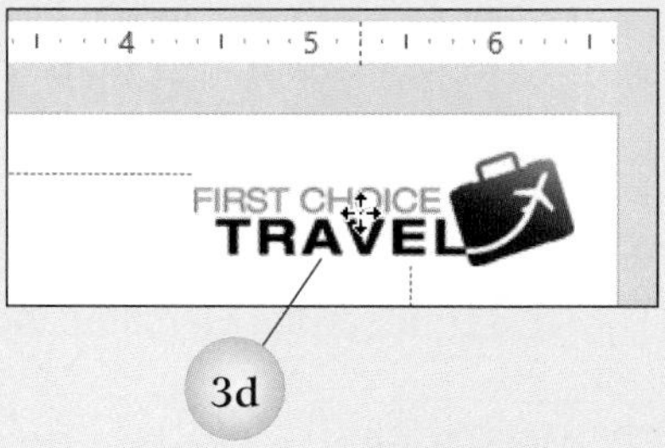

Check Your Work

Creating and Renaming a Custom Slide Layout

Insert Layout

A custom slide layout can be created in Slide Master view and then further customized by inserting or deleting elements and applying formatting to placeholders and text. To create a new slide layout, click the Insert Layout button in the Edit Master group on the Slide Master tab. This inserts in the slide pane a new slide containing a master title placeholder and footer placeholders. Customize the layout by inserting or deleting placeholders and applying formatting to placeholders.

Rename

PowerPoint automatically assigns the name *Custom Layout* to a custom slide layout. If another custom slide layout is created, PowerPoint will name it *1_Custom Layout*, and so on. Consider renaming a custom layout with a name that describes that layout. To rename a layout, make sure the specific slide layout is active and then click the Rename button in the Edit Master group. At the Rename Layout dialog box, type the name for the layout and then click the Rename button.

Inserting Placeholders

Insert Placeholder

Master Layout

A placeholder can be inserted in a predesigned or custom slide layout. Insert a placeholder by clicking the Insert Placeholder button arrow in the Master Layout group and then clicking the specific placeholder option at the drop-down list. If the slide master layout is selected, the Insert Placeholder button is dimmed. If a placeholder is deleted from the slide master, it can be reinserted with options at the Master Layout dialog box. Display this dialog box by clicking the Master Layout button. Any placeholder that has been removed from the slide master displays in the dialog box as an active option with an empty check box. Reinsert the placeholder by clicking the check box to insert a check mark in the box and then clicking OK to close the dialog box.

Creating Custom Prompts

Some placeholders in a custom layout may contain generic text such as *Click to add Master title style* or *Click to edit Master text styles*. In Slide Master view, this generic text can be replaced with custom text. For example, custom text may describe what should be inserted in the placeholder. Insert a custom prompt by clicking the Insert Placeholder button in the Master Layout group on the Slide Master tab and then clicking the type of placeholder to be inserted in the slide. After clicking the placeholder type, the mouse pointer will display as crosshairs. Click and drag in the slide to create the placeholder and then customize the text in the placeholder.

Project 1e **Inserting a Layout and Placeholder** — Part 5 of 6

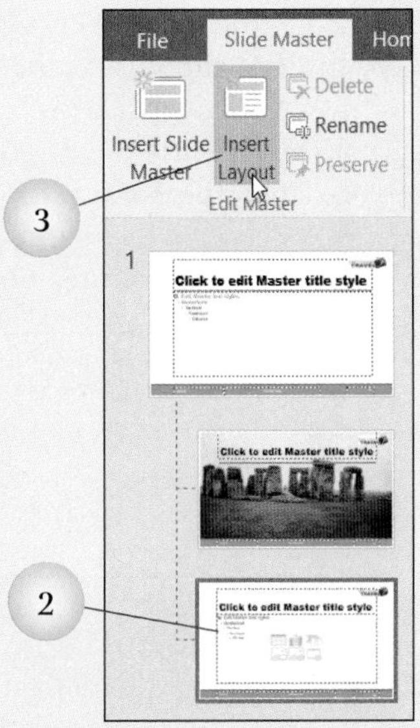

1. With **6-England.pptx** open, click the View tab and then click the Slide Master button in the Master Views group.
2. Click the bottom slide layout thumbnail in the slide thumbnails pane.
3. Click the Insert Layout button in the Edit Master group. (This inserts in the slide pane a new slide with a master title placeholder, the logo, and the footer information.)
4. Remove the footer by clicking the *Footers* check box in the Master Layout group to remove the check mark.
5. Format and move the placeholder by completing the following steps:
   a. Click the *Click to edit Master title style* placeholder border.
   b. Click the Home tab, change the font size to 28 points, apply the Light Blue, Background 2, Darker 50% font color (third column, fourth row in the *Theme Colors* section), and then click the Center button in the Paragraph group.
   c. Move the placeholder so it is positioned along the bottom of the slide, just above the bottom blue border line (as shown below).

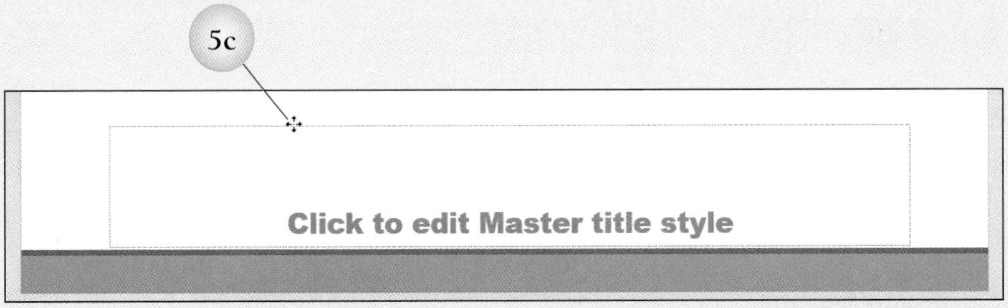

6. Click the Slide Master tab.
7. Insert a picture placeholder by completing the following steps:
   a. Click the Insert Placeholder button arrow.
   b. Click *Picture* at the drop-down list.
   c. Click in the slide to insert a placeholder.
   d. With the Drawing Tools Format tab active, click in the *Shape Height* measurement box and then type 3.5.

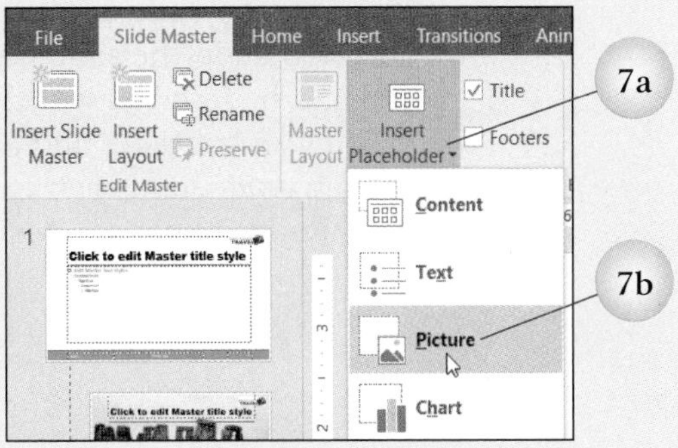

e. Click in the *Shape Width* measurement box, type 12, and then press the Enter key.
f. Drag the placeholder so it is positioned about 0.5 inch below the thin black line in the slide and centered horizontally. (The picture placeholder will overlap the title placeholder.)
g. Click anywhere in the word *Picture* in the placeholder. (This removes the word *Picture* and positions the insertion point in the placeholder.)
h. Type Insert company logo and then click outside of the placeholder.

8. Rename the custom slide layout by completing the following steps:
   a. Click the Rename button in the Edit Master group on the Slide Master tab.
   b. At the Rename Layout dialog box, select the text that displays in the *Layout name* text box and then type Logo.
   c. Click the Rename button.

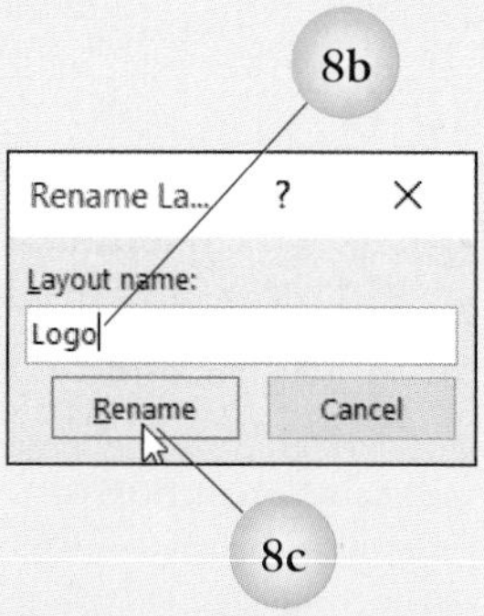

9. Click the Close Master View button.
10. Insert a slide using the new slide layout by completing the following steps:
    a. Make Slide 6 active.
    b. Click the New Slide button arrow.
    c. Click *Logo* at the drop-down list.
    d. Click the Pictures button in the slide.

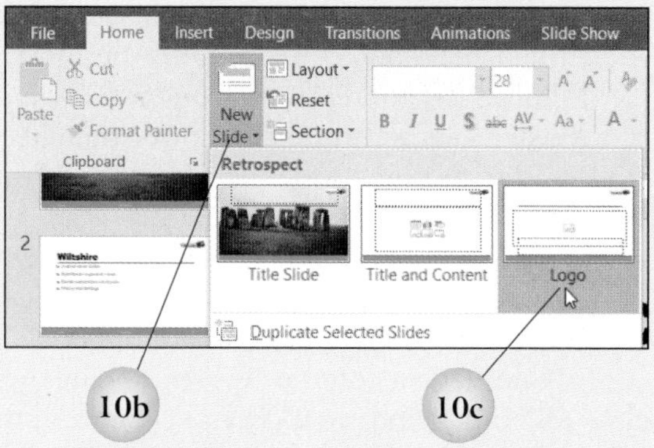

    e. At the Insert Picture dialog box, navigate to the PC6 folder on your storage medium and then double-click ***FCTLogo.jpg***.
    f. Click in the title placeholder and then type Monthly special: 20% discount on Wiltshire tour.
11. Save **6-England.pptx**.

Check Your Work

Inserting a New Slide Master

Insert Slide Master

A PowerPoint presentation can contain more than one slide master (and associated layouts). To insert a new slide master, display the presentation in Slide Master view and then click the Insert Slide Master button in the Edit Master group. This inserts a new slide master and all associated layouts below the existing slide master and layouts in the slide thumbnails pane. A slide master and all associated layouts can also be inserted with a design theme applied. To do this, click below the existing slide master and associated layouts, click the Themes button in the Edit Theme group, and then click the theme at the drop-down gallery. A slide master containing the chosen design theme is inserted below the existing thumbnails.

Preserve

Quick Steps

Preserve a Slide Master

1. Display presentation in Slide Master view.
2. Click slide master thumbnail.
3. Click Preserve button.

Preserving Slide Masters

If all of the slide layouts that follow a slide master are deleted, PowerPoint will automatically delete the slide master. A slide master can be protected from being deleted by preserving the master. To do this, click the slide master thumbnail and then click the Preserve button in the Edit Master group. If a slide master is inserted using the Insert Slide Master button, the Preserve button is automatically active. When a slide master is preserved, a preservation icon displays below the slide number in the slide thumbnails pane.

Changing Page Setup

Click the Slide Size button in the Size group on the Slide Master tab and a drop-down list displays with options for choosing standard or widescreen size. In addition to these two options, the drop-down list also includes the *Custom Slide Size* option. Click this option and the Slide Size dialog box displays. This is the same dialog box covered in Chapter 3. The dialog box contains options for changing slide width, height, and numbering, as well as applying slide orientation to slides, notes, handouts, and outline pages.

Project 1f **Applying a Second Slide Master**

Part 6 of 6

1. With **6-England.pptx** open, preserve the Retrospect slide master by completing the following steps:
   a. Click the View tab and then click the Slide Master button in the Master Views group.
   b. Click the first slide master (*Retrospect Slide Master*) in the slide thumbnails pane.
   c. Click the Preserve button in the Edit Master group. (This inserts a preservation icon below the slide number in the slide thumbnails pane).

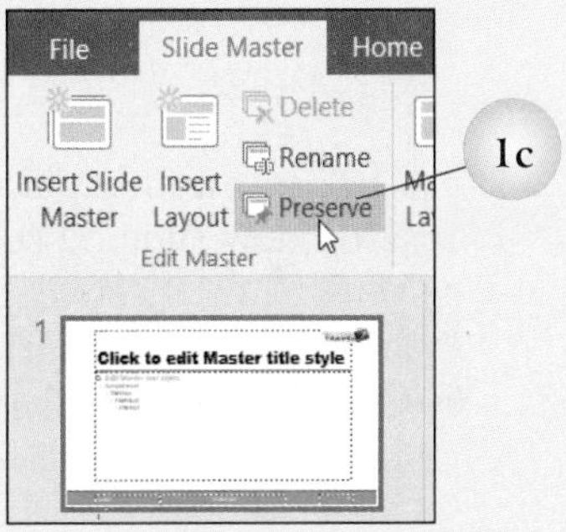

2. Insert a second slide master by completing the following steps:
   a. Click below the bottom slide layout in the slide thumbnails pane. (You want the second slide master and associated layouts to display below the original slide master and not take the place of the original.)
   b. Click the Themes button in the Edit Theme group and then click *Facet* at the drop-down gallery.
   c. Notice that the slide master and associated layouts display in the slide thumbnails pane below the original slide master and associated layouts and that the preservation icon displays below the second slide master.
   d. Click the new slide master (*Facet Slide Master*) in the slide thumbnails pane.
   e. Click the Colors button in the Background group and then click the *Blue* option.
   f. Click the Fonts button and then click the *Arial Black-Arial* option.

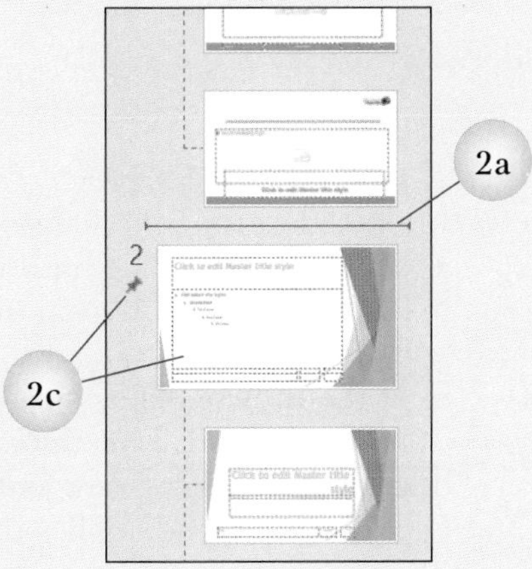

3. Click the first layout below the new slide master (*Title Slide Layout*) and then select and delete the master subtitle placeholder.
4. Click the third layout below the new slide master (*Section Header Layout*), scroll down to the bottom of the slide thumbnails pane, press and hold down the Shift key, click the bottom thumbnail, release the Shift key, and then click the Delete button in the Edit Master group. (This deletes all but two of the layouts associated with the new slide master.)
5. Click the Close Master View button.
6. Insert a new slide by completing the following steps:
   a. Make Slide 7 active.
   b. Click the New Slide button arrow and then click *Title Slide* in the *Facet* section.

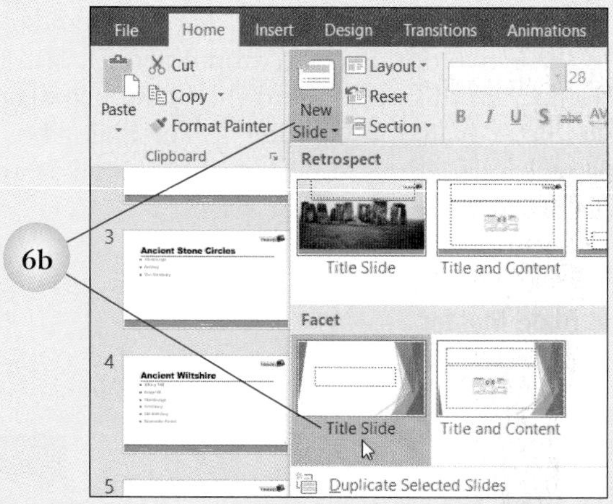

   c. Click in the title placeholder and then type New York City Tour.
7. Insert a new slide by completing the following steps:
   a. With Slide 8 active, click the New Slide button. (This inserts a slide with the Facet Title and Content layout.)
   b. Click in the title placeholder and then type Manhattan Tour.
   c. Click in the text placeholder and then type the following bulleted text:
      Times Square
      Madison Square Garden
      Greenwich Village
      Soho
      Little Italy
      Battery Park
8. Insert slides using the Reuse Slides task pane by completing the following steps:
   a. Click the New Slide button arrow and then click *Reuse Slides* at the drop-down list.
   b. Click the Browse button in the Reuse Slides task pane and then click *Browse File* at the drop-down list.
   c. At the Browse dialog box, navigate to the PC6 folder on your storage medium and then double-click ***FCTNewYork.pptx***.
   d. Click the *Dinner Cruise* slide in the Reuse Slides task pane. (This inserts the slide in the presentation and applies the custom formatting to that slide.)
   e. Click the *City Pass* slide in the Reuse Slides task pane.
   f. Click the *Museum Passes* slide in the Reuse Slides task pane.
   g. Click the Close button in the upper right corner of the Reuse Slides task pane to close the task pane.

9. Assume that the presentation is going to be inserted into a larger presentation and that the starting slide will be Slide 12 (instead of Slide 1). Change the beginning slide number by completing the following steps:
   a. Click the View tab and then click the Slide Master button.
   b. Click the top slide master in the slide thumbnails pane.
   c. Click the Slide Size button in the Size group and then click *Custom Slide Size* at the drop-down list.
   d. At the Slide Size dialog box, select the current number in the *Number slides from* measurement box and then type 12.
   e. Click OK to close the dialog box.

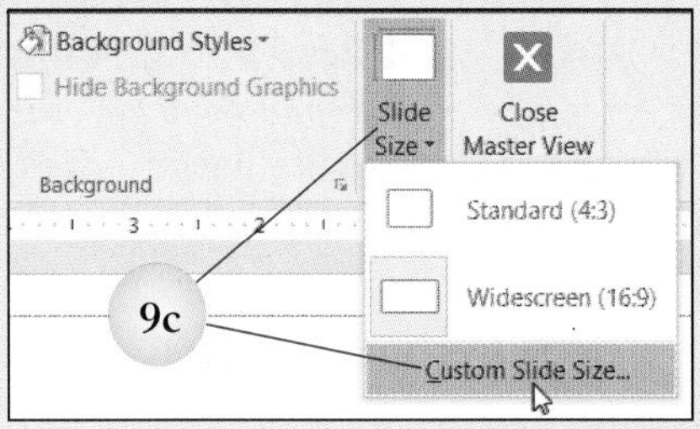

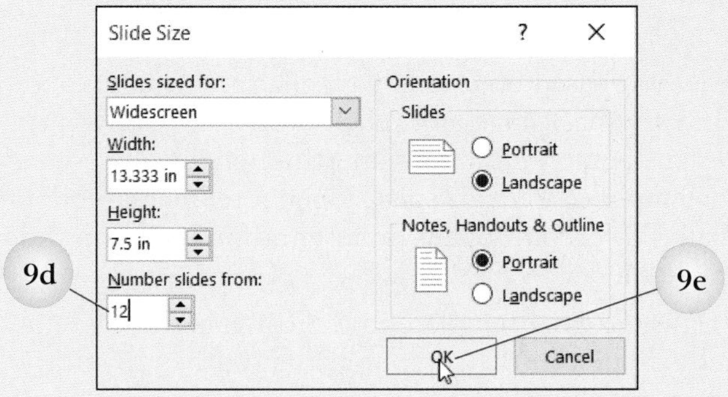

   f. Click the second slide master in the slide thumbnails pane (*Facet Slide Master* thumbnail).
   g. Click the Insert tab and then click the Slide Number button in the Text group.
   h. At the Header and Footer dialog box with the Slide tab selected, click the *Slide number* check box to insert a check mark and then click the Apply to All button.
   i. Click the Slide Master tab.
   j. Click the Close Master View button.
10. Make Slide 12 active (the first slide in the presentation) and then run the slide show.
11. Print the presentation as a handout with six slides displayed horizontally per page.
12. Save and then close **6-England.pptx**.

Check Your Work

Project 2 Save a Template and Create a Travel Presentation with the Template — 4 Parts

You will save a travel presentation as a template and then use that template to create and format a travel presentation. You will insert elements in the presentation in Handout Master view and Notes Master view, change the presentation zoom, and view the presentation in grayscale and black and white.

Preview Finished Project

Tutorial

Saving a Presentation as a Template

Saving a Presentation as a Template

If custom formatting will be used for future presentations, consider saving the presentation as a template. The advantage to saving a presentation as a template is that the template cannot accidentally be overwritten. Save a custom template in the Custom Office Templates folder in the Documents folder on the hard drive. Check to determine the default custom template folder location by displaying the PowerPoint Options dialog box with *Save* selected in the left panel. The *Default personal templates location* option should display the Custom Office Templates folder in the Documents folder as the default location. If this is not the default location, check with your instructor.

Quick Steps

Save a Presentation as a Template

1. Display Save As dialog box.
2. Click *Save as type* option.
3. Click *PowerPoint Template (*.potx)*.
4. Type presentation name.
5. Click Save button.

Open a Presentation Based on a Template

1. Click File tab.
2. Click *New*.
3. Click *PERSONAL*.
4. Double-click template thumbnail.

To save a presentation as a template, display the Save As dialog box, click the *Save as type* option button, and then click *PowerPoint Template (*.potx)* at the drop-down list. Type a name for the template in the *File name* text box and then click the Save button.

To create a presentation based on a template, click the File tab and then click the *New* option. At the New backstage area, click the *PERSONAL* option that displays above the design theme thumbnails and thumbnails for templates saved in the Custom Office Templates folder display. Open a template by double-clicking the template thumbnail. PowerPoint opens a presentation based on the template, not the original template file.

By default, PowerPoint saves a template in the Custom Office Templates folder in the Documents folder on the computer's hard drive. In addition to this folder, a template can be saved to a specific folder and then a presentation based on the template can be opened using File Explorer, which is a file management application included with Microsoft Windows. To use File Explorer, click the File Explorer icon on the taskbar and, at the window that displays, navigate to the folder containing the template and then double-click the template.

If a template is no longer needed, delete the template at the Custom Office Templates folder. Open this folder by displaying the Open dialog box, displaying the Documents folder, and then double-clicking the Custom Office Templates folder. Click the template file to be deleted, click the Organize button, and then click *Delete* at the drop-down list.

Project 2a Saving a Presentation as a Template — Part 1 of 4

Note: If you are using PowerPoint 2016 in a school setting on a network system, you may need to complete Project 2a and 2b on the same day Or, you may need to save a template to your PC6 folder and then use File Explorer to open a presentation based on the template. Check with your instructor for any specific instructions.

1. Open **6-TravelMaster.pptx**.
2. Press F12 to display the Save As dialog box.
3. At the Save As dialog box, type XXXTravelTemplate in the *File name* text box. (Type your initials in place of the *XXX*.)
4. Click the *Save as type* option box and then click *PowerPoint Template (*.potx)* at the drop-down list.
5. Click the Save button.

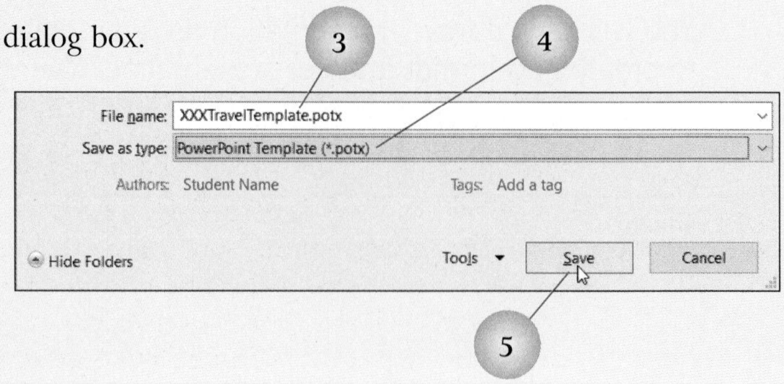

6. Close **XXXTravelTemplate.potx**.
7. Open the template and save it as a presentation by completing the following steps:
   a. Click the File tab and then click the *New* option.
   b. At the New backstage area, click the *PERSONAL* option.
   c. Double-click the ***XXXTravelTemplate*** thumbnail.

8. Save the presentation with the name **6-ParisTour**.

Check Your Work

Tutorial

Customizing the Handout Master

Handout Master

Customizing the Handout Master

When a presentation is printed as handouts or an outline, PowerPoint will automatically print the current date in the upper right corner of the page and the page number in the lower right corner. Customize handouts with options in the Handout Master view. Display a presentation in Handout Master view by clicking the View tab and then clicking the Handout Master button in the Master Views group. Use options on the Handout Master tab to move, size, and format header and footer placeholders; change page orientation; add or remove placeholders; and specify the number of slides to be printed on each page.

With buttons in the Page Setup group, change the handout orientation, display the Slide Size dialog box with options for changing the size and orientation of the handouts page, and specify the number of slides to be printed on the handouts page. By default, a handouts page will contain a header, footer, date, and page number placeholder. Remove any of these placeholders by removing the check mark before the placeholder check boxes in the Placeholders group.

The Edit Theme group contains buttons for changing the theme color, font, and effects. Click the Themes button and the options in the drop-down gallery are dimmed, indicating that the themes are not available for the handouts pages. If a background style is applied to the handout master, theme colors can be changed by clicking the Colors button and then clicking a color theme at the drop-down gallery. Apply theme fonts by clicking the Fonts button and then clicking a font theme at the drop-down gallery.

Background Styles

Apply a background style to the handouts page by clicking the Background Styles button in the Background group and then clicking one of the predesigned styles. Or, click the *Format Background* option at the Background Styles button drop-down list and then make changes at the Format Background task pane. Remove any background graphics by clicking the *Hide Background Graphics* check box to insert a check mark.

Project 2b Customizing the Handout Master

1. With **6-ParisTour.pptx** open and displayed in Normal view, click the New Slide button arrow in the Slides group on the Home tab and then click *Reuse Slides* at the drop-down list.
2. In the Reuse Slides task pane, click the Browse button and then click the *Browse File* option at the drop-down list.
3. Navigate to the PC6 folder on your storage medium and then double-click ***ParisTour.pptx***.
4. Insert the second, third, fourth, and fifth slides from the Reuse Slides task pane into the current presentation.
5. Close the Reuse Slides task pane.
6. Edit the Title Slide Layout in Slide Master view by completing the following steps:
   a. Click the View tab and then click the Slide Master button.
   b. Click the second thumbnail in the slide thumbnails pane (*Title Slide Layout*).
   c. Click the Background Styles button in the Background group and then click *Format Background* at the drop-down list.
   d. At the Format Background task pane, click the File button (below the text *Insert picture from*).
   e. At the Insert Picture dialog box, navigate to the PC6 folder on your storage medium and then double-click ***EiffelTower.jpg***.
   f. Close the Format Background task pane.
   g. If necessary, click the *Hide Background Graphics* check box in the Background group to insert a check mark.
   h. Select the text *Click to edit Master title style*, click the Home tab, click the Font Color button arrow, and then click the *Turquoise, Accent 2, Lighter 60%* option (sixth column, third row in the *Theme Colors* section).
   i. Click the Slide Master tab.
   j. Click the Close Master View button.
   k. Make Slide 1 active and then type Paris Tour in the title placeholder.
   l. Size and move the text placeholder so *Paris Tour* displays in a blue area of the slide (not over the tower).

6d

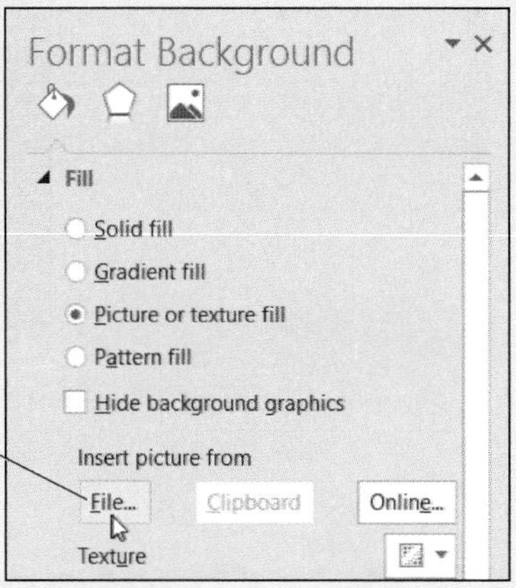

7. Make Slide 5 active and then create a new slide with the Title Slide layout. Type Call Greg at 213-555-4500 in the title placeholder. (Leave the placeholder in the default location.)
8. Save **6-ParisTour.pptx**.
9. Click the View tab and then click the Handout Master button in the Master Views group.

9

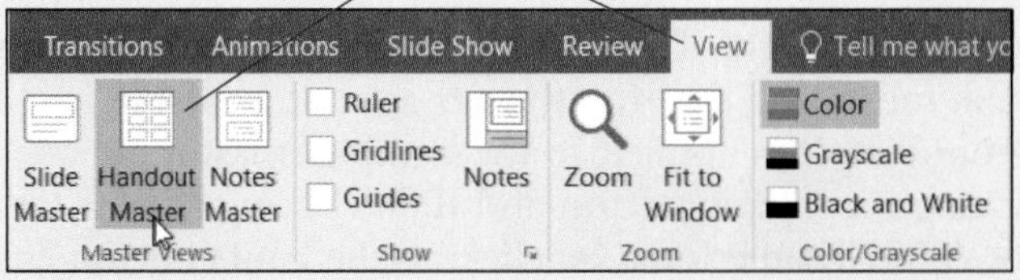

10. Click the Handout Orientation button in the Page Setup group and then click *Landscape* at the drop-down list.

11. Click in the Header placeholder on the page and then type your first and last names.
12. Click in the Footer placeholder and then type Paris Tour.
13. Click the Background Styles button and then click *Style 9* at the drop-down list (first column, third row).
14. Click the Colors button in the Background group and then click the *Blue* option.
15. Click the Fonts button in the Background group, scroll down the drop-down gallery, and then click the *Arial Black-Arial* option.
16. Edit the header text by completing the following steps:
    a. Click in the Header placeholder.
    b. Move the insertion point so it is positioned immediately to the right of the last character in your last name.
    c. Type a comma, press the spacebar, and then type your course number and title.
    d. Click in the handouts page outside of any placeholder.
17. Click the Close Master View button.
18. Save **6-ParisTour.pptx**

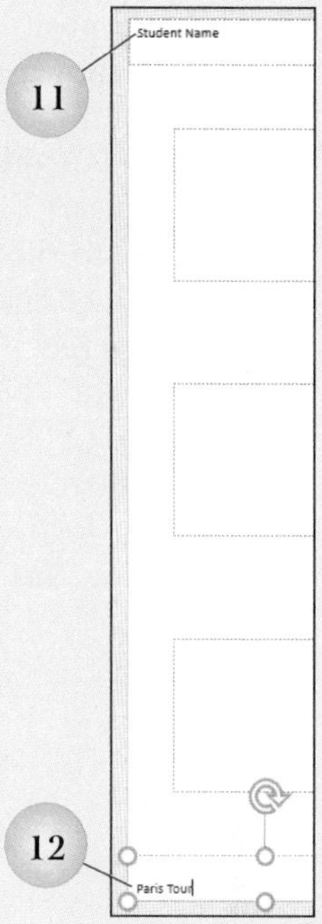

Check Your Work

Tutorial

Customizing the Notes Master

Notes Master

Customizing the Notes Master

If notes are inserted in a presentation, the presentation can be printed as notes pages with the notes printed below the slides. To insert or format text or other elements as notes on all slides in a presentation, consider making the changes in the Notes Master view. Display this view by clicking the View tab and then clicking the Notes Master button in the Master Views group. This displays a notes page along with the Notes Master tab. Many of the buttons and options on this tab are the same as those on the Handout Master tab.

Project 2c Customizing the Notes Master

Part 3 of 4

1. With **6-ParisTour.pptx** open, click the View tab and then click the Notes Master button in the Master Views group.
2. Click the *Body* check box in the Placeholders group to remove the check mark.
3. Click the Fonts button in the Background group, scroll down the drop-down gallery, and then click the *Arial Black-Arial* option.
4. Click the Insert tab.
5. Click the Text Box button in the Text group.
6. Click in the notes page below the slide.
7. Type Visit www.first-choice.emcp.net for a listing of all upcoming tours.

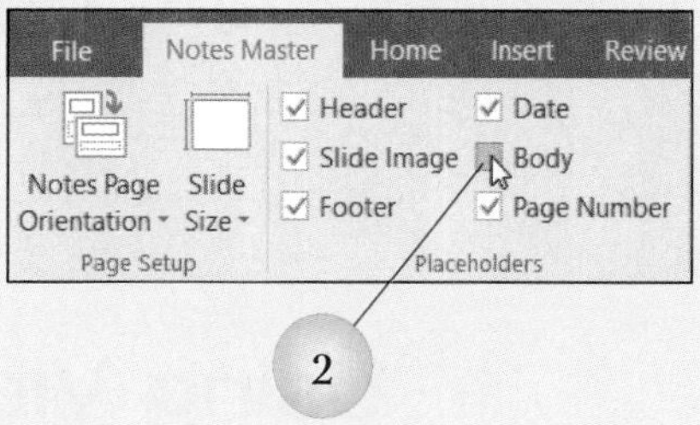

8. Size and position the text box below the slide as shown below and to the right.
9. Click the Insert tab and then click the Pictures button in the Images group.
10. At the Insert Picture dialog box, navigate to the PC6 folder on your storage medium and then double-click ***FCTLogo.jpg***.
11. Change the height of the logo to 0.5 inch. (This changes the width to approximately 1.75 inches.)
12. Drag the logo so it is positioned below the text as shown below.

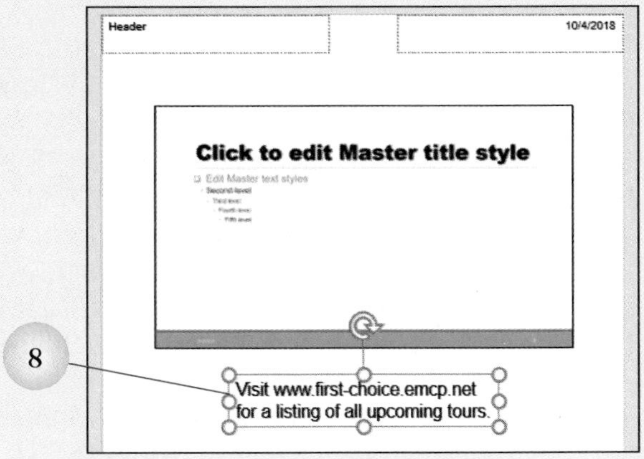

13. Click the Notes Master tab and then click the Close Master View button.
14. Print Slides 2 and 4 as notes pages by completing the following steps:
    a. Display the Print backstage area.
    b. Click the second gallery in the *Settings* category and then click *Notes Pages* in the *Print Layout* section.
    c. Click in the *Slides* text box located below the first gallery in the *Settings* category and then type 2,4.
    d. Click the Print button.
15. Save **6-ParisTour.pptx**.

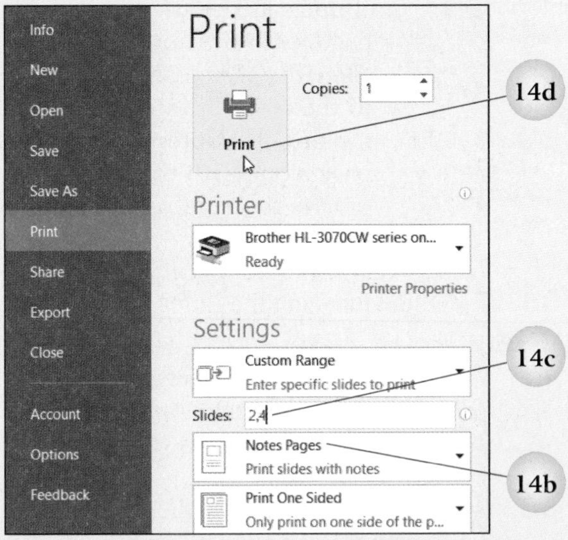

Check Your Work

Using View Tab Options

The View tab contains buttons for displaying a presentation in various views such as Normal, Slide Sorter, Slide Master, Handout Master, and Notes Master. In addition to viewing buttons, the View tab also includes options for showing or hiding the ruler and gridlines; displaying the Notes pane below the slide pane; zooming in or out in the slide; viewing the slide in color, grayscale, or black and white; and working with windows.

Tutorial

Changing the Display of a Slide in the Slide Pane

Zoom

Changing the Zoom

Change the display size of the slide in the slide pane or the slides in the slide thumbnails pane with the Zoom button on the View tab or with the Zoom slider bar at the right side of the Status bar. Click the Zoom button on the View tab and the Zoom dialog box displays. Use options in this dialog box to increase or decrease the display size of slides in the slide pane or slide thumbnails pane.

To change the zoom with the Zoom slider bar, use the mouse to drag the slider bar button to the left to decrease the display size or to the right to increase the display size. Click the Zoom Out button (the minus symbol at the left side of the Zoom slider bar) to decrease the display percentage or click the Zoom In button (the plus symbol at the right side of the Zoom slider bar) to increase the display percentage. Click the Zoom level button, which displays as a percentage number at the right side of the slider bar, and the Zoom dialog box displays.

Managing Windows

New Window

Arrange All

Cascade

Use buttons in the Window group on the View tab to work with presentation windows. Work in two locations in the same presentation by opening the presentation and then opening a new window with the same presentation. This is helpful for viewing and editing slides in two different locations in the presentation. Open a new window by clicking the New Window button in the Window group.

If more than one presentation is open, the presentations can be arranged so a portion of each presentation displays. Click the Arrange All button in the Window group and each open presentation displays as a tile on the screen. Click the Cascade button in the Window group and the open presentations are displayed in a layered manner with the title bar of each presentation visible. Slides can be copied from one presentation to another when the presentations are arranged on the screen by dragging a slide from the slide thumbnails pane in one presentation to the slide thumbnails pane in the other presentation.

Switch Windows

With more than one presentation open, switch between presentations by clicking the Switch Windows button in the Window group. Click this button and a drop-down list with the names of the open presentations displays with a check mark in front of the active presentation. Make another presentation active by clicking the presentation name at the drop-down list.

Move Split

Maximize

Minimize

Restore Down

Increase or decrease the viewing area of each section of the presentation window with the Move Split button. Click this button and the mouse pointer displays as a four-headed arrow. Use the arrow keys on the keyboard to increase or decrease the viewing area of the slide pane and slide thumbnails pane. Click the left mouse button to deactivate the feature. Use the Maximize and Minimize buttons in the upper right corner of the active presentation to change the size of the window. If all open presentations are arranged in the window, click the Maximize button in the active presentation to fill the presentation screen. In addition, the Maximize button changes to the Restore Down button. To return the active presentation back to its size before it was maximized, click the Restore Down button. Click the Minimize button in the active presentation to reduce the presentation to a button that displays on the taskbar.

Viewing in Color and Grayscale

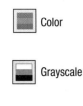

Color

Grayscale

Black and White

By default, the slides in a presentation display in color. This can be changed to grayscale or black and white with buttons in the Color/Grayscale group on the View tab. Click the Grayscale button and the slides in the presentation display in grayscale and the Grayscale tab becomes active. This tab contains a variety of options for changing the grayscale display, such as light grayscale, inverse grayscale, and gray or black with grayscale fill. Return to the color view by clicking the Back to Color View button on the Grayscale tab. Click the Black and White button in the Color/Grayscale group and the slides in the presentation display in black and white and the Black And White tab becomes active. This tab contains many of the same options as the Grayscale tab.

Project 2d **Viewing a Presentation** Part 4 of 4

1. With **6-ParisTour.pptx** open, make Slide 1 active and then click the slide in the slide pane.
2. Click the View tab.
3. Increase and decrease the zoom by completing the following steps:
   a. Click the Zoom button in the Zoom group.
   b. At the Zoom dialog box, click the *33%* option and then click OK.
   c. Click the Zoom button, click the *100%* option in the Zoom dialog box, and then click OK.
   d. Click the Slide 2 thumbnail in the slide thumbnails pane.
   e. Click the Zoom button, click the *66%* option in the Zoom dialog box, and then click OK. (Because the slide was active in the slide thumbnails pane, the percentage display changed for the thumbnails in the pane.)
   f. Position the mouse pointer on the Zoom slider bar button (at the right side of the Status bar), drag the button to the right to increase the size of the slide in the slide pane, and then drag the slider bar to the left to decrease the size of the slide.
   g. Click the Zoom level button (the percentage number at the right side of the Zoom slider bar). This displays the Zoom dialog box.
   h. Click the *100%* option in the Zoom dialog box and then click OK.
   i. Click the Fit to Window button in the Zoom group on the View tab.

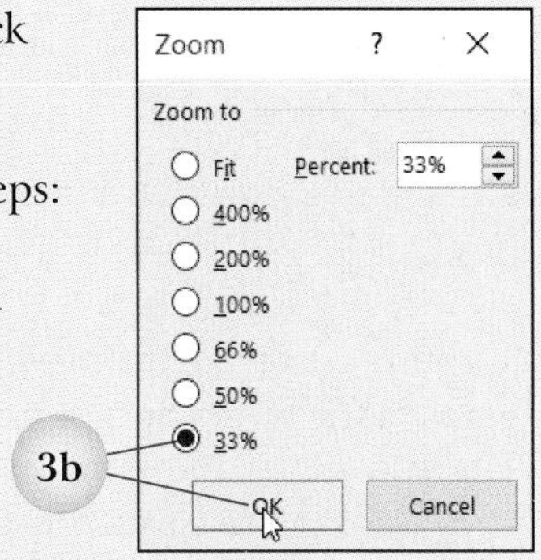

4. View the slides in grayscale by completing the following steps:
   a. Click the Grayscale button in the Color/Grayscale group on the View tab.
   b. Click the slide in the slide pane.
   c. Click the buttons on the Grayscale tab to display the slides in varying grayscale options.
   d. Click the Back To Color View button.

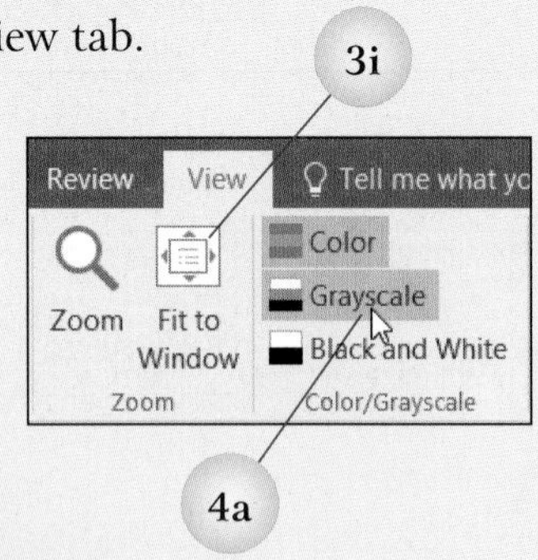

5. View the slides in black and white by completing the following steps:
   a. Click the View tab and then click the Black and White button in the Color/Grayscale group.
   b. Click some of the buttons on the Black And White tab to display the slides with varying black and white options applied.
   c. Click the Back To Color View button.

6. Open another presentation and then arrange the presentations by completing the following steps:
   a. Open **ParisTravelInfo.pptx** from the PC6 folder.
   b. Click the View tab and then click the Cascade button in the Window group. (This arranges the two presentations with the presentations overlapping with the title bar for each presentation visible.)
   c. Click the Switch Windows button in the Window group and then click the *6-ParisTour.pptx* option at the drop-down list.
   d. Click the Arrange All button in the Window group to arrange the two presentations in two side-by-side windows.

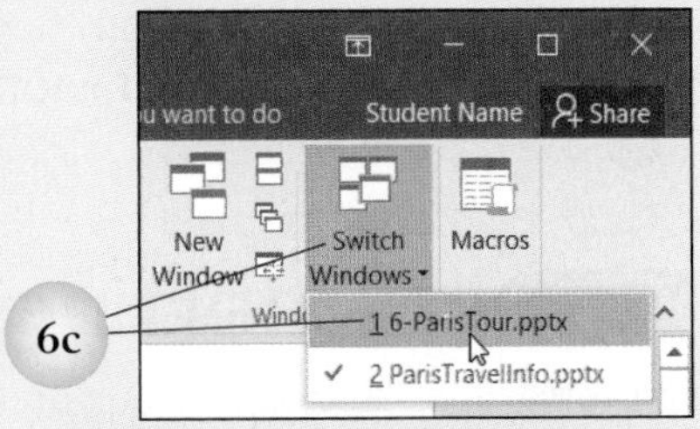

7. Copy a slide from one presentation to another by completing the following steps:
   a. Click Slide 2 (*Accommodations*) in the slide thumbnails pane of **ParisTravelInfo.pptx** and hold down the left mouse button.
   b. Drag the slide so it is positioned below the Slide 5 thumbnail in the slide thumbnails pane in **6-ParisTour.pptx** (an orange line will display) and then release the mouse button.

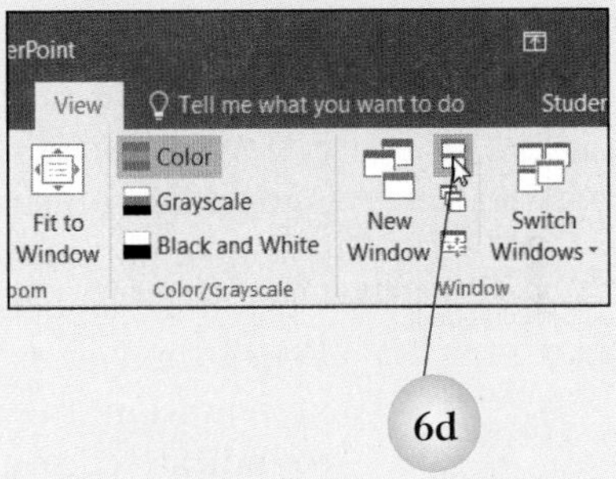

8. Click the Close button in the upper right corner of the **ParisTravelInfo.pptx** file.
9. Click the Maximize button in the upper right corner of the presentation window. (The Maximize button displays immediately to the left of the Close button.)
10. Use the Move Split button by completing these steps:
    a. Click the Move Split button in the Window group. (The mouse displays as a four-headed arrow.)
    b. Press the Right Arrow key on the keyboard several times and notice the slide thumbnails pane increasing in size.
    c. Press the Left Arrow key several times.
    d. Press the Up Arrow key several times and notice that the slide in the slide pane decreases in size and the notes pane displays.
    e. Press the Down Arrow key until the slide in the slide pane returns to the original size and the notes pane has closed.
11. With the View tab active, click the Grayscale button in the Color/Grayscale group and then click the Light Grayscale button in the Change Selected Object group.
12. Print the presentation by completing the following steps:
    a. Display the Print backstage area.
    b. If any text displays in the *Slides* text box, select and then delete the text.
    c. If you are using a color printer, click the *Color* gallery that displays at the bottom of the *Settings* category and then click *Grayscale*. (Skip this step if you are using a black and white printer.)
    d. Click the second gallery in the *Settings* category and then click *4 Slides Horizontal* in the *Handouts* section.
    e. Click the Print button.
13. Click the Back To Color View button on the Grayscale tab.
14. Make Slide 1 active and then run the slide show.
15. Save and then close **6-ParisTour.pptx**.

Check Your Work

Project 3 Insert Action Buttons and Hyperlinks in a Job Search Presentation

5 Parts

You will open a job search presentation and then insert action buttons that display the next slide, the first slide, a website, and another presentation. You will also create a hyperlink from text, a graphic image, and a chart in a slide to a website, a Word document, and another presentation.

Preview Finished Project

Tutorial

Inserting Action Buttons

Quick Steps

Insert an Action Button

1. Make slide active.
2. Click Insert tab.
3. Click Shapes button.
4. Click action button.
5. Click or drag in slide to create button.
6. Make changes at Action Settings dialog box.
7. Click OK.

Hint Apply formatting to an action button with options on the Drawing Tools Format tab.

Inserting Action Buttons

Action buttons are drawn objects on a slide that have a routine attached to them which is activated when the viewer or the presenter clicks the button. For example, an action button can be inserted in a slide that displays the next slide in the presentation, a file in another program, or a specific web page. Creating an action button is a two-step process. The button is drawn in the slide using an Action Button shape in the Shapes button drop-down list and then the action that will take place is defined with options in the Action Settings dialog box. Customize an action button in the same manner as customizing a drawn object. When the viewer or presenter moves the mouse over an action button during a presentation, the pointer changes to a hand with the index finger pointing upward to indicate clicking will result in an action.

To display the available action buttons, click the Insert tab and then click the Shapes button in the Illustrations group. Action buttons display at the bottom of the drop-down list. Hover the mouse pointer over a button and the name and the action it performs will display in a ScreenTip above the button. The action attached to an action button occurs when the button is clicked during the running of the slide show.

Project 3a Inserting Action Buttons

Part 1 of 5

1. Open **JobSearch.pptx** and then save it with the name **6-JobSearch**.
2. Make the following changes to the presentation:
   a. Apply the Dividend design theme.
   b. Click the Insert tab and then click the Header & Footer button in the Text group.
   c. At the Header and Footer dialog box with the Slide tab selected, click the *Date and time* check box and make sure *Update automatically* is selected.
   d. Click the *Slide number* check box to insert a check mark.
   e. Click the Notes and Handouts tab.
   f. Click the *Date and time* check box and make sure *Update automatically* is selected.
   g. Click the *Header* check box to insert a check mark, click in the *Header* text box, and then type the name of your school.
   h. Click the *Footer* check box to insert a check mark, click in the *Footer* text box, and then type your first and last names.
   i. Click the Apply to All button.

3. Insert an action button in Slide 1 that will display the next slide by completing the following steps:
   a. Make sure Slide 1 is active.
   b. Click the Insert tab and then click the Shapes button in the Illustrations group.
   c. Scroll down the drop-down list and then click the *Action Button: Forward or Next* button (second button in the *Action Buttons* group).
   d. Move the crosshairs to the lower right corner of the slide and then drag to create a button that is approximately 0.5 inch in height and width (see below).

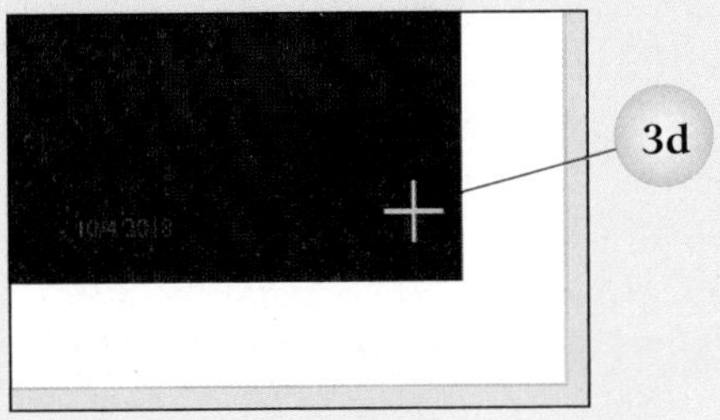

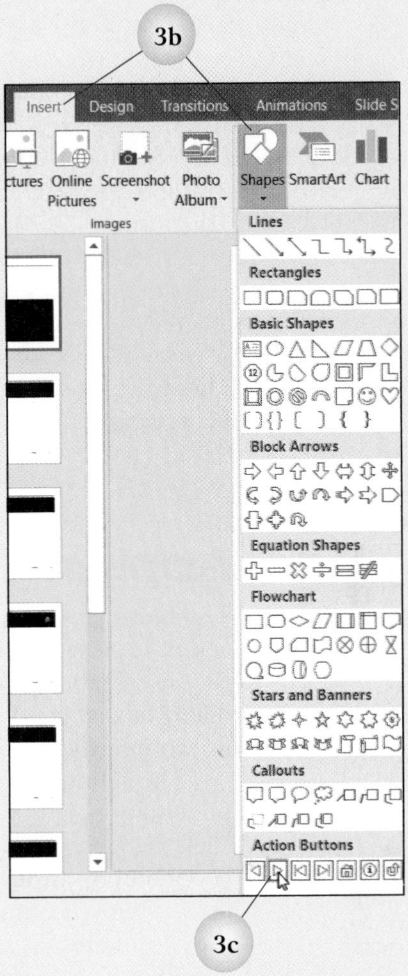

   e. At the Action Settings dialog box, click OK. (The default setting is *Hyperlink to Next Slide*.)
4. Insert an action button in Slide Master view that will display the next slide by completing the following steps:
   a. Display the presentation in Slide Master view.
   b. Click the top slide master thumbnail (*Dividend Slide Master*).
   c. Click the Insert tab and then click the Shapes button in the Illustrations group.
   d. Scroll down the drop-down list and then click the *Action Button: Forward or Next* button (second button in the *Action Buttons* group).
   e. Move the crosshairs to the lower right corner of the slide master and then drag to create a button as shown at the right.

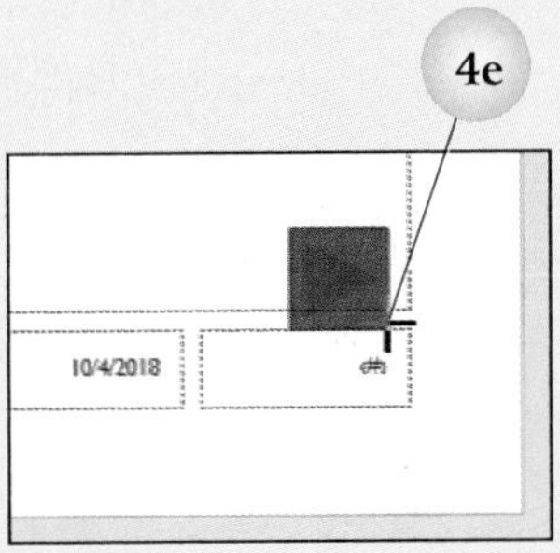

   f. At the Action Settings dialog box, click OK. (The default setting is *Hyperlink to Next Slide*.)
   g. Click the Slide Master tab and then click the Close Master View button.
5. Make Slide 1 active and then run the slide show, clicking the action button to advance slides. When you click the action button on the last slide (Slide 9) nothing happens because it is the last slide. Press the Esc key to end the slide show.
6. Change the action button on Slide 9 by completing the following steps:
   a. Make Slide 9 active.
   b. Click the Insert tab and then click the Shapes button in the Illustrations group.

c. Scroll down the drop-down list and then click the *Action Button: Home* button (fifth button in the *Action Buttons* group).
d. Drag to create a button on top of the previous action button. (Make sure it completely covers the previous action button.)
e. At the Action Settings dialog box with the *Hyperlink to: First Slide* option selected, click OK.
f. Deselect the button.

7. Display Slide 1 in the slide pane and then run the slide show. Navigate through the slide show by clicking the action button. When you click the action button on the last slide, the first slide displays. End the slide show by pressing the Esc key.
8. Save **6-JobSearch.pptx**.

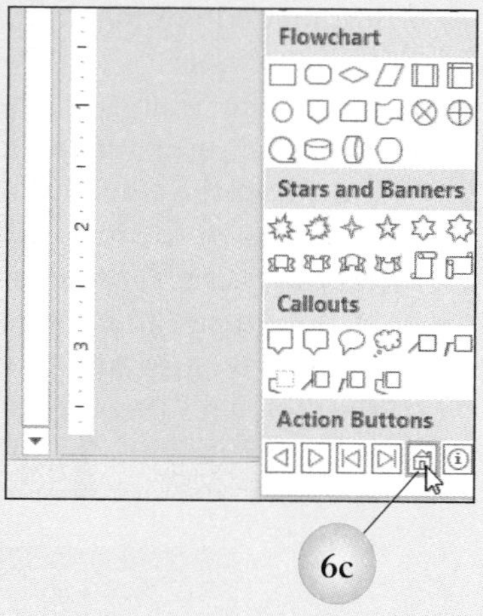

Check Your Work

Tutorial

Applying an Action to an Object

Action

Applying an Action to an Object

The Links group on the Insert tab contains an Action button for specifying an action for a selected object. To use this button, select the object in the slide, click the Insert tab, and then click the Action button. This displays the Action Settings dialog box, which is the same dialog box that displays when an action button is drawn in a slide.

The action button or a selected object can be linked to another PowerPoint presentation, another file, or a website. To link to another PowerPoint presentation, click the *Hyperlink to* option at the Action Settings dialog box, click the *Hyperlink to* option box arrow, and then click *Other PowerPoint Presentation* at the drop-down list. At the Hyperlink to Other PowerPoint Presentation dialog box, navigate to the specific folder, and then double-click the PowerPoint presentation. To link to another file, click the *Hyperlink to* option at the Action Settings dialog box, click the *Hyperlink to* option box arrow, and then click *Other File* at the drop-down list. At the Hyperlink to Other File dialog box, navigate to the specific folder and then double-click the file name. To link to a website, click the *Hyperlink to* option at the Action Settings dialog box, click the *Hyperlink to* option box arrow, and then click *URL* at the drop-down list. At the Hyperlink to URL dialog box, type the web address in the *URL* text box, and then click OK. Other locations that can be linked to using the *Hyperlink to* drop-down list include *Next Slide*, *Previous Slide*, *First Slide*, *Last Slide*, *Last Slide Viewed*, *End Show*, *Custom Show*, *Slide*, and *Other File*.

Project 3b **Linking to Another Presentation and a Website** Part 2 of 5

1. With **6-JobSearch.pptx** open, add an action button that will link to another presentation by completing the following steps:
   a. Make Slide 4 active.
   b. Click the Insert tab and then click the Shapes button in the Illustrations group.
   c. Scroll down the drop-down list and then click *Action Button: Help* (eleventh button in the *Action Buttons* section).

d. Draw the action button to the left of the existing button in the lower right corner of the slide.
e. At the Action Settings dialog box, click the *Hyperlink to* option.
f. Click the *Hyperlink to* option box arrow and then click *Other PowerPoint Presentation* at the drop-down list.
g. At the Hyperlink to Other PowerPoint Presentation dialog box, navigate to the PC6 folder on your storage medium and then double-click ***Contacts.pptx***.
h. At the Hyperlink to Slide dialog box, click OK.
i. Click OK to close the Action Settings dialog box.

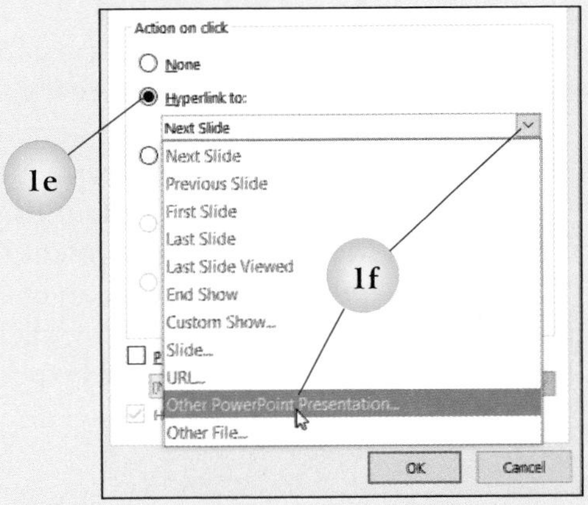

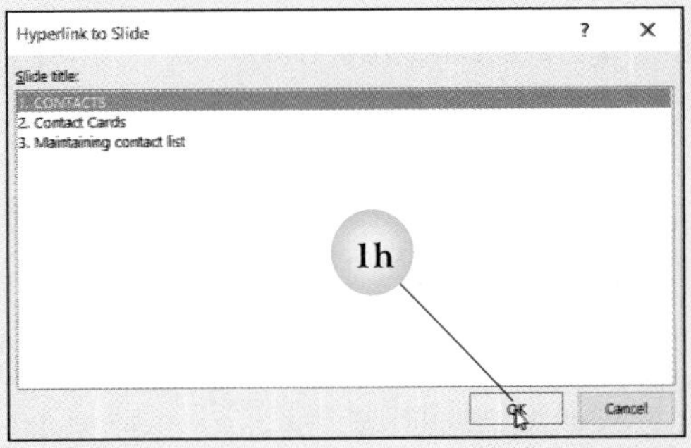

2. Apply an action to the image in Slide 5 that links to a website by completing the following steps:
   a. Make Slide 5 active and then click the image to select it.
   b. Click the Insert tab and then click the Action button in the Links group.
   c. At the Action Settings dialog box, click the *Hyperlink to* option.
   d. Click the *Hyperlink to* option box arrow, and then click *URL* at the drop-down list.
   e. At the Hyperlink to URL dialog box, type www.usajobs.gov in the *URL* text box and then click OK.
   f. Click OK to close the Action Settings dialog box.
   g. Click outside the image to deselect it.

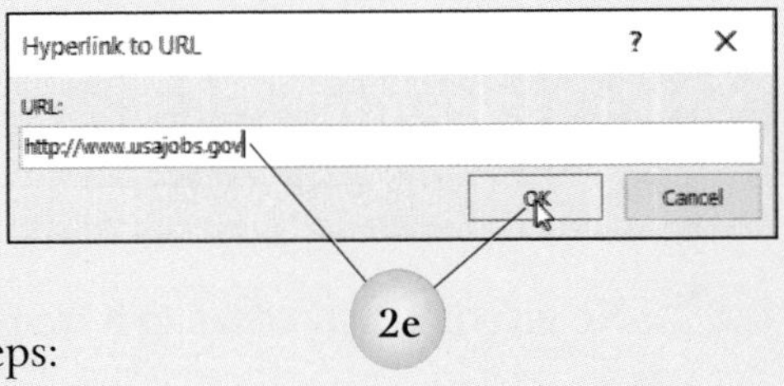

3. Run the slide show by completing the following steps:
   a. Make sure you are connected to the Internet.
   b. Make Slide 1 active.
   c. Click the Slide Show button in the view area on the Status bar.
   d. Navigate through the slide show to Slide 4.
   e. Click the action button in Slide 4 containing the question mark. (This displays Slide 1 of **Contacts.pptx**.)
   f. Navigate through the three slides in **Contacts.pptx**. Continue clicking the mouse button until you return to Slide 4 of **6-JobSearch.pptx**.
   g. Display Slide 5 and then click the image. (If you are connected to the Internet, the job site of the United States Federal Government displays.)
   h. Search for information on a specific job title that interests you and then click a few hyperlinks at the website.
   i. When you have finished viewing the website, close your web browser.
   j. Continue viewing the remainder of the slide show by clicking the action button in the lower right corner of each slide.
   k. When Slide 1 displays, press the Esc key to end the slide show.
4. Save **6-JobSearch.pptx**.

Check Your Work

Tutorial

Inserting Hyperlinks

Hyperlink

Quick Steps

Insert a Hyperlink

1. Click Insert tab.
2. Click Hyperlink button.
3. Make changes at Insert Hyperlink dialog box.
4. Click OK.

Inserting Hyperlinks

Hyperlinks can be created with options at the Action Settings dialog box or with options at the Insert Hyperlink dialog box shown in Figure 6.2. To display this dialog box, select a key word, phrase, or object in a slide, click the Insert tab, and then click the Hyperlink button in the Links group, or press Ctrl + K, which is the keyboard shortcut to display the Insert Hyperlink dialog box. Link to a website, another presentation, a place in the current presentation, a new presentation, or to an email address. To insert a hyperlink to a website or an existing presentation, click the Existing File or Web Page button in the *Link to* group at the Insert Hyperlink dialog box.

Figure 6.2 Insert Hyperlink Dialog Box

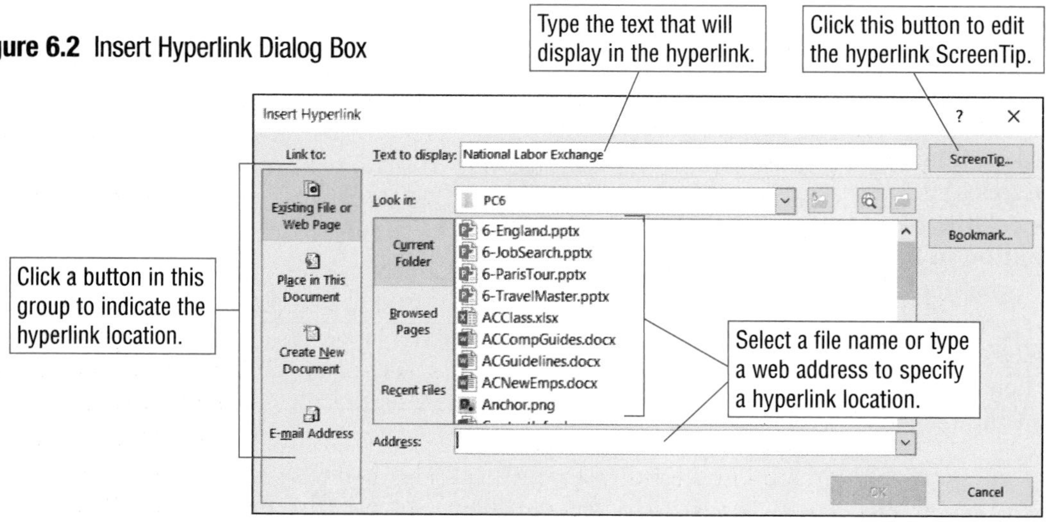

Project 3c **Inserting Hyperlinks to a Website**

Part 3 of 5

1. With **6-JobSearch.pptx** open, insert a new slide by completing the following steps:
   a. Make Slide 5 active.
   b. Click the Home tab.
   c. Click the New Slide button arrow and then click the Title and Content layout option.
   d. Type Internet Job Resources as the slide title.
   e. Click the text placeholder, type National Labor Exchange, press the Enter key, and then type Monster.
2. Add a hyperlink to the National Labor Exchange site by completing the following steps:
   a. Select the text *National Labor Exchange* in Slide 6.
   b. Click the Insert tab and then click the Hyperlink button in the Links group.
   c. At the Insert Hyperlink dialog box, type www.us.jobs in the *Address* text box. (PowerPoint automatically inserts *http://* at the beginning of the address.)
   d. Click OK to close the Insert Hyperlink dialog box.

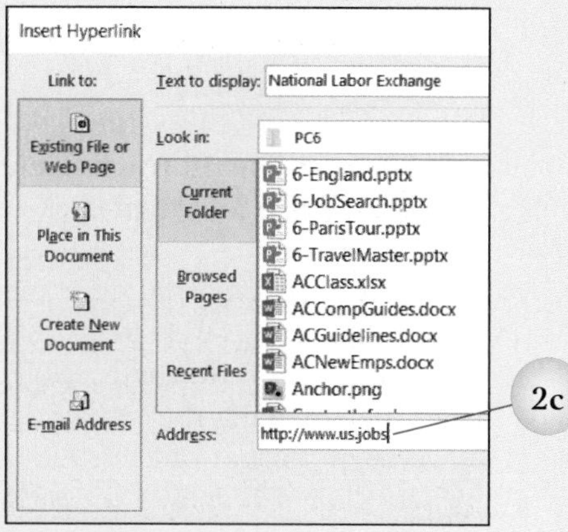

3. Add a hyperlink to the Monster website by completing the following steps:
   a. Select the text *Monster* in Slide 6.
   b. Click the Hyperlink button in the Links group.
   c. At the Insert Hyperlink dialog box, type www.monster.com in the *Address* text box. (PowerPoint automatically inserts *http://* at the beginning of the address.)
   d. Click OK to close the Insert Hyperlink dialog box.
4. Save **6-JobSearch.pptx**.

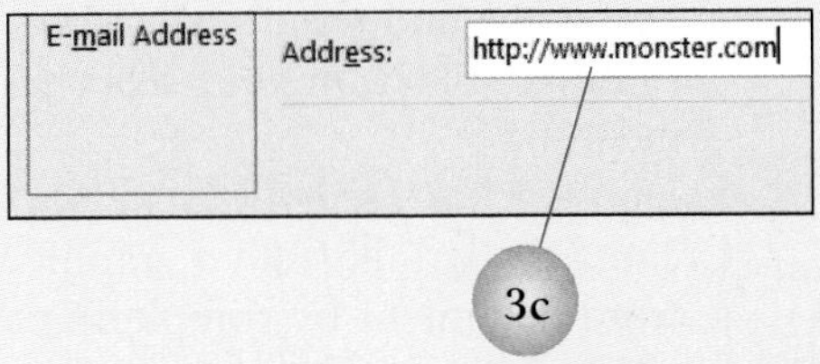

Check Your Work

Hint Hyperlinks are active only when running the slide show, not when creating the presentation.

In addition to linking to a website, a hyperlink can be created that links to another location in the presentation with the Place in This Document button in the *Link to* group at the Insert Hyperlink dialog box. Click the slide to link to in the presentation in the *Select a place in this document* list box. Use the Create New Document button in the Insert Hyperlink dialog box to create a hyperlink to a new presentation. Click this button, type a name for the new presentation, and specify if the new presentation is to be edited now or later.

A graphic such as an image, picture, chart, or text box, can be used as a hyperlink to a file or website. To create a hyperlink with a graphic, select the graphic, click the Insert tab, and then click the Hyperlink button or right-click the graphic and then click *Hyperlink* at the shortcut menu. At the Insert Hyperlink dialog box, specify what to link to and the text to display in the hyperlink.

Insert a hyperlink to an email address using the E-Mail Address button in the *Link to* group in the Insert Hyperlink dialog box. Click the button and the options change in the Insert Hyperlink dialog box. With options that display, type the email address in the *E-mail address* text box, type a subject for the email in the *Subject* text box, and type the text to display in the presentation in the *Text to display* text box. To use this feature, the email address must be set up in Outlook.

Navigate to a hyperlink by clicking the hyperlink in the slide when running the slide show. Hover the mouse over the hyperlink and a ScreenTip displays with the hyperlink. To display specific information in the ScreenTip, click the ScreenTip button in the Insert Hyperlink dialog box, type the text in the Set Hyperlink ScreenTip dialog box, and then click OK.

Project 3d Inserting Hyperlinks to a Website, to Another Presentation, and to a Word Document

Part 4 of 5

1. With **6-JobSearch.pptx** open, make Slide 3 active.
2. Create a link to another presentation by completing the following steps:
   a. Move the insertion point immediately to the right of the word *Picture*, press the Enter key, press Shift + Tab, and then type Resume design.
   b. Select *Resume design*.
   c. Make sure the Insert tab is active and then click the Hyperlink button in the Links group.

d. At the Insert Hyperlink dialog box, make sure the Existing File or Web Page button is selected.
e. If necessary, click the *Look in* option box arrow and then navigate to the PC6 folder on your storage medium.
f. Double-click ***DesignResume.pptx***.

2c

2d

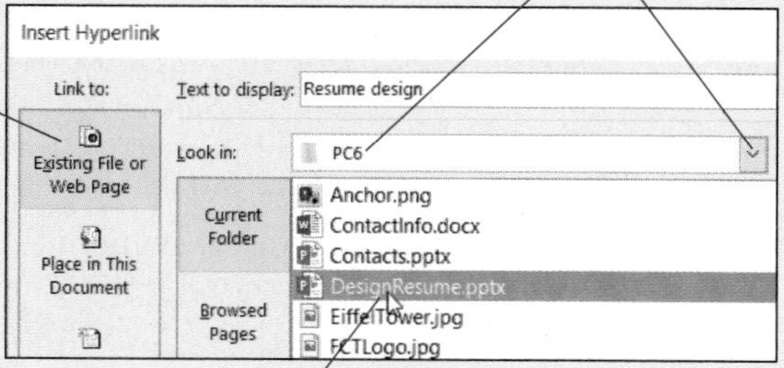

2f

3. Create a hyperlink from a graphic to a Word document by completing the following steps:
a. Make Slide 4 active.
b. Right-click the small image in the upper right corner of the slide and then click *Hyperlink* at the shortcut menu.
c. At the Insert Hyperlink dialog box, make sure the Existing File or Web Page button is selected.
d. If necessary, click the *Look in* option box arrow and then navigate to the PC6 folder on your storage medium.
e. Double-click ***ContactInfo.docx***.

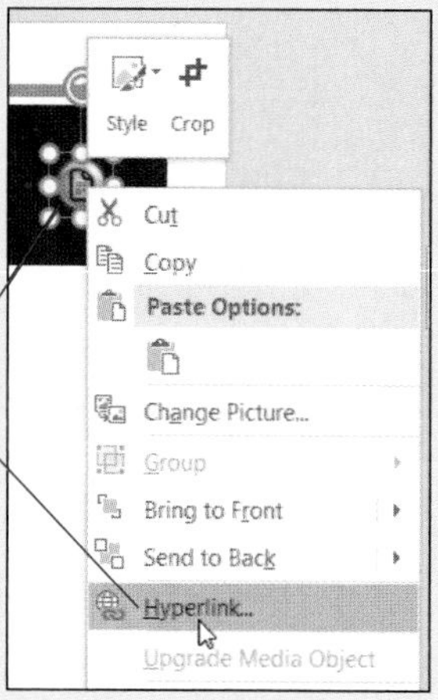

3b

4. Make Slide 6 active and then insert a chart by completing the following steps:
a. Press Ctrl + F12 to display the Open dialog box.
b. Navigate to the PC6 folder on your storage medium and then double-click ***USBLSChart.pptx***.
c. Select the chart.
d. Click the Copy button.
e. Click the PowerPoint button on the taskbar and then click the thumbnail representing **6-JobSearch.pptx**.
f. Click the Paste button.
g. With the chart selected, drag the chart down so it is positioned attractively on the slide.
5. Create a hyperlink from the chart to the United States Bureau of Labor Statistics website by completing the following steps:
a. With the chart selected, click the Hyperlink button in the Links group on the Insert tab.
b. At the Insert Hyperlink dialog box, make sure the Existing File or Web Page button is selected and then type www.bls.gov in the *Address* text box.
c. Click OK to close the Insert Hyperlink dialog box.
6. Hover the mouse pointer on the PowerPoint button on the taskbar, click the thumbnail representing **USBLSChart.pptx**, and then close the presentation.
7. Run the slide show by completing the following steps:
a. Make sure you are connected to the Internet.
b. Make Slide 1 active.
c. Click the Slide Show button in the view area on the Status bar.
d. Navigate through the slides to Slide 3 and then click the Resume design hyperlink in the slide.
e. Run the **DesignResume.pptx** slide show that displays. Continue clicking the mouse button until you return to Slide 3 of **6-JobSearch.pptx**.
f. Click the mouse button to display Slide 4.
g. Display the Word document by clicking the small image in the upper right corner of the slide.

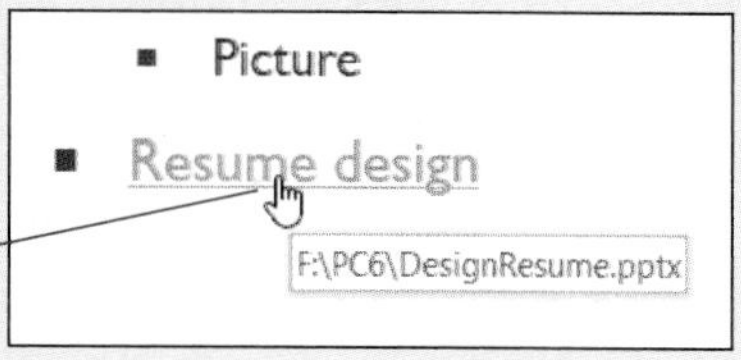

7d

h. Look at the information that displays in the Word document and then click the Close button in the upper right corner of the Word window.
i. Continue running the slide show to Slide 6.
j. At Slide 6, click the National Labor Exchange hyperlink.
k. Scroll through the website and then close the web browser.
l. Click the Monster hyperlink.
m. Scroll through the website and then close the web browser.
n. Click the chart.
o. Scroll through the Bureau of Labor Statistics website and then close the web browser.
p. Continue viewing the remainder of the presentation using the Action buttons. (When Slide 1 displays, press the Esc key to end the slide show.)

8. Save **6-JobSearch.pptx**.

Check Your Work

The hyperlinked text or the hyperlink destination can be edited. To do this, right-click the hyperlink and then click *Edit Hyperlink* at the shortcut menu. At the Edit Hyperlink dialog box, make changes and then close the dialog box. The Edit Hyperlink dialog box contains the same options as the Insert Hyperlink dialog box.

In addition to modifying the hyperlink, the hyperlinked text can be edited. For example, a different font, font size, text color, or text effect can be applied to the hyperlink text. Remove a hyperlink from a slide by right-clicking the hyperlinked text and then clicking *Remove Hyperlink* at the shortcut menu.

Project 3e Modifying, Editing, and Removing a Hyperlink

Part 5 of 5

1. With **6-JobSearch.pptx** open, make Slide 4 active and then modify the hyperlink in the image by completing the following steps:
   a. Right-click the small image in the upper right corner of the slide and then click *Edit Hyperlink* at the shortcut menu.
   b. At the Edit Hyperlink dialog box, click the ScreenTip button in the upper right corner of the dialog box.
   c. At the Set Hyperlink ScreenTip dialog box, type Click this image to display information on typing contact information.
   d. Click OK to close the Set Hyperlink ScreenTip dialog box.
   e. Click OK to close the Edit Hyperlink dialog box.

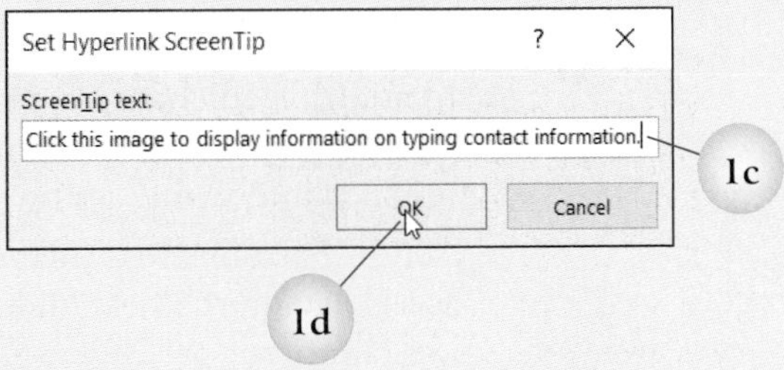

2. Make Slide 3 active and then remove the Resume design hyperlink by right-clicking the hyperlinked text (the text is dimmed and barely visible) and then clicking *Remove Hyperlink* at the shortcut menu.
3. Run the slide show and click the hyperlinks as they appear in the slides.
4. Print the presentation as a handout with six slides displayed horizontally per page.
5. Save and then close **6-JobSearch.pptx**.

Check Your Work

Chapter Summary

- Display a presentation in Slide Master view by clicking the View tab and then clicking the Slide Master button in the Master Views group. In Slide Master view, slide master thumbnails display in the slide thumbnails pane.
- Use buttons in the Background group on the Slide Master tab to change theme colors and fonts, apply a predesigned background style, display the Format Background task pane with options for applying background styles, and hide background graphics.
- Delete a placeholder by clicking in the placeholder, clicking the placeholder border, and then pressing the Delete key.
- Delete a slide master in Slide Master view by clicking the slide master thumbnail in the slide thumbnails pane and then clicking the Delete button in the Edit Master group.
- Create a custom slide layout by clicking the Insert Layout button in the Edit Master group on the Slide Master tab. Rename the custom slide layout with the Rename button in the Edit Master group.
- Insert a placeholder in a slide layout or custom slide layout by clicking the Insert Placeholder button arrow in the Master Layout group on the Slide Master tab and then clicking the desired placeholder at the drop-down list.
- In Slide Master view, create a custom prompt by selecting generic text in a placeholder and then typing the specific text.
- Click the Insert Slide Master button in Slide Master view to insert a new slide master and associated slide layouts. A new slide master can also be inserted by applying a design theme using the Themes button in the Edit Theme group on the Slide Master tab.
- Save a presentation as a template by changing the *Save as type* option at the Save As dialog box to *PowerPoint Template (*.potx)*.
- Open a presentation based on a template by clicking the *PERSONAL* option at the New backstage area and then double-clicking the template thumbnail.
- Customize handouts with options on the Handout Master tab. Display this tab by clicking the Handout Master button on the View tab.
- Customize notes pages with options on the Notes Master tab. Display this tab by clicking the Notes Master button on the View tab.
- In addition to changing views, use buttons on the View tab to show/hide the ruler and/or gridlines; change the zoom display; view slides in color, grayscale, or black and white; and work with multiple windows.
- Action buttons are drawn objects in a slide that have an attached routine, such as displaying the next slide, the first slide, a website, or another PowerPoint presentation.
- Create an action button by clicking the Insert tab, clicking the Shapes button, clicking the specific button at the drop-down list, and then clicking or dragging in the slide to create the button.
- Apply an action to text or an object in a slide by selecting the text or object, clicking the Insert tab, and then clicking the Action button.
- Use options at the Insert Hyperlink dialog box to create a hyperlink to a web page, another presentation, a location within a presentation, a new presentation, or to an email.
- A hyperlink can be created using a graphic and can be modified, edited, or removed.

Commands Review

FEATURE	RIBBON TAB, GROUP/OPTION	BUTTON	KEYBOARD SHORTCUT
action buttons	Insert, Illustrations		
Action Settings dialog box	Insert, Links		
arrange all windows	View, Window		
cascade windows	View, Window		
Handout Master view	View, Master Views		
Insert Hyperlink dialog box	Insert, Links		Ctrl + K
Move split	View, Window		
New backstage area	File, *New*		
Notes Master view	View, Master Views		
Slide Master view	View, Master Views		
Switch Windows	View, Window		
Zoom dialog box	View, Zoom		

Workbook

Chapter study tools and assessment activities are available in the *Workbook* ebook. These resources are designed to help you further develop and demonstrate mastery of the skills learned in this chapter.

Microsoft®

PowerPoint®

Applying Custom Animation and Setting Up Shows

CHAPTER 7

Performance Objectives

Upon successful completion of Chapter 7, you will be able to:

1. Apply, modify, and remove animations
2. Apply a build
3. Animate shapes, images, SmartArt, and chart elements
4. Draw motion paths
5. Set up a slide show
6. Set rehearse timings for slides
7. Hide and unhide slides
8. Use ink tools
9. Create, run, edit, and print a custom slide show
10. Insert and customize audio and video files
11. Create and insert a screen recording

Precheck

Check your current skills to focus your study.

Animation, or movement, can add visual appeal and interest to a slide show when used appropriately. PowerPoint provides a number of animation effects that can be applied to elements in a slide. In this chapter, you will learn how to apply animation effects, use ink tools on slides, insert audio and video files, and make a screen recording to create dynamic presentations.

In some situations, you may want to prepare an automated slide show that runs on a continuous loop. A presentation can be customized to run continuously with a specific amount of time set for each slide to remain on the screen. A custom slide show can be created to present only specific slides in a presentation. In this chapter, you will learn how to prepare automated presentations and how to create and edit custom slide shows.

Data Files

Before beginning chapter work, copy the PC7 folder to your storage medium and then make PC7 the active folder.

SNAP

If you are a SNAP user, launch the Precheck and Tutorials from your Assignments page.

Project 1 **Apply Animation Effects to Elements in a Marketing Presentation** **6 Parts**

You will open a marketing presentation, apply animation effects to the title slide, and then apply animation effects in Slide Master view to the remaining slides. You will remove some of the animation effects and then apply custom animation effects, such as entrance and emphasis effects, to elements in slides.

Tutorial

Applying and Removing Animations

Quick Steps

Apply an Animation

1. Click item.
2. Click Animations tab.
3. Click More Animations button.
4. Click animation at drop-down gallery.

Effects Options

Hint You can animate text, objects, graphics, SmartArt diagrams, charts, hyperlinks, and sound.

Preview

Applying and Removing Animations

Animate items such as text or objects in a slide to add visual interest to a slide show. PowerPoint includes a number of animations that can be applied to items in a slide and the animations can be modified to fit specific needs. For example, an animation can be applied and then customized to display items in a slide one at a time to help the audience focus on each topic or point as it is being presented. An animation can be applied and then customized to specify the direction from which items enter a slide and the rate of speed for the entrance. When considering what animations to apply to a presentation, try not to overwhelm the audience with too much animation. In general, the audience should remember the content of the slide show rather than the visual effects.

To animate an item, click the item, click the Animations tab, click the More Animations button in the Animation group, and then click an animation option at the drop-down gallery. Once an animation is applied, animation effects can be specified using options in the Effect Options button drop-down gallery. Some of the animation effect options may include the direction from which the item appears and whether bulleted text or SmartArt appear as one object, all at once, or by paragraph or object.

Use options in the Timing group on the Animations tab to specify when the animation starts on a slide, the duration of the animation, the delay between animations, and the order in which animations appear on the slide. To view the animation applied to a slide without running the slide show, click the Preview button on the Animations tab and the animation effect displays in the slide in the slide pane. When animation effects are applied to items in a slide, an animation icon displays below the slide number in the slide thumbnails pane.

When inserting or modifying an animation, PowerPoint automatically previews the animation in the slide in the slide pane. This preview feature can be turned off by clicking the Preview button arrow and then clicking *AutoPreview* at the drop-down list to remove the check mark.

Project 1a Applying Animations

Part 1 of 6

1. Open **MarketPres.pptx** and then save it with the name **7-MarketPres**.
2. Make sure Slide 1 is active and then apply animations to the title and subtitle by completing the following steps:
   a. Click in the title *DOUGLAS CONSULTING*.
   b. Click the Animations tab.
   c. Click the *Fade* animation in the Animation group.

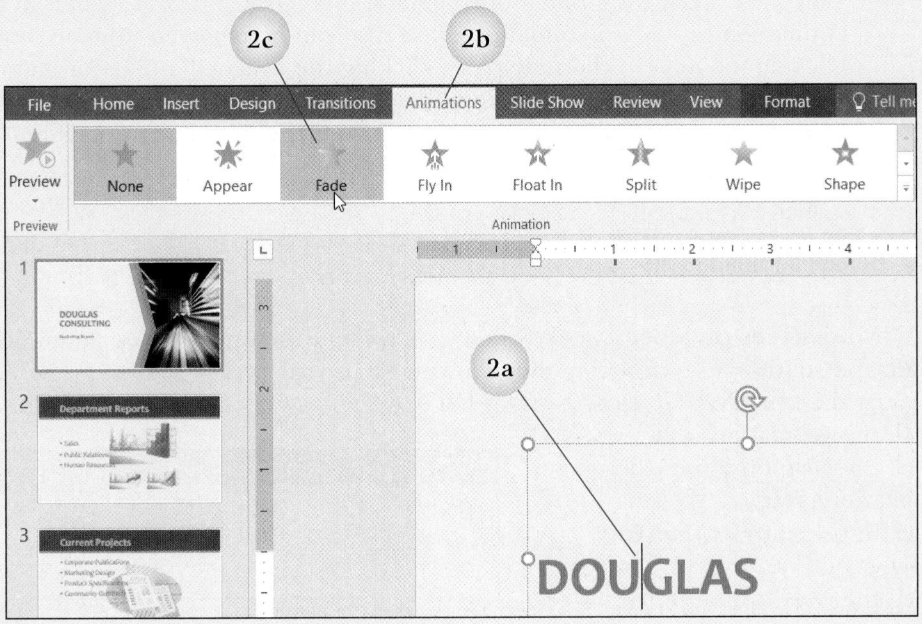

   d. Click in the subtitle *Marketing Report*.
   e. Click the *Fade* animation in the Animation group.
   f. Click the Preview button on the Animations tab to see the animation effects in the slide pane.
3. Apply animations to Slides 2 through 4 in Slide Master view by completing the following steps:
   a. Click the View tab and then click the Slide Master button in the Master Views group.
   b. Click the third slide master layout in the slide thumbnails pane (*Title and Content Layout*).
   c. Click in the text *Click to edit Master title style*.
   d. Click the Animations tab and then click the *Fly In* animation that displays in the Animation group.
   e. Click the Effects Options button in the Animation group and then click *From Top* at the drop-down gallery.
   f. Click in the bulleted text *Click to edit Master text styles*.
   g. Click the *Fly In* animation in the Animation group.
   h. Click the Slide Master tab and then click the Close Master View button.

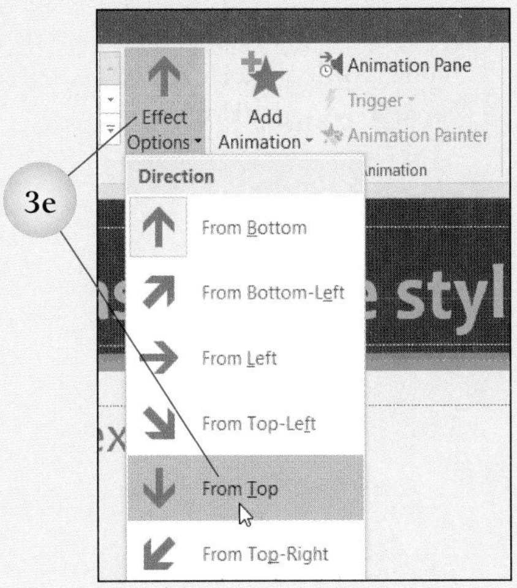

4. Make Slide 1 active and then run the slide show. Click the mouse button to advance items in slides and to move to the next slide. Notice how the bulleted text in Slides 2 through 4 displays one item at a time.
5. Save **7-MarketPres.pptx**.

Quick Steps

Remove an Animation

1. Click item.
2. Click Animations tab.
3. Click *None* option.

To remove an animation effect from an item, click the item in the slide in the slide pane, click the Animations tab, and then click the *None* option in the Animation group. An animation effect also can be removed from an item by clicking the item in the slide pane, clicking the assigned animation number icon, and then pressing the Delete key. To apply a different animation to an item, make sure to delete any existing animations first. If the first animation is not deleted, both animations will be assigned to the item.

Project 1b Removing Animations

Part 2 of 6

1. With **7-MarketPres.pptx** open, make Slide 1 active and then remove the animation from the title and subtitle by completing the following steps:
   a. Click in the title *DOUGLAS CONSULTING*.
   b. Click the Animations tab.
   c. Click the *None* option in the Animation group.
   d. Click in the subtitle *Marketing Report*.
   e. Click the *None* option in the Animation group.

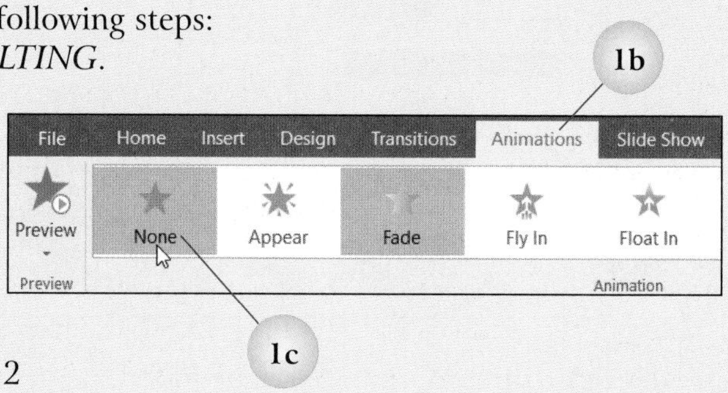

2. Remove the animation effects for Slides 2 through 4 by completing the following steps:
   a. Click the View tab and then click the Slide Master button in the Master Views group.
   b. Click the third slide master layout in the slide thumbnails pane (*Title and Content Layout*).
   c. Click in the text *Click to edit Master title style*.
   d. Click the Animations tab and then click the *None* option in the Animation group.
   e. Click in the text *Click to edit Master text styles*.
   f. Click the *None* option in the Animation group.
   g. Click the Slide Master tab and then click the Close Master View button.
3. Make Slide 1 active and then run the slide show.
4. Save **7-MarketPres.pptx**.

Tutorial

Modifying Animations

Quick Steps

Apply an Animation Effect

1. Click item.
2. Click Animations tab.
3. Click Add Animation button.
4. Click animation effect.

Add Animation

Quick Steps

Apply Effects with Animation Painter

1. Click item.
2. Apply animation effect.
3. Click item with animation effect.
4. Double-click Animation Painter button.
5. Click each item to apply the animation effect.
6. Click Animation Painter button to deactivate it.

Animation Painter

Applying Animation Effects

The Add Animation button in the Advanced Animation group on the Animations tab provides four types of animation effects that can be applied to an item. An effect can be applied that specifies how an item enters and exits the slide, an emphasis can be applied to an item, and a motion path can be created that will dictate the specific pattern for an item to move on, or even off, the slide.

To apply an entrance effect to an item, click the Add Animation button in the Advanced Animation group and then click the animation effect in the *Entrance* section of the drop-down gallery. Customize the entrance effect by clicking the Effect Options button in the Animation group and then clicking the specific entrance effect. Additional entrance effects are available at the Add Entrance Effect dialog box. Display this dialog box by clicking the Add Animation button and then clicking *More Entrance Effects* at the drop-down gallery. Complete similar steps to apply an exit effect and an emphasis effect. Display additional emphasis effects by clicking the Add Animation button and then clicking *More Emphasis Effects*. Display additional exit effects by clicking the Add Animation button and then clicking *More Exit Effects*.

Applying Animations with Animation Painter

An animation that has been applied to one item in a slide can also be applied to other items in the presentation with the Animation Painter. To use the Animation Painter, apply an animation to an item, position the insertion point anywhere in the animated item, and then double-click the Animation Painter button in the Advanced Animation group on the Animations tab. Using the mouse, select or click each additional item in the presentation that should have the same animation. After applying the animation to the items in the presentation, click the Animation Painter button to deactivate it. To apply animation to only one other item in a presentation, click the Animation Painter button once. The first time an item is selected or clicked, the animation is applied and the Animation Painter is deactivated.

Project 1c Applying Animation Effects — Part 3 of 6

1. With **7-MarketPres.pptx** open, apply an animation effect to the title and subtitle in Slide 1 by completing the following steps:
   a. Make Slide 1 active.
   b. Click in the title *DOUGLAS CONSULTING*.
   c. Click the Animations tab.
   d. Click the Add Animation button in the Advanced Animation group and then click the *Wipe* animation in the *Entrance* section of the drop-down gallery.

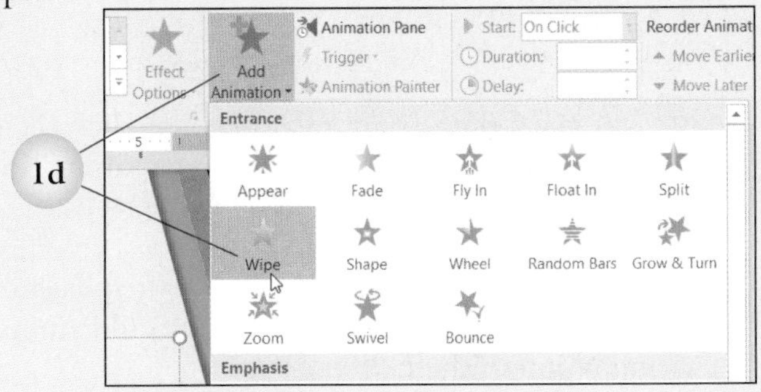

e. Click the Effect Options button in the Animation group and then click *From Top* at the drop-down gallery.
f. Click in the subtitle *Marketing Report*.
g. Click the Add Animation button and then click the *Zoom* animation in the *Entrance* section.

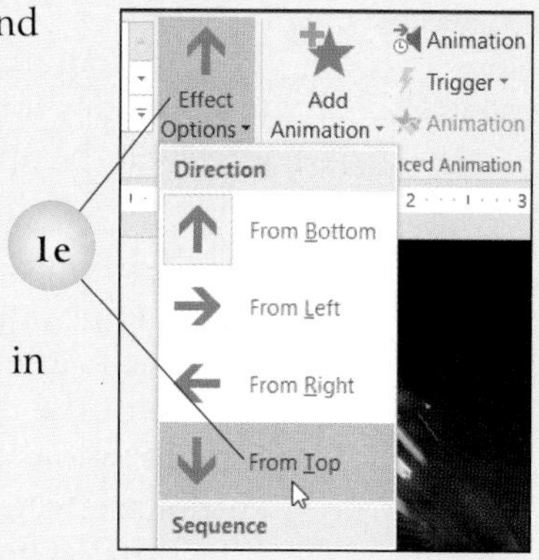

2. Apply an animation effect to the titles in Slides 2 through 4 by completing the following steps:
   a. Click the View tab and then click the Slide Master button in the Master Views group.
   b. Click the third slide master layout in the slide thumbnails pane (*Title and Content Layout*).
   c. Click in the text *Click to edit Master title style*.
   d. Click the Animations tab, click the Add Animation button in the Advanced Animation group, and then click the *More Emphasis Effects* option at the drop-down gallery.
   e. At the Add Emphasis Effect dialog box, click the *Grow With Color* option in the *Moderate* section.
   f. Click OK to close the dialog box.

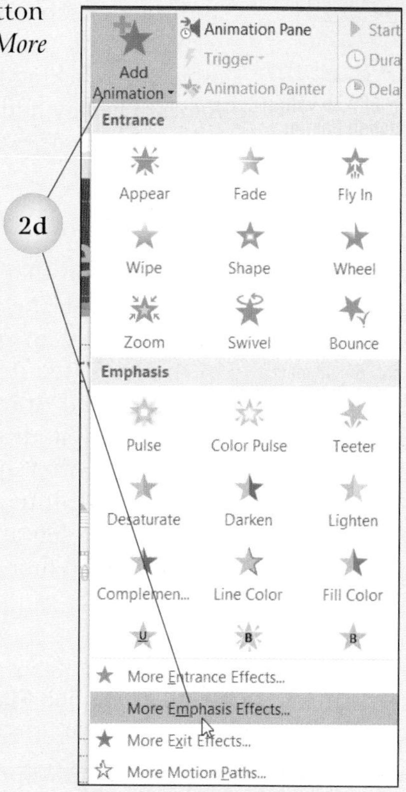

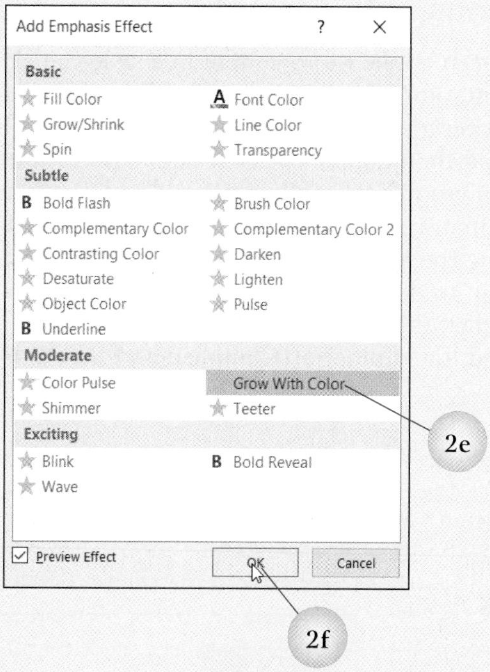

   g. Click the Slide Master tab and then click the Close Master View button.
3. Use the Animation Painter to apply an animation effect to the bulleted text in Slides 2 through 4 by completing the following steps:
   a. Make Slide 2 active.
   b. Click in the bulleted text to make the placeholder active.
   c. Click the Animations tab, click the Add Animation button, and then click the *Split* animation in the *Entrance* section.
   d. Click in the bulleted text.
   e. Double-click the Animation Painter button in the Advanced Animation group.
   f. Make Slide 3 active.

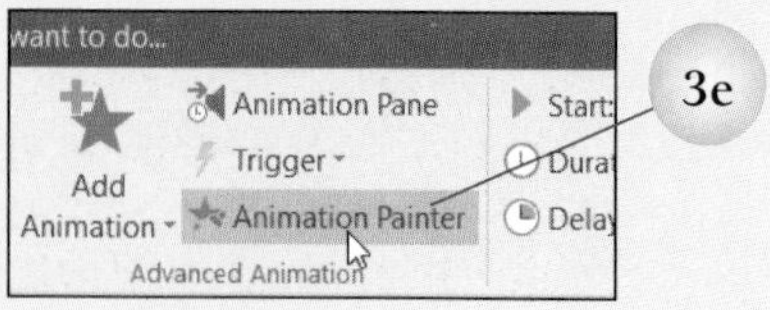

g. Click in the bulleted text. (The mouse pointer displays as an arrow with a paintbrush attached. The animations are applied to all four bulleted items.)
h. Make Slide 4 active and then click in the bulleted text.
i. Click the Animation Painter button to deactivate it.
4. Click the Preview button on the Animations tab to view the animation effects.
5. Run the slide show by clicking the Start From Beginning button on the Quick Access Toolbar. Click the mouse button to advance slide elements and to move to the next slide.
6. Save **7-MarketPres.pptx**.

Modifying Animation Effects

Start

Duration

Delay

An animation effect applied to an item can be modified with options in the Timing group. Use the *Start* option box drop-down list to specify when the item should be inserted in the slide. Generally, items display in a slide when the mouse button is clicked. Click the *Start* option box arrow and then click *With Previous* or *With Next* at the drop-down list to make the item appear in the slide with the previous or next item.

Use the *Duration* measurement box to specify the length of an animation. Click the *Duration* measurement box up arrow to increase the length of time the animation displays on the slide and click the down arrow to decrease the length of time. The duration time also can be changed by selecting the current time in the *Duration* measurement box and then typing a specific time.

Use the *Delay* measurement box to specify the number of seconds an animation delays before playing after the previous animation has finished playing. Click the *Delay* measurement box up arrow to increase the delay time and click the down arrow to decrease the time. The delay time can also be changed by selecting the current time in the *Delay* measurement box and then typing a specific time.

Quick Steps

Reorder an Animation Item
1. Click item in slide.
2. Click Move Earlier button or Move Later button.

Move Earlier

Move Later

Reordering Items

When an animation effect is applied to an item, an animation number displays next to the item in the slide in the slide pane. This number indicates the order in which the item will appear in the slide. When more than one item displays in the slide, the order can be changed with options in the *Reorder Animation* section of the Timing group on the Animations tab. Click the Move Earlier button to move an item before another item or click the Move Later button to move an item after another item.

Project 1d **Removing, Modifying, and Reordering Animation Effects** — Part 4 of 6

1. With **7-MarketPres.pptx** open, make Slide 1 active.
2. Modify the start setting for the animation effect you applied to the slide title by completing the following steps:
   a. Click in the title to activate the placeholder.

b. Click the *Start* option box arrow in the Timing group on the Animations tab.

c. Click *With Previous* at the drop-down list. (The title animation effect will begin as soon as the slide displays, without you having to click the mouse button. Notice that the number *1* located to the left of the item in the slide changes to a 0.)

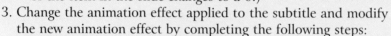

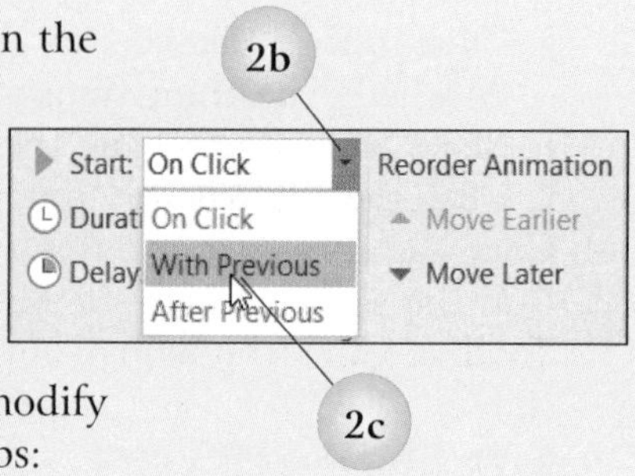

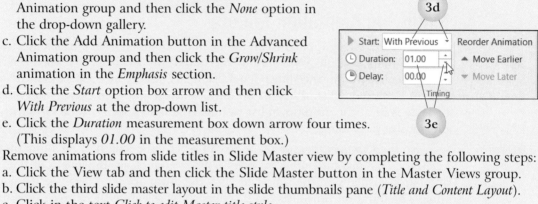

3. Change the animation effect applied to the subtitle and modify the new animation effect by completing the following steps:
   a. Click in the subtitle *Marketing Report*.
   b. Click the More Animations button in the Animation group and then click the *None* option in the drop-down gallery.
   c. Click the Add Animation button in the Advanced Animation group and then click the *Grow/Shrink* animation in the *Emphasis* section.
   d. Click the *Start* option box arrow and then click *With Previous* at the drop-down list.
   e. Click the *Duration* measurement box down arrow four times. (This displays *01.00* in the measurement box.)

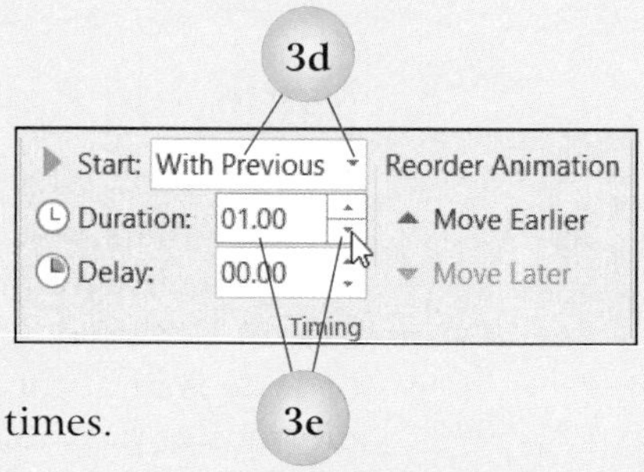

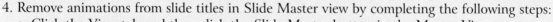

4. Remove animations from slide titles in Slide Master view by completing the following steps:
   a. Click the View tab and then click the Slide Master button in the Master Views group.
   b. Click the third slide master layout in the slide thumbnails pane (*Title and Content Layout*).
   c. Click in the text *Click to edit Master title style*.
   d. Click the Animations tab.
   e. Click the More Animations button in the Animation group and then click the *None* option.
   f. Click the Slide Master tab and then click the Close Master View button.
5. Remove animations from the bulleted text in Slides 2 through 4 by completing the following steps:
   a. Make Slide 2 active.
   b. Click in the bulleted text.
   c. Click the Animations tab and then click the *None* option in the Animation group.
   d. Make Slide 3 active, click in the bulleted text, and then click the *None* option in the Animation group.
   e. Make Slide 4 active, click in the bulleted text, and then click the *None* option in the Animation group.
6. Make Slide 2 active and then apply and customize animation effects by completing the following steps:
   a. Click in the title *Department Reports*.
   b. Click the Add Animation button in the Advanced Animation group and then click the *More Entrance Effects* option at the drop-down gallery.
   c. At the Add Entrance Effect dialog box, scroll down the list box and then click *Spiral In* in the *Exciting* section.
   d. Click OK to close the dialog box.

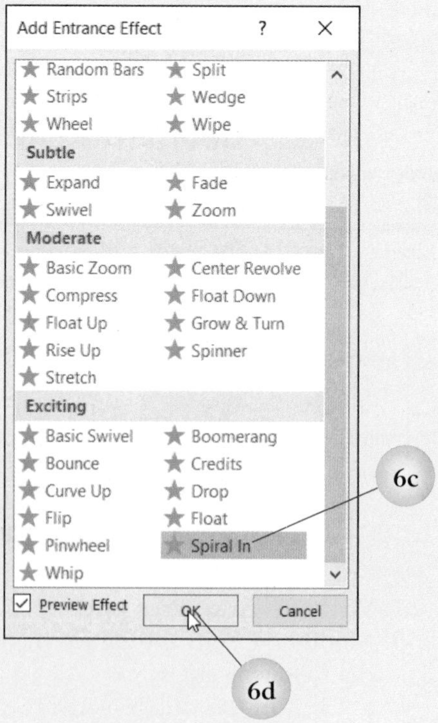

e. Click the bulleted text.
f. Click the Add Animation button and then click the *Zoom* animation in the *Entrance* section.
g. Click the image in the slide.
h. Click the Add Animation button and then click the *Zoom* animation in the *Entrance* section.

7. Click the Preview button at the left side of the Animations tab to view the animation effects.
8. After viewing the animation effects, you decide that you want the image to animate before the bulleted text and you want the animation effects to begin with the previous animation (instead of with a mouse click). With Slide 2 active, complete the following steps:
   a. Click the image. (The number 5 will display outside the upper left corner of the image placeholder because the image is the fifth item to enter the slide.)
   b. Click the Move Earlier button in the *Reorder Animation* section of the Timing group. (The number displayed to the left of the image changes to *2* because you moved the image animation before the three bulleted items.)
   c. Click the *Start* option box arrow in the Timing group and then click *With Previous* at the drop-down list.

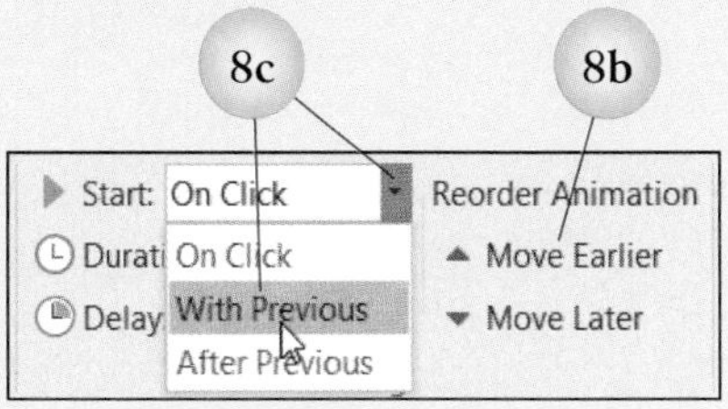

   d. Click in the title *Department Reports*.
   e. Click the *Start* option box arrow in the Timing group and then click *With Previous* at the drop-down list.
9. Make Slide 3 active and then apply the same animation effects you applied in Slide 2. (Do this by completing steps similar to those in Steps 6a through 6h and Steps 8a through 8e.)
10. Make Slide 4 active and then apply the same animation effects you applied to Slide 2. (Do this by completing steps similar to those in Steps 6a through 6f and Steps 8d through 8e.)
11. Make Slide 1 active and then run the slide show.
12. Save **7-MarketPres.pptx**.

Customizing Animation Effects at the Animation Pane

Quick Steps

Reorder Animation Items

1. Click item in Animation Pane.
2. Click Move Earlier button or Move Later button.

Remove an Animation Effect

1. Click item in Animation Pane.
2. Click down arrow.
3. Click *Remove*.

Animation Pane

The Animation Pane provides options for customizing and modifying animation effects. Display the Animation Pane, shown in Figure 7.1, by clicking the Animation Pane button in the Advanced Animation group on the Animations tab. When an animation is applied to an item, the item name or description displays in the Animation Pane. Hover the mouse pointer over an item and a description of the animation effect applied to the item displays in a box below the item. Click the down arrow at the right side of an item in the Animation Pane and a drop-down list displays with options for customizing or removing the animation effect.

When an effect is applied to an item, the item name and/or description displays in the Animation Pane preceded by a number. This number indicates the order in which the item will appear in the slide. When more than one item displays in the Animation Pane, the order of an item can be changed by clicking the item and then clicking the Move Earlier or the Move Later buttons at the top of the Animation Pane.

Figure 7.1 Animation Pane

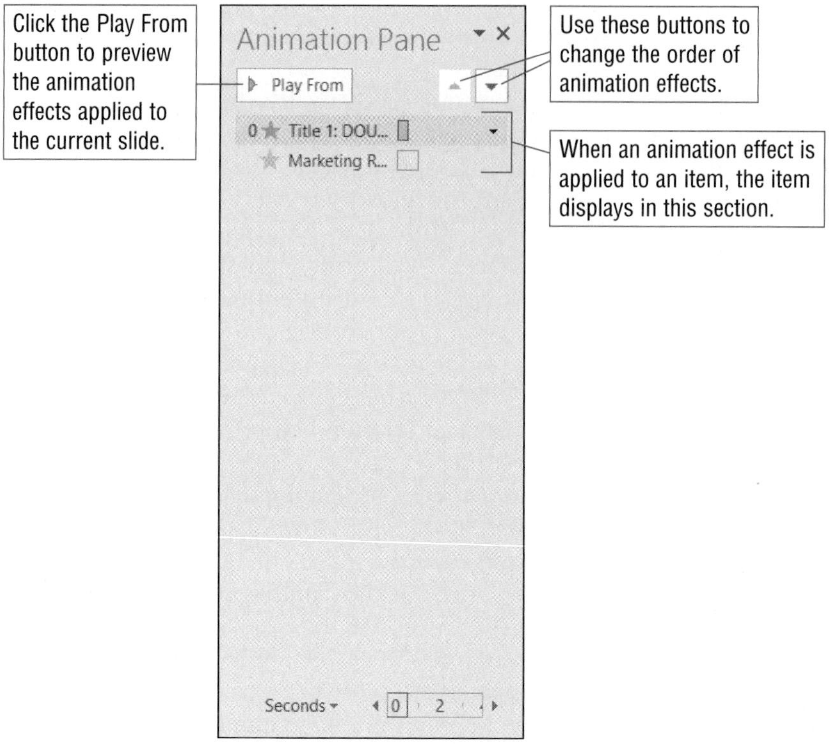
Click the Play From button to preview the animation effects applied to the current slide.
Animation Pane
Play From
Title 1: DOU...
Marketing R...
Seconds
0
2
Use these buttons to change the order of animation effects.
When an animation effect is applied to an item, the item displays in this section.

All animation effects applied to a slide can be played by clicking the Play All button at the top of the pane. (The name of the button varies depending on the contents of the Animation Pane and what is selected in the pane.) The animation effects display in the slide in the slide pane and a time indicator displays along the bottom of the Animation Pane with a vertical line indicating the progression of time (in seconds). Play only the selected animation effect in the Animation Pane by clicking the animation effect in the pane and then clicking the Play From button at the top of the pane.

Project 1e Removing, Customizing, and Reordering Animation Effects in the Animation Pane

Part 5 of 6

1. With **7-MarketPres.pptx** open, make Slide 1 active.
2. Click in the title *DOUGLAS CONSULTING*, click the Animations tab, and then click the *None* option in the Animation group.
3. With the title placeholder selected, click the Add Animation button in the Advanced Animation group and then click the *Grow & Turn* animation in the *Entrance* section.
4. Click the *Duration* measurement box down arrow two times. (This displays *00.50* in the measurement box.)
5. Click in the subtitle *Marketing Report*, click the More Animations button in the Animation group, and then click the *None* option.
6. With the subtitle placeholder selected, click the Add Animation button in the Advanced Animation group and then click the *Grow & Turn* animation in the *Entrance* section.
7. Click the *Duration* measurement box down arrow two times. (This displays *00.50* in the measurement box.)

8. Modify the start setting for the slide title animation effect in the Animation Pane by completing the following steps:
   a. Click the Animation Pane button in the Advanced Animation group on the Animations tab. (This displays the Animation Pane at the right side of the screen.)
   b. Click the Title 1 item in the Animation Pane.
   c. Click the down arrow at the right side of the item and then click *Start With Previous* at the drop-down list.

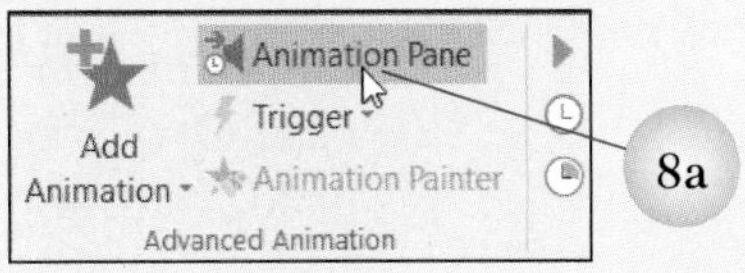

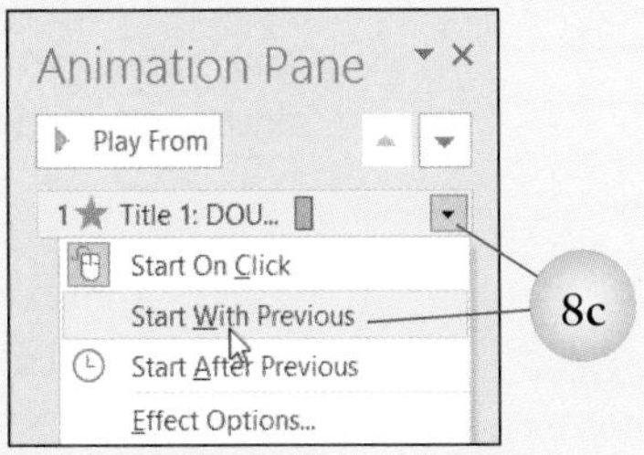

9. Remove animations from slides using the Animation Pane by completing the following steps:
   a. Make Slide 2 active.
   b. Click the Picture 3 item in the Animation Pane.
   c. Click the down arrow at the right side of the item and then click *Remove* at the drop-down list.
   d. Click the image in the slide pane, click the Add Animation button in the Advanced Animation group, and then click the *Pulse* animation in the *Emphasis* section.

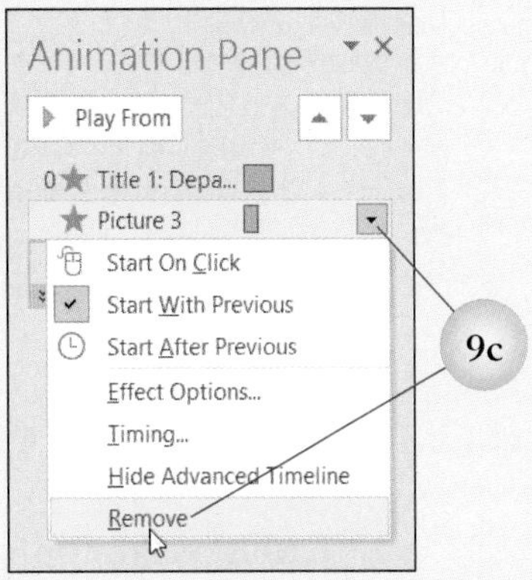

10. Make Slide 3 active and then complete steps similar to those in Steps 9b through 9d to remove the animation effect from the image and add the *Pulse* emphasis animation effect.
11. With the Picture 3 image selected in the Animation Pane, click the Play From button at the top of the pane to view the animation effect applied to the image.
12. Play all animation effects applied to the slide by clicking anywhere in the blank area below the animation effects in the Animation Pane (this deselects the Picture 3 animation effect) and then click the Play All button (previously the Play From button) at the top of the pane.

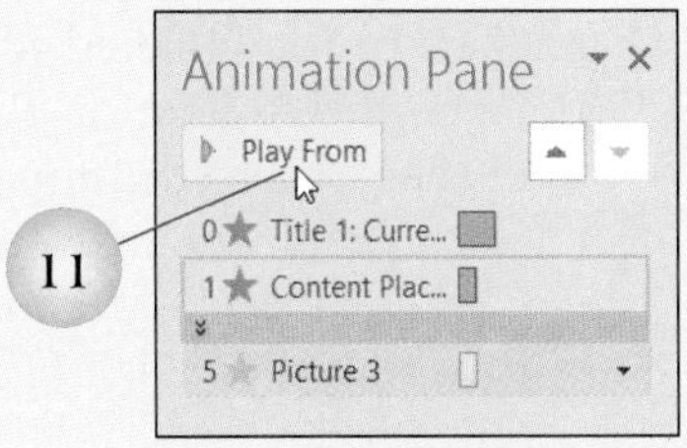

13. After viewing the animation effect, you decide that you want the image to animate before the title and bulleted text and you want the animation effect to begin with the previous animation. With Slide 3 active, complete the following steps:
   a. Click the Picture 3 item in the Animation Pane.
   b. Click the up arrow at the top of the Animation pane two times. (This moves the Picture 3 item above the Title 1 and the Content Placeholder items.)
   c. Click the down arrow at the right side of the Picture 3 item and then click *Start With Previous* at the drop-down list.

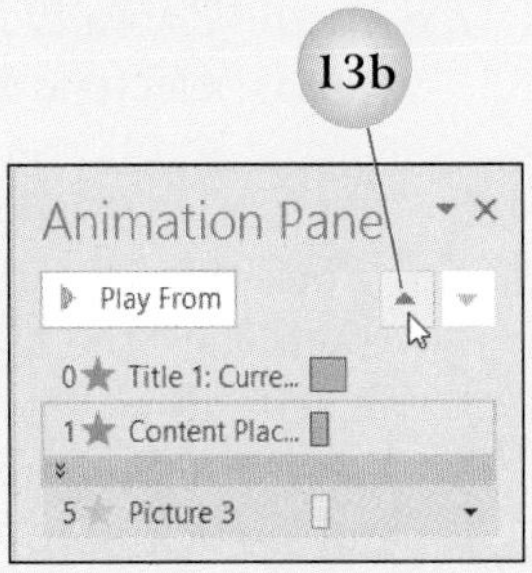

14. Reorder animation effects in Slide 2 to match the changes made to Slide 3.
15. Make Slide 1 active and then run the slide show.
16. Close the Animation Pane.
17. Save **7-MarketPres.pptx**.

Applying Sound to Animations

Enhance an animation by adding a sound to the animation. To apply a sound, click the Animation Pane button to display the Animation Pane, click the animated item in the Animation Pane, click the down arrow at the right side of the item, and then click *Effect Options* at the drop-down list. At the effect options dialog box (the name of the dialog box varies depending on the animation applied) with the Effect tab selected, click the down arrow at the right side of the *Sound* option box and then click a sound at the drop-down list. Sound can also be added to an animation by clicking the animated item in the slide in the slide pane, clicking the Animation group dialog box launcher, and then choosing the sound effect at the dialog box that displays.

Applying a Build

Hint You can group text (in a bulleted text placeholder) at the effect options dialog box by first, second, third, fourth, or fifth levels.

In Project 1a, a build was applied to bulleted text in a slide. A build displays important points on a slide one point at a time, keeping the audience's attention focused on the current point. A build can be further customized by causing a previous point to dim when the next point displays. To customize a build, click the Animation Pane button to display the Animation Pane, click the bulleted item in the Animation Pane, click the down arrow at the right side of the item, and then click *Effect Options* at the drop-down list. At the effect options dialog box (the name of the dialog box will vary) with the Effect tab selected, choose a color option with the *After animation* option box.

Project 1f Applying Sound and a Build to Animations — Part 6 of 6

1. With **7-MarketPres.pptx** open, make Slide 2 active and then apply sound and a build to the bulleted text by completing the following steps:
   a. Click in the bulleted text.
   b. Open the Animation Pane by clicking the Animation Pane button in the Advanced Animation group on the Animations tab.
   c. Click the down arrow at the right side of the Content Placeholder item in the Animation Pane and then click *Effect Options* at the drop-down list.
   d. At the Zoom dialog box, make sure the Effect tab is selected, click the *Sound* option box arrow, scroll down the list box, and then click the *Chime* option.
   e. Click the *After animation* option box arrow and then click the light gray color (last option).
   f. Click OK to close the dialog box.

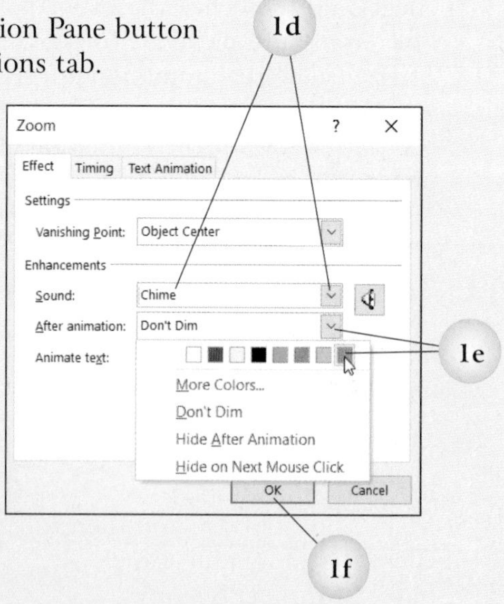

2. Click in the bulleted text in the slide.
3. Double-click the Animation Painter button.
4. Display Slide 3 and then click in the bulleted text.
5. Display Slide 4 and then click in the bulleted text.
6. Click the Animation Painter button to deactivate it.
7. Close the Animation Pane.
8. Make Slide 1 active and then run the slide show.
9. Save and then close **7-MarketPres.pptx**.

Project 2 Apply Custom Animation Effects to Elements in Slides in an Online Learning Presentation

6 Parts

You will open an online learning presentation and then apply animation effects to shapes, an image, elements in SmartArt graphics, and elements in a chart. You will also draw a motion path in a slide.

Preview Finished Project

Animating Shapes and Images

Animate individual shapes or objects, such as images, in a slide in the same way a title or text or objects in a content placeholder are animated. More than one shape can be selected and then the same animation effects can be applied to the shapes. To select more than one shape, click the first shape, press and hold down the Shift key, click any additional shapes, and then release the Shift key.

Project 2a Animating Shapes and an Image

Part 1 of 6

1. Open **OLLearn.pptx** and then save it with the name **7-OLLearn**.
2. Make Slide 8 active (this slide contains one large object with three smaller objects hidden behind it) and then animate objects and apply exit effects by completing the following steps:
   a. Click the Animations tab and then click the Animation Pane button in the Advanced Animation group.
   b. Click the large green shape in the slide.
   c. Click the Add Animation button in the Advanced Animation group and then click the *More Exit Effects* option.
   d. At the Add Exit Effect dialog box, click the *Spiral Out* option in the *Exciting* section. (You will need to scroll down the list to display this option.) Watch the animation effect in the slide and then click OK.

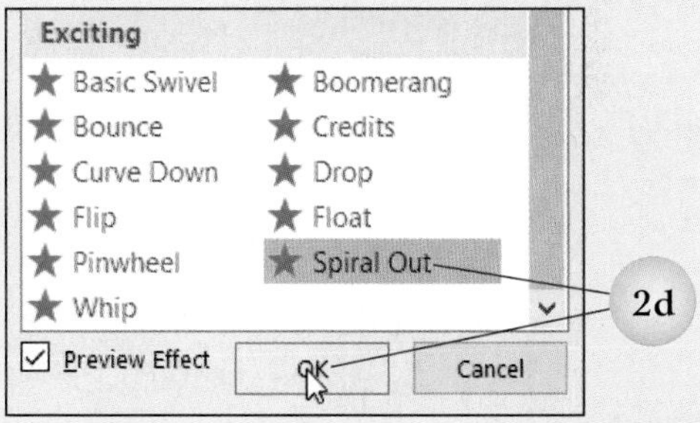

   e. Click the large green shape to select it and then drag it up the slide to display a portion of the three shapes behind.
   f. Click the small shape at the left, click the Add Animation button, and then click the *More Entrance Effects* option.
   g. At the Add Entrance Effect dialog box, click *Spinner* in the *Moderate* section, and then click OK.

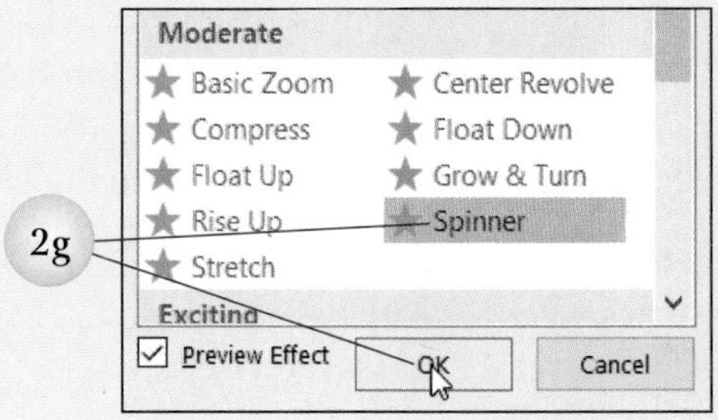

   h. Select the middle shape, press and hold down the Shift key, click the shape at the right, and then release the Shift key. (This selects both shapes.)
   i. Click the Add Animation button and then click the *More Entrance Effects* option.

j. At the Add Entrance Effect dialog box, click *Spinner* in the *Moderate* section and then click OK. (Notice that the two objects are numbered *3* in the Animation Pane and are set to enter the slide at the same time. You will change this in the next step.)
k. Click the small shape at the right, click the down arrow at the right of the *Start* option box in the Timing group, and then click *On Click* at the drop-down list.
l. Apply emphasis to the middle shape by clicking the middle shape, clicking the Add Animation button, and then clicking the *Grow/Shrink* option in the *Emphasis* section of the drop-down gallery.
m. Click the large green shape to select it and then reposition it over the three smaller shapes.
n. Click the Preview button to play the animation effects in the slide.

3. Make Slide 9 active and apply and customize animation effects and change animation order by completing the following steps:
   a. Click anywhere in the text *Online learning continues to evolve!* (this selects the text box), click the Add Animation button, and then click *Grow & Turn* in the *Entrance* section.
   b. Click anywhere in the text *Stay tuned!* (this selects the text box), click the Add Animation button, and then click the *Swivel* option in the *Entrance* section.
   c. Click the image to select it.
   d. Click the Add Animation button and then click the *Spin* animation in the *Emphasis* section.
   e. Click the Effect Options button in the Animation group and then click *Two Spins* at the drop-down gallery.
   f. Click the *Duration* measurement box down arrow until *01.00* displays.
   g. Click the Move Earlier button in the Timing group. This moves the image item in the list box above the *Stay tuned!* text box item.
   h. Click the Preview button to play the animation effects in the slide.
4. Save **7-OLLearn.pptx**.

3e

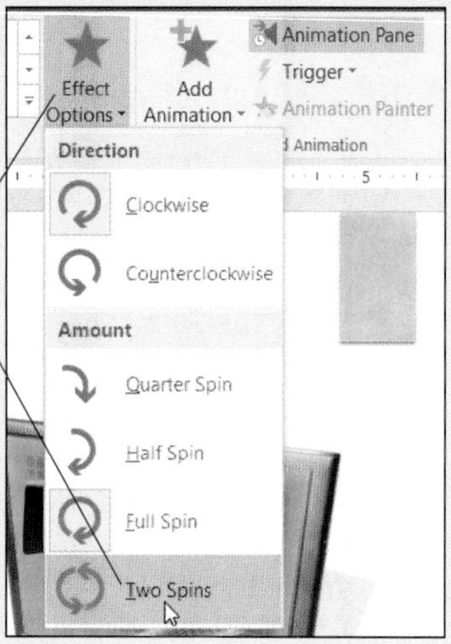

Animating a SmartArt Graphic

Quick Steps

Animate a SmartArt Graphic

1. Click SmartArt graphic.
2. Apply animation effect.
3. Click Effect Options button.
4. Specify sequence.

Animation effects can be applied to a SmartArt graphic and then customized to specify whether the entire SmartArt graphic displays at once or the individual elements in the SmartArt graphic display one at a time. Specify a sequence for displaying elements in a SmartArt graphic with the Effect Options button in the Animation group.

When an animation effect is applied to a SmartArt graphic, animations can be applied to individual elements in the graphic. To do this, click the Effect Options button and then click the *One by One* option at the drop-down list. Display the Animation Pane and then expand the list of SmartArt graphic objects by clicking the small double arrows that display in a gray shaded box below the item in the Animation Pane. Click an individual item in the Animation Pane and then click an animation in the Animation group.

Project 2b **Animating SmartArt** Part 2 of 6

1. With **7-OLLearn.pptx** open, make Slide 4 active and then animate objects in the SmartArt graphic by completing the following steps:
   a. Click the shape in the SmartArt graphic containing the word *Convenient*. (Make sure white sizing handles display around the shape. White sizing handles will also display around the entire SmartArt graphic.)
   b. With the Animations tab active, click the *Float In* animation in the Animation group.
   c. Click the Effect Options button in the Animation group and then click *One by One* at the drop-down gallery. (This will allow you to apply different effects to the objects in the SmartArt graphic.)
   d. Make sure the Animation Pane displays. (If not, click the Animation Pane button in the Advanced Animation group.)
   e. Expand the list of SmartArt graphic objects in the Animation Pane by clicking the small double arrows that display in a gray shaded box below the Content Placeholder item. (This expands the list to display four items.)

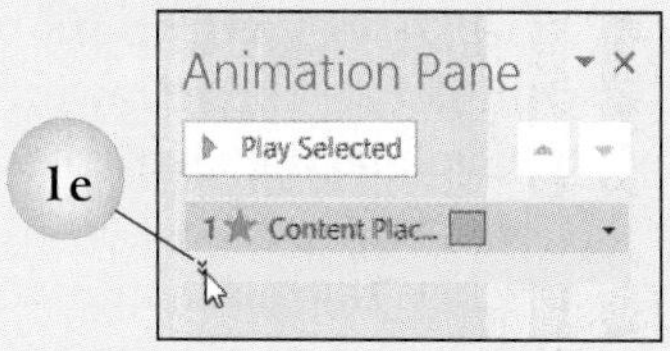

   f. Click the item in the Animation Pane that begins with the number *2*.
   g. Click the More Animations button in the Animation group and then click the *Grow & Turn* animation in the *Entrance* section.
   h. Click the item in the Animation Pane that begins with the number *4*.
   i. Click the More Animations button in the Animation group and then click the *Grow & Turn* animation in the *Entrance* section.
2. Click the Preview button on the Animations tab to view the animation effects applied to the SmartArt graphic objects.
3. Make Slide 6 active and then apply animation effects by completing the following steps:
   a. Click the shape in the SmartArt graphic containing the text *Multi-Media*. (Make sure white sizing handles display around the shape. White sizing handles will also display around the entire SmartArt graphic.)
   b. Click the Add Animation button and then click the *More Entrance Effects* option.
   c. At the Add Entrance Effect dialog box, click the *Circle* option in the *Basic* section.
   d. Click OK to close the dialog box.
   e. Click the Effect Options button in the Animation group and then click *Out* in the *Direction* section of the drop-down list.
   f. Click the Effect Options button again and then click *One by One* in the *Sequence* section of the drop-down list.
   g. Click the *Duration* measurement box down arrow until *00.50* displays.
4. Click the Play Selected button at the top of the Animation Pane to view the animation effects applied to the SmartArt graphic objects.
5. Save **7-OLLearn.pptx**.

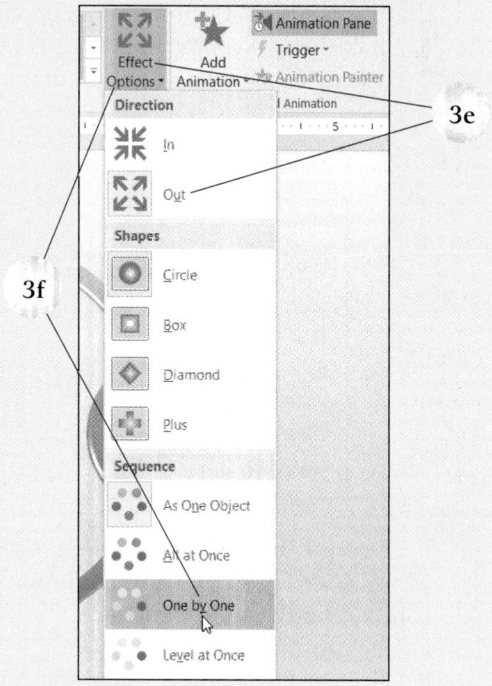

Animating a Chart

Like a SmartArt graphic, a chart or elements in a chart can be animated. Displaying data in a chart may have a more dramatic effect if the chart is animated. Bringing in one element at a time also allows the presenter to discuss each piece of the data as it displays. How the chart is animated in the slide and how the chart elements are grouped can be specified. For example, group chart elements on one object or by series or category. Apply animation to elements in a chart in a manner similar to animating elements in a SmartArt graphic.

Project 2c **Animating Elements in a Chart** — Part 3 of 6

1. With **7-OLLearn.pptx** open, make Slide 3 active and then animate chart elements by completing the following steps:
   a. Click in the chart placeholder to select the chart. (Make sure you do not have a chart element selected and that the Animations tab is active.)
   b. Click the Add Animation button and then click the *More Entrance Effects* option.
   c. At the Add Entrance Effect dialog box, click the *Dissolve In* option in the *Basic* section.
   d. Click OK to close the dialog box.
   e. Make sure the Animation Pane displays and then click the down arrow at the right side of the Content Placeholder item in the list box.
   f. At the drop-down list that displays, click *Effect Options*.
   g. At the Dissolve In dialog box, click the *Sound* option box arrow, scroll down the drop-down list, and then click the *Click* option.
   h. Click the Timing tab.
   i. Click the *Duration* option box arrow and then click *1 seconds (Fast)* at the drop-down list.
   j. Click the Chart Animation tab.
   k. Click the *Group chart* option box arrow and then click *By Category* at the drop-down list.

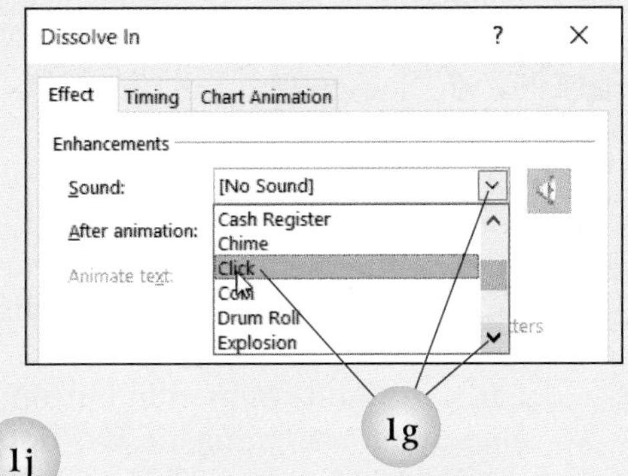

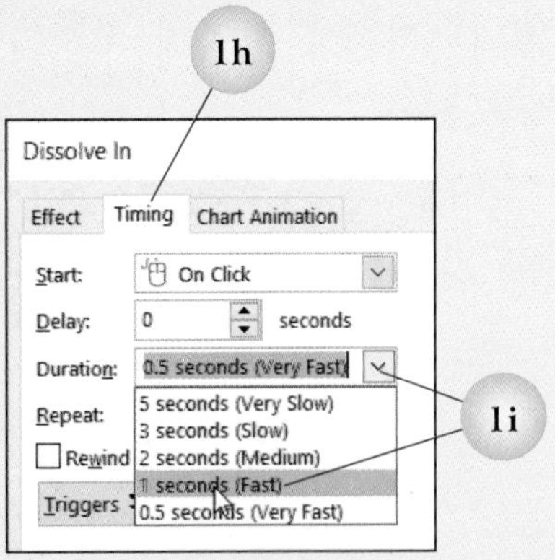

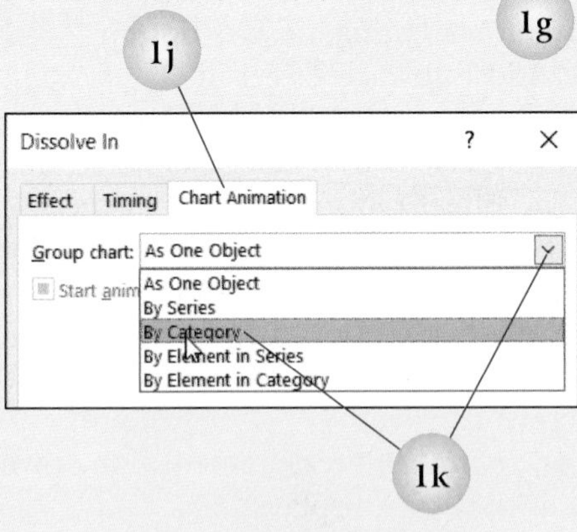

   l. Click OK to close the dialog box.
2. Make Slide 7 active and then apply a build animation effect to the bulleted text by completing the following steps:
   a. Click in the bulleted text.
   b. Click the *Fly In* animation in the Animation group on the Animations tab.

c. Click the Effect Options button and then click *From Right* at the drop-down gallery.
d. Make sure the Animation Pane displays, click the down arrow at the right side of the Content Placeholder item in the pane, and then click *Effect Options* at the drop-down list.
e. At the Fly In dialog box, make sure the Effect tab is selected, click the *After animation* option box arrow, and then click the light green color (second from the right).
f. Click OK to close the dialog box.

3. Save **7-OLLearn.pptx**.

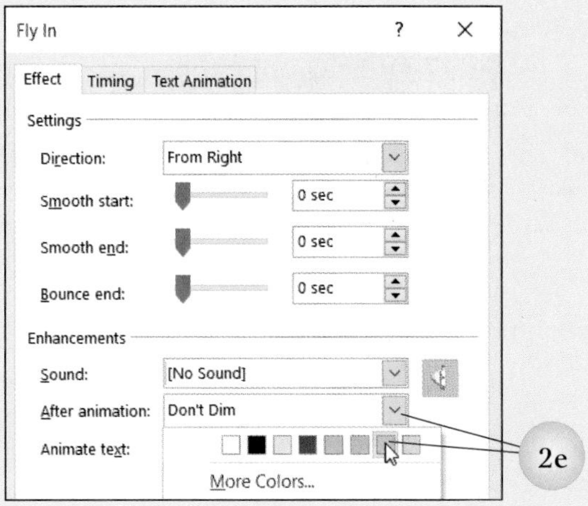

Creating a Motion Path

Quick Steps

Insert a Motion Path
1. Click item in slide.
2. Click Animations tab.
3. Click Add Animation button.
4. Click path in *Motion Paths* section.

Draw a Motion Path
1. Click item in slide.
2. Click Animations tab.
3. Click Add Animation button.
4. Click *Custom Path* in *Motion Paths* section.
5. Drag in slide to create path.
6. Double-click mouse button.

Use options in the *Motion Paths* section of the Add Animation button drop-down gallery to specify a motion path. A motion path is a path created for an object that specifies the movements of the object when running the slide show. Click the Add Animation button in the Advanced Animation group and a gallery of options for drawing a motion path in a specific direction can be found in the *Motion Paths* section. For example, to move an item left in a line when running the slide show, click the Add Animation button in the Advanced Animation group and then click the *Lines* option in the *Motion Paths* section of the drop-down gallery. Click the Effect Options button in the Animation group and then click *Left* at the drop-down gallery. A motion path can also be applied by clicking the Add Animation button, clicking *More Motion Paths* at the drop-down gallery, and then clicking the motion path at the Add Motion Path dialog box.

To draw a motion path freehand, select the object in the slide, click the Add Animation button, and then click the *Custom Path* option in the *Motion Paths* section of the drop-down gallery. Using the mouse, drag in the slide to create the path. When the path is completed, double-click the mouse button.

Project 2d Drawing a Motion Path Part 4 of 6

1. With **7-OLLearn.pptx** open, make Slide 1 active and then apply a motion path to the image by completing the following steps:
   a. Click the image.
   b. Click the Add Animation button and then click the *More Motion Paths* option.
   c. At the Add Motion Path dialog box, scroll down the list box and then click the *Spiral Right* option in the *Lines Curves* section.
   d. Click OK to close the dialog box.
   e. Notice that a spiral line object displays in the slide and a dimmed copy of the image is selected. Hover the mouse pointer over the spiral line until the mouse pointer turns into an arrow with a four-headed arrow attached and then drag the spiral line and dimmed copy of the image so they are positioned over the original image (see the image at the right).

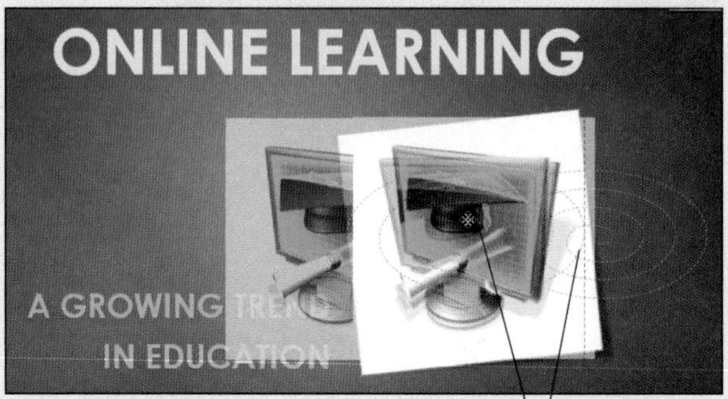

1e

   f. Click the *Start* option box arrow in the Timing group and then click *With Previous* at the drop-down list.
   g. Click the *Duration* measurement box up arrow in the Timing group until *03.00* displays in the measurement box.
   h. Click the *Delay* measurement box up arrow in the Timing group until *01.00* displays in the measurement box.
   i. Click outside the image to deselect it.
2. Make Slide 5 active and then animate the star on the map by completing the following steps:
   a. Click the star object in the slide below the heading *North America*.
   b. Click the Add Animation button, scroll down the drop-down gallery, and then click the *Custom Path* option in the *Motion Paths* section.
   c. Position the mouse pointer (displays as crosshairs) on the star, click and hold down the left mouse button, drag a path through each of the five locations on the map ending back in the original location in the star object, release the mouse button, and then double-click the mouse button.

2a

3. Run the slide show and click the mouse to advance slides and elements on slides as needed.
4. Save **7-OLLearn.pptx**.

Applying a Trigger

Use the Trigger button in the Advanced Animation group to make an animation effect occur by clicking an item on the slide during a slide show. A trigger creates a link between two items and provides additional information about that item. For example, a trigger can be applied to a bulleted item to cause another item, such as a picture or chart, to appear. When running the slide show, hover the mouse pointer

Quick Steps

Apply a Trigger

1. Click object in slide.
2. Click Animations tab.
3. Click Trigger button.
4. Point to *On Click of* and then click trigger item.

Trigger

over the item containing the trigger until the mouse pointer displays as a hand and then click the mouse button to display the trigger item.

The advantage to applying a trigger to an item is that the presenter can control whether or not the item displays when running the slide show. For example, suppose a presentation contains product sales information and the presenter wants to provide additional specific sales data to one group but not another. When presenting to the group that should view the additional sales data, the trigger can be clicked to display the data. When presenting to the other group, the trigger is not clicked, and the sales data remains hidden.

To insert a trigger, apply an animation effect to both items, display the Animation Pane, and then click the item that will become the trigger. Click the Trigger button in the Advanced Animation group, point to *On Click of*, and then click the item to be triggered at the side menu.

Project 2e Inserting Triggers

Part 5 of 6

1. With **7-OLLearn.pptx** open, make Slide 2 active.
2. Apply animation effects to the text and charts by completing the following steps:
   a. Click in the bulleted text.
   b. Click the Animations tab.
   c. Click the *Split* animation in the Animation group.
   d. Select the pie chart at the left. (To do this, click in the chart and then click within the chart border but not on a specific item in the chart. Make sure the chart is selected and not an individual chart element.)
   e. Click the *Split* animation in the Animation group.
   f. Select the middle pie chart and then click the *Split* animation. (Make sure you select the chart and not a chart element.)
   g. Select the pie chart at the right and then click the *Split* animation. (Make sure you select the chart and not a chart element.)
3. Make sure the Animation Pane displays.
4. Apply a trigger to the first bulleted item that, when clicked, will display the chart at the left by completing the following steps:
   a. Click the *Chart 5* item in the Animation Pane.
   b. Click the Trigger button in the Advanced Animation group, point to *On Click of*, and then click *Content Placeholder 2* at the side menu.
   c. Click the *Chart 6* item in the Animation Pane, click the Trigger button, point to *On Click of*, and then click *Content Placeholder 2* at the side menu.
   d. Click the *Chart 7* item in the Animation Pane, click the Trigger button, point to *On Click of*, and then click *Content Placeholder 2* at the side menu.

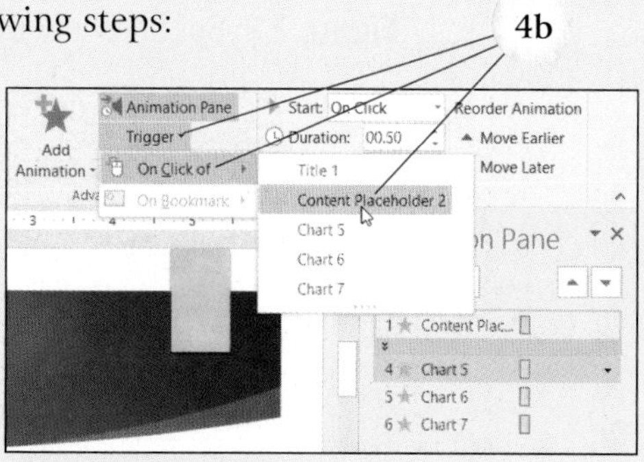

5. Close the Animation Pane.
6. Run the slide show by completing the following steps:
   a. Run the slide show from the beginning and when you get to Slide 2, click the mouse button until the first bulleted item displays (the item that begins with *Traditional*).

Check Your Work

b. Hover your mouse pointer over the bulleted text until the pointer turns into a hand and then click the left mouse button. (This displays the first chart.)
c. Position the mouse pointer anywhere in the white background of the slide and then click the left mouse button to display the second bulleted item (the item that begins with *Hybrid*).

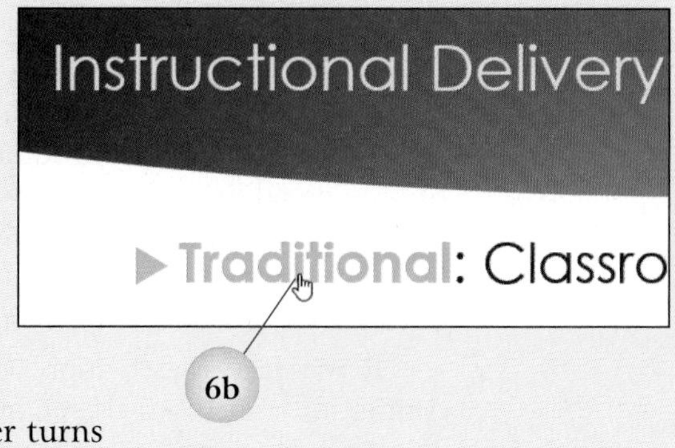

d. Hover your mouse pointer over the text in the second bulleted item until the pointer turns into a hand and then click the left mouse button. (This displays the middle chart.)
e. Position the mouse pointer anywhere in the white background of the slide and then click the left mouse button to display the third bulleted item (the item that begins with *Internet*).
f. Hover your mouse pointer over the text in the third bulleted item until the pointer turns into a hand and then click the left mouse button. (This displays the third chart.)
g. Continue running the remaining slides in the slide show.

7. Save **7-OLLearn.pptx**.
8. Print the presentation as a handout with all nine slides displayed horizontally on the page.

Setting Up a Slide Show

Set Up Slide Show

Control how the presentation displays with options at the Set Up Show dialog box, shown in Figure 7.2. With options at this dialog box, set slide presentation options, specify how slides advance, and set screen resolution. Display the Set Up Show dialog box by clicking the Slide Show tab and then clicking the Set Up Slide Show button in the Set Up group.

Figure 7.2 Set Up Show Dialog Box

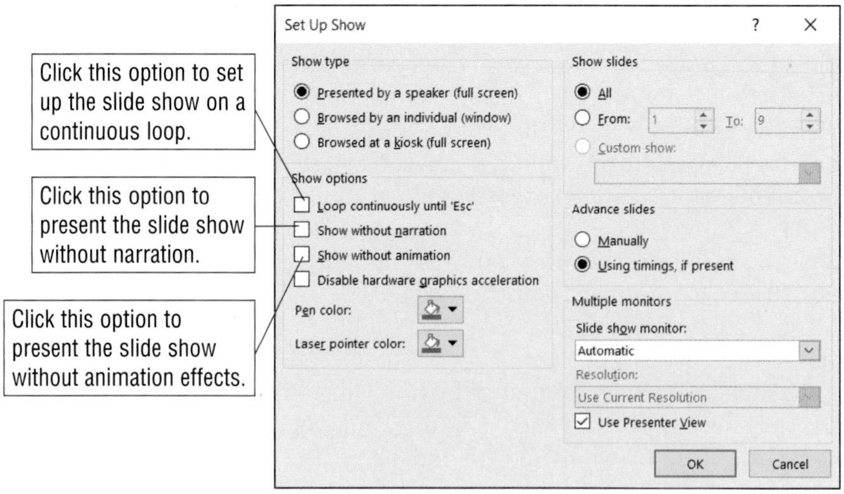

Quick Steps

Run a Slide Show without Animation

1. Click Slide Show tab.
2. Click Set Up Slide Show button.
3. Click *Show without animation.*
4. Click OK.

Running a Slide Show without Animation

A slide show can be run without the animations. To do this, display the Set Up Show dialog box, click the *Show without animation* check box to insert a check mark, and then click OK. Changes made to the Set Up Show dialog box are saved with the presentation.

Project 2f Running a Slide Show without Animation — Part 6 of 6

1. With **7-OLLearn.pptx** open, specify that you want to run the slide show without animation by completing the following steps:
   a. Click the Slide Show tab.
   b. Click the Set Up Slide Show button in the Set Up group.
   c. At the Set Up Show dialog box, click the *Show without animation* check box to insert a check mark.
   d. Click OK to close the dialog box.

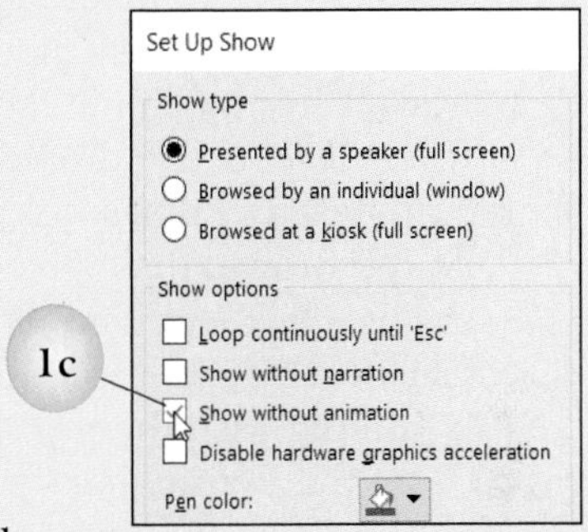

2. Run the slide show to see that the animation effects do not play.
3. Specify that you want the slide show to run with animations by completing the following steps:
   a. Click the Set Up Slide Show button on the Slide Show tab.
   b. At the Set Up Show dialog box, click the *Show without animation* check box to remove the check mark and then click OK.
4. Save and then close **7-OLLearn.pptx**.

Project 3 Prepare a Self-Running Adventure Slide Show, Use Ink Tools, and Create Custom Slide Shows — 7 Parts

You will open a travel tour presentation and then customize it to be an automated slide show set on a continuous loop. You will also hide slides, use ink tools, and create and edit custom slide shows.

Preview Finished Project

Tutorial

Looping a Slide Show Continuously

Quick Steps

Loop a Slide Show Continuously

1. Click Slide Show tab.
2. Click Set Up Slide Show button.
3. Click *Loop continuously until 'Esc'.*
4. Click OK.

Setting Up a Slide Show to Loop Continuously

To advance a slide automatically, insert a check mark in the *After* check box in the Advance Slide section in the Timing group on the Transitions tab and then insert the specific number of seconds in the measurement box. To advance a slide before the specified amount of time has elapsed, leave the check mark in the *On Mouse Click* option. With this option active, the slide will advance after the specified number of seconds or clicking the mouse button will advance the slide sooner. To control the slide show and have slides advanced the specified number of seconds and not allow advancing by clicking the mouse, remove the check mark from the *On Mouse Click* option.

Hint Use an automated slide show to communicate information without a presenter.

In some situations, such as at a trade show or convention, an automated slide show may be needed. An automated slide show is set up on a continuous loop and does not require someone to advance the slides or restart the slide show. To design an automated slide show, display the Set Up Show dialog box and then insert a check mark in the *Loop continuously until 'Esc'* option. With this option active, the slide show will continue running until the Esc key is pressed.

Project 3a Preparing a Self-Running Slide Show

Part 1 of 7

1. Open **AdvTours.pptx** and then save it with the name **7-AdvTours**.
2. Insert slides by completing the following steps:
   a. Click below the last slide thumbnail in the slide thumbnails pane.
   b. Make sure the Home tab is selected, click the New Slide button arrow, and then click *Reuse Slides* at the drop-down list.
   c. At the Reuse Slides task pane, click the Browse button and then click *Browse File*.
   d. At the Browse dialog box, navigate to the PC7 folder on your storage medium and then double-click ***PeruTour.pptx***.
   e. Click each slide in the Reuse Slides task pane in the order in which they display, beginning with the top slide.
   f. Close the Reuse Slides task pane.
3. Add transition and transition sound effects and specify a time for automatically advancing slides by completing the following steps:
   a. Click the Transitions tab.
   b. Click the *On Mouse Click* check box in the Timing group to remove the check mark.
   c. Click the *After* check box to insert a check mark.
   d. Click the *After* measurement box up arrow until *00:05.00* displays.
   e. Click the *Fade* slide transition in the Transition to This Slide group.
   f. Click the *Sound* option box arrow in the Timing group and then click *Breeze* at the drop-down list.
   g. Click the Apply To All button.

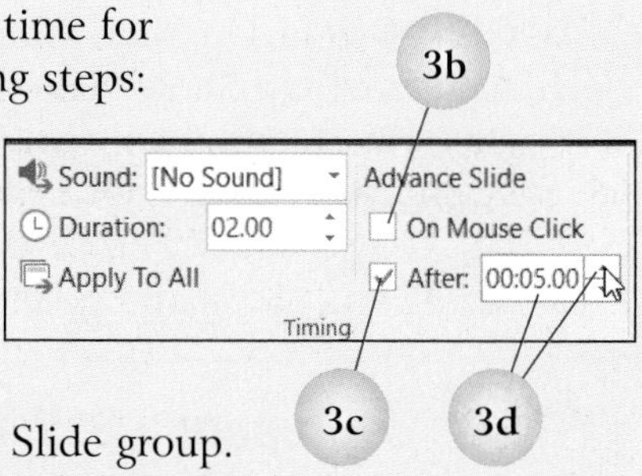

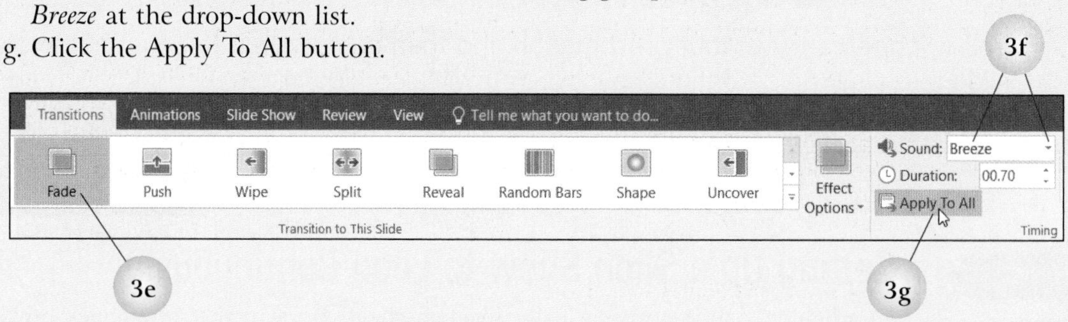

4. Set up the slide show to run continuously by completing the following steps:
   a. Click the Slide Show tab.
   b. Click the Set Up Slide Show button in the Set Up group.
   c. At the Set Up Show dialog box, click the *Loop continuously until 'Esc'* check box to insert a check mark. (Make sure *All* is selected in the *Show slides* section and *Using timings, if present* is selected in the *Advance slides* section.)
   d. Click OK to close the dialog box.

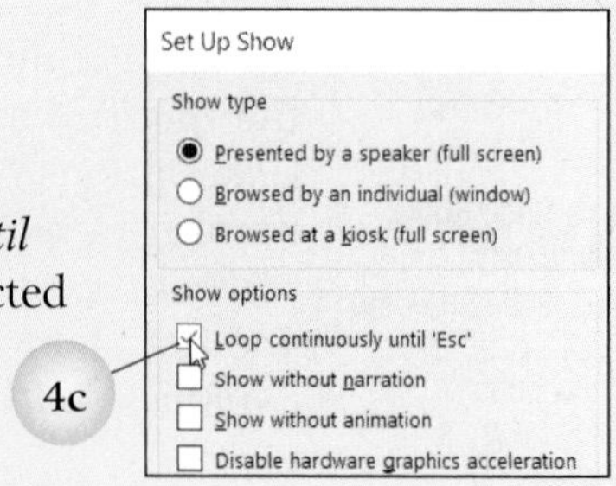

5. Click Slide 1 to select it and then run the slide show. (The slides will advance automatically after five seconds.)
6. After viewing the slide show, press the Esc key on the keyboard.
7. Save **7-AdvTours.pptx**.

Check Your Work

Tutorial

Setting Timings for a Slide Show

Quick Steps

Set Automatic Times for Slides

1. Click Slide Show tab.
2. Click Rehearse Timings button.
3. Using Recording toolbar, specify time for each slide.
4. Click Yes.

Rehearse Timings

Setting Automatic Times for Slides

Applying the same time to all slides is not very practical unless the same amount of text appears on every slide. In most cases, some slides should be left on the screen longer than others. Apply specific times to a slide using buttons on the Recording toolbar. Display this toolbar by clicking the Slide Show tab and then clicking the Rehearse Timings button in the Set Up group. This displays the first slide in the presentation in Slide Show view with the Recording toolbar in the upper left corner of the slide. The buttons on the Recording toolbar are identified in Figure 7.3.

When the slide displays on the screen, the timer on the Recording toolbar begins. Click the Next button on the Recording toolbar when the slide has displayed for the appropriate amount of time. To stop the timer, click the Pause button. Click the Resume Recording button to resume the timer. Use the Repeat button on the Recording toolbar to reset the time for the current slide. Continue through the presentation until the slide show is complete. After the last slide, a confirmation message displays showing the total time for the slide show. At this message, click Yes to set the times for each slide recorded during the rehearsal, or click No to delete the times. A slide show can be run without the rehearsed timings. To run the slide show without the timings, click the Slide Show tab and then click the *Use Timings* check box to remove the check mark.

Hint Enter a specific recording time by selecting the time in the *Slide Time* measurement box, typing the time, and then pressing Enter.

The times applied to slides will display below each slide in the Slide Sorter view. The time that displays below the slide will generally be one second more than the time applied to the slide. So, if 5 seconds were applied to Slide 1, the time *00.06* will display below the slide in Slide Sorter view.

The slide times recorded for individual slides can be edited with the *After* measurement box in the Advance Slide section in the Timing group on the Transitions tab. Make the slide active in the slide pane or click the slide in the Slide Sorter view and then click the up or down arrows to increase or decrease the slide duration.

Figure 7.3 Recording Toolbar

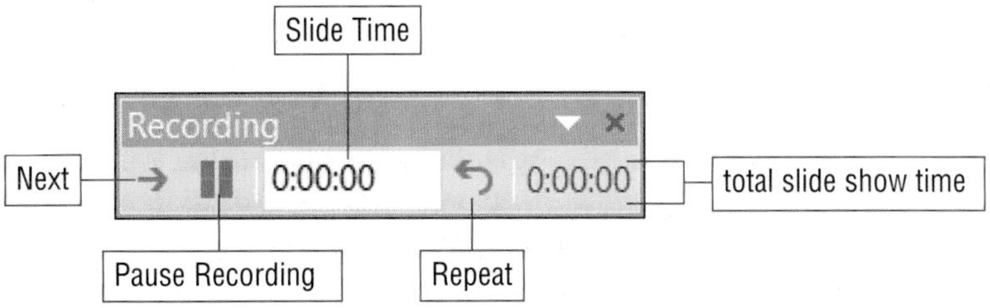

Project 3b Setting Rehearse Timings for Slides

Part 2 of 7

1. With **7-AdvTours.pptx** open, remove the automatic times for slides by completing the following steps:
   a. Click the Slide Show tab.
   b. Click the Set Up Slide Show button.
   c. At the Set Up Show dialog box, click the *Loop continuously until 'Esc'* check box to remove the check mark.
   d. Click OK to close the dialog box.
2. Set times for the slides to display during a slide show by completing the following steps:
   a. Make Slide 1 active.
   b. With the Slide Show tab active, click the Rehearse Timings button in the Set Up group.
   c. The first slide displays in Slide Show view and the Recording toolbar displays. Wait until the time displayed for the current slide reaches :04 (4 seconds) and then click Next. (If you miss the time, click the Repeat button to reset the clock back to 0 for the current slide.)

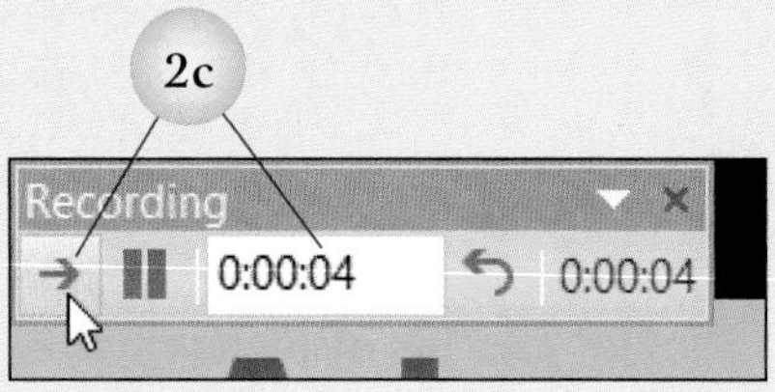

   d. Set the times for the remaining slides as follows:

      Slide 2 = 5 seconds
      Slide 3 = 6 seconds
      Slide 4 = 5 seconds
      Slide 5 = 6 seconds
      Slide 6 = 3 seconds
      Slide 7 = 6 seconds
      Slide 8 = 7 seconds
      Slide 9 = 7 seconds

   e. After the last slide displays, click Yes at the message asking if you want to record the new slide timings. (The slide times may display with one additional second for each.)
   f. If necessary, click the Normal button in the view area on the Status bar.
3. Click the Set Up Slide Show button to display the Set Up Show dialog box, click the *Loop continuously until 'Esc'* check box to insert a check mark, and then click OK to close the dialog box.
4. Run the slide show. (The slide show will start and run continuously.) Watch the slide show until it has started for the second time and then end the show by pressing the Esc key.
5. Save **7-AdvTours.pptx**.

Recording Narration

Quick Steps

Record a Narration

1. Click Slide Show tab.
2. Click Record Slide Show button.
3. Click Start Recording button.
4. Narrate slides.

A narration can be recorded for a presentation that will play when the slide show is running. To record a narration, a microphone must be connected to the computer. To begin the narration, click the Record Slide Show button in the Set Up group on the Slide Show tab. At the Record Slide Show dialog box, click the Start Recording button. The slide show begins and the first slide fills the screen. Begin the narration, clicking the mouse to advance each slide.

Clicking the Record Slide Show button arrow displays a drop-down list with three options. Click the *Start Recording from Beginning* option to begin recording the narration with the first slide in the presentation or click the *Start Recording from Current Slide* option to begin recording the narration with the currently active slide. Position the mouse on the third option, *Clear*, and a side menu displays with options for clearing the timing on the current slide or all slides and clearing the narration from the current slide or all slides.

Record Slide Show

Click the Record Slide Show button on the Slide Show tab and the Record Slide Show dialog box displays. This dialog box contains two options: *Slide and animation timings* and *Narrations and laser pointer*, so that just the slide timings can be recorded, just the narration, or both at the same time.

With the *Slide and animation timings* option active (containing a check mark), PowerPoint will keep track of the timing for each slide. When the slide show runs, the slides will remain on the screen the number of seconds recorded. To narrate a presentation without slides being timed, remove the check mark from the *Slide and animation timings* check box. With the *Narrations and laser pointer* option active (containing a check mark), the narration and laser pointer gestures made with the mouse can be recorded. To make laser pointer gestures, press and hold down the Ctrl key, click and hold down the left mouse button, drag in the slide, and then release the Ctrl key and the mouse button.

The narration in a presentation plays by default when running the slide show. To run the slide show without narration, display the Set Up Show dialog box and then click the *Show without narration* check box in the *Show options* section to insert a check mark.

Project 3c Recording Narration

Part 3 of 7

This is an optional project. Before beginning the project, check with your instructor to determine if you have a microphone available for recording.

1. With **7-AdvTours.pptx** open, save it with the name **7-AdvTours-NarrateSlide.**
2. Make Slide 9 active and then narrate the slide by completing the following steps:
   a. Click the Slide Show tab.
   b. Click the Record Slide Show button arrow in the Set Up group and then click *Start Recording from Current Slide* at the drop-down list.
   c. At the Record Slide Show dialog box, make sure both options contain a check mark and then click the Start Recording button.
   d. Speak the following text into the microphone: *Call Adventure Tours today to receive an additional ten percent savings when you book a Fiji or Peru tour.*
   e. Press the Esc key to end the narration.

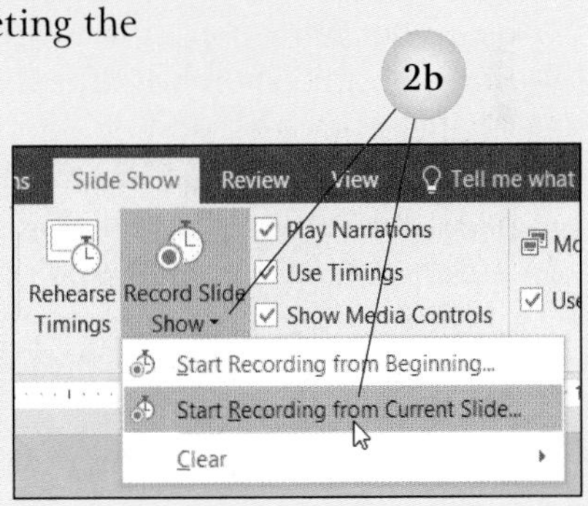

3. Make Slide 1 active and then run the slide show. If your computer has speakers, you will hear your narration when Slide 9 displays. After viewing the slide show at least once, press the Esc key to end it.
4. Save and then close **7-AdvTours-NarrateSlide.pptx**.
5. Open **7-AdvTours.pptx** and then save it with the name **7-AdvTours-Narration**.

6. Remove the timings and the continuous loop option by completing the following steps:
   a. Click the Slide Show tab.
   b. Click the Record Slide Show button arrow, point to *Clear* at the drop-down list, and then click *Clear Timings on All Slides* at the side menu.
   c. Click the Set Up Slide Show button.
   d. At the Set Up Show dialog box, click the *Loop continuously until 'Esc'* check box to remove the check mark.
   e. Click OK to close the dialog box.

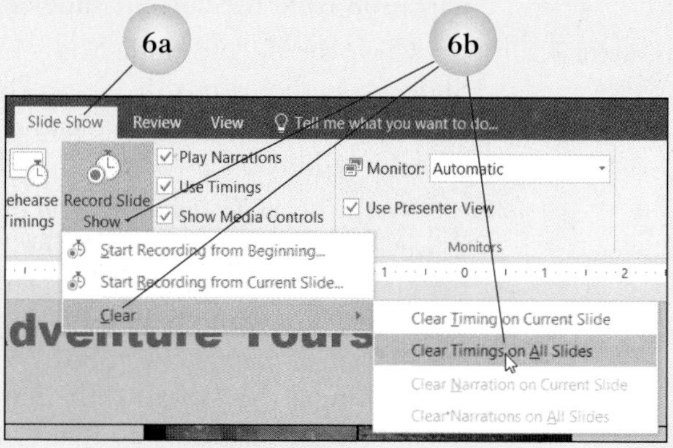

7. Make Slide 1 active and then record narration by completing the following steps:
   a. Click the Record Slide Show button in the Set Up group on the Slide Show tab.
   b. At the Record Slide Show dialog box, make sure both options contain a check mark and then click the Start Recording button.
   c. When the first slide displays, either read the information or provide your own narrative of the slide and then click the left mouse button. (You can also click the Next button on the Recording toolbar that displays in the upper left corner of the slide.)
   d. Continue narrating each slide (either using some of the information in the slides or creating your own narration). Try recording laser pointer gestures by pressing and holding down the Ctrl key, clicking and holding down the left mouse button, dragging in the slide, and then releasing the Ctrl key and the mouse button.
   e. After you narrate the last slide (about accommodations for the Peru tour), the presentation may display in Slide Sorter view.
8. Make Slide 1 active and then run the slide show. If your computer has speakers, you will hear your narration as the slide show runs.
9. Run the slide show without narration by completing the following steps:
   a. Click the Set Up Slide Show button in the Set Up group on the Slide Show tab.
   b. At the Set Up Show dialog box, click the *Show without narration* check box to insert a check mark.
   c. Click OK.
   d. Run the slide show beginning with Slide 1. (The slide show will still run automatically with the timing established when you were recording your narration but without the narration.)
10. Save and then close **7-AdvTours-Narration.pptx**.

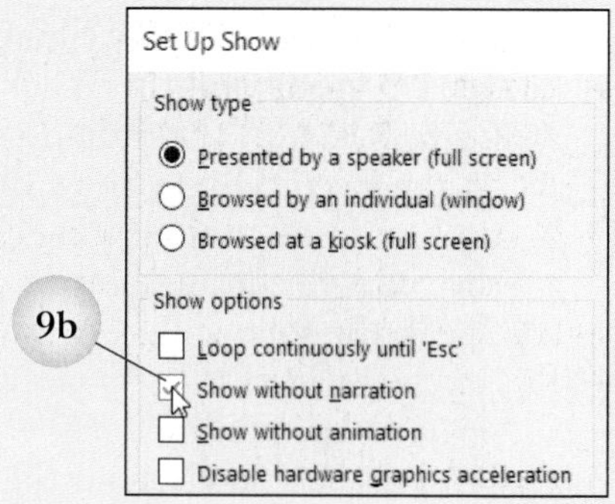

Tutorial

Hiding and Unhiding Slides

Hide Slide

Hiding Slides

A slide show may be presented to a number of different groups or departments. In some situations the presenter may want to hide specific slides in a slide show depending on the audience. To hide a slide in a slide show, make the slide active, click the Slide Show tab, and then click the Hide Slide button in the Set Up group. When a slide is hidden, a slash displays over the slide number in the slide thumbnails pane and the slide in the slide thumbnails pane displays in a dimmed

Quick Steps

Hide/Unhide a Slide

1. Make slide active.
2. Click Slide Show tab.
3. Click Hide Slide button.

manner. The slide is visible in the slide thumbnails pane in Normal view and also in the Slide Sorter view. To remove the hidden icon and redisplay the slide when running a slide show, click the slide in the slide thumbnails pane, click the Slide Show tab, and then click the Hide Slide button.

Managing Monitors

If two monitors are connected to the computer or PowerPoint is running on a laptop with dual-display capabilities, specify which monitor to use when running the slide show with the *Monitor* option in the Monitors group on the Slide Show tab. By default, PowerPoint automatically chooses a monitor to display the slide show. Change the monitor for viewing the slide show by clicking the *Monitor* option box arrow and then clicking the monitor at the drop-down list.

Using Presenter View

Insert a check mark in the *Use Presenter View* check box in the Monitors group on the Slide Show tab if PowerPoint is running on a computer with two monitors or on a laptop with dual-display capabilities. With this option active, the slide show will display in full-screen view on one monitor and in a special speaker view on the other, similar to what is shown in Figure 7.4. The buttons that display below the slide are the same buttons as those that display in Slide Show view. Other options in Presenter View include the display of slide durations, a preview of the next slide in the slide show, a notes pane, and navigation buttons.

Figure 7.4 Presenter View

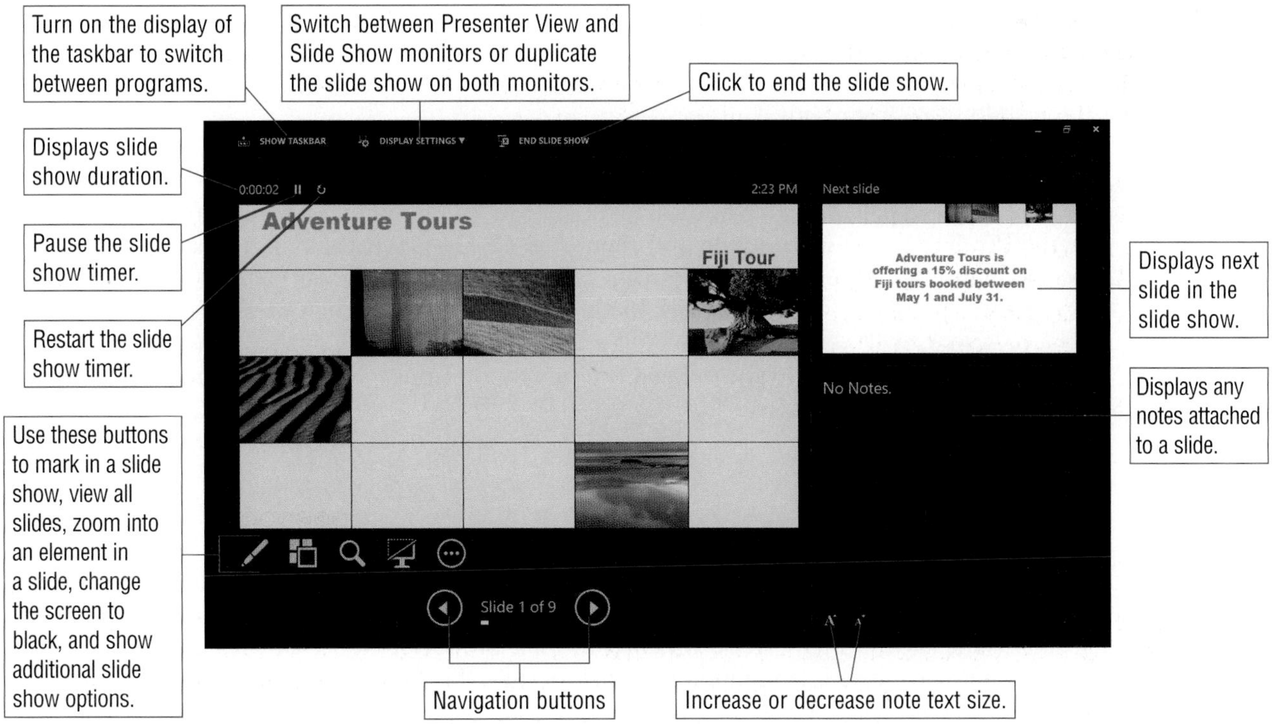

1. Open **7-AdvTours.pptx**.
2. Remove the continuous loop option and remove timings by completing the following steps:
   a. Click the Slide Show tab.
   b. Click the Set Up Slide Show button.
   c. At the Set Up Show dialog box, click the *Loop continuously until 'Esc'* check box to remove the check mark.
   d. Click OK to close the dialog box.
   e. Click the Transitions tab.
   f. Click the *After* measurement box down arrow until *00:00* displays in the box.
   g. Click the *After* check box to remove the check mark.
   h. Click the *On Mouse Click* check box to insert a check mark.
   i. Click the Apply To All button.
3. Hide Slide 2 by completing the following steps:
   a. Click Slide 2 in the slide thumbnails pane.
   b. Click the Slide Show tab and then click the Hide Slide button in the Set Up group.
4. Run the slide show to see that Slide 2 does not display (since it is hidden).
5. Unhide Slide 2 by clicking Slide 2 in the slide thumbnails pane and then clicking the Hide Slide button in the Set Up group on the Slide Show tab.

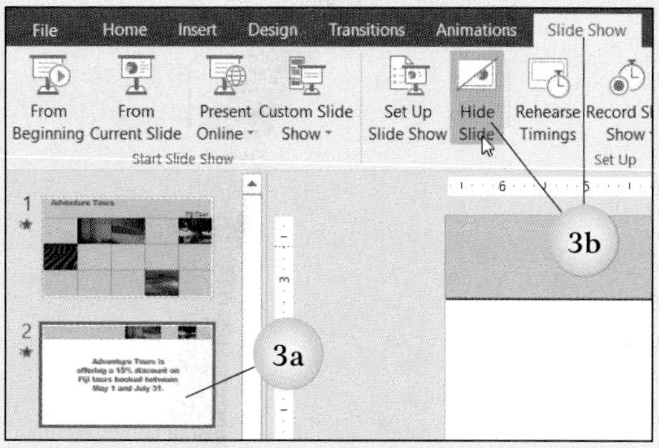

If you have two monitors connected to your computer, you can run the slide show in Presenter View. Complete these optional steps only if you have two monitors connected to your computer.

6. Make sure the Slide Show tab is active and then click the *Use Presenter View* check box in the Monitors group to insert a check mark.
7. Run the slide show from Slide 1.
8. Click the See all slides button below the slide.
9. Click the Slide 3 thumbnail.
10. Click the Return to previous slide button at the bottom of Presenter View to display Slide 2.
11. Click the Pen button below the slide and then click *Highlighter* at the pop-up list.
12. Using the mouse, drag through the text *May 1*.
13. Press the Esc key to turn the highlighter to an arrow pointer, and then press the Esc key to end the presentation.
14. At the message asking if you want to keep the ink annotations, click the Discard button.
15. Save **7-AdvTours.pptx**.

Presenting a Slide Show Online

PowerPoint includes the Present Online feature for sharing a slide show with others over the Internet by sending a link to the people who will view the slide show, which can be watched in their browsers. To use this feature, a network service is required to host the slide show. Microsoft provides the Office Presentation Service, which is available to anyone with a Windows Live ID, such as a OneDrive account, and Microsoft Office 2016.

Quick Steps

Present Online

1. Click Slide Show tab.
2. Click Present Online button.
3. Click CONNECT button.
4. If necessary, enter Windows Live ID user name and password.
5. Click Copy Link hyperlink.
6. Open email.
7. Paste link into email and send email.
8. Click START PRESENTATION button.

Present Online

To present a presentation online, click the Present Online button in the Start Slide Show group on the Slide Show tab. At the Present Online window that displays, click the CONNECT button, and, if necessary, enter a Windows Live ID user name and password. When PowerPoint has connected to an account and prepared the presentation, the Present Online window will display with a unique link PowerPoint created for the presentation. Click the Copy Link hyperlink in the Present Online window to copy the unique link, and then paste the link into an email that will be sent to the people who will be viewing the slide show. If the person presenting the slide show online has an Outlook account, clicking the Send in Email hyperlink opens Outlook and the link can be pasted in the message window.

After everyone has opened the presentation link in a web browser, click the START PRESENTATION button in the Present Online window. People viewing the slide show do not need PowerPoint installed on their computers to view the slide show since the slide show will display through their web browsers. When the slide show has ended, click the End Online Presentation button on the Present Online tab. At the confirmation message that displays, click the End Online Presentation button. The Present Online tab provides options for running the slide show, managing monitors, sharing the slide show through OneNote, and displaying the unique link to send to more people. The Present Online window can also be accessed by clicking the File tab, clicking the *Share* option, clicking *Present Online*, and then clicking the Present Online button.

When presenting a slide show online, the presenter can allow the viewers to download the presentation. To do this, the presenter would click the *Enable remote viewers to download the presentation* check box at the Present Online window before clicking the CONNECT button.

Project 3e Presenting a Slide Show Online — Part 5 of 7

This is an optional project. To complete this project, you will need a Windows Live ID account. Depending on your system configuration and what services are available, these steps will vary.

1. With **7-AdvTours.pptx** open, click the Slide Show tab and then click the Present Online button in the Start Slide Show group.
2. At the Present Online window that displays, click the CONNECT button.
3. If necessary, type your user name and password into the Windows Security dialog box.
4. At the Present Online window with the unique link selected, click the Copy Link hyperlink.
5. Send the link to colleagues by opening your email account, pasting the link into a new message window, and then sending the email to the viewers. Or, if you are using Microsoft Outlook, click the Send in Email hyperlink and Microsoft Outlook opens in a new message window with the link inserted in the message. In Outlook, send the link to people you want to view the presentation.
6. When everyone has received the link, click the START PRESENTATION button at the Present Online window.
7. Run the slide show.
8. When the slide show has ended, press the Esc key and then click the End Online Presentation button on the Present Online tab.
9. At the message that displays telling you that all remote viewers will be disconnected if you continue, click the End Online Presentation button.

Tutorial
Using Ink Tools

Start Inking

Using Ink Tools

Similar to drawing and highlighting in slides during a slide show, as completed in Chapter 1, draw or highlight items in slides in Normal view with options on the Ink Tools Pens tab, as shown in Figure 7.5. Display this tab by clicking the Start Inking button in the Ink group on the Review tab. The Ink Tools Pens tab contains options for drawing and highlighting on slides; erasing markings on slides; selecting multiple options such as ink marks, shapes, and text boxes; selecting a variety of pen and highlighter colors; changing the color and thickness of the pen or highlighter; and converting drawings to shapes. The ink tools feature is useful when using a pen, stylus, or finger when drawing on a tablet or touchscreen computer.

Figure 7.5 Ink Tools Pens Tab

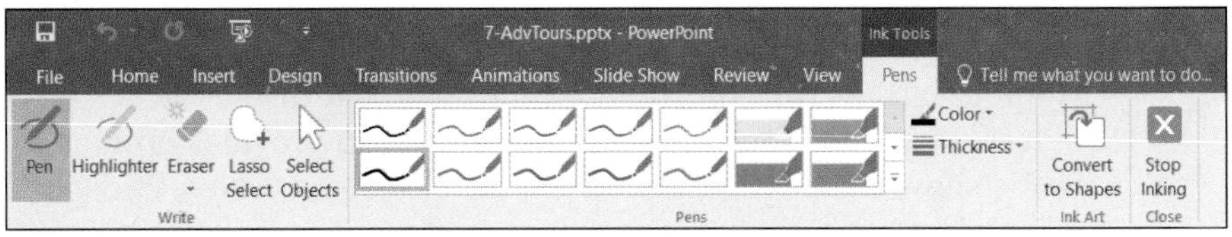

Project 3f Using Ink Tools

Part 6 of 7

1. With **7-AdvTours.pptx** open, make Slide 2 active.
2. Click the Review tab.
3. Click the Start Inking button in the Ink group.
4. With the Ink Tools Pens tab active, draw and highlight on the slide by completing the following steps:
   a. Click the More Pens button in the Pens group.
   b. Click the *Red Pen (1.0 mm)* option at the drop-down list (second column, second row in the *Built-In Pens* section).
   c. Using the mouse, draw a line below the text *15% discount*.

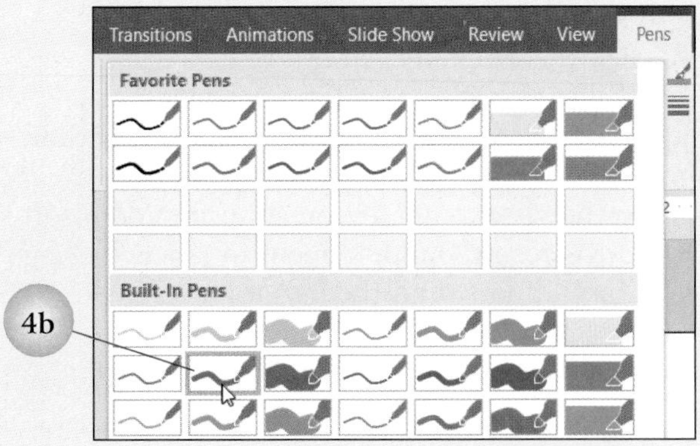

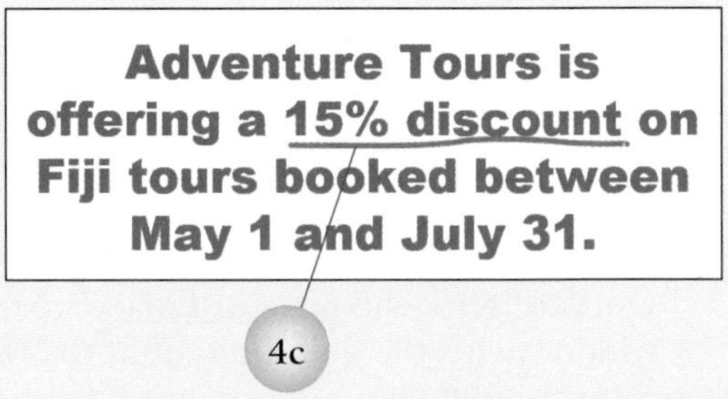

d. Click the More Pens button in the Pens group.
e. Click the *Yellow Highlighter (4.0 mm)* option at the drop-down list (sixth column, first row in the *Favorite Pens* section).
f. Using the mouse, draw through the text *May 1 and July 31.*

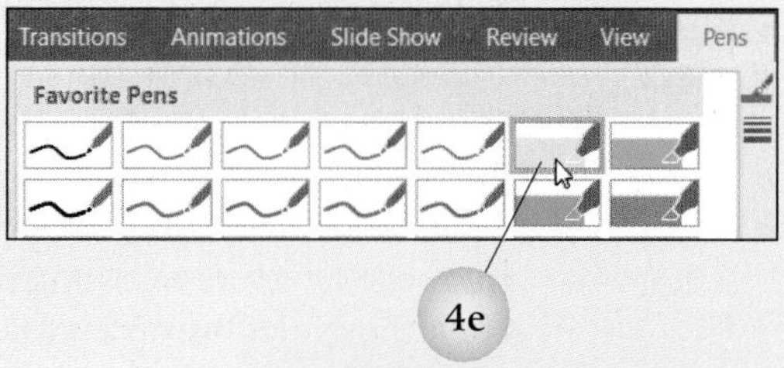

5. Erase drawing and highlighting on the slide by completing the following steps:
   a. Click the Eraser button arrow in the Write group.
   b. Click *Stroke Eraser* at the drop-down list.
   c. Click the mouse pointer (displays with an eraser attached) anywhere in the red line below the text *15% discount.*
   d. Click the Eraser button arrow and then click *Medium Eraser* at the drop-down list.
   e. Using the mouse, which displays as a white box, drag over the text *and July 31.* to erase the yellow highlighting. (The text *May 1* should remain highlighted.)
   f. Press the Esc key to change the mouse pointer to an arrow.

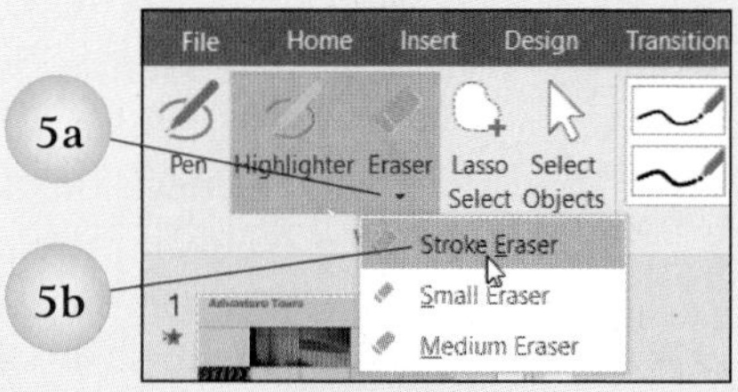

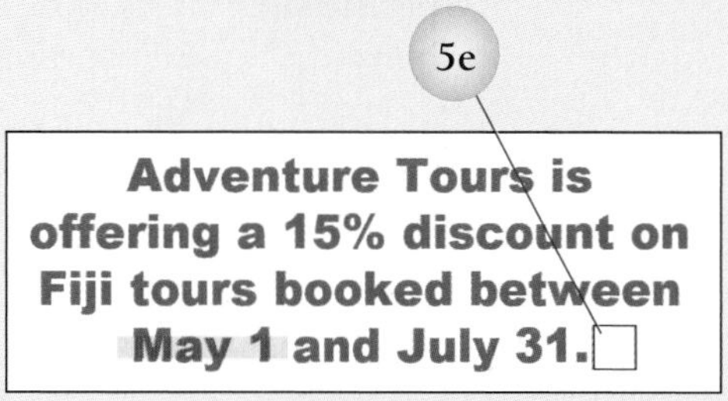

6. Make Slide 5 active.
7. Convert drawings to shapes and select shapes by completing the following steps:
   a. Click the Convert to Shapes button in the Ink Art group.
   b. Click the More Pens button in the Pens group and then click the *Orange Pen (0.35 mm)* option at the drop-down list (first column, third row in the *Built-In Pens* section).
   c. Using the mouse, draw a rectangle around the text *Coral reef* in the second bulleted item. Notice that PowerPoint automatically converted the drawn rectangle into a more precise rectangle. If you are not satisfied with the appearance of the rectangle, click the Undo button on the Quick Access Toolbar two times, select the orange pen again, and then redraw the rectangle.
   d. Click the Select Objects button in the Write group.
   e. Hover the mouse pointer over the orange rectangle until the mouse pointer displays with a four-headed arrow attached and then click the border to select it.
   f. Using the middle sizing handle at the right side of the orange border, drag the border to the right to include the word *cruise.*
   g. Click the Thickness button in the Pens group and then click *4½ pt* at the drop-down gallery.

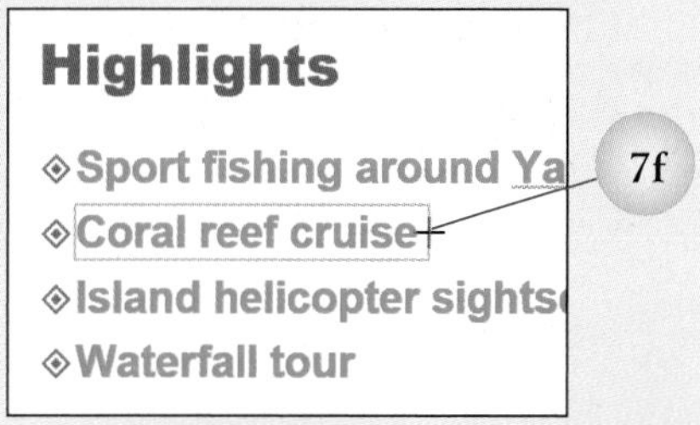

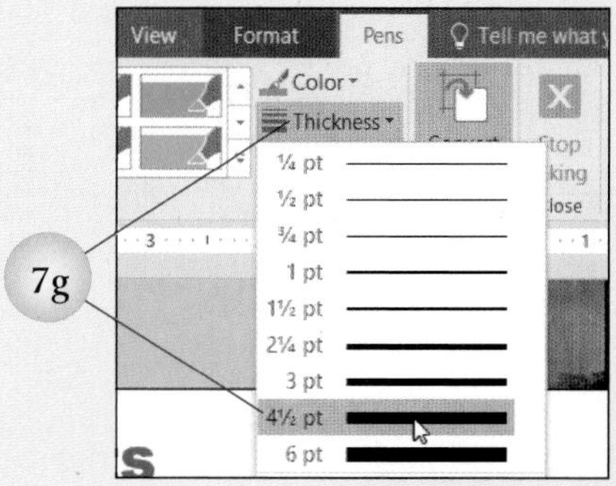

8. Run the slide show to see the highlighting and rectangle applied to the slides.
9. Save **7-AdvTours.pptx**.

Check Your Work

Tutorial

Creating and Running a Custom Slide Show

Custom Slide Show

Quick Steps

Create a Custom Slide Show
1. Click Slide Show tab.
2. Click Custom Slide Show button.
3. Click *Custom Shows*.
4. Click New button.
5. Make changes at Define Custom Show dialog box.
6. Click OK.

Run a Custom Slide Show
1. Click Slide Show tab.
2. Click Custom Slide Show button.
3. Click custom show.

Edit a Custom Slide Show
1. Click Slide Show tab.
2. Click Custom Slide Show button.
3. Click *Custom Shows*.
4. Click custom show's name.
5. Click Edit button.
6. Make changes at Define Custom Show dialog box.
7. Click OK.

Hint Create custom slide shows to customize a presentation for a variety of audiences.

Creating a Custom Slide Show

A custom slide show is a slide show within a slide show. Creating a custom slide show might be useful in situations where only a select number of slides will be presented to a particular audience. To create a custom slide show, click the Slide Show tab, click the Custom Slide Show button in the Start Slide Show group, and then click *Custom Shows* at the drop-down list. At the Custom Shows dialog box, click the New button and the Define Custom Show dialog box displays, similar to what is shown in Figure 7.6.

At the Define Custom Show dialog box, type a name for the custom slide show in the *Slide show name* text box. To insert a slide in the custom slide show, click the check box for the specific slide in the *Slides in presentation* list box to insert a check mark and then click the Add button. This inserts the slide in the *Slides in custom show* list box. Continue in this manner until all specific slides have been added to the custom slide show. A check mark can be inserted in all of the specific slide check boxes first and then clicking the Add button will add all the slides in the *Slides in custom show* list box at once.

To change the order of the slides in the *Slides in custom show* list box, click one of the arrow keys to move the selected slide up or down in the list box. When all slides have been inserted in the *Slides in custom show* list box and are arranged in the desired order, click OK. More than one custom slide show can be created in a presentation.

Running a Custom Slide Show

To run a custom slide show within a slide show, click the Custom Slide Show button on the Slide Show tab and then click the custom slide show's name at the drop-down list. A custom slide show can also be run by displaying the Set Up Show dialog box and then clicking the *Custom show* option. If the presentation contains more than one custom slide show, click the *Custom show* option box arrow and then click the custom slide show's name at the drop-down list.

Figure 7.6 Define Custom Show Dialog Box

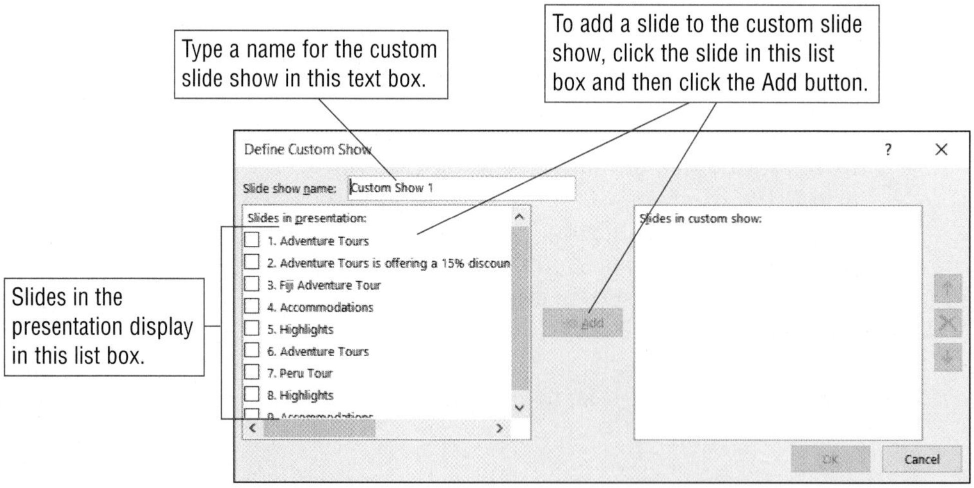

Editing a Custom Slide Show

A custom slide show is saved with the presentation and can be edited. To edit a custom slide show, open the presentation, click the Custom Slide Show button on the Slide Show tab, and then click *Custom Shows* at the drop-down list. At the Custom Shows dialog box, click the custom slide show name to be edited and then click the Edit button. At the Define Custom Show dialog box, make changes to the custom slide show, such as adding or removing slides or changing the order of slides and then click the OK button.

Quick Steps

Print a Custom Slide Show

1. Display Print backstage area.
2. Click first gallery in *Settings* category.
3. Click custom show at drop-down list.
4. Click Print button.

Printing a Custom Slide Show

Print a custom slide show with options in the *Settings* category of the Print backstage area. To do this, click the File tab and then click the *Print* option to display the Print backstage area. Click the first gallery in the Settings category and then click the custom slide show in the *Custom Shows* section.

Project 3g Creating, Editing, and Running Custom Slide Shows — Part 7 of 7

1. With **7-AdvTours.pptx** open, save the presentation with the name **7-AdvTours-Custom**.
2. Create two custom slide shows by completing the following steps:
   a. Click the Slide Show tab, click the Custom Slide Show button, and then click *Custom Shows* at the drop-down list.
   b. At the Custom Shows dialog box, click the New button.
   c. At the Define Custom Show dialog box, select the text in the *Slide show name* text box and then type PeruTourCustom.
   d. Click the Slide 6 check box in the *Slides in presentation* list box to insert a check mark and then click the Add button. (This adds the slide to the *Slides in custom show* list box.)
   e. Click the check boxes for Slides 7, 8, and 9 in the list box to insert check marks and then click the Add button.
   f. Click OK to close the Define Custom Show dialog box.
   g. At the Custom Shows dialog box, click the New button.
   h. At the Define Custom Show dialog box, select the text in the *Slide show name* text box and then type FijiTourCustom.
   i. Add Slides 1 through 5 to the *Slides in custom show* list box.
   j. Click OK to close the dialog box.
   k. Click the Close button to close the Custom Shows dialog box.
3. Run the custom slide shows by completing the following steps:
   a. Click the Custom Slide Show button on the Slide Show tab and then click *PeruTourCustom* at the drop-down list.

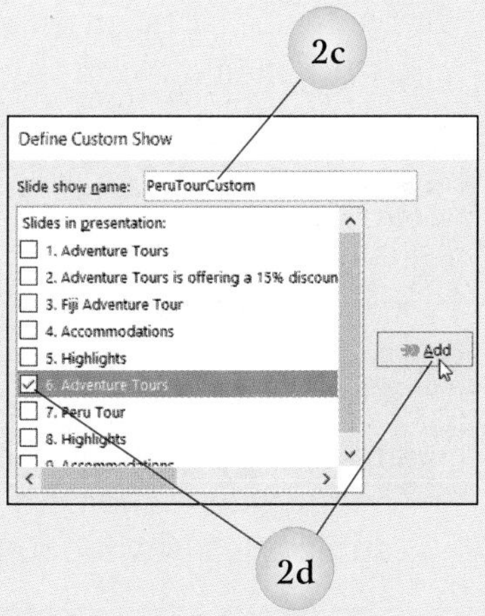

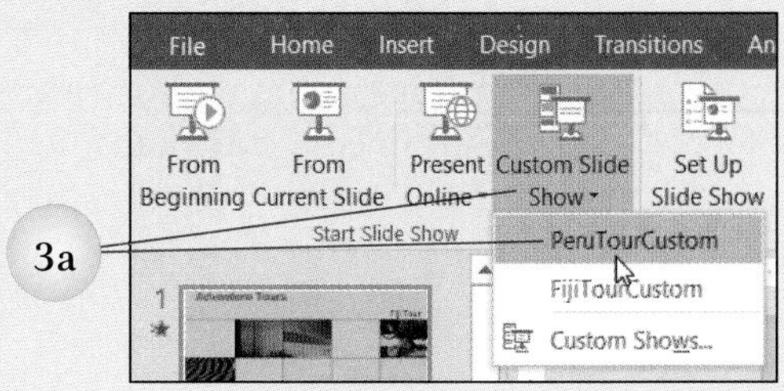

b. Click the left mouse button to advance slides.
c. Click the Custom Slide Show button, click *FijiTourCustom* at the drop-down list, and then view the slide show. (Click the left mouse button to advance the slides.)

4. Edit the FijiTourCustom custom slide show by completing the following steps:
   a. Click the Custom Slide Show button on the Slide Show tab and then click *Custom Shows* at the drop-down list.
   b. At the Custom Shows dialog box, click *FijiTourCustom* in the list box and then click the Edit button.

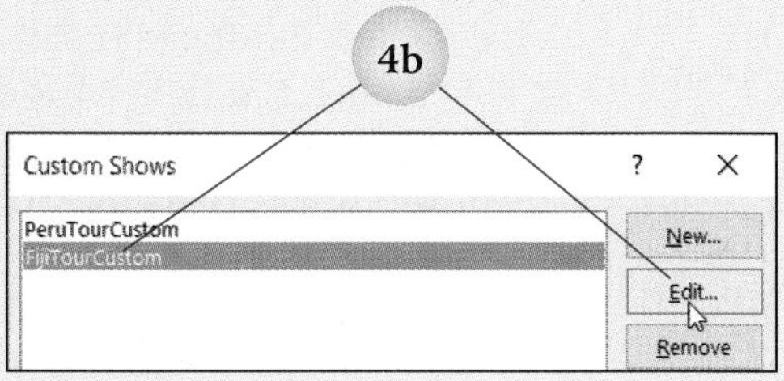

   c. At the Define Custom Show dialog box, click Slide 2 in the *Slides in custom show* list box and then click the Down button at the right side of the list box three times. (This moves the slide to the bottom of the list.)
   d. Click OK to close the dialog box.
   e. Click the Close button to close the Custom Shows dialog box.

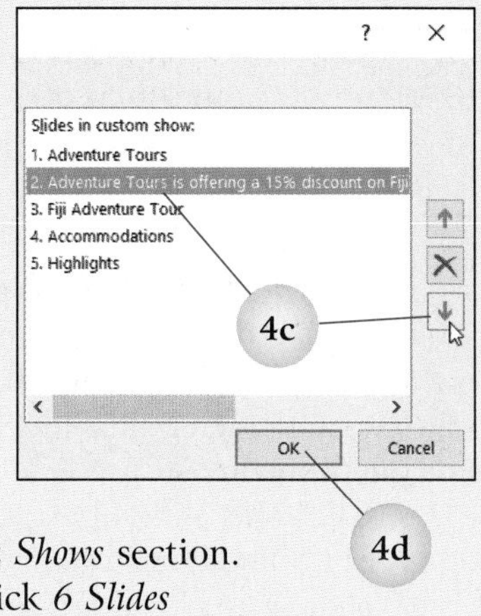

5. Run the FijiTourCustom slide show.
6. Print the FijiTourCustom slide show by completing the following steps:
   a. Click the File tab and then click the *Print* option.
   b. At the Print backstage area, click the first gallery in the *Settings* category and then click *FijiTourCustom* in the *Custom Shows* section.
   c. Click the second gallery in the *Settings* category and then click *6 Slides Horizontal* at the drop-down list.
   d. Click the Print button.
7. Save and then close **7-AdvTours-Custom.pptx**.

Check Your Work

Project 4 Insert Audio and Video Files in an Eco-Tours Presentation 5 Parts

You will open a presentation and then insert an audio file, a video file, and an image with motion. You will also customize the audio and video files to play automatically when running the slide show.

Preview Finished Project

Inserting Audio and Video Files

Adding audio and/or video files to a presentation will turn a slide show into a true multimedia experience for the audience. Including a variety of elements in a presentation will stimulate interest in the slide show and keep the audience motivated.

Tutorial

Inserting and Modifying an Audio File

Audio

Quick Steps

Insert an Audio File

1. Click Insert tab.
2. Click Audio button.
3. Click *Audio on My PC.*
4. Double-click audio file.

Inserting an Audio File

To add an audio file to a presentation, click the Insert tab, click the Audio button in the Media group, and then click *Audio on My PC* at the drop-down list. At the Insert Audio dialog box, navigate to the folder containing the audio file and then double-click the audio file.

If an audio recording device is attached to the computer, audio can be recorded for the presentation by clicking the Audio button and then clicking *Record Audio* at the drop-down list. At the Record Sound dialog box, name the audio, click the Record button, and then record the audio.

When an audio file is inserted in a presentation, the Audio Tools Format tab and the Audio Tools Playback tab display. Click the Audio Tools Format tab and options display that are similar to options on the Picture Tools Format tab. Click the Audio Tools Playback tab and options display for previewing the audio file, inserting a bookmark at a specific time in the audio file, specifying fade in and fade out times, and specifying how to play the audio file.

Project 4a **Inserting an Audio File**

Part 1 of 5

1. Open **EcoTours.pptx** and then save it with the name **7-EcoTours**.
2. Insert an audio file that plays music at the end of the presentation by completing the following steps:
   a. Make Slide 8 active and then click the Insert tab.
   b. Click the Audio button in the Media group, and then click *Audio on My PC* at the drop-down list.
   c. At the Insert Audio dialog box, navigate to the PC7 folder on your storage medium and then double-click ***AudioFile-01.mid***.
   d. With the Audio Tools Playback tab active, click the *Start* option box arrow in the Audio Options group and then click *Automatically* at the drop-down list.
   e. Click the *Loop until Stopped* check box in the Audio Options group to insert a check mark.
   f. Click the *Hide During Show* check box to insert a check mark.
3. Click the Start from Beginning button on the Quick Access Toolbar to run the slide show starting with Slide 1. When the last slide displays, listen to the audio file and then press the Esc key to return to the Normal view.
4. Save **7-EcoTours.pptx**.

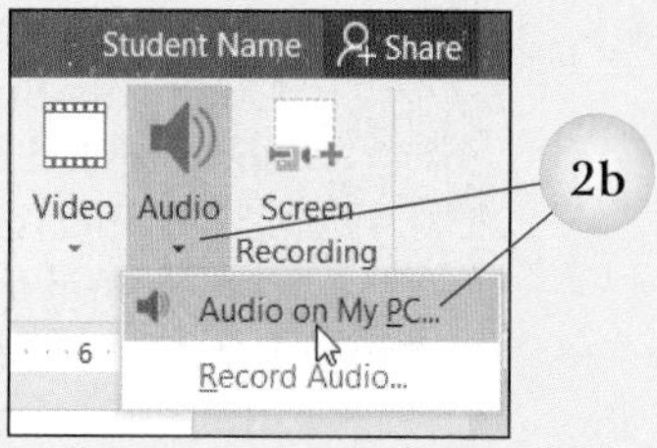

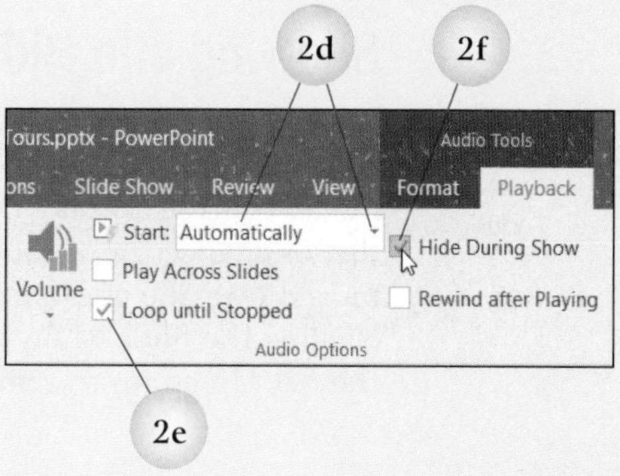

Check Your Work

Tutorial

Inserting and Modifying a Video File

Video

Inserting a Video File

Inserting a video file in a presentation is a similar process to inserting an audio file. Click the Video button in the Media group on the Insert tab and then click *Video on My PC* at the drop-down list to display the Insert Video dialog box. At this dialog box, navigate to the folder containing the video file and then double-click the file.

Quick Steps

Insert a Video File

1. Click Insert tab.
2. Click Video button.
3. Click *Video on My PC*.
4. Double-click video file.

The Video button drop-down list also includes the *Online Video* option. Click this option to display the Insert Video window. At this window, search for videos online using the *YouTube* search option or paste an embedded code into the *From a Video Embed Code* option to insert a video from a website. To embed code from an online video, locate and copy the embedded code of the video, paste the embedded code in the *From a Video Embed Code* section of the Insert Video window, and then click the Insert button. Another way to insert a video in a presentation is to click the Insert Video button in the content placeholder on a slide. This displays the Insert Video window with the additional option to browse for a file on the computer.

When a video file is inserted in a presentation, the Video Tools Format tab and the Video Tools Playback tab display. Click the Video Tools Format tab and options display for adjusting the video file color and frame, applying video styles, and arranging and sizing the video file. Click the Video Tools Playback tab and options display that are similar to the options on the Audio Tools Playback tab. Formatting also can be applied to a video with options in the Format Video task pane.

Optimizing and Compressing Video Files

If a video with an older file format is inserted in a presentation, the Info backstage area may display an Optimize Compatibility button. Optimize compatibility of a video file to increase the likelihood that the video file will play on multiple devices.

Compress Media

When a video file is inserted in a presentation, consider compressing the file to improve playback performance and save disk space. If a presentation contains a video file, the Info backstage area contains the Compress Media button. Click this button and a drop-down list displays with options for specifying the compressed quality of the video. Click the *Presentation Quality* option to save space and maintain the quality of the video. Click the *Internet Quality* option and the compressed video file will be comparable to a video file streamed over the Internet. Choose the last option, *Low Quality*, to compress the file when space is limited, such as when sending the presentation as an email attachment.

Showing and Hiding Media Controls

When a slide with an audio or video file displays during a slide show, media controls appear along the bottom of the audio icon or video window. Use these media controls to play the audio or video file, move to a specific location in the file, or change the volume. The media controls display when the mouse pointer is moved over the audio icon or video window. Media controls can be turned off by clicking the Slide Show tab and then clicking the *Show Media Controls* check box in the Set Up group to remove the check mark.

Project 4b Inserting a Video File in a Presentation

Part 2 of 5

1. With **7-EcoTours.pptx** open, make Slide 8 active.
2. You will insert a video file in the slide that contains audio, so delete the audio file you inserted in Project 4a by clicking the audio file icon that displays in the middle of Slide 8 and then pressing the Delete key.
3. Insert a video file by completing the following steps:
   a. Click the Insert tab.

b. Click the Video button in the Media group and then click *Video on My PC* at the drop-down list.
c. At the Insert Video dialog box, navigate to the PC7 folder on your storage medium and then double-click the file named ***Wildlife.wmv***.
d. Click the Play button in the Preview group (on the left side of the Video Tools Format tab) to preview the video file. (The video plays for approximately 30 seconds.)

4. Format the video by completing the following steps:
   a. Make sure the video image is selected on the slide and the Video Tools Format tab is selected.
   b. Click the *Beveled Frame, Gradient* option in the Video Styles group (fourth option).
   c. Click the Video Shape button in the Video Styles group and then click *Rounded Rectangle* at the drop-down gallery (second option in the *Rectangles* section).
   d. Click the Poster Frame button in the Adjust group and then click *Image from File* at the drop-down list.

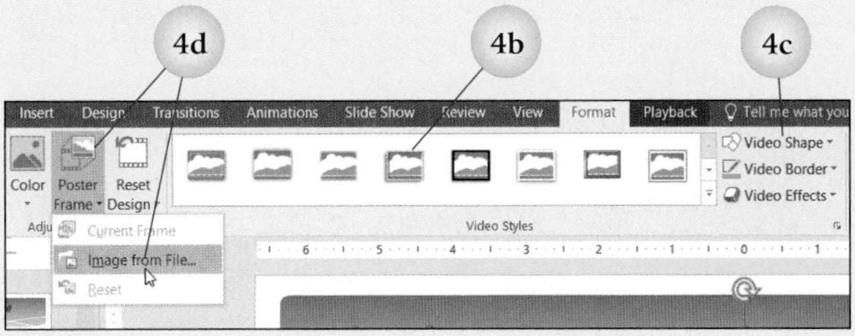

   e. At the Insert Pictures window, click the Browse button to the right of the *From a file* option, navigate to the PC7 folder on your storage medium, and then double-click ***Olympics.jpg***.
   f. Click the Corrections button in the Adjust group and then click *Brightness: 0% (Normal) Contrast: +20%* at the drop-down gallery (third column, fourth row).
   g. Click the Rotate button in the Arrange group and then click *Flip Horizontal* at the drop-down list.
   h. Click the Size group dialog box launcher to display the Format Video task pane.
   i. With the Size & Properties icon selected, make sure the *Size* options display.
   j. Select the current measurement in the *Height* measurement box and then type 4.9.
   k. Click *Position* to display the options.
   l. Select the current measurement in the *Horizontal position* measurement box and then type 2.3.
   m. Select the current measurement in the *Vertical position* measurement box and then type 1.8.

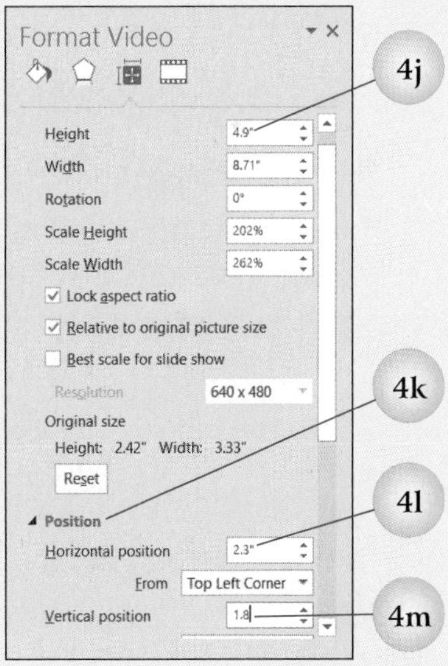

   n. Close the Format Video task pane.
   o. Click the Video Tools Playback tab.
   p. Click the Volume button in the Video Options group and then click *Low* at the drop-down list.
   q. Click the *Loop until Stopped* check box in the Video Options group to insert a check mark.

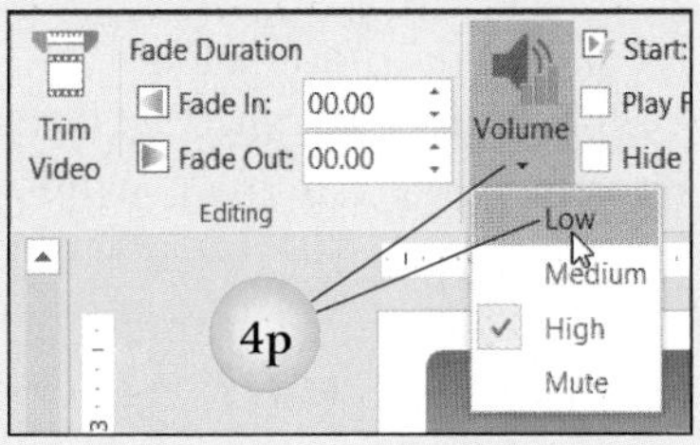

5. Make Slide 1 active and then run the slide show. When the slide containing the video file displays, move the mouse over the video file window and then click the play button at the bottom left side of the window.

6. After viewing the video a couple of times, press the Esc key two times.
7. Specify that you want the video window to fill the slide, the video to automatically start when the slide displays, the video to play only once, and the display of media controls turned off by completing the following steps:
   a. Make sure Slide 8 is active, click the video file window, and then click the Video Tools Playback tab.
   b. Click the *Play Full Screen* check box in the Video Options group to insert a check mark and click the *Loop until Stopped* check box to remove the check mark.
   c. Click the *Start* option box arrow in the Video Options group and then click *Automatically* at the drop-down list.
   d. Click the Slide Show tab.
   e. Click the *Show Media Controls* check box in the Set Up group to remove the check mark.

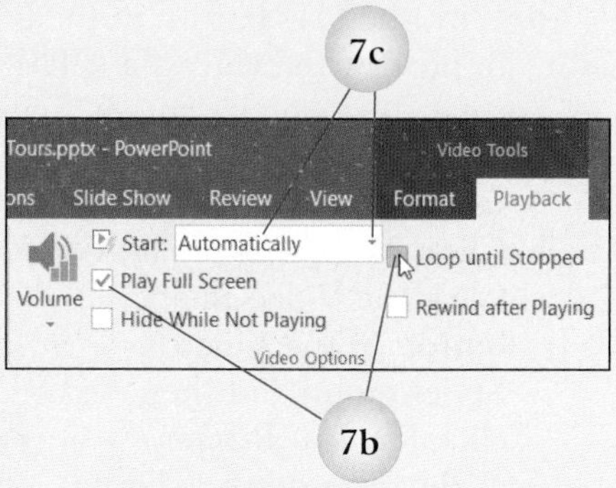

8. Make Slide 1 active and then run the slide show. When the slide displays containing the video, the video will automatically begin. When the video is finished playing, press the Esc key to return to Normal view.
9. Print Slide 8.
10. Compress the video file by completing the following steps:
    a. Make Slide 8 active and then click the video file window.
    b. Click the File tab.
    c. At the Info backstage area, click the Optimize Compatibility button.
    d. When the optimization is complete, click the Close button in the Optimize Media Compatibility dialog box.
    e. Click the Compress Media button and then click *Internet Quality* at the drop-down list.
    f. At the Compress Media dialog box, wait until the compression is complete (notice the progress bar along the bottom of the dialog box) and then the initial size of the video file and the number of megabytes saved by the compression.
    g. Click the Close button to close the dialog box and then click the Back button to return to the presentation.

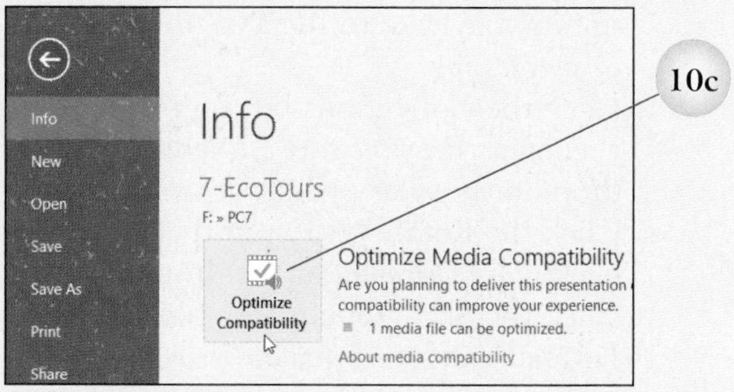

11. Save **7-EcoTours.pptx**.

Complete these optional steps to insert a video from the Internet into a slide.

12. With Slide 8 active, insert a new slide with the Blank layout.
13. Click the Insert tab, click the Video button in the Media group, and then click *Online Video* at the drop-down list.
14. Click in the *Search YouTube* box, type Antarctica wildlife, and then press the Enter key.
15. At the search results window, double-click a video that interests you.
16. Size and position the video window in the slide to better fill the slide.
17. Make Slide 1 active and then run the slide show. When the slide with the video file you inserted displays, click the Play button in the video window. When the video is finished playing, press the Esc key to return to Normal view.
18. Save **7-EcoTours.pptx**.

Check Your Work

Trimming a Video File

Quick Steps

Trim a Video File

1. Insert video file.
2. Click Video Tools Playback tab.
3. Click Trim Video button.
4. Specify start time and/or end time.
5. Click OK.

Trim Video

Use the Trim Video button on the Video Tools Playback tab to trim the beginning and end of a video. This might be helpful in a situation where a portion of the video should be removed that is not pertinent to the message in the presentation. Trimming is limited to a portion of the beginning and end of the video.

To trim a video, insert the video file in the slide, click the Video Tools Playback tab, and then click the Trim Video button in the Editing group. At the Trim Video dialog box, specify the start and/or end time for the video. To trim the start of the video, insert a specific time in the *Start Time* measurement box or drag the green start point marker on the slider bar below the video. Zero in on a very specific starting point by clicking the Next Frame button or the Previous Frame button to move the display of the video a single frame at a time. Complete similar steps to trim the ending of the video except use the red end point marker on the slider bar or insert the specific ending time in the *End Time* measurement box.

Project 4c **Trimming a Video** Part 3 of 5

1. With **7-EcoTour.pptx** open, make Slide 8 active.
2. Trim the first part of the video that shows the running horses by completing the following steps:
   a. Click the video to select it and then click the Video Tools Playback tab.
   b. Click the Trim Video button in the Editing group.
   c. At the Trim Video dialog box, position the mouse pointer on the green start point marker on the slider bar until the pointer displays as a double-headed arrow pointing left and right. Click and hold down the left mouse button, drag the start point marker to approximately the *00:04.0* time, and then release the mouse button.
   d. Click the Next Frame button until the first image of the birds displays and the horses have completely disappeared off the screen. (Depending on where you dragged the start point marker, you may need to click the Previous Frame button.)
   e. Click the OK button.

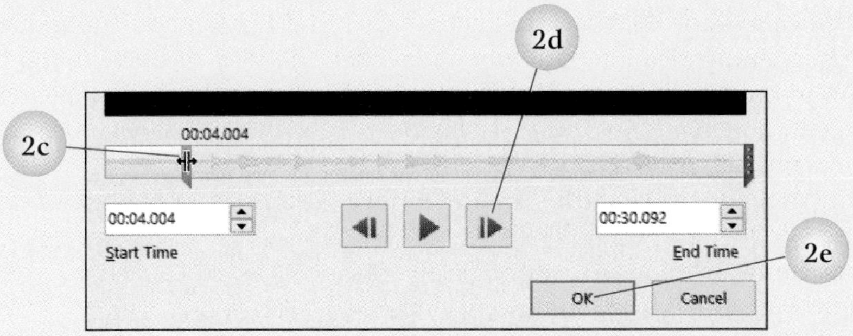

3. Click the *Fade In* measurement box up arrow in the Editing group until *01.00* displays and then click the *Fade Out* measurement box up arrow until *01.00* displays.
4. Run the slide show and then press the Esc key to return to the Normal view.
5. Save **7-EcoTours.pptx**.

Playing an Audio File throughout a Slide Show

An audio file can be inserted in a presentation to play when a specific slide displays when running the slide show. An audio file can also be customized to play continually through all of the slides when running the slide show. Generally, an audio file that plays continually throughout the presentation would be used when setting up an automated presentation.

Play in Background

To specify that the audio file plays throughout the presentation, click the Play in Background button in the Audio Styles group on the Audio Tools Playback tab. When this button is clicked, the *Start* option box in the Audio Options group changes to *Automatically*, and a check mark is inserted in the *Play Across Slides* check box, the *Loop until Stopped* check box, and the *Hide During Show* check box. To make the presentation automated, display the Set Up Show dialog box and then insert a check mark in the *Loop continuously until 'Esc'* check box.

Project 4d Playing an Audio File throughout a Slide Show — Part 4 of 5

1. With **7-EcoTours.pptx** open, make Slide 8 active and then make the following changes:
   a. Select and then delete the video file.
   b. Apply the Title Only slide layout.
   c. Type the title Let the adventure begin! and then change the font size to 54 points and the font color to standard dark blue.
   d. Distribute the title placeholder vertically on the slide. (Do this by clicking the Align button on the Drawing Tools Format tab and then clicking *Distribute Vertically* at the drop-down list.)
2. Make Slide 1 active and then insert an audio file that plays throughout all slides by completing the following steps:
   a. Click the Insert tab, click the Audio button in the Media group, and then click *Audio on My PC* at the drop-down list.
   b. At the Insert Audio dialog box, navigate to the PC7 folder on your storage medium and then double-click ***AudioFile-02.mid***.
   c. With the Audio Tools Playback tab active, click the Play in Background button in the Audio Styles group. (Notice that when you click the Play in Background button, the *Start* option box in the Audio Options group changes to *Automatically*, and a check mark is inserted in the *Play Across Slides* check box, the *Loop until Stopped* check box, and the *Hide During Show* check box.)
   d. Click the Volume button in the Audio Options group and then click *Medium* at the drop-down list.
3. Specify that you want slides to automatically advance after five seconds by completing the following steps:
   a. Click the Transitions tab.
   b. Click the *After* measurement box up arrow in the Timing group until *00:05.00* displays.
   c. Click the *On Mouse Click* check box to remove the check mark.
   d. Click the Apply To All button.

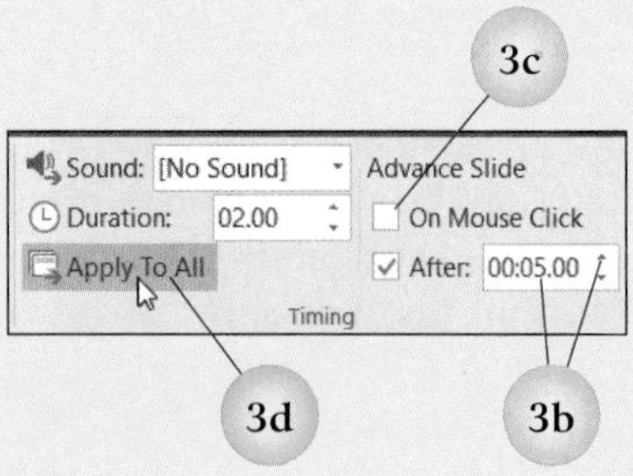

4. Set up the slide show to run continuously by completing the following steps:
   a. Click the Slide Show tab.
   b. Click the Set Up Slide Show button.
   c. At the Set Up Show dialog box, click the *Loop continuously until 'Esc'* check box to insert a check mark.

d. Click OK to close the dialog box.

5. If necessary, make Slide 1 active and then run the slide show. When the slide show begins for the second time, press the Esc key to return to Normal view.
6. Save and then close **7-EcoTours.pptx**.

Check Your Work

Creating a Screen Recording

PowerPoint includes a screen recording feature that will record actions as they are being performed on the screen. A screen recording is automatically inserted into the active slide as a video file, and the Video Tools Format tab and Video Tools Playback tab are available. Format a screen recording in the same manner as formatting a video file.

Screen Recording

Create a screen recording by opening any necessary files (other PowerPoint presentations, different applications, or an Internet browser), clicking the Insert tab, and then clicking the Screen Recording button in the Media group. At the Screen Recording toolbar that displays, click the Select Area button. When the mouse pointer displays as crosshairs, click and hold down the left mouse button, drag to select the screen area that will be used in the screen recording, and then release the mouse button. Once the area is selected, click the Record button on the Screen Recording toolbar, as shown in Figure 7.7. A message will display stating how to end the recording and a countdown to begin the recording. When the countdown is complete, the screen recording will record all mouse movements and actions performed on the screen. Press the Windows logo key + Shift + Q to end the recording. The recording is automatically inserted in the active slide.

A screen recording file is saved with the presentation. To make the recording available for other presentations, save it as a separate file by right-clicking the recording and then clicking *Save Media As* at the shortcut menu. At the Save Media As dialog box, navigate to the desired folder, type a name for the recording in the *File name* text box, and then click the Save button. Insert the recording into a different presentation with the Video button in the Media group.

Figure 7.7 Screen Recording Toolbar

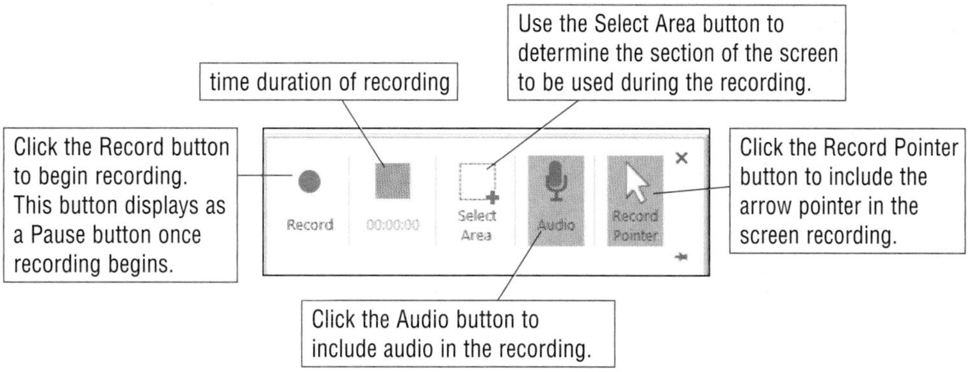

Project 4e **Creating a Screen Recording** Part 5 of 5

1. Open **Animations.pptx** and save it with the name **7-Animations.pptx**.
2. Make Slide 6 active.
3. Open **MotionPath.pptx**. Make sure no other applications are open except for **7-Animations.pptx** and **MotionPath.pptx**.
4. Click the PowerPoint button on the taskbar and then click **7-Animations.pptx**.
5. Create a screen recording of the steps to insert a custom motion path in a slide by completing the following steps:
   a. Click the Insert tab.
   b. Click the Screen Recording button in the Media group.
   c. When the Screen Recording toolbar displays, click the Select Area button.
   d. Using the mouse, drag to select the entire PowerPoint window for the **MotionPath.pptx** file.
   e. Click the Record button on the Screen Recording toolbar.
   f. In the **MotionPath.pptx** window, click the moon image to select it.

5e

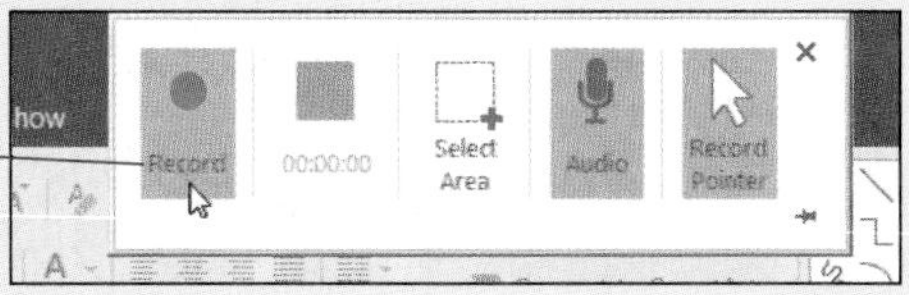

   g. Click the Animations tab.
   h. Click the More Animations button in the Animations group.
   i. Scroll down the drop-down list and then click *Custom Path* in the *Motion Paths* section.
   j. Using the mouse, click and drag the moon around the Earth image, ending in the original location, release the mouse button, and then double-click the mouse button.
   k. Press the Windows logo key + Shift + Q to end the screen recording.
6. Format the screen recording by completing the following steps:
   a. With the Video Tools Format tab active, click in the *Shape Height* measurement box, type 4.5, and then press the Enter key.
   b. Drag the screen recording down so it is positioned below the title and centered vertically on the slide.
7. View the screen recording by clicking the Play button in the Preview group.
8. Save the screen recording to your storage medium by completing the following steps:
   a. Right-click anywhere in the screen recording.
   b. Click the *Save Media as* option at the shortcut menu.
   c. At the Save Media As dialog box, navigate to the PC7 folder on your storage medium.
   d. Type the name 7-Motion in the *File name* text box.
   e. Click the Save button.
9. Make Slide 1 active and then run the slide show. When the slide with the screen recording displays, click the Play button in the video window. When the video is finished playing, press the Esc key to return to Normal view.
10. Print Slide 6.
11. Save and then close **7-Animations.pptx**.
12. Close **MotionPath.pptx** without saving changes.

8b

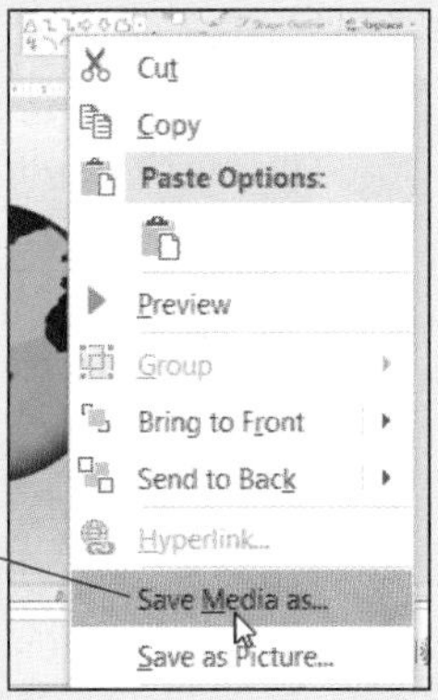

Check Your Work

Chapter Summary

- Apply animation to an item in a slide with options in the Animation group on the Animations tab. Specify animation effects with options from the Effect Options button drop-down gallery.
- Click the Preview button on the Animations tab to view the animation effects without running the slide show.
- Remove an animation effect from an item in a slide by clicking the *None* option in the Animation group on the Animations tab.
- The Add Animation button in the Advanced Animation group on the Animations tab provides four types of animation effects—entrance, exit, emphasis, and motion paths.
- Use the Animation Painter button in the Advanced Animation group on the Animations tab to apply the same animation to items in more than one location in a slide or slides.
- Use options in the Timing group on the Animations tab to determine when an animation starts on a slide, the duration of the animation, the delay between animations, and the order in which animations appear on the slide.
- Use the Animation Pane to customize animation effects. Display the pane by clicking the Animation Pane button in the Advanced Animation group on the Animations tab.
- Apply a sound to an animation with the *Sound* option box at the effect options dialog box with the Effect tab selected. The name of the dialog box varies depending on the animation effect selected.
- A build displays important points on a slide one point at a time. A build can be applied that dims the previous bulleted point with the *After animation* option box at the effect options dialog box with the Effect tab selected.
- Specify a path an item is to follow when it displays on the slide with options in the *Motion Paths* section of the Add Animation button drop-down gallery. To draw a motion path, choose the *Custom path* option at the drop-down gallery.
- Use the Trigger button in the Advanced Animation group to specify that an animation effect occurs during a slide show by clicking an item on the slide.
- Customize a slide show with options in the Set Up Show dialog box. Display the dialog box by clicking the Slide Show tab and then clicking the Set Up Slide Show button.
- To prepare an automated slide show, insert a check mark in the *Loop continuously until 'Esc'* check box at the Set Up Show dialog box.
- To apply specific times to slides, click the Rehearse Timings button in the Set Up group on the Slide Show tab. Use buttons on the Recording toolbar to set, pause, or repeat times.
- To record narration for a presentation, click the Record Slide Show button in the Set Up group on the Slide Show tab and then click the Start Recording button at the Record Slide Show dialog box.
- Hide or unhide a slide in a slide show by clicking the Hide Slide button in the Set Up group on the Slide Show tab.
- Specify on which monitor to run the slide show with the *Monitor* option in the Monitors group on the Slide Show tab.

- If PowerPoint is running on a computer with two monitors or on a laptop with dual-display capabilities, the slide show can be displayed in full-screen view on one monitor and in Presenter view on the other monitor.
- Use the Present Online feature to share a slide show with others over the Internet. Send a link to the people who will view the slide show and then everyone can watch the slide show in their web browsers.
- Draw or highlight text or objects in slides while in Normal view using options on the Ink Tools Pens tab. Display the Ink Tools Pens tab by clicking the Start Inking button in the Ink group on the Review tab.
- Create a custom slide show, which is a slide show within a slide show, with options in the Define Custom Show dialog box.
- To run a custom slide show, click the Custom Slide Show button in the Start Slide Show group on the Slide Show tab and then click the custom show at the drop-down list.
- Print a custom slide show at the Print backstage area by clicking the first gallery in the *Settings* category and then clicking the custom show in the *Custom Shows* section.
- Insert an audio file in a slide by clicking the Audio button in the Media group on the Insert tab and then clicking *Audio on My PC*. Use options on the Audio Tools Format tab and the Audio Tools Playback tab to format and customize the audio file.
- Insert a video file in a slide by clicking the Video button in the Media group on the Insert tab and then clicking *Video on My PC*. Use options on the Video Tools Format tab and the Video Tools Playback tab to format and customize the video file.
- When a slide show runs, media controls display along the bottom of an audio icon or video window in a slide when the mouse is moved over the icon or window. Turn on or off the display of these media controls with the *Show Media Controls* check box in the Set Up group on the Slide Show tab.
- Compress a video file to improve playback performance and save disk space. Compress a video file by clicking the File tab to display the Info backstage area, clicking the Compress Media button, and then clicking the specific compression.
- Use the Trim Video button on the Video Tools Playback tab to trim the beginning and/or end of a video.
- Create and insert a screen recording by clicking the Screen Recording button in the Media group on the Insert tab, selecting the recording area, beginning the recording, and then formating the recording that is inserted in the selected slide.

Commands Review

FEATURE	RIBBON TAB, GROUP/OPTION	BUTTON, OPTION
add animations	Animations, Advanced Animation	
Animation Painter	Animations, Advanced Animation	
Animation Pane	Animations, Advanced Animation	
animations	Animations, Animation	
compress video file	File, *Info*	
Define Custom Show dialog box	Slide Show, Start Slide Show	, *Custom Shows*, New
hide/unhide slide	Slide Show, Set Up	
ink tools	Review, Ink	
insert audio file	Insert, Media	
insert video file	Insert, Media	
optimize video file	File, *Info*	
present online	Slide Show, Start Slide Show	
Recording toolbar	Slide Show, Set Up	
screen recording	Insert, Media	
Set Up Show dialog box	Slide Show, Set Up	
Trim Video dialog box	Video Tools Playback, Editing	

Workbook

Chapter study tools and assessment activities are available in the *Workbook* ebook. These resources are designed to help you further develop and demonstrate mastery of the skills learned in this chapter.

Microsoft®

PowerPoint®

Integrating, Sharing, and Protecting Presentations

CHAPTER 8

Performance Objectives

Upon successful completion of Chapter 8, you will be able to:

1 Import a Word outline into a presentation
2 Copy and paste data between programs and use the Clipboard
3 Share presentations with others
4 Export a presentation to Word
5 Save a presentation in different file formats
6 Embed and link objects
7 Download templates
8 Compare and combine presentations
9 Insert, edit, and delete comments
10 Manage presentation properties
11 Protect a presentation
12 Inspect a presentation and check for accessibility and compatibility issues
13 Manage autosave versions of presentations
14 Customize PowerPoint options

Precheck

Check your current skills to focus your study.

Share data between programs in the Microsoft Office suite by importing and exporting, copying and pasting, copying and embedding, or copying and linking data. The method for sharing data depends on the data and whether it is static or dynamic. Use options in the Share backstage area to share a presentation online or as an email attachment and use options at the Export backstage area to create a video or handout of a presentation and save a presentation in a variety of file formats. If PowerPoint is used in a collaborative environment, comments can be inserted in a presentation and then the presentation can be shared with others. Use options in the Info backstage area to manage presentation properties, password protect a presentation, insert a digital signature, inspect a presentation, and manage versions. In this chapter, you will learn how to complete these tasks as well as how to download design templates from Office.com.

Data Files

Before beginning chapter work, copy the PC8 folder to your storage medium and then make PC8 the active folder.

SNAP

If you are a SNAP user, launch the Precheck and Tutorials from your Assignments page.

Project 1 Import a Word Outline, Save the Presentation in Different File Formats, and Copy and Paste Objects between Programs

9 Parts

You will create a PowerPoint presentation using a Word document, save the presentation in different file formats, and then copy and paste an Excel chart and a Word table into slides in the presentation.

Preview Finished Project

Tutorial

Importing a Word Outline

Quick Steps

Import a Word Outline

1. Open blank presentation.
2. Click New Slide button arrow.
3. Click *Slides from Outline*.
4. Double-click document.

Importing a Word Outline

A Word document containing text formatted as an outline with heading styles can be imported into a PowerPoint presentation. Text formatted with a Heading 1 style becomes the title of a new slide. Text formatted with a Heading 2 style becomes first-level text, paragraphs formatted with a Heading 3 style become second-level text, and so on.

To import a Word outline, open a blank presentation, click the New Slide button arrow in the Slides group on the Home tab, and then click *Slides from Outline* at the drop-down list. At the Insert Outline dialog box, navigate to the folder containing the Word document and then double-click the document. If text in the Word document does not have heading styles applied, PowerPoint creates an outline based on each paragraph of text in the document.

Project 1a Importing a Word Outline

Part 1 of 9

1. At a blank presentation, click the New Slide button arrow in the Slides group on the Home tab and then click *Slides from Outline* at the drop-down list.
2. At the Insert Outline dialog box, navigate to the PC8 folder on your storage medium and then double-click ***ATTopFive.docx***.
3. Click the Design tab and then apply the Parallax design theme.
4. Change the background by completing these steps:
   a. Click the Format Background button in the Customize group on the Design tab.
   b. At the Format Background task pane, click the *Solid fill* option.
   c. Click the Color button and then click the *White, Background 1* option (first column, first row in the *Theme Colors* section).
   d. Click the Apply to All button.
   e. Close the task pane.
5. Delete Slide 1.

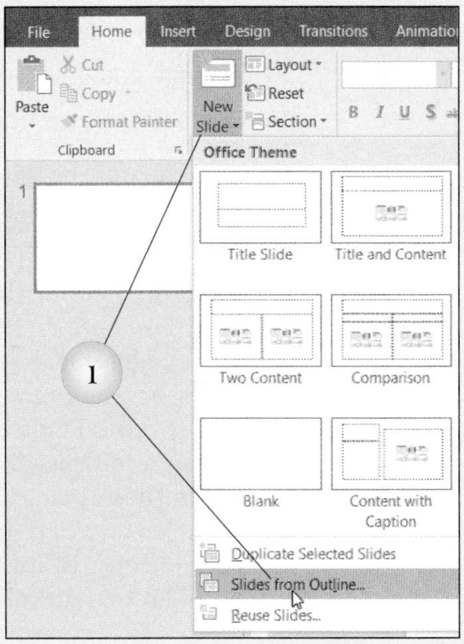

6. Format the new Slide 1 by completing the following steps:
   a. Change the slide layout by clicking the Home tab, clicking the Layout button in the Slides group, and then clicking *Title Only* at the drop-down list.
   b. Drag the placeholder containing the text *Adventure Tours* toward the bottom of the slide and center it horizontally.
   c. Insert the **FCTLogo.jpg**, located in the PC8 folder on your storage medium (do this with the Pictures button on the Insert tab), and then increase the size of the logo so it fills a good portion of the white area of the slide.
7. Make Slide 2 active and then apply the Title Only layout.
8. Make Slide 3 active and then change the bulleted text line spacing to 2.0 lines.
9. Make Slide 4 active and then change the bulleted text line spacing to 1.5 lines.
10. Save the presentation and name it **8-ATTopFive.**

Check Your Work

Tutorial

Copying and Pasting between Programs

Copying and Pasting Data

Use the Copy and Paste buttons in the Clipboard group on the Home tab to copy data such as text or an object from one program and then paste it into another program. For example, in Project 1b, an Excel chart will be copied and then pasted into a PowerPoint slide. A copied object, such as a chart, can be moved and sized like any other object.

Project 1b Copying an Excel Chart to a PowerPoint Slide — Part 2 of 9

1. With **8-ATTopFive.pptx** open, make Slide 2 active.
2. Open Excel and then open **Top5Tours.xlsx**, located in the PC8 folder on your storage medium.
3. Click in the chart to select it. (Make sure you select the chart and not just an element in the chart.)
4. Click the Copy button in the Clipboard group on the Home tab.
5. Close **Top5Tours.xlsx** and then close Excel.
6. In PowerPoint, with Slide 2 active, click the Paste button in the Clipboard group on the Home tab.
7. Move the chart so it is centered below the title *Top Five Destinations*.
8. Display Slide 1 in the slide pane and then run the slide show.
9. Print only Slide 2.
10. Save **8-ATTopFive.pptx**.

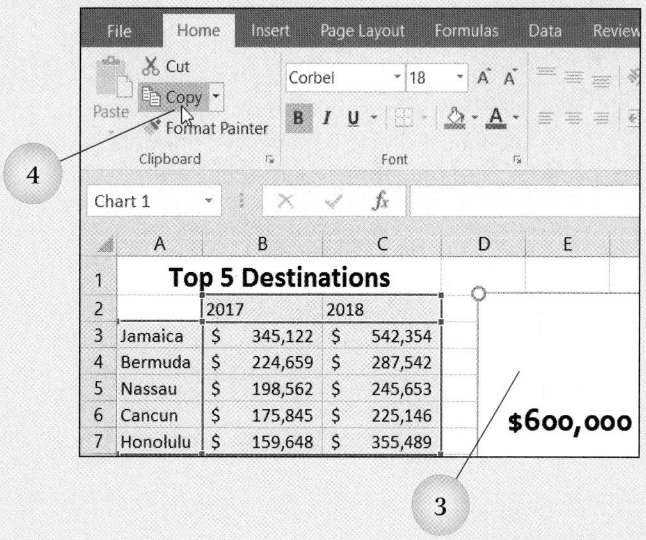

Check Your Work

Hint Click the Options button at the bottom of the Clipboard task pane to customize the display of the task pane.

Use the Clipboard task pane to collect and paste multiple items. Up to 24 different items can be collected and then pasted in various locations. Turn on the display of the Clipboard task pane by clicking the Clipboard group task pane launcher. The Clipboard task pane displays at the left side of the screen.

Select data or an object to be copied and then click the Copy button in the Clipboard group. Continue selecting text or items and clicking the Copy button. To insert an item, position the insertion point in the specific location and then click the item in the Clipboard task pane representing that item. If the copied item is text, the first 50 characters display. When all items are inserted, click the Clear All button to remove any remaining items from the Clipboard task pane. To paste all items from the Clipboard task pane at once, click the Paste All button.

Project 1c Collecting and Pasting Text Between a Document and a Presentation — Part 3 of 9

1. With **8-ATTopFive.pptx** open, make Slide 4 active and then insert a new slide with the Title and Content layout.
2. Click in the title placeholder and then type Spring Treks.
3. Copy text from Word by completing the following steps:
   a. Open Word and then open **AdvTrek.docx**.
   b. Click the Clipboard group task pane launcher to display the Clipboard task pane.
   c. If any data displays in the Clipboard task pane, click the Clear All button at the top of the task pane.
   d. Select the text *Yucatan Adventure – 10 days* (including the paragraph mark following the text—consider turning on the display of nonprinting characters) and then click the Copy button in the Clipboard group.
   e. Select the text *Mexico Adventure – 14 days* and then click the Copy button.
   f. Select the text *Caribbean Highlights – 16 days* and then click the Copy button.
   g. Select the text *California Delights – 7 days* and then click the Copy button.
   h. Select the text *Canyon Adventure – 10 days* and then click the Copy button.
   i. Select the text *Canadian Parks – 12 days* and then click the Copy button.
   j. Select the text *Royal Canadian Adventure – 14 days* and then click the Copy button.
4. Click the PowerPoint button on the taskbar and then paste items from the Clipboard task pane by completing the following steps:
   a. With Slide 5 active, click in the *Click to add text* placeholder.
   b. Click the Clipboard group task pane launcher to display the Clipboard task pane.
   c. Click the *California Delights* item in the Clipboard task pane.
   d. Click the *Canadian Parks* item in the Clipboard task pane.
   e. Click the *Caribbean Highlights* item in the Clipboard task pane.
   f. Click the *Mexico Adventure* item in the Clipboard task pane
   g. Click the *Yucatan Adventure* item in the Clipboard task pane. (Press the Backspace key two times to remove the bullet below *Yucatan Adventure* and the blank line.)
5. Clear the Clipboard task pane by clicking the Clear All button in the upper right corner of the task pane.
6. Close the Clipboard task pane by clicking the Close button (contains an *X*) in the upper right corner of the task pane.
7. Make Slide 1 the active slide and then run the slide show.

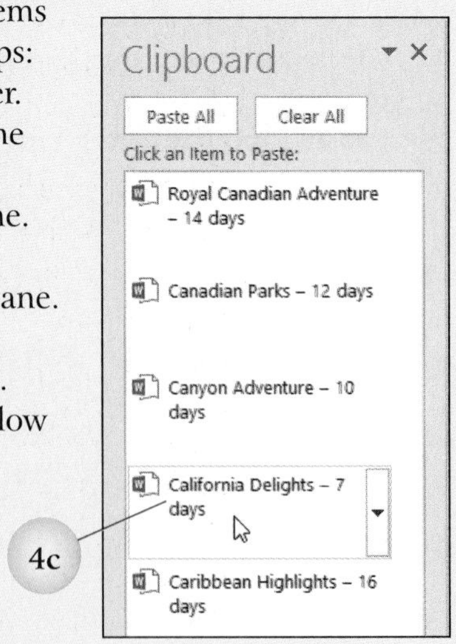

8. Print the presentation as a handout with all slides displayed horizontally on one page. (Make sure the first gallery in the *Settings* category displays as *Print All Slides*.)
9. Save **8-ATTopFive.pptx**.
10. Make Word the active program, close the Clipboard task pane, close **AdvTrek.docx**, and then close Word.

Check Your Work

Sharing Presentations

PowerPoint provides a number of options for sharing presentations between programs, sites on the Internet, other computers, and as attachments. Options for sending and sharing presentations are available at the Share backstage area. Display this backstage area by clicking the File tab and then clicking the *Share* option.

Using the *Share with People* Option

Hint If you have a person's contact information stored, you only have to enter their name in the Invite people text box.

Use the *Share with People* option at the Share backstage area to invite people to view a presentation. To use this feature, the PowerPoint presentation must be saved to a OneDrive account or a shared location such as a website or SharePoint library. (Microsoft SharePoint is a collection of products and software that includes a number of components. If a company or organization uses SharePoint, a presentation can be saved in a library on the organization's SharePoint site so colleagues have a central location for accessing presentations.)

To share a PowerPoint presentation, open the presentation from a OneDrive account (or other shared location) and then click the Share with People button at the Share backstage area. This closes the backstage area and the Share task pane displays at the right side of the screen similar to what is shown in Figure 8.1.

If a presentation is open that is not saved to a OneDrive account, the information at the right side of the Share backstage area will specify that the presentation needs to be saved. To do this, click the Save to Cloud button and, at the Save As backstage area, double-click the OneDrive account. At the Save As dialog box with the OneDrive account folder active and the presentation name in the *File name* text box, click the Save button. With the presentation saved to the OneDrive account, click the File tab, click the *Share* option, and then click the Share with People button. This closes the backstage area and the presentation displays with the Share task pane at the right side of the screen.

In the *Invite people* text box in the Share task pane, type the names or email addresses of people to invite them to view and/or edit the presentation. Type more than one name or email address by separating them with a semicolon. The option box below the *Invite people* text box contains the default setting *Can edit*. At this setting, the people invited will be able to edit the presentation. Change this option to *Can view* if the invited people should only be able to view the presentation.

When all names or email addresses are entered, click the Share button. An email is sent to the email address(es) typed and, in a few moments, the name or names display in the Share task pane. Any time the presentation is opened in the future, displaying the Share backstage area and then clicking the Share with People button will close the backstage area and open the Share task pane in the presentation. To stop sharing the presentation with a person, right-click the person's name in the Share task pane and then click *Remove User* at the shortcut menu.

Figure 8.1 Share Task Pane

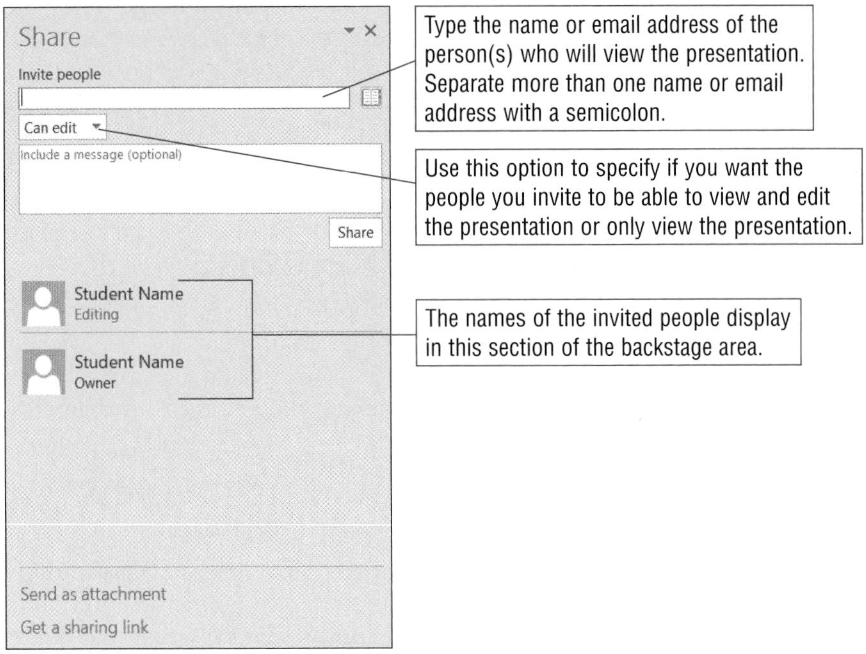
Share
Invite people
Can edit
Include a message (optional)
Share
Student Name
Editing
Student Name
Owner
Send as attachment
Get a sharing link
Type the name or email address of the person(s) who will view the presentation. Separate more than one name or email address with a semicolon.
Use this option to specify if you want the people you invite to be able to view and edit the presentation or only view the presentation.
The names of the invited people display in this section of the backstage area.

Project 1d Inviting People to View Your Presentation

Part 4 of 9

Note: To complete this optional project, you need to be connected to the Internet and have a OneDrive account.

1. With **8-ATTopFive.pptx** open, save the presentation to your OneDrive folder and name it **8-ATTopFive-Shared**. (To do this, click the File tab, click the *Save As* option, and then double-click the OneDrive account in the middle panel. At the Save As dialog box with the OneDrive account folder active, type 8-ATTopFive-Shared in the *File name* text box and then click the Save button.
2. With **8-ATTopFive-Shared.pptx** open, click the File tab and then click the *Share* option.
3. At the Share backstage area with the *Share with People* option selected, click the Share with People button.
4. Type the email address for your instructor and/or the email address of a classmate or friend in the *Invite people* text box in the Share task pane.
5. Click the option box arrow for the option box containing the text *Can edit* and then click *Can view* at the drop-down list.
6. Click the Share button.
7. After a few moments, notice the name(s) that display in the Share task pane.

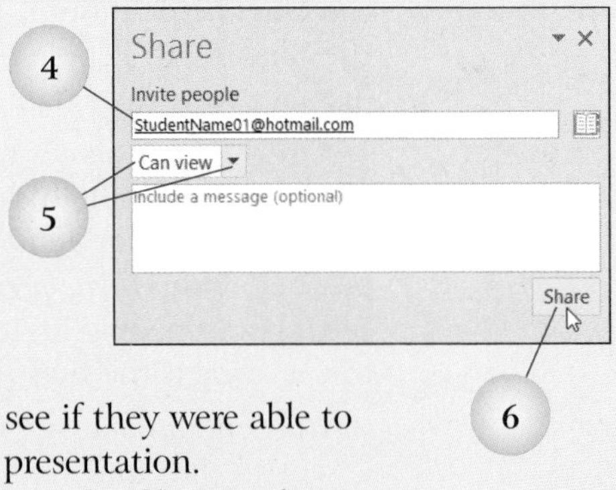
4
5
6
Share
Invite people
StudentName01@hotmail.com
Can view
Include a message (optional)
Share

8. Check with your instructor, classmate, and/or friend to see if they were able to open the email containing the link to your PowerPoint presentation.
9. Remove the name (or one of the names) that displays in the Share task pane by right-clicking the name and then clicking *Remove User* at the shortcut menu.
10. If you have **8-ATTopFive.pptx** saved on a removable device, close **8-ATTopFive-Shared.pptx** saved to your OneDrive folder and then reopen **8-ATTopFive.pptx** from your removable device.

Use the Send as attachment hyperlink that displays near the bottom of the Share task pane to send a copy of the presentation or a PDF version of the presentation as an attachment to the email. The letters PDF stand for *portable document format*, which is a file format developed by Adobe Systems that captures all of the elements of a presentation as an electronic image. To send the presentation as an attachment, an Outlook account must be established.

The Share task pane also contains the Get a sharing link hyperlink that, when clicked, displays options for creating a link for viewing or for editing. Click the Create an edit link button and a link displays for viewing and editing the presentation. Copy the link and paste it an email, instant message, social media site, and so on. To paste a link for viewing the presentation without the ability to edit, click the View-only link button. Copy the link that displays and then paste it in the specific locations.

Using the *Email* Option

Click the *Email* option at the Share backstage area and options display for sending a copy of the presentation as an attachment to an email, sending a link to the presentation, attaching a PDF or XPS copy of the open presentation to an email address, and sending an email as an Internet fax.

As mentioned earlier, to send the presentation as an attachment, an Outlook email account must be established. To create an email that contains a link to the presentation, the presentation must be saved to a OneDrive account or a shared location such as a website or SharePoint library.

Click the Send as PDF button and the presentation is converted to a PDF file and attached to the email. Click the Send as XPS button and the presentation is converted to an XPS file and attached to the email. The XPS file format is a Microsoft file format for publishing content in an easily viewable format. The letters XPS stand for *XML paper specification*, and the letters XML stand for *extensible markup language*, which is a set of rules for encoding presentations electronically. Information displays to the right of both buttons providing a brief description of the formats. Systems that captures all of the elements of a presentation as an electronic image.

Click the Send as Internet Fax button to fax the current presentation without using a fax machine. To use this button, the sender must be signed up with a fax service provider.

Using the *Present Online* Option

Click the *Present Online* option at the Share backstage area to present a presentation through the Office Presentation Service. This process was covered in Chapter 7.

Using the *Publish Slides* Option

Use the *Publish Slides* option at the Share backstage area to save slides in a shared location such as a slide library or a SharePoint site so that other people have access to the presentation and can review or make changes to it.

Project 1e Sending a Presentation as an Email Attachment

Part 5 of 9

Note: Before completing this optional project, check with your instructor to determine if you have Outlook set up as your email provider.

1. With **8-ATTopFive.pptx** open, click the File tab and then click the *Share* option.
2. At the Share backstage area, click the *Email* option and then click the Send as Attachment button.
3. At the Outlook window, type your instructor's email address in the *To* text box.
4. Click the Send button.

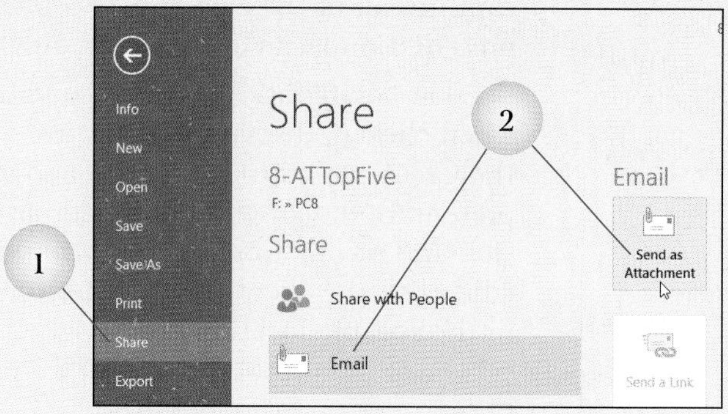

Tutorial

Exporting Presentations

Exporting Presentations

The Export backstage area contains a number of options for saving and exporting a presentation. Options at the Export backstage area include saving a presentation as a PDF or XPS file, creating a video of a presentation, packaging a presentation for a disc, creating handouts, and saving a presentation in a different file format.

Saving a Presentation as a PDF or XPS File

Quick Steps

Save a Presentation as a PDF/XPS File

1. Open presentation.
2. Click File tab.
3. Click *Export* option.
4. Click *Create PDF/XPS Document* option.
5. Click Create PDF/XPS button.
6. Specify PDF or XPS format.
7. Click Publish button.

As explained earlier, the portable document format (PDF) captures all of the elements of a presentation as an electronic image and the XPS format is used for publishing content in an easily viewable format. To save a presentation in PDF or XPS format, click the File tab, click the *Export* option, make sure the *Create PDF/XPS Document* option is selected, and then click the Create PDF/XPS button. This displays the Publish as PDF or XPS dialog box with the *PDF (*.pdf)* option selected in the *Save as type* option box. To save the presentation in XPS format, click the *Save as type* option box and then click *XPS Document (*.xps)* at the drop-down list. At the Save As dialog box, type a name in the *File name* text box and then click the Publish button.

A PDF file can be opened in Adobe Reader, Microsoft Edge, and Microsoft Word. An XPS file can be opened in Adobe Reader, Internet Explorer, and XPS Viewer. One method for opening a PDF or XPS file is to open File Explorer, navigate to the folder containing the file, right-click on the file, and then point to *Open with*. This displays a side menu with the programs that will open the file.

Creating a Video of a Presentation

Quick Steps

Save a Presentation as a Video

1. Open presentation.
2. Click File tab.
3. Click *Export* option.
4. Click *Create a Video* option.
5. Click Create Video button.

Create a video that incorporates all of a presentation's recorded timings and narrations and preserves animations and transitions using the *Create a Video* option. The information at the right side of the Export backstage area describes creating a video and provides a hyperlink to get help on burning a slide show video to a DVD or uploading it to the Web. Click the Get help burning your slide show video to DVD or uploading it to the web hyperlink and information displays on burning a slide show video to disc and publishing a slide show video to YouTube.

Quick Steps

Package a Presentation for CD

1. Open presentation.
2. Click File tab.
3. Click *Export* option.
4. Click *Package Presentation for CD* option.
5. Click Package for CD button.
6. Click Copy to CD button or Copy to Folder button.

Packaging a Presentation

Use the *Package Presentation for CD* option to copy a presentation and include all of the linked files, embedded items, and fonts. Click the *Package Presentation for CD* option and then click the Package for CD button and the Package for CD dialog box displays. At this dialog box, type a name for the CD and specify the files to be copied. The presentation can be copied to a CD or to a specific folder.

Project 1f **Saving a Presentation as PDF and XPS Files, as a Video, and Packaged for a CD**

Part 6 of 9

1. With **8-ATTopFive.pptx** open, save the presentation in PDF format by completing the following steps:
   a. Click the File tab and then click the *Export* option.
   b. Make sure the *Create PDF/XPS Document* option is selected.
   c. Click the Create PDF/XPS button.
   d. At the Publish as PDF or XPS dialog box, make sure the *Save as type* option is set to *PDF (*.pdf)*, insert a check mark in the *Open file after publishing* check box, and then click the Publish button. (In a few moments the presentation displays in PDF format in Adobe Acrobat Reader.)

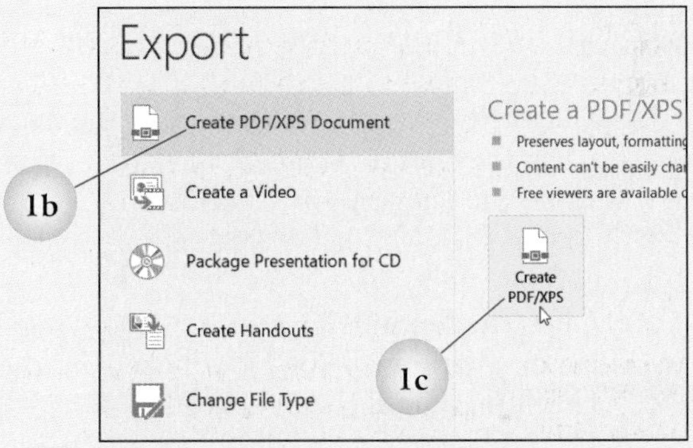

   e. Scroll through the presentation in Adobe Acrobat Reader.
   f. Click the Close button in the upper right corner of the window to close Adobe Acrobat Reader.
2. Save the presentation in XPS format by completing the following steps:
   a. Click the File tab and then click the *Export* option.
   b. With the *Create PDF/XPS Document* option selected, click the Create PDF/XPS button.
   c. At the Publish as PDF or XPS dialog box, click the *Save as type* option box and then click *XPS Document (*.xps)* at the drop-down list.
   d. Make sure the *Open file after publishing* check box contains a check mark and then click the Publish button. (In a few moments the presentation displays in the XPS Viewer.)

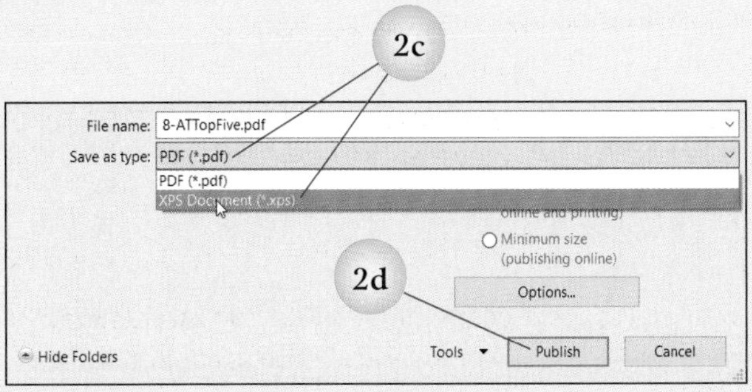

   e. Scroll through the presentation in the XPS Viewer.
   f. Close the XPS viewer by clicking the Close button in the upper right corner of the window.

3. Save **8-ATTopFive.pptx** as a video by completing the following steps:
   a. Click the File tab and then click the *Export* option.
   b. Click the *Create a Video* option.
   c. Click the Create Video button.
   d. At the Save As dialog box, click the Save button. (Saving as a video takes a minute or so. The Status bar displays the saving progress.)

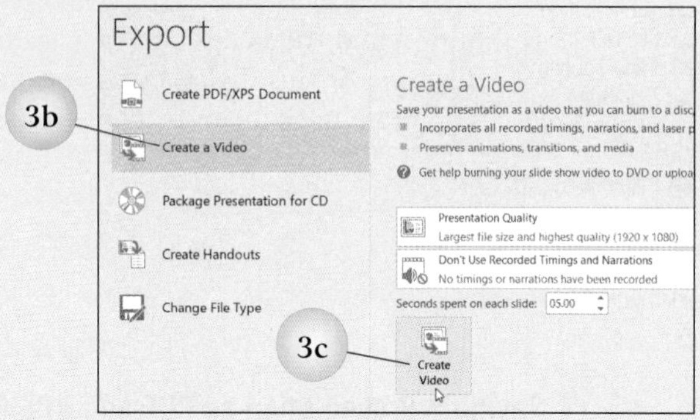

4. When the video has been saved, play the video by completing the following steps:
   a. Click the File Explorer button on the taskbar.
   b. Navigate to the PC8 folder on your storage medium and then double-click *8-ATTopFive.mp4*. (This opens the presentation video in a viewing window.)
   c. Watch the presentation video and, when it is finished, click the Close button in the upper right corner of the window.
   d. Close File Explorer.
5. With **8-ATTopFive.pptx** open, package the presentation by completing the following steps:
   a. Click the File tab and then click the *Export* option.
   b. Click the *Package Presentation for CD* option.
   c. Click the Package for CD button.
   d. At the Package for CD dialog box, select the text in the *Name the CD* text box and type ATTopFiveforCD.
   e. Click the Options button.
   f. At the Options dialog box, make sure the *Embedded TrueType fonts* check box contains a check mark and then click OK.
   g. Click the Copy to Folder button.
   h. At the Copy to Folder dialog box, click the Browse button.
   i. Navigate to the PC8 folder on your storage medium.
   j. Click the Select button.
   k. At the Copy to Folder dialog box, click OK.
   l. At the message asking if you want to include linked files in the presentation, click the Yes button.
   m. When a window displays with the folder name and files, close the window by clicking the Close button in the upper right corner of the window.
   n. Close the Package for CD dialog box by clicking the Close button.

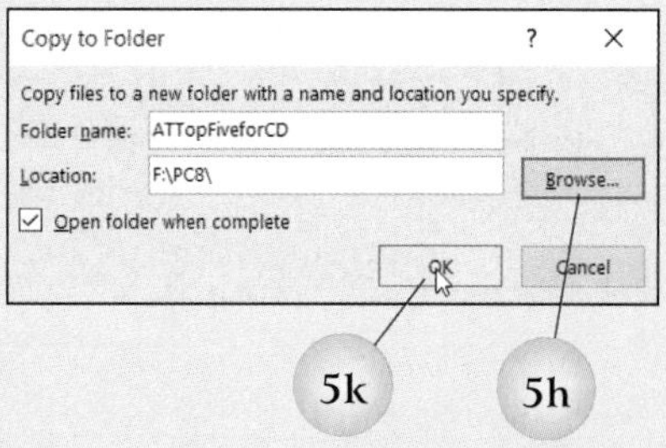

Check Your Work

Exporting a Presentation to a Word Document

Hint Export a presentation to Word to gain greater control over formatting handouts.

Slides can be printed as handouts in PowerPoint; however, exporting a presentation to Word provides greater control over the formatting of the handouts. Use the *Create Handouts* option at the Export backstage area to export a PowerPoint presentation to a Word document. Open the presentation, click the File tab, click the *Export* option, click the *Create Handouts* option, and then click the Create Handouts button. This displays the Send to Microsoft Word dialog box, shown in Figure 8.2. At this dialog box, select the page layout to use in Word and then click OK.

The first four page layout options will export slides as they appear in PowerPoint with lines to the right or below the slides. The last option will export the text only as an outline. Select the *Paste link* option and the Word document will be updated automatically whenever changes are made to the PowerPoint presentation.

Figure 8.2 Send to Microsoft Word Dialog Box

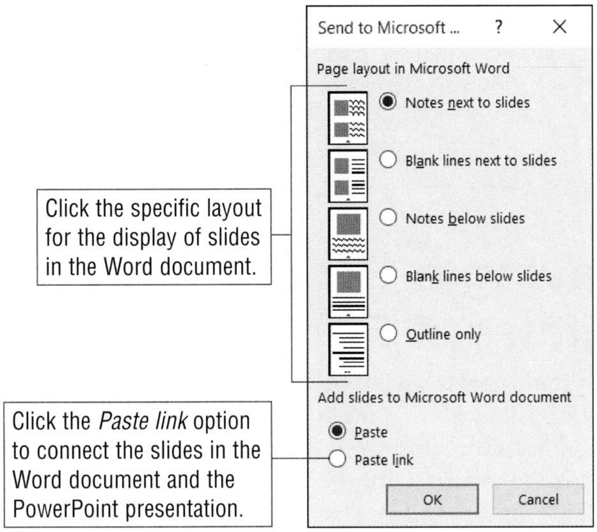

Project 1g **Exporting a Presentation to Word** Part 7 of 9

1. Make sure **8-ATTopFive.pptx** is open, click the File tab, and then click the *Export* option.
2. At the Export backstage area, click the *Create Handouts* option.
3. Click the Create Handouts button.
4. At the Send to Microsoft Word dialog box, click the *Blank lines next to slides* option and then click OK.
5. If necessary, click the Word button on the taskbar.
6. In Word, select the first column (the column that contains *Slide 1*, *Slide 2*, and so on) and then turn on bold formatting. (The presentation was inserted in a table in Word.)

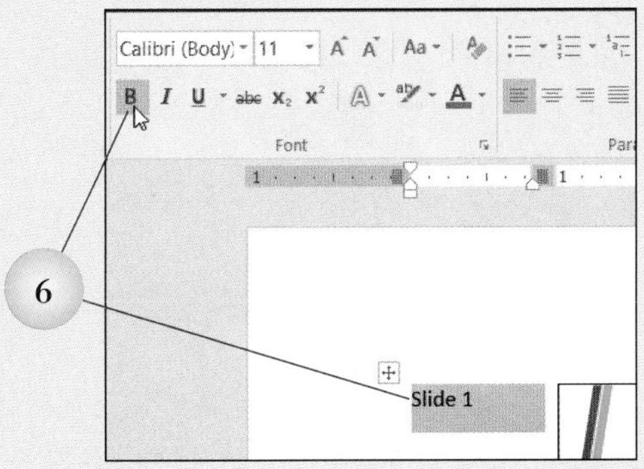

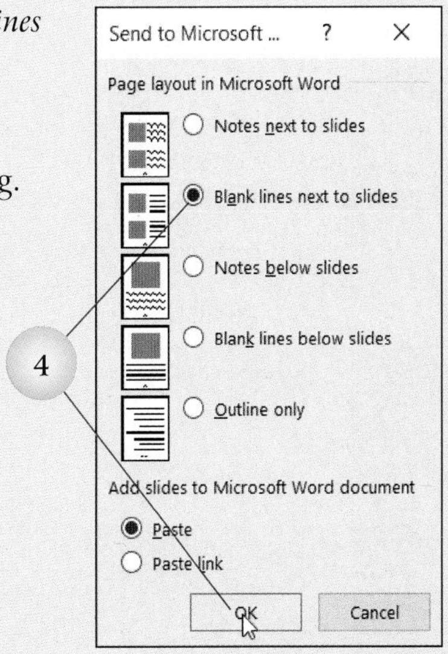

7. Select the third column (contains the lines) and then apply the standard red font color.
8. Save the document and name it **8-ATTopTours**.

9. Print and then close **8-ATTopTours.docx**.
10. Close Word.
11. In PowerPoint, export **8-ATTopFive.pptx** as an outline by completing the following steps:
    a. Click the File tab and then click the *Export* option.
    b. At the Export backstage area, click the *Create Handouts* option.
    c. Click the Create Handouts button.
    d. At the Send to Microsoft Word dialog box, click the *Outline only* option and then click OK.
    e. If necessary, click the Word button on the taskbar.
    f. In Word, scroll through the document and then close Word without saving the document.
12. In PowerPoint, save **8-ATTopFive.pptx**.

Check Your Work

Tutorial

Saving a Presentation in a Different Format

Saving a Presentation in a Different Format

A presentation is saved, by default, as a PowerPoint presentation with the .pptx file extension. If the presentation will be used by someone who is using a different presentation program or a different version of PowerPoint, the presentation may need to be saved in another format. At the Export backstage area, click the *Change File Type* option and the backstage area displays as shown in Figure 8.3.

Figure 8.3 Export Backstage Area with *Change File Type* Option Selected

Click the *Change File Type* option to display options for saving a file in a different format.

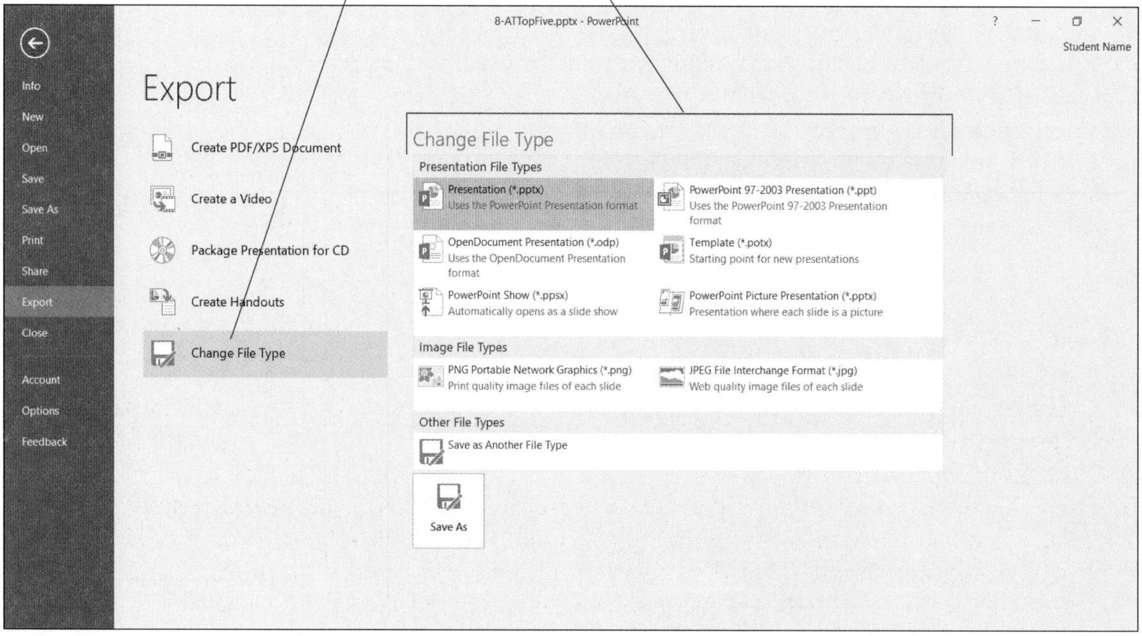

Quick Steps

Save a Presentation in a Different Format

1. Click File tab.
2. Click *Export* option.
3. Click *Change File Type* option.
4. Click format.
5. Click Save As button.

With options in the *Presentation File Types* section, a PowerPoint presentation can be saved with the default file format (.pptx) or in a previous version of PowerPoint. Use the *OpenDocument Presentation (*.odp)* option to save a presentation and make it available to open in other applications. The OpenDocument format enables files to be exchanged, retrieved, and edited with any OpenDocument-compliant software. Save a presentation as a template to use the presentation as a basis for creating other presentations. (Saving a presentation as a template was explained in Chapter 6.) Save a presentation in the PowerPoint Show (*.ppsx) format and the presentation automatically starts when it is opened. When a presentation is saved using the *PowerPoint Picture Presentation (*.pptx)* option, the contents of the presentation are flattened to a single picture per slide. A presentation saved in this format can be opened and viewed but not edited.

Project 1h Saving a Presentation in Different Formats — Part 8 of 9

1. Make sure that **8-ATTopFive.pptx** is open.
2. Save the presentation as a PowerPoint Show by completing the following steps:
   a. Click the File tab and then click the *Export* option.
   b. At the Export backstage area, click the *Change File Type* option.
   c. Click the *PowerPoint Show (*.ppsx)* option in the *Presentation File Types* section and then click the Save As button.

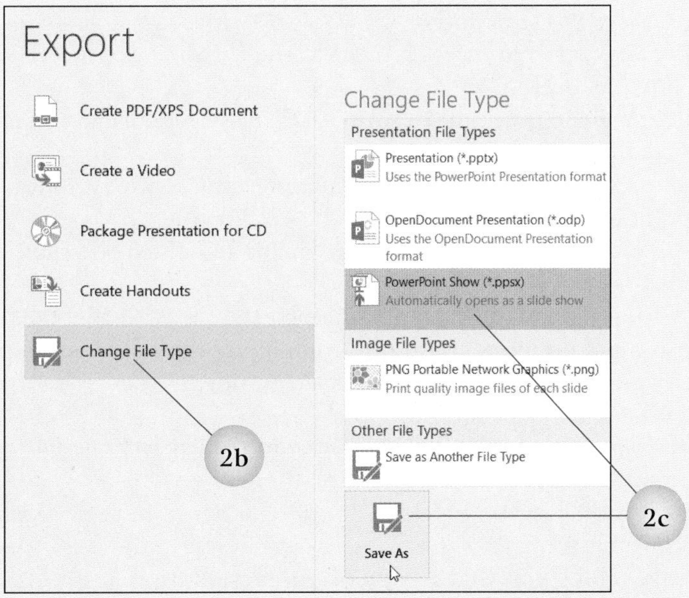

   d. At the Save As dialog box, click the Save button. (This saves the presentation with the file extension *.ppsx*.)
3. Close **8-ATTopFive.ppsx**.
4. Open the **8-ATTopFive.ppsx** file in File Explorer by completing the following steps:
   a. Click the File Explorer button (button containing yellow file folders) on the taskbar.
   b. In File Explorer, double-click the drive representing your storage medium.
   c. Navigate to the PC8 folder on your storage medium and then double-click ***8-ATTopFive.ppsx***.

d. If a *How do you want to open this file?* window displays, double-click the *Microsoft Office PowerPoint Viewer* option in the window. (This starts the presentation in Slide Show view.)
e. Run the slide show.
f. When the slide show has ended, click the left mouse button.
g. Close File Explorer by clicking the File Explorer button on the taskbar and then clicking the Close button in the upper right corner of the window.

5. Open **8-ATTopFive.pptx** (make sure you open the file with the .pptx file extension) and then save it as a previous version of PowerPoint by completing the following steps:
   a. Click the File tab and then click the *Export* option.
   b. Click the *Change File Type* option.
   c. Click *PowerPoint 97-2003 Presentation (*.ppt)* in the *Presentation File Types* section and then click the Save As button.
   d. At the Save As dialog box, type 8-ATTopFive-2003format in the *File name* text box and then click the Save button.
   e. At the Microsoft PowerPoint Compatibility Checker dialog box, click the Continue button.
   f. At the presentation, notice that the file name at the top of the screen displays followed by the words *[Compatibility Mode]*.
6. Close **8-ATTopFive-2003format.ppt**.
7. Open **8-ATTopFive.pptx** (make sure you open the file with the .pptx file extension) and then save it in OpenDocument Presentation format by completing the following steps:
   a. Click the File tab and then click the *Export* option.
   b. Click the *Change File Type* option.
   c. Click *OpenDocument Presentation (*.odp)* in the *Presentation File Types* section and then click the Save As button.
   d. At the Save As dialog box, make sure *8-ATTopFive.odp* displays in the *File name* text box and then click the Save button.
   e. When a message displays stating that the presentation may contain features that are not compatible with the format, click the Yes button.
   f. Run the slide show and notice that formatting remained the same.
8. Close **8-ATTopFive.odp**.
9. Open **8-ATTopFive.pptx** (make sure you open the file with the .pptx file extension) and then save it as a picture presentation by completing the following steps:
   a. Click the File tab and then click the *Export* option.
   b. Click the *Change File Type* option.
   c. Click *PowerPoint Picture Presentation (*.pptx)* in the *Presentation File Types* section and then click the Save As button.
   d. At the Save As dialog box, type 8-ATTopFive-Picture in the *File name* text box and then click the Save button.
   e. At a message telling you that a copy of the presentation has been saved, click OK.
   f. Close **8-ATTopFive.pptx**.
   g. Open **8-ATTopFive-Picture.pptx**.
   h. Click Slide 1 in the slide pane and notice how the entire slide is selected rather than a specific element in the slide. In this format you cannot edit a slide.
10. Close **8-ATTopFive-Picture.pptx**.

Check Your Work

Save slides in a presentation as graphic images in PNG or JPEG format with options in the *Image File Types* section of the Export backstage area. Save slides as PNG images for print quality, and save slides as JPEG images if the slide images will be posted to the Internet. To save a slide or all slides as graphic images, click either the *PNG Portable Network Graphics (*.png)* option or the *JPEG File Interchange Format (*.jpg)* option in the *Image File Types* section and then click the Save As button. At the Save As dialog box, type a name for the slide or presentation and then click the Save button. At the message that displays, click the All Slides button if every slide in the presentation is to be saved as a graphic image or click the Just This One button if only the current slide is to be saved as a graphic image. Click the All Slides button and a message displays indicating that all slides in the presentation were saved as separate files in a folder. The name of the folder is the name typed in the *File name* text box in the Save As dialog box.

Project 1i **Saving Slides as Graphic Images** Part 9 of 9

1. Open **8-ATTopFive.pptx**.
2. Click the File tab and then click the *Export* option.
3. At the Export backstage area, click the *Change File Type* option.
4. Click the *PNG Portable Network Graphics (*.png)* option in the *Image File Types* section and then click the Save As button.
5. At the Save As dialog box, make sure **8-ATTopFive.png** displays in the *File name* text box and then click the Save button.
6. At the message that displays, click the All Slides button.

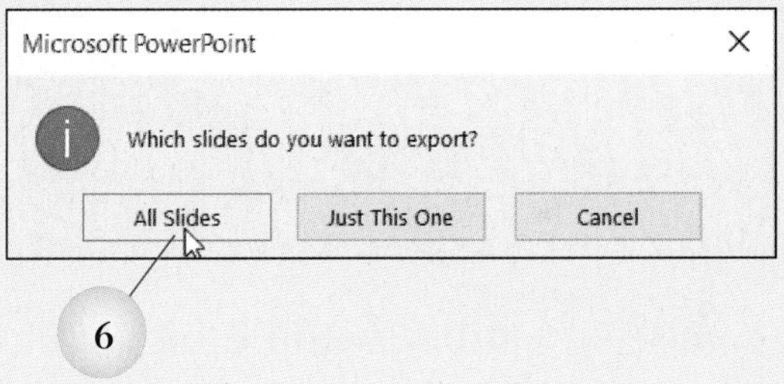

7. At the message telling you that each slide has been saved as a separate file in the 8-ATTopFive.png folder, click OK.
8. Open Word.
9. At a blank document, change the font size to 18 points, turn on bold formatting, change the alignment to center, and then type Adventure Tours.
10. Press the Enter key two times and then insert one of the slides saved in PNG format by completing the following steps:
    a. Click the Insert tab and then click the Pictures button in the Illustrations group.
    b. At the Insert Picture dialog box, navigate to the 8-ATTopFive folder in the PC8 folder on your storage medium and then double-click ***Slide3.PNG***.

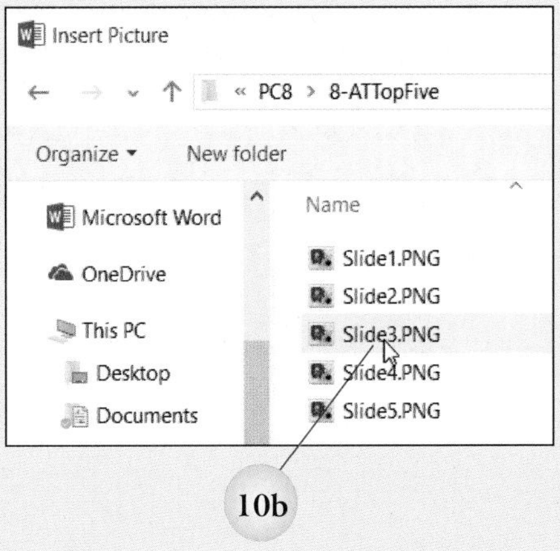

11. Format the image in the document by completing the following steps:
    a. Click in the *Shape Height* measurement box in the Size group on the Picture Tools Format tab, type 2.8, and then press the Enter key.
    b. Click the *Drop Shadow Rectangle* option in the Picture Styles group (fourth option).

12. Press Ctrl + End to move the insertion point to the end of the document, press the Enter key, and then complete steps similar to those in Steps 10 and 11 to insert and format the image Slide4.PNG in the document.
13. Save the document and name it **8-ATTours**.
14. Print and then close **8-ATTours.docx**.
15. Close Word.
16. Capture an image of the Open dialog box and insert the image in a PowerPoint slide by completing the following steps:
    a. Press Ctrl + N to display a new blank presentation.
    b. Click the Layout button in the Slides group on the Home tab and then click *Blank* at the drop-down list.
    c. Press Ctrl + F12 to display the Open dialog box.
    d. At the Open dialog box, navigate to the PC8 folder on your storage medium.
    e. Click the option button at the right side of the *File name* text box (the option button contains the text *All PowerPoint Presentations*) and then click *All Files (*.*)* at the drop-down list.
    f. Make sure all of your project files display. You may need to scroll down the list box to display the files.
    g. Press and hold down the Alt key, press the Print Screen button on your keyboard, and then release the Alt key. (This captures an image of the Open dialog box and not the entire screen.)
    h. Click the Cancel button to close the Open dialog box.
    i. Click the Paste button. (This inserts the image of the Open dialog box into the slide.)
17. Print the slide as a full page slide.
18. Close the presentation without saving it and then close **8-ATTopFive.pptx**.

Check Your Work

Project 2 Embed and Link Excel Charts to a Presentation **3 Parts**

You will open a company funds presentation and then copy an Excel pie chart and embed it in a PowerPoint slide. You will also copy and link an Excel column chart to a slide and then update the chart in Excel.

Preview Finished Project

Embedding and Linking Objects

One of the reasons the Microsoft Office suite is used extensively in business is because it allows data from one program to be seamlessly integrated into another program. For example, a chart depicting sales projections created in Excel can easily be added to a slide in a PowerPoint presentation to the company board of directors on the new budget forecast.

Integration is the process of adding content from other sources to another file. Integrating content is different than simply copying and pasting it. While it makes sense to copy and paste objects from one application to another when the content is not likely to change, if the content is dynamic, the copy and paste method becomes problematic and inefficient. To illustrate this point, assume one of the outcomes from the presentation to the board of directors is a revision to the sales projections, which means that the chart originally created in Excel has to be updated to reflect the new projections. If the first version of the chart was copied and pasted into PowerPoint, it would need to be deleted and then the revised chart in Excel would need to be copied and pasted into the slide again. Both Excel and PowerPoint would need to be opened and edited to reflect this change in projection. In this case, copying and pasting the chart would not be efficient.

To eliminate the inefficiency of the copy and paste method, objects can be integrated between programs. An object can be text in a presentation; data in a table, a chart, a picture, a slide; or any combination of data. The program that was used to create the object is called the *source* and the program the object is linked or embedded to is called the *destination*.

Embedding and linking are two methods for integrating data in addition to the copy and paste method. When an object is embedded, the content in the object is stored in both the source and the destination programs. When editing an embedded object in the destination program, the source program in which the program was created opens. If the content in the object is changed in the source program, the change is not reflected in the destination program and vice versa.

Hint Static data remains the same while dynamic data changes periodically or continually.

Linking inserts a code into the destination file connecting the destination to the name and location of the source object. The object itself is not stored within the destination file. When linking, if a change is made to the content in the source program, the destination program reflects the change automatically. The decision to integrate data by embedding or linking will depend on whether the data is dynamic or static. If the data is dynamic, then linking the object is the most efficient method of integration.

Tutorial

Embedding Objects

Embedding Objects

An object that is embedded is stored in both the source *and* the destination programs. The content of the object can be edited in *either* the source or the destination; however, a change made in one will not be reflected in the other. The difference between copying and pasting and copying and embedding is that embedded objects can be edited with the source program's editing tabs and options.

Quick Steps

Embed an Object

1. Open source program.
2. Select object.
3. Click Copy button.
4. Open destination program.
5. Click Paste button arrow.
6. Click *Paste Special*.
7. Click source of object.
8. Click OK.

Since embedded objects are edited within the source program, the source program must reside on the computer when the presentation is opened for editing. If a presentation will be edited on another computer, check before embedding any objects to verify that the other computer has the same programs.

To embed an object, open both programs and both files. In the source program, click the object and then click the Copy button in the Clipboard group on the Home tab. Click the button on the taskbar representing the destination program file and then position the insertion point at the location where the object is to be embedded. Click the Paste button arrow in the Clipboard group and then click *Paste Special* at the drop-down list. At the Paste Special dialog box, click the source of the object in the *As* list box and then click OK.

Edit an embedded object by double-clicking the object. This displays the object with the source program tabs and options. Make changes and then click outside the object to exit the source program tabs and options. Animation effects can be applied to an embedded object with the same techniques learned in Chapter 7.

Project 2a Embedding an Excel Chart in a Presentation Part 1 of 3

1. Open **FundsPres.pptx** and then save it with the name **8-FundsPres**.
2. Open Excel and then open **Funds01.xlsx**, located in the PC8 folder on your storage medium.
3. Click in the chart to select it. (Make sure the entire chart is selected and not an element in the chart.)
4. Click the Copy button in the Clipboard group on the Home tab.
5. Click the PowerPoint button on the taskbar.
6. Make Slide 4 active.
7. Click the Paste button arrow and then click *Paste Special* at the drop-down list.

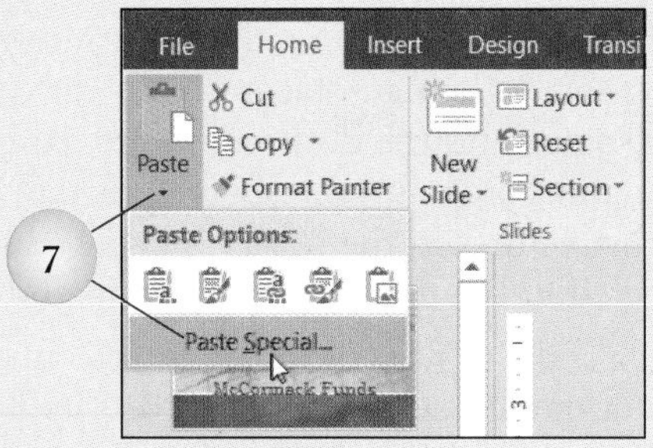

8. At the Paste Special dialog box, click *Microsoft Office Graphic Object* in the *As* list box and then click OK.

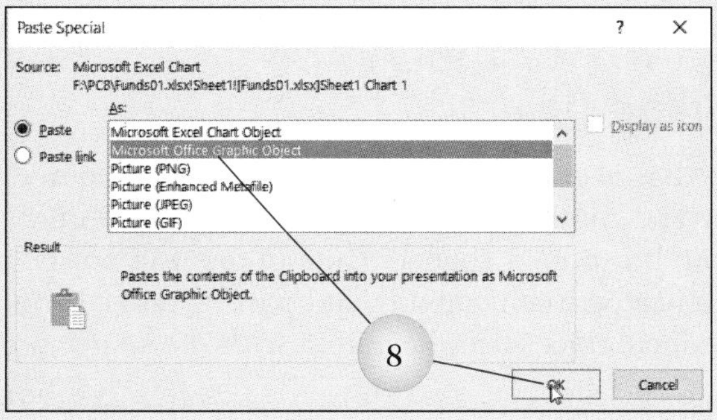

9. Click the Chart Tools Format tab.
10. Change the height of the chart to 5.5 inches and change the width to 9 inches.
11. Center the pie chart in the slide below the title.
12. Save **8-FundsPres.pptx**.
13. Click the Excel button on the taskbar, close the workbook, and then close Excel.

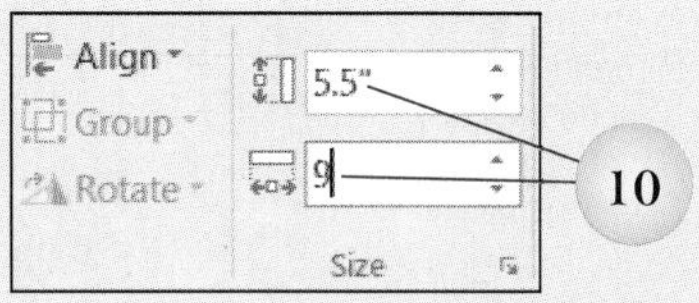

Check Your Work

Tutorial

Linking Objects

Hint Since linking does not increase the size of the file in the destination program, consider linking objects if file size is a consideration.

Linking Objects

If the content of the object to be integrated between programs is likely to change, link the object from the source program to the destination program. Linking the object establishes a direct connection between the source and destination programs. The object is stored in the source program only. The destination program will have a code inserted into it that indicates the name and location of the source of the object. Whenever the presentation containing the link is opened, a message displays saying that the presentation contains links and the user is then prompted to update the links.

Quick Steps

Link an Object

1. Open source program.
2. Select object.
3. Click Copy button.
4. Open destination program.
5. Click Paste button arrow.
6. Click *Paste Special*.
7. Click source of object.
8. Click *Paste link* option.
9. Click OK.

To link an object, open both programs and open both program files. In the source program file, click the object and then click the Copy button in the Clipboard group on the Home tab. Click the button on the taskbar representing the destination program file and then position the insertion point in the desired location. Click the Paste button arrow in the Clipboard group on the Home tab and then click *Paste Special* at the drop-down list. At the Paste Special dialog box, click the source program for the object in the *As* list box, click the *Paste link* option at the left side of the *As* list box, and then click OK.

Project 2b Linking an Excel Chart to a Presentation

Part 2 of 3

1. With **8-FundsPres.pptx** open, open Excel and then open **Funds02.xlsx**, located in the PC8 folder on your storage medium.
2. Save the workbook with the name **8-MMFunds**.
3. Copy and link the chart to a slide in the presentation by completing the following steps:
   a. Click in the chart to select it. (Make sure you select the chart and not just an element in the chart.)
   b. Click the Copy button in the Clipboard group on the Home tab.
   c. Click the PowerPoint button on the taskbar.
   d. Make Slide 5 active.
   e. Click the Paste button arrow and then click *Paste Special* at the drop-down list.
   f. At the Paste Special dialog box, click the *Paste link* option.
   g. Make sure *Microsoft Excel Chart Object* is selected in the *As* list box and then click OK.
   h. Click the Drawing Tools Format tab, change the height of the chart to 5 inches, and then drag the chart so it is centered on the slide.

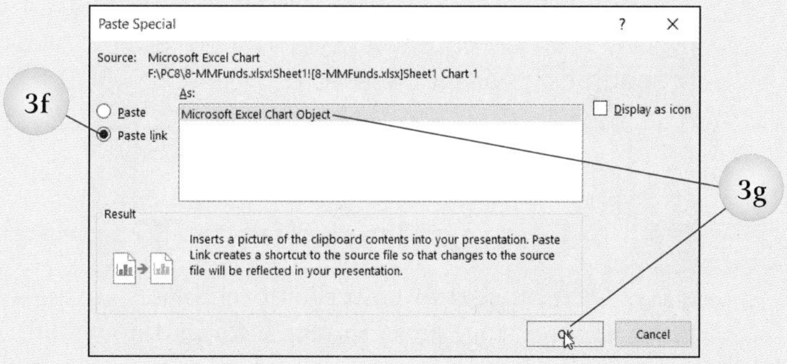

4. Click the Excel button on the taskbar, close **8-MMFunds.xlsx**, and then close Excel.
5. Make Slide 1 active and then run the slide show.
6. Save and then close **8-FundsPres.pptx**.

Check Your Work

Editing Linked Objects

Edit linked objects in the source program in which they were created. Open the document, workbook, or presentation containing the object; make the changes as required; and then save and close the file. If both the source and destination programs are open at the same time, the changed content is reflected immediately in both programs.

Project 2c Editing Linked Data — Part 3 of 3

1. Open Excel and then open **8-MMFunds.xlsx**.
2. Make the changes as indicated to data in the following cells:
   a. Cell B2: Change *13%* to *17%*.
   b. Cell B3: Change *9%* to *12%*.
   c. Cell B6: Change *10%* to *14%*.
3. Click the Save button on the Quick Access Toolbar to save the edited workbook.
4. Close **8-MMFunds.xlsx** and then close Excel.
5. In PowerPoint, open **8-FundsPres.pptx**.
6. At the message telling you that the presentation contains links, click the Update Links button.
7. Make Slide 5 active and then notice the updated changes in the chart data.
8. Print the presentation as a handout with six slides displayed horizontally per page.
9. Save and then close **8-FundsPres.pptx**.

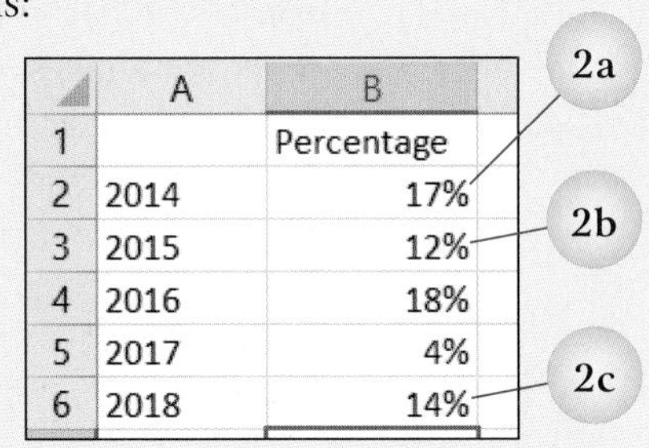

A
B
1 Percentage
2 2014 17%
3 2015 12%
4 2016 18%
5 2017 4%
6 2018 14%
2a
2b
2c

Check Your Work

Project 3 Download and Apply a Design Template to a Presentation and Prepare a Presentation for Sharing — 10 Parts

You will download a design template and apply the template to a company presentation. You will insert, edit, and delete comments in the presentation; modify the presentation properties; inspect the presentation; and encrypt the presentation with a password.

Preview Finished Project

Tutorial

Downloading and Applying a Design Template

Quick Steps

Download a Template
1. Click File tab.
2. Click *New*.
3. Click in search text box.
4. Type key word or phrase.
5. Press Enter.
6. Double-click template.

Downloading Templates

A number of PowerPoint templates are available for downloading at the New backstage area. To search for and download a template, click the File tab and then click the *New* option to display the New backstage area. Click in the search text box, type a keyword or phrase, and then press the Enter key or click the Start searching button at the right side of the search text box. PowerPoint searches the Office.com templates gallery and displays templates that match the key word or phrase. To download a template, double-click the template or click once on the template to display a download window. At this window, read information about the template and view additional template images by clicking the right- or left-pointing arrows that display below the template image. To download the template, click the Create button. When a template is downloaded, a presentation based on the template opens and the downloaded template is added to the New backstage area.

Many presentations opened from a downloaded template contain predesigned slides. Use these slides to help create a presentation or delete the predesigned slides and create a presentation using just the template layouts.

To make the downloaded template (not a customized version of the template) available for future presentations, pin the template to the New backstage area. To do this, display the New backstage area, hover the mouse over the template to be pinned, and then click the push pin that displays. Complete the same steps to unpin a template from the New backstage area.

If a customized template is saved to the Custom Office Templates folder, it can be applied to an existing presentation. To do this, open the presentation, click the Design tab, click the More Themes button in the Themes group, and then click the *Browse for Themes* option at the drop-down list. At the Choose Theme or Themed Document dialog box, navigate to the Custom Office Templates folder in the Documents folder on the computer's hard drive and then double-click the template in the dialog box Content pane.

Project 3a **Downloading and Applying a Design Template** Part 1 of 10

Note: Check with your instructor before downloading a design template. To download a template, you must have access to the Internet and access to the hard drive. If you do not have access to the design template or cannot download it, open ISPres.pptx, save it with the name 8-ISPres, apply a design theme of your choosing, and then continue to Step 13.

1. At a blank PowerPoint screen, click the File tab and then click the *New* option.
2. At the New backstage area, click in the search text box, type marketing plan, and then press the Enter key.
3. Scroll down the backstage list box and view some of the templates.
4. Click in the search text box, type red radial lines, and then press the Enter key.

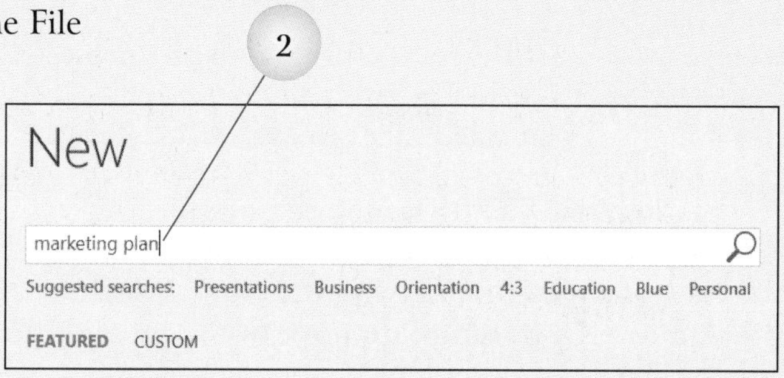

5. Click the *Red radial lines presentation (widescreen)* template.
6. At the template window, view some of the images for the template by clicking the right-pointing arrow below the template image several times.
7. Click the Create button. (This downloads the template and opens a presentation based on the template.)

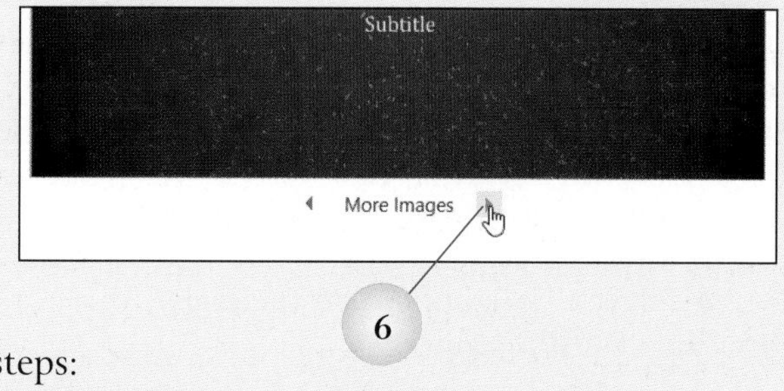

8. Delete the sample slides in the presentation by completing the following steps:
   a. With the first slide selected in the slide thumbnails pane, scroll down the slide thumbnails pane to the last slide, press and hold down the Shift key, click the last slide, and then release the Shift key. (This selects all of the slides in the presentation.)
   b. Press the Delete key. (When you press the Delete key, the slides are deleted and a gray screen displays with the text *Click to add first slide.*)

9. Save the presentation as a template to the Custom Office Templates folder by completing the following steps:
   a. Press the F12 function key to display the Save As dialog box.
   b. Click the *Save as type* option box and then click *PowerPoint Template (*.potx)* at the drop-down list. (Make sure the Custom Office Templates folder in the Documents folder on the computer's hard drive is active.)
   c. Click in the *File name* text box, type XXX-ISTemplate (type your initials in place of the *XXX*) and then click the Save button.

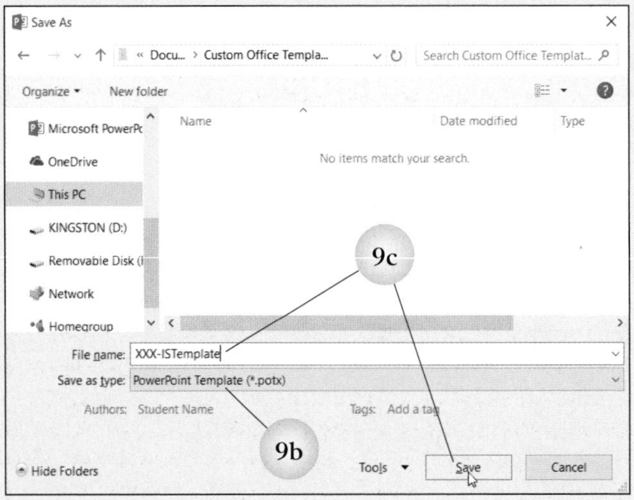

   d. Close the **XXX-ISTemplate.potx** file.
10. Open **ISPres.pptx** from the PC8 folder on your storage medium.
11. Save the presentation with the name **8-ISPres**.
12. Apply **XXX-ISTemplate.potx** to the presentation by completing the following steps:
    a. Click the Design tab.
    b. Click the More Themes button in the Themes group.
    c. Click the *Browse for Themes* option at the drop-down list.
    d. At the Choose Theme or Themed Document dialog box, double-click the *Custom Office Templates* folder in the Content pane.
    e. Double-click ***XXX-ISTemplate.potx*** (where your initial display in place of the ***XXX***).

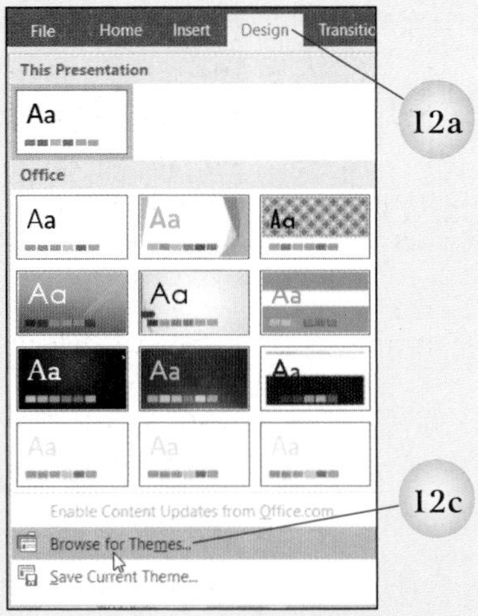

13. Run the slide show.
14. Print the presentation as a handout with all nine slides displayed horizontally on the page.
15. Save **8-ISPres.pptx**.

Check Your Work

Tutorial

Comparing and Combining Presentations

Quick Steps

Compare and Combine Presentations

1. Click Review tab.
2. Click Compare button.
3. Navigate to folder containing presentation to be compared.
4. Click presentation.
5. Click Merge button.
6. Accept or reject changes.
7. Click End Review button.

Compare

Accept

Reject

Previous

Next

Reviewing Pane

End Review

Comparing and Combining Presentations

Use the Compare button in the Compare group on the Review tab to compare two PowerPoint presentations to determine the differences between the presentations. When the presentations are compared, options are available for combining only specific changes, accepting only specific changes, and rejecting some or all of the changes.

To compare and combine presentations, open the first presentation, click the Review tab, and then click the Compare button in the Compare group. This displays the Choose File to Merge with Current Presentation dialog box. At this dialog box, navigate to the folder containing the presentation to be compared with the current presentation, click the presentation name in the Content pane, and then click the Merge button. (The presentation name can also be double-clicked.)

Click the Merge button (or double-click the presentation name) and a Reviewing task pane with the heading *Revisions* displays at the right side of the screen containing changes to slides and the presentation. The *DETAILS* option is selected in the Reviewing task pane and the task pane displays with the *Slide Changes* section and the *Presentation Changes* section. Click a revision that displays in either section of the task pane and the revision mark in the slide or slide thumbnails pane is selected. A revision mark displays in a slide indicating a difference between slides in the two presentations. If a difference occurs to the entire presentation, such as a difference between design themes, a revision mark displays at the left side of the screen near the top of the slide thumbnails pane. Click a revision in the Revisions task pane or click a revision mark in the slide or slide thumbnails pane to expand the revision mark to display a revision check box followed by information about the change.

To accept a change, click the revision check box and then click the Accept button in the Compare group. A change can also be accepted by clicking the Accept button arrow. Clicking the Accept button arrow displays a drop-down list with options to accept the current change, accept all changes to the current slide, or accept all changes to the presentation. To reject a change, click the Reject button in the Compare group. Click the Reject button arrow and options display for rejecting the current change, rejecting all changes to the current slide, or rejecting all changes to the presentation.

Use the Previous and Next buttons in the Compare group to navigate to changes in the presentation. Click the Reviewing Pane button to turn the display of the Reviewing task pane on or off. When finished comparing the presentations, click the End Review button and the review ends and the accept or reject decisions that were made are applied.

Project 3b Comparing and Combining Presentations

Part 2 of 10

1. With **8-ISPres.pptx** open, click the Review tab and then click the Compare button in the Compare group.
2. At the Choose File to Merge with Current Presentation dialog box, navigate to the PC8 folder on your storage medium, click ***ISSalesMeeting.pptx*** in the Content pane, and then click the Merge button in the lower right corner of the dialog box.

3. Notice the Reviewing task pane (with the heading *Revisions*) at the right side of the screen with the *DETAILS* option selected. This option contains a *Slide Changes* section and a *Presentation Changes* section. A message displays in the *Slide Changes* section indicating that the current slide (Slide 1) contains a change to the slide properties and title. The *Presentation Changes* section displays with *Theme (1 - 9)*.
4. Click the *Title 1: International Security* revision that displays in the *Slide Changes* section of the task pane.
5. Click the revision check box that displays before the text *All changes to Title 1* at the right side of the slide in the slide pane to insert a check mark.
6. You do not want to change the title name, so click the Reject button in the Compare group to reject this change.

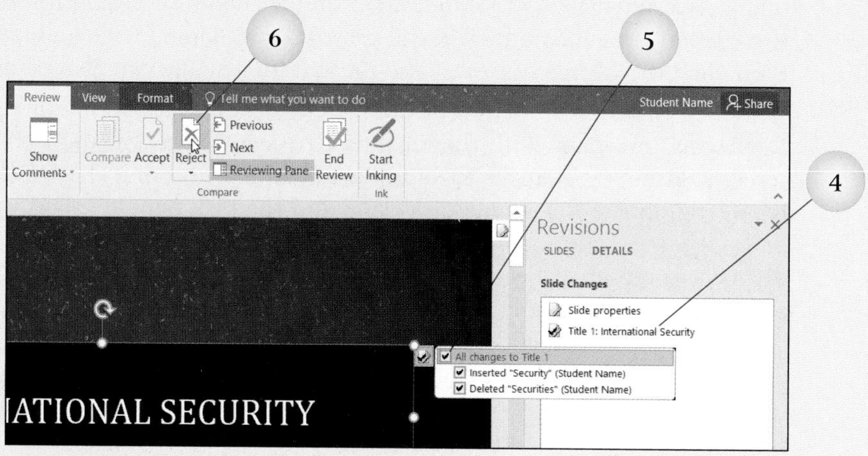

7. Click the Next button.
8. With the chart selected in Slide 3, click the Accept button arrow in the Compare group and then click the *Accept All Changes to This Slide* option.
9. Click the Next button.
10. Accept the remaining changes to the presentation by clicking the Accept button arrow and then click the *Accept All Changes to the Presentation* option.
11. Click the Next button until Slide 9 displays in the slide pane.
12. Notice the check mark at the left of the text *Inserted Picture 3* in Slide 9. This picture was inserted in the slide from **ISSalesMeeting.pptx**.
13. Click the Next button.
14. At the message that displays telling you that was the last change and asking if you want to continue reviewing from the beginning, click the Cancel button.
15. Click the End Review button in the Compare group.
16. At the message asking if you are sure you want to end the review, click the Yes button.
17. Save **8-ISPres.pptx**.

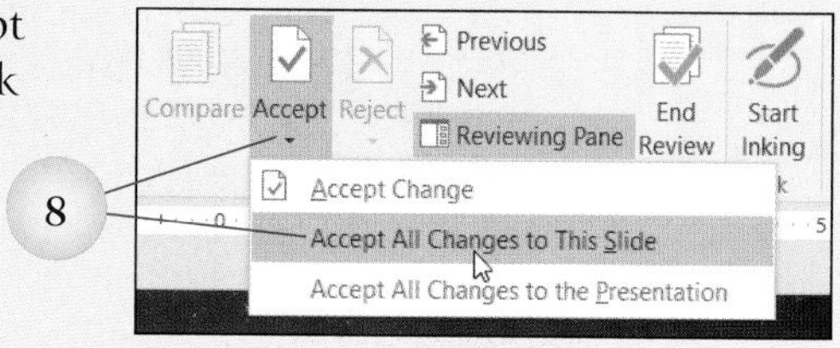

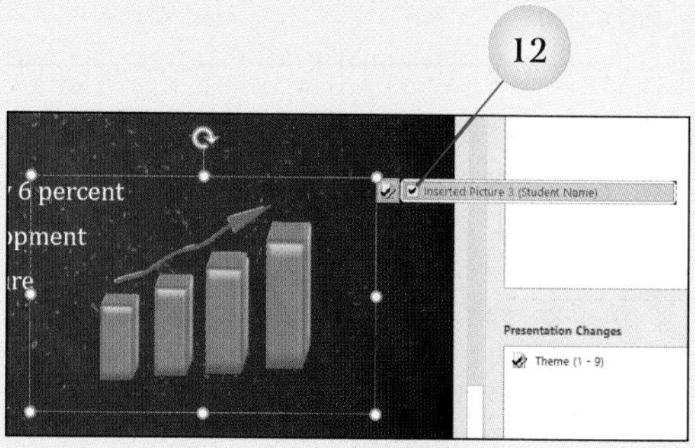

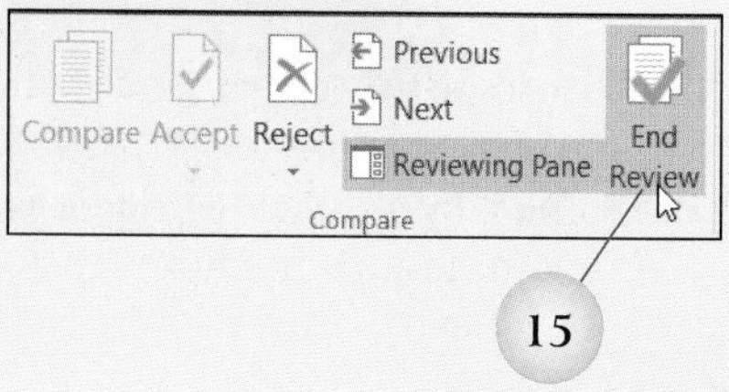

Check Your Work

Tutorial

Inserting and Deleting Comments

Quick Steps

Insert a Comment

1. Click Review tab.
2. Click New Comment button.
3. Type comment text.

New Comment

Next

Previous

Comments

Show Comments

Managing Comments

If a presentation is to be sent to others for review, specific questions or additional information can be included in the presentation by inserting a comment. To insert a comment, display a specific slide and then position the insertion point where the comment is to appear or select an element in the slide on which to comment. Click the Review tab and then click the New Comment button in the Comments group. This displays an orange active icon at the location of the insertion point or next to the selected element and opens the Comments task pane with a text entry box in the pane. Type the comment in the text entry box and then click outside the text entry box, press the Tab key, or press the Enter key.

To insert another comment in the presentation, position the insertion point or select an element in the slide and then click the New button in the Comments task pane or click the New Comment button in the Comments group and then type the comment in the text entry box. To view a comment in a presentation, click the comment icon and then read the information in the Comments task pane.

To move between comments in a presentation, click the Next or Previous buttons in the upper right corner of the Comments task pane. Or, click the Previous or Next buttons in the Comments group on the Review tab.

Other methods for displaying the Comments task pane include clicking the Comments button on the Status bar or clicking the Show Comments button in the Comments group on the Review tab. When the Comments task pane is open, the Show Comments button is active (displays with a gray background). Turn off the display of the Comments task pane by clicking the Comments button on the Status bar, clicking the Show Comments button, or by clicking the Close button in the upper right corner of the Comments task pane.

To print comments, display the Print backstage area and then click the second gallery in the *Settings* category. (This is the gallery containing the text *Full Page Slides*.) At the drop-down list, make sure the *Print Comments and Ink Markup* option is preceded by a check mark. Comments print on a separate page after the presentation is printed.

Project 3c Inserting Comments

Part 3 of 10

1. With **8-ISPres.pptx** open, make Slide 2 active and then insert a comment by completing the following steps:
   a. Position the insertion point immediately to the right of the word *Australia*.
   b. Click the Review tab.
   c. Click the New Comment button in the Comments group.
   d. Type the following in the text entry box in the Comments task pane: Include information on New Zealand division.

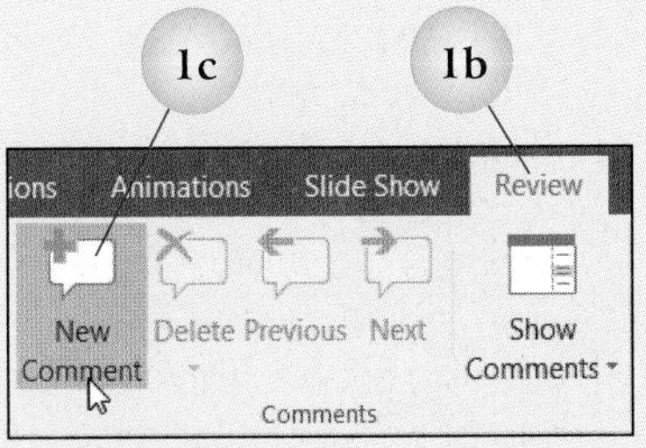

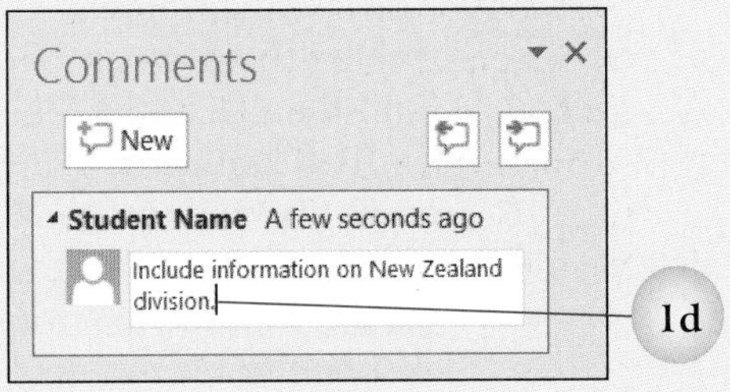

2. Make Slide 3 active and then insert a comment by completing the following steps:
   a. Click in the chart to select it. (Make sure you select the entire chart and not a chart element.)

b. Click the New button in the Comments task pane.
c. Type the following in the text entry box: Include a chart showing profit amounts.

3. Make Slide 5 active, position the insertion point immediately to the right of the word *line* at the end of the third bulleted item, and then insert the comment Provide detailed information on how this goal will be accomplished.
4. Make Slide 8 active, position the insertion point immediately to the right of the word *Singapore* in the second bulleted item, and then insert the comment Who will be managing the Singapore office?
5. Click the Previous button in the Comments task pane to display the comment box in Slide 5.
6. Click the Previous button in the Comments group on the Review tab to display the comment box in Slide 3.
7. Click the Next button in the Comments task pane to display the comment in Slide 5.
8. Click the Next button in the Comments group on the Review tab to display the comment in Slide 8.

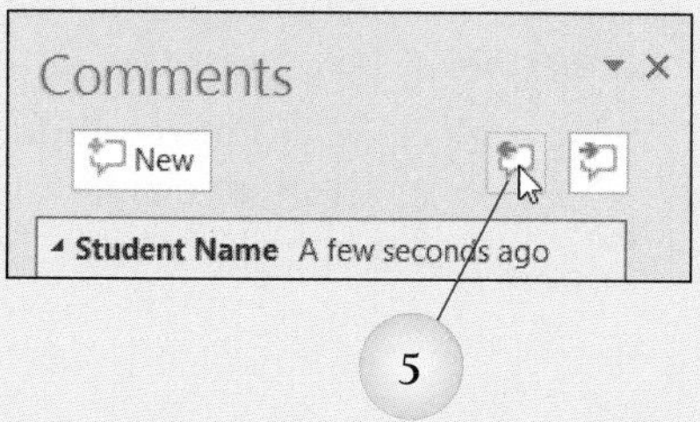

9. Click the Show Comments button in the Comments group on the Review tab to turn off the display of the Comments task pane.

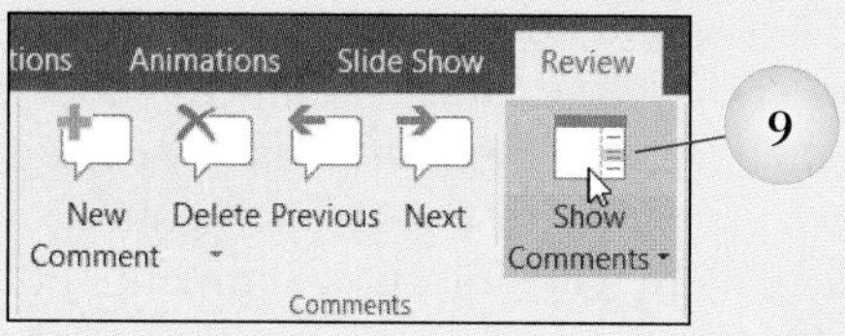

10. Print the presentation and the comments by completing the following steps:
    a. Click the File tab and then click the *Print* option.
    b. At the Print backstage area, click the second gallery in the *Settings* category, make sure the *Print Comments and Ink Markup* option is preceded by a check mark, and then click the *9 Slides Vertical* option.
    c. Click the Print button.
11. Make Slide 1 active and then run the slide show.
12. Save **8-ISPres.pptx**.

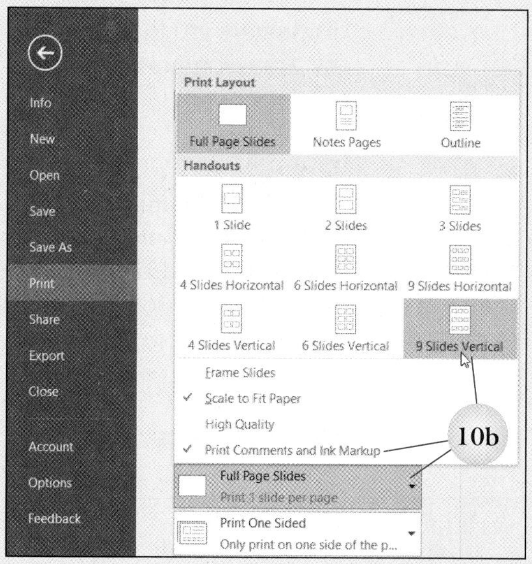

Check Your Work

Hint Move a comment in a slide by selecting the comment icon and then dragging it to the new location.

Delete

To edit a comment, click the comment in the Comments task pane, click in the text entry box and then edit the comment. Reply to a comment by clicking the comment in the Comments task pane, clicking in the reply entry box and then typing the response. To delete a comment from a slide, click the comment icon and then click the Delete button in the Comments task pane or the Delete button in the Comments group on the Review tab. A comment can also be deleted by right-clicking the comment icon and then clicking *Delete Comment* at the shortcut menu. Delete all comments in a presentation by clicking the Delete button arrow in the Comments group and then clicking *Delete All Comments and Ink in This Presentation* at the drop-down list.

Project 3d Editing and Deleting Comments

1. With **8-ISPres.pptx** open, make Slide 8 active and then edit the comment by completing the following steps:
   a. Click the comment icon to the right of *Singapore*. (This displays the Comments task pane.)
   b. Click the comment text in the text entry box in the Comments task pane (this selects the comment text) and then type Check with Sandy Cates to determine who will be appointed branch manager.

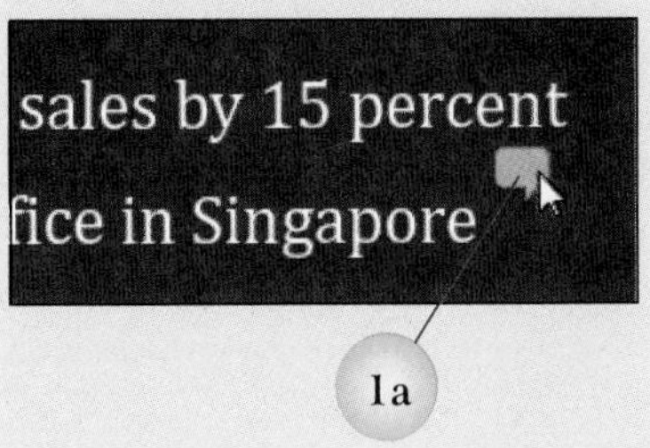

2. Delete the comment in Slide 3 by completing the following steps:
   a. Click the Previous button in the upper right corner of the Comments task pane two times to display Slide 3 and the comment in the slide.
   b. Click the Delete button (contains an *X*) in the upper right corner of the comment box.
3. Close the Comments task pane.
4. Print the presentation as a handout with all nine slides displayed horizontally on the page and make sure the comments print.
5. Save **8-ISPres.pptx**.

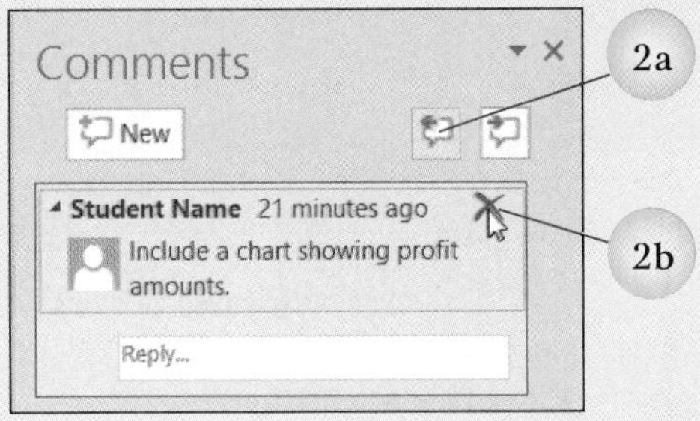

Check Your Work

Tutorial

Managing Presentation Information and Properties

Managing Presentation Information

If a presentation will be distributed or shared with others, check the presentation information and decide if presentation properties should be inserted in the presentation file, if the presentation should be protected with a password, and if the compatibility of the presentation should be checked or versions of the presentation should be accessed. These tasks and others can be completed at the Info backstage area shown in Figure 8.4. Display this backstage area by clicking the File tab and, if necessary, clicking the *Info* option.

Managing Presentation Properties

Each presentation created has certain properties associated with it, such as the type and location of the presentation and when the presentation was created, modified, and accessed. View and modify presentation properties at the Info backstage area and at the Properties dialog box.

Property information about a presentation displays at the right side of the Info backstage area. Add or update a presentation property by hovering the mouse over the information that displays at the right of the property (a rectangular box with a light orange border displays) and then typing the information. In the *Related Dates* section, dates display for when the presentation was created and when it was last modified and printed. The *Related People* section displays the name of the author of the presentation and also contains options for adding additional author names. Click the folder below the *Related Documents* section to display the folder contents where the current presentation is located.

Figure 8.4 Info Backstage Area

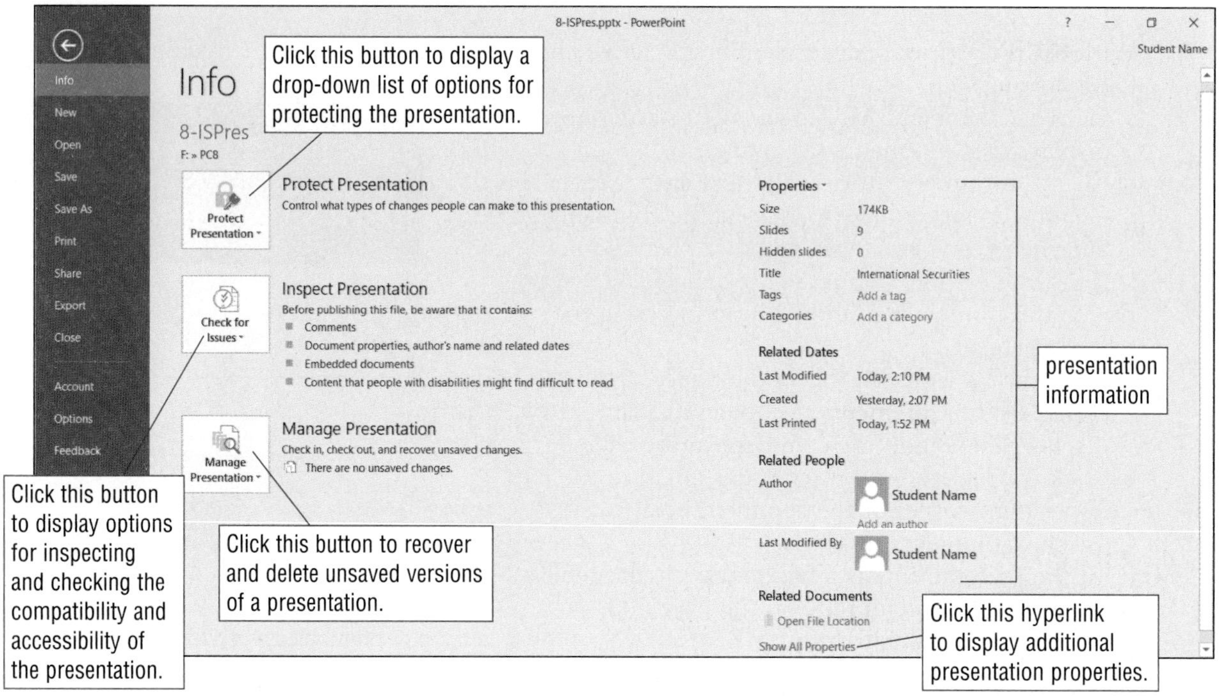

Display additional presentation properties by clicking the Show All Properties hyperlink. Presentation properties also can be managed at the presentations Properties dialog box shown in Figure 8.5. (The name of the dialog box reflects the name of the open presentation.) Display this dialog box by clicking the Properties button at the top of the property information and then clicking *Advanced Properties* at the drop-down list. Inserting text in some of the text boxes can help organize and identify the presentation.

Figure 8.5 Properties Dialog Box

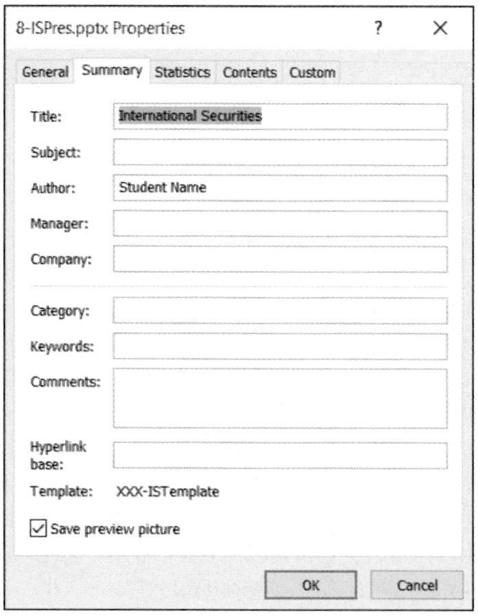

Project 3e Inserting Presentation Properties

Part 5 of 10

1. With **8-ISPres.pptx** open, click the File tab. (This displays the Info backstage area.)
2. At the Info backstage area, hover your mouse over the text *International Securities* at the right of the *Title* property, click the left mouse button (this selects the text), and then type IS Sales Meeting.
3. Display the 8-ISPres.pptx Properties dialog box by clicking the Properties button at the top of the property information and then clicking *Advanced Properties* at the drop-down list.

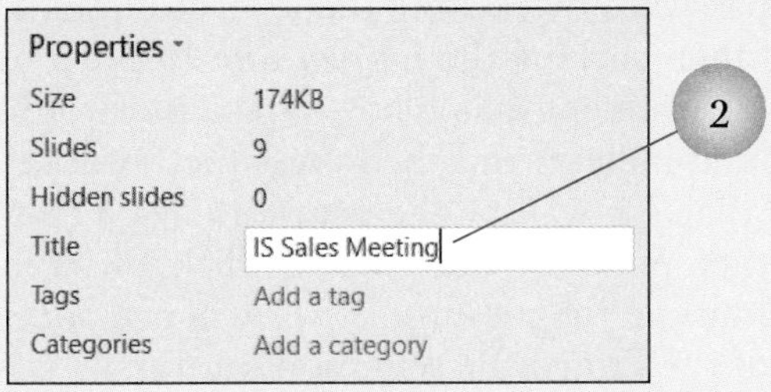

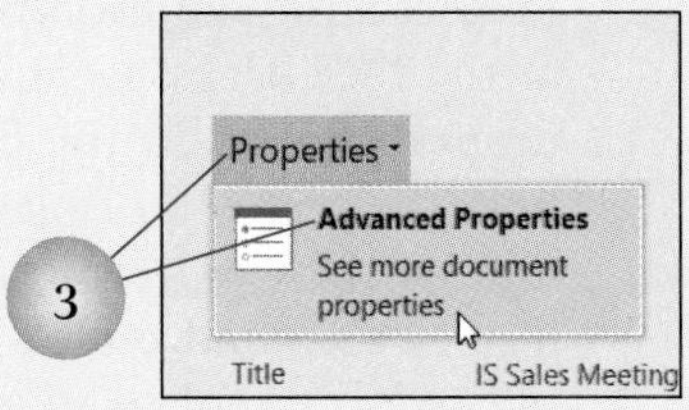

4. At the 8-ISPres.pptx Properties dialog box with the Summary tab selected, press the Tab key (this makes the *Subject* text box active) and then type IS Corporate Sales Meeting.
5. Click in the *Category* text box and then type sales meeting.
6. Press the Tab key to make the *Keywords* text box active and then type International Securities, sales, divisions.
7. Press the Tab key to make the *Comments* text box active and then type This is a presentation prepared for the corporate sales meeting.
8. Click OK to close the dialog box.
9. Save **8-ISPres.pptx**.

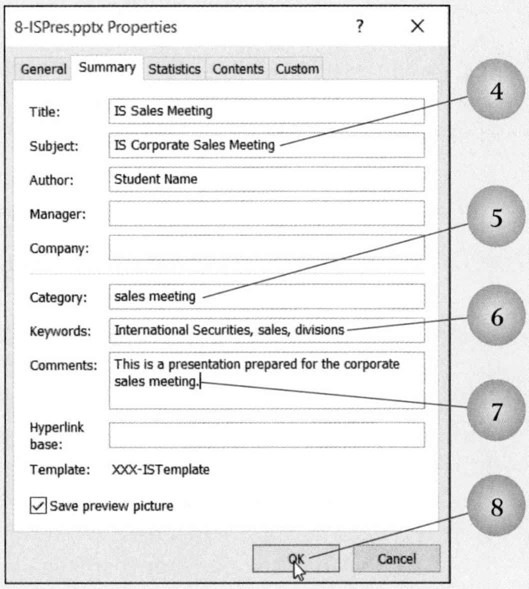

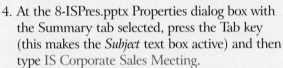

Protecting a Presentation

Protect Presentation

Click the Protect Presentation button in the middle panel at the Info backstage area and a drop-down list displays with the following options: *Mark as Final*, *Encrypt with Password*, and *Add a Digital Signature*. Click the *Mark as Final* option to save the presentation as a read-only presentation. When that option is clicked, a message displays indicating that the presentation will be marked and then saved. At this message, click OK. This displays another message indicating that the presentation has been marked as final and that editing is complete. The message further indicates that when a presentation is marked as final, the status property is set to *Final*; typing, editing commands, and proofing marks are turned off; and that the presentation can be identified by the Mark As Final icon, at the left side of the Status bar. At this message, click OK.

Quick Steps

Mark a Presentation as Final
1. Click File tab.
2. Click Protect Presentation button.
3. Click *Mark as Final.*

After a presentation is marked as final, a message displays above the ruler indicating that the author has marked the presentation as final and includes an Edit Anyway button. Click this button to edit the presentation. When a presentation is marked as final an additional message displays to the right of the Protect Presentation button in the Info backstage area stating "This presentation has been marked as final to discourage editing."

Encrypting a Presentation

Quick Steps

Encrypt a Presentation
1. Click File tab.
2. Click Protect Presentation button.
3. Click *Encrypt with Password.*
4. Type password, press Enter.
5. Type password again, press Enter.

Protect a presentation with a password by clicking the Protect Presentation button at the Info backstage area and then clicking the *Encrypt with Password* option at the drop-down list. At the Encrypt Document dialog box, type a password in the text box (the text will display as round bullets) and then press the Enter key or click OK. At the Confirm Password dialog box, type the password again (the text will display as round bullets) and then press the Enter key or click OK. When a password is applied to a presentation, the message *A password is required to open this document* displays to the right of the Protect Presentation button.

If a presentation is encrypted with a password, keep a copy of the password in a safe place because Microsoft cannot retrieve lost or forgotten passwords. Change a password by removing the original password and then creating a new one. To remove a password, open the password-protected presentation, display the Encrypt Document dialog box, and then remove the password (round bullets) in the *Password* text box.

Project 3f Marking a Presentation as Final and Encrypting with a Password — Part 6 of 10

1. With **8-ISPres.pptx** open, click the File tab.
2. At the Info backstage area, click the Protect Presentation button and then click *Mark as Final* at the drop-down list.
3. At the message telling you the presentation will be marked as final and saved, click OK.
4. At the next message, click OK.
5. Notice the message bar that displays above the ruler.
6. Close the presentation.
7. Open **8-ISPres.pptx**, click the Edit Anyway button on the yellow message bar, and then save the presentation.

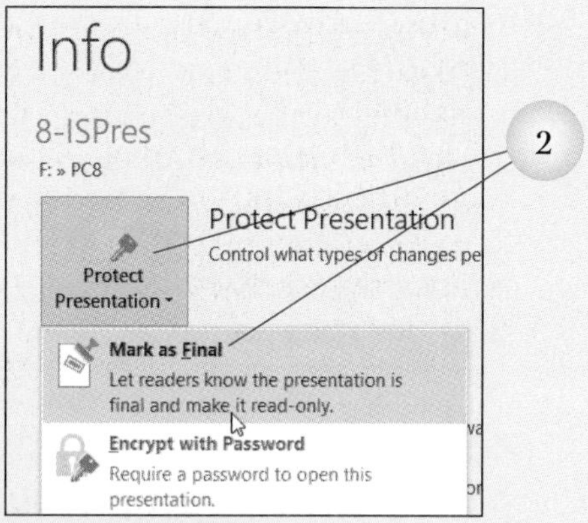

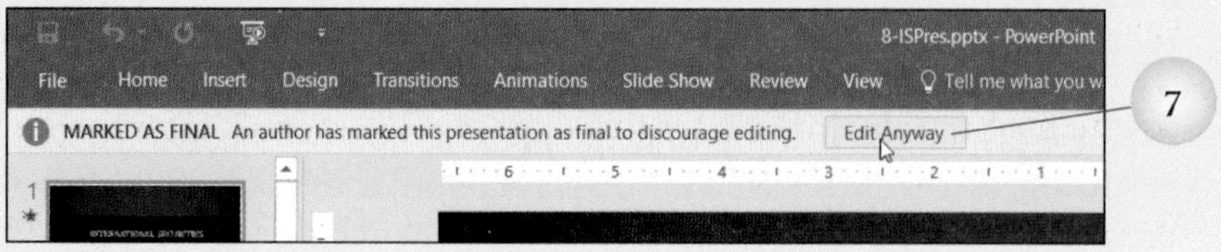

8. Encrypt the presentation with a password by completing the following steps:
   a. Click the File tab, click the Protect Presentation button at the Info backstage area, and then click *Encrypt with Password* at the drop-down list.
   b. At the Encrypt Document dialog box, type your initials in uppercase letters. (Your text will display as round bullets.)
   c. Press the Enter key.
   d. At the Confirm Password dialog box, type your initials again in uppercase letters (your text will display as bullets) and then press the Enter key.

8b
Encrypt Document
Encrypt the contents of this file
Password:
Caution: If you lose or forget the password, it cannot be recovered. It is advisable to keep a list of passwords and their corresponding document names in a safe place. (Remember that passwords are case-sensitive.)
OK
Cancel

9. Click the Back button to return to the presentation.
10. Save and then close **8-ISPres.pptx**.
11. Open **8-ISPres.pptx**. At the Password dialog box, type your initials in uppercase letters and then press the Enter key.
12. Change the password by completing the following steps:
    a. Click the File tab.
    b. At the Info backstage area, click the Protect Presentation button and then click *Encrypt with Password* at the drop-down list.
    c. At the Encrypt Document dialog box, delete the round bullets in the *Password* text box, type your first name in lowercase letters, and then press the Enter key.
    d. At the Confirm Password dialog box, type your first name again in lowercase letters and then press the Enter key.
    e. Press the Esc key to return to the document.
13. Save and then close **8-ISPres.pptx**.
14. Open **8-ISPres.pptx**. At the Password dialog box, type your first name in lowercase letters and then press the Enter key.
15. Remove the password protection by completing the following steps:
    a. Click the File tab.
    b. At the Info backstage area, click the Protect Presentation button and then click *Encrypt with Password* at the drop-down list.
    c. At the Encrypt Document dialog box, delete the round bullets in the *Password* text box and then press the Enter key.
    d. Press the Esc key to return to the presentation.
16. Save **8-ISPres.pptx**.

Adding a Digital Signature

Quick Steps

Add a Digital Signature
1. Click File tab.
2. Click Protect Presentation button.
3. Click *Add a Digital Signature.*
4. Make changes at Sign dialog box.
5. Click OK.

Add a digital signature, which is an electronic stamp that vouches for a presentation's authenticity. When a digital signature is added, the presentation is locked so that it cannot be edited or changed unless the digital signature is removed. To add a digital signature, a digital signature must be obtained from a commercial certification authority. With the commercial digital signature obtained, add it to a presentation by clicking the Protect Presentation button at the Info backstage area and then clicking *Add a Digital Signature* at the drop-down list.

Inspecting a Presentation

Check for Issues

Use options from the Check for Issues button drop-down list at the Info backstage area to inspect a presentation for personal and hidden data and to check a presentation for compatibility and accessibility issues. Click the Check for Issues button and a drop-down list displays with the options *Inspect Document*, *Check Accessibility*, and *Check Compatibility*.

PowerPoint includes a document inspector feature that inspects a presentation for personal data, hidden data, and metadata. Metadata is data that describes other data, such as presentation properties. If a presentation is shared with others, some personal or hidden data may need to be removed before sharing the presentation. To check a presentation for personal or hidden data, click the File tab, click the Check for Issues button at the Info backstage area, and then click the *Inspect Document* option at the drop-down list. This displays the Document Inspector dialog box.

Quick Steps

Inspect a Presentation

1. Click File tab.
2. Click Check for Issues button.
3. Click *Inspect Document*.
4. Remove check marks from items that should not be inspected.
5. Click Inspect button.
6. Click Close button.

By default, the document inspector checks all of the items listed in the dialog box. To exclude items for inspection, remove the check mark preceding the item. For example, if a presentation contains comments and/or ink annotations, click the *Comments and Annotations* check box to remove the check mark. Click the Inspect button toward the bottom of the dialog box, and the document inspector scans the presentation to identify information.

When the inspection is complete, the results display in the dialog box. A check mark before an option indicates that the inspector did not find the specific item. If an exclamation point is inserted before an option, the inspector found and displays a list of the items. To remove the found items, click the Remove All button at the right of the option. Click the Reinspect button to ensure that the specific items were removed and then click the Close button.

Project 3g Inspecting a Presentation — Part 7 of 10

1. With **8-ISPres.pptx** open, click the File tab.
2. At the Info backstage area, click the Check for Issues button and then click *Inspect Document* at the drop-down list.

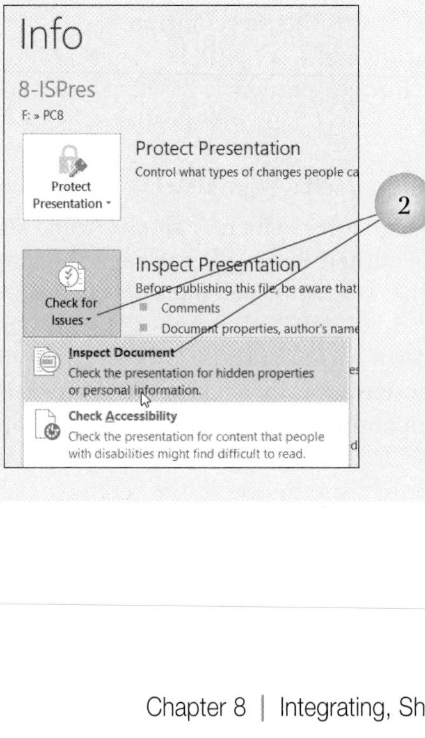

3. At the Document Inspector dialog box, you decide that you do not want to check the presentation for XML data, so click the *Custom XML Data* check box to remove the check mark.

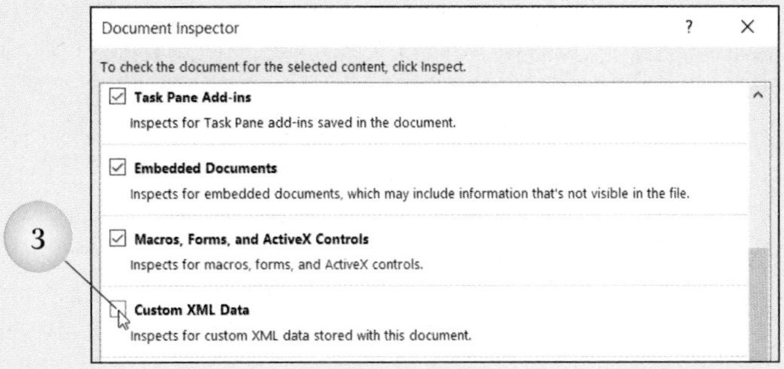

4. Click the Inspect button.
5. Read through the inspection results and then remove all comments by clicking the Remove All button at the right side of the *Comments and Annotations* section.

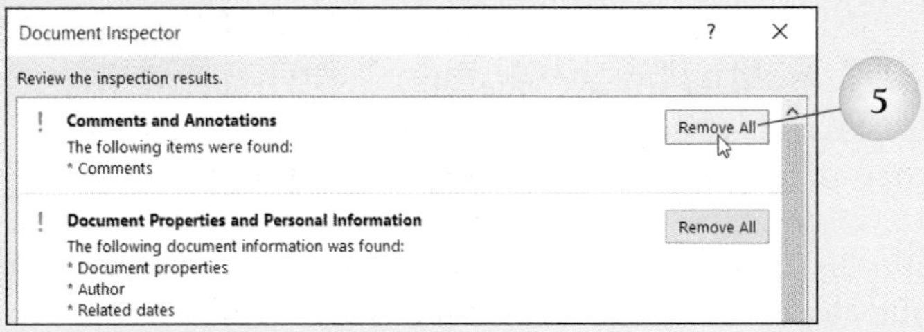

6. Click the Close button to close the Document Inspector dialog box.
7. Click the Back button to return to the presentation. (If necessary, close the Comments task pane.)
8. Save **8-ISPres.pptx**.

Checking the Accessibility of a Presentation

Quick Steps

Check Accessibility

1. Click File tab.
2. Click Check for Issues button.
3. Click *Check Accessibility*.

PowerPoint includes the accessibility checker feature, which checks a presentation for content that a person with disabilities, such as a visual impairment, might find difficult to read. Check the accessibility of a presentation by clicking the Check for Issues button at the Info backstage area and then clicking *Check Accessibility*. The accessibility checker examines the presentation for the most common accessibility problems in PowerPoint presentations and groups them into three categories: errors—content that is unreadable to a person who is blind; warnings—content that is difficult to read; and tips—content that may or may not be difficult to read. The accessibility checker examines the presentation, closes the Info backstage area, and displays the Accessibility Checker task pane.

At the Accessibility Checker task pane, unreadable errors are grouped in the *Errors* section, content that is difficult to read is grouped in the *Warnings* section, and content that may or may not be difficult to read is grouped in the *Tips* section. Select an issue in one of the sections and an explanation of how to fix the issue and why displays at the bottom of the task pane.

1. With **8-ISPres.pptx** open, click the File tab.
2. At the Info backstage area, click the Check for Issues button and then click *Check Accessibility* at the drop-down list.
3. Notice the Accessibility Checker task pane that displays at the right side of the screen. The task pane displays an *Errors* section. Click *Content Placeholder 7 (Slide 3)* in the *Errors* section and then read the information in the task pane describing why and how to fix the error.

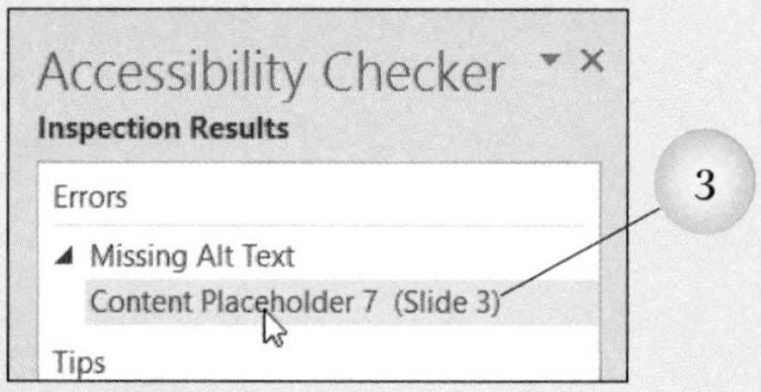

4. Add alternative text (which is a text-based representation of the chart) to the chart by completing the following steps:
   a. Make Slide 3 active, click in the pie chart, right-click the chart border (mouse pointer displays with a four-headed arrow attached), and then click *Format Chart Area* at the shortcut menu.
   b. At the Format Chart Area task pane, click the Size & Properties icon.
   c. Click *Alt Text* to display the options.
   d. Click in the *Title* text box and then type Division Profit Chart.
   e. Click in the *Description* text box and then type Profits: North America, 35%; Europe, 22%; Asia, 17%; Australia, 14%; and Africa, 12%.
   f. Close the Format Chart Area task pane.

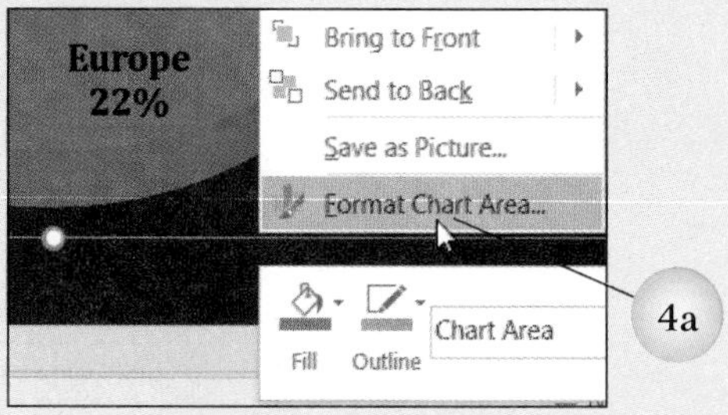

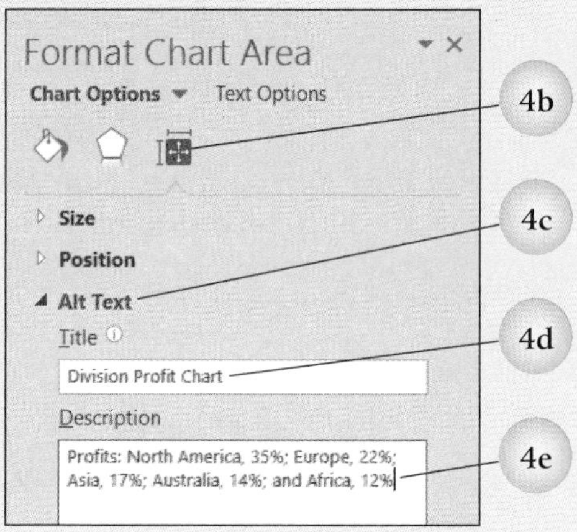

5. Click the remaining item in the Accessibility Checker task pane in the *Tips* section and then read the information in the task pane.
6. Close the Accessibility Checker task pane by clicking the Close button in the upper right corner of the task pane.
7. Save **8-ISPres.pptx**.

Checking the Compatibility of a Presentation

Quick Steps

Check Compatibility

1. Click File tab.
2. Click Check for Issues button.
3. Click *Check Compatibility*.
4. Click OK.

Use the Check for Issues button drop-down option, *Check Compatibility*, to check a presentation and identify elements that are either not supported or will act differently in previous versions of PowerPoint from PowerPoint 97 through PowerPoint 2003.

To run the compatibility checker, open a presentation, display the Info backstage area, click the Check for Issues button, and then click *Check Compatibility* at the drop-down list. This displays the Microsoft PowerPoint Compatibility Checker dialog box that provides a summary of the elements in the presentation that are not compatible with previous versions of PowerPoint and indicates what will happen when the presentation is saved and then opened in a previous version. Click OK to close the dialog box.

Opening an Autosave Presentation

Quick Steps

Open an Autosave Backup Presentation

1. Click File tab.
2. Click presentation name at right of Manage Presentation button.

When working in a presentation, PowerPoint automatically saves the presentation every 10 minutes. This automatic backup feature can be very helpful if the presentation is closed without saving it, or if the power to the computer is disrupted. The automatically saved versions of a presentation are listed to the right of the Manage Presentation button in the Info backstage area. Each autosave presentation displays with *Today*, followed by the time and *(autosave)*. When a presentation is saved and then closed, the autosave backup presentations are deleted.

To open an autosave backup presentation, click the File tab to display the Info backstage area and then click the autosave backup presentation at the right of the Manage Presentation button. The presentation opens as a read-only presentation and a message bar displays above the horizontal ruler that includes a Restore button. Click the Restore button and a message displays indicating that the selected version will overwrite the last saved version. At this message, click OK.

When a presentation is saved, the autosave backup presentations are deleted. However, if a presentation is closed after 10 minutes without saving it or if the power is disrupted, PowerPoint keeps the backup file in the *UnsavedFiles* folder on the hard drive. Access this folder by clicking the Manage Presentation button in the Info backstage area and then clicking *Recover Unsaved Presentations*. At the Open dialog box, double-click the specific backup file to be opened. The *UnsavedFiles* folder can also be displayed by clicking the File tab, clicking the *Open* option, and then clicking the Recover Unsaved Presentations button below the *Recent* option list.

Manage Presentations

Delete an autosave backup file by displaying the Info backstage area, right-clicking the autosave file (to the right of the Manage Presentation button), and then clicking *Delete This Version* at the shortcut menu. At the confirmation message that displays, click the Yes button. To delete all unsaved files from the UnsavedFiles folder, display a blank presentation, click the File tab, click the Manage Presentation button, and then click the *Delete All Unsaved Presentations* option at the drop-down list. At the confirmation message that displays, click the Yes button.

Project 3i Checking the Compatibility of Elements in a Presentation and Managing the Presentation

Part 9 of 10

1. With **8-ISPres.pptx** open, click the File tab.
2. Click the Check for Issues button and then click *Check Compatibility* at the drop-down list.
3. At the Microsoft PowerPoint Compatibility Checker dialog box, read the information in the *Summary* list box.
4. Click OK to close the dialog box.
5. Click the File tab and then check to see if any versions of your presentation display to the right of the Manage Presentation button. If so, click the version (or the first version, if more than one displays). This opens the autosave presentation as read-only.
6. Close the read-only presentation.
7. Click the File tab, click the Manage Presentation button, and then click *Recover Unsaved Presentations* at the drop-down list.

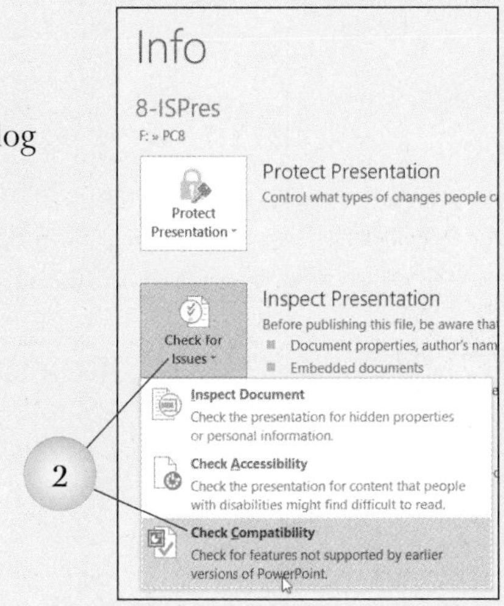

8. At the Open dialog box, check to see if recovered presentation file names display along with the date and time, and then click the Cancel button to close the Open dialog box.
9. Save the presentation.

Tutorial

Customizing PowerPoint Options

Customizing PowerPoint Options

Customize PowerPoint with options at the PowerPoint Options dialog box, shown in Figure 8.6. Display this dialog box by clicking the File tab and then clicking *Options*. Click an option at the left side of the dialog box to display specific options for customizing PowerPoint. For example, click the *General* option in the left panel and options display for turning the display of the Mini toolbar on or off when text is selected, enabling or disabling live preview, and changing the user name and password.

Click the *Proofing* option at the PowerPoint Options dialog box and the dialog box displays with options for customizing the spell checker, such as specifying what should or should not be checked during a spelling check and creating a custom spell check dictionary. Click the AutoCorrect Options button and the AutoCorrect dialog box displays with options for changing how PowerPoint corrects and formats text as it is typed.

Click the *Save* option at the PowerPoint Options dialog box and the dialog box displays with options for customizing how presentations are saved. The format

Figure 8.6 PowerPoint Options Dialog Box

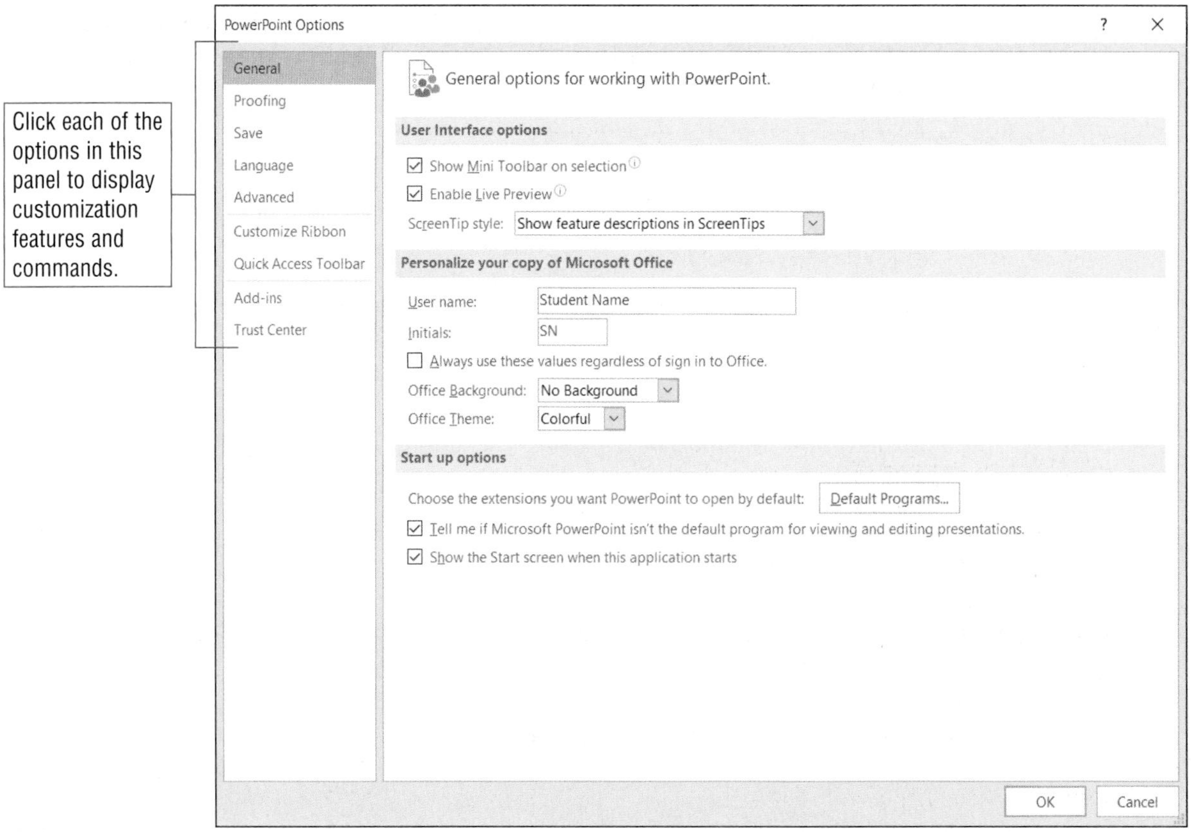

in which files are saved can be changed from the default of *PowerPoint Presentation (*.pptx)* to a macro-enabled PowerPoint presentation, a 97-2003 presentation, a strict open XML presentation, or an OpenDocument presentation. Use other options to specify, by minutes, how often PowerPoint automatically saves a presentation, whether or not to save an autosave version of a presentation if a presentation is closed without first saving it, and a default location for saving presentations.

Project 3j Customizing PowerPoint Options — Part 10 of 10

1. With **8-ISPres.pptx** open, insert new slides in the presentation by completing the following steps:
   a. Click below the bottom slide in the slide thumbnails pane.
   b. Click the New Slide button arrow and then click *Reuse Slides* at the drop-down list.
   c. At the Reuse Slides task pane, click the Browse button and then click *Browse File* at the drop-down list.
   d. At the Browse dialog box, navigate to the PC8 folder on your storage medium and then double-click ***ISPresAfrica.pptx***.
   e. Click each of the three slides in the Reuse Slides task pane to insert the slides into the current presentation.
   f. Close the Reuse Slides task pane.
2. Make Slide 1 active.
3. Change PowerPoint options by completing the following steps:
   a. Click the File tab and then click *Options*.
   b. At the PowerPoint Options dialog box, click the *Save* option in the left panel.
   c. Click the down arrow for the *Save AutoRecover information every* measurement box containing *10* until *1* displays.
   d. Specify that you want presentations saved in the 97-2003 format by clicking the *Save files in this format* option box arrow and then clicking *PowerPoint Presentation 97-2003* at the drop-down list.

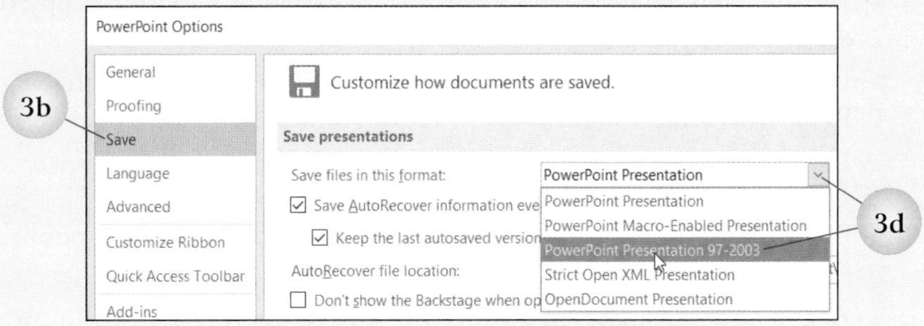

   e. Click the *Proofing* option in the left panel of the PowerPoint Options dialog box.
   f. Click the *Ignore words in UPPERCASE* check box to remove the check mark.
   g. Click the *Ignore words that contain numbers* check box to remove the check mark.
   h. Click OK to close the PowerPoint Options dialog box.
4. Complete a spelling check of the presentation and make changes as needed.

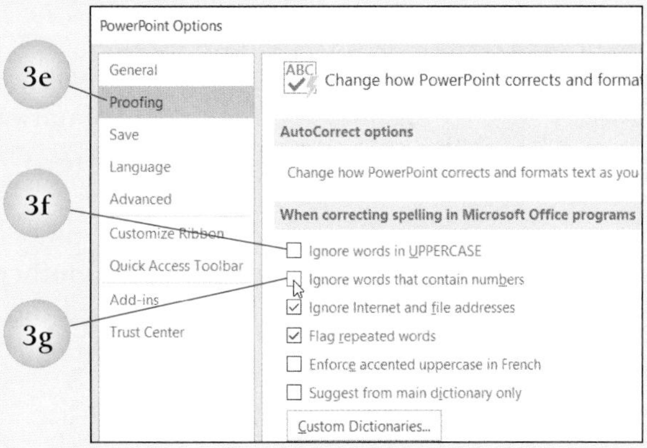

5. Save the presentation, print six slides displayed horizontally per page, and then close the presentation.
6. Press Ctrl + N to open a new blank presentation.
7. Press F12 to display the Save As dialog box.
8. At the Save As dialog box, notice that the *Save as type* option is set to *PowerPoint 97-2003 Presentation (*.ppt)* because you changed the default format at the PowerPoint Options dialog box.
9. Click Cancel to close the dialog box.
10. Display the PowerPoint Options dialog box and then make the following changes:
    a. Click the *Save* option in the left panel.
    b. Change the number in the *Save AutoRecover information every* measurement box to *10*.
    c. Click the *Save files in this format* option box arrow and then click *PowerPoint Presentation* at the drop-down list.
    d. Click the *Proofing* option in the left panel of the PowerPoint Options dialog box.
    e. Click the *Ignore words in UPPERCASE* check box to insert a check mark.
    f. Click the *Ignore words that contain numbers* check box to insert a check mark.
    g. Click OK to close the PowerPoint Options dialog box.
    h. At the message that displays telling you that you are changing the default file format to Office Open XML and asking if you want to change this setting for all Microsoft Office applications, click the No button.
11. Close the blank presentation.

Check Your Work

Chapter Summary

- Create a PowerPoint presentation by importing a Word document containing text with heading styles applied using the *Slides from Outline* option at the New Slides drop-down list.
- Use the Copy and Paste buttons in the Clipboard group to copy data from one program to another.
- Use the Clipboard task pane to collect and paste up to 24 items and paste the items into a presentation or other program files.
- Use options at the Share backstage area to invite people to view and/or edit a presentation, send a presentation as an email attachment or in PDF or XPS file format and as a fax, present a presentation online, and publish slides to a shared location.
- At the Export backstage area, create a PDF or XPS file with a presentation, create a video, package the presentation in a folder or on a CD, and create handouts.
- Click the *Change File Type* option at the Export backstage area and options display for saving a presentation in a different file format such as a previous version of PowerPoint, a PowerPoint show, an OpenDocument presentation, and as graphic images.
- An object created in one program in the Microsoft Office suite can be copied, embedded, or linked in another program in the suite. The program containing the original object is called the *source program* and the program the object is pasted to is called the *destination program*.

- An embedded object is stored in both the source and the destination programs. A linked object is stored in the source program only. Link an object if the contents in the destination program should reflect any changes made to the object stored in the source program.
- Download templates from the Office.com templates gallery at the New backstage area.
- Use the Compare button in the Compare group on the Review tab to compare two presentations to determine the differences between the presentations. Use options in the Compare group to accept or reject differences and display the next or previous change.
- Insert, edit, and delete comments with buttons in the Comments group on the Review tab or with options at the Comments task pane. Display the task pane by clicking the New Comment button or the Show Comments button in the Comments group on the Review tab.
- View and modify presentation properties at the Info backstage area and at the presentation properties dialog box. Display the presentation properties dialog box by clicking the Properties button at the Info backstage area and then clicking *Advanced Properties* at the drop-down list.
- Use options from the Protect Presentation button drop-down list at the Info backstage area to mark a presentation as final, encrypt the presentation with a password, and add a digital signature.
- Use options from the Check for Issues button drop-down list at the Info backstage area to inspect a document for personal and hidden data, check a presentation for content that a person with disabilities, such as a visual impairment, might find difficult to read, and check the compatibility of the presentation with previous versions of PowerPoint.
- PowerPoint automatically saves a presentation every 10 minutes. When a presentation is saved, the autosave backup presentation(s) are deleted.
- Use the Manage Presentation button at the Info backstage area to recover or delete unsaved presentations.
- Customize PowerPoint with options at the PowerPoint Options dialog box. Display this dialog box by clicking the File tab and then clicking *Options*.

Commands Review

FEATURE	RIBBON TAB, GROUP/OPTION	BUTTON, OPTION
Accessibility Checker task pane	File, *Info*	, *Check Accessibility*
Clipboard task pane	Home, Clipboard	
compare presentations	Review, Compare	
Document Inspector dialog box	File, *Info*	, *Inspect Document*
Encrypt Document dialog box	File, *Info*	, *Encrypt with Password*
Export backstage area	File, *Export*	
Insert Outline dialog box	Home, Slides	, *Slides from Outline*

FEATURE	RIBBON TAB, GROUP/OPTION	BUTTON, OPTION
Microsoft PowerPoint Compatibility Checker dialog box	File, *Info*	, *Check Compatibility*
Package for CD dialog box	File, *Export, Package Presentation for CD*	
Paste Special dialog box	Home, Clipboard	, *Paste Special*
Publish as PDF or XPS dialog box	File, *Export, Create PDF/XPS Document*	
Send to Microsoft Word dialog box	File, *Export, Create Handouts*	
Share backstage area	File, *Share*	

Workbook

Chapter study tools and assessment activities are available in the *Workbook* ebook. These resources are designed to help you further develop and demonstrate mastery of the skills learned in this chapter.

Unit assessment activities are also available in the *Workbook*. These activities are designed to help you demonstrate mastery of the skills learned in this unit.

Index

D

E

F

G

H

P

Q

R

S